# THE PHOENIX BOOK
# OF INTERNATIONAL
# RUGBY RECORDS

By the same author
THE BOOK OF ENGLISH INTERNATIONAL RUGBY

# THE PHOENIX BOOK
# OF INTERNATIONAL
# RUGBY RECORDS

## John Griffiths

PHOENIX
HOUSE

J. M. Dent & Sons Ltd
London    Melbourne

First published in Great Britain in 1987
Copyright © John Griffiths 1987

This book is set in Plantin by Gee Graphics Ltd. Printed and bound in Great Britain
by R. J. Acford, Chichester, for Phoenix House, an imprint of
J. M. Dent & Sons Ltd
Aldine House
33 Welbeck Street
London W1M 8LX

British Library Cataloguing in Publication Data

Griffiths, John, 1952 Apr. 8-
    The Phoenix book of international rugby
    records.
    1. Rugby football —— Tournaments ——
    History
I. Title
796.33'375   GV945.5

ISBN 0-460-07003-7

# CONTENTS

# CONTENTS

# ACKNOWLEDGMENTS

This book is the product of a lifelong hobby developed from an interest in rugby first stimulated by the writings of J.B.G. Thomas, E.H.D. Sewell and O.L. Owen. I owe much of my general knowledge of the game's history to the volumes produced by these authors, as well as to the popular *Rugby Football Annuals*, *Wisden's Almanacks*, *Playfair Annuals* and *Rothmans Yearbooks*, which have recorded since before the First War the passing rugby seasons. The following national histories have also been invaluable references:

ENGLAND

*Football: The Rugby Union Game* (Rev. F. Marshall, and updated by L.R. Tosswill)
*History of the Rugby Football Union* (O.L. Owen)
*Centenary History of the RFU* (U.A. Titley and A.R. McWhirter)
*England Rugby* (Barry Bowker)

SCOTLAND

*The Story of Scottish Rugby* (R.J. Phillips)
*The History of Scottish Rugby* (A.M.C. Thorburn)
*The Scottish Rugby Union* (A.M.C. Thorburn)

IRELAND

*The Men in Green* (S. Diffley)
*One Hundred Years of Irish Rugby* (E. van Esbeck)

WALES

*History of Welsh International Rugby* (John Billot)
*The Men in Scarlet* (J.B.G. Thomas)
*Fields of Praise* (D. Smith and G. Williams

FRANCE

*Rugby Français* (G. Gauthey and E. Seidler)
*Les Capes du Matin* (G. Pastre)

SOUTH AFRICA

*History of South African Rugby Football* (I. Difford)
*Springbok Annals* (Dr D.H. Craven)
*The Springboks* (A.C. Parker)
*Springbok Saga* (C. Greyvenstein)

NEW ZEALAND

*History of New Zealand Rugby Football* (A.C. Swan, in two volumes)
*New Zealand International Rugby* (A. H. Carman)
*Men In Black* (R.H. Chester and N.A.C. McMillan, in two volumes)
*The Encyclopaedia of New Zealand Rugby* (R.H. Chester and N.A.C. McMillan)

AUSTRALIA

*Australian Rugby Union: The Game and its Players* (Jack Pollard)

GENERAL

*Rugby Union Football: International Matches* (L. M. Holden)
*The International Rugby Championship* (T.T. Godwin)

Researching a book of this scope takes many years and depends on the assistance and goodwill of a large number of people, as well as delving into numerous primary and secondary sources. I should like to thank the following people and organisations for help:

Auty, Timothy
*Bell's Life in London*
British Museum Newspaper Library
Campbell, Greg
*Cape Argus*
*Cape Times*
Chappin, Brian
Chester, Rod
*Dail Mail*
*Daily Telegraph*
Daly, Desmond
Dalziel, the late Douglas
Davies, Mrs W.J.A.
Donahue, Bob
*Dublin Freeman's Journal*
*Edinburgh Evening News*
General Register Office
*Glasgow Herald*
Griffiths, Phillip
*Irish Sportsman and Farmer*
Jenkins, John
Jenkins, Vivian
Jones, Stephen
*L'Auto*
*Le Figaro*
*L'Equipe*
Lewis, Ron
Murray, Willow
*Port Elizabeth Telegraph*
Potter, the late Alex

*Rand Daily Mail*
*Rugby News*
*Rugby Post*
*Rugby World*
*Scotsman*
Shaw Theatre Public Library
Somerset House
*South African News Weekly*
*South Wales Daily News*
*Sportsman*
Steele, Richard
Stephenson, Mrs G.V.
Sweet, Reg
*Sydney Daily Telegraph*
The *Field*
The *Guardian*
The *Illustrated Sporting and Dramatic News*
The *New Zealand Herald*
The *Times*
*Transvaal Leader*
Vine, Russell
Watford Grammar School
*Welsh Rugby*
*Western Mail*
Westminster Reference Library
Woodward, Jim
Wright, Alfred
*Yorkshire Post*

The chief historian I must thank is Tim Auty, who kindly drew together the list of births and deaths, collating information provided by his large circle of correspondents. Among these John Jenkins, Desmond Daly and Jean-Pierre Bodis supplied numerous British, Irish and French facts respectively.

For some years I have been lucky enough to compile the statistics for the *Rothmans Rugby Yearbook*, and I am grateful to the editors Vivian Jenkins and Stephen Jones for entrusting me with this responsibility. Apart from thanking our contributors to the *Yearbook* I should also like to record my thanks to the past and present secretaries and staffs at the various Union headquarters for their help, particularly regarding the classification of international matches.

And, finally, my thanks to Bill Neill-Hall at Phoenix House for commissioning this edition, skilfully handling the manuscript, and cheerfully and professionally co-ordinating the exercise with calm efficiency.

# PREFACE

The first Rugby World Cup resulted in many changes to the game's international records. The marks for most tries and most conversions in internationals, for most points and conversions in a single international, and for the fastest century of points in internationals all fell during the four weeks of the Cup competition. As a result, many with an interest in the game's statistics wondered whether the landmarks reached in the Cup matches should really count in the world's records. Why, for instance, it was asked, should the England-Japan game played in Australia during the competition count as a match worthy of consideration in the records when the same fixture, played in October 1986 at Twickenham, does not count?

In this new book of international records I have considered *only* those matches for which an International Board country has conferred full official international status on the players participating in such matches – i.e. awarded a full cap. That is the simple qualification for inclusion in this volume.

It will be noticed that over the years different countries have adopted different stances concerning which matches are worthy of full status. During the Second World War, for example, the FFR regarded their games against British and touring sides as full internationals: one therefore has to consider the French players and their contributions to such matches in the lists of major French internationals and records. And it may perhaps come as a surprise to some to learn that prior to the World Cup the world record for points scored in a major international (i.e. one for which an IB nation awarded caps) was held by Guy Camberabero, who kicked 27 points for France against Italy in 1967. It was an interesting coincidence, I thought, that on the same afternoon of the World Cup this record should first be equalled (by Gavin Hastings) and then surpassed by none other than Guy Camberabero's son, Didier, who scored thirty for France against Zimbabwe to keep the record in the family!

The timing of this book has meant that the chief sections had to be completed by early spring 1987. Consequently the records, statistics and text are valid up to the end of the last Northern Hemisphere season, 30 April 1987. Fortunely, however, it has been possible to add a World Cup section later in the book and I hope that the user will find the lists of pre-World Cup records, as well as the subsequent World Cup update, of value.

Finally, a brief note on the divisions within the International sections of the book. As far as possible these divisions have been made to group together matches played during a season or in a Test series. The text accompanying the team lists is intended to describe the leading players, major events or outstanding games relevant to the particular season.

I hope that there are not too many errors in the pages which follow. Certainly I should be grateful to hear of readers' corrections or additions.

John Griffiths
21 June 1987

# AUTHOR'S NOTE

Team line-ups are listed in blocks to show clearly, in any formation from 20- to 15-a-side, the full-backs, threequarters, halves and forwards in that order. Where possible threequarters are given from wing to wing, the fly-half precedes the scrum-half, and forwards are listed from front row to back row. Specialisation has not always existed, however, so it is only since the last war that the prop/hooker/prop/lock/lock/flanker/number-eight/flanker formation so familiar today is given with any certainty. Note too that New Zealand have always played two five-eighths with their scrum-half: these are shown in the half-back blocks in the New Zealand section of the book, as is the "rover" or wing-forward who was employed by the New Zealanders to work their 2-3-2 diamond scrummage in internationals up to 1931.

Concerning scoring, it should be noted that until 1875 international matches were decided by a majority of goals, but from 1876 the try-count was employed to decide a match if teams were level on goals. Scoring by points was not introduced until the late 1880s, a try scoring one point, a conversion two and a dropped goal three. Various experiments were made until 1890-91 when the International Board system was adopted to make scoring uniform in internationals. (For example, in 1889-90 England's two tries against Scotland in Edinburgh counted two points each according to SRU laws, but at Blackheath against Ireland a fortnight later each of England's three tries was only worth a point in accordance with RFU Laws.)

Since the 1890-91 season scoring values have been as follows:

| | Try<br>(T) | Conversion<br>(C) | Drop Goal<br>(DG) | Penalty<br>(PG) | Mark<br>(GM) |
|---|---|---|---|---|---|
| 1890-91 | 1 | 2 | 3 | 2 | 3 |
| 1891-92 to 1892-93 | 2 | 3 | 4 | 3 | 4 |
| 1893-94 to 1904-05 | 3 | 2 | 4 | 3 | 4 |
| 1905-06 to 1947-48 | 3 | 2 | 4 | 3 | 3 |
| 1948-49 to 1970-71 | 3 | 2 | 3 | 3 | 3 |
| 1971-72 to 1976-77 | 4 | 2 | 3 | 3 | 3 |
| 1977-78 to date | 4 | 2 | 3 | 3 | Void |

Note that the penalty goal did not become a scoring device until 1891, and the goal from a mark ceased to exist when the Free Kick clause was introduced in 1977-78. Traditionally, a converted try has been called a goal, usually denoted by the letter G.

Readers will understand that in the Births and Deaths it has been difficult to confirm some dates, while many players' details have yet to be uncovered. I should be grateful to hear of readers' corrections or, better still, additions.

The symbol † is used to indicate a new cap (International Board players only), and an asterisk * shows the player captaining a side.

# ENGLAND INTERNATIONAL TEAMS AND RECORDS

| 1870-71 | 1871-72 | 1872-73 | 1873-74 |
| --- | --- | --- | --- |
| v. SCOTLAND | v. SCOTLAND | v. SCOTLAND | v. SCOTLAND |
| †A. Lyon | A.G. Guillemard | †C.H.R. Vanderspar | †M.J. Brooks |
| †A.G. Guillemard | †W.O. Moberley | †S. Morse | †J.M. Batten |
| †R.R. Osborne | †F.W. Mills | F.W. Mills | |
| | | | H. Freeman 1dg |
| †W. MacLaren | †H. Freeman 1dg | H. Freeman | |
| | | | †W.H. Milton |
| †F. Tobin | *S. Finney 1t | S. Finney | S. Morse |
| †J.E. Bentley | †J.E. Bentley | †C.W. Boyle | †W.E. Collins |
| †J.F. Green | †P. Wilkinson | | |
| | | †W.R.B. Fletcher | †J.S.M. Genth |
| *†F. Stokes | *F. Stokes | *F. Stokes | †E. Kewley |
| †C.W. Sherrard | C.W. Sherrard | †H.A. Lawrence | H.A. Lawrence |
| †B.H. Burns | †T. Batson | J.A. Bush | T. Batson |
| †C.A. Crompton | †F.W. Isherwood 1c | †C.H. Rickards | †W.F.H. Stafford |
| †A. Davenport | †W.W. Pinching | †E.R. Still | †H.A. Bryden |
| †J.M. Dugdale | †J.A. Body | J.A. Body | †C.W. Crosse |
| †A.S. Gibson | †J.E.H. Mackinlay | J.E.H. Mackinlay | †S. Parker |
| †H.J.C. Turner | †J.A. Bush | †E.C. Cheston | E.C. Cheston |
| †R.H. Birkett 1t | †F.B.G.d'Aguilar 1t | †M.W. Marshall | M.W. Marshall |
| †J.H. Luscombe | †F.I. Currey | †H. Marsh | †F.L. Cunliffe |
| †A.St.G. Hamersley | A.St.G. Hamersley 1t | A.St.G. Hamersley | *A.St.G. Hamersley |
| †J.H. Clayton | †F. Luscombe | F. Luscombe | †R. Walker |
| †D.P. Turner | D.P. Turner | D.P. Turner | †D.P. Turner |
| Raeburn Place | Kennington Oval | Glasgow | Kennington Oval |
| LOST | WON | DRAWN | WON |
| Scot.: 1g 1t | Eng.: 1g 1dg 2t | Scot.: Nil | Eng.: 1dg |
| Eng.: 1t | Scot.: 1dg | Engl.: Nil | Scot.: 1t |
| 27 Mar. 1871 | 5 Feb. 1872 | 3 Mar. 1873 | 23 Feb. 1874 |

Until 1877, international matches were played between teams of twenty players. These early matches were dull affairs with the ball rarely reaching the backs, whose chief responsibility was to defend.

Players' preparations for big matches were amusing. J.H. Clayton, following selection for the 1871 match, trained hard for a month before the game, running four miles with a large Newfoundland dog to make the pace every morning in the dark before breakfast. As was then the custom for rugby players, Clayton adhered to a diet of underdone beef and beer.

Among the leading English international players were Fred Stokes of Blackheath, R.H. Birkett, who also won an England soccer cap, and Harold Freeman, the finest drop-kicker of his day. His goals in the 1872 and 1874 matches secured English wins.

| 1874-75 | | 1875-76 | |
| --- | --- | --- | --- |
| v. IRELAND | v. SCOTLAND | v. IRELAND | v. SCOTLAND |
| †A.W. Pearson 1c | A.W. Pearson | †S.H.M. Login | †A.H. Heath |
| †L. Stokes | †L.H. Birkett | A.W. Pearson 1c | A.W. Pearson |
| W.H. Milton | S. Morse | †C.R. Gunner | R.H. Birkett |
| | | A.T. Michell | †J.S. Tetley |
| W.E. Collins | W.E. Collins | | L. Stokes 1c |
| †E.H. Nash 1dg | †W.A.D. Evanson | †C.W.H. Clark 1t | W.E. Collins 1t |
| †A.T. Michell 1t | A.T. Michell | W.E. Collins | †W.C. Hutchinson |
| *H.A. Lawrence | *H.A. Lawrence | †E.B. Turner | |
| †F.R. Adams | F.R. Adams | †E.E. Marriott | F.R. Adams |
| †W.H.H. Hutchinson | W.R.B. Fletcher | W.H.H. Hutchinson | E.C. Cheston |
| T. Batson | J.A. Bush | J.A. Bush | J.A. Bush |
| †E.C. Fraser | R.H. Birkett | †C.C. Bryden | †G.R. Turner |
| †H.J. Graham | H.J. Graham | H.J. Graham | H.J. Graham |
| C.W. Crosse | †J.E. Paul | †J.D.G. Graham | †F.H. Lee 1t |
| J.E.H. MacKinlay | S. Parker | †J. Brewer | †W.C.W. Rawlinson |
| E.C. Cheston 1t | E.C. Cheston | †W. Greg | W. Greg |
| M.W. Marshall | M.W. Marshall | M.W. Marshall | M.W. Marshall |
| †E.S. Perrott | E. Kewley | E. Kewley 1t | E. Kewley |
| F. Luscombe | F. Luscombe | *F. Luscombe | *F. Luscombe |
| R. Walker | J.S.M. Genth | †C.L. Verelst | R. Walker |
| D.P. Turner | D.P. Turner | †A.J. Bulteel | †W.H. Hunt |
| Kennington Oval | Raeburn Place | Leinster C.G. | Kennington Oval |
| WON | DRAWN | WON | WON |
| Eng: 1g 1dg 1t | Scot: Nil | Ire: Nil | Eng: 1g 1t |
| Ire: Nil | Eng: Nil | Eng: 1g 1t | Scot: Nil |
| 15 Feb. 1875 | 8 Mar. 1875 | 13 Dec. 1875 | 6 Mar. 1876 |

England completed the twenty-a-side era with an unbeaten run through 1875 and 1876. Ireland were played for the first time in 1875, at The Oval, and England repaid the visit with a trip to Dublin in December. Both matches were easy for the Englishmen, though the closeness of the Irish marking and a rigid adherence to tight play did not make these matches attractive spectacles.

England had capped 86 players in the first eight matches, and 19 of these appeared three or more times. D.P. Turner, F. Luscombe and M.W. Marshall played in six of the games, more than any of their contemporaries. Turner had failed to win a place in the school side at Rugby, but he became a leading forward of the Richmond club. Later he enjoyed a distinguished army career.

## 1876-77 | | 1877-78 |

| v. IRELAND | v. SCOTLAND | v. SCOTLAND | v. SCOTLAND |
|---|---|---|---|
| L.H. BIRKETT | L.H. BIRKETT | †H.E. KAYLL | †W.J. PENNY 1T |
| L. STOKES 2C | A.W. PEARSON | A.W. PEARSON | A.W. PEARSON 2C |
| | | | |
| †A.N. HORNBY 1T | A.N. HORNBY | A.N. HORNBY | A.N. HORNBY |
| R.H. BIRKETT | L. STOKES | L. STOKES | †H.J. ENTHOVEN |
| | | | |
| W.C. HUTCHINSON 2T | W.A.D. EVANSON | W.A.D. EVANSON | †A.H. JACKSON |
| †P.L.A. PRICE | P.L.A. PRICE | P.L.A. PRICE | †J.L. BELL |
| | | | |
| *E. KEWLEY | *E. KEWLEY | *E. KEWLEY | †H.P. GARDNER 1T |
| F.R. ADAMS 1T | †H.W.T. GARNETT | F.R. ADAMS | C.L. VERELST |
| †R.H. FOWLER | †R. TODD | †F.D. FOWLER | †T. BLATHERWICK |
| M.W. MARSHALL | M.W. MARSHALL | M.W. MARSHALL | *M.W. MARSHALL |
| †G. HARRISON | G. HARRISON | †J.M. BIGGS | A. BUDD |
| W.H. HUNT | W.H. HUNT | †G.F. VERNON | G.F. VERNON |
| †C.J.C. TOUZEL | C.J.C. TOUZEL | †G.T. THOMSON | W.H. HUNT |
| F.H. LEE | C.C. BRYDEN | †E.T. GURDON | †E.F. DAWSON |
| E.B. TURNER | †A.F. LAW | †H. FOWLER | E.B. TURNER 1T |
| | | | |
| Kennington Oval | Raeburn Place | Kennington Oval | Lansdowne Road |
| WON | LOST | DRAWN | WON |
| | | | |
| ENG.: 2G 2T | SCOT.: 1DG | ENG.: NIL | IRE.: NIL |
| IRE.: NIL | ENG.: NIL | SCOT.: NIL | ENG.: 2G 1T |
| | | | |
| 5 Feb. 1877 | 5 Mar. 1877 | 4 Mar. 1878 | 11 Mar. 1878 |

The reduction of players to fifteen-a-side marked the beginnings of modern rugby. Forwards were now found in packs restricted to between eight and ten players, with the result that there were eight fewer men in scrums and mauls; furthermore, the dimensions of the pitch had become settled at around 120 yds by 80 – considerably wider than in the early internationals.

The decrease in numbers and the increase in space encouraged more open football, and the first international played under the new system – against Ireland in 1877 – produced a game in which "from first to last the play was fast and brilliant".

A.N. Hornby was the prominent English back of this period. Later he was to win distinction as captain of both the England cricket and rugby sides.

## 1878-79 | | 1879-80 |

| v. SCOTLAND | v. IRELAND | v. IRELAND | v. SCOTLAND |
|---|---|---|---|
| W.J. PENNY | W.J. PENNY | †T.W. FRY | T.W. FRY 1T |
| †H. HUTH | | A.N. HORNBY | |
| | W.A.D. EVANSON 1T | | †C.H. SAWYER |
| L. STOKES 1C | L. STOKES 1DG,2C | *L. STOKES 1C | *L. STOKES 2C |
| | | †R. HUNT | |
| W.A.D. EVANSON | †H.T. TWYNAM 1T | | †R.T. FINCH |
| †H.H. TAYLOR | †W.E. OPENSHAW | H.T. TWYNAM | H.H. TAYLOR 2T |
| | | A.H. JACKSON | |
| †H.H. SPRINGMAN | †H.D. BATESON | | †C.H. COATES |
| †S. NEAME | S. NEAME | S. NEAME | S. NEAME |
| *F.R. ADAMS | *F.R. ADAMS 1T | †C. GURDON | C. GURDON |
| F.D. FOWLER | J.M. BIGGS | †B. KILNER | †C. PHILLIPS |
| A. BUDD | A. BUDD | G.F. VERNON | G.F. VERNON |
| G. HARRISON | G. HARRISON | †E. WOODHEAD | G. HARRISON |
| †G.W. BURTON 1T | G.W. BURTON | †S.S. ELLIS 1T | G.W. BURTON 1T |
| †H.C. ROWLEY | H.C. ROWLEY 1T | H.C. ROWLEY | H.C. ROWLEY |
| R. WALKER | E.T. GURDON | †E.T. MARKENDALE 1T | E.T. GURDON 1T |
| †N.F. MCLEOD | N.F. MCLEOD | †J.W. SCHOFIELD | R. WALKER |
| | | | |
| Raeburn Place | Kennington Oval | Lansdowne Road | Manchester |
| DRAWN | WON | WON | WON |
| | | | |
| SCOT.: 1DG | ENG.: 2G 2T 1DG | IRE.: 1T | ENG.: 2G 3T |
| ENG.: 1G | IRE.: NIL | ENG.: 1G 1T | SCOT.: 1G |
| | | | |
| 10 Mar. 1879 | 24 Mar. 1879 | 30 Jan. 1880 | 28 Feb. 1880 |

England were the early experts in the fifteen-man game, and between 1878 and 1882 not a game was lost, and no side was fielded without either A.N. Hornby or Lennard Stokes among the backs. Stokes made the perfect complement to Hornby. Stokes had gained a reputation as a superb place-kicker with a prodigious "drop", and as a threequarter he had no equal in tactical appreciation. An athlete of some repute, his faultless handling, powers of jinking and speed-off-the-mark made him the most complete back of his day.

Stokes retired in 1881 as holder of the England cap record (with 12). Incredibly, his 17 conversions in internationals remain an English record.

England's closest match in this period was at Lansdowne Road in 1880. A spirited Irish side lost by only a goal, though it has been reported that the Englishmen were badly shaken-up by a very rough crossing and one of their players was so ill that he was unable to take his place on the field. E. Woodhead, a Yorkshireman studying at Dublin University, was drafted into the side to win a cap in unusual circumstances.

## 1880-81

| v. IRELAND | v. WALES |
|---|---|
| A.N. Hornby | T.W. Fry |
| C.H. Sawyer 1t | R. Hunt 1dg,1t,1c |
| *L. Stokes 2c | *L. Stokes 6c |
| †W.R. Richardson | H.T. Twynam 1t |
| H.H. Taylor 3t | H.H. Taylor 1t |
| †J.I. Ward | †C.P. Wilson |
| †C.W.L. Fernandes | C.W.L. Fernandes 1t |
| C. Gurdon | C. Gurdon |
| C. Phillips | A. Budd 1t |
| G.F. Vernon | †H. Vassall 3t |
| †J.J. Ravenscroft | H. Fowler |
| G.W. Burton | G.W. Burton 4t |
| H.C. Rowley | H.C. Rowley 1t |
| E.T. Gurdon | E.T. Gurdon |
| †W.W. Hewitt | W.W. Hewitt |
| Manchester | Blackheath |
| WON | WON |
| ENG.: 2G 2T | ENG.: 7G 6T 1DG |
| IRE.: NIL | WALES: NIL |
| 5 Feb. 1881 | 19 Feb. 1881 |

## 1881-82

| v. SCOTLAND | v. IRELAND | v. SCOTLAND |
|---|---|---|
| A.N. Hornby | A.N. Hornby | *A.N. Hornby |
| R. Hunt | †W.N. Bolton 1t | W.N. Bolton |
| *L. Stokes 1dg | †E. Beswick | E. Beswick |
| | R. Hunt 1t | |
| H.C. Rowley 1t | | †J.H. Payne |
| †F.T. Wright | H.T. Twynam | H.H. Taylor |
| | H.C. Rowley | |
| C.H. Coates | | C.H. Coates |
| C.W.L. Fernandes | J.I. Ward | †W.M. Tatham |
| C. Gurdon | *C. Gurdon | C. Gurdon |
| A. Budd | †B.B. Middleton | †P.A. Newton |
| H. Vassall | H. Vassall | H. Vassall |
| H. Fowler | †H.G. Fuller | H.G. Fuller |
| G.W. Burton | †J.T. Hunt | J.T. Hunt |
| W.W. Hewitt | G.T. Thomson | G.T. Thomson |
| E.T. Gurdon | †A. Spurling | E.T. Gurdon |
| C. Phillips | W.W. Hewitt | H.C. Rowley |
| Raeburn Place | Lansdowne Road | Manchester |
| DRAWN | DRAWN | LOST |
| SCOT.: 1G 1T | IRE.: 2T | ENG.: NIL |
| ENG.: 1DG 1T | ENG.: 2T | SCOT.: 2T |
| 19 Mar. 1881 | 6 Feb. 1882 | 4 Mar. 1882 |

Disappointing crowds of around 4000 had led the RFU to staging matches in the North of England, and England opened their matches of 1881 at Manchester, where Ireland were soundly beaten by a side in which Hornby and Stokes were still prominent. Among the forwards, the names of the Gurdon brothers, Harry Vassall and A. Budd were to become respected.

Budd and Vassall made their debuts in the first match with Wales, played at Blackheath. The Welsh were so soundly beaten that no fixture was offered in the following season, and Vassall capped his introduction by scoring three tries. (Burton scored four, an international record for a forward.)

Stokes retired after the Scottish match of 1881 to concentrate on a medical career. A crowd of 10,000 surrounded the ropes for his finale, and his dropped goal helped England to draw the match. Following his retirement, England were unable to win a match in 1882.

## 1882-83

| v. WALES | v. IRELAND | v. SCOTLAND |
|---|---|---|
| †A.S. Taylor | A.S. Taylor | †H.B. Tristram |
| W.N. Bolton 1t | W.N. Bolton 1t | W.N. Bolton 1t |
| †A.M. Evanson 2c | A.M. Evanson 1c | A.M. Evanson |
| †C.G. Wade 3t | C.G. Wade 1t | C.G. Wade |
| J.H. Payne | J.H. Payne | J.H. Payne |
| †Al. Rotherham | H.T. Twynam 1t | Al. Rotherham 1t |
| W.M. Tatham | W.M. Tatham 1t | W.M. Tatham |
| †R.S. Kindersley | G. Standing | C. Gurdon |
| †C.S. Wooldridge | C.S. Wooldridge | C.S. Wooldridge |
| H. Vassall | B.B. Middleton | R.S.F. Henderson |
| H.G. Fuller | H.G. Fuller | H.G. Fuller |
| †R.S.F. Henderson 1t | †R.M. Pattisson | R.M. Pattisson |
| G.T. Thomson 1t | G.T. Thomson | G.T. Thomson |
| *E.T. Gurdon | *E.T. Gurdon | *E.T. Gurdon |
| †G. Standing | †E.J. Moore | E.J. Moore |
| St. Helens | Manchester | Raeburn Place |
| WON | WON | WON |
| WALES: NIL | ENG.: 1G 3T | SCOT.: 1T |
| ENG.: 2G 4T | IRE.: 1T | ENG.: 2T |
| 16 Dec. 1882 | 5 Feb. 1883 | 3 Mar. 1883 |

England met the three other Home Countries in 1883, to establish a new but unofficial Championship. And by winning each of the matches, they became first holders of the mythical Triple Crown.

The "find" of the season was Gregory Wade, an Australian scholar at Oxford University. His pace on the wing helped to sink a competent Welsh XV at Swansea, and he followed his three tries against the Welsh with another in a sound win over Ireland.

A narrow victory over Scotland was due in part to Wade's partner on the other wing, W.N. Bolton. In a tight and exciting match at Edinburgh, Bolton scored the winning try under the posts after a good run.

## 1883-84

| v. WALES | v. IRELAND | v. SCOTLAND |
|---|---|---|
| H.B. Tristram | †C.H. Sample 1c | H.B. Tristram |
| | | |
| W.N. Bolton 1c | W.N. Bolton 1t | W.N. Bolton 1c |
| †C.E. Chapman | †H. Wigglesworth | A.M. Evanson |
| C.G. Wade 1t | †H. Fallas | C.G. Wade |
| | | |
| H.T. Twynam 1t | J.H. Payne | H.T. Twynam |
| Al. Rotherham 1t | H.T. Twynam | Al. Rotherham |
| | | |
| W.M. Tatham | W.M. Tatham | W.M. Tatham |
| C. Gurdon | †A. Wood | C. Gurdon |
| C.S. Wooldridge | C.S. Wooldridge | C.S. Wooldridge |
| R.S.F. Henderson | †A. Teggin | R.S.F. Henderson |
| H.G. Fuller | †H. Bell | R.S. Kindersley 1t |
| J.T. Hunt | E.L. Strong | E.L. Strong |
| †E.L. Strong | G.T. Thomson | G.T. Thomson |
| *E.T. Gurdon | *E.T. Gurdon | *E.T. Gurdon |
| †C.J.B. Marriott | C.J.B. Marriott | C.J.B. Marriott |
| | | |
| Leeds | Lansdowne Road | Blackheath |
| WON | WON | WON |
| | | |
| Eng.: 1g 2t | Ire.: Nil | Eng.: 1g |
| Wales: 1g | Eng.: 1g | Scot.: 1t. |
| | | |
| 5 Jan. 1884 | 4 Feb. 1884 | 1 Mar. 1884 |

England continued to dominate the Home Countries in 1884, again securing the Triple Crown. But this season their victories were by narrower margins. The match against Wales was the first international staged in Leeds, and Bolton and Wade, England's stars the previous year, were outstanding. Wade scored one of the tries and Bolton ran 75 yards to set up a try for Rotherham.

England had to thank Bolton for their win over Ireland, his try sealing the match, while his conversion of a controversial try by Kindersley was the difference between two good sides when England met Scotland at the new Blackheath ground, Rectory Field.

The dispute concerning Kindersley's try arose when the Scots claimed that there had been a knock-back on their side. Since this would have given England the advantage anyway, the appeal by the Scots was overruled. Ultimately an International Board was formed to arbitrate such disputes, but the Scots and English argued long and hard over the outcome of this 1884 match, and only two more fixtures in the series were staged before 1890.

## 1884-85 / 1885-86

| 1884-85 | | 1885-86 | | |
|---|---|---|---|---|
| v. WALES | v. IRELAND | v. WALES | v. IRELAND | v. SCOTLAND |
| H.B. Tristram | C.H. Sample | A.S. Taylor | A.S. Taylor | C.H. Sample |
| | | | | |
| †J.J. Hawcridge 1t | J.J. Hawcridge 1t | A.E. Stoddart 1gm | A.E. Stoddart | A.E. Stoddart |
| †A.E. Stoddart | A.E. Stoddart | †R. Robertshaw | R. Robertshaw | R. Robertshaw |
| C.G. Wade 1t | W.N. Bolton 1t | C.G. Wade 1t | C.G. Wade | †E.B. Brutton |
| | | | | |
| J.H. Payne 1c | J.H. Payne | †F. Bonsor | F. Bonsor | F. Bonsor |
| Al. Rotherham | Al. Rotherham | Al. Rotherham | Al. Rotherham | Al. Rotherham |
| | | | | |
| †E.D. Court | †C.H. Horley | †R.E. Inglis | R.E. Inglis | R.E. Inglis |
| R.S. Kindersley 1t | C. Gurdon | C. Gurdon | C. Gurdon | C. Gurdon |
| R.S.F. Henderson | C.S. Wooldridge | †G.L. Jeffery | G.L. Jeffery | G.L. Jeffery |
| A. Teggin 1t | G.T. Thomson | †C.H. Elliot | A. Teggin | A. Teggin |
| G. Harrison | G. Harrison | †W.G. Clibborn | W.G. Clibborn | W.G. Clibborn |
| †H.J. Ryall 1t | H.J. Ryalls | †P.F. Hancock | P.F. Hancock | E. Wilkinson |
| †F. Moss | F. Moss | F. Moss | †N. Spurling | N. Spurling |
| *E.T. Gurdon | *E.T. Gurdon | †E. Wilkinson 1t | E. Wilkinson 1t | *E.T. Gurdon |
| †A.T. Kemble | A.T. Kemble | *C.J.B. Marriott | *C.J.B. Marriott | C.J.B. Marriott |
| | | | | |
| St. Helens | Manchester | Blackheath | Lansdowne Road | Raeburn Place |
| WON | WON | WON | WON | DRAWN |
| | | | | |
| Wales: 1g 1t | Eng.: 2t | Eng.: 1gm 2t | Ire.: Nil | Scot.: Nil |
| Eng.: 1g 4t | Ire.: 1t | Wales: 1g | Eng.: 1t | Eng.: Nil |
| | | | | |
| 3 Jan. 1885 | 7 Feb. 1885 | 2 Jan. 1886 | 6 Feb. 1886 | 13 Mar. 1886 |

Although England remained unbeaten in 1885 and 1886, Scotland twice denied them the Triple Crown. There was no game between the nations in 1885, and the match of 1886, in which E.T. Gurdon led England for the last time, ended in scoreless draw.

Gurdon had been the backbone of the England pack since 1878, graduated to the captaincy in December 1882, and led the side on nine occasions, never losing. He was a robust forward of strong character, and he led his men by example. Later he followed a successful career as a solicitor and was a President of the RFU. He retired as holder of the England cap record, having gained 16. His brother Charles Gurdon was in many of the successful sides of this period too.

A.E. Stoddart, later a noted cricketer, gained the distinction of scoring England's first goal from a mark with his kick in the 1886 match against Wales. C.H. Elliot made the fair catch and nominated Stoddart as kicker.

|  | 1886-87 | | | 1888-89 |
| --- | --- | --- | --- | --- |
|  | v. WALES | v. IRELAND | v. SCOTLAND | v. MAORIS |
| | †S. ROBERTS | S. ROBERTS | H.B. TRISTRAM | †A.V. ROYLE |
| | †J. LE FLEMING | W.N. BOLTON | W.N. BOLTON | †J.W. SUTCLIFFE 1c,1t |
| | R. ROBERTSHAW | †A.ST.L. FAGAN | R. ROBERTSHAW | A.E. STODDART 1t |
| | †R.E. LOCKWOOD | R.E. LOCKWOOD | R.E. LOCKWOOD | R.E. LOCKWOOD |
| | F. BONSOR | †M.T. SCOTT | F. BONSOR | †W.M. SCOTT |
| | *AL. ROTHERHAM | *AL. ROTHERHAM | *AL. ROTHERHAM | *F. BONSOR |
| | †J.L. HICKSON | J.L. HICKSON | J.L. HICKSON | †F. EVERSHED 1t |
| | †R.L. SEDDON | R.L. SEDDON | R.L. SEDDON | †D. JOWETT |
| | G.L. JEFFERY | G.L. JEFFERY | G.L. JEFFERY 1t | †C. ANDERTON |
| | †H.C. BAKER | A. TEGGIN | A. TEGGIN | †H.J. WILKINSON |
| | W.G. CLIBBORN | W.G. CLIBBORN | W.G. CLIBBORN | †H. BEDFORD 2t |
| | E. WILKINSON | A.T. KEMBLE | E. WILKINSON | †W. YIEND |
| | N. SPURLING | †F.E. PEASE | H.H. SPRINGMAN | †J.W. CAVE |
| | †J.H. DEWHURST | J.H. DEWHURST | J.H. DEWHURST | †F. LOWRIE |
| | †C.R. CLEVELAND | C.J.B. MARRIOTT | C.R. CLEVELAND | †A. ROBINSON |
| | Stradey Park | Lansdowne Road | Manchester | Blackheath |
| | DRAWN | LOST | DRAWN | WON |
| | WALES: NIL | IRE.: 2G | ENG.: 1T | ENG.: 1G 4T |
| | ENG.: NIL | ENG.: NIL | SCOT.: 1T | MAORIS: NIL |
| | 8 Jan. 1887 | 5 Feb. 1887 | 5 Mar. 1887 | 16 Feb. 1889 |

Alan Rotherham was England's captain for 1887, but the departure of several leading players had left him with an inexperienced side. As a younger player, Rotherham had demonstrated that halves ought to be an efficient link between forwards and threequarters. Instead of playing for himself, which was the inclination of contemporary opponents, Rotherham preferred to feed his centre-threequarter and became adept at executing the opportune pass, one which made space for an unmarked colleague to collect on the run. By his methods, Rotherham was the prototype of the ideal half and created the standard by which the qualities of later halves became measured.

The RFU's refusal to accept the conditions for a proposed International Board meant that England did not play the other Home Countries in 1888 or 1889. There was a match in 1889, however, against the colourful New Zealand Native side, and England, with a pack of nine new caps, mostly Northerners too, overcame the strong challenge of the Natives in an entertaining match.

|  | 1889-90 | | |
| --- | --- | --- | --- |
|  | v. WALES | v. SCOTLAND | v. IRELAND |
| | †W.G. MITCHELL | W.G. MITCHELL | W.G. MITCHELL |
| | †P.H. MORRISON | P.H. MORRISON | P.H. MORRISON 1t |
| | *A.E. STODDART | †R.L. ASTON | R.L. ASTON |
| | †J. VALENTINE | †J.W. DYSON 1t | *A.E. STODDART 1t |
| | †J. WRIGHT | M.T. SCOTT | M.T. SCOTT |
| | †F.H. FOX | F.H. FOX | †F.W. SPENCE |
| | F. EVERSHED | F. EVERSHED 1t | F. EVERSHED |
| | J.L. HICKSON | *J.L. HICKSON | J.L. HICKSON |
| | †S.M.J. WOODS | S.M.J. WOODS | S.M.J. WOODS |
| | †R.T.D. BUDWORTH | †J. TOOTHILL | J. TOOTHILL |
| | †J.H. ROGERS | J.H. ROGERS | J.H. ROGERS 1t |
| | P.F. HANCOCK | D. JOWETT 1c | D. JOWETT |
| | J.H. DEWHURST | H. BEDFORD | H. BEDFORD |
| | F. LOWRIE | †E. HOLMES | E. HOLMES |
| | A. ROBINSON | A. ROBINSON | A. ROBINSON |
| | Dewsbury | Raeburn Place | Blackheath |
| | LOST 0-1 | WON 6-0 | WON 3-0 |
| | ENG.: NIL | SCOT.: NIL | ENG.: 3T |
| | WALES: 1T | ENG.: 1G 1T | IRE.: NIL |
| | 15 Feb. 1890 | 1 Mar. 1890 | 15 Mar. 1890 |

With the international dispute happily settled, England resumed their home matches at Dewsbury against Wales. In windy, snowy conditions, defeat was suffered at the hands of Wales for the first time. The Welsh victory was due to a wily piece of play by one of their halves and Wright, the English half, became one of the first Englishmen to win just one cap and suffer defeat against the Welsh.

England recovered to regain a share in the Championship title, thanks to wins over Scotland and Ireland. A strong, reliable pack was forming around some notable newcomers: S.M.J. Woods, J.H. Rogers and J.T. Toothill. Woods was an Australian educated in Britain, and, like his skipper A.E. Stoddart, a noted cricketer. Rogers was the first player capped from the Moseley club, and a leading Midland player; while Toothill was a member of a very successful Yorkshire County side. Having earned fame in the rugby game, Toothill later became licensee of a number of Yorkshire hostelries.

Stoddart followed Hornby as a rugby player who captained England at both rugby football and cricket.

## 1890-91

| v. WALES | v. IRELAND | v. SCOTLAND |
|---|---|---|
| W.G. Mitchell | W.G. Mitchell | W.G. Mitchell |
| †P. Christopherson 2T | P.H. Morrison | P. Christopherson |
| *F.H.R. Alderson 2C | *F.H.R. Alderson | *F.H.R. Alderson 1C |
| R.E. Lockwood | R.E. Lockwood 2C,2T | R.E. Lockwood 1T |
| †W.R.M. Leake | W.R.M. Leake | W.R.M. Leake |
| †J. Berry | J. Berry | J. Berry |
| †E.G.H. North | E.G.H. North | E.G.H. North |
| †T. Kent | T. Kent | T. Kent |
| S.M.J. Woods | S.M.J. Woods | S.M.J. Woods |
| J. Toothill | J. Toothill 1T | †E. Bonham-Carter |
| †W.E. Bromet | W.E. Bromet | J.H. Rogers |
| D. Jowett | D. Jowett | D. Jowett |
| R.T.D. Budworth 1T | †L.J. Percival | R.T.D. Budworth |
| †J. Richards | J. Richards | J. Richards |
| †R.P. Wilson | R.P. Wilson 2T | R.P. Wilson |
| Newport | Lansdowne Road | Richmond |
| WON 7-3 | WON 9-0 | LOST 3-9 |
| WALES: 1G | IRE.: NIL | ENG.: 1G |
| ENG.: 2G 1T | ENG.: 2G 3T | SCOT.: 2G 1DG |
| 3 Jan. 1891 | 7 Feb. 1891 | 7 Mar. 1891 |

There was a promising start to the season, with easy wins over Wales and Ireland. Alderson, a product of the Hartlepool Rovers, was appointed captain on his international debut and contributed two fine conversions in the match with Wales. In Dublin, little Richard Lockwood was player of the afternoon, scoring two tries and placing two goals.

The English pack had been praised after their away victories but for the Triple Crown decider, the English forwards were routed and their backs displayed little enterprise. Scotland scored all of their points before a crowd of 15,000 had an English score to cheer.

So, a season which started encouragingly ended with the press describing this as the most disappointing side since 1871.

## 1891-92

| v. WALES | v. IRELAND | v. SCOTLAND |
|---|---|---|
| †W.B. Thomson | †S. Houghton | †T. Coop |
| †G.C. Hubbard 1T | G.C. Hubbard | J.W. Dyson |
| *F.H.R. Alderson 1C,1T | †J. Marsh | *F.H.R. Alderson |
| R.E. Lockwood 2C | R.E. Lockwood | R.E. Lockwood 1C |
| †C. Emmott | †E.W. Taylor | †H. Varley |
| †A. Briggs | A. Briggs | A. Briggs |
| F. Evershed 1T | F. Evershed 1T | F. Evershed |
| T. Kent | T. Kent | T. Kent |
| †A. Allport | *S.M.J. Woods 1C | S.M.J. Woods |
| J. Toothill | J. Toothill | J. Toothill |
| W.E. Bromet | W.E. Bromet | W.E. Bromet 1T |
| W. Yiend | W. Yiend | W. Yiend |
| †J. Pyke | L.J. Percival 1T | †H. Bradshaw |
| †W. Nichol 1T | †A. Ashworth | W. Nichol |
| †E. Bullough | E. Bullough | E. Bullough |
| Blackheath | Manchester | Raeburn Place |
| WON 17-0 | WON 7-0 | WON 5-0 |
| ENG.: 3G 1T | ENG.: 1G 1T | SCOT.: NIL |
| WALES: NIL | IRE.: NIL | ENG.: 1G |
| 2 Jan. 1892 | 6 Feb. 1892 | 5 Mar. 1892 |

This was England's *annus mirabilis*. The Triple Crown was regained, and a 17-0 win over Wales, followed by victories over the Irish and Scots, made England undisputed champions in a season in which they did not concede a point.

There were eight new caps under Alderson for the game against Wales, though it is worthy of note that only Lockwood and Briggs among the backs, and Evershed, Kent, Toothill, Bromet and Yiend among the forwards, played in each of the three matches. Of these five forwards, all but Evershed were playing in the North. Bromet was the captain of Yorkshire, County Champions in 1892, and he was a secure, intelligent forward who was a mainstay of the English packs of the 1890s.

The match against Scotland, despite its importance as a Triple Crown decider, was disappointing. There was too much protracted mauling and a number of fights broke out among the forwards, disrupting the fluency of the game. England fielded thirteen Northerners, and a single try – by Bromet – settled the match.

## 1892-93

| v. WALES | v. IRELAND | v. SCOTLAND |
|---|---|---|
| †E. Field | E. Field | W.G. Mitchell |
| *A.E. Stoddart 1c | J.W. Dyson | *A.E. Stoddart |
| F.H.R. Alderson | R.E. Lockwood | J.W. Dyson |
| R.E. Lockwood | †T. Nicholson | †F.P. Jones |
| †H. Marshall 3t | E.W. Taylor 1t | †C.M. Wells |
| †R.F. de Winton | †H. Duckett | H. Duckett |
| F. Evershed | F. Evershed | F. Evershed |
| †J.H. Greenwell | J.H. Greenwell | †F. Soane |
| S.M.J. Woods | *S.M.J. Woods | †J.J. Robinson |
| J. Toothill | J. Toothill | J. Toothill |
| W.E. Bromet | W.E. Bromet | W.E. Bromet |
| †F.C. Lohden 1t | W. Yiend | W. Yiend |
| H. Bradshaw | H. Bradshaw 1t | H. Bradshaw |
| †T. Broadley | A. Allport | T. Broadley |
| †P. Maud | P. Maud | L.J. Percival |
| Cardiff Arms Park | Lansdowne Road | Leeds |
| LOST 11-12 | WON 4-0 | LOST 0-8 |
| Wales: 1g 1pg 2t | Ire.: Nil | Eng.: Nil |
| Eng.: 1g 3t | Eng.: 2t | Scot.: 2dg |
| 7 Jan. 1893 | 4 Feb. 1893 | 4 Mar. 1893 |

Events off the field shadowed the playing exploits of the England team in 1893. The controversy concerning the payment of players' expenses for time off work and for travelling – Broken Time – reached its climax at the meeting of the RFU. A resolution favouring the compensation of players for loss of earnings failed to obtain a sufficient majority.

For the internationals, the English selectors proved more than usually fickle in their choices. Only Evershed, Toothill, Bromet and Bradshaw were retained for all three matches, and there was tremendous indecision concerning the halves: five different players appearing in three months. Howard Marshall, half-back against Wales, had the peculiar distinction of scoring all three tries in his one and only international appearance, and "Little Billy" Taylor scored one of England's two tries against Ireland before being discarded for the Scottish match. Later Taylor captained his country.

A.E. Stoddart, the England captain, played the last of his ten matches in the defeat by Scotland. During his international career he scored two tries, a conversion and a goal from a mark. A member of the Stock Exchange, he died tragically in 1915.

## 1893-94

| v. WALES | v. IRELAND | v. SCOTLAND |
|---|---|---|
| †J.F. Byrne | J.F. Byrne | J.F. Byrne |
| †F. Firth | F. Firth | F. Firth |
| †C.A. Hooper | C.A. Hooper | C.A. Hooper |
| †S. Morfitt 1t | S. Morfitt | S. Morfitt |
| *R.E. Lockwood 1t,3c | *R.E. Lockwood 1t | †W.J. Jackson |
| C.M. Wells | †R. Wood | C.M. Wells |
| E.W. Taylor 1gm,1t,1c | E.W. Taylor 1c | *E.W. Taylor |
| F. Soane | F. Soane | F. Soane |
| †J. Hall | J. Hall | J. Hall |
| J. Toothill | J. Toothill | †W. Walton |
| †H. Speed | H. Speed | H. Speed |
| †W.E. Tucker | W.E. Tucker | †A.E. Elliott |
| H. Bradshaw 1t | H. Bradshaw | H. Bradshaw |
| T. Broadley | T. Broadley | T. Broadley |
| A. Allport | A. Allport | A. Allport |
| Birkenhead | Blackheath | Raeburn Place |
| WON 24-3 | LOST 5-7 | LOST 0-6 |
| Eng.: 4g 1gm | Eng.: 1g | Scot.: 2t |
| Wales: 1t | Ire.: 1dg 1t | Eng.: Nil |
| 6 Jan. 1894 | 3 Feb. 1894 | 17 Mar. 1894 |

England adopted the Welsh example of playing four threequarters for 1894. Then, with a team containing seven new caps, they overran the Welsh with a fine display on a hard, frosty pitch at the Upper Park, Birkenhead (England's only international match staged in the town).

Once again the North, who had defeated the South in the annual Trial match, supplied the majority of the side, with nine of their players lining up under skipper Dickie Lockwood for the Welsh match. Lockwood's contribution to the win over Wales was matched by that of Taylor, the two players accounting for all but six of England's 24 points.

There were 20,000 present to see Ireland beat England at Blackheath. Lockwood, playing in his last match, scored a try which Taylor converted, but the spoiling tactics of the Irish forwards disrupted the Englishmen and victory for the Irish set them on target for their first Triple Crown.

England were not to find a threequarter of Lockwood's class for another decade. At the height of his career, he was described as "unquestionably the finest all-round threequarter of the present day".

## 1894-95

| v. WALES | v. IRELAND | v. SCOTLAND |
|---|---|---|
| †H. Ward | J.F. Byrne | J.F. Byrne 1PG |
| | | |
| †J.H.C. Fegan | J.H.C. Fegan 1T | J.H.C. Fegan |
| W.B. Thomson 1T | W.B. Thomson | W.B. Thomson |
| †F.A. Leslie-Jones 1T | F.A. Leslie-Jones | †T.H. Dobson |
| †E.M. Baker | E.M. Baker | E.M. Baker |
| | | |
| †R.H.B. Cattell | R.H.B. Cattell | R.H.B. Cattell |
| E.W. Taylor | E.W. Taylor | E.W. Taylor |
| | | |
| †G.M. Carey 1T | G.M. Carey | G.M. Carey |
| *S.M.J. Woods 1T | *S.M.J. Woods | *S.M.J. Woods |
| †H.W. Finlinson | H.W. Finlinson | H.W. Finlinson |
| W.E. Bromet | W.E. Bromet | W.E. Bromet |
| W.E. Tucker | W.E. Tucker | W.E. Tucker |
| †F. Mitchell 1C | F. Mitchell | F. Mitchell |
| †F.O. Poole | F.O. Poole | F.O. Poole |
| †C. Thomas | C. Thomas 1T | C. Thomas |
| | | |
| St. Helens | Lansdowne Road | Richmond |
| WON 14-6 | WON 6-3 | LOST 3-6 |
| | | |
| WALES: 2T | IRE.: 1T | ENG.: 1PG |
| ENG.: 1G 3T | ENG.: 2T | SCOT.: 1PG 1T |
| | | |
| 5 Jan. 1895 | 2 Feb. 1895 | 9 Mar. 1895 |

The feature of the English team in 1895 was their strong pack. The team started slowly in the matches with Wales and Ireland, but thanks to superior scrummaging and fitness were able to become dominant in the tight and provide the foundations for wins.

The showdown of the season was at Richmond, where the English met the unbeaten Scots in a contest to decide the Triple Crown. Severe frost in February and early March had curtailed rugby football in England, with the result that several of the English team were not completely match fit. Nevertheless, before 20,000 people, the Scots displayed superior form throughout a tight match and won by three points.

All of the scoring occurred in the first half. Byrne, the England full-back, landed a penalty (against the run of play) to open the scoring before a similar score tied the points. An astute kick-ahead shortly before half-time caused Byrne difficulty, and the Scottish threequarters took their chance to score a winning try.

## 1895-96

| v. WALES | v. IRELAND | v. SCOTLAND |
|---|---|---|
| S. Houghton | J.F. Byrne 1DG | †R.W. Poole |
| | | |
| S. Morfitt 2T | S. Morfitt | S. Morfitt |
| J. Valentine 1C | J. Valentine | J. Valentine |
| E.M. Baker | E.M. Baker | E.M. Baker |
| †E.F. Fookes 2T | E.F. Fookes | E.F. Fookes |
| | | |
| R.H.B. Cattell 2T | R.H.B. Cattell | R.H.B. Cattell |
| *E.W. Taylor 1C | *E.W. Taylor | C.M. Wells |
| | | |
| G.M. Carey | G.M. Carey | †G.E. Hughes |
| †J. Pinch | J. Pinch | †J.H. Barron |
| †A. Starks | A. Starks | †E. Knowles |
| †L.F. Giblin | L.F. Giblin | H. Speed |
| †J. Rhodes | J. Rhodes | J. Rhodes |
| F. Mitchell 1T | F. Mitchell | *F. Mitchell |
| †J.W. Ward | J.W. Ward | J.W. Ward |
| †W. Whiteley | W.E. Bromet | T. Broadley |
| | | |
| Blackheath | Leeds | Glasgow |
| WON 25-0 | LOST 4-10 | LOST 0-11 |
| | | |
| ENG.: 2G 5T | ENG.: 1DG | SCOT.: 1G 2T |
| WALES: NIL | IRE.: 2G | ENG.: NIL |
| | | |
| 4 Jan. 1896 | 1 Feb. 1896 | 14 Mar. 1896 |

Professionalism in any form had been outlawed by the RFU at their meeting in September 1895, and by-laws were adopted to govern the structure of the game. These laws affected the administration of the game in the north and the result was a breakaway and formation of a Northern Union – later the Rugby League.

The annual North-South match was a truimph for the North, and ten of the side which met Wales were northerners, though several were later to join clubs in the rebel Northern Union. Houghton, the full-back, was an interesting example. He had been capped from Runcorn in 1892, but when he played against Wales this season he had transferred to Birkenhead Wanderers. He was selected for the following match with Ireland, by which time he had rejoined Runcorn, now a Northern Union member. He was promptly discarded.

England's first international following the split resulted in a rousing win over Wales, and suggested that England could fare well without the outlawed players. But disappointing performances against the Irish and Scots showed that such hopes were probably unjustified.

England had to wait until 1910 before winning the Championship again.

## 1896-97

| v. WALES | v. IRELAND | v. SCOTLAND |
|---|---|---|
| J.F. Byrne | J.F. Byrne 2pg | J.F. Byrne 1c,1dg |
| †F.A. Byrne | †G.C. Robinson 1t | G.C. Robinson 1t |
| †T. Fletcher | †W.L. Bunting | W.L. Bunting |
| E.M. Baker | †J.T. Taylor | †O.G. Mackie |
| E.F. Fookes | E.F. Fookes | E.F. Fookes 1t |
| C.M. Wells | †S. Northmore | C.M. Wells |
| *E.W. Taylor | *E.W. Taylor | *E.W. Taylor |
| †F. Jacob | F. Jacob | F. Jacob |
| J.H. Barron | J.H. Barron | J. Pinch |
| †P.J. Ebdon | P.J. Ebdon | E. Knowles |
| †R.F. Oakes | R.F. Oakes | R.F. Oakes |
| †W.B. Stoddart | W.B. Stoddart | W.B. Stoddart |
| †F.M. Stout | F.M. Stout | †H.W. Dudgeon |
| †W. Ashford | W. Ashford | L.F. Giblin |
| †R.H. Mangles | R.H. Mangles | †Jas Davidson |
| Newport | Lansdowne Road | Manchester |
| LOST 0-11 | LOST 9-13 | WON 12-3 |
| WALES: 1G 2T | IRE.: 1GM 3T | ENG.: 1G 1DG 1T |
| ENG.: NIL | ENG.: 2PG 1T | SCOT.: 1T |
| 9 Jan. 1897 | 6 Feb. 1897 | 13 Mar. 1897 |

It was perhaps a sign of the times that, for the match with Wales to open the 1897 season, there were fewer than half the England team from the powerful North. There were, too, as many as 25 players used in the three matches, with sixteen new caps awarded.

Two Northumbrians, Robinson and Taylor (E.W.) were the outstanding players in a season which started with two disappointing defeats before a surprise recovery was staged against Scotland in March. Robinson began his short England career this season. He scored tries in each of his first five matches, and eight in his eight-match career. Robinson was a scratch golfer, a leading Northumberland businessman and later a President of the RFU. E.W. Taylor was also a fine all-round sportsman, and was later a golf pro. This was his last season in the England side, and he led the team to a famous victory in his final game.

The win over Scotland brought the Calcutta Cup to England for the first time for four years. The English pack was able to establish a sound platform in the tight and supply their backs with an ample amount of good possession. Both of the English tries came from the wingers. Scotland had been so confident of victory that they had not brought the Calcutta Cup to Manchester.

## 1897-98

| v. IRELAND | v. SCOTLAND | v. WALES |
|---|---|---|
| *J.F. Byrne 1pg | *J.F. Byrne | *J.F. Byrne 1c |
| G.C. Robinson 1t | †P.W. Stout | P.W. Stout 1t |
| W.L. Bunting | W.L. Bunting | W.L. Bunting |
| O.G. Mackie | †P.M.R. Royds 1t | P.M.R. Royds |
| E.F. Fookes | †W.N. Pilkington | E.F. Fookes 2t |
| †H. Myers | †G.T. Unwin | †R. O'H. Livesay |
| †P.G. Jacob | †Ar. Rotherham | Ar. Rotherham |
| F. Jacob | F. Jacob | F. Jacob |
| †R. Pierce | †J.F. Shaw | J.F. Shaw |
| †F. Shaw | †H.E. Ramsden | H.E. Ramsden |
| R.F. Oakes | R.F. Oakes | R.F. Oakes |
| H.W. Dudgeon | H.W. Dudgeon | H.W. Dudgeon |
| F.M. Stout | F.M. Stout | F.M. Stout 1t |
| †J.H. Blacklock | W. Ashford | W. Ashford |
| †C.E. Wilson | Jas Davidson | Jas Davidson |
| Richmond | Powderhall | Blackheath |
| LOST 6-9 | DRAWN 3-3 | WON 14-7 |
| ENG.: 1PG 1T | SCOT.: 1T | ENG.: 1G 3T |
| IRE.: 1PG 2T | ENG.: 1T | WALES: 1DG 1T |
| 5 Feb. 1898 | 12 Mar. 1898 | 2 Apr. 1898 |

1898 was a season of mixed fortunes for England, with a win, a draw and a loss from three matches. There were difficulties fielding a balanced, steady fifteen, and only six of the players kept their places throughout the season.

J.F. Byrne was the England captain. He was the senior man in an inexperienced side, and his expertise, tactically and technically, was an inspiration to the younger men who played in front of him. He had gained his reputation as a splendid defensive player on the 1896 British tour to South Africa, where he had appeared in every match. Later he was to become a noted industrialist in the Midlands.

The Welsh match, played in April at Blackheath, was to be England's last victory over the Principality for twelve years. As one historian reviewing the 1898 season subsequently wrote, "English rugby was in a bad state, but worse was in store."

## 1898-99

| v. WALES | v. IRELAND | v. SCOTLAND |
| --- | --- | --- |
| †H.T. GAMLIN | J.F. BYRNE | H.T. GAMLIN |
| G.C. ROBINSON 1T | †S. ANDERSON | †J.C. MATTERS |
| P.W. STOUT | P.W. STOUT | P.W. STOUT |
| P.M.R. ROYDS | J.T. TAYLOR | W.L. BUNTING |
| †R. FORREST | E.F. FOOKES | E.F. FOOKES |
| R.O'H. LIVESAY | E.W. TAYLOR | †R.O. SCHWARZ |
| *AR. ROTHERHAM | *AR. ROTHERHAM | *AR. ROTHERHAM |
| F. JACOB | F. JACOB | †R.F.A. HOBBS |
| †G.R. GIBSON | †J.H. SHOOTER | J.H. SHOOTER |
| †J. DANIELL | †A.J.L. DARBY | †A.O. DOWSON |
| R.F. OAKES | C. THOMAS | R.F. OAKES |
| H.W. DUDGEON | H.W. DUDGEON | H.W. DUDGEON |
| †W. MORTIMER | F.M. STOUT | F.M. STOUT |
| †JOS DAVIDSON | J.H. BLACKLOCK | JOS DAVIDSON |
| †C.H. HARPER | JAS DAVIDSON | JAS DAVIDSON |
| St. Helens | Lansdowne Road | Blackheath |
| LOST 3-26 | LOST 0-6 | LOST 0-5 |
| WALES: 4G 2T | IRE.: 1PG 1T | ENG.: NIL |
| ENG.: 1T | ENG.: NIL | SCOT.: 1G |
| 7 Jan. 1899 | 4 Feb. 1899 | 11 Mar. 1899 |

The critics were hard on the England packs of 1899: former player Arthur Budd called them a "rustic collection" and *The Times* referred to the northern element in the pack as "delinquents". For the first time England lost all three matches, and only one try was scored during the season.

The Welsh, starting out on their Golden Era, registered a large win at Swansea and Ireland's victory in Dublin was the first leg of a Triple Crown triumph. England did well to hold the Scots to a goal before 25,000 at Blackheath, and fielded two pairs of brothers in the side: the Stouts of Gloucester and the Cumbrian brothers Davidson.

J.C. Matters, who appeared against Scotland, was considered one of the most splendid centres of the age. Oddly, he was selected to play on the wing in his sole international game, and he had the misfortune to knock forward a pass from which he should have secured a try.

## 1899-1900

| v. WALES | v. IRELAND | v. SCOTLAND |
| --- | --- | --- |
| H.T. GAMLIN | H.T. GAMLIN | H.T. GAMLIN |
| †S.F. COOPPER | G.C. ROBINSON 2T | G.C. ROBINSON |
| †G.W. GORDON- | G.W. GORDON- | G.W. GORDON- |
| SMITH | SMITH 1DG,1T | SMITH |
| †A.T. BRETTARGH | J.T. TAYLOR | W.L. BUNTING |
| †E.T. NICHOLSON 1T | E.T. NICHOLSON | R. FORREST |
| *R.H.B. CATTELL | †J.C. MARQUIS | J.C. MARQUIS |
| †G.H. MARSDEN | G.H. MARSDEN | G.H. MARSDEN |
| †J. BAXTER | J. BAXTER | J. BAXTER |
| †A. COCKERHAM | J.H. SHOOTER | J.H. SHOOTER |
| †J.W. JARMAN | *J. DANIELL | *J. DANIELL |
| †C.T. SCOTT | C.T. SCOTT | †A.F.C.C. LUXMOORE |
| †F.J. BELL | †H. ALEXANDER 1C | H. ALEXANDER |
| †R.W. BELL | R.W. BELL | R.W. BELL |
| †S. REYNOLDS | S. REYNOLDS | S. REYNOLDS |
| †W. COBBY | †A.F. TODD | A.F. TODD |
| Gloucester | Richmond | Inverleith |
| LOST 3-13 | WON 15-4 | DRAWN 0-0 |
| WALES: 2G 1PG | ENG.: 1G 1DG 2T | SCOT.: NIL |
| ENG.: 1T | IRE.: 1DG | ENG.: NIL |
| 6 Jan. 1900 | 3 Feb. 1900 | 10 Mar. 1900 |

England introduced 13 new caps for the start of the 1900 season. Two of the new men, Coopper and Baxter, were to serve various RFU committees for many years. Baxter became Chairman of the England selection committee, where his sound judgment and wide experience were considerable assets, and Coopper served the RFU as Secretary from 1924 to 1947.

After Wales had won decisively in the only international match to have been staged in Gloucester, John Daniell of Cambridge and Somerset became captain and England beat Ireland comfortably before playing a scoreless draw with the Scots.

A crowd of 20,000 were present to see England make their first appearance at Inverleith, the new international ground of the Scottish Rugby Union. Two well-matched sides met in perfect conditions, and for English supporters there was the encouragement of seeing their pack hold the Scottish eight in the tight and loose. Indeed, it was the opinion of many pundits that England should have won the match, and their halves were criticised for failing to make greater use of their threequarters.

## 1900-01

| v. WALES | v. IRELAND | v. SCOTLAND |
|---|---|---|
| †J.W. Sagar | J.W. Sagar | H.T. Gamlin |
| | | |
| †C. Smith | G.C. Robinson 1t | G.C. Robinson 1t |
| †E.J. Vivyan | *W.L. Bunting | *W.L. Bunting |
| *J.T. Taylor | J.T. Taylor | N.S. Cox |
| †E.W. Elliot | E.W. Elliot | E.W. Elliot |
| | | |
| R.O. Schwarz | R.O. Schwarz | †B. Oughtred |
| †E.J. Walton | E.J. Walton | †P.D. Kendall |
| | | |
| †A. O'Neill | A. O'Neill | A. O'Neill |
| †D. Graham | †R.D. Wood | G.R. Gibson |
| A.F.C.C. Luxmoore | †C. Hall | C. Hall |
| C.T. Scott | C.T. Scott | †H.T.F. Weston |
| H. Alexander | H. Alexander 1pg | H. Alexander |
| †N.C. Fletcher | N.C. Fletcher | N.C. Fletcher |
| †C.O.P. Gibson | S. Reynolds | †C.S. Edgar |
| †E.W. Roberts | E.W. Roberts | †B.C. Hartley |
| | | |
| Cardiff Arms Park | Lansdowne Road | Blackheath |
| LOST 0-13 | LOST 6-10 | LOST 3-18 |
| | | |
| WALES: 2G 1T | IRE.: 2G | ENG.: 1T |
| ENG.: NIL | ENG.: 1PG 1T | SCOT.: 3G 1T |
| | | |
| 5 Jan. 1901 | 9 Feb. 1901 | 9 Mar. 1901 |

England used 28 players in 1901, when the improvement shown in the previous season was not maintained. Only four players kept their places throughout the season, Elliot on the wing and Fletcher, Alexander and O'Neill (the first international from Torquay) among the forwards.

Bunting and Gamlin, who only played against Scotland, were the leading English backs of the season. Bunting was a master at Bromsgrove School at this time, and played regularly for the Moseley club. His stylish play and unobtrusive leadership were qualities which impressed the selectors and his final English caps, against the Irish and Scots, were won as captain of the side.

Gamlin was the outstanding English full-back of the era and enhanced his reputation with an impressive display against Scotland. He was a tall and powerful player with a strong tackle which offered no hope of escape to its victim.

## 1901-02

| v. WALES | v. IRELAND | v. SCOTLAND |
|---|---|---|
| H.T. Gamlin | H.T. Gamlin | H.T. Gamlin |
| | | |
| †P.L. Nicholas | R. Forrest | R. Forrest |
| †J.E. Raphael | J.E. Raphael | J.E. Raphael |
| J.T. Taylor | J.T. Taylor | J.T. Taylor 1t |
| S.F. Coopper | S.F. Coopper 1t | †T. Simpson |
| | | |
| B. Oughtred | B. Oughtred | B. Oughtred |
| P.D. Kendall | E.J. Walton | E.J. Walton |
| | | |
| †G. Fraser | G. Fraser | G. Fraser |
| J.J. Robinson 1t | J.J. Robinson | J.J. Robinson |
| †T.H. Willcocks | *J. Daniell | *J. Daniell |
| †L.R. Tosswill | L.R. Tosswill | L.R. Tosswill |
| *H. Alexander 1c | H. Alexander | B.C. Hartley |
| †D.D. Dobson 1t | D.D. Dobson | D.D. Dobson |
| †J. Jewitt | †P.F. Hardwick | P.F. Hardwick |
| †S.G. Williams | S.G. Williams 1t | S.G. Williams 1t |
| | | |
| Blackheath | Leicester | Inverleith |
| LOST 8-9 | WON 6-3 | WON 6-3 |
| | | |
| ENG.: 1G 1T | ENG.: 2T | SCOT.: 1T |
| WALES: 1PG 2T | IRE.: 1T | ENG.: 2T |
| | | |
| 11 Jan. 1902 | 8 Feb. 1902 | 15 Mar. 1902 |

England's form showed a welcome improvement in 1902, victories over Ireland and Scotland following a narrow and unlucky defeat by Wales. Only the antics of the Welsh scrum-half allowed Wales to poach victory in the dying moments of the match. Oughtred was lured into an offside tackle at a scrummage near the English posts and Wales converted the resulting penalty to win by a point.

Few changes were made during the season, though the return of Daniell as skipper strengthened the English pack and added direction to the tactical approach. The experiment of playing an international in the Midlands (at Leicester against Ireland) was described as successful.

The match against Scotland was played in a strong wind, and England built a lead of two tries before facing the elements in the second half. Scotland tried desperately to win after the interval, but a particularly determined performance by Gamlin saved England's line.

## 1902-03

| v. WALES | v. IRELAND | v. SCOTLAND |
|---|---|---|
| H.T. Gamlin | H.T. Gamlin | H.T. Gamlin |
| †J.H. Miles | R. Forrest | T. Simpson |
| J.T. Taylor 1c | J.T. Taylor | †E.I.M. Barrett |
| †R.H. Spooner | A.T. Brettargh | A.T. Brettargh |
| T. Simpson | T. Simpson | R. Forrest 1t |
| *B. Oughtred | *B. Oughtred | †W.V. Butcher |
| †F.C. Hulme | F.C. Hulme | *P.D. Kendall |
| G. Fraser | G. Fraser | N.C. Fletcher |
| R.D. Wood | R.D. Wood | R. Pierce |
| †V.H. Cartwright | V.H. Cartwright | V.H. Cartwright |
| R.F.A. Hobbs | †W.G. Heppell | F.M. Stout |
| †R. Bradley | †B.A. Hill | B.A. Hill |
| D.D. Dobson 1t | D.D. Dobson | D.D. Dobson 1t |
| P.F. Hardwick | P.F. Hardwick | P.F. Hardwick |
| †J. Duthie | S.G. Williams | S.G. Williams |
| St. Helens | Lansdowne Road | Richmond |
| LOST 5-21 | LOST 0-6 | LOST 6-10 |
| WALES: 3G 2T | IRE.: 1PG 1T | ENG.: 2T |
| ENG.: 1G | ENG.: NIL | SCOT.: 1DG 2T |
| 10 Jan. 1903 | 14 Feb. 1903 | 21 Mar. 1903 |

Three defeats from three matches was again England's miserable return in 1903. Selection was fickle with 26 players taking part and only five appearing in each match. Of the newcomers, Cartwright and Hill were to become prominent forwards later in the decade, and both were to lead England.

Among the forwards, Dobson was one of three to play throughout the season. He had the misfortune to be gored by a charging rhinoceros in 1916, whilst serving as a Colonial Officer in Nyasaland. There is a legend that his former schoolmaster, hearing of Dobson's demise, stated that he had always had a weak hand-off.

Several members of the England party which travelled to Dublin for the Irish match are believed to have contracted typhoid fever during their visit. Forrest, a player, and R.S. Whalley of the RFU Committee died of the fever. Oughtred, the captain, was luckier, recovering to lead a successful career as a naval architect.

## 1903-04

| v. WALES | v. IRELAND | v. SCOTLAND |
|---|---|---|
| H.T. Gamlin 1PG | H.T. Gamlin | H.T. Gamlin |
| E.J. Vivyan | E.J. Vivyan 2t,2c | E.J. Vivyan 1t |
| A.T. Brettargh 1t | A.T. Brettargh | A.T. Brettargh |
| †E.W. Dillon | E.W. Dillon | E.W. Dillon |
| E.W. Elliot 2t | T. Simpson 1t | T. Simpson |
| †P.S. Hancock | P.S. Hancock | P.S. Hancock |
| W.V. Butcher | W.V. Butcher | W.V. Butcher |
| †G.H. Keeton | G.H. Keeton | G.H. Keeton |
| †J.G. Milton | J.G. Milton | J.G. Milton |
| V.H. Cartwright | *J. Daniell | *J. Daniell |
| *F.M. Stout 1c | F.M. Stout | F.M. Stout |
| B.A. Hill | B.A. Hill | V.H. Cartwright |
| †N.J. Moore | N.J. Moore 2t | N.J. Moore |
| P.F. Hardwick | P.F. Hardwick | P.F. Hardwick |
| †C.J. Newbold | C.J. Newbold | C.J. Newbold |
| Leicester | Blackheath | Inverleith |
| DRAWN 14-14 | WON 19-0 | LOST 3-6 |
| ENG.: 1G 1PG 2T | ENG.: 2G 3T | SCOT.: 2T |
| WALES: 2G 1GM | IRE.: NIL | ENG.: 1T |
| 9 Jan. 1904 | 13 Feb. 1904 | 19 Mar. 1904 |

The season of 1904 was England's best for many years, and started with an entertaining draw against Wales. A late goal from a mark by the Welsh full-back and some appalling place-kicking by Vivyan, just robbed England of a rare victory over the Welshmen.

John Daniell, in his last season in the side, returned to skipper the team to a large win over Ireland. Daniell was to become an influential RFU Committee member, and his shrewd sporting judgment was a valuable asset to England rugby and cricket selectors for many years.

The disappointment of the season was the narrow failure to beat Scotland in Edinburgh, for victory would have earned England the Championship. Scotland won a protracted forward battle, the English backs were disappointing, and the home side deserved to win by a larger margin.

## 1904-05

| v. WALES | v. IRELAND | v. SCOTLAND |
|---|---|---|
| †S.H. Irvin | †C.F. Stanger-Leathes | J.T. Taylor |
| †F.H. Palmer | T. Simpson | T. Simpson |
| J.E. Raphael | †H.E. Shewring | J.E. Raphael |
| E.W. Dillon | A.T. Brettargh | A.T. Brettargh |
| S.F. Coopper | S.F. Coopper 1t | S.F. Coopper |
| W.V. Butcher | W.V. Butcher | †A.D. Stoop |
| F.C. Hulme | F.C. Hulme | W.V. Butcher |
| †T.A. Gibson | †J. Green | T.A. Gibson |
| †W.L.Y. Rogers | W.L.Y. Rogers | J.G. Milton |
| V.H. Cartwright | V.H. Cartwright | V.H. Cartwright |
| *F.M. Stout | *F.M. Stout | *F.M. Stout |
| B.A. Hill | †G. Vickery | †S.H. Osborne |
| †W.T.C. Cave | †W.M. Grylls | †C.E.L. Hammond |
| †J.L. Mathias | J.L. Mathias | J.L. Mathias |
| C.J. Newbold | C.J. Newbold | CJ. Newbold |
| Cardiff Arms Park | Cork | Richmond |
| LOST 0-25 | LOST 3-17 | LOST 0-8 |
| WALES: 2G 5T | IRE.: 1G 4T | ENG.: NIL |
| ENG.: NIL | ENG.: 1T | SCOT.: 1G 1T |
| 14 Jan. 1905 | 11 Feb. 1905 | 18 Mar. 1905 |

The England side was the weakest in the Championship of 1905, and the season proved one of the most gloomy in history. Players were criticised for a failure to become match fit; the team was pedestrian in attack and vulnerable in defence.

27 players were used in the three matches and it will be noted that, following the retirement of Gamlin, a different full-back was used in each match. Two of the backs, Coopper and Butcher, were consistent and held their positions through the season, and there were three forwards to do likewise: the promising Cartwright, the veteran Frank Stout (as captain) and Newbold.

For the match against Ireland at Cork, it was noted that the team travelled from Dublin to Cork in third-class railway compartments. The RFU were severely criticised for their travel arrangements in the press, one leading critic, writing later, stating that the journey was a byword for discomfort and lack of organisation.

## 1905-06

| v. NZ | v. WALES | v. IRELAND | v. SCOTLAND | v. FRANCE |
|---|---|---|---|---|
| †E.J. Jackett | E.J. Jackett | E.J. Jackett | E.J. Jackett | E.J. Jackett |
| †H.M. Imrie | A.E. Hind | †J.E. Hutchinson | J.E. Raphael 1t | J.E. Raphael |
| †R.E. Godfray | J.E. Raphael | †J.R.P. Sandford | H.E. Shewring | H.E. Shewring |
| H.E. Shewring | H.E. Shewring | †C.H. Milton | †J.G.G. Birkett | J.G.G. Birkett |
| †A.E. Hind | †A. Hudson 1t | A. Hudson | T. Simpson 1t | A. Hudson 4t |
| J.E. Raphael | D.R. Gent | D.R. Gent | †J. Peters | J. Peters 1t |
| †D.R. Gent | †R.A. Jago | R.A. Jago 1t | A.D. Stoop | A.D. Stoop 1t |
| †J. Braithwaite | | | | |
| | †G.E.B. Dobbs | G.E.B. Dobbs | J. Green | J. Green |
| †G. Summerscales | †H.A. Hodges | H.A. Hodges | †R. Dibble | R. Dibble |
| *V.H. Cartwright | *V.H. Cartwright | *V.H. Cartwright | *V.H. Cartwright | *V.H. Cartwright 4c |
| †R.F. Russell | †T.S. Kelly | T.S. Kelly | T.S. Kelly | T.S. Kelly |
| B.A. Hill | †A.L. Kewney | A.L. Kewney | A.L. Kewney | A.L. Kewney 1t |
| C.E.L. Hammond | C.E.L. Hammond | C.E.L. Hammond | C.E.L. Hammond | C.E.L. Hammond |
| J.L. Mathias | †W.A. Mills | W.A. Mills 1t | W.A. Mills 1t | W.A. Mills 1t |
| E.W. Roberts | E.W. Roberts | E.W. Roberts | †C.H. Shaw | †T.B. Hogarth 1t |
| Crystal Palace | Richmond | Leicester | Inverleith | Parc des Princes |
| LOST 0-15 | LOST 3-16 | LOST 6-16 | WON 9-3 | WON 35-8 |
| ENG.: NIL | ENG.: 1T | ENG.: 2T | SCOT.: 1T | FR.: 1G 1T |
| NZ: 5T | WALES: 2G 2T | IRE.: 2G 2T | ENG.: 3T | ENG.: 4G 5T |
| 2 Dec. 1905 | 13 Jan. 1906 | 10 Feb. 1906 | 17 Mar. 1906 | 22 Mar. 1906 |

Two new opponents were added to the fixture list for 1905-06, England losing at the Crystal Palace to the First All Blacks from New Zealand, and winning, at the end of the season, the first international played against France.

Cartwright led England throughout the season and in Jackett England at last found a worthy successor at full-back to Gamlin. Nevertheless, in the Championship, only a win over Scotland broke England's long run of disaster on the field, ending a series of seven defeats. England's win was completely deserved on the day's play, and Peters, the first coloured man to play for England, made a pleasing debut at half-back.

Among the new caps, John Birkett and Bob Dibble enjoyed distinguished rugby careers. Both were excellent players and inspiring leaders who were later invited to captain England. Birkett, the son of a former international, retired in 1912, having established a new record for appearances (with 21). Dibble, a West Countryman, was a farmer who played for Newport in the years following the Great War. In the French match, Hudson's four tries created a new record for an Englishman.

## 1906-07

| v. S.AFRICA | v. FRANCE | v. WALES | v. IRELAND | v. SCOTLAND |
|---|---|---|---|---|
| E.J. Jackett | †H. Lee | E.J. Jackett | E.J. Jackett | E.J. Jackett |
| †F.G. Brooks 1t | †T.B. Batchelor | †F.S. Scott | †W.C. Wilson | W.C. Wilson |
| H.E. Shewring | H.E. Shewring 1t | H.E. Shewring | H.E. Shewring | H.E. Shewring |
| J.G.G. Birkett | J.G.G. Birkett 1dg,1t | J.G.G. Birkett | †A.S. Pickering 1pg | J.G.G. Birkett |
| T. Simpson | †D. Lambert 5t | S.F. Coopper | H.M. Imrie 1t | †A.W. Newton |
| A.D. Stoop | A.D. Stoop | A.D. Stoop | J. Peters | J. Peters 1t |
| R.A. Jago | †T.G. Wedge | R.A. Jago | R.A. Jago | †S.P. Start |
| J. Green | J. Green | J. Green | *J. Green | J. Green |
| R. Dibble | †F.J.V. Hopley | F.J.V. Hopley | J.G. Milton | †G.D. Roberts |
| *V.H. Cartwright | †W.M.B. Nanson 1t | W.M.B. Nanson | †G. Leather | *E.W. Roberts |
| T.S. Kelly | T.S. Kelly | T.S. Kelly | T.S. Kelly | T.S. Kelly |
| B.A. Hill | *B.A. Hill 5c | *B.A. Hill | S.G. Williams | S.G. Williams |
| †A. Alcock | †L.A.N. Slocock 1t | L.A.N. Slocock | L.A.N. Slocock 1t | L.A.N. Slocock |
| W.A. Mills | W.A. Mills | W.A. Mills | W.A. Mills | W.A. Mills |
| C.H. Shaw | C.H. Shaw | C.H. Shaw | C.H. Shaw | C.H. Shaw |
| Crystal Palace | Richmond | St. Helens | Lansdowne Road | Blackheath |
| DRAWN 3-3 | WON 41-13 | LOST 0-22 | LOST 9-17 | LOST 3-8 |
| ENG.: 1T | ENG.: 5G 1DG 4T | WALES: 2G 4T | IRE.: 1G 1GM 3T | ENG.: 1T |
| SA: 1T | FR.: 2G 1PG | ENG.: NIL | ENG.: 1PG 2T | SCOT.: 1G 1T |
| 8 Dec. 1906 | 5 Jan. 1907 | 12 Jan. 1907 | 9 Feb. 1907 | 16 Mar. 1907 |

England made a promising start this season, holding the First Springboks to a draw on a boggy pitch at Crystal Palace, and running up a big win over the French. But they failed to match this early promise in the remaining games, and defeats were suffered at the hands of the other Home nations.

There is an interesting tale in connecton with the selection of the side to meet the South Africans. It is believed that Alcock, a medical student at Guy's, won his cap owing to a clerical error, and at the expense of Slocock, who appeared later in the season.

Shewring, a sturdy centre, was the only back to play in every match, but four excellent forwards, Green of Skipton, Shaw, Kelly and Mills, by their sturdy scrummaging, held their places during the season. Altogether, nine members of the Devon County side were capped this season.

## 1907-08

| v. FRANCE | v. WALES | v. IRELAND | v. SCOTLAND |
|---|---|---|---|
| †A.E. Wood | A.E. Wood 2c | A.E. Wood 2c | †G.H. D'O Lyon |
| D. Lambert 1t | D. Lambert | W.N. Lapage | D. Lambert 2c |
| J.G.G. Birkett 1t | *J.G.G. Birkett 2t | J.G.G. Birkett | J.G.G. Birkett 1t |
| †W.N. Lapage 1t | W.N. Lapage 1t | †H.H. Vassall | W.N. Lapage |
| A. Hudson | A. Hudson | A. Hudson 2t | A. Hudson |
| †G.V. Portus 1t | J. Peters | G.V. Portus | †J. Davey |
| †H.J.H. Sibree | †R.H. Williamson 1t | R.H. Williamson 1t | R.H. Williamson |
| †E.L. Chambers | †R. Gilbert | R. Gilbert | R. Gilbert |
| †F. Boylen | F. Boylen | F. Boylen | F. Boylen |
| *T.S. Kelly | C.E.L. Hammond | *C.E.L Hammond | †T. Woods |
| G.D. Roberts 2c | G.D. Roberts 1c | T.S. Kelly | T.S. Kelly |
| L.A.N. Slocock | L.A.N. Slocock | L.A.N. Slocock | *L.A.N. Slocock 1t |
| R. Dibble | R. Dibble | R. Dibble | R. Dibble |
| W.A. Mills 1t | W.A. Mills | F.J.V. Hopley | †W.L. Oldham |
| †H. Havelock | H. Havelock | H. Havelock | †F.B. Watson |
| Stade Colombes | Bristol City AFC | Richmond | Inverleith |
| WON 19-0 | LOST 18-28 | WON 13-3 | LOST 10-16 |
| FR.: NIL | WALES: 3G 1DG 1PG 2T | ENG.: 2G 1T | SCOT.: 1G 2DG 1T |
| ENG.: 2G 3T | ENG.: 3G 1T | IRE.: 1PG | ENGL.: 2G |
| 1 Jan. 1908 | 18 Jan. 1908 | 8 Feb. 1908 | 21 Mar. 1908 |

England produced good back divisions for their matches of 1908. Wood, a full-back who later turned professional (and who is often confused with the 1904 Blue) was described as "a very fine player", and there were some prolific try-scorers on the wings in Lambert and Hudson. At scrum-half England was well served by Williamson, one of the first English half-backs to appreciate specialisation in his position. Birkett had become established at centre, and for the Irish match was paired with Vassall, the Oxford Blue. Much handicapped by injury, the Irish match was Vassall's solitary appearance for England.

An easy win over the French in Paris was followed by the only international to be staged at Bristol. On a foggy, damp afternoon, Wales won a match in which both fifteens frequently disappeared from sight. The play followed an entertaining, open pattern: a disappointment for the crowd who missed the spectacle of nine tries.

England were too strong for the Irish and travelled to Edinburgh with high hopes of regaining the Calcutta Cup. In a fascinating game, England started with promise before losing by six points.

## 1908-09

| v. AUSTRALIA | v. WALES | v. FRANCE | v. IRELAND | v. SCOTLAND |
|---|---|---|---|---|
| *G.H. D'O LYON | E.J. JACKETT | E.J. JACKETT 2C | E.J. JACKETT | E.J. JACKETT |
| | | | | |
| †E.R. MOBBS 1T | E.R. MOBBS | E.R. MOBBS 1T | †A.C. PALMER 1C,2T | A.C. PALMER 1C |
| †F.N. TARR | F.N. TARR | F.N. TARR 2T | †C.C.G. WRIGHT | C.C.G. WRIGHT |
| †E.W. ASSINDER | E.W. ASSINDER | †R.W. POULTON | R.W. POULTON | R.W. POULTON |
| B.B. BENNETTS | B.B. BENNETTS | T. SIMPSON 1T | E.R. MOBBS 1T | E.R. MOBBS 1T |
| | | | | |
| †A.H. ASHCROFT | T.G. WEDGE | †F. HUTCHINSON 1T | F. HUTCHINSON | F. HUTCHINSON |
| R.H. WILLIAMSON | J. DAVEY | R.H. WILLIAMSON | H.J.H. SIBREE | H.J.H. SIBREE |
| | | | | |
| †J.G. COOPER | J.G. COOPER | †C.A. BOLTON | †H.J.S. MORTON | H.J.S. MORTON |
| R. DIBBLE | *R. DIBBLE | *R. DIBBLE | *R. DIBBLE | *R. DIBBLE |
| A.L. KEWNEY | A.L. KEWNEY | A.L. KEWNEY | A.L. KEWNEY | A.L. KEWNEY |
| †S.H. PENNY | †W.A. JOHNS | W.A. JOHNS 1T | W.A. JOHNS | W.A. JOHNS |
| †A.D. WARRINGTON-MORRIS | A.D. WARRINGTON-MORRIS | A.D. WARRINGTON-MORRIS | †A.J. WILSON | †H.C. HARRISON |
| †F.P. KNIGHT | †E.D. IBBITSON | E.D. IBBITSON | E.D. IBBITSON | E.D. IBBITSON |
| †P.J DOWN | †F.G. HANDFORD | F.G. HANDFORD | F.G. HANDFORD | F.G. HANDFORD |
| W.L. OLDHAM | †H. ARCHER | H. ARCHER | H. ARCHER | F.B. WATSON 1T |
| | | | | |
| Blackheath | Cardiff Arms Park | Leicester | Lansdowne Road | Richmond |
| LOST 3-9 | LOST 0-8 | WON 22-0 | WON 11-5 | LOST 8-18 |
| | | | | |
| ENG.: 1T | WALES: 1G 1T | ENG.: 2G 4T | IRE.: 1G | ENG.: 1G 1T |
| AUST.: 3T | ENG.: NIL | FR.: NIL | ENG.: 1G 2T | SCOT.: 3G 1T |
| | | | | |
| 9 Jan. 1909 | 16 Jan. 1909 | 30 Jan. 1909 | 13 Feb. 1909 | 20 Mar. 1909 |

The general standard of play was improving in England in 1909. The RFU named ten new caps against Australia, a match which England lost and which was the last to be played at Blackheath. But there were sound wins against France and Ireland, and the English forwards were impressive in defeat at Cardiff, where England's performance was their best on Welsh soil since 1895.

The find of the season was Edgar Mobbs, who played in all five matches and scored tries in four. Surprisingly he only appeared for England on two further occasions, but he was a fine sportsman, outstanding threequarter, and a brave soldier when he died in action at Zillebeke in 1917.

Due to a delay in the building of stands at Twickenham, the RFU was obliged to stage the Scotland match at Richmond, the last international played at the Athletic Ground.

## 1909-10

| v. WALES | v. IRELAND | v. FRANCE | v. SCOTLAND |
|---|---|---|---|
| †W.R. JOHNSTON | W.R. JOHNSTON | †C.S. WILLIAMS | W.R. JOHNSTON |
| | | | |
| †F.E. CHAPMAN 1T,1PG,1C | F.E. CHAPMAN | F.E. CHAPMAN 1C | F.E. CHAPMAN 1C |
| †B. SOLOMON 1T | †L.W. HAYWARD | †A.A. ADAMS | †F.M. STOOP |
| J.G.G. BIRKETT | J.G.G. BIRKETT | A. HUDSON 2T | *J.G.G. BIRKETT 2T |
| R.W. POULTON | E.R. MOBBS | *E.R. MOBBS | †P.W. LAWRIE |
| | | | |
| *A.D. STOOP | *A.D. STOOP | †H. COVERDALE | A.D. STOOP |
| D.R. GENT | D.R. GENT | †A.L.H. GOTLEY | A.L.H. GOTLEY |
| | | | |
| H.J.S. MORTON | H.J.S. MORTON | †N.A. WODEHOUSE | R. DIBBLE |
| E.L. CHAMBERS | E.L. CHAMBERS | †J.A.S. RITSON | J.A.S. RITSON 1T |
| †H. BERRY | H. BERRY | H. BERRY 1T | H. BERRY 1T |
| W.A. JOHNS | W.A. JOHNS | W.A. JOHNS | †G.R. HIND |
| †L. HAIGH | L. HAIGH | †E.S. SCORFIELD | L. HAIGH |
| †L.E. BARRINGTON-WARD | L.E. BARRINGTON-WARD | L.E. BARRINGTON-WARD | L.E. BARRINGTON-WARD |
| †D.F. SMITH | D.F. SMITH | †R.H.M. HANDS | R.H.M. HANDS |
| †C.H. PILLMAN | C.H. PILLMAN | C.H. PILLMAN | C.H. PILLMAN |
| | | | |
| Twickenham | Twickenham | Parc des Princes | Inverleith |
| WON 11-6 | DRAWN 0-0 | WON 11-3 | WON 14-5 |
| | | | |
| ENG.: 1G 1PG 1T | ENG.: NIL | FR.: 1T | SCOT.: 1G |
| WALES: 2T | IRE.: NIL | ENG.: 1G 2T | ENG.: 1G 3T |
| | | | |
| 15 Jan. 1910 | 12 Feb. 1910 | 3 Mar. 1910 | 19 Mar. 1910 |

The Championship returned to England at last in 1910, the season in which Twickenham was first opened. The grounds had been acquired by the RFU in 1908 for £5573 and there was a sensational start to the international there against Wales, England scoring from the kick off. Their subsequent victory was the first against Wales since 1898.

The Harlequins club was a force in English rugby circles at this time, and led by Adrian Stoop, one of the finest tactical players of the age, the club played attractive, attacking football. It was splendid judgment on the part of the selectors to pick Stoop as the new English skipper, and give him two of his club colleagues, Birkett and Poulton, in the threequarter line.

Poulton played on the wing against Wales, but later became a more effective centre. Pillman, a new forward, was a key player in England's revival, his wing-forward methods disrupting the harmony of opposition halves.

## 1910-11

| v. WALES | v. FRANCE | v. IRELAND | v. SCOTLAND |
|---|---|---|---|
| †S.H. WILLIAMS | S.H. WILLIAMS | S.H. WILLIAMS | S.H. WILLIAMS |
| †A.D. ROBERTS 1T | A.D. ROBERTS | A.D. ROBERTS | A.D. ROBERTS |
| †J.A. SCHOLFIELD 1T | F.M. STOOP | F.M. STOOP | R.W. POULTON |
| *J.G.G. BIRKETT | *J.G.G. BIRKETT | *J.G.G. BIRKETT | J.G.G. BIRKETT 1T |
| D. LAMBERT 1C | D. LAMBERT 2T,2PG,5C | D. LAMBERT | P.W. LAWRIE 1T |
| A.D. STOOP | A.D. STOOP 1T | A.D. STOOP | A.D. STOOP |
| A.L.H. GOTLEY | A.L.H. GOTLEY | A.L.H. GOTLEY | *A.L.H. GOTLEY |
| R. DIBBLE | R. DIBBLE | G.R. HIND | R. DIBBLE |
| N.A. WODEHOUSE | N.A. WODEHOUSE 1T | N.A. WODEHOUSE | N.A. WODEHOUSE 1T |
| A.L. KEWNEY 1T | A.L. KEWNEY | A.L. KEWNEY | A.L. KEWNEY |
| †J.A. KING | J.A. KING | J.A. KING | J.A. KING |
| †W.E. MANN | W.E. MANN 1T | W.E. MANN | †R.O. LAGDEN 2C |
| L. HAIGH | L. HAIGH | L. HAIGH | L. HAIGH |
| †L.G. BROWN | L.G. BROWN | L.G. BROWN | L.G. BROWN |
| C.H. PILLMAN | C.H. PILLMAN 2T | C.H. PILLMAN | C.H. PILLMAN |
| St. Helen's | Twickenham | Lansdowne Road | Twickenham |
| LOST 11-15 | WON 37-0 | LOST 0-3 | WON 13-8 |
| WALES: 1PG 4T | ENG.: 5G 2PG 2T | IRE.: 1T | ENG.: 2G 1T |
| ENG.: 1G 2T | FR.: NIL | ENG.: NIL | SCOT.: 1G 1T |
| 21 Jan. 1911 | 28 Jan. 1911 | 11 Feb. 1911 | 18 Mar. 1911 |

England's revival continued in 1911, although the side failed to grasp its chances in the away matches at Swansea and Dublin, and narrow defeats ensued. Nevertheless, there was a bright new confidence in the players, the backs ran with panache, the halves played to their centres, and the pack, with Dibble, Wodehouse and Pillman in splendid form, were masters in all four matches.

Five of the seven backs were retained for each match, and there were five members of the Harlequins backs capped for England during the season, F.M. Stoop joining his brother Adrian for the French and Irish games.

The biggest win of the season was over France, and Lambert, who had registered five tries against them in 1907, notched 22 points to create a record for points scored in an England international match. He kicked five conversions, two penalties and touched-down two tries.

## 1911-12

| v. WALES | v. IRELAND | v. SCOTLAND | v. FRANCE |
|---|---|---|---|
| W.R. JOHNSTON | W.R. JOHNSTON | W.R. JOHNSTON | W.R. JOHNSTON |
| F.E. CHAPMAN 1C | A.D. ROBERTS 2T | A.D. ROBERTS | A.D. ROBERTS 1T |
| R.W. POULTON | R.W. POULTON 1T | R.W. POULTON | †M.E. NEALE |
| J.G.G. BIRKETT | J.G.G. BIRKETT 1T | J.G.G. BIRKETT | J.G.G. BIRKETT 1T |
| †H. BROUGHAM 1T | H. BROUGHAM 1T | H. BROUGHAM | H. BROUGHAM 1T |
| A.D. STOOP | H. COVERDALE | A.D. STOOP | H. COVERDALE 1DG |
| †J.A. PYM 1T | J.A. PYM | J.A. PYM | J.A. PYM |
| *R. DIBBLE | *R. DIBBLE | *R. DIBBLE | J.A.S. RITSON |
| N.A. WODEHOUSE | N.A. WODEHOUSE | N.A. WODEHOUSE | *N.A. WODEHOUSE |
| †A.H. MACILWAINE | A.H. MACILWAINE | A.H. MACILWAINE | A.H. MACILWAINE |
| J.A. KING | J.A. KING | J.A. KING | †W.B. HYNES |
| †J.H. EDDISON | J.H. EDDISON | J.H. EDDISON | J.H. EDDISON 1T |
| †R.C. STAFFORD | R.C. STAFFORD | R.C. STAFFORD | R.C. STAFFORD |
| †D HOLLAND | D. HOLLAND | D. HOLLAND 1T | †J.E. GREENWOOD |
| C.H. PILLMAN | A.L. KEWNEY | A.L. KEWNEY | C.H. PILLMAN 1C |
| Twickenham | Twickenham | Inverleith | Parc des Princes |
| WON 8-0 | WON 15-0 | LOST 3-8 | WON 18-8 |
| ENG.: 1G 1T | ENG.: 5T | SCOT.: 1G 1T | FR.: 1G 1T |
| WALES: NIL | IRE.: NIL | ENG.: 1T | ENG.: 1G 1DG 3T |
| 20 Jan. 1912 | 10 Feb. 1912 | 16 Mar. 1912 | 8 Apr. 1912 |

England began with two handsome wins at Twickenham with Bob Dibble as the new leader. Stoop was still at fly-half, and for the Welsh match the Harlequins contributed four of the backs. Stoop played his last England match this year, however, as did Birkett. Both had played important roles in England's return as a rugby power.

Overconfidence denied England the Grand Slam in Edinburgh, where they were favourites to beat an unfancied Scottish side. Scotland played an outstanding game and deserved to overcome the favourites in a fairly rough match. King, the little Headingley forward who was described as a "Pocket Hercules", played for most of the match with two broken ribs, and Johnston, the outstanding Bristol full-back, suffered concussion following heavy tackles.

Dick Stafford, a teenager who played in all four matches this season, died of spinal cancer before the end of the year.

## 1912-13

| v. S.AFRICA | v. WALES | v. FRANCE | v. IRELAND | v. SCOTLAND |
|---|---|---|---|---|
| W.R. Johnston | W.R. Johnston | W.R. Johnston | W.R. Johnston | W.R. Johnston |
| †C.N. Lowe | C.N. Lowe | C.N. Lowe | C.N. Lowe | C.N. Lowe |
| F.M. Stoop | †F.E. Steinthal | F.E. Steinthal | †A.J. Dingle | F.N. Tarr |
| R.W. Poulton 1t | R.W. Poulton 1dg | R.W. Poulton 1t | R.W. Poulton | R.W. Poulton |
| †V.H.M. Coates | V.H.M. Coates 1t | V.H.M. Coates 3t | V.H.M. Coates 2t | V.H.M. Coates |
| †W.J.A. Davies | W.J.A. Davies | W.J.A. Davies | W.J.A. Davies | W.J.A. Davies |
| †W.I. Cheesman | W.I. Cheesman | W.I. Cheesman | W.I. Cheesman | †F.E. Oakeley |
| J.A.S. Ritson | J.A.S. Ritson | J.A.S. Ritson | J.A.S. Ritson 1t | J.A.S. Ritson |
| *N.A. Wodehouse | *N.A. Wodehouse | *N.A. Wodehouse | *N.A. Wodehouse | *N.A. Wodehouse |
| †S.E.J. Smart | S.E.J. Smart | S.E.J. Smart | S.E.J. Smart | S.E.J. Smart |
| J.A. King | J.A. King | J.A. King | J. A. King | J.A. King |
| L.G. Brown | L.G. Brown | L.G. Brown | L.G. Brown | L.G. Brown 1t |
| A.L. Kewney | †G. Ward | G. Ward | †A.E. Kitching | G. Ward |
| J.E. Greenwood | J.E. Greenwood 1c | J.E. Greenwood 1c | J.E. Greenwood 1pg | J.E. Greenwood |
| C.H. Pillman | C.H. Pillman 1t | C.H. Pillman 2t | C.H. Pillman 1t | C.H. Pillman |
| Twickenham | Cardiff Arms Park | Twickenham | Lansdowne Road | Twickenham |
| LOST 3-9 | WON 12-0 | WON 20-0 | WON 15-4 | WON 3-0 |
| ENG.: 1t | WALES: NIL | ENG.: 1G 5t | IRE.: 1DG | ENG.: 1t |
| SA: 2PG 1t | ENG.: 1G 1DG 1t | FR.: NIL | ENG.: 1PG 4t | SCOT.: NIL |
| 4 Jan. 1913 | 18 Jan. 1913 | 25 Jan. 1913 | 8 Feb. 1913 | 15 Mar. 1913 |

1913 marks the true beginning of England's golden era in rugby football, an era which spanned the decade to 1924. Yet the run started with a defeat against the Second Springboks in an epic match best remembered for the cork-screwing runs of the brilliant English centre, Ronnie Poulton.

The team was changed little for the Championship, which started with England's first win at Cardiff in a match in which they scored their first try in the capital since 1893. Among the new English stars were C.N. Lowe and Welsh-born W.J.A. Davies, two backs whose contributions to the England side during the golden era were unsurpassed.

Coates, the Bath wing, enjoyed the service of a smooth threequarter division and scored six tries in the Championship to create a record. A dangerous wing with a devastating hand-off, this was his only season as an international.

## 1913-14

| v. WALES | v. IRELAND | v. SCOTLAND | v. FRANCE |
|---|---|---|---|
| W.R. Johnston | W.R. Johnston | W.R. Johnston | W.R. Johnston |
| C.N. Lowe | C.N. Lowe 2t | C.N. Lowe 3t | C.N. Lowe 3t |
| F.E. Chapman 2c | F.E. Chapman 1c | J.H.D. Watson | J.H.D. Watson 1t |
| *R.W. Poulton | *R.W. Poulton | *R.W. Poulton 1t | *R.W. Poulton 4t |
| †J.H.D. Watson | A.D. Roberts 1t | A.J. Dingle | A.J. Dingle |
| †F.M. Taylor | W.J.A. Davies 1t | W.J.A. Davies | W.J.A. Davies 1t |
| †G.W. Wood | F.E. Oakeley | F.E. Oakeley | F.E. Oakeley |
| †J. Brunton | J. Brunton | J. Brunton | †F le S. Stone |
| †A.G Bull | H.C. Harrison | H.C. Harrison 2c | H.C. Harrison |
| S.E.J. Smart | S.E.J. Smart | S.E.J. Smart | S.E.J. Smart |
| †A.F. Maynard | A.F. Maynard | A.F. Maynard | †R.L. Pillman |
| L.G. Brown 1t | L.G. Brown | L.G. Brown | L.G. Brown |
| G. Ward | G. Ward | G. Ward | A.L. Harrison |
| J.E. Greenwood | †A.L. Harrison | J.E. Greenwood | J.E. Greenwood 6c |
| C.H. Pillman 1t | C.H. Pillman 1t | C.H. Pillman | †A.R.V. Sykes |
| Twickenham | Twickenham | Inverleith | Stade Colombes |
| WON 10-9 | WON 17-12 | WON 16-15 | WON 39-13 |
| ENG.: 2G | ENG.: 1G 4t | SCOT.: 1G 1DG 2t | FR.: 2G 1t |
| WALES: 1G 1DG | IRE.: 1DG 1G 1t | ENG.: 2G 2t | ENG.: 6G 3t |
| 17 Jan. 1914 | 14 Feb. 1914 | 21 Mar. 1914 | 13 Apr. 1914 |

The Triple Crown, Championship and Grand Slam were again won by England in 1914, and Poulton had succeeded Wodehouse as captain. Poulton was regarded by rugby players as a genius on the field. He possessed a magnificent swerve and passed the ball with perfect judgment. C.N. Lowe, on the wing, benefited from this judgment: he scored eight tries during the season to surpass Coates' record of 1913. Poulton was killed in action in Belgium in 1915; he was mourned by a generation of rugby followers.

The victories were hard-earned, particularly those over Wales and Scotland, where the margins were only one point – "a small and artistic margin" commented *The Times* in a summary of the Welsh match.

Pillman, the breakaway forward, had an outstanding season in the pack, until injured in the Scottish match, and he found sterling support for his play in J.E. Greenwood, the Cambridge Blue whose six conversions against France equalled the record set by Len Stokes in 1881.

## 1919-20

| v. WALES | v. FRANCE | v. IRELAND | v. SCOTLAND |
|---|---|---|---|
| † B.S. CUMBERLEGE | †H. MILLETT | B.S. CUMBERLEGE | B.S. CUMBERLEGE |
| C.N. LOWE | C.N. LOWE | C.N. LOWE 1T | C.N. LOWE 1T |
| †E.D.G. HAMMETT | E.D.G. HAMMETT | †E. MYERS 1T | E. MYERS |
| †J.A. KRIGE | †A.M. SMALLWOOD | A.M. SMALLWOOD | E.D.G. HAMMETT |
| †H.L.V. DAY 1T,1C | †W.M. LOWRY | †S.W. HARRIS | S.W. HARRIS 1T |
| H. COVERDALE | W.J.A. DAVIES 1T | W.J.A. DAVIES | W.J.A. DAVIES |
| †C.A. KERSHAW | C.A. KERSHAW | C.A. KERSHAW | C.A. KERSHAW 1T |
| S.E.J. SMART | †F. TAYLOR | F. TAYLOR | S.E.J. SMART |
| †J.R. MORGAN | †G.S. CONWAY | G.S. CONWAY | G.S. CONWAY |
| †W.H.G. WRIGHT | W.H.G. WRIGHT | S.E.J. SMART | †T. WOODS |
| †G. HOLFORD | G. HOLFORD | A.H. MACILWAINE | †A.F. BLAKISTON |
| †L.P.B. MERRIAM | L.P.B. MERRIAM | †A.T. VOYCE | A.T. VOYCE |
| †F.W. MELLISH | F.W. MELLISH | F.W. MELLISH 1T | F.W. MELLISH |
| †W.W. WAKEFIELD | W.W. WAKEFIELD | W.W. WAKEFIELD 1T | W.W. WAKEFIELD |
| *J.E. GREENWOOD | *J.E. GREENWOOD 1PG,1C | *J.E. GREENWOOD 1C | *J.E. GREENWOOD 2C |
| St. Helen's | Twickenham | Lansdowne Road | Twickenham |
| LOST 5-19 | WON 8-3 | WON 14-11 | WON 13-4 |
| WALES: 1G 2DG 1PG 1T | ENG.: 1G 1PG | IRE.: 1G 1PG 1T | ENG.: 2G 1T |
| ENG.: 1G | FR.: 1T | ENG.: 1G 3T | SCOT.: 1DG |
| 17 Jan. 1920 | 31 Jan. 1920 | 14 Feb. 1920 | 20 Mar. 1920 |

Following the war, the England selectors were forced to field an experimental fifteen in 1920, and 40,000 were present on a wet day at Swansea to see the Champions routed by a strong Welsh side. C.A. Kershaw made the first of his sixteen appearances at scrum-half, but it was not until the Irish match that he was partnered by his Navy colleague, Davies. Together the pair were to play 14 times, a record for England, and as a pair they never played on a losing international side.

Lowe, Coverdale, Davies, Smart and Greenwood were players who had been capped before the war, and Greenwood, now captain of Cambridge, was the new England skipper. There were two notable newcomers among the forwards: W.W. Wakefield and A.T. Voyce. Both had distinguished rugby careers as players, and later served the RFU as Committee members of great wisdom, and as Presidents.

W.M. Lowry of Birkenhead Park had a rare experience at Swansea. He was actually photographed as a member of the team, only to be replaced at the last minute by Harold Day. The selectors felt that conditions were more suited to Day's style. Fortunately, Lowry did win his cap later in the season against France.

## 1920-21

| v. WALES | v. IRELAND | v. SCOTLAND | v. FRANCE |
|---|---|---|---|
| B.S. CUMBERLEGE | B.S. CUMBERLEGE 1C | B.S. CUMBERLEGE | B.S. CUMBERLEGE |
| C.N. LOWE 1T | C.N. LOWE 1DG,1T | C.N. LOWE | C.N. LOWE 1T |
| E. MYERS | E. MYERS | A.M. SMALLWOOD | †L.J. CORBETT |
| E.D.G. HAMMETT 1C | E.D.G. HAMMETT | E.D.G. HAMMETT 3C | E.D.G. HAMMETT 2C |
| A.M. SMALLWOOD 2T | A.M. SMALLWOOD | †Q.E.M.A. KING 1T | A.M. SMALLWOOD |
| *W.J.A. DAVIES 1DG | *W.J.A. DAVIES | *W.J.A. DAVIES | *W.J.A. DAVIES |
| C.A. KERSHAW 1T | C.A. KERSHAW | C.A. KERSHAW | C.A. KERSHAW |
| L.G. BROWN | L.G. BROWN 1T | L.G. BROWN 1T | L.G. BROWN |
| A.F. BLAKISTON | A.F. BLAKISTON 1T | A.F. BLAKISTON | A.F. BLAKISTON 1T |
| T. WOODS | T. WOODS | T. WOODS 1T | T. WOODS |
| †R. EDWARDS | R. EDWARDS | R. EDWARDS 1T | R. EDWARDS |
| W.W. WAKEFIELD | W.W. WAKEFIELD | W.W. WAKEFIELD | W.W. WAKEFIELD |
| A.T. VOYCE | A.T. VOYCE | A.T. VOYCE | A.T. VOYCE |
| F.W. MELLISH | F.W. MELLISH | †R. COVE-SMITH | R. COVE-SMITH |
| †E.R. GARDNER | E.R. GARDNER | E.R. GARDNER | G.S. CONWAY |
| Twickenham | Twickenham | Inverleith | Stade Colombes |
| WON 18-3 | WON 15-0 | WON 18-0 | WON 10-6 |
| ENG.: 1G 1DG 3T | ENG.: 1G 1DG 2T | SCOT.: NIL | FR.: 2PG |
| WALES: 1T | IRE.: NIL | ENG.: 3G 1T | ENG.: 2G |
| 15 Jan. 1921 | 12 Feb. 1921 | 19 Mar. 1921 | 28 Mar. 1921 |

The events of 1921 showed that England had recovered more quickly from the war than other Home Nations. The Grand Slam was won without difficulty and seldom has the selection committee had an easier task. The fifteen was virtually unchanged during the season.

A great amount of credit for England's success this season went to the halves. Individually and as a pair, Davies and Kershaw (Dave and K as they were popularly known) were in a different class from their opponents.

Lowe's drop-goal against Ireland was described as the "most delightful" of all. After receiving a pass in midfield, he had raced away towards the corner when, seeing his path blocked, he turned, balanced on his right foot and dropped a goal with his left boot.

## 1921-22

| v. WALES | v. IRELAND | v. FRANCE | v. SCOTLAND |
|---|---|---|---|
| B.S. Cumberlege | †R.C.W. Pickles | R.C.W. Pickles | †J.A. Middleton |
| C.N. Lowe 1t | C.N. Lowe 1t | C.N. Lowe | C.N. Lowe 2t |
| E. Myers | E. Myers | E. Myers | E. Myers |
| E.D.G. Hammett | †M.S. Bradby | M.S. Bradby | A.M. Smallwood |
| H.L.V. Day 1t | A.M. Smallwood 1t | H.L.V. Day 1c,2pg | †I.J. Pitman |
| †V.G. Davies | *W.J.A. Davies | *W.J.A. Davies | *W.J.A. Davies 1t |
| C.A. Kershaw | C.A. Kershaw | C.A. Kershaw | C.A. Kershaw |
| E.R. Gardner | G.S. Conway | G.S. Conway | G.S. Conway 1c |
| †J.S. Tucker | E.R. Gardner 1t | E.R. Gardner | †P.B. William-Powlett |
| *L.G. Brown | †R.F.H. Duncan | R.F.H. Duncan | R.F.H. Duncan |
| G.S. Conway | R. Cove-Smith | R. Cove-Smith | R. Cove-Smith |
| R. Edwards | †J.E. Maxwell-Hyslop 1t | J.E. Maxwell-Hyslop | J.E. Maxwell-Hyslop |
| A.T. Voyce | A.T. Voyce | A.T. Voyce 1t | A.T. Voyce |
| W.W. Wakefield | W.W. Wakefield | W.W. Wakefield | W.W. Wakefield |
| A.F. Blakiston | †H.L. Price | R. Edwards | H.L. Price |
| Cardiff Arms Park | Lansdowne Road | Twickenham | Twickenham |
| LOST 6-28 | WON 12-3 | DRAWN 11-11 | WON 11-5 |
| WALES: 2G 6T | IRE.: 1T | ENG.: 1G 2PG | ENG.: 1G 2T |
| ENG.: 2T | ENG.: 4T | FR.: 1G 2T | SCOT.: 1G |
| 21 Jan. 1922 | 11 Feb. 1922 | 25 Feb. 1922 | 18 Mar. 1922 |

With the majority of the Grand Slam side available, England faced 1922 with confidence. However Davies, the chosen captain, was compelled to withdraw from the team to meet Wales, and the side suffered a very heavy defeat on a muddy ground at Cardiff.

The famous fly-half was restored for the win in Ireland, and there was a lucky escape for England at Twickenham against France. The French were leading 11-6 in the closing minutes of the match when Day was called upon to attempt a long penalty kick. His kick drifted across the face of the goal and Voyce, following up rapidly as always, scored. Day converted to give England a draw and preserve the Twickenham ground record – England having avoided defeat in all Championship matches there since 1910.

England reserved their most convincing performance for the match with Scotland. Before HM King George V and 40,000 spectators, Davies and Lowe shared three tries in a second-half rally which put paid to Scotland's hopes for the Championship.

## 1922-23

| v. WALES | v. IRELAND | v. SCOTLAND | v. FRANCE |
|---|---|---|---|
| †F. Gilbert | F. Gilbert | †T.E. Holliday | T.E. Holliday |
| C.N. Lowe | C.N. Lowe 1t | C.N. Lowe | C.N. Lowe |
| E. Myers | E. Myers | E. Myers | E. Myers |
| L.J. Corbett | L.J. Corbett 1t | †H.M. Locke | H.M. Locke |
| A.M. Smallwood 1dg | A.M. Smallwood 1t | A.M. Smallwood 1t | A.M. Smallwood |
| *W.J.A. Davies | *W.J.A. Davies 1dg | *W.J.A. Davies | *W.J.A. Davies 1dg |
| C.A. Kershaw | C.A. Kershaw | C.A. Kershaw | C.A. Kershaw |
| E.R. Gardner | E.R. Gardner | E.R. Gardner | E.R. Gardner |
| R. Edwards | †F.W. Sanders | F.W. Sanders | F.W. Sanders |
| †W.G.E. Luddington | W.G.E. Luddington | W.G.E. Luddington 1c | W.G.E. Luddington 1c |
| W.W. Wakefield | W.W. Wakefield | W.W. Wakefield | W.W. Wakefield 1t |
| R. Cove-Smith | R. Cove-Smith | R. Cove-Smith | R. Cove-Smith |
| A.T. Voyce | A.T. Voyce 1t | A.T. Voyce 1t | A.T. Voyce |
| G.S. Conway | G.S. Conway 2c | G.S. Conway | G.S. Conway 1t |
| H.L. Price 1t | H.L. Price 1t | A.F. Blakiston | A.F. Blakiston |
| Twickenham | Leicester | Inverleith | Stade Colombes |
| WON 7-3 | WON 23-5 | WON 8-6 | WON 12-3 |
| ENG.: 1DG 1T | ENG.: 2G 1DG 3T | SCOT.: 2T | FR.: 1PG |
| WALES: 1T | IRE.:1G | ENG.: 1G 1T | ENG.: 1G 1DG 1T |
| 20 Jan. 1923 | 10 Feb. 1923 | 17 Mar. 1923 | 2 Apr. 1923 |

The Grand Slam of 1923 was the final flourish for three of England's most famous players. Kershaw and Davies, the Navy halves, retired, and Lowe, the classic right wing, played the last of his 25 consecutive matches – setting a new record for England.

England scraped home against Wales thanks to two unusual scores. From Wakefield's kick-off, the wind blew the ball into the arms of Price, the Leicester forward, who attempted to drop a goal. The Welshmen expected to see the kick fly wide and roll dead, but the ball ballooned back into Price's path and he scored a try before a single Welshman had gained possession. Then, in the second half, when Corbett found himself cramped for space, he swung the ball to Smallwood, who promptly dropped a goal.

England overpowered Ireland at Leicester, the last international in England to be played away from Twickenham. (Incidentally, the full-back, Gilbert, is thought to have been England's oldest-ever player.) In the Paris match, Davies, on his honeymoon too, dropped a goal with virtually his last kick in an international.

## 1923-24

| v. WALES | v. IRELAND | v. FRANCE | v. SCOTLAND |
|---|---|---|---|
| †B.S. Chantrill | B.S. Chantrill | B.S. Chantrill | B.S. Chantrill |
| †H.C. Catcheside 2t | H.C. Catcheside 2t | H.C. Catcheside 1t | H.C. Catcheside 1t |
| L.J. Corbett | L.J. Corbett 1t | L.J. Corbett | L.J. Corbett |
| H.M. Locke 1t | H.P. Jacob | H.M. Locke | H.M. Locke |
| †H.P. Jacob 1t | †R. H. Hamilton-Wickes 1t | H.P. Jacob 3t | H.P. Jacob |
| E. Myers 1t | E. Myers | E. Myers | E. Myers 1t,1dg |
| †A.T. Young | A.T. Young | A.T. Young 1t | A.T. Young |
| R. Edwards | †C.K.T. Faithfull | R. Edwards | R. Edwards |
| †A. Robson | A. Robson | A. Robson | A. Robson |
| W.G.E. Luddington | W.G.E. Luddington | W.G.E. Luddington | W.G.E. Luddington |
| R. Cove-Smith | R. Cove-Smith | R. Cove-Smith | R. Cove-Smith |
| *W.W. Wakefield | *W.W. Wakefield | *W.W. Wakefield | *W.W. Wakefield 1t |
| A.F. Blakiston | A.F. Blakiston | A.F. Blakiston | A.F. Blakiston |
| G.S. Conway 1c | G.S. Conway 1c | G.S. Conway 2c | G.S. Conway 3c |
| A.T. Voyce | A.T. Voyce | A.T. Voyce | A.T. Voyce |
| St. Helen's | Ravenhill | Twickenham | Twickenham |
| WON 17-9 | WON 14-3 | WON 19-7 | WON 19-0 |
| WALES: 3t | IRE.: 1t | ENG.: 2g 3t | ENG.: 3g 1dg |
| ENG.: 1g 4t | ENG.: 1g 3t | FR.: 1dg 1t | SCOT.: NIL |
| 19 Jan. 1924 | 9 Feb. 1924 | 23 Feb. 1924 | 15 Mar. 1924 |

Despite the retirements of leading players, Wakefield led England to another Grand Slam in 1924. The splendid work of the pack won the matches, one critic noting that they outlasted their opponents in each game. Blakiston, Conway and Cove-Smith were outstanding alongside Wakefield and Voyce, and the eight of 1924 must rank among the all-time greats in English rugby.

Myers, formerly capped as a centre, made the transition to fly-half smoothly, forming an effective partnership with the young Cambridge Blue, A.T. Young. Catcheside, in his first season, scored tries in every match of the Championship – a record for an English player – and brought the house down by vaulting over the French full-back in his three-try performance at Twickenham.

The match in Belfast remains England's only visit to the North of Ireland for an international; while the Scots suffered a record defeat by 19 points in a match remembered for Myers' splendid drop-goal and brilliant try.

## 1924-25

| v. NZ | v. WALES | v. IRELAND | v. SCOTLAND | v. FRANCE |
|---|---|---|---|---|
| †J.W. Brough | J.W. Brough | T.E. Holliday | T.E. Holliday | T.E. Holliday |
| R.H. Hamilton-Wickes | R.H. Hamilton-Wickes 1t | R.H. Hamilton-Wickes | R.H. Hamilton-Wickes 1t | R.H. Hamilton-Wickes 1t |
| V.G. Davies | H.M. Locke | H.M. Locke | H.M. Locke | H.M. Locke |
| L.J. Corbett 1pg | L.J. Corbett | L.J. Corbett | L.J. Corbett | L.J. Corbett |
| †J.C. Gibbs | J.C. Gibbs | A.M. Smallwood 2t | A.M. Smallwood | †S.G.U. Considine |
| †H.J. Kittermaster 1t | H.J. Kittermaster 1t | H.J. Kittermaster | E. Myers | E. Myers |
| A.T. Young | †E.J. Massey | E.J. Massey | E.J. Massey | A.T. Young |
| R. Edwards | R. Cove-Smith | R. Cove-Smith | R. Cove-Smith | R. Cove-Smith |
| J.S. Tucker | J.S. Tucker | J.S. Tucker | J.S. Tucker | J.S. Tucker |
| †R.J. Hillard | †R. Armstrong 1pg | †R.G. Lawson | †D.C. Cumming | D.C. Cumming |
| *W.W. Wakefield | A.F. Blakiston | †R.R.F. MacLennan | R.R.F. MacLennan | R.R.F. MacLennan |
| R. Cove-Smith 1t | W.G.E. Luddington | W.G.E. Luddington | W.G.E. Luddington 1pg,1c | W.G.E. Luddington 1gm,2c |
| A.F. Blakiston | †H.G. Periton | A.F. Blakiston | A.F. Blakiston | A.F. Blakiston |
| G.S. Conway 1c | *W.W. Wakefield | *W.W. Wakefield | *W.W. Wakefield 1t | *W.W. Wakefield 1t |
| A.T. Voyce | A.T. Voyce 1t | A.T. Voyce | A.T. Voyce | A.T. Voyce |
| Twickenham | Twickenham | Twickenham | Murrayfield | Stade Colombes |
| LOST 11-17 | WON 12-6 | DRAWN 6-6 | LOST 11-14 | WON 13-11 |
| ENG.: 1g 1pg 1t | ENG.: 1pg 3t | ENG.: 2t | SCOT.: 2g 1dg | FR.: 1g 2t |
| NZ: 1g 1pg 3t | WALES: 2t | IRE.: 2t | ENG.: 1g 1pg 1t | ENG.: 2g 1gm |
| 3 Jan. 1925 | 17 Jan. 1925 | 14 Feb. 1925 | 21 Mar. 1925 | 13 Apr. 1925 |

England's long run of success ended in 1925. A record attendance of 60,000 watched a fascinating match between the All Blacks, in their last match of an unbeaten tour, and England, the reigning Home Champions. The New Zealanders went out to a 14-point lead before Wakefield inspired his men to make a grand recovery and earn considerable honour in a brave defeat.

The remainder of the season was an anti-climax. Owing to many alterations from match to match, the side failed to find the effective combination which had been a feature of the successes in earlier seasons.

England owed much to their forwards for the wins over France and Wales. Wakefield, Voyce and Blakiston were in their sixth season of international football, but they showed considerable skill and magnificent endurance.

## 1925-26

| v. WALES | v. IRELAND | v. FRANCE | v. SCOTLAND |
|---|---|---|---|
| H.C. Catcheside | H.C. Catcheside | T.E. Holliday | T.E. Holliday |
| †H.C. Burton | R.H. Hamilton-Wickes | Sir T.G. Devitt | R.H. Hamilton-Wickes |
| †A.R. Aslett | A.R. Aslett | A.R. Aslett 2t | A.R. Aslett |
| †T.E.S. Francis | T.E.S. Francis 3c | T.E.S. Francis 1c | T.E.S. Francis |
| R.H. Hamilton-Wickes | †Sir T.G. Devitt | J.C. Gibbs | H.L.V. Day |
| H.J. Kittermaster | H.J. Kittermaster | H.J. Kittermaster 1t | H.J. Kittermaster |
| †J.R.B. Worton | A.T. Young 1t | A.T. Young | A.T. Young |
| †R.J. Hanvey | R.J. Hanvey | R.J. Hanvey | R.J. Hanvey |
| J.S. Tucker | J.S. Tucker | J.S. Tucker | J.S. Tucker 1t |
| †E. Stanbury | E. Stanbury | C.K.T. Faithfull | C.K.T. Faithfull |
| A. Robson | †L.W. Haslett 1t | L.W. Haslett | E. Stanbury |
| W.G.E. Luddington | †W.E. Tucker | †J.W.G. Webb | J.W.G. Webb 1t |
| H.G. Periton | H.G. Periton 1t | H.G. Periton | H.G. Periton |
| *W.W. Wakefield 1t | *W.W. Wakefield | *W.W. Wakefield | *W.W. Wakefield |
| A.T. Voyce | A.T. Voyce | A.T. Voyce | A.T. Voyce 1t |
| Cardiff Arms Park | Lansdowne Road | Twickenham | Twickenham |
| DRAWN 3-3 | LOST 15-19 | WON 11-0 | LOST 9-17 |
| WALES: 1T | IRE.: 2G 1PG 2T | ENG.: 1G 2T | ENG.: 3T |
| ENG.: 1T | ENG.: 3G | FR.: NIL | SCOT.: 2G 1DG 1T |
| 16 Jan. 1926 | 13 Feb. 1926 | 27 Feb. 1926 | 20 Mar. 1926 |

Lack of confidence and the difficulty of blending a pack composed of old and new players were the failings of 1926. Wakefield and Voyce were still England's outstanding forwards, neither having lost an inch in pace or skill. Wakefield, in fact, ran with the pace of a threequarter (he had been the RAF quarter-mile champion in 1920), and scored a breathtaking try at Cardiff.

Voyce was fast too, and his acute sense of anticipation and natural exuberance made him the outstanding English wing-forward of the decade. He later served the Gloucester club and the RFU with distinction, and was President of the Union in 1960-61.

The King was present to see Scotland become the first country to win a championship match at the ground. Voyce's try in this match was a memorable effort, the flanker dragging himself over the line with two Scots hanging on to him.

## 1926-27

| v. WALES | v. IRELAND | v. SCOTLAND | v. FRANCE |
|---|---|---|---|
| †K.A. Sellar | K.A. Sellar | K.A. Sellar | †J.N.S. Wallens |
| R.H. Hamilton-Wickes | H.C. Catcheside | H.C. Catcheside | †W. Alexander |
| *L.J. Corbett 1GM,1T | *L.J. Corbett | *L.J. Corbett | *L.J. Corbett |
| H.M. Locke | H.M. Locke | H.M. Locke | †R.A. Buckingham |
| J.C. Gibbs | J.C. Gibbs 1t | J.C. Gibbs 1t | J.C. Gibbs |
| †H.C.C. Laird | H.C.C. Laird 1t | H.C.C. Laird 1t | †C.C. Bishop |
| J.R.B. Worton | A.T. Young | A.T. Young | A.T. Young |
| E. Stanbury 1c,1PG | E. Stanbury 1c | E. Stanbury 1c | E. Stanbury |
| J.S. Tucker | J.S. Tucker | J.S. Tucker | J.S. Tucker |
| R. Cove-Smith | R. Cove-Smith | R. Cove-Smith | R. Cove-Smith |
| G.S. Conway | †D.E. Law | †W.E. Pratten | W.E. Pratten |
| †K.J. Stark | K.J. Stark | K.J. Stark 1PG,1c | K.J. Stark |
| H.G. Periton | H.G. Periton | H.G. Periton | H.G. Periton |
| †T. Coulson | †W.C.T. Eyres | W.W. Wakefield | W.W. Wakefield |
| †J. Hanley | †P.H. Davies | J. Hanley | J. Hanley |
| Twickenham | Twickenham | Murrayfield | Stade Colombes |
| WON 11-9 | WON 8-6 | LOST 13-21 | LOST 0-3 |
| ENG.: 1G 1GM 1PG | ENG.: 1G 1T | SCOT.: 1G 1DG 4T | FR.: 1T |
| WALES: 1PG 2T | IRE.: 1PG 1T | ENG.: 2G 1PG | ENG.: NIL |
| 15 Jan. 1927 | 12 Feb. 1927 | 19 Mar. 1927 | 2 Apr. 1927 |

Illness and injuries handicapped the England pack in 1927 and the side was lucky to avoid the wooden spoon. Wakefield was unable to play until March, and Voyce was sidelined through a thigh injury. The season ended with the first defeat against the French.

Wakefield's international career finished in Paris, his 31 caps creating a new England record (which stood for more than forty years). As a player he was a man of astute leadership and tactical wisdom; as an administrator he was a faithful and enthusiastic servant of the RFU (becoming President), and in business and public life his tireless energy was channelled into Parliamentary service to the Swindon constituency and the Marylebone Division in London. In retirement he was an active skier.

The captain, Len Corbett, ended his England career this season. In the Welsh match he had the unusual distinction of dropping a goal from a mark – England's last in an international. And in that match H.C.C. Laird became England's youngest player, aged just 18 years, 134 days.

## 1927-28

| v. NSW | v. WALES | v. IRELAND | v. FRANCE | v. SCOTLAND |
|---|---|---|---|---|
| K.A. Sellar | K.A. Sellar | K.A. Sellar | K.A. Sellar | †T.W. Brown |
| †W.J. Taylor 1t | W.J. Taylor 1t | W.J. Taylor | W.J. Taylor | W.J. Taylor |
| †C.D. Aarvold | C.D. Aarvold | C.D. Aarvold | C.D. Aarvold | C.D. Aarvold |
| †J.V. Richardson 3c | J.V. Richardson 2c | J.V. Richardson 1dg,1t | J.V. Richardson 3c | J.V. Richardson |
| Sir T.G. Devitt | Sir T.G. Devitt | †G.V. Palmer | G.V. Palmer 2t | G.V. Palmer |
| H.C.C. Laird 1t | H.C.C. Laird 1t | H.C.C. Laird | H.C.C. Laird | H.C.C. Laird 1t |
| A.T. Young | A.T. Young | A.T. Young | A.T. Young | A.T. Young |
| E. Stanbury | E. Stanbury | E. Stanbury | E. Stanbury | E. Stanbury |
| J.S. Tucker 1t | J.S. Tucker | J.S. Tucker | J.S. Tucker | J.S. Tucker |
| *R. Cove-Smith | *R. Cove-Smith | †R.H.W. Sparks | R.H.W. Sparks | R.H.W. Sparks |
| †D. Turquand-Young | D. Turquand-Young | *R. Cove-Smith | *R. Cove-Smith | *R. Cove-Smith |
| K.J. Stark | K.J. Stark | K.J. Stark | K.J. Stark | K.J. Stark |
| †T.M. Lawson | T.M. Lawson | H.G. Periton | H.G. Periton 2t | H.G. Periton |
| T. Coulson | T. Coulson | †F.D. Prentice | F.D. Prentice | F.D. Prentice |
| H.G. Periton 1t | J. Hanley | J. Hanley | J. Hanley | J. Hanley 1t |
| Twickenham | St. Helen's | Lansdowne Road | Twickenham | Twickenham |
| WON 18-11 | WON 10-8 | WON 7-6 | WON 18-8 | WON 6-0 |
| Eng.: 3g 1t | Wales: 1g 1t | Ire.: 2t | Eng.: 3g 1t | Eng.: 2t |
| NSW: 1g 2t | Eng.: 2g | Eng.: 1dg 1t | Fr.: 1g 1t | Scot.: nil |
| 7 Jan. 1928 | 21 Jan. 1928 | 11 Feb. 1928 | 25 Feb. 1928 | 17 Mar. 1928 |

England, with a young back division prepared to play open rugby, enjoyed a triumphant season, recording five wins in five matches for the only time in their history. Of the newcomers, the most notable was C.D. Aarvold. He was an outstanding threequarter destined to win 16 caps, and led the side towards the end of his playing career. As a barrister he later enjoyed a distinguished professional career, becoming a Circuit Judge and the Recorder of London.

For their wins over Wales and Ireland, the English had to thank Richardson for some accurate kicking. He scored 23 points in this his only season in internationals, his eight conversions equalling the record for a season set by Len Stokes back in 1881.

Cove-Smith, who had led the British team to South Africa in 1924, was England's skipper in this successful season. One of the most intelligent forwards of his time, he was to become closely associated with many medical societies and hospitals during his career as a doctor.

## 1928-29

| v. WALES | v. IRELAND | v. SCOTLAND | v. FRANCE |
|---|---|---|---|
| T.W. Brown | T.W. Brown | T.W. Brown | T.W. Brown |
| †R.W. Smeddle | R.W. Smeddle 1t | R.W. Smeddle | C.D. Aarvold 2t |
| C.D. Aarvold | C.D. Aarvold | A.R. Aslett | A.R. Aslett |
| †G.M. Sladen | G.M. Sladen | G.M. Sladen | A.L. Novis |
| †G.S. Wilson 1c | G.S. Wilson 1c | †A.L. Novis 1t | †J.S.R. Reeve |
| H.C.C. Laird | H.C.C. Laird | †S.S.C. Meikle 1t | †R.S. Spong |
| †H. Whitley | A.T. Young | †E.E. Richards | E.E. Richards |
| E. Stanbury | E. Stanbury | E. Stanbury | E. Stanbury 2c |
| J.S. Tucker | J.S. Tucker | †T. Harris | J.S. Tucker |
| †R.T. Foulds | R.T. Foulds | †H. Rew | H. Rew |
| *R. Cove-Smith | *R. Cove-Smith | J.W.G. Webb | †S.A. Martindale |
| †J.W.R. Swayne | D. Turquand-Young | D. Turquand-Young | D. Turquand-Young |
| H.G. Periton | H.G. Periton | *H.G. Periton | *H.G. Periton 1t |
| R.H.W. Sparks | R.H.W. Sparks | R.H.W. Sparks | †C.H.A. Gummer 1t |
| †H. Wilkinson 2t | H. Wilkinson | H. Wilkinson | †E. Coley |
| Twickenham | Twickenham | Murrayfield | Stade Colombes |
| WON 8-3 | LOST 5-6 | LOST 6-12 | WON 16-6 |
| Eng.: 1g 1t | Eng.: 1g | Scot.: 4t | Fr.: 2t |
| Wales: 1t | Ire.: 2t | Eng.: 2t | Eng.: 2g 2t |
| 19 Jan. 1929 | 9 Feb. 1929 | 16 Mar. 1929 | 1 Apr. 1929 |

England possessed a nucleus of veterans in the pack in 1929, but a failure to find an effective blind-side and the loss of form of many leading threequarters meant that England had to surrender the Championship. Several of the tries conceded were the results of poor defence, both Ireland and Scotland coming from behind to register their victories.

Only two of the forwards, Stanbury and Periton, who finished the season as captain, played in every match. Stanbury was an earnest, no-nonsense prop from the West Country who gained 16 England caps, a record for a Devonian. Periton, Irish-born, was an indispensable loose forward, winner of 21 caps and later a member of the Stock Exchange.

Tom Brown of Bristol was the only member of the back division to retain his place. In November 1933 he joined Broughton Rangers Rugby League team for a considerable sum, regretted his decision immediately after and returned his cheque. The RFU refused to reinstate him.

## 1929-30

| v. WALES | v. IRELAND | v. FRANCE | v. SCOTLAND |
|---|---|---|---|
| †J.G. Askew | J.G. Askew | J.G. Askew | †J.C. Hubbard |
| A.L. Novis | A.L. Novis 1t | J.S.R. Reeve 1t | †C.C. Tanner |
| †F.W.S. Malir | F.W.S. Malir | A.L. Novis | F.W.S. Malir |
| †M. Robson | M. Robson | M. Robson 1t | M. Robson |
| J.S.R. Reeve 2t | J.S.R. Reeve | H.P. Jacob | J.S.R. Reeve |
| R.S. Spong | R.S. Spong | R.S. Spong | R.S. Spong |
| †W.H. Sobey | †A. Key | W.H. Sobey | W.H. Sobey |
| †D.A. Kendrew | D.A. Kendrew | H. Rew | H. Rew |
| J.S. Tucker | J.S. Tucker | *J.S. Tucker | *J.S. Tucker |
| †A.H. Bateson | A.H. Bateson | A.H. Bateson | A.H. Bateson |
| *B.H. Black 1pg,1c | B.H. Black | B.H. Black 1c | B.H. Black |
| †J.W. Forrest | J.W. Forrest | J.W. Forrest | J.W. Forrest |
| W.E. Tucker | W.E. Tucker | H. Wilkinson | †P.W.P. Brook |
| †P.D. Howard | P.D. Howard | P.D. Howard | P.D. Howard |
| *H.G. Periton | *H.G. Periton | H.G. Periton 1t | H.G. Periton |
| Cardiff Arms Park | Lansdowne Road | Twickenham | Twickenham |
| WON 11-3 | LOST 3-4 | WON 11-5 | DRAWN 0-0 |
| WALES: 1t | Ire.: 1dg | Eng.: 1g 2t | Eng.: nil |
| Eng.: 1g 1pg 1t | Eng.: 1t | Fr.: 1g | Scot.: nil |
| 18 Jan. 1930 | 8 Feb. 1930 | 22 Feb. 1930 | 15 Mar. 1930 |

England, fielding an experimental side, were the surprise packet of 1930 and secured the Championship, though defeat by a dropped goal in Dublin and a draw with Scotland meant that no Triple Crown was won.

Sam Tucker made a frantic dash by aeroplane across the Bristol Channel on the morning of the Cardiff match to lead a young and relatively inexperienced pack. Bateson and Kendrew gave him support in the front row, and England's victory was their first at the Arms Park since 1913, and only their second since the first visit back in 1893. Tucker's return (due to the late withdrawal of Rew) marked the highlight of the veteran's career, for his powers of motivation were to be rewarded with the captaincy of the side for the matches with France and Scotland.

Of the backs, only Robson, a new cap in the centre, survived the test of four matches. His 35-yard run in the match against France produced the try of the season.

## 1930-31

| v. WALES | v. IRELAND | v. SCOTLAND | v. FRANCE |
|---|---|---|---|
| †L.L. Bedford | L.L. Bedford | †E.C.P. Whiteley | E.C.P. Whiteley |
| J.S.R. Reeve | J.S.R. Reeve | J.S.R. Reeve 2t | R.W. Smeddle 1t |
| †D.W. Burland 1t,1c | D.W. Burland | †J.A. Tallent 2t | J.A. Tallent 1t |
| †M.A. McCanlis | M.A. McCanlis | *C.D. Aarvold | D.W. Burland 1t |
| C.D. Aarvold | †A.C. Harrison | A.C. Harrison | *C.D. Aarvold |
| †T.J.M. Barrington | T.J.M. Barrington | †T.C. Knowles | R.S. Spong |
| †E.B. Pope | †G.J. Dean | E.B. Pope | E.B. Pope |
| H. Rew | †P.C. Hordern | R.H.W. Sparks | R.H.W. Sparks |
| *J.S. Tucker | R.H.W. Sparks | G.G. Gregory | G.G. Gregory |
| †M.S. Bonaventura | †G.G. Gregory | H. Rew | H. Rew |
| B.H. Black 2pg | B.H. Black 1t,1c | B.H. Black 2c,1pg | B.H. Black 1c |
| J.W. Forrest | J.W. Forrest | J.W. Forrest | J.W. Forrest 1c |
| †D.H. Swayne | *P.D. Howard | P.C. Hordern | P.C. Hordern |
| P.D. Howard | †E.H. Harding | P.D. Howard | P.D. Howard |
| †R.F. Davey | †P.E. Dunkley | P.E. Dunkley | P.W.P. Brook |
| Twickenham | Twickenham | Murrayfield | Stade Colombes |
| DRAWN 11-11 | LOST 5-6 | LOST 19-28 | LOST 13-14 |
| Eng.: 1g 2pg | Eng.: 1g | Scot.: 5g 1t | Fr.: 2dg 2t |
| Wales: 1g 1gm 1t | Ire.: 1pg 1t | Eng.: 2g 1pg 2t | Eng.: 2g 1t |
| 17 Jan. 1931 | 14 Feb. 1931 | 21 Mar. 1931 | 6 Apr. 1931 |

Lack of penetration in midfield and an inexperienced pack hampered England this season, and for the first time since the French had become regular opponents, not a single match of the four played was won.

England's wings looked capable of scoring tries but the mechanical passing of the centres failed to draw the opposition in the matches at Twickenham. Later in the season, a new combination of Tallent and Aarvold improved the back play to a marked degree. The threequarters scored seven tries in the last two games, though defeat in Paris, on Easter Monday, was particularly disappointing for them, France overcoming England with a late drop-goal.

Black and Forrest, in the second row, played throughout the season, as they had in the previous year. Forrest was a Serviceman who returned for two appearances in 1934. Black was a South African who had gained his Blue at Oxford in 1929. Sadly he was killed on active service during the summer of 1940. He was a Pilot Officer in the RAF.

## 1931-32

| v. S.AFRICA | v. WALES | v. IRELAND | v. SCOTLAND |
|---|---|---|---|
| †R.J. BARR | R.J. BARR 1C | R.J. BARR | T.W. BROWN |
| | | | |
| C.C. TANNER | C.C. TANNER | C.C. TANNER | C.C. TANNER 1T |
| J.A. TALLENT | R.A. GERRARD | D.W. BURLAND 1T,1C,2PG | D.W. BURLAND 2C |
| †R.A. GERRARD | J.A. TALLENT | R.A. GERRARD | R.A. GERRARD |
| *C.D. AARVOLD | *C.D. AARVOLD | *C.D. AARVOLD | *C.D. AARVOLD 2T |
| | | | |
| R.S. SPONG | R.S. SPONG | †W. ELLIOT | W. ELLIOT |
| W.H. SOBEY | W.H. SOBEY | B.C. GADNEY | B.C. GADNEY |
| | | | |
| †A.D. CARPENTER | †N.L. EVANS | N.L. EVANS | N.L. EVANS |
| †D.J. NORMAN | D.J. NORMAN | †R.S. ROBERTS | G.G. GREGORY |
| G.G. GREGORY | G.G. GREGORY | G.G. GREGORY | †R.J. LONGLAND |
| †C.S.H. WEBB | C.S.H. WEBB | C.S.H. WEBB | C.S.H. WEBB |
| †R.G.S. HOBBS | R.G.S. HOBBS | R.G.S. HOBBS | R.G.S. HOBBS |
| †L.E. SAXBY | L.E. SAXBY · | †A. VAUGHAN-JONES | A. VAUGHAN-JONES |
| †A.J. ROWLEY | E.COLEY 1T | T. HARRIS | B.H. BLACK 1T |
| †J.M. HODGSON | J.M. HODGSON | J.M. HODGSON | J.M. HODGSON |
| | | | |
| Twickenham | St. Helen's | Lansdowne Road | Twickenham |
| LOST 0-7 | LOST 5-12 | WON 11-8 | WON 16-3 |
| | | | |
| ENG.: NIL | WALES: IG IDG IPG | IRE.: IG IPG | ENG.: 2G 2T |
| SA: IDG IT | ENG.: IG | ENG.: IG 2PG | SCOT.: IT |
| | | | |
| 2 Jan. 1932 | 16 Jan. 1932 | 13 Feb. 1932 | 19 Mar. 1932 |

Difficulties finding an adequate front row were eventually resolved in the match with Ireland, and after two opening defeats England recovered sufficiently to claim a share in the International Championship. Behind a slow-heeling pack, Spong and Sobey, who played together for England on five occasions, were unable to produce their best form against South Africa and Wales, and gave way to a younger pair, which included Bernard Gadney of Leicester, for the Irish match.

The highlight of the season was a big win over the Scots. The English forwards overpowered the Scots in the tight and the powerful Burland (who had scored all of the points in the Dublin victory) was a constant intimidation to the visiting backs. Aarvold had a good game on the left wing, scoring two tries.

Ray Longland made his debut this season. He won nineteen caps during the 1930s, ranking as the outstanding English prop of the decade. But for the war and the banishment of the French he would surely have set a new England cap record.

## 1932-33

| v. WALES | v. IRELAND | v. SCOTLAND |
|---|---|---|
| T.W. BROWN | T.W. BROWN | T.W. BROWN |
| | | |
| †L.A. BOOTH | L.A. BOOTH 1T | L.A. BOOTH |
| D.W. BURLAND | D.W. BURLAND | D.W. BURLAND |
| R.A. GERRARD | R.A. GERRARD | R.A. GERRARD |
| *C.D. AARVOLD | *A.L. NOVIS 2T | *A.L. NOVIS |
| | | |
| W. ELLIOT 1T | W. ELLIOT | W. ELLIOT |
| A. KEY | B.C. GADNEY 1T | B.C. GADNEY |
| | | |
| N.L. EVANS | N.L. EVANS | R.J. LONGLAND |
| G.G. GREGORY | G.G. GREGORY | G.G. GREGORY |
| R.J. LONGLAND | D.A. KENDREW 1C | D.A. KENDREW |
| C.S.H. WEBB | C.S.H. WEBB | C.S.H. WEBB |
| †A.D.S. RONCORONI | A.D.S. RONCORONI | A.D.S. RONCORONI |
| A. VAUGHAN-JONES | †W.H. WESTON | W.H. WESTON |
| B.H. BLACK | †C.L. TROOP | C.L. TROOP |
| †R. BOLTON | †E.H. SADLER 1T | E.H. SADLER |
| | | |
| Twickenham | Twickenham | Murrayfield |
| LOST 3-7 | WON 17-6 | LOST 0-3 |
| | | |
| ENG.: IT | ENG.: IG 4T | SCOT.: IT |
| WALES: IDG IT | IRE.: IPG IT | ENG.: NIL |
| | | |
| 21 Jan. 1933 | 11 Feb. 1933 | 18 Mar. 1933 |

Both up front in the tight and in the threequarters, England lacked the speed and cleverness to press for the title in 1933. Poor backing-up deprived them of a win over a young Welsh side at Twickenham, and in a disappointing match at Murrayfield feeble finishing spoiled some good work by Gerrard and Burland.

Gerrard was an unselfish player who made 14 appearances for England before serving King and Country during the war. Courageous in battle as he had been on the field of play, he was an inspiration to his troops and showed determination in leadership. He was killed in action in Libya early in 1943.

The Irish match was the best of the season. Strong running by Novis and Booth on the wings accounted for three of the tries and England's win was their most decisive against Ireland for nine years.

## 1933-34

| v. WALES | v. IRELAND | v. SCOTLAND |
|---|---|---|
| †H.G. Owen-Smith | H.G. Owen-Smith | H.G. Owen-Smith |
| †A.L. Warr 1t | A.L. Warr | L.A. Booth 1t |
| †P. Cranmer | P. Cranmer | P. Cranmer |
| R.A. Gerrard | R.A. Gerrard | R.A. Gerrard |
| †G.W.C. Meikle 2t | G.W.C. Meikle 1t | G.W.C. Meikle 1t |
| W. Elliot | W. Elliot | †C.F. Slow |
| *B.C. Gadney | *B.C. Gadney | *B.C. Gadney |
| R.J. Longland | R.J. Longland | R.J. Longland |
| G.G. Gregory | G.G. Gregory 2c | G.G. Gregory |
| H. Rew | H. Rew | H. Rew |
| †J.C. Wright | J.W. Forrest | J.W. Forrest |
| †J. Dicks | J. Dicks | J. Dicks |
| J.M. Hodgson | W.H. Weston | W.H. Weston |
| P.C. Hordern | J.M. Hodgson | D.A. Kendrew |
| †H.A. Fry | H.A. Fry 2t | H.A. Fry |
| Cardiff Arms Park | Lansdowne Road | Twickenham |
| WON 9-0 | WON 13-3 | WON 6-3 |
| WALES: NIL | IRE.: 1T | ENG.: 2T |
| ENG.: 3T | ENG.: 2G 1T | SCOT.: 1T |
| 20 Jan. 1934 | 10 Feb. 1934 | 17 Mar. 1934 |

England's year. After routing the Welsh pack at Cardiff, England were clearly the better side in Dublin after an anxious opening quarter, and defeated Scotland (though not without some desperately narrow squeaks in the closing stages) to take the Triple Crown for the first time since 1928.

Gadney, the captain, was the supreme tactician behind a pack which was rarely changed. Cranmer showed himself to be a finely balanced runner and the best of Gerrard was seen in defence. Meikle, on the wing, scored tries in each of the matches.

But the principal success of the season was Owen-Smith at full-back. His casual manner and lack of inches were snares for the unwary. He proved an adventurous attacker (setting England on the road to victory with a thrilling run in Dublin) and a devastating tackler (as Beattie discovered to his discomfort in the Scottish game). His rugby career was short – ten caps in three seasons before returning to his native South Africa, where he practised as a doctor.

## 1934-35

| v. WALES | v. IRELAND | v. SCOTLAND |
|---|---|---|
| †H. Boughton 1pg | H. Boughton 3pg,1c | H. Boughton |
| L.A. Booth | L.A. Booth | L.A. Booth 1t |
| P. Cranmer | J. Heaton | P. Cranmer 1dg |
| †J. Heaton | R. Leyland | J. Heaton |
| †R. Leyland | P. Cranmer | R. Leyland |
| †P.L. Candler | J.A. Tallent | †J.R. Auty |
| †J.L. Giles | J.L. Giles 1t | *B.C. Gadney |
| R.J. Longland | R.J. Longland | R.J. Longland |
| †E.S. Nicholson | E.S. Nicholson | E.S. Nicholson |
| *D.A. Kendrew | *D.A. Kendrew | C.S.H. Webb |
| †A.J. Clarke | A.J. Clarke | A.J. Clarke |
| J. Dicks | J. Dicks | J. Dicks |
| †A.G. Cridlan | A.G. Cridlan | A.G. Cridlan |
| †D.T. Kemp | †A.T. Payne | A.T. Payne |
| W.H. Weston | W.H. Weston | W.H. Weston |
| Twickenham | Twickenham | Murrayfield |
| DRAWN 3-3 | WON 14-3 | LOST 7-10 |
| ENG.: 1PG | ENG.: 1G 3PG | SCOT.: 2G |
| WALES: 1T | IRE.: 1T | ENG.: 1DG 1T |
| 19 Jan. 1935 | 9 Feb. 1935 | 16 Mar. 1935 |

England were saved from the wooden spoon in 1935 by the kicking of Boughton. His penalty tied the match with Wales and his four successful goal kicks against the Irish proved the difference between the sides.

During the season England's difficulties were complicated by the problem of finding the best positions for Heaton and Leyland, two of the brilliant back division which helped Lancashire to become County Champions this season. Leyland was picked on the wing for the Welsh and Scottish matches, a position where his talents were wasted. Even when he was tried in his usual centre position, the selectors compounded their indecision by playing Cranmer out of place on the wing.

There were further problems at half, where three different pairs (and three different fly-halves) failed to impress. Only Auty and Gadney in the first half of the Scottish match managed to employ the threequarters to any degree of success in attack, but even their style was cramped by an obstinate Scottish defence later in the game. Only one try was scored by an English threequarter during the season: the worst return since 1905.

## 1935-36

| v. NZ | v. WALES | v. IRELAND | v. SCOTLAND |
|---|---|---|---|
| H.G. Owen-Smith | H.G. Owen-Smith | H.G. Owen-Smith | H.G. Owen-Smith |
| †A. Obolensky 2T | A. Obolensky | A. Obolensky | A. Obolensky |
| R.A. Gerrard | R.A. Gerrard | R.A. Gerrard | R.A. Gerrard |
| P. Cranmer 1DG | P. Cranmer | P. Cranmer | P. Cranmer 1T |
| †H.S. Sever 1T | H.S. Sever | H.S. Sever 1T | H.S. Sever |
| P.L. Candler | P.L. Candler | P.L. Candler | P.L. Candler 1T |
| *B.C. Gadney | *B.C. Gadney | *B.C. Gadney | *B.C. Gadney |
| R.J. Longland | R.J. Longland | R.J. Longland | R.J. Longland |
| E.S. Nicholson | E.S. Nicholson | D.A. Kendrew | †H.B. Toft |
| D.A. Kendrew | D.A. Kendrew | †H.F. Wheatley | J. Dicks |
| A.J. Clarke | A.J. Clarke | A.J. Clarke | P.E. Dunkley |
| C.S.H. Webb | C.S.H. Webb | C.S.H. Webb | C.S.H. Webb |
| W.H. Weston | W.H. Weston | J.M. Hodgson | W.H. Weston |
| P.E. Dunkley | P.E. Dunkley | P.E. Dunkley | P.W.P. Brook |
| †E.A. Hamilton-Hill | E.A. Hamilton-Hill | E.A. Hamilton-Hill | R. Bolton 1T |
| Twickenham | St. Helen's | Lansdowne Road | Twickenham |
| WON 13-0 | DRAWN 0-0 | LOST 3-6 | WON 9-8 |
| Eng.: 1DG 3T | Wales: NIL | Ire.: 2T | Eng.: 3T. |
| NZ: NIL | Eng.: NIL | Eng.: 1T | Scot.: 1G 1PG |
| 4 Jan. 1936 | 18 Jan. 1936 | 8 Feb. 1936 | 21 Mar. 1936 |

The single event to stand above all others in 1936 was the win over New Zealand. A young Russian prince named Obolensky earned eternal fame with two spectacular and unorthodox tries as a crowd of 73,000 saw the All Blacks beaten by a solid pack. Gadney gave an impressive display as captain.

The rest of the season was a disappointment. In the testing atmosphere of St. Helen's, Obolensky was closely marked by the Welsh full-back, and another large crowd saw the two sides who had beaten the All Blacks play a scoreless draw – the first involving England since 1930.

It is a peculiarity of rugby history that Obolensky should create such a name for himself and yet play in only four international matches, his final appearance being in England's sole win of the Championship – against Scotland. Obolensky continued playing until he was killed in a flying training accident in Norfolk in March 1940. But his tries against the All Blacks will never be forgotten.

## 1936-37

| v. WALES | v. IRELAND | v. SCOTLAND |
|---|---|---|
| *H.G. Owen-Smith | *H.G. Owen-Smith | *H.G. Owen-Smith |
| †A.G. Butler | A.G. Butler 1T | †E.J. Unwin 1T |
| P.L. Candler | P.L. Candler | P.L. Candler |
| P. Cranmer | P. Cranmer 1PG | P. Cranmer |
| H.S. Sever 1DG | H.S. Sever 1T | H.S. Sever 1T |
| †T.A. Kemp | T.A. Kemp | †F.J. Reynolds |
| J.L. Giles | J.L. Giles | B.C. Gadney |
| R.J. Longland | R.J. Longland | R.J. Longland |
| H.B. Toft | H.B. Toft | H.B. Toft |
| †R.E. Prescott | R.E. Prescott | H.F. Wheatley |
| †A. Wheatley | A. Wheatley | A. Wheatley |
| †T.F. Huskisson | T.F. Huskisson | T.F. Huskisson |
| W.H. Weston | W.H. Weston | W.H. Weston |
| †D.L.K. Milman | J. Dicks | †J.G. Cook |
| †D.A. Campbell | D.A. Campbell | R. Bolton |
| Twickenham | Twickenham | Murrayfield |
| WON 4-3 | WON 9-8 | WON 6-3 |
| Eng.: 1DG | Eng.: 1PG 2T | Scot.: 1PG |
| Wales: 1T | Ire: 1G 1T | Eng.: 2T |
| 16 Jan. 1937 | 13 Feb. 1937 | 20 Mar. 1937 |

England regained the Triple Crown in 1937, cheerful full-back and former South African Test cricketer Owen-Smith leading the side to three narrow victories. The pack was the best in the Championship and Toft proved to be the most skilful hooker in British rugby this season.

Victory over Wales was due to a freak drop-goal by Sever, who took his chance after the ball had glanced off Prescott's shoulder. Sever was also the matchwinner against Ireland. In the dying minutes he set off on a run from a scrum, swerved past several defenders and launched himself over the Irish line with a tackler on his back. To complete a capital season Sever scored the second of England's tries in the Calcutta Cup win.

Cranmer and Candler were a splendid pair of centres, brilliant in attack and sure in defence. Their fine play was an important factor in England's success.

## 1937-38

| v. WALES | v. IRELAND | v. SCOTLAND |
|---|---|---|
| †H.D. Freakes 1c | †G.W. Parker 6c,1pg | G.W. Parker 3pg |
| E.J. Unwin | E.J. Unwin 1t | E.J. Unwin 1t |
| *P. Cranmer | *P. Cranmer | P. Cranmer |
| †B.E. Nicholson | B.E. Nicholson 1t | P.L. Candler |
| H.S. Sever 1t | H.S. Sever | H.S. Sever |
| P.L. Candler 1t | F.J. Reynolds 1t | F.J. Reynolds 1dg |
| B.C. Gadney | J.L. Giles 1t | J.L. Giles |
| R.J. Longland | R.J. Longland | R.J. Longland |
| H.B. Toft | H.B. Toft | *H.B. Toft |
| H.F. Wheatley | R.E. Prescott 1t | H.F. Wheatley |
| A. Wheatley | †R.M. Marshall 1t | R.M. Marshall |
| T.F. Huskisson | T.F. Huskisson | A. Wheatley |
| W.H. Weston | W.H. Weston | W.H. Weston |
| D.L.K. Milman | D.L.K. Milman | D.L.K. Milman |
| R. Bolton | R. Bolton 1t | †A.A. Brown |
| Cardiff Arms Park | Lansdowne Road | Twickenham |
| LOST 8-14 | WON 36-14 | LOST 16-21 |
| WALES: 1g 2pg 1t | IRE.: 1g 3t | ENG.: 1dg 3pg 1t |
| ENG.: 1g 1t | ENG.: 6g 1pg 1t | SCOT.: 2pg 5t |
| 15 Jan. 1938 | 12 Feb. 1938 | 19 Mar. 1938 |

Peter Cranmer was England's captain at the start of 1938. He won 16 caps for his country and was praised as one of the best centres of the decade. Later he was a shrewd writer and broadcaster on the game.

A gale-force wind made the Welsh match a game of hazards, but there was a high-scoring win in Dublin. England's score of 36 points against Ireland was their highest in an international between the wars, and Parker's six conversions equalled the England match record.

Bert Toft, a master at Manchester Grammar School, became captain for the Scottish match. (After the war he was an erudite rugby correspondent for the *Observer*.) The game, one of the most exciting of the 1930s, was played in perfect conditions in front of 70,000. The lead changed several times before Scotland won a high-scoring contest.

## 1938-39

| v. WALES | v. IRELAND | v. SCOTLAND |
|---|---|---|
| H.D. Freakes | H.D. Freakes | †E.I. Parsons |
| †R.H. Guest | R.H. Guest | R.H. Guest |
| J. Heaton | J. Heaton | J. Heaton 3pg |
| †G.E. Hancock | G.E. Hancock | G.E. Hancock |
| †R.S.L. Carr | R.S.L. Carr | R.S.L. Carr |
| †G.A. Walker | G.A. Walker | T.A. Kemp |
| †P. Cooke | P. Cooke | †J. Ellis |
| R.E. Prescott | R.E. Prescott | R.E. Prescott |
| *H.B. Toft | *H.B. Toft | *H.B. Toft |
| †D.E. Teden 1t | D.E. Teden | D.E. Teden |
| T.F. Huskisson | T.F. Huskisson | T.F. Huskisson |
| H.F. Wheatley | H.F. Wheatley | H.F. Wheatley |
| †J.T.W. Berry | J.T.W. Berry | J.T.W. Berry |
| R.M. Marshall | R.M. Marshall | R.M. Marshall |
| †J.K. Watkins | J.K. Watkins | J.K. Watkins |
| Twickenham | Twickenham | Murrayfield |
| WON 3-0 | LOST 0-5 | WON 9-6 |
| ENG.: 1t | ENG.: NIL | SCOT.: 2t |
| WALES: NIL | IRE.: 1g | ENG.: 3pg |
| 21 Jan. 1939 | 11 Feb. 1939 | 18 Mar. 1939 |

In a mediocre season the selectors were loyal to a threequarter line of three new caps, and one which thus played unchanged throughout the season. There was a solid and experienced English pack, for although Watkins and Berry were new men at international level, both were experienced club and county players. Berry became a President of the RFU.

Teden, the outstanding prop forward in the Championship, scored the only try of the match with Wales, backing-up an English dash led by Watkins. Then an unchanged fifteen was surprisingly outwitted and outmanoeuvred by a lively Irish team.

In the last full international played before the war, England won a dour struggle at Murrayfield, thanks to some magnificent place-kicking by Heaton. His three penalties equalled the record set by Parker against Scotland the previous season. After the war Heaton returned to captain England.

## 1946-47

| v. WALES | v. IRELAND | v. SCOTLAND | v. FRANCE |
|---|---|---|---|
| †A. Gray 1c | A. Gray | A. Gray | †S.C. Newman |
| R.H. Guest | R.H. Guest | †C.B. Holmes 1t | D.W. Swarbrick |
| †N.O. Bennett | J. Heaton | N.O. Bennett 1t | N.O. Bennett |
| †E.K. Scott | †M.P. Donnelly | *J. Heaton 4c | *J. Heaton |
| †D.W. Swarbrick | D.W. Swarbrick | R.H. Guest 1t | R.H. Guest 1t |
| †N.M. Hall 1dg | N.M. Hall | N.M. Hall 1dg | N.M. Hall |
| †W.K.T. Moore | W.K.T. Moore | †J.O. Newton-Thompson | J.O. Newton-Thompson |
| †G.A. Kelly | G.A. Kelly | G.A. Kelly | †G.A. Gibbs |
| †A.P. Henderson | A.P. Henderson | A.P. Henderson 1t | A.P. Henderson |
| †H.W. Walker | H.W. Walker | H.W. Walker | H.W. Walker |
| *†J. Mycock | *J. Mycock | J. Mycock | J. Mycock |
| †S.V. Perry | S.V. Perry | †J. George | J. George |
| †M.R. Steele-Bodger | M.R. Steele-Bodger | M.R. Steele-Bodger | M.R. Steele-Bodger |
| †B.H. Travers | B.H. Travers | †R.H.G. Weighill | R.H.G. Weighill |
| †D.F. White 1t | D.F. White | D.F. White | †V.G. Roberts 1t |
| Cardiff Arms Park | Lansdowne Road | Twickenham | Twickenham |
| WON 9-6 | LOST 0-22 | WON 24-5 | WON 6-3 |
| WALES: 2T | IRE.: 2G 1PG 3T | ENG.: 4G 1DG | ENG.: 2T |
| ENG.: 1G 1DG | ENG.: NIL | SCOT.:1G | FR.: 1PG |
| 18 Jan. 1947 | 8 Feb. 1947 | 15 Mar. 1947 | 19 Apr. 1947 |

A series of Services internationals was played during war-time, followed by an unofficial series, known as the "Victory" Internationals, in 1946. Full internationals resumed in 1947, with England sharing the Championship with Wales.

A drop-goal by Hall, one of a noted St Mary's Hospital midfield trio, robbed Wales of the lead in the second half to set up England's fourth win at Cardiff. The England pack was more than useful – except during the rout in Dublin – and disposed of the Scots with ease on an icy pitch at Twickenham.

The winter of 1947 was severely disrupted by frost and snow. The French match should have been staged in February, but was postponed until late April. Then, a close match was settled in its final moments when Roberts supported a break by Newton-Thompson to score the deciding try.

## 1947-48

| v. AUSTRALIA | v. WALES | v. IRELAND | v. SCOTLAND | v. FRANCE |
|---|---|---|---|---|
| S.C. Newman | S.C. Newman 1pg | †R. Uren 2c | R. Uren 1pg | R. Uren |
| R.H. Guest | R.H. Guest | R.H. Guest 2t | R.H. Guest | M.F. Turner |
| N.O. Bennett | N.O. Bennett | N.O. Bennett | N.O. Bennett | †L.B. Cannell |
| *E.K. Scott | E.K. Scott | *E.K. Scott | *E.K. Scott | †A.C. Towell |
| D.W. Swarbrick | D.W. Swarbrick | C.B. Holmes | †M.F. Turner | C.B. Holmes |
| T.A. Kemp | *T.A. Kemp | †I. Preece | I. Preece | I. Preece |
| †R.J.P. Madge | R.J.P. Madge | R.J.P. Madge | R.J.P. Madge | †P.W. Sykes |
| †E. Evans | G.A. Kelly | G.A. Gibbs | †T.W. Price | T.W. Price |
| †J.H. Keeling | J.H. Keeling | A.P. Henderson | A.P. Henderson | A.P. Henderson |
| H.W. Walker | H.W. Walker | H.W. Walker | H.W. Walker | H.W. Walker |
| J. Mycock | †H.F. Luya | H.F. Luya | H.F. Luya | H.F. Luya |
| S.V. Perry | S.V. Perry | S.V. Perry | S.V. Perry | S.V. Perry |
| M.R. Steele-Bodger | M.R. Steele-Bodger | M.R. Steele-Bodger | M.R. Steele-Bodger | M.R. Steele-Bodger |
| †D.B. Vaughan | D.B. Vaughan | D.B. Vaughan | R.H.G. Weighill | *R.H.G. Weighill |
| B.H. Travers | B.H. Travers | D.F. White | D.B. Vaughan | D.F. White |
| Twickenham | Twickenham | Twickenham | Murrayfield | Stade Colombes |
| LOST 0-11 | DRAWN 3-3 | LOST 10-11 | LOST 3-6 | LOST 0-15 |
| ENG.: NIL | ENG.: 1PG | ENG.: 2G | SCOT.: 2T | FR.: 1G 1DG 2T |
| AUST.: 1G 2T | WALES: 1T | IRE.: 1G 2T | ENG.: 1PG | ENG.: NIL |
| 3 Jan. 1948 | 17 Jan. 1948 | 14 Feb. 1948 | 20 Mar. 1948 | 29 Mar. 1948 |

England finished this season without winning a match and thus fell from joint Champions to holders of the wooden spoon. But the huge post-war interest in rugby can be measured from the fact that more than 70,000 crowded into Twickenham for England's home matches, despite the team's lack of success on the field.

Bob Weighill and M.R. Steele-Bodger were prominent members of the back-row this season. Both served the game with distinction as administrators, Weighill as Secretary of the RFU and Steele-Bodger as a President of the RFU and member of the International Board.

Serious injuries cost England the game at Murrayfield. Madge was compelled to retire with torn ligaments and Scott, the West Country doctor who captained the side, broke his jaw. Even Steele-Bodger, who moved to scrum-half to replace Madge, was in the wars, suffering from concussion.

## 1948-49

| v. WALES | v. IRELAND | v. FRANCE | v. SCOTLAND |
|---|---|---|---|
| †W.B. Holmes | W.B. Holmes 1c | W.B. Holmes 1c | W.B. Holmes |
| †J.A. Gregory | D.W. Swarbrick | R.H. Guest | R.H. Guest 1t |
| L.B. Cannell | L.B. Cannell | L.B. Cannell 1t | L.B. Cannell |
| †C.B. van Ryneveld | C.B. van Ryneveld 1t | C.B. van Ryneveld | C.B. van Ryneveld 2t |
| †T. Danby | †R.D. Kennedy | R.D. Kennedy | R.D. Kennedy 1t |
| *N.M. Hall 1dg | *N.M. Hall | *I. Preece 1dg | *I. Preece |
| †G. Rimmer | G. Rimmer | W.K.T. Moore | W.K.T. Moore |
| T.W. Price | T.W. Price | T.W. Price | T.W. Price |
| A.P. Henderson | A.P. Henderson | †J.H. Steeds | J.H. Steeds |
| †M.J. Berridge | M.J. Berridge | J.M. Kendall-Carpenter | J.M. Kendall-Carpenter |
| H.F. Luya | J. George | †J.R.C. Matthews | J.R.C. Matthews |
| †G.R.D.'a Hosking | G.R.D.'a Hosking | G.R.D.'a Hosking | G.R.D.'a Hosking 1t |
| †E.L. Horsfall | D.B. Vaughan | B.H. Travers | B.H. Travers 2c |
| †B. Braithwaite-Exley | †J.M. Kendall-Carpenter | D.B. Vaughan | D.B. Vaughan |
| V.G. Roberts | V.G. Roberts | V.G. Roberts | V.G. Roberts |
| Cardiff Arms Park | Lansdowne Road | Twickenham | Twickenham |
| LOST 3-9 | LOST 5-14 | WON 8-3 | WON 19-3 |
| WALES: 3T | IRE.: 1G 2PG 1T | ENG.: 1G 1DG | ENG.: 2G 3T |
| ENG.: 1DG | ENG.: 1G | FR.: 1DG | SCOT.: 1PG |
| 15 Jan. 1949 | 12 Feb. 1949 | 26 Feb. 1949 | 19 Mar. 1949 |

There were two inept performances at the start of 1949 before Ivor Preece, a new captain, led a lusty revival in the matches against France and Scotland.

During the season 26 players were used and twelve new caps were recognised. Among the new players was van Ryneveld, a South African scholar at Oxford. His two tries against Scotland were marvellous spectacles, and both stemmed from adventurous counter-attacks by Preece.

Dick Guest, the Waterloo wing first capped ten years earlier, won his last cap this season. Small but polished, he had few chances in his 13 internationals: but for the war he would have won many more caps and scored much more than his 5 tries for England.

## 1949-50

| v. WALES | v. IRELAND | v. FRANCE | v. SCOTLAND |
|---|---|---|---|
| †M.B. Hofmeyr 1c | R. Uren | M.B. Hofmeyr | M.B. Hofmeyr 1pg,1c |
| †J.V. Smith 1t | J.V. Smith | J.V. Smith 1t | J.V. Smith 2t |
| †B. Boobbyer | B. Boobbyer | B. Boobbyer | B. Boobbyer |
| L.B. Cannell | L.B. Cannell | L.B. Cannell | L.B. Cannell |
| †I.J. Botting | I.J. Botting | †J.P. Hyde | J.P. Hyde |
| *I. Preece | *I. Preece | *I. Preece | *I. Preece |
| G. Rimmer | W.K.T. Moore | W.K.T. Moore | W.K.T. Moore |
| J.M. Kendall-Carpenter | J.M. Kendall-Carpenter | J.M. Kendall-Carpenter | †J.L. Baume |
| E. Evans | J.H. Steeds | J.H. Steeds | J.H. Steeds |
| †W.A. Holmes | W.A. Holmes | W.A. Holmes | W.A. Holmes |
| G.R.D.'a Hosking | J.R.C. Matthews | J.R.C. Matthews | J.R.C. Matthews |
| †H.A. Jones | H.A. Jones | H.A. Jones | S.J. Adkins |
| †H.D. Small | H.D. Small | H.D. Small | H.D. Small |
| D.B. Vaughan | †S.J. Adkins | S.J. Adkins | J.M. Kendall-Carpenter |
| †J.J. Cain | V.G. Roberts 1t | V.G. Roberts | V.G. Roberts |
| Twickenham | Twickenham | Stade Colombes | Murrayfield |
| LOST 5-11 | WON 3-0 | LOST 3-6 | LOST 11-13 |
| ENG.: 1G | ENG.: 1T | FR.: 2T | SCOT.: 2G 1T |
| WALES: 1G 1PG 1T | IRE.: NIL | ENG.: 1T | ENG.: 1G 1PG 1T |
| 21 Jan. 1950 | 11 Feb. 1950 | 25 Feb. 1950 | 18 Mar. 1950 |

Controversy was aroused in 1950 by the unusual number of Dominion players – mostly South African but including one All Black – who played for England. The RFU's attitude to leading players from overseas was that such players should be accepted as "one of us" while the man was a resident in England.

Nevertheless, England's reliance on a number of Dominion players did little to enhance their chances of winning the Championship, and only one match – against Ireland – was won during a disappointing season. That win was the first over the Irish since 1938 and was due to a fine break by Preece which led to a try by Roberts.

John Kendall-Carpenter, one of England's finest utility forwards in the post-war seasons, changed from prop to number-eight (then called lock) towards the end of the campaign. Later he served the RFU as President and was an important member of the first International Rugby World Cup Organising Committee.

## 1950-51

| v. WALES | v. IRELAND | v. FRANCE | v. SCOTLAND |
|---|---|---|---|
| †E.N. Hewitt 1c | E.N. Hewitt | E.N. Hewitt | †W.G. Hook 1c |
| †C.G. Woodruff | C.G. Woodruff | C.G. Woodruff | C.G. Woodruff |
| †L.F.L. Oakley | I. Preece | I. Preece | A.C. Towell |
| B. Boobbyer | †J.M. Williams | B. Boobbyer 1t | J.M. Williams |
| V.R. Tindall | V.R. Tindall | V.R. Tindall | V.R. Tindall |
| I. Preece | †E.M.P. Hardy | E.M.P. Hardy | E.M.P. Hardy |
| G. Rimmer | G. Rimmer | G. Rimmer | †D.W. Shuttleworth |
| †R.V. Stirling | R.V. Stirling | R.V. Stirling | R.V. Stirling |
| †T. Smith | E. Evans | E. Evans | E. Evans |
| W.A. Holmes | W.A. Holmes | W.A. Holmes | W.A. Holmes |
| †D.T. Wilkins | D.T. Wilkins | D.T. Wilkins | D.T. Wilkins |
| †J.T. Bartlett | †B.A. Neale | B.A. Neale | B.A. Neale |
| *V.G. Roberts | V.G. Roberts | V.G. Roberts | V.G. Roberts |
| †P.B.C. Moore | *J.M. Kendall-Carpenter | *J.M. Kendall-Carpenter | *J.M. Kendall-Carpenter |
| †G.C. Rittson-Thomas 1t | G.C. Rittson-Thomas | G.C. Rittson-Thomas | D.F. White 1t |
| St. Helen's | Lansdowne Road | Twickenham | Twickenham |
| LOST 5-23 | LOST 0-3 | LOST 3-11 | WON 5-3 |
| Wales: 4g 1t | Ire.: 1pg | Eng.: 1t | Eng.: 1g |
| Eng.: 1g | Eng.: nil | Fr.: 1g 1dg 1t | Scot.: 1t |
| 20 Jan. 1951 | 10 Feb. 1951 | 24 Feb. 1951 | 17 Mar. 1951 |

England found themselves at the bottom of the Championship again in 1951. After a heavy defeat at Swansea – England's last international in that city – there was the consolation of a moral victory over the Irish in Dublin, restricting them to a penalty goal.

France's victory was their first at Twickenham but England managed to salvage some respect from a disappoinitng season with a narrow victory in the Calcutta Cup match. The England side, backs and forwards, showed fresh vigour and determination in a belated revival inspired by the captain, Kendall-Carpenter.

The pairing of the Blackheath and Army halves, Shuttleworth and Hardy, made a deal of difference to the attacking play of the backs, but it was the pack which paved the way for England's win. They foraged enthusiastically in the loose and scrummaged solidly in the tight.

## 1951-52

| v. S.AFRICA | v. WALES | v. SCOTLAND | v. IRELAND | v. FRANCE |
|---|---|---|---|---|
| W.G. Hook | W.G. Hook | †P.J. Collins | P.J. Collins | P.J. Collins |
| †J.E. Woodward | J.E. Woodward 1t | J.E. Woodward 1t | C.E. Winn | C.E. Winn |
| †A.E. Agar | A.E. Agar 1t | A.E. Agar 1dg | A.E. Agar | A.E. Agar |
| L.B. Cannell | L.B. Cannell | B. Boobbyer | B. Boobbyer 1t | B. Boobbyer |
| †C.E. Winn 1t | C.E. Winn | C.E. Winn 1t | †R.C. Bazley | R.C. Bazley |
| *N.M. Hall | *N.M. Hall | *N.M. Hall 2c | *N.M. Hall | *N.M. Hall 2pg |
| G. Rimmer | G. Rimmer | P.W. Sykes | P.W. Sykes | P.W. Sykes |
| W.A. Holmes | †E. Woodgate | W.A. Holmes | W.A. Holmes | W.A. Holmes |
| E. Evans | E. Evans | E. Evans 1t | E. Evans | E. Evans |
| R.V. Stirling | R.V. Stirling | R.V. Stirling | R.V. Stirling | R.V. Stirling |
| J.R.C. Matthews | J.R.C. Matthews | J.R.C. Matthews | J.R.C. Matthews | J.R.C. Matthews |
| D.T. Wilkins | D.T. Wilkins | D.T. Wilkins | D.T. Wilkins | D.T. Wilkins |
| D.F. White | D.F. White | D.F. White | D.F. White | D.F. White |
| J.M. Kendall-Carpenter | J.M. Kendall-Carpenter | J.M. Kendall-Carpenter 1t | J.M. Kendall-Carpenter | J.M. Kendall-Carpenter |
| †A.O. Lewis | A.O. Lewis | A.O. Lewis | A.O. Lewis | A.O. Lewis |
| Twickenham | Twickenham | Murrayfield | Twickenham | Stade Colombes |
| LOST 3-8 | LOST 6-8 | WON 19-3 | WON 3-0 | WON 6-3 |
| Eng.: 1t | Eng.: 2t | Scot.: 1t | Eng.: 1t | Fr.: 1t |
| SA: 1g 1pg | Wales: 1g 1t | Eng.: 2g 1dg 2t | Ire.: nil | Eng.: 2pg |
| 5 Jan. 1952 | 19 Jan. 1952 | 15 Mar. 1952 | 29 Mar. 1952 | 5 Apr. 1952 |

England fielded one of their most effective packs for years in 1952. Eric Evans was reaching the height of his powers as one of the best technical hookers in the British Isles and he was worthily supported by Holmes and Stirling as props. The 3-4-1 formation was now generally in use in international matches, and England's eighth man, Kendall-Carpenter, was the outstanding example of the new back-row player. He was an exceptional coverer and knowledgeable tactician.

Among the backs N.M. Hall, an excellent utility player equally at home at full-back or fly-half, led the side. A first-class tactical kicker, his methods were criticised during the season as being too safety-first. As a runner and creator of openings for his threequarters Hall was sadly lacking, and the new wings, Winn and Woodward, were little danger to defences which marked or tackled hard.

Nevertheless, after two seasons at the bottom of the Championship it was an achievement to win the last three games of the season (after defeats at Twickenham against South Africa and Wales) and finish the season as runners-up in the table.

## 1952-53

| | v. WALES | v. IRELAND | v. FRANCE | v. SCOTLAND |
|---|---|---|---|---|
| | *N.M. HALL 1C | *N.M. HALL 2PG | *N.M. HALL 1C | *N.M. HALL 4C |
| | J.E. WOODWARD 1PG | J.E. WOODWARD | J.E. WOODWARD 1T | J.E. WOODWARD 1T |
| | A.E. AGAR | A.E. AGAR | †J. BUTTERFIELD 1T | J. BUTTERFIELD 1T |
| | L.B. CANNELL 1T | L.B. CANNELL | L.B. CANNELL | †W.P.C. DAVIES |
| | R.C. BAZLEY | R.C. BAZLEY | R.C. BAZLEY | R.C. BAZLEY 2T |
| | †M. REGAN | M. REGAN | M. REGAN | M. REGAN |
| | P.W. SYKES | P.W. SYKES | P.W. SYKES | D.W. SHUTTLEWORTH |
| | W.A. HOLMES | W.A. HOLMES | W.A. HOLMES | W.A. HOLMES |
| | †N.A. LABUSCHAGNE | E. EVANS 1T | E. EVANS 1T | E. EVANS |
| | R.V. STIRLING | R.V. STIRLING | R.V. STIRLING | R.V. STIRLING 1T |
| | S.J. ADKINS | S.J. ADKINS | S.J. ADKINS | S.J. ADKINS 1T |
| | D.T. WILKINS | D.T. WILKINS | D.T. WILKINS | D.T. WILKINS |
| | D.F. WHITE | D.F. WHITE | †D.S. WILSON | D.F. WHITE |
| | J.M. KENDALL-CARPENTER | J.M. KENDALL-CARPENTER | J.M. KENDALL-CARPENTER | J.M. KENDALL-CARPENTER |
| | A.O. LEWIS | A.O. LEWIS | A.O. LEWIS | A.O. LEWIS |
| | Cardiff Arms Park | Lansdowne Road | Twickenham | Twickenham |
| | WON 8-3 | DRAWN 9-9 | WON 11-0 | WON 26-8 |
| | WALES: 1PG | IRE.: 2PG 1T | ENG.: 1G 2T | ENG.: 4G 2T |
| | ENG.: 1G 1PG | ENG.: 2PG 1T | FR.: NIL | SCOT.: 1G 1T |
| | 17 Jan. 1953 | 14 Feb. 1953 | 28 Feb. 1953 | 21 Mar. 1953 |

England captured the title in 1953, their first outright Championship since 1937. With the nucleus of the solid 1952 pack still available, the selectors plumped for greater attacking powers behind the scrum by blooding an adventurous new fly-half from Liverpool, Martin Regan. The introduction of Davies and Butterfield, two splendid all-round centres, made England the most complete side of the Championship.

Hall was now to be found at full-back. He had trained as a medical student at St Mary's Hospital before changing career and becoming a stockbroker. A modest, well-respected man, he died young in 1972. His soccer-style place-kicking (round-the-corner fashion) was regarded as a novelty in 1953, but it certainly came off, for he landed eight kicks at goal during the season.

Magazine-type programmes (first produced for the England v South Africa match in the previous year) were regularly used at Twickenham internationals from this season.

## 1953-54

| | v. WALES | v. NZ | v. IRELAND | v. SCOTLAND | v. FRANCE |
|---|---|---|---|---|---|
| | †I. KING | I. KING | I. KING 1PG,1C | †N. GIBBS 2C | N. GIBBS |
| | J.E. WOODWARD 2T | J.E. WOODWARD | J.E. WOODWARD | J.E. WOODWARD | J.E. WOODWARD |
| | †J.P. QUINN | J.P. QUINN | J.P. QUINN | J.P. QUINN | J.P. QUINN |
| | J. BUTTERFIELD | J. BUTTERFIELD | J. BUTTERFIELD 1T | J. BUTTERFIELD | J. BUTTERFIELD |
| | C.E. WINN 1T | W.P.C. DAVIES | W.P.C. DAVIES | C.E. WINN | C.E. WINN |
| | M. REGAN | M. REGAN | M. REGAN 1T | M. REGAN | M. REGAN |
| | G. RIMMER | G. RIMMER | G. RIMMER | G. RIMMER | †J.E. WILLIAMS |
| | †D.L. SANDERS | D.L. SANDERS | D.L. SANDERS | D.L. SANDERS | D.L. SANDERS |
| | E. EVANS | E. EVANS | E. EVANS | †E. ROBINSON | E. EVANS |
| | *R.V. STIRLING | *R.V. STIRLING | *R.V. STIRLING | *R.V. STIRLING | *R.V. STIRLING |
| | †P.D. YOUNG | P.D. YOUNG | P.D. YOUNG | P.D. YOUNG 1T | P.D. YOUNG |
| | †P.G. YARRANTON | P.G. YARRANTON | P.G. YARRANTON | †J.F. BANCE | V.H. LEADBETTER |
| | D.S. WILSON | D.S. WILSON | D.S. WILSON 1T | D.S. WILSON 2T | D.S. WILSON 1T |
| | J.M. KENDALL-CARPENTER | J.M. KENDALL-CARPENTER | J.M. KENDALL-CARPENTER | †V.H. LEADBETTER | J.M. KENDALL-CARPENTER |
| | †R. HIGGINS | R. HIGGINS | R. HIGGINS | R. HIGGINS | A.O. LEWIS |
| | Twickenham | Twickenham | Twickenham | Murrayfield | Stade Colombes |
| | WON 9-6 | LOST 0-5 | WON 14-3 | WON 13-3 | LOST 3-11 |
| | ENG.: 3T | ENG.: NIL | ENG.: 1G 1PG 2T | SCOT.: 1T | FR.: 1G 1DG 1T |
| | WALES: 1PG 1T | NZ: 1G | IRE.: 1PG | ENG.: 2G 1T | ENG.: 1T |
| | 16 Jan. 1954 | 30 Jan. 1954 | 13 Feb. 1954 | 20 Mar. 1954 | 10 Apr. 1954 |

The chief merit of the English side in 1954 was its will to attack. Regan was again the key player among the backs and his swift breaks brought out the best of a threequarter line which ran with purpose once in its stride. Too often, however, their attacks were carried out under intense pressure – the All Blacks and, at the end of the season, the French deploying their back rows to bottle-up the attacking genius of Regan.

Huge crowds for earlier Welsh visits to Twickenham had compelled the RFU to make the 1954 game between the nations the first all-ticket international at headquarters. England, taking their chances in a close match, went on to beat Ireland (where the pack did none too well) and took the Triple Crown after a decisive victory at Murrayfield.

The ability of the French forwards to take an early advantage up-front against an English pack which looked jaded and unimaginative deprived the English of the Grand Slam. In Paris Kendall-Carpenter played the last of his 23 matches. A schoolmaster by profession, he became Headmaster of Eastbourne College and later Wellington School.

## 1954-55

| v. WALES | v. IRELAND | v. FRANCE | v. SCOTLAND |
|---|---|---|---|
| *N.M. Hall | *N.M. Hall | †H. Scott | †N.S.D. Estcourt |
| J.E. Woodward | J.E. Woodward | †F.D. Sykes | F.D. Sykes 1t |
| J. Butterfield | J. Butterfield | J. Butterfield | J. Butterfield |
| W.P.C. Davies | W.P.C. Davies | W.P.C. Davies | W.P.C. Davies |
| R.C. Bazley | R.C. Bazley | R.C. Bazley | R.C. Bazley |
| †D.G.S. Baker | D.G.S. Baker | D.G.S. Baker | D.G.S. Baker |
| J.E. Williams | J.E. Williams | J.E. Williams | J.E. Williams |
| †D.St.G. Hazell | D.St.G. Hazell | D.St.G. Hazell 2pg | D.St.G. Hazell 1pg |
| N.A. Labuschagne | N.A. Labuschagne | N.A. Labuschagne | N.A. Labuschagne |
| †G.W.D. Hastings | G.W.D. Hastings 1t | G.W.D. Hastings | G.W.D. Hastings |
| P.D. Young | P.D. Young | *P.D. Young | *P.D. Young |
| †J.H. Hancock | J.H. Hancock | P.G. Yarranton | P.G. Yarranton |
| †P.H. Ryan | P.H. Ryan | D.S. Wilson | D.S. Wilson |
| †P.J. Taylor | P.J. Taylor | †I.D.S. Beer | I.D.S. Beer 1t |
| R. Higgins | R. Higgins | R. Higgins 1t | R. Higgins |
| Cardiff Arms Park | Lansdowne Road | Twickenham | Twickenham |
| LOST 0-3 | DRAWN 6-6 | LOST 9-16 | WON 9-6 |
| WALES: 1PG | IRE.: 1PG 1T | ENG.: 2PG 1T | ENG.: 1PG 2T |
| ENG.: NIL | ENG.: 2T | FR.: 2G 2DG | SCOT.: 1PG 1T |
| 22 Jan. 1955 | 12 Feb. 1955 | 26 Feb. 1955 | 19 Mar. 1955 |

Injuries, illness and retirements posed problems for the England selectors this season. There were problems over several of the pack positions as well as the old problem of finding a consistent and reliable goal-kicking full-back. In the event, the selectors fell back on Hall, playing him at full-back as captain.

Six new caps (including five in the forwards) made the trip to Cardiff in the middle of January, only to find the game postponed through heavy snow. The same side eventually played a week later, this time in such wet conditions that the pitch resembled a morass. Defeats at Cardiff and later in Dublin prompted changes for the game with France.

Even then there was no stopping a talented French side. It was only after a grim struggle that the first win of the season, by three points, was gained against the Scots.

## 1955-56

| v. WALES | v. IRELAND | v. SCOTLAND | v. FRANCE |
|---|---|---|---|
| †D.F. Allison 1pg | D.F. Allison 1pg | D.F. Allison | D.F. Allison 2pg |
| †P.B. Jackson | P.B. Jackson 1t | J.E. Woodward | P.B. Jackson |
| J. Butterfield | J. Butterfield 1t | J. Butterfield | J. Butterfield |
| W.P.C. Davies | L.B. Cannell | L.B. Cannell | L.B. Cannell |
| †P.H. Thompson | P.H. Thompson | P.H. Thompson | P.H. Thompson 1t |
| †M.J.K. Smith | M. Regan | M. Regan | M. Regan |
| †R.E.G. Jeeps | J.E. Williams | J.E. Williams 1t | J.E. Williams |
| D.L. Sanders | D.L. Sanders | D.L. Sanders | D.L. Sanders |
| *E. Evans | *E. Evans 1t | *E. Evans | *E. Evans |
| †C.R. Jacobs | C.R. Jacobs | C.R. Jacobs | C.R. Jacobs |
| †J.D. Currie | J.D. Currie 2pg,1c | J.D. Currie 2pg,1c | J.D. Currie |
| †R.W.D. Marques | R.W.D. Marques | R.W.D. Marques | R.W.D. Marques |
| †P.G.D. Robbins | P.G.D. Robbins | P.G.D. Robbins | P.G.D. Robbins |
| †A. Ashcroft | A. Ashcroft | A. Ashcroft | A. Ashcroft |
| V.G. Roberts | V.G. Roberts | V.G. Roberts | V.G. Roberts |
| Twickenham | Twickenham | Murrayfield | Stade Colombes |
| LOST 3-8 | WON 20-0 | WON 11-6 | LOST 9-14 |
| ENG.: 1PG | ENG.: 1G 3PG 2T | SCOT.: 1PG 1T | FR.: 1G 2PG 1T |
| WALES: 1G 1T | IRE.: NIL | ENG.: 1G 2PG | ENG.: 2PG 1T |
| 21 Jan. 1956 | 11 Feb. 1956 | 17 Mar. 1956 | 14 Apr. 1956 |

There were ten new caps under a new captain, Eric Evans of Sale, for the opening game of 1956. Although just two matches were won, the team formed the nucleus of the successful sides which Evans was to lead in following seasons. The pack, it will be noted, was unchanged during the season: indeed in the tight and line-out they had no superiors.

Currie and Marques began a long second-row partnership that was to last for five seasons. Their 22 appearances in tandem became a record partnership for England. Both had made their presence felt in Varsity rugby, Currie at Oxford, Marques at Cambridge, but it was at Harlequins where the two came together in club rugby when at the zeniths of their careers.

Regan returned to the England side after the Welsh defeat, but his flair in attack was diminished, and Butterfield, who had returned from an outstanding tour with the Lions to South Africa, was never quite able to reproduce his best form during the winter.

## 1956-57

| v. WALES | v. IRELAND | v. FRANCE | v. SCOTLAND |
|---|---|---|---|
| D.F. Allison 1PG | †R. Challis 1PG | R. Challis | R. Challis 1PG,2C |
| | | | |
| P.B. Jackson | P.B. Jackson 1T | P.B. Jackson 2T | P.B. Jackson |
| J. Butterfield | J. Butterfield | J. Butterfield | J. Butterfield |
| L.B. Cannell | L.B. Cannell | W.P.C. Davies | W.P.C. Davies 1T |
| P.H. Thompson | P.H. Thompson | P.H. Thompson | P.H. Thompson 1T |
| | | | |
| †R.M. Bartlett | R.M. Bartlett | R.M. Bartlett | R.M. Bartlett |
| R.E.G. Jeeps | R.E.G. Jeeps | R.E.G. Jeeps | R.E.G. Jeeps |
| | | | |
| C.R. Jacobs | C.R. Jacobs | C.R. Jacobs | C.R. Jacobs |
| *E. Evans | *E. Evans | *E. Evans 1T | *E. Evans |
| G.W.D. Hastings | G.W.D. Hastings | G.W.D. Hastings | G.W.D. Hastings |
| J.D. Currie | J.D. Currie | J.D. Currie | J.D. Currie |
| R.W.D. Marques | R.W.D. Marques | R.W.D. Marques | R.W.D. Marques |
| P.G.D. Robbins | P.G.D. Robbins | P.G.D. Robbins | P.G.D. Robbins |
| A. Ashcroft | A. Ashcroft | A. Ashcroft | A. Ashcroft |
| R. Higgins | R. Higgins | R. Higgins | R. Higgins 1T |
| | | | |
| Cardiff Arms Park | Lansdowne Road | Twickenham | Twickenham |
| WON 3-0 | WON 6-0 | WON 9-5 | WON 16-3 |
| | | | |
| WALES: NIL | IRE.: NIL | ENG.: 3T | ENG.: 2G 1PG 1T |
| ENG.: 1PG | ENG.: 1PG 1T | FR.: 1G | SCOT.: 1PG |
| | | | |
| 19 Jan. 1957 | 9 Feb. 1957 | 23 Feb. 1957 | 16 Mar. 1957 |

A series of satisfactory trial matches enabled the selectors to pick a balanced fifteen with a fair sprinkling of experience for the trip to Cardiff at the start of the season. Eleven of the English side had played against Wales in 1956, and the veteran centre Cannell, a doctor, had first played in an international in 1948.

The English backs had a nervous start to the season and penalty kicks assisted England to narrow away wins in Cardiff and Dublin. Then the halves, for the first time, had plenty of time to set their threequarters moving in the French game, and Bartlett was a constant danger to the visiting defence. His brilliant running brought out the best in Jackson on the wing, a tricky runner with a spectacular side-step. Jackson's two tries and one by the captain were enough for England to record their first win over France for four years.

Against Scotland, England played with assurance and their forwards took complete control in the tight and loose. The result was a comfortable victory which secured the Triple Crown and Grand Slam – England's first since 1928.

## 1957-58

| v. WALES | v. AUSTRALIA | v. IRELAND | v. FRANCE | v. SCOTLAND |
|---|---|---|---|---|
| D.F. Allison | †J.G.G. Hetherington 1PG | J.G.G. Hetherington 1PG | †J.S.M. Scott | D.F. Allison |
| | | | | |
| P.B. Jackson | P.B. Jackson 1T | †J.R.C. Young | P.B. Jackson 1T | P.B. Jackson |
| J. Butterfield | J. Butterfield | J. Butterfield | J. Butterfield | J. Butterfield |
| W.P.C. Davies | †M.S. Phillips 1T | M.S. Phillips | M.S. Phillips | M.S. Phillips |
| P.H. Thompson 1T | P.H. Thompson | P.H. Thompson | P.H. Thompson 2T | P.H. Thompson |
| | | | | |
| †J.P. Horrocks-Taylor | J.P. Horrocks-Taylor | R.M. Bartlett | R.M. Bartlett | R.M. Bartlett |
| R.E.G. Jeeps | R.E.G. Jeeps | R.E.G. Jeeps | R.E.G. Jeeps | R.E.G. Jeeps |
| | | | | |
| G.W.D. Hastings | G.W.D. Hastings | G.W.D. Hastings | G.W.D. Hastings 1PG,1C | G.W.D. Hastings 1PG |
| *E. Evans | *E. Evans | *E. Evans | *E. Evans | *E. Evans |
| C.R. Jacobs | C.R. Jacobs | C.R. Jacobs | C.R. Jacobs | C.R. Jacobs |
| J.D. Currie | J.D. Currie | J.D. Currie | J.D. Currie | J.D. Currie |
| R.W.D. Marques | R.W.D. Marques | R.W.D. Marques | R.W.D. Marques | R.W.D. Marques |
| P.G.D. Robbins | P.G.D. Robbins | P.G.D. Robbins | †A.J. Herbert | P.G.D. Robbins |
| A. Ashcroft | A. Ashcroft | A. Ashcroft 1T | A. Ashcroft | A. Ashcroft |
| †R.E. Syrett | R.E. Syrett | R.E. Syrett | R.E. Syrett | A.J. Herbert |
| | | | | |
| Twickenham | Twickenham | Twickenham | Stade Colombes | Murrayfield |
| DRAWN 3-3 | WON 9-6 | WON 6-0 | WON 14-0 | DRAWN 3-3 |
| | | | | |
| ENG.: 1T | ENG.: 2T 1PG | ENG.: 1PG 1T | FR.: NIL | SCOT.: 1PG |
| WALES: 1PG | AUST.: 1PG 1DG | IRE.: NIL | ENG.: 1G 1PG 2T | ENG.: 1PG |
| | | | | |
| 18 Jan. 1958 | 1 Feb. 1958 | 8 Feb. 1958 | 1 Mar. 1958 | 15 Mar. 1958 |

Once again Evans led an outstanding pack and an unbeaten team in 1958. After drawing the opening match of the season England gained their first post-war victory over a Dominion side when Australia were beaten in the closing minutes of a fast, frantic match. With the scores level, Peter Jackson received the ball near the right touchline. He set off on a swerving, feinting run which ended with a dive in the corner for a try.

Following the defeat of Ireland, England reserved their most impressive performance for the French in Paris. In a fantastic first half, Thompson and Jackson, flourishing on the wings of an efficient threequarter line and behind an improving pack, scored three splendid tries to set up England's biggest win against France since 1914.

A disappointing draw at Murrayfield, in which tight marking cancelled out the attacking qualities of England's backs, brought Eric Evans' England career to an end. His thirty appearances stood as a figure exceeded only by W.W. Wakefield.

## 1958-59

| v. WALES | v. IRELAND | v. FRANCE | v. SCOTLAND |
|---|---|---|---|
| J.G.G. Hetherington | J.G.G. Hetherington | J.G.G. Hetherington 1PG | J.G.G. Hetherington |
| P.B. Jackson | P.B. Jackson | P.B. Jackson | P.B. Jackson |
| M.S. Phillips | M.S. Phillips | M.S. Phillips | M.S. Phillips |
| *J. Butterfield | *J. Butterfield | *J. Butterfield | *J. Butterfield |
| P.H. Thompson | P.H. Thompson | P.H. Thompson | P.H. Thompson |
| †A.B.W. Risman | A.B.W. Risman 1PG | A.B.W. Risman | A.B.W. Risman 1PG |
| †S.R. Smith | R.E.G. Jeeps | S.R. Smith | S.R. Smith |
| †L.H. Webb | L.H. Webb | L.H. Webb | L.H. Webb |
| †J.A.S. Wackett | J.A.S. Wackett | †H.O. Godwin | H.O. Godwin |
| †G.J. Bendon | G.J. Bendon | G.J. Bendon | G.J. Bendon |
| J.D. Currie | J.D. Currie | J.D. Currie | J.D. Currie |
| R.W.D. Marques | R.W.D. Marques | R.W.D. Marques | R.W.D. Marques |
| A.J. Herbert | A.J. Herbert | A.J. Herbert | A.J. Herbert |
| †B.J. Wightman | A. Ashcroft | A. Ashcroft | A. Ashcroft |
| R. Higgins | †J.W. Clements | J.W. Clements | J.W. Clements |
| Cardiff Arms Park | Lansdowne Road | Twickenham | Twickenham |
| LOST 0-5 | WON 3-0 | DRAWN 3-3 | DRAWN 3-3 |
| WALES: 1G | IRE.: NIL | ENG.: 1PG | ENG.: 1PG |
| ENG.: NIL | ENG.: 1PG | FR.: 1PG | SCOT.: 1PG |
| 17 Jan. 1959 | 14 Feb. 1959 | 28 Feb. 1959 | 21 Mar. 1959 |

England failed to score a single try in 1959, yet only lost one of their four matches. Jeff Butterfield succeeded Evans as captain, taking a young side of six new caps to Cardiff. On a very muddy surface, and in wet and windy conditions, England were beaten by a Welsh side which maintained an aggressive dominance.

But the English side, the forwards in particular, improved steadily as the season progressed. Currie and Marques had few masters in the lineout and Ashcroft proved to be the best number-eight in the Championship. The unusual incidence of two consecutive drawn games (a penalty apiece in each case) left Butterfield's men joint runners-up in the table.

Nowadays, Butterfield is the manager of the Rugby Club in Hallam Street in London. He won 28 caps in the centre for England, retiring as his country's most-capped back.

## 1959-60

| v. WALES | v. IRELAND | v. FRANCE | v. SCOTLAND |
|---|---|---|---|
| †D. Rutherford 2PG,1C | D. Rutherford 1C | D. Rutherford | D. Rutherford 1PG,3C |
| J.R.C. Young | J.R.C. Young | J.R.C. Young | J.R.C. Young 1T |
| M.S. Phillips | M.S. Phillips | M.S. Phillips | M.S. Phillips |
| †M.P. Weston | M.P. Weston | M.P. Weston 1T | M.P. Weston |
| †J. Roberts 2T | J. Roberts | J. Roberts | J. Roberts 1T |
| †R.A.W. Sharp | R.A.W. Sharp 1DG | R.A.W. Sharp | R.A.W. Sharp 1DG |
| *R.E.G. Jeeps | *R.E.G. Jeeps | *R.E.G. Jeeps | *R.E.G. Jeeps |
| C.R. Jacobs | C.R. Jacobs | C.R. Jacobs | C.R. Jacobs |
| †S.A.M. Hodgson | S.A.M. Hodgson | S.A.M. Hodgson | S.A.M. Hodgson |
| †P.T. Wright | P.T. Wright | P.T. Wright | P.T. Wright |
| R.W.D. Marques | R.W.D. Marques 1T | R.W.D. Marques | R.W.D. Marques |
| J.D. Currie | J.D. Currie | J.D. Currie | J.D. Currie |
| P.G.D. Robbins | P.G.D. Robbins | P.G.D. Robbins | P.G.D. Robbins |
| †W.G.D. Morgan | W.G.D. Morgan | W.G.D. Morgan | W.G.D. Morgan |
| R.E. Syrett | R.E. Syrett | R.E. Syrett | R.E. Syrett 1T |
| Twickenham | Twickenham | Stade Colombes | Murrayfield |
| WON 14-6 | WON 8-5 | DRAWN 3-3 | WON 21-12 |
| ENG.: 1G 2PG 1T | ENG.: 1G 1DG | FR.: 1PG | SCOT.: 3PG 1T |
| WALES: 2PG | IRE.: 1G | ENG.: 1T | ENG.: 3G 1DG 1PG |
| 16 Jan. 1960 | 13 Feb. 1960 | 27 Feb. 1960 | 19 Mar. 1960 |

A new-look England side with seven new caps made a sensational start to the 1960 season. Accurate place-kicking by Rutherford, the Percy Park full-back, and tries by Jim Roberts of Old Millhillians, accelerated England to a 14-0 lead against Wales. The discovery of the match was Richard Sharp at fly-half. He replaced Risman at the last minute but came to be regarded as the player of the season.

The England side, for the only time in its history, was unchanged throughout the season. Thanks to the solidity and expertise of a skilful pack, England were never short of good ball, and once again Currie and Marques were key players in the tight.

The Triple Crown was secured after victory at Murrayfield in another match noted for England's high scoring. Sharp was in brilliant form, receiving a smooth service from Jeeps, his captain and scrum-half, at the heels of a magnificent pack. England's total of 21 points was their highest international score since 1953.

## 1960-61

| v. S.AFRICA | v. WALES | v. IRELAND | v. FRANCE | v. SCOTLAND |
|---|---|---|---|---|
| D. RUTHERFORD | †M.N. GAVINS | †J.G. WILLCOX | J.G. WILLCOX 1c | J.G. WILLCOX |
| | | | | |
| J.R.C. YOUNG | J.R.C. YOUNG 1T | J.R.C. YOUNG | J.R.C. YOUNG | P.B. JACKSON |
| †W.M. PATTERSON | M.S. PHILLIPS | A.B.W. RISMAN 1c | A.B.W. RISMAN | W.M. PATTERSON |
| M.P. WESTON | M.P. WESTON | M.P. WESTON | M.P. WESTON | M.P. WESTON |
| J. ROBERTS | J. ROBERTS | J. ROBERTS 1T | J. ROBERTS | J. ROBERTS 1T |
| | | | | |
| A.B.W. RISMAN | A.B.W. RISMAN | R.A.W. SHARP | R.A.W. SHARP | J.P. HORROCKS-TAYLOR 1PG |
| *R.E.G. JEEPS | *R.E.G. JEEPS | *R.E.G. JEEPS | *R.E.G. JEEPS | *R.E.G. JEEPS |
| | | | | |
| C.R. JACOBS | C.R. JACOBS | C.R. JACOBS | C.R. JACOBS | C.R. JACOBS |
| S.A.M. HODGSON | S.A.M. HODGSON | E. ROBINSON | E. ROBINSON | E. ROBINSON |
| P.T. WRIGHT | P.T. WRIGHT | P.T. WRIGHT | P.T. WRIGHT | P.T. WRIGHT |
| R.W.D. MARQUES | R.W.D. MARQUES | †J. PRICE | †V.S.J. HARDING 1T | V.S.J. HARDING |
| J.D. CURRIE | †R.J. FRENCH | R.J. FRENCH | R.J. FRENCH | R.J. FRENCH |
| P.G.D. ROBBINS | P.G.D. ROBBINS | †D.P. ROGERS 1T | D.P. ROGERS | D.P. ROGERS |
| W.G.D. MORGAN | W.G.D. MORGAN | W.G.D. MORGAN | W.G.D. MORGAN | W.G.D. MORGAN |
| †L.I. RIMMER | L.I. RIMMER | L.I. RIMMER | L.I. RIMMER | L.I. RIMMER |
| | | | | |
| Twickenham | Cardiff Arms Park | Lansdowne Road | Twickenham | Twickenham |
| LOST 0-5 | LOST 3-6 | LOST 8-11 | DRAWN 5-5 | WON 6-0 |
| | | | | |
| ENG.: NIL | WALES: 2T | IRE.: 1G 2PG | ENG.: 1G | ENG.: 1PG 1T |
| SA: 1G | ENG.: 1T | ENG.: 1G 1T | FR.: 1G | SCOT.: NIL |
| | | | | |
| 7 Jan. 1961 | 21 Jan. 1961 | 11 Feb. 1961 | 25 Feb. 1961 | 18 Mar. 1961 |

English hopes of regaining the Championship faded with their third consecutive defeat of the season – the loss to Ireland following narrow defeats against the Springboks and down at Cardiff to Wales.

During the season the selectors were criticised over their inability to decide which player, Risman or Sharp, was better equipped to spearhead the English attack from fly-half. As a compromise they had used both players, preferring Risman as a centre, but with little effect.

For the Scottish match Horrocks-Taylor was reinstated, Sharp having been injured and Risman having gone North. Peter Jackson too was recalled as England gained their only success of the season in a dour struggle at Twickenham. Horrocks-Taylor, whose tactical kicking in the game was faultless, kicked a penalty and helped Roberts to a try.

## 1961-62

| v. WALES | v. IRELAND | v. FRANCE | v. SCOTLAND |
|---|---|---|---|
| J.G. WILLCOX | J.G. WILLCOX | J.G. WILLCOX | J.G. WILLCOX 1PG |
| | | | |
| †A.M. UNDERWOOD | A.M. UNDERWOOD | A.M. UNDERWOOD | †A.C.B. HURST |
| †M.R. WADE | M.R. WADE 1T | M.R. WADE | A.M. UNDERWOOD |
| M.P. WESTON | M.P. WESTON | M.P. WESTON | †J.M. DEE |
| J. ROBERTS | J. ROBERTS 1T | J. ROBERTS | J. ROBERTS |
| | | | |
| R.A.W. SHARP | R.A.W. SHARP 1PG,1T,2C | R.A.W. SHARP | J.P. HORROCKS-TAYLOR |
| *R.E.G. JEEPS | *R.E.G. JEEPS | *R.E.G. JEEPS | *R.E.G. JEEPS |
| | | | |
| †P.E. JUDD | P.E. JUDD | P.E. JUDD | P.E. JUDD |
| S.A.M. HODGSON | S.A.M. HODGSON | S.A.M. HODGSON | S.A.M. HODGSON |
| P.T. WRIGHT | P.T. WRIGHT | P.T. WRIGHT | P.T. WRIGHT |
| V.S.J. HARDING | V.S.J. HARDING | V.S.J. HARDING | V.S.J. HARDING |
| J.D. CURRIE | J.D. CURRIE | J.D. CURRIE | †T.A. PARGETTER |
| D.P. ROGERS | D.P. ROGERS | D.P. ROGERS | P.G.D. ROBBINS |
| P.J. TAYLOR | P.J. TAYLOR | P.J. TAYLOR | P.J. TAYLOR |
| R.E. SYRETT | R.E. SYRETT | R.E. SYRETT | †S.J. PURDY |
| | | | |
| Twickenham | Twickenham | Stade Colombes | Murrayfield |
| DRAWN 0-0 | WON 16-0 | LOST 0-13 | DRAWN 3-3 |
| | | | |
| ENG.: NIL | ENG.: 2G 1PG 1T | FR.: 2G 1T | SCOT.: 1PG |
| WALES: NIL | IRE.: NIL | ENG.: NIL | ENG.: 1PG |
| | | | |
| 20 Jan. 1962 | 10 Feb. 1962 | 24 Feb. 1962 | 17 Mar. 1962 |

England returned a disappointing record in 1962. There was a scoreless draw against Wales – the first between the sides since 1936 – and an uninspiring drawn game at Murrayfield where both sides scored a penalty goal (the third 3-3 draw in the series since 1958). In Paris, France completely outplayed England, who had their goal-line crossed three times. Only the full-back, John Willcox, won praise in that match: his brave tackling on a hard pitch, and his accurate line-kicking, saving England from a heavier defeat.

Sixteen of England's 19 points this season came in an entertaining match against Ireland. The same side which had figured in the drab draw with Wales (and which later was picked *en bloc* for Paris) played attractive attacking football to overcome an inexperienced Irish side.

Sharp was the ideal spearhead for England's backs and a combination pledged to all-out attack ran in three excellent tries. Jeeps was outstanding at scrum-half, and ended his England career at the close of the season. He won 24 caps to create a record for an English scrum-half. Later he was a distinguished sports administrator, and served the RFU as President.

## 1962-63

| v. WALES | v. IRELAND | v. FRANCE | v. SCOTLAND |
|---|---|---|---|
| J.G. WILLCOX | J.G. WILLCOX | J.G. WILLCOX 2PG | J.G. WILLCOX 2C |
| P.B. JACKSON | P.B. JACKSON | P.B. JACKSON | P.B. JACKSON |
| M.S. PHILLIPS 1T | M.S. PHILLIPS | M.S. PHILLIPS | M.S. PHILLIPS |
| M.P. WESTON | M.P. WESTON | M.P. WESTON | M.P. WESTON |
| J. ROBERTS | J. ROBERTS | J. ROBERTS | J. ROBERTS |
| *R.A.W. SHARP 2C,1DG | *R.A.W. SHARP | *R.A.W. SHARP | *R.A.W. SHARP 1T |
| †S.J.S. CLARKE | S.J.S. CLARKE | S.J.S. CLARKE | S.J.S. CLARKE |
| †N.J. DRAKE-LEE | N.J. DRAKE-LEE | N.J. DRAKE-LEE | N.J. DRAKE-LEE 1T |
| †J.D. THORNE | J.D. THORNE | J.D. THORNE | H.O. GODWIN |
| †B.A. DOVEY | B.A. DOVEY | †K.J. WILSON | P.E. JUDD |
| †A.M. DAVIS | A.M. DAVIS | T.A. PARGETTER | A.M. DAVIS |
| †J.E. OWEN 1T | J.E. OWEN | J.E. OWEN | J.E. OWEN |
| D.P. ROGERS | D.P. ROGERS | D.P. ROGERS | D.P. ROGERS |
| B.J. WIGHTMAN | B.J. WIGHTMAN | †D.G. PERRY | D.G. PERRY |
| †D.C. MANLEY | D.C. MANLEY | D.C. MANLEY | D.C. MANLEY |
| Cardiff Arms Park | Lansdowne Road | Twickenham | Twickenham |
| WON 13-6 | DRAWN 0-0 | WON 6-5 | WON 10-8 |
| WALES: 1PG 1T | IRE.: NIL | ENG.: 2PG | ENG.: 2G |
| ENG.: 2G 1DG | ENG.: NIL | FR.: 1G | SCOT.: 1G 1DG |
| 19 Jan. 1963 | 9 Feb. 1963 | 23 Feb. 1963 | 16 Mar. 1963 |

England fielded an experimental side for their opening match of 1963. Seven new caps were in a fifteen which gained England's seventh win at Cardiff. Without being really impressive, the English side acclimatised better to an icy pitch, showed fine qualities in defence, and thanks to some spirited running by Phillips and Sharp managed to score two decisive tries.

The forwards were more sluggish in the mud in Dublin and a scoreless draw prompted the selectors to tinker slightly with the pack. Three changes were made for the French match, though England had to thank the accuracy of Willcox's place-kicking for a narrow victory at Twickenham, his two penalties outpointing a converted French try.

Richard Sharp made a captain's effort to snatch the Calcutta Cup and the Championship late in the Scottish game. With the help of three audacious dummies the Cornishman squeezed through a narrow opening in the Scottish defence for a try which Willcox converted. Sharp's score placed England into the lead for the first time in the match, a lead which was not relinquished.

## 1963

| 1st v. NZ | 2nd v. NZ | v. AUSTRALIA |
|---|---|---|
| †R.W. HOSEN 2PG,1C | R.W. HOSEN 1PG | R.W. HOSEN |
| †J.M. RANSON 1T | J.M. RANSON | F.D. SYKES |
| M.S. PHILLIPS | M.S. PHILLIPS 1T | M.S. PHILLIPS 1T |
| *M.P. WESTON | *M.P. WESTON | *M.P. WESTON |
| J.M. DEE | F.D. SYKES | J.M. RANSON |
| J.P. HORROCKS-TAYLOR | J.P. HORROCKS-TAYLOR | J.P. HORROCKS-TAYLOR |
| S.J.S. CLARKE | S.J.S. CLARKE | S.J.S. CLARKE 1T |
| C.R. JACOBS | C.R. JACOBS | C.R. JACOBS |
| H.O. GODWIN | H.O. GODWIN | H.O. GODWIN 1T |
| P.E. JUDD | P.E. JUDD | P.E. JUDD |
| T.A. PARGETTER | D.G. PERRY | D.G. PERRY |
| A.M. DAVIS | A.M. DAVIS | J.E. OWEN |
| D.P. ROGERS | D.P. ROGERS | D.P. ROGERS |
| D.G. PERRY | B.J. WIGHTMAN | B.J. WIGHTMAN |
| †V.R. MARRIOTT | V.R. MARRIOTT | V.R. MARRIOTT |
| Auckland | Christchurch | Sydney |
| LOST 11-21 | LOST 6-9 | LOST 9-18 |
| NZ: 3G 1DG 1PG | NZ: 1GM 2T | AUST.: 3G 1T |
| ENG.: 1G 2PG | ENG.: 1PG 1T | ENG.: 3T |
| 25 May 1963 | 1 Jun. 1963 | 4 Jan. 1963 |

England were not at full strength when they carried out their first tour to Australasia in the summer of 1963. Mike Weston was captain of a side which became the first Home Union to tour down under.

The side was comprehensively beaten in the first Test in New Zealand, the All Black full-back Don Clarke scoring 15 points after Hosen had given England an early lead. For the second Test, the selectors brought in Frank Sykes, a 35-year-old wing last capped for England in 1955. In their best display of the tour England were unlucky to lose in the dying minutes to a goal from a mark by Clarke. Their pack, with Davis outstanding (despite the discomfort of a dislocated shoulder), won plenty of line-out ball and powered into the rucks and mauls.

The sixth and final match of the tour was played on a waterlogged ground in Sydney. There, after trailing by twelve points at the interval, England staged a second-half recovery in which three tries were scored. But Australia's defence was firm enough to hold on for a first win over England since 1948.

## 1963-64

| v. NZ | v. WALES | v. IRELAND | v. FRANCE | v. SCOTLAND |
|---|---|---|---|---|
| *J.G. WILLCOX | *J.G. WILLCOX | *J.G. WILLCOX 1c | J.G. WILLCOX | J.G. WILLCOX |
| | | | | |
| M.S. PHILLIPS | M.S. PHILLIPS | A.M. UNDERWOOD | R.W. HOSEN 1PG | R.W. HOSEN 1PG |
| M.P. WESTON | M.P. WESTON | M.S. PHILLIPS | M.S. PHILLIPS 1T | M.S. PHILLIPS |
| †R.D. SANGWIN | R.D. SANGWIN | M.P. WESTON | M.P. WESTON | M.P. WESTON |
| J. ROBERTS | J.M. RANSON 1T | J.M. RANSON | J.M. RANSON | J.M. RANSON |
| | | | | |
| J.P. HORROCKS-TAYLOR | J.P. HORROCKS-TAYLOR | †T.J. BROPHY | T.J. BROPHY | T.J. BROPHY |
| S.J.S. CLARKE | S.J.S. CLRKE | S.J.S. CLARKE | S.R. SMITH | S.R. SMITH |
| | | | | |
| P.E. JUDD | C.R. JACOBS | C.R. JACOBS | *C.R. JACOBS | *C.R. JACOBS |
| H.O. GODWIN | S.A.M. HODGSON | H.O. GODWIN | H.O. GODWIN | H.O. GODWIN |
| N.J. DRAKE-LEE | N.J. DRAKE-LEE | N.J. DRAKE-LEE | †D.F.B. WRENCH | D.F.B. WRENCH |
| A.M. DAVIS | A.M. DAVIS | A.M. DAVIS | A.M. DAVIS | A.M. DAVIS |
| J.E. OWEN | †R.E. ROWELL | †C.M. PAYNE | C.M. PAYNE | C.M. PAYNE |
| D.P. ROGERS | D.P. ROGERS | D.P. ROGERS 1T | D.P. ROGERS | D.P. ROGERS 1T |
| D.G. PERRY | D.G. PERRY 1T | D.G. PERRY | †T.G.A.H. PEART | T.G.A.H. PEART |
| V.R. MARRIOTT | †P.J. FORD | P.J. FORD | P.J. FORD | P.J. FORD |
| | | | | |
| Twickenham | Twickenham | Twickenham | Stade Colombes | Murrayfield |
| LOST 0-14 | DRAWN 6-6 | LOST 5-18 | WON 6-3 | LOST 6-15 |
| | | | | |
| ENG.: NIL | ENG.: 2T | ENG.: 1G | FR.: 1T | SCOT.: 3G |
| NZ: 1G 2PG 1T | WALES: 2T | IRE.: 3G 1T | ENG.: 1PG 1T | ENG.: 1PG 1T |
| | | | | |
| 4 Jan. 1964 | 18 Jan. 1964 | 8 Feb. 1964 | 22 Feb. 1964 | 21 Mar. 1964 |

England's poor performances in 1964 were a disappointment, for it was predicted that the side had gained good experience on the Australasian tour where, it was expected, a settled side had developed into a fifteen which would challenge fiercely for the Championship.

Such hopes were dismissed in the match with New Zealand. England's defeat by 14 points at Twickenham was their worst result at the ground since the inaugural match of 1910. Although Wales were held to a draw, several changes were prompted after Ireland's big win at Twickenham. The veteran prop Jacobs, from Northampton, relieved Willcox of the captaincy for the French match, and with the forwards playing soundly England registered their only win of the season. Godwin took six strikes against the head in this match and there were good tactical displays by Smith and Brophy, the halves.

England retained the side for the match with Scotland. But the forward strength was insufficient to match the Scots, who went on to regain the Calcutta Cup for the first time since 1950. Malcolm Phillips made the last of his 25 appearances in the match. He had been an outstanding threequarter in one of England's most talented post-war lines.

## 1964-65

| v. WALES | v. IRELAND | v. FRANCE | v. SCOTLAND |
|---|---|---|---|
| D. RUTHERFORD 1PG | D. RUTHERFORD | D. RUTHERFORD 2PG | D. RUTHERFORD |
| | | | |
| †E.L. RUDD | E.L. RUDD | †A.W. HANCOCK | E.L. RUDD |
| †D.W.A. ROSSER | D.W.A. ROSSER | D.W.A. ROSSER | D.W.A. ROSSER |
| †G.P. FRANKCOM | G.P. FRANKCOM | G.P. FRANKCOM | G.P. FRANKCOM |
| †C.P. SIMPSON | †P.W. COOK | P.W. COOK | A.W. HANCOCK 1T |
| | | | |
| T.J. BROPHY | T.J. BROPHY | M.P. WESTON | M.P. WESTON |
| J.E. WILLIAMS | S.J.S. CLARKE | S.J.S. CLARKE | S.J.S. CLARKE |
| | | | |
| †A.L. HORTON | A.L. HORTON | A.L. HORTON | A.L. HORTON |
| †S.B. RICHARDS | S.B. RICHARDS | S.B. RICHARDS | S.B. RICHARDS |
| N.J. DRAKE-LEE | P.E. JUDD | P.E. JUDD | P.E. JUDD |
| J.E. OWEN | J.E. OWEN | J.E. OWEN | J.E. OWEN |
| R.E. ROWELL | C.M. PAYNE | C.M. PAYNE 1T | C.M. PAYNE |
| D.P. ROGERS | D.P. ROGERS | D.P. ROGERS | D.P. ROGERS |
| *D.G. PERRY | *D.G. PERRY | *D.G. PERRY | *D.G. PERRY |
| †N. SILK | N. SILK | N. SILK | N. SILK |
| | | | |
| Cardiff Arms Park | Lansdowne Road | Twickenham | Twickenham |
| LOST 3-14 | LOST 0-5 | WON 9-6 | DRAWN 3-3 |
| | | | |
| WALES: 1G 1DG 2T | IRE.: 1G | ENG.: 2PG 1T | ENG.: 1T |
| ENG.: 1PG | ENG.: NIL | FR.: 1PG 1T | SCOT.: 1DG |
| | | | |
| 16 Jan. 1965 | 13 Feb. 1965 | 27 Feb. 1965 | 20 Mar. 1965 |

Adverse weather conditions were key factors in England's opening matches of 1965. At Cardiff, in rain and mud, then later in Dublin in a gale-force wind, England were unable to adapt to the conditions and their opponents secured fine wins.

Several changes were made before the French match, the recall of Weston at fly-half ranking as the most significant. His previous appearances had been at centre, but his play at pivot, particularly his masterful tactical kicking, turned this game in England's favour. Hooker Richards took ten strikes against the head and the place-kicking of Don Rutherford, technically one of the soundest full-backs capped for England since the war, was accurate enough to see England home by three points.

HM the Queen was present at Twickenham to watch Hancock seize victory from the Scots with a last-minute try. Scotland led 3-0 in the dying minutes of the match when Weston threw a pass to Hancock on the left and near touch. The Northampton wing then made a scorching dash down the touchline to lunge over at the north end of the ground. It was the longest run for a try ever seen in an international match.

## 1965-66

| v. WALES | v. IRELAND | v. FRANCE | v. SCOTLAND |
|---|---|---|---|
| D. Rutheford 1PG | D. Rutherford 1PG | D. Rutherford | D. Rutherford |
| E.L. Rudd | E.L. Rudd | K.F. Savage | E.L. Rudd |
| †T.G. Arthur | T.G. Arthur | †R.D. Hearn | R.D. Hearn |
| D.W.A. Rosser | †C.W. McFadyean | C.W. McFadyean | C.W. McFadyean 1DG |
| †K.F. Savage | K.F. Savage | A.W. Hancock | K.F. Savage |
| T.J. Brophy | T.J. Brophy | T.J. Brophy | M.P. Weston |
| †Jeremy Spencer | †R.C. Ashby | R.C. Ashby | †T.C. Wintle |
| P.E. Judd | P.E. Judd | P.E. Judd | P.E. Judd |
| †J.V. Pullin | †W.T. Treadwell | W.T. Treadwell | W.T. Treadwell |
| †D.L. Powell | D.L. Powell | A.L. Horton | A.L. Horton |
| C.M. Payne | C.M. Payne | C.M. Payne | C.M. Payne |
| A.M. Davis | J.E. Owen | J.E. Owen | J.E. Owen |
| *D.P. Rogers | *D.P. Rogers | *D.P. Rogers | *D.P. Rogers |
| D.G. Perry 1T | D.G. Perry | D.G. Perry | †G.A. Sherriff |
| †R.B. Taylor | †J.R.H. Greenwood 1T | J.R.H. Greenwood | J.R.H. Greenwood |
| Twickenham | Twickenham | Stade Colombes | Murrayfield |
| LOST 6-11 | DRAWN 6-6 | LOST 0-13 | LOST 3-6 |
| ENG.: 1PG 1T | ENG.: 1PG 1T | FR.: 2G 1T | SCOT.: 1PG 1T |
| WALES: 1G 2PG | IRE.: 1PG 1T | ENG.: NIL | ENG.: 1DG |
| 15 Jan. 1966 | 12 Feb. 1966 | 26 Feb. 1966 | 19 Mar. 1966 |

Three defeats and a draw left England floundering at the bottom of the Championship in 1966 with only one point out of eight – their worst return in the competition since 1948. Altogether 26 players were used, including thirteen new caps and three different scrum-halves.

England's troubles lay principally in the scrum and particularly in the second row. Only against Ireland was the line-out play up to international class. Injuries compounded England's problems in Paris, where Perry, Horton and the skipper Rogers sustained nasty knocks which reduced their effectiveness.

For the Scottish match the selectors brought Weston back at fly-half. His astute tactical kicking gave a fresh edge to the English backs, but even his skills could not persuade the brilliant Scottish forwards to give up a lead gained early in the second half.

## 1966-67

| v. AUSTRALIA | v. IRELAND | v. FRANCE | v. SCOTLAND | v. WALES |
|---|---|---|---|---|
| R.W. Hosen 2PG,1C | R.W. Hosen 1PG,1C | R.W. Hosen 3PG | R.W. Hosen 2PG,3C | R.W. Hosen 4PG |
| †P.B. Glover | K.F. Savage | K.F. Savage | K.F. Savage | K.F. Savage 1T |
| C.W. McFadyean | R.D. Hearn | R.D. Hearn | R.D. Hearn | R.D. Hearn |
| †C.R. Jennins | C.R. Jennins | C.R. Jennins | C.W. McFadyean 2T | C.W. McFadyean |
| K.F. Savage | C.W. McFadyean 1T | C.W. McFadyean | †R.E. Webb 1T | R.E. Webb |
| *R.A.W. Sharp | †J.F. Finlan | J.F. Finlan 1DG | J.F. Finlan 1DG | J.F. Finlan |
| R.C. Ashby 1T | †R.D.A. Pickering | R.D.A. Pickering | R.D.A. Pickering | R.D.A. Pickering |
| P.E. Judd | *P.E. Judd | *P.E. Judd | *P.E. Judd | *P.E. Judd |
| S.B. Richards | S.B. Richards | S.B. Richards | S.B. Richards | S.B. Richards |
| †M.J. Coulman | M.J. Coulman | M.J. Coulman | M.J. Coulman | M.J. Coulman |
| A.M. Davis | †J. Barton | J. Barton | J.N. Pallant | J. Barton 2T |
| †P.J. Larter | †D.E.J. Watt | D.E.J. Watt | D.E.J. Watt | D.E.J. Watt |
| D.P. Rogers | †D.M. Rollitt | D.M. Rollitt | D.P. Rogers | D.P. Rogers |
| G.A. Sherriff | †J.N. Pallant | J.N. Pallant | D.M. Rollitt | D.M. Rollitt |
| J.R.H. Greenwood | R.B. Taylor | R.B. Taylor | R.B. Taylor 1T | R.B. Taylor |
| Twickenham | Lansdowne Road | Twickenham | Twickenham | Cardiff Arms Park |
| LOST 11-23 | WON 8-3 | LOST 12-16 | WON 27-14 | LOST 21-34 |
| ENG.: 1G 2PG | IRE.: 1PG | ENG.: 3PG 1DG | ENG.: 3G 2PG 1DG 1T | WALES: 5G 2PG 1DG |
| AUST.: 1G 3DG 2PG 1T | ENG.: 1G 1PG | FR.: 2G 1DG 1PG | SCOT.: 1G 2PG 1T | ENG.: 4PG 3T |
| 7 Jan. 1967 | 11 Feb. 1967 | 25 Feb. 1967 | 18 Mar. 1967 | 15 Apr. 1967 |

England improved substantially as the season progressed. The selectors responded to the heavy Australian defeat by making wholesale changes for the trip to Dublin and a lucky bounce and fast chase by McFadyean provided England with a late win over the Irish. It marked England's first win in an international match for seven matches and their first over Ireland since 1962.

Two exciting matches at Twickenham followed. After narrowly losing to France, England played inventive football against the Scots and the result was one of the most entertaining games of the year. Scotland were only overtaken in the closing minutes when a flurry of scoring helped England to a comfortable win.

England thus went in search of the Triple Crown at Cardiff in April. The fixture congestion caused by the Wallabies' tour had prompted the authorities to stage the match in the spring. The outcome was a fast, open game, with Wales winning a high-scoring contest. Hosen's four penalties pushed his total of points for the season to 46, a new English record.

## 1967-68

| v. NZ | v. WALES | v. IRELAND | v. FRANCE | v. SCOTLAND |
|---|---|---|---|---|
| D. RUTHERFORD 1C | †R. HILLER 1PG,1C | R. HILLER 2PG | R. HILLER 2PG | R. HILLER 1C,1PG |
| | | | | |
| K.F. SAVAGE | †D.H. PROUT | D.H. PROUT | K.F. SAVAGE | K.F. SAVAGE |
| C.W. McFADYEAN | *C.W. McFADYEAN 1T | *C.W. McFADYEAN | †T.J. BROOKE | T.J. BROOKE |
| †R.H. LLOYD 2T | R.H. LLOYD | R.H. LLOYD | R.H. LLOYD | R.H. LLOYD |
| R.E. WEBB | K.F. SAVAGE | R.E. WEBB | R.E. WEBB | R.E. WEBB |
| | | | | |
| J.F. FINLAN | J.F. FINLAN | J.F. FINLAN 1DG | *M.P. WESTON 1DG | *M.P. WESTON |
| †W.J. GITTINGS | †B.W. REDWOOD 1T | B.W. REDWOOD | R.D.A. PICKERING | R.D.A. PICKERING |
| | | | | |
| A.L. HORTON | †B.W. KEEN | B.W. KEEN | B.W. KEEN | B.W. KEEN |
| H.O. GODWIN | J.V. PULLIN | J.V. PULLIN | J.V. PULLIN | J.V. PULLIN |
| *P.E. JUDD | M.J. COULMAN | M.J. COULMAN | M.J. COULMAN | M.J. COULMAN 1T |
| P.J. LARTER 1PG | †M.J. PARSONS | M.J. PARSONS | M.J. PARSONS | M.J. PARSONS |
| J.E. OWEN | P.J. LARTER | P.J. LARTER | P.J. LARTER | P.J. LARTER |
| D.P. ROGERS | †B.R. WEST | B.R. WEST | B.R. WEST | B.R. WEST |
| G.A. SHERRIFF | †D.J. GAY | D.J. GAY | D.J. GAY | D.J. GAY |
| R.B. TAYLOR | †P.J. BELL | P.J. BELL | P.J. BELL | P.J. BELL |
| | | | | |
| Twickenham | Twickenham | Twickenham | Stade Colombes | Murrayfield |
| LOST 11-23 | DRAWN 11-11 | DRAWN 9-9 | LOST 9-14 | WON 8-6 |
| | | | | |
| ENG.: 1G 1PG 1T | ENG.: 1G 1PG 1T | ENG.: 2PG 1DG | FR.: 1G 1PG 2DG | SCOT.: 1PG 1DG |
| NZ: 4G 1T | WALES: 1G 1DG 1T | IRE.: 3PG | ENG.: 1DG 2PG | ENG.: 1G 1PG |
| | | | | |
| 4 Nov. 1967 | 20 Jan. 1968 | 10 Feb. 1968 | 24 Feb. 1968 | 16 Mar. 1968 |

The selectors had a miserable season in 1968. A heavy defeat by the All Blacks and two undistinguished performances against Wales and Ireland forced them to ring the changes. In all England used 28 players in the five matches and awarded eleven new caps, but only two playes were retained during the season: Lloyd, the brilliant centre who was very highly rated by the New Zealand tourists, and Larter, the big second-row.

Bob Hiller entered international rugby against the Welsh. He was to play 19 times at full-back and score 138 points for England, records which stood for a decade until overhauled by the Leicester full-back, Dusty Hare.

England's best performance was against Scotland, when Mick Weston, the excellent tactical kicker at fly-half, led England on his last appearance in an international. He finished with 29 caps, was later elected to the RFU Selection Committee, and became Chairman of the Selectors.

## 1968-69

| v. IRELAND | v. FRANCE | v. SCOTLAND | v. WALES |
|---|---|---|---|
| R. HILLER 4PG | R. HILLER 3PG,2C | R. HILLER 1C | R. HILLER 3PG |
| | | | |
| †K.J. FIELDING | K.J. FIELDING 1T | K.J. FIELDING¹ | †K.C. PLUMMER |
| †J.S. SPENCER | J.S. SPENCER | J.S. SPENCER | J.S. SPENCER |
| †D.J. DUCKHAM 1T | D.J. DUCKHAM | D.J. DUCKHAM 2T | D.J. DUCKHAM |
| R.E. WEBB | R.E. WEBB 1T | R.E. WEBB | R.E. WEBB |
| | | | |
| J.F. FINLAN | J.F. FINLAN | J.F. FINLAN | J.F. FINLAN |
| T.C. WINTLE | T.C. WINTLE | T.C. WINTLE | T.C. WINTLE |
| | | | |
| D.L. POWELL | D.L. POWELL | D.L. POWELL | D.L. POWELL |
| J.V. PULLIN | J.V. PULLIN | J.V. PULLIN | J.V. PULLEN |
| †K.E. FAIRBROTHER | K.E. FAIRBROTHER | K.E. FAIRBROTHER | K.E. FAIRBROTHER |
| P.J. LARTER | P.J. LARTER | P.J. LARTER | P.J.LARTER |
| †N.E. HORTON | N.E. HORTON | N.E. HORTON | N.E. HORTON |
| D.P. ROGERS | *D.P. ROGERS | *D.P. ROGERS | *D.P. ROGERS |
| D.M. ROLLITT | D.M. ROLLITT 1T | D.M. ROLLITT | D.M. ROLLITT |
| *J.R.H. GREENWOOD | R.B. TAYLOR | R.B. TAYLOR | R.B. TAYLOR |
| | | | |
| Lansdowne Road | Twickenham | Twickenham | Cardiff Arms Park |
| LOST 15-17 | WON 22-8 | WON 8-3 | LOST 9-30 |
| | | | |
| IRE.: 1G 2PG 1DG 1T | ENG.: 2G 3PG 1T | ENG.: 1G 1T | WALES: 3G 2PG 1DG 2T |
| ENG.: 4PG 1T | FR.: 1G 1DG | SCOT.: 1PG | ENG.: 3PG |
| | | | |
| 8 Feb. 1969 | 22 Feb. 1969 | 15 Mar. 1969 | 12 Apr. 1969 |

¹Rep. by †T.J. Dalton

England awarded five new caps for the opening match of 1969, introducing three new threequarters who were to give good service over the following years. Fielding was a powerful, fast Midlands winger whose career was shortened by his decision to join the Rugby League; Spencer was a classical centre who captained England in their Centenary season; and Duckham went on to create a record as England's most capped back, playing 36 times as a centre and wing.

Fielding and Duckham enjoyed successful seasons, scoring four of the English tries. In the Scottish match, however, Fielding was forced to retire with an ankle injury, paving the way for Tim Dalton of Coventry to become the first replacement used by England in an international.

The finale of the season, at Cardiff in April, resulted in an overwhelming defeat by Wales. Although the scores were level at half-time (3-3), Wales coasted to a win by 21 points in the second half, registering their biggest win over England since 1922.

## 1969-70

| v. S.AFRICA | v. IRELAND | v. WALES | v. SCOTLAND | v. FRANCE |
|---|---|---|---|---|
| *R. Hiller 1PG,1C[1] | *R. Hiller 2DG | *R. Hiller 1PG,2C | *R. Hiller 1C | †A.M. Jorden 2C,1PG |
| K.J. Fielding | K.J. Fielding | †M.J. Novak 1T | M.J. Novak | K.J. Fielding |
| J.S. Spencer | J.S. Spencer | J.S. Spencer | J.S. Spencer 1T | J.S. Spencer 1T |
| D.J. Duckham | D.J. Duckham | D.J. Duckham 1T | D.J. Duckham | D.J. Duckham |
| †P.M. Hale | P.M. Hale | P.M. Hale | †M.P. Bulpitt | M.J. Novak |
| †I.R. Shackleton | I.R. Shackleton 1T | I.R. Shackleton | I.R. Shackleton | J.F. Finlan |
| †N.C. Starmer-Smith | N.C. Starmer-Smith | N.C. Starmer-Smith | N.C. Starmer-Smith | N.C. Starmer-Smith |
| †C.B. Stevens | C.B. Stevens | C.B. Stevens | C.B. Stevens | B.K. Jackson |
| J.V. Pullin 1T | J.V. Pullin | J.V. Pullin | J.V. Pullin | J.V. Pullin |
| K.E. Fairbrother | K.E. Fairbrother | K.E. Fairbrother | K.E. Fairbrother | K.E. Fairbrother |
| A.M. Davis | A.M. Davis | A.M. Davis | A.M. Davis | †M.M. Leadbetter |
| P.J. Larter 1T | P.J. Larter | P.J. Larter | P.J. Larter | P.J. Larter |
| B.R. West | B.R. West | B.R. West | B.R. West[1] | *R.B. Taylor 1T |
| R.B. Taylor | R.B. Taylor | R.B. Taylor | R.B. Taylor | †G.F. Redmond |
| †A.L. Bucknall | A.L. Bucknall | A.L. Bucknall | A.L. Bucknall | A.L. Bucknall |
| Twickenham | Twickenham | Twickenham | Murrayfield | Stade Colombes |
| WON 11-8 | WON 9-3 | LOST 13-17 | LOST 5-14 | LOST 13-35 |
| ENG.: 1G 1PG 1T | ENG.: 2DG 1T | ENG.: 2G 1PG | SCOT.: 1G 2PG 1T | FR.: 4G 2DG 1PG 2T |
| SA: 1G 1PG | IRE.: 1PG | WALES: 1G 1DG 3T | ENG.: 1G | ENG.: 2G 1PG |
| 20 Dec. 1969 | 14 Feb. 1970 | 28 Feb. 1970 | 21 Mar. 1970 | 18 Apr. 1970 |
| [1]Rep. by †C.S. Wardlow | | | [1]Rep. by †B.K. Jackson | |

In 1969-70 England adopted a squad system for the first time, naming thirty players for the Springbok encounter. The result was England's first win over the South Africans and there were high hopes that the side would acquit itself with distinction in the Championship. Such hopes were justified in a deserved win over Ireland, Hiller's two remarkable drop-goals from more than forty yards helping England to a six-point victory. England were then comfortably ahead against Wales – by 13-3 – before a dramatic Welsh revival and some weak defensive play allowed the Welshmen to steal a late victory. England's forwards were then unexpectedly outplayed by a lively Scottish pack and, in a panic, the selectors made several changes for the trip to Paris.

The French had a field day! After their promising start to the season England found their hopes totally submerged by a French side in such devastating form that they scored more points against England than any team had in nearly 100 years of matches.

## 1970-71

| v. WALES | v. IRELAND | v. FRANCE | 1st v. SCOT. | 2nd v. SCOT. | v. O'SEAS XV |
|---|---|---|---|---|---|
| †P.A. Rossborough 1PG | R. Hiller 3PG | *R. Hiller 3PG,1C,1T | R. Hiller 1T,3PG | R. Hiller 1PG | R. Hiller 1C,2PG,1T |
| †J.P.A.G. Janion | J.P.A.G. Janion | J.P.A.G. Janion | J.P.A.G. Janion | J.P.A.G. Janion | J.P.A.G. Janion |
| C.S. Wardlow | *J.S. Spencer | C.S. Wardlow | C.S. Wardlow[1] | C.S. Wardlow | *J.S. Spencer |
| J.S. Spencer | C.S. Wardlow | D.J. Duckham | *J.S. Spencer | *J.S. Spencer | D.J. Duckham |
| D.J. Duckham | D.J. Duckham | P.B. Glover | D.J. Duckham | D.J. Duckham | P.B. Glover |
| †I.D. Wright | I.D. Wright | I.D. Wright | †A.R. Cowman | A.R. Cowman 1DG | A.R. Cowman |
| †J.J. Page | J.J. Page | J.J. Page | J.J. Page | N.C. Starmer-Smith | N.C. Starmer-Smith |
| D.L. Powell | D.L. Powell | D.L. Powell | D.L. Powell | D.L. Powell | C.B. Stevens |
| J.V. Pullin | J.V. Pullin | J.V. Pullin | J.V. Pullin | J.V. Pullin | J.V. Pullin |
| K.E. Fairbrother | K.E. Fairbrother | K.E. Fairbrother | †F.E. Cotton | F.E. Cotton | F.E. Cotton |
| P.J. Larter | P.J. Larter | P.J. Larter | P.J. Larter | P.J. Larter | P.J. Larter |
| †B.F. Ninnes | N.E. Horton | N.E. Horton | N.E. Horton | †C.W. Ralston | C.W. Ralston |
| *A.L. Bucknall | A.L. Bucknall | A.L. Bucknall | A.L. Bucknall | A.L. Bucknall | †R.N. Creed |
| †R.C. Hannaford 1T | R.C. Hannaford | R.C. Hannaford | R.B. Taylor | R.B. Taylor | †P.J. Dixon |
| †A. Neary | A. Neary | A. Neary | A. Neary 1T | A. Neary | A. Neary |
| Cardiff Arms Park | Lansdowne Road | Twickenham | Twickenham | Murrayfield | Twickenham |
| LOST 6-22 | WON 9-6 | DRAWN 14-14 | LOST 15-16 | LOST 6-26 | LOST 11-28 |
| WALES: 2G 2DG 1PG 1T | IRE.: 2T | ENG.: 1G 3PG | ENG.: 3PG 2T | SCOT.: 4G 1PG 1T | ENG.: 1G 2PG |
| ENG.: 1PG 1T | ENG.: 3PG | FR.: 1G 1PG 1DG 1T | SCOT.: 2G 1DG 1T | ENG.: 1DG 1PG | OVERSEAS XV: 5G 1T |
| 16 Jan. 1971 | 13 Feb. 1971 | 27 Feb. 1971 | 20 Mar. 1971 | 27 Mar. 1971 | 17 Apr. 1971 |

[1]Rep. by I.D. Wright

Seldom has England been so thoroughly outclassed as they were in their Centenary season, 1971. Two special celebration matches added to the usual round of four Championship matches, yet only one game (and that by three penalty goals to two tries) was won.

England took a side including seven new caps to Cardiff. The team was completely overwhelmed and a couple of changes were made for the Irish game. Most significantly, Bob Hiller was recalled and turned out to be England's matchwinner, kicking three penalties. Even in their subsequent failures, Hiller was the one English player to stand head and shoulders above all others. Altogether he scored 49 points for the season, a new England record, and gained the unique distinction of scoring three full-back tries at Twickenham in one season.

## 1971-72           1972

| v. WALES | v. IRELAND | v. FRANCE | v. SCOTLAND | v. S.AFRICA |
|---|---|---|---|---|
| *R. HILLER 1PG | *R. HILLER 2PG,1C | †P.M. KNIGHT | P.M. KNIGHT | †S.A. DOBLE 4PG,1C |
| J.P.A.G. JANION | K.J. FIELDING | K.J. FIELDING | K.J. FIELDING | P.M. KNIGHT |
| †M.C. BEESE | M.C. BEESE | M.C. BEESE 1T | J.P.A.G. JANION | †P.S. PREECE |
| D.J. DUCKHAM | D.J. DUCKHAM | D.J. DUCKHAM | †G.W. EVANS | J.P.A.G. JANION |
| K.J. FIELDING | R.E. WEBB | R.E. WEBB | D.J. DUCKHAM | †A.J. MORLEY 1T |
| †A.G.B. OLD | A.G.B. OLD | A.G.B. OLD 2PG,1C | A.G.B. OLD 3PG | A.G.B. OLD |
| †J.G. WEBSTER | J.G. WEBSTER | †L.E. WESTON | L.E. WESTON | J.G. WEBSTER |
| C.B. STEVENS | C.B. STEVENS | C.B. STEVENS | C.B. STEVENS | C.B. STEVENS |
| J.V. PULLIN | J.V. PULLIN | J.V. PULLIN | J.V. PULLIN | *J.V. PULLIN |
| †M.A. BURTON | M.A. BURTON | M.A. BURTON | M.A. BURTON | M.A. BURTON |
| †A. BRINN | A. BRINN | J. BARTON | A. BRINN | P.J. LARTER |
| C.W. RALSTON | C.W. RALSTON 1T | C.W. RALSTON | C.W. RALSTON | C.W. RALSTON |
| P.J. DIXON | P.J. DIXON | *P.J. DIXON | *P.J. DIXON | †J.A. WATKINS |
| †A.G. RIPLEY | A.G. RIPLEY | A.G. RIPLEY | A.G. RIPLEY | A.G. RIPLEY |
| A. NEARY | A. NEARY | A. NEARY[1] | A. NEARY | A. NEARY |
| Twickenham | Twickenham | Stade Colombes | Murrayfield | Johannesburg |
| LOST 3-12 | LOST 12-16 | LOST 12-37 | LOST 9-23 | WON 18-9 |
| ENG.: 1PG | ENG.: 1G 2PG | FR.: 5G 1PG 1T | SCOT.: 4PG 1DG 2T | SA: 3PG |
| WALES: 1G 2PG | IRE.: 1G 1T 1PG 1DG | ENG.: 1G 2PG | ENG.: 3PG | ENG.: 1G 4PG |
| 15 Jan. 1972 | 12 Feb. 1972 | 26 Feb. 1972 | 18 Mar. 1972 | 3 June 1972 |

[1]Rep. by †N.O. Martin

For the first time ever, England lost all four of their matches in the International Championship. Bob Hiller was made the scapegoat for defeats against Wales and Ireland, and his passing was mourned by many of the pundits who felt that the English selectors were making a grave error in blooding an inexperienced newcomer for the test in Paris.

The misgivings of the press proved accurate, for England were taken apart in what proved to be the last international staged at Stade Colombes. No other international side had scored 37 points against England before, and defeat by 25 points was England's heaviest since the 0-25 reverse against Wales in 1905.

But there was a remarkable summer tour to South Africa under the captaincy of John Pullin to follow. There, in the only Test of the trip, England surprised the world of rugby by ending an unbeaten tour with a convincing victory, over the mighty Springboks. With four new caps in the side, the English exercised a strong grip on the Test and, thanks to four penalties from Sam Doble, and a corner-try by Alan Morley, a famous win was their just reward.

## 1972-73

| v. NZ | v. WALES | v. IRELAND | v. FRANCE | v. SCOTLAND |
|---|---|---|---|---|
| S.A. DOBLE | S.A. DOBLE 2PG | A.M. JORDEN 1C,1PG | A.M. JORDEN 2PG | A.M. JORDEN 2C |
| A.J. MORLEY | A.J. MORLEY | A.J. MORLEY | †P.J. SQUIRES | P.J. SQUIRES 1T |
| †P.J. WARFIELD | P.J. WARFIELD[1] | P.J. WARFIELD | G.W. EVANS | G.W. EVANS 1T |
| P.S. PREECE | P.S. PREECE | P.S. PREECE | P.S. PREECE | P.S. PREECE |
| D.J. DUCKHAM | D.J. DUCKHAM | D.J. DUCKHAM | D.J. DUCKHAM 2T | D.J. DUCKHAM |
| J.F. FINLAN | A.R. COWMAN 1DG | A.R. COWMAN | †M.J. COOPER | M.J. COOPER |
| J.G. WEBSTER | J.G. WEBSTER | †S.J. SMITH | S.J. SMITH | S.J. SMITH |
| C.B. STEVENS | C.B. STEVENS | C.B. STEVENS | C.B. STEVENS | C.B. STEVENS |
| *J.V. PULLIN | *J.V. PULLIN | *J.V. PULLIN | *J.V. PULLIN | *J.V. PULLIN |
| †W.F. ANDERSON | F.E. COTTON | F.E. COTTON | F.E. COTTON | F.E. COTTON |
| P.J. LARTER | P.J. LARTER | †R.M. UTTLEY | R.M. UTTLEY | R.M. UTTLEY |
| C.W. RALSTON | C.W. RALSTON | C.W. RALSTON | C.W. RALSTON | C.W. RALSTON |
| J.A. WATKINS | J.A. WATKINS | P.J. DIXON | P.J. DIXON | P.J. DIXON 2T |
| A.G. RIPLEY | A.G. RIPLEY | A.G. RIPLEY | A.G. RIPLEY | A.G. RIPLEY |
| A. NEARY | A. NEARY | A. NEARY 1T | A. NEARY | A. NEARY |
| Twickenham | Cardiff Arms Park | Lansdowne Road | Twickenham | Twickenham |
| LOST 0-9 | LOST 9-25 | LOST 9-18 | WON 14-6 | WON 20-13 |
| ENG.: NIL | WALES: 1G 4T 1PG | IRE.: 2G 1DG 1PG | ENG.: 2T 2PG | ENG.: 2G 2T |
| NZ: 1G 1DG | ENG.: 1DG 2PG | ENG.: 1G 1PG | FR.: 1G | SCOT.: 1G 1PG 1T |
| 6 Jan. 1973 | 20 Jan. 1973 | 10 Feb. 1973 | 24 Feb. 1973 | 17 Mar. 1973 |

[1]Rep. by G.W. Evans

England started the season with a spirited effort against the All Blacks. In the end the better side won the match, but England gave a sterling performance in the tight and their backs, despite the tight marking of the New Zealanders, almost fashioned a try for Preece. He actually broke through the All Black defence only to be recalled by the referee for a forward pass.

Disappointments followed in Cardiff and Dublin where England were well beaten by excellent sides, but the first win in the Championship for two years was gained against the French, and England's swift, determined pack outplayed the visitors. The names of Stevens, Pullin, Cotton, Uttley and Ralston were to become regular entries in the English programmes for several seasons, and the back-row trio of Dixon, Neary and Ripley created a record by playing together twelve times in all.

Against Scotland, another impressive display by the English pack laid the foundation for victory, one which enabled England to share in a unique quintuple tie for the Championship.

## 1973      1973-74

| v. NZ | v. AUSTRALIA | v. SCOTLAND | v. IRELAND | v. FRANCE | v. WALES |
|---|---|---|---|---|---|
| P.A. ROSSBOROUGH 2C | P.A. ROSSBOROUGH 2PG,1C | P.A. ROSSBOROUGH 1DG | P.A. ROSSBOROUGH | A.M. JORDEN | †W.H. HARE |
| P.J. SQUIRES 1T | P.J. SQUIRES | P.J. SQUIRES | P.J. SQUIRES 1T | P.J. SQUIRES | P.J. SQUIRES |
| G.W. EVANS¹ | J.P.A.G. JANION | D. ROUGHLEY | D. ROUGHLEY | †K. SMITH | K. SMITH |
| P.S. PREECE | †D. ROUGHLEY | G.W. EVANS | G.W. EVANS | G.W. EVANS 1DG | G.W. EVANS |
| D.J. DUCKHAM | D.J. DUCKHAM | D.J. DUCKHAM | D.J. DUCKHAM | D.J. DUCKHAM 1T | D.J. DUCKHAM 1T |
| A.G.B. OLD | A.G.B. OLD 1T | A.G.B. OLD 1PG | A.G.B. OLD 1C,5PG | A.G.B. OLD 1C,1PG | A.G.B. OLD 2PG,1C |
| J.G. WEBSTER | S.J. SMITH | J.G. WEBSTER | S.J. SMITH | S.J. SMITH | J.G. WEBSTER |
| C.B. STEVENS 1T | C.B. STEVENS | C.B. STEVENS | C.B. STEVENS | C.B. STEVENS | C.B. STEVENS |
| *J.V. PULLIN | *J.V. PULLIN | *J.V. PULLIN | *J.V. PULLIN | *J.V. PULLIN | *J.V.PULLIN |
| F.E. COTTON | F.E. COTTON | F.E. COTTON 1T | F.E. COTTON | M.A. BURTON | M.A. BURTON |
| R.M. UTTLEY | R.M. UTTLEY | N.E. HORTON | R.M. UTTLEY | R.M. UTTLEY | R.M. UTTLEY |
| C.W. RALSTON | C.W. RALSTON | C.W. RALSTON | C.W. RALSTON | C.W. RALSTON | C.W. RALSTON |
| J.A. WATKINS | J.A. WATKINS | P.J. DIXON | P.J. DIXON | P.J. DIXON | P.J. DIXON |
| A.G. RIPLEY | A.G. RIPLEY 1T | A.G. RIPLEY | A.G. RIPLEY | A.G. RIPLEY | A.G. RIPLEY 1T |
| A. NEARY 1T | A. NEARY 1T | A. NEARY 1T | A.NEARY | A. NEARY | A. NEARY |
| Auckland | Twickenham | Murrayfield | Twickenham | Parc des Princes | Twickenham |
| WON 16-10 | WON 20-3 | LOST 14-16 | LOST 21-26 | DRAWN 12-12 | WON 16-12 |
| NZ: 1G 1T | ENG.: 1G 2PG 2T | SCOT.: 1G 2PG 1T | ENG.: 1G 5PG | FR.: 1G 1PG 1DG | ENG.: 1G 2PG 1T |
| ENG.: 2G 1T | AUST.: 1PG | ENG.: 1DG 1PG 2T | IRE.: 2G 2T 1DG 1PG | ENG.: 1G 1PG 1DG | WALES: 1G 2PG |
| 15 Sep. 1973 | 17 Nov. 1973 | 2 Feb. 1974 | 16 Feb. 1974 | 2 Mar. 1974 | 16 Mar. 1974 |

¹Rep. by M.J. Cooper

John Pullin set a remarkable record: by leading England to victory in the only Test of the Autumn tour to New Zealand, and by captaining the side to a win over Australia in November, he became the first international captain in history to win Tests against all three Dominion nations. Disappointment in the Championship followed the win over Australia, but there was the consolation of England's long-awaited first win against Wales since 1963, at the end of the season. England's pack strengthened their claim to being the strongest of the Five Nations, and Ripley had an outstanding match scoring a decisive try from a scrum early in the second half.

Ripley went on to become England's most-capped number-eight, playing 24 times.

## 1974-75

| v. IRELAND | v. FRANCE | v. WALES | v. SCOTLAND |
|---|---|---|---|
| P.A. ROSSBOROUGH | P.A. ROSSBOROUGH 1T,4PG | A.M. JORDEN | A.M. JORDEN |
| P.J. SQUIRES | P.J. SQUIRES | P.J. SQUIRES | P.J. SQUIRES |
| P.J. WARFIELD | P.J. WARFIELD | K. SMITH | P.J. WARFIELD |
| P.S. PREECE | P.S. PREECE | P.S. PREECE | K. SMITH |
| D.J. DUCKHAM | D.J. DUCKHAM 1T | D.J. DUCKHAM | A.J. MORLEY 1T |
| A.G.B. OLD 1C,1DG | M.J. COOPER | M.J. COOPER | †W.N. BENNETT 1PG |
| J.G. WEBSTER | J.G. WEBSTER | J.G. WEBSTER¹ | J.J. PAGE |
| C.B. STEVENS 1T | C.B. STEVENS | C.B. STEVENS | C.B. STEVENS |
| J.V. PULLIN | †P.J. WHEELER | P.J. WHEELER² | J.V. PULLIN |
| *F.E. COTTON | *F.E. COTTON | *F.E. COTTON | M.A. BURTON |
| †W.B. BEAUMONT | R.M. UTTLEY | N.E. HORTON 1T | R.M. UTTLEY |
| C.W. RALSTON | C.W. RALSTON | C.W. RALSTON | C.W. RALSTON |
| P.J. DIXON | J.A. WATKINS | J.A. WATKINS | D.M. ROLLITT |
| A.G. RIPLEY | A.G. RIPLEY | R.M. UTTLEY | A.G. RIPLEY |
| A. NEARY | A. NEARY | A. NEARY | *A. NEARY |
| Lansdowne Road | Twickenham | Cardiff Arms Park | Twickenham |
| LOST 9-12 | LOST 20-27 | LOST 4-20 | WON 7-6 |
| IRE.: 2G | ENG.: 4PG 2T | WALES: 1G 2PG 2T | ENG.: 1PG 1T |
| ENG.: 1G 1DG | FR.: 4G 1PG | ENG.: 1T | SCOT.: 2PG |
| 18 Jan. 1975 | 1 Feb. 1975 | 15 Feb. 1975 | 15 Mar. 1975 |

¹Rep. by S.J. Smith
²Rep. by J.V. Pullin

England started the season with a new coach in John Burgess, a new skipper in Fran Cotton, and a positive attitude which made them favourites to win the Championship. However, their failure to play the open attacking rugby which had been a feature of the final trial, and a series of dreadful defensive lapses, left them clutching the wooden spoon for the third season in four.

The selectors went into the Irish match with an experienced side. Bill Beaumont came in as the only new cap when Uttley withdrew through injury and England led 9-6 at the interval, having faced a stiff breeze. The lively Irish forwards disrupted England's game in the second half and under pressure the English backs yielded a gift try for McCombe to win the game.

The selectors reacted unwisely, making several changes for the visit of France. Peter Wheeler came into the side as the new hooker, winning the first of 41 caps, but France won an entertaining game and their total of 27 points was a new record for them at Twickenham. The recall of two veterans, Page and Rollitt, had much to do with England's sole win of the season, against Scotland.

## 1975

| 1st v. AUSTRALIA | 2nd v. AUSTRALIA |
|---|---|
| †P.E. Butler 1pg,1c | †A.J. Hignell |
| | |
| P.J. Squires 1t | P.J. Squires 1t |
| J.P.A.G. Janion | J.P.A.G. Janion |
| †A.W. Maxwell | P.S. Preece |
| A.J. Morley | A.J. Morley |
| | |
| W.N. Bennett[1] | A.G.B. Old 2c,3pg |
| †P.J. Kingston | P.J. Kingston |
| | |
| †B.G. Nelmes | B.G. Nelmes |
| J.V. Pullin | *J.V. Pullin |
| M.A. Burton | M.A. Burton |
| †N.D. Mantell | †R.M. Wilkinson |
| R.M. Uttley | W.B. Beaumont |
| D.M. Rollitt | D.M. Rollitt |
| A.G. Ripley | A.G. Ripley |
| *A. Neary[2] | R.M. Uttley 1t |
| | |
| Sydney C.G. | Brisbane |
| LOST 9-16 | LOST 21-30 |
| | |
| Aust. 2pg 2dg 1t | Aust. 2g 2pg 3t |
| Eng.: 1g 1pg | Eng.: 2g 3pg |
| | |
| 24 May 1975 | 31 May 1975 |
| | |
| [1]Rep. by †A.J. Wordsworth | |
| [2]Rep. by W.B. Beaumont | |

Although the selectors sent a party of youth and promise, the short tour to Australia was an unmitigated failure. A cruel sequence of injuries reduced the morale of the touring team, and the side failed to achieve any real cohesion.

The English backs were deprived of possession for most of the first Test although Squires scored a fine opportunist's try. The second of the Tests was marred by and unprecedented outburst of thuggery at the start of the match. Burton, having been reprimanded for butting an opponent, was given his marching orders in the second minute of the game for a late tackle. He thus became the first English player to be sent off in an international.

## 1975-76

| v. AUSTRALIA | v. WALES | v. SCOTLAND | v. IRELAND | v. FRANCE |
|---|---|---|---|---|
| A.J. Hignell 3pg,1c | A.J. Hignell 3pg | A.J. Hignell | A.J. Hignell[1] | P.E. Butler 1c,1pg |
| | | | | |
| P.J. Squires | P.J. Squires[1] | K.C. Plummer | K.C. Plummer | K.C. Plummer |
| A.W. Maxwell | A.W. Maxwell | A.W. Maxwell 1t[1] | A.W. Maxwell | A.W. Maxwell |
| †B.J. Corless 1t | †D.A. Cooke | D.A. Cooke | D.A. Cooke | D.A. Cooke |
| D.J. Duckham 1t | D.J. Duckham | D.J. Duckham[2] | †M.A.C. Slemen | M.A.C. Slemen |
| | | | | |
| M.J. Cooper | M.J. Cooper | A.G.B. Old 1c,2pg | A.G.B. Old 4pg | †C.G. Williams |
| †M.S. Lampkowski 1t | M.S. Lampkowski | M.S. Lampkowski | M.S. Lampkowski | S.J. Smith |
| | | | | |
| M.A. Burton | M.A. Burton | M.A. Burton | M.A. Burton | M.A. Burton |
| P.J. Wheeler | P.J. Wheeler | P.J. Wheeler | P.J. Wheeler | J.V. Pullin |
| F.E. Cotton | F.E. Cotton | F.E. Cotton | F.E. Cotton | F.E. Cotton |
| W.B. Beaumont | W.B. Beaumont | W.B. Beaumont | W.B. Beaumont | W.B. Beaumont |
| R.M. Wilkinson | R.M. Wilkinson | R.M. Wilkinson | R.M. Wilkinson | R.M. Wilkinson |
| †M. Keyworth | M. Keyworth | M. Keyworth | M. Keyworth | P.J. Dixon 1t |
| A.G. Ripley | A.G. Ripley | A.G. Ripley | †G.J. Adey | G.J. Adey |
| *A. Neary | *A. Neary | *A. Neary | *A. Neary | *A. Neary |
| | | | | |
| Twickenham | Twickenham | Murrayfield | Twickenham | Parc des Princes |
| WON 23-6 | LOST 9-21 | LOST 12-22 | LOST 12-13 | LOST 9-30 |
| | | | | |
| Eng.: 1g 3pg 2t | Eng.: 3pg | Scot.: 2g 2pg 1t | Eng.: 4pg | Fr.: 3g 3t |
| Aust. 2pg | Wales: 3g 1pg | Eng.: 1g 2pg | Ire.: 2pg 1dg 1t | Eng.: 1g 1pg |
| | | | | |
| 3 Jan. 1976 | 17 Jan. 1976 | 21 Feb. 1976 | 6 Mar. 1976 | 20 Mar. 1976 |
| | | | | |
| | [1]Rep. by P.S. Preece | [1]Rep. by W.N. Bennett | [1]Rep. by B.J. Corless | |
| | | [2]Rep. by †D.M. Wyatt | | |

A new coach prepared the team for the opening match of 1976, Peter Colston. Following a convincing victory over Australia, it was something of a disappointment for England followers to see their side plumb the depths during the rest of the season: all four matches were lost in the Home Internationals for only the second time and just one player, Andy Maxwell, kept his place among the backs during the season. Nevertheless, there were some encouraging performances from the pack. The front five played unchanged and Tony Neary, a dynamic flanker who became England's most-capped player, led the side well.

David Duckham, one of the leading English backs of the 1960s and 1970s ended his international career in the Scottish match.

## 1976-77

| v. SCOTLAND | v. IRELAND | v. FRANCE | v. WALES |
|---|---|---|---|
| A.J. Hignell 2pg,2c | A.J. Hignell | A.J. Hignell 1pg | A.J. Hignell 3pg |
| | | | |
| P.J. Squires | P.J. Squires | P.J. Squires | P.J. Squires |
| B.J. Corless | B.J. Corless | B.J. Corless | B.J. Corless |
| †C.P. Kent 1t | C.P. Kent | C.P. Kent | C.P. Kent |
| M.A.C. Slemen 1t | M.A.C. Slemen | M.A.C. Slemen | M.A.C. Slemen |
| | | | |
| M.J. Cooper | M.J. Cooper 1t | M.J. Cooper | M.J. Cooper |
| †M. Young 1t | M. Young | M. Young¹ | M. Young |
| | | | |
| †R.J. Cowling | R.J. Cowling | R.J. Cowling | R.J. Cowling |
| P.J. Wheeler | P.J. Wheeler | P.J. Wheeler | P.J. Wheeler |
| F.E. Cotton | F.E. Cotton | F.E. Cotton | F.E. Cotton |
| W.B. Beaumont | W.B. Beaumont | W.B. Beaumont | W.B. Beaumont |
| N.E. Horton | N.E. Horton | N.E. Horton | N.E. Horton |
| P.J. Dixon | P.J. Dixon | P.J. Dixon | P.J. Dixon |
| *R.M. Uttley 1t | *R.M. Uttley | *R.M. Uttley | *R.M. Uttley |
| †M. Rafter | A. Neary | M. Rafter | M. Rafter |
| | | | |
| Twickenham | Lansdowne Road | Twickenham | Cardiff Arms Park |
| WON 26-6 | WON 4-0 | LOST 3-4 | LOST 9-14 |
| | | | |
| Eng.: 2g 2pg 2t | Ire.: nil | Eng.: 1pg | Wales: 2pg 2t |
| Scot.: 2pg | Eng.: 1t | Fr.: 1t | Eng.: 3pg |
| | | | |
| 15 Jan. 1977 | 5 Feb. 1977 | 19 Feb. 1977 | 5 Mar. 1977 |

¹Rep. by S.J. Smith

England made a fiery and effective start to 1977 with two wins over Scotland and Ireland. Inspired by the new captain Roger Uttley, the side played to a predetermined pattern which paid dividends. The plan was to back-up the crash-ball runs of centre Charles Kent with some vigorous rucking, then use the second-phase possession to exploit gaps in opposition defences.

The plan worked effectively against Scotland, England securing a record win. The challenge of the Irish was quelled by a second-half try and England would have beaten the French handsomely if Hignell had managed to land his kicks at goal. The full-back was outstanding in defence, but only succeeded with one penalty kick out of six attempts.

The same team was picked for each match, although Rafter was forced to withdraw for the Irish game, Neary replacing him. In a brave attempt to win the Triple Crown at Cardiff, England eventually lost – but by only five points – to a stronger Welsh side.

## 1977-78

| v. FRANCE | v. WALES | v. SCOTLAND | v. IRELAND |
|---|---|---|---|
| W.H. Hare | A.J. Hignell 2pg | †D.W.N. Caplan | D.W.N. Caplan |
| | | | |
| P.J. Squires | P.J. Squires | P.J. Squires 1t | P.J. Squires |
| B.J. Corless | B.J. Corless | B.J. Corless | B.J. Corless |
| A.W. Maxwell¹ | †P.W. Dodge | P.W. Dodge 1pg | P.W. Dodge |
| M.A.C. Slemen | M.A.C. Slemen | M.A.C. Slemen | M.A.C. Slemen 1t |
| | | | |
| A.G.B. Old 2dg | †J.P. Horton | J.P. Horton | J.P. Horton |
| M. Young | M. Young | M. Young 2c | M. Young 1pg,2c |
| | | | |
| R.J. Cowling | B.G. Nelmes | B.G. Nelmes 1t | B.G. Nelmes |
| P.J. Wheeler | P.J. Wheeler | P.J. Wheeler | P.J. Wheeler |
| M.A. Burton | M.A. Burton | F.E. Cotton | F.E. Cotton |
| *W.B. Beaumont | *W.B. Beaumont | *W.B. Beaumont | *W.B. Beaumont |
| N.E. Horton | N.E. Horton | †M.J. Colclough | M.J. Colclough |
| P.J. Dixon² | †R.J. Mordell | P.J. Dixon | P.J. Dixon 1t |
| †J.P. Scott | J.P. Scott | J.P. Scott | J.P. Scott |
| M. Rafter | M. Rafter | M. Rafter | M. Rafter |
| | | | |
| Parc des Princes | Twickenham | Murrayfield | Twickenham |
| LOST 6-15 | LOST 6-9 | WON 15-0 | WON 15-9 |
| | | | |
| Fr.: 2g 1pg | Eng.: 2pg | Scot.: nil | Eng.: 2g 1pg |
| Eng.: 2dg | Wales: 3pg | Eng.: 2g 1pg | Ire.: 1dg 2pg |
| | | | |
| 21 Jan. 1978 | 4 Feb. 1978 | 4 Mar. 1978 | 18 Mar. 1978 |

¹Rep. by C.P. Kent
²Rep. by A. Neary

A system of Divisional matches was added to the Trial schedule prior to the internationals of 1978. There were mixed feelings concerning the use of the matches and the RFU dropped the system for the following season. Nevertheless, England's improvement continued, with Bill Beaumont the new captain. Despite narrow defeats against France and Wales, the English pack showed in all of their matches that they possessed the potential to win a Championship title. There were still problems behind the scrum, however, the injury in Paris to Maxwell (which ended his playing career) coming as a severe blow.

England's win in Scotland was their first at Murrayfield for ten years. Cotton and Dixon returned to the side, strengthening the all-round play of the pack. Colclough and Caplan made impressive debuts, and the same fifteen went on to overcome Ireland in an entertaining game at Twickenham. Once again England's victory was due to their forwards' supremacy in the tight and loose.

Beaumont went on to become England's most popular captain since the 1920s. In an admirable career he led England on 21 occasions and gained eleven victories as captain – all-time records for his nation. He always led by example and had the knack of bringing out the best in his fellows. Injury compelled him to retire in 1982, after he had gained 34 caps.

## 1978-79

| v. NZ | v. SCOTLAND | v. IRELAND | v. FRANCE | v. WALES |
|---|---|---|---|---|
| W.H. HARE 1DG,1PG | A.J. HIGNELL | A.J. HIGNELL | A.J. HIGNELL | A.J. HIGNELL |
| P.J. SQUIRES | P.J. SQUIRES | P.J. SQUIRES | P.J. SQUIRES | P.J. SQUIRES |
| †A.M. BOND | A.M. BOND | A.M. BOND | †R.M. CARDUS | R.M CARDUS |
| P.W. DODGE | P.W. DODGE | P.W. DODGE | P.W. DODGE | P.W. DODGE |
| M.A.C. SLEMEN | M.A.C. SLEMEN 1T | M.A.C. SLEMEN | M.A.C. SLEMEN | M.A.C. SLEMEN |
| J.P. HORTON | W.N. BENNETT 1PG | W.N. BENNETT 1PG,1T | W.N. BENNETT 1PG,1T | W.N. BENNETT 1PG |
| M. YOUNG | M. YOUNG | P.J. KINGSTON | P.J. KINGSTON | P.J. KINGSTON |
| R.J. COWLING | R.J. COWLING | R.J. COWLING | †C.E. SMART | C.E. SMART |
| P.J. WHEELER | P.J. WHEELER | P.J. WHEELER | P.J. WHEELER | P.J. WHEELER |
| B.G. NELMES | †G.S. PEARCE | G.S. PEARCE | G.S. PEARCE | G.S. PEARCE |
| *W.B. BEAUMONT | W.B. BEAUMONT | *W.B. BEAUMONT | *W.B. BEAUMONT | *W.B. BEAUMONT |
| J.P. SCOTT | N.E. HORTON | N.E. HORTON | N.E. HORTON | N.E. HORTON |
| P.J. DIXON | A. NEARY | A. NEARY | A. NEARY | A. NEARY |
| R.M. UTTLEY | *R.M. UTTLEY[1] | J.P. SCOTT | J.P. SCOTT | J.P. SCOTT |
| M. RAFTER | M. RAFTER | M. RAFTER | M. RAFTER | M. RAFTER |
| Twickenham | Twickenham | Lansdowne Road | Twickenham | Cardiff Arms Park |
| LOST 6-16 | DRAWN 7-7 | LOST 7-12 | WON 7-6 | LOST 3-27 |
| ENG.: 1DG 1PG | ENG.: 1PG 1T | IRE.: 1G 1PG 1DG | ENG.: 1PG 1T | WALES: 2G 1DG 3T |
| NZ: 1G 2PG 1T | SCOT.: 1PG 1T | ENG.: 1PG 1T | FR.: 1G | ENG.: 1PG |
| 25 Nov. 1978 | 3 Feb. 1979 | 17 Feb. 1979 | 3 Mar. 1979 | 17 Mar. 1979 |

[1]Rep. by J.P. Scott

Poor midfield play by the backs again upset the sterling efforts of the English forwards in 1979, and a disappointing season ended with just one win (albeit against France) and a draw against Scotland. There was an early season match against the All Blacks in which the ragged liaison between the English halves wrecked the game as a spectacle, yet warned of the problems which lay ahead.

Further difficulties between the halves and a lack of judgment in the centre resulted in undistinguished performances against Scotland and Ireland, though there was a glorious boost to morale from a win over France. Beaumont's inspiring captaincy helped England to raise their game, and a fine performance by Neil Bennett at fly-half led to a narrow victory.

The promise, urgency and power which had been features of the French match, melted in the cauldron of the Arms Park, and Beaumont's men ended second-from-bottom of the Championship table.

## 1979-80

| v. NZ | v. IRELAND | v. FRANCE | v. WALES | v. SCOTLAND |
|---|---|---|---|---|
| W.H. HARE 3PG | W.H. HARE 3C,2PG | W.H. HARE 1PG | W.H. HARE 3PG | W.H. HARE 2PG,2C |
| †J. CARLETON | J. CARLETON | J. CARLETON 1T | J. CARLETON | J. CARLETON 3T |
| A.M. BOND | A.M. BOND[1] | C.R. WOODWARD | C.R. WOODWARD | C.R. WOODWARD |
| †N.J. PRESTON | N.J. PRESTON | N.J. PRESTON 1T | P.W. DODGE | P.W. DODGE |
| M.A.C. SLEMEN | M.A.C. SLEMEN 1T | M.A.C. SLEMEN | M.A.C. SLEMEN | M.A.C. SLEMEN 1T |
| †L. CUSWORTH | J.P. HORTON | J.P. HORTON 2DG | J.P. HORTON | J.P. HORTON |
| S.J. SMITH | S.J. SMITH 1T | S.J. SMITH | S.J. SMITH | S.J. SMITH 1T |
| C.E. SMART | F.E. COTTON | F.E. COTTON | F.E. COTTON | F.E. COTTON |
| P.J. WHEELER | P.J. WHEELER | P.J. WHEELER | P.J. WHEELER | P.J. WHEELER |
| F.E. COTTON | †P.J. BLAKEWAY | P.J. BLAKEWAY | P.J. BLAKEWAY | P.J. BLAKEWAY |
| *W.B. BEAUMONT | *W.B. BEAUMONT | *W.B. BEAUMONT | *W.B. BEAUMONT | *W.B. BEAUMONT |
| M.J. COLCLOUGH | N.E. HORTON | M.J. COLCLOUGH | M.J. COLCLOUGH | M.J. COLCLOUGH |
| A. NEARY | R.M. UTTLEY | R.M. UTTLEY | R.M. UTTLEY[1] | R.M. UTTLEY |
| J.P. SCOTT | J.P. SCOTT 1T | J.P. SCOTT | J.P. SCOTT | J.P. SCOTT |
| M. RAFTER | A. NEARY | A. NEARY | A. NEARY | A. NEARY |
| Twickenham | Twickenham | Parc des Princes | Twickenham | Murrayfield |
| LOST 9-10 | WON 24-9 | WON 17-13 | WON 9-8 | WON 30-18 |
| ENG.: 3PG | ENG.: 3G 2PG | FR.: 1G 1PG 1T | ENG.: 3PG | SCOT.: 2G 2PG |
| NZ: 2PG 1T | IRE.: 3PG | ENG.: 1PG 2DG 2T | WALES: 2T | ENG.: 2G 2PG 3T |
| 24 Nov. 1979 | 19 Jan. 1980 | 2 Feb. 1980 | 16 Feb. 1980 | 15 Mar. 1980 |
| | [1]Rep. by †C.R. Woodward | | [1]Rep. by M. Rafter | |

1980 was England's season. The side gained the Grand Slam for the first time since 1957, the Triple Crown was lifted for the first time since 1960, and the Championship title was England's first outright success for seventeen years.

The season began with a dreary game played on a dreary day against the All Blacks. The North of England had secured a famous win at Otley over the New Zealanders a week before, but the complicated back-row moves which had confused the tourists on that occasion were less effective second-time-round.

After a resounding triumph over Ireland, England proceeded to their first win in Paris for sixteen years. Then, in an ill-tempered match with Wales, the accurate place-kicking of Dusty Hare helped England to a narrow win, before the culmination of the season at Murrayfield. Against the Scots, Carleton became the first England player since 1924 to score three tries in an international, and Neary chose the occasion as a fitting moment to bow-out of international rugby. He had seen the unhappy memories of the 1970s superseded by a magnificent Grand Slam.

## 1980-81

| v. WALES | v. SCOTLAND | v. IRELAND | v. FRANCE |
|---|---|---|---|
| W.H. Hare 5PG,1T | W.H. Hare 3PG,1C | †W.M.H. Rose 1T,1C | W.M.H. Rose 4PG |
| J. Carleton | J. Carleton | J. Carleton | J. Carleton |
| C.R. Woodward | C.R. Woodward 1T | C.R. Woodward | C.R. Woodward |
| P.W. Dodge | P.W. Dodge | P.W. Dodge 1T | P.W. Dodge |
| M.A.C. Slemen | M.A.C. Slemen 1T | M.A.C. Slemen | M.A.C. Slemen |
| J.P. Horton | †G.H. Davies 1T | G.H. Davies | G.H. Davies |
| S.J. Smith | S.J. Smith | S.J. Smith | S.J. Smith |
| F.E. Cotton[1] | C.E. Smart | C.E. Smart | C.E. Smart |
| P.J. Wheeler | P.J. Wheeler | P.J. Wheeler | P.J. Wheeler |
| P.J. Blakeway | P.J. Blakeway | P.J. Blakeway[1] | P.J. Blakeway |
| *W.B. Beaumont | *W.B. Beaumont | *W.B. Beaumont | *W.B. Beaumont |
| M.J. Colclough | M.J. Colclough | M.J. Colclough | M.J. Colclough |
| M. Rafter | †N.C. Jeavons[1] | N.C. Jeavons | N.C. Jeavons |
| J.P. Scott | J.P. Scott | J.P. Scott | J.P. Scott |
| †D.H. Cooke | D.H. Cooke | D.H. Cooke | D.H. Cooke |
| Cardiff Arms Park | Twickenham | Lansdowne Road | Twickenham |
| LOST 19-21 | WON 23-17 | WON 10-6 | LOST 12-16 |
| WALES: 1G 4PG 1DG | ENG.: 1G 3PG 2T | IRE.: 2DG | ENG.: 4PG |
| ENG.: 5PG 1T | SCOT.: 1G 1PG 2T | ENG.: 1G 1T | FR.: 1G 2DG 1T |
| 17 Jan. 1981 | 21 Feb. 1981 | 7 Mar. 1981 | 21 Mar. 1981 |
| [1]Rep. by †A. Sheppard | [1]Rep. by †R. Hesford | [1]Rep. by †G.A.F. Sargent | |

With Neary, Cotton (injured early in the Welsh match) and Uttley absent, the English forward power which had been a key factor in the Grand Slam of the previous season had vanished. England were thus unable to retain the Championship, although they managed rousing wins over Scotland and Ireland and had their moments against Wales and France.

Only a late penalty in front of the posts deprived England of victory in the first match of the season against Wales, and France were winners at Twickenham thanks to a try which strictly should never have been awarded. The French scored from a quick throw-in, but whereas the Law prescribes that only the ball that went into touch may be retrieved by the players for the throw, France took their chance with a ball supplied by a bystander. Nevertheless, France were the better side at Twickenham on the day, and deserved their win.

A curious but promising feature of the season was the enterprise shown by the English backs. Whereas forward skill had been England's strength in the 1970s, players of the calibre of Woodward, Dodge, Carleton, Slemen (England's most-capped wing) and Huw Davies showed considerable flair and pace in attack, qualities which augured well for England's summer tour to Argentina.

## 1981

| 1st v. ARGENTINA | 2nd v. ARGENTINA |
|---|---|
| W.H. Hare 1PG,2C | W.H. Hare 2PG,1C |
| J. Carleton | J. Carleton |
| P.W. Dodge | P.W. Dodge |
| C.R. Woodward 2T | C.R. Woodward |
| †A.H. Swift | A.H. Swift |
| G.H. Davies 1T | G.H. Davies 1T |
| S.J. Smith | S.J. Smith |
| C.E. Smart | C.E. Smart |
| †S.G.F. Mills | S.G.F. Mills |
| G.S. Pearce | G.S. Pearce |
| *W.B. Beaumont | *W.B. Beaumont |
| †J.H. Fidler | J.H. Fidler |
| N.C. Jeavons | N.C. Jeavons |
| J.P. Scott | J.P. Scott |
| M. Rafter | M. Rafter |
| Buenos Aires | Buenos Aires |
| DRAWN 19-19 | WON 12-6 |
| ARG.: 1G 2DG 1PG 1T | ARG.: 1G |
| ENG.: 2G 1PG 1T | ENG.: 1G 2PG |
| 30 May 1981 | 6 Jun. 1981 |

England became the first of the Home Countries to take advantage of a new International Board ruling to the effect that members may award full caps for games against non-IB countries. Caps were awarded for the matches against Argentina.

The tour was a successful venture, England winning six of their seven matches and drawing the other – the first Test. England's pack, in which Fidler and Mills stepped into the positions usually occupied by Peter Wheeler and Colclough, influenced the outcome of the internationals, though the play of Hugo Porta – arguably the best fly-half in the world – was brilliant.

Indeed, only a last-minute try by Woodward from a lovely break by Dodge and a conversion from Hare saved the first Test, and England were grateful to Hare for two penalty goals to decide the second Test.

## 1981-82

| v. AUSTRALIA | v. SCOTLAND | v. IRELAND | v. FRANCE | v. WALES |
|---|---|---|---|---|
| W.M.H. Rose 3pg | W.M.H. Rose 1pg | W.M.H. Rose 3pg,1c | W.H. Hare 5pg,2c | W.H. Hare 3pg |
| J. Carleton | J. Carleton | J. Carleton | J. Carleton 1t | J. Carleton 1t |
| C.R. Woodward | C.R. Woodward | C.R. Woodward | C.R. Woodward 1t | C.R. Woodward |
| P.W. Dodge 1c | P.W. Dodge 2pg | A.M. Bond | P.W. Dodge | P.W. Dodge |
| M.A.C. Slemen[1] | M.A.C. Slemen | M.A.C. Slemen 1t | M.A.C. Slemen | M.A.C. Slemen 1t |
| G.H. Davies | G.H. Davies | G.H. Davies | L. Cusworth | L. Cusworth |
| S.J. Smith | S.J. Smith | *S.J. Smith | *S.J. Smith | *S.J. Smith |
| C.E. Smart | C.E. Smart | C.E. Smart | C.E. Smart | C.E. Smart |
| P.J. Wheeler | P.J. Wheeler | P.J. Wheeler | P.J. Wheeler | P.J. Wheeler |
| G.S. Pearce | G.S. Pearce | P.J. Blakeway | P.J. Blakeway | P.J. Blakeway |
| *W.B. Beaumont | *W.B. Beaumont | †J.P. Syddall | †S. Bainbridge | M.J. Colclough |
| M.J. Colclough | M.J. Colclough | M.J. Colclough | M.J. Colclough | S. Bainbridge |
| N.C. Jeavons 1t | N.C. Jeavons | N.C. Jeavons | N.C. Jeavons[1] | N.C. Jeavons |
| R. Hesford | R. Hesford | J.P. Scott | J.P. Scott | J.P. Scott |
| †P.J. Winterbottom | P.J. Winterbottom | P.J. Winterbottom | P.J. Winterbottom | P.J. Winterbottom |
| Twickenham | Murrayfield | Twickenham | Parc des Princes | Twickenham |
| WON 15-11 | DRAWN 9-9 | LOST 15-16 | WON 27-15 | WON 17-7 |
| ENG.: 1G 3PG | SCOT.: 1DG 2PG | ENG.: 1G 3PG | FR.: 1G 1DG 2PG | ENG.: 3PG 2T |
| AUST.: 1PG 2T | ENG.: 3PG | IRE.: 1G 2PG 1T | ENG.: 2G 5PG | WALES: 1DG 1T |
| 2 Jan. 1982 | 16 Jan. 1982 | 6 Feb. 1982 | 20 Feb. 1982 | 6 Mar. 1982 |
| [1]Rep. by †N.C. Stringer | | | [1]Rep. by R.Hesford | |

During the English revival of the late 1970s and early 1980s, wins over both Scotland and Ireland had been common, with victories over Wales and France more difficult to gain. But in 1982 it was ironical that they now found the wheel turning in the opposite direction. For the Welsh and French were beaten by English sides which played with zest and enterprise, after there had been two disappointing results against Scotland and Ireland.

The season opened with an international against the Wallabies. England fielded just one new cap, the blond, aggressive Headingley flanker Peter Winterbottom. Playing controlled rugby the home side won comfortably, although outscored by two tries to one. The highlight of the afternoon, however, was the spectacular appearance of topless Erica Roe at half-time.

Bill Beaumont played his last international in January, against the Scots. He was injured leading Lancashire to the County Championship just before the Irish match. Acting on medical advice, he subsequently retired from the game and became a popular television and radio personality.

## 1982-83

| v. FRANCE | v. WALES | v. SCOTLAND | v. IRELAND |
|---|---|---|---|
| W.H. Hare 4pg | W.H. Hare 2pg | W.H. Hare 3pg | W.H. Hare 5pg |
| J. Carleton | J. Carleton 1t | J. Carleton | J. Carleton |
| G.H. Davies | G.H. Davies | G.H. Davies | C.R. Woodward |
| P.W. Dodge | P.W. Dodge | P.W. Dodge | P.W. Dodge |
| A.H. Swift | A.H. Swift | A.H. Swift | †D.M. Trick |
| L. Cusworth 1dg | L. Cusworth 1dg | J.P. Horton 1dg | J.P. Horton |
| *S.J. Smith | *S.J. Smith | S.J. Smith | †N.G. Youngs |
| C.E. Smart | C.E. Smart | C.E. Smart | C.E. Smart |
| P.J. Wheeler | S.G.F. Mills | P.J. Wheeler | P.J. Wheeler |
| G.S. Pearce | G.S. Pearce | G.S. Pearce | G.S. Pearce |
| M.J. Colclough[1] | †S.B. Boyle | S.B. Boyle | S.B. Boyle |
| S. Bainbridge | S. Bainbridge | S. Bainbridge | S. Bainbridge |
| N.C. Jeavons | N.C. Jeavons | N.C. Jeavons | N.C. Jeavons |
| J.P. Scott | J.P. Scott | *J.P. Scott | *J.P. Scott |
| P.J. Winterbottom | P.J. Winterbottom | P.J. Winterbottom | P.J. Winterbottom |
| Twickenham | Cardiff Arms Park | Twickenham | Lansdowne Road |
| LOST 15-19 | DRAWN 13-13 | LOST 12-22 | LOST 15-25 |
| ENG.: 4PG 1DG | WALES: 2PG 1DG 1T | ENG.: 3PG 1DG | IRE.: 1G 5PG 1T |
| FR.: 2G 1PG 1T | ENG.: 2PG 1DG 1T | SCOT.: 1G 3PG 1DG 1T | ENG.: 5PG |
| 15 Jan. 1983 | 5 Feb. 1983 | 5 Mar. 1983 | 19 Mar. 1983 |
| [1]Rep. by R. Hesford | | | |

England had become used to fielding an unrivalled set of forwards in previous seasons, but the recent loss of Beaumont, the retirement of Blakeway and the loss through injury of Maurice Colclough, deprived the English scrum of a nucleus of expertise and experience.

Mike Davis ended his reign as England coach, having seen the side to a Grand Slam at the start of his tenure. Speaking philosophically during this wooden spoon season, he remarked: "I have turned wine into water." But his colleagues among the selection committee were heavily criticised this year and much of the blame for England's failures was heaped on their shoulders.

It was surprising to see Slemen overlooked while it was odd to find Cusworth dropped following the draw at Cardiff. There, his close understanding of the play of his Leicester colleagues, Dodge and Hare, had created England's only try of the season.

## 1983-84

| | v. NZ | v. SCOTLAND | v. IRELAND | v. FRANCE | v. WALES |
|---|---|---|---|---|---|
| | W.H. Hare 3PG,1C | W.H. Hare 2PG | W.H. Hare 3PG | W.H. Hare 2C,1T,2PG | W.H. Hare 5PG |
| | J. Carleton[1] | J. Carleton | J. Carleton | J. Carleton | J. Carleton |
| | C.R. Woodward | G.H. Davies | †B. Barley | C.R. Woodward | B. Barley |
| | P.W. Dodge | C.R. Woodward | C.R. Woodward | B. Barley | C.R. Woodward |
| | M.A.C. Slemen | M.A.C. Slemen | †R. Underwood | R. Underwood 1T | R. Underwood |
| | L. Cusworth | L. Cusworth | L. Cusworth 1DG | L. Cusworth | L. Cusworth |
| | N.G. Youngs | N.G. Youngs | N.G. Youngs | N.G. Youngs | N.G. Youngs |
| | †C. White | C. White | C. White[1] | C. White | †P.A.G. Rendall |
| | *P.J. Wheeler | *P.J. Wheeler | *P.J. Wheeler | *P.J. Wheeler | *P.J. Wheeler |
| | G.S. Pearce | G.S. Pearce | P.J. Blakeway | P.J. Blakeway | P.J. Blakeway |
| | M.J. Colclough 1T | M.J. Colclough | M.J. Colclough | M.J. Colclough | M.J. Colclough |
| | S. Bainbridge | S. Bainbridge | S. Bainbridge | S. Bainbridge | S. Bainbridge |
| | †P.D. Simpson | P.D. Simpson | J.P. Hall | J.P. Hall | †A.F. Dun |
| | J.P. Scott | J.P. Scott | J.P. Scott | J.P. Scott | J.P. Scott |
| | P.J. Winterbottom | P.J. Winterbottom[1] | D.H. Cooke | P.J. Winterbottom | P.J. Winterbottom |
| | Twickenham | Murrayfield | Twickenham | Parc des Princes | Twickenham |
| | WON 15-9 | LOST 6-18 | WON 12-9 | LOST 18-32 | LOST 15-24 |
| | ENG.: 1G 3PG | SCOT.: 2G 2PG | ENG.: 3PG 1DG | FR.: 3G 1PG 1DG 2T | ENG.: 5PG |
| | NZ: 1G 1PG | ENG.: 2PG | IRE.: 3PG | ENG.: 2G 2PG | WALES: 1G 4PG 2DG |
| | 19 Nov. 1983 | 4 Feb. 1984 | 18 Feb. 1984 | 3 Mar. 1984 | 17 Mar. 1984 |
| | [1]Rep. by N.C. Stringer | [1]Rep. by †J.P. Hall | [1]Rep. by †S. Redfern | | |

England began the season under new management. Former internationals Derek Morgan and Dick Greenwood took over as Chairman of the Selectors and coach respectively, and for Peter Wheeler, in his final season of international rugby, there was the honour of the captaincy. The new men celebrated their new partnership with a famous win over the All Blacks, England's first against the All Blacks at Twickenham since 1936. Colclough was the outstanding player in a 15-9 win, and scored the decisive try of the game, early in the second half.

At the start of the Championship England were favourites to win the title. But in their first game, against Scotland, a failure to adapt to the conditions and an inability to overcome the disruptive tactics of the Scottish back-row, resulted in a miserable defeat.

The rest of the season, despite a welcome victory over Ireland, was an even greater disappointment. There was a rigid dependance on tight, forward play, and exciting runners such as Underwood and Carleton on the wings were given few chances to show their pace. Underwood, against France, however, created a chance for himself from broken play, and scored an excellent try after France had established a winning lead.

## 1984

| | 1st v. S.AFRICA | 2nd v. S.AFRICA |
|---|---|---|
| | W.H. Hare 4PG | W.H. Hare 3PG |
| | †M.D. Bailey[1] | M.D. Bailey |
| | †J.A. Palmer | J.A. Palmer |
| | G.H. Davies | G.H. Davies |
| | D.M. Trick | A.H. Swift |
| | J.P. Horton 1DG | J.P. Horton |
| | †R.J. Hill | R.J. Hill |
| | †M. Preedy | P.A.G. Rendall |
| | S.G.F. Mills | †S.E. Brain |
| | P.J. Blakeway | G.S. Pearce |
| | *J.P. Scott | *J.P. Scott |
| | J.H. Fidler | J.H. Fidler |
| | J.P. Hall | J.P. Hall[1] |
| | †C.J.S. Butcher | C.J.S. Butcher |
| | P.J. Winterbottom | P.J. Winterbottom |
| | Port Elizabeth | Johannesburg |
| | LOST 15-33 | LOST 9-35 |
| | SA: 3G 5PG | SA: 4G 1PG 2T |
| | ENG.: 4PG 1DG | ENG.: 3PG |
| | 2 Jun. 1984 | 9 Jun. 1984 |
| | [1]Rep. by N.C. Stringer | [1]Rep. by †G.W. Rees |

England took an inexperienced party to South Africa in the summer of 1984. Numerous players were unavailable through injuries or work commitments, and of the seven games played, only four were won.

England's lack of experienced international players was cruelly exposed in the Test matches. South Africa romped away to two easy victories and England's defeat in Johannesburg, by 26 points, was a record losing points margin.

In the first Test the front row was Preedy, Mills and Blakeway – all Gloucester players. This was the first time that a club front row had played in an England team. After the second Test, Dusty Hare announced his retirement from internationals. England's most-capped full-back, he also holds the record for most points in England internationals, his 240 points coming from 25 matches.

## 1984-85

| v. AUSTRALIA | v. ROMANIA | v. FRANCE | v. SCOTLAND | v. IRELAND | v. WALES |
|---|---|---|---|---|---|
| N.C. Stringer | N.C. Stringer[1] | †C.R. Martin | C.R. Martin | C.R. Martin | C.R. Martin |
| | | | | | |
| J. Carleton | †S.T. Smith 1t | S.T. Smith | S.T. Smith 1t | S.T. Smith | S.T. Smith 1t |
| †R.A.P. Lozowski | †K.G. Simms[2] | K.G. Simms | K.G. Simms | K.G. Simms | K.G. Simms |
| B. Barley | *P.W. Dodge | *P.W. Dodge | *P.W. Dodge | *P.W. Dodge | *P.W. Dodge |
| R. Underwood | R. Underwood | R. Underwood | R. Underwood | R. Underwood 1t | R. Underwood |
| | | | | | |
| †S. Barnes 1pg | †C.R. Andrew 2dg,4pg | C.R. Andrew 1dg,2pg | C.R. Andrew 2pg | C.R. Andrew 2pg | C.R. Andrew 2pg,1dg,1c |
| *†N.D. Melville | †R.M. Harding | R.M. Harding | R.M. Harding | N.D. Melville[1] | N.D. Melville |
| | | | | | |
| †G.J. Chilcott | P.J. Blakeway | P.J. Blakeway | P.J. Blakeway | P.J. Blakeway | A. Sheppard |
| S.G.F. Mills[1] | S.E. Brain | S.E. Brain | S.E. Brain | S.E. Brain | S.E. Brain |
| G.S. Pearce | G.S. Pearce | G.S. Pearce | G.S. Pearce | G.S. Pearce | G.S. Pearce |
| J.P. Syddall | †J. Orwin | J. Orwin | J. Orwin | J. Orwin | J. Orwin |
| †N.C. Redman | †W.A. Dooley | W.A. Dooley | W.A. Dooley | W.A. Dooley | W.A. Dooley |
| J.P. Hall | J.P. Hall | J.P. Hall[1] | J.P. Hall | J.P. Hall | J.P. Hall |
| C.J.S. Butcher | R. Hesford | R. Hesford | R. Hesford | R. Hesford | R. Hesford |
| G.W. Rees | D.H. Cooke | D.H. Cooke | D.H. Cooke | D.H. Cooke | D.H. Cooke |
| Twickenham | Twickenham | Twickenham | Twickenham | Lansdowne Road | Cardiff Arms Park |
| LOST 3-19 | WON 22-15 | DRAWN 9-9 | WON 10-7 | LOST 10-13 | LOST 15-24 |
| Eng.: 1pg | Eng.: 4pg 2dg 1t | Eng.: 1dg 2pg | Eng.: 2pg 1t | Ire.: 1dg 2pg 1t | Wales: 2g 3pg 1dg |
| Aust.: 2g 1pg 1t | Rom.: 5pg | Fr.: 3dg | Scot.: 1pg 1t | Eng.: 2pg 1t | Eng.: 1g 2pg 1dg |
| 3 Nov. 1984 | 5 Jan. 1985 | 2 Feb. 1985 | 16 Mar. 1985 | 30 Mar. 1985 | 20 Apr. 1985 |
| [1]Rep. by S.E. Brain | [1]Rep. by S. Barnes | [1]Rep. by †M.C. Teague | | [1]Rep. by R.J. Hill | |
| | [2]Rep. by G.H. Davies | | | | |

England played six internationals during the season, opening with five new caps in the match against Australia. Nigel Melville led the side on his debut, the first England player to do so since Joe Mycock in 1947. England were easily beaten and eleven changes were made for the first ever game against Romania, played in January. Rob Andrew scored eighteen points, a record haul for an Englishman on his debut. Against Wales down in Cardiff the threequarters combined smoothly for Smith to score one of the best tries of the season, and only some dreadful defensive lapses prevented England from gaining their first win at Cardiff since 1963.

One curiosity of the 1984-5 campaign was that the largely experimental party chosen for the summer tour to South Africa in 1984 had all but disappeared from the squad by the end of the domestic season. And altogether England had used 20 new caps in the space of 10 months: an extraordinary statistic.

## 1985

| 1st v. NZ | 2nd v. NZ |
|---|---|
| G.H. Davies | G.H. Davies |
| | |
| S.T. Smith | S.T. Smith |
| *P.W. Dodge | *P.W. Dodge |
| †J.L.B. Salmon | J.L.B. Salmon |
| †M.E. Harrison 1t | M.E. Harrison 1t |
| | |
| S. Barnes 1pg,1c | S. Barnes 2c,1dg |
| N.D. Melville | N.D. Melville[1] |
| | |
| †R.P. Huntsman | R.P. Huntsman |
| S.E. Brain | S.E. Brain |
| G.S. Pearce | G.S. Pearce |
| J. Orwin | J. Orwin[2] |
| S. Bainbridge | S. Bainbridge |
| J.P. Hall | J.P. Hall 1t |
| M.C. Teague 1t | M.C. Teague |
| D.H. Cooke | D.H. Cooke |
| Christchurch | Wellington |
| LOST 13-18 | LOST 15-42 |
| NZ: 6pg | NZ: 3g 3pg 1dg 3t |
| Eng.: 1g 1t 1pg | Eng.: 2g 1dg |
| 1 Jun. 1985 | 8 Jun. 1985 |
| | [1]Rep. by R.J. Hill |
| | [2]Rep. by W.A. Dooley |

As in 1984 England suffered humiliating defeats on their post-season tour, this time in New Zealand. The All Blacks were in devastating form at Wellington, registering a victory by 27 points and inflicting a new record losing margin on England.

Both Martin and Metcalfe, the full-backs selected for the tour, had looked suspect under the high ball in the earlier provincial matches of the tour. Davies played in the position against Otago in the week before the first Test, acquitted himself well, and was nominated for the Test place. He thus became the first man to play full internationals for England in the full-back, centre and fly-half positions.

Jamie Salmon made his debut at Christchurch. He had previously played international rugby for New Zealand, and became the third man to play for England and another IB country. England scored two tries, one by Harrison on his debut, but went down to six penalty goals. Harrison scored another try in the second Test, but this time England were well and truly thrashed.

## 1985-86

| v. WALES | v. SCOTLAND | v. IRELAND | v. FRANCE |
|---|---|---|---|
| G.H. Davies | G.H. Davies[1] | G.H. Davies 1t | G.H. Davies[1] |
| S.T. Smith | S.T. Smith | M.E. Harrison | M.E. Harrison |
| †S.J. Halliday | S.J. Halliday | K.G. Simms | K.G. Simms |
| J.L.B. Salmon | J.L.B. Salmon | †F.J. Clough | F.L. Clough |
| R. Underwood | M.E. Harrison | R. Underwood | R. Underwood |
| C.R. Andrew 6pg,1dg | C.R. Andrew 2pg | C.R. Andrew 3c,1pg | C.R. Andrew |
| *N.D. Melville | *N.D. Melville | *N.D. Melville | *N.D. Melville[2] |
| P.A.G. Rendall | P.A.G. Rendall | G.J. Chilcott | G.J. Chilcott |
| S.E. Brain | S.E. Brain | S.E. Brain | S.E. Brain |
| G.S. Pearce | G.S. Pearce | G.S. Pearce | G.S. Pearce |
| W.A. Dooley | W.A. Dooley | W.A. Dooley | W.A. Dooley 1t |
| M.J. Colclough | M.J. Colclough | M.J. Colclough | M.J. Colclough |
| J.P. Hall | J.P. Hall[2] | P.J. Winterbottom | P.J. Winterbottom |
| †G.L. Robbins | G.L. Robbins | †D. Richards 2t | D. Richards |
| P.J. Winterbottom | P.J. Winterbottom | G.W. Rees | G.W. Rees |
| Twickenham | Murrayfield | Twickenham | Parc des Princes |
| WON 21-18 | LOST 6-33 | WON 25-20 | LOST 10-29 |
| Eng.: 6pg 1dg | Scot.: 3g 5pg | Eng.: 3g‡ 1pg 1t | Fr.: 2g‡ 3pg 2t |
| Wales: 1g 1dg 3pg | Eng.: 2pg | Ire.: 1g 2pg 2t | Eng.: 2pg 1t |
| 18 Jan. 1986 | 15 Feb. 1986 | 1 Mar. 1986 | 15 Mar. 1986 |
| | [1]Rep. by S. Barnes | ‡includes penalty try | [1]Rep. by S. Barnes 2pg |
| | [2]Rep. by N.C. Redman | | [2]Rep. by R.J. Hill ‡includes penalty try |

England resurrected the Divisional Championship in the autumn of 1985 to provide the selectors with a convenient and timely guide to the form of England's leading sixty players. But still there was to be a lack of enterprise and variety in the approach of a conservative national side, which shared third place with Wales in the Championship table.

The side's limitations and weaknesses were cruelly exposed by France and Scotland in England's two matches away from home, though the last-minute victory through Rob Andrew's drop-goal against Wales, and an impressive forward effort against Ireland, gave some crumbs of comfort to England followers desperate for success and anxious to find promise for the World Cup series, some 18 months away.

## 1986-87

| v. IRELAND | v. FRANCE | v. WALES | v. SCOTLAND |
|---|---|---|---|
| W.M.H. Rose[1] | W.M.H. Rose 4pg | W.M.H. Rose 4pg | W.M.H. Rose 1t,2c,3pg |
| M.E. Harrison | M.E. Harrison | M.E. Harrison | *M.E. Harrison 1t |
| J.L.B. Salmon | J.L.B. Salmon | K.G. Simms | S.J. Halliday |
| K.G. Simms | K.G. Simms | J.L.B. Salmon | J.L.B. Salmon |
| R. Underwood | R. Underwood | R. Underwood | R. Underwood |
| C.R. Andrew | C.R. Andrew 1dg | C.R. Andrew | †P.N. Williams |
| *R.J. Hill | *R.J. Hill | *R.J. Hill | R.M. Harding |
| P.A.G. Rendall | P.A.G. Rendall[1] | G.J. Chilcott | P.A.G. Rendall |
| †R.G.R. Dawe | R.G.R. Dawe | R.G.R. Dawe | †B.C. Moore |
| G.S. Pearce | G.S. Pearce | G.S. Pearce | G.S. Pearce |
| N.C. Redman | W.A. Dooley | W.A. Dooley | N.C. Redman |
| †D.A. Cusani | S. Bainbridge | S. Bainbridge | S. Bainbridge |
| J.P. Hall | P.J. Winterbottom | P.J. Winterbottom | J.P. Hall |
| P.D. Simpson | J.P. Hall | J.P. Hall | D. Richards |
| P.J. Winterbottom | G.W. Rees | G.W. Rees | G.W. Rees |
| Lansdowne Road | Twickenham | Cardiff Arms Park | Twickenham |
| LOST 0-17 | LOST 15-19 | LOST 12-19 | WON 21-12 |
| Ire.: 1g 1pg 2t | Eng.: 4pg 1dg | Wales: 5pg 1t | Eng.: 2g‡ 3pg |
| Eng.: NIL | Fr.: 1g 1pg 2dg 1t | Eng.: 4pg | Scot.: 1g 2pg |
| 7 Feb. 1987 | 21 Feb. 1987 | 7 Mar. 1987 | 4 Apr. 1987 |
| [1]Rep. by S. Barnes | [1]Rep. by G.J. Chilcott | | ‡includes penalty try |

1987 was a curious season for English rugby. The hopes of a confident side were shattered in a miserable performance in Dublin, and after changes were made for the game with France, defeat was again England's portion.

Then came the dreadful episode at Cardiff where several English players were involved in foul acts which, though not seen by the referee, were wholeheartedly condemned by the RFU. Setting a fine example to the other Home Nations, the English Union omitted the chief culprits of the Cardiff escapade for the final game of the season. Out went Dawe, Chilcott and Dooley along with Richard Hill, who had captained the fifteen at Cardiff and who thus found himself a scapegoat for failing to control the side.

Mike Harrison, who had led the Northern Division to the Divisional Championship, was installed as England's new skipper to face Scotland. In difficult conditions he led his side to a remarkable triumph and set the side on course for victory by forcing the Scots to concede a penalty try.

# ENGLISH MATCH RECORDS

## Match Results 1871 to 1987

| Match | Date | Opponents | For T | C | D | P | Pts | Against T | C | D | P | Pts | Result | Venue | Captain |
|---|---|---|---|---|---|---|---|---|---|---|---|---|---|---|---|
| 1 | 27.3.1871 | Scotland | 1 | — | — | — | | 2 | 1 | — | — | | Lost | Edinburgh | F. Stokes |
| 2 | 5.2.1872 | Scotland | 3 | 1 | 1 | — | | — | — | 1 | — | | Won | The Oval | F. Stokes |
| 3 | 3.3.1873 | Scotland | — | — | — | — | | — | — | — | — | | Drawn | Glasgow | F. Stokes |
| 4 | 23.2.1874 | Scotland | — | — | 1 | — | | 1 | — | — | — | | Won | The Oval | A. St.G. Hamersley |
| 5 | 15.2.1875 | Ireland | 2 | 1 | 1 | — | | — | — | — | — | | Won | The Oval | Hon. H. A. Lawrence |
| 6 | 8.3.1875 | Scotland | — | — | — | — | | — | — | — | — | | Drawn | Edinburgh | Hon. H. A. Lawrence |
| 7 | 13.12.1875 | Ireland | 2 | 1 | — | — | | — | — | — | — | | Won | Dublin | F. Luscombe |
| 8 | 6.3.1876 | Scotland | 2 | 1 | — | — | | — | — | — | — | | Won | The Oval | F. Luscombe |
| 9 | 5.2.1877 | Ireland | 4 | 2 | — | — | | — | — | — | — | | Won | The Oval | E. Kewley |
| 10 | 5.3.1877 | Scotland | — | — | — | — | | — | — | 1 | — | | Lost | Edinburgh | E. Kewley |
| 11 | 4.3.1878 | Scotland | — | — | — | — | | — | — | — | — | | Drawn | The Oval | E. Kewley |
| 12 | 11.3.1878 | Ireland | 3 | 2 | — | — | | — | — | — | — | | Won | Dublin | M. W. Marshall |
| 13 | 10.3.1879 | Scotland | 1 | 1 | — | — | | — | — | 1 | — | | Drawn | Edinburgh | F. R. Adams |
| 14 | 24.3.1879 | Scotland | 4 | 2 | 1 | — | | — | — | — | — | | Won | The Oval | F. R. Adams |
| 15 | 30.1.1880 | Ireland | 2 | 1 | — | — | | 1 | — | — | — | | Won | Dublin | L. Stokes |
| 16 | 28.2.1880 | Scotland | 5 | 2 | — | — | | 1 | 1 | — | — | | Won | Manchester | L. Stokes |
| 17 | 5.2.1881 | Ireland | 4 | 2 | — | — | | — | — | — | — | | Won | Manchester | L. Stokes |
| 18 | 19.2.1881 | Wales | 13 | 7 | 1 | — | | — | — | — | — | | Won | Blackheath | L. Stokes |
| 19 | 19.3.1881 | Scotland | 1 | — | 1 | — | | 2 | 1 | — | — | | Drawn | Edinburgh | L. Stokes |
| 20 | 6.2.1882 | Ireland | 2 | — | — | — | | 2 | — | — | — | | Drawn | Dublin | C. Gurdon |
| 21 | 4.3.1882 | Scotland | — | — | — | — | | 2 | — | — | — | | Lost | Manchester | A. N. Hornby |
| 22 | 16.12.1882 | Wales | 6 | 2 | — | — | | — | — | — | — | | Won | Swansea | E. T. Gurdon |
| 23 | 5.2.1883 | Ireland | 4 | 1 | — | — | | 1 | — | — | — | | Won | Manchester | E. T. Gurdon |
| 24 | 3.3.1883 | Scotland | 2 | — | — | — | | 1 | — | — | — | | Won | Edinburgh | E. T. Gurdon |
| 25 | 5.1.1884 | Wales | 3 | 1 | — | — | | 1 | 1 | — | — | | Won | Leeds | E. T. Gurdon |
| 26 | 4.2.1884 | Ireland | 1 | 1 | — | — | | — | — | — | — | | Won | Dublin | E. T. Gurdon |
| 27 | 1.3.1884 | Scotland | 1 | 1 | — | — | | 1 | — | — | — | | Won | Blackheath | E. T. Gurdon |
| 28 | 3.1.1885 | Wales | 5 | 1 | — | — | | 2 | 1 | — | — | | Won | Swansea | E. T. Gurdon |
| 29 | 7.2.1885 | Ireland | 2 | — | — | — | | 1 | — | — | — | | Won | Manchester | E. T. Gurdon |
| 30 | 2.1.1886 | Wales | 2 | — | ★ | — | | 1 | 1 | — | — | | Won | Blackheath | C. J. B. Marriott |
| 31 | 6.2.1886 | Ireland | 1 | — | — | — | | — | — | — | — | | Won | Dublin | C. J. B. Marriott |
| 32 | 13.3.1886 | Scotland | — | — | — | — | | — | — | — | — | | Drawn | Edinburgh | E. T. Gurdon |
| 33 | 8.1.1887 | Wales | — | — | — | — | | — | — | — | — | | Drawn | Llanelli | A. Rotherham |
| 34 | 5.2.1887 | Ireland | — | — | — | — | | 2 | 2 | — | — | | Lost | Dublin | A. Rotherham |
| 35 | 5.3.1887 | Scotland | 1 | — | — | — | | 1 | — | — | — | | Drawn | Manchester | A. Rotherham |
| 36 | 16.2.1889 | NZ Natives | 5 | 1 | — | — | 7 | — | — | — | — | 0 | Won | Blackheath | F. Bonsor |
| 37 | 15.2.1890 | Wales | — | — | — | — | 0 | 1 | — | — | — | 1 | Lost | Dewsbury | A. E. Stoddart |
| 38 | 1.3.1890 | Scotland | 2 | 1 | — | — | 6 | — | — | — | — | 0 | Won | Edinburgh | J. L. Hickson |
| 39 | 15.3.1890 | Ireland | 3 | — | — | — | 3 | — | — | — | — | 0 | Won | Blackheath | A. E. Stoddart |
| 40 | 3.1.1891 | Wales | 3 | 2 | — | — | 7 | 1 | 1 | — | — | 3 | Won | Newport | F. H. R. Alderson |
| 41 | 7.2.1891 | Ireland | 5 | 2 | — | — | 9 | — | — | — | — | 0 | Won | Dublin | F. H. R. Alderson |
| 42 | 7.3.1891 | Scotland | 1 | 1 | — | — | 3 | 2 | 2 | 1 | — | 9 | Lost | Richmond | F. H. R. Alderson |
| 43 | 2.1.1892 | Wales | 4 | 3 | — | — | 17 | — | — | — | — | 0 | Won | Blackheath | F. H. R. Alderson |
| 44 | 6.2.1892 | Ireland | 2 | 1 | — | — | 7 | — | — | — | — | 0 | Won | Manchester | S. M. J. Woods |
| 45 | 5.3.1892 | Scotland | 1 | 1 | — | — | 5 | — | — | — | — | 0 | Won | Edinburgh | F. H. R. Alderson |
| 46 | 7.1.1893 | Wales | 4 | 1 | — | — | 11 | 3 | 1 | — | 1 | 12 | Lost | Cardiff | A. E. Stoddart |
| 47 | 4.2.1893 | Ireland | 2 | — | — | — | 4 | — | — | — | — | 0 | Won | Dublin | S. M. J. Woods |
| 48 | 4.3.1893 | Scotland | — | — | — | — | 0 | — | — | 2 | — | 8 | Lost | Leeds | A. E. Stoddart |
| 49 | 6.1.1894 | Wales | 4 | 4 | ★ | — | 24 | 1 | — | — | — | 3 | Won | Birkenhead | R. E. Lockwood |
| 50 | 3.2.1894 | Ireland | 1 | 1 | — | — | 5 | 1 | — | 1 | — | 7 | Lost | Blackheath | R. E. Lockwood |
| 51 | 17.3.1894 | Scotland | — | — | — | — | 0 | 2 | — | — | — | 6 | Lost | Edinburgh | E. W. Taylor |
| 52 | 5.1.1895 | Wales | 4 | 1 | — | — | 14 | 2 | — | — | — | 6 | Won | Swansea | S. M. J. Woods |
| 53 | 2.2.1895 | Ireland | 2 | — | — | — | 6 | 1 | — | — | — | 3 | Won | Dublin | S. M. J. Woods |
| 54 | 9.3.1895 | Scotland | — | — | 1 | — | 3 | 1 | — | — | 1 | 6 | Lost | Richmond | S. M. J. Woods |
| 55 | 4.1.1896 | Wales | 7 | 2 | — | — | 25 | — | — | — | — | 0 | Won | Blackheath | E. W. Taylor |
| 56 | 1.2.1896 | Ireland | — | — | 1 | — | 4 | 2 | 2 | — | — | 10 | Lost | Leeds | E. W. Taylor |
| 57 | 14.3.1896 | Scotland | — | — | — | — | 0 | 3 | 1 | — | — | 11 | Lost | Glasgow | F. Mitchell |
| 58 | 9.1.1897 | Wales | — | — | — | — | 0 | 3 | 1 | — | — | 11 | Lost | Newport | E. W. Taylor |
| 59 | 6.2.1897 | Ireland | 1 | — | — | 2 | 9 | 3 | — | ★ | — | 13 | Lost | Dublin | E. W. Taylor |
| 60 | 13.3.1897 | Scotland | 2 | 1 | 1 | — | 12 | 1 | — | — | — | 3 | Won | Manchester | E. W. Taylor |
| 61 | 5.2.1898 | Ireland | 1 | — | 1 | — | 6 | 2 | — | 1 | — | 9 | Lost | Richmond | J. F. Byrne |
| 62 | 12.3.1898 | Scotland | 1 | — | — | — | 3 | 1 | — | — | — | 3 | Drawn | Edinburgh | J. F. Byrne |
| 63 | 2.4.1898 | Wales | 4 | 1 | — | — | 14 | 1 | — | 1 | — | 7 | Won | Blackheath | J. F. Byrne |
| 64 | 7.1.1899 | Wales | 1 | — | — | — | 3 | 6 | 4 | — | — | 26 | Lost | Swansea | A. Rotherham |
| 65 | 4.2.1899 | Ireland | — | — | — | — | 0 | 1 | — | — | 1 | 6 | Lost | Dublin | A. Rotherham |
| 66 | 11.3.1899 | Scotland | — | — | — | — | 0 | 1 | 1 | — | — | 5 | Lost | Blackheath | A. Rotherham |
| 67 | 6.1.1900 | Wales | 1 | — | — | — | 3 | 2 | 2 | — | 1 | 13 | Lost | Gloucester | R. H. B. Cattell |

★ in the drop-goal column denotes a goal from a mark

| Match | Date | Opponents | For | | | | | Against | | | | | Result | Venue | Captain |
|---|---|---|---|---|---|---|---|---|---|---|---|---|---|---|---|
| | | | T | C | D | P | Pts | T | C | D | P | Pts | | | |
| 68 | 3.2.1900 | Ireland | 3 | 1 | 1 | — | 15 | — | — | 1 | — | 4 | Won | Richmond | J. Daniell |
| 69 | 10.3.1900 | Scotland | — | — | — | — | 0 | — | — | — | — | 0 | Drawn | Edinburgh | J. Daniell |
| 70 | 5.1.1901 | Wales | — | — | — | — | 0 | 3 | 2 | — | — | 13 | Lost | Cardiff | J. T. Taylor |
| 71 | 9.2.1901 | Ireland | 1 | — | — | 1 | 6 | 2 | 2 | — | — | 10 | Lost | Dublin | W. L. Bunting |
| 72 | 9.3.1901 | Scotland | 1 | — | — | — | 3 | 4 | 3 | — | — | 18 | Lost | Blackheath | W. L. Bunting |
| 73 | 11.1.1902 | Wales | 2 | 1 | — | — | 8 | 2 | — | — | 1 | 9 | Lost | Blackheath | H. Alexander |
| 74 | 8.2.1902 | Ireland | 2 | — | — | — | 6 | 1 | — | — | — | 3 | Won | Leicester | J. Daniell |
| 75 | 15.3.1902 | Scotland | 2 | — | — | — | 6 | 1 | — | — | — | 3 | Won | Edinburgh | J. Daniell |
| 76 | 10.1.1903 | Wales | 1 | 1 | — | — | 5 | 5 | 3 | — | — | 21 | Lost | Swansea | B. Oughtred |
| 77 | 14.2.1903 | Ireland | — | — | — | — | 0 | 1 | — | — | 1 | 6 | Lost | Dublin | B. Oughtred |
| 78 | 21.3.1903 | Scotland | 2 | — | — | — | 6 | 2 | — | 1 | — | 10 | Lost | Richmond | P.D. Kendall |
| 79 | 9.1.1904 | Wales | 3 | 1 | — | 1 | 14 | 2 | 2 | ★ | — | 14 | Drawn | Leicester | F. M. Stout |
| 80 | 13.2.1904 | Ireland | 5 | 2 | — | — | 19 | — | — | — | — | 0 | Won | Blackheath | J. Daniell |
| 81 | 19.3.1904 | Scotland | 1 | — | — | — | 3 | 2 | — | — | — | 6 | Lost | Edinburgh | J. Daniell |
| 82 | 14.1.1905 | Wales | — | — | — | — | 0 | 7 | 2 | — | — | 25 | Lost | Cardiff | F. M. Stout |
| 83 | 11.2.1905 | Ireland | 1 | — | — | — | 3 | 5 | 1 | — | — | 17 | Lost | Cork | F. M. Stout |
| 84 | 18.3.1905 | Scotland | — | — | — | — | 0 | 2 | 1 | — | — | 8 | Lost | Richmond | F. M. Stout |
| 85 | 2.12.1905 | New Zealand | — | — | — | — | 0 | 5 | — | — | — | 15 | Lost | Crystal Palace | V. H. Cartwright |
| 86 | 13.1.1906 | Wales | 1 | — | — | — | 3 | 4 | 2 | — | — | 16 | Lost | Richmond | V. H. Cartwright |
| 87 | 10.2.1906 | Ireland | 2 | — | — | — | 6 | 4 | 2 | — | — | 16 | Lost | Leicester | V. H. Cartwright |
| 88 | 17.3.1906 | Scotland | 3 | — | — | — | 9 | 1 | — | — | — | 3 | Won | Edinburgh | V. H. Cartwright |
| 89 | 22.3.1906 | France | 9 | 4 | — | — | 35 | 2 | 1 | — | — | 8 | Won | Paris | V. H. Cartwright |
| 90 | 8.12.1906 | South Africa | 1 | — | — | — | 3 | 1 | — | — | — | 3 | Drawn | Crystal Palace | V. H. Cartwright |
| 91 | 5.1.1907 | France | 9 | 5 | 1 | — | 41 | 2 | 2 | — | 1 | 13 | Won | Richmond | B. A. Hill |
| 92 | 12.1.1907 | Wales | — | — | — | — | 0 | 6 | 2 | — | — | 22 | Lost | Swansea | B. A. Hill |
| 93 | 9.2.1907 | Ireland | 2 | — | — | 1 | 9 | 4 | 1 | ★ | — | 17 | Lost | Dublin | J. Green |
| 94 | 16.3.1907 | Scotland | 1 | — | — | — | 3 | 2 | 1 | — | — | 8 | Lost | Blackheath | E. W. Roberts |
| 95 | 1.1.1908 | France | 5 | 2 | — | — | 19 | — | — | — | — | 0 | Won | Paris | T. S. Kelly |
| 96 | 18.1.1908 | Wales | 4 | 3 | — | — | 18 | 5 | 3 | 1 | 1 | 28 | Lost | Bristol | J. G. G. Birkett |
| 97 | 8.2.1908 | Ireland | 3 | 2 | — | — | 13 | — | — | — | 1 | 3 | Won | Richmond | C.E.L.Hammond |
| 98 | 21.3.1908 | Scotland | 2 | 2 | — | — | 10 | 2 | 1 | 2 | — | 16 | Lost | Edinburgh | L. A. N. Slocock |
| 99 | 9.1.1909 | Australia | 1 | — | — | — | 3 | 3 | — | — | — | 9 | Lost | Blackheath | G. H. D'O. Lyon |
| 100 | 16.1.1909 | Wales | — | — | — | — | 0 | 2 | 1 | — | — | 8 | Lost | Cardiff | R. Dibble |
| 101 | 30.1.1909 | France | 6 | 2 | — | — | 22 | — | — | — | — | 0 | Won | Leicester | R. Dibble |
| 102 | 13.2.1909 | Ireland | 3 | 1 | — | — | 11 | 1 | 1 | — | — | 5 | Won | Dublin | R. Dibble |
| 103 | 20.3.1909 | Scotland | 2 | 1 | — | — | 8 | 4 | 3 | — | — | 18 | Lost | Richmond | R. Dibble |
| 104 | 15.1.1910 | Wales | 2 | 1 | — | 1 | 11 | 2 | — | — | — | 6 | Won | Twickenham | A. D. Stoop |
| 105 | 12.2.1910 | Ireland | — | — | — | — | 0 | — | — | — | — | 0 | Drawn | Twickenham | A. D. Stoop |
| 106 | 3.3.1910 | France | 3 | 1 | — | — | 11 | 1 | — | — | — | 3 | Won | Paris | E. R. Mobbs |
| 107 | 19.3.1910 | Scotland | 4 | 1 | — | — | 14 | 1 | 1 | — | — | 5 | Won | Edinburgh | J. G. G. Birkett |
| 108 | 21.1.1911 | Wales | 3 | 1 | — | — | 11 | 4 | — | — | 1 | 15 | Lost | Swansea | J. G. G. Birkett |
| 109 | 28.1.1911 | France | 7 | 5 | — | 2 | 37 | — | — | — | — | 0 | Won | Twickenham | J. G. G. Birkett |
| 110 | 11.2.1911 | Ireland | — | — | — | — | 0 | 1 | — | — | — | 3 | Lost | Dublin | J. G. G. Birkett |
| 111 | 18.3.1911 | Scotland | 3 | 2 | — | — | 13 | 2 | 1 | — | — | 8 | Won | Twickenham | A. L. H. Gotley |
| 112 | 20.1.1912 | Wales | 2 | 1 | — | — | 8 | — | — | — | — | 0 | Won | Twickenham | R. Dibble |
| 113 | 10.2.1912 | Ireland | 5 | — | — | — | 15 | — | — | — | — | 0 | Won | Twickenham | R. Dibble |
| 114 | 16.3.1912 | Scotland | 1 | — | — | — | 3 | 2 | 1 | — | — | 8 | Lost | Edinburgh | R. Dibble |
| 115 | 8.4.1912 | France | 4 | 1 | 1 | — | 18 | 2 | 1 | — | — | 8 | Won | Paris | N. A. Wodehouse |
| 116 | 4.1.1913 | South Africa | 1 | — | — | — | 3 | 1 | — | — | 2 | 9 | Lost | Twickenham | N. A. Wodehouse |
| 117 | 18.1.1913 | Wales | 2 | 1 | 1 | — | 12 | — | — | — | — | 0 | Won | Cardiff | N. A. Wodehouse |
| 118 | 25.1.1913 | France | 6 | 1 | — | — | 20 | — | — | — | — | 0 | Won | Twickenham | N. A. Wodehouse |
| 119 | 8.2.1913 | Ireland | 4 | — | — | 1 | 15 | — | — | 1 | — | 4 | Won | Dublin | N. A. Wodehouse |
| 120 | 15.3.1913 | Scotland | 1 | — | — | — | 3 | — | — | — | — | 0 | Won | Twickenham | N. A. Wodehouse |
| 121 | 17.1.1914 | Wales | 2 | 2 | — | — | 10 | 1 | 1 | 1 | — | 9 | Won | Twickenham | R. W. Poulton |
| 122 | 14.2.1914 | Ireland | 5 | 1 | — | — | 17 | 2 | 1 | 1 | — | 12 | Won | Twickenham | R. W. Poulton |
| 123 | 21.3.1914 | Scotland | 4 | 2 | — | — | 16 | 3 | 1 | 1 | — | 15 | Won | Edinburgh | R. W. Poulton |
| 124 | 13.4.1914 | France | 9 | 6 | — | — | 39 | 3 | 2 | — | — | 13 | Won | Paris | R. W. Poulton |
| 125 | 17.1.1920 | Wales | 1 | 1 | — | — | 5 | 2 | 1 | 2 | 1 | 19 | Lost | Swansea | J. E. Greenwood |
| 126 | 31.1.1920 | France | 1 | 1 | — | 1 | 8 | 1 | — | — | — | 3 | Won | Twickenham | J. E. Greenwood |
| 127 | 14.2.1920 | Ireland | 4 | 1 | — | — | 14 | 2 | 1 | — | 1 | 11 | Won | Dublin | J. E. Greenwood |
| 128 | 20.3.1920 | Scotland | 3 | 2 | — | — | 13 | — | — | 1 | — | 4 | Won | Twickenham | J. E. Greenwood |
| 129 | 15.1.1921 | Wales | 4 | 1 | 1 | — | 18 | 1 | — | — | — | 3 | Won | Twickenham | W. J. A. Davies |
| 130 | 12.2.1921 | Ireland | 3 | 1 | 1 | — | 15 | — | — | — | — | 0 | Won | Twickenham | W. J. A. Davies |
| 131 | 19.3.1921 | Scotland | 4 | 3 | — | — | 18 | — | — | — | — | 0 | Won | Edinburgh | W. J. A. Davies |
| 132 | 28.3.1921 | France | 2 | 2 | — | — | 10 | — | — | — | 2 | 6 | Won | Paris | W. J. A. Davies |
| 133 | 21.1.1922 | Wales | 2 | — | — | — | 6 | 8 | 2 | — | — | 28 | Lost | Cardiff | L. G. Brown |
| 134 | 11.2.1922 | Ireland | 4 | — | — | — | 12 | 1 | — | — | — | 3 | Won | Dublin | W. J. A. Davies |
| 135 | 25.2.1922 | France | 1 | 1 | — | 2 | 11 | 3 | 1 | — | — | 11 | Drawn | Twickenham | W. J. A. Davies |
| 136 | 18.3.1922 | Scotland | 3 | 1 | — | — | 11 | 1 | 1 | — | — | 5 | Won | Twickenham | W. J. A. Davies |
| 137 | 20.1.1923 | Wales | 1 | — | 1 | — | 7 | 1 | — | — | — | 3 | Won | Twickenham | W. J. A. Davies |
| 138 | 10.2.1923 | Ireland | 5 | 2 | 1 | — | 23 | 1 | 1 | — | — | 5 | Won | Leicester | W. J. A. Davies |
| 139 | 17.3.1923 | Scotland | 2 | 1 | — | — | 8 | 2 | — | — | — | 6 | Won | Edinburgh | W. J. A. Davies |
| 140 | 2.4.1923 | France | 2 | 1 | 1 | — | 12 | — | — | — | 1 | 3 | Won | Paris | W. J. A. Davies |
| 141 | 19.1.1924 | Wales | 5 | 1 | — | — | 17 | 3 | — | — | — | 9 | Won | Swansea | W. W. Wakefield |
| 142 | 9.2.1924 | Ireland | 4 | 1 | — | — | 14 | 1 | — | — | — | 3 | Won | Belfast | W. W. Wakefield |

★ in the drop-goal column denotes a goal from a mark

| Match | Date | Opponents | For T | C | D | P | Pts | Against T | C | D | P | Pts | Result | Venue | Captain |
|---|---|---|---|---|---|---|---|---|---|---|---|---|---|---|---|
| 143 | 23.2.1924 | France | 5 | 2 | — | — | 19 | 1 | — | 1 | — | 7 | Won | Twickenham | W. W. Wakefield |
| 144 | 15.3.1924 | Scotland | 3 | 3 | 1 | — | 19 | — | — | — | — | 0 | Won | Twickenham | W. W. Wakefield |
| 145 | 3.1.1925 | New Zealand | 2 | 1 | — | 1 | 11 | 4 | 1 | — | 1 | 17 | Lost | Twickenham | W. W. Wakefield |
| 146 | 17.1.1925 | Wales | 3 | — | — | 1 | 12 | 2 | — | — | — | 6 | Won | Twickenham | W. W. Wakefield |
| 147 | 14.2.1925 | Ireland | 2 | — | — | — | 6 | 2 | — | — | — | 6 | Drawn | Twickenham | W. W. Wakefield |
| 148 | 21.3.1925 | Scotland | 2 | 1 | — | 1 | 11 | 2 | 2 | 1 | — | 14 | Lost | Edinburgh | W. W. Wakefield |
| 149 | 13.4.1925 | France | 2 | 2 | ★ | — | 13 | 3 | 1 | — | — | 11 | Won | Paris | W. W. Wakefield |
| 150 | 16.1.1926 | Wales | 1 | — | — | — | 3 | 1 | — | — | — | 3 | Drawn | Cardiff | W. W. Wakefield |
| 151 | 13.2.1926 | Ireland | 3 | 3 | — | — | 15 | 4 | 2 | — | 1 | 19 | Lost | Dublin | W. W. Wakefield |
| 152 | 27.2.1926 | France | 3 | 1 | — | — | 11 | — | — | — | — | 0 | Won | Twickenham | W. W. Wakefield |
| 153 | 20.3.1926 | Scotland | 3 | — | — | — | 9 | 3 | 2 | 1 | — | 17 | Lost | Twickenham | W. W. Wakefield |
| 154 | 15.1.1927 | Wales | 1 | 1 | ★ | 1 | 11 | 2 | — | — | 1 | 9 | Won | Twickenham | L. J. Corbett |
| 155 | 12.2.1927 | Ireland | 2 | 1 | — | — | 8 | 1 | — | — | 1 | 6 | Won | Twickenham | L. J. Corbett |
| 156 | 19.3.1927 | Scotland | 2 | 2 | — | 1 | 13 | 5 | 1 | 1 | — | 21 | Lost | Edinburgh | L. J. Corbett |
| 157 | 2.4.1927 | France | — | — | — | — | 0 | 1 | — | — | — | 3 | Lost | Paris | L. J. Corbett |
| 158 | 7.1.1928 | NSW | 4 | 3 | — | — | 18 | 3 | 1 | — | — | 11 | Won | Twickenham | R. Cove-Smith |
| 159 | 21.1.1928 | Wales | 2 | 2 | — | — | 10 | 2 | 1 | — | — | 8 | Won | Swansea | R. Cove-Smith |
| 160 | 11.2.1928 | Ireland | 1 | — | 1 | — | 7 | 2 | — | — | — | 6 | Won | Dublin | R. Cove-Smith |
| 161 | 25.2.1928 | France | 4 | 3 | — | — | 18 | 2 | 1 | — | — | 8 | Won | Twickenham | R. Cove-Smith |
| 162 | 17.3.1928 | Scotland | 2 | — | — | — | 6 | — | — | — | — | 0 | Won | Twickenham | R. Cove-Smith |
| 163 | 19.1.1929 | Wales | 2 | 1 | — | — | 8 | 1 | — | — | — | 3 | Won | Twickenham | R. Cove-Smith |
| 164 | 9.2.1929 | Ireland | 1 | 1 | — | — | 5 | 2 | — | — | — | 6 | Lost | Twickenham | R. Cove-Smith |
| 165 | 16.3.1929 | Scotland | 2 | — | — | — | 6 | 4 | — | — | — | 12 | Lost | Edinburgh | H. G. Periton |
| 166 | 1.4.1929 | France | 4 | 2 | — | — | 16 | 2 | — | — | — | 6 | Won | Paris | H. G. Periton |
| 167 | 18.1.1930 | Wales | 2 | 1 | — | 1 | 11 | 1 | — | — | — | 3 | Won | Cardiff | H. G. Periton |
| 168 | 8.2.1930 | Ireland | 1 | — | — | — | 3 | — | — | 1 | — | 4 | Lost | Dublin | H. G. Periton |
| 169 | 22.2.1930 | France | 3 | 1 | — | — | 11 | 1 | 1 | — | — | 5 | Won | Twickenham | J. S. Tucker |
| 170 | 15.3.1930 | Scotland | — | — | — | — | 0 | — | — | — | — | 0 | Drawn | Twickenham | J. S. Tucker |
| 171 | 17.1.1931 | Wales | 1 | 1 | — | 2 | 11 | 2 | 1 | ★ | — | 11 | Drawn | Twickenham | J. S. Tucker |
| 172 | 14.2.1931 | Ireland | 1 | 1 | — | — | 5 | 1 | — | — | 1 | 6 | Lost | Twickenham | P. D. Howard |
| 173 | 21.3.1931 | Scotland | 4 | 2 | — | 1 | 19 | 6 | 5 | — | — | 28 | Lost | Edinburgh | C. D. Aarvold |
| 174 | 6.4.1931 | France | 3 | 2 | — | — | 13 | 2 | — | 2 | — | 14 | Lost | Paris | C. D. Aarvold |
| 175 | 2.1.1932 | South Africa | — | — | — | — | 0 | 1 | — | 1 | — | 7 | Lost | Twickenham | C. D. Aarvold |
| 176 | 16.1.1932 | Wales | 1 | 1 | — | — | 5 | 1 | 1 | 1 | 1 | 12 | Lost | Swansea | C. D. Aarvold |
| 177 | 13.2.1932 | Ireland | 1 | 1 | — | 2 | 11 | 1 | 1 | — | 1 | 8 | Won | Dublin | C. D. Aarvold |
| 178 | 19.3.1932 | Scotland | 4 | 2 | — | — | 16 | 1 | — | — | — | 3 | Won | Twickenham | C. D. Aarvold |
| 179 | 21.1.1933 | Wales | 1 | — | — | — | 3 | 1 | — | 1 | — | 7 | Lost | Twickenham | C. D. Aarvold |
| 180 | 11.2.1933 | Ireland | 5 | 1 | — | — | 17 | 1 | — | — | 1 | 6 | Won | Twickenham | A. L. Novis |
| 181 | 18.3.1933 | Scotland | — | — | — | — | 0 | 1 | — | — | — | 3 | Lost | Edinburgh | A. L. Novis |
| 182 | 20.1.1934 | Wales | 3 | — | — | — | 9 | — | — | — | — | 0 | Won | Cardiff | B. C. Gadney |
| 183 | 10.2.1934 | Ireland | 3 | 2 | — | — | 13 | 1 | — | — | — | 3 | Won | Dublin | B. C. Gadney |
| 184 | 17.3.1934 | Scotland | 2 | — | — | — | 6 | 1 | — | — | — | 3 | Won | Twickenham | B. C. Gadney |
| 185 | 19.1.1935 | Wales | — | — | — | 1 | 3 | 1 | — | — | — | 3 | Drawn | Twickenham | D. A. Kendrew |
| 186 | 9.2.1935 | Ireland | 1 | 1 | — | 3 | 14 | 1 | — | — | — | 3 | Won | Twickenham | D. A. Kendrew |
| 187 | 16.3.1935 | Scotland | 1 | — | 1 | — | 7 | 2 | 2 | — | — | 10 | Lost | Edinburgh | B. C. Gadney |
| 188 | 4.1.1936 | New Zealand | 3 | — | 1 | — | 13 | — | — | — | — | 0 | Won | Twickenham | B. C. Gadney |
| 189 | 18.1.1936 | Wales | — | — | — | — | 0 | — | — | — | — | 0 | Drawn | Swansea | B. C. Gadney |
| 190 | 8.2.1936 | Ireland | 1 | — | — | — | 3 | 2 | — | — | — | 6 | Lost | Dublin | B. C. Gadney |
| 191 | 21.3.1936 | Scotland | 3 | — | — | — | 9 | 1 | 1 | — | 1 | 8 | Won | Twickenham | B. C. Gadney |
| 192 | 16.1.1937 | Wales | — | — | 1 | — | 4 | 1 | — | — | — | 3 | Won | Twickenham | H. G. Owen-Smith |
| 193 | 13.2.1937 | Ireland | 2 | — | — | 1 | 9 | 2 | 1 | — | — | 8 | Won | Twickenham | H. G. Owen-Smith |
| 194 | 20.3.1937 | Scotland | 2 | — | — | — | 6 | — | — | — | 1 | 3 | Won | Edinburgh | H. G. Owen-Smith |
| 195 | 15.1.1938 | Wales | 2 | 1 | — | — | 8 | 2 | 1 | — | 2 | 14 | Lost | Cardiff | P. Cranmer |
| 196 | 12.2.1938 | Ireland | 7 | 6 | — | 1 | 36 | 4 | 1 | — | — | 14 | Won | Dublin | P. Cranmer |
| 197 | 19.3.1938 | Scotland | 1 | — | 1 | 3 | 16 | 5 | — | — | 2 | 21 | Lost | Twickenham | H. B. Toft |
| 198 | 21.1.1939 | Wales | 1 | — | — | — | 3 | — | — | — | — | 0 | Won | Twickenham | H. B. Toft |
| 199 | 11.2.1939 | Ireland | — | — | — | — | 0 | 1 | 1 | — | — | 5 | Lost | Twickenham | H. B. Toft |
| 200 | 18.3.1939 | Scotland | — | — | — | 3 | 9 | 2 | — | — | — | 6 | Won | Edinburgh | H. B. Toft |
| 201 | 18.1.1947 | Wales | 1 | 1 | 1 | — | 9 | 2 | — | — | — | 6 | Won | Cardiff | J. Mycock |
| 202 | 8.2.1947 | Ireland | — | — | — | — | 0 | 5 | 2 | — | 1 | 22 | Lost | Dublin | J. Mycock |
| 203 | 15.3.1947 | Scotland | 4 | 4 | 1 | — | 24 | 1 | 1 | — | — | 5 | Won | Twickenham | J. Heaton |
| 204 | 19.4.1947 | France | 2 | — | — | — | 6 | 1 | — | — | 1 | 3 | Won | Twickenham | J. Heaton |
| 205 | 3.1.1948 | Australia | — | — | — | — | 0 | 3 | 1 | — | — | 11 | Lost | Twickenham | E. K. Scott |
| 206 | 17.1.1948 | Wales | — | — | 1 | — | 3 | 1 | — | — | — | 3 | Drawn | Twickenham | T. A. Kemp |
| 207 | 14.2.1948 | Ireland | 2 | 2 | — | — | 10 | 3 | 1 | — | — | 11 | Lost | Twickenham | E. K. Scott |
| 208 | 20.3.1948 | Scotland | — | — | — | 1 | 3 | 2 | — | — | — | 6 | Lost | Edinburgh | E. K. Scott |
| 209 | 29.3.1948 | France | — | — | — | — | 0 | 3 | 1 | 1 | — | 15 | Lost | Paris | R. H. G. Weighill |
| 210 | 15.1.1949 | Wales | — | — | 1 | — | 3 | 3 | — | — | — | 9 | Lost | Cardiff | N. M. Hall |
| 211 | 12.2.1949 | Ireland | 1 | 1 | — | — | 5 | 2 | 1 | — | 2 | 14 | Lost | Dublin | N. M. Hall |
| 212 | 26.2.1949 | France | 1 | 1 | 1 | — | 8 | — | — | 1 | — | 3 | Won | Twickenham | I. Preece |
| 213 | 19.3.1949 | Scotland | 5 | 2 | — | — | 19 | 1 | — | — | 1 | 3 | Won | Twickenham | I. Preece |
| 214 | 21.1.1950 | Wales | 1 | 1 | — | — | 5 | 2 | 1 | — | 1 | 11 | Lost | Twickenham | I. Preece |

★ *in the drop-goal column denotes a goal from a mark*

| Match | Date | Opponents | For T | C | D | P | Pts | Against T | C | D | P | Pts | Result | Venue | Captain |
|---|---|---|---|---|---|---|---|---|---|---|---|---|---|---|---|
| 215 | 11.2.1950 | Ireland | 1 | — | — | — | 3 | — | — | — | — | 0 | Won | Twickenham | I. Preece |
| 216 | 25.2.1950 | France | 1 | — | — | — | 3 | 2 | — | — | — | 6 | Lost | Paris | I. Preece |
| 217 | 18.3.1950 | Scotland | 2 | 1 | — | 1 | 11 | 3 | 2 | — | — | 13 | Lost | Edinburgh | I. Preece |
| 218 | 20.1.1951 | Wales | 1 | 1 | — | — | 5 | 5 | 4 | — | — | 23 | Lost | Swansea | V. G. Roberts |
| 219 | 10.2.1951 | Ireland | — | — | — | — | 0 | — | — | — | 1 | 3 | Lost | Dublin | J. M. K. Kendall-Carpenter |
| 220 | 24.2.1951 | France | 1 | — | — | — | 3 | 2 | 1 | 1 | — | 11 | Lost | Twickenham | J. M. K. Kendall-Carpenter |
| 221 | 17.3.1951 | Scotland | 1 | 1 | — | — | 5 | 1 | — | — | — | 3 | Won | Twickenham | J. M. K. Kendall-Carpenter |
| 222 | 5.1.1952 | South Africa | 1 | — | — | — | 3 | 1 | 1 | — | 1 | 8 | Lost | Twickenham | N. M. Hall |
| 223 | 19.1.1952 | Wales | 2 | — | — | — | 6 | 2 | 1 | — | — | 8 | Lost | Twickenham | N. M. Hall |
| 224 | 15.3.1952 | Scotland | 4 | 2 | 1 | — | 19 | 1 | — | — | — | 3 | Won | Edinburgh | N. M. Hall |
| 225 | 29.3.1952 | Ireland | 1 | — | — | — | 3 | — | — | — | — | 0 | Won | Twickenham | N. M. Hall |
| 226 | 5.4.1952 | France | — | — | — | 2 | 6 | 1 | — | — | — | 3 | Won | Paris | N. M. Hall |
| 227 | 17.1.1953 | Wales | 1 | 1 | — | 1 | 8 | — | — | — | 1 | 3 | Won | Cardiff | N. M. Hall |
| 228 | 14.2.1953 | Ireland | 1 | — | — | 2 | 9 | 1 | — | — | 2 | 9 | Drawn | Dublin | N. M. Hall |
| 229 | 28.2.1953 | France | 3 | 1 | — | — | 11 | — | — | — | — | 0 | Won | Twickenham | N. M. Hall |
| 230 | 21.3.1953 | Scotland | 6 | 4 | — | — | 26 | 2 | 1 | — | — | 8 | Won | Twickenham | N. M. Hall |
| 231 | 16.1.1954 | Wales | 3 | — | — | — | 9 | 1 | — | — | 1 | 6 | Won | Twickenham | R. V. Stirling |
| 232 | 30.1.1954 | New Zealand | — | — | — | — | 0 | 1 | 1 | — | — | 5 | Lost | Twickenham | R. V. Stirling |
| 233 | 13.2.1954 | Ireland | 3 | 1 | — | 1 | 14 | — | — | — | 1 | 3 | Won | Twickenham | R. V. Stirling |
| 234 | 20.3.1954 | Scotland | 3 | 2 | — | — | 13 | 1 | — | — | — | 3 | Won | Edinburgh | R. V. Stirling |
| 235 | 10.4.1954 | France | 1 | — | — | — | 3 | 2 | 1 | 1 | — | 11 | Lost | Paris | R. V. Stirling |
| 236 | 22.1.1955 | Wales | — | — | — | — | 0 | 1 | — | — | 1 | 3 | Lost | Cardiff | N. M. Hall |
| 237 | 12.2.1955 | Ireland | 2 | — | — | — | 6 | 1 | — | — | 1 | 6 | Drawn | Dublin | N. M. Hall |
| 238 | 26.2.1955 | France | 1 | — | — | 2 | 9 | 2 | 2 | 2 | — | 16 | Lost | Twickenham | P. D. Young |
| 239 | 19.3.1955 | Scotland | 2 | — | — | 1 | 9 | 1 | — | — | 1 | 6 | Won | Twickenham | P. D. Young |
| 240 | 21.1.1956 | Wales | — | — | — | 1 | 3 | 2 | 1 | — | — | 8 | Lost | Twickenham | E. Evans |
| 241 | 11.2.1956 | Ireland | 3 | 1 | — | 3 | 20 | — | — | — | — | 0 | Won | Twickenham | E. Evans |
| 242 | 17.3.1956 | Scotland | 1 | 1 | — | 2 | 11 | 1 | — | — | 1 | 6 | Won | Edinburgh | E. Evans |
| 243 | 14.4.1956 | France | 1 | — | — | 2 | 9 | 2 | 1 | — | 2 | 14 | Lost | Paris | E. Evans |
| 244 | 19.1.1957 | Wales | — | — | 1 | — | 3 | — | — | — | — | 0 | Won | Cardiff | E. Evans |
| 245 | 9.2.1957 | Ireland | 1 | — | — | 1 | 6 | — | — | — | — | 0 | Won | Dublin | E. Evans |
| 246 | 23.2.1957 | France | 3 | — | — | — | 9 | 1 | 1 | — | — | 5 | Won | Twickenham | E. Evans |
| 247 | 16.3.1957 | Scotland | 3 | 2 | — | 1 | 16 | — | — | — | 1 | 3 | Won | Twickenham | E. Evans |
| 248 | 18.1.1958 | Wales | 1 | — | — | — | 3 | — | — | — | 1 | 3 | Drawn | Twickenham | E. Evans |
| 249 | 1.2.1958 | Australia | 2 | — | — | 1 | 9 | — | — | 1 | 1 | 6 | Won | Twickenham | E. Evans |
| 250 | 8.2.1958 | Ireland | 1 | — | — | 1 | 6 | — | — | — | — | 0 | Won | Twickenham | E. Evans |
| 251 | 1.3.1958 | France | 3 | 1 | — | 1 | 14 | — | — | — | — | 0 | Won | Paris | E. Evans |
| 252 | 15.3.1958 | Scotland | — | — | — | 1 | 3 | — | — | — | 1 | 3 | Drawn | Edinburgh | E. Evans |
| 253 | 17.1.1959 | Wales | — | — | — | — | 0 | 1 | 1 | — | — | 5 | Lost | Cardiff | J. Butterfield |
| 254 | 14.2.1959 | Ireland | — | — | — | 1 | 3 | — | — | — | — | 0 | Won | Dublin | J. Butterfield |
| 255 | 28.2.1959 | France | — | — | — | 1 | 3 | — | — | — | 1 | 3 | Drawn | Twickenham | J. Butterfield |
| 256 | 21.3.1959 | Scotland | — | — | — | 1 | 3 | — | — | — | 1 | 3 | Drawn | Twickenham | J. Butterfield |
| 257 | 16.1.1960 | Wales | 2 | 1 | — | 2 | 14 | — | — | — | 2 | 6 | Won | Twickenham | R. E. G. Jeeps |
| 258 | 13.2.1960 | Ireland | 1 | 1 | 1 | — | 8 | 1 | 1 | — | — | 5 | Won | Twickenham | R. E. G. Jeeps |
| 259 | 27.2.1960 | France | 1 | — | — | — | 3 | — | — | — | 1 | 3 | Drawn | Paris | R. E. G. Jeeps |
| 260 | 19.3.1960 | Scotland | 3 | 3 | 1 | 1 | 21 | 1 | — | — | 3 | 12 | Won | Edinburgh | R. E. G. Jeeps |
| 261 | 7.1.1961 | South Africa | — | — | — | — | 0 | 1 | 1 | — | — | 5 | Lost | Twickenham | R. E. G. Jeeps |
| 262 | 21.1.1961 | Wales | 1 | — | — | — | 3 | 2 | — | — | — | 6 | Lost | Cardiff | R. E. G. Jeeps |
| 263 | 11.2.1961 | Ireland | 2 | 1 | — | — | 8 | 1 | 1 | — | 2 | 11 | Lost | Dublin | R. E. G. Jeeps |
| 264 | 25.2.1961 | France | 1 | 1 | — | — | 5 | 1 | 1 | — | — | 5 | Drawn | Twickenham | R. E. G. Jeeps |
| 265 | 18.3.1961 | Scotland | 1 | — | — | 1 | 6 | — | — | — | — | 0 | Won | Twickenham | R. E. G. Jeeps |
| 266 | 20.1.1962 | Wales | — | — | — | — | 0 | — | — | — | — | 0 | Drawn | Twickenham | R. E. G. Jeeps |
| 267 | 10.2.1962 | Ireland | 3 | 2 | — | 1 | 16 | — | — | — | — | 0 | Won | Twickenham | R. E. G. Jeeps |
| 268 | 24.2.1962 | France | — | — | — | — | 0 | 3 | 2 | — | — | 13 | Lost | Paris | R. E. G. Jeeps |
| 269 | 17.3.1962 | Scotland | — | — | — | 1 | 3 | — | — | — | 1 | 3 | Drawn | Edinburgh | R. E. G. Jeeps |
| 270 | 19.1.1963 | Wales | 2 | 2 | 1 | — | 13 | 1 | — | — | 1 | 6 | Won | Cardiff | R. A. W. Sharp |
| 271 | 9.2.1963 | Ireland | — | — | — | — | 0 | — | — | — | — | 0 | Drawn | Dublin | R. A. W. Sharp |
| 272 | 23.2.1963 | France | — | — | — | 2 | 6 | 1 | 1 | — | — | 5 | Won | Twickenham | R. A. W. Sharp |
| 273 | 16.3.1963 | Scotland | 2 | 2 | — | — | 10 | 1 | 1 | 1 | — | 8 | Won | Twickenham | R. A. W. Sharp |
| 274 | 25.5.1963 | New Zealand | 1 | 1 | — | 2 | 11 | 3 | 3 | 1 | 1 | 21 | Lost | Auckland | M. P. Weston |
| 275 | 1.6.1963 | New Zealand | 1 | — | — | 1 | 6 | 2 | — | ★ | — | 9 | Lost | Christchurch | M. P. Weston |
| 276 | 4.6.1963 | Australia | 3 | — | — | — | 9 | 4 | 3 | — | — | 18 | Lost | Sydney | M. P. Weston |
| 277 | 4.1.1964 | New Zealand | — | — | — | — | 0 | 2 | 1 | — | 2 | 14 | Lost | Twickenham | J. G. Willcox |
| 278 | 18.1.1964 | Wales | 2 | — | — | — | 6 | 2 | — | — | — | 6 | Drawn | Twickenham | J. G. Willcox |
| 279 | 8.2.1964 | Ireland | 1 | 1 | — | — | 5 | 4 | 3 | — | — | 18 | Lost | Twickenham | J. G. Willcox |
| 280 | 22.2.1964 | France | 1 | — | — | 1 | 6 | 1 | — | — | — | 3 | Won | Paris | C. R. Jacobs |
| 281 | 21.3.1964 | Scotland | 1 | — | — | 1 | 6 | 3 | 3 | — | — | 15 | Lost | Edinburgh | C. R. Jacobs |
| 282 | 16.1.1965 | Wales | — | — | — | 1 | 3 | 3 | 1 | 1 | — | 14 | Lost | Cardiff | D. G. Perry |
| 283 | 13.2.1965 | Ireland | — | — | — | — | 0 | 1 | 1 | — | — | 5 | Lost | Dublin | D. G. Perry |

★ in the drop-goal column denotes a goal from a mark

| Match | Date | Opponents | For T | C | D | P | Pts | Against T | C | D | P | Pts | Result | Venue | Captain |
|---|---|---|---|---|---|---|---|---|---|---|---|---|---|---|---|
| 284 | 27.2.1965 | France | 1 | — | — | 2 | 9 | 1 | — | — | 1 | 6 | Won | Twickenham | D. G. Perry |
| 285 | 20.3.1965 | Scotland | 1 | — | — | — | 3 | — | — | 1 | — | 3 | Drawn | Twickenham | D. G. Perry |
| 286 | 15.1.1966 | Wales | 1 | — | — | 1 | 6 | 1 | 1 | — | 2 | 11 | Lost | Twickenham | D. P. Rogers |
| 287 | 12.2.1966 | Ireland | 1 | — | — | 1 | 6 | 1 | — | — | 1 | 6 | Drawn | Twickenham | D. P. Rogers |
| 288 | 26.2.1966 | France | — | — | — | — | 0 | 3 | 2 | — | — | 13 | Lost | Paris | D. P. Rogers |
| 289 | 19.3.1966 | Scotland | — | — | 1 | — | 3 | 1 | — | — | 1 | 6 | Lost | Edinburgh | D. P. Rogers |
| 290 | 7.1.1967 | Australia | 1 | 1 | — | 2 | 11 | 2 | 1 | 3 | 2 | 23 | Lost | Twickenham | R. A. W. Sharp |
| 291 | 11.2.1967 | Ireland | 1 | 1 | — | 1 | 8 | — | — | 1 | — | 3 | Won | Dublin | P. E. Judd |
| 292 | 25.2.1967 | France | — | — | 1 | 3 | 12 | 2 | 2 | 1 | 1 | 16 | Lost | Twickenham | P. E. Judd |
| 293 | 18.3.1967 | Scotland | 4 | 3 | 1 | 2 | 27 | 2 | 1 | — | 2 | 14 | Won | Twickenham | P. E. Judd |
| 294 | 15.4.1967 | Wales | 3 | — | — | 4 | 21 | 5 | 5 | 1 | 2 | 34 | Lost | Cardiff | P. E. Judd |
| 295 | 4.11.1967 | New Zealand | 2 | 1 | — | 1 | 11 | 5 | 4 | — | — | 23 | Lost | Twickenham | P. E. Judd |
| 296 | 20.1.1968 | Wales | 2 | 1 | — | 1 | 11 | 2 | 1 | 1 | — | 11 | Drawn | Twickenham | C. W. McFadyean |
| 297 | 10.2.1968 | Ireland | — | — | 1 | 2 | 9 | — | — | — | 3 | 9 | Drawn | Twickenham | C. W. McFadyean |
| 298 | 24.2.1968 | France | — | — | 1 | 2 | 9 | 1 | 1 | 2 | 1 | 14 | Lost | Paris | M. P. Weston |
| 299 | 16.3.1968 | Scotland | 1 | 1 | — | 1 | 8 | — | — | 1 | 1 | 6 | Won | Edinburgh | M. P. Weston |
| 300 | 8.2.1969 | Ireland | 1 | — | — | 4 | 15 | 2 | 1 | 1 | 2 | 17 | Lost | Dublin | J. R. H. Greenwood |
| 301 | 22.2.1969 | France | 3 | 2 | — | 3 | 22 | 1 | 1 | 1 | — | 8 | Won | Twickenham | D. P. Rogers |
| 302 | 15.3.1969 | Scotland | 2 | 1 | — | — | 8 | — | — | 1 | — | 3 | Won | Twickenham | D. P. Rogers |
| 303 | 12.4.1969 | Wales | — | — | — | 3 | 9 | 5 | 3 | 1 | 2 | 30 | Lost | Cardiff | D. P. Rogers |
| 304 | 20.12.1969 | South Africa | 2 | 1 | — | 1 | 11 | 1 | 1 | — | 1 | 8 | Won | Twickenham | R. Hiller |
| 305 | 14.2.1970 | Ireland | 1 | — | 2 | — | 9 | — | — | — | 1 | 3 | Won | Twickenham | R. Hiller |
| 306 | 28.2.1970 | Wales | 2 | 2 | — | 1 | 13 | 4 | 1 | 1 | — | 17 | Lost | Twickenham | R. Hiller |
| 307 | 21.3.1970 | Scotland | 1 | 1 | — | — | 5 | 2 | 1 | — | 2 | 14 | Lost | Edinburgh | R. Hiller |
| 308 | 18.4.1970 | France | 2 | 2 | — | 1 | 13 | 6 | 4 | 2 | 1 | 35 | Lost | Paris | R. B. Taylor |
| 309 | 16.1.1971 | Wales | 1 | — | — | 1 | 6 | 3 | 2 | 2 | 1 | 22 | Lost | Cardiff | A. L. Bucknall |
| 310 | 13.2.1971 | Ireland | — | — | — | 3 | 9 | 2 | — | — | — | 6 | Won | Dublin | J. S. Spencer |
| 311 | 27.2.1971 | France | 1 | 1 | — | 3 | 14 | 2 | 1 | 1 | 1 | 14 | Drawn | Twickenham | R. Hiller |
| 312 | 20.3.1971 | Scotland | 2 | — | — | 3 | 15 | 3 | 2 | 1 | — | 16 | Lost | Twickenham | J. S. Spencer |
| 313 | 27.3.1971 | Scotland | — | — | 1 | 1 | 6 | 5 | 4 | — | 1 | 26 | Lost | Edinburgh | J. S. Spencer |
| 314 | 17.4.1971 | R.F.U. President's XV | 1 | 1 | — | 2 | 11 | 6 | 5 | — | — | 28 | Lost | Twickenham | J. S. Spencer |
| 315 | 15.1.1972 | Wales | — | — | — | 1 | 3 | 1 | 1 | — | 2 | 12 | Lost | Twickenham | R. Hiller |
| 316 | 12.2.1972 | Ireland | 1 | 1 | — | 2 | 12 | 2 | 1 | 1 | 1 | 16 | Lost | Twickenham | R. Hiller |
| 317 | 26.2.1972 | France | 1 | 1 | — | 2 | 12 | 6 | 5 | — | 1 | 37 | Lost | Paris | P. J. Dixon |
| 318 | 18.3.1972 | Scotland | — | — | — | 3 | 9 | 2 | — | 1 | 4 | 23 | Lost | Edinburgh | P. J. Dixon |
| 319 | 3.6.1972 | South Africa | 1 | 1 | — | 4 | 18 | — | — | — | 3 | 9 | Won | Johannesburg | J. V. Pullin |
| 320 | 6.1.1973 | New Zealand | — | — | — | — | 0 | 1 | 1 | 1 | — | 9 | Lost | Twickenham | J. V. Pullin |
| 321 | 20.1.1973 | Wales | — | — | 1 | 2 | 9 | 5 | 1 | — | 1 | 25 | Lost | Cardiff | J. V. Pullin |
| 322 | 10.2.1973 | Ireland | 1 | 1 | — | 1 | 9 | 2 | 2 | 1 | 1 | 18 | Lost | Dublin | J. V. Pullin |
| 323 | 24.2.1973 | France | 2 | — | — | 2 | 14 | 1 | 1 | — | — | 6 | Won | Twickenham | J. V. Pullin |
| 324 | 17.3.1973 | Scotland | 4 | 2 | — | — | 20 | 2 | 1 | — | 1 | 13 | Won | Twickenham | J. V. Pullin |
| 325 | 15.9.1973 | New Zealand | 3 | 2 | — | — | 16 | 2 | 1 | — | — | 10 | Won | Auckland | J. V. Pullin |
| 326 | 17.11.1973 | Australia | 3 | 1 | — | 2 | 20 | — | — | — | 1 | 3 | Won | Twickenham | J. V. Pullin |
| 327 | 2.2.1974 | Scotland | 2 | — | 1 | 1 | 14 | 2 | 1 | — | 2 | 16 | Lost | Edinburgh | J. V. Pullin |
| 328 | 16.2.1974 | Ireland | 1 | 1 | — | 5 | 21 | 4 | 2 | 1 | 1 | 26 | Lost | Twickenham | J. V. Pullin |
| 329 | 2.3.1974 | France | 1 | 1 | 1 | 1 | 12 | 1 | 1 | 1 | 1 | 12 | Drawn | Paris | J. V. Pullin |
| 330 | 16.3.1974 | Wales | 2 | 1 | — | 2 | 16 | 1 | 1 | — | 2 | 12 | Won | Twickenham | J. V. Pullin |
| 331 | 18.1.1975 | Ireland | 1 | 1 | 1 | — | 9 | 2 | 2 | — | — | 12 | Lost | Dublin | F. E. Cotton |
| 332 | 1.2.1975 | France | 2 | — | — | 4 | 20 | 4 | 4 | — | 1 | 27 | Lost | Twickenham | F. E. Cotton |
| 333 | 15.2.1975 | Wales | 1 | — | — | — | 4 | 3 | 1 | — | 2 | 20 | Lost | Cardiff | F. E. Cotton |
| 334 | 15.3.1975 | Scotland | 1 | — | — | 1 | 7 | — | — | — | 2 | 6 | Won | Twickenham | A. Neary |
| 335 | 24.5.1975 | Australia | 1 | 1 | — | 1 | 9 | 1 | — | 2 | 2 | 16 | Lost | Sydney | A. Neary |
| 336 | 31.5.1975 | Australia | 2 | 2 | — | 3 | 21 | 5 | 2 | — | 2 | 30 | Lost | Brisbane | J. V. Pullin |
| 337 | 3.1.1976 | Australia | 3 | 1 | — | 3 | 23 | — | — | — | 2 | 6 | Won | Twickenham | A. Neary |
| 338 | 17.1.1976 | Wales | — | — | — | 3 | 9 | 3 | 3 | — | 1 | 21 | Lost | Twickenham | A. Neary |
| 339 | 21.2.1976 | Scotland | 1 | 1 | — | 2 | 12 | 3 | 2 | — | 2 | 22 | Lost | Edinburgh | A. Neary |
| 340 | 6.3.1976 | Ireland | — | — | — | 4 | 12 | 1 | — | 1 | 2 | 13 | Lost | Twickenham | A. Neary |
| 341 | 20.3.1976 | France | 1 | 1 | — | 1 | 9 | 6 | 3 | — | — | 30 | Lost | Paris | A. Neary |
| 342 | 15.1.1977 | Scotland | 4 | 2 | — | 2 | 26 | — | — | — | 2 | 6 | Won | Twickenham | R. M. Uttley |
| 343 | 5.2.1977 | Ireland | 1 | — | — | — | 4 | — | — | — | — | 0 | Won | Dublin | R. M. Uttley |
| 344 | 19.2.1977 | France | — | — | 1 | 3 | 9 | 1 | — | — | — | 4 | Lost | Twickenham | R. M. Uttley |
| 345 | 5.3.1977 | Wales | — | — | — | 3 | 9 | 2 | — | — | 2 | 14 | Lost | Cardiff | R. M. Uttley |
| 346 | 21.1.1978 | France | — | — | 2 | — | 6 | 2 | 2 | — | 1 | 15 | Lost | Paris | W. B. Beaumont |
| 347 | 4.2.1978 | Wales | — | — | — | 2 | 6 | — | — | — | 3 | 9 | Lost | Twickenham | W. B. Beaumont |
| 348 | 4.3.1978 | Scotland | 2 | 2 | — | 1 | 15 | — | — | — | — | 0 | Won | Edinburgh | W. B. Beaumont |
| 349 | 18.3.1978 | Ireland | 2 | 2 | — | 1 | 15 | — | — | 1 | 2 | 9 | Won | Twickenham | W. B. Beaumont |
| 350 | 25.11.1978 | New Zealand | — | — | 1 | 1 | 6 | 2 | 1 | — | 2 | 16 | Lost | Twickenham | W. B. Beaumont |
| 351 | 3.2.1979 | Scotland | — | — | — | 1 | 7 | 1 | — | — | 1 | 7 | Drawn | Twickenham | R. M. Uttley |
| 352 | 17.2.1979 | Ireland | 1 | — | — | 1 | 7 | 1 | 1 | 1 | 1 | 12 | Lost | Dublin | W. B. Beaumont |

★ *in the drop-goal column denotes a goal from a mark*

| Match | Date | Opponents | For T | C | D | P | Pts | Against T | C | D | P | Pts | Result | Venue | Captain |
|---|---|---|---|---|---|---|---|---|---|---|---|---|---|---|---|
| 353 | 3.3.1979 | France | 1 | — | — | 1 | 7 | 1 | 1 | — | — | 6 | Won | Twickenham | W. B. Beaumont |
| 354 | 17.3.1979 | Wales | — | — | — | 1 | 3 | 5 | 2 | 1 | — | 27 | Lost | Cardiff | W. B. Beaumont |
| 355 | 24.11.1979 | New Zealand | — | — | — | 3 | 9 | 1 | — | — | 2 | 10 | Lost | Twickenham | W. B. Beaumont |
| 356 | 19.1.1980 | Ireland | 3 | 3 | — | 2 | 24 | — | — | — | 3 | 9 | Won | Twickenham | W. B. Beaumont |
| 357 | 2.2.1980 | France | 2 | — | 2 | 1 | 17 | 2 | 1 | — | 1 | 13 | Won | Paris | W. B. Beaumont |
| 358 | 16.2.1980 | Wales | — | — | — | 3 | 9 | 2 | — | — | — | 8 | Won | Twickenham | W. B. Beaumont |
| 359 | 15.3.1980 | Scotland | 5 | 2 | — | 2 | 30 | 2 | 2 | — | 2 | 18 | Won | Edinburgh | W. B. Beaumont |
| 360 | 17.1.1981 | Wales | 1 | — | — | 5 | 19 | 1 | 1 | 1 | 4 | 21 | Lost | Cardiff | W. B. Beaumont |
| 361 | 21.2.1981 | Scotland | 3 | 1 | — | 3 | 23 | 3 | 1 | — | 1 | 17 | Won | Twickenham | W. B. Beaumont |
| 362 | 7.3.1981 | Ireland | 2 | 1 | — | — | 10 | — | — | 2 | — | 6 | Won | Dublin | W. B. Beaumont |
| 363 | 21.3.1981 | France | — | — | — | 4 | 12 | 2 | 1 | 2 | — | 16 | Lost | Twickenham | W. B. Beaumont |
| 364 | 30.5.1981 | Argentina | 3 | 2 | — | 1 | 19 | 2 | 1 | 2 | 1 | 19 | Drawn | Buenos Aires | W. B. Beaumont |
| 365 | 6.6.1981 | Argentina | 1 | 1 | — | 2 | 12 | 1 | 1 | — | — | 6 | Won | Buenos Aires | W. B. Beaumont |
| 366 | 2.1.1982 | Australia | 1 | 1 | — | 3 | 15 | 2 | — | — | 1 | 11 | Won | Twickenham | W. B. Beaumont |
| 367 | 16.1.1982 | Scotland | — | — | — | 3 | 9 | — | — | 1 | 2 | 9 | Drawn | Edinburgh | W. B. Beaumont |
| 368 | 6.2.1982 | Ireland | 1 | 1 | — | 3 | 15 | 2 | 1 | — | 2 | 16 | Lost | Twickenham | S. J. Smith |
| 369 | 20.2.1982 | France | 2 | 2 | — | 5 | 27 | 1 | 1 | 1 | 2 | 15 | Won | Paris | S. J. Smith |
| 370 | 6.3.1982 | Wales | 2 | — | — | 3 | 17 | 1 | — | 1 | — | 7 | Won | Twickenham | S. J. Smith |
| 371 | 15.1.1983 | France | — | — | 1 | 4 | 15 | 3 | 2 | 0 | 1 | 19 | Lost | Twickenham | S. J. Smith |
| 372 | 5.2.1983 | Wales | 1 | 0 | 1 | 2 | 13 | 1 | 0 | 1 | 2 | 13 | Drawn | Cardiff | S. J. Smith |
| 373 | 5.3.1983 | Scotland | — | — | 1 | 3 | 12 | 2 | 1 | 1 | 3 | 22 | Lost | Twickenham | J. P. Scott |
| 374 | 19.3.1983 | Ireland | — | — | — | 5 | 15 | 2 | 1 | 0 | 5 | 25 | Lost | Dublin | J. P. Scott |
| 375 | 19.11.1983 | New Zealand | 1 | 1 | — | 3 | 15 | 1 | 1 | 0 | 1 | 9 | Won | Twickenham | P. J. Wheeler |
| 376 | 4.2.1984 | Scotland | — | — | — | 2 | 6 | 2 | 2 | 0 | 2 | 18 | Lost | Edinburgh | P. J. Wheeler |
| 377 | 18.2.1984 | Ireland | — | — | 1 | 3 | 12 | — | — | — | 3 | 9 | Won | Twickenham | P. J. Wheeler |
| 378 | 3.3.1984 | France | 2 | 2 | — | 2 | 18 | 5 | 3 | 1 | 1 | 32 | Lost | Paris | P. J. Wheeler |
| 379 | 17.3.1984 | Wales | — | — | — | 5 | 15 | 1 | 1 | 2 | 4 | 24 | Lost | Twickenham | P. J. Wheeler |
| 380 | 2.6.1984 | South Africa | — | — | 1 | 4 | 15 | 3 | 3 | 0 | 5 | 33 | Lost | Port Elizabeth | J. P. Scott |
| 381 | 9.6.1984 | South Africa | — | — | — | 3 | 9 | 6 | 4 | 0 | 1 | 35 | Lost | Johannesburg | J. P. Scott |
| 382 | 3.11.1984 | Australia | — | — | — | 1 | 3 | 3 | 2 | 0 | 1 | 19 | Lost | Twickenham | N. D. Melville |
| 383 | 5.1.1985 | Romania | 1 | — | 2 | 4 | 22 | — | — | — | 5 | 15 | Won | Twickenham | P. W. Dodge |
| 384 | 2.2.1985 | France | — | — | 1 | 2 | 9 | — | — | 3 | — | 9 | Drawn | Twickenham | P. W. Dodge |
| 385 | 16.3.1985 | Scotland | 1 | — | — | 2 | 10 | 1 | — | — | 1 | 7 | Won | Twickenham | P. W. Dodge |
| 386 | 30.3.1985 | Ireland | 1 | — | — | 2 | 10 | 1 | — | 1 | 2 | 13 | Lost | Dublin | P. W. Dodge |
| 387 | 20.4.1985 | Wales | 1 | 1 | 1 | 2 | 15 | 2 | 2 | 1 | 3 | 24 | Lost | Cardiff | P. W. Dodge |
| 388 | 1.6.1985 | New Zealand | 2 | 1 | — | 1 | 13 | — | — | — | 6 | 18 | Lost | Christchurch | P. W. Dodge |
| 389 | 8.6.1985 | New Zealand | 2 | 2 | 1 | — | 15 | 6 | 3 | 1 | 3 | 42 | Lost | Wellington | P. W. Dodge |
| 390 | 18.1.1986 | Wales | — | — | 1 | 6 | 21 | 1 | 1 | 1 | 3 | 18 | Won | Twickenham | N. D. Melville |
| 391 | 15.2.1986 | Scotland | — | — | — | 2 | 6 | 3 | 3 | — | 5 | 33 | Lost | Edinburgh | N. D. Melville |
| 392 | 1.3.1986 | Ireland | 4 | 3 | — | 1 | 25 | 3 | 1 | — | 2 | 20 | Won | Twickenham | N. D. Melville |
| 393 | 15.3.1986 | France | 1 | — | — | 2 | 10 | 4 | 2 | — | 3 | 29 | Lost | Paris | N. D. Melville |
| 394 | 7.2.1987 | Ireland | — | — | — | — | 0 | 3 | 1 | 1 | — | 17 | Lost | Dublin | R. J. Hill |
| 395 | 21.2.1987 | France | — | — | 1 | 4 | 15 | 2 | 1 | 2 | 1 | 19 | Lost | Twickenham | R. J. Hill |
| 396 | 7.3.1987 | Wales | — | — | — | 4 | 12 | 1 | — | — | 5 | 19 | Lost | Cardiff | R. J. Hill |
| 397 | 4.4.1987 | Scotland | 2 | 2 | — | 3 | 21 | 1 | 1 | — | 2 | 12 | Won | Twickenham | M. E. Harrison |

★ in the drop-goal column denotes a goal from a mark

# MATCH RECORDS

## MOST CONSECUTIVE MATCHES WON

| | |
|---|---|
| 10 | *1883* W,I,S *1884* W,I,S *1885* W,I *1886* W,I |
| 9 | *1922* S, *1923* W,I,S,F *1924* W,I,F,S |
| 8 | *1913* W,F,I,S *1914* W,I,S,F |

## MOST CONSECUTIVE MATCHES WITHOUT DEFEAT

| Matches | Wins | Draws | Period |
|---|---|---|---|
| 12 | 10 | 2 | 1882-83 to 1886-87 |
| 11 | 10 | 1 | 1921-22 to 1923-24 |
| 10 | 6 | 4 | 1877-78 to 1881-82 |
| 9 | 7 | 2 | 1956-57 to 1957-58 |
| 8 | 6 | 2 | 1871-72 to 1876-77 |
| 8 | 8 | 0 | 1912-13 to 1913-14 |
| 8 | 7 | 1 | 1951-52 to 1953-54 |

## MOST CONSECUTIVE MATCHES WITHOUT CONCEDING A TRY

| | |
|---|---|
| 10 | between 1874-75 and 1878-79 |
| 6 | between 1956-57 and 1957-58 |
| 4 | in 1912-13 |
| 4 | between 1958-59 and 1959-60 |

## MOST CONSECUTIVE MATCHES WITHOUT CONCEDING A SCORE

| | |
|---|---|
| 5 | between 1874-75 and 1876-77 |

## MOST POINTS IN A MATCH

### By the team

| Pts | Opponents | Venue | Season |
|---|---|---|---|
| 41 | France | Richmond | 1906-07 |
| 39 | France | Paris | 1913-14 |
| 37 | France | Twickenham | 1910-11 |
| 36 | Ireland | Dublin | 1937-38 |
| 35 | France | Paris | 1905-06 |
| 30 | Scotland | Edinburgh | 1979-80 |

*NB England scored heavily in several matches before scoring by points was adopted*

### By a player

| Pts | Player | Opponents | Venue | Season |
|---|---|---|---|---|
| 22 | D. Lambert | France | Twickenham | 1910-11 |
| 21 | C.R. Andrew | Wales | Twickenham | 1985-86 |
| 19 | W.H. Hare | Wales | Cardiff | 1980-81 |
| 19 | W.H. Hare | France | Paris | 1981-82 |
| 18 | C.R. Andrew | Romania | Twickenham | 1984-85 |
| 17 | A.G.B. Old | Ireland | Twickenham | 1973-74 |
| 17 | W.M.H. Rose | Scotland | Twickenham | 1986-87 |
| 16 | P.A. Rossborough | France | Twickenham | 1974-75 |
| 15 | D. Lambert | France | Richmond | 1906-07 |
| 15 | G.W. Parker | Ireland | Dublin | 1937-38 |
| 15 | W.H. Hare | Ireland | Dublin | 1982-83 |
| 15 | W.H. Hare | Wales | Twickenham | 1983-84 |

# MOST TRIES IN A MATCH

## By the team

| T | Opponents | Venue | Season |
|---|---|---|---|
| 13 | Wales | Blackheath | 1880-81 |
| 9 | France | Paris | 1905-06 |
| 9 | France | Richmond | 1906-07 |
| 9 | France | Paris | 1913-14 |
| 7 | Wales | Blackheath | 1895-96 |
| 7 | France | Twickenham | 1910-11 |
| 7 | Ireland | Dublin | 1937-38 |

## By a player

| T | Player | Opponents | Venue | Season |
|---|---|---|---|---|
| 5 | D. Lambert | France | Richmond | 1906-07 |
| 4 | G.W. Burton | Wales | Blackheath | 1880-81 |
| 4 | A. Hudson | France | Paris | 1905-06 |
| 4 | R.W. Poulton | France | Paris | 1913-14 |
| 3 | H.H. Taylor | Ireland | Manchester | 1880-81 |
| 3 | H. Vassall | Wales | Blackheath | 1880-81 |
| 3 | C.G. Wade | Wales | Swansea | 1882-83 |
| 3 | H. Marshall | Wales | Cardiff | 1892-93 |
| 3 | V.H.M. Coates | France | Twickenham | 1912-13 |
| 3 | C.N. Lowe | Scotland | Edinburgh | 1913-14 |
| 3 | C.N. Lowe | France | Paris | 1913-14 |
| 3 | H.P. Jacob | France | Twickenham | 1923-24 |
| 3 | J. Carleton | Scotland | Edinburgh | 1979-80 |

# MOST CONVERSIONS IN A MATCH

## By the team

| C | Opponents | Venue | Season |
|---|---|---|---|
| 7 | Wales | Blackheath | 1880-81 |
| 6 | France | Paris | 1913-14 |
| 6 | Ireland | Dublin | 1937-38 |
| 5 | France | Richmond | 1906-07 |
| 5 | France | Twickenham | 1910-11 |

## By a player

| T | Player | Opponents | Venue | Season |
|---|---|---|---|---|
| 6 | L. Stokes | Wales | Blackheath | 1880-81 |
| 6 | J.E. Greenwood | France | Paris | 1913-14 |
| 6 | G.W. Parker | Ireland | Dublin | 1937-38 |
| 5 | B.A. Hill | France | Richmond | 1906-07 |
| 5 | D. Lambert | France | Twickenham | 1910-11 |
| 4 | V.H. Cartwright | France | Paris | 1905-06 |
| 4 | J. Heaton | Scotland | Twickenham | 1946-47 |
| 4 | N.M. Hall | Scotland | Twickenham | 1952-53 |

# MOST DROPPED GOALS IN A MATCH

## By the team

| DG | Opponents | Venue | Season |
|---|---|---|---|
| 2 | Ireland | Twickenham | 1969-70 |
| 2 | France | Paris | 1977-78 |
| 2 | France | Paris | 1979-80 |
| 2 | Romania | Twickenham | 1984-85 |

## By a player

| DG | Player | Opponents | Venue | Season |
|---|---|---|---|---|
| 2 | R. Hiller | Ireland | Twickenham | 1969-70 |
| 2 | A.G.B. Old | France | Paris | 1977-78 |
| 2 | J.P. Horton | France | Paris | 1979-80 |
| 2 | C.R. Andrew | Romania | Twickenham | 1984-85 |

# MOST PENALTY GOALS IN A MATCH
## By the team

| PG | Opponents | Venue | Season |
|----|-----------|-------|--------|
| 6 | Wales | Twickenham | 1985-86 |
| 5 | Ireland | Twickenham | 1973-74 |
| 5 | Wales | Cardiff | 1980-81 |
| 5 | France | Paris | 1981-82 |
| 5 | Ireland | Dublin | 1982-83 |
| 5 | Wales | Twickenham | 1983-84 |
| 4 | Wales | Cardiff | 1966-67 |
| 4 | Ireland | Dublin | 1968-69 |
| 4 | South Africa | Johannesburg | 1972 |
| 4 | France | Twickenham | 1974-75 |
| 4 | Ireland | Twickenham | 1975-76 |
| 4 | France | Twickenham | 1980-81 |
| 4 | France | Twickenham | 1982-83 |
| 4 | South Africa | Port Elizabeth | 1984 |
| 4 | Romania | Twickenham | 1984-85 |
| 4 | France | Twickenham | 1986-87 |
| 4 | Wales | Cardiff | 1986-87 |

## By a player

| PG | Player | Opponents | Venue | Season |
|----|--------|-----------|-------|--------|
| 6 | C.R. Andrew | Wales | Twickenham | 1985-86 |
| 5 | A.G.B. Old | Ireland | Twickenham | 1973-74 |
| 5 | W.H. Hare | Wales | Cardiff | 1980-81 |
| 5 | W.H. Hare | France | Paris | 1981-82 |
| 5 | W.H. Hare | Ireland | Dublin | 1982-83 |
| 5 | W.H. Hare | Wales | Twickenham | 1983-84 |
| 4 | R.W. Hosen | Wales | Cardiff | 1966-67 |
| 4 | R. Hiller | Ireland | Dublin | 1968-69 |
| 4 | S.A. Doble | South Africa | Johannesburg | 1972 |
| 4 | P.A. Rossborough | France | Twickenham | 1974-75 |
| 4 | A.G.B. Old | Ireland | Twickenham | 1975-76 |
| 4 | W.M.H. Rose | France | Twickenham | 1980-81 |
| 4 | W.H. Hare | France | Twickenham | 1982-83 |
| 4 | W.H. Hare | South Africa | Port Elizabeth | 1984 |
| 4 | C.R. Andrew | Romania | Twickenham | 1984-85 |
| 4 | W.M.H. Rose | France | Twickenham | 1986-87 |
| 4 | W.M.H. Rose | Wales | Cardiff | 1986-87 |

# GOALS FROM MARKS

| ★ | Player | Opponents | Venue | Season |
|---|--------|-----------|-------|--------|
| 1 | A.E. Stoddart | Wales | Blackheath | 1885-86 |
| 1 | E.W. Taylor | Wales | Birkenhead | 1893-94 |
| 1 | W.G.E. Luddington | France | Paris | 1924-25 |
| 1 | L.J. Corbett | Wales | Twickenham | 1926-27 |

# TRY ON DEBUT

| Player | Opponents | Venue | Season |
|--------|-----------|-------|--------|
| R. H. Birkett | Scotland | Edinburgh | 1870-71 |
| S. Finney | Scotland | The Oval | 1871-72 |
| F. B. G. d'Aguilar | Scotland | The Oval | 1871-72 |
| A. T. Michell | Ireland | The Oval | 1874-75 |
| C. W. H. Clark | Ireland | Dublin | 1875-76 |
| F. H. Lee | Scotland | The Oval | 1875-76 |
| A. N. Hornby | Ireland | The Oval | 1876-77 |
| H. P. Gardner | Ireland | Dublin | 1877-78 |
| W. J. Penny | Ireland | Dublin | 1877-78 |
| G. W. Burton | Scotland | Edinburgh | 1878-79 |
| H. T. Twynam | Ireland | The Oval | 1878-79 |
| S. S. Ellis | Ireland | Dublin | 1879-80 |
| E. T. Markendale | Ireland | Dublin | 1879-80 |
| H. Vassall | Wales | Blackheath | 1880-81 |
| W. N. Bolton | Ireland | Dublin | 1881-82 |
| C. G. Wade | Wales | Swansea | 1882-83 |
| R. S. F. Henderson | Wales | Swansea | 1882-83 |
| J. J. Hawcridge | Wales | Swansea | 1884-85 |
| H. J. Ryalls | Wales | Swansea | 1884-85 |
| E. Wilkinson | Wales | Blackheath | 1885-86 |
| J. W. Sutcliffe | NZ Natives | Blackheath | 1888-89 |

| Player | Opponents | Venue | Season |
|---|---|---|---|
| F. Evershed | NZ Natives | Blackheath | 1888-89 |
| H. Bedford | NZ Natives | Blackheath | 1888-89 |
| J. W. Dyson | Scotland | Edinburgh | 1889-90 |
| P. Christopherson | Wales | Newport | 1890-91 |
| G. C. Hubbard | Wales | Blackheath | 1891-92 |
| W. Nichol | Wales | Blackheath | 1891-92 |
| H. Marshall | Wales | Cardiff | 1892-93 |
| F. C. Lohden | Wales | Cardiff | 1892-93 |
| S. Morfitt | Wales | Birkenhead | 1893-94 |
| F. A. Leslie-Jones | Wales | Swansea | 1894-95 |
| G. M. Carey | Wales | Swansea | 1894-95 |
| E. F. Fookes | Wales | Blackheath | 1895-96 |
| G. C. Robinson | Ireland | Dublin | 1896-97 |
| P. M. R. Royds | Scotland | Edinburgh | 1897-98 |
| E. T. Nicholson | Wales | Gloucester | 1899-1900 |
| D. D. Dobson | Wales | Blackheath | 1901-02 |
| A. Hudson | Wales | Richmond | 1905-06 |
| T. B. Hogarth | France | Paris | 1905-06 |
| F. G. Brooks | South Africa | Crystal Palace | 1906-07 |
| D. Lambert | France | Richmond | 1906-07 |
| W. M. B. Nanson | France | Richmond | 1906-07 |
| L. A. N. Slocock | France | Richmond | 1906-07 |
| W. N. Lapage | France | Paris | 1907-08 |
| G. V. Portus | France | Paris | 1907-08 |
| R. H. Williamson | Wales | Bristol | 1907-08 |
| E. R. Mobbs | Australia | Blackheath | 1908-09 |
| F. Hutchinson | France | Leicester | 1908-09 |
| A. C. Palmer | Ireland | Dublin | 1908-09 |
| F. E. Chapman | Wales | Twickenham | 1909-10 |
| B. Solomon | Wales | Twickenham | 1909-10 |
| A. D. Roberts | Wales | Swansea | 1910-11 |
| J. A. Scholfield | Wales | Swansea | 1910-11 |
| H. Brougham | Wales | Twickenham | 1911-12 |
| J. A. Pym | Wales | Twickenham | 1911-12 |
| H. L. V. Day | Wales | Swansea | 1919-20 |
| E. Myers | Ireland | Dublin | 1919-20 |
| Q. E. M. A. King | Scotland | Edinburgh | 1920-21 |
| J. E. Maxwell-Hyslop | Ireland | Dublin | 1921-22 |
| H. C. Catcheside | Wales | Swansea | 1923-24 |
| H. P. Jacob | Wales | Swansea | 1923-24 |
| R. H. Hamilton-Wickes | Ireland | Belfast | 1923-24 |
| H. J. Kittermaster | New Zealand | Twickenham | 1924-25 |
| L. W. Haslett | Ireland | Dublin | 1925-26 |
| W. J. Taylor | New South Wales | Twickenham | 1927-28 |
| H. Wilkinson | Wales | Twickenham | 1928-29 |
| A. L. Novis | Scotland | Edinburgh | 1928-29 |
| S. S. C. Meikle | Scotland | Edinburgh | 1928-29 |
| C. H. A. Gummer | France | Paris | 1928-29 |
| D. W. Burland | Wales | Twickenham | 1930-31 |
| J. A. Tallent | Scotland | Edinburgh | 1930-31 |
| E. H. Sadler | Ireland | Twickenham | 1932-33 |
| A. L. Warr | Wales | Cardiff | 1933-34 |
| G. W. C. Meikle | Wales | Cardiff | 1933-34 |
| A. Obolensky | New Zealand | Twickenham | 1935-36 |
| H. S. Sever | New Zealand | Twickenham | 1935-36 |
| E. J. Unwin | Scotland | Edinburgh | 1936-37 |
| R. M. Marshall | Ireland | Dublin | 1937-38 |
| D. E. Teden | Wales | Twickenham | 1938-39 |
| D. F. White | Wales | Cardiff | 1946-47 |
| C. B. Holmes | Scotland | Twickenham | 1946-47 |
| V. G. Roberts | France | Twickenham | 1946-47 |
| J. V. Smith | Wales | Twickenham | 1949-50 |
| G. C. Rittson-Thomas | Wales | Swansea | 1950-51 |
| C. E. Winn | South Africa | Twickenham | 1951-52 |
| J. Butterfield | France | Twickenham | 1952-53 |
| M. S. Phillips | Australia | Twickenham | 1957-58 |
| J. Roberts | Wales | Twickenham | 1959-60 |
| D. P. Rogers | Ireland | Dublin | 1960-61 |
| V. S. J. Harding | France | Twickenham | 1960-61 |
| J. E. Owen | Wales | Cardiff | 1962-63 |
| J. M. Ranson | New Zealand | Auckland | 1963 |
| J. R. H. Greenwood | Ireland | Twickenham | 1965-66 |
| R. E. Webb | Scotland | Twickenham | 1966-67 |
| R. H. Lloyd | New Zealand | Twickenham | 1967-68 |
| B. W. Redwood | Wales | Twickenham | 1967-68 |
| D. J. Duckham | Ireland | Dublin | 1968-69 |
| M. J. Novak | Wales | Twickenham | 1969-70 |
| R. C. Hannaford | Wales | Cardiff | 1970-71 |
| A. J. Morley | South Africa | Johannesburg | 1972 |
| B. J. Corless | Australia | Twickenham | 1975-76 |
| M. S. Lampkowski | Australia | Twickenham | 1975-76 |
| C. P. Kent | Scotland | Twickenham | 1976-77 |

| Player | | Opponents | Venue | Season |
|---|---|---|---|---|
| M. Young | | Scotland | Twickenham | 1976-77 |
| G. H. Davies | | Scotland | Twickenham | 1980-81 |
| W. M. H. Rose | | Ireland | Dublin | 1980-81 |
| S. T. Smith | | Romania | Twickenham | 1984-85 |
| M. E. Harrison | | New Zealand | Christchurch | 1985 |
| D. Richards | | Ireland | Twickenham | 1985-86 |

## CAPTAIN ON INTERNATIONAL DEBUT

| Player | Opponents | Venue | Season |
|---|---|---|---|
| F. Stokes | Scotland | Edinburgh | 1870-71 |
| F.H.R. Alderson | Wales | Newport | 1890-91 |
| J. Mycock | Wales | Cardiff | 1946-47 |
| N.D. Melville | Australia | Twickenham | 1984-85 |

## TRIES BY FULL-BACKS

| Player | Opponents | Venue | Season |
|---|---|---|---|
| W.J. Penny | Ireland | Dublin | 1877-78 |
| T.W. Fry | Scotland | Manchester | 1879-80 |
| R. Hiller | France | Twickenham | 1970-71 |
| R. Hiller | Scotland | Twickenham | 1970-71 |
| R. Hiller | RFU President's XV | Twickenham | 1970-71 |
| P.A. Rossborough | France | Twickenham | 1974-75 |
| W.H. Hare | Wales | Cardiff | 1980-81 |
| W.M.H. Rose | Ireland | Dublin | 1980-81 |
| W.H. Hare | France | Paris | 1983-84 |
| G.H. Davies | Ireland | Twickenham | 1985-86 |
| W.M.H. Rose | Scotland | Twickenham | 1986-87 |

NB  *There is an account of the 1880-81 match against Ireland which credits A.N. Hornby, the full-back, with a try*

## ALL THE POINTS FOR ENGLAND
## IN A MATCH
### (where more than one scoring action is involved)

| Pts | Player | Opponents | Venue | Season |
|---|---|---|---|---|
| 21 | C.R. Andrew | Wales | Twickenham | 1985-86 |
| 19 | W.H. Hare | Wales | Cardiff | 1980-81 |
| 15 | W.H. Hare | Ireland | Dublin | 1982-83 |
| 15 | W.H. Hare | Wales | Twickenham | 1983-84 |
| 14 | R. Hiller | France | Twickenham | 1970-71 |
| 12 | A.G.B. Old | Ireland | Twickenham | 1975-76 |
| 12 | W.M.H. Rose | France | Twickenham | 1980-81 |
| 12 | W.M.H. Rose | Wales | Cardiff | 1986-87 |
| 11 | D.W. Burland | Ireland | Dublin | 1931-32 |
| 11 | R. Hiller | RFU President's XV | Twickenham | 1970-71 |
| 9 | J. Heaton | Scotland | Edinburgh | 1938-39 |
| 9 | R. Hiller | Wales | Cardiff | 1968-69 |
| 9 | R. Hiller | Ireland | Dublin | 1970-71 |
| 9 | A.G.B. Old | Scotland | Edinburgh | 1971-72 |
| 9 | A.J. Hignell | Wales | Twickenham | 1975-76 |
| 9 | A.J. Hignell | Wales | Cardiff | 1976-77 |
| 9 | W.H. Hare | New Zealand | Twickenham | 1979-80 |
| 9 | W.H. Hare | Wales | Twickenham | 1979-80 |
| 9 | W.H. Hare | South Africa | Johannesburg | 1984 |
| 9 | C.R. Andrew | France | Twickenham | 1984-85 |
| 7 | J.V. Richardson | Ireland | Dublin | 1927-28 |
| 7 | W.N. Bennett | Ireland | Dublin | 1978-79 |
| 7 | W.N. Bennett | France | Twickenham | 1978-79 |
| 6 | A.M. Smallwood | Ireland | Twickenham | 1924-25 |
| 6 | N.M. Hall | France | Paris | 1951-52 |
| 6 | J.G. Willcox | France | Twickenham | 1962-63 |
| 6 | A.G.B. Old | France | Paris | 1977-78 |
| 6 | A.J. Hignell | Wales | Twickenham | 1977-78 |
| 6 | W.H. Hare | New Zealand | Twickenham | 1978-79 |
| 6 | W.H. Hare | Scotland | Edinburgh | 1983-84 |
| 6 | C..R. Andrew | Scotland | Edinburgh | 1985-86 |
| 5 | H.L.V. Day | Wales | Swansea | 1919-20 |
| 5 | B.H. Black | Ireland | Twickenham | 1930-31 |

# INDIVIDUAL RECORDS

## LONGEST CAREER SPANS

| Seasons | Player | Caps | Career span |
|---|---|---|---|
| 13 | J. Heaton | 9 | 1934-35 to 1946-47 |
| 12 | L.G. Brown | 18 | 1910-11 to 1921-22 |
| 12 | N.E. Horton | 20 | 1968-69 to 1979-80 |
| 12 | T.A. Kemp | 5 | 1936-37 to 1947-48 |
| 12 | J.E. Williams | 9 | 1953-54 to 1964-65 |

## MOST CONSECUTIVE CAPS IN A CAREER

| Caps | Player | Opponents |
|---|---|---|
| 36 | J.V. Pullin | *1968* W,I,F,S *1969* I,F,S,W,SA *1970* I,W,S,F *1971* W,I,F,S (1 + 2), P *1972* W,I,F,S,SA *1973* NZ, W,I,F,S,NZ,A *1974* S,I,F,W *1975* I |
| 33 | W.B. Beaumont | *1975* A (1 R + 2) *1976* A,W,S,I,F *1977* S,I,F,W *1978* F,W,S,I,NZ *1979* S,I,F,W,NZ *1980* I,F,W,S *1981* W,S,I,F, Arg. (1 + 2) *1982* A,S |

## MOST CAPS IN A CAREER

| Caps | Player | Career span |
|---|---|---|
| 43 | A. Neary | 1970-71 to 1979-80 |
| 42 | J.V. Pullin | 1965-66 to 1975-76 |
| 41 | P.J. Wheeler | 1974-75 to 1983-84 |
| 36 | D.J. Duckham | 1968-69 to 1975-76 |
| 34 | D.P. Rogers | 1960-61 to 1968-69 |
| 34 | W.B. Beaumont | 1974-75 to 1981-82 |
| 34 | J.P. Scott | 1977-78 to 1984 |
| 32 | P.W. Dodge | 1977-78 to 1985 |
| 31 | W.W. Wakefield | 1919-20 to 1926-27 |
| 31 | F.E. Cotton | 1970-71 to 1980-81 |
| 31 | M.A.C. Slemen | 1975-76 to 1983-84 |
| 31 | G.S. Pearce | 1978-79 to 1986-87 |
| 30 | E. Evans | 1947-48 to 1957-58 |

## MOST POINTS IN A CAREER

| Pts | Player | Matches | Career span |
|---|---|---|---|
| 240 | W.H. Hare | 25 | 1973-74 to 1984 |
| 138 | R. Hiller | 19 | 1967-68 to 1971-72 |
| 98 | A.G.B. Old | 16 | 1971-72 to 1977-78 |
| 89 | C.R. Andrew | 12 | 1984-85 to 1986-87 |
| 82 | W.M.H. Rose | 9 | 1981-82 to 1986-87 |
| 63 | R.W. Hosen | 10 | 1963 to 1966-67 |
| 58 | C.N. Lowe | 25 | 1912-13 to 1922-23 |

## MOST TRIES IN A CAREER

| T | Player | Matches | Career span |
|---|---|---|---|
| 18 | C.N. Lowe | 25 | 1912-13 to 1922-23 |
| 10 | J.G.G. Birkett | 21 | 1905-06 to 1911-12 |
| 10 | D.J. Duckham | 36 | 1968-69 to 1975-76 |

## MOST CONVERSIONS IN A CAREER

| C | Player | Matches | Career span |
|---|--------|---------|-------------|
| 17 | L. Stokes | 12 | 1874-75 to 1880-81 |
| 14 | W.H. Hare | 25 | 1973-74 to 1984 |
| 12 | J.E. Greenwood | 13 | 1911-12 to 1919-20 |
| 12 | R. Hiller | 19 | 1967-68 to 1971-72 |
| 11 | G.S. Conway | 18 | 1919-20 to 1926-27 |

## MOST DROPPED GOALS IN A CAREER

| DG | Player | Matches | Career span |
|----|--------|---------|-------------|
| 6 | C.R. Andrew | 12 | 1984-85 to 1986-87 |
| 4 | J.P. Horton | 13 | 1977-78 to 1984 |
| 3 | W.J.A. Davies | 22 | 1912-13 to 1922-23 |
| 3 | N.M. Hall | 17 | 1946-47 to 1954-55 |
| 3 | R.A.W. Sharp | 14 | 1959-60 to 1966-67 |
| 3 | J.F. Finlan | 13 | 1966-67 to 1972-73 |
| 3 | A.G.B. Old | 16 | 1971-72 to 1977-78 |
| 3 | L. Cusworth | 10 | 1979-80 to 1983-84 |

## MOST PENALTY GOALS IN A CAREER

| PG | Player | Matches | Career span |
|----|--------|---------|-------------|
| 67 | W.H. Hare | 25 | 1973-74 to 1984 |
| 33 | R. Hiller | 19 | 1967-68 to 1971-72 |
| 23 | A.G.B. Old | 16 | 1971-72 to 1977-78 |
| 22 | W.M.H. Rose | 9 | 1981-82 to 1986-87 |
| 21 | C.R. Andrew | 9 | 1984-85 to 1986-87 |
| 17 | R.W. Hosen | 10 | 1963 to 1966-67 |

## MOST MATCHES AS CAPTAIN

| | | |
|---|---|---|
| 21 | W.B. Beaumont | (11 victories) |
| 13 | W.W. Wakefield | ( 7 victories) |
| 13 | N.M. Hall | ( 6 victories) |
| 13 | E. Evans | ( 9 victories) |
| 13 | R.E.G. Jeeps | ( 5 victories) |
| 13 | J.V. Pullin | ( 6 victories) |
| 11 | W.J.A. Davies | (10 victories) |

# SCOTLAND INTERNATIONAL TEAMS AND RECORDS

| 1870-71 | 1871-72 | 1872-73 | 1873-74 |
|---|---|---|---|
| v. ENGLAND | v. ENGLAND | v. ENGLAND | v. ENGLAND |
| †W.D. Brown | W.D. Brown | W.D. Brown | *W.D. Brown |
| †T. Chalmers | T. Chalmers | T. Chalmers | T. Chalmers |
| †A.C. Ross | †L.M. Balfour | †J.L.P. Sanderson | |
| | | | †H.M. Hamilton |
| †T.R. Marshall | T.R. Marshall | †G.B. McClure | T.R. Marshall |
| †W. Cross 1c,1t | †R.P. Maitland | J.L.H. Macfarlane | †W.H. Kidston |
| †J.W. Arthur | | | |
| | J.W. Arthur | W. St Clair-Grant | W. St Clair-Grant |
| | *F.J. Moncreiff | T.R. Marshall | †A.K. Stewart |
| *†F.J. Moncreiff | W. Cross | | |
| †W.J.C. Lyall | | *F.J. Moncreiff | †G. Heron |
| †J.S. Thomson | †H.W. Renny-Tailyour | †H.W. Allen | †A.H. Young |
| †R.W. Irvine | R.W. Irvine | R.W. Irvine | R.W. Irvine |
| †A.H. Robertson | †W. Marshall | †A.G. Petrie | A.G. Petrie |
| †J.F. Finlay | J.F. Finlay | †P. Anton | J.F. Finlay 1t |
| †G. Ritchie | †F.T. Maxwell | †A.T. Wood | A.T. Wood |
| †A. Buchanan 1t | †E.M. Bannerman | E.M. Bannerman | †J. Reid |
| †R. Munro | †J.H. McClure | †C.C. Bryce | C.C. Bryce |
| †A.G. Colville | A.G. Colville | †T.P. Whittington | †T. Neilson |
| †D. Drew | †C.W. Cathcart 1dg | C.W. Cathcart | †J.K. Todd |
| †J.L.H. Macfarlane | J.L.H. Macfarlane | †R.W. Wilson | R.W. Wilson |
| †J. Forsyth | †J. Anderson | †J.P. Davidson | J.P. Davidson |
| †J.A.W. Mein | J.A.W. Mein | J.A.W. Mein | J.A.W. Mein |
| Raeburn Place | Kennington Oval | Glasgow | Kennington Oval |
| WON | LOST | DRAWN | LOST |
| Scot.: 1g 1t | Eng.: 1g 1dg 2t | Scot.: nil | Eng.: 1dg |
| Eng.: 1t | Scot.: 1dg | Eng.: nil | Scot.: 1t |
| 27 Mar. 1871 | 5 Feb. 1872 | 3 Mar. 1873 | 23 Feb. 1874 |

An unofficial association football match between England and Scotland had been played at The Oval in November 1870, but its arrangement and result caused rancour north of the border. The Scots claimed that their side was not truly representative, adding that rugby was the principal version of football played by them. Consequently, a challenge was issued, inviting England to a match in Edinburgh. The challenge led to the 1871 international at Raeburn Place. The Scots proved more efficient in combination, superior in stamina, and deserved to win a match in which all of the scoring occured after half-time. The first try in international rugby was a pushover try credited to Angus Buchanan, who later became a President of the SRU.

| 1874-75 | 1875-76 | 1876-77 | |
|---|---|---|---|
| v. ENGLAND | v. ENGLAND | v. IRELAND | v. ENGLAND |
| *W.D. Brown | †J.S. Carrick | †H.H. Johnston | J.S. Carrick |
| T. Chalmers | T. Chalmers | | H.H. Johnston |
| | | M. Cross 4c | |
| †M. Cross | M. Cross | †R.C. Mackenzie 2dg,3t | M. Cross 1dg |
| †N.J. Finlay | N.J. Finlay | | R.C. Mackenzie |
| H.M. Hamilton | | †E.J. Pocock 1t | |
| | A.K. Stewart | J.R. Hay-Gordon | E.J. Pocock |
| †J.R. Hay-Gordon | †G.Q. Paterson | | J.R. Hay-Gordon |
| J.K. Todd | | †S.H. Smith | |
| | †D.H. Watson | D.H. Watson | D.H. Watson |
| G. Heron | †D. Lang | D. Lang | †T.J. Torrie |
| †D. Robertson | †C. Villar | C. Villar | C. Villar |
| R.W. Irvine | *R.W. Irvine | *R.W. Irvine 1t | *R.W. Irvine |
| A.G. Petrie | A.G. Petrie | A.G. Petrie | A.G. Petrie |
| J.F. Finlay | †J.H.S. Graham | J.H.S. Graham | J.H.S. Graham |
| A.T. Wood | †N.T. Brewis | †H.M. Napier | H.M. Napier |
| J. Reid | J. Reid | J. Reid 1t | J. Reid |
| †A. Marshall | †J.E. Junor | J.E. Junor | J.E. Junor |
| †A. Arthur | A. Arthur | | |
| †G.R. Fleming | G.R. Fleming | Belfast | Raeburn Place |
| †A.B. Finlay | C.W. Cathcart | WON | WON |
| †J.W. Dunlop | D. Drew | | |
| J.A.W. Mein | †W.H. Bolton | Ire.: nil | Scot.: 1dg |
| | | Scot.: 4g 2dg 2t | Eng.: nil |
| Raeburn Place | Kennington Oval | | |
| DRAWN | LOST | 19 Feb. 1877 | 5 Mar. 1877 |
| Scot.: nil | Eng.: 1g 1t | | |
| Eng.: nil | Scot.: nil | | |
| 8 Mar. 1875 | 6 Mar. 1876 | | |

Following the success of 1871, Scotland had to wait until international teams were reduced to fifteens in 1877 before a second win was registered. Then, in their first visit to Ireland, the Scots dominated a match played in a heavy downpour, and scored six tries. Versions of the scorers vary, but several sources credit Mackenzie with three tries and two drop-goals.

Mackenzie and Hay-Gordon were the leading Scottish backs of the 1870s. Mackenzie lived to the ripe age of 89, and was the President of the SRU in the year that Murrayfield opened. The two backs were instrumental in Scotland's win over England at Raeburn Place in 1877. Whereas the 1871 victory had helped to establish the game in Scotland, the triumph of 1877 led to the high public regard for the English international as the major event of the sporting calendar.

| 1877-78 | 1878-79 | | 1879-80 | |
| --- | --- | --- | --- | --- |
| v. ENGLAND | v. IRELAND | v. ENGLAND | v. IRELAND | v. ENGLAND |
| †W.E. MACLAGAN | W.E. MACLAGAN | W.E. MACLAGAN | W.E. MACLAGAN | W.E. MACLAGAN |
| M. CROSS | M. CROSS 1c,1DG | M. CROSS | M. CROSS 1c | M. CROSS 1c |
| N.J. FINLAY | N.J. FINLAY | N.J. FINLAY 1DG | N.J. FINLAY 2DG | N.J. FINLAY |
| †J.A. NEILSON | †W.H. MASTERS | J.A. NEILSON | W.H. MASTERS 1t | W.H. MASTERS |
| †J.A. CAMPBELL | J.A. CAMPBELL | J.A. CAMPBELL | †W.S. BROWN | W.S. BROWN 1t |
| S.H. SMITH | †R. AINSLIE | R. AINSLIE | R. AINSLIE | R. AINSLIE |
| †D.R. IRVINE | D.R. IRVINE | D.R. IRVINE | †C.A.R. STEWART | C.A.R. STEWART |
| †G. MACLEOD | †J.B. BROWN 1t | J.B. BROWN | J.B. BROWN | J.B. BROWN |
| †L.C. AULDJO | †D. SOMERVILLE 1t | †E.N. EWART | E.N. EWART 2t | E.N. EWART |
| *R.W. IRVINE | *R.W. IRVINE | *R.W. IRVINE | *R.W. IRVINE | *R.W. IRVINE |
| A.G. PETRIE | A.G. PETRIE | A.G. PETRIE | A.G. PETRIE | A.G. PETRIE |
| J.H.S. GRAHAM | J.H.S. GRAHAM | J.H.S. GRAHAM | J.H.S. GRAHAM | J.H.S. GRAHAM |
| H.M. NAPIER | H.M. NAPIER | H.M. NAPIER | †D. McCOWAN | D. McCOWAN |
| N.T. BREWIS | N.T. BREWIS | N.T. BREWIS | N.T. BREWIS | N.T. BREWIS |
| J.E. JUNOR | †E.R. SMITH | J.E. JUNOR | †J.G. TAIT | †D.Y. CASSELS |
| Kennington Oval | Belfast | Raeburn Place | Glasgow | Manchester |
| DRAWN | WON | DRAWN | WON | LOST |
| ENG.: NIL | IRE.: NIL | SCOT.: 1DG | SCOT.: 1G 2DG 2T | ENG.: 2G 3T |
| SCOT.: NIL | SCOT.: 1G 1DG 1T | ENG.: 1G | IRE.: NIL | SCOT.: 1G |
| 4 Mar. 1878 | 17 Feb. 1879 | 10 Mar. 1879 | 14 Feb. 1880 | 28 Feb. 1880 |

Scotland enjoyed an unbeaten run of six matches between 1877 and 1880, defeat at Manchester in the first international played in the north of England ending the sequence and coinciding with the retirement of R.W. "Bulldog" Irvine.

Irvine was a robust forward who led the Scots in a strenuous manner for five seasons. Having made his debut as a teenager, he played in the first thirteen Scottish internationals and set a cap record in a career spanning ten seasons. A doctor, he died young, one day short of his 44th birthday.

The 1879 match with England was the first for the Calcutta Cup. The game was unspectacular and finished as a draw. Two Scots, however, Ninian Finlay and W.E. Maclagan, gained distinction for their outstanding contributions. Maclagan was one of the most powerful Scottish backs of the era and he tackled bravely throughout the match, upsetting numerous English attacks. Finlay scored the drop-goal which tied the match. Reports record that he made his successful kick "with a couple of Englishmen hanging on to him".

| 1880-81 | | 1881-82 | |
| --- | --- | --- | --- |
| v. IRELAND | v. ENGLAND | v. IRELAND | v. ENGLAND |
| †T.A. BEGBIE | T.A. BEGBIE 1c | †T. ANDERSON | †J.P. VEITCH |
| W.E. MACLAGAN | W.E. MACLAGAN | W.E. MACLAGAN | W.E. MACLAGAN |
| N.J. FINLAY | N.J. FINLAY | †F. HUNTER | †A. PHILP |
| R.C. MACKENZIE | R.C. MACKENZIE | | |
| | | W.S. BROWN 1t | A.R. DON WAUCHOPE |
| †P.W. SMEATON | †A.R. DON WAUCHOPE | †A.G. GRANT-ASHER | W.S. BROWN |
| J.A. CAMPBELL | J.A. CAMPBELL | | |
| | | G. MACLEOD | A. WALKER |
| D. McCOWAN | R. AINSLIE 1t | *R. AINSLIE | R. AINSLIE 2t |
| †C. REID | C. REID | C. REID | C. REID |
| D.Y. CASSELS | †J.W. FRASER | D.Y. CASSELS | *D.Y. CASSELS |
| *J.H.S. GRAHAM 1t | *J.H.S. GRAHAM | D. SOMERVILLE | †W.A. WALLS |
| †B. ALLAN | D. McCOWAN | D. McCOWAN 1t | D. McCOWAN |
| J.E. JUNOR | †R. MAITLAND | R. MAITLAND | R. MAITLAND |
| †G.H. ROBB | †T. AINSLIE | T. AINSLIE | T. AINSLIE |
| †A. WALKER | †W.A. PETERKIN | †A.F.C. GORE | †J.G. WALKER |
| J.B. BROWN | J.B. BROWN 1t | J.B. BROWN | J.B. BROWN |
| Belfast | Raeburn Place | Glasgow | Manchester |
| LOST | DRAWN | WON | WON |
| IRE.: 1DG | SCOT.: 1G 1T | SCOT.: 2T | ENG.: NIL |
| SCOT.: 1T | ENG.: 1DG 1T | IRE.: NIL | SCOT.: 2T |
| 19 Feb. 1881 | 19 Mar. 1881 | 18 Feb. 1882 | 4 Mar. 1882 |

Maclagan, Ninian Finlay and Mackenzie made history in Belfast in 1881, forming the first three-man threequarter line to appear in an international match. Scotland lost, abandoned the formation for a couple of seasons, but subsequently reverted to the system (in 1884) when it was adopted by the other Home Countries. Finlay won the last of his nine caps in 1881, retiring as the holder of the Scottish international record for dropped goals.

In 1881 Charles Reid, a teenager at Edinburgh Academy, became the first schoolboy forward to appear in an international when he played in Scotland's defeat in Belfast. The Academy had the unique distinction of having players on opposite sides later in the season when F.T. Wright of Lancashire was drafted into the English side for the Calcutta Cup game, another English player having missed the train from London.

Victory at Manchester in 1882 was Scotland's first on English soil, and was due to a splendid pack in which Robert Ainslie was outstanding. Not only did he score a try in each half of the game, his tackling of the English wings halted several dangerous runs.

## 1882-83

| v. WALES | v. IRELAND | v. ENGLAND |
|---|---|---|
| †D.W. Kidston | J.P. Veitch | D.W. Kidston |
| | | |
| W.E. Maclagan 3c | W.E. Maclagan 1c | W.E. Maclagan |
| †D.J. McFarlan 2t | †M.F. Reid | M.F. Reid |
| | | |
| A.R. Don Wauchope 1t | P.W. Smeaton | P.W. Smeaton |
| W.S. Brown | †G.R. Aitchison | W.S. Brown |
| | | |
| A. Walker | A. Walker | A. Walker |
| D. Somerville | D. Somerville 1t | D. Somerville |
| C. Reid | C. Reid 1t | C. Reid 1t |
| *D.Y. Cassels | *D.Y. Cassels | *D.Y. Cassels |
| W.A. Walls | W.A. Walls | W.A. Walls |
| †J.G. Mowat | W.A. Peterkin | J.G. Mowat |
| †J. Jamieson | J. Jamieson | J. Jamieson |
| T. Ainslie | T. Ainslie | T. Ainslie |
| J.G. Walker | D. McCowan | D. McCowan |
| J.B. Brown | J.B. Brown | J.B. Brown |
| Raeburn Place | Belfast | Raeburn Place |
| WON | WON | LOST |
| Scot.: 3g | Ire.: nil | Scot.: 1t |
| Wales: 1g | Scot.: 1g 1t | Eng.: 2t |
| 8 Jan. 1883 | 17 Feb. 1883 | 3 Mar. 1883 |

A narrow defeat against England deprived the Scots of a Triple Crown in 1883. Wales and Ireland were beaten by clear margins, but controversy surrounded the English match at Raeburn Place.

A.R. Don Wauchope was Scotland's outstanding half-back of the early 1880s, and was incapacitated with a knee injury during the season. For the English match, P.W. Smeaton and W.S. Brown appeared as the halves. Both claimed to have scored tries in the game. Brown reckoned that he had dribbled the ball over the line and had controlled his touchdown for a try, while Smeaton thought that he had wriggled over for another. These scores would have been sufficient to give Scotland victory.

David Cassels, a Glasgow iron-master, was Scotland's captain for the season, his last in the international side. Later he was a distinguished President of the Union.

## 1883-84 & 1884-85

| 1883-84 | | | 1884-85 | |
|---|---|---|---|---|
| v. WALES | v. IRELAND | v. ENGLAND | v. WALES | v. IRELAND |
| J.P. Veitch | J.P. Veitch | J.P. Veitch | †P.R. Harrower | J.P. Veitch 1c |
| | | | | |
| *W.E. Maclagan | *W.E. Maclagan | *W.E. Maclagan | *W.E. Maclagan | *W.E. Maclagan |
| D.J. McFarlan | D.J. McFarlan | D.J. McFarlan | †A.E. Stephen | †H.L. Evans |
| †G.C. Lindsay | †E.T. Roland | E.T. Roland | †G. Maitland | G. Maitland |
| | | | | |
| A.R. Don Wauchope | A.R. Don Wauchope 1t | A.R. Don Wauchope | A.R. Don Wauchope | A.R. Don Wauchope 1t |
| A.G. Grant-Asher 1dg | A.G. Grant-Asher 1t | A.G. Grant-Asher | A.G. Grant-Asher | †P.H. Don Wauchope |
| | | | | |
| D. Somerville | †C.W. Berry 2c | C.W. Berry | C.W. Berry | J.G. Tait |
| C. Reid | C. Reid | C. Reid | C. Reid | C. Reid 1t |
| †J. Tod | J. Tod 1t | J. Tod | J. Tod | J. Tod |
| W.A. Walls | W.A. Walls | W.A. Walls | †J.G. Mitchell | J.G. Mitchell |
| W.A. Peterkin | W.A. Peterkin 1t | W.A. Peterkin | W.A. Peterkin | W.A. Peterkin 1t |
| J. Jamieson | J. Jamieson | J. Jamieson 1t | J. Jamieson | J. Jamieson |
| T. Ainslie 1t | T. Ainslie | T. Ainslie | T. Ainslie | T. Ainslie |
| R. Maitland | D. McCowan | D. McCowan | R. Maitland | †T.W. Irvine |
| J.B. Brown | J.B. Brown | J.B. Brown | G.H. Robb | J.B. Brown |
| Newport | Raeburn Place | Blackheath | Glasgow | Raeburn Place |
| WON | WON | LOST | DRAWN | WON |
| Wales: nil | Scot.: 2g 2t | Eng.: 1g | Scot.: nil | Scot.: 1g 2t |
| Scot.: 1dg 1t | Ire.: 1t | Scot.: 1t | Wales: nil | Ire.: nil |
| 12 Jan. 1884 | 16 Feb. 1884 | 1 Mar. 1884 | 10 Jan. 1885 | 7 Mar. 1885 |

Scotland was again deprived of the Triple Crown in 1884, the match with England being noted for the contentious knock-back which led to the winning English goal. The following season Scotland did not meet England, twice beat Ireland (though the first match in Belfast was abandoned after thirty minutes, and has not been included in the foregoing team records), and played a drawn game with Wales.

Among the four new caps for the Welsh match was a London Scot named Pat Harrower. He gained the unique distinction (for a rugby player) of refereeing an FA Cup Final. In 1905 Harrower controlled the final between Aston Villa and Newcastle United.

Patrick and Andrew Don Wauchope, former pupils of Fettes College, played together against Ireland to become the first pair of brothers to form a half-back partnership in an international. Andrew, who was President of the SRU in 1889-90, scored the final try of the match with a brilliant side-stepping run.

## 1885-86

| v. WALES | v. IRELAND | v. ENGLAND |
|---|---|---|
| †F. McINDOE | F. McINDOE | J.P. VEITCH |
| | | |
| †R.H. MORRISON | R.H. MORRISON 2T | R.H. MORRISON |
| D.J. McFARLAN | D.J. McFARLAN 1T,3C | †G.R. WILSON |
| †W.F. HOLMS | A.E. STEPHEN | W.F. HOLMS |
| | | |
| A.R. DON WAUCHOPE 1T | A.G. GRANT-ASHER 1DG | A.G. GRANT-ASHER |
| P.H. DON WAUCHOPE | A.R. DON WAUCHOPE 2T | A.R. DON WAUCHOPE |
| | | |
| †C.J.B. MILNE | C.J.B. MILNE | C.J.B. MILNE |
| C. REID | C. REID | C. REID |
| J. TOD 1T | J. TOD | J. TOD |
| †J. FRENCH | †D.A. MACLEOD | D.A. MACLEOD |
| †A.T. CLAY 1T | A.T. CLAY | A.T. CLAY |
| W.A. WALLS | W.A. WALLS | W.A. WALLS |
| †W.M. MACLEOD 2C | W.M. MACLEOD | †M.C. MAEWAN |
| T.W. IRVINE | T.W. IRVINE | T.W. IRVINE |
| *J.B. BROWN | *J.B. BROWN | *J.B. BROWN |
| Cardiff Arms Park | Raeburn Place | Raeburn Place |
| WON | WON | DRAWN |
| WALES: NIL | SCOT.: 3G 1DG 2T | SCOT.: NIL |
| SCOT.: 2G 1T | IRE.: NIL | ENG.: NIL |
| 9 Jan. 1886 | 20 Feb. 1886 | 13 Mar. 1886 |

The four home Unions met in Dublin in February 1886 to discuss the dispute arising from the England-Scotland match of 1884. The Scots acknowledged England's victory, hence insuring the future of the Calcutta Cup series. But they also insisted on the formation of an International Board to settle such disputes, an idea accepted in principle by the other Unions, though agreed with reservations by the delegates of the RFU.

J.B. Brown led Scotland to a share in the Championship. This was his last season in international rugby and he retired with 18 caps, to set a new Scottish record.

There were satisfying wins over Wales and Ireland, but a scoreless draw with England prevented Scotland gaining the Triple Crown. Scotland were the better side in the dour struggle for the Calcutta Cup, forcing England to touch down in defence twice, having a try by Wilson disallowed, and seeing Morrison fail to touch down after crossing the English line.

## 1886-87

| v. IRELAND | v. WALES | v. ENGLAND |
|---|---|---|
| W.F. HOLMS | †A.W.C. CAMERON | W.F. HOLMS |
| | | |
| W.E. MACLAGAN 1T | W.E. MACLAGAN 1T | W.E. MACLAGAN |
| D.J. McFARLAN | G.C. LINDSAY 5T | G.C. LINDSAY |
| †A.N. WOODROW | A.N. WOODROW 2C | A.N. WOODROW |
| | | |
| †C.E. ORR | C.E. ORR 1T | C.E. ORR |
| P.H. DON WAUCHOPE | P.H. DON WAUCHOPE 1T | P.H. DON WAUCHOPE |
| | | |
| C.W. BERRY 1C,1GM | C.W. BERRY 2C | C.W. BERRY |
| *C. REID | *C. REID 1T | *C. REID |
| †H.T. KER | H.T. KER | H.T. KER |
| J. FRENCH | J. FRENCH | J. FRENCH |
| A.T. CLAY | A.T. CLAY | A.T. CLAY |
| †D.S. MORTON 1T | D.S. MORTON 1T | D.S. MORTON 1T |
| M.C. McEWAN 1T | M.C. McEWAN 1T | M.C. McEWAN |
| T.W. IRVINE | T.W. IRVINE | T.W. IRVINE |
| †R.G. MACMILLAN | R.G. MACMILLAN 1T | R.G. MACMILLAN |
| Belfast | Raeburn Place | Manchester |
| WON | WON | DRAWN |
| IRE.: NIL | SCOT.: 4G 8T | ENG.: 1T |
| SCOT.: 1G 1GM 2T | WALES: NIL | SCOT.: 1T |
| 19 Feb. 1887 | 26 Feb. 1887 | 5 Mar. 1887 |

Scotland scored fifteen tries to nil in the Irish and Welsh matches of 1887. Charles Reid was the new skipper of an experienced side which went on to win the Championship, Scotland's first outright title success. The pack was unchanged for the three matches.

The opening score of the Irish match was Scotland's first goal from a mark in an international. Then in the Welsh match, which had been postponed in January, George Lindsay, one of the first rugby players to turn his hand to journalism, set a world record (which stands 100 years later) by running in five tries. Scotland thus started as favourites for the Calcutta Cup contest, where victory would have earned the Triple Crown. But England's forwards outplayed the Scottish pack

Douglas Morton scored tries in each of his first three internationals, a unique record for a Scottish forward. Later he was a President of the SRU.

| 1887-88 | | 1888-89 | |
| v. WALES | v. IRELAND | v. WALES | v. IRELAND |
| --- | --- | --- | --- |
| †H.F.T. Chambers | H.F.T. Chambers | H.F.T. Chambers | H.F.T. Chambers |
| W.E. Maclagan | W.E. Maclagan | †J.H. Marsh | J.H. Marsh |
| †H.J. Stevenson | H.J. Stevenson | H.J. Stevenson | H.J. Stevenson 1dg |
| †M.M. Duncan | D.J. McFarlan 1t | W.F. Holms | W.F. Holms |
| C.E. Orr | C.E. Orr | C.E. Orr 1t | C.E. Orr |
| †C.F.P. Fraser | *A.R. Don Wauchope | C.F.P. Fraser | †D.G. Anderson |
| C.W. Berry | C.W. Berry 1c | †A. Methuen | A. Methuen |
| *C. Reid | C. Reid | †J.D. Boswell | J.D Boswell |
| †L.E. Stevenson | H.T. Ker | H.T. Ker 1t | †J.G. McKendrick |
| †A. Duke | A. Duke | A. Duke | A. Duke |
| A.T. Clay | †A. Malcolm | †W. Auld | †J.E. Orr |
| D.S. Morton | D.S. Morton | *D.S. Morton | *D.S. Morton |
| M.C. McEwan | M.C. McEwan | M.C. McEwan | M.C. McEwan |
| T.W. Irvine | T.W. Irvine | †W.A. McDonald | T.W. Irvine |
| †T.B. White | T.B. White | T.B. White | †A.I. Aitken |
| Newport | Raeburn Place | Raeburn Place | Belfast |
| LOST | WON | WON | WON |
| Wales: 1t | Scot.: 1g | Scot.: 2t | Ire.: nil |
| Scot.: nil | Ire.: nil | Wales: nil | Scot.: 1dg |
| 4 Feb. 1888 | 10 Mar. 1888 | 2 Feb. 1889 | 16 Feb 1889 |

The international dispute concerning England's participation in the proposed IB raged on in 1888 and 1889: consequently there were no games for the Calcutta Cup.

Charles Reid ended his international career in Scotland's win over Ireland in 1888. A doctor, Reid played twenty times for Scotland to set a record for a forward. Another doctor, J.H. Marsh, who first appeared as a threequarter in 1889, became the first Scotland player to turn out for two countries when he later played for England. Marsh gained his degree at Edinburgh University, but later returned to the Manchester area, where he practised as a GP for nearly forty years.

Scotland were unbeaten in 1889. There was a narrow win over Ireland in Belfast. Playing with the wind and the slope in the first half, Scotland scraped to victory thanks to a drop-goal by Stevenson before the interval. Stevenson was an outstanding utility back who played with aplomb as a centre and full-back.

| 1889-90 | | |
| v. WALES | v. IRELAND | v. ENGLAND |
| --- | --- | --- |
| †G. MacGregor | G. MacGregor | G. MacGregor |
| *W.E. Maclagan 1t | *W.E. Maclagan | *W.E. Maclagan |
| H.J. Stevenson | H.J. Stevenson | H.J. Stevenson |
| G.R. Wilson | G.R. Wilson | G.R. Wilson |
| C.E. Orr | C.E. Orr | C.E. Orr |
| D.G. Anderson 1t | D.G. Anderson | D.G. Anderson |
| †F.W.J. Goodhue | F.W.J. Goodhue | F.W.J. Goodhue |
| J.D. Boswell | J.D. Boswell 1dg | J.D. Boswell |
| W. Auld | H.T. Ker | H.T. Ker |
| A. Duke | A. Duke | D.S. Morton |
| J.E. Orr | J.E. Orr 1t | J.E. Orr |
| †A. Dalgleish | D.S. Morton | A. Dalgleish |
| M.C. McEwan 1c,1t | M.C. McEwan | M.C. McEwan |
| †I. MacIntyre | I. MacIntyre | I. MacIntyre |
| R.G. MacMillan | R.G. MacMillan | R.G. MacMillan |
| Cardiff Arms Park | Raeburn Place | Raeburn Place |
| WON 5-1 | WON 4-0 | LOST 0-4 |
| Wales: 1t | Scot.: 1dg 1t | Scot.: nil |
| Scot.: 1g 2t | Ire.: nil | Eng.: 1g 1t |
| 1 Feb. 1890 | 22 Feb. 1890 | 1 Mar. 1890 |

For the fifth time in seven years, Scotland were deprived of the Triple Crown by England, and had to be content with a share in the Championship. The Scottish backs were unchanged for the three matches and Maclagan, now a veteran, returned to skipper the side and win the last of his 25 caps, thus creating a new record. A London stockbroker, he was one of the early stalwarts of the London Scottish side, while his career span of thirteen seasons in the Scottish side stood as a record for nearly sixty years.

Among the new caps for the Welsh match was Gregor MacGregor, a former Uppingham pupil who became one of the finest wicketkeepers in England. In addition to gaining 13 rugby caps, he appeared in eight Test matches, and made 17 dismissals. Another new cap, Adam Dalgleish, was the first playing member of a Border club to be capped. A millworker, he weighed less than 12 stone and was a renowned dribbler.

Scotland called on 17 players during the season, sound teamwork paving the way for good wins over Wales and Ireland. It was recorded, however, that Scotland were deservedly beaten by England, only the anticipation and tackling of Stevenson in defence saving the Scots from a larger defeat.

## 1890-91

| v. WALES | v. IRELAND | v. ENGLAND |
|---|---|---|
| H.J. Stevenson 1dg | H.J. Stevenson | H.J. Stevenson |
| | | |
| †P.R. Clauss 2t | P.R. Clauss 1t | P.R. Clauss 1dg |
| G. MacGregor | G. MacGregor 1t | G. MacGregor 2c |
| †W. Neilson 1dg | G.R. Wilson | W. Neilson 1t |
| | | |
| C.E. Orr 1t | C.E. Orr | C.E. Orr |
| D.G. Anderson | †W. Wotherspoon 3t | D.G. Anderson |
| | | |
| F.W.J. Goodhue 1t | F.W.J. Goodhue | F.W.J. Goodhue |
| J.D. Boswell 1t | J.D. Boswell 3c | J.D. Boswell |
| †H.T.O. Leggatt 1t | H.T.O. Leggatt | H.T.O. Leggatt |
| †G.T. Neilson | G.T. Neilson | G.T. Neilson |
| J.E. Orr 1t | J.E. Orr | J.E. Orr 1t |
| A. Dalgleish | A. Dalgleish | W.R. Gibson |
| *M.C. McEwan 1c | *M.C. McEwan 1dg | *M.C. McEwan |
| I. MacIntyre | I. MacIntyre | I. MacIntyre |
| R.G. MacMillan | †W.R. Gibson | R.G. MacMillan |
| | | |
| Raeburn Place | Belfast | Richmond |
| WON 15-0 | WON 14-0 | WON 9-3 |
| | | |
| Scot.: 1g 2dg 6t | Ire.: nil | Eng.: 1g |
| Wales: nil | Scot.: 3g 1dg 2t | Scot.: 1dg 2g |
| | | |
| 7 Feb. 1891 | 21 Feb. 1891 | 7 Mar. 1891 |

Two pairs of brothers appeared in the Scottish fifteens of 1891. The Neilsons made their debuts against Wales and the Orrs, who had first appeared together in 1889, were key members of a side which won the Triple Crown for the first time. The former were Merchistonians who became Presidents of the SRU. W. Neilson was a noted barrister who enjoyed a long and successful life, while his brother became an ironmaster.

Scotland amassed 12 tries in their two opening games. Reporters seem to vary in their accounts of these matches, different scoring versions appearing in different newspapers. The details provided here are those given in the most reliable of the Scottish dailies, though it is amusing to note that the Cardiff press completely ignored one of the Scottish tries in the Welsh match!

The match at Richmond for the Triple Crown attracted 20,000. Clauss gave Scotland a super start, dropping a neat goal after eight minutes. Soon after the interval, Scotland went further ahead when J.E. Orr crossed at the posts for MacGregor to convert, and another try was obtained by W. Neilson following some intricate passing between Anderson and MacGregor, the outstanding Scottish backs.

## 1891-92

| v. WALES | v. IRELAND | v. ENGLAND |
|---|---|---|
| H.J. Stevenson | H.J. Stevenson | H.J. Stevenson |
| | | |
| P.R. Clauss | †J.C. Woodburn | P.R. Clauss |
| †G.T. Campbell 1t | G.T. Campbell | G.T. Campbell |
| W. Neilson | W. Neilson | W. Neilson |
| | | |
| *C.E. Orr | *C.E. Orr | *C.E. Orr |
| D.G. Anderson | W. Wotherspoon | D.G. Anderson |
| | | |
| F.W.J. Goodhue | F.W.J. Goodhue | F.W.J. Goodhue |
| J.D. Boswell 1t,1c | J.D. Boswell | J.D. Boswell |
| H.T.O. Leggatt | H.T.O. Leggatt | M.C. McEwan |
| G.T. Neilson | †N.F. Henderson | G.T. Neilson |
| J.E. Orr | J.E. Orr | J.E. Orr |
| A. Dalgleish | W.A. McDonald | W.A. McDonald |
| W.R. Gibson | W.R. Gibson | W.R. Gibson |
| †J.N. Millar | J.N. Millar 1t | J.N. Millar |
| R.G. MacMillan | R.G. MacMillan | R.G. MacMillan |
| | | |
| Swansea | Raeburn Place | Raeburn Place |
| WON 7-2 | WON 2-0 | LOST 0-5 |
| | | |
| Wales: 1t | Scot.: 1t | Scot.: nil |
| Scot.: 1g 1t | Ire.: nil | Eng.: 1g |
| | | |
| 6 Feb. 1892 | 20 Feb. 1892 | 5 Mar. 1892 |

Scotland were well off for forwards in 1892. Goodhue, Boswell, Leggatt, Orr, McEwan and MacMillan were automatic choices for a number of seasons, and the forwards were responsible for all but one of Scotland's scores this season.

Boswell was the man-of-the-match at Swansea. Educated at Loretto, Rugby and Oxford, he had an unusual talent for dropping goals and was a very accurate place-kicker. His barnstorming play resulted in the equalising score against Wales, and he converted another try later in the match to increase Scotland's lead. Boswell later captained the team, became a Writer to the Signet, and was President of the SRU in 1898-9.

The Irish match ended in a snow-storm. Boswell dropped a goal which the referee disallowed, and in the end Scotland were lucky to win by a single try by yarn merchant John Millar. England beat Scotland in the Triple Crown match, one noted for the frequent stoppages for players to receive attentions to injuries, some caused by rough play.

## 1892-93

| v. WALES | v. IRELAND | v. ENGLAND |
|---|---|---|
| A.W.C. CAMERON | H.J. STEVENSON | H.J. STEVENSON |
| †D.D. ROBERTSON | G.T. CAMPBELL | G.T. CAMPBELL 1DG |
| G. MacGREGOR | G. MacGREGOR | G. MacGREGOR |
| †J.J. GOWANS | W. NEILSON | W. NEILSON |
| †R.C. GREIG | †J.W. SIMPSON | J.W. SIMPSON |
| W. WOTHERSPOON | †W.P. DONALDSON | W. WOTHERSPOON |
| †H.F. MENZIES | H.F. MENZIES | H.T.O. LEGGATT |
| †T.L. HENDRY | T.L. HENDRY | T.L. HENDRY |
| H.T.O. LEGGATT | *J.D. BOSWELL | *J.D. BOSWELL 1DG |
| G.T. NEILSON | †J.M. BISHOP | †R.S. DAVIDSON |
| †W.B. COWNIE | W.B. COWNIE | W.B. COWNIE |
| A. DALGLEISH | J.E. ORR | J.E. ORR |
| W.R. GIBSON | W.R. GIBSON | W.R. GIBSON |
| J.N. MILLAR | †D. FISHER | †T.M. SCOTT |
| *R.G. MacMILLAN | †J.R. FORD | R.G. MacMILLAN |
| Raeburn Place | Belfast | Leeds |
| LOST 0-9 | DRAWN 0-0 | WON 8-0 |
| SCOT.: NIL | IRE.: NIL | ENG.: NIL |
| WALES: 1PG 3T | SCOT.: NIL | SCOT.: 2DG |
| 4 Feb. 1893 | 18 Feb. 1893 | 4 Mar. 1893 |

Scotland were well beaten by the Welsh, who employed the four threequarter system to good effect, and there were five changes to the six backs before the second game of the season in Ireland. Up front, J.D. Boswell took over from MacMillan as captain, and altogether the Scottish selectors made eleven changes.

Awful weather reduced the Irish match to a muddy long-drawn-out battle between the forwards. The conditions made safe handling almost impossible and the backs were mainly required for defence. The Scottish backs fielded and cleared with surprising ease on the slippery surface and the new halves, Donaldson and Simpson, made splendid debuts. Simpson played for the Royal HSFP, but curiously was never a pupil of the school. He was educated at Dollar Academy, became a doctor in Edinburgh, and was President of the SRU in 1904-5. Donaldson had a rather chequered international career, appearing sporadically up to 1899. He was one of the first half-backs to perfect the screw kick back to touch, and was a rather dour player.

The only victory of the season was over England by two dropped goals. Boswell, described as "florid and stout almost to rotundity" dropped one of the goals, G.T. Campbell gaining the other.

## 1893-94

| v. WALES | v. IRELAND | v. ENGLAND |
|---|---|---|
| †J. ROGERSON | A.W.C. CAMERON | G. MacGREGOR |
| J.J. GOWANS | G. MacGREGOR | J.J. GOWANS |
| *G. MacGREGOR | W. WOTHERSPOON | W. NEILSON |
| G.T. CAMPBELL | G.T. CAMPBELL | G.T. CAMPBELL |
| †H.T.S. GEDGE | H.T.S. GEDGE | H.T.S. GEDGE |
| J.W. SIMPSON | J.W. SIMPSON | J.W. SIMPSON |
| W. WOTHERSPOON | W.P. DONALDSON | W. WOTHERSPOON |
| H.F. MENZIES | H.T.O. LEGGATT | H.T.O. LEGGATT |
| †J.B. WRIGHT | *J.D. BOSWELL | *J.D. BOSWELL 2T |
| †W.M.C. McEWAN | †A.H. ANDERSON | W.M.C. McEWAN |
| W.B. COWNIE | W.B. COWNIE | W.B. COWNIE |
| A. DALGLEISH | A. DALGLEISH | H.F. MENZIES |
| W.R. GIBSON | W.R. GIBSON | W.R. GIBSON |
| G.T. NEILSON | G.T. NEILSON | †W.G. NEILSON |
| R.G. MacMILLAN | R.G. MacMILLAN | R.G. MacMILLAN |
| Newport | Lansdowne Road | Raeburn Place |
| LOST 0-7 | LOST 0-5 | WON 6-0 |
| WALES: 1DG 1T | IRE.: 1G | SCOT.: 2T |
| SCOT.: NIL | SCOT.: NIL | ENG.: NIL |
| 3 Feb. 1894 | 24 Feb. 1894 | 17 Mar. 1894 |

Scotland joined the other Home Unions in employing four threequarters in 1894, but could not master the system and suffered defeats in Newport and Dublin. Scotland had often complained about the poor state of the playing surfaces on their biennial visits to Belfast to play Ireland, but the 1894 trip to Dublin marked Scotland's first visit to the south of the country. There, in beautiful weather, the destructive tactics of the Irish completely disrupted the rhythm of the Scottish backs, and Ireland deserved their narrow victory. Boswell, in his last season in the international side, nearly dropped a goal from a mark.

Boswell's career ended with a splendid win over England, the Scots' first Calcutta Cup triumph at home. Boswell scored the two tries which settled the match, led his forwards shrewdly, and set a fine individual example to the side.

London Scottish provided the four Scottish threequarters for the Welsh and English matches (though Gowans and Neilson were principally associated with Cambridge University during the season, while Gedge, then at Oxford, played for Edinburgh Wanderers during the Easter vacation). W.M.C. McEwan and W.G. Neilson, brothers of former caps, were capped as schoolboys. McEwan, who later played for South Africa, was a pupil of Edinburgh Academy; Neilson was at Merchiston.

## 1894-95

| v. WALES | v. IRELAND | v. ENGLAND |
|---|---|---|
| †A.R. SMITH 1c | A.R. SMITH | A.R. SMITH |
| | | |
| J.J. GOWANS 1t | J.J. GOWANS | J.J. GOWANS |
| W. NEILSON | W. NEILSON | W. NEILSON |
| G.T. CAMPBELL | G.T. CAMPBELL 1t | G.T. CAMPBELL |
| †R. WELSH | R. WELSH 1t | R. WELSH |
| | | |
| J.W. SIMPSON | J.W. SIMPSON | J.W. SIMPSON |
| †M. ELLIOT | P.R. CLAUSS | W.P. DONALDSON |
| | | |
| †J.H. DODS | J.H. DODS | J.H. DODS |
| †H.O. SMITH | J.N. MILLAR | J.N. MILLAR |
| W.M.C. McEWAN | T.L. HENDRY | W.M.C. McEWAN |
| W.B. COWNIE | W.B. COWNIE | W.B. COWNIE |
| T.M. SCOTT | T.M. SCOTT | T.M. SCOTT |
| *W.R. GIBSON | W.R. GIBSON | W.R. GIBSON |
| G.T. NEILSON | G.T. NEILSON | G.T. NEILSON 1t,1pg |
| R.G. MacMILLAN | *R.G. MacMILLAN | *R.G. MacMILLAN |
| | | |
| Raeburn Place | Raeburn Place | Richmond |
| WON 5-4 | WON 6-0 | WON 6-3 |
| | | |
| SCOT.: 1G | SCOT.: 2T | ENG.: 1PG |
| WALES: 1GM | IRE.: NIL | SCOT.: 1PG 1T |
| | | |
| 26 Jan. 1895 | 2 Mar. 1895 | 9 Mar. 1895 |

R.G. MacMillan, a 29-year-old former pupil of Merchiston, led Scotland to their second Triple Crown in 1895. MacMillan was a leading forward of the London Scottish side, whom he also captained, and had settled in the south after becoming an underwriter with Lloyd's of London. His side contained a good blend of youth and experience and few changes were made in the three matches.

Both Wales and Ireland were beaten with little difficulty and the Calcutta Cup match was billed as the showdown of the season, the two sides searching for the Triple Crown. There had been slight anxiety over one of the Scottish half-back positions, and following the Irish match, Clauss lost his place to Donaldson.

In a match confined to the forwards it was the superior fitness of the Scots which proved crucial in the closing stages. They were impressive in combined play, with the forwards favouring the classic Scottish dribbling tactics. And Donaldson was the perfect foil to his pack, preserving their fitness with some astute tactical kicking.

The penalty goal by George Neilson was Scotland's first in an international match.

## 1895-96 / 1896-97

| v. WALES | v. IRELAND | v. ENGLAND | v. IRELAND | v. ENGLAND |
|---|---|---|---|---|
| A.R. SMITH | A.R. SMITH | G. MacGREGOR | A.R. SMITH | A.R. SMITH |
| | | | | |
| G.T. CAMPBELL | G.T. CAMPBELL | G.T. CAMPBELL | G.T. CAMPBELL | †A.M. BUCHER 1t |
| †A.B. TIMMS | J.J. GOWANS | J.J. GOWANS 1t | W. NEILSON | W. NEILSON |
| †T. SCOTT | †C.J.N. FLEMING | C.J.N. FLEMING 1t | C.J.N. FLEMING | †A.W. ROBERTSON |
| R. WELSH | W. NEILSON | H.T.S. GEDGE 1t | T. SCOTT | T. SCOTT |
| | | | | |
| J.W. SIMPSON | J.W. SIMPSON | M. ELLIOT | R.C. GREIG | J.W. SIMPSON |
| †D. PATTERSON | W.P. DONALDSON | W.P. DONALDSON | M. ELLIOT | M. ELLIOT |
| | | | | |
| J.H. DODS | J.H. DODS | J.H. DODS | J.H. DODS | J.H. DODS |
| H.O. SMITH | H.O. SMITH | H.O. SMITH | †A.S. LAIDLAW | A. BALFOUR |
| W.M.C. McEWAN | W.M.C. McEWAN | W.M.C. McEWAN | W.M.C. McEWAN | W.M.C. McEWAN |
| †J.H. COUPAR | J.H. COUPAR | T.M. SCOTT 1c | T.M. SCOTT 1pg,1c | T.M. SCOTT |
| T.M. SCOTT | †G.O. TURNBULL | G.O. TURNBULL | G.O. TURNBULL 1t | G.O. TURNBULL |
| †M.C. MORRISON | M.C. MORRISON | M.C. MORRISON | M.C. MORRISON | M.C. MORRISON |
| *G.T. NEILSON | *G.T. NEILSON | *G.T. NEILSON | †R.C. STEVENSON | R.C. STEVENSON |
| †A. BALFOUR | A. BALFOUR | A. BALFOUR | *R.G. MacMILLAN | *R.G. MacMILLAN |
| | | | | |
| Cardiff Arms Park | Lansdowne Road | Hampden Park | Powderhall Gds | Manchester |
| LOST 0-6 | DRAWN 0-0 | WON 11-0 | WON 8-3 | LOST 3-12 |
| | | | | |
| WALES: 2T | IRE.: NIL | SCOT.: 1G 2T | SCOT.: 1G 1PG | ENG.: 1G 1DG 1T |
| SCOT.: NIL | SCOT.: NIL | ENG.: NIL | IRE.: 1T | SCOT.: 1T |
| | | | | |
| 25 Jan. 1896 | 15 Feb. 1896 | 14 Mar. 1896 | 20 Feb. 1897 | 13 Mar. 1897 |

Scotland placed an experimental fifteen in the field for the match with Wales, sending six new caps down to Cardiff. The pack was less experienced than in previous seasons, though Mark Morrison was a forward destined for greatness. Altogether he was to play in 23 internationals, captaining the side on fifteen occasions – a Scottish record which lasted for seventy years. Strong and resolute, he was first capped as an 18-year-old.

Scotland's best performance of 1896 was against England. Their marauding forwards wheeled the English in the scrummages, dribbled at speed in the open, and created enough good possession for their threequarters to secure three splendid tries.

Only two matches were played in 1897, the SRU refusing to play the Welsh. The Welsh Union had endorsed a fund set up to present to their star player, Arthur Gould, who was about to retire. The Scots objected to the action, claiming it as an act of professionalism.

Alex Laidlaw, capped against Ireland in 1897, became the first Scottish international to join the Northern Union. A stonemason, he signed professional for Bradford two years after gaining his cap.

| 1897-98 | | 1898-99 | | |
| v. IRELAND | v. ENGLAND | v. IRELAND | v. WALES | v. ENGLAND |
|---|---|---|---|---|
| †J.M. REID | J.M. REID | J.M. REID | †H. ROTTENBURG | H. ROTTENBURG |
| | | | | |
| †R.T. NEILSON | R.T. NEILSON | G.T. CAMPBELL | H.T.S. GEDGE 1DG,1T | H.T.S. GEDGE |
| †E. SPENCER | †T.A. NELSON | R.T. NEILSON | †G.A.W. LAMOND 1DG | G.A.W. LAMOND |
| *A.R. SMITH | *A.R. SMITH | †D.B. MONYPENNY | D.B. MONYPENNY 1T | D.B. MONYPENNY |
| T. SCOTT 2T | T. SCOTT | T. SCOTT | T. SCOTT | T. SCOTT |
| | | | | |
| †J.T. MABON | J.T. MABON | J.T. MABON | J.W. SIMPSON | J.W. SIMPSON |
| M. ELLIOT | M. ELLIOT | *W.P. DONALDSON 1PG | R.T. NEILSON | †J.I. GILLESPIE 1T |
| | | | | |
| †A. MACKINNON | A. MACKINNON | A. MACKINNON | A. MACKINNON | A. MACKINNON |
| H.O. SMITH | H.O. SMITH | H.O. SMITH | H.O. SMITH 1T | H.O. SMITH |
| W.M.C. MCEWAN | W.M.C. MCEWAN 1T | W.M.C. MCEWAN | W.M.C. MCEWAN | W.M.C. MCEWAN |
| T.M. SCOTT 1C | T.M. SCOTT | J.H. COUPAR | †W.J. THOMSON 1GM | W.J. THOMSON 1C |
| †J.M. DYKES | J.M. DYKES | †L. HARVEY | J.M. DYKES | J.M. DYKES |
| M.C. MORRISON | M.C. MORRISON | M.C. MORRISON | R.C. STEVENSON | R.C. STEVENSON |
| †R. SCOTT | R.C. STEVENSON | R.C. STEVENSON | *M.C. MORRISON | *M.C. MORRISON |
| †G.C. KERR | G.C. KERR | G.C. KERR | G.C. KERR | G.C. KERR |
| | | | | |
| Belfast | Powderhall Gds. | Inverleith | Inverleith | Blackheath |
| WON 8-0 | DRAWN 3-3 | LOST 3-9 | WON 21-10 | WON 5-0 |
| | | | | |
| IRE.: NIL | SCOT.: 1T | SCOT.: 1PG | SCOT.: 1GM 2DG 3T | ENG.: NIL |
| SCOT.: 1G 1T | ENG.: 1T | IRE.: 3T | WALES: 2G | SCOT.: 1G |
| | | | | |
| 19 Feb. 1898 | 12 Mar. 1898 | 18 Feb. 1899 | 4 Mar. 1899 | 11 Mar. 1899 |

Scotland refused to play the Welsh again in 1898, fielded eight new caps for the match with Ireland, and ended an unbeaten season with a draw against England at the Powderhall Gardens, the scene of many famous sprint races.

Allan Smith was Scotland's captain for 1898. As a full-back he had been an outstanding tackler with an exceptional reach and a long kick. The Scottish selectors, however, now decided to pick him as a centre, a position where he had had lesser experience (although as an Oxford undergraduate he had won a Blue on the wing). His defence proved as sound as usual and his rather awkward running style certainly deceived the Irish, for Smith was very hard to tackle and made several unexpected bursts.

The highlight of 1899 was the opening of Inverleith, Scotland's national ground. The Welsh match was postponed to March because of poor weather, so the Irish were the SRU's first guests at the ground. Although the Scots lost to the Irish, the season ended on a high note with wins over both Wales and England.

| 1899-1900 | | |
| v. WALES | v. IRELAND | v. ENGLAND |
|---|---|---|
| H. ROTTENBURG | H. ROTTENBURG | H. ROTTENBURG |
| | | |
| †J.E. CRABBIE | †W.H. WELSH | W.H. WELSH |
| A.B. TIMMS | A.B. TIMMS | G.T. CAMPBELL |
| †W.H. MORRISON | A.R. SMITH | A.R. SMITH |
| T. SCOTT | T. SCOTT | T. SCOTT |
| | | |
| †F.H. FASSON | J.T. MABON | J.I. GILLESPIE |
| J.I. GILLESPIE | R.T. NEILSON | R.T. NEILSON |
| | | |
| T.M. SCOTT | *T.M. SCOTT | A. MACKINNON |
| †F.W. HENDERSON | F.W. HENDERSON | H.O. SMITH |
| W.M.C. MCEWAN | †J.R.C. GREENLEES | W.M.C. MCEWAN |
| †D.R. BEDELL-SIVRIGHT | R. SCOTT | R. SCOTT |
| J.M. DYKES 1T | J.M. DYKES | †L.H.I. BELL |
| *M.C. MORRISON | †J.A. CAMPBELL | *M.C. MORRISON |
| W.J. THOMSON | †W.P. SCOTT | W.P. SCOTT |
| G.C. KERR | G.C. KERR | G.C. KERR |
| | | |
| St. Helen's | Lansdowne Road | Inverleith |
| LOST 3-12 | DRAWN 0-0 | DRAWN 0-0 |
| | | |
| WALES: 4T | IRE.: NIL | SCOT.: NIL |
| SCOT.: 1T | SCOT.: NIL | ENG.: NIL |
| | | |
| 27 Jan. 1900 | 24 Feb. 1900 | 10 Mar. 1900 |

Scotland failed to win a match in 1900, but had the unusual record of playing two consecutive scoreless draws. Allan Smith, who had been unavailable in 1898-99 due to a round-the-world tour, returned to win his last caps against Ireland and England. Smith then concentrated on an education career. He became a tutor at Borough Road Training College in London, was later appointed to HMI, and from 1908-26 he was the Headmaster of his former school, Loretto.

The side contained a number of veterans and eight others joined Smith in retirement at the end of the season. Among the leading players to stand down were G.T. Campbell, a gifted, speedy and resolute runner who finished with 17 caps, and R.T. Neilson, last of the four brothers to play for Scotland.

Most famous of the new men was D.R. Bedell-Sivright. He gained 22 caps and was one of the first Scottish forwards to play in the role of wing-forward. An amazing dribbler, he was relentless on the attack and sound in defence.

## 1900-01

| v. WALES | v. IRELAND | v. ENGLAND |
|---|---|---|
| †A.W. Duncan | A.W. Duncan | A.W. Duncan |
| | | |
| W.H. Welsh | W.H. Welsh 2t | W.H. Welsh 1t |
| A.B. Timms | A.B. Timms | A.B. Timms 1t |
| †P. Turnbull 1t | P. Turnbull | P. Turnbull |
| †A.N. Fell 1t | A.N. Fell | A.N. Fell 1t |
| | | |
| F.H. Fasson | F.H. Fasson | †R.M. Neill |
| J.I. Gillespie 2c,2t | J.I. Gillespie 1t | J.I. Gillespie 1t,3c |
| | | |
| †J. Ross | J. Ross | J. Ross |
| †A.B. Flett 1c | A.B. Flett | A.B. Flett |
| †A. Frew | A. Frew | A. Frew |
| D.R. Bedell-Sivright | D.R. Bedell-Sivright | D.R. Bedell-Sivright |
| J.M. Dykes | J.M. Dykes | J.M. Dykes |
| *M.C. Morrison | *M.C. Morrison | *M.C. Morrison |
| †R.S. Stronach | †F.P. Dods | R.S. Stronach |
| †J.A. Bell | J.A. Bell | J.A. Bell |
| | | |
| Inverleith | Inverleith | Blackheath |
| WON 18-8 | WON 9-5 | WON 18-3 |
| | | |
| SCOT.: 3G 1T | SCOT.: 3T | ENG.: 1T |
| WALES: 1G 1T | IRE.: 1G | SCOT.: 3G 1T |
| | | |
| 9 Feb. 1901 | 23 Feb. 1901 | 9 Mar. 1901 |

Eight new caps appeared at the start of the Scots' Triple Crown season. All of the backs and nine of the side against Wales were from Edinburgh clubs.

Welsh and Fell scored five tries on the wings. Fell, a New Zealander, was studying a postgraduate medicine course at Edinburgh University and was described as "fleet, graceful and finished" in a side which played spectacular football. At half-back, J.I. Gillespie understood the intricacies of the four threequarter game and practised the new combined game most effectively. A prolific scorer, he landed five goals and ran in four tries in the Triple Crown matches. Scotland used only 17 players during the season.

## 1901-02

| v. WALES | v. IRELAND | v. ENGLAND |
|---|---|---|
| A.W. Duncan | A.W. Duncan | A.W. Duncan |
| | | |
| W.H. Welsh 1t | W.H. Welsh | W.H. Welsh |
| A.B. Timms | †A.S. Drybrough | A.B. Timms |
| P. Turnbull | P. Turnbull | P. Turnbull |
| A.N. Fell | J.E. Crabbie | A.N. Fell 1t |
| | | |
| F.H. Fasson | R.M. Neill | F.H. Fasson |
| J.I. Gillespie 1c | J.I. Gillespie | †E.D. Simson |
| | | |
| †W.E. Kyle | W.E. Kyle | W.E. Kyle |
| A.B. Flett | A.B. Flett | H.O. Smith |
| J.R.C. Greenlees | J.R.C. Greenlees | J.R.C. Greenlees |
| D.R. Bedell-Sivright | D.R. Bedell-Sivright | D.R. Bedell-Sivright |
| J. Ross | †H.H. Bullmore | J.M. Dykes |
| *M.C. Morrison | *M.C. Morrison | *M.C. Morrison |
| †J.V. Bedell-Sivright | W.P. Scott | W.P. Scott |
| J.A. Bell | J.A. Bell | J.A. Bell |
| | | |
| Cardiff Park Arms | Belfast | Inverleith |
| LOST 5-14 | LOST 0-5 | LOST 3-6 |
| | | |
| WALES: 1G 3T | IRE.: 1G | SCOT.: 1T |
| SCOT.: 1G | SCOT.: NIL | ENG.: 2T |
| | | |
| 1 Feb. 1902 | 22 Feb. 1902 | 15 Mar. 1902 |

It was difficult to explain Scotland's demise in 1902. The nucleus of the young successful Triple Crown side remained, but injuries to the wings considerably reduced the side's scoring potential. The backs continued to play attractive football. Turnball ran and swerved with effortless ease while Timms, an Australian, was a finely balanced attacker who timed passes to perfection.

Welsh scored an outstanding try against Wales. Receiving the ball near half-way he glided past the defence to curve gently around behind the goal. Later in the English match he was the victim of a heavy tackle which ended his playing career. A doctor, he became President of the SRU in 1938-9 and died, in his 93rd year, in 1972.

Fell was injured against Wales and had to stand down for the visit to Belfast. He returned for the Calcutta Cup (when six of the backs were Edinburgh University men) and scored a sparkling try. But Scotland's defeat was the third of the season – Scotland's first whitewash in the Championship.

## 1902-03

| v. WALES | v. IRELAND | v. ENGLAND |
|---|---|---|
| †W.T. FORREST | W.T. FORREST | W.T. FORREST |
| | | |
| A.N. FELL | J.E. CRABBIE 1T | A.N. FELL |
| A.B. TIMMS 1PG | A.S. DRYBROUGH | A.B. TIMMS 1DG |
| †H.J. ORR | H.J. ORR | H.J. ORR |
| J.E. CRABBIE | †C. FRANCE | †J.S. MACDONALD |
| | | |
| †J. KNOX | J. KNOX | J. KNOX |
| E.D. SIMSON | E.D. SIMSON | E.D. SIMSON 1T |
| | | |
| W.E. KYLE 1T | W.E. KYLE | W.E. KYLE |
| †L. WEST | L. WEST | L. WEST |
| J.R.C. GREENLEES | J.R.C. GREENLEES | *J.R.C. GREENLEES |
| D.R. BEDELL-SIVRIGHT | D.R. BEDELL-SIVRIGHT | J. ROSS |
| †N. KENNEDY | N. KENNEDY | N. KENNEDY |
| *M.C. MORRISON | *M.C. MORRISON | †J.D. DALLAS 1T |
| W.P. SCOTT | W.P. SCOTT | W.P. SCOTT |
| †A.G. CAIRNS | A.G. CAIRNS | A.G. CAIRNS |
| | | |
| Inverleith | Inverleith | Richmond |
| WON 6-0 | WON 3-0 | WON 10-6 |
| | | |
| SCOT.: 1PG 1T | SCOT.: 1T | ENG.: 2T |
| WALES: NIL | IRE.: NIL | SCOT.: 1DG 2T |
| | | |
| 7 Feb. 1903 | 28 Feb. 1903 | 21 Mar. 1903 |

The Scots bounced back to win the Triple Crown in 1903. Among the six new caps in the victory over Wales was W.T. Forrest, a devastating tackler who enjoyed taking risks on the field. He was a Hawick player but later helped Kelso, his home town. A major in the KOSB, he was killed in action in Gaza in 1917.

The matches resulted in narrow wins, though the dazzling back play which had been features of Scotland's successes in 1901 was no longer apparent, and with the break up of the exciting Edinburgh University back division, Scotland now turned to their pack for inspiration.

Morrison, a seasoned campaigner and captain, had sterling support from established forwards such as Greenlees, Bedell-Sivright and Scott, and found new strength in the youth of West, Kyle and Cairns, players who were to hold their places for several seasons.

## 1903-04

| v. WALES | v. IRELAND | v. ENGLAND |
|---|---|---|
| W.T. FORREST | W.T. FORREST | W.T. FORREST |
| | | |
| †G.E. CRABBIE | A.B. TIMMS 1T | A.B. TIMMS |
| †L.M. MACLEOD | L.M. MACLEOD | L.M. MACLEOD |
| H.J. ORR 1T | H.J. ORR 1T | J.S. MACDONALD 1T |
| J.S. MACDONALD | J.S. MACDONALD 2C,1T | J.E. CRABBIE 1T |
| | | |
| E.D. SIMSON | E.D. SIMSON 1T | E.D. SIMSON |
| †A.A. BISSETT | J.I. GILLESPIE | J.I. GILLESPIE |
| | | |
| W.E. KYLE | W.E. KYLE | W.E. KYLE |
| G.O. TURNBULL | †J.B. WATERS | J.B. WATERS |
| †E.J. ROSS | †W.M. MILNE | W.M. MILNE |
| D.R. BEDELL-SIVRIGHT | D.R. BEDELL-SIVRIGHT 1T | D.R. BEDELL-SIVRIGHT |
| L.H.I. BELL | L.H.I. BELL | †H.N. FLETCHER |
| *M.C. MORRISON | *M.C. MORRISON | *M.C. MORRISON |
| W.P. SCOTT | W.P. SCOTT | W.P. SCOTT |
| A.G. CAIRNS | A.G. CAIRNS | A.G. CAIRNS |
| | | |
| St Helen's | Lansdowne Road | Inverleith |
| LOST 3-21 | WON 19-3 | WON 6-3 |
| | | |
| WALES: 3G 1PG 1T | IRE.: 1T | SCOT.: 2T |
| SCOT.: 1T | SCOT.: 2G 3T | ENG.: 1T |
| | | |
| 6 Feb. 1904 | 27 Feb. 1904 | 19 Mar. 1904 |

Mark Morrison, in his last year as an international, led Scotland to the Championship, despite a heavy defeat at the beginning of the season in Wales. Simson, Lewis MacLeod, Orr and J.S. MacDonald, a South African studying medicine at Edinburgh University, formed part of a good, fast back division which accounted for seven of Scotland's tries.

Four changes were made after the defeat at Swansea and the match with England was regarded as the most important game of the season. It turned out to be a protracted forward battle in which the Scots deserved their victory.

Scotland played with a stiff breeze in their favour in the first half and Gillespie and MacLeod combined to create a try for Crabbie after 15 minutes. (Crabbie's brother George, incidentally, had played against Wales.) England equalised early in the second half but MacDonald crossed for the winning try in the corner on the point of no-side, following a long period of Scottish pressure.

## 1904-05

| v. WALES | v. IRELAND | v. ENGLAND |
|---|---|---|
| W.T. Forrest | W.T. Forrest 1c | †D.G. Schulze |
| | | |
| J.E. Crabbie | †W.T. Ritchie | W.T. Richie |
| L.M. MacLeod | L.M. MacLeod | G.A.W. Lamond |
| †J.L. Forbes | A.B. Timms 1t | *A.B. Timms |
| J.S. MacDonald | †R. H. McCowat | †T. Elliot |
| | | |
| E.D. Simson | E.D. Simson | E.D. Simson 1t |
| †P. Munro | P. Munro | P. Munro |
| | | |
| W.E. Kyle | W.E. Kyle | W.E. Kyle |
| †A.W. Little 1t | L. West | L. West |
| W.M. Milne | W.M. Milne | †J.C. MacCallum |
| R.S. Stronach | R.S. Stronach | R.S. Stronach 1t |
| H.N. Fletcher | †M.R. Dickson | †H.G. Monteith |
| †A. Ross | A. Ross | A. Ross |
| *W.P. Scott | *W.P. Scott | W.P. Scott 1c |
| A.G. Cairns | A.G. Cairns | A.G. Cairns |
| Inverleith | Inverleith | Richmond |
| LOST 3-6 | LOST 5-11 | WON 8-0 |
| SCOT.: 1T | SCOT.: 1G | ENG.: NIL |
| WALES: 2T | IRE.: 1G 2T | SCOT.: 1G 1T |
| 4 Feb. 1905 | 25 Feb. 1905 | 18 Mar. 1905 |

W.P. Scott, a Glaswegian distiller, took over as captain in 1905, Morrison having retired to concentrate on his farming commitments. Scott's side included four new caps and was narrowly beaten by Wales in a match which marked the end of MacDonald's international career. He returned to Africa soon after leaving university and served as a doctor in the Southern Rhodesia Medical Service. Among the new men, Patrick Munro was destined to become one of Scotland's leading halves before World War I. He gained 13 caps, was praised as one of the finest all-weather players and was later the MP for Llandaff and Barry. He was killed while serving with the Home Guard in 1942.

E.D. Simson was the outstanding Scottish player of the season. A plucky defender, he possessed the ability to make the classic half-back break from the scrum, and scored several excellent tries in his international career. Against England he gathered the ball from a rush and skipped past his opposite number for the decisive score of the match. Simson was a doctor and died young in India.

There were four new caps for the English match. Schulze played 13 times to become Scotland's most-capped full-back before the war, Elliot was only the second Border back capped for Scotland, and Monteith and MacCallum played soundly on their debuts.

## 1905-06

| v. NZ | v. WALES | v. IRELAND | v. ENGLAND |
|---|---|---|---|
| †J.G. Scoular | J.G. Scoular | J.G. Scoular | J.G. Scoular |
| | | | |
| †T. Sloan | T. Sloan | A.B.H.L. Purves | A.B.H.L. Purves 1t |
| L.M. MacLeod | †W.C. Church | J.L. Forbes | J.L. Forbes |
| †K.G. MacLeod | K.G. MacLeod 1pg | †M.W. Walter | M.W. Walter |
| †J.T. Simson | †A.B.H.L. Purves | K G. MacLeod 1gm | K.G. MacLeod |
| | | | |
| E.D. Simson 1dg | E.D. Simson | E.D. Simson | E.D. Simson |
| P. Munro | P. Munro | P. Munro 1t | P. Munro |
| †L.L. Greig | | | |
| | H.G. Monteith | H.G. Monteith | H.G. Monteith |
| L. West | *L. West | *L. West | *L. West |
| J.C. MacCallum 1t | J.C. MacCallum | J.C. MacCallum 2c | J.C. MacCallum |
| *D.R. Bedell-Sivright | D.R. Bedell-Sivright | D.R. Bedell-Sivright 1t | D.R. Bedell-Sivright |
| W.E. Kyle | W.E. Kyle | W.E. Kyle | W.E. Kyle |
| †W.L. Russell | W.L. Russell | W.L. Russell | W.L. Russell |
| W.P. Scott | W.P. Scott | W.P. Scott | W.P. Scott |
| †J.M. Mackenzie | A.G. Cairns | A.G. Cairns | A.G. Cairns |
| Inverleith | Cardiff Arms Park | Lansdowne Road | Inverleith |
| LOST 7-12 | LOST 3-9 | WON 13-6 | LOST 3-9 |
| SCOT.: 1DG 1T | WALES: 3T | IRE.: 2T | SCOT.: 1T |
| NZ: 4T | SCOT.: 1PG | SCOT.: 2G 1GM | ENG.: 3T |
| 18 Nov. 1905 | 3 Feb. 1906 | 24 Feb. 1906 | 17 Mar. 1906 |

1905-06 was a disappointing season with just one win from four matches. The highlight of the winter was the encounter with the first New Zealand team, and Scotland gave the All Blacks an interesting contest.

The Scottish selectors had decided to counter the New Zealanders' unusual formation by fielding eight backs and seven new men were behind the scrum. Kenneth MacLeod was included alongside his brother. Kenneth was a mere teenager at the time but his lightning pace and powerful kicking impressed the tourists.

Scotland led for much of the game. Simson opened the scoring with a drop-goal and MacCallum scored a try from a rush just before the interval. L.M. MacLeod sustained an ankle injury but it was not until the closing ten minutes that New Zealand scored two tries to secure victory.

## 1906-07

| S. AFRICA | v. WALES | v. IRELAND | v. ENGLAND |
|---|---|---|---|
| J.G. SCOULAR | T. SLOAN | D.G. SCHULZE | D.G. SCHULZE |
| K.G. MACLEOD 1T | K.G. MACLEOD | K.G. MACLEOD | K.G. MACLEOD |
| T. SLOAN | †D.G. MACGREGOR | D.G. MACGREGOR | D.G. MACGREGOR |
| M.W. WALTER | M.W. WALTER | M.W. WALTER | T. SLOAN |
| A.B.H.L. PURVES 1T | A.B.H.L. PURVES 1T | A.B.H.L. PURVES 1T | A.B.H.L. PURVES 1T |
| *L.L. GREIG | E.D. SIMSON | E.D. SIMSON | E.D. SIMSON 1T |
| P. MUNRO | *L.L. GREIG | *P. MUNRO | *P. MUNRO |
| H.G. MONTEITH | H.G. MONTEITH 1T | H.G. MONTEITH | †J.M.B. SCOTT |
| †I.C. GEDDES | I.C. GEDDES | I.C. GEDDES 3C | I.C. GEDDES 1C |
| J.C. MACCALLUM | J.C. MACCALLUM | J.C. MACCALLUM | J.C. MACCALLUM |
| D.R. BEDELL-SIVRIGHT | D.R. BEDELL-SIVRIGHT | D.R. BEDELL-SIVRIGHT | D.R. BEDELL-SIVRIGHT |
| †G.M. FREW | G.M. FREW | G.M. FREW 1T | G.M. FREW |
| †L.M. SPIERS | L.M. SPIERS | L.M. SPIERS | L.M. SPIERS |
| W.P. SCOTT | W.P. SCOTT | W.P. SCOTT | W.P. SCOTT |
| †W.H. THOMSON | †G.A. SANDERSON | G.A. SANDERSON 1T | G.A. SANDERSON |
| Hampden Park | Inverleith | Inverleith | Blackheath |
| WON 6-0 | WON 6-3 | WON 15-3 | WON 8-3 |
| SCOT.: 2T | SCOT.: 2T | SCOT.: 3G | ENG.: 1T |
| SA: NIL | WALES: 1PG | IRE.: 1PG | SCOT.: 1G 1T |
| 17 Nov. 1906 | 2 Feb. 1907 | 23 Feb. 1907 | 16 Mar. 1907 |

A tight defence, a vigorous pack, and two wings of genuine pace were the chief factors in Scotland's marvellous run of success during 1906-07. The touring Springboks were beaten by two second-half tries on a muddy pitch at Hampden Park, and in front of a record crowd of 30,000. One of the tries was scored by K.G. MacLeod, following a cross-kick by Munro. Showing tremendous pace, K.G. caught the kick and raced through the mud for what the late E.H.D. Sewell described as an "impossible try".

MacLeod won ten caps before he was 21, might have played for Scotland as a schoolboy at Fettes had his headmaster given permission of the selectors to use the young pupil, but eventually gave up the game in 1908 following the sudden death from appendicitis of his brother Lewis.

The Triple Crown was added to the famous South Africa victory to give Scotland four wins from four matches. Alec Purves, playing on the left wing (another former pupil of Fettes), scored tries in each of the matches.

## 1907-08

| v. WALES | v. IRELAND | v. ENGLAND |
|---|---|---|
| D.G. SCHULZE | D.G. SCHULZE | D.G. SCHULZE 1DG |
| A.B.H.L. PURVES 1T | A.B.H.L. PURVES | A.B.H.L. PURVES 1DG |
| M.W. WALTER | M.W. WALTER | †C.M. GILRAY |
| T. SLOAN | K.G. MACLEOD 1PG,1C,1T | K.G. MACLEOD 2T |
| †H. MARTIN | H. MARTIN 1T | H. MARTIN |
| *L.L. GREIG | *L.L. GREIG | †J. ROBERTSON |
| †G. CUNNINGHAM | G. CUNNINGHAM | †A.L. WADE |
| D.R. BEDELL-SIVRIGHT | D.R. BEDELL-SIVRIGHT | W.E. KYLE |
| J.C. MACCALLUM | J.C. MACCALLUM | J.C. MACCALLUM |
| L.M. SPIERS | L.M. SPIERS | L.M. SPIERS |
| I.C. GEDDES 1C | †J.S. WILSON | *I.C. GEDDES 1C |
| †G.C. GOWLLAND | G.A. SANDERSON | H.G. MONTEITH |
| J.M.B. SCOTT | J.M.B. SCOTT | J.M.B. SCOTT |
| †J.A. BROWN | J.A. BROWN | †A.L. ROBERTSON |
| G.M. FREW | G.M. FREW | G.M. FREW |
| St. Helen's | Lansdowne Road | Inverleith |
| LOST 5-6 | LOST 11-16 | WON 16-10 |
| WALES: 2T | IRE.: 2G 2T | SCOT.: 1G 2DG 1T |
| SCOT.: 1G | SCOT.: 1G 1PG 1T | ENG.: 2G |
| 1 Feb. 1908 | 29 Feb. 1908 | 21 Mar. 1908 |

Purves' try in the opening game of 1908 gave him an unusual record for Scotland: he had scored tries in six consecutive matches stretching back to the English game of 1906. Scotland could not retain the Championship due to a narrow defeat at Swansea, though reports indicate that both Purves and Walter should have gained tries against the Welshmen.

Louis Greig, a brilliant all-round half, captained the Scots again at the start of the season. A Naval officer, he was one of the first United Services players to gain international recognition, though in the years preceding the first war the Services were to find an increasing number of their men capped by the Home Countries. Greig was later awarded a KBE.

The only win of the season, against England, was memorable for a late drop-goal by Schulze. The lead changed several times during the game and Scotland were just 12-10 ahead when Schulze kicked the decisive goal.

## 1908-09

| v. WALES | v. IRELAND | v. ENGLAND |
|---|---|---|
| D.G. Schulze | D.G. Schulze | D.G. Schulze |
| H. Martin | J.T. Simson | H. Martin |
| C.M. Gilray | T. Sloan | C.M. Gilray 1t |
| †A.W. Angus | †J. Pearson | J.Pearson |
| J.T. Simson | †R.H. Lindsay-Watson 1t | J.T. Simson 1t |
| G. Cunningham 1pg | J.M. Tennent | *G. Cunningham 3c |
| †J.M. Tennent | †J.R. McGregor 1t | J.M. Tennent 2t |
| W.E. Kyle | W.E. Kyle 1t | W.E. Kyle |
| J.C. MacCallum | J.C. MacCallum | J.C. MacCallum |
| A. Ross | A. Ross | †J. Reid-Kerr |
| J.S. Wilson | †C.D. Stuart | †A.R. Moodie |
| G.C. Gowlland | †W.E. Lely | G.C. Gowlland |
| *J.M.B. Scott | *J.M.B. Scott | J.M.B. Scott |
| J.M. Mackenzie | J.M. Mackenzie | J.M. Mackenzie |
| G.M. Frew | G.M. Frew | G.M. Frew |
| Inverleith | Inverleith | Richmond |
| LOST 3-5 | WON 9-3 | WON 18-8 |
| SCOT.: 1PG | SCOT.: 3T | ENG.: 1G 1T |
| WALES: 1G | IRE.: 1PG | SCOT.: 3G 1T |
| 6 Feb. 1909 | 27 Feb. 1909 | 20 Mar. 1909 |

Scotland were runners-up to Wales in the Championship of 1909. A poor match in which several Scots were in the wars was lost to Wales after George Cunningham had given Scotland the lead with a penalty goal early in the second half. But from a period of sustained pressure Wales scored their winning try and conversion, ten minutes before no-side.

Ireland were well-beaten but a dispute with the RFU concerning the payment of expenses to the touring Wallabies placed the Calcutta Cup match in jeopardy. The Scots had refused to meet the tourists and objected to the fact that they had received three shillings in daily expenses. Happily the dispute was resolved in time for the game to go ahead and Cunningham, the Scottish captain, spearheaded his side to a convincing victory.

Sir George Cunningham, as he became, was one of the first Scottish international halves to specialise at fly-half. In 1911 he entered the Indian Civil Service after playing in eight international matches.

## 1909-10

| v. FRANCE | v. WALES | v. IRELAND | v. ENGLAND |
|---|---|---|---|
| †F.G. Buchanan | D.G. Schulze | D.G. Schulze | D.G. Schulze |
| J.T. Simson | J.T. Simson | †D.G. Macpherson | D.G. Macpherson 1t |
| A.W. Angus 1t | A.W. Angus | M.W. Walter 2t | A.W. Angus |
| J. Pearson | J. Pearson | J. Pearson | J. Pearson |
| †I.P.M. Robertson 2t | †W.R. Sutherland | †J.D. Dobson 1t | W.R. Sutherland |
| *G. Cunningham | J.M. Tennent | *G. Cunningham | *G. Cunningham |
| J.M. Tennent 3t | †E. Milroy | †A.B. Lindsay | J.M. Tennent |
| †R.C. Stevenson | W.E. Kyle | R.C. Stevenson | R.C. Stevenson |
| J.C. MacCallum 3c | J.C. MacCallum | J.C. MacCallum 1c | J.C. MacCallum 1c |
| L.M. Spiers | L.M. Spiers | †C.H. Abercrombie | C.H. Abercrombie |
| C.D. Stuart | C.D. Stuart | C.D. Stuart 1t | C.D. Stuart |
| G.C. Gowlland 1t | G.C. Gowlland | G.C. Gowlland | G.C. Gowlland |
| J.M.B. Scott | J.M.B. Scott | J.M.B. Scott | J.M.B. Scott |
| A.R. Moodie | J.M. Mackenzie | J.M. Mackenzie | J.M. Mackenzie |
| G.M. Frew | *G.M. Frew | G.M. Frew | L.M. Spiers |
| Inverleith | Cardiff Arms Park | Belfast | Inverleith |
| WON 27-0 | LOST 0-14 | WON 14-0 | LOST 5-14 |
| SCOT.: 3G 4T | WALES: 1G 3T | IRE.: NIL | SCOT.: 1G |
| FR.: NIL | SCOT.: NIL | SCOT.: 1G 3T | ENG.: 1G 3T |
| 22 Jan. 1910 | 5 Feb. 1910 | 26 Feb. 1910 | 19 Mar. 1910 |

Scotland opened the season with their first international against France. Although the side is regarded as a full Scotland team the SRU did not award caps to the players. Nevertheless, the match has always been included in international records and for the purpose of uniformity with the other Home Unions, the players participating are duly recognised in this book of records.

The Watsonians club, one of the strongest in Scotland at the time, supplied the entire threequarter line. From 1909 until the war hardly a Scottish side took the field without either Pearson or Angus as one of the centres, though Simson and Robertson had to be content with fewer international appearances.

Angus was a resolute runner whose 18 matches for Scotland spanned twelve seasons. He played after the war as captain, his alertness and capacity to take the stray chance unaltered by his increasing years. Pearson was a smaller man, a secure handler, and an excellent cricketer too. He joined the Army in August 1914 and left for the Front on his 26th birthday in February 1915. A Private in the 9th Royal Scots, he fell in action at Hooge, Belgium, less than three months later.

## 1910-11

| v. FRANCE | v. WALES | v. IRELAND | v. ENGLAND |
|---|---|---|---|
| †H.B. Tod | D.G. Schulze | †A. Greig | C. Ogilvy |
| W.R. Sutherland | †D.M. Grant | D.M. Grant | †S.S.L. Steyn |
| F.G. Buchanan | F.G. Buchanan | †C. Ogilvy | †R.F. Simson 1t |
| A.W. Angus | A.W. Angus | A.W. Angus 1t | G. Cunningham 1c |
| J. Pearson 1dg | †J.M. Macdonald | J.T. Simson 1t | W.R. Sutherland 1t |
| *P. Munro 1t | *P. Munro 1dg | *P. Munro 1dg | †J.Y.M. Henderson |
| †F.L. Osler | F.L. Osler | A.B. Lindsay | E. Milroy |
| R.C. Stevenson | R.C. Stevenson | R.C. Stevenson | †D.McL. Bain |
| †F.H. Turner 1c | F.H. Turner 1t | F.H. Turner | F.H. Turner |
| †R. Fraser | R. Fraser | R. Fraser | R. Fraser |
| C.H. Abercrombie 1t | C.H. Abercrombie | C.D. Stuart | C.D. Stuart |
| †A.M. Stevenson | †A.R. Ross | G.M. Frew | G.M. Frew |
| J.M.B. Scott | J.M.B. Scott 1t | J.M.B. Scott | †W.R. Hutchison |
| A.R. Moodie | J.M. Mackenzie | J.M. Mackenzie | †J. Dobson |
| J.C. MacCallum 1t | A.L. Robertson | J.C. MacCallum | *J.C. MacCallum |
| Stade Colombes | Inverleith | Inverleith | Twickenham |
| LOST 15-16 | LOST 10-32 | LOST 10-16 | LOST 8-13 |
| FR.: 2G 2T | SCOT.: 1DG 2T | SCOT.: 1DG 2T | ENG.: 2G 1T |
| SCOT.: 1G 1DG 2T | WALES: 2G 1DG 6T | IRE.: 2G 2T | SCOT.: 1G 1T |
| 2 Jan. 1911 | 4 Feb. 1911 | 25 Feb. 1911 | 18 Mar. 1911 |

1911 was a season of unmitigated disaster. For a start there was the humiliation of defeat against the young French in Paris, and this was followed by Scotland's heaviest defeat (until then) by Wales, at Inverleith. The remaining matches were also lost, leaving Scotland with four losses from four games for the first time.

Sixteen new internationals were used in the four games, and only F.H. Turner was to win more than a dozen selections for his country, though David Bain played eleven games before war intervened. Both Turner and Bain were among the numerous Scottish casualties of war. Bain was a captain in the Gordon Highlanders who fell in action near Festubert in 1915; Turner was killed in the trenches near Kemmel in the same year.

The Calcutta Cup match was Scotland's first trip to Twickenham. It is recorded that some of the visiting players were unable to find the ground entrance and had to walk through allotments to gain access!

## 1911-12

| v. FRANCE | v. WALES | v. IRELAND | v. ENGLAND |
|---|---|---|---|
| †W.M. Dickson | W.M. Dickson | C. Ogilvy | W.M. Dickson |
| W.R. Sutherland 2t | W.R. Sutherland | S.S.L. Steyn | W.R. Sutherland 1t |
| A.W. Angus | A.W. Angus | A.W. Angus | †W. Burnet |
| J. Pearson 1pg,1t | J. Pearson | C.M. Gilray | A.W. Angus |
| †J.G. Will 1t | J.G. Will 2t | J.G. Will 1t | J.G. Will |
| †A.W. Gunn 1t | A.W. Gunn | A.W. Gunn | †J.L. Boyd |
| †J. Hume | E. Milroy | E. Milroy | E. Milroy |
| *J.C. MacCallum | *J.C. MacCallum | *J.C. MacCallum 1c | *J.C. MacCallum 1c |
| †R.D. Robertson | A.L. Robertson | A.L. Robertson | A.L. Robertson |
| †W.D.C.L. Purves | W.D.C.L. Purves | W.D.C.L. Purves | †C.M. Usher 1t |
| †D.D. Howie | D.D. Howie | D.D. Howie | D.D. Howie |
| D.McL. Bain | D.McL. Bain | C.C.P. Hill | D.McL. Bain |
| †C.C.P. Hill | J.M.B. Scott | J.M.B. Scott | J.M.B. Scott |
| J. Dobson | J. Dobson | J. Dobson | J. Dobson |
| F.H. Turner 1t,5c | F.H. Turner | F.H. Turner 1t | F.H. Turner |
| Inverleith | St. Helens | Lansdowne Road | Inverleith |
| WON 31-3 | LOST 6-21 | LOST 8-10 | WON 8-3 |
| SCOT.: 5G 1PG 1T | WALES: 2G 2DG 1T | IRE.: 1DG 1PG 1T | SCOT.: 1G 1T |
| FR.: 1T | SCOT.: 2T | SCOT.: 1G 1T | ENG.: 1T |
| 20 Jan. 1912 | 3 Feb. 1912 | 24 Feb. 1912 | 16 Mar. 1912 |

Scotland selected eight new players for the French match of 1912. For a number of years before the war the SRU regarded the encounter with France as an extra trial match for the internationals with the Home Countries. One of the new men, J.G. Will, was a very fast, determined runner who scored tries in each of his first three internationals. Turner converted five of the tries against the French to set a new Scottish record.

The side was captained by J.C. MacCallum, who was one of the strongest all-round Scottish forwards of the era. Described as a "gifted player", he played the last of his 26 internationals against England this season, passing the cap record previously held by W.E. Maclagan.

Scotland ended the year with an exciting win over England. Charles Usher scored the winning try on his debut, and MacCallum bowed out of the Scottish side by converting and completing the scoring.

## 1912-13

| v. S. AFRICA | v. FRANCE | v. WALES | v. IRELAND | v. ENGLAND |
|---|---|---|---|---|
| W.M. Dickson | W.M. Dickson | W.M. Dickson | W.M. Dickson | †W.M. Wallace |
| W.R. Sutherland | †W.A. Stewart 3t | W.A. Stewart | W.A. Stewart 4t | †J.B. Sweet |
| A.W. Angus | A.W. Angus | A.W. Angus | J. Pearson | J. Pearson |
| A.W. Gunn | †R.E. Gordon 2t | R.E. Gordon | R.E. Gordon | †E.G. Loudoon-Shand |
| J. Pearson | W.R. Sutherland | W.R. Sutherland | W.R. Sutherland | W.R. Sutherland |
| J.L. Boyd | A.W. Gunn | †J.H. Bruce-Lockhart | †T.C. Bowie 1t | T.C. Bowie |
| E. Milroy | E. Milroy | E. Milroy | E. Milroy | E. Milroy |
| †P.C.B. Blair | P.C.B. Blair | P.C.B. Blair | P.C.B. Blair | P.C.B. Blair |
| A.L. Robertson | †G.A. Ledingham | A.L. Robertson | A.L. Robertson | A.L. Robertson |
| W.D.C.L. Purves | C.M. Usher | C.M. Usher | C.M. Usher 1t | C.M. Usher |
| D.D. Howie | D.D. Howie | D.D. Howie | W.D.C.L. Purves 1t | W.D.C.L. Purves |
| D.McL. Bain | D.McL. Bain | D.McL. Bain | D.McL. Bain | D.McL. Bain |
| J.M.B. Scott | †J.B. McDougall | J.M.B. Scott | J.M.B. Scott | J.M.B. Scott |
| J. Dobson | C.H. Abercrombie | C.H. Abercrombie | †G.H.H.P. Maxwell | G.H.H.P. Maxwell |
| *F.H. Turner | *F.H. Turner 3c | *F.H. Turner | *F.H. Turner 4c | *F.H. Turner |
| Inverleith LOST 0-16 | Parc des Princes WON 21-3 | Inverleith LOST 0-8 | Inverleith WON 29-14 | Twickenham LOST 0-3 |
| SCOT.: NIL SA: 2G 2T | FR.: 1T SCOT.: 3G 2T | SCOT.: NIL WALES: 1G 1T | SCOT.: 4G 3T IRE.: 2G 1DG | ENG.: 1T SCOT.: NIL |
| 23 Nov. 1912 | 1 Jan. 1913 | 1 Feb. 1913 | 22 Feb. 1913 | 15 Mar. 1913 |

Freddie Turner was Scotland's captain in the five matches of 1912-13. The Springboks, making their second trip to Scotland, won comfortably at Inverleith, thus avenging the defeat at Hampden Park in 1906.

W.A. Stewart, a Tasmanian born at Launceston, burst onto the scene in the game with France, scoring three tries on the wing. But the match was marred by the riotous reaction of the French crowd to some of the decisions made by the English referee, Mr Baxter. The Scots refused to play the French the following season and the series did not continue until 1920.

There is an amusing story concerning the Scottish full-back Dickson, who appeared in this game. Dickson was quite deaf and misinterpreted the French reaction to be a sporting appreciation of Scotland's play! As a full-back he was not so easy to mislead: he was sound and clever in defence and a splendid kicker. A keen motor-sport enthusiast, he occasionally raced at Brooklands. After joining the Argyll and Sutherland Highlanders to serve in France, he was killed in action at the front in September 1915.

## 1913-14

| v. WALES | v. IRELAND | v. ENGLAND |
|---|---|---|
| W.M. Wallace | W.M. Wallace | W.M. Wallace |
| J.G. Will | J.G. Will | J.G. Will 2t |
| W.R. Sutherland | †J.R. Warren | A.W. Angus |
| †R.M. Scobie | R.M. Scobie | R.M. Scobie |
| W.A. Stewart 1t | J.B. Sweet | †J.L. Huggan 1t |
| †A.T. Sloan | T.C. Bowie | T.C. Bowie 1dg |
| †A.S. Hamilton | *E. Milroy | *E. Milroy |
| †A.M. Stewart | A.D. Laing | A.D. Laing |
| †A.D. Laing 1c | F.H. Turner | F.H. Turner 1c |
| †A. Wemyss | A. Weymss | C.M. Usher |
| A.R. Ross | A.R. Ross | A.R. Ross |
| *D.McL. Bain | D.McL. Bain | †I.M. Pender |
| †A.W. Symington | J.B.McDougall | A.W. Symington |
| G.H.H.P. Maxwell | G.H.H.P. Maxwell | G.H.H.P. Maxwell |
| †D.G. Donald | D.G. Donald | †E.T. Young |
| Cardiff Arms Park LOST 5-24 | Lansdowne Road LOST 0-6 | Inverleith LOST 15-16 |
| WALES:2G 2DG 1PG 1T SCOT.: 1G | IRE.: 2T SCOT.: NIL | SCOT.: 1G 1DG 2T ENG.: 2G 2T |
| 7 Feb. 1914 | 28 Feb. 1914 | 21 Mar. 1914 |

Scotland were defeated in all three matches in 1914, there being no game with the French. Eight new caps were awarded at the start of the season but the side failed miserably against Wales and several changes were necessary for the Irish match. Only six players retained their places for the three matches.

Andrew "Jock" Wemyss won his cap against Wales. In later years he was a distinguished writer and broadcaster on rugby football and one of the committee members of the Barbarians club. Despite losing an eye in the war, he continued playing for Scotland in the 1920s, along with other 1914 caps A.W. Angus, A.T. Sloan, A.S. Hamilton, J.B. McDougall, C.M. Usher, A.D. Laing, J. Hume, and G.H.H.P. Maxwell.

The match at Inverleith was very exciting, England winning by a single point. Scotland at last found a settled pack and with Turner hooking accurately the backs received their best possession of the season and the wings ran in three tries.

## 1919-20

| v. FRANCE | v. WALES | v. IRELAND | v. ENGLAND |
|---|---|---|---|
| †G.L. Pattullo | G.L. Pattullo | G.L. Pattullo | G.L. Pattullo |
| | | | |
| †G.B. Crole 1t | G.B. Crole | G.B. Crole 2t | G.B. Crole |
| †E.C. Fahmy | E.C. Fahmy | A.T. Sloan | J.H. Bruce-Lockhart 1dg |
| *A.W. Angus | A.W. Angus | A.W. Angus 1t | A.W. Angus |
| A.T. Sloan | †E.B. Mackay | †A. Browning 1t | A.T. Sloan |
| | | | |
| A.S. Hamilton | A.T. Sloan 1t | E.C. Fahmy | E.C. Fahmy |
| J. Hume | †J.A.R. Selby | J.A.R. Selby | †C.S. Nimmo |
| | | | |
| †F. Kennedy | F. Kennedy 2pg | F. Kennedy 1pg,2c | F. Kennedy |
| †R.A. Gallie | R.A. Gallie | R.A. Gallie | R.A. Gallie |
| †D.D. Duncan | D.D. Duncan | D.D. Duncan | D.D. Duncan |
| †W.A.K. Murray | †N.C. Macpherson | N.C. Macpherson | N.C. Macpherson |
| A.D. Laing 1c | A.D. Laing | A.D. Laing | G.H.H.P. Maxwell |
| †G. Thom | G. Thom | G. Thom | A. Wemyss |
| C.M. Usher | *C.M. Usher | *C.M. Usher | *C.M. Usher |
| A. Wemyss | G.H.H.P. Maxwell | W.A.K. Murray | G. Thom |
| | | | |
| Parc des Princes | Inverleith | Inverleith | Twickenham |
| won 5-0 | won 9-5 | won 19-0 | lost 4-13 |
| | | | |
| Fr.: nil | Scot.: 2pg 1t | Scot.: 2g 1pg 2t | Eng.: 2g 1t |
| Scot.: 1g | Wales: 1g | Ire.: nil | Scot.: 1dg |
| | | | |
| 1 Jan. 1920 | 7 Feb. 1920 | 28 Feb. 1920 | 20 Mar. 1920 |

Scotland recovered fairly quickly after the Armistice, despite the fact that six of those who had appeared in the last match of 1914 were killed in action. Three matches were won but Scotland fell to England at the last hurdle to the Triple Crown, and the Championship was thus shared with the Welsh and English.

Charles Usher, one of several pre-war caps, succeeded Angus as captain for the Welsh game. Born in Wimbledon, he was educated at Merchiston and the Royal Military Academy before leading an Army career. He was a typical Scottish forward, skilful and conscientious in the scrum, dashing in the loose, and a clever dribbler. He died in 1981, in his 90th year.

G.H.H.P. Maxwell, another pre-war cap to return to the side in 1920, was one of the largest forwards to play for Scotland before modern times. He measured over 6 ft and his weight exceeded 16 stones. He played 13 times between 1913 and 1922 and was noted for his remarkable kicking powers.

## 1920-21

| v. FRANCE | v. WALES | v. IRELAND | v. ENGLAND |
|---|---|---|---|
| †H.H. Forsayth | H.H. Forsayth | H.H. Forsayth | H.H. Forsayth |
| | | | |
| †J.H. Carmichael | A.T. Sloan 1t | †J.W.S. McCrow | A.T. Sloan |
| †A.L. Gracie | A.L. Gracie | A.L. Gracie | †C.J.G. Mackenzie |
| †A.E. Thomson | A.E. Thomson 1t | A.T. Sloan | A.E. Thomson |
| †I.J. Kilgour | J.H. Carmichael | J.H. Carmichael | A.L. Gracie |
| | | | |
| *A.T. Sloan | †R.L.H. Donald | R.L.H. Donald | R.L.H. Donald |
| J. Hume | *J. Hume | *J. Hume 2t | *J. Hume |
| | | | |
| R.A. Gallie | R.S. Cumming | R.A. Gallie | R.A. Gallie |
| †R.S. Cumming | †J.C.R. Buchanan 1t | J.C.R. Buchanan | J.C.R. Buchanan |
| †J.M. Bannerman | J.M. Bannerman | J.M. Bannerman | J.M. Bannerman |
| J.B. McDougall | R.A. Gallie | J.B. McDougall | J.B. McDougall |
| A.D. Laing | †G. Douglas | G.H.H.P. Maxwell 1c | F. Kennedy |
| W.A.K. Murray | C.M. Usher | †J.L. Stewart | C.M. Usher |
| G.H.H.P. Maxwell | †J.N. Shaw | J.N. Shaw | G.H.H.P. Maxwell |
| N.C. Macpherson | G.H.H.P. Maxwell 1c,1pg | †G.M. Murray | N.C. Macpherson |
| | | | |
| Inverleith | St. Helens | Lansdowne Road | Inverleith |
| lost 0-3 | won 14-8 | lost 8-9 | lost 0-18 |
| | | | |
| Scot.: nil | Wales: 2dg | Ire.: 3t | Scot.: nil |
| Fr.: 1t | Scot.: 1g 1pg 2t | Scot.: 1g 1t | Eng.: 3g 1t |
| | | | |
| 22 Jan. 1921 | 5 Feb. 1921 | 26 Feb. 1921 | 19 Mar. 1921 |

Disappointment was mixed with a rare success in 1921. The Scots fielded seven new caps for the opening match of the season, against France at Inverleith. Five of the backs, including the entire threequarter line, were new. But the French won on their merits and numerous changes were made before the side played Wales.

However the shock caused by that first French victory in Scotland was forgotten after the triumph at Swansea, Scotland's first win in Wales for 29 years. Maxwell's place-kicking and an electrifying sprint by Sloan near the end helped the Scots to a famous victory in which the huge crowd frequently spilled over the sidelines and on to the field of play.

John Bannerman was the most illustrious of the Scottish newcomers. He was a teenager when first capped but went on to win 37 caps and set a new appearance record for Scotland. A fine dribbler, hard tackler and dynamic leader, he was the outstanding Scottish forward between the wars.

## 1921-22

| v. FRANCE | v. WALES | v. IRELAND | v. ENGLAND |
|---|---|---|---|
| †W.C. JOHNSTON | H.H. FORSAYTH | H.H. FORSAYTH | H.H. FORSAYTH |
| A. BROWNING 1T | A. BROWNING 1PG,2T | A. BROWNING | E.B. MACKAY |
| †G.P.S. MACPHERSON | †R.C. WARREN | R.C. WARREN | G.P.S. MACPHERSON |
| A.L. GRACIE | A.L. GRACIE | A.L. GRACIE | A.L. GRACIE |
| †E.H. LIDDELL | E.H. LIDDELL | E.H. LIDDELL 1T | †J.M. TOLMIE |
| †J.C. DYKES | G.P.S. MACPHERSON | G.P.S. MACPHERSON | J.C. DYKES 1T |
| J. HUME | †W.E. BRYCE | W.E. BRYCE 1T | W.E. BRYCE |
| †A.K. STEVENSON | †W.G. DOBSON | W.G. DOBSON | W.G. DOBSON |
| †D.M. BERTRAM | D.M. BERTRAM | D.M. BERTRAM | D.M. BERTRAM 1C |
| A. WEMYSS | A. WEMYSS | A. WEMYSS | J.C.R. BUCHANAN |
| J.M. BANNERMAN | J.M. BANNERMAN | J.M. BANNERMAN | J.M. BANNERMAN |
| †D.S. DAVIES | D.S. DAVIES | D.S. DAVIES | D.S. DAVIES |
| †J.R. LAWRIE | J.R. LAWRIE | J.R. LAWRIE | J.R. LAWRIE |
| *C.M. USHER | *C.M. USHER | *C.M. USHER | *C.M. USHER |
| G.H.H.P. MAXWELL | J.C.R. BUCHANAN | J.C.R. BUCHANAN | G.H.H.P. MAXWELL |
| Stade Colombes | Inverleith | Inverleith | Twickenham |
| DRAWN 3-3 | DRAWN 9-9 | WON 6-3 | LOST 5-11 |
| FR.: 1T | SCOT.: 1PG 2T | SCOT.: 2T | ENG.: 1G 2T |
| SCOT.: 1T | WALES: 1G 1DG | IRE.: 1T | SCOT.: 1G |
| 2 Jan. 1922 | 4 Feb. 1922 | 25 Feb. 1922 | 18 Mar. 1922 |

Charles Usher returned to lead the side in 1922. He had a useful mix of youth behind the scrum and experience up front, and the side was beaten only once, at Twickenham at the end of the season.

Phil Macpherson, Eric Liddell, J.C. Dykes and Willie Bryce were notable debutants in the backs. Liddell was the subject of the film "Chariots of Fire" and of course a very famous athlete. Macpherson and Dykes, as midfield backs, were to play a significant part in the Scottish successes later in the 1920s, and Willie Bryce, the Selkirk scrum-half, was the ideal half-back whose quick service and deadly burst from the scrum made him the perfect match for Kershaw, the outstanding English scrum-half.

The two scrum-halves were in opposition at Twickenham. Despite an early try by Dykes, the English pack outplayed the Scots and the visiting backs were unable to play the attacking tactics which had brought a good win in difficult conditions against Ireland.

## 1922-23

| v. FRANCE | v. WALES | v. IRELAND | v. ENGLAND |
|---|---|---|---|
| †D. DRYSDALE 2C | D. DRYSDALE 1C | D. DRYSDALE | D. DRYSDALE |
| E.H. LIDDELL 1T | E.H. LIDDELL 1T | E.H. LIDDELL | E.H. LIDDELL |
| *A.L. GRACIE | *A.L. GRACIE 1T | *A.L. GRACIE 1T | *A.L. GRACIE 1T |
| †E. McLAREN 2T | E. McLAREN | E. McLAREN | E. McLAREN 1T |
| †A.C. WALLACE | A. BROWNING | A. BROWNING 1T,2C | A. BROWNING |
| †S.B. McQUEEN | S.B. McQUEEN | S.B. McQUEEN 1T | S.B. McQUEEN |
| W.E. BRYCE 1T | W.E. BRYCE | W.E. BRYCE | W.E. BRYCE |
| †D.S. KERR | D.S. KERR | N.C. MACPHERSON | N.C. MACPHERSON |
| D.M. BERTRAM | D.M. BERTRAM | D.M. BERTRAM | D.M. BERTRAM |
| A.K. STEVENSON | A.K. STEVENSON | J.C.R. BUCHANAN | J.C.R. BUCHANAN |
| J.M. BANNERMAN | J.M. BANNERMAN | J.M. BANNERMAN | J.M. BANNERMAN |
| †L.M. STUART | L.M. STUART 1T | L.M. STUART | L.M. STUART |
| J.C.R. BUCHANAN | J.C.R. BUCHANAN | †R.S. SIMPSON | A.K. STEVENSON |
| D.S. DAVIES | D.S. DAVIES | D.S. DAVIES | D.S. DAVIES |
| J.R. LAWRIE | J.R. LAWRIE | J.R. LAWRIE | J.R. LAWRIE |
| Inverleith | Cardiff Arms Park | Lansdowne Road | Inverleith |
| WON 16-3 | WON 11-8 | WON 13-3 | LOST 6-8 |
| SCOT.: 2G 2T | WALES: 1G 1PG | IRE.: 1T | SCOT.: 2T |
| FR.: 1GM | SCOT.: 1G 2T | SCOT.: 2G 1T | ENG.: 1G 1T |
| 20 Jan. 1923 | 3 Feb. 1923 | 24 Feb. 1923 | 17 Mar. 1923 |

Scotland were building a formidable side and three good wins marked the start of the 1923 Championship. Leslie Gracie, a superlative centre with pace and a devastating swerve, led the side in style, scored the winning try in Cardiff (in a match long referred to as "Gracie's match"), and scored further tries against Ireland and England.

Altogether the backs were responsible for eleven of Scotland's twelve tries during the season, and both Gracie and Liddell were very close to scoring a thirteenth try in the closing moments of a tense struggle against England at Inverleith. The lasting power of the Scottish forwards did not quite match the stamina of the English pack, however, and the Scots had to be content to finish as runners-up in the Championship.

Dan Drysdale started his long international career in 1923. His sure fielding, superb positional sense, and accurate touch-kicking were qualities which the Scottish selectors relied upon through 26 games. First in a distinguished line of Heriot's full-backs, Drysdale became a timber merchant and was President of the SRU in 1951-2.

## 1923-24

| v. FRANCE | v. WALES | v. IRELAND | v. ENGLAND |
|---|---|---|---|
| D. DRYSDALE | D. DRYSDALE 1PG,4C | D. DRYSDALE 2C | D. DRYSDALE |
| †C.E.W.C. MACKINTOSH | †I.S. SMITH 3T | I.S.SMITH | I.S. SMITH |
| A.L. GRACIE | G.P.S. MACPHERSON 1T | G.G. AITKEN | G.P.S. MACPHERSON |
| E. MCLAREN | †G.G. AITKEN | J.C. DYKES | G.G. AITKEN |
| A.C. WALLACE 1T | A.C. WALLACE 1T | †R.K. MILLAR | A.C. WALLACE |
| †H. WADDELL 1DG | H. WADDELL 1T | H. WADDELL 2T | H. WADDELL |
| W.E. BRYCE | W.E. BRYCE 1T | W.E. BRYCE | W.E. BRYCE |
| †R.A. HOWIE | R.A. HOWIE | R.A. HOWIE | R.A. HOWIE |
| †A. ROSS | D. M. BERTRAM 1T | D.M. BERTRAM 1T | D.M. BERTRAM |
| D.S. KERR | A. ROSS | †R.G. HENDERSON | D.S. DAVIES |
| J.M. BANNERMAN | J.M. BANNERMAN | J.M. BANNERMAN | J.M. BANNERMAN |
| L.M. STUART | *J.C.R. BUCHANAN | *J.C.R. BUCHANAN | R.G. HENDERSON |
| †K.G.P. HENDRIE | †A.C. GILLIES | J.R. LAWRIE | *J.C.R. BUCHANAN |
| D.S. DAVIES 1PG | K.G.P. HENDRIE | K.G.P. HENDRIE | A.C. GILLIES |
| *J.C.R. BUCHANAN | J.R. LAWRIE | A.C. GILLIES | J.R. LAWRIE |
| Stade Pershing | Inverleith | Inverleith | Twickenham |
| LOST 10-12 | WON 35-10 | WON 13-8 | LOST 0-19 |
| FR.: 4T | SCOT.: 4G 1PG 4T | SCOT.: 2G 1T | ENG.: 3G 1DG |
| SCOT.: 1PG 1DG 1T | WALES: 2G | IRE.: 1G 1T | SCOT.: NIL |
| 1 Jan. 1924 | 2 Feb. 1924 | 23 Feb. 1924 | 15 Mar. 1924 |

Despite the fact that many of the previous season's successful side were still available, Scotland failed to make much impact in the Championship. The defeat in Paris was a nasty shock and blame was heaped on the Scottish side for underestimating the opposition.

It was no surprise, therefore, to see six changes made before the Welsh match at Inverleith. Gracie was unavailable and Scotland thus fielded a club threequarter line, Oxford University supplying Smith (who on his debut romped away for three tries), Aitken (who had been capped for New Zealand in 1921), Wallace (an Australian), and Macpherson, an established centre threequarter of considerable skill and polish.

Scotland's win over a weak Welsh side stands as the highest Scottish victory over the Welsh, but the Scots were unable to repeat their good play in the Calcutta Cup match and England in turn inflicted a record winning margin over the Scots. The Scottish forwards lacked strength at Twickenham, their scrummaging was inept, and the tackling of the backs was very sloppy.

## 1924-25

| v. FRANCE | v. WALES | v. IRELAND | v. ENGLAND |
|---|---|---|---|
| D. DRYSDALE 1C | D. DRYSDALE 1DG,1C | *D. DRYSDALE 1C | D. DRYSDALE 1C |
| A.C. WALLACE 2T | A.C. WALLACE 2T | A.C. WALLACE 1T | A.C. WALLACE 1T |
| *G.P.S. MACPHERSON | *G.P.S. MACPHERSON | G.G. AITKEN | G.G. AITKEN |
| G.G. AITKEN | G.G. AITKEN | J.C. DYKES 1C | *G.P.S. MACPHERSON |
| I.S. SMITH 4T | I.S. SMITH 4T | I.S. SMITH | I.S. SMITH |
| J.C. DYKES | J.C. DYKES | H. WADDELL 1DG | H. WADDELL 1DG |
| †J.B. NELSON | J.B. NELSON | J.B. NELSON | J.B. NELSON 1T |
| †W.H. STEVENSON | R.A. HOWIE | R.A. HOWIE | R.A. HOWIE |
| †J. GILCHRIST | †J.C.H. IRELAND | J.C.H. IRELAND | J.C.H. IRELAND |
| J.C.R. BUCHANAN | D.S. DAVIES | D.S. DAVIES | D.S. DAVIES |
| J.M. BANNERMAN | J.M. BANNERMAN | J.M. BANNERMAN | J.M. BANNERMAN |
| †D.J. MACMYN | D.J. MACMYN | D.J. MACMYN 1T | D.J. MACMYN |
| †J.R. PATERSON | J.R. PATERSON | J.R. PATERSON | J.R. PATERSON |
| A.C. GILLIES 1T,1C | A.C. GILLIES | J.C.R. BUCHANAN | A.C. GILLIES 1C |
| †J.W. SCOTT | J.W. SCOTT | J.W. SCOTT | J.W. SCOTT |
| Inverleith | St. Helens | Lansdowne Road | Murrayfield |
| WON 25-4 | WON 24-14 | WON 14-8 | WON 14-11 |
| SCOT.: 2G 5T | WALES: 1G 1PG 2T | IRE.: 1G 1PG | SCOT.: 2G 1DG |
| FR.: 1DG | SCOT.: 1G 1DG 5T | SCOT.: 2G 1DG | ENG.: 1G 1PG 1T |
| 24 Jan. 1925 | 7 Feb. 1925 | 28 Feb. 1925 | 21 Mar. 1925 |

Scotland won the Grand Slam for the first time in 1924-5. The backs enjoyed a marvellous season, scoring fifteen tries behind a young pack which displayed remarkable staying powers. Seven new caps were awarded during the season. Of these, Nelson was a consistent scrum-half who went on to play 25 times, a Scottish record, MacMyn, Paterson and Scott were forwards who played regularly for several seasons, and Jimmy Ireland was a brewer who became Scotland's most outstanding hooker of the decade.

The Oxford threequarter line fashioned the easy victories over France and Wales, but there was a keen finish to the Irish match. Herbert Waddell, Nelson's club partner at half, dropped a late goal to quell the fiery finish of a spirited Irish side. Waddell became a stockbroker, President of the Barbarians club, and was President of the SRU in 1963-4. His son Gordon also played for Scotland.

In the first match to be played at Murrayfield, Scotland's young pack showed true grit against their English counterparts, and with the aid of another drop-goal by Waddell, the Triple Crown, Championship and Grand Slam were secured in a close contest.

## 1925-26

| v. FRANCE | v. WALES | v. IRELAND | v. ENGLAND |
|---|---|---|---|
| *D. DRYSDALE 1C | *D. DRYSDALE 1C | *D. DRYSDALE | *D. DRYSDALE |
| | | | |
| I.S. SMITH | I.S. SMITH | I.S. SMITH | I.S. SMITH 2T |
| †R.M. KINNEAR | R.M. KINNEAR | R.M. KINNEAR | J.C. DYKES 1DG |
| J.C. DYKES | J.C. DYKES | J.C. DYKES | W.M. SIMMERS |
| A.C. WALLACE 3T | †W.M. SIMMERS | W.M. SIMMERS | †G.M. BOYD |
| | | | |
| H. WADDELL | H. WADDELL 1T | H. WADDELL | H. WADDELL 1T,2C |
| J.B. NELSON | J.B. NELSON | J.B. NELSON | J.B. NELSON |
| | | | |
| †W.V. BERKELEY | G.M. MURRAY | D.S. KERR | D.S. KERR |
| J.C.H. IRELAND | J.C.H. IRELAND | J.C.H. IRELAND | J.C.H. IRELAND |
| D.S. DAVIES | D.S. DAVIES | D.S. DAVIES | D.S. DAVIES |
| D.J. MACMYN 1T | D.J. MACMYN | D.J. MACMYN | D.J. MACMYN |
| J.M. BANNERMAN 1T | J.M. BANNERMAN | J.M. BANNERMAN | J.M. BANNERMAN |
| J.W. SCOTT | J.W. SCOTT | †J. GRAHAM | J. GRAHAM |
| A.C. GILLIES 1PG | A.C. GILLIES 1PG | J.W. SCOTT | J.W. SCOTT |
| J.R. PATERSON | J.R. PATERSON | J.R. PATERSON | J.R. PATERSON |
| Stade Colombes | Murrayfield | Murrayfield | Twickenham |
| WON 20-6 | WON 8-5 | LOST 0-3 | WON 17-9 |
| FR.: 1PG 1T | SCOT.: 1G 1PG | SCOT.: NIL | ENG.: 3T |
| SCOT.: 1G 1PG 4T | WALES: 1G | IRE.: 1T | SCOT.: 2G 1DG 1T |
| 2 Jan. 1926 | 6 Feb. 1926 | 27 Feb. 1926 | 20 Mar. 1926 |

Scotland were Champions again in 1926, though Ireland became the first international team to win at Murrayfield, and so prevented the Scots winning the Triple Crown. The nucleus of the Grand Slam team was retained, but the pack found greater difficulty winning possession than in the 1925 campaign, and fewer tries were scored by the backs.

The brilliant Oxford threequarter line had been disbanded. Macpherson had gone to America to study at Yale, Wallace returned to Australia, and Aitken was also abroad. Only Ian Smith remained and his two tries at Twickenham helped Scotland to their first victory at the ground, and their first win on English soil for fifteen years.

Waddell and Nelson presided with calm and efficiency over the threequarters. Waddell had a good season, his try against Wales winning the match. He cut clean through the defence with a lovely dummy and break and Drysdale, Scotland's accomplished full-back and their captain, kicked the important conversion for an 8-5 win.

## 1926-27

| v. FRANCE | v. WALES | v. IRELAND | v. ENGLAND |
|---|---|---|---|
| D. DRYSDALE | D. DRYSDALE | D. DRYSDALE | *D. DRYSDALE |
| | | | |
| I.S. SMITH 2T | †E.G. TAYLOR | I.S. SMITH | I.S. SMITH 2T |
| *G.P.S. MACPHERSON | *G.P.S. MACPHERSON | *G.P.S. MACPHERSON | G.P.S. MACPHERSON 1T |
| J.C. DYKES | J.C. DYKES | J.C. DYKES | J.C. DYKES 1T |
| W.M. SIMMERS | W.M. SIMMERS | W.M. SIMMERS | W.M. SIMMERS |
| | | | |
| H. WADDELL 2T | H. WADDELL | H. WADDELL | H. WADDELL 1DG |
| J.B. NELSON | J.B. NELSON | J.B. NELSON | J.B. NELSON |
| | | | |
| †J.W. ALLAN | D.S. KERR 1T | D.S. KERR | D.S. KERR |
| J.C.H. IRELAND | J.C.H. IRELAND | J.C.H. IRELAND | J.C.H. IRELAND |
| D.S. DAVIES | D.S. DAVIES | D.S. DAVIES | J.W. SCOTT 1T |
| J.W. SCOTT | J.W. SCOTT | J.W. SCOTT | J.M. BANNERMAN |
| J.M. BANNERMAN | J.M. BANNERMAN | J.M. BANNERMAN | D.J. MACMYN |
| J.R. PATERSON | J.R. PATERSON | J.R. PATERSON | J.R. PATERSON |
| A.C. GILLIES 4C,1PG | A.C. GILLIES 1C | A.C. GILLIES | A.C. GILLIES 1C |
| J. GRAHAM | J. GRAHAM | J. GRAHAM | J. GRAHAM |
| Murrayfield | Cardiff Arms Park | Lansdowne Road | Murrayfield |
| WON 23-6 | WON 5-0 | LOST 0-6 | WON 21-13 |
| SCOT.: 4G 1PG | WALES: NIL | IRE.: 2T | SCOT.: 1G 1DG 4T |
| FR.: 2T | SCOT.: 1G | SCOT.: NIL | ENG.: 2G 1PG |
| 22 Jan. 1927 | 5 Feb. 1927 | 26 Feb. 1927 | 19 Mar. 1927 |

Scotland again shared the Championship, winning three matches but failing against Ireland. The pack contained numerous splendid forwards, but their scrummaging and marking in the line-out was loose, and the side had to rely on brilliant back play to beat France. Phil Macpherson returned to captain the side. As a centre he played with grace and assurance, passed skilfully with accuracy and judgment, and created two clear-cut openings for Ian Smith to score tries against France.

The Irish match in Dublin was played in the most awful conditions, and it was probably Ireland's luck in winning the toss which settled the match – their points coming before the teams were frozen rigid by a stiff wind carrying icy rain.

A.C. Gillies kicked six conversions during the season, a fine achievement for a forward. He was a gifted all-round forward who could place goals from anywhere inside opponents' halves. A doctor, he won a dozen caps and placed eleven goals (three of them penalties) in his international career.

## 1927-28

| v. NSW | v. FRANCE | v. WALES | v. IRELAND | v. ENGLAND |
|---|---|---|---|---|
| *D. DRYSDALE 2C | *D. DRYSDALE | D. DRYSDALE | *D. DRYSDALE 1C | *D. DRYSDALE |
| | | | | |
| E.G. TAYLOR | G.P.S. MACPHERSON | †J. GOODFELLOW | J. GOODFELLOW | J. GOODFELLOW |
| †R.F. KELLY | R.F. KELLY | G.P.S. MACPHERSON | †J.W.G. HUME | G.P.S. MACPHERSON |
| J.C. DYKES | J.C. DYKES 2T | R.F. KELLY | J.C. DYKES | W.M. SIMMERS |
| W.M. SIMMERS | W.M. SIMMERS | W.M. SIMMERS | W.M. SIMMERS | R.F. KELLY |
| | | | | |
| †H.D. GREENLEES | H.D. GREENLEES | H.D. GREENLEES | †H. LIND | †A.H. BROWN |
| †P.S. DOUTY | P.S. DOUTY 1T | P.S. DOUTY | J.B. NELSON | J.B. NELSON |
| | | | | |
| †W.G. FERGUSON | W.G. FERGUSON | W.G. FERGUSON | J.W. ALLAN | L.M. STUART |
| †W.N. ROUGHEAD | W.N. ROUGHEAD | W.N. ROUGHEAD | W.N. ROUGHEAD | W.N. ROUGHEAD |
| J.W. SCOTT | W.B. WELSH | †J.H. FERGUSON | D.S. KERR 1T | D.S. KERR |
| J.M. BANNERMAN | J.M. BANNERMAN | *J.M. BANNERMAN | J.M. BANNERMAN | J.M. BANNERMAN |
| D.J. MACMYN | D.J. MACMYN | J.W. SCOTT | W.G. FERGUSON | W.G. FERGUSON |
| J. GRAHAM 1T | J. GRAHAM | J.R. PATERSON | J. GRAHAM | J. GRAHAM |
| †W.B. WELSH 1T | J.W. SCOTT 1T | W.B. WELSH | W.B. WELSH | J.W. SCOTT |
| J.R. PATERSON | J.R. PATERSON 1T | J. GRAHAM | J.R. PATERSON | J.R. PATERSON |
| | | | | |
| Murrayfield | Stade Colombes | Murrayfield | Murrayfield | Twickenham |
| WON 10-8 | WON 15-6 | LOST 0-13 | LOST 5-13 | LOST 0-6 |
| | | | | |
| SCOT.: 2G | FR.: 2T | SCOT.: NIL | SCOT.: 1G | ENG.: 2T |
| NSW: 1G 1T | SCOT.: 5T | WALES: 2G 1T | IRE.: 2G 1T | SCOT.: NIL |
| | | | | |
| 17 Dec. 1927 | 2 Jan. 1928 | 4 Feb. 1928 | 25 Feb. 1928 | 17 Mar. 1928 |

The "Waratahs", tourists from New South Wales captained by former Scottish cap A.C. Wallace, visited Scotland in 1927. The international was an exciting affair between two even packs. In the end the excellent individual play of Simmers created two tries for Scottish forwards and the goal kicks enabled Scotland to win by two points.

Max Simmers was a loyal servant to Scottish rugby for many years. As a wing or centre he gained 28 consecutive caps and his thrustful running produced five international tries. He was a chartered accountant by profession, was President of the SRU in 1956-7, and had the pleasure of watching his son play for Scotland in the late 1960s.

Scotland's previous Championship successes and their win over NSW made them favourites to retain the title in 1928. But after an easy victory over the French, injuries and loss of form among the backs compelled the selectors to field an experimental side for the last three matches of the winter. Only Simmers and Drysdale represented the backs in each of the season's games.

## 1928-29

| v. FRANCE | v. WALES | v. IRELAND | v. ENGLAND |
|---|---|---|---|
| *D. DRYSDALE | †T.G. AITCHISON | T.G. AITCHISON | T.G. AITCHISON |
| | | | |
| I.S. SMITH | I.S. SMITH | I.S. SMITH 1T | I.S. SMITH 2T |
| G.G. AITKEN | †T.G. BROWN | G.P.S. MACPHERSON 1T | G.P.S. MACPHERSON |
| J.C. DYKES | J.C DYKES 1PG | J.C. DYKES 1C | W.M. SIMMERS |
| W.M. SIMMERS | W.M. SIMMERS | W.M. SIMMERS 1T | †C.H.C. BROWN 1T |
| | | | |
| A.H. BROWN 1PG | A.H. BROWN 1DG | H.D. GREENLEES | H.D. GREENLEES |
| J.B. NELSON | J.B. NELSON | J.B. NELSON | J.B. NELSON 1T |
| | | | |
| †R.T. SMITH | R.T. SMITH | R.T. SMITH | R.T. SMITH |
| †H.S. MACKINTOSH | H.S. MACKINTOSH | H.S. MACKINTOSH | H.S. MACKINTOSH |
| J.W. ALLAN | J.W. ALLAN | J.W. ALLAN 1C | J.W. ALLAN |
| J.M. BANNERMAN | *J.M. BANNERMAN | W.V. BERKELEY | J.W. SCOTT |
| †J. BEATTIE | J. BEATTIE | *J.M. BANNERMAN 1T | *J.M. BANNERMAN |
| J.R. PATERSON 1T | J.R. PATERSON | J.R. PATERSON | J.R. PATERSON |
| W.V. BERKELEY | W.V. BERKELEY | W.B. WELSH | W.B. WELSH |
| †K.M. WRIGHT | K.M. WRIGHT | K.M. WRIGHT | K.M. WRIGHT |
| | | | |
| Murrayfield | St. Helens | Lansdowne Road | Murrayfield |
| WON 6-3 | LOST 7-14 | WON 16-7 | WON 12-6 |
| | | | |
| SCOT.: 1PG 1T | WALES: 1G 3T | IRE.: 1DG 1T | SCOT.: 4T |
| FR.: 1T | SCOT.: 1DG 1PG | SCOT.: 2G 2T | ENG.: 2T |
| | | | |
| 19 Jan. 1929 | 2 Feb. 1929 | 23 Feb. 1929 | 16 Mar. 1929 |

Scotland were the champions again in 1929, though defeat at Swansea cost them the Triple Crown. There was a revival of the traditional style of Scottish forward play, Bannerman inspiring the pack by his excellent individual example. Four of the forwards were drawn from the competitive teams of the Border League: Jock Beattie of Hawick gained the first of his 23 caps against France, alongside J.W. Allan, the Melrose kicking specialist, and another new cap, R.T. Smith of Kelso. Another Hawick man, W.B. Welsh, returned to the side for the Irish and English matches.

J.C. Dykes, a reliable attacking player with sound defence, was laid out in the Irish match, the last of his 20 games for Scotland.

The return of Ian Smith added a new edge to the attacking potential of the backs, and in the Irish and English games, when he was reunited with his old Oxford contemporary Macpherson, he regained his old form and scored three tries.

## 1929-30

| v. FRANCE | v. WALES | v. IRELAND | v. ENGLAND |
|---|---|---|---|
| †R.W. Langrish | R.C. Warren | R.C. Warren | R.C. Warren |
| | | | |
| I.S. Smith | I.S. Smith | I.S. Smith | D.J.St.C. Ford |
| *G.P.S. Macpherson | *G.P.S. Macpherson | *G.P.S. Macpherson 1t | †J.E. Hutton |
| J.W.G. Hume | †T.M. Hart | W.M. Simmers | *G.P.S. Macpherson |
| W.M. Simmers 1t | W.M. Simmers 2t | †D.J.St.C. Ford 1t | W.M. Simmers |
| | | | |
| †W.D. Emslie | H. Waddell 1dg | T.M. Hart | H.D. Greenlees |
| J.B. Nelson | J.B. Nelson | J.B. Nelson | J.B. Nelson |
| | | | |
| R.T. Smith | R.T. Smith | R.T. Smith | H.S. Mackintosh |
| H.S. Mackintosh | H.S. Mackintosh | W.N. Roughead | W.N. Roughead |
| J.W. Allan | †R.A. Foster | H.S. Mackintosh | J.W. Allan |
| †J. Stewart | F.H. Waters 1c | L.M. Stuart | L.M. Stuart |
| J.W. Scott | J. Beattie | W.C.C. Agnew | W.B. Welsh |
| †F.H. Waters | †W.C.C. Agnew | F.H. Waters 1t,1c | F.H. Waters |
| †R. Rowand | R. Rowand | J. Graham | J. Graham |
| W.B. Welsh | W.B. Welsh | W.B. Welsh | †A.H. Polson |
| | | | |
| Stade Colombes | Murrayfield | Murrayfield | Twickenham |
| LOST 3-7 | WON 12-9 | LOST 11-14 | DRAWN 0-0 |
| | | | |
| FRANCE: IDG IT | SCOT.: IG IDG IT | SCOT.: IG 2T | ENG.: NIL |
| SCOT.: IT | WALES: IG IDG | IRE.: IG 3T | SCOT.: NIL |
| | | | |
| 1 Jan. 1930 | 1 Feb. 1930 | 22 Feb. 1930 | 15 Mar. 1930 |

Scotland opened the 1930 season with high hopes of retaining the Championship, for their side appeared to have available a convincing blend of youth and experience. However the season turned out to be very disappointing. There was only one victory and the wooden spoon went north for the first time since 1911 (though Scotland had shared bottom place in more recent seasons).

Macpherson as captain, Simmers, and the durable J.B. Nelson were the only backs to figure in each match. Macpherson was one of the finest players ever to appear in the blue jersey. He was an unselfish player who created numerous opportunities for his wings, won 26 caps, and led Scotland on twelve occasions. He became a distinguished merchant banker and was appointed director of Kleinwort, Benson Lonsdale in 1960.

Herbert Waddell made a brief return to win his 15th and final cap against Wales. In the final minutes of the match he dropped a goal from in front of the posts to win the game. It was his fifth drop-goal in internationals, creating a Scottish record.

## 1930-31

| v. FRANCE | v. WALES | v. IRELAND | v. ENGLAND |
|---|---|---|---|
| R.W. Langrish | R.W. Langrish | R.W. Langrish | A.W. Wilson |
| | | | |
| I.S. Smith | I.S. Smith | I.S. Smith | I.S. Smith 2t |
| J.E. Hutton | G.P.S. Macpherson | W.M. Simmers | *G.P.S. Macpherson |
| †A.W. Wilson | W.M. Simmers | A.W. Wilson | D.J.St.C. Ford 1t |
| W.M. Simmers | †G. Wood | G. Wood | W.M. Simmers |
| | | | |
| H. Lind | H. Lind | H. Lind | H. Lind |
| J.B. Nelson | J.B. Nelson | J.B. Nelson | †W.R. Logan 1t |
| | | | |
| J.W. Allan 2pg | J.W. Allan 1c | J.W. Allan 1c | J.W. Allan 5c |
| *W.N. Roughead | *W.N. Roughead | *W.N. Roughead | W.N. Roughead |
| H.S. Mackintosh | H.S. Mackintosh | H.S. Mackintosh 1t | H.S. Mackintosh 2t |
| J. Beattie | J. Beattie | J. Beattie | J. Beattie |
| †A. McLaren | A.W. Walker | A.W. Walker | A.W. Walker |
| †A.W. Walker | †D. Crichton-Miller 2t | D. Crichton-Miller | D. Crichton-Miller |
| †J.S. Wilson | J.S. Wilson | J.S. Wilson | J.S. Wilson |
| W.B. Welsh | W.B. Welsh | W.B. Welsh | W.B. Welsh |
| | | | |
| Murrayfield | Cardiff Arms Park | Lansdowne Road | Murrayfield |
| WON 6-4 | LOST 8-13 | LOST 5-8 | WON 28-19 |
| | | | |
| SCOT.: 2PG | WALES: 2G IT | IRE.: IG IT | SCOT.: 5G IT |
| FR.: IDG | SCOT.: IG IT | SCOT.: IG | ENG.: 2G IPG 2T |
| | | | |
| 24 Jan. 1931 | 7 Feb. 1931 | 28 Feb. 1931 | 21 Mar. 1931 |

W.N. Roughead, a scholar of Rugby School and Oxford University, was Scotland's captain at the start of 1931. A huge crowd of 50,000 saw the Scots gain a lucky win over the French in perfect conditions, two penalties by J.W. Allan resulting in a narrow 6-4 victory.

Allan was a solid scrummager who usually propped in his 17 internationals. His place-kicking earned him a position in the record books this season, for his seven conversions (five against England) surpassed the previous record for a season and stood until Peter Dods kicked eight in 1984. Allan was a male nurse.

Donald Crichton-Miller, a Monmouth schoolmaster at the time, made an auspicious debut against Wales. A brilliant loose forward with sound positional sense and immense speed, he later returned as Headmaster to Fettes College, his former school.

## 1931-32

| v. S. AFRICA | v. WALES | v. IRELAND | v. ENGLAND |
|---|---|---|---|
| †T.H.B. LAWTHER | T.H.B. LAWTHER | †A.H.M. HUTTON | †A.S. DYKES |
| | | | |
| I.S. SMITH | I.S. SMITH | *W.M. SIMMERS 1T | I.S. SMITH 1T |
| G.P.S. MACPHERSON | *W.M. SIMMERS | D.J.ST.C. FORD | *G.P.S. MACPHERSON |
| *W.M. SIMMERS | D.J.ST.C. FORD | G. WOOD 1T | G. WOOD |
| †J.E. FORREST | G. WOOD | I.S. SMITH | W.M. SIMMERS |
| | | | |
| H. LIND 1T | H. LIND | W.D. EMSLIE | H. LIND |
| W.R. LOGAN | W.R. LOGAN | W.R. LOGAN | †J.P. MACARTHUR |
| | | | |
| J.W. ALLAN | H.S. MACKINTOSH | R.A. FOSTER | R. ROWAND |
| H.S. MACKINTOSH | W.N. ROUGHEAD | H.S. MACKINTOSH | H.S. MACKINTOSH |
| R.A. FOSTER | J.W. ALLAN | J.W. ALLAN 1C | R.A. FOSTER |
| J. BEATTIE | J. BEATTIE | J. BEATTIE | J. BEATTIE |
| †M.S. STEWART | M.S. STEWART | M.S. STEWART | †F.A. WRIGHT |
| F.H. WATERS | F.H. WATERS | W.B. WELSH | J.S. WILSON |
| W.B. WELSH | W.B. WELSH | F.H. WATERS | †G.F. RITCHIE |
| J. GRAHAM | J. GRAHAM | A.W. WALKER | W.B. WELSH |
| | | | |
| Murrayfield | Murrayfield | Murrayfield | Twickenham |
| LOST 3-6 | LOST 0-6 | LOST 8-20 | LOST 3-16 |
| | | | |
| SCOT.: 1T | SCOT.: NIL | SCOT.: 1G 1T | ENG.: 2G 2T |
| SA: 2T | WALES: 1PG 1T | IRE.: 4G | SCOT.: 1T |
| | | | |
| 16 Jan. 1932 | 6 Feb. 1932 | 27 Feb. 1932 | 19 Mar. 1932 |

The season was Scotland's most miserable for years. There was a nucleus of Border forwards in the pack, and their splendid effort in testing conditions against the Springbok pack impressed the pundits. But the side failed to reproduce its best form against the Home Nations, and three matches were lost.

Only two of the backs (the veterans Smith and Simmers), and three of the forwards played in each of the four matches. Two of these forwards were the Hawick stalwarts, Beattie and Welsh. The other forward to keep his place was H.S. Mackintosh, a graduate of Glasgow University who became Director of Education in the city. At the time he was the enthusiastic leader of the successful West of Scotland side.

In the match with Ireland, Emslie sustained an ankle injury and was forced to retire. Subsequently the Scots crashed to their worst defeat against Ireland.

## 1932-33

| v. WALES | v. ENGLAND | v. IRELAND |
|---|---|---|
| †D.I. BROWN | D.I. BROWN | D.I. BROWN |
| | | |
| *I.S. SMITH 1T | *I.S. SMITH | *I.S. SMITH |
| †H.D.B. LORRAINE | H.D.B. LORRAINE | H.D.B. LORRAINE |
| H. LIND | H. LIND | H. LIND 1DG |
| †K.C. FYFE 1PG,1C | K.C. FYFE 1T | †P.M.S. GEDGE |
| | | |
| †K.L.T. JACKSON 1T | K.L.T. JACKSON | K.L.T. JACKSON 1DG |
| W.R. LOGAN | W.R. LOGAN | W.R. LOGAN |
| | | |
| †J.A. WATERS | J.A. WATERS | J.A. WATERS |
| †J.M. RITCHIE | J.M. RITCHIE | J.M. RITCHIE |
| †J.R. THOM | J.R. THOM | J.R. THOM |
| J. BEATTIE | J. BEATTIE | J. BEATTIE |
| M.S. STEWART | M.S. STEWART | M.S. STEWART |
| R. ROWAND | R. ROWAND | R. ROWAND |
| †J.McL. HENDERSON | J.McL. HENDERSON | J.McL. HENDERSON |
| W.B. WELSH | W.B. WELSH | W.B. WELSH |
| | | |
| St. Helen's | Murrayfield | Lansdowne Road |
| WON 11-3 | WON 3-0 | WON 8-6 |
| | | |
| WALES: 1T | SCOT.: 1T | IRE.: 2T |
| SCOT.: 1G 1PG 1T | ENG.: NIL | SCOT.: 2DG |
| | | |
| 4 Feb. 1933 | 18 Mar. 1933 | 1 Apr. 1933 |

This was Ian Smith's last season in international rugby, and he had the honour of leading the side to the Triple Crown. Smith retired with 24 tries in his 32 internationals, a try total which still stands as a world record for matches between International Board nations.

Scotland fielded a young side with eight new men against Wales. The side displayed fine team spirit and keenness at Swansea, and they were rewarded by the fourth Scottish win at St Helen's. Smith scored his last try in internationals to give his side the lead in this match, and the dynamic forwards ensured that that lead was never relinquished.

An appalling blizzard caused the postponement of the Irish match in Dublin, so England were Scotland's second opponents of the season. The match was a dour struggle in which Scotland were just the livelier side. A try by K.C. Fyfe, just before the interval, was the only score of the game. The Irish game was eventually staged in April, and Harry Lind's late drop-goal gave the Scots the Triple Crown for the first time since 1925.

## 1933-34

| v. WALES | v. IRELAND | v. ENGLAND |
|---|---|---|
| †K.W. Marshall | K.W. Marshall | K.W. Marshall |
| †R.W. Shaw | R.W. Shaw 1c | R.W. Shaw 1t |
| †R.C.S. Dick | R.C.S. Dick 2t | R.C.S. Dick |
| *H. Lind | H. Lind | H. Lind |
| †J. Park | †J.A. Crawford 1t | K.C. Fyfe |
| K.L.T. Jackson | †J.L. Cotter | J.L. Cotter |
| W.R. Logan 1t | W.R. Logan | W.R. Logan |
| †W.A. Burnet | J.W. Allan 1pg,1c | J.W. Allan |
| †L.B. Lambie | †G.S. Cottington | G.S. Cottington |
| J.M. Ritchie 1pg | J.M. Ritchie | J.M. Ritchie |
| †J.D. Lowe | J. Beattie | J. Beattie |
| M.S. Stewart | *M.S. Stewart | *M.S. Stewart |
| R. Rowand | L.B. Lambie | L.B. Lambie |
| J.A. Waters | J.A. Waters | J.A. Waters |
| †D.A. Thom | †J.G. Watherston | J.G. Watherston |
| Murrayfield | Murrayfield | Twickenham |
| LOST 6-13 | WON 16-9 | LOST 3-6 |
| SCOT.: 1PG 1T | SCOT.: 2G 1PG 1T | ENG.: 2T |
| WALES: 2G 1T | IRE.: 3T | SCOT.: 1T |
| 3 Feb. 1934 | 24 Feb. 1934 | 17 Mar. 1934 |

The absence of Beattie handicapped Scotland at the beginning of the campaign, and a side of eight new caps was well beaten by Wales. D.I. Brown had been an outstanding success at full-back during the Triple Crown year, but injuries dogged him in 1934 and he never again played for Scotland. K.W. Marshall, the Edinburgh Academical who was South African by birth, proved an able deputy. Of the other new players Charles Dick and Wilson Shaw were to become leading Scottish players of the pre-war era.

The side improved as the season progressed. Beattie returned for the Irish match, adding considerable strength to a pack which boasted a formidable front five. M.S. Stewart, later a President of the SRU, became captain and led the side to a convincing win over Ireland.

There was an exciting finish to the Calcutta Cup game. Wilson Shaw gave Scotland the lead with a try created by Lind and Dick, but England equalised before half-time. The scores were still level as the match went into injury time. Lind, a brilliant opportunist, made several dashing breaks but failed to pierce the English defence. Then, against the run of play, the English wing gathered a bouncing ball to race away for the deciding try.

## 1934-35

| v. WALES | v. IRELAND | v. ENGLAND |
|---|---|---|
| K.W. Marshall | K.W. Marshall | K.W. Marshall |
| †W.G.S. Johnston | W.G.S. Johnston | J.E. Forrest |
| R.C.S. Dick | R.C.S. Dick | R.C.S. Dick |
| R.W. Shaw 1t | H. Lind | †W.C.W. Murdoch |
| *K.C. Fyfe | K.C. Fyfe 1c | K.C. Fyfe 1t,2c |
| †C.F. Grieve | *R.W. Shaw 1t | *R.W. Shaw |
| W.R. Logan | W.R. Logan | W.R. Logan |
| †R.O. Murray | †A.S.B. McNeill | R.O. Murray |
| G.S. Cottington | G.S. Cottington | †P.W. Tait |
| †R.M. Grieve | R.M. Grieve | R.M. Grieve |
| J. Beattie | J. Beattie | J. Beattie |
| W.A. Burnet | W.A. Burnet | W.A. Burnet |
| L.A. Lambie | L.B. Lambie | L.B. Lambie 1t |
| J.A. Waters | J.A. Waters | J.A. Waters |
| D.A. Thom 1t | D.A. Thom | D.A. Thom |
| Cardiff Arms Park | Lansdowne Road | Murrayfield |
| LOST 6-10 | LOST 5-12 | WON 10-7 |
| WALES: 1DG 2T | IRE.: 4T | SCOT.: 2G |
| SCOT.: 2T | SCOT.: 1G | ENG.: 1DG 1T |
| 2 Feb. 1935 | 23 Feb. 1935 | 16 Mar. 1935 |

There were difficulties fielding a settled front row in 1935. Only Grieve, the sturdy Kelso builder at prop, played in the front row throughout the season, although the back five were unchanged, with Jock Beattie still the dominating character of the pack. Among his colleagues were the Selkirk master butcher, Jock Waters; Lambie, the Glasgow brewery representative; and David Thom, a dashing wing-forward who became President of the SRU in 1965-6.

The selectors experimented with Wilson Shaw this season. Previously capped on the wing, he appeared at centre against Wales and was finally chosen in his best position, fly-half, for the two closing matches of the season. Shaw had a fine game against England, and had a hand in each of Scotland's two tries.

Ken Fyfe, a former Cambridge Blue who later emigrated to South Africa, was the man of the match against England. Shaw initiated the move which created space for Fyfe to kick ahead and score Scotland's first try. Fyfe converted and later converted a try scored by Lambie.

## 1935-36

| v. NZ | v. WALES | v. IRELAND | v. ENGLAND |
|---|---|---|---|
| †J.M. KERR | K.W. MARSHALL | J.M. KERR | J.M. KERR |
| J.E. FORREST | W.C.W. MURDOCH | W.C.W. MURDOCH 1DG | R.W. SHAW 1T |
| R.C.S. DICK 1T | *R.C.S. DICK | *R.C.S. DICK | R.C.S. DICK |
| W.C.W. MURDOCH 1C | †H.M. MURRAY 1T | H.M. MURRAY | H. LIND |
| K.C. FYFE 1T | K.C. FYFE | †R.J.E. WHITWORTH | K.C. FYFE 1PG,1C |
| *R.W. SHAW | R.W. SHAW | R.W. SHAW | C.F. GRIEVE |
| W.R. LOGAN | W.R. LOGAN | W.R. LOGAN | W.R. LOGAN |
| R.M. GRIEVE | R.M. GRIEVE | R.M. GRIEVE | R.M. GRIEVE |
| †G.L. GRAY | †W.A.H. DRUITT | W.A.H. DRUITT | G.S. COTTINGTON |
| †G.D. SHAW | J.A. WATERS | J.A. WATERS | W.A.H. DRUITT |
| J. BEATTIE | J. BEATTIE | J. BEATTIE | *J. BEATTIE |
| W.A. BURNET | W.A. BURNET | W.A. BURNET | W.A. BURNET |
| L.B. LAMBIE | †M.McG. COOPER | M.McG. COOPER | †R.W. BARRIE |
| J.A. WATERS | †P.L. DUFF | P.L. DUFF | J.A. WATERS |
| D.A. THOM | G.D. SHAW | †V.G. WESTON | V.G. WESTON |
| Murrayfield | Murrayfield | Murrayfield | Twickenham |
| LOST 8-18 | LOST 3-13 | LOST 4-10 | LOST 8-9 |
| SCOT.: 1G 1T | SCOT.: 1T | SCOT.: 1DG | ENG.: 3T |
| NZ: 3G 1T | WALES: 2G 1T | IRE.: 1DG 2T | SCOT.: 1G 1PG |
| 23 Nov. 1935 | 1 Feb. 1936 | 22 Feb. 1936 | 21 Mar. 1936 |

Scotland were unable to win a match in 1936, despite playing their part in an exciting, fast contest against the All Blacks early in the season. Then at Murrayfield on an overcast November day, a huge crowd saw the Scots take the lead through a try by Fyfe. There was an injury to Murdoch shortly afterwards, and although he continued to play he was very dazed and the Scots were forced to rearrange their side in order to cover the backs. The All Blacks took full advantage of Scotland's resulting weakness and gained a comfortable victory.

For the rest of the season there were difficulties finding a balanced front row. Grieve was a solid prop once again, but the selection of Waters, a number-eight moved up to prop, was not a success.

Two veterans, Lind and Beattie, played their final internationals against England. Beattie was given the captaincy for the day in the Calcutta Cup match, and inspired his men to their best performance of the season. Lind, an unobtrusive player with the ability to make an electrifying break, won 16 caps as a centre and fly-half during a span of nine seasons.

## 1936-37

| v. WALES | v. IRELAND | v. ENGLAND |
|---|---|---|
| J.M. KERR | J.M. KERR | K.W. MARSHALL |
| W.G.S. JOHNSTON | W.G.S. JOHNSTON | W.G.S. JOHNSTON |
| R.C.S. DICK 2T | †I. SHAW 1DG | R.W. SHAW |
| †D.J. MACRAE | D.J. MACRAE | D.J. MACRAE |
| R.W. SHAW 1T | R.W. SHAW | †R.H. DRYDEN |
| †W.A. ROSS | †R.B. BRUCE-LOCKHART | W.A. ROSS |
| *W.R. LOGAN | *W.R. LOGAN | *W.R. LOGAN |
| †M.M. HENDERSON | M.M. HENDERSON | M.M. HENDERSON |
| G.L. GRAY | G.L. GRAY | G.L. GRAY |
| †W.M. INGLIS | W.M. INGLIS | W.M. INGLIS |
| †G.B. HORSBURGH | G.B. HORSBURGH | G.B. HORSBURGH |
| †G.L. MELVILLE | G.L. MELVILLE | G.L. MELVILLE |
| †W.B. YOUNG | W.B. YOUNG | W.B. YOUNG |
| J.A. WATERS | J.A. WATERS | J.A. WATERS |
| G.D. SHAW 2C | G.D. SHAW | G.D. SHAW 1PG |
| St. Helen's | Lansdowne Road | Murrayfield |
| WON 13-6 | LOST 4-11 | LOST 3-6 |
| WALES: 2T | IRE.: 1G 2T | SCOT.: 1PG |
| SCOT.: 2G 1T | SCOT.: 1DG | ENG.: 2T |
| 6 Feb. 1937 | 27 Feb. 1937 | 20 Mar. 1937 |

Ross Logan, a veteran scrum-half, was Scotland's captain for 1937. He had succeeded Jimmy Nelson at the base of the scrum way back in 1931, ended his international career after the English match, having won 20 caps, and won renown for his quick and long service to the backs. A graduate of Edinburgh University, Logan became a farmer and was later President of the SRU.

Logan had a competent pack to rely on at the start of the season, and there was an encouraging win at Swansea. The pack played without change throughout the season, but undoubtedly their finest achievement was in outwitting the Welsh. The tigerish play of Duncan Shaw and the experienced Waters in the loose set up a couple of Scotland's tries at Swansea, Wilson Shaw and Charles Dick exercising the admirable qualities of directness and resolution in their running to convert these half-chances into tries.

Dick was unavailable for the last two games. Against Ireland and England the youthful Scottish pack regularly gained possession, but without an adequate spearhead and against secure defences, Scotland were unable to repeat the fine form shown at Swansea, and the season ended in disappointment.

## 1937-38

| v. WALES | v. IRELAND | v. ENGLAND |
|---|---|---|
| †G. ROBERTS | G. ROBERTS | G. ROBERTS |
| †A.H. DRUMMOND | A.H. DRUMMOND 1PG,1T | †W.N. RENWICK 2T |
| R.C.S. DICK | R.C.S. DICK | R.C.S. DICK 1T |
| D.J. MACRAE | D.J. MACRAE 1T | D.J. MACRAE |
| †J.G.S. FORREST | J.G.S. FORREST 2T | J.G.S. FORREST |
| *R.W. SHAW | *R.W. SHAW | *R.W. SHAW 2T |
| †T.F. DORWARD | T.F. DORWARD 1DG | T.F. DORWARD |
| †J.B. BORTHWICK | J.B. BORTHWICK | †W.F. BLACKADDER |
| †J.D.H. HASTIE | J.D.H. HASTIE | J.D.H. HASTIE |
| W.M. INGLIS | W.M. INGLIS | W.M. INGLIS |
| G.B. HORSBURGH | G.B. HORSBURGH | G.B. HORSBURGH |
| †A. ROY | A. ROY | A. ROY |
| W.B. YOUNG | W.B. YOUNG | W.B. YOUNG |
| P.L. DUFF | P.L. DUFF | P.L. DUFF |
| †W.H. CRAWFORD 1T,1C,1PG | W.H. CRAWFORD 2C | W.H. CRAWFORD 2PG |
| Murrayfield | Murrayfield | Twickenham |
| WON 8-6 | WON 23-14 | WON 21-16 |
| SCOT.: 1G 1PG | SCOT.: 2G 1DG 1PG 2T | ENG.: 1DG 3PG 1T |
| WALES: 2T | IRE.: 1G 3T | SCOT.: 2PG 5T |
| 5 Feb. 1938 | 26 Feb. 1938 | 19 Mar. 1938 |

Wilson Shaw, restored at fly-half, captained Scotland in 1938 and was a key member of the side which regained the Triple Crown. He blended a side of eight new caps into a winning team against Wales, though a late penalty accounted for Scotland's victory.

Following that narrow win, Scotland featured in two high-scoring matches against Ireland and England. Nine tries were scored, all by the backs, and it was noted in the *Rugby Football Annual* that proper use of a fast set of midfield backs such as Shaw, Dick and Macrae kept alive the lesson that attack has its triumphs.

The Triple Crown match at Twickenham was an outstanding spectacle of open rugby. In perfect conditions a crowd of 70,000 watched an exciting match in which the lead changed hands several times. With the game in the balance it was a breathless, swerving run by Shaw which produced the decisive score three minutes from no-side.

## 1938-39

| v. WALES | v. IRELAND | v. ENGLAND |
|---|---|---|
| G. ROBERTS | †W.M. PENMAN | G. ROBERTS |
| †J.B. CRAIG | J.R.S. INNES 1T | J.R.S. INNES |
| D.J. MACRAE | D.J. MACRAE | D.J. MACRAE |
| †J.R.S. INNES | *R.W. SHAW | *R.W. SHAW 1T |
| W.N. RENWICK | K.C. FYFE | W.C.W. MURDOCH 1T |
| *R.W. SHAW | R.B. BRUCE-LOCKHART | R.B. BRUCE-LOCKHART |
| †W.R.C. BRYDON | T.F. DORWARD | T.F. DORWARD |
| †G.H. GALLIE | †I.C. HENDERSON | I.C. HENDERSON |
| †R.W.F. SAMPSON | †I.N. GRAHAM | I.N. GRAHAM |
| †W. PURDIE | W. PURDIE | W. PURDIE |
| G.B. HORSBURGH | G.B. HORSBURGH | G.B. HORSBURGH |
| A. ROY | A. ROY | A. ROY |
| W.B. YOUNG | W.B. YOUNG | W.B. YOUNG |
| P.L. DUFF | †D.K.A. MACKENZIE | D.K.A. MACKENZIE |
| W.H. CRAWFORD 1PG | G.D. SHAW | W.H. CRAWFORD |
| Cardiff Arms Park | Lansdowne Road | Murrayfield |
| LOST 3-11 | LOST 3-12 | LOST 6-9 |
| WALES: 1G 1PG 1T | IRE.: 1PG 1GM 2T | SCOT.: 2T |
| SCOT.: 1PG | SCOT.: 1T | ENG.: 3PG |
| 4 Feb. 1939 | 25 Feb. 1939 | 18 Mar. 1939 |

Medical commitments prevented Charles Dick from playing in 1939, and there were further difficulties when the nominated replacement, J.G.S. Forrest, fell out through injury. Forrest had played effectively on the wing in the previous season, and scored two tries against Ireland. During the war he served as a sub-lieutenant in the RNVR, but was killed in action in September 1942.

Scotland's fall from grace was attributed to their failure to recruit a sound pack. There were difficulties finding a solid front row, the forwards were consistently beaten in the scrummages and line-outs, and even in the loose the traditional Scottish virtues of aggression and dribbling skill were at a premium.

As a result, a talented back division, starved of good possession, was unable to create many scoring chances. At Murrayfield, in the defeat by England, Macrae, Innes and Murdoch showed considerable dash and pace against a pedestrian English attack. But their forwards were so out-scrummaged that chances were limited, and England scraped home by three penalties to two tries.

## 1946-47

| v. FRANCE | v. WALES | v. IRELAND | v. ENGLAND |
|---|---|---|---|
| *†K.I. GEDDES 1PG | *K.I. GEDDES 1c,1PG | K.I. GEDDES | K.I. GEDDES 1c |
| †T.G.H. JACKSON | T.G.H. JACKSON | W.D. MacLENNAN | T.G.H. JACKSON 1T |
| †C.W. DRUMMOND | C.W. DRUMMOND | C.W. DRUMMOND | C.W. DRUMMOND |
| †C.R. BRUCE | C.R. BRUCE | C.R. BRUCE | W.H. MUNRO |
| †W.D. MacLENNAN | †D.D. MACKENZIE | D.D. MACKENZIE | D.D. MACKENZIE |
| †I.J.M. LUMSDEN | I.J.M LUMSDEN | *†W.H. MUNRO | *C.R. BRUCE |
| †A.W. BLACK | A.W. BLACK | †E. ANDERSON | E. ANDERSON |
| †T.P.L. McGLASHAN | I.C. HENDERSON | T.P.L. McGLASHAN | T.P.L. McGLASHAN |
| I.C. HENDERSON | R.W.F. SAMPSON | †A.T. FISHER | A.T. FISHER |
| †A.G.M. WATT | †R. AITKEN | †H.H. CAMPBELL | H.H. CAMPBELL |
| †G.L. CAWKWELL | D.W. DEAS | A.G.M. WATT | I.C. HENDERSON |
| †J.M. HUNTER | †F.H. COUTTS | F.H. COUTTS | F.H. COUTTS |
| †W.I.D. ELLIOT | W.I.D. ELLIOT 1T | †D.D. VALENTINE | D.D. VALENTINE |
| †D.W. DEAS | A.G.M. WATT | †J.B. LEES | D.I. McLEAN |
| †J.H. ORR | J.H. ORR | †D.I. McLEAN | W.I.D. ELLIOT |
| Stade Colombes | Murrayfield | Murrayfield | Twickenham |
| LOST 3-8 | LOST 8-22 | LOST 0-3 | LOST 5-24 |
| FR.: 1G 1T | SCOT.: 1G 1PG | SCOT.: NIL | ENG.: 4G 1DG |
| SCOT.: 1PG | WALES: 2G 1PG 3T | IRE.: 1T | SCOT.: 1G |
| 1 Jan. 1947 | 1 Feb. 1947 | 22 Feb. 1947 | 15 Mar. 1947 |

A high standard of combined play had made Scotland the outstanding peformers in the unofficial "Victory" internationals of 1945-6, but they failed to reproduce such form in 1947, and all four matches were lost in the Championship.

There were weak points at half-back and in the front five tight positions of the scrummage. Three different pairings were made in the pivot positions, while six different front-row players appeared. Two of these, farmer Ian Henderson and Ralph Sampson, had appeared for Scotland before the war. Henderson was picked at hooker, prop and second row during the season and was one of the few successes of the Scottish side. Sampson had earned the DFC and DSO during a distinguished service career.

Two of Scotland's new wing-forwards were to enjoy sucessful rugby careers. Douglas Elliot, another farmer, played 29 times up to 1954. He was a sure tackler and efficient destroyer of attacks, but he also possessed good handling skills and had the ability to combine effectively with his backs. David Valentine made his name as a Rugby League player. After gaining two caps in 1947 he signed for Huddersfield. In a long career, he gained a Rugby League Cup-winners medal and led Great Britain to victory in the first Rugby League World Cup tournament in 1954.

## 1947-48

| v. AUSTRALIA | v. FRANCE | v. WALES | v. IRELAND | v. ENGLAND |
|---|---|---|---|---|
| I.J.M. LUMSDEN | W.C.W. MURDOCH 2PG | W.C.W. MURDOCH | W.C.W. MURDOCH | W.C.W. MURDOCH |
| T.G.H. JACKSON | T.G.H. JACKSON 1T | T.G.H. JACKSON | T.G.H. JACKSON | T.G.H. JACKSON |
| *J.R.S. INNES | *J.R.S. INNES | *J.R.S. INNES | *J.R.S. INNES | *J.R.S. INNES |
| †T. WRIGHT | C.W. DRUMMOND | †A. CAMERON | C.W. DRUMMOND | †L. BRUCE-LOCKHART |
| †C. McDONALD 1PG | D.D. MACKENZIE | D.D. MACKENZIE | D.D. MACKENZIE | C.W. DRUMMOND 1T |
| †D.P. HEPBURN 1DG | D.P. HEPBURN | D.P. HEPBURN | D.P. HEPBURN | D.P. HEPBURN |
| †W.D. ALLARDICE | W.D. ALLARDICE | W.D. ALLARDICE | W.D. ALLARDICE | A.W. BLACK |
| †R.M. BRUCE | R.M. BRUCE | L.R. CURRIE | †S. COLTMAN | H.H. CAMPBELL |
| †G.G. LYALL | G.G. LYALL | G.G. LYALL | G.G. LYALL | G.G. LYALL |
| I.C. HENDERSON | †W.P. BLACK | R.M. BRUCE | I.C. HENDERSON | I.C. HENDERSON |
| †L.R. CURRIE | L.R. CURRIE | J.C. DAWSON | H.H. CAMPBELL | †R. FINLAY |
| †J.C. DAWSON | J.C. DAWSON | W.P. BLACK | L.R. CURRIE | W.P. BLACK |
| W.I.D. ELLIOT | W.I.D. ELLIOT | W.I.D. ELLIOT | W.I.D. ELLIOT | W.I.D. ELLIOT |
| A.G.M. WATT | A.G.M. WATT | A.G.M. WATT | W.P. BLACK | J.B. LEES |
| J.B. LEES | J.B. LEES | J.B. LEES | R.M. BRUCE | W.B. YOUNG 1T |
| Murrayfield | Murrayfield | Cardiff Arms Park | Lansdowne Road | Murrayfield |
| LOST 7-16 | WON 9-8 | LOST 0-14 | LOST 0-6 | WON 6-3 |
| SCOT.: 1DG 1PG | SCOT.: 2PG 1T | WALES: 1G 1PG 2T | IRE.: 2T | SCOT.: 2T |
| AUST. 2G 2T | FR.: 1G 1PG | SCOT.: NIL | SCOT.: NIL | ENG.: 1PG |
| 22 Nov. 1947 | 24 Jan. 1948 | 7 Feb. 1948 | 28 Feb. 1948 | 20 Mar. 1948 |

There was little improvement in the Scottish forward play in 1948, though one or two changes in the backs resulted in encouraging wins over France and England. The Scots opened the season in November with a match against the Australians. Late withdrawals gave the fifteen a makeshift look, but new fly-half Hepburn gave a fine all-round performance and combined effectively with Allardice. Scotland's failure to win good possession deprived the backs of attacking opportunities, and in the end the tourists won comfortably by four tries to nil.

The assistance of two pre-war caps, Innes and Murdoch, added experience to the side for the Championship matches. Murdoch's international career thus spanned fourteen seasons, a record for a Scot. Innes was a doctor and became President of the SRU in 1973-4.

The recall of another pre-war international, W.B. Young, led to victory against England. With the scores level, Young gathered the ball at the back of a lineout and charged through several defenders to score the winning try 15 minutes from no-side.

## 1948-49

| v. FRANCE | v. WALES | v. IRELAND | v. ENGLAND |
|---|---|---|---|
| I.J.M. Lumsden | I.J.M. Lumsden | I.J.M. Lumsden | I.J.M. Lumsden |
| T.G.H. Jackson | T.G.H. Jackson | T.G.H. Jackson | T.G.H. Jackson |
| †L.G. Gloag | L.G. Gloag 1t | L.G. Gloag | L.G. Gloag |
| D.P. Hepburn | D.P. Hepburn | D.P. Hepburn | D.P. Hepburn |
| †D.W.C. Smith | D.W.C. Smith 1t | D.W.C. Smith | D.W.C. Smith |
| C.R. Bruce | C.R. Bruce | C.R. Bruce | C.R. Bruce |
| W.D. Allardice 1c | W.D. Allardice | W.D. Allardice 1pg | W.D. Allardice |
| J.C. Dawson | J.C. Dawson | J.C. Dawson | †S.T.H. Wright |
| †J.G. Abercrombie | J.G. Abercrombie | J.G. Abercrombie | †J.A.R. MacPhail |
| S. Coltman | S. Coltman | S. Coltman | S. Coltman |
| L.R. Currie | L.R. Currie | L.R. Currie | L.R. Currie |
| †G.A. Wilson | G.A. Wilson | †A.M. Thomson | G.A. Wilson 1pg |
| W.I.D. Elliot 1t | W.I.D. Elliot | W.I.D. Elliot | W.I.D. Elliot |
| †P.W. Kininmonth 1t | P.W. Kininmonth | P.W. Kininmonth | P.W. Kininmonth |
| *†D.H. Keller | *D.H. Keller | *D.H. Keller | *D.H. Keller |
| Stade Colombes | Murrayfield | Murrayfield | Twickenham |
| WON 8-0 | WON 6-5 | LOST 3-13 | LOST 3-19 |
| Fr.: NIL | Scot.: 2t | Scot.: 1pg | Eng.: 2g 3t |
| Scot.: 1g 1t | Wales: 1g | Ire.: 2g 1pg | Scot.: 1pg |
| 15 Jan. 1949 | 5 Feb. 1949 | 26 Feb. 1949 | 19 Mar. 1949 |

Scotland opened the season with six new caps, relying upon exiles and university men. Indeed, less than half of the side who faced the French were playing for Scottish clubs at the time of the match. Doug Keller, an Australian who had played against the Scots the previous season, became the new captain on his debut. Keller had returned to Britain following the 1947-8 Wallabies' tour in order to study at Guy's Hospital.

The Scots flattered to deceive in winning the two opening matches before losing heavily to Ireland and England. The Scots devised a clever trap to ensnare the Welsh backs at Murrayfield. A defensive net comprising the two halves and two loose forwards repeatedly and mercilessly caught the Welsh backs as openings were sought. Eventually the Scottish backs, with limited possession, scored two fine tries to beat Wales by a point.

Peter Kininmonth, a London broker, made the first of his 21 appearances this season. He was an intelligent back-row expert who was mobile in the loose and handled safely and accurately in attack.

## 1949-50

| v. FRANCE | v. WALES | v. IRELAND | v. ENGLAND |
|---|---|---|---|
| †G. Burrell | G. Burrell | G. Burrell | †T. Gray 2c |
| D.W.C. Smith | D.W.C. Smith | †D.M. Scott | D.M. Scott |
| †R. MacDonald 1t | R. MacDonald | R. MacDonald | R. MacDonald |
| †D.A. Sloan | D.A. Sloan | C.W. Drummond | D.A. Sloan 2t |
| C.W. Drummond | C.W. Drummond | D.W.C. Smith | C.W. Drummond |
| L. Bruce-Lockhart 1c | L. Bruce-Lockhart | A. Cameron | A. Cameron |
| †A.F. Dorward | A.W. Black | A.W. Black | A.W. Black |
| J.C. Dawson | J.C. Dawson | J.C. Dawson | J.C. Dawson |
| J.G. Abercrombie | J.G. Abercrombie | J.G. Abercrombie | J.G. Abercrombie 1t |
| †G.M. Budge 1t | G.M. Budge | G.M. Budge | G.M. Budge |
| †R. Gemmill | R. Gemmill | R. Gemmill | R. Gemmill |
| †D.E. Muir | D.E. Muir | D.E. Muir | D.E. Muir |
| *W.I.D. Elliot | *W.I.D. Elliot | *W.I.D. Elliot | W.I.D. Elliot |
| P.W. Kininmonth | P.W. Kininmonth | P.W. Kininmonth | *P.W. Kininmonth |
| D.H. Keller | D.H. Keller | D.H. Keller | †H. Scott |
| Murrayfield | St. Helen's | Lansdowne Road | Murrayfield |
| WON 8-5 | LOST 0-12 | LOST 0-21 | WON 13-11 |
| Scot.: 1g 1t | Wales: 1dg 1pg 2t | Ire.: 3g 2pg | Scot.: 2g 1t |
| Fr.: 1g | Scot.: NIL | Scot.: NIL | Eng.: 1g 1pg 1t |
| 14 Jan. 1950 | 4 Feb. 1950 | 25 Feb. 1950 | 18 Mar. 1950 |

Scotland fielded seven new caps against France, and they went on to finish as runners-up in the Championship. Douglas Elliot, as the new captain, instilled a disciplined approach and the selectors made few adjustments during the season.

George Burrell was among the new caps for the French match. Apart from playing international rugby, he later became an international referee, was appointed manager for the 1977 British and Irish Lions tour, and served as President of the SRU in 1985-6.

Scotland regained the Calcutta Cup in a match full of excitement. It was a superb last-minute conversion by new cap Tom Gray which produced a Scottish victory in wet, muddy conditions. Gray was a surprise choice for the match, for he had been playing club rugby for Northampton as a fly-half. Aged 33 years, he proved a model of steadiness at full-back and thus became the oldest first cap to play for Scotland.

## 1950-51

| v. FRANCE | v. WALES | v.IRELAND | v.ENGLAND |
|---|---|---|---|
| T. Gray 2PG | †I.H.M. Thomson 1PG,1C | I.H.M. Thomson 1C | T. Gray |
| | | | |
| †A.D. Cameron | †R.A. Gordon 2T | †K.J. Dalgleish | K.J. Dalgleish |
| †I.D.F. Coutts | D.A. Sloan | D.A. Sloan 1T | D.A. Sloan |
| †F.O. Turnbull | D.M. Scott | D.M. Scott | D.M. Scott |
| †D.M. Rose 2T | D.M. Rose | D.M. Rose | D.M. Rose |
| | | | |
| A. Cameron | A. Cameron | A. Cameron | A. Cameron 1T |
| †I.A. Ross | I.A. Ross | I.A. Ross | I.A. Ross |
| | | | |
| J.C. Dawson | J.C. Dawson 1T | J.C. Dawson | J.C. Dawson |
| †N.G.R. Mair | N.G.R. Mair | N.G.R. Mair | N.G.R. Mair |
| †R.L. Wilson | R.L. Wilson | R.L. Wilson | R.L. Wilson |
| †H.M. Inglis | H.M. Inglis 1C | H.M. Inglis | H.M. Inglis |
| R. Gemmill | R. Gemmill | R. Gemmill | W.P. Black |
| W.I.D. Elliot | W.I.D. Elliot | W.I.D. Elliot | W.I.D. Elliot |
| *P.W. Kininmonth | *P.W. Kininmonth 1DG | *P.W. Kininmonth | *P.W. Kininmonth |
| †J.J. Hegarty | †R.C. Taylor | R.C. Taylor | R.C. Taylor |
| | | | |
| Stade Colombes | Murrayfield | Murrayfield | Twickenham |
| LOST 12-14 | WON 19-0 | LOST 5-6 | LOST 3-5 |
| | | | |
| Fr.: 1G 2PG 1T | Scot.: 2G 1DG 1PG 1T | Scot.: 1G | Eng.: 1G |
| Scot.: 2PG 2T | Wales: NIL | Ire.: 1DG 1T | Scot.: 1T |
| | | | |
| 13 Jan. 1951 | 3 Feb. 1951 | 24 Feb. 1951 | 17 Mar. 1951 |

Scotland, under Peter Kininmonth's leadership, had to share the wooden spoon in 1951. But their sole win of the season, the massacre of Wales, was described as the most famous "David and Goliath" act in international rugby history.

Wales were the Grand Slam holders and had already thrashed England before their fateful journey to Murrayfield. In front of 80,000 spectators, the Scots constantly harassed Wales and the forwards slowly gained the upper-hand at forward and at half-back. A penalty goal by Thomson was the only score of the first half.

Then midway through the second half, Kininmonth fielded a loose Welsh kick and dropped a magnificent goal from beyond the Welsh 25. It was the turning point of the match and the inspired Scots added three further tries to win by 19 points.

## 1951-52

| v. S. AFRICA | v. FRANCE | v. WALES | v. IRELAND | v. ENGLAND |
|---|---|---|---|---|
| G. Burrell | I.H.M. Thomson 2PG,1C | I.H.M. Thomson | I.H.M. Thomson 1PG,1C | †N.W.Cameron |
| | | | | |
| †J.G.M. Hart | R.A. Gordon | R.A. Gordon | R.A. Gordon | R.A. Gordon |
| D.M. Scott | †I.F. Cordial 1T | I.F. Cordial | I.F. Cordial | I.F. Cordial |
| F.O. Turnbull | †J.L. Allan | J.L. Allan | J.L. Allan | I.D.F. Coutts |
| D.M. Rose | D.M. Scott | D.M. Scott | D.M. Scott | †T.G. Weatherstone |
| | | | | |
| *A. Cameron | †J.N.G. Davidson | J.N.G. Davidson | J.N.G. Davidson 1T | J.N.G. Davidson |
| A.F. Dorward | †A.K. Fulton | A.F. Dorward | A.F. Dorward | *A.F. Dorward |
| | | | | |
| J.C. Dawson | J.C. Dawson | J.C. Dawson | J.C. Dawson | J.C. Dawson |
| J.A.R. MacPhail | †N.M. Munnoch | N.M. Munnoch | N.M. Munnoch | J. Fox |
| R.L. Wilson | †J. Fox | J. Fox | J. Fox | †J.M. Inglis |
| †J. Johnston | J. Johnston | J. Johnston | J. Johnston | J. Johnston 1T |
| H.M. Inglis | †M. Walker | D.E. Muir | D.E. Muir | D.E. Muir |
| W.I.D. Elliot | W.I.D. Elliot | W.I.D. Elliot | W.I.D. Elliot | W.I.D. Elliot |
| P.W. Kininmonth | *P.W. Kininmonth | H.M. Inglis | H.M. Inglis | †J.P. Friebe |
| R.C. Taylor | †J.T. Greenwood | *P.W. Kininmonth | *P.W. Kininmonth | †D.S. Gilbert-Smith |
| | | | | |
| Murrayfield | Murrayfield | Cardiff Arms Park | Lansdowne Road | Murrayfield |
| LOST 0-44 | LOST 11-13 | LOST 0-11 | LOST 8-12 | LOST 3-19 |
| | | | | |
| Scot.: NIL | Scot.: 1G 2PG | Wales: 1G 2PG | Ire.: 1PG 3T | Scot.: 1T |
| SA.: 7G 1DG 2T | Fr.: 2G 1PG | Scot.: NIL | Scot.: 1G 1PG | Eng.: 2G 1DG 2T |
| | | | | |
| 24 Nov. 1951 | 12 Jan. 1952 | 2 Feb. 1952 | 23 Feb. 1952 | 15 Mar. 1952 |

1951-2 went down as Scotland's worst season on record. Five matches were lost, 99 points conceded, and Scotland's record defeat by South Africa was a rugby disaster which the nation took several years to overcome.

There were numerous changes following the South African debacle. Six of the backs did not survive for the French match, and the seventh, Scott, was transferred from the centre to the wing. Less drastic action was taken with the forwards and three men, Dawson, Johnston and the reliable Douglas Elliot, were the only Scots to appear in all five of the international matches.

John Hart, who won his only cap for Scotland in the match with the Springboks, became Honorary Secretary of the International Board.

## 1952-53

| v. FRANCE | v. WALES | v. IRELAND | v. ENGLAND |
|---|---|---|---|
| N.W. CAMERON 1c | N.W. CAMERON | I.H.M. THOMSON 1c | I.H.M. THOMSON 1c |
| | | | |
| K.J. DALGLEISH | R.A. GORDON | T.G. WEATHERSTONE | T.G. WEATHERSTONE 1T |
| D.M. SCOTT | K.J. DALGLEISH | *A. CAMERON | *A. CAMERON |
| D.A. SLOAN | J.L. ALLAN | †D. CAMERON | D. CAMERON |
| D.M. ROSE 1T | D.M. ROSE | D.W.C. SMITH | †J.S. SWAN |
| | | | |
| J.N.G. DAVIDSON | J.N.G. DAVIDSON | L.BRUCE-LOCKHART | L.BRUCE-LOCKHART |
| *A.F. DORWARD | *A.F. DORWARD | †K.M. SPENCE | A.F. DORWARD |
| | | | |
| †B.E. THOMSON | B.E. THOMSON | B.E. THOMSON | J.C. DAWSON |
| †J.H.F. KING | J.H.F. KING | †G.C. HOYER-MILLAR | J.H.F. KING |
| R.L. WILSON | R.L. WILSON | †J.H. WILSON | R.L. WILSON |
| †J.H. HENDERSON | J.H. HENDERSON | J.H. HENDERSON 1T,1PG | J.H. HENDERSON 1T |
| J.J. HEGARTY | J.J. HEGARTY | J.J. HEGARTY | J.J. HEGARTY |
| †A.R. VALENTINE | A.R. VALENTINE | A.R. VALENTINE | †W. KERR |
| †D.C. McDONALD | D.C. McDONALD | †E.H. HENRIKSEN | †W.L.K. COWIE |
| †K.H.D. McMILLAN | K.H.D. McMILLAN | K.H.D. McMILLAN | K.H.D. McMILLAN |
| | | | |
| Stade Colombes | Murrayfield | Murrayfield | Twickenham |
| LOST 5-11 | LOST 0-12 | LOST 8-26 | LOST 8-26 |
| | | | |
| FR.: 1G 1DG 1PG | SCOT.: NIL | SCOT.: 1G 1PG | ENG.: 4G 2T |
| SCOT.: 1G | WALES: 1PG 3T | IRE.: 4G 2T | SCOT.: 1G 1T |
| | | | |
| 10 Jan. 1953 | 7 Feb. 1953 | 28 Feb. 1953 | 21 Mar. 1953 |

The pundits attributed Scotland's combined failures on the rugby field to lack of intense competion among the Scottish clubs and an over-emphasis on seven-a-side football. In their four losses of 1953, there was a distinct lack of expertise in the scrummaging, and the tackling power of the backs was far below the standard expected at international level.

Arthur Dorward and Angus Cameron, two of Scotland's finest servants in the gloomy years of the early 1950s, shared the captaincy during the season. At a time when Scotland's attacking potential was extremely limited, both were valued for their astute tactical kicking.

Doctor Douglas Smith, a native of Aberdeen who played for London Scottish, won the last of his eight Scottish caps against Ireland. Later, in 1971, he was the manager of the victorious British and Irish Lions team which toured New Zealand, and he was awarded the OBE for his part in the Lions' success.

## 1953-54

| v. FRANCE | v. NZ | v. IRELAND | v. ENGLAND | v. WALES |
|---|---|---|---|---|
| †J.C. MARSHALL | J.C. MARSHALL | J.C. MARSHALL | J.C. MARSHALL | J.C. MARSHALL |
| | | | | |
| J.S. SWAN | J.S. SWAN | J.S. SWAN | J.S. SWAN | J.S. SWAN |
| A.D. CAMERON | †M.K. ELGIE | M.K. ELGIE | M.K. ELGIE 1T | M.K. ELGIE |
| D. CAMERON | D. CAMERON | D. CAMERON | D. CAMERON | A.D. CAMERON |
| T.G. WEATHERSTONE | T.G. WEATHERSTONE | T.G. WEATHERSTONE | T.G. WEATHERSTONE | T.G. WEATHERSTONE |
| | | | | |
| *J.N.G. DAVIDSON | †G.T. ROSS | G.T. ROSS | G.T. ROSS | G.T. ROSS |
| A.K. FULTON | †L.P. MacLACHLAN | L.P. MacLACHLAN | L.P. MacLACHLAN | L.P. MacLACHLAN |
| | | | | |
| T.P.L. McGLASHAN | T.P.L. McGLASHAN | T.P.L. McGLASHAN | T.P.L. McGLASHAN | T.P.L. McGLASHAN |
| †R.K.G. MacEWEN | R.K.G. MacEWEN | R.K.G. MacEWEN | J.H.F. KING | R.K.G. MacEWEN |
| †H.F. McLEOD | H.F. McLEOD | H.F. McLEOD | H.F. McLEOD | H.F. McLEOD |
| †E.A.J. FERGUSSON | E.A.J. FERGUSSON | E.A.J. FERGUSSON | E.A.J. FERGUSSON | E.A.J. FERGUSSON |
| †E.J.S. MICHIE | E.J.S. MICHIE | E.J.S. MICHIE | E.J.S. MICHIE | †J.W.Y. KEMP |
| †A. ROBSON | *W.I.D. ELLIOT | *W.I.D. ELLIOT | *W.I.D. ELLIOT | *W.I.D. ELLIOT |
| P.W. KININMONTH | P.W. KININMONTH | P.W. KININMONTH | P.W. KININMONTH | P.W. KININMONTH |
| J.H. HENDERSON | J.H. HENDERSON | J.H. HENDERSON | J.H. HENDERSON | J.H. HENDERSON 1T |
| | | | | |
| Murrayfield | Murrayfield | Ravenhill | Murrayfield | St.Helen's |
| LOST 0-3 | LOST 0-3 | LOST 0-6 | LOST 3-13 | LOST 3-15 |
| | | | | |
| SCOT.: NIL | SCOT.: NIL | IRE.: 2T | SCOT.: 1T | WALES: 1PG 4T |
| FR.: 1T | NZ: 1PG | SCOT.: NIL | ENG.: 2G 1T | SCOT.: 1T |
| | | | | |
| 9 Jan. 1954 | 13 Feb. 1954 | 27 Feb. 1954 | 20 Mar. 1954 | 10 Apr. 1954 |

Scotland again finished with the wooden spoon, but there were two splendid fighting performances against France and New Zealand. Veteran Douglas Elliot inspired a fine revival of spirited Scottish forward play, especially in the loose against the All Blacks. In the end the tourists were thankful to win by a penalty to nil.

Although the high morale produced by these early games failed to inspire victories later in the season, there was a marked improvement in the tackling and defence of the side. Marshall proved to be a sound full-back, Weatherstone and Swan had few opportunities in attack but defended stoutly when required, and Kim Elgie, a South African who later played Test cricket against New Zealand, was a hard-running centre with the ability to kick goals.

Another South African, J.H. "Chick" Henderson, played the last of his nine internationals for Scotland against Wales. An Oxford graduate, he later returned to South Africa as an Industrial Engineer and became well-known for his broadcasts of South African rugby and cricket matches.

## 1954-55

| v. FRANCE | v. WALES | v. IRELAND | v. ENGLAND |
|---|---|---|---|
| A. CAMERON | *A. CAMERON | †R.W.T. CHISHOLM | R.W.T. CHISHOLM |
| | | | |
| J.S. SWAN | †A.R. SMITH 1T | A.R. SMITH | A.R. SMITH |
| M.K. ELGIE | M.K. ELGIE 1PG,1C | M.K. ELGIE 2PG | M.K. ELGIE |
| †M.L. GRANT | †R.G. CHARTERS | R.G. CHARTERS | R.G. CHARTERS |
| T.G. WEATHERSTONE | J.S. SWAN | J.S. SWAN 1T | J.S. SWAN |
| | | | |
| †J.T. DOCHERTY | J.T. DOCHERTY 1DG | *A. CAMERON 1DG | *A. CAMERON 1PG,1T |
| A.F. DORWARD | †J.A. NICHOL 1T | J.A. NICHOL | J.A. NICHOL |
| | | | |
| H.F. McLEOD | H.F. McLEOD | H.F. McLEOD | H.F. McLEOD |
| †W.K.L. RELPH | W.K.L. RELPH | W.K.L. RELPH | W.K.L. RELPH |
| †I.R. HASTIE | †T. ELLIOT | T. ELLIOT | T. ELLIOT |
| J.J. HEGARTY | E.J.S. MICHIE | E.J.S. MICHIE | E.J.S. MICHIE |
| J.W.Y. KEMP | J.W.Y. KEMP | J.W.Y. KEMP | J.W.Y. KEMP |
| †H. DUFFY | †W.S. GLEN | †I.A.A. MacGREGOR | I.A.A. MacGREGOR |
| *J.T. GREENWOOD | J.T. GREENWOOD | J.T. GREENWOOD | J.T. GREENWOOD |
| A. ROBSON | A. ROBSON | A. ROBSON | A. ROBSON |
| | | | |
| Stade Colombes | Murrayfield | Murrayfield | Twickenham |
| LOST 0-15 | WON 14-8 | WON 12-3 | LOST 6-9 |
| | | | |
| FR.: 4T 1PG | SCOT.: 1G 1DG 1PG 1T | SCOT.: 1DG 2PG 1T | ENG.: 1PG 2T |
| SCOT.: NIL | WALES: 1G 1T | IRE.: 1PG | SCOT.: 1PG 1T |
| | | | |
| 8 Jan. 1955 | 5 Feb. 1955 | 26 Feb. 1955 | 19 Mar. 1955 |

The long, grim series of defeats – 17 in all – ended with a triumph at Murrayfield against a strong Welsh fifteen. Following a loss in Paris, sweeping changes were made before the Welsh game and Angus Cameron, now playing at full-back (after winning previous caps at centre and fly-half) became captain.

Arthur Smith, on his debut, scored a brilliant try against the Welsh, setting Scotland on the path to a famous victory. He went on to win 33 caps for Scotland, captained the side fifteen times, and scored 58 points (including twelve tries) in his international career. He retired after captaining the 1962 Lions to South Africa.

Scotland beat Ireland for the first time since 1938 and there was talk of a new-found spirit which had captured Scottish rugby. Despite a marvellous display by Angus Cameron against England, however, the Scots could not engineer a Triple Crown victory at Twickenham.

## 1955-56

| v. FRANCE | v. WALES | v. IRELAND | v. ENGLAND |
|---|---|---|---|
| R.W.T. CHISHOLM | R.W.T. CHISHOLM | R.W.T. CHISHOLM | R.W.T. CHISHOLM |
| | | | |
| A.R. SMITH 1PG | A.R. SMITH | A.R. SMITH 1T | A.R. SMITH 1PG |
| *A. CAMERON 1PG | *A. CAMERON 1PG | †T. McCLUNG 2C | J.T. DOCHERTY |
| †K.R. MacDONALD | K.R. MacDONALD | K.R. MacDONALD | †G.D. STEVENSON 1T |
| J.S. SWAN | J.S. SWAN | J.S. SWAN | J.S. SWAN |
| | | | |
| M.L. GRANT | M.L. GRANT | *A. CAMERON | T. McCLUNG |
| †N.M. CAMPBELL | N.M. CAMPBELL | A.F. DORWARD | A.F. DORWARD |
| | | | |
| H.F. McLEOD | H.F. McLEOD | H.F. McLEOD | H.F. McLEOD |
| R.K.G. MacEWEN | R.K.G. MacEWEN | R.K.G. MacEWEN | R.K.G. MacEWEN |
| T. ELLIOT | T. ELLIOT | T. ELLIOT | T. ELLIOT |
| E.J.S. MICHIE | E.J.S. MICHIE | E.J.S. MICHIE 1T | E.J.S. MICHIE |
| J.W.Y. KEMP 2T | J.W.Y. KEMP | J.W.Y. KEMP | J.W.Y. KEMP |
| I.A.A. MacGREGOR | I.A.A. MacGREGOR | I.A.A. MacGREGOR | I.A.A. MacGREGOR |
| J.T. GREENWOOD | J.T. GREENWOOD | J.T. GREENWOOD | *J.T. GREENWOOD |
| A. ROBSON | A. ROBSON | A. ROBSON | A. ROBSON |
| | | | |
| Murrayfield | Cardiff Arms Park | Lansdowne Road | Murrayfield |
| WON 12-0 | LOST 3-9 | LOST 10-14 | LOST 6-11 |
| | | | |
| SCOT.: 2PG 2T | WALES: 3T | IRE.: 1G 3T | SCOT.: 1PG 1T |
| FR.: NIL | SCOT.: 1PG | SCOT.: 2G | ENG.: 1G 2PG |
| | | | |
| 14 Jan. 1956 | 4 Feb. 1956 | 25 Feb. 1956 | 17 Mar. 1956 |

The Scottish forwards, favouring the old-fashioned 3-2-3 scrummage formation, were unchanged throughout the season. However, weakness in midfield and failures to take penalty points, often at crucial moments, deprived the Scots of success.

Splendid scrummaging and dash in the loose delighted the Scottish supporters who studied the French match. Hamish Kemp, the Glasgow grain merchant, scored two tries in Scotland's twelve-point victory, the only win of the season. Kemp eventually retired in 1960, after winning 27 caps.

There had been reservations concerning the form of Angus Cameron early in the Championship. His tactical kicking was as accurate as ever, but many critics felt his lack of pace was stifling Scotland's enterprise in midfield. He was injured in the Irish game, which turned out to be the last of his 17 appearances for Scotland.

## 1956-57

| v. FRANCE | v. WALES | v. IRELAND | v. ENGLAND |
|---|---|---|---|
| †K.J.F. SCOTLAND 1DG,1PG | K.J.F. SCOTLAND 1PG | K.J.F. SCOTLAND 1PG | K.J.F. SCOTLAND 1PG |
| A.R. SMITH | A.R. SMITH 1T | *A.R. SMITH | A.R. SMITH |
| †E. McKEATING | E. McKEATING | T. McCLUNG | T. McCLUNG |
| G.D. STEVENSON | K.R. MacDONALD | K.R. MacDONALD | K.R. MacDONALD |
| J.S. SWAN | J.S. SWAN | †J.L.F. ALLAN | J.L.F. ALLAN |
| M.L. GRANT | T. McCLUNG | †J.M. MAXWELL | †G.H. WADDELL |
| A.F. DORWARD | A.F. DORWARD 1DG | A.F. DORWARD | A.F. DORWARD |
| H.F. McLEOD | H.F. McLEOD | H.F. McLEOD | H.F. McLEOD |
| R.K.G. MacEWEN | R.K.G. MacEWEN | R.K.G. MacEWEN | R.K.G. MacEWEN |
| T. ELLIOT | T. ELLIOT | T. ELLIOT | T. ELLIOT |
| E.J.S. MICHIE | E.J.S. MICHIE | E.J.S. MICHIE | E.J.S. MICHIE |
| J.W.Y. KEMP | J.W.Y. KEMP | J.W.Y. KEMP | J.W.Y. KEMP |
| I.A.A. MacGREGOR | I.A.A. MacGREGOR | I.A.A. MacGREGOR | G.K. SMITH |
| *J.T. GREENWOOD | *J.T. GREENWOOD | †G.K. SMITH | *J.T. GREENWOOD |
| A. ROBSON | A. ROBSON | A. ROBSON | A. ROBSON |
| Stade Colombes | Murrayfield | Murrayfield | Twickenham |
| WON 6-0 | WON 9-6 | LOST 3-5 | LOST 3-16 |
| FR.: NIL | SCOT.: 1DG 1PG 1T | SCOT.: 1PG | ENG.: 2G 1PG 1T |
| SCOT.: 1DG 1PG | WALES: 1PG 1T | IRE.: 1G | SCOT.: 1PG |
| 12 Jan. 1957 | 2 Feb. 1957 | 23 Feb. 1957 | 16 Mar. 1957 |

K.J.F. Scotland, a full-back from Heriot's FP, scored all of Scotland's points on his debut to become the first Scot since W.H. Crawford in 1938 to score all the points in a win. Scotland (the player) was an accomplished full-back with a gift for attack. He won 27 caps in a long career, and led Scotland in 1963.

The Scottish pack created a record in 1957, too. By playing together against France and Wales, they did so for the sixth time in internationals, a feat never achieved by any side prior to this date.

Arthur Dorward played his last game for Scotland this season. A scrum-half like his brother (T.F. Dorward, who was killed during the war), his towering drop-goal against the Welsh inspired the Scots to a 9-6 win.

## 1957-58

| v. FRANCE | v. WALES | v. AUSTRALIA | v. IRELAND | v. ENGLAND |
|---|---|---|---|---|
| R.W.T. CHISHOLM 1PG,1C | R.W.T. CHISHOLM | R.W.T. CHISHOLM | R.W.T. CHISHOLM | K.J.F. SCOTLAND |
| *A.R. SMITH | *A.R. SMITH 1PG | *A.R. SMITH 2PG | *A.R. SMITH 1T | †C. ELLIOT 1PG |
| G.D. STEVENSON 1T | G.D. STEVENSON | G.D. STEVENSON 1T | G.D. STEVENSON | G.D. STEVENSON |
| J.T. DOCHERTY | J.T. DOCHERTY | J.T. DOCHERTY | J.T. DOCHERTY | J.T. DOCHERTY |
| J.S. SWAN | T.G. WEATHERSTONE | T.G. WEATHERSTONE 1T | T.G. WEATHERSTONE 1T | T.G. WEATHERSTONE |
| G.H. WADDELL | G.H. WADDELL | G.H. WADDELL | G.H. WADDELL | G.H. WADDELL |
| †J.A.T. RODD | J.A.T. RODD | J.A.T. RODD | J.A.T. RODD | J.A.T. RODD |
| H.F. McLEOD | H.F. McLEOD | H.F. McLEOD | H.F. McLEOD | H.F. McLEOD |
| †N.S. BRUCE | R.K.G. MacEWEN | N.S. BRUCE | N.S. BRUCE | N.S. BRUCE |
| I.R. HASTIE 1T | T. ELLIOT | T. ELLIOT | T. ELLIOT | I.R. HASTIE |
| †M.W. SWAN | M.W. SWAN | M.W. SWAN | M.W. SWAN | M.W. SWAN |
| J.W.Y. KEMP | J.W.Y. KEMP | J.W.Y. KEMP | J.W.Y. KEMP | J.W.Y. KEMP |
| G.K. SMITH | G.K. SMITH | G.K. SMITH | J.T. GREENWOOD | *J.T. GREENWOOD |
| J.T. GREENWOOD | J.T. GREENWOOD | J.T. GREENWOOD | D.C. McDONALD | D.C. McDONALD |
| †M.A. ROBERTSON | A. ROBSON | A. ROBSON | A. ROBSON | A. ROBSON |
| Murrayfield | Cardiff Arms Park | Murrayfield | Lansdowne Road | Murrayfield |
| WON 11-9 | LOST 3-8 | WON 12-8 | LOST 6-12 | DRAWN 3-3 |
| SCOT.: 1G 1PG 1T | WALES: 1G 1T | SCOT.: 2PG 2T | IRE.: 2PG 2T | SCOT.: 1PG |
| FR.: 2PG 1T | SCOT.: 1PG | AUST.: 1G 1T | SCOT.: 2T | ENG.: 1PG |
| 11 Jan. 1958 | 1 Feb. 1958 | 15 Feb. 1958 | 1 Mar. 1958 | 15 Mar. 1958 |

Scotland fielded a settled side this season. There were several new caps in the pack against France, a new scrum-half partner for Gordon Waddell, and an experienced threequarter line. Their victory over the French, in a close game, made an encouraging start to the season.

There was the customary defeat at Cardiff (where Scotland had not won since 1927) before Arthur Smith's place-kicking changed the course of a close match with Australia. Australia were leading by 8-6 when Smith kicked a tremendous penalty goal from half-way early in the second half. The Australians were visibly demoralised by this kick, the Scots raised their game, and a fine attack initiated by Waddell resulted in a try for Stevenson. Scotland were disappointed to lose in Dublin and shared a draw – a penalty goal apiece – with England.

Norman Bruce, an Army officer, played the first of his 31 matches for Scotland against France. A skilful hooker, he was always prominent in the loose and his speed and mobility in open play brought him three tries in his international career. He retired as Scotland's most-capped hooker.

## 1958-59

| v. FRANCE | v. WALES | v. IRELAND | v. ENGLAND |
|---|---|---|---|
| K.J.F. SCOTLAND | K.J.F. SCOTLAND 1PG | K.J.F. SCOTLAND 1PG | K.J.F. SCOTLAND 1PG |
| A.R. SMITH | A.R. SMITH | A.R. SMITH | A.R. SMITH |
| T. McCLUNG | T. McCLUNG | T. McCLUNG | †J.A.P. SHACKLETON |
| †I.H.P. LAUGHLAND | G.D. STEVENSON | G.D. STEVENSON | G.D. STEVENSON |
| C. ELLIOT | T.G. WEATHERSTONE | T.G. WEATHERSTONE | T.G. WEATHERSTONE |
| G.H. WADDELL | G.H. WADDELL | G.H. WADDELL | *G.H. WADDELL |
| †S. COUGHTRIE | S. COUGHTRIE | S. COUGHTRIE | S. COUGHTRIE |
| H.F. McLEOD | H.F. McLEOD | H.F. McLEOD | H.F. McLEOD |
| N.S. BRUCE | N.S. BRUCE 1T | N.S. BRUCE | N.S. BRUCE |
| I.R. HASTIE | I.R. HASTIE | I.R. HASTIE | †D.M.D. ROLLO |
| M.W. SWAN | M.W. SWAN | M.W. SWAN | †F.H. TEN BOS |
| J.W.Y. KEMP | J.W.Y. KEMP | J.W.Y. KEMP | J.W.Y. KEMP |
| G.K. SMITH | G.K. SMITH | G.K. SMITH | G.K. SMITH |
| *J.T. GREENWOOD | *J.T. GREENWOOD | *J.T. GREENWOOD | †J.A. DAVIDSON |
| A. ROBSON | A. ROBSON | A. ROBSON | A. ROBSON |
| Stade Colombes | Murrayfield | Murrayfield | Twickenham |
| LOST 0-9 | WON 6-5 | LOST 3-8 | DRAWN 3-3 |
| FR.: 2DG 1T | SCOT.: 1PG 1T | SCOT.: 1PG | ENG.: 1PG |
| SCOT.: NIL | WALES: 1G | IRE.: 1G 1PG | SCOT.: 1PG |
| 10 Jan. 1959 | 7 Feb. 1959 | 28 Feb. 1959 | 21 Mar. 1959 |

1959 was a dour season for Scotland. They finished with the wooden spoon, scored just twelve points from four matches, and managed only one try. Nevertheless, there were splendid performances by the pack, particularly against Wales and England, and a new scrum-half, Stan Coughtrie, provided Waddell and the backs with a quick, accurate service. Close marking often prevented the backs from gaining much ground, but the general feeling in Scotland at the close of the season was one of optimism. Emergency measures were necessary before the Welsh match. A freeze had gripped the country at the start of February, but thanks to an anti-freeze plan the Murrayfield pitch was firm but playable on a cold day. Waddell and Smith made some exciting runs as Scotland gained their only win of the season. (At the end of the season the SRU laid an electric blanket at Murrayfield.)

Jim Greenwood was Scotland's captain in his last season of international competition. A schoolmaster by profession, he was to become one of Britain's most respected coaches in the 1970s and 1980s. And as a lecturer at Loughborough he formed the college rugby team into a first-class English club side.

## 1959-60 / 1960

| v. FRANCE | v. WALES | v. IRELAND | v. ENGLAND | v. S.AFRICA |
|---|---|---|---|---|
| K.J.F. SCOTLAND | K.J.F. SCOTLAND | K.J.F. SCOTLAND 1DG | K.J.F. SCOTLAND 3PG | R.W.T. CHISHOLM |
| *A.R. SMITH 2T | *A.R. SMITH | A.R. SMITH | A.R. SMITH 1T | A.R. SMITH 2C,1T |
| †J.J. McPARTLIN | J.J. McPARTLIN | G.D. STEVENSON | G.D. STEVENSON | G.D. STEVENSON |
| I.H.P. LAUGHLAND | I.H.P. LAUGHLAND | I.H.P. LAUGHLAND | I.H.P. LAUGHLAND | †P.J. BURNET |
| C. ELLIOT 1PG,1C | G.D. STEVENSON | †R.H. THOMSON 1T | R.H. THOMSON | R.H. THOMSON |
| †G. SHARP | T. McCLUNG | *G.H. WADDELL | *G.H. WADDELL | *G.H. WADDELL |
| J.A.T. RODD | J.A.T. RODD | †R.B. SHILLINGLAW | R.B. SHILLINGLAW | R.B. SHILLINGLAW |
| D.M.D. ROLLO | D.M.D. ROLLO | D.M.D. ROLLO | D.M.D. ROLLO | D.M.D. ROLLO |
| N.S. BRUCE | N.S. BRUCE | N.S. BRUCE | N.S. BRUCE | N.S. BRUCE 1T |
| H.F. McLEOD | H.F. McLEOD | H.F. McLEOD | H.F. McLEOD | H.F. McLEOD |
| F.H. TEN BOS | F.H. TEN BOS | †T.O. GRANT | T.O. GRANT | F.H. TEN BOS |
| J.W.Y. KEMP | J.W.Y. KEMP | J.W.Y. KEMP | J.W.Y. KEMP | J.W.Y. KEMP |
| G.K. SMITH | G.K. SMITH | G.K. SMITH | G.K. SMITH | †W. HART |
| †K.R.F. BEARNE | K.R.F. BEARNE | J.A. DAVIDSON | J.A. DAVIDSON | T.O. GRANT |
| A. ROBSON | †C.E.B. STEWART | †D.B. EDWARDS | D.B. EDWARDS | D.B. EDWARDS |
| Murrayfield | Cardiff Arms Park | Lansdowne Road | Murrayfield | Port Elizabeth |
| LOST 11-13 | LOST 0-8 | WON 6-5 | LOST 12-21 | LOST 10-18 |
| SCOT.: 1G 1PG 1T | WALES: 1G 1PG | IRE.: 1G | SCOT.: 3PG 1T | SA: 3G 1T |
| FR.: 2G 1T | SCOT.: NIL | SCOT.: 1DG 1T | ENG.: 3G 1DG 1PG | SCOT.: 2G |
| 9 Jan. 1960 | 6 Feb. 1960 | 27 Feb. 1960 | 19 Mar. 1960 | 30 Apr. 1960 |

Although the season was a disappointing one in terms of results, there was a sweet victory over Ireland to savour, and Scotland played a significant part in two attractive, open games with France and England. Rugby internationals of the late 1950s and early 1960s were frequently uninspiring contests between close-marking, defensive sides. But the Scotland-France game turned out to be a fast, exciting spectacle and five splendid tries were scored. Later, also at Murrayfield, another four tries were scored in the Calcutta Cup game. Here, England's early lead was sufficient to outpoint a late Scottish rally.

The match in Dublin provided Scotland's second win over Ireland since the war, and it was their first success there since 1933. Ken Scotland joined the threequarter line to help put new cap Thomson over for a try, and later dropped the decisive goal.

At the end of the season the Scots made a short tour to South Africa, becoming the first Home nation to undertake such a trip. In the Test match (the opening game of the tour) Bruce scored near the posts in the first minute, but a strong Springbok pack slowly gained the initiative and Scotland went down by 10-18 at Port Elizabeth. At least it was a great improvement on the result of 1951.

## 1960-61

| v. FRANCE | v. S.AFRICA | v. WALES | v. IRELAND | v. ENGLAND |
|---|---|---|---|---|
| K.J.F. Scotland | K.J.F. Scotland 1c | K.J.F. Scotland | K.J.F. Scotland 2c,1pg | K.J.F. Scotland |
| A.R. Smith | *A.R. Smith 1t | *A.R. Smith 1t | *A.R. Smith | *A.R. Smith |
| †R.C. Cowan | E.McKeating | E. McKeating | E. McKeating | E.McKeating |
| G.D. Stevenson | G.D. Stevenson | G.D. Stevenson | G.D. Stevenson | G.D. Stevenson |
| R.H. Thomson | R.H. Thomson | R.H. Thomson | R.H. Thomson | R.H. Thomson |
| *G.H. Waddell | I.H.P. Laughland | I.H.P. Laughland | I.H.P. Laughland | I.H.P. Laughland |
| R.B. Shillinglaw | R.B. Shillinglaw | †A.J. Hastie | A.J. Hastie | A.J. Hastie |
| H.F. McLeod | H.F. McLeod | H.F. McLeod | H.F. McLeod | H.F. McLeod |
| N.S. Bruce | N.S. Bruce | N.S. Bruce | N.S. Bruce | N.S. Bruce |
| D.M.D. Rollo | D.M.D. Rollo | D.M.D. Rollo | D.M.D. Rollo | D.M.D. Rollo |
| F.H. ten Bos | F.H. ten Bos | F.H. ten Bos | F.H. ten Bos | F.H. ten Bos |
| †M.J. Campbell-Lamerton | M.J. Campbell-Lamerton | M.J. Campbell-Lamerton | M.J. Campbell-Lamerton | J. Douglas |
| G.K. Smith | G.K. Smith | G.K. Smith | G.K. Smith | †J.C. Brash |
| †J. Douglas | J. Douglas | J. Douglas | J. Douglas 1t | G.K. Smith |
| C.E.B. Stewart | †K.I. Ross | K.I. Ross | K.I. Ross 2t | K.I. Ross |
| Stade Colombes | Murrayfield | Murrayfield | Murrayfield | Twickenham |
| LOST 0-11 | LOST 5-12 | WON 3-0 | WON 16-8 | LOST 0-6 |
| Fr.: 1G 1DG 1PG | Scot.: 1G | Scot.: 1T | Scot.: 2G 1PG 1T | Eng.: 1PG 1T |
| Scot.: NIL | S.A.: 2PG 2T | Wales: NIL | Ire.: 1G 1T | Scot.: NIL |
| 7 Jan. 1961 | 21 Jan. 1961 | 11 Feb. 1961 | 25 Feb. 1961 | 18 Mar. 1961 |

Scotland fielded only twenty players this season. There were two sterling performances at the beginning of the campaign, against France and South Africa, and the try scored by Arthur Smith against the Springboks was the only time the tourists' goal-line was crossed in five international matches. Two good wins then followed at Murrayfield. On a wet, windy day against Wales, Ken Scotland made one of his timely runs into the threequarter line, drew the Welsh defence, and sent Smith over in the corner for the only score. In the Irish match, the back-row were outstanding and Douglas and Ross scored three tries in a 16-8 victory.

John Douglas had a remarkable distinction in 1979: he was the owner of Grand National winner Rubstic. No doubt many of his former colleagues in this Scottish fifteen benefited from a flutter on his horse.

Scotland's hopes of the Triple Crown were dashed at Twickenham, where Campbell-Lamerton had to withdraw. Ken Scotland, usually so reliable with his place-kicking, missed four penalties and Scotland had to finish the season content with two Championship wins.

## 1961-62

| v. FRANCE | v. WALES | v. IRELAND | v. ENGLAND |
|---|---|---|---|
| K.J.F. Scotland | K.J.F. Scotland 1c | K.J.F. Scotland 2pg,1c | K.J.F. Scotland 1pg |
| *A.R. Smith 1pg | *A.R. Smith | *A.R. Smith 2t | *A.R. Smith |
| J.J. McPartlin | J.J. McPartlin | J.J. McPartlin | J.J. McPartlin |
| I.H.P. Laughland | I.H.P. Laughland | I.H.P. Laughland | I.H.P. Laughland |
| R.C. Cowan | R.C. Cowan | R.C. Cowan 1t | R.C. Cowan |
| G.H. Waddell | G.H. Waddell | G.H. Waddell | G.H. Waddell |
| J.A.T. Rodd | S. Coughtrie | S. Coughtrie 1dg | S. Coughtrie |
| H.F. McLeod | H.F. McLeod | H.F. McLeod | H.F. McLeod |
| N.S. Bruce | N.S. Bruce | N.S. Bruce | N.S. Bruce |
| D.M.D. Rollo | D.M.D. Rollo | †R. Steven | D.M.D. Rollo |
| F.H. ten Bos | F.H. ten Bos 1t | F.H. ten Bos | F.H. ten Bos |
| M.J. Campbell-Lamerton | M.J. Campbell-Lamerton | M.J. Campbell-Lamerton | M.J. Campbell-Lamerton |
| †R.J.C. Glasgow | R.J.C. Glasgow 1t | R.J.C. Glasgow | R.J.C. Glasgow |
| J. Douglas | J. Douglas | J. Douglas | J. Douglas |
| K.I. Ross | K.I. Ross | K.I. Ross | K.I. Ross |
| Murrayfield | Cardiff Arms Park | Lansdowne Road | Murrayfield |
| LOST 3-11 | WON 8-3 | WON 20-6 | DRAWN 3-3 |
| Scot.: 1PG | Wales: 1DG | Ire.: 1PG 1T | Scot.: 1PG |
| Fr.: 1G 2PG | Scot.: 1G 1T | Scot.: 1G 1DG 2PG 2T | Eng.: 1PG |
| 13 Jan. 1962 | 3 Feb. 1962 | 24 Feb. 1962 | 17 Mar. 1962 |

Ron Glasgow, a schoolmaster, came into the Scottish side against France, winning his first cap at 31. He had first played in a trial back in 1955, while at Jordanhill Training College, but Scotland had been well-served for back-row men in the interim.

Glasgow made a name for himself now, however, scoring Scotland's opening try in a famous victory in the mud at Cardiff. Only 17 players were used by the Scots and their season was only spoiled by a draw against England at Murrayfield. Their five points – two wins and a draw – in the Championship was the best Scottish performance in the competition since before World War II.

Several leading players appeared for the last time in Scottish colours. Arthur Smith and Gordon Waddell, a talented fly-half with a rare tactical sense, were the leading backs to go, while among the forwards H.F. McLeod finished his career with 40 caps to set a new Scottish record. McLeod won his caps at prop during an unbroken run of nine seasons – a record bearing testimony to his remarkable consistency and fitness, and one which was rewarded with an OBE in the 1963 New Year's Honours.

## 1962-63

| v. FRANCE | v. WALES | v. IRELAND | v. ENGLAND |
|---|---|---|---|
| *K.J.F. Scotland 1DG,1PG,1C | *K.J.F. Scotland | †C.F. Blaikie | C.F. Blaikie |
| | | | |
| R.H. Thomson 1T | R.H. Thomson | R.H. Thomson | C. Elliot |
| J.A.P. Shackleton | J.A.P. Shackleton | I.H.P. Laughland | †B.C. Henderson |
| †D.M. White | D.M. White | D.M. White | D.M. White |
| G.D. Stevenson | G.D. Stevenson | G.D. Stevenson | R.H. Thomson |
| | | | |
| I.H.P. Laughland | I.H.P. Laughland | *K.J.F. Scotland | *K.J.F. Scotland 1DG |
| S. Coughtrie | S. Coughtrie | S. Coughtrie 1PG | S. Coughtrie 1C |
| | | | |
| †A.C.W. Boyle | A.C.W. Boyle | A.C.W. Boyle | †J.B. Neill |
| N.S. Bruce | N.S. Bruce | N.S. Bruce | N.S. Bruce |
| D.M.D. Rollo | D.M.D. Rollo | D.M.D. Rollo | D.M.D. Rollo |
| F.H. ten Bos | F.H. ten Bos | F.H. ten Bos | F.H. ten Bos |
| M.J. Campbell-Lamerton | M.J. Campbell-Lamerton | M.J. Campbell-Lamerton | M.J. Campbell-Lamerton |
| †W.R.A. Watherston | W.R.A. Watherston | W.R.A. Watherston | K.I. Ross |
| J. Douglas | J. Douglas | J. Douglas | †J.P. Fisher |
| K.I. Ross | K.I. Ross | R.J.C. Glasgow | R.J.C. Glasgow 1T |
| | | | |
| Stade Colombes | Murrayfield | Murrayfield | Twickenham |
| WON 11-6 | LOST 0-6 | WON 3-0 | LOST 8-10 |
| | | | |
| Fr.: 1DG 1PG | Scot.: NIL | Scot.: 1PG | Eng.: 2G |
| Scot.: 1G 1DG 1PG | Wales: 1DG 1PG | Eng.: NIL | Scot.: 1G 1DG |
| | | | |
| 12 Jan. 1963 | 2 Feb. 1963 | 23 Feb. 1963 | 16 Mar. 1963 |

There were seven London Scottish players in the side which gained a belated victory in Paris, Scotland's first there since 1957. With the scores level in injury time, Laughland hooked an attempted drop-goal. But Thomson raced across from the right wing to gather a bouncing ball and scored to the left of the posts for Ken Scotland to convert.

After the unexpected defeat by Wales at Murrayfield, Ken Scotland was moved to fly-half. Against Ireland a single penalty kicked by Coughtrie put Scotland in the running for the Championship, but after leading by eight points at Twickenham, their hopes were dashed by Richard Sharp's winning try for England.

Frans ten Bos played the last of his 17 internationals against England. A management consultant, he formed with Campbell-Lamerton one of the heaviest second-row combinations ever to play for Scotland. They played together in twelve internationals.

## 1963-64

| v. FRANCE | v. NZ | v. WALES | v. IRELAND | v. ENGLAND |
|---|---|---|---|---|
| †S. Wilson 2C | S. Wilson | S. Wilson | S. Wilson 2PG | S. Wilson 3C |
| | | | | |
| C. Elliot | C. Elliot | C. Elliot | C. Elliot | C. Elliot |
| B.C. Henderson | J.A.P. Shackleton | J.A.P. Shackleton | B.C. Henderson | B.C. Henderson |
| I.H.P. Laughland 1T | I.H.P. Laughland | I.H.P. Laughland 1T | I.H.P. Laughland | I.H.P. Laughland |
| R.H. Thomson 1T | R.H. Thomson | R.H. Thomson | †W.D. Jackson | G.D. Stevenson |
| | | | | |
| G. Sharp | G. Sharp | G. Sharp | †D.H. Chisholm | D.H. Chisholm |
| J.A.T. Rodd | J.A.T. Rodd | J.A.T. Rodd | A.J. Hastie | A.J. Hastie |
| | | | | |
| D.M.D. Rollo | D.M.D. Rollo | D.M.D. Rollo | D.M.D. Rollo | D.M.D. Rollo |
| N.S. Bruce | N.S. Bruce | N.S. Bruce | N.S. Bruce | N.S. Bruce 1T |
| *J.B. Neill | *J.B. Neill | *J.B. Neill | *J.B. Neill | *J.B. Neill |
| †W.J. Hunter | W.J. Hunter | W.J. Hunter | P.C. Brown | P.C. Brown |
| †P.C. Brown | P.C. Brown | P.C. Brown | M.J. Campbell-Lamerton | M.J. Campbell-Lamerton |
| †J.W. Telfer | J.W. Telfer | J.W. Telfer | J.W. Telfer | J.P. Fisher |
| T.O. Grant | T.O. Grant | T.O. Grant | J.P. Fisher | J.W. Telfer 1T |
| J.P. Fisher | J.P. Fisher | J.P. Fisher | R.J.C. Glasgow | R.J.C. Glasgow 1T |
| | | | | |
| Murrayfield | Murrayfield | Cardiff Arms Park | Lansdowne Road | Murrayfield |
| WON 10-0 | DRAWN 0-0 | LOST 3-11 | WON 6-3 | WON 15-6 |
| | | | | |
| Scot.: 2G | Scot.: NIL | Wales: 1G 1PG 1T | Ire.: 1PG | Scot.: 3G |
| Fr.: NIL | N.Z.: NIL | Scot.: 1T | Scot.: 2PG | Eng.: 1PG 1T |
| | | | | |
| 4 Jan. 1964 | 18 Jan. 1964 | 1 Feb. 1964 | 22 Feb. 1964 | 21 Mar. 1964 |

This was Scotland's most successful season since 1938. Not only were the Fifth All Blacks held to a scoreless draw, the Scots also shared the Championship with Wales. A side with four new caps opened the season against France. The Scots took few risks, relying on their forward strength to keep the game tight, and the backs grasped their opportunities from mistakes made by their opponents. A late try by Thomson, from an interception, and two conversions by the new full-back resulted in victory.

Stewart Wilson, the Oxford University full-back, proved a reliable and adventurous successor to Ken Scotland. His agility and excellent kicking were qualities which served Scotland well in 22 internationals, and he also led the team on four occasions. The only disappointment of the season was a poor performance against Wales at Cardiff. Wilson's place-kicking was decisive in Dublin and the side played their best football to regain the Calcutta Cup at Murrayfield. In a match in which forwards and backs were clear masters of their English opponents, Scotland retained the famous Cup for the first time since 1950.

## 1964-65

| v. FRANCE | v. WALES | v. IRELAND | v. ENGLAND | v. S.AFRICA |
|---|---|---|---|---|
| K.J.F. Scotland 1c | S. Wilson 2pg | S. Wilson 1pg | *S. Wilson | *S. Wilson 1c |
| | | | | |
| C. Elliot | C. Elliot | C. Elliot | D.J. Whyte | D.J. Whyte |
| B.C. Henderson 2t | B.C. Henderson | B.C. Henderson | B.C. Henderson | J.A.P. Shackleton 1t |
| I.H.P. Laughland | I.H.P. Laughland | J.A.P. Shackleton | I.H.P. Laughland | I.H.P. Laughland |
| G.D. Stevenson | †D.J. Whyte | D.J. Whyte | W.D. Jackson | W.D. Jackson |
| | | | | |
| †B.M. Simmers | B.M. Simmers 2dg | I.H.P. Laughland 1dg | D.H. Chisholm 1dg | D.H. Chisholm 1dg |
| J.A.T. Rodd | J.A.T. Rodd | J.A.T. Rodd | A.J. Hastie | A.J. Hastie |
| | | | | |
| D.M.D. Rollo | D.M.D. Rollo | D.M.D. Rollo | D.M.D. Rollo | D.M.D. Rollo |
| †F.A.L. Laidlaw | F.A.L. Laidlaw | F.A.L. Laidlaw | F.A.L. Laidlaw | F.A.L. Laidlaw |
| *J.B. Neill | †N. Suddon | N. Suddon | N. Suddon | N. Suddon |
| †P.K. Stagg | P.K. Stagg | P.C. Brown | P.K. Stagg | P.K. Stagg |
| M.J. Campbell-Lamerton | *M.J. Campbell-Lamerton | *M.J. Campbell-Lamerton | M.J. Campbell-Lamerton | M.J. Campbell-Lamerton |
| J.P. Fisher | J.P. Fisher | J.P. Fisher | J.P. Fisher | J.P. Fisher |
| J.W. Telfer | J.W. Telfer | J.W. Telfer | P.C. Brown | P.C. Brown |
| †D. Grant | R.J.C. Glasgow | R.J.C. Glasgow | D. Grant | D. Grant |
| | | | | |
| Stade Colombes | Murrayfield | Murrayfield | Twickenham | Murrayfield |
| LOST 8-16 | LOST 12-14 | LOST 6-16 | DRAWN 3-3 | WON 8-5 |
| | | | | |
| Fr.: 2G 2T | Scot.: 2DG 2PG | Scot.: 1DG 1PG | Eng.: 1T | Scot.: 1G 1DG |
| Scot.: 1G 1T | Wales: 1G 2PG 1T | Ire.: 2G 1T 1DG | Scot.: 1DG | S.A: 1G |
| | | | | |
| 9 Jan. 1965 | 6 Feb. 1965 | 27 Feb. 1965 | 20 Mar. 1965 | 17 Apr. 1965 |

Scotland's results show a draw in the Championship match with England and a solitary win, at the end of the season, against the touring South Africans. Yet the suggestion that the side which had shared the Championship in the previous season was disintegrating, was countered by the fact that the Scots did not enjoy the best of luck in their matches.

They were well-beaten in Paris by a superb French side, but it was a late corner-try which pipped them in the match with Wales, and a memorable try by Hancock deprived them of the Calcutta Cup after the Scots had led for most of that game.

Chisholm and Hastie, who had first appeared together for Scotland in Dublin in 1964, confirmed their promise as Scotland's finest half-back pair in the last two games of the season. The Melrose club pair, they were selected together on thirteen occasions: twice more than the Glasgow Academicals pair of J.B. Nelson and Herbert Waddell in the 1920s. Chisholm's drop-goal was the deciding score of the match against South Africa.

## 1965-66

| v. FRANCE | v. WALES | v. IRELAND | v. ENGLAND |
|---|---|---|---|
| *S. Wilson | *S. Wilson 1pg | S. Wilson 1c | C.F. Blaikie 1pg |
| | | | |
| †A.J.W. Hinshelwood | A.J.W. Hinshelwood | A.J.W. Hinshelwood 2t | A.J.W. Hinshelwood |
| B.C. Henderson | B.C. Henderson | B.C. Henderson | B.C. Henderson |
| I.H.P. Laughland | I.H.P. Laughland | *I.H.P. Laughland | *I.H.P. Laughland |
| D.J. Whyte 1t | D.J. Whyte | D.J. Whyte | D.J. Whyte 1t |
| | | | |
| D.H. Chisholm | †J.W.C. Turner | D.H. Chisholm | D.H. Chisholm |
| A.J. Hastie | A.J. Hastie | A.J. Hastie | A.J. Hastie |
| | | | |
| D.M.D. Rollo | D.M.D. Rollo | D.M.D. Rollo | D.M.D. Rollo |
| F.A.L. Laidlaw | F.A.L. Laidlaw | F.A.L. Laidlaw | F.A.L. Laidlaw |
| †J.D. MacDonald | J.D. MacDonald | J.D. MacDonald | J.D. MacDonald |
| P.K. Stagg | P.K. Stagg | P.K. Stagg | P.K. Stagg |
| M.J. Campbell-Lamerton | M.J. Campbell-Lamerton | M.J. Campbell-Lamerton | M.J. Campbell-Lamerton |
| J.P. Fisher | J.P. Fisher | J.P. Fisher | J.P. Fisher |
| J.W. Telfer | J.W. Telfer | J.W. Telfer | J.W. Telfer |
| D. Grant | D. Grant | D. Grant 1t | D. Grant |
| | | | |
| Murrayfield | Cardiff Arms Park | Lansdowne Road | Murrayfield |
| DRAWN 3-3 | LOST 3-8 | WON 11-3 | WON 6-3 |
| | | | |
| Scot.: 1T | Wales: 1G 1T | Ire.: 1PG | Scot.: 1PG 1T |
| Fr.: 1PG | Scot.: 1PG | Scot.: 1G 2T | Eng.: 1DG |
| | | | |
| 15 Jan. 1966 | 5 Feb. 1966 | 26 Feb. 1966 | 19 Mar. 1966 |

Scotland enjoyed a reasonably successful season, losing only once (and in appalling conditions at Cardiff). The Scottish selectors would have fielded the same fifteen throughout the season, but in Cardiff, Chisholm was unavailable, and Blaikie came in for Stewart Wilson at Murrayfield. The Scottish pack was unchanged for the Championship for the first time since 1956.

Mike Campbell-Lamerton gained the last of his 23 caps in the victory over England. He was an Army officer, weighed over 17½ stones, and stood 6ft 4½ins, one of the largest forwards of his day. Another Scot, Peter Stagg, was over 6ft 8ins, giving his side a distinct advantage in the line-out. Furthermore, the Scottish back-row of Fisher, Telfer and Grant were outstanding in the loose and set up the winning tries in both the Irish and English matches.

Jock Turner, the young Gala fly-half who stood in for Chisholm at Cardiff, went on to gain 20 caps for Scotland. An insurance inspector, he was a useful utility back who appeared at centre, full-back and fly-half in international matches.

## 1966-67

| v. AUSTRALIA | v. FRANCE | v. WALES | v. IRELAND | v. ENGLAND |
|---|---|---|---|---|
| S. WILSON 1PG,1C | S. WILSON 2PG | S. WILSON 1C | S. WILSON 1PG | S. WILSON 2PG,1C |
| | | | | |
| A.J.W. HINSELWOOD | A.J.W. HINSELWOOD | A.J.W. HINSELWOOD 1T | A.J.W. HINSELWOOD | A.J.W. HINSELWOOD 1T |
| J.W.C. TURNER | J.W.C. TURNER | J.W.C. TURNER | J.W.C. TURNER | J.W.C. TURNER 1T |
| B.M. SIMMERS | B.M. SIMMERS 1DG | B.M. SIMMERS | †R.B. WELSH | R.B. WELSH |
| D.J. WHYTE | D.J. WHYTE | D.J. WHYTE | D.J. WHYTE | D.J. WHYTE |
| | | | | |
| D.H. CHRISHOLM 1T | D.H. CHRISHOLM | D.H. CHRISHOLM 1DG | B.M. SIMMERS | I.H.P. LAUGHLAND |
| A.J. HASTIE | A.J. HASTIE | A.J. HASTIE | A.J. HASTIE | †I.G. McCRAE |
| | | | | |
| N. SUDDON | J.D. MacDONALD | J.D. MacDONALD | J.D. MacDONALD | J.D. MacDONALD |
| F.A.L. LAIDLAW | F.A.L. LAIDLAW | F.A.L. LAIDLAW | F.A.L. LAIDLAW | F.A.L. LAIDLAW |
| D.M.D. ROLLO | D.M.D. ROLLO | D.M.D. ROLLO | †A.B. CARMICHAEL | D.M.D. ROLLO |
| P.K. STAGG | P.K. STAGG | P.K. STAGG | P.K. STAGG | P.K. STAGG |
| P.C. BROWN | W.J. HUNTER | W.J. HUNTER | W.J. HUNTER | W.J. HUNTER |
| *J.P. FISHER | *J.P. FISHER | *J.P. FISHER | *J.P. FISHER | *J.P. FISHER |
| †A.H.W. BOYLE 1T | A.H.W. BOYLE | J.W. TELFER 1T | J.W. TELFER | J.W. TELFER |
| D. GRANT | D. GRANT | D. GRANT | D. GRANT | D. GRANT |
| Murrayfield | Stade Colombes | Murrayfield | Murrayfield | Twickenham |
| WON 11-5 | WON 9-8 | WON 11-5 | LOST 3-5 | LOST 14-27 |
| SCOT.: 1G 1PG 1T | FR.: 1G 1T | SCOT.: 1G 1PG 1T | SCOT.: 1PG | ENG.: 3G 2PG 1DG 1T |
| AUS.: 1G | SCOT.: 2PG 1DG | WALES: 1G | IRE.: 1G | SCOT.: 1G 2PG 1T |
| 17 Dec. 1966 | 14 Jan. 1967 | 4 Feb. 1967 | 25 Feb. 1967 | 18 Mar. 1967 |

The Scots made a promising start to the season, inspired by some excellent performances by Chisholm at fly-half. He scored an outstanding try against the Australians, deceiving the defence with a feint and a swerve. Then, against Wales, he dropped a goal to put his side ahead, worried the Welsh defence with some astute tactical kicking, and used his centres cleverly in attack.

The Scottish pack was splendid in the tight play. Frank Laidlaw, the Melrose joiner, was one of the best hookers in Britain at the time, and few opponents had the better of him at the set-pieces. Scotland's loose trio of Fisher, Telfer and Grant were an experienced unit who played together through eight internationals, and their play in combination with scrum-half Hastie was excellent. A well-planned move featuring Hastie and Telfer brought the decisive score against the Welsh.

Against Ireland, Pringle Fisher was the Scottish star. His fine all-round play at the rear of the line-out enabled the Scottish backs to play an expansive game. However the Irish tackled fiercely and Mike Gibson spearheaded numerous dangerous counter-attacks. One such attack, from a line-out, set up Ireland's winning try midway through the second half. England were the only side to outplay the Scots up front, their second-half pressure leading to Scotland's heaviest defeat of the season.

## 1967-68

| v. NZ | v. FRANCE | v. WALES | v. IRELAND | v. ENGLAND |
|---|---|---|---|---|
| S. WILSON | S. WILSON 1PG | S. WILSON | S. WILSON 2PG | S. WILSON 1PG |
| | | | | |
| A.J.W. HINSHELWOOD | A.J.W. HINSHELWOOD | A.J.W. HINSHELWOOD | A.J.W. HINSHELWOOD | A.J.W. HINSHELWOOD |
| J.W.C. TURNER | J.W.C. TURNER | J.W.C. TURNER | J.W.C. TURNER | J.W.C. TURNER |
| †J.N.M. FRAME | J.N.M. FRAME | J.N.M. FRAME | J.N.M. FRAME | J.N.M. FRAMCE |
| †R.R. KEDDIE | †G.J. KEITH 1T | G.J. KEITH | †C.G. HODGSON | C.G. HODGSON |
| | | | | |
| D.H. CHISHOLM 1DG | D.H. CHISHOLM | D.H. CHISHOLM | D.H. CHISHOLM | †I. ROBERTSON |
| A.J. HASTIE | A.J. HASTIE | A.J. HASTIE | I.G. McCRAE | †G.C. CONNELL 1DG |
| | | | | |
| A.B. CARMICHAEL | A.B. CARMICHAEL | A.B. CARMICHAEL | A.B. CARMICHAEL | A.B. CARMICHAEL |
| F.A.L. LAIDLAW | F.A.L. LAIDLAW | F.A.L. LAIDLAW | F.A.L. LAIDLAW | †D.T. DEANS |
| D.M.D. ROLLO | D.M.D. ROLLO | D.M.D. ROLLO | D.M.D. ROLLO | N. SUDDON |
| P.K. STAGG | P.K. STAGG | P.K. STAGG | P.K. STAGG | P.K. STAGG |
| †G.W.E. MITCHELL | G.W.E. MITCHELL | G.W.E. MITCHELL | †A.F. McHARG | A.F. McHARG |
| *J.P. FISHER | *J.P. FISHER | *J.P. FISHER | *J.P. FISHER | J.P. FISHER |
| A.H.W. BOYLE | A.H.W. BOYLE | A.H.W. BOYLE | A.H.W. BOYLE | *J.W. TELFER |
| D. GRANT | D. GRANT | †T.G. ELLIOT | †R.J. ARNEIL | R.J. ARNEIL |
| Murrayfield | Murrayfield | Cardiff Arms Park | Lansdowne Road | Murrayfield |
| LOST 3-14 | LOST 6-8 | LOST 0-5 | LOST 6-14 | LOST 6-8 |
| SCOT.: 1DG | SCOT.: 1PG 1T | WALES: 1G | IRE.: 1G 1PG 2T | SCOT.: 1PG 1DG |
| NZ.: 1G 2PG 1T | FR.: 1G 1T | SCOT.: NIL | SCOT.: 2PG | ENG.: 1G 1PG |
| 2 Dec. 1967 | 13 Jan. 1968 | 3 Feb. 1968 | 24 Feb. 1968 | 16 Mar. 1968 |

This was Scotland's most disappointing season for 14 years. All five matches were lost, there were 11 new caps introduced during the season, and altogether 26 different players appeared in Scotland's internationals.

David Rollo, a durable farmer from the Howe of Fife club, appeared in the last of his 40 internationals for Scotland when he played against Ireland. He thus equalled Hugh McLeod's record number of caps for Scotland. Chisholm and Hastie appeared together for the last time against Wales at Cardiff. During their 13-match partnership, they had played on the winning side eight times and featured in drawn games twice.

Another loyal servant of Scottish rugby played his last international against England. Stewart Wilson, Scotland's place-kicking full-back, finished his career with 68 points from ten conversions and sixteen penalty goals. His penalty-goal haul stood as a Scottish career record until overtaken by Andy Irvine.

## 1968-69

| v. AUSTRALIA | v. FRANCE | v. WALES | v. IRELAND | v. ENGLAND |
|---|---|---|---|---|
| C.F. Blaikie 2pg | C.F. Blaikie 1pg | C.F. Blaikie 1pg | C.F. Blaikie | C.F. Blaikie |
| | | | | |
| A.J.W. Hinshelwood 1t | A.J.W. Hinshelwood | A.J.W. Hinshelwood | A.J.W. Hinshelwood | †W.C.C. Steele |
| J.W.C. Turner | J.W.C. Turner | J.N.M. Frame | J.N.M. Frame | J.N.M. Frame |
| †C.W.W. Rea | C.W.W. Rea | C.W.W. Rea | C.W.W. Rea[1] | I. Robertson |
| W.D. Jackson | W.D. Jackson | W.D. Jackson | W.D. Jackson | W.D. Jackson |
| | | | | |
| †C.M. Telfer | C.M. Telfer | C.M. Telfer | C.M. Telfer | C.M. Telfer |
| G.C. Connell | G.C. Connell[1] | I.G. McCrae | †R.C. Allan | G.C. Connell |
| | | | | |
| N. Suddon | N. Suddon | N. Suddon | N. Suddon | †J. McLauchlan |
| F.A.L. Laidlaw | F.A.L. Laidlaw | F.A.L. Laidlaw | F.A.L. Laidlaw | F.A.L. Laidlaw |
| A.B. Carmichael | A.B. Carmichael | A.B. Carmichael | A.B. Carmichael | A.B. Carmichael |
| P.K. Stagg | P.K. Stagg | P.K. Stagg | P.C. Brown | P.C. Brown 1pg |
| A.F. McHarg | A.F. McHarg | A.F. McHarg | A.F. McHarg | A.F. McHarg |
| T.G. Elliot | T.G. Elliot | T.G. Elliot | †W. Lauder | W. Lauder |
| *J.W. Telfer | *J.W. Telfer 1t | *J.W. Telfer | *J.W. Telfer[2] | *J.W. Telfer |
| R.J. Arneil | R.J. Arneil | R.J. Arneil | R.J. Arneil | R.J. Arneil |
| | | | | |
| Murrayfield | Stade Colombes | Murrayfield | Murrayfield | Twickenham |
| WON 9-3 | WON 6-3 | LOST 3-17 | LOST 0-16 | LOST 3-8 |
| | | | | |
| Scot.: 2pg 1t | Fr.: 1pg | Scot.: 1pg | Scot.: nil | Eng.: 1g 1t |
| Aust.: 1pg | Scot.: 1pg 1t | Wales: 1g 2pg 2t | Ire.: 2g 2t | Scot.: 1pg |
| | | | | |
| 2 Nov. 1968 | 11 Jan. 1969 | 1 Feb. 1969 | 22 Feb. 1969 | 15 Mar. 1969 |

[1]Rep. by I.G. McCrae

[1]Rep. by †W.G. McDonald
[2]Rep. by P.K. Stagg

There was an encouraging start to the season. In the first match of the season, against Australia, Scotland brought to an end a miserable sequence of seven consecutive international defeats. It was Scotland's first match under the new dispensation law which restricted direct kicking to touch. However there was only one try for the crowd to savour, though the two new men, Telfer and Rea, played a prominent role in its execution.

Telfer was one of the finest attacking fly-halves produced by the Border area. A finely balanced runner with the ability to kick shrewdly in attack and defence, he played 17 internationals and was later chosen to coach the national side. Rea, a history graduate, joined the BBC, where his rugby broadcasts became noted for their shrewd insights and sensible summaries.

Gordon McCrae became the first replacement used by Scotland when he substituted for Connell in the first half against France.

## 1969-70

| v. S.AFRICA | v. FRANCE | v. WALES | v. IRELAND | v. ENGLAND |
|---|---|---|---|---|
| †I.S.G. Smith 1pg,1t | I.S.G. Smith 1t | I.S.G. Smith | I.S.G. Smith 1c | I.S.G. Smith |
| | | | | |
| †A.G. Biggar | A.G. Biggar | †M.A. Smith | M.A. Smith 1t | M.A. Smith |
| J.N.M. Frame | J.N.M. Frame | J.N.M. Frame | J.N.M. Frame | J.N.M. Frame |
| C.W.W. Rea | C.W.W. Rea | C.W.W. Rea | C.W.W. Rea | J.W.C. Turner 1t |
| A.J.W. Hinshelwood | A.J.W. Hinshelwood | A.J.W. Hinshelwood | A.G. Biggar | A.G. Biggar 1t |
| | | | | |
| I. Robertson | I. Robertson | I. Robertson 1t,1dg | I. Robertson 1dg | I. Robertson |
| †D.S. Paterson | G.C. Connell | †R.G. Young | D.S. Paterson | D.S. Paterson |
| | | | | |
| J. McLauchlan | J. McLauchlan | J. McLauchlan | N. Suddon | N. Suddon |
| F.A.L. Laidlaw | F.A.L. Laidlaw | F.A.L. Laidlaw | F.A.L. Laidlaw | *F.A.L. Laidlaw |
| A.B. Carmichael | A.B. Carmichael | A.B. Carmichael | A.B. Carmichael | A.B. Carmichael |
| P.K. Stagg | P.K. Stagg | P.K. Stagg | P.K. Stagg | P.K. Stagg |
| †G.L. Brown | G.L. Brown | P.C. Brown[1] | G.L. Brown | G.L. Brown |
| W. Lauder | W. Lauder 2pg | W. Lauder 1pg | W. Lauder 1t | T.G. Elliot |
| *J.W. Telfer | *J.W. Telfer | *J.W. Telfer | *J.W. Telfer | P.C. Brown 2pg,1c |
| R.J. Arneil | R.J. Arneil | R.J. Arneil | R.J. Arneil | R.J. Arneil |
| | | | | |
| Murrayfield | Murrayfield | Cardiff Arms Park | Lansdowne Road | Murrayfield |
| WON 6-3 | LOST 9-11 | LOST 9-18 | LOST 11-16 | WON 14-5 |
| | | | | |
| Scot.: 1t 1pg | Scot.: 2pg 1t | Wales: 3g 1t | Ire.: 2g 2t | Scot.: 1g 2pg 1t |
| SA: 1pg | Fr.: 1g 1dg 1t | Scot.: 1dg 1pg 1t | Scot.: 1g 1dg 1t | Eng.: 1g |
| | | | | |
| 6 Dec. 1969 | 10 Jan. 1970 | 7 Feb. 1970 | 28 Feb. 1970 | 21 Mar. 1970 |

[1]Rep. by G.L. Brown

Scotland finished with the wooden spoon in 1970, despite beating the Sixth Springboks in the first international of the season. It was Scotland's third success against South Africa, and stemmed from a clever threequarter move which included the Scottish full-back. With the scores level, and with time running out, Robertson and Frame combined to send Ian Smith crashing over for a try to the right of the posts. Smith, an army dentist, thus gained the distinction of becoming the first full-back to score a try for Scotland in an international. What is more, he repeated the feat a month later in the match with France.

In Cardiff, Scotland had first use of a strong wind, but their nine-point lead was insufficient against a Welsh pack which totally dominated the game after half-time. History was made just after the interval when Gordon Brown came on to replace his brother.

Altogether, the Brown brothers gained 57 caps. Peter, a chartered accountant, later captained Scotland and will be remembered for his ungainly (yet most effective) place-kicking style. Gordon was an uncompromising lock who played a major part in the British and Irish Lions triumphant tour to South Africa in 1974.

## 1970 — 1970-71

| v. AUSTRALIA | v. FRANCE | v. WALES | v. IRELAND | 1st v. ENGLAND | 2nd v. ENGLAND |
|---|---|---|---|---|---|
| J.W.C. Turner | I.S.G. Smith 1PG[1] | I.S.G. Smith | I.S.G. Smith | †A.R. Brown | A.R. Brown 4C |
| M.A. Smith | W.C.C. Steele 1T | W.C.C. Steele | W.C.C. Steele | W.C.C. Steele | W.C.C. Steele 1T |
| J.N.M. Frame | J.N.M. Frame | J.N.M. Frame | J.N.M. Frame 1T | J.N.M. Frame[1] | J.N.M. Frame 2T |
| C.W.W. Rea | C.W.W. Rea | C.W.W. Rea 1T | A.G. Biggar | C.W.W. Rea 1T | C.W.W. Rea 1T |
| A.G. Biggar | A.G. Biggar | A.G. Biggar | †R.S.M. Hannah | A.G. Biggar | A.G. Biggar |
| I. Robertson | J.W.C. Turner | J.W.C. Turner | J.W.C. Turner | J.W.C. Turner | J.W.C. Turner |
| D.S. Paterson | D.S. Paterson | D.S. Paterson | D.S. Paterson | D.S. Paterson 1T,1DG | D.S. Paterson |
| N. Suddon | J. McLauchlan | J. McLauchlan | J. McLauchlan | J. McLauchlan | J. McLauchlan |
| *F.A.L. Laidlaw | F.A.L. Laidlaw | F.A.L. Laidlaw | F.A.L. Laidlaw | †Q. Dunlop | Q. Dunlop |
| A.B. Carmichael | A.B. Carmichael | A.B. Carmichael 1T | A.B. Carmichael | A.B. Carmichael | A.B. Carmichael |
| P.K. Stagg | A.F. McHarg | A.F. McHarg | A.F. McHarg | A.F. McHarg | A.F. McHarg |
| G.L. Brown | G.L. Brown | G.L. Brown | G.L. Brown | G.L. Brown | G.L. Brown[1] |
| W. Lauder 1PG | †N.A. MacEwan | N.A. MacEwan | N.A. MacEwan | N.A. MacEwan | N.A. MacEwan |
| †G.K. Oliver | *P.C. Brown 1C | *P.C. Brown 4PG | *P.C. Brown 1C | *P.C. Brown 1T,2C | *P.C. Brown 1T,1PG |
| R.J. Arneil | R.J. Arneil | R.J. Arneil | R.J. Arneil | R.J. Arneil | R.J. Arneil |
| Sydney C.G | Stade Colombes | Murrayfield | Murrayfield | Twickenham | Murrayfield |
| LOST 3-23 | LOST 8-13 | LOST 18-19 | LOST 5-17 | WON 16-15 | WON 26-6 |
| Aust.: 1G 1PG 5T | Fr.: 2G 1PG | Scot.: 4PG 2T | Scot.: 1G | Eng.: 3PG 2T | Scot.: 4G 1PG 1T |
| Scot.: 1PG | Scot.: 1G 1PG | Wales: 2G 1PG 2T | Ire.: 1G 2PG 2T | Scot.: 2G 1DG 1T | Eng.: 1DG 1PG |
| 6 Jun. 1970 | 16 Jan. 1971 | 6 Feb. 1971 | 27 Feb. 1971 | 20 Mar. 1971 | 27 Mar. 1971 |
| | [1]Rep. by B.M. Simmers | | | [1]Rep. by †A.S. Turk | [1]Rep. by †G.M. Strachan |

Scotland undertook a short tour of Australia in the summer of 1970. Six matches were played, three were won, but the single Test resulted in a heavy defeat by twenty points. There were seven changes made to the side for the opening game of the 1971 Championship, Peter Brown succeeding tour skipper Frank Laidlaw as captain.

The Scots were well beaten by France and Ireland, but featured in an exciting match with Wales. In a game in which the lead changed several times, Chris Rea made an aggressive break from open play to place the Scots 18-14 ahead with little time to go. Peter Brown's conversion struck an upright, Wales fought back to score in the corner, and a dramatic last-minute conversion gave Wales the game. A month later Scotland, and Rea in particular, had good reason to forget the narrow defeat by Wales. At Twickenham, Rea's last-minute try was converted by Brown for the Scots to secure their first win in England since 1938. To prove that this win was no fluke, the Scots hammered England a week later in a celebration match to mark the centenary of international rugby.

## 1971-72

| v. FRANCE | v. WALES | v. ENGLAND |
|---|---|---|
| A.R. Brown 1C | A.R. Brown | A.R. Brown 1PG |
| W.C.C. Steele | W.C.C. Steele | W.C.C. Steele |
| J.N.M. Frame 1T | J.N.M. Frame | J.N.M. Frame |
| †J.M. Renwick 1T | J.M. Renwick 1PG | J.M. Renwick |
| A.G. Biggar | A.G. Biggar[1] | L.G. Dick |
| C.M. Telfer 1T,1DG | C.M. Telfer | C.M. Telfer 1DG |
| I.G. McCrae[1] | D.S. Paterson | A.J.M. Lawson |
| J. McLauchlan | J. McLauchlan | J. McLauchlan |
| †R.L. Clark | R.L. Clark 1T | R.L. Clark |
| A.B. Carmichael | A.B. Carmichael | A.B. Carmichael |
| A.F. McHarg | †I.A. Barnes | A.F. McHarg |
| G.L. Brown | G.L. Brown | G.L. Brown |
| N.A. McEwan | N.A. McEwan | N.A. McEwan 1T |
| *P.C. Brown 1PG | *P.C. Brown 1PG,1C | *P.C. Brown 3PG,1T |
| R.J. Arneil | R.J. Arneil | R.J. Arneil |
| Murrayfield | Cardiff Arms Park | Murrayfield |
| WON 20-9 | LOST 12-35 | WON 23-9 |
| Scot.: 1G 1PG 1DG 2T | Wales: 3G 3PG 2T | Scot.: 1DG 4PG 2T |
| Fr.: 1G 1PG | Scot.: 1G 2PG | Eng.: 3PG |
| 15 Jan. 1972 | 5 Feb. 1972 | 18 Mar. 1972 |
| [1]Rep. by †A.J.M. Lawson | [1]Rep. by †L.G. Dick | |

The internal political problems in Ireland caused the SRU to cancel their visit to Dublin. As a result, the Championship was left incomplete for the first time since the war. Jim Renwick made an impressive debut against France. He scored a splendid try, showed considerable flair in attack, and was compared by some with Mike Gibson, the famous Irish midfield player. The comparison was justified: in a long, successful career Renwick went on to become Scotland's most-capped player, appearing in 52 internationals. He is also the most-capped centre in the world.

Peter Brown led Scotland to victory (for a third time) against England. Not since Mark Morrison at the turn of the century had a Scottish captain led his side to three wins against England.

## 1972-73

| v. NZ | v. FRANCE | v. WALES | v. IRELAND | v. ENGLAND | v. OVERSEAS XV |
|---|---|---|---|---|---|
| †A.R. IRVINE 2PG | A.R. IRVINE | A.R. IRVINE | A.R. IRVINE | A.R. IRVINE 1C | A.R. IRVINE 1PG,2C |
| W.C.C. STEELE | W.C.C. STEELE | W.C.C. STEELE 1T | W.C.C. STEELE | W.C.C. STEELE 2T | †A.D. GILL 2T |
| †I.W. FORSYTH | I.W. FORSYTH | I.R. McGEECHAN | I.R. McGEECHAN 1DG | I.R. McGEECHAN | I.R. McGEECHAN[1] |
| J.M. RENWICK | J.M. RENWICK | I.W. FORSYTH | I.W. FORSYTH 1T | I.W. FORSYTH | I.W. FORSYTH |
| †D. SHEDDEN | D. SHEDDEN | D. SHEDDEN | D. SHEDDEN | D. SHEDDEN | D. SHEDDEN 1T |
| †I.R. McGEECHAN 1DG | I.R. McGEECHAN 1DG | C.M. TELFER 1T | C.M. TELFER | C.M. TELFER | C.M. TELFER 1T |
| I.G. McCRAE | A.J.M. LAWSON 1T | †D.W. MORGAN 1C | D.W. MORGAN 2DG,2PG | D.W. MORGAN 1PG | D.W. MORGAN |
| J. McLAUCHLAN | J. McLAUCHLAN | *J. McLAUCHLAN | *J. McLAUCHLAN[1] | *J. McLAUCHLAN | *J. McLAUCHLAN |
| R.L. CLARK | R.L. CLARK | R.L. CLARK | R.L. CLARK | R.L. CLARK | R.L. CLARK |
| A.B. CARMICHAEL | A.B. CARMICHAEL | A.B. CARMICHAEL | A.B. CARMICHAEL | A.B. CARMICHAEL | A.B. CARMICHAEL |
| A.F. McHARG | A.F. McHARG | A.F. McHARG | A.F. McHARG | A.F. McHARG | A.F. McHARG 1T |
| G.L. BROWN | †R.W.J. WRIGHT | P.C. BROWN | P.C. BROWN | P.C. BROWN | G.L. BROWN |
| N.A. MacEWAN | N.A. MacEWAN | N.A. MacEWAN | N.A. MacEWAN | N.A. MacEWAN | N.A. MacEWAN |
| *P.C. BROWN | *P.C. BROWN 2PG | G.M. STRACHAN | G.M. STRACHAN | G.M. STRACHAN | P.C. BROWN |
| R.J. ARNEIL | W. LAUDER | †J.G. MILLICAN | J.G. MILLICAN | J.G. MILLICAN[1] | G.M. STRACHAN |
| Murrayfield | Parc des Princes | Murrayfield | Murrayfield | Twickenham | Murrayfield |
| LOST 9-14 | LOST 13-16 | WON 10-9 | WON 19-14 | LOST 13-20 | WON 27-16 |
| SCOT.: 2PG 1DG | FR.: 3PG 1DG 1T | SCOT.: 1G 1T | SCOT.: 1T 2PG 3DG | ENG.: 2G 2T | SCOT.: 2G 1PG 3T |
| NZ: 1G 2T | SCOT.: 2PG 1DG 1T | WALES: 3PG | IRE.: 2T 2PG | SCOT.: 1G 1PG 1T | O/s.XV: 2G 1T |
| 16 Dec. 1972 | 13 Jan. 1973 | 3 Feb. 1973 | 24 Feb. 1973 | 17 Mar. 1973 | 31 Mar. 1973 |
| | | | [1]Rep. by †R.D.H. Bryce | [1]Rep. by G.L. Brown | [1]Rep. by J.N.M. Frame |

This was the Centenary season of the SRU, and it was celebrated with an extra international against the SRU President's Overseas XV. In an exciting match with the All Blacks, full-back Andy Irvine and fly-half Ian McGeechan were new caps. Both were to enjoy long international careers: Irvine played 51 times for Scotland, more than any other Scottish full-back; and McGeechan appeared 32 times as a centre or fly-half. Both were splendid attacking players who could also turn matches through their kicking abilities. Irvine retired as a leading points-scorer in international rugby while McGeechan created a record for Scotland by dropping seven goals in his career. (John Rutherford has subsequently broken the record.)

Another leading Scottish kicker, Douglas Morgan, came into the side which gained a surprising, yet deserved victory over Wales. Morgan was an astute tactician and his six international drop-goals placed him second to McGeechan in the list of leading Scottish drop-goal scorers.

## 1973-74

| v. WALES | v. ENGLAND | v. IRELAND | v. FRANCE |
|---|---|---|---|
| A.R. IRVINE | A.R. IRVINE 1C,1T,2PG | A.R. IRVINE 2PG | A.R. IRVINE 2PG,1C |
| A.D. GILL | A.D. GILL | A.D. GILL | A.D. GILL |
| J.M. RENWICK | J.M. RENWICK | J.M. RENWICK | J.M. RENWICK |
| I.R. McGEECHAN | I.R. McGEECHAN | I.R. McGEECHAN | †M.D. HUNTER |
| L.G. DICK | L.G. DICK | L.G. DICK | L.G. DICK 1T |
| C.M. TELFER | C.M. TELFER | C.M. TELFER | I.R. McGEECHAN |
| A.J.M. LAWSON | A.J.M. LAWSON | D.W. MORGAN | D.W. MORGAN 1PG |
| *J. McLAUCHLAN | *J. McLAUCHLAN | *J. McLAUCHLAN | *J. McLAUCHLAN |
| †D.F. MADSEN | D.F. MADSEN | D.F. MADSEN | D.F. MADSEN |
| A.B. CARMICHAEL | A.B. CARMICHAEL | A.B. CARMICHAEL | A.B. CARMICHAEL |
| G.L. BROWN | G.L. BROWN | G.L. BROWN | G.L. BROWN |
| A.F. McHARG | A.F. McHARG | A.F. McHARG | A.F. McHARG 1T |
| N.A. MacEWAN | N.A. MacEWAN | N.A. MacEWAN | N.A. MacEWAN[1] |
| †W.S. WATSON | W.S. WATSON | W.S. WATSON | W.S. WATSON |
| W. LAUDER | W. LAUDER 1T | W. LAUDER | W. LAUDER |
| Cardiff Arms Park | Murrayfield | Lansdowne Road | Murrayfield |
| LOST 0-6 | WON 16-14 | LOST 6-9 | WON 19-6 |
| WALES: 1G | SCOT.: 1G 2PG 1T | IRE.: 1G 1PG | SCOT.: 1G 3PG 1T |
| SCOT.: NIL | ENG.: 2T 1DG 1PG | SCOT.: 2PG | FR.: 1PG 1DG |
| 19 Jan. 1974 | 2 Feb. 1974 | 2 Mar. 1974 | 16 Mar. 1974 |
| | | | [1]Rep. by I.A. Barnes |

By winning their two home matches, Scotland were able to feature as joint runners-up in the Championship. McLauchlan, Carmichael, Brown and McHarg were experienced experts in a formidable Scottish front five, and there was no occasion when Scotland lacked for possession from the set-pieces. It was a failure by the backs which was so disappointing in the away games. In the match with Ireland, which was the Championship decider, the Scottish pack had a brilliant second half but the only points registered were two penalties, kicked with a stiff wind, by Andy Irvine. The game against England was the most interesting of the season, and produced a last-minute victory for the Scots. England were leading 14-13, going into injury time. Then, from 40 yards and near touch, Irvine converted a penalty to thwart the visitors.

## 1974-75

| v. IRELAND | v. FRANCE | v. WALES | v. ENGLAND |
|---|---|---|---|
| A.R. Irvine 2PG | A.R. Irvine 3PG | A.R. Irvine | A.R. Irvine |
| | | | |
| W.C.C. Steele 1T | W.C.C. Steele | W.C.C. Steele | W.C.C. Steele |
| J.M. Renwick 1T | J.M. Renwick | J.M. Renwick | J.M. Renwick |
| †D.L. Bell | D.L. Bell | D.L. Bell | D.L. Bell |
| L.G. Dick | L.G. Dick | L.G. Dick | L.G. Dick |
| | | | |
| I.R. McGeechan 1DG | I.R. McGeechan | I.R. McGeechan 1DG | I.R. McGeechan |
| D.W. Morgan 1DG | D.W. Morgan | D.W. Morgan 3PG | D.W. Morgan 2PG |
| | | | |
| *J. McLauchlan | *J. McLauchlan | *J. McLauchlan | *J. McLauchlan |
| D.F. Madsen | D.F. Madsen | D.F. Madsen | D.F. Madsen |
| A.B. Carmichael | A.B. Carmichael | A.B. Carmichael | A.B. Carmichael |
| A.F. McHarg | A.F. McHarg | A.F. McHarg | A.F. McHarg |
| G.L. Brown | G.L. Brown | G.L. Brown | G.L. Brown |
| †M.A. Biggar | M.A. Biggar | M.A. Biggar | M.A. Biggar |
| †D.G. Leslie | D.G. Leslie | D.G. Leslie | D.G. Leslie |
| W. Lauder | W. Lauder | N.A. MacEwan | N.A. MacEwan[1] |
| | | | |
| Murrayfield | Parc des Princes | Murrayfield | Twickenham |
| WON 20-13 | LOST 9-10 | WON 12-10 | LOST 6-7 |
| | | | |
| SCOT.: 2PG 2DG 2T | FR.: 1PG 1DG 1T | SCOT.: 3PG 1DG | ENG.: 1PG 1T |
| IRE.: 1G 1PG 1T | SCOT.: 3PG | WALES: 2PG 1T | SCOT.: 2PG |
| | | | |
| 1 Feb. 1975 | 15 Feb. 1975 | 1 Mar. 1975 | 15 Mar. 1975 |
| | | | [1]Rep. by I.A. Barnes |

Scotland started the 1975 season with an encouraging win over Ireland, the Champions of 1974. Drop-goals by the halves, tries by Steele and Renwick following good threequarter play, and accurate place-kicking by Irvine set up this victory, and, despite a narrow defeat in Paris, success against Wales (in front of 104,000 spectators) kept the Scots in the hunt for the Championship.

The encounter with England at Twickenham turned out to be a disappointment. Scotland were denied the Triple Crown in a drab game, played on a wet and gloomy day. The Scots had the better of play until England went ahead early in the second half. A harmless kick bounced spitefully over Irvine's shoulder and the English wing dashed in to score the decisive try of the match.

It was the fourth time since the war that England had prevented Scotland gaining the Triple Crown at Twickenham.

## 1975 / 1975-76

| v. NZ | v. AUSTRALIA | v. FRANCE | v. WALES | v. ENGLAND | v. IRELAND |
|---|---|---|---|---|---|
| †B.H. Hay[1] | B.H. Hay | B.H. Hay | A.R. Irvine 1T | A.R. Irvine 2PG,2C | A.R. Irvine 4PG |
| | | | | | |
| A.R. Irvine | A.R. Irvine | A.R. Irvine | W.C.C. Steele | W.C.C. Steele | W.C.C. Steele |
| J.M. Renwick | J.M. Renwick 1T | J.M. Renwick 1PG | J.M. Renwick | A.G. Cranston | A.G. Cranston |
| †G.A. Birkett | I.R. McGeechan | I.R. McGeechan | †A.G. Cranston | I.R. McGeechan | I.R. McGeechan |
| L.G. Dick | L.G. Dick 1T | L.G. Dick | D. Shedden | D. Shedden[1] | D. Shedden |
| | | | | | |
| I.R. McGeechan | C.M. Telfer | C.M. Telfer | I.R. McGeechan | †R. Wilson | R. Wilson 1DG |
| D.W. Morgan | D.W. Morgan 1C | D.W. Morgan 1DG | D.W. Morgan 1C | A.J.M. Lawson 2T | A.J.M. Lawson |
| | | | | | |
| *J. McLauchlan | *J. McLauchlan | *J. McLauchlan | *J. McLauchlan | *J. McLauchlan | *J. McLauchlan |
| †C.D. Fisher | C.D. Fisher | D.F. Madsen | C.D. Fisher | C.D. Fisher | C.D. Fisher |
| A.B. Carmichael | A.B. Carmichael | A.B. Carmichael | A.B. Carmichael | A.B. Carmichael | A.B. Carmichael |
| I.A. Barnes | A.F. McHarg | A.F. McHarg | A.F. McHarg | †A.J. Tomes | A.J. Tomes |
| A.F. McHarg | G.L. Brown | G.L. Brown | G.L. Brown | G.L. Brown | G.L. Brown |
| D.G. Leslie | W. Lauder | W. Lauder | M.A. Biggar | M.A. Biggar | M.A. Biggar |
| W.S. Watson | †G.Y. Mackie | G.Y. Mackie | G.Y. Mackie | A.F. McHarg | A.F. McHarg |
| W. Lauder | D.G. Leslie | D.G. Leslie | D.G. Leslie | D.G. Leslie 1T | D.G. Leslie |
| | | | | | |
| Auckland | Murrayfield | Murrayfield | Cardiff Arms Park | Murrayfield | Lansdowne Road |
| LOST 0-24 | WON 10-3 | LOST 6-13 | LOST 6-28 | WON 22-12 | WON 15-6 |
| | | | | | |
| NZ: 4G | SCOT.: 1G 1T | SCOT.: 1PG 1DG | WALES: 2G 3PG 1DG 1T | SCOT.: 2G 2PG 1T | IRE.: 2PG |
| SCOT.: NIL | AUST.: 1PG | FR.: 3PG 1T | SCOT.: 1G | ENG.: 1G 2PG | SCOT.: 4PG 1DG |
| | | | | | |
| 14 Jun. 1975 | 6 Dec. 1975 | 10 Jan. 1976 | 7 Feb. 1976 | 21 Feb. 1976 | 20 Mar. 1976 |
| [1]Rep. by W.C.C. Steele | | | | [1]Rep. by J.M. Renwick | |

Scotland toured New Zealand in the summer of 1975, winning four of the seven matches played. The strength of the side lay in its powerful scrummaging, but an inflexible tactical approach limited their appeal to the New Zealand crowds. In the sole Test of the tour, the Scots were heavily beaten on a saturated pitch.

Scotland's front five had been unchanged for eight matches during 1974 and 1975, but following their first appearances together in the 1976 Championship, against France, there were signs that their scrummaging had become less effective, and for the rest of the season Colin Fisher, who replaced Madsen in the matches against Australia and New Zealand, regained his position as hooker. Furthermore, following the defeat in Cardiff, it was felt that McHarg's style of play would be more appropriate at number eight, and a new lock, Alan Tomes, was introduced.

Two good wins followed. A pulsating match for the Calcutta Cup produced four tries, two by Alan Lawson. Scotland's deciding score was by Leslie, midway through the second half. He took advantage of a lucky bounce after a charge-down and raced twenty yards for a try. The win in Dublin was less spectacular, but did give Scotland their first away victory since 1971.

## 1976-77

| v. ENGLAND | v. IRELAND | v. FRANCE | v. WALES |
|---|---|---|---|
| A.R. IRVINE 2PG | A.R. IRVINE 2PG | A.R. IRVINE 1PG | A.R. IRVINE 1T,1C |
|  |  |  |  |
| W.C.C. STEELE | †W.B.B. GAMMELL 2T | W.B.B. GAMMELL | W.B.B. GAMMELL |
| *I.R. McGEECHAN | *I.R. McGEECHAN | *I.R. McGEECHAN | J.M. RENWICK |
| A.G. CRANSTON | J.M. RENWICK | J.M. RENWICK | A.G. CRANSTON |
| L.G. DICK | D. SHEDDEN | D. SHEDDEN | D. SHEDDEN |
|  |  |  |  |
| R. WILSON | R. WILSON | R. WILSON | *I.R. McGEECHAN 1DG |
| A.J.M. LAWSON | D.W. MORGAN 1DG | D.W. MORGAN | D.W. MORGAN |
|  |  |  |  |
| †J. AITKEN | J. AITKEN | J. AITKEN | J. McLAUCHLAN |
| D.F. MADSEN | D.F. MADSEN 1T | D.F. MADSEN | D.F. MADSEN |
| A.B. CARMICHAEL | †N.E.K. PENDER¹ | A.B. CARMICHAEL | A.B. CARMICHAEL |
| A.J. TOMES | I.A. BARNES | I.A. BARNES | I.A. BARNES |
| A.F. McHARG | A.F. McHARG | A.F. McHARG | A.F. McHARG |
| W. LAUDER | M.A. BIGGAR | M.A. BIGGAR | M.A. BIGGAR |
| †D.S.M. MacDONALD | D.S.M. MacDONALD | D.S.M. MacDONALD | D.S.M. MacDONALD |
| †A.K. BREWSTER | W.S. WATSON | W.S. WATSON | W.S. WATSON |
|  |  |  |  |
| Twickenham | Murrayfield | Parc des Princes | Murrayfield |
| LOST 6-26 | WON 21-18 | LOST 3-23 | LOST 9-18 |
|  |  |  |  |
| ENG.: 2G 2PG 2T | SCOT.: 2PG 1DG 3T | FR.: 2G 1PG 2T | SCOT.: 1G 1DG |
| SCOT.: 2PG | IRE.: 1G 3PG 1DG | SCOT.: 1PG | WALES: 2G 2PG |
|  |  |  |  |
| 15 Jan. 1977 | 19 Feb. 1977 | 5 Mar. 1977 | 19 Mar. 1977 |
|  | ¹Rep. by A.B. Carmichael |  |  |

Two events before the start of the international season affected Scotland's fortunes in 1977. In October David Leslie injured his back and was out of contention for an international place. Then Gordon Brown, Scotland's key lock, was sent off in December while playing in an inter-district match, and his subsequent suspension ruled him out for most of the international season.

The heavy defeats at Twickenham and Parc des Princes were Scotland's biggest losing points margins against England and France respectively. And it was the first time since 1971 that Scotland had lost three Championship games during a season.

Bill Gammell, a burly 15-stone wing from Edinburgh Wanderers, had a memorable debut against Ireland. Making good use of his limited opportunities he scored two tries to help his side to a narrow win.

## 1977-78

| v. IRELAND | v. FRANCE | v. WALES | v. ENGLAND |
|---|---|---|---|
| B.H. HAY | A.R. IRVINE 1T¹ | B.H. HAY | A.R. IRVINE |
|  |  |  |  |
| A.R. IRVINE | B.H. HAY | W.B.B. GAMMELL | W.B.B. GAMMELL |
| J.M. RENWICK | J.M. RENWICK | J.M. RENWICK 1T | J.M. RENWICK |
| I.R. McGEECHAN | I.R. McGEECHAN | A.G. CRANSTON | A.G. CRANSTON |
| D. SHEDDEN | D. SHEDDEN 1T² | D. SHEDDEN¹ | B.H. HAY |
|  |  |  |  |
| R. WILSON | R. WILSON | I.R. McGEECHAN | † R.W. BREAKEY |
| *D.W. MORGAN 3PG | *D.W. MORGAN 1DG,1PG,1C | *D.W. MORGAN 2PG | *D.W. MORGAN |
|  |  |  |  |
| J. McLAUCHLAN | J. McLAUCHLAN | J. McLAUCHLAN | J. McLAUCHLAN |
| D.F. MADSEN | †C.T. DEANS | C.T. DEANS | C.T. DEANS |
| A.B. CARMICHAEL | N.E.K. PENDER | N.E.K. PENDER | N.E.K. PENDER |
| A.J. TOMES | A.J. TOMES | A.F. McHARG | A.J. TOMES |
| A.F. McHARG | A.F. McHARG | A.J. TOMES 1T | †D. GRAY |
| M.A. BIGGAR | M.A. BIGGAR | M.A. BIGGAR | M.A. BIGGAR |
| D.S.M. MacDONALD | G.Y. MACKIE | D.S.M. MacDONALD | D.S.M. MacDONALD |
| †C.B. HEGARTY | C.B. HEGARTY | C.B. HEGARTY | C.B. HEGARTY |
|  |  |  |  |
| Lansdowne Road | Murrayfield | Cardiff Arms Park | Murrayfield |
| LOST 9-12 | LOST 16-19 | LOST 14-22 | LOST 0-15 |
|  |  |  |  |
| IRE.: 1G 2PG | SCOT.: 1G 1PG 1DG 1T | WALES: 1PG 1DG 4T | SCOT.: NIL |
| SCOT.:3PG | FR.: 1G 3PG 1T | SCOT.: 2PG 2T | ENG.: 2G 1PG |
|  |  |  |  |
| 21 Jan. 1978 | 4 Feb. 1978 | 18 Feb. 1978 | 4 Mar. 1978 |
|  | ¹Rep. by A.G. Cranston | ¹Rep. by C.G. Hogg |  |
|  | ²Rep. by †C.G. Hogg |  |  |

This was Scotland's worst international season since 1968. Every match was lost, though only three points separated the sides at the end of the Irish and French matches. Sandy Carmichael's international career ended after the Irish match. Educated at Loretto, he played in fifty international matches, retiring as the most-capped Scottish player and the world's most-capped prop. An outstanding scrummager, he had been a key member of the 1971 Lions to New Zealand. Then in the match with Canterbury shortly before the first Test, he had been the victim of one of the worst acts of thuggery seen on a rugby field. He suffered a multiple fracture of the cheekbone, and his injuries were so severe that he was unable to take any further part in the tour.

Brian Hegarty, who made his debut against Ireland, was the son of the 1951 cap John Hegarty.

## 1978-79

| v. NZ | v. WALES | v. ENGLAND | V. IRELAND | v. FRANCE |
|---|---|---|---|---|
| A.R. IRVINE 1C | A.R. IRVINE 3PG,1T | A.R. IRVINE 1PG | A.R. IRVINE 1PG,1T | A.R. IRVINE 1PG,1C,1T |
| †K.W. ROBERTSON | K.W. ROBERTSON | K.W. ROBERTSON | K.W. ROBERTSON 1T | K.W. ROBERTSON 1T |
| J.M. RENWICK | J.M. RENWICK | J.M. RENWICK | J.M. RENWICK | J.M. RENWICK |
| A.G. CRANSTON | *I.R. McGEECHAN | *I.R. McGEECHAN | *I.R. McGEECHAN | *I.R. McGEECHAN |
| B.H. HAY 1T | B.H. HAY | B.H. HAY | B.H. HAY | B.H. HAY |
| *I.R. McGEECHAN 1DG | †J.Y. RUTHERFORD | J.Y. RUTHERFORD 1T | J.Y. RUTHERFORD | J.Y. RUTHERFORD |
| A.J.M. LAWSON | A.J.M. LAWSON | A.J.M. LAWSON | A.J.M. LAWSON | A.J.M. LAWSON |
| J. McLAUCHLAN | J. McLAUCHLAN | J. McLAUCHLAN | J. McLAUCHLAN | J. McLAUCHLAN |
| C.T. DEANS | C.T. DEANS | C.T. DEANS | C.T. DEANS | C.T. DEANS |
| †R.F. CUNNINGHAM | R.F. CUNNINGHAM | R.F. CUNNINGHAM | †I.G. MILNE | I.G. MILNE |
| A.J. TOMES | A.J. TOMES | A.J. TOMES | A.J. TOMES | A.J. TOMES |
| A.F. McHARG | A.F. McHARG | A.F. McHARG | D. GRAY | D. GRAY |
| M.A. BIGGAR | M.A. BIGGAR | M.A. BIGGAR | M.A. BIGGAR | M.A. BIGGAR |
| D.G. LESLIE[1] | I.K. LAMBIE | I.K. LAMBIE | W.S. WATSON | W.S. WATSON |
| †G. DICKSON | G. DICKSON | G. DICKSON | G. DICKSON | G. DICKSON 1T |
| Murrayfield | Murrayfield | Twickenham | Murrayfield | Parc des Princes |
| LOST 9-18 | LOST 13-19 | DRAWN 7-7 | DRAWN 11-11 | LOST 17-21 |
| SCOT.: 1G 1DG | SCOT.: 3PG 1T | ENG.: 1PG 1T | SCOT.: 1PG 2T | FR.: 2PG 1DG 3T |
| NZ: 2G 2PG | WALES: 1G 3PG 1T | SCOT.: 1PG 1T | IRELAND:1PG 2T | SCOT: 1G 1PG 2T |
| 9 Dec. 1978 | 20 Jan. 1979 | 3 Feb. 1979 | 3 Mar. 1979 | 17 Mar. 1979 |

[1] Rep. by †I.K. Lambie

Scotland took the wooden spoon, failing to win a match, yet their heaviest defeat in the Championship was only by six points. The side had plenty of experience and the new fly-half, John Rutherford, proved to be an exciting prospect. Both forwards and backs had their high moments, but a failing of the side was the inability to hit form together or to play with consistency.

Irvine became the second full-back in international history to score three tries in a season (equalling Bob Hiller's record in 1971). Furthermore, he took his haul of tries to seven, more than any other international full-back.

Alastair McHarg retired as Scotland's most-capped lock. He played the last of his 44 games against England (though two of his appearances had been at number eight). One of the most popular members of the Scottish sides of the 1970s, his international career spanned twelve seasons.

## 1979-80

| v. NZ | v. IRELAND | v. FRANCE | v. WALES | v. ENGLAND |
|---|---|---|---|---|
| A.R. IRVINE 2PG | A.R. IRVINE 1PG,2C | A.R. IRVINE 2T,2PG,1C | A.R. IRVINE 1C | *A.R. IRVINE 2PG,2C |
| K.W. ROBERTSON | †S. MUNRO | S. MUNRO | K.W. ROBERTSON | K.W. ROBERTSON |
| J.M. RENWICK | J.M. RENWICK | J.M. RENWICK 1C | J.M. RENWICK 1T | J.M. RENWICK |
| †D.I. JOHNSTON | D.I. JOHNSTON 2T | D.I. JOHNSTON | D.I. JOHNSTON | D.I. JOHNSTON |
| B.H. HAY | B.H. HAY | B.H. HAY | B.H. HAY | B.H. HAY[1] |
| J.Y. RUTHERFORD | J.Y. RUTHERFORD | J.Y. RUTHERFORD 1T | †B.M. GOSSMAN | J.Y. RUTHERFORD 1T |
| A.J.M. LAWSON | †R.J. LAIDLAW | R.J. LAIDLAW | R.J. LAIDLAW[1] | R.J. LAIDLAW |
| *J. McLAUCHLAN | †J.N. BURNETT | J.N. BURNETT | J.N. BURNETT | J.N. BURNETT |
| C.T. DEANS | C.T. DEANS | C.T. DEANS[1] | K.G. LAWRIE | K.G. LAWRIE |
| I.G. MILNE | I.G. MILNE | I.G. MILNE | †N.A. ROWAN | N.A. ROWAN |
| A.J. TOMES | †W. CUTHBERTSON | A.J. TOMES | A.J. TOMES | A.J. TOMES 1T |
| D. GRAY | D. GRAY | D. GRAY | D. GRAY | D. GRAY |
| M.A. BIGGAR | *M.A. BIGGAR | *M.A. BIGGAR | *M.A. BIGGAR | D.G. LESLIE |
| I.K. LAMBIE | †J.R. BEATTIE | J.R. BEATTIE | J.R. BEATTIE | J.R. BEATTIE |
| G. DICKSON | A.K. BREWSTER | A.K. BREWSTER | G. DICKSON | M.A. BIGGAR |
| Murrayfield | Lansdowne Road | Murrayfield | Cardiff Arms Park | Murrayfield |
| LOST 6-20 | LOST 15-22 | WON 22-14 | LOST 6-17 | LOST 18-30 |
| SCOT.: 2PG | IRELAND: 1G 1DG 3PG 1T | SCOT.: 2G 2PG 1T | WALES: 1G 1PG 2T | SCOT.: 2G 2PG |
| NZ: 2G 2T | SCOT.: 2G 1PG | FR.: 1PG 1DG 2T | SCOT.: 1G | ENG.: 2G 2PG 3T |
| 10 Nov. 1979 | 2 Feb. 1980 | 16 Feb. 1980 | 1 Mar. 1980 | 15 Mar. 1980 |
| | [1] Rep. by †K.G. Lawrie | | [1] Rep. by A.J.M. Lawson | [1] Rep. by †J.S. Gossman |

Scotland shared the wooden spoon with France in 1980. The long run without success ended in a win, the first for 13 matches, against the French. But there were few crumbs of comfort for their followers in the remaining matches of the season.

Ian McLauchlan played the last of his 43 internationals for Scotland against the All Blacks in November. His career spanned twelve seasons, he captained Scotland a record number of times (19), and he used his 16-stone, 5ft 9ins frame with splendid technical know-how. His strong physique and excellent technique earned for him the nickname "Mighty Mouse". Later he was a keen marathon runner, and he has become the Scottish rugby correspondent for *The Times*. Two of the finds of the season were David Johnston, an exciting centre with rare attacking adventure, and John Beattie. The latter's storming play in the loose and skill at the tail of the line-out carried him straight into the 1980 Lions team.

## 1980-81

| v. FRANCE | v. WALES | v. ENGLAND | v. IRELAND |
|---|---|---|---|
| *A.R. IRVINE 1PG | *A.R. IRVINE 1T‡ | *A.R. IRVINE 1C,1PG | *A.R. IRVINE 1PG |
| | | | |
| S. MUNRO | S. MUNRO | S. MUNRO 2T | S. MUNRO |
| J.M. RENWICK 1C | J.M. RENWICK 1PG,2C | J.M. RENWICK | J.M. RENWICK |
| K.W. ROBERTSON | K.W. ROBERTSON | K.W. ROBERTSON | K.W. ROBERTSON |
| B.H. HAY | B.H. HAY | B.H. HAY | B.H. HAY 1T |
| | | | |
| J.Y. RUTHERFORD 1T | J.Y. RUTHERFORD | J.Y. RUTHERFORD | J.Y. RUTHERFORD 1DG |
| R.J. LAIDLAW | R.J. LAIDLAW | R.J. LAIDLAW | R.J. LAIDLAW |
| | | | |
| J. AITKEN | J. AITKEN | J. AITKEN | J. AITKEN |
| C.T. DEANS | C.T. DEANS | C.T. DEANS | C.T. DEANS |
| N.A. ROWAN | N.A. ROWAN | N.A. ROWAN | N.A. ROWAN |
| A.J. TOMES | W. CUTHBERTSON | W. CUTHBERTSON | W. CUTHBERTSON |
| D. GRAY | A.J. TOMES 1T | A.J. TOMES | A.J. TOMES |
| †J.H. CALDER | J.H. CALDER | J.H. CALDER 1T | J.H. CALDER |
| J.R. BEATTIE | J.R. BEATTIE | J.R. BEATTIE | J.R. BEATTIE |
| G. DICKSON | D.G. LESLIE | D.G. LESLIE | D.G. LESLIE |
| | | | |
| Parc des Princes | Murrayfield | Twickenham | Murrayfield |
| LOST 9-16 | WON 15-6 | LOST 17-23 | WON 10-9 |
| | | | |
| FR.: 1G 2PG 1T | SCOT.: 2G‡ 1PG | ENG.: 1G 3PG 2T | SCOT.: 1PG 1DG 1T |
| SCOT.: 1G 1PG | WALES: 2PG | SCOT.: 1G 1PG 2T | IRE.: 1G 1PG |
| | | | |
| 17 Jan. 1981 | 7 Feb. 1981 | 21 Feb. 1981 | 21 Mar. 1981 |

‡Includes penalty try

Jim Telfer was Scotland's new coach for 1981, and his side finished as joint-runners-up in the Championship – their best performance since finishing joint-second in 1975. The two home matches were won, and the victory over Wales in a thrilling contest was the highlight of the season.

The emergence of Rutherford and Laidlaw as world-class half-backs brought a new dimension to the attacking edge of the rest of the back division, and Andy Irvine, the world's finest full-back, had plenty of chances to exhibit his brilliant skills as a runner. Although there was a lack of scrummaging power in the tight, the loose forward trio of Calder, Leslie and Beattie was the best in the Home Countries. Scotland were in the process of building an excellent team.

Andy Irvine has been credited with the penalty try scored by the Scots against Wales. He was impeded by the Welsh fly-half just as a try seemed inevitable: David Burnett, one of the best referees on the international panel, was in a good position to award the penalty try, the first ever scored in the long history of the International Championship, and the first ever awarded to Scotland.

## 1981       1981

| 1st v. NZ | 2nd v. NZ | v. ROMANIA |
|---|---|---|
| *A.R. IRVINE | *A.R. IRVINE 1C,2PG | *A.R. IRVINE 4PG |
| | | |
| S. MUNRO | S. MUNRO | S. MUNRO |
| A.G. CRANSTON | A.G. CRANSTON | J.M. RENWICK |
| J.M. RENWICK | J.M. RENWICK 1DG | D.I. JOHNSTON |
| B.H. HAY | B.H. HAY 1T | K.W. ROBERTSON |
| | | |
| J.Y. RUTHERFORD | J.Y. RUTHERFORD | R. WILSON |
| R.J. LAIDLAW | R.J. LAIDLAW | R.J. LAIDLAW |
| | | |
| J. AITKEN | J. AITKEN | J. AITKEN |
| C.T. DEANS 1T | C.T. DEANS | C.T. DEANS |
| I.G. MILNE | I.G. MILNE | I. G. MILNE |
| W. CUTHBERTSON | W. CUTHBERTSON | W. CUTHBERTSON |
| A.J. TOMES | A.J. TOMES | A.J. TOMES |
| D.G. LESLIE | D.G. LESLIE | J.H. CALDER |
| †I.A.M. PAXTON | I.A. M. PAXTON | I.A.M. PAXTON |
| J.H. CALDER | J.H. CALDER | D.G. LESLIE |
| | | |
| Dunedin | Auckland | Murrayfield |
| LOST 4-11 | LOST 15-40 | WON 12-6 |
| | | |
| NZ: 1PG 2T | NZ: 6G 1T | SCOT.: 4PG |
| SCOT.: 1T | SCOT.: 1G 2PG 1DG | ROM.: 2PG |
| | | |
| 13 Jun. 1981 | 20 Jun. 1981 | 26 Sept. 1981 |

Scotland's eight-match tour to New Zealand resulted in five wins, two defeats. In addition to the loss of the Tests, the Scots were also beaten by Wellington. The tour was well-managed and Jim Telfer made positive use of the talent available. The side played some fine attacking rugby towards the end of the first Test, unleashing their backs after a subdued first sixty minutes. However, the tight defence and well-organised cover of the All Blacks' back row stopped the Scots from scoring.

The only serious setback of the tour was the record defeat in the second Test at Auckland. Admittedly the New Zealanders accelerated away from the Scots in the last ten minutes (scoring three tries), to gain their biggest winning points margin over the Scots. But up to half-time the Scots actually dominated the loose play, and only trailed 6-10 at the interval.

In September, the Scots entertained the Romanians, and thus became the first of the Home Unions to award caps for an international against the Continentals. The match at Murrayfield was played in wet, awful conditions, and neither side could score a try. Irvine's four penalty goals took him past Don Clarke's world record aggregate of points, but Scotland deserved their victory.

## 1981-82

| v. AUSTRALIA | v. ENGLAND | v. IRELAND | v. FRANCE | v. WALES |
|---|---|---|---|---|
| *A.R. Irvine 1c,5pg | *A.R. Irvine 2pg | *A.R. Irvine 1c | *A.R. Irvine 3pg | *A.R. Irvine 4c |
| K.W. Robertson | K.W. Robertson | K.W. Robertson | K.W. Robertson | †J.A. Pollock 1t |
| J.M. Renwick 1t | J.M. Renwick | J.M. Renwick 2pg | J.M. Renwick 1dg | J.M. Renwick 1dg,1t |
| D.I. Johnston | D.I. Johnston | D.I. Johnston | D.I. Johnston | D.I. Johnston 1t |
| †G.R.T. Baird | G.R.T. Baird | G.R.T. Baird | G.R.T. Baird | G.R.T. Baird |
| J.Y. Rutherford 1dg | J.Y. Rutherford 1dg | J.Y. Rutherford 1t | J.Y. Rutherford 1t | J.Y. Rutherford 1dg |
| R.J. Laidlaw | R.J. Laidlaw | R.J. Laidlaw | R.J. Laidlaw | R.J. Laidlaw |
| J. Aitken | J. Aitken | J. Aitken | J. Aitken | J. Aitken |
| C.T. Deans | C.T. Deans | C.T. Deans | C.T. Deans | C.T. Deans |
| I.G. Milne | I.G. Milne | I.G. Milne | I.G. Milne | I.G. Milne |
| W. Cuthbertson | W. Cuthbertson | W. Cuthbertson | W. Cuthbertson | W. Cuthbertson |
| A.J. Tomes | A.J. Tomes | A.J. Tomes | A.J. Tomes | A.J. Tomes |
| J.H. Calder | J.H. Calder | J.H. Calder | J.H. Calder | J.H. Calder 1t |
| I.A.M. Paxton | I.A.M. Paxton | I.A.M. Paxton | I.A.M. Paxton | I.A.M. Paxton¹ |
| D.G. Leslie | D.G. Leslie | †R.E. Paxton | †D.B. White | D.B. White 1t |
| Murrayfield | Murrayfield | Lansdowne Road | Murrayfield | Cardiff Arms Park |
| WON 24-15 | DRAWN 9-9 | LOST 12-21 | WON 16-7 | WON 34-18 |
| Scot.: 1G 5PG 1DG | Scot.: 2PG 1DG | Ire.: 6PG 1DG | Scot.: 3PG 1DG 1T | Wales: 1G 4PG |
| Aust.: 1PG 3T | Eng.: 3PG | Scot.: 1G 2PG | Fr.: 1PG 1T | Scot.: 4G 2DG 1T |
| 19 Dec. 1981 | 16 Jan. 1982 | 20 Feb. 1982 | 6 Mar. 1982 | 20 Mar. 1982 |
| | | | | ¹Rep. by G. Dickson |

Scotland's performance in the 1982 Championship was encouraging. The side played open, attacking rugby and was served by a strong, determined pack which had few masters. The only disappointment of the season was in Dublin, where the side lost to an Irish fifteen which kicked seven goals. In the victory over Australia, Irvine's seventeen points created a new record for most points by a Scot in an international, while the half-backs, Laidlaw and Rutherford, extended their Scottish partnership to 14 matches, thus passing the previous partnership record of Chisholm and Hastie.

Scotland's win at Cardiff was the major achievement of the season. It was Scotland's first win in Cardiff in twenty years, and the manner and style with which it was accomplished won the generous applause of the Welsh spectators. Wales were totally destroyed, fore and aft, in a thrilling match.

## 1982

| 1st v. AUSTRALIA | 2nd v. AUSTRALIA |
|---|---|
| *A.R. Irvine 1pg,1c | *A.R. Irvine 3pg |
| K.W. Robertson 1t | K.W. Robertson |
| †R.J. Gordon | R.J. Gordon |
| D.I. Johnston | D.I. Johnston |
| G.R.T. Baird | G.R.T. Baird |
| J.Y. Rutherford 1dg | J.Y. Rutherford |
| R.J. Laidlaw | R.J. Laidlaw |
| †G.M. McGuinness | G.M. McGuinness |
| C.T. Deans | C.T. Deans |
| I.G. Milne | I.G. Milne |
| W. Cuthbertson | W. Cuthbertson |
| A.J. Tomes | A.J. Tomes |
| J.H. Calder | J.H. Calder |
| I.A.M. Paxton | I.A.M. Paxton¹ |
| D.B. White | D.B. White |
| Ballymore | Sydney C.G. |
| WON 12-7 | LOST 9-33 |
| Aust.: 1PG 1T | Aust.: 3G 5PG |
| Scot.: 1G 1PG 1DG | Scot.: 3PG |
| 4 Jul. 1982 | 10 Jul. 1982 |
| | ¹Rep. by R.E. Paxton |

The summer tour to Australia in 1982 was Scotland's most successful to date. For the first time Scotland won an international on tour, Irvine's team defeating the Wallabies in a tight, rather disappointing spectacle at Brisbane.

Altogether the side undertook nine matches, but lost two of the tour games and the final international. The powerful Queensland team, and Sydney, beat the tourists at the start of the trip, but coach Jim Telfer did a grand job with the forwards before that first Test victory at the Ballymore ground.

Telfer's men were well-beaten in the second Test, however. The forwards were unable to dominate to the extent enjoyed in the first Test, and the Wallabies ran-in three fine tries. Irvine made his last appearance for Scotland in this match, and thus retired as the most-capped Scottish international, having played 51 times and scored 273 points – another Scottish (and world) record.

## 1982-83

| v. IRELAND | v. FRANCE | v. WALES | v. ENGLAND |
|---|---|---|---|
| †P.W. Dods 2PG | P.W. Dods 1PG,1C | P.W. Dods 3PG,1C | P.W. Dods 3PG,1C |
| K.W. Robertson | K.W. Robertson 1T | K.W. Robertson | J.A. Pollock |
| J.M. Renwick 1DG | J.M. Renwick | J.M. Renwick 1T | J.M. Renwick |
| D.I. Johnston | D.I. Johnston | D.I. Johnston | K.W. Robertson 1DG |
| G.R.T. Baird | G.R.T. Baird | G.R.T. Baird | G.R.T. Baird |
| R. Wilson | B.M. Gossman 2DG | B.M. Gossman | J.Y. Rutherford |
| *R.J. Laidlaw 1T | *R.J. Laidlaw | *R.J. Laidlaw | R.J. Laidlaw 1T |
| G.M. McGuinness | J. Aitken | J. Aitken | *J. Aitken |
| C.T. Deans | C.T. Deans | C.T. Deans | C.T. Deans |
| I.G. Milne | I.G. Milne | I.G. Milne | I.G. Milne |
| W. Cuthbertson | W. Cuthbertson | W. Cuthbertson | †T.J. Smith 1T |
| A.J. Tomes | A.J. Tomes | A.J. Tomes | I.A.M. Paxton |
| J.H. Calder | J.H. Calder | J.H. Calder | J.H. Calder |
| I.A.M. Paxton | J.R. Beattie | J.R. Beattie | J.R. Beattie |
| D.G. Leslie | D.G. Leslie | D.G. Leslie | D.G. Leslie |
| Murrayfield | Parc des Princes | Murrayfield | Twickenham |
| LOST 13-15 | LOST 15-19 | LOST 15-19 | WON 22-12 |
| Scot.: 2PG 1DG 1T | Fr.: 1G 3PG 1T | Scot.: 1G 3PG | Eng.: 3PG 1DG |
| Ire.: 1G 3PG | Scot.: 1G 1PG 2DG | Wales: 1G 3PG 1T | Scot.: 1G 3PG 1DG 1T |
| 15 Jan. 1983 | 5 Feb. 1983 | 19 Feb. 1983 | 5 Mar. 1983 |

The loss of Rutherford (who had undergone a shoulder operation) was a blow to Scotland's prospects. Laidlaw took over from Irvine as captain, but the added responsibility seemed to hamper his play and at length he relinquished the job in favour of Aitken.

Scotland's best performance of the season was against England, when Rutherford was restored at fly-half. The forwards rucked and mauled with such commitment that the English pack were put under constant pressure. Laidlaw had his best match of the campaign, and scored the decisive try early in the second half, which Dods converted. Near the end the new lock, Tom Smith, flopped over the English line from a line-out to complete Scotland's fourth win at Twickenham.

## 1983-84

| v. NZ | v. WALES | v. ENGLAND | v. IRELAND | v. FRANCE | v. ROMANIA |
|---|---|---|---|---|---|
| P.W. Dods 5PG | P.W. Dods 1PG,2C | P.W. Dods 2PG,2C | P.W. Dods 1T,3C,2PG | P.W. Dods 5PG,1C | P.W. Dods 1T,1C,3PG |
| J.A. Pollock 1T | S. Munro | K.W. Robertson | J.A. Pollock | J.A. Pollock | J.A. Pollock |
| †A.E. Kennedy | D.I. Johnston | A.E. Kennedy 1T[1] | K.W. Robertson 1T | K.W. Robertson | J.M. Renwick |
| D.I. Johnston | A.E. Kennedy | D.I. Johnston 1T | D.I. Johnston | D.I. Johnston | D.I. Johnston |
| G.R.T. Baird | G.R.T. Baird | G.R.T. Baird | G.R.T. Baird | G.R.T. Baird | K.W. Robertson 1DG |
| J.Y. Rutherford 2DG | J.Y. Rutherford | J.Y. Rutherford | J.Y. Rutherford | J.Y. Rutherford | J.Y. Rutherford |
| R.J. Laidlaw | R.J. Laidlaw | R.J. Laidlaw | R.J. Laidlaw 2T[1] | R.J. Laidlaw | R.J. Laidlaw |
| *J. Aitken | *J. Aitken 1T | *J. Aitken | *J. Aitken | *J. Aitken | *J. Aitken |
| C.T. Deans | C.T. Deans | C.T. Deans | C.T. Deans | C.T. Deans | †G.J. Callander |
| I.G. Milne | I.G. Milne | I.G. Milne | I.G. Milne | I.G. Milne | N.A. Rowan |
| W. Cuthbertson | W. Cuthbertson | W. Cuthbertson[2] | †A.J. Campbell | A.J. Campbell | A.J. Campbell |
| T.J. Smith | A.J. Tomes | A.J. Tomes | A.J. Tomes | A.J. Tomes | A.J. Tomes |
| J.H. Calder | J.H. Calder | J.H. Calder | J.H. Calder | J.H. Calder 1T | †S.K. McGaughey |
| I.A.M. Paxton | I.A.M. Paxton 1T | I.A.M. Paxton | I.A.M. Paxton | I.A.M. Paxton | J.R. Beattie |
| J.R. Beattie | D.G. Leslie | D.G. Leslie | D.G. Leslie | D.G. Leslie | D.G. Leslie 1T |
| Murrayfield | Cardiff Arms Park | Murrayfield | Lansdowne Road | Murrayfield | Bucharest |
| DRAWN 25-25 | WON 15-9 | WON 18-6 | WON 32-9 | WON 21-12 | LOST 22-28 |
| Scot.: 5PG 2DG 1T | Wales: 1G 1PG | Scot.: 2G 2PG | Ire.: 1G 1PG | Scot.: 1G 5PG | Rom.: 2G 3PG 1DG 1T |
| NZ: 2G 3PG 1T | Scot.: 2G 1PG | Eng.: 2PG | Scot.: 3G‡ 2PG 2T | Fr.: 1G 1PG 1DG | Scot.: 1G 3PG 1DG 1T |
| 12 Nov. 1983 | 21 Jan. 1984 | 4 Feb. 1984 | 3 Mar. 1984 | 17 Mar. 1984 | 20 May 1984 |

[1]Rep. by J.A. Pollock
[2]Rep. by J.R. Beattie

[1]Rep. by †I.G. Hunter
‡includes a penalty try

Scotland's busiest domestic season for years started with a hectic 25-25 draw against the All Blacks – the highest-scoring draw ever between International Board countries. Then the Scots went on to their first Grand Slam since 1925, and their first Triple Crown triumph since 1938. The pack was superb in the set-pieces, with the loose trio of Calder, Paxton and Leslie excelling in open play. This fine pack was supported by outstanding backs, spearheaded by Laidlaw and Rutherford.

The team's best display was in Dublin, where the Irish were completely overwhelmed in the first half, Scotland building a lead of 22 points. The Grand Slam decider with France was a controversial episode, the argumentative and indisciplined French conceding too many penalties to Peter Dods, who kicked fifty points in the Championship, creating a new Scottish record.

Curiously the side was well-beaten in Bucharest in the spring. Jim Renwick returned to win his 52nd cap, thus becoming Scotland's most-capped player, but his expertise could not help his side to a victory in a match played in almost unbearable heat.

## 1984-85

| v. AUSTRALIA | v. IRELAND | v. FRANCE | v. WALES | v. ENGLAND |
|---|---|---|---|---|
| P.W. Dods 4PG | P.W. Dods 4PG | P.W. Dods 1PG | P.W. Dods 1PG,2C | P.W. Dods 1PG |
| †P.D. Steven | G.R.T. Baird | P.D. Steven | P.D. Steven | P.D. Steven |
| A.E. Kennedy | †K.T. Murray | K.T. Murray | K.T. Murray[1] | D.S. Wyllie |
| K.W. Robertson | K.W. Robertson 1DG | K.W. Robertson | K.W. Robertson | K.W. Robertson 1T |
| G.R.T. Baird | †I. Tukalo | J.A. Pollock | G.R.T. Baird | G.R.T. Baird |
| †D.S. Wyllie | J.Y. Rutherford | J.Y. Rutherford | J.Y. Rutherford 2DG | J.Y. Rutherford |
| *R.J. Laidlaw | *R.J. Laidlaw | R.J. Laidlaw[1] | I.G. Hunter | I.G. Hunter |
| †A.D.G. Mackenzie | G.M. McGuinness | G.M. McGuinness | G.M. McGuinness | G.M. McGuinness |
| C.T. Deans | C.T. Deans | C.T. Deans | C.T. Deans | C.T. Deans |
| I.G. Milne | N.A. Rowan | I.G. Milne | I.G. Milne | I.G. Milne |
| W. Cuthbertson | A.J. Campbell | A.J. Campbell | A.J. Campbell | A.J. Campbell |
| A.J. Tomes | T.J. Smith | T.J. Smith | A.J. Tomes | A.J. Tomes |
| J.H. Calder | J.H. Calder | J.H. Calder | J.H. Calder | J. Jeffrey |
| J.R. Beattie | J.R. Beattie[1] | I.A.M. Paxton | I.A.M. Paxton 2T | I.A.M. Paxton |
| †J. Jeffrey | J. Jeffrey | *D.G. Leslie | *D.G. Leslie | *D.G. Leslie |
| Murrayfield | Murrayfield | Parc des Princes | Murrayfield | Twickenham |
| LOST 12-37 | LOST 15-18 | LOST 3-11 | LOST 21-25 | LOST 7-10 |
| SCOT.: 4PG | SCOT.: 4PG 1DG | FR.: 1PG 2T | SCOT.: 2G 2DG 1PG | ENG.: 2PG 1T |
| AUS.: 3G 5PG 1T | IRE.: 2G 1DG 1PG | SCOT.: 1PG | WALES: 1G 1DG 4PG 1T | SCOT.: 1PG 1T |
| 8 Dec. 1984 | 2 Feb. 1985 | 16 Feb. 1985 | 2 Mar. 1985 | 16 Mar. 1985 |
| | [1]Rep. by I.A.M. Paxton | [1]Rep. by I.G. Hunter | [1]Rep. by D.S. Wyllie | |

Scotland went from the Grand Slam to the wooden spoon, losing all of their matches in 1985. Colin Telfer succeeded Jim Telfer as Scottish coach, and it was decided that, at 37, Jim Aitken (who had led the Scots to five victories and a draw in his seven games as captain) was too old to retain a place in the front row. Scotland's scrummaging was visibly weaker than in the previous year.

Despite their four defeats in the Championship, the Scots participated in several exciting matches. The matches with Ireland, Wales and England could so easily have resulted in Scottish wins, and even in Paris the margin of defeat was only eight points.

Rutherford's two drop-goals against Wales took him ahead of McGeechan's Scottish career record, and his partnership with Roy Laidlaw was extended to a new Scottish record of 25 partnerships.

## 1985-86

| v. FRANCE | v. WALES | v. ENGLAND | v. IRELAND | v. ROMANIA |
|---|---|---|---|---|
| †A.G. Hastings 6PG | A.G. Hastings 1T,1PG | A.G. Hastings 5PG,3C | A.G. Hastings 2PG | A.G. Hastings 5PG,3C |
| †M.D.F. Duncan | M.D.F. Duncan 1T | M.D.F. Duncan 1T | K.W. Robertson | M.D.F. Duncan |
| D.I. Johnston | D.I. Johnston | D.I. Johnston | D.I. Johnston | D.I. Johnston |
| †S. Hastings | S. Hastings | S. Hastings 1T | S. Hastings | S. Hastings 1T |
| G.R.T. Baird | G.R.T. Baird | G.R.T. Baird | G.R.T. Baird | G.R.T. Baird |
| J.Y. Rutherford | J.Y. Rutherford | J.Y. Rutherford 1T | J.Y. Rutherford | J.Y. Rutherford |
| R.J. Laidlaw | R.J. Laidlaw | R.J. Laidlaw | R.J. Laidlaw 1T | R.J. Laidlaw |
| †D.M.B. Sole | D.M.B. Sole | A.K. Brewster | A.K. Brewster | A.K. Brewster |
| *C.T. Deans | *C.T. Deans | *C.T. Deans | *C.T. Deans | *C.T. Deans 1T |
| I.G. Milne | I.G. Milne | I.G. Milne | I.G. Milne | I.G. Milne |
| A.J. Campbell | A.J. Campbell | A.J. Campbell | A.J. Campbell | A.J. Campbell |
| †J.R.E. Campbell-Lamerton | I.A.M. Paxton | I.A.M. Paxton | I.A.M. Paxton | I.A.M. Paxton |
| J. Jeffrey | J. Jeffrey 1T | J. Jeffrey | J. Jeffrey | J. Jeffrey 1T |
| J.R. Beattie | J.R. Beattie | J.R. Beattie | J.R. Beattie | J.R. Beattie |
| †F. Calder | F. Calder | F. Calder | F. Calder | F. Calder |
| Murrayfield | Cardiff Arms Park | Murrayfield | Lansdowne Road | Bucharest |
| WON 18-17 | LOST 15-22 | WON 33-6 | WON 10-9 | WON 33-18 |
| SCOT.: 6PG | WALES: 5PG 1DG 1T | SCOT.: 3G 5PG | IRE.: 1G,1PG | ROM.: 1DG 5PG |
| FR.: 2PG 1DG 2T | SCOT.: 1PG 3T | ENG.: 2PG | SCOT.: 2PG 1T | SCOT.: 3G 5PG |
| 18 Jan. 1986 | 1 Feb. 1986 | 15 Feb. 1986 | 15 Mar. 1986 | 29 Mar. 1986 |

Scotland enjoyed a successful season, sharing the Championship with France. Much of the credit for Scotland's triumph went to new coach Derrick Grant, whose shrewd approach to selection – he had the courage to blood six new caps against France – and sound guidance of the team made him a worthy successor to Colin and Jim Telfer.

Gavin Hastings equalled the world record of six penalty goals for a match on his debut, and in so doing created a new Scottish record for points in an international. Then, against England at Murrayfield, he broke his own Scottish record by scoring 21 points in a total of 33 – Scotland's highest-ever score in the Calcutta Cup. By the end of the season Hastings had scored 14 penalties and 52 points in the Championship, two new Scottish records.

Scott Hastings made his debut with his brother Gavin against France. They were the first pair of brothers to play together on their debuts for Scotland since William and George Neilson first appeared in 1891.

## 1986-87

| v. IRELAND | v. FRANCE | v. WALES | v. ENGLAND |
|---|---|---|---|
| A.G. HASTINGS 1C | A.G. HASTINGS 4PG,1C | A.G. HASTINGS 2PG,2C | A.G. HASTINGS 2PG,1C |
| M.D.F. DUNCAN | M.D.F. DUNCAN | M.D.F. DUNCAN | M.D.F. DUNCAN |
| D.S. WYLLIE | D.S. WYLLIE[1] | K.W. ROBERTSON | K.W. ROBERTSON 1T |
| S. HASTINGS | S. HASTINGS 1T | S. HASTINGS | G.R.T. BAIRD |
| I. TUKALO 1T | I. TUKALO | I. TUKALO | I. TUKALO |
| J.Y. RUTHERFORD 2DG | J.Y. RUTHERFORD | J.Y. RUTHERFORD 1DG | J.Y. RUTHERFORD |
| R.J. LAIDLAW 1T | R.J. LAIDLAW | R.J. LAIDLAW | R.J. LAIDLAW |
| D.M.B. SOLE | D.M.B. SOLE | D.M.B. SOLE | D.M.B. SOLE |
| *C.T. DEANS | *C.T. DEANS | *C.T. DEANS | *C.T. DEANS |
| I.G. MILNE | I.G. MILNE | I.G. MILNE | I.G. MILNE |
| A.J. TOMES | A.J. TOMES | D.B. WHITE | D.B. WHITE |
| I.A.M. PAXTON | I.A.M. PAXTON | I.A.M. PAXTON | I.A.M. PAXTON |
| J. JEFFREY | J. JEFFREY | J. JEFFREY 1T | J. JEFFREY |
| J.R. BEATTIE | J.R. BEATTIE 1T | J.R. BEATTIE 1T | J.R. BEATTIE[1] |
| F. CALDER | F. CALDER | F. CALDER | F. CALDER |
| Murrayfield | Parc des Princes | Murrayfield | Twickenham |
| WON 16-12 | LOST 22-28 | WON 21-15 | LOST 12-21 |
| SCOT.: 1G 2DG 1T | FR.: 3PG 1DG 4T | SCOT.: 2G 2PG 1DG | ENG.: 2G‡ 3PG |
| IRE.: 1G 1DG 1PG | SCOT.: 1G 4PG 1T | WALES: 1G 2PG 1DG | SCOT.: 1G 2PG |
| 21 Feb. 1987 | 7 Mar. 1987 | 21 Mar. 1987 | 4 Apr. 1987 |
| | [1]Rep. by K.W. Robertson | | [1]Rep. by A.J. Tomes ‡includes penalty try |

Scotland opened the season as strong challengers for the Championship title. Their selectors' policy of picking light yet mobile, athletic forwards paid off handsomely in two fine wins against Ireland and Wales. Indeed, to the Welsh the Scots conceded weight advantage but still managed to outplay their opponents and opened the scoring with a memorable push-over try.

But the wet, heavy conditions at Twickenham were not to the liking of the visitors, and against a revived England side the Scots were unable to establish the clear dominance enjoyed at the line-out in their early-season matches. Consequently, Laidlaw and Rutherford, playing together for the 34th time in an international (a world record) were unable to take command of a match for which victory would have brought Scotland the Triple Crown.

Gavin Hastings brought up his century of points in internationals with a towering early penalty goal against England. Only in his ninth international appearance, Hastings thus became the fastest century-maker within IB countries.

# SCOTTISH MATCH RECORDS

## Match Results 1871 to 1987

| Match | Date | Opponents | For T | C | D | P | Pts | Against T | C | D | P | Pts | Result | Venue | Captain |
|---|---|---|---|---|---|---|---|---|---|---|---|---|---|---|---|
| 1 | 27.3.1871 | England | 2 | 1 | — | — |  | 1 | — | — | — |  | Won | Edinburgh | F. J. Moncreiff |
| 2 | 5.2.1872 | England | — | — | 1 | — |  | 3 | 1 | 1 | — |  | Lost | The Oval | F. J. Moncreiff |
| 3 | 3.3.1873 | England | — | — | — | — |  | — | — | — | — |  | Drawn | Glasgow | F. J. Moncreiff |
| 4 | 23.2.1874 | England | 1 | — | — | — |  | — | — | 1 | — |  | Lost | The Oval | W. D. Brown |
| 5 | 8.3.1875 | England | — | — | — | — |  | — | — | — | — |  | Drawn | Edinburgh | W. D. Brown |
| 6 | 6.3.1876 | England | — | — | — | — |  | 2 | 1 | — | — |  | Lost | The Oval | R. W. Irvine |
| 7 | 19.2.1877 | Ireland | 6 | 4 | 2 | — |  | — | — | — | — |  | Won | Belfast | R. W. Irvine |
| 8 | 5.3.1877 | England | — | — | 1 | — |  | — | — | — | — |  | Won | Edinburgh | R. W. Irvine |
| 9 | 4.3.1878 | England | — | — | — | — |  | — | — | — | — |  | Drawn | The Oval | R. W. Irvine |
| 10 | 17.2.1879 | Ireland | 2 | 1 | 1 | — |  | — | — | — | — |  | Won | Belfast | R. W. Irvine |
| 11 | 10.3.1879 | England | — | — | 1 | — |  | 1 | 1 | — | — |  | Drawn | Edinburgh | R. W. Irvine |
| 12 | 14.2.1880 | Ireland | 3 | 1 | 2 | — |  | — | — | — | — |  | Won | Glasgow | R. W. Irvine |
| 13 | 28.2.1880 | England | 1 | 1 | — | — |  | 5 | 2 | — | — |  | Lost | Manchester | R. W. Irvine |
| 14 | 19.2.1881 | Ireland | 1 | — | — | — |  | — | — | 1 | — |  | Lost | Belfast | J. H. S. Graham |
| 15 | 19.3.1881 | England | 2 | 1 | — | — |  | 1 | — | 1 | — |  | Drawn | Edinburgh | J. H. S. Graham |
| 16 | 18.2.1882 | Ireland | 2 | — | — | — |  | — | — | — | — |  | Won | Glasgow | R. Ainslie |
| 17 | 4.3.1882 | England | 2 | — | — | — |  | — | — | — | — |  | Won | Manchester | D. Y. Cassels |
| 18 | 8.1.1883 | Wales | 3 | 3 | — | — |  | 1 | 1 | — | — |  | Won | Edinburgh | D. Y. Cassels |
| 19 | 17.2.1883 | Ireland | 2 | 1 | — | — |  | — | — | — | — |  | Won | Belfast | D. Y. Cassels |
| 20 | 3.3.1883 | England | 1 | — | — | — |  | 2 | — | — | — |  | Lost | Edinburgh | D. Y. Cassels |
| 21 | 12.1.1884 | Wales | 1 | — | 1 | — |  | — | — | — | — |  | Won | Newport | W. E. Maclagan |
| 22 | 16.2.1884 | Ireland | 4 | 2 | — | — |  | 1 | — | — | — |  | Won | Edinburgh | W. E. Maclagan |
| 23 | 1.3.1884 | England | 1 | — | — | — |  | 1 | 1 | — | — |  | Lost | Blackheath | W. E. Maclagan |
| 24 | 10.1.1885 | Wales | — | — | — | — |  | — | — | — | — |  | Drawn | Glasgow | W. E. Maclagan |
| 25 | 7.3.1885 | Ireland | 3 | 1 | — | — |  | — | — | — | — |  | Won | Edinburgh | W. E. Maclagan |
| 26 | 9.1.1886 | Wales | 3 | 2 | — | — |  | — | — | — | — |  | Won | Cardiff | J. B. Brown |
| 27 | 20.2.1886 | Ireland | 5 | 3 | 1 | — |  | — | — | — | — |  | Won | Edinburgh | J. B. Brown |
| 28 | 13.3.1886 | England | — | — | — | — |  | — | — | — | — |  | Drawn | Edinburgh | J. B. Brown |
| 29 | 19.2.1887 | Ireland | 3 | 1 | ★ | — |  | — | — | — | — |  | Won | Belfast | C. Reid |
| 30 | 26.2.1887 | Wales | 12 | 4 | — | — |  | — | — | — | — |  | Won | Edinburgh | C. Reid |
| 31 | 5.3.1887 | England | 1 | — | — | — |  | 1 | — | — | — |  | Drawn | Manchester | C. Reid |
| 32 | 4.2.1888 | Wales | — | — | — | — |  | 1 | — | — | — |  | Lost | Newport | C. Reid |
| 33 | 10.3.1888 | Ireland | 1 | 1 | — | — |  | — | — | — | — |  | Won | Edinburgh | A. R. Don Wauchope |
| 34 | 2.2.1889 | Wales | 2 | — | — | — |  | — | — | — | — |  | Won | Edinburgh | D. S. Morton |
| 35 | 16.2.1889 | Ireland | — | — | 1 | — |  | — | — | — | — |  | Won | Belfast | D. S. Morton |
| 36 | 1.2.1890 | Wales | 3 | 1 | — | — | 8 | 1 | — | — | — | 2 | Won | Cardiff | W. E. Maclagan |
| 37 | 22.2.1890 | Ireland | 1 | — | 1 | — | 5 | — | — | — | — | 0 | Won | Edinburgh | M. C. McEwan |
| 38 | 1.3.1890 | England | — | — | — | — | 0 | 2 | 1 | — | — | 6 | Lost | Edinburgh | W. E. Maclagan |
| 39 | 7.2.1891 | Wales | 7 | 1 | 2 | — | 15 | — | — | — | — | 0 | Won | Edinburgh | M. C. McEwan |
| 40 | 21.2.1891 | Ireland | 5 | 3 | 1 | — | 14 | — | — | — | — | 0 | Won | Belfast | M. C. McEwan |
| 41 | 7.3.1891 | England | 2 | 2 | 1 | — | 9 | 1 | 1 | — | — | 3 | Won | Richmond | M. C. McEwan |
| 42 | 6.2.1892 | Wales | 2 | 1 | — | — | 7 | 1 | — | — | — | 2 | Won | Swansea | C. E. Orr |
| 43 | 20.2.1892 | Ireland | 1 | — | — | — | 2 | — | — | — | — | 0 | Won | Edinburgh | C. E. Orr |
| 44 | 5.3.1892 | England | — | — | — | — | 0 | 1 | 1 | — | — | 5 | Lost | Edinburgh | C. E. Orr |
| 45 | 4.2.1893 | Wales | — | — | — | — | 0 | 3 | — | — | 1 | 9 | Lost | Edinburgh | R. G. Macmillan |
| 46 | 18.2.1893 | Ireland | — | — | — | — | 0 | — | — | — | — | 0 | Drawn | Belfast | J. D. Boswell |
| 47 | 4.3.1893 | England | — | — | 2 | — | 8 | — | — | — | — | 0 | Won | Leeds | J. D. Boswell |
| 48 | 3.2.1894 | Wales | — | — | — | — | 0 | 1 | — | 1 | — | 7 | Lost | Newport | R. G. Macmillan |
| 49 | 24.2.1894 | Ireland | — | — | — | — | 0 | 1 | 1 | — | — | 5 | Lost | Dublin | J. D. Boswell |
| 50 | 17.3.1894 | England | 2 | — | — | — | 6 | — | — | — | — | 0 | Won | Edinburgh | J. D. Boswell |
| 51 | 26.1.1895 | Wales | 1 | 1 | — | — | 5 | — | — | ★ | — | 4 | Won | Edinburgh | W. R. Gibson |
| 52 | 2.3.1895 | Ireland | 2 | — | — | — | 6 | — | — | — | — | 0 | Won | Edinburgh | R. G. Macmillan |
| 53 | 9.3.1895 | England | 1 | — | — | 1 | 6 | — | — | — | 1 | 3 | Won | Richmond | R. G. Macmillan |
| 54 | 25.1.1896 | Wales | — | — | — | — | 0 | 2 | — | — | — | 6 | Lost | Cardiff | G. T. Neilson |
| 55 | 15.2.1896 | Ireland | — | — | — | — | 0 | — | — | — | — | 0 | Drawn | Dublin | G. T. Neilson |
| 56 | 14.3.1896 | England | 3 | 1 | — | — | 11 | — | — | — | — | 0 | Won | Glasgow | G. T. Neilson |
| 57 | 20.2.1897 | Ireland | 1 | 1 | — | 1 | 8 | 1 | — | — | — | 3 | Won | Edinburgh | R. G. Macmillan |
| 58 | 13.3.1897 | England | 1 | — | — | — | 3 | 2 | 1 | 1 | — | 12 | Lost | Manchester | R. G. Macmillan |
| 59 | 19.2.1898 | Ireland | 2 | 1 | — | — | 8 | — | — | — | — | 0 | Won | Belfast | A. R. Smith |
| 60 | 12.3.1898 | England | 1 | — | — | — | 3 | 1 | — | — | — | 3 | Drawn | Edinburgh | A. R. Smith |
| 61 | 18.2.1899 | Ireland | — | — | — | 1 | 3 | 3 | — | — | — | 9 | Lost | Edinburgh | W. P. Donaldson |
| 62 | 4.3.1899 | Wales | 3 | — | 2★ | — | 21 | 2 | 2 | — | — | 10 | Won | Edinburgh | M. C. Morrison |
| 63 | 11.3.1899 | England | 1 | 1 | — | — | 5 | — | — | — | — | 0 | Won | Blackheath | M. C. Morrison |
| 64 | 27.1.1900 | Wales | 1 | — | — | — | 3 | 4 | — | — | — | 12 | Lost | Swansea | M. C. Morrison |
| 65 | 24.2.1900 | Ireland | — | — | — | — | 0 | — | — | — | — | 0 | Drawn | Dublin | T. M. Scott |
| 66 | 10.3.1900 | England | — | — | — | — | 0 | — | — | — | — | 0 | Drawn | Edinburgh | M. C. Morrison |
| 67 | 9.2.1901 | Wales | 4 | 3 | — | — | 18 | 2 | 1 | — | — | 8 | Won | Edinburgh | M. C. Morrison |
| 68 | 23.2.1901 | Ireland | 3 | — | — | — | 9 | 1 | 1 | — | — | 5 | Won | Edinburgh | M. C. Morrison |
| 69 | 9.3.1901 | England | 4 | 3 | — | — | 18 | 1 | — | — | — | 3 | Won | Blackheath | M. C. Morrison |
| 70 | 1.2.1902 | Wales | 1 | 1 | — | — | 5 | 4 | 1 | — | — | 14 | Lost | Cardiff | M. C. Morrison |

*in the drop-goal column denotes a goal from a mark

| Match | Date | Opponents | For | | | | | Against | | | | | Result | Venue | Captain |
|---|---|---|---|---|---|---|---|---|---|---|---|---|---|---|---|
| | | | T | C | D | P | Pts | T | C | D | P | Pts | | | |
| 71 | 22.2.1902 | Ireland | — | — | — | — | 0 | 1 | 1 | — | — | 5 | Lost | Belfast | M. C. Morrison |
| 72 | 15.3.1902 | England | 1 | — | — | — | 3 | 2 | — | — | — | 6 | Lost | Edinburgh | M. C. Morrison |
| 73 | 7.2.1903 | Wales | 1 | — | — | 1 | 6 | — | — | — | — | 0 | Won | Edinburgh | M. C. Morrison |
| 74 | 28.2.1903 | Ireland | 1 | — | — | — | 3 | — | — | — | — | 0 | Won | Edinburgh | M. C. Morrison |
| 75 | 21.3.1903 | England | 2 | — | 1 | — | 10 | 2 | — | — | — | 6 | Won | Richmond | J. R. C. Greenlees |
| 76 | 6.2.1904 | Wales | 1 | — | — | — | 3 | 4 | 3 | — | 1 | 21 | Lost | Swansea | M. C. Morrison |
| 77 | 27.2.1904 | Ireland | 5 | 2 | — | — | 19 | 1 | — | — | — | 3 | Won | Dublin | M. C. Morrison |
| 78 | 19.3.1904 | England | 2 | — | — | — | 6 | 1 | — | — | — | 3 | Won | Edinburgh | M. C. Morrison |
| 79 | 4.2.1905 | Wales | 1 | — | — | — | 3 | 2 | — | — | — | 6 | Lost | Edinburgh | W. P. Scott |
| 80 | 25.2.1905 | Ireland | 1 | 1 | — | — | 5 | 3 | 1 | — | — | 11 | Lost | Edinburgh | W. P. Scott |
| 81 | 18.3.1905 | England | 2 | 1 | — | — | 8 | — | — | — | — | 0 | Won | Richmond | A. B. Timms |
| 82 | 18.11.1905 | New Zealand | 1 | — | 1 | — | 7 | 4 | — | — | — | 12 | Lost | Edinburgh | D. R. Bedell-Sivright |
| 83 | 3.2.1906 | Wales | — | — | — | 1 | 3 | 3 | — | — | — | 9 | Lost | Cardiff | L. West |
| 84 | 24.2.1906 | Ireland | 2 | 2 | ★ | — | 13 | 2 | — | — | — | 6 | Won | Dublin | L. West |
| 85 | 17.3.1906 | England | 1 | — | — | — | 3 | 3 | — | — | — | 9 | Lost | Edinburgh | L. West |
| 86 | 17.11.1906 | South Africa | 2 | — | — | — | 6 | — | — | — | — | 0 | Won | Glasgow | L. L. Greig |
| 87 | 2.2.1907 | Wales | 2 | — | — | — | 6 | — | — | — | 1 | 3 | Won | Edinburgh | L. L. Greig |
| 88 | 23.2.1907 | Ireland | 3 | 3 | — | — | 15 | — | — | — | 1 | 3 | Won | Edinburgh | P. Munro |
| 89 | 16.3.1907 | England | 2 | 1 | — | — | 8 | 1 | — | — | — | 3 | Won | Blackheath | P. Munro |
| 90 | 1.2.1908 | Wales | 1 | 1 | — | — | 5 | 2 | — | — | — | 6 | Lost | Swansea | L. L. Greig |
| 91 | 29.2.1908 | Ireland | 2 | 1 | — | 1 | 11 | 4 | 2 | — | — | 16 | Lost | Dublin | L. L. Greig |
| 92 | 21.3.1908 | England | 2 | 1 | 2 | — | 16 | 2 | 2 | — | — | 10 | Won | Edinburgh | I. C. Geddes |
| 93 | 6.2.1909 | Wales | — | — | — | 1 | 3 | 1 | 1 | — | — | 5 | Lost | Edinburgh | J. M. B. Scott |
| 94 | 27.2.1909 | Ireland | 3 | — | — | — | 9 | — | — | — | 1 | 3 | Won | Edinburgh | J. M. B. Scott |
| 95 | 20.3.1909 | England | 4 | 3 | — | — | 18 | 2 | 1 | — | — | 8 | Won | Richmond | G. Cunningham |
| 96 | 22.1.1910 | France | 7 | 3 | — | — | 27 | — | — | — | — | 0 | Won | Edinburgh | G. Cunningham |
| 97 | 5.2.1910 | Wales | — | — | — | — | 0 | 4 | 1 | — | — | 14 | Lost | Cardiff | G. M. Frew |
| 98 | 26.2.1910 | Ireland | 4 | 1 | — | — | 14 | — | — | — | — | 0 | Won | Belfast | G. Cunningham |
| 99 | 19.3.1910 | England | 1 | 1 | — | — | 5 | 4 | 1 | — | — | 14 | Lost | Edinburgh | G. Cunningham |
| 100 | 2.1.1911 | France | 3 | 1 | 1 | — | 15 | 4 | 2 | — | — | 16 | Lost | Paris | P. Munro |
| 101 | 4.2.1911 | Wales | 2 | — | 1 | — | 10 | 8 | 2 | 1 | — | 32 | Lost | Edinburgh | P. Munro |
| 102 | 25.2.1911 | Ireland | 2 | — | 1 | — | 10 | 4 | 2 | — | — | 16 | Lost | Edinburgh | P. Munro |
| 103 | 18.3.1911 | England | 2 | 1 | — | — | 8 | 3 | 2 | — | — | 13 | Lost | Twickenham | J. C. MacCallum |
| 104 | 20.1.1912 | France | 6 | 5 | — | 1 | 31 | 1 | — | — | — | 3 | Won | Edinburgh | J. C. MacCallum |
| 105 | 3.2.1912 | Wales | 2 | — | — | — | 6 | 3 | 2 | 2 | — | 21 | Lost | Swansea | J. C. MacCallum |
| 106 | 24.2.1912 | Ireland | 2 | 1 | — | — | 8 | 1 | — | 1 | 1 | 10 | Lost | Dublin | J. C. MacCallum |
| 107 | 16.3.1912 | England | 2 | 1 | — | — | 8 | 1 | — | — | — | 3 | Won | Edinburgh | J. C. MacCallum |
| 108 | 23.11.1912 | South Africa | — | — | — | — | 0 | 4 | 2 | — | — | 16 | Lost | Edinburgh | F. H. Turner |
| 109 | 1.1.1913 | France | 5 | 3 | — | — | 21 | 1 | — | — | — | 3 | Won | Paris | F. H. Turner |
| 110 | 1.2.1913 | Wales | — | — | — | — | 0 | 2 | 1 | — | — | 8 | Lost | Edinburgh | F. H. Turner |
| 111 | 22.2.1913 | Ireland | 7 | 4 | — | — | 29 | 2 | 2 | 1 | — | 14 | Won | Edinburgh | F. H. Turner |
| 112 | 15.3.1913 | England | — | — | — | — | 0 | 1 | — | — | — | 3 | Lost | Twickenham | F. H. Turner |
| 113 | 7.2.1914 | Wales | 1 | 1 | — | — | 5 | 3 | 2 | 2 | 1 | 24 | Lost | Cardiff | D. M. Bain |
| 114 | 28.2.1914 | Ireland | — | — | — | — | 0 | 2 | — | — | — | 6 | Lost | Dublin | E. Milroy |
| 115 | 21.3.1914 | England | 3 | 1 | 1 | — | 15 | 4 | 2 | — | — | 16 | Lost | Edinburgh | E. Milroy |
| 116 | 1.1.1920 | France | 1 | 1 | — | — | 5 | — | — | — | — | 0 | Won | Paris | A. W. Angus |
| 117 | 7.2.1920 | Wales | 1 | — | — | 2 | 9 | 1 | 1 | — | — | 5 | Won | Edinburgh | C. M. Usher |
| 118 | 28.2.1920 | Ireland | 4 | 2 | — | 1 | 19 | — | — | — | — | 0 | Won | Edinburgh | C. M. Usher |
| 119 | 20.3.1920 | England | — | — | 1 | — | 4 | 3 | 2 | — | — | 13 | Lost | Twickenham | C. M. Usher |
| 120 | 22.1.1921 | France | — | — | — | — | 0 | 1 | — | — | — | 3 | Lost | Edinburgh | A. T. Sloan |
| 121 | 5.2.1921 | Wales | 3 | 1 | — | 1 | 14 | — | — | 2 | — | 8 | Won | Swansea | J. Hume |
| 122 | 26.2.1921 | Ireland | 2 | 1 | — | — | 8 | 3 | — | — | — | 9 | Lost | Dublin | J. Hume |
| 123 | 19.3.1921 | England | — | — | — | — | 0 | 4 | 3 | — | — | 18 | Lost | Edinburgh | J. Hume |
| 124 | 2.1.1922 | France | 1 | — | — | — | 3 | 1 | — | — | — | 3 | Drawn | Paris | C. M. Usher |
| 125 | 4.2.1922 | Wales | 2 | — | — | 1 | 9 | 1 | 1 | 1 | — | 9 | Drawn | Edinburgh | C. M. Usher |
| 126 | 25.2.1922 | Ireland | 2 | — | — | — | 6 | 1 | — | — | — | 3 | Won | Edinburgh | C. M. Usher |
| 127 | 18.3.1922 | England | 1 | 1 | — | — | 5 | 3 | 1 | — | — | 11 | Lost | Twickenham | C. M. Usher |
| 128 | 20.1.1923 | France | 4 | 2 | — | — | 16 | — | — | ★ | — | 3 | Won | Edinburgh | A. L. Gracie |
| 129 | 3.2.1923 | Wales | 3 | 1 | — | — | 11 | 1 | 1 | — | 1 | 8 | Won | Cardiff | A. L. Gracie |
| 130 | 24.2.1923 | Ireland | 3 | 2 | — | — | 13 | 1 | — | — | — | 3 | Won | Dublin | A. L. Gracie |
| 131 | 17.3.1923 | England | 2 | — | — | — | 6 | 2 | 1 | — | — | 8 | Lost | Edinburgh | A. L. Gracie |
| 132 | 1.1.1924 | France | 1 | — | 1 | 1 | 10 | 4 | — | — | — | 12 | Lost | Paris | J. C. R. Buchanan |
| 133 | 2.2.1924 | Wales | 8 | 4 | — | 1 | 35 | 2 | 2 | — | — | 10 | Won | Edinburgh | J. C. R. Buchanan |
| 134 | 23.2.1924 | Ireland | 3 | 2 | — | — | 13 | 2 | 1 | — | — | 8 | Won | Edinburgh | J. C. R. Buchanan |
| 135 | 15.3.1924 | England | — | — | — | — | 0 | 3 | 3 | 1 | — | 19 | Lost | Twickenham | J. C. R. Buchanan |
| 136 | 24.1.1925 | France | 7 | 2 | — | — | 25 | — | — | 1 | — | 4 | Won | Edinburgh | G.P.S. Macpherson |
| 137 | 7.2.1925 | Wales | 6 | 1 | 1 | — | 24 | 3 | 1 | — | 1 | 14 | Won | Swansea | G.P.S. Macpherson |
| 138 | 28.2.1925 | Ireland | 2 | 2 | 1 | — | 14 | 1 | 1 | — | 1 | 8 | Won | Dublin | D. Drysdale |
| 139 | 21.3.1925 | England | 2 | 2 | 1 | — | 14 | 2 | 1 | — | 1 | 11 | Won | Edinburgh | G.P.S. Macpherson |
| 140 | 2.1.1926 | France | 5 | 1 | — | 1 | 20 | 1 | — | — | 1 | 6 | Won | Paris | D. Drysdale |
| 141 | 6.2.1926 | Wales | 1 | 1 | — | 1 | 8 | 1 | 1 | — | — | 5 | Won | Edinburgh | D. Drysdale |
| 142 | 27.2.1926 | Ireland | — | — | — | — | 0 | 1 | — | — | — | 3 | Lost | Edinburgh | D. Drysdale |

*in the drop-goal column denotes a goal from a mark

| Match | Date | Opponents | For | | | | | Against | | | | | Result | Venue | Captain |
|---|---|---|---|---|---|---|---|---|---|---|---|---|---|---|---|
| | | | T | C | D | P | Pts | T | C | D | P | Pts | | | |
| 143 | 20.3.1926 | England | 3 | 2 | 1 | — | 17 | 3 | — | — | — | 9 | Won | Twickenham | D. Drysdale |
| 144 | 22.1.1927 | France | 4 | 4 | — | 1 | 23 | 2 | — | — | — | 6 | Won | Edinburgh | G.P.S. Macpherson |
| 145 | 5.2.1927 | Wales | 1 | 1 | — | — | 5 | — | — | — | — | 0 | Won | Cardiff | G.P.S. Macpherson |
| 146 | 26.2.1927 | Ireland | — | — | — | — | 0 | 2 | — | — | — | 6 | Lost | Dublin | G.P.S. Macpherson |
| 147 | 19.3.1927 | England | 5 | 1 | 1 | — | 21 | 2 | 2 | — | 1 | 13 | Won | Edinburgh | D. Drysdale |
| 148 | 17.12.1927 | N.S.W. | 2 | 2 | — | — | 10 | 2 | 1 | — | — | 8 | Won | Edinburgh | D. Drysdale |
| 149 | 2.1.1928 | France | 5 | — | — | — | 15 | 2 | — | — | — | 6 | Won | Paris | D. Drysdale |
| 150 | 4.2.1928 | Wales | — | — | — | — | 0 | 3 | 2 | — | — | 13 | Lost | Edinburgh | J. M. Bannerman |
| 151 | 25.2.1928 | Ireland | 1 | 1 | — | — | 5 | 3 | 2 | — | — | 13 | Lost | Edinburgh | D. Drysdale |
| 152 | 17.3.1928 | England | — | — | — | — | 0 | 2 | — | — | — | 6 | Lost | Twickenham | D. Drysdale |
| 153 | 19.1.1929 | France | 1 | — | — | 1 | 6 | 1 | — | — | — | 3 | Won | Edinburgh | D. Drysdale |
| 154 | 2.2.1929 | Wales | — | — | 1 | 1 | 7 | 4 | 1 | — | — | 14 | Lost | Swansea | J. M. Bannerman |
| 155 | 23.2.1929 | Ireland | 4 | 2 | — | — | 16 | 1 | — | 1 | — | 7 | Won | Dublin | J. M. Bannerman |
| 156 | 16.3.1929 | England | 4 | — | — | — | 12 | 2 | — | — | — | 6 | Won | Edinburgh | J. M. Bannerman |
| 157 | 1.1.1930 | France | 1 | — | — | — | 3 | 1 | — | 1 | — | 7 | Lost | Paris | G.P.S. Macpherson |
| 158 | 1.2.1930 | Wales | 2 | 1 | 1 | — | 12 | 1 | 1 | 1 | — | 9 | Won | Edinburgh | G.P.S. Macpherson |
| 159 | 22.2.1930 | Ireland | 3 | 1 | — | — | 11 | 4 | 1 | — | — | 14 | Lost | Edinburgh | G.P.S. Macpherson |
| 160 | 15.3.1930 | England | — | — | — | — | 0 | — | — | — | — | 0 | Drawn | Twickenham | G.P.S. Macpherson |
| 161 | 24.1.1931 | France | — | — | — | 2 | 6 | — | — | 1 | — | 4 | Won | Edinburgh | W. N. Roughead |
| 162 | 7.2.1931 | Wales | 2 | 1 | — | — | 8 | 3 | 2 | — | — | 13 | Lost | Cardiff | W. N. Roughead |
| 163 | 28.2.1931 | Ireland | 1 | 1 | — | — | 5 | 2 | 1 | — | — | 8 | Lost | Dublin | W. N. Roughead |
| 164 | 21.3.1931 | England | 6 | 5 | — | — | 28 | 4 | 2 | — | 1 | 19 | Won | Edinburgh | G.P.S. Macpherson |
| 165 | 16.1.1932 | South Africa | 1 | — | — | — | 3 | 2 | — | — | — | 6 | Lost | Edinburgh | W. M. Simmers |
| 166 | 6.2.1932 | Wales | — | — | — | — | 0 | 1 | — | — | 1 | 6 | Lost | Edinburgh | W. M. Simmers |
| 167 | 27.2.1932 | Ireland | 2 | 1 | — | — | 8 | 4 | 4 | — | — | 20 | Lost | Edinburgh | W. M. Simmers |
| 168 | 19.3.1932 | England | 1 | — | — | — | 3 | 4 | 2 | — | — | 16 | Lost | Twickenham | G.P.S. Macpherson |
| 169 | 4.2.1933 | Wales | 2 | 1 | — | 1 | 11 | 1 | — | — | — | 3 | Won | Swansea | I. S. Smith |
| 170 | 18.3.1933 | England | 1 | — | — | — | 3 | — | — | — | — | 0 | Won | Edinburgh | I. S. Smith |
| 171 | 1.4.1933 | Ireland | — | — | 2 | — | 8 | 2 | — | — | — | 6 | Won | Dublin | I. S. Smith |
| 172 | 3.2.1934 | Wales | 1 | — | — | 1 | 6 | 3 | 2 | — | — | 13 | Lost | Edinburgh | H. Lind |
| 173 | 24.2.1934 | Ireland | 3 | 2 | — | 1 | 16 | 3 | — | — | — | 9 | Won | Edinburgh | M. S. Stewart |
| 174 | 17.3.1934 | England | 1 | — | — | — | 3 | 2 | — | — | — | 6 | Lost | Twickenham | M. S. Stewart |
| 175 | 2.2.1935 | Wales | 2 | — | — | — | 6 | 2 | — | 1 | — | 10 | Lost | Cardiff | K. C. Fyfe |
| 176 | 23.2.1935 | Ireland | 1 | 1 | — | — | 5 | 4 | — | — | — | 12 | Lost | Dublin | R. W. Shaw |
| 177 | 16.3.1935 | England | 2 | 2 | — | — | 10 | 1 | — | 1 | — | 7 | Won | Edinburgh | R. W. Shaw |
| 178 | 23.11.1935 | New Zealand | 2 | 1 | — | — | 8 | 4 | 3 | — | — | 18 | Lost | Edinburgh | R. W. Shaw |
| 179 | 1.2.1936 | Wales | 1 | — | — | — | 3 | 3 | 2 | — | — | 13 | Lost | Edinburgh | R. C. S.Dick |
| 180 | 22.2.1936 | Ireland | — | — | 1 | — | 4 | 2 | — | 1 | — | 10 | Lost | Edinburgh | R. C. S. Dick |
| 181 | 21.3.1936 | England | 1 | 1 | — | 1 | 8 | 3 | — | — | — | 9 | Lost | Twickenham | J. A. Beattie |
| 182 | 6.2.1937 | Wales | 3 | 2 | — | — | 13 | 2 | — | — | — | 6 | Won | Swansea | W. R. Logan |
| 183 | 27.2.1937 | Ireland | — | — | 1 | — | 4 | 3 | 1 | — | — | 11 | Lost | Dublin | W. R. Logan |
| 184 | 20.3.1937 | England | — | — | 1 | — | 3 | 2 | — | — | — | 6 | Lost | Edinburgh | W. R. Logan |
| 185 | 5.2.1938 | Wales | 1 | 1 | — | 1 | 8 | 2 | — | — | — | 6 | Won | Edinburgh | R. W. Shaw |
| 186 | 26.2.1938 | Ireland | 4 | 2 | 1 | 1 | 23 | 4 | 1 | — | — | 14 | Won | Edinburgh | R. W. Shaw |
| 187 | 19.3.1938 | England | 5 | — | — | 2 | 21 | 1 | — | 1 | 3 | 16 | Won | Twickenham | R. W. Shaw |
| 188 | 4.2.1939 | Wales | — | — | — | 1 | 3 | 2 | 1 | — | 1 | 11 | Lost | Cardiff | R. W. Shaw |
| 189 | 25.2.1939 | Ireland | 1 | — | — | — | 3 | 2 | — | ★ | 1 | 12 | Lost | Dublin | R. W. Shaw |
| 190 | 18.3.1939 | England | 2 | — | — | — | 6 | — | — | — | 3 | 9 | Lost | Edinburgh | R. W. Shaw |
| 191 | 1.1.1947 | France | — | — | — | 1 | 3 | 2 | 1 | — | — | 8 | Lost | Paris | K. I. Geddes |
| 192 | 1.2.1947 | Wales | 1 | 1 | — | 1 | 8 | 5 | 2 | — | 1 | 22 | Lost | Edinburgh | K. I. Geddes |
| 193 | 22.2.1947 | Ireland | — | — | — | — | 0 | 1 | — | — | — | 3 | Lost | Edinburgh | W. H. Munro |
| 194 | 15.3.1947 | England | 1 | 1 | — | — | 5 | 4 | 4 | 1 | — | 24 | Lost | Edinburgh | C. R. Bruce |
| 195 | 22.11.1947 | Australia | — | — | 1 | 1 | 7 | 4 | 2 | — | — | 16 | Lost | Edinburgh | J. R. S. Innes |
| 196 | 24.1.1948 | France | 1 | — | — | 2 | 9 | 1 | 1 | — | 1 | 8 | Won | Edinburgh | J. R. S. Innes |
| 197 | 7.2.1948 | Wales | — | — | — | — | 0 | 3 | 1 | — | 1 | 14 | Lost | Cardiff | J. R. S. Innes |
| 198 | 28.2.1948 | Ireland | — | — | — | — | 0 | 2 | — | — | — | 6 | Lost | Dublin | J. R. S. Innes |
| 199 | 20.3.1948 | England | 2 | — | — | — | 6 | — | — | — | 1 | 3 | Won | Edinburgh | J. R. S. Innes |
| 200 | 15.1.1949 | France | 2 | 1 | — | — | 8 | — | — | — | — | 0 | Won | Paris | D. H. Keller |
| 201 | 5.2.1949 | Wales | 2 | — | — | — | 6 | 1 | 1 | — | — | 5 | Won | Edinburgh | D. H. Keller |
| 202 | 26.2.1949 | Ireland | — | — | — | 1 | 3 | 2 | 2 | — | 1 | 13 | Lost | Edinburgh | D. H. Keller |
| 203 | 19.3.1949 | England | — | — | — | 1 | 3 | 6 | 3 | — | — | 24 | Lost | Twickenham | D. H. Keller |
| 204 | 14.1.1950 | France | 2 | 1 | — | — | 8 | 1 | 1 | — | — | 5 | Won | Edinburgh | W. I. D. Elliot |
| 205 | 4.2.1950 | Wales | — | — | — | — | 0 | 2 | — | 1 | 1 | 12 | Lost | Swansea | W. I. D. Elliot |
| 206 | 25.2.1950 | Ireland | — | — | — | — | 0 | 3 | 3 | — | 2 | 21 | Lost | Dublin | W. I. D. Elliot |
| 207 | 18.3.1950 | England | 3 | 2 | — | — | 13 | 2 | 1 | — | 1 | 11 | Won | Edinburgh | P. W. Kininmonth |
| 208 | 13.1.1951 | France | 2 | — | — | 2 | 12 | 2 | 1 | — | 2 | 14 | Lost | Paris | P. W. Kininmonth |
| 209 | 3.2.1951 | Wales | 3 | 2 | 1 | 1 | 19 | — | — | — | — | 0 | Won | Edinburgh | P. W. Kininmonth |

★ in the drop-goal column denotes a goal from a mark

| Match | Date | Opponents | For T C D P Pts | Against T C D P Pts | Result | Venue | Captain |
|---|---|---|---|---|---|---|---|
| 210 | 24.2.1951 | Ireland | 1 1 — — 5 | 1 — 1 — 6 | Lost | Edinburgh | P. W. Kininmonth |
| 211 | 17.3.1951 | England | 1 — — — 3 | 1 1 — — 5 | Lost | Twickenham | P. W. Kininmonth |
| 212 | 24.11.1951 | South Africa | — — — — 0 | 9 7 1 — 44 | Lost | Edinburgh | A. Cameron |
| 213 | 12.1.1952 | France | 1 1 — 2 11 | 2 2 — 1 13 | Lost | Edinburgh | P. W. Kininmonth |
| 214 | 2.2.1952 | Wales | — — — — 0 | 1 1 — 2 11 | Lost | Cardiff | P. W. Kininmonth |
| 215 | 23.2.1952 | Ireland | 1 1 — 1 8 | 3 — — 1 12 | Lost | Dublin | P. W. Kininmonth |
| 216 | 15.3.1952 | England | 1 — — — 3 | 4 2 1 — 19 | Lost | Edinburgh | A. F. Dorward |
| 217 | 10.1.1953 | France | 1 1 — — 5 | 1 1 1 1 11 | Lost | Paris | A. F. Dorward |
| 218 | 7.2.1953 | Wales | — — — — 0 | 3 — — 1 12 | Lost | Edinburgh | A. F. Dorward |
| 219 | 28.2.1953 | Ireland | 1 1 — 1 8 | 6 4 — — 26 | Lost | Edinburgh | A. Cameron |
| 220 | 21.3.1953 | England | 2 1 — — 8 | 6 4 — — 26 | Lost | Twickenham | A. Cameron |
| 221 | 9.1.1954 | France | — — — — 0 | 1 — — — 3 | Lost | Edinburgh | J. N. G. Davidson |
| 222 | 13.2.1954 | New Zealand | — — — — 0 | — — — 1 3 | Lost | Edinburgh | W. I. D. Elliot |
| 223 | 27.2.1954 | Ireland | — — — — 0 | 2 — — — 6 | Lost | Belfast | W. I. D. Elliot |
| 224 | 20.3.1954 | England | 1 — — — 3 | 3 2 — — 13 | Lost | Edinburgh | W. I. D. Elliot |
| 225 | 10.4.1954 | Wales | 1 — — — 3 | 4 — — 1 15 | Lost | Swansea | W. I. D. Elliot |
| 226 | 8.1.1955 | France | — — — — 0 | 4 — — 1 15 | Lost | Paris | J. T. Greenwood |
| 227 | 5.2.1955 | Wales | 2 1 1 1 14 | 2 1 — — 8 | Won | Edinburgh | A. Cameron |
| 228 | 26.2.1955 | Ireland | 1 — 1 2 12 | — — — 1 3 | Won | Edinburgh | A. Cameron |
| 229 | 19.3.1955 | England | 1 — — 1 6 | 2 — — 1 9 | Lost | Twickenham | A. Cameron |
| 230 | 14.1.1956 | France | 2 — — 2 12 | — — — — 0 | Won | Edinburgh | A. Cameron |
| 231 | 4.2.1956 | Wales | — — — 1 3 | 3 — — — 9 | Lost | Cardiff | A. Cameron |
| 232 | 25.2.1956 | Ireland | 2 2 — — 10 | 4 1 — — 14 | Lost | Dublin | A. Cameron |
| 233 | 17.3.1956 | England | 1 — — 1 6 | 1 1 — 2 11 | Lost | Edinburgh | J. T. Greenwood |
| 234 | 12.1.1957 | France | — — 1 1 6 | — — — — 0 | Won | Paris | J. T. Greenwood |
| 235 | 2.2.1957 | Wales | 1 — 1 1 9 | 1 — — 1 6 | Won | Edinburgh | J. T. Greenwood |
| 236 | 23.2.1957 | Ireland | — — — 1 3 | 1 1 — — 5 | Lost | Edinburgh | A. R. Smith |
| 237 | 16.3.1957 | England | — — — 1 3 | 3 2 — 1 16 | Lost | Twickenham | J. T. Greenwood |
| 238 | 11.1.1958 | France | 2 1 — 1 11 | 1 — — 2 9 | Won | Edinburgh | A. R. Smith |
| 239 | 1.2.1958 | Wales | — — — 1 3 | 2 1 — — 8 | Lost | Cardiff | A. R. Smith |
| 240 | 15.2.1958 | Australia | 2 — — 2 12 | 2 1 — — 8 | Won | Edinburgh | A. R. Smith |
| 241 | 1.3.1958 | Ireland | 2 — — — 6 | 2 — — 2 12 | Lost | Dublin | A. R. Smith |
| 242 | 15.3.1958 | England | — — — 1 3 | — — — 1 3 | Drawn | Edinburgh | J. T. Greenwood |
| 243 | 10.1.1959 | France | — — — — 0 | 1 — 2 — 9 | Lost | Paris | J. T. Greenwood |
| 244 | 7.2.1959 | Wales | 1 — — 1 6 | 1 1 — — 5 | Won | Edinburgh | J. T. Greenwood |
| 245 | 28.2.1959 | Ireland | — — — 1 3 | 1 1 — 1 8 | Lost | Edinburgh | J. T. Greenwood |
| 246 | 21.3.1959 | England | — — — 1 3 | — — — 1 3 | Drawn | Twickenham | G. H. Waddell |
| 247 | 9.1.1960 | France | 2 1 — 1 11 | 3 2 — — 13 | Lost | Edinburgh | A. R. Smith |
| 248 | 6.2.1960 | Wales | — — — — 0 | 1 1 — 1 8 | Lost | Cardiff | A. R. Smith |
| 249 | 27.2.1960 | Ireland | 1 — 1 — 6 | 1 1 — — 5 | Won | Dublin | G. H. Waddell |
| 250 | 19.3.1960 | England | 1 — — 3 12 | 3 3 1 1 21 | Lost | Edinburgh | G. H. Waddell |
| 251 | 30.4.1960 | South Africa | 2 2 — — 10 | 4 3 — — 18 | Lost | Port Elizabeth | G. H. Waddell |
| 252 | 7.1.1961 | France | — — — — 0 | 1 1 1 1 11 | Lost | Paris | G. H. Waddell |
| 253 | 21.1.1961 | South Africa | 1 1 — — 5 | 2 — — 2 12 | Lost | Edinburgh | A. R. Smith |
| 254 | 11.2.1961 | Wales | 1 — — — 3 | — — — — 0 | Won | Edinburgh | A. R. Smith |
| 255 | 25.2.1961 | Ireland | 3 2 — 1 16 | 2 1 — — 8 | Won | Edinburgh | A. R. Smith |
| 256 | 18.3.1961 | England | — — — — 0 | 1 — — 1 6 | Lost | Twickenham | A. R. Smith |
| 257 | 13.1.1962 | France | — — — 1 3 | 1 1 — 2 11 | Lost | Edinburgh | A. R. Smith |
| 258 | 3.2.1962 | Wales | 2 1 — — 8 | — — 1 — 3 | Won | Cardiff | A. R. Smith |
| 259 | 24.2.1962 | Ireland | 3 1 1 2 20 | 1 — — 1 6 | Won | Dublin | A. R. Smith |
| 260 | 17.3.1962 | England | — — — 1 3 | — — — 1 3 | Drawn | Edinburgh | A. R. Smith |
| 261 | 12.1.1963 | France | 1 1 1 1 11 | — — 1 1 6 | Won | Paris | K. J. F. Scotland |
| 262 | 2.2.1963 | Wales | — — — — 0 | — — 1 1 6 | Lost | Edinburgh | K. J. F. Scotland |
| 263 | 23.2.1963 | Ireland | — — — 1 3 | — — — — 0 | Won | Edinburgh | K. J. F. Scotland |
| 264 | 16.3.1963 | England | 1 1 1 — 8 | 2 2 — — 10 | Lost | Twickenham | K. J. F. Scotland |
| 265 | 4.1.1964 | France | 2 2 — — 10 | — — — — 0 | Won | Edinburgh | J. B. Neill |
| 266 | 18.1.1964 | New Zealand | — — — — 0 | — — — — 0 | Drawn | Edinburgh | J. B. Neill |
| 267 | 1.2.1964 | Wales | 1 — — — 3 | 2 1 — 1 11 | Lost | Cardiff | J. B. Neill |
| 268 | 22.2.1964 | Ireland | — — 2 6 | — — — 1 3 | Won | Dublin | J. B. Neill |
| 269 | 21.3.1964 | England | 3 3 — — 15 | 1 — — 1 6 | Won | Edinburgh | J. B. Neill |
| 270 | 9.1.1965 | France | 2 1 — — 8 | 4 2 — — 16 | Lost | Paris | J. B. Neill |
| 271 | 6.2.1965 | Wales | — — 2 2 12 | 2 1 — 2 14 | Lost | Edinburgh | M. J. Campbell-Lamerton |
| 272 | 27.2.1965 | Ireland | — — 1 1 6 | 3 2 1 — 16 | Lost | Edinburgh | M. J. Campbell-Lamerton |
| 273 | 20.3.1965 | England | — — 1 — 3 | 1 — — — 3 | Drawn | Twickenham | S. Wilson |
| 274 | 17.4.1965 | South Africa | 1 1 1 — 8 | 1 1 — — 5 | Won | Edinburgh | S. Wilson |
| 275 | 15.1.1966 | France | 1 — — — 3 | — — — 1 3 | Drawn | Edinburgh | S. Wilson |
| 276 | 5.2.1966 | Wales | — — — 1 3 | 2 1 — — 8 | Lost | Cardiff | S. Wilson |
| 277 | 26.2.1966 | Ireland | 3 1 — — 11 | — — — 1 3 | Won | Dublin | I. H. P. Laughland |
| 278 | 19.3.1966 | England | 1 — — 1 6 | — — 1 — 3 | Won | Edinburgh | I. H. P. Laughland |
| 279 | 17.12.1966 | Australia | 2 1 — 1 11 | 1 1 — — 5 | Won | Edinburgh | J. P. Fisher |

| Match | Date | Opponents | For T | C | D | P | Pts | Against T | C | D | P | Pts | Result | Venue | Captain |
|---|---|---|---|---|---|---|---|---|---|---|---|---|---|---|---|
| 280 | 14.1.1967 | France | — | — | 1 | 2 | 9 | 2 | 1 | — | — | 8 | Won | Paris | J. P. Fisher |
| 281 | 4.2.1967 | Wales | 2 | 1 | 1 | — | 11 | 1 | 1 | — | — | 5 | Won | Edinburgh | J. P. Fisher |
| 282 | 25.2.1967 | Ireland | — | — | — | 1 | 3 | 1 | 1 | — | — | 5 | Lost | Edinburgh | J. P. Fisher |
| 283 | 18.3.1967 | England | 2 | 1 | — | 2 | 14 | 4 | 3 | 1 | 2 | 27 | Lost | Twickenham | J. P. Fisher |
| 284 | 2.12.1967 | New Zealand | — | — | 1 | — | 3 | 2 | 1 | — | 2 | 14 | Lost | Edinburgh | J. P. Fisher |
| 285 | 13.1.1968 | France | 1 | — | — | 1 | 6 | 2 | 1 | — | — | 8 | Lost | Edinburgh | J. P. Fisher |
| 286 | 3.2.1968 | Wales | — | — | — | — | 0 | 1 | 1 | — | — | 5 | Lost | Cardiff | J. P. Fisher |
| 287 | 24.2.1968 | Ireland | — | — | — | 2 | 6 | 3 | 1 | — | 1 | 14 | Lost | Dublin | J. P. Fisher |
| 288 | 16.3.1968 | England | — | — | 1 | 1 | 6 | 1 | 1 | — | 1 | 8 | Lost | Edinburgh | J. W. Telfer |
| 289 | 2.11.1968 | Australia | 1 | — | — | 2 | 9 | — | — | — | 1 | 3 | Won | Edinburgh | J. W. Telfer |
| 290 | 11.1.1969 | France | 1 | — | — | 1 | 6 | — | — | — | 1 | 3 | Won | Paris | J. W. Telfer |
| 291 | 1.2.1969 | Wales | — | — | — | 1 | 3 | 3 | 1 | — | 2 | 17 | Lost | Edinburgh | J. W. Telfer |
| 292 | 22.2.1969 | Ireland | — | — | — | — | 0 | 4 | 2 | — | — | 16 | Lost | Edinburgh | J. W. Telfer |
| 293 | 15.3.1969 | England | — | — | — | 1 | 3 | 2 | 1 | — | — | 8 | Lost | Twickenham | J. W. Telfer |
| 294 | 6.12.1969 | South Africa | 1 | — | — | 1 | 6 | — | — | — | 1 | 3 | Won | Edinburgh | J. W. Telfer |
| 295 | 10.1.1970 | France | 1 | — | — | 2 | 9 | 2 | 1 | 1 | — | 11 | Lost | Edinburgh | J. W. Telfer |
| 296 | 7.2.1970 | Wales | 1 | — | 1 | 1 | 9 | 4 | 3 | — | — | 18 | Lost | Cardiff | J. W. Telfer |
| 297 | 28.2.1970 | Ireland | 2 | 1 | 1 | — | 11 | 4 | 2 | — | — | 16 | Lost | Dublin | J. W. Telfer |
| 298 | 21.3.1970 | England | 2 | 1 | — | 2 | 14 | 1 | 1 | — | — | 5 | Won | Edinburgh | F. A. L. Laidlaw |
| 299 | 6.6.1970 | Australia | — | — | — | 1 | 3 | 6 | 1 | — | 1 | 23 | Lost | Sydney | F. A. L. Laidlaw |
| 300 | 16.1.1971 | France | 1 | 1 | — | 1 | 8 | 2 | 2 | — | 1 | 13 | Lost | Paris | P. C. Brown |
| 301 | 6.2.1971 | Wales | 2 | — | — | 4 | 18 | 4 | 2 | — | 1 | 19 | Lost | Edinburgh | P. C. Brown |
| 302 | 27.2.1971 | Ireland | 1 | 1 | — | — | 5 | 3 | 1 | — | 2 | 17 | Lost | Edinburgh | P. C. Brown |
| 303 | 20.3.1971 | England | 3 | 2 | 1 | — | 16 | 2 | — | — | 3 | 15 | Won | Twickenham | P. C. Brown |
| 304 | 27.3.1971 | England | 5 | 4 | — | 1 | 26 | — | — | 1 | 1 | 6 | Won | Edinburgh | P. C. Brown |
| 305 | 15.1.1972 | France | 3 | 1 | 1 | 1 | 20 | 1 | 1 | — | 1 | 9 | Won | Edinburgh | P. C. Brown |
| 306 | 5.2.1972 | Wales | 1 | 1 | — | 2 | 12 | 5 | 3 | — | 3 | 35 | Lost | Cardiff | P. C. Brown |
| 307 | 18.3.1972 | England | 2 | — | 1 | 4 | 23 | — | — | — | 3 | 9 | Won | Edinburgh | P. C. Brown |
| 308 | 16.12.1972 | New Zealand | — | — | 1 | 2 | 9 | 3 | 1 | — | — | 14 | Lost | Edinburgh | P. C. Brown |
| 309 | 13.1.1972 | France | 1 | — | 1 | 2 | 13 | 1 | — | 1 | 3 | 16 | Lost | Paris | P. C. Brown |
| 310 | 3.2.1973 | Wales | 2 | 1 | — | — | 10 | — | — | — | 3 | 9 | Won | Edinburgh | J. McLauchlan |
| 311 | 24.2.1973 | Ireland | 1 | — | 3 | 2 | 19 | 2 | — | — | 2 | 14 | Won | Edinburgh | J. McLauchlan |
| 312 | 17.3.1973 | England | 2 | 1 | — | 1 | 13 | 4 | 2 | — | — | 20 | Lost | Twickenham | J. McLauchlan |
| 313 | 31.3.1973 | SRU President's XV | 5 | 2 | — | 1 | 27 | 3 | 2 | — | — | 16 | Won | Edinburgh | J. McLauchlan |
| 314 | 19.1.1974 | Wales | — | — | — | — | 0 | 1 | 1 | — | — | 6 | Lost | Cardiff | J. McLauchlan |
| 315 | 2.2.1974 | England | 2 | 1 | — | 2 | 16 | 2 | — | 1 | 1 | 14 | Won | Edinburgh | J. McLauchlan |
| 316 | 2.3.1974 | Ireland | — | — | — | 2 | 6 | 1 | 1 | — | 1 | 9 | Lost | Dublin | J. McLauchlan |
| 317 | 16.3.1974 | France | 2 | 1 | — | 3 | 19 | — | — | 1 | 1 | 6 | Won | Edinburgh | J. McLauchlan |
| 318 | 1.2.1975 | Ireland | 2 | — | 2 | 2 | 20 | 2 | 1 | — | 1 | 13 | Won | Edinburgh | J. McLauchlan |
| 319 | 15.2.1975 | France | — | — | — | 3 | 9 | 1 | — | 1 | 1 | 10 | Lost | Paris | J. McLauchlan |
| 320 | 1.3.1975 | Wales | — | — | 1 | 3 | 12 | 1 | — | — | 2 | 10 | Won | Edinburgh | J. McLauchlan |
| 321 | 15.3.1975 | England | — | — | — | 2 | 6 | 1 | — | — | 1 | 7 | Lost | Twickenham | J. McLauchlan |
| 322 | 14.6.1975 | New Zealand | — | — | — | — | 0 | 4 | 4 | — | — | 24 | Lost | Auckland | J. McLauchlan |
| 323 | 6.12.1975 | Australia | 2 | 1 | — | — | 10 | — | — | — | 1 | 3 | Won | Edinburgh | J. McLauchlan |
| 324 | 10.1.1976 | France | — | — | 1 | 1 | 6 | 1 | — | — | 3 | 13 | Lost | Edinburgh | J. McLauchlan |
| 325 | 7.2.1976 | Wales | 1 | 1 | — | — | 6 | 3 | 2 | 1 | 3 | 28 | Lost | Cardiff | J. McLauchlan |
| 326 | 21.2.1976 | England | 3 | 2 | — | 2 | 22 | 1 | 1 | — | 2 | 12 | Won | Edinburgh | J. McLauchlan |
| 327 | 20.3.1976 | Ireland | — | — | 1 | 4 | 15 | — | — | — | 2 | 6 | Won | Dublin | J. McLauchlan |
| 328 | 15.1.1977 | England | — | — | — | 2 | 6 | 4 | 2 | — | 2 | 26 | Lost | Twickenham | I. R. McGeechan |
| 329 | 19.2.1977 | Ireland | 3 | — | 1 | 2 | 21 | 1 | 1 | 1 | 3 | 18 | Won | Edinburgh | I. R. McGeechan |
| 330 | 5.3.1977 | France | — | — | 1 | 3 | 3 | 4 | 2 | — | 1 | 23 | Lost | Paris | I. R. McGeechan |
| 331 | 19.3.1977 | Wales | 1 | 1 | 1 | — | 9 | 2 | 2 | — | 2 | 18 | Lost | Edinburgh | I. R. McGeechan |
| 332 | 21.1.1978 | Ireland | — | — | — | 3 | 9 | 1 | 1 | — | 2 | 12 | Lost | Dublin | D. W. Morgan |
| 333 | 4.2.1978 | France | 2 | 1 | 1 | 1 | 16 | 2 | 1 | — | 3 | 19 | Lost | Edinburgh | D. W. Morgan |
| 334 | 18.2.1978 | Wales | 2 | — | — | 2 | 14 | 4 | — | 1 | 1 | 22 | Lost | Cardiff | D. W. Morgan |
| 335 | 4.3.1978 | England | — | — | — | — | 0 | 2 | 2 | — | 1 | 15 | Lost | Edinburgh | D. W. Morgan |
| 336 | 9.12.1978 | New Zealand | 1 | 1 | 1 | — | 9 | 2 | 2 | — | 2 | 18 | Lost | Edinburgh | I. R. McGeechan |
| 337 | 20.1.1979 | Wales | 1 | — | — | 3 | 13 | 2 | 1 | — | 3 | 19 | Lost | Edinburgh | I. R. McGeechan |
| 338 | 3.2.1979 | England | 1 | — | — | 1 | 7 | 1 | — | — | 1 | 7 | Drawn | Twickenham | I. R. McGeechan |
| 339 | 3.3.1979 | Ireland | 2 | — | — | 1 | 11 | 2 | — | — | 1 | 11 | Drawn | Edinburgh | I. R. McGeechan |
| 340 | 17.3.1979 | France | 3 | 1 | — | 1 | 17 | 3 | — | 1 | 2 | 21 | Lost | Paris | I. R. McGeechan |
| 341 | 10.11.1979 | New Zealand | — | — | — | 2 | 6 | 4 | 2 | — | — | 20 | Lost | Edinburgh | J. McLauchlan |
| 342 | 2.2.1980 | Ireland | 2 | 2 | — | 1 | 15 | 2 | 1 | 1 | 3 | 22 | Lost | Dublin | M. A. Biggar |
| 343 | 16.2.1980 | France | 3 | 2 | — | 2 | 22 | 2 | — | 1 | 1 | 14 | Won | Edinburgh | M. A. Biggar |
| 344 | 1.3.1980 | Wales | 1 | 1 | — | — | 6 | 3 | 1 | — | 1 | 17 | Lost | Cardiff | M. A. Biggar |
| 345 | 15.3.1980 | England | 2 | 2 | — | 2 | 18 | 5 | 2 | — | 2 | 30 | Lost | Edinburgh | A. R. Irvine |
| 346 | 17.1.1981 | France | 1 | 1 | — | 1 | 9 | 2 | 1 | — | 2 | 16 | Lost | Paris | A. R. Irvine |
| 347 | 7.2.1981 | Wales | 2 | 2 | — | 1 | 15 | — | — | — | 2 | 6 | Won | Edinburgh | A. R. Irvine |
| 348 | 21.2.1981 | England | 3 | 1 | — | 1 | 17 | 3 | 1 | — | 3 | 23 | Lost | Twickenham | A. R. Irvine |
| 349 | 21.3.1981 | Ireland | 1 | — | 1 | 1 | 10 | 1 | 1 | — | 1 | 9 | Won | Edinburgh | A. R. Irvine |
| 350 | 13.6.1981 | New Zealand | 1 | — | — | — | 4 | 2 | — | — | 1 | 11 | Lost | Dunedin | A. R. Irvine |

| Match | Date | Opponents | For T | C | D | P | Pts | Against T | C | D | P | Pts | Result | Venue | Captain |
|---|---|---|---|---|---|---|---|---|---|---|---|---|---|---|---|
| 351 | 20.6.1981 | New Zealand | 1 | 1 | 1 | 2 | 15 | 7 | 6 | — | — | 40 | Lost | Auckland | A. R. Irvine |
| 352 | 26.9.1981 | Romania | — | — | — | 4 | 12 | — | — | — | 2 | 6 | Won | Edinburgh | A. R. Irvine |
| 353 | 19.12.1981 | Australia | 1 | 1 | 1 | 5 | 24 | 3 | — | — | 1 | 15 | Won | Edinburgh | A. R. Irvine |
| 354 | 16.1.1982 | England | — | — | 1 | 2 | 9 | — | — | — | 3 | 9 | Drawn | Edinburgh | A. R. Irvine |
| 355 | 20.2.1982 | Ireland | 1 | 1 | — | 2 | 12 | — | — | 1 | 6 | 21 | Lost | Dublin | A. R. Irvine |
| 356 | 6.3.1982 | France | 1 | — | 1 | 3 | 16 | 1 | — | — | 1 | 7 | Won | Edinburgh | A. R. Irvine |
| 357 | 20.3.1982 | Wales | 5 | 4 | 2 | — | 34 | 1 | 1 | — | 4 | 18 | Won | Cardiff | A. R. Irvine |
| 358 | 4.7.1982 | Australia | 1 | 1 | 1 | 1 | 12 | 1 | — | — | 1 | 7 | Won | Brisbane | A. R. Irvine |
| 359 | 10.7.1982 | Australia | — | — | — | 3 | 9 | 3 | 3 | — | 5 | 33 | Lost | Sydney | A. R. Irvine |
| 360 | 15.1.1983 | Ireland | 1 | — | 1 | 2 | 13 | 1 | 1 | — | 3 | 15 | Lost | Edinburgh | R. J. Laidlaw |
| 361 | 5.2.1983 | France | 1 | 1 | 2 | 1 | 15 | 2 | 1 | — | 3 | 19 | Lost | Paris | R. J. Laidlaw |
| 362 | 19.2.1983 | Wales | 1 | 1 | — | 3 | 15 | 2 | 1 | — | 3 | 19 | Lost | Edinburgh | R. J. Laidlaw |
| 363 | 5.3.1983 | England | 2 | i | 1 | 3 | 22 | — | — | 1 | 3 | 12 | Won | Twickenham | J. Aitken |
| 364 | 12.11.1983 | New Zealand | 1 | — | 2 | 5 | 25 | 3 | 2 | — | 3 | 25 | Drawn | Edinburgh | J. Aitken |
| 365 | 21.1.1984 | Wales | 2 | 2 | — | 1 | 15 | 1 | 1 | — | 1 | 9 | Won | Cardiff | J. Aitken |
| 366 | 4.2.1984 | England | 2 | 2 | — | 2 | 18 | — | — | — | 2 | 6 | Won | Edinburgh | J. Aitken |
| 367 | 3.3.1984 | Ireland | 5 | 3 | — | 2 | 32 | 1 | 1 | — | 1 | 9 | Won | Dublin | J. Aitken |
| 368 | 17.3.1984 | France | 1 | 1 | — | 5 | 21 | 1 | 1 | 1 | 1 | 12 | Won | Edinburgh | J. Aitken |
| 369 | 20.5.1984 | Romania | 2 | 1 | 1 | 3 | 22 | 3 | 2 | 1 | 3 | 28 | Lost | Bucharest | J. Aitken |
| 370 | 8.12.1984 | Australia | — | — | — | 4 | 12 | 4 | 3 | — | 5 | 37 | Lost | Edinburgh | R. J. Laidlaw |
| 371 | 2.2.1985 | Ireland | — | — | 1 | 4 | 15 | 2 | 2 | 1 | 1 | 18 | Lost | Edinburgh | R. J. Laidlaw |
| 372 | 16.2.1985 | France | — | — | — | 1 | 3 | 2 | — | — | 1 | 11 | Lost | Paris | D. G. Leslie |
| 373 | 2.3.1985 | Wales | 2 | 2 | 2 | 1 | 21 | 2 | 1 | 1 | 4 | 25 | Lost | Edinburgh | D. G. Leslie |
| 374 | 16.3.1985 | England | 1 | — | — | 1 | 7 | 1 | — | — | 2 | 10 | Lost | Twickenham | D. G. Leslie |
| 375 | 17.1.1986 | France | — | — | — | 6 | 18 | 2 | — | 1 | 2 | 17 | Won | Edinburgh | C. T. Deans |
| 376 | 1.2.1986 | Wales | 3 | — | — | 1 | 15 | 1 | — | 1 | 5 | 22 | Lost | Cardiff | C. T. Deans |
| 377 | 15.2.1986 | England | 3 | 3 | — | 5 | 33 | — | — | — | 2 | 6 | Won | Edinburgh | C. T. Deans |
| 378 | 15.3.1986 | Ireland | 1 | — | — | 2 | 10 | 1 | 1 | — | 1 | 9 | Won | Dublin | C. T. Deans |
| 379 | 30.3.1986 | Romania | 3 | 3 | — | 5 | 33 | — | — | 1 | 5 | 18 | Won | Bucharest | C. T. Deans |
| 380 | 21.2.1987 | Ireland | 2 | 1 | 2 | — | 16 | 1 | 1 | 1 | 1 | 12 | Won | Edinburgh | C. T. Deans |
| 381 | 7.3.1987 | France | 2 | 1 | — | 4 | 22 | 4 | — | 1 | 3 | 28 | Lost | Paris | C. T. Deans |
| 382 | 21.3.1987 | Wales | 2 | 2 | 1 | 2 | 21 | 1 | 1 | 1 | 2 | 15 | Won | Edinburgh | C. T. Deans |
| 383 | 4.4.1987 | England | 1 | 1 | — | 2 | 12 | 2 | 2 | — | 3 | 21 | Lost | Twickenham | C. T. Deans |

# MATCH RECORDS

## MOST CONSECUTIVE MATCHES WON

| | |
|---|---|
| 6 | *1925* F,W,I,E  *1926*  F,W |
| 5 | *1888* I  *1889*  W,I  *1890* W,I |
| 5 | *1891* W,I,E  *1892*  W,I |
| 5 | *1966* I,E,A,  *1967*  F,W |

## MOST CONSECUTIVE MATCHES WITHOUT DEFEAT

| Matches | Wins | Draws | Period |
|---|---|---|---|
| 8 | 5 | 3 | 1884-85 to 1886-87 |
| 6 | 6 | 0 | 1924-25 to 1925-26 |
| 6 | 4 | 2 | 1876-77 to 1879-80 |
| 6 | 5 | 1 | 1982-83 to 1983-84 |

## MOST CONSECUTIVE MATCHES WITHOUT CONCEDING A TRY

| | |
|---|---|
| 7 | between 1884-85 and 1886-87 |
| 4 | between 1876-77 and 1878-79 |
| 4 | between 1893-94 and 1894-95 |
| 4 | between 1961-62 and 1962-63 |

## MOST CONSECUTIVE MATCHES WITHOUT CONCEDING A SCORE

| | |
|---|---|
| 7 | between 1884-85 and 1886-87 |

# MOST POINTS IN A MATCH
## By the team

| Pts | Opponents | Venue | Season |
|-----|-----------|-------|--------|
| 35 | Wales | Edinburgh | 1923-24 |
| 33 | England | Edinburgh | 1985-86 |
| 33 | Romania | Bucharest | 1985-86 |
| 34 | Wales | Cardiff | 1981-82 |
| 32 | Ireland | Dublin | 1983-84 |
| 31 | France | Edinburgh | 1911-12 |

*NB Scotland scored heavily in several matches before scoring by points was adopted*

## By a player

| Pts | Player | Opponents | Venue | Season |
|-----|--------|-----------|-------|--------|
| 21 | A.G. Hastings | England | Edinburgh | 1985-86 |
| 21 | A.G. Hastings | Romania | Bucharest | 1985-86 |
| 18 | A.G. Hastings | France | Edinburgh | 1985-86 |
| 17 | A.R. Irvine | Australia | Edinburgh | 1981-82 |
| 17 | P.W. Dods | France | Edinburgh | 1983-84 |
| 16 | A.R. Irvine | France | Edinburgh | 1979-80 |
| 16 | P.W. Dods | Ireland | Dublin | 1983-84 |
| 15 | P.W. Dods | New Zealand | Edinburgh | 1983-84 |
| 15 | P.W. Dods | Romania | Bucharest | 1984 |

# MOST TRIES IN A MATCH
## By the team

| T | Opponents | Venue | Season |
|---|-----------|-------|--------|
| 12 | Wales | Edinburgh | 1886-87 |
| 8 | Wales | Edinburgh | 1923-24 |
| 7 | France | Edinburgh | 1924-25 |
| 7 | Wales | Edinburgh | 1890-91 |
| 7 | France | Edinburgh | 1909-10 |
| 7 | Ireland | Edinburgh | 1912-13 |
| 6 | Ireland | Belfast | 1876-77 |
| 6 | France | Edinburgh | 1911-12 |
| 6 | Wales | Swansea | 1924-25 |
| 6 | England | Edinburgh | 1930-31 |

## By a player

| T | Player | Opponents | Venue | Season |
|---|--------|-----------|-------|--------|
| 5 | G.C. Lindsay | Wales | Edinburgh | 1886-87 |
| 4 | W.A. Stewart | Ireland | Edinburgh | 1912-13 |
| 4 | I.S. Smith | France | Edinburgh | 1924-25 |
| 4 | I.S. Smith | Wales | Swansea | 1924-25 |
| 3 | R.C. MacKenzie | Ireland | Belfast | 1876-77 |
| 3 | W. Wotherspoon * | Ireland | Belfast | 1890-91 |
| 3 | J.M. Tennent | France | Edinburgh | 1909-10 |
| 3 | W.A. Stewart | France | Paris | 1912-13 |
| 3 | I.S. Smith | Wales | Edinburgh | 1923-24 |
| 3 | A.C. Wallace | France | Paris | 1925-26 |

*(* There is an account of this match in which Wotherspoon is credited with only two tries).*

# MOST CONVERSIONS IN A MATCH
## By the team

| C | Opponents | Venue | Season |
|---|-----------|-------|--------|
| 5 | France | Edinburgh | 1911-12 |
| 5 | England | Edinburgh | 1930-31 |
| 4 | Ireland | Belfast | 1876-77 |
| 4 | Wales | Edinburgh | 1886-87 |
| 4 | Ireland | Edinburgh | 1912-13 |
| 4 | Wales | Edinburgh | 1923-24 |
| 4 | France | Edinburgh | 1926-27 |
| 4 | England | Edinburgh | 1970-71 |
| 4 | Wales | Cardiff | 1981-82 |

## By a player

| C | Player | Opponents | Venue | Season |
|---|--------|-----------|-------|--------|
| 5 | F.H. Turner | France | Edinburgh | 1911-12 |
| 5 | J.W. Allan | England | Edinburgh | 1930-31 |
| 4 | M. Cross | Ireland | Belfast | 1876-77 |
| 4 | F.H. Turner | Ireland | Edinburgh | 1912-13 |
| 4 | D. Drysdale | Wales | Edinburgh | 1923-24 |
| 4 | A.C. Gillies | France | Edinburgh | 1926-27 |
| 4 | A.R. Brown | England | Edinburgh | 1970-71 |
| 4 | A.R. Irvine | Wales | Cardiff | 1981-82 |

# MOST DROPPED GOALS IN A MATCH

## By the team

| DG | Opponents | Venue | Season |
|----|-----------|-------|--------|
| 3 | Ireland | Edinburgh | 1972-73 |
| 2 | Wales | Edinburgh | 1984-85 |
| 2 | Ireland | Belfast | 1876-77 |
| 2 | Ireland | Glasgow | 1879-80 |
| 2 | Wales | Edinburgh | 1890-91 |
| 2 | England | Leeds | 1892-93 |
| 2 | Wales | Edinburgh | 1898-99 |
| 2 | England | Edinburgh | 1907-08 |
| 2 | Ireland | Dublin | 1932-33 |
| 2 | Wales | Edinburgh | 1964-65 |
| 2 | Ireland | Edinburgh | 1974-75 |
| 2 | Wales | Cardiff | 1981-82 |
| 2 | France | Paris | 1982-83 |
| 2 | New Zealand | Edinburgh | 1983-84 |
| 2 | Ireland | Edinburgh | 1986-87 |

## By a player

| DG | Player | Opponents | Venue | Season |
|----|--------|-----------|-------|--------|
| 2 | R.C. MacKenzie | Ireland | Belfast | 1876-77 |
| 2 | N.J. Finlay | Ireland | Glasgow | 1879-80 |
| 2 | B.M. Simmers | Wales | Edinburgh | 1964-65 |
| 2 | D.W. Morgan | Ireland | Edinburgh | 1972-73 |
| 2 | B.M. Gossman | France | Paris | 1982-83 |
| 2 | J.Y. Rutherford | New Zealand | Edinburgh | 1983-84 |
| 2 | J.Y. Rutherford | Wales | Edinburgh | 1984-85 |
| 2 | J.Y. Rutherford | Ireland | Edinburgh | 1986-87 |

# MOST PENALTY GOALS IN A MATCH

## By the team

| PG | Opponents | Venue | Season |
|----|-----------|-------|--------|
| 6 | France | Edinburgh | 1985-86 |
| 5 | Australia | Edinburgh | 1981-82 |
| 5 | New Zealand | Edinburgh | 1983-84 |
| 5 | France | Edinburgh | 1983-84 |
| 5 | England | Edinburgh | 1985-86 |
| 5 | Romania | Bucharest | 1985-86 |
| 4 | Wales | Edinburgh | 1970-71 |
| 4 | England | Edinburgh | 1971-72 |
| 4 | Ireland | Dublin | 1975-76 |
| 4 | Romania | Edinburgh | 1981-82 |
| 4 | Australia | Edinburgh | 1984-85 |
| 4 | Ireland | Edinburgh | 1984-85 |
| 4 | France | Paris | 1986-87 |

## By a player

| PG | Player | Opponents | Venue | Season |
|---|---|---|---|---|
| 6 | A.G. Hastings | France | Edinburgh | 1985-86 |
| 5 | A.R. Irvine | Australia | Edinburgh | 1981-82 |
| 5 | P.W. Dods | New Zealand | Edinburgh | 1983-84 |
| 5 | P.W. Dods | France | Edinburgh | 1983-84 |
| 5 | A.G. Hastings | England | Edinburgh | 1985-86 |
| 5 | A.G. Hastings | Romania | Bucharest | 1985-86 |
| 4 | P.C. Brown | Wales | Edinburgh | 1970-71 |
| 4 | A.R. Irvine | Ireland | Dublin | 1975-76 |
| 4 | A.R. Irvine | Romania | Edinburgh | 1981-82 |
| 4 | P.W. Dods | Australia | Edinburgh | 1984-85 |
| 4 | P.W. Dods | Ireland | Edinburgh | 1984-85 |
| 4 | A.G. Hastings | France | Paris | 1986-87 |

## GOALS FROM MARKS

| * | Player | Opponents | Venue | Season |
|---|---|---|---|---|
| 1 | C.W. Berry | Ireland | Belfast | 1886-87 |
| 1 | W.J. Thomson | Wales | Edinburgh | 1898-99 |
| 1 | K.G. MacLeod | Ireland | Dublin | 1905-06 |

## TRY ON DEBUT

| Player | Opponents | Venue | Season |
|---|---|---|---|
| A. Buchanan | England | Edinburgh | 1870-71 |
| W. Cross | England | Edinburgh | 1870-71 |
| R. C. MacKenzie | Ireland | Belfast | 1876-77 |
| E. J. Pocock | Ireland | Belfast | 1876-77 |
| J. B. Brown | Ireland | Belfast | 1878-79 |
| D. Somerville | Ireland | Belfast | 1878-79 |
| D. J. Macfarlan | Wales | Edinburgh | 1882-83 |
| A. T. Clay | Wales | Cardiff | 1885-86 |
| D. S. Morton | Ireland | Belfast | 1886-87 |
| H. T. O. Leggatt | Wales | Edinburgh | 1890-91 |
| P. R. Clauss | Wales | Edinburgh | 1890-91 |
| W. Wotherspoon | Ireland | Belfast | 1890-91 |
| G. T. Campbell | Wales | Swansea | 1891-92 |
| A. M. Bucher | England | Manchester | 1896-97 |
| J. I. Gillespie | England | Blackheath | 1898-99 |
| P. Turnbull | Wales | Edinburgh | 1900-01 |
| A. N. Fell | Wales | Edinburgh | 1900-01 |
| J. D. Dallas | England | Richmond | 1902-03 |
| A. W. Little | Wales | Edinburgh | 1904-05 |
| R. H. Lindsay-Watson | Ireland | Edinburgh | 1908-09 |
| J. R. McGregor | Ireland | Edinburgh | 1908-09 |
| I. P. M. Robertson | France | Edinburgh | 1909-10 |
| J. D. Dobson | Ireland | Belfast | 1909-10 |
| R. F. Simson | England | Twickenham | 1910-11 |
| J. G. Will | France | Edinburgh | 1911-12 |
| A. W. Gunn | France | Edinburgh | 1911-12 |
| C. M. Usher | England | Edinburgh | 1911-12 |
| W. A. Stewart | France | Paris | 1912-13 |
| R. E. Gordon | France | Paris | 1912-13 |
| T. C. Bowie | Ireland | Edinburgh | 1912-13 |
| J. L. Huggan | England | Edinburgh | 1913-14 |
| G. B. Crole | France | Paris | 1919-20 |
| A. Browning | Ireland | Edinburgh | 1919-20 |
| J. C. R. Buchanan | Wales | Swansea | 1920-21 |
| E. McLaren | France | Edinburgh | 1922-23 |
| I. S. Smith | Wales | Edinburgh | 1923-24 |
| W. B. Welsh | New South Wales | Edinburgh | 1927-28 |
| C. H. C. Brown | England | Edinburgh | 1928-29 |
| D. J. StC. Ford | Ireland | Edinburgh | 1929-30 |
| D. Crichton-Miller | Wales | Cardiff | 1930-31 |
| W. R. Logan | England | Edinburgh | 1930-31 |
| K. L. T. Jackson | Wales | Swansea | 1932-33 |
| J. A. Crawford | Ireland | Edinburgh | 1933-34 |
| H. M. Murray | Wales | Edinburgh | 1935-36 |
| W. H. Crawford | Wales | Edinburgh | 1937-38 |
| W. N. Renwick | England | Twickenham | 1937-38 |
| P. W. Kininmonth | France | Paris | 1948-49 |
| R. Macdonald | France | Edinburgh | 1949-50 |
| G. M. Budge | France | Edinburgh | 1949-50 |
| D. M. Rose | France | Paris | 1950-51 |
| R. A. Gordon | Wales | Edinburgh | 1950-51 |

| Player | Opponents | Venue | Season |
|---|---|---|---|
| I. F. Cordial | France | Edinburgh | 1951-52 |
| A. R. Smith | Wales | Edinburgh | 1954-55 |
| J. A. Nichol | Wales | Edinburgh | 1954-55 |
| G. D. Stevenson | England | Edinburgh | 1955-56 |
| R. H. Thomson | Ireland | Dublin | 1959-60 |
| A. H. W. Boyle | Australia | Edinburgh | 1966-67 |
| G. J. Keith | France | Edinburgh | 1967-68 |
| I. S. G. Smith | South Africa | Edinburgh | 1969-70 |
| J. M. Renwick | France | Edinburgh | 1971-72 |
| A. D. Gill | President's XV | Edinburgh | 1972-73 |
| W. B. B. Gammell | Ireland | Edinburgh | 1976-77 |
| J. A. Pollock | Wales | Cardiff | 1981-82 |
| T. J. Smith | England | Twickenham | 1982-83 |

## CAPTAIN ON INTERNATIONAL DEBUT

| Player | Opponents | Venue | Season |
|---|---|---|---|
| F. J. Moncreiff | England | Edinburgh | 1870-71 |
| K. I. Geddes | France | Paris | 1946-47 |
| W. H. Munro | Ireland | Edinburgh | 1946-47 |
| D. H. Keller | France | Paris | 1948-49 |

## TRIES BY FULL-BACKS

| Player | Opponents | Venue | Season |
|---|---|---|---|
| I.S.G. Smith | South Africa | Edinburgh | 1969-70 |
| I.S.G. Smith | France | Edinburgh | 1969-70 |
| A.R. Irvine | England | Edinburgh | 1973-74 |
| A.R. Irvine | Wales | Cardiff | 1975-76 |
| A.R. Irvine | Wales | Edinburgh | 1976-77 |
| A.R. Irvine | France | Edinburgh | 1977-78 |
| A.R. Irvine | Wales | Edinburgh | 1978-79 |
| A.R. Irvine | Ireland | Edinburgh | 1978-79 |
| A.R. Irvine | France | Paris | 1978-79 |
| A.R. Irvine (2) | France | Edinburgh | 1979-80 |
| A.R. Irvine * | Wales | Edinburgh | 1980-81 |
| P.W. Dods | Ireland | Dublin | 1983-84 |
| P.W. Dods | Romania | Bucharest | 1984 |
| A.G. Hastings | Wales | Cardiff | 1985-86 |

* denotes a penalty try.

## ALL THE POINTS FOR SCOTLAND
## IN A MATCH
### (where more than one scoring action is involved)

| Pts | Player | Opponents | Venue | Season |
|---|---|---|---|---|
| 18 | A.G. Hastings | France | Edinburgh | 1985-86 |
| 13 | A.R. Irvine | Wales | Edinburgh | 1978-79 |
| 12 | P.W. Dods | Australia | Edinburgh | 1984-85 |
| 12 | A.R. Irvine | Romania | Edinburgh | 1981-82 |
| 9 | A.R. Irvine | Australia | Sydney | 1982 |
| 9 | D.W. Morgan | Ireland | Dublin | 1977-78 |
| 9 | A.R. Irvine | France | Paris | 1974-75 |
| 9 | A. Browning | Wales | Edinburgh | 1921-22 |
| 8 | W.H. Crawford | Wales | Edinburgh | 1937-38 |
| 6 | J.D. Boswell | England | Edinburgh | 1893-94 |
| 6 | G.T. Neilson | England | Richmond | 1894-95 |
| 6 | J.W. Allan | France | Edinburgh | 1930-31 |
| 6 | A. Cameron | England | Twickenham | 1954-55 |
| 6 | K.J.F. Scotland | France | Paris | 1956-57 |
| 6 | S. Wilson | Ireland | Dublin | 1963-64 |
| 6 | S. Wilson | Ireland | Dublin | 1967-68 |
| 6 | I.S.G. Smith | South Africa | Edinburgh | 1969-70 |
| 6 | A.R. Irvine | Ireland | Dublin | 1973-74 |
| 6 | A.R. Irvine | England | Twickenham | 1976-77 |
| 6 | A.R. Irvine | New Zealand | Edinburgh | 1979-80 |

# INDIVIDUAL RECORDS

## LONGEST CAREER SPANS

| Seasons | Player | Caps | Career Span |
|---|---|---|---|
| 14 | W.C.W. Murdoch | 9 | 1934-35 to 1947-48 |
| 13 | W.E. Maclagan | 25 | 1877-78 to 1889-90 |
| 12 | A.W. Angus | 18 | 1908-09 to 1919-20 |
| 12 | W.B. Young | 10 | 1936-37 to 1947-48 |
| 12 | A.B. Carmichael | 50 | 1966-67 to 1977-78 |
| 12 | A.F. McHarg | 44 | 1967-68 to 1978-79 |
| 12 | J. McLauchlan | 43 | 1968-69 to 1979-80 |
| 12 | A.J.Tomes | 44 | 1975-76 to 1986-87 |

## MOST CONSECUTIVE CAPS IN A CAREER

| Caps | Player | Opponents |
|---|---|---|
| 49 | A.B. Carmichael | 1967 NZ  1968  F,W,I,E,A,  1969  F,W,I,E,SA  1970  F,W,I,E,A  1971  F,W,I,E(1 + 2)  1972  F,W,E,NZ  1973  F,W,I,E,P  1974  W,E,I,F  1975  I,F,W,E,NZ,A  1976  F,W,E,I  1977  E,I(R),F,W  1978  I |
| 40 | H.F. McLeod | 1954  F,NZ,I,E,W  1955  F,W,I,E  1956  F,W,I,E  1957  F,W,I,E  1958  F,W,A,I,E  1959  F,W,I,E  1960  F,W,I,E,SA  1961  F,SA,W,I,E  1962  F,W,I,E |

## MOST CAPS IN A CAREER

| Caps | Player | Career span |
|---|---|---|
| 52 | J.M. Renwick | 1971-72 to 1984 |
| 51 | A.R. Irvine | 1972-73 to 1982 |
| 50 | A.B. Carmichael | 1966-67 to 1977-78 |
| 48 | C.T. Deans | 1977-78 to 1986-87 |
| 44 | A.F. McHarg | 1967-68 to 1978-79 |
| 44 | A.J. Tomes | 1975-76 to 1986-87 |
| 43 | J. McLauchlan | 1968-69 to 1979-80 |
| 41 | J.Y. Rutherford | 1978-79 to 1986-87 |
| 40 | H.F. McLeod | 1953-54 to 1961-62 |
| 40 | D.M.D. Rollo | 1958-59 to 1967-68 |
| 40 | R.J. Laidlaw | 1979-80 to 1986-87 |
| 37 | J.M. Bannerman | 1920-21 to 1928-29 |
| 37 | I.G. Milne | 1978-79 to 1986-87 |
| 36 | K.W. Robertson | 1978-79 to 1986-87 |

## MOST POINTS IN A CAREER

| Pts | Player | Matches | Career span |
|---|---|---|---|
| 273 | A.R. Irvine | 51 | 1972-73 to 1982 |
| 150 | P.W. Dods | 15 | 1982-83 to 1984-85 |
| 107 | A.G. Hastings | 9 | 1985-86 to 1986-87 |
| 72 | I.S. Smith | 32 | 1923-24 to 1932-33 |
| 71 | K.J.F. Scotland | 27 | 1956-57 to 1964-65 |
| 71 | D.W. Morgan | 21 | 1972-73 to 1977-78 |

## MOST TRIES IN A CAREER

| T | Player | Matches | Career span |
|---|---|---|---|
| 24 | I.S. Smith | 32 | 1923-24 to 1932-33 |
| 12 | A.R. Smith | 33 | 1954-55 to 1961-62 |
| 11 | A.C. Wallace | 9 | 1922-23 to 1925-26 |
| 10* | A.R. Irvine | 51 | 1972-73 to 1982 |

* Irvine's total includes one penalty try.

## MOST CONVERSIONS IN A CAREER

| C | Player | Matches | Career span |
|---|--------|---------|-------------|
| 25 | A.R. Irvine | 51 | 1972-73 to 1982 |
| 18 | D. Drysdale | 26 | 1922-23 to 1928-29 |
| 14 | F.H. Turner | 15 | 1910-11 to 1913-14 |
| 11 | A.G. Hastings | 9 | 1985-86 to 1986-87 |
| 10 | S. Wilson | 22 | 1963-64 to 1967-68 |

## MOST DROPPED GOALS IN A CAREER

| DG | Player | Matches | Career span |
|----|--------|---------|-------------|
| 12 | J.Y. Rutherford | 41 | 1978-79 to 1986-87 |
| 7 | I.R. McGeechan | 32 | 1972-73 to 1978-79 |
| 6 | D.W. Morgan | 21 | 1972-73 to 1977-78 |
| 5 | H. Waddell | 15 | 1923-24 to 1929-30 |

## MOST PENALTY GOALS IN A CAREER

| PG | Player | Matches | Career span |
|----|--------|---------|-------------|
| 61 | A.R. Irvine | 51 | 1972-73 to 1982 |
| 38 | P.W. Dods | 15 | 1982-83 to 1984-85 |
| 27 | A.G. Hastings | 9 | 1985-86 to 1986-87 |
| 16 | S. Wilson | 22 | 1963-64 to 1967-68 |

## MOST MATCHES AS CAPTAIN

| | | |
|---|---|---|
| 19 | J. McLauchlan | (10 victories) |
| 15 | M.C. Morrison | (9 victories) |
| 15 | A.R. Smith | (6 victories) |
| 15 | A.R. Irvine | (7 victories) |
| 12 | G.P.S. Macpherson | (7 victories) |
| 11 | D. Drysdale | (8 victories) |

# IRELAND INTERNATIONAL
# TEAMS AND RECORDS

| 1874-75 v. ENGLAND | 1875-76 v. ENGLAND | 1876-77 v. ENGLAND | 1876-77 v. SCOTLAND |
|---|---|---|---|
| †R.B. WALKINGTON | R.B. WALKINGTON | R.B. WALKINGTON | †G.M. SHAW |
| †H.L. COX | †H. MOORE | *R. GALBRAITH | H. MOORE |
| †R.J. BELL | †E.W. HOBSON | †H. BROWN | R.B. WALKINGTON |
| †A.P. CRONYN | B.N. CASEMENT | †F.W. KIDD | F.W. KIDD |
| †J. MYLES | *R.J. BELL | †A.M. WHITESTONE | †J. HERON |
| †R. GALBRAITH | A.P. CRONYN | †T.G. GORDON | T.G. GORDON |
| †E.N. MCILWAINE | | | |
| | R. GALBRAITH | †H.W. JACKSON | †J. CURRELL |
| †W.S. ALLEN | H.L. COX | H.L. COX | H.L. COX |
| †R.M. MAGINNESS | R.M. MAGINNESS | W. FINLAY | W. FINLAY |
| †A. COMBE | †J. IRELAND | J. IRELAND | J.A. MCDONALD |
| †F.T. HEWSON | †W.A. CUSCADEN | †W.H. WILSON | *W.H. WILSON |
| †G. ANDREWS | G. ANDREWS | †H.G. EDWARDS | †H.W. MURRAY |
| †E. GALBRAITH | †R. GREER | †H.C. KELLY | H.C. KELLY |
| *†G.H. STACK | †A.J. WESTBY | †T. BROWN | T. BROWN |
| †W.H. ASH | W.H. ASH | †W.J. HAMILTON | W.H. ASH |
| †J.A. MCDONALD | J.A. MCDONALD | | |
| †M. BARLOW | †W. FINLAY | | |
| †H.D. WALSH | H.D. WALSH | | |
| †W. GAFFIKIN | †D.T. ARNOTT | | |
| †B.N. CASEMENT | E.N. MCILWAINE | | |
| KENNINGTON OVAL — LOST | LEINSTER C.G. — LOST | KENNINGTON OVAL — LOST | BELFAST — LOST |
| ENG.: 1G 1DG 1T | IRE.: NIL | ENG.: 2G 2T | IRE.: NIL |
| IRE.: NIL | ENG.: 1G 1T | IRE.: NIL | SCOT.: 4G 2DG 2T |
| 15 Feb. 1875 | 13 Dec. 1875 | 5 Feb. 1877 | 19 Feb. 1877 |

An Irish Football Union was founded in Dublin in November 1874, and a Northern Football Union of Ireland was formed in Belfast in January 1875. For Ireland's first international in February 1875, a compromise was arranged so that each Union nominated ten players, but several of those selected failed to turn up for the game, most who did had never previously seen one another, and backs were forced to play as forwards and vice-versa. With such haphazard organisation it was perhaps not surprising that Ireland should lose the first game, and the next nine matches played.

George Stack was the first Irish captain. He gained his MA at Dublin University in 1875 and was one of nine Trinity men in the first XX. A tall man with a bushy beard, he was one of the few early Irish players able to kick a rugby ball with any skill. He was an important figure in the IFU committee until he accidentally poisoned himself with an overdose of chloral in November 1876.

Abraham Cronyn was the outstanding Irish player of the 1870s. A fine runner, hard tackler and useful punter, he appeared as a forward and a back. Later he joined the Army, serving as an officer in the 97th Regiment.

| 1877-78 v. ENGLAND | 1878-79 v. SCOTLAND | 1878-79 v. ENGLAND | 1879-80 v. ENGLAND | 1879-80 v. SCOTLAND |
|---|---|---|---|---|
| *R.B. WALKINGTON | R.B. WALKINGTON | | R.B. WALKINGTON | R.B. WALKINGTON |
| | †T. HARRISON | | | |
| †R.N. MATIER | | †W.J. WILLIS | A.M. WHITESTONE | T. HARRISON |
| F.W. KIDD | †J.C. BAGOT | J.C. BAGOT | J.C. BAGOT | J.C. BAGOT |
| | R.N. MATIER | | | |
| †G.L. FAGAN | | A.M. WHITESTONE | †W.T. HERON | W.T. HERON |
| T.G. GORDON | A.M. WHITESTONE | J. HERON | †M. JOHNSTON | M. JOHNSTON |
| | †W.J. GOULDING | | | |
| †E.W.D. CROKER | | B.N. CASEMENT | †A.J. FORREST | A.J. FORREST |
| †W.D. MOORE | †W.E.A. CUMMINS | †J.R. BRISTOW | †F. KENNEDY | A.P. CRONYN |
| †F. SCHUTE | †A.M. ARCHER | F. SCHUTE | †A. MILLAR | A. MILLAR |
| H.W. MURRAY | H.C. KELLY | H.W. MURRAY | *H.C. KELLY | *H.C. KELLY |
| W. FINLAY | W. FINLAY | W. FINLAY | J.W. TAYLOR | J.W. TAYLOR |
| J.A. MCDONALD | J.A. MCDONALD | †J.J. KEON | J.A. MCDONALD | W. FINLAY |
| H.G. EDWARDS | †J.W. TAYLOR | †J.L. CUPPAIDGE | J.L. CUPPAIDGE 1T | J.L. CUPPAIDGE |
| H.C. KELLY | †*W.C. NEVILLE | *W.C. NEVILLE | R.W. HUGHES | R.W. HUGHES |
| †R.W. HUGHES | †G. SCRIVEN | G. SCRIVEN | G. SCRIVEN | G. SCRIVEN |
| †W. GRIFFITHS | †H. PURDON | H. PURDON | H. PURDON | †W.A. WALLIS |
| Lansdowne Road — LOST | Belfast — LOST | Kennington Oval — LOST | Lansdowne Road — LOST | Glasgow — LOST |
| IRE.: NIL | IRE.: NIL | ENG.: 2G 1DG 2T | IRE.: 1T | SCOT.: 1G 2DG 2T |
| ENG.: 1T 2G | SCOT.: 1G 1DG 1T | IRE.: NIL | ENG.: 1G 1T | IRE.: NIL |
| 11 Mar. 1878 | 17 Feb. 1879 | 24 Mar. 1879 | 30 Jan. 1880 | 14 Feb. 1880 |

In the period 1878-80, Ireland blooded two young forwards who were to become leading internationals. A.J. Forrest, a skilful dribbler, was a young player straight from Cheltenham College when he won his first cap in 1880. He went on to play in seven internationals and captained the side in 1881, when aged only 21. R.W. Hughes was another fine forward, renowned for his tremendous shoving in the scrums. He played the last of his twelve internationals in 1886.

Hugh Kelly, reputedly "a magnificent man, six feet or so", was the captain against England in 1880 when Ireland's first score in an international was made. J.L. Cuppaidge, a doctor who later emigrated to Queensland, was the scorer of a try under the posts. But Walkington ("who trembled from head to toe") failed to convert.

Walkington played the last of his ten internationals in 1882, in which year he was also President of the Irish Rugby Football Union. He retired as the first Irish cap-record holder. His younger brother, D.B., played for Ireland between 1887 and 1891.

| | 1880-81 | | 1881-82 | | |
| --- | --- | --- | --- | --- | --- |
| | v. ENGLAND | v. SCOTLAND | v. WALES | v. ENGLAND | v. SCOTLAND |
| | T. HARRISON | †R.E. McLEAN | R.E. McLEAN | R.B. WALKINGTON | R.B. WALKINGTON |
| | †W. PEIRCE | W.W. PIKE | †J.R. ATKINSON | R.E. McLEAN | R.E. McLEAN |
| | W.W. PIKE | J.C. BAGOT 1DG | †T.St.G. McCARTHY | †E.J. WOLFE | J.R. ATKINSON |
| | | | †W.W. FLETCHER | W.W. PIKE | †R.W. MORROW |
| | †H.F. SPUNNER | H.F. SPUNNER | †E.H. GREENE | M. JOHNSTON 1T | W.W. FLETCHER |
| | M. JOHNSTON | M. JOHNSTON | †G.C. BENT | G.C. BENT | †J. PEDLOW |
| | *A.J. FORREST | *A.J. FORREST | *A.J. FORREST | A.J. FORREST | †A.C. O'SULLIVAN |
| | †D.R. BROWNING | D.R. BROWNING | †J.M. KENNEDY | *J.W. TAYLOR | *J.W. TAYLOR |
| | †J.C.S. BURKITT | J.W. TAYLOR | F. KENNEDY | †R. NELSON | R. NELSON |
| | F. KENNEDY | †J. JOHNSTON | H.B. MORELL | H.B. MORELL | †J.B.W. BUCHANAN |
| | †H.B. MORELL | H.B. MORELL | †E.A. McCARTHY | W.E.A. CUMMINS | W. FINLAY |
| | W.E.A. CUMMINS | J.A. McDONALD | W.A. WALLIS | J.A. McDONALD | J.A. McDONALD |
| | W.A. WALLIS | W.A. WALLIS | †A.J. DOWNING | R.W. HUGHES | R.W. HUGHES |
| | †A.R. McMULLEN | A.R. McMULLEN | †F.S. HEUSTON | †T.R. JOHNSON-SMYTH | G. SCRIVEN |
| | G. SCRIVEN | R.W. HUGHES | †R.G. THOMPSON | †O.S. STOKES 1T | J. JOHNSTON |
| | H. PURDON | H. PURDON | | | |
| | Manchester | Belfast | Landowne Road | Lansdowne Road | Glasgow |
| | LOST | WON | LOST | DRAWN | LOST |
| | ENG.: 2G 2T | IRE.: 1DG | IRE.: NIL | IRE.: 2T | SCOT.: 2T |
| | IRE.: NIL | SCOT.: 1T | Wales: 2G 2T | ENG.: 2T | IRE.: NIL |
| | 5 Feb. 1881 | 19 Feb. 1881 | 28 Jan. 1882 | 6 Feb. 1881 | 18 Feb. 1881 |

In 1880-81 the various Irish footballing Unions, with centres now established in Leinster, Munster and Ulster, united to form the IRFU and Ireland's first international win soon followed. John Bagot dropped the winning goal against Scotland at Belfast.

Ten new caps were in the Irish XV which met Wales for the first time in January 1882. The Irish side was a makeshift one, ten of those originally selected having withdrawn, and their problems were compounded when Kennedy retired injured after 30 minutes. Atkinson too was in the wars with a nose injury. The correspondent of the *Irish Times* was disgusted with his team, referring to the "dormant apathy" of the fifteen.

By all accounts Ireland should have won the 1882 game with England. The official result was a draw but the final Irish try by Meredith Johnston was followed by a conversion by McLean. To the dismay of the crowd the kick was disallowed by one of the umpires, a Mr Nugent, and Ireland had to settle for a draw.

| | 1882-83 | | 1883-84 | | |
| --- | --- | --- | --- | --- | --- |
| | v. ENGLAND | v. SCOTLAND | v. ENGLAND | v. SCOTLAND | v. WALES |
| | R.W. MORROW | R.W. MORROW | R.W. MORROW | †J.M. O'SULLIVAN | R.W. MORROW |
| | R.E. McLEAN | R.E. McLEAN | R.E. McLEAN | R.E. McLEAN | E.H. GREENE |
| | †R.H. SCOVELL | W.W. PIKE | R.H. SCOVELL | †G.H. WHEELER | J. PEDLOW |
| | | | †D.J. ROSS | †L.M. MacINTOSH 1T | |
| | W.W. FLETCHER | A.M. WHITESTONE | | | H.F. SPUNNER |
| | †J.P. WARREN | †S.R. COLLIER | M. JOHNSTON | M. JOHNSTON | †R.G. WARREN |
| | | | †W.W. HIGGINS | W.W. HIGGINS | |
| | †S.A.M. BRUCE | S.A.M. BRUCE | | | †R.O.N. HALL |
| | A.J. FORREST 1T | *G. SCRIVEN | S.A.M. BRUCE | †W. KELLY | †A.J. HAMILTON |
| | J.W. TAYLOR | J.W. TAYLOR | †F.H. LEVIS | †T.H.M. HOBBS | J.M. KENNEDY |
| | A. MILLAR | W.A. WALLIS | †H.M. BRABAZON | †A. GORDON | *†H.G. COOK |
| | †D.F. MOORE | D.F. MOORE | D.F. MOORE | †J.F. MAGUIRE | D.F. MOORE |
| | †H. KING | H. KING | J.B.W. BUCHANAN | J.B.W. BUCHANAN | †F.W. MOORE |
| | J.A. McDONALD | J.A. McDONALD | *J.A. McDONALD | *J.A. McDONALD | †W.S. COLLIS |
| | R.W. HUGHES | R.W. HUGHES | R.W. HUGHES | R.W. HUGHES | †L. MOYERS |
| | F.S. HEUSTON | F.S. HEUSTON | †W.G. RUTHERFORD | W.G. RUTHERFORD | †W.E. JOHNSTONE |
| | *G. SCRIVEN | R. NELSON | O.S. STOKES | J. JOHNSTON | †J. FITZGERALD |
| | Manchester | Belfast | Lansdowne Road | Raeburn Place | Cardiff Arms Park |
| | LOST | LOST | LOST | LOST | LOST |
| | ENG.: 1G 3T | IRE.: NIL | IRE.: NIL | SCOT.: 2G 2T | WALES: 1DG 2T |
| | IRE.: 1T | SCOT.: 1G 1T | ENG.: 1G | IRE.: 1T | IRE.: NIL |
| | 5 Feb. 1883 | 17 Feb. 1883 | 4 Feb. 1884 | 16 Feb. 1884 | 12 Apr. 1884 |

George Scriven was the Irish captain in 1883. Educated at Repton school in England, he was a student at Dublin University when first capped, and President of the IRFU in his season as skipper. He qualified as a doctor, was the referee in the famous Calcutta Cup match of 1884, and served the Union as President for a second term in 1885-6.

He was succeeded as captain by J.A. McDonald, another doctor. This was McDonald's last season in internationals, and he retired as the Irish cap-record holder, having appeared in 13 matches since 1875. He was on the small, light side for a forward, but his qualities in the loose-play and his tremendous stamina never waned during his long career. A Chairman of the BMA Council in later years, he died in Taunton in his 79th year in 1928.

It is known that the 1884 Irish side against Wales is a matter of conjecture! Ireland arrived in Cardiff short of players and were "loaned" two Welshmen, Purdon and H.M. Jordan. No accurate record exists of the men who were replaced and the list above is the side which is compatible with lists of Irish international players given in annuals and yearbooks down the years. R.O.N. Hall, incidentally, seems to have been a *nom de plume* for a player named Hallaran of Dublin University. Hall's name has always appeared in lists, and another Irish player named Eames, is listed as playing in several newspaper reports of the match.

## 1884-85

| v. ENGLAND | v. SCOTLAND |
| --- | --- |
| G.H. Wheeler | R.W. Morrow |
| | |
| R.E. McLean | D.J. Ross |
| †J.P. Ross | J.P. Ross |
| E.H. Greene 1T | E.H. Greene |
| | |
| †E.C. Crawford | †D.V. Hunter |
| R.G. Warren | R.G. Warren |
| | |
| †H.J. Neill | H.J. Neill |
| †T. Shanahan | T. Shanahan |
| T.H.M. Hobbs | †J. Thompson |
| †T.R. Lyle | T.R. Lyle |
| F.W. Moore | F.W. Moore |
| †R.M. Bradshaw | R.M. Bradshaw |
| R.W. Hughes | J.Johnston |
| *W.G. Rutherford | †W. Hogg |
| †T.C. Allen | *A.J. Forrest |
| | |
| Manchester | Raeburn Place |
| LOST | LOST |
| | |
| Eng.: 2T | Scot.: 1G 2T |
| Ire.: 1T | Ire.: NIL |
| | |
| 7 Feb. 1885 | 7 Mar. 1885 |

## 1885-86

| v. ENGLAND | v. SCOTLAND |
| --- | --- |
| R.W. Morrow | R.W. Morrow |
| | |
| D.J. Ross | D.J. Ross |
| J.P. Ross | *J.P. Ross |
| E.H. Greene | †M.J. Carpendale |
| | |
| *M. Johnston | †J.F Ross |
| R.G. Warren | †R.W. Herrick |
| | |
| †J. Chambers | J. Chambers |
| T. Shanahan | F.W. Moore |
| †V.C. le Fanu | V.C. le Fanu |
| T.R. Lyle | †J. McMordie |
| H.M. Brabazon | †F.H. Miller |
| J. Johnston | †J. Waites |
| R.W. Hughes | R. Nelson |
| W.G. Rutherford | H.J. Neill |
| †R.H. Massy-Westropp | †F.O. Stoker |
| | |
| Lansdowne Road | Raeburn Place |
| LOST | LOST |
| | |
| Ire.: NIL | Scot.: 3G 1DG 2T |
| Eng.: 1T | Ire.: NIL |
| | |
| 6 Feb. 1886 | 20 Feb. 1886 |

Ireland's run of twelve matches without a win extended to the end of the 1886 season, although Ireland took an early lead in the 1885 game with England. The match was played at Manchester and many of the Irish XV were reported to be very sea-sick following a rough crossing. Nevertheless, Greene, the Irish 100-yards sprint champion, gained a try in the first minute. England eventually won by two tries to one, though Ireland nearly equalised in the second half when playing with the slope.

The match in Belfast against Scotland in 1885 was abandoned after 30 minutes, and a full replay took place in Edinburgh two weeks later. Those who appeared in Belfast were not awarded caps.

R.G. Warren at half-back was the finest Irish back of his day. A stocky player, he was a strong tackler and resolute charger who won 15 caps before retiring in 1890. He became President of the IRFU and was appointed Honorary Secretary of the International Board in 1897.

## 1886-87

| v. ENGLAND | v. SCOTLAND | v. WALES |
| --- | --- | --- |
| †D.B. Walkington | J.M. O'Sullivan | D.B. Walkington |
| | | |
| †C.R. Tillie 1T | C.R. Tillie | M.J. Carpendale |
| †D.F. Rambaut 2C | D.F. Rambaut | D.F. Rambaut |
| †R. Montgomery 1T | R. Montgomery | R. Montgomery 3T |
| | | |
| †J.H. McLaughlin | J.H. McLaughlin | †P.J. O'Connor |
| *R.G. Warren | *R.G. Warren | *R.G. Warren |
| | | |
| J. Chambers | J. Chambers | J. Chambers |
| †J.S. Dick | J.S. Dick | J.S. Dick |
| V.C. le Fanu | †C.M. Moore | V.C. le Fanu |
| T.R. Lyle | T.R. Lyle | †T. Taggart |
| †E.J. Walsh | E.J. Walsh | E.J. Walsh |
| J. Johnston | J. Johnston | J. Johnston |
| †R. Stevenson | R. Stevenson | R. Stevenson |
| H.J. Neill | H.J. Neill | H.J. Neill |
| †J. Macauley | J. Macauley | †W. Davison |
| | | |
| Lansdowne Road | Belfast | Birkenhead |
| WON | LOST | LOST |
| | | |
| Ire.: 2G | Ire.: NIL | Wales: 1DG 1T |
| Eng.: NIL | Scot.: 1G 1GM 2T | Ire.: 3T |
| | | |
| 5 Feb. 1887 | 19 Feb. 1887 | 12 Mar. 1887 |

The major event of the season was Ireland's win against England. There were nine new caps in a side well-led by Warren. The side was determined to win and Macauley of Limerick could only obtain leave of absence from his job as a miller's agent by getting married! He thus became the first married man to play for Ireland.

The Irish forwards hustled their opponents all over the field, while the backs tackled with resolution and ran with pace. The wings Tillie and Montgomery scored the tries and Rambaut, the Irish 120-yards hurdles champion, placed two goals. These conversions were the first scored by Ireland in an international.

Financial difficulties prevented the IRFU travelling to Wales for the 1887 match. As a result the game was staged in Birkenhead where, according to the scoring laws then in vogue, Ireland's three tries were not good enough to win against a try and a drop-goal. During the match Montgomery became the first Irishman to score three tries in an international.

### 1887-88 / 1888-89

| v. WALES | v. SCOTLAND | v. MAORIS | v. SCOTLAND | v. WALES |
|---|---|---|---|---|
| D.B. WALKINGTON | R.W. MORROW | †T. EDWARDS | †L.J. HOLMES | L.J. HOLMES |
| C.R. TILLIE | C.R. TILLIE | †D.C. WOODS 1T | D.C. WOODS | R.A. YEATES |
| D.F. RAMBAUT 1c | †A. WALPOLE | A. WALPOLE | †R.A. YEATES | †R. DUNLOP |
| M.J. CARPENDALE 1DG | M.J. CARPENDALE | †M.J. BULGER | †B.T. PEDLOW | B.T. PEDLOW |
| J.H. McLAUGHLIN | J.H. McLAUGHLIN | †J. STEVENSON 1c | J. STEVENSON | †A.C. McDONNELL 1T |
| R.G. WARREN 1T | R.G. WARREN | *R.G. WARREN | *R.G. WARREN | *R.G. WARREN |
| †R.H. MAYNE | R.H. MAYNE | †H.W. ANDREWS | H.W. ANDREWS | H.W. ANDREWS |
| T. SHANAHAN 1T | T. SHANAHAN | †E.G. FORREST | E.G. FORREST | E.G. FORREST |
| †W. EKIN | W. EKIN | †J.H. O'CONOR | †L.C. NASH | V.C. LE FANU |
| †J. MOFFATT | J. MOFFATT | J. MOFFATT | J. MOFFATT | †J. COTTON 1T |
| C.M. MOORE | C.M. MOORE | †J.N. LYTLE | †C.R.R. STACK | J.N. LYTLE |
| †E.W. STOKER | E.W. STOKER | J. WAITES 1T | †T.M. DONOVAN | J. WAITES |
| W.G. RUTHERFORD | V.C. LE FANU | R. STEVENSON | R. STEVENSON | R. STEVENSON |
| *H.J. NEILL | *H.J. NEILL | †J.S. JAMESON | J.S. JAMESON | J.S. JAMESON |
| F.O. STOKER | †W.A. MORTON | F.O. STOKER | F.O. STOKER | †H.A. RICHEY |
| Lansdowne Road | Raeburn Place | Lansdowne Road | Belfast | St Helen's |
| WON | LOST | LOST | LOST | WON |
| IRE.: IG IDG IT | SCOT.: IG | IRE.: IG IT | IRE.: NIL | WALES: NIL |
| WALES: NIL | IRE.: NIL | MAORIS: 4G IT | SCOT.: IDG | IRE.: 2T |
| 3 Mar. 1888 | 10 Mar. 1888 | 1 Dec. 1888 | 16 Feb. 1889 | 2 Mar. 1889 |

The deadlock concerning the composition of the International Board prevented Ireland playing the English in 1888 and 1889. Ireland were experimenting tactically at this time, the selection committee considering the question of wing-forward play. R.G. Warren, the influential half-back, favoured employing Shanahan in such a role for the 1888 Welsh match, apparently the first instance of a forward gaining selection specifically to fill a winging position.

Shanahan played with rare fire, set up Ireland's first try by Warren, and concluded Ireland's first win against Wales with a try. It will be noted that the Irish backs were those who had figured in the first victory over England in 1887.

Although four of Ireland's leading players were unable to play, there were 3000 present to see Ireland's first international against overseas opponents – the Maoris – in December 1888. Warren elected to make first use of a stiff breeze, but his side failed to capitalise on the conditions and the Maoris, after a lacklustre display in the first two-thirds of the game, came from behind to win by scoring five tries.

### 1889-90

| v. SCOTLAND | v. WALES | v. ENGLAND |
|---|---|---|
| †H.P. GIFFORD | D.B. WALKINGTON | D.B. WALKINGTON |
| R. DUNLOP | R. DUNLOP 1T | R. DUNLOP |
| †R.W. JOHNSTON | R.W. JOHNSTON | R.W. JOHNSTON |
| T. EDWARDS | T. EDWARDS | T. EDWARDS |
| A.C. McDONNELL | A.C. McDONNELL | †B.B. TUKE |
| *R.G. WARREN | *R.G. WARREN | *R.G. WARREN |
| J. MOFFATT | J. MOFFATT | J.N. LYTLE |
| E.G. FORREST | †H.T. GALBRAITH | E.G. FORREST |
| J. WAITES | J. WAITES | J. WAITES |
| J.H. O'CONOR | J.H. O'CONOR | J.H. O'CONOR |
| R. STEVENSON | R. STEVENSON | R. STEVENSON |
| †J. ROCHE | J. ROCHE 1c | J. ROCHE |
| †E.F. DORAN | E.F. DORAN | V.C. LE FANU |
| H.A. RICHEY | L.C. NASH | L.C. NASH |
| †W.J.N. DAVIS | W.J.N. DAVIS | W.J.N. DAVIS |
| Raeburn Place | Lansdowne Road | Blackheath |
| LOST 0-5 | DRAWN 3-3 | LOST 0-3 |
| SCOT.: IDG IT | IRE.: IG | ENG.: 3T |
| IRE.: NIL | WALES: IG | IRE.: NIL |
| 22 Feb.1890 | 1 Mar.1890 | 15 Mar. 1890 |

A criticism of Irish rugby in 1890 was that whereas their backs were fast and improving rapidly, their best forwards were players who were too small to compete on equal terms with their opponents in international matches. The Irish preoccupation with winging-forwards, it was observed, left the pack without a centre to its scrummage.

Nevertheless, the performances against Scotland and Wales were sound, and only the English at Blackheath beat the Irish by any substantial margin. The English match was played in the middle of March, due to the late settlement of the international dispute. It appears that there was a blunder concerning the arrangements for the Irish accommodation at Blackheath: the side was forced to walk the streets for half a night in search of hotel accommodation prior to the game!

V.C. le Fanu returned to the Irish side for the English match. A tall, ginger-headed man, he had learned the game at Haileybury and Cambridge, where he won Blues in 1884-5-6. As a player he was quick-thinking, sure-handed and a devastating tackler, but towards the end of his career he played a looser forward game, and fell out of favour with the selectors after 1892, having gained eleven caps.

## 1890-91

| v. ENGLAND | v. SCOTLAND | v. WALES |
|---|---|---|
| *D.B. WALKINGTON | *D.B. WALKINGTON | D.B. WALKINGTON 1DG |
| | | |
| R. DUNLOP | R. DUNLOP | R. DUNLOP |
| †S. LEE | S. LEE | S. LEE 1T |
| R. MONTGOMERY | †H.G. WELLS | H.G. WELLS |
| | | |
| A.C. McDONNELL | †E.D. CAMERON | E.D. CAMERON |
| B.B. TUKE | B.B. TUKE | †R. PEDLOW |
| | | |
| J.N. LYTLE | J.N. LYTLE | †T. FOGARTY |
| E.G. FORREST | †R.D. STOKES | R.D. STOKES |
| J. WAITES | J. MOFFATT | F.O. STOKER |
| J.H. O'CONOR | J.H. O'CONOR | J.S. JAMESON |
| †C.V. ROOKE | †G. COLLOPY | *R. STEVENSON |
| J. ROCHE | J. ROCHE | J. ROCHE |
| V.C.LE FANU | †E.F. FRAZER | C.V. ROOKE |
| L.C. NASH | L.C. NASH | L.C. NASH |
| W.J.N. DAVIS | W.J.N. DAVIS | W.J.N. DAVIS |
| | | |
| Lansdowne Road | Belfast | Stradey Park |
| LOST 0-9 | LOST 0-14 | LOST 4-6 |
| | | |
| IRE.: NIL | IRE.: NIL | WALES: 1G 1DG |
| ENG.: 2G 3T | SCOT.: 3G 1DG 2T | IRE.: 1DG 1T |
| | | |
| 7 Feb. 1891 | 21 Feb. 1891 | 7 Mar. 1891 |

This was Ireland's worst season since 1884. All three matches were lost and England and Scotland inflicted very heavy defeats on the Irish. D.B. Walkington, at the end of his international career, led the side in these defeats. A solicitor, he won eight caps and in bright conditions was reputedly the best full-back produced by Ireland before the turn of the century. By all accounts he was very short-sighted, however, occasionally wore a monocle on the field, and "in the dark" it was reported "his delicate sight tells terribly against him".

Charles Rooke made his debut as a teenager against England. He was an aggressive player who specialised in fast, accurate, dribbling away from the side of the scrummage, and is recognised as the father of the modern wing-forward. A minister, he played in 19 internationals, and his 18 consecutive caps from March 1891 to 1897 created an Irish record.

Sam Lee was the other new cap against England. His career lasted to 1898 and, like Rooke, he gained 19 caps. A wonderful kicker and runner, he had the fine knack of intercepting passes between opposing backs, was a gifted passer, and possessed the rare qualities of perfect timing and judgment.

## 1891-92

| v. ENGLAND | v. SCOTLAND | v. WALES |
|---|---|---|
| †T. PEEL | T. PEEL | T. PEEL |
| | | |
| R. DUNLOP | R. DUNLOP | T. EDWARDS |
| S. LEE | S. LEE | S. LEE |
| †W. GARDINER | W. GARDINER | R. MONTGOMERY |
| | | |
| †T. THORNHILL | T. THORNHILL | T. THORNHILL |
| B.B. TUKE | †F.E. DAVIES | F.E. DAVIES 1T |
| | | |
| *V.C. LE FANU | *V.C. LE FANU | *V.C. LE FANU |
| †T.J. JOHNSTON | T.J. JOHNSTON | T.J. JOHNSTON |
| E.J. WALSH | E.J. WALSH | E.J. WALSH 2T |
| †A.K. WALLIS | A.K. WALLIS | A.K. WALLIS |
| J.S. JAMESON | G. COLLOPY | J.S. JAMESON |
| †R.E. SMITH | †A.D. CLINCH | J. ROCHE 1C |
| J.H. O'CONOR | E.F. FRAZER | J.H. O'CONOR |
| W.J.N. DAVIS | W.J.N. DAVIS | R. STEVENSON |
| C.V. ROOKE | C.V. ROOKE | C.V. ROOKE |
| | | |
| Manchester | Raeburn Place | Lansdowne Road |
| LOST 0-7 | LOST 0-2 | WON 9-0 |
| | | |
| ENG.: 1G 1T | SCOT.: 1T | IRE.: 1G 2T |
| IRE.: NIL | IRE.: NIL | WALES: NIL |
| | | |
| 6 Feb. 1892 | 20 Feb. 1892 | 5 Mar. 1892 |

Ireland's away matches ended in defeats, but for the game against Wales in Dublin 5000 excited spectators assembled to see the wooden spoon decider. Irish forward play was improving and certainly their ferocious mauling and spirited work in the open earned the victory over the Welsh. Their style was not subtle, more brawn than brain attending their approach, but it was effective.

Edward Walsh was the man-of-the-match against Wales. As a young man he was the Irish High Jump and Hurdles champion, and would have made an outstanding threequarter. However he had very poor eyesight so was compelled to play as a forward. He won seven caps and in the Welsh match he became the first Irish forward to score two tries in an international.

In his professional life Walsh became the Accountant General to the Supreme Court of Ireland.

## 1892-93

| v. ENGLAND | v. SCOTLAND | v. WALES |
|---|---|---|
| †S. GARDINER | S. GARDINER | †W. SPARROW |
| T. EDWARDS | †L.H. GWYNN | R. DUNLOP |
| *S. LEE | *S. LEE | *S. LEE |
| W. GARDINER | W. GARDINER | W. GARDINER |
| T. THORNHILL | †W.S. BROWN | W.S. BROWN |
| F.E. DAVIES | F.E. DAVIES | F.E. DAVIES |
| †R. JOHNSTON | †B. O'BRIEN | B. O'BRIEN |
| T.J. JOHNSTON | T.J. JOHNSTON | R. JOHNSTON |
| E.J. WALSH | E.G. FORREST | E.G. FORREST |
| A.K. WALLIS | †H. FORREST | A.K. WALLIS |
| †H. LINDSAY | H. LINDSAY | H. LINDSAY |
| †M.S. EGAN | J.S. JAMESON | †R.W. HAMILTON |
| J.H. O'CONOR | J.H. O'CONOR | A.D. CLINCH |
| R. STEVENSON | R. STEVENSON | R. STEVENSON |
| C.V. ROOKE | C.V. ROOKE | C.V. ROOKE |
| Lansdowne Road | Belfast | Stradey Park |
| LOST 0-4 | DRAWN 0-0 | LOST 0-2 |
| IRE.: NIL | IRE.: NIL | WALES: IT |
| ENG.: 2T | SCOT.: NIL | IRE.: NIL |
| 4 Feb. 1893 | 18 Feb. 1893 | 11 Mar. 1893 |

Ireland finished with the wooden spoon again, despite the inspiring leadership of Sam Lee. More than 7000 were present for the English match in Dublin, where a feature of the game was the strong all-round play of the Irish backs. Their threequarters passed accurately in attack and Edwards and Lee tackled bravely in defence.

Awful weather reduced the Scottish game to a muddy slog between two packs and there was much criticism concerning the Ballynafeigh ground in Belfast, after the match. Many of the previous internationals played at the ground had been muddy, scrambling affairs and one critic referred to the ground as "Ballynafeigh Bog".

Robert Johnston played his two Irish matches this season. Educated at King William's, Isle of Man, he became an army officer and gained the Victoria Cross at Elandslaagte during the Boer War.

## 1893-94

| v. ENGLAND | v. SCOTLAND | v. WALES |
|---|---|---|
| W. SPARROW | †P.J. GRANT | P.J. GRANT |
| H.G. WELLS | H.G. WELLS 1T | R. DUNLOP |
| S. LEE | S. LEE | S. LEE |
| W. GARDINER | W. GARDINER | W. GARDINER |
| L.H. GWYNN | L.H. GWYNN | L.H. GWYNN |
| W.S. BROWN | W.S. BROWN | W.S. BROWN |
| B.B. TUKE | B.B. TUKE | B.B. TUKE |
| J.N. LYTLE 1T | J.N. LYTLE 1C | J.N. LYTLE 1PG |
| †J.H. LYTLE | J.H. LYTLE | J.H. LYTLE |
| †G. WALMSLEY | †A.T.W. BOND | A.T.W. BOND |
| J.H. O'CONOR | J.H. O'CONOR | J.H. O'CONOR |
| H. LINDSAY | H. LINDSAY | H. LINDSAY |
| *E.G. FORREST 1DG | *E.G. FORREST | *E.G. FORREST |
| †T.J. CREAN | T.J. CREAN | T.J. CREAN |
| C.V. ROOKE | C.V. ROOKE | C.V. ROOKE |
| Blackheath | Lansdowne Road | Belfast |
| WON 7-5 | WON 5-0 | WON 3-0 |
| ENG.: IG | IRE.: IG | IRE.: IPG |
| IRE.: IDG IT | SCOT.: NIL | WALES: NIL |
| 3 Feb. 1894 | 24 Feb. 1894 | 10 Mar. 1894 |

Ireland adopted the four threequarter system in 1894, and won the Triple Crown for the first time. Edward Forrest, a Dublin doctor and an experienced international, was the captain and his last-minute drop-goal decided the match with England.

Against the Scots, Ireland's forwards played an effective, spoiling game using the dribble away from the scrum as their chief attacking weapon. In the backs the individual brilliance of Gwynn and Lee posed many problems to the Scots. The winning score came in the dying moments. The Irish forwards charged-down a Scottish kick, led the ball downfield in a rush, and Tuke, Gardiner and Gwynn combined to send Wells tearing in for a try.

When Ireland beat Wales, once again the Ballynafeigh ground in Belfast resembled a morass. The only score was a penalty goal kicked by John Lytle after ten minutes, the Welsh forwards falling off-side. It was Ireland's first penalty goal in an international.

## 1894-95

| v. ENGLAND | v. SCOTLAND | v. WALES |
|---|---|---|
| †G.R. Symes | †J. Fulton | J. Fulton |
| | | |
| W. Gardiner | W. Gardiner | W. Gardiner |
| S. Lee | †A. Montgomery | S. Lee |
| †T.H. Stevenson | J.T. Magee | T.H. Stevenson |
| †J.T. Magee | †J. O'Connor | †A.P. Gwynn |
| | | |
| †A.M. Magee 1t | A.M. Magee | A.M. Magee |
| B.B. Tuke | B.B. Tuke | †M. G. Delany |
| | | |
| T.J. Johnston | †E.H. McIlwaine | E.H. McIlwaine |
| H. Lindsay | †W. O'Sullivan | J.H. Lytle |
| †A.A. Brunker | W.J.N. Davis | A.A. Brunker |
| *J.H. O'Conor | M.S.Egan | *E.G. Forrest |
| †H.C. McCoull | H.C. McCoull | H.C. McCoull |
| A.D. Clinch | A.D. Clinch | A.D. Clinch |
| T.J. Crean | T.J. Crean | T.J. Crean 1t |
| C.V. Rooke | *C.V. Rooke | C.V. Rooke |
| | | |
| Lansdowne Road | Raeburn Place | Cardiff Arms Park |
| LOST 3-6 | LOST 0-6 | LOST 3-5 |
| | | |
| IRE.: 1T | SCOT.: 2T | WALES: 1G |
| ENG.: 2T | IRE.: NIL | IRE.: 1T |
| | | |
| 2 Feb. 1895 | 2 Mar. 1895 | 16 Mar. 1895 |

Ireland slumped to the wooden spoon in 1895, many of the successful Triple Crown side having retired or lost form. Only half of the Irish forwards kept their places for the three internationals, while of the backs, just A.M. Magee and William Gardiner, a flax manufacturer from Belfast, played throughout the season.

Magee went on to play 26 consecutive matches for Ireland, retiring as Ireland's most-capped player after winning a 27th cap against Wales in 1904. He was a brilliant half-back who preferred to play at right-half, and through his dodgy, unorthodox running, turned many matches in Ireland's favour. Although he was highly individualistic in his play, he was a useful defender and saved many tries with his ankle-tap tackling. Joe Magee, who won caps this season, was his elder brother.

Tom Crean was a powerful forward who demonstrated his drive in the Welsh match at Cardiff. A long throw-in on the Welsh line was caught by Crean, who stormed through a tackle and stretched his frame across the line for a try. He displayed the same courage in war: he was decorated with the Victoria Cross for bravery during the Boer War (1901) and was awarded the DSO in 1915.

## 1895-96     1896-97

| v. ENGLAND | v. SCOTLAND | v. WALES | v. ENGLAND | v. SCOTLAND |
|---|---|---|---|---|
| J. Fulton | †G.H. McAllan | G.H. McAllan | J. Fulton | †P.E. O'Brien-Butler |
| | | | | |
| W. Gardiner | W. Gardiner | W. Gardiner | W. Gardiner 2t | W. Gardiner |
| *S. Lee | *S. Lee | *S. Lee | S. Lee | L.H. Gwynn |
| T.H. Stevenson 1t | T.H. Stevenson | T.H. Stevenson | T.H. Stevenson | T.H.Stevenson |
| †L.Q. Bulger 2c | L.Q. Bulger | L.Q. Bulger 1c | L.Q. Bulger 1gm,1t | L.Q. Bulger 1t |
| | | | | |
| A.M. Magee | A.M. Magee | A.M. Magee | A.M. Magee | A.M. Magee |
| †G.G. Allen | G.G. Allen | G.G. Allen | G.G. Allen | G.G. Allen |
| | | | | |
| J.H. O'Conor | J.H. O'Conor | J.H. O'Conor | †J.E. McIlwaine | J.E. McIlwaine |
| J.H. Lytle | J.H. Lytle | J.H. Lytle 1t | J.H. Lytle | J.H. Lytle |
| †W.G. Byron | W.G. Byron | W.G. Byron | W.G. Byron | W.G. Byron |
| H. Lindsay | H. Lindsay | H. Lindsay | †M. Ryan | M. Ryan |
| †J. Sealy 1t | J. Sealy | J. Sealy | †J. Ryan | J. Sealy |
| A.D. Clinch | A.D. Clinch | A.D. Clinch | A.D. Clinch | A.D. Clinch |
| T.J. Crean | T.J. Crean | T.J. Crean 1t | *E.G. Forrest | *E.G. Forrest |
| C.V. Rooke | C.V. Rooke | C.V. Rooke | C.V. Rooke | C.V. Rooke |
| | | | | |
| Leeds | Lansdowne Road | Lansdowne Road | Lansdowne Road | Powderhall |
| WON 10-4 | DRAWN 0-0 | WON 8-4 | WON 13-9 | LOST 3-8 |
| | | | | |
| ENG.: 1DG | IRE.: NIL | IRE.: 1G 1T | IRE.: 1GM 3T | SCOT.: 1G 1PG |
| IRE.: 2G | SCOT.: NIL | WALES: 1DG | ENG.: 2PG 1T | IRE.: 1T |
| | | | | |
| 1 Feb. 1896 | 15 Feb. 1896 | 14 Mar. 1896 | 6 Feb. 1897 | 20 Feb. 1897 |

Ireland were the champions in 1896, a scoreless draw with Scotland depriving them of the Triple Crown. Sam Lee skippered the side which showed just one change during the season. For the first time the forwards played together through three matches, and the threequarters and halves were also unchanged.

John Fulton, manager of a Belfast woollen mill, was Ireland's full-back in 16 matches between 1895 and 1904. But he lost his place after Ireland's victory over England in 1896, giving way for George McAllan of the Royal School, Dungannon, to become the first schoolboy to play for Ireland. The young full-back made a fine break in the second half of the Scottish match, only a wayward pass to Gardiner preventing a certain score.

There was no match with Wales in 1897 when the dispute concerning Arthur Gould was raging. In Ireland's win over England Larry Bulger became the first Irishman to place a goal from a mark in an international. A doctor, like his brother Michael, capped in 1888, he also represented Ireland at athletics.

## 1897-98

| v. ENGLAND | v. SCOTLAND | v. WALES |
|---|---|---|
| P.E. O'BRIEN-BUTLER | P.E. O'BRIEN-BUTLER | J. FULTON |
| †F.C. PURSER | F.C. PURSER | F.C. PURSER |
| *S. LEE | †F.F.S. SMITHWICK | F.F.S. SMITHWICK |
| L.H. GWYNN | L.H. GWYNN | *W. GARDINER |
| L.Q. BULGER 1PG | L.Q. BULGER | L.Q BULGER 1PG |
| A.M. MAGEE 1T | A.M. MAGEE | A.M. MAGEE |
| G.G. ALLEN | *G.G. ALLEN | †A. BARR |
| W.G. BYRON | W.G. BYRON | W.G. BYRON |
| J.E. McILWAINE | J.E. McILWAINE | J.E. McILWAINE |
| †J.G. FRANKS | J.G. FRANKS | J.G. FRANKS |
| M. RYAN | M. RYAN | M. RYAN |
| J. RYAN | J. RYAN | J. RYAN |
| J.H. LYTLE | J.H. LYTLE | †T.J. LITTLE |
| H. LINDSAY 1T | H. LINDSAY | H. LINDSAY |
| †J.L. DAVIS | J.L. DAVIS | †T. McCARTHY |
| Richmond | Belfast | Limerick |
| WON 9-6 | LOST 0-8 | LOST 3-11 |
| ENG.: 1PG 1T | IRE.: NIL | IRE.: 1PG |
| IRE.: 1PG 2T | SCOT.: 1G 1T | WALES: 1G 1PG 1T |
| 5 Feb. 1898 | 19 Feb. 1898 | 19 Mar. 1898 |

Ireland opened the season with a good win at Richmond, their fourth win in five matches against England. It was Sam Lee's last game for Ireland though victory was due to the skill and finish of his pack in the loose play and the expert tactical command exerted by Magee and Allen at half. Magee, with a typical burst of wizardry, won the match with a try in the last minute.

The Scottish match was the first played in Belfast since the 1894 game with Wales at Ballynafeigh. The Irish authorities had wisely decided to transfer Belfast fixtures to the Balmoral Showgrounds, and more than 10,000 fans, a record for Belfast, attended to see Ireland succumb to two second-half tries.

The Welsh match was played in Limerick, the first Irish centre outside Dublin or Belfast to stage an international. The Irish side was much-altered through injury and, although Bulger opened the scoring with a penalty, the Irish forwards were well beaten in the tight and loose. Wales won and it was reported that the Irish spectators had much to cheer and learn from the Welsh approach.

## 1898-99

| v. ENGLAND | v. SCOTLAND | v. WALES |
|---|---|---|
| J. FULTON | P.E. O'BRIEN-BUTLER | P.E. O'BRIEN-BUTLER |
| †I.G. DAVIDSON | †G.P. DORAN | G.P. DORAN 1T |
| †G.R.A. HARMAN | †C. REID 1T | G.R.A. HARMAN |
| †J.B. ALLISON | J.B. ALLISON | C. REID |
| †W.H. BROWN | †E.F. CAMPBELL 1T | E.F. CAMPBELL |
| *A.M. MAGEE 1PG | *A.M. MAGEE | *A.M. MAGEE |
| G.G. ALLEN 1T | A. BARR | G.G. ALLEN |
| W.G. BYRON | W.G. BYRON | W.G. BYRON |
| J.E. McILWAINE | J.H. LYTLE | J.E. McILWAINE |
| †T. AHEARNE | †A.W.D. MEARES | A.W.D. MEARES |
| M. RYAN | M. RYAN | M. RYAN |
| J. RYAN | J. RYAN | J. RYAN |
| H.C. McCOULL | T.J. LITTLE | T.J. LITTLE |
| J. SEALY | J. SEALY 1T | J. SEALY |
| †T.M.W. McGOWN | T.M.W. McGOWN | †C.C.H. MORIARTY |
| Lansdowne Road | Inverleith | Cardiff Arms Park |
| WON 6-0 | WON 9-3 | WON 3-0 |
| IRE.: 1PG 1T | SCOT.: 1PG | WALES: NIL |
| ENG.: NIL | IRE.: 3T | IRE.: 1T |
| 4 Feb. 1899 | 18 Feb. 1899 | 18 Mar. 1899 |

Louis Magee led Ireland to their second Triple Crown in 1899. By now he had formed a fruitful partnership at half-back with Allen, and both scored in Ireland's opening success of the season against England. Magee landed a penalty (though some reports credit Fulton with the score) and Allen scored a try, bouncing the ball in from touch and gathering it himself to dive over. This appears to have been a trick of the game in the 1890s, one frequently employed by Welsh half-backs.

Magee created two tries for Reid and Campbell against Scotland, Ireland winning comfortably, but it was Doran who earned the Triple Crown with the only try of the match against Wales in Cardiff. Even so, Ireland's captain managed to stamp his mark on the game with a try-saving tackle in the last minute. The Welsh threequarters looked certain to score, but Magee came up like a whirlwind and pulled down the likely scorer with a tackle from behind. The match was Ireland's first success at Cardiff and there were several occasions when play was interrupted by spectators bursting over the railings to invade the pitch.

George Harman played in this Triple Crown side. The longest-lived of all rugby international players, he was a doctor and died at Totnes in Devon in December 1975, aged 101.

## 1899-1900

| v. ENGLAND | v. SCOTLAND | v. WALES |
|---|---|---|
| P.E. O'Brien-Butler | †C.A. Boyd | J. Fulton |
| G.P. Doran | I.G. Davidson | I.G. Davidson |
| J.B. Allison 1DG | J.B. Allison | J.B. Allison |
| C. Reid | †B.R.W. Doran | B.R.W. Doran |
| E.F. Campbell | G.P. Doran | E.F. Campbell |
| *A.M. Magee | *A.M. Magee | *A.M. Magee |
| †J.H. Ferris | J.H. Ferris | J.H. Ferris |
| †S.T. Irwin | S.T. Irwin | S.T. Irwin |
| †C.E. Allen | C.E. Allen | C.E. Allen |
| J. Sealy | J. Sealy | †T.A. Harvey |
| †P.C. Nicholson | P.C. Nicholson | P.C. Nicholson |
| M. Ryan | M. Ryan | M. Ryan |
| †J.J. Coffey | J. Ryan | J. Ryan |
| A.W.D. Meares | T.J. Little | A.W.D. Meares |
| †F. Gardiner | F. Gardiner | T.J. Little |
| Richmond | Lansdowne Road | Belfast |
| LOST 4-15 | DRAWN 0-0 | LOST 0-3 |
| ENG.: 1G 1DG 2T | IRE.: NIL | IRE.: NIL |
| IRE.: 1DG | SCOT.: NIL | WALES: 1T |
| 3 Feb. 1900 | 24 Feb. 1900 | 17 Mar. 1900 |

Ireland finished with the wooden spoon in 1900, losing two matches and drawing in cold conditions with Scotland. The fifteen failed to register a try during the season for the first time since 1893, and the only score in three matches was a drop-goal by J.B. Allison against England. Allison had been capped as a teenager in 1899.

There were two pairs of brothers in the Irish side against Scotland. Bert and "Blucher" Doran were solicitors from Dublin who played as threequarters, while John and Michael Ryan were Tipperary farmers who gained 31 caps between them. The Ryans were hard, uncompromising forwards: both were strong, fast and terrors to their opponents, though apt to fade towards the ends of matches.

John Ryan was a keen breeder of racehorses. One of his successes was Tipperary Tim, who won the 1928 Grand National with a starting price of 100-1.

## 1900-01

| v. ENGLAND | v. SCOTLAND | v. WALES |
|---|---|---|
| J. Fulton | C.A. Boyd | C.A. Boyd |
| I.G. Davidson 1T | I.G. Davidson | I.G. Davidson 1T |
| J.B. Allison | J.B. Allison | J.B. Allison |
| B.R.W. Doran | B.R.W. Doran 1T | B.R.W. Doran |
| †A.E. Freear | A.E. Freear | A.E. Freear 1T |
| *A.M. Magee | *A.M. Magee | *A.M. Magee |
| A. Barr | A. Barr | †H.H. Ferris |
| S.T. Irwin 2C | †H.A.S. Irvine 1C | S.T. Irwin |
| C.E. Allen | C.E. Allen | C.E. Allen |
| †A.G. Heron | T.A. Harvey | T.A. Harvey |
| †P. Healey | P. Healey | P. Healey |
| M.Ryan | M. Ryan | M. Ryan |
| J. Ryan | J. Ryan | J. Ryan 1T |
| T.J. Little | T.J. Little | J.J. Coffey |
| F. Gardiner 1T | T.M.W. McGown | F. Gardiner |
| Lansdowne Road | Inverleith | St. Helen's |
| WON 10-6 | LOST 5-9 | LOST 9-10 |
| IRE.: 2G | SCOT.: 3T | WALES: 2G |
| ENG.: 1PG 1T | IRE.: 1G | IRE.: 3T |
| 9 Feb. 1901 | 23 Feb. 1901 | 16 Mar. 1901 |

The highlight of the season was a splendid win against England before 8000 spectators. Although Magee was injured quite early in the match, the play of the Irish halves was an inspiration to their forwards. The Irish pack broke quickly from scrums, played with their traditional fire, and disrupted the English halves.

Ian Davidson, a hard-running wing from Belfast who later emigrated to British Columbia, scored Ireland's first try, and Fred Gardiner, a linen manufacturer from Armagh, gained the second from a charged-down kick. Gardiner won 22 caps for Ireland, playing as a forward and as a half-back.

The Irish failed to beat Scotland and Wales, but the threequarter line remained intact for the international season and scored four tries in the three matches, equalling the record of 1897.

## 1901-02

| v. ENGLAND | v. SCOTLAND | v. WALES |
|---|---|---|
| *J. FULTON | *J. FULTON | J. FULTON |
| | | |
| I.G. DAVIDSON | I.G. DAVIDSON | I.G. DAVIDSON |
| J.B. ALLISON | J.B. ALLISON | J.B. ALLISON |
| B.R.W. DORAN | B.R.W. DORAN | B.R.W. DORAN |
| †C.C. FITZGERALD | G.P. DORAN 1T | G.P. DORAN |
| | | |
| A.M. MAGEE | A.M. MAGEE | *A.M. MAGEE |
| †H.H. CORLEY | H.H. CORLEY 1C | H.H. CORLEY |
| | | |
| S.T. IRWIN | S.T. IRWIN | S.T. IRWIN |
| †A. TEDFORD | A. TEDFORD | A. TEDFORD |
| T.A. HARVEY | T.A. HARVEY | T.A. HARVEY |
| P. HEALEY | P. HEALEY | P. HEALEY |
| †G.T. HAMLET | G.T. HAMLET | G.T. HAMLET |
| J. RYAN | †J.C. PRINGLE | J.C. PRINGLE |
| J.J. COFFEY | J.J. COFFEY | J.J. COFFEY |
| F. GARDINER 1T | F. GARDINER | F. GARDINER |
| | | |
| Leicester | Belfast | Lansdowne Road |
| LOST 3-6 | WON 5-0 | LOST 0-15 |
| | | |
| ENG.: 2T | IRE.: 1G | IRE.: NIL |
| IRE.: 1T | SCOT.: NIL | WALES: 1G 1DG 2T |
| | | |
| 8 Feb. 1902 | 22 Feb. 1902 | 8 Mar. 1902 |

Ireland fielded one of their strongest packs to date. The eight held England's good forwards at Leicester, though Ryan was made the scapegoat for England's winning try near the end of the match. The try had resulted from a lineout close to the Irish line, and Ryan was the only forward dropped during the season. His place went to John Pringle, a Royal Engineer from Belfast.

The Irish pack dominated the Scots in Belfast, Doran scoring a classic try from a round of passing by the threequarters in the second half, but Ireland were well beaten by Wales in the championship decider in Dublin.

Hamlet and Tedford made their debuts against England. Hamlet was a clever dribbler who often led the rushes in the loose, but he was also a solid scrummager. His 30 appearances between 1902-11 set a new Irish cap record, and he later served the IRFU as President. Alfred Tedford, a Belfast linen merchant, won 23 consecutive caps up to 1908, and, like Hamlet, became a President of the IRFU.

## 1902-03

| v. ENGLAND | v. SCOTLAND | v. WALES |
|---|---|---|
| J. FULTON | J. FULTON | J. FULTON |
| | | |
| †H.J. ANDERSON | H.J. ANDERSON | †G. BRADSHAW |
| †D.R. TAYLOR | J.B. ALLISON | †J.C. PARKE |
| †G.A.D. HARVEY | G.A.D. HARVEY | C. REID |
| C.C. FITZGERALD | C.C. FITZGERALD | G.P. DORAN |
| | | |
| A.M. MAGEE | A.M. MAGEE | A.M. MAGEE |
| *H.H. CORLEY 1PG | *H.H. CORLEY | *H.H. CORLEY |
| | | |
| M. RYAN 1T | C.E. ALLEN | C.E. ALLEN |
| A. TEDFORD | A. TEDFORD | A. TEDFORD |
| T.A. HARVEY | †JOS. WALLACE | JOS. WALLACE |
| P. HEALEY | P. HEALEY | P. HEALEY |
| G.T. HAMLET | G.T. HAMLET | G.T. HAMLET |
| †R.S. SMYTH | R.S. SMYTH | T.A. HARVEY |
| J.J. COFFEY | J.J. COFFEY | J.J. COFFEY |
| F. GARDINER | S.T. IRWIN | F. GARDINER |
| | | |
| Lansdowne Road | Inverleith | Cardiff Arms Park |
| WON 6-0 | LOST 0-3 | LOST 0-18 |
| | | |
| IRE.: 1PG 1T | SCOT.: 1T | WALES: 6T |
| ENG.: NIL | IRE.: NIL | IRE.: NIL |
| | | |
| 14 Feb. 1903 | 28 Feb. 1903 | 14 Mar. 1903 |

There were four new caps in the Irish side which beat England. Henry Corley, a recent graduate of Dublin University, was the captain and played brilliantly. He opened the scoring with a long penalty after the English fowards had been caught offside, and Mick Ryan scored a try from a forward rush.

Whereas the great Louis Magee favoured the right- and left-half tradition for half-back play, Corley was one of the first Irish players to specialise as a fly-half. Corley was a brilliant attacking player and a splendid drop-kicker who played eight times for Ireland, captaining the side in five of his games. He was also a talented cricketer and later a leading international referee.

A troubled sea-crossing was blamed for Ireland's disappointing game in Edinburgh. The backs failed to combine effectively in attack and the pack ran out of steam early in the second half – a common failing of many Irish packs of the time. J.C. Parke, a thrustful runner and useful kicker, came in for the first of his twenty caps against Wales. He was also a brilliant tennis player, and represented Britain on numerous occasions in the Davis Cup.

## 1903-04

| v. ENGLAND | v. SCOTLAND | v. WALES |
|---|---|---|
| J. FULTON | J. FULTON | †M.F. LANDERS |
| | | |
| †C.G. ROBB | C.G. ROBB | C.G. ROBB |
| J.C. PARKE | J.C. PARKE | J.C. PARKE 1c |
| *H.H. CORLEY | *H.H. CORLEY | G.A.D. HARVEY |
| G.P. DORAN | †J.E. MOFFATT 1T | †H.B. THRIFT 1T |
| | | |
| †T.T.H. ROBINSON | T.T.H. ROBINSON | A.M. MAGEE |
| †F.A. KENNEDY | †E.D. CADDELL | F.A. KENNEDY |
| | | |
| A. TEDFORD | A. TEDFORD | A. TEDFORD 2T |
| C.E. ALLEN | C.E. ALLEN | *C.E. ALLEN |
| JOS. WALLACE | JOS. WALLACE | JOS. WALLACE 1T |
| †JAS. WALLACE | JAS. WALLACE | †H.J. MILLAR |
| R.S. SMYTH | G.T. HAMLET | G.T. HAMLET |
| M. RYAN | M. RYAN | †R.W. EDWARDS |
| J. RYAN | P. HEALEY | †H.J. KNOX |
| F. GARDINER | F. GARDINER | F. GARDINER |
| | | |
| Blackheath | Lansdowne Road | Belfast |
| LOST 0-19 | LOST 3-19 | WON 14-12 |
| | | |
| ENG.: 2G 3T | IRE.: 1T | IRE.: 1G 3T |
| IRE.: NIL | SCOT.: 2G 3T | WALES: 4T |
| | | |
| 13 Feb. 1904 | 27 Feb. 1904 | 12 Mar. 1904 |

Ireland were well beaten by England and Scotland and made eight changes for the Welsh match, recalling Magee at half. The match, at Belfast, turned out to be the game of the season.

It was Magee's last appearance for Ireland and he made the opening for Tedford, the outstanding forward of the match, to score the first try of the game. Ireland led 6-3 at half-time, the versatile Joe Wallace scoring from a long pass. But Wales recovered in the second half and went into a 12-6 lead before Robb had to leave the field. Ireland were thus reduced to fourteen men and Wallace was withdrawn from the pack to cover Robb's wing.

Adversity inspired Ireland to stage a thrilling comeback. Thrift charged across for a try after an Irish kick had been deflected, and then a cross-kick by Wallace confused the Welsh full-back. It was Tedford who gathered the ball from an eccentric bounce, and he levelled the scores with a try beneath the posts. Parke kicked the winning goal.

## 1904-05

| v. ENGLAND | v. SCOTLAND | v. WALES |
|---|---|---|
| M.F. LANDERS | M.F. LANDERS | M.F. LANDERS |
| | | |
| H.B. THRIFT | H.B. THRIFT | H.B. THRIFT |
| †B. MACLEAR 1T,1c | B. MACLEAR 1c | B. MACLEAR |
| G.A.D. HARVEY | G.A.D. HARVEY | J.C. PARKE |
| J.E. MOFFATT 2T | J.E. MOFFATT 1T | J.E. MOFFATT |
| | | |
| T.T.H. ROBINSON | T.T.H. ROBINSON | T.T.H. ROBINSON 1T |
| E.D. CADDELL | E.D. CADDELL | E.D. CADDELL |
| | | |
| A. TEDFORD | A. TEDFORD 1T | A. TEDFORD |
| *C.E. ALLEN 1T | *C.E. ALLEN | *C.E. ALLEN |
| JOS. WALLACE 1T | JOS. WALLACE 1T | JOS. WALLACE |
| H.J. MILLAR | H.J. MILLAR | H.J. MILLAR |
| G.T. HAMLET | G.T. HAMLET | G.T. HAMLET |
| †H.G. WILSON | H.G. WILSON | H.G. WILSON |
| H.J. KNOX | H.J. KNOX | H.J. KNOX |
| J.J. COFFEY | J.J. COFFEY | J.J. COFFEY |
| | | |
| Cork | Inverleith | St. Helen's |
| WON 17-3 | WON 11-5 | LOST 3-10 |
| | | |
| IRE.: 1G 4T | SCOT.: 1G | WALES: 2G |
| ENG.: 1T | IRE.: 1G 2T | IRE.: 1T |
| | | |
| 11 Feb. 1905 | 25 Feb. 1905 | 11 Mar. 1905 |

An English soldier stationed in Munster made his debut for Ireland against England at Cork. His name was Basil Maclear and he stamped his authority and class on the match by creating two tries in the first half and scoring another after the interval. *The Times* summarised his qualities thus: "His defence was very fine, he fitted in well to the passing game . . . displayed a fine turn of speed and . . . was very difficult to stop." Maclear went on to play eleven games for Ireland and scored four tries in internationals.

The match in Cork was the first international played in the city, and attracted a crowd of 12,000 which payed record gate money of £900.

Maclear was the key player in the win against Scotland too, and the try he created for Moffatt gave that player his fourth touchdown in three internationals – an Irish record. In the match for the Triple Crown at Swansea, Ireland's pack were subdued by a strong Welsh unit and a brilliant Welsh back division succeeded in holding Maclear's genius in check.

## 1905-06

| v. NZ | v. ENGLAND | v. SCOTLAND | v. WALES |
|---|---|---|---|
| M.F. Landers | †G.J. Henebrey | G.J. Henebrey | G.J. Henebrey |
| H.B. Thrift | H.B. Thrift | C.G. Robb 1t | H.B. Thrift 1t |
| B. Maclear | †F. Casement | F. Casement | F. Casement |
| J.C. Parke | J.C. Parke | J.C. Parke 1t | J.C. Parke |
| C.G. Robb | H.J. Anderson | H.J. Anderson | B. Maclear 1t |
| T.T.H. Robinson | B. Maclear 1c,1t | B. Maclear | E.D. Caddell |
| E.D. Caddell | E.D. Caddell | E.D. Caddell | W.B.Purdon |
| Jos. Wallace | †W.B. Purdon 1t | W.B. Purdon |  |
|  |  |  | A. Tedford |
| A. Tedford | A. Tedford 2t | A. Tedford | *C.E. Allen |
| *C.E. Allen | *C.E. Allen | *C.E. Allen | Jos. Wallace 1t |
| †H.S. Sugars | F. Gardiner 1c | F. Gardiner | F. Gardiner 1c |
| G.T. Hamlet | †M. White | M. White | M. White |
| H.G. Wilson | H.G. Wilson | H.G. Wilson | H.G. Wilson |
| H.J. Knox | H.J. Knox | H.J. Knox | H.J. Knox |
| J.J. Coffey | J.J. Coffey | J.J. Coffey | J.J. Coffey |
| Lansdowne Road | Leicester | Lansdowne Road | Belfast |
| LOST 0-15 | WON 16-6 | LOST 6-13 | WON 11-6 |
| IRE.: NIL | ENG.: 2T | IRE.: 2T | IRE.: 1G 2T |
| NZ: 3G | IRE.: 2G 2T | SCOT.: 2G 1GM | WALES: 2T |
| 25 Nov. 1905 | 10 Feb. 1906 | 24 Feb. 1906 | 10 Mar. 1906 |

Ireland were easily beaten by the First All Blacks but, impressed by the New Zealand method, fielded seven forwards with Basil Maclear as rover (referred to as "flying man" in press reports) for the subsequent matches with England and Scotland.

The gamble was successful against England. The Irish halves Caddell and Purdon ran like ghosts, Casement and Anderson were prominent in the combined play, and Tedford in the pack capped a splendid performance with two tries. Against Scotland, however, the formation handicapped the Irish backs, the pack was outshoved, and for a time Maclear was forced to push in the scrummages.

For the Welsh game Ireland reverted to the traditional eight-forward formation and gained a remarkable victory against overwhelming odds. Ireland lost both of their halves and finished the match with only 13 men, forwards Joe Wallace and Fred Gardiner deputising behind the scrum. Maclear had his part in this victory, making some telling dashes, tackling steadily, and scoring a try after perfect Irish passing.

## 1906-07

| v. S.AFRICA | v. ENGLAND | v. SCOTLAND | v. WALES |
|---|---|---|---|
| G.J. Henebrey | †C. Thompson | C. Thompson | †W.P. Hinton |
| H.B. Thrift | H.B. Thrift 1t | H.B. Thrift | H.B. Thrift |
| †R.P.C. Gotto | B. Maclear | T.J. Greeves | T.J. Greeves |
| J.C. Parke 1pg | J.C. Parke 1c,1gm | J.C. Parke 1pg | J.C. Parke |
| B. Maclear 1t | †T.J. Greeves | B. Maclear | B. Maclear |
| T.T.H. Robinson | T.T.H. Robinson | T.T.H. Robinson | T.T.H. Robinson |
| E.D. Caddell | E.D. Caddell 2t | E.D. Caddell | †F.M.W. Harvey |
| A. Tedford | *A. Tedford 1t | A. Tedford | A. Tedford |
| *C.E. Allen | †R.E. Forbes | *C.E. Allen | *C.E. Allen |
| H.S. Sugars 2t | †W.St.J. Cogan | W.St.J. Cogan | H.J. Knox |
| G.T. Hamlet | G.T. Hamlet | G.T. Hamlet | G.T. Hamlet |
| M. White | M. White | H.S. Sugars | M. White |
| †G. McIldowie | †J.A. Sweeney | J.A. Sweeney | J.A. Sweeney |
| H.G. Wilson | H.G. Wilson | H.G. Wilson | H.G. Wilson |
| J.J. Coffey | J.J. Coffey | F. Gardiner | F. Gardiner |
| Belfast | Lansdowne Road | Inverleith | Cardiff Arms Park |
| LOST 12-15 | WON 17-9 | LOST 3-15 | LOST 0-29 |
| IRE.: 1PG 3T | IRE.: 1G 1GM 3T | SCOT.: 3G | WALES:2G 1PG 1DG 4T |
| SA: 1PG 4T | ENG.: 1PG 2T | IRE.: 1PG | IRE.: NIL |
| 24 Nov. 1906 | 9 Feb. 1907 | 23 Feb. 1907 | 9 Mar. 1907 |

The season opened with outstanding performances against the First Springboks and England. An exciting match was narrowly lost to the South Africans. Ireland trailed 3-12 at half-time, but after the interval they were brilliant. Parke kicked a penalty before Maclear made the run of the match. The Cork soldier gathered the ball in his own half before making a breathtaking dash the length of the pitch for a sensational try. Ireland actually equalised moments later when Sugars dribbled over the line from a wheeled scrum, but the Springboks won with a subsequent try scored by one of their wings.

Tedford captained Ireland to their third successive victory over England in Dublin, and scored the sixth try of his international career in Ireland's big win. His try-record stood until J.P. Quinn scored nine in the seasons before the first war. There was a disappointing finish to the season, the side losing to Scotland and by a record margin to Wales.

This was Maclear's last season in the Irish side. Born in Portsmouth, he had learned the game at Bedford School before entering the Royal Dublin Fusiliers from Sandhurst. He served in the Boer War but was killed in action toward the end of the second battle of Ypres in May 1915.

## 1907-08

| v. ENGLAND | v. SCOTLAND | v. WALES |
|---|---|---|
| W.P. HINTON | W.P. HINTON 1C | W.P. HINTON |
| | | |
| *H.B. THRIFT | H.B. THRIFT 2T | H.B. THRIFT |
| †G.C.P. BECKETT | G.C.P. BECKETT 1T | G.C.P. BECKETT |
| J.C. PARKE 1PG | *J.C. PARKE 1C | *J.C. PARKE 1C |
| C. THOMPSON | C. THOMPSON 1T | C. THOMPSON |
| | | |
| †H.R. ASTON | E.D. CADDELL | E.D. CADDELL |
| †F.N.B. SMARTT | F.N.B. SMARTT | H.R. ASTON 1T |
| | | |
| A. TEDFORD | A. TEDFORD | A. TEDFORD |
| †T. SMYTH | T. SMYTH | T. SMYTH |
| †B.A. SOLOMONS | B.A. SOLOMONS | B.A. SOLOMONS |
| †T.G. HARPUR | T.G. HARPUR | T.G. HARPUR |
| G.T. HAMLET | G.T. HAMLET | G.T. HAMLET |
| H.G. WILSON | H.G. WILSON | H.G. WILSON |
| †E. McG. MORPHY | H.J. KNOX | J.J. COFFEY |
| †C. ADAMS | F. GARDINER | F. GARDINER |
| | | |
| Richmond | Lansdowne Road | Belfast |
| LOST 3-13 | WON 16-11 | LOST 5-11 |
| ENG.: 2G 1T | IRE.: 2G 2T | IRE.: 1G |
| IRE.: 1PG | SCOT.: 1G 1PG 1T | WALES: 1G 2T |
| 8 Feb. 1908 | 29 Feb. 1908 | 14 Mar. 1908 |

This was W.P. Hinton's first full season at full-back for Ireland. Altogether he won 16 caps, establishing himself as his nation's leading full-back before the first war. Hinton was a player of immense courage, an accurate fielder and tackler, with the ability to kick safely with each foot. Afterwards he served the IRFU as President.

Ireland's selectors fielded a settled side in the Championship, but there was only one success in these matches. Five of the backs and six of the forwards played throughout the season.

Tom Smyth, a fast, determined runner, made his debut against England. He won 14 caps, captained Ireland against Wales in 1910, and was the skipper of the first truly representative British touring team which went to South Africa in 1910. A doctor who played for Malone, he later practised in Wales, and played regularly for the Newport club when the side enjoyed a very successful run. He died young, in his forties, in London in 1928.

## 1908-09

| v. ENGLAND | v. SCOTLAND | v. WALES | v. FRANCE |
|---|---|---|---|
| W.P. HINTON | W.P. HINTON | G.J. HENEBREY | G.J. HENEBREY |
| | | | |
| H.B. THRIFT | H.B. THRIFT | H.B. THRIFT | H.B. THRIFT |
| J.C. PARKE 1T | J.C. PARKE 1PG | J.C. PARKE 1C | J.C. PARKE 1PG,1C |
| C. THOMPSON | C. THOMPSON | T.J. GREEVES | C. THOMPSON 2T |
| †E.C. DEANE | †R.M. MAGRATH | C. THOMPSON 1T | T.J. GREEVES |
| | | | |
| †G. PINION 1C | G. PINION | G. PINION | G. PINION |
| F.N.B. SMARTT | *F. GARDINER | †F.M. McCORMAC | †J.J. O'CONNOR 1T |
| | | | |
| †M.G. GARRY | M.G. GARRY | M.G. GARRY | M.G. GARRY |
| T. SMYTH | T. SMYTH | T. SMYTH | C. ADAMS |
| B.A. SOLOMONS | B.A. SOLOMONS | B.A. SOLOMONS | B.A. SOLOMONS |
| †O.J.S. PIPER | O.J.S. PIPER | O.J.S. PIPER | O.J.S. PIPER |
| G.T. HAMLET | G.T. HAMLET | *G.T. HAMLET | G.T. HAMLET |
| H.G. WILSON | H.G. WILSON | H.G. WILSON | *F. GARDINER 1C,1T |
| C. ADAMS | †J.C. BLACKHAM | J.C. BLACKHAM | J.C. BLACKHAM |
| *F. GARDINER | †T. HALPIN | T. HALPIN | T. HALPIN |
| | | | |
| Lansdowne Road | Inverleith | St. Helen's | Lansdowne Road |
| LOST 5-11 | LOST 3-9 | LOST 5-18 | WON 19-8 |
| IRE.: 1G | SCOT.: 3T | WALES: 3G 1T | IRE.: 2G 1PG 2T |
| ENG.: 1G 2T | IRE.: 1PG | IRE.: 1G | FR.: 1G 1T |
| 13 Feb. 1909 | 27 Feb. 1909 | 13 Mar. 1909 | 20 Mar. 1909 |

This was a disappointing season with only one win in four matches. Two of Ireland's senior backs, Thrift and Parke, played for the last time in the French match, Ireland's first against the youngest of the International Board nations.

Thrift was a wing-threequarter abundantly blessed with resource and resolution. A stout defender and an alert opportunist, he played 18 times in internationals and scored five tries. Educated at Dublin HS and Dublin University, he became a professor at Trinity and served the IRFU as President in 1923-4. Parke was a fine place-kicker whose five penalty goals in internationals stood as an Irish career record until broken by George Stephenson in 1927.

Oliver Piper, who made his debut against England, was one of the rare band of Irish international players born in Wales. A member of a circus family, he was born at Aberavon in 1886. He won eight Irish caps and was a member of Tom Smyth's British touring team to South Africa in 1910.

## 1909-10

| v. ENGLAND | v. SCOTLAND | v. WALES | v. FRANCE |
|---|---|---|---|
| W.P. HINTON | W.P. HINTON | W.P. HINTON | W.P. HINTON |
| †J.P. QUINN | J.P. QUINN | †C.T. O'CALLAGHAN | C.T. O'CALLAGHAN |
| †A.R. FOSTER | A.R. FOSTER | A.S. TAYLOR | A.R. FOSTER |
| †A.S. TAYLOR | A.S. TAYLOR | †R.K. LYLE | R.K. LYLE |
| C. THOMPSON | C. THOMPSON | C. THOMPSON | C. THOMPSON 1T |
| †R.A. LLOYD | R.A. LLOYD | †A.N. McCLINTON | A.N. McCLINTON 1C |
| †H.M. READ | H.M. READ | F.M. McCORMAC | F.M. McCORMAC |
| G. McILDOWIE | G. McILDOWIE | G. McILDOWIE 1T | †W.J. BEATTY |
| T. SMYTH | T. SMYTH | *T. SMYTH | T. SMYTH 1T |
| B.A. SOLOMONS | B.A. SOLOMONS | B.A. SOLOMONS | *G.T. HAMLET |
| O.J.S. PIPER | O.J.S. PIPER | O.J.S. PIPER | O.J.S. PIPER |
| *G.T. HAMLET | *G.T. HAMLET | †W.S. SMYTH | W.S. SMYTH |
| †W.F. RIORDAN | †H. MOORE | H.G. WILSON | C. ADAMS |
| J.C. BLACKHAM | J.C. BLACKHAM | J.C. BLACKHAM | J.J. COFFEY |
| T. HALPIN | T. HALPIN | T. HALPIN | †W. TYRRELL |
| Twickenham | Belfast | Lansdowne Road | Parc des Princes |
| DRAWN 0-0 | LOST 0-14 | LOST 3-19 | WON 8-3 |
| ENG.: NIL | IRE.: NIL | IRE.: 1T | FR.: 1T |
| IRE.: NIL | SCOT.: 1G 3T | WALES: 1DG 5T | IRE.: 1G 1T |
| 12 Feb. 1910 | 26 Feb. 1910 | 12 Mar. 1910 | 28 Mar. 1910 |

Ireland's best performance of 1910 was holding England to a scoreless draw at the new RFU ground at Twickenham. The Irish fielded six new caps in a side which should have become the first visitors to win at the ground. The forwards, who played with traditional fire and passion, lasted the pace well. They scrummaged with rare control, foraged eagerly, and dribbled the ball away to the opposing backs from the tight play. Only some poor handling among the backs spoiled several scoring opportunities.

The rest of the season was disappointing. Scotland and Wales beat Ireland comfortably and even in Paris, on their first visit to France, the Irish side struggled to win by a narrow margin. John Coffey, a Dublin civil servant, went along to see the side off for France, but when one of the side failed to turn up, he made the journey instead and duly won his 19th and last cap.

Dicky Lloyd and Harry Read, the Dublin University halves, were the first truly specialist half-backs selected to play for Ireland. Lloyd, a drop-goal expert who was also a brilliant tactician, was the fly-half. He gained 19 caps in a career which spanned the war, scored 75 points to create an Irish career record, and dropped seven goals in International Championship matches, a record which was not equalled until the Welshman Barry John finished his career in 1972. Read, who was Lloyd's partner in 13 matches (creating another Irish record), was a President of the IRFU later, but like Lloyd was a talented cricketer.

## 1910-11

| v. ENGLAND | v. SCOTLAND | v. WALES | v. FRANCE |
|---|---|---|---|
| W.P. HINTON | W.P. HINTON 1C | W.P. HINTON | F.M.W. HARVEY |
| C.T. O'CALLAGHAN | C.T. O'CALLAGHAN 1T | C.T. O'CALLAGHAN | C.T. O'CALLAGHAN 1T |
| A.R. FOSTER | A.R. FOSTER 1T | A.R. FOSTER | A.R. FOSTER |
| †A.R.V. JACKSON | A.R.V. JACKSON | A.R.V. JACKSON | A.R.V. JACKSON 2T |
| J.P. QUINN | J.P. QUINN 1T | J.P. QUINN | J.P. QUINN 1T |
| R.A. LLOYD | R.A. LLOYD 1C | R.A. LLOYD | R.A. LLOYD 1DG,3C |
| H.M. READ | H.M. READ | H.M. READ | H.M. READ |
| M.G. GARRY | M.G. GARRY | M.G. GARRY | †R.I. GRAHAM |
| T. SMYTH 1T | T. SMYTH | T. SMYTH | P.J. SMYTH |
| †S.B.B. CAMPBELL | S.B.B. CAMPBELL | S.B.B. CAMPBELL | S.B.B. CAMPBELL |
| †P.J. SMYTH | P.J. SMYTH | H. MOORE | H. MOORE |
| *G.T. HAMLET | *G.T. HAMLET | *G.T. HAMLET | *G.T. HAMLET |
| C. ADAMS | C. ADAMS 1T | C. ADAMS | C. ADAMS |
| †M.R. HEFFERNAN | M.R. HEFFERNAN | M.R. HEFFERNAN | M.R. HEFFERNAN 1T |
| T. HALPIN | T. HALPIN | T. HALPIN | T. HALPIN |
| Lansdowne Road | Inverleith | Cardiff Arms Park | Cork |
| WON 3-0 | WON 16-10 | LOST 0-16 | WON 25-5 |
| IRE.: 1T | SCOT.: 1DG 2T | WALES: 2G 1PG 1T | IRE.: 3G 1DG 2T |
| ENG.: NIL | IRE.: 2G 2T | IRE.: NIL | FR.: 1G |
| 11 Feb. 1911 | 25 Feb. 1911 | 11 Mar. 1911 | 25 Mar. 1911 |

Ireland called on 17 players for their successful campaign of 1911. A last-minute try against England and an exciting victory over Scotland pointed to a Triple Crown decider with Wales, who were also unbeaten. The match at Cardiff was such a magnet for public attention that, wrote one critic, "those who couldn't squeeze into the enclosure sought vantage points outside and took so many risks . . . that a number . . . had to be taken to hospital, some of them seriously injured".

Wales won the match comfortably, though Ireland were compelled to play with 14 men for part of the game, Hinton retiring with a first-half injury and Campbell withdrawing from the pack to act as an extra back.

France were soundly beaten at Cork to enable Ireland to finish as runners-up in the Championship. F.M.W. Harvey, previously capped at half-back in 1907, replaced Hinton at full-back for this game. He gained the Victoria Cross in 1917, and later emigrated to Canada. He died at Calgary in 1980, a few days before his 92nd birthday.

## 1911-12

| v. FRANCE | v. ENGLAND | v. SCOTLAND | v. WALES |
|---|---|---|---|
| W.P. HINTON | W.P. HINTON | †R.A. WRIGHT | W.P. HINTON |
| | | | |
| †C.V. MacIVOR | C.V. MacIVOR | C.V. MacIVOR | C.V. MacIVOR 1T |
| A.S. TAYLOR 1T | †M. ABRAHAM | M. ABRAHAM | M. ABRAHAM |
| A.R. FOSTER 1T | *A.R. FOSTER | A.R. FOSTER 1T | A.R. FOSTER |
| C.T. O'CALLAGHAN | J.P. QUINN | J.P. QUINN | J.P. QUINN |
| | | | |
| *R.A. LLOYD 1T,1C | R.A. LLOYD | *R.A. LLOYD 1DG,1PG | *R.A. LLOYD 1DG,1C |
| H.M. READ | H.M. READ | H.M. READ | H.M. READ |
| | | | |
| W.J. BEATTY | T. SMYTH | †G.S. BROWN | G.S. BROWN 1T |
| †R. HEMPHILL | R. HEMPHILL | R. HEMPHILL | R. HEMPHILL |
| S.B.B. CAMPBELL | S.B.B. CAMPBELL | S.B.B. CAMPBELL | S.B.B. CAMPBELL |
| H. MOORE | H. MOORE | H. MOORE | H. MOORE |
| †G. McCONNELL | G. McCONNELL | C. ADAMS | C. ADAMS |
| †W.V. EDWARDS | W.V. EDWARDS | R. d'A. PATTERSON | R. d'A. PATTERSON |
| †R. d'A. PATTERSON | †G.V. KILLEEN | G.V. KILLEEN | G.V. KILLEEN |
| T. HALPIN | T. HALPIN | T. HALPIN | W.J. BEATTY |
| | | | |
| Parc des Princes | Twickenham | Lansdowne Road | Belfast |
| WON 11-6 | LOST 0-15 | WON 10-8 | WON 12-5 |
| | | | |
| FR.: 2T | ENG.: 5T | IRE.: 1DG 1PG 1T | IRE.: 1G 1DG 1T |
| IRE.: 1G 2T | IRE.: NIL | SCOT.: 1G 1T | WALES: 1G |
| | | | |
| 1 Jan. 1912 | 10 Feb. 1912 | 24 Feb. 1912 | 9 Mar. 1912 |

Ireland were joint champions with England. Three matches were won but the side was well beaten at Twickenham and had to rely on Dicky Lloyd's kicking to see them home against Scotland. Lloyd landed a penalty for a scrummage offence, dropped a lovely goal, and narrowly failed to convert a try by the Derry threequarter Foster. Foster, incidentally, was one of the few Irishmen to play before and after the Great War. He won 17 caps in a career lasting from 1910 to 1921.

Wales were defeated in Belfast when Ireland gave their best performance of the season. It was the first Irish success against Wales for six years, and Lloyd again dropped a goal to help his side to victory.

One of the Irish scorers against Wales was C.V. MacIvor. He was an engineering student at Dublin University, but died tragically as a result of a rugby injury. In October 1913 he was playing in a practice match and dived on the ball to smother a rush. His head struck another player's boot, but he continued to play for several minutes before retiring without assistance. He collapsed and died of concussion on reaching his home.

## 1912-13

| v. S.AFRICA | v. ENGLAND | v. SCOTLAND | v. WALES | v. FRANCE |
|---|---|---|---|---|
| †C.P. STUART | †G. YOUNG | †J.W. McCONNELL | †A.W.P. TODD | A.W.P. TODD |
| | | | | |
| †R. WATSON | C.V. MacIVOR | C.V. MacIVOR | †G.H. WOOD | C.V. MacIVOR |
| †G.W. HOLMES | G.W. HOLMES | G.W. HOLMES | A.R.V. JACKSON | A.R.V. JACKSON |
| †J.B. MINCH | J.B. MINCH | J.B. MINCH | †A.L. STEWART 1T | A.L. STEWART |
| M. ABRAHAM | J.P. QUINN | †F. BENNETT | J.P. QUINN 1T | J.P. QUINN 3T |
| | | | | |
| *R.A. LLOYD | *R.A. LLOYD 1DG | *R.A. LLOYD 1DG,2C | *R.A. LLOYD 2C,1PG | *R.A. LLOYD 3C |
| H.M. READ | H.M. READ | H..M. READ | †S.E. POLDEN | S.E. POLDEN |
| | | | | |
| G.S. BROWN | †J.E. FINLAY | J.E. FINLAY | J.E. FINLAY | G. McCONNELL |
| †R.B. BURGESS | W. TYRRELL | W. TYRRELL | W. TYRRELL | W. TYRRELL 2T |
| S.B.B. CAMPBELL | S.B.B. CAMPBELL | S.B.B. CAMPBELL | G. McCONNELL | S.B.B. CAMPBELL |
| H. MOORE | †E.W. JEFFARES | E.W. JEFFARES | †P. O'CONNELL | P. O'CONNELL |
| C. ADAMS | G.V. KILLEEN | G.V. KILLEEN | G.V. KILLEEN | G.V. KILLEEN |
| R. d'A. PATTERSON | R. d'A. PATTERSON | R. d'A. PATTERSON | R. d'A. PATTERSON | R. d'A. PATTERSON 1T |
| †F.G. SCHUTE | F.G. SCHUTE | F.G. SCHUTE 1T | C. ADAMS | C. ADAMS |
| †J.J. CLUNE | †P. STOKES | P. STOKES 1T | J.J. CLUNE | J.J. CLUNE |
| | | | | |
| Lansdowne Road | Lansdowne Road | Inverleith | St. Helen's | Cork |
| LOST 0-38 | LOST 4-15 | LOST 14-29 | LOST 13-16 | WON 24-0 |
| | | | | |
| IRE.: NIL | IRE.: 1DG | SCOT.: 4G 3T | WALES: 2G 1PG 1T | IRE.: 3G 3T |
| SA: 4G 6T | ENG.: 1PG 4T | IRE.: 2G 1DG | IRE.: 2G 1PG | FR.: NIL |
| | | | | |
| 30 Nov. 1912 | 8 Feb. 1913 | 22 Feb. 1913 | 8 Mar. 1913 | 24 Mar. 1913 |

Loss of form of several members of the Championship side meant that the Irish selectors were forced to field an experimental side in 1912-13. Seven new caps were awarded for the season's opening international against the Springboks. In a record defeat, Ireland conceded ten tries and eight changes were made to the side for the Home internationals.

The match in Cork against France was played in the morning, so that the 8000 spectators and players could attend Cork races in the afternoon. At the course the teams were regaled to a champagne luncheon by the racecourse executive. Joseph Quinn, a Dublin University medical student, scored three tries against the French, equalling the record for most tries by an Irishman in an international. Quinn was a real flyer, quick off the mark and sharp to grasp an opportunity. His career record of nine tries stood as an Irish record until the advent of George Stephenson. Quinn won a Military Cross during the Great War.

Dicky Lloyd's haul of 25 points in the Championship season remained an Irish record for 36 years.

## 1913-14

| v. FRANCE | v. ENGLAND | v. SCOTLAND | v. WALES |
|---|---|---|---|
| A.W.P. Todd | †F.P. Montgomery | F.P. Montgomery | F.P. Montgomery |
| G.H. Wood | A.R. Foster | *A.R. Foster | *A.R. Foster 1T |
| A.R.V. Jackson | A.R.V. Jackson 1T | A.R.V. Jackson | A.R.V. Jackson |
| A.L. Stewart | J.B. Minch | J.B. Minch | M. Abraham |
| J.P. Quinn 1T | J.P. Quinn 1T | J.P. Quinn 1T | †J.T. Brett |
| *R.A. Lloyd 1c | *R.A. Lloyd 1DG,1c | †H.W. Jack | H.W. Jack |
| S.E. Polden | †V. McNamara | V. McNamara 1T | V. McNamara |
| †J.C.A. Dowse | †J. Taylor | J. Taylor | J. Taylor |
| W. Tyrrell 1T | W. Tyrrell | W. Tyrrell | W. Tyrrell |
| †J.S. Parr | J.S. Parr | J.S. Parr | J.S. Parr |
| P. O'Connell | P. O'Connell | P. O'Connell | P. O'Connell |
| C. Adams | C. Adams | C. Adams | J.J. Clune |
| J.J. Clune | J.J. Clune | J.C.A. Dowse | J.C.A. Dowse |
| †W.P. Collopy | W.P. Collopy | W.P. Collopy | W.P. Collopy |
| P. Stokes | G.V. Killeen | G.V. Killeen | G.V. Killeen |
| Parc des Princes | Twickenham | Lansdowne Road | Belfast |
| WON 8-6 | LOST 12-17 | WON 6-0 | LOST 3-11 |
| FR.: 2T | ENG.: 1G 4T | IRE.: 2T | IRE.: 1T |
| IRE.: 1G 1T | IRE.: 1G 1DG 1T | SCOT.: NIL | WALES: 1G 2T |
| 1 Jan. 1914 | 14 Feb. 1914 | 28 Feb. 1914 | 14 Mar. 1914 |

The Irish pack of 1914 was regarded as one of the roughest ever. It was led by a Belfast medical student, William Tyrrell, who later became a distinguished doctor. Tyrrell also gained the DSO (with bar) and Croix de Guerre during the Great War, and reached the rank of Air-Vice-Marshall in the RAF. A water-polo international too, he served the IRFU as President in 1950-51, and was knighted in 1944.

Tyrrell's pack paved the ways to victory in Paris and against Scotland, but their rough methods were countered in Belfast by an equally rough Welsh pack. The match has often been described as the "dirtiest" ever played between the nations, though as so often is the case in such circumstances, the combatants later became firm friends off the field.

Frank Montgomery, another Belfast medical student, was an invaluable asset to his side at full-back. In the match with Wales his play in difficult conditions was brilliant. His catching, fielding and kicking were described as "of the very best".

## 1919-20

| v. ENGLAND | v. SCOTLAND | v. WALES | v. FRANCE |
|---|---|---|---|
| †W.E. Crawford | W.E. Crawford | W.E. Crawford | W.E. Crawford |
| †J.A.N. Dickson 1T | C.H. Bryant | J.A.N. Dickson | J.A.N. Dickson |
| †T. Wallace | *T. Wallace | *T. Wallace | †G.V. Stephenson |
| †W.J. Cullen | †P.J. Roddy | W. Duggan | P.J. Roddy |
| †C.H. Bryant | †B.A.T. McFarland | B.A.T. McFarland 1DG | B.A.T. McFarland |
| *R.A. Lloyd 1T,1c,1PG | †W. Duggan | †W. Cunningham | *R.A. Lloyd 1DG |
| †A.K. Horan | †J.B. O'Neill | A.K. Horan | S.E. Polden |
| †N. Butler | †A.H. Price | †M.J. Bradley | M.J. Bradley |
| †H.H. Coulter | H.H. Coulter | H.H. Coulter | A.H. Price 1T |
| W.S. Smyth | †A.W. Courtney | A.W. Courtney | A.W. Courtney |
| J.E. Finlay | J.E. Finlay | J.E. Finlay | †J.T. Smyth |
| †R.Y. Crichton | R.Y. Crichton | R.Y. Crichton | R.Y. Crichton |
| †W.D. Doherty | W.D. Doherty | W.D. Doherty | †D. Browne |
| †W.J. Roche | W.J. Roche | †H.N. Potterton | W.J. Roche |
| P. Stokes | P. Stokes | P. Stokes | P. Stokes |
| Lansdowne Road | Inverleith | Cardiff Arms Park | Lansdowne Road |
| LOST 11-14 | LOST 0-19 | LOST 4-28 | LOST 7-15 |
| IRE.: 1G 1PG 1T | SCOT.: 2G 1PG 2T | WALES: 3G 1DG 3T | IRE.: 1DG 1T |
| ENG.: 1G 3T | IRE.: NIL | IRE.: 1DG | FR.: 5T |
| 14 Feb. 1920 | 28 Feb. 1920 | 13 Mar. 1920 | 3 Apr. 1920 |

Dicky Lloyd returned to lead Ireland after the war, and he had a team of eleven new caps against England. Although he continued to play with all his old guile, his forwards were comprehensively beaten by a faster, more skilful English pack. Nevertheless, Lloyd's kicking and tactical command permitted Ireland to lead for much of the match. He scored a first-half penalty, created a try for Dickson, and then converted a try of his own to give the Irish an eleven-point lead half an hour from no-side. England finally overcame the Irish pack, however, and their expected victory was obtained from four good tries.

Two of Ireland's leading personalities between the wars made their debuts during the season. Ernie Crawford won the first of his 30 caps at full-back against England. He was a clever player who made careful use of conditions, often outwitted opponents with acts of pure genius, and carried the burden of captaincy on 15 occasions, creating an Irish record. An accountant, he was President of the IRFU in 1957-58.

George Stephenson went on to win 42 caps, another Irish record, and in so doing proved himself to be the most complete threequarter in British rugby during the 1920s. His record of 14 international tries for Ireland has yet to be overtaken.

## 1920-21

| v. ENGLAND | v. SCOTLAND | v. WALES | v. FRANCE |
|---|---|---|---|
| W.E. Crawford | W.E. Crawford | W.E. Crawford | W.E. Crawford |
| | | | |
| †D.J. Cussen | D.J. Cussen 1t | D.J. Cussen | D.J. Cussen |
| G.V. Stephenson | G.V. Stephenson 1t | G.V. Stephenson | G.V. Stephenson |
| A.R. Foster | A.R. Foster | A.R. Foster | †T.G. Wallis 2c |
| †H.S.T. Cormac | H.S.T. Cormac | H.S.T. Cormac | †C.T. Davidson |
| | | | |
| W. Cunningham | W. Cunningham 1t | W. Cunningham | W. Cunningham |
| †T. Mayne | T. Mayne | H.W. Jack | T. Mayne |
| | | | |
| *W.D. Doherty | *W.D. Doherty | *W.D. Doherty | *W.D. Doherty |
| †T.A. McClelland | T.A. McClelland | T.A. McClelland | T.A. McClelland |
| A.W. Courtney | A.W. Courtney | A.W. Courtney | A.W. Courtney |
| †J.J. Bermingham | J.J. Bermingham | J.J. Bermingham | J.J. Bermingham |
| †C.F.G.T. Hallaran | C.F.G.T. Hallaran | C.F.G.T. Hallaran | R.Y. Crichton |
| W.P. Collopy | W.P. Collopy | W.P. Collopy | W.P. Collopy |
| †N.M. Purcell | N.M. Purcell | N.M. Purcell | N.M. Purcell |
| P. Stokes | P. Stokes | †J.K.S. Thompson | P. Stokes 2t |
| | | | |
| Twickenham | Lansdowne Road | Balmoral | Stade Colombes |
| LOST 0-15 | WON 9-8 | LOST 0-6 | LOST 10-20 |
| | | | |
| Eng.: 1G 1DG 2T | Ire.: 3T | Ire.: Nil | Fr.: 4G |
| Ire.: Nil | Scot.: 1G 1T | Wales: 1PG 1T | Ire.: 2G |
| | | | |
| 12 Feb. 1921 | 26 Feb. 1921 | 12 Mar. 1921 | 9 Apr. 1921 |

Denis Cussen of Co. Limerick came into the Irish side in 1921. An Irish athletics international and a doctor, he was one of the fastest wings produced by Ireland between the wars and scored five tries in a career which lasted until 1927.

Playing behind a robust pack, Cussen opened the Irish scoring in his country's only win of the season, against Scotland in Dublin. The match was a close affair and only second-half tries by Stephenson and Cunningham permitted Ireland to come from behind and win by a point. Cunningham later emigrated to Johannesburg and during the 1924 British tour to South Africa he was co-opted to the team when injuries depleted the squad. His form was good enough to win for him a place in one of the Test matches of the series.

Two of the Irish regulars in the pack, Paddy Stokes and Billy Collopy, were stalwarts who had played before the war. Billy captained Ireland in 1922 (and once more in 1924), played alongside his brother Dick in 1923 and 1924, and was the son of George Collopy, who had been capped back in 1891. Stokes was another doctor. As a forward he proved to be a prolific try-scorer, gaining four in his international career.

## 1921-22

| v. ENGLAND | v. SCOTLAND | v. WALES | v. FRANCE |
|---|---|---|---|
| W.E. Crawford | W.E. Crawford | B.A.T. McFarland | †J.W. Stewart |
| | | | |
| T.G. Wallis 1t | T.G. Wallis | T.G. Wallis 1c | T.G. Wallis 1c,1pg |
| †D.B. Sullivan | D.B. Sullivan | D.B. Sullivan | D.B. Sullivan |
| G.V. Stephenson | G.V. Stephenson | G.V. Stephenson | G.V. Stephenson 1t |
| D.J. Cussen | †H.W.V. Stephenson | H.W.V. Stephenson | H.W.V. Stephenson |
| | | | |
| †J.R. Wheeler | J.R. Wheeler | J.R. Wheeler | J.R. Wheeler |
| W. Cunningham | †J.A.B. Clarke 1t | J.A.B. Clarke | J.A.B. Clarke |
| | | | |
| M.J. Bradley | M.J. Bradley | M.J. Bradley | M.J. Bradley |
| T.A. McClelland | †J.D. Egan | T.A. McClelland | T.A. McClelland |
| †S. McVicker | S. McVicker | S. McVicker | S. McVicker |
| C.F.G.T. Hallaran | C.F.G.T. Hallaran | C.F.G.T. Hallaran | J.C. Gillespie |
| R.Y. Crichton | †I. Popham | I. Popham | I. Popham |
| *W.P. Collopy | *W.P. Collopy | *W.P. Collopy | *W.P. Collopy |
| †R.H. Owens | R.H. Owens | P. Stokes 1t | P. Stokes |
| J.K.S. Thompson | J.K.S. Thompson | †J.C. Gillespie | J.K.S. Thompson |
| | | | |
| Lansdowne Road | Inverleith | St. Helen's | Lansdowne Road |
| LOST 3-12 | LOST 3-6 | LOST 5-11 | WON 8-3 |
| | | | |
| Ire.: 1T | Scot.: 2T | Wales: 1G 2T | Ire.: 1G 1PG |
| Eng.: 4T | Ire.: 1T | Ire.: 1G | Fr.: 1T |
| | | | |
| 11 Feb. 1922 | 25 Feb. 1922 | 11 Mar. 1922 | 8 Apr. 1922 |

Only a narrow victory over France at the end of the season saved Ireland from a Championship whitewash. The fifteen was unable to blend as successfully as the selectors had wished, although few changes in personnel were deemed necessary.

Among the new players, Harry Stephenson played on the wing outside his brother. Harry's career of 14 caps was interrupted by Naval service, which took him to South Africa where he appeared in Provincial matches. In his international career he scored four tries.

At fly-half, Dr J.R. Wheeler began a long association with international rugby. Although he won just five Irish caps, he became a very distinguished referee, taking charge of six championship matches between 1929 and 1933. He was elected President of the IRFU in 1959-60.

## 1922-23

| v. ENGLAND | v. SCOTLAND | v. WALES | v. FRANCE |
|---|---|---|---|
| W.E. CRAWFORD 1c | W.E. CRAWFORD | W.E. CRAWFORD 1c | W.E. CRAWFORD 1c |
| †R.O. McCLENAHAN | R.O. McCLENAHAN | R.O. McCLENAHAN | D.J. CUSSEN |
| †F. JACKSON | G.V. STEPHENSON | G.V. STEPHENSON | G.V. STEPHENSON |
| G.V. STEPHENSON | J.B. GARDINER | J.B. GARDINER | J.B. GARDINER |
| D.J. CUSSEN | D.J. CUSSEN 1T | D.J. CUSSEN 1T | †A.C. DOUGLAS 1T |
| †W.H. HALL | W.H. HALL | W.H. HALL | W.H. HALL |
| †J.B. GARDINER | W. CUNNINGHAM | W. CUNNINGHAM | J.A.B. CLARKE |
| M.J. BRADLEY | M.J. BRADLEY | M.J. BRADLEY | M.J. BRADLEY |
| T.A. McCLELLAND 1T | T.A. McCLELLAND | T.A. McCLELLAND | T.A. McCLELLAND 1T |
| †R. COLLOPY | R. COLLOPY | R. COLLOPY | R. COLLOPY |
| C.F.G.T. HALLARAN | †P.E.F. DUNN | †J.D. CLINCH | C.F.G.T. HALLARAN |
| †D.M. CUNNINGHAM | D.M. CUNNINGHAM | D.M. CUNNINGHAM | I. POPHAM |
| †J. MAHONY | W.P. COLLOPY | W.P. COLLOPY | W.P. COLLOPY |
| †R.D. GRAY | R.D. GRAY | R.Y. CRICHTON | R.Y. CRICHTON |
| *J.K.S. THOMPSON | *J.K.S. THOMPSON | *J.K.S. THOMPSON | *J.K.S. THOMPSON |
| Leicester | Lansdowne Road | Lansdowne Road | Stade Colombes |
| LOST 5-23 | LOST 3-13 | WON 5-4 | LOST 8-14 |
| ENG.: 2G IDG 3T | IRE.: IT | IRE.: IG | FR.: IG 3T |
| IRE.: IG | SCOT.: 2G IT | WALES: IDG | IRE.: IG IT |
| 10 Feb. 1923 | 24 Feb. 1923 | 10 Mar. 1923 | 14 Apr. 1923 |

The continued failures of the Irish XV prompted the selectors to chop and change too often to allow young players to gain valuable experience of international rugby. In all, 23 players were used in four matches, but only the game against Wales ended in a victory, Ireland's first win against Wales for eleven years.

James Gardiner of Belfast was first capped against England as a scrum-half, though his twelve other international appearances were as a threequarter. He emigrated to Rhodesia during the 1920s, became a cattle-rancher and played as a centre for Rhodesia against Maurice Brownlie's 1928 All-Black touring team.

J.D. Clinch, an outstanding personality on and off the field, won the first of his 30 caps against Wales. Clinch was a fast, fiery loose forward who tackled relentlessly and dribbled the ball skilfully. The son of former international A.D. Clinch, J.D. became a doctor and continued to support Irish rugby right up to his death in 1981.

## 1923-24

| v. FRANCE | v. ENGLAND | v. SCOTLAND | v. WALES |
|---|---|---|---|
| *W.E. CRAWFORD | *W.E. CRAWFORD | J.W. STEWART | *W.E. CRAWFORD 2c |
| H.W.V. STEPHENSON | H.W.V. STEPHENSON | H.W.V. STEPHENSON | H.W.V. STEPHENSON 1T |
| G.V. STEPHENSON 1T | G.V. STEPHENSON | G.V. STEPHENSON 1c,2T | G.V. STEPHENSON |
| J.B. GARDINER | J.B. GARDINER | J.B. GARDINER | J.B. GARDINER |
| †A.P. ATKINS 1T | A.C. DOUGLAS 1T | A.C. DOUGLAS | †T.R. HEWITT 1T |
| W.H. HALL | J.R. WHEELER | W.H. HALL | †F.S. HEWITT 1T |
| †J.C. McDOWELL | J.A.B. CLARKE | J.A.B. CLARKE | J.A.B. CLARKE |
| †J. McVICKER | J. McVICKER | J. McVICKER | J. McVICKER |
| T.A. McCLELLAND | T.A. McCLELLAND | T.A. McCLELLAND | T.A. McCLELLAND |
| R. COLLOPY | R. COLLOPY | R. COLLOPY | R. COLLOPY |
| C.F.G.T. HALLARAN | C.F.G.T. HALLARAN | C.F.G.T. HALLARAN | C.F.G.T. HALLARAN |
| †W.R.F. COLLIS | †I.M.B. STUART | I.M.B. STUART | W.R.F. COLLIS |
| W.P. COLLOPY | W.P. COLLOPY | *W.P. COLLOPY | W.P. COLLOPY |
| R.Y. CRICHTON | R.Y. CRICHTON | R.Y. CRICHTON | R.Y. CRICHTON |
| J.D. CLINCH | J.D. CLINCH | J.D. CLINCH | J.D. CLINCH |
| Lansdowne Road | Ravenhill | Inverleith | Cardiff Arms Park |
| WON 6-0 | LOST 3-14 | LOST 8-13 | WON 13-10 |
| IRE.: 2T | IRE.: IT | SCOT.: 2G IT | WALES: IDG 2T |
| FR.: NIL | ENG.: IG 3T | IRE.: IG IT | IRE.: 2G IT |
| 26 Jan. 1924 | 9 Feb. 1924 | 23 Feb. 1924 | 8 Mar. 1924 |

Ireland enjoyed their best season since 1914, gaining wins over France and Wales. In Dublin tries by George Stephenson and dental student Alfred Atkins secured victory over France. Atkins was later suspended by the IRFU for taking part (without payment) in a Rugby League match for Huddersfield. Though an amateur, he was never reinstated.

Tries by the Hewitt brothers – the first time brothers had scored tries for Ireland in an international match – set up the win against Wales. Frank Hewitt, who was only 17 years and 5 months old at the time of the match, became the youngest player ever to win a cap for Ireland, and uniquely there were three sets of brothers in the Irish side. The Stephensons lined up alongside the Hewitts in the backs, while Dick Collopy (who later turned professional and played Rugby League for Huddersfield) and Billy Collopy were in the front line of the pack.

To complete the extensive family ties of that Irish XV, which was the first to win at Cardiff since 1899, Jim McVicker had two brothers who were capped by Ireland, and W.R.F. Collis was the son of the 1884 cap, W.S. Collis.

## 1924-25

| v. NZ | v. FRANCE | v. ENGLAND | v. SCOTLAND | v. WALES |
|---|---|---|---|---|
| W.E. Crawford | *W.E. Crawford 1PG | *W.E. Crawford | *W.E. Crawford 1PG,1C | *W.E. Crawford |
| | | | | |
| H.W.V. Stephenson | H.W.V. Stephenson | H.W.V. Stephenson 1T | H.W.V. Stephenson 1T | H.W.V. Stephenson 1T |
| *G.V. Stephenson | G.V. Stephenson 1T | J.B. Gardiner | G.V. Stephenson | †T.J. Millin 1T |
| J.B. Gardiner | J.B. Gardiner 1T | T.R. Hewitt 1T | J.B. Gardiner | J.B. Gardiner |
| T.R. Hewitt | T.R. Hewitt | G.V. Stephenson | T.R. Hewitt | G.V. Stephenson 1PG,2C,1T |
| | | | | |
| F.S. Hewitt | F.S. Hewitt | F.S. Hewitt | F.S. Hewitt | †E.O'D. Davy |
| J.C. McDowell | †M. Sugden | M. Sugden | M. Sugden | M. Sugden |
| | | | | |
| J. McVicker | J. McVicker | J. McVicker | J. McVicker | J. McVicker |
| T.A. McClelland | M.J. Bradley | D.M. Cunningham | M.J. Bradley | M.J. Bradley |
| R. Collopy | R. Collopy | R. Collopy | R. Collopy | R. Collopy |
| †A.W. Spain | C.F.G.T. Hallaran | R.Y. Crichton | R.Y. Crichton | †S.J. Cagney |
| W.R.F. Collis | W.R.F. Collis | W.R.F. Collis | W.R.F. Collis | †R.S. Flood |
| †T.N. Brand | D.M. Cunningham | †W.F. Browne | W.F. Browne | W.F. Browne 1T |
| R.Y. Crichton | R.D. Gray | †G.R. Beamish | G.R. Beamish | G.R. Beamish |
| J.D. Clinch | J.D. Clinch | J.D. Clinch | J.D. Clinch | D.M. Cunningham |
| | | | | |
| Lansdowne Road | Stade Colombes | Twickenham | Lansdowne Road | Ravenhill |
| LOST 0-6 | WON 9-3 | DRAWN 6-6 | LOST 8-14 | WON 19-3 |
| | | | | |
| IRE.: NIL | FR.: 1T | ENG.: 2T | IRE.: 1G 1PG | IRE.: 2G 1PG 2T |
| NZ: 1PG 1T | IRE.: 1PG 2T | IRE.: 2T | SCOT.: 2G 1DG | WALES: 1T |
| | | | | |
| 1 Nov. 1924 | 1 Jan. 1925 | 14 Feb. 1925 | 28 Feb. 1925 | 14 Mar. 1925 |

Ireland gave the invincible All Blacks a hard game in torrential rain. The Irish pack was strong and more than held the big New Zealanders, and there was no score at half time. In the second half, however, the All Blacks did go ahead after Harry Stephenson was caught near his own goal, and minutes later a penalty stretched the visitors' lead to six points.

Ireland's promise was maintained in a good win over France and a creditable draw at Twickenham, in which George Stephenson was selected out of position on the wing to enable Tom Hewitt to experiment as a centre. Scotland won in Dublin, but Ireland's best performance of the season was a record win over Wales at Ravenhill, the IRFU's new international ground in Belfast (which had opened in 1924 for the England game).

Two famous backs made their debuts. Mark Sugden, an English-born scrum-half, was a brilliant individualist, and was particularly dangerous breaking on the blindside of the scrum near opponents' try-lines. He played 28 times for Ireland, forming a smooth link with new fly-half Eugene Davy (34 caps) on 19 occasions, a new Irish record for a pair of halves.

## 1925-26

| v. FRANCE | v. ENGLAND | v. SCOTLAND | v. WALES |
|---|---|---|---|
| *W.E. Crawford | *W.E. Crawford | *W.E. Crawford | *W.E. Crawford |
| | | | |
| D.J. Cussen | D.J. Cussen 2T | D.J. Cussen | D.J. Cussen |
| G.V. Stephenson 2T,1PG | G.V. Stephenson 1T,1PG,2C | G.V. Stephenson | G.V. Stephenson 1PG,1C |
| T.R. Hewitt 1C | F.S. Hewitt 1T | T.R. Hewitt | T.R. Hewitt |
| †R.L. Hamilton | T.R. Hewitt | †J.H. Gage 1T | J.H. Gage |
| | | | |
| E.O'D. Davy | E.O'D. Davy | E.O'D. Davy | E.O'D. Davy |
| M. Sugden | M. Sugden | M. Sugden | M. Sugden |
| | | | |
| R.D. Gray | S.J. Cagney | M.J. Bradley | M.J. Bradley |
| M.J. Bradley | M.J. Bradley | A.M. Buchanan | A.M. Buchanan |
| †J.McF. Neill | †A.M. Buchanan | W.F. Browne | W.F. Browne |
| S.J. Cagney | C.F.G.T. Hallaran | S.J. Cagney | S.J. Cagney |
| W.R.F. Collis | J.L. Farrell | J. McVicker | J. McVicker |
| C.F.G.T. Hallaran | J.D. Clinch | J.D. Clinch | J.D. Clinch |
| J. McVicker | J. McVicker | †C.J. Hanrahan | C.J. Hanrahan 1T |
| †J.L. Farrell | †C.T. Payne | J.L. Farrell | J.L. Farrell |
| | | | |
| Belfast | Lansdowne Road | Murrayfield | St. Helen's |
| WON 11-0 | WON 19-15 | WON 3-0 | LOST 8-11 |
| | | | |
| IRE.: 1G 1PG 1T | IRE.: 2G 1PG 2T | SCOT.: NIL | WALES: 1G 2T |
| FR.: NIL | ENG.: 3G | IRE.: 1T | IRE.: 1G 1PG |
| | | | |
| 23 Jan. 1926 | 13 Feb. 1926 | 27 Feb. 1926 | 13 Mar. 1926 |

This was Ireland's finest side of the inter-war years. The team shared the Championship with Scotland, and failed by a whisker to lift the Triple Crown. At Swansea, a last-minute drop at goal by Tom Hewitt curved away from the goal, so Ireland's bid for the mythical crown failed at the last hurdle.

The season began with a comfortable victory over France and an exciting win against England in Dublin, where a capacity crowd saw a match of seven tries. The genius of Sugden, the irrepressible Clinch, and the steady influence of George Stephenson and Ernie Crawford helped Ireland to their first win over England since 1911 in a game played at a blistering pace.

Ireland became the first visitors to win at Murrayfield. A second-half try in the corner by Jack Gage secured victory on a wet, heavy pitch. Gage was a South African by birth and later played for the Sprinkboks in the Test series of 1933 against Australia. He only played four times for Ireland, but was on the winning side on three occasions.

## 1926-27

| v. FRANCE | v. ENGLAND | v. SCOTLAND | v. WALES |
|---|---|---|---|
| *W.E. CRAWFORD | *W.E. CRAWFORD | *W.E. CRAWFORD | *W.E. CRAWFORD |
| D.J. CUSSEN | D.J. CUSSEN | J.B. GANLY 1T | J.B. GANLY 2T |
| G.V. STEPHENSON 1PG,1C | G.V. STEPHENSON 1PG | G.V. STEPHENSON | G.V. STEPHENSON 1PG,2C,2T |
| †J.M. ATKINSON | F.S. HEWITT | F.S. HEWITT | F.S. HEWITT |
| †J.B. GANLY | J.B. GANLY | J.H. GAGE | J.H. GAGE |
| E.O'D. DAVY 1T | E.O'D. DAVY | E.O'D. DAVY | E.O'D. DAVY |
| †P.F. MURRAY | M. SUGDEN | M. SUGDEN | M. SUGDEN |
| M.J. BRADLEY | C.J. HANRAHAN | C.J. HANRAHAN | C.J. HANRAHAN |
| J.L. FARRELL | C.T. PAYNE | C.T. PAYNE | M.J. BRADLEY |
| J. McVICKER | J. McVICKER | J. McVICKER | J. McVICKER |
| C.T. PAYNE | J.L. FARRELL | J.L. FARRELL | J.L. FARRELL |
| S.J. CAGNEY | †H. McVICKER 1T | H. McVICKER | H. McVICKER |
| J.D. CLINCH | †T.O. PIKE | T.O. PIKE 1T | T.O. PIKE |
| †N.G. ROSS | N.G. ROSS | A.M. BUCHANAN | A.M. BUCHANAN |
| W.F. BROWNE | W.F. BROWNE | W.F. BROWNE | W.F. BROWNE |
| Stade Colombes | Twickenham | Lansdowne Road | Lansdowne Road |
| WON 8-3 | LOST 6-8 | WON 6-0 | WON 19-9 |
| FR.: 1T | ENG.: 1G 1T | IRE.: 2T | IRE.: 2G 1PG 2T |
| IRE.: 1G 1PG | IRE.: 1PG 1T | SCOT.: NIL | WALES: 1G 1DG |
| 1 Jan. 1927 | 12 Feb. 1927 | 26 Feb. 1927 | 12 Mar. 1927 |

For the second year running, Ireland shared the Championship with Scotland. The backs were secure in defence, confident in attack; and the forwards, though light by Irish standards, possessed great stamina and pace. W.F. Browne led the pack with style. His vitality and impetus made him the outstanding forward of the season, and his display against Wales, when the Welsh halves were completely stifled by his wing-forward play, was the key to Ireland's big win. An army officer and one of the most popular players of his generation, "Horsey" Browne only played eleven times for Ireland before his death, aged 28, in 1931.

The match against Scotland marked the opening of the new East Stand at Lansdowne Road. But the dreadful weather conditions reduced the spectators and players to misery. The teams were covered in mud and became indistinguishable, and several of the players and officials suffered extreme discomfort.

James Ganly, a cattle salesman who also played cricket and tennis for Ireland, had a successful baptism on the Irish side, scoring three tries during the season. Equally at home in the centre or on the wing, this remarkable sportsman scored seven tries and one penalty goal in his twelve Irish matches.

## 1927-28

| v. NSW | v. FRANCE | v. ENGLAND | v. SCOTLAND | v. WALES |
|---|---|---|---|---|
| A.C. DOUGLAS | J.W. STEWART | J.W. STEWART | J.W. STEWART | J.W. STEWART |
| J.B. GANLY 1PG | J.B. GANLY 2T | H.W.V. STEPHENSON | †R.M. BYERS | R.M. BYERS |
| J.M. ATKINSON | †R.V.M. ODBERT | J.B. GANLY | J.B. GANLY 1T | J.B. GANLY 1T |
| *G.V. STEPHENSON | *G.V. STEPHENSON | *G.V. STEPHENSON | *G.V. STEPHENSON 1T,2C | *G.V. STEPHENSON 2C |
| H.W.V. STEPHENSON | †J.E. ARIGHO 2T | J.E. ARIGHO 1T | A.C. DOUGLAS | J.E. ARIGHO 2T |
| E.O'D. DAVY | E.O'D. DAVY | E.O'D. DAVY | E.O'D. DAVY 1T | E.O'D. DAVY |
| M. SUGDEN | M. SUGDEN | M. SUGDEN 1T | M. SUGDEN | M. SUGDEN |
| C.J. HANRAHAN | C.J. HANRAHAN | C.J. HANRAHAN | C.J. HANRAHAN | J. McVICKER |
| J.L. FARRELL | J.L. FARRELL | C.T. PAYNE | C.T. PAYNE | C.T. PAYNE |
| J. McVICKER | T.O. PIKE | T.O. PIKE | T.O. PIKE | T.O. PIKE |
| C.T. PAYNE | C.T. PAYNE | J.L. FARRELL | J.L. FARRELL | J.L. FARRELL |
| H. McVICKER | H. McVICKER | S.J. CAGNEY | S.J. CAGNEY | S.J. CAGNEY |
| T.O. PIKE | †T. BRAMWELL | W.F. BROWNE | W.F. BROWNE | †J.P. MULLANE |
| A.M. BUCHANAN | G.R. BEAMISH | G.R. BEAMISH | G.R. BEAMISH | G.R. BEAMISH |
| W.F. BROWNE | J.D. CLINCH | J.D. CLINCH | J.D. CLINCH | J.D. CLINCH |
| Lansdowne Road | Belfast | Lansdowne Road | Murrayfield | Cardiff Arms Park |
| LOST 3-5 | WON 12-8 | LOST 6-7 | WON 13-5 | WON 13-10 |
| IRE.: 1PG | IRE.: 4T | IRE.: 2T | SCOT.: 1G | WALES: 2G |
| NSW: 1G | FR.: 1G 1T | ENG.: 1DG 1T | IRE.: 2G 1T | IRE.: 2G 1T |
| 12 Nov. 1927 | 28 Jan. 1928 | 11 Feb. 1928 | 25 Feb. 1928 | 10 Mar. 1928 |

For the third year in succession Ireland won three of their four matches in the Championship. Indeed, had current scoring values applied in 1928 the Irish should have won the Grand Slam, for their two tries would outscore a drop-goal and try nowadays. But a defeat by 6-7 in Dublin left the Irish as runners-up to their conquerers, the English.

Jack Arigho burst on the scene scoring two tries against France, and ended the season with five tries from three games to establish an Irish record. He was a winger of genuine pace who also played courageously in defence. He tackled well, kicked adroitly on the run, and possessed remarkable speed off the mark.

George Beamish returned to gain a regular place this season. A powerful scrummager with a magnificent physique, altogether Beamish played 25 times for Ireland and instilled his forwards with a restraint which permitted them to play a constructive, disciplined type of game, hitherto unknown to Irish packs. Later he captained the side to a share in the Championship in 1932. He was also the skipper of the East Midlands XV which was the only side to defeat the Springboks touring side of 1931-2.

## 1928-29

| v. FRANCE | v. ENGLAND | v. SCOTLAND | v. WALES |
|---|---|---|---|
| J.W. STEWART | J.W. STEWART | J.W. STEWART | J.W. STEWART |
| | | | |
| J.B. GANLY | R.M. BYERS | R.M. BYERS | R.M. BYERS |
| *G.V. STEPHENSON 1T | *G.V. STEPHENSON | J.B. GANLY | *G.V. STEPHENSON |
| P.F. MURRAY | P.F. MURRAY | P.F. MURRAY | †M.P. CROWE |
| J.E. ARIGHO | J.E. ARIGHO | J.E. ARIGHO 1T | J.E. ARIGHO |
| | | | |
| E.O'D. DAVY 1T | E.O'D. DAVY 1T | *E. O'D. DAVY 1DG | E.O'D. DAVY 1T |
| M. SUGDEN | M. SUGDEN 1T | M. SUGDEN | M. SUGDEN |
| | | | |
| C.J. HANRAHAN | C.J. HANRAHAN | C.J. HANRAHAN | J.L. FARRELL |
| J.P. MULLANE | †H.C. BROWNE | H.C. BROWNE | C.T. PAYNE |
| C.T. PAYNE | S.J. CAGNEY | †J.S. SYNGE | H.C. BROWNE 1C |
| J.L. FARRELL | J.L. FARRELL | J.L. FARRELL | C.J. HANRAHAN |
| †M.J. DUNNE | M.J. DUNNE | M.J. DUNNE | †M. DEERING |
| J.D. CLINCH | J.D. CLINCH | J.D. CLINCH | J.D. CLINCH |
| G.R. BEAMISH | G.R. BEAMISH | G.R. BEAMISH | G.R. BEAMISH |
| S.J. CAGNEY | C.T. PAYNE | S.J. CAGNEY | S.J. CAGNEY |
| Stade Colombes | Twickenham | Lansdowne Road | Belfast |
| WON 6-0 | WON 6-5 | LOST 7-16 | DRAWN 5-5 |
| FR.: NIL | ENG.: 1G | IRE.: 1DG 1T | IRE.: 1G |
| IRE.: 2T | IRE.: 2T | SCOT.: 2G 2T | WALES: 1G |
| 31 Dec. 1928 | 9 Feb. 1929 | 23 Feb. 1929 | 9 Mar. 1929 |

Highlight of the season was Ireland's first win at Twickenham. The side had its limitations, but deserved victory by a narrow margin in an exciting game. Storming play by the Irish forwards forced England onto the defensive at the start of the match, and Davy gathered a loose ball near the English line to open the scoring after three minutes. In the second half Sugden scored the second and decisive try from a scrum. He opted for a blindside dash, beat the defence with a dummy, and scored in the corner.

George Stephenson suffered a rib injury at Twickenham and was ruled out of the Scottish match, his first absence from the international side since his debut in 1920. Eugene Davy took over as captain in Dublin, but without Stephenson's skill and experience in midfield, the Irish back play was unusually diffident and Scotland gained a sound victory.

Morgan Crowe, a dashing centre who won 13 caps, made his debut against Wales. He became a doctor and saw both his brother (Phil in 1935) and son (Jim in 1974) capped for Ireland. Mark Deering, the Wicklow forward and farmer who played against Wales, was another with extensive family rugby connections: his brother Seamus was capped in 1935, and his nephew in 1974.

## 1929-30

| v. FRANCE | v. ENGLAND | v. SCOTLAND | v. WALES |
|---|---|---|---|
| †E.W.F. DE VERE HUNT | †F.W. WILLIAMSON | F.W. WILLIAMSON | F.W. WILLIAMSON |
| | | | |
| J.B. GANLY | *G.V. STEPHENSON | *G.V. STEPHENSON | *G.V. STEPHENSON |
| *G.V. STEPHENSON | E.O'D. DAVY | E.O'D. DAVY 3T | E.O'D. DAVY 1DG |
| P.F. MURRAY | M.P. CROWE | M.P. CROWE 1T | M.P. CROWE |
| J.E. ARIGHO | J.E. ARIGHO | J.E. ARIGHO | J.E. ARIGHO |
| | | | |
| E.O.'D. DAVY | P.F. MURRAY 1DG | P.F. MURRAY 1C | P.F. MURRAY 1PG |
| M. SUGDEN | M. SUGDEN | M. SUGDEN | M. SUGDEN |
| | | | |
| C.J. HANRAHAN | C.J. HANRAHAN | C.J. HANRAHAN | C.J. HANRAHAN |
| M.J. DUNNE | M.J. DUNNE | M.J. DUNNE | M.J. DUNNE |
| C.T. PAYNE | †H.O'H. O'NEILL | H.O'H. O'NEILL | H.O'H. O'NEILL |
| †C. CARROLL | C.T. PAYNE | C.T. PAYNE | C.T. PAYNE |
| J.L. FARRELL | J.L. FARRELL | J.L. FARRELL | J.L. FARRELL |
| J. McVICKER | †N.F. MURPHY | †T.C. CASEY | N.F. MURPHY |
| G.R. BEAMISH | †W.J. McCORMICK | G.R. BEAMISH | G.R. BEAMISH |
| J.D. CLINCH | J.D. CLINCH | J.D. CLINCH | J.D. CLINCH |
| Ravenhill | Lansdowne Road | Murrayfield | St. Helen's |
| LOST 0-5 | WON 4-3 | WON 14-11 | LOST 7-12 |
| IRE.: NIL | IRE.: 1DG | SCOT.: 1G 2T | WALES: 1PG 3T |
| FR.: 1G | ENG.: 1T | IRE.: 1G 3T | IRE.: 1DG 1PG |
| 25 Jan. 1930 | 8 Feb. 1930 | 22 Feb. 1930 | 8 Mar. 1930 |

George Stephenson played the last of his 42 internationals against Wales, and had captained the side on 13 occasions. He settled in England, practising as a psychiatrist in Hertfordshire.

Stephenson's team were joint runners-up in the Championship, beating both England (by a drop-goal) and Scotland, but losing at Ravenhill to France. They missed the Triple Crown in Swansea, where a powerful Irish pack was subdued by a livelier Welsh unit. In the match at Murrayfield, Eugene Davy equalled the record for most tries by an Irish player in an international. He became the first Irishman since J.P. Quinn (in 1913) to score three tries in a match.

## 1930-31

| v. FRANCE | v. ENGLAND | v. SCOTLAND | v. WALES |
|---|---|---|---|
| †J.T. Egan | J.T. Egan | †J.C. Entrican | †D.P. Morris |
| | | | |
| †E.J. Lightfoot | E.J. Lightfoot | E.J. Lightfoot | E.J. Lightfoot |
| P.F. Murray | E.O'D. Davy | E.O'D. Davy | E.O'D. Davy |
| M.P. Crowe | †L.B. McMahon 1t | M.P. Crowe | M.P. Crowe |
| J.E. Arigho | J.E. Arigho | J.E. Arigho | J.E. Arigho |
| | | | |
| E.O'D. Davy | P.F. Murray 1pg | P.F. Murray 1c | P.F. Murray |
| *M. Sugden | *M. Sugden | *M. Sugden 1t | *M. Sugden |
| | | | |
| C.J. Hanrahan | †V.J. Pike | V.J. Pike 1t | V.J. Pike |
| †H.H.C. Withers | H.H.C. Withers | H.H.C. Withers | H.H.C. Withers |
| J.L. Farrell | J.L. Farrell | J.L. Farrell | J.L. Farrell |
| †J.A.E. Siggins | J.A.E. Siggins | J.A.E. Siggins | J.A.E. Siggins 1t |
| †J. Russell | J. Russell | J. Russell | J. Russell |
| N.F. Murphy | N.F. Murphy | N.F. Murphy | N.F. Murphy |
| G.R. Beamish | G.R. Beamish | G.R. Beamish | G.R. Beamish |
| J.D. Clinch | J.D. Clinch | J.D. Clinch | J.D. Clinch |
| Stade Colombes | Twickenham | Lansdowne Road | Ravenhill |
| LOST 0-3 | WON 6-5 | WON 8-5 | LOST 3-15 |
| Fr.: 1t | Eng.: 1g | Ire.: 1g 1t | Ire.: 1t |
| Ire.: nil | Ire.: 1pg 1t | Scot.: 1g | Wales: 1g 1dg 2t |
| 1 Jan. 1931 | 14 Feb. 1931 | 28 Feb. 1931 | 14 Mar. 1931 |

Ireland fielded a splendid pack with a fine mix of experience and youth. Jack Siggins and Victor Pike, a player from a big Irish rugby family, were new men among the forwards, and both were to serve their country admirably for several seasons. Siggins went on to win 24 consecutive caps in the engine-room of the Irish scrummage, while Pike was an expert front-ranker who played in 13 internationals.

The Lansdowne club provided Ireland's threequarter line for the two matches with Scotland and Wales (and for the game in 1932 against South Africa). No other Irish club has yet given an entire threequarter line for an international.

Once again Wales prevented the Irish from winning the Triple Crown. Ireland were comprehensively beaten in Belfast, but did lose Morgan Crowe through injury. Jack Arigho, who moved into the centre to cover for Crowe, played with such panache that one pundit was inclined to write that he very nearly beat Wales on his own.

## 1931-32

| v. S. AFRICA | v. ENGLAND | v. SCOTLAND | v. WALES |
|---|---|---|---|
| J.T. Egan | D.P. Morris | †E.C. Ridgeway | E.C. Ridgeway |
| | | | |
| E.J. Lightfoot | E.J. Lightfoot | E.J. Lightfoot 2t | E.J. Lightfoot 1t |
| E.O'D. Davy | P.F. Murray 1pg, 1c | M.P. Crowe | M.P. Crowe |
| M.P. Crowe | E.W.F. de Vere Hunt | E.W.F. de Vere Hunt 1t | E.W.F. de Vere Hunt |
| J.E. Arigho | †S.L. Waide 1t | S.L. Waide 1t | S.L. Waide 1t |
| | | | |
| L.B. McMahon 1pg | E.O'D. Davy | E.O'D. Davy | E.O'D. Davy |
| P.F. Murray | †M.D. Sheehan | P.F. Murray 4c | P.F. Murray |
| | | | |
| H.H.C. Withers | T.C. Casey | C.J. Hanrahan | C.J. Hanrahan |
| V.J. Pike | V.J. Pike | V.J. Pike | V.J. Pike |
| J.L. Farrell | J.L. Farrell | J.L. Farrell | J.L. Farrell |
| J. Russell | M.J. Dunne | M.J. Dunne | M.J. Dunne |
| J.A.E. Siggins | J.A.E. Siggins | J.A.E. Siggins | J.A.E. Siggins |
| N.F. Murphy | N.F. Murphy | N.F. Murphy | N.F. Murphy |
| *G.R. Beamish | *G.R. Beamish | *G.R. Beamish | *G.R. Beamish |
| J.D. Clinch | †W.McC. Ross | W.McC. Ross | W.McC. Ross 2t |
| Lansdowne Road | Lansdowne Road | Murrayfield | Cardiff Arms Park |
| LOST 3-8 | LOST 8-11 | WON 20-8 | WON 12-10 |
| Ire.: 1pg | Ire.: 1g 1pg | Scot.: 1g 1t | Wales: 1dg 2t |
| SA: 1g 1t | Eng.: 1g 2pg | Ire.: 4g | Ire.: 4t |
| 19 Dec. 1931 | 13 Feb. 1932 | 27 Feb. 1932 | 12 Mar. 1932 |

Ireland's failure to find a competent place-kicker cost them dearly against the Springboks. Altogether the Irish had 13 kicks at goal, but only one effort, by McMahon, resulted in points and was sufficient to give Ireland a slender lead at half-time. In the second half of a match of no particular distinction, the big Springbok forwards dominated their counterparts, and despite relentless Irish spoiling two tries were enough to sink Ireland's hopes.

Jack Arigho and J.D. Clinch ended their careers after the South African game. Shaun Waide, the young Oxford undergraduate, succeeded Arigho, and promptly equalled an Irish record (set by J.E. Moffatt in 1905) by scoring tries in each of his first three internationals – and all before winning a Blue! Bill Ross, a medical student from Belfast, followed the great Clinch at wing-forward, and helped lay the foundations of Ireland's win at Cardiff by scoring two tries. By depriving Wales of the Triple Crown, the Irish were thus entitled to share the International Championship.

Paul Murray, a versatile back who played at centre, fly-half and scrum-half during his 19 appearances for Ireland, kicked a record four conversions at Murrayfield against Scotland. Murray was a doctor who had the pleasure to see his son play for Ireland in 1963, and he was President of the IRFU in 1965-66.

## 1932-33

| v. ENGLAND | v. WALES | v. SCOTLAND |
|---|---|---|
| †R.H. Pratt | R.H. Pratt | R.H. Pratt |
| | | |
| E.J. Lightfoot | E.J. Lightfoot | E.J. Lightfoot |
| L.B. McMahon | M.P. Crowe | M.P. Crowe 1t |
| E.W.F. de Vere Hunt 1t | †R.J. Barnes 1t | †P.B. Coote |
| S.L. Waide | S.L. Waide | †J.J. O'Connor |
| | | |
| *E.O'D. Davy | *E.O'D. Davy 1dg | *E.O'D. Davy |
| P.F. Murray 1pg | P.F. Murray | P.F. Murray 1t |
| | | |
| G.R. Beamish | G.R. Beamish | G.R. Beamish |
| M.J. Dunne | M.J. Dunne | M.J. Dunne |
| H.O'H. O'Neill | H.O'H. O'Neill | H.O'H. O'Neill |
| J.A.E. Siggins | J.A.E. Siggins 1pg | J.A.E. Siggins |
| J. Russell | J. Russell | J. Russell |
| N.F. Murphy | †C.E. Beamish | C.E. Beamish |
| V.J. Pike | V.J. Pike | V.J. Pike |
| W.McC. Ross | W.McC. Ross | W.McC. Ross |
| Twickenham | Ravenhill | Lansdowne Road |
| LOST 6-17 | WON 10-5 | LOST 6-8 |
| Eng.: 1G 4T | Ire.: 1DG 1PG 1T | Ire.: 2T |
| Ire.: 1PG 1T | Wales: 1G | Scot.: 2DG |
| 11 Feb. 1933 | 11 Mar. 1933 | 1 Apr. 1933 |

Ireland scored most points of the four competing nations in the 1933 Championship, but also conceded most. At Twickenham the forwards kept up a rumbustious assault which threatened to sweep aside the English pack in the first twenty minutes, but the visitors began to fade, and the final result was a total rout of the Irish, fore and aft. Noel Murphy, the diminutive flanker from Cork, was dropped for the next match after winning 11 caps. He became President of the IRFU in 1960-61, when his son Noel junior, also a flanker, was a regular member of the Irish side.

Wales were defeated at Ravenhill and in the delayed match with Scotland (which had been postponed from February because of the snow), the Irish pack lasted the pace much better than at Twickenham. The Irish centres pinned down their opponents with some stern tackling, Davy kicked cleverly, and Crowe and Murray scored two good tries. Alas, in 1933 two drop-goals were valued more than two tries, and so Ireland had to surrender a share in the Championship to the all-conquering Scots.

Charles Beamish, who made his debut against Wales, was a younger brother of George Beamish. He gave splendid service during a dozen internationals up to 1938, and had a distinguished war record with the RAF, winning the DFC in 1940.

## 1933-34

| v. ENGLAND | v. SCOTLAND | v. WALES |
|---|---|---|
| R.H. Pratt | R.H. Pratt | †D.J. Langan |
| | | |
| J.J. O'Connor | †D.J. Lane | D.J. Lane |
| M.P. Crowe | †N.H. Lambert | N.H. Lambert |
| †J.V. Reardon | J.V. Reardon | †A.H. Bailey |
| L.B. McMahon | J.J. O'Connor 1t | J.J. O'Connor |
| | | |
| E.O'D. Davy | †J.L. Reid | J.L. Reid |
| †G.J. Morgan 1t | G.J. Morgan | G.J. Morgan |
| | | |
| †S. Walker | S. Walker | †N.F. McGrath |
| V.J. Pike | V.J. Pike | V.J. Pike |
| †M.E. Bardon | C.E. Beamish | †J. Megaw |
| J. Russell | J. Russell 2t | J. Russell |
| *J.A.E. Siggins | *J.A.E. Siggins | *J.A.E. Siggins |
| †C.R.A. Graves | C.R.A. Graves | C.R.A. Graves |
| M.J. Dunne | M.J. Dunne | M.J. Dunne |
| W.McC. Ross | W.McC. Ross | C.E. Beamish |
| Lansdowne Road | Murrayfield | St. Helen's |
| LOST 3-13 | LOST 9-16 | LOST 0-13 |
| Ire.: 1T | Scot.: 2G 1PG 1T | Wales: 2G 1T |
| Eng.: 2G 1T | Ire.: 3T | Ire.: NIL |
| 10 Feb. 1934 | 24 Feb. 1934 | 10 Mar. 1934 |

This was Ireland's least successful season since 1920. Jack Siggins' men were heavily beaten in each match, though, as the *Rugby Football Annual* noted, "The pack as a whole were mastered only once, and that in the scrummage, by the solid, competent English eight." Nevertheless, the indecision of the selectors did leave the midfield with grave weaknesses.

At Swansea the side played well for seven-eighths of the match, but when Langan (who later became President of the Texaco Oil Company) broke his collarbone in the closing stages, the Welsh ran in three tries in the last five minutes.

George Morgan, an outstanding all-round scrum-half, scored a try on his debut against England, played in every match up to the outbreak of the war, and accompanied the British and Irish Lions on the 1938 tour to South Africa. It is a remarkable fact that from 1925 to 1939 Ireland called on just four men to play at scrum-half. One of these, Danaher Sheehan, appeared once only.

## 1934-35

| v. ENGLAND | v. SCOTLAND | v. WALES |
|---|---|---|
| D.P. Morris | D.P. Morris | D.P. Morris |
| | | |
| D.J. Lane | D.J. Lane | †J.I. Doyle 1t |
| †P.M. Crowe | A.H. Bailey 1t | A.H. Bailey 1pg |
| E.C. Ridgeway | E.C. Ridgeway 1t | E.C. Ridgeway |
| J.J. O'Connor 1t | J.J. O'Connor 1t | J.J. O'Connor |
| | | |
| A.H. Bailey | †V.A. Hewitt | V.A. Hewitt |
| G.J. Morgan | G.J. Morgan | G.J. Morgan |
| | | |
| C.E. Beamish | C.E. Beamish | C.E. Beamish |
| C.R.A. Graves | C.R.A. Graves | C.R.A. Graves |
| S. Walker | S. Walker | S. Walker |
| J. Russell | J. Russell | J. Russell |
| †S.J. Deering | S.J. Deering | S.J. Deering |
| †H.J.M. Sayers | H.J.M. Sayers | H.J.M. Sayers |
| *J.A.E. Siggins | *J.A.E. Siggins | *J.A.E. Siggins 1pg |
| †P.J. Lawlor | P.J. Lawlor 1t | P.J. Lawlor |
| Twickenham | Lansdowne Road | Ravenhill |
| LOST 3-14 | WON 12-5 | WON 9-3 |
| Eng.: 1g 3pg | Ire.: 4t | Ire.: 2pg 1t |
| Ire.: 1t | Scot.: 1g | Wales: 1pg |
| 9 Feb. 1935 | 23 Feb. 1935 | 9 Mar. 1935 |

Ireland regained the International Championship as outright winners for the first time since 1899. The selectors' faith in retaining Siggins as captain paid off, for despite defeat in the opening match of the season at Twickenham, the side underwent few changes and improved as the season progressed. The match at Twickenham was a game of penalties, and Ireland were unlucky to find their captain in poor form with his boots. Not so the England full-back, however: who had four successful kicks at goal.

Victor Hewitt, member of the famous Belfast rugby family, entered the side for the game with Scotland. He made an excellent impression on his debut, forming an efficient link between forwards and backs.

At Ravenhill, against Wales in the Championship decider, Ireland were unfortunate to lose O'Connor, an engineering student at UC Cork, after five minutes. Playing with 14 men, the Irish had to thank the magnificent superiority of their forwards for a well-deserved victory. Aidan Bailey, described as the greatest defensive centre in British rugby, tackled his opposite number out of the game and kicked one of the Irish penalty goals. A law student at UC Dublin, Bailey had earned his cap as a teenager the previous season. He went on to gain 13 caps altogether.

## 1935-36

| v. NZ | v. ENGLAND | v. SCOTLAND | v. WALES |
|---|---|---|---|
| D.P. Morris | G.L. Malcolmson | G.L. Malcolmson | G.L. Malcolmson |
| | | | |
| †C.V. Boyle | C.V. Boyle 1t | C.V. Boyle | C.V. Boyle |
| A.H. Bailey 1pg | L.B. McMahon | L.B. McMahon 1t | A.H. Bailey |
| †G.L. Malcolmson | A.H. Bailey 1t | A.H. Bailey | L.B. McMahon |
| J.J. O'Connor | †F.G. Moran | J.J. O'Connor | J.J. O'Connor |
| | | | |
| V.A. Hewitt | V.A. Hewitt | V.A. Hewitt 1dg | V.A. Hewitt |
| G.J. Morgan | G.J. Morgan | G.J. Morgan | G.J. Morgan |
| | | | |
| †T.B. Dunn | S. Walker | S. Walker 1t | S. Walker |
| C.R.A. Graves | C.R.A. Graves | C.R.A. Graves | C.R.A. Graves |
| †C. O'N. Wallis | C.E. Beamish | C.E. Beamish | C.E. Beamish |
| S. Walker | J. Russell | J. Russell | J. Russell |
| S.J. Deering | S.J. Deering | S.J. Deering | S.J. Deering |
| C.E. Beamish 1t | †R. Alexander | R. Alexander | R. Alexander |
| *J.A.E. Siggins 1pg | *J.A.E. Siggins | *J.A.E. Siggins | *J.A.E. Siggins |
| W.McC. Ross | H.J.M. Sayers | H.J.M. Sayers | H.J.M. Sayers |
| Lansdowne Road | Lansdowne Road | Murrayfield | Cardiff Arms Park |
| LOST 9-17 | WON 6-3 | WON 10-4 | LOST 0-3 |
| Ire.: 2pg 1t | Ire.: 2t | Scot.: 1dg | Wales: 1pg |
| NZ: 1g 2pg 2t | Eng.: 1t | Ire.: 1dg 2t | Ire.: nil |
| 7 Dec. 1935 | 8 Feb. 1936 | 22 Feb. 1936 | 14 Mar. 1936 |

Ireland gave a good account of themselves in defeat against the All Blacks. Their side possessed strong forwards with Walker, Graves and Siggins outstanding, but found the New Zealand backs superior in attack. However, Ireland fought hard and trailed by only 9-11, with thirty minutes left for play. Eventually the New Zealanders added two further penalties, but though beaten, the Irish were far from disgraced.

Irish back play improved during the season. Bailey showed himself to be an enterprising and thrustful centre, with a useful ability to place penalty goals, and his combination with McMahon made the finest centre-pairing in the Home nations. After a hesitant start in Dublin against England, the Irish came through to win in the second half, Bailey getting the decisive score with a fine run through the centre. Sammy Walker, a tremendous forward who later captained the 1938 Lions to South Africa, and whose lively radio commentaries entertained a generation of listeners, scored the first try in Ireland's easy win against Scotland.

So Ireland, once again, found Wales their last hurdle to a Triple Crown. At Cardiff, before a huge attendance, the Irish pack were guilty of overconfidence and found themselves subdued by a determined Welsh unit. Both sides were pinned down by tight marking, and a penalty goal, kicked by the Welsh full-back, was the only score of the match.

## 1936-37

| v. ENGLAND | v. SCOTLAND | v. WALES |
|---|---|---|
| G.L. MALCOLMSON | G.L. MALCOLMSON | G.L. MALCOLMSON |
| | | |
| F.G. MORAN 2T | F.G. MORAN 1T | F.G. MORAN |
| L.B. MCMAHON | L.B. MCMAHON 1T | L.B. MCMAHON |
| A.H. BAILEY 1C | A.H. BAILEY 1C | A.H. BAILEY 1T |
| C.V. BOYLE | C.V. BOYLE | C.V. BOYLE |
| | | |
| †G.E. CROMEY | G.E. CROMEY | G.E. CROMEY |
| *G.J. MORGAN | *G.J. MORGAN | *G.J. MORGAN |
| | | |
| S. WALKER | S. WALKER | S. WALKER 1C |
| †T.S. CORKEN | T.S. CORKEN | T.S. CORKEN |
| C.R.A. GRAVES | C.R.A. GRAVES | †E. RYAN |
| J. RUSSELL | J. RUSSELL | †C.J. REIDY |
| S.J. DEERING | S.J. DEERING | †R.B. MAYNE |
| R. ALEXANDER | R. ALEXANDER 1T | R. ALEXANDER |
| J.A.E. SIGGINS | J.A.E. SIGGINS | J.A.E. SIGGINS |
| P.J. LAWLOR | P.J. LAWLOR | P.J. LAWLOR |
| | | |
| Twickenham | Lansdowne Road | Ravenhill |
| LOST 8-9 | WON 11-4 | WON 5-3 |
| | | |
| ENG.: 1PG 2T | IRE.: 1G 2T | IRE.: 1G |
| IRE.: 1G 1T | SCOT.: 1DG | WALES: 1PG |
| | | |
| 13 Feb. 1937 | 27 Feb. 1937 | 3 Apr. 1937 |

Penalty goals, or rather their failure to kick them, cost Ireland dearly this season. In an exciting match at Twickenham the Irish were pipped by a point, despite the fact that Fred Moran scored two spectacular tries and Aidan Bailey kicked a conversion – Ireland's first successful conversion for five years and fifteen games. But in the last minute of the Twickenham game, Ireland were awarded a penalty, which they failed to kick. The miss cost them the Triple Crown and Championship, which went to England.

Solid defence, a good pack and speedy threequarters saw Ireland to victory on a sleety day against Scotland. Moran scored another try – he went on to score six tries in his nine internationals – and Bob Alexander, the Belfast policeman, got another in a win by seven points. During the war, Alexander served as a captain in the Royal Inniskilling Fusiliers, but was killed in action in 1943.

The selectors made three changes in the pack for the Welsh match, substituting the experience of Graves, Russell and Deering with the youth of Ryan, Reidy and Blair Mayne. Mayne gained six caps before winning the DSO (with two bars) during World War II. A snowstorm in March had caused the Welsh match to be postponed until April, and Ireland's narrow victory was achieved through a controversial try by Aidan Bailey, converted by Walker.

## 1937-38

| v. ENGLAND | v. SCOTLAND | v. WALES |
|---|---|---|
| P.M. CROWE 1C | †R.G. CRAIG | R.G. CRAIG |
| | | |
| †M.J. DALY 1T | F.G. MORAN 1T | F.G. MORAN 1T |
| A.H. BAILEY 1T | A.H. BAILEY | †H.R. MCKIBBIN 1C |
| L.B. MCMAHON | L.B. MCMAHON | †J.D. TORRENS |
| †V.J. LYTTLE | J.J. O'CONNOR | C.V. BOYLE |
| | | |
| G.E. CROMEY 1T | G.E. CROMEY 1T | G.E. CROMEY |
| *G.J. MORGAN | *G.J. MORGAN 1T | G.J. MORGAN |
| | | |
| E. RYAN | E. RYAN | C.E. BEAMISH |
| C.R.A. GRAVES | C.R.A. GRAVES | C.R.A. GRAVES |
| †D.B. O'LOUGHLIN | †H. KENNEDY | H. KENNEDY |
| S. WALKER | †D. TIERNEY | D. TIERNEY |
| R.B. MAYNE 1T | D.B. O'LOUGHLIN 1T | R.B. MAYNE |
| R. ALEXANDER | R. ALEXANDER | D.B. O'LOUGHLIN |
| †J.W.S. IRWIN | S. WALKER 1C | *S. WALKER |
| J. MEGAW | J.W.S. IRWIN | H.J.M. SAYERS |
| | | |
| Lansdowne Road | Murrayfield | St. Helen's |
| LOST 14-36 | LOST 14-23 | LOST 5-11 |
| | | |
| IRE.: 1G 3T | SCOT.: 2G 1DG 1PG 2T | WALES: 1G 1PG 1T |
| ENG.: 6G 1PG 1T | IRE.: 1G 3T | IRE.: 1G |
| | | |
| 12 Feb. 1938 | 26 Feb. 1938 | 12 Mar. 1938 |

Ireland's backs scored seven tries during the season, their best return since 1932, yet the side failed to win a match. In a series of high-scoring matches, their 28 points against England and Scotland were not good enough to win matches which were full of open and exciting play. The problem with the Irish side was a lack of determined defence, and the seven tries conceded to England in Dublin stands as the record number of tries against Ireland in an International Championship match.

Cromey and Morgan formed a sound partnership at half and played together in nine matches before the war. Cromey was a Belfast student who became a minister, scored tries in the defeats by England and Scotland, and went to South Africa with Morgan as his partner on the 1938 Lions tour.

Harry McKibbin, a law student in Belfast, and Des Torrens (who was later a successful trainer of greyhounds) came in to stiffen the centre of the Irish threequarter line against Wales. Their inclusion was a success and Ireland were ahead of the Welsh until injury forced Cromey to retire, and Torrens was shifted up to fly-half. Wales took advantage of Ireland's misfortune, and with O'Loughlin having to cover a gap on the wing, the depleted Irish pack were unable to stop Wales winning by six points.

## 1938-39

| v. ENGLAND | v. SCOTLAND | v. WALES |
|---|---|---|
| †C.J. Murphy | C.J. Murphy | C.J. Murphy |
| | | |
| F.G. Moran | F.G. Moran 1t | F.G. Moran |
| H.R. McKibbin 1c | H.R. McKibbin 1pg | H.R. McKibbin |
| J.D. Torrens | J.D. Torrens 1t | J.D. Torrens |
| V.J. Lyttle | V.J. Lyttle | C.V. Boyle |
| | | |
| G.E. Cromey | G.E. Cromey | G.E. Cromey |
| *G.J. Morgan | *G.J. Morgan | *G.J. Morgan |
| | | |
| D. Tierney | †T.A. Headon | T.A. Headon |
| †C. Teehan | C. Teehan | C. Teehan |
| †J.G. Ryan | J.G. Ryan | J.G. Ryan |
| D.B. O'Loughlin | D.B. O'Loughlin | D.B. O'Loughlin |
| R.B. Mayne | R.B. Mayne | R.B. Mayne |
| R. Alexander | R. Alexander | R. Alexander |
| J.W.S. Irwin 1t | J.W.S. Irwin | J.W.S. Irwin |
| H.J.M. Sayers | H.J.M. Sayers 1gm | H.J.M. Sayers |
| | | |
| Twickenham | Lansdowne Road | Ravenhill |
| WON 5-0 | WON 12-3 | LOST 0-7 |
| | | |
| Eng.: NIL | Ire.: 1pg 1gm 2t | Ire.: NIL |
| Ire.: 1g | Scot.: 1t | Wales: 1dg 1t |
| | | |
| 11 Feb. 1939 | 25 Feb. 1939 | 11 Mar. 1939 |

The last Championship before World War II ended in an indecisive tie between Ireland, Wales and England. Ireland had supplied a large number of players for the 1938 British tour of South Africa and their selectors were so confident of the team's potential that Sam Walker, the big, strong forward who had led the Lions, was left out of the side. At Twickenham a young pack dominated the Englishmen and won through a try scored by Sinclair Irwin, son of a former Irish international. Harry McKibbin converted.

McKibbin was the first of a large Belfast rugby family to win international honours. His brother was capped as a forward soon after the war, and his two sons played for Ireland as threequarters in the 1970s. Harry toured South Africa with the Lions twice, as a player in 1938 and as assistant manager in 1962, and served the IRFU as President in its Centenary season, 1974-75.

Mike Sayers, with Ireland's last goal from a mark in an international, helped the side to victory against Scotland. Tries by Moran and Torrens and a penalty by McKibbin completed a comfortable victory, but Wales deprived Ireland of the Triple Crown by winning the last international to be staged before the outbreak of war.

## 1946-47

| v. FRANCE | v. ENGLAND | v. SCOTLAND | v. WALES |
|---|---|---|---|
| *C.J. Murphy | *C.J. Murphy | †J.A.D. Higgins | J.A.D. Higgins |
| | | | |
| †B.T. Quinn | †B.R. O'Hanlon 2t | B.R. O'Hanlon | B.R. O'Hanlon |
| †K.N. Quinn | †J.D.E. Monteith | *J.D.E. Monteith | *J.D.E. Monteith |
| †J. Harper | J. Harper | J. Harper | †M.F. Lane |
| †B. Mullan 1pg,1c | B. Mullan 2c,1pg,2t | B. Mullan 1t | B. Mullan |
| | | | |
| †J.W. Kyle | J.W. Kyle | J.W. Kyle | J.W. Kyle |
| †R. Carroll | †E. Strathdee | E. Strathdee | E. Strathdee |
| | | | |
| †M.R. Neely | M.R. Neely | M.R. Neely | M.R. Neely |
| †K.D. Mullen | K.D. Mullen | K.D. Mullen | K.D. Mullen |
| †J.C. Daly | J.C. Daly | J.C. Daly | J.C. Daly |
| †C.P. Callan | C.P. Callan | C.P. Callan | C.P. Callan |
| †E. Keeffe | E. Keeffe | E. Keeffe | E. Keeffe |
| †J.W. McKay 1t | J.W. McKay 1t | J.W. McKay | J.W. McKay |
| †R.D. Agar | R.D. Agar | R.D. Agar | R.D. Agar |
| †D.J. Hingerty | D.J. Hingerty | D.J. Hingerty | D.J. Hingerty |
| | | | |
| Lansdowne Road | Lansdowne Road | Murrayfield | St. Helen's |
| LOST 8-12 | WON 22-0 | WON 3-0 | LOST 0-6 |
| | | | |
| Ire.: 1g 1pg | Ire.: 2g 1pg 3t | Scot.: NIL | Wales: 1pg 1t |
| Fr.: 4t | Eng.: NIL | Ire.: 1t | Ire.: NIL |
| | | | |
| 25 Jan. 1947 | 8 Feb. 1947 | 22 Feb. 1947 | 29 Mar. 1947 |

During the war an Irish XV played five matches against British Army sides, winning one. Then, in the Victory series of 1945-6, matches were played against England, Scotland, Wales and France, Ireland losing all four. When full internationals restarted in 1947, only Con Murphy, a Dublin accountant, at full-back, had previously won a full cap. He was also captain of a side which opened the season with two home matches, each played in windy conditions.

The French were fit enough and strong enough to stage a comeback after trailing by five points, having faced the wind. Admittedly Mullen, the Irish hooker, was injured during the second half, but the French deserved their victory and scored four tries. Against England, however, the Irish success derived from the superiority of its light forwards and the opportunism of their alert backs, who scored four tries. It was the biggest victory ever gained by Ireland over England.

Spectators armed with shovels had cleared Murrayfield of its snow and straw covering during the morning of the Scotland-Ireland match. The only score of the game, a try by Mullan from a blindside break by Strathdee, set Ireland up for a Triple Crown tie with Wales. But, as so often in the past, Wales deprived the Irish of glory.

## 1947-48

| v. AUSTRALIA | v. FRANCE | v. ENGLAND | v. SCOTLAND | v. WALES |
|---|---|---|---|---|
| J.A.D. Higgins | J.A.D. Higgins | †J.A. Mattsson | J.A.D. Higgins | J.A.D. Higgins |
| †W.D. McKee | B.R. O'Hanlon | B.R. O'Hanlon | B.R. O'Hanlon | B.R. O'Hanlon |
| K.N. Quinn 1PG | W.D. McKee | W.D. McKee 1T | W.D. McKee | W.D. McKee |
| †P.J. Reid | P.J. Reid 1T | P.J. Reid | †M. O'Flanagan | P.J. Reid |
| †K.P. O'Flanagan | B. Mullan 2C,1T | B. Mullan 1C | B. Mullan 1T | B. Mullan 1T |
| J.W. Kyle | J.W. Kyle | J.W. Kyle 1T | J.W. Kyle 1T | J.W. Kyle |
| *E. Strathdee | *E. Strathdee | †H. de Lacy | H. de Lacy | E. Strathdee |
| †J.C. Corcoran | J.C. Corcoran | J.C. Daly | J.C. Daly | J.C. Daly 1T |
| K.D. Mullen | K.D. Mullen | *K.D. Mullen | *K.D. Mullen | *K.D. Mullen |
| †A.A. McConnell | A.A. McConnell | A.A. McConnell | A.A. McConnell | A.A. McConnell |
| †R.W. Wilkinson | C.P. Callan | C.P. Callan | C.P. Callan | C.P. Callan |
| †J.E. Nelson | E. Keeffe | J.E. Nelson | J.E. Nelson | J.E. Nelson |
| J.W. McKay | J.W. McKay | J.W. McKay 1T | J.W. McKay | J.W. McKay |
| E. Keeffe | R.D. Agar | †D.J. O'Brien | D.J. O'Brien | D.J. O'Brien |
| †D. McCourt | †J.S. McCarthy 1T | J.S. McCarthy | J.S. McCarthy | J.S. McCarthy |
| Lansdowne Road | Stade Colombes | Twickenham | Lansdowne Road | Ravenhill |
| LOST 3-16 | WON 13-6 | WON 11-10 | WON 6-0 | WON 6-3 |
| IRE.: 1PG | FR.: 2T | ENG.: 2G | IRE.: 2T | IRE.: 2T |
| AUST.: 2G 2T | IRE.: 2G 1T | IRE.: 1G 2T | SCOT.: NIL | WALES: 1T |
| 6 Dec. 1947 | 1 Jan. 1948 | 14 Feb. 1948 | 28 Feb. 1948 | 13 Mar. 1948 |

Ireland won the Triple Crown for the first time since 1899, and the Grand Slam, yet there was little to suggest in their feeble display against the Australians that this should become so successful a season. Five changes and a couple of positional adjustments were made before the opening game of the Championship. Then, in a splendid performance against a useful French XV, Ireland overcame a side which dominated most of the play. At Twickenham, Karl Mullen, a medical student, was appointed captain. Immediately there was an improvement in the Irish tactical approach: the forwards adopted a more scientific attitude to the tight and loose play, and the backs, realising their limitations, played shrewdly in defence but snapped up chances when they were presented. The style became known as "Triple Crown Rugby", and helped Ireland to dominate international rugby until 1952.

Jack Kyle, another medical student, was the guiding genius among the backs. He went on to become the world's most capped player, gaining 46 caps in a career which spanned twelve seasons.

At last, against Wales, that trophy returned to Ireland. Kyle's brilliance and the power of the Irish pack placed Wales under great pressure in the first half, but the scores were level at the interval. Ireland's tactics in the second half were to kick and harry, and hope that the Welsh would make errors. It was from just such an error that Daly, who later joined Huddersfield in the Rugby League, followed up to score the winning try. There were great scenes of jubilation at Ravenhill at no-side.

## 1948-49

| v. FRANCE | v. ENGLAND | v. SCOTLAND | v. WALES |
|---|---|---|---|
| †G.W. Norton 3PG | G.W. Norton 2PG,1C | G.W. Norton 1PG,2C | G.W. Norton 1C |
| M.F. Lane | M.F. Lane | M.F. Lane | M.F. Lane |
| W.D. McKee | W.D. McKee 1T | W.D. McKee | W.D. McKee |
| †T.J. Gavin | T.J. Gavin | †N.J. Henderson | N.J. Henderson |
| B.R. O'Hanlon | B.R. O'Hanlon 1T | B.R. O'Hanlon | B.R. O'Hanlon |
| J.W. Kyle | J.W. Kyle | J.W. Kyle | J.W. Kyle |
| †T.J. Cullen | E. Strathdee | E. Strathdee | E. Strathdee |
| †T. Clifford | T. Clifford | T. Clifford | T. Clifford |
| *K.D. Mullen | *K.D. Mullen | *K.D. Mullen | *K.D. Mullen |
| A.A. McConnell | A.A. McConnell | †J.L. Griffin | J.L. Griffin |
| C.P. Callan | C.P. Callan | R.D. Agar | R.D. Agar |
| J.E. Nelson | J.E. Nelson | J.E. Nelson | J.E. Nelson |
| J.W. McKay | J.W. McKay | J.W. McKay | J.W. McKay |
| D.J. O'Brien | D.J. O'Brien | D.J. O'Brien | D.J. O'Brien |
| J.S. McCarthy | J.S. McCarthy | J.S. McCarthy 2T | J.S. McCarthy 1T |
| Lansdowne Road | Lansdowne Road | Murrayfield | St. Helen's |
| LOST 9-16 | WON 14-5 | WON 13-3 | WON 5-0 |
| IRE.: 3PG | IRE.: 1G 2PG 1T | SCOT.: 1PG | WALES: NIL |
| FR.: 2G 2PG | ENG.: 1G | IRE.: 2G 1PG | IRE.: 1G |
| 29 Jan. 1949 | 12 Feb. 1949 | 26 Feb. 1949 | 12 Mar. 1949 |

Again Ireland made an unpromising start to the season (losing to France this time), but as in the previous year they finished the Championship as winners and added the Triple Crown. Mullen was captain and continued to adopt the principles which had guided Ireland to success in 1948. The paths to victory over England and Scotland proved easier than in the previous year, for in George Norton Ireland had found a place-kicker of unerring accuracy. His 26-point haul for the season exceeded by one point the record established by Dicky Lloyd back in 1913.

Kyle was again the tactical spearhead, ably served by Strathdee at half-back. Later Strathdee was to combine successfully the somewhat unlikely dual professions of Presbyterian minister and sports journalist, and showed the versatility of his character which had been so useful to Irish rugby sides. A useful combination in the back row had much to do with Ireland's success this season as well, the trio of McCarthy, O'Brien and McKay supporting Kyle's attacks brilliantly and defending stoutly.

## 1949-50

| v. FRANCE | v. ENGLAND | v. SCOTLAND | v. WALES |
|---|---|---|---|
| G.W. NORTON | G.W. NORTON | G.W. NORTON 2PG,3C | G.W. NORTON 1PG |
| M.F. LANE | M.F. LANE | M.F. LANE | M.F. LANE |
| W.D. McKEE | W.D. McKEE | †R.J.H. UPRICHARD | R.J.H. UPRICHARD |
| N.J. HENDERSON | †G.C. PHIPPS | J.J. BLAYNEY 1T | G.C. PHIPPS |
| B.R. O'HANLON | †L. CROWE | L. CROWE 1T | L. CROWE |
| J.W. KYLE | J.W. KYLE | J.W. KYLE | J.W. KYLE |
| †J.H. BURGES 1PG | J.H. BURGES | R. CARROLL | R. CARROLL |
| T. CLIFFORD | T. CLIFFORD | T. CLIFFORD | T. CLIFFORD |
| *K.D. MULLEN | *K.D. MULLEN | *K.D. MULLEN | *K.D. MULLEN |
| †D. McKIBBIN | D. McKIBBIN | D. McKIBBIN | D. McKIBBIN |
| J.E. NELSON | J.E. NELSON | J.E. NELSON | J.E. NELSON |
| R.D. AGAR | R.D. AGAR | †J.U. MOLONY | R.D. AGAR |
| J.W. McKAY | J.W. McKAY | J.W. McKAY | J.W. McKAY |
| D.J. O'BRIEN | D.J. O'BRIEN | D.J. O'BRIEN | D.J. O'BRIEN |
| †A.B. CURTIS | A.B. CURTIS | A.B. CURTIS 1T | J.S. McCARTHY |
| Stade Colombes | Twickenham | Lansdowne Road | Ravenhill |
| DRAWN 3-3 | LOST 0-3 | WON 21-0 | LOST 3-6 |
| FR.: 1DG | ENG.: 1T | IRE.: 3G 2PG | IRE.: 1PG |
| IRE.: 1PG | IRE.: NIL | SCOT.: NIL | WALES: 2T |
| 28 Jan. 1950 | 11 Feb. 1950 | 25 Feb. 1950 | 11 Mar. 1950 |

Karl Mullen's side began the season as hot favourites to retain both Championship and Triple Crown. The side against France was built around the successful 1949 team, though McCarthy was forced to withdraw through injury and Kyle had a new and untried partner in Burges. The match in Paris was played in uncomfortable, freezing conditions. Ireland looked most dangerous when their centres were attacking, but lack of support and poor finishing deprived them of tries. In the end a last-minute penalty was sufficient to earn a draw.

Although England and Wales defeated the Irish, there was a brilliant display against the Scots. Mullen's plan was to subdue and tire the heavier Scots in the first half. Once this had been accomplished the Scottish defence cracked under pressure and the floodgates opened in the second half, Ireland registering their biggest winning points margin over Scotland.

Norton played immaculately for Ireland at full-back. His catching and tackling were superb and his place-kicking brought him a further 15 points. He only played eleven internationals, a shoulder injury sustained in the 1951 match against Scotland ending his playing career.

## 1950-51

| v. FRANCE | v. ENGLAND | v. SCOTLAND | v. WALES |
|---|---|---|---|
| G.W. NORTON | G.W. NORTON | G.W. NORTON | †A. McMORROW |
| †C.S. GRIFFIN | C.S. GRIFFIN | W.H.J. MILLAR | W.H.J. MILLAR |
| N.J. HENDERSON 1PG | N.J. HENDERSON | N.J. HENDERSON 1DG | N.J. HENDERSON |
| †R.R. CHAMBERS | R.R. CHAMBERS | R.R. CHAMBERS | R.R. CHAMBERS |
| M.F. LANE | †W.H.J. MILLAR | M.F. LANE | M.F. LANE |
| J.W. KYLE | J.W. KYLE | J.W. KYLE | J.W. KYLE 1T |
| †J.A. O'MEARA | J.A. O'MEARA | J.A. O'MEARA | J.A. O'MEARA |
| T. CLIFFORD 1T | T. CLIFFORD | D. McKIBBIN | D. McKIBBIN |
| *K.D. MULLEN | *K.D. MULLEN | *K.D. MULLEN | *K.D. MULLEN |
| †J.H. SMITH | J.H. SMITH | J.H. SMITH | J.H. SMITH |
| J.E. NELSON 1T | J.E. NELSON | †P.J. LAWLER | J.E. NELSON |
| D. McKIBBIN | D. McKIBBIN 1PG | †J.R. BRADY | J.R. BRADY |
| J.W. McKAY | J.W. McKAY | J.W. McKAY | J.W. McKAY |
| D.J. O'BRIEN | D.J. O'BRIEN | D.J. O'BRIEN 1T | D.J. O'BRIEN |
| J.S. McCARTHY | J.S. McCARTHY | J.S. McCARTHY | J.S. McCARTHY |
| Lansdowne Road | Lansdowne Road | Murrayfield | Cardiff Arms Park |
| WON 9-8 | WON 3-0 | WON 6-5 | DRAWN 3-3 |
| IRE.: 1PG 2T | IRE.: 1PG | SCOT.: 1G | WALES: 1PG |
| FR.: 1G 1T | ENG.: NIL | IRE.: 1DG 1T | IRE.: 1T |
| 27 Jan. 1951 | 10 Feb. 1951 | 24 Feb. 1951 | 10 Mar. 1951 |

The pundits attributed Ireland's success in 1951 to a well-balanced pack, ably led by Mullen; and to the outstanding play in attack and defence of Jack Kyle. Ireland regained the Championship, but a draw at Cardiff in their last game of the season deprived them of the Triple Crown and Grand Slam.

All of the matches were close, though the win over Scotland was Ireland's greatest achievement, for the loss of Norton after only 15 minutes was a handicap with which few sides would have coped. Kyle's play was noteworthy in this match. His tactical kicking was an inspiration to a depleted pack, his covering and tackling saved Ireland's line a couple of times, and his flair in attack paved the way for a blind-side try by O'Brien. Kyle's individual genius was again evident at Cardiff, his elusive running bringing him a superb try.

John O'Meara won the first of his 22 caps against France. A student at UC Cork, he qualified as a solicitor. During his long rugby career he partnered Jack Kyle on 19 occasions to equal the record established by Davy and Sugden between the wars.

## 1951-52

| v. S.AFRICA | v. FRANCE | v. SCOTLAND | v. WALES | v. ENGLAND |
|---|---|---|---|---|
| †J.G.M.W. Murphy 1c | †J.R. Notley 1c | J.G.M.W. Murphy | J.G.M.W. Murphy 1pg | J.G.M.W. Murphy |
| W.D. McKee | G.C. Phipps | W.H.J. Millar | W.H.J. Millar | †M.F. Hillary |
| N.J. Henderson | N.J. Henderson 1t,1pg | N.J. Henderson 1pg,1t | N.J. Henderson | N.J. Henderson |
| †A.W. Browne 1t | R.R. Chambers | J.R. Notley | R.R. Chambers | G.C. Phipps |
| M.F. Lane | M.F. Lane | M.F. Lane 1t | G.C. Phipps | †N. Bailey |
| J.W. Kyle | J.W. Kyle | J.W. Kyle 1t | J.W. Kyle | J.W. Kyle |
| J.A. O'Meara | J.A. O'Meara | J.A. O'Meara | J.A. O'Meara | J.A. O'Meara |
| T. Clifford | T. Clifford | T. Clifford | T. Clifford | †W.A. O'Neill |
| K.D. Mullen | K.D. Mullen | K.D. Mullen | K.D. Mullen | †R. Roe |
| J.H. Smith | J.H. Smith | J.H. Smith | J.H. Smith | J.H. Smith |
| P.J. Lawler | P.J. Lawler | P.J. Lawler | P.J. Lawler | P.J. Lawler |
| †R.H. Thompson | R.H. Thompson | †A.F. O'Leary | A.F. O'Leary | A.F. O'Leary |
| J.W. McKay | J.W. McKay | †M.J. Dargan | M.J. Dargan | †P.J. Kavanagh |
| *D.J. O'Brien | *D.J. O'Brien | *D.J. O'Brien | *D.J. O'Brien | *D.J. O'Brien |
| J.S. McCarthy | J.S. McCarthy 1t | J.S. McCarthy | J.S. McCarthy | J.S. McCarthy |
| Lansdowne Road | Stade Colombes | Lansdowne Road | Lansdowne Road | Twickenham |
| LOST 5-17 | WON 11-8 | WON 12-8 | LOST 3-14 | LOST 0-3 |
| Ire.: 1g | Fr.: 1g 1pg | Ire.: 1pg 3t | Ire.: 1pg | Eng.: 1t |
| SA: 1g 1dg 3t | Ire.: 1g 1pg 1t | Scot.: 1g 1pg | Wales: 1g 1pg 2t | Ire.: nil |
| 8 Dec. 1951 | 26 Jan. 1952 | 23 Feb. 1952 | 8 Mar. 1952 | 29 Mar. 1952 |

Karl Mullen, after leading Ireland a record-equalling 15 times, was succeeded as captain by Des O'Brien, the number eight forward who was playing for Cardiff at the time. O'Brien had been the most improved player in British rugby in 1951, and he packed down now at the rear of the best scrummaging unit in the Home Countries.

Ireland's lack of weight in the forwards was exposed by heavier packs, however, and the brilliance which McKay, McCarthy and O'Brien had previously shown in loose play was of little avail against the Springboks. To a lesser extent against Wales and England at the end of the season, the Irish forwards were again subdued in the loose, though Mullen's successor at hooker, Robin Roe, made a promising debut at Twickenham, revealing the same technical expertise which had been the hallmark of Mullen's play.

Apart from the half-backs, the only other Irish back to play throughout the season was Noel Henderson. He was a strong-running, hard-tackling centre who appeared 40 times for Ireland up to 1959. Henderson scored 57 points during his career, captained Ireland on eleven occasions, and became an executive with an oil company. He was Jack Kyle's brother-in-law.

## 1952-53

| v. FRANCE | v. ENGLAND | v. SCOTLAND | v. WALES |
|---|---|---|---|
| †R.J. Gregg 2c | R.J. Gregg | R.J. Gregg 4c | R.J. Gregg |
| M.F. Lane | M.F. Lane | †S.J. Byrne 3t | S.J. Byrne 1t |
| N.J. Henderson | N.J. Henderson 2pg | N.J. Henderson | N.J. Henderson |
| K.N. Quinn | K.N. Quinn | K.N. Quinn | †A.C. Pedlow |
| †M. Mortell 1t | M. Mortell 1t | M. Mortell 1t | M. Mortell |
| *J.W. Kyle 1t | *J.W. Kyle | *J.W. Kyle | *J.W. Kyle |
| J.A. O'Meara | J.A. O'Meara | J.A. O'Meara | J.A. O'Meara |
| W.A. O'Neill | W.A. O'Neill | W.A. O'Neill | W.A. O'Neill |
| R. Roe | R. Roe | R. Roe | R. Roe |
| †F.E. Anderson | F.E. Anderson | F.E. Anderson | F.E. Anderson |
| P.J. Lawler 1t | †T.E. Reid | T.E. Reid | T.E. Reid |
| J.R. Brady | J.R. Brady | J.R. Brady | J.R. Brady |
| †W.E. Bell | W.E. Bell | W.E. Bell | W.E. Bell |
| †J.R. Kavanagh | J.R. Kavanagh | J.R. Kavanagh 1t | J.R. Kavanagh |
| J.S. McCarthy 1t | J.S. McCarthy | J.S. McCarthy 1t | †G.F. Reidy |
| Ravenhill | Lansdowne Road | Murrayfield | St. Helen's |
| WON 16-3 | DRAWN 9-9 | WON 26-8 | LOST 3-5 |
| Ire.: 2g 2t | Ire.: 2pg 1t | Scot.: 1g 1pg | Wales: 1g |
| Fr.: 1dg | Eng.: 2pg 1t | Ire.: 4g 2t | Ire.: 1t |
| 24 Jan. 1953 | 14 Feb. 1953 | 28 Feb. 1953 | 14 Mar. 1953 |

Ireland fielded a strong side, but a narrow defeat at Swansea prevented them from sharing the Championship with England (with whom they had drawn). The new players showed considerable promise, particularly the four new backs. Mortell equalled the records of Shaun Waide and J.E. Moffatt by scoring tries in each of his first three matches; against Scotland, Gregg equalled Paul Murray's record of four conversions in an international; and in the same match, Seamus Byrne scored three tries on his debut.

Cecil Pedlow, another newcomer, went on to gain 30 Irish caps as a centre and wing in a career which spanned eleven seasons. Pedlow was a versatile sportsman who also played squash for Ireland, was a member of the 1955 Lions to South Africa, and scored 31 points in his rugby internationals. He became a dentist.

Ireland's total of 26 points against Scotland was their highest in a Championship match. One of their tries was scored by Ronnie Kavanagh, a student at UC Dublin who went on to become Ireland's most-capped forward at the time of his retirement. He was a mobile loose forward, won 35 caps, and also played water-polo for Ireland. His brother Patrick was capped in 1952 and 1955.

## 1953-54

| v. NZ | v. FRANCE | v. ENGLAND | v. SCOTLAND | v. WALES |
|---|---|---|---|---|
| J.G.M.W. Murphy | R.J. Gregg | R.J. Gregg | R.J. Gregg | †P.J. Berkery |
| | | | | |
| M. Mortell | M. Mortell | M. Mortell | M. Mortell 2t | M. Mortell |
| N.J. Henderson 1pg | N.J. Henderson | N.J. Henderson | N.J. Henderson | N.J. Henderson 1pg |
| A.C. Pedlow | A.C. Pedlow | A.C. Pedlow | †R.P. Godfrey | R.P. Godfrey |
| †J.T. Gaston | J.T. Gaston | J.T. Gaston | J.T. Gaston | J.T. Gaston 1t |
| | | | | |
| *J.W. Kyle | *J.W. Kyle | †W.J. Hewitt | †S. Kelly | S. Kelly 1pg |
| J.A. O'Meara | J.A. O'Meara | J.A. O'Meara | J.A. O'Meara | †H. McCracken |
| | | | | |
| W.A. O'Neill | F.E. Anderson | F.E. Anderson | F.E. Anderson | F.E. Anderson |
| F.E. Anderson | R. Roe | R. Roe | R. Roe | R. Roe |
| J.H. Smith | J.H. Smith | †B.G.M. Wood | B.G.M. Wood | J.H. Smith |
| P.J. Lawler | T.E. Reid | P.J. Lawler | P.J. Lawler | J.R. Brady |
| R.H. Thompson | R.H. Thompson | R.H. Thompson | R.H. Thompson | R.H. Thompson |
| J.R. Kavanagh | G.F. Reidy | G.F. Reidy | G.F. Reidy | G.F. Reidy |
| T.E. Reid | J.E. Nelson | †J. Murphy-O'Connor 1pg | J.R. Kavanagh | J.R. Kavanagh |
| J.S. McCarthy | J.S. McCarthy | *J.S. McCarthy | *J.S. McCarthy | *J.S. McCarthy |
| | | | | |
| Lansdowne Road | Stade Colombes | Twickenham | Ravenhill | Lansdowne Road |
| LOST 3-14 | LOST 0-8 | LOST 3-14 | WON 6-0 | LOST 9-12 |
| | | | | |
| IRE.: 1PG | FR.: 1G 1T | ENG.: 1G 1PG 2T | IRE.: 2T | IRE.: 2PG 1T |
| NZ: 1G 1DG 1PG 1T | IRE.: NIL | IRE.: 1PG | SCOT.: NIL | WALES: 1DG 3PG |
| | | | | |
| 9 Jan. 1954 | 23 Jan. 1954 | 13 Feb. 1954 | 27 Feb. 1954 | 13 Mar. 1954 |

This was Ireland's least successful season since 1938. Of five matches played, only one game was won, and the loss through injury of Jack Kyle, who had appeared in 32 consecutive internationals since the war, was greatly felt. His substitute at Twickenham was John Hewitt, but Hewitt was unable to back up a good forward effort against the English and he subsequently made way for Kelly, the Lansdowne fly-half.

Ireland's only success of the season was against Scotland in the last international to be staged in Belfast. The introduction of Kelly and Godfrey in midfield added a fresh edge to the Irish backs and Kelly revealed a dangerous turn of pace, carving out several neat openings. Mortell, with tries in each half, was Ireland's scorer in their ninth consecutive win against the Scots.

Gordon Wood, a strong Garryowen prop, entered the Irish side this season. He went on to collect 29 caps in a long, distinguished career, and was a member of the 1959 Lions team which toured Australasia.

## 1954-55

| v. FRANCE | v. ENGLAND | v. SCOTLAND | v. WALES |
|---|---|---|---|
| †W.R. Tector | W.R. Tector | W.R. Tector | P.J. Berkery |
| | | | |
| S.J. Byrne | †R.E. Roche | R.E. Roche | A.C. Pedlow |
| N.J. Henderson 1pg | N.J. Henderson 1pg | N.J. Henderson | N.J. Henderson 1pg |
| †A.J.F. O'Reilly | A.J.F. O'Reilly | A.J.F. O'Reilly | A.J.F. O'Reilly |
| A.C. Pedlow | A.C. Pedlow 1t | A.C. Pedlow | J.T. Gaston |
| | | | |
| J.W. Kyle | J.W. Kyle | S. Kelly 1pg | J.W. Kyle |
| J.A. O'Meara | J.A. O'Meara | †S.J. McDermott | S.J. McDermott |
| | | | |
| F.E. Anderson | F.E. Anderson | F.E. Anderson | F.E. Anderson |
| R. Roe | R. Roe | R. Roe | R. Roe |
| †P.J. O'Donoghue | P.J. O'Donoghue | P.J. O'Donoghue | P.J. O'Donoghue |
| *R.H. Thompson | T.E. Reid | T.E. Reid | *R.H. Thompson |
| †W.J. O'Connell | †M.N. Madden | M.N. Madden | M.N. Madden |
| †M.J. Cunningham | M.J. Cunningham | M.J. Cunningham | M.J. Cunningham |
| J.R. Kavanagh | J.R. Kavanagh | *R.H. Thompson | †G.R.P. Ross |
| J.S. McCarthy | *J.S. McCarthy | †D.A. MacSweeney | P.J. Kavanagh |
| | | | |
| Lansdowne Road | Lansdowne Road | Murrayfield | Cardiff Arms Park |
| LOST 3-5 | DRAWN 6-6 | LOST 3-12 | LOST 3-21 |
| | | | |
| IRE.: 1PG | IRE.: 1PG 1T | SCOT.: 2PG 1DG 1T | WALES: 3G 1PG 1T |
| FR.: 1G | ENG.: 2T | IRE.: 1PG | IRE.: 1PG |
| | | | |
| 22 Jan. 1955 | 12 Feb. 1955 | 26 Feb. 1955 | 12 Mar. 1955 |

A big, strong teenager, recently out of school, entered the Irish side in 1955. He was to become a legend in his own time, respected as an exceptionally swift threequarter and cherished for outstanding wit and extrovert personality. His name was Tony O'Reilly, he went on to score four tries for Ireland in his 29 appearances, and his international career spanned 16 seasons, a world record.

O'Reilly's baptism could not prevent Ireland from finishing with the wooden spoon. A young pack gave a good account of itself against France and there were suggestions of an Irish bid for the Triple Crown. However, uncertainty at half-back and a lack of direction up front offset the early season promise. Kyle and O'Meara were dropped (with disastrous results) for the game against Scotland, and at Cardiff the Irish were routed towards the end of the match.

Robin Thompson, a Belfast graduate food chemist, captained the side and was honoured with the captaincy of the 1955 Lions to South Africa. A fine forward, Thompson played once more for Ireland (in 1956) before joining Warrington in the Rugby League.

## 1955-56

| v. FRANCE | v. ENGLAND | v. SCOTLAND | v. WALES |
|---|---|---|---|
| †J.M. McKelvey | J.M. McKelvey | P.J. Berkery | P.J. Berkery |
| †S.V.J. Quinlan | S.V.J. Quinlan | W.J. Hewitt | S.V.J. Quinlan |
| A.J.F. O'Reilly 1T | A.J.F. O'Reilly | *N.J. Henderson 1T | *N.J. Henderson |
| A.C. Pedlow 1PG,1C | A.C. Pedlow | A.J.F. O'Reilly 1T | A.J.F. O'Reilly |
| J.T. Gaston | J.T. Gaston | A.C. Pedlow 1C | A.C. Pedlow 1PG,1C |
| J.W. Kyle | J.W. Kyle | J.W. Kyle 1T | J.W. Kyle 1DG |
| †A.A. Mulligan | A.A. Mulligan | J.A. O'Meara 1T | J.A. O'Meara |
| †W.B.C. Fagan | W.B.C. Fagan | W.B.C. Fagan | P.J. O'Donoghue |
| R. Roe | R. Roe | R. Roe | R. Roe |
| B.G.M. Wood | B.G.M. Wood | B.G.M. Wood | B.G.M. Wood |
| P.J. Lawler | P.J. Lawler | †B.N. Guerin | R.H. Thompson |
| T.E. Reid | T.E. Reid | †L.M. Lynch | J.R. Brady |
| M.J. Cunningham | †N. Feddis | M.J. Cunningham | M.J. Cunningham 1T |
| †A.G. Kennedy | J.R. Kavanagh | J.R. Kavanagh | †T. McGrath |
| *†J.S. Ritchie | *J.S. Ritchie | †C.T.J. Lydon | J.R. Kavanagh |
| Stade Colombes | Twickenham | Lansdowne Road | Lansdowne Road |
| LOST 8-14 | LOST 0-20 | WON 14-10 | WON 11-3 |
| FR.: 1G 2PG 1T | ENG.: 1G 3PG 2T | IRE.: 1G 3T | IRE.: 1G 1DG 1PG |
| IRE.: 1G 1PG | IRE.: NIL | SCOT.: 2G | WALES: 1PG |
| 28 Jan. 1956 | 11 Feb. 1956 | 25 Feb. 1956 | 10 Mar. 1956 |

Jim Ritchie, a Belfast-born engineer playing for London Irish, was given his first cap and made captain for the match in Paris, becoming the first captain to lead the Irish team on his debut since H.G. Cook in 1884. His presence could not inspire the Irish to victory, however, and after the disaster at Twickenham, Ritchie and seven others were dropped as the selectors made wholesale changes for the match with Scotland.

In the backs, Henderson returned as captain, Kyle was reunited with O'Meara, and Pedlow transferred to the wing. Scotland were beaten in an exciting match and the experiments of the selectors were deemed successful, the backs scoring four tries.

Ireland's revival continued during the Welsh match. Robin Thompson had recovered from injuries sustained on the tour of South Africa and was recalled as pack leader. His splendid leadership had much to do with Ireland's second-half display against the Welsh, who were seeking the Triple Crown. Ireland's forwards completely dominated a tired Welsh pack after the interval, and Kyle revelled in the wealth of good possession supplied by his scrum-half. He dropped a goal to level the scores, Pedlow added a penalty, and Cunningham set the seal on a famous victory with a storming try.

## 1956-57

| v. FRANCE | v. ENGLAND | v. SCOTLAND | v. WALES |
|---|---|---|---|
| P.J. Berkery | P.J. Berkery | P.J. Berkery 1C | P.J. Berkery |
| A.J.F. O'Reilly | A.J.F. O'Reilly | R.E. Roche | R.E. Roche |
| *N.J. Henderson | *N.J. Henderson | A.J.F. O'Reilly | A.J.F. O'Reilly |
| A.C. Pedlow 1C,1PG | A.C. Pedlow | *N.J. Henderson | *N.J. Henderson |
| †N.H. Brophy 1T | N.H. Brophy | A.C. Pedlow | A.C. Pedlow 1C |
| J.W. Kyle 1T | J.W. Kyle | J.W. Kyle | J.W. Kyle |
| A.A. Mulligan | A.A. Mulligan | A.A. Mulligan | A.A. Mulligan |
| P.J. O'Donoghue | P.J. O'Donoghue | †J.I. Brennan | J.I. Brennan |
| R. Roe | R. Roe | R. Roe | R. Roe |
| B.G.M. Wood | B.G.M. Wood | B.G.M. Wood | B.G.M. Wood |
| T.E. Reid | T.E. Reid | T.E. Reid | T.E. Reid |
| J.R. Brady | J.R. Brady | J.R. Brady | J.R. Brady |
| †H.S. O'Connor | H.S. O'Connor | H.S. O'Connor | H.S. O'Connor |
| †P.J.A. O'Sullivan | P.J.A. O'Sullivan | P.J.A. O'Sullivan 1T | P.J.A. O'Sullivan |
| J.R. Kavanagh | J.R. Kavanagh | J.R. Kavanagh | J.R. Kavanagh 1T |
| Lansdowne Road | Lansdowne Road | Murrayfield | Cardiff Arms Park |
| WON 11-6 | LOST 0-6 | WON 5-3 | LOST 5-6 |
| IRE.: 1G 1PG 1T | IRE.: NIL | SCOT.: 1PG | WALES: 2PG |
| FR.: 2PG | ENG.: 1PG 1T | IRE.: 1G | IRE.: 1G |
| 26 Jan. 1957 | 9 Feb. 1957 | 23 Feb. 1957 | 9 Mar. 1957 |

Ireland had as good a set of backs as any side in the 1957 Championship. Mulligan was a mature young footballer of considerable skill, and his adaptability brought out the best in Kyle, who was now a veteran. Nevertheless, Kyle's try against France was one of the best of his long career. The defence of the Irish backs was impeccable, and only one try was conceded during the season.

Unfortunately the Irish forwards were unable to dominate their opponents to any extent, and the possession enjoyed by the Irish backs was limited. Reid played well at the line-out, there was plenty of lively activity in the loose, and the Irish back-row snapped up small opportunities to score tries at Murrayfield and Cardiff.

A kick by Kyle resulted in a try by O'Sullivan against Scotland, and Berkery's conversion won the game. At Cardiff the Irish back-row smothered the Welsh backs out of the game, and from a Welsh mistake Ron Kavanagh scored a try which Pedlow converted to give his side a lead. Ireland were held in the tight, however, and a penalty by the Welsh full-back defeated the visitors.

## 1957-58

| v. AUSTRALIA | v. ENGLAND | v. SCOTLAND | v. WALES | v. FRANCE |
|---|---|---|---|---|
| P.J. BERKERY | P.J. BERKERY | P.J. BERKERY 1PG | J.G.M.W. MURPHY | *N.J. HENDERSON 2PG |
| | | | | |
| A.J.F. O'REILLY | A.J.F. O'REILLY | A.J.F. O'REILLY | S.V.J. QUINLAN | A.J.F. O'REILLY |
| *N.J. HENDERSON 1T | *N.J. HENDERSON | *N.J. HENDERSON 1PG | *N.J. HENDERSON 1PG | †D.C. GLASS |
| †D. HEWITT | D. HEWITT | D. HEWITT | A.J.F. O'REILLY | D. HEWITT |
| A.C. PEDLOW 1PG | A.C. PEDLOW | A.C. PEDLOW 2T | A.C. PEDLOW | A.C. PEDLOW |
| | | | | |
| J.W. KYLE | J.W. KYLE | J.W. KYLE | †M.A.F. ENGLISH | M.A.F. ENGLISH |
| A.A. MULLIGAN | A.A. MULLIGAN | A.A. MULLIGAN | J.A. O'MEARA 1T | A.A. MULLIGAN |
| | | | | |
| P.J. O'DONOGHUE | P.J. O'DONOGHUE | P.J. O'DONOGHUE | P.J. O'DONOGHUE | †S. MILLAR |
| †A.R. DAWSON 1T | A.R. DAWSON | A.R. DAWSON | A.R. DAWSON | A.R. DAWSON |
| B.G.M. WOOD | B.G.M. WOOD | B.G.M. WOOD | B.G.M. WOOD | B.G.M. WOOD |
| †J.B. STEVENSON | J.B. STEVENSON | J.B. STEVENSON | J.B. STEVENSON | J.B. STEVENSON |
| †W.A. MULCAHY | W.A. MULCAHY | W.A. MULCAHY | W.A. MULCAHY | W.A. MULCAHY |
| †J.A. DONALDSON | J.A. DONALDSON | J.A. DONALDSON | J.A. DONALDSON | †E.L. BROWN |
| J.R. KAVANAGH | J.R. KAVANAGH | J.R. KAVANAGH | J.R. KAVANAGH | T. McGRATH |
| †N.A.A. MURPHY | N.A.A. MURPHY | N.A.A. MURPHY | N.A.A. MURPHY | N.A.A. MURPHY |
| | | | | |
| Lansdowne Road | Twickenham | Lansdowne Road | Lansdowne Road | Stade Columbes |
| WON 9-6 | LOST 0-6 | WON 12-6 | LOST 6-9 | LOST 6-11 |
| | | | | |
| IRE.: 1PG 2T | ENG.: 1PG 1T | IRE.: 2PG 2T | IRE.: 1PG 1T | FR.: 1G 1DG 1PG |
| AUST.: 2T | IRE.: NIL | SCOT.: 2T | WALES: 3T | IRE.: 2PG |
| | | | | |
| 18 Jan. 1958 | 8 Feb. 1958 | 1 Mar. 1958 | 15 Mar. 1958 | 19 Apr. 1958 |

Ireland fielded six new caps for the match with Australia. David Hewitt was a young, exciting runner from Belfast who went on to gain 18 caps, and three of the new forwards were to become household names in Irish rugby during the following decade. In the front row Ron Dawson, a Dublin architect, was an expert hooker whose qualities as a leader earned him the captaincy of the 1959 Lions to Australasia; Bill Mulcahy was a medical student who subsequently gained 35 caps; and Noel Murphy played 41 times in the back row before returning to international rugby as Irish team coach.

The victory over Australia was Ireland's first success against a touring team. Conditions were wet and windy and the tourists led by three points as the match approached its end. Then Henderson played a captain's part. A towering punt by the skipper bisected the tourists' defence and Dawson, following up at speed, touched down for a try. Then Hewitt latched onto an interception and sent Henderson away on a long and thrilling run to win the match with a memorable try. Ireland's only win in the Championship was against Scotland, in a match which marked the end of the great Jack Kyle's international career.

## 1958-59

| v. ENGLAND | v. SCOTLAND | v. WALES | v. FRANCE |
|---|---|---|---|
| N.J. HENDERSON | N.J. HENDERSON | N.J. HENDERSON | N.J. HENDERSON |
| | | | |
| A.C. PEDLOW | A.J.F. O'REILLY | A.J.F. O'REILLY 1T | A.J.F. O'REILLY |
| †J.F. DOOLEY | J.F. DOOLEY 1T | J.F. DOOLEY | †M.K. FLYNN |
| A.J.F. O'REILLY | D. HEWITT 1PG,1C | D. HEWITT 1PG | D. HEWITT 1PG |
| N.H. BROPHY | N.H. BROPHY | N.H. BROPHY | N.H. BROPHY 1T |
| | | | |
| M.A.F. ENGLISH | M.A.F. ENGLISH | W.J. HEWITT | M.A.F. ENGLISH 1DG |
| A.A. MULLIGAN | A.A. MULLIGAN | A.A. MULLIGAN | A.A. MULLIGAN |
| | | | |
| B.G.M. WOOD | B.G.M. WOOD | B.G.M. WOOD | B.G.M. WOOD |
| *A.R. DAWSON | *A.R. DAWSON | *A.R. DAWSON | *A.R. DAWSON |
| S. MILLAR | S. MILLAR | S. MILLAR | S. MILLAR |
| W.A. MULCAHY | W.A. MULCAHY | W.A. MULCAHY | W.A. MULCAHY |
| †M.G. CULLITON | M.G. CULLITON | M.G. CULLITON | M.G. CULLITON |
| N.A.A. MURPHY | N.A.A. MURPHY | N.A.A. MURPHY | N.A.A. MURPHY |
| P.J.A. O'SULLIVAN | P.J.A. O'SULLIVAN | P.J.A. O'SULLIVAN | P.J.A. O'SULLIVAN |
| J.R. KAVANAGH | J.R. KAVANAGH | J.R. KAVANAGH | J.R. KAVANAGH |
| | | | |
| Lansdowne Road | Murrayfield | Cardiff Arms Park | Lansdowne Road |
| LOST 0-3 | WON 8-3 | LOST 6-8 | WON 9-5 |
| | | | |
| IRE.: NIL | SCOT.: 1PG | WALES: 1G 1T | IRE.: 1DG 1PG 1T |
| ENG.: 1PG | IRE.: 1G 1PG | IRE.: 1PG 1T | FR.: 1G |
| | | | |
| 14 Feb. 1959 | 28 Feb. 1959 | 14 Mar. 1959 | 18 Apr. 1959 |

The Irish were unlucky to lose to England. Their forwards earned plenty of good possession, but the tactical approach of the backs was ineffective. The extent of their enterprise was tossing the ball to O'Reilly in the centre, and expecting the big man to burst through the opposition. Effective tackling by the visitors prevented Ireland's plan working. Even so, Ireland did not deserve to lose.

David Hewitt scored all of the points in Ireland's win at Murrayfield, and the Irish led for most of a muddy game at Cardiff. They were on top and six points ahead until half way through the second period of the match, when Wales were transformed from lethargic mediocrity into adventurous combination. Two late tries and a conversion enabled the Welsh to win by two points. There had been a sensational start to this match. Henderson kicked off to the left, away from the forwards, and Brophy gathered the ball in full stride. He raced deep into the Welsh half and as he was tackled by the Welsh fly-half Brophy passed inwards to Murphy, who appeared to score a try. However, the referee ordered a line-out despite the fact that the touch-judge had not raised his flag.

Playing with confidence and tremendous spirit, Ireland beat the champions, France, in the final game of the season.

## 1959-60

| v. ENGLAND | v. SCOTLAND | v. WALES | v. FRANCE |
|---|---|---|---|
| †T.J. KIERNAN 1c | T.J. KIERNAN | T.J. KIERNAN | T.J. KIERNAN |
| †W.W. BORNEMANN | W.W. BORNEMANN | W.W. BORNEMANN | A.C. PEDLOW |
| A.C. PEDLOW | †J.C. WALSH | A.C. PEDLOW | M.K. FLYNN |
| D. HEWITT | D. HEWITT 1c | D. HEWITT | D. HEWITT |
| A.J.F. O'REILLY | A.C. PEDLOW | D.C. GLASS | N.H. BROPHY 2T |
| M.A.F. ENGLISH | M.A.F. ENGLISH | S. KELLY 2PG | S. KELLY |
| *A.A. MULLIGAN | *A.A. MULLIGAN | *A.A. MULLIGAN | A.A. MULLIGAN |
| B.G.M. WOOD | B.G.M. WOOD 1T | B.G.M. WOOD | B.G.M. WOOD |
| †B. McCALLAN | B. McCALLAN | †L.G. BUTLER | *A.R. DAWSON |
| S. MILLAR | S. MILLAR | S. MILLAR | S. MILLAR |
| W.A. MULCAHY | W.A. MULCAHY | W.A. MULCAHY | †P.J. COSTELLO |
| M.G. CULLITON 1T | M.G. CULLITON | M.G. CULLITON | M.G. CULLITON |
| N.A.A. MURPHY | N.A.A. MURPHY | N.A.A. MURPHY 1T | N.A.A. MURPHY |
| T. McGRATH | T. McGRATH | T. McGRATH | T. McGRATH |
| J.R. KAVANAGH | J.R. KAVANAGH | J.R. KAVANAGH | J.R. KAVANAGH |
| Twickenham | Lansdowne Road | Lansdowne Road | Stade Colombes |
| LOST 5-8 | LOST 5-6 | LOST 9-10 | LOST 6-23 |
| ENG.: 1G 1DG | IRE.: 1G | IRE.: 2PG 1T | FR.: 1G 3DG 3T |
| IRE.: 1G | SCOT.: 1DG 1T | WALES: 2G | IRE.: 2T |
| 13 Feb. 1960 | 27 Feb. 1960 | 12 Mar. 1960 | 9 Apr. 1960 |

Ireland took the wooden spoon, losing all four Championship matches for the first time since 1920. Three of the defeats were by very narrow margins, but in Paris in the spring the side was overwhelmed.

Tom Kiernan, the UC Cork student, won the first of his 54 Irish caps in the match with England. His long career lasted until 1973, by which time he had become the most capped full-back in the world. One of the most popular players of his generation, he led Ireland on a record number of 24 occasions, and was the skipper of the 1968 British and Irish Lions tour to South Africa.

O'Reilly was badly injured during the English match, and was unable to take part in the last three games of the season. His successor in the threequarter line was Jerry Walsh, a medical student from Cork. Walsh was a balanced runner and strong tackler who kept his place in the Irish sides of the 1960s, and won 26 caps in a distinguished career.

## 1960-61

| v. S.AFRICA | v. ENGLAND | v. SCOTLAND | v. WALES | v. FRANCE |
|---|---|---|---|---|
| T.J. KIERNAN 1PG | T.J. KIERNAN | T.J. KIERNAN | T.J. KIERNAN | T.J. KIERNAN 1PG |
| W.W. BORNEMANN | †R.J. McCARTEN | A.C. PEDLOW | N.H. BROPHY | A.J.F. O'REILLY |
| J.C. WALSH | D. HEWITT | D. HEWITT 1T | D. HEWITT | D. HEWITT |
| A.C. PEDLOW | J.C. WALSH | J.C. WALSH | D.C. GLASS | J.C. WALSH |
| N.H. BROPHY | A.J.F. O'REILLY | N.H. BROPHY | R.J. McCARTEN | R.J. McCARTEN |
| †W.K. ARMSTRONG | W.K. ARMSTRONG | M.A.F. ENGLISH | M.A.F. ENGLISH | M.A.F. ENGLISH |
| A.A. MULLIGAN | †J.W. MOFFETT 2PG,1c | J.W. MOFFETT 1c | A.A. MULLIGAN | A.A. MULLIGAN |
| S. MILLAR | S. MILLAR | S. MILLAR | S. MILLAR | S. MILLAR |
| *A.R. DAWSON | *A.R. DAWSON | *A.R. DAWSON | *A.R. DAWSON | *A.R. DAWSON |
| B.G.M. WOOD | B.G.M. WOOD | B.G.M. WOOD | B.G.M. WOOD | B.G.M. WOOD |
| W.A. MULCAHY | W.A. MULCAHY | W.A. MULCAHY | W.A. MULCAHY | †J.T. NESDALE |
| M.G. CULLITON | M.G. CULLITON | M.G. CULLITON | †C.J. DICK | C.J. DICK |
| N.A.A. MURPHY | N.A.A. MURPHY | N.A.A. MURPHY | N.A.A. MURPHY | †D. SCOTT |
| P.J.A. O'SULLIVAN | P.J.A. O'SULLIVAN | P.J.A. O'SULLIVAN | J.R. KAVANAGH | J.R. KAVANAGH |
| J.R. KAVANAGH | J.R. KAVANAGH 1T | J.R. KAVANAGH 1T | M.G. CULLITON | M.G. CULLITON |
| Lansdowne Road | Lansdowne Road | Murrayfield | Cardiff Arms Park | Lansdowne Road |
| LOST 3-8 | WON 11-8 | LOST 8-16 | LOST 0-9 | LOST 3-15 |
| IRE.: 1PG | IRE.: 1G 2PG | SCOT.: 2G 1PG 1T | WALES: 2PG 1T | IRE.: 1PG |
| SA: 1G 1T | ENG.: 1G 1T | IRE.: 1G 1T | IRE.: NIL | FR.: 2DG 2PG 1T |
| 17 Dec. 1960 | 11 Feb. 1961 | 25 Feb. 1961 | 11 Mar. 1961 | 15 Apr. 1961 |

The season up to mid-February was rich in promise. Against the Springboks, Ireland led at the interval and only lost in injury time, the tourists scoring a pushover try. Then, before 50,000 spectators, the Irish forwards played an outstanding game against the English. Backed up by some splendid place-kicking by Moffett, Ireland gained a three-point victory, their first international win for six matches. Moffett, a late replacement for the injured Andy Mulligan, had played most of his rugby as a centre and wing-forward, but his eight points from a penalty and two conversions were crucial.

A rapid decline followed. The forwards were outplayed at Murrayfield, the side lacked fire in a poor match at Cardiff, and a disappointing second-half display against France resulted in a defeat which left Ireland as holders of the wooden spoon for the second season running.

The selectors did not escape blame for Ireland's misfortunes. They were criticised for some ill-judged decisions, particularly concerning the selection of the backs. Only Tom Kierman played in all five matches, the selectors chopped and changed both Pedlow and O'Reilly from wing to centre and vice-versa, and the most controversial move of the season was the dropping of Bill Mulcahy, Ireland's leading tight forward, for the match with France.

## 1961 | 1961-62

| v. S.AFRICA | v. ENGLAND | v. SCOTLAND | v. FRANCE | v. WALES |
|---|---|---|---|---|
| T.J. Kiernan 1c,1t,1pg | T.J. Kiernan | F.G. Gilpin | F.G. Gilpin | *T.J. Kiernan |
| | | | | |
| A.J.F. O'Reilly | †L.P.F. L'Estrange | W.R. Hunter 1pg,1t | W.R. Hunter | W.R. Hunter |
| J.C. Walsh | M.K. Flynn | M.K. Flynn | D. Hewitt | A.C. Pedlow |
| †K.J. Houston | †W.R. Hunter | D. Hewitt | M.K. Flynn | M.K. Flynn |
| W.J. Hewitt | N.H. Brophy | N.H. Brophy | †N.F. Byrne | N.H. Brophy |
| | | | | |
| D.C. Glass | †F.G. Gilpin | †G.G. Hardy | M.A.F. English | M.A.F. English 1dg |
| A.A. Mulligan | †J.T.M. Quirke | J.T.M. Quirke | †J.C. Kelly | J.C. Kelly |
| | | | | |
| S. Millar | S. Millar | S. Millar | S. Millar | †M.P. O'Callaghan |
| *A.R. Dawson | †J.S. Dick | A.R. Dawson | A.R. Dawson | A.R. Dawson |
| B.G.M. Wood | †R.J. McLoughlin | R.J. McLoughlin | R.J. McLoughlin | †P.J. Dwyer |
| W.A. Mulcahy | *W.A. Mulcahy | *W.A. Mulcahy | *W.A. Mulcahy | *W.A. Mulcahy |
| C.J. Dick | †W.J. McBride | W.J. McBride | W.J. McBride | W.J. McBride |
| D. Scott | †P.N. Turley | D. Scott | J.R. Kavanagh | P.J.A. O'Sullivan |
| T. McGrath | †M.L. Hipwell | M.L. Hipwell | P.J.A. O'Sullivan | C.J. Dick |
| J.R. Kavanagh | N.A.A. Murphy | M.G. Culliton | M.G. Culliton | †M.D. Kiely |
| | | | | |
| Cape Town | Twickenham | Lansdowne Road | Stade Colombes | Lansdowne Road |
| LOST 8-24 | LOST 0-16 | LOST 6-20 | LOST 0-11 | DRAWN 3-3 |
| | | | | |
| SA: 3G 1PG 2T | ENG.: 2G 1PG 1T | IRE.: 1PG 1T | FR.: 1G 2T | IRE.: 1DG |
| IRE.: 1G 1PG | IRE.: NIL | SCOT.: 1G 1DG 2PG 2T | IRE.: NIL | WALES: 1PG |
| | | | | |
| 13 May 1961 | 10 Feb. 1962 | 24 Feb. 1962 | 14 Apr. 1962 | 17 Nov. 1962 |

Ireland undertook a short four-match tour to South Africa in May 1961. The side played enterprising, attacking rugby and won three of the matches with ease. Tom Kiernan was the leading scorer, and scored all of Ireland's points in the defeat in the international. Curiously, the match with South Africa was the first match of the tour: later touring sides were to learn the lesson of this rather disastrous choice of itinerary, and programmes for subsequent tours were more carefully devised.

In the Test at Cape Town, Tom Kiernan became the first Irish full back to score a try in an international. He entered the threequarter line to join a passing movement, and completed the attack with a splendid try beneath the posts.

The Championship was another poor campaign, with Ireland losing every match and scoring just nine points, their lowest ever tally for a season since the introduction of scoring by points. Bill McBride was one of nine new caps at Twickenham. A wonderful forward, he went on to win 63 caps for Ireland, a record for a forward, and captained the side from 1973 to 1975. In 1974 he was the skipper of the British and Irish Lions team which toured South Africa.

## 1962-63

| v. FRANCE | v. ENGLAND | v. SCOTLAND | v. WALES |
|---|---|---|---|
| *T.J. Kiernan 1c | †B.D.E. Marshall | T.J. Kiernan | T.J. Kiernan 2pg,1c |
| | | | |
| W.R. Hunter | W.R. Hunter | W.R. Hunter | A.J.F. O'Reilly |
| A.C. Pedlow | J.C. Walsh | J.C. Walsh | J.C. Walsh |
| A.J.F. O'Reilly 1t | P.J. Casey | P.J. Casey | P.J. Casey 1t |
| †P.J. Casey | N.H. Brophy | A.J.F. O'Reilly | N.H. Brophy |
| | | | |
| †J.B. Murray | M.A.F. English | M.A.F. English | M.A.F. English 1dg |
| J.C. Kelly | J.C. Kelly | J.C. Kelly | J.C. Kelly |
| | | | |
| S. Millar | S. Millar | S. Millar | S. Millar |
| A.R. Dawson | A.R. Dawson | A.R. Dawson | A.R. Dawson |
| P.J. Dwyer | R.J. McLoughlin | R.J. McLoughlin | R.J. McLoughlin |
| W.A. Mulcahy | *W.A. Mulcahy | *W.A. Mulcahy | *W.A. Mulcahy |
| W.J. McBride | W.J. McBride | W.J. McBride | W.J. McBride |
| P.J.A. O'Sullivan | †E.P. McGuire | E.P. McGuire | E.P. McGuire |
| C.J. Dick | C.J. Dick | C.J. Dick | C.J. Dick |
| M.D. Kiely | M.D. Kiely | M.D. Kiely | M.D. Kiely |
| | | | |
| Lansdowne Road | Lansdowne Road | Murrayfield | Cardiff Arms Park |
| LOST 5-24 | DRAWN 0-0 | LOST 0-3 | WON 14-6 |
| | | | |
| FR.: 3G 2DG 1T | IRE.: NIL | SCOT.: 1PG | WALES: 1DG 1T |
| IRE.: 1G | ENG.: NIL | IRE.: NIL | IRE.: 1G 1DG 2PG |
| | | | |
| 26 Jan. 1963 | 9 Feb. 1963 | 23 Feb. 1963 | 9 Mar. 1963 |

Ireland played Wales twice in 1962-63! The first match took place in November, but is shown in the records as belonging to the 1961-62 season. The game was originally planned for March 1962, but was postponed due to an outbreak of smallpox in South Wales. It was rearranged for the following autumn and resulted in a dour draw.

The second match against Wales, played in March 1963, was a different matter altogether, bringing Ireland their second win in eighteen internationals since 1959, their first in Wales since 1949, and the first at Cardiff since 1932.

The strength of the side was the pack, in which six players retained their places throughout the Championship. The scrummaging power derived from Bill Mulcahy and Bill McBride, who were to play together 17 times in the second row, creating an Irish record for such a combination.

## 1963-64

| v. NZ | v. ENGLAND | v. SCOTLAND | v. WALES | v. FRANCE |
|---|---|---|---|---|
| T.J. KIERNAN 1c | T.J. KIERNAN 3c | T.J. KIERNAN 1PG | †F.S. KEOGH 2PG | F.S. KEOGH |
| †J.J. FORTUNE 1T | P.J. CASEY 1T | P.J. CASEY | P.J. CASEY | P.J. CASEY 1T |
| P.J. CASEY | J.C. WALSH | M.K. FLYNN | M.K. FLYNN | M.K. FLYNN |
| J.C. WALSH | M.K. FLYNN 2T | J.C. WALSH | J.C. WALSH | J.C. WALSH |
| †A.T.A. DUGGAN | J.J. FORTUNE | K.J. HOUSTON | K.J. HOUSTON | A.T.A. DUGGAN |
| M.A.F. ENGLISH | †C.M.H. GIBSON | C.M.H. GIBSON | C.M.H. GIBSON | C.M.H. GIBSON 1DG |
| *J.C. KELLY | J.C. KELLY | J.C. KELLY | J.C. KELLY | J.C. KELLY |
| P.J. DWYER | M.P. O'CALLAGHAN | P.J. DYWER | P.J. DWYER | S. MILLAR |
| A.R. DAWSON | A.R. DAWSON | A.R. DAWSON | †P. LANE | A.R. DAWSON |
| R.J. McLOUGHLIN | R.J. McLOUGHLIN | R.J. McLOUGHLIN | †T.A. MORONEY | M.P. O'CALLAGHAN |
| W.J. McBRIDE | W.J. McBRIDE | W.J. McBRIDE | †M.W. LEAHY | W.J. McBRIDE |
| W.A. MULCAHY | *W.A. MULCAHY | *W.A. MULCAHY | *W.A. MULCAHY | *W.A. MULCAHY |
| E.P. McGUIRE | E.P. McGUIRE | E.P. McGUIRE | E.P. McGUIRE | E.P. McGUIRE |
| P.J.A. O'SULLIVAN | M.G. CULLITON | M.G. CULLITON | M.G. CULLITON | M.G. CULLITON |
| N.A.A. MURPHY | N.A.A. MURPHY 1T | N.A.A. MURPHY | N.A.A. MURPHY | N.A.A. MURPHY |
| Lansdowne Road | Twickenham | Lansdowne Road | Lansdowne Road | Stade Colombes |
| LOST 5-6 | WON 18-5 | LOST 3-6 | LOST 6-15 | LOST 6-27 |
| IRE.: IG | ENG.: IG | IRE.: IPG | IRE.: 2PG | FR.: 3G IDG 3T |
| NZ: IPG IT | IRE.: 3G IT | SCOT.: 2PG | WALES: 3G | IRE.: IDG IT |
| 7 Dec. 1963 | 8 Feb. 1964 | 22 Feb. 1964 | 7 Mar. 1964 | 11 Apr. 1964 |

Ireland very nearly registered their first win over New Zealand in their opening game of the season. A lively Irish side gave the All Blacks a fright, led for much of the match, and only saw that lead vanish in the closing minutes, the All Blacks scoring a late penalty.

The first match of the Championship was at Twickenham, where a young Cambridge undergraduate, Mike Gibson, burst into international rugby with a scintillating display of dashing fly-half play. Gibson played a great part in Ireland's victory by 18-5 and the Irish were enthusiastic regarding their chances of a Triple Crown following this first win at Twickenham since 1948.

The side was plagued by injuries, however, and went down in the mud to a strong Scottish side whose pack found the conditions to their liking. Ireland were unlucky to lose Ray McLoughlin's expertise after only five minutes against the Scots, a painful knee-injury reducing him to a passenger and ruling him out of the fifteen for the remainder of the season. In the final two matches, the confidence of the side vanished, the Welsh and then the French taking advantage of ill-chosen Irish packs and recording 42 points.

## 1964-65

| v. FRANCE | v. ENGLAND | v. SCOTLAND | v. WALES | v. S.AFRICA |
|---|---|---|---|---|
| T.J. KIERNAN | T.J. KIERNAN 1c | T.J. KIERNAN 2c | T.J. KIERNAN 1PG,1c | T.J. KIERNAN 2PG |
| P.J. CASEY | P.J. CASEY | P.J. CASEY | D. HEWITT | K.J. HOUSTON |
| J.C. WALSH | M.K. FLYNN | J.C. WALSH | J.C. WALSH | J.C. WALSH |
| M.K. FLYNN | K.J. HOUSTON | M.K. FLYNN | M.K. FLYNN 1T | M.K. FLYNN |
| K.J. HOUSTON | †P.J. McGRATH | P.J. McGRATH 1T | P.J. McGRATH | P.J. McGRATH 1T |
| C.M.H. GIBSON | C.M.H. GIBSON | C.M.H. GIBSON 1DG | C.M.H. GIBSON | C.M.H. GIBSON |
| †R.M. YOUNG | R.M. YOUNG | R.M. YOUNG 1T | R.M. YOUNG | R.M. YOUNG |
| †S. MacHALE | S. MacHALE | S. MacHALE | S. MacHALE | S. MacHALE |
| †K.W. KENNEDY | K.W. KENNEDY | K.W. KENNEDY | K.W. KENNEDY | K.W. KENNEDY |
| *R.J. McLOUGHLIN | *R.J. McLOUGHLIN | *R.J. McLOUGHLIN | *R.J. McLOUGHLIN | *R.J. McLOUGHLIN |
| W.J. McBRIDE | W.J. McBRIDE | W.J. McBRIDE | W.J. McBRIDE | W.J. McBRIDE |
| W.A. MULCAHY | W.A. MULCAHY | W.A. MULCAHY | W.A. MULCAHY | W.A. MULCAHY |
| †M.G. DOYLE 1T | M.G. DOYLE | M.G. DOYLE | M.G. DOYLE | M.G. DOYLE |
| †R.A. LAMONT | R.A. LAMONT 1T | †C.H. WALL | C.H. WALL | R.A. LAMONT |
| N.A.A. MURPHY | N.A.A. MURPHY | N.A.A. MURPHY 1T | N.A.A. MURPHY | N.A.A. MURPHY |
| Lansdowne Road | Lansdowne Road | Murrayfield | Cardiff Arms Park | Lansdowne Road |
| DRAWN 3-3 | WON 5-0 | WON 16-6 | LOST 8-14 | WON 9-6 |
| IRE.: IT | IRE.: IG | SCOT.: IPG IDG | WALES: IG IDG IPG IT | IRE.: 2PG IT |
| FR.: IT | ENG.: NIL | IRE.: 2G IDG IT | IRE.: IG IPG | SA: IPG IT |
| 23 Jan. 1965 | 13 Feb. 1965 | 27 Feb. 1965 | 13 Mar. 1965 | 6 Apr. 1965 |

Ray McLoughlin, a chemical engineer who went on to gain 40 Irish caps, captained Ireland in their most successful season since 1953. He was a deep thinker about the game and a forceful motivator, and the team benefited from his solid scrummaging. Five new caps were awarded for the match with France, each of them playing a prominent role in Ireland's draw, a result which upset the predictions of the pundits. The Irish forwards played with fierce determination and one of the new men, Mick Doyle, opened the scoring with a try following a forceful rush by the entire pack. Doyle was to become a regular member of the Irish back row for four seasons, and returned more recently to the international scene as Ireland's coach.

Dental student Roger Young was the find of the season among the backs. He played with the calm authority of a veteran in defence and spun out an immaculate service to the brilliant Gibson from the set pieces. Young went on to play 26 games for Ireland, two short of Mark Sugden's record for a scrum-half.

Wins followed over England and Scotland, but in the Triple Crown decider at Cardiff, Ireland were subdued in the mud by a determined Welsh eight, and missed early chances to collect penalty points. In April, however, the disappointment over the Welsh defeat was dissipated when Ireland defeated South Africa for the first time.

## 1965-66

| v. FRANCE | v. ENGLAND | v. SCOTLAND | v. WALES |
|---|---|---|---|
| T.J. KIERNAN 1DG | T.J. KIERNAN 1PG | T.J. KIERNAN 1PG | *T.J. KIERNAN |
| W.R. HUNTER | W.R. HUNTER | W.R. HUNTER | A.T.A. DUGGAN |
| J.C. WALSH | M.K. FLYNN | M.K. FLYNN | F.P.K. BRESNIHAN 1T |
| M.K. FLYNN | †F.P.K. BRESNIHAN | J.C. WALSH | J.C. WALSH |
| P.J. McGRATH | P.J. McGRATH 1T | P.J. McGRATH | P.J. McGRATH |
| C.M.H. GIBSON 1PG | C.M.H. GIBSON | C.M.H. GIBSON | C.M.H. GIBSON 1PG 1DG |
| R.M. YOUNG | R.M. YOUNG | R.M. YOUNG | R.M. YOUNG |
| S. MacHALE | S. MacHALE | S. MacHALE | S. MacHALE |
| K.W. KENNEDY | K.W. KENNEDY | †A.M. BRADY | K.W. KENNEDY |
| *R.J. McLOUGHLIN | *R.J. McLOUGHLIN | *R.J. McLOUGHLIN | R.J. McLOUGHLIN |
| †M.G. MOLLOY | M.G. MOLLOY | †O.C. WALDRON | O.C. WALDRON |
| W.J. McBRIDE | W.J. McBRIDE | W.J. McBRIDE | W.J. McBRIDE |
| M.G. DOYLE | M.G. DOYLE | M.G. DOYLE | M.G. DOYLE |
| R.A. LAMONT | R.A. LAMONT | R.A. LAMONT | R.A. LAMONT |
| N.A.A. MURPHY | N.A.A. MURPHY | N.A.A. MURPHY | N.A.A. MURPHY |
| Stade Colombes | Twickenham | Lansdowne Road | Lansdowne Road |
| LOST 6-11 | DRAWN 6-6 | LOST 3-11 | WON 9-6 |
| FR.: 1G 1PG 1T | ENG.: 1PG 1T | IRE.: 1PG | IRE.: 1DG 1PG 1T |
| IRE.: 1PG 1DG | IRE.: 1PG 1T | SCOT.: 1G 2T | WALES: 1PG 1T |
| 29 Jan. 1966 | 12 Feb. 1966 | 26 Feb. 1966 | 12 Mar. 1966 |

Mick Molloy was the only new cap in an experienced Irish side at the start of the season. He formed a successful partnership with Bill McBride in the engine-room of the scrum, and teamed up with the famous Ulsterman on 26 occasions in the second row, a record partnership for Ireland.

McLoughlin remained as captain. He had imbued the side with such determination and spirit in the previous season that it was felt that Ireland had both the confidence and skill to dominate the International Championship. However, the defeat in Paris against a brilliant French XV was the beginning of a decline which was only checked after the unlucky McLoughlin had been relieved of the captaincy.

The defeat of Wales, who were seeking the Triple Crown, was a satisfying way for the Irish to celebrate the end of the season. In an exciting and tense match, young Barry Bresnihan, a promising centre and UCD medical student, frustrated the Welsh when he capitalised on a defensive error late in the match to score the winning try.

## 1966-67

| v. AUSTRALIA | v. ENGLAND | v. SCOTLAND | v. WALES | v. FRANCE |
|---|---|---|---|---|
| T.J. KIERNAN 1PG | T.J. KIERNAN 1PG | T.J. KIERNAN 1C | T.J. KIERNAN | T.J. KIERNAN 1PG |
| A.T.A. DUGGAN 1T | †R.D. SCOTT | A.T.A. DUGGAN | A.T.A. DUGGAN 1T | R.D. SCOTT |
| F.P.K. BRESNIHAN | F.P.K. BRESNIHAN | F.P.K. BRESNIHAN | F.P.K. BRESNIHAN | F.P.K. BRESNIHAN |
| †H.H. REA | J.C. WALSH | J.C. WALSH | J.C. WALSH | J.C. WALSH |
| P.J. McGRATH | N.H. BROPHY | N.H. BROPHY | N.H. BROPHY | N.H. BROPHY |
| C.M.H. GIBSON 2DG,1T | C.M.H. GIBSON | C.M.H. GIBSON | C.M.H. GIBSON | C.M.H. GIBSON |
| †B.F. SHERRY | B.F. SHERRY | B.F. SHERRY | R.M. YOUNG | R.M. YOUNG |
| †P. O'CALLAGHAN | P. O'CALLAGHAN | S. MacHALE | S. MacHALE | S. MacHALE |
| K.W. KENNEDY | K.W. KENNEDY | K.W. KENNEDY | K.W. KENNEDY | K.W. KENNEDY |
| T.A. MORONEY | T.A. MORONEY | †S.A. HUTTON | S.A. HUTTON | S.A. HUTTON |
| W.J. McBRIDE | W.J. McBRIDE | W.J. McBRIDE | W.J. McBRIDE | W.J. McBRIDE |
| M.G. MOLLOY | M.G. MOLLOY | M.G. MOLLOY | M.G. MOLLOY | M.G. MOLLOY 1T |
| M.G. DOYLE | M.G. DOYLE | M.G. DOYLE | M.G. DOYLE | M.G. DOYLE |
| †K.G. GOODALL | K.G. GOODALL | K.G. GOODALL | K.G. GOODALL | K.G. GOODALL |
| *N.A.A. MURPHY | *N.A.A. MURPHY | *N.A.A. MURPHY 1T | *N.A.A. MURPHY | *N.A.A. MURPHY |
| Lansdowne Road | Lansdowne Road | Murrayfield | Cardiff Arms Park | Lansdowne Road |
| WON 15-8 | LOST 3-8 | WON 5-3 | WON 3-0 | LOST 6-11 |
| IRE.: 2DG 1PG 2T | IRE.: 1PG | SCOT.: 1PG | WALES: NIL | IRE.: 1PG 1T |
| AUST.: 1G 1DG | ENG.: 1G 1PG | IRE.: 1G | IRE.: 1T | FR.: 1G 2DG |
| 21 Jan. 1967 | 11 Feb. 1967 | 25 Feb. 1967 | 11 Mar. 1967 | 15 Apr. 1967 |

Gibson, Kennedy and Murphy were Ireland's heroes in a fine victory against the Australian tourists. Gibson played with outstanding poise. He tackled and covered ubiquitously in defence, distributed the ball sensibly in attack, and contributed two dropped goals and a brilliant individual try to Ireland's total of 15 points. His overall control at fly-half was due to an excellent forward effort, and the credit for victory really belonged to Murphy's pack. As captain, the flanker set a dynamic example: he was fast in the loose, steady in the tight play, and bottled up the threat of Australia's excellent halves with numerous smother tackles. Kennedy took several strikes against the head.

Kennedy earned 45 caps for Ireland in a career which spanned ten seasons. Twice his exceptional technical skills were recognised by the Lions' selectors: he went to Australia and New Zealand with the 1966 team and was a member of the outstanding 1974 Lions team to South Africa.

The Championship matches were close affairs. The side lost to a last-minute try against England; Goodall and Murphy scrambled over from a lineout to settle the match at Murrayfield; and Duggan's try in a gale-force wind was sufficient to beat the Welsh. France won the match in Dublin, depriving Ireland of a share in the championship.

| 1967 | 1967-68 | | | |
| v. AUSTRALIA | v. FRANCE | v. ENGLAND | v. SCOTLAND | v. WALES |
| --- | --- | --- | --- | --- |
| *T.J. KIERNAN 1DG,1C | *T.J. KIERNAN | *T.J. KIERNAN 3PG | *T.J. KIERNAN 1PG,1C | *T.J. KIERNAN 1PG |
| A.T.A. DUGGAN | A.T.A. DUGGAN | A.T.A. DUGGAN | A.T.A. DUGGAN 2T | A.T.A. DUGGAN |
| J.C. WALSH 1T | †B.A.P. O'BRIEN | B.A.P. O'BRIEN | B.A.P. O'BRIEN | F.P.K. BRESNIHAN |
| P.J. McGRATH 1T | F.P.K. BRESNIHAN | F.P.K. BRESNIHAN | F.P.K. BRESNIHAN 1T | †L.M. HUNTER |
| N.H. BROPHY | R.D. SCOTT | R.D. SCOTT | R.D. SCOTT | †J.C.M. MORONEY |
| C.M.H. GIBSON | †W.M. McCOMBE 2PG | C.M.H. GIBSON | C.M.H. GIBSON | C.M.H. GIBSON 1DG |
| B.F. SHERRY | B.F. SHERRY | B.F. SHERRY | J.T.M. QUIRKE | R.M. YOUNG |
| P. O'CALLAGHAN | P. O'CALLAGHAN | P. O'CALLAGHAN | P. O'CALLAGHAN | P. O'CALLAGHAN |
| K.W. KENNEDY | K.W. KENNEDY | A.M. BRADY | A.M. BRADY | A.M. BRADY |
| S.A. HUTTON | S. MILLAR | S. MILLAR | S. MILLAR | S. MILLAR |
| W.J. McBRIDE | W.J. McBRIDE | W.J. McBRIDE | W.J. McBRIDE | W.J. McBRIDE |
| M.G. MOLLOY | M.G. MOLLOY | M.G. MOLLOY | M.G. MOLLOY | M.G. MOLLOY |
| M.G. DOYLE | M.G. DOYLE | M.G. DOYLE | M.G. DOYLE | M.G. DOYLE 1T |
| †T.A.P. MOORE | M.L. HIPWELL | K.G. GOODALL | K.G. GOODALL | K.G. GOODALL |
| K.G. GOODALL | K.G. GOODALL | †T.J. DOYLE | T.J. DOYLE | T.J. DOYLE |
| Sydney | Stade Colombes | Twickenham | Lansdowne Road | Lansdowne Road |
| WON 11-5 | LOST 6-16 | DRAWN 9-9 | WON 14-6 | WON 9-6 |
| AUST.: 1G | FR.: 2G 1DG 1PG | ENG.: 2PG 1DG | IRE.: 1G 1PG 2T | IRE.: 1DG 1PG 1T |
| IRE.: 1G 1DG 1T | IRE.: 2PG | IRE.: 3PG | SCOT.: 2PG | WALES: 1DG 1PG |
| 13 May 1967 | 27 Jan. 1968 | 10 Feb. 1968 | 24 Feb. 1968 | 9 Mar. 1968 |

Eugene Davy and Des McKibbin, both former caps, led the Irish management on the first Irish visit to Australia in the summer of 1967. The international at Sydney resulted in a fine win, Ireland's third in a row against the Wallabies.

Ireland proved the best of the Home nations in the 1968 Championship, losing only to France and thus finishing as runners-up. Ireland were not without their problems, it should be added. Before the game Mike Gibson had been laid low with a viral infection which developed into pneumonia, and was forced to miss his first international since his debut. And during the match the Irish pack was hamstrung by crippling injuries to Kennedy and Molloy. Kennedy's knee injury ruled him out of the side for the remainder of the season.

| 1968-69 | | | | |
| v. AUSTRALIA | v. FRANCE | v. ENGLAND | v. SCOTLAND | v. WALES |
| --- | --- | --- | --- | --- |
| *T.J. KIERNAN 1C | *T.J. KIERNAN | *T.J. KIERNAN 2PG,1C | *T.J. KIERNAN | *T.J. KIERNAN 2PG,1C |
| J.C.M. MORONEY 1C | A.T.A. DUGGAN | A.T.A. DUGGAN | A.T.A. DUGGAN 1T | A.T.A. DUGGAN |
| F.P.K. BRESNIHAN 1T | F.P.K. BRESNIHAN | F.P.K. BRESNIHAN 1T | F.P.K. BRESNIHAN 1T | F.P.K. BRESNIHAN |
| L.M. HUNTER | H.H. REA | C.M.H. GIBSON | C.M.H. GIBSON 1T | C.M.H. GIBSON 1T |
| †J.J. TYDINGS | J.C.M.MORONEY 1T,1C,3PG | J.C.M. MORONEY | J.C.M. MORONEY 2C | J.C.M. MORONEY |
| C.M.H. GIBSON | †B.J. McGANN 1DG | B.J. McGANN 1DG | B.J. McGANN 1T | B.J. McGANN |
| R.M. YOUNG | R.M. YOUNG | R.M. YOUNG[1] | R.M. YOUNG | R.M. YOUNG |
| S. MILLAR | S. MILLAR | S. MILLAR | S. MILLAR | S. MILLAR |
| K.W. KENNEDY | K.W. KENNEDY | K.W. KENNEDY | K.W. KENNEDY | K.W. KENNEDY |
| O.C. WALDRON | P. O'CALLAGHAN | P. O'CALLAGHAN | P. O'CALLAGHAN | P. O'CALLAGHAN |
| W.J. McBRIDE | W.J. McBRIDE | W.J. McBRIDE | W.J. McBRIDE | W.J. McBRIDE |
| M.G. MOLLOY | M.G. MOLLOY | M.G. MOLLOY | M.G. MOLLOY | M.G. MOLLOY |
| M.G. DOYLE | †J.C. DAVIDSON | J.C. DAVIDSON | J.C. DAVIDSON | J.C. DAVIDSON |
| M.L. HIPWELL | K.G. GOODALL | K.G. GOODALL | K.G. GOODALL[1] | M.L. HIPWELL |
| K.G. GOODALL 1T | N.A.A. MURPHY[1] | N.A.A. MURPHY 1T | N.A.A. MURPHY | N.A.A. MURPHY |
| Lansdowne Road | Lansdowne Road | Lansdowne Road | Murrayfield | Cardiff Arms Park |
| WON 10-3 | WON 17-9 | WON 17-15 | WON 16-0 | LOST 11-24 |
| IRE.: 2G | IRE.: 1G 1DG 3PG | IRE.: 1G 2PG 1DG 1T | SCOT.: NIL | WALES: 3G 1DG 1PG 1T |
| AUST.: 1T | FR.: 2PG 1T | ENG.: 4PG 1T | IRE.: 2G 2T | IRE.: 1G 2PG |
| 26 Oct. 1968 | 25 Jan. 1969 | 8 Feb. 1969 | 22 Feb. 1969 | 8 Mar. 1969 |
|  | [1]Rep. by M.L. Hipwell | [1]Rep. by †C. Grimshaw | [1]Rep. by M.L. Hipwell |  |

Ireland's unbeaten sequence of seven matches between February 1968 and March 1969 was a record run which prompted critics to call this side Ireland's best-ever. Yet the Triple Crown and Grand Slam eluded them in a rough match at Cardiff in which Noel Murphy was felled by a punch to the jaw. Wales went on to win the Triple Crown and Championship with Ireland runners-up.

Ireland's successful run was due to a powerful pack. The front five were among the best forwards ever to play for Ireland and they were backed by a balanced threequarter line and skilful halves. Mike Gibson moved into the centre to accommodate Barry McGann, an accomplished all-round footballer, at fly-half.

In the match with France, Mick Hipwell became the first Irishman to win a cap as a substitute, and in the same match John Moroney scored fourteen points, a new record individual contribution for an Irish international.

## 1969-70

| v. S.AFRICA | v. FRANCE | v. ENGLAND | v. SCOTLAND | v. WALES |
|---|---|---|---|---|
| *T.J. KIERNAN 1C,1PG | *T.J. KIERNAN | *T.J. KIERNAN 1PG | *T.J. KIERNAN 2C | *T.J. KIERNAN 1PG,1C |
| A.T.A. DUGGAN 1T | A.T.A. DUGGAN | A.T.A. DUGGAN | A.T.A. DUGGAN | A.T.A. DUGGAN 1T |
| F.P.K. BRESNIHAN | F.P.K. BRESNIHAN | F.P.K. BRESNIHAN | F.P.K. BRESNIHAN | F.P.K. BRESNIHAN |
| C.M.H. GIBSON | C.M.H. GIBSON | C.M.H. GIBSON | C.M.H. GIBSON 1T | C.M.H. GIBSON |
| †W.J. BROWN | W.J. BROWN | A.J.F. O'REILLY | W.J. BROWN 1T | W.J. BROWN |
| B.J. McGANN | B.J. McGANN | B.J. McGANN | B.J. McGANN | B.J. McGANN 1DG |
| R.M. YOUNG | R.M. YOUNG | R.M. YOUNG | R.M. YOUNG | R.M. YOUNG |
| S. MILLAR | S. MILLAR | S. MILLAR | S. MILLAR | S. MILLAR |
| K.W. KENNEDY | K.W. KENNEDY | K.W. KENNEDY | K.W. KENNEDY | K.W. KENNEDY |
| P. O'CALLAGHAN | P. O'CALLAGHAN | P. O'CALLAGHAN | P. O'CALLAGHAN | P. O'CALLAGHAN |
| †C.E. CAMPBELL | M.G. MOLLOY | M.G. MOLLOY | M.G. MOLLOY 1T | M.G. MOLLOY |
| W.J. McBRIDE | W.J. McBRIDE | W.J. McBRIDE | W.J. McBRIDE | W.J. McBRIDE |
| R.A. LAMONT | R.A. LAMONT | R.A. LAMONT | R.A. LAMONT | R.A. LAMONT |
| K.G. GOODALL | K.G. GOODALL | K.G. GOODALL | K.G. GOODALL 1T | K.G. GOODALL 1T |
| †J.F. SLATTERY | J.F. SLATTERY | J.F. SLATTERY | J.F. SLATTERY | J.F. SLATTERY |
| Lansdowne Road | Stade Colombes | Twickenham | Lansdowne Road | Lansdowne Road |
| DRAWN 8-8 | LOST 0-8 | LOST 3-9 | WON 16-11 | WON 14-0 |
| IRE.: 1G 1PG | FR.: 1G 1DG | ENG.: 2DG 1T | IRE.: 2G 2T | IRE.: 1G 1DG 1PG 1T |
| SA: 1G 1PG | IRE.: NIL | IRE.: 1PG | SCOT.: 1G 1DG 1T | WALES: NIL |
| 10 Jan. 1970 | 24 Jan. 1970 | 14 Feb. 1970 | 28 Feb. 1970 | 14 Mar. 1970 |

After two good campaigns in 1968 and 1969, and with the majority of the previous season's players available, a promising season for the Irish was predicted. However, after a last-minute equaliser (in the form of a penalty kicked by Kiernan) against South Africa, the team was surprisingly beaten by France and England. Ireland's true form was not revealed until the end of the season in two stirring wins in Dublin, first against Scotland and then, against Wales, who were seeking the Triple Crown.

Tony O'Reilly made an extraordinary return to international rugby at Twickenham. He had not appeared for Ireland since 1963 but was called into the side on the eve of the match when Bill Brown was declared unfit. O'Reilly had actually contributed the main article to the match programme! He had little to do during the game, however, and suffered slight concussion after a collision.

Fergus Slattery, entered the Irish side for the match against the Springboks. He was to enjoy a long career in the international side, gaining 61 caps during 14 seasons and setting a world record for number of appearances as an international flanker.

## 1970-71

| v. FRANCE | v. ENGLAND | v. SCOTLAND | v. WALES |
|---|---|---|---|
| *T.J. KIERNAN[1] | B.J. O'DRISCOLL | B.J. O'DRISCOLL | B.J. O'DRISCOLL |
| A.T.A. DUGGAN | A.T.A. DUGGAN 1T | A.T.A. DUGGAN 2T | A.T.A. DUGGAN |
| F.P.K. BRESNIHAN | F.P.K. BRESNIHAN | F.P.K. BRESNIHAN | F.P.K. BRESNIHAN |
| C.M.H. GIBSON | *C.M.H. GIBSON | *C.M.H. GIBSON 2PG,1C | *C.M.H. GIBSON 3PG |
| †E.L. GRANT 1T | E.L. GRANT 1T | E.L. GRANT 1T | E.L. GRANT |
| B.J. McGANN | B.J. McGANN | B.J. McGANN | B.J. McGANN |
| R.M. YOUNG | R.M. YOUNG | R.M. YOUNG | R.M. YOUNG |
| R.J. McLOUGHLIN | R.J. McLOUGHLIN | R.J. McLOUGHLIN | R.J. McLOUGHLIN |
| K.W. KENNEDY | K.W. KENNEDY | K.W. KENNEDY | K.W. KENNEDY |
| †J.F. LYNCH | J.F. LYNCH | J.F. LYNCH | J.F. LYNCH |
| W.J. McBRIDE | W.J. McBRIDE | W.J. McBRIDE | W.J. McBRIDE |
| M.G. MOLLOY | M.G. MOLLOY | M.G. MOLLOY | M.G. MOLLOY |
| M.L. HIPWELL | M.L. HIPWELL | M.L. HIPWELL | M.L. HIPWELL |
| †D.J. HICKIE | D.J. HICKIE | D.J. HICKIE | D.J. HICKIE |
| J.F. SLATTERY | J.F. SLATTERY | J.F. SLATTERY | J.F. SLATTERY |
| Lansdowne Road | Lansdowne Road | Murrayfield | Cardiff Arms Park |
| DRAWN 9-9 | LOST 6-9 | WON 17-5 | LOST 9-23 |
| IRE.: 2PG 1T | IRE.: 2T | SCOT.: 1G | WALES: 1G 2PG 1DG 3T |
| FR.: 2PG 1DG | ENG.: 3PG | IRE.: 1G 2PG 2T | IRE.: 3PG |
| 30 Jan. 1971 | 13 Feb. 1971 | 27 Feb. 1971 | 13 Mar. 1971 |

[1]Rep. by †B.J. O'Driscoll 2PG

For the second year running the Irish selectors used only 16 players. Tom Kiernan cracked a fibula in a collision with Mike Gibson against France, and his replacement, Barry O'Driscoll (for so long a reserve), retained his place for the remainder of the season.

Lynch and Grant were new caps. Lynch contributed his expertise to an excellent pack of scrummagers, and his skill during the season was rewarded with a place among the Lions' tour party to New Zealand. Grant, like Mortell in 1953 and Shaun Waide in 1932, scored tries in each of his first three international matches. Admittedly some believed that Grant's try against England, which resulted from an interception and 75-yard dash, should have been disallowed for a knock forward.

Gibson's brilliance in New Zealand on tour with the Lions later that summer confirmed that he was the world's finest centre.

## 1971-72

| 1st v. FRANCE | v. ENGLAND | 2nd v. FRANCE |
|---|---|---|
| *T.J. KIERNAN 2PG | *T.J. KIERNAN 1PG,1C | *T.J. KIERNAN 3C,2PG |
| †T.O. GRACE | T.O. GRACE 1T | A.T.A. DUGGAN 1T |
| C.M.H. GIBSON | C.M.H. GIBSON | C.M.H. GIBSON |
| M.K. FLYNN | M.K. FLYNN 1T | M.K. FLYNN 1T |
| †A.W. McMASTER | A.W. McMASTER | A.W. McMASTER |
| B.J. McGANN | B.J. McGANN 1DG | B.J. McGANN |
| †J.J. MOLONEY 1T | J.J. MOLONEY | J.J. MOLONEY 1T |
| R.J. McLOUGHLIN 1T | R.J. McLOUGHLIN | R.J. McLOUGHLIN |
| K.W. KENNEDY | K.W. KENNEDY | K.W. KENNEDY |
| J.F. LYNCH | J.F. LYNCH | J.F. LYNCH |
| W.J. McBRIDE | W.J. McBRIDE | W.J. McBRIDE |
| †C.F.P. FEIGHERY | C.F.P. FEIGHERY | C.F.P. FEIGHERY |
| †S.A. McKINNEY | S.A. McKINNEY | S.A. McKINNEY |
| D.J. HICKIE | D.J. HICKIE | M.L. HIPWELL |
| J.F. SLATTERY | J.F. SLATTERY | J.F. SLATTERY |
| Stade Colombes | Twickenham | Lansdowne Road |
| WON 14-9 | WON 16-12 | WON 24-14 |
| FR.: 1G 1PG | ENG.: 1G 2PG | IRE.: 3G 2PG |
| IRE.: 2PG 2T | IRE.: 1G 1DG 1PG 1T | FR.: 1G 2T |
| 29 Jan. 1972 | 12 Feb. 1972 | 29 Apr. 1972 |

Johnny Moloney, who went on to gain 27 Irish caps (appearing on the wing towards the end of his career), replaced Roger Young (who had emigrated to South Africa), and scored a try on his debut in Paris. It was the first Irish win at Colombes since 1952, and was due to a magnificent forward effort. The flankers subdued the French halves and Ken Kennedy had a marvellous match. He was outstanding in the loose and hooked with excellent technique to take the tight-head count in the scrummages.

Kevin Flynn, recalled after a six-year absence, sliced through a narrow chink in the English defence to score the winning try, in injury time, at Twickenham. It was a lively game which marked Tom Kiernan's 50th appearance for Ireland, and contained some splendid place-kicking by the great man, as well as a fine individual try by Tom Grace, the new wing.

But for Ireland the season was one of bitter disappointment. The political strife within the country compelled both the Scottish and Welsh Unions to cancel their visits, and the International Championship was left incomplete, with Wales and Ireland unbeaten. France provided additional international opposition late in April in a game which was outside the Championship, but for which both nations awarded caps. Ireland won the match comfortably.

## 1972-73

| v. NZ | v. ENGLAND | v. SCOTLAND | v. WALES | v. FRANCE |
|---|---|---|---|---|
| *T.J. KIERNAN | *T.J. KIERNAN | *T.J. KIERNAN 1T | †A.H. ENSOR | A.H. ENSOR 1PG |
| T.O. GRACE 1T | T.O. GRACE 1T | T.O. GRACE | T.O. GRACE | †S.P. DENNISON |
| M.K. FLYNN | †R.A. MILLIKEN 1T | R.A. MILLIKEN | R.A. MILLIKEN | R.A. MILLIKEN |
| C.M.H. GIBSON | C.M.H. GIBSON | C.M.H. GIBSON | C.M.H. GIBSON 1T | C.M.H. GIBSON 1PG |
| A.W. McMASTER | A.W. McMASTER | A.W. McMASTER 1T | A.W. McMASTER | A.W. McMASTER |
| B.J. McGANN 2PG | B.J. McGANN 1PG,1DG,2C | B.J. McGANN 2PG | B.J. McGANN 2PG,1C | †M.A.M. QUINN |
| J.J. MOLONEY | J.J. MOLONEY | J.J. MOLONEY | J.J. MOLONEY | J.J. MOLONEY |
| R.J. McLOUGHLIN | R.J. McLOUGHLIN | R.J. McLOUGHLIN | R.J. McLOUGHLIN | R.J. McLOUGHLIN |
| K.W. KENNEDY | K.W. KENNEDY | K.W. KENNEDY | K.W. KENNEDY | K.W. KENNEDY |
| J.F. LYNCH | J.F. LYNCH | J.F. LYNCH | J.F. LYNCH | †R.J. CLEGG |
| W.J. McBRIDE | W.J. McBRIDE | W.J. McBRIDE | *W.J. McBRIDE | *W.J. McBRIDE |
| †K.M.A. MAYS | K.M.A. MAYS | K.M.A. MAYS | K.M.A. MAYS | M.G. MOLLOY |
| J.C. DAVIDSON | †J.H. BUCKLEY | J.H. BUCKLEY | S.A. McKINNEY | S.A. McKINNEY |
| T.A.P. MOORE | T.A.P. MOORE | T.A.P. MOORE | T.A.P. MOORE | T.A.P. MOORE |
| J.F. SLATTERY | J.F. SLATTERY | J.F. SLATTERY | J.F. SLATTERY | J.F. SLATTERY |
| Lansdowne Road | Lansdowne Road | Murrayfield | Cardiff Arms Park | Lansdowne Road |
| DRAWN 10-10 | WON 18-9 | LOST 14-19 | LOST 12-16 | WON 6-4 |
| IRE.: 2PG 1T | IRE.: 2G 1PG 1DG | SCOT.: 3DG 2PG 1T | WALES: 1G 2PG 1T | IRE.: 2PG |
| NZ: 1G 1T | ENG.: 1G 1PG | IRE.: 2PG 2T | IRE.: 1G 2PG | FR.: 1T |
| 20 Jan. 1973 | 10 Feb. 1973 | 24 Feb. 1973 | 10 Mar. 1973 | 14 Apr. 1973 |

Ireland's first partial success against the All Blacks – a draw – was gained against the odds. The New Zealanders dominated the game but allowed Ireland to stage a dramatic comeback: a late penalty goal by McGann, followed by a memorable try from Grace, tied the scores in injury time.

The English XV were greeted with a lasting ovation when they honoured their fixture in Dublin. Hospitality did not extend to the field of play, however, and the English pack were overrun by an eager Irish unit in which Kennedy was outstanding. Milliken, a promising, forceful centre from Bangor, capped a fine debut by scoring a try.

The Scottish match was Tom Kiernan's last for Ireland (and he celebrated by scoring a try). He retired as his country's leading points-scorer (158), their most-capped player (54), and most experienced international captain (24). Tony Ensor, his successor, and Mike Gibson, kicked the penalties which defeated France in April to give Ireland a share in a unique quintuple tie.

## 1973-74

| v. FRANCE | v. WALES | v. ENGLAND | v. SCOTLAND |
|---|---|---|---|
| A.H. Ensor 2PG | A.H. Ensor 3PG | A.H. Ensor 1PG | A.H. Ensor |
| | | | |
| †V.A. Becker | V.A. Becker | T.O. Grace | T.O. Grace |
| C.M.H. Gibson | C.M.H. Gibson | C.M.H. Gibson 2T,2C | C.M.H. Gibson 1C |
| R.A. Milliken | R.A. Milliken | R.A. Milliken | R.A. Milliken 1T |
| A.W. McMaster | †P.J. Lavery | A.W. McMaster | A.W. McMaster |
| | | | |
| M.A.M. Quinn | M.A.M. Quinn | M.A.M. Quinn 1DG | M.A.M. Quinn |
| J.J. Moloney | J.J. Moloney | J.J. Moloney 1T | J.J. Moloney |
| | | | |
| R.J. McLoughlin[1] | R.J. McLoughlin | R.J. McLoughlin | R.J. McLoughlin |
| K.W. Kennedy | K.W. Kennedy | K.W. Kennedy | K.W. Kennedy |
| J.F. Lynch | J.F. Lynch | J.F. Lynch | J.F. Lynch |
| *W.J. McBride | *W.J. McBride | *W.J. McBride | *W.J. McBride |
| †M.I. Keane | M.I. Keane | M.I. Keane | M.I. Keane |
| S.A. McKinney | †S.M. Deering | S.A. McKinney | S.A. McKinney 1PG |
| T.A.P. Moore | T.A.P. Moore | T.A.P. Moore 1T | T.A.P. Moore |
| J.F. Slattery | J.F. Slattery | J.F. Slattery | J.F. Slattery |
| Parc des Princes | Lansdowne Road | Twickenham | Lansdowne Road |
| LOST 6-9 | DRAWN 9-9 | WON 26-21 | WON 9-6 |
| Fr.: 1G 1PG | Ire.: 3PG | Eng.: 1G 5PG | Ire.: 1G 1PG |
| Ire.: 2PG | Wales: 1G 1PG | Ire.: 2G 1PG 1DG 2T | Scot.: 2PG |
| 19 Jan. 1974 | 2 Feb. 1974 | 16 Feb. 1974 | 2 Mar. 1974 |

[1]Rep. by †P.J. Agnew

Ireland became champions for the first time since 1951, winning two matches and drawing with Wales. This was the first season of the "double-header" fixture arrangements for the International Championship, and the Irish were first to complete their programme of matches. Consequently they had to wait two weeks to see France and Wales beaten in the season's final round of matches before celebrating their title triumph.

It was a just reward for four of Ireland's most experienced citizens: Ray McLoughlin, Bill McBride, Mike Gibson and Ken Kennedy. Each had made considerable contributions to Irish sides over the previous decade, and their presence in this successful team made Ireland popular champions.

## 1974-75

| v. O'SEAS XV | v. NZ | v. ENGLAND | v. SCOTLAND | v. FRANCE | v. WALES |
|---|---|---|---|---|---|
| A.H. Ensor | A.H. Ensor 2PG | A.H. Ensor | A.H. Ensor | A.H. Ensor 1T | A.H. Ensor |
| | | | | | |
| T.O. Grace | T.O. Grace | T.O. Grace | T.O. Grace 1T | T.O. Grace 1T | T.O. Grace |
| C.M.H. Gibson 2PG,2C[1] | R.A. Milliken | R.A. Milliken | R.A. Milliken | R.A. Milliken | R.A. Milliken |
| R.A. Milliken | †J.F. Crowe | C.M.H. Gibson 1T | C.M.H. Gibson | C.M.H. Gibson | C.M.H. Gibson |
| A.W. McMaster | †P. Parfrey | S.P. Dennison | S.P. Dennison 1T | A.W. McMaster | A.W. McMaster |
| | | | | | |
| M.A.M. Quinn | M.A.M. Quinn | W.M. McCombe 1T,2C | W.M. McCombe 1PG,1C | W.M. McCombe 2C,1PG,2DG | W.M. McCombe |
| J.J. Moloney | J.J. Moloney | J.J. Moloney | J.J. Moloney | J.J. Moloney | J.J. Moloney |
| | | | | | |
| R.J. McLoughlin | R.J. McLoughlin | R.J. McLoughlin | R.J. McLoughlin | R.J. McLoughlin | R.J. McLoughlin |
| K.W. Kennedy | K.W. Kennedy | †P.C. Whelan | P.C. Whelan | K.W. Kennedy | K.W. Kennedy |
| J.F. Lynch | J.F. Lynch | R.J. Clegg | R.J. Clegg | R.J. Clegg | R.J. Clegg |
| *W.J. McBride | *W.J. McBride | *W.J. McBride | *W.J. McBride | *W.J. McBride 1T | *W.J. McBride |
| M.I. Keane | M.I. Keane | M.I. Keane | M.I. Keane | M.I. Keane | M.I. Keane |
| S.A. McKinney 1T | S.A. McKinney | S.A. McKinney | S.A. McKinney | †M.J.A. Sherry | M.J.A. Sherry |
| T.A.P. Moore | T.A.P. Moore | †W.P. Duggan | W.P. Duggan | W.P. Duggan | W.P. Duggan 1T |
| J.F. Slattery 1T | J.F. Slattery | J.F. Slattery | J.F. Slattery | J.F. Slattery | J.F. Slattery |
| Lansdowne Road | Lansdowne Road | Lansdowne Road | Murrayfield | Lansdowne Road | Cardiff Arms Park |
| DRAWN 18-18 | LOST 6-15 | WON 12-9 | LOST 13-20 | WON 25-6 | LOST 4-32 |
| Ire.: 2G 2PG | Ire.: 2PG | Ire.: 2G | Scot.: 2PG 2DG 2T | Ire.: 2G 1PG 2DG 1T | Wales: 3G 2PG 2T |
| O/seas XV: 2G 2PG | NZ: 1G 3PG | Eng.: 1G 1DG | Ire.: 1G 1PG 1T | Fr.: 1PG 1DG | Ire.: 1T |
| 7 Sep. 1974 | 23 Nov. 1974 | 18 Jan. 1975 | 1 Feb. 1975 | 1 Mar. 1975 | 15 Mar. 1975 |

[1]Rep. by †A. Doherty

Ireland celebrated their Centenary season in 1974-5, playing two additional internationals early in the autumn to mark the occasion. The President's XV, led by Gareth Edwards, provided stiff opposition in September and an entertaining game ended in a high-scoring draw. Later the All Blacks, special guests of the IRFU in November, put Ireland under too much pressure for the result of the international ever to be in doubt, but Ireland's experienced team gave a good performance in losing by nine points.

For the Championship, Willie Duggan was brought in at number eight against England. He was to become Ireland's most-capped number eight, playing there 39 times (and twice as a flanker) in a career which spanned ten seasons.

The total of 25 points against France equalled Ireland's highest points total against the French, originally set before the Great War. McCombe kicked 13 points in the game, bringing his contribution for the season to 26 points and thus equalling the record for a season set by George Norton in 1949. Furthermore, Bill McBride played the last of his 63 internationals for Ireland in March at Cardiff. Upon his retirement he was the world's most-capped player.

## 1975-76

| v. AUSTRALIA | v. FRANCE | v. WALES | v. ENGLAND | v. SCOTLAND |
|---|---|---|---|---|
| A.H. Ensor | A.H. Ensor | A.H. Ensor | A.H. Ensor | L.A. Moloney |
| T.O. Grace | T.O. Grace | *T.O. Grace | *T.O. Grace 1T | *T.O. Grace |
| †J.A. McIlrath | J.A. McIlrath | P.J. Lavery[1] | †J.A. Brady | J.A. Brady |
| *C.M.H. Gibson | *C.M.H. Gibson | C.M.H. Gibson | C.M.H. Gibson | C.M.H. Gibson[1] |
| A.W. McMaster 1T | A.W. McMaster | A.W. McMaster | †S.E.F. Blake-Knox | S.E.F. Blake-Knox |
| †S.O. Campbell | B.J. McGann | B.J. McGann 3PG | B.J. McGann 2PG,1DG | B.J. McGann 2PG |
| †J.C. Robbie 2PG | J.C. Robbie 1PG | †D.M. Canniffe | D.M. Canniffe | J.J. Moloney |
| P.J. Agnew | †P.A. Orr | P.A. Orr | P.A. Orr | P.A. Orr |
| †J.L. Cantrell | J.L. Cantrell | J.L. Cantrell | J.L. Cantrell | J.L. Cantrell |
| †F.M. McLoughlin | P. O'Callaghan | P. O'Callaghan | P. O'Callaghan | P. O'Callaghan |
| M.I. Keane | M.I. Keane | M.I. Keane | M.I. Keane | M.I. Keane |
| M.G. Molloy | †B.O. Foley | †R.F. Hakin | B.O. Foley | R.F. Hakin |
| S.A. McKinney | S.A. McKinney | S.A. McKinney | S.A. McKinney | S.A. McKinney |
| W.P. Duggan | W.P. Duggan | W.P. Duggan | †H.W. Steele | W.P. Duggan |
| J.F. Slattery | S.M. Deering | S.M. Deering | S.M. Deering | S.M. Deering |
| Lansdowne Road | Parc des Princes | Lansdowne Road | Twickenham | Lansdowne Road |
| LOST 10-20 | LOST 3-26 | LOST 9-34 | WON 13-12 | LOST 6-15 |
| Ire.: 2PG 1T | Fr.: 2G 2PG 2T | Ire.: 3PG | Eng.: 4PG | Ire.: 2PG |
| Aust.: 1G 2PG 2T | Ire.: 1PG | Wales: 3G 4PG 1T | Ire.: 2PG 1DG 1T | Scot.: 4PG 1DG |
| 17 Jan. 1976 | 7 Feb. 1976 | 21 Feb. 1976 | 6 Mar. 1976 | 20 Mar. 1976 |
| | | [1]Rep. by †L.A. Moloney | | [1]Rep. by †C.H. McKibbin |

Feidlim McLoughlin, brother of the former Irish captain Ray McLoughlin, became the oldest first cap for Ireland when he was picked to play against Australia. At the time of the match he was a few days short of being 34½.

The selectors had problems fielding a balanced side in the wake of the retirements of McBride, McLoughlin and Kennedy, and the absences through injury of Slattery and Milliken. The return of Barry McGann improved the side's scoring power, but this fine player and popular character had lost much of his old attacking potential, and the backs had few opportunities to shine. Similarly, the recall of Mick Molloy was deemed an unsuccessful experiment, and he was dropped after the Australian game.

## 1976 / 1976-77

| v. NZ | v. WALES | v. ENGLAND | v. SCOTLAND | v. FRANCE |
|---|---|---|---|---|
| A.H. Ensor | †F. Wilson | F. Wilson | F. Wilson | A.H. Ensor |
| *T.O. Grace | *T.O. Grace | *T.O. Grace | *T.O. Grace | *T.O. Grace[1] |
| C.M.H. Gibson | †A.R. McKibbin | A.R. McKibbin | A.R. McKibbin | †R.G.A. Finn |
| J.A. McIlrath | J.A. McIlrath | J.A. McIlrath | C.M.H. Gibson 1T,1C,2PG | C.M.H. Gibson 1PG |
| A.W. McMaster | †D. St.J. Bowen | D. St.J. Bowen | D. St.J. Bowen | †A.C. McLennan |
| B.J. McGann 1PG | C.M.H. Gibson 3PG | C.M.H. Gibson | M.A.M. Quinn 1PG,1DG | M.A.M. Quinn 1PG |
| J.C. Robbie | †R.J.M. McGrath | R.J.M. McGrath | J.C. Robbie | J.C. Robbie[2] |
| P.A. Orr | P.A. Orr | P.A. Orr | P.A. Orr | P.A. Orr |
| P.C. Whelan | P.C. Whelan | P.C. Whelan | P.C. Whelan | P.C. Whelan |
| P. O'Callaghan | †T.A.O. Feighery | T.A.O. Feighery | †E.M.J. Byrne | E.M.J. Byrne |
| R.F. Hakin | M.I. Keane | M.I. Keane | M.I. Keane | M.I. Keane |
| M.I. Keane | R.F. Hakin[1] | R.F. Hakin | †C.W. Murtagh | R.F. Hakin |
| S.A. McKinney | S.A. McKinney | S.A. McKinney | S.A. McKinney | H.W. Steele |
| W.P. Duggan | W.P. Duggan | W.P. Duggan | W.P. Duggan | W.P. Duggan |
| J.C. Davidson | S.M. Deering | S.M. Deering | J.F. Slattery | J.F. Slattery |
| Wellington | Cardiff Arms Park | Lansdowne Road | Murrayfield | Lansdowne Road |
| LOST 3-11 | LOST 9-25 | LOST 0-4 | LOST 18-21 | LOST 6-15 |
| NZ: 1PG 2T | Wales: 2G 2PG 1DG 1T | Ire.: NIL | Scot.: 2PG 1DG 3T | Ire.: 2PG |
| Ire.: 1PG | Ire.: 3PG | Eng.: 1T | Ire.: 1G 3PG 1DG | Fr.: 1G 3PG |
| 5 Jun. 1976 | 15 Jan. 1977 | 5 Feb. 1977 | 19 Feb. 1977 | 19 Mar. 1977 |
| | [1]Rep. by B.O. Foley | | | [1]Rep. by S.E.F. Blake-Knox |
| | | | | [2]Rep. by R.J.M. McGrath |

Under the management of Kevin Quilligan, and with T.W. Meates as coach, Ireland made their first visit to New Zealand in the summer of 1976. In the only Test of the tour, Moss Keane and Willie Duggan played in the best tradition of New Zealand forward aggression, setting an inspiring example to their tough and energetic colleagues in the Irish pack.    The Championship season which followed was a miserable failure. All four matches were lost, only six players retained their places throughout the campaign, and at Cardiff, Willie Duggan became the first Irishman to be sent off in an international. He had been the outstanding player on the field up to the moment during the 38th minute of the first half when he punched Allan Martin.

## 1977-78

| v. SCOTLAND | v. FRANCE | v. WALES | v. ENGLAND |
|---|---|---|---|
| A.H. Ensor[1] | A.H. Ensor | A.H. Ensor | A.H. Ensor |
| T.O. Grace | C.M.H. Gibson | C.M.H. Gibson | C.M.H. Gibson |
| A.R. McKibbin | A.R. McKibbin | A.R. McKibbin | A.R. McKibbin |
| [†]P.P. McNaughton | P.P. McNaughton | P.P. McNaughton | P.P. McNaughton |
| A.C. McLennan | A.C. McLennan | A.C. McLennan | A.C. McLennan |
| [†]A.J.P. Ward 2PG,1C | A.J.P. Ward 3PG | A.J.P. Ward 3PG,1DG | A.J.P. Ward 1DG,2PG |
| *J.J. Moloney | *J.J. Moloney | *J.J. Moloney 1T | *J.J. Moloney |
| P.A. Orr | P.A. Orr | P.A. Orr | P.A. Orr |
| P.C. Whelan | P.C. Whelan | P.C. Whelan | P.C. Whelan |
| [†]M.P. Fitzpatrick | E.M.J. Byrne | E.M.J. Byrne | E.M.J. Byrne |
| M.I. Keane | M.I. Keane | M.I. Keane | M.I. Keane |
| [†]D.E. Spring | H.W. Steele | H.W. Steele | H.W. Steele |
| [†]J.B. O'Driscoll[2] | S.A. McKinney | S.A. McKinney | S.A. McKinney |
| W.P. Duggan | W.P. Duggan | W.P. Duggan | W.P. Duggan |
| J.F. Slattery | J.F. Slattery | J.F. Slattery | J.F. Slattery |
| Lansdowne Road | Parc des Princes | Lansdowne Road | Twickenham |
| WON 12-9 | LOST 9-10 | LOST 16-20 | LOST 9-15 |
| IRE.: 1G 2PG | FR.: 2PG 1T | IRE.: 3PG 1DG 1T | ENG.: 2G 1PG |
| SCOT.: 3PG | IRE.: 3PG | WALES: 4PG 2T | IRE.: 1DG 2PG |
| 21 Jan. 1978 | 18 Feb. 1978 | 4 Mar. 1978 | 18 Mar. 1978 |
| [1]Rep. by L.A. Moloney | | | |
| [2]Rep. by S.A. McKinney 1T | | | |

Ireland made a marginal improvement in 1978, boosted by the emergence of Tony Ward as a brilliant place-kicker with an eye for an opening in attack. He kicked 38 points to establish a new Irish record for points in a Championship season, and equalled the Five Nations records of Roger Hosen and Phil Bennett.

The match in Paris should never have been staged. The pitch was frozen hard after a spell of very cold weather, and conditions were extremely dangerous. The French Union, as host Union, exercised their right to play the match, despite the objections of players, referee and the IRFU Committee. In a close match, Ireland held a very strong French pack in the tight, and Tony Ward just failed to win the match in injury time with a drop at goal.

## 1978-79

| v. NZ | v. FRANCE | v. WALES | v. ENGLAND | v. SCOTLAND |
|---|---|---|---|---|
| L.A. Moloney | [†]R.M. Spring | R.M. Spring | R.M. Spring | [†]W.R.J. Elliott |
| [†]T.J. Kennedy | T.J. Kennedy | T.J. Kennedy | [†]M.C. Finn[1] | C.M.H. Gibson |
| A.R. McKibbin | A.R. McKibbin | A.R. McKibbin | A.R. McKibbin | A.R. McKibbin |
| C.M.H. Gibson | P.P. McNaughton | P.P. McNaughton | P.P. McNaughton | P.P. McNaughton |
| A.C. McLennan | A.C. McLennan | A.C. McLennan 1T | A.C. McLennan 1T | A.C. McLennan |
| A.J.P. Ward 2PG | A.J.P. Ward 3PG | A.J.P. Ward 3PG,2C | A.J.P. Ward 1PG,1DG,1C | A.J.P. Ward 1PG |
| [†]C.S. Patterson | C.S. Patterson | C.S. Patterson 1T | C.S. Patterson | C.S. Patterson 2T |
| P.A. Orr | P.A. Orr | P.A. Orr | P.A. Orr | P.A. Orr |
| P.C. Whelan | P.C. Whelan | P.C. Whelan | P.C. Whelan | P.C. Whelan |
| E.M.J. Byrne | [†]G.A.J. McLoughlin | G.A.J. McLoughlin | G.A.J. McLoughlin | G.A.J. McLoughlin |
| M.I. Keane | M.I. Keane | M.I. Keane | M.I. Keane | M.I. Keane |
| D.E. Spring | H.W. Steele | H.W. Steele | H.W. Steele | D.E. Spring |
| J.F. Slattery | [†]C.C. Tucker | C.C. Tucker | W.P. Duggan | W.P. Duggan |
| W.P. Duggan | [†]M.E. Gibson | M.E.Gibson | M.E. Gibson | M.E. Gibson |
| *S.M. Deering | *J.F. Slattery | *J.F. Slattery | *J.F. Slattery | *J.F. Slattery |
| Lansdowne Road | Lansdowne Road | Cardiff Arms Park | Lansdowne Road | Murrayfield |
| LOST 6-10 | DRAWN 9-9 | LOST 21-24 | WON 12-7 | DRAWN 11-11 |
| IRE.: 2PG | IRE.: 3PG | WALES: 2G 4PG | IRE.: 1G 1PG 1DG | SCOT.: 1PG 2T |
| NZ: 2DG 1T | FR.: 1G 1PG | IRE.: 2G 3PG | ENG.: 1PG 1T | IRE.: 1PG 2T |
| 4 Nov. 1978 | 20 Jan. 1979 | 3 Feb. 1979 | 17 Feb. 1979 | 3 Mar. 1979 |
| | | | [1]Rep. by T.J. Kennedy | |

After Munster had become the first Irish side to beat the All Blacks in October, there were high hopes that Ireland could repeat the performance a few days later. But in a disappointing international, the tourists gained an injury-time victory thanks to a try in the corner following a line-out. After Christmas, Ireland were the most improved side in the Championship.

Tony Ward had another successful season as place-kicker, though a moment's indecision when attempting a drop at goal in the dying minutes of the French match cost Ireland a famous victory (and, indeed, a share in the Championship).

## 1979

| 1st v. AUST. | 2nd v. AUST. |
|---|---|
| †R.C. O'Donnell[1] | R.C. O'Donnell |
| | |
| J.J. Moloney | J.J. Moloney |
| C.M.H. Gibson | C.M.H. Gibson |
| P.P. McNaughton | P.P. McNaughton |
| T.J. Kennedy | T.J. Kennedy |
| | |
| S.O. Campbell 4PG,2C,1DG | S.O. Campbell 2DG,1PG |
| C.S. Patterson 2T | C.S. Patterson |
| | |
| P.A. Orr | P.A. Orr |
| †C.F. Fitzgerald | C.F. Fitzgerald |
| G.A.J. McLoughlin | G.A.J. McLoughlin |
| M.I. Keane | M.I. Keane |
| H.W. Steele | H.W. Steele |
| *J.F. Slattery | *J.F. Slattery |
| W.P. Duggan | W.P. Duggan |
| J.B. O'Driscoll | J.B. O'Driscoll |
| | |
| Brisbane | Sydney |
| WON 27-12 | WON 9-3 |
| | |
| Aust.: 1G 2PG | Aust.: 1PG |
| Ire.: 2G 4PG 1DG | Ire.: 1PG 2DG |
| | |
| 3 Jun. 1979 | 16 Jun. 1979 |
| [1]Rep. by †F.N.G. Ennis | |

Ireland's second tour of Australia took place in the summer of 1979. The side was led by Fergus Slattery and included a nucleus of very experienced players supported by a handful of promising new men. Ciaran Fitzgerald, who went on to become a popular, inspiring and successful captain of Ireland, made his debut in the first of the Tests; and the other cap was Rodney O'Donnell at full-back, whose courageous displays won the admiration of the Australian pundits.

The same Irish side was fielded for the two internationals, and many back in Britain and Ireland were surprised to see Ollie Campbell preferred to Tony Ward. Campbell fully justified his promotion, however, setting a new Irish record for points scored in an international, with his 19 points in the first Test. Ireland's score of 27 points was also a record points total for an international.

## 1979-80

| v. ENGLAND | v. SCOTLAND | v. FRANCE | v. WALES |
|---|---|---|---|
| †K.A. O'Brien | R.C. O'Donnell | R.C. O'Donnell | R.C. O'Donnell |
| | | | |
| T.J. Kennedy | T.J. Kennedy 1T | T.J. Kennedy | T.J. Kennedy |
| A.R. McKibbin | A.R. McKibbin | †D.G. Irwin | D.G. Irwin 1T |
| P.P. McNaughton[1] | P.P. McNaughton | P.P. McNaughton | P.P. McNaughton |
| A.C. McLennan | J.J. Moloney | A.C. McLennan 1T | J.J. Moloney |
| | | | |
| S.O. Campbell 3PG | S.O. Campbell 3PG,1C,1DG | S.O. Campbell 3PG,1C,1DG | S.O. Campbell 3C,1PG |
| C.S. Patterson | C.S. Patterson | C.S. Patterson | C.S. Patterson |
| | | | |
| P.A. Orr | P.A. Orr | P.A. Orr | P.A. Orr |
| C.F. Fitzgerald | C.F. Fitzgerald | C.F. Fitzgerald | C.F. Fitzgerald 1T |
| G.A.J. McLoughlin | M.P. Fitzpatrick | M.P. Fitzpatrick | M.P. Fitzpatrick |
| M.I. Keane | J.J. Glennon | B.O. Foley | M.I. Keane |
| †J.J. Glennon | M.I. Keane 1T | M.I. Keane | B.O. Foley |
| J.B. O'Driscoll | J.B. O'Driscoll | J.B. O'Driscoll[1] | J.B. O'Driscoll 1T |
| W.P. Duggan | D.E. Spring | D.E. Spring | D.E. Spring |
| *J.F. Slattery | *J.F. Slattery | *J.F. Slattery | *J.F. Slattery |
| | | | |
| Twickenham | Lansdowne Road | Parc des Princes | Lansdowne Road |
| LOST 9-24 | WON 22-15 | LOST 18-19 | WON 21-7 |
| | | | |
| Eng.: 3G 2PG | Ire.: 1G 3PG 1DG 1T | Fr.: 1G 2PG 1DG 1T | Ire.: 3G 1PG |
| Ire.: 3PG | Scot.: 2G 1PG | Ire.: 1G 3PG 1DG | Wales: 1PG 1T |
| | | | |
| 19 Jan. 1980 | 2 Feb. 1980 | 1 Mar. 1980 | 15 Mar. 1980 |
| [1]Rep. by †I.J. Burns | | [1]Rep. by C.C. Tucker | |

The season saw two new Irish records established, though there were only two wins from the four matches. Ireland's 70 points were their highest ever for the International Championship, and 46 of these came from the trusty boot of Ollie Campbell. His haul was a record, not only to Ireland but also for the Five Nations Championship.

Ciaran Fitzgerald established himself as the leading Irish hooker, and his play in the loose was outstanding. In a narrow defeat in Paris, the Irish supporters felt that Fitzgerald had scored a perfectly legitimate try in the closing minutes – one which would have ensured an Irish victory. However his effort was disallowed by the referee. The season concluded with a triumph. Wales, the reigning champions, were surprisingly beaten by an Irish side which was fitter, faster and determined to gain victory. This time Fitzgerald got his try, through a fine piece of opportunism following a charged-down Welsh clearance.

## 1980-81

| v. FRANCE | v. WALES | v. ENGLAND | v. SCOTLAND |
|---|---|---|---|
| †H.P. MacNeill 1T | H.P. MacNeill 1T | H.P. MacNeill 1DG | H.P. MacNeill |
| †F.P. Quinn | F.P. Quinn | F.P. Quinn | †K.J. Hooks |
| D.G. Irwin | D.G. Irwin | D.G. Irwin | D.G. Irwin 1T |
| P.P. McNaughton | S.O. Campbell | S.O. Campbell 1DG | S.O. Campbell 1PG,1C |
| A.C. McLennan | A.C. McLennan | A.C. McLennan | A.C. McLennan |
| S.O. Campbell 3PG | A.J.P. Ward | A.J.P. Ward | A.J.P. Ward |
| J.C. Robbie | J.C. Robbie | J.C. Robbie | J.C. Robbie |
| P.A. Orr | P.A. Orr | P.A. Orr | P.A. Orr |
| P.C. Whelan | P.C. Whelan | P.C. Whelan | J.L. Cantrell |
| M.P. Fitzpatrick | M.P. Fitzpatrick | M.P. Fitzpatrick | M.P. Fitzpatrick |
| M.I. Keane | M.I. Keane | M.I. Keane | M.I. Keane |
| B.O. Foley | D.E. Spring[1] | B.O. Foley | B.O. Foley |
| J.B. O'Driscoll | J.B. O'Driscoll | J.B. O'Driscoll | J.B. O'Driscoll |
| W.P. Duggan | W.P. Duggan | W.P. Duggan | W.P. Duggan |
| *J.F. Slattery | *J.F. Slattery 1T | *J.F. Slattery | *J.F. Slattery |
| Lansdowne Road | Cardiff Arms Park | Lansdowne Road | Murrayfield |
| LOST 13-19 | LOST 8-9 | LOST 6-10 | LOST 9-10 |
| IRE.: 3PG 1T | WALES: 2PG 1DG | IRE.: 2DG | SCOT.: 1PG 1DG 1T |
| FR.: 3PG 2DG 1T | IRE.: 2T | ENG.: 1G 1T | IRE.: 1G 1PG |
| 7 Feb. 1981 | 21 Feb. 1981 | 7 Mar. 1981 | 21 Mar. 1981 |
|  | [1]Rep. by M.E. Gibson |  |  |

Ireland began the season as hot favourites to win the Championship. They ended the season with the wooden spoon, having lost all four of their matches for the first time since 1977. The side was full of promise and experience, especially in the scrummage, where more than half of the players were in their thirties. However the new coach, Tom Kiernan, had a bitterly disappointing season.

Hugo MacNeill made his debut against France and celebrated his selection with a spectacular second-half score. After some slick Irish passing, MacNeill popped up on the left wing to race away for a try. He scored another try at Cardiff, dropped a goal against England, and played with such poise and anticipation that he was acclaimed as the discovery of the season.

To accommodate both Tony Ward and Ollie Campbell, the Irish selectors used Campbell at centre with Ward in the pivot position. Their form at Cardiff was rich in promise, though there were few opportunities in the subsequent games against England and Scotland for the critics to gauge whether or not the experiment was a success.

## 1981

| 1st v. S.AFRICA | 2nd v. S.AFRICA |
|---|---|
| †J.J. Murphy[1] | K.A. O'Brien 1T |
| T.J. Kennedy | T.J. Kennedy |
| D.G. Irwin | D.G. Irwin |
| S.O. Campbell 2C,1PG[2] | P.M. Dean[1] |
| A.C. McLennan 1T | A.C. McLennan |
| †P.M. Dean | M.A.M. Quinn 2PG |
| R.J.M. McGrath 1T | R.J.M. McGrath |
| P.A. Orr | P.A. Orr |
| J.L. Cantrell | J.L. Cantrell |
| G.A.J. McLoughlin | G.A.J. McLoughlin |
| †J.J. Holland | J.J. Holland |
| B.O. Foley | B.O. Foley |
| *J.F. Slattery | *J.F. Slattery |
| W.P. Duggan | W.P. Duggan |
| J.B. O'Driscoll | J.B. O'Driscoll |
| Cape Town | Durban |
| LOST 15-23 | LOST 10-12 |
| SA: 1G 3PG 2T | SA: 1PG 3DG |
| IRE.: 2G 1PG | IRE.: 2PG 1T |
| 30 May 1981 | 6 Jun. 1981 |
| [1]Rep. by K.A. O'Brien | [1]Rep. by J.A. Hewitt |
| [2]Rep. by †J.A. Hewitt |  |

Despite extensive condemnation of their intentions, the IRFU fulfilled a promise to tour South Africa in the summer of 1981. Many of the tourists resigned their jobs when employers refused to grant leave of absence for the tour, while the Irish Union faced both political and ecclesiastical opposition to the visit from within their own country.

Of the seven matches played, four were lost, including both of the internationals. Injuries dogged Ollie Campbell, who played only twice on tour, and Mick Quinn, whose last caps had been won in 1977, was flown out as a late replacement for Campbell.

Quinn appeared in the second Test where Ireland very nearly squared the series. Ireland led 10-6 in the second half, thanks to Quinn's kicking and storming play by the forwards. Two late drop-goals by the Springbok fly-half finally defeated the Irish.

## 1981-82

| v. AUSTRALIA | v. WALES | v. ENGLAND | v. SCOTLAND | v. FRANCE |
|---|---|---|---|---|
| H.P. MacNeill | H.P. MacNeill | H.P. MacNeill 1t | H.P. MacNeill | H.P. MacNeill |
| †T.M. Ringland | T.M. Ringland 1t | T.M. Ringland | M.C. Finn | T.M. Ringland |
| D.G. Irwin | D.G. Irwin[1] | M.J. Kiernan | M.J. Kiernan | M.J. Kiernan |
| P.M. Dean | P.M. Dean[2] | P.M. Dean | P.M. Dean | P.M. Dean |
| T.J. Kennedy | M.C. Finn 2t | M.C. Finn | †K.D. Crossan | M.C. Finn |
| A.J.P. Ward 4pg | S.O. Campbell 1c,2pg | S.O. Campbell 2pg,1c | S.O. Campbell 6pg,1dg | S.O. Campbell 3pg |
| R.J.M. McGrath | R.J.M. McGrath | R.J.M. McGrath | R.J.M. McGrath | R.J.M. McGrath |
| P.A. Orr | P.A. Orr | P.A. Orr | P.A. Orr | P.A. Orr |
| J.L. Cantrell | *C.F. Fitzgerlad | *C.F. Fitzgerald | *C.F. Fitzgerald | *C.F. Fitzgerald |
| M.P. Fitzpatrick | G.A.J. McLoughlin | G.A.J. McLoughlin 1t | G.A.J. McLoughlin | G.A.J. McLoughlin |
| B.O. Foley | M.I. Keane | M.I. Keane | M.I. Keane | M.I. Keane |
| †D.G. Lenihan | D.G. Lenihan | D.G. Lenihan | D.G. Lenihan | D.G. Lenihan |
| J.B. O'Driscoll | J.F. Slattery | J.F. Slattery | J.F. Slattery | J.F. Slattery |
| W.P. Duggan | W.P. Duggan | W.P. Duggan | W.P. Duggan | J.B. O'Driscoll |
| *J.F. Slattery | J.B. O'Driscoll | J.B. O'Driscoll | J.B. O'Driscoll | †R.K. Kearney |
| Lansdowne Road | Lansdowne Road | Twickenham | Lansdowne Road | Parc des Princes |
| LOST 12-16 | WON 20-12 | WON 16-15 | WON 21-12 | LOST 9-22 |
| IRE.: 4PG | IRE.: 1G 2PG 2T | ENG.: 1G 3PG | IRE.: 6PG 1DG | FR.: 1G 4PG 1T |
| AUST.: 3PG 1DG 1T | WALES: 1G 1PG 1DG | IRE.: 1G 2PG 1T | SCOT.: 1G 2PG | IRE.: 3PG |
| 21 Nov. 1981 | 23 Jan. 1982 | 6 Feb. 1982 | 20 Feb. 1982 | 20 Mar. 1982 |

[1]Rep. by †M.J. Kiernan
[2]Rep. by J.J. Murphy

Fergus Slattery led Ireland for the 17th time in the match against Australia. The game was Ireland's seventh successive defeat, their worst international run since the early 1960s, and provided the visitors with their only Test win of the tour. Consequently, Ireland began the Championship as underdogs.

But a new captain, Ciaran Fitzgerald, infused an experienced side with fresh enthusiasm, commanded the respect of his senior players, and led by example on the field. The result was that Ireland won the Triple Crown for the first time since 1949.

Ollie Campbell kicked himself into the record books: 46 points (for the second time) and 13 penalty goals to create Championship records; six penalties against Scotland to equal the world record for an international; and 21 points in the same match to create a new mark for most points in an international by an Irish player.

## 1982-83

| v. SCOTLAND | v. FRANCE | v. WALES | v. ENGLAND |
|---|---|---|---|
| H.P. MacNeill | H.P. MacNeill | H.P. MacNeill 1pg | H.P. MacNeill |
| T.M. Ringland | T.M. Ringland | T.M. Ringland | T.M. Ringland |
| D.G. Irwin | D.G. Irwin | D.G. Irwin | D.G. Irwin |
| M.J. Kiernan 1t | M.J. Kiernan | M.J. Kiernan | M.J. Kiernan |
| M.C. Finn | M.C. Finn 2t | M.C. Finn | M.C. Finn |
| S.O. Campbell 1c,3pg | S.O. Campbell 1c,4pg | S.O. Campbell 2pg | S.O. Campbell 5pg,1t,1c[1] |
| R.J.M. McGrath | R.J.M. McGrath | R.J.M. McGrath | R.J.M. McGrath |
| P.A. Orr | P.A. Orr | P.A. Orr | P.A. Orr |
| *C.F. Fitzgerald | *C.F. Fitzgerald | *C.F. Fitzgerald | *C.F. Fitzgerald |
| G.A.J. McLoughlin | G.A.J. McLoughlin | G.A.J. McLoughlin | G.A.J. McLoughlin |
| D.G. Lenihan | D.G. Lenihan | D.G. Lenihan | D.G. Lenihan |
| M.I. Keane | M.I. Keane | M.I. Keane | M.I. Keane |
| J.F. Slattery | J.F. Slattery | J.F. Slattery | J.F. Slattery 1t |
| W.P. Duggan | W.P. Duggan | W.P. Duggan | W.P. Duggan |
| J.B. O'Driscoll | J.B. O'Driscoll | J.B. O'Driscoll | J.B. O'Driscoll |
| Murrayfield | Lansdowne Road | Cardiff Arms Park | Lansdowne Road |
| WON 15-13 | WON 22-16 | LOST 9-23 | WON 25-15 |
| SCOT.: 2PG 1DG 1T | IRE.: 1G 4PG 1T | WALES: 1G 3PG 2T | IRE.: 1G 5PG 1T |
| IRE.: 1G 3PG | FR.: 1G 2PG 1T | IRE.: 3PG | ENG.: 5PG |
| 15 Jan. 1983 | 19 Feb. 1983 | 5 Mar. 1983 | 19 Mar. 1983 |

[1]Rep. by A.J.P. Ward

Ireland's veteran pack again proved their ability to meet the challenges of younger forwards, and the team went on to retain the Championship, sharing the title with the French. Ollie Campbell was the chief scorer, registering 52 points in the four matches to set a new Five Nations record. His 14 penalty goals were also a new record for the Championship, and his 21 points against England equalled the individual record for most points by an Irishman in an international.    For the first time in Irish rugby history the same fifteen players were used in the four Championship matches. Fitzgerald again led the side with spirit and his leadership qualities were recognised by the Lions selectors, who made him skipper for the tour to New Zealand.

## 1983-84

| v. FRANCE | v. WALES | v. ENGLAND | v. SCOTLAND |
|---|---|---|---|
| H.P. MacNeill | H.P. MacNeill | H.P. MacNeill | J.J. Murphy 1c,1pg |
| | | | |
| T.M. Ringland | T.M. Ringland | T.M. Ringland | T.M. Ringland |
| D.G. Irwin | D.G. Irwin | M.J. Kiernan | M.J. Kiernan 1t |
| †R.J.M. Moroney | R.J.M. Moroney | M.C. Finn | M.C. Finn |
| K.D. Crossan | K.D. Crossan | K.D. Crossan | K.D. Crossan |
| | | | |
| S.O. Campbell 4pg | S.O. Campbell 3pg | A.J.P. Ward 3pg | A.J.P. Ward¹ |
| R.J.M. McGrath | R.J.M. McGrath | †J.A.P. Doyle | J.A.P. Doyle |
| | | | |
| P.A. Orr | P.A. Orr | P.A. Orr | P.A. Orr |
| *C.F. Fitzgerald | *C.F. Fitzgerald¹ | H.T. Harbison | H.T. Harbison |
| G.A.J. McLoughlin | †J.J. McCoy | †D.C. Fitzgerald | D.C. Fitzgerald |
| M.I. Keane | M.I. Keane | M.I. Keane | M.I. Keane |
| D.G. Lenihan | D.G. Lenihan | D.G. Lenihan | D.G. Lenihan |
| J.F. Slattery | †W.R. Duncan | W.R. Duncan | J.B. O'Driscoll |
| W.P. Duggan | W.P. Duggan | *W.P. Duggan | *W.P. Duggan |
| J.B. O'Driscoll | J.B. O'Driscoll | J.B. O'Driscoll | †D.G. McGrath |
| | | | |
| Parc des Princes | Lansdowne Road | Twickenham | Lansdowne Road |
| LOST 12-25 | LOST 9-18 | LOST 9-12 | LOST 9-32 |
| | | | |
| Fr.: 1g 4pg 1dg 1t | Ire.: 3pg | Eng.: 1dg 3pg | Ire.: 1g 1pg |
| Ire.: 4pg | Wales: 1g 4pg | Ire.: 3pg | Scot.: 3g‡ 2pg 2t |
| | | | |
| 21 Jan. 1984 | 4 Feb. 1984 | 18 Feb. 1984 | 3 Mar. 1984 |
| | ¹Rep. by †H.T. Harbison | | ¹Rep. by †H.C. Condon ‡includes a penalty try |

The Irish pack, for some seasons labelled with a "Dad's Army" tag, broke records in Paris, but lost heavily to a faster side. By playing together for their eighth time the pack established a record which is unlikely to be surpassed; the mean age of the eight in Paris was 31 years, 10 months, another record; and the loose forwards Slattery, O'Driscoll and Duggan played for the 19th time, creating another world record for official matches between 1B nations. Following the defeat in Paris, the selectors dropped McLoughlin and the long-serving Slattery. The campaign ended in a whitewash, with Scotland registering their highest points total and their highest winning margin against Ireland.

## 1984-85

| v. AUSTRALIA | v. SCOTLAND | v. FRANCE | v. WALES | v. ENGLAND |
|---|---|---|---|---|
| H.P. MacNeill | H.P. MacNeill | H.P. MacNeill | H.P. MacNeill | H.P. MacNeill |
| | | | | |
| T.M. Ringland | T.M. Ringland 2t | T.M. Ringland | T.M. Ringland 1t | T.M. Ringland |
| †B.J. Mullin | B.J. Mullin | R.J.M. Moroney | B.J. Mullin | B.J. Mullin 1t |
| M.C. Finn | M.J. Kiernan 2c,1dg,1pg | M.J. Kiernan 5pg | M.J. Kiernan 3pg,2c | M.J. Kiernan 2pg,1dg |
| M.J. Kiernan 3pg | K.D. Crossan | K.D. Crossan | K.D. Crossan 1t | K.D. Crossan |
| | | | | |
| P.M. Dean | P.M. Dean | P.M. Dean | P.M. Dean | P.M. Dean |
| †M.T. Bradley | M.T. Bradley | M.T. Bradley | M.T. Bradley | M.T. Bradley |
| | | | | |
| P.A. Orr | P.A. Orr | P.A. Orr | P.A. Orr | P.A. Orr |
| *C.F. Fitzgerald | *C.F. Fitzgerald | *C.F. Fitzgerald | *C.F. Fitzgerald | *C.F. Fitzgerald |
| J.J. McCoy | J.J. McCoy | J.J. McCoy | J.J. McCoy | J.J. McCoy |
| D.G. Lenihan | D.G. Lenihan | D.G. Lenihan | D.G. Lenihan | D.G. Lenihan |
| †W.A. Anderson | W.A. Anderson | W.A. Anderson | W.A. Anderson | W.A. Anderson |
| †P.M. Matthews | P.M. Matthews | P.M. Matthews¹ | P.M. Matthews | P.M. Matthews |
| R.K. Kearney | †B.J. Spillane | B.J. Spillane² | B.J. Spillane | B.J. Spillane |
| †W.J. Sexton | †N.J. Carr | N.J. Carr | N.J. Carr | N.J. Carr |
| | | | | |
| Lansdowne Road | Murrayfield | Lansdowne Road | Cardiff Arms Park | Lansdowne Road |
| LOST 9-16 | WON 18-15 | DRAWN 15-15 | WON 21-9 | WON 13-10 |
| | | | | |
| Ire.: 3pg | Scot.: 4pg 1dg | Ire.: 5pg | Wales: 1g 1dg | Ire.: 1dg 2pg 1t |
| Aust.: 3dg 1pg 1t | Ire.: 2g 1dg 1pg | Fr.: 2g 1pg | Ire.: 2g 3pg | Eng.: 2pg 1t |
| | | | | |
| 10 Nov. 1984 | 2 Feb. 1985 | 2 Mar. 1985 | 16 Mar. 1985 | 30 Mar. 1985 |
| | | ¹Rep. by M.P. Fitzpatrick ²Rep. by †B.W. McCall | | |

Ireland bounced back from the wooden spoon position and a defeat against a brilliant Australian side to win the Triple Crown and Championship. Mick Doyle replaced Bill McBride as coach and inspired the side to adopt an exciting, open approach. The team was unbeaten and only a draw with France deprived them of the Grand Slam.

Dean and Bradley, the new halves, forged a sound understanding and the emergence of Michael Kiernan as an accurate kicker had an important effect on Ireland's success. He scored 47 points in the Championship and his late drop-goal against England won the match and brought Ireland their sixth Triple Crown. It was the view of Sean Diffley, leading Irish rugby critic, that this was the most highly skilled all-round team ever produced by Ireland.

## 1985-86

| v. FRANCE | v. WALES | v. ENGLAND | v. SCOTLAND |
|---|---|---|---|
| H.P. MacNeill | H.P. MacNeill | H.P. MacNeill | H.P. MacNeill |
| | | | |
| T.M. Ringland | T.M. Ringland 1t | T.M. Ringland 1t | T.M. Ringland 1t |
| B.J. Mullin | B.J. Mullin | B.J. Mullin | B.J. Mullin |
| M.J. Kiernan 3pg | M.J. Kiernan 1c 2pg | M.J. Kiernan 1c 2pg | M.J. Kiernan 1pg 1c |
| M.C. Finn | M.C. Finn | K.D. Crossan | K.D. Crossan |
| | | | |
| P.M. Dean | P.M. Dean | †R.P. Keyes | A.J.P. Ward |
| M.T. Bradley | M.T. Bradley | M.T. Bradley | M.T. Bradley |
| | | | |
| P.A. Orr | †A.P. Kennedy | A.P. Kennedy | P.A. Orr |
| *C.F. Fitzgerald | *C.F. Fitzgerald | *C.F. Fitzgerald | *C.F. Fitzgerald |
| J.J. McCoy | D.C. Fitzgerald | D.C. Fitzgerald | D.C. Fitzgerald |
| D.G. Lenihan | D.G. Lenihan | B.W. McCall 1t | B.W. McCall |
| W.A. Anderson | J.J. Holland | D.G. Lenihan | D.G. Lenihan |
| R.K. Kearney | R.K. Kearney | R.D. Morrow | R.D. Morrow |
| B.J. Spillane | B.J. Spillane | B.J. Spillane | W.A. Anderson |
| †R.D. Morrow | N.J. Carr | N.J. Carr | N.J. Carr |
| | | | |
| Parc des Princes | Lansdowne Road | Twickenham | Lansdowne Road |
| LOST 9-29 | LOST 12-19 | LOST 20-25 | LOST 9-10 |
| | | | |
| Fr.: 1g 4pg 1dg 2t | Ire.: 1g 2pg | Eng.: 3g‡ 1pg 1t | Ire.: 1g 1pg |
| Ire.: 3pg | Wales: 1g 3pg 1t | Ire.: 1g 2pg 2t | Scot.: 2pg 1t |
| | | | |
| 1 Feb. 1986 | 15 Feb. 1986 | 1 Mar. 1986 | 15 Mar. 1986 |

‡includes penalty try.

Ireland, with a dozen of the previous season's Championship players available, and still under the thoughtful guidance of coach Mick Doyle and skipper Ciaran Fitzgerald, started the season with a heavy defeat in Paris. The Championship went from bad to worse thereafter and the side finished whitewashed holders of the wooden spoon for the second time in three seasons.

Among the few performances for Irish supporters to savour were the continued lineout expertise of Lenihan, probably the best line jumper of the British players in the Championship; the rapid development of the attacking potential of young Mullin in the centre; and the three tries scored by Ringland in consecutive matches.

The match at Twickenham was played on one of the bitterest days for rugby for many years. South-East England was trapped in a cold snap which had frozen the surrounds of a Twickenham pitch well-insulated from frost. But the game was staged as scheduled, despite a snowfall in the early hours of the morning of the match, and Ireland made a considerable contribution to a high-scoring contest played in difficult conditions.

## 1986-87

| v. ROMANIA | v. ENGLAND | v. SCOTLAND | v. FRANCE | v. WALES |
|---|---|---|---|---|
| H.P. MacNeill 1t | H.P. MacNeill | H.P. MacNeill | H.P. MacNeill | H.P. MacNeill |
| | | | | |
| T.M. Ringland | T.M. Ringland | T.M. Ringland | T.M. Ringland 1t | T.M. Ringland |
| B.J. Mullin 2t | B.J. Mullin | B.J. Mullin | B.J. Mullin | B.J. Mullin 1t |
| M.J. Kiernan 2pg 7c | M.J. Kiernan 1t 1c 1pg | M.J. Kiernan 1pg 1dg 1c | M.J. Kiernan 1pg 1c | M.J. Kiernan 1pg 2c |
| K.D. Crossan 3t | K.D. Crossan 1t | K.D. Crossan | K.D. Crossan | K.D. Crossan |
| | | | | |
| P.M. Dean 2t | P.M. Dean | P.M. Dean | P.M. Dean | P.M. Dean 1t |
| M.T. Bradley 1t | M.T. Bradley | M.T. Bradley | M.T. Bradley 1t | M.T. Bradley |
| | | | | |
| P.A. Orr | P.A. Orr | P.A. Orr | P.A. Orr | P.A. Orr |
| H.T. Harbison | H.T. Harbison | H.T. Harbison | H.T. Harbison | H.T. Harbison |
| D.C. Fitzgerald | D.C. Fitzgerald | D.C. Fitzgerald | D.C. Fitzgerald | D.C. Fitzgerald |
| *D.G. Lenihan | *D.G. Lenihan | *D.G. Lenihan 1t | *D.G. Lenihan | *D.G. Lenihan |
| W.A. Anderson 1t | J.J. Glennon | J.J. Glennon | J.J. Glennon | W.A. Anderson |
| P.M. Matthews | P.M. Matthews 1t | P.M. Matthews | B.J. Spillane | P.M. Matthews |
| M.E. Gibson | W.A. Anderson | W.A. Anderson | W.A. Anderson | B.J. Spillane |
| N.J. Carr | N.J. Carr | N.J. Carr | P.M. Matthews | N.J. Carr |
| | | | | |
| Lansdowne Road | Lansdowne Road | Murrayfield | Lansdowne Road | Cardiff Arms Park |
| WON 60-0 | WON 17-0 | LOST 12-16 | LOST 13-19 | WON 15-11 |
| | | | | |
| Ire.: 7g 3t 2pg | Ire.: 1g 1pg 2t | Scot.: 1g 2dg 1t | Ire.: 1g 1pg 1t | Wales: 1pg 2t |
| Rom.: nil | Eng.: nil | Ire.: 1g 1dg 1pg | Fr.: 1g 3pg 1t | Ire.: 2g 1pg |
| | | | | |
| 1 Nov. 1986 | 7 Feb. 1987 | 21 Feb. 1987 | 21 Mar. 1987 | 4 Apr. 1987 |

Ireland began their World Cup preparations with a record-breaking performance against Romania in Dublin. Awarding caps for the first time against non-IB opponents, the IRFU thus conferred full official status on this international.

Ireland's total of sixty points matched the IB record (set by France in 1967) for the highest score in a match, the margin of victory was a new world record, and Kiernan and Crossan became Irish record-holders. Kiernan kicked seven conversions in the match and Crossan's three tries equalled the Irish record held by several players.

After a convincing start in the Championship there were disappointing defeats before the Irish succeeded against Wales in Cardiff. The victory had especial significance: not only was it Ireland's second consecutive win at Cardiff, it enabled Ireland to set off for the World Cup as favourites to qualify as winners from a group in which the only other seeded nation was Wales.

# IRISH MATCH RESULTS

## Match Results 1875 to 1987

| Match | Date | Opponents | For T | C | D | P | Pts | Against T | C | D | P | Pts | Result | Venue | Captain |
|---|---|---|---|---|---|---|---|---|---|---|---|---|---|---|---|
| 1 | 15.2.1875 | England | — | — | — | — |  | 2 | 1 | 1 | — |  | Lost | The Oval | G. Stack |
| 2 | 13.12.1875 | England | — | — | — | — |  | 2 | 1 | — | — |  | Lost | Dublin | R. J. Bell |
| 3 | 5.2.1877 | England | — | — | — | — |  | 4 | 2 | — | — |  | Lost | The Oval | R. Galbraith |
| 4 | 19.2.1877 | Scotland | — | — | — | — |  | 6 | 4 | 2 | — |  | Lost | Belfast | W. H. Wilson |
| 5 | 11.3.1878 | England | — | — | — | — |  | 3 | 2 | — | — |  | Lost | Dublin | R. B. Walkington |
| 6 | 17.2.1879 | Scotland | — | — | — | — |  | 2 | 1 | 1 | — |  | Lost | Belfast | W. C. Neville |
| 7 | 24.3.1879 | England | — | — | — | — |  | 4 | 2 | 1 | — |  | Lost | The Oval | W. C. Neville |
| 8 | 30.1.1880 | England | 1 | — | — | — |  | 2 | 1 | — | — |  | Lost | Dublin | H. C. Kelly |
| 9 | 14.2.1880 | Scotland | — | — | — | — |  | 3 | 1 | 2 | — |  | Lost | Glasgow | H. C. Kelly |
| 10 | 5.2.1881 | England | — | — | — | — |  | 4 | 2 | — | — |  | Lost | Manchester | A. J. Forrest |
| 11 | 19.2.1881 | Scotland | — | — | 1 | — |  | 1 | — | — | — |  | Won | Belfast | A. J. Forrest |
| 12 | 28.1.1882 | Wales | — | — | — | — |  | 4 | 2 | — | — |  | Lost | Dublin | A. J. Forrest |
| 13 | 6.2.1882 | England | 2 | — | — | — |  | 2 | — | — | — |  | Drawn | Dublin | J. W. Taylor |
| 14 | 18.2.1882 | Scotland | — | — | — | — |  | 2 | — | — | — |  | Lost | Glasgow | J. W. Taylor |
| 15 | 5.2.1883 | England | 1 | — | — | — |  | 4 | 1 | — | — |  | Lost | Manchester | G. Scriven |
| 16 | 17.2.1883 | Scotland | — | — | — | — |  | 2 | 1 | — | — |  | Lost | Belfast | G. Scriven |
| 17 | 4.2.1884 | England | — | — | — | — |  | 1 | 1 | — | — |  | Lost | Dublin | J. A. McDonald |
| 18 | 16.2.1884 | Scotland | 1 | — | — | — |  | 4 | 2 | — | — |  | Lost | Edinburgh | J. A. McDonald |
| 19 | 12.4.1884 | Wales | — | — | — | — |  | 2 | — | 1 | — |  | Lost | Cardiff | H. G. Cook |
| 20 | 7.2.1885 | England | 1 | — | — | — |  | 2 | — | — | — |  | Lost | Manchester | W. G. Rutherford |
| 21 | 7.3.1885 | Scotland | — | — | — | — |  | 3 | 1 | — | — |  | Lost | Edinburgh | A. J. Forrest |
| 22 | 6.2.1886 | England | — | — | — | — |  | 1 | — | — | — |  | Lost | Dublin | M. Johnston |
| 23 | 20.2.1886 | Scotland | — | — | — | — |  | 5 | 3 | 1 | — |  | Lost | Edinburgh | J. P. Ross |
| 24 | 5.2.1887 | England | 2 | 2 | — | — |  | — | — | — | — |  | Won | Dublin | R. G. Warren |
| 25 | 19.2.1887 | Scotland | — | — | — | — |  | 3 | 1 | ★ | — |  | Lost | Belfast | R. G. Warren |
| 26 | 12.3.1887 | Wales | 3 | — | — | — |  | 1 | — | — | — |  | Won | Birkenhead | R. G. Warren |
| 27 | 3.3.1888 | Wales | 2 | 1 | 1 | — |  | — | — | — | — |  | Won | Dublin | H. J. Neill |
| 28 | 10.3.1888 | Scotland | — | — | — | — |  | 1 | 1 | — | — |  | Lost | Edinburgh | H. J. Neill |
| 29 | 1.12.1888 | New Zealand Natives | 2 | 1 | — | — |  | 5 | 1 | — | — |  | Lost | Dublin | R. G. Warren |
| 30 | 16.2.1889 | Scotland | — | — | — | — |  | — | — | 1 | — |  | Lost | Belfast | R. G. Warren |
| 31 | 2.3.1889 | Wales | 2 | — | — | — |  | — | — | — | — |  | Won | Swansea | R. G. Warren |
| 32 | 22.2.1890 | Scotland | — | — | — | — | 0 | 1 | — | 1 | — | 5 | Lost | Edinburgh | R. G. Warren |
| 33 | 1.3.1890 | Wales | 1 | 1 | — | — | 3 | 1 | 1 | — | — | 3 | Drawn | Dublin | R. G. Warren |
| 34 | 15.3.1890 | England | — | — | — | — | 0 | 3 | — | — | — | 3 | Lost | Blackheath | R. G. Warren |
| 35 | 7.2.1891 | England | — | — | — | — | 0 | 5 | 2 | — | — | 9 | Lost | Dublin | D. B. Walkington |
| 36 | 21.2.1891 | Scotland | — | — | — | — | 0 | 5 | 3 | 1 | — | 14 | Lost | Belfast | D. B. Walkington |
| 37 | 7.3.1891 | Wales | 1 | — | 1 | — | 4 | 1 | 1 | 1 | — | 6 | Lost | Llanelli | R. Stevenson |
| 38 | 6.2.1892 | England | — | — | — | — | 0 | 2 | 1 | — | — | 7 | Lost | Manchester | V. C. le Fanu |
| 39 | 20.2.1892 | Scotland | — | — | — | — | 0 | 1 | — | — | — | 2 | Lost | Edinburgh | V. C. le Fanu |
| 40 | 5.3.1892 | Wales | 3 | 1 | — | — | 9 | — | — | — | — | 0 | Won | Dublin | V. C. le Fanu |
| 41 | 4.2.1893 | England | — | — | — | — | 0 | 2 | — | — | — | 4 | Lost | Dublin | S. Lee |
| 42 | 18.2.1893 | Scotland | — | — | — | — | 0 | — | — | — | — | 0 | Drawn | Belfast | S. Lee |
| 43 | 11.3.1893 | Wales | — | — | — | — | 0 | 1 | — | — | — | 2 | Lost | Llanelli | S. Lee |
| 44 | 3.2.1894 | England | 1 | — | 1 | — | 7 | 1 | 1 | — | — | 5 | Won | Blackheath | E. G. Forrest |
| 45 | 24.2.1894 | Scotland | 1 | 1 | — | — | 5 | — | — | — | — | 0 | Won | Dublin | E. G. Forrest |
| 46 | 10.3.1894 | Wales | — | — | — | 1 | 3 | — | — | — | — | 0 | Won | Belfast | E. G. Forrest |
| 47 | 2.2.1895 | England | 1 | — | — | — | 3 | 2 | — | — | — | 6 | Lost | Dublin | J. H. O'Conor |
| 48 | 2.3.1895 | Scotland | — | — | — | — | 0 | 2 | — | — | — | 6 | Lost | Edinburgh | C. V. Rooke |
| 49 | 16.3.1895 | Wales | 1 | — | — | — | 3 | 1 | 1 | — | — | 5 | Lost | Cardiff | E. G. Forrest |
| 50 | 1.2.1896 | England | 2 | 2 | — | — | 10 | — | — | 1 | — | 4 | Won | Leeds | S. Lee |
| 51 | 15.2.1896 | Scotland | — | — | — | — | 0 | — | — | — | — | 0 | Drawn | Dublin | S. Lee |
| 52 | 14.3.1896 | Wales | 2 | 1 | — | — | 8 | — | — | 1 | — | 4 | Won | Dublin | S. Lee |
| 53 | 6.2.1897 | England | 3 | — | ★ | — | 13 | 1 | — | — | 2 | 9 | Won | Dublin | E. G. Forrest |
| 54 | 20.2.1897 | Scotland | 1 | — | — | — | 3 | 1 | 1 | — | 1 | 8 | Lost | Edinburgh | E. G. Forrest |
| 55 | 5.2.1898 | England | 2 | — | — | 1 | 9 | 1 | — | — | 1 | 6 | Won | Richmond | S. Lee |
| 56 | 19.2.1898 | Scotland | — | — | — | — | 0 | 2 | 1 | — | — | 8 | Lost | Belfast | G. G. Allen |
| 57 | 19.3.1898 | Wales | — | — | — | 1 | 3 | 2 | 1 | — | 1 | 11 | Lost | Limerick | W. Gardiner |
| 58 | 4.2.1899 | England | 1 | — | — | 1 | 6 | — | — | — | — | 0 | Won | Dublin | L. M. Magee |
| 59 | 18.2.1899 | Scotland | 3 | — | — | — | 9 | — | — | — | 1 | 3 | Won | Edinburgh | L. M. Magee |
| 60 | 18.3.1899 | Wales | 1 | — | — | — | 3 | — | — | — | — | 0 | Won | Cardiff | L. M. Magee |
| 61 | 3.2.1900 | England | — | — | 1 | — | 4 | 3 | 1 | 1 | — | 15 | Lost | Richmond | L. M. Magee |
| 62 | 24.2.1900 | Scotland | — | — | — | — | 0 | — | — | — | — | 0 | Drawn | Dublin | L. M. Magee |
| 63 | 17.3.1900 | Wales | — | — | — | — | 0 | 1 | — | — | — | 3 | Lost | Belfast | L. M. Magee |
| 64 | 9.2.1901 | England | 2 | 2 | — | — | 10 | 1 | — | — | 1 | 6 | Won | Dublin | L. M. Magee |
| 65 | 23.2.1901 | Scotland | 1 | 1 | — | — | 5 | 3 | — | — | — | 9 | Lost | Edinburgh | L. M. Magee |
| 66 | 16.3.1901 | Wales | 3 | — | — | — | 9 | 2 | 2 | — | — | 10 | Lost | Swansea | L. M. Magee |
| 67 | 8.2.1902 | England | 1 | — | — | — | 3 | 2 | — | — | — | 6 | Lost | Leicester | J. Fulton |
| 68 | 22.2.1902 | Scotland | 1 | 1 | — | — | 5 | — | — | — | — | 0 | Won | Belfast | J. Fulton |
| 69 | 8.3.1902 | Wales | — | — | — | — | 0 | 3 | 1 | 1 | — | 15 | Lost | Dublin | L. M. Magee |

*in the drop-goal column denotes a goal from a mark

| Match | Date | Opponents | For T | C | D | P | Pts | Against T | C | D | P | Pts | Result | Venue | Captain |
|---|---|---|---|---|---|---|---|---|---|---|---|---|---|---|---|
| 70 | 14.2.1903 | England | 1 | — | — | 1 | 6 | — | — | — | — | 0 | Won | Dublin | H. H. Corley |
| 71 | 28.2.1903 | Scotland | — | — | — | — | 0 | 1 | — | — | — | 3 | Lost | Edinburgh | H. H. Corley |
| 72 | 14.3.1903 | Wales | — | — | — | — | 0 | 6 | — | — | — | 18 | Lost | Cardiff | H. H. Corley |
| 73 | 13.2.1904 | England | — | — | — | — | 0 | 5 | 2 | — | — | 19 | Lost | Blackheath | H. H. Corley |
| 74 | 27.2.1904 | Scotland | 1 | — | — | — | 3 | 5 | 2 | — | — | 19 | Lost | Dublin | H. H. Corley |
| 75 | 12.3.1904 | Wales | 4 | 1 | — | — | 14 | 4 | — | — | — | 12 | Won | Belfast | C. E. Allen |
| 76 | 11.2.1905 | England | 5 | 1 | — | — | 17 | 1 | — | — | — | 3 | Won | Cork | C. E. Allen |
| 77 | 25.2.1905 | Scotland | 3 | 1 | — | — | 11 | 1 | 1 | — | — | 5 | Won | Edinburgh | C. E. Allen |
| 78 | 11.3.1905 | Wales | 1 | — | — | — | 3 | 2 | 2 | — | — | 10 | Lost | Swansea | C. E. Allen |
| 79 | 25.11.1905 | New Zealand | — | — | — | — | 0 | 3 | 3 | — | — | 15 | Lost | Dublin | C. E. Allen |
| 80 | 10.2.1906 | England | 4 | 2 | — | — | 16 | 2 | — | — | — | 6 | Won | Leicester | C. E. Allen |
| 81 | 24.2.1906 | Scotland | 2 | — | — | — | 6 | 2 | 2 | ★ | — | 13 | Lost | Dublin | C. E. Allen |
| 82 | 10.3.1906 | Wales | 3 | 1 | — | — | 11 | 2 | — | — | — | 6 | Won | Belfast | C. E. Allen |
| 83 | 24.11.1906 | South Africa | 3 | — | — | 1 | 12 | 4 | — | — | 1 | 15 | Lost | Belfast | C. E. Allen |
| 84 | 9.2.1907 | England | 4 | 1 | ★ | — | 17 | 2 | — | — | 1 | 9 | Won | Dublin | A. Tedford |
| 85 | 23.2.1907 | Scotland | — | — | — | 1 | 3 | 3 | 3 | — | — | 15 | Lost | Edinburgh | C. E. Allen |
| 86 | 9.3.1907 | Wales | — | — | — | — | 0 | 6 | 2 | 1 | 1 | 29 | Lost | Cardiff | C. E. Allen |
| 87 | 8.2.1908 | England | — | — | — | 1 | 3 | 3 | 2 | — | — | 13 | Lost | Richmond | H. B. Thrift |
| 88 | 29.2.1908 | Scotland | 4 | 2 | — | — | 16 | 2 | 1 | — | 1 | 11 | Won | Dublin | J. C. Parke |
| 89 | 14.3.1908 | Wales | 1 | 1 | — | — | 5 | 3 | 1 | — | — | 11 | Lost | Belfast | J. C. Parke |
| 90 | 13.2.1909 | England | 1 | 1 | — | — | 5 | 3 | 1 | — | — | 11 | Lost | Dublin | F. Gardiner |
| 91 | 27.2.1909 | Scotland | — | — | — | 1 | 3 | 3 | — | — | — | 9 | Lost | Edinburgh | F. Gardiner |
| 92 | 13.3.1909 | Wales | 1 | 1 | — | — | 5 | 4 | 3 | — | — | 18 | Lost | Swansea | G.T. Hamlet |
| 93 | 20.3.1909 | France | 4 | 2 | — | 1 | 19 | 2 | 1 | — | — | 8 | Won | Dublin | F. Gardiner |
| 94 | 12.2.1910 | England | — | — | — | — | 0 | — | — | — | — | 0 | Drawn | Twickenham | G. T. Hamlet |
| 95 | 26.2.1910 | Scotland | — | — | — | — | 0 | 4 | 1 | — | — | 14 | Lost | Belfast | G. T. Hamlet |
| 96 | 12.3.1910 | Wales | 1 | — | — | — | 3 | 5 | — | 1 | — | 19 | Lost | Dublin | T. Smyth |
| 97 | 28.3.1910 | France | 2 | 1 | — | — | 8 | 1 | — | — | — | 3 | Won | Paris | G. T. Hamlet |
| 98 | 11.2.1911 | England | 1 | — | — | — | 3 | — | — | — | — | 0 | Won | Dublin | G. T. Hamlet |
| 99 | 25.2.1911 | Scotland | 4 | 2 | — | — | 16 | 2 | — | 1 | — | 10 | Won | Edinburgh | G. T. Hamlet |
| 100 | 11.3.1911 | Wales | — | — | — | — | 0 | 3 | 2 | — | 1 | 16 | Lost | Cardiff | G. T. Hamlet |
| 101 | 25.3.1911 | France | 5 | 3 | 1 | — | 25 | 1 | 1 | — | — | 5 | Won | Cork | G. T. Hamlet |
| 102 | 1.1.1912 | France | 3 | 1 | — | — | 11 | 2 | — | — | — | 6 | Won | Paris | R. A. Lloyd |
| 103 | 10.2.1912 | England | — | — | — | — | 0 | 5 | — | — | — | 15 | Lost | Twickenham | A. R. Foster |
| 104 | 24.2.1912 | Scotland | 1 | — | 1 | 1 | 10 | 2 | 1 | — | — | 8 | Won | Dublin | R. A. Lloyd |
| 105 | 9.3.1912 | Wales | 2 | 1 | 1 | — | 12 | 1 | 1 | — | — | 5 | Won | Belfast | R. A. Lloyd |
| 106 | 30.11.1912 | South Africa | — | — | — | — | 0 | 10 | 4 | — | — | 38 | Lost | Dublin | R. A. Lloyd |
| 107 | 8.2.1913 | England | — | — | 1 | — | 4 | 4 | — | — | 1 | 15 | Lost | Dublin | R. A. Lloyd |
| 108 | 22.2.1913 | Scotland | 2 | 2 | 1 | — | 14 | 7 | 4 | — | — | 29 | Lost | Edinburgh | R. A. Lloyd |
| 109 | 8.3.1913 | Wales | 2 | 2 | — | 1 | 13 | 3 | 2 | — | 1 | 16 | Lost | Swansea | R. A. Lloyd |
| 110 | 24.3.1913 | France | 6 | 3 | — | — | 24 | — | — | — | — | 0 | Won | Cork | R. A. Lloyd |
| 111 | 1.1.1914 | France | 2 | 1 | — | — | 8 | 2 | — | — | — | 6 | Won | Paris | R. A. Lloyd |
| 112 | 14.2.1914 | England | 2 | 1 | 1 | — | 12 | 5 | 1 | — | — | 17 | Lost | Twickenham | R. A. Lloyd |
| 113 | 28.2.1914 | Scotland | 2 | — | — | — | 6 | — | — | — | — | 0 | Won | Dublin | A. R. Foster |
| 114 | 14.3.1914 | Wales | 1 | — | — | — | 3 | 3 | 1 | — | — | 11 | Lost | Belfast | A. R. Foster |
| 115 | 14.2.1920 | England | 2 | 1 | — | 1 | 11 | 4 | 1 | — | — | 14 | Lost | Dublin | R. A. Lloyd |
| 116 | 28.2.1920 | Scotland | — | — | — | — | 0 | 4 | 2 | — | 1 | 19 | Lost | Edinburgh | T. Wallace |
| 117 | 13.3.1920 | Wales | — | — | 1 | — | 4 | 6 | 3 | 1 | — | 28 | Lost | Cardiff | T. Wallace |
| 118 | 3.4.1920 | France | 1 | — | 1 | — | 7 | 5 | — | — | — | 15 | Lost | Dublin | R. A. Lloyd |
| 119 | 12.2.1921 | England | — | — | — | — | 0 | 3 | 1 | 1 | — | 15 | Lost | Twickenham | W. D. Doherty |
| 120 | 26.2.1921 | Scotland | 3 | — | — | — | 9 | 2 | 1 | — | — | 8 | Won | Dublin | W. D. Doherty |
| 121 | 12.3.1921 | Wales | — | — | — | — | 0 | 1 | — | — | 1 | 6 | Lost | Belfast | W. D. Doherty |
| 122 | 9.4.1921 | France | 2 | 2 | — | — | 10 | 4 | 4 | — | — | 20 | Lost | Paris | W. D. Doherty |
| 123 | 11.2.1922 | England | 1 | — | — | — | 3 | 4 | — | — | — | 12 | Lost | Dublin | W. P. Collopy |
| 124 | 25.2.1922 | Scotland | 1 | — | — | — | 3 | 2 | — | — | — | 6 | Lost | Edinburgh | W. P. Collopy |
| 125 | 11.3.1922 | Wales | 1 | 1 | — | — | 5 | 3 | 1 | — | — | 11 | Lost | Swansea | W. P. Collopy |
| 126 | 8.4.1922 | France | 1 | 1 | — | 1 | 8 | 1 | — | — | — | 3 | Won | Dublin | W. P. Collopy |
| 127 | 10.2.1923 | England | 1 | 1 | — | — | 5 | 5 | 2 | 1 | — | 23 | Lost | Leicester | J. K. S. Thompson |
| 128 | 24.2.1923 | Scotland | 1 | — | — | — | 3 | 3 | 2 | — | — | 13 | Lost | Dublin | J. K. S. Thompson |
| 129 | 10.3.1923 | Wales | 1 | 1 | — | — | 5 | — | — | 1 | — | 4 | Won | Dublin | J. K. S. Thompson |
| 130 | 14.4.1923 | France | 2 | 1 | — | — | 8 | 4 | 1 | — | — | 14 | Lost | Paris | J. K. S. Thompson |
| 131 | 26.1.1924 | France | 2 | — | — | — | 6 | — | — | — | — | 0 | Won | Dublin | W. E. Crawford |
| 132 | 9.2.1924 | England | 1 | — | — | — | 3 | 4 | 1 | — | — | 14 | Lost | Belfast | W. E. Crawford |
| 133 | 23.2.1924 | Scotland | 2 | 1 | — | — | 8 | 3 | 2 | — | — | 13 | Lost | Edinburgh | W. P. Collopy |
| 134 | 8.3.1924 | Wales | 3 | 2 | — | — | 13 | 2 | 1 | — | — | 8 | Won | Cardiff | W. E. Crawford |
| 135 | 1.11.1924 | New Zealand | — | — | — | — | 0 | 1 | — | — | 1 | 6 | Lost | Dublin | G. V. Stephenson |
| 136 | 1.1.1925 | France | 2 | — | — | 1 | 9 | 1 | — | — | — | 3 | Won | Paris | W. E. Crawford |
| 137 | 14.2.1925 | Engpand | 2 | — | — | — | 6 | 2 | — | — | — | 6 | Drawn | Twickenham | W. E. Crawford |
| 138 | 28.2.1925 | Scotland | 1 | 1 | — | 1 | 8 | 2 | 2 | 1 | — | 14 | Lost | Dublin | W. E. Crawford |
| 139 | 14.3.1925 | Wales | 4 | 2 | — | 1 | 19 | 1 | — | — | — | 3 | Won | Belfast | W. E. Crawford |

*in the drop-goal column denotes a goal from a mark

| Match | Date | Opponents | For T C D P Pts | Against T C D P Pts | Result | Venue | Captain |
|---|---|---|---|---|---|---|---|
| 140 | 23.1.1926 | France | 2 1 — 1 11 | — — — — 0 | Won | Belfast | W. E. Crawford |
| 141 | 13.2.1926 | England | 4 2 — 1 19 | 3 3 — — 15 | Won | Dublin | W. E. Crawford |
| 142 | 27.2.1926 | Scotland | 1 — — — 3 | — — — — 0 | Won | Edinburgh | W. E. Crawford |
| 143 | 13.3.1926 | Wales | 1 1 — 1 8 | 3 1 — — 11 | Lost | Swansea | W. E. Crawford |
| 144 | 1.1.1927 | France | 1 1 — 1 8 | 1 — — — 3 | Won | Paris | W. E. Crawford |
| 145 | 12.2.1927 | England | 1 — 1 6 | 2 1 — — 8 | Lost | Twickenham | W. E. Crawford |
| 146 | 26.2.1927 | Scotland | 2 — — 6 | — — — — 0 | Won | Dublin | W. E. Crawford |
| 147 | 12.3.1927 | Wales | 4 2 — 1 19 | 1 1 1 — 9 | Won | Dublin | W. E. Crawford |
| 148 | 12.11.1927 | New South Wales | — — — 1 3 | 1 1 — — 5 | Lost | Dublin | G. V. Stephenson |
| 149 | 28.1.1928 | France | 4 — — — 12 | 2 1 — — 8 | Won | Belfast | G. V. Stephenson |
| 150 | 11.2.1928 | England | 2 — — — 6 | 1 — 1 — 7 | Lost | Dublin | G. V. Stephenson |
| 151 | 25.2.1928 | Scotland | 3 2 — — 13 | 1 1 — — 5 | Won | Edinburgh | G. V. Stephenson |
| 152 | 10.3.1928 | Wales | 3 2 — — 13 | 2 2 — — 10 | Won | Cardiff | G. V. Stephenson |
| 153 | 31.12.1928 | France | 2 — — — 6 | — — — — 0 | Won | Paris | G. V. Stephenson |
| 154 | 9.2.1929 | England | 2 — — — 6 | 1 1 — — 5 | Won | Twickenham | G. V. Stephenson |
| 155 | 23.2.1929 | Scotland | 1 — 1 — 7 | 4 2 — — 16 | Lost | Dublin | E. O'D. Davy |
| 156 | 9.3.1929 | Wales | 1 1 — — 5 | 1 1 — — 5 | Drawn | Belfast | G. V. Stephenson |
| 157 | 25.1.1930 | France | — — — — 0 | 1 1 — — 5 | Lost | Belfast | G. V. Stephenson |
| 158 | 8.2.1930 | England | — — 1 — 4 | 1 — — — 3 | Won | Dublin | G. V. Stephenson |
| 159 | 22.2.1930 | Scotland | 4 1 — — 14 | 3 1 — — 11 | Won | Edinburgh | G. V. Stephenson |
| 160 | 8.3.1930 | Wales | — — 1 1 7 | 3 — — 1 12 | Lost | Swansea | G. V. Stephenson |
| 161 | 1.1.1931 | France | — — — — 0 | 1 — — — 3 | Lost | Paris | M. Sugden |
| 162 | 14.2.1931 | England | 1 — — 1 6 | 1 1 — — 5 | Won | Twickenham | M. Sugden |
| 163 | 28.2.1931 | Scotland | 2 1 — — 8 | 1 1 — — 5 | Won | Dublin | M. Sugden |
| 164 | 14.3.1931 | Wales | 1 — — — 3 | 3 1 1 — 15 | Lost | Belfast | M. Sugden |
| 165 | 19.12.1931 | South Africa | — — — 1 3 | 2 1 — — 8 | Lost | Dublin | G. R. Beamish |
| 166 | 13.2.1932 | England | 1 1 — 1 8 | 1 1 — 2 11 | Lost | Dublin | G. R. Beamish |
| 167 | 27.2.1932 | Scotland | 4 4 — — 20 | 2 1 — — 8 | Won | Edinburgh | G. R. Beamish |
| 168 | 12.3.1932 | Wales | 4 — — — 12 | 2 — 1 — 10 | Won | Cardiff | G. R. Beamish |
| 169 | 11.2.1933 | England | 1 — — 1 6 | 5 1 — — 17 | Lost | Twickenham | E. O'D. Davy |
| 170 | 11.3.1933 | Wales | 1 — 1 1 10 | 1 1 — — 5 | Won | Belfast | E. O'D. Davy |
| 171 | 1.4.1933 | Scotland | 2 — — — 6 | — — 2 — 8 | Lost | Dublin | E. O'D. Davy |
| 172 | 10.2.1934 | England | 1 — — — 3 | 3 2 — — 13 | Lost | Dublin | J. A. E. Siggins |
| 173 | 24.2.1934 | Scotland | 3 — — — 9 | 3 2 — 1 16 | Lost | Edinburgh | J. A. E. Siggins |
| 174 | 10.3.1934 | Wales | — — — — 0 | 3 2 — — 13 | Lost | Swansea | J. A. E. Siggins |
| 175 | 9.2.1935 | England | 1 — — — 3 | 1 1 — 3 14 | Lost | Twickenham | J. A. E. Siggins |
| 176 | 23.2.1935 | Scotland | 4 — — — 12 | 1 1 — — 5 | Won | Dublin | J. A. E. Siggins |
| 177 | 9.3.1935 | Wales | 1 — — 2 9 | — — 1 3 | Won | Belfast | J. A. E. Siggins |
| 178 | 7.12.1935 | New Zealand | 1 — — 2 9 | 3 1 — 2 17 | Lost | Dublin | J. A. E. Siggins |
| 179 | 8.2.1936 | England | 2 — — — 6 | 1 — — — 3 | Won | Dublin | J. A. E. Siggins |
| 180 | 22.2.1936 | Scotland | 2 — 1 — 10 | — — 1 — 4 | Won | Edinburgh | J. A. E. Siggins |
| 181 | 14.3.1936 | Wales | — — — — 0 | 1 — — 1 3 | Lost | Cardiff | J. A. E. Siggins |
| 182 | 13.2.1937 | England | 2 1 — — 8 | 2 — — 1 9 | Lost | Twickenham | G. J. Morgan |
| 183 | 27.2.1937 | Scotland | 3 1 — — 11 | — — 1 — 4 | Won | Dublin | G. J. Morgan |
| 184 | 3.4.1937 | Wales | 1 1 — — 5 | — — — 1 3 | Won | Belfast | G. J. Morgan |
| 185 | 12.2.1938 | England | 4 1 — — 14 | 7 6 — 1 36 | Lost | Dublin | G. J. Morgan |
| 186 | 26.2.1938 | Scotland | 4 1 — — 14 | 4 2 1 1 23 | Lost | Edinburgh | G. J. Morgan |
| 187 | 12.3.1938 | Wales | 1 1 — — 5 | 2 1 — 1 11 | Lost | Swansea | S. Walker |
| 188 | 11.2.1939 | England | 1 1 — — 5 | — — — — 0 | Won | Twickenham | G. J. Morgan |
| 189 | 25.2.1939 | Scotland | 2 — ★ 1 12 | 1 — — — 3 | Won | Dublin | G. J. Morgan |
| 190 | 11.3.1939 | Wales | — — — — 0 | 1 — 1 — 7 | Lost | Belfast | G. J. Morgan |
| 191 | 25.1.1947 | France | 1 1 — 1 8 | 4 — — — 12 | Lost | Dublin | C. J. Murphy |
| 192 | 8.2.1947 | England | 5 2 — 1 22 | — — — — 0 | Won | Dublin | C. J. Murphy |
| 193 | 22.2.1947 | Scotland | 1 — — — 3 | — — — — 0 | Won | Edinburgh | J. D. E. Monteith |
| 194 | 29.3.1947 | Wales | — — — — 0 | 1 — — 1 6 | Lost | Swansea | J. D. E. Monteith |
| 195 | 6.12.1947 | Australia | — — — 1 3 | 4 2 — — 16 | Lost | Dublin | E. Strathdee |
| 196 | 1.1.1948 | France | 3 2 — — 13 | 2 — — — 6 | Won | Paris | E. Strathdee |
| 197 | 14.2.1948 | England | 3 1 — — 11 | 2 2 — — 10 | Won | Twickenham | K. D. Mullen |
| 198 | 28.2.1948 | Scotland | 2 — — — 6 | — — — — 0 | Won | Dublin | K. D. Mullen |
| 199 | 13.3.1948 | Wales | 2 — — — 6 | 1 — — — 3 | Won | Belfast | K. D. Mullen |
| 200 | 29.1.1949 | France | — — — 3 9 | 2 2 — 2 16 | Lost | Dublin | K. D. Mullen |
| 201 | 12.2.1949 | England | 2 1 — 2 14 | 1 1 — — 5 | Won | Dublin | K. D. Mullen |
| 202 | 26.2.1949 | Scotland | 2 2 — 1 13 | — — — 1 3 | Won | Edinburgh | K. D. Mullen |
| 203 | 12.3.1949 | Wales | 1 1 — — 5 | — — — — 0 | Won | Swansea | K. D. Mullen |
| 204 | 28.1.1950 | France | — — — 1 3 | — — 1 — 3 | Drawn | Paris | K. D. Mullen |
| 205 | 11.2.1950 | England | — — — — 0 | 1 — — — 3 | Lost | Twickenham | K. D. Mullen |
| 206 | 25.2.1950 | Scotland | 3 3 — 2 21 | — — — — 0 | Won | Dublin | K. D. Mullen |
| 207 | 11.3.1950 | Wales | — — — 1 3 | 2 — — — 6 | Lost | Belfast | K. D. Mullen |
| 208 | 27.1.1951 | France | 2 — — 1 9 | 2 1 — — 8 | Won | Dublin | K. D. Mullen |
| 209 | 10.2.1951 | England | 1 — — 1 3 | — — — — 0 | Won | Dublin | K. D. Mullen |
| 210 | 24.2.1951 | Scotland | 1 — 1 — 6 | 1 1 — — 5 | Won | Edinburgh | K. D. Mullen |
| 211 | 10.3.1951 | Wales | 1 — — — 3 | — — — 1 3 | Drawn | Cardiff | K. D. Mullen |
| 212 | 8.12.1951 | South Africa | 1 1 — — 5 | 4 1 1 — 17 | Lost | Dublin | D. J. O'Brien |

*in the drop-goal column denotes a goal from a mark

| Match | Date | Opponents | For T | C | D | P | Pts | Against T | C | D | P | Pts | Result | Venue | Captain |
|---|---|---|---|---|---|---|---|---|---|---|---|---|---|---|---|
| 213 | 26.1.1952 | France | 2 | 1 | — | 1 | 11 | 1 | 1 | — | 1 | 8 | Won | Paris | D. J. O'Brien |
| 214 | 23.2.1952 | Scotland | 3 | — | — | 1 | 12 | 1 | 1 | — | 1 | 8 | Won | Dublin | D. J. O'Brien |
| 215 | 8.3.1952 | Wales | — | — | — | 1 | 3 | 3 | 1 | — | 1 | 14 | Lost | Dublin | D. J. O'Brien |
| 216 | 29.3.1952 | England | — | — | — | — | 0 | 1 | — | — | — | 3 | Lost | Twickenham | D. J. O'Brien |
| 217 | 24.1.1953 | France | 4 | 2 | — | — | 16 | — | — | 1 | — | 3 | Won | Belfast | J. W. Kyle |
| 218 | 14.2.1953 | England | 1 | — | — | 2 | 9 | 1 | — | — | 2 | 9 | Drawn | Dublin | J. W. Kyle |
| 219 | 28.2.1953 | Scotland | 6 | 4 | — | — | 26 | 1 | 1 | — | 1 | 8 | Won | Edinburgh | J. W. Kyle |
| 220 | 14.3.1953 | Wales | 1 | — | — | — | 3 | 1 | 1 | — | — | 5 | Lost | Swansea | J. W. Kyle |
| 221 | 9.1.1954 | New Zealand | — | — | — | 1 | 3 | 2 | 1 | 1 | 1 | 14 | Lost | Dublin | J. W. Kyle |
| 222 | 23.1.1954 | France | — | — | — | — | 0 | 2 | 1 | — | — | 8 | Lost | Paris | J. W. Kyle |
| 223 | 13.2.1954 | England | — | — | — | 1 | 3 | 3 | 1 | — | 1 | 14 | Lost | Twickenham | J. S. McCarthy |
| 224 | 27.2.1954 | Scotland | 2 | — | — | — | 6 | — | — | — | — | 0 | Won | Belfast | J. S. McCarthy |
| 225 | 13.3.1954 | Wales | 1 | — | — | 2 | 9 | — | — | 1 | 3 | 12 | Lost | Dublin | J. S. McCarthy |
| 226 | 22.1.1955 | France | — | — | — | 1 | 3 | 1 | 1 | — | — | 5 | Lost | Dublin | R. H. Thompson |
| 227 | 12.2.1955 | England | 1 | — | — | 1 | 6 | 2 | — | — | — | 6 | Drawn | Dublin | J. S. McCarthy |
| 228 | 26.2.1955 | Scotland | — | — | — | 1 | 3 | 1 | — | 1 | 2 | 12 | Lost | Edinburgh | R. H. Thompson |
| 229 | 12.3.1955 | Wales | — | — | — | 1 | 3 | 4 | 3 | — | 1 | 21 | Lost | Cardiff | R. H. Thompson |
| 230 | 28.1.1956 | France | 1 | 1 | — | 1 | 8 | 2 | 1 | — | 2 | 14 | Lost | Paris | J. S. Ritchie |
| 231 | 11.2.1956 | England | — | — | — | — | 0 | 3 | 1 | — | 3 | 20 | Lost | Twickenham | J. S. Ritchie |
| 232 | 25.2.1956 | Scotland | 4 | 1 | — | — | 14 | 2 | 2 | — | — | 10 | Won | Dublin | N. J. Henderson |
| 233 | 10.3.1956 | Wales | 1 | 1 | 1 | 1 | 11 | — | — | — | 1 | 3 | Won | Dublin | N. J. Henderson |
| 234 | 26.1.1957 | France | 2 | 1 | — | 1 | 11 | 2 | — | — | — | 6 | Won | Dublin | N. J. Henderson |
| 235 | 9.2.1957 | England | — | — | — | — | 0 | 1 | — | — | 1 | 6 | Lost | Dublin | N. J. Henderson |
| 236 | 23.2.1957 | Scotland | 1 | 1 | — | — | 5 | — | — | — | 1 | 3 | Won | Edinburgh | N. J. Henderson |
| 237 | 9.3.1957 | Wales | 1 | 1 | — | — | 5 | — | — | — | 2 | 6 | Lost | Cardiff | N. J. Henderson |
| 238 | 18.1.1958 | Australia | 2 | — | — | 1 | 9 | 2 | — | — | — | 6 | Won | Dublin | N. J. Henderson |
| 239 | 8.2.1958 | England | — | — | — | — | 0 | 1 | — | — | 1 | 6 | Lost | Twickenham | N. J. Henderson |
| 240 | 1.3.1958 | Scotland | 2 | — | — | 2 | 12 | 2 | — | — | — | 6 | Won | Dublin | N. J. Henderson |
| 241 | 15.3.1958 | Wales | 1 | — | — | 1 | 6 | 3 | — | — | — | 9 | Lost | Dublin | N. J. Henderson |
| 242 | 19.4.1958 | France | — | — | — | 2 | 6 | 1 | 1 | 1 | 1 | 11 | Lost | Paris | N. J. Henderson |
| 243 | 14.2.1959 | England | — | — | — | — | 0 | — | — | — | 1 | 3 | Lost | Dublin | A. R. Dawson |
| 244 | 28.2.1959 | Scotland | 1 | 1 | — | 1 | 8 | — | — | — | 1 | 3 | Won | Edinburgh | A. R. Dawson |
| 245 | 14.3.1959 | Wales | 1 | — | — | 1 | 6 | 2 | 1 | — | — | 8 | Lost | Cardiff | A. R. Dawson |
| 246 | 18.4.1959 | France | — | 1 | 1 | 1 | 9 | 1 | 1 | — | — | 5 | Won | Dublin | A. R. Dawson |
| 247 | 13.2.1960 | England | 1 | 1 | — | — | 5 | 1 | 1 | 1 | — | 8 | Lost | Twickenham | A. A. Mulligan |
| 248 | 27.2.1960 | Scotland | 1 | 1 | — | — | 5 | 1 | — | 1 | — | 6 | Lost | Dublin | A. A. Mulligan |
| 249 | 12.3.1960 | Wales | 1 | — | — | 2 | 9 | 2 | 2 | — | — | 10 | Lost | Dublin | A. A. Mulligan |
| 250 | 9.4.1960 | France | 2 | — | — | — | 6 | 4 | 1 | 3 | — | 23 | Lost | Paris | A. R. Dawson |
| 251 | 17.12.1960 | South Africa | — | — | — | 1 | 3 | 2 | 1 | — | — | 8 | Lost | Dublin | A. R. Dawson |
| 252 | 11.2.1961 | England | 1 | 1 | — | 2 | 11 | 2 | 1 | — | — | 8 | Won | Dublin | A. R. Dawson |
| 253 | 25.2.1961 | Scotland | 2 | 1 | — | — | 8 | 3 | 2 | — | 1 | 16 | Lost | Edinburgh | A. R. Dawson |
| 254 | 11.3.1961 | Wales | — | — | — | — | 0 | 1 | — | — | 2 | 9 | Lost | Cardiff | A. R. Dawson |
| 255 | 15.4.1961 | France | — | — | — | 1 | 3 | 1 | — | 2 | 2 | 15 | Lost | Dublin | A. R. Dawson |
| 256 | 13.5.1961 | South Africa | 1 | 1 | — | 1 | 8 | 5 | 3 | — | 1 | 24 | Lost | Cape Town | A. R. Dawson |
| 257 | 10.2.1962 | England | — | — | — | — | 0 | 3 | 2 | — | 1 | 16 | Lost | Twickenham | W. A. Mulcahy |
| 258 | 24.2.1962 | Scotland | 1 | — | — | 1 | 6 | 3 | 1 | 1 | 2 | 20 | Lost | Dublin | W. A. Mulcahy |
| 259 | 14.4.1962 | France | — | — | — | — | 0 | 3 | 1 | — | — | 11 | Lost | Paris | W. A. Mulcahy |
| 260 | 17.11.1962 | Wales | — | — | 1 | — | 3 | — | — | — | 1 | 3 | Drawn | Dublin | W. A. Mulcahy |
| 261 | 26.1.1963 | France | 1 | 1 | — | — | 5 | 4 | 3 | 2 | — | 24 | Lost | Dublin | T. J. Kiernan |
| 262 | 9.2.1963 | England | — | — | — | — | 0 | — | — | — | — | 0 | Drawn | Dublin | W. A. Mulcahy |
| 263 | 23.2.1963 | Scotland | — | — | — | — | 0 | — | — | — | 1 | 3 | Lost | Edinburgh | W. A. Mulcahy |
| 264 | 9.3.1963 | Wales | 1 | 1 | 1 | 2 | 14 | 1 | — | 1 | — | 6 | Won | Cardiff | W. A. Mulcahy |
| 265 | 7.12.1963 | New Zealand | 1 | 1 | — | — | 5 | 1 | — | — | 1 | 6 | Lost | Dublin | J. C. Kelly |
| 266 | 8.2.1964 | England | 4 | 3 | — | — | 18 | 1 | 1 | — | — | 5 | Won | Twickenham | W. A. Mulcahy |
| 267 | 22.2.1964 | Scotland | — | — | — | 1 | 3 | — | — | — | 2 | 6 | Lost | Dublin | W. A. Mulcahy |
| 268 | 7.3.1964 | Wales | — | — | — | 2 | 6 | 3 | 3 | — | — | 15 | Lost | Dublin | W. A. Mulcahy |
| 269 | 11.4.1964 | France | 1 | — | 1 | — | 6 | 6 | 3 | 1 | — | 27 | Lost | Paris | W. A. Mulcahy |
| 270 | 23.1.1965 | France | — | — | — | — | 3 | 1 | — | — | — | 3 | Drawn | Dublin | R. J. McLoughlin |
| 271 | 13.2.1965 | England | 1 | 1 | — | — | 5 | — | — | — | — | 0 | Won | Dublin | R. J. McLoughlin |
| 272 | 27.2.1965 | Scotland | 3 | 2 | 1 | — | 16 | — | — | 1 | 1 | 6 | Won | Edinburgh | R. J. McLoughlin |
| 273 | 13.3.1965 | Wales | 1 | 1 | — | 1 | 8 | 2 | 1 | 1 | 1 | 14 | Lost | Cardiff | R. J. McLoughlin |
| 274 | 6.4.1965 | South Africa | 1 | — | — | 2 | 9 | 1 | — | — | 1 | 6 | Won | Dublin | R. J. McLoughlin |
| 275 | 29.1.1966 | France | — | — | 1 | 1 | 6 | 2 | 1 | — | 1 | 11 | Lost | Paris | R. J. McLoughlin |
| 276 | 12.2.1966 | England | 1 | — | — | 1 | 6 | 1 | — | — | 1 | 6 | Drawn | Twickenham | R. J. McLoughlin |
| 277 | 26.2.1966 | Scotland | — | — | — | 1 | 3 | 3 | 1 | — | 1 | 11 | Lost | Dublin | R. J. McLoughlin |
| 278 | 12.3.1966 | Wales | 1 | — | 1 | 1 | 9 | 1 | — | — | 1 | 6 | Won | Dublin | T. J. Kiernan |
| 279 | 21.1.1967 | Australia | 2 | — | 2 | 1 | 15 | 1 | 1 | 1 | — | 8 | Won | Dublin | N. A. A. Murphy |
| 280 | 11.2.1967 | England | — | — | — | 1 | 3 | 1 | 1 | — | 1 | 8 | Lost | Dublin | N. A. A. Murphy |
| 281 | 25.2.1967 | Scotland | 1 | 1 | — | — | 5 | — | — | — | 1 | 3 | Won | Edinburgh | N. A. A. Murphy |
| 282 | 11.3.1967 | Wales | 1 | — | — | — | 3 | — | — | — | — | 0 | Won | Cardiff | N. A. A. Murphy |
| 283 | 15.4.1967 | France | 1 | 1 | — | 1 | 6 | 1 | 1 | 2 | — | 11 | Lost | Dublin | N. A. A. Murphy |
| 284 | 13.5.1967 | Australia | 2 | 1 | 1 | — | 11 | 1 | 1 | — | — | 5 | Won | Sydney | T. J. Kiernan |
| 285 | 27.1.1968 | France | — | — | — | 2 | 6 | 2 | 2 | 1 | 1 | 16 | Lost | Paris | T. J. Kiernan |

*in the drop-goal column denotes a goal from a mark

| Match | Date | Opponents | For | | | | | Against | | | | | Result | Venue | Captain |
|---|---|---|---|---|---|---|---|---|---|---|---|---|---|---|---|
| | | | T | C | D | P | Pts | T | C | D | P | Pts | | | |
| 286 | 10.2.1968 | England | — | — | — | 3 | 9 | — | — | 1 | 2 | 9 | Drawn | Twickenham | T. J. Kiernan |
| 287 | 24.2.1968 | Scotland | 3 | 1 | — | 1 | 14 | — | — | — | 2 | 6 | Won | Dublin | T. J. Kiernan |
| 288 | 9.3.1968 | Wales | 1 | — | 1 | 1 | 9 | — | — | 1 | 1 | 6 | Won | Dublin | T. J. Kiernan |
| 289 | 26.10.1968 | Australia | 2 | 2 | — | — | 10 | 1 | — | — | — | 3 | Won | Dublin | T. J. Kiernan |
| 290 | 25.1.1969 | France | 1 | 1 | 1 | 3 | 17 | 1 | — | — | 2 | 9 | Won | Dublin | T. J. Kiernan |
| 291 | 8.2.1969 | England | 2 | 1 | 1 | 2 | 17 | 1 | — | — | 4 | 15 | Won | Dublin | T. J. Kiernan |
| 292 | 22.2.1969 | Scotland | 4 | 2 | — | — | 16 | — | — | — | — | 0 | Won | Edinburgh | T. J. Kiernan |
| 293 | 8.3.1969 | Wales | 1 | 1 | — | 2 | 11 | 4 | 3 | 1 | 1 | 24 | Lost | Cardiff | T. J. Kiernan |
| 294 | 10.1.1970 | South Africa | 1 | 1 | — | 1 | 8 | 1 | 1 | — | 1 | 8 | Drawn | Dublin | T. J. Kiernan |
| 295 | 24.1.1970 | France | — | — | — | — | 0 | 1 | 1 | 1 | — | 8 | Lost | Paris | T. J. Kiernan |
| 296 | 14.2.1970 | England | — | — | — | 1 | 3 | 1 | — | 2 | — | 9 | Lost | Twickenham | T. J. Kiernan |
| 297 | 28.2.1970 | Scotland | 4 | 2 | — | — | 16 | 2 | 1 | 1 | — | 11 | Won | Dublin | T. J. Kiernan |
| 298 | 14.3.1970 | Wales | 2 | 1 | 1 | 1 | 14 | — | — | — | — | 0 | Won | Dublin | T. J. Kiernan |
| 299 | 30.1.1971 | France | 1 | — | — | 2 | 9 | — | — | 1 | 2 | 9 | Drawn | Dublin | T. J. Kiernan |
| 300 | 13.2.1971 | England | 2 | — | — | — | 6 | — | — | — | 3 | 9 | Lost | Dublin | C. M. H. Gibson |
| 301 | 27.2.1971 | Scotland | 3 | 1 | — | 2 | 17 | 1 | 1 | — | — | 5 | Won | Edinburgh | C. M. H. Gibson |
| 302 | 13.3.1971 | Wales | — | — | — | 3 | 9 | 4 | 1 | 1 | 2 | 23 | Lost | Cardiff | C. M. H. Gibson |
| 303 | 29.1.1972 | France | 2 | — | — | 2 | 14 | 1 | 1 | — | 1 | 9 | Won | Paris | T. J. Kiernan |
| 304 | 12.2.1972 | England | 2 | 1 | 1 | 1 | 16 | 1 | 1 | — | 2 | 12 | Won | Twickenham | T. J. Kiernan |
| 305 | 29.4.1972 | France | 3 | 3 | — | 2 | 24 | 3 | 1 | — | — | 14 | Won | Dublin | T. J. Kiernan |
| 306 | 20.1.1973 | New Zealand | 1 | — | — | 2 | 10 | 2 | 1 | — | — | 10 | Drawn | Dublin | T. J. Kiernan |
| 307 | 10.2.1973 | England | 2 | 2 | 1 | 1 | 18 | 1 | 1 | — | 1 | 9 | Won | Dublin | T. J. Kiernan |
| 308 | 24.2.1973 | Scotland | 2 | — | — | 2 | 14 | 1 | — | 3 | 2 | 19 | Lost | Edinburgh | T. J. Kiernan |
| 309 | 10.3.1973 | Wales | 1 | 1 | — | 2 | 12 | 2 | 1 | — | 2 | 16 | Lost | Cardiff | W. J. McBride |
| 310 | 14.4.1973 | France | — | — | — | 2 | 6 | 1 | — | — | — | 4 | Won | Dublin | W. J. McBride |
| 311 | 19.1.1974 | France | — | — | — | 2 | 6 | 1 | 1 | — | 1 | 9 | Lost | Paris | W. J. McBride |
| 312 | 2.2.1974 | Wales | — | — | — | 3 | 9 | 1 | 1 | — | 1 | 9 | Drawn | Dublin | W. J. McBride |
| 313 | 16.2.1974 | England | 4 | 2 | 1 | 1 | 26 | 1 | 1 | — | 5 | 21 | Won | Twickenham | W. J. McBride |
| 314 | 2.3.1974 | Scotland | 1 | 1 | — | 1 | 9 | — | — | — | 2 | 6 | Lost | Edinburgh | W. J. McBride |
| 315 | 7.9.1974 | IRFU President's Fifteen | 2 | 2 | — | 2 | 18 | 2 | 2 | — | 2 | 18 | Drawn | Dublin | W. J. McBride |
| 316 | 23.11.1974 | New Zealand | — | — | — | 2 | 6 | 1 | 1 | — | 3 | 15 | Lost | Dublin | W. J. McBride |
| 317 | 18.1.1975 | England | 2 | 2 | — | — | 12 | 1 | 1 | 1 | — | 9 | Won | Dublin | W. J. McBride |
| 318 | 1.2.1975 | Scotland | 2 | 1 | — | 1 | 13 | 2 | — | 2 | 2 | 20 | Lost | Edinburgh | W. J. McBride |
| 319 | 1.3.1975 | France | 3 | 2 | 2 | 1 | 25 | — | — | 1 | 1 | 6 | Won | Dublin | W. J. McBride |
| 320 | 15.3.1975 | Wales | 1 | — | — | — | 4 | 5 | 3 | — | 2 | 32 | Lost | Cardiff | W. J. McBride |
| 321 | 17.1.1976 | Australia | 1 | — | — | 2 | 10 | 3 | 1 | — | 2 | 20 | Lost | Dublin | C. M. H. Gibson |
| 322 | 7.2.1976 | France | — | — | — | 1 | 3 | 4 | 2 | — | 2 | 26 | Lost | Paris | C. M. H. Gibson |
| 323 | 21.2.1976 | Wales | — | — | — | 3 | 9 | 4 | 3 | — | 4 | 34 | Lost | Dublin | T. O. Grace |
| 324 | 6.3.1976 | England | 1 | — | 1 | 2 | 12 | — | — | — | 4 | 12 | Won | Twickenham | T. O. Grace |
| 325 | 20.3.1976 | Scotland | — | — | — | 2 | 6 | — | — | 1 | 4 | 15 | Lost | Dublin | T. O. Grace |
| 326 | 5.6.1976 | New Zealand | — | — | — | 1 | 3 | 2 | — | — | 1 | 11 | Lost | Wellington | T. O. Grace |
| 327 | 15.1.1977 | Wales | — | — | — | 3 | 9 | 3 | 2 | 1 | 2 | 25 | Lost | Cardiff | T. O. Grace |
| 328 | 5.2.1977 | England | — | — | — | — | 0 | 1 | — | — | — | 4 | Lost | Dublin | T. O. Grace |
| 329 | 19.2.1977 | Scotland | 1 | 1 | 1 | 3 | 18 | 3 | — | 1 | 2 | 21 | Lost | Edinburgh | T. O. Grace |
| 330 | 19.3.1977 | France | — | — | — | 2 | 6 | 1 | 1 | — | 3 | 15 | Lost | Dublin | T. O. Grace |
| 331 | 21.1.1978 | Scotland | 1 | 1 | — | 2 | 12 | — | — | — | 3 | 9 | Won | Dublin | J. J. Moloney |
| 332 | 18.2.1978 | France | — | — | — | 3 | 9 | 1 | — | — | 2 | 10 | Lost | Paris | J. J. Moloney |
| 333 | 4.3.1978 | Wales | 1 | — | 1 | 3 | 16 | 2 | — | — | 4 | 20 | Lost | Dublin | J. J. Moloney |
| 334 | 18.3.1978 | England | — | — | 1 | 2 | 9 | 2 | 2 | — | 1 | 15 | Lost | Twickenham | J. J. Moloney |
| 335 | 4.11.1978 | New Zealand | — | — | — | 2 | 6 | 1 | — | 2 | — | 10 | Lost | Dublin | S. M. Deering |
| 336 | 20.1.1979 | France | — | — | — | 3 | 9 | 1 | 1 | — | 1 | 9 | Drawn | Dublin | J. F. Slattery |
| 337 | 3.2.1979 | Wales | 2 | 2 | — | 3 | 21 | 2 | 2 | — | 4 | 24 | Lost | Cardiff | J. F. Slattery |
| 338 | 17.2.1979 | England | 1 | 1 | 1 | 1 | 12 | 1 | — | — | 1 | 7 | Won | Dublin | J. F. Slattery |
| 339 | 3.3.1979 | Scotland | 2 | — | — | 1 | 11 | 2 | — | — | 1 | 11 | Drawn | Edinburgh | J. F. Slattery |
| 340 | 3.6.1979 | Australia | 2 | 2 | 1 | 4 | 27 | 1 | 1 | — | 1 | 12 | Won | Brisbane | J. F. Slattery |
| 341 | 16.6.1979 | Australia | — | — | 2 | 1 | 9 | — | — | — | 1 | 3 | Won | Sydney | J. F. Slattery |
| 342 | 19.1.1980 | England | — | — | — | 3 | 9 | 3 | 3 | — | 2 | 24 | Lost | Twickenham | J. F. Slattery |
| 343 | 2.2.1980 | Scotland | 2 | 1 | 1 | 3 | 22 | 2 | — | 1 | 1 | 15 | Won | Dublin | J. F. Slattery |
| 344 | 1.3.1980 | France | 1 | 1 | 1 | 3 | 18 | 2 | 1 | 1 | 2 | 19 | Lost | Paris | J. F. Slattery |
| 345 | 15.3.1980 | Wales | 3 | 3 | — | 1 | 21 | 1 | — | — | 1 | 7 | Won | Dublin | J. F. Slattery |
| 346 | 7.2.1981 | France | 1 | — | — | 3 | 13 | 1 | — | 2 | 3 | 19 | Lost | Dublin | J. F. Slattery |
| 347 | 21.2.1981 | Wales | 2 | — | — | — | 8 | — | — | 1 | 2 | 9 | Lost | Cardiff | J. F. Slattery |
| 348 | 7.3.1981 | England | — | — | 2 | — | 6 | 2 | 1 | — | — | 10 | Lost | Dublin | J. F. Slattery |
| 349 | 21.3.1981 | Scotland | 1 | 1 | — | 1 | 9 | 1 | — | 1 | 1 | 10 | Lost | Edinburgh | J. F. Slattery |
| 350 | 30.5.1981 | South Africa | 2 | 2 | — | 1 | 15 | 3 | 1 | — | 3 | 23 | Lost | Cape Town | J. F. Slattery |
| 351 | 6.6.1981 | South Africa | 1 | — | — | 2 | 10 | — | — | 3 | 1 | 12 | Lost | Durban | J. F. Slattery |
| 352 | 21.11.1981 | Australia | — | — | — | 4 | 12 | 1 | — | 1 | 3 | 16 | Lost | Dublin | J. F. Slattery |
| 353 | 23.1.1982 | Wales | 3 | 1 | — | 2 | 20 | 1 | 1 | 1 | 1 | 12 | Won | Dublin | C. F. Fitzgerald |
| 354 | 6.2.1982 | England | 2 | 1 | — | 2 | 16 | 1 | 1 | — | 3 | 15 | Won | Twickenham | C. F. Fitzgerald |

*in the drop-goal column denotes a goal from a mark

| Match | Date | Opponents | For | | | | | Against | | | | | Result | Venue | Captain |
|---|---|---|---|---|---|---|---|---|---|---|---|---|---|---|---|
| | | | T | C | D | P | Pts | T | C | D | P | Pts | | | |
| 355 | 20.2.1982 | Scotland | — | — | 1 | 6 | 21 | 1 | 1 | — | 2 | 12 | Won | Dublin | C. F. Fitzgerald |
| 356 | 20.3.1982 | France | — | — | — | 3 | 9 | 2 | 1 | — | 4 | 22 | Lost | Paris | C. F. Fitzgerald |
| 357 | 15.1.1983 | Scotland | 1 | 1 | — | 3 | 15 | 1 | — | 1 | 2 | 13 | Won | Edinburgh | C. F. Fitzgerald |
| 358 | 19.2.1983 | France | 2 | 1 | — | 4 | 22 | 2 | 1 | — | 2 | 16 | Won | Dublin | C. F. Fitzgerald |
| 359 | 5.3.1983 | Wales | — | — | — | 3 | 9 | 3 | 1 | — | 3 | 23 | Lost | Cardiff | C. F. Fitzgerald |
| 360 | 19.3.1983 | England | 2 | 1 | — | 5 | 25 | — | — | — | 5 | 15 | Won | Dublin | C. F. Fitzgerald |
| 361 | 21.1.1984 | France | — | — | — | 4 | 12 | 2 | 1 | 1 | 4 | 25 | Lost | Paris | C. F. Fitzgerald |
| 362 | 4.2.1984 | Wales | — | — | — | 3 | 9 | 1 | 1 | — | 4 | 18 | Lost | Dublin | C. F. Fitzgerald |
| 363 | 18.2.1984 | England | — | — | — | 3 | 9 | 1 | — | 1 | 3 | 12 | Lost | Twickenham | W. P. Duggan |
| 364 | 3.3.1984 | Scotland | 1 | 1 | — | 1 | 9 | 5 | 3 | — | 2 | 32 | Lost | Dublin | W. P. Duggan |
| 365 | 10.11.1984 | Australia | — | — | — | 3 | 9 | 1 | — | 3 | 1 | 16 | Lost | Dublin | C. F. Fitzgerald |
| 366 | 2.2.1985 | Scotland | 2 | 2 | 1 | 1 | 18 | — | — | 1 | 4 | 15 | Won | Edinburgh | C. F. Fitzgerald |
| 367 | 2.3.1985 | France | — | — | — | 5 | 15 | 2 | 2 | — | 1 | 15 | Drawn | Dublin | C. F. Fitzgerald |
| 368 | 16.3.1985 | Wales | 2 | 2 | — | 3 | 21 | 1 | 1 | 1 | — | 9 | Won | Cardiff | C. F. Fitzgerald |
| 369 | 30.3.1985 | England | 1 | — | 1 | 2 | 13 | 1 | — | — | 2 | 10 | Won | Dublin | C. F. Fitzgerald |
| 370 | 1.2.1986 | France | — | — | — | 3 | 9 | 3 | 1 | 1 | 4 | 29 | Lost | Paris | C. F. Fitzgerald |
| 371 | 15.2.1986 | Wales | 1 | 1 | — | 2 | 12 | 2 | 1 | — | 3 | 19 | Lost | Dublin | C. F. Fitzgerald |
| 372 | 1.3.1986 | England | 3 | 1 | — | 2 | 20 | 4 | 3 | — | 1 | 25 | Lost | Twickenham | C. F. Fitzgerald |
| 373 | 15.3.1986 | Scotland | 1 | 1 | — | 1 | 9 | 1 | — | — | 2 | 10 | Lost | Dublin | C. F. Fitzgerald |
| 374 | 1.11.1986 | Romania | 10 | 7 | — | 2 | 60 | — | — | — | — | 0 | Won | Dublin | D. G. Lenihan |
| 375 | 7.2.1987 | England | 3 | 1 | — | 1 | 17 | — | — | — | — | 0 | Won | Dublin | D. G. Lenihan |
| 376 | 21.2.1987 | Scotland | 1 | 1 | 1 | 1 | 12 | 2 | 1 | 2 | — | 16 | Lost | Edinburgh | D. G. Lenihan |
| 377 | 21.3.1987 | France | 2 | 1 | — | 1 | 13 | 2 | 1 | — | 3 | 19 | Lost | Dublin | D. G. Lenihan |
| 378 | 4.4.1987 | Wales | 2 | 2 | — | 1 | 15 | 2 | — | — | 1 | 11 | Won | Cardiff | D. G. Lenihan |

# MATCH RECORDS

## MOST CONSECUTIVE MATCHES WON

6    *1968* S,W,A *1969* F,E,S

## MOST CONSECUTIVE MATCHES WITHOUT DEFEAT

| Matches | Wins | Draws | Period |
|---|---|---|---|
| 7 | 6 | 1 | 1967-68 to 1968-69 |
| 5 | 4 | 1 | 1971-72 to 1972-73 |

## MOST CONSECUTIVE MATCHES WITHOUT CONCEDING A TRY

| | |
|---|---|
| 3 | in 1895-96 |
| 3 | in 1898-99 |
| 3 | between 1948-49 and 1949-50 |
| 3 | between 1969-70 and 1970-71 |
| 3 | in 1967-68 |

## MOST CONSECUTIVE MATCHES WITHOUT CONCEDING A SCORE

| | |
|---|---|
| 2 | in 1893-94 |
| 2 | in 1946-47 |
| 2 | in 1986-87 |

## MOST POINTS IN A MATCH

### By the team

| Pts | Opponents | Venue | Season |
|---|---|---|---|
| 60 | Romania | Dublin | 1986-87 |
| 27 | Australia | Brisbane | 1979 |
| 26 | England | Twickenham | 1973-74 |
| 26 | Scotland | Edinburgh | 1952-53 |
| 25 | France | Cork | 1910-11 |
| 25 | France | Dublin | 1974-75 |
| 25 | England | Dublin | 1982-83 |

## By a player

| Pts | Player | Opponents | Venue | Season |
|---|---|---|---|---|
| 21 | S. O. Campbell | Scotland | Dublin | 1981-82 |
| 21 | S. O. Campbell | England | Dublin | 1982-83 |
| 20 | M. J. Kiernan | Romania | Dublin | 1986-87 |
| 19 | S. O. Campbell | Australia | Brisbane | 1979 |
| 15 | M. J. Kiernan | France | Dublin | 1984-85 |
| 14 | J. C. M. Moroney | France | Dublin | 1968-69 |
| 14 | S. O. Campbell | France | Dublin | 1982-83 |
| 14 | S. O. Campbell | France | Paris | 1979-80 |

# MOST TRIES IN A MATCH

## By the team

| T | Opponents | Venue | Season |
|---|---|---|---|
| 10 | Romania | Dublin | 1986-87 |
| 6 | France | Cork | 1912-13 |
| 6 | Scotland | Edinburgh | 1952-53 |
| 5 | England | Cork | 1904-05 |
| 5 | France | Cork | 1910-11 |
| 5 | England | Dublin | 1946-47 |

## By a player

| T | Player | Opponents | Venue | Season |
|---|---|---|---|---|
| 3 | R. Montgomery* | Wales | Birkenhead | 1886-87 |
| 3 | J. P. Quinn | France | Cork | 1912-13 |
| 3 | E. O'D. Davy | Scotland | Edinburgh | 1929-30 |
| 3 | S. J. Byrne | Scotland | Edinburgh | 1952-53 |
| 3 | K. D. Crossan | Romania | Dublin | 1986-87 |

(* There is an account of this match in which Montgomery is credited with only two tries.)

# MOST CONVERSIONS IN A MATCH

## By the team

| C | Opponents | Venue | Season |
|---|---|---|---|
| 7 | Romania | Dublin | 1986-87 |
| 4 | Scotland | Edinburgh | 1931-32 |
| 4 | Scotland | Edinburgh | 1952-53 |
| 3 | France | Cork | 1910-11 |
| 3 | France | Cork | 1912-13 |
| 3 | Scotland | Dublin | 1949-50 |
| 3 | England | Twickenham | 1963-64 |
| 3 | France | Dublin | 1971-72 |
| 3 | Wales | Dublin | 1979-80 |

## By a player

| C | Player | Opponents | Venue | Season |
|---|---|---|---|---|
| 7 | M. J. Kiernan | Romania | Dublin | 1986-87 |
| 4 | P. F. Murray | Scotland | Edinburgh | 1931-32 |
| 4 | R. J. Gregg | Scotland | Edinburgh | 1952-53 |
| 3 | R. A. Lloyd | France | Cork | 1910-11 |
| 3 | R. A. Lloyd | France | Cork | 1912-13 |
| 3 | G. W. Norton | Scotland | Dublin | 1949-50 |
| 3 | T. J. Kiernan | England | Twickenham | 1963-64 |
| 3 | T. J. Kiernan | France | Dublin | 1971-72 |
| 3 | S. O. Campbell | Wales | Dublin | 1979-80 |

# MOST DROPPED GOALS IN A MATCH

## By the team

| DG | Opponents | Venue | Season |
|---|---|---|---|
| 2 | Australia | Dublin | 1966-67 |
| 2 | France | Dublin | 1974-75 |
| 2 | Australia | Sydney | 1979 |
| 2 | England | Dublin | 1980-81 |

## By a player

| DG | Player | Opponents | Venue | Season |
|---|---|---|---|---|
| 2 | C. M. H. Gibson | Australia | Dublin | 1966-67 |
| 2 | W. M. McCombe | France | Dublin | 1974-75 |
| 2 | S. O. Campbell | Australia | Sydney | 1979 |

# MOST PENALTY GOALS IN A MATCH

## By the team

| PG | | Opponents | Venue | Season |
|---|---|---|---|---|
| 6 | | Scotland | Dublin | 1981-82 |
| 5 | | England | Dublin | 1982-83 |
| 5 | | France | Dublin | 1984-85 |
| 4 | | Australia | Brisbane | 1979 |
| 4 | | Australia | Dublin | 1981-82 |
| 4 | | France | Dublin | 1982-83 |
| 4 | | France | Paris | 1983-84 |

## By a player

| PG | Player | Opponents | Venue | Season |
|---|---|---|---|---|
| 6 | S. O. Campbell | Scotland | Dublin | 1981-82 |
| 5 | S. O. Campbell | England | Dublin | 1982-83 |
| 5 | M. J. Kiernan | France | Dublin | 1984-85 |
| 4 | S. O. Campbell | Australia | Brisbane | 1979 |
| 4 | A. J. P. Ward | Australia | Dublin | 1981-82 |
| 4 | S. O. Campbell | France | Dublin | 1982-83 |
| 4 | S. O. Campbell | France | Paris | 1983-84 |

# GOALS FROM MARKS

| * | Player | Opponents | Venue | Season |
|---|---|---|---|---|
| 1 | L. Q. Bulger | England | Dublin | 1896-97 |
| 1 | J. C. Parke | England | Dublin | 1906-07 |
| 1 | H. J. M. Sayers | Scotland | Dublin | 1938-39 |

# TRY ON DEBUT

| Player | Opponents | Venue | Season |
|---|---|---|---|
| O. S. Stokes | England | Dublin | 1881-82 |
| L. M. MacIntosh | Scotland | Edinburgh | 1883-84 |
| C. R. Tillie | England | Dublin | 1886-87 |
| R. Montgomery | England | Dublin | 1886-87 |
| D. C. Woods | N.Z.Natives | Dublin | 1888-89 |
| A. C. McDonnell | Wales | Swansea | 1888-89 |
| J. Cotton | Wales | Swansea | 1888-89 |
| A. M. Magee | England | Dublin | 1894-95 |
| J. Sealy | England | Leeds | 1895-96 |
| E. F. Campbell | Scotland | Edinburgh | 1898-99 |
| C. Reid | Scotland | Edinburgh | 1898-99 |
| J. E. Moffatt | Scotland | Dublin | 1903-04 |
| H. B. Thrift | Wales | Belfast | 1903-04 |
| B. Maclear | England | Cork | 1904-05 |
| W. B. Purdon | England | Leicester | 1905-06 |
| J. J. O'Connor | France | Dublin | 1908-09 |
| A. L. Stewart | Wales | Swansea | 1912-13 |
| J. A. N. Dickson | England | Dublin | 1919-20 |
| J. A. B. Clarke | Scotland | Edinburgh | 1921-22 |
| A. C. Douglas* | France | Paris | 1922-23 |
| A. P. Atkins | France | Dublin | 1923-24 |
| T. Hewitt | Wales | Cardiff | 1923-24 |
| F. S. Hewitt | Wales | Cardiff | 1923-24 |
| T. J. Millin | Wales | Belfast | 1924-25 |
| J. H. Gage | Scotland | Edinburgh | 1925-26 |
| H. McVicker | England | Twickenham | 1926-27 |
| J. E. Arigho | France | Belfast | 1927-28 |
| L. B. McMahon | England | Twickenham | 1930-31 |
| S. L. Waide | England | Dublin | 1931-32 |
| R. J. Barnes | Wales | Belfast | 1932-33 |
| G. J. Morgan | England | Dublin | 1933-34 |
| J. I. Doyle | Wales | Belfast | 1934-35 |

| Player | Opponents | Venue | Season |
|---|---|---|---|
| M. J. Daly | England | Dublin | 1937-38 |
| J. W. McKay | France | Dublin | 1946-47 |
| B. O'Hanlon | England | Dublin | 1946-47 |
| J. S. McCarthy | France | Paris | 1947-48 |
| J. Blayney | Scotland | Dublin | 1949-50 |
| A. W. Browne | South Africa | Dublin | 1951-52 |
| M. Mortell | France | Belfast | 1952-53 |
| S. J. Byrne | Scotland | Edinburgh | 1952-53 |
| N. H. Brophy | France | Dublin | 1956-57 |
| A. R. Dawson | Australia | Dublin | 1957-58 |
| J. J. Fortune | New Zealand | Dublin | 1963-64 |
| M. G. Doyle | France | Dublin | 1964-65 |
| E. L. Grant | France | Dublin | 1970-71 |
| J. J. Moloney | France | Paris | 1971-72 |
| R. A. Milliken | England | Dublin | 1972-73 |
| H. P. MacNeill | France | Dublin | 1980-81 |

(* Some accounts credit J.B. Gardiner with the try instead of Douglas.)

## CAPTAIN ON INTERNATIONAL DEBUT

| Player | Opponents | Venue | Season |
|---|---|---|---|
| G. H. Stack | England | The Oval | 1874-75 |
| W. C. Neville | Scotland | Belfast | 1878-79 |
| H. G. Cook | Wales | Cardiff | 1883-84 |
| J. S. Ritchie | France | Paris | 1955-56 |

## TRIES BY FULL-BACKS

| Player | Opponents | Venue | Season |
|---|---|---|---|
| T. J. Kiernan | South Africa | Cape Town | 1961 |
| T. J. Kiernan | Scotland | Edinburgh | 1972-73 |
| A. H. Ensor | France | Dublin | 1974-75 |
| H. P. MacNeill | France | Dublin | 1980-81 |
| H. P. MacNeill | Wales | Cardiff | 1980-81 |
| K. A. O'Brien | South Africa | Durban | 1981 |
| H. P. MacNeill | England | Twickenham | 1981-82 |
| H. P. McNeill | Romania | Dublin | 1986-87 |

## ALL THE POINTS FOR IRELAND IN A MATCH
### (where more than one scoring action is involved)

| Pts | Player | Opponents | Venue | Season |
|---|---|---|---|---|
| 21 | S. O. Campbell | Scotland | Dublin | 1981-82 |
| 15 | M. J. Kiernan | France | Dublin | 1984-85 |
| 12 | A. J. P. Ward | Australia | Dublin | 1981-82 |
| 12 | S. O. Campbell | France | Paris | 1983-84 |
| 9 | G. W. Norton | France | Dublin | 1948-49 |
| 9 | T. J. Kiernan | England | Twickenham | 1967-68 |
| 9 | C. M. H. Gibson | Wales | Cardiff | 1970-71 |
| 9 | A. H. Ensor | Wales | Dublin | 1973-74 |
| 9 | B. J. McGann | Wales | Dublin | 1975-76 |
| 9 | C. M. H. Gibson | Wales | Cardiff | 1976-77 |
| 9 | A. J. P. Ward | France | Paris | 1977-78 |
| 9 | S. O. Campbell | Australia | Sydney | 1979 |
| 9 | S. O. Campbell | England | Twickenham | 1979-80 |
| 9 | S. O. Campbell | France | Paris | 1981-82 |
| 9 | A. J. P. Ward | England | Twickenham | 1977-78 |
| 9 | A. J. P. Ward | France | Dublin | 1978-79 |
| 9 | S. O. Campbell | Wales | Dublin | 1983-84 |
| 9 | A. J. P. Ward | England | Twickenham | 1983-84 |
| 9 | M. J. Kiernan | Australia | Dublin | 1984-85 |
| 9 | M. J. Kiernan | France | Paris | 1985-86 |
| 8 | G. V. Stephenson | Scotland | Edinburgh | 1923-24 |
| 8 | T. J. Kiernan | South Africa | Cape Town | 1961 |
| 6 | M. Mortell | Scotland | Belfast | 1953-54 |
| 6 | N. J. Henderson | France | Paris | 1957-58 |
| 6 | N. H. Brophy | France | Paris | 1959-60 |
| 6 | W. R. Hunter | Scotland | Dublin | 1961-62 |

| Pts | Player | Opponents | Venue | Season |
|---|---|---|---|---|
| 6 | F. S. Keogh | Wales | Dublin | 1963-64 |
| 6 | W. M. McCombe | France | Paris | 1967-68 |
| 6 | A. H. Ensor | France | Paris | 1973-74 |
| 6 | A. H. Ensor | New Zealand | Dublin | 1974-75 |
| 6 | B. J. McGann | Scotland | Dublin | 1975-76 |
| 6 | A. J. P. Ward | New Zealand | Dublin | 1978-79 |

# INDIVIDUAL RECORDS

## LONGEST CAREER SPANS

| Seasons | Player | Caps | Career Span |
|---|---|---|---|
| 16 | C. M. H. Gibson | 69 | 1963-64 to 1979 |
| 16 | A. J. F. O'Reilly | 29 | 1954-55 to 1969-70 |
| 15 | M. K. Flynn | 22 | 1958-59 to 1972-73 |
| 15 | J. F. Slattery | 61 | 1969-70 to 1983-84 |
| 14 | T. J. Kiernan | 54 | 1959-60 to 1972-73 |
| 14 | R. J. McLoughlin | 40 | 1961-62 to 1974-75 |
| 14 | W. J. McBride | 63 | 1961-62 to 1974-75 |
| 13 | S. Millar | 37 | 1957-58 to 1969-70 |

## MOST CONSECUTIVE CAPS IN A CAREER

| Caps | Player | Opponents |
|---|---|---|
| 52 | W. J. McBride | 1964 F 1965 F,E,S,W,SA 1966 F,E,S,W 1967 A,E,S,W,F,A 1968 F,E,S,W,A 1969 F,E,S,W 1970 SA,F,E,S,W 1971 F,E,S,W 1972 F,E,F 1973 NZ,E S W F 1974 F,W,E,S,P,NZ 1975 E,S,F,W |
| 49 | P. A. Orr | 1976 F,W,E,S,NZ 1977 W,E,S,F 1979 S,F,W,E,NZ 1979 F,W,E,S,A (1 + 2) 1980 E,S,F,W 1981 F,W,E,S,SA (1+ 2), A 1982 W,E,S,F 1983 S,F,W,E 1984 F,W,E,S,A 1985 S,F,W,E 1986 F |

## MOST CAPS IN A CAREER

| Caps | Player | Career span |
|---|---|---|
| 69 | C. M. H. Gibson | 1963-64 to 1979 |
| 63 | W. J. McBride | 1961-62 to 1974-75 |
| 61 | J. F Slattery | 1969-70 to 1983-84 |
| 55 | P. A. Orr | 1975-76 to 1986-87 |
| 54 | T. J. Kiernan | 1959-60 to 1972-73 |
| 51 | M. I. Keane | 1973-74 to 1983-84 |
| 46 | J. W. Kyle | 1946-47 to 1957-58 |
| 45 | K. W. Kennedy | 1964-65 to 1974-75 |
| 42 | G. V. Stephenson | 1919-20 to 1929-30 |
| 41 | N. A. A. Murphy | 1957-58 to 1968-69 |
| 41 | W. P. Duggan | 1974-75 to 1983-84 |
| 40 | N. J. Henderson | 1948-49 to 1958-59 |
| 40 | R. J. McLoughlin | 1961-62 to 1974-75 |
| 37 | S. Millar | 1957-58 to 1969-70 |
| 35 | J. R. Kavanagh | 1952-53 to 1961-62 |
| 35 | W. A. Mulcahy | 1957-58 to 1964-65 |

## MOST POINTS IN A CAREER

| Pts | Player | Matches | Career span |
|---|---|---|---|
| 217 | S. O. Campbell | 22 | 1975-76 to 1983-84 |
| 158 | T. J. Kiernan | 54 | 1959-60 to 1972-73 |
| 143 | M. J. Kiernan | 24 | 1981-82 to 1986-87 |
| 112 | C. M. H. Gibson | 69 | 1963-64 to 1979 |
| 98 | A. J. P. Ward | 17 | 1977-78 to 1985-86 |
| 89 | G. V. Stephenson | 42 | 1919-20 to 1929-30 |
| 75 | R. A. Lloyd | 19 | 1909-10 to 1919-20 |
| 72 | B. J. McGann | 25 | 1968-69 to 1976 |

## MOST TRIES IN A CAREER

| T | Player | Matches | Career span |
|---|---|---|---|
| 14 | G. V. Stephenson | 42 | 1919-20 to 1929-30 |
| 11 | A. T. A. Duggan | 25 | 1963-64 to 1971-72 |
| 9 | J. P. Quinn | 15 | 1909-10 to 1913-14 |
| 9 | C. M. H. Gibson | 69 | 1963-64 to 1979 |

## MOST CONVERSIONS IN A CAREER

| C | Player | Matches | Career span |
|---|---|---|---|
| 26 | T. J. Kiernan | 54 | 1959-60 to 1972-73 |
| 19 | M. J. Kiernan | 24 | 1981-82 to 1986-87 |
| 16 | R. A. Lloyd | 19 | 1909-10 to 1919-20 |
| 15 | S. O. Campbell | 22 | 1975-76 to 1983-84 |
| 13 | G. V. Stephenson | 42 | 1919-20 to 1929-30 |

## MOST DROPPED GOALS IN A CAREER

| DG | Player | Matches | Career span |
|---|---|---|---|
| 7 | R. A. Lloyd | 19 | 1909-10 to 1919-20 |
| 7 | S. O. Campbell | 22 | 1975-76 to 1983-84 |
| 6 | C. M. H. Gibson | 69 | 1963-64 to 1979 |
| 6 | B. J. McGann | 25 | 1968-69 to 1976 |

## MOST PENALTY GOALS IN A CAREER

| PG | Player | Matches | Career span |
|---|---|---|---|
| 54 | S. O. Campbell | 22 | 1975-76 to 1983-84 |
| 31 | T. J. Kiernan | 54 | 1959-60 to 1972-73 |
| 28 | M. J. Kiernan | 24 | 1981-82 to 1986-87 |
| 24 | A. J. P. Ward | 17 | 1977-78 to 1985-86 |

## MOST MATCHES AS CAPTAIN

| | | |
|---|---|---|
| 24 | T. J. Kiernan | (14 victories) |
| 19 | C. F. Fitzgerald | ( 9 victories) |
| 17 | J. F. Slattery | ( 5 victories) |
| 15 | W. E. Crawford | (10 victories) |
| 15 | K. D. Mullen | (10 victories) |
| 13 | G. V. Stephenson | ( 7 victories) |
| 12 | R. A. Lloyd | ( 5 victories) |
| 12 | W. J. McBride | ( 5 victories) |
| 11 | C. E. Allen | ( 5 victories) |
| 11 | N. J. Henderson | ( 6 victories) |
| 11 | A. R. Dawson | ( 3 victories) |
| 11 | W. A. Mulcahy | ( 2 victories) |

# WALES INTERNATIONAL
# TEAMS AND RECORDS

| 1880-81 | 1881-82 | 1882-83 | |
| v. ENGLAND | v. IRELAND | v. ENGLAND | v. SCOTLAND |
| --- | --- | --- | --- |
| †C.H. NEWMAN | *†C.P. LEWIS 2c | *C.P. LEWIS | *C.P. LEWIS 1c |
| †R.H.B. SUMMERS | †S.S. CLARK | †D.H. BOWEN | |
| | | | W.B. NORTON |
| *†J.A. BEVAN | †W.B. NORTON | W.B. NORTON | C.H. NEWMAN |
| †E. PEAKE | †W.F. EVANS 1T | †J. CLARE | |
| | G.F. HARDING | †D. GWYNN | W.F. EVANS |
| †L. WATKINS | | | G.F. HARDING |
| †E.J. LEWIS | C.H. NEWMAN | C.H. NEWMAN | |
| | †R.H. BRIDIE 1T | E. TREHARNE | †J.A. JONES |
| †B.E. GIRLING | | | †A. GRIFFIN |
| †T.A. REES | †H.C. VINCENT | †J.H. JUDSON | J.H. JUDSON 1T |
| †F.T. PURDON | F.T. PURDON | F.T. PURDON | F.T. PURDON |
| †G.F. HARDING | †R. GOULD | R. GOULD | R. GOULD |
| †R.D.G. WILLIAMS | †T. BAKER-JONES 1T | T. BAKER-JONES | T. BAKER-JONES |
| †B.B. MANN | †T.J.S. CLAPP 1T | T.J.S. CLAPP | T.J.S. CLAPP |
| †E. TREHARNE | W.D. PHILLIPS | G.F. HARDING | †H.S. LYNE |
| †G. DARBISHIRE | †G.L. MORRIS | G.L. MORRIS | G.L. MORRIS |
| †W.D. PHILLIPS | †T. WILLIAMS | †A. CATTELL | A. CATTELL |
| Blackheath | Lansdowne Road | St. Helen's | Raeburn Place |
| LOST | WON | LOST | LOST |
| ENG: 7G 6T 1DG | IRE.: NIL | WALES: NIL | SCOT.: 3G |
| WALES: NIL | WALES: 2G 2T | ENG.: 2G 4T | WALES: 1G |
| 19 Feb. 1881 | 28 Jan. 1882 | 16 Dec. 1882 | 8 Jan. 1883 |

A South Wales Football Union had existed in the 1870s and selected sides to meet English counties and other visitors from the British Isles. However, the first Welsh XV at Blackheath in 1881 appears to have been a private selection chosen by Richard Mullock of Newport, and was clearly not representative of the true playing strength of Welsh rugby. As a result of Wales' humiliating defeat, a Welsh Football Union was founded in Neath in March 1881, and Mullock was installed as Secretary.

England declined to meet Wales in the following season, though a match at Newport against the North of England took place two weeks prior to the first international with Ireland. The *Irish Times* reports that many ladies attended the game in Dublin, including two who had travelled over with the Welsh team. But it was an acrimonious match, frequently interrupted by dispute. Wales ran out winners and Tom Baker-Jones, a Newport solicitor, scored the first try for Wales in international rugby, running in from a scrum after 26 minutes.

The WFU had difficulties persuading players to travel for away matches in these early years. Vincent (a student at Dublin University) and Griffin (of Edinburgh University) were last-minute caps against Ireland (1882) and Scotland (1883) respectively, and the team group photographed before that Scottish match shows just 13 players. Some confusion exists as to whether R.H. Bridie, who had played in 1882, appeared against the Scots in 1883.

| 1883-84 | | | 1884-85 | |
| v. ENGLAND | v. SCOTLAND | v. IRELAND | v. ENGLAND | v. SCOTLAND |
| --- | --- | --- | --- | --- |
| C.P. LEWIS 1c | C.P. LEWIS | †T.M. BARLOW | †A.J. GOULD 1c | A.J. GOULD |
| †C.P. ALLEN 1T | C.P. ALLEN | W.B. NORTON 1T | †H.M. JORDAN 2T | H.M. JORDAN |
| W.B. NORTON | W.B. NORTON | †F.E. HANCOCK | F.E. HANCOCK | F.E. HANCOCK |
| C.G. TAYLOR | C.G. TAYLOR | C.G. TAYLOR | C.G. TAYLOR | C.G. TAYLOR |
| *C.H. NEWMAN | *C.H. NEWMAN | †W.J.W. STADDEN 1DG | *C.H. NEWMAN | *C.H. NEWMAN |
| †W.H. GWYNN | W.H. GWYNN | W.H. GWYNN | W.H. GWYNN | W.H. GWYNN |
| †J.S. SMITH | T. BAKER-JONES | J.S. SMITH | J.S. SMITH | †E.P. ALEXANDER |
| †H.J. SIMPSON | H.J. SIMPSON | *H.J. SIMPSON | †E.S. RICHARDS | †A.F. HILL |
| †F.G. ANDREWS | F.G. ANDREWS | †S.J. GOLDSWORTHY | S.J. GOLDSWORTHY | S.J. GOLDSWORTHY |
| R. GOULD | R. GOULD | R. GOULD | R. GOULD | R. GOULD |
| †F.L. MARGRAVE | F.L. MARGRAVE | †W.B. RODERICK | T. BAKER-JONES | T. BAKER-JONES |
| T.J.S. CLAPP | T.J.S. CLAPP | T.J.S. CLAPP 1T | T.J.S. CLAPP | T.J.S. CLAPP |
| H.S. LYNE | H.S. LYNE | H.S. LYNE | H.S. LYNE | †D. MORGAN |
| G.L. MORRIS | G.L. MORRIS | †J.T. HINTON | †L.C. THOMAS | L.C. THOMAS |
| W.D. PHILLIPS | W.D. PHILLIPS | W.D. PHILLIPS | †E.M. ROWLAND | W.H. THOMAS |
| Leeds | Newport | Cardiff Arms Park | St. Helen's | Glasgow |
| LOST | LOST | WON | LOST | DRAWN |
| ENG.: 1G 2T | WALES: NIL | WALES: 1DG 2T | WALES: 1G 1T | SCOT.: NIL |
| WALES: 1G | SCOT.: 1DG 1T | IRE.: NIL | ENG.: 1G 4T | WALES: NIL |
| 5 Jan. 1884 | 12 Jan. 1884 | 12 Apr. 1884 | 3 Jan. 1885 | 10 Jan. 1885 |

Interest in rugby football grew in South Wales during the mid-1880s, thanks mainly to the rivalry between the major clubs participating in the South Wales Cup competition. Big ties regularly attracted greater attendances than international matches.

Tom Clapp, for instance, led Newport to victory in 1885. He had been born of a well-known West of England family before moving to Nantyglo, where he made his name as a robust footballer, capable of playing as a back or forward. He was to become the backbone of these early Welsh packs, retiring in 1888 after setting a Welsh cap record. A solicitor, he emigrated to America.

Arthur Gould, the first rugby player to be hero-worshipped from West Wales to East Wales, made his debut at full-back against England in 1885. As a centre he was to become the outstanding Welsh threequarter of the following decade, and his 18 matches as captain of Wales remains a Welsh record. "Shorty" Jordan scored two tries on his debut against England. At Cardiff in 1884, he and Frank Purdon had played for Ireland when the Irish arrived several players short for the Welsh international.

## 1885-86 | 1886-87

| v. ENGLAND | v. SCOTLAND | v. ENGLAND | v. SCOTLAND | v. IRELAND |
|---|---|---|---|---|
| D.H. Bowen | D.H. Bowen | D.H. Bowen | †H. Hughes | S.S. Clark |
| | | | | |
| †W.M. Douglas | W.M. Douglas | W.M. Douglas | W.M. Douglas | G.E. Bowen |
| A.J. Gould | A.J. Gould | A.J. Gould | A.J. Gould | A.J. Gould 1DG |
| C.G. Taylor 1C | *F.E. Hancock | C.G. Taylor | D. Gwynn | C.G. Taylor |
| | C.G. Taylor | | | |
| | | | | |
| *C.H. Newman | | *C.H. Newman | †G.E. Bowen | †J.G. Lewis |
| W.J.W. Stadden 1T | †A.A. Mathews | †O.J. Evans | O.J. Evans | W.J.W. Stadden |
| | W.J.W. Stadden | | | |
| | | | | |
| E.P. Alexander | | E.P. Alexander | E.S. Richards | E.P. Alexander |
| A.F. Hill | A.F. Hill | †T.W. Lockwood | T.W. Lockwood | T.W. Lockwood |
| †E. Roberts | E.P. Alexander | †A.J. Hybart | †W.E.O. Williams | W.E.O. Williams |
| R. Gould | T.J.S. Clapp | R. Gould | *R. Gould | E. Roberts |
| †G.A. Young | G.A. Young | †A.F. Bland | A.F. Bland | A.F. Bland |
| †D.H. Lewis | D.H. Lewis | T.J.S. Clapp | T.J.S. Clapp | *T.J.S. Clapp |
| D. Morgan | D. Morgan | D. Morgan | D. Morgan | D. Morgan 1T |
| †W.A. Bowen | W.A. Bowen | W.A. Bowen | W.A. Bowen | W.A. Bowen |
| W.H. Thomas | W.H. Thomas | W.H. Thomas | W.H. Thomas | †W.H. Towers |
| | | | | |
| Blackheath | Cardiff Arms Park | Stradey Park | Raeburn Place | Birkenhead |
| LOST | LOST | DRAWN | LOST | WON |
| | | | | |
| ENG.: 1GM 2T | WALES: NIL | WALES: NIL | SCOT.: 4G 8T | WALES: 1DG 1T |
| WALES: 1G | SCOT.: 2G 1T | ENG. NIL | WALES: NIL | IRE.: 3T |
| | | | | |
| 2 Jan. 1886 | 9 Jan. 1886 | 8 Jan. 1887 | 26 Feb. 1887 | 12 Mar. 1887 |

Charles Taylor, a naval engineering officer, was recognised as the finest place- and drop-kicker in the Welsh side of the 1880s. He went on to play nine times and was a member of the first four-man threequarter line to appear in an international.

The Cardiff club had been experimenting with four threequarters for a couple of seasons before the Welsh first used the system in 1886 against Scotland. Frank Hancock, a member of the famous Somerset brewing family, had so impressed Cardiff with his play that, in order to keep Hancock in the team and accommodate other useful backs, it was decided to use four threequarters.

Having proved the effectiveness of the new system at Cardiff, the Welsh selectors at length entrusted Hancock with the captaincy of the national side, so that he could direct the four threequarter system from the middle. But against the nine mighty Scottish forwards, the Welsh eight were so overrun at Cardiff that, at half time, Harry Bowen, the Bynea schoolmaster and Llanelli's brilliant full-back, was put into the pack. In the reshuffle, Gould was moved to full-back: a move which it is said provoked his abhorrence of the four threequarter system for the rest of his career.

## 1887-88 | 1888-89

| v. SCOTLAND | v. IRELAND | v. MAORIS | v. SCOTLAND | v. IRELAND |
|---|---|---|---|---|
| †E.J. Roberts | E.J. Roberts | †E.J. Webb 1C | H. Hughes | E.J. Roberts |
| | | | | |
| G.E. Bowen | †C.S. Arthur | †G. Thomas 1T | H.M. Jordan | †A.C. Davies |
| A.J. Gould | G.E. Bowen | †N.W. Biggs | †E.H. Bishop | *A.J. Gould |
| †T.J. Pryce-Jenkins 1T | T.J. Pryce-Jenkins | C.S. Arthur | E.J. Webb | †T. Morgan |
| | | †R.M. Garrett | R.M. Garrett | N.W. Biggs |
| | | | | |
| O.J. Evans | O.J. Evans | C.J. Thomas | C.J. Thomas | C.J. Thomas |
| W.J.W. Stadden | †C.J. Thomas | W.J.W. Stadden | †R. Evans | †G. Griffiths |
| | | | | |
| †R.W. Powell | R.W. Powell | | | |
| A.F. Hill | A.F. Hill | *A.F. Hill | *A.F. Hill | D. Griffiths |
| †Q.D. Kedzlie | Q.D. Kedzlie | †S.H. Nicholls | S.H. Nicholls | S.H. Nicholls |
| †J. Meredith | J. Meredith | †J. Hannan 1T | J. Hannan | J. Hannan |
| A.F. Bland | A.F. Bland | A.F. Bland | †D.W. Evans | D.W. Evans |
| *T.J.S. Clapp | *T.J.S. Clapp | †C.T. Harding | C.T. Harding | C.T. Harding |
| †W.H. Howells | W.H. Howells | †D. Griffiths | W.E.O. Williams | D. Morgan |
| †T. Williams | T. Williams | W.A. Bowen | W.A. Bowen | W.A. Bowen |
| W.H. Thomas | W.H. Thomas | W.H. Towers 1T | †R.L. Thomas | R.L. Thomas |
| | | | | |
| Newport | Lansdowne Road | St. Helen's | Raeburn Place | St. Helen's |
| WON | LOST | WON | LOST | LOST |
| | | | | |
| WALES: 1T | IRE.: 1G 1DG 1T | WALES: 1G 2T | SCOT.: 2T | WALES: NIL |
| SCOT.: NIL | WALES: NIL | MAORIS: NIL | WALES: NIL | IRE.: 2T |
| | | | | |
| 4 Feb. 1888 | 3 Mar. 1888 | 22 Dec. 1888 | 2 Feb. 1889 | 2 Mar. 1889 |

Tom Pryce-Jenkins, a flamboyant personality who had settled in medical practice in London, came in for the match with Scotland in 1888, and won the game with a dash down the touchline for a try in the first half. Jacques McCarthy, the caustic Irish critic, described the remainder of the match in his unique style: "Wales then killed [the game] by lying on the ball, kicking out of play and every other trick and dodge that the rules have not provided against, as prostitution of a noble, fair and chivalrous game."

Young Norman Biggs of Cardiff made his debut against the New Zealand Native team in December 1888, becoming the youngest man to win a Welsh cap, at 18 years, 1 month. The Welsh had discarded the four threequarter system after the events at Cardiff in the 1886 match with Scotland, but the system was used for the Maoris game and proved so successful that it was decided to persevere with what has become Wales' greatest contribution to the game.

The International Board dispute meant that there were no international matches with England in 1888 and 1889. Wales failed against Scotland in 1889 and there were two defeats against useful Irish sides.

## 1889-90

| v. SCOTLAND | v. ENGLAND | v. IRELAND |
|---|---|---|
| †W.J. BANCROFT | W.J. BANCROFT | W.J. BANCROFT 1C |
| | | |
| †D.P.M. LLOYD | D.P.M. LLOYD | G. THOMAS |
| A.J. GOULD 1T | *A.J. GOULD | *A.J. GOULD |
| R.M. GARRETT | R.M. GARRETT | R.M. GARRETT |
| C.J. THOMAS | D. GWYNN | D. GWYNN |
| | | |
| †E. JAMES | C.J. THOMAS | C.J. THOMAS 1T |
| W.J.W. STADDEN | W.J.W. STADDEN 1T | †H.M. INGLEDEW |
| | | |
| *A.F. HILL | D.W. EVANS | A.F. HILL |
| W.E.O. WILLIAMS | W.E.O. WILLIAMS | D.W. EVANS |
| J. MEREDITH | J. MEREDITH | †T.C. GRAHAM |
| A.F. BLAND | A.F. BLAND | A.F. BLAND |
| J. HANNAN | J. HANNAN | J. HANNAN |
| †S. THOMAS | S. THOMAS | R.L. THOMAS |
| W.A. BOWEN | W.A. BOWEN | W.A. BOWEN |
| †W. RICE-EVANS | W.H. THOMAS | W.H. THOMAS |
| | | |
| Cardiff Arms Park | Dewsbury | Lansdowne Road |
| LOST 1-5 | WON 1-0 | DRAWN 3-3 |
| | | |
| WALES: 1T | ENG.: NIL | IRE.: 1G |
| SCOT.: 1G 2T | WALES: 1T | WALES 1G |
| | | |
| 1 Feb. 1890 | 15 Feb. 1890 | 1 Mar. 1890 |

Billy Bancroft of Swansea made the first of his 33 consecutive appearances in the match against Scotland. His long career was to span twelve seasons and his flair and attacking spirit were qualities which served Wales admirably during some notable victories. In his long career he took every place kick offered to the Welsh in international matches – a remarkable record.

The International dispute was finally settled in February, and when England and Wales met at Dewsbury on a hard, frosty pitch, Wales gained their first victory over the English. A single try, early in the second half and scored by Bill Stadden from a "bounce-in" to a line-out, sealed Wales' famous victory.

Tom Graham, Newport's captain in their invincible season of 1891-2, made his Welsh debut in the Irish match on St David's Day. A thoughtful leader and an intelligent, mobile forward, Graham was to prove an invaluable asset to the Welsh packs of the 1890s.

## 1890-91

| v. ENGLAND | v. SCOTLAND | v. IRELAND |
|---|---|---|
| W.J. BANCROFT 1C | W.J. BANCROFT | W.J. BANCROFT 1DG,1C |
| | | |
| D.P.M. LLOYD | G. THOMAS | D.P.M. LLOYD |
| C.S. ARTHUR | R.M. GARRETT | R.M. GARRETT |
| D. GWYNN | D. GWYNN | C.J. THOMAS |
| †T.W.R. PEARSON 1T | †W.M. McCUTCHEON | T.W.R. PEARSON |
| | | |
| C.J. THOMAS | †R.B. SWEET-ESCOTT | E. JAMES |
| H.M. INGLEDEW | H.M. INGLEDEW | †D. JAMES |
| | | |
| †P. BENNETT | P. BENNETT | †J. SAMUEL |
| D.W. EVANS | S.H. NICHOLLS | †C.B. NICHOLL |
| †H. PACKER | T.C. GRAHAM | T.C. GRAHAM |
| W. RICE-EVANS | W. RICE-EVANS | †J.T. DEACON |
| J. HANNAN | †D.J. DANIEL | †D. SAMUEL 1T |
| R.L. THOMAS | R.L. THOMAS | R.L. THOMAS |
| *W.A. BOWEN | W.A. BOWEN | S. THOMAS |
| †E.V. PEGGE | *W.H. THOMAS | *W.H. THOMAS |
| | | |
| Newport | Raeburn Place | Stradey Park |
| LOST 3-7 | LOST 0-15 | WON 6-4 |
| | | |
| WALES: 1G | SCOT.: 1G 2DG 6T | WALES: 1G 1DG |
| ENG.: 2G 1T | WALES: NIL | IRE.: 1DG 1T |
| | | |
| 3 Jan. 1891 | 7 Feb. 1891 | 7 Mar. 1891 |

Wales were unable to field a settled side. Arthur Gould, backbone of the Welsh threequarters, was away on business in the West Indies, and only Rowland Thomas, the Whitland doctor who had (with Tom Pryce-Jenkins) been a leading force in the formation of the London Welsh RFC during his student days in London, played in the pack throughout the season.

England and Scotland outplayed Wales, who were hamstrung by an inefficient pair of halves. For the Irish match, the darting Swansea halves, Dai and Evan James, were drafted in and immediately there was an improvement in Welsh back play. Two pairs of brothers, the Jameses and the Samuels from Morriston, appeared in the Irish match.

A number of noted players made their debuts during the season. Tom Pearson scored a try in his first international, the beginning of a career which lasted until 1903. And in the pack, Harry Packer began a long association with international rugby which culminated in the 1920s with his invitation to manage the 1924 British team to South Africa. C.B. Nicholl went on to play 15 times as an uncompromising forward. Later a schoolmaster, Nicholl was a founder member of the famous Barbarians club.

## 1891-92

| v. ENGLAND | v. SCOTLAND | v. IRELAND |
| --- | --- | --- |
| W.J. Bancroft | W.J. Bancroft | W.J. Bancroft |
| T.W.R. Pearson | T.W.R. Pearson | N.W. Biggs |
| *A.J. Gould | *A.J. Gould | *A.J. Gould |
| R.M. Garrett | †J.C. Rees | †G.H. Gould |
| W.M. McCutcheon | W.M. McCutcheon | †F.E. Nicholls |
| †H.P. Phillips | E. James | E. James |
| †G.R. Rowles | D. James | D. James |
| †F. Mills | F. Mills | F. Mills |
| C.B. Nicholl | C.B. Nicholl | C.B. Nicholl |
| T.C. Graham | T.C. Graham | P. Bennett |
| J.T. Deacon | J.T. Deacon | J.T. Deacon |
| J. Hannan | J. Hannan 1t | J. Hannan |
| R.L. Thomas | P. Bennett | †H.T. Day |
| †A.W. Boucher | A.W. Boucher | A.W. Boucher |
| †W.H. Watts | W.H. Watts | W.H. Watts |
| Blackheath | St. Helen's | Lansdowne Road |
| LOST 0-17 | LOST 2-7 | LOST 0-9 |
| ENG.: 3G 1T | WALES: 1T | IRE.: 1G 2T |
| WALES: NIL | SCOT.: 1G 1T | WALES: NIL |
| 2 Jan. 1892 | 6 Feb. 1892 | 5 Mar. 1892 |

Although the results of the Welsh side in 1892 were very disappointing, there was plenty of promise in the forwards and experience among the backs. Arthur Gould, Bancroft, Pearson and Garrett were the senior backs, but somehow their combined efforts were not good enough to hold an excellent English side at Blackheath.

Jim Hannan, a Newport boilermaker, was a key member of his club's successful pack. One of the strongest scrummagers of the era, he was an expert at wheeling the scrum, a tactic which was highly effective in the 1890s. It was from a rush following a wheel near the Scottish line that Hannan opened the scoring with a try against Scotland at Swansea. It was Wales' sole score of the season.

Four new forwards who were to feature regularly in Welsh packs of the decade appeared for the first time in 1892. Frank Mills, a tall Swansea undertaker with a fine physique, came in with two of the invincible Newport pack, Wallace Watts and Arthur Boucher, for the English game. For speed, cleverness and all round forward ability Watts and Boucher were without peer. Harry Day, a carpenter and another Newport forward in the Jim Hannan mould, made his debut against Ireland.

## 1892-93

| v. ENGLAND | v. SCOTLAND | v. IRELAND |
| --- | --- | --- |
| W.J. Bancroft 1c,1pg | W.J. Bancroft 1pg | W.J. Bancroft |
| N.W. Biggs 1t | N.W. Biggs 1t | N.W. Biggs |
| *A.J. Gould 2t | *A.J. Gould | *A.J. Gould |
| J.C. Rees | G.H. Gould 1t | G.H. Gould 1t |
| W.M. McCutcheon | W.M. McCutcheon 1t | W.M. McCutcheon |
| H.P. Phillips | H.P. Phillips | H.P. Phillips |
| †F.C. Parfitt | F.C. Parfitt | F.C. Parfitt |
| F. Mills | F. Mills | F. Mills |
| C.B. Nicholl | C.B. Nicholl | C.B. Nicholl |
| T.C. Graham | T.C. Graham | T.C. Graham |
| A.F. Hill | A.F. Hill | A.F. Hill |
| J. Hannan | J. Hannan | J. Hannan |
| H.T. Day | H.T. Day | D. Samuel |
| A.W. Boucher | A.W. Boucher | A.W. Boucher |
| W.H. Watts | W.H. Watts | W.H. Watts |
| Cardiff Arms Park | Raeburn Place | Stradey Park |
| WON 12-11 | WON 9-0 | WON 2-0 |
| WALES: 1G 1PG 2T | SCOT.: NIL | WALES: 1T |
| ENG.: 1G 3T | WALES: 1PG 3T | SCOT.: NIL |
| 7 Jan. 1893 | 4 Feb. 1893 | 11 Mar. 1893 |

Wales won the Triple Crown for the first time in 1893. Two of the key factors in the side's success were their brilliant pack, and the skilful use of the four threequarter system. The pack comprised eight athletes who had the height, weight and strength to master the essential scrummaging and jumping tasks; but they also backed-up and passed with the skills of threequarters.

The match against England was played in the middle of a very bitter, cold, frosty spell. Portable fires were kept burning during the day and night before the match, thawing the ground sufficiently for the game to go ahead, but leaving several large, soft and darkened patches across the pitch. Wales won an exciting game by a late penalty goal, converted by Bancroft with a drop-kick from near the English 25. It was the first penalty goal kicked in an international match.

Great enthusiasm preceded the match with Ireland. The newspapers of the day carried stories of supporters' interest, and such was the fervour for the game that it is recorded that two young men from the fishing town of Tenby walked to Llanelli – some forty miles – to see the Triple Crown match. Wales' victory was a triumph for the four threequarter system, a typical bout of Welsh passing working the overlap for Bert Gould, Arthur's brother, to sprint over for the only try of the match.

## 1893-94

| v. ENGLAND | v. SCOTLAND | v. IRELAND |
|---|---|---|
| W.J. BANCROFT | W.J. BANCROFT | W.J. BANCROFT |
| | | |
| N.W. BIGGS | †W.L. THOMAS | N.W. BIGGS |
| *A.J. GOULD | *A.J. GOULD | †J.E. ELLIOTT |
| J.C. REES | †D. FITZGERALD 1DG,1T | D. FITZGERALD |
| W.M. McCUTCHEON | T.W.R. PEARSON | T.W.R. PEARSON |
| | | |
| H.P. PHILLIPS | H.P. PHILLIPS | R.B. SWEET-ESCOTT |
| F.C. PARFITT 1T | F.C. PARFITT | F.C. PARFITT |
| | | |
| F. MILLS | F. MILLS | F. MILLS |
| C.B. NICHOLL | C.B. NICHOLL | †F. HUTCHINSON |
| T.C. GRAHAM | T.C. GRAHAM | †D.W. NICHOLL |
| A.F. HILL | A.F. HILL | *A.F. HILL |
| J. HANNAN | J. HANNAN | J. HANNAN |
| D.J. DANIEL | D.J. DANIEL | D.J. DANIEL |
| A.W. BOUCHER | H.T. DAY | H.T. DAY |
| W.H. WATTS | W.H. WATTS | W.H. WATTS |
| | | |
| Birkenhead | Newport | Belfast |
| LOST 3-24 | WON 7-0 | LOST 0-3 |
| | | |
| ENG.: 4G 1GM | WALES: 1T 1DG | IRE.: 1PG |
| WALES: 1T | SCOT.: NIL | WALES: NIL |
| | | |
| 6 Jan. 1894 | 3 Feb. 1894 | 10 Mar. 1894 |

The Welsh side against England in 1894 showed just one change from the XV which had defeated England in the Triple Crown year, David Daniel, the Llanelli brewery-worker, replacing Harry Day. Wales were trounced on an icy pitch at Birkenhead, but there is every reason to suspect that the team was a divided one, and that a rift among the forwards reduced the effectiveness of the side.

Arthur Gould had requested his forwards to concentrate on heeling in the scrums, so that the backs had plenty of opportunity to run the ball. But Frank Hill questioned Gould's wisdom, and put his massive weight and strength into wheeling the scrums, working against the efforts of packleader Jim Hannan, who naturally wanted to support the wishes of his captain.

Surprisingly, there were only three changes for the Scottish match, with the forwards retained en bloc. However, Arthur Boucher was forced to withdraw and Harry Day was called into the side, one drawn entirely from the big four South Wales clubs of Newport, Llanelli, Swansea and Cardiff. Fitzgerald won the game singlehanded, but Wales were unable to overcome the Irish on a boggy pitch in Belfast.

## 1894-95

| v. ENGLAND | v. SCOTLAND | v. IRELAND |
|---|---|---|
| W.J. BANCROFT | W.J. BANCROFT 1GM | W.J. BANCROFT 1C |
| | | |
| W.L. THOMAS | †E. LLOYD | W.L. THOMAS |
| *A.J. GOULD | *A.J. GOULD | *A.J. GOULD |
| †O. BADGER | O. BADGER | O. BADGER |
| T.W.R. PEARSON | T.W.R. PEARSON | T.W.R. PEARSON 1T |
| | | |
| †S.H. BIGGS | S.H. BIGGS | †D. MORGAN |
| †B. DAVIES | F.C. PARFITT | R.B. SWEET-ESCOTT |
| | | |
| F. MILLS | F. MILLS | F. MILLS |
| C.B. NICHOLL | C.B. NICHOLL | C.B. NICHOLL |
| T.C. GRAHAM 1T | T.C. GRAHAM | †A.M. JENKIN |
| †T.H. JACKSON | H. PACKER | H. PACKER |
| J. HANNAN | J. HANNAN | J. HANNAN |
| †W.J. ELSEY 1T | †E.E. GEORGE | E.E. GEORGE |
| A.W. BOUCHER | A.W. BOUCHER | A.W. BOUCHER |
| W.H. WATTS | †T. POOK | W.H. WATTS |
| | | |
| St. Helen's | Raeburn Place | Cardiff Arms Park |
| LOST 6-14 | LOST 4-5 | WON 5-3 |
| | | |
| WALES: 2T | SCOT.: 1G | WALES: 1G |
| ENG.: 1G 3T | WALES: 1GM | IRE.: 1T |
| | | |
| 5 Jan. 1895 | 26 Jan. 1895 | 16 Mar. 1895 |

The great Welsh backs of the Triple Crown year had either retired or lost form by 1895, with only Bancroft and the captain, Gould, remaining from the famous team of 1893. Most of the old guard were still good enough to win places in the pack, however, though the livelier English forwards outplayed their respected rivals in the loose at Swansea, where a huge crowd of about 20,000 had assembled.

By this time heeling out from the scrum to allow the backs to run and handle at speed had become the focal point of the game in Wales, and large crowds attracted by fine, open football were not uncommon in the Principality.

At international level, however, the strength of Welsh forward play had fallen away considerably by the middle years of the 1890s. In Edinburgh, the Scottish forwards dominated their opponents to the extent that the Welsh backs were completely bottled up for the afternoon, though the brilliant full-back, Billy Bancroft, managed to keep Wales in contention with a goal from a mark from near the touchline. A brilliant sixty-yard run to the Taff end of the ground won the match with Ireland. Pearson was the scorer after inventive play by the Welsh threequarters had created an overlap for him.

## 1895-96

| v. ENGLAND | v. SCOTLAND | v. IRELAND |
|---|---|---|
| W.J. Bancroft | W.J. Bancroft | W.J. Bancroft |
| †C.A. Bowen | C.A. Bowen 1t | C.A. Bowen |
| *A.J. Gould | *A.J. Gould 1t | *A.J. Gould 1dg |
| O. Badger | †E.G. Nicholls | E.G. Nicholls |
| †F.H. Dauncey | F.H. Dauncey | F.H. Dauncey |
| D. Morgan | S.H. Biggs | †G.L. Lloyd |
| B. Davies | F.C. Parfitt | F.C. Parfitt |
| F. Mills | F. Hutchinson | F. Hutchinson |
| C.B. Nicholl | C.B. Nicholl | C.B. Nicholl |
| A.M. Jenkin | †J. Evans | J. Evans |
| H. Packer | H. Packer | H. Packer |
| †S.H. Ramsey | †W. Morris | W. Morris |
| E.E. George | †W. Davies | †F. Miller |
| A.W. Boucher | †W. Cope | A.W. Boucher |
| W.H. Watts | †D. Evans | D. Evans |
| Blackheath | Cardiff Arms Park | Lansdowne Road |
| LOST 0-25 | WON 6-0 | LOST 4-8 |
| ENG.: 2G 5T | WALES: 2T | IRE.: 1G 1T |
| WALES: NIL | SCOT.: NIL | WALES: 1DG |
| 4 Jan. 1896 | 25 Jan. 1896 | 14 Mar. 1896 |

The failure of the Welsh forwards against England compelled the Welsh selectors to ring the changes in the pack. They turned to a new kind of forward, one who could carry out all of the necessary scrummaging and jumping duties, but one who could also take and hand out "rough stuff". Such forwards became known as "the Rhondda-type of forward": these were men who were not prepared to be subdued or intimidated by the actions of opponents.

Six new forwards were drafted into the pack against Scotland. Jack Evans, a miner, and Bill Morris, a plasterer, were Llanelli forwards who steered the new Welsh policy into practice. They found support in Dai Evans, a brawny policeman from Pembrokeshire, stationed in Penygraig, at the heart of the Rhondda. A side short in experience caused a considerable stir by defeating the Scots at Cardiff. This was the fifteen which, in many ways, forged the template which was to bring Wales repeated success during the following decade.

Second-half tries scored by Bowen and Gould from typical Welsh handling movements sealed the game against the Scots, but the Welsh forward approach was no match for the kick-and-rush tactics adopted by the Irish in Dublin. Wales were well beaten and Lloyd, the new fly-half, had a torrid time trying to stem the Irish attacks.

| 1896-97 | 1897-98 | |
|---|---|---|
| v. ENGLAND | v. IRELAND | v. ENGLAND |
| W.J. Bancroft 1c | *W.J. Bancroft 1c,1pg | *W.J. Bancroft |
| C.A. Bowen | †H.V.P. Huzzey 1t | H.V.P. Huzzey 1dg,1t |
| *A.J. Gould | †W. Jones | W. Jones |
| E.G. Nicholls | E.G. Nicholls | E.G. Nicholls |
| T.W.R. Pearson 1t | T.W.R. Pearson | T.W.R. Pearson |
| S.H. Biggs | S.H. Biggs | S.H. Biggs |
| †D. Jones 1t | J.E. Elliott | J.E. Elliott |
| †F.H. Cornish | F.H. Cornish | F.H. Cornish |
| †R. Hellings | R. Hellings | R. Hellings |
| J. Evans | †H. Davies | H. Davies |
| H. Packer | †J.G. Boots | J.G. Boots |
| W. Morris | †W.H. Alexander | W.H. Alexander |
| †J. Rhapps | D.J. Daniel | D.J. Daniel |
| A.W. Boucher 1t | †T. Dobson 1t | T. Dobson |
| D. Evans | †J. Booth | D. Evans |
| Newport | Limerick | Blackheath |
| WON 11-0 | WON 11-3 | LOST 7-14 |
| WALES: 1G 2T | IRE.: 1PG | ENG.: 1G 3T |
| ENG.: NIL | WALES: 1G 1PG 1T | WALES: 1DG 1T |
| 9 Jan. 1897 | 19 Mar. 1898 | 2 Apr. 1898 |

Arthur Gould retired after leading Wales to a decisive win over England at Newport. He had set a record number of 27 caps and been the leading player of his generation – the first Welsh "superstar". His admirers contributed to a testimonial fund which was set up with the permission of the Welsh Football Union. But the International Board regarded the move as an act of professionalism, and refused to play against Wales until their Union sorted out the matter or pledged never again to select Gould for an international. The Union stood by Gould, steadfastly refusing to give such an undertaking, and many believed that Wales would never play international matches again.

But Gould had no wish to continue as a player and he resolved the issue himself by stating that he had no wish to return to the international fifteen. The matter was thus resolved and Wales played Ireland and England in the spring of 1898.

## 1898-99

| v. ENGLAND | v. SCOTLAND | v. IRELAND |
|---|---|---|
| *W.J. BANCROFT 4C | *W.J. BANCROFT 2C | *W.J. BANCROFT |
| | | |
| H.V.P. HUZZEY 2T | H.V.P. HUZZEY | H.V.P. HUZZEY |
| †R.T. SKRIMSHIRE | R.T. SKRIMSHIRE | R.T. SKRIMSHIRE |
| E.G. NICHOLLS | E.G. NICHOLLS | E.G. NICHOLLS |
| †W.M. LLEWELLYN 4T | W.M. LLEWELLYN 1T | W.M. LLEWELLYN |
| | | |
| E. JAMES | G.L. LLOYD 1T | G.L. LLOYD |
| D. JAMES | S.H. BIGGS | S.H. BIGGS |
| | | |
| †J.J. HODGES | J.J. HODGES | J.J. HODGES |
| †G.F. SCRINE | R. HELLINGS | R. HELLINGS |
| †A. BRICE | A. BRICE | A. BRICE |
| †W.H. PARKER | W.H. PARKER | J.G. BOOTS |
| W.H. ALEXANDER | W.H. ALEXANDER | W.H. ALEXANDER |
| D.J. DANIEL | G.F. SCRINE | D.J. DANIEL |
| T. DOBSON | T. DOBSON | F.H. CORNISH |
| †J. BLAKE | J. BLAKE | J. BLAKE |
| | | |
| St. Helen's | Inverleith | Cardiff Arms Park |
| WON 26-3 | LOST 10-21 | LOST 0-3 |
| | | |
| WALES: 4G 2T | SCOT.: 1GM 2DG 3T | WALES: NIL |
| ENG.: 1T | WALES: 2G | IRE.: 1T |
| | | |
| 7 Jan. 1899 | 4 Mar. 1899 | 18 Mar. 1899 |

Wales made an auspicious start to the season, demolishing a weak English side at Swansea and inflicting a record defeat on their opponents. Willie Llewellyn, from Tonypandy, and a player with the junior club Llwynypia, shot to fame by scoring four tries on his debut. By the following year he had gone to study pharmacy in London, where he turned out for London Welsh. Resourceful in defence and effective in attack, Llewellyn went on to play 20 times for Wales, creating a career record of 16 international tries.

Welsh halves were renowned for their entertaining play at this time. The legerdemain and constant change of relative positions practised by the James brothers completely confused the English halves, but soon after that game the brothers accepted £200 down and match fees of £2 to play rugby league for Broughton. Llewellyn Lloyd, Newport's outstanding fly-half, played in the last two games of the season.

Jehoida Hodges, Bob Brice and the formidable George Boots were the finest forwards in the Welsh pack. They came shoulder to shoulder for the Irish match at Cardiff, but could not prevent their opponents winning the Triple Crown.

## 1899-1900

| v. ENGLAND | v. SCOTLAND | v. IRELAND |
|---|---|---|
| *W.J. BANCROFT 1PG,2C | *W.J. BANCROFT | *W.J. BANCROFT |
| | | |
| W.M. LLEWELLYN | W.M. LLEWELLYN 2T | W.M. LLEWELLYN |
| †G. DAVIES | G. DAVIES | G. DAVIES 1T |
| †D. REES | E.G. NICHOLLS 1T | E.G. NICHOLLS |
| †W.J. TREW 1T | W.J. TREW | W.J. TREW |
| | | |
| G.L. LLOYD | G.L. LLOYD | S.H. BIGGS |
| †L.A. PHILLIPS | L.A. PHILLIPS | L.A. PHILLIPS |
| | | |
| J.J. HODGES | J.J. HODGES | J.J. HODGES |
| R. HELLINGS 1T | †G. DOBSON | R. HELLINGS |
| A. BRICE | A. BRICE | A. BRICE |
| J.G. BOOTS | J.G. BOOTS | J.G. BOOTS |
| †R. THOMAS | R. THOMAS | R. THOMAS |
| F. MILLER | F. MILLER | F. MILLER |
| †W.H. WILLIAMS | W.H. WILLIAMS 1T | W.H. WILLIAMS |
| J. BLAKE | J. BLAKE | J. BLAKE |
| | | |
| Gloucester | St. Helen's | Belfast |
| WON 13-3 | WON 12-3 | WON 3-0 |
| | | |
| ENG.: 1T | WALES: 4T | IRE.: NIL |
| WALES: 2G 1PG | SCOT.: 1T | WALES: 1T |
| | | |
| 6 Jan. 1900 | 27 Jan. 1900 | 17 Mar. 1900 |

Wales won the Triple Crown in 1900, the captain Billy Bancroft becoming the first Welshman to play in two Triple Crown winning sides. The triumph marked the beginning of an eleven-year golden era for Wales, a period in which the Principality gained the Triple Crown on six occasions, won three Grand Slams, and became virtually invincible at home. (The 1906 Springboks were the only international team to win in Wales between 1900 and 1913.)

The success of Bancroft's fifteen depended on hard forwards who constantly heeled the ball in the scrummages for their brilliant backs to use in attack. Five of the seven Welsh tries were scored from attractive bouts of threequarter passing. Nicholls was a finely balanced runner in the centre who passed the ball with immaculate judgment; while Trew of Swansea began a long career in the Welsh side by appearing on the wing and scoring a try on debut at Gloucester.

## 1900-01

| v. ENGLAND | v. SCOTLAND | v. IRELAND |
|---|---|---|
| *W.J. BANCROFT 2c | *W.J. BANCROFT 1c | *W.J. BANCROFT 2c |
| W.M. LLEWELLYN | W.M. LLEWELLYN | W.M. LLEWELLYN |
| G. DAVIES | G. DAVIES | G. DAVIES |
| E.G. NICHOLLS 1T | E.G. NICHOLLS | E.G. NICHOLLS |
| W.J. TREW | W.J. TREW | †R.T. GABE |
| G.L. LLOYD | G.L. LLOYD 1T | †R. JONES |
| †J. JONES | L.A. PHILLIPS | †R.M. OWEN |
| J.J. HODGES 1T | J.J. HODGES | †R. (BOB) JONES |
| R. HELLINGS | R. HELLINGS | G.F. SCRINE |
| A. BRICE | A. BRICE | A. BRICE |
| J.G. BOOTS | J.G. BOOTS 1T | J.G. BOOTS |
| R. THOMAS | W.H. ALEXANDER | W.H. ALEXANDER 2T |
| F. MILLER | F. MILLER | F. MILLER |
| W.H. WILLIAMS 1T | H. DAVIES | H. DAVIES |
| J. BLAKE | J. BLAKE | J. BLAKE |
| Cardiff Arms Park | Inverleith | St. Helen's |
| WON 13-0 | LOST 8-18 | WON 10-9 |
| WALES: 2G 1T | SCOT.: 3G 1T | WALES: 2G |
| ENG.: NIL | WALES: 1G 1T | IRE.: 3T |
| 5 Jan. 1901 | 9 Feb. 1901 | 16 Mar. 1901 |

There were high hopes that Wales would retain the Triple Crown in 1901, Bancroft's last season in the international side. The nucleus of the 1900 pack was again available and England were soundly beaten at Cardiff. However, there was disappointment in victory: Bancroft played poorly and the forwards, led by Dick Hellings, lacked cohesion in the tight.

Nevertheless, the side showed only two changes for the visit to Scotland, where the fears voiced after the English match were shown to be justified. Wales caved in towards the end of the Scottish game, losing by ten points.

Three of the new caps at Swansea were to become household names in Welsh rugby history. Dick Owen went on to gain 35 caps and surpass Bill Bancroft's appearance record for Wales. His half-back partner Dick Jones, also from Swansea, played only 15 times, but there was an opinion that Owen carried his partner into the international team. Rhys Gabe played 24 matches, forming a superlative combination with Nicholls in the centre of the Welsh threequarter line.

## 1901-02

| v. ENGLAND | v. SCOTLAND | v. IRELAND |
|---|---|---|
| †J. STRAND-JONES 1PG | J. STRAND-JONES 1c | J. STRAND-JONES |
| W.M. LLEWELLYN | W.M. LLEWELLYN 2T | W.M. LLEWELLYN 1T |
| R.T. GABE 1T | R.T. GABE 2T | R.T. GABE |
| *E.G. NICHOLLS | *E.G. NICHOLLS | *E.G. NICHOLLS 1T,1DG |
| †E. MORGAN | E. MORGAN | E. MORGAN |
| R. JONES | G.L. LLOYD | G.L. LLOYD 1T |
| R.M. OWEN | R.M. OWEN | R.M. OWEN |
| J.J. HODGES | J.J. HODGES | J.J. HODGES |
| †W. JOSEPH | W. JOSPEH | W. JOSEPH |
| A. BRICE | A. BRICE | A. BRICE 1c |
| J.G. BOOTS | J.G. BOOTS | J.G. BOOTS |
| †D. JONES | D. JONES | D. JONES |
| †A.F. HARDING | A.F. HARDING | A.F. HARDING |
| †N. WALTERS | †H. JONES | H. JONES |
| †W.T. OSBORNE 1T | W.T. OSBORNE | W.T. OSBORNE |
| Blackheath | Cardiff Arms Park | Lansdowne Road |
| WON 9-8 | WON 14-5 | WON 15-0 |
| ENG.: 1G 1T | WALES: 1G 3T | IRE.: NIL |
| WALES: 1PG 2T | SCOT.: 1G | WALES: 1G 1DG 2T |
| 11 Jan. 1902 | 1 Feb. 1902 | 8 Mar. 1902 |

Wales won the Triple Crown under the captaincy of Gwyn Nicholls. Nicholls was an Englishman by birth, but had joined the Cardiff club as a teenager in the early 1890s, distinguishing himself as a threequarter rich in promise and one of exceptional judgment. He went on to play 24 times for Wales and captained the side ten times during the first half of the Golden Era. With Rhys Gabe, Willie Llewellyn and Teddy Morgan he formed the most famous threequarter line of all time, a line which played together on seven occasions. Morgan made his debut against England. He was a player of great pace with the resource to beat opponents in one-to-one situations, and his 14 tries (in 16 matches) included the gem which defeated the First All Blacks in 1905. Only the cheek of scrum-half Dickie Owen helped Wales to steal victory over England. Five minutes from no-side, Owen tricked his opponent into an offside tackle under the shadow of the English posts. New full-back Jack Strand-Jones kicked the penalty goal which gave Wales victory by a point.

The Welsh threequarters ensured comfortable victories over Scotland and Ireland, scoring six tries in the two matches.

## 1902-03

| v. ENGLAND | v. SCOTLAND | v. IRELAND |
|---|---|---|
| J. STRAND-JONES 3C | J. STRAND-JONES | †H.B. WINFIELD |
| †W.F. JOWETT | †W.R. ARNOLD | W.M. LLEWELLYN 2T |
| R.T. GABE | R.T. GABE | R.T. GABE 1T |
| D. REES | D. REES | *E.G. NICHOLLS |
| *T.W.R. PEARSON 1T | W.J. TREW | E. MORGAN 2T |
| G.L. LLOYD | *G.L. LLOYD | G.L. LLOYD |
| R.M. OWEN 1T | R.M. OWEN | R.M. OWEN |
| J.J. HODGES 3T | J.J. HODGES | J.J. HODGES |
| W. JOSEPH | W. JOSEPH | W. JOSEPH |
| A. BRICE | A. BRICE | A. BRICE 1T |
| J.G. BOOTS | J.G. BOOTS | J.G. BOOTS |
| D. JONES | D. JONES | D. JONES |
| A.F. HARDING | A.F. HARDING | A.F. HARDING |
| †G. TRAVERS | G. TRAVERS | G. TRAVERS |
| W.T. OSBORNE | W.T. OSBORNE | W.T. OSBORNE |
| St Helen's | Inverleith | Cardiff Arms Park |
| WON 21-5 | LOST 0-6 | WON 18-0 |
| WALES: 3G 2T | SCOT.: 1PG 1T | WALES: 6T |
| ENG.: 1G | WALES: NIL | IRE.: NIL |
| 10 Jan. 1903 | 7 Feb. 1903 | 14 Mar. 1903 |

The Welsh forwards were unchanged during the season, despite being well beaten in Scotland in difficult conditions. The defeat cost Wales the Triple Crown and the Championship, for the team played most stylishly in beating England and Ireland.

George Travers, a scientific forward who became the first specialist Welsh international hooker, gained the first of his 25 caps against England. His selection in 1903 was remarkable for the fact that he was then playing with Pill Harriers, a second-class side based in the Newport Docks area. His long international career lasted until 1911, and in the 1930s he had the pleasure to see his son, also a hooker, capped for Wales. Travers senior died on Boxing Day 1945, listening to an exciting commentary on one of the New Zealand Kiwi matches in Wales.

## 1903-04

| v. ENGLAND | v. SCOTLAND | v. IRELAND |
|---|---|---|
| H.B. WINFIELD 2C,1GM | H.B. WINFIELD 3C,1PG | H.B. WINFIELD |
| W.M. LLEWELLYN 1T | *W.M. LLEWELLYN | *W.M. LLEWELLYN |
| R.T. GABE | R.T. GABE 1T | R.T. GABE 1T |
| *E.G. NICHOLLS | †C.C. PRITCHARD | C.C. PRITCHARD 1T |
| E. MORGAN 1T | E. MORGAN 1T | E. MORGAN 2T |
| R. JONES | R. JONES 1T | R. JONES |
| R.M. OWEN | R.M. OWEN | R.M. OWEN |
| J.J. HODGES | J.J. HODGES | †T.S. BEVAN |
| W. JOSEPH | W. JOSEPH | †H. JONES |
| A. BRICE | A. BRICE 1T | A. BRICE |
| J.G. BOOTS | †D.H. DAVIES | †C.M. PRITCHARD |
| S.H. RAMSEY | †E. THOMAS | E. THOMAS |
| A.F. HARDING | A.F. HARDING | A.F. HARDING |
| †J. EVANS | †W. O'NEILL | W. O'NEILL |
| †D.J. THOMAS | †H.V. WATKINS | H.V. WATKINS |
| Leicester | St. Helen's | Belfast |
| DRAWN 14-14 | WON 21-3 | LOST 12-14 |
| ENG.: 1G 1PG 2T | WALES: 3G 1PG 1T | IRE.: 1G 3T |
| WALES: 2G 1GM | SCOT.: 1T | WALES: 4T |
| 9 Jan. 1904 | 6 Feb. 1904 | 12 Mar. 1904 |

Bert Winfield, one of the finest kickers to play full-back for Wales, saved the match against England with a late goal from a mark. The English were leading by four points when Joseph, the Swansea forward, caught a loose kick and claimed the fair catch. Winfield, from a position just inside the English half, banged the goal over with ease. Wales were rather unlucky to finish the match with a draw. A late bout of passing by their threequarters created an overlap for Morgan to score. The referee, however, judged the final pass to have been forward.

Scotland were comprehensively beaten up front in the match at Swansea, and the Welsh backs revelled in the grand possession earned by their pack, scoring three tries.

In Belfast, Wales were deprived of victory by another controversial refereeing decision. Ireland had fought back with only fourteen men to gain a two-point lead, having trailed Wales by six points. Fly half Dick Jones crossed for a try which both Irish and Welsh teams had thought was perfectly fair. The referee, Crawford Findlay of Scotland (who had earlier controlled the English match), disallowed the score, and thus Wales were denied a share of the Championship.

## 1904-05

| v. ENGLAND | v. SCOTLAND | v. IRELAND |
|---|---|---|
| G. DAVIES 2c | G. DAVIES | G. DAVIES 2c |
| *W.M. LLEWELLYN 1T | *W.M. LLEWELLYN 2T | *W.M. LLEWELLYN |
| R.T. GABE 1T | R.T. GABE | R.T. GABE |
| D. REES | D. REES | E.G. NICHOLLS |
| E. MORGAN 2T | E. MORGAN | E. MORGAN 1T |
| R. JONES 1T | W.J. TREW | †W. JONES 1T |
| R.M. OWEN | R.M. OWEN | R.M. OWEN |
| J.J. HODGES | J.J. HODGES | J.J. HODGES |
| G. TRAVERS | G. TRAVERS | G. TRAVERS |
| W. JOSEPH | W. JOSEPH | W. JOSEPH |
| A.F. HARDING 1T | A.F. HARDING | A.F. HARDING |
| D. JONES | D. JONES | D. JONES |
| C.M. PRITCHARD | C.M. PRITCHARD | †J.F. WILLIAMS |
| W. O'NEILL | W. O'NEILL | W. O'NEILL |
| H.V. WATKINS 1T | H.V. WATKINS | H.V. WATKINS |
| Cardiff Arms Park | Inverleith | St. Helen's |
| WON 25-0 | WON 6-3 | WON 10-3 |
| WALES: 2G 5T | SCOT.: 1T | WALES: 2G |
| ENG.: NIL | WALES: 2T | IRE.: 1T |
| 14 Jan. 1905 | 4 Feb. 1905 | 11 Mar. 1905 |

Wales regained the Triple Crown, opening the season with a resounding victory over a very weak English side. The dazzling speed of a brilliant back division and the ruthless efficiency of a skilful pack combined to sink the Englishmen to the tune of 25 points.

Dai "Tarw" Jones, the Treherbert miner turned policeman, Charles Pritchard, a Newport wine merchant who died within two months of going to the Western Front in 1916, and Billy O'Neill, a Cardiff docker, joined seasoned campaigners Harding, Joseph, Hodges and Travers in a formidable Welsh pack.

Willie Llewellyn scored the winning try in Edinburgh to give Wales their first win at the Inverleith ground, and at Swansea tries by new cap Wyndham Jones and winger Teddy Morgan brought Wales the Triple Crown for the fourth time.

## 1905-06

| v. NZ | v. ENGLAND | v. SCOTLAND | v. IRELAND |
|---|---|---|---|
| H.B. WINFIELD | H.B. WINFIELD 2c | H.B. WINFIELD | H.B. WINFIELD |
| W.M. LLEWELLYN | †H.T. MADDOCK 1T | H.T. MADDOCK 1T | H.T. MADDOCK |
| R.T. GABE | R.T. GABE | C.C. PRITCHARD 1T | R.T. GABE 1T |
| *E.G. NICHOLLS | *E.G. NICHOLLS | *E.G. NICHOLLS | *E.G. NICHOLLS |
| E. MORGAN 1T | E. MORGAN 1T | E. MORGAN | E. MORGAN 1T |
| †P.F. BUSH | P.F. BUSH | †R.A. GIBBS | R.A. GIBBS |
| R.M. OWEN | R.M. OWEN | W.J. TREW | R.M. OWEN |
| C.C. PRITCHARD | C.C. PRITCHARD | R.M. OWEN | |
| | | | J.J. HODGES |
| J.J. HODGES | J.J. HODGES 1T | J.J. HODGES 1T | G. TRAVERS |
| G. TRAVERS | G. TRAVERS | G. TRAVERS | W. JOSEPH |
| W. JOSEPH | W. JOSEPH | W. JOSEPH | A.F. HARDING |
| A.F. HARDING | A.F. HARDING | A.F. HARDING | †J. POWELL |
| D. JONES | D. JONES | D. JONES | †T.H. EVANS |
| J.F. WILLIAMS | H.V. WATKINS | J.F. WILLIAMS | †D. WESTACOTT |
| C.M. PRITCHARD | C.M. PRITCHARD 1T | C.M. PRITCHARD | C.M. PRITCHARD |
| Cardiff Arms Park | Richmond | Cardiff Arms Park | Belfast |
| WON 3-0 | WON 16-3 | WON 9-3 | LOST 6-11 |
| WALES: 1T | ENG.: 1T | WALES: 3T | IRE.: 1G 2T |
| NZ: NIL | WALES: 2G 2T | SCOT.: 1PG | WALES: 2T |
| 16 Dec. 1905 | 13 Jan. 1906 | 3 Feb. 1906 | 10 Mar. 1906 |

Probably the most famous win in Welsh international rugby history was gained at the beginning of this season. The New Zealanders were drawing towards the end of their first tour of Britain when they met Wales at Cardiff in December. The visitors were unbeaten, and Wales were holders of the Triple Crown: the Championship of the World was at stake. On a dry, still day Wales scored the only try of the game ten minutes before the interval. The score was the result of a pre-planned move, one worked out by little Dickie Owen. It involved Bush, Nicholls and Llewellyn in a decoy move to the right while Owen fed Cliff Pritchard from a scrum. Pritchard had been selected as an extra half to combat the unusual New Zealand formation. He received a reverse pass from the scrum-half, and with the opposition committed to Bush and Co., there was just enough space for Pritchard and Gabe to send Teddy Morgan haring over at the left corner of the town end of the field.

For the Championship season Wales persisted with the formation which had helped them to victory over the All Blacks, but after a defeat in Scotland in 1907, the new plan was laid to rest.

Hopkin Maddock and Reg Gibbs entered the side against England and Scotland respectively. Both were to become prolific scorers. Maddock scored 170 tries for London Welsh, a club record which stands to this day, and Gibbs set a new Welsh try scoring record with 17 touch-downs in his 16 internationals. Neither could prevent Ireland, with only 13 men for most of the match, denying Wales the Triple Crown in Belfast.

## 1906-07

| v. S.AFRICA | v. ENGLAND | v. SCOTLAND | v. IRELAND |
|---|---|---|---|
| †J.C.M. DYKE | †D.B. DAVIES | H.B. WINFIELD 1PG | H.B. WINFIELD 2C,1PG |
| †J.L. WILLIAMS | J.L. WILLIAMS 2T | J.L. WILLIAMS | J.L. WILLIAMS 3T |
| R.T. GABE | R.T. GABE | R.T. GABE | *R.T. GABE1T |
| *E.G. NICHOLLS | †J. EVANS | J.. EVANS | J. EVANS |
| E. MORGAN | H.T. MADDOCK 2T | H.T. MADDOCK | †D.P. JONES 1T |
| P.F. BUSH | R.A. GIBBS 1T,1C | R.A. GIBBS | P.F. BUSH 1T,1DG |
| R.M. OWEN | W.J. TREW | *W.J. TREW | †R.J. DAVID |
|  | *R.M. OWEN | R.M. OWEN |  |
| †J.C. JENKINS | | | J. WATTS |
| G. TRAVERS | †J. WATTS | †J. WATTS | G. TRAVERS |
| W. JOSEPH | G. TRAVERS | G. TRAVERS | W.H. DOWELL |
| A.F. HARDING | †W.H. DOWELL | W.H. DOWELL | J.A. BROWN |
| D. JONES | †J.A. BROWN 1T | J.A. BROWN | A.F. HARDING |
| †E.J.R. THOMAS | T.H. EVANS | T.H. EVANS | T.H. EVANS |
| J.F. WILLIAMS | W. O'NEILL | †J. WEBB | W. O'NEILL |
| C.M. PRITCHARD | C.M. PRITCHARD | C.M. PRITCHARD | C.M. PRITCHARD |
| St. Helen's | St. Helen's | Inverleith | Cardiff Arms Park |
| LOST 0-11 | WON 22-0 | LOST 3-6 | WON 29-0 |
| WALES: NIL | WALES: 2G 4T | SCOT.: 2T | WALES: 2G 1PG 1DG 4T |
| SA: 1G 2T | SA: nil | WALES: 1PG | IRE: NIL |
| 1 Dec. 1906 | 12 Jan. 1907 | 2 Feb. 1907 | 9 Mar. 1907 |

Gwyn Nicholls was tempted out of retirement to lead Wales for a last time against the first Springboks. But there was to be no repeat of the wonderful triumph over the New Zealanders, and the South Africans gained the distinction of becoming the only international side to lower Welsh colours in Wales during the Golden Era.

There were positive signals of the deterioration of the Welsh pack, with several of the old stalwarts reaching the close of their careers, and for the match with England three new forwards were introduced, Dai Jones, Joseph and Harding losing their places.

Wales beat England by a convincing margin, Maddock and J.L. Williams scoring four of the six Welsh tries. Williams, an official at the Cardiff Coal Exchange, went on to equal Reg Gibbs' record of 17 tries for Wales. A product of Cowbridge GS, Williams was noted for his sidestep and his swerve inwards, though much of his success was due to the supreme skill and judgment of his centre and club colleague, Rhys Gabe.

## 1907-08

| v. ENGLAND | v. SCOTLAND | v. FRANCE | v. IRELAND |
|---|---|---|---|
| H.B. WINFIELD 2C,1PG | H.B. WINFIELD | H.B. WINFIELD 2C,1PG | *H.B. WINFIELD 1C |
| J.L. WILLIAMS | J.L. WILLIAMS 1T | *E. MORGAN 2T | J.L. WILLIAMS 2T |
| R.T. GABE 2T | R.T. GABE | R.T. GABE | R.T. GABE |
| W.J. TREW 1T | W.J. TREW 1T | W.J. TREW 2T | W.J. TREW |
| R.A. GIBBS 1T | R.A. GIBBS | R.A. GIBBS 1C,4T | R.A. GIBBS 1T |
| P.F. BUSH 1DG,1C,1T | P.F. BUSH | R. JONES1T | R. JONES |
| †T.H. VILE | T.H. VILE | R.M. OWEN | R.M. OWEN |
| J. WATTS | J. WATTS | J. WATTS | J. WATTS |
| G. TRAVERS | *G. TRAVERS | G. TRAVERS | G. TRAVERS |
| W.H. DOWELL | W.H. DOWELL | W.H. DOWELL | W.H. DOWELL |
| J.A. BROWN | J.A. BROWN | J.A. BROWN | J. WEBB |
| *A.F. HARDING | A.F. HARDING | E.J.R. THOMAS | E.J.R. THOMAS |
| J. WEBB | J. WEBB | J. WEBB | T.H. EVANS |
| W. O'NEILL | W. O'NEILL | W. O'NEILL | W. O'NEILL |
| C.M. PRITCHARD | †G. HAYWARD | G. HAYWARD | G. HAYWARD |
| Bristol | St. Helen's | Cardiff Arms Park | Belfast |
| WON 28-18 | WON 6-5 | WON 36-4 | WON 11-5 |
| ENG.: 3G 1T | WALES: 2T | WALES: 3G 1PG 6T | IRE: 1G |
| WALES: 3G 1DG 1PG 2T | SCOT.: 1G | FR: 1DG | WALES: 1G 2T |
| 18 Jan. 1908 | 1 Feb. 1908 | 2 Mar. 1908 | 14 Mar. 1908 |

By winning the Triple Crown and their first international match against France, Wales became the first nation to gain the Grand Slam. George Hayward proved to be a versatile loose forward, one of the first specialist flankers to win selection in the position in the Welsh team. His defence was sound and his strength was his ability to support and combine with his scrum-half.

The threequarters played with panache, the Swansea utility back Billy Trew settling splendidly in the centre. The threes scored 17 tries in the four Championship matches, Gibbs creating a record by scoring six for the season, and equalling the match record of Willie Llewellyn by scoring four in the game with France.

The backs were spearheaded by Percy Bush against England and Scotland. He was an audacious fly-half who had been much respected by the All Blacks, but there was a criticism that his genius was too erratic, and that he did not relish playing at half-back with Dickie Owen, Wales' principal scrum-half. It will be noted that Bush's partner for the opening matches was Tommy Vile, the talented Newport scrum-half: both gave way for Jones and Owen, the Swansea pair, to return for the final two games.

## 1908-09

| v. AUSTRALIA | v. ENGLAND | v. SCOTLAND | v. FRANCE | v. IRELAND |
|---|---|---|---|---|
| H.B. WINFIELD 1PG | †J. BANCROFT 1C | J. BANCROFT 1C | J. BANCROFT 6C | J. BANCROFT 3C |
| | | | | |
| J.L. WILLIAMS | J.L. WILLIAMS 1T | J.L. WILLIAMS | J.L. WILLIAMS 2T | J.L. WILLIAMS |
| †J.P. JONES | J.P. JONES | J.P. JONES | J.P. JONES 2T | J.P. JONES 1T |
| *W.J. TREW | *W.J. TREW | *W.J. TREW 1T | *W.J. TREW 1C,3T | *W.J. TREW 1T |
| †P.L. HOPKINS 1T | P.L. HOPKINS 1T | †A.M. BAKER | A.M. BAKER 3T | P.L. HOPKINS 1T |
| | | | | |
| R. JONES | R. JONES | R. JONES | R. JONES | R. JONES |
| R.M. OWEN | R.M. OWEN | R.M. OWEN | R.M. OWEN | R.M. OWEN |
| | | | | |
| J. WATTS | J.A. BROWN | J. WATTS | J. WATTS 1T | J. WATTS 1T |
| G. TRAVERS 1T | G. TRAVERS | G. TRAVERS | †T.C. LLOYD | G. TRAVERS |
| G. HAYWARD | G. HAYWARD | E. THOMAS | E. THOMAS | E. THOMAS |
| J. WEBB | J. WEBB | J. WEBB | J. WEBB | J. WEBB |
| †P.D. WALLER | P.D. WALLER | P.D. WALLER | P.D. WALLER | P.D. WALLER |
| T.H. EVANS | T.H. EVANS | T.H. EVANS | T.H. EVANS | T.H. EVANS |
| †I. MORGAN | I. MORGAN | I. MORGAN | I. MORGAN | I. MORGAN |
| D.J. THOMAS | †J.H. BLACKMORE | E.J.R. THOMAS | †R. THOMAS | R. THOMAS |
| | | | | |
| Cardiff Arms Park | Cardiff Arms Park | Inverleith | Stade Colombes | St. Helen's |
| WON 9-6 | WON 8-0 | WON 5-3 | WON 47-5 | WON 18-5 |
| | | | | |
| WALES: 1PG 2T | WALES: 1G 1T | SCOT.: 1PG | FR.: 1G | WALES: 3G 1T |
| AUST.: 2T | ENG.: NIL | WALES: 1G | WALES: 7G 4T | IRE.: 1G |
| | | | | |
| 12 Dec. 1908 | 16 Jan. 1909 | 6 Feb. 1909 | 23 Feb. 1909 | 13 Mar. 1909 |

Wales retained the Triple Crown and Grand Slam in 1909, beating the first tourists from Australia before the start of the Championship season. The Australians lacked the finesse and crowd-drawing enterprise of their predecessors, the Springboks and All Blacks, but there was a crowd of 30,000 present to see Bert Winfield, in the last of his 16 internationals, decide the match with a penalty goal in the second half. Winfield was the first tactical kicker to perfect the screw kick to touch, a device which he used cleverly both in attack and defence.

His successor at full back, Jack Bancroft, was the younger brother of the great Billy. Bancroft junior represented Wales 18 times up to the outbreak of the Great War, displaying pluck and sound positional sense on the field. But his chief contribution to the Welsh side was a record number of points. His 88 points from 38 conversions and four penalty goals remained a Welsh record until surpassed by Barry John in 1972.

J.P. (Jack) Jones, one of three brilliant brothers who played in the Pontypool threequarter line, made his debut in the side this season. His elder brother, D.P. (Ponty) was capped against Ireland in 1907, and a third member of the family played one match in 1913. But Jack was the most outstanding of the three, and his 14 caps spanned the war years.

## 1909-10

| v. FRANCE | v. ENGLAND | v. SCOTLAND | v. IRELAND |
|---|---|---|---|
| J. BANCROFT 1PG,8C | J. BANCROFT | J. BANCROFT 1C | J. BANCROFT |
| | | | |
| H.T. MADDOCK 2T | P.L. HOPKINS | A.M. BAKER 1T | J.L. WILLIAMS 3T |
| J.P. JONES 1T | J.P. JONES | †W.J. SPILLER 1T | W.J. SPILLER |
| *W.J. TREW 1T | *W.J. TREW | *W.J. TREW | †L.M. DYKE 1T |
| R.A. GIBBS 3T | R.A. GIBBS 1T | R.A. GIBBS | *R.A. GIBBS 1T |
| | | | |
| R. JONES | R. JONES | P.F. BUSH | P.F. BUSH 1DG |
| R.M. OWEN | R.M. OWEN | †W.L. MORGAN | T.H. VILE |
| | | | |
| †B. GRONOW 1T | B. GRONOW | B. GRONOW | B. GRONOW |
| †J.J. PULLMAN | †J. PUGSLEY | J. PUGSLEY 1T | J. PUGSLEY |
| E. THOMAS | †H. JARMAN | H. JARMAN | H. JARMAN |
| J. WEBB | J. WEBB 1T | J. WEBB | J. WEBB |
| P.D. WALLER | C.M. PRITCHARD | †E. JENKINS | E. JENKINS |
| T.H. EVANS | T.H. EVANS | T.H. EVANS | T.H. EVANS |
| I. MORGAN 2T | I. MORGAN | I. MORGAN 1T | I. MORGAN |
| C.M. PRITCHARD | D.J. THOMAS | D.J. THOMAS | D.J. THOMAS |
| | | | |
| St. Helen's | Twickenham | Cardiff Arms Park | Lansdowne Road |
| WON 49-14 | LOST 6-11 | WON 14-0 | WON 19-3 |
| | | | |
| WALES: 8G 1PG 2T | ENG.: 1G 1PG 1T | WALES: 1G 3T | IRE.: 1T |
| FR.: 1G 2PG 1T | WALES: 2T | SCOT.: NIL | WALES: 1DG 5T |
| | | | |
| 1 Jan. 1910 | 15 Jan. 1910 | 5 Feb. 1910 | 12 Mar. 1910 |

The season began on New Year's Day with an overwhelming victory over the hapless French. Jack Bancroft created a match record for a Welshman, scoring 19 of the 49 points – a record which has since been equalled but not surpassed. But Wales' run of eleven international victories was ended on their first visit to the RFU's new ground at Twickenham. The match marked the close of a record run of victories, and was Wales' first defeat by England since 1898.

Jones and Owen, who had been the architects of many of Wales' wins during the three previous seasons, were dropped for the Scottish match, Bush returning with his club partner, W.L. Morgan (a younger brother of Teddy Morgan). The season concluded with comfortable wins over Scotland and Ireland, but Wales had to be content to finish the season as runners-up to England.

Billy Spiller, a policeman from St Fagans, played the first of his ten Welsh internationals against Scotland, scoring a try on his debut. A talented all-round sportsman (who scored the first century for Glamorgan in first-class cricket), Spiller was a dependable centre with a penchant for the crash-tackle and an ability to drop goals from difficult positions.

## 1910-11

| v. ENGLAND | v. SCOTLAND | v. FRANCE | v. IRELAND |
|---|---|---|---|
| J. Bancroft | F.W. Birt | J. Bancroft 3c | J. Bancroft 2c,1pg |
| J.L. Williams | J.L. Williams 2t | *J.L. Williams 1t | J.L. Williams |
| W.J. Spiller 1t | W.J. Spiller 1dg,2t | W.J. Spiller | W.J. Spiller |
| †F.W. Birt 1pg | L.M. Dyke 2c | L.M. Dyke | L.M. Dyke |
| R.A. Gibbs 1t | R.A. Gibbs 3t | R.A. Gibbs | R.A. Gibbs 1t |
| *W.J. Trew | *W.J. Trew | W.J. Trew | *W.J. Trew |
| R.M. Owen | R.M. Owen | R.M. Owen 1t | R.M. Owen |
| †W. Perry | G. Travers | G. Travers | G. Travers |
| J. Pugsley 1t | J. Pugsley | J. Pugsley | J. Pugsley |
| H. Jarman | †J. Birch | J. Birch | †W.G. Evans |
| J. Webb | J. Webb | J. Webb | J. Webb 1t |
| †A.P. Coldrick | A.P. Coldrick | R. Thomas | A.P. Coldrick |
| T.H. Evans | T.H. Evans | T.H. Evans | T.H. Evans 1t |
| I. Morgan 1t | R. Thomas 1t | I. Morgan 1t | I. Morgan |
| D.J. Thomas | D.J. Thomas | D.J. Thomas | D.J. Thomas |
| St. Helen's | Inverleith | Parc des Princes | Cardiff Arms Park |
| WON 15-11 | WON 32-10 | WON 15-0 | WON 16-0 |
| WALES: 1PG 4T | SCOT.: 1DG 2T | FR.: NIL | WALES: 2G 1PG 1T |
| ENG.: 1G 2T | WALES: 2G 1DG 6T | WALES: 3G | IRE.: NIL |
| 21 Jan. 1911 | 4 Feb. 1911 | 28 Feb. 1911 | 11 Mar. 1911 |

Scotland had been the chief threat to Welsh supremacy during the early years of the Golden Era. Now, as the ageing Welsh halves Trew and Owen reached the ends of their long careers, the rising promise of English international rugby posed the greatest problems for the Welsh. But in 1911, Wales managed to scrape home against the English in an evenly contested match. It was a sign of the times that the Welsh threequarters, who had led the world for combined play during the previous decade, were reckoned by the press to have been inferior to the English threequarters.

Yet Wales went on to gain the Triple Crown and Grand Slam, their last such success for 39 years. Cardiff supplied the entire threequarter line for the last three games, only Fred Birt of Newport preventing them playing against England.

Birt was the outstanding Newport threequarter of the day, though he was equally at home as a full-back. He had learned the game as a very young lad, having watched the peerless Arthur Gould practise in a field near to Birt's house. Birt became ball-retriever for Gould and studied the master's methods assiduously.

## 1911-12

| v. ENGLAND | v. SCOTLAND | v. IRELAND | v. FRANCE |
|---|---|---|---|
| J. Bancroft | J. Bancroft 2c | *J. Bancroft 1c | †H. Thomas 1c |
| J.P. Jones | †R.C.S. Plummer 1t | R.C.S. Plummer | R.C.S. Plummer 1t |
| W.J. Spiller | †W.A. Davies | W.A. Davies 1t | W.J. Spiller |
| F.W. Birt | F.W. Birt 1dg | F.W. Birt | J.P. Jones 1t |
| †E.G. Davies | †G.L. Hirst 1t | †B.R. Lewis | E.G. Davies 2t |
| †J.M.C. Lewis | W.J. Trew 1dg | †W.J. Martin | W.J. Martin |
| *R.M. Owen | *R.M. Owen | T.H. Vile | *T.H. Vile |
| †G. Stephens | G. Stephens | G. Stephens | G. Stephens |
| †H. Uzzell | H. Uzzell | H. Uzzell | H. Uzzell |
| †L.C. Trump | L.C. Trump | L.C. Trump | L.C. Trump |
| J. Webb | J. Webb | †A.E. Merry | A.E. Merry |
| A.P. Coldrick | A.P. Coldrick | †T. Williams | A.P. Coldrick |
| R. Thomas | R. Thomas | †H. Hiams | H. Hiams |
| †H.J. Davies | I. Morgan 1t | †W.J. Jenkins | W.J. Jenkins |
| D.J. Thomas | H.J. Davies | †F. Hawkins | F. Hawkins |
| Twickenham | St. Helen's | Belfast | Newport |
| LOST 0-8 | WON 21-6 | LOST 5-12 | WON 14-8 |
| ENG.: 1G 1T | WALES: 2G 2DG 1T | IRE.: 1G 1DG 1T | WALES: 1G 3T |
| WALES: NIL | SCOT.: 2T | WALES: 1G | FR.: 1G 1T |
| 20 Jan. 1912 | 3 Feb. 1912 | 9 Mar. 1912 | 25 Mar. 1912 |

This was Dickie Owen's last season and he captained the team at Twickenham, where Wales were narrowly beaten by a competent English fifteen. Wales selected four new forwards for the English match, but a young pack won plenty of possession for Owen and the Welsh backs to exploit. There was a criticism concerning the selection of the side, however, the pundits arguing that Owen preferred to play with his Swansea colleague Ivor Morgan, a wing forward, to provide ample cover for Owen's tricks and ploys in attack. Morgan's absence hampered Owen, who was given a roasting by the English halves and wing-forwards.

Glyn Stephens, a mining engineer from Neath, won the first of his ten caps against the English. He was one of only three forwards to play throughout the season, and went on to earn a reputation as a strong, stylish forward. He later became a committee member of the WRU, serving as President in 1956-7, when his son (J.R.G. [Rees] Stephens) captained Wales.

Defeat in Belfast, after a stirring win against a good Scottish team, came as a disappointment to the Welsh supporters. The side which played in Ireland contained seven new caps, and it is believed that several of the players originally chosen for the trip declined to play for a variety of reasons.

## 1912-13

| v. S.AFRICA | v. ENGLAND | v. SCOTLAND | v. FRANCE | v. IRELAND |
|---|---|---|---|---|
| †R.F. WILLIAMS | R.F. WILLIAMS | R.F. WILLIAMS | †G. GETHING | J. BANCROFT 2c,1pg |
| | | | | |
| R.C.S. PLUMMER | R.C.S. PLUMMER | †H. LEWIS | H. LEWIS | H. LEWIS |
| W.J. SPILLER | W.J. SPILLER | †TUAN JONES 1t | J.P. JONES | *J.P. JONES 1t |
| F.W. BIRT | F.W. BIRT | *W.J. TREW | *W.J. TREW | W.P. GEEN |
| †W.P. GEEN | W.P. GEEN | G.L. HIRST | †M. LEWIS | B.R. LEWIS 2t |
| | | | | |
| †H.W. THOMAS | H.W. THOMAS | J.M.C. LEWIS 1t,1c | J.M.C. LEWIS 1t,1c | J.M.C. LEWIS |
| *T.H. VILE | *T.H. VILE | †R. LLOYD | R. LLOYD | R. LLOYD |
| | | | | |
| G. STEPHENS | G. STEPHENS | G. STEPHENS | G. STEPHENS | G. STEPHENS |
| †H. WETTER | H. WETTER | H. UZZELL | H. UZZELL | H. UZZELL |
| †P. JONES | P. JONES | P. JONES | P. JONES | W.J. JENKINS |
| †J.L. MORGAN | J.L. MORGAN | †J.A. DAVIES | J.A. DAVIES 1t | J.A. DAVIES |
| †F. ANDREWS | F. ANDREWS | F. ANDREWS | T. WILLIAMS 1t | F. ANDREWS |
| R. THOMAS | R. THOMAS | †R. RICHARDS | R. RICHARDS | R. RICHARDS |
| †H. HOLLINGDALE | H. HOLLINGDALE | W.J. JENKINS | T.C. LLOYD | T.C. LLOYD |
| †F.L. PERRETT | F.L. PERRETT | F.L. PERRETT | F.L. PERRETT | F.L. PERRETT |
| Cardiff Arms Park | Cardiff Arms Park | Inverleith | Parc des Princes | St. Helen's |
| LOST 0-3 | LOST 0-12 | WON 8-0 | WON 11-8 | WON 16-13 |
| WALES: NIL | WALES: NIL | SCOT.: NIL | FR.: 1G 1T | WALES: 2G 1PG 1T |
| SA: 1PG | ENG.: 1G 1DG 1T | WALES: 1G 1T | WALES: 1G 2T | IRE.: 2G 1PG |
| 14 Dec. 1912 | 18 Jan. 1913 | 1 Feb. 1913 | 27 Feb. 1913 | 8 Mar. 1913 |

A young team containing nine new caps made a brave attempt to beat the second Springboks at Cardiff. But fears amongst the Welsh public that their great run of success had come to an end were justified, the visitors winning by a first-half penalty goal from near the Welsh posts. It was the first Welsh defeat at Cardiff since 1899.

Worse was to follow. Against England, the Welsh lost by twelve points in muddy, wet conditions. It was England's first win at Cardiff and their first in Wales since 1895: the first Golden Era of Welsh rugby had ended.

Billy Trew returned as captain against Scotland and France, but a groin injury sustained in the Paris international virtually ended his career. His span of fourteen seasons set a Welsh record (later equalled by his contemporary Tommy Vile). Only two players appeared in all five of the matches this season. Glyn Stephens excelled in the lineout and received sterling support from his clubmate, Fred Perrett. Perrett joined Leeds in the Rugby League before the following season had started, but his playing career was shortened by the war. He registered with a London unit of the Army, served in France, but died of wounds in a casualty clearing-station in December 1918, less than a month after the Armistice.

## 1913-14

| v. ENGLAND | v. SCOTLAND | v. FRANCE | v. IRELAND |
|---|---|---|---|
| J. BANCROFT 1c | J. BANCROFT 2c,1pg | J. BANCROFT 5c | R.F. WILLIAMS |
| | | | |
| H. LEWIS | †I.T. DAVIES 1t | I.T. DAVIES | I.T. DAVIES 1t |
| †W.J. WATT 1t | †J.J. WETTER 1t | J.J. WETTER 2t | J.J. WETTER 1t |
| †W.H. EVANS | W.H. EVANS | W.H. EVANS 1t | W.H. EVANS |
| G.L. HIRST 1dg | G.L. HIRST 1t,1dg | G.L. HIRST 1t | G.L. HIRST |
| | | | |
| J.M.C. LEWIS | J.M.C. LEWIS 1dg | J.M.C. LEWIS | J.M.C. LEWIS 1c |
| R. LLOYD | R. LLOYD | R. LLOYD | R. LLOYD |
| | | | |
| †J.B. JONES | J.B. JONES | J.B. JONES | J.B. JONES 1t |
| H. UZZELL | H. UZZELL | H. UZZELL 2t | H. UZZELL |
| P. JONES | P. JONES | P. JONES | P. JONES |
| *J.A. DAVIES | *J.A. DAVIES | *J.A. DAVIES 1t | *J. A. DAVIES |
| T. WILLIAMS | T. WILLIAMS | T. WILLIAMS | T. WILLIAMS |
| †D. WATTS | D. WATTS | D. WATTS | D. WATTS |
| T.C. LLOYD | T.C. LLOYD | T.C. LLOYD | T.C. LLOYD |
| †E. MORGAN | E. MORGAN | E. MORGAN | E. MORGAN |
| Twickenham | Cardiff Arms Park | St. Helen's | Belfast |
| LOST 9-10 | WON 24-5 | WON 31-0 | WON 11-3 |
| ENG.: 2G | WALES:2G 2DG 1PG 1T | WALES: 5G 2T | IRE.: 1T |
| WALES: 1G 1DG | SCOT.: 1G | FR.: NIL | WALES: 1G 2T |
| 17 Jan. 1914 | 7 Feb. 1914 | 2 Mar. 1914 | 14 Mar. 1914 |

The England-Wales match was the key to the Championship. By winning through the "small and artistic" margin of one point, England were able to proceed to the Grand Slam, leaving Wales as runners-up in the table. The Welsh were unlucky. Their solid pack so completely dominated up front that it was a wonder that England gained sufficient possession to score. Reports of the match emphasise the traditional reversal of roles – the English backs playing brilliantly on scant rations, while the Welsh centres, lacking judgment, failing to create sufficient openings for their wings to score.

Jack Wetter, the young Newport utility back, was introduced for the Scottish match. He began his career as a first-class centre with superb defensive qualities and the ability to beat an opponent in attack. He created an unusual record in 1914, scoring tries in each of his first three internationals. After the war he played as an outside half, but tended to overdo the kick-to-touch.

The side was led by a clergyman, the Rev. Alban Davies. During his long career he turned out for Llanelli, Swansea, Cardiff, London Welsh and Oxford University. His pack was a robust collection, known as the "Terrible Eight". It was reported that these "furies in red jerseys . . . fought to a standstill the militant Irish pack", Wales winning a very rough match in Belfast.

| 1919 | 1919-20 | | | |
| v. NZ ARMY | v. ENGLAND | v. SCOTLAND | v. FRANCE | v. IRELAND |
|---|---|---|---|---|
| †E. Davies | †J. Rees | J. Rees | J. Rees | J. Rees |
| | | | | |
| †M.G. Thomas | †W.J. Powell 1t | W.J. Powell | W.J. Powell 1t | W.J. Powell |
| †E.B. Rees | †A. Jenkins | A. Jenkins 1t,1c | A. Jenkins | A. Jenkins 1t,1dg,2c |
| †J. Shea 1pg | J. Shea 1t,2dg,1pg,1c | J. Shea | J.P. Jones | J.P. Jones |
| †T.J. Nicholas | †B.S. Evans | †B. Williams | B. Williams 1t | B. Williams 3t |
| | | | | |
| W.J. Martin | J.J. Wetter | J.J. Wetter | J.J. Wetter | J.J. Wetter 1c |
| †I.J. Fowler | †B. Beynon | B. Beynon | †F. Reeves | F. Reeves |
| | | | | |
| *G. Stephens | †C.W. Jones | C.W. Jones | C.W. Jones | †D.E. Morgan |
| †D.G. Francis | *H. Uzzell | *H. Uzzell | *H. Uzzell | *H. Uzzell |
| †W. Morris | †J. Williams | J. Williams | J. Williams | J. Williams |
| †J. Jones | J. Jones | J. Jones | †R. Huxtable | R. Huxtable |
| †J. Whitfield | J. Whitfield | J. Whitfield | J. Whitfield | J. Whitfield 1t |
| †W.T. Havard | †S. Morris | S. Morris | S. Morris | S. Morris |
| †A. Rees | †G. Oliver | G. Oliver | G. Oliver | G. Oliver |
| †T. Parker | T. Parker | T. Parker | W. Morris | T. Parker 1t |
| | | | | |
| St. Helen's | St. Helen's | Inverleith | Stade Colombes | Cardiff Arms Park |
| LOST 3-6 | WON 19-5 | LOST 5-9 | WON 6-5 | WON 28-4 |
| | | | | |
| WALES: 1PG | WALES: 1G 2DG 1PG 1T | SCOT.: 2PG 1T | FR.: 1G | WALES: 3G 1DG 3T |
| NZ ARMY: 2PG | ENG.: 1G | WALES: 1G | WALES: 2T | IRE.: 1DG |
| | | | | |
| 21 Apr. 1919 | 17 Jan. 1920 | 7 Feb. 1920 | 17 Feb. 1920 | 13 Mar. 1920 |

Wales fielded thirteen new caps for an official match played in April 1919, against a team of New Zealand Army players. Glyn Stephens was the only pre-war cap among the forwards, and he led the side in a disappointing match decided by penalty goals, the New Zealanders scoring two to one by Jerry Shea.

When Championship matches were resumed in 1920, Shea made a great impact on the game at Swansea against England. He became the first Welshman to score a try, conversion, penalty and drop-goal in a match, and scored a total of 16 points in all. But Shea's major fault was his individualism. He simply tried to do too much, and it was said of him that he would more often have achieved more had he done less. In trying to repeat his scoring feats against the Scots, he was regularly caught in possession by a sound Scottish defence. Wales were beaten, and the defeat cost them the Triple Crown and Grand Slam.

For the French and Irish matches, Jack Jones returned instead of Shea, and by playing to his wings the experienced centre created four tries for Wick Powell and Bryn Williams in two matches. Victories enabled Wales to share the Championship with England and Scotland.

| 1920-21 | | | |
| v. ENGLAND | v. SCOTLAND | v. FRANCE | v. IRELAND |
|---|---|---|---|
| J. Rees | J. Rees | †B.O. Male | J. Rees |
| | | | |
| †J. Ring 1t | M.G. Thomas | M.G. Thomas | M.G. Thomas 1t |
| J.P. Jones | A. Jenkins 2dg | A. Jenkins 2pg | †D. Davies |
| J. Shea | †P.E.R. Baker-Jones | †H.G. Davies | H.G. Davies |
| †T. Johnson | †F. Evans | T. Johnson | T. Johnson 1pg |
| | | | |
| *J. J. Wetter | †W. Bowen | W. Bowen | J.M.C. Lewis |
| F. Reeves | *T.H. Vile | †T. Williams | †A. Brown |
| | | | |
| D.E. Morgan | D.E. Morgan | D.E. Morgan | W. Morris |
| †S.L. Attewell | S.L. Attewell | S.L. Attewell | †A. Baker |
| †D.W. Edwards | J. Williams | J. Williams 1t | J. Williams |
| †D. Marsden-Jones | J. Jones | J. Jones | J. Jones |
| J. Whitfield | †T. Roberts | T. Roberts | T. Roberts |
| †W. Hodder | W. Hodder | W. Hodder 1t | †F.J. Prosser |
| †S. Winmill | S. Winmill | S. Winmill | S. Winmill |
| T. Parker | T. Parker | *T. Parker | *T. Parker |
| | | | |
| Twickenham | St. Helen's | Cardiff Arms Park | Belfast |
| LOST 3-18 | LOST 8-14 | WON 12-4 | WON 6-0 |
| | | | |
| ENG.: 1G 1DG 3T | WALES: 2DG | WALES: 2PG 2T | IRE.: NIL |
| WALES: 1T | SCOT.: 1G 1PG 2T | FR.: 1DG | WALES: 1PG 1T |
| | | | |
| 15 Jan. 1921 | 5 Feb. 1921 | 26 Feb. 1921 | 12 Mar. 1921 |

The Welsh selectors had much to brood over this season. Wales' heaviest defeat since the 1890s against England was followed by sweeping changes and another defeat at Swansea, against Scotland. The side was not allowed to settle, and only two players retained their positions during the season, Tom Parker, the big Swansea forward, and Stanley Winmill, the Cross Keys captain.

Parker was a steelworker who had first made an impression as a member of the successful Swansea side of 1913. He played 15 times for Wales after the war, striking his colleagues as a sound all-round forward with the ability to lead by example. His qualities were further recognised in the French match, when he was appointed captain of the Welsh side, and promptly inspired an inexperienced side to victory. In all he led Wales seven times, and was never captain of a losing international side.

Winmill was the backbone of the Cross Keys side during the club's zenith. He captained the club from 1912 to 1923, a period in which the side won one hundred of the 136 games played. Winmill, known as "Docker", was a collier at the Nine Mile Point Mine near Cross Keys.

## 1921-22

| v. ENGLAND | v. SCOTLAND | v. IRELAND | v. FRANCE |
|---|---|---|---|
| J. REES 2C | †F. SAMUEL 1C | F. SAMUEL 1C | F. SAMUEL |
| †C. RICHARDS 1T | C. RICHARDS | C. RICHARDS | C.RICHARDS |
| †I. EVANS 1T | I. EVANS 1DG | I. EVANS 1T | I. EVANS 1T |
| B.S. EVANS | B.S. EVANS | B.S. EVANS | A. JENKINS 1C |
| †F. PALMER 1T | F. PALMER | F. PALMER | B.S. EVANS |
| W. BOWEN 1T | W. BOWEN 1T | W. BOWEN | W. BOWEN |
| †W.J. DELAHAY 1T | W.J. DELAHAY | W.J. DELAHAY | W.J. DELAHAY |
| †T. JONES | T. JONES | T. JONES | T. JONES |
| †J.G. STEPHENS | J.G. STEPHENS | J.G. STEPHENS | J.G. STEPHENS |
| †W. CUMMINS | W. CUMMINS | W. CUMMINS | W. CUMMINS 1T |
| J. WHITFIELD 1T | J. WHITFIELD | J. WHITFIELD 2T | J. WHITFIELD 1T |
| T. ROBERTS | T. ROBERTS | T. ROBERTS | T. ROBERTS |
| S. MORRIS | S. MORRIS | S. MORRIS | S. MORRIS |
| †D.D. HIDDLESTONE 1T | D.D. HIDDLESTONE | D.D. HIDDLESTONE | D.D. HIDDLESTONE |
| *T. PARKER 1T | *T. PARKER | *T. PARKER | *T. PARKER |
| Cardiff Arms Park | Inverleith | St. Helen's | Stade Colombes |
| WON 28-6 | DRAWN 9-9 | WON 11-5 | WON 11-3 |
| WALES: 2G 6T | SCOT.: 1PG 2T | WALES: 1G 2T | FR.: 1T |
| ENG.: 2T | WALES: 1G 1DG | IRE.: 1G | WALES: 1G 2T |
| 21 Jan. 1922 | 4 Feb. 1922 | 11 Mar. 1922 | 23 Mar. 1922 |

Tom Parker's unbeaten team won the Championship outright, Wales' first outright title since 1911. Incessant rain in the week prior to the English match turned the Arms Park into a patch of slime, but the sub-aqua experts in the Welsh pack revelled in the wet conditions and helped Wales to their biggest victory over England since 1907. Dai Hiddlestone, a veteran at 31, was the star of the Welsh pack. A wing forward, he utterly destroyed the English half-back play and capped a fine debut by scoring a try. By all accounts Hiddlestone credited his great stamina and fitness to his dog, who set the pace for Dai on training runs!

Islwyn Evans, a clever runner and a shrewd kicker, saved Wales' bacon at Inverleith. Scotland looked set for victory when Evans dropped a superb goal right at the end of the match. Evans had scored a try against the English, and his tries against Ireland and France brought his contribution of points in his only season of international rugby to thirteen.

Jack Whitfield, the Newport fitter who had learned the game with the famous wartime Pill Harriers side, was the outstanding tight forward of the era. He was very fast for a big man, and reports imply that he was an agile man with the necessary strength of a forward, but the kicking and handling skills of a threequarter.

## 1922-23

| v. ENGLAND | v. SCOTLAND | v. FRANCE | v. IRELAND |
|---|---|---|---|
| J. REES | B.O. MALE | J. REES 1PG | J. REES |
| †W.R. HARDING | W.R. HARDING | W.R. HARDING 1T | W.R. HARDING |
| †R.A. CORNISH | R.A. CORNISH | M.G. THOMAS 1T | †T. COLLINS |
| A. JENKINS | A. JENKINS 1C,1PG | A. JENKINS 2C | *A. JENKINS |
| T. JOHNSON | T. JOHNSON | T. JOHNSON | †J. POWELL 1DG |
| *J.M.C. LEWIS | *J.M.C. LEWIS 1T | †D.E. JOHN | D.E. JOHN |
| W.J. DELAHAY | W.J. DELAHAY | W.J. DELAHAY | W.J. DELAHAY |
| †S.G. THOMAS | S.G. THOMAS | S.G. THOMAS | S.G. THOMAS |
| A. BAKER | A. BAKER | A. BAKER 1T | A. BAKER |
| †D.G. DAVIES | D.G. DAVIES | †D. PASCOE | D. PASCOE |
| †J.F. THOMPSON | †J.L. JENKINS | J.L. JENKINS | †H.S. DAVIES |
| T. ROBERTS | T. ROBERTS | †M. WILLIAMS | †T.L. RICHARDS |
| S. MORRIS | S. MORRIS | S. MORRIS | S. MORRIS |
| †G. MICHAEL 1T | G. MICHAEL | G. MICHAEL | †J.H. DAVIES |
| T. PARKER | T. PARKER | *T. PARKER | †W.J. RADFORD |
| Twickenham | Cardiff Arms Park | St. Helen's | Lansdowne Road |
| LOST 3-7 | LOST 8-11 | WON 16-8 | LOST 4-5 |
| ENG.: 1T 1DG | WALES: 1G 1PG | WALES: 2G 1PG 1T | IRE.: 1G |
| WALES: 1T | SCOT.: 1G 2T | FR.: 1G 1T | WALES: 1DG |
| 20 Jan. 1923 | 3 Feb. 1923 | 24 Feb. 1923 | 10 Mar. 1923 |

Welsh rugby fell into a decline in 1923, and only three matches were won (all against the French) between 1923 and 1925. A substantial cause of the decline was the system used for selecting the international teams. Thirteen district representatives were given the responsibility for choosing the Welsh side, and in order to retain respect in their districts they were expected to push the cause of their "local" players. A glance through the sides of the early 1920s shows the numerous changes in personnel which probably resulted from such parochialism.

But there were still outstanding players to be found in South Wales, even in this period of disappointment. Albert Jenkins, the beloved hero of Llanelli; Rowe Harding, a product of Gowerton Grammar School and a champion sprinter in the Teddy Morgan class; and the Cardiff pair of Arthur Cornish and Tom Johnson, were a threequarter line of enormous potential. But as a quartet they were never again together after the defeat.

Admittedly the selectors cannot be blamed for the unusual composition of the Welsh XV in Dublin. The Irish "Troubles" were at their height, and it is known that several of those originally chosen to play in the match declined invitations to travel. Each member of the Welsh fifteen was insured for £1,000.

## 1923-24

| v. ENGLAND | v. SCOTLAND | v. IRELAND | v. FRANCE |
|---|---|---|---|
| *J. REES | B.O. MALE 2c | B.O. MALE | M.A. ROSSER |
| | | | |
| M.G. THOMAS | †H.J. DAVIES | W.R. HARDING | *W.R. HARDING |
| R.A. CORNISH | †J.E. EVANS | *J.J. WETTER | †A.R. STOCK |
| †D.H. DAVIES | †M.A. ROSSER | †T. EVANS | †J. JONES |
| T. JOHNSON 1T | T. JOHNSON | C. RICHARDS 1T | †E. FINCH 1T |
| | | | |
| †A. OWEN 1T | †V.M. GRIFFITHS 1T | V.M. GRIFFITHS | V.M. GRIFFITHS 1DG |
| †E. WATKINS | E. WATKINS | E. WATKINS 1DG | E. WATKINS |
| | | | |
| T. JONES 1T | T. JONES | †D. PARKER | D. PARKER |
| †C.H. PUGH | C.H. PUGH | C.H. PUGH 1T | C.H. PUGH |
| †J.I. MORRIS | J.I. MORRIS | †J.H. GORE | J.H. GORE |
| †I. THOMAS | *J. WHITFIELD | J. WHITFIELD | †A.R. RICKARD 1T |
| †A.C. EVANS | D.G. FRANCIS | A.C. EVANS | A.C. EVANS |
| S. MORRIS | S. MORRIS | †W.J. JONES | S. MORRIS |
| †W.J. OULD | W.J. OULD | †R. RANDALL | R. RANDALL |
| †I.E. JONES | I.E. JONES 1T | †G.F. HATHWAY | G.F. HATHWAY |
| | | | |
| St. Helen's | Inverleith | Cardiff Arms Park | Stade Colombes |
| LOST 9-17 | LOST 10-35 | LOST 10-13 | WON 10-6 |
| | | | |
| WALES: 3T | SCOT.: 4G 1PG 4T | WALES: 1DG 2T | FR.: 2T |
| ENG.: 1G 4T | WALES: 2G | IRE.: 2G 1T | WALES: 1DG 2T |
| | | | |
| 19 Jan. 1924 | 2 Feb. 1924 | 8 Mar. 1924 | 27 Mar. 1924 |

Welsh rugby sank to its international nadir in February 1924 when, after losing to England, the Scots inflicted the heaviest-ever defeat on Wales and, in so doing, ran up a record highest score against an unlucky Welsh side. Wales were completely overwhelmed, and there is a story which reflects the hopelessness of Wales' efforts in the match, which runs as follows. Wales were 22 points down at half time when skipper Jack Whitfield of Newport turned to his colleague Tom Jones and asked: "What shall we do?" Jones paused for a moment before delivering his considered reply: "Stick a pin in the ball and let's go home."

Ten changes were made for the game at Cardiff against Ireland, where Jack Wetter, now aged 34, returned as captain the side. In an exciting match played before the Prince of Wales and the Duke of York, a young Irish side inflicted Wales' fourth consecutive international defeat. The season ended in Paris where, in a match played on a Thursday, a dropped goal by Vincent Griffiths, the talented Newport fly-half, separated the teams.

## 1924-25

| v. NZ | v. ENGLAND | v. SCOTLAND | v. FRANCE | v. IRELAND |
|---|---|---|---|---|
| T. JOHNSON | *T. JOHNSON | T. JOHNSON | T. JOHNSON | †D.N. ROCYN-JONES |
| | | | | |
| W.R. HARDING | †W.P. JAMES 1T | W.P. JAMES | W.R. HARDING | W.R. HARDING |
| A.R. STOCK | R.A. CORNISH | R.A. CORNISH 1T | *R.A. CORNISH | D. DAVIES |
| A. JENKINS | †EVAN WILLIAMS | EVAN WILLIAMS | H.G. DAVIES | †B.R. TURNBULL 1T |
| E. FINCH | †C. THOMAS 1T | C. THOMAS | E. FINCH 2T | E. FINCH |
| | | | | |
| *J.J. WETTER | †W.J. HOPKINS | W.J. HOPKINS 1T | E. WILLIAMS | W.J. DELAHAY |
| †E. WILLIAMS | W.J. DELAHAY | W.J. DELAHAY | W.J. DELAHAY 1T | †A. JOHN |
| W.J. DELAHAY | | | | |
| | D. PARKER | D. PARKER 1PG,1C | D. PARKER 1C | D. PARKER |
| D. PARKER | C.H. PUGH | C.H. PUGH | †G.E. BEYNON | G.E. BEYNON |
| C.H. PUGH | J.H. GORE | †S.D. LAWRENCE | †W. LEWIS | S.D. LAWRENCE |
| J.H. GORE | †B. PHILLIPS | B. PHILLIPS | B. PHILLIPS | B. PHILLIPS |
| D. MARSDEN-JONES | C. WILLIAMS | †R.C. HERRERA | R.C. HERRERA | R.C. HERRERA |
| †C. WILLIAMS | S. MORRIS | *S. MORRIS | S. MORRIS | †J. BROWN |
| S. MORRIS | †W.I. JONES | W.I. JONES 1T | W.I. JONES | *W.I. JONES |
| D.D. HIDDLESTONE | †I. RICHARDS | I. RICHARDS | I. RICHARDS | †S. HINAM |
| | | | | |
| St. Helen's | Twickenham | St. Helen's | Cardiff Arms Park | Ravenhill |
| LOST 0-19 | LOST 6-12 | LOST 14-24 | WON 11-5 | LOST 3-19 |
| | | | | |
| WALES: NIL | ENG.: 1PG 3T | WALES: 1G 1PG 2T | WALES: 1G 2T | IRE.: 2G 1PG 2T |
| NZ: 2G 1PG 2T | WALES: 2T | SCOT.: 1G 1DG 5T | FR.: 1G | WALES: 1T |
| | | | | |
| 29 Nov. 1924 | 17 Jan. 1925 | 7 Feb. 1925 | 28 Feb. 1925 | 14 Mar. 1925 |

There was a long overdue reform of the system regarding the selection of the Welsh side for 1924-25. The WRU Committee agreed that five selectors should choose the national side in the future, and "The Big Five", as the columnist W.J. Hoare (Old Stager) named them, picked their first team for the match against the Second All Blacks in November 1924. Wales fielded eight backs in an attempt to counter the unique New Zealand formation (as in 1905), but the All Blacks were part-way through an invincible tour, and the Welsh were soundly beaten.

Matters were little better in the Championship. Aberavon supplied four of the fifteen against England, including Hopkins, James and Evan Williams among the backs. By the end of the season the selectorial axe had fallen on these three, though Bryn Phillips, their club colleague, was one of only three in the pack to play throughout the Championship. Phillips found permanent support from Dai Parker, a useful place-kicker from Swansea, and from hooker Idris Jones of Cambridge and Llanelli. Jones became an academic and held many important posts with the NCB.

Bobby Delahay, the Cardiff builder and carpenter who had won his previous caps at scrum-half, was chosen at fly-half for Wales' first visit to the new Irish ground at Ravenhill in Belfast. But this was an uncalculated risk by the selectors, Wales crashing to a record defeat against the Irish.

## 1925-26

| v. ENGLAND | v. SCOTLAND | v. IRELAND | v. FRANCE |
|---|---|---|---|
| †D.B. EVANS | †W.A. EVERSON 1C | †T.E. REES 1C | T.E. REES |
|  |  |  |  |
| *W.R. HARDING | †W.C. POWELL | *W.R. HARDING 1T | W.R. HARDING |
| R.A. CORNISH | *R.A. CORNISH | R.A. CORNISH | R.A. CORNISH 1DG |
| A.R. STOCK | A.R. STOCK | W.J. DELAHAY | *W.J. DELAHAY |
| †G.E. ANDREWS 1T | G.E. ANDREWS | †C.F. ROWLANDS | E. FINCH |
|  |  |  |  |
| †R. JONES | R. JONES | †W.H. LEWIS | R. JONES |
| W.J. DELAHAY | W.J. DELAHAY | W.C. POWELL | W.C. POWELL |
|  |  |  |  |
| †T.W. LEWIS | S.D. LAWRENCE | S.D. LAWRENCE | S.D. LAWRENCE |
| †D.L. JONES | D.L. JONES | D.L. JONES | D.L. JONES |
| †T. HOPKINS | T. HOPKINS | T. HOPKINS 1T | T. HOPKINS |
| B. PHILLIPS | †E. WATKINS | E. WATKINS | E. WATKINS 1T |
| R.C. HERRERA | R.C. HERRERA 1T | R.C. HERRERA 1T | R.C. HERRERA |
| †D.M. JENKINS | D.M. JENKINS | D.M. JENKINS | D.M. JENKINS |
| †J.H. JOHN | J.H. JOHN | J.H. JOHN | J.H. JOHN |
| S. HINAM | S. HINAM | S. HINAM | S. HINAM |
| Cardiff Arms Park | Murrayfield | St. Helen's | Stade Colombes |
| DRAWN 3-3 | LOST 5-8 | WON 11-8 | WON 7-5 |
| WALES: 1T | SCOT.: 1G 1PG | WALES: 1G 2T | FR.: 1G |
| ENG.: 1T | WALES: 1G | IRE.: 1G 1PG | WALES: 1DG 1T |
| 16 Jan. 1926 | 6 Feb. 1926 | 13 Mar. 1926 | 5 Apr. 1926 |

The Welsh sides of the early 1920s had consisted mainly of colliers and steelworkers, but the financial attractions offered by the accursed Rugby League scouts lured many of Wales' finest players away to the North of England. Players such as Johnny Ring, Joe Thompson and Jim Sullivan (a former Cardiff full-back who had not been capped), were Welshmen who were to become household names in the League. And by 1926 the problem of economic decline had been the catalyst for many more Welsh international Union players to join the professional ranks. (In the 1926 Rugby League match with England, more than 70 per cent of the Welsh League side were recent former Union caps.)

It was perhaps a sign of the times that the Welsh pack against England at Cardiff in 1926 contained six policemen, and just one collier – Tom Hopkins of Ystradgynlais. The red-headed Hopkins graduated via his village team to the Swansea side, and kept his place for the four Championship matches. The loyal Hopkins turned down thirteen offers to join the professional ranks, decisions which he never regretted, right up to his death in Ystradgynlais in 1980.

It was a try by Hopkins, and a majestic display by the new quicksilver fly-half, Windsor Lewis, which brought Wales victory over Ireland. It was Wales' first win against a Home Nation for exactly four years.

## 1926-27

| v. ENGLAND | v. SCOTLAND | v. FRANCE | v. IRELAND |
|---|---|---|---|
| B.O. MALE 1PG | *B.O. MALE | B.O. MALE 2C | B.O. MALE |
|  |  |  |  |
| W.R. HARDING 1T | W.R. HARDING | W.R. HARDING 2T | W.R. HARDING |
| †J. ROBERTS | J. ROBERTS | J. ROBERTS 2T | J. ROBERTS |
| *B.R. TURNBULL | B.R. TURNBULL | †W.G. MORGAN 1T | W.G. MORGAN 1T |
| G.E. ANDREWS 1T | †J.D. BARTLETT | G.E. ANDREWS 1T | G.E. ANDREWS |
|  |  |  |  |
| W.H. LEWIS | †E.G. RICHARDS | W.H. LEWIS | W.H. LEWIS 1DG |
| W.C. POWELL | W.J. DELAHAY | *W.C. POWELL | *W.C. POWELL 1C |
|  |  |  |  |
| T.W. LEWIS | T.W. LEWIS | †J. BURNS | J. BURNS |
| D.L. JONES | †E.M. JENKINS | E.M. JENKINS | E.M. JENKINS |
| S.D. LAWRENCE | W.A. WILLIAMS | W.A. WILLIAMS | W.A. WILLIAMS |
| †H.T. PHILLIPS | H.T. PHILLIPS | H.T. PHILLIPS | H.T. PHILLIPS |
| R.C. HERRERA | †T. ARTHUR | T. ARTHUR | T. ARTHUR |
| †W.G. THOMAS | W.G. THOMAS | W.G. THOMAS 1T | W.G. THOMAS |
| J.H. JOHN | J.H. JOHN | J.H. JOHN | J.H. JOHN |
| †W.A. WILLIAMS | I.E. JONES | I.E. JONES | I.E. JONES |
| Twickenham | Cardiff Arms Park | St. Helen's | Lansdowne Road |
| LOST 9-11 | LOST 0-5 | WON 25-7 | LOST 9-19 |
| ENG.: 1G 1GM 1PG | WALES: NIL | WALES: 2G 5T | IRE.: 2G 1PG 2T |
| WALES: 1PG 2T | SCOT.: 1G | FR.: 1DG 1T | WALES: 1G 1DG |
| 15 Jan. 1927 | 5 Feb. 1927 | 26 Feb. 1927 | 12 Mar. 1927 |

Three of Wales' finest forwards of the decade made their debuts in 1927. Tom Arthur and "Ned" Jenkins, officers in the Glamorgan Police, won their caps at Cardiff against Scotland. Arthur was a hardworking scrummager who excelled at the line-out, while Jenkins had the strength and muscle expected of a Welsh discus and shott-putt champion.

The third of these forwards was a student from Swansea University, Watcyn Thomas. A tall, strapping forward, Thomas' speed and skill were best utilised in the back row, but it was as captain, later in his career, that his exploits were seen to best advantage. At Twickenham in 1933, he was to exercise his schoolmasterly authority with calm sense, welding a youthful back division and a strong pack into the first Welsh team to win at Twickenham. Thomas' career of 14 caps ended in 1933, but he was rated the best forward opponent by the 1936 All Blacks, who could not understand how the Welsh selectors afforded to overlook his abilities.

Guy Morgan and John Roberts (who later became a missionary in China) played shrewdly in Paris in Wales' only win of the season. Each of the threequarters scored tries, a feat performed only twice before (also against the French, in 1909 and 1910).

## 1927-28

| v. NSW | v. ENGLAND | v. SCOTLAND | v. IRELAND | v. FRANCE |
|---|---|---|---|---|
| T.E. REES 1c | T.E. REES | *B.O. MALE 2c | B.O. MALE | *B.O. MALE |
| †D. JONES | *W.R. HARDING | W.C. POWELL | W.C. POWELL | J. ROBERTS |
| J. ROBERTS | J. ROBERTS | J. ROBERTS 1T | J. ROBERTS | W.R. JONES |
| †W.R. JONES | B.R. TURNBULL | A. JENKINS 1T | *A. JENKINS 1T | B.R. TURNBULL |
| E. FINCH 1T | J.D. BARTLETT 1T | J.D. BARTLETT | E. FINCH | †E.G. DAVIES |
| W.H. LEWIS 1T | D.E. JOHN 1T | D.E. JOHN 1T | D.E. JOHN 1T | W.H. LEWIS |
| †T. HARRIS | A. JOHN | A. JOHN | A. JOHN | W.C. POWELL 1T |
| †D.R. JENKINS | †A. SKYM | A. SKYM | A. SKYM | A. SKYM |
| †F.A. BOWDLER | F.A. BOWDLER | F.A. BOWDLER | F.A. BOWDLER | F.A. BOWDLER |
| E.M. JENKINS | E.M. JENKINS | E.M. JENKINS | E.M. JENKINS | E.M. JENKINS |
| H.T. PHILLIPS | H.T. PHILLIPS | H.T. PHILLIPS | H.T. PHILLIPS | H.T. PHILLIPS |
| †A.S. BROUGHTON | †C. PRITCHARD | C. PRITCHARD | C. PRITCHARD | C. PRITCHARD |
| †IORWERTH JONES | IORWERTH JONES | IORWERTH JONES | IORWERTH JONES | IORWERTH JONES |
| †T.H. HOLLINGDALE | T.H. HOLLINGDALE | T.H. HOLLINGDALE | T.H. HOLLINGDALE | T.H. HOLLINGDALE |
| *I.E. JONES | I.E. JONES 1c | I.E. JONES | I.E. JONES 2c | I.E. JONES |
| Cardiff Arms Park | St. Helen's | Murrayfield | Cardiff Arms Park | Stade Colombes |
| LOST 8-18 | LOST 8-10 | WON 13-0 | LOST 10-13 | LOST 3-8 |
| WALES: 1G 1T | WALES: 1G 1T | WALES: 2G 1T | WALES: 2G | FR.: 1G 1T |
| NSW: 3G 1T | ENG.: 2G | SCOT.: NIL | IRE.: 2G 1T | WALES: 1T |
| 26 Nov. 1927 | 21 Jan. 1928 | 4 Feb. 1928 | 10 Mar. 1928 | 9 Apr. 1928 |

Wales opened the season with eight new caps in the side which met the Waratahs, tourists from New South Wales. Ifor Jones, the outstanding Welsh wing-forward of the 1920s, was the Welsh captain. He played only 16 games for Wales, but he was unsurpassed for speed in attack, and was one of the safest handlers in the side. He was one of seven Llanelli players capped for Wales during the season.

Apart from a first Welsh victory at Murrayfield, there was little for their supporters to relish in a season which concluded with the first defeat by France. Albert Jenkins, having scored tries in the triumph in Scotland and against Ireland, was made the scapegoat of Wales' defeat at Cardiff by the Irish, and he never played again in the international side.

Like his Llanelli colleague Ifor Jones, Jenkins never gained half of the caps he should have won. At his best he was described as the most attractive and impressive centre of the era; and he became a legend in West Wales, where thousands of spectators were regularly delighted by his dashing play. Jenkins won 13 caps.

## 1928-29

| v. ENGLAND | v. SCOTLAND | v. FRANCE | v. IRELAND |
|---|---|---|---|
| †J.A. BASSETT | J.A. BASSETT | J.A. BASSETT | J.A. BASSETT |
| †J.C. MORLEY 1T | J. ROBERTS 2T | J. ROBERTS | J. ROBERTS |
| J. ROBERTS | †H.M. BOWCOTT | H.M. BOWCOTT | H.M. BOWCOTT |
| W.G. MORGAN | *W.G. MORGAN 1T | *W.G. MORGAN | *W.G. MORGAN |
| E.G. DAVIES | J.C. MORLEY | J.C. MORLEY | J.C. MORLEY |
| †W. ROBERTS | †F.L. WILLIAMS | F.L. WILLIAMS | F.L. WILLIAMS 1T |
| W.C. POWELL | W.C. POWELL | W.C. POWELL | W.C. POWELL |
| D.R. JENKINS | †R. BARRELL | R. BARRELL 1T | R. BARRELL |
| F.A. BOWDLER | F.A. BOWDLER | F.A. BOWDLER | F.A. BOWDLER |
| †H. JONES | H. JONES | D. PARKER 1c | D. PARKER 1c |
| T. ARTHUR | T. ARTHUR | T. ARTHUR 1T | T. ARTHUR |
| C. PRITCHARD | C. PRITCHARD | C. PRITCHARD | C. PRITCHARD |
| W.G. THOMAS | †H. PEACOCK 1T | H. PEACOCK | H. PEACOCK |
| †R. JONES | A.S. BROUGHTON | E.M. JENKINS | †A. LEMON |
| *I.E. JONES | I.E. JONES 1c | I.E. JONES | I.E. JONES |
| Twickenham | St. Helen's | Cardiff Arms Park | Ravenhill |
| LOST 3-8 | WON 14-7 | WON 8-3 | DRAWN 5-5 |
| ENG.: 1G 1T | WALES: 1G 3T | WALES: 1G 1T | IRE.: 1G |
| WALES: 1T | SCOT.: 1DG 1PG | FR.: 1T | WALES: 1G |
| 19 Jan. 1929 | 2 Feb. 1929 | 23 Feb. 1929 | 9 Mar. 1929 |

Wales' reward for two wins and a draw was second place in the Championship of 1929. The side lost to a fast English fifteen at Twickenham – their eighth consecutive defeat at the RFU's headquarters – but sound selectorial judgment brought together a talented and successful back division for the remainder of the season.

Bassett, Morley, Bowcott and Frank Williams were to become the backbone of a strong Welsh back division whose enterprise and skills reminded followers of the halcyon days of the Golden Era. Morley possessed an effective swerve and perfected a talent for beating opponents with a sudden change of pace. He won 14 caps for Wales before signing professional with Wigan in 1932. Bowcott, like Guy Morgan, was a university man who was a complete footballer. Later his excellent footballing judgment benefited Welsh selection panels, and he was President of the WRU in 1974-75.

Jack Bassett played 15 times for Wales and inspired the side to the Championship in 1931, and a shared title in 1932. A police officer in the Glamorgan Constabulary, he maintained rigidly the laws governing full-back play: he always tackled the man with the ball; his defensive and positional duties were undertaken with care; and he used the long torpedo kick to touch with accuracy.

## 1929-30

| v. ENGLAND | v. SCOTLAND | v. IRELAND | v. FRANCE |
|---|---|---|---|
| J.A. Bassett | J.A. Bassett | *J.A. Bassett 1PG | †T. Scourfield |
| | | | |
| †A. Hickman | †R.W. Boon | †H. Jones 1T | H. Jones |
| *H.M. Bowcott | †G.G. Jones 1T,1DG | W.G. Morgan | *W.G. Morgan 1DG |
| †T.E. Jones-Davies 1T | B.R. Turnbull | T.E. Jones-Davies | †E.C. Davey |
| J.C. Morley | E.G. Davies | J.C. Morley | R.W. Boon |
| | | | |
| F.L. Williams | F.L. Williams | F.L. Williams | F.L. Williams |
| †D.E.A. Roberts | W.C. Powell | W.C. Powell | W.C. Powell 1DG |
| | | | |
| A. Skym | A. Skym | A. Skym 1T | A. Skym 1T |
| F.A. Bowdler | †H.C. Day | H.C. Day | H.C. Day |
| D. Parker | †D. Thomas | D. Thomas | †E.L. Jones |
| T. Arthur | T. Arthur | T. Arthur 1T | T. Arthur |
| E.M. Jenkins | E.M. Jenkins | E.M. Jenkins | E.M. Jenkins |
| †W.T. Thomas | H. Peacock | H. Peacock | H. Peacock |
| T. H. Hollingdale | A. Lemon | A. Lemon | A. Lemon |
| I.E. Jones | *I.E. Jones 1C | †N. Fender | N. Fender |
| | | | |
| Cardiff Arms Park | Murrayfield | St. Helen's | Stade Colombes |
| LOST 3-11 | LOST 9-12 | WON 12-7 | WON 11-0 |
| | | | |
| WALES: 1T | SCOT.: 1G 1DG 1T | WALES: 1PG 3T | FR.: NIL |
| ENG.: 1G 1PG 1T | WALES: 1G 1DG | IRE.: 1DG 1PG | WALES: 2DG 1T |
| | | | |
| 18 Jan. 1930 | 1 Feb. 1930 | 8 Mar. 1930 | 21 Apr. 1930 |

Ifor Jones was dropped after leading Wales in a last-minute defeat in Scotland, though the British Lions selectors showed their faith in his abilities by inviting him to tour Australasia in the summer. On tour he was highly rated by the New Zealand public, and it is one of the lasting mysteries of Welsh rugby history that Jones never again played for Wales. He did become a committee member of the WRU, however, and was elected to the Presidency for 1968-69.

Cardiff supplied the entire threequarter line at Murrayfield, Ronnie Boon and Graham Jones (a product of Llandovery College) winning first caps alongside Bernard Turnbull and Gwyn Davies. Boon was an opportunist capable of winning matches single-handed. He went on to gain a dozen caps and won everlasting fame for his drop-goal and try at Twickenham in 1933, scores which secured Wales' first win at the ground.

The match in Paris was notorious for its brutality. Day, the hooker, had to retire in order to have his lip stitched, and many stoppages were necessary as the referee was forced to reproach the packs for provocative play. Edgar Jones and Claude Davey were new caps in a game later referred to as the "Battle of Colombes".

## 1930-31

| v. ENGLAND | v. SCOTLAND | v. FRANCE | v. IRELAND |
|---|---|---|---|
| *J.A. Bassett 1C | *J.A. Bassett 2C | *J.A. Bassett 5C | *J.A. Bassett 1C |
| | | | |
| R.W. Boon | R.W. Boon 1T | R.W. Boon | R.W. Boon |
| E.C. Davey | E.C. Davey | E.C. Davey 1T | E.C. Davey 1T |
| T.E. Jones-Davies 1T | T.E. Jones-Davies | F.L. Williams 1T | F.L. Williams |
| J.C. Morley 1T | J.C. Morley 1T | J.C. Morley | J.C. Morley 2T |
| | | | |
| H.M. Bowcott | H.M. Bowcott | †A.R. Ralph 2T | A.R. Ralph 1DG |
| W.C. Powell 1GM | W.C. Powell | W.C. Powell 1DG | W.C. Powell |
| | | | |
| A. Skym | A. Skym | A. Skym | A. Skym |
| H.C. Day | H.C. Day | †D.R. James | D.R. James |
| †T.B. Day | T.B. Day | T.B. Day | T.B. Day |
| T. Arthur | T. Arthur | T. Arthur 1T | T. Arthur |
| E.M. Jenkins | E.M. Jenkins | E.M. Jenkins | E.M. Jenkins |
| W.G. Thomas | W.G. Thomas 1T | †J. Lang 1T | J. Lang |
| A. Lemon | A. Lemon | A. Lemon | A. Lemon |
| N. Fender | N. Fender | N. Fender 1T | N. Fender |
| | | | |
| Twickenham | Cardiff Arms Park | St Helen's | Ravenhill |
| DRAWN 11-11 | WON 13-8 | WON 35-3 | WON 15-3 |
| | | | |
| ENG.: 1G 2PG | WALES: 2G 1T | WALES: 5G 1DG 2T | IRE.: 1T |
| WALES: 1G 1GM 1T | SCOT.: 1G 1T | FR.: 1T | WALES: 1G 1DG 2T |
| | | | |
| 17 Jan. 1931 | 7 Feb. 1931 | 28 Feb. 1931 | 14 Mar. 1931 |

The Twickenham bogey was still operating against Wales in 1931, when England salvaged a draw with virtually the last kick of the match. But Wales went on to complete an unbeaten season and won the Championship outright for the first time since 1922. The threequarters were good finishers and recorded nine tries, while skipper Jack Bassett landed nine conversions with some accurate place-kicking.

Claude Davey was the best of the threequarters this season. His crash-tackling in defence was crucial in the close matches with England and Scotland, and his devastating bursts for the line brought him important tries in the wins over France and Ireland. He went on to win 24 caps in a long career, and had the distinction of leading Wales to victory over the All Blacks in 1935.

Raymond Ralph's brief international career began in the match with France, when he marked a promising debut by scoring two tries and carving out numerous openings for his threequarters. Only twice Ralph played in a losing Welsh side, before moving North in August 1933 to join Leeds Rugby League club.

## 1931-32

| v. S.AFRICA | v. ENGLAND | v. SCOTLAND | v. IRELAND |
|---|---|---|---|
| *J.A. BASSETT | *J.A. BASSETT 1C,1PG | *J.A. BASSETT 1PG | *J.A. BASSETT |
| R.W. BOON | R.W. BOON 1DG,1T | R.W. BOON 1T | R.W. BOON |
| E.C. DAVEY | E.C. DAVEY | E.C. DAVEY | E.C. DAVEY 1T |
| F.L. WILLIAMS | F.L. WILLIAMS | F.L. WILLIAMS | F.L. WILLIAMS |
| J.C. MORLEY | J.C. MORLEY | J.C. MORLEY | J.C. MORLEY |
| A.R. RALPH | A.R. RALPH | A.R. RALPH | A.R. RALPH 1DG,1T |
| W.C. POWELL | W.C. POWELL | W.C. POWELL | W.C. POWELL |
| A. SKYM | A. SKYM | A. SKYM | A. SKYM |
| F.A. BOWDLER | F.A. BOWDLER | F.A. BOWDLER | F.A. BOWDLER |
| T.B. DAY | T.B. DAY | T.B. DAY | T.B. DAY |
| T. ARTHUR | D. THOMAS | D. THOMAS | D. THOMAS |
| E.M. JENKINS | E.M. JENKINS | E.M. JENKINS | E.M. JENKINS |
| A. LEMON | A. LEMON | A. LEMON | A. LEMON |
| W.G. THOMAS | W.G. THOMAS | W.G. THOMAS | W.G. THOMAS |
| †W. DAVIES 1T | W. DAVIES | W. DAVIES | W. DAVIES |
| St. Helen's | St. Helen's | Murrayfield | Cardiff Arms Park |
| LOST 3-8 | WON 12-5 | WON 6-0 | LOST 10-12 |
| WALES: 1T | WALES: 1G 1DG 1PG | SCOT.: NIL | WALES: 1DG 2T |
| SA: 1G 1T | ENG.: 1G | WALES: 1PG 1T | IRE.: 4T |
| 5 Dec. 1931 | 16 Jan. 1932 | 6 Feb. 1932 | 12 Mar. 1932 |

In December 1931 Wales, the Northern Hemisphere champions, were narrowly beaten in the mud at Swansea by the South Africans. It was a match billed as the World Championship decider. The Welsh pack was one of the best fielded between the wars, and gave the massive Springbok forwards a difficult time. The old brigade of Jenkins, Arthur and Thomas were joined by a solid front row comprising Archie Skym (a Cardiff policeman), Arthur Bowdler (a miner at Cwmcarn), and Tom Day, the refinery-worker from Skewen. Bowdler was a skilful hooker who found reliable support from Day and Skym, two strong all-round scrummagers.

For the first time Wales were unchanged during a Championship season. England and Scotland were beaten thanks to careful place-kicking by Bassett and the opportunism of Boon, but the side narrowly failed to gain the Triple Crown, losing to Ireland on a fine day at Cardiff. Poor Jack Bassett had a disappointing end to his career. He failed to convert a try by Ralph and saw a perverse bounce enable the Irish left wing to run the length of the pitch to score the deciding try.

## 1932-33

| v. ENGLAND | v. SCOTLAND | v. IRELAND |
|---|---|---|
| †V.G.J. JENKINS | †G. BAYLISS | V.G.J. JENKINS 1C |
| R.W. BOON 1T,1DG | A. HICKMAN | R.W. BOON |
| E.C. DAVEY | E.C. DAVEY | G.G. JONES |
| †W. WOOLLER | W. WOOLLER | F.L. WILLIAMS |
| †A.H. JONES | A.H. JONES | W. WOOLLER |
| H.M. BOWCOTT | †R.R. MORRIS | H.M. BOWCOTT 1T |
| †M.J.L. TURNBULL | †B. EVANS | M.J.L. TURNBULL |
| A. SKYM | A. SKYM | A. SKYM |
| †B. EVANS | B. EVANS | F.A. BOWDLER |
| E.L. JONES | E.L. JONES | E.L. JONES |
| T. ARTHUR | T. ARTHUR 1T | †W.J. MOORE |
| D. THOMAS | D. THOMAS | R. BARRELL |
| †R.B. JONES | R.B. JONES | A. LEMON |
| *W.G. THOMAS | *W.G. THOMAS | *W.G. THOMAS |
| †I. ISAAC | I. ISAAC | †L.M. REES |
| Twickenham | St. Helen's | Ravenhill |
| WON 7-3 | LOST 3-11 | LOST 5-10 |
| ENG.: 1T | WALES: 1T | IRE.: 1DG 1PG 1T |
| WALES: 1DG 1T | SCOT.: 1G 1PG 1T | WALES: 1G |
| 21 Jan. 1933 | 4 Feb. 1933 | 11 Mar. 1933 |

In 1933, and at the tenth attempt, Wales achieved their first victory at Twickenham. The courageous play of a back division full of university men, and the inspiring leadership of Watcyn Thomas were the vital factors in this long-awaited success. Vivian Jenkins, winning the first of his fourteen caps at full-back, defended brilliantly for Wales in the first half, his sure tackling and safe kicking to touch inspiring the backs and forwards in front of him. England led by a try at the interval, but Boon snatched the lead for Wales early in the second half with a drop-goal. The same player sealed Wales' victory near the end of the match with a try, after Davey had drawn the English full-back to create an overlap.

Wales retained the same fifteen for the match at Swansea, but several late withdrawals upset the balance of the backs. Viv Jenkins had an arm injury and was replaced by Gwyn Bayliss, and when Maurice Turnbull was forced to withdraw, the selectors took the unusual step of asking Harry Bowcott to stand down so that a club pair, Ron Morris and Bryn Evans of Swansea, could operate. Wales were easily beaten.

High jinks by some of the players on the boat to Belfast incurred the wrath of WRU officials and probably cost Wales the game with Ireland. Jenkins was outstanding in defence and Bowcott scored the try of the season near the end of the game.

## 1933-34

| v. ENGLAND | v. SCOTLAND | v. IRELAND |
|---|---|---|
| †B. Howells | V.G.J. Jenkins 2c | V.G.J. Jenkins 2c,1t |
| | | |
| †B.T.V. Cowey | B.T.V. Cowey 2t | B.T.V. Cowey 1t |
| E.C. Davey | *E.C. Davey | *E.C. Davey |
| †J.I. Rees | J.I. Rees 1t | J.I. Rees |
| †G.R. Rees-Jones | G.R. Rees-Jones | †A.H. Bassett |
| | | |
| †C.W. Jones | C.W. Jones | C.W. Jones |
| †D.D. Evans | †W.H. Jones | W.H. Jones |
| | | |
| †C.R. Davies | †D.R. Prosser | D.R. Prosser |
| *†J.R. Evans | †I. Evans | I. Evans |
| †W.H. Truman | T.B. Day | T.B. Day |
| †G. Hughes | G. Hughes | G. Hughes |
| D. Thomas | †W. Ward | W. Ward |
| †G. Prosser | G. Prosser | G. Prosser |
| †K.W.J. Jones | J. Lang | J. Lang |
| †A.M. Rees | †A. Fear | A. Fear 1t |
| | | |
| Cardiff Arms Park | Murrayfield | St. Helen's |
| LOST 0-9 | WON 13-6 | WON 13-0 |
| | | |
| WALES: NIL | SCOT.: 1PG 1T | WALES: 2G 1T |
| ENG.: 3T | WALES: 2G 1T | IRE.: NIL |
| | | |
| 20 Jan. 1934 | 3 Feb. 1934 | 10 Mar. 1934 |

The Welsh selectors, relying heavily on exiles, introduced thirteen new caps for the game with England. But the pack was completely outplayed by a solid English eight and Jones and Evans, two tiny halves, were overwhelmed by a lively English back row. Thus many of the 50,000 spectators, including some 5,000 seated in a splendid new grandstand on the north touchline, were disappointed to see Wales fail against England at Cardiff for only the third time.

Five of the new caps at Cardiff were never chosen for Wales again, and for the Scottish match the selectors turned to players who had proved themselves in the testing conditions of Welsh club rugby. Claude Davey was given the captaincy and his tackling, together with Viv Jenkins' steadiness, helped Wales to a convincing win in Edinburgh.

Jenkins was the leading full-back in British rugby during the decade. A safe tackler, reliable touch-finder and immaculate catcher (as one would expect of a Glamorgan wicket-keeper), he was also a player of vision and imagination. His forays into the threequarter line created openings for wings to score, and against Ireland he created his own piece of history by becoming the first Welshman (and the first player in a Championship match) to score an international try from full-back.

## 1934-35

| v. ENGLAND | v. SCOTLAND | v. IRELAND |
|---|---|---|
| V.G.J. Jenkins | V.G.J. Jenkins 1DG | †T.O. James 1PG |
| | | |
| B.T.V. Cowey | J.I. Rees | G.R. Rees-Jones |
| *E.C. Davey | *E.C. Davey | *E.C. Davey |
| W. Wooller 1t | W. Wooller 1t | W. Wooller |
| A.H. Bassett | A.H. Bassett | A.H. Bassett |
| | | |
| C.W. Jones | C.W. Jones 1t | C.W. Jones |
| W.C. Powell | W.C. Powell | W.C. Powell |
| | | |
| E.L. Jones | †T.J. Rees | T.J. Rees |
| †C.D. Murphy | C.D. Murphy | C.D. Murphy |
| T.B. Day | T.B. Day | T.B. Day |
| W.H. Truman | †T. Williams | T. Williams |
| D. Thomas | D. Thomas | D. Thomas |
| A. Skym | A. Fear | A. Fear |
| J. Lang | J. Lang | J. Lang |
| A.M. Rees | A.M. Rees | A.M. Rees |
| | | |
| Twickenham | Cardiff Arms Park | Ravenhill |
| DRAWN 3-3 | WON 10-6 | LOST 3-9 |
| | | |
| ENG.: 1PG | WALES: 1DG 2T | IRE.: 2PG 1T |
| WALES: 1T | SCOT.: 2T | WALES: 1PG |
| | | |
| 19 Jan. 1935 | 2 Feb. 1935 | 9 Mar. 1935 |

Wilf Wooller, another sportsman who distinguished himself by playing County Cricket for Glamorgan (as well as leading them to the County Championship in 1948), was at his best as a long-striding runner in the centre in 1935. His try at Twickenham, early in the second half, was the product of a dazzling break by Cliff Jones. But Welsh hopes of victory were dispelled when Wales were lured offside at a scrummage and the English full-back levelled the scores with a penalty.

A remarkable drop-goal by Jenkins and two spectacular tries by Wooller and Jones helped Wales to victory over Scotland. Jones was an elusive runner who was described as the most brilliant fly-half of the 1930s. He formed an impressive attacking combination with Wilf Wooller, but injuries restricted his appearances and he was capped only thirteen times for Wales. He later served on the WRU selection committee, and was made President of the Union for the Centenary season, 1980-81.

Wick Powell's amazing career in the Welsh jersey finished in Belfast. He won the first of his 27 caps in 1926, and was one of the biggest men to play for Wales as a scrum-half. His taste for the unorthodox, his long passes, and his thrustful running away from the base of the scrummage made him a very difficult opponent.

## 1935-36

| v. NZ | v. ENGLAND | v. SCOTLAND | v. IRELAND |
|---|---|---|---|
| V.G.J. Jenkins 2c | V.G.J. Jenkins | V.G.J. Jenkins 2c | V.G.J. Jenkins 1pg |
| G.R. Rees-Jones 2t | G.R. Rees-Jones | J.I. Rees | *J.I. Rees |
| *E.C. Davey 1t | W. Wooller | *E.C. Davey 1t | †W.T.H. Davies |
| J.I. Rees | *J.I. Rees | W. Wooller 1t | W. Wooller |
| W. Wooller | †B.E.W. McCall | B.E.W. McCall | B.E.W. McCall |
| C.W. Jones | C.W. Jones | C.W. Jones 1t | C.W. Jones |
| †H. Tanner | H. Tanner | H. Tanner | H. Tanner |
| T.J. Rees | T.J. Rees | T.J. Rees | T.J. Rees |
| †D.J. Tarr | B. Evans | B. Evans | B. Evans |
| †H. Payne | T. Williams | T. Williams | T. Williams |
| T. Williams | †G. Williams | G. Williams | G. Williams |
| †E. Watkins | †H.W. Thomas | H.W. Thomas | H.W. Thomas |
| G. Prosser | †E.C. Long | E.C. Long | E.C. Long |
| J. Lang | J. Lang | J. Lang | J. Lang |
| A.M. Rees | A.M. Rees | A.M. Rees | A.M. Rees |
| Cardiff Arms Park | St. Helen's | Murrayfield | Cardiff Arms Park |
| WON 13-12 | DRAWN 0-0 | WON 13-3 | WON 3-0 |
| WALES: 2G 1T | WALES: NIL | SCOT.: 1T | WALES: 1PG |
| NZ: 1G 1DG 1T | ENG.: NIL | WALES: 2G 1T | IRE.: NIL |
| 21 Dec. 1935 | 18 Jan. 1936 | 1 Feb. 1936 | 14 Mar. 1936 |

This was the outstanding Welsh team of the years between the wars. Not only were the All Blacks beaten at Cardiff, but Wales went on to complete an unbeaten season and thus won the Championship. The contest with the All Blacks was thrilling. Wales led 10-3 early in the second half, but a spirited recovery by the visitors took them into a two-point lead at 12-10 with time running out. Then the huge crowd was stunned into silence when hooker Don Tarr was stretchered off with a broken neck. Surely there was no hope of Welsh success now? But then Wooller punted high and over the New Zealand line. The ball bounced eccentrically, Wooller overran the ball and many thought that Wales' chance was gone. Rees-Jones had followed too, however, and he got the touch-down which gave Wales victory by "that lovely point", as Arthur Rees, Welsh pack-leader, referred to Wales' margin of victory.

The match with England, who had also defeated the All Blacks, was a scoreless draw. Wales then gained an easy win in Edinburgh before meeting Ireland in the Championship decider.

The ground was filled to its capacity, the 70,000 crowd spilling over the railings and on to the pitch. The Welsh forwards were architects of victory, subduing the rousing Irish forwards, just as they had the New Zealanders. A penalty after twenty minutes, kicked by Viv Jenkins from under the shadow of the North Stand and towards the Taff end of the ground, was the score which settled the match and secured the Championship for Wales.

## 1936-37

| v. ENGLAND | v. SCOTLAND | v. IRELAND |
|---|---|---|
| V.G.J. Jenkins | T.O. James | †W.G.S. Legge 1pg |
| †W.H. Clement | W.H. Clement | W.H. Clement |
| *E.C. Davey | *J.I. Rees | E.C. Davey |
| W. Wooller 1t | W. Wooller 2t | *W. Wooller |
| J.I. Rees | †W.H. Hopkin | J.I. Rees |
| W.T.H. Davies | R.R. Morris | W.T.H. Davies |
| H. Tanner | H. Tanner | H. Tanner |
| T.J. Rees | T.J. Rees | †I. Bennett |
| B. Evans | †W.H. Travers | W.H. Travers |
| †E. Evans | T. Williams | T. Williams |
| †D.L. Thomas | †H. Rees | H. Rees |
| H.W. Thomas | H.W. Thomas | H.W. Thomas |
| E.C. Long | E.C. Long | †A.R. Taylor |
| J. Lang | E. Watkins | E. Watkins |
| A.M. Rees | A.M. Rees | A.M. Rees |
| Twickenham | St. Helen's | Ravenhill |
| LOST 3-4 | LOST 6-13 | LOST 3-5 |
| ENG.: 1DG | WALES: 2T | IRE.: 1G |
| WALES: 1T | SCOT.: 2G 1T | WALES: 1PG |
| 16 Jan. 1937 | 6 Feb. 1937 | 3 Apr. 1937 |

Willie Davies and Haydn Tanner, the Gowerton cousins who had helped Swansea to become the first British club to beat a New Zealand side in 1935, were the Welsh halves against England. Tanner was an outstanding scrum-half, strong on the burst from the scrummage and sound in defence, and his 25 Welsh caps spanned a record 14 seasons. Davies was a classical fly-half whose talents were widely appreciated in Rugby League circles after the war.

Wales' slow-heeling pack hampered the attacking skills of the backs, and Wilf Wooller's try was not good enough to beat an English drop-goal. A rare mis-kick by Vivian Jenkins had glanced off an Englishman's shoulder, giving one of the English backs the space and time to drop a decisive goal.

Jenkins did not retain his place for the remaining matches of the season. Defeats at Swansea and in Belfast left Wales without a point in the Championship for the first time since 1892.

## 1937-38

| v. ENGLAND | v. SCOTLAND | v. IRELAND |
|---|---|---|
| V.G.J. JENKINS 1C,2PG | V.G.J. JENKINS | W.G.S. LEGGE 1C |
| | | |
| W.H. CLEMENT | W.H. CLEMENT | W.H. CLEMENT 1T |
| E.C. DAVEY | J.I. REES | E.C. DAVEY |
| J.I. REES 1T | W. WOOLLER | J.I. REES |
| A.H. BASSETT | A.H. BASSETT | W. WOOLLER 1PG |
| | | |
| *C.W. JONES | *C.W. JONES | *C.W. JONES |
| H. TANNER | H. TANNER | H. TANNER |
| | | |
| H. REES | H. REES | H. REES |
| W.H. TRAVERS | W.H. TRAVERS | W.H. TRAVERS |
| †M.E. MORGAN | M.E. MORGAN | M.E. MORGAN |
| †F.L. MORGAN | F.L. MORGAN | F.L. MORGAN |
| E. WATKINS | E. WATKINS | E. WATKINS |
| †A. McCARLEY 1T | A. McCARLEY 2T | A. McCARLEY |
| †W. VICKERY | W. VICKERY | W. VICKERY |
| A.M. REES | A.M. REES | A.R. TAYLOR 1T |
| | | |
| Cardiff Arms Park | Murrayfield | St. Helen's |
| WON 14-8 | LOST 6-8 | WON 11-5 |
| | | |
| WALES: 1G 2PG 1T | SCOT.: 1G 1PG | WALES: 1G 1PG 1T |
| ENG.: 1G 1T | WALES: 2T | IRE.: 1G |
| | | |
| 15 Jan. 1938 | 5 Feb. 1938 | 12 Mar. 1938 |

Walter Vickery, whose father had played for England in 1905, joined Allan McCarley, the Neath flanker, and the experienced Arthur Rees, an officer in the Metropolitan Police, in a splendid back row. Rees was the most-respected Welsh loose forward of the late 1930s, while McCarley's three tries during the season fell one short of Jack Whitfield's record of four tries by a Welsh forward, set in 1922.

Cliff Jones, who had been injured in 1937, returned as captain. He and Vivian Jenkins judged the strong wind to perfection at Cardiff against England. Their tactical kicking, in attack and in defence, were important factors in Wales' success. Jenkins also landed three fine goals.

Wales were the better side at Murrayfield, but lost to a last-minute penalty goal awarded in front of the posts when Harry Rees was caught lying over the ball. That defeat cost Wales the Triple Crown.

## 1938-39

| v. ENGLAND | v. SCOTLAND | v. IRELAND |
|---|---|---|
| V.G.J. JENKINS | †C.H. DAVIES | C.H. DAVIES |
| | | |
| †F.J.V. FORD | †E.L. JONES | †C. MATTHEWS |
| †D.I. DAVIES | †M.J. DAVIES 1T | M.J. DAVIES |
| *W. WOOLLER | *W. WOOLLER 1PG,1C | *W. WOOLLER |
| †S.A. WILLIAMS | S.A. WILLIAMS | S.A. WILLIAMS |
| | | |
| W.T.H. DAVIES | W.T.H. DAVIES | W.T.H. DAVIES 1DG,1T |
| H. TANNER | H. TANNER | H. TANNER |
| | | |
| †W.E.N. DAVIES | W.E.N. DAVIES | W.E.N. DAVIES |
| W.H. TRAVERS | W.H. TRAVERS 1T | W.H. TRAVERS |
| M.E. MORGAN | †L. DAVIES | †V.J. LAW |
| F.L. MORGAN | †R.E. PRICE | R.E. PRICE |
| E. WATKINS | E. WATKINS | L. DAVIES |
| †C. CHALLINOR | E.C. LONG | E.C. LONG |
| W. VICKERY | †L. MANFIELD | L. MANFIELD |
| A.R. TAYLOR | E. EVANS | E. EVANS |
| | | |
| Twickenham | Cardiff Arms Park | Ravenhill |
| LOST 0-3 | WON 11-3 | WON 7-0 |
| | | |
| ENG.: 1T | WALES: 1G 1PG 1T | IRE.: NIL |
| WALES: NIL | SCOT.: 1PG | WALES: 1DG 1T |
| | | |
| 21 Jan. 1939 | 4 Feb. 1939 | 11 Mar. 1939 |

Vivian Jenkins retired from international rugby after Wales lost narrowly to England. He became the world's most distinguished rugby writer after the war. The hallmarks of his reports of matches and appraisals of players were accuracy, fairness and a deep love for the game and its characters.

Howard Davies, the Swansea full-back (who later played for Llanelli), succeeded Jenkins and was one of only four players (Haydn Tanner, Les Manfield and "Bunner" Travers were the others) to appear for Wales before and after the Second World War.

Wins against Scotland and Ireland gave Wales a share in the International Championship. The match in Belfast was a personal triumph for Willie Davies. He scored all of the Welsh points (including Wales' last drop-goal valued at four points) in a win which deprived Ireland of the Triple Crown.

## 1946-47

| v. ENGLAND | v. SCOTLAND | v. FRANCE | v. IRELAND |
|---|---|---|---|
| C.H. Davies | C.H. Davies | C.H. Davies | C.H. Davies |
| †K.J. Jones | K.J. Jones 2t | K.J. Jones | K.J. Jones |
| †J. Matthews | B.L. Williams 1t | B.L. Williams | B.L. Williams |
| †W.B. Cleaver | W.B. Cleaver 1t | W.L.T. Williams | W.L.T. Williams |
| †W.L.T. Williams | W.L.T. Williams 1t | †P. Rees | P. Rees |
| †B.L. Williams | †G. Davies | W.B. Cleaver | W.B. Cleaver |
| *H. Tanner | *H. Tanner | *H. Tanner | *H. Tanner |
| †D. Jones | †W.J. Evans | D. Jones | D. Jones |
| †R.E. Blakemore | †W. Gore | W. Gore | W. Gore |
| †G.W. Bevan | †C. Davies | C. Davies | C. Davies |
| †S. Williams | S. Williams | S. Williams | S. Williams |
| †G.W. Parsons | †W.E. Tamplin 2c,1pg | W.E. Tamplin 1pg | W.E. Tamplin 1pg |
| †O. Williams | O. Williams | †R.T. Evans | R.T. Evans 1t |
| †J.R.G. Stephens 1t | J.R.G. Stephens | J.R.G. Stephens | J.R.G. Stephens |
| †G. Evans 1t | G. Evans | G. Evans | G. Evans |
| Cardiff Arms Park | Murrayfield | Stade Colombes | St. Helen's |
| LOST 6-9 | WON 22-8 | WON 3-0 | WON 6-0 |
| WALES: 2T | SCOT.: 1G 1PG | FR.: NIL | WALES: 1PG 1T |
| ENG.: 1G 1DG | WALES: 2G 1PG 3T | WALES: 1PG | IRE.: NIL |
| 18 Jan. 1947 | 1 Feb. 1947 | 22 Mar. 1947 | 29 Mar. 1947 |

Three of Wales' most respected players emerged in the first season after the war to help Wales to a share in the International Championship. Ken Jones played on the Welsh right wing in every game for exactly ten seasons, and ended in 1957 with a record 44 caps for his country. His tally of 17 tries also equalled the career record for a Welsh international player.

Bleddyn Williams, first capped against England as an outside half, was the most accomplished centre threequarter of his generation. His sidestep and his powerful running brought him seven tries in 22 appearances for Wales. He was also a successful international captain, leading Wales to five wins and no defeats between 1953 and 1955.

Rees Stephens' career spanned eleven seasons, during which he won 32 caps as a lock/number eight, creating a record number of appearances for a Welsh forward. He was a member of the brave Welsh eight which took on a tough French pack in a bruising battle in Paris in March. Wales were happy to win the match by a single penalty goal.

## 1947-48

| v. AUSTRALIA | v. ENGLAND | v. SCOTLAND | v. FRANCE | v. IRELAND |
|---|---|---|---|---|
| W.B. Cleaver | †R.F. Trott | R.F. Trott | R.F. Trott | R.F. Trott |
| K.J. Jones | K.J. Jones 1t | K.J. Jones 1t | K.J. Jones | K.J. Jones |
| B.L. Williams | B.L. Williams | B.L. Williams 1t | B.L. Williams | B.L. Williams 1t |
| J. Matthews | W.B. Cleaver | W.B. Cleaver | W.B. Cleaver | W.B. Cleaver |
| W.L.T. Williams | J. Matthews | J. Matthews 1t | J. Matthews | W.L.T. Williams |
| G. Davies | G. Davies | G. Davies | G. Davies | G. Davies |
| †H. Greville | *H. Tanner | *H. Tanner | *H. Tanner | *H. Tanner |
| †E. Davies | †L. Anthony | L. Anthony | L. Anthony | E. Davies |
| †M. James | M. James | M. James | M. James | M. James |
| C. Davies | C. Davies | C. Davies | C. Davies | C. Davies |
| †J.A. Gwilliam | †W.D. Jones | S. Williams | S. Williams | J.A. Gwilliam |
| *W.E. Tamplin 2pg | W.E. Tamplin | W.E. Tamplin 1c,1pg | W.E. Tamplin | J.R.G. Stephens |
| O. Williams | O. Williams | O. Williams | O. Williams 1pg | O. Williams |
| L. Manfield | L. Manfield | L. Manfield | L. Manfield | L. Manfield |
| G. Evans | G. Evans | G. Evans | G. Evans | G. Evans |
| Cardiff Arms Park | Twickenham | Cardiff Arms Park | St. Helen's | Ravenhill |
| WON 6-0 | DRAWN 3-3 | WON 14-0 | LOST 3-11 | LOST 3-6 |
| WALES: 2PG | ENG.: 1PG | WALES: 1G 1PG 2T | WALES: 1PG | IRE.: 2T |
| AUST.: NIL | WALES: 1T | SCOT.: NIL | FR.: 1G 2T | WALES: 1T |
| 20 Dec. 1947 | 17 Jan. 1948 | 7 Feb. 1948 | 21 Feb. 1948 | 13 Mar. 1948 |

Cardiff were the leading club in British rugby in 1947-48, and it was fitting that 11 of their successful side should represent Wales during the season. There were ten from the club in the Welsh teams against England, Scotland and France, but following France's first international win on Welsh soil, the selectors broadened their view for the trip to Belfast, and four changes were made.

Against Australia, Billy Cleaver became the first man since Charlie Newman (in the 1880s) to play full-back, threequarter and half-back for Wales. A fine tactical kicker, Cleaver's talents were highly regarded by the Welsh public, and he was a member of the only international side to beat the Wallabies during their tour of Britain. Two penalties by Tamplin, the Welsh captain, were sufficient to sink the tourists, but hopes of a successful season for Wales were dashed at Twickenham, where Wales were unlucky to draw with a weak English team.

John Gwilliam, a Cambridge student who later became a schoolmaster and Headmaster of Birkenhead School, made his debut in the Australian match. Adopting a thoughtful and analytical tactical approach, he captained Wales to nine victories in the early 1950s, his prizes including two Triple Crowns and two Grand Slams.

## 1948-49

| v. ENGLAND | v. SCOTLAND | v. IRELAND | v. FRANCE |
|---|---|---|---|
| R.F. Trott | R.F. Trott 1c | R.F. Trott | R.F. Trott |
| | | | |
| K.J. Jones | K.J. Jones | K.J. Jones | K.J. Jones 1t |
| B.L. Williams | B.L. Williams 1t | B.L. Williams | †M.C. Thomas |
| J. Matthews | J. Matthews | J. Matthews | J. Matthews |
| W.L.T. Williams 2t | †T. Cook | T. Cook | †W.C. Major |
| | | | |
| G. Davies | G. Davies | W.B. Cleaver | G. Davies |
| *H. Tanner | *H. Tanner | *H. Tanner | *H. Tanner |
| | | | |
| D. Jones | D. Jones | D. Jones | D. Jones |
| W.H. Travers | W.H. Travers | W.H. Travers | W.H. Travers |
| †E. Coleman | E. Coleman | E. Coleman | C. Davies |
| †D.J. Hayward | J.A. Gwilliam | J.A. Gwilliam | J.A. Gwilliam |
| †A. Meredith 1t | A. Meredith | A. Meredith | D.J. Hayward |
| †W.R. Cale | W.R. Cale | W.R. Cale | †R.C.C. Thomas |
| J.A. Gwilliam | J.R.G. Stephens | J.R.G. Stephens | J.R.G. Stephens |
| G. Evans | G. Evans | G. Evans | †P. Stone |
| | | | |
| Cardiff Arms Park | Murrayfield | St. Helen's | Stade Colombes |
| WON 9-3 | LOST 5-6 | LOST 0-5 | LOST 3-5 |
| | | | |
| WALES: 3T | SCOT.: 2T | WALES: NIL | FR.: 1G |
| ENG.: 1DG | WALES: 1G | IRE.: 1G | WALES: 1T |
| | | | |
| 15 Jan. 1949 | 5 Feb. 1949 | 12 Mar. 1949 | 26 Mar. 1949 |

Wales ended a very disappointing season with three narrow defeats and the wooden spoon. The campaign started with a spirited win against England, Les Williams scoring two cracking tries and Glyn Davies displaying a wide variety of fly-half skills, both in attack and defence.

But Williams, a teacher, converted to Rugby League (signing for Hunslet) soon after the match, depriving an excellent threequarter line of a fine finisher and swift runner. At Murrayfield the Welsh midfield backs were constantly disrupted by a subtle Scottish back-row trap, and a season which had started with such promise ended in tatters with disappointing performances against Ireland and France.

This was the first season that Welsh international teams wore white shorts.

## 1949-50

| v. ENGLAND | v. SCOTLAND | v. IRELAND | v. FRANCE |
|---|---|---|---|
| †B.L. Jones 1PG,1c | B.L. Jones 1PG | †G. Williams | G. Williams |
| | | | |
| K.J. Jones | K.J. Jones 1t | K.J. Jones 1t | K.J. Jones 2t |
| M.C. Thomas | M.C. Thomas 1t | B.L. Jones | B.L. Jones 1PG,3c |
| J. Matthews | J. Matthews | J. Matthews | J. Matthews 1t |
| †T.J. Brewer | W.C. Major | M.C. Thomas 1t | M.C. Thomas |
| | | | |
| W.B. Cleaver | W.B. Cleaver 1DG | W.B. Cleaver | W.B. Cleaver |
| †W.R. Willis | W.R. Willis | W.R. Willis | W.R. Willis |
| | | | |
| †J.D. Robins | J.D. Robins | J.D. Robins | J.D. Robins |
| †D.M. Davies | D.M. Davies | D.M. Davies | D.M. Davies |
| C. Davies 1t | C. Davies | C. Davies | C. Davies |
| †E.R. John | E.R. John | E.R. John | E.R. John 1t |
| D.J. Hayward | D.J. Hayward | D.J. Hayward | D.J. Hayward |
| W.R. Cale 1t | W.R. Cale | W.R. Cale | W.R. Cale |
| *J.A. Gwilliam | *J.A. Gwilliam | *J.A. Gwilliam | *J.A. Gwilliam |
| R.T. Evans | R.T. Evans | R.T. Evans | R.T. Evans |
| | | | |
| Twickenham | St. Helen's | Ravenhill | Cardiff Arms Park |
| WON 11-5 | WON 12-0 | WON 6-3 | WON 21-0 |
| | | | |
| ENG.: 1G | WALES: 1DG 1PG 2T | IRE.: 1PG | WALES: 3G 1PG 1T |
| WALES: 1G 1PG 1T | SCOT.: NIL | WALES: 2T | FR.: NIL |
| | | | |
| 21 Jan. 1950 | 4 Feb. 1950 | 11 Mar. 1950 | 25 Mar. 1950 |

Following late withdrawals by Rees Stephens and Bleddyn Williams, John Gwilliam became captain of a hastily rearranged team against England, leading Wales to their second win at Twickenham since 1910. Lewis Jones, the youngest of a team which included six new caps, played like a veteran on his debut, and kicked a penalty and conversion in Wales' win by six points.

The team played to its strengths throughout the season and went on to regain the Triple Crown and Grand Slam for the first time for 39 years. D.M. Davies, a Somerset policeman, was an expert hooker who found ample support from two strong props. Clifton Davies, a miner from Kenfig Hill, had established himself as the finest prop in the Principality, and he was joined by John Robins, a PE specialist, in a front row which dominated the scrummages in each of the season's matches. In the second row, Roy John was an outstanding jumper who controlled the line-outs. Two shrewd halves in Billy Cleaver and newcomer Rex Willis were thus able to dictate tactically, and revelled in a plentiful supply of possession.

The most exciting match of the year was in Belfast, where Wales won narrowly thanks to tries by Ken Jones, and by Malcolm Thomas in the last minute. Undoubtedly the best of the side was seen in the match against France, however, when four tries were scored in a convincing victory. But the successes of the season were marred by the deaths of 80 Welsh supporters who were killed when their aircraft crashed on their return from the Irish match.

## 1950-51

| v. ENGLAND | v. SCOTLAND | v. IRELAND | v. FRANCE |
|---|---|---|---|
| G. WILLIAMS | G. WILLIAMS | G. WILLIAMS | G. WILLIAMS |
| | | | |
| K.J. JONES 1T | K.J. JONES | K.J. JONES | K.J. JONES 1T |
| B.L. JONES 4C | B.L. JONES | B.L. WILLIAMS | M.C. THOMAS |
| J. MATTHEWS 2T | J. MATTHEWS | J. MATTHEWS | *J. MATTHEWS |
| M.C. THOMAS 2T | M.C. THOMAS | M.C. THOMAS | †H. MORRIS |
| | | | |
| G. DAVIES | G. DAVIES | †C.I. MORGAN | C.I. MORGAN |
| W.R. WILLIS | W.R. WILLIS | W.R. WILLIS | W.R. WILLIS |
| | | | |
| J.D. ROBINS | J.D. ROBINS | J.D. ROBINS | J.D. ROBINS |
| D.M. DAVIES | D.M. DAVIES | D.M. DAVIES | D.M. DAVIES |
| C. DAVIES | C. DAVIES | C. DAVIES | †W.O.G. WILLIAMS |
| E.R. JOHN | E.R. JOHN | †B.O. EDWARDS 1PG | E.R. JOHN |
| D.J. HAYWARD | D.J. HAYWARD | D.J. HAYWARD | D.J. HAYWARD |
| †P.D. EVANS | †A. FORWARD | E.R. JOHN | ?P.D. EVANS |
| *J.A. GWILLIAM | *J.A. GWILLIAM | *J.A. GWILLIAM | J.R.G. STEPHENS |
| R.T. EVANS | R.T. EVANS | R.T. EVANS | R.T. EVANS |
| | | | |
| St. Helen's | Murrayfield | Cardiff Arms Park | Stade Colombes |
| WON 23-5 | LOST 0-19 | DRAWN 3-3 | LOST 3-8 |
| | | | |
| WALES: 4G 1T | SCOT.: 2G 1DG 1PG 1T | WALES: 1PG | FR.: 1G 1PG |
| ENG.: 1G | WALES: NIL | IRE.: 1T | WALES: 1T |
| | | | |
| 20 Jan. 1951 | 3 Feb. 1951 | 10 Mar. 1951 | 7 Apr. 1951 |

Wales opened the season in convincing style by overwhelming a weak English side at Swansea, and there were high hopes that the Triple Crown would be won for the second successive season. But a fifteen which showed just one change from the victorious side at Swansea suffered a disastrous defeat by 19 points in Scotland. The Welsh side, containing 11 British Lions, was completely outplayed in the second half as Wales crashed to their heaviest defeat for 26 years.

The selectors delayed announcing the side for the Irish match, but eventually named three changes for the game at Cardiff. Roy John was moved to flanker to accommodate big Ben Edwards at lock, and Cliff Morgan came in for Glyn Davies at fly-half. A penalty by Edwards, in his only international, helped Wales to a draw.

Morgan eventually gained 29 caps, a record for a Welsh stand-off. During the 1950s he was acknowledged as the world's finest fly-half, and he enjoyed successes against every major nation at international level. Tremendous speed-off-the-mark and a deceptive change of pace on the outside burst were the hallmarks of his attacking play. He preferred to run the ball rather than to kick, and it is remarkable to note that he never dropped a goal for Wales in his long career.

## 1951-52

| v. S.AFRICA | v. ENGLAND | v. SCOTLAND | v. IRELAND | v. FRANCE |
|---|---|---|---|---|
| G. WILLIAMS | G. WILLIAMS | G. WILLIAMS | G. WILLIAMS | G. WILLIAMS |
| | | | | |
| K.J. JONES | K.J. JONES 2T | K.J. JONES 1T | K.J. JONES 1T | K.J. JONES |
| B.L. WILLIAMS 1T | †A.G. THOMAS | B.L. WILLIAMS | A.G. THOMAS | B.L. JONES 2PG |
| M.C. THOMAS | M.C. THOMAS 1C | M.C. THOMAS 2PG,1C | M.C. THOMAS | M.C. THOMAS |
| B.L. JONES | B.L. JONES | A.G. THOMAS | B.L. JONES 1PG,1C | †D.H. PHILLIPS |
| | | | | |
| C.I. MORGAN | C.I. MORGAN | C.I. MORGAN | C.I. MORGAN | A.G. THOMAS 1DG |
| W.R. WILLIS | W.R. WILLIS | W.R. WILLIS | †W.A. WILLIAMS | W.A. WILLIAMS |
| | | | | |
| D.J. HAYWARD | D.J. HAYWARD | D.J. HAYWARD | D.J. HAYWARD | D.J. HAYWARD |
| D.M. DAVIES | D.M. DAVIES | D.M. DAVIES | D.M. DAVIES | D.M. DAVIES |
| W.O.G. WILLIAMS | W.O.G. WILLIAMS | W.O.G. WILLIAMS | W.O.G. WILLIAMS | W.O.G. WILLIAMS |
| E.R. JOHN | E.R. JOHN | E.R. JOHN | E.R. JOHN | E.R. JOHN |
| J.R.G. STEPHENS | J.R.G. STEPHENS | J.R.G. STEPHENS | J.R.G. STEPHENS 1T | J.R.G. STEPHENS |
| †L. BLYTH | L. BLYTH | L. BLYTH | R.C.C. THOMAS 1T | R.C.C. THOMAS |
| *J.A. GWILLIAM | *J.A. GWILLIAM | *J.A. GWILLIAM | *J.A. GWILLIAM | *J.A. GWILLIAM |
| A. FORWARD | A. FORWARD | A. FORWARD | A. FORWARD | A. FORWARD |
| | | | | |
| Cardiff Arms Park | Twickenham | Cardiff Arms Park | Lansdowne Road | St. Helen's |
| LOST 3-6 | WON 8-6 | WON 11-0 | WON 14-3 | WON 9-5 |
| | | | | |
| WALES: 1T | ENG.: 2T | WALES: 1G 2PG | IRE.: 1PG | WALES: 2PG 1DG |
| SA: 1DG 1T | WALES: 1G 1T | SCOT.: NIL | WALES: 1G 1PG 2T | FR.: 1G |
| | | | | |
| 22 Dec. 1951 | 19 Jan. 1952 | 2 Feb. 1952 | 8 Mar. 1952 | 22 Mar. 1952 |

In an attempt to strengthen the scrummage for the encounter with the Fourth Springboks, Don Hayward, the Newbridge lock, was converted (with success) into a prop forward. Wales lost to the tourists in a tight struggle, but the pack played soundly throughout the season and deserved commendation for its part in the retention of the Triple Crown and Grand Slam.

Cliff Morgan, after a disappointing performance against the Springboks (in which he tended, for once, to overdo his kicking), was the catalyst who inspired a lively back division in the Championship matches. Ken Jones scored four tries during the season, including a spectacular effort at Twickenham, while Malcolm Thomas and Lewis Jones contributed vital points with some accurate place-kicking.

Jones signed professional with Leeds Rugby League club in October 1952. He became the outstanding Rugby League figure of the decade, and his accurate goal-kicking helped him to establish numerous records.

## 1952-53

| v. ENGLAND | v. SCOTLAND | v. IRELAND | v. FRANCE |
|---|---|---|---|
| †T.J. Davies 1PG | T.J. Davies 1PG | T.J. Davies 1C | T.J. Davies |
| | | | |
| K.J. Jones | K.J. Jones 1T | K.J. Jones | K.J. Jones |
| B.L. Williams | *B.L. Williams 2T | *B.L. Williams | *B.L. Williams |
| M.C. Thomas | A.G. Thomas | A.G. Thomas | A.G. Thomas |
| †G.M. Griffiths | G.M. Griffiths | G.M. Griffiths 1T | G.M. Griffiths 2T |
| | | | |
| †R. Burnett | C.I. Morgan | C.I. Morgan | C.I. Morgan |
| W.A. Williams | W.R. Willis | †T. Lloyd | T. Lloyd |
| | | | |
| J.D. Robins | †C.C. Meredith | J.D. Robins | J.D. Robins |
| †G. Beckingham | G. Beckingham | D.M. Davies | D.M. Davies |
| W.O.G. Williams | W.O.G. Williams | W.O.G. Williams | W.O.G. Williams |
| E.R. John | E.R. John | E.R. John | E.R. John |
| J.R.G. Stephens | J.R.G. Stephens | J.R.G. Stephens | J.R.G. Stephens |
| †W.D. Johnson | R.C.C. Thomas | R.C.C. Thomas | R.C.C. Thomas |
| *J.A. Gwilliam | †R.J. Robins | J.A. Gwilliam | J.A. Gwilliam |
| †S. Judd | S. Judd | S. Judd | S. Judd |
| Cardiff Arms Park | Murrayfield | St. Helen's | Stade Colombes |
| LOST 3-8 | WON 12-0 | WON 5-3 | WON 6-3 |
| WALES: 1PG | SCOT.: NIL | WALES: 1G | FR.: 1PG |
| ENG.: 1G 1PG | WALES: 1PG 3T | IRE.: 1T | WALES: 2T |
| 17 Jan. 1953 | 7 Feb. 1953 | 14 Mar. 1953 | 28 Mar. 1953 |

Terry Davies, having impressed the Welsh selectors with his performances for his village side, Bynea, and later Devonport Services and Swansea, began his career in Wales' defeat at Cardiff. He went on to become the finest Welsh full-back of the 1950s, but his career was frequently interrupted by serious injuries, and his final tally of caps was only 21. Nevertheless, he impressed with his excellent tackling and touch-finding, and he scored fifty points with accurate place-kicking. His total included a new Welsh career record of twelve penalty goals.

The Welsh backs, without Cliff Morgan, were disappointing against England, and despite Roy John's brilliance in the line-out, Wales were unable to create tries. Six changes were made before the Scottish match, and the return of Morgan and Willis at half back, with the inclusion of Clem Thomas in the back row, brought Wales their first win in Edinburgh since 1947.

Victories over Ireland and France, in which the Welsh packs were architects of success, left Wales as runners-up in the Championship. Gareth Griffiths, the new Cardiff left wing, completed the season with three tries in these last two games.

## 1953-54

| v. NZ | v. ENGLAND | v. IRELAND | v. FRANCE | v. SCOTLAND |
|---|---|---|---|---|
| G. Williams | G. Williams | †V. Evans 3PG | V. Evans 2C,3PG | V. Evans 1PG |
| | | | | |
| K.J. Jones 1T | K.J. Jones | K.J. Jones | K.J. Jones | *K.J. Jones |
| *B.L. Williams | A.G. Thomas | A.G. Thomas | A.G. Thomas | B.L. Williams |
| G.M. Griffiths | †G. John | †J.D. Thomas 1DG | G.M. Griffiths 1T | G.M. Griffiths |
| †G. Rowlands 2C,1PG | G. Rowlands 1T,1PG | G.M. Griffiths | G. Rowlands | †H.R. Williams 1T |
| | | | | |
| C.I. Morgan | C.I. Morgan | C.I. Morgan | G. John | C.I. Morgan 1T |
| W.R. Willis | W.R. Willis | W.R. Willis | *W.R. Willis | W.R. Willis |
| | | | | |
| C.C. Meredith | C.C. Meredith | C.C. Meredith | C.C. Meredith | C.C. Meredith |
| D.M. Davies | D.M. Davies | †B.V. Meredith | B.V. Meredith | B.V. Meredith 1T |
| W.O.G. Williams | W.O.G. Williams | W.O.G. Williams | W.O.G. Williams 1T | W.O.G. Williams |
| E.R. John | E.R. John | †R.H. Williams | R.H. Williams | R.H. Williams 1T |
| J.R.G. Stephens | *J.R.G. Stephens | *J.R.G. Stephens | R.J. Robins | R.J. Robins |
| R.C.C. Thomas | R.C.C. Thomas | R.C.C. Thomas | R.C.C. Thomas | R.C.C. Thomas |
| J.A. Gwilliam | J.A. Gwilliam | †L.H. Jenkins | S. Judd | S. Judd |
| S. Judd 1T | S. Judd | †B. Sparks | †L.M. Davies | L.M. Davies |
| Cardiff Arms Park | Twickenham | Lansdowne Road | Cardiff Arms Park | St. Helen's |
| WON 13-8 | LOST 6-9 | WON 12-9 | WON 19-13 | WON 15-3 |
| WALES: 2G 1PG | ENG.: 3T | IRE.: 2PG 1T | WALES: 2G 3PG | WALES: 1PG 4T |
| NZ: 1G 1PG | WALES: 1PG 1T | WALES: 3PG 1DG | FR.: 2G 1PG | SCOT.: 1T |
| 19 Dec. 1953 | 16 Jan. 1954 | 13 Mar. 1954 | 27 Mar. 1954 | 10 Apr. 1954 |

An exciting late try by Ken Jones, following an unorthodox cross-kick from a line-out by Clem Thomas, helped Wales to their third win over the All Blacks in December 1953. Cardiff had beaten the tourists earlier in the season, and the nucleus of the successful club side was selected for the international.

Injuries disrupted Wales at Twickenham, where England scraped home through a corner try in injury time. But Wales won their remaining matches to share the Championship with France and England. Ireland were beaten thanks to a fine drop-goal by Neath centre Denzil Thomas. He never again played for Wales, having the misfortune to find several other top-rate centres in contention for Welsh selection during his career.

The match with Scotland was the last to be staged at the St. Helen's ground in Swansea. Ken Jones equalled the record of 35 Welsh caps previously set in 1912 by Dicky Owen, and Viv Evans, the veteran Neath full-back, created a record by finishing the season with 25 points. He had won his three caps at the age of 34 years.

## 1954-55

| v. ENGLAND | v. SCOTLAND | v. IRELAND | v. FRANCE |
|---|---|---|---|
| †A.B. Edwards 1pg | A.B. Edwards | †G.D. Owen 3c,1pg | G.D. Owen 2c,2pg |
| | | | |
| K.J. Jones | K.J. Jones | K.J. Jones | K.J. Jones |
| *B.L. Williams | A.G. Thomas | A.G. Thomas | A.G. Thomas 1t |
| †G.T. Wells | G.T. Wells | G.M. Griffiths 1t | G.M. Griffiths |
| T.J. Brewer | T.J. Brewer 2t | H. Morris 1t | H. Morris 1t |
| | | | |
| C.I. Morgan | C.I. Morgan | C.I. Morgan 1t | C.I. Morgan |
| W.R. Willis | *W.R. Willis | W.R. Willis | W.R. Willis |
| | | | |
| C.C. Meredith | C.C. Meredith | C.C. Meredith 1t | C.C. Meredith |
| B.V. Meredith | B.V. Meredith | B.V. Meredith | B.V. Meredith |
| W.O.G. Williams | W.O.G. Williams | W.O.G. Williams | W.O.G. Williams |
| J.R.G. Stephens | R.H. Williams | R.H. Williams | R.H. Williams |
| R.J. Robins | R.J. Robins | R.J. Robins | R.J. Robins |
| †N.G. Davies | R.C.C. Thomas | R.C.C. Thomas | †C.D. Williams |
| S. Judd | J.R.G. Stephens 1c | *J.R.G. Stephens | *J.R.G. Stephens |
| B. Sparks | S. Judd | L.M. Davies | B. Sparks |
| | | | |
| Cardiff Arms Park | Murrayfield | Cardiff Arms Park | Stade Colombes |
| WON 3-0 | LOST 8-14 | WON 21-3 | WON 16-11 |
| | | | |
| WALES: 1PG | SCOT.: 1G 1PG 1DG 1T | WALES: 3G 1PG 1T | FR.: 1G 1DG 1PG |
| ENG.: NIL | WALES: 1G 1T | IRE.: 1PG | WALES: 2G 2PG |
| | | | |
| 22 Jan. 1955 | 5 Feb. 1955 | 12 Mar. 1955 | 26 Mar. 1955 |

A heavy snowfall compelled the WRU to postpone the English match for a week. Even then, a sudden thaw and steady drizzle combined to make the pitch very wet and muddy when the sides did meet, and there were few passages of open play for the crowd to savour. An uneventful match resulted in a narrow Welsh victory, Arthur Edwards (a late replacement for Garfield Owen) kicking a penalty goal from an easy position after ten minutes.

Rex Willis succeeded Bleddyn Williams as captain for the Scottish match. Willis played 21 times for Wales, forming a particularly productive partnership with his clubmate Cliff Morgan. But at Murrayfield there was a repeat of the 1951 surprise, the Scots staging a remarkable second-half rally to beat Wales by six points. For the first hour of the Irish match, there was little to suggest that the side would proceed to share the International Championship. But making good use of a gusting wind, and inspired by a zig-zagging run and try by Cliff Morgan, Wales played marvellous rugby to score 18 points in as many minutes. The French were unbeaten when Rees Stephens led his side to victory. The architects of the success were the powerful Welsh forwards, who denied the dangerous French backs the ball. Wales shared the title with the French for the second year running.

## 1955-56

| v. ENGLAND | v. SCOTLAND | v. IRELAND | v. FRANCE |
|---|---|---|---|
| G.D. Owen 1c | G.D. Owen | G.D. Owen 1pg | G.D. Owen 1c |
| | | | |
| K.J. Jones | K.J. Jones | K.J. Jones | K.J. Jones |
| †H.P. Morgan | H.P. Morgan 1t | H.P. Morgan | H.P. Morgan |
| M.C. Thomas | M.C. Thomas | M.C. Thomas | M.C. Thomas |
| †C.L. Davies 1t | C.L. Davies 1t | C.L. Davies | G. Rowlands |
| | | | |
| *C.I. Morgan | *C.I. Morgan 1t | *C.I. Morgan | *C.I. Morgan |
| †D.O. Brace | D.O. Brace | D.O. Brace | D.O. Brace |
| | | | |
| C.C. Meredith | †T.R. Prosser | C.C. Meredith | T.R. Prosser |
| B.V. Meredith | B.V. Meredith | B.V. Meredith | B.V. Meredith |
| W.O.G. Williams | W.O.G. Williams | W.O.G. Williams | †R. Richards |
| R.H. Williams | R.H. Williams | R.H. Williams | L.H. Jenkins |
| R.J. Robins 1t | J.R.G. Stephens | J.R.G. Stephens | J.R.G. Stephens |
| R.C.C. Thomas | R.C.C. Thomas | R.C.C. Thomas | C.D. Williams 1t |
| L.H. Jenkins | L.H. Jenkins | L.H. Jenkins | R.J. Robins |
| B. Sparks | B. Sparks | B. Sparks | †G.K. Whitson |
| | | | |
| Twickenham | Cardiff Arms Park | Lansdowne Road | Cardiff Arms Park |
| WON 8-3 | WON 9-3 | LOST 3-11 | WON 5-3 |
| | | | |
| ENG.: 1PG | WALES: 3T | IRE.: 1G 1PG 1DG | WALES: 1G |
| WALES: 1G 1T | SCOT.: 1PG | WALES: 1PG | FR.: 1T |
| | | | |
| 21 Jan. 1956 | 4 Feb. 1956 | 10 Mar. 1956 | 24 Mar. 1956 |

The Welsh front five of C.C. Meredith, B.V. Meredith, W.O. Williams, R.H. Williams and Robins played together for the sixth time in the match at Twickenham. These five had been the backbone of the successful 1955 British and Irish Lions in South Africa, but there were signs in the game with England that the power of the Welsh scrummaging was waning. Despite a victory for Cliff Morgan's side, the Welsh pack was subdued in the tight and the loose by a strong English eight. Opportunism by the back row led to Wales' first score, a try by Robins; and Lynn Davies slithered over in the corner for the second after a forty-yard dash.

Wales went on to gain the Championship, but a setback was the surprise defeat in Dublin. A penalty by Owen gave Wales the lead in the first half, and the enthusiastic Welsh supporters among the crowd thought that the Triple Crown was within grasp. But the storming play of the Irish pack unsettled Wales after the interval, and the visitors returned disappointed.

The selectors, panicked into making several changes for the France match, breathed a sigh of relief when Wales scraped home by two points against the French. A controversial try by the veteran flanker Derek Williams, converted by Owen, decided the match. Many believed that Williams had touched down beyond the dead-ball line at the Taff-end of the ground.

## 1956-57

| v. ENGLAND | v. SCOTLAND | v. IRELAND | v. FRANCE |
|---|---|---|---|
| T.J. Davies | T.J. Davies 1pg | T.J. Davies 2pg | T.J. Davies 2c,1pg |
| | | | |
| †W.G. Howells | K.J. Jones | W.G. Howells | H.R. Williams |
| *M.C. Thomas | *M.C. Thomas | †G. Powell | G. Powell |
| G.M. Griffiths | G.M. Griffiths | †C.A.H. Davies | G.T. Wells |
| †K. Maddocks | W.G. Howells | G.T. Wells | W.G. Howells 1t |
| | | | |
| C.I. Morgan | C.I. Morgan | C.I. Morgan | C.I. Morgan |
| D.O. Brace | †L.H. Williams | L.H. Williams | L.H. Williams |
| | | | |
| C.C. Meredith | C.C. Meredith | †C.H. Morgan | C.H. Morgan |
| B.V. Meredith | B.V. Meredith | B.V. Meredith | B.V. Meredith 1t |
| T.R. Prosser | T.R. Prosser | T.R. Prosser | T.R. Prosser 1t |
| R.H. Williams | R.H. Williams | R.H. Williams | R.H. Williams |
| J.R.G. Stephens | J.R.G. Stephens | *J.R.G. Stephens | *J.R.G. Stephens |
| R.C.C. Thomas | †R.H. Davies 1t | R.H. Davies | R.H. Davies |
| R.J. Robins | R.J. Robins | R.J. Robins | R.J. Robins |
| †R. O'Connor | B. Sparks | †J. Faull | J. Faull 1t |
| | | | |
| Cardiff Arms Park | Murrayfield | Cardiff Arms Park | Stade Colombes |
| LOST 0-3 | LOST 6-9 | WON 6-5 | WON 19-13 |
| | | | |
| WALES: NIL | SCOT.: 1DG 1PG 1T | WALES: 2PG | FR.: 2G 1T |
| ENG.: 1PG | WALES: 1PG 1T | IRE.: 1G | WALES: 2G 1PG 2T |
| | | | |
| 19 Jan. 1957 | 2 Feb. 1957 | 9 Mar. 1957 | 23 Mar. 1957 |

Terry Davies, having recovered from serious injury, returned as Welsh full-back. But the season began miserably as Wales failed to score tries in three consecutive matches. There were narrow defeats against England and Scotland, but Davies' two penalties in the mud against Ireland were sufficient to bring Wales their first Championship points of the season. The Welsh backs, with Cliff Morgan and Lloyd Williams in attacking mood, had a field-day in Paris, and in a fast-flowing game Wales scored four tries.

Ken Jones played his last match at Murrayfield. His Welsh record of 44 appearances had become a world record, surpassing the 42 caps of Ireland's George Stephenson. And among the pack, Bryn Meredith was on his way to creating a new Welsh record of appearances for a forward. Meredith had first attracted the attentions of the Welsh selectors as a student in an outstanding St. Luke's College (Exeter) fifteen. Later, as a qualified schoolmaster, he played for London Welsh and Newport, winning 34 caps as a hooker.

Russell Robins, an expert number eight forward, played the last of his internationals for Wales against France. A player of immense promise and considerable skill, he turned professional and joined Leeds Rugby League club in 1958.

## 1957-58

| v. AUSTRALIA | v. ENGLAND | v. SCOTLAND | v. IRELAND | v. FRANCE |
|---|---|---|---|---|
| T.J. Davies 1pg | T.J. Davies 1pg | T.J. Davies 1c | †A.J. Priday | T.J. Davies 1pg |
| | | | | |
| †J. Collins 1t | J. Collins | J. Collins 1t | †C. Roberts 1t | C. Roberts |
| G.T. Wells | M.C. Thomas | M.C. Thomas | M.C. Thomas | M.C. Thomas |
| C.A.H. Davies | C.A.H. Davies | C.A.H. Davies | C.A.H. Davies | C.R. James |
| H.R. Williams | G.T. Wells | G.T. Wells 1t | †H. Nicholls | J. Collins 1t |
| | | | | |
| †C.R. James 1dg | C.I. Morgan | C.I. Morgan | C.I. Morgan | C.I. Morgan |
| †T.W. Evans | L.H. Williams | L.H.Williams | L.H. Williams | L.H.williams |
| | | | | |
| †D. Devereux | D. Devereux | D. Devereux | †J.D. Evans | J.D. Evans |
| B.V. Meredith | B.V. Meredith | B.V. Meredith | B.V. Meredith 1t | G. Beckingham |
| T.R. Prosser | T.R. Prosser | T.R. Prosser | T.R. Prosser | T.R. Prosser |
| R.H. Williams | R.H. Williams | R.H. Williams | R.H. Williams | R.H. Williams |
| †W.R. Evans | W.R. Evans | W.R. Evans | W.R. Evans | W.R. Evans |
| R.H. Davies | *R.C.C. Thomas | *R.C.C. Thomas | *R.C.C. Thomas | *R.C.C. Thomas |
| J. Faull | J. Faull | J. Faull | J. Faull | J. Faull |
| *R.C.C. Thomas | †H.J. Morgan | H.J. Morgan | H.J. Morgan 1t | H.J. Morgan |
| | | | | |
| Cardiff Arms Park | Twickenham | Cardiff Arms Park | Lansdowne Road | Cardiff Arms Park |
| WON 9-3 | DRAWN 3-3 | WON 8-3 | WON 9-6 | LOST 6-16 |
| | | | | |
| WALES: 1DG 1PG 1T | ENG.: 1T | WALES: 1G 1T | IRE.: 1PG 1T | WALES: 1PG 1T |
| AUST.: 1T | WALES: 1PG | SCOT.: 1PG | WALES: 3T | FR.: 2G 2DG |
| | | | | |
| 4 Jan. 1958 | 18 Jan. 1958 | 1 Feb. 1958 | 15 Mar. 1958 | 29 Mar. 1958 |

Llanelli supplied Wales with six players for the match against Australia. Rhys Williams, who became chairman of the Welsh selectors and was the outstanding Welsh lock of the late 1950s, was in the pack, with Terry Davies, Cyril Davies, Ray Williams, Wynne Evans and Carwyn James among the backs.

James was to become a legend in his own time. Although his career as a fly-half was overshadowed by that of Cliff Morgan, James became the world's leading coach of the 1970s, guiding both the British Lions (1971) and Llanelli (1972) to victories over the All Blacks. Since his death in Holland in January 1983, British rugby has struggled to regain its superiority over the French and Southern Hemisphere countries, which it enjoyed during James' decade of influence.

A draw with England, and France's first win at Cardiff, left Wales as runners-up in the International Championship. Cliff Morgan, who retired following the French match, joined the BBC and has become one of the Corporation's leading executives.

## 1958-59

| v. ENGLAND | v. SCOTLAND | v. IRELAND | v. FRANCE |
|---|---|---|---|
| T.J. Davies 1c | T.J. Davies 1c | T.J. Davies 1c | T.J. Davies 1pg |
| J. Collins | J. Collins | J. Collins | J. Collins |
| †H.J. Davies | H.J. Davies | M.C. Thomas | †J.E. Hurrell |
| †M.J. Price | M.J. Price 1t | M.J. Price 1t | M.J. Price |
| †D.I.E. Bebb 1t | D.I.E. Bebb | D.I.E. Bebb | D.I.E. Bebb |
| †C. Ashton | C. Ashton | C. Ashton 1t | M.C. Thomas |
| L.H. Williams | L.H. Williams | L.H. Williams | †W. Watkins |
| †D.R. Main | D.R. Main | D.R. Main | D.R. Main |
| B.V. Meredith | B.V. Meredith | B.V. Meredith | B.V. Meredith |
| T.R. Prosser | T.R. Prosser | T.R. Prosser | T.R. Prosser |
| R.H. Williams | R.H. Williams | R.H. Williams | R.H. Williams |
| †I. Ford | I. Ford | †D.J.E. Harris | D.J.E. Harris |
| *R.C.C. Thomas | *R.C.C. Thomas | *R.C.C. Thomas | *R.C.C. Thomas |
| J. Faull | J. Faull | J. Faull | †G.D. Davidge |
| †J. Leleu | J. Leleu | H.J. Morgan | H.J. Morgan |
| Cardiff Arms Park | Murrayfield | Cardiff Arms Park | Stade Colombes |
| WON 5-0 | LOST 5-6 | WON 8-6 | LOST 3-11 |
| WALES: 1G | SCOT.: 1PG 1T | WALES: 1G 1T | FR.: 1G 1PG 1T |
| ENG.: NIL | WALES: 1G | IRE.: 1PG 1T | WALES: 1PG |
| 17 Jan. 1959 | 7 Feb. 1959 | 14 Mar. 1959 | 4 Apr. 1959 |

1959 was a season of low-scoring internationals, and Wales' tally of 21 points was their smallest in the Championship for ten years. The winter was also noted for its climatic extremes: the matches in Cardiff were played in remarkably wet, muddy conditions; the match in Scotland was staged in the middle of a cold, frosty spell; yet in Paris, the temperature soared to 75°F for the Welsh game with France.

Wales had a sound pack, ably led by the Swansea blind-side Clem Thomas, who was in his final season in the Welsh team. He gained 26 caps in a career which spanned eleven seasons. Following his distinguished playing days, Thomas became a respected critic whose observations regarding rugby appeared in the *Guardian* and the *Observer*.

Dewi Bebb and Malcolm Price made their debuts against England. Bebb, who scored the only try of the match at Cardiff, was one of Wales' "favourite" wings. He was a popular player who created his own opportunities: he appeared on the left wing 34 times, scoring eleven tries. Price scored tries in the Scottish and Irish matches and enjoyed a successful summer tour with the Lions to New Zealand. Later, in the winter of 1962, he turned professional, joining Oldham Rugby League club.

## 1959-60

| v. ENGLAND | v. SCOTLAND | v. IRELAND | v. FRANCE |
|---|---|---|---|
| T.J. Davies 2pg | †N. Morgan 1c,1pg | N. Morgan 2c | N. Morgan 1c,1pg |
| J. Collins | †F.C. Coles | F.C. Coles | F.C. Coles |
| †G.W. Lewis | G.W. Lewis | †B.J. Jones | B.J. Jones |
| M.J. Price | M.J. Price | M.J. Price | M.J. Price |
| D.I.E. Bebb | D.I.E. Bebb 1t | D.I.E. Bebb | D.I.E. Bebb |
| C. Ashton | C. Ashton | C. Ashton | †T.B. Richards |
| †C. Evans | D.O. Brace | *D.O. Brace 1t | D.O. Brace |
| †L.J. Cunningham | L.J. Cunningham | L.J. Cunningham | L.J. Cunningham |
| B.V. Meredith | *B.V. Meredith | †N.R. Gale | *B.V. Meredith |
| T.R. Prosser | T.R. Prosser | T.R. Prosser | T.R. Prosser |
| *R.H. Williams | D.J.E. Harris | D.J.E. Harris | D.J.E. Harris |
| †G.W. Payne | G.W. Payne | G.W. Payne | J. Faull |
| †B. Cresswell | B. Cresswell | B. Cresswell 1t | B. Cresswell 1t |
| J. Faull | G.D. Davidge | G.D. Davidge | G.D. Davidge |
| H.J. Morgan | G.K. Whitson | G.K. Whitson | J. Leleu |
| Twickenham | Cardiff Arms Park | Lansdowne Road | Cardiff Arms Park |
| LOST 6-14 | WON 8-0 | WON 10-9 | LOST 8-16 |
| ENG.: 1G 2PG 1T | WALES: 1G 1PG | IRE.: 2PG 1T | WALES: 1G 1PG |
| WALES: 2PG | SCOT.: NIL | WALES: 2G | FR.: 2G 2T |
| 16 Jan. 1960 | 6 Feb. 1960 | 12 Mar. 1960 | 26 Mar. 1960 |

Seven of the 1959 British Lions touring team appeared in the Welsh side at Twickenham. But a Welsh side full of experience and enthusiasm, captained by the lock Rhys Williams, were easily beaten by a young lively English team. Wales found themselves fourteen points in arrears at the interval, and only two penalties by Terry Davies in the second half added a touch of respectability to the final score. The selectors wielded the axe. Six changes were made for the game against Scotland, and Newport supplied five of the Welsh team, including the entire back row.

Wales defeated an ordinary Scottish side, but were lucky to win by a point in Dublin. The forwards were outplayed by a sound Irish eight, and the weaknesses of the pack were eventually exposed by the French, who won their third successive match against Wales, by defeating the Principality at Cardiff. Bryan Richards, one of the most talented Welsh fly-halves of the day, played his only game for Wales against France. He enjoyed enormous success in club rugby with Swansea and London Welsh, and later joined the staff at Rugby School as and Economics master. Geoffrey Windsor Lewis, son of the former Welsh fly-half of the 1920s, won two caps this season from Richmond. He is the present secretary of the Barbarians.

## 1960-61

| v. S. AFRICA | v. ENGLAND | v. SCOTLAND | v. IRELAND | v. FRANCE |
|---|---|---|---|---|
| *T.J. DAVIES | *T.J. DAVIES | *T.J. DAVIES | A.J. PRIDAY | T.J. DAVIES |
| †D.P. EVANS | †P.M. REES | P.M. REES | P.M. REES | J. COLLINS |
| C.A.H. DAVIES | C.A.H. DAVIES | †G.R. BRITTON | †D. THOMAS | †H.J. MAINWARING |
| †H.M. ROBERTS | H.M. ROBERTS | H.M. ROBERTS | H.M. ROBERTS | H.M. ROBERTS |
| D.I.E. BEBB | D.I.E. BEBB 2T | D.I.E. BEBB | D.I.E. BEBB | D.I.E. BEBB 1T |
| †K.H.L. RICHARDS | K.H.L. RICHARDS | K.H.L. RICHARDS | K.H.L. RICHARDS 1T,2PG | K.H.L. RICHARDS |
| †A. O'CONNOR | A. O'CONNOR | A. O'CONNOR | *D.O. BRACE | *L.H. WILLIAMS |
| T.R. PROSSER | †P.E.J. MORGAN | P.E.J. MORGAN | T.R. PROSSER | T.R. PROSSER |
| B.V. MEREDITH | B.V. MEREDITH | B.V. MEREDITH | B.V. MEREDITH | †W.J. THOMAS |
| †K.D. JONES | K.D. JONES | K.D. JONES | K.D. JONES | P.E.J. MORGAN |
| D.J.E. HARRIS | D.J.E. HARRIS | D.J.E. HARRIS | †B. PRICE | B. PRICE |
| W.R. EVANS | W.R. EVANS | W.R. EVANS | W.R. EVANS | W.R. EVANS |
| G.D. DAVIDGE | G.D. DAVIDGE | G.D. DAVIDGE | G.D. DAVIDGE | †A.I.E. PASK 1T |
| †D. NASH | D. NASH | D. NASH | D. NASH | D. NASH |
| J. LELEU | H.J. MORGAN | H.J. MORGAN | H.J. MORGAN | H.J. MORGAN |
| Cardiff Arms Park | Cardiff Arms Park | Murrayfield | Cardiff Arms Park | Stade Colombes |
| LOST 0-3 | WON 6-3 | LOST 0-3 | WON 9-0 | LOST 6-8 |
| WALES: NIL | WALES: 2T | SCOT.: 1T | WALES: 1T 2PG | FR.: 1G 1T |
| SA: 1PG | ENG.: 1T | WALES: NIL | IRE.: NIL | WALES: 2T |
| 3 Dec. 1960 | 21 Jan. 1961 | 11 Feb. 1961 | 11 Mar. 1961 | 25 Mar. 1961 |

Terry Davies was the Welsh captain against South Africa. But his gamble of playing into the elements in the first half just failed to produce a Welsh victory, and in a dour game in appalling weather conditions, the South Africans scraped home.

There was an entertaining match against England at Cardiff, where both teams fulfilled a promise to play open, attractive football. Wales deserved to win but had to thank the speed and determination of Dewi Bebb, who scored two tries, for their victory. Cyril Davies, an adventurous centre, was badly injured during the match, and his loss was a considerable setback to the team's attacking hopes. The customary defeat at Murrayfield was followed by a most uninteresting match against Ireland in which Ken Richards, a prolific scorer of points for his club, kicked two penalties and touched down for a try in Wales' win by nine points.

Ray Prosser played the last of his 22 matches for Wales in the defeat in Paris. One of the best loved of Welsh forwards, he became a leading committee-man at his Pontypool club, and coached the successful Pontypool sides of recent times. A solid scrummager, he was also a useful forager in the loose and excelled at the front of the line out.

## 1961-62

| v. ENGLAND | v. SCOTLAND | v. FRANCE | v. IRELAND |
|---|---|---|---|
| †K. COSLETT | K. COSLETT | K. COSLETT 1PG | †G.T.R. HODGSON 1PG |
| †D.R.R. MORGAN | D.R.R. MORGAN | D.R.R. MORGAN | D.R.R. MORGAN |
| †D.K. JONES | D.K. JONES | D.K. JONES | D.K. JONES |
| M.J. PRICE | H.M. ROBERTS | H.M. ROBERTS | †D.B. DAVIES |
| D.I.E. BEBB | D.I.E. BEBB | D.I.E. BEBB | D.I.E. BEBB |
| †A. REES | A. REES 1DG | A. REES | C. ASHTON |
| *L.H. WILLIAMS | *L.H. WILLIAMS | A. O'CONNOR | A. O'CONNOR |
| L.J. CUNNINGHAM | L.J. CUNNINGHAM | L.J. CUNNINGHAM | L.J. CUNNINGHAM |
| B.V. MEREDITH | B.V. MEREDITH | *B.V. MEREDITH | *B.V. MEREDITH |
| K.D. JONES | †D. GREENSLADE | K.D. JONES | †J. WARLOW |
| B. PRICE | B. PRICE | D. NASH | W.R. EVANS |
| W.R. EVANS | W.R. EVANS | †K.A. ROWLANDS | K.A. ROWLANDS |
| R.H. DAVIES | R.H. DAVIES | G.D. DAVIDGE | †J. DAVIES |
| A.I.E. PASK | A.I.E. PASK | A.I.E. PASK | A.I.E. PASK |
| H.J. MORGAN | H.J. MORGAN | H.J. MORGAN | H.J. MORGAN |
| Twickenham | Cardiff Arms Park | Cardiff Arms Park | Lansdowne Road |
| DRAWN 0-0 | LOST 3-8 | WON 3-0 | DRAWN 3-3 |
| ENG.: NIL | WALES: 1DG | WALES: 1PG | IRE.: 1DG |
| WALES: NIL | SCOT.: 1G 1T | FR.: NIL | WALES: 1PG |
| 20 Jan. 1962 | 3 Feb. 1962 | 24 Mar. 1962 | 17 Nov. 1962 |

Ken Jones, an exciting young Llanelli centre who had enjoyed a very successful run in the Welsh Secondary Schools side, came into the Welsh fifteen against England. But Jones and the rest of the Welsh backs were unable to find sufficient room to make any telling breaks, and the match ended in a scoreless draw for the first time since 1936.

Wales played poorly in wet conditions against Scotland, and the result was the first Scottish victory at Cardiff since 1927. Kingsley Jones was unable to take his place against Scotland owing to injury, and his continued unavailability forced the selectors to turn to Neath's Ron Waldron for the match with Ireland. However, an epidemic of smallpox in South Wales caused the postponement of the match (and it was eventually played as a "hangover match" in November 1962), and by the time the selectors reconvened to consider the side to meet France, Jones had reported fit and the unlucky Waldron was dropped.

New cap Keith Rowlands and loose forward Alun Pask inspired the Welsh pack to overcome the dangerous French, and a penalty goal kicked by Coslett (who later had a long and successful Rugby League career) gave Wales their sole victory of the season, and the first against France since 1957. Wales failed to score a try during the season.

## 1962-63

| v. ENGLAND | v. SCOTLAND | v. IRELAND | v. FRANCE |
|---|---|---|---|
| G.T.R. Hodgson 1pg | G.T.R. Hodgson 1pg | G.T.R. Hodgson | G.T.R. Hodgson 1pg |
| D.R.R. Morgan | D.R.R. Morgan | D.R.R. Morgan | D.R.R. Morgan |
| D.K. Jones | †R. Evans | R. Evans | D.K. Jones |
| D.B. Davies | D.B. Davies | H.M. Roberts | R. Evans |
| D.I.E. Bebb | †W.J. Morris | W.J. Morris | D.I.E. Bebb |
| †D. Watkins | D. Watkins | D. Watkins 1dg | D. Watkins |
| *†D.C.T. Rowlands | *D.C.T. Rowlands 1dg | *D.C.T. Rowlands | *D.C.T. Rowlands |
| †D. Williams | D. Williams | D. Williams | D. Williams |
| N.R. Gale | N.R. Gale | N.R. Gale | W.J. Thomas |
| K.D. Jones | K.D. Jones | K.D. Jones | †C.H. Norris |
| B. Price | B. Price | K.A. Rowlands | B. Price |
| †B.E. Thomas | B.E. Thomas | B.E. Thomas | B.E. Thomas |
| A.I.E. Pask | †G. Jones | G. Jones 1t | G. Jones |
| †R.C.B. Michaelson | A.I.E. Pask | A.I.E. Pask | A.I.E. Pask |
| †D.J. Hayward 1t | H.J. Morgan | H.J. Morgan | H.J. Morgan |
| Cardiff Arms Park | Murrayfield | Cardiff Arms Park | Stade Colombes |
| LOST 6-13 | WON 6-0 | LOST 6-14 | LOST 3-5 |
| Wales: 1pg 1t | Scot.: Nil | Wales: 1t 1dg | Fr.: 1g |
| Eng.: 2g 1dg | Wales: 1pg 1dg | Ire.: 1g 1dg 2pg | Wales: 1pg |
| 19 Jan. 1963 | 2 Feb. 1963 | 9 Mar. 1963 | 23 Mar. 1963 |

Wales fielded an experimental side with six new caps against England. There were new halves in David Watkins and Clive Rowlands, who captained Wales in his debut, and four new forwards, but a sluggish Welsh pack were unable to master a lively English side. Rowlands was criticised for adopting an inflexible tactical approach, though he was to become the Welsh hero two weeks later when he kicked Wales to their first win in Edinburgh for ten years, in a match of 111 line-outs.

Only 45,000 spectators saw the Irish match at Cardiff, the smallest attendance at the Arms Park for many seasons. They watched Ireland gain their first win at Cardiff for 31 years and it was the first time since 1928 that Wales had lost two home matches in the Championship. Few Welsh supporters made the trip to Paris, where Wales lost to a mediocre French side.

It was the first time since 1949 that Wales had finished with the wooden spoon.

## 1963-64

| v. NZ | v. ENGLAND | v. SCOTLAND | v. IRELAND | v. FRANCE |
|---|---|---|---|---|
| G.T.R. Hodgson | G.T.R. Hodgson | G.T.R. Hodgson | G.T.R. Hodgson | G.T.R. Hodgson |
| D.R.R. Morgan | †David Weaver | †S.J. Watkins | S.J. Watkins 1t | S.J. Watkins 1t |
| D.K. Jones | D.K. Jones | D.K. Jones | †S.J. Dawes 1t | S.J. Dawes |
| †J.R. Uzzell | †K. Bradshaw | K. Bradshaw 1t,1c,1pg | K. Bradshaw 3c | K. Bradshaw 1c,2pg |
| D.I.E. Bebb | D.I.E. Bebb 2t | D.I.E. Bebb | P.M. Rees | D.I.E. Bebb |
| D. Watkins | D. Watkins | D. Watkins | D. Watkins 1t | D. Watkins |
| *D.C.T. Rowlands | *D.C.T. Rowlands | *D.C.T. Rowlands | *D.C.T. Rowlands | *D.C.T. Rowlands |
| L.J. Cunningham | L.J. Cunningham | L.J. Cunningham | L.J. Cunningham | L.J. Cunningham |
| N.R. Gale | N.R. Gale | N.R. Gale | N.R. Gale | N.R. Gale |
| K.D. Jones | D. Williams | D. Williams | D. Williams | D. Williams |
| B. Price | B. Price | B. Price | B. Price | B. Price |
| B.E. Thomas | B.E. Thomas | B.E. Thomas 1t | B.E. Thomas | B.E. Thomas |
| †A. Thomas | A. Thomas | †G.J. Prothero | G.J. Prothero | G.J. Prothero |
| A.I.E. Pask | A.I.E. Pask | A.I.E. Pask | A.I.E. Pask | A.I.E. Pask |
| D.J. Hayward | †J.T. Mantle | D.J. Hayward | D.J. Hayward | D.J. Hayward |
| Cardiff Arms Park | Twickenham | Cardiff Arms Park | Lansdowne Road | Cardiff Arms Park |
| LOST 0-6 | DRAWN 6-6 | WON 11-3 | WON 15-6 | DRAWN 11-11 |
| Wales: Nil | Eng.: 2t | Wales: 1g 1pg 1t | Ire.: 2pg | Wales: 1g 2pg |
| NZ: 1pg 1dg | Wales: 2t | Scot.: 1t | Wales: 3g | Fr.: 1g 2pg |
| 21 Dec. 1963 | 18 Jan. 1964 | 1 Feb. 1964 | 7 Mar. 1964 | 21 Mar. 1964 |

For the first time, Wales were beaten in an international at Cardiff by New Zealand. This defeat prompted a call for Welsh rugby to undertake a complete review of its approach to the development of the game. There were murmurings of approval for the suggestion that coaches should be appointed to guide the Welsh clubs towards an approach that would enable Wales to compete again on equal terms with the nations from the Southern Hemisphere.

To an extent these ideas were forgotten as Wales proceeded to take a share in the Championship with Scotland. After falling into arrears early in the game at Twickenham, the side bounced back to a draw, thanks to two fine tries by Bebb. Scotland were overcome by a good Welsh pack, and in Dublin there were signs in the last quarter of the match that the Welsh threequarters were beginning to play with style and confidence.

But the game with France showed that Wales had flattered to deceive in their Championship matches. A weak French side led by eight points at one stage, and Wales had to rely on some fine place-kicking by Keith Bradshaw to snatch a draw.

|  | 1964 | 1964-65 | | | |
|---|---|---|---|---|---|
|  | v. S. AFRICA | v. ENGLAND | v. SCOTLAND | v. IRELAND | v. FRANCE |
|  | G.T.R. Hodgson | †T.G. Price 1c | T.G. Price 1c,2pg | T.G. Price 1c,1pg,1dg | T.G. Price 2c |
|  | D.K. Jones | S.J. Watkins 2t | S.J. Watkins 1t | S.J. Watkins | S.J. Watkins 1t |
|  | S.J. Dawes | S.J. Dawes | S.J. Dawes | S.J. Dawes | S.J. Dawes 1t |
|  | K. Bradshaw 1pg | J.R. Uzzell | J.R. Uzzell | J.R. Uzzell | J.R. Uzzell |
|  | D.I.E. Bebb | D.I.E. Bebb | D.I.E. Bebb | D.I.E. Bebb 1t | D.I.E. Bebb 1t |
|  | D. Watkins | D. Watkins 1dg | D. Watkins | D. Watkins 1t | D. Watkins |
|  | *D.C.T. Rowlands | *D.C.T. Rowlands | *D.C.T. Rowlands | *D.C.T. Rowlands | *D.C.T. Rowlands |
|  | L.J. Cunningham | D. Williams | D. Williams | D. Williams | D. Williams |
|  | N.R. Gale | N.R. Gale | N.R. Gale 1t | N.R. Gale | N.R. Gale |
|  | D. Williams | †R. Waldron | R. Waldron | R. Waldron | R. Waldron |
|  | B. Price | B. Price | B. Price | B. Price | B. Price |
|  | B.E. Thomas | B.E. Thomas | †W.J. Morris | K.A. Rowlands | K.A. Rowlands |
|  | A.I.E. Pask | G.J. Prothero | G.J. Prothero | G.J. Prothero | G.J. Prothero |
|  | J.T. Mantle | A.I.E. Pask | A.I.E. Pask | A.I.E. Pask | A.I.E. Pask |
|  | D.J. Hayward | H.J. Morgan 1t | H.J. Morgan | H.J. Morgan | H.J. Morgan |
|  | Durban | Cardiff Arms Park | Murrayfield | Cardiff Arms Park | Stade Colombes |
|  | LOST 3-24 | WON 14-3 | WON 14-12 | WON 14-8 | LOST 13-22 |
|  | SA: 3g 1dg 2pg | Wales: 1g 1dg 2t | Scot.: 2dg 2pg | Wales: 1g 1dg 1pg 1t | Fr.: 2g 1dg 1pg 2t |
|  | Wales: 1pg | Eng.: 1pg | Wales: 1g 2pg 1t | Ire.: 1g 1pg | Wales: 2g 1t |
|  | 23 May 1964 | 16 Jan. 1965 | 6 Feb. 1965 | 13 Mar. 1965 | 27 Mar. 1965 |

At the request of the SARB, who were celebrating the 75th Anniversary of organised rugby in the Dominion, Wales undertook a five-match tour in the summer of 1964. The matches provided the first major test for new laws designed to make the game more open and attractive, but Wales failed to adapt to these laws on tour and two of the matches were lost. Defeat in the Test at Durban by 21 points was Wales' worst result at international level since 1924. After the tour the WRU created a panel to investigate both the weaknesses in Welsh rugby and the future for coaching in the Principality.

The Welsh side responded by winning the Triple Crown for the first time for thirteen years. David Watkins had his best season, the new laws enabling him to display his attacking talents more effectively than before. Wales played fluently to beat England; had to thank Norman Gale for a late corner try for victory in Scotland; and faced Ireland in the match of the season.

Both sides were seeking the Triple Crown, but a fine display by Terry Price helped Wales to victory. Price converted a try by David Watkins just before half-time, kicked a late penalty to seal the match, and in between dropped a splendid goal from forty yards. In an extraordinary match in Paris, Wales trailed 0-22 at the interval, but eventually pulled back to lose by only nine points.

|  | 1965-66 | | | |
|---|---|---|---|---|
|  | v. ENGLAND | v. SCOTLAND | v. IRELAND | v. FRANCE |
|  | T.G. Price 1c,2pg | G.T.R. Hodgson | G.T.R. Hodgson | G.T.R. Hodgson |
|  | S.J. Watkins | S.J. Watkins | S.J. Watkins | S.J. Watkins 1t |
|  | D.K. Jones | D.K. Jones 2t | D.K. Jones | D.K. Jones |
|  | K. Bradshaw | K. Bradshaw 1c | K. Bradshaw 1pg | K. Bradshaw 2pg |
|  | †L. Davies | L. Davies | L. Davies | D.I.E. Bebb |
|  | D. Watkins | D. Watkins | D. Watkins | D. Watkins |
|  | †R.A. Lewis | R.A. Lewis | R.A. Lewis | R.A. Lewis |
|  | D. Williams | D. Williams | D. … | C.H. Norris |
|  | N.R. Gale | N.R. Gale | N.R. Gale | N.R. Gale |
|  | †D.J. Lloyd | D.J. Lloyd | D.J. Lloyd | D.J. Lloyd |
|  | B. Price | B. Price | B. Price | B. Price |
|  | B.E. Thomas | B.E. Thomas | B.E. Thomas | W.J. Morris |
|  | G.J. Prothero | G.J. Prothero | G.J. Prothero 1· | G.J. Prothero |
|  | *A.I.E. Pask 1t | *A.I.E. Pask | *A.I.E. Pask | *A.I.E. Pask |
|  | H.J. Morgan | H.J. Morgan | H.J. Morgan | H.J. Morgan |
|  | Twickenham | Cardiff Arms Park | Lansdowne Road | Cardiff Arms Park |
|  | WON 11-6 | WON 8-3 | LOST 6-9 | WON 9-8 |
|  | Eng.: 1pg 1t | Wales: 1g 1t | Ire.: 1dg 1pg 1t | Wales: 2pg 1t |
|  | Wales: 1g 2pg | Scot.: 1pg | Wales: 1pg 1t | Fr.: 1g 1t |
|  | 15 Jan. 1966 | 5 Feb. 1966 | 12 Mar. 1966 | 26 Mar. 1966 |

Clive Rowlands was surprisingly dropped for the opening match of 1966, after leading Wales in fourteen consecutive matches. He had often incurred criticism for adopting a limited tactical approach, but his achievements had been considerable: two championships and a Triple Crown. Later he coached the successful Welsh side from 1969 to 1974.

Alun Pask succeeded Rowlands as captain and became the fourth man to lead Wales to victory at Twickenham. The captain scored a spectacular one-handed try in the corner and Terry Price kicked three good goals. David Watkins and Ken Jones were outstanding in wet, muddy conditions against the Scots and many expected Wales to regain the Triple Crown in Dublin. However, Ireland played with vigour and determination to deny Pask's men the triple triumph.

With the Championship still at stake in Cardiff, Wales and France engaged in an exciting contest filled with incidents. Bradshaw had to kick two penalties to bring Wales back into the game after France had led by eight points after a dozen minutes. Then, ten minutes from the end, Stuart Watkins intercepted a French pass on his own 25. He set off on a seventy-yard run along the right touchline to score a memorable try which won the Championship title outright for the second successive season.

## 1966-67

| v. AUSTRALIA | v. SCOTLAND | v. IRELAND | v. FRANCE | v. ENGLAND |
|---|---|---|---|---|
| T.G. PRICE 1C,1PG | T.G. PRICE 1C | G.T.R. HODGSON | T.G. PRICE 1C,2PG | †K.S. JARRETT 5C,2PG,1T |
| S.J. WATKINS | S.J. WATKINS 1T | S.J. WATKINS | S.J. WATKINS | S.J. WATKINS |
| S.J. DAWES 1T | †W.H. RAYBOULD | W.H. RAYBOULD | W.H. RAYBOULD | W.H. RAYBOULD 1DG |
| †T.G.R. DAVIES | T.G.R. DAVIES | T.G.R. DAVIES | T.G.R. DAVIES | T.G.R. DAVIES 2T |
| D.I.E. BEBB | D.I.E. BEBB | D.I.E. BEBB | D.I.E. BEBB 1T | D.I.E. BEBB 1T |
| †B. JOHN | B. JOHN | *D. WATKINS | *D. WATKINS 1DG | *D. WATKINS |
| R.A. LEWIS | †W.G. HULLIN | R.A. LEWIS | †G.O. EDWARDS | G.O. EDWARDS |
| D. WILLIAMS | †J.P. O'SHEA | J.P. O'SHEA | D. WILLIAMS | D. WILLIAMS |
| N.R. GALE | †B.I. REES | B.I. REES | B.I. REES | N.R. GALE |
| D.J. LLOYD | D.J. LLOYD | D.J. LLOYD | D.J. LLOYD | D.J. LLOYD |
| B. PRICE | B. PRICE | B. PRICE | B. PRICE | B. PRICE |
| †W.D. THOMAS | †W.T. MAINWARING | W.T. MAINWARING | W.T. MAINWARING | W.T. MAINWARING |
| †K.J. BRADDOCK | K.J. BRADDOCK | K.J. BRADDOCK | †R.E. JONES | R.E. JONES |
| *A.I.E. PASK | *A.I.E. PASK | A.I.E. PASK | †W.D. MORRIS | W.D. MORRIS 1T |
| H.J. MORGAN 1T | †J. TAYLOR | J. TAYLOR | J. TAYLOR | J. TAYLOR |
| Cardiff Arms Park | Murrayfield | Cardiff Arms Park | Stade Colombes | Cardiff Arms Park |
| LOST 11-14 | LOST 5-11 | LOST 0-3 | LOST 14-20 | WON 34-21 |
| WALES: 1G 1PG 1T | SCOT.: 1G 1DG 1T | WALES: NIL | FR.: 1G 1PG 2DG 2T | WALES: 5G 2PG 1DG |
| AUST.: 1G 1PG 1DG 1T | WALES: 1G | IRELAND: 1T | WALES: 1G 2PG 1DG | ENG.: 4PG 3T |
| 3 Dec. 1966 | 4 Feb. 1967 | 11 Mar. 1967 | 1 Apr. 1967 | 15 Apr. 1967 |

Four consecutive defeats brought to an end Wales' good run of the mid-1960s. The season was one of transition, the selectors blooding fourteen new caps in their five matches. Of these, several, including Gerald Davies, Gareth Edwards, Barry John and John Taylor were to become legends in the game. Taylor, a product of Watford GS in Hertfordshire and Loughborough Colleges, replaced Haydn Morgan, who had won the last of his 27 Welsh caps in the defeat by Australia. Taylor went on to gain 26 caps in the first part of Wales' second golden era, and formed with Dai Morris of Neath an effective wing-forward duo.

Barry John and Gerald Davies were players of incomparable grace and excellence. John was a fly-half who "ghosted" past defenders while Davies was a player capable of creating his own scores from seemingly impossible situations. Davies went on to establish with Gareth Edwards a new Welsh try record, each scoring twenty tries. Edwards won 53 consecutive caps before retiring as one of the world's greatest all-time scrum-halves.

The match with England, which resulted in Wales' only win of the campaign, was a personal triumph for the young Newport player, Keith Jarrett. In a sensational debut he equalled the Welsh record of 19 points in an international, his tally including a marvellous try from a forty-yard run.

## 1967-68

| v. NZ | v. ENGLAND | v. SCOTLAND | v. IRELAND | v. FRANCE |
|---|---|---|---|---|
| †P.J. WHEELER | P.J. WHEELER | †D. REES | D. REES 1PG | D. REES 2PG |
| S.J. WATKINS | S.J. WATKINS | S.J. WATKINS | W.K. JONES | W.K. JONES 1T |
| W.H. RAYBOULD | K.S. JARRETT 1C | K.S. JARRETT 1C | *S.J. DAWES | S.J. DAWES |
| †I. HALL | T.G.R. DAVIES | T.G.R DAVIES | W.H. RAYBOULD | W.H. RAYBOULD |
| †W.K. JONES | W.K. JONES | W.K. JONES 1T | †M.C.R. RICHARDS | M.C.R. RICHARDS |
| B. JOHN 1DG | B. JOHN 1DG | B. JOHN | B. JOHN | B. JOHN |
| G.O. EDWARDS | G.O. EDWARDS 1T | *G.O. EDWARDS | G.O. EDWARDS 1DG | *G.O. EDWARDS |
| D. WILLIAMS | D. WILLIAMS | J.P. O'SHEA | J.P. O'SHEA | J.P. O'SHEA |
| *N.R. GALE 1PG | *N.R. GALE | †J. YOUNG | J. YOUNG | J. YOUNG |
| B.E. THOMAS | †W.B. JAMES | D.J. LLOYD | D.J. LLOYD | D.J. LLOYD |
| †M. WILTSHIRE | M. WILTSHIRE | M. WILTSHIRE | †I.C. JONES | M. WILTSHIRE |
| W.T. MAINWARING | W.T. MAINWARING | W.D. THOMAS | W.D. THOMAS | W.D. THOMAS |
| †W.D. HUGHES | W.D. MORRIS | W.D. MORRIS | W.D. MORRIS | W.D. MORRIS |
| †J.J. JEFFERY | †R. WANBON 1T | R.E. JONES | R.E. JONES | R.E. JONES |
| J. TAYLOR | †A.J. GRAY | A.J. GRAY | J. TAYLOR | J. TAYLOR |
| Cardiff Arms Park | Twickenham | Cardiff Arms Park | Lansdowne Road | Cardiff Arms Park |
| LOST 6-13 | DRAWN 11-11 | WON 5-0 | LOST 6-9 | LOST 9-14 |
| WALES: 1DG 1PG | ENG.: 1G 1PG 1T | WALES: 1G | IRE.: 1DG 1PG 1T | WALES: 2PG 1T |
| NZ: 2G 1PG | WALES: 1G 1DG 1T | SCOT.: NIL | WALES: 1DG 1PG | FR.: 1G 1DG 1PG 1T |
| 11 Nov. 1967 | 20 Jan. 1968 | 3 Feb. 1968 | 9 Mar. 1968 | 23 Mar. 1968 |

Against the All Blacks, in dismal conditions at Cardiff, Barry John and Gareth Edwards played together for the first time in an international. The pair were to feature together 23 times for Wales (and four times for the victorious 1971 British Test team, once for the 1968 Lions against South Africa), steering both their country and the Lions to many successes.

Norman Gale, the durable Llanelli hooker, led Wales in the matches with New Zealand and England. Wales were unable to capitalise on their chances to kick penalty goals against the All Blacks, so in desperation Gale decided to kick for goal himself when an opportunity was offered late in the match. Gale duly became the only hooker to land a penalty for Wales in an international.

Gareth Edwards, who became the youngest man (at twenty years of age) to captain Wales when he led the side to victory over Scotland, was awarded a remarkable drop-goal against Ireland. Many of the players and the majority of the crowd had seen his effort sail wide of the goal, but the referee accepted the kick.

## 1968-69

| v. SCOTLAND | v. IRELAND | v. FRANCE | v. ENGLAND |
|---|---|---|---|
| †J.P.R. WILLIAMS | J.P.R. WILLIAMS | J.P.R. WILLIAMS | J.P.R. WILLIAMS |
| S.J. WATKINS | S.J. WATKINS 1T | S.J. WATKINS | S.J. WATKINS |
| K.S. JARRETT 1C,2PG | K.S. JARRETT 3C,1PG | K.S. JARRETT 1C | K.S. JARRETT 3C,2PG |
| T.G.R. DAVIES | T.G.R. DAVIES | T.G.R. DAVIES¹ | S.J. DAWES |
| M.C.R. RICHARDS 1T | M.C.R. RICHARDS | M.C.R. RICHARDS 1T | M.C.R. RICHARDS 4T |
| B. JOHN 1T | B. JOHN 1DG | B. JOHN | B. JOHN 1DG,1T |
| G.O. EDWARDS 1T | G.O. EDWARDS | G.O.EDWARDS 1T | *G.O. EDWARDS |
| D. WILLIAMS | D. WILLIAMS 1T | D. WILLIAMS | D. WILLIAMS |
| J. YOUNG | J. YOUNG | J. YOUNG | J. YOUNG |
| D.J. LLOYD | D.J. LLOYD | D.J. LLOYD | D.J. LLOYD |
| *B. PRICE | *B. PRICE | *B. PRICE | W.D. THOMAS |
| B.E. THOMAS | B.E. THOMAS | B.E. THOMAS | B.E. THOMAS |
| W.D. MORRIS | W.D. MORRIS 1T | W.D. MORRIS | W.D. MORRIS |
| †T.M. DAVIES | T.M. DAVIES | T.M. DAVIES | T.M. DAVIES |
| J. TAYLOR | J. TAYLOR 1T | J. TAYLOR | J. TAYOR |
| Murrayfield | Cardiff Arms Park | Stade Colombes | Cardiff Arms Park |
| WON 17-3 | WON 24-11 | DRAWN 8-8 | WON 30-9 |
| SCOT.: 1PG | WALES: 3G 1DG 1PG 1T | FR.: 1G 1PG | WALES: 3G 2PG 1DG 2T |
| WALES: 1G 2PG 2T | IRE.: 1G 2PG | WALES: 1G 1T | ENG.: 3PG |
| 1 Feb. 1969 | 8 Mar. 1969 | 22 Mar. 1969 | 12 Apr. 1969 |

¹Rep. by †P. Bennett

Under the control of coach Clive Rowlands, the Welsh team and reserves met frequently during the season, and the benefits of a squad system were immediately seen when Wales won the Triple Crown and Championship. The team played impressive, attractive rugby and the backs developed a confidence in open play which helped to bring them eleven tries. The side was backed up by the place-kicking of Keith Jarrett, who scored 31 points in the four matches, a new Welsh record for the Championship.

The old North Stand at Cardiff had been demolished as part of the WRU's plans to redevelop the stadium. Consequently only 29,000 were present to see the fine performances against Ireland and England. Wales registered their biggest win against England for 47 years, and Maurice Richards became the first Welsh player since 1899 to score four tries in an international against England.

J.P.R. Williams made his debut against Scotland. He went on to become Wales' most-capped player, making 55 appearances in a career spanning twelve years. In 1969 the Australian Law regarding the restriction of direct kicking into touch was adopted by the International Board. Williams was to become the world's leading full-back during the following decade, exploiting the new Law in an imaginative, enterprising fashion.

## 1969

| 1st v. NZ | 2nd v. NZ | v. AUSTRALIA |
|---|---|---|
| J.P.R. WILLIAMS | J.P.R. WILLIAMS | J.P.R. WILLIAMS |
| S.J. WATKINS | T.G.R. DAVIES | T.G.R. DAVIES 1T |
| K.S. JARRETT | K.S. JARRETT 2PG,1T | K.S. JARRETT 2C,2PG |
| T.G.R. DAVIES | S.J. DAWES | S.J. DAWES |
| M.C.R.RICHARDS | M.C.R. RICHARDS 1T | M.C.R. RICHARDS |
| B. JOHN | B. JOHN | B. JOHN |
| G.O. EDWARDS | G.O. EDWARDS | G.O. EDWARDS |
| D.WILLIAMS | D. WILLIAMS | D. WILLIAMS |
| J. YOUNG¹ | N.R. GALE | N.R. GALE |
| D.J. LLOYD | B.E. THOMAS | D.J. LLOYD |
| *B. PRICE | *B. PRICE | *B. PRICE |
| B.E. THOMAS | W.D. THOMAS | W.D. THOMAS |
| W.D. MORRIS | W.D. MORRIS | W.D. MORRIS 1T |
| T.M. DAVIES | T.M. DAVIES | T.M. DAVIES |
| J. TAYLOR | W.D. HUGHES | J. TAYLOR 1T |
| Christchurch | Auckland | Sydney C.G. |
| LOST 0-19 | LOST 12-33 | WON 19-16 |
| WALES: NIL | WALES: 2PG 2T | WALES: 2G 2PG 1T |
| NZ: 2G 1PG 2T | NZ: 3G 5PG 1DG | AUST.: 2G 2DG |
| 31 May 1969 | 14 Jun. 1969 | 21 Jun. 1969 |

¹Rep. by N.R. Gale

Wales were completely overwhelmed by the All Blacks in the two international matches on their first tour to New Zealand. The Welshmen were dominated in the scrums and line-outs, and conceded seven tries and 52 points in the Tests.

Norman Gale regained his place as Welsh hooker when Jeff Young had his jaw fractured in a fracas during the Christchurch Test. In an attempt to bolster the front row for the second Test, Brian Thomas, the Neath lock, was shifted to prop, the position in which he had been capped against New Zealand in 1967.

This was the stage in his career when Gerald Davies transferred from the centre to right wing. Davies played 35 times as a wing following his eleven appearances as a centre, and his 46 caps remain a record for a Welsh threequarter.

## 1969-70

| v. S. AFRICA | v. SCOTLAND | v. ENGLAND | v. IRELAND | v. FRANCE |
|---|---|---|---|---|
| J.P.R. WILLIAMS | J.P.R. WILLIAMS | J.P.R.WILLIAMS 1C,1T | J.P.R. WILLIAMS | J.P.R.WILLIAMS 2PG,1C |
| | | | | |
| P. BENNETT | †L.T.D. DANIEL 1T,1C | S.J. WATKINS | S.J. WATKINS | †R. MATHIAS |
| S.J. DAWES | S.J. DAWES 1T | S.J. DAWES | S.J. DAWES | *S.J. DAWES |
| W.H. RAYBOULD | P. BENNETT | W.H. RAYBOULD | W.H. RAYBOULD | †A.J. LEWIS |
| I. HALL | I. HALL | I. HALL | †K. HUGHES | J.L. SHANKLIN¹ |
| | | | | |
| B. JOHN | B. JOHN | B. JOHN 1T,1DG | B. JOHN | P. BENNETT |
| *G.O. EDWARDS 1PG,1T | *G.O EDWARDS 2C | *G.O. EDWARDS¹ | *G.O. EDWARDS | G.O. EDWARDS |
| | | | | |
| D. WILLIAMS | D. WILLIAMS | D. WILLIAMS | D. WILLIAMS | D.J. LLOYD |
| †V.C. PERRINS | V.C. PERRINS | J. YOUNG | J. YOUNG | J. YOUNG |
| †D.B. LLEWELLYN | D.B. LLEWELLYN 1T | D.B. LLEWELLYN | D.B. LLEWELLYN | D.B. LLEWELLYN |
| †T.G. EVANS | T.G. EVANS | T.G. EVANS | T.G. EVANS | †I.S. GALLACHER |
| W.D. THOMAS | W.D. THOMAS | W.D. THOMAS | W.D. THOMAS | W.D. THOMAS |
| W.D. MORRIS | W.D. MORRIS 1T | W.D. MORRIS | W.D. MORRIS | W.D. MORRIS 1T |
| T.M. DAVIES | T.M. DAVIES | T.M. DAVIES 1T | T.M. DAVIES | T.M. DAVIES |
| W.D. HUGHES | W.D. HUGHES | W.D. HUGHES | W.D. HUGHES | J. TAYLOR |
| | | | | |
| Cardiff Arms Park | Cardiff Arms Park | Twickenham | Lansdowne Road | Cardiff Arms Park |
| DRAWN 6-6 | WON 18-9 | WON 17-13 | LOST 0-14 | WON 11-6 |
| | | | | |
| WALES: 1PG 1T | WALES: 3G 1T | ENG.: 2G 1PG | IRE.: 1G 1PG 1DG 1T | WALES: 1G 2PG |
| SA: 1PG 1T | SCOT.: 1DG 1PG 1T | WALES: 1G 1DG 3T | WALES: NIL | FR.: 2T |
| | | | | |
| 24 Jan. 1970 | 7 Feb. 1970 | 28 Feb. 1970 | 14 Mar. 1970 | 4 Apr. 1970 |
| | | ¹Rep. by †Ray Hopkins 1T | | ¹Rep. by W.H. Raybould |

There were frequent changes to the threequarter line this season, where Gerald Davies was unavailable due to exams. Nevertheless, a last-minute corner try by Gareth Edwards against South Africa; a controlled forward effort on a windy day against Scotland; and a brilliant recovery led by substitute Ray Hopkins at Twickenham, kept Wales' unbeaten record intact. But then in Dublin, with the Triple Crown at stake, the Welsh had one of those days when everyone plays below form.

Wales' reward for victory in the last match of the season, however, was a share in the Championship with France. Phil Bennett, whose previous appearances had been at wing and centre, partnered Gareth Edwards for the first time in this match. Together they played 25 times for Wales and four times for the British Lions in internationals against IB nations, establishing a world record.

## 1970-71

| v. ENGLAND | v. SCOTLAND | v. IRELAND | v. FRANCE |
|---|---|---|---|
| J.P.R. WILLIAMS 1PG | J.P.R. WILLIAMS | J.P.R. WILLIAMS | J.P.R. WILLIAMS |
| | | | |
| T.G.R. DAVIES 2T | T.G.R. DAVIES 1T | T.G.R. DAVIES 2T | T.G.R. DAVIES |
| *S.J. DAWES | *S.J. DAWES | *S.J. DAWES | *S.J. DAWES |
| A.J. LEWIS | I. HALL | A.J. LEWIS | A.J. LEWIS |
| †J.C. BEVAN 1T | J.C. BEVAN | J.C. BEVAN | J.C. BEVAN |
| | | | |
| B. JOHN 2DG | B. JOHN 1T,1PG,1C | B. JOHN 2PG,1DG,1C | B. JOHN 1T,1PG |
| G.O. EDWARDS | G.O. EDWARDS 1T | G.O. EDWARDS 2T | G.O. EDWARDS 1T |
| | | | |
| D. WILLIAMS | D. WILLIAMS | D. WILLIAMS | D. WILLIAMS |
| J. YOUNG | J. YOUNG | J. YOUNG | J. YOUNG |
| D.B. LLEWELLYN | D.B. LLEWELLYN | D.B. LLEWELLYN | D.B. LLEWELLYN |
| †M.G. ROBERTS | M.G. ROBERTS | M.G. ROBERTS | M.G. ROBERTS |
| W.D. THOMAS | W.D. THOMAS | W.D.THOMAS | W.D. THOMAS |
| W.D. MORRIS | W.D. MORRIS | W.D. MORRIS | W.D. MORRIS |
| T.M. DAVIES | T.M. DAVIES | T.M. DAVIES | T.M. DAVIES |
| J. TAYLOR 2C | J. TAYLOR 1T,1C | J. TAYLOR | J. TAYLOR |
| | | | |
| Cardiff Arms Park | Murrayfield | Cardiff Arms Park | Stade Colombes |
| WON 22-6 | WON 19-18 | WON 23-9 | WON 9-5 |
| | | | |
| WALES:2G 1T 2DG 1PG | SCOT.: 2T 4PG | WALES: 1G 3T 2PG 1DG | FR.: 1G |
| ENG.: 1T 1PG | WALES: 2G 2T 1PG | IRE.: 3PG | WALES: 2T 1PG |
| | | | |
| 16 Jan. 1971 | 6 Feb. 1971 | 13 Mar. 1971 | 27 Mar. 1971 |

This was a Welsh team of all the talents. An experienced pack dominated their opponents. Behind them was a back-line which exuded confidence and possessed immense skill. Edwards and John exercised complete tactical control to propel Wales to the Triple Crown and Grand Slam, finding support from a wonderfully entertaining threequarter line (and full-back) who were all capable of transforming defence into spectacular offence. In the view of many eminent observers this was the finest side Wales ever produced. Fortunate to avoid injury, only sixteen players were needed to complete this successful campaign, and the side was also lucky to find in John Dawes a captain whose gifts of leadership exceeded his considerable talents as a passer and runner.

## 1971-72

| | v. ENGLAND | v. SCOTLAND | v. FRANCE |
|---|---|---|---|
| | J.P.R. WILLIAMS 1T | J.P.R. WILLIAMS[1] | J.P.R. WILLIAMS |
| | T.G.R. DAVIES | T.G.R. DAVIES 1T | T.G.R. DAVIES 1T |
| | †R.T.E. BERGIERS | R.T.E. BERGIERS 1T | R.T.E. BERGIERS |
| | A.J. LEWIS | A.J. LEWIS | A.J. LEWIS |
| | J.C. BEVAN | J.C. BEVAN | J.C. BEVAN 1T |
| | B. JOHN 1C,2PG | B. JOHN 3PG,3C | B. JOHN 4PG |
| | G.O. EDWARDS | G.O. EDWARDS 2T | G.O. EDWARDS |
| | *D.J. LLOYD | *D.J. LLOYD | *D.J. LLOYD |
| | J. YOUNG | J. YOUNG | J. YOUNG |
| | D.B. LLEWELLYN | D.B. LLEWELLYN | D.B. LLEWELLYN |
| | W.D. THOMAS | W.D. THOMAS | W.D. THOMAS |
| | T.G. EVANS | T.G. EVANS | T.G. EVANS |
| | W.D. MORRIS | W.D. MORRIS | W.D. MORRIS |
| | T.M. DAVIES | T.M. DAVIES | T.M. DAVIES[1] |
| | J. TAYLOR | J. TAYLOR 1T | J. TAYLOR |
| | Twickenham | Cardiff Arms Park | Cardiff Arms Park |
| | WON 12-3 | WON 35-12 | WON 20-6 |
| | ENG.: 1PG | WALES: 3G 3PG 2T | WALES: 4PG 2T |
| | WALES: 1G 2PG | SCOT.: 1G 2PG | FR.: 2PG |
| | 15 Jan. 1972 | 5 Feb. 1972 | 25 Mar. 1972 |
| | | [1]Rep. by P. Bennett | [1]Rep. by †D.L. Quinnell |

The Welsh side of 1972 was unaltered in their Championship matches, but political strife in Ireland prevented the WRU from fulfilling their fixture in Dublin. As a result, the Welsh side, on the brink of a second successive Grand Slam and Triple Crown, were denied the opportunity of playing against an unbeaten Irish side.

Wales fielded ten players who had been members of the successful 1971 British and Irish Lions, and a team of considerable experience and supreme skills won their three matches with style. Barry John scored 35 points, creating a new record for a Welshman in a Championship season, and passed Jack Bancroft's Welsh career record with his fourth penalty against the French. Then, in May, John announced his retirement from rugby. At the age of 27 he was still in his prime, but chose to stand down with grace, having been described as the outstanding player in world rugby.

## 1972-73

| | v. NZ | v. ENGLAND | v. SCOTLAND | v. IRELAND | v. FRANCE |
|---|---|---|---|---|---|
| | J.P.R. WILLIAMS | J.P.R. WILLIAMS | J.P.R. WILLIAMS | J.P.R. WILLIAMS | J.P.R. WILLIAMS |
| | T.G.R. DAVIES | T.G.R. DAVIES 1T | T.G.R. DAVIES | T.G.R. DAVIES | T.G.R. DAVIES |
| | R.T.E. BERGIERS | R.T.E. BERGIERS | R.T.E. BERGIERS | R.T.E. BERGIERS | R.T.E. BERGIERS |
| | J.L. SHANKLIN | *A.J. LEWIS 1T | *A.J. LEWIS | *A.J. LEWIS | A.J. LEWIS[1] |
| | J.C. BEVAN 1T | J.C. BEVAN 2T | J.C. BEVAN | J.L. SHANKLIN 1T | J.L. SHANKLIN |
| | P. BENNETT 4PG | P. BENNETT 1C | P. BENNETT 2PG | P. BENNETT 2PG,1C | P. BENNETT 1DG |
| | G.O. EDWARDS | G.O. EDWARDS 1T | G.O. EDWARDS | G.O. EDWARDS 1T | *G.O. EDWARDS |
| | †G. SHAW | G. SHAW | G. SHAW | G. SHAW | G. SHAW |
| | J. YOUNG | J. YOUNG | J. YOUNG | J. YOUNG | J. YOUNG |
| | D.B. LLEWELLYN | D.J. LLOYD | D.J. LLOYD | †P.D. LLEWELLYN | P.D. LLEWELLYN |
| | *W.D. THOMAS | W.D. THOMAS | W.D. THOMAS | W.D. THOMAS | W.D. THOMAS |
| | D.L. QUINNELL | D.L. QUINNELL | D.L. QUINNELL | M.G. ROBERTS | M.G. ROBERTS |
| | W.D. MORRIS | W.D. MORRIS | W.D. MORRIS | W.D. MORRIS | J. TAYLOR |
| | T.M. DAVIES | T.M. DAVIES | T.M. DAVIES | T.M. DAVIES | T.M. DAVIES |
| | J. TAYLOR | J. TAYLOR 1PG | J. TAYLOR 1PG | J. TAYLOR | †T.P. DAVID |
| | Cardiff Arms Park | Cardiff Arms Park | Murrayfield | Cardiff Arms Park | Parc des Princes |
| | LOST 16-19 | WON 25-9 | LOST 9-10 | WON 16-12 | LOST 3-12 |
| | WALES: 4PG 1T | WALES: 1G 1PG 4T | SCOT.: 1G 1T | WALES: 1G 2PG 1T | FR.: 1DG 3PG |
| | NZ: 5PG 1T | ENG.: 1DG 2PG | WALES: 3PG | IRE.: 1G 2PG | WALES: 1DG |
| | 2 Dec. 1972 | 20 Jan. 1973 | 3 Feb. 1973 | 10 Mar. 1973 | 24 Mar. 1973 |
| | | | | | [1]Rep. by †J.J. Williams |

A slow start in which they conceded ten points cost Wales an exciting game with the All Blacks. The sides were evenly matched, but a succession of technical infringements by the Welsh front-row allowed Karam to kick New Zealand into a big lead. Wales managed a late rally in the second half, and J.P.R. Williams was unlucky to have a try disallowed. As the tourists became rattled they resorted to late tackles and high tackles. Bennett narrowly failed to tie the match with a kick at goal in the last minute.

At the start of the Championship Wales were well-organised up front, with excellent halves to dictate the tactics, and an entertaining threequarter line. In a final flourish at Cardiff, the Welsh demolished England with two late tries, one by Bevan materialising from a breathless move in which every Welsh back handled the ball. Surprisingly, the Welsh found themselves dominated in the scrummages and line-outs in Scotland, and succumbed to their first Championship defeat in ten matches. The expertise of Edwards and the fine finishing of Jim Shanklin brought an encouraging win against Ireland, but in Paris the Welsh failed to play with any zest and defeat left them with a meaningless share in a Quintuple Tie in the Championship.

## 1973-74

| v. AUSTRALIA | v. SCOTLAND | v. IRELAND | v. FRANCE | v. ENGLAND |
|---|---|---|---|---|
| J.P.R. WILLIAMS | J.P.R. WILLIAMS | J.P.R. WILLIAMS | J.P.R. WILLIAMS | †W.R. BLYTH |
| | | | | |
| T.G.R. DAVIES 1T | T.G.R. DAVIES | †C.F.W. REES | T.G.R. DAVIES | T.G.R. DAVIES |
| K. HUGHES | K. HUGHES | I. HALL | I. HALL | R.T.E. BERGIERS |
| R.T.E. BERGIERS | I. HALL | †A.A.J. FINLAYSON | A.A.J. FINLAYSON | A.A.J. FINLAYSON |
| J.J. WILLIAMS | J.J. WILLIAMS | J.J. WILLIAMS 1T | J.J. WILLIAMS 1T | J.J. WILLIAMS |
| | | | | |
| P. BENNETT 4PG | P. BENNETT 1C | P. BENNETT 1C,1PG | P. BENNETT 3PG | P. BENNETT 2PG,1C |
| *G.O. EDWARDS[1] | *G.O. EDWARDS | *G.O. EDWARDS | *G.O. EDWARDS 1DG | *G.O. EDWARDS |
| | | | | |
| G. SHAW | G. SHAW | †W.P.J. WILLIAMS | W.P.J. WILLIAMS | G. SHAW |
| †R.W. WINDSOR 1T | R.W. WINDSOR | R.W. WINDSOR | R.W. WINDSOR | R.W. WINDSOR |
| P.D. LLEWELLYN | P.D. LLEWELLYN | G. SHAW | G. SHAW | P.D. LLEWELLYN |
| †A.J. MARTIN | A.J. MARTIN | A.J. MARTIN | †I.R. ROBINSON | I.R. ROBINSON[1] |
| D.L. QUINNELL | D.L. QUINNELL | †G.A.D. WHEEL | D.L. QUINNELL | W.D. THOMAS |
| W.D. MORRIS 1T | W.D. MORRIS | W.D. MORRIS | W.D. MORRIS | W.D. MORRIS |
| T.M. DAVIES | T.M. DAVIES | T.M. DAVIES | T.M. DAVIES | T.M. DAVIES 1T |
| T.P. DAVID | †T.J. COBNER 1T | T.J. COBNER | T.J. COBNER | T.J. COBNER |
| | | | | |
| Cardiff Arms Park | Cardiff Arms Park | Lansdowne Road | Cardiff Arms Park | Twickenham |
| WON 24-0 | WON 6-0 | DRAWN 9-9 | DRAWN 16-16 | LOST 12-16 |
| | | | | |
| WALES: 3T 4PG | WALES: 1G | IRE.: 3PG | WALES: 3PG 1DG 1T | ENG.: 1G 2PG 1T |
| AUST.: NIL | SCOT.: NIL | WALES: 1G 1PG | FR.: 3PG 1DG 1T | WALES: 1G 2PG |
| | | | | |
| 10 Nov. 1973 | 19 Jan. 1974 | 2 Feb. 1974 | 16 Feb. 1974 | 16 Mar. 1974 |
| | | | | |
| [1]Rep. by †R.C. Shell | | | | [1]Rep. by G.A.D. Wheel |

Wales overpowered the Wallabies in November, the home pack using a five-stone advantage to good effect. Bobby Windsor, the Pontypool hooker, celebrated his debut with a splendid try and won the tight head count by 3-1.

In the Championship the side struggled to live up to its high reputation. Another new Pontypool forward, Terry Cobner, was outstanding in the pack and scored the only try of the match in his debut against Scotland. Draws against Ireland and France kept Welsh hopes of the Championship alive, but at Twickenham England deserved their first win over Wales for eleven years.

Two key forwards from the first half of this Welsh golden era played for the last time at Twickenham. Dai Morris had gained 34 caps and become Wales' most capped flanker, while Delme Thomas ended his international career with 25 caps.

## 1974-75

| v. FRANCE | v. ENGLAND | v. SCOTLAND | v. IRELAND |
|---|---|---|---|
| J.P.R. WILLIAMS | J.P.R. WILLIAMS | J.P.R. WILLIAMS | J.P.R. WILLIAMS |
| | | | |
| T.G.R. DAVIES 1T | T.G.R. DAVIES 1T | T.G.R. DAVIES | T.G.R. DAVIES 1T |
| †S.P. FENWICK 1T,1PG,1C | S.P. FENWICK 1T | S.P. FENWICK 2PG[1] | R.T.E. BERGIERS 1T |
| †R.W.R. GRAVELL | R.W.R. GRAVELL | R.W.R. GRAVELL | R.W.R. GRAVELL |
| J.J. WILLIAMS | J.J. WILLIAMS 1T | J.J. WILLIAMS | J.J. WILLIAMS 1T |
| | | | |
| †J.D. BEVAN | J.D. BEVAN | J.D. BEVAN[2] | P. BENNETT 2PG,3C |
| G.O. EDWARDS 1T | G.O. EDWARDS | G.O. EDWARDS | G.O. EDWARDS 1T |
| | | | |
| †A.G. FAULKNER | A.G. FAULKNER | A.G. FAULKNER | A.G. FAULKNER 1T |
| R.W. WINDSOR | R.W. WINDSOR | R.W. WINDSOR | R.W. WINDSOR |
| †G. PRICE 1T | G. PRICE | G. PRICE | G. PRICE |
| A.J. MARTIN | A.J. MARTIN 1C,2PG | A.J. MARTIN | A.J. MARTIN |
| G.A.D. WHEEL | G.A.D. WHEEL[1] | M.G. ROBERTS | G.A.D. WHEEL |
| T.J. COBNER 1T | T.J. COBNER | T.J. COBNER | T.J. COBNER |
| *T.M. DAVIES | *T.M. DAVIES | *T.M. DAVIES | *T.M. DAVIES |
| †T.P. EVANS | T.P. EVANS | T.P. EVANS 1T | T.P. EVANS |
| | | | |
| Parc des Princes | Cardiff Arms Park | Murrayfield | Cardiff Arms Park |
| WON 25-10 | WON 20-4 | LOST 10-12 | WON 32-4 |
| | | | |
| FR.: 2PG 1T | WALES: 1G 2PG 2T | SCOT.: 3PG 1DG | WALES: 3G 2PG 2T |
| WALES: 1G 1PG 4T | ENG.: 1T | WALES: 2PG 1T | IRE.: 1T |
| | | | |
| 18 Jan. 1975 | 15 Feb. 1975 | 1 Mar. 1975 | 15 Mar. 1975 |
| | | | |
| | [1]Rep. by D.L. Quinnell | [1]Rep. by W.R. Blyth | |
| | | [2]Rep. by P. Bennett | |

Mervyn Davies, the world's leading number eight forward, took over the Welsh captaincy with John Dawes succeeding Clive Rowlands as national team coach. Six new caps were named for the season's opening international in Paris, and for the first time an entire club front-row played for Wales. Pontypool supplied the trio of Price, Windsor and Faulkner, as well as Terry Cobner in the pack. These four were the cornerstone of a magnificent pack which paved the way for Wales' biggest victory in Paris since 1911.

Another powerful forward effort enabled Wales to overwhelm England in the first half at Cardiff, the Welsh backs showing a refreshing readiness to run the ball in an entertaining manner. In Scotland, however, injuries to Bevan and Fenwick upset the balance of the back division and, although Wales scored the only try of the match, Scotland deserved their victory.

The fifteen produced its finest display of the season against Ireland, running up a record Welsh total of 32 points for matches against the Irish. Bennett, Bergiers and Gravell inspired five tries by a team which deserved its outright Championship title.

## 1975-76

| v. AUSTRALIA | v. ENGLAND | v. SCOTLAND | v. IRELAND | v. FRANCE |
|---|---|---|---|---|
| J.P.R. WILLIAMS | J.P.R. WILLIAMS 2T | J.P.R. WILLIAMS | J.P.R. WILLIAMS | J.P.R. WILLIAMS |
| J.J. WILLIAMS 3T | T.G.R. DAVIES | T.G.R. DAVIES | T.G.R. DAVIES 2T | T.G.R. DAVIES |
| R.W.R. GRAVELL | R.W.R. GRAVELL | R.W.R. GRAVELL | R.W.R. GRAVELL | R.W.R. GRAVELL |
| S.P. FENWICK 1PG,2C | S.P. FENWICK 3C | S.P. FENWICK 1DG | S.P. FENWICK | S.P. FENWICK 2PG |
| C.F.W. REES | J.J. WILLIAMS | J.J. WILLIAMS 1T | J.J. WILLIAMS | J.J. WILLIAMS 1T |
| J.D. BEVAN 1DG | P. BENNETT | P. BENNETT 3PG,2C | P. BENNETT 3C,1T,3PG | P. BENNETT 2PG |
| G.O. EDWARDS 1T | G.O. EDWARDS 1T | G.O. EDWARDS 1T | G.O. EDWARDS 1T | G.O. EDWARDS |
| A.G. FAULKNER | A.G. FAULKNER | A.G. FAULKNER | A.G. FAULKNER | A.G. FAULKNER |
| R.W. WINDSOR | R.W. WINDSOR | R.W. WINDSOR | R.W. WINDSOR | R.W. WINDSOR |
| G. PRICE | G. PRICE | G. PRICE | G. PRICE | G. PRICE[1] |
| A.J. MARTIN 1C | A.J. MARTIN 1PG | A.J. MARTIN | A.J. MARTIN 1PG | A.J. MARTIN 1PG |
| G.A.D. WHEEL | G.A.D. WHEEL | G.A.D. WHEEL | G.A.D. WHEEL | G.A.D. WHEEL |
| T.J. COBNER | T.J. COBNER | T.J. COBNER | T.P. DAVID | T.P. DAVID |
| *T.M. DAVIES | *T.M. DAVIES | *T.M. DAVIES | *T.M. DAVIES | *T.M. DAVIES |
| T.P. EVANS | T.P. EVANS | T.P. EVANS 1T | T.P. EVANS | T.P. EVANS |
| Cardiff Arms Park WON 28-3 | Twickenham WON 21-9 | Cardiff Arms Park WON 28-6 | Lansdowne Road WON 34-9 | Cardiff Arms Park WON 19-13 |
| WALES: 3G 1PG 1DG 1T AUST.: 1PG | ENG.: 3PG WALES 3G 1PG | WALES: 2G 3PG 1DG 1T SCOT.: 1G | IRE.: 3PG WALES: 3G 4PG 1T | WALES: 5PG 1T FR.: 1G 1PG 1T |
| 20 Dec. 1975 | 17 Jan. 1976 | 7 Feb. 1976 | 21 Feb. 1976 | 6 Mar. 1976 |

[1]Rep. by [†]F.M.D. Knill

Wales began their four "Crowning Years" with five wins in 1976. During the course of their Triple Crown and Grand Slam season records tumbled. The side scored 102 points in the Championship, and Phil Bennett notched up 38 points for the season, including 19 in the game in Dublin to equal the match records of Jack Bancroft and Keith Jarrett. Bennett also overtook the previous career record held by Barry John, while Gareth Edwards became the first man to score eighteen tries for Wales.

Against England, J.P.R. Williams became the most-capped full-back in Welsh history, passing the 75-year-old record of Billy Bancroft. Victory against Ireland in the Triple Crown match was Wales' first win in Dublin for a dozen years, and their total of 34 points was a record Welsh tally against Ireland.

The Grand Slam decider with France was a tense match with a hectic climax. Wales came from behind to lead by 19-13. Then in the closing stages, it seemed likely that the French right wing would score. But a shoulder-charge by J.P.R. Williams poleaxed the Frenchman and ensured the Welsh Grand Slam. Weeks later, however, captain Mervyn Davies' career ended when he suffered a brain haemorrhage in a Swansea club match. His 38 caps established a new record for a Welsh forward, and his 46 appearances (which include eight Tests for the Lions) are a world record for a number eight.

## 1976-77

| v. IRELAND | v. FRANCE | v. ENGLAND | v. SCOTLAND |
|---|---|---|---|
| J.P.R. WILLIAMS 1T | J.P.R. WILLIAMS | J.P.R. WILLIAMS 1T | J.P.R. WILLIAMS |
| T.G.R. DAVIES 1T | T.G.R. DAVIES[1] | T.G.R. DAVIES | T.G.R. DAVIES |
| S.P. FENWICK 1DG | S.P. FENWICK 3PG | S.P. FENWICK 2PG | S.P. FENWICK |
| [†]D.H. BURCHER | D.H. BURCHER | D.H. BURCHER | D.H. BURCHER |
| J.J. WILLIAMS | J.J. WILLIAMS | J.J. WILLIAMS | J.J. WILLIAMS 1T |
| *P. BENNETT 2PG,2C | *P. BENNETT | *P. BENNETT | *P. BENNETT 1T,2PG,2C |
| G.O. EDWARDS | G.O. EDWARDS | G.O. EDWARDS 1T | G.O. EDWARDS |
| G. SHAW | G. SHAW | [†]C. WILLIAMS | C.WILLIAMS |
| R.W. WINDSOR | R.W. WINDSOR | R.W. WINDSOR | R.W. WINDSOR |
| G. PRICE | G. PRICE | G. PRICE | G. PRICE |
| A.J. MARTIN | A.J. MARTIN | A.J. MARTIN | A.J. MARTIN |
| G.A.D. WHEEL | D.L. QUINNELL | G.A.D. WHEEL | G.A.D. WHEEL |
| T.P. EVANS[1] | T.J. COBNER | T.J. COBNER | T.J. COBNER |
| [†]J. SQUIRE | J. SQUIRE | D.L. QUINNELL | D.L. QUINNELL |
| [†]R.C. BURGESS 1T | R.C. BURGESS | R.C. BURGESS | R.C. BURGESS |
| Cardiff Arms Park WON 25-9 | Parc des Princes LOST 9-16 | Cardiff Arms Park WON 14-9 | Murrayfield WON 18-9 |
| WALES: 2G 2PG 1DG 1T IRE.: 3PG | FR.: 1G 2PG 1T WALES: 3PG | WALES: 2PG 2T ENG.: 3PG | SCOT.: 1G 1DG WALES: 2G 2PG |
| 15 Jan. 1977 | 5 Feb. 1977 | 5 Mar. 1977 | 19 Mar. 1977 |

[1]Rep. by D.L. Quinnell

[1]Rep. by [†]G.L. Evans

Phil Bennett led Wales to their second successive Triple Crown in 1977, but the side was well beaten in Paris by a French side which went on to take the Grand Slam. Wales thus finished as runners-up in the Championship: something which no Triple Crown winner had experienced before. The match with Ireland was very close until the superiority of the Welsh forwards began to tell in the last quarter. Then the backs paved the way for two excellent tries by Gerald Davies and J.P.R. Williams, and Burgess, the Ebbw Vale flanker, scored a try on his debut. But Wales' victory was marred by the sending-off just before half time of Geoff Wheel, the Swansea lock. He became the first Welsh player to be ordered from the field in an international.

## 1977-78

| v. ENGLAND | v. SCOTLAND | v. IRELAND | v. FRANCE |
|---|---|---|---|
| J.P.R. WILLIAMS | J.P.R. WILLIAMS | J.P.R. WILLIAMS | J.P.R. WILLIAMS |
| | | | |
| T.G.R. DAVIES | T.G.R. DAVIES | T.G.R. DAVIES | J.J. WILLIAMS |
| R.W.R. GRAVELL | R.W.R. GRAVELL 1T | R.W.R. GRAVELL | R.W.R. GRAVELL |
| S.P. FENWICK | S.P. FENWICK 1T | S.P. FENWICK 1T,4PG | S.P. FENWICK 1DG |
| J.J. WILLIAMS | J.J. WILLIAMS | J.J. WILLIAMS 1T | G.L. EVANS |
| | | | |
| *P. BENNETT 3PG | *P. BENNETT 1DG,1PG | *P. BENNETT | *P. BENNETT 2T,1C |
| G.O. EDWARDS | G.O. EDWARDS 1T | G.O. EDWARDS | G.O. EDWARDS 1DG |
| | | | |
| A.G. FAULKNER | A.G. FAULKNER | A.G. FAULKNER | A.G. FAULKNER |
| R.W. WINDSOR | R.W. WINDSOR | R.W. WINDSOR | R.W. WINDSOR |
| G. PRICE | G. PRICE | G. PRICE | G. PRICE |
| A.J. MARTIN | A.J. MARTIN | A.J. MARTIN | A.J. MARTIN |
| G.A.D. WHEEL | G.A.D. WHEEL | G.A.D. WHEEL | G.A.D. WHEEL |
| J. SQUIRE | T.J. COBNER | J. SQUIRE | J. SQUIRE |
| D.L. QUINNELL | D.L. QUINNELL 1T | D.L. QUINNELL | D.L. QUINNELL |
| T.J. COBNER | J. SQUIRE | T.J. COBNER | T.J. COBNER |
| Twickenham | Cardiff Arms Park | Lansdowne Road | Cardiff Arms Park |
| WON 9-6 | WON 22-14 | WON 20-16 | WON 16-7 |
| ENG.: 2PG | WALES: 1PG 1DG 4T | IRE.: 3PG 1DG 1T | WALES: 1G 2DG 1T |
| WALES: 3PG | SCOT.: 2PG 2T | WALES: 4PG 2T | FR.: 1DG 1T |
| 4 Feb. 1978 | 18 Feb. 1978 | 4 Mar. 1978 | 18 Mar. 1978 |

Wales became the first nation to win three consecutive Triple Crowns, and by beating France in a grand finale at Cardiff, added the Grand Slam for the eighth time, a record. Both of Wales' away matches were tight encounters in which Edward's tactical expertise, J.P.R. Williams' sound defence, and the determined approach of a seasoned threequarter line were just sufficient to secure wins.

Against Scotland, Gareth Edwards scored his twentieth (and last) try for Wales, but for his final appearance in the Welsh jersey, against France, he produced one of the best performances of his long and brilliant career. His tactical kicking and his service to Bennett inspired the Welsh side to a victory by nine points, after France had led 7-0 earlier in the match.

Bennett too made an impressive contribution to the Grand Slam match, his final game for Wales. He scored two splendid tries and a conversion, ending his international career with a record 166 points for Wales and a world record total of 210 points in 29 matches for Wales and eight for the Lions.

## 1978

| 1st v. AUSTRALIA | 2nd v. AUSTRALIA |
|---|---|
| J.P.R. WILLIAMS | †A.J. DONOVAN[1] |
| | |
| T.G.R. DAVIES 1T | *T.G.R. DAVIES 1T |
| R.W.R. GRAVELL | R.W.R. GRAVELL |
| S.P. FENWICK | S.P. FENWICK |
| J.J. WILLIAMS | J.J. WILLIAMS |
| | |
| †W.G. DAVIES | W.G. DAVIES 2PG,1DG |
| †D.B. WILLIAMS 1T | †T.D. HOLMES 1T |
| | |
| A.G. FAULKNER | A.G. FAULKNER |
| R.W. WINDSOR | R.W. WINDSOR |
| G. PRICE | G. PRICE[2] |
| A.J. MARTIN | A.J. MARTIN |
| G.A.D. WHEEL | G.A.D. WHEEL |
| *T.J. COBNER | S.M. LANE |
| D.L. QUINNELL | †C.E. DAVIS |
| J. SQUIRE[1] | J.P.R. WILLIAMS |
| Brisbane | Sydney C.G. |
| LOST 8-18 | LOST 17-19 |
| AUST.: 1G 4PG | AUST.: 3PG 2DG 1T |
| WALES: 2T | WALES: 2PG 1DG 2T |
| 11 Jun. 1978 | 17 Jun. 1978 |
| [1] Rep. by †S.M. Lane | [1] Rep. by G.L. Evans |
| | [2] Rep. by †S.J. Richardson |

Under the management of Clive Rowlands and John Dawes, Wales undertook a nine-match tour of Australia in the summer of 1978. The tourists, champions of the Northern Hemisphere, not only had their pride dented by competent Australian sides in the Tests, but also lost to Sydney and Australian Capital Territory in the tour matches.

Tries by Gerald Davies in each of the internationals brought his career total level with Gareth Edwards' record of twenty. And in the Test at Sydney, for which J.P.R. Williams was orginally selected as a flanker, the Welsh threequarter line of Davies, Gravell, Fenwick and J.J. Williams appeared together for the twelfth and final time in an international.

Gareth Davies and Terry Holmes proved suitable successors to Phil Bennett and Gareth Edwards. Holmes displayed considerable strength and courage at Sydney, barging over for a try on his debut. But the match was marred by rough play. Price had his jaw broken after three minutes, Donovan's replacement Gareth Evans sustained a fractured cheekbone in his first tackle, and J.J. Williams had to hobble around with a twisted ankle.

## 1978-79

| v. NZ | v. SCOTLAND | v. IRELAND | v. FRANCE | v. ENGLAND |
|---|---|---|---|---|
| *J.P.R. WILLIAMS | *J.P.R. WILLIAMS | *J.P.R. WILLIAMS | *J.P.R. WILLIAMS | *J.P.R. WILLIAMS[1] |
| J.J. WILLIAMS | †H.E. REES 1T | H.E. REES | H.E. REES | H.E. REES 1T |
| R.W.R. GRAVELL | R.W.R. GRAVELL | R.W.R. GRAVELL | †D.S. RICHARDS | D.S. RICHARDS 1T |
| S.P. FENWICK 1PG | S.P. FENWICK 3PG,1C | S.P. FENWICK 4PG,2C | S.P. FENWICK 3PG | S.P. FENWICK 1C |
| C.F.W. REES | J.J. WILLIAMS | J.J. WILLIAMS | J.J. WILLIAMS | J.J. WILLIAMS 1T |
| W.G. DAVIES 3PG | W.G. DAVIES | W.G. DAVIES | W.G. DAVIES | W.G. DAVIES 1DG |
| T.D. HOLMES | T.D. HOLMES 1T | T.D. HOLMES | T.D. HOLMES 1T | T.D. HOLMES |
| A.G. FAULKNER | A.G. FAULKNER | A.G. FAULKNER | A.G. FAULKNER | S.J. RICHARDSON |
| R.W. WINDSOR | R.W. WINDSOR | R.W. WINDSOR | R.W. WINDSOR | †A.J. PHILLIPS |
| G. PRICE | G. PRICE | G. PRICE | G. PRICE | G. PRICE |
| A.J. MARTIN | A.J. MARTIN | A.J. MARTIN 1T | A.J. MARTIN | A.J. MARTIN 1C |
| G.A.D. WHEEL | G.A.D. WHEEL | G.A.D. WHEEL[1] | †B.G. CLEGG | M.G. ROBERTS 1T |
| †P. RINGER | P. RINGER | P. RINGER 1T | P. RINGER | P. RINGER 1T |
| D.L. QUINNELL | D.L. QUINNELL | D.L. QUINNELL | D.L. QUINNELL | D.L. QUINNELL |
| J. SQUIRE | J. SQUIRE | J. SQUIRE | J. SQUIRE | J. SQUIRE |
| Cardiff Arms Park | Murrayfield | Cardiff Arms Park | Parc des Princes | Cardiff Arms Park |
| LOST 12-13 | WON 19-13 | WON 24-21 | LOST 13-14 | WON 27-3 |
| WALES: 4PG | SCOT.: 3PG 1T | WALES: 2G 4PG | FR.: 2PG 2T | WALES: 2G 1DG 3T |
| NZ: 3PG 1T | WALES: 1G 3PG 1T | IRE.: 2G 3PG | WALES: 3PG 1T | ENG.: 1PG |
| 11 Nov. 1978 | 20 Jan. 1979 | 3 Feb. 1979 | 17 Feb. 1979 | 17 Mar. 1979 |
| | | [1]Rep. by S.M. Lane | | [1]Rep. by †C. Griffiths |

This was an experimental side which was not expected to achieve any glittering prizes. The departures of Bennett, Edwards, Gerald Davies and Cobner, it was felt, would leave Wales too short of experience for the encounter with the All Blacks. But a young, spirited side led by J.P.R. Williams gave the New Zealanders a stiff test at Cardiff, where the all-round kicking skills of Gareth Davies kept Wales in the lead until the final moments of the game.

Elgan Rees and Paul Ringer were worthy successors to Gerald Davies and Terry Cobner. Rees scored important tries against Scotland and England, while Ringer's storming play and pace in the loose brought him tries against Ireland and England. The famed Pontypool front row played together for a record 19th time in the international in Paris.

The "Decade of the Dragon" ended with a convincing win over England at Cardiff. Composure at half-back, complete dominance up front, and committed defence enabled Wales to run away to their biggest win over the English since 1905, and brought Wales the Championship title as well as a fourth Triple Crown in four years.

## 1979-80

| v. FRANCE | v. ENGLAND | v. SCOTLAND | v. IRELAND |
|---|---|---|---|
| W.R. BLYTH | W.R. BLYTH | W.R. BLYTH 1C | W.R. BLYTH 1T |
| H.E. REES 1T | H.E. REES 1T | H.E. REES | H.E. REES |
| D.S. RICHARDS 1T | D.S. RICHARDS | D.S. RICHARDS 1T | D.S. RICHARDS |
| S.P. FENWICK | S.P. FENWICK | S.P. FENWICK 1PG | S.P. FENWICK 1PG |
| †L. KEEN | L. KEEN | L. KEEN 1T | L. KEEN |
| W.G. DAVIES 1C | W.G. DAVIES | W.G. DAVIES[1] | P.J. MORGAN |
| T.D. HOLMES 1T | T.D. HOLMES | T.D. HOLMES 1T | T.D. HOLMES |
| C. WILLIAMS | C. WILLIAMS | C. WILLIAMS | C. WILLIAMS |
| A.J. PHILLIPS | A.J. PHILLIPS | A.J. PHILLIPS | A.J. PHILLIPS |
| G. PRICE 1T | G. PRICE | G. PRICE | G. PRICE |
| A.J. MARTIN | A.J. MARTIN | A.J. MARTIN | A.J. MARTIN |
| G.A.D. WHEEL | G.A.D. WHEEL | G.A.D. WHEEL | G.A.D. WHEEL |
| P. RINGER | P. RINGER | S.M. LANE | S.M. LANE |
| †E.T. BUTLER | E.T. BUTLER | E.T. BUTLER | E.T. BUTLER |
| *J. SQUIRE | *J. SQUIRE 1T | *J. SQUIRE | *J. SQUIRE |
| Cardiff Arms Park | Twickenham | Cardiff Arms Park | Lansdowne Road |
| WON 18-9 | LOST 8-9 | WON 17-6 | LOST 7-21 |
| WALES: 1G 3T | ENG.: 3PG | WALES: 1G 1PG 2T | IRE.: 3G 1PG |
| FR.: 1G 1DG | WALES: 2T | SCOT.: 1G | WALES: 1PG 1T |
| 19 Jan. 1980 | 16 Feb. 1980 | 1 Mar. 1980 | 15 Mar. 1980 |
| | | [1]Rep. by †P.J. Morgan | |

Wales, under the guidance of new coach John Lloyd, began the season by setting a record. Their win against France was their 23rd consecutive home match without defeat in the Championship, and passed the previous record of 22 successive wins against the Five Nations, set between 1900-1912 during the first golden era of Welsh rugby.

But the French match was soured by rough play, and French allegations of violence by the Welsh were not totally unjustified. In Wales' next game, against England in a match built up by the press as the showdown of the season, further thuggery (for which both sides were equally responsible) culminated in the expulsion of Paul Ringer after he had committed a late tackle.

Understandably, the WRU issued a strong statement to the effect that better behaviour on the field was expected of its international representatives. But the side showed unnecessary restraint in the match with Scotland, despite a convincing victory, and a season which had started full of promise ended in a disappointing performance in Dublin.

## 1980-81

| v. NZ | v. ENGLAND | v. SCOTLAND | v. IRELAND | v. FRANCE |
|---|---|---|---|---|
| J.P.R. WILLIAMS | J.P.R. WILLIAMS | J.P.R. WILLIAMS | G. EVANS 2PG | G. EVANS 1C,3PG |
| | | | | |
| H.E. REES[1] | R.A. ACKERMAN | R.A. ACKERMAN | D.S. RICHARDS | C.F.W. REES |
| D.S. RICHARDS | D.S. RICHARDS | D.S. RICHARDS | R.W.R. GRAVELL | R.W.R. GRAVELL |
| *S.P. FENWICK 1PG | *S.P. FENWICK 1C,4PG | *S.P. FENWICK 2PG | P.J. MORGAN[1] | D.S. RICHARDS 1T |
| †R.A. ACKERMAN | †D.L. NICHOLAS | D.L. NICHOLAS[1] | D.L. NICHOLAS | D.L. NICHOLAS |
| | | | | |
| W.G. DAVIES | W.G. DAVIES 1DG | W.G. DAVIES | †G.P. PEARCE 1DG | G.P. PEARCE |
| T.D. HOLMES | D.B. WILLIAMS | D.B. WILLIAMS | †G. WILLIAMS | G. WILLIAMS |
| | | | | |
| C. WILLIAMS | †I. STEPHENS | I. STEPHENS | I. STEPHENS | I. STEPHENS |
| A.J. PHILLIPS | A.J. PHILLIPS | A.J. PHILLIPS | A.J. PHILLIPS | A.J. PHILLIPS |
| G. PRICE | G. PRICE | G. PRICE | G. PRICE | G. PRICE |
| D.L. QUINNELL | C.E. DAVIS 1T | C.E. DAVIS | A.J. MARTIN | A.J. MARTIN |
| A.J. MARTIN | G.A.D. WHEEL | G.A.D. WHEEL | G.A.D. WHEEL | G.A.D. WHEEL |
| P. RINGER | †J.R. LEWIS | J.R. LEWIS | J.R. LEWIS | J.R. LEWIS |
| †G.P. WILLIAMS | G.P. WILLIAMS | G.P. WILLIAMS | *J. SQUIRE | *J. SQUIRE |
| J. SQUIRE[2] | J. SQUIRE | J. SQUIRE | R.C. BURGESS | R.C. BURGESS |
| | | | | |
| Cardiff Arms Park | Cardiff Arms Park | Murrayfield | Cardiff Arms Park | Parc des Princes |
| LOST 3-23 | WON 21-19 | LOST 6-15 | WON 9-8 | LOST 15-19 |
| | | | | |
| WALES: 1PG | WALES: 1G 4PG 1DG | SCOT.: 2G 1PG | WALES: 2PG 1DG | FR.: 5PG 1T |
| NZ: 2G 1PG 2T | ENG.: 5PG 1T | WALES: 2PG | IRE.: 2T | WALES: 1G 3PG |
| | | | | |
| 1 Nov. 1980 | 17 Jan. 1981 | 7 Feb. 1981 | 21 Feb. 1981 | 7 Mar. 1981 |
| | | | | |
| [1]Rep. by P.J. Morgan | | [1]Rep. by †G. Evans | [1]Rep. by A.J. Donovan | |
| [2]Rep. by E.T. Butler | | | | |

To celebrate their Centenary season, the WRU invited the All Blacks for a short tour which concluded with an international at Cardiff. The tourists won all of the games, routing Wales in the Test by twenty points.

J.P.R. Williams, who had announced his retirement from representative football in 1979, returned for three matches at the start of the season, extending his Welsh cap total to 55, a new Welsh record.

Fenwick was dropped after the defeat at Murrayfield. He had been a dependable threequarter during the later stages of the "Crowning Years", and his useful place-kicking had contributed to many Welsh victories. Altogether he had scored 152 points in his 30 appearances, and had become Wales' most-capped centre.

## 1981-82

| v. AUSTRALIA | v. IRELAND | v. FRANCE | v. ENGLAND | v. SCOTLAND |
|---|---|---|---|---|
| G. EVANS 3PG,1C | G. EVANS 1C,1PG | G. EVANS 6PG | G. EVANS | G. EVANS 4PG,1C |
| | | | | |
| R.A. ACKERMAN | R.A. ACKERMAN | R.A. ACKERMAN | R.A. ACKERMAN | R.A. ACKERMAN |
| †P.C.T. DANIELS | D.S. RICHARDS | D.S. RICHARDS | R.W.R. GRAVELL | R.W.R. GRAVELL |
| A.J. DONOVAN | P.C.T. DANIELS | R.W.R. GRAVELL | A.J. DONOVAN | A.J. DONOVAN |
| C.F.W. REES | C.F.W. REES | C.F.W. REES | C.F.W. REES | C.F.W. REES |
| | | | | |
| *W.G. DAVIES 1DG | *W.G. DAVIES[1] | *W.G. DAVIES | *W.G. DAVIES 1DG | *W.G. DAVIES |
| T.D. HOLMES | T.D. HOLMES 1T | T.D. HOLMES 1T | T.D. HOLMES[1] | G. WILLIAMS |
| | | | | |
| I. STEPHENS | I. STEPHENS | I. STEPHENS | I. STEPHENS | I. STEPHENS |
| A.J. PHILLIPS | A.J. PHILLIPS | A.J. PHILLIPS | A.J. PHILLIPS | A.J. PHILLIPS |
| G. PRICE | G. PRICE | G. PRICE | G. PRICE | G. PRICE |
| †R.D. MORIARTY 1T | G.A.D. WHEEL | †S. SUTTON | S. SUTTON | †R.L. NORSTER |
| G.A.D. WHEEL | R.D. MORIARTY | R.D. MORIARTY | R.D. MORIARTY | R.D. MORIARTY |
| †M. DAVIES | M. DAVIES | R.C. BURGESS | R.C. BURGESS | R.C. BURGESS |
| J. SQUIRE | J. SQUIRE | J. SQUIRE | J. SQUIRE | E.T. BUTLER 1T |
| G.P. WILLIAMS | G.P. WILLIAMS | J.R. LEWIS | J.R. LEWIS 1T | J.R. LEWIS |
| | | | | |
| Cardiff Arms Park | Lansdowne Road | Cardiff Arms Park | Twickenham | Cardiff Arms Park |
| WON 18-13 | LOST 12-20 | WON 22-12 | LOST 7-17 | LOST 18-34 |
| | | | | |
| WALES: 1G 3PG 1DG | IRE.: 1G 2PG 2T | WALES: 6PG 1T | ENG.: 3PG 2T | WALES: 1G 4PG |
| AUST.: 1G 1PG 1T | WALES: 1G 1PG 1DG | FR.: 1G 2PG | WALES: 1DG 1T | SCOT.: 4G 2DG 1T |
| | | | | |
| 5 Dec. 1981 | 23 Jan. 1982 | 6 Feb. 1982 | 6 Mar. 1982 | 20 Mar. 1982 |
| | [1]Rep. by G.P. Pearce 1DG | | [1]Rep. by G. Williams | |

The season started with a convincing victory over the Australians. In an entertaining game, the Welsh captain Gareth Davies exercised a tight tactical control of events and Richard Moriarty, a new cap at lock, made an impressive impact in the tight and loose. Indeed, his try following brilliant play by the Welsh backs gave Wales the initiative to overtake the Wallabies, who had led 13-6 at the time of Moriarty's vital score.

But Gareth Davies' side was disappointing in the Championship, and finished with the wooden spoon for the first time since 1967. Against France, in the only Championship success of the season, Gwyn Evans equalled the world record of six penalty goals in a match, but defeat by Scotland in March ended Wales' record run of 27 home matches in the Championship without loss.

Geoff Wheel, the Swansea tool-maker, played the last of his 32 games in the postponed match with Ireland. Wheel's immense upper-body strength made him the outstanding mauler of his generation, and he had partnered Allan Martin, the Aberavon lineout expert, on 27 occasions to create a second-row record for Wales.

## 1982-83

| v. ENGLAND | v. SCOTLAND | v. IRELAND | v. FRANCE |
|---|---|---|---|
| †M.A. Wyatt 2PG | M.A. Wyatt 3PG,1C | M.A. Wyatt 3PG,1C,1T | M.A. Wyatt 1C[1] |
| | | | |
| H.E. Rees | H.E. Rees 1T | H.E. Rees 1T | H.E. Rees |
| D.S. Richards | D.S. Richards | R.A. Ackerman | R.A. Ackerman |
| †M.G. Ring | R.A. Ackerman | D.S. Richards | G. Evans 1PG |
| C.F.W. Rees | C.F.W. Rees | C.F.W. Rees | C.F.W. Rees |
| | | | |
| †M. Dacey 1DG | M. Dacey | M. Dacey | M. Dacey |
| T.D. Holmes | T.D. Holmes | T.D. Holmes 1T | T.D. Holmes |
| | | | |
| C. Williams | †S.T. Jones 1T | S.T. Jones | S.T. Jones |
| †W.J. James | W.J. James | W.J. James | W.J. James |
| G. Price | †I.H. Eidman | G. Price | G. Price |
| R.L. Norster | R.L. Norster | S.J. Perkins | S.J. Perkins |
| R.D. Moriarty | †S.J. Perkins | R.L. Norster | R.L. Norster |
| J. Squire 1T | J. Squire | J. Squire | J. Squire 1T |
| *E.T. Butler | *E.T. Butler | *E.T. Butler | *E.T. Butler |
| †D.F. Pickering | D.F. Pickering | D.F. Pickering | D.F. Pickering |
| | | | |
| Cardiff Arms Park | Murrayfield | Cardiff Arms Park | Parc des Princes |
| DRAWN 13-13 | WON 19-15 | WON 23-9 | LOST 9-16 |
| | | | |
| WALES: 2PG 1DG 1T | SCOT.: 1G 3PG | WALES: 1G 3PG 2T | FR.: 3PG 1DG 1T |
| ENG.: 2PG 1DG 1T | WALES: 1G 3PG 1T | IRE.: 3PG | WALES: 1G 1DG |
| | | | |
| 5 Feb. 1983 | 19 Feb. 1983 | 5 Mar. 1983 | 19 Mar. 1983 |
| | | | [1]Rep. by †R. Donovan |

The Welsh side improved in 1983. John Bevan, the former Welsh fly-half, followed John Lloyd as coach and he set out to choose a back line which would move the ball at every opportunity. But against England, and behind a hesitant pack, fly-half Malcolm Dacey was forced into an unaccustomed kicking role, and there was a clamour for the reinstatement of Gareth Davies after Wales escaped with a draw against England at Cardiff.

But Bevan retained the same tactical plan for the game at Murrayfield, and with a reshaped pack the Welsh team registered their first away win in the Championship for four years.

In Paris, however, with France on the verge of the Championship too, the Welsh pack was subdued by a powerful scrummaging unit. Norster and Squire were excellent in the line-out and the loose, and Holmes played like a ninth forward. But despite the magnificent efforts of these three, Wales were overcome and finished in third place in the Championship.

## 1983-84

| v. ROMANIA | v. SCOTLAND | v. IRELAND | v. FRANCE | v. ENGLAND |
|---|---|---|---|---|
| G. Evans 2PG | †H. Davies 1PG,1C | H. Davies 2PG,1C | H. Davies 1T,1C,2PG | H. Davies 1C,4PG |
| | | | | |
| †M.H. Titley | M.H. Titley 1T | M.H. Titley | M.H. Titley | M.H. Titley |
| R.A. Ackerman | R.A. Ackerman | R.A. Ackerman 1T | R.A. Ackerman | R.A. Ackerman |
| †B. Bowen | B. Bowen | B. Bowen 2PG | B. Bowen | B. Bowen |
| †A.M. Hadley | A.M. Hadley | A.M. Hadley | A.M. Hadley | A.M. Hadley 1T |
| | | | | |
| M. Dacey[1] | M. Dacey | M. Dacey | M. Dacey | M. Dacey 2DG |
| †R. Giles | †M.H.J. Douglas | M.H.J. Douglas | M.H.J. Douglas | T.D. Holmes |
| | | | | |
| S.T. Jones | S.T. Jones | I. Stephens | I. Stephens | I. Stephens |
| W.J. James | W.J. James | *†M.J. Watkins | *M.J. Watkins | *M.J. Watkins |
| I.H. Eidman | †R. Morgan | I.H. Eidman | I.H. Eidman | I.H. Eidman |
| S.J. Perkins | S.J. Perkins | S.J. Perkins | S.J. Perkins | S.J. Perkins |
| †T.W. Shaw | R.L. Norster | R.L. Norster | R.L. Norster | R.L. Norster |
| D.F. Pickering | R.D. Moriarty | R.D. Moriarty | R.D. Moriarty | R.D. Moriarty |
| *E.T. Butler | *E.T. Butler | E.T. Butler | E.T. Butler 1T | E.T. Butler |
| †M. Brown | D.F. Pickering | D.F. Pickering | D.F. Pickering | D.F. Pickering |
| | | | | |
| Bucharest | Cardiff Arms Park | Lansdowne Road | Cardiff Arms Park | Twickenham |
| LOST 6-24 | LOST 9-15 | WON 18-9 | LOST 16-21 | WON 24-15 |
| | | | | |
| ROM.: 1G 2PG 3T | WALES: 1G 1PG | IRE.: 3PG | WALES: 1G 2PG 1T | ENG.: 5PG |
| WALES: 2PG | SCOT.: 2G 1PG | WALES: 1G 4PG | FR.: 1G 4PG 1DG | WALES: 1G 2DG 4PG |
| | | | | |
| 12 Nov. 1983 | 21 Jan. 1984 | 4 Feb. 1984 | 18 Feb. 1984 | 17 Mar. 1984 |
| [1]Rep. by D.S. Richards | | | | |

The depressing decline of Welsh rugby was emphasised in the Principality's first official international against Romania in Bucharest in November. The Welsh pack was completely overwhelmed and a brittle defence was unable to cope with the giant marauding Romanian forwards, who created four tries.

Finally, after intense criticism for their apparent intransigence, the Welsh selectors restructured the pack around a new captain, following the defeat against Scotland. Mike Watkins became only the fourth man to lead Wales on debut, and his men responded to his example by winning in Dublin. A spectacular try by Ackerman and accurate place-kicking by Howell Davies (who scored 39 points in the season, a new Welsh record), brought Wales their first success in Dublin since 1978.

Defeat by France in a hectic match meant that Wales had lost both home internationals for the first time since 1963. But then, with Terry Holmes fit again, the season ended with a promising Welsh victory against England.

## 1984-85

| v. AUSTRALIA | v. SCOTLAND | v. IRELAND | v. FRANCE | v. ENGLAND |
|---|---|---|---|---|
| M.A. Wyatt 1PG,1C | M.A. Wyatt 4PG,1C | M.A. Wyatt 1C | †P.H. Thorburn 1PG | P.H. Thorburn 3PG,2C |
| | | | | |
| M.H. Titley | M.H. Titley | M.H. Titley | P.I. Lewis | P.I. Lewis |
| R.A. Ackerman | R.A. Ackerman | R.A. Ackerman | R.A. Ackerman | R.A. Ackerman |
| M.G. Ring | M.G. Ring | M.G. Ring | M.G. Ring | †K. Hopkins |
| †P.I. Lewis | P.I. Lewis | P.I. Lewis 1T | A.M. Hadley | A.M. Hadley |
| | | | | |
| M. Dacey | W.G. Davies 1DG | W.G. Davies 1DG | W.G. Davies | †J. Davies 1DG,1T |
| †D.J. Bishop 1T | *T.D. Holmes | *T.D. Holmes | *T.D. Holmes | *T.D. Holmes |
| | | | | |
| I. Stephens[1] | J. Whitefoot | J. Whitefoot | J. Whitefoot | J. Whitefoot |
| *M.J. Watkins | W.J. James | W.J. James | W.J. James | W.J. James |
| I.H. Eidman | I.H. Eidman | I.H. Eidman | †S. Evans | S. Evans |
| S.J. Perkins | S.J. Perkins | S.J. Perkins | S.J. Perkins | S.J. Perkins |
| R.L. Norster | R.L. Norster | R.L. Norster | R.L. Norster | R.L. Norster |
| †A.E. Davies | †M.S. Morris | M.S. Morris | M.S. Morris | G.J. Roberts 1T |
| E.T. Butler | R.D. Moriarty | R.D. Moriarty | R.D. Moriarty[1] | †P.T. Davies |
| D.F. Pickering | D.F. Pickering 2T | D.F. Pickering | D.F. Pickering | D.F. Pickering |
| | | | | |
| Cardiff Arms Park | Murrayfield | Cardiff Arms Park | Parc des Princes | Cardiff Arms Park |
| LOST 9-28 | WON 25-21 | LOST 9-21 | LOST 3-14 | WON 24-15 |
| | | | | |
| WALES: 1G 1PG | SCOT.: 2G 2DG 1PG | WALES: 1G 1DG | FR.: 2PG 2T | WALES: 2G 3PG 1DG |
| AUST.: 3G 2PG 1T | WALES: 1G 1DG 4PG 1T | IRE.: 2G 3PG | WALES: 1PG | ENG.: 1G 2PG 1DG |
| | | | | |
| 24 Nov. 1984 | 2 Mar. 1985 | 16 Mar. 1985 | 30 Mar. 1985 | 20 Apr. 1985 |
| | | | | |
| [1]Rep. by †J. Whitefoot | | | [1]Rep. by G.J. Roberts | |

Mike Watkins, Eddie Butler and Gareth Davies, three former Welsh captains, announced their retirements from international football during the season. Graham Price, Squire and David Richards had made similar decisions in the previous season and there was speculation among critics and supporters that the Welsh squad system was beginning to command too much of players' time, and was becoming counter-productive. These feelings were endorsed by Price in a controversial autobiography, in which he accused the coaching hierarchy of mismanagement. The Australians inflicted a humiliating defeat on the side at Cardiff, Ireland won at the ground for the first time since 1967, and France ran up their biggest-ever winning margin over the Welsh.

However, a glimmer of hope flickered at the end of the season. With a new fly-half and a pack rejuvenated by the inclusion of Stuart Evans, Phil Davies and Gareth Roberts, Wales at last satisfied their supporters by defeating England convincingly.

## 1985-86

| v. FIJI | v. ENGLAND | v. SCOTLAND | v. IRELAND | v. FRANCE |
|---|---|---|---|---|
| P.H. Thorburn 3C 2PG | P.H. Thorburn 3PG 1C | P.H. Thorburn 5PG | P.H. Thorburn 3PG 1C | P.H. Thorburn 5PG |
| | | | | |
| M.H. Titley 1T | P.I. Lewis | P.I. Lewis 1T | P.I. Lewis 1T | M.H. Titley |
| R.A. Ackerman | †J.A. Devereux | J.A. Devereux | J.A. Devereux | J.A. Devereux |
| B. Bowen | B. Bowen 1T | B. Bowen | B. Bowen | B. Bowen |
| A.M. Hadley 1T | A.M. Hadley | A.M. Hadley 1T | A.M. Hadley | A.M. Hadley |
| | | | | |
| J. Davies | J. Davies 1DG | J. Davies 1DG | J. Davies | J. Davies |
| *T.D. Holmes[1] 1T | †R.N. Jones | R.N. Jones | R.N. Jones | R.N. Jones |
| | | | | |
| J. Whitefoot | J. Whitefoot | J. Whitefoot | J. Whitefoot | J. Whitefoot |
| W.J. James 1T | W.J. James | W.J. James | W.J. James | W.J. James |
| I.H. Eidman | I.H. Eidman | I.H. Eidman | I.H. Eidman | I.H. Eidman |
| S.J. Perkins | S.J. Perkins | S.J. Perkins | S.J. Perkins | S.J. Perkins |
| R.L. Norster | †D.R. Waters | D.R. Waters | D.R. Waters | D.R. Waters |
| M. Davies | M. Brown | M. Brown | †W.P. Moriarty | W.P. Moriarty |
| P.T. Davies 2T | P.T. Davies | P.T. Davies | P.T. Davies 1T | P.T. Davies |
| D.F. Pickering 1T | *D.F. Pickering | *D.F. Pickering | *D.F. Pickering | *D.F. Pickering |
| | | | | |
| Cardiff Arms Park | Twickenham | Cardiff Arms Park | Lansdowne Road | Cardiff Arms Park |
| WON 40-3 | LOST 18-21 | WON 22-15 | WON 19-12 | LOST 15-23 |
| | | | | |
| WALES: 3G 2PG 4T | ENG.: 6PG 1DG | WALES: 5PG 1DG 1T | IRE.: 1G 2PG | WALES: 5PG |
| FIJI: 1PG | WALES: 1G 1DG 3PG | SCOT.: 1PG 3T | WALES: 1G 3PG 1T | FR.: 2G 1DG 2T |
| | | | | |
| 9 Nov. 1985 | 18 Jan. 1986 | 1 Feb. 1986 | 15 Feb. 1986 | 1 Mar. 1986 |
| | | | | |
| [1]Rep. by R. Giles | | | | |

The opening match of the season resulted in Wales' biggest win in an international since 1909. Fiji were routed on a heavy pitch in a match for which the WRU awarded full caps. Captain Terry Holmes fired Wales to forty points, scoring a try on the way, in what turned out to be his last match for Wales. Before the Championship season started, Holmes joined Bradford Northern in the Rugby League for a fee reported as £80,000.

But Tony Gray, the new Welsh national coach, set about guiding Wales into the Championship by choosing an exciting new back-line full of enterprise and youth, but the imposed absence (on disciplinary grounds) of Richard Moriarty and Robert Norster took much of the edge off the Welsh forward play.

Paul Thorburn, Neath's full-back, kicked 16 penalty goals to create a new International Championship record for a season. His total included a phenomenal goal from seventy yards against Scotland.

## 1986

| v. FIJI | v. TONGA | v. WEST. SAMOA |
|---|---|---|
| M. Dacey 3PG | M. Dacey 1PG 1C | M. Dacey 2C 3PG |
| | | |
| M.H. Titley | M.H. Titley | M.H. Titley 1T |
| B. Bowen 1C | B. Bowen 2PG | B. Bowen 1T |
| J.A. Devereux | J.A. Devereux | J.A. Devereux 1T |
| A.M. Hadley 1T | A.M. Hadley[1] | G.M.C. Webbe |
| | | |
| J. Davies 1DG 1T | J. Davies | J. Davies 1DG |
| R.N. Jones | R.N. Jones | R.N. Jones |
| | | |
| J. Whitefoot | J. Whitefoot | J. Whitefoot |
| W.J. James | W.J. James | W.J. James |
| S. Evans | S. Evans | S. Evans |
| R.D. Moriarty | *R.D. Moriarty | *R.D. Moriarty 1T |
| R.L. Norster | R.L. Norster | R.L. Norster |
| W.P. Moriarty | W.P. Moriarty 1T | W.P. Moriarty |
| P.T. Davies | P.T. Davies | P.T. Davies |
| *D.F. Pickering[1] | M. Brown[2] | M. Brown |
| | | |
| Suva | Nuku' Alofa | Apia |
| WON 22-15 | WON 15-7 | WON 32-14 |
| | | |
| Fiji: 2G 1PG | Tonga: 1PG 1T | W.Samoa: 2PG 2T |
| Wales: 1G 1DG 3PG 1T | Wales: 1G 3PG | Wales: 2G 3PG 1DG 2T |
| | | |
| 31 May 1986 | 12 Jun. 1986 | 14 Jun. 1986 |
| [1]Rep. by M. Brown | [1]Rep. by †G.M.C. Webbe | |
| | [2]Rep. by †H.D. Richards | |

In the summer of 1986, Wales undertook a six-match tour of the Southern Pacific as part of their preparations for the World Cup the following year. Five of the games were won, including full Tests against Fiji, Tonga and Western Samoa, and the first Welsh rugby tour since 1978 was regarded as a success.

Among the more interesting features of the Test series were the use of Malcolm Dacey out of position at full-back, the introduction of Glen Webbe on the wing, and the strong leadership qualities revealed by Richard Moriarty. The Swansea forward emerged as a thoughtful captain when David Pickering was concussed in the Fiji match. Moriarty led the side for the remainder of the tour, and was joined in the international side by his brother Paul. They became the first pair of brothers to play together for Wales since the Thomases packed down together at Twickenham in 1937.

## 1986-87

| v. FRANCE | v. ENGLAND | v. SCOTLAND | v. IRELAND |
|---|---|---|---|
| P.H. Thorburn[1] 3PG | M.A. Wyatt 5PG | M.A. Wyatt 2PG 1C | M.A. Wyatt 1PG |
| | | | |
| G.M.C. Webbe | G.M.C. Webbe | G.M.C. Webbe | I.C. Evans 1T |
| J.A. Devereux | J.A. Devereux | J.A. Devereux | J.A. Devereux |
| K. Hopkins | K. Hopkins | K. Hopkins | M.G. Ring |
| †I.C. Evans | I.C. Evans | I.C. Evans[1] | A.M. Hadley |
| | | | |
| J. Davies | J. Davies | J. Davies 1DG | J. Davies |
| R.N. Jones | R.N. Jones | R.N. Jones | R.N. Jones |
| | | | |
| J. Whitefoot | J. Whitefoot | J. Whitefoot | J. Whitefoot |
| †K. Phillips | W.J. James | W.J. James | *W.J. James |
| S. Evans | S. Evans 1T | †P. Francis | †S.W. Blackmore |
| S. Sutton | S. Sutton | S. Sutton | S. Sutton |
| R.L. Norster | R.L. Norster | R.L. Norster | R.L. Norster 1T |
| W.P. Moriarty | W.P. Moriarty | W.P. Moriarty | W.P. Moriarty |
| P.T. Davies | P.T. Davies[1] | †M. Jones 1T | P.T. Davies |
| *D.F. Pickering | *D.F. Pickering | *D.F. Pickering | R.G. Collins |
| | | | |
| Parc des Princes | Cardiff Arms Park | Murrayfield | Cardiff Arms Park |
| LOST 9-16 | WON 19-12 | LOST 15-21 | LOST 11-15 |
| | | | |
| Fr.: 1G 2PG 1T | Wales: 5PG 1T | Scot.: 2G 2PG 1DG | Wales: 1PG 2T |
| Wales: 3PG | Eng.: 4PG | Wales: 1G 2PG 1DG | Ire.: 2G 1PG |
| | | | |
| 7 Feb. 1987 | 21 Feb. 1987 | 21 Mar. 1987 | 4 Apr. 1987 |
| [1]Rep. by M. Dacey | [1]Rep. by †R.G. Collins | [1]Rep. by A.M. Hadley | |

Wales failed to impress as contenders for the Championship and at the end of the season their hopes of World Cup success were probably lowest of the five main European nations. The absence through injury of Richard Moriarty, and the subsequent injury to Stuart Evans (who had been the main pillar in impressive Welsh forward performances against France and England) left Wales bereft of scrummaging power.

Of the new Welsh players the most promising prospect was Llanelli threequarter Ieuan Evans. His try against Ireland, the product of an excellent break by Robert Jones and good support by Collins, was the single highlight of a disappointing season. Failure to win the Championship meant that Wales had suffered eight seasons without a title to celebrate: their longest run of Championship disappointment since the dark days before 1893, when Welsh rugby was in its infancy.

# WELSH MATCH RECORDS

## Match Results 1881 to 1987

| Match | Date | Opponents | For T | C | D | P | Pts | Against T | C | D | P | Pts | Result | Venue | Captain |
|---|---|---|---|---|---|---|---|---|---|---|---|---|---|---|---|
| 1 | 19.2.1881 | England | — | — | — | — | | 13 | 7 | 1 | — | | Lost | Blackheath | J. A. Bevan |
| 2 | 28.1.1882 | Ireland | 4 | 2 | — | — | | — | — | — | — | | Won | Dublin | C. P. Lewis |
| 3 | 16.12.1882 | England | — | — | — | — | | 6 | 2 | — | — | | Lost | Swansea | C. P. Lewis |
| 4 | 8.1.1883 | Scotland | 1 | 1 | — | — | | 3 | 3 | — | — | | Lost | Edinburgh | C. P. Lewis |
| 5 | 5.1.1884 | England | 1 | 1 | — | — | | 3 | 1 | — | — | | Lost | Leeds | C. H. Newman |
| 6 | 12.1.1884 | Scotland | — | — | — | — | | 1 | — | 1 | — | | Lost | Newport | C. H. Newman[1] |
| 7 | 12.4.1884 | Ireland | 2 | — | 1 | — | | — | — | — | — | | Won | Cardiff | H. J. Simpson |
| 8 | 3.1.1885 | England | 2 | 1 | — | — | | 5 | 1 | — | — | | Lost | Swansea | C. H. Newman |
| 9 | 10.1.1885 | Scotland | — | — | — | — | | — | — | — | — | | Drawn | Glasgow | C. H. Newman |
| 10 | 2.1.1886 | England | 1 | 1 | — | — | | 2 | — | ★ | — | | Lost | Blackheath | C. H. Newman |
| 11 | 9.1.1886 | Scotland | — | — | — | — | | 3 | 2 | — | — | | Lost | Cardiff | F. E. Hancock |
| 12 | 8.1.1887 | England | — | — | — | — | | — | — | — | — | | Drawn | Llanelli | C. H. Newman |
| 13 | 26.2.1887 | Scotland | — | — | — | — | | 12 | 4 | — | — | | Lost | Edinburgh | R. Gould |
| 14 | 12.3.1887 | Ireland | 1 | — | 1 | — | | 3 | — | — | — | | Won | Birkenhead | T. J. S. Clapp |
| 15 | 4.2.1888 | Scotland | 1 | — | — | — | | — | — | — | — | | Won | Newport | T. J. S. Clapp |
| 16 | 3.3.1888 | Ireland | — | — | — | — | | 2 | 1 | 1 | — | | Lost | Dublin | T. J. S. Clapp |
| 17 | 22.12.1888 | New Zealand Natives | 3 | 1 | — | — | | — | — | — | — | | Won | Swansea | A. F. Hill |
| 18 | 2.2.1889 | Scotland | — | — | — | — | | 2 | — | — | — | | Lost | Edinburgh | A. F. Hill |
| 19 | 2.3.1889 | Ireland | — | — | — | — | | 2 | — | — | — | | Lost | Swansea | A. J. Gould |
| 20 | 1.2.1890 | Scotland | 1 | — | — | — | 1 | 3 | 1 | — | — | 5 | Lost | Cardiff | A. F. Hill |
| 21 | 15.2.1890 | England | 1 | — | — | — | 1 | — | — | — | — | 0 | Won | Dewsbury | A. J. Gould |
| 22 | 1.3.1890 | Ireland | 1 | 1 | — | — | 3 | 1 | 1 | — | — | 3 | Drawn | Dublin | A. J. Gould |
| 23 | 3.1.1891 | England | 1 | 1 | — | — | 3 | 3 | 2 | — | — | 7 | Lost | Newport | W. A. Bowen |
| 24 | 7.2.1891 | Scotland | — | — | — | — | 0 | 7 | 1 | 2 | — | 15 | Lost | Edinburgh | W. H. Thomas |
| 25 | 7.3.1891 | Ireland | 1 | 1 | 1 | — | 6 | 1 | — | 1 | — | 4 | Won | Llanelli | W. H. Thomas |
| 26 | 2.1.1892 | England | — | — | — | — | 0 | 4 | 3 | — | — | 17 | Lost | Blackheath | A. J. Gould |
| 27 | 6.2.1892 | Scotland | 1 | — | — | — | 2 | 2 | 1 | — | — | 7 | Lost | Swansea | A. J. Gould |
| 28 | 5.3.1892 | Ireland | — | — | — | — | 0 | 3 | 1 | — | — | 9 | Lost | Dublin | A. J. Gould |
| 29 | 7.1.1893 | England | 3 | 1 | — | 1 | 12 | 4 | 1 | — | — | 11 | Won | Cardiff | A. J. Gould |
| 30 | 4.2.1893 | Scotland | 3 | — | — | 1 | 9 | — | — | — | — | 0 | Won | Edinburgh | A. J. Gould |
| 31 | 11.3.1893 | Ireland | 1 | — | — | — | 2 | — | — | — | — | 0 | Won | Llanelli | A. J. Gould |
| 32 | 6.1.1894 | England | 1 | — | — | — | 3 | 4 | 4 | ★ | — | 24 | Lost | Birkenhead Park | A. J. Gould |
| 33 | 3.2.1894 | Scotland | 1 | — | 1 | — | 7 | — | — | — | — | 0 | Won | Newport | A. J. Gould |
| 34 | 10.3.1894 | Ireland | — | — | — | — | 0 | — | — | 1 | — | 3 | Lost | Belfast | A. F. Hill |
| 35 | 5.1.1895 | England | 2 | — | — | — | 6 | 4 | 1 | — | — | 14 | Lost | Swansea | A. J. Gould |
| 36 | 26.1.1895 | Scotland | — | — | ★ | — | 4 | 1 | 1 | — | — | 5 | Lost | Edinburgh | A. J. Gould |
| 37 | 16.3.1895 | Ireland | 1 | 1 | — | — | 5 | 1 | — | — | — | 3 | Won | Cardiff | A. J. Gould |
| 38 | 4.1.1896 | England | — | — | — | — | 0 | 7 | 2 | — | — | 25 | Lost | Blackheath | A. J. Gould |
| 39 | 25.1.1896 | Scotland | 2 | — | — | — | 6 | — | — | — | — | 0 | Won | Cardiff | A. J. Gould |
| 40 | 14.3.1896 | Ireland | — | — | 1 | — | 4 | 2 | 1 | — | — | 8 | Lost | Dublin | A. J. Gould |
| 41 | 9.1.1897 | England | 3 | 1 | — | — | 11 | — | — | — | — | 0 | Won | Newport | A. J. Gould |
| 42 | 19.3.1898 | Ireland | 2 | 1 | — | 1 | 11 | — | — | — | 1 | 3 | Won | Limerick | W. J. Bancroft |
| 43 | 2.4.1898 | England | 1 | — | 1 | — | 7 | 4 | 1 | — | — | 14 | Lost | Blackheath | W. J. Bancroft |
| 44 | 7.1.1899 | England | 6 | 4 | — | — | 26 | 1 | — | — | — | 3 | Won | Swansea | W. J. Bancroft |
| 45 | 4.3.1899 | Scotland | 2 | 2 | — | — | 10 | 3 | — | 2★ | — | 21 | Lost | Edinburgh | W. J. Bancroft |
| 46 | 18.3.1899 | Ireland | — | — | — | — | 0 | 1 | — | — | — | 3 | Lost | Cardiff | W. J. Bancroft |
| 47 | 6.1.1900 | England | 2 | 2 | — | 1 | 13 | 1 | — | — | — | 3 | Won | Gloucester | W. J. Bancroft |
| 48 | 27.1.1900 | Scotland | 4 | — | — | — | 12 | 1 | — | — | — | 3 | Won | Swansea | W. J. Bancroft |
| 49 | 17.3.1900 | Ireland | 1 | — | — | — | 3 | — | — | — | — | 0 | Won | Belfast | W. J. Bancroft |
| 50 | 5.1.1901 | England | 3 | 2 | — | — | 13 | — | — | — | — | 0 | Won | Cardiff | W. J. Bancroft |
| 51 | 9.2.1901 | Scotland | 2 | 1 | — | — | 8 | 4 | 3 | — | — | 18 | Lost | Edinburgh | W. J. Bancroft |
| 52 | 16.3.1901 | Ireland | 2 | 2 | — | — | 10 | 3 | — | — | — | 9 | Won | Swansea | W. J. Bancroft |
| 53 | 11.1.1902 | England | 2 | — | — | 1 | 9 | 2 | 1 | — | — | 8 | Won | Blackheath | E. G. Nicholls |
| 54 | 1.2.1902 | Scotland | 4 | 1 | — | — | 14 | 1 | 1 | — | — | 5 | Won | Cardiff | E. G. Nicholls |
| 55 | 8.3.1902 | Ireland | 3 | 1 | 1 | — | 15 | — | — | — | — | 0 | Won | Dublin | E. G. Nicholls |
| 56 | 10.1.1903 | England | 5 | 3 | — | — | 21 | 1 | 1 | — | — | 5 | Won | Swansea | T. W. Pearson |
| 57 | 7.2.1903 | Scotland | — | — | — | — | 0 | 1 | — | 1 | — | 6 | Lost | Edinburgh | G. L. Lloyd |
| 58 | 14.3.1903 | Ireland | 6 | — | — | — | 18 | — | — | — | — | 0 | Won | Cardiff | E. G. Nicholls |
| 59 | 9.1.1904 | England | 2 | 2 | ★ | — | 14 | 3 | 1 | — | 1 | 14 | Drawn | Leicester | E. G. Nicholls |
| 60 | 6.2.1904 | Scotland | 4 | 3 | — | 1 | 21 | 1 | — | — | — | 3 | Won | Swansea | W. M. Llewellyn |
| 61 | 12.3.1904 | Ireland | 4 | — | — | — | 12 | 4 | 1 | — | — | 14 | Lost | Belfast | W. M. Llewellyn |
| 62 | 14.1.1905 | England | 7 | 2 | — | — | 25 | — | — | — | — | 0 | Won | Cardiff | W. M. Llewellyn |
| 63 | 4.2.1905 | Scotland | 2 | — | — | — | 6 | 1 | — | — | — | 3 | Won | Edinburgh | W. M. Llewellyn |
| 64 | 11.3.1905 | Ireland | 2 | 2 | — | — | 10 | 1 | — | — | — | 3 | Won | Swansea | W. M. Llewellyn |
| 65 | 16.12.1905 | New Zealand | 1 | — | — | — | 3 | — | — | — | — | 0 | Won | Cardiff | E. G. Nicholls |
| 66 | 13.1.1906 | England | 4 | 2 | — | — | 16 | 1 | — | — | — | 3 | Won | Richmond | E. G. Nicholls |

★in the drop-goal column denotes a goal from a mark.
[1]There is pictorial evidence that C. P. Lewis may have led Wales v Scotland 1884, instead of Newman.

| Match | Date | Opponents | For T | C | D | P | Pts | Against T | C | D | P | Pts | Result | Venue | Captain |
|---|---|---|---|---|---|---|---|---|---|---|---|---|---|---|---|
| 67 | 3.2.1906 | Scotland | 3 | — | — | — | 9 | — | — | — | 1 | 3 | Won | Cardiff | E. G. Nicholls |
| 68 | 10.3.1906 | Ireland | 2 | — | — | — | 6 | 3 | 1 | — | — | 11 | Lost | Belfast | E. G. Nicholls |
| 69 | 1.12.1906 | South Africa | — | — | — | — | 0 | 3 | 1 | — | — | 11 | Lost | Swansea | E. G. Nicholls |
| 70 | 12.1.1907 | England | 6 | 2 | — | — | 22 | — | — | — | — | 0 | Won | Swansea | R. M. Owen |
| 71 | 2.2.1907 | Scotland | — | — | 1 | — | 3 | 2 | — | — | — | 6 | Lost | Edinburgh | W. J. Trew |
| 72 | 9.3.1907 | Ireland | 6 | 2 | 1 | 1 | 29 | — | — | — | — | 0 | Won | Cardiff | R. T. Gabe |
| 73 | 18.1.1908 | England | 5 | 3 | 1 | 1 | 28 | 4 | 3 | — | — | 18 | Won | Bristol | A. F. Harding |
| 74 | 1.2.1908 | Scotland | 2 | — | — | — | 6 | 1 | 1 | — | — | 5 | Won | Swansea | G. Travers |
| 75 | 2.3.1908 | France | 9 | 3 | — | 1 | 36 | — | 1 | — | — | 4 | Won | Cardiff | E. T. Morgan |
| 76 | 14.3.1908 | Ireland | 3 | 1 | — | — | 11 | 1 | 1 | — | — | 5 | Won | Belfast | H. B. Winfield |
| 77 | 12.12.1908 | Australia | 2 | — | — | 1 | 9 | 2 | — | — | — | 6 | Won | Cardiff | W. J. Trew |
| 78 | 16.1.1909 | England | 2 | 1 | — | — | 8 | — | — | — | — | 0 | Won | Cardiff | W. J. Trew |
| 79 | 6.2.1909 | Scotland | 1 | 1 | — | — | 5 | — | — | — | 1 | 3 | Won | Edinburgh | W. J. Trew |
| 80 | 23.2.1909 | France | 11 | 7 | — | — | 47 | 1 | 1 | — | — | 5 | Won | Paris | W. J. Trew |
| 81 | 13.3.1909 | Ireland | 4 | 3 | — | — | 18 | 1 | 1 | — | — | 5 | Won | Swansea | W. J. Trew |
| 82 | 1.1.1910 | France | 10 | 8 | — | 1 | 49 | 2 | 1 | — | 2 | 14 | Won | Swansea | W. J. Trew |
| 83 | 15.1.1910 | England | 2 | — | — | — | 6 | 2 | 1 | — | 1 | 11 | Lost | Twickenham | W. J. Trew |
| 84 | 5.2.1910 | Scotland | 4 | 1 | — | — | 14 | — | — | — | — | 0 | Won | Cardiff | W. J. Trew |
| 85 | 12.3.1910 | Ireland | 5 | — | 1 | — | 19 | 1 | — | — | — | 3 | Won | Dublin | R. A. Gibbs |
| 86 | 21.1.1911 | England | 4 | — | — | 1 | 15 | 3 | 1 | — | — | 11 | Won | Swansea | W. J. Trew |
| 87 | 4.2.1911 | Scotland | 8 | 2 | 1 | — | 32 | 2 | — | 1 | — | 10 | Won | Edinburgh | W. J. Trew |
| 88 | 28.2.1911 | France | 3 | 3 | — | — | 15 | — | — | — | — | 0 | Won | Paris | J. L. Williams |
| 89 | 11.3.1911 | Ireland | 3 | 2 | — | 1 | 16 | — | — | — | — | 0 | Won | Cardiff | W. J. Trew |
| 90 | 20.1.1912 | England | — | — | — | — | 0 | 2 | 1 | — | — | 8 | Lost | Twickenham | R. M. Owen |
| 91 | 3.2.1912 | Scotland | 3 | 2 | 2 | — | 21 | 2 | — | — | — | 6 | Won | Swansea | R. M. Owen |
| 92 | 9.3.1912 | Ireland | 1 | 1 | — | — | 5 | 2 | 1 | 1 | — | 12 | Lost | Belfast | J. Bancroft |
| 93 | 25.3.1912 | France | 4 | 1 | — | — | 14 | 2 | 1 | — | — | 8 | Won | Newport | T. H. Vile |
| 94 | 14.12.1912 | South Africa | — | — | — | — | 0 | — | — | — | 1 | 3 | Lost | Cardiff | T. H. Vile |
| 95 | 18.1.1913 | England | — | — | — | — | 0 | 2 | 1 | 1 | — | 12 | Lost | Cardiff | T. H. Vile |
| 96 | 1.2.1913 | Scotland | 2 | 1 | — | — | 8 | — | — | — | — | 0 | Won | Edinburgh | W. J. Trew |
| 97 | 27.2.1913 | France | 3 | 1 | — | — | 11 | 2 | 1 | — | — | 8 | Won | Paris | W. J. Trew |
| 98 | 8.3.1913 | Ireland | 3 | 2 | — | 1 | 16 | 2 | 2 | — | 1 | 13 | Won | Swansea | J. P. Jones |
| 99 | 17.1.1914 | England | 1 | 1 | 1 | — | 9 | 2 | 2 | — | — | 10 | Lost | Twickenham | J. A. Davies |
| 100 | 7.2.1914 | Scotland | 3 | 2 | 2 | 1 | 24 | 1 | 1 | — | — | 5 | Won | Cardiff | J. A. Davies |
| 101 | 2.3.1914 | France | 7 | 5 | — | — | 31 | — | — | — | — | 0 | Won | Swansea | J. A. Davies |
| 102 | 14.3.1914 | Ireland | 3 | 1 | — | — | 11 | 1 | — | — | — | 3 | Won | Belfast | J. A. Davies |
| 103 | 21.4.1919 | New Zealand Army | — | — | — | — | 3 | — | — | — | 2 | 6 | Lost | Swansea | G. Stephens |
| 104 | 17.1.1920 | England | 2 | 1 | 2 | 1 | 19 | 1 | 1 | — | — | 5 | Won | Swansea | H. Uzzell |
| 105 | 7.2.1920 | Scotland | 1 | 1 | — | — | 5 | 1 | — | 2 | — | 9 | Lost | Edinburgh | H. Uzzell |
| 106 | 17.2.1920 | France | 2 | — | — | — | 6 | 1 | 1 | — | — | 5 | Won | Paris | H. Uzzell |
| 107 | 13.3.1920 | Ireland | 6 | 3 | 1 | — | 28 | — | — | 1 | — | 4 | Won | Cardiff | H. Uzzell |
| 108 | 15.1.1921 | England | 1 | — | — | — | 3 | 4 | 1 | 1 | — | 18 | Lost | Twickenham | J. J. Wetter |
| 109 | 5.2.1921 | Scotland | — | — | 2 | — | 8 | 3 | 1 | — | 1 | 14 | Lost | Swansea | T. H. Vile |
| 110 | 26.2.1921 | France | 2 | — | — | 2 | 12 | — | — | 1 | — | 4 | Won | Cardiff | T. Parker |
| 111 | 12.3.1921 | Ireland | 1 | — | — | 1 | 6 | — | — | — | — | 0 | Won | Belfast | T. Parker |
| 112 | 21.1.1922 | England | 8 | 2 | — | — | 28 | 2 | — | — | — | 6 | Won | Cardiff | T. Parker |
| 113 | 4.2.1922 | Scotland | 1 | 1 | 1 | — | 9 | 2 | — | 1 | — | 9 | Drawn | Edinburgh | T. Parker |
| 114 | 11.3.1922 | Ireland | 3 | 1 | — | — | 11 | 1 | 1 | — | — | 5 | Won | Swansea | T. Parker |
| 115 | 23.3.1922 | France | 3 | 1 | — | — | 11 | 1 | — | — | — | 3 | Won | Paris | T. Parker |
| 116 | 20.1.1923 | England | 1 | — | — | — | 3 | 1 | — | 1 | — | 7 | Lost | Twickenham | J. M. C. Lewis |
| 117 | 3.2.1923 | Scotland | 1 | 1 | — | 1 | 8 | 3 | 1 | — | — | 11 | Lost | Cardiff | J. M. C. Lewis |
| 118 | 24.2.1923 | France | 3 | 2 | — | 1 | 16 | 2 | 1 | — | — | 8 | Won | Swansea | T. Parker |
| 119 | 10.3.1923 | Ireland | — | — | 1 | — | 4 | 1 | 1 | — | — | 5 | Lost | Dublin | A. Jenkins |
| 120 | 19.1.1924 | Wales | 3 | — | — | — | 9 | 5 | 1 | — | — | 17 | Lost | Swansea | J. Rees |
| 121 | 2.2.1924 | Scotland | 2 | 2 | — | — | 10 | 8 | 4 | — | 1 | 35 | Lost | Edinburgh | J. Whitfield |
| 122 | 8.3.1924 | Ireland | 2 | — | 1 | — | 10 | 3 | 2 | — | — | 13 | Lost | Cardiff | J. J. Wetter |
| 123 | 27.3.1924 | France | 2 | — | 1 | — | 10 | 2 | — | — | — | 6 | Won | Paris | W. R. Harding |
| 124 | 29.11.1924 | New Zealand | — | — | — | — | 0 | 4 | 2 | — | 1 | 19 | Lost | Swansea | J. J. Wetter |
| 125 | 17.1.1925 | England | 2 | — | — | — | 6 | 3 | — | — | 1 | 12 | Lost | Twickenham | T. Johnson |
| 126 | 7.2.1925 | Scotland | 3 | 1 | — | 1 | 14 | 6 | 1 | 1 | — | 24 | Lost | Swansea | S. Morris |
| 127 | 28.2.1925 | France | 3 | 1 | — | — | 11 | 1 | 1 | — | — | 5 | Won | Cardiff | R. A. Cornish |
| 128 | 14.3.1925 | Ireland | 1 | — | — | — | 3 | 4 | 2 | — | 1 | 19 | Lost | Belfast | W. I. Jones |
| 129 | 16.1.1926 | England | 1 | — | — | — | 3 | 1 | — | — | — | 3 | Drawn | Cardiff | W. R. Harding |
| 130 | 6.2.1926 | Scotland | 1 | 1 | — | — | 5 | 1 | 1 | — | 1 | 8 | Lost | Edinburgh | R. A. Cornish |
| 131 | 13.3.1926 | Ireland | 3 | 1 | — | — | 11 | 1 | 1 | — | 1 | 8 | Won | Swansea | W. R. Harding |
| 132 | 5.4.1926 | France | 1 | — | 1 | — | 7 | 1 | 1 | — | — | 5 | Won | Paris | W. J. Delahay |
| 133 | 15.1.1927 | England | 2 | — | — | 1 | 9 | 1 | 1 | ★ 1 | 1 | 11 | Lost | Twickenham | B. R. Turnbull |
| 134 | 5.2.1927 | Scotland | — | — | — | — | 0 | 1 | 1 | — | — | 5 | Lost | Cardiff | B.O. Male |
| 135 | 26.2.1927 | France | 7 | 2 | — | — | 25 | 1 | — | 1 | — | 7 | Won | Swansea | W. C. Powell |
| 136 | 12.3.1927 | Ireland | 1 | 1 | 1 | — | 9 | 4 | 2 | — | 1 | 19 | Lost | Dublin | W. C. Powell |
| 137 | 26.11.1927 | New South Wales | 2 | 1 | — | — | 8 | 4 | 3 | — | — | 18 | Lost | Cardiff | I. E. Jones |

★in the drop-goal column denotes a goal from a mark.

| Match | Date | Opponents | For T | C | D | P | Pts | Against T | C | D | P | Pts | Result | Venue | Captain |
|---|---|---|---|---|---|---|---|---|---|---|---|---|---|---|---|
| 138 | 21.1.1928 | England | 2 | 1 | — | — | 8 | 2 | 2 | — | — | 10 | Lost | Swansea | W. R. Harding |
| 139 | 4.2.1928 | Scotland | 3 | 2 | — | — | 13 | — | — | — | — | 0 | Won | Edinburgh | B. O. Male |
| 140 | 10.3.1928 | Ireland | 2 | 2 | — | — | 10 | 3 | 2 | — | — | 13 | Lost | Cardiff | A. Jenkins |
| 141 | 9.4.1928 | France | 1 | — | — | — | 3 | 2 | 1 | — | — | 8 | Lost | Paris | B. O. Male |
| 142 | 19.1.1929 | England | 1 | — | — | — | 3 | 2 | 1 | — | — | 8 | Lost | Twickenham | I. E. Jones |
| 143 | 2.2.1929 | Scotland | 4 | 1 | — | — | 14 | — | — | 1 | 1 | 7 | Won | Swansea | W. G. Morgan |
| 144 | 23.2.1929 | France | 2 | 1 | — | — | 8 | 1 | — | — | — | 3 | Won | Cardiff | W. G. Morgan |
| 145 | 9.3.1929 | Ireland | 1 | 1 | — | — | 5 | 1 | 1 | — | — | 5 | Drawn | Belfast | W. G. Morgan |
| 146 | 18.1.1930 | England | 1 | — | — | — | 3 | 2 | 1 | — | 1 | 11 | Lost | Cardiff | H. M. Bowcott |
| 147 | 1.2.1930 | Scotland | 1 | 1 | 1 | — | 9 | 2 | 1 | 1 | — | 12 | Lost | Edinburgh | I. E. Jones |
| 148 | 8.3.1930 | Ireland | 3 | — | — | 1 | 12 | — | — | 1 | 1 | 7 | Won | Swansea | J. Bassett |
| 149 | 21.4.1930 | France | 1 | — | 2 | — | 11 | — | — | — | — | 0 | Won | Paris | W. G. Morgan |
| 150 | 17.1.1931 | England | 2 | 1 | ★ | — | 11 | 1 | 1 | — | 2 | 11 | Drawn | Twickenham | J. Bassett |
| 151 | 7.2.1931 | Scotland | 3 | 2 | — | — | 13 | 2 | 1 | — | — | 8 | Won | Cardiff | J. Bassett |
| 152 | 28.2.1931 | France | 7 | 5 | 1 | — | 35 | 1 | — | — | — | 3 | Won | Swansea | J. Bassett |
| 153 | 14.3.1931 | Ireland | 3 | 1 | 1 | — | 15 | 1 | — | — | — | 3 | Won | Belfast | J. Bassett |
| 154 | 5.12.1931 | South Africa | 1 | — | — | — | 3 | 2 | 1 | — | — | 8 | Lost | Swansea | J. Bassett |
| 155 | 16.1.1932 | England | 1 | 1 | 1 | 1 | 12 | 1 | 1 | — | — | 5 | Won | Swansea | J. Bassett |
| 156 | 6.2.1932 | Scotland | 1 | — | — | 1 | 6 | — | — | — | — | 0 | Won | Edinburgh | J. Bassett |
| 157 | 12.3.1932 | Ireland | 2 | — | 1 | — | 10 | 4 | — | — | — | 12 | Lost | Cardiff | J. Bassett |
| 158 | 21.1.1933 | England | 1 | — | 1 | — | 7 | 1 | — | — | — | 3 | Won | Twickenham | W. G. Thomas |
| 159 | 4.2.1933 | Scotland | 1 | — | — | — | 3 | 2 | 1 | — | 1 | 11 | Lost | Swansea | W. G. Thomas |
| 160 | 11.3.1933 | Ireland | 1 | 1 | — | — | 5 | 1 | — | 1 | 1 | 10 | Lost | Belfast | W. G. Thomas |
| 161 | 20.1.1934 | England | — | — | — | — | 0 | 3 | — | — | — | 9 | Lost | Cardiff | J. R. Evans |
| 162 | 3.2.1934 | Scotland | 3 | 2 | — | — | 13 | 1 | — | — | 1 | 6 | Won | Edinburgh | E. C. Davey |
| 163 | 10.3.1934 | Ireland | 3 | 2 | — | — | 13 | — | — | — | — | 0 | Won | Swansea | E. C. Davey |
| 164 | 19.1.1935 | England | 1 | — | — | — | 3 | — | — | — | 1 | 3 | Drawn | Twickenham | E. C. Davey |
| 165 | 2.2.1935 | Scotland | 2 | — | 1 | — | 10 | 2 | — | — | — | 6 | Won | Cardiff | E. C. Davey |
| 166 | 9.3.1935 | Ireland | — | — | — | 1 | 3 | 1 | — | — | 2 | 9 | Lost | Belfast | E. C. Davey |
| 167 | 21.12.1935 | New Zealand | 3 | 2 | — | — | 13 | 2 | 1 | 1 | — | 12 | Won | Cardiff | E. C. Davey |
| 168 | 18.1.1936 | England | — | — | — | — | 0 | — | — | — | — | 0 | Drawn | Swansea | J. I. Rees |
| 169 | 1.2.1936 | Scotland | 3 | 2 | — | — | 13 | 1 | — | — | — | 3 | Won | Edinburgh | E. C. Davey |
| 170 | 14.3.1936 | Ireland | — | — | — | 1 | 3 | — | — | — | — | 0 | Won | Cardiff | J. I. Rees |
| 171 | 16.1.1937 | England | 1 | — | — | — | 3 | — | — | 1 | — | 4 | Lost | Twickenham | E. C.Davey |
| 172 | 6.2.1937 | Scotland | 2 | — | — | — | 6 | 3 | 2 | — | — | 13 | Lost | Swansea | J. I. Rees |
| 173 | 3.4.1937 | Ireland | — | — | — | 1 | 3 | 1 | 1 | — | — | 5 | Lost | Belfast | W. Wooller |
| 174 | 15.1.1938 | England | 2 | 1 | — | 2 | 14 | 2 | 1 | — | — | 8 | Won | Cardiff | C. W. Jones |
| 175 | 5.2.1938 | Scotland | 2 | — | — | — | 6 | 1 | 1 | — | 1 | 8 | Lost | Edinburgh | C. W. Jones |
| 176 | 12.3.1938 | Ireland | 2 | 1 | — | 1 | 11 | 1 | 1 | — | — | 5 | Won | Swansea | C. W. Jones |
| 177 | 21.1.1939 | England | — | — | — | — | 0 | 1 | — | — | — | 3 | Lost | Twickenham | W. Wooller |
| 178 | 4.2.1939 | Scotland | 2 | 1 | — | 1 | 11 | — | — | — | 1 | 3 | Won | Cardiff | W. Wooller |
| 179 | 11.3.1939 | Ireland | 1 | — | 1 | — | 7 | — | — | — | — | 0 | Won | Belfast | W. Wooller |
| 180 | 18.1.1947 | England | 2 | — | — | — | 6 | 1 | 1 | 1 | — | 9 | Lost | Cardiff | H. Tanner |
| 181 | 1.2.1947 | Scotland | 5 | 2 | — | 1 | 22 | 1 | 1 | — | 1 | 8 | Won | Edinburgh | H. Tanner |
| 182 | 22.3.1947 | France | — | — | — | 1 | 3 | — | — | — | — | 0 | Won | Paris | H. Tanner |
| 183 | 29.3.1947 | Ireland | 1 | — | — | 1 | 6 | — | — | — | — | 0 | Won | Swansea | H. Tanner |
| 184 | 20.12.1947 | Australia | — | — | — | 2 | 6 | — | — | — | — | 0 | Won | Cardiff | W. E. Tamplin |
| 185 | 17.1.1948 | England | 1 | — | — | — | 3 | — | — | — | 1 | 3 | Drawn | Twickenham | H. Tanner |
| 186 | 7.2.1948 | Scotland | 3 | 1 | — | 1 | 14 | — | — | — | — | 0 | Won | Cardiff | H. Tanner |
| 187 | 21.2.1948 | France | — | — | — | 1 | 3 | 3 | 1 | — | — | 11 | Lost | Swansea | H. Tanner |
| 188 | 13.3.1948 | Ireland | 1 | — | — | — | 3 | 2 | — | — | — | 6 | Lost | Belfast | H. Tanner |
| 189 | 15.1.1949 | England | 3 | — | — | — | 9 | — | — | 1 | — | 3 | Won | Cardiff | H. Tanner |
| 190 | 5.2.1949 | Scotland | 1 | — | — | — | 3 | 2 | — | — | — | 6 | Lost | Edinburgh | H. Tanner |
| 191 | 12.3.1949 | Ireland | — | — | — | — | 0 | 1 | 1 | — | — | 5 | Lost | Swansea | H. Tanner |
| 192 | 26.3.1949 | France | 1 | — | — | — | 3 | 1 | 1 | — | — | 5 | Lost | Paris | H. Tanner |
| 193 | 21.1.1950 | England | 2 | 1 | — | 1 | 11 | 1 | 1 | — | — | 5 | Won | Twickenham | J. A. Gwilliam |
| 194 | 4.2.1950 | Scotland | 2 | — | 1 | 1 | 12 | — | — | — | — | 0 | Won | Swansea | J. A. Gwilliam |
| 195 | 11.3.1950 | Ireland | 2 | — | — | — | 6 | — | — | — | 1 | 3 | Won | Belfast | J. A. Gwilliam |
| 196 | 25.3.1950 | France | 4 | 3 | — | 1 | 21 | — | — | — | — | 0 | Won | Cardiff | J. A. Gwilliam |
| 197 | 20.1.1951 | England | 5 | 4 | — | — | 23 | 1 | 1 | — | — | 5 | Won | Swansea | J. A. Gwilliam |
| 198 | 3.2.1951 | Scotland | — | — | — | — | 0 | 3 | 2 | 1 | 1 | 19 | Lost | Edinburgh | J. A. Gwilliam |
| 199 | 10.3.1951 | Ireland | — | — | — | 1 | 3 | 1 | — | — | — | 3 | Drawn | Cardiff | J. A. Gwilliam |
| 200 | 7.4.1951 | France | 1 | — | — | — | 3 | 1 | 1 | — | 1 | 8 | Lost | Paris | J. Matthews |
| 201 | 22.12.1951 | South Africa | 1 | — | — | — | 3 | 1 | — | 1 | — | 6 | Lost | Cardiff | J. A. Gwilliam |
| 202 | 19.1.1952 | England | 2 | 1 | — | — | 8 | 2 | — | — | — | 6 | Won | Twickenham | J. A. Gwilliam |
| 203 | 2.2.1952 | Scotland | 1 | 1 | — | 2 | 11 | — | — | — | — | 0 | Won | Cardiff | J. A. Gwilliam |
| 204 | 8.3.1952 | Ireland | 3 | 1 | — | 1 | 14 | — | — | — | 1 | 3 | Won | Dublin | J. A. Gwilliam |
| 205 | 22.3.1952 | France | — | — | 1 | 2 | 9 | 1 | 1 | — | — | 5 | Won | Swansea | J. A. Gwilliam |
| 206 | 17.1.1953 | England | — | — | — | 1 | 3 | 1 | 1 | — | 1 | 8 | Lost | Cardiff | J. A. Gwilliam |
| 207 | 7.2.1953 | Scotland | 3 | — | — | 1 | 12 | — | — | — | — | 0 | Won | Edinburgh | B. L. Williams |
| 208 | 14.3.1953 | Ireland | 1 | 1 | — | — | 5 | 1 | — | — | — | 3 | Won | Swansea | B. L. Williams |
| 209 | 28.3.1953 | France | 2 | — | — | — | 6 | — | — | — | 1 | 3 | Won | Paris | B. L. Williams |
| 210 | 19.12.1953 | New Zealand | 2 | 2 | — | 1 | 13 | 1 | 1 | — | 1 | 8 | Won | Cardiff | B. L. Williams |
| 211 | 16.1.1954 | England | 1 | — | — | 1 | 6 | 3 | — | — | — | 9 | Lost | Twickenham | J. R. G. Stephens |

★in the drop-goal column denotes a goal from a mark.

| Match | Date | Opponents | For | | | | | Against | | | | | Result | Venue | Captain |
|---|---|---|---|---|---|---|---|---|---|---|---|---|---|---|---|
| | | | T | C | D | P | Pts | T | C | D | P | Pts | | | |
| 212 | 13.3.1954 | Ireland | — | — | 1 | 3 | 12 | 1 | — | — | 2 | 9 | Won | Dublin | J. R. G. Stephens |
| 213 | 27.3.1954 | France | 2 | 2 | — | 3 | 19 | 2 | 2 | — | 1 | 13 | Won | Cardiff | W. R. Willis |
| 214 | 10.4.1954 | Scotland | 4 | — | — | 1 | 15 | 1 | — | — | — | 3 | Won | Swansea | K. J. Jones |
| 215 | 22.1.1955 | England | — | — | — | 1 | 3 | — | — | — | — | 0 | Won | Cardiff | B. L. Williams |
| 216 | 5.2.1955 | Scotland | 2 | 1 | — | — | 8 | 2 | 1 | 1 | 1 | 14 | Lost | Edinburgh | W. R. Willis |
| 217 | 12.3.1955 | Ireland | 4 | 3 | — | 1 | 21 | — | — | — | 1 | 3 | Won | Cardiff | J. R. G. Stephens |
| 218 | 26.3.1955 | France | 2 | 2 | — | 2 | 16 | 1 | 1 | 1 | 1 | 11 | Won | Paris | J. R. G. Stephens |
| 219 | 21.1.1956 | England | 2 | 1 | — | — | 8 | — | — | — | 1 | 3 | Won | Twickenham | C. I. Morgan |
| 220 | 4.2.1956 | Scotland | 3 | — | — | — | 9 | 1 | — | — | 1 | 3 | Won | Cardiff | C. I. Morgan |
| 221 | 10.3.1956 | Ireland | — | — | — | 1 | 3 | 1 | 1 | 1 | 1 | 11 | Lost | Dublin | C. I. Morgan |
| 222 | 24.3.1956 | France | 1 | 1 | — | — | 5 | 1 | — | — | — | 3 | Won | Cardiff | C. I. Morgan |
| 223 | 19.1.1957 | England | — | — | — | — | 0 | — | — | — | 1 | 3 | Lost | Cardiff | M. C. Thomas |
| 224 | 2.2.1957 | Scotland | 1 | — | — | 1 | 6 | 1 | — | 1 | 1 | 9 | Lost | Edinburgh | M. C. Thomas |
| 225 | 9.3.1957 | Ireland | — | — | 2 | — | 6 | 1 | 1 | — | — | 5 | Won | Cardiff | J. R. G. Stephens |
| 226 | 23.3.1957 | France | 4 | 2 | — | 1 | 19 | 3 | 2 | — | — | 13 | Won | Paris | J. R. G. Stephens |
| 227 | 4.1.1958 | Australia | 1 | — | 1 | 1 | 9 | 1 | — | — | — | 3 | Won | Cardiff | R. C. C. Thomas |
| 228 | 18.1.1958 | England | — | — | — | 1 | 3 | 1 | — | — | — | 3 | Drawn | Twickenham | R. C. C. Thomas |
| 229 | 1.2.1958 | Scotland | 2 | 1 | — | — | 8 | — | — | — | 1 | 3 | Won | Cardiff | R. C. C. Thomas |
| 230 | 15.3.1958 | Ireland | 3 | — | — | — | 9 | 1 | — | — | 1 | 6 | Won | Dublin | R. C. C. Thomas |
| 231 | 29.3.1958 | France | 1 | — | — | 1 | 6 | 2 | 2 | 2 | — | 16 | Lost | Cardiff | R. C. C. Thomas |
| 232 | 17.1.1959 | England | 1 | 1 | — | — | 5 | — | — | — | — | 0 | Won | Cardiff | R. C. C. Thomas |
| 233 | 7.2.1959 | Scotland | 1 | 1 | — | — | 5 | 1 | — | — | 1 | 6 | Lost | Edinburgh | R. C. C. Thomas |
| 234 | 14.3.1959 | Ireland | 2 | 1 | — | — | 8 | 1 | — | — | 1 | 6 | Won | Cardiff | R. C. C. Thomas |
| 235 | 4.4.1959 | France | — | — | — | 1 | 3 | 2 | 1 | — | 1 | 11 | Lost | Paris | R. C. C. Thomas |
| 236 | 16.1.1960 | England | — | — | — | 2 | 6 | 2 | 1 | — | 2 | 14 | Lost | Twickenham | R. H. Williams |
| 237 | 6.2.1960 | Scotland | 1 | 1 | — | 1 | 8 | — | — | — | — | 0 | Won | Cardiff | B. V. Meredith |
| 238 | 12.3.1960 | Ireland | 2 | 2 | — | — | 10 | 1 | — | — | 2 | 9 | Won | Dublin | D. O. Brace |
| 239 | 26.3.1960 | France | 1 | 1 | — | 1 | 8 | 4 | 2 | — | — | 16 | Lost | Cardiff | B. V.Meredith |
| 240 | 3.12.1960 | South Africa | — | — | — | — | 0 | — | — | — | 1 | 3 | Lost | Cardiff | T. J. Davies |
| 241 | 21.1.1961 | England | 2 | — | — | — | 6 | 1 | — | — | — | 3 | Won | Cardiff | T. J. Davies |
| 242 | 11.2.1961 | Scotland | — | — | — | — | 0 | 1 | — | — | — | 3 | Lost | Edinburgh | T. J. Davies |
| 243 | 11.3.1961 | Ireland | 1 | — | — | 2 | 9 | — | — | — | — | 0 | Won | Cardiff | D. O. Brace |
| 244 | 25.3.1961 | France | 2 | — | — | — | 6 | 2 | 1 | — | — | 8 | Lost | Paris | L. H. Williams |
| 245 | 20.1.1962 | England | — | — | — | — | 0 | — | — | — | — | 0 | Drawn | Twickenham | L. H. Williams |
| 246 | 3.2.1962 | Scotland | — | — | 1 | — | 3 | 2 | 1 | — | — | 8 | Lost | Cardiff | L. H. Williams |
| 247 | 24.3.1962 | France | — | — | — | 1 | 3 | — | — | — | — | 0 | Won | Cardiff | B. V. Meredith |
| 248 | 17.11.1962 | Ireland | — | — | — | 1 | 3 | — | — | 1 | — | 3 | Drawn | Dublin | B. V. Meredith |
| 249 | 19.1.1963 | England | 1 | — | — | 1 | 6 | 2 | 2 | 1 | — | 13 | Lost | Cardiff | D.C.T. Rowlands |
| 250 | 2.2.1963 | Scotland | — | — | 1 | 1 | 6 | — | — | — | — | 0 | Won | Edinburgh | D.C.T. Rowlands |
| 251 | 9.3.1963 | Ireland | 1 | — | 1 | — | 6 | 1 | 1 | 1 | 2 | 14 | Lost | Cardiff | D.C.T. Rowlands |
| 252 | 23.3.1963 | France | — | — | — | 1 | 3 | 1 | 1 | — | — | 5 | Lost | Paris | D.C.T. Rowlands |
| 253 | 21.12.1963 | New Zealand | — | — | — | — | 0 | — | — | 1 | 1 | 6 | Lost | Cardiff | D.C.T. Rowlands |
| 254 | 18.1.1964 | England | 2 | — | — | — | 6 | 2 | — | — | — | 6 | Drawn | Twickenham | D.C.T. Rowlands |
| 255 | 1.2.1964 | Scotland | 2 | 1 | — | 1 | 11 | 1 | — | — | — | 3 | Won | Cardiff | D.C.T. Rowlands |
| 256 | 7.3.1964 | Ireland | 3 | 3 | — | — | 15 | — | — | — | 2 | 6 | Won | Dublin | D.C.T. Rowlands |
| 257 | 21.3.1964 | France | 1 | 1 | — | 2 | 11 | 1 | 1 | — | 2 | 11 | Drawn | Cardiff | D.C.T. Rowlands |
| 258 | 23.5.1964 | South Africa | — | — | — | 1 | 3 | 3 | 3 | 1 | 2 | 24 | Lost | Durban | D.C.T. Rowlands |
| 259 | 16.1.1965 | England | 3 | 1 | 1 | — | 14 | — | — | — | 1 | 3 | Won | Cardiff | D.C.T. Rowlands |
| 260 | 6.2.1965 | Scotland | 2 | 1 | — | 2 | 14 | — | — | 2 | 2 | 12 | Won | Edinburgh | D.C.T. Rowlands |
| 261 | 13.3.1965 | Ireland | 2 | 1 | 1 | 1 | 14 | 1 | 1 | — | 1 | 8 | Won | Cardiff | D.C.T. Rowlands |
| 262 | 27.3.1965 | France | 3 | 2 | — | — | 13 | 4 | 2 | 1 | 1 | 22 | Lost | Paris | D.C.T. Rowlands |
| 263 | 15.1.1966 | England | 1 | 1 | — | 2 | 11 | 1 | — | — | 1 | 6 | Won | Twickenham | A. E. I. Pask |
| 264 | 5.2.1966 | Scotland | 2 | 1 | — | — | 8 | — | — | — | 1 | 3 | Won | Cardiff | A. E. I. Pask |
| 265 | 12.3.1966 | Ireland | 1 | — | — | 1 | 6 | 1 | — | 1 | 1 | 9 | Lost | Dublin | A. E. I. Pask |
| 266 | 26.3.1966 | France | 1 | — | — | 2 | 9 | 2 | 1 | — | — | 8 | Won | Cardiff | A. E. I. Pask |
| 267 | 3.12.1966 | Australia | 2 | 1 | — | 1 | 11 | 2 | 1 | 1 | 1 | 14 | Lost | Cardiff | A. E. I. Pask |
| 268 | 4.2.1967 | Scotland | 1 | 1 | — | — | 5 | 2 | 1 | 1 | — | 11 | Lost | Edinburgh | A. E. I. Pask |
| 269 | 11.3.1967 | Ireland | — | — | — | — | 0 | 1 | — | — | — | 3 | Lost | Cardiff | D. Watkins |
| 270 | 1.4.1967 | France | 1 | 1 | 1 | 2 | 14 | 3 | 1 | 2 | 1 | 20 | Lost | Paris | D. Watkins |
| 271 | 15.4.1967 | England | 5 | 5 | 1 | 2 | 34 | 3 | — | — | 4 | 21 | Won | Cardiff | D. Watkins |
| 272 | 11.11.1967 | New Zealand | — | — | 1 | 1 | 6 | 2 | 2 | — | 1 | 13 | Lost | Cardiff | N. R. Gale |
| 273 | 20.1.1968 | England | 2 | 1 | 1 | — | 11 | 2 | 1 | — | 1 | 11 | Drawn | Twickenham | N. R. Gale |
| 274 | 3.2.1968 | Scotland | 1 | 1 | — | — | 5 | — | — | — | — | 0 | Won | Cardiff | G. O. Edwards |
| 275 | 9.3.1968 | Ireland | — | — | 1 | 1 | 6 | 1 | — | 1 | 1 | 9 | Lost | Dublin | S. J. Dawes |
| 276 | 23.3.1968 | France | 1 | — | — | 2 | 9 | 2 | 1 | 1 | 1 | 14 | Lost | Cardiff | G. O. Edwards |
| 277 | 1.2.1969 | Scotland | 3 | 1 | — | 2 | 17 | — | — | — | 1 | 3 | Won | Edinburgh | B. Price |
| 278 | 8.3.1969 | Ireland | 4 | 3 | 1 | 1 | 24 | 1 | 1 | — | 2 | 11 | Won | Cardiff | B. Price |
| 279 | 22.3.1969 | France | 2 | 1 | — | — | 8 | 1 | 1 | — | 1 | 8 | Drawn | Paris | B. Price |
| 280 | 12.4.1969 | England | 5 | 3 | 1 | 2 | 30 | — | — | — | 3 | 9 | Won | Cardiff | G. O. Edwards |
| 281 | 31.5.1969 | New Zealand | — | — | — | — | 0 | 4 | 2 | — | 1 | 19 | Lost | Christchurch | B. Price |
| 282 | 14.6.1969 | New Zealand | 2 | — | — | 2 | 12 | 3 | 3 | 1 | 5 | 33 | Lost | Auckland | B. Price |
| 283 | 21.6.1969 | Australia | 3 | 2 | — | 2 | 19 | 2 | 2 | — | 2 | 16 | Won | Sydney | B. Price |
| 284 | 24.1.1970 | South Africa | 1 | — | — | 1 | 6 | 1 | — | — | 1 | 6 | Drawn | Cardiff | G. O. Edwards |

| Match | Date | Opponents | For | | | | | Against | | | | | Result | Venue | Captain |
|---|---|---|---|---|---|---|---|---|---|---|---|---|---|---|---|
| | | | T | C | D | P | Pts | T | C | D | P | Pts | | | |
| 285 | 7.2.1970 | Scotland | 4 | 3 | — | — | 18 | 1 | — | 1 | 1 | 9 | Won | Cardiff | G. O. Edwards |
| 286 | 28.2.1970 | England | 4 | 1 | 1 | — | 17 | 2 | 2 | — | 1 | 13 | Won | Twickenham | G. O. Edwards |
| 287 | 14.3.1970 | Ireland | — | — | — | — | 0 | 2 | 1 | 1 | 1 | 14 | Lost | Dublin | G. O. Edwards |
| 288 | 4.4.1970 | France | 1 | 1 | — | 2 | 11 | 2 | — | — | — | 6 | Won | Cardiff | S. J. Dawes |
| 289 | 16.1.1971 | England | 3 | 2 | 2 | 1 | 22 | 1 | — | — | 1 | 6 | Won | Cardiff | S. J. Dawes |
| 290 | 6.2.1971 | Scotland | 4 | 2 | — | 1 | 19 | 2 | — | — | 4 | 18 | Won | Edinburgh | S. J. Dawes |
| 291 | 13.3.1971 | Ireland | 4 | 1 | 1 | 2 | 23 | — | — | — | 3 | 9 | Won | Cardiff | S. J. Dawes |
| 292 | 27.3.1971 | France | 2 | — | — | 1 | 9 | 1 | 1 | — | — | 5 | Won | Paris | S. J. Dawes |
| 293 | 15.1.1972 | England | 1 | 1 | — | 2 | 12 | — | — | — | 1 | 3 | Won | Twickenham | D. J. Lloyd |
| 294 | 5.2.1972 | Scotland | 5 | 3 | — | 3 | 35 | 1 | 1 | — | 2 | 12 | Won | Cardiff | D. J. Lloyd |
| 295 | 25.3.1972 | France | 2 | — | — | 4 | 20 | — | — | — | 2 | 6 | Won | Cardiff | D. J. Lloyd |
| 296 | 2.12.1972 | New Zealand | 1 | — | — | 4 | 16 | 1 | — | — | 5 | 19 | Lost | Cardiff | W. D. Thomas |
| 297 | 20.1.1973 | England | 5 | 1 | — | 1 | 25 | — | — | 1 | 2 | 9 | Won | Cardiff | A. J. L. Lewis |
| 298 | 3.2.1973 | Scotland | — | — | — | 3 | 9 | 2 | 1 | — | — | 10 | Lost | Edinburgh | A. J. L. Lewis |
| 299 | 10.3.1973 | Ireland | 2 | 1 | — | 2 | 16 | 1 | 1 | — | 2 | 12 | Won | Cardiff | A. J. L. Lewis |
| 300 | 24.3.1973 | France | — | — | 1 | — | 3 | — | — | 1 | 3 | 12 | Lost | Paris | G. O. Edwards |
| 301 | 10.11.1973 | Australia | 3 | — | — | 4 | 24 | — | — | — | — | 0 | Won | Cardiff | G. O. Edwards |
| 302 | 19.1.1974 | Scotland | 1 | 1 | — | — | 6 | — | — | — | — | 0 | Won | Cardiff | G. O. Edwards |
| 303 | 2.2.1974 | Ireland | 1 | 1 | — | 1 | 9 | — | — | — | 3 | 9 | Drawn | Dublin | G. O. Edwards |
| 304 | 16.2.1974 | France | 1 | — | 1 | 3 | 16 | 1 | — | 1 | 3 | 16 | Drawn | Cardiff | G. O. Edwards |
| 305 | 16.3.1974 | England | 1 | — | — | 2 | 12 | 2 | 1 | — | 2 | 16 | Lost | Twickenham | G. O. Edwards |
| 306 | 18.1.1975 | France | 5 | 1 | — | 1 | 25 | 1 | — | — | 2 | 10 | Won | Paris | T. M. Davies |
| 307 | 15.2.1975 | England | 3 | 1 | — | 2 | 20 | 1 | — | — | — | 4 | Won | Cardiff | T. M. Davies |
| 308 | 1.3.1975 | Scotland | 1 | — | — | 2 | 10 | — | — | 1 | 3 | 12 | Lost | Edinburgh | T. M. Davies |
| 309 | 15.3.1975 | Ireland | 5 | 3 | — | 2 | 32 | 1 | — | — | — | 4 | Won | Cardiff | T. M. Davies |
| 310 | 20.12.1975 | Australia | 4 | 3 | 1 | 1 | 28 | — | — | — | 1 | 3 | Won | Cardiff | T. M. Davies |
| 311 | 17.1.1976 | England | 3 | 3 | — | 1 | 21 | — | — | — | 3 | 9 | Won | Twickenham | T. M. Davies |
| 312 | 7.2.1976 | Scotland | 3 | 2 | 1 | 3 | 28 | 1 | 1 | — | — | 6 | Won | Cardiff | T. M. Davies |
| 313 | 21.2.1976 | Ireland | 4 | 3 | — | 4 | 34 | — | — | — | 3 | 9 | Won | Dublin | T. M. Davies |
| 314 | 6.3.1976 | France | 1 | — | — | 5 | 19 | 2 | 1 | — | 1 | 13 | Won | Cardiff | T. M. Davies |
| 315 | 15.1.1977 | Ireland | 3 | 2 | 1 | 2 | 25 | — | — | — | 3 | 9 | Won | Cardiff | P. Bennett |
| 316 | 5.2.1977 | France | — | — | — | 3 | 9 | 2 | 1 | — | 2 | 16 | Lost | Paris | P. Bennett |
| 317 | 5.3.1977 | England | 2 | — | — | 2 | 14 | — | — | — | 3 | 9 | Won | Cardiff | P. Bennett |
| 318 | 19.3.1977 | Scotland | 2 | 2 | — | 2 | 18 | 1 | 1 | 1 | — | 9 | Won | Edinburgh | P. Bennett |
| 319 | 4.2.1978 | England | — | — | — | 3 | 9 | — | — | — | 2 | 6 | Won | Twickenham | P. Bennett |
| 320 | 18.2.1978 | Scotland | 4 | — | 1 | 1 | 22 | 2 | — | — | 2 | 14 | Won | Cardiff | P. Bennett |
| 321 | 4.3.1978 | Ireland | 2 | — | — | 4 | 20 | 1 | — | 1 | 3 | 16 | Won | Dublin | P. Bennett |
| 322 | 18.3.1978 | France | 2 | 1 | 2 | — | 16 | 1 | — | 1 | — | 7 | Won | Cardiff | P. Bennett |
| 323 | 11.6.1978 | Australia | 2 | — | — | — | 8 | 1 | 1 | — | 4 | 18 | Lost | Brisbane | T. J. Cobner |
| 324 | 17.6.1978 | Australia | 2 | — | 1 | 2 | 17 | 1 | — | 2 | 3 | 19 | Lost | Sydney | T. G. R. Davies |
| 325 | 11.11.1978 | New Zealand | — | — | — | 4 | 12 | 1 | — | — | 3 | 13 | Lost | Cardiff | J. P. R. Williams |
| 326 | 20.1.1979 | Scotland | 2 | 1 | — | 3 | 19 | 1 | — | — | 3 | 13 | Won | Edinburgh | J. P. R. Williams |
| 327 | 3.2.1979 | Ireland | 2 | 2 | — | 4 | 24 | 2 | 2 | — | 3 | 21 | Won | Cardiff | J. P. R. Williams |
| 328 | 17.2.1979 | France | 1 | — | — | 3 | 13 | 2 | — | — | 2 | 14 | Lost | Paris | J. P. R. Williams |
| 329 | 17.3.1979 | England | 5 | 2 | 1 | — | 27 | — | — | — | 1 | 3 | Won | Cardiff | J. P. R. Williams |
| 330 | 19.1.1980 | France | 4 | 1 | — | — | 18 | 1 | 1 | 1 | — | 9 | Won | Cardiff | J. Squire |
| 331 | 16.2.1980 | England | 2 | — | — | — | 8 | — | — | — | 3 | 9 | Lost | Twickenham | J. Squire |
| 332 | 1.3.1980 | Scotland | 3 | 1 | — | 1 | 17 | 1 | 1 | — | — | 6 | Won | Cardiff | J. Squire |
| 333 | 15.3.1980 | Ireland | 1 | — | — | 1 | 7 | 3 | 3 | — | 1 | 21 | Lost | Dublin | J. Squire |
| 334 | 1.11.1980 | New Zealand | — | — | — | 1 | 3 | 4 | 2 | — | 1 | 23 | Lost | Cardiff | S. P. Fenwick |
| 335 | 17.1.1981 | England | 1 | 1 | 1 | 4 | 21 | 1 | — | — | 5 | 19 | Won | Cardiff | S. P. Fenwick |
| 336 | 7.2.1981 | Scotland | — | — | — | 2 | 6 | 2 | 2 | — | 1 | 15 | Lost | Edinburgh | S. P. Fenwick |
| 337 | 21.2.1981 | Ireland | — | — | 1 | 2 | 9 | 2 | — | — | — | 8 | Won | Cardiff | J. Squire |
| 338 | 7.3.1981 | France | 1 | 1 | — | 3 | 15 | 1 | — | — | 5 | 19 | Lost | Paris | J. Squire |
| 339 | 5.12.1981 | Australia | 1 | 1 | 1 | 3 | 18 | 2 | 1 | — | 1 | 13 | Won | Cardiff | W. G. Davies |
| 340 | 23.1.1982 | Ireland | 1 | 1 | 1 | 1 | 12 | 3 | 1 | — | 2 | 20 | Lost | Dublin | W. G. Davies |
| 341 | 6.2.1982 | France | 1 | — | — | 6 | 22 | 1 | 1 | — | 2 | 12 | Won | Cardiff | W. G. Davies |
| 342 | 6.3.1982 | England | 1 | — | 1 | — | 7 | 2 | — | — | 3 | 17 | Lost | Twickenham | W. G. Davies |
| 343 | 20.3.1982 | Scotland | 1 | 1 | — | 4 | 18 | 5 | 4 | 2 | — | 34 | Lost | Cardiff | W. G. Davies |
| 344 | 5.2.1983 | England | 1 | — | 1 | 2 | 13 | 1 | — | 1 | 2 | 13 | Drawn | Cardiff | E. T. Butler |
| 345 | 19.2.1983 | Scotland | 2 | 1 | — | 3 | 19 | 1 | 1 | — | 3 | 15 | Won | Edinburgh | E. T. Butler |
| 346 | 5.3.1983 | Ireland | 3 | 1 | — | 3 | 23 | — | — | — | 3 | 9 | Won | Cardiff | E. T. Butler |
| 347 | 19.3.1983 | France | 1 | 1 | 1 | — | 9 | 1 | — | 1 | 3 | 16 | Lost | Paris | E. T. Butler |
| 348 | 12.11.1983 | Romania | — | — | — | 2 | 6 | 4 | 1 | — | 2 | 24 | Lost | Bucharest | E. T. Butler |
| 349 | 21.1.1984 | Scotland | 1 | 1 | — | 1 | 9 | 2 | 2 | — | 1 | 15 | Lost | Cardiff | E. T. Butler |
| 350 | 4.2.1984 | Ireland | 1 | 1 | — | 4 | 18 | — | — | — | 3 | 9 | Won | Dublin | M. J. Watkins |
| 351 | 18.2.1984 | France | 2 | 1 | — | 2 | 16 | 1 | 1 | 1 | 4 | 21 | Lost | Cardiff | M. J. Watkins |
| 352 | 17.3.1984 | England | 1 | 1 | 2 | 4 | 24 | — | — | — | 5 | 15 | Won | Twickenham | M. J. Watkins |
| 353 | 24.11.1984 | Australia | 1 | 1 | — | 1 | 9 | 4 | 3 | — | 2 | 28 | Lost | Cardiff | M. J. Watkins |
| 354 | 2.3.1985 | Scotland | 2 | 1 | 1 | 4 | 25 | 2 | 2 | 2 | 1 | 21 | Won | Edinburgh | T. D. Holmes |
| 355 | 16.3.1985 | Ireland | 1 | 1 | 1 | — | 9 | 2 | 2 | — | 3 | 21 | Lost | Cardiff | T. D. Holmes |
| 356 | 30.3.1985 | France | — | — | — | 1 | 3 | 2 | — | — | 2 | 14 | Lost | Paris | T. D. Holmes |
| 357 | 20.4.1985 | England | 2 | 2 | 1 | 3 | 24 | 1 | 1 | 1 | 2 | 15 | Won | Cardiff | T. D. Holmes |
| 358 | 9.11.1985 | Fiji | 7 | 3 | — | 2 | 40 | — | — | — | 1 | 3 | Won | Cardiff | T. D. Holmes |
| 359 | 17.1.1986 | England | 1 | 1 | 1 | 3 | 18 | — | — | 1 | 6 | 21 | Lost | Twickenham | D. F. Pickering |
| 360 | 1.2.1986 | Scotland | 1 | — | 1 | 5 | 22 | 3 | — | — | 1 | 15 | Won | Cardiff | D. F. Pickering |
| 361 | 15.2.1986 | Ireland | 2 | 1 | — | 3 | 19 | 1 | 1 | — | 2 | 12 | Won | Dublin | D. F. Pickering |

| Match | Date | Opponents | For T | C | D | P | Pts | Against T | C | D | P | Pts | Result | Venue | Captain |
|---|---|---|---|---|---|---|---|---|---|---|---|---|---|---|---|
| **362** | 1.3.1986 | France | — | — | — | 5 | 15 | 4 | 2 | 1 | — | 23 | Lost | Cardiff | D. F. Pickering |
| **363** | 31.5.1986 | Fiji | 2 | 1 | 1 | 3 | 22 | 2 | 2 | — | 1 | 15 | Won | Suva | D. F. Pickering |
| **364** | 12.6.1986 | Tonga | 1 | 1 | — | 3 | 15 | 1 | — | — | 1 | 7 | Won | Nuku'alofa | R. D. Moriarty |
| **365** | 14.6.1986 | W. Samoa | 4 | 2 | 1 | 3 | 32 | 2 | — | — | 2 | 14 | Won | Apia | R. D. Moriarty |
| **366** | 7.2.1987 | France | — | — | — | 3 | 9 | 2 | 1 | — | 2 | 16 | Lost | Paris | D. F. Pickering |
| **367** | 7.3.1987 | England | 1 | — | — | 5 | 19 | — | — | — | 4 | 12 | Won | Cardiff | D. F. Pickering |
| **368** | 21.3.1987 | Scotland | 1 | 1 | 1 | 1 | 12 | 2 | 2 | 1 | 2 | 21 | Lost | Edinburgh | D. F. Pickering |
| **369** | 4.4.1987 | Ireland | 2 | — | — | 1 | 11 | 2 | 2 | — | 1 | 15 | Lost | Cardiff | W. J. James |

# MATCH RECORDS

## MOST CONSECUTIVE MATCHES WON

| | |
|---|---|
| 11 | *1907* I *1908* E,S,F,I,A *1909* E,S,F,I *1910* F |
| 8 | *1970* F *1971* E,S,I,F *1972* E,S,F |
| 7 | *1975* I,A *1976* E,S,I,F *1977* I |

## MOST CONSECUTIVE MATCHES WITHOUT DEFEAT

| Matches | Wins | Draws | Period |
|---|---|---|---|
| 11 | 11 | 0 | 1906-07 to 1909-10 |
| 8 | 8 | 0 | 1969-70 to 1971-72 |
| 7 | 7 | 0 | 1974-75 to 1976-77 |

## MOST CONSECUTIVE MATCHES WITHOUT CONCEDING A TRY

| | |
|---|---|
| 5 | between 1946-47 and 1947-48 |
| 4 | between 1972-73 and 1973-74 |
| 3 | in 1949-40 |

## MOST CONSECUTIVE MATCHES WITHOUT CONCEDING A SCORE

| | |
|---|---|
| 3 | between 1946-47 and 1947-48 |

## MOST POINTS IN A MATCH
### By the team

| Pts | Opponents | Venue | Season |
|---|---|---|---|
| 49 | France | Swansea | 1909-10 |
| 47 | France | Paris | 1908-09 |
| 40 | Fiji | Cardiff | 1985-86 |
| 36 | France | Cardiff | 1907-08 |
| 35 | Scotland | Cardiff | 1971-72 |
| 35 | France | Swansea | 1930-31 |
| 34 | England | Cardiff | 1966-67 |
| 34 | Ireland | Dublin | 1975-76 |
| 32 | Scotland | Edinburgh | 1910-11 |
| 32 | Ireland | Cardiff | 1974-75 |
| 32 | Western Samoa | Apia | 1986 |
| 31 | France | Swansea | 1913-14 |
| 30 | England | Cardiff | 1968-69 |

## By a player

| Pts | Player | Opponents | Venue | Season |
|-----|--------|-----------|-------|--------|
| 19 | J. Bancroft | France | Swansea | 1909-10 |
| 19 | K. S. Jarrett | England | Cardiff | 1966-67 |
| 19 | P. Bennett | Ireland | Dublin | 1975-76 |
| 18 | G. Evans | France | Cardiff | 1981-82 |
| 16 | J. Shea | England | Swansea | 1919-20 |
| 16 | S. P. Fenwick | Ireland | Dublin | 1977-78 |
| 16 | S. P. Fenwick | Ireland | Cardiff | 1978-79 |
| 15 | B. John | Scotland | Cardiff | 1971-72 |
| 15 | M. A. Wyatt | Ireland | Cardiff | 1982-83 |
| 15 | P. H. Thorburn | Scotland | Cardiff | 1985-86 |
| 15 | P. H. Thorburn | France | Cardiff | 1985-86 |
| 15 | M. A. Wyatt | England | Cardiff | 1986-87 |

# MOST TRIES IN A MATCH
## By the team

| T | Opponents | Venue | Season |
|---|-----------|-------|--------|
| 11 | France | Paris | 1908-09 |
| 10 | France | Swansea | 1909-10 |
| 9 | France | Cardiff | 1907-08 |
| 8 | Scotland | Edinburgh | 1910-11 |
| 8 | England | Cardiff | 1921-22 |
| 7 | England | Cardiff | 1904-05 |
| 7 | France | Swansea | 1913-14 |
| 7 | France | Swansea | 1926-27 |
| 7 | France | Swansea | 1930-31 |
| 7 | Fiji | Cardiff | 1985-86 |
| 6 | England | Swansea | 1898-99 |
| 6 | Ireland | Cardiff | 1902-03 |
| 6 | England | Swansea | 1906-07 |
| 6 | Ireland | Cardiff | 1906-07 |
| 6 | Ireland | Cardiff | 1919-20 |

## By a player

| T | Player | Opponents | Venue | Season |
|---|--------|-----------|-------|--------|
| 4 | W. M. Llewellyn | England | Swansea | 1898-99 |
| 4 | R. A. Gibbs | France | Cardiff | 1907-08 |
| 4 | M. C. R. Richards | England | Cardiff | 1968-69 |
| 3 | J. J. Hodges | England | Swansea | 1902-03 |
| 3 | J. L. Williams | Ireland | Cardiff | 1906-07 |
| 3 | A. M. Baker | France | Paris | 1908-09 |
| 3 | W. J. Trew | France | Paris | 1908-09 |
| 3 | R. A. Gibbs | France | Swansea | 1909-10 |
| 3 | J. L. Williams | Ireland | Dublin | 1909-10 |
| 3 | R. A. Gibbs | Scotland | Edinburgh | 1910-11 |
| 3 | B. Williams | Ireland | Cardiff | 1919-20 |
| 3 | J. J. Williams | Australia | Cardiff | 1975-76 |

# MOST CONVERSIONS IN A MATCH
## By the team

| C | Opponents | Venue | Season |
|---|-----------|-------|--------|
| 8 | France | Swansea | 1909-10 |
| 7 | France | Paris | 1908-09 |
| 5 | France | Swansea | 1913-14 |
| 5 | France | Swansea | 1930-31 |
| 5 | England | Cardiff | 1966-67 |

## By a player

| C | Player | Opponents | Venue | Season |
|---|--------|-----------|-------|--------|
| 8 | J. Bancroft | France | Swansea | 1909-10 |
| 6 | J. Bancroft | France | Paris | 1908-09 |
| 5 | J. Bancroft | France | Swansea | 1913-14 |
| 5 | J. Bassett | France | Swansea | 1930-31 |
| 5 | K. S. Jarrett | England | Cardiff | 1966-67 |
| 4 | W. J. Bancroft | England | Swansea | 1898-99 |
| 4 | B. L. Jones | England | Swansea | 1950-51 |

# MOST DROPPED GOALS IN A MATCH

## By the team

| DG | Opponents | Venue | Season |
|----|-----------|-------|--------|
| 2 | Scotland | Swansea | 1911-12 |
| 2 | Scotland | Cardiff | 1913-14 |
| 2 | England | Swansea | 1919-20 |
| 2 | Scotland | Swansea | 1920-21 |
| 2 | France | Paris | 1929-30 |
| 2 | England | Cardiff | 1970-71 |
| 2 | France | Cardiff | 1977-78 |
| 2 | England | Twickenham | 1983-84 |

## By a player

| DG | Player | Opponents | Venue | Season |
|----|--------|-----------|-------|--------|
| 2 | J. Shea | England | Swansea | 1919-20 |
| 2 | A. Jenkins | Scotland | Swansea | 1920-21 |
| 2 | B. John | England | Cardiff | 1970-71 |
| 2 | M. Dacey | England | Twickenham | 1983-84 |

# MOST PENALTY GOALS IN A MATCH

## By the team

| PG | Opponents | Venue | Season |
|----|-----------|-------|--------|
| 6 | France | Cardiff | 1981-82 |
| 5 | France | Cardiff | 1975-76 |
| 5 | Scotland | Cardiff | 1985-86 |
| 5 | France | Cardiff | 1985-86 |
| 5 | England | Cardiff | 1986-87 |
| 4 | France | Cardiff | 1971-72 |
| 4 | New Zealand | Cardiff | 1972-73 |
| 4 | Australia | Cardiff | 1973-74 |
| 4 | Ireland | Dublin | 1975-76 |
| 4 | Ireland | Dublin | 1977-78 |
| 4 | New Zealand | Cardiff | 1978-79 |
| 4 | Ireland | Cardiff | 1978-79 |
| 4 | England | Cardiff | 1980-81 |
| 4 | Scotland | Cardiff | 1981-82 |
| 4 | Ireland | Dublin | 1983-84 |
| 4 | England | Twickenham | 1983-84 |
| 4 | Scotland | Edinburgh | 1984-85 |

## By a player

| PG | Player | Opponents | Venue | Season |
|----|--------|-----------|-------|--------|
| 6 | G. Evans | France | Cardiff | 1981-82 |
| 5 | P. H. Thorburn | France | Cardiff | 1985-86 |
| 5 | P. H. Thorburn | Scotland | Cardiff | 1985-86 |
| 5 | M. A. Wyatt | England | Cardiff | 1986-87 |
| 4 | B. John | France | Cardiff | 1971-72 |
| 4 | P. Bennett | New Zealand | Cardiff | 1972-73 |
| 4 | P. Bennett | Australia | Cardiff | 1973-74 |
| 4 | S. P. Fenwick | Ireland | Dublin | 1977-78 |
| 4 | S. P. Fenwick | Ireland | Cardiff | 1978-79 |
| 4 | S. P. Fenwick | England | Cardiff | 1980-81 |
| 4 | G. Evans | Scotland | Cardiff | 1981-82 |
| 4 | H. Davies | England | Twickenham | 1983-84 |
| 4 | M. A. Wyatt | Scotland | Edinburgh | 1984-85 |

# GOALS FROM MARKS

| * | Player | Opponents | Venue | Season |
|---|--------|-----------|-------|--------|
| 1 | W. J. Bancroft | Scotland | Edinburgh | 1894-95 |
| 1 | H. B. Winfield | England | Leicester | 1903-04 |
| 1 | W. C. Powell | England | Twickenham | 1930-31 |

| Player | Opponents | Venue | Season |
|---|---|---|---|
| T. Baker-Jones | Ireland | Dublin | 1881-82 |
| W. F. Evans | Ireland | Dublin | 1881-82 |
| R. H. Bridie | Ireland | Dublin | 1881-82 |
| T. J. S. Clapp | Ireland | Dublin | 1881-82 |
| C. P. Allen | England | Leeds | 1883-84 |
| H. M. Jordan | England | Swansea | 1884-85 |
| T. J. Pryce-Jenkins | Scotland | Newport | 1887-88 |
| J. Hannan | N. Z. Natives | Swansea | 1888-89 |
| G. Thomas | N. Z. Natives | Swansea | 1888-89 |
| T. W. Pearson | England | Newport | 1890-91 |
| D. Samuel | Ireland | Llanelli | 1890-91 |
| G. D. Fitzgerald | Scotland | Newport | 1893-94 |
| W. J. Elsey | England | Swansea | 1894-95 |
| D. Jones | England | Newport | 1896-97 |
| H. V. P. Huzzey | Ireland | Limerick | 1897-98 |
| T. Dobson | Ireland | Limerick | 1897-98 |
| W. M. Lewellyn | England | Swansea | 1898-99 |
| W. J. Trew | England | Gloucester | 1899-1900 |
| W. T. Osborne | England | Blackheath | 1901-02 |
| W. Jones | Ireland | Swansea | 1904-05 |
| H. T. Maddock | England | Richmond | 1905-06 |
| J. A. Brown | England | Swansea | 1906-07 |
| D. P. Jones | Ireland | Cardiff | 1906-07 |
| P. L. Hopkins | Australia | Cardiff | 1908-09 |
| B. Gronow | France | Swansea | 1909-10 |
| W. J. Spiller | Scotland | Cardiff | 1909-10 |
| L. M. Dyke | Ireland | Dublin | 1909-10 |
| R. C. S. Plummer | Scotland | Swansea | 1911-12 |
| G. L. Hirst | Scotland | Swansea | 1911-12 |
| J. P. ("Tuan") Jones | Scotland | Edinburgh | 1912-13 |
| W. J. Watts | England | Twickenham | 1913-14 |
| J. J. Wetter | Scotland | Cardiff | 1913-14 |
| I. T. Davies | Scotland | Cardiff | 1913-14 |
| W. J. Powell | England | Swansea | 1919-20 |
| J. Ring | England | Twickenham | 1920-21 |
| I. Evans | England | Cardiff | 1921-22 |
| C. Richards | England | Cardiff | 1921-22 |
| F. Palmer | England | Cardiff | 1921-22 |
| W. J. Delahay | England | Cardiff | 1921-22 |
| D. D. Hiddlestone | England | Cardiff | 1921-22 |
| G. M. Michael | England | Twickenham | 1922-23 |
| A. Owen | England | Swansea | 1923-24 |
| V. M. Griffiths | Scotland | Edinburgh | 1923-24 |
| E. Finch | France | Paris | 1923-24 |
| A. R. Rickard | France | Paris | 1923-24 |
| W. P. James | England | Twickenham | 1924-25 |
| C. Thomas | England | Twickenham | 1924-25 |
| B. R. Turnbull | Ireland | Belfast | 1924-25 |
| G. E. Andrews | England | Cardiff | 1925-26 |
| W. G. Morgan | France | Swansea | 1926-27 |
| J. C. Morley | England | Twickenham | 1928-29 |
| H. Peacock | Scotland | Swansea | 1928-29 |
| T. E. Jones-Davies | England | Cardiff | 1929-30 |
| G. G. Jones | Scotland | Edinburgh | 1929-30 |
| H. Jones | Ireland | Swansea | 1929-30 |
| A. R. Ralph | France | Swansea | 1930-31 |
| J. Lang | France | Swansea | 1930-31 |
| W. Davies | South Africa | Swansea | 1931-32 |
| A. McCarley | England | Cardiff | 1937-38 |
| M. J. Davies | Scotland | Cardiff | 1938-39 |
| J. R. G. Stephens | England | Cardiff | 1946-47 |
| G. Evans | England | Cardiff | 1946-47 |
| A. Meredith | England | Cardiff | 1948-49 |
| H. R. Williams | Scotland | Swansea | 1953-54 |
| C. L. Davies | England | Twickenham | 1955-56 |
| R. H. Davies | Scotland | Edinburgh | 1956-57 |
| J. R. Collins | Australia | Cardiff | 1957-58 |
| C. Roberts | Ireland | Dublin | 1957-58 |
| D. I. E. Bebb | England | Cardiff | 1958-59 |
| A. I. E. Pask | France | Paris | 1960-61 |
| D. J. Hayward | England | Cardiff | 1962-63 |
| S. J. Dawes | Ireland | Dublin | 1963-64 |
| K. S. Jarrett | England | Cardiff | 1966-67 |
| R. Wanbon | England | Twickenham | 1967-68 |
| L. T. D. Daniel | Scotland | Cardiff | 1969-70 |
| R. Hopkins | Engpland | Twickenham | 1969-70 |
| J. C. Bevan | England | Cardiff | 1970-71 |
| R. W. Windsor | Australia | Cardiff | 1973-74 |
| T. J. Cobner | Scotland | Cardiff | 1973-74 |
| S. P. Fenwick | France | Paris | 1974-75 |
| G. Price | France | Paris | 1974-75 |
| R. C. Burgess | Ireland | Cardiff | 1976-77 |

| Player | Opponents | Venue | Season |
|---|---|---|---|
| D. B. Williams | Australia | Brisbane | 1978 |
| T. D. Holmes | Australia | Sydney | 1978 |
| H. E. Rees | Scotland | Edinburgh | 1978-79 |
| R. D. Moriarty | Australia | Cardiff | 1981-82 |
| S. T. Jones | Scotland | Edinburgh | 1982-83 |
| D. J. Bishop | Australia | Cardiff | 1984-85 |
| J. Davies | England | Cardiff | 1984-85 |
| M. Jones | Scotland | Edinburgh | 1986-87 |

# CAPTAIN ON INTERNATIONAL DEBUT

| Player | Opponents | Venue | Season |
|---|---|---|---|
| J. A. Bevan | England | Blackheath | 1880-81 |
| C. P. Lewis | Ireland | Dublin | 1881-82 |
| J. R. Evans | England | Cardiff | 1933-34 |
| D. C. T. Rowlands | England | Cardiff | 1962-63 |
| M. J. Watkins | Ireland | Dublin | 1983-84 |

# TRIES BY FULL-BACKS

| Player | Opponents | Venue | Season |
|---|---|---|---|
| V. G. J. Jenkins | Ireland | Swansea | 1933-34 |
| K. S. Jarrett | England | Cardiff | 1966-67 |
| J. P. R. Williams | England | Twickenham | 1969-70 |
| J. P. R. Williams | England | Twickenham | 1971-72 |
| J. P. R. Williams (2) | England | Twickenham | 1975-76 |
| J. P. R. Williams | Ireland | Cardiff | 1976-77 |
| J. P. R. Williams | England | Cardiff | 1976-77 |
| W. R. Blyth | Ireland | Dublin | 1979-80 |
| M. A. Wyatt | Ireland | Cardiff | 1982-83 |
| H. Davies | France | Cardiff | 1983-84 |

# ALL THE POINTS FOR WALES IN A MATCH
## (where more than one scoring action is involved)

| Pts | Player | Opponents | Venue | Season |
|---|---|---|---|---|
| 15 | P. H. Thorburn | France | Cardiff | 1985-86 |
| 9 | K. H. L. Richards | Ireland | Cardiff | 1960-61 |
| 9 | S. P. Fenwick | France | Paris | 1976-77 |
| 9 | P. Bennett | England | Twickenham | 1977-78 |
| 9 | P. H. Thorburn | France | Paris | 1986-87 |
| 8 | A. Jenkins | Scotland | Swansea | 1920-21 |
| 7 | G. D. Fitzgerald | Scotland | Newport | 1893-94 |
| 7 | H. V. P. Huzzey | England | Blackheath | 1897-98 |
| 7 | R. W. Boom | England | Twickenham | 1932-33 |
| 7 | W. T. H. Davies | Ireland | Belfast | 1938-39 |
| 6 | W. M. Llewellyn | Scotland | Edinburgh | 1904-05 |
| 6 | W. Wooller | Scotland | Swansea | 1936-37 |
| 6 | A. McCarley | Scotland | Edinburgh | 1937-38 |
| 6 | W. E. Tamplin | Australia | Cardiff | 1947-48 |
| 6 | G. M. Griffiths | France | Paris | 1952-53 |
| 6 | G. Rowlands | England | Twickenham | 1953-54 |
| 6 | T. J. Davies | Ireland | Cardiff | 1956-57 |
| 6 | T. J. Davies | England | Twickenham | 1959-60 |
| 6 | D. I. E. Bebb | England | Cardiff | 1960-61 |
| 6 | D. I. E. Bebb | England | Twickenham | 1963-64 |
| 6 | G. O. Edwards | South Africa | Cardiff | 1969-70 |
| 6 | S. P. Fenwick | Scotland | Edinburgh | 1980-81 |
| 6 | G. Evans | Romania | Bucharest | 1983-84 |
| 5 | A. Jenkins | Scotland | Edinburgh | 1919-20 |

# INDIVIDUAL RECORDS

## LONGEST CAREER SPANS

| Seasons | Player | Caps | Career Span |
|---|---|---|---|
| 14 | W. J. Trew | 29 | 1899-1900 to 1912-13 |
| 14 | T. H. Vile | 8 | 1907-08 to 1920-21 |
| 14 | H. Tanner | 25 | 1935-36 to 1948-49 |
| 13 | A. J. Gould | 27 | 1884-85 to 1896-97 |
| 13 | T. W. Pearson | 13 | 1890-91 to 1902-03 |
| 13 | J. P. Jones | 14 | 1908-09 to 1920-21 |
| 13 | W. H. Travers | 12 | 1936-37 to 1948-49 |
| 13 | J. P. R. Williams | 55 | 1968-69 to 1980-81 |

## MOST CONSECUTIVE CAPS IN A CAREER

| Caps | Player | Opponents |
|---|---|---|
| 53 | G. O. Edwards | 1967 F,E,NZ 1968 E,S,I,F 1969 S,I,F,E, NZ (1 and 2), A 1970 SA,S,E,I,F 1971 E,S,I, F 1972 E,S,F,NZ 1973 E,S,I,F,A 1974 S,I,F,E 1975 F,E,S,I,A 1976 E,S,I,F 1977 I,F,E,S 1978 E,S,I,F |
| 43 | K. J. Jones | 1947 E,S,F,I,A 1948 E,S,F,I 1949 E,S,I,F 1950 E,S,I,F 1951 E,S,I,F,SA 1952 E,S,I,F 1953 E,S,I,F,NZ 1954 E,I,F,S 1955 E,S,I,F 1956 E,S,I,F |

## MOST CAPS IN A CAREER

| Caps | Player | Career Span |
|---|---|---|
| 55 | J. P. R. Williams | 1968-69 to 1980-81 |
| 53 | G. O. Edwards | 1966-67 to 1977-78 |
| 46 | T. G. R. Davies | 1966-67 to 1978 |
| 44 | K. J. Jones | 1946-47 to 1956-57 |
| 41 | G. Price | 1974-75 to 1982-83 |
| 38 | T. M. Davies | 1968-69 to 1975-76 |
| 36 | D. Williams | 1962-63 to 1970-71 |
| 35 | R. M. Owen | 1900-01 to 1911-12 |
| 34 | B. V. Meredith | 1953-54 to 1961-62 |
| 34 | D. I. E. Bebb | 1958-59 to 1966-67 |
| 34 | W. D. Morris | 1966-67 to 1973-74 |
| 34 | A. J. Martin | 1973-74 to 1980-81 |
| 33 | W. J. Bancroft | 1889-90 to 1900-01 |
| 32 | B. Price | 1960-61 to 1969 |
| 32 | J. R. G. Stephens | 1946-47 to 1956-57 |
| 32 | G. A. D. Wheel | 1973-74 to 1981-82 |

## MOST POINTS IN A CAREER

| Pts | Player | Matches | Career Span |
|---|---|---|---|
| 166 | P Bennett | 29 | 1968-69 to 1977-78 |
| 152 | S. P. Fenwick | 30 | 1974-75 to 1980-81 |
| 90 | B. John | 25 | 1966-67 to 1971-72 |
| 89 | P. H. Thorburn | 8 | 1984-85 to 1986-87 |
| 88 | J. Bancroft | 18 | 1908-09 to 1913-14 |
| 88 | G. O. Edwards | 53 | 1966-67 to 1977-78 |
| 81 | M. A. Wyatt | 10 | 1982-83 to 1986-87 |
| 74 | G. Evans | 10 | 1980-81 to 1983-84 |
| 73 | K. S. Jarrett | 10 | 1966-67 to 1969 |
| 72 | T. G. R. Davies | 46 | 1966-67 to 1978 |

## MOST TRIES IN A CAREER

| T | Player | Matches | Career Span |
|---|--------|---------|-------------|
| 20 | G. O. Edwards | 53 | 1966-67 to 1977-78 |
| 20 | T. G. R. Davies | 46 | 1966-67 to 1978 |
| 17 | R. A. Gibbs | 16 | 1905-06 to 1910-11 |
| 17 | J. L. Williams | 17 | 1905-06 to 1910-11 |
| 17 | K. J. Jones | 44 | 1946-47 to 1956-57 |
| 16 | W. M. Lewellyn | 20 | 1898-99 to 1905-06 |
| 14 | E. Morgan | 16 | 1901-02 to 1907-08 |
| 12 | J. J. Williams | 30 | 1972-73 to 1978-79 |
| 11 | W. J. Trew | 29 | 1899-1900 to 1912-13 |
| 11 | R. T. Gabe | 24 | 1900-01 to 1907-08 |
| 11 | D. I. E. Bebb | 34 | 1958-59 to 1966-67 |

## MOST CONVERSIONS IN A CAREER

| C | Player | Matches | Career Span |
|---|--------|---------|-------------|
| 38 | J. Bancroft | 18 | 1908-09 to 1913-14 |
| 20 | W. J. Bancroft | 33 | 1889-90 to 1900-01 |
| 18 | P. Bennett | 29 | 1968-69 to 1977-78 |
| 17 | K. S. Jarrett | 10 | 1966-67 to 1969 |
| 14 | H. B. Winfield | 15 | 1902-03 to 1908-09 |
| 11 | S. P. Fenwick | 30 | 1974-75 to 1980-81 |
| 10 | J. A. Bassett | 15 | 1928-29 to 1931-32 |
| 10 | V. G. J. Jenkins | 14 | 1932-33 to 1938-39 |

## MOST DROPPED GOALS IN A CAREER

| DG | Player | Matches | Career Span |
|----|--------|---------|-------------|
| 8 | B. John | 25 | 1966-67 to 1971-72 |
| 7 | W. G. Davies | 21 | 1978 to 1984-85 |
| 6 | J. Davies | 13 | 1984-85 to 1986-87 |
| 3 | P. F. Bush | 8 | 1905-06 to 1909-10 |
| 3 | A. Jenkins | 14 | 1919-20 to 1927-28 |
| 3 | G. O. Edwards | 53 | 1966-67 to 1977-78 |
| 3 | S. P. Fenwick | 30 | 1974-75 to 1980-81 |
| 3 | M. Dacey | 13 | 1982-83 to 1986 |

## MOST PENALTY GOALS IN A CAREER

| PG | Player | Matches | Career Span |
|----|--------|---------|-------------|
| 36 | P. Bennett | 29 | 1968-69 to 1977-78 |
| 35 | S. P. Fenwick | 30 | 1974-75 to 1980-81 |
| 25 | P. H. Thorburn | 8 | 1984-85 to 1986-87 |
| 22 | G. Evans | 10 | 1980-81 to 1983-84 |
| 21 | M. A. Wyatt | 10 | 1982-83 to 1986-87 |
| 13 | B. John | 25 | 1966-67 to 1971-72 |
| 12 | T. J. Davies | 21 | 1952-53 to 1960-61 |
| 11 | K. S. Jarrett | 10 | 1966-67 to 1969 |

## MOST MATCHES AS CAPTAIN

| | | |
|---|---|---|
| 18 | A. J. Gould | (8 victories) |
| 14 | D. C. T. Rowlands | (6 victories) |
| 14 | W. J. Trew | (12 victories) |
| 13 | J. A. Gwilliam | (9 victories) |
| 13 | G. O. Edwards | (6 victories) |
| 12 | H. Tanner | (5 victories) |
| 11 | W. J. Bancroft | (7 victories) |
| 10 | E. G. Nicholls | (7 victories) |

# FRANCE INTERNATIONAL
# TEAMS AND RECORDS

| 1905-06 | | 1906-07 |
| --- | --- | --- |
| v. NZ | v. ENGLAND | v. ENGLAND |
| †W.H. CRICHTON | W.H. CRICHTON | †H. ISAAC |
| †G. LANE | *G. LANE | G. LANE |
| †H. LEVEE | †E. LESIEUR 1T | †H. MARTIN |
| †R. SAGOT | E.W. LEWIS | P. MACLOS 1PG,2C |
| †PUJOL | †P. MACLOS | †C. VAREILLES |
| *†H. AMAND | †T. VARVIER | A. HUBERT |
| †A. LACASSAGNE | †A. HUBERT | A. LACASSAGNE |
| †A. VERGES | A. VERGES | A. VERGES |
| †P. DEDEYN | †MAURIN | †G. POIRIER |
| †A. BRANLAT 1C | A. BRANLAT 1C | †P. MAURIAT |
| †G. JEROME 1T | G. JEROME | †M. GIACCARDY |
| †A.H. MUHR | A.H. MUHR 1T | A.H. MUHR 1T |
| †M. COMMUNEAU | M. COMMUNEAU | *M. COMMUNEAU 1T |
| †N. CESSIEUX 1T | †P. GAUDERMEN | †C. BEAURIN |
| †J. DUFOURCQ | J. DUFOURCQ | J. DUFOURCQ |
| Parc des Princes | Parc des Princes | Richmond |
| LOST 8-38 | LOST 8-35 | LOST 13-41 |
| FR.: 1G 1T | FR.: 1G 1T | ENG.: 5G 1DG 4T |
| NZ: 4G 6T | ENG.: 4G 5T | FR.: 2G 1PG |
| 1 Jan. 1906 | 22 Mar. 1906 | 5 Jan. 1907 |

Cyril Rutherford, a Scot who settled in France and joined the Racing Club de Paris in 1897, was a moving force behind France's recognition as a leading rugby nation. He had been a useful player, appearing for his club in the French Championship finals of 1900 and 1902, and he had captained France in an international against Canada in 1902. (This was one of several unofficial French matches played prior to 1906, when official games began with a match against the All Blacks.) Rutherford later became secretary of the French Rugby Federation (the FFR) and secured regular official fixtures with the International Board nations.

Three of France's early players were emigrants. Two Englishmen, Lewis and Crichton, were members of the Le Havre club. Lewis, a British Army officer, was an experienced player who had featured in French club rugby since the early 1890s, but little is known of Crichton. Allan Muhr, a forward who scored tries in two of the first three French matches, was from Chicago. He had originally come to France to study, but stayed to act as an interpreter. At the outset of the Second World War he joined the American Red Cross, but was arrested by the Germans and deported to Hamburg where he died.

| 1907-08 | | 1908-09 | | |
| --- | --- | --- | --- | --- |
| v. ENGLAND | v. WALES | v. ENGLAND | v. WALES | v. IRELAND |
| H. ISAAC | H. MARTIN | †J. CAUJOLLE | †E. DE JOUVENCEL | E. DE JOUVENCEL |
| E. LESIEUR | E. LESIEUR | E. LESIEUR | E. LESIEUR | †F. MOURONVAL |
| G. LANE | G. LANE | †H. HOUBLAIN | R. SAGOT 1T | E. LESIEUR |
| R. SAGOT | †M. LEUVIELLE | T. VARVIER | T. VARVIER | †M. BURGUN |
| C. VAREILLES | C. VAREILLES 1DG | G. LANE | G. LANE | G. LANE 1T |
| A. HUBERT | A. HUBERT | †A. THEURIET | A. THEURIET | †C. MARTIN |
| †A. MAYSONNIE | A. MAYSONNIE | A. HUBERT | A. HUBERT | A. HUBERT |
| P. MAURIAT | P. MAURIAT | †G. FOURCADE | G. FOURCADE | †J. GOMMES |
| †G. BORCHARD | †A. MASSE | R. DUVAL | †P. DUPRE | P. GUILLEMIN |
| †P. GUILLEMIN | P. GUILLEMIN | P. GUILLEMIN | P. MAURIAT 1C | P. MAURIAT 1C |
| †R. DUVAL | R. DUVAL | A. MASSE | A. MASSE | †M. LEGRAIN |
| †H. MOURE | A. BRANLAT | *M. COMMUNEAU | *M. COMMUNEAU | *M. COMMUNEAU |
| *M. COMMUNEAU | *M. COMMUNEAU | †J. ICARD | J. ICARD | †M. HOURDEBAIGT 1T |
| C. BEAURIN | J. DUFOURCQ | G. BORCHARD | G. BORCHARD | G. BORCHARD |
| †R. DE MALMANN | R. DE MALMANN | R. DE MALMANN | R. DE MALMANN | R. DE MALMANN |
| Stade Colombes | Cardiff Arms Park | Leicester | Stade Colombes | Lansdowne Road |
| LOST 0-19 | LOST 4-36 | LOST 0-22 | LOST 5-47 | LOST 8-19 |
| FR.: NIL | WALES: 3G 1PG 6T | ENG.: 2G 4T | FR.: 1G | IRE.: 2G 1PG 2T |
| ENG.: 2G 3T | FR.: 1DG | FR.: NIL | WALES: 7G 4T | FR.: 1G 1T |
| 1 Jan. 1908 | 2 Mar. 1908 | 30 Jan. 1909 | 23 Feb. 1909 | 20 Mar. 1909 |

France suffered big defeats in 1908 and 1909, years in which Wales and Ireland were added to the fixture list. Vareilles, who later established himself as a planter in Indochina, scored France's only points in 1908 with a first-half drop-goal at Cardiff. Lesieur, Lane and Hubert were the only backs to play in each match.

Lane was an engineer who played 16 games for France. Solid, swift and with a good sense of anticipation, Lane was killed in action in September 1914. Lesieur was the French 100m champion in 1906, and a Parisian for long associated with the Stade Francais club. Elegant, fast and the scorer of two tries in 12 internationals, Lesieur was decorated for valour during the Great War, and maintained an interest in French rugby until his death in 1985.

The leading French player before the First War was Marcel Communeau. He set a record number of 21 appearances and led the side 13 times (including the occasion in 1911 when France gained their first victory). An engineer, he had won his first cap in 1906 when playing for his club's second fifteen.

## 1909-10

| v. WALES | v. SCOTLAND | v. ENGLAND | v. IRELAND |
|---|---|---|---|
| †J. MENRATH 1c,2PG | †J. COMBE | J. COMBE | J. COMBE |
| | | | |
| *G. LANE | E. LESIEUR | E. LESIEUR | †J. DE MUISON |
| M. BURGUN | †J. DEDET | G. LANE | J. DEDET |
| H. HOUBLAIN | M. BURGUN | C. VAREILLES | M. BURGUN |
| †M. BRUNEAU | C. VAREILLES | M. BRUNEAU | E. LESIEUR |
| | | | |
| C. MARTIN | C. MARTIN | J. DEDET | †ROUJAS |
| A. MAYSONNIE | A. THEURIET | †G. LATERRADE | G. LATERRADE |
| | | | |
| †R. BOUDREAU | R. BOUDREAU | G. THEVENOT | G. THEVENOT |
| †J. ANDURAN | †J. CADENAT | J. CADENAT | M. LEGRAIN |
| †G. THEVENOT | *M. COMMUNEAU | *M. COMMUNEAU 1T | *M. COMMUNEAU |
| M. HOURDEBAIGT | M. HOURDEBAIGT | M. HOURDEBAIGT | M. HOURDEBAIGT |
| P. MAURIAT 1T | P. MAURIAT | P. MAURIAT | P. MAURIAT |
| A. MASSE | A. MASSE | A. MASSE | A. MASSE |
| †L. LAFITTE 1T | L. LAFITTE | R. DE MALMANN | R. DE MALMANN |
| P. GUILLEMIN | P. GUILLEMIN | P. GUILLEMIN | P. GUILLEMIN 1T |
| | | | |
| Swansea | Inverleith | Parc des Princes | Parc des Princes |
| LOST 14-49 | LOST 0-27 | LOST 3-11 | LOST 3-8 |
| | | | |
| WALES: 8G 1PG 2T | SCOT.: 3G 4T | FR.: 1T | FR.: 1T |
| FR.: 1G 2PG 1T | FR.: NIL | ENG.: 1G 2T | IRE.: 1G 1T |
| | | | |
| 1 Jan. 1910 | 22 Jan. 1910 | 3 Mar. 1910 | 27 Mar. 1910 |

France had problems for the trip to Swansea and there is a legend that Joe Anduran, a picture-gallery assistant, was invited at the last minute to join the team, as a result of a chance meeting with Cyril Rutherford, who was desperate to fill a vacancy in the side. Anduran, who never again played for France, was killed in action in the Great War.

There were two good home performances at the end of the season. Against England the French backs were impressive and Laterrade, a schoolmaster, made an impressive debut at the heels of a lively pack. Furthermore, Combe was a sound, consistent full-back whose tackling persistently upset English attacks.

Ireland were made to struggle for victory in the season's concluding match. Combe again pleased the crowd with his fine tackling, and the threequarters marked the Irish backs tightly. Pierre Guillemin, the tallest of the French forwards, scored a try in France's narrow defeat. He was one of four players to compete in each match of France's first complete season in the International Championship. Guillemin was another Great War casualty.

## 1910-11

| v. SCOTLAND | v. ENGLAND | v. WALES | v. IRELAND |
|---|---|---|---|
| J. COMBE | †F.X. DUTOUR | T. VARVIER | F.X. DUTOUR 1c |
| | | | |
| †P. FAILLIOT 2T | E. LESIEUR | P. FAILLIOT | P. FAILLIOT 1T |
| M. BURGUN | M. BURGUN | J. DEDET | J. DEDET |
| †A. FRANQUENELLE | T. VARVIER | †C. DU SOUICH | C. DU SOUICH |
| G. LANE | †G. CHARPENTIER | G. LANE | E. LESIEUR |
| | | | |
| †G. PEYROUTOU 1T | G. PEYROUTOU | *R. DUVAL | R. DUVAL |
| G. LATERRADE 1T | G. LATERRADE | A. THEURIET | G. LATERRADE |
| | | | |
| P. MAURIAT | P. MAURIAT | P. MAURIAT | G. BORCHARD |
| †J. BAVOZET | J. BAVOZET | J. BAVOZET | †R. PAOLI |
| P. GUILLEMIN | P. GUILLEMIN | P. GUILLEMIN | †R. MONNIER |
| †F. FORGUES | F. FORGUES | F. FORGUES | P. MAURIAT |
| *M. COMMUNEAU | *M. COMMUNEAU | †R. DUFOUR | *M. COMMUNEAU |
| †P. DECAMPS 2c | R. DUVAL | J. CADENAT | J. CADENAT |
| †P. MOUNICQ | P. MOUNICQ | P. MOUNICQ | P. MOUNICQ |
| M. LEGRAIN | M. LEGRAIN | M. LEGRAIN | M. LEGRAIN |
| | | | |
| Stade Colombes | Twickenham | Parc des Princes | Cork |
| WON 16-15 | LOST 0-37 | LOST 0-15 | LOST 5-25 |
| | | | |
| FR.: 2G 2T | ENG.: 5G 2T 2PG | FR.: NIL | IRE.: 3G 1DG 2T |
| SCOT.: 1G 1DG 2T | FR.: NIL | WALES: 3G | FR.: 1G |
| | | | |
| 2 Jan. 1911 | 28 Jan. 1911 | 28 Feb. 1911 | 25 Mar. 1911 |

France beat Scotland at the start of the season to record their first international victory. The French backs were the architects of a fine win. Peyroutou and Laterrade combined effectively at half-back and cleverly brought the best out of a fast threequarter line. Many observers noted that for a first time France played with collective purpose, abandoning the happy-go-lucky approach which had characterised their early international performances.

Peyroutou and Laterrade each scored, but the French hero was Pierre Failliot, whose two tries were achieved with style. He ran with the pace which had made him a French champion athlete over 100m, 200m and 400m, and once in flight he was extremely difficult to stop. The second of his tries, converted by Decamps, put the French into the safety of a 16-12 lead.

Failliot and Lane were unable to travel to London for France's first visit to Twickenham. (Indeed numerous difficulties concerning the persuasion of players to travel to away fixtures confronted French selectors before the Great War.) France lost the rest of their matches in 1911, though in Cork another try by Failliot enabled the side to lead 5-0 at half time.

## 1911-12

| | v. IRELAND | v. SCOTLAND | v. WALES | v. ENGLAND |
|---|---|---|---|---|
| | T. VARVIER | F.X. DUTOUR | F.X. DUTOUR | F.X. DUTOUR |
| | P. FAILLIOT | P. FAILLIOT | E. LESIEUR 1T | P. FAILLIOT 1T |
| | G. LANE | M. BURGUN | *G. LANE | *G. LANE |
| | †D. IHINGOUE | D. IHINGOUE | †J. SENTILLES | J. SENTILLES |
| | †J. DUFAU 1T | J. DUFAU | J. DUFAU | J. DUFAU 1T |
| | M. BURGUN | *J. DEDET | G. CHARPENTIER | G. CHARPENTIER |
| | †L. LARRIBEAU | L. LARRIBEAU | L. LARRIBEAU 1T | L. LARRIBEAU |
| | †J.C. DE BEYSSAC | J.C. DE BEYSSAC | †J. FORESTIER | M. MONNIOT |
| | P. MAURIAT | †E. VALLOT | †A. PASCAREL | A. PASCAREL |
| | P. MOUNICQ | R. MONNIER | †P. THIL | P. THIL |
| | R. PAOLI 1T | R. PAOLI | J. CADENAT | J. CADENAT |
| | *M. COMMUNEAU | P. MAURIAT | †M. MONNIOT | P. MOUNICQ |
| | †M. BOYAU | M. BOYAU | M. BOYAU 1C | M. BOYAU 1C |
| | †J. DOMERCQ | J. DOMERCQ | F. FORGUES | F. FORGUES |
| | F. FORGUES | M. COMMUNEAU 1T | M. COMMUNEAU | M. COMMUNEAU |
| | Parc des Princes | Inverleith | Newport | Parc des Princes |
| | LOST 6-11 | LOST 3-31 | LOST 8-14 | LOST 8-18 |
| | FR.: 2T | SCOT.: 5G 1PG 1T | WALES: 1G 3T | FR.: 1G 1T |
| | IRE.: 1G 2T | FR.: 1T | FR.: 1G 1T | ENG.: 1PG 1DG 4T |
| | 1 Jan. 1912 | 20 Jan. 1912 | 25 Mar. 1912 | 8 Apr. 1912 |

All four matches were lost, but the margins of defeat against Ireland, Wales and England were narrow and there was agreement that French rugby had made great strides since 1906.

Larribeau, the scrum-half, was one of two backs who played in each match. He gained international recognition from Périgueux, where he completed his military service. He was a small man endowed with an exceptional pass which permitted his fly-half to stand 25-30 metres from the scrummage. He gained seven caps before the war, in which he served as a sergeant in the Infantry. Larribeau was killed leading his men courageously near Poivre in December 1916.

The evergreen Communeau and Boyau were the only forwards to play throughout the Championship. Boyau was from an aristocratic family of French landowners, an excellent cyclist, and a rugby footballer in the Corinthian tradition. A mobile forward, he gained a reputation as one of the leading wing-forwards of the day. During the Great War Boyau served as a pilot, but he was shot down and killed in 1918. By all accounts, most of France mourned the death of one of their noble sporting knights.

## 1912-13

| | v. SCOTLAND | v. S.AFRICA | v. ENGLAND | v. WALES | v. IRELAND |
|---|---|---|---|---|---|
| | F.X. DUTOUR | J. CAUJOLLE | J. CAUJOLLE | †J. SEMMARTIN | J. SEMMARTIN |
| | L. LARRIBEAU | †G. ANDRE 1C | G. ANDRE | G. ANDRE 1T | G. ANDRE |
| | J. SENTILLES | M. BRUNEAU 1T | J. DEDET | P. JAUREGUY | J. DEDET |
| | *G. LANE | J. SENTILLES | M. BURGUN | A. FRANQUENELLE | A. FRANQUENELLE |
| | †P. JAUREGUY | P. JAUREGUY | P. FAILLIOT | P. FAILLIOT 1T | P. JAUREGUY |
| | M. BURGUN | †A. CHATEAU | M. BRUNEAU | †C. BIOUSSA | C. BIOUSSA |
| | †M. HEDEMBAIGHT | M. HEDEMBAIGHT | A. THEURIET | †P. STRUXIANO 1C | P. STRUXIANO |
| | P. MAURIAT | P. MAURIAT | †M. FAVRE | M. FAVRE | †C. TAVERNIER |
| | A. PASCAREL | A. PASCAREL | A. PASCAREL | P. THIL | A. PASCAREL |
| | †J. SEBEDIO 1T | P. THIL | P. THIL | P. MAURIAT | P. MAURIAT |
| | P. THIL | P. MOUNICQ | P. MOUNICQ | †J. PODEVIN | J. PODEVIN |
| | M. LEUVIELLE | *M. LEUVIELLE | *M. LEUVIELLE | *M. LEUVIELLE | J. CADENAT |
| | M. LEGRAIN | M. LEGRAIN | M. LEGRAIN | M. BOYAU | †A. EUTROPE |
| | P. MOUNICQ | M. COMMUNEAU | M. COMMUNEAU | M. COMMUNEAU | M. LEGRAIN |
| | F. FORGUES | F. FORGUES | J. SEBEDIO | F. FORGUES | *M. BOYAU |
| | Parc des Princes | Bordeaux | Twickenham | Parc des Princes | Cork |
| | LOST 3-21 | LOST 5-35 | LOST 0-20 | LOST 8-11 | LOST 0-24 |
| | FR.: 1T | FR.: 1G | ENG.: 1G 5T | FR.: 1G 1T | FR.: NIL |
| | SCOT.: 3G 2T | SA: 4G 1PG 4T | FR.: NIL | WALES: 1G 2T | IRE.: 3G 3T |
| | 1 Jan. 1913 | 11 Jan. 1913 | 25 Jan. 1913 | 27 Feb. 1913 | 24 Mar. 1913 |

French rugby fell under a cloud at the start of the season, as a result of a riot during and after the France-Scotland match. The game in France was controlled by the Union des Sociétés Françaises des Sports Athlétique until 1920, and as a result of the commotion and an assault on the referee, the Scots broke relations with this body, declining to host the match scheduled for 1914.

Fortunately, there were no further riot scenes at Bordeaux for the first official match against South Africa. The tourists, who had amassed 55 points against France in an unofficial match in 1907, were again comfortable winners in a match which marked the debut of Géo André, one of France's leading sportsmen.

André played seven successive matches until the outbreak of the war, but gained additional fame as an athlete, representing France at the Olympics between 1908 and 1924. As a wing he ran with an unusual action, a legacy of his expertise as a hurdler, and he was a difficult opponent to halt. A Great-War flying ace, he volunteered for action in the Second War, and died a hero in North Africa in May 1943, aged 54.

## 1913-14

| | v. IRELAND | v. WALES | v. ENGLAND |
|---|---|---|---|
| | †R. Lasserre | J. Caujolle | J. Caujolle |
| | †R. Lacoste 1t | R. Lacoste | R. Lacoste |
| | †F. Poydebasque | †L. Besset | L. Besset 2c |
| | †G. Pierrot | G. Pierrot | G. Pierrot |
| | G. André 1t | G. André | G. André 1t |
| | C. Bioussa | F. Poydebasque | M. Burgun |
| | L. Larribeau | M. Hedembaight | L. Larribeau |
| | J.C. de Beyssac | J.C. de Beyssac | †E. Iguinitz |
| | †F. Faure | F. Faure | F. Faure |
| | †M.F. Lubin-Lebrere | M.F. Lubin-Lebrere | M.F. Lubin-Lebrere 1t |
| | †P. Lavaud | †R. Desvouges | *M. Leuvielle |
| | †J.M. Arnal | J.M. Arnal | J.C. de Beyssac |
| | *F. Forgues | P. Lavaud | †Capmau 1t |
| | J. Sebedio | *M. Leuvielle | †P. Bascou |
| | M. Legrain | M. Legrain | F. Forgues |
| | Parc des Princes | Swansea | Stade Colombes |
| | LOST 6-8 | LOST 0-31 | LOST 13-39 |
| | Fr.: 2t | Wales: 5g 2t | Fr.: 2g 1t |
| | Ire.: 1g 1t | Fr.: nil | Eng.: 6g 3t |
| | 1 Jan. 1914 | 2 Mar. 1914 | 13 Apr. 1914 |

France nearly beat Ireland in 1914. Larribeau and Bioussa made clever use of the blind-side to create a try for Lacoste in the first half, and André added another early in the second half. But a spirited Irish rally in which eight points were scored just pipped the French when victory appeared to be within their grasp. The match was played in snow.

Forgues, the captain against Ireland, and Conilh de Beyssac, were excellent forwards whose careers were ended by the war. Forgues was a Basque who had been a founder of the Bayonne club, and he made 11 appearances for France. One of the most talented wing-forwards of his era, he helped to make his club one of the most exciting in France by imposing an open, entertaining style of play based on rapid, accurate passing between backs and forwards. De Beyssac was reputed to be the most complete French forward before the war. A skilful dribbler, he was a good line-out technician and a sound scrummager.

Despite conceding 16 tries in the last two matches, Jean Caujolle was respected as the first great French full-back. Solidly built, he was a steady catcher, a determined tackler, and had a long, accurate kick. He made five appearances between 1909 and 1914.

## 1919-20

| | v. SCOTLAND | v. ENGLAND | v. WALES | v. IRELAND |
|---|---|---|---|---|
| | †A. Chilo | †T. Cambre | T. Cambre | T. Cambre |
| | †A. Jaureguy | A. Jaureguy | A. Jaureguy 1t | A. Jaureguy 2t |
| | R. Lasserre | †B. Lavigne | B. Lavigne | †F. Borde |
| | †R. Crabos | R. Crabos 1t | R. Crabos | R. Crabos |
| | †P. Serre | P. Serre | A. Chilo | †R. Got 2t |
| | †E. Billac | E. Billac | E. Billac | E. Billac |
| | *P. Struxiano | *P. Struxiano | *P. Struxiano 1c | *P. Struxiano |
| | M.F. Lubin-Lebrere | M.F. Lubin-Lebrere | M.F. Lubin-Lebrere | M.F. Lubin-Lebrere |
| | †P. Pons | P. Pons | P. Pons | †W. Gayraud 1t |
| | J. Sebedio | †E. Soulie | †M. Biraben | M. Biraben |
| | †L. Puech | L. Puech | R. Thierry | L. Puech |
| | †A. Cassayet | A. Cassayet | A. Cassayet | E. Soulie |
| | †R. Thierry | R. Thierry | †G. Constant | J. Sebedio |
| | †R. Marchand | †A. Guichemerre | R. Marchand | †P. Moureu |
| | †J. Laurent | J. Laurent | J. Laurent | †J. Larrieu |
| | Parc des Princes | Twickenham | Stade Colombes | Lansdowne Road |
| | LOST 0-5 | LOST 3-8 | LOST 5-6 | WON 15-7 |
| | Fr.: nil | Eng.: 1g 1pg | Fr.: 1g | Ire.: 1dg 1t |
| | Scot.: 1g | Fr.: 1t | Wales: 2t | Fr.: 5t |
| | 1 Jan. 1920 | 31 Jan. 1920 | 17 Feb. 1920 | 3 Apr. 1920 |

More than twenty former French internationals were killed in action during the Great War. The game, however, continued to flourish in France, with war-time competitions for juniors drawing large crowds in the south, and unofficial matches against a noted NZ Army team allowing the French to measure the advances made by the national side. In 1917 a French Selection lost 13-14 to the New Zealanders, while a French XV were beaten 10-16 by the same side in 1919.

When full internationals resumed in 1920, France were a considerable force in the Championship. Only narrow margins separated the French from the Scots, English and Welsh, before in April they won abroad (in Ireland) for the first time.

The French scored three tries in the first ten minutes and never relinquished a winning lead. The backs were outstanding and the first try (by Gayraud) was the culmination of a marvellous bout of passing by the halves and threequarters. The five tries established a new French try-record for an international match.

## 1920-21

| v. AMERICA | v. SCOTLAND | v. WALES | v. ENGLAND | v. IRELAND |
|---|---|---|---|---|
| T. CAMBRE | †J. CLEMENT | J. CLEMENT | J. CLEMENT | R. LASSERRE |
| A. JAUREGUY 1T | †J. LOBIES | J. LOBIES | J. LOBIES | †J. BAQUET |
| F. BORDE 1T | F. BORDE | F. BORDE | F. BORDE | †H. JEANGRAND |
| R. CRABOS | *R. CRABOS | *R. CRABOS | *R. CRABOS 2PG | *R. CRABOS 4C |
| R. GOT 1T | R. GOT | R. GOT | †E. CAYREFOURCQ | †M. DE LABORDERIE |
| E. BILLAC 1T | E. BILLAC 1T | E. BILLAC | †A. BOUSQUET | A. BOUSQUET |
| *P. STRUXIANO 1C | †R. PITEU | R. PITEU | R. PITEU | R. PITEU 2T |
| M.F. LUBIN-LEBRERE | M.F. LUBIN-LEBRERE | G. COSCOLL | P. MOUREU | E. SOULIE |
| J. LARRIEU | P. PONS | P. PONS | †C.A. GONNET | C.A. GONNET |
| M. BIRABEN | M. BIRABEN | M. BIRABEN | M. BIRABEN | M. BIRABEN |
| P. MOUREU | †G. COSCOLL | P. MOURE | L. PUECH | L. PUECH |
| A. CASSAYET | E. SOULIE | A. CASSAYET | A. CASSAYET | A. CASSAYET 1T |
| E. SOULIE | †F. VAQUER | F. VAQUER | E. SOULIE | P. MOUREU |
| R. THIERRY | †J. BOUBEE | J. LARRIEU | J. BOUBEE | J. BOUBEE 1T |
| J. SEBEDIO | R. LASSERRE | R. LASSERRE 1DG | A. GUICHEMERRE | A. GUICHEMERRE |
| Stade Colombes | Inverleith | Cardiff Arms Park | Stade Colombes | Stade Colombes |
| WON 14-5 | WON 3-0 | LOST 4-12 | LOST 6-10 | WON 20-10 |
| FR.: 1G 3T | SCOT.: NIL | WALES: 2PG 2T | FR.: 2PG | FR.: 4G |
| AMER.: 1G | FR.: 1T | FR.: 1DG | ENG.: 2G | IRE.: 2G |
| 10 Oct. 1920 | 22 Jan. 1921 | 26 Feb. 1921 | 28 Mar. 1921 | 9 Apr. 1921 |

1920-1 was an important season for France. In October the national side met America in a full international to decide the Olympic gold medal. Fielding the nucleus of the XV which had beaten Ireland in the spring, the French secured the Olympic title, defeating an American side which adopted the unusual diamond scrummage favoured by the New Zealanders. In the same month the FFR became the controlling body of French rugby.

In the Championship France won two matches. Billac, a Basque who helped to establish a French tradition for lively attacking fly-halves, scored the only try in the win against Scotland; and four tries, all converted by René Crabos, gave France their second consecutive win against Ireland in April.

Crabos was to become an important figure in French rugby. An outstanding player in 17 internationals, he was the moving force of a talented, swift threequarter line in which Got and Jauréguy were smooth runners on the wings, and in which Borde was usually Crabos' centre partner. A broken leg sustained in the 1924 match with Ireland ended Crabos' playing career, but he later became a leading administrator of the FFR.

## 1921-22

| v. SCOTLAND | v. ENGLAND | v. WALES | v. IRELAND |
|---|---|---|---|
| J. CLEMENT | J. CLEMENT | J. CLEMENT | J. CLEMENT |
| A. JAUREGUY 1T | †A. LAFOND | A. JAUREGUY 1T | R. GOT |
| F. BORDE | †R. RAMIS | F. BORDE | R. RAMIS |
| *R. CRABOS | *R. CRABOS 1C | *R. CRABOS | *R. CRABOS |
| R. GOT | R. GOT 1T | R. GOT | M. DE LABORDERIE |
| †J. PASCOT | J. PASCOT | E. BILLAC | J. PASCOT 1T |
| R. PITEU | R. PITEU | R. PITEU | R. PITEU |
| M.F. LUBIN-LEBRERE | E. SOULIE | M.F. LUBIN-LEBRERE | M. BIRABEN |
| P. PONS | C.A. GONNET | C.A. GONNET | †L. BEGUET |
| M. BIRABEN | M. BIRABEN | E. SOULIE | E. SOULIE |
| A. CASSAYET | M.F. LUBIN-LEBRERE | A. CASSAYET | †J. BERNON |
| P. MOUREU | J. SEBEDIO | P. MOUREU | P. MOUREU |
| †F. CAHUC | J. BOUBEE | J. BOUBEE | †J. ETCHEPARE |
| J. SEBEDIO | A. CASSAYET 1T | F. VAQUER | †N. SICART |
| R. LASSERRE | R. LASSERRE 1T | R. LASSERRE | R. LASSERRE |
| Stade Colombes | Twickenham | Stade Colombes | Lansdowne Road |
| DRAWN 3-3 | DRAWN 11-11 | LOST 3-11 | LOST 3-8 |
| FR.: 1T | ENG.: 1G 2PG | FR.: 1T | IRE.: 1G 1PG |
| SCOT.: 1T | FR.: 1G 2T | WALES: 1G 2T | FR.: 1T |
| 2 Jan. 1922 | 25 Feb. 1922 | 23 Mar. 1922 | 8 Apr. 1922 |

France began the season with two draws, failing by a whisker to become the first team to win a Championship match at Twickenham. Two of France's leading threequarters, Jauréguy and Borde, were unavailable for the English match, their places going to two teenagers: Lafond (a grandfather of J.B Lafond, capped in 1984 as a wing), and Roger Ramis. Good line-out play by the French forwards gave their backs ample possession, but their scrummaging was rather ragged.

France were joint wooden-spoon holders with Ireland. Only Lasserre played in the pack throughout the season. He was a remarkable player who appeared as full-back, centre and wing-forward in a career which spanned the Great War and brought him 15 caps.

Jean Clément was the best French full-back of the early 1920s. His Charlie Chaplin appearance belied his footballing ability, for he was an imperturbable defender with an extraordinary sense of anticipation.

## 1922-23

| v. SCOTLAND | v. WALES | v. ENGLAND | v. IRELAND |
|---|---|---|---|
| J. CLEMENT | J. CLEMENT | †C. MAGNANOU | J. CLEMENT |
| A. JAUREGUY | A. JAUREGUY | A. JAUREGUY | A. JAUREGUY 2T |
| F. BORDE | R. RAMIS | †A. BEHOTEGUY | F. BORDE |
| *R. CRABOS | *H. BEHOTEGUY | *R. SALINIE | *R. CRABOS |
| †M. LALANDE | M. LALANDE 1T | †M. LOUSTEAU | M. LALANDE |
| J. PASCOT | †C. LACAZEDIEU | E. BILLAC | C. LACAZEDIEU |
| †C. DUPONT | C. DUPONT | R. PITEU | C. DUPONT |
| L. BEGUET 1GM | L. BEGUET 1C | L. BEGUET 1PG | L. BEGUET 1T,1C |
| †J. BAYARD | J. BAYARD | J. BAYARD | J. LARRIEU |
| J. BERNON | P. MOUREU | P. MOUREU | P. MOUREU 1T |
| P. MOUREU | †J. CASTETS | J. CASTETS | J. CASTETS |
| A. CASSAYET | A. CASSAYET | A. CASSAYET | A. CASSAYET |
| J. LARRIEU | J. LARRIEU | J. LARRIEU | †H. FARGUES |
| J. SEBEDIO | †J. ETCHEBERRY | J. BOUBEE | J. ETCHEBERRY |
| A. GUICHEMERRE | *R. LASSERRE 1T | *R. LASSERRE | J. BOUBEE |
| Inverleith | Swansea | Stade Colombes | Stade Colombes |
| LOST 3-16 | LOST 8-16 | LOST 3-12 | WON 14-8 |
| SCOT.: 2G 2T | WALES: 2G 1T 1PG | FR.: 1PG | FR.: 1G 3T |
| FR.: 1GM | FR.: 1G 1T | ENG.: 1G 1DG 1T | IRE.: 1G 1T |
| 20 Jan. 1923 | 24 Feb. 1923 | 2 Apr. 1923 | 14 Apr. 1923 |

A failing of French rugby in its infancy was the lack of sound combination in the pack. The forwards, individually, were skilful, athletic performers who were backed by ingenious halves and threequarters whose chief virtue was speed. But ragged scrummaging and ponderous play in the loose comdemned their backs to operate at a disadvantage.

Borde, an elegant and forceful centre of slender build, sustained a broken hand against Scotland, and he was out of action until April, when he was reunited with two other mainstays of French backplay, Crabos and Jauréguy, against Ireland. France twice came from behind in this match, two tries by Jauréguy enabling them to gain their third win in four years against the Irish.

Jauréguy was often described as the best French wing of the period between the wars. He formed with Borde a formidable wing for both Toulouse and France, Borde's incomparable eye for an opening and astonishing speed off the mark creating numerous tries for Jauréguy. Later a French selector, Jauréguy won 31 caps and created a career record by scoring 14 international tries.

## 1923-24

| v. SCOTLAND | v. IRELAND | v. ENGLAND | v. WALES | v. ROMANIA | v. AMERICA |
|---|---|---|---|---|---|
| †E. BESSET | †L. PARDO | L. PARDO | †E. BONNES | E. BONNES | E. BONNES |
| A. JAUREGUY 1T | †M. BESSON | †J. BALLARIN 1T | A. JAUREGUY | A. JAUREGUY 4T | A. JAUREGUY |
| A. BEHOTEGUY | A. BEHOTEGUY | *F. BORDE | †A. DUPOUY | A. BEHOTEGUY 1PG,2T | A. BEHOTEGUY |
| *R. CRABOS | *R. CRABOS | A. BEHOTEGUY 1DG | A. BEHOTEGUY 1T | A. DUPOUY 2T | †J. VAYSSE |
| †L. CLUCHAGUE | R. GOT | R. GOT | R. GOT | R. GOT 2T | R. GOT |
| †H. GALAU 1T | H. GALAU | H. GALAU | H. GALAU | A. BOUSQUET | H. GALAU 1T |
| C. DUPONT | C. DUPONT | R. PITEU | C. DUPONT | C. DUPONT | C. DUPONT |
| †L. LEPATEY | L. LEPATEY | L. LEPATEY | J. ETCHEBERRY | †R. ARAOU | J. ETCHEBERRY |
| C.A. GONNET | L. BEGUET | C.A. GONNET | J. BAYARD | J. BAYARD | J. BAYARD |
| L. BEGUET | †J. DANION | L. BEGUET | P. MOUREU | L. BEGUET 1PG,7C,1T | L. BEGUET |
| P. MOUREU 1T | P. MOUREU | P. MOUREU | M.F. LUBIN-LEBRERE 1T | A. CASSAYET | A. CASSAYET |
| A. CASSAYET | E. PIQUIRAL | A. CASSAYET | *A. CASSAYET | E. PIQUIRAL | M.F. LUBIN-LEBRERE |
| †E. PIQUIRAL 1T | †E. RIBERE | E. PIQUIRAL | E. PIQUIRAL | †G. GERINTES 1T | A. BIOUSSA |
| J. ETCHEBERRY | J. ETCHEBERRY | J. ETCHEBERRY | †A. BIOUSSA | J. ETCHEBERRY 1T | E. PIQUIRAL |
| R. LASSERRE | R. LASSERRE | †F. CLAUZEL | F. CLAUZEL | *R. LASSERRE | *R. LASSERRE |
| Stade Pershing | Lansdowne Road | Twickenham | Stade Colombes | Stade Colombes | Stade Colombes |
| WON 12-10 | LOST 0-6 | LOST 7-19 | LOST 6-10 | WON 59-3 | LOST 3-17 |
| FR.: 4T | IRE.: 2T | ENG.: 2G 3T | FR.: 2T | FR.: 7G 6T 2PG | FR.: 1T |
| SCOT.: 1PG 1DG 1T | FR.: NIL | FR.: 1DG 1T | WALES: 2T 1DG | ROM.: 1PG | AMER.: 1G 4T |
| 1 Jan. 1924 | 26 Jan. 1924 | 23 Feb. 1924 | 27 Mar. 1924 | 4 May 1924 | 18 May 1924 |

There was an auspicious start to the season. Pierre Moureu, one of the most complete French forwards of his generation, scored the winning try against Scotland from a rush in the closing minutes of the game, but then French rugby fell into rapid decline.

Their problems began in Dublin, where the lack of a specialist hooker and injury to Crabos marked the beginning of a long and disappointing run of failure in the Championship. The leadership of Crabos (who was appointed President of the FFR in 1952) was greatly missed in the defeats by Wales and England, though the forwards had the better of the Welsh eight in difficult conditions at Colombes.

France were silver medallists in the Olympic tournament held in Paris in 1924. Against Romania (whom the French had first played in an unofficial international in 1919), France established numerous records. In a win by 59-3, they reached their highest total in an international, winning by a record margin. In addition, Louis Béguet, a solid front-row player with an accurate place-kick, scored 20 points while Jauréguy marked four tries – both French international records. But in the Olympic final the French were well beaten by an American XV represented by the Stanford University team.

## 1924-25

| v. IRELAND | v. NZ | v. SCOTLAND | v. WALES | v. ENGLAND |
|---|---|---|---|---|
| A. CHILO | A. CHILO | †J. DUCOUSSO | J. DUCOUSSO 1c | J. DUCOUSSO 1c |
| A. JAUREGUY | A. JAUREGUY | †F. RAYMOND | †A. BRINGEON | L. CLUCHAGUE 1T |
| *F. BORDE | J. BALLARIN | J. BALLARIN | C. MAGNANOU | C. MAGNANOU |
| †M. BAILLETTE | M. BAILLETTE | M. BAILLETTE | M. DE LABORDERIE 1T | M. DE LABORDERIE |
| M. BESSON | †R. HALET | R. HALET | R. HALET | M. BESSON 1T |
| †Y. DU MANOIR | Y. DU MANOIR | Y. DU MANOIR 1DG | Y. DU MANOIR | Y. DU MANOIR |
| R. PITEU | R. PITEU | C. DUPONT | R. PITEU | *R. PITEU |
| †C. MONTADE | C. MONTADE | C. MONTADE | C. MONTADE | P. MOUREU |
| †C. MARCET | C. MARCET | C. MARCET | C. MARCET | C. MARCET |
| †A. MAURY | A. MAURY | A. MAURY | A. MAURY | A. MAURY |
| M.F. LUBIN-LEBRERE | J. BOUBEE | A. LAURENT | A. LAURENT | A. LAURENT |
| A. CASSAYET | *A. CASSAYET 1T | *A. CASSAYET | †R. LEVASSEUR | R. LEVASSEUR |
| G. GERINTES | †A. LAURENT | J. BOUBEE | †E. BARTHE | E. BARTHE 1T |
| E. RIBERE 1T | E. RIBERE 1T | E. RIBERE | *A. CASSAYET | E. PIQUIRAL |
| A. BIOUSSA | A. BIOUSSA | A. BIOUSSA | F. CLAUZEL | A. BIOUSSA |
| Stade Colombes | Toulouse | Inverleith | Cardiff Arms Park | Stade Colombes |
| LOST 3-9 | LOST 6-30 | LOST 4-25 | LOST 5-11 | LOST 11-13 |
| FR.: 1T | FR.: 2T | SCOT.: 2G 5T | WALES: 1G 2T | FR.: 1G 2T |
| IRE.: 2T 1PG | NZ: 3G 5T | FR.: 1DG | FR.: 1G | ENG.: 2G 1PG |
| 1 Jan. 1925 | 18 Jan. 1925 | 24 Jan. 1925 | 28 Feb. 1925 | 13 Apr. 1925 |

This was France's most disappointing season since the war. The focus of French rugby attention in the 1920s was the club Championship, and the intense rivalry which the competition induced distracted players' concentration from the International Championship. The importance of club matches incited players to acts of ill-discipline, prompted some clubs to transgress the Laws governing amateurism, while other players consistently declined invitations to play for France.

In 1925, for instance, Roger Ramis, first capped in 1922, was the most skilful player in French rugby. Yet he repeatedly refused to play for his country, preserving his fitness for club rugby. He captained Perpignan in 1924 when the club reached the Championship final, and led the side to victory in the final of 1925. Furthermore, the Béhotéguy brothers (two fine Basque centres) and Jean Etcheberry, a tireless loose forward, were under suspension and not considered for the French XV.

Thirty-one players were capped during the five defeats, Lubin-Lebrère, a powerful tight forward who was a leading personality before and after the Great War (in which he lost an eye), winning the last of his 15 caps against Ireland. Only Yves du Manoir, Marcet and Maury played in each of the matches. Du Manoir was a wonderful all-round sportsman who excelled at motor sports, watersports and tennis. He was killed in a flying accident in 1928, aged 24.

## 1925-26

| v. SCOTLAND | v. IRELAND | v. ENGLAND | v. WALES |
|---|---|---|---|
| †L. DESTARAC | L. DESTARAC | L. DESTARAC | L. DESTARAC |
| A. JAUREGUY | †C. DULAURANS | A. JAUREGUY | *A. JAUREGUY |
| †L. CHAPUIS | †V. GRAULE | F. BORDE | M. BAILLETTE |
| C. MAGNANOU | †R. GRACIET | A. BEHOTEGUY | R. GRACIET |
| M. BESSON | †J. REVILLON | J. REVILLON | M. BESSON |
| Y. DU MANOIR | J. PASCOT | V. GRAULE | V. GRAULE |
| †LLARY | †B. BERGES | R. PITEU | †H. LAFFONT |
| A. MAURY | A. MAURY | A. MAURY | C. MONTADE |
| C.A. GONNET 1PG | C.A. GONNET | C.A. GONNET | C.A. GONNET 1c |
| J. ETCHEBERRY | C. MARCET | C. MARCET | †J. SAYROU |
| †A. PUIG | E. PIQUIRAL | A. PUIG | A. LAURENT |
| *A. CASSAYET | *A. CASSAYET | *A. CASSAYET | A. CASSAYET |
| E. RIBERE | E. RIBERE | J. ETCHEBERRY | E. RIBERE |
| E. PIQUIRAL 1T | J. ETCHEBERRY | E. PIQUIRAL | E. PIQUIRAL |
| A. BIOUSSA | A. BIOUSSA | A. BIOUSSA | G. GERINTES 1T |
| Stade Colombes | Ravenhill | Twickenham | Stade Colombes |
| LOST 6-20 | LOST 0-11 | LOST 0-11 | LOST 5-7 |
| FR.: 1PG 1T | IRE.: 1G 1PG 1T | ENG.: 1G 2T | FR.: 1G |
| SCOT.: 1G 1PG 4T | FR.: NIL | FR.: NIL | WALES: 1DG 1T |
| 2 Jan. 1926 | 23 Jan. 1926 | 27 Feb. 1926 | 5 Apr. 1926 |

The French were left with the wooden spoon, failing to win a match. The club Championship continued to attract the attentions of players, and whereas the competition had helped to spread the popularity of the game – more than 1000 new clubs having been formed since the war – few competent coaches emerged to instruct players in the basics of the game.

However, there was a perceptible advance during the international season, and the French gave sound performances against England and Wales, having found a steady full-back in Destarac, a dangerous runner in Graule and an impressive pack.

Gonnet, a supple, talented hooker who won 16 caps, was the most experienced member of the front row. An all-round sportsman who was a boxer and swimmer of note, Gonnet later became a journalist. And in the back row, Piquiral and Ribère were two intelligent forwards who won more than fifty caps. Piquiral was an innovator who became an effective captain of RCF in Paris. Ribère was the French cap-record-holder between the wars, appearing 34 times as an athletic flanker with the pace of a threequarter and a secure defence.

## 1926-27

| v. MAORIS | v. IRELAND | v. SCOTLAND | v. WALES | v. ENGLAND |
|---|---|---|---|---|
| L. DESTARAC | †M. PIQUEMAL | M. PIQUEMAL | L. DESTARAC | L. DESTARAC |
| *A. JAUREGUY | *A. JAUREGUY | †R. HOUDET | R. HOUDET | E. VELLAT 1T |
| J. VAYSSE | M. BESSON | V. GRAULE | V. GRAULE | A. BEHOTEGUY |
| M. BAILLETTE | M. BAILLETTE | R. GRACIET | M. BAILLETTE | †G. GERALD |
| †E. VILA | †E. VELLAT | J. REVILLON | F. RAYMOND | *A. JAUREGUY |
| †J. SOURGENS | Y. DU MANOIR | *Y. DU MANOIR | †A. VERGER 1DG | A. VERGER |
| †E. BADER | E. BADER | E. BADER | †P. CARBONNE | C. DUPONT |
| J. ETCHEBERRY | J. ETCHEBERRY | J. ETCHEBERRY | J. ETCHEBERRY | †A. LOURY |
| C.A. GONNET | C.A. GONNET | C.A. GONNET | C.A. GONNET | C.A. GONNET |
| J. SAYROU | †R. HUTIN | R. HUTIN 1T | R. HUTIN | †J. MORERE |
| †R. BOUSQUET | R. BOUSQUET | R. BOUSQUET | R. BOUSQUET | R. BOUSQUET |
| A. CASSAYET | A. CASSAYET | A. CASSAYET | *A. CASSAYET | †J. GALIA |
| †A. PREVOST | A. PREVOST | A. PREVOST | A. PREVOST 1T | †A. CAZENAVE |
| E. PIQUIRAL | E. PIQUIRAL | E. PIQUIRAL 1T | E. PIQUIRAL | E. PIQUIRAL |
| E. RIBERE 1T | E. RIBERE 1T | E. RIBERE | E. RIBERE | E. RIBERE |
| Stade Colombes | Stade Colombes | Murrayfield | Swansea | Stade Colombes |
| LOST 3-12 | LOST 3-8 | LOST 6-23 | LOST 7-25 | WON 3-0 |
| FR.: 1T | FR.: 1T | SCOT.: 4G 1PG | WALES: 2G 5T | FR.: 1T |
| MAORIS: 4T | IRE.: 1G 1PG | FR.: 2T | FR.: 1DG 1T | ENG.: NIL |
| 26 Dec. 1926 | 1 Jan. 1927 | 22 Jan. 1927 | 26 Feb. 1927 | 2 Apr. 1927 |

The FFR invited the NZ Maoris to France during the winter. Altogether the tourists played 31 matches, of which half took place in Britain, and the focal point of the visit was the international in Paris on Boxing Day. France were beaten, lost their first three matches in the Championship, but ended the season with a memorable win against England. The only score of the match came after eleven minutes when Béhotéguy thundered through a square defence to send Vellat over for a try.

Aimé Cassayet, one of the finest French forwards of the 1920s, played his final match against Wales. A painful illness prevented his participation in the English game, and he died in May, mourned by players, officials and followers of the game throughout the world.

Cassayet was an incomparable lock forward, always close to the ball in the loose, sound in the scrummage, and an expert in the line-out. He gained 31 caps for France, a record at the time of his death, and led the side in eight internationals.

## 1927

| v. GERMANY | v. GERMANY |
|---|---|
| L. DESTARAC 3C | L. DESTARAC 2C |
| E. VELLAT 2T | E. VELLAT 2T |
| *A. BEHOTEGUY | *A. BEHOTEGUY 1T |
| R. GRACIET 1T | M. BAILLETTE |
| R. HOUDET 2T | G. GERALD |
| A. VERGER | J. PASCOT |
| C. DUPONT | C. DUPONT |
| A. LOURY | A. LOURY |
| C.A. GONNET | †F. CAMICAS |
| J. MORERE | J. ETCHEBERRY |
| J. GALIA 1T | J. GALIA |
| R. BOUSQUET 1T | †M. LARRIEU |
| A. CAZENAVE 1T | E. PIQUIRAL |
| E. PIQUIRAL | †P. DESCAMPS |
| E. RIBERE | E. RIBERE 1T |
| Stade Colombes | Frankfurt |
| WON 30-5 | LOST 16-17 |
| FR.: 3G 5T | FR.: 2G 2T |
| GER.: 1G | GER.: 1G 1PG 3T |
| 17 Apr. 1927 | 15 May 1927 |

After inviting the Maoris to tour during the winter, the FFR showed considerable initiative in the spring, undertaking matches against three continental countries, Romania, Spain and Germany. The French B team defeated the Romanians 44-3 in Paris, and the Spaniards lost 6-66 in Madrid in a match which was not accorded full offiicial status by the FFR.

Two official matches, in Paris and Frankfurt, were played against Germany, Mr W.H. Jackson of the RFU acting as referee. Before 20,000 spectators the French found the Germans competent in the scrums and line-outs at Colombes, but the brittle defence of the visiting backs enabled France to run-in eight tries.

However, the return match in Germany resulted in a surprising French defeat, the Germans deriving inspiration from a brilliant 17-year-old scrum half. Morère, the Toulouse prop, and a couple of other leading French players, were unavailable owing to club commitments (the match taking place on the same day as the French Championship semi-finals), but nine of the side who had beaten England a month earlier were in action.

## 1927-28

| v. SCOTLAND | v. NS WALES | v. IRELAND | v. ENGLAND | v. GERMANY | v. WALES |
|---|---|---|---|---|---|
| †L. Magnol | †L. Pellissier | L. Pellissier | L. Pellissier | L. Pellissier | L. Pellissier |
| *A. Jaureguy | *A. Jaureguy | †J. Jardel | *A. Jaureguy 1t | *A. Jaureguy | *A. Jaureguy |
| G. Gerald | A. Behoteguy 1c | *A. Behoteguy 1c | A. Behoteguy | A. Behoteguy | A. Behoteguy 1c |
| †J. Coulon | H. Behoteguy | H. Behoteguy 1t | H. Behoteguy | H. Behoteguy | H. Behoteguy |
| C. Dulaurans | E. Vellat | F. Raymond | J. Jardel | R. Houdet 2t | R. Houdet 2t |
| †H. Haget 1t | C. Lacazedieu | A. Verger | A. Verger 1c | A. Verger 1c | A. Verger |
| †G. Daudignon | C. Dupont | C. Lacazedieu | †L. Serin | C. Dupont | C. Dupont |
| A. Loury | A. Loury | A. Loury | †J. Hauc | J. Hauc 1t | H. Lacaze |
| F. Camicas | †G. Vaills | F. Camicas | F. Camicas | F. Camicas | F. Camicas |
| J. Morere | J. Morere | †J. Duhau | J. Sayrou | J. Sayrou | J. Sayrou |
| †A. Camel 1t | A. Camel 1t | A. Camel | A. Camel | A. Camel | A. Camel |
| J. Galia | J. Galia | †H. Lacaze | J. Galia 1t | H. Lacaze | †R. Majerus |
| A. Cazenave | A. Cazenave | R. Bonamy | A. Bioussa | A. Bioussa 1t | A. Bioussa |
| †G. Branca | †R. Bonamy 1t | J. Galia | E. Piquiral | A. Cazenave | J. Galia |
| E. Ribere | E. Ribere | E. Ribere 1t | E. Ribere | E. Ribere | E. Ribere |
| Stade Colombes | Stade Colombes | Ravenhill | Twickenham | Hanover | Stade Colombes |
| LOST 6-15 | LOST 8-11 | LOST 8-12 | LOST 8-18 | WON 14-3 | WON 8-3 |
| Fr.: 2T | Fr.: 1G 1T | Ire.: 4T | Eng.: 3G 1T | Ger.: 1PG | Fr.: 1G 1T |
| Scot.: 5T | NSW: 1G 2T | Fr.: 1G 1T | Fr.: 1G 1T | Fr.: 1G 3T | Wales: 1T |
| 2 Jan. 1928 | 22 Jan. 1928 | 28 Jan. 1928 | 25 Feb. 1928 | 18 Mar. 1928 | 9 Apr. 1928 |

Six matches were played in 1928, but only two players, Ribère and André Camel, appeared in each match. Camel was a tall, muscular lock forward whose speed in the loose and strength in the tight made him the outstanding French second-row player of his generation. In an international career which lasted until 1935, he won 16 caps, and was joined by his elder brother Marcel in the French pack of 1929.

Two others, Jean Galia and hooker Camicas, played in the four Championship matches. Galia was a Catalan who was one of the most gifted all-round French forwards between the wars. He gained 20 caps before arousing controversy in the 1930s. After leaving the Quillan club in 1930 to join Villeneuve, he was suspected of breaches of the amateur code and the FFR disqualified him in 1933. He then founded Rugby League football in France and was the first manager, selector and captain of the French XIII.

Robert Houdet was the star of France's two wins at the end of the season. His two tries in Hanover helped France to defeat Germany, and he scored each of the tries against Wales in France's first win against the Principality. Camel was injured early in the Welsh match, the French playing with 14 men for most of the game. Houdet's winning try resulted from clever play by Verger, Jauréguy and the Béhotéguy brothers.

## 1928-29

| v. IRELAND | v. SCOTLAND | v. WALES | v. ENGLAND | v. GERMANY |
|---|---|---|---|---|
| M. Piquemal | L. Magnol | L. Magnol | L. Magnol | M. Piquemal |
| *A. Jaureguy | *A. Jaureguy | †A. Domec | *A. Jaureguy | †A. Duche 3c,1t |
| G. Gerald | G. Gerald | *A. Behoteguy | A. Behoteguy | G. Gerald |
| †G. Caussarieu | A. Behoteguy 1t | G. Gerald | G. Gerald | M. Baillette 2t |
| R. Houdet | R. Houdet | C. Dulaurans | R. Houdet 1t | †Soler 2t |
| †R. Sarrade | C. Magnanou | C. Magnanou | R. Graciet | †A. Cutzach |
| C. Dupont | C. Lacazedieu | L. Serin | L. Serin | L. Serin |
| J. Hauc | J. Hauc | R. Bousquet | R. Bousquet | J. Hauc 1t |
| F. Camicas | F. Camicas | F. Camicas | F. Camicas | G. Vaills |
| H. Lacaze | J. Sayrou | J. Sayrou | J. Sayrou | J. Sayrou |
| J. Galia | A. Camel | A. Camel | A. Camel | A. Camel |
| R. Majerus | R. Majerus | H. Lacaze | J. Galia | †P. Barrere |
| A. Bioussa | A. Bioussa | A. Bioussa | A. Bioussa | †A. Clady |
| G. Branca | G. Branca | †M. Camel 1t | M. Camel | J. Galia |
| E. Ribere | †J. Auge | J. Auge | E. Ribere 1t | *E. Ribere |
| Stade Colombes | Murrayfield | Cardiff Arms Park | Stade Colombes | Stade Colombes |
| LOST 0-6 | LOST 3-6 | LOST 3-8 | LOST 6-16 | WON 24-0 |
| Fr.: NIL | Scot.: 1PG 1T | Wales: 1G 1T | Fr.: 2T | Fr.: 3G 3T |
| Ire.: 2T | Fr.: 1T | Fr.: 1T | Eng.: 2G 2T | Ger.: NIL |
| 31 Dec. 1928 | 17 Jan. 1929 | 23 Feb. 1929 | 1 Apr. 1929 | 28 Apr. 1929 |

The season was one of disappointment, though each of the defeats in the Championship was by a narrow margin. However, at Colombes, at the end of April, the Germans were soundly beaten by an experimental side containing five new caps, and captained for the first time by Ribère.

Jauréguy played his last international against England, so did André Béhotéguy, the smiling Basque who had featured in winning French sides against Wales, England and Scotland during an international career which spanned seven seasons.

Béhotéguy was a swift, incisive runner in the best Basque tradition, and a complete all-round athlete. He had been a French champion oarsman as well as an athletics international, and formed with his elder brother Henri, who had a devastating swerve, an effective centre-pairing for Bayonne, Cognac and France. More than thirty years passed before another pair of brothers, the Bonifaces, occupied the French centre positions.

## 1929-30

| v. SCOTLAND | v. IRELAND | v. ENGLAND | v. GERMANY | v. WALES |
|---|---|---|---|---|
| M. PIQUEMAL | M. PIQUEMAL | M. PIQUEMAL | M. PIQUEMAL | M. PIQUEMAL |
| R. HOUDET | †J. TAILLANTOU | R. HOUDET | J. TAILLANTOU 3T | J. TAILLANTOU |
| G. GERALD | G. GERALD | G. GERALD | G. GERALD | G. GERALD |
| M. BAILLETTE | M. BAILLETTE | M. BAILLETTE | M. BAILLETTE | R. GRACIET |
| †R. SAMATAN | R. SAMATAN 1T | R. SAMATAN | R. SAMATAN 1T | R. SAMATAN |
| C. MAGNANOU 1DG | C. MAGNANOU | C. MAGNANOU | H. HAGET 1PG | C. MAGNANOU |
| L. SERIN | L. SERIN | L. SERIN 1T | L. SERIN | L. SERIN |
| †A. AMBERT | A. AMBERT 1C | A. AMBERT 1C | A. AMBERT 2C,1T | R. BOUSQUET |
| †C. BIGOT | J. DUHAU | C. BIGOT | †L. FABRE | A. AMBERT |
| †J. CHOY | J. CHOY | J. CHOY | J. CHOY | J. CHOY |
| A. CAMEL | A. CAMEL | A. CAMEL | A. CAMEL | A. CAMEL |
| R. MAJERUS | R. MAJERUS | R. MAJERUS | R. MAJERUS 2T | R. MAJERUS |
| A. BIOUSSA 1T | A. BIOUSSA | A. BIOUSSA | *A. BIOUSSA 1T | A. BIOUSSA |
| J. GALIA | J. GALIA | J. GALIA | J. GALIA | J. GALIA |
| *E. RIBERE | *E. RIBERE | *E. RIBERE | J. DUHAU | *E. RIBERE |
| Stade Colombes | Ravenhill | Twickenham | Berlin | Stade Colombes |
| WON 7-3 | WON 5-0 | LOST 5-11 | WON 31-0 | LOST 0-11 |
| FR.: 1DG 1T | IRE.: NIL | ENG.: 1G 2T | GER.: NIL | FR.: NIL |
| SCOT.: 1T | FR.: 1G | FR.: 1G | FR.: 2G 6T 1PG | WALES: 2DG 1T |
| 1 Jan. 1930 | 25 Jan. 1930 | 22 Feb. 1930 | 6 Apr. 1930 | 21 Apr. 1930 |

Ribère's leadership and skilful play by the French forwards in the loose enabled France to win their two opening internationals for the first time. Against the Scots, Magnanou was the architect of a fine victory. He made an opening for Bioussa to score at the start of the match, and his drop-goal in the dying minutes sealed a deserved French win.

Magnanou was one of the first French fly-halves to be noted for his excellent all-round abilities as a kicker, but he was also a brave defensive player, despite a slim build. In Belfast, his quick, accurate passing enabled Baillette to open a gap for Samatan to run sixty yards for the only try of the match with Ireland.

Though defeated at Twickenham, the French still had a chance to win the Championship by beating Wales in Paris. But the lure of the title clouded their playing judgment and the game degenerated into a savage brawl with several exchanges of the boot and fist. The FFR were so disappointed by the reactions of their team that one of the forwards was promised that he would never again be chosen for an international.

## 1930-31

| v. IRELAND | v. SCOTLAND | v. WALES | v. ENGLAND | v. GERMANY |
|---|---|---|---|---|
| †M. SAVY | M. SAVY | M. SAVY | M. SAVY | †M. GUIRAL 4C |
| R. SAMATAN | R. SAMATAN | R. SAMATAN | R. SAMATAN | R. SAMATAN 1T |
| G. GERALD | G. GERALD | †P. CLEMENT | G. GERALD 1DG | G. GERALD |
| M. BAILLETTE | M. BAILLETTE | †M. VIGERIE | M. BAILLETTE 1DG | V. GRAULE |
| †L. AUGRAS | L. AUGRAS | L. AUGRAS | †P. GUELORGUET | P. GUELORGUET 2T |
| †L. SERVOLE | L. SERVOLE 1DG | L. SERVOLE | L. SERVOLE | L. SERVOLE |
| L. SERIN | †M. ROUSIE | L. SERIN | L. SERIN | M. ROUSIE 2T |
| J. DUHAU | J. DUHAU | J. DUHAU | R. SCOHY | R. SCOHY 1T |
| †M. PORRA | †R. SCOHY | R. SCOHY | †R. NAMUR | R. NAMUR |
| J. CHOY | †A. DUCLOS | M. RODRIGO | †H. BUISSON | H. BUISSON |
| †M. RODRIGO | J. GALIA | P. BARRERE | E. CAMO | E. CAMO |
| A. CLADY | A. CLADY | †C. PETIT 1T | A. CLADY 1T | A. CLADY 1T,1C |
| C. BIGOT | C. BIGOT | E. CAMO | †R. TRIVIAUX | R. TRIVIAUX |
| †E. CAMO | E. CAMO | J. GALIA | J. GALIA 1T | J. GALIA |
| *E. RIBERE 1T | *E. RIBERE | *E. RIBERE | *E. RIBERE | *E. RIBERE 1T |
| Stade Colombes | Murrayfield | Swansea | Stade Colombes | Stade Colombes |
| WON 3-0 | LOST 4-6 | LOST 3-35 | WON 14-13 | WON 34-0 |
| FR.: 1T | SCOT.: 2PG | WALES: 5G 1DG 2T | FR.: 2DG 2T | FR.: 5G 3T |
| IRE.: NIL | FR.: 1DG | FR.: 1T | ENG.: 2G 1T | GER.: NIL |
| 1 Jan. 1931 | 24 Jan. 1931 | 28 Feb. 1931 | 6 Apr. 1931 | 19 Apr. 1931 |

Events off the field governed the season. In January, ten of the leading French clubs broke away from the FFR to form their own Union, with the intention of competing for a separate club Championship. A couple of other clubs joined the "rebels" later in the season.

Disturbed by these events and rumours of professionalism, the four Home Unions met in February 1931 and passed a resolution stating that relations with France would not be resumed until the control and conduct of the game in the country had been placed on a satisfactory basis. The FFR thus honoured their 1931 commitments, despite the uncertainty concerning the international future of the game in France. And, as if to prove a point, the French side enjoyed a good season in the Championship, winning their two home matches and losing by only two penalty goals to the Scots.

In April, in the last game against England for sixteen years, the French came from behind on three occasions to win. The forwards were excellent, Camo standing out as a line-out expert with plenty of energy in the loose. Rousié, who became a leading Rugby League player in the 1930s, scored two fine tries and took a firm tactical grip on the match with Germany.

| 1932 | 1933 | 1934 | 1935 | 1936 | |
|---|---|---|---|---|---|
| v. GERMANY | v. GERMANY | v. GERMANY | v. GERMANY | 1st v. GERMANY | 2nd v GERMANY |
| M. GUIRAL | M. GUIRAL | E. CHAUD 1c | E. CHAUD 1pg,3c | M. SAVY | †F. SAHUC |
| †E. CHAUD 1c,1t | †F. RAYNAUD 2t | A. DULUC 1t | A. VIGNEAU 1t | †P. GESCHWIND 1t | P. GESCHWIND 1t |
| M. BAILLETTE 1t | A. BARBAZANGES | †J. DESCLAUX 1c,1t | J. CODERC | J. CODERC | †F. BERGEZE |
| †J. CODERC 1t | J. CODERC 1t | J. CODERC | J. DESCLAUX | *J. DESCLAUX 2t | *J. DESCLAUX |
| †R. FINAT 2t | R. FINAT 3t | P. CUSSAC | †M. CELHAY 2t | M. CELHAY 1t | †P. MILLIAND |
| †A. BARBAZANGES | †J. DAGUERRE | *L. SERVOLE | *L. SERVOLE | †G. LIBAROS | †E. ELISSALDE |
| M. ROUSIE 1pg | M. ROUSIE | †F. LOMBARD | †P. BOYER | †P. THIERS 1c | P. THIERS |
| †J. GRIFFARD | †P. ESCAFFRE | P. ESCAFFRE 1t | J. CHOY | †F. DAGUERRE 1t | J. CHOY 1t |
| †M. LAURENT | †E. AINCIART | E. AINCIART | E. AINCIART | †A. ROCHON | †J. CLAVE |
| †A. POTEL | M. LAURENT | M. LAURENT | M. LAURENT | M. LAURENT | A. GOYARD |
| E. CAMO | J. GRIFFARD | J. GRIFFARD | A. CAMEL | A. GOYARD | L. COGNET |
| †L. COGNET | J. CHOY | J. CHOY | †J. DOROT | †E. ITHURRA | E. ITHURRA |
| †R. CLAUDEL | H. DE MALHERBE 2t | R. CLAUDEL | †F. RAYNAL | L. COGNET | F. RAYNAL |
| †H. DE MALHERBE | J. DUHAU 1pg,1t,4c | †L. DUPONT | L. DUPONT | L. DUPONT | L. DUPONT |
| *E. RIBERE | *E. RIBERE | †A. BLAIN | †J. BLOND | F. RAYNAL 1c | J. BLOND |
| Frankfurt | Parc des Princes | Hanover | Parc des Princes | Berlin | Hanover |
| WON 20-4 | WON 38-17 | WON 13-9 | WON 18-3 | WON 19-14 | WON 6-3 |
| GER.: 1DG | FR.: 4G 1PG 5T | GER.: 1G 1DG | FR.: 3G 1PG | GER.: 1G 1PG 2T | GER.: 1T |
| FR.: 1G 1PG 4T | GER.: 2G 1T 1DG | FR.: 2G 1T | GER.: 1T | FR.: 2G 3T | FR.: 2T |
| 17 Apr. 1932 | 26 Mar. 1933 | 25 Mar. 1934 | 24 Mar. 1935 | 17 May 1936 | 1 Nov. 1936 |

Deprived of matches with International Board countries, France turned to the Continent for competition. The series of matches with Germany, begun in 1927, sustained the French during the early years of the 1930s, and six wins were recorded. Furthermore, at the instigation of the French and German Federations, FIRA, a European Union to promote international rugby on the Continent, was formed in January 1934.

Two of the leading French players of these years were Joseph (Jep) Desclaux and Marcel Laurent. Desclaux was one of the finest attacking midfield players produced by France before the Second War. Equally comfortable as a centre or fly-half, his first nine caps were gained before 1939, when he passed to the Rugby League. (He played in the first French international Rugby League side to defeat England, at St Helens in 1939.) Then, during the war, when restrictions on League players playing Union were relaxed, Desclaux was recalled to play in a winning team against the British Army.

Marcel Laurent was a sound front-row player who won five caps before becoming a distinguished FFR official in the post-war years. As manager, he led various French tours overseas, he was a member of the national selection committee, and served the Union as a vice-president and committee member until 1984.

| 1937 | | 1938 | | |
|---|---|---|---|---|
| v. GERMANY | v. ITALY | 1st v. GERMANY | v. ROMANIA | 2nd v. GERMANY |
| †H. MASSE | †M. BONNUS 1dg | M. BONNUS | M. BONNUS | M. BONNUS |
| P. MILLIAND 2t | P. MILLIAND 1t | M. CELHAY | †R. CAUNEGRE 1t | R. CAUNEGRE 1t |
| F. BERGEZE 2t | F. BERGEZE 1t | F. BERGEZE | †A. RAPIN | F. BERGEZE 1t |
| *J. DESCLAUX | †M. DEYGAS | *J. DESCLAUX | F. BERGEZE | *J. DESCLAUX 1c |
| M. CELHAY 1t | M. CELHAY 4t | †R. CALS | †R. LE GOFF 1t | R. LE GOFF |
| †G. LAVAIL | *J. DESCLAUX 3c | †J. CHASSAGNE | *J. DESCLAUX 1c | †G. VASSAL |
| P. THIERS 3c | P. THIERS 3c | P. THIERS | G. VASSAL | P. THIERS |
| A. GOYARD | A. GOYARD 1t | A. GOYARD | A. GOYARD | A. GOYARD |
| E. AINCIART | E. AINCIART | E. AINCIART | J. CLAVE | J. CLAVE |
| †P. DAULOUEDE | P. DAULOUEDE | P. DAULOUEDE | †E. DOUSSEAU | R. LOMBARTEIX |
| E. ITHURRA | †A. DELQUE 2t | A. DELQUE | A. DELQUE | A. DELQUE |
| †D. AGUILAR | †E. FABRE | E. FABRE | †R. LOMBARTEIX | E. FABRE |
| F. RAYNAL 1t | F. RAYNAL | J. BLOND | J. BLOND 1t | J. BLOND |
| L. COGNET | L. COGNET | †J.-B. LEFORT | L. DUPONT | L. DUPONT |
| J. BLOND 1t | F. LOMBARD | †H. CLARAC | †R. AROTCA | †J. PALAT |
| Parc des Princes | Parc des Princes | Frankfurt | Bucharest | Bucharest |
| WON 27-6 | WON 43-5 | LOST 0-3 | WON 11-8 | WON 8-5 |
| FR.: 3G 4T | FR.: 6G 1DG 3T | GER.: 1PG | ROM.: 1G 1PG | FR.: 1G 1T |
| GER.: 1T 1PG | ITALY: 1G | FR.: NIL | FR.: 1G 2T | GER.: 1G |
| 18 Apr. 1937 | 17 Oct. 1937 | 27 Mar. 1938 | 15 May 1938 | 19 May 1938 |

The internationals in the spring and autumn of 1937, against Germany and Italy respectively, resulted in easy wins for a French side led by Desclaux. Maurice Celhay, a tall, strapping wing, was a prolific try-scorer and his four tries against Italy equalled the French match record set by Jauréguy in 1924. Altogether, Celhay scored eight tries for France in his six matches.

After losing by a penalty goal to Germany in Frankfurt in the early spring of 1938, the French recovered to win an interesting triangular tournament (involving Germany and Romania) held in Bucharest in May. Robert Caunègre scored decisive tries in each of the matches to help France to two narrow wins. (The Germans were runners-up in the tournament, beating Romania by a single score.)

In 1939 the four Home Unions announced that relations would be renewed with the FFR. Consequently, the international fixtures proposed for 1939-40 included the French, though of course the outbreak of war meant that the programme was abandoned, and seven years passed before the full Five-Nations Championship was resumed.

| | 1940 | 1945 | |
|---|---|---|---|
| | v. GB | v. BRITISH ARMY | v. BRITISH EMPIRE |
| | M. BONNUS | †R. MINJAT | †L. ROUFFIA |
| | †R. TOURTE | †R. GENESTE | †J. CHABAN-DELMAS |
| | G. LIBAROS | †L. JUNQUAS | L. JUNQUAS |
| | E. ELISSALDE | †J. DAUGER 2T | J. DAUGER |
| | M. CELHAY | †G. BALADIE 1T | G. BALADIE |
| | G. LAVAIL | J. DESCLAUX 1C | †A. ALVAREZ |
| | †H. PEYRELADE | †Y.R. BERGOUGNAN | †G. COMBES |
| | P. DAULOUEDE | †J. MASSARE | J. MASSARE 1T |
| | †R. PAUL | †A. JARRASSE | †J. VILLAGRA |
| | †F. MERET | †J. PRIN-CLARY 1T | J. PRIN-CLARY |
| | †J. DUTREY | †A. MOGA | A. MOGA |
| | †M. TUCOO-CHALAT | †R. SORO | R. SORO |
| | †L. FERRAND | †J. PRAT 2C | J. PRAT 1PG |
| | †P. CHARTON | †A. SAHUC 1T | A. SAHUC |
| | *P. THIERS 1PG | *P. THIERS | *P. THIERS |
| | Parc des Princes | Parc des Princes | Richmond |
| | LOST 3-36 | WON 21-9 | LOST 6-27 |
| | FR.: 1PG | FR.: 3G 2T | EMP.: 3G 4T |
| | GB: 6G 2T | ARMY: 3T | FR.: 1PG 1T |
| | 25 Feb. 1940 | 1 Jan. 1945 | 28 Apr. 1945 |

Although unable to participate in Championship matches, a series of wartime matches between France and British and Empire combinations of players drawn from the Forces, were given full-cap status by the FFR. The first of these games was played in Paris in the winter of 1940, when a British Army XV (comprising seven English, four Welsh, three Irish and one Scottish international) scored eight tries (including three by Wilf Wooller) in front of 25,000 spectators.

Then, in 1945, France fielded 13 new caps to beat a British Army XV at Parc des Princes. Many of these players were to form the backbone of the French teams which contested the Championship in post-war seasons, and only Desclaux and Pierre Thiers had played for pre-war French teams.

Thiers had originally appeared as a scrum-half, his large, powerful frame allowing him to serve his backs with a long, accurate pass. But he was a fine athlete and skilful all-round player, and he successfully made the transition to loose forward during the war years. Altogether, he won nine caps between 1936 and 1945, leading France three times. His last international was the first visit to Britain by the French XV since 1931.

| 1945-46 | | | | |
|---|---|---|---|---|
| v. WALES | v. BE SERVICES | v. IRELAND | v. NZ ARMY | v. WALES |
| L. ROUFFIA | A. ALVAREZ | A. ALVAREZ | A. ALVAREZ | L. ROUFFIA |
| †H. DUTRAIN | H. DUTRAIN | H. DUTRAIN | E. PEBEYRE 1T | †J. LASSEGUE |
| *L. JUNQUAS | *L. JUNQUAS | *L. JUNQUAS | *L. JUNQUAS | *L. JUNQUAS |
| G. BALADIE | †A. KAEMPF | G. BALADIE | †M. SORRONDO | M. TERRAU 2T |
| †E. PEBEYRE | G. BALADIE 1T | E. PEBEYRE | G. BALADIE 1T | E. PEBEYRE |
| †M. TERRAU | M. TERRAU | M. TERRAU | M. TERRAU 1T | A. ALVAREZ 1DG |
| Y.R. BERGOUGNAN | Y.R. BERGOUGNAN 1DG | Y.R. BERGOUGNAN 1DG | Y.R. BERGOUGNAN | Y.R. BERGOUGNAN |
| J. MASSARE | J. MASSARE | J. MASSARE | J. PRIN-CLARY | J. MASSARE |
| *M. VOLOT | M. VOLOT | M. VOLOT | M. VOLOT | M. VOLOT |
| J. PRIN-CLARY | J. PRIN-CLARY | J. PRIN-CLARY | †E. BUZY | E. BUZY |
| A. MOGA | A. MOGA | A. MOGA | A. MOGA | A. MOGA |
| R. SORO | R. SORO | R. SORO | R. SORO | J. PRIN-CLARY |
| J. PRAT | J. PRAT 1T | J. PRAT | J. PRAT | J. PRAT 1C |
| †G. BASQUET | G. BASQUET | G. BASQUET | G. BASQUET | G. BASQUET |
| †J. MATHEU | J. MATHEU | J. MATHEU | J. MATHEU | J. MATHEU |
| Swansea | Parc des Princes | Lansdowne Road | Stade Colombes | Stade Colombes |
| LOST 0-8 | WON 10-0 | WON 4-3 | LOST 9-14 | WON 12-0 |
| WALES: 1G 1T | FR.: 1DG 2T | IRE.: 1PG | FR.: 3T | FR.: 1G 1DG 1T |
| FR.: NIL | BES: NIL | FR.: 1DG | KIWIS: 1G 1PG 2T | WALES: NIL |
| 22 Dec. 1945 | 1 Jan. 1946 | 26 Jan. 1946 | 10 Mar. 1946 | 22 Apr. 1946 |

France played five "Victory" internationals in 1945-6, the FFR awarding full caps to the players taking part (although the Home Unions did not recognise these games as official internationals). Louis Junquas, an exciting centre with a commitment to attacking, enterprising play, led the French to three victories against an Empire Services XV, Ireland and Wales.

Jean Prat, Basquet and Matheu, the French back-row trio, went on to play together in 22 French sides, creating a world record. Prat and Basquet were subsequent French captains whose achievements helped to push France to the fore in international rugby. Prat retired in 1955, having made 51 appearances for his country, a new French record.

Albert Moga and Robert Soro, two huge forwards, formed the French second row on 21 occasions, missing only one match between 1945 and 1950. Moga was the solid line-expert of the duo; Soro his dashing, athletic foil.

## 1946-47

| | v. SCOTLAND | v. IRELAND | v. WALES | v. ENGLAND |
|---|---|---|---|---|
| | A. ALVAREZ | A. ALVAREZ | A. ALVAREZ | A. ALVAREZ |
| | E. PEBEYRE | E. PEBEYRE | E. PEBEYRE | E. PEBEYRE |
| | *L. JUNQUAS | *L. JUNQUAS | *L. JUNQUAS | *L. JUNQUAS |
| | M. SORRONDO | M. SORRONDO 1T | M. SORRONDO | M. SORRONDO |
| | J. LASSEGUE 1T | J. LASSEGUE 2T | J. LASSEGUE | H. DUTRAIN |
| | M. TERRAU 1T | M. TERRAU | M. TERRAU | M. TERRAU |
| | Y.R. BERGOUGNAN | Y.R. BERGOUGNAN | Y.R. BERGOUGNAN | Y.R. BERGOUGNAN |
| | J. PRIN-CLARY | J. PRIN-CLARY | J. PRIN-CLARY | †L. CARON |
| | †M. JOL | M. JOL | M. JOL | M. JOL |
| | E. BUZY | E. BUZY | E. BUZY | E. BUZY |
| | A. MOGA | A. MOGA | A. MOGA | A. MOGA |
| | R. SORO | R. SORO | R. SORO | R. SORO |
| | J. PRAT 1C | J. PRAT 1T | J. PRAT | J. PRAT 1PG |
| | G. BASQUET | G. BASQUET | G. BASQUET | G. BASQUET |
| | J. MATHEU | J. MATHEU | J. MATHEU | J. MATHEU |
| | Stade Colombes | Lansdowne Road | Stade Colombes | Twickenham |
| | WON 8-3 | WON 12-8 | LOST 0-3 | LOST 3-6 |
| | FR.: 1G 1T | IRE.: 1G 1PG | FR.: NIL | ENG.: 2T |
| | SCOT.: 1PG | FR.: 4T | WALES: 1PG | FR.: 1PG |
| | 1 Jan. 1947 | 25 Jan. 1947 | 22 Mar. 1947 | 19 Apr. 1947 |

France were strong contenders for the Championship in 1947. The side which had established itself during the "Victory" internationals became a settled combination of forward strength and attacking threequarter flair and opened the season with wins against Scotland and Ireland.

Jean Lassègue, a powerful runner who was nicknamed "The Buffalo", was a skilful, determined winger of rare effectiveness. His three tries at the start of the season were significant contributions to the French victories, but following the defeat by Wales in Paris, Lassègue made way for Dutrain for the match against England at Twickenham, which had been postponed in February owing to snow.

France (who used only 17 players) conceded just three tries in the season, an excellent record for which their full-back, Alvarez, deserved commendation. He was a shrewd player with a deep tactical understanding of the game. Brilliant in defence, he also had a penchant for attack which was later put to use at fly-half. Alvarez was one of the most popular and most respected French players of the late 1940s, and he later became a French selector.

## 1947-48

| | v. IRELAND | v. AUSTRALIA | v. SCOTLAND | v. WALES | v. ENGLAND |
|---|---|---|---|---|---|
| | L. ROUFFIA | A. ALVAREZ 2C | A. ALVAREZ 1C | A. ALVAREZ 1C | A. ALVAREZ 1C |
| | †M. POMATHIOS | M. POMATHIOS 1T | M. POMATHIOS | M. POMATHIOS 1T | M. POMATHIOS 1T |
| | M. TERRAU | †P. DIZABO | P. DIZABO | M. TERRAU 1T | M. TERRAU |
| | M. SORRONDO | M. TERRAU | L. JUNQUAS | L. JUNQUAS | P. DIZABO |
| | †P. JEANJEAN | †R. LACAUSSADE | R. LACAUSSADE 1T | J. LASSEGUE | †M. SIMAN |
| | A. ALVAREZ | †L. BORDENAVE | L. BORDENAVE | L. BORDENAVE | L. BORDENAVE |
| | †G. DUFAU | G. DUFAU | Y.R. BERGOUGNAN | Y.R. BERGOUGNAN | Y.R. BERGOUGNAN 1DG |
| | L. CARON | L. CARON | †P. ARISTOUY | L. CARON | L. CARON |
| | †L. MARTIN | L. MARTIN | L. MARTIN | L. MARTIN | L. MARTIN |
| | E. BUZY | E. BUZY | E. BUZY | E. BUZY | E. BUZY |
| | A. MOGA | A. MOGA | A. MOGA | A. MOGA | A. MOGA |
| | R. SORO 1T | R. SORO | R. SORO | R. SORO | R. SORO 1T |
| | J. PRAT | J. PRAT | J. PRAT 1PG | J. PRAT | J. PRAT 1T |
| | *G. BASQUET 1T | *G. BASQUET 2T | *G. BASQUET | *G. BASQUET 1T | *G. BASQUET |
| | J. MATHEU | J. MATHEU | J. MATHEU | J. MATHEU | J. MATHEU |
| | Stade Colombes | Stade Colombes | Murrayfield | Swansea | Stade Colombes |
| | LOST 6-13 | WON 13-6 | LOST 8-9 | WON 11-3 | WON 15-0 |
| | FR.: 2T | FR.: 2G 1T | SCOT.: 2PG 1T | WALES: 1PG | FR.: 1G 1DG 2T |
| | IRE.: 2G 1T | AUST.: 2PG | FR.: 1G 1PG | FR.: 1G 2T | ENG.: NIL |
| | 1 Jan. 1948 | 11 Jan. 1948 | 24 Jan. 1948 | 21 Feb. 1948 | 29 Mar. 1948 |

France opened the season with five players who were new to the Championship (though Rouffia had played in a "Victory" international in 1946). The side was built around a heavy pack which dictated tactics in the tight but which could not pierce a determined Irish defence. Although France dominated throughout the match, they were unable to improve on two early second-half tries, and Ireland secured victory against the run of play.

The selectors wisely retained the same pack for the encounter with the Wallabies, but made adjustments among the backs. The result was France's first-ever success against a Dominion side, and the new strength of French rugby was reflected by the fact that they were the only international side to score tries against the tourists.

The French pack established a clear superiority against Scotland, despite losing by a point, and finished the season with convincing wins over Wales and England. The success in Swansea was their first on Welsh soil, and again stemmed from forward dominance backed up by tight marking. Pomathios, the finest French wing of the immediate post-war era, scored tries in the final two games, and his skiful play at Swansea so impressed the Welsh crowd that he was chaired from the field at the end of the game.

## 1948-49

| v. SCOTLAND | v. IRELAND | v. ENGLAND | v. WALES |
|---|---|---|---|
| †N. BAUDRY | N. BAUDRY | A. ALVAREZ 1DG | N. BAUDRY |
| M. POMATHIOS | M. POMATHIOS | M. POMATHIOS | M. POMATHIOS |
| P. DIZABO | P. DIZABO | P. DIZABO | P. DIZABO |
| M. TERRAU | H. DUTRAIN | H. DUTRAIN | H. DUTRAIN |
| M. SIMAN | J. LASSEGUE 1T | J. LASSEGUE | J. LASSEGUE 1T |
| L. BORDENAVE | A. ALVAREZ | †J. PILON | A. ALVAREZ 1C |
| Y.R. BERGOUGNAN | G. DUFAU | Y.R. BERGOUGNAN | G. DUFAU |
| L. CARON | L. CARON | L. CARON | L. CARON |
| M. JOL | M. JOL | M. JOL | M. JOL |
| E. BUZY | E. BUZY | E. BUZY | E. BUZY |
| A. MOGA | A. MOGA | A. MOGA | A. MOGA |
| R. SORO | R. SORO | R. SORO | R. SORO |
| J. PRAT | J. PRAT 2PG,2C | J. PRAT | J. PRAT |
| *G. BASQUET | *G. BASQUET 1T | *G. BASQUET | *G. BASQUET |
| J. MATHEU | J. MATHEU | J. MATHEU | J. MATHEU |
| Stade Colombes | Lansdowne Road | Twickenham | Stade Colombes |
| LOST 0-8 | WON 16-9 | LOST 3-8 | WON 5-3 |
| FR.: NIL | IRE.: 3PG | ENG.: 1G 1DG | FR.: 1G |
| SCOT.: 1G 1T | FR.: 2G 2PG | FR.: 1DG | WALES: 1T |
| 15 Jan. 1949 | 29 Jan. 1949 | 27 Feb. 1949 | 26 Mar. 1949 |

France was blessed with an outstanding, mobile pack capable of winning good ball in the tight and certain to impress in the loose. But a failure to find an effective midfield combination at threequarter cost the French the match with Scotland, and several attempts were made to introduce wider attacking potential during the season. The recall of Lassègue was a successful move, but generally the back play remained disappointing and the side was unable to challenge seriously for Championship honours.

Six members of the pack had played unchanged for three successive seasons and twelve Championship matches, an unusual record. And Basquet had become established as an inspiring captain who led by personal example. Altogether he skippered France on 24 occasions, a record surpassed by only Jean-Pierre Rives.

The French back play was more enterprising in Paris against Wales, though sound defence by the Welsh full-back prevented his side suffering a heavy defeat. Only a second-half try by Lassègue, converted by Alvarez, enabled France to win, but their victory gave them two consecutive wins over Wales for the first time in the series.

## 1949

| 1st v. ARGENTINA | 2nd v. ARGENTINA |
|---|---|
| N. BAUDRY | N. BAUDRY 1DG |
| M. POMATHIOS | R. GENESTE |
| †F. DESCLAUX | F. DESCLAUX |
| H. DUTRAIN | P. DIZABO |
| J. LASSEGUE | M. POMATHIOS 1T |
| M. TERRAU | M. TERRAU |
| Y.R. BERGOUGNAN | Y.R. BERGOUGNAN |
| L. CARON 1T | P. ARISTOUY |
| M. JOL | M. JOL |
| E. BUZY | E BUZY |
| A. MOGA | A. MOGA |
| R. SORO | R. SORO |
| J. PRAT 1C | *J. PRAT 1PG,1T |
| *G. BASQUET | †F. LACRAMPE |
| J. MATHEU | J. MATHEU |
| Buenos Aires | Buenos Aires |
| WON 5-0 | WON 12-3 |
| ARG.: NIL | ARG.: 1T |
| FR.: 1G | FR.: 2T 1DG 1PG |
| 28 Aug. 1949 | 4 Sept. 1949 |

The FFR undertook their first official tour in the summer of 1949, a party of 23 players visiting Argentina under the management of René Crabos and Adolphe Jauréguy. Nine matches were played, including two official Tests, and all of the matches were won.

The FFR was invited to send a French referee with the party, but the Federation elected not to and the internationals were handled by Argentinians, John Knox and Oscar Noon. Knox was of Scots parentage and had been a prominent player in his youth. Also a very good cricketer, he had toured Britain with the combined South American side of 1932.

Yves Bergougnan, an exceptionally tall but talented scrum-half, made the last of his 17 French appearances in the second Test against Argentina. Intelligent, lissom and with a remarkable ability to drop goals from awkward angles, Bergougnan possessed a long and accurate pass. But his career was dogged by shoulder injuries, and he was only 25 at the time of his final international.

## 1949-50

| v. SCOTLAND | v. IRELAND | v. ENGLAND | v. WALES |
|---|---|---|---|
| †R. ARCALIS | R. ARCALIS | †G. BRUN | G. BRUN |
| M. SIMAN | M. SIMAN | M. SIMAN | M. SIMAN |
| P. DIZABO | P. DIZABO | P. LAUGA | P. LAUGA |
| †J. MERQUEY 1T | J. MERQUEY | J. MERQUEY | J. MERQUEY |
| M. POMATHIOS | M. POMATHIOS | †F. CAZENAVE 1T | M. POMATHIOS |
| †P. LAUGA | P. LAUGA 1DG | J. PILON 1T | †F. FOURNET |
| G. DUFAU | †P. LASAOSA | G. DUFAU | G. DUFAU |
| †P. LAVERGNE | R. BIENES | R. BIENES | R. BIENES |
| L. MARTIN | †P. PASCALIN | P. PASCALIN | P. PASCALIN |
| †R. FERRIEN | R. FERRIEN | R. FERRIEN | R. FERRIEN |
| P. ARISTOUY | P. ARISTOUY | P. ARISTOUY | P. ARISTOUY |
| †F. BONNUS | F. BONNUS | F. BONNUS | F. BONNUS |
| J. PRAT 1C | J. PRAT | J. PRAT | J. PRAT |
| *G. BASQUET | *G. BASQUET | *G. BASQUET | *G. BASQUET |
| †R. BIENES | †D. HERICE | J. MATHEU | J. MATHEU |
| Murrayfield | Stade Colombes | Stade Colombes | Cardiff Arms Park |
| LOST 5-8 | DRAWN 3-3 | WON 6-3 | LOST 0-21 |
| SCOT.: 1G 1T | FR.: 1DG | FR.: 2T | WALES: 3G 1PG 1T |
| FR.: 1G | IRE.: 1PG | ENG.: 1T | FR.: NIL |
| 14 Jan. 1950 | 28 Jan. 1950 | 25 Feb. 1950 | 25 Mar. 1950 |

The French fielded an experimental fifteen in 1950, several of their leading forwards having retired or lost form. During the season the French packs aligned themselves in the increasingly fashionable 3-4-1 formation; but their only successes were in holding a strong Irish side to a draw in freezing conditions in Paris, and beating England.

Lauga and Pilon bombarded the English with drop-goal attempts in Paris, though it was thanks to two tries that victory was achieved in heavy conditions. Brun, in his debut, had a busy afternoon, but proved a valuable asset to his side. His tackling and fielding were sure, and his perfectly timed entries to the threequarter line caused many problems for the English defence. Brun was such an exciting, fast runner that he later occupied the centre and wing positions in the national side.

France were unusually lethargic at Cardiff, losing to a formidable Welsh side by 21 points. France did well until half-time, but the loss of Prat and Bienes through injuries permitted the Welsh to overwhelm the visiting pack, who were out-hooked, outpushed and overrun.

## 1950-51

| v. SCOTLAND | v. IRELAND | v. ENGLAND | v. WALES |
|---|---|---|---|
| A. ALVAREZ | R. ARCALIS | R. ARCALIS | R. ARCALIS |
| †A. PORTHAULT 1T | M. POMATHIOS | A. PORTHAULT | A. PORTHAULT |
| M. TERRAU | †M. PRAT | G. BRUN | G. BRUN |
| G. BRUN | †G. BELLETANTE | G. BELLETANTE | G. BELLETANTE |
| M. POMATHIOS | †D. OLIVE 1T | M. POMATHIOS | M. POMATHIOS |
| †J. CARABIGNAC | J. CARABIGNAC | A. ALVAREZ | A. ALVAREZ 1PG,1T |
| G. DUFAU | G. DUFAU | G. DUFAU | G. DUFAU |
| †R. BERNARD | R. BERNARD | R. BERNARD | R. BERNARD |
| P. PASCALIN | P. PASCALIN | P. PASCALIN | P. PASCALIN |
| R. BIENES | †P. BERTRAND 1C | P. BERTRAND | P. BERTRAND |
| †L. MIAS 1T | L. MIAS | L. MIAS | L. MIAS |
| †H. FOURES | H. FOURES | H. FOURES | H. FOURES |
| J. PRAT 2PG,1C | R. BIENES | J. PRAT 1T,1C,1DG | J. PRAT 1C |
| *G. BASQUET | *G. BASQUET | *G. BASQUET 1T | *G. BASQUET |
| J. MATHEU | J. MATHEU 1T | R. BIENES | R. BIENES |
| Stade Colombes | Lansdowne Road | Twickenham | Stade Colombes |
| WON 14-12 | LOST 8-9 | WON 11-3 | WON 8-3 |
| FR.: 1G 2PG 1T | IRE.: 1PG 2T | ENG.: 1T | FR.: 1G 1PG |
| SCOT.: 2PG 2T | FR.: 1G 1T | FR.: 1G 1DG 1T | WALES: 1T |
| 13 Jan. 1951 | 27 Jan. 1951 | 24 Feb. 1951 | 7 Apr. 1951 |

France gained three victories in 1951, losing unluckily by a single point to Ireland, and thus finished as runners-up in the International Championship for the first time. Prat, their outstanding flanker, was absent in Dublin through influenza, otherwise his ability to kick goals could have given the French the Grand Slam.

Prat returned, and in excellent form, for France's first ever win at Twickenham. In a match played in awful conditions, he contributed a try, a conversion and a drop-goal to a memorable victory.

The French forwards were dominant against Wales and the architects of a success which owed much to two second-half scores, Wales having led at the interval. Mias, a schoolmaster, was the youngest member of the pack. After a promising start to his career, he lost form in the mid-1950s, became overweight, and was dropped from the French XV after gaining 17 caps. Then he changed profession, concentrated on studies to become a doctor, and later regained his zest and commitment for international rugby. Resuming his international career in 1957-8, he went on to lead France to her famous successes in South Africa, and was the French skipper who led the side to its first outright Five-Nations title in 1959.

## 1951-52

| v. SCOTLAND | v. IRELAND | v. S.AFRICA | v. WALES | v. ENGLAND | v. ITALY |
|---|---|---|---|---|---|
| †R. Labarthete | G. Brun | †P. Guilleux | G. Brun | G. Brun | P. Guilleux |
| | | | | | |
| G. Brun | A. Porthault | G. Brun | M. Pomathios 1t | M. Pomathios 1t | G. Brun |
| M. Prat | M. Prat | †J. Mauran | J. Mauran | J. Mauran | R. Martine |
| †R. Martine | R. Martine | M. Prat | M. Prat | M. Prat | J. Mauran |
| F. Cazenave | D. Olive | †J. Colombier | J. Colombier | J. Colombier | †L. Roge 1t |
| | | | | | |
| †R. Furcade | †A. Labazuy | J. Carabignac 1dg | J. Carabignac | J. Carabignac | †M. Lecointre |
| P. Lasaosa | P. Lasaosa | G. Dufau | G. Dufau | P. Lasaosa | P. Lasaosa |
| | | | | | |
| R. Bienes | R. Bienes | R. Bienes | R. Bienes | R. Bienes | R. Bienes 1t |
| †P. Labadie | P. Labadie | P. Labadie | P. Labadie | P. Labadie | P. Labadie |
| †R. Brejassou | R. Brejassou | R. Brejassou | R. Brejassou | R. Brejassou | †A. Sanac |
| †F. Varenne | L. Mias | L. Mias | L. Mias | L. Mias | L. Mias |
| †B. Chevallier | B. Chevallier | B. Chevallier | B. Chevallier | B. Chevallier | B. Chevallier |
| J. Prat 1t,2c,1pg | J. Prat 1t,1c,1pg | J. Prat | J. Prat 1c | J. Prat | J. Prat 2pg,1c |
| *G. Basquet 1t | *G. Basquet | *G. Basquet | *G. Basquet | *G. Basquet | *G. Basquet 1t |
| †J.R. Bourdeu | J.R. Bourdeu | J.R. Bourdeu | J.R. Bourdeu | J.R. Bourdeu | J.R. Bourdeu |
| Murrayfield | Stade Colombes | Stade Colombes | Swansea | Stade Colombes | Milan |
| WON 13-11 | LOST 8-11 | LOST 3-25 | LOST 5-9 | LOST 3-6 | WON 17-8 |
| SCOT.: 1G 2PG | FR.: 1G 1PG | FR.: 1DG | WALES: 1DG 2PG | FR.: 1T | ITALY: 1G 1PG |
| FR.: 2G 1PG | IRE.: 1G 1PG 1T | SA: 2G 1PG 4T | FR.: 1G | ENG.: 2PG | FR.: 1G 2PG 2T |
| 12 Jan. 1952 | 26 Jan. 1952 | 16 Feb. 1952 | 22 Mar. 1952 | 5 Apr. 1952 | 17 May 1952 |

The season began with the French recording a first-ever victory at Murrayfield. As at Twickenham the previous year, all of the French scoring was executed by their senior players, Basquet and Prat. Prat was outstanding. He kicked a penalty goal, backed-up a storming run by his younger brother Maurice, which yielded a try at the posts, and played a part in a blindside break in the second-half to create the decisive try for Basquet.

But the season ended in disappointment, following a narrow defeat against Ireland. The French selectors made wholesale changes among the backs for the match with the Springboks. Carabignac, a chubby fly-half with a liking for drops at goal (three successes in his seven internationals to equal the career record of Bergougnan) opened the scoring against the tourists, but the French pack was overpowered by the strength of the tourists' forwards and the French finished well beaten.

Pomathios scored tries in the defeats by Wales and England before the French, fielding three new caps, beat Italy in Milan during May. The Italians proved to be strong members of FIRA in the 1950s and 1960s, regularly beating the Romanians. The French recognised the value of playing their FIRA neighbours, awarding full caps for the annual matches with the Italians (up to 1967), and later for the matches with Romania.

## 1952-53

| v. SCOTLAND | v. IRELAND | v. ENGLAND | v. WALES | v. ITALY |
|---|---|---|---|---|
| †J. Rouan | J. Rouan | G. Brun | †M. Vannier | G. Brun |
| | | | | |
| A. Porthault | A. Porthault | J.R. Bourdeu | M. Pomathios | A. Porthault 2t |
| J. Dauger | J. Mauran | J. Mauran | †J. Galy | †J.H. Pargade |
| M. Prat | M. Prat | M. Prat | G. Brun | F. Desclaux 1dg,2c |
| M. Pomathios | M. Pomathios | L. Roge | L. Roge | L. Roge |
| | | | | |
| J. Carabignac 1dg | J. Carabignac 1dg | †A. Haget | †L. Bidart | R. Martine |
| G. Dufau | G. Dufau | G. Dufau | G. Dufau | †J. Darrieusecq |
| | | | | |
| P. Bertrand 1pg,1c | P. Bertrand | P. Bertrand | P. Bertrand 1pg | P. Bertrand 1pg |
| P. Labadie | P. Labadie | †J. Arrieta | J. Arrieta | P. Labadie |
| A. Sanac | R. Bienes | †R. Carrere | R. Brejassou | R. Carrere |
| L. Mias | L. Mias | R. Brejassou | L. Mias | L. Mias |
| †P. Tignol | A. Sanac | B. Chevallier | B. Chevallier | B. Chevallier |
| *J. Prat | *J. Prat | *J. Prat | *J. Prat | *J. Prat 1dg |
| R. Bienes | P. Tignol | †M. Celaya | M.Celaya | M. Celeya |
| J.R. Bourdeu 1t | J.R. Bourdeu | R. Bienes | †H. Domec | H. Domec 1t |
| Stade Colombes | Ravenhill | Twickenham | Stade Colombes | Lyon |
| WON 11-5 | LOST 3-16 | LOST 0-11 | LOST 3-6 | WON 22-8 |
| FR.: 1G 1DG 1PG | IRE.: 2G 2T | ENG.: 1G 2T | FR.: 1PG | FR.: 2G 2DG 1PG 1T |
| SCOT.: 1G | FR.: 1DG | FR.: NIL | WALES: 2T | ITALY: 1G 1PG |
| 10 Jan. 1953 | 24 Jan. 1953 | 28 Feb. 1953 | 28 Mar. 1953 | 26 Apr. 1953 |

Malpractices surrounding the French Club Championship surfaced again in the early 1950s, with the four Home Unions threatening to repeat the excommunications of 1931. Following a letter from the Home Unions Committee, dated July 1952, the French promised to discontinue the Championship. However, the promise was never carried out and the issue was forgotten.

Jean Dauger made his sole Five-Nations appearance against Scotland, at the age of 33. As a teenager before the war he had been a Rugby League international. But during the war he built an excellent reputation as a brilliant attacking centre with Bayonne, and he won two caps in 1945 against Service teams. However, his previous League connections may have dissuaded the selectors from fielding him in matches against Home Unions. Later, Dauger was a distinguished French rugby writer.

France's only victories were against Scotland and Italy. Carabignac was criticised for this lack of pace in Belfast and he lost his place to Haget, whose father had played for France in 1928 (the first father/son combination to be capped for France).

## 1953-54

| v. SCOTLAND | v. IRELAND | v. NZ | v. WALES | v. ENGLAND | v. ITALY |
|---|---|---|---|---|---|
| M. VANNIER | M. VANNIER | †H. CLAVERIE | H. CLAVERIE | †P. ALBALADEJO | P. ALBALADEJO |
| M. POMATHIOS | F. CAZENAVE | F. CAZENAVE | F. CAZENAVE | F. CAZENAVE | †J. LEPATEY 2T |
| †J. BOUQUET | M. PRAT 2T | M. PRAT | M. PRAT | M. PRAT 1T | M. PRAT 1T |
| R. MARTINE | R. MARTINE | R. MARTINE | R. MARTINE 1T | R. MARTINE | A. BONIFACE 1T |
| L. ROGE | †A. BONIFACE | A. BONIFACE | A. BONIFACE | A. BONIFACE 1T | †G. MURILLO 2T |
| A. LABAZUY | A. HAGET | A. HAGET | A. LABAZUY | A. HAGET | R. MARTINE |
| G. DUFAU | G. DUFAU | G. DUFAU | G. DUFAU | G. DUFAU | G. DUFAU |
| R. BIENES | R. BIENES | R. BIENES | R. BIENES | R. BIENES | A. DOMENECH |
| P. LABADIE | P. LABADIE | P. LABADIE | P. LABADIE | P. LABADIE | †J. BENETIERE |
| R. BREJASSOU 1T | R. BREJASSOU | R. BREJASSOU | †A. DOMENECH | A. DOMENECH | †J. BICHENDARITZ |
| L. MIAS | L. MIAS | L. MIAS | L. MIAS | A. SANAC | R. BAULON |
| B. CHEVALLIER | B. CHEVALLIER | B. CHEVALLIER | B. CHEVALLIER | R. BAULON | M. CELAYA |
| *J. PRAT | *J. PRAT 1C | *J. PRAT 1T | *J. PRAT 2C,1PG | *J. PRAT 1DG,1C | †G. LARREGUY 1T |
| †R. BAULON | M. CELAYA | R. BAULON | R. BAULON 1T | M. CELAYA | *J. PRAT 6C,2PG |
| H. DOMEC | H. DOMEC | H. DOMEC | H. DOMEC | H. DOMEC | H. DOMEC |
| Murrayfield | Stade Colombes | Stade Colombes | Cardiff Arms Park | Stade Colombes | Rome |
| WON 3-0 | WON 8-0 | WON 3-0 | LOST 13-19 | WON 11-3 | WON 39-12 |
| SCOT.: NIL | FR.: 1G 1T | FR.: 1T | WALES: 2G 3PG | FR.: 1G 1DG 1T | ITALY: 2PG 2T |
| FR.: 1T | IRE.: NIL | NZ: NIL | FR.: 2G 1PG | ENG.: 1T | FR.: 2PG 6G 1T |
| 9 Jan. 1954 | 23 Jan. 1954 | 27 Feb. 1954 | 27 Mar. 1954 | 10 Apr. 1954 | 24 Apr. 1954 |

The season was an important milestone in the history of French rugby. For the first time France shared the Championship, winning three of their matches, and beat the All Blacks.

The success of the side derived from an energetic pack and an enterprising threequarter line, reliably and imaginatively harnessed by Dufau, a splendid scrum-half with the agility of a tiger. Prat, Baulon and Domec formed a trio of swift destroyers whose quickness onto man and ball forced opponents into error. Against New Zealand, Domec dispossessed the scrum-half to enable Baulon to make a run towards the All Blacks' line. When challenged, Baulon found Prat at his shoulder to score the winning try of the match.

Intense spoiling, tight marking and skilful tactical kicking were features of the Championship wins. Although the backs ran and handled efficiently, they failed to draw their markers in these matches. However, in Rome the backs had a field day and the threequarters scored six tries. The match marked Boniface's debut as a centre, a position in which he was to establish himself as the best attacking player in France.

## 1954

| 1st v. ARGENTINA | 2nd v. ARGENTINA |
|---|---|
| M. VANNIER 2C,2PG | M. VANNIER 3C,2DG,1PG |
| A. BONIFACE | L. ROGE 1T |
| G. MURILLO 1T | A. BONIFACE 2T |
| †J. MEYNARD | R. MARTINE |
| L. ROGE | †A. MOREL 1T |
| †R. BASAURI | A. HAGET |
| †P. DANOS 1DG | P. DANOS |
| *R. BIENES 2T | *R. BIENES 1T |
| J. BENETIERE | P. LABADIE |
| J. BICHENDARITZ | J. BICHENDARITZ |
| B. CHEVALLIER | †H. LAZIES |
| †P. CAPITANI | P. CAPITANI |
| †Y. DUFFAUT | Y. DUFFAUT |
| M. CELAYA | M. CELAYA |
| †J. BARTHE | J. BARTHE |
| Buenos Aires | Buenos Aires |
| WON 22-8 | WON 30-3 |
| ARG.: 1G 1PG | ARG.: 1T |
| FR.: 2G 1DG 2PG 1T | FR.: 3G 2DG 1PG 2T |
| 29 Aug. 1954 | 12 Sept. 1954 |

The second French tour of Argentina took place in the summer of 1954. A party of 22 players was managed by former internationals René Crabos and Marcel Laurent, and eleven matches, including two full internationals, were played and won on the tour.

In the absence of Jean Prat, René Biènes, who had just led his club Cognac to the French club championship final, and who had played an important part in France's Five-Nations success during the winter, was appointed tour captain. Biènes won medals for bravery with the French Resistance during the war, before forcing his way into the national side as an inexhaustible loose forward. Mobile, powerful and excellent in the line-out, Biènes subsequently made the transition to prop, and went on to gain 29 caps.

France blooded eight new caps in the two Tests, though only three, Danos, Barthe and Laziès, later gained recognition against IB nations. Danos and Barthe became key players in France's famous teams of the late 1950s. Danos had to wait until the great Dufau passed from the side before winning a regular place in the national team; while Barthe established himself as an outstanding number-eight, before joining the Rugby League.

## 1954-55

| v. SCOTLAND | v. IRELAND | v. ENGLAND | v. WALES | v. ITALY |
|---|---|---|---|---|
| M. VANNIER 1PG | M. VANNIER 1C | M. VANNIER 2C | M. VANNIER 1PG,1C | M. VANNIER 2PG,3C |
| A. BONIFACE 1T | A. BONIFACE | †H. RANCOULE | H. RANCOULE | †J. CHIBERRY |
| M. PRAT | M. PRAT | M. PRAT | M. PRAT 1DG | P. LASAOSA |
| L. ROGE | L. ROGE | J. BOUQUET | R. MARTINE | M. PRAT |
| J. LEPATEY | J. LEPATEY | J. LEPATEY | J. LEPATEY | H. RANCOULE 2T |
| R. MARTINE | R. MARTINE | A. HAGET | A. HAGET | A. HAGET |
| G. DUFAU 1T | G. DUFAU | G. DUFAU | G. DUFAU | G. DUFAU 1T |
| R. BREJASSOU | R. BREJASSOU | R. BREJASSOU | R. BREJASSOU | H. LAZIES |
| P. LABADIE | P. LABADIE | P. LABADIE | P. LABADIE | †M. ESCOMMIER |
| A. DOMENECH 1T | A. DOMENECH 1T | A. DOMENECH | A. DOMENECH | R. BREJASSOU |
| J. BARTHE | M. CELAYA | M. CELAYA 1T | M. CELAYA | M. CELAYA |
| B. CHEVALLIER | B. CHEVALLIER | B. CHEVALLIER | B. CHEVALLIER | B. CHEVALLIER |
| *J. PRAT 1T | *J. PRAT | *J. PRAT 2DG | *J. PRAT | *J. PRAT |
| M. CELAYA | R. BAULON | R. BAULON 1T | R. BAULON 1T | †T. MANTEROLA |
| H. DOMEC | H. DOMEC | H. DOMEC | H. DOMEC | R. BAULON 1T |
| Stade Colombes | Lansdowne Road | Twickenham | Stade Colombes | Grenoble |
| WON 15-0 | WON 5-3 | WON 16-9 | LOST 11-16 | WON 24-0 |
| FR.: 4T 1PG | IRE.: 1PG | ENG.: 2PG 1T | FR.: 1G 1DG 1PG | FR.: 3G 2PG 1T |
| SCOT.: NIL | FR.: 1G | FR.: 2G 2DG | WALES: 2G 2PG | ITALY: NIL |
| 8 Jan. 1955 | 22 Jan. 1955 | 26 Feb. 1955 | 26 Mar. 1955 | 10 Apr. 1955 |

The rise of French rugby, which owed much to the expertise and personality of Jean Prat, continued under his captaincy in 1955. The team won its first three matches with little difficulty. Prat was supported by a rich blend of experience, balance and speed, only a slight hesitancy at fly-half depriving the side of all-round excellence.

The Grand Slam beckoned as France entertained Wales at Colombes in the fianl match of the Championship. But in front of a record crowd of 62,000, France had their confidence shaken in the first half of a fascinating game. Facing the wind France conceded eleven points, but despite an irresistible rally after the interval their elan was insufficient to force victory. France thus shared the title with Wales.

Jean Prat made his final appearance in the side which trounced Italy. The legendary "Monsieur Rugby" retired having established a career record of 139 points for France, including five drop-goals – a remarkable feat for a wing forward. For his club Lourdes, he played in six winning Championship sides up to 1958, captained the club in seven finals, and later coached Lourdes to adopt the open, flowing style he had enjoyed in his playing days.

## 1955-56

| v. SCOTLAND | v. IRELAND | v. WALES | v. ITALY | v. ENGLAND |
|---|---|---|---|---|
| M. VANNIER | M. VANNIER 1DG,1C | M. VANNIER | M. VANNIER 2C,1PG | M. VANNIER |
| †J. DUPUY | A. BONIFACE 1T | J. DUPUY | L. ROGE 2T | J. DUPUY 1T |
| A. BONIFACE | M. PRAT | M. PRAT | M. PRAT | J. BOUQUET |
| †G. STENER | G. STENER | A. BONIFACE | A. BONIFACE | G. STENER |
| †S. TORREILLES | J. DUPUY | L. ROGE | J. DUPUY | L. ROGE |
| J. BOUQUET | J. BOUQUET 1DG | J. BOUQUET | J. BOUQUET | A. LABAZUY 2PG,1C |
| *G. DUFAU | *G. DUFAU | *G. DUFAU | *G. DUFAU | †G. PAUTHE 1T |
| R. BIENES | R. BIENES | R. BIENES | R. BIENES | R. BIENES |
| †R. VIGIER | P. LABADIE | R. VIGIER | R. VIGIER | R. VIGIER |
| A. DOMENECH | A. DOMENECH | A. DOMENECH | A. DOMENECH | A. DOMENECH |
| †G. ROUCARIES | M. CELAYA | M. CELAYA | M. CELAYA | *M. CELAYA |
| B. CHEVALLIER | B. CHEVALLIER | B. CHEVALLIER | B. CHEVALLIER | B. CHEVALLIER |
| †J. CARRERE | H. DOMEC | H. DOMEC | H. DOMEC | J. BARTHE |
| M. CELAYA | J. BARTHE | J. BARTHE | J. BARTHE | H. LAZIES |
| R. BAULON | R. BAULON 1T | R. BAULON 1T | R. BAULON 1T | R. BAULON |
| Murrayfield | Stade Colombes | Cardiff Arms Park | Padua | Stade Colombes |
| LOST 0-12 | WON 14-8 | LOST 3-5 | WON 16-3 | WON 14-9 |
| SCOT.: 2PG 2T | FR.: 1G 2DG 1T | WALES: 1G | ITALY: 1T | FR.: 1G 2PG 1T |
| FR.: NIL | IRE.: 1G 1T | FR.: 1T | FR.: 2G 1PG 1T | ENG.: 2PG 1T |
| 14 Jan. 1956 | 28 Jan. 1956 | 24 Mar. 1956 | 2 Apr. 1956 | 14 Apr. 1956 |

Gérard Dufau, who gained 38 caps in a career which stretched from 1948 to 1957, establishing a record for a French scrum-half, succeeded Prat as captain and led a side which again made a serious challenge for the Championship. Only the difference between a converted try and unconverted try at Cardiff prevented the side taking a share in the title.

The team improved as the season developed. At Murrayfield, in wet, miserable conditions and after a thousand-mile journey, the French, fielding six new caps, were unable to settle and were well beaten by Scotland. The pack was strengthened for the Irish match, and the return of Maurice Prat added a new dimension to the French midfield play. Few changes were made until Dufau withdrew from the side which met and beat England. The new French halves kicked skilfully and the new scrum-half Pauthe celebrated his only international appearance by scoring a decisive try in the second half.

Jean Dupuy made his debut against Scotland. An exceptionally tough, fast player, he set a record by playing 39 internationals as a wing for France, and in his 40 matches (one of which was as a centre) he created a new French career record of 19 tries, though only six of these were against IB nations.

## 1956-57

| v. CZECHOSLOVAKIA | v. SCOTLAND | v. IRELAND | v. ENGLAND | v. WALES |
|---|---|---|---|---|
| J. MEYNARD 2c,2pg | M. VANNIER | M. VANNIER 2pg | M. VANNIER 1c | M. VANNIER |
| A. BONIFACE 1t | A. BONIFACE | †C. DARROUY | C. DARROUY 1t | C. DARROUY |
| †R. MONIE 1t | M. PRAT | M. PRAT | J. BOUQUET | M. PRAT 1t |
| M. PRAT 1t | L. ROGE | A. BONIFACE | R. MONIE | A. BONIFACE |
| J. DUPUY 1t | J. DUPUY | J. DUPUY | J. DUPUY | J. DUPUY 1t |
| J. BOUQUET | J. BOUQUET | A. HAGET | A. HAGET | J. BOUQUET 2c |
| †G. GAUBY | G. DUFAU | G. DUFAU | G. DUFAU | G. DUFAU |
| A. SANAC | H. LAZIES | A. SANAC | A. SANAC | A. SANAC 1t |
| R. VIGIER | R. VIGIER | P. LABADIE | R. VIGIER | R. VIGIER |
| A. DOMENECH 1t | A. DOMENECH | A. DOMENECH | A. DOMENECH | A. DOMENECH |
| B. CHEVALLIER | A. SANAC | *M. CELAYA | *M. CELAYA | *M. CELAYA |
| †F. MONCLA | B. CHEVALLIER | †M. HOCHE | M. HOCHE | M. HOCHE |
| R. BAULON | J. BARTHE | F. MONCLA | F. MONCLA | F. MONCLA |
| *M. CELAYA 1t | *M. CELAYA | J. BARTHE | J. BARTHE | J. BARTHE |
| J. BARTHE | R. BAULON | R. BAULON | J. CARRERE | J. CARRERE |
| Toulouse | Stade Colombes | Lansdowne Road | Twickenham | Stade Colombes |
| WON 28-3 | LOST 0-6 | LOST 6-11 | LOST 5-9 | LOST 13-19 |
| FR.: 2G 2PG 4T | FR.: 1DG 1PG | IRE.: 1G 1PG 1T | ENG.: 3T | FR.: 2G 1T |
| CZECH.: 1PG | SCOT.: NIL | FR.: 2PG | FR.: 1G | WALES: 2G 1PG 2T |
| 16 Dec. 1956 | 12 Jan. 1957 | 26 Jan. 1957 | 23 Feb. 1957 | 23 Mar. 1957 |

After defeating Czechoslovakia in a match in which each threequarter scored a try, the French were whitewashed in the Championship for the first time since 1929 (and for the only time since the Second War).

A pack of heavy forwards and a back division of pace and determination – the nucleus of the side which had overcome the Czechs – faced Scotland. The match started in conditions ideal for running and handling, and to the liking of the French backs. But heavy rain, which began after only five minutes, ruined the playing conditions and suited the Scots, who went on to win by a penalty goal and a drop-goal to nil. Similar conditions in Dublin, where the French showed several changes, again deprived the backs the opportunity of playing an expansive game.

But after losing to England, France finished in a blaze of glory, joining with Wales in the season's most open match. Both sides upheld a commitment to play attractive football, and French enterprise was rewarded at the end of the game by a splendid try featuring the pack. Domenech and Moncla, two fast, mobile forwards who were key members of the French pack for several seasons, participated in a flowing forward movement which culminated in a try for Sanac.

## 1957

| v. ITALY | 1st v. ROMANIA | 2nd v. ROMANIA |
|---|---|---|
| M. VANNIER 2c | M. VANNIER 4pg,1dg | M. VANNIER 6c,1t,1pg |
| C. DARROUY 2t | C. DARROUY | G. MAUDUY |
| M. PRAT | M. PRAT | A. BONIFACE 2t |
| J. DUPUY 2t | †C. VIGNES 1t | J. BOUQUET |
| †G. MAUDUY 2t | G. MAUDUY | J. DUPUY 3t |
| A. HAGET 1t | A. HAGET | C. VIGNES |
| *G. DUFAU | *G. DUFAU | P. DANOS |
| A. SANAC | T. MANTEROLA | †A. QUAGLIO |
| R. VIGIER | R. VIGIER | R. VIGIER 1t |
| A. DOMENECH 1t | A. DOMENECH | A. DOMENECH |
| †P. CASSAGNE 5c | †R. NORMAND | L. MIAS |
| M. HOCHE | M. HOCHE | *M. CELAYA |
| †R. DARRACQ | J. BARTHE | M. CRAUSTE 1t |
| R. BAULON | †M. CRAUSTE | J. BARTHE |
| F. MONCLA | F. MONCLA | J. CARRERE |
| Agen | Bucharest | Bordeaux |
| WON 38-6 | WON 18-15 | WON 39-0 |
| FR.: 7G 1T | ROM.: 3PG 2DG | FR.: 6G 1PG 2T |
| ITALY: 1PG 1T | FR.: 4PG 1DG 1T | ROM.: NIL |
| 21 Apr. 1957 | 19 May 1957 | 15 Dec. 1957 |

In the spring following the Championship there was an easy victory over the Italians before Romania, in front of 95,000 spectators in Bucharest, gave France a scare in an intense game settled in the dying moments. The Romanians were superbly fit and their pack played as well as any of the Home Nation packs in the Championship. They led 9-6 at the interval. Midway through the second half they were 15-6 ahead, but some splendid kicking by Vannier, including a penalty goal off the crossbar from 40 metres and only three minutes from no-side, saved French honour.

Worries concerning shady club transfers, accusations of shamateurism, and rumours that French players were offered £20 each by the Romanians during the Bucharest visit, again threatened the future of France's relations with the Home Unions during the summer of 1957.

Fortunately these fears were allayed and the following season opened with a return match against Romania, played in Bordeaux. Mias returned for this game with a brief to "lead, weld and galvanise" a French pack which had Celaya as captain. But Mias' influence was clearly evident in Bordeaux, where the forwards were outstanding, Boniface and Dupuy shared five tries, and Vannier became the first French full-back to score a try in an international.

## 1957-58

| v. SCOTLAND | v. ENGLAND | v. AUSTRALIA | v. WALES | v. ITALY | v. IRELAND |
|---|---|---|---|---|---|
| M. VANNIER 2PG | M. VANNIER | M. VANNIER | M. VANNIER 2DG | M. VANNIER 1C,1PG | M. VANNIER 1DG |
| G. MAUDUY | G. MAUDUY | H. RANCOULE 1T | H. RANCOULE | H. RANCOULE | H. RANCOULE |
| A. BONIFACE | A. BONIFACE | M. PRAT 1DG | M. PRAT | †A. MARQUESUZAA | *M. PRAT |
| J. BOUQUET | C. VIGNES | R. MARTINE | R. MARTINE | R. MARTINE | R. MARTINE |
| J. DUPUY 1T | J. DUPUY | †P. TARRICQ | P. TARRICQ 1T | P. TARRICQ | P. TARRICQ |
| C. VIGNES | J. BOUQUET | A. LABAZUY 1DG,2C | A. LABAZUY 2C | A. HAGET | A. LABAZUY 1PG,1C |
| P. DANOS | P. DANOS | †P. LACROIX | †P. LACROIX | P. DANOS 1T | P. DANOS 1T |
| A. QUAGLIO | A. QUAGLIO | A. QUAGLIO 1T | A. QUAGLIO | A. DOMENECH | A. QUAGLIO |
| R. VIGIER | R. VIGIER | R. VIGIER | R. VIGIER | R. VIGIER | R. VIGIER |
| A. DOMENECH | A. DOMENECH | †A. ROQUES | A. ROQUES | A. ROQUES | A. ROQUES |
| L. MIAS | L. MIAS | L. MIAS | L. MIAS | *M. CELAYA | L. MIAS |
| *M. CELAYA | *M. CELAYA | *M. CELAYA | *M. CELAYA | †B. MOMMEJAT 1T | B. MOMMEJAT |
| M. CRAUSTE | M. CRAUSTE | M. CRAUSTE 1T | M. CRAUSTE | M. CRAUSTE | M. CRAUSTE |
| J. BARTHE | J. BARTHE | J. BARTHE | J. BARTHE | J. BARTHE | J. BARTHE |
| J. CARRERE | H. DOMEC | H. DOMEC | H. DOMEC | H. DOMEC | H. DOMEC |
| Murrayfield | Stade Colombes | Stade Colombes | Cardiff Arms Park | Naples | Stade Colombes |
| LOST 9-11 | LOST 0-14 | WON 19-0 | WON 16-6 | WON 11-3 | WON 11-6 |
| SCOT.: 1G 1PG 1T | FR.: NIL | FR.: 2G 2DG 1T | WALES: 1PG 1T | ITALY: 1PG | FR.: 1G 1DG 1PG |
| FR.: 2PG 1T | ENG.: 1G 1PG 2T | AUST.: NIL | FR.: 2G 2DG | FR.: 1G 1PG 1T | IRE.: 2PG |
| 11 Jan. 1958 | 1 Mar. 1958 | 9 Mar. 1958 | 29 Mar. 1958 | 7 Apr. 1958 | 19 Apr. 1958 |

This was a significant season in French rugby. The pack, with Mias to harness the individual talents of the forwards into an effective, combined force, were promising at Murrayfield and, after a slow start against England, played well in the second half at Colombes. But the alarming collapse of the French defence in Paris had permitted England to win by 14 points, and in desperation (for it was their sixth consecutive Championship defeat) the French selectors turned to the Lourdes back division, including the entire club threequarter line, for the match with the Wallabies.

In front of only 15,000 spectators, the rousing play of the French forwards was complemented by dashing back play, and 14 of the side which thrashed Australia travelled to Cardiff to play in a famous victory against the Welsh. It was the first French success at the ground since the beginning of fixtures in 1908. Wales were outplayed by the combination and skill of the French forwards in the second half. Labazuy flourished among his Lourdes colleagues and his fine tactical and place-kicking played as important a role in the French victory as Mias' leadership and expert line-out control. The season ended with less emphatic victories against Italy and Ireland, but a leading French critic was encouraged to write that there had been a distinct effort by the side to open up the game, arresting the stultifying process which had set in upon Jean Prat's retirement from international rugby.

## 1958

| 1st v. S.AFRICA | 2nd v. S.AFRICA |
|---|---|
| †P. LACAZE | P. LACAZE 1PG,1DG |
| J. DUPUY | J. DUPUY |
| A. MARQUESUZAA | A. MARQUESUZAA |
| G. STENER | R. MARTINE 1DG |
| H. RANCOULE | G. STENER |
| R. MARTINE | A. HAGET |
| P. DANOS 1DG | P. DANOS |
| A. QUAGLIO | A. QUAGLIO |
| R. VIGIER | R. VIGIER |
| A. ROQUES | A. ROQUES |
| *L. MIAS | *L. MIAS |
| B. MOMMEJAT | B. MOMMEJAT |
| F. MONCLA | F. MONCLA |
| J. BARTHE | J. BARTHE |
| J. CARRERE | J. CARRERE |
| Cape Town | Johannesburg |
| DRAWN 3-3 | WON 9-5 |
| SA: 1T | SA: 1G |
| FR.: 1DG | FR.: 2DG 1PG |
| 26 Jul. 1958 | 16 Aug. 1958 |

French rugby continued its triumphant march during the summer of 1958, on its first tour to South Africa. Although the tourists won only half of their matches, they took the series against South Africa, drawing the first Test and defeating the Springboks 9-5 in the last match at Johannesburg.

Several leading French players were unable to tour, and the side was also crippled by injuries and sickness. Casaux, a utility player who was a late replacement for Maurice Prat, broke his collar-bone in training before the first match, and did not play a single game on tour; and Lepatey underwent an appendicitis operation which ruled him out of the tour.

But the French made light of their troubles, installed Mias as captain when Celaya was injured, and became the first team since 1896 to win a Test series in South Africa. In Johannesburg, Mias' team trailed 3-5 in the second half, and only some miraculous covering by Jean Barthe prevented South Africa moving into a winning lead. But the French forwards maintained a vigorous challenge to their heavy opponents and gained sufficient possession for Lacaze (who played with a painful injury) and Martine to drop decisive goals.

## 1958-59

| v. SCOTLAND | v. ENGLAND | v. ITALY | v. WALES | v. IRELAND |
|---|---|---|---|---|
| P. LACAZE 2DG | P. LACAZE | P. LACAZE | P. LACAZE | P. LACAZE 1C |
| H. RANCOULE | C. DARROUY | H. RANCOULE 1T | H. RANCOULE | †S. MERICQ |
| J. BOUQUET | A. BONIFACE | J. BOUQUET 1T | J. BOUQUET | J. BOUQUET |
| A. MARQUESUZAA | A. MARQUESUZAA | A. MARQUESUZAA | A. MARQUESUZAA | †L. CASAUX |
| J. DUPUY | J. DUPUY | J. DUPUY 2T | J. DUPUY | J. DUPUY 1T |
| A. LABAZUY | A. LABAZUY 1PG | A. LABAZUY 2C,1PG | A. LABAZUY 1PG,1C | †C. MANTOULAN |
| P. DANOS | P. DANOS | P. DANOS | P. DANOS | P. DANOS |
| A. QUAGLIO | A. QUAGLIO | A. QUAGLIO | A. QUAGLIO | A. QUAGLIO |
| R. VIGIER | R. VIGIER | R. VIGIER | R. VIGIER | R. VIGIER |
| A. ROQUES | A. ROQUES | A. DOMENECH | A. ROQUES | A. ROQUES |
| *L. MIAS | M. CELAYA | *L. MIAS | *L. MIAS | *L. MIAS |
| B. MOMMEJAT | B. MOMMEJAT | B. MOMMEJAT | B. MOMMEJAT | B. MOMMEJAT |
| M. CELAYA | M. CRAUSTE | M. CRAUSTE | M. CRAUSTE | J. CARRERE |
| J. BARTHE | *J. BARTHE | J. BARTHE | J. BARTHE | M. CRAUSTE |
| F. MONCLA 1T | F. MONCLA | F. MONCLA 1T | F. MONCLA 2T | F. MONCLA |
| Stade Colombes | Twickenham | Nantes | Stade Colombes | Lansdowne Road |
| WON 9-0 | DRAWN 3-3 | WON 22-0 | WON 11-3 | LOST 5-9 |
| FR.: 2DG 1T | ENG.: 1PG | FR.: 2G 1PG 3T | FR.: 1G 1PG 1T | IRE.: 1DG 1PG 1T |
| SCOT.: NIL | FR.: 1PG | ITALY: NIL | WALES: 1PG | FR.: 1G |
| 10 Jan. 1959 | 28 Feb. 1959 | 29 Mar. 1959 | 4 Apr. 1959 | 18 Apr. 1959 |

Earlier French sides had scored more points and gained more victories in Championship seasons, but this side, led by Mias, became the first to win the Five Nations title outright. The success was the culmination of a happy series of victories (dating back to March 1958) in which a refreshing new dimension was added to the international scene by the ebullient French. Fast interpassing between forwards who peeled from line-outs in a formidable wedge-shaped pattern launched many attacks from which dynamic backs (as well as mobile forwards) were able to penetrate opponents' defences.

Forward dominance was the key to France's success, and an experienced pack had no superiors in the Championship, despite the surprising setback in Dublin after the title had been secured. But the astute tactical punting and accurate place-kicking of Labazuy was also an important factor in the French triumph. Significantly, subsequent French sides have rarely lacked a big-kicking fly-half able to place goals.

The title was won in Paris against Wales before 55,000 partisan French supporters. On a very hot day the best was seen of the French forwards as attackers, and Mias was chaired from the ground after the match.

## 1959-60

| v. SCOTLAND | v. ENGLAND | v. WALES | v. IRELAND | v. ITALY |
|---|---|---|---|---|
| M. VANNIER 2C | M. VANNIER 1PG | M. VANNIER 1C | M. VANNIER | M. VANNIER 4C |
| L. ROGE | L. ROGE | S. MERICQ 1T | J. DUPUY | H. RANCOULE 1T |
| J. BOUQUET | J. BOUQUET | J. BOUQUET | J. BOUQUET 1C | G. BONIFACE |
| A. MARQUESUZAA | A. MARQUESUZAA | †G. BONIFACE | G. BONIFACE | L. CASAUX 2T |
| S. MERICQ 1T | S. MERICQ | J. DUPUY 1T | H. RANCOULE 1T | J. DUPUY |
| R. MARTINE | R. MARTINE | P. ALBALADEJO 1C | P. ALBALADEJO 3DG | P. ALBALADEJO 2DG |
| P. DANOS | P. DANOS | P. LACROIX 1T | P. LACROIX | P. LACROIX |
| A. DOMENECH | A. DOMENECH | A. DOMENECH | A. DOMENECH 1T | A. DOMENECH |
| †J. DE GREGORIO | J. DE GREGORIO | J. DE GREGORIO | J. DE GREGORIO | J. DE GREGORIO |
| A. ROQUES | A. ROQUES | A. ROQUES | A. ROQUES | A. ROQUES |
| M. CELAYA | M. CELAYA | †H. LARRUE | H. LARRUE | H. LARRUE |
| B. MOMMEJAT | B. MOMMEJAT | †J.-P. SAUX | B. MOMMEJAT | J.-P. SAUX |
| *F. MONCLA 1T | *F. MONCLA | *F. MONCLA | *F. MONCLA 1T | M. CRAUSTE |
| M. CRAUSTE | M. CRAUSTE | M. CELAYA 1T | M. CELAYA 1T | G.S. MEYER 1T |
| †G.S. MEYER 1T | G.S. MEYER | M. CRAUSTE | M. CRAUSTE | *F. MONCLA |
| Murrayfield | Stade Colombes | Cardiff Arms Park | Stade Colombes | Treviso |
| WON 13-11 | DRAWN 3-3 | WON 16-8 | WON 23-6 | WON 26-0 |
| SCOT.: 1G 1PG 1T | FR.: 1PG | WALES: 1G 1PG | FR.: 1G 3DG 3T | ITALY: NIL |
| FR.: 2G 1T | ENG.: 1T | FR.: 2G 2T | IRE.: 2T | FR.: 4G 2DG |
| 9 Jan. 1960 | 27 Feb. 1960 | 26 Mar. 1960 | 9 Apr. 1960 | 17 Apr. 1960 |

France were unbeaten for the first time in the Championship, though they were held to a draw by England and thus shared the title. Vannier, who had recovered from torn ligaments sustained early in the South African trip, kicked the goal which saved France's bacon against England. A gifted player with a flair for attack, Vannier made 43 appearances in French internationals, establishing a record for a full-back. In addition, his haul of 180 points, which included eight drop-goals, created new French career records. (Vannier was born at Etain on the Meuse. He is one of the few leading French players to have originated from the north.)

Several changes, including the return of Albaladéjo, first capped in 1954, and the introduction of the younger Boniface brother, were made for the match in Cardiff. France played brilliantly. Their technique in the tight was excellent and their speed and fluency in the loose threatened to overrun the Welsh.

Amazing fitness, accurate handling and perpetual support as the side moved forward were features of an impressive win against Ireland. The victory brought France 55 points for the Championship, a French record, and Albaladéjo established a new world record by dropping three goals in the match. A week later he kicked two more in the French demolition of Italy.

## 1960

| v. ROMANIA | 1st v. ARGENTINA | 2nd v. ARGENTINA | 3rd v. ARGENTINA |
|---|---|---|---|
| M. VANNIER 1c | M. VANNIER 5c | †R. BRETHES 1pg | M. VANNIER 4c,1dg |
| | | | |
| H. RANCOULE | H. RANCOULE | H. RANCOULE | J. DUPUY 2t |
| G. BONIFACE | G. BONIFACE 1t | G. BONIFACE 2t | G. BONIFACE 1t |
| J. BOUQUET | A. MARQUESUZAA 1t | †M. LACOME | R. MARTINE |
| S. MEYER | J. DUPUY | †J. OTHATS | J. OTHATS |
| | | | |
| P. ALBALADEJO | P. DIZABO | P. DIZABO 1dg | P. DIZABO 1t |
| P. LACROIX | P. LACROIX 1t | P. LACROIX | P. LACROIX 1t |
| | | | |
| A. DOMENECH | A. DOMENCH 2t | A. DOMENECH | A. DOMENECH |
| J. DE GREGORIO | J. DE GREGORIO 1t | J. DE GREGORIO | †J. ROLLET |
| †R. BARRIERE | A. ROQUES | A. ROQUES | A. ROQUES |
| H. LARRUE | H. LARRUE 1t | H. LARRUE | H. LARRUE |
| B. MOMMEJAT | J-P. SAUX | J-P. SAUX | M. CELAYA |
| M. CRAUSTE | M. CRAUSTE | G.S. MEYER | M. CRAUSTE |
| M. CELAYA | M. CELAYA 2t | M. CELAYA | †R. CRANCEE 1t |
| *F. MONCLA | *F. MONCLA | *F. MONCLA | *F. MONCLA |
| Bucharest | Buenos Aires | Buenos Aires | Buenos Aires |
| LOST 5-11 | WON 37-3 | WON 12-3 | WON 29-6 |
| ROM.: 1G 2DG | ARG.: 1PG | ARG.: 1T | ARG.: 2PG |
| FR.: 1G | FR.: 5G 4T | FR.: 1DG 1PG 2T | FR.: 4G 1DG 2T |
| 5 Jun. 1960 | 23 Jul. 1960 | 6 Aug. 1960 | 17 Aug. 1960 |

In 1960, the Championship was followed by a hectic spring and summer in which France played four matches. The Romanians, full of vitality and eager to impress their FIRA colleagues, surprised a tired French side by the improvement made in their standard of play since the heavy defeat of 1957. Victory in Bucharest earned for the Romanians a permanent place in subsequent French international fixture arrangements, the matches usually taking place as a trial for their Championship commitments.

In the summer a party of 25 players undertook a twelve-match tour of South America, winning each game. For the third time René Crabos accompanied the team, with Marcel Laurent as manager. Bernard Marie, the leading French referee, was invited by the Argentinians to control some of the tour matches and he took charge of the first and last Tests of the three-game series.

One of the most interesting selections for the tour was Pierre Dizabo, first capped as a teenager in 1948. His promising career was interrupted by illness, but he gradually recovered to play at fly-half in the three Tests of this tour.

## 1960-61

| v. SCOTLAND | v. S.AFRICA | v. ENGLAND | v. WALES | v. ITALY | v. IRELAND |
|---|---|---|---|---|---|
| R. MARTINE | M. VANNIER | M. VANNIER 1c | M. VANNIER 1c | M. VANNIER 1pg,1c | M. VANNIER 1pg |
| | | | | | |
| †J. GACHASSIN | H. RANCOULE | H. RANCOULE | H. RANCOULE | H. RANCOULE 1t | S. MERICQ |
| G. BONIFACE 1t | G. BONIFACE | G. BONIFACE | G. BONIFACE 1t | G. BONIFACE 1t | G. BONIFACE |
| J. BOUQUET | J. BOUQUET | J. BOUQUET | J. BOUQUET | J. BOUQUET 1t | J. BOUQUET 1dg |
| J. DUPUY | J. DUPUY | J. DUPUY | G. MAUDUY | G. MAUDUY | J. GACHASSIN 1t |
| | | | | | |
| P. ALBALADEJO 1dg,1pg,1c | P. ALBALADEJO | P. ALBALADEJO | P. ALBALADEJO | R. MARTINE | P. ALBALADEJO 1dg,1pg |
| P. LACROIX | P. LACROIX | P. LACROIX | P. LACROIX | †M. PUGET | P. LACROIX |
| | | | | | |
| A. DOMENECH | A. DOMENECH | A. DOMENECH | A. DOMENECH | A. DOMENECH 1t | A. DOMENECH |
| J. DE GREGORIO | J. DE GREGORIO | J. DE GREGORIO | J. DE GREGORIO | J. DE GREGORIO | J. DE GREGORIO |
| A. ROQUES | A. ROQUES | A. ROQUES | A. ROQUES | A. ROQUES | A. ROQUES |
| M. CELAYA | †G. BOUGUYON | G. BOUGUYON | G. BOUGUYON | G. BOUGUYON | G. BOUGUYON |
| †L. ECHAVE | J-P. SAUX | J-P. SAUX | J-P. SAUX 1t | J-P. SAUX | J-P. SAUX |
| M. CRAUSTE | M. CRAUSTE | M. CRAUSTE 1t | M. CRAUSTE | M. CRAUSTE | M. CRAUSTE |
| R. CRANCEE | M. CELAYA | M. CELAYA | M. CELAYA | M. CELAYA | M. CELAYA |
| *F. MONCLA | *F. MONCLA | *F. MONCLA | *F. MONCLA | *F. MONCLA | *F. MONCLA |
| Stade Colombes | Stade Colombes | Twickenham | Stade Colombes | Chambéry | Lansdowne Road |
| WON 11-0 | DRAWN 0-0 | DRAWN 5-5 | WON 8-6 | WON 17-0 | WON 15-3 |
| FR.: 1G 1DG 1PG | FR.: NIL | ENG.: 1G | FR.: 1G 1T | FR.: 1G 1PG 3T | IRE.: 1PG |
| SCOT.: NIL | SA.: NIL | FR.: 1G | WALES: 2T | ITALY: NIL | FR.: 2DG 2PG 1T |
| 7 Jan. 1961 | 18 Feb. 1961 | 25 Feb. 1961 | 25 Mar. 1961 | 2 Apr. 1961 | 15 Apr. 1961 |

France were unbeaten champions in 1961 and shared a scoreless draw with the fifth Springboks in Paris. By the end of the season, their exciting brand of football – labelled "Champagne Rugby" – had brought just one defeat in matches with IB nations in a stretch of 18 games dating back to March 1958. Victories had been achieved against six of the major nations, and the proposed tour to New Zealand, scheduled for the summer, would be a contest for an unofficial "World Title".

The only man to have featured in each of France's 18 matches was Alfred Roques. A convert from soccer, Roques did not gain his first cap until he was 33 years of age, but became a legend in French rugby. He was named the best prop forward in world rugby as a result of his powerful play and technique on the tour of South Africa, and went on to make 30 international appearances.

The scoring power of the side was less impressive than in the previous season. 29 of the 56 points scored were from goal-kicks and only Guy Boniface lived up to his reputation among the backs. A steady, sound defender, he also revealed a good eye for an opening and his speed through narrow gaps brought him three tries. Another back, Roger Martine, who had first appeared in 1952, made his final appearance against Scotland. As a valuable utility back, he had been a faithful servant to French rugby.

## 1961

| 1st v. NZ | 2nd v. NZ | 3rd v. NZ | v. AUSTRALIA |
|---|---|---|---|
| M. Vannier | †C. Lacaze | C. Lacaze | M. Vannier |
| | | | |
| H. Rancoule | H. Rancoule | J. Pique | C. Lacaze |
| G. Boniface | G. Boniface | G. Boniface | J. Pique 1t |
| A. Boniface | †J. Pique | A. Boniface | A. Boniface |
| †G. Calvo | J. Dupuy 1t | G. Calvo | †S. Plantey |
| | | | |
| P. Albaladejo 2dg | P. Albaladejo | †G. Camberabero | P. Albaladejo 2dg |
| P. Lacroix | P. Lacroix | P. Lacroix | P. Lacroix 1t |
| | | | |
| †P. Cazals | G. Bouguyon | G. Bouguyon | G. Bouguyon 1t |
| †J. Laudouar | J. Laudouar | J. Rollet | J. Rollet |
| A. Domenech | A. Domenech | A. Domenech | P. Cazals |
| G. Bouguyon | M. Celaya | †M. Cassiede | M. Cassiede |
| J-P. Saux | J-P. Saux | J-P. Saux | J-P. Saux |
| M. Crauste | M. Crauste | M. Crauste 1t | *M. Crauste |
| M. Celaya | †R. Lefevre | M. Celaya | A. Domenech |
| *F. Moncla | *F. Moncla | *F. Moncla | M. Celaya |
| | | | |
| Auckland | Wellington | Christchurch | Sydney |
| LOST 6-13 | LOST 3-5 | LOST 3-32 | WON 15-8 |
| | | | |
| NZ.: 2G 1DG | NZ.: 1G | NZ.: 4G 3PG 1T | AUS.: 1G 1PG |
| FR.: 2DG | FR.: 1T | FR.: 1T | FR.: 2DG 3T |
| | | | |
| 22 Jul. 1961 | 5 Aug. 1961 | 19 Aug. 1961 | 26 Aug. 1961 |

François Moncla led the French side to Australasia in 1961. His authority and personal courage had made him the natural successor to Mias in 1960, and he went on to lead France in 18 consecutive internationals, including the three Tests with New Zealand. Altogether he made 31 appearances for France, and scored seven tries as a wing-forward of exceptional pace and ability.

But he was made the scapegoat for France's failures in New Zealand. The tour, the first to New Zealand by a European Union, was a disappointment from the outset. Numerous players (including the great Roques) were unavailable before Marcel Laurent and Guy Basquet, the managers, left France with a team of 30 players. On the field the side was unprepared for the overwhelming power of New Zealand forward play, though indifferent defence and some ill-luck concerning injuries and illness also contributed to the French difficulties.

Problems adopting the best combination up front meant that Domenech, Bourguyon and Celaya were used as utility men in the Tests. Domenech, one of the most versatile and mobile of forwards during the rise of French rugby in the 1950s, adapted admirably to the back row in the Australiian Test. Altogether he played 52 internationals, breaking the record of Jean Prat.

## 1961-62

| v. ROMANIA | v. SCOTLAND | v. ENGLAND | v. WALES | v. IRELAND | v. ITALY |
|---|---|---|---|---|---|
| C. Lacaze 1c | L. Casaux | C. Lacaze | C. Lacaze | C. Lacaze 1t | C. Lacaze |
| | | | | | |
| J. Dupuy | H. Rancoule 1t | H. Rancoule | H. Rancoule | H. Rancoule | H. Rancoule |
| G. Boniface | J. Bouquet | A. Boniface | A. Boniface | A. Boniface | A. Boniface 1pg |
| A. Boniface | J. Pique | J. Bouquet | J. Bouquet | J. Bouquet | J. Pique |
| C. Darrouy | J. Dupuy | J. Dupuy | J. Dupuy | J. Dupuy | J. Dupuy |
| | | | | | |
| J. Bouquet | P. Albaladejo 2pg,1c | P. Albaladejo 2c | P. Albaladejo | P. Albaladejo 1c | S. Plantey |
| P. Lacroix | *P. Lacroix | *P. Lacroix | *P. Lacroix | *P. Lacroix | †C. Laborde |
| | | | | | |
| P. Cazals | A. Roques | A. Roques | A. Roques | A. Roques | A. Domenech |
| J. Laudouar | J. de Gregorio | J. de Gregorio | J. de Gregorio | J. Laudouar | J. Rollet |
| A. Domenech | A. Domenech | A. Domenech | A. Domenech | A. Domenech | A. Roques |
| †R. le Bourhis | B. Mommejat | B. Mommejat | B. Mommejat | B. Mommejat 1t | B. Mommejat |
| M. Cassiede | J-P. Saux | J-P. Saux | J-P. Saux | J-P. Saux | J-P. Saux 1t |
| †H. Marracq 1t | †R. Gensane | R. Gensane | R. Gensane | R. Gensane | *M. Crauste |
| M. Celaya | †H. Romero | H. Romero | H. Romero | H. Romero | H. Romero |
| *M. Crauste | M. Crauste | M. Crauste 3t | M. Crauste | M. Crauste 1t | R. Gensane |
| | | | | | |
| Bayonne | Murrayfield | Stade Colombes | Cardiff Arms Park | Stade Colombes | Brescia |
| DRAWN 5-5 | WON 11-3 | WON 13-0 | LOST 0-3 | WON 11-0 | WON 6-3 |
| | | | | | |
| FR.: 1G | SCOT.: 1PG | FR.: 2G 1T | WALES: 1PG | FR.: 1G 2T | ITALY: 1PG |
| ROM.: 1G | FR.: 1G 2PG | ENG.: NIL | FR.: NIL | IRE.: NIL | FR.: 1PG 1T |
| | | | | | |
| 12 Nov. 1961 | 13 Jan. 1962 | 24 Feb. 1962 | 24 Mar. 1962 | 14 Apr. 1962 | 22 Apr. 1962 |

France fielded an experimental pack for the match with Romania. Five of the forwards had only six caps between them, Domenech, Crauste and Celaya having to exercise their experience to hold the Romanians to a dour draw. The match was Celaya's last for France. During 50 internationals he gave inestimable service to the side as an all-round forward. Twelve times French captain in a career spanning nearly a decade, he had renounced the honour when he felt the responsibility of the post was detracting from his efficiency as a player.

Although the French reigned as champions for the fourth consecutive season, the side was defeated at Cardiff – their first reverse in the Championship since 1959. Nevertheless, splendid displays at Murrayfield and against England (where Crauste equalled the Championship record of three tries by a forward, set in 1903) confirmed the French as worthy title winners. Lacaze, younger brother of Pierre Lacaze (who had been the outstanding success of the 1958 French trip to South Africa before joining the Rugby League), became the first French full-back to score a try in a Five-Nations match when he crossed against Ireland.

The season concluded with the slimmest-ever victory over Italy, and there were signs that the adventurous Gallic spirit which had captivated audiences for four years was beginning to fade.

## 1962-63

| v. ROMANIA | v. SCOTLAND | v. IRELAND |
|---|---|---|
| †J.P. Razat | J.P. Razat | J.P. Razat |
| †M. Arino | †P. Besson | P. Besson |
| G. Boniface | G. Boniface | G. Boniface 1t |
| A. Boniface | A. Boniface 1dg | A. Boniface 1dg |
| C. Laborde | C. Darrouy | C. Darrouy 3t |
| G. Camberabero | P. Albaladejo 1pg | P. Albaladejo 3c,1dg |
| *P. Lacroix | *P. Lacroix | *P. Lacroix |
| A. Domenech | F. Mas | F. Mas |
| J. Laudouar | J. de Gregorio | J. Rollet |
| †F. Mas | A. Roques | †F. Zago |
| B. Mommejat | B. Mommejat | B. Mommejat |
| †M. Lira | J-P. Saux | J-P. Saux |
| M. Crauste | R. Gensane | M. Lira |
| H. Romero | †J. Fabre | J. Fabre |
| R. Gensane | M. Crauste | M. Crauste |
| Bucharest | Stade Colombes | Lansdowne Road |
| LOST 0-3 | LOST 6-11 | WON 24-5 |
| Rom.: 1pg | Fr.: 1dg 1pg | Ire.: 1g |
| Fr.: nil | Scot.: 1g 1dg 1pg | Fr.: 3g 2dg 1t |
| 11 Nov. 1962 | 12 Jan. 1963 | 26 Jan. 1963 |

## 1962-63

| v. ENGLAND | v. WALES | v. ITALY |
|---|---|---|
| †P. Dedieu | C. Lacaze | P. Dedieu 1c |
| P. Besson | C.Darrouy | J. Dupuy 2t |
| G. Boniface 1t | G. Boniface 1t | G. Boniface |
| A. Boniface | A. Boniface | A. Boniface |
| C. Darrouy | J. Dupuy | C. Darrouy 1t |
| P. Albaladejo 1c | P. Albaladejo 1c | P. Albaladejo |
| *P. Lacroix | *P. Lacroix | †J.C. Lasserre |
| F. Mas | F. Mas | A. Domenech |
| R. Rebujent | J. de Gregorio | J. de Gregorio |
| F. Zago | A. Domenech | J-P. Saux |
| M. Lira | B. Mommejat | †J. le Droff |
| J-P. Saux | †R. Fite | R. Fite |
| J. Fabre | M. Lira | M. Lira 1t |
| H. Romero | J. Fabre | J. Fabre |
| M. Crauste | M. Crauste | *M. Crauste |
| Twickenham | Stade Colombes | Grenoble |
| LOST 5-6 | WON 5-3 | WON 14-12 |
| Eng.: 2pg | Fr.: 1g | Fr.: 1g 3t |
| Fr.: 1g | Wales: 1pg | Italy: 2pg 2t |
| 23 Feb. 1963 | 23 Mar. 1963 | 14 Apr. 1963 |

Pierre Lacroix, a skilful scrum-half capable of effective liaison with the back-row, continued to lead the side in 1963. The season opened with a struggle in Bucharest, where the French, fielding four new caps, lost by a penalty goal. For all their excellent successes against IB nations between 1958 and 1962, it was an extraordinary fact that during this phase France had failed to overcome the Romanians. In three matches, France twice lost in Bucharest but managed a draw in Bayonne in 1961.

The French were eased into second place in the Championship, losing to Scotland and at Twickenham. Their most convincing display was in Dublin, where Darrouy, recalled to the French side after sporadic appearances since 1957, equalled the French record for matches against IB nations, scoring three tries. The handling and passing of the French were spectacular, with the Boniface brothers in impressive form.

Guy Boniface scored the only tries of the English and Welsh matches, and it required a combined team effort before the Italians were beaten in the final match at Grenoble. Italy led 12-6 with five minutes of play remaining. Two late tries (one converted by Dedieu) and inspiring play by Crauste eventually saved France from defeat.

## 1963-64

| v. ROMANIA | v. SCOTLAND | v. NZ | v. ENGLAND |
|---|---|---|---|
| J.P. RAZAT | C. LACAZE | C. LACAZE | C. LACAZE |
| J. GACHASSIN 1T | J. GACHASSIN | J. GACHASSIN | J. GACHASSIN |
| G. BONIFACE | G. BONIFACE | J. PIQUE | J. PIQUE |
| A. BONIFACE | A. BONIFACE | A. BONIFACE | A. BONIFACE |
| J. DUPUY 1T | J. DUPUY | C. DARROUY | C. DARROUY 1T |
| C. LACAZE | P. ALBALADEJO | P. ALBALADEJO 1PG | †J.C. HIQUET |
| C. LABORDE | J.C. LASSERRE | J.C. LASSERRE | J.C. LASSERRE |
| †L. ABADIE | J.C. BEREJNOI | †J.B. AMESTOY | J.B. AMESTOY |
| †J.M. CABANIER | J.M. CABANIER | J. DE GREGORIO | J. DE GREGORIO |
| †J.C. BEREJNOI | †J. BAYARDON | J. BAYARDON | J. BAYARDON |
| J. LE DROFF | †B. DAUGA | B. DAUGA | B. DAUGA |
| M. LIRA | J. LE DROFF | J. LE DROFF | J. LE DROFF |
| †J.J. RUPERT | J.J. RUPERT | A. HERRERO | A. HERRERO |
| †A. HERRERO | *J. FABRE | *J. FABRE | *J. FABRE |
| *M. CRAUSTE | M. CRAUSTE | M. CRAUSTE | M. CRAUSTE |
| Toulouse | Murrayfield | Stade Colombes | Stade Colombes |
| DRAWN 6-6 | LOST 0-10 | LOST 3-12 | LOST 3-6 |
| FR.: 2T | SCOT.: 2G | FR.: 1PG | FR.: 1T |
| ROM.: 1DG 1T | FR.: NIL | NZ: 1PG 1DG 2T | ENG.: 1PG 1T |
| 15 Dec. 1963 | 4 Jan. 1964 | 8 Feb. 1964 | 22 Feb. 1964 |

## 1963-64

| v. WALES | v. ITALY | v. IRELAND |
|---|---|---|
| P. DEDIEU | P. DEDIEU | P. DEDIEU 1DG |
| J. GACHASSIN | J. GACHASSIN | J. GACHASSIN |
| J. PIQUE | A. BONIFACE 1T | J. PIQUE |
| A. BONIFACE | J. PIQUE | †M. ARNAUDET 1T |
| C. DARROUY | C. DARROUY | C. DARROUY 2T |
| P. ALBALADEJO 2PG,1C | P. ALBALADEJO 3PG | P. ALBALADEJO 3C |
| J.C. LASSERRE | J.C. LASSERRE | J.C. LASSERRE |
| J.C. BEREJNOI | J.C. BEREJNOI | J.C. BEREJNOI |
| †Y. MENTHILLER | Y. MENTHILLER | †A. ABADIE |
| †A. GRUARIN | A. GRUARIN | A. GRUARIN |
| B. DAUGA | B. DAUGA | B. DAUGA |
| A. HERRERO | A. HERRERO | A. HERRERO 1T |
| †M. SITJAR | M. SITJAR | M. SITJAR |
| M. LIRA | M. LIRA | M. LIRA 1T |
| *M. CRAUSTE 1T | *M. CRAUSTE | *M. CRAUSTE 1T |
| Cardiff Arms Park | Parma | Stade Colombes |
| DRAWN 11-11 | WON 12-3 | WON 27-6 |
| WALES: 1G 2PG | ITALY: 1DG | FR.: 3G 1DG 3T |
| FR.: 1G 2PG | FR.: 3PG 1T | IRE.: 1DG 1T |
| 21 Mar. 1964 | 29 Mar. 1964 | 11 Apr. 1964 |

France had a busy season in 1963-64, playing seven full internationals. The matches against their usual Continental opponents, Romania and Italy, were difficult games in which the French were lucky to avoid defeats. The Romanians in particular gave an impressive performance at Toulouse, earning a draw by playing football of the style adopted by French clubs in the club Championship.

It was not a successful season, though several new tight forwards were blooded and came through their initial international tests with credit. Altogether, France used 28 players in the Five Nations Championship, and only four figured in each match. These were Jean Gachassin, a jack-in-the-box of a wing whose speed and versatility were later utilised at centre, fly-half and full back; J-C Lasserre, the successor to Lacroix at scrum-half; Dauga, a new lock; and Michel Crauste, a veteran loose forward who took over the captaincy at Cardiff.

Dauga and Crauste went on to create French appearance records. Crauste was a complete player with exceptional temperament, and during his long career he played in 63 full internationals for France. Dauga, the rising star of the season, was a hard, uncompromising forward who went on to equal Crauste's remarkable record.

## 1964

| | v. S.AFRICA | v. FIJI | v. ROMANIA |
|---|---|---|---|
| | P. Dedieu | P. Dedieu 3c | P. Dedieu |
| | J. Gachassin | J. Gachassin | J. Gachassin 1t |
| | †J.P. Capdouze | J.P. Capdouze 2t | J.P. Capdouze |
| | J. Pique | J. Pique | J. Pique |
| | C. Darrouy 1t | C. Darrouy 2t | C. Darrouy |
| | P. Albaladejo 1pg,1c | P. Albaladejo | G. Camberabero 1t,1dg |
| | C. Laborde | J.C. Lasserre | †L. Camberabero |
| | J.C. Berejnoi | J.C. Berejnoi | J.C. Berejnoi |
| | Y. Menthiller | J.M. Cabanier | Y. Menthiller |
| | A. Gruarin | A. Gruarin | A. Gruarin |
| | B. Dauga | B. Dauga | B. Dauga |
| | †W. Spanghero | W. Spanghero | W. Spanghero |
| | M. Lira | J.J. Rupert 1t | M. Sitjar |
| | A. Herrero | A. Herrero | A. Herrero |
| | *M. Crauste | *M. Crauste | *M. Crauste |
| | Springs | Stade Colombes | Bucharest |
| | WON 8-6 | WON 21-3 | WON 9-6 |
| | SA: 1t 1pg | Fr.: 3g 2t | Rom.: 1pg 1t |
| | Fr.: 1g 1pg | Fiji: 1t | Fr.: 1dg 2t |
| | 25 Jul. 1964 | 17 Oct. 1964 | 29 Nov. 1964 |

In the summer of 1964, France undertook their second tour to South Africa, Serge Saulnier leading a party of 25 players with Jean Prat assistant manager. The side won five of its six matches, losing to Western Province but winning the only Test of the tour. The French margin of victory in the international was narrow, but the side played controlled rugby and the final score flattered the South Africans. Walter Spanghéro, who was described by M. Saulnier as "a sensational revelation" on the South Africa tour, helped France assert their dominance in the two internationals of the autumn, against the Fijians and Romania. The matches were valuable build-up tests for the Championship, and France's win against the Romanians was their first in Bucharest since 1957.

Pierre Albaladéjo announced his retirement from international rugby after the Fijian game. A balanced runner with the ability to kick well off both feet, he played 30 times for France, scoring 104 points and including 12 drop-goals, a new French career record. The Cambérabéro brothers from La Voulte came together for the game with Romania: the first pair of brothers to form the French half-back partnership in an international.

## 1964-65

| | v. SCOTLAND | v. IRELAND | v. ENGLAND | v. WALES | v. ITALY |
|---|---|---|---|---|---|
| | P. Dedieu 2c | P. Dedieu | P. Dedieu 1pg | P. Dedieu 1pg,2c | C. Lacaze 3c |
| | J. Gachassin 1t | J. Gachassin | J. Gachassin | J. Pique | J. Pique |
| | G. Boniface | G. Boniface | G. Boniface | G. Boniface 2t | G. Boniface 1t |
| | J. Pique 1t | J. Pique | J. Pique | A. Boniface | A. Boniface |
| | C. Darrouy 2t | C. Darrouy 1t | C. Darrouy 1t | †A. Campaes | C. Darrouy 2t |
| | J.P. Capdouze | J.P. Capdouze | J.P. Capdouze | J. Gachassin | J. Gachassin |
| | L. Camberabero | L. Camberabero | C. Laborde | J.C. Lasserre 1dg | J.C. Lasserre |
| | J.C. Berejnoi | J.C. Berejnoi | J.C. Berejnoi | J.C. Berejnoi | J.C. Berejnoi |
| | J.M. Cabanier | J.M. Cabanier | Y. Menthiller | J.M. Cabanier 1t | J.M. Cabanier |
| | A. Gruarin | A. Gruarin | A. Gruarin | A. Gruarin | A. Gruarin 1t |
| | B. Dauga | B. Dauga | B. Dauga | B. Dauga | B. Dauga |
| | W. Spanghero | W. Spanghero | W. Spanghero | W. Spanghero | W. Spanghero |
| | M. Lira | M. Lira | J.J. Rupert | J.J. Rupert | J.J. Rupert 1t |
| | A. Herrero | A. Herrero | A. Herrero | A. Herrero 1t | *M. Crauste |
| | *M. Crauste | *M. Crauste | *M. Crauste | *M. Crauste | M. Sitjar |
| | Stade Colombes | Lansdowne Road | Twickenham | Stade Colombes | Pau |
| | WON 16-8 | DRAWN 3-3 | LOST 6-9 | WON 22-13 | WON 21-0 |
| | Fr.: 2g 2t | Ire.: 1t | Eng.: 2pg 1t | Fr.: 2g 1pg 1dg 2t | Fr.: 3g 2t |
| | Scot.: 1g 1t | Fr.: 1t | Fr.: 1pg 1t | Wales: 2g 1t | Italy: nil |
| | 9 Jan. 1965 | 23 Jan. 1965 | 27 Feb. 1965 | 27 Mar. 1965 | 18 Apr. 1965 |

France opened the Five-Nations Championship as hot favourites to win the title. The successes of the summer and autumn had precipitated talk of a new team ready to win the Grand Slam. Certainly the side fulfilled its promise with a spectacular triumph against the Scots, but there followed the disappointment of a draw in a hard, physical battle in Dublin, and the mystery of a defeat at Twickenham against a mediocre English side which surprisingly subdued the French pack.

Then, playing gala rugby, the French exploited the new laws (giving backs greater space at the set-pieces, particularly the line-out) with colourful efficiency to tear Wales, the champions no less, apart to the tune of 22 points in the first half of the match in Paris.

Bernard Marie, touch-judge during the France-Wales game, had the distinction of becoming the first Frenchman to control a Championship match when he replaced the Irish official, Mr Gilliland, who had the misfortune to twist an ankle just before the interval in this game. M. Marie refereed so efficiently in the second half that French officials were subsequently invited to become regular members of the Championship panel.

## 1965-66

| v. ROMANIA | v. SCOTLAND | v. IRELAND |
|---|---|---|
| C. LACAZE | C. LACAZE 1PG | C. LACAZE 1PG,1C |
| | | |
| P. BESSON | J. GACHASSIN | J. GACHASSIN |
| G. BONIFACE 2T | G. BONIFACE | G. BONIFACE |
| A. BONIFACE 1C | A. BONIFACE | A. BONIFACE |
| C. DARROUY | C. DARROUY | C. DARROUY 2T |
| | | |
| J. GACHASSIN | †J.C. ROQUES | J.C. ROQUES |
| J.C. LASSERRE | M. PUGET | M. PUGET |
| | | |
| J.C. BEREJNOI | J.C. BEREJNOI | J.C. BEREJNOI |
| J.M. CABANIER | J.M. CABANIER | J.M. CABANIER |
| †A. ABADIE | A. GRUARIN | A. GRUARIN |
| B. DAUGA | †E. CESTER | E. CESTER |
| W. SPANGHERO | W. SPANGHERO | W. SPANGHERO |
| M. SITJAR | J.J. RUPERT | J.J. RUPERT |
| M. LIRA | B. DAUGA | B. DAUGA |
| *M. CRAUSTE | *M. CRAUSTE | *M. CRAUSTE |
| Lyon | Murrayfield | Stade Colombes |
| WON 8-3 | DRAWN 3-3 | WON 11-6 |
| FR.: 1G 1T | SCOT.: 1T | FR.: 1G 1PG 1T |
| ROM.: 1DG | FR.: 1PG | IRE.: 1DG 1PG |
| 28 Nov. 1965 | 15 Jan. 1966 | 29 Jan. 1966 |

## 1965-66

| v. ENGLAND | v. WALES | v. ITALY |
|---|---|---|
| C. LACAZE 2C | C. LACAZE 1C | C. LACAZE 3C,1DG |
| | | |
| †B. DUPRAT | B. DUPRAT 1T | B. DUPRAT |
| G. BONIFACE | G. BONIFACE | †J. MASO 1T |
| A. BONIFACE 1T | A. BONIFACE | †J.C. LAGRANGE 1T |
| C. DARROUY | C. DARROUY | C. DARROUY 1T |
| | | |
| J. GACHASSIN 1T | J. GACHASSIN | J.C. ROQUES |
| L. CAMBERABERO | L. CAMBERABERA | M. PUGET |
| | | |
| I.C. BEREJNOI | J.C. BEREJNOI | J.C. BEREJNOI |
| J.M. CABANIER | J.M. CABANIER | J.M. CABANIER |
| †A. GRUARIN 1T | A. GRUARIN | A. GRUARIN |
| E. CESTER | B. DAUGA | B. DAUGA 1T |
| W. SPANGHERO | W. SPANGHERO | W. SPANGHERO |
| J.J. RUPERT | J.J. RUPERT 1T | J.J. RUPERT |
| B. DAUGA | A. HERRERO | A. HERRERO |
| *M. CRAUSTE | *M. CRAUSTE | *M. CRAUSTE |
| Stade Colombes | Cardiff Arms Park | Naples |
| WON 13-0 | LOST 8-9 | WON 21-0 |
| FR.: 2G 1T | WALES: 2PG 1T | ITALY: NIL |
| ENG.: NIL | FR.: 1G 1T | FR.: 3G 1DG 1T |
| 26 Feb. 1966 | 26 Mar. 1966 | 9 Apr. 1966 |

The season began with the customary tight match with the Romanians, the French winning thanks to two tries by Guy Boniface. The season was the last for the two brothers who had become the most exciting centre pairing in international rugby. Together they had played 18 times for France, a world record which still stands (though Ray Gravell and Steve Fenwick, who played together 17 times for Wales, hold the record for matches between IB nations).

France were leading contenders for the Championship in the spring, and led at Cardiff by eight points after ten minutes. French fans thought the title was a formality, especially with a stiff breeze to assist their side in the second half. But a couple of Welsh penalty goals and a famous try by the Welsh right-wing placed the home side into a precarious one-point lead.

Then, in the dying seconds of the match, Lacaze was presented with the opportunity of winning the Championship with a penalty kick at goal, from near touch. His kick appeared at first to be on target, but the wind sent the ball past the upright and the Championship went to Wales. Crauste announced his international retirement after leading France to a convincing win in Naples against Italy.

## 1966-67

| v. ROMANIA | v. SCOTLAND | v. AUSTRALIA | v. ENGLAND |
|---|---|---|---|
| C. Lacaze 1PG | C. Lacaze | J. Gachassin | C. Lacaze |
| | | | |
| B. Duprat 1T | B. Duprat 1T | B. Duprat | B. Duprat 1T |
| J. Maso | J. Maso | †J.P. Mir | †J.P. Lux |
| †C. Dourthe | C. Dourthe | C. Dourthe | C. Dourthe 1T |
| *C. Darrouy | *C. Darrouy | *C. Darrouy | *C. Darrouy |
| | | | |
| J.C. Roques | J. Gachassin 1c | G.Camberabero 4PG,1DG,1c | G.Camberabero 1PG,1DG,2c |
| J.C. Lasserre | J.C. Lasserre | L. Camberabero 1T | L. Camberabero |
| | | | |
| J.C. Berejnoi | J.C. Berejnoi | J.C. Berejnoi | J.C. Berejnoi |
| J.M. Cabanier | J.M. Cabanier | J.M. Cabanier | J.M. Cabanier |
| A. Gruarin | A. Gruarin | A. Gruarin | A. Gruarin |
| B. Dauga | B. Dauga | B. Dauga | B. Dauga |
| W. Spanghero | W. Spanghero | W. Spanghero | W. Spanghero |
| †C. Carrere | J.P. Salut | M. Sitjar | M. Sitjar |
| A. Herrero | A. Herrero | A. Herrero | A. Herrero |
| †J.P. Salut 1T | C. Carrere 1T | C. Carrere | C. Carrere |
| Bucharest | Stade Colombes | Stade Colombes | Twickenham |
| WON 9-3 | LOST 8-9 | WON 20-14 | WON 16-12 |
| ROM.: 1PG | FR.: 1G 1T | FR.: 1G 4PG 1DG | ENG.: 3PG 1DG |
| FR.: 1PG 2T | SCOT.: 2PG 1DG | AUST.: 1G 1DG 1PG 1T | FR.: 2G 1DG 1PG |
| 27 Nov. 1966 | 14 Jan. 1967 | 11 Feb. 1967 | 25 Feb. 1967 |

## 1966-67

| v. ITALY | v. WALES | v. IRELAND |
|---|---|---|
| †P. Villepreux | J. Gachassin | P. Villepreux |
| | | |
| M. Arnaudet 3T | M. Arnaudet | J. Gachassin |
| J. Gachassin 2T | J.P. Lux | J.P. Lux |
| J.P. Lux 1T | C. Dourthe 1T | C. Dourthe |
| *C. Darrouy 1T | *C. Darrouy | *C. Darrouy |
| | | |
| G. Camberabero 9c,2PG,1DG | G. Camberabero 2DG,1PG,1c,1T | G. Camberabero 2DG,1c |
| L. Camberabero | L. Camberabero | L. Camberabero |
| | | |
| J.C. Berejnoi | J.C. Berejnoi | J.C. Berejnoi |
| J.M. Cabanier 1T | J.M. Cabanier | J.M. Cabanier 1T |
| A. Gruarin | A. Gruarin | A. Gruarin |
| B. Dauga 1T | E. Cester | A. Herrero |
| †J. Fort | J. Fort | J. Fort |
| M. Sitjar 1T | M. Sitjar | M. Sitjar |
| A. Herrero | B. Dauga 1T | B. Dauga |
| J.J. Rupert 1T | C. Carrere | C. Carrere |
| Toulon | Stade Colombes | Lansdowne Road |
| WON 60-13 | WON 20-14 | WON 11-6 |
| FR.: 9G 2PG 1DG 2T | FR.: 1G 2DG 1PG 2T | IRE.: 1PG 1T |
| ITALY: 2G 1T | WALES: 1G 2PG 1DG | FR.: 1G 2DG |
| 26 Mar. 1967 | 1 Apr. 1967 | 15 Apr. 1967 |

France enjoyed their most successful season for five years. Seven internationals were played, six were won and the sole defeat, by Scotland in Paris, was by a single point. The team were outright winners of the International Championship for the fourth time.

France were lucky to find imaginative new centres to replace the Boniface brothers. Maso, Dourthe and Lux were stylish players whose attacking play and sense of anticipation created some spectacular tries during the season. Dourthe, in particular, impressed the crowd at Twickenham, scoring from an electrifying run involving several swerves and sidesteps.

Guy Cambérabéro established several new records. His five dropped-goals and 32 points in the Championship were milestones for a French player, his drop-goal feat standing as a Championship record today. And in the massacre of Italy at Toulon, the diminutive fly-half created a new French match record by scoring 27 points. The Italians were completely overwhelmed and subsequent French matches with Italy were not regarded as full internationals.

## 1967

| 1st v. S.AFRICA | 2nd v. S.AFRICA | 3rd v. S. AFRICA | 4th v. S. AFRICA |
|---|---|---|---|
| C. LACAZE | P. VILLEPREUX 1PG | C. LACAZE 1PG | C. LACAZE |
| † A. QUILIS | B. DUPRAT | B. DUPRAT | †J. CRAMPAGNE |
| C. DOURTHE 1T | C. DOURTHE | C. DOURTHE | J. P. LUX |
| J. P. LUX | J. P. LUX | †J. TRILLO 1T | J. TRILLO |
| *C. DARROUY | *C. DARROUY | †J. LONDIOS | *C. DARROUY |
| G. CAMBERABERO | †J. L. DEHEZ | G.CAMBERABERO 2DG,2C | G. CAMBERABERO 1PG |
| M. PUGET | †G. SUTRA | M. PUGET | M. PUGET |
| †J. M. ESPONDA | J. M. ESPONDA | *J. FORT | J. FORT |
| J. M. CABANIER | †J. C. MALBET | J. M. CABANIER 1T | J. C. MALBET |
| A. ABADIE | †M. LASSERRE | A. ABADIE | A. ABADIE |
| J. FORT | J. FORT | B. DAUGA | B. DAUGA |
| W. SPANGHERO | †A. PLANTEFOL | A. PLANTEFOL | A. PLANTEFOL |
| M. SITJAR | M. SITJAR | C. CARRERE | C. CARRERE |
| B. DAUGA | B. DAUGA | M. LASSERRE | W. SPANGHERO 1T |
| C. CARRERE | W. SPANGHERO | W. SPANGHERO | A. QUILIS |
| Durban | Bloemfontein | Johannesburg | Cape Town |
| LOST 3-26 | LOST 3-16 | WON 19-14 | DRAWN 6-6 |
| SA: 4G 1PG 1T | SA: 2G 1PG 1T | SA: 1G 2PG 1T | SA: 1DG 1PG |
| FR.: 1T | FR.: 1PG | FR.: 2G 2DG 1PG | FR.: 1PG 1T |
| 15 Jul. 1967 | 22 Jul. 1967 | 29 Jul. 1967 | 12 Aug. 1967 |

The touring party to South Africa in the summer of 1967 comprised 30 players under the management of Marcel Batigne, Marcel Laurent and André Garrigues. The side undertook thirteen matches, losing four (including two of the Tests) and drawing the final Test.

The team was trounced in the opening Test of the series, in Durban, but played its best rugby at Johannesburg in a desperate attempt to save the series in the third Test. Fort, a powerful tight forward who led the pack with vigour and determination, was the captain of the side in the absence of Darrouy, who was skipper of the party. The French, playing tightly and relying on the kicking skills of Cambérabéro and Lacaze (who drop-kicked a towering penalty goal from half-way), kept their hopes of tieing the series alive with a five-point win. But a draw in Cape Town, in which the French scored the only try of the match, enabled the Springboks to win a series against the French for the first time.

Christian Darrouy, whose 40 international appearances spanned a decade, played his last match for France in the Cape Town Test. He retired with 23 international tries to his credit (including 14 against International Board countries), a French career record which still stands.

## 1967-68

| v. NZ | v. ROMANIA | v. SCOTLAND | v. IRELAND |
|---|---|---|---|
| P. Villepreux 3pg | C. Lacaze 1pg,1c,1dg | C. Lacaze | P. Villepreux 1pg,2c |
| †J.M. Capendeguy | J.M. Capendeguy 1t | B. Duprat 1t | B. Duprat |
| C. Dourthe | J.P. Lux | J. Maso | J.P. Lux |
| J. Trillo | J. Trillo | J. Trillo | J. Trillo |
| A. Campaes 1t | †J.J. Lenient | A. Campaes 1t | A. Campaes 1t |
| J. Gachassin 1dg | J. Maso | G. Camberabero 1c | J. Gachassin 1dg |
| M. Puget | †J.H. Mir | L. Camberabero | J.H. Mir |
| A. Abadie | J.C. Berejnoi | A. Abadie | A. Abadie |
| J.M. Cabanier | J.M. Cabanier | J.M. Cabanier | J.M. Cabanier |
| A. Gruarin | J.M. Esponda | A. Gruarin | A. Gruarin |
| B. Dauga | A. Plantefol | B. Dauga | B. Dauga 1t |
| A. Plantefol | B. Dauga | E. Cester | E. Cester |
| A. Quilis | J.J. Rupert | J.J. Rupert | J.P. Salut |
| W. Spanghero | A. Herrero | W. Spanghero | W. Spanghero |
| *C. Carrere | *C. Carrere | *C. Carrere | *C. Carrere |
| Stade Colombes | Nantes | Murrayfield | Stade Colombes |
| LOST 15-21 | WON 11-3 | WON 8-6 | WON 16-6 |
| Fr.: 3pg 1dg 1t | Fr.: 1g 1pg 1dg | Scot.: 1pg 1t | Fr.: 2g 1dg 1pg |
| NZ: 3g 1pg 1t | Rom.: 1pg | Fr.: 1g 1t | Ire.: 2pg |
| 25 Nov. 1967 | 10 Dec. 1967 | 13 Jan. 1968 | 27 Jan. 1968 |

## 1967-68

| v. ENGLAND | v. WALES | v. CZECHOSLOVAKIA |
|---|---|---|
| C. Lacaze 1dg | C. Lacaze | P. Villepreux 1t,2c |
| †J.M. Bonal | J.M. Bonal | J.M. Bonal |
| J.P. Lux | J. Maso | J.P. Lux 2t |
| J. Gachassin 1t | C. Dourthe | J. Maso |
| A. Campaes | A. Campaes | A. Campaes |
| G.Camberabero 1pg,1c | G.Camberabero 1dg,1pg,1c | C. Lacaze |
| L. Camberabero 1dg | L. Camberabero 1t | M. Puget |
| †J.C. Noble | J.C. Noble | M. Lasserre |
| †M. Yachvili | M. Yachvili | M. Yachvili |
| M. Lasserre | M. Lasserre | J.C. Noble |
| A. Plantefol | A. Plantefol | A. Plantefol 1t |
| E. Cester | E. Cester | E. Cester |
| J.P. Salut | W. Spanghero | J.P. Salut |
| W. Spanghero | †M. Greffe | M. Greffe |
| *C. Carrere | *C. Carrere 1t | *C. Carrere 1t |
| Stade Colombes | Cardiff Arms Park | Prague |
| WON 14-9 | WON 14-9 | WON 19-6 |
| Fr.: 1g 2dg 1pg | Wales: 2pg 1t | Czech.: 1pg 1t |
| Eng.: 1dg 2pg | Fr.: 1g 1pg 1dg 1t | Fr.: 2g 3t |
| 24 Feb. 1968 | 23 Mar. 1968 | 5 May 1968 |

France returned from South Africa to face a busy representative programme in Europe. The opening match of the autumn was against a strong New Zealand team and in a tough, bruising game the French provided brave resistance to the visitors. Early in the second half, Villepreux actually placed his side into the lead, but a ten-minute purple-patch in which the All Blacks scored as many points effectively sank French hopes.

But the side went on to make history after defeating Romania in Nantes. For the first time France won the International Grand Slam. The victories were hard-earned and many French critics bemoaned the fact that the side did not show a commitment to the "Total Rugby" so long proposed by leading French rugby coaches and critics. Nevertheless, there were great celebrations following the triumph in the mud and rain at Cardiff.

Guy Cambérabéro played his last international at Cardiff. He had won his first cap as understudy to Albaladéjo on the 1961 tour to New Zealand, and made occasional appearances in the side before establishing himself as the regular French fly-half in 1967. In his 14 internationals he amassed 110 points, including 11 drop-goals.

## 1968

| 1st v. NZ | 2nd v. NZ | 3rd v. NZ | v. AUSTRALIA |
|---|---|---|---|
| P. VILLEPREUX 2PG | P. VILLEPREUX 1PG | P. VILLEPREUX | P. VILLEPREUX 1c[1] |
| †A. PIAZZA | J. M. BONAL | J. M. BONAL | A. PIAZZA |
| J. MASO | J. MASO | C. DOURTHE 1DG | J. P. LUX |
| J. TRILLO | J. TRILLO | J. TRILLO 1T | J. TRILLO |
| A. CAMPAES | A. CAMPAES | J.P. LUX 1T | A. CAMPAES |
| *C. LACAZE 1DG | †C. BOUJET | J. MASO | J. MASO |
| M. PUGET | *M. PUGET | †J. L. BEROT | J. L. BEROT |
| J. M. ESPONDA | J. M. ESPONDA | J. C. NOBLE | J. C. NOBLE |
| †J.P. BAUX | J. P. BAUX | M. YACHVILI | M. YACHVILI |
| †J. IRACABAL | J. IRACABAL | M. LASSERRE | M. LASSERRE |
| B. DAUGA | B. DAUGA | B. DAUGA | B. DAUGA |
| E. CESTER | A. PLANTEFOL | E. CESTER | E. CESTER |
| J. P. SALUT | †B. DUTIN | †M. BILLIERE | B. DUTIN |
| W. SPANGHERO | W. SPANGHERO | W. SPANGHERO | W. SPANGHERO 1T |
| M. GREFFE | M. GREFFE | *C. CARRERE 1T | *C. CARRERE |
| LOST 9-12 | LOST 3-9 | LOST 12-19 | LOST 10-11 |
| Christchurch | Wellington | Auckland | Sydney |
| NZ: 3PG 1T | NZ: 3PG | NZ: 2G 2PG 1DG | AUST.: 1G 1PG 1DG |
| FR.: 1DG 2PG | FR.: 1PG | FR.: 3T 1DG | FR.: 2G |
| 13 Jul. 1968 | 27 Jul. 1968 | 10 Aug. 1968 | 17 Aug. 1968 |

[1]Rep. by C.
Boujet 1T,1c

The eighth major overseas tour undertaken by the FFR was to New Zealand and Australia in the summer of 1968. The tour was the worst completed by the French up to that date: the side which travelled with the Grand Slam title returning after 14 matches with a whitewash in the four Tests against New Zealand and Australia.

In New Zealand the French were bedevilled by injuries, the most critical of these being the indisposition of Carrère, the popular French captain, who twisted an ankle just before the first Test. Claude Lucaze, a veteran of the 1961 tour to New Zealand, led the team in Carrère's absence at Christchurch, but he gave way to Marcel Puget for the second Test, with Boujet coming in at fly-half for his first cap in Wellington.

Boujet, a 25-year-old science teacher, became the first French player to be capped as a replacement when he substituted for Pierre Villepreux in Sydney. In the same match he scored a try from full-back with an elusive run, and converted his try. But his efforts were not sufficient to prevent Australia gaining victory by a point. It was the first time that France had lost an international against Australia (though the "Waratahs", tourists from New South Wales, did beat France in a full international in 1928).

## 1968

| 1st v. S.AFRICA | 2nd v. S.AFRICA | v. ROMANIA |
|---|---|---|
| †H. MAGOIS | H. MAGOIS | H. MAGOIS |
| J. M. BONAL 1T | J. P. LUX | J. M. BONAL 1T |
| C. DOURTHE | C. DOURTHE | J. MASO |
| J. P. LUX | †A. RUIZ | A. RUIZ |
| P. BESSON | J. M. BONAL | †J. SILLIERES |
| C. BOUJET | †L. PARIES 1DG,1c | L. PARIES 1c,3PG |
| *M. PUGET | *M. PUGET 1DG | M. PUGET |
| M. LASSERRE | M. LASSERRE | J. C. NOBLE |
| J. P. BAUX | J. P. BAUX | M. YACHVILI |
| J. IRACABAL | J. M. ESPONDA | J. M. ESPONDA |
| B. DAUGA 2T | B. DAUGA | B. DAUGA |
| E. CESTER | E. CESTER 1T | E. CESTER |
| †C. CHENEVAY | B. DUTIN | B. DUTIN |
| W. SPANGHERO | W. SPANGHERO | W. SPANGHERO |
| M. GREFFE | †D. BONTEMPS | *C. CARRERE |
| Bordeaux | Stade Colombes | Bucharest |
| LOST 9-12 | LOST 11-16 | LOST 14-15 |
| FR.: 3T | FR.: 1G 2DG | ROM.: 4PG 1DG |
| SA: 4PG | SA: 2G 1T 1PG | FR.: 1G 3PG |
| 9 Nov. 1968 | 16 Nov. 1968 | 1 Dec. 1968 |

France had a busy autumn, entertaining a side from South Africa which played two Tests, and travelling to Bucharest for the annual fixture with Romania. France lost all three matches – their astonishing run of defeats following the Grand Slam success extending to seven matches. Reasons for France's poor record were the failure to adapt to the new laws (involving the direct kicking-to-touch restriction), the lack of an authoritative pair of halves, and a surfeit of international competition.

The two-match series with South Africa broke new ground. For the first time an International Board country made a short tour exclusively to France. The Springboks were forced to work hard for their success in the series and had to thank their place-kicker for victory in Bordeaux, where France were unlucky to lose to four penalty goals after scoring three tries.

The Romanians showed a good understanding of the new touch-kicking law to beat the French by a point. Irimescu, a kicking centre-threequarter, landed all of the Romanian points from four penalties and a drop-goal.

## 1968-69

| v. SCOTLAND | v. IRELAND | v. ENGLAND | v. WALES |
|---|---|---|---|
| P. VILLEPREUX 1PG | P. VILLEPREUX 2PG | P. VILLEPREUX | P. VILLEPREUX 1PG,1C |
| J.M. BONAL | J.M. BONAL | †B. MORAITIS | B. MORAITIS |
| J.P. LUX | J. MASO | J.P. LUX | C. DOURTHE |
| J. MASO | J. TRILLO 1T | J. TRILLO | J. TRILLO |
| A. CAMPAES | J.P. LUX | J.M. BONAL 1T | A. CAMPAES 1T |
| J. GACHASSIN | J. GACHASSIN | C. LACAZE 1C,1DG | J. MASO |
| J.L. BEROT | J.L. BEROT | *M. PUGET | G. SUTRA |
| J.M. ESPONDA | M. LASSERRE¹ | M. LASSERRE | †J.L. AZARETE |
| M. YACHVILI | M. YACHVILI | †C. SWIERCZINSKI | †R. BENESIS |
| J. IRACABAL | J. IRACABAL | J. M. ESPONDA | J. IRACABAL |
| M. LASSERRE | B. DAUGA | A. PLANTEFOL | A. PLANTEFOL |
| E. CESTER | E. CESTER | E. CESTER | E. CESTER |
| W. SPANGHERO | J.P. SALUT | †P. BIEMOURET | P. BIEMOURET |
| B. DAUGA | W. SPANGHERO | B. DAUGA | *W. SPANGHERO |
| *C. CARRERE | *C. CARRERE | †M. HAUSER | †G. VIARD |
| Stade Colombes | Lansdowne Road | Twickenham | Stade Colombes |
| LOST 3-6 | LOST 9-17 | LOST 8-22 | DRAWN 8-8 |
| FR.: 1PG | IRE.: 1G 1DG 3PG | ENG.: 2G 3PG 1T | FR.: 1G 1PG |
| SCOT.: 1T 1PG | FR.: 2PG 1T | FR.: 1G 1DG | WALES: 1G 1T |
| 11 Jan. 1969 | 25 Jan. 1969 | 22 Feb. 1969 | 22 Mar. 1969 |

¹Rep. by J.M. Esponda

The extraordinary run of French defeats continued in the International Championship. The side finished with the wooden spoon, their worst record in the competition since 1957. Altogether 29 players were used in the four matches, with only Villepreux, at full-back, and Cester, the lock, gaining the selectors' confidence throughout the season.

Jean Gachassin won the last of his 32 French caps in the defeat by Ireland. His commitment to adventurous rugby made him a favourite with French crowds during his long career, and his versatility enabled him to set an unusual record unlikely to be broken, for he holds the unique distinction of having appeared in every back position (except scrum-half) in an international for France.

The defeat at Twickenham was France's tenth consecutive international reverse, their worst run since the fourteen successive defeats suffered in the mid-1920s. For the game with Wales, Walter Spanghéro was appointed captain. His direct approach to the captaincy inspired the French to hold Wales in a hard but exciting game.

## 1969-70

| v. ROMANIA | v. SCOTLAND | v. IRELAND | v. WALES | v. ENGLAND |
|---|---|---|---|---|
| P. VILLEPREUX | P. VILLEPREUX | P. VILLEPREUX | P. VILLEPREUX | P. VILLEPREUX 1PG,4C,1DG |
| †R. BOURGAREL | R. BOURGAREL | R. BOURGAREL | †J. CANTONI 1T | R. BOURGAREL 1T |
| †A. MAROT | A. MAROT | A. MAROT | A. MAROT | J. TRILLO 1T |
| J. TRILLO | J.P. LUX 1T | J.P. LUX | J. P. LUX | J. P. LUX 1T |
| J.M. BONAL | J. SILLIERES | J. SILLIERES 1T | J.M. BONAL 1T | J.M. BONAL 1T |
| J.L. DEHEZ 1C,2PG,1DG | L. PARIES 1DG,1C | L. PARIES 1DG,1C | L. PARIES | J.L. BEROT 1DG,1T |
| *M. PUGET | G. SUTRA | G. SUTRA | M. PUGET | †M. PEBEYRE |
| J.L. AZARETE | J.L. AZARETE | J.L. AZARETE | J.L. AZARETE | M. LASSERRE |
| R. BENESIS | R. BENESIS | R. BENESIS | R. BENESIS | R. BENESIS |
| J. IRACABAL | J. IRACABAL | J. IRACABAL | J. IRACABAL | J. IRACABAL |
| †J.P. BASTIAT | J.P. BASTIAT | J.P. BASTIAT | J.P. BASTIAT | J. LE DROFF |
| †M. SAVITSKY | E. CESTER | E. CESTER | E. CESTER | E. CESTER |
| M. YACHVILI | G. VIARD | P. BIEMOURET | P. BIEMOURET | P. BIEMOURET |
| B. DAUGA 1T | B. DAUGA 1T | B. DAUGA | B. DAUGA | B. DAUGA 1T |
| †P. DARBOS | *C. CARRERE | *C. CARRERE | *C. CARRERE | *C. CARRERE |
| Tarbes | Murrayfield | Stade Colombes | Cardiff Arms Park | Stade Colombes |
| WON 14-9 | WON 11-9 | WON 8-0 | LOST 6-11 | WON 35-13 |
| FR.: 1G 2PG 1DG | SCOT.: 2PG 1T | FR. 1G 1DG | WALES: 1G 2PG | FR.: 4G 2DG 1PG 2T |
| ROM.: 2PG 1DG | FR.: 1G 1DG 1T | IRE.: NIL | FR.: 2T | ENG.: 2G 1PG |
| 14 Dec. 1969 | 10 Jan. 1970 | 24 Jan. 1970 | 4 Apr. 1970 | 18 Apr. 1970 |

France ended their bitterly disappointing run of defeats with three good wins to open the 1969-70 international season. There was a fair sprinkling of youth and experience in the side which beat Romania at Tarbes in December, and the nucleus of that team opened the Championship with victories against Scotland and Ireland.

Then a long wait followed until April and the game with Wales at Cardiff. There, France was beaten by a lively Welsh side which took its opportunities and capitalised upon some uncharacteristic French errors. With the possibility of a share in the Championship remaining, the French selectors exercised restraint when they convened to pick the side to meet England. In the end six changes were made – conservative by comparison with French selection in 1969 – and only one new cap was introduced, Pebeyre at scrum-half. (His father had been capped just after the war.) England were completely submerged in Paris by a French side in such devastating form that more points were scored against England in this match than any side had achieved in 100 years of international rugby. France thus finished the season as joint-champions with Wales.

## 1970-71

| v. ROMANIA | v. SCOTLAND | v. IRELAND | v. ENGLAND | v. WALES |
|---|---|---|---|---|
| P. VILLEPREUX 1C,3PG | P. VILLEPREUX 1T,1PG,2C | P. VILLEPREUX 2PG | P. VILLEPREUX 1PG,1C | P. VILLEPREUX 1C |
| R. BOURGAREL | J. SILLIERES 1T | J. SILLIERES | J. SILLIERES | R. BOURGAREL |
| J. TRILLO | J. TRILLO | J. TRILLO | †R. BERTRANNE 1T | R. BERTRANNE |
| J.P. LUX | J.P. LUX | J.P. LUX | J.P. LUX | J.P. LUX |
| J. CANTONI | J. CANTONI | J. CANTONI | J. CANTONI 1T | J. CANTONI |
| J.L. BEROT | J.L. BEROT | J.L. BEROT 1DG | J.L. BEROT 1DG | J.L. BEROT |
| M. PEBEYRE 1T | †M. BARRAU | M. PEBEYRE | M. BARRAU | M. BARRAU |
| J.L. AZARETE | J.L. AZARETE | J.L. AZARETE | J.L. AZARETE | J. IRACABAL |
| R. BENESIS | R. BENESIS | R. BENESIS | R. BENESIS | R. BENESIS |
| J. IRACABAL | †M. ETCHEVERRY | M. ETCHEVERRY | M. LASSERRE | M. LASSERRE |
| W. SPANGHERO | J.P. BASTIAT | J.P. BASTIAT | W. SPANGHERO | W. SPANGHERO |
| J. LE DROFF | J. LE DROFF | J. LE DROFF | †C. SPANGHERO | C. SPANGHERO |
| A. QUILIS | †D. DUBOIS | A. QUILIS | M. YACHVILI | P. BIEMOURET |
| *B. DAUGA | *B. DAUGA | *B. DAUGA | B. DAUGA | B. DAUGA 1T |
| G. VIARD | G. VIARD | G. VIARD | *C. CARRERE | *C. CARRERE |
| Bucharest | Stade Colombes | Lansdowne Road | Twickenham | Stade Colombes |
| WON 14-3 | WON 13-8 | DRAWN 9-9 | DRAWN 14-14 | LOST 5-9 |
| ROM.: 1PG | FR.: 2G 1PG | IRE.: 2PG 1T | ENG.: 1G 3PG | FR.: 1G |
| FR.: 1G 3PG | SCOT.: 1G 1PG | FR.: 2PG 1DG | FR.: 1G 1PG 1DG 1T | WALES: 1PG 2T |
| 29 Nov. 1970 | 16 Jan. 1971 | 30 Jan. 1971 | 27 Feb. 1971 | 27 Mar. 1971 |

France were second to Wales in the 1971 Championship. A good win in Bucharest, under the captaincy of Dauga, was followed with the first French home success against Scotland for six years. But draws against Ireland and England, and a struggle with Wales which resulted in a French defeat, ended their Championship challenge.

Twenty-six players were used in the Five-Nations matches, though there was greater ease at half-back in this French side than at any time since the retirement of the Cambérabéro brothers. Berot, previously used as a scrum-half, settled well into his duties at fly-half, forming a fruitful partnership with the new man, Max Barrau.

Two of the newcomers at Twickenham were Roland Bertranne, who scored a try on his debut and went on to become the most-capped French international player; and Claude Spanghéro, younger brother of Walter. The brothers formed the French second row against both England and Wales: the first time brothers had done so in an international for France.

## 1971

| 1st v. S.AFRICA | 2nd v. S.AFRICA | 1st v. AUSTRALIA | 2nd v. AUSTRALIA | v. ROMANIA |
|---|---|---|---|---|
| A. MAROT | J. CANTONI 1DG | P. VILLEPREUX 1PG | P. VILLEPREUX 4PG,1C | P. VILLEPREUX 3PG,3C |
| R. BOURGAREL | R. BOURGAREL | R. BERTRANNE 1T | R. BERTRANNE | A. DUBERTRAND 1T |
| *J. TRILLO 1T | J. TRILLO | J. TRILLO | J. TRILLO | C. DOURTHE 1T |
| J. MASO | J. MASO¹ | J. P. LUX | J. P. LUX | J. MASO 1T |
| J. CANTONI | R. BERTRANNE 1T | J. CANTONI | †A. DUBERTRAND | J. CANTONI 1T |
| J.L. BEROT 2PG | J.L. BEROT 1C | J.L. BEROT | J.L. BEROT | J.L. BEROT |
| M. PEBEYRE | M. PEBEYRE | M. PEBEYRE | †J. M. AGUIRRE | †R. ASTRE |
| J. IRACABAL | J. IRACABAL | J. IRACABAL | †J. P. HORTOLAND | †A. VAQUERIN |
| M. YACHVILI | M. YACHVILI | M. YACHVILI | R. BENESIS | R. BENESIS |
| J.L. AZARETE | J.L. AZARETE | J.L. AZARETE | †J.L. MARTIN | J.L. MARTIN |
| C. SPANGHERO | C. SPANGHERO | C. SPANGHERO | C. SPANGHERO | C. SPANGHERO |
| †A. ESTEVE | J. P. BASTIAT | E. CESTER | *B. DAUGA | *B. DAUGA |
| P. BIEMOURET | P. BIEMOURET | P. BIEMOURET | †V. BOFFELLI 1T | †O. SAISSET |
| B. DAUGA | *B. DAUGA | *B. DAUGA | †Y. BUONOMO | Y. BUONOMO |
| W. SPANGHERO | †J. C. SKRELA | J. C. SKRELA 1T | J. C. SKRELA | V. BOFFELLI |
| Bloemfontein | Durban | Toulouse | Stade Colombes | Beziers |
| LOST 9-22 | DRAWN 8-8 | LOST 11-13 | WON 18-9 | WON 31-12 |
| SA: 2G 3PG 1DG | SA: 1G 1DG | FR.: 1PG 2T | FR.: 1G 4PG | FR.: 3G 3PG 1T |
| FR.: 1T 2PG | FR.: 1G 1DG | AUST.: 1G 1PG 1T | AUST.: 3PG | ROM.: 1GM 1PG 2DG |
| 12 Jun. 1971 | 19 Jun. 1971 | 20 Nov. 1971 | 27 Nov. 1971 | 11 Dec. 1971 |

¹Rep. by C. Dourthe

The fourth French tour of South Africa took place in the summer of 1971. The party of 28 players was skippered by Christian Carrère, managed by Elie Pebeyre, and had Michel Celaya and Fernand Cazenave (both former caps) as assistant managers. Nine matches were played, seven won, one drawn and one lost. The team was praised for its commitment to open, attacking rugby, but suffered from injuries. Barrau had leg tendons torn in the opening game and was unable to participate further in the tour, and Villepreux, France's brilliant full-back, completed just one match.

France lost the Test series. In the first Test the Springboks placed the visitors under intense pressure, and the French were frustrated at being unable to play their natural running game and lost quite heavily. The drawn second Test was marred by an ugly punch-up, described as "the ugliest ever seen in an internaitonal".

The tour was followed by a busy late autumn programme in which the French played three internationals. The series with the Australians, who were on a short tour of France, was drawn, the French making seven changes after losing the Test at Toulouse. Six Béziers players came into the side to face Romania. France, having trailed by six points after half an hour, began to play fifteen-man football in the second half and overwhelmed the Romanians 31-12, their best result against them since 1957.

## 1971-72

| v. SCOTLAND | v. IRELAND | v. ENGLAND | v. WALES | 2nd v. IRELAND |
|---|---|---|---|---|
| P. VILLEPREUX 1C,1PG | P. VILLEPREUX 1C,1PG | P. VILLEPREUX 1PG,5C | *P. VILLEPREUX 2PG | P. VILLEPREUX 1C |
| R. BERTRANNE | R. BERTRANNE | B. DUPRAT 2T | B. DUPRAT | A. DUBERTRAND |
| J. TRILLO | C. DOURTHE | J. MASO | J. MASO | C. DOURTHE |
| J. P. LUX | J. P. LUX 1T | J. P. LUX 1T | J. P. LUX | J. P. LUX 1T |
| J. CANTONI | J. CANTONI | J. SILLIERES 1T | J. SILLIERES | B. DUPRAT 2T |
| J.L. BEROT | J.L. BEROT | J.L. BEROT | J.L. BEROT | A. MAROT |
| J. M. AGUIRRE | R. ASTRE | M. BARRAU | M. BARRAU | †J. FOUROUX |
| A. VAQUERIN | A. VAQUERIN | J.L. AZARETE | J.L. AZARETE | J.L. AZARETE |
| R. BENESIS | R. BENESIS | R. BENESIS | R. BENESIS | R. BENESIS |
| J.L. MARTIN | J.L. MARTIN | J. IRACABAL | J. IRACABAL | J. IRACABAL |
| J.P. BASTIAT | A. ESTEVE | A. ESTEVE | A. ESTEVE | A. ESTEVE |
| *B. DAUGA 1T | *B. DAUGA | C. SPANGHERO | C. SPANGHERO | C. SPANGHERO |
| O. SAISSET | O. SAISSET | P. BIEMOURET 1T | P. BIEMOURET | P. BIEMOURET |
| C. SPANGHERO | Y. BUONOMO | *W. SPANGHERO 1T | B. DAUGA | *W. SPANGHERO |
| V. BOFFELLI | V. BOFFELLI¹ | J. C. SKRELA | J. C. SKRELA | J. C. SKRELA |
| Murrayfield | Stade Colombes | Stade Colombes | Cardiff Arms Park | Lansdowne Road |
| LOST 9-20 | LOST 9-14 | WON 37-12 | LOST 6-20 | LOST 14-24 |
| SCOT.: 1G 1PG 1DG 2T | FR.: 1G 1PG | FR.: 5G 1PG 1T | WALES: 4PG 2T | IRE.: 3G 2PG |
| FR.: 1G 1PG | IRE.: 2T 2PG | ENG.: 1G 2PG | FR.: 2PG | FR.: 1G 2T |
| 15 Jan. 1972 | 29 Jan. 1972 | 26 Feb. 1972 | 25 Mar. 1972 | 29 Apr. 1972 |

¹Rep. by J.C. Skrela

Although Wales and Scotland were unable to fulfil their fixtures in Ireland, France met each of the Home Nations as usual in the Championship, and played an extra match in Dublin at the request of the IRFU. Full caps were awarded for the extra game.

Four defeats in five matches disappointed the French press and public, and there was caustic criticism of the selectors for their reliance on the Béziers club players. As many as seven of the side against Ireland in Paris, including five forwards, were from Béziers, the French club champions of 1971 (and later 1972). The club style, so effective in the domestic championship, was unsuccessful at international level and there were demands for the fifteen-man style for which France had been striving since the dawn of the Mias era.

The pundits were partially satisfied when England were demolished by a side showing ten changes from that beaten by Ireland. Only one Béziers player (Estève) survived the chop, as France ran up their highest score against an IB nation; and Villepreux marked another milestone for France in matches with IB countries by kicking five conversions. Altogether he converted seven tries for France in the championship season, a French record.

## 1972 | 1972

| 1st v. AUSTRALIA | 2nd v. AUSTRALIA | v. ROMANIA |
|---|---|---|
| P. VILLEPREUX 1C | P. VILLEPREUX 1C | †M. DROITECOURT |
| B. DUPRAT | C. DOURTHE | J.P. LUX |
| J. TRILLO | J. TRILLO | C. DOURTHE |
| C. DOURTHE | J. MASO 2T | J. TRILLO 1T |
| J.P. LUX 2T | J.P. LUX | A. CAMPAES |
| J.L. BEROT¹ | H. CABROL 1C | †J.P. ROMEU 1C,3PG |
| M. BARRAU | M. BARRAU | J. FOUROUX |
| A. VAQUERIN | †J. C. ROSSIGNOL | J.L. AZARETE |
| R. BENESIS | †A. LUBRANO | R. BENESIS |
| J.L. AZARETE | J. IRACABAL | J. IRACABAL |
| C. SPANGHERO | C. SPANGHERO | E. CESTER |
| J.P. BASTIAT | A. ESTEVE | A. ESTEVE |
| O. SAISSET 1T | O. SAISSET | M. YACHVILI |
| *W. SPANGHERO | *W. SPANGHERO 1T | *W. SPANGHERO |
| J. C. SKRELA | P. BIEMOURET | P. BIEMOURET |
| Sydney | Brisbane | Constantza |
| DRAWN 14-14 | WON 16-15 | WON 15-6 |
| AUST.: 2PG 2T | AUST.: 5PG | FR.: 1G 3PG |
| FR.: 1G 2T | FR.: 2G 1T | ROM.: 2PG |
| 17 Jun. 1972 | 25 Jun. 1972 | 26 Nov. 1972 |

Rep. by †H. Cabrol

A party of 27 players, managed by René Dassé and with Michel Celaya and Fernand Cazenave as assistants, made the first full French tour of Australia in 1972. (Previous visits had been supplements to tours to New Zealand.)

In terms of results the tour was a roaring success. Of nine matches played, none was lost, and in the two-Test series France were held to a draw in Sydney before winning a week later in Brisbane. The match marked the final appearance of Pierre Villepreux. In his 34 appearances he had gained a reputation as a sound defender with a commitment to attacking play. One of the best French full-backs ever fielded, he scored 166 points in internationals, setting a new record of 133 points for France against IB nations.

In the prelude to the International Championship, France won at Constantza against Romania in a match which was decided by the towering kicks (punts and place-kicks) of the new French fly-half, Romeu. Spanghéro remained as captain of a promising side which had experience and expertise up front, pace and youth in the backs.

## 1972-73

| v. SCOTLAND | v. NZ | v. ENGLAND | v. WALES | v. IRELAND |
|---|---|---|---|---|
| J. Cantoni | J. Cantoni[1] | M. Droitecourt | J. M. Aguirre | J.M. Aguirre |
| | | | | |
| J.P. Lux | R. Bertranne 1t | R. Bertranne 1t | †J.F. Phliponneau 1t | J.F. Phliponneau 1t |
| C. Dourthe 1t | C. Dourthe 1t | C. Dourthe | †C. Badin | C. Badin |
| J. Trillo | J.P. Lux | J. Trillo | J. Maso | J. Maso |
| R. Bourgarel | A. Campaes | J. P. Lux | J. Cantoni | J. Cantoni |
| | | | | |
| J.P. Romeu 3pg,1dg | J.P. Romeu 1pg,1c | J.P. Romeu 1c | J.P. Romeu 3pg,1dg | J.P. Romeu |
| M. Barrau | M. Barrau | M. Barrau[1] | M. Pebeyre | M. Barrau |
| | | | | |
| A. Vaquerin | J.L. Azarete | †A. Darrieussecq | J.L. Azarete | J.L. Azarete |
| A. Lubrano | R. Benesis | R. Benesis | R. Benesis | R. Benesis |
| J. Iracabal | J. Iracabal | J. Iracabal | J. Iracabal | J. Iracabal |
| E. Cester | E. Cester | J. P. Bastiat | E. Cester | E. Cester |
| A. Esteve | A. Esteve | A. Esteve | *W. Spanghero | A. Esteve |
| O. Saisset | O. Saisset | O. Saisset | J.C. Skrela | O. Saisset |
| *W. Spanghero | *W. Spanghero | *W. Spanghero | O. Saisset | *W. Spanghero |
| P. Biemouret | P. Biemouret | P. Biemouret | P. Biemouret | P. Biemouret |
| | | | | |
| Parc des Princes | Parc des Princes | Twickenham | Parc des Princes | Lansdowne Road |
| WON 16-13 | WON 13-6 | LOST 6-14 | WON 12-3 | LOST 4-6 |
| | | | | |
| Fr.: 1t 3pg 1dg | Fr.: 1g 1pg 1t | Eng.: 2pg 2t | Fr.: 3pg 1dg | Ire.: 2pg |
| Scot.: 1t 2pg 1dg | NZ: 2pg | Fr.: 1g | Wales: 1dg | Fr.: 1t |
| | | | | |
| 13 Jan. 1973 | 10 Feb. 1973 | 24 Feb. 1973 | 24 Mar. 1973 | 14 Apr. 1973 |
| | [1]Rep. by M. Droitecourt | [1]Rep. by R. Astre | | |

The French played their first international (and several others up to 1921) at Parc des Princes. By 1973 the ground had been redeveloped as an £8 million concrete palace, owned by the City of Paris and French Government, and for joint use by the FFR and its soccer equivalent. The match with Scotland was the first international in the ground's new surrounds, and, fittingly, France won, though mainly thanks to Romeu's goal-kicking.

The French followed this with victory over a New Zealand side reaching the end of a long tour. Inspiring captaincy by Spanghéro and the scheming brilliance of Barrau at the heels of a mobile pack were the features of France's win. But the side's inconsistency was exposed at Twickenham and again in Dublin, where Romeu's failure to level the scores with a last-minute conversion deprived France of the Championship. Spanghéro, having led France ten times in his 51 internationals, retired at the end of the season.

## 1973-74

| v. JAPAN | v. ROMANIA | v. IRELAND | v. WALES | v. ENGLAND | v. SCOTLAND |
|---|---|---|---|---|---|
| J.M. Aguirre 1t | J.M. Aguirre | J.M. Aguirre 1c | J.M. Aguirre | M. Droitecourt | M. Droitecourt |
| | | | | | |
| R. Bertranne 1t | R. Bertranne 1t | R. Bertranne | R. Bertranne | R. Bertranne | †J. F. Gourdon |
| †G. Delaigue 1t | G. Delaigue | C. Dourthe | †J. Pecune | J. Pecune | J. Pecune |
| J. Maso | J. Maso | J.P. Lux | J.P. Lux 1t | J.P. Lux | J.P. Lux |
| †N. Seguier | N. Seguier | A. Dubertrand | A. Dubertrand | A. Dubertrand | R. Bertranne |
| | | | | | |
| H. Cabrol 3c | J.P. Romeu 1dg | J.L. Berot 1pg | J.P. Romeu 3pg,1dg | J.P. Romeu 1t,1c,1pg,1dg | J.P. Romeu 1pg,1dg |
| *M. Barrau 1t | *M. Barrau | *M. Barrau | J. Fouroux | J. Fouroux | M. Barrau |
| | | | | | |
| †J. Rougerie | J.L. Azarete | J.L. Azarete | A. Vaquerin | A. Vaquerin | A. Vaquerin |
| R. Benesis | R. Benesis | R. Benesis | R. Benesis | R. Benesis | R. Benesis |
| J. Iracabal | †J. Costantino | J. Iracabal | J. Iracabal | J. Iracabal | J. Iracabal |
| E. Cester | E. Cester | A. Esteve | A. Esteve | A. Esteve | A. Esteve |
| †M. Sappa | M. Sappa | E. Cester | *E. Cester | *E. Cester | *E. Cester |
| J.C. Skrela 1t | J.C. Skrela | O. Saisset[1] | J.C. Skrela | J.C. Skrela | J.C. Skrela |
| O. Saisset 1t | O. Saisset | C. Spanghero | C. Spanghero | C. Spanghero | C. Spanghero |
| V. Boffelli | V. Boffelli | V. Boffelli 1t | V. Boffelli | V. Boffelli | V. Boffelli |
| | | | | | |
| Bordeaux | Valence | Parc des Princes | Cardiff Arms Park | Parc des Princes | Murrayfield |
| WON 30-18 | WON 7-6 | WON 9-6 | DRAWN 16-16 | DRAWN 12-12 | LOST 6-19 |
| | | | | | |
| Fr.: 3g 3t | Fr.: 1dg 1t | Fr.: 1g 1pg | Wales: 3pg 1dg 1t | Fr.: 1g 1pg 1dg | Scot.: 1g 3pg 1t |
| Japan: 2pg 3t | Rom.: 2pg | Ire.: 2pg | Fr.: 3pg 1dg 1t | Eng.: 1g 1pg 1dg | Fr.: 1pg 1dg |
| | | | | | |
| 27 Oct. 1973 | 11 Nov. 1973 | 19 Jan. 1974 | 16 Feb. 1974 | 2 Mar. 1974 | 16 Mar. 1974 |
| | | [1]Rep. by †D. Kaczorowski | | | |

The Japanese played four games in France after their seven-match tour of England and Wales in the autumn of 1973. The final match, against France, was granted full international status by the FFR. Only a late surge of points brought France success: the tourists led 10-7 at the interval and were still in contention at 15-16 with twenty minutes to go.

France then scraped home by a point against the Romanians, thanks to a drop-goal from Romeu and a try by Bertranne, and opened the International Championship with a last-minute win by a penalty goal against Ireland. Two draws followed, against Wales and England, before Championship hopes were evaporated by a storming Scottish forward display in Edinburgh. The French crashed to their heaviest defeat against the Scots since 1927. The popular, powerful French front-row of Iraçabal, Azarète and Bénésis played together for the last time in an international in the match with Ireland. Since 1969 this formidable trio had been France's front row in 14 international matches, two games short of the French record set by Domenech, de Grégorio and Roques in the early 1960s.

## 1974

| 1st v. ARGENTINA | 2nd v. ARGENTINA | v. ROMANIA | 1st v. S.AFRICA | 2nd v. S.AFRICA |
|---|---|---|---|---|
| M. Droitecourt | J.M. Aguirre | J.M. Aguirre | J.M. Aguirre | M. Droitecourt[1] |
| J.F. Gourdon | J.F. Gourdon 2t | J.F. Gourdon 1t | J.F. Gourdon | J.F. Gourdon 1t |
| *C. Dourthe 1t | C. Dourthe 1t | R. Bertranne | C. Dourthe | C. Dourthe 1t |
| J.P. Lux | J.P. Lux | †J.M. Etchenique | J.M. Etchenique | R. Bertranne |
| R. Bertranne 1t | R. Bertranne 1t | †L. Desnoyer | R. Bertranne 1t | A. Dubertrand |
| J.P. Romeu 1c,2pg | J.P. Romeu 3c,3pg | J.P. Romeu 2pg | J.P. Romeu | H. Cabrol |
| J. Fouroux 1t | J. Fouroux | *J. Fouroux | *J. Fouroux | *J. Fouroux |
| A. Vaquerin | A. Vaquerin | A. Vaquerin | A. Vaquerin | A. Vaquerin[2] |
| †A. Paco | A. Paco | A. Paco | A. Paco | A. Paco |
| J. Iracabal | J. Iracabal | J.L. Azarete | J.L. Azarete | J.L. Azarete |
| †G. Senal | G. Senal | G. Senal | G. Senal | G. Senal |
| †F. Haget | F. Haget | A. Esteve | A. Esteve | A. Esteve |
| J.C. Skrela | *O. Saisset | J.C. Skrela | O. Saisset | O. Saisset |
| J.P. Bastiat | J.P. Bastiat | C.Spanghero | C. Spanghero | J.P. Bastiat |
| V. Boffelli | V. Boffelli | V. Boffelli | V. Boffelli | V. Boffelli |
| Buenos Aires | Buenos Aires | Bucharest | Toulouse | Parc des Princes |
| WON 20-15 | WON 31-27 | LOST 10-15 | LOST 4-14 | LOST 8-10 |
| Arg.: 1g 3pg | Arg.: 1g 7pg | Rom.: 1g 3pg | Fr.: 1t | Fr.: 2t |
| Fr.: 1g 2pg 2t | Fr.: 3g 3pg 1t | Fr.: 2pg 1t | SA: 3pg 1t | SA: 2pg 1t |
| 20 Jun. 1974 | 29 Jun. 1974 | 13 Oct. 1974 | 23 Nov. 1974 | 30 Nov. 1974 |

[1] Rep. by J.P. Romeu
[2] Rep. by J. Iraçabal

The French tour of Argentina in the summer of 1974 was managed by Marcel Laurent, with Henri Fourès and Jean Desclaux, a thoughtful coach, as assistants. The tour party of 28 players won each of its eight matches, but had to struggle for victories in both of the Tests.

French preparations for the Championship involved a heavy autumn schedule in which Romania and South Africa (twice) beat them. The defeat in Bucharest was unlucky, but a lack of composure and some poor kicking by Romeu let the side down badly in the first Test with the Springboks, watched by a meagre crowd of 20,000. The selectors reacted with caution, making few changes for the game in Paris. There France showed considerable improvement and were unlucky to lose. Dourthe scrambled over for a try in injury time, but Cabrol's failure to convert gave the Springboks a 2-0 win in the series and the distinction of becoming the first side to win at the new Parc des Princes ground.

## 1974-75

| v. WALES | v. ENGLAND | v. SCOTLAND | v. IRELAND |
|---|---|---|---|
| †M. Taffary 2pg | M. Taffary | M. Taffary | M. Taffary |
| J.F. Gourdon 1t[1] | J.F. Gourdon 1t | J.F. Gourdon | J.F. Gourdon |
| C. Dourthe | *C. Dourthe | *C. Dourthe 1t | †F. Sangalli |
| R. Bertranne | J.M. Etchenique 1t | R. Bertranne | R. Bertranne |
| J.P. Lux | R. Bertranne | †J.L. Averous | J. L. Averous |
| J.P. Romeu | L. Paries 1pg,4c | L. Paries 1pg | L. Paries 1pg,1dg |
| *J. Fouroux | R. Astre | R. Astre 1dg | *R. Astre |
| A. Vaquerin | A. Vaquerin | A. Vaquerin | A. Vaquerin |
| A. Paco | A. Paco | †J.L. Ugartemendia | J.L. Ugartemendia |
| J.L. Azarete | †G. Cholley | G. Cholley | G. Cholley |
| G. Senal | A. Esteve | A. Guilbert | A. Guilbert |
| A. Esteve | †A. Guilbert 1t | C. Spanghero | C. Spanghero |
| O. Saisset[2] | †J.P. Rives | J.P. Rives | J.P. Rives |
| J.P. Bastiat | C. Spanghero 1t | V. Boffelli | V. Boffelli |
| V. Boffelli | J.C. Skrela | J.C. Skrela | J.C. Skrela |
| Parc des Princes | Twickenham | Parc des Princes | Lansdowne Road |
| LOST 10-25 | WON 27-20 | WON 10-9 | LOST 6-25 |
| Fr.: 1t 2pg | Eng.: 4pg 2t | Fr.: 1pg 1dg 1t | Ire.: 2g 2dg 1pg 1t |
| Wales: 4t 1pg 1g | Fr.: 4g 1pg | Scot.: 3pg | Fr.: 1dg 1pg |
| 18 Jan. 1975 | 1 Feb. 1975 | 15 Feb. 1975 | 1 Mar. 1975 |

[1] Rep. by J. Cantoni
[2] Rep. by J.C. Skrela

The disappointment over the three autumn defeats turned to despair after France were well beaten by the Welsh in Paris. But the resilience of French rugby was clearly illustrated when, in the next international, a team showing eight changes (and a positional change) and which included three new caps in the pack, scored 27 points in an entertaining win over England.

Rives was among the newcomers, and stamped his personality on the match with an active performance in the loose. A narrow victory in Paris against Scotland was followed by a poor display in Dublin, where France conceded 25 points.     Jean-Pierre Lux, one of France's most consistent threequarters between 1967 and 1975, played the last of his 47 internationals against Wales. A dentist, he formed a formidable partnership, either as a wing or centre, with his club colleague Dourthe, and retired as France's leading centre, having appeared in the position in 38 of his internationals.

## 1975

| 1st v. S.AFRICA | 2nd v. S.AFRICA | 1st v. ARGENTINA | 2nd v. ARGENTINA | v. ROMANIA |
|---|---|---|---|---|
| M. Droitecourt | M. Droitecourt | M. Droitecourt 1T | M. Droitecourt 1T | M. Droitecourt |
| †D. Harize 1T | D. Harize | J. Pecune 2T | J. Pecune | J.F. Gourdon |
| R. Bertranne | R. Bertranne | R. Bertranne | R. Bertranne 1T | R. Bertranne |
| F. Sangalli | F. Sangalli | C.F. Badin | J.M. Etchenique | J. Pecune 1T |
| J.L. Averous 1T | J.L. Averous | A. Dubertrand | A. Dubertrand | A. Dubertrand 3T |
| †J.P. Pesteil 1PG,3C | J.P. Romeu 3PG,1DG,1C | J.P. Romeu 1C,1PG | J.P. Romeu 2C,1T,4PG | J.P. Romeu 1PG,3C |
| *R. Astre | *R. Astre | *J. Fouroux 1T | *R. Astre 1T | *J. Fouroux 1T |
| †R. Paparemborde 1T | R. Paparemborde 1T | G. Cholley | G. Cholley | G. Cholley |
| †Y. Brunet | M. Yachvili | A. Paco | A. Paco | A. Paco |
| G. Cholley | G. Cholley | R. Paparemborde | R. Paparemborde | R. Paparemborde |
| A. Guilbert | F. Haget | F. Haget | F. Haget | F. Haget |
| †M. Palmie | M. Palmie | M. Palmie | M. Palmie | M. Palmie |
| J.C. Skrela 1T | J.C. Skrela | J.P. Rives 1T | J.P. Rives | J.P. Rives |
| †G. Rousset | A. Guilbert | J.P. Bastiat | J.P. Bastiat | J.P. Bastiat 1PG,1T |
| †P. Peron | P. Peron | J.C. Skrela 1T | J.C. Skrela 1T | J.C. Skrela |
| Bloemfontein | Pretoria | Lyon | Parc des Princes | Bordeaux |
| LOST 25-38 | LOST 18-33 | WON 29-6 | WON 36-21 | WON 36-12 |
| SA: 3G 4PG 2T | SA: 2G 7PG | FR.: 1G 1PG 5T | FR.: 2G 4PG 3T | FR.: 3G 3T 2PG |
| FR.: 3G 1PG 1T | FR.: 1G 1DG 3PG | ARG.: 2PG | ARG.: 1G 5PG | ROM.:3PG 1DG |
| 21 Jun. 1975 | 28 Jun. 1975 | 19 Oct. 1975 | 25 Oct. 1975 | 23 Nov. 1975 |

The summer tour to South Africa saw the emergence of Paparemborde as a sturdy scrummager, of Palmié as a robust all-round forward, and confirmed the promise shown earlier by younger men such as Haget, Guilbert and Cholley. Several of these men were to become key members of a formidable French pack in the seasons that followed. Thirty-one players made the trip (including a young forward who was to gain world recognition for his marvellous handling skills and mobility, Jean-Luc Joinel) under the charge of Marcel Batigne and Michel Celaya. The French won six of the eleven tour games, losing the Test series in two high-scoring internationals.

Three decisive victories followed at home in the autumn. An unchanged pack won plenty of good possession and 17 tries were scored in the three games, France averaging 34 points per game. Features of the autumn's matches were the assured play and reliable place-kicking of Romeu, and the effective leadership of Fouroux.

## 1975-76

| v. SCOTLAND | v. IRELAND | v. WALES | v. ENGLAND |
|---|---|---|---|
| M. Droitecourt | M. Droitecourt | M. Droitecourt[1] | J.M. Aguirre[1] |
| J.F. Gourdon | J.F. Gourdon | J.F. Gourdon 1T | J.F. Gourdon 1T |
| R. Bertranne | R. Bertranne | R. Bertranne | R. Bertranne |
| F. Sangalli | J. Pecune 1T | J. Pecune | J. Pecune |
| A. Dubertrand 1T | J.L. Averous | J.L. Averous 1T | J.L. Averous |
| J.P. Romeu 3PG | J.P. Romeu 1PG,1C | J.P. Romeu 1PG,1C | J.P. Romeu 1T,3C |
| *J. Fouroux | *J. Fouroux 1T | *J. Fouroux | *J. Fouroux 1T |
| G. Cholley | G. Cholley 1T | G. Cholley | G. Cholley |
| A. Paco | A. Paco | A. Paco | A. Paco |
| R. Paparemborde | R. Paparemborde | R. Paparemborde | R. Paparemborde 2T |
| F. Haget | †J.F. Imbernon | J.F. Imbernon | J.F. Imbernon |
| M. Palmie | M. Palmie | M. Palmie | M. Palmie |
| J.P. Rives | J.P. Rives 1T | J.P. Rives | J.P. Rives |
| J.P. Bastiat | J.P. Bastiat 1PG,1C | J.P. Bastiat | J.P. Bastiat 1T |
| J.C. Skrela | J.C. Skrela | J.C. Skrela | J.C. Skrela |
| Murrayfield | Parc des Princes | Cardiff Arms Park | Parc des Princes |
| WON 13-6 | WON 26-3 | LOST 13-19 | WON 30-9 |
| Scot.: 1PG 1DG | FR.: 2G 2PG 2T | Wales: 5PG 1T | FR.: 3G 3T |
| FR.: 3PG 1T | IRE.: 1PG | FR.: 1G 1PG 1T | ENG.: 1G 1PG |
| 10 Jan. 1976 | 7 Feb. 1976 | 6 Mar. 1976 | 20 Mar. 1976 |
| | | [1]Rep. by J.M. Aguirre | [1]Rep. by †R. Berges-Cau |

A talented side inspiringly led by Fouroux and benefiting from a skilful and powerful pack, challenged strongly for the Championship title in 1976. The dividends of the tour to South Africa and the intensive practice and preparation for the matches in the autumn, paid off at the start of the year. France's seven-point win at Murrayfield was their biggest in Scotland for fourteen years, and was followed by the rout of the Irish in Paris.

The French back row was outstanding in the Irish match. Skréla and Rives put the visiting backs under immense pressure and were tireless workers in the loose, while Bastiat, a huge number-eight, completely dominated the line-out. An unchanged side, with hopes high, set off for Cardiff and the game which held the key to the title. But France were thwarted in a grand game.

At the end of the season the side ran riot against a weak English side. The French pack displayed enormous power at the scrums and in the rucks and mauls. One of Paparemborde's two tries resulted from a pushover, and Bastiat forced his way across the line from a scrummage. The 30 points scored in the match boosted France's total to 82 for the season – a new French record in the International Championship.

## 1976

| v. AMERICA | 1st v. AUSTRALIA | 2nd v. AUSTRALIA | v. ROMANIA |
|---|---|---|---|
| J.M. AGUIRRE | M. DROITECOURT 3C | J.M. AGUIRRE 1T,2C,1PG | J.M. AGUIRRE 1C,2PG |
| A. DUBERTRAND[1] | D. HARIZE | D. HARIZE 1T | D. HARIZE |
| R. BERTRANNE | R. BERTRANNE 1T | R. BERTRANNE 1T | R. BERTRANNE |
| J. PECUNE | F. SANGALLI | F. SANGALLI | F. SANGALLI |
| J.L. AVEROUS 1T | J.L. AVEROUS | J.L. AVEROUS 1T | J.L. AVEROUS |
| J.P. ROMEU 1T,3C,5PG | A. MAROT | J.P. PESTEIL | J.P. PESTEIL |
| *J. FOUROUX | *J. FOUROUX | *R. ASTRE 1DG | *R. ASTRE |
| A. VAQUERIN | G. CHOLLEY 1T | A. VAQUERIN | A. VAQUERIN |
| A. PACO | A. PACO | A. PACO | A. PACO |
| R. PAPAREMBORDE | R. PAPAREMBORDE 1T | R. PAPAREMBORDE | R. PAPAREMBORDE |
| J.F. IMBERNON | J.F. IMBERNON[1] | G. CHOLLEY 1T | G. CHOLLEY |
| M. PALMIE | A. GUILBERT | [1]G. GASPAROTTO | G. GASPAROTTO |
| J.P. RIVES | J.P. RIVES | J.P. RIVES 1T | J.P. RIVES |
| G. ROUSSET 1T | J.P. BASTIAT | J.P. BASTIAT | J.P. BASTIAT 1T |
| J.C. SKRELA | J.C. SKRELA | J.C. SKRELA | J.C. SKRELA |
| Chicago | Bordeaux | Parc des Princes | Bucharest |
| WON 33-14 | WON 18-15 | WON 34-6 | LOST 12-15 |
| AMER.:2PG 2T | FR.: 3G | FR.: 2G 1PG 1DG 4T | ROM.: 1DG 3T |
| FR.: 3G 5PG | AUST.: 4PG 1DG | AUST.: 2PG | FR.: 1G 2PG |
| 12 Jun. 1976 | 24 Oct. 1976 | 30 Oct. 1976 | 14 Nov. 1976 |
| [1]Rep. by | [1]Rep. by A. Vaquerin | | |
| [†]J. Cimarosti | | | |

Four major internationals were undertaken in the summer and autumn of 1976. A party of 22 players, managed by Marcel Batigne, made a short tour to the United States, playing three games including a full international against the American national side. It was France's first full international with the Americans since the Olympic Final of 1924. The Americans played skilfully in the Test and trailed by just 10-15 at the interval, but excellent kicking by Romeu took the visitors clear in the second half.

The French took the two-Test series at home against Australia with a convincing display in the second match at Paris. Breathtaking interplay between forwards and backs resulted in an avalanche of French points in the second half. France's 34-6 win was their biggest ever against an IB Nation.

But French pride was severely dented a fortnight later when the same team which had overwhelmed Australia were beaten in Bucharest. France were leading 12-0 ten minutes after the interval before Romania scored three tries and a drop-goal.

## 1976-77

| v. WALES | v. ENGLAND | v. SCOTLAND | v. IRELAND |
|---|---|---|---|
| J.M. AGUIRRE | J.M. AGUIRRE | J.M. AGUIRRE | J.M. AGUIRRE 2PG,1C |
| D. HARIZE 1T | D. HARIZE | D. HARIZE 1T | D. HARIZE |
| R. BERTRANNE | R. BERTRANNE | R. BERTRANNE 1T | R. BERTRANNE |
| F. SANGALLI | F. SANGALLI 1T | F. SANGALLI | F. SANGALLI |
| J.L. AVEROUS | J.L. AVEROUS | J.L. AVEROUS | J.L. AVEROUS |
| J.P. ROMEU 2PG,1C | J.P. ROMEU | J.P. ROMEU 1PG,2C | J.P. ROMEU 1PG |
| *J. FOUROUX | *J. FOUROUX | *J. FOUROUX | *J. FOUROUX |
| G. CHOLLEY | G. CHOLLEY | G. CHOLLEY | G. CHOLLEY |
| A. PACO | A. PACO | A. PACO 1T | A. PACO |
| R. PAPAREMBORDE | R. PAPAREMBORDE | R. PAPAREMBORDE 1T | R. PAPAREMBORDE |
| J.F. IMBERNON | J.F. IMBERNON | J.F. IMBERNON | J.F. IMBERNON |
| M. PALMIE | M. PALMIE | M. PALMIE | M. PALMIE |
| J.P. RIVES | J.P. RIVES | J.P. RIVES | J.P. RIVES |
| J.P. BASTIAT | J.P. BASTIAT | J.P. BASTIAT | J.P. BASTIAT 1T |
| J.C. SKRELA 1T | J.C. SKRELA | J.C. SKRELA | J.C. SKRELA |
| Parc des Princes | Twickenham | Parc des Princes | Lansdowne Road |
| WON 16-9 | WON 4-3 | WON 23-3 | WON 15-6 |
| FR.: 1G 2PG 1T | ENG.: 1PG | FR.:2G 1PG 2T | IRE.: 2PG |
| WALES: 3PG | FR.: 1T | SCOT.: 1PG | FR.: 1G 3PG |
| 5 Feb. 1977 | 19 Feb. 1977 | 5 Mar. 1977 | 19 Mar. 1977 |

Jacques Fouroux, nicknamed "Napoleon", led France to their second Grand Slam in 1977. The match with Wales, it was felt, would hold the key to the Championship, and so it proved. The French dominated the game. Their forwards were on top in all departments, with the loose trio of Rives, Skréla and Bastiat exerting a tight rein on the Welsh backs.

The Welsh hurdle successfully negotiated, the French reckoned that the rest of their Championship would be plain sailing. But they had to work extremely hard for victory at Twickenham. After a scoreless first half, the French went ahead ten minutes into the second half when Aguirre, an adventurous full-back with the speed and ability to beat the cleverest of defences, made an opening for Sangalli to score. England kicked a penalty later and pressed hard for a score in the final ten minutes of the match. Convincing wins followed against Scotland and in Ireland, and a spectacular try scored by Bastiat, after good team work in a sweeping seventy-metre movement, capped the display in Dublin.

For the first time France fielded an unchanged team throughout the Championship. Only two other sides have accomplished this unusual record : the English fifteen of 1960, and the Irish side of 1983.

## 1977

| 1st v. ARGENTINA | 2nd v. ARGENTINA | 1st v. NZ | 2nd v. NZ |
|---|---|---|---|
| J.M. Aguirre 1PG | J.M. Aguirre 6PG | J.M. Aguirre | J.M. Aguirre |
| †D. Bustaffa 1T | D. Bustaffa | D. Bustaffa | D. Bustaffa |
| R. Bertranne 1T | R. Bertranne | R. Bertranne | R. Bertranne |
| F. Sangalli | F. Sangalli | F. Sangalli | F. Sangalli |
| J.L. Averous | M. Droitecourt | †G. Noves | G. Noves |
| J.P. Romeu 1DG,4PG | J.P. Romeu | J.P. Romeu 3PG,1DG,1C | J.P. Romeu 1PG |
| *J. Fouroux | *J. Fouroux | *J. Fouroux | *J. Fouroux |
| G. Cholley | G. Cholley | G. Cholley | G. Cholley |
| Y. Brunet | C. Swierczinski | A. Paco | A. Paco |
| R. Paparemborde | A. Vaquerin | R. Paparemborde 1T | R. Paparemborde |
| J.F. Imbernon | J.F. Imbernon | J.F. Imbernon | J.F. Imbernon |
| M. Palmie | M. Palmie | M. Palmie | M. Palmie |
| J.P. Rives | J.P. Rives | †J.L. Joinel | †J. Gasc |
| A. Guilbert | A. Guilbert | A. Guilbert | A. Guilbert |
| J.C. Skrela | J.C. Skrela | J.C. Skrela | J.C. Skrela |
| Buenos Aires | Buenos Aires | Toulouse | Parc des Princes |
| WON 26-3 | DRAWN 18-18 | WON 18-13 | LOST 3-15 |
| ARG.: 1PG | ARG.: 6PG | FR.: 1G 1DG 3PG | FR.: 1PG |
| FR.: 1DG 5PG 2T | FR.: 6PG | NZ: 2PG 1DG 1T | NZ: 1G 2PG 1DG |
| 25 Jun. 1977 | 2 Jul. 1977 | 11 Nov. 1977 | 19 Nov. 1977 |

France made their fifth tour of Argentina in the summer of 1977. Fouroux continued as captain and six of the seven matches played were won. In the final game of the tour, the second of the Tests at Buenos Aires, the French were held to a draw. Hugo Porta, the Argentinian fly-half, and Aguirre each kicked six penalty goals, equalling the world record set by Don Clarke in 1959 for New Zealand against the British Isles.

Apart from a spectacular win against a Buenos Aires selection in the opening match of the tour, the French depended on the kicking of Romeu and the power of a formidable set of forwards to create scoring opportunities. Rives and Skréla were the outstanding successes of the tour, causing havoc in the loose with their hard-tackling disruption of the Argentinian back-play.

During the autumn, there was a rare success against the All Blacks in the first Test of a short series. At Toulouse, the place-kicking of Romeu and a first-half try by Paparemborde (following a towering punt by the fly-half) were sufficient to beat-off the challenge of a young and inexperienced side. But the French played indifferently in victory and defeat followed a week later in Paris, and the series was shared.

## 1977-78

| v. ROMANIA | v. ENGLAND | v. SCOTLAND | v. IRELAND | v. WALES |
|---|---|---|---|---|
| J.M. Aguirre | J.M. Aguirre 1PG,2C | J.M. Aguirre 3PG,1C | J.M. Aguirre 2PG | J.M. Aguirre |
| J.L. Averous | J.F. Gourdon | J.F. Gourdon | †L. Bilbao | D. Bustaffa |
| R. Bertranne | R. Bertranne | R. Bertranne | R. Bertranne | R. Bertranne |
| †C. Belascain | C. Belascain | C. Belascain | C. Belascain | C. Belascain |
| G. Noves | J.L. Averous 1T | J.L. Averous | J.L. Averous | G. Noves |
| J.P. Romeu 3PG | †B. Vivies | B. Vivies | B. Vivies | B. Vivies 1DG |
| *J. Fouroux | †J. Gallion 1T | J. Gallion 1T | J. Gallion 1T | J. Gallion |
| G. Cholley | G. Cholley | G. Cholley | G. Cholley | G. Cholley |
| A. Paco | A. Paco | A. Paco | A. Paco | A. Paco |
| †P. Dospital | R. Paparemborde | R. Paparemborde | R. Paparemborde | R. Paparemborde |
| M. Sappa | J.F. Imbernon | M. Palmie | M. Palmie | F. Haget |
| M. Palmie | M. Palmie | F. Haget 1T | F. Haget | M. Palmie |
| J.P. Rives | J.P. Rives | J.P. Rives | J.P. Rives | J.P. Rives |
| A. Guilbert | *J.P. Bastiat | *J.P. Bastiat | *J.P. Bastiat | *J.P. Bastiat |
| J.C. Skrela | J.C. Skrela | J.C. Skrela | J.C. Skrela | J.C. Skrela 1T |
| Clermont Ferrand | Parc des Princes | Murrayfield | Parc des Princes | Cardiff Arms Park |
| WON 9-6 | WON 15-6 | WON 19-16 | WON 10-9 | LOST 7-16 |
| FR.: 3PG | FR.: 2G 1PG | SCOT.: 1G 1DG 1PG 1T | FR.: 2PG 1T | WALES: 1G 2DG 1T |
| ROM.: 1PG 1DG | ENG.: 2DG | FR.: 1G 3PG 1T | IRE.: 3PG | FR.: 1DG 1T |
| 10 Dec. 1977 | 21 Jan. 1978 | 4 Feb. 1978 | 18 Feb. 1978 | 19 Mar. 1978 |

The winter of 1977-78 was not a pleasant one for the international side. Controversy surrounded the relation between the selectors and the coach, and it was evident that the coach was not given the players he required to practise the type of tactical approach he favoured. As a result there was an unwelcome dependence on forward play, backed by a kicking fly-half and defensive backs.

Fouroux retired after leading France to victory in a try-less match with Romania. In 21 of his 27 internationals he captained France, becoming the first man to lead France against each of the other members of the International Board. His partner in many of these matches, Jean-Pierre Romeu, also played his last game against Romania. In 34 matches Romeu had become France's most prolific international scorer, obtaining 265 points in full internationals, of which 139 were scored against IB nations.

Under the captaincy of Bastiat the French finished the season as runners-up in the Championship to the Welsh. Gallion, the new scrum-half, created an unusual French record by scoring tries in each of his first three internationals, while the pack which beat England in the opening game of the season was playing together for an unprecedented eighth time.

| 1978 | 1978-79 | | | |
| v. ROMANIA | v. IRELAND | v. WALES | v. ENGLAND | v. SCOTLAND |
| --- | --- | --- | --- | --- |
| J.M. AGUIRRE 2PG | J.M. AGUIRRE 1PG,1C | J.M. AGUIRRE 2PG | J.M. AGUIRRE 1C | J.M. AGUIRRE 1PG |
| D. BUSTAFFA | L. BILBAO | J.F. GOURDON 2T | J.F. GOURDON | J.F. GOURDON |
| R. BERTRANNE | R. BERTRANNE | R. BERTRANNE | R. BERTRANNE | R. BERTRANNE |
| C. BELASCAIN | C. BELASCAIN | C. BELASCAIN | C. BELASCAIN | C. BELASCAIN 1T |
| G. NOVES | G. NOVES | G. NOVES | †F. COSTES 1T | F. COSTES |
| †A. CAUSSADE 1DG | A. CAUSSADE 1T | A. CAUSSADE | A. CAUSSADE | †R. AGUERRE 1DG,1PG |
| †Y. LAFARGE | J. GALLION | J. GALLION | J. GALLION | J. GALLION |
| G. CHOLLEY | G. CHOLLEY | A. VAQUERIN | A. VAQUERIN | G. CHOLLEY |
| A. PACO | A. PACO | A. PACO | A. PACO | A. PACO |
| R. PAPAREMBORDE | R. PAPAREMBORDE | R. PAPAREMBORDE | R. PAPAREMBORDE | R. PAPAREMBORDE |
| F. HAGET | F. HAGET | F. HAGET | F. HAGET | F. HAGET |
| J.F. IMBERNON | J.F. IMBERNON | †A. MALEIG | A. MALEIG | †J.F. MARCHAL |
| *J.P. RIVES | *J.P. RIVES | *J.P. RIVES | *J.P. RIVES | *J.P. RIVES |
| †M. CLEMENTE | A. GUILBERT | A. GUILBERT | A. GUILBERT | †Y. MALQUIER 2T |
| J.L. JOINEL | J.L. JOINEL | J.L. JOINEL | J.L. JOINEL | J.L. JOINEL |
| Bucharest | Lansdowne Road | Parc des Princes | Twickenham | Parc des Princes |
| WON 9-6 | DRAWN 9-9 | WON 14-13 | LOST 6-7 | WON 21-17 |
| ROM.: 2PG | IRE.: 3PG | FR.: 2PG 2T | ENG.: 1PG 1T | FR.: 1DG 2PG 3T |
| FR.: 2PG 1DG | FR.: 1G 1PG | WALES: 3PG 1T | FR.: 1G | SCOT.: 1G 1PG 2T |
| 3 Dec. 1978 | 20 Jan. 1979 | 17 Feb. 1979 | 3 Mar. 1979 | 17 Mar. 1979 |

France played seven matches in Canada and the Far East during the late summer of 1978, but the contests against Japan and Canada do not rank as full internationals in the official FFR lists. Nevertheless, the tour was a successful venture and of the younger players, Lafarge and Aguerre were first capped the following winter.

Having proved an admirable leader on tour, Bastiat badly sprained a knee in a club match and Rives had the captaincy thrust upon him for the Romanian Test. Rives was to become an outstanding leader, and went on to match Wilson Whineray's world record of leading his nation in 30 games against IB countries. (Rives also captained France in four other full internationals.)

The season was one of transition as French officials aimed for a return to the "Champagne Rugby" style of the early 1960s. There was a call for a more mobile and cohesive pack to replace the devotees to the powerful scrummaging/tight-forward school of the mid-1970s, and by finishing as runners-up to Wales in the Championship, the side went some way towards achieving this goal. A noted trio of Paparemborde, Paco and Cholley played together for the 21st and last time against Scotland – a French front-row record.

| 1979 | |
| 1st v. NZ | 2nd v. NZ |
| --- | --- |
| J.M. AGUIRRE 1C | J.M. AGUIRRE 1PG |
| F. COSTES | F. COSTES |
| †P. MESNY 1T | P. MESNY |
| †D. CODORNIOU | D. CODORNIOU 1T |
| J.L. AVEROUS | J.L. AVEROUS 1T |
| A. CAUSSADE 1DG | A. CAUSSADE 1DG,1C,1T |
| Y. LAFARGE | J. GALLION 1T |
| †G. COLOMINE | R. PAPAREMBORDE |
| †P. DINTRANS | P. DINTRANS |
| R. PAPAREMBORDE | †D. DUBROCA |
| F. HAGET | F. HAGET |
| †P. SALAS | A. MALEIG |
| *J.P. RIVES | *J.P. RIVES |
| †C. BEGUERIE | P. SALAS |
| J.L. JOINEL | J.L. JOINEL |
| Christchurch | Auckland |
| LOST 9-23 | WON 24-19 |
| NZ: 1G 3PG 2T | NZ: 1G 3PG 1T |
| FR.: 1G 1DG | FR.: 1G 1PG 1DG 3T |
| 7 Jul. 1979 | 14 Jul. 1979 |

There was a short tour to Fiji and New Zealand (and a match against Tahiti on the journey home) during the summer of 1979. A party of 26 players, managed by Yves Noé with Fernand Cazenave as assistant, and coached by Jean Desclaux and Jean Piqué, enjoyed a happy and successful trip.

During the tour Rives' entertaining attitude to the game became established through his positive approach to the captaincy. Victory at all cost was a maxim ignored as Rives imbued his side with a spirit of adventure, one which paid capital dividends in the second Test of the New Zealand series. At Auckland the French were inspired by the non-stop actions of Rives and Joinel, and in a sparkling display of attacking rugby, the visitors ran in four tries to record their first international victory on New Zealand soil.

The backs ran and passed with pace and accuracy at Auckland and the match was referred to as one of the best internationals ever seen in New Zealand. Altogether the side played nine matches, winning six of them.

### 1979 / 1979-80

| v. ROMANIA | v. WALES | v. ENGLAND | v. SCOTLAND | v. IRELAND |
|---|---|---|---|---|
| J.M. Aguirre 1PG,1DG,2C | J.M. Aguirre | †S. Gabernet | S. Gabernet 1PG,1T | J.M. Aguirre 1C,2PG |
| J.F. Gourdon | D. Bustaffa | D. Bustaffa | D. Bustaffa | J.F. Gourdon 2T |
| R. Bertranne 1T | R. Bertranne | R. Bertranne | R. Bertranne | R. Bertranne |
| D. Codorniou 1T | D. Codorniou | D. Codorniou | D. Codorniou | D. Codorniou |
| F. Costes | F. Costes | J.L. Averous 1T | J.L. Averous | F. Costes |
| A. Caussade 2PG,1C | A. Caussade 1DG,1C | A. Caussade 1PG,1C | A. Caussade 1DG | †P. Pedeutour 1DG |
| J. Gallion | J. Gallion | J. Gallion | J. Gallion 1T | J. Gallion |
| P. Salas | P. Salas | P. Salas | A. Vaquerin | A. Vaquerin |
| P. Dintrans | A. Paco | P. Dintrans | P. Dintrans | P. Dintrans |
| R. Paparemborde | R. Paparemborde | R. Paparemborde | R. Paparemborde | P. Dospital |
| F. Haget | F. Haget | †Y. Duhard | F. Haget | F. Haget |
| J.F. Marchal | J.F. Marchal 1T | A. Maleig | J.F. Marchal | J.F. Marchal |
| *J.P. Rives | *J.P. Rives | *J.P. Rives 1T | *J.P. Rives | *J.P. Rives |
| †J. Cristina | A. Maleig | †M. Carpentier | M. Clemente | M. Clemente |
| J.L. Joinel 1T | J.L. Joinel | J.L. Joinel | J.L. Joinel | J.L. Joinel |
| Montauban | Cardiff Arms Park | Parc des Princes | Murrayfield | Parc des Princes |
| WON 30-12 | LOST 9-18 | LOST 13-17 | LOST 14-22 | WON 19-18 |
| FR.: 3G 1DG 3PG | WALES: 1G 3T | FR.: 1G 1PG 1T | SCOT.: 2G 2PG 1T | FR.: 1G 2PG 1DG 1T |
| ROM.: 3PG 1DG | FR.: 1G 1DG | ENG.: 1PG 2DG 2T | FR.: 1PG 1DG 2T | IRE.: 1G 3PG 1DG |
| 2 Dec. 1979 | 19 Jan. 1980 | 2 Feb. 1980 | 16 Feb. 1980 | 1 Mar. 1980 |

France's "spirit of Auckland" was in evidence at Montauban in the opening international of the 1979-80 winter. For the first time since 1976, France registered a try against the Romanians, and the style with which the French overwhelmed their opponents suggested that they should be installed as favourites for the International Championship.

But the "spirit" evaporated in the opening twenty minutes of a bruising match at Cardiff. The French selectors announced changes for the game against England, but defeat was again their result despite Rives' faith in open, attacking football. Salas, who had appeared in all three rows of the scrum in the space of five matches, was eventually replaced by a specialist prop, and at length the team brought off its single win of the Championship by beating Ireland in Paris.

For the first time since 1969, France finished with the wooden spoon.

### 1980-81

| v. S.AFRICA | v. ROMANIA | v. SCOTLAND | v. IRELAND | v. WALES | v. ENGLAND |
|---|---|---|---|---|---|
| †S. Blanco | S. Blanco | S. Gabernet 1PG | S. Gabernet 1PG | S. Gabernet 1T,2PG | S. Gabernet |
| D. Bustaffa | D. Bustaffa | S. Blanco 1T | A. Caussade | S. Blanco | S. Blanco |
| R. Bertranne | P. Mesny | R. Bertranne 1T | R. Bertranne | R. Bertranne[1] | R. Bertranne |
| P. Mesny | R. Bertranne | D. Codorniou | P. Mesny[1] | D. Codorniou | D. Codorniou |
| †L. Pardo | L. Pardo | L. Pardo | L. Pardo 1T | L. Pardo | L. Pardo 1T |
| B. Vivies 3PG,1C | B. Vivies | B. Vivies 1PG[1] | †G. Laporte 2PG,2DG | G. Laporte 3PG | G. Laporte 2DG,1C |
| †J.P. Elissalde | J.P. Elissalde | †P. Berbizier | P. Berbizier | P. Berbizier | P. Berbizier |
| †J.P. Wolff | †M. Cremaschi | P. Dospital | P. Dospital | P. Dospital | P. Dospital |
| P. Dintrans 1T | P. Dintrans | P. Dintrans | P. Dintrans | P. Dintrans | P. Dintrans |
| R. Paparemborde | *R. Paperemborde | R. Paparemborde | R. Paparemborde | R. Paparemborde | R. Paparemborde |
| M. Carpentier | A. Maleig | †D. Revallier | D. Revallier | D. Revallier | D. Revallier |
| A. Maleig | J.P. Wolff | J.F. Imbernon | J.F. Imbernon | J.F. Imbernon | J.F. Imbernon |
| *J.P. Rives | †J.P. Fauvel | *J.P. Rives | *J.P. Rives | *J.P. Rives | *J.P. Rives |
| J.L. Joinel | M. Carpentier | M. Carpentier | M. Carpentier | J.L. Joinel | J.L. Joinel |
| †P. Lacans | †E. Buchet | J.L. Joinel | J.L. Joinel | P. Lacans | P. Lacans 1T |
| Pretoria | Bucharest | Parc des Princes | Lansdowne Road | Parc des Princes | Twickenham |
| LOST 15-37 | LOST 0-15 | WON 16-9 | WON 19-13 | WON 19-15 | WON 16-12 |
| SA: 4G 3PG 1T | ROM.: 1G 3PG | FR.: 1G 2PG 1T | IRE.: 3PG 1T | FR.: 5PG 1T | ENG.: 4PG |
| FR.: 1G 3PG | FR.: NIL | SCOT.: 1G 1PG | FR.: 3PG 2DG 1T | WALES: 1G 3PG | FR.: 1G 2DG 1T |
| 8 Nov. 1980 | 23 Nov. 1980 | 17 Jan. 1981 | 7 Feb. 1981 | 7 Mar. 1981 | 21 Mar. 1981 |
| | | [1]Rep. by A. Caussade 1C | [1]Rep. by Y. Lafarge | [1]Rep. by P. Mesny | |

France made a hastily arranged tour of South Africa in the late autumn of 1980, playing four matches including an international at Pretoria. Yves Noé was the manager, with Michel Celaya and Jean Piqué as assistants, of a party comprising 25 players. The French won plenty of admiration for their enterprising style, but in the Test they were overpowered by a massive Springbok pack which set up five tries.

An unbalanced side was well beaten by the Romanians, and the vice-chairman of selectors, Elie Pebeyre, was replaced for the Championship season. Furthermore, Jacques Fouroux was appointed national coach in place of Michel Celaya.

Then, with typical Gallic unpredictability, France proceeded to win their third Grand Slam, and seventh outright Championship title. The strength of the side was its powerful scrummaging and imaginative backs, though Laporte's contribution of 29 goal points, including four drop-goals, was an important factor in the side's success.

## 1981

| 1st v. AUSTRALIA | 2nd v. AUSTRALIA | v. ROMANIA | 1st v. NZ | 2nd v. NZ |
|---|---|---|---|---|
| S. Gabernet 1PG,1C | S. Gabernet | S. Gabernet 2PG | S. Gabernet 1DG | S. Gabernet |
| †M. Fabre | S. Blanco | M. Fabre | M. Fabre | M. Fabre |
| P. Mesny 1T | P. Mesny | P. Mesny | R. Bertranne | R. Bertranne |
| L. Pardo | D. Codorniou | R. Bertranne | P. Mesny | P. Mesny |
| S. Blanco 1PG | J.L. Averous | S. Blanco 1T | S. Blanco | S. Blanco 1PG |
| B. Vivies 1DG | †M. Sallefranque 1DG | G. Laporte 1DG | G. Laporte 2PG | G. Laporte 1PG |
| J.P. Elissalde¹ | J.P. Elissalde 1DG,1T | J.P. Elissalde 1T | P. Berbizier | P. Berbizier |
| P. Salas | J.P. Wolff | M. Cremaschi | M. Cremaschi | M. Cremaschi¹ |
| P. Dintrans | P. Dintrans | P. Dintrans | P. Dintrans | P. Dintrans |
| *R. Paparemborde | R. Paparemborde | *R. Paparemborde | *R. Paparemborde | *R. Paparemborde |
| †A. Lorieux | L. Rodriguez | A. Lorieux | A. Lorieux | A. Lorieux |
| D. Revallier | D. Revallier | D. Revallier | D. Revallier | D. Revallier |
| †D. Erbani | *J.P. Rives | L. Rodriguez | L. Rodriguez | L. Rodriguez |
| M. Carpentier | D. Erbani | J.L. Joinel | D. Erbani | D. Erbani |
| †L. Rodriguez | P. Lacans 1T | P. Lacans | J.L. Joinel | J.L. Joinel |
| Brisbane | Sydney | Narbonne | Toulouse | Parc des Princes |
| LOST 15-17 | LOST 14-24 | WON 17-9 | LOST 9-13 | LOST 6-18 |
| AUST.: 1G 1PG 2T | AUST.: 2G 4PG | FR.: 2PG 1DG 2T | FR.: 2PG 1DG | FR.: 2PG |
| FR.: 1G 2PG 1DG | FR.: 2DG 2T | ROM.: 3PG | NZ: 2PG 1DG 1T | NZ: 2G 2PG |
| 5 Jul. 1981 | 11 Jul. 1981 | 1 Nov. 1981 | 14 Nov. 1981 | 21 Nov. 1981 |
| ¹Rep. by †A. Mournet | | | | ¹Rep. by D. Dubroca |

France had a busy summer and autumn programme in 1981. A party of 28 players, managed by Yves Noé and accompanied by coaches Jacques Fouroux and Jean Piqué, made a nine-match tour of Australia. Six matches were won but in the important Test series France were beaten 2-0, and the team also lost to a Sydney combination early in the tour.

The dominance of the Southern Hemisphere over their Northern counterparts was further demonstrated by the ease with which the All Blacks won both Tests of their short tour to France in the autumn. The French paid the penalty for fielding too inexperienced a pack against a strong New Zealand scrummage. Sandwiched between the two Test series, France did manage a win at Narbonne against the Romanians.

Roland Bertranne, one of France's most skilful and complete threequarters of all time, played his last international in the Paris Test against the All Blacks. In a career which spanned a decade, he established a new French appearance record, playing 69 matches, of which 52 were against IB nations.

## 1981-82

| v. WALES | v. ENGLAND | v. SCOTLAND | v. IRELAND |
|---|---|---|---|
| M. Sallefranque 1C,1PG | M. Sallefranque 1C,2PG | M. Sallefranque 1PG | S. Gabernet 2PG,1C |
| S. Blanco 1T | S. Blanco | S. Blanco | M. Fabre |
| †P. Perrier | P. Perrier | P. Perrier | P. Mesny 1T |
| C. Belascain | C. Belascain | C. Belascain | C. Belascain¹ |
| L. Pardo | L. Pardo 1T | L. Pardo | S. Blanco 2PG,1T |
| †J.P. Lescarboura | J.P. Lescarboura 1DG | J.P. Lescarboura | J.P. Lescarboura |
| †G. Martinez 1PG | G. Martinez | G. Martinez | P. Berbizier |
| M. Cremaschi | J.P. Wolff | M. Cremaschi | P. Dospital |
| P. Dintrans | P. Dintrans | P. Dintrans | P. Dintrans |
| R. Paparemborde | D. Dubroca | D. Dubroca | R. Paparemborde |
| A. Lorieux | M. Carpentier | D. Revallier | D. Revallier |
| D. Revallier | L. Rodriguez | L. Rodriguez | J.F. Imbernon |
| *J.P. Rives | *J.P. Rives | *J.P. Rives 1T | *J.P. Rives |
| L. Rodriguez | J.L. Joinel | M. Carpentier | J.L. Joinel |
| P. Lacans | E. Buchet | J.L. Joinel | L. Rodriguez |
| Cardiff Arms Park | Parc des Princes | Murrayfield | Parc des Princes |
| LOST 12-22 | LOST 15-27 | LOST 7-16 | WON 22-9 |
| WALES: 6PG 1T | FR.: 1G 2PG 1DG | SCOT.: 3PG 1DG 1T | FR.: 1G 4PG 1T |
| FR.: 1G 2PG | ENG.: 2G 5PG | FR.: 1PG 1T | IRE.: 3PG |
| 6 Feb. 1982 | 20 Feb. 1982 | 6 Mar. 1982 | 20 Mar. 1982 |
| | | | ¹Rep. by P. Perrier |

France scored more tries than any of their opponents in the Five Nations Championship, yet finished bracketed with Wales in the wooden spoon place. At the start of the season, the French were confident that their young, new backs, mostly from the Basque region, would set the side on the road to a second successive Grand Slam. But the French pack lacked the strength to beat the Welsh in the tight at Cardiff, and their weakness in presenting Wales with numerous penalty kicks at goal enabled the Welsh to win by a convincing (though flattering) margin.

Many changes were made as the season progressed, and it was not until the match against the Champions (Ireland) that the pack resembled the successful Grand Slam combination of 1982. Then, with an impressive display of running, handling and forward power, the French returned to winning ways. The threequarters produced some spectacular touches and the try by Blanco, following a chip ahead and sprint to the Irish line, was the culmination of a clever attack initiated by Lescarboura.

## 1982

| v. ROMANIA | 1st v. ARGENTINA | 2nd v. ARGENTINA |
|---|---|---|
| S. Blanco | S. Blanco 1t,1pg | S. Blanco 1t |
| M. Fabre 1t | P. Sella 2t | P. Sella |
| †P. Sella | P. Mesny | P. Mesny |
| †P. Chadebach | P. Chadebach | P. Chadebach |
| †P. Esteve | P. Esteve 1t | P. Esteve[1] |
| †D. Camberabero 1c,1dg | D. Camberabero 1dg,1pg | D. Camberabero 1pg,1c |
| P. Berbizier | *G. Martinez | *G. Martinez |
| P. Dospital | P. Dospital | P. Dospital |
| P. Dintrans | P. Dintrans | P. Dintrans |
| R. Paparemborde | R. Paparemborde | R. Paparemborde |
| D. Revallier | D. Revallier | P. Salas |
| †J. Condom | †J.C. Orso | J.C. Orso |
| *J.P. Rives | †T. Janeczek | T. Janeczek |
| J.L. Joinel[1] | D. Erbani | D. Erbani |
| L. Rodriguez | E. Buchet | E. Buchet |
| Bucharest | Toulouse | Parc des Princes |
| LOST 9-13 | WON 25-12 | WON 13-6 |
| Rom.: 2pg 1dg 1t | Fr.: 2pg 1dg 4t | Fr.: 1g 1pg 1t |
| Fr.: 1g 1dg | Arg.: 1g 2pg | Arg.: 2dg |
| 31 Oct. 1982 | 14 Nov. 1982 | 20 Nov. 1982 |
| [1]Rep. by E. Buchet | | [1]Rep. by †J. Begu 1t |

In Bucharest, France fielded five new caps for the match with Romania. An interesting selection was that of Didier Cambérabéro, son of the former French fly-half, Guy Cambérabéro. In the first half in Bucharest, Camérabéro junior demonstrated that he had inherited his father's kicking genius, a drop-goal and conversion of a try by Fabre giving France a slender lead. But a failure by the fly-half (and Blanco) to take penalty chances cost France dearly, and the Romanians (who kicked three goals) steamed to a 13-9 win – their fourth in Bucharest against France in five matches since 1974.

Good wins achieved in the two Tests against Argentina, prompted Fouroux to conclude that he had a promising side to contest the forthcoming Championship. The selectors stood by the side beaten in Bucharest, and their patience with the threequarters paid dividends in each of the Tests with Argentina. Sella, transferred from centre to wing, scored twice in the first Test and made a telling break for Bégu, a replacement wing, to score a memorable try in the second.

## 1982-83

| v. ENGLAND | v. SCOTLAND | v. IRELAND | v. WALES |
|---|---|---|---|
| S. Blanco 2c | S. Blanco 3pg,1c | S. Blanco 2pg,1c,1t | S. Blanco 3pg |
| P. Sella 1t | P. Sella | P. Sella | P. Sella |
| C. Belascain | D. Codorniou | C. Belascain | D. Codorniou |
| D. Codorniou | C. Belascain | D. Codorniou | C. Belascain |
| P. Esteve 1t | P. Esteve 2t | P. Esteve 1t | P. Esteve 1t |
| D. Camberabero 1pg | †C. Delage | C. Delage | D. Camberabero 1dg |
| G. Martinez | P. Berbizier | P. Berbizier | G. Martinez |
| P. Dospital | P. Dospital | P. Dospital | P. Dospital |
| P. Dintrans | †J.L. Dupont | †B. Herrero | P. Dintrans |
| R. Paparemborde 1t | R. Paparemborde | R. Paparemborde | R. Paparemborde |
| J.C. Orso | J. Condom | J. Condom | J. Condom |
| J. Condom | J.C. Orso | J.F. Imbernon | J.F. Imbernon |
| *J.P. Rives | *J.P. Rives | *J.P. Rives | *J.P. Rives |
| J.L. Joinel | J.L. Joinel | J.L. Joinel | J.L. Joinel |
| L. Rodriguez | L. Rodriguez[1] | D. Erbani | D. Erbani |
| Twickenham | Parc des Princes | Lansdowne Road | Parc des Princes |
| WON 19-15 | WON 19-15 | LOST 16-22 | WON 16-9 |
| Eng.: 4pg 1dg | Fr.: 1g 3pg 1t | Ire.: 1g 4pg 1t | Fr.: 3pg 1dg 1t |
| Fr.: 2g 1pg 1t | Scot.: 1g 1pg 2dg | Fr.: 1g 2pg 1t | Wales: 1g 1dg |
| 15 Jan. 1983 | 5 Feb. 1983 | 19 Feb. 1983 | 19 Mar. 1983 |
| | [1]Rep. by D. Erbani | | |

France were the best side in the 1983 Five Nations competition, though their defeat in a ding-dong battle at Lansdowne Road forced them to share the title with the Irish. There was a welcome consistency in the selection of the side, and a brilliant back division was allowed to settle and develop. The centres passed the ball with a precision and speed unmatched by any of the British backs, and the pace of two very fast wings and Blanco at full-back was often sufficient to produce tries.

Patrick Estève scored five tries in the Championship, a new French record, and became the first Frenchman to score a try in each match of a Championship campaign. (Only Carston Catcheside of England in 1924 and A.C. Wallace of Scotland in 1925 had previously performed such a feat.)

Robert Paparemborde played his last international for France in the hard-earned victory against Wales which brought the Championship. Paparemborde had played 55 times, including 42 games against IB nations, to become France's most-capped prop. But, more remarkably, he had also scored 8 tries in his internationals, equalling the record for a French front-row forward which had been set by Domenech in the 1960s.

## 1983

| 1st v. AUSTRALIA | 2nd v. AUSTRALIA | v. ROMANIA |
|---|---|---|
| †J.B. Lafond 1DG[1] | S. Gabernet 1PG | S. Gabernet |
| | | |
| †P. Lagisquet | P. Lagisquet | P. Lagisquet 1T |
| P. Sella | P. Sella | P. Sella |
| D. Codorniou | D. Codorniou | D. Codorniou |
| P. Esteve | P. Esteve 1T | P. Esteve 1T |
| | | |
| J.P. Lescarboura 3PG,1DG | J.P. Lescarboura 1C,2PG | J.P. Lescarboura 1DG,1T,2C,1PG |
| J. Gallion | J. Gallion | J. Gallion 1T |
| | | |
| M. Cremaschi | M. Cremaschi[1] | M. Cremaschi |
| P. Dintrans | P. Dintrans | P. Dintrans |
| †J.P. Garuet | J.P. Garuet | J.P. Garuet |
| J. Condom | J. Condom | J. Condom |
| J.C. Orso | A. Lorieux | A. Lorieux |
| *J.P. Rives | *J.P. Rives | *J.P. Rives |
| J.L. Joinel | J.L. Joinel | J.L. Joinel |
| D. Erbani | D. Erbani | D. Erbani |
| | | |
| Clermont Ferrand | Parc des Princes | Toulouse |
| DRAWN 15-15 | WON 15-6 | WON 26-15 |
| | | |
| FR.: 3PG 2DG | FR.: 1G 3PG | FR.: 2G 2T 1DG 1PG |
| AUS. 1G 2DG 1PG | AUS.: 1PG 1DG | ROM.: 2G 1PG |
| | | |
| 13 Nov. 1983 | 19 Nov. 1983 | 4 Dec. 1983 |
| | [1]Rep. by B. Viviès, then by L. Pardo | [1]Rep. by †P.E. Detrez |

There was a two-Test series with the touring Australians to open France's international season in 1983-84. The Australians possessed a well-organised defence, but there was a surprising lack of penetration among their backs and only one try was scored by the Wallabies in the two Tests. (France also managed just one try.) After a dull draw in Clermont Ferrand in the first Test, France won the series at Paris a week later, thanks to a powerful display by their forwards. The side which had beaten Australia was unchanged for the match with Romania, and ran in four tries in a convincing performance to win.

A rare event took place in the opening Test with the Australians, when J.B. Lafond, the full-back, was injured. He was replaced by Viviès early in the second half, and when Viviès had to retire just before no-side, there was the unusual sight of a replacement replacing a replacement, Pardo substituting.

## 1983-84

| v. IRELAND | v. WALES | v. ENGLAND | v. SCOTLAND |
|---|---|---|---|
| S. Blanco | S. Blanco | S. Blanco | S. Blanco |
| | | | |
| P. Lagisquet | P. Lagisquet | J. Begu 1T | J. Begu |
| P. Sella 1T | P. Sella 1T | P. Sella 1T | P. Sella |
| D. Codorniou | D. Codorniou | D. Codorniou 1T | D. Codorniou |
| P. Esteve | P. Esteve | P. Esteve 1T | P. Esteve |
| | | | |
| J.P. Lescarboura 1DG,4PG,1C | J.P. Lescarboura 4PG,1DG,1C | J.P. Lescarboura 1PG,3C,1DG | J.P. Lescarboura 1PG,1C,1DG |
| J. Gallion 1T | J. Gallion | J. Gallion 1T | J. Gallion 1T[1] |
| | | | |
| M. Cremaschi | M. Cremaschi | P. Dospital | P. Dospital |
| P. Dintrans | P. Dintrans | P. Dintrans | P. Dintrans |
| J.P. Garuet | D. Dubroca | D. Dubroca | D. Dubroca |
| A. Lorieux | A. Lorieux | A. Lorieux[1] | F. Haget |
| J. Condom | J. Condom | J. Condom | J. Condom |
| *J.P. Rives | *J.P. Rives | *J.P. Rives | *J.P. Rives |
| J.L. Joinel | J.L. Joinel | J.L. Joinel | J.C. Orso |
| L. Rodriguez | D. Erbani | D. Erbani | J.L Joinel |
| | | | |
| Parc des Princes | Cardiff Arms Park | Parc des Princes | Murrayfield |
| WON 25-12 | WON 21-16 | WON 32-18 | LOST 12-21 |
| | | | |
| FR.: 1G 4PG 1DG 1T | WALES: 1G 2PG 1T | FR.: 3G 1PG 1DG 2T | SCOT. 1G 5PG |
| IRE.: 4PG | FR.: 1G 4PG 1DG | ENG.: 2G 2PG | FR.: 1G 1PG 1DG |
| | | | |
| 21 Jan. 1984 | 18 Feb. 1984 | 3 Mar. 1984 | 17 Mar. 1984 |
| | | [1]Rep. by J.C. Orso | [1]Rep. by P. Berbizier |

For the second consecutive year, France were the best side in the Five Nations Championship. They crushed Ireland in Paris, where Garuet became the first French player to be sent off in an international, and each threequarter scored in the splendid win against England. But at Murrayfield, after an outstanding first half, French impetuosity and indiscipline cost them the Championship. Like the French, the Scots were seeking the Grand Slam. But in a tense match, France's inability to control their reactions – both to playing situations and decisions by the referee – presented the home side with numerous kicks at goal. Thus Rives, in his final international, had to be content to see his side finish as runners-up.

The total of 90 points marked a French record for the Championship, while Lescarboura created two new Five-Nations records: becoming the first player to drop a goal in each of his country's games, and scoring 54 points to pass the previous highest total of Ireland's Ollie Campbell.

## 1984

| 1st v. NZ | 2nd v. NZ |
|---|---|
| S. BLANCO 1T | S. BLANCO |
| | |
| P. LAGISQUET | P. LAGISQUET |
| D. CODORNIOU | D. CODORNIOU[1] |
| P. SELLA | P. SELLA |
| P. ESTEVE | P. ESTEVE |
| | |
| J.P. LESCARBOURA | J.P. LESCARBOURA |
| 1DG,1C | 2PG,2T |
| P. BERBIZIER | P. BERBIZIER |
| | |
| P. DOSPITAL | P. DOSPITAL |
| *P. DINTRANS | *P. DINTRANS |
| J.P. GARUET | J.P. GARUET |
| F. HAGET | F. HAGET |
| J. CONDOM | J. CONDOM |
| L. RODRIGUEZ | L. RODRIGUEZ |
| J.C. ORSO | J.L. JOINEL |
| J.L. JOINEL | †J. GRATTON |
| | |
| Christchurch | Auckland |
| LOST 9-10 | LOST 18-31 |
| | |
| NZ: 2PG 1T | NZ: 2G 5PG 1T |
| FR.: 1G 1DG | FR.: 2PG 3T |
| | |
| 16 Jun. 1984 | 23 Jun. 1984 |

[1]Rep. by †E.
Bonneval 1T

Managed by Yves Noé and coached by Jacques Fouroux, France sent a party of 27 players to New Zealand in the summer of 1984. The side won each of its six provincial matches, attracting big New Zealand crowds with its daring, exciting brand of open rugby. Rather unluckily, the French failed to win either of the two Tests.

The French pack played steadily against a strong New Zealand combination in the first Test, but the tight marking constrained the French backs and it was not until the final quarter of the match that the threequarters managed to break their shackles and transfer the ball with fluency. But despite several drop-shots at goal in the dying minutes by Lescarboura, the French were unable to snatch victory. Lescarboura's failure to land goal points cost France dearly in the Auckland Test. Both sides scored three tries though New Zealand landed five penalties to Lescarboura's two.

## 1984-85

| v. ROMANIA | v. ENGLAND | v. SCOTLAND | v. IRELAND | v. WALES |
|---|---|---|---|---|
| S. BLANCO | S. BLANCO | S. BLANCO 2T | S. BLANCO | S. BLANCO |
| | | | | |
| P. ESTEVE | P. ESTEVE | L. PARDO | L. PARDO | E. BONNEVAL |
| P. SELLA 1T | P. SELLA | P. SELLA | P. SELLA | P. SELLA |
| D. CODORNIOU | D. CODORNIOU | D. CODORNIOU | D. CODORNIOU 1T | D. CODORNIOU |
| †B. LAVIGNE | B. LAVIGNE | P. ESTEVE | P. ESTEVE 1T | P. ESTEVE 1T |
| | | | | |
| J.P. LESCARBOURA | J.P. LESCARBOURA | J.P. LESCARBOURA | J.P. LESCARBOURA | J.P. LESCARBOURA |
| 1T,2PG,2C | 3DG | 1PG | 2C,1PG | 2PG |
| J. GALLION | J. GALLION | J. GALLION | J. GALLION | J. GALLION 1T |
| | | | | |
| P. DOSPITAL | P. DOSPITAL | P. DOSPITAL | P. DOSPITAL | P. DOSPITAL |
| *P. DINTRANS | *P. DINTRANS | *P. DINTRANS | *P. DINTRANS | *P. DINTRANS |
| J.P. GARUET | J.P. GARUET | J.P. GARUET | J.P. GARUET | J.P. GARUET |
| F. HAGET | F. HAGET | F. HAGET | F. HAGET[1] | J.C ORSO |
| J. CONDOM | J. CONDOM | J. CONDOM | J. CONDOM | J. CONDOM |
| J. GRATTON | J. GRATTON | J. GRATTON | J. GRATTON | J. GRATTON |
| D. ERBANI | D. ERBANI | J.L. JOINEL | J.L. JOINEL | J.L. JOINEL |
| L. RODRIGUEZ | L. RODRIGUEZ | L. RODRIGUEZ | L. RODRIGUEZ | L. RODRIGUEZ[1] |
| | | | | |
| Bucharest | Twickenham | Parc des Princes | Lansdowne Road | Parc des Princes |
| WON 18-3 | DRAWN 9-9 | WON 11-3 | DRAWN 15-15 | WON 14-3 |
| | | | | |
| ROM.: 1PG | ENG.: 1DG 2PG | FR.: 1PG 2T | IRE.: 5PG | FR.: 2PG 2T |
| FR.: 2G 2PG | FR.: 3DG | SCOT.: 1PG | FR.: 2G 1PG | WALES: 1PG |
| | | | | |
| 11 Nov. 1984 | 2 Feb. 1985 | 16 Feb. 1985 | 2 Mar. 1985 | 30 Mar. 1985 |
| | | | [1]Rep. by J.C. Orso | [1]Rep. by D. Erbani |

France undertook a short tour of the Far East in the early autumn of 1984, winning their provincial matches and two Tests (for which full caps were not awarded) by huge margins. Fouroux having successfully coached the side in three overseas tours, returned to France to succeed Guy Basquet as chairman of the selectors.

In the Championship his men were outstanding, though after recording their biggest ever away win over Romania, it was disappointing to draw at Twickenham against England. All of France's points were scored by Lescarboura, who dropped three goals to equal the world record for an international match, but the memory of Estève crossing the goal-line only to see the ball knocked out of his grasp while in the act of scoring will haunt French followers (and Estève) for many years.

A draw in Dublin (where France scored two tries and Ireland relied on penalty goals) let Ireland in to take the Championship.

## 1985

| 1st v. ARGENTINA | 2nd v. ARGENTINA |
|---|---|
| S. BLANCO 1T | S. BLANCO 1T |
| J.B. LAFOND 1T | J.B. LAFOND |
| P. SELLA | D. CODORNIOU 1T |
| D. CODORNIOU | P. SELLA |
| E. BONNEVAL | L. PARDO |
| J.P. LESCARBOURA 2PG,1C | J. P. LESCARBOURA 2C,1PG |
| P. BERBIZIER | P. BERBIZIER 1T |
| P. DOSPITAL | †H. CHABOWSKI |
| *P. DINTRANS | *P. DINTRANS |
| J.P. GARUET | D. DUBROCA |
| A. LORIEUX | †T. PICARD[1] |
| J. CONDOM | J. CONDOM |
| J. GRATTON | J. GRATTON |
| J.L. JOINEL | D. ERBANI 1T |
| †E. CHAMP | E. CHAMP |
| Buenos Aires | Buenos Aires |
| LOST 16-24 | WON 23-15 |
| ARG.: 2G 1DG 3PG | ARG.: 1G 3PG |
| FR.: 1G 2PG 1T | FR.: 2G 1PG 2T |
| 22 Jun. 1985 | 29 Jun. 1985 |
|  | [1]Rep. by A. Lorieux |

The sixth French tour of Argentina took place in the summer of 1985. With Jacques Fouroux in charge as coach, the tourists played seven matches, winning six but losing the first international against the Agentinians. It was the first occasion that a French side had been beaten in Argentina, though the South Americans had drawn with France in the second international of the 1977 series.

Following the first Test defeat, Fouroux rearranged his front five for the second Test. Dubroca, who had been unable to break the Dospital, Dintrans, Garuet combination for eight international matches, regained his place at tight-head prop, and played solidly in a French victory in which four tries, three of them by the backs, were registered. Fouroux was happier to see his men play with increased commitment and splendid style, though their victory did not become certain until the closing moment of the match.

## 1985-86

| v. SCOTLAND | v. IRELAND | v. WALES | v. ENGLAND | v. ROMANIA |
|---|---|---|---|---|
| S. BLANCO | S. BLANCO 1PG | S. BLANCO 1T | S. BLANCO 1T | S. BLANCO |
| J.B. LAFOND | J.B. LAFOND 1DG | J.B. LAFOND 2T | J.B. LAFOND | J.B. LAFOND[1] |
| P. SELLA 1T | P. SELLA 1T | P. SELLA 1T | P. SELLA 1T | P. SELLA 1T |
| P. CHADEBACH | P. CHADEBACH | †D. CHARVET | D. CHARVET | D. CHARVET 1T |
| P. ESTEVE | P. ESTEVE | E. BONNEVAL | E. BONNEVAL | E. BONNEVAL 1T |
| G. LAPORTE 2PG,1DG | G. LAPORTE 1C,3PG | G. LAPORTE 2C,1DG | G. LAPORTE 3PG,2C,1T | G. LAPORTE 1PG,1C |
| P. BERBIZIER 1T | P. BERBIZIER 1T | P. BERBIZIER | P. BERBIZIER | P. BERBIZIER |
| †P. MAROCCO | P. MAROCCO 1T | P. MAROCCO | P. MAROCCO | P. MAROCCO |
| *D. DUBROCA | *D. DUBROCA | *D. DUBROCA | *D. DUBROCA | *D. DUBROCA |
| J.P. GARUET | J.P. GARUET | J.P. GARUET | J.P. GARUET | J.P. GARUET |
| F. HAGET | F. HAGET | F. HAGET | F. HAGET | F. HAGET |
| J. CONDOM | J. CONDOM | J. CONDOM | J. CONDOM | J. CONDOM |
| J. GRATTON | E. CHAMP | E. CHAMP | E. CHAMP | E. CHAMP[2] |
| J.L. JOINEL | J.L. JOINEL | J.L. JOINEL | J.L. JOINEL | J.L. JOINEL |
| D. ERBANI | D. ERBANI | E. CHAMP | D. ERBANI | D. ERBANI 1T |
| Murrayfield | Parc des Princes | Cardiff Arms Park | Parc des Princes | Lille |
| LOST 17-18 | WON 29-9 | WON 23-15 | WON 29-10 | WON 25-13 |
| SCOT.: 6PG | FR.: 1G 4PG 1DG 2T | WALES: 5PG | FR.: 2G‡ 3PG 2T | FR.: 1G 1PG 4T |
| FR.: 2PG 1DG 2T | IRE.: 3PG | FR.: 2G 1DG 2T | ENG.: 2PG 1T | ROM.: 1G 1PG 1T |
| 18 Jan. 1986 | 1 Feb. 1986 | 1 Mar. 1986 | 15 Mar. 1986 | 12 Apr. 1986 |
|  |  |  | ‡Includes a penalty try | [1]Rep. by P. Lagisquet 1T [2]Rep. by T. Picard |

Dubroca successfully made the unusual switch from prop to hooker, and captained France in the absence (through injury) of Dintrans. But, as in 1984, one or two indiscretions by their players and irresponsible reactions to refereeing decisions cost France the match at Murrayfield. They were the more entertaining side, scored a spectacularly unorthodox try in the first minute of the match, and proceeded to win their three other Championship games with ease and in fine style. Yet the six penalties conceded at Murrayfield forced the French to share the Championship title with Scotland.

Sella, whose threequarter play was a shining example to modern backs and a pleasure to spectators, became the second Frenchman (and only the fourth man in the history of the tournament) to score tries in each Championship match. In addition, Blanco scored his tenth international try as a full-back (equalling the world record of Andy Irvine), while Laporte secured 17 points in the victory over England, matching the French record for points scored against an IB nation.

## 1986

| 1st v. ARGENTINA | 2nd v. ARGENTINA | v. AUSTRALIA | v. NZ |
|---|---|---|---|
| †J. BIANCHI | S. BLANCO | S. BLANCO 2T | S. BLANCO |
| | | | |
| P. LAGISQUET | P. LAGISQUET | P. LAGISQUET | P. LAGISQUET |
| P. SELLA | P. SELLA 1T | P. SELLA 1T | P. SELLA |
| D. CHARVET | †M. ANDRIEU | D. CHARVET | D. CHARVET |
| E. BONNEVAL 1T | E. BONNEVAL | E. BONNEVAL | M. ANDRIEU |
| | | | |
| G. LAPORTE 3PG | J.P. LESCARBOURA 2PG 2C 1T | J.P. LESCARBOURA[1] | J.P. LESCARBOURA 3DG |
| *P. BERBIZIER | J. GALLION | P. BERBIZIER | P. BERBIZIER |
| | | | |
| P. MAROCCO | P. MAROCCO | P. MAROCCO[2] | P.E. DETREZ |
| B. HERRERO | *D. DUBROCA 1T | *D. DUBROCA 1T | *D. DUBROCA |
| J.P. GARUET[1] | P.E. DETREZ | †C. PORTOLAN | J.P. GARUET |
| F. HAGET | T. PICARD | F. HAGET | F. HAGET |
| J. CONDOM | J. CONDOM | †P. SERRIERE | J. CONDOM |
| E. CHAMP | E. CHAMP | E. CHAMP | E. CHAMP |
| L. RODRIGUEZ | J.L. JOINEL | J.L. JOINEL | D. ERBANI |
| J.L. JOINEL | D. ERBANI | L. RODRIGUEZ | J. GRATTON |
| | | | |
| Buenos Aires | Buenos Aires | Sydney | Christchurch |
| LOST 13-15 | WON 22-9 | LOST 14-27 | LOST 9-18 |
| | | | |
| ARG.: 1G 3PG | ARG.: 3PG | AUST.: 1G 6PG 1DG | NZ: 1G 1PG 3DG |
| FR.: 3PG 1T | FR.: 2G 2PG 1T | FR.: 1G 2T | FR.: 3DG |
| | | | |
| 31 May 1986 | 7 Jun. 1986 | 21 Jun. 1986 | 28 Jun. 1986 |
| [1]Rep. by P.E. Detrez | | [1]Rep. by G. Laporte 1c | |
| | | [2]Rep. by P.E. Detrez | |

France's preparations for the inaugural World Cup began with a punishing World tour of South America, Australia and New Zealand during the summer of 1986. Four internationals were played on the tour, the French losing three but squaring the series with Argentina in an impressive second Test win in Buenos Aires. Though beaten in the Test against the Australians, the French did score three tries (including two by Blanco from full-back) to Australia's one.

Against an extremely inexperienced New Zealand side the French were well beaten and had only Lescarboura's three dropped goals to remember from a poor match. Lescarboura thus became the first French player to drop three goals in two international matches.

## 1986

| v. ROMANIA | 1st v. NZ | 2nd v. NZ |
|---|---|---|
| S. BLANCO 1T | S. BLANCO | S. BLANCO |
| | | |
| †P. BEROT 1T 2PG 1C | P. BEROT 1PG | P. BEROT 2PG 1C |
| P. SELLA | P. SELLA 1T | P. SELLA |
| E. BONNEVAL | E. BONNEVAL | D. CHARVET 1T |
| M. ANDRIEU 1T | M. ANDRIEU | E. BONNEVAL |
| | | |
| J.P. LESCARBOURA | J.P. LESCARBOURA[1] | F. MESNEL |
| P. BERBIZIER | P. BERBIZIER | P. BERBIZIER |
| | | |
| H. CHABOWSKI | H. CHABOWSKI | †P. ONDARTS |
| *D. DUBROCA | *D. DUBROCA | *D. DUBROCA |
| J.P. GARUET | J.P. GARUET | J.P. GARUET |
| A. LORIEUX | A. LORIEUX | A. LORIEUX 1T |
| J. CONDOM | J. CONDOM | J. CONDOM |
| E. CHAMP | E. CHAMP | E. CHAMP |
| †A. CARMINATI | A. CARMINATI[2] | L. RODRIGUEZ |
| L. RODRIGUEZ | L. RODRIGUEZ | D. ERBANI |
| | | |
| Bucharest | Toulouse | Nantes |
| WON 20-3 | LOST 7-19 | WON 16-3 |
| | | |
| ROM.: 1PG | FR.: 1PG 1T | FR.: 1G 2PG 1T |
| FR.: 1G 2PG 2T | NZ: 3PG 2DG 1T | NZ: 1PG |
| | | |
| 25 Oct. 1986 | 8 Nov. 1986 | 15 Nov. 1986 |
| | [1]Rep. by †F. Mesnel | |
| | [2]Rep. by D. Erbani | |

France completed 1986 with three autumn Tests, one against Romania and two with the All Blacks. During the calendar year, the French had thus contested the remarkable number of twelve major internationals, of which seven were won.

The match in Bucharest was a success for new cap Berot. The Agen full-back, capped as a wing, scored twelve points including a debut try, while Blanco, the world's leading full-back as a try-scorer, stretched his record to 13 tries. (He has also scored four tries as a wing.)

Following the resounding New Zealand win at Toulouse, there was much criticism of French coach Jacques Fouroux. But the wily Fouroux responded magnificently to his critics by inspiring his side to a grand forward effort and deserved victory in Nantes. The French win by 13 points represented a new record winning points margin for France against New Zealand.

## 1986-87

| v. WALES | v. ENGLAND | v. SCOTLAND | v. IRELAND |
|---|---|---|---|
| S. Blanco | S. Blanco 1dg | S. Blanco | S. Blanco[1] |
| | | | |
| P. Berot 2pg 1c | P. Berot 1pg 1c | P. Berot 3pg 1t | P. Berot 3pg 1c |
| P. Sella | P. Sella 1t | P. Sella | P. Sella |
| D. Charvet | D. Charvet | D. Charvet | D. Charvet |
| E. Bonneval 1t | E. Bonneval 1t | E. Bonneval 3t | E. Bonneval |
| | | | |
| F. Mesnel 1t | F. Mesnel 1dg | F. Mesnel 1dg | F. Mesnel |
| P. Berbizier | P. Berbizier | P. Berbizier | P. Berbizier |
| | | | |
| P. Ondarts | P. Ondarts | P. Ondarts | P. Ondarts |
| *D. Dubroca | *D. Dubroca | *D. Dubroca | *D. Dubroca |
| J.P. Garuet | J.P. Garuet | J.P. Garuet | J.P. Garuet |
| A. Lorieux | A. Lorieux | F. Haget | F. Haget |
| J. Condom | J. Condom | J. Condom | J. Condom |
| E. Champ | E. Champ | E. Champ | E. Champ 2t |
| L. Rodriguez | L. Rodriguez | L. Rodriguez | L. Rodriguez |
| D. Erbani | D. Erbani | D. Erbani | D. Erbani |
| | | | |
| Parc des Princes | Twickenham | Parc des Princes | Lansdowne Road |
| WON 16-9 | WON 19-15 | WON 28-22 | WON 19-13 |
| | | | |
| FR.: 1G 2PG 1T | FR.: 1G 1PG 2DG 1T | FR.: 3PG 1DG 4T | FR.: 1G 3PG 1T |
| WALES: 3PG | ENG.: 4PG 1DG | SCOT.: 1G 4PG 1T | IRE.: 1G 1PG 1T |
| | | | |
| 7 Feb. 1987 | 21 Feb. 1987 | 7 Mar. 1987 | 21 Mar. 1987 |

[1]Rep. by J.B. Lafond

France completed their World Cup preparations by winning the Five Nations Championship. Daniel Dubroca, a quiet yet extremely effective captain, steered the French to their Fourth Grand Slam and their eighth outright Championship title.

The pack was outstanding, and numerous attacking ploys were initiated by the athletic and dynamic back row of Champ, Rodriguez and Erbani. Berbizier marshalled the side efficiently from the base of the scrum and was the team's chief play-maker. The threequarters were carefully served by Mesnel too, while Blanco continued to counter-attack audaciously from full-back.

Bonneval's five tries equalled the French record total for a Championship season, and his hat-trick against Scotland was the first by a Frenchman in the Championship since 1963. In the forwards Haget, recalled through the injury to Lorieux, equalled the record career span of 13 seasons as a French player. He had first served France in Argentina in 1974 when Fouroux, now the successful coach, had been the scrum-half.

# FRENCH MATCH RECORDS

## Match Results 1906 to 1987

| Match | Date | Opponents | For | | | | | Against | | | | | Result | Venue | Captain |
|---|---|---|---|---|---|---|---|---|---|---|---|---|---|---|---|
| | | | T | C | D | P | Pts | T | C | D | P | Pts | | | |
| 1 | 1.1.1906 | New Zealand | 2 | 1 | — | — | 8 | 10 | 4 | — | — | 38 | Lost | Parc des Princes | H. Amand |
| 2 | 22.3.1906 | England | 2 | 1 | — | — | 8 | 9 | 4 | — | — | 35 | Lost | Parc des Princes | G. Lane |
| 3 | 5.1.1907 | England | 2 | 2 | — | 1 | 13 | 9 | 5 | 1 | — | 41 | Lost | Richmond | M. Communeau |
| 4 | 1.1.1908 | England | — | — | — | — | 0 | 5 | 2 | — | — | 19 | Lost | Colombes | M. Communeau |
| 5 | 2.3.1908 | Wales | — | — | 1 | — | 4 | 9 | 3 | — | 1 | 36 | Lost | Cardiff | M. Communeau |
| 6 | 30.1.1909 | England | — | — | — | — | 0 | 6 | 2 | — | — | 22 | Lost | Leicester | M. Communeau |
| 7 | 23.2.1909 | Wales | 1 | 1 | — | — | 5 | 11 | 7 | — | — | 47 | Lost | Colombes | M. Communeau |
| 8 | 20.3.1909 | Ireland | 2 | 1 | — | — | 8 | 4 | 2 | — | 1 | 19 | Lost | Dublin | M. Communeau |
| 9 | 1.1.1910 | Wales | 2 | 1 | — | 2 | 14 | 10 | 8 | — | 1 | 49 | Lost | Swansea | G. Lane |
| 10 | 22.1.1910 | Scotland | — | — | — | — | 0 | 7 | 3 | — | — | 27 | Lost | Edinburgh | M. Communeau |
| 11 | 3.3.1910 | England | 1 | — | — | — | 3 | 3 | 1 | — | — | 11 | Lost | Parc des Princes | M. Communeau |
| 12 | 27.3.1910 | Ireland | 1 | — | — | — | 3 | 2 | 1 | — | — | 8 | Lost | Parc des Princes | M. Communeau |
| 13 | 2.1.1911 | Scotland | 4 | 2 | — | — | 16 | 3 | 1 | 1 | — | 15 | Won | Colombes | M. Communeau |
| 14 | 28.1.1911 | England | — | — | — | — | 0 | 7 | 5 | — | 2 | 37 | Lost | Twickenham | M. Communeau |
| 15 | 28.2.1911 | Wales | — | — | — | — | 0 | 3 | 3 | — | — | 15 | Lost | Parc des Princes | R. Duval |
| 16 | 25.3.1911 | Ireland | 1 | 1 | — | — | 5 | 5 | 3 | 1 | — | 25 | Lost | Cork | M. Communeau |
| 17 | 1.1.1912 | Ireland | 2 | — | — | — | 6 | 3 | 1 | — | — | 11 | Lost | Parc des Princes | M. Communeau |
| 18 | 20.1.1912 | Scotland | 1 | — | — | — | 3 | 6 | 5 | — | 1 | 31 | Lost | Edinburgh | J. Dedet |
| 19 | 25.3.1912 | Wales | 2 | 1 | — | — | 8 | 4 | 1 | — | — | 14 | Lost | Newport | G. Lane |
| 20 | 8.4.1912 | England | 2 | 1 | — | — | 8 | 4 | — | 1 | 1 | 18 | Lost | Parc des Princes | G. Lane |
| 21 | 1.1.1913 | Scotland | 1 | — | — | — | 3 | 5 | 3 | — | — | 21 | Lost | Parc des Princes | G. Lane |
| 22 | 11.1.1913 | South Africa | 1 | 1 | — | — | 5 | 8 | 4 | — | 1 | 35 | Lost | Bordeaux | M. Leuvielle |
| 23 | 25.1.1913 | England | — | — | — | — | 0 | 6 | 1 | — | — | 20 | Lost | Twickenham | M. Leuvielle |
| 24 | 27.2.1913 | Wales | 2 | 1 | — | — | 8 | 3 | 1 | — | — | 11 | Lost | Parc des Princes | M. Leuvielle |
| 25 | 24.3.1913 | Ireland | — | — | — | — | 0 | 6 | 3 | — | — | 24 | Lost | Cork | M. Boyau |
| 26 | 1.1.1914 | Ireland | 2 | — | — | — | 6 | 2 | 1 | — | — | 8 | Lost | Parc des Princes | F. Forgues |
| 27 | 2.3.1914 | Wales | — | — | — | — | 0 | 7 | 5 | — | — | 31 | Lost | Swansea | M. Leuvielle |
| 28 | 13.4.1914 | England | 3 | 2 | — | — | 13 | 9 | 6 | — | — | 39 | Lost | Colombes | M. Leuvielle |
| 29 | 1.1.1920 | Scotland | — | — | — | — | 0 | 1 | 1 | — | — | 5 | Lost | Parc des Princes | P. Struxiano |
| 30 | 31.1.1920 | England | 1 | — | — | — | 3 | 1 | 1 | — | 1 | 8 | Lost | Twickenham | P. Struxiano |
| 31 | 17.2.1920 | Wales | 1 | 1 | — | — | 5 | 2 | — | — | — | 6 | Lost | Colombes | P. Struxiano |
| 32 | 3.4.1920 | Ireland | 5 | — | — | — | 15 | 1 | — | 1 | — | 7 | Won | Dublin | P. Struxiano |
| 33 | 10.10.1920 | United States | 4 | 1 | — | — | 14 | 1 | 1 | — | — | 5 | Won | Colombes | P. Struxiano |
| 34 | 22.1.1921 | Scotland | 1 | — | — | — | 3 | — | — | — | — | 0 | Won | Edinburgh | R. Crabos |
| 35 | 26.2.1921 | Wales | — | — | 1 | — | 4 | 2 | — | 2 | — | 12 | Lost | Cardiff | R. Crabos |
| 36 | 28.3.1921 | England | — | — | — | 2 | 6 | 2 | 2 | — | — | 10 | Lost | Colombes | R. Crabos |
| 37 | 9.4.1921 | Ireland | 4 | 4 | — | — | 20 | 2 | 2 | — | — | 10 | Won | Colombes | R. Crabos |
| 38 | 2.1.1922 | Scotland | 1 | — | — | — | 3 | 1 | — | — | — | 3 | Drawn | Colombes | R. Crabos |
| 39 | 25.2.1922 | England | 3 | 1 | — | — | 11 | 1 | 1 | — | 2 | 11 | Drawn | Twickenham | R. Crabos |
| 40 | 23.3.1922 | Wales | 1 | — | — | — | 3 | 3 | 1 | — | — | 11 | Lost | Colombes | R. Crabos |
| 41 | 8.4.1922 | Ireland | 1 | — | — | — | 3 | 1 | 1 | — | 1 | 8 | Lost | Dublin | R. Crabos |
| 42 | 20.1.1923 | Scotland | — | — | ★ | — | 3 | 4 | 2 | — | — | 16 | Lost | Edinburgh | R. Crabos |
| 43 | 24.2.1923 | Wales | 2 | 1 | — | — | 8 | 3 | 2 | — | — | 16 | Lost | Swansea | R. Lasserre |
| 44 | 2.4.1923 | England | — | — | — | 1 | 3 | 2 | 1 | 1 | — | 12 | Lost | Colombes | R. Lasserre |
| 45 | 14.4.1923 | Ireland | 4 | 1 | — | — | 14 | 2 | 1 | — | — | 8 | Won | Colombes | R. Crabos |
| 46 | 1.1.1924 | Scotland | 4 | — | — | — | 12 | 1 | — | 1 | 1 | 10 | Won | Stade Pershing | R. Crabos |
| 47 | 26.1.1924 | Ireland | — | — | — | — | 0 | 2 | — | — | — | 6 | Lost | Dublin | R. Crabos |
| 48 | 23.2.1924 | England | 1 | — | 1 | — | 7 | 5 | 2 | — | — | 19 | Lost | Twickenham | F. Borde |
| 49 | 27.3.1924 | Wales | 2 | — | — | — | 6 | 2 | 1 | — | 10 | Lost | Colombes | A. Cassayet |
| 50 | 4.5.1924 | Romania | 13 | 7 | — | 2 | 59 | — | — | — | 1 | 3 | Won | Colombes | R. Lasserre |
| 51 | 18.5.1924 | United States | 1 | — | — | — | 3 | 5 | 1 | — | — | 17 | Lost | Colombes | R. Lasserre |
| 52 | 1.1.1925 | Ireland | 1 | — | — | — | 3 | 2 | — | 1 | — | 9 | Lost | Colombes | F. Borde |
| 53 | 18.1.1925 | New Zealand | 2 | — | — | — | 6 | 8 | 3 | — | — | 30 | Lost | Toulouse | A. Cassayet |
| 54 | 24.1.1925 | Scotland | — | — | 1 | — | 4 | 7 | 2 | — | — | 25 | Lost | Edinburgh | A. Cassayet |
| 55 | 28.2.1925 | Wales | 1 | 1 | — | — | 5 | 3 | 1 | — | — | 11 | Lost | Cardiff | A. Cassayet |
| 56 | 13.4.1925 | England | 3 | 1 | — | — | 11 | 2 | 2 | — | 1 | 13 | Lost | Colombes | R. Piteu |

*in the drop-goal column denotes a goal from a mark

| Match | Date | Opponents | For T | C | D | P | Pts | Against T | C | D | P | Pts | Result | Venue | Captain |
|---|---|---|---|---|---|---|---|---|---|---|---|---|---|---|---|
| 57 | 2.1.1926 | Scotland | 1 | — | — | 1 | 6 | 5 | 1 | — | 1 | 20 | Lost | Colombes | A. Cassayet |
| 58 | 23.1.1926 | Ireland | — | — | — | — | 0 | 2 | 1 | — | 1 | 11 | Lost | Belfast | A. Cassayet |
| 59 | 27.2.1926 | England | — | — | — | — | 0 | 3 | 1 | — | — | 11 | Lost | Twickenham | A. Cassayet |
| 60 | 5.4.1926 | Wales | 1 | 1 | — | — | 5 | 1 | — | 1 | — | 7 | Lost | Colombes | A. Jauréguy |
| 61 | 26.12.1926 | Maoris | 1 | — | — | — | 3 | 4 | — | — | — | 12 | Lost | Colombes | A. Jauréguy |
| 62 | 1.1.1927 | Ireland | 1 | — | — | — | 3 | 1 | 1 | — | 1 | 8 | Lost | Colombes | A. Jauréguy |
| 63 | 22.1.1927 | Scotland | 2 | — | — | — | 6 | 4 | 4 | — | 1 | 23 | Lost | Edinburgh | Y. du Manoir |
| 64 | 26.2.1927 | Wales | 1 | — | 1 | — | 7 | 7 | 2 | — | — | 25 | Lost | Swansea | A. Cassayet |
| 65 | 2.4.1927 | England | 1 | — | — | — | 3 | — | — | — | — | 0 | Won | Colombes | A. Jauréguy |
| 66 | 17.4.1927 | Germany | 8 | 3 | — | — | 30 | 1 | 1 | — | — | 5 | Won | Colombes | A. Béhotéguy |
| 67 | 15.5.1927 | Germany | 4 | 2 | — | — | 16 | 4 | 1 | — | 1 | 17 | Lost | Frankfurt | A. Béhotéguy |
| 68 | 2.1.1928 | Scotland | 2 | — | — | — | 6 | 5 | — | — | — | 15 | Lost | Colombes | A. Jauréguy |
| 69 | 22.1.1928 | New South Wales | 2 | 1 | — | — | 8 | 3 | 1 | — | — | 11 | Lost | Colombes | A. Jauréguy |
| 70 | 28.1.1928 | Ireland | 2 | 1 | — | — | 8 | 4 | — | — | — | 12 | Lost | Belfast | A. Béhotéguy |
| 71 | 25.2.1928 | England | 2 | 1 | — | — | 8 | 4 | 3 | — | — | 18 | Lost | Twickenham | A. Jauréguy |
| 72 | 18.3.1928 | Germany | 4 | 1 | — | — | 14 | — | — | — | 1 | 3 | Won | Hanover | A. Jauréguy |
| 73 | 9.4.1928 | Wales | 2 | 1 | — | — | 8 | 1 | — | — | — | 3 | Won | Colombes | A. Jauréguy |
| 74 | 31.12.1928 | Ireland | — | — | — | — | 0 | 2 | — | — | — | 6 | Lost | Colombes | A. Jauréguy |
| 75 | 17.1.1929 | Scotland | 1 | — | — | — | 3 | 1 | — | — | 1 | 6 | Lost | Edinburgh | A. Jauréguy |
| 76 | 23.2.1929 | Wales | 1 | — | — | — | 3 | 2 | 1 | — | — | 8 | Lost | Cardiff | A. Béhotéguy |
| 77 | 1.4.1929 | England | 2 | — | — | — | 6 | 4 | 2 | — | — | 16 | Lost | Colombes | A. Jauréguy |
| 78 | 28.4.1929 | Germany | 6 | 3 | — | — | 24 | — | — | — | — | 0 | Won | Colombes | E. Ribère |
| 79 | 1.1.1930 | Scotland | 1 | — | 1 | — | 7 | 1 | — | — | — | 3 | Won | Colombes | E. Ribère |
| 80 | 25.1.1930 | Ireland | 1 | 1 | — | — | 5 | — | — | — | — | 0 | Won | Belfast | E. Ribère |
| 81 | 22.2.1930 | England | 1 | 1 | — | — | 5 | 3 | 1 | — | — | 11 | Lost | Twickenham | E. Ribère |
| 82 | 6.4.1930 | Germany | 8 | 2 | — | 1 | 31 | — | — | — | — | 0 | Won | Berlin | A. Bioussa |
| 83 | 21.4.1930 | Wales | — | — | — | — | 0 | 1 | — | 2 | — | 11 | Lost | Colombes | E. Ribère |
| 84 | 1.1.1931 | Ireland | 1 | — | — | — | 3 | — | — | — | — | 0 | Won | Colombes | E. Ribère |
| 85 | 24.1.1931 | Scotland | — | — | 1 | — | 4 | — | — | — | 2 | 6 | Lost | Edinburgh | E. Ribère |
| 86 | 28.2.1931 | Wales | 1 | — | — | — | 3 | 7 | 5 | 1 | — | 35 | Lost | Swansea | E. Ribère |
| 87 | 6.4.1931 | England | 2 | — | 2 | — | 14 | 3 | 2 | — | — | 13 | Won | Colombes | E. Ribère |
| 88 | 19.4.1931 | Germany | 8 | 5 | — | — | 34 | — | — | — | — | 0 | Won | Colombes | E. Ribère |
| 89 | 17.4.1932 | Germany | 5 | 1 | — | 1 | 20 | — | — | 1 | — | 4 | Won | Frankfurt | E. Ribère |
| 90 | 26.3.1933 | Germany | 9 | 4 | — | 1 | 38 | 3 | 2 | 1 | — | 17 | Won | Parc des Princes | E. Ribère |
| 91 | 25.3.1934 | Germany | 3 | 2 | — | — | 13 | 1 | 1 | 1 | — | 9 | Won | Hanover | L. Servole |
| 92 | 24.3.1935 | Germany | 3 | 3 | — | 1 | 18 | 1 | — | — | — | 3 | Won | Parc des Princes | L. Servole |
| 93 | 17.5.1936 | Germany | 5 | 2 | — | — | 19 | 3 | 1 | — | 1 | 14 | Won | Berlin | J. Desclaux |
| 94 | 1.11.1936 | Germany | 2 | — | — | — | 6 | 1 | — | — | — | 3 | Won | Hanover | J. Desclaux |
| 95 | 18.4.1937 | Germany | 7 | 3 | — | — | 27 | 1 | — | — | 1 | 6 | Won | Parc des Princes | J. Desclaux |
| 96 | 17.10.1937 | Italy | 9 | 6 | 1 | — | 43 | 1 | 1 | — | — | 5 | Won | Parc des Princes | J. Desclaux |
| 97 | 27.3.1938 | Germany | — | — | — | — | 0 | 1 | — | 1 | — | 3 | Lost | Frankfurt | J. Desclaux |
| 98 | 15.5.1938 | Romania | 3 | 1 | — | — | 11 | 1 | 1 | — | 1 | 8 | Won | Bucharest | J. Desclaux |
| 99 | 19.5.1938 | Germany | 2 | 1 | — | — | 8 | 1 | 1 | — | — | 5 | Won | Bucharest | J. Desclaux |
| 100 | 25.2.1940 | Great Britain | — | — | 1 | — | 3 | 8 | 6 | — | — | 36 | Lost | Parc des Princes | P. Thiers |
| 101 | 1.1.1945 | British Army | 5 | 3 | — | — | 21 | 3 | — | — | — | 9 | Won | Parc des Princes | P. Thiers |
| 102 | 28.4.1945 | British Empire | 1 | — | 1 | — | 6 | 7 | 3 | — | — | 27 | Lost | Richmond | P. Thiers |
| 103 | 22.12.1945 | Wales | — | — | — | — | 0 | 2 | 1 | — | — | 8 | Lost | Swansea | L. Junquas |
| 104 | 1.1.1946 | British Empire | 2 | — | 1 | — | 10 | — | — | — | — | 0 | Won | Parc des Princes | L. Junquas |
| 105 | 26.1.1946 | Ireland | — | — | 1 | — | 4 | — | — | — | 1 | 3 | Won | Dublin | L. Junquas |
| 106 | 10.3.1946 | Kiwis | 3 | — | — | — | 9 | 3 | 1 | — | 1 | 14 | Lost | Colombes | L. Junquas |
| 107 | 22.4.1946 | Wales | 2 | 1 | 1 | — | 12 | — | — | — | — | 0 | Won | Colombes | L. Junquas |
| 108 | 1.1.1947 | Scotland | 2 | 1 | — | — | 8 | 1 | — | — | — | 3 | Won | Colombes | L. Junquas |
| 109 | 25.1.1947 | Ireland | 4 | — | — | — | 12 | 1 | 1 | — | 1 | 8 | Won | Dublin | L. Junquas |
| 110 | 22.3.1947 | Wales | — | — | — | — | 0 | 1 | — | — | — | 3 | Lost | Colombes | L. Junquas |
| 111 | 19.4.1947 | England | — | — | 1 | — | 3 | 2 | — | — | — | 6 | Lost | Twickenham | L. Junquas |
| 112 | 1.1.1948 | Ireland | 2 | — | — | — | 6 | 3 | 2 | — | — | 13 | Lost | Colombes | G. Basquet |
| 113 | 11.1.1948 | Australia | 3 | 2 | — | — | 13 | — | — | — | 2 | 6 | Won | Colombes | G. Basquet |
| 114 | 24.1.1948 | Scotland | 1 | 1 | — | 1 | 8 | 1 | — | — | 2 | 9 | Lost | Edinburgh | G. Basquet |
| 115 | 21.2.1948 | Wales | 3 | 1 | — | — | 11 | 1 | — | — | — | 3 | Won | Swansea | G. Basquet |
| 116 | 29.3.1948 | England | 3 | 1 | 1 | — | 15 | — | — | — | — | 0 | Won | Colombes | G. Basquet |
| 117 | 15.1.1949 | Scotland | — | — | — | — | 0 | 2 | 1 | — | — | 8 | Lost | Colombes | G. Basquet |
| 118 | 29.1.1949 | Ireland | 2 | 2 | — | 2 | 16 | — | — | — | 3 | 9 | Won | Dublin | G. Basquet |
| 119 | 27.2.1949 | England | — | — | 1 | — | 3 | 1 | 1 | 1 | — | 8 | Lost | Twickenham | G. Basquet |
| 120 | 26.3.1949 | Wales | 1 | 1 | — | — | 5 | 1 | — | — | — | 3 | Won | Colombes | G. Basquet |
| 121 | 28.8.1949 | Argentina | 1 | 1 | — | — | 5 | — | — | — | — | 0 | Won | Buenos Aires | G. Basquet |
| 122 | 4.9.1949 | Argentina | 2 | — | 1 | 1 | 12 | 1 | — | — | — | 3 | Won | Buenos Aires | J. Prat |
| 123 | 14.1.1950 | Scotland | 1 | 1 | — | — | 5 | 2 | 1 | — | — | 8 | Lost | Edinburgh | G. Basquet |
| 124 | 28.1.1950 | Ireland | — | — | 1 | — | 3 | — | — | — | 1 | 3 | Drawn | Colombes | G. Basquet |
| 125 | 25.2.1950 | England | 2 | — | — | — | 6 | 1 | — | — | — | 3 | Won | Colombes | G. Basquet |
| 126 | 25.3.1950 | Wales | — | — | — | — | 0 | 4 | 3 | — | 1 | 21 | Lost | Cardiff | G. Basquet |

| Match | Date | Opponents | For T | C | D | P | Pts | Against T | C | D | P | Pts | Result | Venue | Captain |
|---|---|---|---|---|---|---|---|---|---|---|---|---|---|---|---|
| 127 | 13.1.1951 | Scotland | 2 | 1 | — | 2 | 14 | 2 | — | — | 2 | 12 | Won | Colombes | G. Basquet |
| 128 | 27.1.1951 | Ireland | 2 | 1 | — | — | 8 | 2 | — | — | 1 | 9 | Lost | Dublin | G. Basquet |
| 129 | 24.2.1951 | England | 2 | 1 | 1 | — | 11 | 1 | — | — | — | 3 | Won | Twickenham | G. Basquet |
| 130 | 7.4.1951 | Wales | 1 | 1 | — | 1 | 8 | 1 | — | — | — | 3 | Won | Colombes | G. Basquet |
| 131 | 12.1.1952 | Scotland | 2 | 2 | — | 1 | 13 | 1 | 1 | — | 2 | 11 | Won | Edinburgh | G. Basquet |
| 132 | 26.1.1952 | Ireland | 1 | 1 | — | 1 | 8 | 2 | 1 | — | 1 | 11 | Lost | Colombes | G. Basquet |
| 133 | 16.2.1952 | South Africa | — | — | 1 | — | 3 | 6 | 2 | — | 1 | 25 | Lost | Colombes | G. Basquet |
| 134 | 22.3.1952 | Wales | 1 | 1 | — | — | 5 | — | — | 1 | 2 | 9 | Lost | Swansea | G. Basquet |
| 135 | 5.4.1952 | England | 1 | — | — | — | 3 | — | — | — | 2 | 6 | Lost | Colombes | G. Basquet |
| 136 | 17.5.1952 | Italy | 3 | 1 | — | 2 | 17 | 1 | 1 | — | 1 | 8 | Won | Milan | G. Basquet |
| 137 | 10.1.1953 | Scotland | 1 | 1 | 1 | 1 | 11 | 1 | 1 | — | — | 5 | Won | Colombes | J. Prat |
| 138 | 24.1.1953 | Ireland | — | — | 1 | — | 3 | 4 | 2 | — | — | 16 | Lost | Belfast | J. Prat |
| 139 | 28.2.1953 | England | — | — | — | — | 0 | 3 | 1 | — | — | 11 | Lost | Twickenham | J. Prat |
| 140 | 28.3.1953 | Wales | — | — | 1 | 3 |  | 2 | — | — | — | 6 | Lost | Colombes | J. Prat |
| 141 | 26.4.1953 | Italy | 3 | 2 | 2 | 1 | 22 | 1 | 1 | — | 1 | 8 | Won | Lyon | J. Prat |
| 142 | 9.1.1954 | Scotland | 1 | — | — | — | 3 | — | — | — | — | 0 | Won | Edinburgh | J. Prat |
| 143 | 23.1.1954 | Ireland | 2 | 1 | — | — | 8 | — | — | — | — | 0 | Won | Colombes | J. Prat |
| 144 | 27.2.1954 | New Zealand | 1 | — | — | — | 3 | — | — | — | — | 0 | Won | Colombes | J. Prat |
| 145 | 27.3.1954 | Wales | 2 | 2 | — | 1 | 13 | 2 | 2 | — | 3 | 19 | Lost | Cardiff | J. Prat |
| 146 | 10.4.1954 | England | 2 | 1 | 1 | — | 11 | 1 | — | — | — | 3 | Won | Colombes | J. Prat |
| 147 | 24.4.1954 | Italy | 7 | 6 | — | 2 | 39 | 2 | — | — | 2 | 12 | Won | Rome | J. Prat |
| 148 | 29.8.1954 | Argentina | 3 | 2 | 1 | 2 | 22 | 1 | 1 | — | 1 | 8 | Won | Buenos Aires | R. Bienès |
| 149 | 12.9.1954 | Argentina | 5 | 3 | 2 | 1 | 30 | 1 | — | — | — | 3 | Won | Buenos Aires | R. Bienès |
| 150 | 8.1.1955 | Scotland | 4 | — | — | 1 | 15 | — | — | — | — | 0 | Won | Colombes | J. Prat |
| 151 | 22.1.1955 | Ireland | 1 | 1 | — | — | 5 | — | — | — | 1 | 3 | Won | Dublin | J. Prat |
| 152 | 26.2.1955 | England | 2 | 2 | — | — | 16 | 1 | — | — | 2 | 9 | Won | Twickenham | J. Prat |
| 153 | 26.3.1955 | Wales | 1 | 1 | 1 | 1 | 11 | 2 | 2 | — | 2 | 16 | Lost | Colombes | J. Prat |
| 154 | 10.4.1955 | Italy | 4 | 3 | — | 2 | 24 | — | — | — | — | 0 | Won | Grenoble | J. Prat |
| 155 | 14.1.1956 | Scotland | — | — | — | — | 0 | 2 | — | — | 2 | 12 | Lost | Edinburgh | G. Dufau |
| 156 | 28.1.1956 | Ireland | 2 | 1 | 2 | — | 14 | 2 | 1 | — | — | 8 | Won | Colombes | G. Dufau |
| 157 | 24.3.1956 | Wales | 1 | — | — | — | 3 | 1 | 1 | — | — | 5 | Lost | Cardiff | G. Dufau |
| 158 | 2.4.1956 | Italy | 3 | 2 | — | 1 | 16 | 1 | — | — | — | 3 | Won | Padua | G. Dufau |
| 159 | 14.4.1956 | England | 2 | 1 | — | 2 | 14 | 1 | — | — | 2 | 9 | Won | Colombes | M. Celaya |
| 160 | 16.12.1956 | Czechoslovakia | 6 | 2 | — | 2 | 28 | — | — | — | 1 | 3 | Won | Toulouse | M. Celaya |
| 161 | 12.1.1957 | Scotland | — | — | — | — | 0 | — | — | 1 | 1 | 6 | Lost | Colombes | M. Celaya |
| 162 | 26.1.1957 | Ireland | — | — | — | 2 | 6 | 2 | 1 | — | 1 | 11 | Lost | Dublin | M. Celaya |
| 163 | 23.2.1957 | England | 1 | 1 | — | — | 5 | 3 | — | — | — | 9 | Lost | Twickenham | M. Celaya |
| 164 | 23.3.1957 | Wales | 3 | 2 | — | — | 13 | 4 | 2 | — | 1 | 19 | Lost | Colombes | M. Celaya |
| 165 | 21.4.1957 | Italy | 8 | 7 | — | — | 38 | 1 | — | — | 1 | 6 | Won | Agen | G. Dufau |
| 166 | 19.5.1957 | Romania | 1 | — | 1 | 4 | 18 | — | — | 2 | 3 | 15 | Won | Bucharest | G. Dufau |
| 167 | 15.12.1957 | Romania | 8 | 6 | — | 1 | 39 | — | — | — | — | 0 | Won | Bordeaux | M. Celaya |
| 168 | 11.1.1958 | Scotland | 1 | — | — | 2 | 9 | 2 | 1 | — | 1 | 11 | Lost | Edinburgh | M. Celaya |
| 169 | 1.3.1958 | England | — | — | — | — | 0 | 3 | 1 | — | 1 | 14 | Lost | Colombes | M. Celaya |
| 170 | 9.3.1958 | Australia | 3 | 2 | 2 | — | 19 | — | — | — | — | 0 | Won | Colombes | M. Celaya |
| 171 | 29.3.1958 | Wales | 2 | 2 | 2 | — | 16 | 1 | — | — | 1 | 6 | Won | Cardiff | M. Celaya |
| 172 | 7.4.1958 | Italy | 2 | 1 | — | 1 | 11 | — | — | — | 1 | 3 | Won | Naples | M. Celaya |
| 173 | 19.4.1958 | Ireland | 1 | 1 | 1 | 1 | 11 | — | — | — | 2 | 6 | Won | Colombes | M. Prat |
| 174 | 26.7.1958 | South Africa | — | — | 1 | — | 3 | 1 | — | — | — | 3 | Drawn | Cape Town | L. Mias |
| 175 | 16.8.1958 | South Africa | — | — | 2 | 1 | 9 | 1 | 1 | — | — | 5 | Won | Johannesburg | L. Mias |
| 176 | 10.1.1959 | Scotland | 1 | — | 2 | — | 9 | — | — | — | — | 0 | Won | Colombes | L. Mias |
| 177 | 28.2.1959 | England | — | — | 1 | 3 |  | — | — | — | 1 | 3 | Drawn | Twickenham | J. Barthe |
| 178 | 29.3.1959 | Italy | 5 | 2 | — | 1 | 22 | — | — | — | — | 0 | Won | Nantes | L. Mias |
| 179 | 4.4.1959 | Wales | 2 | 1 | — | 1 | 11 | — | — | — | 1 | 3 | Won | Colombes | L. Mias |
| 180 | 18.4.1959 | Ireland | 1 | 1 | — | — | 5 | 1 | — | 1 | 1 | 9 | Lost | Dublin | L. Mias |
| 181 | 9.1.1960 | Scotland | 3 | 2 | — | — | 13 | 2 | 1 | — | 1 | 11 | Won | Edinburgh | F. Moncla |
| 182 | 27.2.1960 | England | — | — | 1 | 3 |  | 1 | — | — | — | 3 | Drawn | Colombes | F. Moncla |
| 183 | 26.3.1960 | Wales | 4 | 2 | — | — | 16 | 1 | 1 | — | 1 | 8 | Won | Cardiff | F. Moncla |
| 184 | 9.4.1960 | Ireland | 4 | 1 | 3 | — | 23 | 2 | — | — | — | 6 | Won | Colombes | F. Moncla |
| 185 | 17.4.1960 | Italy | 4 | 4 | 2 | — | 26 | — | — | — | — | 0 | Won | Tréviso | F. Moncla |
| 186 | 5.6.1960 | Romania | 1 | 1 | — | — | 5 | 1 | 1 | 2 | — | 11 | Lost | Bucharest | F. Moncla |
| 187 | 23.7.1960 | Argentina | 9 | 5 | — | — | 37 | — | — | — | 1 | 3 | Won | Buenos Aires | F. Moncla |
| 188 | 6.8.1960 | Argentina | 2 | — | 1 | 1 | 12 | 1 | — | — | — | 3 | Won | Buenos Aires | F. Moncla |
| 189 | 17.8.1960 | Argentina | 6 | 4 | 1 | — | 29 | — | — | — | 2 | 6 | Won | Buenos Aires | F. Moncla |
| 190 | 7.1.1961 | Scotland | 1 | 1 | 1 | 1 | 11 | — | — | — | — | 0 | Won | Colombes | F. Moncla |
| 191 | 18.2.1961 | South Africa | — | — | — | — | 0 | — | — | — | — | 0 | Drawn | Colombes | F. Moncla |
| 192 | 25.2.1961 | England | 1 | 1 | — | — | 5 | 1 | 1 | — | — | 5 | Drawn | Twickenham | F. Moncla |
| 193 | 25.3.1961 | Wales | 2 | 1 | — | — | 8 | 1 | — | — | — | 3 | Won | Colombes | F. Moncla |
| 194 | 2.4.1961 | Italy | 4 | 1 | — | 1 | 17 | — | — | — | — | 0 | Won | Chambéry | F. Moncla |
| 195 | 15.4.1961 | Ireland | 1 | — | 2 | 2 | 15 | — | — | — | 1 | 3 | Won | Dublin | F. Moncla |
| 196 | 22.7.1961 | New Zealand | — | — | 2 | — | 6 | 2 | 2 | 1 | — | 13 | Lost | Auckland | F. Moncla |
| 197 | 5.8.1961 | New Zealand | 1 | — | — | — | 3 | 1 | 1 | — | — | 5 | Lost | Wellington | F. Moncla |

| Match | Date | Opponents | For | | | | | Against | | | | | Result | Venue | Captain |
|---|---|---|---|---|---|---|---|---|---|---|---|---|---|---|---|
| | | | T | C | D | P | Pts | T | C | D | P | Pts | | | |
| 198 | 19.8.1961 | New Zealand | 1 | — | — | — | 3 | 5 | 4 | — | 3 | 32 | Lost | Christchurch | F. Moncla |
| 199 | 26.8.1961 | Australia | 3 | — | 2 | — | 15 | 1 | 1 | — | 1 | 8 | Won | Sydney | M. Crauste |
| 200 | 12.11.1961 | Romania | 1 | 1 | — | — | 5 | 1 | 1 | — | — | 5 | Drawn | Bayonne | M. Crauste |
| 201 | 13.1.1962 | Scotland | 1 | 1 | — | 2 | 11 | — | — | — | 1 | 3 | Won | Edinburgh | P. Lacroix |
| 202 | 24.2.1962 | England | 3 | 2 | — | — | 13 | — | — | — | — | 0 | Won | Colombes | P. Lacroix |
| 203 | 24.3.1962 | Wales | — | — | — | — | 0 | — | — | — | 1 | 3 | Lost | Cardiff | P. Lacroix |
| 204 | 14.4.1962 | Ireland | 3 | 1 | — | — | 11 | — | — | — | — | 0 | Won | Colombes | P. Lacroix |
| 205 | 22.4.1962 | Italy | 1 | — | — | 1 | 6 | — | — | — | 1 | 3 | Won | Brescia | M. Crauste |
| 206 | 11.11.1962 | Romania | — | — | — | — | 0 | — | — | — | 1 | 3 | Lost | Bucharest | P. Lacroix |
| 207 | 12.1.1963 | Scotland | — | — | 1 | 1 | 6 | 1 | 1 | 1 | 1 | 11 | Lost | Colombes | P. Lacroix |
| 208 | 26.1.1963 | Ireland | 4 | 3 | 2 | — | 24 | 1 | 1 | — | — | 5 | Won | Dublin | P. Lacroix |
| 209 | 23.2.1963 | England | 1 | 1 | — | — | 5 | — | — | — | 2 | 6 | Lost | Twickenham | P. Lacroix |
| 210 | 23.3.1963 | Wales | 1 | 1 | — | — | 5 | — | — | — | 1 | 3 | Won | Colombes | P. Lacroix |
| 211 | 14.4.1963 | Italy | 4 | 1 | — | — | 14 | 2 | — | — | 2 | 12 | Won | Grenoble | M. Crauste |
| 212 | 15.12.1963 | Romania | 2 | — | — | — | 6 | 1 | — | 1 | — | 6 | Drawn | Toulouse | M. Crauste |
| 213 | 4.1.1964 | Scotland | — | — | — | — | 0 | 2 | 2 | — | — | 10 | Lost | Edinburgh | J. Fabre |
| 214 | 8.2.1964 | New Zealand | — | — | — | 1 | 3 | 2 | — | 1 | 1 | 12 | Lost | Colombes | J. Fabre |
| 215 | 22.2.1964 | England | 1 | — | — | — | 3 | 2 | — | — | 1 | 6 | Lost | Colombes | J. Fabre |
| 216 | 21.3.1964 | Wales | 1 | 1 | — | 2 | 11 | 1 | 1 | — | 2 | 11 | Drawn | Cardiff | M. Crauste |
| 217 | 29.3.1964 | Italy | — | — | — | 3 | 12 | — | — | 1 | — | 3 | Won | Parma | M. Crauste |
| 218 | 11.4.1964 | Ireland | 6 | 3 | 1 | — | 27 | 1 | — | 1 | — | 6 | Won | Colombes | M. Crauste |
| 219 | 25.7.1964 | South Africa | 1 | 1 | — | 1 | 8 | 1 | — | — | 1 | 6 | Won | Springs | M. Crauste |
| 220 | 17.10.1964 | Fiji | 5 | 3 | — | — | 21 | 1 | — | — | — | 3 | Won | Colombes | M. Crauste |
| 221 | 29.11.1964 | Romania | 2 | — | 1 | — | 9 | 1 | — | — | 1 | 6 | Won | Bucharest | M. Crauste |
| 222 | 9.1.1965 | Scotland | 4 | 2 | — | — | 16 | 2 | 1 | — | — | 8 | Won | Colombes | M. Crauste |
| 223 | 23.1.1965 | Ireland | 1 | — | — | — | 3 | 1 | — | — | — | 3 | Drawn | Dublin | M. Crauste |
| 224 | 27.2.1965 | England | 1 | — | — | 1 | 6 | 1 | — | — | 2 | 9 | Lost | Twickenham | M. Crauste |
| 225 | 27.3.1965 | Wales | 4 | 2 | 1 | 1 | 22 | 3 | 2 | — | — | 13 | Won | Colombes | M. Crauste |
| 226 | 18.4.1965 | Italy | 5 | 3 | — | — | 21 | — | — | — | — | 0 | Won | Pau | M. Crauste |
| 227 | 28.11.1965 | Romania | 2 | 1 | — | — | 8 | — | — | 1 | — | 3 | Won | Lyon | M. Crauste |
| 228 | 15.1.1966 | Scotland | — | — | 1 | — | 3 | 1 | — | — | — | 3 | Drawn | Edinburgh | M. Crauste |
| 229 | 29.1.1966 | Ireland | 2 | 1 | — | 1 | 11 | — | — | 1 | 1 | 6 | Won | Colombes | M. Crauste |
| 230 | 26.2.1966 | England | 3 | 2 | — | — | 13 | — | — | — | — | 0 | Won | Colombes | M. Crauste |
| 231 | 26.3.1966 | Wales | 2 | 1 | — | — | 8 | 1 | — | — | 2 | 9 | Lost | Cardiff | M. Crauste |
| 232 | 9.4.1966 | Italy | 4 | 3 | 1 | — | 21 | — | — | — | — | 0 | Won | Naples | M. Crauste |
| 233 | 27.11.1966 | Romania | 2 | — | — | 1 | 9 | — | — | — | 1 | 3 | Won | Bucharest | C. Darrouy |
| 234 | 14.1.1967 | Scotland | 2 | 1 | — | — | 8 | — | — | 1 | 2 | 9 | Lost | Colombes | C. Darrouy |
| 235 | 11.2.1967 | Australia | 1 | 1 | 1 | 4 | 20 | 2 | 1 | 1 | 1 | 14 | Won | Colombes | C. Darrouy |
| 236 | 25.2.1967 | England | 2 | 2 | 1 | 1 | 16 | — | — | 1 | 3 | 12 | Won | Twickenham | C. Darrouy |
| 237 | 26.3.1967 | Italy | 11 | 9 | 1 | 2 | 60 | 3 | 2 | — | — | 13 | Won | Toulon | C. Darrouy |
| 238 | 1.4.1967 | Wales | 3 | 1 | 2 | 1 | 20 | 1 | 1 | 1 | 2 | 14 | Won | Colombes | C. Darrouy |
| 239 | 15.4.1967 | Ireland | 1 | 1 | 2 | — | 11 | 1 | — | — | 1 | 6 | Won | Dublin | C. Darrouy |
| 240 | 15.7.1967 | S.A. | 1 | — | — | — | 3 | 5 | 4 | — | 1 | 26 | Lost | Durban | C. Darrouy |
| 241 | 22.7.1967 | S.A. | — | — | — | 1 | 3 | 3 | 2 | — | 1 | 16 | Lost | Bloemfontein | C. Darrouy |
| 242 | 29.7.1967 | S.A. | 2 | 2 | 2 | 1 | 19 | 2 | 1 | — | 2 | 14 | Won | Johannesburg | J. Fort |
| 243 | 12.8.1967 | S.A. | 1 | — | — | 1 | 6 | — | — | 1 | 1 | 6 | Drawn | Cape Town | C. Darrouy |
| 244 | 25.11.1967 | New Zealand | 1 | — | 1 | 3 | 15 | 4 | 3 | — | 1 | 21 | Lost | Colombes | C. Carrère |
| 245 | 10.12.1967 | Romania | 1 | 1 | 1 | 1 | 11 | — | — | — | 1 | 3 | Won | Nantes | C. Carrère |
| 246 | 13.1.1968 | Scotland | 2 | 1 | — | — | 8 | 1 | — | — | 1 | 6 | Won | Edinburgh | C. Carrère |
| 247 | 27.1.1968 | Ireland | 2 | 2 | 1 | 1 | 16 | — | — | — | 2 | 6 | Won | Colombes | C. Carrère |
| 248 | 24.2.1968 | England | 1 | 1 | 2 | 1 | 14 | — | — | 1 | 2 | 9 | Won | Colombes | C. Carrère |
| 249 | 23.3.1968 | Wales | 2 | 1 | 1 | 1 | 14 | 1 | — | — | 2 | 9 | Won | Cardiff | C. Carrère |
| 250 | 5.5.1968 | Czechoslovakia | 5 | 2 | — | — | 19 | 1 | — | — | 1 | 6 | Won | Prague | C. Carrère |
| 251 | 13.7.1968 | New Zealand | — | — | 1 | 2 | 9 | 1 | — | — | 3 | 12 | Lost | Christchurch | C. Lacaze |
| 252 | 27.7.1968 | New Zealand | — | — | — | 1 | 3 | — | — | — | 3 | 9 | Lost | Wellington | M. Puget |
| 253 | 10.8.1968 | New Zealand | 3 | — | 1 | — | 12 | 2 | 2 | 1 | 2 | 19 | Lost | Auckland | C. Carrère |
| 254 | 17.8.1968 | Australia | 2 | 2 | — | — | 10 | 1 | 1 | 1 | 1 | 11 | Lost | Sydney | C. Carrère |
| 255 | 9.11.1968 | S.A. | 3 | — | — | — | 9 | — | — | — | 4 | 12 | Lost | Bordeaux | M. Puget |
| 256 | 16.11.1968 | S.A. | 1 | 1 | 2 | — | 11 | 3 | 2 | — | 1 | 16 | Lost | Colombes | M. Puget |
| 257 | 1.12.1968 | Romania | 1 | 1 | — | 3 | 14 | — | — | 1 | 4 | 15 | Lost | Bucharest | C. Carrère |
| 258 | 11.1.1969 | Scotland | — | — | 1 | — | 3 | 1 | — | — | 1 | 6 | Lost | Colombes | C. Carrère |
| 259 | 25.1.1969 | Ireland | 1 | — | — | 2 | 9 | 1 | 1 | 1 | 3 | 17 | Lost | Dublin | C. Carrère |
| 260 | 22.2.1969 | England | 1 | 1 | 1 | — | 8 | 3 | 2 | — | 3 | 22 | Lost | Twickenham | M. Puget |
| 261 | 22.3.1969 | Wales | 1 | 1 | — | 1 | 8 | 2 | 1 | — | — | 8 | Drawn | Colombes | W. Sphanghéro |
| 262 | 14.12.1969 | Romania | 1 | 1 | 1 | 2 | 14 | — | — | 1 | 2 | 9 | Won | Tarbes | M. Puget |
| 263 | 10.1.1970 | Scotland | 2 | 1 | 1 | — | 11 | 1 | — | — | 2 | 9 | Won | Edinburgh | C. Carrère |
| 264 | 24.1.1970 | Ireland | 1 | 1 | 1 | — | 8 | — | — | — | — | 0 | Won | Colombes | C. Carrère |
| 265 | 4.4.1970 | Wales | 2 | — | — | — | 6 | 1 | 1 | — | 2 | 11 | Lost | Cardiff | C. Carrère |
| 266 | 18.4.1970 | England | 6 | 4 | 2 | 1 | 35 | 2 | 2 | — | 1 | 13 | Won | Colombes | C. Carrère |
| 267 | 29.11.1970 | Romania | 1 | 1 | — | 3 | 14 | — | — | — | 1 | 3 | Won | Bucharest | B. Dauga |
| 268 | 16.1.1971 | Scotland | 2 | 2 | — | 1 | 13 | 1 | 1 | — | 1 | 8 | Won | Colombes | B. Dauga |
| 269 | 30.1.1971 | Ireland | — | — | 1 | 2 | 9 | 1 | — | — | 2 | 9 | Drawn | Dublin | B. Dauga |

| Match | Date | Opponents | For T | C | D | P | Pts | Against T | C | D | P | Pts | Result | Venue | Captain |
|---|---|---|---|---|---|---|---|---|---|---|---|---|---|---|---|
| 270 | 27.2.1971 | England | 2 | 1 | 1 | 1 | 14 | 1 | 1 | — |  | 3 | 14 | Drawn | Twickenham | C. Carrère |
| 271 | 27.3.1971 | Wales | 1 | 1 | — | — | 5 | 2 | — | — | 1 | 9 | | Lost | Colombes | C. Carrère |
| 272 | 12.6.1971 | South Africa | 1 | — | — | 2 | 9 | 2 | 2 | 1 | 3 | 22 | Lost | Bloemfontein | J. Trillo |
| 273 | 19.6.1971 | South Africa | 1 | 1 | 1 | — | 8 | 1 | 1 | 1 | — | 8 | Drawn | Durban | B. Dauga |
| 274 | 20.11.1971 | Australia | 2 | — | — | 1 | 11 | 2 | 1 | — | 1 | 13 | Lost | Toulouse | B. Dauga |
| 275 | 27.11.1971 | Australia | 1 | 1 | — | 4 | 18 | — | — | — | 3 | 9 | Won | Colombes | B. Dauga |
| 276 | 11.12.1971 | Romania | 4 | 3 | — | 3 | 31 | — | — | 2* | 1 | 12 | Won | Beziers | B. Dauga |
| 277 | 15.1.1972 | Scotland | 1 | 1 | — | 1 | 9 | 3 | 1 | 1 | 1 | 20 | Lost | Edinburgh | B. Dauga |
| 278 | 29.1.1972 | Ireland | 1 | 1 | — | 1 | 9 | 2 | — | — | 2 | 14 | Lost | Colombes | B. Dauga |
| 279 | 26.2.1972 | England | 6 | 5 | — | 1 | 37 | 1 | 1 | — | 2 | 12 | Won | Colombes | W. Spanghéro |
| 280 | 25.3.1972 | Wales | — | — | — | 2 | 6 | 2 | — | — | 4 | 20 | Lost | Cardiff | P. Villepreux |
| 281 | 29.4.1972 | Ireland | 3 | 1 | — | — | 14 | 3 | 3 | — | 2 | 24 | Lost | Dublin | W. Spanghéro |
| 282 | 17.6.1972 | Australia | 3 | 1 | — | — | 14 | 2 | — | — | 2 | 14 | Drawn | Sydney | W. Spanghéro |
| 283 | 25.6.1972 | Australia | 3 | 2 | — | — | 16 | — | — | — | 5 | 15 | Won | Brisbane | W. Spanghéro |
| 284 | 26.11.1972 | Romania | 1 | 1 | — | 3 | 15 | — | — | — | 2 | 6 | Won | Constanza | W. Spanghéro |
| 285 | 13.1.1973 | Scotland | 1 | 1 | 1 | 3 | 16 | 1 | — | 1 | 2 | 13 | Won | Parc des Princes | W. Spanghéro |
| 286 | 10.2.1973 | New Zealand | 2 | 1 | — | 1 | 13 | — | — | — | 2 | 6 | Won | Parc des Princes | W. Spanghéro |
| 287 | 24.2.1973 | England | 1 | 1 | — | — | 6 | 2 | — | — | 2 | 14 | Lost | Twickenham | W. Spanghéro |
| 288 | 24.3.1973 | Wales | — | — | 1 | 3 | 12 | — | — | 1 | — | 3 | Won | Parc des Princes | W. Spanghéro |
| 289 | 14.4.1973 | Ireland | 1 | — | — | — | 4 | — | — | — | 2 | 6 | Lost | Dublin | W. Spanghéro |
| 290 | 27.10.1973 | Japan | 6 | 3 | — | — | 30 | 3 | — | — | 2 | 18 | Won | Bordeaux | M. Barrau |
| 291 | 11.11.1973 | Romania | 1 | — | 1 | — | 7 | — | — | — | 2 | 6 | Won | Valence | M. Barrau |
| 292 | 19.1.1974 | Ireland | 1 | 1 | — | 1 | 9 | — | — | — | 2 | 6 | Won | Parc des Princes | M. Barrau |
| 293 | 16.2.1974 | Wales | 1 | — | 1 | 3 | 16 | 1 | — | 1 | 3 | 16 | Drawn | Cardiff | E. Cester |
| 294 | 2.3.1974 | England | 1 | 1 | 1 | 1 | 12 | 1 | 1 | 1 | 1 | 12 | Drawn | Parc des Princes | E. Cester |
| 295 | 16.3.1974 | Scotland | — | — | 1 | 1 | 6 | 2 | 1 | — | 3 | 19 | Lost | Edinburgh | E. Cester |
| 296 | 20.6.1974 | Argentina | 3 | 1 | — | 2 | 20 | 1 | 1 | — | 3 | 15 | Won | Buenos Aires | C. Dourthe |
| 297 | 29.6.1974 | Argentina | 4 | 3 | — | 3 | 31 | 1 | 1 | — | 7 | 27 | Won | Buenos Aires | O. Saisset |
| 298 | 13.10.1974 | Romania | 1 | — | — | 2 | 10 | 1 | 1 | — | 3 | 15 | Lost | Bucharest | J. Fouroux |
| 299 | 23.11.1974 | South Africa | 1 | — | — | — | 4 | 1 | — | — | 3 | 13 | Lost | Toulouse | J. Fouroux |
| 300 | 30.11.1974 | South Africa | 2 | — | — | — | 8 | 1 | — | — | 2 | 10 | Lost | Parc des Princes | J. Fouroux |
| 301 | 18.1.1975 | Wales | 1 | — | — | 2 | 10 | 5 | 1 | — | 1 | 25 | Lost | Parc des Princes | J. Fouroux |
| 302 | 1.2.1975 | England | 4 | 4 | — | 1 | 27 | 2 | — | — | 4 | 20 | Won | Twickenham | C. Dourthe |
| 303 | 15.2.1975 | Scotland | 1 | — | 1 | 1 | 10 | — | — | — | 3 | 9 | Won | Parc des Princes | C. Dourthe |
| 304 | 1.3.1975 | Ireland | — | — | 1 | 1 | 6 | 3 | 2 | 2 | 1 | 25 | Lost | Dublin | R. Astre |
| 305 | 21.6.1975 | South Africa | 4 | 3 | — | 1 | 25 | 5 | 3 | — | 4 | 38 | Lost | Bloemfontein | R. Astre |
| 306 | 28.6.1975 | South Africa | 1 | 1 | 1 | 3 | 18 | 2 | 2 | — | 7 | 33 | Lost | Pretoria | R. Astre |
| 307 | 19.10.1975 | Argentina | 6 | 1 | — | 1 | 29 | — | — | — | 2 | 6 | Won | Lyon | J. Fouroux |
| 308 | 25.10.1975 | Argentina | 5 | 2 | — | 4 | 36 | 1 | 1 | — | 5 | 21 | Won | Parc des Princes | R. Astre |
| 309 | 23.11.1975 | Romania | 6 | 3 | — | 2 | 36 | — | — | 1 | 3 | 12 | Won | Bordeaux | J. Fouroux |
| 310 | 10.1.1976 | Scotland | 1 | — | — | 3 | 13 | — | — | 1 | 1 | 6 | Won | Edinburgh | J. Fouroux |
| 311 | 7.2.1976 | Ireland | 4 | 2 | — | 2 | 26 | — | — | — | 1 | 3 | Won | Parc des Princes | J. Fouroux |
| 312 | 6.3.1976 | Wales | 2 | 1 | — | 1 | 13 | 1 | — | — | 5 | 19 | Lost | Cardiff | J. Fouroux |
| 313 | 20.3.1976 | England | 6 | 3 | — | — | 30 | 1 | 1 | — | 1 | 9 | Won | Parc des Princes | J. Fouroux |
| 314 | 12.6.1976 | United States | 3 | 3 | — | 5 | 33 | 2 | — | — | 2 | 14 | Won | Chicago | J. Fouroux |
| 315 | 24.10.1976 | Australia | 3 | 3 | — | — | 18 | — | — | 1 | 4 | 15 | Won | Bordeaux | J. Fouroux |
| 316 | 30.10.1976 | Australia | 6 | 2 | 1 | 1 | 34 | — | — | — | 2 | 6 | Won | Parc des Princes | R. Astre |
| 317 | 14.11.1976 | Romania | 1 | 1 | — | 2 | 12 | 3 | — | 1 | — | 15 | Lost | Bucharest | R. Astre |
| 318 | 5.2.1977 | Wales | 2 | 1 | — | 2 | 16 | — | — | — | 3 | 9 | Won | Parc des Princes | J. Fouroux |
| 319 | 19.2.1977 | England | 1 | — | — | — | 4 | — | — | — | 1 | 3 | Won | Twickenham | J. Fouroux |
| 320 | 5.3.1977 | Scotland | 4 | 2 | — | 1 | 23 | — | — | — | 1 | 3 | Won | Parc des Princes | J. Fouroux |
| 321 | 19.3.1977 | Ireland | 1 | 1 | — | 3 | 15 | — | — | — | 2 | 6 | Won | Dublin | J. Fouroux |
| 322 | 25.6.1977 | Argentina | 2 | — | 1 | 5 | 26 | — | — | — | 1 | 3 | Won | Buenos Aires | J. Fouroux |
| 323 | 2.7.1977 | Argentina | — | — | — | 6 | 18 | — | — | — | 6 | 18 | Drawn | Buenos Aires | J. Fouroux |
| 324 | 11.11.1977 | New Zealand | 1 | 1 | 1 | 3 | 18 | 1 | — | 1 | 2 | 13 | Won | Toulouse | J. Fouroux |
| 325 | 19.11.1977 | New Zealand | — | — | — | 1 | 3 | 1 | 1 | 1 | 2 | 15 | Lost | Parc des Princes | J. Fouroux |

*in the drop-goal column denotes a goal from a mark

| Match | Date | Opponents | For | | | | | Against | | | | | Result | Venue | Captain |
|---|---|---|---|---|---|---|---|---|---|---|---|---|---|---|---|
| | | | T | C | D | P | Pts | T | C | D | P | Pts | | | |
| 326 | 10.12.1977 | Romania | — | — | — | 3 | 9 | — | — | 1 | 1 | 6 | Won | Clermont Ferrand | J. Fouroux |
| 327 | 21.1.1978 | England | 2 | 2 | — | 1 | 15 | — | — | 2 | — | 6 | Won | Parc des Princes | J. P. Bastiat |
| 328 | 4.2.1978 | Scotland | 2 | 1 | — | 3 | 19 | 2 | 1 | 1 | 1 | 16 | Won | Edinburgh | J. P. Bastiat |
| 329 | 18.2.1978 | Ireland | 1 | — | — | 2 | 10 | — | — | — | 3 | 9 | Won | Parc des Princes | J. P. Bastiat |
| 330 | 19.3.1978 | Wales | 1 | — | 1 | — | 7 | 2 | 1 | 2 | — | 16 | Lost | Cardiff | J. P. Bastiat |
| 331 | 3.12.1978 | Romania | — | — | 1 | 2 | 9 | — | — | — | 2 | 6 | Won | Bucharest | J. P. Rives |
| 332 | 20.1.1979 | Ireland | 1 | 1 | — | 1 | 9 | — | — | — | 3 | 9 | Drawn | Dublin | J. P. Rives |
| 333 | 17.2.1979 | Wales | 2 | — | — | 2 | 14 | 1 | — | — | 3 | 13 | Won | Parc des Princes | J. P. Rives |
| 334 | 3.3.1979 | England | 1 | 1 | — | — | 6 | 1 | — | — | 1 | 7 | Lost | Twickenham | J. P. Rives |
| 335 | 17.3.1979 | Scotland | 3 | — | 1 | 2 | 21 | 3 | 1 | — | 1 | 17 | Won | Parc des Princes | J. P. Rives |
| 336 | 7.7.1979 | New Zealand | 1 | 1 | 1 | — | 9 | 3 | 1 | — | 3 | 23 | Lost | Christchurch | J. P. Rives |
| 337 | 14.7.1979 | New Zealand | 4 | 1 | 1 | 1 | 24 | 2 | 1 | — | 3 | 19 | Won | Auckland | J. P. Rives |
| 338 | 2.12.1979 | Romania | 3 | 3 | 1 | 3 | 30 | — | — | 1 | 3 | 12 | Won | Montauban | J. P. Rives |
| 339 | 19.1.1980 | Wales | 1 | 1 | 1 | — | 9 | 4 | 1 | — | — | 18 | Lost | Cardiff | J. P. Rives |
| 340 | 2.2.1980 | England | 2 | 1 | — | 1 | 13 | 2 | — | 2 | 1 | 17 | Lost | Parc des Princes | J. P. Rives |
| 341 | 16.2.1980 | Scotland | 2 | — | 1 | 1 | 14 | 3 | 2 | — | 2 | 22 | Lost | Edinburgh | J. P. Rives |
| 342 | 1.3.1980 | Ireland | 2 | 1 | 1 | 2 | 19 | 1 | 1 | 1 | 3 | 18 | Won | Parc des Princes | J. P. Rives |
| 343 | 8.11.1980 | South Africa | 1 | 1 | — | 3 | 15 | 5 | 4 | — | 3 | 37 | Lost | Pretoria | J. P. Rives |
| 344 | 23.11.1980 | Romania | — | — | — | — | 0 | 1 | 1 | — | 3 | 15 | Lost | Bucharest | R. Paparemborde |
| 345 | 17.1.1981 | Scotland | 2 | 1 | — | 2 | 16 | 1 | 1 | — | 1 | 9 | Won | Parc des Princes | J. P. Rives |
| 346 | 7.2.1981 | Ireland | 1 | — | 2 | 3 | 19 | 1 | — | — | 3 | 13 | Won | Dublin | J. P. Rives |
| 347 | 7.3.1981 | Wales | 1 | — | — | 5 | 19 | 1 | 1 | — | 3 | 15 | Won | Parc des Princes | J. P. Rives |
| 348 | 21.3.1981 | England | 2 | 1 | 2 | — | 16 | — | — | — | 4 | 12 | Won | Twickenham | J. P. Rives |
| 349 | 5.7.1981 | Australia | 1 | 1 | 1 | 2 | 15 | 3 | 1 | — | 1 | 17 | Lost | Brisbane | R. Paparemborde |
| 350 | 11.7.1981 | Australia | 2 | — | 1 | 2 | 14 | 2 | 2 | — | 4 | 24 | Lost | Sydney | J. P. Rives |
| 351 | 1.11.1981 | Romania | 2 | — | 1 | 2 | 17 | — | — | — | 3 | 9 | Won | Narbonne | R. Paparemborde |
| 352 | 14.11.1981 | New Zealand | — | — | 1 | 2 | 9 | 1 | — | 1 | 2 | 13 | Lost | Toulouse | R. Paparemborde |
| 353 | 21.11.1981 | New Zealand | — | — | — | 2 | 6 | 2 | 2 | — | 2 | 18 | Lost | Parc des Princes | R. Paparemborde |
| 354 | 6.2.1982 | Wales | 1 | 1 | — | 2 | 12 | 1 | — | — | 6 | 22 | Lost | Cardiff | J. P. Rives |
| 355 | 20.2.1982 | England | 1 | 1 | 1 | 2 | 15 | 2 | 2 | — | 5 | 27 | Lost | Parc des Princes | J. P. Rives |
| 356 | 6.3.1982 | Scotland | 1 | — | — | 1 | 7 | 1 | — | 1 | 3 | 16 | Lost | Edinburgh | J. P. Rives |
| 357 | 20.3.1982 | Ireland | 2 | 1 | — | 4 | 22 | — | — | — | 3 | 9 | Won | Parc des Princes | J. P. Rives |
| 358 | 31.10.1982 | Romania | 1 | 1 | 1 | — | 9 | 1 | — | 1 | 2 | 13 | Lost | Bucharest | J. P. Rives |
| 359 | 14.11.1982 | Argentina | 4 | — | 1 | 2 | 25 | 1 | 1 | — | 2 | 12 | Won | Toulouse | G. Martinez |
| 360 | 20.11.1982 | Argentina | 2 | 1 | — | 1 | 13 | — | — | 2 | — | 6 | Won | Parc des Princes | G. Martinez |
| 361 | 15.1.1983 | England | 3 | 2 | — | 1 | 19 | — | — | 1 | 4 | 15 | Won | Twickenham | J. P. Rives |
| 362 | 5.2.1983 | Scotland | 2 | 1 | — | 3 | 19 | 1 | 1 | 2 | 1 | 15 | Won | Parc des Princes | J. P. Rives |
| 363 | 19.2.1983 | Ireland | 2 | 1 | — | 2 | 16 | 2 | 1 | — | 4 | 22 | Lost | Dublin | J. P. Rives |
| 364 | 19.3.1983 | Wales | 1 | — | 1 | 3 | 16 | 1 | 1 | 1 | — | 9 | Won | Parc des Princes | J. P. Rives |
| 365 | 13.11.1983 | Australia | — | — | 2 | 3 | 15 | 1 | 1 | 2 | 1 | 15 | Drawn | Clermont Ferrand | J. P. Rives |
| 366 | 19.11.1983 | Australia | 1 | 1 | — | 3 | 15 | — | — | 1 | 1 | 6 | Won | Parc des Princes | J. P. Rives |
| 367 | 4.12.1983 | Romania | 4 | 2 | 1 | 1 | 26 | 2 | 2 | — | 1 | 15 | Won | Toulouse | J. P. Rives |
| 368 | 21.1.1984 | Ireland | 2 | 1 | 1 | 4 | 25 | — | — | — | 4 | 12 | Won | Parc des Princes | J. P. Rives |
| 369 | 18.2.1984 | Wales | 1 | 1 | 1 | 4 | 21 | 2 | 1 | — | 2 | 16 | Won | Cardiff | J. P. Rives |
| 370 | 3.3.1984 | England | 5 | 3 | 1 | 1 | 32 | 2 | 2 | — | 2 | 18 | Won | Parc des Princes | J. P. Rives |
| 371 | 17.3.1984 | Scotland | 1 | 1 | 1 | 1 | 12 | 1 | 1 | — | 5 | 21 | Lost | Edinburgh | J. P. Rives |
| 372 | 16.6.1984 | New Zealand | 1 | 1 | 1 | — | 9 | 1 | — | — | 2 | 10 | Lost | Christchurch | P. Dintrans |
| 373 | 23.6.1984 | New Zealand | 3 | — | — | 2 | 18 | 3 | 2 | — | 5 | 31 | Lost | Auckland | P. Dintrans |
| 374 | 11.11.1984 | Romania | 2 | 2 | — | 2 | 18 | — | — | — | 1 | 3 | Won | Bucharest | P. Dintrans |
| 375 | 2.2.1985 | England | — | — | 3 | — | 9 | — | — | 1 | 2 | 9 | Drawn | Twickenham | P. Dintrans |
| 376 | 16.2.1985 | Scotland | 2 | — | — | 1 | 11 | — | — | — | 1 | 3 | Won | Parc des Princes | P. Dintrans |
| 377 | 2.3.1985 | Ireland | 2 | 2 | — | 1 | 15 | — | — | — | 5 | 15 | Drawn | Dublin | P. Dintrans |
| 378 | 30.3.1985 | Wales | 2 | — | — | 2 | 14 | — | — | — | 1 | 3 | Won | Parc des Princes | P. Dintrans |

| Match | Date | Opponents | For T | C | D | P | Pts | Against T | C | D | P | Pts | Result | Venue | Captain |
|-------|------|-----------|-------|---|---|---|-----|-----------|---|---|---|-----|--------|-------|---------|
| 379 | 22.6.1985 | Argentina | 2 | 1 | — | 2 | 16 | 2 | 2 | 1 | 3 | 24 | Lost | Buenos Aires | P. Dintrans |
| 380 | 29.6.1985 | Argentina | 4 | 2 | — | 1 | 23 | 1 | 1 | — | 3 | 15 | Won | Buenos Aires | P. Dintrans |
| 381 | 18.1.1986 | Scotland | 2 | — | 1 | 2 | 17 | — | — | — | 6 | 18 | Lost | Edinburgh | D. Dubroca |
| 382 | 1.2.1986 | Ireland | 3 | 1 | 1 | 4 | 29 | — | — | — | 3 | 9 | Won | Parc des Princes | D. Dubroca |
| 383 | 1.3.1986 | Wales | 4 | 2 | 1 | — | 23 | — | — | — | 5 | 15 | Won | Cardiff | D. Dubroca |
| 384 | 15.3.1986 | England | 4 | 2 | — | 3 | 29 | 1 | — | — | 2 | 10 | Won | Parc des Princes | D. Dubroca |
| 385 | 12.4.1986 | Romania | 5 | 1 | — | 1 | 25 | 2 | 1 | — | 1 | 13 | Won | Lille | D. Dubroca |
| 386 | 31.5.1986 | Argentina | 1 | — | — | 3 | 13 | 1 | 1 | — | 3 | 15 | Lost | Buenos Aires | P. Berbizier |
| 387 | 7.6.1986 | Argentina | 3 | 2 | — | 2 | 22 | — | — | — | 3 | 9 | Won | Buenos Aires | D. Dubroca |
| 388 | 21.6.1986 | Australia | 3 | 1 | — | — | 14 | 1 | 1 | 1 | 6 | 27 | Lost | Sydney | D. Dubroca |
| 389 | 28.6.1986 | New Zealand | — | — | 3 | — | 9 | 1 | 1 | 3 | 1 | 18 | Lost | Christchurch | D. Dubroca |
| 390 | 25.10.1986 | Romania | 3 | 1 | — | 2 | 20 | — | — | — | 1 | 3 | Won | Bucharest | D. Dubroca |
| 391 | 8.11.1986 | New Zealand | 1 | — | — | 1 | 7 | 1 | — | 2 | 3 | 19 | Lost | Toulouse | D. Dubroca |
| 392 | 15.11.1986 | New Zealand | 2 | 1 | — | 2 | 16 | — | — | — | 1 | 3 | Won | Nantes | D. Dubroca |
| 393 | 7.2.1987 | Wales | 2 | 1 | — | 2 | 16 | — | — | — | 3 | 9 | Won | Parc des Princes | D. Dubroca |
| 394 | 21.2.1987 | England | 2 | 1 | 2 | 1 | 19 | — | — | 1 | 4 | 15 | Won | Twickenham | D. Dubroca |
| 395 | 7.3.1987 | Scotland | 4 | — | 1 | 3 | 28 | 2 | 1 | — | 4 | 22 | Won | Parc des Princes | D. Dubroca |
| 396 | 21.3.1987 | Ireland | 2 | 1 | — | 3 | 19 | 2 | 1 | — | 1 | 13 | Won | Dublin | D. Dubroca |

# MATCH RECORDS

## MOST CONSECUTIVE MATCHES WON

| | |
|---|---|
| 10 | *1931* E,G *1932* G *1933* G *1934* G *1935* G *1936* G *1,2* *1937* G,It |
| 7 | *1954* E, It, Arg *1,2* *1955* S, I, E |

## MOST CONSECUTIVE MATCHES WITHOUT DEFEAT

| Matches | Wins | Draws | Period |
|---------|------|-------|--------|
| 10 | 10 | 0 | 1930-31 to 1937-38 |
| 10 | 8 | 2 | 1957-58 to 1958-59 |
| 9 | 7 | 2 | 1960 to 1960-61 |
| 8 | 6 | 2 | 1963-64 to 1964-65 |
| 7 | 7 | 0 | 1953-54 to 1954-55 |
| 7 | 6 | 1 | 1976-77 to 1977-78 |
| 7 | 6 | 1 | 1982-83 to 1983-84 |

## MOST CONSECUTIVE MATCHES WITHOUT CONCEDING A TRY

| | |
|---|---|
| 6 | between 1961-62 and 1962-63 |
| 6 | between 1976-77 and 1977 |
| 5 | in 1984-85 |
| 4 | in 1958-59 |

## MOST CONSECUTIVE MATCHES WITHOUT CONCEDING A SCORE

| | |
|---|---|
| 3 | in 1953-54 |

# MOST POINTS IN A MATCH
## By the team

| Pts | Opponents | Venue | Season |
|---|---|---|---|
| 60 | Italy | Toulon | 1966-67 |
| 59 | Romania | Paris | 1923-24 |
| 43 | Italy | Paris | 1937-38 |
| 39 | Italy | Rome | 1953-54 |
| 39 | Romania | Bordeaux | 1957-58 |
| 38 | Germany | Paris | 1932-33 |
| 38 | Italy | Agen | 1956-57 |
| 37 | Argentina | Buenos Aires | 1960 |
| 37 | England | Paris | 1971-72 |
| 36 | Argentina | Paris | 1975-76 |
| 36 | Romania | Bordeaux | 1975-76 |
| 35 | England | Paris | 1969-70 |

## By a player

| Pts | Player | Opponents | Venue | Season |
|---|---|---|---|---|
| 27 | G. Cambérabero | Italy | Toulon | 1966-67 |
| 25 | J-P Romeu | United States | Chicago | 1976 |
| 20 | L. Beguet | Romania | Paris | 1923-24 |
| 20 | J-P Romeu | Argentina | Paris | 1975-76 |
| 18 | J. Prat | Italy | Rome | 1953-54 |
| 18 | M. Vannier | Romania | Bordeaux | 1957-58 |
| 18 | J-M Aguirre | Argentina | Buenos Aires | 1977 |
| 17 | G. Cambérabero | Australia | Paris | 1966-67 |
| 17 | J-P Lescarboura | Ireland | Paris | 1983-84 |
| 17 | J-P Lescarboura | Wales | Cardiff | 1983-84 |
| 17 | G. Laporte | England | Paris | 1985-86 |
| 15 | M. Vannier | Argentina | Buenos Aires | 1954 |
| 15 | M. Vannier | Romania | Bucharest | 1956-57 |
| 15 | P. Villepreux | Romania | Beziers | 1971-72 |
| 15 | J-P Romeu | Argentina | Buenos Aires | 1974 |
| 15 | J-P Romeu | Argentina | Buenos Aires | 1977 |

# MOST TRIES IN A MATCH
## By the team

| T | Opponents | Venue | Season |
|---|---|---|---|
| 13 | Romania | Paris | 1923-24 |
| 11 | Italy | Toulon | 1966-67 |
| 9 | Germany | Paris | 1932-33 |
| 9 | Italy | Paris | 1937-38 |
| 9 | Argentina | Buenos Aires | 1960 |
| 8 | Germany | Paris | 1926-27 |
| 8 | Germany | Berlin | 1929-30 |
| 8 | Germany | Paris | 1930-31 |
| 8 | Italy | Agen | 1956-57 |
| 8 | Romania | Bordeaux | 1957-58 |
| 7 | Germany | Paris | 1936-37 |
| 7 | Italy | Rome | 1953-54 |

## By a player

| T | Player | Opponents | Venue | Season |
|---|---|---|---|---|
| 4 | A. Jauréguy | Romania | Paris | 1923-24 |
| 4 | M. Celhay | Italy | Paris | 1937-38 |
| 3 | J. Taillantou | Germany | Berlin | 1929-30 |
| 3 | R. Finat | Germany | Paris | 1932-33 |
| 3 | J. Dupuy | Romania | Bordeaux | 1957-58 |
| 3 | M.Crauste | England | Paris | 1961-62 |
| 3 | C. Darrouy | Ireland | Dublin | 1962-63 |
| 3 | M. Arnaudet | Italy | Toulon | 1966-67 |
| 3 | A. Dubertrand | Romania | Bordeaux | 1975-76 |
| 3 | E. Bonneval | Scotland | Paris | 1986-87 |

# MOST CONVERSIONS IN A MATCH
## By the team

| C | Opponents | Venue | Season |
|---|---|---|---|
| 9 | Italy | Toulon | 1966-67 |
| 7 | Romania | Paris | 1923-24 |
| 7 | Italy | Agen | 1956-57 |
| 6 | Italy | Paris | 1937-38 |
| 6 | Italy | Rome | 1953-54 |
| 6 | Romania | Bordeaux | 1957-58 |
| 5 | Germany | Paris | 1930-31 |
| 5 | Argentina | Buenos Aires | 1960 |
| 5 | England | Paris | 1971-72 |

## By a player

| C | Player | Opponents | Venue | Season |
|---|---|---|---|---|
| 9 | G. Cambérabero | Italy | Toulon | 1966-67 |
| 7 | L. Beguet | Romania | Paris | 1923-24 |
| 6 | J. Prat | Italy | Rome | 1953-54 |
| 6 | M. Vannier | Romania | Bordeaux | 1957-58 |
| 5 | P. Cassagne | Italy | Agen | 1956-57 |
| 5 | M. Vannier | Argentina | Buenos Aires | 1960 |
| 5 | P. Villepreux | England | Paris | 1971-72 |

# MOST DROPPED GOALS IN A MATCH
## By the team

| DG | Opponents | Venue | Season |
|---|---|---|---|
| 3 | Ireland | Paris | 1959-60 |
| 3 | England | Twickenham | 1984-85 |
| 3 | New Zealand | Christchurch | 1986 |

## By a player

| DG | Player | Opponents | Venue | Season |
|---|---|---|---|---|
| 3 | P. Albaladéjo | Ireland | Paris | 1959-60 |
| 3 | J-P Lescarboura | England | Twickenham | 1984-85 |
| 3 | J-P Lescarboura | New Zealand | Christchurch | 1986 |

# MOST PENALTY GOALS IN A MATCH
## By the team

| PG | Opponents | Venue | Season |
|---|---|---|---|
| 6 | Argentina | Buenos Aires | 1977 |
| 5 | United States | Chicago | 1976 |
| 5 | Argentina | Buenos Aires | 1977 |
| 5 | Wales | Paris | 1980-81 |
| 4 | Romania | Bucharest | 1956-57 |
| 4 | Australia | Paris | 1966-67 |
| 4 | Australia | Paris | 1971-72 |
| 4 | Argentina | Paris | 1975-76 |
| 4 | Ireland | Paris | 1981-82 |
| 4 | Ireland | Paris | 1983-84 |
| 4 | Wales | Cardiff | 1983-84 |
| 4 | Ireland | Paris | 1985-86 |

## By a player

| PG | Player | Opponents | Venue | Season |
|---|---|---|---|---|
| 6 | J-M Aguirre | Argentina | Buenos Aires | 1977 |
| 5 | J-P Romeu | United States | Chicago | 1976 |
| 4 | M. Vannier | Romania | Bucharest | 1956-57 |
| 4 | G. Cambérabero | Australia | Paris | 1966-67 |
| 4 | P. Villepreux | Australia | Paris | 1971-72 |
| 4 | J-P Romeu | Argentina | Paris | 1975-76 |
| 4 | J-P Romeu | Argentina | Buenos Aires | 1977 |
| 4 | J-P Lescarboura | Ireland | Paris | 1983-84 |
| 4 | J-P Lescarboura | Wales | Cardiff | 1983-84 |

# GOALS FROM MARKS

| * | Player | Opponents | Venue | Season |
|---|--------|-----------|-------|--------|
| 1 | L. Beguet | Scotland | Edinburgh | 1922-23 |

# TRY ON DEBUT

| Player | Opponents | Venue | Season |
|--------|-----------|-------|--------|
| N. Cessieux | New Zealand | Paris | 1905-06 |
| G. Jérôme | New Zealand | Paris | 1905-06 |
| E. Lesieur | England | Paris | 1905-06 |
| M. Hourdebaight | Ireland | Dublin | 1908-09 |
| R. Laffitte | Wales | Swansea | 1909-10 |
| P. Failliot | Scotland | Paris | 1910-11 |
| J. Dufau | Ireland | Paris | 1911-12 |
| J. Sebedio | Scotland | Paris | 1912-13 |
| J. Lacoste | Ireland | Paris | 1913-14 |
| M. Capmau | England | Paris | 1913-14 |
| W. Gayraud | Ireland | Dublin | 1919-20 |
| R. Got | Ireland | Dublin | 1919-20 |
| H. Galau | Scotland | Paris | 1923-24 |
| E. Piquiral | Scotland | Paris | 1923-24 |
| J. Ballarin | England | Twickenham | 1923-24 |
| G. Gerintes | Romania | Paris | 1923-24 |
| H. Haget | Scotland | Paris | 1927-28 |
| A. Camel | Scotland | Paris | 1927-28 |
| R. Bonamy | N.S.W. | Paris | 1927-28 |
| A. Duche | Germany | Paris | 1928-29 |
| M. Soler | Germany | Paris | 1928-29 |
| C. Petit | Wales | Swansea | 1930-31 |
| E. Chaud | Germany | Frankfurt | 1931-32 |
| J. Coderc | Germany | Frankfurt | 1931-32 |
| R. Finat | Germany | Frankfurt | 1931-32 |
| F. Raynaud | Germany | Paris | 1932-33 |
| A. Duluc | Germany | Hanover | 1933-34 |
| J. Desclaux | Germany | Hanover | 1933-34 |
| A. Vigneau | Germany | Paris | 1934-35 |
| M. Celhay | Germany | Paris | 1934-35 |
| F. Daguerre | Germany | Berlin | 1935-36 |
| P. Geschwind | Germany | Berlin | 1935-36 |
| A. Delque | Italy | Paris | 1937-38 |
| R. Caunègre | Romania | Bucharest | 1937-38 |
| R. le Goff | Romania | Bucharest | 1937-38 |
| J. Dauger | British Army | Paris | 1944-45 |
| G. Baladie | British Army | Paris | 1944-45 |
| J. Prin-Clary | British Army | Paris | 1944-45 |
| A. Sahuc | British Army | Paris | 1944-45 |
| J. Merquey | Scotland | Edinburgh | 1949-50 |
| F. Cazenave | England | Paris | 1949-50 |
| A. Porthault | Scotland | Paris | 1950-51 |
| L. Mias | Scotland | Paris | 1950-51 |
| D. Olive | Ireland | Dublin | 1950-51 |
| L. Roge | Italy | Milan | 1951-52 |
| J. Lepatey | Italy | Rome | 1953-54 |
| G. Murillo | Italy | Rome | 1953-54 |
| G. Larreguy | Italy | Rome | 1953-54 |
| A. Morel | Argentina | Buenos Aires | 1954 |
| G. Pauthe | England | Paris | 1955-56 |
| R. Monie | Czechoslovakia | Toulouse | 1956-57 |
| G. Mauduy | Italy | Agen | 1956-57 |
| C. Vignes | Romania | Bucharest | 1956-57 |
| B. Mommejat | Italy | Naples | 1957-58 |
| G-S. Meyer | Scotland | Edinburgh | 1959-60 |
| R. Crancée | Argentina | Buenos Aires | 1960 |
| H. Marracq | Romania | Bayonne | 1961-62 |
| M. Arnaudet | Ireland | Paris | 1963-64 |
| J. Maso | Italy | Naples | 1965-66 |
| J-C Lagrange | Italy | Naples | 1965-66 |
| J-P Salut | Romania | Bucharest | 1966-67 |
| J. Trillo | South Africa | Johannesburg | 1967 |
| J. Cantoni | Wales | Cardiff | 1969-70 |
| R. Bertranne | England | Twickenham | 1970-71 |
| V. Boffelli | Australia | Paris | 1971-72 |
| G. Delaigue | Japan | Bordeaux | 1973-74 |
| A. Guilbert | England | Twickenham | 1974-75 |
| D. Harize | South Africa | Bloemfontein | 1975 |
| R. Paparemborde | South Africa | Bloemfontein | 1975 |
| D. Bustaffa | Argentina | Buenos Aires | 1977 |
| J. Gallion | England | Paris | 1977-78 |

| Player | Opponents | Venue | Season |
|--------|-----------|-------|--------|
| F. Costes | England | Twickenham | 1978-79 |
| Y. Malquier | Scotland | Paris | 1978-79 |
| P. Mesny | New Zealand | Christchurch | 1979 |
| J. Bégu | Argentina | Paris | 1982-83 |
| E. Bonneval | New Zealand | Auckland | 1984 |
| P. Berot | Romania | Bucharest | 1986-87 |

## CAPTAIN ON INTERNATIONAL DEBUT

| Player | Opponents | Venue | Season |
|--------|-----------|-------|--------|
| H. Amand | New Zealand | Paris | 1905-06 |

(This is the only instance. Louis Junquas was captain on his debut in the Five Nations Championship, against Scotland in 1946-47. However, he had won several caps prior to his Championship debut.)

## TRIES BY FULL-BACKS

| Player | Opponents | Venue | Season |
|--------|-----------|-------|--------|
| M. Vannier | Romania | Bordeaux | 1957-58 |
| C. Lacaze | Ireland | Paris | 1961-62 |
| P. Villepreux | Czechoslovakia | Prague | 1967-68 |
| C. Boujet ★ | Australia | Sydney | 1968 |
| P. Villepreux | Scotland | Paris | 1970-71 |
| J-M Aguirre | Japan | Bordeaux | 1973-74 |
| M. Droitecourt | Argentina | Lyon | 1975-76 |
| M. Droitecourt | Argentina | Paris | 1975-76 |
| J-M Aguirre | Australia | Paris | 1976-77 |
| S. Gabernet | Scotland | Edinburgh | 1979-80 |
| S. Gabernet | Wales | Paris | 1980-81 |
| S. Blanco | Argentina | Toulouse | 1982-83 |
| S. Blanco | Argentina | Paris | 1982-83 |
| S. Blanco | Ireland | Dublin | 1982-83 |
| S. Blanco | New Zealand | Christchurch | 1984 |
| S. Blanco(2) | Scotland | Paris | 1984-85 |
| S. Blanco | Argentina | Buenos Aires | 1985 |
| S. Blanco | Argentina | Buenos Aires | 1985 |
| S. Blanco | Wales | Cardiff | 1985-86 |
| S. Blanco | England | Paris | 1985-86 |
| S. Blanco(2) | Australia | Sydney | 1986 |
| S. Blanco | Romania | Bucharest | 1986-87 |

★ *Boujet scored his try as a replacement for Villepreux.*

## ALL THE POINTS FOR FRANCE IN A MATCH
### (where more than one scoring action is involved)

| Pts | Player | Opponents | Venue | Season |
|-----|--------|-----------|-------|--------|
| 18 | J-M Aguirre | Argentina | Buenos Aires | 1977 |
| 12 | J-P Romeu | Wales | Paris | 1972-73 |
| 12 | J-P Romeu | England | Paris | 1973-74 |
| 9 | J-P Romeu | Romania | Clermont Ferrand | 1977-78 |
| 9 | J-P Lescarboura | England | Twickenham | 1984-85 |
| 9 | J-P Lescarboura | New Zealand | Christchurch | 1986 |
| 8 | J. Prat | Ireland | Paris | 1951-52 |
| 6 | R. Crabos | England | Paris | 1920-21 |
| 6 | M. Vannier | Ireland | Dublin | 1956-57 |
| 6 | P. Albaladéjo | New Zealand | Auckland | 1961 |
| 6 | J-P Romeu | Scotland | Edinburgh | 1973-74 |
| 6 | L. Pariès | Ireland | Dublin | 1974-75 |

# INDIVIDUAL RECORDS

## LONGEST CAREER SPANS

| Seasons | Player | Caps | Career Span |
|---|---|---|---|
| 13½ | P. Dizabo | 13 | 1947-48 to 1960 |
| 13½ | F. Haget | 38 | 1974 to 1986-87 |
| 13 | A. Boniface | 48 | 1953-54 to 1965-66 |
| 12 | M-F Lubin-Lebrère | 15 | 1913-14 to 1924-25 |

## MOST CONSECUTIVE CAPS IN A CAREER

| Caps | Player | Opponents |
|---|---|---|
| 46 | R. Bertranne | *1973* J,R *1974* I,W,E,S,Arg 1,2, R, SA 1,2 *1975* W,E,S,I, SA 1,2, Arg 1,2,R *1976* S,I, W,E,US, A 1,2, R *1977* W,E,S,I, Arg 1,2, NZ 1,2, R *1978* E,S,I,W,R *1979* I,W,E,S |
| 44 | M. Crauste | *1960* Arg 3 *1961* S,SA,E,W,It,I, NZ 1,2,3, A,R *1962* S,E,W,I,It,R *1963* S,I,E,W,It,R *1964* S,NZ,E,W,It,I,SA,Fj,R *1965* S,I,E,W,It, R *1966* S,I,E,W,It |

## MOST CAPS IN A CAREER

| Caps | Player | Career Span |
|---|---|---|
| 69 | R. Bertranne | 1970-71 to 1981-82 |
| 63 | B. Dauga | 1963-64 to 1971-72 |
| 63 | M. Crauste | 1956-57 to 1965-66 |
| 59 | J-P Rives | 1974-75 to 1983-84 |
| 55 | R. Paparemborde | 1975 to 1982-83 |
| 52 | A. Domenech | 1953-54 to 1962-63 |
| 51 | J. Prat | 1944-45 to 1954-55 |
| 51 | W. Spanghéro | 1964 to 1972-73 |
| 50 | M. Celaya | 1952-53 to 1961-62 |
| 50 | J-L Joinel | 1977-78 to 1986-87 |
| 49 | S. Blanco | 1980 to 1986-87 |
| 48 | A. Boniface | 1953-54 to 1965-66 |
| 47 | J-P Lux | 1966-67 to 1974-75 |
| 46 | J-C Skréla | 1971 to 1977-78 |

## MOST POINTS IN A CAREER

| Pts | Player | Matches | Career Span |
|---|---|---|---|
| 265 | J-P Romeu | 34 | 1972-73 to 1977-78 |
| 187 | J-P Lescarboura | 25 | 1981-82 to 1986-87 |
| 180 | M. Vannier | 43 | 1952-53 to 1961 |
| 166 | P. Villepreux | 34 | 1966-67 to 1972 |
| 139 | J. Prat | 51 | 1944-45 to 1954-55 |
| 123 | J-M Aguirre | 39 | 1971-72 to 1979-80 |
| 121 | S. Blanco | 49 | 1980 to 1986-87 |
| 110 | G. Cambérabero | 14 | 1961 to 1967-68 |
| 104 | P. Albaladéjo | 30 | 1953-54 to 1964-65 |
| 101 | G. Laporte | 13 | 1980-81 to 1986 |

# MOST TRIES IN A CAREER

| T | Player | Matches | Career Span |
|---|--------|---------|-------------|
| 23 | C. Darrouy | 40 | 1956-57 to 1967 |
| 19 | J. Dupuy | 40 | 1955-56 to 1963-64 |
| 17 | S. Blanco | 49 | 1980 to 1986-87 |
| 17 | R. Bertranne | 69 | 1970-71 to 1981-82 |
| 16 | P. Sella | 39 | 1982-83 to 1986-87 |
| 15 | G. Boniface | 35 | 1959-60 to 1965-66 |
| 14 | A. Jauréguy | 31 | 1919-20 to 1928-29 |
| 12 | J-P Lux | 47 | 1966-67 to 1974-75 |
| 12 | J-F Gourdon | 22 | 1973-74 to 1979-80 |
| 11 | A. Boniface | 48 | 1953-54 to 1965-66 |
| 11 | P. Estève | 23 | 1982-83 to 1985-86 |
| 10 | M. Crauste | 63 | 1956-57 to 1965-66 |
| 10 | C. Dourthe | 33 | 1966-67 to 1974-75 |
| 10 | J. Gallion | 27 | 1977-78 to 1986 |

# MOST CONVERSIONS IN A CAREER

| C | Player | Matches | Career Span |
|---|--------|---------|-------------|
| 45 | M. Vannier | 43 | 1952-53 to 1961 |
| 29 | P. Villepreux | 34 | 1966-67 to 1972 |
| 27 | J-P Romeu | 34 | 1972-73 to 1977-78 |
| 26 | J. Prat | 51 | 1944-45 to 1954-55 |
| 19 | G. Cambérabero | 14 | 1961 to 1967-68 |
| 19 | J-P Lescarboura | 25 | 1981-82 to 1986-87 |

# MOST DROPPED GOALS IN A CAREER

| DG | Player | Matches | Career Span |
|----|--------|---------|-------------|
| 14 | J-P Lescarboura | 25 | 1981-82 to 1986-87 |
| 12 | P. Albaladéjo | 30 | 1953-54 to 1964-65 |
| 11 | G. Cambérabero | 14 | 1961 to 1967-68 |
| 9 | J-P Romeu | 34 | 1972-73 to 1977-78 |
| 8 | M. Vannier | 43 | 1952-53 to 1961 |
| 7 | G. Laporte | 13 | 1980-81 to 1986 |

# MOST PENALTY GOALS IN A CAREER

| PG | Player | Matches | Career Span |
|----|--------|---------|-------------|
| 56 | J-P Romeu | 34 | 1972-73 to 1977-78 |
| 33 | P. Villepreux | 34 | 1966-67 to 1972 |
| 29 | J-P Lescarboura | 25 | 1981-82 to 1986-87 |
| 28 | J-M Aguirre | 39 | 1971-72 to 1979-80 |
| 21 | M. Vannier | 43 | 1952-53 to 1961 |
| 20 | G. Laporte | 13 | 1980-81 to 1986 |
| 15 | J. Prat | 51 | 1944-45 to 1954-55 |

# MOST MATCHES AS CAPTAIN

| 34 | J-P Romeu | (19 victories) |
|----|-----------|----------------|
| 24 | G. Basquet | (12 victories) |
| 22 | M. Crauste | (15 victories) |
| 21 | J. Fouroux | (14 victories) |
| 18 | F. Moncla | (11 victories) |
| 18 | C. Carrère | (9 victories) |
| 17 | J. Prat | (12 victories) |
| 15 | D. Dubroca | (11 victories) |
| 13 | M. Communeau | (1 victory) |
| 12 | R. Crabos | (4 victories) |
| 12 | A. Jauréguy | (3 victories) |
| 12 | E. Ribère | (8 victories) |
| 12 | M. Celaya | (6 victories) |

# SOUTH AFRICA
# INTERNATIONAL
# TEAMS AND RECORDS

## 1891

| 1st v. GB | 2nd v. GB | 3rd v. GB |
|---|---|---|
| †B. DUFF | B. DUFF | B. DUFF |
| †H.C. BOYES | H.C. BOYES | †A.J. HARTLEY |
| †J.T. VIGNE | J.T. VIGNE | J.T. VIGNE |
| †M.C. VAN BUUREN | †A. DE KOCK | †C. VERSFELD |
| †A.R. RICHARDS | A.R. RICHARDS | *A.R. RICHARDS |
| †F.H. GUTHRIE | †J.M. POWELL | F.H. GUTHRIE |
| *†H.H. CASTENS | *†R.C. SNEDDEN | †C.W. CHIGNELL |
| †W.M. BISSET | †W. TRENERY | W.M. BISSET |
| †J. MERRY | R. SHAND | R. SHAND |
| †F. HAMILTON | †D. SMITH | †J. MCKENDRICK |
| †M. VERSFELD | M. VERSFELD | M. VERSFELD |
| †J.S. LOUW | J.S. LOUW | J.S. LOUW |
| †M. DEVENISH | †B.H. HEATLIE | B.H. HEATLIE |
| †E. ALEXANDER | E. ALEXANDER | †C.G. VAN RENEN |
| †E.M.M. LITTLE | †C.W. SMITH | E.M.M. LITTLE |
| Port Elizabeth | Kimberley | Cape Town |
| LOST 0-4 | LOST 0-3 | LOST 0-4 |
| SA: NIL | SA: NIL | SA: NIL |
| GB: 1G 1T | GB: 1GM | GB: 1G 1T |
| 30 Jul. 1891 | 29 Aug. 1891 | 5 Sep. 1891 |

The South African Rugby Board was formed in 1889, and one of the Board's earliest ideas was to invite a British side to visit South Africa. In September 1890, the RFU seriously discussed the idea at a meeting in the presence of Mr J Richards of Cape Town, who was an Old Leysian and on a visit to England. At length the idea of the tour was approved, a side was selected and Cecil Rhodes, Prime Minister of the Cape Colony, guaranteed to pay any loss incurred by the British tourists.

For the three Tests of 1891, the Union staging the match was responsible for the selection of the team. Herbert Castens, a 26-year-old from Port Elizabeth, became the first South African skipper. A graduate of Oxford University, where he had won Blues in 1886 and 1887, Castens was a fast and intelligent forward who also led the first South African cricket side to England in 1894. A barrister by profession, he became Chief Secretary to the Administrator of Rhodesia from 1899. He also gained the unusual distinction of refereeing the final Test of the 1891 series.

The standard of South African forward play was good, but their backs were very small by comparison with the faster, strapping British backs. Alf Richards, a dynamic half-back from Cape Town, was the most impressive of the South African backs, and captained the side in the third Test.

## 1896

| 1st v. GB | 2nd v. GB | 3rd v. GB | 4th v. GB |
|---|---|---|---|
| †D. LYONS | †D. COPE 1C | T.A. SAMUELS | T.A. SAMUELS |
| †P.S.T. JONES | †T.A. SAMUELS 2T | P.S.T. JONES 1T | P.S.T. JONES |
| †J.H. ANDERSON | †H.H. FORBES | J.H. ANDERSON | J.H. ANDERSON |
| †F.T.D. ASTON | †W.S. TABERER | †A.W. POWELL | F.T.D. ASTON |
| †E. OLVER | *F.T.D. ASTON | *F.T.D. ASTON | †T. HEPBURN 1C |
| *†F.R. MYBURGH | †A. LARARD | †W. COTTY | A. LARARD 1T |
| F.H. GUTHRIE | †G.ST.L. DEVENISH | J.M. POWELL | †T. ETLINGER |
| †J.J. WESSELS | J.J. WESSELS | J.J. WESSELS | †H.A. CLOETE |
| †P. SCOTT | P. SCOTT | P. SCOTT | P. SCOTT |
| †P.J. MEYER | †A.M. BESWICK | A.M. BESWICK | A.M. BESWICK |
| †M. BREDENKAMP | †J.H. CROSBY | M. BREDENKAMP | †P. DE WAAL |
| †F.W. DOUGLASS | †C. DEVENISH | †D.J. THEUNISSEN | †H.D. VAN BROCKHUIZEN |
| B.H. HEATLIE | †T. MELLETT | †E.W. KELLY | *B.H. HEATLIE |
| C.G. VAN RENEN | †J.B. ANDREW | †P.J. DORMEHL | C.G. VAN RENEN |
| †H.C. GORTON | C.W. SMITH | C.W. SMITH | P.J. DORMEHL |
| Port Elizabeth | Johannesburg | Kimberley | Cape Town |
| LOST 0-8 | LOST 8-17 | LOST 3-9 | WON 5-0 |
| SA: NIL | SA: 1G 1T | SA: 1T | SA: 1G |
| GB: 1G 1T | GB: 2G 1DG 1T | GB: 1G 1DG | GB: NIL |
| 30 Jul. 1896 | 22 Aug. 1896 | 29 Aug. 1896 | 5 Sep. 1896 |

As in 1891, the selection of the Test side was left to the centre which staged the match, and a glance at the four Test sides which faced the tourists reveals that only Ferdie Aston, a brother of R.L.Aston, the famous English centre who had played in each match of the 1891 tour by the British side, and P. Scott appeared in the four Tests.

Despite losing the series, the South Africans had the consolation of winning their first international in the final Test at Cape Town. There were eleven Western Province players and four Transvaalers in the winning side, and it is also interesting to note that the occasion was the first on which South Africa wore green shirts. The match was noted for the fine display of the South African forwards, who scrummaged solidly in the tight and dribbled with control in the loose. The only try came in the first half when Anderson sent Larard beneath the posts for a try converted by Hepburn.

Three of this South African side became Test cricketers: P.S.T.Jones, A.W.Powell and J.H.Anderson, who led the 1902 side in the second Test against Australia.

## 1903

| 1st v. GB | 2nd v. GB | 3rd v. GB |
|---|---|---|
| †C.H. JONES | C.H. JONES | W. VAN RENEN |
| | | |
| †J. BARRY | J. BARRY | J. BARRY 1T |
| †W. VAN RENEN | †S. ASHLEY | †H.W. CAROLIN |
| †J.D. KRIGE | †S.C. DE MELKER | J.D. KRIGE |
| †A.O. MORKEL | †B. GIBBS | †J.A. LOUBSER |
| | | |
| †F.J. DOBBIN 1T | F.J. DOBBIN | †H.H. FERRIS |
| J.M. POWELL | *J.M. POWELL | †T.E.C. HOBSON |
| | | |
| *†A. FREW | †J.S. JACKSON | †A. REID 1T |
| W.M.C. McEWAN | †H. D. METCALF | W.M.C. McEWAN |
| †J.H. SINCLAIR 1T | †G. CRAMPTON | †J.A. ANDERSON |
| †J.W.E. RAAFF | J.W.E. RAAFF | †P.J. ROOS |
| †C. BROWN | C. BROWN | C. BROWN |
| B.H. HEATLIE 2C | †W.C. MARTHEZE | *B.H. HEATLIE 1C |
| †P.A.R.O. NEL | P.A.R.O. NEL | P.A.R.O. NEL |
| †E.J.C. PARTRIDGE | †C. CURRIE | †J. BOTHA |
| | | |
| Johannesburg | Kimberley | Cape Town |
| DRAWN 10-10 | DRAWN 0-0 | WON 8-0 |
| | | |
| SA: 2G | SA: NIL | SA: 1G 1T |
| GB: 2G | GB: NIL | GB: NIL |
| | | |
| 26 Aug. 1903 | 5 Sep. 1903 | 12 Sep. 1903 |

Following drawn Tests at Johannesburg and Kimberley, South Africa beat the British tourists in the final Test to win their first ever international series in 1903. The selectors were criticised for choosing Van Renen, a centre, out of position at full-back; and for selecting Carolin (a half-back) in the threequarters. But following a scoreless first half in which Van Renen defended skilfully in wet and difficult conditions, the South Africans took the series with a try by Barry and one by Reid, following an opening made by Hobson.

Heatlie was appointed captain for the second and third Tests, though he stood down from the side at Kimberley to return to Cape Town to attend the birth of his second son. Like Jack Powell, Heatlie had played in 1891 against the British, and their Test career spans of thirteen seasons remain South African international records. Heatlie was considered (by his contemporaries) the greatest forward produced by South Africa.

Of the South Africans capped in this series, McEwan and Frew had previously played for Scotland, while Partridge, one of the forwards in the first Test, was a regular player for both the Blackheath and Newport clubs in Britain.

## 1906-07

| v. SCOTLAND | v. IRELAND | v. WALES | v. ENGLAND |
|---|---|---|---|
| †A.F.W. MARSBERG | †S.J. JOUBERT 1PG | A.F.W. MARSBERG | S.J. JOUBERT |
| | | | |
| †A.C. STEGMANN | A.C. STEGMANN 1T | S.J. JOUBERT 1T,1C | A.F.W. MARSBERG |
| †H.A. DE VILLIERS | †J.G. HIRSCH | H.A. DE VILLIERS | H.A. DE VILLIERS |
| J.D. KRIGE | J.D. KRIGE 1T | J.D. KRIGE | S. C. DE MELKER |
| J.A. LOUBSER | J.A. LOUBSER 2T | J.A. LOUBSER 1T | J.A. LOUBSER |
| | | | |
| *H.W. CAROLIN | †D.C. JACKSON | D.C. JACKSON | D.C. JACKSON |
| F.J. DOBBIN | H.W. CAROLIN | F.J. DOBBIN | F.J. DOBBIN |
| | | | |
| †W.A.G. BURGER | W.A.G. BURGER | W.A.G. BURGER | †W.A. MILLAR 1T |
| †H.J. DANEEL | H.J. DANEEL | H.J. DANEEL | H.J. DANEEL |
| †D.J. BRINK | A.F. BURDETT | D.J. BRINK | D.J. BRINK |
| †D. BROOKS | *P.J. ROOS | *P.J. ROOS | *P.J. ROOS |
| J.W.E. RAAFF | †D.F.T. MORKEL | J.W.E. RAAFF 1T | J.W.E. RAAFF |
| †A.F. BURDETT | W.C. MARTHEZE | W.C. MARTHEZE | D.F.T. MORKEL |
| †W.S. MORKEL | W.S. MORKEL | W.S. MORKEL | W.S. MORKEL |
| †D.S. MARE | †P.A. LE ROUX | P.A. LE ROUX | P.A. LE ROUX |
| | | | |
| Hampden Park | Belfast | Swansea | Crystal Palace |
| LOST 0-6 | WON 15-12 | WON 11-0 | DRAWN 3-3 |
| | | | |
| SCOT.: 2T | IRE.: 1PG 3T | WALES: NIL | ENG.: 1T |
| SA: NIL | SA: 1PG 4T | SA: 1G 2T | SA: 1T |
| | | | |
| 17 Nov. 1906 | 24 Nov. 1906 | 1 Dec. 1906 | 8 Dec. 1906 |

The selection of South Africa's first team to tour abroad was based on the performances of those competing in the 1906 Currie Cup tournament, and the names of the tourists were first given on the screen at the Empire Theatre in Johannesburg on the last Saturday night of the competition. Western Province, the Cup winners, provided the bulk of the players, and Paul Roos, a schoolmaster who had not participated in the Currie Cup games, was included in the party and subsequently elected skipper.

The team did not quite capture the attention of the British public to the extent that the First All Blacks, who toured a year earlier, had. Nevertheless, the "Springbokken" (or Springboks) as the side was named, enjoyed an unbeaten run up to the first of the internationals. The tourists fielded the Stellenbosch quartet of Loubser, Stegmann, Krige and de Villiers against Scotland, but the Test (played in awful conditions) was lost and the four were never again selected en-bloc for a Test. Against Ireland, Krige (the finest of the Springbok midfield players), Stegmann and Loubser scored four of the tries in a 15-12 win; while Krige's brilliance at Swansea paved the way for first-half scores by Joubert and Loubser as the tourists recorded their finest result of the tour. The final Test was played in dreadful conditions at Crystal Palace. The Springboks relied on their forwards for inspiration, but in a match of missed chances the tourists had to settle for a draw.

## 1910

| 1st v. GB | 2nd v. GB | 3rd v. GB |
|---|---|---|
| †P.A. MARSBERG | †P. ALLPORT | P. ALLPORT 1T |
| | | |
| †C.H.L. HAHN 1T | C.H.L. HAHN | C.H.L. HAHN |
| J.G. HIRSCH | †R.R. LUYT | R.R. LUYT |
| †D.I. DE VILLIERS 1T | D.I. DE VILLIERS | D.I. DE VILLIERS |
| J.A. LOUBSER | †W.J. MILLS 1T | J.A. LOUBSER |
| | | |
| †F.P. LUYT 1T | F.P. LUYT | F.P. LUYT 1T |
| F.J. DOBBIN | †R.C.B. VAN RYNEVELD | R.C.B. VAN RYNEVELD |
| | | |
| †A.E. WILLIAMS | *W.A. MILLAR | *W.A. MILLAR |
| †N.R.F.G. HOWE-BROWNE | N.R.F.G. HOWE-BROWNE | N.R.F.G. HOWE-BROWNE |
| †N. CROSBY | W.A.G. BURGER | N. CROSBY |
| †H.W. WALKER | H.W. WALKER | H.W. WALKER |
| J.W.E. RAAFF | †G.D. ROOS | G.D. ROOS 1T |
| *D.F.T. MORKEL 1T,1C | T.M. MOLL | D.F.T. MORKEL 1PG,3C |
| †C.E. RIORDAN | †T.M. MOLL | †W.H. MORKEL |
| †M. DAVIDSON | C.E. RIORDAN | |
| | †A.C. LOMBARD | †H.J. REYNECKE 1T |
| | | |
| Johannesburg | Port Elizabeth | Cape Town |
| WON 14-10 | LOST 3-8 | WON 21-5 |
| | | |
| SA: 1G 3T | SA: 1T | SA: 3G 1PG 1T |
| GB: 1DG 2T | GB: 1G 1T | GB: 1G |
| | | |
| 6 Aug. 1910 | 27 Aug. 1910 | 3 Sep. 1910 |

The selection system for the 1910 Tests was complex: three five-man panels nominated the teams, with the host Unions appointing two selectors and the two other Test centres nominating one selector. Griqualand, which no longer staged a Test, was allowed one panel member.

Douglas Morkel, who served South African sides from 1906 to 1913, captained the Springboks at Johannesburg. A prodigious kicker, his try and conversion helped his side to a narrow victory in the first Test, though he was succeeded as skipper by Billy Millar for the rest of the series. Following his inspiring play in leading the Springboks to victory in this 1910 series, Millar was appointed captain of the Second Springboks to Britain in 1912.

The 1910 series was settled with a convincing Springbok win in a bruising last Test at Cape Town. Percy Allport, a splendid utility player who had appeared with distinction as a threequarter for his club, became the first South African full-back to score a try in an international with a fine solo effort after fielding a stray kick near the half-way line.

## 1912-13

| v. SCOTLAND | v. IRELAND | v. WALES | v. ENGLAND | v. FRANCE |
|---|---|---|---|---|
| †P.G. MORKEL 1C | P.G. MORKEL 3C | P.G. MORKEL | P.G. MORKEL | P.G. MORKEL |
| | | | | |
| †J.A. STEGMANN 2T | J.A. STEGMANN 3T | J.A. STEGMANN | J.A. STEGMANN | J.A. STEGMANN |
| R.R. LUYT | R.R. LUYT | R.R. LUYT | R.R. LUYT | R.R. LUYT 1T |
| †J.W.H. MORKEL | J.W.H. MORKEL 2T | J.W.H. MORKEL | J.W.H. MORKEL 1T | J.W.H. MORKEL 1T,2C |
| †E.E. MCHARDY 1T | E.E. MCHARDY 3T | E.E. MCHARDY | E.E. MCHARDY | E.E. MCHARDY 2T |
| | | | | |
| F.P. LUYT | F.P. LUYT 1C | F.P. LUYT | F.P. LUYT | †J.H. IMMELMAN |
| *F.J. DOBBIN | F.J. DOBBIN | F.J. DOBBIN | †J.D. MCCULLOCH | J.D. MCCULLOCH |
| | | | | |
| †J.D. LUYT | *W.A. MILLAR 1T | *W.A. MILLAR | J.D. LUYT | *W.A. MILLAR |
| †S.H. LEDGER | S.H. LEDGER | G. THOMPSON | S.H. LEDGER | S.H. LEDGER 1T |
| †G. THOMPSON | G. THOMPSON | J.D. LUYT | †E.H. SHUM | J.D. LUYT |
| †T.F. VAN VUUREN | T.F. VAN VUUREN | T.F. VAN VUUREN | T.F. VAN VUUREN | T.F. VAN VUUREN |
| †J.A.J. FRANCIS | J.A.J. FRANCIS 1T | J.A.J. FRANCIS | J.A.J. FRANCIS | J.A.J. FRANCIS 1T |
| D.F.T. MORKEL 1C | D.F.T. MORKEL | D.F.T. MORKEL 1PG | *D.F.T. MORKEL 2PG | D.F.T. MORKEL 2T,1PG,2C |
| W.H. MORKEL 1T | W.H. MORKEL | W.H. MORKEL | W.H. MORKEL | W.H. MORKEL 1T |
| †A.S. KNIGHT | A.S. KNIGHT | A.S. KNIGHT | A.S. KNIGHT | A.S. KNIGHT |
| | | | | |
| Inverleith | Landowne Road | Cardiff Arms Park | Twickenham | Bordeaux |
| WON 16-0 | WON 38-0 | WON 3-0 | WON 9-3 | WON 38-5 |
| | | | | |
| SCOT.: NIL | IRE.: NIL | WALES: NIL | ENG.: 1T | FR.: 1G |
| SA: 2G 2T | SA: 4G 6T | SA: 1PG | SA: 2PG 1T | SA: 4G 1PG 5T |
| | | | | |
| 23 Nov. 1912 | 30 Nov. 1912 | 14 Dec. 1912 | 4 Jan. 1913 | 11 Jan. 1913 |

The Second Springboks to Britain were one of the most successful touring sides ever to play in the Northern Hemisphere. The side was one of all-round strength and won each of its five international matches – a feat performed only once since – and several Springbok records were established on the tour.

Jan Stegmann, a dentist who became South Africa's oldest surviving international player, and Boetie McHardy, each scored three tries in South Africa's record win against Ireland, while McHardy finished the tour with six Test tries to create a new South African career record which stood until the 1930s. And in the official Test against France, Douglas Morkel made a new record for an individual by scoring 13 points at Bordeaux.

The match against England was the stiffest game of the tour. Only two long-range penalties by Douglas Morkel settled a close game after Jack Morkel, a neat threequarter who proved to be the most capable of the Springboks centres, opened the scoring with a try following clever work by his co-centre, Dick Luyt. The try tied the scores, Poulton having scored for England. Like Poulton, Jack Morkel died on active service. As a trooper with the Mounted Brigade Scout Corps, Jack Morkel died of dysentery in East Africa in 1916, aged twenty-four.

## 1921

| 1st v. NZ | 2nd v. NZ | 3rd v. NZ |
|---|---|---|
| P.G. MORKEL 1C | P.G. MORKEL 1DG,1C | P.G. MORKEL |
| †A.J. VAN HEERDEN 1T | †W.C. ZELLER | A.J. VAN HEERDEN |
| †W.A. CLARKSON | W.A. CLARKSON | †S.S.F. STRAUSS |
| †C. DU P. MEYER | †W.D. SENDIN 1T | †J.S. DE KOCK |
| †H.W. MORKEL | H.W. MORKEL | W.C. ZELLER |
| †W.D. TOWNSEND | C. DU P. MEYER | C. DU P. MEYER |
| †J.P. MICHAU | J.P. MICHAU | J.P. MICHAU |
| †P.J. MOSTERT | P.J. MOSTERT | F.W. MELLISH |
| †T.L. KRUGER | T.L. KRUGER | P.J. MOSTERT |
| †F.W. MELLISH | †N.J. DU PLESSIS | N. J. DU PLESSIS |
| †J.M. MICHAU | †G.W. VAN ROOYEN | G. W. VAN ROOYEN |
| †H.J. MORKEL | †J.A. MORKEL | J.A. MORKEL |
| †H.H. SCHOLTZ | †M. ELLIS | M. ELLIS |
| *W.H. MORKEL | *W.H. MORKEL | *W.H. MORKEL |
| †A.P. WALKER | H.H. SCHOLTZ | A.P. WALKER |
| Dunedin | Auckland | Wellington |
| LOST 5-13 | WON 9-5 | DRAWN 0-0 |
| NZ: 2G 1T | NZ: 1G | NZ: NIL |
| SA: 1G | SA: 1G 1DG | SA: NIL |
| 13 Aug. 1921 | 27 Aug. 1921 | 17 Sep. 1921 |

The first tour to Australasia took place in 1921. Theo Pienaar was the captain of a side which played 24 games in Australia and New Zealand and which lost twice. The tour party comprised 29 players, though five were members of the remarkable Morkel family, and two of the family, W.H. "Boy" Morkel and Gerhard Morkel, gained the distinction of playing international rugby before and after the Great War.

The first series between the world's greatest rugby nations was drawn – a suitable reflection of the strengths of the two sides. At Dunedin, in torrential rain, the Springboks went ahead through a try by Attie van Heerden, but were outplayed by the clever New Zealand backs. The series was tied at Auckland, thanks to a huge drop-goal by Gerhard Morkel, before at Wellington, in heavy rain once again, a scoreless draw before 18,000 spectators completed a famous series.

Van Heerden, the first man to score a try in a New Zealand-South Africa Test, was an exceptional sprinter and represented South Africa as an athlete in the Olympics. In October 1923, having graduated from Stellenbosch University, he became one of the first Springboks to turn professional when he joined Wigan. He enjoyed a successful Rugby League career, and with George van Rooyan, a huge forward who also figured in the 1921 series, he gained a RL Cup-winners medal in 1924 (scoring a try in the final), and a Championship medal in 1926.

## 1924

| 1st v. GB | 2nd v. GB | 3rd v. GB | 4th v. GB |
|---|---|---|---|
| †J.C. TINDALL | †N.J.S. BOSMAN | N.J.S. BOSMAN | N.J.S. BOSMAN |
| †K.T. STARKE | K.T. STARKE 1T | K.T. STARKE | K.T. STARKE 2T,1DG |
| *†P.K. ALBERTYN | *P.K. ALBERTYN 1T | *P.K. ALBERTYN | *P.K. ALBERTYN |
| W.A. CLARKSON | †J.J.N. BESTER | J.S. DE KOCK | J.J.N. BESTER 1T |
| †J. AUCAMP 1T | J. AUCAMP | †J.T. SLATER | J.T. SLATER 1T |
| †B.L. OSLER 1DG | B.L. OSLER 1PG,1C | B.L. OSLER | B.L. OSLER |
| †W.H. MYBURGH | †D.R. TRUTER | †D. DEVINE | D.R. TRUTER |
| P.J. MOSTERT | P.J. MOSTERT 1T | †B.E. VAN DER PLANK | B.E. VAN DER PLANK |
| T.L. KRUGER | T.L. KRUGER | T.L. KRUGER | T.L. KRUGER |
| F.W. MELLISH | F.W. MELLISH | F.W. MELLISH | F.W. MELLISH |
| †C. PAYN | C. PAYN | N.J. DU PLESSIS | J.B. LA GRANGE |
| N.J. DU PLESSIS | N.J. DU PLESSIS | †J.B. LA GRANGE | P.J. MOSTERT |
| A.P. WALKER | A.P. WALKER | A.P. WALKER | A.P. WALKER |
| M. ELLIS | M. ELLIS | M. ELLIS | M. ELLIS |
| †N.J.V. VAN DRUTEN | N.J.V. VAN DRUTEN 1T | N.J.V. VAN DRUTEN 1T | N.J.V. VAN DRUTEN |
| Durban | Johannesburg | Port Elizabeth | Cape Town |
| WON 7-3 | WON 17-0 | DRAWN 3-3 | WON 16-9 |
| SA: 1DG 1T | SA: 1G 1PG 3T | SA: 1T | SA: 1DG 4T |
| GB: 1T | GB: NIL | GB: 1T | GB: 1PG 2T |
| 16 Aug. 1924 | 23 Aug. 1924 | 13 Sep. 1924 | 20 Sep. 1924 |

The 1924 Springboks possessed a seasoned pack of skilful, heavy forwards who laid the foundation for a convincing win in the Test series. Bennie Osler, a magnificent kicker who was to spearhead the Springbok attack for a decade, came into the side at Durban and opened the scoring with a drop-goal which set South Africa on the way to a narrow first Test success. After playing 17 consecutive Tests, Osler retired in 1933 as the leading Springbok cap holder, and his tally of 46 points in internationals established a new South African international record.

Frank Mellish, who had first appeared in 1921, was South Africa's third dual rugby international. As a Blackheath player shortly after the War, in which he was awarded the MC for bravery at the Battle of Ypres, Mellish won six caps for England and played in their 1921 Grand Slam side. He was later a South African selector and was the manager of the 1951 Springboks to England.

Pieter Albertyn captained South Africa in the series. A tall, strapping sprinter, Albertyn had practised dentistry in England and been invited to appear in England trials before he returned to South Africa.

## 1928

| | 1st v. NZ | 2nd v. NZ | 3rd v. NZ | 4th v. NZ |
|---|---|---|---|---|
| | J.C. TINDALL | J.C. TINDALL | J.C. TINDALL | J.C. TINDALL |
| | †J.P. PRINSLOO | †N.S. TOD | †H.P.K. DE JONGH 1T | †P.K. MORKEL |
| | †S.G. OSLER | †J.A.R. DOBIE | †W.P. ROUSSEAU | W.P. ROUSSEAU |
| | B.A. DUFFY | †J.C. VAN DER WESTHUIZEN | J.C. VAN DER WESTHUIZEN | J.C. VAN DER WESTHUIZEN 1T |
| | J.T. SLATER 1T | †G.H. BRAND | G.H. BRAND | †J.A. VAN NIEKERK |
| | B.L. OSLER 2DG,2PG | B.L. OSLER 1PG | B.L. OSLER 1C | B.L. OSLER 1C |
| | †P. DE VILLIERS | D. DEVINE | P. DE VILLIERS | P. DE VILLIERS |
| | *P.J. MOSTERT | *P.J. MOSTERT 1GM | †M.M. LOUW | M.M. LOUW |
| | T.L. KRUGER | T.L. KRUGER | *P.J. MOSTERT | *P.J. MOSTERT |
| | †S.P. VAN WYK | H.J. POTGIETER | †J.F. OLIVER | J.F. OLIVER |
| | †H.J. POTGIETER | S.P. VAN WYK | P.J. NEL 1T | A.F. DU TOIT |
| | †P.J. NEL | P.J. NEL | †A.F. DU TOIT | P.J. NEL |
| | †N.F. PRETORIUS | N.F. PRETORIUS | N.F. PRETORIUS | N.F. PRETORIUS |
| | †G.M. DANEEL | G.M. DANEEL | G.M. DANEEL 1T | G.M. DANEEL |
| | N.J.V. VAN DRUTEN | N.J.V. VAN DRUTEN | N.J.V. VAN DRUTEN | N.J.V. VAN DRUTEN |
| | Durban | Johannesburg | Port Elizabeth | Cape Town |
| | WON 17-0 | LOST 6-7 | WON 11-6 | LOST 5-13 |
| | SA: 2DG 2PG 1T | SA: 1GM 1PG | SA: 1G 2T | SA: 1G |
| | NZ: NIL | NZ: 1DG 1PG | NZ: 2T | NZ: 1T 2PG 1DG |
| | 30 Jun. 1928 | 21 Jul. 1928 | 18 Aug. 1928 | 1 Sep. 1928 |

For most of the twentieth century, rugby has been dominated by either New Zealand or South Africa and the 1928 series was built-up in the press as the World Championship decider. But, as in 1921, the rubber was tied.

The strength of the Springboks' side was its great pack, which was built on the foundation of an experienced and solid trio comprising Mostert, Kruger and Van Druten, three survivors from 1924. Mostert, a clerk, was the captain in the series and at Johannesburg, in the second Test, became the only Springbok ever to kick a goal from a mark in an international. His effort followed a New Zealand drop-out and opened the scoring. But in a tight match in which the 2-3-2 scrummage of the All Blacks overcame the 3-4-1 and 3-3-2 formations adopted by the Springboks, the visitors tied the series through a late drop-goal.

South Africa wore white shorts for the first time when they took the field at Port Elizabeth for the third Test. M.M. "Boy" Louw made his debut in this match. Later he bcame one of the most powerful front rankers ever produced by SA and set a new appearance record by winning 18 caps. Immensely strong, he helped his side to victory on his debut but could not prevent New Zealand levelling the rubber at Cape Town.

## 1931-32

| | v. WALES | v. IRELAND | v. ENGLAND | v. SCOTLAND |
|---|---|---|---|---|
| | G.H. BRAND | G.H. BRAND | G.H. BRAND 1DG | G.H. BRAND |
| | †M. ZIMERMAN | M. ZIMERMAN 1T | M. ZIMERMAN | M. ZIMERMAN |
| | †B.G. GRAY | †F.W. WARING 1T | B.G. GRAY | B.G. GRAY |
| | †J. WHITE | J.C. VAN DER WESTHUIZEN | F.W. WARING | J.H. VAN DER WESTHUIZEN |
| | †F.D. VENTER | †J.H. VAN DER WESTHUIZEN | J.H. VAN DER WESTHUIZEN | F.D. VENTER |
| | *B.L. OSLER 1C | *B.L. OSLER 1C | *B.L. OSLER | *B.L. OSLER 1T |
| | †D.H. CRAVEN | D.H. CRAVEN | P. DE VILLIERS | D.H. CRAVEN 1T |
| | P.J. MOSTERT | P.J. MOSTERT | P.J. MOSTERT | P.J. MOSTERT |
| | †H.G. KIPLING | H.G. KIPLING | H.G. KIPLING | H.G. KIPLING |
| | M.M. LOUW | M.M. LOUW | M.M. LOUW | M.M. LOUW |
| | †W.F. BERGH 1T | W.F. BERGH | W.F. BERGH 1T | W.F. BERGH |
| | P.J. NEL | P.J. NEL | P.J. NEL | P.J. NEL |
| | †A.J. VAN DER MERWE | †J.N. BIERMAN | †L.C. STRACHAN | L.C. STRACHAN |
| | G.M. DANEEL 1T | G.M. DANEEL | G.M. DANEEL | G.M. DANEEL |
| | †J.A.J. MCDONALD | J.A.J. MCDONALD | J.A.J. MCDONALD | J.A.J. MCDONALD |
| | Swansea | Lansdowne Road | Twickenham | Murrayfield |
| | WON 8-3 | WON 8-3 | WON 7-0 | WON 6-3 |
| | WALES: 1T | IRE.: 1PG | ENG.: NIL | SCOT.: 1T |
| | SA: 1G 1T | SA: 1G 1T | SA: 1DG 1T | SA: 2T |
| | 5 Dec. 1931 | 19 Dec. 1931 | 2 Jan. 1932 | 16 Jan. 1932 |

A well-drilled pack adopting a 3-4-1 formation and backed by a tactical genius in Bennie Osler, the captain, made the Third Springboks to Britain a highly successful combination.

Osler's immaculate tactical kicking and his unerring sense for weakness in opposition defences steered the side towards its fine record. Osler's pack was an admirable servant, gaining plenty of good possession for him to work the touchline with ruthless precision. Only near the opposition's goal-line did Osler release his backs, a tactic which led the pundits to criticise his rather dour methods. Nevertheless, the side drew large crowds in Britain: the mean attendance at club/representative matches was 22,500, and an average of 53,000 spectators attended the four Tests.

Danie Craven was the most notable of the Springbok newcomers, earning his international colours before winning a Provincial cap. Craven played 16 times for South Africa before the Second War, appearing in Tests as a fly-half, scrum-half, centre and loose forward. As an innovative coach, thoughtful manager and President of the SARB, he has remained at the fore of South African rugby for more than fifty years.

## 1933

| 1st v. AUSTRALIA | 2nd v. AUSTRALIA | 3rd v. AUSTRALIA | 4th v. AUSTRALIA | 5th v. AUSTRALIA |
| --- | --- | --- | --- | --- |
| G.H. BRAND 1PG,1C | G.H. BRAND 1PG | G.H. BRAND 1C | †B.C. REID | J. WHITE |
| †J.H. GAGE | †P.J. LYSTER | F.D. VENTER | J. WHITE 1T | P.J. LYSTER |
| F.W. WARING | F.G. TURNER | F.W. WARING | F.W. WARING | F.W. WARING |
| J. WHITE | J. WHITE | J. WHITE | D.H. CRAVEN | B.G. GRAY |
| †F.G. TURNER | F.W. WARING 1T | F.G. TURNER 1T | G.H. BRAND 1PG | G.H. BRAND 1DG |
| B.L. OSLER 1T | *B.L. OSLER | B.L. OSLER 1DG | B.L. OSLER 1C | B.L. OSLER |
| D.H. CRAVEN 1T | D.H. CRAVEN | D.H. CRAVEN | P. DE VILLIERS | D.H. CRAVEN |
| †S.C. LOUW | S.C. LOUW | S.C. LOUW | S.C. LOUW 1T | S.C. LOUW |
| H.G. KIPLING | H.G. KIPLING | H.G. KIPLING | H.G. KIPLING | H.G. KIPLING |
| M.M. LOUW | M.M. LOUW | M.M. LOUW 1T | M.M. LOUW | M.M. LOUW |
| *P.J. NEL | V. GEERE | V. GEERE | V. GEERE | V. GEERE |
| †V. GEERE | †P.J. VISSER | *P.J. NEL | *P.J. NEL | *P.J. NEL |
| †G. D'ALTON | †L.B. HATTINGH | †W.H. CLARKE | †J.T. APSEY | J.T. APSEY |
| W.F. BERGH 2T | W.F. BERGH | W.F. BERGH | W.F. BERGH | W.F. BERGH |
| †I.L. FRONEMAN | †J.L. NYKAMP | †F.C. SMOLLAN | F.C. SMOLLAN | F.C. SMOLLAN |
| Cape Town | Durban | Johannesburg | Port Elizabeth | Bloemfontein |
| WON 17-3 | LOST 6-21 | WON 12-3 | WON 11-0 | LOST 4-15 |
| SA: 1G 1PG 3T | SA: 1PG 1T | AUST.: 1T | SA: 1G 1PG 1T | SA: 1DG |
| AUST.: 1PG | AUST.: 3G 1PG 1T | SA: 1G 1DG 1T | AUST.: NIL | AUST.: 1G 1DG 2T |
| 8 Jul. 1933 | 22 Jul. 1933 | 12 Aug. 1933 | 26 Aug. 1933 | 2 Sep. 1933 |

The first Tests between South Africa and Australia took place in a protracted series of five matches played in 1933. The opening Test of the series saw the Springboks continue the winning run started in Britain 18 months earlier. A heavy but skilful pack ground the Australians into the dust in an ill-tempered game at Cape Town.

But the tourists staged a recovery at Durban in the second Test and inflicted the heaviest defeat suffered by South Africa since their entry to internationals in 1891. Phil Nel, who had led South Africa at Cape Town, had to stand down through injury for the Durban Test, Osler resuming the captaincy. Having tired of caustic criticism of his dour methods, Osler apparently opted to adopt a more expansive approach. But this led to disaster and the Australians were able to run in four splendid tries.

Freddie Turner made his debut on the wing at Cape Town as a late replacement, becoming (at 19 years, three months) the youngest South African to appear in a Test. A versatile back, he played 11 tests and scored 29 points. His co-wing at Cape Town, Jack Gage, was a dual international, having played for Ireland in 1926 and 1927.

## 1937

| 1st v. AUSTRALIA | 2nd v. AUSTRALIA | 1st v. NZ | 2nd v. NZ | 3rd v. NZ |
| --- | --- | --- | --- | --- |
| G.H. BRAND 1PG | G.H. BRAND 4C | F.G. TURNER | G.H. BRAND 1PG,2C | G.H. BRAND 1C |
| †D.O. WILLIAMS | D.O. WILLIAMS 1T | D.O. WILLIAMS 1T | D.O. WILLIAMS | D.O. WILLIAMS 1T |
| †L. BABROW | L. BABROW 1T | L. BABROW | L. BABROW | L. BABROW 2T |
| J. WHITE | J. WHITE 1T | J. WHITE 1DG | J. WHITE | †G.P. LOCHNER |
| F.G. TURNER | F.G. TURNER | P.J. LYSTER | F.G. TURNER 1T | F.G. TURNER 1T |
| D.H. CRAVEN | †D.F. VAN DER VYVER | *D.H. CRAVEN | †T.A. HARRIS | T.A. HARRIS |
| P. DE VILLIERS | P. DE VILLIERS | P. DE VILLIERS | D.H. CRAVEN | D.H. CRAVEN |
| S.C. LOUW | †H.J. MARTIN | S.C. LOUW | S.C. LOUW | S.C. LOUW |
| †J.W. LOTZ | J.W. LOTZ | J.W. LOTZ | J.W. LOTZ | J.W. LOTZ |
| M.M. LOUW | M.M. LOUW | †C.B. JENNINGS | M.M. LOUW | M.M. LOUW |
| *P.J. NEL | W.F. BERGH 1T | W.F. BERGH | *P.J. NEL | *P.J. NEL |
| †M.A. VAN DEN BERGH | *P.J. NEL | M.A. VAN DEN BERGH | M.A. VAN DEN BERGH | M.A. VAN DEN BERGH |
| L.C. STRACHAN | L.C. STRACHAN | L.C. STRACHAN | L.C. STRACHAN | L.C. STRACHAN |
| W.F. BERGH 1T | D.H. CRAVEN | G.L. VAN REENEN | W.F. BERGH | W.F. BERGH 1T |
| †W.E. BASTARD 1T | †G.L. VAN REENEN 2T | W.E. BASTARD | W.E. BASTARD 1T | W.E. BASTARD |
| Sydney | Sydney | Wellington | Christchurch | Auckland |
| WON 9-5 | WON 26-17 | LOST 7-13 | WON 13-6 | WON 17-6 |
| AUST.: 1G | AUST.: 1G 2PG 2T | NZ: 1DG 2PG 1T | NZ: 2T | NZ: 2PG |
| SA: 1PG 2T | SA: 4G 2T | SA: 1DG 1T | SA: 2G 1PG | SA: 1G 4T |
| 26 Jun. 1937 | 17 Jul. 1937 | 14 Aug. 1937 | 4 Sep. 1937 | 25 Sep. 1937 |

Philip Nel's tourists of 1937 were regarded as the finest Springboks prior to the Second War. The side established numerous scoring records on the tour, impressed their hosts with the sheer power and expertise of their scrummaging, and became the first team to win a rubber in a New Zealand–South Africa series. The tour began well with an impressive march through Australia, though there was a setback at Sydney where a strong NSW side upset the tourists to the tune of 17-6. South Africa won the two Tests, however, and in a breathless first half at Sydney ran up 26 points against Australia in the second of the Tests.

Good wins in the early provincial matches in New Zealand enabled the Springboks to enter the first Test with confidence. Later, after defeat, over-confidence was blamed for their surprise defeat, though the side which lost at Wellington certainly had an unusual balance. Nel, the captain and inspiration of the side was left out; Craven, the expert scrum-half who had become the world's leading exponent of the dive pass, played at fly-half; and Boy Louw and Gerry Brand, two key players, were injured. Louw, Brand and Nel returned for the remainder of the series and Craven was able to resume his duties at the base of the scrum with Tony Harris, a diminutive, elusive and outstanding fly-half as partner. Brand's excellent place-kicking, Craven's immaculate service from a magnificent pack and tries from Turner and Williams, two hard-running wings, swept South Africa to victory in the series and to the title of unofficial "World Champions".

## 1938

| 1st v. GB | 2nd v. GB | 3rd v. GB |
|---|---|---|
| G.H. BRAND 2PG,4C | F.G. TURNER 2C,2PG | †G.A.C. SMITH |
| | | |
| D.O. WILLIAMS 2T | D.O. WILLIAMS | D.O. WILLIAMS |
| †P. DE WET | P. DE WET | P. DE WET |
| G.P. LOCHNER | G.P. LOCHNER 1T | F.G. TURNER 1T,2C,1PG |
| F.G. TURNER | †J.L.A. BESTER 1T | J.L.A. BESTER 1T |
| | | |
| T.A. HARRIS 1T | T.A. HARRIS | T.A. HARRIS |
| *D.H. CRAVEN | *D.H. CRAVEN | *D.H. CRAVEN |
| | | |
| S.C. LOUW 1T | S.C. LOUW | S.C. LOUW |
| J.W. LOTZ | J.W. LOTZ | J.W. LOTZ 1T |
| M.M. LOUW | M.M. LOUW | M.M. LOUW |
| W.F. BERGH | W.F. BERGH | W.F. BERGH |
| †A.R. SHERIFF | A.R. SHERIFF | A.R. SHERIFF |
| †B.A. DU TOIT | B.A. DU TOIT 1T | B.A. DU TOIT |
| L.C. STRACHAN | L.C. STRACHAN | L.C. STRACHAN |
| W.E. BASTARD | J.T. APSEY | W.E. BASTARD |
| Johannesburg | Port Elizabeth | Cape Town |
| WON 26-12 | WON 19-3 | LOST 16-21 |
| SA: 4G 2PG | SA: 2G 2PG 1T | SA: 2G 1PG 1T |
| GB: 4PG | GB: 1T | GB: 1G 1DG 1PG 3T |
| 6 Aug. 1938 | 3 Sep. 1938 | 10 Sep. 1938 |

This was one of the most thrilling series seen in South Africa. The British Lions and the Springboks joined in a rubber which produced open, attractive rugby which was enjoyed by spectators, players and officials of both sides. The Springboks had the edge up front, their huge front row of the Louw brothers and Lotz each over six feet in height showing the excellent form which had impressed the All Blacks a year earlier, and South Africa deserved to take the series 2-1 after three high-scoring Tests.

Some extraordinary place-kicking by Brand helped the Springboks to a 26-12 win at Johannesburg. His contribution of 14 points equalled the SA Test record (established by Bennie Osler at Durban in 1928). However, Brand was injured just before the second Test, and in a reshuffle Freddie Turner moved to full-back and assumed the duties of first place-kicker. In a match played in sweltering heat, the Springboks were convincing winners with Turner helping to secure the rubber by kicking ten points.

Ferdie Bergh played the last of his 17 consecutive Tests in the defeat in the last Test at Cape Town, his career tally of seven Test tries standing as a South African record for thirty years. Later a successful company director, Bergh was the popular manager of the 1960-61 Springboks to Britain.

## 1949

| 1st v. NZ | 2nd v. NZ | 3rd v. NZ | 4th v. NZ |
|---|---|---|---|
| †J.H. VAN DER SCHYFF | J.H. VAN DER SCHYFF | J.H. VAN DER SCHYFF | J.H. VAN DER SCHYFF |
| | | | |
| †F.P. MARAIS | F.P. MARAIS | F.P. DUVENAGE | C. MOSS |
| †M.T. LATEGAN | M.T. LATEGAN 1T | M.T. LATEGAN | M.T. LATEGAN |
| †F.P. DUVENAGE | †R.A.M. VAN SCHOOR | R.A.M. VAN SCHOOR | R.A.M. VAN SCHOOR |
| †C. MOSS | C. MOSS | C. MOSS | †E. M. GERAGHTY |
| | | | |
| †J.D. BREWIS | J.D. BREWIS 1DG,1T | J.D. BREWIS | J.D. BREWIS 1DG |
| †J.J. WAAL | †P.A. DU TOIT | P.A. DU TOIT | P.A. DU TOIT 1T |
| | | | |
| †A. GEFFIN 5PG | A. GEFFIN 1PG | A. GEFFIN 3PG | A. GEFFIN 1PG,1C |
| †R.P. JORDAAN | R.P. JORDAAN | R.P. JORDAAN | R.P. JORDAAN |
| †C.J. VAN JAARSVELD | †A.C. KOCH | A.C. KOCH | A.C. KOCH |
| *†F. DU PLESSIS | *F. DU PLESSIS | *F. DU PLESSIS | †W.H.M. BARNARD |
| †H.V. KOCH | H.V. KOCH | †P.J. GEEL | H.V. KOCH |
| †L.J. STRYDOM | L.J. STRYDOM | H.V. KOCH | †P. MALAN |
| †H.S.V. MULLER | H.S.V. MULLER | H.S.V. MULLER | H.S.V. MULLER |
| †B.S. VAN DER MERWE | †J.A. DU RAND | J.A. DU RAND | *†B.J. KENYON |
| Cape Town | Johannesburg | Durban | Port Elizabeth |
| WON 15-11 | WON 12-6 | WON 9-3 | WON 11-8 |
| SA: 5PG | SA: 2T 1DG 1PG | SA: 3PG | SA: 1G 1PG 1DG |
| NZ: 1G 1PG 1DG | NZ: 1PG 1DG | NZ: 1T | NZ: 1G 1T |
| 16 Jul. 1949 | 13 Aug. 1949 | 3 Sep. 1949 | 17 Sep. 1949 |

South Africa fielded 15 new caps for their first post-war Test. The side was a strong combination which outgunned the All Blacks fore and aft, but relied heavily on the remarkable kicking powers of Geffin to win matches. The All Blacks, who were whitewashed in the series, saw Geffin create a new South African scoring record in the first Test (by kicking fifteen points from five penalties), and his 32 points in the rubber created a record for a New Zealand-South Africa series.

Felix du Plessis, nephew of the 1921 Springbok and father of Morné du Plessis, captained the side in the three opening Tests. But the outstanding player of the series was Hennie Muller, the Springbok number-eight. Supremely fit, he was to dominate South African forward play in 13 Tests up to 1953, establishing himself as the model loose forward of the modern game.

Du Rand, a versatile forward and van Schoor, a hard-tackling, resolute centre, became the first Rhodesians capped by South Africa. Van Schoor formed a useful centre partnership with Lategan, the pair appearing together a record ten times in Tests. Another player, Brewis, became the outstanding fly-half in world rugby in the immediate post-war era and also featured in a record partnership (with P.A. du Toit). He played in ten winning international sides during his career and his five drop-goals established a new Springbok career record, beating the four drop-goals scored by Bennie Osler between the wars.

## 1951-52

| v. SCOTLAND | v. IRELAND | v. WALES | v. ENGLAND | v. FRANCE |
|---|---|---|---|---|
| †J.U. Buchler | J.U. Buchler | J.U. Buchler | J.U. Buchler | J.U. Buchler |
| F.P. Marais | P.G.A. Johnstone | P.G.A. Johnstone | P.G.A. Johnstone | P.G.A. Johnstone 2t,1pg,1c |
| R.A.M. van Schoor 1t | R.A.M. van Schoor 1t | R.A.M. van Schoor | R.A.M. van Schoor | R.A.M. van Schoor |
| M.T. Lategan 1t | M.T. Lategan | M.T. Lategan | M.T. Lategan | M.T. Lategan |
| †P.G.A. Johnstone | †J.K. Ochse 1t | J.K. Ochse 1t | J.K. Ochse | J.K. Ochse |
| J.D. Brewis 1dg | J.D. Brewis 1dg | J.D. Brewis 1dg | J.D. Brewis | J.D. Brewis |
| P.A. du Toit | P.A. du Toit | P.A. du Toit | P.A. du Toit 1t | P.A. du Toit |
| A. Geffin 7c | A. Geffin 1c | A. Geffin | †H.P.J. Bekker | H.P.J. Bekker |
| †W.H. Delport 1t | W.H. Delport | W.H. Delport | W.H. Delport | W.H. Delport 1t |
| A.C. Koch 2t | A.C. Koch | A.C. Koch | A.C. Koch | A.C. Koch |
| J.A. du Rand 1t | J.A. du Rand | J.A. du Rand | J.A. du Rand | J.A. du Rand |
| †E.E. Dinkelmann 1t | E.E. Dinkelmann | W.H.M. Barnard | E.E. Dinkelmann | E.E. Dinkelmann 1t |
| †S.P. Fry | S.P. Fry | S.P. Fry | S.P. Fry | S.P. Fry |
| *H.S.V. Muller 1t | *H.S.V. Muller | *H.S.V. Muller | *H.S.V. Muller 1pg,1c | *H.S.V. Muller 1t,1c |
| †C.J. van Wyk 1t | C.J. van Wyk 2t | C.J. van Wyk | C.J. van Wyk | C.J. van Wyk 1t |
| Murrayfield | Lansdowne Road | Cardiff Arms Park | Twickenham | Stade Colombes |
| WON 44-0 | WON 17-5 | WON 6-3 | WON 8-3 | WON 25-3 |
| SCOT.: NIL | IRE.: 1G | WALES: 1T | ENG.: 1T | FR.: 1DG |
| SA: 7G 1DG 2T | SA: 1G 1DG 3T | SA: 1T 1DG | SA: 1G 1PG | SA: 2G 1PG 4T |
| 24 Nov. 1951 | 8 Dec. 1951 | 22 Dec. 1951 | 5 Jan. 1952 | 16 Feb. 1952 |

The Fourth Springboks to Britain, managed by Frank Mellish and Danie Craven, and led by Basil Kenyon, were popular tourists both on and off the field, and emulated their predecessors of 1912 by winning all five Tests. The team won 30 of its 31 matches (losing to London Counties), relying on a powerful, mobile pack for possession, finding Brewis and du Toit an efficient link to a competent threequarter line, and depending on a reliable defensive full-back in Buchler.

Kenyon, who was injured early in the tour, was succeeded as captain by Muller, and the big forward had a splendid series at the helm. The Scots were overwhelmed by 44 points in the first of the internationals. Seven of the nine tries scored at Murrayfield were by forwards and Geffin landed a record seven conversions. After a slow start in Dublin, the Springboks staged a fine second half display in which Ochse scored a good try. Narrow victories over Wales (in which Ochse scored another splendid try) and England followed before the side departed for the four-match French leg of the tour. Then, in a grand finale, the side set the seal on a triumphant tour with an exhilarating win by 25-3 against France.

## 1953

| 1st v. AUSTRALIA | 2nd v. AUSTRALIA | 3rd v. AUSTRALIA | 4th v. AUSTRALIA |
|---|---|---|---|
| J.U. Buchler 1pg,1c | J.U. Buchler | J.U. Buchler | J.U. Buchler 1dg |
| F.P. Marais 1t,1pg,1c | F.P. Marais 1c | †R.P. Bekker 1t | R.P. Bekker |
| R.A.M. van Schoor | R.A.M. van Schoor | R.A.M. van Schoor | R.A.M. van Schoor |
| M.T. Lategan 1t | M.T. Lategan | †D. Rossouw 1t | D. Rossouw |
| J.K. Ochse | J.K. Ochse 1t | †R.S. Hoffman | J.K. Ochse |
| J.D. Brewis | †A.I. Kirkpatrick | †I.J. Rens 3c | I.J. Rens 2pg,2c,1dg |
| †J.S.A. Oelofse 1t | J.S.A. Oelofse | J.S.A. Oelofse | J.S.A. Oelofse 1t |
| H.P.J. Bekker | H.P.J. Bekker | H.P.J. Bekker 1t | H.P.J. Bekker |
| W.H. Delport | W.H. Delport | W.H. Delport | W.H. Delport |
| A.C. Koch | A.C. Koch | †H.N. Walker | A.C. Koch 1t |
| J.A. du Rand 1t | J.A. du Rand 1t | J.A. du Rand | J.A. du Rand |
| E.E. Dinkelmann | E.E. Dinkelmann | †J.A.J. Pickard | J.A.J. Pickard |
| S.P. Fry | S.P. Fry | S.P. Fry | S.P. Fry |
| *H.S.V. Muller 1t | *H.S.V. Muller | *H.S.V. Muller | *H.S.V. Muller |
| C.J. van Wyk | C.J. van Wyk 1t | C.J. van Wyk 1t | C.J. van Wyk |
| Johannesburg | Cape Town | Durban | Port Elizabeth |
| WON 25-3 | LOST 14-18 | WON 18-8 | WON 22-9 |
| SA: 2G 2PG 3T | SA: 1G 3T | SA: 3G 1T | SA: 2G 2DG 2PG |
| AUST.: 1PG | AUST.: 3G 1T | AUST.: 1G 1PG | AUST.: 1T 2PG |
| 22 Aug. 1953 | 5 Sep. 1953 | 19 Sep. 1953 | 26 Sep. 1953 |

For the opening Test against the 1953 Wallabies, the Springboks fielded the same pack which had overcome the French in Paris a year earlier. In fact, the fifteen was drawn entirely from players who had toured Britain, with Oelofse, a talented but injury-prone scrum-half, the only new Test player. Muller, having struggled to regain his fitness after the long British tour, continued as captain.

The loose style of the Wallabies rubbed off on the usually conservative South African public, and there was much clamour in the press and among supporters for the Springboks to shake off the kicking tactics which were the cornerstone of South African rugby success. In the first Test the Springboks had few problems in winning by 22 points, setting a record winning margin for a home Test. But at Cape Town, after establishing a sound lead, the Springboks amazingly suffered their first Test defeat for 15 years. In their desire to play to the crowd and adopt a more imaginative approach, the South Africans decided to keep the ball in play as far as possible. This was to the liking of the Wallabies and a fine rally was capped by a last-minute winning try.

Six new men appeared at Durban where the Springbok forwards dominated the match, and an easy win at Port Elizabeth, in which Rens scored 13 points, gave South Africa victory in the rubber. Muller retired after this series, having led South Africa in nine Tests, a new Springbok record.

## 1955

| 1st v. BRITISH ISLES | 2nd v. BRITISH ISLES | 3rd v. BRITISH ISLES | 4th v. BRITISH ISLES |
|---|---|---|---|
| J.H. van der Schyff 2PG,2C | †R.G. Dryburgh 1T,2C | R.G. Dryburgh 2PG | R.G. Dryburgh 2C |
| †T.P.D. Briers 2T | T.P.D. Briers 1T | T.P.D. Briers | T.P.D. Briers 2T |
| †D.J. Sinclair | D.J. Sinclair | D.J. Sinclair | D.J. Sinclair |
| †K.T. Van Vollenhoven | †W. Rosenberg 1T | W. Rosenberg | W. Rosenberg |
| †J.J.N. Swart 1T | K.T. Van Vollenhoven 3T | K.T. Van Vollenhoven | K.T. Van Vollenhoven 1T |
| †C.A. Uylate | C.A. Ulyate | C.A. Ulyate | C.A. Ulyate 1DG,1T |
| †T.A. Gentles | T.A. Gentles | †C.F. Strydom | T.A. Gentles |
| †A.J.J. du Plooy | H.P.J. Bekker | H.P.J. Bekker | H.P.J. Bekker |
| †C.M. Kroon | †A.J. van der Merwe | A.J. van der Merwe | A.J. van der Merwe |
| A.C. Koch 1T | A.C. Koch | A.C. Koch | A.C. Koch |
| J.A. du Rand | J.A. du Rand | J.A. du Rand | J.A. du Rand |
| †J.T. Claassen | J.T. Claassen | J.T. Claassen | J.T. Claassen |
| *S.P. Fry | *S.P. Fry | *S.P. Fry | *S.P. Fry |
| †D.F. Retief | D.F. Retief | †G.P. Lochner | D.F. Retief 1T |
| C.J. van Wyk | †D.S.P. Ackermann 1T | D.S.P. Ackermann | D.S.P. Ackermann |
| Johannesburg | Cape Town | Pretoria | Port Elizabeth |
| LOST 22-23 | WON 25-9 | LOST 6-9 | WON 22-8 |
| SA: 2G 2PG 2T | SA: 2G 5T | SA: 2PG | SA: 2G 1DG 3T |
| B.Is.: 4G 1T | B. Is.: 1PG 2T | B. Is.: 1PG 1DG 1T | B. Is.: 1G 1T |
| 6 Aug. 1955 | 20 Aug. 1955 | 3 Sep. 1955 | 24 Sep. 1955 |

For the first time since 1928 the Springboks were held in a home Test series. A crowd estimated officially at 90,000, a world record, witnessed a high-scoring and exciting first Test in which the Springboks staged a fine recovery to turn a 12-point deficit into near victory. With the score delicately set at 22-23, full-back van der Schyff (last capped in 1949) sent a last-minute kick wide.

South Africa made several changes for the second Test at Cape Town, moving van Vollenhoven out to the wing. His transfer was a success, for he went on to equal the SA Test record by scoring three tries in a match as the Springboks coasted to a convincing win.

Defeat at Pretoria meant that South Africa had to win at Port Elizabeth to save the rubber. The decisive score came early in the second half when Gentles, the smallest man ever to play for South Africa, broke from a scrum to create a try under the posts for Ulyate. The conversion stretched them two scores ahead of the Lions, and further tries resulted in a sound victory.

## 1956

| 1st v. AUSTRALIA | 2nd v. AUSTRALIA | 1st v. NZ | 2nd v. NZ | 3rd v. NZ | 4th v. NZ |
|---|---|---|---|---|---|
| *†S.S. Viviers 1PG | J.U. Buchler | R.G. Dryburgh 1PG | *S.S. Viviers 1C | *S.S. Viviers 2C | *S.S. Viviers 1C |
| P.G.A. Johnstone | R.G. Dryburgh 1T | P.G.A. Johnstone | T.P.D. Briers | T.P.D. Briers | T.P.D. Briers |
| †P.E. Montini | P.E. Montini | †B.F. Howe 1T | A.I. Kirkpatrick | W. Rosenberg 1T | P.G.A. Johnstone |
| †J.J. Nel 1T | J.J. Nel | J.J. Nel | J.J. Nel | J.J. Nel | J.J. Nel |
| K.T. van Vollenhoven | K.T. van Vollenhoven 1DG | †J.G.H. du Preez | P.G.A. Johnstone | K.T. van Vollenhoven | R.G. Dryburgh 1T |
| †B.D. Pfaff | *S.S. Viviers | C.A. Ulyate | C.A. Ulyate | C.A. Ulyate | B.F. Howe |
| C.F. Strydom | C.F. Strydom | C.F. Strydom | T.A. Gentles | T.A. Gentles | C.F. Strydom |
| H.P.J. Bekker | H.P.J. Bekker | H.P.J. Bekker | H.P.J. Bekker | H.P.J. Bekker | H.P.J. Bekker |
| A.J. van der Merwe | A.J. van der Merwe | A.J. van der Merwe | A.J. van der Merwe | A.J. van der Merwe | A.J. van der Merwe |
| A.C. Koch | H.N. Walker | H.N. Walker | A.C. Koch | A.C. Koch | H.N. Walker |
| J.A. du Rand | J.A. du Rand | *J.A. du Rand | J.A. du Rand 1T | J.A. du Rand | J.A. du Rand |
| J.T. Claassen | J.T. Claassen | J.T. Claassen | J.T. Claassen | J.T. Claassen | J.T. Claassen |
| G.P. Lochner | D.F. Retief 1T | D.F. Retief | D.F. Retief 1T | D.S.P. Ackermann | D.F. Retief |
| D.F. Retief 1T | G.P. Lochner | G.P. Lochner | J.A.J. Pickard | D.F. Retief | G.P. Lochner |
| D.S.P. Ackermann | D.S.P. Ackermann | D.S.P. Ackermann | G.P. Lochner | G.P. Lochner 1T | †J.J. Starke |
| Sydney | Brisbane | Dunedin | Wellington | Christchurch | Auckland |
| WON 9-0 | WON 9-0 | LOST 6-10 | WON 8-3 | LOST 10-17 | LOST 5-11 |
| Aust.: NIL | Aust.: NIL | NZ: 2G | NZ: 1T | NZ: 1G 2PG 2T | NZ: 1G 2PG |
| SA: 1PG 2T | SA: 1DG 2T | SA: 1T 1PG | SA: 1G 1T | SA: 2G | SA: 1G |
| 26 May 1956 | 2 Jun. 1956 | 14 Jul. 1956 | 4 Aug. 1956 | 18 Aug. 1956 | 1 Sep. 1956 |

Under the management of Dr Danie Craven and the captaincy of S.S. Viviers, 32 players (including two replacements) took part in a 29-match tour of Australia and New Zealand in 1956. Altogether six of the matches were lost, three of them Tests, and for the first time in 60 years the Springboks lost a Test rubber, the All Blacks winning the series 3-1. The Springboks won both Tests against the Wallabies comfortably, but found the New Zealand forwards too strong in the subsequent Tests. The tourists sorely missed Basie van Wyk, the 31-year-old flanker who had scored six Test tries in his long career. He sustained a fractured leg in Australia before the first match of the tour, and never again wore the Springbok jersey.

J.A. "Salty" du Rand, who captained the team in the first Test with the All Blacks when Viviers was indisposed, went on to become the most-capped Springbok, earning his 21st cap at Auckland. He also established a Springbok second-row partnership record with Claassen, for the pair played together ten times in Tests. Van Vollenhoven, who had made a meteoric rise to fame in 1955, later joined St Helens in the English Rugby League. There he set a club record by scoring 62 tries in 1958-9, and in a long, successful career gained Rugby League Cup-winners and Championship-winners medals.

## 1958

| 1st v. FRANCE | 2nd v. FRANCE |
|---|---|
| †M.C. Gerber | M.C. Gerber 1c |
| | |
| †J. Prinsloo | J. Prinsloo |
| W. Rosenberg | †J. Kaminer |
| J.J. Nel | †A. Skene |
| †W.L. Fourie | W.L. Fourie 1t |
| | |
| A.I. Kirkpatrick | J.J. Nel |
| C.F. Strydom | T.A. Gentles |
| | |
| †P.S. du Toit | P.S. du Toit |
| A.J. van der Merwe | †G.F. Malan |
| A.C. Koch | A.C. Koch |
| †J. Steenkamp | J.A.J. Pickard |
| *J.T. Claassen | *J.T. Claassen |
| †G.H. van Zyl | †L.U. Schmidt |
| G.P. Lochner 1t | G.P. Lochner |
| †H.J.M. Pelser | D.S.P. Ackermann |
| | |
| Cape Town | Johannesburg |
| DRAWN 3-3 | LOST 5-9 |
| | |
| SA: 1t | SA: 1g |
| Fr.: 1dg | Fr.: 1pg 2dg |
| | |
| 26 Jul. 1958 | 16 Aug. 1958 |

There were seven new caps in the Springbok side for the first Test at Cape Town, and J.T. Claassen, an outstanding second-row forward who later managed the 1981 Springboks to New Zealand, was captain for the two-match series.

At Cape Town, the match was drawn. Ian Kirkpatrick, previously capped in 1953 (once) and 1956 (once) was brought in at fly-half for the game, but his rather dour tactics turned the game into a disappointing spectacle for the crowd. France led by a drop-goal at the interval, but it was expected that South Africa would benefit from a fresh breeze in the second half, and win handsomely. But the Springboks played miserably. Their only score was a try in the right corner by Lochner, following a diagonal kick by Nel. In the end, South Africa were happy to play defensively for a draw.

There were seven changes and a positional adjustment for the Test at Johannesburg. Jeremy Nel was transferred from centre to fly-half and created the first try of the match when his break enabled Fourie to gallop over for a try converted by Gerber. South Africa led 5-3 at half-time but two second-half drop-goals by France took the sting out of the Springbok attack and for the first time since 1896 they were defeated in a Test series on their own soil.

## 1960

| v. SCOTLAND | 1st v. NZ | 2nd v. NZ | 3rd v. NZ | 4th v. NZ |
|---|---|---|---|---|
| M.C. Gerber 3c | *R.G. Dryburgh 1c | *R.G. Dryburgh | †L.G. Wilson | L.G. Wilson |
| | | | | |
| †J.P. Engelbrecht | †M.J.G. Antelme | M.J.G. Antelme | M.J.G. Antelme | M.J.G. Antelme |
| A.I. Kirkpatrick | A.I. Kirkpatrick | A.I. Kirkpatrick | A.I. Kirkpatrick | A.I. Kirkpatrick |
| †J.L. Gainsford | J.L. Gainsford | J.L. Gainsford | J.L. Gainsford | J.L. Gainsford |
| †R.J. Twigge | †H.J. van Zyl 2t | H.J. van Zyl | H.J. Van Zyl | H.J. van Zyl |
| | | | | |
| †D.A. Stewart | †K. Oxlee | K. Oxlee 1t | K. Oxlee 1t | K. Oxlee |
| †F.W. Gericke 1t | †R.J. Lockyear 1c,1pg | R.J. Lockyear | R.J. Lockyear 2pg,1c | R.J. Lockyear 1pg,1c |
| | | | | |
| †D.N. Holton | P.S. du Toit | P.S. du Toit | P.S. du Toit | P.S. du Toit |
| A.J. van der Merwe | G.F. Malan | A.J. van der Merwe | G.F. Malan | G.F. Malan |
| †M.J. Bekker | A.C. Koch | A.C. Koch | †S.P. Kuhn | S.P. Kuhn |
| †P.B. Allen | †A.S. Malan | A.S. Malan | *A.S. Malan | *A.S. Malan |
| J.T. Claassen | J.T. Claassen | J.T. Claassen | J.T. Claassen | †H.S. van der Merwe |
| G.H. van Zyl 2t | G.H. van Zyl | G.H. van Zyl | G.H. van Zyl | G.H. van Zyl |
| †D.J. Hopwood | †J.A. Nel | J.A. Nel | D.J. Hopwood | D.J. Hopwood |
| *†D.C. van Jaarsveldt 1t | H.J.M. Pelser | H.J.M. Pelser | H.J.M. Pelser | H.J.M. Pelser 1t |
| | | | | |
| Port Elizabeth | Johannesburg | Cape Town | Bloemfontein | Port Elizabeth |
| WON 18-10 | WON 13-0 | LOST 3-11 | DRAWN 11-11 | WON 8-3 |
| | | | | |
| SA: 3g 1t | SA: 2g 1pg | SA: 1t | SA: 1g 2pg | SA: 1g 1pg |
| Scot.: 2g | NZ: NIL | NZ: 1g 1pg 1dg | NZ: 1p 2pg | NZ: 1pg |
| | | | | |
| 30 Apr. 1960 | 25 Jun. 1960 | 23 Jul. 1960 | 13 Aug. 1960 | 27 Aug. 1960 |

The 1960 season was one of the busiest in South Africa since the five-Test series of 1933. Again five Tests were played, the chief attraction being the four-match series with New Zealand, but there was also an early season warm-up against Scotland, who thus became the first individual British Union to visit the Southern Hemisphere. Des van Jaarsveldt, in his only international, became the first Rhodesian to skipper South Africa, and led the Springboks to a comfortable win in a match which marked the debuts of Engelbrecht, Gainsford, Stewart and Hopwood, four leading Springboks of the 1960s.

For the series with the All Blacks, Roy Dryburgh was captain and he led an experimental side to victory by 13 points at Johannesburg. However, the brilliant kicking of the New Zealand full-back tied the series in the second Test and four changes were made by the South African selectors for the third Test.

Avril Malan became captain, at 23 the youngest man to skipper the Springboks. Malan's side drew the Test but there was only one change, prompted by the illness of Claassen, for the decider at Port Elizabeth. There, after a tight first half, it was thanks to Martin Pelser, a one-eyed Transvaal flanker who hurled himself over near the posts for a try converted by Lockyear, that South Africa gained victory by 8-3, and thus won the rubber by 2-1.

## 1960-61

| v. WALES | v. IRELAND | v. ENGLAND | v. SCOTLAND | v. FRANCE |
|---|---|---|---|---|
| L.G. WILSON | L.G. WILSON | L.G. WILSON | D.A. STEWART | L.G. WILSON |
| J.P. ENGELBRECHT | J.P. ENGELBRECHT | J.P. ENGELBRECHT | J.P. ENGELBRECHT | J.P. ENGELBRECHT |
| A.I. KIRKPATRICK | A.I. KIRKPATRICK | A.I. KIRKPATRICK | A.I. KIRKPATRICK | A.I. KIRKPATRICK |
| J.L. GAINSFORD | J.L. GAINSFORD 1T | J.L. GAINSFORD | J.L. GAINSFORD | J.L. GAINSFORD |
| †F. du T. ROUX | H.J. van ZYL | H.J. van ZYL | H.J. van ZYL | M.J.G. ANTELME |
| K. OXLEE 1PG | K. OXLEE | D.A. STEWART | K. OXLEE | D.A. STEWART |
| †P. de W. UYS | R.J. LOCKYEAR 1C | P. de W. UYS | P. de W. UYS | R.J. LOCKYEAR |
| P.S. du TOIT | P.S. du TOIT | P.S. du TOIT | P.S. du TOIT | P.S. du TOIT |
| †R.A. HILL | R.A. HILL | G.F. MALAN | G.F. MALAN | G.F. MALAN |
| S.P. KUHN | S.P. KUHN | S.P. KUHN | S.P. KUHN | S.P. KUHN |
| *A.S. MALAN | *A.S. MALAN | *A.S. MALAN | *A.S. MALAN | *A.S. MALAN |
| J.T. CLAASSEN | J.T. CLAASSEN | J.T. CLAASSEN | J.T. CLAASSEN 1T | J.T. CLAASSEN |
| G.H. van ZYL | G.H. van ZYL 1T | G.H. van ZYL | G.H. van ZYL | G.H. van ZYL |
| D.J. HOPWOOD | H.J.M. PELSER | D.J. HOPWOOD | D.J. HOPWOOD 1T | D.J. HOPWOOD |
| H.J.M. PELSER | †A.P. BAARD | †F.C.H. du PREEZ 1C | F.C.H. du PREEZ 2PG | H.J.M. PELSER |
| Cardiff Arms Park WON 3-0 | Lansdowne Road WON 8-3 | Twickenham WON 5-0 | Murrayfield WON 12-5 | Stade Colombes DRAWN 0-0 |
| WALES: NIL SA.: 1PG | IRE.: 1PG SA.: 1G 1T | ENG.: NIL SA.: 1G | SCOT.: 1G SA.: 2PG 2T | FR.: NIL SA.: NIL |
| 3 Dec. 1960 | 17 Dec. 1960 | 7 Jan. 1961 | 21 Jan. 1961 | 18 Feb. 1961 |

The 1960-61 Springboks played 34 matches in the Northern Hemisphere, losing only once, in their last game of the British tour against the Barbarians. The side adopted a "subdue and penetrate" principle on the field, and with their huge forwards to master the tight and loose phases, it was a pity that their schemes did not admit a more expansive approach to back play.

Claassen, Avril Malan (the captain) and Hopwood, an impressive number-eight, were world-class forwards who were outstanding in the four Test wins in Britain. The victory which gave the Springboks most pleasure was at Cardiff against Wales, for here they not only defeated a strong side but also showed immense character in overcoming appalling conditions. Ireland were beaten thanks to a late pushover try and Doug Hopwood's try settled the English match. Frik du Preez, who went on to set a Springbok appearance record, playing 38 Tests, made his debut at Twickenham and converted Hopwood's try. At Murrayfield, he landed two penalties in the Springboks' best Test win of the tour.

The final match, against France, was a bruising battle in which Claassen and Malan dominated the line-outs. France, however, were outstanding in the scrummages and always dangerous in the loose, and in the final analysis it was agreed that the draw was a fitting reflection of the game.

## 1961

| v. IRELAND | 1st v. AUSTRALIA | 2nd v. AUSTRALIA |
|---|---|---|
| L.G. WILSON | L.G. WILSON | L.G. WILSON 1DG |
| †B.P. van ZYL 2T | J.P. ENGELBRECHT 1T | J.P. ENGELBRECHT |
| D.A. STEWART | F. du T. ROUX | F. du T. ROUX 1T |
| †C.M. GREENWOOD 2T | J.L. GAINSFORD 1T | J.L. GAINSFORD |
| H.J. van ZYL | H.J. van ZYL 3T | H.J. van ZYL 1T |
| †C.F. NIMB 3C,1PG | K. OXLEE 1T | K. OXLEE 1T,1C,3PG |
| P. de W. UYS | P. de W. UYS | P. de W. UYS |
| P.S. du TOIT | P.S. du TOIT | P.S. du TOIT |
| R.A. HILL | R.A. HILL | R.A. HILL |
| S.P. KUHN | S.P. KUHN | S.P. KUHN |
| †P.J. van ZYL | F.C.H. du PREEZ | F.C.H. du PREEZ |
| *J.T. CLAASSEN | *J.T. CLAASSEN 2C | *J.T. CLAASSEN |
| G.H. van ZYL | G.H. van ZYL | G.H. van ZYL |
| D.J. HOPWOOD 1T | D.J. HOPWOOD 1T | D.J. HOPWOOD |
| H.J.M. PELSER | H.J.M. PELSER 1T | H.J.M. PELSER |
| Cape Town WON 24-8 | Johannesburg WON 28-3 | Port Elizabeth WON 23-11 |
| SA: 3G 2T 1PG IRE.: 1G 1PG | SA: 2G 6T AUS.: 1PG | SA: 1G 2T 3PG 1DG AUST.: 1G 2PG |
| 13 May 1961 | 5 Aug. 1961 | 12 Aug. 1961 |

Playing relaxed football and forsaking the power rugby which had been the feature of their approach in Britain, the South African side entertained their supporters in three high-scoring Tests in 1961. Ireland were visitors to Cape Town in May and before 35,000 spectators found the Springboks in irrepressible form. South Africa, with a team of four van Zyls, awarded four new Test caps, though only Greenwood had not toured with Avril Malan's side to Britain.

Two of the new caps, Ben-Piet van Zyl and Greenwood (who a month later joined Wakefield Trinity Rugby League club in England), scored two tries, benefiting from some outstanding centre play by Dave Stewart. Charles Nimb, in his only Test match, scored nine points with four successful goal-kicks.

The powerful Springbok forwards were too strong for the Wallabies in the two-Test series which followed in August. At Johannesburg the Springboks romped home by eight tries, setting a new record for a Test in South Africa, and Hennie van Zyl equalled the South African Test record by scoring three of the tries. Two of the other try-scorers at Johannesburg were Engelbrecht and John Gainsford. Both went on to score eight Test tries, establishing a new Springbok career record.

## 1962

| 1st v. BRITISH ISLES | 2nd v. BRITISH ISLES | 3rd v. BRITISH ISLES | 4th v. BRITISH ISLES |
|---|---|---|---|
| L.G. WILSON | L.G. WILSON | L.G. WILSON | L.G. WILSON |
| F.DU T. ROUX | J.P. ENGELBRECHT | J.P. ENGELBRECHT | J.P. ENGELBRECHT |
| †M.R.K. WYNESS | M.R.K. WYNESS | M.R.K. WYNESS | M.R.K. WYNESS 1T |
| J.L. GAINSFORD 1T | J.L. GAINSFORD | J.L. GAINSFORD | J.L. GAINSFORD 1T |
| †O.B. TAYLOR | F.DU T. ROUX | F.DU T. ROUX | F.DU T. ROUX 2T |
| K. OXLEE | K. OXLEE 1PG | K. OXLEE 1C,1T,1PG | K. OXLEE 5C,2PG |
| P.DE W. UYS | †D.J. DE VILLIERS | D.J. DE VILLIERS | P.DE W. UYS |
| †J.L. MYBURGH | †C.E. BEZUIDENHOUT | C.E. BEZUIDENHOUT | C.E. BEZUIDENHOUT |
| G.F. MALAN | G.F. MALAN | G.F. MALAN | R.A. HILL |
| S.P. KUHN | S.P. KUHN | S.P. KUHN | S.P. KUHN |
| A.S. MALAN | F.C.H. DU PREEZ | F.C.H. DU PREEZ | F.C.H. DU PREEZ |
| *J.T. CLAASSEN | *J.T. CLAASSEN | *J.T. CLAASSEN | *J.T. CLAASSEN 1T |
| G.H. VAN ZYL | †J.P.F. BOTHA | J.P.F. BOTHA | J.P.F. BOTHA |
| D.J. HOPWOOD | D.J. HOPWOOD | D.J. HOPWOOD | D.J. HOPWOOD |
| F.C.H. DU PREEZ | L.U. SCHMIDT | G.H. VAN ZYL | G.H. VAN ZYL 1T |
| Johannesburg | Durban | Cape Town | Bloemfontein |
| DRAWN 3-3 | WON 3-0 | WON 8-3 | WON 34-14 |
| SA: 1T | SA: 1PG | SA: 1G 1PG | SA: 5G 2PG 1T |
| B.Is.: 1T | B.Is.: NIL | B. Is.: 1DG | B. Is.: 1G 1PG 2T |
| 23 Jun. 1962 | 21 Jul. 1962 | 4 Aug. 1962 | 25 Aug. 1962 |

Keith Oxlee, a representative from Natal, was the key player for South Africa in the Test series with the British Lions. A talented fly-half who was a sound tactical kicker with a sharp eye for an opening, it was Oxlee's ability to land points from place-kicks which settled the series. After a drawn first Test, Oxlee won the series by scoring all of the points in the second and third Tests.

For once the Springboks were well held in the tight by a competent Lions scrummage. Throughout the series, however, it was clear that the South Africans were superior in the loose, and du Preez, Hopwood, Hugo van Zyl and Botha exposed the weaknesses of the British backs with ruthless efficiency.

The final Test resulted in a handsome Springbok win by twenty points. Spearheaded by Oxlee, who received a fast, efficient service from Uys, the South Africans produced a magnificent five-minute spell after half-time when 13 points were added. Backs and forwards ran and handled with amazing pace and dexterity, and Oxlee's contribution of 16 points was a new Test record for South Africa. It had taken him just 13 Tests to score 53 points – two points short of Gerry Brand's South African career record.

## 1963

| 1st v. AUSTRALIA | 2nd v. AUSTRALIA | 3rd v. AUSTRALIA | 4th v. AUSTRALIA |
|---|---|---|---|
| L.G. WILSON | L.G. WILSON | L.G. WILSON | L.G. WILSON |
| †J.T. TRUTER | J.P. ENGELBRECHT | J.P. ENGELBRECHT | G.D. CILLIERS |
| D.A. STEWART | M.R.K. WYNESS | D.A. STEWART | D.A. STEWART |
| J.L. GAINSFORD | J.L. GAINSFORD | J.L. GAINSFORD | J.L. GAINSFORD 1T |
| †G.D. CILLIERS 1T | F.DU T. ROUX | G.D. CILLIERS | †C.W. DIRKSEN |
| K. OXLEE 1C,2PG | K. OXLEE 1C | †N.M. RILEY | K. OXLEE 2PG,2C |
| P.DE W. UYS | P.DE W. UYS | †C.M. SMITH 3PG | C.M. SMITH |
| †D.J. PUTTER | D.J. PUTTER | †J.F.K. MARAIS | J.L. MYBURGH |
| *G.F. MALAN | *G.F. MALAN | R.A. HILL | *G.F. MALAN 1T |
| S.P. KUHN | S.P. KUHN | S.P. KUHN | D.J. PUTTER |
| A.S. MALAN | A.S. MALAN | *A.S. MALAN | †J.P. NAUDE 1PG,1T |
| F.C.H. DU PREEZ | H.S. VAN DER MERWE | H.S. VAN DER MERWE | H.S. VAN DER MERWE |
| J.A. NEL | J.A. NEL | †J. SCHOEMANN | J. SCHOEMANN |
| D.J. HOPWOOD | D.J. HOPWOOD | †J. PRINSLOO | D.J. HOPWOOD |
| †T.P. BEDFORD 1T | T.P. BEDFORD | T.P. BEDFORD | T.P. BEDFORD |
| Pretoria | Cape Town | Johannesburg | Port Elizabeth |
| WON 14-3 | LOST 5-9 | LOST 9-11 | WON 22-6 |
| SA: 1G 2PG 1T | SA: 1G‡ | SA: 3PG | SA: 2G 3PG 1T |
| AUST.: 1T | AUST.: 1PG 1DG 1T | AUST.: 1G 1DG 1PG | AUST. 1PG 1DG |
| 13 Jul. 1963 | 10 Aug. 1963 | 24 Aug. 1963 | 7 Sep. 1963 |
| | ‡includes penalty try | | |

There were few signs in the Springboks' first Test victory that this series would be such a struggle for the South Africans to rescue. At Pretoria, Tom Bedford, a dynamic loose forward who was to play in 25 Tests in a distinguished career, scored a try on his debut, while Keith Oxlee's eight points made him South Africa's leading points-scorer in Tests. The Springboks coasted to a 14-3 win.

But at Cape Town the Wallabies staged a fine comeback to level the series. Early in the match South Africa were awarded their first penalty try in a Test when Bedford was obstructed by Ellwood in a chase following a kick by Engelbrecht. Then an injury sustained by Uys upset the rhythm of the Springboks and the Australians, carefully nursed by their captain, went on to win 9-5. The Springbok selectors reacted by dropping Oxlee and several others for the Test at Ellis Park, where an inexperienced side, committed to dour, ten-man rugby tactics, never looked capable of creating try-scoring opportunities.

For the final match, the Springbok selectors made wholesale changes, including the replacement of the entire front row. Abe Malan returned as skipper instead of Avril Malan, and together with coach Hennie Muller induced the side to play in a more relaxed style. The Test was tight for the first 70 minutes and delicately balanced at 6-6. Then, in an exciting final flourish, the Springboks added sixteen points to preserve their honour and the series.

| | 1964 | | 1965 | |
|---|---|---|---|---|
| | v. WALES | v. FRANCE | v. IRELAND | v. SCOTLAND |
| | L.G. WILSON 1DG | L.G. WILSON | L.G. WILSON | L.G. WILSON |
| | J.P. ENGELBRECHT | J.P. ENGELBRECHT | J.P. ENGELBRECHT | J.P. ENGELBRECHT 1T |
| | D.A. STEWART | D.A. STEWART 1PG,1T | †W.J. MANS 1T | W.J. MANS 1C |
| | J.L. GAINSFORD | J.L. GAINSFORD | J.L. GAINSFORD | J.L. GAINSFORD |
| | C.W. DIRKSEN | J.T. TRUTER | C.W. DIRKSEN | C.W. DIRKSEN |
| | K. OXLEE 2PG,3C | †M.J. LAWLESS | D.A. STEWART 1PG | †J.H. BARNARD |
| | C.M. SMITH 1T | *C.M. SMITH | D.J. DE VILLIERS | †D.J.J. DE VOS |
| | J.L. MYBURGH | J.L. MYBURGH | J.F.K. MARAIS | J.F.K. MARAIS |
| | *G.F. MALAN | †D.C. WALTON | D.C. WALTON | D.C. WALTON |
| | J.F.K. MARAIS 1T | J.F.K. MARAIS | S.P. KUHN | S.P. KUHN |
| | A.S. MALAN | H.S. VAN DER MERWE | *A.S. MALAN | *A.S. MALAN |
| | †G. CARELSE | G. CARELSE | G. CARELSE | G. CARELSE |
| | F.C.H. DU PREEZ | F.C.H. DU PREEZ | J. SCHOEMANN | J. SCHOEMANN |
| | D.J. HOPWOOD 1T | D.J. HOPWOOD | T.P. BEDFORD | D.J. HOPWOOD |
| | T.P. BEDFORD | T.P. BEDFORD | †M.R. SUTER | M.R. SUTER |
| | Durban | Springs | Lansdowne Road | Murrayfield |
| | WON 24-3 | LOST 6-8 | LOST 6-9 | LOST 5-8 |
| | SA: 3G 2PG 1DG | SA: 1PG 1T | IRE.: 2PG 1T | SCOT.: 1G 1DG |
| | WALES: 1PG | FR.: 1G 1PG | SA: 1PG 1T | SA: 1G |
| | 23 May 1964 | 25 Jul. 1964 | 10 Apr. 1965 | 17 Apr. 1965 |

The year 1964 marked the 75th Jubilee Anniversary of the founding of the SARB and Wales were invited to tour the country at the start of the Springbok season. In the only Test of the tour the Welsh subdued the Springboks for three-quarters of the match, but an extraordinary drop-goal by Lionel Wilson from 50 yards and midway through the second half, set the home side on course for a record win against Wales. The Springbok pack improved as the game progressed and Oxlee contributed twelve points.

But this win was to be the Springboks' last for eight Tests. France repeated their triumph of 1958 by winning the only Test of their tour at Springs. Stewart scored a penalty and a late try in a match described as the worst ever seen in South Africa.

Then, on a short tour to Ireland and Scotland in April 1965, the Springboks failed to win a match, losing four games (including the two internationals) and drawing one. Avril Malan was named tour captain by the SARB, who overruled the selectors' choice of Doug Hopwood. Dave Stewart, capped as a full-back, centre and fly-half, played his last Test in Dublin, scoring a penalty against the Irish; and Avril Malan, warrior of 16 Tests, never played again in a Test following the defeat at Murrayfield.

| 1965 | | | | | |
|---|---|---|---|---|---|
| 1st v. AUSTRALIA | 2nd v. AUSTRALIA | 1st v. NZ | 2nd v. NZ | 3rd v. NZ | 4th v. NZ |
| L.G. WILSON | L.G. WILSON | L.G. WILSON | L.G. WILSON | L.G. WILSON | L.G. WILSON |
| J.P. ENGELBRECHT 2T | J.P. ENGELBRECHT | J.P. ENGELBRECHT | J.P. ENGELBRECHT | J.P. ENGELBRECHT | J.P. ENGELBRECHT |
| J.L. GAINSFORD | J.L. GAINSFORD 1T | F. DU T. ROUX | F. DU T. ROUX | F. DU T. ROUX | F. DU T. ROUX |
| F. DU T. ROUX | F. DU T. ROUX | J.L. GAINSFORD | J.L. GAINSFORD | J.L. GAINSFORD 2T | J.L. GAINSFORD |
| †G.S. BRYNARD | J.T. TRUTER 1T | G.S. BRYNARD | G.S. BRYNARD | G.S. BRYNARD 2T | G.S. BRYNARD |
| J.H. BARNARD | J.H. BARNARD | K. OXLEE 1DG | K. OXLEE | J.H. BARNARD | J.H. BARNARD |
| *C.M. SMITH | *C.M. SMITH | *D.J. DE VILLIERS | *C.M. SMITH | *D.J. DE VILLIERS | *D.J. DE VILLIERS |
| †W.H. PARKER | W.H. PARKER | †C.G.P. VAN ZYL | C.G.P. VAN ZYL | C.G.P. VAN ZYL | C.G.P. VAN ZYL |
| G.F. MALAN | G.F. MALAN | G.F. MALAN | G.F. MALAN | D.C. WALTON | D.C. WALTON |
| †A.W. MACDONALD | J.F.K. MARAIS | A.W. MACDONALD | A.W. MACDONALD | A.W. MACDONALD | A.W. MACDONALD |
| J.P. NAUDE 1PG,1C | J.P. NAUDE 1C | J.P. NAUDE | †C.P. GOOSEN | J.P. NAUDE 1PG,2C | J.P. NAUDE 1PG |
| †P.H. BOTHA | P.H. BOTHA | F.C.H. DU PREEZ | F.C.H. DU PREEZ | F.C.H. PREEZ | F.C.H. DU PREEZ |
| J. SCHOEMANN | J.A. NEL | J. SCHOEMANN | J. SCHOEMANN | J.A. NEL | J.A. NEL |
| T.P. BEDFORD | T.P. BEDFORD | J.A. NEL | J.A. NEL | D.J. HOPWOOD | D.J. HOPWOOD |
| F.C.H. DU PREEZ | F.C.H. DU PREEZ | †J.H. ELLIS | J.H. ELLIS | J.H. ELLIS | J.H. ELLIS |
| Sydney | Brisbane | Wellington | Dunedin | Christchurch | Auckland |
| LOST 11-18 | LOST 8-12 | LOST 3-6 | LOST 0-13 | WON 19-16 | LOST 3-20 |
| AUST.: 2T 4PG | AUST.: 4PG | NZ: 2T | NZ: 2G 1T | NZ: 2G 1PG 1T | NZ: 1G 4T 1DG |
| SA: 1G 1T 1PG | SA: 1G 1T | SA: 1DG | SA: NIL | SA: 2G 1PG 2T | SA: 1PG |
| 19 Jun. 1965 | 26 Jun. 1965 | 31 Jul. 1965 | 21 Aug. 1965 | 4 Sep. 1965 | 18 Sep. 1965 |

This was called South Africa's "Black Year". Following the disappointments of the tour to Britain, the Springboks undertook a long tour of Australasia under the management of J.F. Louw with Hennie Muller as coach. There was criticism of the choice of Dawie de Villiers and Nelie Smith as captain and vice-captain. Both were scrum-halves and the critics were sceptical that no natural forward leader had been given any responsibility for evolving a tactical plan up front.

Disaster followed the side on the field and both Tests in Australia were lost. The young de Villiers, who missed these Tests, found additional problems in NZ where his side were out-scrummaged at Wellington (in the first Test). At Dunedin – SA's seventh successive Test defeat – Lionel Wilson played heroically in defeat, and coach Muller was left wondering how to stem the threat of the All Black forwards. But Springbok pride was restored in a 19-16 win at Christchurch. However, the New Zealanders secured the series by capitalising on a chapter of Springbok errors in the second half of the final Test, and South Africa crashed to their heaviest defeat at the hands of the All Blacks.

The series marked the ends of the careers of two famous Springboks. Lionel Wilson, a veteran of 17 Tests and the most consistent defensive full-back produced by SA, retired as the most-capped Springbok in the position. And Keith Oxlee, dropped after the Dunedin defeat, finished as his nation's leading points-scorer, with 88 in his Tests.

## 1967

| 1st v. FRANCE | 2nd v. FRANCE | 3rd v. FRANCE | 4th v. FRANCE |
|---|---|---|---|
| †H.O. DE VILLIERS 4C,1PG | H.O. DE VILLIERS 2C | H.O. DE VILLIERS | H.O. DE VILLIERS 1PG |
| J.P. ENGELBRECHT | J.P. ENGELBRECHT 1T | J.P. ENGELBRECHT | J.P. ENGELBRECHT |
| †E. OLIVIER | E. OLIVIER 1T | E. OLIVIER 1T | E. OLIVIER |
| J.L. GAINSFORD | J.L. GAINSFORD | J.L. GAINSFORD | †S.H. NOMIS |
| C.W. DIRKSEN 2T | C.W. DIRKSEN 1T | C.W. DIRKSEN | C.W. DIRKSEN |
| †P.J. VISAGIE | P.J. VISAGIE | P.J. VISAGIE 1C | P.J. VISAGIE 1DG |
| *D.J. DE VILLIERS | *D.J. DE VILLIERS | *D.J. DE VILLIERS | *D.J. DE VILLIERS |
| †G.J.M. KOTZE | G.J.M. KOTZE | G.J.M. KOTZE | G.J.M. KOTZE |
| †G. PITZER | G. PITZER | G. PITZER | G. PITZER |
| †J.B. NEETHLING | J.B. NEETHLING | J.B. NEETHLING | J.B. NEETHLING |
| J.P. NAUDE | J.P. NAUDE 1PG | J.P. NAUDE 2PG | J.P. NAUDE |
| G. CARELSE | G. CARELSE | G. CARELSE | F.C.H. DE PREEZ |
| †P.J.F. GREYLING 2T | P.J.F. GREYLING | P.J.F. GREYLING | P.J.F. GREYLING |
| †A.N. DE WAAL | A.N. DE WAAL | A.N. DE WAAL | A.N. DE WAAL |
| J.H. ELLIS 1T | J.H. ELLIS | J.H. ELLIS 1T | J.H. ELLIS |
| Durban | Bloemfontein | Johannesburg | Cape Town |
| WON 26-3 | WON 16-3 | LOST 14-19 | DRAWN 6-6 |
| SA: 4G 1T 1PG | SA: 2G 1PG 1T | SA: 1G 2PG 1T | SA: 1PG 1DG |
| FR.: 1T | FR.: 1PG | FR.: 2G 2DG 1PG | FR.: 1PG 1T |
| 15 Jun. 1967 | 22 Jul. 1967 | 29 Jul. 1967 | 12 Aug. 1967 |

The All Blacks were due to tour South Africa in 1967, but the inflexible political stance adopted by the late Dr H.F. Verwoerd, who had pointed out in a speech at Loskop Dam in 1965 that Maoris would not be admitted if selected, led to the cancellation of the tour. As a result the French stepped in to undertake a four-Test series.

A fresh selection panel awarded eight new caps for the first Test at Durban. Commitment up front, strength and pace in the back row, and competence among the backs were features of South Africa's big win by 23 points. Not surprisingly, the selectors remained loyal to their experimental side, and the same fifteen routed the French at Bloemfontein and faced them again at Ellis Park for the third Test. However, following a surprise defeat at Johannesburg, for the fourth Test the selectors made two changes, ending the illustrious career of John Gainsford, their most-capped centre, and recalling du Preez at lock. Although the Test was drawn, the Springboks were able to celebrate, for it was their first series success against the French.

Two notable Springbok newcomers were Henry de Villiers and Piet Visagie. De Villiers proved the most exciting attacking fullback in world rugby before serious injury brought a premature end to his career, while Visagie established himself as a complete footballer and went on to create a new Springbok Test record by scoring 130 points in 25 internationals.

## 1968

| 1st v. BRITISH ISLES | 2nd v. BRITISH ISLES | 3rd v. BRITISH ISLES | 4th v. BRITISH ISLES |
|---|---|---|---|
| †R.L. GOULD | R.L. GOULD | R.L. GOULD | R.L. GOULD 1DG |
| J.P. ENGELBRECHT | J.P. ENGELBRECHT | G.S. BRYNARD | G.S. BRYNARD |
| E. OLIVIER | E. OLIVIER | E. OLIVIER | E. OLIVIER 1T |
| S.H. NOMIS | S.H. NOMIS | F. DU T. ROUX | F. DU T. ROUX 1T |
| C.W. DIRKSEN | C.W. DIRKSEN | S.H. NOMIS | S.H. NOMIS 1T |
| P.J. VISAGIE 2PG,2C | P.J. VISAGIE 1PG | P.J. VISAGIE 1PG,1C | P.J. VISAGIE 2C |
| *D.J. DE VILLIERS 1T | *D.J. DE VILLIERS | *D.J. DE VILLIERS | *D.J. DE VILLIERS |
| J.L. MYBURGH | J.L. MYBURGH | J.L. MYBURGH | J.B. NEETHLING |
| G. PITZER | G. PITZER | G. PITZER | G. PITZER |
| J.F.K. MARAIS | J.F.K. MARAIS | J.F.K. MARAIS | J.F.K. MARAIS |
| J.P. NAUDE 2PG,1T | J.P. NAUDE 1PG | J.P. NAUDE 1PG | J.P. NAUDE |
| F.C.H. DU PREEZ 1T | F.C.H. DU PREEZ | F.C.H. DU PREEZ | F.C.H. DU PREEZ |
| P.J.F. GREYLING | †M.J. LOURENS | M.J. LOURENS 1T | M.J. LOURENS |
| T.P. BEDFORD | T.P. BEDFORD | T.P. BEDFORD | T.P. BEDFORD |
| J.H. ELLIS | J.H. ELLIS | J.H. ELLIS | J.H. ELLIS 1T |
| Pretoria | Port Elizabeth | Cape Town | Johannesburg |
| WON 25-20 | DRAWN 6-6 | WON 11-6 | WON 19-6 |
| SA: 2G 4PG 1T | SA: 2PG | SA: 1G 2PG | SA: 2G 2T 1DG |
| B.Is.: 1G 5PG | B.Is.: 2PG | B.Is.: 2PG | B.Is.: 2PG |
| 8 Jun. 1968 | 22 Jun. 1968 | 13 Jul. 1968 | 27 Jul. 1968 |

The South African public still had doubts that their national side had recovered from the dreadful run of defeats suffered in 1964-65. Optimists pointed out that a fresh side had demolished the French in the opening Tests of the previous year, but the sceptics were quite quick to retort that the same side had been unable to win either of the two last Tests.

But the South Africans proved against the Lions that they were once again contenders for the title "World Champions". In an undistinguished rubber, the Springboks won 3-0, the second Test finishing as a draw. The notable feature of the Tests was the emergence of Visagie as a sound tactician at fly-half, and his haul of 22 points was a significant factor in the Springboks' success. Naude, a huge lock, supported Visagie as placekicker, landing several long-range goals in his tally of 15 points for the series.

Other features of the series were a storming run from a line-out by du Preez for a try in the first Test; some strong and entertaining running by Mannetjies Roux in the final Test when three of the Springbok tries were scored by threequarters; and the unobtrusive but sound generalship of de Villiers as captain. The fair-haired scrum-half went on to lead the Springboks 22 times, a South African record.

## 1968

| 1st v. FRANCE | 2nd v. FRANCE |
|---|---|
| H.O. DE VILLIERS | H.O. DE VILLIERS |
| | |
| J.P. ENGELBRECHT | J.P. ENGELBRECHT 1T |
| E. OLIVIER | E. OLIVIER |
| F. DU T. ROUX | F. DU T. ROUX |
| S.H. NOMIS | S.H. NOMIS 1T |
| | |
| P.J. VISAGIE 4PG | P.J. VISAGIE 1PG,2C |
| *D.J. DE VILLIERS | *D.J. DE VILLIERS 1T |
| | |
| J.L. MYBURGH | J.L. MYBURGH |
| G. PITZER | G. PITZER |
| J.F.K. MARAIS | J.F.K. MARAIS |
| F.C.H. DU PREEZ | F.C.H. DU PREEZ |
| G. CARELSE | G. CARELSE |
| P.J.F. GREYLING | P.J.F. GREYLING |
| T.P. BEDFORD | T.P. BEDFORD |
| J.H. ELLIS | J.H. ELLIS |
| | |
| Bordeaux | Stade Colombes |
| WON 12-9 | WON 16-11 |
| | |
| FR.: 3T | FR.: 1G 2DG |
| SA: 4PG | SA: 2G 1T 1PG |
| | |
| 9 Nov. 1968 | 16 Nov. 1968 |

With Fritz Eloff as manager, J.F.Claassen assistant manager, and Dawie de Villiers skipper, the Springboks completed a six-match tour of France in the autumn of 1968. Five of the matches were won, but between two narrow Test victories the Springboks were defeated on French soil for the first time, losing 3-11 to a SW France selection.

The Springboks played carefully in both Tests, and had to thank the clinical tactical and place-kicking of Visagie for success in the series. He coolly kicked four penalties at Bordeaux to sink the French, who scored three tries; and on a miserable day in Paris a week later he landed seven more points in a narrow Springbok win by 16-11.

One of the heroes at Stade Colombes was full-back Henry de Villiers. Loss of form had cost him his Test spot for the series against the Lions earlier in the year, but he returned to brilliant form in the more difficult conditions of France in November.

## 1969

| 1st v. AUSTRALIA | 2nd v. AUSTRALIA | 3rd v. AUSTRALIA | 4th v. AUSTRALIA |
|---|---|---|---|
| H.O. DE VILLIERS | H.O. DE VILLIERS | H.O. DE VILLIERS | H.O. DE VILLIERS |
| | | | |
| J.P. ENGELBRECHT | J.P.ENGELBRECHT 2T | †G.H. MULLER | G.H. MULLER |
| E. OLIVIER | E. OLIVIER | E. OLIVIER | E. OLIVIER 2T |
| F. DU T. ROUX 1T | F. DU T. ROUX | F. DU T. ROUX | F. DU T. ROUX 1T |
| S.H. NOMIS 2T | S.H. NOMIS | S.H. NOMIS | S.H. NOMIS |
| | | | |
| P.J. VISAGIE 3PG,3C | P.J. VISAGIE 2C,1T,1PG | P.J. VISAGIE 1T,1PG,1C | P.J. VISAGIE 2PG,2C |
| *D.J. DE VILLIERS¹ | P. DE W. UYS | D.J.J. DE VOS | *D.J. DE VILLIERS |
| | | | |
| J.L. MYBURGH | J.L.MYBURGH | J.L. MYBURGH | J.L. MYBURGH |
| D.C. WALTON | D.C. WALTON | G. PITZER | G. PITZER |
| J.F.K. MARAIS | J.F.K. MARAIS | J.F.K. MARAIS | J.F.K. MARAIS |
| F.C.H. DU PREEZ | F.C.H. DU PREEZ | †A.E. DE WET | A.E. DE WET |
| G. CARELSE | G. CARELSE | G. CARELSE | G. CARELSE |
| P.J.F. GREYLING 1T | P.J.F. GREYLING | P.J.F. GREYLING | P.J.F. GREYLING |
| T.P. BEDFORD | *T.P. BEDFORD | *T.P. BEDFORD | T.P. BEDFORD |
| J.H. ELLIS 1T | J.H. ELLIS | J.H. ELLIS 1T | J.H. ELLIS |
| | | | |
| Johannesburg | Durban | Cape Town | Bloemfontein |
| WON 30-11 | WON 16-9 | WON 11-3 | WON 19-8 |
| | | | |
| SA: 3G 3PG 2T | SA: 2G 1PG 1T | SA: 1G 1PG 1T | SA: 2G 2PG 1T |
| AUST.: 1G 2PG | AUST.: 3PG | AUST.: 1PG | AUST.: 1G 1PG |
| | | | |
| 2 Aug. 1969 | 16 Aug. 1969 | 6 Sep. 1969 | 20 Sep. 1969 |
| ¹Rep. by P. de W. Uys | | | |

The Springbok pack of 1969, coached by Avril Malan, was one of the strongest ever fielded. The front row rolled back the Wallabies in the Tests and for the first time since 1949 all of the four Tests of a home series were won.

South Africa would have fielded the same side for the two opening Tests of the rubber, but skipper de Villiers injured his collar-bone at Johannesburg and the veteran Piet Uys, who became the first replacement used by SA in an international, held his place for the second Test. Tom Bedford took over as captain, becoming the third Natal player to captain the Springboks (following Phil Nel and Roy Dryburgh), but at Durban the Springboks struggled to dominate the line-outs, and a surprise announcement by the selectors was the dropping of du Preez for the third Test. Engelbrecht, after 33 Tests – a record for a Springbok wing – was also dropped, making way for the young and much-rated Gert Muller.

Visagie's kicking guided South Africa to victory in the third Test, and with the rubber safe and de Villiers back as captain, the Spingboks wrapped up the series with a convincing win at Bloemfontein. Visagie created two records with his last kick of the match, the conversion of Olivier's second try. He passed by one point the previous South African career record of 88 points set by Keith Oxlee, and finished with 43 points in the rubber, a new world record for a four-Test series.

## 1969-70

| v. SCOTLAND | v. ENGLAND | v. IRELAND | v. WALES |
|---|---|---|---|
| H.O. DE VILLIERS | H.O. DE VILLIERS | H.O. DE VILLIERS 1PG,1C | H.O. DE VILLIERS 1PG |
| S.H. NOMIS | S.H. NOMIS | S.H. NOMIS | S.H. NOMIS 1T |
| †O.A. ROUX | O.A. ROUX | O.A. ROUX | O.A. ROUX |
| E. OLIVIER | E. OLIVIER¹ | F. DU T. ROUX | †J.P. VAN DER MERWE |
| G.H. MULLER¹ | A.E. VAN DER WATT | A.E. VAN DER WATT | G.H. MULLER |
| P.J. VISAGIE 1PG | P.J. VISAGIE 1C,1PG | M.J. LAWLESS | M.J. LAWLESS |
| D.J.J. DE VOS | *D.J. DE VILLIERS | *D.J. DE VILLIERS | *D.J. DE VILLIERS |
| J.B. NEETHLING | J.L. MYBURGH | J.L. MYBURGH | J.L. MYBURGH |
| †C.H. COCKRELL | D.C. WALTON | C.H. COCKRELL | C.H. COCKRELL |
| J.F.K. MARAIS | J.F.K. MARAIS | J.F.K. MARAIS | J.F.K. MARAIS |
| F.C.H. DU PREEZ | A.E. DE WET | F.C.H. DU PREEZ | F.C.H. DU PREEZ |
| G. CARELSE | †I.J. DE KLERK | I.J. DE KLERK | I.J. DE KLERK |
| P.J.F. GREYLING | P.J.F. GREYLING 1T | P.J.F. GREYLING 1T | P.J.F. GREYLING |
| *T.P. BEDFORD | T.P. BEDFORD | T.P. BEDFORD | T.P. BEDFORD |
| J.H. ELLIS | †A.J. BATES | J.H. ELLIS | J.H. ELLIS |
| Murrayfield | Twickenham | Lansdowne Road | Cardiff Arms Park |
| LOST 3-6 | LOST 8-11 | DRAWN 8-8 | DRAWN 6-6 |
| SCOT.: 1PG 1T | ENG.: 1G 1PG 1T | IRE.: 1G 1PG | WALES: 1PG 1T |
| SA: 1PG | SA: 1G 1PG | SA: 1G 1PG | SA: 1PG 1T |
| 6 Dec. 1969 | 20 Dec. 1969 | 10 Jan. 1970 | 24 Jan. 1970 |
| ¹Rep. by †A.E. van der Watt | ¹Rep. by M.J. Lawless | | |

The Sixth Springboks were the last official South African international side to tour Britain. Their matches were played under difficult circumstances, the players experiencing extreme harassment from anti-apartheid demonstrators.

For the first time the Springboks failed to win a single Test on a major tour. The constant protests against the side naturally meant that few players enjoyed the visit, and the strains of the tour accounted (in part) for the Springboks' poor international record. Visagie lost form as a place-kicker, disliking the softer, muddier British grounds, and there was a dearth of enterprise among the Springboks' backs. The Springboks had ill-luck with injuries to hookers on this tour, and replacement, Cockrell, had to hook in the opening Test against Scotland. He had only been in Britain ten days and was outhooked by his opponent as the Springboks went down, rather surprisingly, against the Scots. A well-prepared English side deserved victory at Twickenham, but lucky last-minute scores by both Ireland and Wales left the final tour internationals drawn.

## 1970

| 1st v. NZ | 2nd v. NZ | 3rd v. NZ | 4th v. NZ |
|---|---|---|---|
| †I.D. McCALLUM 1C,2PG | I.D. McCALLUM 1C,1PG | I.D. McCALLUM 2PG,1C | I.D. McCALLUM 1C,4PG |
| S.H. NOMIS 1T | S.H. NOMIS | S.H. NOMIS | S.H. NOMIS |
| F. DU T. ROUX | F. DU T. ROUX | F. DU T. ROUX | F. DU T. ROUX |
| †J.S. JANSEN | J.S. JANSEN 1T | J.S. JANSEN | J.S. JANSEN |
| G.H. MULLER | G.H. MULLER | G.H. MULLER 2T | G.H. MULLER 1T |
| P.J. VISAGIE 1DG | P.J. VISAGIE | P.J. VISAGIE | P.J. VISAGIE 1T |
| *D.J. DE VILLIERS 1T | *D.J. DE VILLIERS | *D.J. DE VILLIERS | *D.J. DE VILLIERS |
| J.B. NEETHLING | J.B. NEETHLING | J.L. MYBURGH | J.L. MYBURGH |
| †J.F.B. VAN WYK | J.F.B. VAN WYK¹ | J.F.B. VAN WYK | J.F.B. VAN WYK |
| J.F.K. MARAIS | J.F.K. MARAIS | J.F.K. MARAIS | J.F.K. MARAIS |
| F.C.H. DU PREEZ | F.C.H. DU PREEZ | F.C.H. DU PREEZ | F.C.H. DU PREEZ |
| †J.J. SPIES | J.J. SPIES | J.J. SPIES | J.J. SPIES |
| P.J.F. GREYLING | P.J.F. GREYLING | P.J.F. GREYLING | P.J.F. GREYLING |
| A.J. BATES | A.J. BATES | J.A. NEL | J.A. NEL |
| J.H. ELLIS | J.H. ELLIS | J.H. ELLIS | J.H. ELLIS |
| Pretoria | Cape Town | Port Elizabeth | Johannesburg |
| WON 17-6 | LOST 8-9 | WON 14-3 | WON 20-17 |
| SA: 1G 2PG 1DG 1T | SA: 1G 1PG | SA: 1G 2PG 1T | SA: 1G 4PG 1T |
| NZ: 1PG 1T | NZ: 1PG 2T | NZ: 1PG | NZ: 1G 4PG |
| 25 Jul. 1970 | 8 Aug. 1970 | 29 Aug. 1970 | 12 Sep. 1970 |
| | ¹Rep. by †R.W. Barnard | | |

Dr Verwoerd having been succeeded as Prime Minister, the South Africans accepted that change in their policies regarding touring sides had to be made, and for the 1970 tour by the New Zealanders, Maoris were welcomed as tourists for the first time. The All Blacks came as favourites to win the rubber: they had dominated world rugby during the decade of the 1960s, while South Africa were still on the rebound following their demoralising tour of Britain.

But once again the Springboks, who used only 18 players in the entire series, foiled the All Blacks. The rubber was all-square after the Cape Town Test, and for the decisive third Test the South African selectors took the extraordinary step of recalling "Lofty" Nel as number-eight. At 36, Nel thus became the oldest Springbok to play in a Test. But the selectors' gamble paid off. Splendid left-footed place-kicking by McCallum and three fine tries by Muller on the wing steered them to success by 3-1 in one of the most exciting series in South African rugby history.

## 1971

| 1st v. FRANCE | 2nd v. FRANCE | 1st v. AUSTRALIA | 2nd v. AUSTRALIA | 3rd v. AUSTRALIA |
|---|---|---|---|---|
| I.D. McCallum 3PG,2C | I.D. McCallum 1C | I.D. McCallum 1PG,2C | I.D. McCallum 1PG,1C | I.D. McCallum |
| | | | | |
| S.H. Nomis | S.H. Nomis | S.H. Nomis | S.H. Nomis | S.H. Nomis |
| J.S. Jansen | J.S. Jansen | J.S. Jansen | J.S. Jansen | J.S. Jansen |
| †P.A. Cronje | P.A. Cronje 1T | P.A. Cronje | P.A. Cronje | P.A. Cronje 1T |
| G.H. Muller 1T | G.H. Muller | †J.T. Viljoen 1T | J.T. Viljoen 1T | J.T. Viljoen |
| | | | | |
| P.J. Visagie 1DG | P.J. Visagie 1DG | P.J. Visagie 1DG | P.J. Visagie 2T | P.J. Visagie 1T,1PG,3C |
| †J.F. Viljoen 1T | J.F. Viljoen | J.F. Viljoen 1T | J.F. Viljoen | J.F. Viljoen |
| | | | | |
| †J.T. Sauermann | J.T. Sauermann | J.T. Sauermann | †M.J. Louw | M.J. Louw |
| J.F.B. van Wyk | J.F.B. van Wyk | J.F.B. van Wyk | J.F.B. van Wyk | J.F.B. van Wyk |
| *J.F.K. Marais | *J.F.K. Marais | *J.F.K. Marais | *J.F.K. Marais | *J.F.K. Marais |
| F.C.H. du Preez | F.C.H. du Preez | F.C.H. du Preez | F.C.H. du Preez | F.C.H. du Preez |
| †J.G. Williams | J.G. Williams | J.G. Williams | J.G. Williams | J.G. Williams |
| P.J.F. Greyling | P.J.F. Greyling | P.J.F. Greyling | P.J.F. Greyling | P.J.F. Greyling |
| T.P. Bedford | T.P. Bedford | †M. du Plessis | M. du Plessis | M. du Plessis |
| J.H. Ellis | J.H. Ellis | J.H. Ellis 1T | J.H. Ellis | J.H. Ellis 1T |
| | | | | |
| Bloemfontein | Durban | Sydney | Brisbane | Sydney |
| WON 22-9 | DRAWN 8-8 | WON 19-11 | WON 14-6 | WON 18-6 |
| | | | | |
| SA: 2G 1DG 3PG | SA: 1G 1DG | AUST.: 1G 2PG | AUST.: 1PG 1DG | AUST.: 1PG 1T |
| Fr.: 2PG 1T | Fr.: 1G 1DG | SA: 2G 1PG 1DG 1T | SA: 1G 1PG 2T | SA: 3G 1PG |
| | | | | |
| 12 Jun. 1971 | 19 Jun. 1971 | 17 Jul. 1971 | 31 Jul. 1971 | 7 Aug. 1971 |

The Springboks of 1971 were regarded as the finest for years. Five Tests were played, four won, and for the first time South Africa made a tour of Australia only. (Previous tours had been part of a combined tour of Australia and New Zealand.) With "Flappie" Lochner as manager, the side enjoyed an invincible run of thirteen games on a visit marred by political demonstrations. Much of the credit for the side's success went to coach Johan Claassen, who prepared a super-fit side which concentrated on the basic skills and adopted the subdue and penetrate philosophy which had always served the Springboks well in the past.

Four new caps opened the season against France. The veteran prop Hannes Marais took over as captain from de Villers, who had retired after establishing a Springbok record with 25 appearances at scrum-half, and Marais led his men to a decisive victory at Bloemfontein. The draw at Durban was disappointing, however, a flare up of fisticuffs overshadowing a match which should have gone on record for the outstanding back play of both teams. Complete forward mastery and the tactical control of Visagie guided the Springboks to three convincing wins in the Tests in Australia.

## 1972       1974

| v. ENGLAND | 1st v. BRITISH ISLES | 2nd v. BRITISH ISLES | 3rd v. BRITISH ISLES | 4th v. BRITISH ISLES |
|---|---|---|---|---|
| †R.A. Carlson | I.D. McCallum | I.D. McCallum[1] | O.A. Roux | O.A. Roux |
| | | | | |
| S.H. Nomis | †C.F. Pope | C.F. Pope | C.F. Pope | C.F. Pope |
| J.S. Jansen | †J.J. Oosthuizen | †J.C.P. Snyman | †J.J.J. Schlebusch | J.J.J. Schlebusch |
| O.A. Roux | †P.J.M. Whipp | P.J.M. Whipp | P.A. Cronje | P.A. Cronje 1T |
| G.H. Muller | G.H. Muller | †J.S. Germishuys | G.H. Muller | G.H. Muller |
| | | | | |
| †D.S.L. Snyman 3PG | D.S.L. Snyman 1DG | †G.R. Bosch 2PG,1DG | J.C.P. Snyman 3PG | J.C.P. Snyman 3PG |
| J.F. Viljoen | †R.J. McCallum | †P.C.R. Bayvel | †G.H.H Sonnekus | P.C.R. Bayvel |
| | | | | |
| †N. Bezuidenhout | J.T. Sauermann | N. Bezuidenhout | N. Bezuidenhout | N. Bezuidenhout[1] |
| J.F.B. van Wyk | J.F.B. van Wyk | †C.A. Frederickson | J.F.B. van Wyk | J.F.B. van Wyk |
| J.T. Sauermann | *J.F.K. Marais | *J.F.K. Marais | *J.F.K. Marais | *J.F.K. Marais |
| J.G. Williams | J.G. Williams | J.G. Williams | †J.L. van Heerden[1] | J.G. Williams |
| †P.G. du Plessis | †K.B.H. de Klerk | K.B.H. de Klerk | †J. de Bruyn | J.L. van Heerden |
| *P.J.F. Greyling | †J.H.H. Coetzee | M. du Plessis | †T.T. Fourie | J.L. Kritzinger |
| A.J. Bates | M. du Plessis | †D.A. MacDonald | †J.L. Kritzinger | †C.J. Grobler |
| J.H. Ellis | J.H. Ellis | J.H. Ellis | J.H. Ellis | J.H. Ellis |
| | | | | |
| Johannesburg | Cape Town | Pretoria | Port Elizabeth | Johannesburg |
| LOST 9-18 | LOST 3-12 | LOST 9-28 | LOST 9-26 | DRAWN 13-13 |
| | | | | |
| SA: 3PG | SA: 1DG | SA: 2PG 1DG | SA: 3PG | SA: 3PG 1T |
| Eng.: 1G 4PG | B.Is.: 3PG 1DG | B.Is.: 1G 4T 1PG 1DG | B.Is.: 1G 2T 2PG 2DG | B.Is.: 1G 1PG 1T |
| | | | | |
| 3 Jun. 1972 | 8 Jun. 1974 | 22 Jun. 1974 | 13 Jul. 1974 | 27 Jul. 1974 |
| | | [1]Rep. by D.S.L. Snyman, then by †M.L. Vogel | [1]Rep. by K.B.H. de Klerk | [1]Rep. by †J.C.J. Stander |

1972 and 1974 were years in which the supremacy of the British over South Africa on the rugby field was clearly established. An underrated English side, which had finished bottom of the Five-Nations table, stunned the rugby world by defeating the Springboks 18-9 in the only Test of the 1972 tour at Johannesburg.

Then, in 1974, the Lions were undefeated in a four-Test series, winning three and drawing the final game of the rubber. It was the first time since 1896 that the Springboks had lost a Test series to the British.

Altogether 33 Springboks appeared in the Test series, Vogel gaining the unusual distinction of replacing a replacement when he came on as full-back in the second half of the Pretoria Test. Rearrangements made to the team by selectors seeking the best permutation of talent available prevented a settled Springbok side developing, and many of their problems (despite a hectic draw at Ellis Park) were unresolved by the close of the series.

| | 1974 | | 1975 | |
|---|---|---|---|---|
| | 1st v. FRANCE | 2nd v. FRANCE | 1st v. FRANCE | 2nd v. FRANCE |
| | D.S.L. SNYMAN | D.S.L. SNYMAN | D.S.L. SNYMAN 1PG,1C | D.S.L. SNYMAN |
| | †W.P. STAPELBERG 1T | W.P. STAPELBERG 1T | C.F. POPE 1T | C.F. POPE |
| | †I.W. ROBERTSON | I.W. ROBERTSON | J.J. OOSTHUIZEN 1T | J.J. OOSTHUIZEN |
| | J.J. OOSTHUIZEN | J.J. OOSTHUIZEN | P.J.M. WHIPP 1T | J.J.J. SCHLEBUSCH |
| | †C. FOURIE 1PG | C. FOURIE | C. FOURIE | C. FOURIE 1T,1PG |
| | G.R. BOSCH 2PG | G.R. BOSCH 2PG | G.R. BOSCH 3PG,2C | G.R. BOSCH 6PG,2C |
| | P.C.R. BAYVEL | P.C.R. BAYVEL | P.C.R. BAYVEL | P.C.R. BAYVEL |
| | N. BEZUIDENHOUT | N. BEZUIDENHOUT | N. BEZUIDENHOUT | N. BEZUIDENHOUT |
| | †R.J. COCKRELL | R.J. COCKRELL[1] | R.J. COCKRELL 1T | R.J. COCKRELL |
| | *J.F.K. MARAIS | *J.F.K. MARAIS | †D.S. VAN DEN BERG | D.S. VAN DEN BERG |
| | J.G. WILLIAMS | J.G. WILLIAMS | K.B.H. DE KLERK | K.B.H. DE KLERK |
| | J.L. VAN HEERDEN | J.L. VAN HEERDEN | J.L. VAN HEERDEN | J.L. VAN HEERDEN[1] |
| | J.L. KRITZINGER | J.L. KRITZINGER | J.L. KRITZINGER | J.L. KRITZINGER |
| | M. DU PLESSIS | M. DU PLESSIS | *M. DU PLESSIS | *M. DU PLESSIS 1T |
| | J.H. ELLIS | J.H. ELLIS | C.J. GROBLER 1T | C.J. GROBLER |
| | Toulouse | Parc des Princes | Bloemfontein | Pretoria |
| | WON 13-4 | WON 10-8 | WON 38-25 | WON 33-18 |
| | FR.: 1T | FR.: 2T | SA: 3G 2T 4PG | SA: 2G 7PG |
| | SA: 3PG 1T | SA: 2PG 1T | FR.: 3G 1PG 1T | FR.: 1G 1DG 3PG |
| | 23 Nov. 1974 | 30 Nov. 1974 | 21 Jun. 1975 | 28 Jun. 1975 |
| | | [1]Rep. by †A. Bestbier | | [1]Rep. by J.H.H. Coetzee |

South Africa's next four Tests were against France. In November a party managed by J.S. le Roux and captained by Marais played nine matches in France, winning eight but losing to a regional selection at Angoulême. The two Tests in France were close encounters in which the defensive play of Dawie Snyman at full-back, the determined running of Stapelberg and Fourie on the wings, and the good understanding of Bayvel and Bosch at half-back, augured well for the future of Springbok rugby. Seven months later the Springboks were hosts to the French. In a high-scoring two-match series, the South Africans were happy to secure their fourth consecutive win over the French. Morné du Plessis took over as captain for the series, becoming (with his father Felix) the first son/father combination to lead South Africa. At Pretoria, Bosch established a new record by scoring 22 points in a Test, his six penalty goals equalling the world record for an international.

| | 1976 | | | | 1977 |
|---|---|---|---|---|---|
| | 1st. v. NZ | 2nd v. NZ | 3rd v. NZ | 4th v. NZ | v. WORLD INV XV |
| | I.W. ROBERTSON 1DG | D.S.L. SNYMAN | D.S.L. SNYMAN 1DG | I.W. ROBERTSON | D.S.L. SNYMAN 1T |
| | †E.F.W. KRANTZ 1T | C.F. POPE | C.F. POPE | C.F. POPE | †H.L. POTGIETER 1T |
| | J.J. OOSTHUIZEN | J.J. OOSTHUIZEN | J.J. OOSTHUIZEN 1T | J.J. OOSTHUIZEN | †D.C. FRONEMAN |
| | P.J.M. WHIPP | I.W. ROBERTSON | P.J.M. WHIPP | P.J.M. WHIPP | †C. WAGENAAR |
| | J.S. GERMISHUYS 1T | J.S. GERMISHUYS | J.S. GERMISHUYS | J.S. GERMISHUYS | J.S. GERMISHUYS 1T |
| | G.R. BOSCH 1PG,1C[1] | G.R. BOSCH 3PG | G.R. BOSCH 2PG,1C | G.R. BOSCH 2PG,1DG,1C | †R. BLAIR 5PG,3C |
| | P.C.R. BAYVEL | P.C.R. BAYVEL | P.C.R. BAYVEL | P.C.R. BAYVEL | †B.J. WOLMARANS 1T |
| | J.C.J. STANDER | J.C.J. STANDER | J.C.J. STANDER | J.C.J. STANDER | N. BEZUIDENHOUT |
| | R.J. COCKRELL | R.J. COCKRELL | J.F.B. VAN WYK | J.F.B. VAN WYK | R.J. COCKRELL |
| | D.S. VAN DEN BERG | D.S. VAN DEN BERG | †J.H.P. STRAUSS | J.H.P. STRAUSS | †D.C. DU PLESSIS |
| | J.G. WILLIAMS | J.G. WILLIAMS[1] | K.B.H. DE KLERK | K.B.H. DE KLERK | †L.C. MOOLMAN |
| | J.L. VAN HEERDEN | J.L. VAN HEERDEN | J.L. VAN HEERDEN | J.L. VAN HEERDEN | J.L. VAN HEERDEN |
| | J.H.H. COETZEE | J.H.H. COETZEE | J.H.H. COETZEE | J.H.H. COETZEE | M.T.S. STOFBERG 2T |
| | *M. DU PLESSIS | *M. DU PLESSIS | *M. DU PLESSIS | *M. DU PLESSIS | *M. DU PLESSIS |
| | J.H. ELLIS | †M.T.S. STOFBERG | M.T.S. STOFBERG | J.L. KRITZINGER 1T | †P.E. VELDSMAN |
| | Durban | Bloemfontein | Cape Town | Johannesburg | Pretoria |
| | WON 16-7 | LOST 9-15 | WON 15-10 | WON 15-14 | WON 45-24 |
| | SA: 1G 1T 1PG 1DG | SA: 3PG | SA: 1G 2PG 1DG | SA: 1G 2PG 1DG | SA: 3G 5PG 3T |
| | NZ: 1PG 1T | NZ: 1G 2PG 1DG | NZ: 2PG 1T | NZ: 1PG 1DG 2T | WORLD: 4G |
| | 24 Jul. 1976 | 14 Aug. 1976 | 4 Sep. 1976 | 18 Sep. 1976 | 27 Aug. 1977 |
| | [1]Rep. by †W.J. de Wet Ras | [1]Rep. by K.B.H. de Klerk | | | |

The 1976 series with the All Blacks was as tight and gruelling as any between the two great rivals of world rugby. South Africa won an extremely tense series by the narrowest of margins, taking the rubber with a one-point victory in the final Test. But there was very little open play in a series between two well-matches sides. Bosch ran a tight regime at fly-half and gave little ball to his threequarters. Nevertheless his 33 points in the Tests had a telling effect on the series, especially as the New Zealanders had no recognised kicker; while Morné du Plessis' inspiring leadership also proved a vital factor in South Africa's success.

Jan Ellis bowed out of Test rugby after the first win at Durban. A tall, red-headed flanker with blistering pace, Ellis was a veteran of 38 Tests, equalling the Springbok record.

In 1977, to mark the reopening of a refurbished Loftus Versfeld stadium in Pretoria, a World XV was invited to play in a Test which was accorded full international status by the SARB. In a high-scoring South African victory, Robbie Blair created a world record for a player on his Test debut, scoring 21 points.

## 1980

| 1st v. S.AMERICA | 2nd v. S.AMERICA |
|---|---|
| †P. Edwards | P. Edwards[1] |
| †R.H. Mordt 1t | R.H. Mordt |
| P.J.M. Whipp | P.J.M. Whipp |
| †W. du Plessis | W. du Plessis[2] |
| J.S. Germishuys 1t | J.S. Germishuys |
| †H.E. Botha 1dg,1pg,3c | H.E. Botha 3dg,1pg,1c |
| †T.D. du Plessis 1t | T.D. du Plessis |
| J.H.P. Strauss | D.C. du Plessis |
| C.A. Frederickson | C.A. Frederickson |
| †R.B. Prentis | R.B. Prentis |
| K.B.H. de Klerk | K.B.H. de Klerk |
| L.C. Moolman | L.C. Moolman |
| †R.J. Louw | R.J. Louw |
| *M. du Plessis | *M. du Plessis 1t |
| M.T.S. Stofberg | M.T.S. Stofberg |
| Johannesburg | Durban |
| WON 24-9 | WON 18-9 |
| SA: 3G 1PG 1DG | SA: 1G 1PG 3DG |
| S.Am.: 1G 1PG | S.Am.: 3PG |
| 26 April 1980 | 3 May 1980 |

[1]Rep. by †Z.M.J. Pienaar
[2]Rep. by W.J. de Wet Ras

## 1980

| 1st v. BRITISH ISLES | 2nd v. BRITISH ISLES | 3rd v. BRITISH ISLES | 4th v. BRITISH ISLES |
|---|---|---|---|
| Z.M.J. Pienaar | Z.M.J. Pienaar 1t | Z.M.J. Pienaar | Z.M.J. Pienaar 2pg |
| R.H. Mordt | R.H. Mordt | R.H. Mordt | R.H. Mordt |
| †D.J. Smith | D.J. Smith | D.J. Smith | D.J. Smith |
| W. du Plessis 1t | W. du Plessis | W. du Plessis | W. du Plessis 1t |
| J.S. Germishuys 1t | J.S. Germishuys 1t | J.S. Germishuys 1t | J.S. Germishuys |
| H.E. Botha 3c | H.E. Botha 2c,2pg | H.E. Botha 1dg,1pg,1c | H.E. Botha 1pg |
| †D.J. Serfontein 1t | D.J. Serfontein | D.J. Serfontein | D.J. Serfontein |
| R.B. Prentis | R.B. Prentis | R.B. Prentis | R.B. Prentis |
| †W.J.H. Kahts | W.J.H. Kahts | W.J.H. Kahts[1] | E. Malan |
| †M. le Roux | M. le Roux | M. le Roux | M. le Roux |
| L.C. Moolman | L.C. Moolman | L.C. Moolman | L.C. Moolman |
| J.L. van Heerden 1t | K.B.H. de Klerk | J.L. van Heerden | J.L. van Heerden |
| M.T.S. Stofberg | M.T.S. Stofberg 1t | M.T.S. Stofberg | M.T.S. Stofberg |
| *M. du Plessis | *M. du Plessis | *M. du Plessis | *M. du Plessis |
| R.J. Louw 1t | R.J. Louw 1t[1] | R.J. Louw | R.J. Louw |
| Cape Town | Bloemfontein | Port Elizabeth | Pretoria |
| WON 26-22 | WON 26-19 | WON 12-10 | LOST 13-17 |
| SA 3G 2T | SA: 2G 2PG 2T | SA: 1G 1PG 1DG | SA: 3PG 1T |
| B.Is.: 5PG 1DG 1T | B.Is.: 1G 3PG 1T | B.Is.: 2PG 1T | B.Is.: 1G 1PG 2T |
| 31 May 1980 | 14 Jun. 1980 | 28 Jun. 1980 | 12 Jul. 1980 |

[1]Rep. †M.B. Burger (2nd v. British Isles)
[1]Rep. by †E. Malan (3rd v. British Isles)

Deprived of Test opposition for four seasons, South Africa returned to international commitments in 1980, a season which turned out to be the longest and busiest in their history. In order to prepare for their forthcoming series with the Lions, the Springboks invited a team of South American (principally of Argentine origin) for a two-Test series which was granted full international status.

Seven new caps were awarded for the first Test played at the Wanderers ground in Johannesburg. Naas Botha, a superb kicker, proved a prolific scorer of points, breaking the South African drop-goal record by landing three in the Durban Test.

Against the Lions, the Springboks deserved to take the series 3-1. But each match was a close contest between sides boasting two strong, well-drilled packs. In the end it was the outstanding counter-attacking of the new full-back, Gysie Pienaar, and the running of Germishuys (who scored tries in each of the first three Tests) which helped the Springboks to their narrow victories.

## 1980 | 1980

| 3rd v. S.AMERICA | 4th v. S.AMERICA | v. FRANCE |
|---|---|---|
| Z.M.J. Pienaar | Z.M.J. Pienaar | Z.M.J. Pienaar 1t |
| R.H. Mordt | R.H. Mordt 2t | R.H. Mordt |
| †D.M. Gerber 1t | D.M. Gerber 1t | W. du Plessis |
| W. du Plessis | W. du Plessis | D.M. Gerber |
| J.S. Germishuys | J.S. Germishuys 2t | J.S. Germishuys 1t |
| H.E. Botha 1dg,1pg,2c | H.E. Botha 3c | H.E. Botha 3pg,4c |
| D.J. Serfontein | D.J. Serfontein | D.J. Serfontein 1t |
| R.B. Prentis | R.B. Prentis | R.B. Prentis |
| W.J.H. Kahts | W.J.H. Kahts | W.J.H. Kahts 1t |
| M. le Roux | M. le Roux | M. le Roux |
| J.L. van Heerden | L.C. Moolman | L.C. Moolman |
| L.C. Moolman | J.L. van Heerden | J.L. van Heerden |
| *M.T.S. Stofberg 1t | M.T.S. Stofberg | M.T.S. Stofberg 1t |
| M.B. Burger 1t | *M. du Plessis 1t | *M. du Plessis |
| R.J. Louw | R.J. Louw | R.J. Louw |
| Montevideo | Santiago | Pretoria |
| WON 22-13 | WON 30-16 | WON 37-15 |
| S.Am.: 1G 1DG 1T | S.Am.: 1G 1PG 1DG 1T | SA: 4G 3PG 1T |
| SA.: 2G 1PG 1DG 1T | SA.: 3G 3T | Fr.: 1G 3PG |
| 18 Oct. 1980 | 26 Oct. 1980 | 8 Nov. 1980 |

The second half of the 1980 Springbok Test season followed the domestic Currie Cup competition. Although the original itinerary had shown Buenos Aires as the venue for the Tests, the tour was subsequently confined to Paraguay, Uruguay and Chile. Nevertheless, the South American Test side consisted entirely of Argentinians.

There was only one new cap in the Springbok line-up for the first Test: Danie Gerber. To date he has been one of the outstanding centres in world rugby, his aggressive running and prolific try scoring having thrilled crowds in both hemispheres. Only 3,000 spectators were present at Montevideo, though double this number attended the second Test, for which Morné du Plessis returned as captain of a side which gave an improved all-round performance to win 30-16 in Santiago.

South Africa's ninth Test of the season was played against France at Pretoria in November. Running the ball from all quarters, the Springboks displayed marvellous combination to score five tries. Germishuys completed a fine personal season by scoring his seventh try of the year and his ninth Test try to establish a new Springbok career record.

## 1981

| 1st v. IRELAND | 2nd v. IRELAND | 1st v. NZ | 2nd v. NZ | 3rd v. NZ | v. AMERICA |
|---|---|---|---|---|---|
| Z.M.J. PIENAAR | Z.M.J. PIENAAR | Z.M.J. PIENAAR | Z.M.J. PIENAAR | Z.M.J. PIENAAR[1] | J.W. HEUNIS |
| E.F.W. KRANTZ | R.H. MORDT | R.H. MORDT | R.H. MORDT | R.H. MORDT 3T | R.H. MORDT 3T |
| D.M. GERBER 2T | D.M. GERBER | D.M. GERBER | D.M. GERBER | D.M. GERBER | D.M. GERBER |
| †E.G. TOBIAS | E.G. TOBIAS | W. DU PLESSIS | W. DU PLESSIS[1] | W. DU PLESSIS[2] | J.J. BECK 1T |
| J.S. GERMISHUYS | J.S. GERMISHUYS | †D.S. BOTHA | J.S. GERMISHUYS 1T | J.S. GERMISHUYS | J.S. GERMISHUYS 2T |
| H.E. BOTHA 3PG,1C | H.E. BOTHA 1PG,3DG | H.E. BOTHA 1DG,1C | H.E. BOTHA 5PG,1C,1DG | H.E. BOTHA 2PG,2C | H.E. BOTHA 3C |
| D.J. SERFONTEIN | D.J. SERFONTEIN | D.J. SERFONTEIN | D.J. SERFONTEIN | D.J. SERFONTEIN | D.J. SERFONTEIN |
| R.B. PRENTIS | R.B. PRENTIS | †H.J. VAN ASWEGAN | †P.R. VAN DER MERWE | P.R. VAN DER MERWE | P.R. VAN DER MERWE |
| W.J.H. KAHTS | W.J.H. KAHTS | R.J. COCKRELL | W.J.H. KAHTS[2] | R.J. COCKRELL | R.J. COCKRELL |
| M. LE ROUX[1] | O.W. OOSTHUIZEN | †P.G. DU TOIT | O.W. OOSTHUIZEN | O.W. OOSTHUIZEN | O.W. OOSTHUIZEN |
| K.B.H. DE KLERK | K.B.H. KLERK | †H.J. BEKKER 1T | †J. DE V. VISSER | H.J. BEKKER | J. DE V. VISSER |
| L.C. MOOLMAN | L.C. MOOLMAN | L.C. MOOLMAN | L.C. MOOLMAN | L.C. MOOLMAN | L.C. MOOLMAN |
| R.J. LOUW 1T | R.J. LOUW | †E. JANSEN | †S.B. GELDENHUYS | S.B. GELDENHUYS | S.B. GELDENHUYS 1T |
| *†W. CLAASSEN | *W. CLAASSEN | R.J. LOUW | *W. CLAASSEN | *W. CLAASSEN | *W. CLAASSEN |
| M.T.S. STOFBERG | M.T.S. STOFBERG | *M.T.S. STOFBERG | M.T.S. STOFBERG | R.J. LOUW | M.T.S. STOFBERG[1] |
| Cape Town | Durban | Christchurch | Wellington | Auckland | Glenville, N.Y. |
| WON 23-15 | WON 12-10 | LOST 9-14 | WON 24-12 | LOST 22-25 | WON 38-7 |
| SA: 1G 3PG 2T | SA: 1PG 3DG | NZ: 1G 2T | NZ: 4PG | NZ: 1G 4PG 1DG 1T | AM: 1PG 1T |
| IRE.: 2G 1PG | IRE.: 2PG 1T | SA: 1G 1DG | SA: 1G 5PG 1DG | SA: 2G 2PG 1T | SA: 3G 5T |
| 30 May 1981 | 6 Jun. 1981 | 15 Aug. 1981 | 29 Aug. 1981 | 12 Sep. 1981 | 26 Sep. 1981 |
| [1]Rep. by †O.W. Oosthuizen | | | [1]Rep. by †J.J. Beck [2]Rep by R.J. Cockrell | [1]Rep. by †J.W. Heunis [2]Rep by J.J. Beck | [1]Rep. by M.B. Burger 1T |

Six Tests were played in another busy season in 1981. Ireland, despite strong political opposition by the Dublin Government, fulfilled a promise to tour early in the season, and gave the Springboks a stiff trial for their subsequent series in New Zealand. Errol Tobias became the first coloured player to appear in an international when he took the field against Ireland; and Abe Williams, an SARF official, accompanied the Springbok tour party to New Zealand as assistant manager.

The kicking of Naas Botha was a major factor in the series with Ireland. He kicked eleven points in the first of the Tests, and scored all of South Africa's points at Cape Town, equalling the world record by dropping three goals. In New Zealand, Botha's kicking was again significant in the internationals, his twenty points in Wellington squaring the series after the Springboks had been defeated in the first of the Tests. But a series dogged by anti-apartheid demonstrations was decided by the last kick of the tour when NZ triumphed 25-22 thanks to a last-minute penalty.

The final leg of the Springboks' tour was a week in America, where a Test match took place on a deserted polo field at Glenville, New York. The American Eagles played well up to half-time, but the Springboks asserted their authority on the match in the second half. Mordt became the first Springbok to score hat-tricks in consecutive internationals.

## 1982

| 1st v. S.AMERICA | 2nd v. S.AMERICA |
|---|---|
| J.W. HEUNIS 1PG | J.W. HEUNIS |
| R.H. MORDT 2T | R.H. MORDT |
| W. DU PLESSIS 1T | W. DU PLESSIS |
| D.M. GERBER 3T | D.M. GERBER 1T |
| †C.J. DU PLESSIS 1T | C.J. DU PLESSIS |
| H.E. BOTHA 6C,1DG | H.E. BOTHA 2PG,1C |
| D.J. SERFONTEIN | D.J. SERFONTEIN |
| P.G. DU TOIT | P.G. DU TOIT |
| W.J.H. KAHTS | W.J.H. KAHTS |
| O.W. OOSTHUIZEN 1T | O.W. OOSTHUIZEN |
| M.T.S STOFBERG | M.T.S STOFBERG |
| L.C. MOOLMAN | L.C. MOOLMAN |
| S.B. GELDENHUYS | S.B. GELDENHUYS |
| *W. CLAASSEN | *W. CLAASSEN |
| R.J. LOUW | R.J. LOUW |
| Pretoria | Bloemfontein |
| WON 50-18 | LOST 12-21 |
| SA: 6G 1PG 1DG 2T | SA: 1G 2PG |
| S.AM: 1G 4PG | S.AM: 1G 4PG 1DG |
| 27 Mar. 1982 | 3 Apr. 1982 |

A touring party of 42 players, drawn from Chile, Paraguay, Argentina and Uruquay, made a short tour of South Africa very early in the 1982 season. Two internationals were played against a side drawn entirely from the Argentinian players in the tour party. South Africa quickly gained the ascendancy up front in the first Test, and had few problems running up fifty points, the highest South African score in an official international. Botha extended his Springbok Test career record by fifteen points and Gerber equalled the South African Test record with three tries. But the same Springbok side was amazingly defeated in Bloemfontein a week later. Concentrating on the areas of the game where they had been inferior in the first Test, the Jaguars staged a remarkable improvement to level the series with a 21-12 win, their outstanding fly-half Hugo Porta scoring all of the side's points.

| **1984** | | **1984** | |
|---|---|---|---|
| 1st v. ENGLAND | 2nd v. ENGLAND | 1st v. S.AMERICA | 2nd v. S.AMERICA |
| J.W. Heunis 5PG,3C | J.W. Heunis 3C,1PG | J.W. Heunis 1T | J.W. Heunis |
| | | | |
| †A.P. Williams | A.P. Williams | R.H. Mordt | R.H. Mordt 1T |
| D.M. Gerber 1T | D.M. Gerber 3T | D.M. Gerber 1C,1T | D.M. Gerber 1T |
| †J.V. Villet | J.V. Villet | †M. du Plessis | M. du Plessis |
| C.J. du Plessis 1T | C.J. du Plessis | C.J. du Plessis | C.J. du Plessis 1T |
| | | | |
| E.G. Tobias | E.G. Tobias 1C,1T | E.G. Tobias 2PG,2C | E.G. Tobias 2PG |
| D.J. Serfontein | D.J. Serfontein | *D.J. Serfontein 1T | *D.J. Serfontein |
| | | | |
| O.W. Oosthuizen | O.W. Oosthuizen | †A.S. Barnard | A.S. Barnard |
| †C.D. Rogers | C.D. Rogers | C.D. Rogers | C.D. Rogers |
| P.G. du Toit | P.G. du Toit | †J.A. Strauss | J.A. Strauss |
| †S.W.P. Burger | S.W.P. Burger | L.C. Moolman | L.C. Moolman |
| †R.G. Visagie | R.G. Visagie | R.G. Visagie | R.G. Visagie |
| R.J. Louw 1T | R.J. Louw | R.J. Louw 1T | R.J. Louw |
| G.H.H. Sonnekus | G.H.H. Sonnekus 1T | †N.V.H. Mallett 1T | N.V.H. Mallett |
| *M.T.S. Stofberg | *M.T.S. Stofberg 1T | †P.S. Ferreira | P.S. Ferreira 1T |
| | | | |
| Port Elizabeth | Johannesburg | Pretoria | Cape Town |
| WON 33-15 | WON 35-9 | WON 32-15 | WON 22-13 |
| | | | |
| SA: 3G 5PG | SA: 4G 1PG 2T | SA: 3G 2T 2PG | SA: 4T 2PG |
| Eng.: 4PG 1DG | Eng.: 3PG | S.Am.: 2G 1PG | S.Am. 3PG 1T |
| | | | |
| 2 Jun. 1984 | 9 Jun. 1984 | 20 Oct. 1984 | 27 Oct. 1984 |

The Springboks powered to four easy Test victories in 1984. England, making their second tour of South Africa, were outplayed in the two internationals in early June and South Africa's win by 35-9 was their highest total and their biggest winning margin ever recorded against the English. The match in Johannesburg was the first in the refurbished Ellis Park stadium, and Gerber marked the occasion by scoring three tries, becoming only the second Springbok to score two hat-tricks in internationals.

The series with the Jaguars was an opportunity for the Springbok selectors to experiment with their team, and consolidate their preparations for the scheduled tour by the All Blacks in 1985. Divan Serfontein, the lively Western Province scrum-half, took over from Stofberg as captain and led the side with considerable panache. Both of the Tests were won by comfortable margins, and by scoring two tries Danie Gerber succeeded Germishuys as the principal Springbok try-scorer in Tests.

Two of the team played their final Tests at Cape Town. Ray Mordt, an outstanding wing, and Rob Louw, a menacing flanker who had scored five international tries, left South Africa during the 1985-86 season to play Rugby League in England.

| **1986** | | | |
|---|---|---|---|
| 1st v. NZ CAV. | 2nd v. NZ CAV. | 3rd v. NZ CAV. | 4th v. NZ CAV. |
| J.W. Heunis | J.W. Heunis | J.W. Heunis | J.W. Heunis |
| | | | |
| †J. Reinach | J. Reinach 1T | J. Reinach 1T | J. Reinach[1] |
| D.M. Gerber | D.M. Gerber | D.M. Gerber 1T | D.M. Gerber |
| M.J. du Plessis | M.J. du Plessis | M.J. du Plessis | M.J. du Plessis 1DG |
| C.J. du Plessis 1T | C.J. du Plessis | C.J. du Plessis | C.J. du Plessis |
| | | | |
| *H.E. Botha 3PG 2DG 1C | *H.E. Botha 4PG 1C | *H.E. Botha 1T 3PG 4C | *H.E. Botha 5PG 1C |
| †C. Ferreira | C. Ferreira | †G.D. Wright | G.D. Wright 1T |
| | | | |
| A.S. Barnard | A.S. Barnard | †F.S. Erasmus | F.S. Erasmus |
| †U.L. Schmidt | U.L. Schmidt | U.L. Schmidt 1T | U.L. Schmidt |
| P.R. van der Merwe | P.R. van der Merwe | †P.E. Kruger | P.E. Kruger |
| S.W.P. Burger | S.W.P. Burger | S.W.P. Burger | S.W.P. Burger |
| L.C. Moolman | L.C. Moolman | L.C. Moolman | L.C. Moolman |
| †W.J. Bartmann | W.J. Bartmann | W.J. Bartmann | W.J. Bartmann |
| †J.C. Breedt | J.C. Breedt | J.C. Breedt | J.C. Breedt |
| †G.P. Smal | G.P. Smal | G.P. Smal | G.P. Smal |
| | | | |
| Cape Town | Durban | Pretoria | Johannesburg |
| WON 21-15 | LOST 18-19 | WON 33-18 | WON 24-10 |
| | | | |
| SA: 1G 3PG 2DG | SA: 1G 4PG | SA: 4G 3PG | SA: 1G 1DG 5PG |
| NZ Cav.: 1G‡ 3PG | NZ Cav.: 1G 3PG 1T | NZ Cav.: 1G 1DG 3PG | NZ Cav.: 2PG 1T |
| | | | |
| 10 May 1986 | 17 May 1986 | 24 May 1986 | 31 May 1986 |
| | | | [1]Rep. by †H.L. Muller |

The South Africans had been due to entertain New Zealand in 1985, but a New Zealand High Court ruling prevented an official tour by the All Blacks. However, in 1986 a New Zealand rebel side, comprising 31 players and known as the Cavaliers, toured the Republic and played a four-Test series against the full Springbok side.

As a spectacle the series was disappointing. The Springbok captain Naas Botha was served quality possession by a powerful, mobile pack. But the pivot constantly neglected his talented threequarters, choosing to kick far more often than feed his backs. Nevertheless he was very largely responsible for guiding his side to victory, and in amassing 69 points, he created a new record for the total number of points in a Test series.

# SOUTH AFRICAN MATCH RECORDS

## MATCH RESULTS 1891 to 1987

| Match | Date | Opponents | For: T | C | D | P | Pts | Against: T | C | D | P | Pts | Result | Venue | Captain |
|---|---|---|---|---|---|---|---|---|---|---|---|---|---|---|---|
| 1 | 30.7.1891 | G.B. | — | — | — | — | 0 | 2 | 1 | — | — | 4 | Lost | Port Elizabeth | H. H. Castens |
| 2 | 29.8.1891 | G.B. | — | — | — | — | 0 | — | — | ★ | — | 3 | Lost | Kimberley | R. C. Snedden |
| 3 | 5.9.1891 | G.B. | — | — | — | — | 0 | 2 | 1 | — | — | 4 | Lost | Cape Town | A. R. Richards |
| 4 | 30.7.1896 | G.B. | — | — | — | — | 0 | 2 | 1 | — | — | 8 | Lost | Port Elizabeth | F. R. Myburgh |
| 5 | 22.8.1896 | G.B. | 2 | 1 | — | — | 8 | 3 | 2 | 1 | — | 17 | Lost | Johannesburg | F. T. D. Aston |
| 6 | 29.8.1896 | G.B. | 1 | — | — | — | 3 | 1 | 1 | 1 | — | 9 | Lost | Kimberley | F. T. D. Aston |
| 7 | 5.9.1896 | G.B. | 1 | 1 | — | — | 5 | — | — | — | — | 0 | Won | Cape Town | B. H. Heatlie |
| 8 | 26.8.1903 | G.B. | 2 | 2 | — | — | 10 | 2 | 2 | — | — | 10 | Drawn | Johannesburg | A. Frew |
| 9 | 5.9.1903 | G.B. | — | — | — | — | 0 | — | — | — | — | 0 | Drawn | Kimberley | J. M. Powell |
| 10 | 12.19.1903 | G.B. | 2 | 1 | — | — | 8 | — | — | — | — | 0 | Won | Cape Town | B. H. Heatlie |
| 11 | 17.11.1906 | Scotland | — | — | — | — | 0 | 2 | — | — | — | 6 | Lost | Glasgow | H. W. Carolin |
| 12 | 24.11.1906 | Ireland | 4 | — | — | 1 | 15 | 3 | — | — | 1 | 12 | Won | Belfast | P. J. Roos |
| 13 | 1.12.1906 | Wales | 3 | 1 | — | — | 11 | — | — | — | — | 0 | Won | Swansea | P. J. Roos |
| 14 | 8.12.1906 | England | 1 | — | — | — | 3 | 1 | — | — | — | 3 | Drawn | Crystal Palace | P. J. Roos |
| 15 | 6.8.1910 | G.B. | 4 | 1 | — | — | 14 | 2 | — | 1 | — | 10 | Won | Johannesburg | D. F. T. Morkel |
| 16 | 27.8.1910 | G.B. | 1 | — | — | — | 3 | 2 | 1 | — | — | 8 | Lost | Port Elizabeth | W. A. Millar |
| 17 | 3.9.1910 | G.B. | 4 | 3 | — | 1 | 21 | 1 | 1 | — | — | 5 | Won | Cape Town | W. A. Millar |
| 18 | 23.11.1912 | Scotland | 4 | 2 | — | — | 16 | — | — | — | — | 0 | Won | Edinburgh | F. J. Dobbin |
| 19 | 30.11.1912 | Ireland | 10 | 4 | — | — | 38 | — | — | — | — | 0 | Won | Dublin | W. A. Millar |
| 20 | 14.12.1912 | Wales | — | — | — | 1 | 3 | — | — | — | — | 0 | Won | Cardiff | W. A. Millar |
| 21 | 4.1.1913 | England | 1 | — | — | 2 | 9 | 1 | — | — | — | 3 | Won | Twickenham | D. F. T. Morkel |
| 22 | 11.1.1913 | France | 9 | 4 | — | 1 | 38 | 1 | 1 | — | — | 5 | Won | Bordeaux | W. A. Millar |
| 23 | 13.8.1921 | New Zealand | 1 | 1 | — | — | 5 | 3 | 2 | — | — | 13 | Lost | Dunedin | W. H. Morkel |
| 24 | 27.8.1921 | New Zealand | 1 | 1 | 1 | — | 9 | 1 | 1 | — | — | 5 | Won | Auckland | W. H. Morkel |
| 25 | 17.9.1921 | New Zealand | — | — | — | — | 0 | — | — | — | — | 0 | Drawn | Wellington | W. H. Morkel |
| 26 | 16.8.1924 | G.B. | 1 | — | 1 | — | 7 | 1 | — | — | — | 3 | Won | Durban | P. K. Albertyn |
| 27 | 23.8.1924 | G.B. | 4 | 1 | — | 1 | 17 | — | — | — | — | 0 | Won | Johannesburg | P. K. Albertyn |
| 28 | 13.9.1924 | G.B. | 1 | — | — | — | 3 | 1 | — | — | — | 3 | Drawn | Port Elizabeth | P. K. Albertyn |
| 29 | 20.9.1924 | G.B. | 4 | — | 1 | — | 16 | 2 | — | — | 1 | 9 | Won | Cape Town | P. K. Albertyn |
| 30 | 30.6.1928 | New Zealand | 1 | — | 2 | 2 | 17 | — | — | — | — | 0 | Won | Durban | P. J. Mostert |
| 31 | 21.7.1928 | New Zealand | — | — | ★ | 1 | 6 | — | — | 1 | 1 | 7 | Lost | Johannesburg | P. J. Mostert |
| 32 | 18.8.1928 | New Zealand | 3 | 1 | — | — | 11 | 2 | — | — | — | 6 | Won | Port Elizabeth | P. J. Mostert |
| 33 | 1.9.1928 | New Zealand | 1 | 1 | — | — | 5 | 1 | — | 1 | 2 | 13 | Lost | Cape Town | P. J. Mostert |
| 34 | 5.12.1931 | Wales | 2 | 1 | — | — | 8 | 1 | — | — | — | 3 | Won | Swansea | B. L. Osler |
| 35 | 19.12.1931 | Ireland | 2 | 1 | — | — | 8 | 1 | — | — | 1 | 3 | Won | Dublin | B. L. Osler |
| 36 | 2.1.1932 | England | 1 | — | 1 | — | 7 | 1 | — | — | — | 0 | Won | Twickenham | B. L. Osler |
| 37 | 16.1.1932 | Scotland | 2 | — | — | — | 6 | 1 | — | — | — | 3 | Won | Edinburgh | B. L. Osler |
| 38 | 8.7.1933 | Australia | 4 | 1 | — | 1 | 17 | — | — | — | 1 | 3 | Won | Cape Town | P. J. Nel |
| 39 | 22.7.1933 | Australia | 1 | — | — | 1 | 6 | 4 | 3 | — | 1 | 21 | Lost | Durban | B. L. Osler |
| 40 | 12.8.1933 | Australia | 2 | 1 | 1 | — | 12 | 1 | — | — | — | 3 | Won | Johannesburg | P. J. Nel |
| 41 | 26.8.1933 | Australia | 2 | 1 | — | 1 | 11 | — | — | — | — | 0 | Won | Port Elizabeth | P. J. Nel |
| 42 | 2.9.1933 | Australia | — | — | 1 | — | 4 | 3 | 1 | 1 | — | 15 | Lost | Bloemfontein | P. J. Nel |
| 43 | 26.6.1937 | Australia | 2 | — | — | 1 | 9 | 1 | 1 | — | — | 5 | Won | Sydney | P. J. Nel |
| 44 | 17.7.1937 | Australia | 6 | 4 | — | — | 26 | 3 | 1 | — | 2 | 17 | Won | Sydney | P. J. Nel |
| 45 | 14.8.1937 | New Zealand | 1 | — | 1 | — | 7 | 1 | — | 1 | 2 | 13 | Lost | Wellington | D. H. Craven |
| 46 | 4.9.1937 | New Zealand | 2 | 2 | — | 1 | 13 | 2 | — | — | — | 6 | Won | Christchurch | P. J. Nel |
| 47 | 25.9.1937 | New Zealand | 5 | 1 | — | — | 17 | — | — | — | 2 | 6 | Won | Auckland | P. J. Nel |
| 48 | 6.8.1938 | G.B. | 4 | 4 | — | 2 | 26 | — | — | — | 4 | 12 | Won | Johannesburg | D. H. Craven |
| 49 | 3.9.1938 | G.B. | 3 | 2 | — | 2 | 19 | 1 | — | — | — | 3 | Won | Port Elizabeth | D. H. Craven |
| 50 | 10.9.1938 | G.B. | 3 | 2 | — | 1 | 16 | 4 | 1 | 1 | 1 | 21 | Lost | Cape Town | D. H. Craven |
| 51 | 16.7.1949 | New Zealand | — | — | — | 5 | 15 | 1 | 1 | 1 | 1 | 11 | Won | Cape Town | F. du Plessis |
| 52 | 13.8.1949 | New Zealand | 2 | — | 1 | 1 | 12 | — | — | 1 | 1 | 6 | Won | Johannesburg | F. du Plessis |
| 53 | 3.9.1949 | New Zealand | — | — | — | 3 | 9 | — | — | — | 1 | 3 | Won | Durban | F. du Plessis |
| 54 | 17.9.1949 | New Zealand | 1 | 1 | 1 | 1 | 11 | 2 | 1 | — | — | 8 | Won | Port Elizabeth | B. J. Kenyon |
| 55 | 24.11.1951 | Scotland | 9 | 7 | 1 | — | 44 | — | — | — | — | 0 | Won | Edinburgh | H. S. V. Muller |
| 56 | 8.12.1951 | Ireland | 4 | 1 | 1 | — | 17 | 1 | 1 | — | — | 5 | Won | Dublin | H. S. V. Muller |
| 57 | 22.12.1951 | Wales | 1 | — | 1 | — | 6 | 1 | — | — | — | 3 | Won | Cardiff | H. S. V. Muller |

*in the drop-goal column denotes a goal from a mark

| Match | Date | Opponents | For | | | | | Against | | | | | Result | Venue | Captain |
|---|---|---|---|---|---|---|---|---|---|---|---|---|---|---|---|
| | | | T | C | D | P | Pts | T | C | D | P | Pts | | | |
| 58 | 5.1.1952 | England | 1 | 1 | — | 1 | 8 | 1 | — | — | — | 3 | Won | Twickenham | H. S. V. Muller |
| 59 | 16.2.1952 | France | 6 | 2 | — | 1 | 25 | — | — | 1 | — | 3 | Won | Colombes | H. S. V. Muller |
| 60 | 22.8.1953 | Australia | 5 | 2 | — | 2 | 25 | — | — | 1 | — | 3 | Won | Johannesburg | H. S. V. Muller |
| 61 | 5.9.1953 | Australia | 4 | 1 | — | — | 14 | 4 | 3 | — | — | 18 | Lost | Cape Town | H. S. V. Muller |
| 62 | 19.9.1953 | Australia | 4 | 3 | — | — | 18 | 1 | 1 | — | 1 | 8 | Won | Durban | H. S. V. Muller |
| 63 | 26.9.1953 | Australia | 2 | 2 | 2 | 2 | 22 | 1 | — | — | 2 | 9 | Won | Port Elizabeth | H. S. V. Muller |
| 64 | 6.8.1955 | British Isles | 4 | 2 | — | 2 | 22 | 5 | 4 | — | — | 23 | Lost | Johannesburg | S. P. Fry |
| 65 | 20.8.1955 | British Isles | 7 | 2 | — | — | 25 | 2 | — | — | 1 | 9 | Won | Cape Town | S. P. Fry |
| 66 | 3.9.1955 | British Isles | — | — | — | 2 | 6 | 1 | — | 1 | 1 | 9 | Lost | Pretoria | S. P. Fry |
| 67 | 24.9.1955 | British Isles | 5 | 2 | 1 | — | 22 | 2 | 1 | — | — | 8 | Won | Port Elizabeth | S. P. Fry |
| 68 | 26.5.1956 | Australia | 2 | — | — | 1 | 9 | — | — | — | — | 0 | Won | Sydney | S. S. Viviers |
| 69 | 2.6.1956 | Australia | 2 | — | 1 | — | 9 | — | — | — | — | 0 | Won | Brisbane | S. S. Viviers |
| 70 | 14.7.1956 | New Zealand | 1 | — | — | 1 | 6 | 2 | 2 | — | — | 10 | Lost | Dunedin | J. A. du Rand |
| 71 | 4.8.1956 | New Zealand | 2 | 1 | — | — | 8 | 1 | — | — | — | 3 | Won | Wellington | S. S. Viviers |
| 72 | 18.8.1956 | New Zealand | 2 | 2 | — | — | 10 | 3 | 1 | — | 2 | 17 | Lost | Christchurch | S. S. Viviers |
| 73 | 1.9.1956 | New Zealand | 1 | 1 | — | — | 5 | 1 | 1 | — | 2 | 11 | Lost | Auckland | S. S. Viviers |
| 74 | 26.7.1958 | France | 1 | — | — | — | 3 | — | — | 1 | — | 3 | Drawn | Cape Town | J. T. Claassen |
| 75 | 16.8.1958 | France | 1 | 1 | — | — | 5 | — | — | 2 | 1 | 9 | Lost | Johannesburg | J. T. Claassen |
| 76 | 30.4.1960 | Scotland | 4 | 3 | — | — | 18 | 2 | 2 | — | — | 10 | Won | Port Elizabeth | D. C. van Jaarsveldt |
| 77 | 25.6.1960 | New Zealand | 2 | 2 | — | 1 | 13 | — | — | — | — | 0 | Won | Johannesburg | R. G. Dryburgh |
| 78 | 23.7.1960 | New Zealand | 1 | — | — | — | 3 | 1 | 1 | 1 | 1 | 11 | Lost | Cape Town | R. G. Dryburgh |
| 79 | 13.8.1960 | New Zealand | 1 | 1 | — | 2 | 11 | 1 | 1 | — | 2 | 11 | Drawn | Bloemfontein | A. S. Malan |
| 80 | 27.8.1960 | New Zealand | 1 | 1 | — | 1 | 8 | — | — | — | 1 | 3 | Won | Port Elizabeth | A. S. Malan |
| 81 | 3.12.1960 | Wales | — | — | — | 1 | 3 | — | — | — | — | 0 | Won | Cardiff | A. S. Malan |
| 82 | 17.12.1960 | Ireland | 2 | 1 | — | — | 8 | — | — | — | 1 | 3 | Won | Dublin | A. S. Malan |
| 83 | 7.1.1961 | England | 1 | 1 | — | — | 5 | — | — | — | — | 0 | Won | Twickenham | A. S. Malan |
| 84 | 21.1.1961 | Scotland | 2 | — | — | 2 | 12 | 1 | 1 | — | — | 5 | Won | Edinburgh | A. S. Malan |
| 85 | 18.2.1961 | France | — | — | — | — | 0 | — | — | — | — | 0 | Drawn | Colombes | A. S. Malan |
| 86 | 13.5.1961 | Ireland | 5 | 3 | — | 1 | 24 | 1 | 1 | — | 1 | 8 | Won | Cape Town | J. T. Claassen |
| 87 | 5.8.1961 | Australia | 8 | 2 | — | — | 28 | — | — | — | 1 | 3 | Won | Johannesburg | J. T. Claassen |
| 88 | 12.8.1961 | Australia | 3 | 1 | 1 | 3 | 23 | 1 | 1 | — | 2 | 11 | Won | Port Elizabeth | J. T. Claassen |
| 89 | 23.6.1962 | British Isles | 1 | — | — | — | 3 | 1 | — | — | — | 3 | Drawn | Johannesburg | J. T. Claassen |
| 90 | 21.7.1962 | British Isles | — | — | 1 | — | 3 | — | — | — | — | 0 | Won | Durban | J. T. Claassen |
| 91 | 4.8.1962 | British Isles | 1 | 1 | — | 1 | 8 | — | — | 1 | — | 3 | Won | Cape Town | J. T. Claassen |
| 92 | 25.8.1962 | British Isles | 6 | 5 | — | 2 | 34 | 3 | 1 | — | 1 | 14 | Won | Bloemfontein | J. T. Claassen |
| 93 | 13.7.1963 | Australia | 2 | 1 | — | 2 | 14 | 1 | — | — | — | 3 | Won | Pretoria | G. F. Malan |
| 94 | 10.8.1963 | Australia | 1 | 1 | — | — | 5 | 1 | — | 1 | 1 | 9 | Lost | Cape Town | G. F. Malan |
| 95 | 24.8.1963 | Australia | — | — | — | 3 | 9 | 1 | 1 | 1 | 1 | 11 | Lost | Johannesburg | A. S. Malan |
| 96 | 7.9.1963 | Australia | 3 | 2 | — | 3 | 22 | — | — | 1 | 1 | 6 | Won | Port Elizabeth | G. F. Malan |
| 97 | 23.5.1964 | Wales | 3 | 3 | 1 | 2 | 24 | 1 | — | — | 1 | 3 | Won | Durban | G. F. Malan |
| 98 | 25.7.1964 | France | 1 | — | — | 1 | 6 | 1 | 1 | — | 1 | 8 | Lost | Springs | C. M. Smith |
| 99 | 10.4.1965 | Ireland | 1 | — | — | 1 | 6 | 1 | — | — | 2 | 9 | Lost | Dublin | A. S. Malan |
| 100 | 17.4.1965 | Scotland | 1 | 1 | — | — | 5 | 1 | 1 | 1 | — | 8 | Lost | Edinburgh | A. S. Malan |
| 101 | 19.6.1965 | Australia | 2 | 1 | — | 1 | 11 | 2 | — | — | 4 | 18 | Lost | Sydney | C. M. Smith |
| 102 | 26.6.1965 | Australia | 2 | 1 | — | — | 8 | — | — | — | 4 | 12 | Lost | Brisbane | C. M. Smith |
| 103 | 31.7.1965 | New Zealand | — | — | 1 | — | 3 | 2 | — | — | — | 6 | Lost | Wellington | D. J. de Villiers |
| 104 | 21.8.1965 | New Zealand | — | — | — | — | 0 | 3 | 2 | — | — | 13 | Lost | Dunedin | C. M. Smith |
| 105 | 4.9.1965 | New Zealand | 4 | 2 | — | 1 | 19 | 3 | 2 | — | 1 | 16 | Won | Christchurch | D. J. de Villiers |
| 106 | 18.9.1965 | New Zealand | — | — | — | 1 | 3 | 5 | 1 | 1 | — | 20 | Lost | Auckland | D. J. de Villiers |
| 107 | 15.7.1967 | France | 5 | 4 | — | 1 | 26 | 1 | — | — | — | 3 | Won | Durban | D. J. de Villiers |
| 108 | 22.7.1967 | France | 3 | 2 | — | 1 | 16 | — | — | — | 1 | 3 | Won | Bloemfontein | D. J. de Villiers |
| 109 | 29.7.1967 | France | 2 | 1 | — | 2 | 14 | 2 | 2 | 2 | 1 | 19 | Lost | Johannesburg | D. J. de Villiers |
| 110 | 12.8.1967 | France | — | — | 1 | 1 | 6 | 1 | — | — | 1 | 6 | Drawn | Cape Town | D. J. de Villiers |
| 111 | 8.6.1968 | British Isles | 3 | 2 | — | 4 | 25 | 1 | 1 | — | 5 | 20 | Won | Pretoria | D. J. de Villiers |
| 112 | 22.6.1968 | British Isles | — | — | — | 2 | 6 | — | — | — | 2 | 6 | Drawn | Port Elizabeth | D. J. de Villiers |
| 113 | 13.7.1968 | British Isles | 1 | 1 | — | 2 | 11 | — | — | — | 2 | 6 | Won | Cape Town | D. J. de Villiers |
| 114 | 27.7.1968 | British Isles | 4 | 2 | 1 | — | 19 | — | — | — | 2 | 6 | Won | Johannesburg | D. J. de Villiers |
| 115 | 9.11.1968 | France | — | — | — | 4 | 12 | 3 | — | — | — | 9 | Won | Bordeaux | D. J. de Villiers |
| 116 | 16.11.1968 | France | 3 | 2 | — | 1 | 16 | 1 | 1 | 2 | — | 11 | Won | Colombes | D. J. de Villiers |
| 117 | 2.8.1969 | Australia | 5 | 3 | — | 3 | 30 | 1 | 1 | — | 2 | 11 | Won | Johannesburg | D. J. de Villiers |
| 118 | 16.8.1969 | Australia | 3 | 2 | — | 1 | 16 | — | — | — | 3 | 9 | Won | Durban | T. P. Bedford |
| 119 | 6.9.1969 | Australia | 2 | 1 | — | 1 | 11 | 1 | — | — | 1 | 3 | Won | Cape Town | T. P. Bedford |
| 120 | 20.9.1969 | Australia | 3 | 2 | — | 1 | 19 | 1 | — | — | 1 | 8 | Won | Bloemfontein | D. J. de Villiers |
| 121 | 6.12.1969 | Scotland | — | — | — | 1 | 3 | 1 | — | — | 1 | 6 | Lost | Edinburgh | T. P. Bedford |
| 122 | 20.12.1969 | England | 1 | 1 | — | 1 | 8 | 2 | 1 | — | 1 | 11 | Lost | Twickenham | D. J. de Villiers |
| 123 | 10.1.1970 | Ireland | 1 | 1 | — | 1 | 8 | 1 | 1 | — | 1 | 8 | Drawn | Dublin | D. J. de Villiers |
| 124 | 24.1.1970 | Wales | 1 | — | — | 1 | 6 | 1 | — | — | 1 | 6 | Drawn | Cardiff | D. J. de Villiers |

| Match | Date | Opponents | For T | C | D | P | Pts | Against T | C | D | P | Pts | Result | Venue | Captain |
|---|---|---|---|---|---|---|---|---|---|---|---|---|---|---|---|
| 125 | 25.7.1970 | New Zealand | 2 | 1 | 1 | 2 | 17 | 1 | — | — | 1 | 6 | Won | Pretoria | D. J. de Villiers |
| 126 | 8.8.1970 | New Zealand | 1 | 1 | — | 1 | 8 | 2 | — | — | 1 | 9 | Lost | Cape Town | D. J. de Villiers |
| 127 | 29.8.1970 | New Zealand | 2 | 1 | — | 2 | 14 | — | — | — | 1 | 3 | Won | Port Elizabeth | D. J. de Villiers |
| 128 | 12.9.1970 | New Zealand | 2 | 1 | — | 4 | 20 | 1 | 1 | — | 4 | 17 | Won | Johannesburg | D. J. de Villiers |
| 129 | 12.6.1971 | France | 2 | 2 | 1 | 3 | 22 | 1 | — | — | 2 | 9 | Won | Bloemfontein | J. F. K. Marais |
| 130 | 19.6.1971 | France | 1 | 1 | 1 | — | 8 | 1 | 1 | 1 | — | 8 | Drawn | Durban | J. F. K. Marais |
| 131 | 17.7.1971 | Australia | 3 | 2 | 1 | 1 | 19 | 1 | 1 | — | 2 | 11 | Won | Sydney | J. F. K. Marais |
| 132 | 31.7.1971 | Australia | 3 | 1 | — | 1 | 14 | — | — | 1 | 1 | 6 | Won | Brisbane | J. F. K. Marais |
| 133 | 7.8.1971 | Australia | 3 | 3 | — | 1 | 18 | 1 | — | — | 1 | 6 | Won | Sydney | J. F. K. Marais |
| 134 | 3.6.1972 | England | — | — | — | 3 | 9 | 1 | 1 | — | 4 | 18 | Lost | Johannesburg | P. J. F. Greyling |
| 135 | 8.6.1974 | British Isles | — | — | 1 | — | 3 | — | — | 1 | 3 | 12 | Lost | Cape Town | J. F. K. Marais |
| 136 | 22.6.1974 | British Isles | — | — | 1 | 2 | 9 | 5 | 1 | 1 | 1 | 28 | Lost | Pretoria | J. F. K. Marais |
| 137 | 13.7.1974 | British Isles | — | — | — | 3 | 9 | 3 | 1 | 2 | 2 | 26 | Lost | Pt Elizabeth | J. F. K. Marais |
| 138 | 27.7.1974 | British Isles | 1 | — | — | 3 | 13 | 2 | 1 | — | 1 | 13 | Drawn | Johannesburg | J. F. K. Marais |
| 139 | 23.11.1974 | France | 1 | — | — | 3 | 13 | 1 | — | — | — | 4 | Won | Toulouse | J. F. K. Marais |
| 140 | 30.11.1974 | France | 1 | — | — | 2 | 10 | 2 | — | — | — | 8 | Won | Parc des Princes | J. F. K. Marais |
| 141 | 21.6.1975 | France | 5 | 3 | — | 4 | 38 | 4 | 3 | — | 1 | 25 | Won | Bloemfontein | M. du Plessis |
| 142 | 28.6.1975 | France | 2 | 2 | — | 7 | 33 | 1 | 1 | 1 | 3 | 18 | Won | Pretoria | M. du Plessis |
| 143 | 24.7.1976 | New Zealand | 2 | 1 | 1 | 1 | 16 | 1 | — | — | 1 | 7 | Won | Durban | M. du Plessis |
| 144 | 14.8.1976 | New Zealand | — | — | — | 3 | 9 | 1 | 1 | 1 | 2 | 15 | Lost | Bloemfontein | M. du Plessis |
| 145 | 4.9.1976 | New Zealand | 1 | 1 | 1 | 2 | 15 | 1 | — | — | 2 | 10 | Won | Cape Town | M. du Plessis |
| 146 | 18.9.1976 | New Zealand | 1 | 1 | 1 | 2 | 15 | 2 | — | 1 | 1 | 14 | Won | Johannesburg | M. du Plessis |
| 147 | 27.8.1977 | World XV | 6 | 3 | — | 5 | 45 | 4 | 4 | — | — | 24 | Won | Pretoria | M. du Plessis |
| 148 | 26.4.1980 | South America | 3 | 3 | 1 | 1 | 24 | 1 | 1 | — | 1 | 9 | Won | Johannesburg | M. du Plessis |
| 149 | 3.5.1980 | Sth America | 1 | 1 | 3 | 1 | 18 | — | — | — | 3 | 9 | Won | Durban | M. du Plessis |
| 150 | 31.5.1980 | British Isles | 5 | 3 | — | — | 26 | 1 | — | 1 | 5 | 22 | Won | Cape Town | M. du Plessis |
| 151 | 14.6.1980 | British Isles | 4 | 2 | — | 2 | 26 | 2 | 1 | — | 3 | 19 | Won | Bloemfontein | M. du Plessis |
| 152 | 28.6.1980 | British Isles | 1 | 1 | 1 | 1 | 12 | 1 | — | — | 2 | 10 | Won | Port Elizabeth | M. du Plessis |
| 153 | 12.7.1980 | British Isles | 1 | — | — | 3 | 13 | 3 | 1 | — | 1 | 17 | Lost | Pretoria | M. du Plessis |
| 154 | 18.10.1980 | Sth America | 3 | 2 | 1 | 1 | 22 | 2 | 1 | 1 | — | 13 | Won | Montevideo | M. T. S. Stofberg |
| 155 | 25.10.1980 | Sth America | 6 | 3 | — | — | 30 | 2 | 1 | 1 | 1 | 16 | Won | Santiago | M. du Plessis |
| 156 | 8.11.1980 | France | 5 | 4 | — | 3 | 37 | 1 | 1 | — | 3 | 15 | Won | Pretoria | M. du Plessis |
| 157 | 30.5.1981 | Ireland | 3 | 1 | — | 3 | 23 | 2 | 2 | — | 1 | 15 | Won | Cape Town | W. Claassen |
| 158 | 6.6.1981 | Ireland | — | — | 3 | 1 | 12 | 1 | — | — | 2 | 10 | Won | Durban | W. Claassen |
| 159 | 15.8.1981 | New Zealand | 1 | 1 | 1 | — | 9 | 3 | 1 | — | — | 14 | Lost | Christchurch | M. T. S. Stofberg |
| 160 | 29.8.1981 | New Zealand | 1 | 1 | 1 | 5 | 24 | — | — | — | 4 | 12 | Won | Wellington | W. Claassen |
| 161 | 12.9.1981 | New Zealand | 3 | 2 | — | 2 | 22 | 2 | 1 | 1 | 4 | 25 | Lost | Auckland | W. Claassen |
| 162 | 26.9.1981 | U.S. | 8 | 3 | — | — | 38 | 1 | — | — | 1 | 7 | Won | New York | W. Claassen |
| 163 | 27.3.1982 | Sth America | 8 | 6 | 1 | 1 | 50 | 1 | 1 | — | 4 | 18 | Won | Pretoria | W. Claassen |
| 164 | 3.4.1982 | Sth America | 1 | 1 | — | 2 | 12 | 1 | 1 | 1 | 4 | 21 | Lost | Bloemfontein | W. Claassen |
| 165 | 2.6.1984 | England | 3 | 3 | — | 5 | 33 | — | — | 1 | 4 | 15 | Won | Port Elizabeth | M. T. S. Stofberg |
| 166 | 9.6.1984 | England | 6 | 4 | — | 1 | 35 | — | — | — | 3 | 9 | Won | Johannesburg | M. T. S. Stofberg |
| 167 | 20.10.1984 | Sth America | 5 | 3 | — | 2 | 32 | 2 | 2 | — | 1 | 15 | Won | Pretoria | D. J. Serfontein |
| 168 | 27.10.1984 | Sth America | 4 | — | — | 2 | 22 | 1 | — | — | 3 | 13 | Won | Cape Town | D. J. Serfontein |
| 169 | 10.5.1986 | NZ Cavaliers | 1 | 1 | 2 | 3 | 21 | 1 | 1 | — | 3 | 15 | Won | Cape Town | H. E. Botha |
| 170 | 17.5.1986 | NZ Cavaliers | 1 | 1 | — | 4 | 18 | 2 | 1 | — | 3 | 19 | Lost | Durban | H. E. Botha |
| 171 | 24.5.1986 | NZ Cavaliers | 4 | 4 | — | 3 | 33 | 1 | 1 | 1 | 3 | 18 | Won | Pretoria | H. E. Botha |
| 172 | 31.5.1986 | NZ Cavaliers | 1 | 1 | 1 | 5 | 24 | 1 | — | — | 2 | 10 | Won | Johannesburg | H. E. Botha |

# MATCH RECORDS

## MOST CONSECUTIVE MATCHES WON

| | |
|---|---|
| 10 | *1949* NZ 1,2,3,4  *1951* S,I,W  *1952* E,F  *1953* A 1 |
| 8 | *1968* BI 3,4 F 1,2  *1969* A 1,2,3,4 |
| 8 | *1976* NZ 3,4  *1977* Wld  *1980* S Am 1,2,BI 1,2,3 |
| 6 | *1910* GB 3  *1912* S,I,W  1913 E,F |

## MOST CONSECUTIVE MATCHES WITHOUT DEFEAT

| Matches | Wins | Draws | Period |
|---|---|---|---|
| 15 | 12 | 3 | 1960 to 1963 |
| 11 | 9 | 2 | 1967 to 1969 |
| 10 | 10 | 0 | 1949 to 1953 |
| 8 | 8 | 0 | 1968 to 1969 |
| 8 | 8 | 0 | 1976 to 1980 |
| 7 | 5 | 2 | 1921 to 1928 |
| 7 | 6 | 1 | 1970 to 1971 |
| 6 | 6 | 0 | 1910 to 1912-13 |
| 6 | 5 | 1 | 1974 to 1976 |

## MOST CONSECUTIVE MATCHES WITHOUT CONCEDING A TRY

| | |
|---|---|
| 4 | between 1960 to 1960-61 |
| 3 | in 1912-13 |
| 3 | in 1968 |

## MOST CONSECUTIVE MATCHES WITHOUT CONCEDING A SCORE

| | |
|---|---|
| 3 | in 1912-13 |

## MOST POINTS IN A MATCH
### By the team

| Pts | Opponents | Venue | Season |
|---|---|---|---|
| 50 | S America | Pretoria | 1982 |
| 45 | World XV | Pretoria | 1977 |
| 44 | Scotland | Edinburgh | 1951-52 |
| 38 | Ireland | Dublin | 1912-13 |
| 38 | France | Bordeaux | 1912-13 |
| 38 | France | Bloemfontein | 1975 |
| 38 | United States | New York | 1981 |
| 37 | France | Pretoria | 1980 |
| 35 | England | Johannesburg | 1984 |
| 34 | British Isles | Bloemfontein | 1962 |
| 33 | France | Pretoria | 1975 |
| 33 | England | Port Elizabeth | 1984 |
| 33 | NZ Cavaliers | Pretoria | 1986 |
| 32 | S America | Pretoria | 1984 |
| 30 | Australia | Johannesburg | 1969 |
| 30 | S America | Santiago | 1980 |

## By a player

| Pts | Player | Opponents | Venue | Season |
|---|---|---|---|---|
| 22 | G. R. Bosch | France | Pretoria | 1975 |
| 21 | R. Blair | World XV | Pretoria | 1977 |
| 21 | J. W. Heunis | England | Port Elizabeth | 1984 |
| 21 | H. E. Botha | NZ Cavaliers | Pretoria | 1986 |
| 20 | H. E. Botha | New Zealand | Wellington | 1981 |
| 17 | H. E. Botha | France | Pretoria | 1980 |
| 17 | H. E. Botha | NZ Cavaliers | Cape Town | 1986 |
| 17 | H. E. Botha | NZ Cavaliers | Johannesburg | 1986 |
| 16 | K. Oxlee | British Isles | Bloemfontein | 1962 |
| 15 | A. Geffin | New Zealand | Cape Town | 1949 |
| 15 | P. J. Visagie | Australia | Johannesburg | 1969 |
| 15 | H. E. Botha | S America | Pretoria | 1982 |

# MOST TRIES IN A MATCH
## By the team

| T | Opponents | Venue | Season |
|---|---|---|---|
| 10 | Ireland | Dublin | 1912-13 |
| 9 | France | Bordeaux | 1912-13 |
| 9 | Scotland | Edinburgh | 1951-52 |
| 8 | Australia | Johannesburg | 1961 |
| 8 | United States | New York | 1981 |
| 8 | S America | Pretoria | 1982 |
| 7 | British Isles | Cape Town | 1955 |
| 6 | Australia | Sydney | 1937 |
| 6 | France | Paris | 1951-52 |
| 6 | British Isles | Bloemfontein | 1962 |
| 6 | World XV | Pretoria | 1977 |
| 6 | S America | Santiago | 1980 |
| 6 | England | Johannesburg | 1984 |

## By a player

| T | Player | Opponents | Venue | Season |
|---|---|---|---|---|
| 3 | E. E. McHardy | Ireland | Dublin | 1912-13 |
| 3 | J. A. Stegmann | Ireland | Dublin | 1912-13 |
| 3 | K. T. van Vollenhoven | British Isles | Cape Town | 1955 |
| 3 | H. J. van Zyl | Australia | Johannesburg | 1961 |
| 3 | R. H. Mordt | New Zealand | Auckland | 1981 |
| 3 | R. H. Mordt | United States | New York | 1981 |
| 3 | D. M. Gerber | S America | Pretoria | 1982 |
| 3 | D. M. Gerber | England | Johannesburg | 1984 |

# MOST CONVERSIONS IN A MATCH
## By the team

| C | Opponents | Venue | Season |
|---|---|---|---|
| 7 | Scotland | Edinburgh | 1951-52 |
| 6 | S America | Pretoria | 1982 |
| 5 | British Isles | Bloemfontein | 1962 |
| 4 | Ireland | Dublin | 1912-13 |
| 4 | France | Bordeaux | 1912-13 |
| 4 | Australia | Sydney | 1937 |
| 4 | Great Britain | Johannesburg | 1938 |
| 4 | France | Durban | 1967 |
| 4 | France | Pretoria | 1980 |
| 4 | England | Johannesburg | 1984 |
| 4 | NZ Cavaliers | Pretoria | 1986 |

## By a player

| C | Player | Opponents | Venue | Season |
|---|---|---|---|---|
| 7 | A. Geffin | Scotland | Edinburgh | 1951-52 |
| 6 | H. E. Botha | S America | Pretoria | 1982 |
| 5 | K. Oxlee | British Isles | Bloemfontein | 1962 |
| 4 | G. H. Brand | Australia | Sydney | 1937 |
| 4 | G. H. Brand | Great Britain | Johannesburg | 1938 |
| 4 | H. O. de Villiers | France | Durban | 1967 |
| 4 | H. E. Botha | France | Pretoria | 1980 |
| 4 | H. E. Botha | NZ Cavaliers | Pretoria | 1986 |

# MOST DROPPED GOALS IN A MATCH
## By the team

| DG | Opponents | Venue | Season |
|---|---|---|---|
| 3 | S America | Durban | 1980 |
| 3 | Ireland | Durban | 1981 |

## By a player

| DG | Player | Opponents | Venue | Season |
|---|---|---|---|---|
| 3 | H. E. Botha | S America | Durban | 1980 |
| 3 | H. E. Botha | Ireland | Durban | 1981 |
| 2 | B. L. Osler | New Zealand | Durban | 1928 |
| 2 | H. E. Botha | NZ Cavaliers | Cape Town | 1986 |

# MOST PENALTY GOALS IN A MATCH
## By the team

| PG | Opponents | Venue | Season |
|---|---|---|---|
| 7 | France | Pretoria | 1975 |
| 5 | New Zealand | Cape Town | 1949 |
| 5 | World XV | Pretoria | 1977 |
| 5 | New Zealand | Wellington | 1981 |
| 5 | England | Port Elizabeth | 1984 |
| 5 | NZ Cavaliers | Johannesburg | 1986 |
| 4 | British Isles | Pretoria | 1968 |
| 4 | France | Bordeaux | 1968 |
| 4 | New Zealand | Johannesburg | 1970 |
| 4 | France | Bloemfontein | 1975 |
| 4 | NZ Cavaliers | Durban | 1986 |

## By a player

| PG | Player | Opponents | Venue | Season |
|---|---|---|---|---|
| 6 | G. R. Bosch | France | Pretoria | 1975 |
| 5 | A. Geffin | New Zealand | Cape Town | 1949 |
| 5 | R. Blair | World XV | Pretoria | 1977 |
| 5 | H. E. Botha | New Zealand | Wellington | 1981 |
| 5 | J. W. Heunis | England | Port Elizabeth | 1974 |
| 5 | H. E. Botha | NZ Cavaliers | Johannesburg | 1986 |
| 4 | P. J. Visagie | France | Bordeaux | 1968 |
| 4 | I. D. McCallum | New Zealand | Johannesburg | 1970 |
| 4 | H. E. Botha | NZ Cavaliers | Durban | 1986 |

# GOALS FROM MARKS

| * | Player | Opponents | Venue | Season |
|---|---|---|---|---|
| 1 | P. J. Mostert | New Zealand | Johannesburg | 1928 |

# TRY ON DEBUT

| Player | Opponents | Venue | Season |
|---|---|---|---|
| T. A. Samuels | Great Britain | Johannesburg | 1896 |
| F. J. Dobbin | Great Britain | Johannesburg | 1903 |
| J. H. Sinclair | Great Britain | Johannesburg | 1903 |
| A. Reid | Great Britain | Cape Town | 1903 |
| W. A. Millar | England | Crystal Palace | 1906-07 |
| C. H. L. Hahn | Great Britain | Johannesburg | 1910 |
| D. I. de Villiers | Great Britain | Johannesburg | 1910 |
| F. P. Luyt | Great Britain | Johannesburg | 1910 |
| W. J. Mills | Great Britain | Port Elizabeth | 1910 |
| H. J. Reynecke | Great Britain | Cape Town | 1910 |
| J. A. Stegmann | Scotland | Edinburgh | 1912-13 |
| E. E. McHardy | Scotland | Edinburgh | 1912-13 |
| A. J. van Heerden | New Zealand | Dunedin | 1921 |
| W. D. Sendin | New Zealand | Auckland | 1921 |
| J. Aucamp | Great Britain | Durban | 1924 |
| H. P. K. de Jongh | New Zealand | Port Elizabeth | 1928 |
| W. F. Bergh | Wales | Swansea | 1931-32 |
| F. W. Waring | Ireland | Dublin | 1931-32 |

| Player | Opponents | Venue | Season |
|---|---|---|---|
| W. E. Bastard | Australia | Sydney | 1937 |
| G. L. van Reenan | Australia | Sydney | 1937 |
| J. L. A. Bester | New Zealand | Port Elizabeth | 1938 |
| W. Delport | Scotland | Edinburgh | 1951-52 |
| E. E. Dinkelmann | Scotland | Edinburgh | 1951-52 |
| C. J. van Wyk | Scotland | Edinburgh | 1951-52 |
| J. K. Ochse | Ireland | Dublin | 1951-52 |
| J. S. A. Oelofse | Australia | Johannesburg | 1955 |
| R. P. Bekker | Australia | Durban | 1953 |
| D. Rossouw | Australia | Durban | 1953 |
| J. J. N. Swart | British Isles | Johannesburg | 1955 |
| T. P. D. Briers | British Isles | Johannesburg | 1955 |
| D. S. P. Ackermann | British Isles | Cape Town | 1955 |
| R. G. Dryburgh | British Isles | Cape Town | 1955 |
| W. Rosenberg | British Isles | Cape Town | 1955 |
| J. J. Nel | Australia | Sydney | 1956 |
| B. F. Howe | New Zealand | Dunedin | 1956 |
| F. W. Gericke | Scotland | Port Elizabeth | 1960 |
| D. C. van Jaarsveldt | Scotland | Port Elizabeth | 1960 |
| H. J. van Zyl | New Zealand | Johannesburg | 1960 |
| B. P. van Zyl | Ireland | Cape Town | 1961 |
| C. M. Greenwood | Ireland | Cape Town | 1961 |
| T. P. Bedford | Australia | Pretoria | 1963 |
| G. Cilliers | Australia | Pretoria | 1963 |
| J. P. Naude | Australia | Port Elizabeth | 1963 |
| W. J. Mans | Ireland | Dublin | 1964-65 |
| P. J. F. Greyling | France | Durban | 1967 |
| J. F. Viljoen | France | Bloemfontein | 1971 |
| J. T. Viljoen | Australia | Sydney | 1971 |
| W. P. Stapelberg | France | Toulouse | 1974-75 |
| E. F. W. Krantz | New Zealand | Durban | 1976 |
| H. L. Potgieter | World XV | Pretoria | 1977 |
| B. J. Wolmarans | World XV | Pretoria | 1977 |
| R. H. Mordt | S America | Johannesburg | 1980 |
| T. D. du Plessis | S America | Johannesburg | 1980 |
| D. J. Serfontein | British Isles | Cape Town | 1980 |
| D. M. Gerber | S America | Montevideo | 1980 |
| H. J. Bekker | New Zealand | Christchurch | 1981 |
| C. J. du Plessis | S America | Pretoria | 1982 |
| N. V. H. Mallett | S America | Pretoria | 1984 |

## CAPTAIN ON INTERNATIONAL DEBUT

| Player | Opponents | Venue | Season |
|---|---|---|---|
| H. H. Castens | Great Britain | Port Elizabeth | 1891 |
| R. C. Snedden | Great Britain | Kimberley | 1891 |
| F. T. D. Aston | Great Britain | Port Elizabeth | 1896 |
| A. Frew | Great Britain | Johannesburg | 1903 |
| P. K. Albertyn | Great Britain | Durban | 1924 |
| F. du Plessis | New Zealand | Cape Town | 1949 |
| B. J. Kenyon | New Zealand | Port Elizabeth | 1949 |
| S. S. Viviers | Australia | Sydney | 1956 |
| D. C. van Jaarsveldt | Scotland | Port Elizabeth | 1960 |
| W. Claassen | Ireland | Cape Town | 1981 |

## TRIES BY FULL-BACKS

| Player | Opponents | Venue | Season |
|---|---|---|---|
| P. Allport | Great Britain | Cape Town | 1910 |
| R. G. Dryburgh | British Isles | Cape Town | 1955 |
| D. S. L. Snyman | World XV | Pretoria | 1977 |
| Z. M. J. Pienaar | British Isles | Bloemfontein | 1980 |
| Z. M. J. Pienaar | France | Pretoria | 1980 |
| J. W. Heunis | S America | Pretoria | 1984 |

# ALL THE POINTS FOR SOUTH AFRICA
## IN A MATCH
### (where more than one scoring action is involved)

| Pts | Player | Opponents | Venue | Season |
|---|---|---|---|---|
| 15 | A. Geffin | New Zealand | Cape Town | 1949 |
| 12 | P. J. Visagie | France | Bordeaux | 1968 |
| 12 | H. E. Botha | Ireland | Durban | 1981 |
| 9 | A. Geffin | New Zealand | Durban | 1949 |
| 9 | C. M. Smith | Australia | Johannesburg | 1963 |
| 9 | D. S. L. Snyman | England | Johannesburg | 1972 |
| 9 | G. R. Bosch | British Isles | Pretoria | 1974 |
| 9 | J. C. P. Snyman | British Isles | Port Elizabeth | 1974 |
| 9 | G. R. Bosch | New Zealand | Bloemfontein | 1976 |
| 8 | K. Oxlee | British Isles | Cape Town | 1962 |
| 6 | R. G. Dryburgh | British Isles | Pretoria | 1955 |
| 6 | D. A. Stewart | France | Springs | 1964 |

# INDIVIDUAL RECORDS

## LONGEST CAREER SPANS

| Seasons | Player | Caps | Career Span |
|---|---|---|---|
| 13 | J. M. Powell | 4 | 1891 to 1903 |
| 13 | B. H. Heatlie | 6 | 1891 to 1903 |
| 12 | W. H. Morkel | 9 | 1910 to 1921 |
| 12 | A. C. Koch | 22 | 1949 to 1960 |
| 12 | J. F. K. Marais | 35 | 1963 to 1974 |
| 12 | J. H. Ellis | 38 | 1965 to 1976 |

## MOST CONSECUTIVE CAPS IN A CAREER

| Caps | Player | Opponents |
|---|---|---|
| 25 | S. H. Nomis | 1967 F 4  1968 BI 1,2,3,4, F 1,2  1969 A 1,2,3,4  1969-70   S,E,I,W  1970   NZ 1,2,3,4  1971 F 1,2, A 1,2,3  1972 E |

## MOST CAPS IN A CAREER

| Caps | Player | Career Span |
|---|---|---|
| 38 | F. C. H. du Preez | 1960-61 to 1971 |
| 38 | J. H. Ellis | 1965 to 1976 |
| 35 | J. F. K. Marais | 1963 to 1974 |
| 33 | J. P. Engelbrecht | 1960 to 1969 |
| 33 | J. L. Gainsford | 1960 to 1967 |
| 28 | J. T. Claassen | 1955 to 1962 |
| 27 | L. G. Wilson | 1960 to 1965 |
| 27 | F. du T. Roux | 1960-61 to 1970 |

## MOST POINTS IN A CAREER

| Pts | Player | Matches | Career Span |
|---|---|---|---|
| 242 | H. E. Botha | 21 | 1980 to 1986 |
| 130 | P. J. Visagie | 25 | 1967 to 1971 |
| 89 | G. R. Bosch | 9 | 1974 to 1976 |
| 88 | K. Oxlee | 19 | 1960 to 1965 |
| 62 | I. D. McCallum | 11 | 1970 to 1974 |
| 62 | D. M. Gerber | 19 | 1980 to 1986 |
| 55 | G. H. Brand | 16 | 1928 to 1938 |

## MOST TRIES IN A CAREER

| T | Player | Matches | Career Span |
|---|---|---|---|
| 15 | D. M. Gerber | 19 | 1980 to 1986 |
| 12 | J. S. Germishuys | 20 | 1974 to 1981 |
| 12 | R. H. Mordt | 18 | 1980 to 1984 |
| 8 | J. L. Gainsford | 33 | 1960 to 1967 |
| 8 | J. P. Engelbrecht | 33 | 1960 to 1969 |

## MOST CONVERSIONS IN A CAREER

| C | Player | Matches | Career Span |
|---|---|---|---|
| 41 | H. E. Botha | 21 | 1980 to 1986 |
| 20 | P. J. Visagie | 25 | 1967 to 1971 |
| 14 | K. Oxlee | 19 | 1960 to 1965 |
| 13 | G. H. Brand | 16 | 1928 to 1938 |
| 10 | I. D. McCallum | 11 | 1970 to 1974 |
| 9 | A. Geffin | 7 | 1949 to 1951-52 |

## MOST DROPPED GOALS IN A CAREER

| DG | Player | Matches | Career Span |
|---|---|---|---|
| 14 | H. E. Botha | 21 | 1980 to 1986 |
| 5 | J. D. Brewis | 10 | 1949 to 1953 |
| 5 | P. J. Visagie | 25 | 1967 to 1971 |
| 4 | B. L. Osler | 17 | 1924 to 1933 |

## MOST PENALTY GOALS IN A CAREER

| PG | Player | Matches | Career Span |
|---|---|---|---|
| 38 | H. E. Botha | 21 | 1980 to 1986 |
| 23 | G. R. Bosch | 9 | 1974 to 1976 |
| 19 | P. J. Visagie | 25 | 1967 to 1971 |
| 14 | K. Oxlee | 19 | 1960 to 1965 |
| 14 | I. D. McCallum | 11 | 1970 to 1974 |
| 10 | A. Geffin | 7 | 1949 to 1951-52 |

## MOST MATCHES AS CAPTAIN

| | | |
|---|---|---|
| 22 | D. J. de Villiers | (13 victories) |
| 15 | M. du Plessis | (13 victories) |
| 11 | J. F. K. Marais | (6 victories) |
| 10 | A. S. Malan | (5 victories) |
| 9 | H. S. V. Muller | (8 victories) |
| 9 | J. T. Claassen | (6 victories) |
| 8 | P. J. Nel | (7 victories) |

# NEW ZEALAND
# INTERNATIONAL
# TEAMS AND RECORDS

| 1903 v. AUSTRALIA | 1904 v. GB | 1905 v. AUSTRALIA |
|---|---|---|
| †W.J. Wallace 2GM,1PG,1C | R.W. McGregor | †H.S. Turtill |
| †A. Asher 1T | W.J. Wallace 1PG | †D.G. Macpherson |
| †R.W. McGregor 1T | †E.T. Harper | †R. Bennet |
| †D. McGregor | D. McGregor 2T | †C.M. Gilray |
| †M.E. Wood | M.E. Wood | †E. Wrigley 1T |
| *†J. Duncan | *†J.W. Stead | †W.E. Smith |
| †H.A.D. Kiernan | †P. Harvey | †G.F. Burgess |
| †D. Gallaher | D. Gallaher | A.F. McMinn 2T |
| †G.A. Tyler 1T | G.A. Tyler | †E.H. Dodd |
| †D.K. Udy | †F.A. McMinn | †E.L. Watkins |
| †R.J. Cooke | †W.S. Glenn | *†J.C. Spencer |
| †B.J. Fanning | B.J. Fanning | †E.G. Purdue |
| †A.J. Long | †T. Cross | T. Cross 1T |
| †G.W. Nicholson | G.W. Nicholson | †C.A. Purdue |
| †A.F. McMinn | †C.E. Seeling | †A.R.H. Francis 1C |
| Sydney | Wellington | Dunedin |
| WON 22-3 | WON 9-3 | WON 14-3 |
| AUST.: 1PG | NZ: 2T 1PG | NZ: 1G 3T |
| NZ: 1G 1PG 2GM 2T | GB: 1PG | AUS.: 1T |
| 15 Aug. 1903 | 13 Aug. 1904 | 2 Sep. 1905 |

New Zealand had a long series of matches with Australian states, and a New Zealand Native team, known as the Maoris, had played internationals on a tour of Britain in 1888-9, before the first full international match took place in 1903, against Australia. The match was played in Sydney and resulted in a resounding win for New Zealand. As host to the British tourists a year later, they scored a second success, while in 1905 the Australians suffered defeat at Dunedin against what should be regarded as a New Zealand third XV, the leading players having embarked on a visit to Britain, France and North America.

New Zealand's scrum formation comprised seven forwards packing in a diamond pattern. Because the ball was heeled so swiftly, an eighth forward was used to insert the ball at scrummages, and a separate half-back employed as scrum-half. The eighth man, who was called a "rover", also acted as a wing-forward. The back formation favoured by New Zealanders was one which admitted three threequarters with an extra back permanently stationed between the centre threequarter and the fly-half. This extra back became known as the five-eighth, or, later, the second five-eighth (with the fly-half being labelled first five-eighth).

Billy Wallace, was the last survivor of the 1903 Test. His two goals from marks in that Test are unique in international rugby history, and he was to set an all-time record in 1905-6 by scoring 230 points on the All Blacks tour of Britain and France.

## 1905-06

| v. SCOTLAND | v. IRELAND | v. ENGLAND | v. WALES | v. FRANCE |
|---|---|---|---|---|
| †G.A. Gillett | W.J. Wallace 3C | G.A. Gillett | G.A. Gillett | †E.E. Booth |
| W.J. Wallace | †H.J. Mynott | D. McGregor 4T | D. McGregor | †H.L. Abbott 2T,1C |
| †R.G. Deans | R.G. Deans 2T | R.G. Deans | R.G. Deans | W.J. Wallace 3T,2C |
| †G.W. Smith 2T | G.W. Smith | W.J. Wallace | W.J. Wallace | E.T. Harper 2T |
| †J. Hunter | J. Hunter | J. Hunter | J. Hunter | J. Hunter 2T |
| J.W. Stead | *J.W. Stead | J.W. Stead | H.J. Mynott | H.J. Mynott |
| †F. Roberts | F. Roberts | F. Roberts | F. Roberts | J.W. Stead |
| *D. Gallaher | G.A. Gillett | *D. Gallaher | *D. Gallaher | *D. Gallaher |
| †S.T. Casey | S.T. Casey | S.T. Casey | S.T. Casey | †W.H.C. Mackrell |
| G.A. Tyler | G.A. Tyler | G.A. Tyler | G.A. Tyler | G.A. Tyler 1C |
| †A. McDonald | A. McDonald 1T | F.T. Glasgow | F.T. Glasgow | F.T. Glasgow 1T |
| †W. Cunningham 1T | W. Cunningham | †F. Newton 1T | F. Newton | W. Cunningham |
| †J.M. O'Sullivan | C.E. Seeling | J.M. O'Sullivan | J.M. O'Sullivan | F. Newton |
| C.E. Seeling | J.M. O'Sullivan | C.E. Seeling | C.E. Seeling | C.E. Seeling |
| †F.T. Glasgow 1T | F.T. Glasgow | A. McDonald | A. McDonald | W.S. Glenn |
| Inverleith | Lansdowne Road | Crystal Palace | Cardiff Arms Park | Parc des Princes |
| WON 12-7 | WON 15-0 | WON 15-0 | LOST 0-3 | WON 38-8 |
| SCOT.: 1DG 1T | IRE.: NIL | ENG.: NIL | WALES: 1T | FR.: 1G 1T |
| NZ: 4T | NZ: 3G | NZ: 5T | NZ: NIL | NZ: 4G 6T |
| 18 Nov. 1905 | 25 Nov. 1905 | 2 Dec. 1905 | 16 Dec. 1905 | 1 Jan. 1906 |

There can be no doubt that the wonderful prestige enjoyed by New Zealand in rugby circles stems from the triumphant tour by Dave Gallaher's team in 1905-6. This stylish side attracted huge crowds everywhere in Britain and ran up some big scores. Indeed, one newspaper, ignorant of New Zealand's rugby prowess, recorded their opening tour result as a 6-55 defeat.

The first three internationals were contests in which the New Zealanders held the upper hand. George Smith, an outstanding hurdler and powerful runner, scored two tries in the victory against Scotland; Bob Deans, a graceful centre who died less than three years after the tour, was the matchwinner against Ireland; and Duncan McGregor scored four tries against England to establish a New Zealand Test record never since equalled. Only against a strong Welsh side were the All Blacks, as the side had been nicknamed by the British press, defeated on tour. And even at Cardiff controversy subsequently surrounded the match, a legend (which persists to this day) arising that Bob Deans should have been awarded an equalising try in the second half.

Gallaher, a most charming and tactful skipper, gracefully acknowledged the defeat, however. An Irishman by birth, he retired from rugby after the tour and was killed in action, serving in Belgium during the Great War.

## 1907

| 1st v. AUSTRALIA | 2nd v. AUSTRALIA | 3rd v. AUSTRALIA |
|---|---|---|
| E.E. BOOTH | J.T.H. COLMAN | E.E. BOOTH |
| †F.C. FRYER | F.C. FRYER | F.C. FRYER |
| †F.E. MITCHINSON 3T | F.E. MITCHINSON | F.E. MITCHINSON 1T |
| W.J. WALLACE 4C | W.J. WALLACE 2T,1C | W.J. WALLACE 1C |
| *J. HUNTER | *J. HUNTER | *J. HUNTER |
| H.J. MYNOTT | H.J. MYNOTT | H.J. MYNOTT |
| F. ROBERTS | F. ROBERTS | F. ROBERTS |
| †J.T.H. COLMAN¹ | G.A. GILLETT | G.A. GILLETT |
| S.T. CASEY | S.T. CASEY | S.T. CASEY |
| A. McDONALD | E. HUGHES | E. HUGHES |
| C.E. SEELING 1T | G.W. NICHOLSON | G.W. NICHOLSON |
| W. CUNNINGHAM | W. CUNNINGHAM | W. CUNNINGHAM |
| A.R.H. FRANCIS 1T | W. JOHNSTON | W. JOHNSTON |
| †W. JOHNSTON | A.R.H. FRANCIS 1T | A.R.H. FRANCIS |
| †E. HUGHES 1T | C.E. SEELING 1T | J.M. O'SULLIVAN |
| Sydney | Brisbane | Sydney |
| WON 26-6 | WON 14-5 | DRAWN 5-5 |
| AUS.: 1PG 1GM | AUST.: 1G | AUST.: 1G |
| NZ: 4G 2T | NZ: 1G 3T | NZ: 1G |
| 20 Jul. 1907 | 3 Aug. 1907 | 10 Aug. 1907 |

¹Rep. by J.C. Spencer

Thirteen of the famous 1905 tourists were among a party of players who toured Australia in 1907. The Test series was won by the New Zealanders who took the two opening Tests of the rubber before drawing the final game at Sydney. Their captain was Jimmy Hunter, a sinuous runner who was one of the first outstanding second five-eighths to play for New Zealand.

Charles Seeling, one of the most powerful of the forwards, scored tries in each of the first two Tests. Later he became one of the first New Zealanders to play Rugby League in England, where he enjoyed a long and successful career at Wigan.

Ned Hughes of Southland became the oldest All Black to appear in an international when, in 1921 and at the age of forty, he was recalled to play against the Springboks. (In 1910 he had actually been banned for playing Rugby League, but was reinstated following the Great War.) His record international career span of fifteen seasons was subsequently equalled by Colin Meads.

During the first Test, J.C. Spencer became the first substitute to be used in international rugby (as a result of an informal agreement between New Zealand and Australia permitting the replacement of injured players for this and some other series between them). It was not until 1968 that the International Board ruled to allow replacements in all international rugby.

## 1908

| 1st v. ANGLO-WELSH | 2nd v. ANGLO-WELSH | 3rd v. ANGLO-WELSH |
|---|---|---|
| J.T.H. COLMAN | W.J. WALLACE | J.T.H. COLMAN 1C |
| †D. CAMERON 1T | D. CAMERON | D. CAMERON |
| F.E. MITCHINSON 2T | F.E. MITCHINSON | R.G. DEANS 1T |
| †H.D. THOMSON 1T | F.C. FRYER | F.E. MITCHINSON 3T |
| J. HUNTER 1T | *J. HUNTER | J. HUNTER 1T |
| *J.W. STEAD | †G.D. GRAY | *J.W. STEAD |
| F. ROBERTS 2T,1PG,1C | †P.J. BURNS | F. ROBERTS |
| G.A. GILLETT 2C | †D.C. HAMILTON | G.A. GILLETT 1T |
| S.T. CASEY | †W.J. REEDY | W.J. REEDY |
| E. HUGHES | †P.C. MURRAY | F.T. GLASGOW 1T |
| †A. WILSON | A. WILSON | C.E. SEELING |
| W. CUNNINGHAM | W. CUNNINGHAM | W. CUNNINGHAM |
| A.R.H. FRANCIS 1C | A.R.H. FRANCIS 1PG | A.R.H. FRANCIS 1T |
| A. McDONALD | †A.M. PATERSON | A.M. PATERSON |
| C.E. SEELING | C.E. SEELING | †H.O. HAYWARD 1T |
| Dunedin | Wellington | Auckland |
| WON 32-5 | DRAWN 3-3 | WON 29-0 |
| A-WELSH: 1G | A-WELSH: 1T | A-WELSH: NIL |
| NZ: 4G 1PG 3T | NZ: 1PG | NZ: 1G 8T |
| 6 Jun. 1908 | 27 Jun. 1908 | 25 Jul. 1908 |

The defection of many leading players to the Rugby League code had given the NZRFU a trying time, but the visit of an Anglo-Welsh side in 1908 gave the Union game a much-needed fillip.

Only three new caps were in the New Zealand line-up for the first Test, in which the All Black forwards dominated the tight and loose. Casey, Cunningham, Seeling and McDonald were experienced experts from the 1905 tour and they were backed by a threequarter line of pace and intelligence. Altogether the backs scored seven tries as the All Blacks ran up their highest total for a home Test. Sensing their clear dominance over the visitors, the selectors fielded a young and experimental side for the drawn second Test, but reverted to the men of experience for another resounding win in the last Test at Auckland.

Billy Wallace played the last of his eleven Tests at Wellington, cartilage injuries prematurely ending his career. He was the first New Zealand cap record holder and his 53 points in Tests stood as a New Zealand career record until the advent of Bob Scott after the Second World War.

## 1910

| 1st v. AUSTRALIA | 2nd v. AUSTRALIA | 3rd v. AUSTRALIA |
|---|---|---|
| †M.J. O'Leary | †J. Ryan | M.J. O'Leary 2c |
| P.J. Burns | L.B. Stohr | L.B. Stohr 2t |
| F.E. Mitchinson | P.J. Burns | P.J. Burns 2t |
| †L.B. Stohr | †W.J. Mitchell | W.J. Mitchell 1t |
| †W.B. Fuller 1t | F.E. Mitchinson | F.E. Mitchinson 1t |
| H.J. Mynott | W.B. Fuller | H.J. Mynott |
| *F. Roberts | *F. Roberts | *F. Roberts |
| †G.F. McKellar | H.E. Avery | H.E. Avery |
| †J.R. Maguire | J.R. Maguire | J.R. Maguire |
| †J. Ridland | J. Ridland | J. Ridland |
| A.M. Paterson | A.M. Paterson | A.M. Paterson 1t |
| †H. Paton | †D.A. Evans | H. Paton 1t |
| A.R.H. Francis | A.R.H. Francis | A.R.H. Francis |
| A. Wilson 1t | A. Wilson | A. Wilson |
| †H.E. Avery | G.F. McKellar | G.F. McKellar |
| Sydney | Sydney | Sydney |
| WON 6-0 | LOST 0-11 | WON 28-13 |
| AUST.: NIL | AUST.: 1G 2T | AUST.: 2G 1PG |
| NZ: 2T | NZ: NIL | NZ 2G 6T |
| 25 Jun. 1910 | 27 Jun. 1910 | 2 Jul. 1910 |

There were only four reasonably experienced players among the 22 tourists who visited Australia in 1910. Mynott and Roberts had been members of the famous 1905 team, Mitchinson had played several Tests as a threequarter, and Francis, a useful place-kicker, had been a regular All Black for five years. Roberts, a clerk from Wellington who had played in 29 of the 32 matches of the 1905 tour to Britain, was the captain of the tourists.

But a team of eight new caps just deserved victory over Australia in the opening Test. Fine support play by Wilson resulted in a try midway through the second half, and a controlled forward rush later in the game produced a try by Fuller. Two days later, in the second Test, New Zealand struggled to gain possession and were well beaten.

For the third and decisive Test of the rubber, the selectors fell back on 14 of the side which had succeeded in the first Test. In warm conditions the Australians defended well up to half time, when they trailed by only one point. But the All Blacks, inspired by an impressive display from their skipper, went on to register eight tries in a 28-13 win which secured the rubber.

## 1913

| 1st v. AUSTRALIA | 2nd v. AUSTRALIA | 3rd v. AUSTRALIA | v. ALL AMERICA |
|---|---|---|---|
| †J.E. Cuthill | *M.J. O'Leary 1DG,3C | *M.J. O'Leary 1c | J.E. Cuthill |
| †T.W. Lynch 3t | †J.V. Macky | †E.A.P. Cockroft | A.J. McGregor 1t |
| †R.W. Roberts 3c,1t | †J.A.S. Baird | P.J. Burns | R.W. Roberts 3t |
| †A.J. McGregor | †J.D. Stewart | J.D. Stewart | F.E. Mitchinson 1c |
| †J.R. McKenzie 2t | †A.P. Spillane | A.P. Spillane | J.R. McKenzie 2t |
| G.D. Gray 1t | †W.M. Geddes | †J.T. Tilyard | G.D. Gray 2t |
| H.M. Taylor[1] | †C. Brown 1t | C. Brown | H.M. Taylor |
| H.V. Murray 1t | †R. Taylor 1t | R. Taylor | H.V. Murray 2t |
| †H. Dewar | †E.W. Hasell 1t | E.W. Hasell | †M.J. Cain |
| †P. Williams | †W.C. Francis | W.C. Francis | G.M.V. Sellars |
| †A.J. Downing | †W. Cummings 1t | W. Cummings | A.J. Downing |
| †H. Atkinson | †C.T. Gillespie | †A.H.N. Fanning 1t | J.T. Wylie 1t |
| †J.T. Wylie | †J. McNeece | J. McNeece | †J.B. Graham 4c |
| *A. McDonald | †J. Barrett | J. Barrett | *A. McDonald 1c,2t |
| †G.M.V. Sellars | A. Wilson 1t | A. Wilson | H. Dewar |
| Wellington | Dunedin | Christchurch | Berkeley |
| WON 30-5 | WON 25-13 | LOST 5-16 | WON 51-3 |
| NZ: 3G 5T | NZ: 3G 1DG 2T | NZ: 1G | ALL-AM.: 1PG |
| AUST.: 1G | AUST.: 2G 1T | AUST.: 2G 2T | NZ: 6G 7T |
| 6 Sep. 1913 | 13 Sep. 1913 | 20 Sep. 1913 | 15 Nov. 1913 |

[1]Rep. by F.E. Mitchinson

New Zealand fielded two distinct sides in 1913. A party of 23 players undertook a 16-match tour of North America, winning every match, and the team which faced Australia at Wellington in the first Test was selected from members of the tour party. The side, which included 13 new caps, was led by Alex McDonald, a brewery-worker from Otago. A veteran of the 1905 tour to Britain, McDonald played in all but three of the matches in North America, and led New Zealand to their record international victory (51-3) in the Test at Berkeley. The American side was drawn from the strong Californian clubs and universities.

Back home a second All Blacks side disputed the remaining Tests of the series with Australia. A side of 13 new caps, led by Mick O'Leary, decisively won the second Test but were then beaten at Christchurch. O'Leary was rated one of the best utility backs produced by New Zealand before the war, his excellent line-kicking demoralising numerous opposing forwards.

Frank Mitchinson played his last Test in California, retiring with ten Test tries to his credit, a New Zealand career record which stood for sixty years.

## 1914

| 1st v. AUSTRALIA | 2nd v. AUSTRALIA | 3rd v. AUSTRALIA |
|---|---|---|
| †J.G. O'BRIEN | E.A.P. COCKROFT | E.A.P. COCKROFT |
| | | |
| T.W. LYNCH | T.W. LYNCH 1T | T.W. LYNCH |
| *R.W. ROBERTS | *R.W. ROBERTS 1T | *R.W. ROBERTS 2T,1C |
| H.M. TAYLOR | H.M. TAYLOR 3T | H.M. TAYLOR 1T |
| | | |
| J. RYAN | J. RYAN | J. RYAN |
| †R.S. BLACK | J.R. McKENZIE | J.R. McKENZIE 1T |
| †E.J. ROBERTS | E.J. ROBERTS 1C | E.J. ROBERTS 1C |
| J.B. GRAHAM 1C | H.V. MURRAY | H.V. MURRAY |
| | | |
| M.J. CAIN | M.J. CAIN | M.J. CAIN |
| W.C. FRANCIS | W.C. FRANCIS | W.C. FRANCIS 2T |
| A. WILSON | A. WILSON | A. WILSON |
| †J.G. IRVINE | J.G. IRVINE | J.G. IRVINE |
| A.J. DOWNING | A.J. DOWNING | A.J. DOWNING |
| J. McNEECE 1T | J. McNEECE | J. McNEECE |
| †J.A. BRUCE | J.A. BRUCE | J.B. GRAHAM |
| Sydney | Brisbane | Sydney |
| WON 5-0 | WON 17-0 | WON 22-7 |
| AUST.: NIL | AUST.: NIL | AUST.: IDG IT |
| NZ: IG | NZ: IG 4T | NZ: 2G 4T |
| 18 Jul. 1914 | 1 Aug. 1914 | 15 Aug. 1914 |

A party of 23 players made an invincible tour of Australia in 1914. The ten victories included three Test wins, the All Blacks' threequarters enjoying a good service from an efficient pack and scoring eight of the international tries.

Dick Roberts, a farmer from the Waimate Plains, was the captain on this tour. An excellent threequarter, he was one of the outstanding New Zealand centres before the war, possessing pace, strength and excellent judgment. These qualities were particularly apparent at Brisbane in the second Test, where his vision in attack created several of the five tries scored by the All Blacks.

The final Test of the series was played shortly after war broke out in Europe. Numerous New Zealand rugby players later joined the forces and fought with honour for the peace of the Commonwealth. Twelve international players fell in action, three of whom had featured in the 1914 Tests: James McNeece, who scored the only try of the first Test; "Doolan" Downing; and Bob Black. Black died on the Somme in 1916, aged 23: the youngest age at which a New Zealand Test player has died.

## 1921

| 1st v. S.AFRICA | 2nd v. S.AFRICA | 3rd v. S.AFRICA |
|---|---|---|
| †C.N. KINGSTONE | C.N. KINGSTONE | C.N. KINGSTONE |
| | | |
| †P.W. STOREY 1T | P.W. STOREY | †S.K. SIDDELLS |
| *†G.G. AITKEN | *G.G. AITKEN | M.F. NICHOLLS |
| †J. STEEL 1T | J. STEEL | J. STEEL |
| | | |
| †M.F. NICHOLLS 2C | M.F. NICHOLLS 1C | †K.D. IFWERSON |
| †C.E.O. BADELEY | C.E.O. BADELEY | †W.R. FEA |
| †H.E. NICHOLLS | E.J. ROBERTS | *E.J. ROBERTS |
| †J.G. DONALD | J.G. DONALD | E.A. BELLISS |
| | | |
| E. HUGHES | E. HUGHES | R.D. FOGARTY |
| †W.D. DUNCAN | W.D. DUNCAN | W.D. DUNCAN |
| †R.D. FOGARTY | †A.L. McLEAN 1T | A.L. McLEAN |
| †J.E. MOFFITT | J.E. MOFFITT | J.E. MOFFITT |
| †J. RICHARDSON | J. RICHARDSON | J. RICHARDSON |
| †E.A. BELLISS 1T | E.A. BELLISS | †C.J.C. FLETCHER |
| †A. WHITE | †A.H. WEST | A.H. WEST |
| Dunedin | Auckland | Wellington |
| WON 13-5 | LOST 5-9 | DRAWN 0-0 |
| NZ: 2G IT | NZ: IG | NZ: NIL |
| SA: IG | SA: IG IDG | SA: NIL |
| 13 Aug. 1921 | 27 Aug. 1921 | 17 Sep. 1921 |

The New Zealand team which faced the Springboks in the first Test ever played between the two sides consisted of fourteen new caps led by George Aitken, the Wellington centre. Aitken was a student who later won a Rhodes Scholarship, gaining rugby Blues at Oxford in the 1920s and forming an all-Oxford threequarter line for Scotland when that nation won the Grand Slam in 1925. Hughes, the only former cap in the first Test line up, is reputed to have been 40 years of age at the time of this series, thus becoming the oldest New Zealand international player – a record which still stands.

The Nicholls brothers were among the backs in the opening Test victory at Dunedin. Mark Nicholls, the five-eighth, became New Zealand's most outstanding allround back between the wars. As an instigator of attacks he was without peer in New Zealand rugby during the 1920s, and his judgment and timing impressed the British critics during the 1924-5 tour. Nicholls was also a prolific scorer of points and his 48 in ten Tests included two drop-goals – a New Zealand record which stood until the 1960s.

The series was an exciting rubber which attracted intense public interest. In all 83,000 spectators attended the three Tests, and no doubt thousands more would have turned out at Wellington for the drawn final Test (which left the rubber tied) had weather conditions been kinder.

## 1924-25

| v. IRELAND | v. WALES | v. ENGLAND | v. FRANCE |
|---|---|---|---|
| †G. NEPIA | G. NEPIA | G. NEPIA | G. NEPIA |
| | | | |
| †K.S. SVENSON 1T | J. STEEL | J. STEEL 1T | J. STEEL 1T |
| †F.W. LUCAS | A.E. COOKE | A.E. COOKE | F.W. LUCAS |
| †A.H. HART | K.S. SVENSON 1T | K.S. SVENSON 1T | K.S. SVENSON 1T |
| | | | |
| †A.E. COOKE | M.F. NICHOLLS 1PG,2C | M.F. NICHOLLS 1PG,1C | A.E. COOKE 2T |
| M.F. NICHOLLS 1PG | †N.P. MCGREGOR | N.P. MCGREGOR | M.F. NICHOLLS 3C |
| †W.C. DALLEY | †J.J. MILL | J.J. MILL | J.J. MILL |
| †J.H. PARKER | J.H. PARKER | J.H. PARKER 1T | *†C.G. PORTER 1T |
| | | | |
| †Q. DONALD | Q. DONALD | Q. DONALD | Q. DONALD |
| †W.R. IRVINE | W.R. IRVINE 2T | W.R. IRVINE | W.R. IRVINE 1T |
| †M.J. BROWNLIE | M.J. BROWNLIE 1T | M.J. BROWNLIE 1T | M.J. BROWNLIE |
| †R.R. MASTERS | R.R. MASTERS | R.R. MASTERS | R.R. MASTERS |
| *J. RICHARDSON | *J. RICHARDSON | C.J. BROWNLIE | C.J. BROWNLIE |
| A. WHITE | †C.J. BROWNLIE | A. WHITE | A. WHITE 1T |
| †L.F. CUPPLES | L.F. CUPPLES | *J. RICHARDSON | J. RICHARDSON 1T |
| | | | |
| Lansdowne Road | Swansea | Twickenham | Toulouse |
| WON 6-0 | WON 19-0 | WON 17-11 | WON 30-6 |
| | | | |
| IRE.: NIL | WALES: NIL | ENG.: 1G 1PG 1T | FR.: 2T |
| NZ: 1PG 1T | NZ: 2G 1PG 2T | NZ: 1G 1PG 3T | NZ: 3G 5T |
| | | | |
| 1 Nov. 1924 | 29 Nov. 1924 | 3 Jan. 1925 | 18 Jan. 1925 |

The Second All Blacks to tour Britain and France were strong in every position and won all 30 of their matches, including the four Tests. (Scotland, who were Champions in 1924-25, however, were unable to give the All Blacks any fixtures.) The side was led by Cliff Porter, a manufacturer from the Hutt Valley who was one of the finest "rovers" produced by New Zealand. A knee injury and fine performances by Jim Parker, Porter's rival for the "rover" position, confined the skipper's Test appearances to the French match.

The superior scrummaging technique and the extraordinary pace of an adventurous threequarter line were the strengths of this famous side. Svenson, a perfect wing, scored the only try of the Irish Test, and went on to score tries in each of the tour internationals (a feat equalled only once since on British soil, by Mark Ella in 1984). Wales were decisively outplayed at Swansea and the All Blacks won an exciting match at Twickenham in which Cyril Brownlie gained the dubious distinction of becoming the first player to be sent off in an international match.

## 1928

| 1st v. S.AFRICA | 2nd v. S.AFRICA | 3rd v. S.AFRICA | 4th v. S.AFRICA |
|---|---|---|---|
| †D.F. LINDSAY | D.F. LINDSAY 1PG | D.F. LINDSAY | H.T. LILBURNE |
| | | | |
| †B.A. GRENSIDE | B.A. GRENSIDE | B.A. GRENSIDE 1T | B.A. GRENSIDE |
| †S.R. CARLETON | S.R. CARLETON | S.R. CARLETON | F.W. LUCAS |
| †A.C.C. ROBILLIARD | A.C.C. ROBILLIARD | A.C.C. ROBILLIARD | A.C.C. ROBILLIARD |
| | | | |
| †W.A. STRANG | W.A. STRANG 1DG | L.M. JOHNSON | M.F. NICHOLLS 1DG,2PG |
| †L.M. JOHNSON | L.M. JOHNSON | †H.T. LILBURNE | L.M. JOHNSON |
| W.C. DALLEY | W.C. DALLEY | W.C. DALLEY | W.C. DALLEY |
| †G. SCRIMSHAW | R.T. STEWART | R.T. STEWART 1T | R.T. STEWART |
| | | | |
| †J.P. SWAIN | J.P. SWAIN | J.P. SWAIN | J.P. SWAIN 1T |
| †S. HADLEY | S. HADLEY | S. HADLEY | S. HADLEY |
| †I.H. FINLAYSON | I.H. FINLAYSON | I.H. FINLAYSON | I.H. FINLAYSON |
| †G.T. ALLEY | G.T. ALLEY | G.T. ALLEY | †I.H. HARVEY |
| *M.J. BROWNLIE | *M.J. BROWNLIE | *M.J. BROWNLIE | *M.J. BROWNLIE |
| †W.E. HAZLETT | W.E. HAZLETT | W.E. HAZLETT | W.E. HAZLETT |
| †R.T. STEWART | †R.G. MCWILLIAMS | R.G. MCWILLIAMS | R.G. MCWILLIAMS |
| | | | |
| Durban | Johannesburg | Port Elizabeth | Cape Town |
| LOST 0-17 | WON 7-6 | LOST 6-11 | WON 13-5 |
| | | | |
| SA: 2PG 2DG 1T | SA: 1GM 1PG | SA: 1G 2T | SA: 1G |
| NZ: NIL | NZ: 1PG 1DG | NZ: 2T | NZ: 1DG 2PG 1T |
| | | | |
| 30 Jun. 1928 | 21 Jul. 1928 | 18 Aug. 1928 | 1 Sep. 1928 |

Maurice Brownlie, an automatic selection as forward for most New Zealand teams of the 1920s, was the captain of the first All Blacks team to visit South Africa. The side was considered to be one of the strongest ever to leave New Zealand.

New Zealand were outgunned at Durban in the first Test, however. During the 1920s New Zealand rugby operated a dispensation which prescribed that kicking to touch could only be done from certain areas of the field. The All Blacks consequently found that lack of expertise in the important tactical aspects of line-kicking placed them at a disadvantage in Test rugby. Furthermore, Brownlie's men were surprisingly outplayed at the scrummages in Durban, and the final defeat by 17 points represents what is still New Zealand's biggest losing margin in a Test.

For the second Test the selectors made just one change, but a significant tactical development was the use of Stewart, the "rover", as an additional front-ranker at scrums. This reduced the overwhelming Springbok forward advantage, and in a tight match the All Blacks levelled the series.

## 1929

| | 1st v. AUSTRALIA | 2nd v. AUSTRALIA | 3rd v. AUSTRALIA |
|---|---|---|---|
| | G. Nepia[1] 1PG,1C | S.R. Carleton | J.M. Tuck |
| | †A.C. Waterman | A.C. Waterman | L.S. Hook |
| | S.R. Carleton | L.S. Hook | J.C. Stringfellow 1T |
| | †J.H. Geddes | B.A. Grenside 1T | B.A. Grenside 1T |
| | †C.J. Oliver 1T | C.J. Oliver[1] | S.R. Carleton |
| | *H.T. Lilburne | H.T. Lilburne | H.T. Lilburne 2C |
| | †J.M. Tuck | J.M. Tuck | †E.T. Leys |
| | †L.S. Hook | *C.G. Porter 1T | *C.G. Porter |
| | †A.I. Cottrell | A.I. Cottrell | A.I. Cottrell |
| | †K.H. Reid | †B.P. Palmer | K.H. Reid |
| | †W.B. Reside | †A.L. Kivell | E.M. Snow |
| | †W.T.C. Sonntag | W.T.C. Sonntag | W.T.C. Sonntag |
| | †W.R. Heke | W.R. Heke | W.R. Heke |
| | R.G. McWilliams | R.G. McWilliams | A.L. Kivell |
| | †E.M. Snow | E.M. Snow | R.G. McWilliams 1T |
| | Sydney | Brisbane | Sydney |
| | LOST 8-9 | LOST 9-17 | LOST 13-15 |
| | AUST.: 2PG 1T | AUST.: 1G 2PG 2T | AUST.: 3PG 2T |
| | NZ: 1G 1PG | NZ: 1PG 2T | NZ: 2G 1T |
| | 6 Jul. 1929 | 20 Jul. 1929 | 27 Jul. 1929 |
| | [1]Rep. by †J.C. Stringfellow | [1]Rep. by †R.T. Cundy 1PG | |

New South Wales was the only state side to continue playing Rugby Union rules in Australia immediately after the Great War. Numerous representative matches were played by the All Blacks against the state, but the NZRFU has not classified these contests as full internationals. By 1929, however, Queensland and Victoria had resumed the game and the tour by the All Blacks included the first full Test series between the two Australasian nations since 1914.

The All Blacks were led by Cliff Porter, but illness and injuries dogged his side, while the unavailability of class players such as Nicholls, Cooke and Lucas deprived the backs of considerable attacking potential. Porter only played in the last four games; Dalley, the expert half-back who led the side at the start of the tour, was injured in the second game; and Nepia took no further part in the tour after being crocked in the first Test. For the first time New Zealand lost all three Tests of a series and it was their first defeat in a rubber against Australia.

## 1930 / 1931

| 1st v. GB | 2nd v. GB | 3rd v. GB | 4th v. GB | 1931 v. AUSTRALIA |
|---|---|---|---|---|
| G. Nepia | G. Nepia | G. Nepia | G. Nepia | †R.G. Bush 4PG,1C |
| †G.F. Hart 1T | G.F. Hart 1T | G.F. Hart | G.F. Hart | G.F. Hart 1T |
| F.W. Lucas | F.W. Lucas | A.E. Cooke | A.E. Cooke 2T | †J.R. Page |
| †D.J. Oliver | D.J. Oliver 1T | F.W. Lucas 1T | F.W. Lucas | †N. Ball 1T |
| A.E. Cooke | A.E. Cooke | M.F. Nicholls 1DG | H.T. Lilburne | H.T. Lilburne |
| H.T. Lilburne | M.F. Nicholls 1GM,2C | W.A. Strang 1C | W.A. Strang 1T,2C | *W.A. Strang |
| J.J. Mill | †M.M.N. Corner | M.M.N. Corner | M.M.N. Corner | M.M.N. Corner |
| *C.G. Porter | *C.G. Porter | *C.G. Porter | *C.G. Porter 2T | †F. Solomon |
| A.I. Cottrell | A.I. Cottrell | A.I. Cottrell | A.I. Cottrell | A.I. Cottrell |
| W.R. Irvine | †J. Hore | J. Hore | J. Hore | †E.M. Jessep |
| I.H. Finlayson | I.H. Finlayson | W.E. Hazlett | W.E. Hazlett | †G.B. Purdue |
| †E.R.G. Steere | E.R.G. Steere | E.R.G. Steere | E.R.G. Steere | E.R.G. Steere |
| R.G. McWilliams | R.G. McWilliams | R.G. McWilliams | R.G. McWilliams | †D.S. Max |
| W.E. Hazlett | W.E. Hazlett | †H.F. McLean 2T | H.F. McLean | †T.C. Metcalfe |
| †W. Batty | R.T. Stewart | W. Batty | W. Batty 1T | W. Batty |
| Dunedin | Christchurch | Auckland | Wellington | Auckland |
| LOST 3-6 | WON 13-10 | WON 15-10 | WON 22-8 | WON 20-13 |
| NZ: 1T | NZ: 2G 1GM | NZ: 1G 1DG 2T | NZ: 2G 4T | NZ: 1G 4PG 1T |
| GB: 2T | GB: 2G | GB: 2G | GB: 1G 1PG | AUST.: 2G 1T |
| 21 Jun. 1930 | 5 Jul. 1930 | 26 Jul. 1930 | 9 Aug. 1930 | 12 Sep. 1931 |

The first fully representative British side to visit New Zealand played a four-Test rubber in 1930, winning the first but losing the last three to a side full of expertise and containing a good mix of youth and experience.

The British tour was surrounded by controversy. The Lions' manager, Mr Baxter, constantly attacked the New Zealand "rover" principle, arguing that such obstructive use of the wing-forward was contrary to the spirit of the game. In an amendment to the scrummaging laws, the International Board subsequently framed a new rule prescribing that front rows had to contain three players. The amendment took effect in 1932, so that the All Blacks who faced Australia at Auckland in 1931 were the last to adopt the 2-3-2 "rover" formation.

The match with Australia in 1931 was the first for the Bledisloe Cup, which had been presented by the Governor-General, Baron Bledisloe, for competition between the Wallabies and All Blacks. New Zealand became first holders thanks to some outstanding place-kicking by Ron Bush. In his only Test appearance he became the first international player to kick four penalties in a game, and his 14 points created a new record contribution for a New Zealander in a Test.

| 1932 | | | 1934 | |
|---|---|---|---|---|
| 1st v. AUSTRALIA | 2nd v. AUSTRALIA | 3rd v. AUSTRALIA | 1st v. AUSTRALIA | 2nd v. AUSTRALIA |
| H.T. Lilburne | †A.H. Collins 1pg | A.H. Collins 2c | A.H. Collins 1c | H.T. Lilburne |
| †G.A.H. Bullock-Douglas 1t | G.A.H. Bullock-Douglas 2t | G.A.H. Bullock-Douglas | G.A.H. Bullock-Douglas | G.A.H. Bullock-Douglas |
| †T.H.C. Caughey | H.R. Pollock 1c,1dg | T.H.C. Caughey | T.H.C. Caughey | T.H.C. Caughey |
| †A.C. Procter | N. Ball 1t | N. Ball | G.F. Hart | †E.C. Holder |
| †H.R. Pollock 1dg,2c | †G.D. Innes | H.R. Pollock 1c | C.J. Oliver | †J.L. Griffiths |
| J.R. Page | J.R. Page 1t | J.R. Page | *J.R. Page | J.R. Page |
| *†F.D. Kilby | *F.D. Kilby | *F.D. Kilby 1t | M.M.N. Corner | *F.D. Kilby |
| A.I. Cottrell | A.I. Cottrell | A.I. Cottrell | †A. Lambourn | A. Lambourn |
| E.M. Jessep | B.P. Palmer | B.P. Palmer 1t | †W.E. Hadley | W.E. Hadley |
| J. Hore 1t | J. Hore | J. Hore | J. Hore 1t | J. Hore 1t |
| G.B. Purdue 1t | G.B. Purdue | G.B. Purdue | †R.M. McKenzie | †R.R. King |
| E.R.G. Steere | †R.L. Clarke | R.L. Clarke | †A. Knight 1t | D.S. Max |
| †J.E. Manchester | J.E. Manchester | J.E. Manchester 1t | J.E. Manchester | J.E. Manchester |
| T.C. Metcalfe | F. Solomon | F. Solomon 1t | H.F. McLean | †H. Mataira |
| H.F. McLean | H.F. McLean | H.F. McLean 1t | D.S. Max 1t | †E.F. Barry |
| Sydney | Brisbane | Sydney | Sydney | Sydney |
| LOST 17-22 | WON 21-3 | WON 21-13 | LOST 11-25 | DRAWN 3-3 |
| AUST.: 2G 2PG 2T | AUST.: 1T | AUST.: 2G 1T | AUST.: 2G 3PG 2T | AUST.: 1T |
| NZ: 2G 1DG 1T | NZ: 1G 1PG 1DG 3T | NZ: 3G 2T | NZ: 1G 2T | NZ: 1T |
| 2 Jul. 1932 | 16 Jul. 1932 | 23 Jul. 1932 | 11 Aug. 1934 | 25 Aug. 1934 |

The New Zealand team of 1932 adopted the three-fronted scrum, Evan Jessep becoming the first man to hook on his own for the All Blacks. Australia-born, Jessep had moved to New Zealand as an infant, but soon after appearing in this 1932 series he moved to Melbourne where he represented Victoria and was selected for the Australian Test side of 1934.

Despite losing the first Test of the 1932 series, New Zealand recorded two brilliant wins in the later Tests of the rubber. Frank Kilby, a Southland banker, was the skipper on the 1932 tour, gaining the unusual distinction of captaining his country on his Test debut.

Two years later Kilby led another All Black side to Australia. The 1934 team won six of its matches, but in losing the first Test and drawing the second had to surrender the Bledisloe Cup to the Wallabies. Kilby, who was injured early in the tour and missed the first Test, became a leading rugby administrator and was the manager of the Fifth All Black side to visit Britain, in 1963-64.

| 1935-36 | | | |
|---|---|---|---|
| v. SCOTLAND | v. IRELAND | v. WALES | v. ENGLAND |
| †G.D.M. Gilbert 3c | G.D.M. Gilbert 2pg,1c | G.D.M. Gilbert 1dg,1c | G.D.M. Gilbert |
| G.F. Hart | G.F. Hart 1t | G.F. Hart | N.A. Mitchell |
| C.J. Oliver | C.J. Oliver 1t | N.A. Mitchell | C.J. Oliver |
| †N.A. Mitchell | N.A. Mitchell 1t | N. Ball 2t | N. Ball |
| T.H.C. Caughey 3t | T.H.C. Caughey | C.J. Oliver | T.H.C. Caughey |
| J.L. Griffiths | J.L. Griffiths | J.L. Griffiths | †E.W.T. Tindill |
| †B.S. Sadler | B.S. Sadler | B.S. Sadler | M.M.N. Corner |
| A. Lambourn | A. Lambourn | A. Lambourn | A. Lambourn |
| W.E. Hadley 1t | W.E. Hadley | W.E. Hadley | W.E. Hadley |
| J. Hore | †D. Dalton | D. Dalton | J. Hore |
| †S.T. Reid | S.T. Reid | S.T. Reid | S.T. Reid |
| R.R. King | R.R. King | R.R. King | R.R. King |
| *J.E. Manchester | *J.E. Manchester | *J.E. Manchester | H.F. McLean |
| †A. Mahoney | A. Mahoney | A. Mahoney | A. Mahoney |
| R.M. McKenzie | H.F. McLean | H.F. McLean | *J.E. Manchester |
| Murrayfield | Lansdowne Road | Cardiff Arms Park | Twickenham |
| WON 18-8 | WON 17-9 | LOST 12-13 | LOST 0-13 |
| SCOT.: 1G 1T | IRE.: 2PG 1T | WALES: 2G 1T | ENG.: 1DG 3T |
| NZ: 3G 1T | NZ: 1G 2PG 2T | NZ: 1G 1DG 1T | NZ: NIL |
| 23 Nov. 1935 | 7 Dec. 1935 | 21 Dec. 1935 | 4 Jan. 1936 |

The Third All Blacks, captained by loose-forward Jack Manchester, were a popular side and drew large crowds in Britain. The All Blacks were unable to master several of their British opponents at scrummaging, however, and the advent of the three-fronted scrum had clearly set New Zealand rugby back several years.

Nevertheless, Manchester's team started the internationals successfully, defeating Scotland and Ireland by convincing scores. "Pat" Caughey, normally a centre, occupied the second five-eighth berth in the opening Tests, and scored a hat-trick of tries against the Scots. A successful businessman in later years, Caughey was knighted in 1972 for his services to the Auckland Hospital Board.

Injury forced Caughey to withdraw from the Welsh international, in which the All Blacks were narrowly beaten at Cardiff, but he returned with a new cap, Eric Tindill, as his five-eighth partner for the match with England. At Twickenham, in the last match of the tour, the New Zealanders found themselves outplayed, and finished with a tour record of 24 wins, three defeats and a draw. Tindill, incidentally, became the only sportsman to represent his country at rugby and cricket, as well as referee and umpire rugby and cricket Tests.

## 1936

| 1st v. AUSTRALIA | 2nd v. AUSTRALIA |
| --- | --- |
| H.R. POLLOCK 1C | H.R. POLLOCK 1PG,4C |
| G.F. HART 1T | G.F. HART 2T |
| T.H.C. CAUGHEY | N.A. MITCHELL 2T |
| †J.M. WATT 1T | J.M. WATT 1T |
| †B.A. KILLEEN | *J.L. GRIFFITHS |
| *J.L. GRIFFITHS | †C.C. GILLIES |
| B.S. SADLER | B.S. SADLER |
| †E.S. JACKSON | E.S. JACKSON |
| W.E. HADLEY 1T | W.E. HADLEY |
| D. DALTON | D. DALTON |
| S.T. REID | S.T. REID 2T |
| R.R. KING | R.R. KING |
| R.M. McKENZIE | †R.H. WARD |
| †J.G. RANKIN | J.G. RANKIN 2T |
| †J. WELLS | J. WELLS |
| Wellington | Dunedin |
| WON 11-6 | WON 38-13 |
| NZ: 1G 2T | NZ: 4G 1PG 5T |
| AUST.: 1PG 1T | AUST.: 2G 1PG |
| 5 Sep. 1936 | 12 Sep. 1936 |

## 1937

| 1st v. S.AFRICA | 2nd v. S.AFRICA | 3rd v. S.AFRICA |
| --- | --- | --- |
| †J.M. TAYLOR | J.M. TAYLOR | J.M. TAYLOR |
| †J. DICK 1T | J. DICK | J.L. SULLIVAN |
| †J.L. SULLIVAN | J.L. SULLIVAN 2T | N.A. MITCHELL |
| †D.G. COBDEN | †W.J. PHILLIPS | T.H.C. CAUGHEY |
| †J.A. HOOPER | J.A. HOOPER | J.A. HOOPER |
| †D. TREVATHAN 1DG,2PG | D. TREVATHAN | D. TREVATHAN 2PG |
| †H.J. SIMON | H.J. SIMON | H.J. SIMON |
| E.S. JACKSON | E.S. JACKSON | E.S. JACKSON |
| A. LAMBOURN | A. LAMBOURN | A. LAMBOURN |
| D. DALTON | D. DALTON | D. DALTON |
| S.T. REID | S.T. REID | S.T. REID |
| *R.R. KING | *R.R. KING | *R.R. KING |
| R.H. WARD | J.G. RANKIN | R.H. WARD |
| †A.A. PARKHILL | A.A. PARKHILL | A.A. PARKHILL |
| R.M. McKENZIE | R.M. McKENZIE | R.M. McKENZIE |
| Wellington | Christchurch | Auckland |
| WON 13-7 | LOST 6-13 | LOST 6-17 |
| NZ: 2PG 1DG 1T | NZ: 2T | NZ: 2PG |
| SA: 1DG 1T | SA: 2G 1PG | SA: 1G 4T |
| 14 Aug. 1937 | 4 Sep. 1937 | 25 Sep. 1937 |

The 1936 New Zealand team which relieved Australia of the Bledisloe Cup was an experimental side. The home selectors clearly used the series as a trial for the contest a year later with the Springboks and seven new caps were awarded. For the All Blacks, the emergence of a sound and solid front row comprising Jackson, Lambourn and Dalton was an encouraging feature, and with King and Reid firmly established in the second row, it was felt that New Zealand could look forward to the Springbok series with confidence.

That confidence appeared to be justified when, a year later, the All Blacks, fielding an all-new back division, won the opening Test against South Africa. The fine kicking of Dave Trevathan and the fine play of the pack enabled the All Blacks to gain a surprise victory by 13-7. This win was made the more remarkable by the fact that Cobden was injured in the first half, Ward transferred to the wing, and the forwards played for threequarters of the game with seven men.

Few changes were made for the remainder of the series, but two victories by South Africa meant that for the first time a series between New Zealand and South Africa was decided – the previous two rubbers having been tied.

## 1938

| 1st v. AUSTRALIA | 2nd v. AUSTRALIA | 3rd v. AUSTRALIA |
| --- | --- | --- |
| J.M. TAYLOR 2PG,3C | J.M. TAYLOR 2C | J.M. TAYLOR 2PG,1C |
| W.J. PHILLIPS | W.J. PHILLIPS 1T | J. DICK |
| *N.A. MITCHELL | *N.A. MITCHELL 1T | J.L. SULLIVAN |
| †T.C. MORRISON | T.C. MORRISON 1DG | T.C. MORRISON |
| J.L. SULLIVAN 1T | J.L. SULLIVAN | J.L. GRIFFITHS |
| †T. BERGHAN | T. BERGHAN | T. BERGHAN |
| †C.K. SAXTON 2T | C.K. SAXTON | C.K. SAXTON 1T |
| †V.L. GEORGE | V.L. GEORGE | V.L. GEORGE |
| †C.E. QUAID | C.E. QUAID | A. LAMBOURN |
| D. DALTON | D. DALTON | E.S. JACKSON |
| R.R. KING | R.R. KING | R.R. KING |
| †H.M. MILLIKEN | H.M. MILLIKEN 1T | H.M. MILLIKEN |
| R.M. McKENZIE | R.M. McKENZIE | *R.M. McKENZIE |
| A.A. PARKHILL 1T | A.A. PARKHILL | A.A. PARKHILL |
| †A.W. BOWMAN | A.W. BOWMAN 1T | A.W. BOWMAN 1T |
| Sydney | Brisbane | Sydney |
| WON 24-9 | WON 20-14 | WON 14-6 |
| AUST.: 3PG | AUST.: 1G 1PG 2T | AUST.: 1PG 1T |
| NZ: 3G 2PG 1T | NZ: 2G 1DG 2T | NZ: 1G 2PG 1T |
| 23 Jul. 1938 | 6 Aug. 1938 | 13 Aug. 1938 |

"Brushy" Mitchell, a deceptive threequarter with the confidence and ability to take on and beat opposing defenders, led the team to Australia in 1938. This was the last international team to represent New Zealand before the war, and by winning each of its nine matches (and thus retaining the Bledisloe Cup), All Black rugby could at least claim to have recovered from some serious setbacks suffered during the early 1930s.

Charles Saxton, an impressive scrum-half with a long and efficient service, was the outstanding back of this side, though he was well served by a solid, uncompromising pack. During the war Saxton rose to the rank of major and became captain of the "Kiwis" side which toured Britain in 1945-46. Later a leading rugby administrator, Saxton was the popular manager of the exciting 1967 All Blacks to Britain. Another member of the 1938 All Blacks, John Sullivan, became a distinguished administrator, his long association with the NZRFU culminating in his Chairmanship from 1969-77, when he was elected a life member.

The final Test at Sydney was New Zealand's sixtieth official international since 1903. Of this total, forty matches were won, four drawn and only sixteen were lost.

|  | 1946 |  | 1947 |  |
|---|---|---|---|---|
|  | 1st v. AUSTRALIA | 2nd v. AUSTRALIA | 1st v. AUSTRALIA | 2nd v. AUSTRALIA |
|  | †R.W.H. Scott 5c | R.W.H. Scott 3pg,1c | R.W.H. Scott 2c | R.W.H. Scott 3pg,3c |
|  | †J.M. Dunn | †E.G. Boggs | †J.K. McLean | M.P. Goddard |
|  | †J.B. Smith 1t | †M.P. Goddard | M.P. Goddard | J.B. Smith |
|  | †W.G. Argus 2t | W.G. Argus | W.G. Argus 1t | W.G. Argus 1t[1] |
|  | †R.R. Elvidge | R.R. Elvidge 1t | *F.R. Allen | *F.R. Allen |
|  | *†F.R. Allen | *F.R. Allen | †M.B.R. Couch | †J.C. Kearney 1t |
|  | †J.S. Haig 1t | J.S. Haig | †P.L. Tetzlaff | P.L. Tetzlaff |
|  | †P.K. Rhind | P.K. Rhind | †J.G. Simpson | J.G. Simpson |
|  | †E.H. Catley | J.A. McRae | E.H. Catley | E.H. Catley |
|  | †H.F. Frazer[1] | H.F. Frazer | †R.A. Dalton | R.A. Dalton |
|  | †K.G. Elliott 1t | †T.A. Budd | L.A. Grant | L.A. Grant |
|  | †C. Willocks | C. Willocks | H.F. Frazer 1t | H.F. Frazer |
|  | †R.M. White 1t | R.M. White | R.M. White | R.M. White |
|  | †J. Finlay 1t | K.G. Elliott | †N.H. Thornton | N.H. Thornton 1pg |
|  | †M.J. McHugh | M.J. McHugh | †K.D. Arnold 1t | K.D. Arnold |
|  | Dunedin | Auckland | Brisbane | Sydney |
|  | WON 31-8 | WON 14-10 | WON 13-5 | WON 27-14 |
|  | NZ: 5G 2T | NZ: 1G 3PG | AUST.: 1G | AUST.: 1G 3PG |
|  | AUST.: 1G 1T | AUST.: 2G | NZ: 2G‡ 1T | NZ: 3G 4PG |
|  | 14 Sep. 1946 | 28 Sep. 1946 | 14 Jun. 1947 | 28 Jun. 1947 |
|  | [1]Rep. by †J.A. McCrae |  | ‡includes penalty try | [1]Rep. by †D.F. Mason 1t |

New Zealand rugby quickly recovered from the disruptions caused by war. Although no full internationals had been played since 1938, a successful tour of Britain by the NZEF (Kiwis) had taken place immediately after the war and many of that popular and skilful side formed the core of New Zealand's first international side against Australia in 1946. The All Blacks opened their post-war Tests with a convincing win at Dunedin in which Bob Scott, by kicking five conversions, set an All Black international record. His fine place-kicking also sealed the second match of the two-Test series.

Fred Allen led the 1946 All Blacks. A former "Kiwi", he was regarded as the finest New Zealand five-eighth since the days of Mark Nicholls. A beautifully balanced player, he later gained immense respect as an innovative coach with the vision and ability to motivate sides to play entertaining, attractive yet winning rugby.

Allen also led the 1947 All Blacks to Australia. Eight of the nine matches were won, including both of the Tests. Once again Bob Scott captured the headlines, registering a new New Zealand record by scoring fifteen points in the Test at Sydney.

|  | 1949 |  |  |  |  |
|---|---|---|---|---|---|
| 1st v. S.AFRICA | 2nd v. S.AFRICA | 1st v. AUSTRALIA | 3rd v. S.AFRICA | 4th v. S.AFRICA | 2nd v. AUSTRALIA |
| R.W.H. Scott 1pg,1c | R.W.H. Scott 1pg | †R.W. Orr | R.W.H. Scott | R.W.H. Scott 1c | J.W. Kelly |
| E.G. Boggs | †W.A. Meates | †G.J.T. Moore 1t | W.A. Meates | W.A. Meates | J.K. McLean |
| R.R. Elvidge | R.R. Elvidge | *J.B. Smith | M.P. Goddard 1t | M.P. Goddard | *J.B. Smith 1dg |
| †P. Henderson 1t | P. Henderson | †J.W. Kelly 1pg | P. Henderson | P. Henderson | †R.A. Roper 1t |
| *F.R. Allen | *F.R. Allen | †R.L. Dobson | *R.R. Elvidge | *R.R. Elvidge 1t | †T.R. O'Callaghan 1pg |
| J.C. Kearney 1dg | J.C. Kearney 1dg | M.B.R. Couch | J.C. Kearney | †G.W. Delamore | M.B.R. Couch |
| †L.T. Savage | L.T. Savage | †V.D. Bevan | †N.W. Black | L.T. Savage | V.D. Bevan |
| J.G. Simpson | J.G. Simpson | †H.W. Wilson | J.G. Simpson | J.G. Simpson | †D.H. O'Donnell |
| E.H. Catley | E.H. Catley | †A.M. Hughes | E.H. Catley | E.H. Catley | A.M. Hughes |
| †K.L. Skinner | K.L. Skinner | †W.J. Mumm | K.L. Skinner | K.L. Skinner | †J.G. Bond |
| †L.R. Harvey | L.R. Harvey | †R.A. White | L.R. Harvey | L.R. Harvey | R.A. White |
| C. Willocks | H.F. Frazer | †R.F. Bryers | C. Willocks | C. Willocks | T.A. Budd |
| L.A. Grant | L.A. Grant | †W.A. Lunn | †P.J.B. Crowley | P.J.B. Crowley | W.A. Lunn |
| N.H. Thornton | †P. Johnstone | †R.C. Stuart | M.J. McHugh | †D.L. Christian | †H.C.B. Rowley |
| †J.R. McNab | J.R. McNab | †A.W. Blake | J.R. McNab | P. Johnstone 1t | R.C. Stuart |
| Cape Town | Johannesburg | Wellington | Durban | Port Elizabeth | Auckland |
| LOST 11-15 | LOST 6-12 | LOST 6-11 | LOST 3-9 | LOST 8-11 | LOST 9-16 |
| SA: 5PG | SA: 1PG 1DG 2T | NZ: 1PG 1T | SA: 3PG | SA: 1G 1PG 1DG | NZ: 1PG 1DG 1T |
| NZ: 1G 1PG 1DG | NZ: 1PG 1DG | AUST.: 1G 2T | NZ: 1T | NZ: 1G 1T | AUST.: 2G 1PG 1T |
| 16 Jul. 1949 | 13 Aug. 1949 | 3 Sep. 1949 | 3 Sep. 1949 | 17 Sep. 1949 | 24 Sep. 1949 |

1949 was the "Black Year" of New Zealand rugby history. Six Tests were played and all were lost, four to South Africa and two against Australia. Uniquely, the series ran parallel, the South African tour taking place at the same time as the home rubber with Australia, and the first Test against Australia was staged on the same day as the third Test in South Africa.

Fred Allen's side in South Africa was unlucky to be whitewashed in the rubber. The first and third Tests were decided by penalty goals, the All Blacks scoring the only tries. Unfortunately, Bob Scott, who had earned a reputation as an accurate place-kicker, had a disappointing series and managed just four successful goal kicks.

Smith, Couch and Bevan, three exciting Maori backs who, because of their race, were excluded from the tour party to South Africa, formed the attacking spearhead of the New Zealand sides which played Australia. Smith, a baker from North Auckland, had been a distinguished member of the 1945-46 "Kiwi" side and led the All Blacks in their narrow defeats against Australia. It was the first time that New Zealand had failed to win a home rubber with Australia.

## 1950

| 1st v. BRITISH ISLES | 2nd v. BRITISH ISLES | 3rd v. BRITISH ISLES | 4th v. BRITISH ISLES |
|---|---|---|---|
| R.W.H. Scott 1PG | R.W.H. Scott | R.W.H. Scott 1PG | R.W.H. Scott 1DG,1C |
| | | | |
| W.A. Meates | W.A. Meates | W.A. Meates | W.A. Meates |
| R.A. Roper 1T | R.A. Roper 1T | R.A. Roper | R.A. Roper |
| †N.P. Cherrington | P. Henderson | P. Henderson | P. Henderson 1T |
| | | | |
| *R.R. Elvidge 1T | *R.R. Elvidge | *R.R. Elvidge 1T | †J.M. Tanner |
| †G.E. Beatty | †L.S. Haig 1C | L.S. Haig | L.S. Haig |
| V.D. Bevan | V.D. Bevan | V.D. Bevan | V.D. Bevan |
| | | | |
| J.G. Simpson | J.G. Simpson | J.G. Simpson | H.W. Wilson 1T |
| A.M. Hughes | A.M. Hughes | A.M. Hughes | A.M. Hughes |
| K.L. Skinner | K.L. Skinner | K.L. Skinner | K.L. Skinner |
| R.A. White | R.A. White | R.A. White | R.A. White |
| L.R. Harvey | L.R. Harvey | L.R. Harvey | L.R. Harvey |
| P.J.B. Crowley | P.J.B. Crowley 1T | P.J.B. Crowley | P.J.B. Crowley |
| P. Johnstone | P. Johnstone | P. Johnstone | †G.G. Mexted |
| J.R. McNab | J.R. McNab | J.R. McNab | *P. Johnstone |
| | | | |
| Dunedin | Christchurch | Wellington | Auckland |
| DRAWN 9-9 | WON 8-0 | WON 6-3 | WON 11-8 |
| | | | |
| NZ: 1PG 2T | NZ: 1G 1T | NZ: 1PG 1T | NZ: 1G 1DG 1T |
| B.Is.: 1PG 2T | B.Is.: NIL | B.Is.: 1PG | B.Is.: 1G 1PG |
| | | | |
| 27 May 1950 | 10 Jun. 1950 | 1 Jul. 1950 | 29 Jul. 1950 |

The series with the Lions was won 3-0, with the opening Test drawn. Each of the matches was a close contest, though the New Zealand forwards improved as the rubber progressed, and the Lions had to be content to live off approximately 30 per cent of the possession in the final Tests of the series.

Ron Elvidge was the All Blacks' skipper. A clever tactical player, Elvidge combined aggressive defence with forceful attack to create a reputation as New Zealand's most formidable midfield back of the era. He scored a decisive try at Dunedin and in the third Test returned, following treatment to a head wound, to score a memorable equalising try.

The Test in Auckland was a stirring match and easily the best of the series. The All Blacks built up a secure lead of 11-3 through tries by Wilson and Henderson. One was converted by Scott, who also dropped a remarkable goal. But the Lions played boldly in the closing stages to create a splendid try by their right wing, and only steady forward play by the New Zealand pack prevented further tries by the Lions.

## 1951 / 1952

| 1st v. AUSTRALIA | 2nd v. AUSTRALIA | 3rd v. AUSTRALIA | 1st v. AUSTRALIA | 2nd v. AUSTRALIA |
|---|---|---|---|---|
| †M.S. Cockerill 1PG,1C | M.S. Cockerill 1C | M.S. Cockerill 2C | R.H. Bell 1PG | †N.J.G. Bowden 1PG |
| | | | | |
| †P. Erceg | P. Erceg | P. Erceg | P. Erceg | R.H. Bell |
| J.M. Tanner | J.M. Tanner | J.M. Tanner 1T | †A.E.G. Elsom | A.E.G. Elsom |
| †R.A. Jarden | R.A. Jarden 2T | †R.H. Bell 1T | R.A. Jarden | R.A. Jarden 1PG |
| | | | | |
| T.W. Lynch | T.W. Lynch 1DG,1T | T.W. Lynch 1T | †J.T. Fitzgerald 1T | †S.G. Bremner |
| L.S. Haig | L.S. Haig | L.S. Haig 1T | †J. Hotop | J. Hotop 1DG,1T |
| †L.B. Steele | L.B. Steele | L.B. Steele | †A.R. Reid | †K. Davis |
| | | | | |
| H.W. Wilson | H.W. Wilson | H.W. Wilson | †B.P. Eastgate | B.P. Eastgate |
| †N.L. Wilson | N.L. Wilson 1T | N.L. Wilson | †I.B. Irvine | †I.A. Hammond |
| K.L. Skinner 1T | K.L. Skinner | K.L. Skinner | *K.L. Skinner | *K.L. Skinner |
| R.A. White | R.A. White | R.A. White | R.A. White 1T | R.A. White |
| †R.H. Duff | R.H. Duff | R.H. Duff | R.H. Duff | R.H. Duff |
| †C.E. Robinson | C.E. Robinson | C.E. Robinson | C.E. Robinson | C.E. Robinson 1T |
| *P. Johnstone | *P. Johnstone | W.A. McCaw | †H.C. McLaren | K.F. Meates |
| †W.A. McCaw | W.A. McCaw | *P. Johnstone | †K.F. Meates | †J.R. Skeen |
| | | | | |
| Sydney | Sydney | Brisbane | Christchurch | Wellington |
| WON 8-0 | WON 17-11 | WON 16-6 | LOST 9-14 | WON 15-8 |
| | | | | |
| AUST.: NIL | AUST.: 1G 1PG 1T | AUST.: 2PG | NZ: 1PG 2T | NZ: 2PG 1DG 2T |
| NZ: 1G 1PG | NZ: 1G 1DG 3T | NZ: 2G 2T | AUST.: 1G 1DG 2T | AUST.: 1G 1PG |
| | | | | |
| 23 Jun. 1951 | 7. Jul. 1951 | 21 Jul. 1951 | 6 Sep. 1952 | 13 Sep. 1952 |

Thirteen of the twenty players who played in the series against the Lions in 1950 never again appeared in an international, and there were nine new caps consequently in the side which faced Australia at Sydney in the first Test of 1951. Peter Johnstone captained an inexperienced team on an invincible tour of thirteen matches.

Ron Jarden scored two tries in his first Test series. A member of the 1951 New Zealand universities side to Australia, Jarden remained in the country for the tour by the international side. A strong runner with an accurate left-footed kick, he scored 42 points (including seven tries) in his 16 internationals and created a New Zealand career record by scoring 145 tries in 134 first-class matches. A successful businessman, Jarden died young in 1977, aged 47.

Kevin Skinner, a former amateur boxer and a prop of considerable expertise, led New Zealand in a drawn series with the Wallabies in 1952. His pack was well beaten in the first Test but the rucking was more efficient at Wellington. Despite a tied rubber, New Zealand retained the Bledisloe Cup.

## 1953-54

| v. WALES | v. IRELAND | v. ENGLAND | v. SCOTLAND | v. FRANCE |
|---|---|---|---|---|
| R.W.H. SCOTT | R.W.H. SCOTT 1DG,1PG,1C | R.W.H. SCOTT 1C | R.W.H. SCOTT 1PG | R.W.H. SCOTT |
| A.E.G.ELSOM | †M.J. DIXON | M.J. DIXON | M.J. DIXON | M.J. DIXON |
| J.M. TANNER | †C.J. LOADER | C.J. LOADER | C.J. LOADER | C.J. LOADER |
| R.A. JARDEN 1PG,1C | R.A. JARDEN | R.A. JARDEN | R.A. JARDEN | R.A. JARDEN |
| †B.B.J. FITZPATRICK | B.B.J. FITZPATRICK | †D.D. WILSON | D.D. WILSON | B.B.J. FITZPATRICK |
| L.S. HAIG | †R.G. BOWERS | L.S. HAIG | L.S. HAIG | R.G. BOWERS |
| K. DAVIS | K. DAVIS | K. DAVIS | K. DAVIS | K. DAVIS |
| †I.J. CLARKE | †H.L. WHITE | H.L. WHITE | B.P. EASTGATE | H.L. WHITE |
| †R.C. HEMI | R.C. HEMI | R.C. HEMI | R.C. HEMI | R.C. HEMI |
| K.L. SKINNER | K.L. SKINNER | K.L. SKINNER | K.L. SKINNER | K.L. SKINNER |
| †G.N. DALZELL | G.N. DALZELL | G.N. DALZELL 1T | G.N. DALZELL | G.N. DALZELL |
| R.A. WHITE | R.A. WHITE | R.A. WHITE | R.A. WHITE | R.A. WHITE |
| *R.C. STUART | †D.O. OLIVER | †P.F. JONES | P.F. JONES | *R.C. STUART |
| W.A. McCAW | *R.C. STUART 1T | *R.C. STUART | *R.C. STUART | W.A. McCAW |
| †W.H. CLARK 1T | W.H. CLARK 1T | W.H. CLARK | W.H. CLARK | D.O. OLIVER |
| Cardiff Arms Park | Lansdowne Road | Twickenham | Murrayfield | Stade Colombes |
| LOST 8-13 | WON 14-3 | WON 5-0 | WON 3-0 | LOST 0-3 |
| WALES: 2G 1PG | IRE.: 1PG | ENG.: NIL | SCOT.: NIL | FR.: 1T |
| NZ: 1G 1PG | NZ: 1G 1PG 1DG 1T | NZ: 1G | NZ: 1PG | NZ: NIL |
| 19 Dec. 1953 | 9 Jan. 1954 | 30 Jan. 1954 | 13 Feb. 1954 | 27 Feb. 1954 |

The Fourth All Blacks, led by Bob Stuart, a surprise choice as skipper, were one of the most popular New Zealand sides to tour Britain. Stuart had not played for New Zealand since 1949, but his style of captaincy was applauded by the critics. He set high standards on the field, and in the demanding round of off-the-field activities his courteous, thoughtful disposition helped to make the side such a popular one with the British press and public.

In the internationals, the All Blacks won comfortably against Ireland but struggled to beat both Scotland and England. Against Wales, in the opening Test of the trip, the All Blacks had attacked for most of the game before losing to a converted try, scored five minutes from no-side. A cross-kick bounced fortuitously into the path of the Welsh right wing who scored.

In the final Test of the tour the All Blacks were beaten by a French side which marked tightly. The game marked the end of the Test career of Bob Scott. His final career tally of 74 points in Tests represented a new New Zealand record.

## 1955

| 1st v. AUSTRALIA | 2nd v. AUSTRALIA | 3rd v. AUSTRALIA |
|---|---|---|
| †K.C. STUART | P.T. WALSH | P.T. WALSH |
| †R.M. SMITH | †T. KATENE | A.E.G. ELSOM |
| A.E.G. ELSOM | A.E.G. ELSOM 1DG | †R.H. BROWN |
| R.A. JARDEN 1T,2C,1PG | R.A. JARDEN 1T,1C | R.A. JARDEN 1T |
| †P.T. WALSH | †W.N. GRAY | W.N. GRAY |
| †W.R. ARCHER | W.R. ARCHER | J. HOTOP |
| †L.J. TOWNSEND | K. DAVIS | L.J. TOWNSEND |
| †M.W. IRWIN | M.W. IRWIN | H.L. WHITE |
| R.C. HEMI | R.C. HEMI | R.C. HEMI |
| †I.M.H. VODANOVICH 1T | I.M.H. VODANOVICH | I.M.H. VODANOVICH |
| †P.S. BURKE | R.H. DUFF | R.H. DUFF |
| R.A. WHITE | R.A. WHITE | R.A. WHITE |
| P.F. JONES | P.F. JONES | †J.B. BUXTON |
| *I.J. CLARKE | *I.J. CLARKE | *I.J. CLARKE |
| W.H. CLARK 1T | W.H. CLARK | †S.F. HILL |
| Wellington | Dunedin | Auckland |
| WON 16-8 | WON 8-0 | LOST 3-8 |
| NZ: 2G 1PG 1T | NZ: 1G 1DG | NZ: 1T |
| AUST.: 1G 1PG | AUST.: NIL | AUST.: 1G 1T |
| 20 Aug. 1955 | 3 Sep. 1955 | 17 Sep. 1955 |

Eight new caps were included in the first Test side at Wellington. Of these, Stuart was the younger brother of Bob Stuart, captain of the 1953-54 All Blacks; Pat Walsh was a versatile Maori who went on to create a unique New Zealand record by appearing as full-back, wing, centre and five-eighth in Tests; and Ivan Vodanovich, a durable prop, became a leading administrator and influential national coach. Ian Clarke, who had made his debut as a prop on the British tour, was appointed captain of the side, and appeared now at number-eight.

New Zealand won the first Test comfortably but there were doubts concerning the strength of the pack following victory in the second. Bob Duff, a powerful line-out expert who formed an effective partnership with "Tiny" White, had returned for the Test at Dunedin. Unavailable for the British tour, and temporarily retired in 1954, his recall was a measure taken with a view to strengthening the All Blacks' pack against the powerful threat of the Springbok forwards, who were due to tour the following year.

New Zealand played creative rugby in the final Test of the tour and at last their forwards combined most effectively. It was the opinion of the pundits that they performed better even in defeat than they had earlier in the series, and there was general satisfaction that the All Blacks could look forward to their forthcoming series against South Africa with confidence.

## 1956

| 1st v. S.AFRICA | 2nd v. S.AFRICA | 3rd v. S.AFRICA | 4th v. S.AFRICA |
|---|---|---|---|
| P.T. WALSH | P.T. WALSH | †D.B. CLARKE 2PG,1C | D.B. CLARKE 2PG,1C |
| M.J. DIXON | M.J. DIXON | M.J. DIXON 1T | M.J. DIXON |
| R.H. BROWN | R.H. BROWN 1T | R.H. BROWN | P.T. WALSH |
| R.A. JARDEN 1T,2C | R.A. JARDEN | R.A. JARDEN 1T | R.A. JARDEN |
| W.N. GRAY | W.N. GRAY | W.N. GRAY | W.N. GRAY |
| W.R. ARCHER | S.G. BREMNER | W.R. ARCHER | R.H. BROWN |
| *†P.B. VINCENT | *P.B. VINCENT | A.R. REID | A.R. REID |
| M.W. IRWIN | †F.S. McATAMNEY | K.L. SKINNER | K.L. SKINNER |
| R.C. HEMI | †D. YOUNG | R.C. HEMI | R.C. HEMI |
| I.J. CLARKE | I.J. CLARKE | I.J. CLARKE | I.J. CLARKE |
| R.H. DUFF | R.H. DUFF | *R.H. DUFF | *R.H. DUFF |
| R.A. WHITE 1T | R.A. WHITE | R.A. WHITE 1T | R.A. WHITE |
| J.B. BUXTON | W.H. CLARK | W.H. CLARK | W.H. CLARK |
| S.F. HILL | †I.N. MacEWAN | P.F. JONES | P.F. JONES 1T |
| †D.N. McINTOSH | D.N. McINTOSH | S.F. HILL | S.F. HILL |
| Dunedin | Wellington | Christchurch | Auckland |
| WON 10-6 | LOST 3-8 | WON 17-10 | WON 11-5 |
| NZ: 2G | NZ: 1T | NZ: 1G 2PG 2T | NZ: 1G 2PG |
| SA: 1PG 1T | SA: 1G 1T | SA: 2G | SA: 1G |
| 14 Jul. 1956 | 4 Aug. 1956 | 18 Aug. 1956 | 1 Sep. 1956 |

The fifth series between New Zealand and South Africa was the first New Zealand success in a rubber: the All Blacks winning three of the Tests and losing one. Part of the reason for the All Blacks' success had been the careful selection applied in the previous season: fourteen of the players who had appeared in the 1955 series with Australia faced the Springboks in 1956.

The start of the series followed the patterns of the 1921, 1928 and 1937 rubbers, each side winning one of the two opening Tests. For the decisive third Test in 1956, New Zealand introduced a young goal-kicking wonder from Waikato named Don Clarke, recalled Kevin Skinner at prop, two years after he had announced his retirement, and handed responsibility for the team to Bob Duff. Clarke, who went on to become the most prolific scorer of points in world rugby (207 in his 31 Tests, including a world record of six penalties in the match against the British Isles at Dunedin in 1959) made a significant contribution to the 17-10 win at Christchurch, kicking eight points.

Clarke kicked another eight points in the memorable fourth Test, but the oustanding event of that game was the try scored by Peter Jones early in the second half. He gathered the ball in broken play, some 35 yards from the Springbok line, and outpaced the defence to arc round behind the goal. The try decided the series, so that it was on a note of triumph that Jarden, "Tiny" White (after 23 consecutive Tests), Kevin Skinner and Bob Duff ended their Test careers.

| 1957 | | 1958 | | |
|---|---|---|---|---|
| 1st v. AUSTRALIA | 2nd v. AUSTRALIA | 1st v. AUSTRALIA | 2nd v. AUSTRALIA | 3rd v. AUSTRALIA |
| D.B. CLARKE 3PG,2C | D.B. CLARKE 1GM,2C | D.B. CLARKE 2C | †D.L. ASHBY | D.B. CLARKE 4PG,1C |
| M.J. DIXON | M.J. DIXON 1T | †R.R. COSSEY | †J.R. WATT | P.T. WALSH |
| †R.F. McMULLEN 1T | R.F. McMULLEN 1T | P.T. WALSH 2T | P.T. WALSH | T.R. LINEEN |
| P.T. WALSH 1T | P.T. WALSH | R.F. McMULLEN 1T | R.F. McMULLEN | R.F. McMULLEN |
| †T.R. LINEEN | T.R. LINEEN | T.R. LINEEN | T.R. LINEEN | R.H. BROWN |
| R.H. BROWN | R.H. BROWN 1DG,1T | R.H. BROWN | R.H. BROWN 1T | †A.H. CLARKE |
| *A.R. REID | *A.R. REID | K. DAVIS | K. DAVIS | K. DAVIS |
| †W.J. WHINERAY | W.J. WHINERAY | *W.J. WHINERAY 2T | *W.J. WHINERAY | *W.J. WHINERAY |
| R.C. HEMI 1T | R.C. HEMI | D. YOUNG | D. YOUNG | D. YOUNG |
| I.J. CLARKE | I.J. CLARKE | I.J. CLARKE | M.W. IRWIN | I.J. CLARKE |
| I.N. MacEWAN 1T | I.N. MacEWAN | I.N. MacEWAN | I.N. MacEWAN | I.N. MacEWAN |
| S.F. HILL | S.F. HILL | C.E. MEADS | C.E. MEADS | S.F. HILL |
| †C.E. MEADS | C.E. MEADS 1T | P.F. JONES 1T | P.F. JONES | C.E. MEADS 1T |
| P.S. BURKE | P.S. BURKE | †D.J. GRAHAM 1T | D.J. GRAHAM | P.F. JONES |
| D.N. McINTOSH | D.N. McINTOSH | †T.D. COUGHLAN | †E.A.R. PICKERING | †W.D. GILLESPIE |
| Sydney | Brisbane | Wellington | Christchurch | Auckland |
| WON 25-11 | WON 22-9 | WON 25-3 | LOST 3-6 | WON 17-8 |
| AUST.: 1G 2PG | AUST.: 2PG 1T | NZ: 2G 5T | NZ: 1T | NZ: 1G 4PG |
| NZ: 2G 3PG 2T | NZ: 2G 1GM 1DG 2T | AUST.: 1T | AUST.: 1PG 1T | AUST.: 1G 1PG |
| 25 May 1957 | 1 Jun. 1957 | 23 Aug. 1958 | 6 Sep. 1958 | 20 Sep. 1958 |

New Zealand made a 13-match tour of Australia in 1957, winning every match, including the two Tests. The same fifteen took part in the two convincing international victories, games which marked the debuts of Wilson Whineray and Colin Meads, two of the world's leading forwards in the following decade.

Whineray went on to captain New Zealand in 30 internationals between 1958 and 1965, a world record for matches between International Board nations. A knowledgeable tactician, astute motivator and perfect ambassador for the game in his off-the-field duties, Whineray led New Zealand to the unofficial title of World Champions in the 1960s, recording wins against every member of the International Board except Scotland.

Meads, who began his Test career as a flanker, went on to become the world's most capped player (with 55 caps). But it was as a powerful, mobile and aggressive lock that he earned his reputation as the greatest forward in world rugby during the 1960s, and became an All Black legend.

## 1959

| 1st v. BRITISH ISLES | 2nd v. BRITISH ISLES | 3rd v. BRITISH ISLES | 4th v. BRITISH ISLES |
|---|---|---|---|
| D.B. CLARKE **6PG** | D.B. CLARKE **1C,1T** | D.B. CLARKE **1DG,1PG,2C** | D.B. CLARKE **2PG** |
| †B.E. McPHAIL | †E.S. DIACK | R.F. McMULLEN | B.E. McPHAIL |
| R.F. McMULLEN | R.F. McMULLEN | R.H. BROWN | T.R. LINEEN |
| P.T. WALSH | †R.W. CAULTON **2T** | R.W. CAULTON **2T** | R.W. CAULTON |
| T.R. LINEEN | T.R. LINEEN | T.R. LINEEN | A.H. CLARKE |
| R.H. BROWN | †J.F. McCULLOUGH | J.F. McCULLOUGH | J.F. McCULLOUGH |
| †R.J. URBAHN | †K.C. BRISCOE | R.J. URBAHN **1T** | R.J. URBAHN |
| *W.J. WHINERAY | *W.J. WHINERAY | *W.J. WHINERAY | *W.J. WHINERAY |
| R.C. HEMI | †D.S. WEBB | R.C. HEMI | R.C. HEMI |
| I.J. CLARKE | I.J. CLARKE | M.W. IRWIN | M.W. IRWIN |
| I.N. MacEWAN | I.N. MacEWAN | I.N. MacEWAN | C.E. MEADS |
| S.F. HILL | S.F. HILL | S.F. HILL | S.F. HILL |
| †B.E.L. FINLAY | C.E. MEADS | C.E. MEADS **1T** | E.A.R. PICKERING |
| P.F. JONES | †R.J. CONWAY | R.J. CONWAY | R.J. CONWAY |
| E.A.R. PICKERING | †K.R. TREMAIN | K.R. TREMAIN | K.R. TREMAIN |
| Dunedin | Wellington | Christchurch | Auckland |
| WON 18-17 | WON 11-8 | WON 22-8 | LOST 6-9 |
| NZ: 6PG | NZ: 1G 2T | NZ: 2G 1PG 1DG 2T | NZ: 2PG |
| B.Is.: 1G 1PG 3T | B.Is.: 1G 1PG | B.Is.: 1G 1PG | B.Is.: 3T |
| 18 Jul. 1959 | 15 Aug. 1959 | 29 Aug. 1959 | 19 Sep. 1959 |

The series against the Lions was won 3-1, but all bar the third Test were very close contests in which the match-winning abilities of full-back Don Clarke were crucial. Altogether he notched 39 points for the series, a New Zealand individual record.

In the first Test, before a record Dunedin crowd of 41,000, Clarke kicked six penalty goals including a last-minute effort to win the match by a single point. Then, in the second Test at Wellington, Clarke scored the winning try a minute from no-side when he made the extra man on a blind-side move from a scrum. He thus became the first All Black full-back to score a try in a Test match.

Ralph Caulton, an elegant runner of considerable pace, made his debut at Wellington, scoring two tries, a feat he repeated in the next Test. Always quick to grasp scoring opportunities, he established himself as the leading New Zealand wing of the early 1960s, and went on to score eight tries in his Test career.

## 1960

| 1st v. S.AFRICA | 2nd v. S.AFRICA | 3rd v. S.AFRICA | 4th v. S.AFRICA |
|---|---|---|---|
| D.B. CLARKE | D.B. CLARKE **1DG,1PG,1C** | D.B. CLARKE **2PG,1C** | D.B. CLARKE **1PG** |
| J.R. WATT | J.R. WATT | J.R. WATT | J.R. WATT |
| †T.P.A. O'SULLIVAN | †K.F. LAIDLAW | K.F. LAIDLAW | R.F. McMULLEN |
| R.W. CAULTON | R.F. McMULLEN | R.F. McMULLEN **1T** | R.W. CAULTON |
| T.R. LINEEN | T.R. LINEEN | T.R. LINEEN | K.F. LAIDLAW |
| A.H. CLARKE | †S.R. NESBIT | S.R. NESBIT | †W.A. DAVIES |
| K.C. BRISCOE | K.C. BRISCOE | K.C. BRISCOE | K.C. BRISCOE |
| *W.J. WHINERAY | *W.J. WHINERAY | *W.J. WHINERAY | *W.J. WHINERAY |
| D. YOUNG | D. YOUNG | D. YOUNG | D. YOUNG |
| M.W. IRWIN | I.J. CLARKE | I.N. MacEWAN | I.J. CLARKE |
| C.E. MEADS | †R.H. HORSLEY | R.H. HORSLEY | R.H. HORSLEY |
| I.N. MacEWAN | I.N. MacEWAN | C.E. MEADS | I.N. MacEWAN |
| P.F. JONES | D.J. GRAHAM | D.J. GRAHAM | C.E. MEADS |
| R.J. CONWAY | C.E. MEADS **1T** | R.J. CONWAY | R.J. CONWAY |
| K.R. TREMAIN | K.R. TREMAIN | K.R. TREMAIN | K.R. TREMAIN |
| Johannesburg | Cape Town | Bloemfontein | Port Elizabeth |
| LOST 0-13 | WON 11-3 | DRAWN 11-11 | LOST 3-8 |
| SA: 2G 1PG | SA: 1T | SA: 1G 2PG | SA: 1G 1PG |
| NZ: NIL | NZ: 1G 1PG 1DG | NZ: 1G 2PG | NZ: 1PG |
| 25 Jun. 1960 | 23 Jul. 1960 | 13 Aug. 1960 | 27 Aug. 1960 |

The All Blacks made a 26-match tour of South Africa in 1960. There was much public comment concerning the ethics of the trip, the exclusion of Maoris on racial grounds stirring much contentious debate. The rugby authorities bowed to the apartheid laws, however, and the tour went ahead as scheduled with the All Blacks winning 20 matches: but no subsequent New Zealand team visited South Africa without Maoris.

The series was an exciting one with the Springboks clinching the rubber early in the second half of the final Test. New Zealand, thumped 13-0 in the opening Test (in which Peter Jones, one of the fastest loose forwards to appear for New Zealand, played his last international), bounced back to win the second Test in Cape Town. Colin Meads, at number-eight, scored a try and Don Clarke made up the difference with three successful goal kicks. The third Test was drawn leaving the Springboks, the better all-round team, to take the rubber in front of 60,000 at Port Elizabeth.

This was the first full series in which Kelvin Tremain played. A prolific try-scorer with nine tries in his 38 Tests, he became New Zealand's most capped flanker in a brilliant career which spanned ten seasons.

## 1961

| 1st v. FRANCE | 2nd v. FRANCE | 3rd v. FRANCE |
|---|---|---|
| D.B. CLARKE 1DG,2C | D.B. CLARKE 1C | D.B. CLARKE 3PG,4C |
| †D.W. McKAY 1T | D.W. McKAY | D.W. McKAY |
| T.P.A. O'SULLIVAN 1T | †P.F. LITTLE | P.F. LITTLE 1T |
| J.R. WATT | R.W. CAULTON | J.R. WATT |
| R.H. BROWN | R.H. BROWN | R.H. BROWN |
| †T.N. WOLFE | T.N. WOLFE | T.N. WOLFE |
| †D.M. CONNOR | D.M. CONNOR | D.M. CONNOR |
| *W.J. WHINERAY | *W.J. WHINERAY | *W.J. WHINERAY |
| D. YOUNG | D. YOUNG | D. YOUNG |
| I.J. CLARKE | I.J. CLARKE | I.J. CLARKE |
| C.E. MEADS | C.E. MEADS | C.E. MEADS 1T |
| I.N. MacEWAN | I.N. MacEWAN | I.N. MacEWAN |
| †S.T. MEADS | K.R. TREMAIN 1T | K.R. TREMAIN 1T |
| †V.M. YATES | V.M. YATES | V.M. YATES 1T |
| D.J. GRAHAM | D.J. GRAHAM | D.J. GRAHAM 1T |
| Auckland | Wellington | Christchurch |
| WON 13-6 | WON 5-3 | WON 32-3 |
| NZ: 2G 1DG | NZ: 1G | NZ: 4G 3PG 1T |
| FR.: 2DG | FR.: 1T | FR.: 1T |
| 22 Jul. 1961 | 5 Aug. 1961 | 19 Aug. 1961 |

New Zealand played host to the French in 1961. The first individual European nation to tour New Zealand, the French came as the undisputed champions of the Northern Hemisphere, having won the Five Nations title for three consecutive seasons. However, they found New Zealanders difficult to master and the rugged All Black forwards were more than a match for their French counterparts.

In the Tests, the French were outplayed in the tight and loose and, like the Lions two years earlier, were demoralised by the phenomenal place-kicking of Don Clarke. The Waikato full-back provided the seven points which separated the sides in the first Test, kicked the conversions of Tremain's try to decide the second Test, and finished the series by scoring 17 points in the crushing victory at Christchurch.

For the first time two sets of brothers appeared together in a New Zealand Test team, the Clarkes of Waikato teaming up with the Meads forwards from the King Country in the Auckland Test.

## 1962      1962

| 1st v. AUSTRALIA | 2nd v. AUSTRALIA | 1st v. AUSTRALIA | 2nd v. AUSTRALIA | 3rd v. AUSTRALIA |
|---|---|---|---|---|
| D.B. CLARKE 1DG,1PG,1C | D.B. CLARKE 2PG,1C | D.B. CLARKE 2PG | D.B. CLARKE 1PG | D.B. CLARKE 2C |
| J.R. WATT | J.R. WATT 1T | †P.J. MORRISSEY 1T | P.J. MORRISSEY | P.J. MORRISSEY 1T |
| T.P.A. O'SULLIVAN | P.F. LITTLE | P.F. LITTLE | R.C. MORETON | P.F. LITTLE |
| †T.R. HEEPS | T.R. HEEPS | T.R. HEEPS | T.R. HEEPS | T.R. HEEPS 1T |
| R.H. BROWN | T.P.A. O'SULLIVAN | †R.C. MORETON | W.A. DAVIES | W.A. DAVIES |
| †B.A. WATT 2T | T.N. WOLFE | T.N. WOLFE | B.A. WATT | †M.A. HEREWINI 1DG,1T |
| D.M. CONNOR | D.M. CONNOR | D.M. CONNOR | D.M. CONNOR | D.M. CONNOR |
| *W.J. WHINERAY | *W.J. WHINERAY | *W.J. WHINERAY | *W.J. WHINERAY | *W.J. WHINERAY |
| D. YOUNG | D. YOUNG | D. YOUNG | †J.N. CREIGHTON | D. YOUNG |
| I.J. CLARKE | I.J. CLARKE | I.J. CLARKE | †J.M. LE LIEVRE | †B.T. THOMAS |
| C.E. MEADS | C.E. MEADS | C.E. MEADS | S.T. MEADS | C.E. MEADS |
| I.N. MacEWAN 1T | I.N. MacEWAN | I.N. MacEWAN | I.N. MacEWAN | S.T. MEADS |
| K.R. TREMAIN 1T | K.R. TREMAIN | K.R. TREMAIN | D.J. GRAHAM | W.J. NATHAN |
| D.J. GRAHAM | D.J. GRAHAM | D.J. GRAHAM | †K.A. NELSON | K.A. NELSON |
| †W.J. NATHAN | W.J. NATHAN 1T | W.J. NATHAN | W.J. NATHAN | D.J. GRAHAM |
| Brisbane | Sydney | Wellington | Dunedin | Auckland |
| WON 20-6 | WON 14-5 | DRAWN 9-9 | WON 3-0 | WON 16-8 |
| AUST.: 2PG | AUST.: 1G | NZ: 2PG 1T | NZ: 1PG | NZ: 2G 1DG 1T |
| NZ: 1G 1PG 1DG 3T | NZ: 1G 2PG 1T | AUST.: 3PG | AUST.: NIL | AUST.: 1G 1PG |
| 26 May 1962 | 4 Jun. 1962 | 25 Aug. 1962 | 8 Sep. 1962 | 22 Sep. 1962 |

New Zealand played five Tests against Australia in 1962, a home and away series of internationals between the two nations taking place for the first time. The All Blacks made a ten-match tour in May and June, losing narrowly to a strong NSW state side but winning two Tests and the remainder of the tour games. Later in the season Australia visited New Zealand, losing the Test rubber 0-2, but drawing the Test at Wellington.

Among the new caps in 1962 were two popular and skilful Maori players, Waka Nathan and Mac Herewini. Nathan was an outstanding loose forward described by Colin Meads as a "most virile runner with the ball". Injuries restricted Nathan's international appearances to 14 Tests during the 1960s. Herewini burst onto the scene with a drop-goal and a try following a characteristic jinking break in the Test at Auckland. A fine kicker and elusive runner, he was an able pivot who revelled behind a very impressive All Black pack during the decade.

Des Connor, the All Black scrum-half of 1962, was a shrewd tactician and excellent all-round player who had earlier been capped by Australia. In the mid-1960s he returned to Australia and became a national selector.

## 1963

| 1st v. ENGLAND | 2nd v. ENGLAND |
|---|---|
| D.B. CLARKE 1T,1DG,1PG,3C | D.B. CLARKE 1GM |
| D.W. McKAY | D.W. McKAY 1T |
| †I.N. UTTLEY | I.N. UTTLEY |
| R.W. CAULTON 2T | R.W. CAULTON |
| T.N. WOLFE | P.T. WALSH 1T |
| B.A. WATT | B.A. WATT |
| D.M. CONNOR | D.M. CONNOR |
| *W.J. WHINERAY | *W.J. WHINERAY |
| D. YOUNG | D. YOUNG |
| I.J. CLARKE | I.J. CLARKE |
| C.E. MEADS | C.E. MEADS |
| †A.J. STEWART | A.J. STEWART |
| W.J. NATHAN | W.J. NATHAN |
| D.J. GRAHAM | D.J. GRAHAM |
| K.R. TREMAIN | K.R. TREMAIN |
| Auckland | Christchurch |
| WON 21-11 | WON 9-6 |
| NZ: 3G 1DG 1PG | NZ: 1GM 2T |
| ENG.: 1G 2PG | ENG.: 1PG 1T |
| 25 May 1963 | 1 Jun. 1963 |

The two-Test series with England was the first against a visiting country from the British Isles. England were the Five Nations champions, but found the strength, power and efficiency of New Zealand's forward play too great, and the All Blacks easily won both Tests.

Don Clarke had an outstanding game in the first, totalling 15 points from four different scoring actions. (Jerry Shea, the Welsh centre in 1920, and Lewis Jones in 1950, had been the only previous players to score a try, penalty, conversion and drop-goal in an international.) Clarke was the match-winner in the second Test at Christchurch too, kicking a goal from a mark from 65 yards to give New Zealand a 9-6 victory. That was the last goal from a mark to be registered in an international match between IB nations, for the scoring device was abolished in 1977 when the free-kick clause entered the Laws.

Don Clarke and Ian Clarke became New Zealand's most capped Test players at Christchurch, passing the previous record of 23 matches set by R.A. White. Although Ian later toured Britain with the Fifth All Blacks, he never again played in an international match, and his Test record was soon surpassed by his brother.

## 1963-64

| v. IRELAND | v. WALES | v. ENGLAND | v. SCOTLAND | v. FRANCE |
|---|---|---|---|---|
| D.B. CLARKE 1PG | D.B. CLARKE 1PG | D.B. CLARKE 2PG,1C | D.B. CLARKE | D.B. CLARKE |
| †M.J. DICK | M.J. DICK | M.J. DICK | M.J. DICK | M.J. DICK |
| P.F. LITTLE | P.F. LITTLE | P.F. LITTLE | P.F. LITTLE | P.F. LITTLE |
| R.W. CAULTON | R.W. CAULTON | R.W. CAULTON 1T | R.W. CAULTON | R.W. CAULTON 1T |
| †D.A. ARNOLD | D.A. ARNOLD | D.A. ARNOLD | M.A. HEREWINI | D.A. ARNOLD |
| M.A. HEREWINI | B.A. WATT 1DG | B.A. WATT | B.A. WATT | M.A. HEREWINI 1PG |
| K.C. BRISCOE | K.C. BRISCOE | K.C. BRISCOE | K.C. BRISCOE | †C.R. LAIDLAW 1DG |
| *W.J. WHINERAY | *W.J. WHINERAY | *W.J. WHINERAY | *W.J. WHINERAY | *W.J. WHINERAY |
| D. YOUNG | D. YOUNG | D. YOUNG | D. YOUNG | D. YOUNG |
| †K.F. GRAY | K.F. GRAY | K.F. GRAY | K.F. GRAY | K.F. GRAY 1T |
| C.E. MEADS | C.E. MEADS | C.E. MEADS 1T | C.E. MEADS | C.E. MEADS |
| A.J. STEWART | A.J. STEWART | A.J. STEWART | A.J. STEWART | A.J. STEWART |
| D.J. GRAHAM | D.J. GRAHAM | D.J. GRAHAM | D.J. GRAHAM | W.J. NATHAN |
| S.T. MEADS | K.R. TREMAIN | †B.J. LOCHORE | B.J. LOCHORE | K.R. TREMAIN |
| K.R. TREMAIN 1T | W.J. NATHAN | K.R. TREMAIN | K.R. TREMAIN | D.J. GRAHAM |
| Lansdowne Road | Cardiff Arms Park | Twickenham | Murrayfield | Stade Colombes |
| WON 6-5 | WON 6-0 | WON 14-0 | DRAWN 0-0 | WON 12-3 |
| IRE.: 1G | WALES: NIL | ENG.: NIL | SCOT.: NIL | FR.: 1PG |
| NZ: 1PG 1T | NZ: 1PG 1DG | NZ: 1G 2PG 1T | NZ: NIL | NZ: 1PG 1DG 2T |
| 7 Dec. 1963 | 21 Dec. 1963 | 4 Jan. 1964 | 18 Jan. 1964 | 8 Feb. 1964 |

The Fifth All Blacks were an impressive combination of strength and expertise at forward, and scoring power behind. Admittedly there were no outstanding halves or midfield players, but the backs displayed competence in all of their matches and found in Dick and Caulton wings of genuine pace who scored many tries. Last but not least, Don Clarke lived up to his reputation as the world's leading place-kicker.

But the side, which lost just once (to Newport) in 34 matches, struggled to win their internationals and were held by a determined Scottish side in a scoreless draw at Murrayfield. The success which gave the team most joy was against Wales at Cardiff – the All Blacks' first win against Wales at the ground in four attempts. Don Clarke kicked an early penalty and with the tourists' forwards well on top, Watt added a drop-goal in the second half.

Whineray was a popular and effective captain and his leadership was described as "second to none of the great captains who have come from overseas". In the final tour match against the Barbarians he was given a generous ovation at Cardiff after he had scored the last try of a memorable match.

## 1964

| 1st v. AUSTRALIA | 2nd v. AUSTRALIA | 3rd v. AUSTRALIA |
|---|---|---|
| †M. WILLIMENT 2PG,1C | D.B. CLARKE 3C | D.B. CLARKE 1C |
| | | |
| †I.S.T. SMITH | I.S.T. SMITH | I.S.T. SMITH |
| R.C. MORETON 1DG | †R.E. RANGI 1T | R.E. RANGI |
| R.W. CAULTON | R.W. CAULTON | R.W. CAULTON |
| | | |
| †J.L. COLLINS | R.C. MORETON 1T | R.C. MORETON |
| B.A. WATT | †P.H. MURDOCH 1T | P.H. MURDOCH 1T |
| C.R. LAIDLAW | D.M. CONNOR | D.M. CONNOR |
| | | |
| K.F. GRAY | K.F. GRAY 1T | K.F. GRAY |
| †B.E. MCLEOD 1T | B.E. MCLEOD | B.E. MCLEOD |
| B.T. THOMAS | B.T. THOMAS | B.T. THOMAS |
| C.E. MEADS | C.E. MEADS | S.T. MEADS |
| S.T. MEADS | S.T. MEADS | A.J. STEWART |
| K.R. TREMAIN | K.R. TREMAIN | K.R. TREMAIN |
| *D.J. GRAHAM | *D.J. GRAHAM | C.E. MEADS |
| †D.W. CLARK | D.W. CLARK | *D.J. GRAHAM |
| | | |
| Dunedin | Christchurch | Wellington |
| WON 14-9 | WON 18-3 | LOST 5-20 |
| | | |
| NZ: 1G 1DG 2PG | NZ: 3G 1T | NZ: 1G |
| AUST.: 2PG 1T | AUST.: 1T | AUST.: 1G 3PG 1DG 1T |
| | | |
| 15 Aug. 1964 | 22 Aug. 1964 | 29 Aug. 1964 |

New Zealand retained the Bledisloe Cup in 1964, winning the first two Tests of the rubber with Australia but losing the final game of the series by 15 points in Wellington.

John Graham, an intelligent loose forward, skippered the All Blacks, succeeding Wilson Whineray, who had chosen to restrict his football to club games for 1964. Graham proved to be a shrewd leader who, following his 22 Tests, became a successful schoolmaster. Since 1973, he has been the Headmaster of the Auckland Grammar School.

Bruce McLeod was among the new caps in the first Test at Dunedin, and scored a try on his debut. A mobile, powerful hooker, he went on to win 24 caps, creating a new record for a New Zealand hooker, and was a member of the All Black front row throughout the late 1960s, when the side had the best pack in world rugby.

## 1965

| 1st v. S.AFRICA | 2nd v. S.AFRICA | 3rd v. S.AFRICA | 4th v. S.AFRICA |
|---|---|---|---|
| M. WILLIMENT | M. WILLIMENT 2C | M. WILLIMENT 1PG,2C | †W.F. MCCORMICK 1C |
| | | | |
| †W.M. BIRTWISTLE 1T | W.M. BIRTWISTLE | W.M. BIRTWISTLE | W.M. BIRTWISTLE 1T |
| R.E. RANGI | R.E. RANGI 1T | R.E. RANGI 1T | R.E. RANGI |
| I.S.T. SMITH | I.S.T. SMITH | M.J. DICK | I.S.T. SMITH 2T |
| | | | |
| J.L. COLLINS | R.C. MORETON | R.C. MORETON 1T | J.L. COLLINS |
| P.H. MURDOCH | P.H. MURDOCH | P.H. MURDOCH | M.A. HEREWINI 1DG |
| C.R. LAIDLAW | C.R. LAIDLAW | C.R. LAIDLAW | C.R. LAIDLAW |
| | | | |
| *W.J. WHINERAY | *W.J. WHINERAY | *W.J. WHINERAY | *W.J. WHINERAY |
| B.E. MCLEOD | B.E. MCLEOD 1T | B.E. MCLEOD | B.E. MCLEOD |
| K.F. GRAY | K.F. GRAY | K.F. GRAY | K.F. GRAY 1T |
| C.E. MEADS | C.E. MEADS | C.E. MEADS | C.E. MEADS |
| S.T. MEADS | S.T. MEADS | S.T. MEADS | S.T. MEADS |
| K.R. TREMAIN 1T | K.R. TREMAIN 1T | K.R. TREMAIN 1T | K.R. TREMAIN |
| B.J. LOCHORE | B.J. LOCHORE | B.J. LOCHORE | B.J. LOCHORE |
| R.J. CONWAY | R.J. CONWAY | R.J. CONWAY | R.J. CONWAY 1T |
| | | | |
| Wellington | Dunedin | Christchurch | Auckland |
| WON 6-3 | WON 13-0 | LOST 16-19 | WON 20-3 |
| | | | |
| NZ: 2T | NZ: 2G 1T | NZ: 2G 1PG 1T | NZ: 1G 1DG 4T |
| SA: 1DG | SA: NIL | SA: 2G 1PG 2T | SA: 1PG |
| | | | |
| 31 Jul. 1965 | 21 Aug. 1965 | 4 Sep. 1965 | 18 Sep. 1965 |

The return of Wilson Whineray as captain, and impressive forward displays by the New Zealand pack, which was unchanged for the four-match series, were key factors in the All Blacks' success against South Africa in 1965. The rubber was won 3-1, with the New Zealanders reserving their most outstanding performance for the decisive final Test of the series in Auckland.

Chris Laidlaw gained a regular place in the side this season, his quick, accurate passing supplying the backs with a wealth of good possession. He went on to play in twenty Tests before retiring to follow a career as a diplomat.

Laidlaw impressed the touring Sprinkboks by his interaction with his back row. Tremain and Lochore in particular enjoyed a brilliant series, and the former scored tries in each of the first three Tests, his effort at Wellington deciding a close match.

|  | 1966 |  |  | 1967 |
| --- | --- | --- | --- | --- |
| 1st v. BRITISH ISLES | 2nd v. BRITISH ISLES | 3rd v. BRITISH ISLES | 4th v. BRITISH ISLES | v. AUSTRALIA |
| M. WILLIMENT 2PG,1T,1C | M. WILLIMENT 1PG,2C | M. WILLIMENT 2PG,2C | M. WILLIMENT 1PG,3C | M. WILLIMENT 2PG,4C |
| I.S.T. SMITH | I.S.T. SMITH | I.S.T. SMITH | M.J. DICK 1T | M.J. DICK |
| R.E. RANGI | R.E. RANGI | R.E. RANGI | R.E. RANGI | †W.L. DAVIS 1T |
| †A.G. STEEL | A.G. STEEL 1T | A.G. STEEL 1T | A.G. STEEL 1T | A.G. STEEL 2T |
| †I.R. MACRAE | I.R. MACRAE | I.R. MACRAE | I.R. MACRAE 1T | I.R. MACRAE |
| M.A. HEREWINI 1DG | M.A. HEREWINI | M.A. HEREWINI | M.A. HEREWINI 1DG | M.A. HEREWINI 1DG |
| C.R. LAIDLAW | C.R. LAIDLAW | C.R. LAIDLAW | C.R. LAIDLAW | †S.M. GOING |
| †E.J. HAZLETT | E.J. HAZLETT | E.J. HAZLETT | E.J. HAZLETT | †B.L. MULLER |
| B.E. MCLEOD 1T | B.E. MCLEOD | B.E. MCLEOD | B.E. MCLEOD | †J. MAJOR |
| K.F. GRAY | K.F. GRAY | K.F. GRAY | K.F. GRAY | E.J. HAZLETT |
| C.E. MEADS | C.E. MEADS 1T | C.E. MEADS | C.E. MEADS | †S.C. STRAHAN |
| S.T. MEADS | S.T. MEADS | S.T. MEADS | S.T. MEADS | C.E. MEADS |
| W.J. NATHAN | W.J. NATHAN | W.J. NATHAN 2T | W.J. NATHAN 1T | W.J. NATHAN |
| *B.J. LOCHORE 1T | *B.J. LOCHORE | *B.J. LOCHORE | *B.J. LOCHORE | *B.J. LOCHORE |
| K.R. TREMAIN | K.R. TREMAIN 1T | K.R. TREMAIN | K.R. TREMAIN | K.R. TREMAIN 1T |
| Dunedin | Wellington | Christchurch | Auckland | Wellington |
| WON 20-3 | WON 16-12 | WON 19-6 | WON 24-11 | WON 29-9 |
| NZ: 1G 2PG 1DG 2T | NZ: 2G 1PG 1T | NZ: 2G 2PG 1T | NZ: 3G 1PG 1DG 1T | NZ: 4G 2PG 1DG |
| B.Is.: 1PG | B.Is.: 1DG 3PG | B.Is.: 2T | B.Is.: 1G 1PG 1T | AUST: 1PG 2T |
| 16 Jul. 1966 | 6 Aug. 1966 | 27 Aug. 1966 | 10 Sep. 1966 | 19 Aug. 1967 |

The All Blacks of 1966 were one of the strongest sides ever to represent New Zealand. They succeeded in winning a Test series 4-0 against the Lions for the first time, and used only 16 players in the rubber.

A solid front row, an experienced second row, and an outstanding loose trio (which registered five tries during the series) dominated the tight and loose play in the four Tests. Behind there were exciting backs, spearheaded by Laidlaw and Herewini; and Steel, a dynamic flyer on the wing, scored three tries in his first international series. Finally, at full-back, Williment proved to be the perfect successor to Don Clarke, for he scored 37 points, just two short of Clarke's record set against the 1959 Lions.

In 1967, to celebrate the 75th anniversary of the NZRFU, an Australian side played a Test against the All Blacks at Wellington. More than 300 former All Blacks were invited to attend a match which ended in an entertaining and convincing victory.

|  | 1967 |  |  |
| --- | --- | --- | --- |
| v. ENGLAND | v. WALES | v. FRANCE | v. SCOTLAND |
| W.F. MCCORMICK 4C | W.F. MCCORMICK 1PG,2C | W.F. MCCORMICK 1PG,3C | W.F. MCCORMICK 2PG,1C |
| M.J. DICK 1T | M.J. DICK | M.J. DICK 1T | W.M. BIRTWISTLE |
| W.L. DAVIS | W.L. DAVIS 1T | W.L. DAVIS | W.L. DAVIS 1T |
| W.M. BIRTWISTLE 1T | W.M. BIRTWISTLE 1T | A.G. STEEL 1T | A.G. STEEL |
| I.R. MACRAE | I.R. MACRAE | I.R. MACRAE | I.R. MACRAE 1T |
| †E.W. KIRTON 2T | E.W. KIRTON | E.W. KIRTON | E.W. KIRTON |
| C.R. LAIDLAW 1T | C.R. LAIDLAW | S.M. GOING 1T | C.R. LAIDLAW |
| B.L. MULLER | B.L. MULLER | B.L. MULLER | †A.E. HOPKINSON |
| B.E. MCLEOD | B.E. MCLEOD | B.E. MCLEOD | B.E. MCLEOD |
| E.J. HAZLETT | K.F. GRAY | K.F. GRAY | K.F. GRAY |
| S.C. STRAHAN | S.C. STRAHAN | S.C. STRAHAN | S.C. STRAHAN |
| C.E. MEADS | C.E. MEADS | C.E. MEADS | C.E. MEADS |
| †G.C. WILLIAMS | G.C. WILLIAMS | G.C. WILLIAMS | G.C. WILLIAMS |
| *B.J. LOCHORE | *B.J. LOCHORE | *B.J. LOCHORE | *B.J. LOCHORE |
| K.R. TREMAIN | K.R. TREMAIN | †I.A. KIRKPATRICK 1T | K.R. TREMAIN |
| Twickenham | Cardiff Arms Park | Stade Colombes | Murrayfield |
| WON 23-11 | WON 13-6 | WON 21-15 | WON 14-3 |
| ENG.: 1G 1PG 1T | WALES: 1PG 1DG | FR.: 3PG 1DG 1T | SCOT.: 1DG |
| NZ: 4G 1T | NZ: 2G 1PG | NZ: 3G 1PG 1T | NZ: 1G 2PG 1T |
| 4 Nov. 1967 | 11 Nov. 1967 | 25 Nov. 1967 | 2 Dec. 1967 |

This was the first New Zealand team to undertake a shorter tour of Britain. The All Blacks' scheduled tour of South Africa earlier this year had been cancelled and the visit to Britain was arranged as a replacement tour. One of the most attractive and popular sides to emerge from New Zealand, the Sixth All Blacks had Fred Allen, a former Test captain, as coach. Coaching became an important facet of rugby from the late 1960s and Allen was one of the first influential coaches in the modern game.

With excellent players available in 1967, Allen was able to blend individual flair with appeciation of the basic skills to produce rugby played to a pattern but without being stereotyped. In addition to the traditional strengths of New Zealand rugby – forward power – Allen was fortunate to possess imaginative midfield players capable of creating scoring opportunities, as well as brilliant halves in Going, Laidlaw and Kirton. At full-back, McCormick proved a valuable asset in defence and was a prolific scorer.

The side was unbeaten in 15 matches and won all four Tests handsomely. There were no matches in Ireland, however, owing to a foot-and-mouth epidemic, and the only disappointment of the tour was the sending-off of Colin Meads in the Scotland match.

| 1968 | | | | |
|---|---|---|---|---|
| 1st v. AUSTRALIA | 2nd v. AUSTRALIA | 1st v. FRANCE | 2nd v. FRANCE | 3rd v. FRANCE |
| W.F. McCormick 1PG,3C | W.F. McCormick 2PG,2C | W.F. McCormick 3PG | W.F. McCormick 3PG | W.F. McCormick 2PG,2C |
| †G.S. Thorne | G.S. Thorne 1T | G.S. Thorne | G.S. Thorne | †O.G. Stephens |
| W.L. Davis | W.L. Davis 1T‡ | W.L. Davis | I.R. MacRae | G.S. Thorne |
| A.G. Steel 1T | A.G. Steel | †M.W. O'Callaghan | M.W. O'Callaghan | M.W. O'Callaghan |
| †W.D. Cottrell | W.D. Cottrell | I.R. MacRae | W.D. Cottrell | W.D. Cottrell 1DG |
| E.W. Kirton 1T | E.W. Kirton | E.W. Kirton 1T | E.W. Kirton | E.W. Kirton |
| C.R. Laidlaw 1T | *C.R. Laidlaw | C.R. Laidlaw | C.R. Laidlaw | S.M. Going 2T |
| K.F. Gray | A.E. Hopkinson | A.E. Hopkinson | A.E. Hopkinson | A.E. Hopkinson |
| B.E. McLeod | B.E. McLeod | B.E. McLeod | B.E. McLeod | B.E. McLeod |
| B.L. Muller | †A.J. Kreft | B.L. Muller | K.F. Gray | K.F. Gray |
| C.E. Meads | C.E. Meads | C.E. Meads | C.E. Meads | C.E. Meads |
| S.C. Strahan | S.C. Strahan | S.C. Strahan | S.C. Strahan | S.C. Strahan |
| †T.N. Lister | T.N. Lister 1T | *K.R. Tremain | K.R. Tremain | K.R. Tremain |
| *B.J. Lochore¹ | I.A. Kirkpatrick | I.A. Kirkpatrick | *B.J. Lochore | *B.J. Lochore |
| K.R. Tremain | G.C. Williams | T.N. Lister | I.A. Kirkpatrick | I.A. Kirkpatrick |
| Sydney | Brisbane | Christchurch | Wellington | Auckland |
| WON 27-11 | WON 19-18 | WON 12-9 | WON 9-3 | WON 19-12 |
| AUST.:1G 2PG | AUST.: 5PG 1T | NZ:1T 3PG | NZ: 3PG | NZ: 2G 2PG 1DG |
| NZ: 3G 1PG 3T | NZ: 2G‡ 2PG 1T | FR.: 1DG 2PG | FR.: 1PG | FR.: 1DG 3T |
| 15 Jun. 1968 | 22 Jun. 1968 | 13 Jul. 1968 | 27 Jul. 1968 | 10 Aug. 1968 |
| ¹Rep. by I.A. Kirkpatrick 3T | ‡includes penalty try | | | |

Fred Allen completed his three years as national coach with an unbeaten tour of Australia and victory in each of three Tests against the visiting French, who were Grand Slam winners in the 1968 Five Nations Championship. During his tenure, Allen's side won every Test played to earn the title of unofficial World Champions. In addition, Allen had won high praise for his commitment to total rugby, and numerous influential coaches attempted to imitate his approach in the years which followed.

For various series between Australia and New Zealand in the past an informal agreement permitting the replacement of injured players had operated. But Ian Kirkpatrick became the first New Zealand replacement to appear in a Test since an official International Board ruling on substitutes had been passed in 1968.

An outstanding loose forward, Kirkpatrick replaced Lochore in the 25th minute of the Test at Sydney and miraculously went on to score a hat-trick of tries, a record for an All Black forward in an international. Altogether, Kirkpatrick played 39 times and created a New Zealand international record by scoring 16 tries in a distinguished career.

| 1969 | |
|---|---|
| 1st v. WALES | 2nd v. WALES |
| W.F. McCormick 1PG,2C | W.F.McCormick 1DG,5PG,3C |
| M.J. Dick 1T | M.J. Dick |
| W.L. Davis | W.L. Davis |
| G.S. Thorne | †G.R. Skudder 1T |
| I.R. MacRae | I.R. MacRae 1T |
| E.W. Kirton | E.W. Kirton |
| S.M. Going | S.M. Going |
| K.F. Gray 1T | A.E. Hopkinson |
| B.E. McLeod 1T | B.E. McLeod |
| B.L. Muller | K.F. Gray |
| C.E. Meads | C.E. Meads |
| †A.E. Smith | A.E. Smith |
| T.N. Lister | T.N. Lister |
| *B.J. Lochore 1T | *B.J. Lochore |
| I.A. Kirkpatrick | I.A. Kirkpatrick 1T |
| Christchurch | Auckland |
| WON 19-0 | WON 33-12 |
| NZ: 2G 1PG 2T | NZ: 3G 5PG 1DG |
| WALES: NIL | WALES: 2PG 2T |
| 31 May 1969 | 14 Jun. 1969 |

The All Blacks were too strong for Wales, the Five Nations Champions, who made their first tour to New Zealand in 1969. The Welsh had a difficult itinerary, playing the first of two Tests within a week of their arrival in the country.

The forward play of the All Blacks was too powerful for the Welsh. At Christchurch, two of the front row, Gray and McLeod, scored tries as New Zealand coasted to victory by 19 points. For the second of the Tests, New Zealand selected an unchanged side, but injuries to Thorne and Muller compelled them to make two changes. In another convincing victory, McCormick stole the headlines by scoring 24 points in the match, beating the 58-year-old record of Englishman Dan Lambert, who had scored 22 points against the French.

Ken Gray, a big, durable prop from Wellington, played the last of his 24 Tests at Auckland. He was a cornerstone of the successful pack of the 1960s, a pack which has come to be regarded as one of the best New Zealand scrums of all time.

## 1970

| 1st v. S.AFRICA | 2nd v. S.AFRICA | 3rd v. S.AFRICA | 4th v. S.AFRICA |
|---|---|---|---|
| W.F. McCormick 1PG | W.F. McCormick 1PG | W.F. McCormick | †G.F. Kember 4PG,1C |
| M.J. Dick | B.G. Williams | G.S. Thorne | M.J. Dick |
| G.S. Thorne | W.L. Davis | B.G. Williams 1PG | G.S. Thorne |
| †B.G. Williams 1T | G.S. Thorne | †H.P. Milner | B.G. Williams 1T |
| I.R. MacRae | I.R. MacRae | I.R. MacRae | I.R. MacRae |
| W.D. Cottrell | E.W. Kirton | E.W. Kirton | †B.D.M. Furlong |
| C.R. Laidlaw¹ | C.R. Laidlaw 1T | C.R. Laidlaw | S.M. Going |
| B.L. Muller | B.L. Muller | †N.W. Thimbleby | †K. Murdoch |
| B.E. McLeod | B.E. McLeod | †R.A. Urlich | R.A. Urlich |
| A.E. Hopkinson | A.E. Hopkinson | A.E. Hopkinson | B.L. Muller |
| S.C. Strahan | S.C. Strahan | S.C. Strahan | A.R. Sutherland |
| A.E. Smith | †A.R. Sutherland | C.E. Meads | C.E. Meads |
| I.A. Kirkpatrick | I.A. Kirkpatrick 1T | I.A. Kirkpatrick | I.A. Kirkpatrick |
| *B.J. Lochore | *B.J. Lochore | *B.J. Lochore | *B.J. Lochore |
| T.N. Lister | †A.J. Wyllie | A.J. Wyllie | T.N. Lister |
| Pretoria | Cape Town | Port Elizabeth | Johannesburg |
| LOST 6-17 | WON 9-8 | LOST 3-14 | LOST 17-20 |
| SA: 1G 2PG 1DG 1T | SA: 1G 1PG | SA: 1G 2PG 1T | SA: 1G 4PG 1T |
| NZ: 1PG 1T | NZ: 1PG 2T | NZ: 1PG | NZ: 1G 4PG |
| 25 Jul. 1970 | 8 Aug. 1970 | 29 Aug. 1970 | 12 Sep. 1970 |

¹Rep. by S.M. Going

The fourth All Blacks to tour South Africa were led by Brian Lochore, a Masterton farmer of immense fitness, impenetrable resolution and considerable expertise. One of the most complete back row forwards ever to represent New Zealand, Lochore led his country with dignity in 18 internationals between 1966 to 1970. He was the winning skipper in 15 of these Tests,

The All Blacks, shrewdly coached by former international Ivan Vodanovich, had an unbeaten run of ten matches up to the first Test. But a broken arm sustained by Colin Meads in the provincial match against Eastern Transvaal robbed the tourists of their leading tight forward, and his absence was sorely felt as the All Blacks succumbed to a 6-17 defeat at Pretoria.

Meads recovered to play in the two final Tests of the series, the All Blacks having tied the rubber with a narrow win at Cape Town. But the presence of the world's leading forward could not prevent New Zealand making crucial errors in Port Elizabeth and Johannesburg. With a three-point win before 67,000 spectators at Ellis Park, the Springboks took the rubber 3-1.

## 1971

| 1st v. BRITISH ISLES | 2nd v. BRITISH ISLES | 3rd v. BRITISH ISLES | 4th v. BRITISH ISLES |
|---|---|---|---|
| W.F. McCormick 1PG | †L.W. Mains 1PG,2C | L.W. Mains 1T | L.W. Mains 2PG,1C |
| †B.A. Hunter | B.A. Hunter | B.A. Hunter | K.R. Carrington |
| B.G. Williams | †H.T. Joseph | H.T. Joseph | M.G. Duncan |
| †K.R. Carrington | B.G. Williams 1T‡ | K.R. Carrington | B.G. Williams |
| W.D. Cottrell | W.D. Cottrell | W.D. Cottrell | †P.C. Gard |
| †R.E. Burgess | R.E. Burgess 2T | R.E. Burgess¹ | W.D. Cottrell 1T |
| S.M. Going | S.M. Going 1T | S.M. Going | S.M. Going |
| B.L. Muller | B.L. Muller | B.L. Muller | B.L. Muller |
| †R.W. Norton | R.W. Norton | R.W. Norton | R.W. Norton |
| †R.A. Guy | R.A. Guy | R.A. Guy | R.A. Guy |
| †P.J. Whiting | P.J. Whiting | B.J. Lochore | P.J. Whiting |
| *C.E. Meads | *C.E. Meads | *C.E. Meads | *C.E. Meads |
| †A.M. McNaughton | I.A. Kirkpatrick 1T | I.A. Kirkpatrick | I.A. Kirkpatrick |
| A.R. Sutherland | A.J. Wyllie | A.J. Wyllie | A.J. Wyllie |
| I.A. Kirkpatrick | A.M. McNaughton | A.M. McNaughton | T.N. Lister 1T |
| Dunedin | Christchurch | Wellington | Auckland |
| LOST 3-9 | WON 22-12 | LOST 3-13 | DRAWN 14-14 |
| NZ: 1PG | NZ: 2G‡ 1PG 3T | NZ: 1T | NZ: 1G 2PG 1T |
| B.Is.: 2PG 1T | B.Is.: 1DG 1PG 2T | B.Is.: 2G 1DG | B.Is.: 1G 2PG 1DG |
| 26 Jun. 1971 | 10 Jul. 1971 | 31 Jul. 1971 | 14 Aug. 1971 |
| | ‡includes penalty try | ¹Rep. by †M.G. Duncan | |

Colin Meads ended his career as the world's leading cap-holder, and his span of 15 seasons in Test rugby equalled the New Zealand record set by Ned Hughes in 1921. However, the Lions of 1971 were the best ever to tour New Zealand and Meads became the first All Black captain to lead his nation to defeat in a Test series with the British.

Following the Lions' victory in the first Test, Fergie McCormick was dropped after 16 games as full-back. A reliable defensive player, he was a prolific points-scorer whose 121 points in Tests left him second only to Don Clarke in the list of New Zealand international match scorers.

Held by the Lions' forwards and outplayed by their outstanding backs, there were few successes among the New Zealand players. One to stand out, however, was the All Black fly-half, Bob Burgess. An exciting, balanced runner with a sharp eye for an opening, he scored two excellent tries in the victory at Christchurch and impressed the British players by his attacking approach. Injured in the third Test, he was unable to play in the decisive drawn game at Auckland.

## 1972

| 1st v. AUSTRALIA | 2nd v. AUSTRALIA | 3rd v. AUSTRALIA |
|---|---|---|
| †T.J. MORRIS 1DG,3C | T.J. MORRIS 2C,2PG | T.J. MORRIS 4C,2PG |
| | | |
| B.G. WILLIAMS 1T | B.G. WILLIAMS 1T | B.G. WILLIAMS 1T |
| †B.J. ROBERTSON | †G.S. SIMS | B.J. ROBERTSON |
| †D.A. HALES | D.A. HALES | D.A. HALES |
| | | |
| †R.M. PARKINSON | R.M. PARKINSON | R.M. PARKINSON |
| †J.P. DOUGAN 1T | †J.L. JAFFRAY | R.E. BURGESS |
| S.M. GOING 1T | S.M. GOING | S.M. GOING 1T |
| | | |
| †J.D. MATHESON | J.D. MATHESON | J.D. MATHESON |
| R.W. NORTON | R.W. NORTON | R.W. NORTON |
| †G.J. WHITING | G.J. WHITING | K. MURDOCH |
| S.C. STRAHAN | S.C. STRAHAN | S.C. STRAHAN |
| P.J. WHITING 1T | P.J. WHITING 1T | P.J. WHITING 1T |
| *I.A. KIRKPATRICK | *I.A. KIRKPATRICK 2T | *I.A. KIRKPATRICK 1T |
| A.R. SUTHERLAND 1T | A.R. SUTHERLAND 1T | A.R. SUTHERLAND 1T |
| †A.I. SCOWN | A.I. SCOWN | A.I. SCOWN 1T |
| | | |
| Wellington | Christchurch | Auckland |
| WON 29-6 | WON 30-17 | WON 38-3 |
| | | |
| NZ: 3G 2T 1DG | NZ: 2G 2PG 3T | NZ: 4G 2PG 2T |
| AUST.: 2PG | AUST.: 1G 1DG 2T | AUST.: 1PG |
| | | |
| 19 Aug. 1972 | 2 Sep. 1972 | 16 Sep. 1972 |

There was an internal tour in the early part of the 1972 season, a party of 21 players winning all nine matches under the captaincy of Ian Kirkpatrick, Meads' successor as skipper. Jack Gleeson was the manager/coach for the tour.

Most of the players who figured in the tour were included in the Test series in which New Zealand overwhelmed the Wallabies later in the season. The All Black forwards dominated the three Tests, but there was a feeling of dissatisfaction with the play of the backs. It was felt that, given such splendid possession by the pack, the backs should have created more scoring opportunities. Trevor Morris, a Nelson schoolmaster who was gaining All Black honours at the age of 30, kicked 33 points to create a new record for a New Zealander in a series against Australia.

The third Test at Auckland was the first to be broadcast live on New Zealand television. Nevertheless a crowd of 43,000 turned out at Eden Park to watch the home side win 38-3 – a new record-winning-points-margin for the All Blacks against an International Board nation.

## 1972-73 / 1973

| v. WALES | v. SCOTLAND | v. ENGLAND | v. IRELAND | v. FRANCE | v. ENGLAND |
|---|---|---|---|---|---|
| †J.F. KARAM 5PG | J.F. KARAM 1C | J.F. KARAM 1C | J.F. KARAM 1C | J.F. KARAM 2PG | †R.N. LENDRUM 1C |
| | | | | | |
| B.G. WILLIAMS | B.G. WILLIAMS | B.G. WILLIAMS 1DG | B.G. WILLIAMS | B.G. WILLIAMS | B.G. WILLIAMS |
| D.A. HALES | B.J. ROBERTSON | B.J. ROBERTSON | B.J. ROBERTSON | B.J. ROBERTSON | I.A. HURST 1T |
| †G.B. BATTY | G.B. BATTY 1T | G.B. BATTY | G.B. BATTY | G.B. BATTY | G.B. BATTY 1T |
| | | | | | |
| R.M. PARKINSON | R.M. PARKINSON | R.M. PARKINSON | †I.A. HURST | I.A. HURST | R.M. PARKINSON[1] |
| R.E. BURGESS | †I.N. STEVENS | I.N. STEVENS | R.E. BURGESS | R.E. BURGESS | J.P.DOUGAN |
| S.M. GOING | S.M.GOING 1T | S.M. GOING | S.M. GOING 1T | S.M. GOING | S.M. GOING |
| | | | | | |
| J.D. MATHESON | J.D. MATHESON[1] | G.J. WHITING | G.J. WHITING | G.J. WHITING | K.K. LAMBERT |
| R.W. NORTON | R.W. NORTON | R.W. NORTON | R.W. NORTON | R.W. NORTON | R.W. NORTON |
| K. MURDOCH 1T | G.J. WHITING | K.K. LAMBERT | K.K. LAMBERT | K.K. LAMBERT | †M.G. JONES |
| †H.H. MACDONALD | P.J. WHITING | H.H. MACDONALD | P.J. WHITING | P.J. WHITING | H.H. MACDONALD |
| P.J. WHITING | H.H. MACDONALD | P.J. WHITING | H.H. MACDONALD | H.H. MACDONALD | S.C. STRAHAN |
| A.J. WYLLIE[1] | *I.A. KIRKPATRICK | A.J. WYLLIE | *I.A. KIRKPATRICK | *I.A. KIRKPATRICK | †K.W. STEWART |
| A.R. SUTHERLAND | A.J. WYLLIE 1T | A.R. SUTHERLAND | A.R. SUTHERLAND | A.R. SUTHERLAND | A.J. WYLLIE |
| *I.A. KIRKPATRICK | A.I. SCOWN | *I.A. KIRKPATRICK 1T | A.J. WYLLIE 1T | A.J. WYLLIE | *I.A. KIRKPATRICK |
| | | | | | |
| Cardiff Arms Park | Murrayfield | Twickenham | Lansdowne Road | Parc des Princes | Auckland |
| WON 19-16 | WON 14-9 | WON 9-0 | DRAWN 10-10 | LOST 6-13 | LOST 10-16 |
| | | | | | |
| WALES: 4PG 1T | SCOT.: 1DG 2PG | ENG.: NIL | IRE.: 2PG 1T | FR.: 1G 1PG 1T | NZ: 1G 1T |
| NZ: 5PG 1T | NZ: 1G 2T | NZ: 1G 1DG | NZ: 1G 1T | NZ: 2PG | ENG.: 2G 1T |
| | | | | | |
| 2 Dec. 1972 | 16 Dec. 1972 | 6 Jan. 1973 | 20 Jan. 1973 | 10 Feb. 1973 | 15 Sep. 1973 |
| [1]Rep. by A.I. Scown | [1]Rep. by †K.K. Lambert | | | | [1]Rep. by †T.G. Morrison |

Ian Kirkpatrick led the Seventh All Blacks to Britain and France in 1972. Although the side lacked the popularity of most of its predecessors to Britain, and found difficulty matching up to the high playing standards set by Lochore's brilliant side of 1967, Kirkpatrick had the pleasure of avenging the defeats suffered at the hands of the Lions in 1971.

Forward power, exceptional talent on the wings (where Bryan Williams and Grant Batty proved world-class performers), and accurate place-kicking by new full-back Joe Karam, were the qualities which helped the All Blacks to wins over Wales, Scotland and England. In addition, Sid Going was a constant threat to British back divisions with his probing runs from the base of the scrum and his clever interaction with his back-row men. Even Going's fine individual try in Dublin could not inspire New Zealand to victory against the Irish, however, and in the final Test the All Blacks were well beaten by a determined French side.

In September 1973 the All Blacks found themselves well beaten again, this time by an unfancied England side. The All Blacks' display was described as "the poorest in an international for years", and was their first Test defeat at Auckland since 1959.

| | 1974 | | | 1974 | 1975 |
|---|---|---|---|---|---|
| | 1st v. AUSTRALIA | 2nd v. AUSTRALIA | 3rd v. AUSTRALIA | v. IRELAND | v. SCOTLAND |
| | J.F. Karam 1pg | J.F. Karam 2pg,1c | J.F. Karam 2c | J.F. Karam 1t,3pg,1c | J.F. Karam 4c |
| | B.G. Williams | B.G. Williams | B.G. Williams | B.G. Williams | B.G. Williams 2t |
| | B.J. Robertson | B.J. Robertson | B.J. Robertson | B.J. Robertson | †W.M. Osborne |
| | G.B. Batty | †J.S McLachlan | G.B. Batty 1t | G.B. Batty | G.B. Batty |
| | I.A. Hurst | I.A. Hurst 1t | †J.E. Morgan | J.E. Morgan | J.L. Jaffray |
| | †D.J. Robertson 1t | D.J. Robertson | D.J. Robertson | D.J. Robertson | D.J. Robertson 1t |
| | †B.M. Gemmell | B.M. Gemmell | I.N. Stevens 1t | S.M. Going | S.M. Going |
| | †W.K. Bush | W.K. Bush | †A.J. Gardiner | K.K. Lambert | W.K. Bush |
| | R.W. Norton | R.W. Norton | R.W. Norton | R.W. Norton | R.W. Norton |
| | †K.J. Tanner | K.J. Tanner | K.J. Tanner | K.J. Tanner | K.J. Tanner |
| | †J.A. Callesen | J.A. Callesen | J.A. Callesen | H.H. Macdonald | H.H. Macdonald 1t |
| | P.J. Whiting | P.J. Whiting | P.J. Whiting | P.J. Whiting | J.A. Callesen |
| | I.A. Kirkpatrick 1t | I.A. Kirkpatrick | I.A. Kirkpatrick 1t | I.A. Kirkpatrick | I.A. Kirkpatrick |
| | *†A.R. Leslie | *A.R. Leslie 1t | *A.R. Leslie | *A.R. Leslie | *A.R. Leslie |
| | K.W. Stewart | K.W. Stewart | K.W. Stewart | K.W. Stewart | K.W. Stewart |
| | Sydney | Brisbane | Sydney | Lansdowne Road | Auckland |
| | WON 11-6 | DRAWN 16-16 | WON 16-6 | WON 15-6 | WON 24-0 |
| | Aust.: 1g | Aust.: 1g 2pg 1t | Aust.: 2pg | Ire.: 2pg | NZ: 4g |
| | NZ: 1pg 2t | NZ: 1g 2pg 1t | NZ: 2g 1t | NZ: 1g 3pg | Scot.: nil |
| | 25 May 1974 | 1 Jun. 1974 | 8 Jun. 1974 | 23 Nov. 1974 | 14 Jun. 1975 |

A team of 25 players undertook a twelve-match tour of Australia and Fiji in 1974. Retirements and the unavailability of several players compelled the All Blacks to field six new caps for the first Test in Sydney, with Andy Leslie becoming the third post-war All Black to lead the side on international debut. The New Zealanders won the series 2-0, drawing the Test at Brisbane.

Later in the year the All Blacks were guests of the Irish Rugby Union, who invited the New Zealanders to share in their Centenary celebrations. In the only Test of the tour the All Blacks were comfortable winners.

There was only one international played by New Zealand in 1975 – against the touring Scots. The match took place in trying conditions at Auckland, rain forming mini lakes on the playing surface. The All Blacks handled well in the circumstances to win by four tries, each converted by Karam. A dependable full-back with a superb big-match temperament, Karam switched to Rugby League the following season, having scored 65 points in his ten Tests.

| | 1976 | 1976 | | | |
|---|---|---|---|---|---|
| | v. IRELAND | 1st v. S.AFRICA | 2nd v. S.AFRICA | 3rd v. S.AFRICA | 4th v. S.AFRICA |
| | L.W. Mains 1pg | D.J. Robertson | †C.L. Fawcett | C.L. Fawcett | D.J. Robertson |
| | B.G. Williams | B.G. Williams 1pg | B.G. Williams | B.G. Williams 2pg | B.G. Williams 1pg |
| | B.J. Robertson 1t | B.J. Robertson | B.J. Robertson | B.J. Robertson 1t | B.J. Robertson |
| | †N.A. Purvis | G.B. Batty | G.B. Batty[1] | G.B. Batty | G.B. Batty[1] |
| | J.L. Jaffray | J.L. Jaffray 1t | J.E. Morgan 1t | J.E. Morgan | J.E. Morgan[2] |
| | D.J. Robertson | †O.D. Bruce | O.D. Bruce 1dg | D.J. Robertson | O.D. Bruce 1dg |
| | †L.J. Davis[1] | S.M. Going | S.M. Going 2pg,1c | S.M. Going | S.M. Going 1t |
| | W.K. Bush | K.J. Tanner | †B.R. Johnstone | †P.C. Harris | K.K. Lambert |
| | R.W. Norton | R.W. Norton | R.W. Norton | R.W. Norton | R.W. Norton |
| | K.J. Tanner | K.K. Lambert | W.K. Bush | K.K. Lambert | W.K. Bush |
| | H.H. Macdonald | P.J. Whiting | P.J. Whiting | P.J. Whiting | †F.J. Oliver |
| | P.J. Whiting | H.H. Macdonald | H.H. Macdonald | H.H. Macdonald | P.J. Whiting |
| | I.A. Kirkpatrick 1t | I.A. Kirkpatrick | I.A. Kirkpatrick | I.A. Kirkpatrick | I.A. Kirkpatrick 1t |
| | *A.R. Leslie | *A.R. Leslie | *A.R. Leslie | *A.R. Leslie | *A.R. Leslie |
| | K.W. Stewart | K.W. Stewart | †K.A. Eveleigh | K.W. Stewart | K.A. Eveleigh |
| | Wellington | Durban | Bloemfontein | Cape Town | Johannesburg |
| | WON 11-3 | LOST 7-16 | WON 15-9 | LOST 10-15 | LOST 14-15 |
| | NZ: 1pg 2t | SA: 1g 1pg 1dg 1t | SA: 3pg | SA: 1g 2pg 1dg | SA: 1g 1dg 2pg |
| | Ire.: 1pg | NZ: 1pg 1t | NZ: 1g 1dg 2pg | NZ: 2pg 1t | NZ: 1dg 1pg 2t |
| | 5 Jun. 1976 | 24 Jul. 1976 | 14 Aug. 1976 | 4 Sep. 1976 | 18 Sep. 1976 |
| | [1]Rep. by S.M. Going | | [1]Rep. by W.M. Osborne | | [1]Rep. by †T.W. Mitchell [2]Rep. by W.M. Osborne |

Laurie Mains, first capped against the 1971 Lions, was recalled for the early season Test against the Irish, but although selected for the tour to South Africa, he lost his place to Duncan Robertson and Kit Fawcett in the series with the Springboks.

New Zealand regarded the Irish Test as a warm up for the rubber in South Africa. The victory over Ireland did little to bolster confidence for the tour: the match was disappointing and few of the players taking part enhanced their reputations. Nevertheless, when the party to tour South Africa was announced, every member of the victorious side was included.

The series was lost 1-3 to the Springboks, but the All Blacks were a little unlucky not to finish the rubber with honours even. The lack of a consistent goal-kicker in the Tests was a real handicap, Sid Going and Bryan Williams sharing these responsibilities but with limited success. (Curiously, Mains, who scored 132 points on the tour, did not appear in a Test.) And in the final international they were beaten by a point thanks to a late penalty goal kicked by the Springbok fly-half.

## 1977

| 1st v. BRITISH ISLES | 2nd v. BRITISH ISLES | 3rd v. BRITISH ISLES | 4th v. BRITISH ISLES |
|---|---|---|---|
| †C.P. FARRELL | C.P. FARRELL | †B.W. WILSON 2PG,1C | B.W. WILSON 2PG |
| | | | |
| B.G. WILLIAMS 2C | B.G. WILLIAMS 3PG | B.G. WILLIAMS | B.G. WILLIAMS |
| B.J. ROBERTSON | W.M. OSBORNE | B.J. ROBERTSON 1DG | B.J. ROBERTSON |
| G.B. BATTY 1T | †N.M. TAYLOR | †B.R. FORD | B.R. FORD[1] |
| | | | |
| W.M. OSBORNE | J.L. JAFFRAY | W.M. OSBORNE | W.M. OSBORNE |
| D.J. ROBERTSON | O.D. BRUCE | O.D. BRUCE | O.D. BRUCE |
| S.M. GOING 1T | S.M. GOING | L.J. DAVIS | L.J. DAVIS |
| | | | |
| B.R. JOHNSTONE 1T | B.R. JOHNSTONE | †J.T. McELDOWNEY | J.T. McELDOWNEY[2] |
| *R.W. NORTON | *R.W. NORTON | *R.W. NORTON | *R.W. NORTON |
| K.K. LAMBERT | W.K. BUSH | W.K. BUSH | K.K. LAMBERT |
| F.J. OLIVER | F.J. OLIVER | F.J. OLIVER | F.J. OLIVER |
| †A.M. HADEN | A.M. HADEN | A.M. HADEN 1T | A.M. HADEN |
| K.A. EVELEIGH | K.A. EVELEIGH | †G.N.K. MOURIE | G.N.K. MOURIE |
| †L.G. KNIGHT | L.G. KNIGHT | L.G. KNIGHT | L.G. KNIGHT 1T |
| I.A. KIRKPATRICK | I.A. KIRKPATRICK | I.A. KIRKPATRICK 1T | I.A. KIRKPATRICK |
| | | | |
| Wellington | Christchurch | Dunedin | Auckland |
| WON 16-12 | LOST 9-13 | WON 19-7 | WON 10-9 |
| | | | |
| NZ: 2G 1T | NZ: 3PG | NZ: 1G 2PG 1DG 1T | NZ: 1T 2PG |
| B.Is.: 4PG | B.Is.: 3PG 1T | B.Is.: 1PG 1T | B.Is.: 1G 1PG |
| | | | |
| 18 Jun. 1977 | 9 Jul. 1977 | 30 Jul. 1977 | 13 Aug. 1977 |

[1]Rep. by N.M. Taylor
[2]Rep. by W.K. Bush

The All Blacks were lucky to win this series. 2-1 ahead in the rubber when they met the Lions in the final Test, the New Zealanders were trailing 6-9 as the match entered injury time. But then a kick ahead by Bill Osborne caused the Lions confusion and the ball bounced luckily for Knight to gather and race over in the corner. Outscrummaged in the series, the All Blacks had shown great determination and stamina to win a rubber which the Lions should at least have drawn.

Three famous All Blacks of the 1970s made their final Test appearances during the series. Sid Going, for so long a thorn in the flesh to British sides, played the last of his 29 internationals (a record for an All Black scrum-half) at Christchurch; Grant Batty announced his retirement due to a recurring knee injury; and Ian Kirkpatrick played his 39th and final Test at Auckland.

Andy Haden, who went on to become the second All Black to appear in more than forty Tests, and Graham Mourie, later an influential captain, were among the eight new players capped during the series.

## 1977

| 1st v. FRANCE | 2nd v. FRANCE |
|---|---|
| †B.J. McKECHNIE 1PG | B.J. McKECHNIE 1DG,1PG,1C |
| | |
| B.G. WILLIAMS 1PG,1T[1] | N.M. TAYLOR |
| B.J. ROBERTSON 1DG | B.J. ROBERTSON |
| †S.S. WILSON | S.S. WILSON 1T |
| | |
| N.M. TAYLOR | W.M. OSBORNE |
| O.D. BRUCE | O.D. BRUCE |
| †M.W. DONALDSON | M.W. DONALDSON |
| | |
| B.R. JOHNSTONE | B.R. JOHNSTONE |
| †J.E. BLACK | †A.G. DALTON |
| †G.A. KNIGHT[2] | G.A. KNIGHT |
| A.M. HADEN | A.M. HADEN |
| F.J. OLIVER | F.J. OLIVER |
| L.G. KNIGHT | L.G. KNIGHT |
| †G.A. SEEAR | G.A. SEEAR 1PG |
| *G.N.K. MOURIE | *G.N.K. MOURIE |
| | |
| Toulouse | Parc des Princes |
| LOST 13-18 | WON 15-3 |
| | |
| FR.: 1G 3PG 1DG | FR.: 1PG |
| NZ: 2PG 1DG 1T | NZ: 1G 2PG 1DG |
| | |
| 11 Nov. 1977 | 19 Nov. 1977 |

[1]Rep. by W.M. Osborne
[2]Rep. by †R.L. Stuart

Graham Mourie, the Taranaki flanker, had led a New Zealand team on a tour of Argentina in 1976, just before gaining his cap against the Lions. In late 1977, he was appointed captain of the All Blacks party which toured Italy and France. The team played nine games, winning eight. Mourie and Jack Gleeson, the coach, formed a harmonious and productive partnership, and although the series with France was shared, a young and experimental side was judged to have come through the tour with credit.

Stuart Wilson made his Test debut at Toulouse. Another, like Mourie, to have earned his spurs in the 1976 tour of Argentina, Wilson became the outstanding wing in New Zealand rugby during the following decade. His pace and opportunism brought him 19 tries in his 34 Tests, a new career record for an All Black international.

## 1978

| 1st v. AUSTRALIA | 2nd v. AUSTRALIA | 3rd v. AUSTRALIA |
|---|---|---|
| B.W. Wilson 3PG | B.W. Wilson 1PG,2C | B.W. Wilson |
| | | |
| S.S. Wilson | S.S. Wilson 1T | S.S. Wilson 1T |
| B.J. Robertson | B.J. Robertson | B.J. Robertson |
| B.G. Williams 1T | B.G. Williams | B.G. Williams |
| | | |
| N.M. Taylor | N.M. Taylor 1T | N.M. Taylor |
| O.D. Bruce | O.D. Bruce 1DG[1] | B.J. McKechnie 2PG,1C |
| M.W. Donaldson | M.W. Donaldson | M.W. Donaldson |
| | | |
| †J.C. Ashworth | J.C. Ashworth | J.C. Ashworth 1T |
| A.G. Dalton | A.G. Dalton | A.G. Dalton |
| G.A. Knight | G.A. Knight | G.A. Knight |
| A.M. Haden | A.M. Haden | A.M. Haden |
| *F.J. Oliver | *F.J. Oliver | *F.J. Oliver |
| †B.G. Ashworth | B.G. Ashworth | †R.G. Myers |
| G.A. Seear | G.A. Seear 1T | G.A. Seear |
| †L.M. Rutledge | L.M. Rutledge | L.M. Rutledge |
| Wellington | Christchurch | Auckland |
| WON 13-12 | WON 22-6 | LOST 16-30 |
| NZ: 3PG 1T | NZ: 2G 1PG 1DG 1T | NZ: 1G 2PG 1T |
| AUST.: 1G 2PG | AUST.: 1PG 1DG | AUST.: 2G 1PG 1DG 3T |
| 19 Aug. 1978 | 26 Aug. 1978 | 9 Sep. 1978 |
| | [1]Rep. by B.J. McKechnie | |

The All Blacks were hosts to Australia for a three-Test series. Lucky to win the opening game of the rubber, the New Zealanders fielded an unchanged side to gain an emphatic win at Christchurch in difficult conditions. Frank Oliver, who had stepped into Graham Mourie's shoes as captain when the flanker withdrew from the Wellington Test with a back injury, led the side shrewdly, though the All Blacks conceded 30 points in the final Test at Auckland. This represents the highest score registered against the All Blacks in more than eighty years of Test rugby.

John Ashworth gained his first cap at Wellington. A rugged, determined scrummager, he formed a formidable front row with Dalton and Gary Knight. To date the trio has played together twenty times in Tests: a world record for matches between International Board nations.

The Test at Auckland was refereed by Mr D.H. Millar of Otago: the last New Zealander to referee a home All Black Test. In subsequent years neutral referees were appointed to control Test series in New Zealand.

## 1978

| v. IRELAND | v. WALES | v. ENGLAND | v. SCOTLAND |
|---|---|---|---|
| †C.J. Currie | C.J. Currie[1] | B.J. McKechnie 2PG,1C | B.J. McKechnie 2PG,2C |
| | | | |
| S.S. Wilson | S.S. Wilson 1T | S.S. Wilson | S.S. Wilson |
| W.M. Osborne | B.J. Robertson | B.J. Robertson | B.J. Robertson 1T |
| B.R. Ford[1] | B.G. Williams | B.G. Williams | B.G. Williams |
| | | | |
| N.M. Taylor | W.M. Osborne | W.M. Osborne | W.M. Osborne |
| O.D. Bruce 2DG | O.D. Bruce | O.D. Bruce | O.D. Bruce |
| M.W. Donaldson | †D.S. Loveridge | M.W. Donaldson | M.W. Donaldson |
| | | | |
| B.R. Johnstone | B.R. Johnstone | B.R. Johnstone 1T | B.R. Johnstone |
| A.G. Dalton 1T | A.G. Dalton | A.G. Dalton | A.G. Dalton |
| W.K. Bush | W.K. Bush | G.A. Knight | G.A. Knight |
| A.M. Haden | A.M. Haden | A.M. Haden | A.M. Haden |
| F.J. Oliver | F.J. Oliver | F.J. Oliver 1T | F.J. Oliver |
| *G.N.K. Mourie | *G.N.K. Mourie | *G.N.K. Mourie | *G.N.K. Mourie |
| G.A. Seear | G.A. Seear | G.A. Seear | G.A. Seear 1T |
| L.M. Rutledge | L.M. Rutledge | L.M. Rutledge | L.M. Rutledge |
| Lansdowne Road | Cardiff Arms Park | Twickenham | Murrayfield |
| WON 10-6 | WON 13-12 | WON 16-6 | WON 18-9 |
| IRE.: 2PG | WALES: 4PG | ENG.: 1PG 1DG | SCOT.: 1G 1DG |
| NZ: 2DG 1T | NZ: 3PG 1T | NZ: 1G 2PG 1T | NZ: 2G 2PG |
| 4 Nov. 1978 | 11 Nov. 1978 | 25 Nov. 1978 | 9 Dec. 1978 |
| [1]Rep. by B.G. Williams | [1]Rep. by B.J. McKechnie 3PG | | |

Graham Mourie's All Blacks of 1978 created history by becoming the first New Zealand touring side to beat England, Scotland, Ireland and Wales on the same tour. This was a splendid team of all-round strength, much of its success deriving from the astute captaincy of Mourie. There was also thoughtful, tactical appreciation instilled into the side by a fine coach, Jack Gleeson.

In the Tests, a late try by Dalton sealed the Irish match, another late score (by McKechnie) secured a narrow win over Wales, and forward mastery paved the way for successes against England and Scotland. In Dublin, Doug Bruce created a New Zealand record by dropping two goals in an international. Bryan Williams, a powerful runner and useful place-kicker, played the last of his 38 Tests at Murrayfield. The most capped All Black back at the time of his retirement, he had impressed critics throughout the world during an international career which realised 71 points (including ten tries).

|  | 1979 |  | 1979 |  |
|---|---|---|---|---|
| 1st v. FRANCE | 2nd v. FRANCE | v. AUSTRALIA | v. SCOTLAND | v. ENGLAND |
| B.W. Wilson 1c,3pg | B.W. Wilson 1c,3pg | B.W. Wilson 1pg | †R.G. Wilson 2c | R.G. Wilson 2pg |
| S.S. Wilson 1t | S.S. Wilson 1t | S.S. Wilson | S.S. Wilson 1t | B.R. Ford |
| B.J. Robertson | B.J. Robertson | B.J. Robertson | G.R. Cunningham | S.S. Wilson |
| †M.G. Watts 1t | M.G. Watts | †G.R. Cunningham | †B.G. Fraser | B.G. Fraser |
| J.L. Jaffray | J.L. Jaffray | M.B. Taylor 1dg | M.B. Taylor | G.R. Cunningham |
| †M.B. Taylor | M.B. Taylor | B.J. McKechnie | †E.J. Dunn 1t | M.B. Taylor |
| M.W. Donaldson 1t | M.W. Donaldson | M.W. Donaldson | D.S. Loveridge 1t[1] | D.S. Loveridge |
| B.R. Johnstone | B.R. Johnstone | W.K. Bush | B.R. Johnstone | B.R. Johnstone |
| A.G. Dalton | A.G. Dalton | J.E. Black | A.G. Dalton | †P.H. Sloane |
| G.A. Knight | G.A. Knight | G.A. Knight | †J.E. Spiers | J.E. Spiers |
| A.M. Haden | A.M. Haden | A.M. Haden | †J.K. Fleming | J.K. Fleming 1t |
| F.J. Oliver[1] | F.J. Oliver | †M.J. McCool | A.M. Haden | A.M. Haden |
| L.M. Rutledge | L.M. Rutledge | L.M. Rutledge | K.W. Stewart | K.W. Stewart |
| G.A. Seear | G.A. Seear | G.A. Seear | †M.G. Mexted 1t | M.G. Mexted |
| *G.N.K. Mourie | *G.N.K. Mourie 1t | *G.N.K. Mourie | *G.N.K. Mourie | *G.N.K. Mourie |
| Christchurch | Auckland | Sydney | Murrayfield | Twickenham |
| WON 23-9 | LOST 19-24 | LOST 6-12 | WON 20-6 | WON 10-9 |
| NZ: 1g 3pg 2t | NZ: 1g 3pg 1t | Aust.: 3pg 1dg | Scot.: 2pg | Eng.: 3pg |
| Fr.: 1g 1dg | Fr.: 1g 1pg 1dg 3t | NZ: 1pg 1dg | NZ: 2g 2t | NZ: 2pg 1t |
| 7 Jul. 1979 | 14 Jul. 1979 | 28 Jul. 1979 | 10 Nov. 1979 | 24 Nov. 1979 |
| [1]Rep. by †W.G. Graham |  |  | [1]Rep. by M.W Donaldson |  |

This was a mixed year for the All Blacks, who played twice at home against France, visited Australia for a single Test in Sydney (on account of a policy in which the New Zealand and Australian Unions agreed to play a Test with each other every season that no tour between the nations was scheduled), and made a short tour of England and Scotland before Christmas.

Graham Mourie captained in all five Tests, though an experimental side was well beaten at Auckland and surrendered the Bledisloe Cup (for the first time since 1949) in a dour match at Sydney. A side containing six new caps scored four tries in a convincing win against Scotland, however, and England were narrowly beaten in an uninspiring Test at Twickenham.

Murray Mexted, who scored a fine try from a line-out on his Test debut, is the son of 1950 All Black Graham Mexted. Mexted junior enjoyed a successful career as a mobile, intelligent number-eight, becoming New Zealand's most-capped player in that position.

|  | 1980 |  | 1980 |
|---|---|---|---|
| 1st v. AUSTRALIA | 2nd v. AUSTRALIA | 3rd v. AUSTRALIA | v. WALES |
| †B.W. Codlin 3pg | B.W. Codlin 2pg,1c | B.W. Codlin 2pg | †D.L. Rollerson 1pg,2c |
| S.S. Wilson | †T.M. Twigden | T.M. Twigden[1] | S.S. Wilson |
| G.R. Cunningham | B.J. Robertson | B.J. Robertson | B.J. Robertson |
| M.G. Watts | M.G. Watts | B.G. Fraser 1t | B.G. Fraser 1t |
| M.B. Taylor | G.R. Cunningham | †L.M. Cameron | W.M. Osborne |
| †W.R. Smith | M.B. Taylor | †N.H. Allen | N.H. Allen 1t |
| *D.S. Loveridge | *D.S. Loveridge | *D.S. Loveridge | D.S. Loveridge |
| J.C. Ashworth | J.C. Ashworth | J.C. Ashworth | †R.C. Ketels |
| †H.R. Reid | H.R. Reid 1t | J.E. Black | H.R. Reid 1t |
| G.A. Knight | G.A. Knight | G.A. Knight | G.A. Knight |
| A.M. Haden | A.M. Haden | A.M. Haden | A.M. Haden |
| J.K. Fleming | J.K. Fleming | J.K. Fleming | †G. Higginson |
| †M.W. Shaw | M.W. Shaw | L.M. Rutledge | *G.N.K. Mourie 1t |
| M.G. Mexted | M.G. Mexted | M.G. Mexted[2] | M.G. Mexted |
| L.M. Rutledge | L.M. Rutledge | †G.R. Hines | M.W. Shaw |
| Sydney | Brisbane | Sydney | Cardiff Arms Park |
| LOST 9-13 | WON 12-9 | LOST 10-26 | WON 23-3 |
| Aust.: 1g 1dg 1t | Aust.: 1g 1pg | Aust.: 2g 1pg 1dg 2t | Wales: 1pg |
| NZ: 3pg | NZ: 1g 2pg | NZ: 2pg 1t | NZ: 2g 1pg 2t |
| 21 Jun. 1980 | 28 Jun. 1980 | 12 Jul. 1980 | 1 Nov. 1980 |
|  |  | [1]Rep. by M.G. Watts |  |
|  |  | [2]Rep. by M.W. Shaw |  |

The disappointment of New Zealand's failure to regain the Bledisloe Cup on the tour to Australia was offset by the highly successful trip to Wales in October, when the All Blacks were guests for the WRU's Centenary.

Unfortunately, several of the leading players were unable to make the trip to Australia. Loveridge captained the side in the absence of Mourie, but further ill-luck befell the tourists when Stuart Wilson, Bernie Fraser and Wayne Smith suffered injuries. Defeat in the Test series meant that, for the first time, New Zealand had failed at consecutive attempts to win the Bledisloe Cup.

A stronger side completed the tour of Wales with a huge win by twenty points in the Test. One of the best players at Cardiff was Nicky Allen, the creative Counties five-eighth. Alas, in 1984 Allen was the victim of a tragic accident sustained on the rugby field: in a tackle whilst playing in a club game in NSW, he lost consciousness after striking his head on the ground, and died from the effects of serious head injuries.

## 1981

| 1st v. SCOTLAND | 2nd v. SCOTLAND | 1st v. S.AFRICA | 2nd v. S.AFRICA | 3rd v. S.AFRICA |
|---|---|---|---|---|
| †A.R. HEWSON 1PG | A.R. HEWSON 2T,6C | A.R. HEWSON¹ | A.R. HEWSON 4PG | A.R. HEWSON 3PG |
| S.S. WILSON 1T | S.S. WILSON 3T | †F.A. WOODMAN | F.A. WOODMAN | S.S. WILSON 1T |
| B.J. ROBERTSON | B.J. ROBERTSON 1T | S.S. WILSON 1T² | S.S. WILSON | L.M. CAMERON |
| B.G. FRASER | B.G. FRASER | B.G. FRASER | B.G. FRASER | B.G. FRASER |
| †A.C.R. JEFFERD | A.C.R. JEFFERD | A.C.R. JEFFERD | L.M. CAMERON | †S.T. POKERE |
| E.J. DUNN | D.L. ROLLERSON | D.L. ROLLERSON 1C,1T | D.L. ROLLERSON | D.L. ROLLERSON 1DG,1PG,1C |
| D.S. LOVERIDGE 1T | D.S. LOVERIDGE | D.S. LOVERIDGE | D.S. LOVERIDGE | D.S. LOVERIDGE¹ |
| R.C. KETELS | R.C. KETELS | J.C. ASHWORTH | J.C. ASHWORTH | J.C. ASHWORTH |
| A.G. DALTON | A.G. DALTON | *A.G. DALTON | *A.G. DALTON | *A.G. DALTON |
| G.A. KNIGHT | G.A. KNIGHT | G.A. KNIGHT | †G.A.J. BURGESS | G.A. KNIGHT 1T |
| †H. RICKIT | H. RICKIT | G. HIGGINSON | F.J. OLIVER | †G.W. WHETTON |
| G. HIGGINSON | A.M. HADEN | A.M. HADEN | A.M. HADEN | A.M. HADEN |
| M.W. SHAW | M.W. SHAW | M.W. SHAW 1T | M.W. SHAW | †G.H. OLD |
| M.G. MEXTED | M.G. MEXTED | M.G. MEXTED | M.G. MEXTED | M.G. MEXTED |
| *G.N.K. MOURIE | *G.N.K. MOURIE 1T | K.W. STEWART | K.W. STEWART | †F.N.K. SHELFORD |
| Dunedin | Auckland | Christchurch | Wellington | Auckland |
| WON 11-4 | WON 40-15 | WON 14-9 | LOST 12-24 | WON 25-22 |
| NZ: 1PG 2T | NZ: 6G 1T | NZ: 1G 2T | NZ: 4PG | NZ: 1G 4PG 1DG 1T |
| SCOT.: 1T | SCOT.: 1G 1DG 2PG | SA: 1G 1DG | SA.: 1G 1DG 5PG | SA: 2G 2PG 1T |
| 13 Jun. 1981 | 20 Jun. 1981 | 15 Aug. 1981 | 29 Aug. 1981 | 12 Sep. 1981 |
| | | ¹Rep. by B.J. McKechnie ²Rep. by L.M. Cameron | | ¹Rep. by M.W. Donaldson |

New Zealand played five home Tests for the first time this season. The Scots were beaten in a two-Test series in June, and two months later the All Blacks won an exciting series with the Springboks by the last kick of the rubber. New full-back Allan Hewson was the find of the series. In the huge victory against Scotland at Auckland – New Zealand's highest score in a Test for 68 years – Hewson became the first New Zealander to convert six tries in a Test, and the first New Zealand full-back to score two tries in an international. Bruce Robertson stepped down from Test rugby following the Scottish internationals, declaring that he would not play against South Africa for moral reasons. In a brilliant career dating from 1972, he had become his nation's most-capped centre.

## 1981

| v. ROMANIA | 1st v. FRANCE | 2nd v. FRANCE |
|---|---|---|
| A.R. HEWSON 1PG | A.R. HEWSON 2PG,1DG | A.R. HEWSON 2PG,2C |
| S.S. WILSON | S.S. WILSON 1T | F.A. WOODMAN |
| †J.L.B. SALMON 1T | J.L.B. SALMON | S.S. WILSON 1T |
| B.G. FRASER | B.G. FRASER | B.G. FRASER¹ |
| L.M. CAMERON | †A.M. STONE | A.M. STONE |
| D.L. ROLLERSON 1DG | B.J. McKECHNIE¹ | D.L. ROLLERSON |
| D.S. LOVERIDGE | D.S. LOVERIDGE | D.S. LOVERIDGE |
| R.C. KETELS | R.C. KETELS | †T.T. KOTEKA |
| *A.G. DALTON 1T | A.G. DALTON | A.G. DALTON |
| J.E. SPIERS | J.E. SPIERS | J.E. SPIERS |
| G.W. WHETTON | G.W. WHETTON | G.W. WHETTON |
| A.M. HADEN | A.M. HADEN | A.M. HADEN |
| M.W. SHAW | *G.N.K. MOURIE | M.W. SHAW 1T‡ |
| M.G. MEXTED¹ | M.G. MEXTED | M.G. MEXTED |
| F.N.K. SHELFORD | M.W. SHAW | *G.N.K. MOURIE |
| Bucharest | Toulouse | Parc des Princes |
| WON 14-6 | WON 13-9 | WON 18-6 |
| ROMANIA: 1PG 1DG | FR.: 2PG 1DG | FR.: 2PG |
| NZ: 1PG 1DG 2T | NZ: 2PG 1DG 1T | NZ: 2G‡ 2PG |
| 24 Oct. 1981 | 14 Nov. 1981 | 21 Nov. 1981 |
| ¹Rep. by G.H. Old | ¹Rep. by D.L. Rollerson | ¹Rep. by J.L.B. Salmon ‡Includes penalty try |

The All Blacks, led by Graham Mourie, undertook a ten-match tour of Europe in October and November. The Test with Romania was given full international status by the NZRFU, and the new opponents proved difficult to overcome. Two gruelling Tests followed in France, where the All Blacks' forward dominance helped them to deserved victories. Jamie Salmon, an English-born centre who had been playing provincial rugby for Wellington, made his debut against Romania, scoring a try. Later he played for the Harlequins club in London, and became the first New Zealand Test player to be capped by England when he played against the All Blacks in 1985.

## 1982

| 1st v. AUSTRALIA | 2nd v. AUSTRALIA | 3rd v. AUSTRALIA |
|---|---|---|
| A.R. Hewson | A.R. Hewson | A.R. Hewson |
| 1PG,2C | 2PG,1C | 1T,2C,5PG,1DG |
| | | |
| S.S. Wilson | S.S. Wilson | S.S. Wilson |
| S.T. Pokere 1T | S.T. Pokere | S.T. Pokere |
| B.G. Fraser 1T | B.G. Fraser 1T | B.G. Fraser |
| | | |
| W.M. Osborne | N.M. Taylor | W.M. Osborne |
| W.R. Smith | W.R. Smith | W.R. Smith 1DG |
| D.S. Loveridge | D.S. Loveridge | D.S. Loveridge |
| | | |
| J.C. Ashworth | J.C. Ashworth | T.T. Koteka |
| A.G. Dalton | A.G. Dalton | A.G. Dalton |
| G.A. Knight | G.A. Knight | G.A. Knight |
| G. Higginson | A.M. Haden | A.M. Haden |
| A.M. Haden[1] | G. Higginson | G.W. Whetton |
| M.W. Shaw | M.W. Shaw 1T | M.W. Shaw 1T |
| M.G. Mexted 1T | M.G. Mexted | M.G. Mexted |
| *G.N.K. Mourie 1T | *G.N.K. Mourie | *G.N.K. Mourie |
| Christchurch | Wellington | Auckland |
| WON 23-16 | LOST 16-19 | WON 33-18 |
| NZ: 2G 1PG 2T | NZ: 1G 2PG 1T | NZ: 2G 5PG 2DG |
| AUST.: 1G 2PG 1T | AUST.: 1G 3PG 1T | AUST.: 1G 3PG 1DG |
| 14 Aug. 1982 | 28 Aug. 1982 | 11 Sep. 1982 |

[1]Rep. by G.H. Old

New Zealand regained the Bledisloe Cup, winning the rubber with Australia 2-1. The series generated much interest, partly because at full strength the All Blacks were a formidable combination, but also because the Wallabies played exciting, attacking football which thrilled New Zealand crowds. 52,000, a record for an Australia-New Zealand Test in New Zealand, attended the final Test at Auckland.

Several interesting milestones were reached in the series: New Zealand played its 200th international in the opening Test at Christchurch; Allan Hewson created a new world record by scoring 26 points in the Test at Auckland; and for the first time New Zealand completed a Test series without introducing a single new cap.

Mark Shaw had a brilliant series for the All Blacks. Indeed, his uncompromising style in the loose and his fitness and speed in support helped make the back row of Shaw, Mexted and Mourie one of the most formidable in world rugby in the early 1980s.

## 1983

| 1st v. BRITISH ISLES | 2nd v. BRITISH ISLES | 3rd v. BRITISH ISLES | 4th v. BRITISH ISLES |
|---|---|---|---|
| A.R. Hewson 3PG,1DG | A.R. Hewson 1PG,1C | A.R. Hewson 3PG,1C | A.R. Hewson 1T,4C,2PG |
| | | | |
| S.S. Wilson | S.S. Wilson | S.S. Wilson 1T | S.S. Wilson 3T |
| S.T. Pokere | S.T. Pokere | S.T. Pokere | S.T. Pokere |
| B.G. Fraser | B.G. Fraser | B.G. Fraser | B.G. Fraser |
| | | | |
| †W.T. Taylor | W.T. Taylor | W.T. Taylor | W.T. Taylor |
| †I.T.W. Dunn | W.R. Smith | W.R. Smith[1] | I.T.W. Dunn |
| D.S. Loveridge | D.S. Loveridge 1T | D.S. Loveridge | D.S. Loveridge |
| | | | |
| J.C. Ashworth | J.C. Ashworth | J.C. Ashworth | J.C. Ashworth |
| *A.G. Dalton | *A.G. Dalton | *A.G. Dalton | *A.G. Dalton |
| G.A. Knight | G.A. Knight | G.A. Knight | G.A. Knight |
| G.W. Whetton | G.W. Whetton | G.W. Whetton | G.W. Whetton |
| A.M. Haden | A.M. Haden | A.M. Haden | A.M. Haden 1T |
| M.W. Shaw 1T | M.W. Shaw | M.W. Shaw | M.W. Shaw |
| M.G. Mexted | M.G. Mexted | M.G. Mexted | M.G. Mexted |
| †M.J.B. Hobbs | M.J.B. Hobbs | M.J.B. Hobbs | M.J.B. Hobbs 1T |
| Christchurch | Wellington | Dunedin | Auckland |
| WON 16-12 | WON 9-0 | WON 15-8 | WON 38-6 |
| NZ: 3PG 1DG 1T | NZ: 1G 1PG | NZ: 1G 3PG | NZ: 4G 2PG 2T |
| B.Is.: 3PG 1DG | B.Is.: NIL | B.Is.: 2T | B.Is.: 2PG |
| 4 Jun. 1983 | 18 Jun. 1983 | 2 Jul. 1983 | 16 Jul. 1983 |

[1]Rep. by A.M. Stone

The selectors named three new caps for the opening Test of the series against the Lions – Jock Hobbs entered the side at flanker, Graham Mourie having retired; and there were two new five-eighths, each of whom had elder brothers who were New Zealand internationals: Ian Dunn was a brother of Eddie (1979); Warwick Taylor was the brother of Murray (1979).

As in 1966, New Zealand won the rubber 4-0, and other parallels with the 1966 series were that the same pack was retained for each Test and only 16 players were selected for the four Tests (though a seventeenth, Stone of Waikato, was required as a replacement at Dunedin).

This was one of the finest New Zealand sides since the 1960s. In addition to forward power in the tight and dominance in the loose – traditional strengths of New Zealand rugby – the 1983 backs displayed imagination in their attacking play, accurate handling skills and deadly finishing. Wilson, in particular, enjoyed a successful series, his tally of four tries helping him to become the leading New Zealand try-scorer in international matches.

| 1983 | 1983 | |
| --- | --- | --- |
| v. AUSTRALIA | v. SCOTLAND | v. ENGLAND |
| A.R. Hewson 4PG,1C | †R.M. Deans 3PG,2C | R.M. Deans 1C,1PG |
| S.S. Wilson | *S.S. Wilson | *S.S. Wilson |
| S.T. Pokere | S.T. Pokere | S.T. Pokere |
| B.G. Fraser | B.G. Fraser 2T | B.G. Fraser |
| W.T. Taylor 1T | W.T. Taylor[1] | C.I. Green |
| I.T.W. Dunn | W.R. Smith | W.R. Smith |
| D.S. Loveridge | †A.J. Donald | A.J. Donald |
| J.C. Ashworth | †B. McGrattan | B. McGrattan |
| *A.G. Dalton | H.R. Reid | H.R. Reid |
| G.A. Knight | †S. Crichton | S. Crichton[1] |
| G. Higginson | †G.J. Braid | G.J. Braid |
| A.M. Haden | †A. Anderson | A. Anderson |
| M.W. Shaw | M.W. Shaw | M.W. Shaw |
| M.G. Mexted | M.G. Mexted | M.G. Mexted |
| M.J.B. Hobbs | M.J.B. Hobbs 1T | M.J.B. Hobbs |
| Sydney | Murrayfield | Twickenham |
| WON 18-8 | DRAWN 25-25 | LOST 9-15 |
| AUST.: 2T | SCOT.: 2DG 5PG 1T | ENG. 1G 3PG |
| NZ: 1G 4PG | NZ: 2G 3PG 1T | NZ: 1G 1PG |
| 20 Aug. 1983 | 12 Nov. 1983 | 19 Nov. 1983 |
| | [1]Rep. by ‡C.I. Green | [1]Rep. by †M.G. Davie 1T |

Following the victories over the Lions, the All Blacks retained the Bledisloe Cup with a sound win against Australia at Sydney – New Zealand's first Test success at the ground since 1974.

The All Blacks were scheduled to tour Argentina late in 1983, but difficulties concerning visas forced the NZRFU to cancel the proposed tour. Instead, a tour of eight games in England and Scotland was arranged, but the unavailability of seven of the players who had featured in the five wins against the Lions and Australia meant that an inexperienced party undertook the tour.

For the first time, a New Zealand team failed to win a Test on a tour of Britain, Stuart Wilson's team drawing with Scotland and losing to England at Twickenham – New Zealand's first defeat in Britain since December 1953. The English match also marked the end of Wilson's distinguished career.

| 1984 | | 1984 | | |
| --- | --- | --- | --- | --- |
| 1st v. FRANCE | 2nd v. FRANCE | 1st v. AUSTRALIA | 2nd v. AUSTRALIA | 3rd v. AUSTRALIA |
| A.R. Hewson 2PG | A.R. Hewson 5PG,2C | A.R. Hewson 2PG,1DG | R.M. Deans 5PG | R.M. Deans 5PG,1C |
| †J.J. Kirwan | J.J. Kirwan | B.W. Smith[1] | †M. Clamp | M. Clamp 1T |
| S.T. Pokere | S.T. Pokere | C.I. Green | S.T. Pokere 1T | S.T. Pokere |
| †B.W. Smith | B.W. Smith 1T | B.G. Fraser | C.I. Green | C.I. Green |
| W.T. Taylor 1T | W.T. Taylor 1T | W.T. Taylor | W.T. Taylor | A.M. Stone 1T |
| W.R. Smith | W.R. Smith | W.R. Smith | W.R. Smith | W.R. Smith |
| A.J. Donald | A.J. Donald | A.J. Donald | A.J. Donald | A.J. Donald |
| J.C. Ashworth | J.C. Ashworth | J.C. Ashworth | J.C. Ashworth | J.C. Ashworth |
| *A.G. Dalton | *A.G. Dalton 1T | *A.G. Dalton | *A.G. Dalton | *A.G. Dalton |
| G.A. Knight | G.A. Knight | G.A. Knight | G.A. Knight | G.A. Knight |
| G.W. Whetton | G.W. Whetton | G.W. Whetton | A. Anderson | G.W. Whetton |
| A.M. Haden | A.M. Haden | A. Anderson | G.W. Whetton | A. Anderson |
| M.W. Shaw | M.W. Shaw | M.W. Shaw[2] | F.N.K. Shelford | M.J.B. Hobbs[1] |
| M.G. Mexted | M.G. Mexted | M.G. Mexted | M.G. Mexted | M.G. Mexted |
| M.J.B. Hobbs | M.J.B. Hobbs | M.J.B. Hobbs | M.J.B. Hobbs | F.N.K. Shelford |
| Christchurch | Auckland | Sydney | Brisbane | Sydney |
| WON 10-9 | WON 31-18 | LOST 9-16 | WON 19-15 | WON 25-24 |
| NZ: 2PG 1T | NZ: 2G 5PG 1T | AUST.: 1G 1PG 1DG 1T | AUST.: 1G 3PG | AUST.: 1G 6PG |
| FR.: 1G 1DG | FR.: 2PG 3T | NZ: 2PG 1DG | NZ: 5PG 1T | NZ: 1G 5PG 1T |
| 16 Jun. 1984 | 23 Jun. 1984 | 21 Jul. 1984 | 4 Aug. 1984 | 18 Aug. 1984 |
| | | [1]Rep. by R.M. Deans [2]Rep. by †A.J. Whetton | | [1]Rep. by A.J. Whetton |

New Zealand opened the season with two new caps, Kirwan and Smith on the wings, in the Test against France at Christchurch. A narrow victory by a point was due to the ill-luck of the French, who really deserved victory. Several times in injury time the French fly-half went close with drops at goal, and once Berbizier knocked-on when the goal-line was at his mercy. Stronger forward play and two opportunist tries by Smith and Taylor enabled the All Blacks to win comfortably at Auckland.

Later in the season Dalton led his side on a 14-match tour of Australia in which the All Blacks won 13 of the games. In the Test series the Australians won against an ill-prepared All Black side at Sydney before superior forward play by the New Zealanders helped to level the series in the second Test. Then, in a tense final Test punctuated by too many penalty kicks (of which eleven were successful), the All Blacks retained the Bledisloe Cup with a 25-24 win. At Sydney, history was made when Alan Whetton replaced Mark Shaw and joined his brother in the All Black pack: they became the first twins to appear together for New Zealand in a Test.

## 1985 | | | 1985 |

| 1st v. ENGLAND | 2nd v. ENGLAND | v. AUSTRALIA | 1st v. ARGENTINA | 2nd v. ARGENTINA |
|---|---|---|---|---|
| †K.J. CROWLEY 6PG | K.J. CROWLEY 3PG,3C | K.J. CROWLEY 2PG | K.J. CROWLEY 1C,1T,4PG | K.J. CROWLEY 1PG,1C |
| J.J. KIRWAN | J.J. KIRWAN 1T | J.J. KIRWAN | J.J. KIRWAN 2T | J.J. KIRWAN 2T |
| S.T. POKERE | S.T. POKERE | S.T. POKERE | †V.L.J. SIMPSON | V.L.J. SIMPSON |
| C.I. GREEN | C.I. GREEN 2T | C.I. GREEN 1T | C.I. GREEN | C.I. GREEN 1T |
| W.T. TAYLOR | W.T. TAYLOR | W.T. TAYLOR | W.T. TAYLOR | W.T. TAYLOR |
| W.R. SMITH | W.R. SMITH 1DG | W.R. SMITH | †G.J. FOX 1DG | W.R. SMITH |
| †D.E. KIRK | D.E. KIRK | D.E. KIRK | D.E. KIRK | D.S. LOVERIDGE |
| J.C. ASHWORTH | J.C. ASHWORTH | J.C. ASHWORTH | B. McGRATTAN | B. McGRATTAN |
| *A.G. DALTON | *A.G. DALTON | *A.G. DALTON | H.R. REID | H.R. REID |
| G.A. KNIGHT | G.A. KNIGHT | G.A. KNIGHT | †S.C. McDOWELL | S.C. McDOWELL |
| †M.J. PIERCE | M.J. PIERCE | M.J. PIERCE | A.M. HADEN | A.M. HADEN |
| G.W. WHETTON | G.W. WHETTON | G.W. WHETTON | M.J. PIERCE[1] | G.W. WHETTON |
| M.W. SHAW | M.W. SHAW 1T | M.W. SHAW[1] | M.W. SHAW | M.W. SHAW |
| M.G. MEXTED | M.G. MEXTED 1T | M.G. MEXTED | M.G. MEXTED | M.G MEXTED 1T |
| M.J.B. HOBBS | M.J.B. HOBBS 1T | M.J.B. HOBBS | *M.J.B. HOBBS 1T | *M.J.B. HOBBS |
| Christchurch | Wellington | Auckland | Buenos Aires | Buenos Aires |
| WON 18-13 | WON 42-15 | WON 10-9 | WON 33-20 | DRAWN 21-21 |
| NZ: 6PG | NZ: 3G 3PG 1DG 3T | NZ: 2PG 1T | ARG.: 3PG 1DG 2T | ARG.: 4PG 3DG |
| ENG.: 1G 1PG 1T | ENG.: 2G 1DG | AUST.: 1G 1PG | NZ: 1G 4PG 1DG 3T | NZ: 1G 1PG 3T |
| 1 Jun. 1985 | 8 Jun. 1985 | 29 Jun. 1985 | 26 Oct. 1985 | 2 Nov. 1985 |
| | | [1]Rep. by A.J. Whetton | [1]Rep. by A.J. Whetton | |

A weak England side provided New Zealand's first international opposition of the season. In the opening Test at Christchurch, however, the English acquitted themselves well, but despite scoring the only tries of the Test found themselves outpointed by New Zealand's new full-back, Kieran Crowley. Crowley scored all 18 of his side's points, becoming the first player to kick six penalty goals on debut in an international.

New Zealand ran up a record total for a home Test by scoring 42 points in the second international at Wellington. Then, a few weeks later in Auckland, an unchanged side struggled in a dour match with Australia to retain the Bledisloe Cup.

The NZRFU were due to send a side to South Africa later in the season, but a cancellation was forced on technical grounds. Instead, New Zealand undertook a full-scale tour of Argentina, and played their first official Tests against the Pumas in October and November. The standard of Argentine rugby was high and the All Blacks, after winning a high-scoring first Test, were happy to finish the tour with a 21-21 draw in the second of the internationals.

## 1986

| v. FRANCE | 1st v. AUSTRALIA | 2nd v. AUSTRALIA | 3rd v. AUSTRALIA |
|---|---|---|---|
| †G.J.L. COOPER 1DG 1PG 1C | G.J.L. COOPER 2PG 1C | G.J.L. COOPER 2PG 1DG | K.J. CROWLEY 3PG |
| J.J. KIRWAN | J.J. KIRWAN | J.J. KIRWAN | J.J. KIRWAN |
| †J.T. STANLEY | J.T. STANLEY | J.T. STANLEY | J.T. STANLEY |
| †T.J. WRIGHT | T.J. WRIGHT | C.I. GREEN | C.I. GREEN |
| A.M. STONE | A.M. STONE | W.T. TAYLOR | A.M. STONE |
| †F.M. BOTICA 2DG | F.M. BOTICA | F.M. BOTICA | F.M. BOTICA[1] |
| *D.E. KIRK | *D.E. KIRK | *D.E. KIRK 1T | *D.E. KIRK |
| B. McGRATTAN | B. McGRATTAN | S.C. McDOWELL | S.C. McDOWELL |
| †S.B.T. FITZPATRICK | S.B.T. FITZPATRICK | H.R. REID | H.R. REID |
| †K.G. BOROEVICH | K.G. BOROEVICH | G.A. KNIGHT | G.A. KNIGHT |
| †A.T. EARL | †M.W. SPEIGHT | G.W. WHETTON | G.W. WHETTON |
| †G. MacPHERSON | †B.L. ANDERSON | M.J. PIERCE | M.J. PIERCE |
| †B.A. HARVEY | A.T. EARL | A.J. WHETTON | M.W. SHAW |
| †M.R. BREWER 1T | M.R. BREWER | M.R. BREWER | M.R. BREWER |
| †M. BROOKE-COWDEN | M. BROOKE-COWDEN 1T | M.J.B. HOBBS | M.J.B. HOBBS |
| Christchurch | Wellington | Dunedin | Auckland |
| WON 18-9 | LOST 12-13 | WON 13-12 | LOST 9-22 |
| NZ: 1G 1PG 3DG | NZ: 1G 2PG | NZ: 2PG 1DG 1T | NZ: 3PG |
| FR.: 3DG | AUS.: 1G 1PG 1T | AUS.: 3PG 1DG | AUS.: 1G 4PG 1T |
| 28 Jun. 1986 | 9 Aug. 1986 | 23 Aug. 1986 | 6 Sep. 1986 |
| | | | [1]Rep. by †M.J. Berry |

31 of New Zealand's leading players had visited South Africa in May under the name of 'Cavaliers'. The tour had been arranged outside the jurisdiction of the NZRFU, but the Union subsequently launched an inquiry to investigate whether International Board Laws had been breached by the tourists, and each of the 31 players was banned from selection for the first Test of the New Zealand season. Thus a side of 11 new caps, and with an average age of 23, took the field against France, the European champions, at Christchurch. But the young All Blacks were inspired to play well above their reputations and an early drop-goal by Cooper and a storming try by Brewer set the All Blacks on course for a fine win.

In the series which followed with Australia, New Zealand rehabilitated several of the South African tourists, but their plans and preparations for the World Cup were severely dented by an athletic and well-organised Wallaby side which went on to win the Bledisloe Cup. It was New Zealand's first defeat in a home Test series with Australia since 1949.

## 1986

| 1st v. FRANCE | 2nd v. FRANCE |
|---|---|
| K.J. CROWLEY 3PG 1DG | K.J. CROWLEY 1PG |
| | |
| J.J. KIRWAN | J.J. KIRWAN |
| J.T. STANLEY | J.T. STANLEY |
| C.I. GREEN | C.I. GREEN |
| | |
| A.M. STONE 1DG | A.M. STONE |
| F.M. BOTICA | F.M. BOTICA |
| D.E. KIRK | D.E. KIRK |
| | |
| S.C. McDOWELL | S.C. McDOWELL |
| S.B.T. FITZPATRICK | S.B.T. FITZPATRICK |
| †J.A. DRAKE | J.A. DRAKE |
| G.W. WHETTON | M.J. PIERCE |
| M.J. PIERCE | G.W. WHETTON[1] |
| M.R. BREWER | M.R. BREWER |
| †W.T. SHELFORD 1T | W.T. SHELFORD[2] |
| *M.J.B. HOBBS | *M.J.B. HOBBS |

| Toulouse | Nantes |
|---|---|
| WON 19-7 | LOST 3-16 |
| FR.: 1PG 1T | FR.: 1G 2PG 1T |
| NZ: 3PG 2DG 1T | NZ: 1PG |
| 8 Nov. 1986 | 15 Nov. 1986 |

[1]Rep. by A.T. Earl
[2]Rep. by K.G. Boroevich

New Zealand made an impressive start to their short continental tour in the autumn of 1986, winning their first seven matches. The nucleus of the side was young and inexperienced, though the tourists emerged from the tour with a creditable record and sufficient promise to augur well for New Zealand's World Cup challenge.

Jock Hobbs proved an astute captain whose concentration on control in the tight and loose paved the way for a sound victory in the opening Test at Toulouse. The French were never permitted to settle and with the All Black back row dominant, the threat of the exciting French threequarters was completely stifled.

New Zealand fielded the same fifteen, including an all-Auckland front-row, for the second Test at Nantes a week later. But this time, with fitness doubts over a couple of players, and two injuries compelling substitutions during the match, the All Blacks found themselves surprisingly beaten at their own controlled game. In victory, France had inflicted their biggest winning points margin ever against the All Blacks.

# NEW ZEALAND MATCH RECORDS

## MATCH RESULTS 1903 to 1987

| Match | Date | Opponents | T | C | D | P | Pts | T | C | D | P | Pts | Result | Venue | Captain |
|---|---|---|---|---|---|---|---|---|---|---|---|---|---|---|---|
| | | | | | For | | | | | Against | | | | | |
| 1 | 15.8.1903 | Australia | 3 | 1 | ** | | 1 22 | — | — | — | | 1 3 | Won | Sydney | J. Duncan |
| 2 | 13.8.1904 | Great Britain | 2 | — | — | | 1 9 | — | — | — | | 1 3 | Won | Wellington | J. W. Stead |
| 3 | 2.9.1905 | Australia | 4 | 1 | — | — | 14 | 1 | — | — | — | 3 | Won | Dunedin | J. C. Spencer |
| 4 | 18.11.1905 | Scotland | 4 | — | — | — | 12 | 1 | — | 1 | — | 7 | Won | Edinburgh | D. Gallaher |
| 5 | 25.11.1905 | Ireland | 3 | 3 | — | — | 15 | — | — | — | — | 0 | Won | Dublin | J. W. Stead |
| 6 | 2.12.1905 | England | 5 | — | — | — | 15 | — | — | — | — | 0 | Won | Crystal Palace | D. Gallaher |
| 7 | 16.12.1905 | Wales | — | — | — | — | 0 | 1 | — | — | — | 3 | Lost | Cardiff | D. Gallaher |
| 8 | 1.1.1906 | France | 10 | 4 | — | — | 38 | 2 | 1 | — | — | 8 | Won | Parc des Princes | D. Gallaher |
| 9 | 20.7.1907 | Australia | 6 | 4 | — | — | 26 | — | — | * | 1 | 6 | Won | Sydney | J. Hunter |
| 10 | 3.8.1907 | Australia | 4 | 1 | — | — | 14 | 1 | 1 | — | — | 5 | Won | Brisbane | J. Hunter |
| 11 | 10.8.1907 | Australia | 1 | 1 | — | — | 5 | 1 | 1 | — | — | 5 | Drawn | Sydney | J. Hunter |
| 12 | 6.6.1908 | Anglo Welsh | 7 | 4 | — | 1 | 32 | 1 | 1 | — | — | 5 | Won | Dunedin | J. W. Stead |
| 13 | 27.6.1908 | Anglo Welsh | — | — | — | 1 | 3 | 1 | — | — | — | 3 | Drawn | Wellington | J. Hunter |
| 14 | 25.7.1908 | Anglo Welsh | 9 | 1 | — | — | 29 | — | — | — | — | 0 | Won | Auckland | J. W. Stead |
| 15 | 25.6.1910 | Australia | 2 | — | — | — | 6 | — | — | — | — | 0 | Won | Sydney | F. Roberts |
| 16 | 27.6.1910 | Australia | — | — | — | — | 0 | 3 | 1 | — | 1 | 11 | Lost | Sydney | F. Roberts |
| 17 | 2.7.1910 | Australia | 8 | 2 | — | — | 28 | 2 | 2 | — | 1 | 13 | Won | Sydney | F. Roberts |
| 18 | 6.9.1913 | Australia | 8 | 3 | — | — | 30 | 1 | 1 | — | — | 5 | Won | Wellington | A. McDonald |
| 19 | 13.9.1913 | Australia | 5 | 3 | 1 | — | 25 | 3 | 2 | — | — | 13 | Won | Dunedin | M. J. O'Leary |
| 20 | 20.9.1913 | Australia | 1 | 1 | — | — | 5 | 4 | 2 | — | — | 16 | Lost | Christchurch | M. J. O'Leary |
| 21 | 15.11.1913 | America | 13 | 6 | — | — | 51 | — | — | — | 1 | 3 | Won | Berkeley | A. McDonald |
| 22 | 18.7.1914 | Australia | 1 | 1 | — | — | 5 | — | — | — | — | 0 | Won | Sydney | R. W. Roberts |
| 23 | 1.8.1914 | Australia | 5 | 1 | — | — | 17 | — | — | — | — | 0 | Won | Brisbane | R. W. Roberts |
| 24 | 15.8.1914 | Australia | 6 | 2 | — | — | 22 | 1 | — | 1 | — | 7 | Won | Sydney | R. W. Roberts |
| 25 | 13.8.1921 | S.A. | 3 | 2 | — | — | 13 | 1 | 1 | — | — | 5 | Won | Dunedin | G. G. Aitken |
| 26 | 27.8.1921 | S.A. | 1 | 1 | — | — | 5 | 1 | 1 | 1 | — | 9 | Lost | Auckland | G. G. Aitken |
| 27 | 17.9.1921 | S.A. | — | — | — | — | 0 | — | — | — | — | 0 | Drawn | Wellington | E. J. Roberts |
| 28 | 1.11.1924 | Ireland | 1 | — | 1 | — | 6 | — | — | — | — | 0 | Won | Dublin | J. Richardson |
| 29 | 29.11.1924 | Wales | 4 | 2 | — | 1 | 19 | — | — | — | — | 0 | Won | Swansea | J. Richardson |
| 30 | 3.1.1925 | England | 4 | 1 | — | 1 | 17 | 2 | 1 | — | 1 | 11 | Won | Twickenham | J. Richardson |
| 31 | 18.1.1925 | France | 8 | 3 | — | — | 30 | 2 | — | — | — | 6 | Won | Toulouse | C. G. Porter |
| 32 | 30.6.1928 | S.A. | — | — | — | — | 0 | 1 | — | 2 | 2 | 17 | Lost | Durban | M. J. Brownlie |
| 33 | 21.7.1928 | S.A. | — | — | 1 | 1 | 7 | — | — | * | 1 | 6 | Won | Johannesburg | M. J. Brownlie |
| 34 | 18.8.1928 | S.A. | 2 | — | — | — | 6 | 3 | 1 | — | — | 11 | Lost | Port Elizabeth | M. J. Brownlie |
| 35 | 1.9.1928 | S.A. | 1 | — | 1 | 2 | 13 | 1 | 1 | — | — | 5 | Won | Cape Town | M. J. Brownlie |
| 36 | 6.7.1929 | Australia | 1 | 1 | — | 1 | 8 | 1 | — | — | 2 | 9 | Lost | Sydney | H. T. Lilburne |
| 37 | 20.7.1929 | Australia | 2 | — | — | 1 | 9 | 3 | 1 | — | 2 | 17 | Lost | Brisbane | C. G. Porter |
| 38 | 27.7.1929 | Australia | 3 | 2 | — | — | 13 | 2 | — | — | 3 | 15 | Lost | Sydney | C. G. Porter |
| 39 | 21.6.1930 | Great Britain | 1 | — | — | — | 3 | 2 | — | — | — | 6 | Lost | Dunedin | C. G. Porter |
| 40 | 5.7.1930 | Great Britain | 2 | 2 | * | — | 13 | 2 | 2 | — | — | 10 | Won | Christchurch | C. G. Porter |
| 41 | 26.7.1930 | Great Britain | 3 | 1 | 1 | — | 15 | 2 | 2 | — | — | 10 | Won | Auckland | C. G. Porter |
| 42 | 9.8.1930 | Great Britain | 6 | 2 | — | — | 22 | 1 | 1 | — | 1 | 8 | Won | Wellington | C. G. Porter |
| 43 | 12.9.1931 | Australia | 2 | 1 | — | 4 | 20 | 3 | 2 | — | — | 13 | Won | Auckland | W. A. Strang |
| 44 | 2.7.1932 | Australia | 3 | 2 | 1 | — | 17 | 4 | 2 | — | 2 | 22 | Lost | Sydney | F. D. Kilby |
| 45 | 16.7.1932 | Australia | 4 | 1 | 1 | 1 | 21 | 1 | — | — | — | 3 | Won | Brisbane | F. D. Kilby |
| 46 | 23.7.1932 | Australia | 5 | 3 | — | — | 21 | 3 | 2 | — | — | 13 | Won | Sydney | F. D. Kilby |
| 47 | 11.8.1934 | Australia | 3 | 1 | — | — | 11 | 4 | 2 | — | 3 | 25 | Lost | Sydney | J. R. Page |
| 48 | 25.8.1934 | Australia | 1 | — | — | — | 3 | 1 | — | — | — | 3 | Drawn | Sydney | F. D. Kilby |
| 49 | 23.11.1935 | Scotland | 4 | 3 | — | — | 18 | 2 | 1 | — | — | 8 | Won | Edinburgh | J. E. Manchester |
| 50 | 7.12.1935 | Ireland | 3 | 1 | — | 2 | 17 | 1 | — | — | 2 | 9 | Won | Dublin | J. E. Manchester |
| 51 | 21.12.1935 | Wales | 2 | 1 | 1 | — | 12 | 3 | 2 | — | — | 13 | Lost | Cardiff | J. E. Manchester |
| 52 | 4.1.1936 | England | — | — | — | — | 0 | 3 | — | 1 | — | 13 | Lost | Twickenham | J. E. Manchester |
| 53 | 5.9.1936 | Australia | 3 | 1 | — | — | 11 | 1 | — | — | 1 | 6 | Won | Wellington | J. L. Griffiths |
| 54 | 12.9.1936 | Australia | 9 | 4 | — | 1 | 38 | 2 | 2 | — | 1 | 13 | Won | Dunedin | J. L. Griffiths |
| 55 | 14.8.1937 | S.A. | 1 | — | 1 | 2 | 13 | 1 | — | 1 | — | 7 | Won | Wellington | R. R. King |
| 56 | 4.9.1937 | S.A. | 2 | — | — | — | 6 | 2 | 2 | — | 1 | 13 | Lost | Christchurch | R. R. King |
| 57 | 25.9.1937 | S.A. | — | — | — | 2 | 6 | 5 | 1 | — | — | 17 | Lost | Auckland | R. R. King |
| 58 | 23.7.1938 | Australia | 4 | 3 | — | 2 | 24 | — | — | — | 3 | 9 | Won | Sydney | N. A. Mitchell |
| 59 | 6.8.1938 | Australia | 4 | 2 | 1 | — | 20 | 3 | 1 | — | 1 | 14 | Won | Brisbane | N. A. Mitchell |
| 60 | 13.8.1938 | Australia | 2 | 1 | — | 2 | 14 | 1 | — | — | 1 | 6 | Won | Sydney | R. M. McKenzie |
| 61 | 14.9.1946 | Australia | 7 | 5 | — | — | 31 | 2 | 1 | — | — | 8 | Won | Dunedin | F. R. Allen |
| 62 | 28.9.1946 | Australia | 1 | 1 | — | 3 | 14 | 2 | 2 | — | — | 10 | Won | Auckland | F. R. Allen |
| 63 | 14.6.1947 | Australia | 3 | 2 | — | — | 13 | 1 | 1 | — | — | 5 | Won | Brisbane | F. R. Allen |
| 64 | 28.6.1947 | Australia | 3 | 3 | — | 4 | 27 | 1 | 1 | — | 3 | 14 | Won | Sydney | F. R. Allen |
| 65 | 16.7.1949 | S.A. | 1 | 1 | 1 | 1 | 11 | — | — | — | 5 | 15 | Lost | Cape Town | F. R. Allen |

*in the drop-goal column denotes a goal from a mark

| Match | Date | Opponents | For | | | | | Against | | | | | Result | Venue | Captain |
|---|---|---|---|---|---|---|---|---|---|---|---|---|---|---|---|
| | | | T | C | D | P | Pts | T | C | D | P | Pts | | | |
| 66 | 13.8.1949 | S.A. | — | — | 1 | 1 | 6 | 2 | — | 1 | 1 | 12 | Lost | Johannesburg | F. R. Allen |
| 67 | 3.9.1949 | Australia | 1 | — | — | 1 | 6 | 3 | 1 | — | — | 11 | Lost | Wellington | J. B. Smith |
| 68 | 3.9.1949 | S.A. | 1 | — | — | — | 3 | — | — | — | 3 | 9 | Lost | Durban | R. R. Elvidge |
| 69 | 17.9.1949 | S.A. | 2 | 1 | — | — | 8 | 1 | 1 | 1 | 1 | 11 | Lost | Port Elizabeth | R. R. Elvidge |
| 70 | 24.9.1949 | Australia | 1 | — | 1 | 1 | 9 | 3 | 2 | — | 1 | 16 | Lost | Auckland | J. B. Smith |
| 71 | 27.5.1950 | British Isles | 2 | — | — | 1 | 9 | 2 | — | — | 1 | 9 | Drawn | Dunedin | R. R. Elvidge |
| 72 | 10.6.1950 | British Isles | 2 | 1 | — | — | 8 | — | — | — | — | 0 | Won | Christchurch | R. R. Elvidge |
| 73 | 1.7.1950 | British Isles | 1 | — | — | 1 | 6 | — | — | — | 1 | 3 | Won | Wellington | R. R. Elvidge |
| 74 | 29.7.1950 | British Isles | 2 | 1 | 1 | — | 11 | 1 | 1 | — | 1 | 8 | Won | Auckland | P. Johnstone |
| 75 | 23.6.1951 | Australia | 1 | 1 | — | 1 | 8 | — | — | — | — | 0 | Won | Sydney | P. Johnstone |
| 76 | 7.7.1951 | Australia | 4 | 1 | 1 | — | 17 | 2 | 1 | — | 1 | 11 | Won | Sydney | P. Johnstone |
| 77 | 21.7.1951 | Australia | 4 | 2 | — | — | 16 | — | — | — | 2 | 6 | Won | Brisbane | P. Johnstone |
| 78 | 6.9.1952 | Australia | 2 | — | — | 1 | 9 | 3 | 1 | 1 | — | 14 | Lost | Christchurch | K. L. Skinner |
| 79 | 13.9.1952 | Australia | 2 | — | 1 | 2 | 15 | 1 | 1 | — | 1 | 8 | Won | Wellington | K. L. Skinner |
| 80 | 19.12.1953 | Wales | 1 | 1 | — | 1 | 8 | 2 | 2 | — | 1 | 13 | Lost | Cardiff | R. C. Stuart |
| 81 | 9.1.1954 | Ireland | 2 | 1 | 1 | 1 | 14 | — | — | — | 1 | 3 | Won | Dublin | R. C. Stuart |
| 82 | 30.1.1954 | England | 1 | 1 | — | — | 5 | — | — | — | — | 0 | Won | Twickenham | R. C. Stuart |
| 83 | 13.2.1954 | Scotland | — | — | — | 1 | 3 | — | — | — | — | 0 | Won | Edinburgh | R. C. Stuart |
| 84 | 27.2.1954 | France | — | — | — | — | 0 | 1 | — | — | — | 3 | Lost | Paris | R. C. Stuart |
| 85 | 20.8.1955 | Australia | 3 | 2 | — | 1 | 16 | 1 | 1 | — | 1 | 8 | Won | Wellington | I. J. Clarke |
| 86 | 3.9.1955 | Australia | 1 | 1 | 1 | — | 8 | — | — | — | — | 0 | Won | Dunedin | I. J. Clarke |
| 87 | 17.9.1955 | Australia | 1 | — | — | — | 3 | 2 | 1 | — | — | 8 | Lost | Auckland | I. J. Clarke |
| 88 | 14.7.1956 | S.A. | 2 | 2 | — | — | 10 | 1 | — | — | 1 | 6 | Won | Dunedin | P. B. Vincent |
| 89 | 4.8.1956 | S.A. | 1 | — | — | — | 3 | 2 | 1 | — | — | 8 | Lost | Wellington | P. B. Vincent |
| 90 | 18.8.1956 | S.A. | 3 | 1 | — | 2 | 17 | 2 | 2 | — | — | 10 | Won | Christchurch | R. H. Duff |
| 91 | 1.9.1956 | S.A. | 1 | 1 | — | 2 | 11 | 1 | 1 | — | — | 5 | Won | Auckland | R. H. Duff |
| 92 | 25.5.1957 | Australia | 4 | 2 | — | 3 | 25 | 1 | 1 | — | 2 | 11 | Won | Sydney | A. R. Reid |
| 93 | 1.6.1957 | Australia | 4 | 2 | 1* | — | 22 | 1 | — | — | 2 | 9 | Won | Brisbane | A.R. Reid |
| 94 | 23.8.1958 | Australia | 7 | 2 | — | — | 25 | 1 | — | — | — | 3 | Won | Wellington | W. J. Whineray |
| 95 | 6.9.1958 | Australia | 1 | — | — | — | 3 | 1 | — | — | 1 | 6 | Lost | Christchurch | W. J. Whineray |
| 96 | 20.9.1958 | Australia | 1 | 1 | — | 4 | 17 | 1 | 1 | — | 1 | 8 | Won | Auckland | W. J. Whineray |
| 97 | 18.7.1959 | British Isles | — | — | — | 6 | 18 | 4 | 1 | — | 1 | 17 | Won | Dunedin | W. J. Whineray |
| 98 | 15.8.1959 | British Isles | 3 | 1 | — | — | 11 | 1 | 1 | — | 1 | 8 | Won | Wellington | W. J. Whineray |
| 99 | 29.8.1959 | British Isles | 4 | 2 | 1 | 1 | 22 | 1 | 1 | — | 1 | 8 | Won | Christchurch | W. J. Whineray |
| 100 | 19.9.1959 | British Isles | — | — | — | 2 | 6 | 3 | — | — | — | 9 | Lost | Auckland | W. J. Whineray |
| 101 | 25.6.1960 | S.A. | — | — | — | — | 0 | 2 | 2 | — | 1 | 13 | Lost | Johannesburg | W. J. Whineray |
| 102 | 23.7.1960 | S.A. | 1 | 1 | 1 | 1 | 11 | — | — | — | 1 | 3 | Won | Cape Town | W. J. Whineray |
| 103 | 13.8.1960 | S.A. | 1 | 1 | — | 2 | 11 | 1 | 1 | — | 2 | 11 | Drawn | Bloemfontein | W. J. Whineray |
| 104 | 27.8.1960 | S.A. | — | — | — | 1 | 3 | 1 | 1 | — | 1 | 8 | Lost | Port Elizabeth | W. J. Whineray |
| 105 | 22.7.1961 | France | 2 | 2 | 1 | — | 13 | — | — | 2 | — | 6 | Won | Auckland | W. J. Whineray |
| 106 | 5.8.1961 | France | 1 | 1 | — | — | 5 | 1 | — | — | — | 3 | Won | Wellington | W. J. Whineray |
| 107 | 19.8.1961 | France | 5 | 4 | — | 3 | 32 | 1 | — | — | — | 3 | Won | Christchurch | W. J. Whineray |
| 108 | 26.5.1962 | Australia | 4 | 1 | 1 | 1 | 20 | — | — | — | 2 | 6 | Won | Brisbane | W. J. Whineray |
| 109 | 4.6.1962 | Australia | 2 | 1 | — | 2 | 14 | 1 | 1 | — | — | 5 | Won | Sydney | W. J. Whineray |
| 110 | 25.8.1962 | Australia | 1 | — | — | 2 | 9 | — | — | — | 3 | 9 | Drawn | Wellington | W. J. Whineray |
| 111 | 8.9.1962 | Australia | — | — | — | 1 | 3 | — | — | — | — | 0 | Won | Dunedin | W. J. Whineray |
| 112 | 22.9.1962 | Australia | 3 | 2 | 1 | — | 16 | 1 | 1 | — | 1 | 8 | Won | Auckland | W. J. Whineray |
| 113 | 25.5.1963 | England | 3 | 3 | 1 | 1 | 21 | 1 | 1 | — | 2 | 11 | Won | Auckland | W. J. Whineray |
| 114 | 1.6.1963 | England | 2 | — | * | — | 9 | 1 | — | — | 1 | 6 | Won | Christchurch | W. J. Whineray |
| 115 | 7.12.1963 | Ireland | 1 | — | — | 1 | 6 | 1 | 1 | — | — | 5 | Won | Dublin | W. J. Whineray |
| 116 | 21.12.1963 | Wales | — | — | 1 | 1 | 6 | — | — | — | — | 0 | Won | Cardiff | W. J. Whineray |
| 117 | 4.1.1964 | England | 2 | 1 | — | 2 | 14 | — | — | — | — | 0 | Won | Twickenham | W. J. Whineray |
| 118 | 18.1.1964 | Scotland | — | — | — | — | 0 | — | — | — | — | 0 | Drawn | Edinburgh | W. J. Whineray |
| 119 | 8.2.1964 | France | 2 | — | 1 | 1 | 12 | — | — | — | 1 | 3 | Won | Colombes | W. J. Whineray |
| 120 | 15.8.1964 | Australia | 1 | 1 | 1 | 2 | 14 | 1 | — | — | 2 | 9 | Won | Dunedin | D. J. Graham |
| 121 | 22.8.1964 | Australia | 4 | 3 | — | — | 18 | 1 | — | — | — | 3 | Won | Christchurch | D. J. Graham |
| 122 | 29.8.1964 | Australia | 1 | 1 | — | — | 5 | 2 | 1 | 1 | 3 | 20 | Lost | Wellington | D. J. Graham |
| 123 | 31.7.1965 | S.A. | 2 | — | — | — | 6 | — | — | — | 1 | 3 | Won | Wellington | W. J. Whineray |
| 124 | 21.8.1965 | S.A. | 3 | 2 | — | — | 13 | — | — | — | — | 0 | Won | Dunedin | W. J. Whineray |
| 125 | 4.9.1965 | S.A. | 3 | 2 | — | 1 | 16 | 4 | 2 | — | 1 | 19 | Lost | Christchurch | W. J. Whineray |
| 126 | 18.9.1965 | S.A. | 5 | 1 | 1 | — | 20 | — | — | — | 1 | 3 | Won | Auckland | W. J. Whineray |
| 127 | 16.7.1966 | British Isles | 3 | 1 | 1 | 2 | 20 | — | — | — | 1 | 3 | Won | Dunedin | B. J. Lochore |
| 128 | 6.8.1966 | British Isles | 3 | 2 | — | 1 | 16 | — | — | 1 | 3 | 12 | Won | Wellington | B. J. Lochore |
| 129 | 27.8.1966 | British Isles | 3 | 2 | — | 2 | 19 | 2 | — | — | — | 6 | Won | Christchurch | B. J. Lochore |
| 130 | 10.9.1966 | British Isles | 4 | 3 | 1 | 1 | 24 | 2 | 1 | — | 1 | 11 | Won | Auckland | B. J. Lochore |
| 131 | 19.8.1967 | Australia | 4 | 4 | 1 | 2 | 29 | 2 | — | — | 1 | 9 | Won | Wellington | B. J. Lochore |
| 132 | 4.11.1967 | England | 5 | 4 | — | — | 23 | 2 | 1 | — | 1 | 11 | Won | Twickenham | B. J. Lochore |
| 133 | 11.11.1967 | Wales | 2 | 2 | — | 1 | 13 | — | — | 1 | 1 | 6 | Won | Cardiff | B. J. Lochore |
| 134 | 25.11.1967 | France | 4 | 3 | — | 1 | 21 | 1 | — | 1 | 3 | 15 | Won | Colombes | B. J. Lochore |
| 135 | 2.12.1967 | Scotland | 2 | 1 | — | 2 | 14 | 1 | — | 1 | — | 3 | Won | Edinburgh | B. J. Lochore |
| 136 | 15.6.1968 | Australia | 6 | 3 | — | 1 | 27 | 1 | 1 | — | 2 | 11 | Won | Sydney | B. J. Lochore |
| 137 | 22.6.1968 | Australia | 3 | 2 | — | 2 | 19 | 1 | — | — | 5 | 18 | Won | Brisbane | C. R. Laidlaw |
| 138 | 13.7.1968 | France | 1 | — | — | 3 | 12 | — | — | 1 | 2 | 9 | Won | Christchurch | K. R. Tremain |
| 139 | 27.7.1968 | France | — | — | — | 3 | 9 | — | — | — | 1 | 3 | Won | Wellington | B. J. Lochore |
| 140 | 10.8.1968 | France | 2 | 2 | 1 | 2 | 19 | 3 | — | 1 | — | 12 | Won | Auckland | B. J. Lochore |
| 141 | 31.5.1969 | Wales | 4 | 2 | — | 1 | 19 | — | — | — | — | 0 | Won | Christchurch | B. J. Lochore |
| 142 | 14.6.1969 | Wales | 3 | 3 | 1 | 5 | 33 | 2 | — | — | 2 | 12 | Won | Auckland | B. J. Lochore |
| 143 | 25.7.1970 | S.A. | 1 | — | — | 1 | 6 | 2 | 1 | 1 | 2 | 17 | Lost | Pretoria | B. J. Lochore |
| 144 | 8.8.1970 | S.A. | 2 | — | — | 1 | 9 | 1 | 1 | — | 1 | 8 | Won | Cape Town | B. J. Lochore |
| 145 | 29.8.1970 | S.A. | — | — | — | 1 | 3 | 2 | 1 | — | 2 | 14 | Lost | Port Elizabeth | B. J. Lochore |

★ in the drop-goal column denotes a goal from a mark

| Match | Date | Opponents | For T | C | D | P | Pts | Against T | C | D | P | Pts | Result | Venue | Captain |
|---|---|---|---|---|---|---|---|---|---|---|---|---|---|---|---|
| 146 | 12.9.1970 | S.A. | 1 | 1 | — | | 4 17 | 2 | 1 | — | | 4 20 | Lost | Johannesburg | B. J. Lochore |
| 147 | 26.6.1971 | British Isles | — | — | — | 1 | 3 | 1 | — | — | | 2 9 | Lost | Dunedin | C. E. Meads |
| 148 | 10.7.1971 | British Isles | 5 | 2 | — | 1 | 22 | 2 | — | 1 | 1 | 12 | Won | Christchurch | C. E. Meads |
| 149 | 31.7.1971 | British Isles | 1 | — | — | | 3 | 2 | 2 | 1 | — | 13 | Lost | Wellington | C. E. Meads |
| 150 | 14.8.1971 | British Isles | 2 | 1 | — | 2 | 14 | 1 | 1 | 1 | 2 | 14 | Drawn | Auckland | C. E. Meads |
| 151 | 19.8.1972 | Australia | 5 | 3 | 1 | — | 29 | — | — | — | | 2 6 | Won | Wellington | I. A. Kirkpatrick |
| 152 | 2.9.1972 | Australia | 5 | 2 | — | 2 | 30 | 3 | 1 | 1 | — | 17 | Won | Christchurch | I. A. Kirkpatrick |
| 153 | 16.9.1972 | Australia | 6 | 4 | — | 2 | 38 | — | — | — | 1 | 3 | Won | Auckland | I. A. Kirkpatrick |
| 154 | 2.12.1972 | Wales | 1 | — | — | 5 | 19 | 1 | — | — | 4 | 16 | Won | Cardiff | I. A. Kirkpatrick |
| 155 | 16.12.1972 | Scotland | 3 | 1 | — | 1 | 14 | — | — | 1 | 2 | 9 | Won | Edinburgh | I. A. Kirkpatrick |
| 156 | 6.1.1973 | England | 1 | 1 | 1 | | 9 | — | — | — | — | 0 | Won | Twickenham | I. A. Kirkpatrick |
| 157 | 20.1.1973 | Ireland | 2 | 1 | — | — | 10 | 1 | — | — | 2 | 10 | Drawn | Dublin | I. A. Kirkpatrick |
| 158 | 10.2.1973 | France | — | — | — | 2 | 6 | 2 | 1 | — | 1 | 13 | Lost | Parc des Princes | I. A. Kirkpatrick |
| 159 | 15.9.1973 | England | 2 | 1 | — | — | 10 | 3 | 2 | — | | 16 | Lost | Auckland | I. A. Kirkpatrick |
| 160 | 25.5.1974 | Australia | 2 | — | — | 1 | 11 | 1 | 1 | — | | 6 | Won | Sydney | A. R. Leslie |
| 161 | 1.6.1974 | Australia | 2 | 1 | — | 2 | 16 | 2 | 1 | — | 2 | 16 | Drawn | Brisbane | A. R. Leslie |
| 162 | 8.6.1974 | Australia | 3 | 2 | — | | 16 | — | — | — | 2 | 6 | Won | Sydney | A. R. Leslie |
| 163 | 23.11.1974 | Ireland | 1 | 1 | — | 3 | 15 | — | — | — | 2 | 6 | Won | Dublin | A. R. Leslie |
| 164 | 14.6.1975 | Scotland | 4 | 4 | — | — | 24 | — | — | — | — | 0 | Won | Auckland | A. R. Leslie |
| 165 | 5.6.1976 | Ireland | 2 | — | — | 1 | 11 | — | — | — | 1 | 3 | Won | Wellington | A. R. Leslie |
| 166 | 24.7.1976 | S.A. | 1 | — | — | 1 | 7 | 2 | 1 | 1 | 1 | 16 | Lost | Durban | A. R. Leslie |
| 167 | 14.8.1976 | S.A. | 1 | 1 | 1 | 2 | 15 | — | — | — | 3 | 9 | Won | Bloemfontein | A. R. Leslie |
| 168 | 4.9.1976 | S.A. | 1 | — | — | 2 | 10 | 1 | 1 | 1 | 2 | 15 | Lost | Cape Town | A. R. Leslie |
| 169 | 18.9.1976 | S.A. | 2 | — | 1 | 1 | 14 | 1 | 1 | 1 | 2 | 15 | Lost | Johannesburg | A. R. Leslie |
| 170 | 18.6.1977 | British Isles | 3 | 2 | — | — | 16 | — | — | — | 4 | 12 | Won | Wellington | R. W. Norton |
| 171 | 9.7.1977 | British Isles | — | — | — | 3 | 9 | 1 | — | — | 3 | 13 | Lost | Christchurch | R. W. Norton |
| 172 | 30.7.1977 | British Isles | 2 | 1 | 1 | 2 | 19 | 1 | — | — | 1 | 7 | Won | Dunedin | R. W. Norton |
| 173 | 13.8.1977 | British Isles | 1 | — | — | 2 | 10 | 1 | 1 | — | 1 | 9 | Won | Auckland | R. W. Norton |
| 174 | 11.11.1977 | France | 1 | — | — | 2 | 13 | 1 | 1 | 1 | 3 | 18 | Lost | Toulouse | G. N. K. Mourie |
| 175 | 19.11.1977 | France | 1 | 1 | 1 | 2 | 15 | — | — | — | 1 | 3 | Won | Parc des | G. N. K. Mourie |
| 176 | 19.8.1978 | Australia | 1 | — | — | 3 | 13 | 1 | 1 | — | 2 | 12 | Won | Wellington | F. J. Oliver |
| 177 | 26.8.1978 | Australia | 3 | 2 | 1 | 1 | 22 | — | — | 1 | 1 | 6 | Won | Christchurch | F. J. Oliver |
| 178 | 9.9.1978 | Australia | 2 | 1 | — | 2 | 16 | 5 | 2 | 1 | 1 | 30 | Lost | Auckland | F. J. Oliver |
| 179 | 4.11.1978 | Ireland | 1 | — | 2 | — | 10 | — | — | — | 2 | 6 | Won | Dublin | G. N. K. Mourie |
| 180 | 11.11.1978 | Wales | 1 | — | — | 3 | 13 | — | — | — | 4 | 12 | Won | Cardiff | G. N. K. Mourie |
| 181 | 25.11.1978 | England | 2 | 1 | — | 2 | 16 | 1 | — | — | 1 | 6 | Won | Twickenham | G. N. K. Mourie |
| 182 | 9.12.1978 | Scotland | 2 | 2 | — | 2 | 18 | 1 | 1 | 1 | — | 9 | Won | Edinburgh | G. N. K. Mourie |
| 183 | 7.7.1979 | France | 3 | 1 | — | 3 | 23 | 1 | 1 | 1 | — | 9 | Won | Christchurch | G. N. K. Mourie |
| 184 | 14.7.1979 | France | 2 | 1 | — | 3 | 19 | 4 | 1 | 1 | 1 | 24 | Lost | Auckland | G. N. K. Mourie |
| 185 | 28.7.1979 | Australia | — | — | 1 | 1 | 6 | — | — | — | 1 | 3 12 | Lost | Sydney | G. N. K. Mourie |
| 186 | 10.11.1979 | Scotland | 4 | 2 | — | — | 20 | — | — | — | 2 | 6 | Won | Edinburgh | G. N. K. Mourie |
| 187 | 24.11.1979 | England | 1 | — | — | 2 | 10 | — | — | — | 3 | 9 | Won | Twickenham | G. N. K. Mourie |
| 188 | 21.6.1980 | Australia | — | — | — | 3 | 9 | 2 | 1 | — | 1 | 13 | Lost | Sydney | D. S. Loveridge |
| 189 | 28.6.1980 | Australia | 1 | 1 | — | 2 | 12 | 1 | 1 | — | 1 | 9 | Won | Brisbane | D. S. Loveridge |
| 190 | 12.7.1980 | Australia | 1 | — | — | 2 | 10 | 4 | 2 | 1 | 1 | 26 | Lost | Sydney | D. S. Loveridge |
| 191 | 1.11.1980 | Wales | 4 | 2 | — | 1 | 23 | — | — | — | 1 | 3 | Won | Cardiff | G. N. K. Mourie |
| 192 | 13.6.1981 | Scotland | 2 | — | — | 1 | 11 | 1 | — | — | — | 4 | Won | Dunedin | G. N. K. Mourie |
| 193 | 20.6.1981 | Scotland | 7 | 6 | — | — | 40 | 1 | 1 | 1 | 2 | 15 | Won | Auckland | G. N. K. Mourie |
| 194 | 15.8.1981 | S.A. | 3 | 1 | — | — | 14 | 1 | 1 | 1 | — | 9 | Won | Christchurch | A. G. Dalton |
| 195 | 29.8.1981 | S.A. | — | — | — | 4 | 12 | 1 | 1 | 1 | 5 | 24 | Lost | Wellington | A. G. Dalton |
| 196 | 12.9.1981 | S.A. | 2 | 1 | 1 | 4 | 25 | 3 | 2 | — | 2 | 22 | Won | Auckland | A. G. Dalton |
| 197 | 24.10.1981 | Romania | 2 | — | 1 | 1 | 14 | — | — | 1 | 1 | 6 | Won | Bucharest | A. G. Dalton |
| 198 | 14.11.1981 | France | 1 | — | 1 | 2 | 13 | — | — | 1 | 2 | 9 | Won | Toulouse | G. N. K. Mourie |
| 199 | 21.11.1981 | France | 2 | 2 | — | 2 | 18 | — | — | — | 2 | 6 | Won | Parc des Princes | G. N. K. Mourie |
| 200 | 14.8.1982 | Australia | 4 | 2 | — | 1 | 23 | 2 | 1 | — | 2 | 16 | Won | Christchurch | G. N. K. Mourie |
| 201 | 28.8.1982 | Australia | 2 | 1 | — | 2 | 16 | 2 | 1 | — | 3 | 19 | Lost | Wellington | G. N. K. Mourie |
| 202 | 11.9.1982 | Australia | 2 | 2 | 2 | 5 | 33 | 1 | 1 | 1 | 3 | 18 | Won | Auckland | G. N. K. Mourie |
| 203 | 4.6.1983 | British Isles | 1 | — | 1 | 3 | 16 | — | — | 1 | 3 | 12 | Won | Christchurch | A. G. Dalton |
| 204 | 18.6.1983 | British Isles | 1 | 1 | — | 1 | 9 | — | — | — | — | 0 | Won | Wellington | A. G. Dalton |
| 205 | 2.7.1983 | British Isles | 1 | 1 | — | 3 | 15 | 2 | — | — | — | 8 | Won | Dunedin | A. G. Dalton |
| 206 | 16.7.1983 | British Isles | 6 | 4 | — | 2 | 38 | — | — | — | 2 | 6 | Won | Auckland | A. G. Dalton |
| 207 | 20.8.1983 | Australia | 1 | 1 | — | 4 | 18 | 2 | — | — | — | 8 | Won | Sydney | A. G. Dalton |
| 208 | 12.11.1983 | Scotland | 3 | 2 | — | 3 | 25 | 1 | — | 2 | 5 | 25 | Drawn | Edinburgh | S. S. Wilson |
| 209 | 19.11.1983 | England | 1 | 1 | — | 1 | 9 | 1 | 1 | — | 3 | 15 | Lost | Twickenham | S. S. Wilson |
| 210 | 16.6.1984 | France | 1 | — | — | 2 | 10 | 1 | 1 | 1 | — | 9 | Won | Christchurch | A. G. Dalton |
| 211 | 23.6.1984 | France | 3 | 2 | — | 5 | 31 | 3 | — | — | 2 | 18 | Won | Auckland | A. G. Dalton |
| 212 | 21.7.1984 | Australia | — | — | 1 | 2 | 9 | 2 | 1 | 1 | 1 | 16 | Lost | Sydney | A. G. Dalton |
| 213 | 4.8.1984 | Australia | 1 | — | — | 5 | 19 | 1 | 1 | — | 3 | 15 | Won | Brisbane | A. G. Dalton |
| 214 | 18.8.1984 | Australia | 2 | 1 | — | 5 | 25 | 1 | 1 | — | 6 | 24 | Won | Sydney | A. G. Dalton |
| 215 | 1.6.1985 | England | — | — | — | 6 | 18 | 2 | 2 | 1 | 1 | 13 | Won | Christchurch | A. G. Dalton |
| 216 | 8.6.1985 | England | 6 | 3 | 1 | 3 | 42 | 2 | 2 | 1 | — | 15 | Won | Wellington | A. G. Dalton |
| 217 | 29.6.1985 | Australia | 1 | — | — | 2 | 10 | 1 | 1 | — | 1 | 9 | Won | Auckland | A. G. Dalton |
| 218 | 26.10.1985 | Argentina | 4 | 1 | 1 | 4 | 33 | 2 | — | 1 | 3 | 20 | Won | Buenos Aires | M. J. B. Hobbs |
| 219 | 2.11.1985 | Argentina | 4 | 1 | — | 1 | 21 | — | — | 3 | 4 | 21 | Drawn | Buenos Aires | M. J. B. Hobbs |
| 220 | 28.6.1986 | France | 1 | 1 | 3 | 1 | 18 | — | — | 3 | — | 9 | Won | Christchurch | D. E. Kirk |
| 221 | 9.8.1986 | Australia | 1 | 1 | — | 2 | 12 | 2 | 1 | — | 1 | 13 | Lost | Wellington | D. E. Kirk |
| 222 | 23.8.1986 | Australia | 1 | — | 1 | 2 | 13 | 1 | — | 1 | 3 | 12 | Won | Dunedin | D. E. Kirk |
| 223 | 6.9.1986 | Australia | — | — | — | 3 | 9 | 2 | 1 | — | 4 | 22 | Lost | Auckland | D. E. Kirk |
| 224 | 8.11.1986 | France | 1 | — | 2 | 3 | 19 | 1 | — | — | 1 | 7 | Won | Toulouse | M. J. B. Hobbs |
| 225 | 15.11.1986 | France | — | — | — | 1 | 3 | 2 | 1 | — | 2 | 16 | Lost | Nantes | M. J. B. Hobbs |

# MATCH RECORDS

## MOST CONSECUTIVE MATCHES WON

| | |
|---|---|
| 17 | *1965* SA 4   *1966* BI 1,2,3,4   *1967* A,E,W,F,S   *1968* A 1,2 F1,2,3   *1969* W 1,2 |
| 7 | *1938* A 1,2,3   *1946* A 1,2   *1947* A 1,2 |
| 7 | *1962* A 4,5   *1963* E 1,2   *1963-64* I,W,E |

## MOST CONSECUTIVE MATCHES WITHOUT DEFEAT

| Matches | Wins | Draws | Period |
|---|---|---|---|
| 17 | 15 | 2 | 1961 to 1964 |
| 17 | 17 | 0 | 1965 to 1969 |
| 8 | 6 | 2 | 1905-06 to 1910 |
| 8 | 6 | 2 | 1971 to 1972-73 |
| 8 | 7 | 1 | 1984 to 1985 |

## MOST CONSECUTIVE MATCHES WITHOUT CONCEDING A TRY

| | |
|---|---|
| 4 | in 1963-64 |
| 4 | between 1974 and 1976 |

## MOST CONSECUTIVE MATCHES WITHOUT CONCEDING A SCORE

| | |
|---|---|
| 3 | between 1921 and 1924-25 |
| 3 | in 1963-64 |

## MOST POINTS IN A MATCH
### By the team

| Pts | Opponents | Venue | Season |
|---|---|---|---|
| 51 | United States | Berkeley | 1913 |
| 42 | England | Wellington | 1985 |
| 40 | Scotland | Auckland | 1981 |
| 38 | France | Paris | 1905-06 |
| 38 | Australia | Dunedin | 1936 |
| 38 | Australia | Auckland | 1972 |
| 38 | British Isles | Auckland | 1983 |
| 33 | Wales | Auckland | 1969 |
| 33 | Australia | Auckland | 1982 |
| 33 | Argentina | Buenos Aires | 1985 |
| 32 | Anglo Welsh | Dunedin | 1908 |
| 32 | France | Christchurch | 1961 |
| 31 | Australia | Dunedin | 1946 |
| 31 | France | Auckland | 1984 |
| 30 | Australia | Wellington | 1913 |
| 30 | France | Toulouse | 1924-25 |
| 30 | Australia | Christchurch | 1972 |

## By a player

| Pts | Player | Opponents | Venue | Season |
|-----|--------|-----------|-------|--------|
| 26 | A. R. Hewson | Australia | Auckland | 1982 |
| 24 | W. F. McCormick | Wales | Auckland | 1969 |
| 20 | A. R. Hewson | Scotland | Auckland | 1981 |
| 19 | A. R. Hewson | France | Auckland | 1984 |
| 18 | A. R. Hewson | British Isles | Auckland | 1983 |
| 18 | D. B. Clarke | British Isles | Dunedin | 1959 |
| 18 | K. J. Crowley | England | Christchurch | 1985 |
| 18 | K. J. Crowley | Argentina | Buenos Aires | 1985 |
| 17 | D. B. Clarke | France | Christchurch | 1961 |
| 17 | R. M. Deans | Australia | Sydney | 1984 |
| 15 | R. W. H. Scott | Australia | Sydney | 1947 |
| 15 | J. F. Karam | Wales | Cardiff | 1972-73 |
| 15 | J. F. Karam | Ireland | Dublin | 1974-75 |
| 15 | R. M. Deans | Australia | Brisbane | 1984 |
| 15 | K. J. Crowley | England | Wellington | 1985 |

# MOST TRIES IN A MATCH

## By the team

| T | Opponents | Venue | Season |
|---|-----------|-------|--------|
| 13 | United States | Berkeley | 1913 |
| 10 | France | Paris | 1905-06 |
| 9 | Anglo Welsh | Auckland | 1908 |
| 9 | Australia | Dunedin | 1936 |
| 8 | Australia | Sydney | 1910 |
| 8 | Australia | Wellington | 1913 |
| 8 | France | Toulouse | 1924-25 |
| 7 | Anglo Welsh | Dunedin | 1908 |
| 7 | Australia | Dunedin | 1946 |
| 7 | Australia | Wellington | 1958 |
| 7 | Scotland | Auckland | 1981 |

## By a player

| T | Player | Opponents | Venue | Season |
|---|--------|-----------|-------|--------|
| 4 | D. McGregor | England | Crystal Palace | 1905-06 |
| 3 | W. J. Wallace | France | Paris | 1905-06 |
| 3 | F. E. Mitchinson | Australia | Sydney | 1907 |
| 3 | F. E. Mitchinson | Anglo Welsh | Auckland | 1908 |
| 3 | T. W. Lynch | Australia | Wellington | 1913 |
| 3 | R. W. Roberts | United States | Berkeley | 1913 |
| 3 | H. M. Taylor | Australia | Brisbane | 1914 |
| 3 | T. H. C. Caughey | Scotland | Edinburgh | 1935-36 |
| 3 | I. A. Kirkpatrick | Australia | Sydney | 1968 |
| 3 | S. S. Wilson | Scotland | Auckland | 1981 |
| 3 | S. S. Wilson | British Isles | Auckland | 1983 |

# MOST CONVERSIONS IN A MATCH

## By the team

| C | Opponents | Venue | Season |
|---|-----------|-------|--------|
| 6 | United States | Berkeley | 1913 |
| 6 | Scotland | Auckland | 1981 |
| 5 | Australia | Dunedin | 1946 |

## By a player

| C | Player | Opponents | Venue | Season |
|---|--------|-----------|-------|--------|
| 6 | A. R. Hewson | Scotland | Auckland | 1981 |
| 5 | R. W. H. Scott | Australia | Dunedin | 1946 |
| 4 | W. J. Wallace | Australia | Sydney | 1907 |
| 4 | J. B. Graham | United States | Berkeley | 1913 |
| 4 | H. R. Pollock | Australia | Dunedin | 1936 |
| 4 | D. B. Clarke | France | Christchurch | 1961 |
| 4 | M. Williment | Australia | Wellington | 1967 |
| 4 | W. F. McCormick | England | Twickenham | 1967-68 |
| 4 | T. J. Morris | Australia | Auckland | 1972 |
| 4 | J. F. Karam | Scotland | Auckland | 1975 |
| 4 | A. R. Hewson | British Isles | Auckland | 1983 |

# MOST DROPPED GOALS IN A MATCH

## By the team

| DG | Opponents | Venue | Season |
|----|-----------|-------|--------|
| 3 | France | Christchurch | 1986 |
| 2 | Ireland | Dublin | 1978-79 |
| 2 | Australia | Auckland | 1982 |
| 2 | France | Toulouse | 1986-87 |

## By a player

| DG | Player | Opponents | Venue | Season |
|----|--------|-----------|-------|--------|
| 2 | O. D. Bruce | Ireland | Dublin | 1978-79 |
| 2 | F. M. Botica | France | Christchurch | 1986 |

# MOST PENALTY GOALS IN A MATCH

## By the team

| PG | Opponents | Venue | Season |
|----|-----------|-------|--------|
| 6 | British Isles | Dunedin | 1959 |
| 6 | England | Christchurch | 1985 |
| 5 | Wales | Auckland | 1969 |
| 5 | Wales | Cardiff | 1972-73 |
| 5 | Australia | Auckland | 1982 |
| 5 | France | Auckland | 1984 |
| 5 | Australia | Brisbane | 1984 |
| 5 | Australia | Sydney | 1984 |
| 4 | Australia | Auckland | 1931 |
| 4 | Australia | Sydney | 1947 |
| 4 | Australia | Auckland | 1958 |
| 4 | South Africa | Johannesburg | 1970 |
| 4 | South Africa | Wellington | 1981 |
| 4 | South Africa | Auckland | 1981 |
| 4 | Australia | Sydney | 1983 |
| 4 | Argentina | Buenos Aires | 1985 |

## By a player

| PG | Player | Opponents | Venue | Season |
|----|--------|-----------|-------|--------|
| 6 | D. B. Clarke | British Isles | Dunedin | 1959 |
| 6 | K. J. Crowley | England | Christchurch | 1985 |
| 5 | W. F. McCormick | Wales | Auckland | 1969 |
| 5 | J. F. Karam | Wales | Cardiff | 1972-73 |
| 5 | A. R. Hewson | Australia | Auckland | 1982 |
| 5 | A. R. Hewson | France | Auckland | 1984 |
| 5 | R. M. Deans | Australia | Brisbane | 1984 |
| 5 | R. M. Deans | Australia | Sydney | 1984 |
| 4 | R. G. Bush | Australia | Auckland | 1931 |
| 4 | D. B. Clarke | Australia | Auckland | 1958 |
| 4 | G. F. Kember | South Africa | Johannesburg | 1970 |
| 4 | A. R. Hewson | South Africa | Wellington | 1981 |
| 4 | A. R. Hewson | Australia | Sydney | 1983 |
| 4 | K. J. Crowley | Argentina | Buenos Aires | 1985 |

# GOALS FROM MARKS

| ★ | Player | Opponents | Venue | Season |
|---|--------|-----------|-------|--------|
| 2 | W. J. Wallace | Australia | Sydney | 1903 |
| 1 | M. F. Nicholls | British Isles | Christchurch | 1930 |
| 1 | D. B. Clarke | Australia | Brisbane | 1957 |
| 1 | D. B. Clarke | England | Christchurch | 1963 |

# TRY ON DEBUT

| Player | Opponents | Venue | Season |
|---|---|---|---|
| A. Asher | Australia | Sydney | 1903 |
| R. McGregor | Australia | Sydney | 1903 |
| G. A. Tyler | Australia | Sydney | 1903 |
| E. Wrigley | Australia | Dunedin | 1905 |
| G. W. Smith | Scotland | Edinburgh | 1905-06 |
| W. Cunningham | Scotland | Edinburgh | 1905-06 |
| F. T. Glasgow | Scotland | Edinburgh | 1905-06 |
| F. Newton | England | Crystal Palace | 1905-06 |
| H. L. Abbott | France | Paris | 1905-06 |
| E. Hughes | Australia | Sydney | 1907 |
| F. E. Mitchinson | Australia | Sydney | 1907 |
| D. Cameron | Anglo Welsh | Dunedin | 1908 |
| H. D. Thomson | Anglo Welsh | Dunedin | 1908 |
| H. O. Hayward | Anglo Welsh | Auckland | 1908 |
| W. B. Fuller | Australia | Sydney | 1910 |
| T. W. Lynch | Australia | Wellington | 1913 |
| R. W. Roberts | Australia | Wellington | 1913 |
| J. R. McKenzie | Australia | Wellington | 1913 |
| H. V. Murray | Australia | Wellington | 1913 |
| C. Brown | Australia | Dunedin | 1913 |
| R. Taylor | Australia | Dunedin | 1913 |
| E. W. Hasell | Australia | Dunedin | 1913 |
| W. Cummings | Australia | Dunedin | 1913 |
| A. H. N. Fanning | Australia | Christchurch | 1913 |
| P. W. Storey | South Africa | Dunedin | 1921 |
| J. Steel | South Africa | Dunedin | 1921 |
| E. A. Belliss | South Africa | Dunedin | 1921 |
| A. L. McLean | South Africa | Auckland | 1921 |
| K. S. Svenson | Ireland | Dublin | 1924-25 |
| C. G. Porter | France | Paris | 1924-25 |
| C. J. Oliver | Australia | Sydney | 1929 |
| G. F. Hart | Great Britain | Dunedin | 1930 |
| H. F. McLean | Great Britain | Auckland | 1930 |
| N. Ball | Australia | Auckland | 1931 |
| G. A. H. Bullock-Douglas | Australia | Sydney | 1932 |
| A. Knight | Australia | Sydney | 1934 |
| J. M. Watt | Australia | Wellington | 1936 |
| J. Dick | South Africa | Wellington | 1937 |
| C. K. Saxton | Australia | Sydney | 1938 |
| J. B. Smith | Australia | Dunedin | 1946 |
| W. G. Argus | Australia | Dunedin | 1946 |
| J. S. Haig | Australia | Dunedin | 1946 |
| K. G. Elliott | Australia | Dunedin | 1946 |
| R. M. White | Australia | Dunedin | 1946 |
| J. Finlay | Australia | Dunedin | 1946 |
| K. D. Arnold | Australia | Brisbane | 1947 |
| D. F. Mason | Australia | Sydney | 1947 |
| J. C. Kearney | Australia | Sydney | 1947 |
| P. Henderson | South Africa | Cape Town | 1949 |
| G. J. T. Moore | Australia | Wellington | 1949 |
| R. A. Roper | Australia | Auckland | 1949 |
| R. H. Bell | Australia | Brisbane | 1951 |
| J. T. Fitzgerald | Australia | Christchurch | 1952 |
| W. H. Clark | Wales | Cardiff | 1953-54 |
| I. M. H. Vodanovich | Australia | Wellington | 1955 |
| R. F. McMullen | Australia | Sydney | 1957 |
| D. J. Graham | Australia | Wellington | 1958 |
| R. W. Caulton | British Isles | Wellington | 1959 |
| D. W. McKay | France | Auckland | 1961 |
| B. A. Watt | Australia | Brisbane | 1962 |
| P. J. Morrissey | Australia | Wellington | 1962 |
| M. A. Herewini | Australia | Auckland | 1962 |
| B. E. McLeod | Australia | Dunedin | 1964 |
| R. E. Rangi | Australia | Christchurch | 1964 |
| P. H. Murdoch | Australia | Christchurch | 1964 |
| W. M. Birtwistle | South Africa | Wellington | 1965 |
| W. L. Davis | Australia | Wellington | 1967 |
| E. W. Kirton | England | Twickenham | 1967-68 |
| I. A. Kirkpatrick | France | Paris | 1967-68 |
| G. R. Skudder | Wales | Auckland | 1969 |
| B. G. Williams | South Africa | Pretoria | 1970 |
| J. P. Dougan | Australia | Wellington | 1972 |
| D. J. Robertson | Australia | Sydney | 1974 |
| M. G. Watts | France | Christchurch | 1979 |
| E. J. Dunn | Scotland | Edinburgh | 1979-80 |
| M. G. Mexted | Scotland | Edinburgh | 1979-80 |
| J. L. B. Salmon | Romania | Bucharest | 1981-82 |
| M. G. Davie | England | Twickenham | 1983-84 |
| M. R. Brewer | France | Christchurch | 1986 |
| W. T. Shelford | France | Toulouse | 1986-87 |

## CAPTAIN ON INTERNATIONAL DEBUT

| Player | Opponents | Venue | Season |
|---|---|---|---|
| J. Duncan | Australia | Sydney | 1903 |
| J. W. Stead | Great Britain | Wellington | 1904 |
| J. C. Spencer | Australia | Auckland | 1905 |
| G. G. Aitken | South Africa | Dunedin | 1921 |
| C. G. Porter | France | Toulouse | 1924-25 |
| F. D. Kilby | Australia | Sydney | 1932 |
| F. R. Allen | Australia | Dunedin | 1946 |
| P. B. Vincent | South Africa | Dunedin | 1956 |
| A. R. Leslie | Australia | Sydney | 1974 |

## TRIES BY FULL-BACKS

| Player | Opponents | Venue | Season |
|---|---|---|---|
| D. B. Clarke | British Isles | Wellington | 1959 |
| D. B. Clarke | England | Auckland | 1963 |
| M. Williment | British Isles | Dunedin | 1966 |
| L. W. Mains | British Isles | Wellington | 1971 |
| J. F. Karam | Ireland | Dublin | 1974-75 |
| A. R. Hewson (2) | Scotland | Auckland | 1981 |
| A. R. Hewson | Australia | Auckland | 1982 |
| A. R. Hewson | British Isles | Auckland | 1983 |
| K. J. Crowley | Argentina | Buenos Aires | 1985 |

## ALL THE POINTS FOR NEW ZEALAND IN A MATCH
### (where more than one scoring action is involved)

| Pts | Player | Opponents | Venue | Season |
|---|---|---|---|---|
| 18 | D. B. Clarke | British Isles | Dunedin | 1959 |
| 18 | K. J. Crowley | England | Christchurch | 1985 |
| 15 | J. F. Karam | Ireland | Dublin | 1974-75 |
| 12 | A. R. Hewson | South Africa | Wellington | 1981 |
| 9 | W. F. McCormick | France | Wellington | 1968 |
| 9 | B. G. Williams | British Isles | Christchurch | 1977 |
| 9 | B. W. Codlin | Australia | Sydney | 1980 |
| 9 | A. R. Hewson | Australia | Sydney | 1984 |
| 9 | K. J. Crowley | Australia | Auckland | 1986 |
| 6 | J. L. Sullivan | South Africa | Christchurch | 1937 |
| 6 | D. Trevathan | South Africa | Auckland | 1937 |
| 6 | D. B. Clarke | British Isles | Auckland | 1959 |
| 6 | J. F. Karam | France | Paris | 1972-73 |

# INDIVIDUAL RECORDS

## LONGEST CAREER SPANS

| Seasons | Player | Caps | Career Span |
|---|---|---|---|
| 15 | E. Hughes | 6 | 1907 to 1921 |
| 15 | C. E. Meads | 55 | 1957 to 1971 |
| 11 | S. M. Going | 29 | 1967 to 1977 |
| 11 | I. A. Kirkpatrick | 39 | 1967 to 1977 |

## MOST CONSECUTIVE CAPS IN A CAREER

| Caps | Player | Opponents |
|---|---|---|
| 38 | I. A. Kirkpatrick | *1968* A 1(R),2, F 1,2,3 *1969* W 1,2 *1970* SA 1,2,3,4 *1971* BI 1,2,3,4 *1972* A 1,2,3 *1972-73* W,S,E,I,F *1973* E *1974* A 1,2,3,I *1975* S *1976* I, SA 1,2,3,4 *1977* BI 1,2,3,4 |
| 34 | M. G. Mexted | *1979-80* S,E *1980* A 1,2,3 *1980-81* W *1981* S 1,2 SA 1,2,3 *1981-82* R, F 1,2 *1982* A 1,2,3 *1983* BI 1,2,3,4,A *1983-84* S,E *1984* F 1,2, A 1,2,3 *1985* E 1,2,A, Arg 1,2 |

# MOST CAPS IN A CAREER

| Caps | Player | Career Span |
|------|--------|-------------|
| 55 | C. E. Meads | 1957 to 1971 |
| 41 | A. M. Haden | 1977 to 1985 |
| 39 | I. A. Kirkpatrick | 1967 to 1977 |
| 38 | K. R. Tremain | 1959 to 1968 |
| 38 | B. Williams | 1970 to 1978-79 |
| 36 | G. A. Knight | 1977-78 to 1986 |
| 35 | A. G. Dalton | 1977-78 to 1985 |
| 34 | B. J. Robertson | 1982 to 1981 |
| 34 | S. S. Wilson | 1977-78 to 1983-84 |
| 34 | M. G. Mexted | 1979-80 to 1985 |

# MOST POINTS IN A CAREER

| Pts | Player | Matches | Career Span |
|-----|--------|---------|-------------|
| 207 | D. B. Clarke | 31 | 1956 to 1964 |
| 201 | A. R. Hewson | 19 | 1981 to 1984 |
| 121 | W. F. McCormick | 15 | 1965 to 1971 |
| 86 | K. J. Crowley | 8 | 1985 to 1986-87 |
| 76 | S. S. Wilson | 34 | 1977-78 to 1983-84 |
| 74 | R. W. H. Scott | 17 | 1946 to 1953-54 |
| 71 | B. G. Williams | 38 | 1970 to 1978-79 |
| 70 | M. Williment | 9 | 1964 to 1967 |
| 65 | J. F. Karam | 10 | 1972-73 to 1975 |

# MOST TRIES IN A CAREER

| T | Player | Matches | Career Span |
|---|--------|---------|-------------|
| 19 | S. S. Wilson | 34 | 1977-78 to 1983-84 |
| 16 | I. A. Kirkpatrick | 39 | 1967 to 1977 |
| 10 | F. E. Mitchinson | 11 | 1907 to 1913 |
| 10 | S. M. Going | 29 | 1967 to 1977 |
| 10* | B. G. Williams | 38 | 1970 to 1978-79 |
| 9 | K. R. Tremain | 38 | 1959 to 1968 |

* Williams' total includes a penalty try scored against the British Isles in 1971.

# MOST CONVERSIONS IN A CAREER

| C | Player | Matches | Career Span |
|---|--------|---------|-------------|
| 33 | D. B. Clarke | 31 | 1956 to 1964 |
| 23 | W. F. McCormick | 15 | 1965 to 1971 |
| 22 | A. R. Hewson | 19 | 1981 to 1984 |
| 17 | M. Williment | 9 | 1964 to 1967 |
| 16 | R. W. H. Scott | 17 | 1946 to 1953-54 |
| 12 | W. J. Wallace | 11 | 1903 to 1908 |

# MOST DROPPED GOALS IN A CAREER

| DG | Player | Matches | Career Span |
|----|--------|---------|-------------|
| 5 | D. B. Clarke | 31 | 1956 to 1964 |
| 5 | M. A. Herewini | 10 | 1962 to 1967 |
| 5 | O. D. Bruce | 14 | 1976 to 1978-79 |
| 4 | A. R. Hewson | 19 | 1981 to 1984 |

# MOST PENALTY GOALS IN A CAREER

| PG | Player | Matches | Career Span |
|----|--------|---------|-------------|
| 43 | A. R. Hewson | 19 | 1981 to 1984 |
| 38 | D. B. Clarke | 31 | 1956 to 1964 |
| 24 | W. F. McCormick | 15 | 1965 to 1971 |
| 23 | K. J. Crowley | 8 | 1985 to 1986-87 |
| 15 | B. W. Wilson | 8 | 1977 to 1979 |
| 14 | R. M. Deans | 5 | 1983-84 to 1984 |
| 13 | J. F. Karam | 10 | 1972-73 to 1975 |

## MOST MATCHES AS CAPTAIN

| | | |
|---|---|---|
| 30 | W. J. Whineray | (22 victories) |
| 19 | G. K. N. Mourie | (15 victories) |
| 18 | B. J. Lochore | (15 victories) |
| 17 | A. G. Dalton | (15 victories) |
| 10 | A. R. Leslie | ( 6 victories) |
| 9 | I. A. Kirkpatrick | ( 6 victories) |

# AUSTRALIA INTERNATIONAL TEAMS AND RECORDS

## 1899

| 1st v. GB | 2nd v. GB | 3rd v. GB | 4th v. GB |
|---|---|---|---|
| †R.H. McCowan | *R.H. McCowan | †W.G. Cobb | W.G. Cobb |
| | | | |
| †C.J. White | †T. Ward | †S.W. Miller | R.H. McCowan |
| *†F.L. Row | †A.R. Henry | *F.L. Row | *F.L. Row |
| †S.A. Spragg 2c,1t | S.A. Spragg | S.A. Spragg 2t,2c | S.A. Spragg |
| | | | |
| †W.T. Evans 1t | W.T. Evans | P.M. Ward | P.M. Ward |
| †P.M. Ward | P.M. Ward | †I.C. O'Donnell | I.C. O'Donnell |
| †A.S. Gralton | †E.W. Currie | †A. Boyd | A.S. Gralton |
| | | | |
| †J. Carson | W.H. Tanner | †W. Webb | W. Webb |
| †W.H. Tanner | †C.S. Graham | †G.F. Bouffler | †J.M. O'Donnell |
| †W. Davis | C.S. Ellis | P.J. Carew | P.J. Carew |
| †H. Marks | H. Marks | W. Davis | W. Davis |
| †P.J. Carew | P.J. Carew | C.S. Ellis | C.S. Ellis |
| †C.S. Ellis | †A.C. Corfe | †R.F.D. Barton | †W.R. Hardcastle |
| †A.J. Colton | †R.L. Challoner | A.J. Colton | †J.H. Sampson |
| †A.J. Kelly 1t | †N.O. Street | †S.B. Boland | S.B. Boland |
| | | | |
| Sydney | Brisbane | Sydney | Sydney |
| WON 13-3 | LOST 0-11 | LOST 10-11 | LOST 0-13 |
| | | | |
| AUST.: 2G 1T | AUST. NIL | AUST.: 2G | AUST.: NIL |
| GB: 1T | GB: 1G 2T | GB: 1G 2T | GB: 2G 1PG |
| | | | |
| 24 Jun. 1899 | 22 Jul. 1899 | 5 Aug. 1899 | 12 Aug. 1899 |

Sides from Britain and New Zealand had played matches against New South Wales and Queensland since the 1880s before Australia fielded their first Test side in 1899 against the British tourists of that year. The Australian sides were selected by the State authorities hosting the Tests, and the teams lined out with the three threequarters and second five-eighth formation favoured in New Zealand.

In the first Test at Sydney the Australians won handsomely. "The pace of our forwards killed them and that is how the Test was won," summarised Mr H.A. Langley of the Australian committee. The Australians scored three tries in front of 28,000 spectators, to win 13-3. The first try resulted from a missed drop at goal by Evans. In the follow-up, however, Kelly, Colton and Davis swooped for a try credited to Kelly (though some sources give the score to Colton).

Frank Row was nominated captain for the three Sydney Tests, giving way to Robert McCowan for the Test in Brisbane. Row's tackling and defensive play inspired the first victory, but his side were unable to hold the British in the later matches. Row became a leading Australian banker, and his younger brother Norman was an Australian cap in 1907.

| 1903 | 1904 | | |
|---|---|---|---|
| v. NZ | 1st v. GB | 2nd v. GB | 3rd v. GB |
| †J.W. Maund | †A. Verge | A. Verge | C.E. Redwood |
| | | | |
| C.E. Redwood | C.J. White | *S.M. Wickham | †Fred Nicholson |
| †S.A. Riley | †J.A. Hindmarsh | †P.P. Carmichael | †F.C. Futter |
| *†S.M. Wickham 1pg | S.M. Wickham | †D.J. McLean | *S.M. Wickham |
| C.J. White | C.E. Redwood | C.E. Redwood | D.J. McLean |
| | | | |
| †L.J. Evans | L.J. Evans | †J. Manning | L.J. Evans |
| A.S. Gralton | †R.L. Baker | R.L. Baker | †F.G. Finley |
| | | | |
| †A. Burdon | A. Burdon | A. Burdon 1t | †J.H. Meibusch |
| †E.R. Larkin | †E. Dore | †A.M. Oxlade | A.M. Oxlade |
| †Frank Nicholson | *Frank Nicholson | †A. McE. Oxenham | E.W. Richards |
| †J.E. Joyce | †E.W. Richards | †A. McKinnon | †E.J. Dixon |
| †D. Lutge | D. Lutge | D. Lutge | D. Lutge |
| W.R. Hardcastle | †T. Colton | T. Colton | †J.M. White |
| S.B. Boland | †P.B. Walsh | P.B. Walsh | H.A. Judd |
| †H.A. Judd | H.A. Judd | H.A. Judd | P.B. Walsh |
| | | | |
| Sydney | Sydney | Brisbane | Sydney |
| LOST 3-22 | LOST 0-17 | LOST 3-17 | LOST 0-16 |
| | | | |
| AUST.: 1PG | AUST.: NIL | AUST.: 1T | AUST.: NIL |
| NZ: 1G 2GM 1PG 2T | GB: 2G 1DG 1T | GB: 1GM 1DG 3T | GB: 2G 2T |
| | | | |
| 15 Aug. 1903 | 2 Jul. 1904 | 23 Jul. 1904 | 30 Jul. 1904 |

The mean attendance for the four Tests played in Australia in 1903 and 1904 was 26,000, with a record crowd of 34,000 present to watch the opening Test of the 1904 series with the British. Although the Australians failed to win a single Test, several brillant players emerged.

Stan Wickham, Charles Redwood and Denis Lutge, a wharf labourer who proved to be the toughest of the Australian forwards, played in all four Tests. Wickham and Redwood were talented threequarters who were equally dangerous as centres or wings. The former was noted for an extraordinary sidestep and was a prolific points-scorer in club and State matches. He had few opportunities to shine in his brief Test career, however, but was later a respected administrator and accompanied the first Australian team to Britain in 1908. Redwood was the best defensive player for Australia in 1904, his fine tackling earning his selection as full-back for the final Test of the series.

Redwood was one of three New Zealanders who appeared in the Test at Sydney in 1903 against New Zealand. Bill Hardcastle, who had been one of the five trans-Tasman representatives in the 1899 Test side, and Syd Riley, a furniture dealer in Sydney, were the other New Zealanders to play against their native land.

| 1905 | 1907 | | |
| --- | --- | --- | --- |
| v. NZ | 1st v. NZ | 2nd v. NZ | 3rd v. NZ |
| †A.P. Penman | P. P. Carmichael 1pg,1gm | W. Dix | W. Dix |
| | | | |
| *S.M. Wickham | †G.W. Watson | †C.E. Parkinson | C.J. Russell |
| †L.M. Smith | F.B. Smith | F.B. Smith | F.B. Smith |
| †F.B. Smith | †W. Dix | C.J. Russell | E.F. Mandible |
| D.J. McLean 1t | †C.J. Russell | †H.H. Messenger 1t,1c | H.H. Messenger 1c |
| | | | |
| †E.A. Anlezark | †C.H. McKivat | †E.F. Mandible | C.H. McKivat |
| †M.J. Dore | †F. Wood | F. Wood | F. Wood 1t |
| | | | |
| A. Burdon | †J.S.H. Rosewell[1] | *A.M. Oxlade | J.S.H. Rosewell |
| A.M. Oxlade | †T.S. Griffin | A. McE. Oxenham | T.S. Griffin |
| †J.C. Clarken | †J.T. Barnett[2] | J.T. Barnett | J.T. Barnett |
| E.W. Richards | *†P.H. Burge | P.H. Burge | *P.H. Burge |
| H.A. Judd | †P.A. McCue | †W.D. Canniffe | P.A. McCue |
| †W.A. Hirschberg | †N.E. Row | J.A. Fihelly | N.E. Row |
| †B.I. Swannell | †J.C. Hughes | E.W. Richards | J.C. Hughes |
| †B.C. Lucas | †P. Flanagan | P. Flanagan | †A.B. Burge |
| | | | |
| Dunedin | Sydney | Brisbane | Sydney |
| LOST 3-14 | LOST 6-26 | LOST 5-14 | DRAWN 5-5 |
| | | | |
| NZ: 1G 3T | AUST.: 1GM 1PG | AUST.: 1G | AUST.: 1G |
| AUST.: 1T | NZ: 4G 2T | NZ: 1G 3T | NZ: 1G |
| | | | |
| 2 Sep. 1905 | 20 Jul. 1907 | 3 Aug. 1907 | 10 Aug. 1907 |

[1]Rep. by †R.H. Graves
[2]Rep. by E.W. Richards

Rugby football gained immense popularity in Australia during the early years of the century, and the 1907 All Blacks possessed tremendous drawing power. They won the Test series 2-0, drew the final Test at Sydney, and many attendance records were set. The mean attendance at the Tests was 34,000, and a record crowd of 49,327 watched the match between New South Wales and the tourists played in Sydney on 13 July. Blair Swannell, a member of the first Australian side to play a Test abroad (in New Zealand in 1905), was an Englishman who had played for Britain in Australia in 1899 and 1904. He settled in Australia soon after the 1904 tour. During the Great War he served as a major in the AIF, and was killed in action at Gallipoli in 1915.

Although the IB agreement regarding the use of replacements in Tests was not signed until 1968, there was an informal arrangement between Australia and New Zealand allowing replacements in certain Tests between them.

| 1908-09 | |
| --- | --- |
| v. WALES | v. ENGLAND |
| P.P. Carmichael | P.P. Carmichael |
| | |
| C.J. Russell 1t | C.J. Russell 2t |
| †J. Hickey | J. Hickey |
| E.F. Mandible | W.S. Prentice |
| †D.B. Carroll | W. Dix |
| | |
| †W.S. Prentice | †A.J.M. McCabe |
| C.H. McKivat | *C.H. McKivat |
| | |
| T.S. Griffin | †K.A. Gavin |
| †R.R. Craig | N.E. Row 1t |
| J.T. Barnett | J.T. Barnett |
| A.B. Burge | P.A. McCue |
| †C.A. Hammand | C.A. Hammand |
| P.A. McCue | †M. McArthur |
| †T.J. Richards 1t | T.J. Richards |
| *†H.M. Moran | †S.A. Middleton |
| | |
| Cardiff Arms Park | Blackheath |
| LOST 6-9 | WON 9-3 |
| | |
| WALES: 1PG 2T | ENG.: 1T |
| AUST.: 2T | AUST.: 3T |
| | |
| 12 Dec. 1908 | 9 Jan. 1909 |

The first tour to Britain undertaken by an Australian side was in 1908-09. A side which became known as the Wallabies (although their shirts were blue and embroidered with the Waratah, emblem of the NSW State team) was captained by Dr "Paddy" Moran.

There were no matches in Ireland or Scotland, the IRFU and SRU having resented the RFU's attitude regarding the invitation of the Australian side. Moran, who led the side in an exciting but narrow defeat against Wales, was chaired from the ground by a Cardiff crowd which appreciated the captain's part in a fine Australian display. Later, at Blackheath, an Achilles-tendon injury forced Moran to miss the Test against England, a game which the Wallabies won by three tries to one.

During the tour the Australians entered the 1908 Olympic Games, winning the rugby tournament in a final against Cornwall, the English County Champions. A member of the winning side was Dan Carroll, an elusive winger who later emigrated to America and served with the US Army in the Great War. Carroll was later a member of the 1920 American Olympic rugby side, and coached the side which won the Gold Medal in 1924.

## 1910

| 1st v. NZ | 2nd v. NZ | 3rd v. NZ |
|---|---|---|
| †L.J. Dwyer | L.J. Dwyer | L.J. Dwyer |
| | | |
| †A.R. Dunbar | A.R. Dunbar | A.R. Dunbar |
| †J.D. Campbell | J.D. Campbell | J.D. Campbell |
| W.S. Prentice | W.S. Prentice | W.S. Prentice |
| †H. Gilbert | H. Gilbert 2t | H. Gilbert 1t |
| | | |
| †C.H. Hodgens | C.H. Hodgens 1t | C.H. Hodgens |
| F. Wood | F. Wood | F. Wood |
| | | |
| †H.W. George | H.W. George | H.W. George |
| T.S. Griffin | T.S. Griffin | †S.H. Slater |
| J.C. Clarken | J.C. Clarken | J.C. Clarken |
| †P.J. Murphy | P.J. Murphy | P.J. Murphy |
| †F.R.V. Timbury | F.R.V. Timbury | L.J. Reynolds |
| N.E. Row | N.E. Row 1c | N.E. Row 1pg,1t,2c |
| *S.A. Middleton | *S.A. Middleton | *S.A. Middleton |
| †E.H. Farmer | †R. Stuart | R. Stuart |
| | | |
| Sydney | Sydney | Sydney |
| LOST 0-6 | WON 11-0 | LOST 13-28 |
| | | |
| AUST.: NIL | AUST.: 1G 2T | AUST.: 2G 1PG |
| NZ: 2T | NZ: NIL | NZ: 2G 6T |
| | | |
| 25 Jun. 1910 | 27 Jun. 1910 | 2 Jul. 1910 |

The season which followed the Wallabies' return from Britain was a purely domestic one for Australia, but by the time the All Blacks arrived for the 1910 series a mass defection to Rugby League had taken place. Consequently there were nine new caps in the side which faced New Zealand in the first Test.

Despite losing, the Australian selectors made just one change for the second Test, two days later. And thanks to a fine display by their attacking backs, Australia levelled the series and registered their first win against New Zealand. Bert Gilbert, a strong-running wing and fine finisher of passing movements, scored two of Australia's tries in an 11-0 victory. Gilbert scored again in the third Test before joining the Rugby League, where he enjoyed a long, successful career. He later played for the Hull club in England, leading their Cup-winning side of 1914 before returning in 1915 to Sydney, where he became curator at the SCG.

Norman Row's ten points in the third match equalled the Australian Test record (set by Stephen Spragg in the third Test against Great Britain in 1899), and for the first time Australia fielded an unchanged back division for a Test series.

| 1912 | 1913 | | |
|---|---|---|---|
| v. ALL-AMERICA | 1st v. NZ | 2nd v. NZ | 3rd v. NZ |
| A.R. Dunbar | †M.J. McMahon 1c | †R.J. Simpson 2c | *L.J. Dwyer |
| | | | |
| †L.S. Meibusch 2t | †D.C. Suttor | D.C. Suttor 1t | D.C. Suttor 2t |
| L.J. Dwyer | †H.A. Jones | H.A. Jones 2t | H.A. Jones 1t |
| *W.S. Prentice 1pg | †L.W. Wogan | L.W. Wogan | L.W. Wogan |
| †R.W. Adamson | †E.T.A. Carr 1t | E.T.A. Carr | E.T.A. Carr |
| | | | |
| D.B. Carroll 1t | †W.G. Tasker | W.G. Tasker | W.G. Tasker |
| †A.S.B. Walker | F. Wood | F. Wood | F. Wood |
| | | | |
| H.W. George | H.W. George | †D.J. Horodam | †D. Williams |
| T.S. Griffin | †C. O'Donnell | C. O'Donnell | H.W. George |
| †W.T. Watson | W.T. Watson | W.T. Watson | W.T. Watson |
| †E.J. Fahey | *E.J. Fahey | *E.J. Fahey | C. Wallach |
| †G.H. Pugh | †C. Wallach | P.J. Murphy | P.J. Murphy |
| T.J. Richards | †E.W. Cody | E.W. Cody | E.W. Cody |
| †W. Murphy | †F. Thompson | F. Thompson | F. Thompson 1t |
| †A. Kent | P.J. Murphy | †B.D. Hughes | B.D. Hughes 2c |
| | | | |
| Berkeley | Wellington | Dunedin | Christchurch |
| WON 12-8 | LOST 5-30 | LOST 13-25 | WON 16-5 |
| | | | |
| ALL-AM.: 1G 1PG | NZ: 3G 5T | NZ: 3G 1DG 2T | NZ: 1G |
| AUST.: 1PG 3T | AUST.: 1G | AUST.: 2G 1T | AUST.: 2G 2T |
| | | | |
| 16 Nov. 1912 | 6 Sep. 1913 | 13 Sep. 1913 | 20 Sep. 1913 |

The only full-scale tour of North America by Australia took place in 1912. A side of 24 players completed 16 matches, winning 11 but losing five (including all three of the games in Canada). The side departed Sydney on 7 September, travelled via New Zealand in the *Moana*, and arrived on 3 October.

Australia won the sole Test of the tour, 12-8. No caps were awarded at the time to a young side, though the Test was retrospectively granted full international status by the ARU. One of the more experienced players in the side was Ward Prentice, a skilful ball-player and inspiring captain, whose fine example helped his side in the last 15 minutes of the Test to recover from a 0-8 deficit. Loose forward Tom Richards, who had gained a reputation as a globetrotter since his Test debut in 1908, returned from England (and having represented the 1910 British side in South Africa) just before the side sailed for America. Proving his fitness, he was appointed vice-captain to Prentice.

Many of the 1912 tourists were selected for the tour of New Zealand the following season. Larry Dwyer, a reliable full-back with excellent positional sense and a long kick, led the side, but missed the first two Tests through injury. Nevertheless, he returned for the game at Christchurch, leading Australia to a sound 16-5 victory – their highest score in a Test match (until 1928).

## 1914

| 1st v. NZ | 2nd v. NZ | 3rd v. NZ |
|---|---|---|
| L.J. Dwyer | L.J. Dwyer | †B. McN. Beith |
| | | |
| E.T.A. Carr | E.T.A. Carr | E.T.A. Carr |
| †J.P. Flynn | *J.P. Flynn | L.J. Dwyer 1dg |
| L.W. Wogan | L.W. Wogan | L.W. Wogan 1t |
| †E. Francis | E. Francis | †M. Massey-Westropp |
| | | |
| W.G. Tasker | W.G. Tasker | W.G. Tasker |
| *F. Wood | F. Wood | *F. Wood |
| | | |
| H.W. George | †W. Morrissey | H.W. George |
| D. Williams | D. Williams | D. Williams |
| W.T. Watson | †S.D. Kreutzer | †C.W. Prentice |
| †W.H. Baker | P.J. Murphy | E.J. Fahey |
| F. Thompson | C. Wallach | C. Wallach |
| †J. Thompson | W.H. Baker | P.J. Murphy |
| P.J. Murphy | †R. Birt | W.H. Baker |
| C. Wallach | F. Thompson | F. Thompson |
| | | |
| Sydney | Brisbane | Sydney |
| LOST 0-5 | LOST 0-17 | LOST 7-22 |
| | | |
| AUST.: NIL | AUST.: NIL | AUST.: 1dg 1t |
| NZ: 1g | NZ: 1g 4t | NZ: 2g 4t |
| | | |
| 18 Jul. 1914 | 1 Aug. 1914 | 15 Aug. 1914 |

Frederick Wood, a veteran scrum-half first capped in 1907, was recalled to lead Australia in the Tests at Sydney in 1914, against New Zealand. A side which included four new caps faced the All Blacks in the first Test, but a converted try gained by the New Zealanders in the second half was the decisive score of a close match.

In an attempt to square the series at Brisbane, the Australian selectors gave the captaincy to J.P. Flynn, a half-back whose two international appearances were as a centre. Flynn was only twenty at the time (though two years earlier he had proved his footballing ability on the Australian tour to North America), becoming the youngest player ever to lead Australia in a Test. Later he became a leading Australian selector.

Harald Baker, who appeared as a forward in the three Tests, was a brother of the former cap R.L. Baker. Both were outstanding all-round sportsmen, the sons of an Irish gold prospector who had settled in Australia during the 1850s. The Bakers adhered strictly to amateur sporting principles, gaining distinction in the fields of boxing, swimming and wrestling as well as Rugby Union.

## 1927-28

| v. IRELAND | v. WALES | v. SCOTLAND | v. ENGLAND | v. FRANCE |
|---|---|---|---|---|
| †A.W. Ross | A.W. Ross | A.W. Ross | A.W. Ross | A.W. Ross |
| | | | | |
| †E.E. Ford | E.E. Ford | E.E. Ford 1t | E.E. Ford 2t | E.E. Ford 1t |
| *†A.C. Wallace 1t | †S.C. King 1t | S.C. King | S.C. King | S.C. King |
| †C.H.T. Towers | †W.B.J. Sheehan 1t | W.B.J. Sheehan | C.H.T. Towers 1t | C.H.T. Towers 1t |
| †A.J. Bowers | *A.C. Wallace 2t | *A.C. Wallace | *A.C. Wallace | *A.C. Wallace 1t |
| | | | | |
| †T. Lawton 1c | T. Lawton 3c | T. Lawton 1c | T. Lawton 1c | T. Lawton 1c |
| †F.W. Meagher | F.W. Meagher | †S.J. Malcolm | S.J. Malcolm | S.J. Malcolm |
| | | | | |
| †H.F. Woods | H.F. Woods | H.F. Woods | H.F. Woods | †M.R. Blair |
| †J.G. Blackwood | J.G. Blackwood | J.G. Blackwood | J.G. Blackwood | J.G. Blackwood |
| †P.B. Judd | P.B. Judd | P.B. Judd | P.B. Judd | †J.L. Tancred |
| †G.P. Storey | G.P. Storey | G.P. Storey | G.P. Storey | G.P. Storey |
| †A.N. Finlay | A.N. Finlay | A.N. Finlay | A.N. Finlay | †C.L. Fox |
| †A.J. Tancred | A.J. Tancred | A.J. Tancred | †E.N. Greatorex | E.N. Greatorex |
| †J.A. Ford | J.A. Ford | J.A. Ford 1t | J.A. Ford | A.N. Finlay |
| †J.W. Breckenridge | J.W. Breckenridge | J.W. Breckenridge | J.W. Breckenridge | J.W. Breckenridge |
| | | | | |
| Dublin | Cardiff Arms Park | Murrayfield | Twickenham | Stade Colombes |
| WON 5-3 | WON 18-8 | LOST 8-10 | LOST 11-18 | WON 11-8 |
| | | | | |
| IRE.: 1pg | WALES: 1g 1t | SCOT.: 2g | ENG.: 3g 1t | FR.: 1g 1t |
| AUST.: 1g | AUST.: 3g 1t | AUST.: 1g 1t | AUST.: 1g 2t | AUST.: 1g 2t |
| | | | | |
| 12 Nov. 1927 | 26 Nov. 1927 | 17 Dec. 1927 | 7 Jan. 1928 | 22 Jan. 1928 |

No Rugby Union was played in Queensland between 1919 and 1929, leaving New South Wales as the principal State side to play representative matches against IB nations in the 1920s. A particularly successful tour was made to Britain in 1927-28 by a team known as the Waratahs (drawn almost entirely from the Sydney suburbs). In 1986 Mr John Dedrick, the Executive Director of the ARU, was happy to confirm that his Union had retrospectively granted international Test status to the five Tests played by these popular tourists. Hence the inclusion of these matches as part of Australia's Test record.

Captained by A.C. "Johnnie" Wallace, the former Scottish international, the Waratahs (who played in the blue jerseys of the NSW State side) were a happy band of tourists whose devotion to flowing football earned them many supporters in Britain. This side, which won three of its Tests, was the first from Australia to play in Ireland, Scotland and France.

Wylie Breckenridge, a wholehearted loose forward who appeared in each of the internationals, became an influential Australian rugby administrator. An accountant by profession, he adopted a shrewd approach to his duties as selector and as President of the ARU. In the late 1960s he did so much to persuade the International Board to adopt the restricted kicking-to-touch Law.

## 1929

| 1st v. NZ | 2nd v. NZ | 3rd v. NZ |
|---|---|---|
| A.W. Ross | †R.E. Westfield | R.E. Westfield |
| | | |
| E.E. Ford | †G.H. McGhie 1t | E.E. Ford |
| S.C. King | S.C. King | S.C. King 1t |
| C.H.T. Towers[1] | †G.S. Sturtridge | C.H.T. Towers 1pg |
| †G.C. Gordon 1t | †O.C. Crossman 1t | G.H. McGhie |
| | | |
| *T. Lawton 2pg | *T. Lawton 2pg,1c | *T. Lawton 2pg |
| S.J. Malcolm | S.J. Malcolm | S.J. Malcolm |
| | | |
| †W.H. Cerutti | W.H. Cerutti | W.H. Cerutti |
| †E.T. Bonis | E.T. Bonis | E.T. Bonis |
| †E.G. Thompson | E.G. Thompson | E.G. Thompson |
| †H.A. Hamalainen | H.A. Hamalainen | H.A. Hamalainen |
| A.N. Finlay | A.N. Finlay | A.N. Finlay[1] |
| †J.R.L. Palfreyman | †R.B. Loudon | †W.N. Ives |
| J.A. Ford | J.A. Ford 1t | J.A. Ford 1t |
| J.W. Breckenridge | J.W. Breckenridge | J.W. Breckenridge |
| | | |
| Sydney | Brisbane | Sydney |
| WON 9-8 | WON 17-9 | WON 15-13 |
| | | |
| AUST.: 2pg 1t | AUST.: 1g 2pg 2t | AUST.: 3pg 2t |
| NZ: 1g 1pg | NZ: 1pg 2t | NZ: 2g 1t |
| | | |
| 6 Jul. 1929 | 20 Jul. 1929 | 27 Jul. 1929 |
| [1]Rep. by †A.C. Thorpe | | [1]Rep. by G.P. Storey |

State rugby was revived in Queensland in 1929 and the first Australian national side to play New Zealand for fifteen years was selected in 1929. For the only time in their history Australia won all three Tests of a series with NZ, and many of the fine Waratah team which had toured Britian became the backbone of the Test side.

Tom Lawton, a fine fly-half who had won Oxford Blues in 1921-22-23, was the Australian captain. A balanced runner with a deceptive weaving action, he was also a useful place-kicker. His twenty points in the series created a new Australian record, and his penalties in the Sydney Tests were the vital goals which produced narrow victories.

Gordon Sturtridge, a medical student who made his debut in the second of the internationals, was the first player capped direct from Victoria. As a student at Melbourne University he had played a big part in the successful rise of Rugby Union in the State. Sturtridge, a Queenslander by birth, later specialised as a gynaecologist and was a consultant at Northampton Hospital in England. He appeared regularly for the Northampton club as a sound, all-round back.

## 1930 | 1931

| v. GB | v. MAORIS | v. NZ |
|---|---|---|
| A.W. Ross | A.W. Ross 1c,1pg | A.W. Ross 2c |
| | | |
| O.C. Crossman | †W.H. Hemingway | W.H. Hemingway |
| S.C. King | C.H.T. Towers | C.H.T. Towers 2t |
| C.H.T. Towers | †H.V. Herd | †D.L. Cowper 1t |
| G.H. McGhie 1t | †H.A. Tolhurst | H.A. Tolhurst |
| | | |
| *T. Lawton | †J.C. Steggall 1t | J.C. Steggall |
| S.J. Malcolm 1t | †W.G. Bennett | *S.J. Malcolm |
| | | |
| W.H. Cerutti | W.H. Cerutti | W.H. Cerutti |
| E.T. Bonis | E.T. Bonis 1t | E.T. Bonis |
| E.G. Thompson | M.R. Blair | M.R. Blair |
| A.N. Finlay | P.B. Judd 1t | P.B. Judd |
| G.P. Storey | †M.C. White | M.C. White |
| J.R.L. Palfreyman | †O.L. Bridle | J.R.L. Palfreyman |
| J.A. Ford | †T.D. Perrin | T.D. Perrin |
| J.W. Breckenridge | *†J.G. Clark | J.G. Clark |
| | | |
| Sydney | Palmerston North | Auckland |
| WON 6-5 | WON 14-3 | LOST 13-20 |
| | | |
| AUST.: 2t | MAORIS: 1t | NZ: 1g 4pg 1t |
| GB: 1g | AUST.: 1g 1pg 2t | AUST.: 2g 1t |
| | | |
| 30 Aug. 1930 | 9 Sep. 1931 | 12 Sep. 1931 |

A team containing no new caps gained a famous victory over the touring British Lions in the sole Test of 1930. Lawton inspired his side to victory, creating a try for Syd Malcolm in the first half and engineering the move which led to McGhie's try in the second half. (Only 5'2", McGhie was one of the smallest men to represent Australia.)

Syd Malcolm, an astute and competitive scrum-half who had made a name for himself on tour with the 1927-28 Waratahs, captained the Australian side which toured New Zealand in 1931 – the first visit by a full Australian team for 18 years. Malcolm's team won only three of its ten matches, finding New Zealand forward play extremely difficult to master.

Two Tests were played within three days. (The ARU has given full international status to the match against the NZ Maoris played at Palmerston North, which the Wallabies won 14-3.) The Saturday following the Maori match, the tourists lost 13-20 against New Zealand, despite scoring three tries to two. "Dave" Cowper, a Victorian whose determined running brought him nine caps in the 1930s, scored a try on his debut at Auckland. His son Bob Cowper was a noted Australian Test cricketer in the 1960s.

## 1932

| 1st v. NZ | 2nd v. NZ | 3rd v. NZ |
|---|---|---|
| J.C. STEGGALL | A.W. ROSS | A.W. ROSS 1C |
| | | |
| D.L. COWPER 1T | D.L. COWPER | W.H. HEMINGWAY 1T |
| G.S. STURTRIDGE | S.C. KING | J.C. STEGGALL |
| S.C. KING | G.S. STURTRIDGE | D.L. COWPER 1C,1T |
| †W.J. WHITE | J.C. STEGGALL 1T | †R.T.G. LINDSAY |
| | | |
| *T. LAWTON 2PG,2C | *T. LAWTON | G.S. STURTRIDGE |
| S.J. MALCOLM | S.J. MALCOLM | *S.J. MALCOLM |
| | | |
| W.H. CERUTTI 2T | W.H. CERUTTI | W.H. CERUTTI |
| E.T. BONIS | E.T. BONIS | E.T. BONIS |
| †E.W. LOVE | E.W. LOVE | E.W. LOVE |
| †G.M. COOKE | G.M. COOKE | G.M. COOKE |
| †G.V. BLAND | G.V. BLAND | G.V. BLAND |
| O.L. BRIDLE 1T | O.L. BRIDLE | O.L. BRIDLE 1T |
| M.C. WHITE | M.C. WHITE | †E.E. DUNLOP |
| J.G. CLARK | J.G. CLARK | J.R.L. PALFREYMAN |
| | | |
| Sydney | Brisbane | Sydney |
| WON 22-17 | LOST 3-21 | LOST 13-21 |
| | | |
| AUST.: 2G 2PG 2T | AUST.: 1T | AUST.: 2G 1T |
| NZ: 2G 1DG 1T | NZ: 1G 1PG 1DG 3T | NZ: 3G 2T |
| | | |
| 2 Jul. 1932 | 16 Jul. 1932 | 23 Jul. 1932 |

Australia began the 1932 Test series with a fine win over New Zealand at Sydney. A side containing four new caps and spearheaded by Tom Lawton trailed 5-8 at the interval, but accurate place-kicking by Lawton and two splendid tries by front-ranker Cerutti helped the Australians to a convincing victory.

Cerutti was a tough, uncompromising prop of Italian parentage who played 17 times for Australia. He formed with Ted Bonis a formidable partnership in the front row, and the pair became respected by New Zealand rugby players. Bonis played in 21 Tests, an Australian Test record until the 1950s, and missed only three internationals played by his country between 1929 and the war.

Lawton's career ended after the heavy defeat at Brisbane, his 44 points in Tests standing as an Australian career record until the 1960s. Cooke, who made his debut at Sydney, played in 13 Tests up to January 1948, a remarkable span of 16 seasons as an Australian international. His record was later equalled by Tony Miller in the 1960s.

## 1933

| 1st v. S.AFRICA | 2nd v. S.AFRICA | 3rd v. S.AFRICA | 4th v. S.AFRICA | 5th v. S.AFRICA |
|---|---|---|---|---|
| J.C. STEGGALL | J.C. STEGGALL | J.C. STEGGALL | J.C. STEGGALL | *A.W. ROSS 1C |
| | | | | |
| †A.D. MCLEAN | A.D. MCLEAN | A.D. MCLEAN | A.D. MCLEAN | A.D. MCLEAN |
| *D.L. COWPER | *D.L. COWPER | *D.L. COWPER 1T | D.L. COWPER | D.L. COWPER 1DG |
| G.S. STURTRIDGE | G.S. STURTRIDGE 1T | G.S. STURTRIDGE | G.S. STURTRIDGE | J.C. STEGGALL 1T |
| †J.D. KELAHER | J.D. KELAHER | J.D. KELAHER | J.D. KELAHER | J.D. KELAHER 1T |
| | | | | |
| †R.R. BIILMANN 1PG | R.R. BIILMANN 1PG,3C | R.R. BIILMANN | R.R. BIILMANN | G.S. STURTRIDGE |
| W.G. BENNETT | W.G. BENNETT 1T | W.G. BENNETT | *S.J. MALCOLM | S.J. MALCOLM |
| | | | | |
| W.H. CERUTTI | W.H. CERUTTI 1T | W.H. CERUTTI | W.H. CERUTTI | W.H. CERUTTI |
| E.T. BONIS | E.T. BONIS | E.T. BONIS | E.T. BONIS | E.T. BONIS |
| M.C. WHITE | M.C. WHITE | M.C. WHITE | M.C. WHITE | M.C. WHITE |
| †W.G.S. WHITE | W.G.S. WHITE | W.G.S. WHITE | W.G.S. WHITE | W.G.S. WHITE |
| G.M. COOKE | G.M. COOKE | G.M. COOKE | G.V. BLAND | G.V. BLAND |
| G.V. BLAND | R.B. LOUDON 1T | R.B. LOUDON | R.B. LOUDON | R.B. LOUDON |
| †W.A.R. MACKNEY | G.V. BLAND | A.J. HODGSON | A.J. HODGSON | W.A.R. MACKNEY |
| J.G. CLARK | †A.J. HODGSON | O.L. BRIDLE | O.L. BRIDLE | O.L. BRIDLE 1T |
| | | | | |
| Cape Town | Durban | Johannesburg | Port Elizabeth | Bloemfontein |
| LOST 3-17 | WON 21-6 | LOST 3-12 | LOST 0-11 | WON 15-4 |
| | | | | |
| SA: 1G 1PG 3T | SA: 1PG 1T | SA: 1G 1DG 1T | SA: 1G 1PG 1T | SA: 1DG |
| AUST.: 1PG | AUST.: 3G 1PG 1T | AUST.: 1T | AUST.: NIL | AUST.: 1G 1DG 2T |
| | | | | |
| 8 Jul. 1933 | 22 Jul. 1933 | 12 Aug. 1933 | 26 Aug. 1933 | 2 Sep. 1933 |

Australia broke new ground in 1933, sending the international team on a 23-match tour of South Africa. The side, which comprised 15 NSW players, 11 from Queensland and three Victorians, won 12 of the matches, drew one and lost ten. The five-Test rubber was lost 2-3, but the Wallabies played open, attacking rugby which endeared them to the South African rugby public. The Wallabies passed and handled attractively, their backs receiving plenty of support from light, fast loose forwards and hard tight forwards who held their own in the scrummages. For the first time the Wallabies used the 3-4-1 forward formation.

The tourists were bedevilled by injuries, however. Neither their captain Alec Ross nor vice-captain Syd Malcolm played in a Test until the defeat at Port Elizabeth. Ross, a gifted full-back with a fine positional sense, underwent an appendectomy early in the tour, and Malcolm was hampered by a shoulder injury sustained in the fourth game of the tour. In their absence Cowper became the first Victorian to lead Australia. He led the side to a famous 21-6 win at Durban, an Australian record winning-points margin for an international. Ron Biilmann, a sinewy fly-half of Dutch descent, succeeded Tom Lawton as Australia's chief play-maker and place-kicker. He enjoyed a succesful tour until badly injured early in the fourth Test, and his three conversions at Durban equalled the Australian Test record.

| 1934 | | 1936 | | |
| --- | --- | --- | --- | --- |
| 1st v. NZ | 2nd v. NZ | 1st v. NZ | 2nd v. NZ | v. MAORIS |
| *A.W. Ross 3PG,2C | *A.W. Ross | †R. Rankin 1PG | †K.P. Storey | R. Rankin 1PG,3C |
| A.D. McLean 1T | A.D. McLean | A.D. McLean | A.D. McLean | A.D. McLean 3T |
| C.H.T. Towers 2T | C.H.T. Towers | †R.E.M. McLaughlin 1T | R.E.M. McLaughlin 1T[1] | J.D. Kelaher 1T |
| †E.S. Hayes | E.S. Hayes | T.P. Pauling | R. Rankin 1PG,2C | O.L. Bridle |
| J.D. Kelaher | J.D. Kelaher | J.D. Kelaher | K.D. Kelaher | †R.W. Dorr |
| †L.S. Lewis | L.S. Lewis | †V.S. Richards | L.S. Lewis | V.S. Richards 1T |
| S.J. Malcolm | S.J. Malcolm | †E. de C. Gibbons | E. de C. Gibbons | E. de C. Gibbons 1C |
| †E.M. Jessep | E.M. Jessep | *R.J. Walden | *R.J. Walden | W.H. Cerutti |
| E.T. Bonis | E.T. Bonis | E.T. Bonis | E.T. Bonis | E.T. Bonis |
| †J.V. Bermingham | J.V. Bermingham | †J.H. Malone | J.H. Malone | J.H. Malone |
| W.G.S. White | W.G.S. White | W.G.S. White | W.G.S. White | W.G.S. White |
| E.E. Dunlop | †R.J. Walden | †F.E. Hutchinson | F.E. Hutchinson | A.J. Hodgson |
| O.L. Bridle 1T | O.L. Bridle | O.L. Bridle | O.L. Bridle 1T | †K.M. Ramsay 1T |
| A.J. Hodgson | R.B. Loudon 1T | †R.L.F. Kelly | R.L.F. Kelly | R.L.F. Kelly 1C |
| W.A.R. Mackney | W.A.R. Mackney | A.J. Hodgson | A.J. Hodgson | *R.J. Walden |
| Sydney | Sydney | Wellington | Dunedin | Palmerston North |
| WON 25-11 | DRAWN 3-3 | LOST 6-11 | LOST 13-38 | WON 31-6 |
| AUST.: 2G 3PG 2T | AUST.: 1T | NZ: 1G 2T | NZ: 4G 1PG 5T | MAORIS: 1PG 1T |
| NZ: 1G 2T | NZ: 1T | AUST.: 1PG 1T | AUST.: 2G 1PG | AUST.: 5G 1PG 1T |
| 11 Aug. 1934 | 25 Aug. 1934 | 5 Sep. 1936 | 12 Sep. 1936 | 23 Sep. 1936 |

[1]Rep. by V.S. Richards

Dr Alec Ross retained the captaincy in 1934, becoming the first man to lead Australia to a Bledisloe Cup triumph. Ross played an important part in the two-Test series success, contributing a record 13 points in the opening match at Sydney, where Australia's total of 25 points was their highest ever.

"Dooney" Hayes, a versatile back who made his Test debut in the 1934 series, was selected to captain the Wallabies to New Zealand in 1936. As on the South African tour three years earlier, however, the Australians were unlucky concerning injuries. Hayes and Cerutti missed both New Zealand Tests and injuries were so common that Pauling and Bridle, two strapping forwards, played as centres for part of the tour.

Doug McLean, who played in all five Tests of 1934-6, was an outstanding wing who had come to prominence on the 1933 tour to South Africa. His strong running and powerful hand-off helped him to score three tries (an Australian record) in the final Test of the 1936 tour, against the NZ Maoris. Doug McLean later switched to League, where he enjoyed a successful career, and a younger brother (Bill) captained the Wallabies after the war.

| 1937 | | 1938 | | |
| --- | --- | --- | --- | --- |
| 1st v. S.AFRICA | 2nd v. S.AFRICA | 1st v. NZ | 2nd v. NZ | 3rd v. NZ |
| R. Rankin | R. Rankin 2PG,1C | R. Rankin | R. Rankin | †M. Clifford |
| R.W. Dorr | †F.W.H. O'Brien 1T | †M.G. Carpenter 3PG | M.G. Carpenter 2T,1PG,1C | F.W.H. O'Brien |
| *C.H.T. Towers 1T,1C | *C.H.T. Towers | L.S. Lewis | E.S. Hayes | E.S. Hayes 1PG |
| T.P. Pauling | †J.D.C. Hammon | E.S. Hayes | †W.P.J. Ide | W.P.J. Ide |
| J.D. Kelaher | J.D. Kelaher 1T | †J. Howard | J. Howard | J.D. Kelaher |
| V.S. Richards | †P.K. Collins | V.S. Richards | P.K. Collins 1T | P.K. Collins |
| †J.M.S. McShane | J.M.S. McShane | †C.G. Stone | †C. Ramalli | C. Ramalli |
| W.H. Cerutti | W.H. Cerutti | *V.W. Wilson | *V.W. Wilson | *V.W. Wilson |
| E.T. Bonis | †A.H. Stone | E.T. Bonis | A.H. Stone | A.H. Stone |
| J.V. Bermingham | J.H. Malone | K.M. Ramsay | †C.W.P. Lang | C.W.P. Lang |
| †V.W. Wilson | V.W. Wilson | R.L.F. Kelly | R.L.F. Kelly | K.M. Ramsay 1T |
| †E.E. Hutchinson | E.E. Hutchinson | F.E. Hutchinson | †C.I.A. Monti | F.E. Hutchinson |
| R.L.F. Kelly | R.L.F. Kelly | A.J. Hodgson | B.D. Oxlade | B.D. Oxlade |
| K.M. Ramsay | A.J. Hodgson 1T | †F.R. Kerr | A.J. Hodgson | A.J. Hodgson |
| †K.S. Windon | K.S. Windon | †B.D. Oxlade | †J.C. McDonald | J.C. McDonald |
| Sydney | Sydney | Sydney | Brisbane | Sydney |
| LOST 5-9 | LOST 17-26 | LOST 9-24 | LOST 14-20 | LOST 6-14 |
| AUST.: 1G | AUST.: 1G 2PG 2T | AUST.: 3PG | AUST.: 1G 1PG 2T | AUST.: 1PG 1T |
| SA: 1PG 2T | SA: 4G 2T | NZ: 3G 2PG 1T | NZ: 2G 1DG 2T | NZ: 1G 2PG 1T |
| 26 Jun. 1937 | 17 Jul. 1937 | 23 Jul. 1938 | 6 Aug. 1938 | 13 Aug. 1938 |

Cyril Towers, one of Australia's finest ever threequarters, was recalled to skipper the side in 1937 against South Africa. He played with all of his old guile and skill in the first Test at Sydney, where the dour Springboks won by four points. In a match of 120 line-outs, Towers scored Australia's try and converted it. Although well beaten in the second Test, Towers did have the satisfaction of leading NSW to victory by 17-6 over the tourists in a match played on a wet, slippery surface at Sydney.

Hayes, a former cap; Boyd Oxlade, a brilliant line-out expert; Aub Hodgson and new captain V.W. Wilson were the only Australians who played in each of the 1938 Tests. Hodgson was the outstanding personality of Australian rugby in the 1930s. A veteran of 11 Tests, he was a heavy, crash-tackling loose forward who maintained a lively interest in the game up to his death in 1982. Wilson was a university graduate who brought an appropriate studious tactical approach to Australian rugby. He led the 1939-40 Wallabies to Britain, but the declaration of war soon after his team's arrival caused the cancellation of the tour.

|  | 1946 | | | 1947 | |
| --- | --- | --- | --- | --- | --- |
|  | 1st v. NZ | v. MAORIS | 2nd v. NZ | 1st v. NZ | 2nd v. NZ |
|  | †B.J.C. Piper | B.J.C. Piper | B.J.C. Piper 2c | B.J.C. Piper 1c | †J.C. Windsor |
|  | †J.W.T. MacBride | †J.M. Stone | J.M. Stone | J.W.T. MacBride | J.W.T. MacBride |
|  | †A.P. Johnson | A.P. Johnson | J.W.T. MacBride 1t | M.L. Howell | †T.K. Bourke |
|  | †T. Allan 1t[1] | T. Allan | T. Allan | †A.K. Walker | T. Allan 3pg,1c |
|  | †C.C. Eastes 1t | J.W.T. MacBride | C.C. Eastes 1t | C.C. Eastes | C.C. Eastes |
|  | †J.F. Cremin | †D.P. Bannon | J.F. Cremin | J.F. Cremin | †N.A. Emery |
|  | †B.G. Schulte | B.G. Schulte | †C.T. Burke | C.T. Burke | C.T. Burke |
|  | †R.E. McMaster | R.E. McMaster | R.E. McMaster | R.E. McMaster | R.E. McMaster |
|  | †W.L. Dawson | †D.C. Furness | W.L. Dawson | †K.H. Kearney | K.H. Kearney |
|  | †E. Tweedale[2] | E. Freeman | E. Tweedale | †D.H. Keller | E. Tweedale |
|  | †P.A. Hardcastle | P.A. Hardcastle | P.A. Hardcastle | *P.A. Hardcastle | †D.F. Kraefft |
|  | *†W.M. McLean | †B.G. Hamilton | G.M. Cooke | W.M. McLean | †N.M. Shehadie |
|  | †A.E. Livermore 1c | A.E. Livermore | *W.M. McLean | †R.G.W. Cornforth 1t | *W.M. McLean 1t |
|  | †A.J. Buchan | K.S. Windon | A.J. Buchan | A.J. Buchan | G.M. Cooke |
|  | †C.J. Windon | *W.M. McLean | C.J. Windon | C.J. Windon | A.J. Buchan |
|  | Dunedin | Hamilton | Auckland | Brisbane | Sydney |
|  | LOST 8-31 | LOST 0-20 | LOST 10-14 | LOST 5-13 | LOST 14-27 |
|  | NZ: 5G 2T | MAORIS: 1G 1PG 4T | NZ: 1G 3PG | AUST.: 1G | AUST.: 1G 3PG |
|  | AUST.: 1G 1T | AUST.: NIL | AUST.: 2G | NZ: 2G 1T | NZ: 3G 4PG |
|  | 14 Sep. 1946 | 25 Sep. 1946 | 28 Sep. 1946 | 14 Jun. 1947 | 28 Jun. 1947 |

[1] Rep. by †M.L. Howell
[2] Rep. by E. Freeman

Australia were beaten in each of their first five Tests following the war. There were 17 new caps (including the replacements Howell and Freeman) used in the opening Test of 1946, though two of those capped on the tour of New Zealand, Keith Windon and Graham Cooke, had been Test players before the war.

The 1947 side which lost to New Zealand at Brisbane contained two interesting dual internationals, Doug Keller and Alan Walker. Keller was a versatile forward who was successfully converted from a prop into a flanker on the 1947-8 Wallabies tour of Britain. At the end of that tour he continued his medical studies at Guy's Hospital, played for London Scottish and won selection for the Scottish international side. In 1949 he captained the Scots, masterminding a memorable victory against Wales. Walker reached the top level as a rugby player and cricketer: the only man to represent Australia at both sports. A medium left-arm bowler, he toured South Africa with Hassett's team in 1949-50, but failed to gain Test selection.

Nick Shehadie, who made his debut in the Sydney Test in 1947, became Australia's leading forward during the following decade and established a record as his country's most-capped player, appearing in 30 Tests up to 1958.

## 1947-48

|  | v. SCOTLAND | v. IRELAND | v. WALES | v. ENGLAND | v. FRANCE |
| --- | --- | --- | --- | --- | --- |
|  | B.J.C. Piper 2c | B.J.C. Piper | B.J.C. Piper | B.J.C. Piper | B.J.C. Piper |
|  | †A.E.J. Tonkin 1t | A.E.J. Tonkin 1t | A.E.J. Tonkin | A.E.J. Tonkin 1c | A.E.J. Tonkin 2pg |
|  | *T. Allan | M.L. Howell | *T. Allan | *T. Allan | *T. Allan |
|  | M.L. Howell 1t | *T. Allan 1t,1c | M.L. Howell | A.K. Walker 1t | A.K. Walker |
|  | J.W.T. MacBride | J.W.T. MacBride | J.W.T. MacBride | J.W.T. MacBride | J.W.T. MacBride |
|  | N.A. Emery | N.A. Emery | N.A. Emery | N.A. Emery | N.A. Emery |
|  | C.T. Burke | C.T. Burke 1t | C.T. Burke | C.T. Burke | C.T. Burke |
|  | †E.H. Davis | R.E. McMaster 1c | R.E. McMaster | N.M. Shehadie | N.M. Shehadie |
|  | K.H. Kearney 1t | K.H. Kearney | K.H. Kearney | K.H. Kearney | K.H. Kearney |
|  | E. Tweedale | E. Tweedale | E.H. Davis | E. Tweedale | E. Tweedale |
|  | D.F. Kraefft | D.F. Kraefft | D.F. Kraefft | D.F. Kraefft | D.F. Kraefft |
|  | G.M. Cooke 1t | G.M. Cooke | G.M. Cooke | G.M. Cooke | G.M. Cooke |
|  | D.H. Keller | D.H. Keller | D.H. Keller | D.H. Keller | D.H. Keller |
|  | A.J. Buchan | A.J. Buchan | A.J. Buchan | A.J. Buchan | A.J. Buchan |
|  | C.J. Windon | C.J. Windon 1t | C.J. Windon | C.J. Windon 2t | C.J. Windon |
|  | Murrayfield | Lansdowne Road | Cardiff Arms Park | Twickenham | Stade Colombes |
|  | WON 16-7 | WON 16-3 | LOST 0-6 | WON 11-0 | LOST 6-13 |
|  | SCOT.: 1PG 1DG | IRE.: 1PG | WALES: 2PG | ENG.: NIL | FR.: 2G 1T |
|  | AUST.: 2G 2T | AUST.: 2G 2T | AUST.: NIL | AUST.: 1G 2T | AUST.: 2PG |
|  | 22 Nov. 1947 | 6 Dec. 1947 | 20 Dec. 1947 | 3 Jan. 1948 | 11 Jan. 1948 |

The Third Wallabies who toured Britain under Bill McLean were a popular side on and off the field. In their play they had a well-organised cover defence, and when their backs were in possession the accent was on attack.

Possibly the most outstanding win of the tour was against England. At Twickenham the Wallabies scored three tries, including a fine solo effort by Walker towards the end of the game. He punted the ball ahead from his own 25, gathered it on the bounce and outpaced a converging defence along the left touchline. After a neat swerve past the English full-back, he touched down in the corner for a try which consolidated the Australians' narrow lead. The tourists were hampered by injuries but, despite a difficult programme, lost only six of their 35 matches. McLean, an original member of the Wallaby side selected to make the 1939-40 tour, broke a leg against the Combined Services at Twickenham and had to pass the Captaincy to Trevor Allan.

| 1949 | | | 1949 | |
|---|---|---|---|---|
| 1st v. MAORIS | 2nd v. MAORIS | 3rd v. MAORIS | 1st v. NZ | 2nd v. NZ |
| B.J.C. PIPER | B.J.C. PIPER 1C | B.J.C. PIPER 3C | R.M. CAWSEY 1C | R.M. CAWSEY 1C |
| †J.S. MARSHALL | †J.R. FOGARTY 1T | J.R. FOGARTY | †C.C. DAVIS | H.J. SOLOMON 1T |
| *T. ALLAN | *T. ALLAN | *T. ALLAN | *T. ALLAN | *T. ALLAN 1PG,1C |
| †J. BLOMLEY | J. BLOMLEY | J. BLOMLEY 1T | J. BLOMLEY | J. BLOMLEY |
| C.C. EASTES | C.C. EASTES | †H.J. SOLOMON | †R.L. GARNER 2T | R.L. GARNER |
| †E.G. BROAD | N.A. EMERY | N.A. EMERY | N.A. EMERY | N.A. EMERY 1T |
| †R.M. CAWSEY | C.T. BURKE | C.T. BURKE | C.T. BURKE | C.T. BURKE |
| †A.J. BAXTER | A.J. BAXTER | A.J. BAXTER | A.J. BAXTER | A.J. BAXTER |
| †N.V. COTTRELL | N.V. COTTRELL | N.V. COTTRELL | N.V. COTTRELL | N.V. COTTRELL |
| E.H. DAVIS | E.H. DAVIS | E. TWEEDALE | †B.J. WILSON | B.J. WILSON |
| E. TWEEDALE | E. TWEEDALE | P.A. HARDCASTLE | N.M. SHEHADIE | N.M. SHEHADIE |
| N.M. SHEHADIE | N.M. SHEHADIE | N.M. SHEHADIE | †R.P. MOSSOP | R.P. MOSSOP |
| †K.A. CROSS | †J.D. BROCKHOFF | J.D. BROCKHOFF 2T | C.J. WINDON 1T | C.J. WINDON 1T |
| †P.B. HARVEY | P.B. HARVEY | A.J. BUCHAN | K.A. CROSS | K.A. CROSS |
| C.J. WINDON 1T | C.J. WINDON 1T | C.J. WINDON 1T | J.D. BROCKHOFF | J.D. BROCKHOFF |
| Sydney | Brisbane | Sydney | Wellington | Auckland |
| LOST 3-12 | DRAWN 8-8 | WON 18-3 | WON 11-6 | WON 16-9 |
| AUST.: 1T | AUST.: 1G 1T | AUST.: 3G 1T | NZ: 1PG 1T | NZ: 1DG 1PG 1T |
| MAORIS: 4T | MAORIS: 1G 1PG | MAORIS: 1PG | AUST.: 1G 2T | AUST.: 2G 1PG 1T |
| 4 Jun. 1949 | 11 Jun. 1949 | 25 Jun. 1949 | 3 Sep. 1949 | 24 Sep. 1949 |

Trevor Allan, a brilliant footballer who ran straight, handled carefully and possessed tremendous acceleration, led Australia in the five Tests of 1949. Early in the season his side struggled to tie an exciting series with a strong Maori side, but the Wallabies made a successful tour of New Zealand later in the year and regained the Bledisloe Cup with good wins at Wellington and Auckland.

Allan's centre partner for the five Test was John Blomley, a doctor who made numerous openings for his wings. Solomon and Garner, who had played for the Australian Universities earlier in the season, impressed the New Zealand public with their determined running and abilities to snap up chances. Of the forwards, Rex Mossop impressed at the line-out, worked hard in the tight and promised, at just 21 years of age, to be Australia's brightest forward prospect for years.

But Australian Rugby Union was to suffer cruel blows in the 1950s as many of their leading players, Allan and Mossop among them, turned to League. Allan captained Australia a record ten times before sailing for England in 1950 to play for Leigh RL club. Mossop joined the same club several months later. Both enjoyed happy League careers and eventually returned to Australia, becoming the country's leading television rugby commentators.

| 1950 | | 1951 | | |
|---|---|---|---|---|
| 1st v. BRITISH IS. | 2nd v. BRITISH IS. | 1st v. NZ | 2nd v. NZ | 3rd v. NZ |
| †W.C. GARDNER 2PG | †P.P.S. COSTELLO | †P.R. ROTHWELL | P.R. ROTHWELL 1PG,1C | P.R. ROTHWELL 1PG |
| †P.D. THOMPSON | A.E.J. TONKIN | †E.T. STAPLETON | E.T. STAPLETON | E.T. STAPLETON |
| A.K. WALKER | A.K. WALKER | †K.E. GUDSELL | K.E. GUDSELL | †M.J. TATE |
| J. BLOMLEY | J. BLOMLEY | H.J. SOLOMON | H.J. SOLOMON | K.E. GUDSELL |
| †E.F. HILLS | E.F. HILLS | C.C. DAVIS | C.C. DAVIS | C.C. DAVIS |
| H.J. SOLOMON | H.J. SOLOMON | †R.M. TOOTH | R.M. TOOTH 1T | R.M. TOOTH |
| C.T. BURKE | C.T. BURKE 1T | C.T. BURKE | C.T. BURKE | C.T. BURKE |
| †F.J.C. McCARTHY | N.M. SHEHADIE | A.J. BAXTER | A.J. BAXTER | T.N. BETTS |
| *N.V. COTTRELL | *N.V. COTTRELL | N.V. COTTRELL | N.V. COTTRELL | N.V. COTTRELL 1PG |
| †K.M. GORDON | K.M. GORDON | N.M. SHEHADIE | †T.N. BETTS | N.M. SHEHADIE |
| N.M. SHEHADIE | R.G.W. CORNFORTH | †A.S. CAMERON | A.S. CAMERON | A.S. CAMERON |
| R.P. MOSSOP | R.P. MOSSOP | †C.J. PRIMMER | N.M. SHEHADIE 1T | C.J. PRIMMER |
| †D.I. MacMILLAN | D.I. MacMILLAN | C.J. WINDON | *C.J. WINDON | *C.J. WINDON |
| K.A. CROSS | K.A. CROSS | R.P. MOSSOP | K.A. CROSS | K.A. CROSS |
| J.D. BROCKHOFF | J.D. BROCKHOFF | *†K.C. WINNING | J.D. BROCKHOFF | J.D. BROCKHOFF |
| Brisbane | Sydney | Sydney | Sydney | Brisbane |
| LOST 6-19 | LOST 3-24 | LOST 0-8 | LOST 11-17 | LOST 6-16 |
| AUST.: 2PG | AUST.: 1T | AUST.: NIL | AUST.: 1G 1PG 1T | AUST.: 2PG |
| BIS: 2G 2PG 1DG | BIS: 3G 1PG 2T | NZ: 1G 1PG | NZ: 1G 1DG 3T | NZ: 2G 2T |
| 19 Aug. 1950 | 26 Aug. 1950 | 23 Jun. 1951 | 7 Jul. 1951 | 21 Jul. 1951 |

These were black years for Australian rugby, the defections of Allan and Mossop to League adding to the disappointment of five Test losses against the Lions and All Blacks. The Australians were well beaten by a strong British side which had already completed the New Zealand leg of a long tour. Trounced in Brisbane, the Australian selectors made a couple of changes for the second Test in Sydney, including a positional switch involving Shehadie, who went from second row to prop. Even the expert scrummaging of this fine forward could not prevent a second big defeat, however, the Australians going down by 21 points – their worst performance against a British side up to that date.

In the following season the Australians were whitewashed by a strong New Zealand side. Alan Cameron, a 20-year-old line-out expert from NSW, began a long Test career in the first Test at Sydney. Altogether he gained 20 caps before retiring after the Wallabies tour of Britain in 1958.

Colin Windon, who captained the Australians in the last two Tests against New Zealand (having missed the games with the Lions) went on to play 20 times for his country. A fast, aggressive loose forward, he scored eleven tries in internationals, creating a new Australian Test career record.

| 1952 | | 1952 | |
|---|---|---|---|
| 1st v. FIJI | 2nd v. FIJI | 1st v. NZ | 2nd v. NZ |
| P.R. ROTHWELL | †R. COLBERT | R. COLBERT | R. COLBERT |
| | | | |
| E.T. STAPLETON 1T | E.T. STAPLETON 1T | E.T. STAPLETON 1T | E.T. STAPLETON |
| *H.J. SOLOMON 1T | *H.J. SOLOMON 1DG | *H.J. SOLOMON 1DG | *H.J. SOLOMON |
| †H.S. BARKER 1PG | H.S. BARKER | H.S. BARKER 1T | H.S. BARKER |
| †G.G. JONES 1T | G.G. JONES | †J.M. O'NEILL | J.M. O'NEILL |
| | | | |
| M.J. TATE | M.J. TATE | M.J. TATE | M.J. TATE |
| †B.P. COX | B.P. COX 1T | B.P. COX | B.P. COX |
| | | | |
| †R.A.L. DAVIDSON | R.A.L. DAVIDSON | R.A.L. DAVIDSON | R.A.L. DAVIDSON |
| N.V. COTTRELL | N.V. COTTRELL | N.V. COTTRELL 1C | N.V. COTTRELL 1PG,1C |
| †W.I. HATHERELL | W.I. HATHERELL | A.J. BAXTER | A.J. BAXTER |
| N.M. SHEHADIE | N.M. SHEHADIE 1T | A.R. MILLER | N.M. SHEHADIE |
| A.S. CAMERON | A.S. CAMERON | A.S. CAMERON | A.S. CAMERON |
| †B.B. JOHNSON 1T | B.B. JOHNSON | C.J. WINDON 1T | C.J. WINDON 1T |
| †A.R. MILLER | A.R. MILLER | B.B. JOHNSON | A.R. MILLER |
| C.J. WINDON | C.J. WINDON 1T | K.A. CROSS | B.B. JOHNSON |
| | | | |
| Sydney | Sydney | Christchurch | Wellington |
| WON 15-9 | LOST 15-17 | WON 14-9 | LOST 8-15 |
| | | | |
| AUST.: 1PG 4T | AUST.: 1DG 4T | NZ: 1PG 2T | NZ: 2PG 1DG 2T |
| FIJI: 1PG 2T | FIJI: 1G 2PG 1DG 1T | AUST.: 1G 1DG 2T | AUST.: 1G 1PG |
| | | | |
| 26 Jul. 1952 | 9 Aug. 1952 | 6 Sep. 1952 | 13 Sep. 1952 |

John Solomon, a fifth-year medical student, was entrusted with the captaincy in 1952. Only 22 at the time, he had already played six Tests (as a wing, centre and fly-half), before taking over at Sydney for the opening Test of the first Fijian tour of Australia. The ARU, finding its finances in a difficult position, had taken the gamble of inviting the Fijians in the hope that the drawing-power of the Islanders would enhance their bank balance. The gamble paid off. The Fijians pulled in huge crowds during their ten-match tour, played unorthodox yet attractive rugby which helped to restore the game's prestige among the Australian public, and finished a successful tour with just one defeat.

Solomon, having proved his ability as captain, was appointed leader of the Wallabies who toured New Zealand later in 1952. Setting a fine example (with a neat drop-goal) he skippered his side to victory in the Test at Christchurch – Australia's first Test win against an IB nation for three years.

Tony Miller, whose Australian Test career spanned a record-equalling 16 seasons, made his debut as a number-eight against Fiji before transferring to lock in New Zealand. He established an electrical business which prevented him from participating in several Wallaby tours. Nevertheless, at the time of his final Test he had won 41 caps, setting a new Australian record.

| 1953 | | | |
|---|---|---|---|
| 1st v. S.AFRICA | 2nd v. S.AFRICA | 3rd v. S.AFRICA | 4th v. S.AFRICA |
| †T.L. SWEENEY 1PG | R. COLBERT 2C | R. COLBERT 1C | R. COLBERT |
| | | | |
| E.T. STAPLETON | E.T. STAPLETON 1C,1T | E.T. STAPLETON | E.T. STAPLETON 1T |
| *H.J. SOLOMON | *H.J. SOLOMON | *H.J. SOLOMON 1PG | H.S. BARKER 2PG |
| †J.A. PHIPPS | J.A. PHIPPS | J.A. PHIPPS | J.A. PHIPPS |
| G.G. JONES | G.G. JONES 1T | G.G. JONES | G.G. JONES |
| | | | |
| M.J. TATE | †S.W. BROWN | S.W. BROWN | S.W. BROWN |
| †J.M. BOSLER | C.T. BURKE | C.T. BURKE | C.T. BURKE |
| | | | |
| N.M. SHEHADIE | N.M. SHEHADIE | N.M. SHEHADIE | *N.M. SHEHADIE |
| †J.J. WALSH | J.J. WALSH | J.J. WALSH | J.J. WALSH |
| R.A.L. DAVIDSON | †C.F. FORBES | C.F. FORBES | C.F. FORBES |
| A.S. CAMERON | A.S. CAMERON | A.S. CAMERON | A.S. CAMERON |
| A.R. MILLER | A.R. MILLER | A.R. MILLER | A.R. MILLER |
| †N.M. HUGHES | N.M. HUGHES | N.M. HUGHES | N.M. HUGHES |
| †J.C. CARROLL | B.B. JOHNSON 1T | B.B. JOHNSON | B.B. JOHNSON |
| K.A. CROSS | K.A. CROSS 1T | K.A. CROSS 1T | K.A. CROSS |
| | | | |
| Johannesburg | Cape Town | Durban | Port Elizabeth |
| LOST 3-25 | WON 18-14 | LOST 8-18 | LOST 9-22 |
| | | | |
| SA: 2G 2PG 3T | SA: 1G 3T | SA: 3G 1T | SA: 2G 2PG 2DG |
| AUST.: 1PG | AUST.: 3G 1T | AUST.: 1G 1PG | AUST.: 2PG 1T |
| | | | |
| 22 Aug. 1953 | 5 Sep. 1953 | 19 Sep. 1953 | 26 Sep. 1953 |

Twenty of the side which had shared the series in New Zealand the year before were included in John Solomon's team to South Africa in 1953. With Wylie Breckenridge and A.C. Wallace (two stalwarts of the 1920s) as manager and coach respectively, the Wallabies set out to play the exciting passing game which had been a characteristic of their previous tour of 1933. The tourists clocked up 450 points on their visit, playing to their wingers, Stapleton and Garth Jones, who were both even-timers.

Well beaten at Johannesburg in the first Test, the Wallabies gained a memorable injury-time win in the second at Newlands. Trailing 13-14, the Australians began a threequarter movement deep inside their own 25. At length Garth Jones received the ball seventy yards from the Springbok line, and set off on a long race with Muller, the Springbok captain. Jones outpaced him along the touchline and skirted behind the goal for a famous try, converted into an 18-14 victory by Colbert.

The Wallabies struggled in the final two Tests, eventually losing the rubber 1-3. Solomon missed the last international and only played once more for Australia before a badly dislocated shoulder brought a premature end to his career.

| 1954 | | 1955 | | |
| --- | --- | --- | --- | --- |
| 1st v. FIJI | 2nd v. FIJI | 1st v. NZ | 2nd v. NZ | 3rd v. NZ |
| R.M. Tooth 1c | R.M. Tooth | R.M. Tooth 1c | †R. Phelps | R. Phelps |
| E.T. Stapleton | †G.R. Horsley | E.T. Stapleton 1pg | E.T. Stapleton | E.T. Stapleton 1c,1t |
| J.A. Phipps 1t | J.A. Phipps | J.A. Phipps | †P.J. Phipps | J.A. Phipps |
| H.S. Barker 1c,1pg | H.S. Barker 2c,2pg | C.T. Burke | R.M. Tooth | G.W.G. Davis |
| G.G. Jones 1t | G.G. Jones | G.G. Jones 1t | G.G. Jones | G.G. Jones |
| M.J. Tate 1t | M.J. Tate | *H.J. Solomon | †G.W.G. Davis | R.M. Tooth |
| C.T. Burke | B.P. Cox | B.P. Cox | C.T. Burke | C.T. Burke |
| *N.M. Shehadie | *N.M. Shehadie 1t | N.M. Shehadie | N.M. Shehadie | N.M. Shehadie |
| †T.P. Mooney | T.P. Mooney | †J.R. Cross | J.R. Cross | J.R. Cross |
| C.F. Forbes | T.N. Betts | †N.J. Adams | †D.J. Strachan | D.J. Strachan |
| A.R. Miller | A.R. Miller | A.S. Cameron | *A.S. Cameron | *A.S. Cameron |
| A.S. Cameron 1t | A.S. Cameron | A.R. Miller | A.R. Miller | A.R. Miller |
| †J.J. Pashley | J.J. Pashley | †J.E. Thornett | J.E. Thornett | J.E. Thornett |
| K.A. Cross 1t | K.A. Cross 1t | B.B. Johnson | B.B. Johnson | N.M. Hughes 1t |
| †V.W. Heinrich | V.W. Heinrich | N.M. Hughes | N.M. Hughes | K.A. Cross |
| Brisbane | Sydney | Wellington | Dunedin | Auckland |
| WON 22-19 | LOST 16-18 | LOST 8-16 | LOST 0-8 | WON 8-3 |
| AUST.: 2G 1PG 3T | AUST.: 2G 2PG | NZ: 2G 1PG 1T | NZ: 1G 1DG | NZ: 1T |
| FIJI: 2G 1PG 2T | FIJI: 4PG 2T | AUST.: 1G 1PG | AUST.: NIL | AUST. 1G 1T |
| 5 Jun. 1954 | 26 Jun. 1954 | 20 Aug. 1955 | 3 Sep. 1955 | 17 Sep. 1955 |

The second Fijian team proved as popular and talented as their predecessors in 1952. The Islanders played 17 matches, winning 15 but losing to NSW early in the tour and to Australia in the first Test. It was the sound tackling of full-back Dick Tooth and a vigorous display by a determined Australian pack which decided the opening Test at Brisbane; but at Sydney in the final Test the accurate place-kicking of Ranavue, the Fijian full-back, squared the rubber.

The following season John Solomon took the Eighth Australian side to New Zealand. Having led the 1952 side, he thus became the first Australian to captain two teams to NZ. His side won ten of its 13 matches in 1955, but lost the Test rubber 1-2. Solomon was injured shortly after the first Test, in which Garth Jones scored a marvellous try, and Cameron took over as captain for the remainder of the series.

Tight defence and controlled forward play enabled the Wallabies to win the last international of the series. The pack was one of the best to represent Australia during the 1950s: Shehadie, Cameron, Miller, Cross and young John Thornett all went on to gain 19 or more caps in distinguished careers. Thornett, whose first series this was, gained 37 caps during the following decade and led Australia a record number of 16 times.

| 1956 | | 1957 | |
| --- | --- | --- | --- |
| 1st v. S.AFRICA | 2nd v. S.AFRICA | 1st v. NZ | 2nd v. NZ |
| J.M. O'Neill | J.M. O'Neill | †T.G.P. Curley | T.G.P. Curley |
| R. Phelps | R. Phelps | †A.R. Morton | A.R. Morton 1t |
| J.A. Phipps | J.A. Phipps | R. Phelps | R. Phelps |
| †S.W. White | S.W. White | †J.M. Potts | J.M. Potts |
| G.G. Jones | †B.T. Roberts | †K.J. Donald | †B. Ford |
| †A.G.R. Sheil | C.T. Burke | *R.M. Tooth 2pg,1c | *R.M. Tooth 2pg |
| C.T. Burke | B.P. Cox | B.P. Cox | B.P. Cox |
| C.F.Forbes | C.F. Forbes | R.A.L. Davidson | R.A.L.Davidson |
| †J.V. Brown | J.V. Brown | J.V. Brown | J.V. Brown |
| N.M. Shehadie | N.M. Shehadie | †F.M. Elliott | N.M. Shehadie |
| *A.S. Cameron | *A.S. Cameron | A.S. Cameron | †N.B. Latimer |
| A.R. Miller | A.R. Miller | A.R. Miller | A.R. Miller |
| J.E. Thornett | J.E. Thornett | K.A. Cross 1t | K.A. Cross |
| N.M. Hughes | N.M. Hughes | †P.T. Fenwicke | †W.J. Gunther |
| K.A. Cross | K.A. Cross | †C.R. Wilson | †D.M. Emanuel |
| Sydney | Brisbane | Sydney | Brisbane |
| LOST 0-9 | LOST 0-9 | LOST 11-25 | LOST 9-22 |
| AUST.: NIL | AUST.: NIL | AUST.: 1G 2PG | AUST.: 2PG 1T |
| SA: 1PG 2T | SA: 1DG 2T | NZ: 2G 3PG 2T | NZ: 2G 1DG 1GM 2T |
| 26 May 1956 | 2 Jun. 1956 | 25 May 1957 | 1 Jun. 1957 |

Australia received tours by South Africa and New Zealand in 1956/57, playing and losing four Test matches. The seasons marked the passing of two of Australia's outstanding half-backs of the post-war seasons, Cyril Burke and Brian Cox.

Burke, veteran of 26 Tests, played his last internationals against the Springboks in 1956. Principally a scrum-half, whose strong breaks from the base of the scrummage made useful openings for his fellow-backs, he could also play elsewhere behind the forwards. Brian Cox, despite living in the shadow of Burke, still managed to gain nine caps as a scrum-half with an exceptionally long pass. After finishing his international career against the All Blacks in 1957, he had the pleasure of watching his two sons play together for Australia in the 1981-82 Wallaby tour of Britain.

Dick Tooth, an experienced and versatile back, captained Australia in 1957 against New Zealand. A doctor who became a distinguished Sydney surgeon, he was an accomplished player with an astute tactical sense. His failure to lead Australia to victory over the All Blacks, however, may have influenced the Australian selectors who chose the side to tour Britain in 1957-58.

## 1957-58

| v. WALES | v. IRELAND | v. ENGLAND | v. SCOTLAND | v. FRANCE |
|---|---|---|---|---|
| T.G.P. CURLEY | T.G.P. CURLEY | T.G.P. CURLEY 1DG | T.G.P. CURLEY | T.G.P. CURLEY |
| K.J. DONALD | K.J. DONALD | K.J. DONALD | K.J. DONALD 1T | A.R. MORTON |
| †J.K. LENEHAN | S.W. WHITE | J.K. LENEHAN 1PG | J.K. LENEHAN 1C | J.K. LENEHAN |
| J.M. POTTS | J.M. POTTS | S.W. WHITE | S.W. WHITE | R. PHELPS |
| R. PHELPS | R. PHELPS 1T | R. PHELPS | R. PHELPS | †O.G. FOX |
| †A.J. SUMMONS | A.J. SUMMONS 1T | A.J. SUMMONS | A.J. SUMMONS | †R.M. HARVEY |
| †D.M. CONNOR | D.M. CONNOR | D.M. CONNOR | D.M. CONNOR | D.M. CONNOR |
| N.M. SHEHADIE | N.M. SHEHADIE | †G.N. VAUGHAN | G.N. VAUGHAN | G.N. VAUGHAN |
| J.V. BROWN | J.V. BROWN | J.V. BROWN | J.V. BROWN | J.V. BROWN |
| *R.A.L. DAVIDSON | *R.A.L. DAVIDSON | *R.A.L. DAVIDSON | *R.A.L. DAVIDSON | *R.A.L. DAVIDSON |
| A.R. MILLER 1T | A.S. CAMERON | A.R. MILLER | A.R. MILLER | A.R. MILLER |
| D.M. EMANUEL | D.M. EMANUEL | D.M. EMANUEL | D.M. EMANUEL | D.M. EMANUEL |
| J.E. THORNETT | J.E. THORNETT | N.M. HUGHES | †E.M. PURKISS | †K. YANZ |
| N.M. HUGHES | N.M. HUGHES | †K.J. RYAN | N.M. HUGHES | N.M. HUGHES |
| P.T. FENWICKE | P.T. FENWICKE | P.T. FENWICKE | J.E. THORNETT 1T | J.E. THORNETT |
| Cardiff Arms Park | Lansdowne Road | Twickenham | Murrayfield | Stade Colombes |
| LOST 3-9 | LOST 6-9 | LOST 6-9 | LOST 8-12 | LOST 0-19 |
| WALES: 1PG 1DG 1T | IRE.: 1PG 2T | ENG.: 1PG 2T | SCOT.: 2PG 2T | FR.: 2G 2DG 1T |
| AUST.: 1T | AUST.: 2T | AUST.: 1PG 1DG | AUST.: 1G 1T | AUST.: NIL |
| 4 Jan. 1958 | 18 Jan. 1958 | 1 Feb. 1958 | 15 Feb. 1958 | 9 Mar. 1958 |

The Fourth Wallabies to Britain, captained by schoolmaster Bob Davidson, were popular tourists but had a disappointing record on the field, losing nearly half of their matches and suffering defeat in each of the five internationals. The forwards were competent in the tight play, but failings of the side were in the loose, where there was a slowness to grasp opportunities, and in back play. Throughout the tour there was criticism of the Wallabies' poor alignment in attack, a fault which the tactical awareness of Dick Tooth (had he been included) could have rectified.

Although the side had a miserable international record, the losses to Ireland, England and Scotland were by narrow margins and the results of careless Australian indiscretions and expensive tactical misjudgements. Only the French outplayed the tourists, scoring 19 points against a tired, jaded side in an eventful second half at Stade Colombes.

The two teenaged full-backs Terry Curley and Jim Lenehan were among the few players to distinguish themselves on tour. Curley played reliably in defence in 24 matches in Britain, while Lenehan finished the tour as top scorer, having been converted into a centre when Jim Phipps sustained a broken leg early in the tour. Lenehan, a most versatile player, went on to gain 24 caps and score 46 points in his international career to set a new Australian record.

## 1958

| 1st v. MAORIS | 2nd v. MAORIS | 3rd v. MAORIS |
|---|---|---|
| T.G.P. CURLEY | J.K. LENEHAN | J.K. LENEHAN |
| †A.F. McC. BOYD | K.J. DONALD 1PG | K.J. DONALD 2PG |
| J.K. LENEHAN 4PG | †P.M. JAMES | P.M. JAMES |
| R. PHELPS | S.W. WHITE | S.W. WHITE |
| A.R. MORTON 1T | A.R. MORTON | A.R. MORTON |
| †B.G. WELLS | A.J. SUMMONS | R.M. HARVEY |
| †D.L. LOGAN | *D.M. CONNOR | *D.M. CONNOR |
| G.N. VAUGHAN | G.N. VAUGHAN | G.N. VAUGHAN |
| †R.W. MEADOWS | R.W. MEADOWS | R.W. MEADOWS |
| *R.A.L. DAVIDSON | †K.K. LARKIN | K.K. LARKIN |
| A.R. MILLER | A.R. MILLER | A.R. MILLER |
| D.M. EMANUEL | D.M. EMANUEL | D.M. EMANUEL |
| E.M. PURKISS | J.E. THORNETT | J.E. THORNETT |
| K.J. RYAN | †J.H. CARROLL | J.H. CARROLL |
| J.J. PASHLEY | J.J. PASHLEY | J.J. PASHLEY |
| Brisbane | Sydney | Melbourne |
| WON 15-14 | DRAWN 3-3 | LOST 6-13 |
| AUST.: 4PG 1T | AUST.: 1PG | AUST.: 2PG |
| MAORIS: 1G 2PG 1T | MAORIS: 1PG | MAORIS: 2G 1T |
| 14 Jun. 1958 | 28 Jun. 1958 | 5 Jul. 1958 |

## 1958

| 1st v. NZ | 2nd v. NZ | 3rd v. NZ |
|---|---|---|
| T.G.P. CURLEY | T.G.P. CURLEY 1PG | T.G.P. CURLEY 1PG,1C |
| E.T. STAPLETON | A.R. MORTON 1T | A.R. MORTON |
| R. PHELPS | †A.R. KAY | †T.J. BAXTER |
| †B.J. ELLWOOD 1T | B.J. ELLWOOD | B.J. ELLWOOD |
| A.R. MORTON | R. PHELPS | R. PHELPS |
| A.J. SUMMONS | A.J. SUMMONS | A.J. SUMMONS |
| D.M. CONNOR | D.M. CONNOR | D.M. CONNOR |
| †K.J. ELLIS | K.J. ELLIS | K.J. ELLIS |
| R.W. MEADOWS | R.W. MEADOWS | R.W. MEADOWS |
| †P.K. DUNN | P.K. DUNN | P.K. DUNN |
| J.H. CARROLL | J.H. CARROLL | J.H. CARROLL 1T |
| †J.P.L. WHITE | J.P.L. WHITE | J.P.L. WHITE |
| *C.R. WILSON | *C.R. WILSON | *C.R. WILSON |
| K.J. RYAN | K.J. RYAN | K.J. RYAN |
| †D.R. LOWTH | J.E. THORNETT | J.E. THORNETT |
| Wellington | Christchurch | Auckland |
| LOST 3-25 | WON 6-3 | LOST 8-17 |
| NZ: 2G 5T | NZ: 1T | NZ: 1G 4PG |
| AUST.: 1T | AUST.: 1PG 1T | AUST.: 1G 1PG |
| 23 Aug. 1958 | 6 Sep. 1958 | 20 Sep. 1958 |

This was Australia's busiest international season since their first Test was staged in 1899. Six Tests were played, three each against the Maoris (Australia's last Tests against them to date) and New Zealand. A last-minute penalty by Lenehan, one of his record four for the Test, gave Australia victory by a point in the first match against the Maoris and ended a depressing run of nine consecutive international defeats. A draw in heavy conditions at Sydney was a fair result for the second Test, but the Maoris squared the rubber by winning convincingly at Melbourne in fine weather.

Des Connor, a talented scrum-half who later played for New Zealand, captained Australia against the Maoris and handed over the leadership to Charles Wilson (a medical student) for the Wallabies' tour to New Zealand.

Wilson's side, a modest mix of youth and experience, lost the rubber 1-2 but won the second Test thanks to a brilliant try by Alan Morton, who used his powerful frame to bump past several tacklers for a last-minute try at Christchurch. Morton became a Physical Education expert and a noted rugby coach in Western Australia.

## 1959

| 1st v. BRITISH IS. | 2nd v. BRITISH IS. |
|---|---|
| J.K. LENEHAN | J.K. LENEHAN |
| A.R. MORTON | A.R. MORTON |
| J.M. POTTS | A.R. KAY |
| †L.J. DIETT | L.J. DIETT |
| K.J. DONALD 2PG | K.J. DONALD 1PG |
| A.J. SUMMONS | A.J. SUMMONS |
| D.M. CONNOR | D.M. CONNOR |
| K.J. ELLIS | K.J. ELLIS |
| †P.G. JOHNSON | P.G. JOHNSON |
| P.K. DUNN | P.K. DUNN |
| A.R. MILLER | A.R. MILLER |
| J.H. CARROLL | J.H. CARROLL |
| J.E. THORNETT | J.E. THORNETT |
| †R. OUTTERSIDE | R. OUTTERSIDE |
| *P.T. FENWICKE | *P.T. FENWICKE |
| Brisbane | Sydney |
| LOST 6-17 | LOST 3-24 |
| AUST.: 2PG | AUST.: 1PG |
| BIs.: 1G 1DG 2PG 1T | BIs.: 3G 1PG 2T |
| 6 Jun. 1959 | 13 Jun. 1959 |

An Australian side full of experience was confident of beating the Lions in the two-Test series which was staged as a prelude to the British tour of New Zealand. However the Australians were beaten with considerable ease in both matches.

Three new caps were awarded at Brisbane. Diett, a student teacher of considerable rugby promise, was the only new back, and he was joined by Peter Johnson and Bob Outterside in the pack. Outterside, a teacher, had toured South Africa with the 1953 Wallabies but had to wait six years before gaining Test selection. Johnson, an agile hooker, went on to become Australia's most capped player, appearing in 42 Tests during a long international career.

Australia named the same fifteen for the second Test, but Potts stood down to study for impending Law examinations and his place was occupied by Kay, an Army sapper who had played in the winning Australian side against New Zealand at Christchurch in 1958. Ken Donald, a medical student, scored all of Australia's points in the series, landing three penalty goals.

|  | 1961 |  |  | 1961 |  | 1961 |
|---|---|---|---|---|---|---|
| 1st v. FIJI | 2nd v. FIJI | 3rd v. FIJI | 1st v. S.AFRICA | 2nd v. S.AFRICA | v. FRANCE |
| R. PHELPS 1T | R. PHELPS | R. PHELPS | J.K. LENEHAN | J.K. LENEHAN | J.K. LENEHAN |
| †M.A. CLEARY 1T | M.A. CLEARY 2T | M.A. CLEARY | M.A. CLEARY | M.A. CLEARY 1T | M.A. CLEARY |
| †R.J. LISLE 1T | R.J. LISLE | R.J. LISLE 1T | R.J. LISLE | R. PHELPS | R. PHELPS |
| †H.F. ROBERTS | B.J. ELLWOOD 1T | B.J. ELLWOOD | B.J. ELLWOOD | H.F. ROBERTS | B.J. ELLWOOD 1PG,1C |
| †E. MAGRATH 1T | †R.T. POTTER | †A. TURNBULL | R. PHELPS | E. MAGRATH | E. MAGRATH |
| †J.H. DOWSE 3C | J.H. DOWSE 2PG,1C | H.F. ROBERTS | J.H. DOWSE 1PG | J.H. DOWSE 2PG,1C | H.F. ROBERTS |
| *†K.W. CATCHPOLE 1T | *K.W. CATCHPOLE | *K.W. CATCHPOLE | *K.W. CATCHPOLE | *K.W. CATCHPOLE | *K.W. CATCHPOLE |
| J.P.L. WHITE | J.P.L. WHITE | J.P.L. WHITE | J.P.L. WHITE | J.P.L. WHITE | J.P.L. WHITE |
| P.G. JOHNSON | P.G. JOHNSON | P.G. JOHNSON | P.G. JOHNSON | P.G. JOHNSON | P.G. JOHNSON |
| A.R. MILLER | A.R. MILLER | A.R. MILLER | J.E. THORNETT | A.R. MILLER | A.R. MILLER |
| †D.G. MacDOUGALL | J.E. THORNETT | J.E. THORNETT | D.G. MacDOUGALL | J.E. THORNETT | J.E. THORNETT |
| †R.N. THORNETT 1T | †R.J. HEMING | R.J. HEMING | R.N. THORNETT | R.N. THORNETT | R.N. THORNETT |
| †E.L. HEINRICH | E.L. HEINRICH | E.L. HEINRICH | T.W. REID | E.L. HEINRICH | E.L. HEINRICH 1T |
| †J.F. O'GORMAN | R.N. THORNETT | R.N. THORNETT | R.J. HEMING | R.J. HEMING | R.J. HEMING |
| †T.W. REID | T.W. REID 1T | T.W. REID | J.F. O'GORMAN | J.F. O'GORMAN | J.F. O'GORMAN |
| Brisbane | Sydney | Melbourne | Johannesburg | Port Elizabeth | Sydney |
| WON 24-6 | WON 20-14 | DRAWN 3-3 | LOST 3-28 | LOST 11-23 | LOST 8-15 |
| AUST.: 3G 3T | AUST.: 1G 2PG 3T | AUST.: 1T | SA: 2G 6T | SA: 1G 1DG 3PG 2T | AUST.: 1G 1PG |
| FIJI: 2PG | FIJI: 1G 1PG 2T | FIJI: 1T | AUS.: 1PG | AUST.: 1G 2PG | FR.: 3T 2DG |
| 10 Jun. 1961 | 17 Jun. 1961 | 1 Jul. 1961 | 5 Aug. 1961 | 12 Aug. 1961 | 26 Aug. 1961 |

This was one of Australia's busiest ever international seasons. They won two matches at home in an entertaining series with the Fijians, were trounced twice in South Africa, and ended the season losing to France on a waterlogged pitch in Sydney.

In the opening Test of the season the play of the new threequarters was encouraging, and schoolmaster Jim Lisle and Michael Cleary scored tries in a 24-6 victory which set Australia on the path to a first home rubber success since 1934. Both Cleary and Lisle later enjoyed long and successful careers in Australian Rugby League circles, and Cleary became a noted New South Wales politician in the 1980s.

Ken Catchpole, Australia's most talented scrum-half, won his first caps this season, gaining the rare distinction of captaining his country on his Test debut. He went on to win 27 caps at scrum-half, where his ability to pass quickly from the base of the scrummage enabled his backs to elude opposing flankers and make openings for their wings.

| 1962 | | 1962 | | |
| --- | --- | --- | --- | --- |
| 1st v. NZ | 2nd v. NZ | 1st v. NZ | 2nd v. NZ | 3rd v. NZ |
| R. Phelps | *J.K. Lenehan | J.K. Lenehan | J.K. Lenehan | J.K. Lenehan 1T |
| †E.S. Boyce | E.S. Boyce | †K.P. Walsham | J.A. Douglas | J.A. Douglas |
| B.J. Ellwood | R. Phelps | B.J. Ellwood | †R.J.P. Marks | R.J.P. Marks |
| †P.R.I. Scott 2PG | P.R.I. Scott 1c | †J.S. Boyce | B.J. Ellwood | B.J. Ellwood |
| †L.C. McDermott | L.C. McDermott | †J.A. Douglas | J.S. Boyce | J.S. Boyce |
| †N.J.D. Storey | B.J. Ellwood | †P.F. Hawthorne | P.F. Hawthorne | P.F. Hawthorne |
| K.W. Catchpole | K.W. Catchpole | †K.V. McMullen | K.W. Catchpole | K.V. McMullen |
| J.P.L. White | J.P.L. White | J.P.L. White | J.P.L. White | J.P.L. White |
| *P.G. Johnson | P.G. Johnson | P.G. Johnson | P.G. Johnson | P.G. Johnson |
| A.R. Miller | A.R. Miller | †J.E. Freedman | J.E. Freedman | J.E. Freedman |
| †J.M. Miller | R.N. Thornett 1T | *J.E. Thornett | *J.E. Thornett | *J.E. Thornett |
| †P.D. Perrin | J.E. Thornett | R.N. Thornett | R.N. Thornett | R.N. Thornett |
| E.L. Heinrich | E.L. Heinrich | E.L. Heinrich | †C.P. Crittle | C.P. Crittle |
| R.N. Thornett | R.J. Heming | R.J. Heming | R.J. Heming | R.J. Heming |
| T.W. Reid | J.F. O'Gorman | †G.A. Chapman 3PG | G.A. Chapman | G.A. Chapman 1PG,1c |
| Brisbane | Sydney | Wellington | Dunedin | Auckland |
| LOST 6-20 | LOST 5-14 | DRAWN 9-9 | LOST 0-3 | LOST 8-16 |
| AUST.: 2PG | AUST.: 1G | NZ: 2PG 1T | NZ: 1PG | NZ: 2G 1DG 1T |
| NZ: 1G 1DG 1PG 3T | NZ: 1G 2PG 1T | AUST.: 3PG | AUST.: NIL | AUST.: 1G 1PG |
| 26 May 1962 | 4 Jun. 1962 | 25 Aug. 1962 | 8 Sep. 1962 | 22 Sep. 1962 |

Australia played two series against New Zealand in 1962. In May/June at home they participated in two sternly contested matches which resulted in wins for the All Blacks. The week before the first of the Tests, however, New South Wales struck an encouraging blow for Australian rugby by defeating the All Blacks 12-11 in Sydney.

The second of the Tests, in Sydney, marked the final international appearance of Rod Phelps, a versatile utility back who had featured as a centre, wing and full-back in his 23 Tests. A dentist, Phelps was the first Australian full-back to score a try in a Test when he crossed in the 1961 Test against the Fijians at Brisbane.

Jim Lenehan, Australia's first-choice full-back following Terry Curley's premature retirement (to join the Marist Brotherhood) repeated Phelps' feat with a try against New Zealand at Auckland in the final Test of Australia's late-season tour. Though beaten in the series, a significant feature of the trip was the thoughtful leadership of new captain John Thornett.

| 1963 | | 1963 | | |
| --- | --- | --- | --- | --- |
| v. ENGLAND | 1st v. S.AFRICA | 2nd v. S.AFRICA | 3rd v. S.AFRICA | 4th v. S.AFRICA |
| †P.F. Ryan 3c | P.F. Ryan | †T.V. Casey 1PG | T.V. Casey 1PG,1DG,1c | T.V. Casey 1PG |
| K.P. Walsham 1T | †J.L. Williams | R.J.P. Marks | J.L. Williams 1T | J.L. Williams |
| R.J.P. Marks | B.J. Ellwood | B.J. Ellwood | B.J. Ellwood | B.J. Ellwood |
| †P.A. Jones 1T | P.A. Jones | †I.E. Moutray | R.J.P. Marks | R.J.P. Marks |
| J.S. Boyce | J.S. Boyce | J.S. Boyce 1T | J.S. Boyce | J.S. Boyce |
| P.F. Hawthorne | P.F. Hawthorne | P.F. Hawthorne 1DG | P.F. Hawthorne | P.F. Hawthorne 1DG |
| K.V. McMullen | K.V. McMullen 1T | K.W. Catchpole | K.W. Catchpole | K.W. Catchpole |
| J.P.L. White | J.P.L. White | J.P.L. White | J.P.L. White | J.P.L. White |
| P.G. Johnson | P.G. Johnson | P.G. Johnson | P.G. Johnson | P.G. Johnson |
| †L.R. Austin | J.E. Freedman | *J.E. Thornett | *J.E. Thornett | *J.E. Thornett |
| *J.E. Thornett | J.M. Miller | R.J. Heming | R.J. Heming | R.J. Heming |
| J.M. Miller | *J.E. Thornett | C.P. Crittle | C.P. Crittle | C.P. Crittle |
| E.L. Heinrich 1T | E.L. Heinrich | †J. Guerassimoff | J. Guerassimoff | J. Guerassimoff |
| J.F. O'Gorman | J.F. O'Gorman | J.F. O'Gorman | J.F. O'Gorman | J.F. O'Gorman |
| †G.V. Davis 1T | G.V. Davis | G.V. Davis | G.V. Davis | G.V. Davis |
| Sydney | Pretoria | Cape Town | Johannesburg | Port Elizabeth |
| WON 18-9 | LOST 3-14 | WON 9-5 | WON 11-9 | LOST 6-22 |
| AUST.: 3G 1T | SA: 1G 2PG 1T | SA: 1G | SA: 3PG | SA: 2G 3PG 1T |
| ENG.: 3T | AUST.: 1T | AUST. 1PG 1DG 1T | AUST.: 1G 1DG 1PG | AUST.: 1PG 1DG |
| 4 Jun. 1963 | 13 Jul. 1963 | 10 Aug. 1963 | 24 Aug. 1963 | 7 Sep. 1963 |

This was Australia's most successful season since the late 1940s, with three victories resulting from five Tests. Early in June the English tourists were beaten by a young side which adopted an attractive approach in awful conditions at the Sydney Sports Ground. Inspired by some brilliant half-back play, the Australians scored four tries to win 18-9, their first home victory against an International Board country since 1934.

A young team which adopted a thoughtful approach to their rugby then enjoyed a tremendous tour of South Africa, where for the first time the Wallabies shared the spoils of a rubber with the Springboks. Careful defence, imaginative backs, splendid loose forwards and some accurate kicking by full-back Terry Casey were the chief reasons for the side's success. (Casey had been called into the tour side when Lenehan, an original choice, was injured and unable to undertake the trip.) Only a late surge of typical Springbok power play in the Port Elizabeth Test prevented the Wallabies winning the rubber.

Thornett's inspiring leadership was another key factor in Australia's success. He was to guide his nation back into the reckoning as a major rugby power in the 1960s, captaining the side in 15 consecutive Tests and on the tour of Britain in 1966-67.

## 1964

| 1st v. NZ | 2nd v. NZ | 3rd v. NZ |
|---|---|---|
| T.V. CASEY 2PG | T.V. CASEY | T.V. CASEY 3PG,1C |
| | | |
| E.S. BOYCE | E.S. BOYCE | E.S. BOYCE 2T |
| †R.E. HONAN | R.E. HONAN | R.J.P. MARKS |
| R.J.P. MARKS 1T | R.J.P. MARKS 1T | B.J. ELLWOOD |
| J.S. BOYCE | †D.N. GRIMMOND | J.S. BOYCE |
| | | |
| P.F. HAWTHORNE | P.F. HAWTHORNE | P.F. HAWTHORNE 1DG |
| K.W. CATCHPOLE | K.W. CATCHPOLE | K.W. CATCHPOLE |
| | | |
| J.P.L. WHITE | J.P.L. WHITE | J.P.L. WHITE |
| P.G. JOHNSON | P.G. JOHNSON | P.G. JOHNSON |
| *J.E. THORNETT | *J.E. THORNETT | *J.E. THORNETT |
| R.J. HEMING | R.J. HEMING | R.J. HEMING |
| C.P. CRITTLE | C.P. CRITTLE | C.P. CRITTLE |
| J. GUERASSIMOFF | J. GUERASSIMOFF | J. GUERASSIMOFF |
| †D.J. O'NEILL | D.J. O'NEILL | †D.J. SHEPHERD |
| G.V. DAVIS | G.V. DAVIS | G.V. DAVIS |
| Dunedin | Christchurch | Wellington |
| LOST 9-14 | LOST 3-18 | WON 20-5 |
| NZ: 1G 2PG 1DG | NZ: 3G 1T | NZ: 1G |
| AUST.: 2PG 1T | AUST.: 1T | AUST.: 1G 3PG 1DG 1T |
| 15 Aug. 1964 | 22 Aug. 1964 | 29 Aug. 1964 |

John Thornett's team which visited New Zealand in 1964 lost four of its first seven matches, including the first two Tests, and was in danger of becoming the worst side to tour the country.

But before the final Test, team manager Mr Alan Roper brought his side together for an intensive series of preparations and team talks which resulted in the Wallabies taking the field at Wellington with fresh resolution. Thornett elected to face a breeze in the first half, and a clever try by Stewart Boyce pushed the Australians into the lead (3-0) at the interval. In the second half, with Hawthorne outstanding and the Wallabies forcing the All Blacks to make errors, the hosts were routed 20-5, and a famous Australian victory turned Thornett's side into heroes.

Jim and Stewart Boyce, who played together as wingers in the Tests at Dunedin and Wellington, were the first twins to play in an international for Australia.

| 1965 | | 1966 | |
|---|---|---|---|
| 1st v. S.AFRICA | 2nd v. S.AFRICA | 1st v. BRITISH IS. | 2nd. v. BRITISH IS. |
| J.K. LENEHAN 1T | J.K. LENEHAN 2PG | P.F. RYAN | P.F. RYAN |
| | | | |
| E.S. BOYCE 1T | E.S. BOYCE | †G. RUEBNER 1PG,1C | G. RUEBNER |
| R.J.P. MARKS | R.J.P. MARKS | †R.K. TRIVETT | †J.E. BRASS |
| B.J. ELLWOOD 4PG | B.J. ELLWOOD 2PG | B.J. ELLWOOD | R.K. TRIVETT |
| J.S. BOYCE | J.S. BOYCE | †A.M. CARDY | A.M. CARDY |
| | | | |
| P.F. HAWTHORNE | P.F. HAWTHORNE | P.F. HAWTHORNE | P.F. HAWTHORNE |
| K.W. CATCHPOLE | K.W. CATCHPOLE | K.W. CATCHPOLE | K.W. CATCHPOLE |
| | | | |
| J.P.L. WHITE | J.P.L. WHITE | *J.E. THORNETT | *J.E. THORNETT |
| P.G. JOHNSON | P.G. JOHNSON | P.G. JOHNSON | P.G. JOHNSON |
| *J.E. THORNETT | *J.E. THORNETT | A.R. MILLER 1T | A.R. MILLER |
| R.J. HEMING | R.J. HEMING | R.J. HEMING | R.J. HEMING |
| C.P. CRITTLE | C.P. CRITTLE | C.P. CRITTLE | C.P. CRITTLE |
| J.F. O'GORMAN | J.F. O'GORMAN | J. GUERASSIMOFF | J. GUERASSIMOFF |
| D.J. SHEPHERD | D.J. SHEPHERD | D.J. SHEPHERD | D.J. SHEPHERD |
| G.V. DAVIS | J. GUERASSIMOFF | G.V. DAVIS | G.V. DAVIS |
| Sydney | Brisbane | Sydney | Brisbane |
| WON 18-11 | WON 12-8 | LOST 8-11 | LOST 0-31 |
| AUST.: 4PG 2T | AUST.: 4PG | AUST.: 1G 1PG | AUST.: NIL |
| SA: 1G 1T 1PG | SA: 1G 1T | BIs.: 1G 1PG 1T | BIs.: 5G 1DG 1PG |
| 19 Jun. 1965 | 26 Jun. 1965 | 28 May 1966 | 4 Jun. 1966 |

Barely 8000 had watched Australia's rugby revival at Sydney against England in 1963: there were 45,946 at Sydney to see the first Test against the Springboks in 1965, a tribute to the improvement made by the international team under John Thornett.

In a series dominated by penalties (and marred by some curious refereeing decisions), the Australians pleased their success-thirsty public by winning a series against the Springboks for the first time. Beres Ellwood, an outstanding threequarter who played 20 times for Australia, kicked four penalty goals in the opening Test and two more to help Australia recover from a 0-8 deficit to win the second Test. Ellwood was dropped after the Lions won the Sydney Test in 1966.

Australia's excellent halves Catchpole and Hawthorne, who played in the Tests of 1965 and 1966, were partners in a record 17 internationals before Hawthorne passed to Rugby League. A skilful fly-half, he had dropped nine goals in his 21 Tests, and went on to become an outstanding League player.

## 1966-67

| v. WALES | v. SCOTLAND | v. ENGLAND | v. IRELAND | v. FRANCE |
|---|---|---|---|---|
| J.K. LENEHAN 1T,1PG | J.K. LENEHAN 1C | J.K. LENEHAN 1PG,1C | J.K. LENEHAN 1C | J.K. LENEHAN |
| | | | | |
| E.S. BOYCE | E.S. BOYCE | E.S. BOYCE | E.S. BOYCE 1T | E.S. BOYCE |
| R.J.P. MARKS | R.J.P. MARKS | R.J.P. MARKS | R.J.P. MARKS | R.J.P. MARKS |
| J.E. BRASS | J.E. BRASS 1T | J.E. BRASS 1T | J.E. BRASS | J.E. BRASS |
| A.M. CARDY 1T | A.M. CARDY | A.M. CARDY | A.M. CARDY | A.M. CARDY |
| | | | | |
| P.F. HAWTHORNE 1DG,1C | †P.R. GIBBS | P.F. HAWTHORNE 3DG,1PG | P.F. HAWTHORNE 1DG | P.F. HAWTHORNE 1DG,1PG,1C |
| *K.W. CATCHPOLE | *K.W. CATCHPOLE | *K.W. CATCHPOLE 1T | *K.W. CATCHPOLE | K.W. CATCHPOLE |
| | | | | |
| J.M. MILLER | J.M. MILLER | J.M. MILLER | A.R. MILLER | *J.E. THORNETT |
| P.G. JOHNSON | P.G. JOHNSON | P.G. JOHNSON | P.G. JOHNSON | P.G. JOHNSON 1T |
| A.R. MILLER | A.R. MILLER | †R.B. PROSSER | R.B. PROSSER | A.R. MILLER |
| †R.G. TEITZEL | R.G. TEITZEL | R.G. TEITZEL | R.G. TEITZEL | R.G. TEITZEL |
| R.J. HEMING | P.C. CRITTLE | P.C. CRITTLE | P.C. CRITTLE | R.J. HEMING |
| †M.P. PURCELL | M.P. PURCELL | J. GUERASSIMOFF | J. GUERASSIMOFF | J. GUERASSIMOFF |
| J.F. O'GORMAN | J.F. O'GORMAN | J.F. O'GORMAN | J.F. O'GORMAN | J.F. O'GORMAN |
| G.V. DAVIS | G.V. DAVIS | G.V. DAVIS | G.V. DAVIS | G.V. DAVIS 1T |
| Cardiff Arms Park | Murrayfield | Twickenham | Lansdowne Road | Stade Colombes |
| WON 14-11 | LOST 5-11 | WON 23-11 | LOST 8-15 | LOST 14-20 |
| WALES: 1G 1PG 1T | SCOT.: 1G 1PG 1T | ENG.: 1G 2PG | IRE.: 1PG 2DG 2T | FR.: 1G 4PG 1DG |
| AUST.: 1G 1PG 1DG 1T | AUST.: 1G | AUST.: 1G 3DG 2PG 1T | AUST.: 1G 1DG | AUST.: 1G 1PG 1DG 1T |
| 3 Dec. 1966 | 17 Dec. 1966 | 7 Jan. 1967 | 21 Jan. 1967 | 11 Feb. 1967 |

The Fifth Wallabies to Britain brought a fresh commitment to bright, open rugby, and gained memorable wins in the internationals at Cardiff and Twickenham. Their backs relied on short, sharp, accurate passing to stretch opposing defences until overlaps appeared. Fired by Catchpole's quick service, their tactics often led to spectacular tries, none more so than Lenehan's effort in the corner which defeated Wales.

Hawthorne masterminded the victory over England, equalling the world international record by dropping three goals in the match. He finished the Test series with six drop-goals – a remarkable feat.

John Thornett, one of the rare band of overseas players to tour Britain twice ten years apart, had an unlucky tour (as in 1957 when he had suffered from hepatitis). An attack of impetigo sidelined him on this trip and he stood down from all but the last international of the tour.

| 1967 | 1967 |
|---|---|
| v. IRELAND | v. NZ |
| J.K. LENEHAN 1C | †R.C.S. MANNING |
| | |
| E.S. BOYCE | †I.J. PROCTOR |
| R.J.P. MARKS | †P.V. SMITH |
| J.E. BRASS | J.E. BRASS |
| †R.A. HOW | †R.P. BATTERHAM 1PG,2T |
| | |
| P.F. HAWTHORNE | P.F. HAWTHORNE |
| *K.W. CATCHPOLE 1T | *K.W. CATCHPOLE |
| | |
| R.B. PROSSER | R.B. PROSSER |
| P.G. JOHNSON | P.G. JOHNSON |
| A.R. MILLER | A.R. MILLER |
| M.P. PURCELL | †A.M.F. ABRAHAMS |
| R.G. TEITZEL | R.G. TEITZEL |
| †H.A. ROSE | †J.L. SAYLE |
| J.F. O'GORMAN | H.A. ROSE |
| G.V. DAVIS | G.V. DAVIS |
| Sydney | Wellington |
| LOST 5-11 | LOST 9-29 |
| AUST.: 1G | NZ: 4G 2PG 1DG |
| IRE.: 1G 1DG 1T | AUST.: 1PG 2T |
| 13 May 1967 | 19 Aug. 1967 |

The only home Test of the season was against Ireland, who were on their first short tour of Australia. The international at Sydney took place a week after New South Wales had walloped the tourists 21-9. The Australian selectors were criticised for leaving out some of the successful State side, and fuel was added to the pundits' argument when the Irish ran out clear winners of a dreary Test dominated by unimaginative kicking.

Jim Lenehan, in his last Test, had a disappointing match and missed a penalty kick and drop at goal attempt which were well within his compass.

A very young group, containing only eleven of the thirty who had toured Britain in 1966-7, undertook a brief visit to New Zealand in August. The side were guests of the NZRFU, who were celebrating their 75th anniversary. In the only Test of the visit Australia, fielding six new caps, were trounced 9-29, Rod Batterham, in his Test debut, scoring all of the Australian points.

| 1968 | | | 1968 | |
|---|---|---|---|---|
| 1st v. NZ | 2nd v. NZ | v. FRANCE | v. IRELAND | v. SCOTLAND |
| †A.N. McGill 2PG,1C | A.N. McGill 5PG | A.N. McGill 1PG,1C | B.D. Honan | B.D. Honan |
| †J.W. Cole | J.W. Cole | J.W. Cole | J.W. Cole | J.W. Cole |
| J.E. Brass[1] | B.D. Honan | P.V. Smith 1T | P.V. Smith | P.V. Smith |
| P.V. Smith | P.V. Smith[1] | J.E. Brass | J.E. Brass | J.E. Brass 1PG |
| A.M. Cardy 1T | A.M. Cardy | B.D. Honan | †T.R. Forman | T.R. Forman |
| †J.P. Ballesty | J.P. Ballesty | J.P. Ballesty 1DG | J.P. Ballesty 1T | J.P. Ballesty |
| *K.W. Catchpole[2] | J.N.B. Hipwell 1T | J.N.B. Hipwell | J.N.B. Hipwell | J.N.B. Hipwell |
| †J.R. Roxburgh | J.R. Roxburgh | J.R. Roxburgh | R.B. Prosser | †K.R. Bell |
| P.G. Johnson | *P.G. Johnson | *P.G. Johnson | *P.G. Johnson | *P.G. Johnson |
| R.B. Prosser | R.B. Prosser | R.B. Prosser | †R.V. Turnbull | R.B. Prosser |
| A.M.F. Abrahams | †S.C. Gregory | S.C. Gregory | N.P. Reilly | N.P. Reilly |
| †N.P. Reilly | N.P. Reilly | N.P. Reilly | S.C. Gregory | S.C. Gregory |
| G.V. Davis | G.V. Davis | G.V. Davis | H.A. Rose | H.A. Rose |
| †D.A. Taylor | D.A. Taylor | D.A. Taylor | D.A. Taylor | D.A. Taylor |
| H.A. Rose | H.A. Rose | H.A. Rose | G.V. Davis | G.V. Davis |
| Sydney | Ballymore | Sydney | Lansdowne Road | Murrayfield |
| LOST 11-27 | LOST 18-19 | WON 11-10 | LOST 3-10 | LOST 3-9 |
| AUST.: 1G 2PG | AUST.: 5PG 1T | AUST.: 1G 1PG 1DG | IRE.: 2G | SCOT.: 2PG 1T |
| NZ: 3G 1PG 3T | NZ: 2G 2PG 1T | FR.: 2G | AUST.: 1T | AUST.: 1PG |
| 15 Jun. 1968 | 22 Jun. 1968 | 17 Aug. 1968 | 26 Oct. 1968 | 2 Nov. 1968 |

[1]Rep. by †B.D. Honan
[2]Rep. by †J.N.B. Hipwell

(2nd v. NZ) [1]Rep. by †A.M. Pope

Ken Catchpole's career ended during the first Test of the season against New Zealand. Just before half-time he was dragged from a ruck, sustained a groin injury and was stretchered off. It was a sad end to a fine career. As a scrum-half Catchpole rarely employed the dive pass, preferring to remain on his feet at all times and concentrating on transferring the ball quickly to create overlaps. His example was to influence leading coaches during the following decade. Another splendid scrum-half John Hipwell, who went on to win 35 caps, becoming Australia's most-capped half-back, succeeded Catchpole. His first complete Test was against New Zealand at the new Brisbane rugby ground, Ballymore Park. Australia lost by a point in a match dominated by penalty goals. McGill kicked five to create a new Australian Test record of 15 points for the match. The Australian dispensation law, one which restricted direct kicking to touch, became universally adopted in September 1968, and the short tour of the Wallabies was eagerly anticipated in Britain. It was believed that Australian experience of the rule would show the way for the British to exploit the new law with expertise. But the Australians were a disappointing side, lost both of the Tests, and revealed few subtleties regarding the law.

| 1969 | | 1969 | | |
|---|---|---|---|---|
| v. WALES | 1st v. S.AFRICA | 2nd v. S.AFRICA | 3rd v. S.AFRICA | 4th v. S.AFRICA |
| A.N. McGill 1T,2PG,2C | A.N. McGill | A.N. McGill | A.N. McGill | A.N. McGill |
| J.W. Cole | J.W. Cole | J.W. Cole | J.W. Cole | J.W. Cole |
| †G.A. Shaw | P.V. Smith[1] | B.D. Honan | J.P. Ballesty 1PG | B.D. Honan |
| P.V. Smith 1T | B.D. Honan | †S.O. Knight | B.D. Honan | S.O. Knight 1T |
| T.R. Forman | T.R. Forman 1T | T.R. Forman | T.R. Forman | T.R. Forman |
| J.P. Ballesty | †R.G. Rosenblum 2PG,1C | J.P. Ballesty 3PG | R.G. Rosenblum | J.P. Ballesty 1PG,1C |
| J.N.B. Hipwell | J.N.B. Hipwell | J.N.B. Hipwell | J.N.B. Hipwell | J.N.B. Hipwell |
| J.R. Roxburgh | J.R. Roxburgh | J.R. Roxburgh | J.R. Roxburgh | J.R. Roxburgh |
| †P. Darveniza | †B.S. Taafe | P. Darveniza | P. Darveniza | P. Darveniza |
| R.B. Prosser | R.B. Prosser | R.B. Prosser | R.B. Prosser | R.B. Prosser |
| N.P. Reilly | S.C. Gregory | N.P. Reilly | S.C. Gregory | N.P. Reilly |
| A.M.F. Abrahams | †O.F. Butler | O.F. Butler | N.P. Reilly | A.J. Skinner |
| *G.V. Davis | *G.V. Davis | *G.V. Davis | *G.V. Davis | *G.V. Davis |
| †A.J. Skinner | H.A. Rose | H.A. Rose | H.A. Rose | H.A. Rose |
| H.A. Rose | N.P. Reilly | †R.J. Kelleher | R.J. Kelleher | †B.S. McDonald |
| Sydney | Johannesburg | Durban | Cape Town | Bloemfontein |
| LOST 16-19 | LOST 11-30 | LOST 9-16 | LOST 3-11 | LOST 8-19 |
| AUST.: 2G 2PG | SA: 3G 3PG 2T | SA: 2G 1PG 1T | SA: 1G 1PG 1T | SA: 2G 2PG 1T |
| WALES: 2G 2PG 1T | AUST.: 1G 2PG | AUST.: 3PG | AUST.: 1PG | AUST.: 1G 1PG |
| 21 Jun. 1969 | 2 Aug. 1969 | 16 Aug. 1969 | 6 Sep. 1969 | 20 Sep. 1969 |

[1]Rep. by G.A. Shaw

Greg Davis became Australia's captain against Wales in 1969. Born and bred in New Zealand, Davis came to Australia in 1963 and was capped in the same year. A fearless loose forward of great pace and considerable tactical awareness, Davis played 39 Tests, the last 16 as captain (to equal John Thornett's record). Later he returned to New Zealand but died of a brain tumour in 1979.

Davis' side had a disappointing tour of South Africa, where for the first time on a long tour the Wallabies failed to win a Test. A young side foraged energetically in the loose but found the Springboks too heavy and too strong to overcome in the set pieces.

Geoff Shaw, a powerful runner who went on to become Australia's most-capped centre, made his debut as a teenager in the Test against Wales. In his 27 Tests, which spanned the decade, he used his burly frame to create numerous openings for his wings.

|  | 1970 | 1971 |  |  |
| --- | --- | --- | --- | --- |
|  | v. SCOTLAND | 1st v. S.AFRICA | 2nd v. S.AFRICA | 3rd v. S.AFRICA |
|  | A.N. McGill 1PG,1c | A.N. McGill 2PG,1c | A.N. McGill 1PG,1DG | A.N. McGill |
|  | J.W. Cole 2T | J.W. Cole | J.W. Cole | J.W. Cole 1T |
|  | S.O. Knight | S.O. Knight | S.O. Knight | S.O. Knight |
|  | G.A. Shaw | G.A. Shaw | G.A. Shaw | G.A. Shaw |
|  | R.P. Batterham 2T | †J.I. Taylor | †J.J. McLean | J.J. McLean 1PG |
|  | R.G. Rosenblum 1T | †G.C. Richardson | G.C. Richardson | G.C. Richardson |
|  | J.N.B. Hipwell 1T | J.N.B. Hipwell | J.N.B. Hipwell | †M.J. Barry |
|  | J.R. Roxburgh | J.L. Howard | R.A. Smith | R.B. Prosser |
|  | P.G. Johnson | P.G. Johnson | P.G. Johnson | †R.J. Thompson |
|  | †J.L. Howard | R.B. Prosser | R.B. Prosser | †S.G. MacDougall |
|  | O.F. Butler | †R.A. Smith | †G. Fay | S.C. Gregory |
|  | A.J. Skinner | S.C. Gregory | O.F. Butler | O.F. Butler |
|  | B.S. McDonald | †P.D. Sullivan | P.D. Sullivan | P.D. Sullivan |
|  | H.A. Rose | †R.A. McLean 1T | R.A. McLean | R.A. McLean |
|  | *G.V. Davis | *G.V. Davis | *G.V. Davis | *G.V. Davis |
|  | Sydney | Sydney | Ballymore | Sydney |
|  | WON 23-3 | LOST 11-19 | LOST 6-14 | LOST 6-18 |
|  | AUST.: 1G 1PG 5T | AUST.: 1G 2PG | AUST.: 1PG 1DG | AUST.: 1PG 1T |
|  | SCOT.: 1PG | SA: 2G 1DG 1PG 1T | SA: 1G 1PG 2T | SA: 3G 1PG |
|  | 6 Jun. 1970 | 17 Jul. 1971 | 31 Jul. 1971 | 7 Aug. 1971 |

Australian rugby met with mixed fortunes in 1970 and 1971. Scotland toured the country in 1970, finding the quality of the Australian game very high. New South Wales and Queensland each defeated the tourists, and in the sole Test of the season Australia ran in six tries at Sydney.

Hipwell and Rosenblum combined smoothly to activate a dynamic threequarter line, and in the second half Shaw and Knight repeatedly pierced a weak defence to send their wingers over for three tries (to add to one scored by Batterham in the first half). Fittingly, the halves scored a try in each half too as Australia registered their best Test win for 34 years.

But the elation which followed the win of 1970 quickly evaporated the next season when Australia were mastered by an invincible Springbok force. Lacking confidence, the home players were unable to deal effectively with fit, mobile opponents who coasted to each of their three Test wins.

|  | 1971 |  | 1972 |  |
| --- | --- | --- | --- | --- |
|  | 1st v. FRANCE | 2nd v. FRANCE | 1st v. FRANCE | 2nd v. FRANCE |
|  | A.N. McGill 1c | A.N. McGill 1PG | A.N. McGill | A.N. McGill |
|  | J.W. Cole | J.W. Cole | J.I. Taylor 1T | J.I. Taylor |
|  | G.A. Shaw | G.A. Shaw | †D.R. Burnet | D.R. Burnet |
|  | †R.D. L'Estrange 2T | R.D. L'Estrange | †D.S. Rathie | D.S. Rathie |
|  | J.J. McLean 1PG | J.J. McLean 2PG | J.J. McLean | J.J. McLean |
|  | †R.L. Fairfax | R.L. Fairfax | R.L. Fairfax 2PG | R.L. Fairfax 5PG |
|  | J.N.B. Hipwell | J.N.B. Hipwell | J.N.B. Hipwell | J.N.B. Hipwell¹ |
|  | R.B. Prosser | R.B. Prosser | D.A. Dunworth¹ | D.A. Dunworth |
|  | P.G. Johnson | P.G. Johnson¹ | B.S. Taafe 1T | B.S. Taafe |
|  | †D.A. Dunworth | D.A. Dunworth | R.B. Prosser | R.B. Prosser |
|  | S.C. Gregory | S.C. Gregory | S.C. Gregory | S.C. Gregory |
|  | O.F. Butler | O.F. Butler | R.A. Smith | R.A. Smith |
|  | P.D. Sullivan | P.D. Sullivan | P.D. Sullivan | P.D. Sullivan |
|  | R.A. McLean | R.A. McLean | †M.R. Cocks | M.R. Cocks |
|  | *G.V. Davis | *G.V. Davis | *G.V. Davis | *G.V. Davis |
|  | Toulouse | Stade Colombes | Sydney | Ballymore |
|  | WON 13-11 | LOST 9-18 | DRAWN 14-14 | LOST 15-16 |
|  | FR.: 1PG 2T | FR.: 1G 4PG | AUST.: 2PG 2T | AUST.: 5PG |
|  | AUST.: 1G 1PG 1T | AUST.: 3PG | FR.: 1G 2T | FR.: 2G 1T |
|  | 20 Nov. 1971 | 27 Nov. 1971 | 17 Jun. 1972 | 25 Jun. 1972 |
|  |  | ¹Rep. by R.J. Thompson | ¹Rep. by J.L. Howard | ¹Rep. by †G.O. Grey |

The first independent Australian tour of France took place in November 1971. The Wallabies had visited the country before, but only as part of broader tours to the Northern Hemisphere.

Australia fielded a side of three new caps for the first Test at Toulouse. Of these, Fairfax proved a dashing fly-half of remarkable pace, while L'Estrange complemented a promising debut by scoring two tries in a remarkable win over the French. A week later, in Peter Johnson's final appearance for Australia, the same fifteen were beaten by a better-organised French side which took extreme care to blot out the threat posed by Fairfax.

The following season opened with a return visit from the French. After a drawn first Test, the Australians were beaten by a point in a close match in Brisbane. Fairfax kicked five penalty goals in the match, equalling Arthur McGill's Australian Test record. The fair-haired Fairfax later joined the Rugby League.

## 1972

| 1st v. NZ | 2nd v. NZ | 3rd v. NZ | v. FIJI |
|---|---|---|---|
| A.N. McGILL | A.N. McGILL | A.N. McGILL | R.L. FAIRFAX 1DG |
| | | | |
| J.W. COLE | J.W. COLE 1T | J.W. COLE | J.I. TAYLOR |
| D.R. BURNET | D.R. BURNET | D.R. BURNET | D.R. BURNET 1T |
| R.D. L'ESTRANGE | R.D. L'ESTRANGE | R.D. L'ESTRANGE | †P.G. ROWLES |
| J.J. McLEAN 2PG | J.J. McLEAN 2T,1C | J.J. McLEAN 1PG | J.J. McLEAN |
| | | | |
| R.L. FAIRFAX | G.C. RICHARDSON 1DG | G.C. RICHARDSON | G.C. RICHARDSON |
| G.O. GREY | G.O. GREY | G.O. GREY | †J.R. CORNES¹ |
| | | | |
| †B.R. BROWN | J.L. HOWARD | B.R. BROWN | R.A. SMITH |
| †M.E. FRENEY | M.E. FRENEY | M.E. FRENEY | R.J. THOMPSON 1C,1T |
| R.B. PROSSER | R.B. PROSSER | R.B. PROSSER | R.B. PROSSER |
| R.A. SMITH | B.D. STUMBLES | R.A. SMITH | †R.N. WOOD |
| G. FAY | G. FAY | G. FAY | B.D. STUMBLES 1T |
| P.D. SULLIVAN¹ | P.D. SULLIVAN | M.R. COCKS | *P.D. SULLIVAN 1T |
| †A.M. GELLING | M.R. COCKS | B.D. STUMBLES | A.M. GELLING |
| *G.V. DAVIS | *G.V. DAVIS¹ | *G.V. DAVIS | M.R. COCKS |
| | | | |
| Wellington | Christchurch | Auckland | Suva |
| LOST 6-29 | LOST 17-30 | LOST 3-38 | WON 21-19 |
| | | | |
| NZ: 3G 1DG 2T | NZ: 2G 2PG 3T | NZ: 4G 2PG 2T | FIJI: 1G 3PG 1T |
| AUST.: 2PG | AUST.: 1G 1DG 2T | AUST.: 1PG | AUST.: 1G 1DG 3T |
| | | | |
| 19 Aug. 1972 | 2 Sep. 1972 | 16 Sep. 1972 | 19 Sep. 1972 |
| | | | |
| ¹Rep. by †B.D. Stumbles | ¹Rep. by R.A. Smith | | ¹Rep. by G.O. Grey |

Australian rugby reached its post-war nadir on the late-season tour of New Zealand. Greg Davis, in his final international season, led a side which had exciting backs but which lacked experienced tight forwards. The team was overwhelmed by the All Blacks and just avoided defeat in Suva in a full Test against Fiji – Australia's first Test against non-International Board opponents for eleven years, and their first Test in Fiji.

Bob Templeton, the national coach, had few illusions concerning the uphill task Australia faced before it could stand near the top of the rugby world. He recognised the need to increase players' concentration during major matches, noted Australians' shortcomings in ruck and line-out techniques, and began a search for large, athletic forwards.

Roy Prosser retired after the win in Suva. His expertise in the front row, mobility in the loose and fine technique as a mauler made him an automatic choice for 25 Tests, the record number of Test appearances by an Australian prop forward.

## 1973 / 1973

| 1st v. TONGA | 2nd v. TONGA | v. WALES | v. ENGLAND |
|---|---|---|---|
| A.N. McGILL 2C | A.N. McGILL 1PG | R.L. FAIRFAX | R.L. FAIRFAX 1PG |
| | | | |
| J.W. COLE 1T | J.W. COLE 1T | O.G. STEPHENS | †L.E. MONAGHAN |
| R.D. L'ESTRANGE | R.D. L'ESTRANGE | R.D. L'ESTRANGE | R.D. L'ESTRANGE |
| †T.R. STEGMAN | T.R. STEGMAN | G.A. SHAW | G.A. SHAW |
| †O.G. STEPHENS 2T | O.G. STEPHENS | J.J. McLEAN | J.J. McLEAN |
| | | | |
| G.C. RICHARDSON 1DG,1T | G.C. RICHARDSON | G.C. RICHARDSON | P.G. ROWLES |
| J.N.B. HIPWELL 1T | †E.N. TINDALL 1T | J.N.B. HIPWELL | *J.N.B. HIPWELL |
| | | | |
| †R. GRAHAM | R. GRAHAM | R. GRAHAM | R. GRAHAM |
| M.E. FRENEY | †C.M. CARBERRY | M.E. FRENEY | C.M. CARBERRY¹ |
| J.L. HOWARD | J.L. HOWARD | J.L. HOWARD | S.G. MacDOUGALL |
| S.C. GREGORY | S.C. GREGORY | S.C. GREGORY | S.C. GREGORY |
| G. FAY 1DG | G. FAY | G. FAY | G. FAY |
| *P.D. SULLIVAN | *P.D. SULLIVAN | M.R. COCKS | M.R. COCKS |
| M.R. COCKS | M.R. COCKS | †A.A. SHAW | A.A. SHAW |
| †M.E. LOANE | M.E. LOANE | *P.D. SULLIVAN | †B.R. BATTISHALL |
| | | | |
| Sydney | Ballymore | Cardiff Arms Park | Twickenham |
| WON 30-12 | LOST 11-16 | LOST 0-24 | LOST 3-20 |
| | | | |
| AUST.: 2G 2DG 3T | AUST.: 1PG 2T | WALES: 4PG 3T | ENG.: 1G 2PG 2T |
| TONGA: 2G | TONGA: 4T | AUST.: NIL | AUST.: 1PG |
| | | | |
| 23 Jun. 1973 | 30 Jun. 1973 | 10 Nov. 1973 | 17 Nov. 1973 |
| | | | ¹Rep. by M.E. Freney |

The only Tongan side to play Test rugby against Australia appeared for a short tour in 1973. The ARU granted full Test status to the two-match international series (which was shared), and in subsequent years made similar gestures for the Tests played with Japan, Argentina and Italy. As well as continuing to meet America and Fiji on a full international basis, increasing their international ties, it was argued, would enable Australia to improve their rugby at the highest level. But defeat by four tries to two in Brisbane and a disastrous short tour to England and Wales at the end of the season, when just two of the eight matches played were won, left Australian rugby followers even more desperate for success.

Arthur McGill, a wiry, reliable full-back who played 21 times for Australia, finished his international career in 1973, having established a new Australian international Test career record by scoring 72 points. Russell Fairfax, an attacking player of immense promise who followed McGill as full-back in Britain, switched to League in 1974, a sad loss for Australian Rugby Union.

## 1974

| 1st v. NZ | 2nd v. NZ | 3rd v. NZ |
|---|---|---|
| L.E. Monaghan | L.E. Monaghan 1T | L.E. Monaghan |
| | | |
| J.W. Cole | J.W. Cole | J.W. Cole |
| R.D. L'Estrange | R.D. L'Estrange | R.D. L'Estrange |
| G.A. Shaw | G.A. Shaw | G.A. Shaw |
| J.J. McLean | O.G. Stephens | O.G. Stephens |
| | | |
| †P.E. McLean 1C | P.E. McLean 2PG,1C | P.E. McLean 2PG |
| *J.N.B. Hipwell | *J.N.B. Hipwell 1T | *J.N.B. Hipwell |
| | | |
| S.G. MacDougall | S.G. MacDougall | S.G. MacDougall |
| †P.A. Horton | P.A. Horton | P.A. Horton |
| †J.E.C. Meadows | R. Graham | R. Graham |
| G. Fay | G. Fay | G. Fay |
| †R.A. Davis | R.A. Davis | R.A. Davis |
| †J.K. Lambie | †G. Cornelsen | G. Cornelsen |
| M.E. Loane | J.K. Lambie | J.K. Lambie |
| †R.A. Price 1T | R.A. Price | R.A. Price |
| | | |
| Sydney | Ballymore | Sydney |
| LOST 6-11 | DRAWN 16-16 | LOST 6-16 |
| | | |
| AUST.: 1G | AUST.: 1G 2PG 1T | AUST.: 2PG |
| NZ: 1PG 2T | NZ: 1G 2PG 1T | NZ: 2G 1T |
| | | |
| 25 May 1974 | 1 Jun. 1974 | 8 Jun. 1974 |

In 1874 a Rugby Union had been formed in Sydney to place the administration and rulings of the game in Australia on an organised basis. 1974 was regarded as the centenary, and an All Black side undertook a major tour as part of the celebrations.

The customary rash of retirements and defections to League left Australia to field an inexperienced side of several new caps for the opening Test. In awful conditions the visitors eventually won a close match and only three changes were made to the Australian side for the Brisbane Test. There Australia forced a creditable draw after trailing 6-16, and Paul McLean just failed to win the match with his conversion attempt after the final try. 37,000, the biggest rugby crowd at Sydney for eight years, watched New Zealand clinch the series with a 16-6 win in the third Test.

Paul and Jeff McLean, who played together in the first Test, were goal-kicking brothers. Jeff's career was cut short through a leg injury, but Paul became Australia's leading scorer in Tests, collecting 260 points in a fine career of thirty internationals.

## 1975

| 1st v. ENGLAND | 2nd v. ENGLAND | 1st v. JAPAN | 2nd v. JAPAN |
|---|---|---|---|
| †R.C. Brown 2PG,1DG | R.C. Brown 1C,1PG | P.E. McLean 1PG,5C,2T | †J.C. Hindmarsh |
| | | | |
| L.E. Monaghan | L.E. Monaghan 1T | D.H. Osborne 1T | †J.R. Ryan 3T |
| †L.J. Weatherstone | L.J. Weatherstone 1T | L.J. Weatherstone | L.J. Weatherstone |
| G.A. Shaw | G.A. Shaw | G.A. Shaw | *G.A. Shaw 2T |
| †D.H. Osborne | D.H. Osborne | †I.J. Robertson 2T | I.J. Robertson |
| | | | |
| †K.J. Wright 1DG | K.J. Wright 1C,1PG | K.J. Wright 1T | P.E. McLean 6C,2PG |
| *J.N.B. Hipwell | *J.N.B. Hipwell | *J.N.B. Hipwell¹ | R.G. Hauser 1T |
| | | | |
| S.G. MacDougall | S.G. MacDougall | S.C. Finnane | S.C. Finnane |
| P.A. Horton | P.A. Horton | P.A. Horton | P.A. Horton |
| †S.C. Finnane | R. Graham | R. Graham | R. Graham |
| R.A. Smith | R.A. Smith 1T | R.A. Smith | †B.W. Mansfield |
| G. Fay | G. Fay 1T | G. Fay | R.A. Smith |
| A.A. Shaw | A.A. Shaw | M.R. Cocks | A.A. Shaw 1T |
| M.E. Loane 1T | M.E. Loane | M.E. Loane | G. Cornelsen |
| R.A. Price | R.A. Price 1T | R.A. Price | R.A. Price 1T |
| | | | |
| Sydney | Ballymore | Sydney | Ballymore |
| WON 16-9 | WON 30-21 | WON 37-7 | WON 50-25 |
| | | | |
| AUST.: 2PG 2DG 1T | AUST.: 2G 2PG 3T | AUST.: 5G 1PG 1T | AUST.: 6G 2PG 2T |
| ENG.: 1G 1PG | ENG.: 2G 3PG | JAPAN: 1PG 1T | JAPAN: 1G 1PG 4T |
| | | | |
| 24 May 1975 | 31 May 1975 | 2 Aug. 1975 | 17 Aug. 1975 |
| | | ¹Rep. by †R.G. Hauser | |

This was Australia's most successful post-war season, the side winning four consecutive Tests for the first time since 1929-1931. England were well beaten in each of the Tests, the Australian backs treating the 40,000 spectators at Sydney to some exciting running and handling. At Brisbane the Test was marred by an ugly brawl near the start which resulted in the sending-off of an English forward. Australia took full advantage of their numerical superiority, and in scoring thirty points created a new Australian record total for a match against International Board teams.

Japan, on their first full visit of Australia in August, entertained the crowds at the Tests with some unorthodox moves and ruses. But they found the Australians too powerful to contain. McLean's 21 points at Sydney, his six conversions at Brisbane and Australia's 50 points were new Test match records for the Aussies.

John Ryan, a bullocking runner on the wing, was another record-breaker at Brisbane, scoring three tries. In his brief career before joining League, Ryan had the unique distinction of scoring tries in all six of his internationals.

## 1975-76

| v. SCOTLAND | v. WALES | v. ENGLAND | v. IRELAND | v. USA |
|---|---|---|---|---|
| P.E. McLean 1PG | P.E. McLean 1PG | P.E. McLean 2PG | P.E. McLean 2PG,1C | J.C. Hindmarsh 4PG |
| †P.G. Batch | P.G. Batch | P.G. Batch | J.R. Ryan 1T | J.R. Ryan 1T |
| R.D. L'Estrange | R.D. L'Estrange | †W.A. McKid | R.D. L'Estrange | R.D. L'Estrange |
| †J. Berne[1] | G.A. Shaw | *G.A. Shaw | *G.A. Shaw | *G.A. Shaw |
| L.E. Monaghan | L.E. Monaghan | L.E. Monaghan | L.E. Monaghan | L.E. Monaghan |
| J.C. Hindmarsh | J.C. Hindmarsh | L.J. Weatherstone | L.J. Weatherstone 1T | K.J. Wright |
| *J.N.B. Hipwell | *J.N.B. Hipwell[1] | R.G. Hauser | R.G. Hauser | R.G. Hauser |
| J.E.C. Meadows | J.E.C. Meadows | S.C. Finnane | J.E.C. Meadows | J.E.C. Meadows |
| P.A. Horton | P.A. Horton | P.A. Horton | C.M. Carberry | C.M. Carberry |
| R. Graham | R. Graham | S.G. MacDougall | R. Graham | R. Graham |
| G. Fay | R.A. Smith | R.A. Smith | G. Fay | G. Fay |
| R.A. Smith | G. Fay | D.W. Hillhouse | R.A. Smith | R.A. Smith |
| G. Cornelsen | J.K. Lambie[2] | G. Cornelsen | G.K. Pearse | G.K. Pearse 1T |
| †D.W. Hillhouse | G. Cornelsen | M.E. Loane | M.E. Loane | A.A. Shaw |
| A.A. Shaw | A.A. Shaw | A.A. Shaw | A.A. Shaw 1T | R.A. Price 1T |
| Murrayfield | Cardiff Arms Park | Twickenham | Lansdowne Road | Los Angeles |
| LOST 3-10 | LOST 3-28 | LOST 6-23 | WON 20-10 | WON 24-12 |
| SCOT.: 1G 1T | WALES: 3G 1PG 1DG 1T | ENG.: 1G 3PG 2T | IRE.: 2PG 1T | USA: 4PG |
| AUST.: 1PG | AUST.: 1PG | AUST.: 2PG | AUST.: 1G 2PG 2T | AUST.: 4PG 3T |
| 6 Dec. 1975 | 20 Dec. 1975 | 3 Jan. 1976 | 17 Jan. 1976 | 31 Jan. 1976 |
| [1]Rep. by L.J. Weatherstone | [1]Rep. by R.G. Hauser [2]Rep. by †G.K. Pearse | | | |

The Sixth Wallabies to Britain were expertly managed by solicitor (and former cap) Ross Turnbull, and imaginatively coached by Dave Brockhoff, a former flanker who had won eight caps soon after the war. But John Hipwell, as captain, was injured in the Welsh Test and missed most of the rest of the tour, and several colleagues were also unlucky to miss Tests through injury.

The forward play improved considerably as the tour progressed. Garrick Fay proved the strongest of the tight forwards and elicited the praise of the British pundits. In a fine career he went on to win 24 caps, and holds the unique record for an Australian forward of dropping a goal in an international (against Tonga in 1973).

Laurie Monaghan, a skilful utility back; Reg Smith, a solid and robust tight forward; and Tony Shaw, an outstanding loose forward were the only players to retain their places in each of the tour's five Tests.

## 1976 / 1976

| 1st v. FIJI | 2nd v. FIJI | 3rd v. FIJI | 1st v. FRANCE | 2nd v. FRANCE |
|---|---|---|---|---|
| J.C. Hindmarsh | J.C. Hindmarsh | J.C. Hindmarsh | J.C. Hindmarsh | J.C. Hindmarsh |
| P.G. Batch 2T | P.G. Batch | P.G. Batch 1T | P.G. Batch | P.G. Batch |
| *G.A. Shaw | *G.A. Shaw | *G.A. Shaw[1] | K.J. Wright | K.J. Wright |
| W.A. McKid | †G.G. Shambrook | G.G. Shambrook | *G.A. Shaw | *G.A. Shaw |
| J.R. Ryan 1T | J.R. Ryan 2T | J.R. Ryan 1T | L.E. Monaghan | †P.J. Crowe |
| P.E. McLean 2PG | P.E. McLean 2C,2PG,1DG | P.E. McLean 5PG | P.E. McLean 4PG,1DG | P.E. McLean 2PG |
| R.G. Hauser | R.G. Hauser | R.G. Hauser | R.G. Hauser | R.G. Hauser |
| J.E.C. Meadows | D.A. Dunworth | J.E.C. Meadows | J.E.C. Meadows | J.E.C. Meadows |
| C.M. Carberry | C.M. Carberry | C.M. Carberry | P.A. Horton | P.A. Horton |
| R. Graham | R. Graham | R. Graham | R. Graham | R. Graham |
| D.W. Hillhouse | D.W. Hillhouse | D.W. Hillhouse | D.W. Hillhouse | D.W. Hillhouse |
| R.A. Smith | R.A. Smith | R.A. Smith | R.A. Smith | R.A. Smith |
| G.K. Pearse 1T | G.K. Pearse | G.K. Pearse 1T | A.A. Shaw | A.A. Shaw |
| M.E. Loane | M.E. Loane | M.E. Loane | M.E. Loane | M.E. Loane |
| A.A. Shaw | A.A. Shaw | A.A. Shaw | G. Cornelsen | G. Cornelsen |
| Sydney | Ballymore | Sydney | Bordeaux | Parc des Princes |
| WON 22-6 | WON 21-9 | WON 27-17 | LOST 15-18 | LOST 6-34 |
| AUST.: 2PG 4T | AUST.: 2G 2PG 1DG | AUST.: 5PG 3T | FR.: 3G | FR.: 2G 1PG 1DG 4T |
| FIJI: 1G | FIJI: 3PG | FIJI: 1G 1PG 2T | AUST.: 4PG 1DG | AUST.: 2PG |
| 12 Jun. 1976 | 19 Jun. 1976 | 26 Jun. 1976 | 24 Oct. 1976 | 30 Oct. 1976 |
| | | [1]Rep. by †M.A. Ellem | | |

Three wins against Fiji extended Australia's home winning run to seven successive Tests. The Fijian side, hailed on arrival as the best side to come from the Islands, failed to fulfil its potential and eight of the thirteen tour games were lost.

The Fijians also blotted their copybook by their unprecedented behaviour during the second half of the third Test. Referee Mr Cooney had sent off Sovau, the Fijian prop, for kicking scrum-half Rod Hauser. In protest at the referee's decision the entire Fijian side walked off the pitch, one of their players allegedly picking up some mud from the ground and throwing it at the referee. At length the Fijian manager persuaded his side to resume the game.

Later in the year Geoff Shaw led the Wallabies on a ten-match tour of France and Italy. No doubt tired from the effects of months of continuous international competition, the tourists lost six of their games (including the two Tests). The defeat in Paris was Australia's biggest ever against France, and in Milan five days afterwards the visitors just escaped (winning 16-15) the humiliation of losing to Italy. For the Italian "international", no caps were awarded.

## 1978

| 1st v. WALES | 2nd v. WALES | 1st v. NZ | 2nd v. NZ | 3rd v. NZ |
|---|---|---|---|---|
| L.E. MONAGHAN | L.E. MONAGHAN 1DG | L.E. MONAGHAN | P.E. McLEAN¹ | G. RICHARDS |
| | | | | |
| P.G. BATCH | P.G. BATCH | P.G. BATCH 1T | P.G. BATCH | P.G. BATCH |
| †A.G. SLACK | A.G. SLACK | A.G. SLACK | W.A. McKID | W.A. McKID |
| †M. KNIGHT | M. KNIGHT | M. KNIGHT | A.G. SLACK | K.J. WRIGHT 1PG,1C |
| P.J. CROWE 1T | P.J. CROWE | †S.F. STREETER | †B.J. MOON | B.J. MOON |
| | | | | |
| P.E. McLEAN 4PG,1C | P.E. McLEAN 3PG,1DG | K.J. WRIGHT 2PG,1C | K.J. WRIGHT 1DG,1PG | †T.C. MELROSE 1DG,1C |
| R.G. HAUSER | R.G. HAUSER | J.N.B. HIPWELL | J.N.B. HIPWELL | J.N.B. HIPWELL |
| | | | | |
| S.C. FINNANE | S.C. FINNANE | J.E.C. MEADOWS | J.E.C. MEADOWS | J.E.C. MEADOWS |
| P.A. HORTON | P.A. HORTON | P.A. HORTON | P.A. HORTON | P.A. HORTON |
| †S.J. PILECKI | S.J. PILECKI | S.J. PILECKI | S.J. PILECKI | †C.B. HANDY |
| D.W. HILLHOUSE | D.W. HILLHOUSE | G. FAY | P.W. McLEAN | G. FAY |
| G. FAY | G. FAY | †P.W. McLEAN | G. FAY | P.W. McLEAN |
| *A.A. SHAW | *A.A. SHAW | *A.A. SHAW | *A.A. SHAW | G.K. PEARSE 1T |
| M.E. LOANE | M.E. LOANE 1T | G. CORNELSEN | G. CORNELSEN | G. CORNELSEN 4T |
| G. CORNELSEN | G. CORNELSEN | G.K. PEARSE | G.K. PEARSE | *A.A. SHAW |
| Ballymore | Sydney | Wellington | Christchurch | Auckland |
| WON 18-8 | WON 19-17 | LOST 12-13 | LOST 6-22 | WON 30-16 |
| AUST.: 1G 4PG | AUST.: 3PG 2DG 1T | NZ: 3PG 1T | NZ: 2G 1PG 1DG 1T | NZ: 1G 2PG 1T |
| WALES: 2T | WALES: 2PG 1DG 2T | AUST.: 1G 2PG | AUST.: 1PG 1DG | AUST.: 2G 1PG 1DG 3T |
| 11 Jun. 1978 | 17 Jun. 1978 | 19 Aug. 1978 | 26 Aug. 1978 | 9 Sep. 1978 |
| | | | ¹Rep. by †G. Richards | |

Australia showed considerable purpose and dedication in maintaining their impressive unbeaten home record with two fine wins against Wales, the Five Nations Grand Slam Champions. Later, in New Zealand, despite losing the Test rubber, the Australians proved their worth as a major rugby force with a convincing 30-16 Test win at Auckland.

Daryl Haberecht as coach and Tony Shaw, the new captain, concentrated on providing a firm forward platform in the Welsh matches. Backed up by splendid place-kicking from Paul McLean (26 points in two Tests) they succeeded in their aim against Wales, though there was a cry for more open play from the Australian public.

In New Zealand, after several injuries, the Australians at last fulfilled their wish to play fifteen-man rugby. In the Auckland Test the back line ran and handled magnificently, and cleverly interacted with the dynamic back row. Cornelsen set a new Australian Test record scoring four tries, and became the first forward since 1881 to cross the line four times in an international.

## 1979

| 1st v. IRELAND | 2nd v. IRELAND | v. NZ | 1st v. ARGENTINA | 2nd v. ARGENTINA |
|---|---|---|---|---|
| †B.P. COOKE | L.E. MONAGHAN | P.E. McLEAN 3PG | P.E. McLEAN 2PG | P.E. McLEAN 1PG,1C |
| | | | | |
| L.E. MONAGHAN | P.J. CROWE | P.J. CROWE | P.J. CROWE 1T | P.G. BATCH 1T |
| W.A. McKID | W.A. McKID | A.G. SLACK | †M.D. O'CONNOR | M.D. O'CONNOR |
| T.C. MELROSE | T.C. MELROSE | G.A. SHAW | A.G. SLACK | A.G. SLACK |
| B.J. MOON 1T | B.J. MOON | B.J. MOON | B.J. MOON | B.J. MOON 2T |
| | | | | |
| P.E. McLEAN 2PG,1C | P.E. McLEAN 1PG | T.C. MELROSE 1DG | T.C. MELROSE 1DG | T.C. MELROSE |
| R.G. HAUSER | R.G. HAUSER | †P.J. CARSON | †P.A. COX | P.A. COX |
| | | | | |
| J.E.C. MEADOWS | J.E.C. MEADOWS | C.B. HANDY | S.J. PILECKI | S.J. PILECKI |
| †W.S. ROSS | W.S. ROSS | P.A. HORTON | P.A. HORTON | W.S. ROSS |
| S.J. PILECKI | S.J. PILECKI | S.J. PILECKI | C.B. HANDY | C.B. HANDY |
| P.W. McLEAN | P.W. McLEAN | P.W. McLEAN | P.W. McLEAN | P.W. McLEAN |
| G. FAY | †K.S. BESOMO | A.A. SHAW | A.A. SHAW | A.A. SHAW |
| *A.A. SHAW | *A.A. SHAW | †A.A. STEWART | A.A. STEWART | A.A. STEWART |
| M.E. LOANE | M.E. LOANE | *M.E. LOANE | *M.E. LOANE | *M.E. LOANE |
| G. CORNELSEN | G. CORNELSEN | G. CORNELSEN | G. CORNELSEN | G. CORNELSEN |
| Ballymore | Sydney | Sydney | Buenos Aires | Buenos Aires |
| LOST 12-27 | LOST 3-9 | WON 12-6 | LOST 13-24 | WON 17-12 |
| AUST.: 1G 2PG | AUST.: 1PG | AUST.: 3PG 1DG | ARG.: 2G 1PG 3DG | ARG.: 1G 1PG 1DG |
| IRE.: 2G 4PG 1DG | IRE.: 1PG 2DG | NZ: 1PG 1DG | AUST.: 2PG 1DG 1T | AUST.: 1G 1PG 2T |
| 3 Jun. 1979 | 16 Jun. 1979 | 28 Jul. 1979 | 27 Oct. 1979 | 3 Nov. 1979 |

Australia's proud home record was destroyed by a competent Irish side early in the 1979 season. The Australians failed to respond to the ten-man game adopted by the Irish visitors, and although there was little to choose between the sides in the Tests, Ireland's superior place-kicking enabled them to become the first side for five years to win a Test in Australia.

The best Australian form of the season was shown in the Test against New Zealand. A superb display by the home forwards bustled the All Blacks to a 12-6 defeat, giving Australia its first hold on the Bledisloe Cup since 1949.

In October, Australia played its inaugural Tests against Argentina. The Wallabies thrilled the South American crowds with their quick transfers along the threequarter line and their direct running. Beaten by a superior pack in the first of the two Tests, the Wallabies squared the series with a 17-12 win in which they showed their best form of the tour.

## 1980

| | v. FIJI | 1st v. NZ | 2nd v. NZ | 3rd v. NZ |
|---|---|---|---|---|
| | *P.E. McLean 3PG,1DG,1C | †R.G. Gould 1C | R.G. Gould 1PG,1C | R.G. Gould 2C,1PG |
| | †M.C. Martin 1T | M.C. Martin 1T | M.C. Martin | †P.C. Grigg 2T |
| | M.D. O'Connor | M.J. Hawker 1T | M.J. Hawker | M.J. Hawker |
| | A.G. Slack | M.D. O'Connor | M.D. O'Connor | M.D. O'Connor 1T |
| | B.J. Moon 1T | B.J. Moon | B.J. Moon 1T | B.J. Moon |
| | †M.J. Hawker | †M.G. Ella 1DG | M.G. Ella | M.G. Ella 1DG |
| | P.A. Cox | P.A. Cox | P.A. Cox | P.J. Carson 1T |
| | †A.M. D'Arcy | S.J. Pilecki | S.J. Pilecki | A.M. D'Arcy |
| | W.S. Ross | W.S. Ross | W.S. Ross | W.S. Ross |
| | S.J. Pilecki | C.B. Handy | C.B. Handy | †D.J. Curran |
| | †M.J. Mathers | S.A. Williams | S.A. Williams¹ | P.W. McLean |
| | †S.A. Williams¹ | D. Hall | D. Hall | *A.A. Shaw |
| | A.A. Shaw | S.P. Poidevin | S.P. Poidevin | S.P. Poidevin |
| | †D. Hall | G. Cornelsen | G. Cornelsen | D. Hall |
| | †S.P. Poidevin | *A.A. Shaw | *A.A. Shaw | G. Cornelsen |
| | Suva | Sydney | Ballymore | Sydney |
| | WON 22-9 | WON 13-9 | LOST 9-12 | WON 26-10 |
| | FIJI: 2PG 1DG | AUST.: 1G 1DG 1T | AUST.: 1G 1PG | AUST.: 2G 1PG 1DG 2T |
| | AUST.: 1G 3PG 1DG 1T | NZ: 3PG | NZ: 1G 2PG | NZ: 2PG 1T |
| | 24 May 1980 | 21 Jun. 1980 | 28 Jun. 1980 | 12 Jul. 1980 |

¹Rep. by P.W. McLean

¹Rep. by M.J. Mathers

To prepare for the forthcoming Test series against the All Blacks, the ARU sent the Wallabies on a short tour to Fiji in May. A young side containing a fair sprinkling of the former Australian Schoolboys side (which had enjoyed a successful tour to Britain in 1977-78) played attractive, open football to score 93 points in their three wins. The side comfortably won the Test in Suva.

In June and July Australia rightly felt that a dramatic new era in their rugby history was beginning. Inspired by a genius named Mark Ella, they retained the Bledisloe Cup by defeating New Zealand 2-1 in the three-Test series. The side was named the most exciting to represent Australia since the 1927-28 Waratahs.

At Sydney, in the final Test of the season, the Australian backs revealed a striking combination of pace, ingenuity and flair to register their biggest-ever winning margin against New Zealand. The backs scored four tries as 48,698 spectators – an attendance record for an Australian Test – saw the All Blacks crushed 26-10.

## 1981 — 1981-82

| 1st v. FRANCE | 2nd v. FRANCE | v. IRELAND | v. WALES | v. SCOTLAND | v. ENGLAND |
|---|---|---|---|---|---|
| G. Richards 1PG | P.E. McLean 4PG,2C | R.G. Gould 1DG | R.G. Gould | R.G. Gould | P.E. McLean 1PG |
| M.C. Martin | M.C. Martin | M.D. O'Connor 1T | †M.H. Cox 1T | M.H. Cox | M.D. O'Connor |
| M.D. O'Connor 1T | M.D. O'Connor 1T | A.G. Slack | A.G. Slack 1T | A.G. Slack 1T | A.G. Slack |
| M.J. Hawker | M.J. Hawker | M.J. Hawker | M.J. Hawker¹ | P.E. McLean 1PG | M.J. Hawker |
| B.J. Moon 1T | B.J. Moon | B.J. Moon | B.J. Moon | B.J. Moon 1T | B.J. Moon 2T |
| P.E. McLean 1C | M.G. Ella | P.E. McLean 3PG | P.E. McLean 1PG,1C | M.G. Ella | M.G. Ella |
| J.N.B. Hipwell | J.N.B. Hipwell | J.N.B. Hipwell | J.N.B. Hipwell² | P.A. Cox | J.N.B. Hipwell |
| A.M. D'Arcy | A.M. D'Arcy | J.E.C. Meadows | A.M. D'Arcy | J.E.C. Meadows | J.E.C. Meadows |
| C.M. Carberry | C.M. Carberry | C.M. Carberry | C.M. Carberry | C.M. Carberry | C.M. Carberry |
| D.J. Curran | D.J. Curran | A.M. D'Arcy | D.J. Curran | A.M. D'Arcy | A.M. D'Arcy |
| D. Hall | D. Hall 1T | *A.A. Shaw | *A.A. Shaw | *A.A. Shaw | S.A. Williams |
| S.A. Williams | S.A. Williams | P.W. McLean | P.W. McLean | P.W. McLean | P.W. McLean |
| S.P. Poidevin 1T | S.P. Poidevin | S.P. Poidevin | G. Cornelsen | S.P. Poidevin 1T | S.P. Poidevin |
| M.E. Loane | M.E. Loane | M.E. Loane | M.E. Loane | M.E. Loane | *M.E. Loane |
| *A.A. Shaw | *A.A. Shaw | G. Cornelsen | S.P. Poidevin | G. Cornelsen | G. Cornelsen |
| Ballymore | Sydney | Lansdowne Road | Cardiff Arms Park | Murrayfield | Twickenham |
| WON 17-15 | WON 24-14 | WON 16-12 | LOST 13-18 | LOST 15-24 | LOST 11-15 |
| AUST.: 1G 1PG 2T | AUST.: 2G 4PG | IRE.: 4PG | WALES: 1G 3PG 1DG | SCOT.: 1G 5PG 1DG | ENG.: 1G 3PG |
| FR.: 1G 2PG 1DG | FR.: 2DG 2T | AUST.: 3PG 1DG 1T | AUST.: 1G 1PG 1T | AUST.: 1PG 3T | AUST.: 1PG 2T |
| 5 Jul. 1981 | 11 Jul. 1981 | 21 Nov. 1981 | 5 Dec. 1981 | 19 Dec. 1981 | 2 Jan. 1982 |

¹Rep. by M.C. Martin

²Rep. by P.A. Cox

The Australian rugby year began with another home series success, this time against the French. The return of John Hipwell after a three-year absence, outstanding loose forward play, and reliable kicking by Paul McLean were features of the two Test wins.

The Wallabies thus set out for their tour of Britain with an outstanding reputation. But Tony Shaw's side found the softer footing of British grounds difficult to adjust to, and only one of the first matches was won. In the Tests the side was unable to contain opposing forwards, though the seven tries scored by the threequarters in these matches showed just what might have occurred had the pack been able to gain possession from the tight. Slack and Moon in particular were skilful runners and handlers.

## 1982

| 1st v. SCOTLAND | 2nd v. SCOTLAND | 1st v. NZ | 2nd v. NZ | 3rd v. NZ |
|---|---|---|---|---|
| †G.J. ELLA | R.G. GOULD 2T | R.G. GOULD 2PG,1C | R.G. GOULD 3PG,1C | R.G. GOULD 1T,1C,3PG |
| | | | | |
| M.J. HAWKER 1T,1PG | P.C. GRIGG | P.C. GRIGG | P.C. GRIGG | P.C. GRIGG |
| M.D. O'CONNOR | M.D. O'CONNOR 1T | †G.A. ELLA | G.A. ELLA 1T | A.G. SLACK |
| A.G. SLACK | M.J. HAWKER | M.J. HAWKER 1T | M.J. HAWKER | M.J. HAWKER 1DG |
| B.J. MOON | B.J. MOON | †D.I. CAMPESE 1T | D.I. CAMPESE 1T | D.I. CAMPESE |
| | | | | |
| M.G. ELLA | P.E. McLEAN 5PG,3C | *M.G. ELLA | *M.G. ELLA | *M.G. ELLA |
| P.A. COX | P.A. COX | P.A. COX | P.A. COX | P.A. COX |
| | | | | |
| A.M. D'ARCY | A.M. D'ARCY | †J.E. COOLICAN | J.E.C. MEADOWS | J.E.C. MEADOWS |
| W.S. ROSS | W.S. ROSS | †B.P. MALOUF | †L.R. WALER | L.R. WALKER |
| S.J. PILECKI | S.J. PILECKI | †A.J. McINTYRE | A.J. McINTYRE | A.J. McINTYRE |
| D. HALL | D. HALL | D. HALL | D. HALL[1] | †P. CLEMENTS |
| P.W. McLEAN | P.W. McLEAN | S.A. WILLIAMS | S.A. WILLIAMS | S.A. WILLIAMS |
| A.A. SHAW | A.A. SHAW | C. ROCHE | C. ROCHE | C. ROCHE |
| *M.E. LOANE | *M.E. LOANE | †P.W. LUCAS | P.W. LUCAS | P.W. LUCAS |
| †C. ROCHE | C. ROCHE | S.P. POIDEVIN | S.P. POIDEVIN | S.P. POIDEVIN |
| | | | | |
| Ballymore | Sydney | Christchurch | Wellington | Auckland |
| LOST 7-12 | WON 33-9 | LOST 16-23 | WON 19-16 | LOST 18-33 |
| | | | | |
| AUST.: 1PG 1T | AUST.: 3G 5PG | NZ: 2G 1PG 2T | NZ: 1G 2PG 1T | NZ: 2G 5PG 2DG |
| SCOT.: 1G 1PG 1DG | SCOT.: 3PG | AUST.: 1G 2PG 1T | AUST.: 1G 3PG 1T | AUST.: 1G 3PG 1DG |
| | | | | |
| 4 Jul. 1982 | 10 Jul. 1982 | 14 Aug. 1982 | 28 Aug. 1982 | 11 Sep. 1982 |
| | | | [1]Rep. by †S.A.G. Cutler | |

Bob Dwyer was appointed coach in 1982. Although the side for the first Test against Scotland was narrowly defeated, the returns of Gould and McLean for the second enabled Australia to run up their highest-ever score against International Board nations. The 33-9 win included 21 points by Paul McLean – another record for matches against International Board teams.

Mark Ella, a brilliant running fly-half who attracted large crowds to matches, led the Wallabies on their 14-match tour to New Zealand later in the season. Despite the unavailability of numerous leading players, Ella's side, containing 17 uncapped men, developed into a sound scrummaging combination backed by an attacking line of skill and flair. Only lack of experience cost the Wallabies the Test series, and the record of ten wins from the 14 matches was considered an encouraging return for a young side.

Gary, Glen and Mark Ella all appeared in Tests this season: the first trio of brothers to be capped for Australia.

## 1983

| v. USA | 1st v. ARGENTINA | 2nd v. ARGENTINA | v. NZ |
|---|---|---|---|
| R.G. GOULD 4C[1] | R.G. GOULD | D.I. CAMPESE 1PG,3C,1T | D.I. CAMPESE |
| | | | |
| D.I. CAMPESE 1C,4T | D.I. CAMPESE 1PG | P.C. GRIGG | P.C. GRIGG |
| A.G. SLACK 2T | A.G. SLACK | A.G. SLACK | A.G. SLACK 1T |
| M.J. HAWKER | M.J. HAWKER | M.J. HAWKER | M.J. HAWKER |
| B.J. MOON | B.J. MOON | B.J. MOON 2T | B.J. MOON |
| | | | |
| *M.G. ELLA 1DG | *M.G. ELLA | *M.G. ELLA | *M.G. ELLA |
| †D. VAUGHAN | D. VAUGHAN[1] | A.J. PARKER | A.J. PARKER |
| | | | |
| J.E.C. MEADOWS | D.J. CURRAN | J.E.C. MEADOWS | J.E.C. MEADOWS |
| W.S. ROSS 1T | W.S. ROSS | W.S. ROSS | W.S. ROSS |
| S.J. PILECKI | S.J. PILECKI | S.J. PILECKI | S.J. PILECKI |
| D.W. HILLHOUSE | D. HALL | D.W. HILLHOUSE | D.W. HILLHOUSE |
| S.A. WILLIAMS | D.W. HILLHOUSE | S.A. WILLIAMS | S.A. WILLIAMS |
| C. ROCHE 1T | C. ROCHE | C. ROCHE 1T | C. ROCHE |
| D. HALL | †D. CODEY[2] | D. HALL | D. HALL |
| S.P. POIDEVIN | S.P. POIDEVIN | S.P. POIDEVIN 1T‡ | S.P. POIDEVIN 1T |
| | | | |
| Sydney | Ballymore | Sydney | Sydney |
| WON 49-3 | LOST 3-18 | WON 29-13 | LOST 8-18 |
| | | | |
| AUST.: 5G 1DG 4T | AUST.: 1PG | AUST.: 3G‡ 1PG 2T | AUST.: 2T |
| US: 1PG | ARG.: 2G 1PG 1DG | ARG.: 2PG 1DG 1T | NZ: 1G 4PG |
| | | | |
| 9 Jul. 1983 | 31 Jul. 1983 | 7 Aug. 1983 | 20 Aug. 1983 |
| [1]Rep. by †R.G. Hanley 1T | [1]Rep. by †A.J. Parker | ‡includes penalty try | |
| | [2]Rep. by S.A. Williams | | |

Australia had two convincing wins and two defeats in their home matches. Against the United States, Australia's first home Test with the Americans, nine tries were scored in a free-flowing game. David Campese, scored four of the tries to match the Australian Test record. Victory by 46 points was also a record winning margin for Australia in an international.

In the first Test against the Argentinians, the Australians found themselves outscrummaged. (One of the Argentinians, Enriqué Rodriguez, later settled in Australia and has become a regular member of the Wallaby Test side.) The return of veteran prop John Meadows and a controversial penalty-try decision helped Australia to square the series with a 29-13 win at Sydney.

In August, despite scoring two splendid tries, the home side was beaten by a New Zealand team which kicked four penalty goals, whereas Australia rued the two conversion failures and two missed penalty kicks which would have drawn the match.

## 1983

| v. ITALY | 1st v. FRANCE | 2nd v. FRANCE |
|---|---|---|
| G.J. ELLA | R.G. GOULD | R.G. GOULD |
| D.I. CAMPESE 3C,1PG | D.I. CAMPESE 1PG,1C | D.I. CAMPESE 1PG |
| A.G. SLACK | G.A. ELLA | G.A. ELLA |
| M.J. HAWKER 2T | M.J. HAWKER 1DG | M.J. HAWKER |
| B.J. MOON 1T¹ | B.J. MOON | B.J. MOON |
| *M.G. ELLA 1T | *M.G. ELLA 1DG | *M.G. ELLA 1DG |
| D. VAUGHAN | D. VAUGHAN | D. VAUGHAN |
| †M.A. HARDING | A.J. McINTYRE | A.J. McINTYRE |
| †M.I. McBAIN | M.I. McBAIN¹ | T.A. LAWTON |
| J.E. COOLICAN | J.E. COOLICAN | J.E. COOLICAN |
| S.A. WILLIAMS 1T | S.A. WILLIAMS | S.A. WILLIAMS |
| D.W. HILLHOUSE | D.W. HILLHOUSE | D.W. HILLHOUSE |
| C. ROCHE | C. ROCHE 1T | C. ROCHE |
| D. HALL | †S.N. TUYNMAN | S.N. TUYNMAN |
| S.P. POIDEVIN | S.P. POIDEVIN | S.P. POIDEVIN |
| Rovigo | Clermont-Ferrand | Parc des Princes |
| WON 29-7 | DRAWN 15-15 | LOST 6-15 |
| ITALY: 1PG 1T | FR.: 3PG 2DG | FR.: 1G 3PG |
| AUST.: 3G 1PG 2T | AUST.: 1G 2DG 1PG | AUST.: 1PG 1DG |
| 22 Oct. 1983 | 13 Nov. 1983 | 19 Nov. 1983 |
| | ¹Rep. by R.G. Hanley | ¹Rep. by †T.A. Lawton |

Mark Ella led a team, managed by Dr Charles Wilson and coached by Bob Dwyer, on an 11-match tour of Europe at the end of 1983. Two matches were played and won in Italy (including Australia's first official Test against the Italians in Rovigo) before the team concentrated on a difficult tour of France.

A heavy defeat at Agen, just before the first of the Tests against France, upset the tactical approach of Ella's team. It was noticeable at Clermont-Ferrand that the Wallabies were more intent on tight defence instead of the running rugby which had been their style in previous seasons. Although Australia scored the only try of the game, five successful French kicks at goal left the first Test drawn.

In Paris six days later, where the French held a faint advantage up front, a similar match to the first Test produced a deserved French win, though Australia's failure to score penalty points emphasised coach Dwyer's dire need of a specialist place-kicker.

## 1984                    1984

| v. FIJI | 1st v. NZ | 2nd v. NZ | 3rd v. NZ |
|---|---|---|---|
| D.I. CAMPESE 1T | R.G. GOULD 1DG | R.G. GOULD | R.G. GOULD |
| P.C. GRIGG | D.I. CAMPESE | D.I. CAMPESE 1PG | D.I. CAMPESE 1PG,1T |
| *A.G. SLACK | *A.G. SLACK | *A.G. SLACK | *A.G. SLACK |
| †M.P. LYNAGH 3PG | M.J. HAWKER | M.J. HAWKER | M.J. HAWKER |
| B.J. MOON | B.J. MOON 1T | B.J. MOON | B.J. MOON |
| M.G. ELLA 1DG | M.G. ELLA 1PG,1C | M.G. ELLA 1T,1C,2PG | M.G. ELLA 5PG,1C |
| P.A. COX | P.A. COX | P.A. COX | P.A. COX |
| †E.E. RODRIGUEZ | E.E. RODRIGUEZ | E.E. RODRIGUEZ | E.E. RODRIGUEZ |
| T.A. LAWTON | T.A. LAWTON | T.A. LAWTON | T.A. LAWTON |
| A.J. McINTYRE | A.J. McINTYRE | A.J. McINTYRE | A.J. McINTYRE |
| †N.G. HOLT | S.A.G. CUTLER | S.A.G. CUTLER | S.A.G. CUTLER |
| †W.A. CAMPBELL | S.A. WILLIAMS | S.A. WILLIAMS | S.A. WILLIAMS |
| S.P. POIDEVIN | S.P. POIDEVIN | S.P. POIDEVIN | S.P. POIDEVIN |
| †R.J. REYNOLDS | R.J. REYNOLDS 1T | R.J. REYNOLDS | R.J. REYNOLDS |
| C. ROCHE | C. ROCHE | C. ROCHE | C. ROCHE |
| Suva | Sydney | Ballymore | Sydney |
| WON 16-3 | WON 16-9 | LOST 15-19 | LOST 24-25 |
| FIJI: 1PG | AUST.: 1G 1PG 1DG 1T | AUST.: 1G 3PG | AUST.: 1G 6PG |
| AUST.: 3PG 1DG 1T | NZ: 1DG 2PG | NZ: 5PG 1T | NZ: 1G 5PG 1T |
| 9 Jun. 1984 | 21 Jul. 1984 | 4 Aug. 1984 | 18 Aug. 1984 |

Alan Jones, man of many talents, succeeded Bob Dwyer as Australian coach for 1984, taking advantage of an early season opportunity to tour Fiji (where the Test was easily won) to prepare a side to face the All Blacks.

In what turned out to be a fascinating and exciting series, the All Blacks retained the Bledisloe Cup by winning the rubber 2-1, but not without a stern fight. The Australians took advantage of an underprepared New Zealand team to win the first Test comfortably, despite some poor goal-kicking by Campese. Then, in the second Test, after leading 12-0, a match which developed into a goal-kicking contest ended with the All Blacks squaring the series. In the final Test at Sydney, before 44,000 spectators, Ella's failure to drop last-minute goals, after his forwards had dominated the line-outs, enabled New Zealand to win a close match by a single point. For the first time, Australia fielded an unchanged fifteen for a three-Test series.

## 1984

| v. ENGLAND | v. IRELAND | v. WALES | v. SCOTLAND |
|---|---|---|---|
| R.G. GOULD | R.G. GOULD | R.G. GOULD 2PG,3C | R.G. GOULD |
| D.I. CAMPESE | M.P. BURKE | P.C. GRIGG | P.C. GRIGG |
| *A.G. SLACK | *A.G. SLACK | *A.G. SLACK | *A.G. SLACK |
| M.P. LYNAGH 1T,2C,1PG | M.P. LYNAGH 1DG,1PG | M.P. LYNAGH 1T | M.P. LYNAGH 5PG,3C |
| B.J. MOON[1] | D.I. CAMPESE | D.I. CAMPESE | D.I. CAMPESE 2T |
| M.G. ELLA 1T | M.G. ELLA 2DG,1T | M.G. ELLA 1T | M.G. ELLA 1T |
| †N.C. FARR-JONES | N.C. FARR-JONES | N.C. FARR-JONES | N.C. FARR-JONES 1T |
| E.E. RODRIGUEZ | E.E. RODRIGUEZ | E.E. RODRIGUEZ | E.E. RODRIGUEZ |
| T.A. LAWTON | T.A. LAWTON | T.A. LAWTON 1T | T.A. LAWTON |
| A.J. McINTYRE | A.J. McINTYRE | A.J. McINTYRE | A.J. McINTYRE |
| S.A. WILLIAMS | S.A. WILLIAMS | S.A. WILLIAMS | S.A. WILLIAMS |
| S.A.G. CUTLER | S.A.G. CUTLER | S.A.G. CUTLER | S.A.G. CUTLER |
| S.P. POIDEVIN 1T | S.P. POIDEVIN | S.P. POIDEVIN | S.P. POIDEVIN |
| S.N. TUYNMAN | S.N. TUYNMAN | S.N. TUYNMAN 1T | S.N. TUYNMAN |
| D. CODEY | C. ROCHE | D. CODEY | D. CODEY |
| Twickenham | Lansdowne Road | Cardiff Arms Park | Murrayfield |
| WON 19-3 | WON 16-9 | WON 28-9 | WON 37-12 |
| ENG.: 1PG | IRE.: 3PG | WALES: 1G 1PG | SCOT.: 4PG |
| AUST.: 2G 1PG 1T | AUST.: 1PG 3DG 1T | AUST.: 3G 2PG 1T | AUST.: 3G 5PG 1T |
| 3 Nov. 1984 | 10 Nov. 1984 | 24 Nov. 1984 | 8 Dec. 1984 |

[1]Rep. by †M.P. Burke

Under the management of Dr Charles Wilson and coaching of Alan Jones, Australian rugby reached its zenith late in 1984 on a very successful tour of Britain. Andrew Slack, a thrusting threequarter who has become Australia's most-capped centre, led the Wallabies to a Grand Slam – victories in all four Tests of the tour.

For once the Australian backs succeeded in playing their natural flowing game on the soft British grounds. Furthermore, for a first time they were able to boast a powerful pack capable of subduing the best British forwards. And with Michael Lynagh to kick goals – he scored 42 points in the four Tests – this was one of the most complete all-round sides ever to tour Britain.

Mark Ella was the key player among the backs. Most of the Australians' successful moves originated from him, and he became the first overseas player to score tries in each Test of a series against the four Home Unions.

## 1985

| 1st v. CANADA | 2nd v. CANADA | v. NZ | 1st v. FIJI | 2nd v. FIJI |
|---|---|---|---|---|
| †J.W. BLACK | J.W. BLACK | R.G. GOULD | J.W. BLACK | G.J. ELLA |
| P.C. GRIGG 2T | P.C. GRIGG 1T | P.C. GRIGG | P.C. GRIGG 1T | P.C. GRIGG 1T |
| †N. KASSULKE 1T | N. KASSULKE[1] | J.W. BLACK 1T | M.P. BURKE | M.P. BURKE |
| †T.A. LANE 2T | T.A. LANE | T.A. LANE | †B. PAPWORTH 1T | B. PAPWORTH |
| M.P. BURKE 2T | M.P. BURKE 3T | M.P. BURKE | D.I. CAMPESE 1DG | D.I. CAMPESE 2T |
| M.P. LYNAGH 7C,3PG | M.P. LYNAGH 3C,2PG,1DG | M.P. LYNAGH 1C,1PG | †D. KNOX 3C,3PG,2DG | D. KNOX 1C,3PG |
| N.C. FARR-JONES 1T | N.C. FARR-JONES 1T | N.C. FARR-JONES | N.C. FARR-JONES 2T | N.C. FARR-JONES |
| E.E. RODRIGUEZ | E.E. RODRIGUEZ | E.E. RODRIGUEZ | E.E. RODRIGUEZ | †C.A. LILLICRAP |
| T.A. LAWTON | T.A. LAWTON | T.A. LAWTON | T.A. LAWTON 1T | M.I. McBAIN |
| A.J. McINTYRE | A.J. McINTYRE | A.J. McINTYRE | A.J. McINTYRE | A.J. McINTYRE 1T |
| S.A.G. CUTLER | S.A.G. CUTLER 1T | S.A.G. CUTLER | S.A.G. CUTLER 1T | S.A.G. CUTLER 1T |
| *S.A. WILLIAMS | *S.A. WILLIAMS | *S.A. WILLIAMS | *S.A. WILLIAMS | *S.A. WILLIAMS |
| S.P. POIDEVIN | S.P. POIDEVIN | S.P. POIDEVIN | S.P. POIDEVIN | S.P. POIDEVIN |
| S.N. TUYNMAN | S.N. TUYNMAN 1T | S.N. TUYNMAN | R.J. REYNOLDS 1T | R.J. REYNOLDS |
| †W.J. CALCRAFT 1T | D. CODEY | D. CODEY | S.N. TUYNMAN | S.N. TUYNMAN |
| Sydney | Ballymore | Auckland | Ballymore | Sydney |
| WON 59-3 | WON 43-15 | LOST 9-10 | WON 52-28 | WON 31-9 |
| AUST.: 7G 3PG 2T | AUST.: 3G 2PG 1DG 4T | NZ: 2PG 1T | AUST.: 3G 3PG 3DG 4T | AUST.: 1G 3PG 4T |
| CAN.:1DG | CAN.: 1G 3PG | AUST.: 1G 1PG | FIJI: 3G 2PG 1T | FIJI: 2PG 1DG |
| 15 Jun. 1985 | 23 Jun. 1985 | 29 Jun. 1985 | 10 Aug. 1985 | 17 Aug. 1985 |

[1]Rep. by G.J. Ella

This was the highest-scoring international season in Australia's rugby history. In five Tests the Australians notched 194 points, passing 50 points in two of the Tests. The total of 59 in the first Test against Canada is Australia's highest for a Test match, and Lynagh's contribution of 23 points for the game created a new individual Australian record.

But the victories over Canada and Fiji were hollow, for in the major Test of the season the Australians were narrowly defeated by the All Blacks in Auckland.

Steve Williams, an athletic lock forward who overcame serious jaw injuries earlier in his career, captained the Australians this season. He was the first regular lock to captain his nation since John Thornett's leadership in the early 1960s, though Tony Shaw (a regular loose forward) had captained the side from lock on the 1981-82 tour of Britain.

## 1986

| v. ITALY | v. FRANCE | 1st v. ARGENTINA | 2nd v. ARGENTINA |
|---|---|---|---|
| R.G. GOULD | D.I. CAMPESE 1T | D.I. CAMPESE 1T | D.I. CAMPESE 2T |
| | | | |
| D.I. CAMPESE 2T | M.P. BURKE | P.C. GRIGG 1T | P.C. GRIGG |
| *A.G. SLACK[1] | *A.G. SLACK | M.P. BURKE | M.P. BURKE |
| B. PAPWORTH | †M.T. COOK | B. PAPWORTH 2T | B. PAPWORTH |
| B.J. MOON 1T | B.J. MOON | B.J. MOON | B.J. MOON |
| | | | |
| M.P. LYNAGH 1PG 6C | M.P. LYNAGH 6PG 1DG 1C | M.P. LYNAGH 5PG 4C | M.P. LYNAGH 4PG 1C |
| N.C. FARR-JONES | N.C. FARR-JONES | N.C. FARR-JONES | N.C. FARR-JONES |
| | | | |
| E.E. RODRIGUEZ | E.E. RODRIGUEZ | E.E. RODRIGUEZ | E.E. RODRIGUEZ |
| T.A. LAWTON[2] | T.A. LAWTON | T.A. LAWTON | T.A. LAWTON |
| A.J. McINTYRE 1T | A.J. McINTYRE | A.J. McINTYRE | A.J. McINTYRE |
| S.A.G. CUTLER | S.A.G. CUTLER | R.J. REYNOLDS | R.J. REYNOLDS |
| W.A. CAMPBELL | W.A. CAMPBELL | W.A. CAMPBELL | W.A. CAMPBELL |
| S.P. POIDEVIN | S.P. POIDEVIN | *S.P. POIDEVIN | *S.P. POIDEVIN |
| S.N. TUYNMAN 1T | S.N. TUYNMAN | S.N. TUYNMAN | S.N. TUYNMAN 1T[1] |
| W.J. CALCRAFT | D. CODEY | D. CODEY | W.J. CALCRAFT |
| | | | |
| Brisbane | Sydney | Brisbane | Sydney |
| WON 39-18 | WON 27-14 | WON 39-19 | WON 26-0 |
| | | | |
| AUS.: 6G 1PG | AUS.: 1G 1DG 6PG | AUS.: 4G 5PG | AUS.: 1G 4PG 2T |
| ITALY: 2G 2PG | FR.: 1G 2T | ARG.: 2G 1PG 1T | ARG.: NIL |
| | | | |
| 1 Jun. 1986 | 21 Jun. 1986 | 6 Jul. 1986 | 12 Jul. 1986 |
| | [1]Rep. by M.P. Burke 1T | | [1]Rep. by †D. Frawley |
| | [2]Rep. by M.I. McBain | | |

The season began with four home Tests, against Italy, France and Argentina. Australia, who won all of these Tests in preparation for their late-season tour of New Zealand, recalled Brendon Moon and former skipper Andrew Slack for the internationals.

In the convincing win against France, the Five Nations joint-Champions, the Australians were outscored on tries but won thanks to some brilliant place-kicking by Michael Lynagh, who equalled his own Australian Test record of scoring 23 points in a game, and matched the world Test record by kicking six penalties.

Some splendid tries by Campese, more accurate place-kicking by Lynagh, and expert tight play by the forwards were the features of the two wins over Argentina. Tom Lawton in particular had four fine matches. Australia's most consistent hooker since the retirement of Peter Johnson, Lawton is a grandson of the famous Australian fly-half of the 1920s and 1930s.

## 1986

| 1st v. NZ | 2nd v. NZ | 3rd v. NZ |
|---|---|---|
| D. CAMPESE 1T | D.I. CAMPESE | †A. LEEDS 1T |
| | | |
| P.C. GRIGG | P.C. GRIGG | D.I. CAMPESE 1T |
| *A.G. SLACK | *A.G. SLACK | *A.G. SLACK |
| B. PAPWORTH | B. PAPWORTH | B. PAPWORTH |
| M.P. BURKE 1T | M.P. BURKE | M.P. BURKE |
| | | |
| M.P. LYNAGH 1PG 1C | M.P. LYNAGH 1DG 3PG | M.P. LYNAGH 4PG 1C |
| N.C. FARR-JONES | N.C. FARR-JONES | N.C. FARR-JONES |
| | | |
| E.E. RODRIGUEZ | E.E. RODRIGUEZ | E.E. RODRIGUEZ |
| T.A. LAWTON | T.A. LAWTON | T.A. LAWTON |
| †M.N. HARTILL | M.N. HARTILL | M.N. HARTILL |
| S.A.G. CUTLER | S.A.G. CUTLER | S.A.G. CUTLER |
| W.A. CAMPBELL | W.A. CAMPBELL | W.A. CAMPBELL |
| S.N. TUYNMAN | †J.S. MILLER | J.S. MILLER |
| R.J. REYNOLDS | S.N. TUYNMAN | S.N. TUYNMAN 1T |
| S.P. POIDEVIN | S.P. POIDEVIN | W.J. CALCRAFT |
| | | |
| Wellington | Dunedin | Auckland |
| WON 13-12 | LOST 12-13 | WON 22-9 |
| | | |
| NZ: 1G 2PG | NZ: 1DG 2PG 1T | NZ: 3PG |
| AUS.: 1G 1PG 1T | AUS.: 3PG 1DG | AUS.: 1G 4PG 1T |
| | | |
| 9 Aug. 1986 | 23 Aug. 1986 | 6 Sep. 1986 |

Alan Jones, the influential Australian coach, propelled his talented side to their first Bledisloe Cup triumph in New Zealand since 1949, and thus catapulted the Wallabies to the position of firm favourites for the 1987 World Cup.

Firm control in the tight, excellent support play by the forwards in the loose, and imaginative tactical direction from Lynagh in midfield enabled the Wallabies to establish their superiority in the first and third Tests, and thus lay the foundations for the series victory.

Lynagh ended the season by scoring his 200th Test point, and in only his 15th Test, placing him second to Paul McLean in the order of Australian Test points scorers. And Campese's important try at Auckland was his 21st in Tests, a record for an Australian.

# AUSTRALIAN MATCH RECORDS

## Match Results 1899 to 1987

| Match | Date | Opponents | For T C D P Pts | Against T C D P Pts | Result | Venue | Captain |
|---|---|---|---|---|---|---|---|
| 1 | 24.6.1899 | G.B. | 3 2 — — 13 | 1 — — — 3 | Won | Sydney | F. L. Row |
| 2 | 22.7.1899 | G.B. | — — — — 0 | 3 1 — — 11 | Lost | Brisbane | R. H. McCowan |
| 3 | 5.8.1899 | G.B. | 2 2 — — 10 | 3 1 — — 11 | Lost | Sydney | F. L. Row |
| 4 | 12.8.1899 | G.B. | — — — — 0 | 2 2 — 1 13 | Lost | Sydney | F. L. Row |
| 5 | 15.8.1903 | N.Z. | — — 1 — 3 | 3 1 ** 1 22 | Lost | Sydney | S. M. Wickham |
| 6 | 2.7.1904 | G.B. | — — — — 0 | 3 2 1 — 17 | Lost | Sydney | F. Nicholson |
| 7 | 23.7.1904 | G.B. | 1 — — — 3 | 3 — 1* — 17 | Lost | Brisbane | S. M. Wickham |
| 8 | 30.7.1904 | G.B. | — — — — 0 | 4 2 — — 16 | Lost | Sydney | S. M. Wickham |
| 9 | 2.9.1905 | N.Z. | 1 — — — 3 | 4 1 — — 14 | Lost | Dunedin | S. M. Wickham |
| 10 | 20.7.1907 | N.Z. | — — * 1 6 | 6 4 — — 26 | Lost | Sydney | P. H. Burge |
| 11 | 3.8.1907 | N.Z. | 1 1 — — 5 | 4 1 — — 14 | Lost | Brisbane | A. M. Oxlade |
| 12 | 10.8.1907 | N.Z. | 1 1 — — 5 | 1 1 — — 5 | Drawn | Sydney | P. H. Burge |
| 13 | 12.12.1908 | Wales | 2 — — — 6 | 2 — 1 — 9 | Lost | Cardiff | H. M. Moran |
| 14 | 9.1.1909 | England | 3 — — — 9 | 1 — — — 3 | Won | Blackheath | C. H. McKivat |
| 15 | 25.6.1910 | N.Z. | — — — — 0 | 2 — — — 6 | Lost | Sydney | S. A. Middleton |
| 16 | 27.6.1910 | N.Z. | 3 1 — — 11 | — — — — 0 | Won | Sydney | S. A. Middleton |
| 17 | 2.7.1910 | N.Z. | 2 2 — 1 13 | 8 2 — — 28 | Lost | Sydney | S. A. Middleton |
| 18 | 16.11.1912 | America | 3 — — 1 12 | 1 1 — 1 8 | Won | Berkeley | W. S. Prentice |
| 19 | 6.9.1913 | N.Z. | 1 1 — — 5 | 8 3 — — 30 | Lost | Wellington | E. J. Fahey |
| 20 | 13.9.1913 | N.Z. | 3 2 — — 13 | 5 3 1 — 25 | Lost | Dunedin | E. J. Fahey |
| 21 | 20.9.1913 | N.Z. | 4 2 — — 16 | 1 1 — — 5 | Won | Christchurch | E. J. Fahey |
| 22 | 18.7.1914 | N.Z. | — — — — 0 | 1 1 — — 5 | Lost | Sydney | F. Wood |
| 23 | 1.8.1914 | N.Z. | — — — — 0 | 5 1 — — 17 | Lost | Brisbane | J. P. Flynn |
| 24 | 15.8.1914 | N.Z. | 1 — 1 — 7 | 6 2 — — 22 | Lost | Sydney | F. Wood |
| 25 | 12.11.1927 | Ireland | 1 1 — — 5 | — — — 1 3 | Won | Dublin | A. C. Wallace |
| 26 | 26.11.1927 | Wales | 4 3 — — 18 | 2 1 — — 8 | Won | Cardiff | A. C. Wallace |
| 27 | 17.12.1927 | Scotland | 2 1 — — 8 | 2 2 — — 10 | Lost | Murrayfield | A. C. Wallace |
| 28 | 7.1.1928 | England | 3 1 — — 11 | 4 3 — — 18 | Lost | Twickenham | A. C. Wallace |
| 29 | 22.1.1928 | France | 3 1 — — 11 | 2 1 — — 8 | Won | Paris | A. C. Wallace |
| 30 | 6.7.1929 | N.Z. | 1 — — 2 9 | 1 1 — 1 8 | Won | Sydney | T. Lawton |
| 31 | 20.7.1929 | N.Z. | 3 1 — 2 17 | 2 — — 1 9 | Won | Brisbane | T. Lawton |
| 32 | 27.7.1929 | N.Z. | 2 — — 3 15 | 3 2 — — 13 | Won | Sydney | T. Lawton |
| 33 | 30.8.1930 | G.B. | 2 — — — 6 | 1 1 — — 5 | Won | Sydney | T. Lawton |
| 34 | 9.9.1931 | N.Z. Maoris | 3 1 — 1 14 | 1 — — — 3 | Won | Palmerston N. | J. G. Clark |
| 35 | 12.9.1931 | N.Z. | 3 2 — — 11 | 2 1 — 4 20 | Lost | Auckland | S. J. Malcolm |
| 36 | 2.7.1932 | N.Z. | 4 2 — 2 22 | 3 2 1 — 17 | Won | Sydney | T. Lawton |
| 37 | 16.7.1932 | N.Z. | 1 — — — 3 | 4 1 1 1 21 | Lost | Brisbane | T. Lawton |
| 38 | 23.7.1932 | N.Z. | 3 2 — — 13 | 5 3 — — 21 | Lost | Sydney | S. J. Malcolm |
| 39 | 8.7.1933 | S.Africa | — — 1 — 3 | 4 1 — 1 17 | Lost | Cape Town | D. L. Cowper |
| 40 | 22.7.1933 | S.Africa | 4 3 — 1 21 | 1 — — 1 6 | Won | Durban | D. L. Cowper |
| 41 | 12.8.1933 | S.Africa | 1 — — — 3 | 2 1 1 — 12 | Lost | Johannesburg | D. L. Cowper |
| 42 | 26.8.1933 | S.Africa | — — — — 0 | 2 1 — 1 11 | Lost | Port Elizabeth | S. J. Malcolm |
| 43 | 2.9.1933 | S.Africa | 3 1 1 — 15 | — — 1 — 4 | Won | Bloemfontein | A. W. Ross |
| 44 | 11.8.1934 | N.Z. | 4 2 — 3 25 | 3 1 — — 11 | Won | Sydney | A. W. Ross |
| 45 | 25.8.1934 | N.Z. | 1 — — — 3 | 1 — — — 3 | Drawn | Sydney | A. W. Ross |
| 46 | 5.9.1936 | N.Z. | 1 — — 1 6 | 3 1 — — 11 | Lost | Wellington | R. J. Walden |
| 47 | 12.9.1936 | N.Z. | 2 2 — 1 13 | 9 4 — 1 38 | Lost | Dunedin | R. J. Walden |
| 48 | 23.9.1936 | N.Z. Maoris | 6 5 — 1 31 | 1 — — 1 6 | Won | Palmerston N. | R. J. Walden |
| 49 | 26.6.1937 | S.Africa | 1 1 — — 5 | 2 — — 1 9 | Lost | Sydney | C. H. T. Towers |
| 50 | 17.7.1937 | S.Africa | 3 1 — 2 17 | 6 4 — — 26 | Lost | Sydney | C. H. T. Towers |
| 51 | 23.7.1938 | N.Z. | — — — 3 9 | 4 3 — 2 24 | Lost | Sydney | V. W. Wilson |
| 52 | 6.8.1938 | N.Z. | 3 1 — 1 14 | 4 2 1 — 20 | Lost | Brisbane | V. W. Wilson |
| 53 | 13.8.1938 | N.Z. | 1 — — 1 6 | 2 1 — 2 14 | Lost | Sydney | V. W. Wilson |
| 54 | 14.9.1946 | N.Z. | 2 1 — — 8 | 7 5 — — 31 | Lost | Dunedin | W. M. McLean |
| 55 | 25.9.1946 | N.Z. Maoris | — — — — 0 | 5 1 — 1 20 | Lost | Hamilton | W. M. McLean |
| 56 | 28.9.1946 | N.Z. | 2 2 — — 10 | 1 1 — 3 14 | Lost | Auckland | W. M. McLean |
| 57 | 14.6.1947 | N.Z. | 1 1 — — 5 | 3 2 — — 13 | Lost | Brisbane | P. A. Hardcastle |
| 58 | 28.6.1947 | N.Z. | 1 1 — 3 14 | 3 3 — 4 27 | Lost | Sydney | W. M. McLean |
| 59 | 22.11.1947 | Scotland | 4 2 — — 16 | — — 1 1 7 | Won | Murrayfield | T. Allan |
| 60 | 6.12.1947 | Ireland | 4 2 — — 16 | — — — 1 3 | Won | Dublin | T. Allan |
| 61 | 20.12.1947 | Wales | — — — — 0 | — — — 2 6 | Lost | Cardiff | T. Allan |
| 62 | 3.1.1948 | England | 3 1 — — 11 | — — — — 0 | Won | Twickenham | T. Allan |
| 63 | 11.1.1948 | France | — — — 2 6 | 3 2 — — 13 | Lost | Paris | T. Allan |
| 64 | 4.6.1949 | N.Z. Maoris | 1 — — — 3 | 4 — — — 12 | Lost | Sydney | T. Allan |
| 65 | 11.6.1949 | N.Z. Maoris | 2 1 — — 8 | 1 1 — 1 8 | Drawn | Brisbane | T. Allan |

* in the drop-goal column denotes a goal from a mark

| Match | Date | Opponents | T | C | D | P | Pts | T | C | D | P | Pts | Result | Venue | Captain |
|---|---|---|---|---|---|---|---|---|---|---|---|---|---|---|---|
| 66 | 25.6.1949 | N.Z. Maoris | 4 | 3 | — | — | 18 | — | — | — | 1 | 3 | Won | Sydney | T. Allan |
| 67 | 3.9.1949 | N.Z. | 3 | 1 | — | — | 11 | 1 | — | — | 1 | 6 | Won | Wellington | T. Allan |
| 68 | 24.9.1949 | N.Z. | 3 | 2 | — | 1 | 16 | 1 | — | 1 | 1 | 9 | Won | Auckland | T. Allan |
| 69 | 19.8.1950 | British Is. | — | — | — | 2 | 6 | 2 | 2 | 1 | 2 | 19 | Lost | Brisbane | N. V. Cottrell |
| 70 | 26.8.1950 | British Is. | 1 | — | — | — | 3 | 5 | 3 | — | 1 | 24 | Lost | Sydney | N. V. Cottrell |
| 71 | 23.6.1951 | N.Z. | — | — | — | — | 0 | 1 | 1 | — | 1 | 8 | Lost | Sydney | K. C. Winning |
| 72 | 7.7.1951 | N.Z. | 2 | 1 | — | 1 | 11 | 4 | 1 | 1 | — | 17 | Lost | Sydney | C. J. Windon |
| 73 | 21.7.1951 | N.Z. | — | — | — | 2 | 6 | 4 | 2 | — | — | 16 | Lost | Brisbane | C. J. Windon |
| 74 | 26.7.1952 | Fiji | 4 | — | — | 1 | 15 | 2 | — | — | 1 | 9 | Won | Sydney | H. J. Solomon |
| 75 | 9.8.1952 | Fiji | 4 | — | 1 | — | 15 | 2 | 1 | 1 | 2 | 17 | Lost | Sydney | H. J. Solomon |
| 76 | 6.9.1952 | N.Z. | 3 | 1 | 1 | — | 14 | 2 | — | — | 1 | 9 | Won | Christchurch | H. J. Solomon |
| 77 | 13.9.1952 | N.Z. | 1 | 1 | — | 1 | 8 | 2 | — | 1 | 2 | 15 | Lost | Wellington | H. J. Solomon |
| 78 | 22.8.1953 | S.Africa | — | — | 1 | 3 |  | 5 | 2 | — | 2 | 25 | Lost | Johannesburg | H. J. Solomon |
| 79 | 5.9.1953 | S.Africa | 4 | 3 | — | 18 |  | 4 | 1 | — | — | 14 | Won | Cape Town | H. J. Solomon |
| 80 | 19.9.1953 | S.Africa | 1 | 1 | — | 1 | 8 | 4 | 3 | — | — | 18 | Lost | Durban | H. J. Solomon |
| 81 | 26.9.1953 | S.Africa | 1 | — | — | 2 | 9 | 2 | 2 | 2 | 2 | 22 | Lost | Port Elizabeth | N. M. Shehadie |
| 82 | 5.6.1954 | Fiji | 5 | 2 | — | 1 | 22 | 4 | 2 | — | 1 | 19 | Won | Brisbane | N. M. Shehadie |
| 83 | 26.6.1954 | Fiji | 2 | 2 | — | 2 | 16 | 2 | — | — | 4 | 18 | Lost | Sydney | N. M. Shehadie |
| 84 | 20.8.1955 | N.Z. | 1 | 1 | — | 1 | 8 | 3 | 2 | — | 1 | 16 | Lost | Wellington | H. J. Solomon |
| 85 | 3.9.1955 | N.Z. | — | — | — | — | 0 | 1 | 1 | 1 | 1 | 8 | Lost | Dunedin | A. S. Cameron |
| 86 | 17.9.1955 | N.Z. | 2 | 1 | — | — | 8 | 1 | — | — | — | 3 | Won | Auckland | A. S. Cameron |
| 87 | 26.5.1956 | S.Africa | — | — | — | — | 0 | 2 | — | 1 | — | 9 | Lost | Sydney | A. S. Cameron |
| 88 | 2.6.1956 | S.Africa | — | — | — | — | 0 | 2 | — | 1 | — | 9 | Lost | Brisbane | A. S. Cameron |
| 89 | 25.5.1957 | N.Z. | 1 | 1 | — | 2 | 11 | 4 | 2 | — | 3 | 25 | Lost | Sydney | R. M. Tooth |
| 90 | 1.6.1957 | N.Z. | 1 | — | — | 2 | 9 | 4 | 2 | 1* | — | 22 | Lost | Brisbane | R. M. Tooth |
| 91 | 4.1.1958 | Wales | 1 | — | — | — | 3 | 1 | — | 1 | 1 | 9 | Lost | Cardiff | R. A. L. Davidson |
| 92 | 18.1.1958 | Ireland | 2 | — | — | — | 6 | 2 | — | 1 | — | 9 | Lost | Dublin | R. A. L. Davidson |
| 93 | 1.2.1958 | England | — | — | 1 | 1 | 6 | 2 | — | 1 | — | 9 | Lost | Twickenham | R. A. L. Davidson |
| 94 | 15.2.1958 | Scotland | 2 | 1 | — | — | 8 | 2 | — | — | 2 | 12 | Lost | Murrayfield | R. A. L. Davidson |
| 95 | 9.3.1958 | France | — | — | — | — | 0 | 3 | 2 | 2 | — | 19 | Lost | Paris | R. A. L. Davidson |
| 96 | 14.6.1958 | N.Z. Maoris | 1 | — | — | 4 | 15 | 2 | 1 | — | 2 | 14 | Won | Brisbane | R. A. L. Davidson |
| 97 | 28.6.1958 | N.Z. Maoris | — | — | — | 1 | 3 | — | — | — | 1 | 3 | Drawn | Sydney | D. M. Connor |
| 98 | 5.7.1958 | N.Z. Maoris | — | — | — | 2 | 6 | 3 | 2 | — | — | 13 | Lost | Melbourne | D. M. Connor |
| 99 | 23.8.1958 | N.Z. | 1 | — | — | — | 3 | 7 | 2 | — | — | 25 | Lost | Wellington | C. R. Wilson |
| 100 | 6.9.1958 | N.Z. | 1 | — | — | 1 | 6 | 1 | — | — | — | 3 | Won | Christchurch | C. R. Wilson |
| 101 | 20.9.1958 | N.Z. | 1 | 1 | — | 1 | 8 | 1 | 1 | — | 4 | 17 | Lost | Auckland | C. R. Wilson |
| 102 | 6.6.1959 | British Is. | — | — | — | 2 | 6 | 2 | 1 | 1 | 2 | 17 | Lost | Brisbane | P. T. Fenwicke |
| 103 | 13.6.1959 | British Is. | — | — | — | 1 | 3 | 5 | 3 | — | 1 | 24 | Lost | Sydney | P. T. Fenwicke |
| 104 | 10.6.1961 | Fiji | 6 | 3 | — | — | 24 | — | — | — | 2 | 6 | Won | Brisbane | K. W. Catchpole |
| 105 | 17.6.1961 | Fiji | 4 | 1 | — | 2 | 20 | 3 | 1 | — | 1 | 14 | Won | Sydney | K. W. Catchpole |
| 106 | 1.7.1961 | Fiji | 1 | — | — | — | 3 | 1 | — | — | — | 3 | Drawn | Melbourne | K. W. Catchpole |
| 107 | 5.8.1961 | S.Africa | — | — | — | 1 | 3 | 8 | 2 | — | — | 28 | Lost | Johannesburg | K. W. Catchpole |
| 108 | 12.8.1961 | S.Africa | 1 | 1 | — | 2 | 11 | 3 | 1 | 1 | 3 | 23 | Lost | Port Elizabeth | K. W. Catchpole |
| 109 | 26.8.1961 | France | 1 | 1 | — | 1 | 8 | 3 | — | 2 | — | 15 | Lost | Sydney | K. W. Catchpole |
| 110 | 26.5.1962 | N.Z. | — | — | — | 2 | 6 | 4 | 1 | 1 | 1 | 20 | Lost | Brisbane | P. G. Johnson |
| 111 | 4.6.1962 | N.Z. | 1 | 1 | — | — | 5 | 2 | 1 | — | 2 | 14 | Lost | Sydney | J. K. Lenehan |
| 112 | 25.8.1962 | N.Z. | — | — | — | 3 | 9 | 1 | — | — | 2 | 9 | Drawn | Wellington | J. E. Thornett |
| 113 | 8.9.1962 | N.Z. | — | — | — | — | 0 | — | — | — | 1 | 3 | Lost | Dunedin | J. E. Thornett |
| 114 | 22.9.1962 | N.Z. | 1 | 1 | — | 1 | 8 | 3 | 2 | 1 | — | 16 | Lost | Auckland | J. E. Thornett |
| 115 | 4.6.1963 | England | 4 | 3 | — | — | 18 | 3 | — | — | — | 9 | Won | Sydney | J. E. Thornett |
| 116 | 13.7.1963 | S.Africa | 1 | — | — | 3 | 9 | 2 | 1 | — | 2 | 14 | Lost | Pretoria | J. E. Thornett |
| 117 | 10.8.1963 | S.Africa | 1 | — | 1 | 1 | 9 | 1 | 1 | — | — | 5 | Won | Cape Town | J. E. Thornett |
| 118 | 24.8.1963 | S.Africa | 1 | 1 | 1 | 1 | 11 | — | — | — | 3 | 9 | Won | Johannesburg | J. E. Thornett |
| 119 | 7.9.1963 | S.Africa | — | — | 1 | 1 | 6 | 3 | 2 | — | 3 | 22 | Lost | Port Elizabeth | J. E. Thornett |
| 120 | 15.8.1964 | N.Z. | 1 | — | — | 2 | 9 | 1 | 1 | 1 | 2 | 14 | Lost | Dunedin | J. E. Thornett |
| 121 | 22.8.1964 | N.Z. | 1 | — | — | — | 3 | 4 | 3 | — | — | 18 | Lost | Christchurch | J. E. Thornett |
| 122 | 29.8.1964 | N.Z. | 2 | 1 | 1 | 3 | 20 | 1 | 1 | — | — | 5 | Won | Wellington | J. E. Thornett |
| 123 | 19.6.1965 | S.Africa | 2 | — | — | 4 | 18 | 2 | 1 | — | 1 | 11 | Won | Sydney | J. E. Thornett |
| 124 | 26.6.1965 | S.Africa | — | — | — | 4 | 12 | 2 | 1 | — | — | 8 | Won | Brisbane | J. E. Thornett |
| 125 | 28.5.1966 | British Is. | 1 | 1 | — | 1 | 8 | 2 | 1 | — | 1 | 11 | Lost | Sydney | J. E. Thornett |
| 126 | 4.6.1966 | British Is. | — | — | — | — | 0 | 5 | 5 | 1 | 1 | 31 | Lost | Brisbane | J. E. Thornett |
| 127 | 3.12.1966 | Wales | 2 | 1 | 1 | 1 | 14 | 2 | 1 | — | 1 | 11 | Won | Cardiff | K. W. Catchpole |
| 128 | 17.12.1966 | Scotland | 1 | 1 | — | — | 5 | 2 | 1 | — | 1 | 11 | Lost | Murrayfield | K. W. Catchpole |
| 129 | 7.1.1967 | England | 2 | 1 | 3 | 2 | 23 | 1 | 1 | — | 2 | 11 | Won | Twickenham | K. W. Catchpole |
| 130 | 21.1.1967 | Ireland | 1 | 1 | — | 2 | 11 | 2 | — | 2 | 1 | 15 | Lost | Dublin | K. W. Catchpole |
| 131 | 11.2.1967 | France | 2 | 1 | 1 | 1 | 14 | 1 | 1 | 1 | 4 | 20 | Lost | Paris | J. E. Thornett |
| 132 | 13.5.1967 | Ireland | 1 | 1 | — | — | 5 | 2 | 1 | 1 | — | 11 | Lost | Sydney | K. W. Catchpole |
| 133 | 19.8.1967 | N.Z. | 2 | — | — | 1 | 9 | 4 | 4 | 1 | 2 | 29 | Lost | Wellington | K. W. Catchpole |
| 134 | 15.6.1968 | N.Z. | 1 | 1 | — | 2 | 11 | 6 | 3 | — | 1 | 27 | Lost | Sydney | K. W. Catchpole |
| 135 | 22.6.1968 | N.Z. | 1 | — | — | 5 | 18 | 3 | 2 | — | 2 | 19 | Lost | Brisbane | P. G. Johnson |
| 136 | 17.8.1968 | France | 1 | 1 | 1 | 1 | 11 | 2 | 2 | — | — | 10 | Won | Sydney | P. G. Johnson |
| 137 | 26.10.1968 | Ireland | 1 | — | — | — | 3 | 2 | 2 | — | — | 10 | Lost | Dublin | P. G. Johnson |
| 138 | 2.11.1968 | Scotland | — | — | — | 1 | 3 | 1 | — | — | 2 | 9 | Lost | Murrayfield | P. G. Johnson |
| 139 | 21.6.1969 | Wales | 2 | 2 | — | 2 | 16 | 3 | 2 | — | 2 | 19 | Lost | Sydney | G. V. Davis |

* in the drop-goal column denotes a goal from a mark

| Match | Date | Opponents | For | | | | | Against | | | | | Result | Venue | Captain |
|---|---|---|---|---|---|---|---|---|---|---|---|---|---|---|---|
| | | | T | C | D | P | Pts | T | C | D | P | Pts | | | |
| 140 | 2.8.1969 | S.Africa | 1 | 1 | — | 2 | 11 | 5 | 3 | — | 3 | 30 | Lost | Johannesburg | G. V. Davis |
| 141 | 16.8.1969 | S.Africa | — | — | — | 3 | 9 | 3 | 2 | — | 1 | 16 | Lost | Durban | G. V. Davis |
| 142 | 6.9.1969 | S.Africa | — | — | — | 1 | 3 | 2 | 1 | — | 1 | 11 | Lost | Cape Town | G. V. Davis |
| 143 | 20.9.1969 | S.Africa | 1 | 1 | — | 1 | 8 | 3 | 2 | — | 2 | 19 | Lost | Bloemfontein | G. V. Davis |
| 144 | 6.6.1970 | Scotland | 6 | 1 | — | 1 | 23 | — | — | — | 1 | 3 | Won | Sydney | G. V. Davis |
| 145 | 17.7.1971 | S.Africa | 1 | 1 | — | 2 | 11 | 3 | 2 | 1 | 1 | 19 | Lost | Sydney | G. V. Davis |
| 146 | 31.7.1971 | S.Africa | — | — | 1 | 1 | 6 | 3 | 1 | — | 1 | 14 | Lost | Brisbane | G. V. Davis |
| 147 | 7.8.1971 | S.Africa | 1 | — | — | 1 | 6 | 3 | 3 | — | 1 | 18 | Lost | Sydney | G. V. Davis |
| 148 | 20.11.1971 | France | 2 | 1 | — | 1 | 13 | 2 | — | — | 1 | 11 | Won | Toulouse | G. V. Davis |
| 149 | 27.11.1971 | France | — | — | — | 3 | 9 | 1 | 1 | — | 4 | 18 | Lost | Paris | G. V. Davis |
| 150 | 17.6.1972 | France | 2 | — | — | 2 | 14 | 3 | 1 | — | — | 14 | Drawn | Sydney | G. V. Davis |
| 151 | 25.6.1972 | France | — | — | — | 5 | 15 | 3 | 2 | — | — | 16 | Lost | Brisbane | G. V. Davis |
| 152 | 19.8.1972 | N.Z. | — | — | — | 2 | 6 | 5 | 3 | 1 | — | 29 | Lost | Wellington | G. V. Davis |
| 153 | 2.9.1972 | N.Z. | 3 | 1 | 1 | — | 17 | 5 | 2 | — | 2 | 30 | Lost | Christchurch | G. V. Davis |
| 154 | 16.9.1972 | N.Z. | — | — | — | 1 | 3 | 6 | 4 | — | 2 | 38 | Lost | Auckland | G. V. Davis |
| 155 | 19.9.1972 | Fiji | 4 | 1 | 1 | — | 21 | 2 | 1 | — | 3 | 19 | Won | Suva | P. D. Sullivan |
| 156 | 23.6.1973 | Tonga | 5 | 2 | 2 | — | 30 | 2 | 2 | — | — | 12 | Won | Sydney | P. D. Sullivan |
| 157 | 30.6.1973 | Tonga | 2 | — | — | 1 | 11 | 4 | — | — | — | 16 | Lost | Brisbane | P. D. Sullivan |
| 158 | 10.11.1973 | Wales | — | — | — | — | 0 | 3 | — | — | 4 | 24 | Lost | Cardiff | P. D. Sullivan |
| 159 | 17.11.1973 | England | — | — | — | 1 | 3 | 3 | 1 | — | 2 | 20 | Lost | Twickenham | J. N. B. Hipwell |
| 160 | 25.5.1974 | N.Z. | 1 | 1 | — | — | 6 | 2 | — | — | 1 | 11 | Lost | Sydney | J. N. B. Hipwell |
| 161 | 1.6.1974 | N.Z. | 2 | 1 | — | 2 | 16 | 2 | 1 | — | 2 | 16 | Drawn | Brisbane | J. N. B. Hipwell |
| 162 | 8.6.1974 | N.Z. | — | — | — | 2 | 6 | 3 | 2 | — | 2 | 16 | Lost | Sydney | J. N. B. Hipwell |
| 163 | 24.5.1975 | England | 1 | — | 2 | 2 | 16 | 1 | 1 | — | 1 | 9 | Won | Sydney | J. N. B. Hipwell |
| 164 | 31.5.1975 | England | 5 | 2 | — | 2 | 30 | 2 | 2 | — | 3 | 21 | Won | Brisbane | J. N. B. Hipwell |
| 165 | 2.8.1975 | Japan | 6 | 5 | — | 1 | 37 | 1 | — | — | 1 | 7 | Won | Sydney | J. N. B. Hipwell |
| 166 | 17.8.1975 | Japan | 8 | 6 | — | 2 | 50 | 5 | 1 | — | 1 | 25 | Won | Brisbane | G. A. Shaw |
| 167 | 6.12.1975 | Scotland | — | — | — | 1 | 3 | 2 | 1 | — | 1 | 10 | Lost | Murrayfield | J. N. B. Hipwell |
| 168 | 20.12.1975 | Wales | — | — | — | 1 | 3 | 4 | 3 | 1 | 1 | 28 | Lost | Cardiff | J. N. B. Hipwell |
| 169 | 3.1.1976 | England | — | — | — | 2 | 6 | 3 | 1 | — | 3 | 23 | Lost | Twickenham | G. A. Shaw |
| 170 | 17.1.1976 | Ireland | 3 | 1 | — | 2 | 20 | 1 | — | — | 2 | 10 | Won | Dublin | G. A. Shaw |
| 171 | 31.1.1976 | U.S. | 3 | — | — | 4 | 24 | — | — | — | 4 | 12 | Won | Lost Angeles | G. A. Shaw |
| 172 | 12.6.1976 | Fiji | 4 | — | — | 2 | 22 | 1 | 1 | — | — | 6 | Won | Sydney | G. A. Shaw |
| 173 | 19.6.1976 | Fiji | 2 | 2 | 1 | 2 | 21 | — | — | — | 3 | 9 | Won | Brisbane | G. A. Shaw |
| 174 | 26.6.1976 | Fiji | 3 | — | — | 5 | 27 | 3 | 1 | — | 1 | 17 | Won | Sydney | G. A. Shaw |
| 175 | 24.10.1976 | France | — | — | 1 | 4 | 15 | 3 | 3 | — | — | 18 | Lost | Bordeaux | G. A. Shaw |
| 176 | 30.10.1976 | France | — | — | — | 2 | 6 | 6 | 2 | 1 | 1 | 34 | Lost | Paris | G. A. Shaw |
| 177 | 11.6.1978 | Wales | 1 | 1 | — | 4 | 18 | 2 | — | — | — | 8 | Won | Brisbane | A. A. Shaw |
| 178 | 17.6.1978 | Wales | 1 | — | 2 | 3 | 19 | 2 | — | 1 | 2 | 17 | Won | Sydney | A. A. Shaw |
| 179 | 19.8.1978 | N.Z. | 1 | 1 | — | 2 | 12 | 1 | — | — | 3 | 13 | Lost | Wellington | A. A. Shaw |
| 180 | 26.8.1978 | N.Z. | — | — | 1 | 1 | 6 | 3 | 2 | 1 | 1 | 22 | Lost | Christchurch | A. A. Shaw |
| 181 | 9.9.1978 | N.Z. | 5 | 2 | 1 | 1 | 30 | 2 | 1 | — | 2 | 16 | Won | Auckland | A. A. Shaw |
| 182 | 3.6.1979 | Ireland | 1 | 1 | — | 2 | 12 | 2 | 2 | 1 | 4 | 27 | Lost | Brisbane | A. A. Shaw |
| 183 | 16.6.1979 | Ireland | — | — | — | 1 | 3 | — | — | 2 | 1 | 9 | Lost | Sydney | A. A. Shaw |
| 184 | 28.7.1979 | N.Z. | — | — | 1 | 3 | 12 | — | — | — | 1 | 6 | Won | Sydney | M. E. Loane |
| 185 | 27.10.1979 | Argentina | 1 | — | 1 | 2 | 13 | 2 | 2 | 3 | 1 | 24 | Lost | Buenos Aires | M. E. Loane |
| 186 | 3.11.1979 | Argentina | 3 | 1 | — | 1 | 17 | 1 | 1 | 1 | 1 | 12 | Won | Buenos Aires | M. E. Loane |
| 187 | 24.5.1980 | Fiji | 2 | 1 | 1 | 3 | 22 | — | — | 1 | 2 | 9 | Won | Suva | P. E. McLean |
| 188 | 21.6.1980 | N.Z. | 2 | 1 | 1 | — | 13 | — | — | — | 3 | 9 | Won | Sydney | A. A. Shaw |
| 189 | 28.6.1980 | N.Z. | 1 | 1 | — | 1 | 9 | 1 | 1 | — | 2 | 12 | Lost | Brisbane | A. A. Shaw |
| 190 | 12.7.1980 | N.Z. | 4 | 2 | 1 | 1 | 26 | 1 | — | — | 2 | 10 | Won | Sydney | A. A. Shaw |
| 191 | 5.7.1981 | France | 3 | 1 | — | 1 | 17 | 1 | 1 | 1 | 2 | 15 | Won | Brisbane | A. A. Shaw |
| 192 | 11.7.1981 | France | 2 | 2 | — | 4 | 24 | 2 | — | 2 | — | 14 | Won | Sydney | A. A. Shaw |
| 193 | 21.11.1981 | Ireland | 1 | — | 1 | 3 | 16 | — | — | — | 4 | 12 | Won | Dublin | A. A. Shaw |
| 194 | 5.12.1981 | Wales | 2 | 1 | — | 1 | 13 | 1 | 1 | 1 | 3 | 18 | Lost | Cardiff | A. A. Shaw |
| 195 | 19.12.1981 | Scotland | 3 | — | — | 1 | 15 | 1 | 1 | 1 | 5 | 24 | Lost | Murrayfield | A. A. Shaw |
| 196 | 2.1.1982 | England | 2 | — | — | 1 | 11 | 1 | 1 | — | 3 | 15 | Lost | Twickenham | M.E. Loane |
| 197 | 4.7.1982 | Scotland | 1 | — | — | 1 | 7 | 1 | 1 | 1 | 1 | 12 | Lost | Brisbane | M.E. Loane |
| 198 | 10.7.1982 | Scotland | 3 | 3 | — | 5 | 33 | — | — | — | 3 | 9 | Won | Sydney | M. E. Loane |
| 199 | 14.8.1982 | N.Z. | 2 | 1 | — | 2 | 16 | 4 | 2 | — | 1 | 23 | Lost | Christchurch | M. G. Ella |
| 200 | 28.8.1982 | N.Z. | 2 | 1 | — | 3 | 19 | 2 | 1 | — | 2 | 16 | Won | Wellington | M. G. Ella |
| 201 | 11.9.1982 | N.Z. | 1 | 1 | 1 | 3 | 18 | 2 | 2 | 2 | 5 | 33 | Lost | Auckland | M. G. Ella |
| 202 | 9.7.1983 | United States | 9 | 5 | 1 | — | 49 | — | — | — | 1 | 3 | Won | Sydney | M. G. Ella |
| 203 | 31.7.1983 | Argentina | — | — | — | 1 | 3 | 2 | 2 | 1 | 1 | 18 | Lost | Brisbane | M. G. Ella |
| 204 | 7.8.1983 | Argentina | 5 | 3 | — | 1 | 29 | 1 | — | 1 | 2 | 13 | Won | Sydney | M. G. Ella |
| 205 | 20.8.1983 | N.Z. | 2 | — | — | — | 8 | 1 | 1 | — | 4 | 18 | Lost | Sydney | M. G. Ella |
| 206 | 22.10.1983 | Italy | 5 | 3 | — | 1 | 29 | 1 | — | — | 1 | 7 | Won | Rovigo | M. G. Ella |
| 207 | 13.11.1983 | France | 1 | 1 | 2 | 1 | 15 | — | — | 2 | 3 | 15 | Drawn | Clermont-Ferrand | M. G. Ella |
| 208 | 19.11.1983 | France | — | — | 1 | 1 | 6 | 1 | 1 | — | 3 | 15 | Lost | Paris | M. G. Ella |
| 209 | 9.6.1984 | Fiji | 1 | — | 1 | 3 | 16 | — | — | — | 1 | 3 | Won | Suva | A. G. Slack |
| 210 | 21.7.1984 | N.Z. | 2 | 1 | 1 | 1 | 16 | — | — | 1 | 2 | 9 | Won | Sydney | A. G. Slack |
| 211 | 4.8.1984 | N.Z. | 1 | 1 | — | 3 | 15 | 1 | — | — | 5 | 19 | Lost | Brisbane | A. G. Slack |
| 212 | 18.8.1984 | N.Z. | 1 | 1 | — | 6 | 24 | 2 | 1 | — | 5 | 25 | Lost | Sydney | A. G. Slack |
| 213 | 3.11.1984 | England | 3 | 2 | — | 1 | 19 | 1 | — | — | 1 | 3 | Won | Twickenham | A. G. Slack |
| 214 | 10.11.1984 | Ireland | 1 | — | 3 | 1 | 16 | — | — | — | 3 | 9 | Won | Dublin | A. G. Slack |
| 215 | 24.11.1984 | Wales | 4 | 3 | — | 2 | 28 | 1 | 1 | — | 1 | 9 | Won | Cardiff | A. G. Slack |
| 216 | 8.12.1984 | Scotland | 4 | 3 | — | 5 | 37 | — | — | — | 4 | 12 | Won | Murrayfield | A. G. Slack |
| 217 | 15.6.1985 | Canada | 9 | 7 | — | 3 | 59 | — | — | 1 | — | 3 | Won | Sydney | S. A. Williams |

| Match | Date | Opponents | For T C D P Pts | Against T C D P Pts | Result | Venue | Captain |
|-------|------|-----------|-----------------|---------------------|--------|-------|---------|
| 218 | 23.6.1985 | Canada | 7 3 1 2 43 | 1 1 — 3 15 | Won | Brisbane | S. A. Williams |
| 219 | 29.6.1985 | N.Z. | 1 1 — 1 9 | 1 — — 2 10 | Lost | Auckland | S. A. Williams |
| 220 | 10.8.1985 | Fiji | 7 3 3 3 52 | 4 3 — 2 28 | Won | Brisbane | S. A. Williams |
| 221 | 17.8.1985 | Fiji | 5 1 — 3 31 | — — 1 2 9 | Won | Sydney | S. A. Williams |
| 222 | 1.6.1986 | Italy | 6 6 — 1 39 | 2 2 — 2 18 | Won | Brisbane | A. G. Slack |
| 223 | 21.6.1986 | France | 1 1 1 6 27 | 3 1 — — 14 | Won | Sydney | A. G. Slack |
| 224 | 6.7.1986 | Argentina | 4 4 — 5 39 | 3 2 — 1 19 | Won | Brisbane | S. P. Poidevin |
| 225 | 12.7.1986 | Argentina | 3 1 — 4 26 | — — — — 0 | Won | Sydney | S. P. Poidevin |
| 226 | 9.8.1986 | N.Z. | 2 1 — 1 13 | 1 1 — 2 12 | Won | Wellington | A. G. Slack |
| 227 | 23.8.1986 | N.Z. | — — 1 3 12 | 1 — 1 2 13 | Lost | Dunedin | A. G. Slack |
| 228 | 6.9.1986 | N.Z. | 2 1 — 4 22 | — — — 3 9 | Won | Auckland | A. G. Slack |

# MATCH RECORDS

## MOST CONSECUTIVE MATCHES WON

| | |
|---|---|
| 7 | *1985* Fj 1,2  *1986* It, F, Arg 1,2, NZ 1 |
| 6 | *1927-28* F  *1929* NZ 1,2,3  *1930* GB  *1931* M |
| 6 | *1984* E,I,W,S  *1985* C 1,2 |
| 5 | *1975-76* I,US  *1976* Fj 1,2,3 |

## MOST CONSECUTIVE MATCHES WITHOUT DEFEAT

| Matches | Wins | Draws | Period |
|---------|------|-------|--------|
| 7 | 7 | 0 | 1985 to 1986 |
| 6 | 6 | 0 | 1927-28 to 1931 |
| 6 | 6 | 0 | 1984 to 1985 |
| 5 | 5 | 0 | 1975-76 to 1976 |

## MOST CONSECUTIVE MATCHES WITHOUT CONCEDING A TRY

|   |   |
|---|---|
| 4 | in 1947-48 |

## MOST CONSECUTIVE MATCHES WITHOUT CONCEDING A SCORE

*(Australia has only won three matches without conceding a score: v NZ at Sydney 1910; v E at Twickenham 1948; v Arg at Sydney 1986).*

## MOST POINTS IN A MATCH
### By the team

| Pts | Opponents | Venue | Seasons |
|-----|-----------|-------|---------|
| 59 | Canada | Sydney | 1985 |
| 52 | Fiji | Brisbane | 1985 |
| 50 | Japan | Brisbane | 1975 |
| 49 | United States | Sydney | 1983 |
| 43 | Canada | Brisbane | 1985 |
| 39 | Italy | Brisbane | 1986 |
| 39 | Argentina | Brisbane | 1986 |
| 37 | Japan | Sydney | 1975 |
| 37 | Scotland | Edinburgh | 1984-85 |
| 33 | Scotland | Sydney | 1982 |
| 31 | NZ Maoris | Palmerston North | 1936 |
| 31 | Fiji | Sydney | 1985 |
| 30 | Tonga | Sydney | 1973 |
| 30 | England | Brisbane | 1975 |
| 30 | New Zealand | Auckland | 1978 |

## By a player

| Pts | Player | Opponents | Venue | Season |
|---|---|---|---|---|
| 23 | M.P. Lynagh | Canada | Sydney | 1985 |
| 23 | M.P. Lynagh | France | Sydney | 1986 |
| 23 | M.P. Lynagh | Argentina | Brisbane | 1986 |
| 21 | P.E. McLean | Japan | Sydney | 1975 |
| 21 | P.E. McLean | Scotland | Sydney | 1982 |
| 21 | M.P. Lynagh | Scotland | Edinburgh | 1984-85 |
| 21 | D. Knox | Fiji | Brisbane | 1985 |
| 18 | P.E. McLean | Japan | Brisbane | 1975 |
| 18 | D.I. Campese | United States | Sydney | 1983 |
| 17 | M.G. Ella | New Zealand | Sydney | 1984 |
| 16 | G. Cornelsen | New Zealand | Auckland | 1978 |
| 16 | P.E. McLean | France | Sydney | 1981 |
| 15 | A.N. McGill | New Zealand | Brisbane | 1968 |
| 15 | R.L. Fairfax | France | Brisbane | 1972 |
| 15 | P.E. McLean | Fiji | Sydney | 1976 |
| 15 | P.E. McLean | France | Bordeaux | 1976-77 |
| 15 | R.G. Gould | New Zealand | Auckland | 1982 |
| 15 | M.P. Lynagh | Canada | Brisbane | 1985 |
| 15 | M.P. Lynagh | Italy | Brisbane | 1986 |

# MOST TRIES IN A MATCH
## By the team

| T | Opponents | Venue | Season |
|---|---|---|---|
| 9 | United States | Sydney | 1983 |
| 9 | Canada | Sydney | 1985 |
| 8 | Japan | Brisbane | 1975 |
| 7 | Canada | Brisbane | 1985 |
| 7 | Fiji | Brisbane | 1985 |
| 6 | NZ Maoris | Palmerston North | 1936 |
| 6 | Fiji | Brisbane | 1961 |
| 6 | Scotland | Sydney | 1970 |
| 6 | Japan | Sydney | 1975 |
| 6 | Italy | Brisbane | 1986 |

## By a player

| T | Player | Opponents | Venue | Season |
|---|---|---|---|---|
| 4 | D.I. Campese | United States | Sydney | 1983 |
| 4 | G. Cornelsen | New Zealand | Auckland | 1978 |
| 3 | M.P. Burke | Canada | Brisbane | 1985 |
| 3 | J.R. Ryan | Japan | Brisbane | 1975 |
| 3 | A.D. McLean | NZ Maoris | Palmerston North | 1936 |

# MOST CONVERSIONS IN A MATCH
## By the team

| C | Opponents | Venue | Season |
|---|---|---|---|
| 7 | Canada | Sydney | 1985 |
| 6 | Japan | Brisbane | 1975 |
| 6 | Italy | Brisbane | 1986 |
| 5 | NZ Maoris | Palmerston North | 1936 |
| 5 | Japan | Sydney | 1975 |
| 5 | United States | Sydney | 1983 |
| 4 | Argentina | Brisbane | 1986 |

## By a player

| C | Player | Opponents | Venue | Season |
|---|---|---|---|---|
| 7 | M.P. Lynagh | Canada | Sydney | 1985 |
| 6 | P.E. McLean | Japan | Brisbane | 1975 |
| 6 | M.P. Lynagh | Italy | Brisbane | 1986 |
| 5 | P.E. McLean | Japan | Sydney | 1975 |
| 4 | R.G. Gould | United States | Sydney | 1983 |
| 4 | M.P. Lynagh | Argentina | Brisbane | 1986 |

# MOST DROPPED GOALS IN A MATCH

## By the team

| DG | Opponents | Venue | Season |
|---|---|---|---|
| 3 | England | Twickenham | 1966-67 |
| 3 | Ireland | Dublin | 1984-85 |
| 3 | Fiji | Brisbane | 1985 |
| 2 | Tonga | Sydney | 1973 |
| 2 | England | Sydney | 1975 |
| 2 | Wales | Sydney | 1978 |
| 2 | France | Clermont Ferrand | 1983-84 |

## By a player

| DG | Player | Opponents | Venue | Season |
|---|---|---|---|---|
| 3 | P.F. Hawthorne | England | Twickenham | 1966-67 |
| 2 | M.G. Ella | Ireland | Dublin | 1984-85 |
| 2 | D. Knox | Fiji | Brisbane | 1985 |

# MOST PENALTY GOALS IN A MATCH

## By the team

| PG | Opponents | Venue | Season |
|---|---|---|---|
| 6 | New Zealand | Sydney | 1984 |
| 6 | France | Sydney | 1986 |
| 5 | New Zealand | Brisbane | 1968 |
| 5 | France | Brisbane | 1972 |
| 5 | Fiji | Sydney | 1976 |
| 5 | Scotland | Sydney | 1982 |
| 5 | Scotland | Edinburgh | 1984-85 |
| 5 | Argentina | Brisbane | 1986 |

## By a player

| PG | Player | Opponents | Venue | Season |
|---|---|---|---|---|
| 6 | M.P. Lynagh | France | Sydney | 1986 |
| 5 | A.N. McGill | New Zealand | Brisbane | 1968 |
| 5 | R.L. Fairfax | France | Brisbane | 1972 |
| 5 | P.E. McLean | Fiji | Sydney | 1976 |
| 5 | P.E. McLean | Scotland | Sydney | 1982 |
| 5 | M.G. Ella | New Zealand | Sydney | 1984 |
| 5 | M.P. Lynagh | Scotland | Edinburgh | 1984-85 |
| 5 | M.P. Lynagh | Argentina | Brisbane | 1986 |

# GOALS FROM MARKS

| * | Player | Opponents | Venue | Season |
|---|---|---|---|---|
| 1 | P.P. Carmichael | New Zealand | Sydney | 1907 |

# TRY ON DEBUT

| Player | Opponents | Venue | Season |
|---|---|---|---|
| S.A. Spragg | Great Britain | Sydney | 1899 |
| W.T. Evans | Great Britain | Sydney | 1899 |
| A.J. Kelly | Great Britain | Sydney | 1899 |
| H.H. Messenger | New Zealand | Brisbane | 1907 |
| T.J. Richards | Wales | Cardiff | 1908-09 |
| L.S. Meibusch | United States | Berkeley | 1912 |
| E.T.A. Carr | New Zealand | Wellington | 1913 |
| A.C. Wallace | Ireland | Dublin | 1927-28 |
| S.C. King | Wales | Cardiff | 1927-28 |
| W.B.J. Sheehan | Wales | Cardiff | 1927-28 |
| G.C. Gordon | New Zealand | Sydney | 1929 |
| O.C. Crossman | New Zealand | Brisbane | 1929 |
| G.H. McGhie | New Zealand | Brisbane | 1929 |
| J.C. Steggall | NZ Maoris | Palmerston North | 1931 |
| D.L. Cowper | New Zealand | Auckland | 1931 |
| R.E.M. McLaughlin | New Zealand | Wellington | 1936 |
| K.M. Ramsay | NZ Maoris | Palmerston North | 1936 |
| F.W.H. O'Brien | South Africa | Sydney | 1937 |

| Player | Opponents | Venue | Season |
|---|---|---|---|
| C.C. Eastes | New Zealand | Dunedin | 1946 |
| T. Allan | New Zealand | Dunedin | 1946 |
| R.G.W. Cornforth | New Zealand | Brisbane | 1947 |
| A.E.J. Tonkin | Scotland | Edinburgh | 1947-48 |
| J.R. Fogarty | NZ Maoris | Brisbane | 1949 |
| R.L. Garner | New Zealand | Wellington | 1949 |
| G.G.Jones | Fiji | Sydney | 1952 |
| B.B. Johnson | Fiji | Sydney | 1952 |
| B.J. Ellwood | New Zealand | Wellington | 1958 |
| M.A. Cleary | Fiji | Brisbane | 1961 |
| R.J. Lisle | Fiji | Brisbane | 1961 |
| E. Magrath | Fiji | Brisbane | 1961 |
| K.W. Catchpole | Fiji | Brisbane | 1961 |
| R.N. Thornett | Fiji | Brisbane | 1961 |
| P.A. Jones | England | Sydney | 1963 |
| G.V. Davis | England | Sydney | 1963 |
| R.P. Batterham | New Zealand | Wellington | 1967 |
| R.A. McLean | South Africa | Sydney | 1971 |
| R.D. L'Estrange | France | Toulouse | 1971-72 |
| O.G. Stephens | Tonga | Sydney | 1973 |
| E.N. Tindall | Tonga | Brisbane | 1973 |
| R.A. Price | New Zealand | Sydney | 1974 |
| I.J. Robertson | Japan | Sydney | 1975 |
| J.R. Ryan | Japan | Brisbane | 1975 |
| M.C. Martin | Fiji | Suva | 1980 |
| P.C. Grigg | New Zealand | Sydney | 1980 |
| M.H. Cox | Wales | Cardiff | 1981-82 |
| D.I. Campese | New Zealand | Christchurch | 1982 |
| R.G. Hanley | United States | Sydney | 1983 |
| T.A. Lane | Canada | Sydney | 1985 |
| N. Kassulke | Canada | Sydney | 1985 |
| W.J. Calcraft | Canada | Sydney | 1985 |
| B. Papworth | Fiji | Brisbane | 1985 |
| A. Leeds | New Zealand | Auckland | 1986 |

## CAPTAIN ON INTERNATIONAL DEBUT

| Player | Opponent | Venue | Season |
|---|---|---|---|
| F.L. Row | Great Britain | Sydney | 1899 |
| S.M. Wickham | New Zealand | Sydney | 1903 |
| P.H. Burge | New Zealand | Sydney | 1907 |
| H.M. Moran | Wales | Cardiff | 1908-09 |
| A.C. Wallace | Ireland | Dublin | 1927-28 |
| J.G. Clark | NZ Maoris | Palmerston North | 1931 |
| W.M. McLean | New Zealand | Dunedin | 1946 |
| K.C. Winning | New Zealand | Sydney | 1951 |
| K.W. Catchpole | Fiji | Brisbane | 1961 |

## TRIES BY FULL-BACKS

| Player | Opponents | Venue | Season |
|---|---|---|---|
| R. Phelps | Fiji | Brisbane | 1961 |
| J.K. Lenehan | New Zealand | Auckland | 1962 |
| J.K. Lenehan | South Africa | Sydney | 1965 |
| J.K. Lenehan | Wales | Cardiff | 1966-67 |
| A.N. McGill | Wales | Sydney | 1969 |
| L.E. Monaghan | New Zealand | Brisbane | 1974 |
| P.E. McLean (2) | Japan | Sydney | 1975 |
| R.G. Gould (2) | Scotland | Sydney | 1982 |
| R.G. Gould | New Zealand | Auckland | 1982 |
| R.G. Hanley* | United States | Sydney | 1983 |
| D.I. Campese | Argentina | Sydney | 1983 |
| D.I. Campese | Fiji | Suva | 1984 |
| D.I. Campese | France | Sydney | 1986 |
| D.I. Campese | Argentina | Brisbane | 1986 |
| D.I. Campese (2) | Argentina | Sydney | 1986 |

(* Hanley had come on as a replacement)

## ALL THE POINTS FOR AUSTRALIA
## IN A MATCH
### (where more than one scoring action is involved)

| Pts | Player | Opponents | Venue | Season |
|-----|--------|-----------|-------|--------|
| 15 | R.L. Fairfax | France | Brisbane | 1972 |
| 15 | P.E. McLean | France | Bordeaux | 1976-77 |
| 12 | M.P. Lynagh | New Zealand | Dunedin | 1986 |
| 10 | S.M. Wickham | Great Britain | Sydney | 1899 |
| 9 | M.G. Carpenter | New Zealand | Sydney | 1938 |
| 9 | G.A. Chapman | New Zealand | Wellington | 1962 |
| 9 | R.P. Batterham | New Zealand | Wellington | 1967 |
| 9 | J.P. Ballesty | South Africa | Durban | 1969 |
| 7 | M.J. Hawker | Scotland | Brisbane | 1982 |
| 6 | P.P. Carmichael | New Zealand | Sydney | 1907 |
| 6 | A.E.J. Tonkin | France | Paris | 1947-48 |
| 6 | W.C. Gardner | British Isles | Brisbane | 1950 |
| 6 | K.J. Donald | NZ Maoris | Melbourne | 1958 |
| 6 | K.J. Donald | British Isles | Brisbane | 1959 |
| 6 | P.R.I. Scott | New Zealand | Brisbane | 1962 |
| 6 | A.N. McGill | South Africa | Brisbane | 1971 |
| 6 | J.J. McLean | New Zealand | Wellington | 1972 |
| 6 | P.E. McLean | New Zealand | Sydney | 1974 |
| 6 | P.E. McLean | England | Twickenham | 1975-76 |
| 6 | P.E. McLean | France | Paris | 1976-77 |
| 6 | K.J. Wright | New Zealand | Christchurch | 1978 |
| 5 | H.H. Messenger | New Zealand | Brisbane | 1907 |
| 5 | C.H.T. Towers | South Africa | Sydney | 1937 |

# INDIVIDUAL RECORDS

## LONGEST CAREER SPANS

| Seasons | Player | Caps | Career Span |
|---------|--------|------|-------------|
| 16½ | G.M. Cooke | 13 | 1932 to 1947-48 |
| 16 | A.R. Miller | 41 | 1952 to 1967 |
| 14½ | J.N.B. Hipwell | 36 | 1968 to 1981-82 |
| 13½ | P.G. Johnson | 42 | 1959 to 1971-72 |
| 12½ | J.E. Thornett | 37 | 1955 to 1966-67 |
| 11½ | N.M. Shehadie | 30 | 1947 to 1957-58 |
| 11 | C.T. Burke | 26 | 1946 to 1956 |

## MOST CONSECUTIVE CAPS IN A CAREER

| Caps | Player | Opponents |
|------|--------|-----------|
| 37 | P.G. Johnson | 1959 BI 1,2  1961 Fj 1,2,3, SA 1,2, F  1962 NZ 1,2,3,4,5  1963 E, SA 1,2,3,4  1964 NZ 1,2,3  1965 SA 1,2  1966 BI 1,2  1966-67 W,S,E,I,F  1967 I, NZ  1968 NZ 1,2, F  1968-69 I,S |

## MOST CAPS IN A CAREER

| Caps | Player | Career Span |
|------|--------|-------------|
| 42 | P. G. Johnson | 1959 to 1971-72 |
| 41 | A. R. Miller | 1952 to 1967 |
| 40 | S. P. Poidevin | 1980 to 1986 |
| 39 | G. V. Davis | 1963 to 1972 |
| 37 | J. E. Thornett | 1955 to 1966-67 |
| 36 | J. N. B. Hipwell | 1968 to 1981-82 |
| 36 | A. A. Shaw | 1973-74 to 1982 |
| 35 | B. J. Moon | 1978 to 1986 |
| 32 | A. G. Slack | 1978 to 1986 |
| 30 | N. M. Shehadie | 1947 to 1957-58 |
| 30 | P. E. McLean | 1974 to 1982 |

# MOST POINTS IN A CAREER

| Pts | Player | Matches | Career Span |
|---|---|---|---|
| 260 | P.E. McLean | 30 | 1974 to 1982 |
| 200 | M.P. Lynagh | 15 | 1984 to 1986 |
| 124 | D.I. Campese | 27 | 1982 to 1986 |
| 82 | R.G. Gould | 23 | 1980 to 1986 |
| 78 | M.G. Ella | 25 | 1980 to 1984-85 |
| 72 | A.N. McGill | 21 | 1968 to 1973 |
| 56 | B.J. Moon | 35 | 1978 to 1986 |

# MOST TRIES IN A CAREER

| T | Player | Matches | Career Span |
|---|---|---|---|
| 21 | D.I. Campese | 27 | 1982 to 1986 |
| 14 | B.J. Moon | 35 | 1978 to 1986 |
| 11 | C.J. Windon | 20 | 1946 to 1952 |
| 9 | J.R. Ryan | 6 | 1975 to 1976 |

# MOST CONVERSIONS IN A CAREER

| C | Player | Matches | Career Span |
|---|---|---|---|
| 30 | M.P. Lynagh | 15 | 1984 to 1986 |
| 27 | P.E. McLean | 30 | 1974 to 1982 |
| 14 | R.G. Gould | 23 | 1980 to 1986 |
| 10 | T. Lawton | 11 | 1927-28 to 1932 |
| 9 | B.J.C. Piper | 12 | 1946 to 1949 |
| 9 | A.N. McGill | 21 | 1968 to 1973 |

# MOST DROPPED GOALS IN A CAREER

| DG | Player | Matches | Career Span |
|---|---|---|---|
| 9 | P.F. Hawthorne | 21 | 1962 to 1967 |
| 8 | M.G. Ella | 25 | 1980 to 1984-85 |
| 4 | P.E. McLean | 30 | 1974 to 1982 |
| 4 | M. P. Lynagh | 15 | 1984 to 1986 |

# MOST PENALTY GOALS IN A CAREER

| PG | Player | Matches | Career Span |
|---|---|---|---|
| 62 | P.E. McLean | 30 | 1974 to 1982 |
| 40 | M.P. Lynagh | 15 | 1984 to 1986 |
| 16 | A.N. McGill | 21 | 1968 to 1973 |
| 12 | R.G. Gould | 23 | 1980 to 1986 |

# MOST MATCHES AS CAPTAIN

| | | |
|---|---|---|
| 16 | J.E. Thornett | ( 6 victories) |
| 16 | G. V. Davis | ( 2 victories) |
| 15 | A. A. Shaw | ( 8 victories) |
| 13 | K. W. Catchpole | ( 4 victories) |
| 13 | A. G. Slack | (10 victories) |
| 10 | T. Allan | ( 6 victories) |
| 10 | M. G. Ella | ( 4 victories) |

# BRITISH/IRISH COMBINED
# INTERNATIONAL
# TEAMS AND RECORDS

## 1891

| 1st v. S.AFRICA | 2nd v. S.AFRICA | 3rd v. S.AFRICA |
|---|---|---|
| †W.G. Mitchell | W.G. Mitchell 1GM | W.G. Mitchell |
| | | |
| †P.R. Clauss | P.R. Clauss | P.R. Clauss |
| †R.L. Aston 1T | R.L. Aston | R.L. Aston 1T |
| *†W.E. Maclagan | *W.E. Maclagan | *W.E. Maclagan 1T |
| | | |
| †A. Rotherham 1C | †H. Marshall | H. Marshall |
| †W. Wotherspoon | †E. Bromet | A. Rotherham 1C |
| | | |
| †W.E. Bromet | W.E. Bromet | W.E. Bromet |
| †J.H. Gould | J.H. Gould | E. Bromet |
| †J. Hammond | J. Hammond | J. Hammond |
| †P.F. Hancock | P.F. Hancock | P.F. Hancock |
| †R.G. Macmillan | R.G. Macmillan | R.G. Macmillan |
| †C. Simpson | †W.E. Mayfield | W.E. Mayfield |
| †A.A. Surtees | A.A. Surtees | A.A. Surtees |
| †R. Thompson | R. Thompson | R. Thompson |
| †T.S. Whittaker 1T | T.S. Whittaker | T.S. Whittaker |
| Port Elizabeth | Kimberley | Cape Town |
| WON 4-0 | WON 3-0 | WON 4-0 |
| SA: NIL | SA: NIL | SA: NIL |
| GB: 1G 1T | GB: 1GM | GB: 1G 1T |
| 30 Jul. 1891 | 29 Aug. 1891 | 5 Sep. 1891 |

A British side had visited Australasia in 1888, but the RFU refused to patronise that tour (arranged by two English professional cricketers named Shaw and Shrewsbury), and no Test matches were played. However, the tour of 1891, underwritten by Cecil Rhodes, was given the blessing of the RFU, and three international matches were played and won by a side captained by Bill Maclagan, the former Scottish international.

The side enjoyed a successful tour, winning all of its twenty matches and conceding just one point – a try in the opening match against Cape clubs. All of the British players were from English or Scottish clubs, half were (or became) international players for their countries, and many of the uncapped members of the squad were former Cambridge Blues.

The team travelled the vast distances between match centres by horse-drawn carriages, as trains lacked dining facilities at this time. But the wearisome journeys could not have tired the British players too greatly: one, R.L. Aston, who played in every match, scored the remarkable total of thirty tries. At 15 stones he was regarded with awe by his smaller opponents, and used his speed and size to score tries in two of the three Tests.

## 1896

| 1st v. S.AFRICA | 2nd v. S.AFRICA | 3rd v. S.AFRICA | 4th v. S.AFRICA |
|---|---|---|---|
| †C.A. Boyd | †J.T. Magee | †A.W.D. Meares | A.W.D. Meares |
| | | | |
| †L.Q. Bulger 1T | L.Q. Bulger | L.Q. Bulger | J.T. Magee |
| †J.F. Byrne 1C | J.F. Byrne 2C | J.F. Byrne 1DG,1C | J.F. Byrne |
| †O.G. Mackie | O.G. Mackie 1DG | O.G. Mackie 1T | O.G. Mackie |
| †R. Johnston | R. Johnston | R. Johnston | L.Q. Bulger |
| | | | |
| †M. Mullineux | †S.P. Bell | S.P. Bell | S.P. Bell |
| †A.M. Magee | A.M. Magee | A.M. Magee | A.M. Magee |
| | | | |
| †R.C. Mullins | *J. Hammond | R.C. Mullins | *J. Hammond |
| †A.F. Todd | A.F. Todd 1T | A.F. Todd | A.F. Todd |
| †W. Mortimer | W. Mortimer | W. Mortimer | W. Mortimer |
| P.F. Hancock | P.F. Hancock 1T | P.F. Hancock | P.F. Hancock |
| †W.J. Carey 1T | W.J. Carey | W.J. Carey | W.J. Carey |
| †J. Sealy | J. Sealy | J. Sealy | J. Sealy |
| †A.D. Clinch | A.D. Clinch | A.D. Clinch | A.D. Clinch |
| *†T.J. Crean | T.J. Crean 1T | *T.J. Crean | T.J. Crean |
| Port Elizabeth | Johannesburg | Kimberley | Cape Town |
| WON 8-0 | WON 17-8 | WON 9-3 | LOST 0-5 |
| SA: NIL | SA: 1G 1T | SA: 1T | SA: 1G |
| GB: 1G 1T | GB: 2G 1DG 1T | GB: 1G 1DG | GB: NIL |
| 30 Jul. 1896 | 22 Aug. 1896 | 29 Aug. 1896 | 5 Sep. 1896 |

University students formed the backbone of the second British side to visit South Africa. Ireland was well-represented on this tour, though neither Scotland nor Wales contributed players. Of the 21 matches played, 19 were won, one was drawn and the final Test of the four-match series with the South Africans was lost. Johnny Hammond, who never played for England, was the captain of the side. He and P.F. Hancock were the only survivors of the 1891 tour party.

Tom Crean acted as deputy to Hammond, leading the British side in two of the Tests and some of the provincial matches. Crean was a dynamic personality on and off the field, and always in the thick of the action. Later he won a VC (as did Robert Johnston, another Irishman in the party) during the Boer War.

Walter Carey and R.C. Mullins were Oxford Blues (nominated by their university for the tour) who played in the Test series. Mullins was a South African by birth who later practised medicine in Grahamstown. Carey became the Bishop of Bloemfontein between the world wars. He coined the famous motto of the Barbarians: "Rugby is a game for gentlemen in all classes, but for no bad sportsman in any class."

## 1899

| 1st v. AUSTRALIA | 2nd v. AUSTRALIA | 3rd v. AUSTRALIA | 4th v. AUSTRALIA |
|---|---|---|---|
| †E. MARTELLI | †C.E.K. THOMPSON | C.E.K. THOMPSON | C.E.K. THOMPSON |
| | | | |
| †A.M. BUCHER | H.G.S. GRAY | A.M. BUCHER 2T | A.M. BUCHER 1T |
| †E.G. NICHOLLS 1T | †A.B. TIMMS | A.B. TIMMS | A.B. TIMMS |
| †C.Y. ADAMSON | E.G. NICHOLLS 1T | E.G. NICHOLLS | E.G. NICHOLLS |
| †G.P. DORAN | G.P. DORAN | †E.T. NICHOLSON | E.T. NICHOLSON |
| | | | |
| *M. MULLINEUX | C.Y. ADAMSON 1T,1C | C.Y. ADAMSON 1C | C.Y. ADAMSON 1T,1PG,2C |
| †G. COOKSON | G. COOKSON | G. COOKSON | G. COOKSON |
| | | | |
| †F.M. STOUT | *F.M. STOUT | *F.M. STOUT | *F.M. STOUT |
| †J.W. JARMAN | J.W. JARMAN | J.W. JARMAN | J.W. JARMAN |
| †T.M.W. McGOWN | T.M.W. McGOWN | T.M.W. McGOWN | T.M.W. McGOWN |
| †J.S. FRANCOMBE | †G.V. EVERS | G.V. EVERS | G.V. EVERS |
| †H.G.S. GRAY | †B.I. SWANNELL | B.I. SWANNELL | B.I. SWANNELL |
| †F.C. BELSON | †W. JUDKINS | W. JUDKINS | W. JUDKINS |
| †A. AYRE-SMITH | A. AYRE-SMITH 1T | A. AYRE-SMITH | A. AYRE-SMITH |
| †G.R. GIBSON | G.R. GIBSON | G.R. GIBSON | G.R. GIBSON |
| | | | |
| Sydney | Brisbane | Sydney | Sydney |
| LOST 3-13 | WON 11-0 | WON 11-10 | WON 13-0 |
| | | | |
| AUST.: 2G 1T | AUST.: NIL | AUST.: 2G | AUST.: NIL |
| GB: 1T | GB: 1G 2T | GB: 1G 2T | GB: 2G 1PG |
| | | | |
| 24 Jun. 1899 | 22 Jul. 1899 | 5 Aug. 1899 | 12 Aug. 1899 |

In 1899, for the only occasion to date, a British rugby tour to Australia took place. The Revd Mullineaux, an Oxford graduate and member of the 1896 tour party, skippered the side which, for the first time, included players from each of the four Home countries. The side lost three of its 21 matches but succeeded in winning the Test series 3-1. With a fine disregard for the other nations, the Australian newspapers (as well as some of the British dailies) referred to the tourists as "the English football team".

Gwyn Nicholls, who became the outstanding centre in British rugby during the early years of the twentieth century, was the first Welshman to play in a Test for a British side, and scored a try in the opening Test. Adamason, the side's utility back and a former Durham County player, was the leading goal-kicker in the party and his ten points in the fourth Test were a record for a British touring side in a Test match.

The British side, a combination full of emerging representative players, was far from a full-strength British side. However, the players, by their steadfast commitment to the passing game, gave rugby in Australia a tremendous boost.

## 1903

| 1st v. S.AFRICA | 2nd v. S.AFRICA | 3rd v. S.AFRICA |
|---|---|---|
| †E.M. HARRISON | †R.M. NEILL | R.M. NEILL |
| | | |
| †I.G. DAVIDSON | †E.F. WALKER | E.F. WALKER |
| †R.T. SKRIMSHIRE 1T | R.T. SKRIMSHIRE | R.T. SKRIMSHIRE |
| †L.L. GREIG | L.L. GREIG | L.L. GREIG |
| †G.F. COLLETT | G.F. COLLETT | G.F. COLLETT |
| | | |
| †J.I. GILLESPIE 2C | J.I. GILLESPIE | J.I. GILLESPIE |
| †P.S. HANCOCK | P.S. HANCOCK | P.S. HANCOCK |
| | | |
| F.M. STOUT | F.M. STOUT | F.M. STOUT |
| †JOS. WALLACE | JOS. WALLACE | JOS. WALLACE |
| †T.A. GIBSON | T.A. GIBSON | T.A. GIBSON |
| †R.S. SMYTH | R.S. SMYTH | R.S. SMYTH |
| †A. TEDFORD | A. TEDFORD | A. TEDFORD |
| *†M.C. MORRISON | *M.C. MORRISON | *M.C. MORRISON |
| †W.P. SCOTT | W.P. SCOTT | W.P. SCOTT |
| †W.T.C. CAVE 1T | W.T.C. CAVE | W.T.C. CAVE |
| | | |
| Johannesburg | Kimberley | Cape Town |
| DRAWN 10-10 | DRAWN 0-0 | LOST 0-8 |
| | | |
| SA: 2G | SA: NIL | SA: 1G 1T |
| GB: 2G | GB: NIL | GB: NIL |
| | | |
| 26 Aug. 1903 | 5 Sep. 1903 | 12 Sep. 1903 |

The third British side to South Africa, led by the experienced Scottish skipper Mark Morrison, lacked a first-rate full-back and found difficulty adjusting to the hard grounds and the handicap of playing at high altitude – problems which were to be faced by most subsequent British tourists. Nevertheless, the main achievement of Morrison's side was in holding a much-improved South African side to draws in the opening Tests of the series.

Greig, Gillespie and Neill, three Scottish half-backs, were among the outstanding tour players. But weaknesses in the threequarter line, as well as at full-back, led to Greig and Neill appearing out of their natural positions in the Tests. Reg Skrimshire, the only Welshman among the party, was the only other threequarter to enhance his reputation on the tour.

Skrimshire was highly regarded by the South Africans. He played in all but one of the tour matches and finished the trip as Britain's leading scorer. Later he played provincial rugby for the Western Province of South Africa before returning to England to practise as a Civil Engineer. One of the last survivors of this tour Skrimshire died at Worthing in 1963, aged 85.

## 1904

| 1st v. AUSTRALIA | 2nd v. AUSTRALIA | 3rd v. AUSTRALIA | v. NZ |
|---|---|---|---|
| †C.F. Stanger-Leathes | A.B. O'Brien 1t | A.B. O'Brien 1c | A.B. O'Brien |
| | | | |
| †W.M. Llewellyn 2t | W.M. Llewellyn 1t | W.M. Llewellyn 1t | P.F. McEvedy |
| †A.B. O'Brien 1c | R.T. Gabe | R.T. Gabe 1t | W.M. Llewellyn |
| †R.T. Gabe | †P.F. McEvedy | P.F. McEvedy | R.T. Gabe |
| †E. Morgan | *E. Morgan | *E. Morgan 1t | *E. Morgan |
| | | | |
| †P.F. Bush 1t,1dg | P.F. Bush 1dg,1gm,1t | P.F. Bush 1c | P.F. Bush |
| †F.C. Hulme | †T.H. Vile | T.H. Vile | T.H. Vile |
| | | | |
| *†D.R. Bedell-Sivright | †R.W. Edwards | R.W. Edwards | R.J. Rogers |
| †D.H. Traill | D.H. Traill | D.H. Traill | D.H. Traill |
| †D.D. Dobson | D.D. Dobson | D.D. Dobson | D.D. Dobson |
| †T.S. Bevan | T.S. Bevan | T.S. Bevan | T.S. Bevan |
| †S.McK. Saunders | S.McK. Saunders | †B.F. Massey | R.W. Edwards |
| †S.N. Crowther | S.N. Crowther | S.N. Crowther | S.N. Crowther |
| B.I. Swannell | B.I. Swannell | B.I. Swannell 1t | B.I. Swannell |
| †A.F. Harding 1c | A.F. Harding | A.F. Harding | A.F. Harding 1pg |
| | | | |
| Sydney | Brisbane | Sydney | Wellington |
| WON 17-0 | WON 17-3 | WON 16-0 | LOST 3-9 |
| | | | |
| AUST.: NIL | AUST.: 1T | AUST.: NIL | NZ: 1PG 2T |
| GB: 2G 1DG 1T | GB: 1GM 1DG 3T | GB: 2G 2T | GB: 1PG |
| | | | |
| 2 Jul. 1904 | 23 Jul. 1904 | 30 Jul. 1904 | 13 Aug. 1904 |

"Darkie" Bedell-Sivright, a seasoned Scottish international, led the British side which toured Australia and New Zealand in 1904. More than one half of his side were or became international players, and for the first time a substantial Welsh contingent took part in the tour.

The British side, with an outstanding back division, swept to victory in the three Tests of the series in Australia. However, they found the forward strength of New Zealand rugby too powerful in the Test at Wellington, a story repeated many times during the subsequent eighty years.

Tommy Vile's remarkable international career was to span 21 years. He formed a sound understanding with Percy Bush and the pair, together with the other Welsh backs Llewellyn, Gabe and Morgan (who captained the side in three of the Tests) were highly respected by the New Zealand and Australian followers. Vile went on to play for Wales, gained his last cap in 1921, and became a leading international referee during the decade which followed his playing retirement.

## 1908

| 1st v. NZ | 2nd v. NZ | 3rd v. NZ |
|---|---|---|
| †E.J. Jackett | E.J. Jackett | E.J. Jackett |
| | | |
| †J.L. Williams | J.L. Williams | †F.E. Chapman |
| †J.P. Jones | J.P. Jones 1t | J.P. Jones |
| †H.H. Vassall | H.H. Vassall | H.H. Vassall |
| †R.A. Gibbs 1t | P.F. McEvedy | P.F. McEvedy |
| | | |
| †J. Davey | †J.P. (Tuan) Jones | J.P. (Tuan) Jones |
| †H. Laxon | †W.L. Morgan | W.L. Morgan |
| | R.A. Gibbs | |
| †W.L. Oldham | | E. Morgan |
| †R. Dibble | †T.W. Smith | R. Dibble |
| †F.S. Jackson 1c | R. Dibble | †J.F. Williams |
| †P.J. Down | P.J. Down | P.J. Down |
| †H.A. Archer | H.A. Archer | T.W. Smith |
| †J.A.S. Ritson | †E. Morgan | H.A. Archer |
| †G.V. Kyrke | †G.R. Hind | G.R. Hind |
| *A.F. Harding | *A.F. Harding | *A.F. Harding |
| | | |
| Dunedin | Wellington | Auckand |
| LOST 5-32 | DRAWN 3-3 | LOST 0-29 |
| | | |
| NZ: 4G 1PG 3T | NZ: 1PG | NZ: 1G 8T |
| A-Welsh: 1G | A-Welsh: 1T | A-Welsh: NIL |
| | | |
| 6 Jun. 1908 | 27 Jun. 1908 | 25 Jul. 1908 |

With the Irish and Scottish declining to support the tour to Australia and New Zealand in 1908, the side became known as the "Anglo-Welsh" and was captained by A.F. "Boxer" Harding, an experienced Welsh forward who had toured with the 1904 British side. Later Harding emigrated to New Zealand, as did F.S. Jackson of Leicester, a forward who played in the Dunedin Test. In addition Tuan Jones, a medical student from Pontypool, was to settle in Melbourne, Australia, where he practised medicine for many years.

The Anglo-Welsh were overwhelmed in the Tests at Dunedin and Auckland, but escaped with a draw in the second Test, when New Zealand fielded virtually their second fifteen. It will be noted that, for the drawn Test, the visitors copied the unusual New Zealand scrummage custom of using only seven forwards. The Cardiff wing, Reggie Gibbs, appeared as an extra half-back.

Patrick McEvedy, a survivor of the 1904 touring side, played in two of the Tests for the visitors. He was a New Zealander by birth and after qualifying as a doctor in London during the 1900s, he returned to New Zealand the year after this tour. A useful utility back, McEvedy became a leading adminstrator and was President of the NZRFU at the time of his death.

## 1910

| 1st v. S.AFRICA | 2nd v. S.AFRICA | 3rd v. S.AFRICA |
|---|---|---|
| †S.H. WILLIAMS | S.H. WILLIAMS | S.H. WILLIAMS |
| | | |
| †A.R. FOSTER 1T | A.R. FOSTER | †A.M. BAKER |
| *J.P. JONES 1DG | J.P. JONES | J.P. JONES |
| K.B. WOOD | J.A. SPOORS 1T | K.B. WOOD |
| †M.E. NEALE | M.E. NEALE 1T | M.E. NEALE |
| | | |
| †J.A. SPOORS 1T | †C.H. PILLMAN 1C | J.A. SPOORS 1T |
| †G.A.M. ISHERWOOD | G.A.M. ISHERWOOD | G.A.M. ISHERWOOD |
| | | |
| †D.F. SMITH | D.F. SMITH | D.F. SMITH |
| †R.C. STEVENSON | R.C. STEVENSON | R.C. STEVENSON |
| †O.J.S. PIPER | *†T. SMYTH | *T. SMYTH |
| †F.G. HANDFORD | F.G. HANDFORD | F.G. HANDFORD |
| †H. JARMAN | H. JARMAN | H. JARMAN |
| †J. WEBB | J. WEBB | J. WEBB |
| †T.J. RICHARDS | T.J. RICHARDS | C.H. PILLMAN 1C |
| †P.D. WALLER | P.D. WALLER | P.D. WALLER |
| | | |
| Kimberley | Port Elizabeth | Cape Town |
| LOST 10-14 | WON 8-3 | LOST 5-21 |
| | | |
| SA: 1G 3T | SA: 1T | SA: 3G 1T 1PG |
| GB: 1DG 2T | GB: 1G 1T | GB: 1G |
| | | |
| 6 Aug. 1910 | 27 Aug. 1910 | 3 Sep. 1910 |

The British side of 1910, led by the Irish forward Tom Smyth, was the first team officially representative of the Four Home Unions, though many of the leading British players were unable to undertake the tour. Newport supplied seven players and altogether two-thirds of the tourists were or became international players for their Home Unions. Furthermore, Tom Richards, a globetrotting loose forward, had played for Australia before taking part for the British in this series.

C.H. Pillman, the outstanding Blackheath player who was one of the pioneers of modern loose-forward play, was the tourist who most impressed the South Africans. A fast, strong runner with the skills of a threequarter, Pillman was a versatile player who was even pressed into action at Port Elizabeth as a fly-half. In the British victory he initiated both of the tries and converted one.

Stanley Williams, the England full-back who was a native of Rogerstone in Gwent and one of the many Newport players in the party, together with Jack Jones (who had toured New Zealand with the 1908 team) were the other successes of the tour. Williams proved a reliable defensive player with a useful left-foot kick, whereas Jones was described by South African experts as a grand exponent of centre play. Another midfield player, Jack Spoors, had the distinction of scoring tries in each Test of the series.

## 1924

| 1st v. S.AFRICA | 2nd v. S.AFRICA | 3rd v. S.AFRICA | 4th v. S.AFRICA |
|---|---|---|---|
| †D. DRYSDALE | D. DRYSDALE | D. DRYSDALE | D. DRYSDALE |
| | | | |
| †I.S. SMITH | I.S. SMITH | †S.W. HARRIS | S.W. HARRIS 1T |
| †R.M. KINNEAR | R.M. KINNEAR | R.M. KINNEAR | R.M. KINNEAR |
| †R.B. MAXWELL | †H.J. DAVIES | †V.M. GRIFFITHS | V.M. GRIFFITHS |
| †W. WALLACE | †W.R. HARDING | W.R. HARDING | W.R. HARDING |
| | | | |
| †H. WADDELL | H. WADDELL | †W. CUNNINGHAM 1T | H. WADDELL |
| †H. WHITLEY 1T | †A.T. YOUNG | H. WHITLEY | H. WHITLEY |
| | | | |
| *†R. COVE-SMITH | *R. COVE-SMITH | *R. COVE-SMITH | *R. COVE-SMITH |
| †A.F. BLAKISTON | A.F. BLAKISTON | A.F. BLAKISTON | A.F. BLAKISTON |
| †N.C. MACPHERSON | N.C. MACPHERSON | N.C. MACPHERSON | N.C. MACPHERSON |
| †R.A. HOWIE | R.A. HOWIE | R.A. HOWIE | R.A. HOWIE |
| †D.S. DAVIES | D.S. DAVIES | D.S. DAVIES | D.S. DAVIES |
| †T.N. BRAND | T.N. BRAND | †A.T. VOYCE | A.T. VOYCE 1PG,1T |
| †D. MARSDEN-JONES | D. MARSDEN-JONES | †R.G. HENDERSON | R.G. HENDERSON |
| †J.M. MCVICKER | †K.G.P. HENDRIE | J.M. MCVICKER | J.M. MCVICKER |
| | | | |
| Durban | Johannesburg | Port Elizabeth | Cape Town |
| LOST 3-7 | LOST 0-17 | DRAWN 3-3 | LOST 9-16 |
| | | | |
| SA: 1DG 1T | SA: 1G 3T 1PG | SA: 1T | SA: 1DG 4T |
| GB: 1T | GB: NIL | GB: 1T | GB: 1PG 2T |
| | | | |
| 16 Aug. 1924 | 23 Aug. 1924 | 13 Sep. 1924 | 20 Sep. 1924 |

The former Newport and Wales international Harry Packer was the popular manager of the 1924 British tourists. There was great difficulty finding a suitable party to undertake the tour, a number of leading internationals declaring themselves unavailable. At length Cove-Smith, the England forward, led a party of 29 players, of whom 80 per cent played for their Home Nations.

The side was one of the unluckiest ever to tour South Africa. There was an abnormal number of injuries and there were times when the management struggled to place fifteen fit men on the field. Two of the characters of the party were Tom Voyce and Jammie Clinch, dynamic loose-forwards of considerable ability. At times, when Dan Drysdale (the only fit full-back in the party for much of the tour) was rested, Voyce and Clinch deputised as full-backs. Harold Davies, the Newport and Wales centre, and W.Cunningham, the former Irish half who had emigrated to South Africa, later joined the British tourists as replacements.

Cunningham was the British scorer in their best Test-showing of the tour – the third at Port Elizabeth. It was also in this match that the British pack dominated their huge Springbok opponents. The visitors regularly heeled the ball in the scrums, giving their backs plenty of scope to attack. Sound defence, however, meant that the British had to be content with a draw. The other Tests were clear South African victories.

## 1930

| 1st v. NZ | 2nd v. NZ | 3rd v. NZ | 4th v. NZ | v. AUSTRALIA |
|---|---|---|---|---|
| †J.A. Bassett | J.A. Bassett | J.A. Bassett | J.A. Bassett | J.A. Bassett |
| | | | | |
| †J.C. Morley 1t | J.C. Morley | J.C. Morley | A.L. Novis 1t | C.D. Aarvold |
| †H.M. Bowcott | H.M. Bowcott | H.M. Bowcott 1t | H.M. Bowcott | H.M. Bowcott |
| *†C.D. Aarvold | C.D. Aarvold 2t | *C.D. Aarvold 1t | *C.D. Aarvold | A.L. Novis 1t |
| †J.S.R. Reeve 1t | †A.L. Novis | J.S.R. Reeve | J.S.R. Reeve | J.S.R. Reeve |
| | | | | |
| †R.S. Spong | R.S. Spong | R.S. Spong | R.S. Spong | R.S. Spong |
| †P.F. Murray | P.F. Murray | †H. Poole | P.F. Murray | P.F. Murray |
| | | | | |
| †H. Rew | H. Rew | H. Rew | H. Rew | H.O'H. O'Neill |
| †D. Parker | D. Parker | D. Parker | D. Parker 1pg | †S.A. Martindale |
| †H.O'H. O'Neill | H.O'H. O'Neill | H.O'H. O'Neill | H.O'H. O'Neill | J.L. Farrell |
| †J.L. Farrell | J.L. Farrell | J.L. Farrell | J.L. Farrell | D. Parker |
| †B.H. Black | *F.D. Prentice 2c | J.M. Hodgson | †W.B. Welsh | *F.D. Prentice 1c |
| †J.M. Hodgson | B.H. Black | B.H. Black 1c | B.H. Black 1c | B.H. Black |
| †G.R. Beamish | G.R. Beamish | G.R. Beamish | G.R. Beamish | G.R. Beamish |
| †I.E. Jones | I.E. Jones | I.E. Jones 1c | I.E. Jones | I.E. Jones |
| | | | | |
| Dunedin | Christchurch | Auckland | Wellington | Sydney |
| WON 6-3 | LOST 10-13 | LOST 10-15 | LOST 8-22 | LOST 5-6 |
| | | | | |
| NZ: 1t | NZ: 2g 1gm | NZ: 1g 1dg 2t | NZ: 2g 4t | AUST.: 2t |
| GB: 2t | GB: 2g | GB: 2g | GB: 1g 1pg | GB: 1g |
| | | | | |
| 21 Jun. 1930 | 5 Jul. 1930 | 26 Jul. 1930 | 9 Aug. 1930 | 30 Aug. 1930 |

The British side of 1930, one of the first to be known as the "Lions", was a popular party which attracted large crowds in New Zealand. The backs, spearheaded by Roger Spong, an attacking runner with a shrewd tactical appreciation, played attractive football. There were plenty of seasoned forwards in the side too, but the stronger, more scientific New Zealand forwards proved difficult to overcome in the Test series.

Ivor Jones, the Llanelli and Wales flanker, was outstanding among the forwards and created the Lions' winning try at Dunedin in the first Test. With the scores level and time running out, Jones intercepted a pass by the New Zealand half-back. Sprinting away from the cover the Welshman drew Nepia perfectly to send his compatriot Morley flying along the touchline for the deciding try. The Lions lost the remaining Tests in New Zealand, and were narrowly beaten in the only international against Australia.

The touring side was competently led by Doug Prentice of England (who later became Secretary to the RFU), and well managed by Mr J. Baxter. But Mr Baxter's outspoken opinions regarding the ploys of the New Zealand wing-forwards upset New Zealand followers. Mr Baxter's criticisms were later studied by the International Board, and the upshot was a change to the hooking law which brought to an end the 2-3-2 scrum formation favoured by the All Blacks.

## 1938

| 1st v. S.AFRICA | 2nd v. S.AFRICA | 3rd v. S.AFRICA |
|---|---|---|
| †V.G.J. Jenkins 3pg | †C.F. Grieve | C.F. Grieve 1dg |
| | | |
| †E.J. Unwin | E.J. Unwin | E.L. Jones 1t |
| †D.J. Macrae | †B.E. Nicholson | J.L. Giles |
| †H.R. McKibbin | H.R. McKibbin | H.R. McKibbin 1c,1pg |
| †E.L. Jones | †C.V. Boyle | C.V. Boyle |
| | | |
| †F.J. Reynolds | F.J. Reynolds | †G.E. Cromey |
| †J.L. Giles | †H. Tanner | †G.J. Morgan |
| | | |
| †M.E. Morgan | M.E. Morgan | C.R.A. Graves |
| †C.R.A. Graves | †W.H. Travers | W.H. Travers |
| †G.T. Dancer | G.T. Dancer | G.T. Dancer 1t |
| *†S. Walker | *S. Walker | *S. Walker |
| †R.B. Mayne | R.B. Mayne | R.B. Mayne |
| †A.R. Taylor 1pg | A.R. Taylor | P.L. Duff 1t |
| †W.G. Howard | †P.L. Duff 1t | †J.A. Waters |
| †R. Alexander | R. Alexander | R. Alexander 1t |
| | | |
| Johannesburg | Port Elizabeth | Cape Town |
| LOST 12-26 | LOST 3-19 | WON 21-16 |
| | | |
| SA: 4g 2pg | SA: 2g 2pg 1t | SA: 2g 1pg 1t |
| GB: 4pg | GB: 1t | GB: 1g 1dg 1pg 3t |
| | | |
| 6 Aug. 1938 | 3 Sep. 1938 | 10 Sep. 1938 |

South Africa was the strongest rugby-playing nation of the world in the immediate pre-war years. Consequently the tour by the 1938 Lions, who were led by Sam Walker and who lost only six of 23 matches, was regarded as a sporting success. As usual, it was impossible to send a fully representative side, but the party of 29 included 24 players who gained international status.

Despite immense injury problems – three different scrum-halves, for instance, appeared in the Tests – the tourists impressed their hosts by their willingness to play open football. Vivian Jenkins, the Lions' vice-captain, kicked three huge penalty goals, a new record for a British player in a Test, at Johannesburg, but the massive Springbok forwards, who constantly opted for scrums instead of line-outs, dominated in the tight and paved the way for four tries. At Port Elizabeth, injuries sustained by Nicholson and Reynolds considerably weakened the Lions and it was not surprising that the visitors went down by 16 points in the second Test.

But a week later, in the last Test, Walker's side made a remarkable second-half recovery to win 21-16, after trailing by ten points at the interval. The victory – Britain's first in South Africa since 1910 – must have given particular satisfaction to the Irish, who supplied eight men to the winning side.

## 1950

| 1st v. NZ | 2nd v. NZ | 3rd v. NZ | 4th v. NZ | 1st v. AUSTRALIA | 2nd v. AUSTRALIA |
|---|---|---|---|---|---|
| †W.B. Cleaver | W.B. Cleaver | W.B. Cleaver | †B.L. Jones 1pg,1c | B.L. Jones 2c,2pg,1dg,1t | B.L. Jones 1pg,1c |
| †K.J. Jones 1t | K.J. Jones | †N.J. Henderson | K.J. Jones 1t | †D.W.C. Smith | R. MacDonald 1t |
| †J. Matthews | J. Matthews | J. Matthews | J. Matthews | J. Matthews | J. Matthews |
| †I. Preece | †B.L. Williams | *B.L. Williams | *B.L. Williams | *B.L. Williams 1t | B.L. Williams |
| †R. MacDonald | †M.C. Thomas | M.C. Thomas | †M.F. Lane | M.C. Thomas | M.F. Lane |
| †J.W. Kyle 1t | J.W. Kyle | J.W. Kyle | J.W. Kyle | J.W. Kyle | J.W. Kyle 1t |
| †A.W. Black | A.W. Black | †G. Rimmer | †W.R. Willis | W.R. Willis | W.R. Willis |
| †J.D. Robins 1pg | J.D. Robins | J.D. Robins 1pg | †G.M. Budge | J.D. Robins | J.D. Robins 2c |
| *K.D. Mullen | *K.D. Mullen | †D.M. Davies | D.M. Davies | D.M. Davies | *K.D. Mullen |
| †T. Clifford | T. Clifford | T. Clifford | *C. Davies | T. Clifford | T. Clifford |
| †D.J. Hayward | D.J. Hayward | D.J. Hayward | J.E. Nelson | J.E. Nelson | J.E. Nelson 2t |
| †E.R. John | E.R. John | †J.E. Nelson | E.R. John | †J.R.G. Stephens | J.R.G. Stephens |
| †R.T. Evans | R.T. Evans | R.T. Evans | R.T. Evans | R.T. Evans | R.T. Evans |
| †P.W. Kininmonth | P.W. Kininmonth | E.R. John | P.W. Kininmonth | E.R. John | E.R. John 1t |
| †J.W. McKay | J.W. McKay | J.W. McKay | J.W. McKay | J.W. McKay | J.W. McKay |
| Dunedin DRAWN 9-9 | Christchurch LOST 0-8 | Wellington LOST 3-6 | Auckland LOST 8-11 | Brisbane WON 19-6 | Sydney WON 24-3 |
| NZ: 1pg 2t BI: 1pg 2t | NZ: 1g 1t BI: NIL | NZ: 1pg 1t BI: 1pg | NZ: 1g 1dg 1t BI: 1g 1pg | AUST.: 2pg BI: 2g 1dg 2pg | AUST.: 1t BI: 3g 1pg 2t |
| 27 May 1950 | 10 Jun. 1950 | 1 Jul. 1950 | 29 Jul. 1950 | 19 Aug. 1950 | 26 Aug. 1950 |

The 1950 Lions, led by Karl Mullen, were one of the most fully representative combinations to represent the four Home Unions. For the first time every member of the British squad was an international player before the series with New Zealand started, and there were thirteen Welshmen in the party, including Lewis Jones who was sent out to join the side as a replacement.

As in 1930, the British backs were applauded everywhere for their readiness to play open, attacking rugby. Jack Kyle, Bleddyn Williams and Ken Jones (who scored two thrilling tries in the Tests) were players who lived up to the brilliant reputations they had gained at home. But the power of the New Zealand forwards was immense, and in the final three Tests the British packs were out-scrummaged in the tight and overwhelmed by efficient ruckers in the second-phase.

The Australian portion of the tour provided the Lions with the opportunity of unleashing their backs, and 150 points were scored in six matches. Both of the Tests were easily won, with Lewis Jones creating a then British Test record by scoring 16 points in Sydney.

## 1955

| 1st v. S.AFRICA | 2nd v. S.AFRICA | 3rd v. S.AFRICA | 4th v. S.AFRICA |
|---|---|---|---|
| †A. Cameron 4c | A. Cameron 1pg | †D.G.S. Baker 1pg | D.G.S. Baker |
| †A.J.F. O'Reilly 1t | A.J.F. O'Reilly | G.M. Griffiths | G.M. Griffiths |
| †J. Butterfield 1t | J. Butterfield 1t | J. Butterfield 1t,1dg | J. Butterfield |
| †W.P.C. Davies | W.P.C. Davies | W.P.C. Davies | A.J.F. O'Reilly 1t |
| †A.C. Pedlow 1t | †G.M. Griffiths | A.J.F. O'Reilly | A.C. Pedlow 1c |
| †C.I. Morgan 1t | C.I. Morgan | *C.I. Morgan | C.I. Morgan |
| †R.E.G. Jeeps | R.E.G. Jeeps | R.E.G. Jeeps | R.E.G. Jeeps |
| †W.O.G. Williams | W.O.G. Williams | W.O.G. Williams | W.O.G. Williams |
| †B.V. Meredith | B.V. Meredith 1t | B.V. Meredith | B.V. Meredith |
| †C.C. Meredith | C.C. Meredith | C.C. Meredith | C.C. Meredith |
| †R.H. Williams | R.H. Williams | R.H. Williams | R.H. Williams |
| *†R.H. Thompson | *R.H. Thompson | T.E. Reid | *R.H. Thompson |
| †R. Higgins | R.J. Robins | †R.C.C. Thomas | R.C.C. Thomas |
| †R.J. Robins | †T.E. Reid | R.J. Robins | R.J. Robins |
| †J.T. Greenwood 1t | J.T. Greenwood | J.T. Greenwood | J.T. Greenwood 1t |
| Johannesburg WON 23-22 | Cape Town LOST 9-25 | Pretoria WON 9-6 | Port Elizabeth LOST 8-22 |
| SA: 2g 2pg 2t BI: 4g 1t | SA: 2g 5t BI: 1pg 2t | SA: 2pg BI: 1dg 1pg 1t | SA: 2g 1dg 3t BI: 1g 1t |
| 6 Aug. 1955 | 20 Aug. 1955 | 3 Sep. 1955 | 24 Sep. 1955 |

Once again a strong, fully representative Lions party was selected for the 1955 tour. The traditional strength of British rugby, its backs, maintained the attacking principles laid down by their predecessors in 1950, but this time Britain was able to boast a fit, mobile and powerful pack capable of holding the huge Springbok forwards on their own grounds.

The side benefited from a strong Welsh influence, and six of the pack, Cliff Morgan (as captain) and Gareth Griffiths (who had joined the squad as a replacement) appeared in the successful third Test side when the Lions ensured a share in the rubber and thus became the first British side since 1896 to avoid defeat in a series in South Africa.

The quality of rugby played by the Lions attracted about 230,000 to the four Tests, and a new world record of 95,000 spectators watched the exciting first Test at Johannesburg, where the British succeeded by 23-22, though the Springboks did miss a last-minute conversion.

## 1959

| 1st v. AUSTRALIA | 2nd v. AUSTRALIA | 1st v. NZ | 2nd v. NZ | 3rd v. NZ | 4th v. NZ |
|---|---|---|---|---|---|
| †K.J.F. Scotland 1DG | K.J.F. Scotland 1PG,1C | K.J.F. Scotland | †T.J. Davies 1PG,1C | K.J.F. Scotland | T.J. Davies |
| †P.B. Jackson | P.B. Jackson | P.B. Jackson 1T | †J.R.C. Young 1T | P.B. Jackson | P.B. Jackson 1T |
| †D. Hewitt 2PG | D. Hewitt 2C | M.J. Price 2T | M.C. Thomas | M.J. Price | D. Hewitt |
| †M.J. Price | M.J. Price 2T | D. Hewitt 1PG | †W.M. Patterson | D. Hewitt 1T | K.J.F. Scotland |
| A.J.F. O'Reilly 1T | A.J.F. O'Reilly 1T | A.J.F. O'Reilly 1T | A.J.F. O'Reilly | A.J.F. O'Reilly | A.J.F. O'Reilly 1T |
| †A.B.W. Risman 1C | A.B.W. Risman 1T | A.B.W. Risman 1C | M.J. Price | †J.P. Horrocks-Taylor | A.B.W. Risman 1T |
| R.E.G. Jeeps | R.E.G. Jeeps | R.E.G. Jeeps | R.E.G. Jeeps | R.E.G. Jeeps | †A.A. Mulligan |
| †H.F. McLeod | H.F. McLeod | H.F. McLeod | H.F. McLeod | H.F. McLeod | H.F. McLeod |
| *†A.R. Dawson | *A.R. Dawson 1T | *A.R. Dawson | *A.R. Dawson | *A.R. Dawson | *A.R. Dawson |
| †S. Millar | S. Millar | †B.G.M. Wood | S. Millar | B.G.M. Wood | †T.R. Prosser |
| †W.A. Mulcahy | †W.R. Evans | R.H. Williams | R.H. Williams | R.H. Williams | R.H. Williams |
| R.H. Williams | R.H. Williams | W.R. Evans | W.R. Evans | W.R. Evans | W.A. Mulcahy |
| †A. Ashcroft | †N.A.A. Murphy | N.A.A. Murphy | A. Ashcroft | G.K. Smith | N.A.A. Murphy |
| †J. Faull | †R.W.D. Marques | J. Faull | R.W.D. Marques | J. Faull 1PG,1C | J. Faull |
| †G.K. Smith 1T | G.K. Smith | G.K. Smith | N.A.A. Murphy | †H.J. Morgan | H.J. Morgan |
| Brisbane WON 17-6 | Sydney WON 24-3 | Dunedin LOST 17-18 | Wellington LOST 8-11 | Christchurch LOST 8-22 | Auckland WON 9-6 |
| Aust.: 2PG BI: 1G 1DG 2PG 1T | Aust.: 1PG BI: 3G 1PG 2T | NZ: 6PG BI: 1G 1PG 3T | NZ: 1G 2T BI: 1G 1PG | NZ: 2G 1DG 1PG 2T BI: 1G 1PG | NZ: 2PG BI: 3T |
| 6 Jun. 1959 | 13 Jun. 1959 | 18 Jul. 1959 | 15 Aug. 1959 | 29 Aug. 1959 | 19 Sep. 1959 |

In its analysis of the Lions tour of Australasia, the *Playfair Rugby Annual* commented: "The 1959 Lions, as in the tradition of their predecessors, achieved great things even though they lost the Test rubber in New Zealand by three matches to one." The side was a popular one which continued the open, attacking style adopted by the 1950 and 1955 Lions. However, there were still problems gaining possession against a very strong New Zealand pack, and the Lions had the misfortune to lose by six penalty goals to four tries in the opening Test of the series at Dunedin.

Tony O'Reilly, who had toured South Africa in 1955 as a teenager, was the outstanding personality. In all he scored 22 tries on tour, a record for a British team, and his career total of six tries in Tests played on the 1955 and 1959 tours remains a British record. Bev Risman was the Lions' spearhead in attack, but injuries kept him out for part of the tour. It was significant that his return for the final Test transformed the Lions into a winning side, Risman, O'Reilly and Jackson scoring tries in a 9-6 win.

Ronnie Dawson, the young Irish skipper of the Lions, captained the side in six Tests, a British international record.

## 1962

| 1st v. S.AFRICA | 2nd v. S.AFRICA | 3rd v. S.AFRICA | 4th v. S.AFRICA |
|---|---|---|---|
| †J.G. Willcox | J.G. Willcox | †T.J. Kiernan | J.G. Willcox 1C,1PG |
| *†A.R. Smith | *A.R. Smith | *A.R. Smith | †R.C. Cowan 1T |
| †D.K. Jones 1T | D.K. Jones | D.K. Jones | M.P. Weston |
| †M.P. Weston | M.P. Weston | M.P. Weston | D. Hewitt |
| †N.H. Brophy | †D.I.E. Bebb | D.I.E. Bebb | N.H. Brophy |
| †G.H. Waddell | G.H. Waddell | †R.A.W. Sharp 1DG | R.A.W. Sharp |
| R.E.G. Jeeps | R.E.G. Jeeps | R.E.G. Jeeps | *R.E.G. Jeeps |
| S. Millar | S. Millar | S. Millar | S. Millar |
| B.V. Meredith | B.V. Meredith | B.V. Meredith | B.V. Meredith |
| †K.D. Jones | K.D. Jones | K.D. Jones | K.D. Jones |
| W.A. Mulcahy | W.A. Mulcahy | W.A. Mulcahy | K.A. Rowlands 1T |
| †K.A. Rowlands | K.A. Rowlands | †W.J. McBride | W.J. McBride |
| †D.P. Rogers | A.E.I. Pask | A.E.I. Pask | W.A. Mulcahy |
| †M.J. Campbell-Lamerton | M.J. Campbell-Lamerton | M.J. Campbell-Lamerton | M.J. Campbell-Lamerton 1T |
| †A.E.I. Pask | †H.J. Morgan | H.J. Morgan | D.P. Rogers |
| Johannesburg DRAWN 3-3 | Durban LOST 0-3 | Cape Town LOST 3-8 | Bloemfontein LOST 14-34 |
| SA: 1T BI: 1T | SA: 1PG BI: NIL | SA: 1G 1PG BI: 1DG | SA: 5G 2PG 1T BI: 1G 1PG 2T |
| 23 Jun. 1962 | 21 Jul. 1962 | 4 Aug. 1962 | 25 Aug. 1962 |

The 1962 Lions tour of South Africa was marred by injuries. Several players were so severely crocked that for most of the series the British were unable to field their strongest side. Hodgson broke his leg in his first match of the tour; David Nash was injured in the third match and took no further active role; while Richard Sharp, the spearhead of the Lions' attack, was so heavily laid-out in the match against Northern Transvaal (on the eve of the opening Test) that he was unable to resume playing until half-way through the series.

Nevertheless, the British side put up a brave show to draw the first Test and only narrowly lost the second. Ken Jones, the oustanding centre in British rugby in 1962, scored a memorable try at Johannesburg to level the scores in the first of the Tests, but he was criticised in the later Tests for squandering opportunities by overdoing his solo efforts.

Beset by injury and tired at the close of a long tour, the Lions caved in during the second half of the fourth Test and lost by twenty points – a new record losing points margin for a fully representative British Test team.

## 1966

| 1st v. AUSTRALIA | 2nd v. AUSTRALIA | 1st v. NZ | 2nd v. NZ | 3rd v. NZ | 4th v. NZ |
|---|---|---|---|---|---|
| †D. RUTHERFORD 1PG,1C | †S. WILSON 1PG,5C | S. WILSON 1PG | S. WILSON 3PG | S. WILSON | S. WILSON 1PG,1C |
| †S.J. WATKINS | S.J. WATKINS | †C.W. McFADYEAN | †A.J.W. HINSHELWOOD | S.J. WATKINS | A.J.W. HINSHELWOOD 1T |
| D.K. JONES | D.K. JONES 2T | D.K. JONES | C.W. McFADYEAN | C.W. McFADYEAN | C.W. McFADYEAN 1T |
| M.P. WESTON | M.P. WESTON | †C.M.H. GIBSON | C.M.H. GIBSON | C.M.H. GIBSON | C.M.H. GIBSON |
| D.I.E. BEBB | D.I.E. BEBB 1T | D.I.E. BEBB | D.I.E. BEBB | D.I.E. BEBB | D.I.E. BEBB |
| †D. WATKINS | D. WATKINS 1DG,1T | D. WATKINS | *D. WATKINS 1DG | D. WATKINS 1T | *D. WATKINS |
| †R.M. YOUNG | R.M. YOUNG | R.M. YOUNG | †A.R. LEWIS | A.R. LEWIS | A.R. LEWIS |
| †D. WILLIAMS | D. WILLIAMS | D. WILLIAMS | D. WILLIAMS | W.D. THOMAS | D. WILLIAMS |
| †K.W. KENNEDY 1T | K.W. KENNEDY | K.W. KENNEDY | †F.A.L. LAIDLAW | F.A.L. LAIDLAW | K.W. KENNEDY |
| †R.J. McLOUGHLIN 1T | R.J. McLOUGHLIN | †C.H. NORRIS | C.H. NORRIS | C.H. NORRIS | R.J. McLOUGHLIN |
| *M.J. CAMPBELL-LAMERTON | *M.J. CAMPBELL-LAMERTON | B. PRICE | †W.D. THOMAS | *M.J. CAMPBELL-LAMERTON | W.J. McBRIDE |
| †B. PRICE | B. PRICE | *M.J. CAMPBELL-LAMERTON | W.J. McBRIDE | W.J. McBRIDE | B. PRICE |
| †J.W. TELFER | J.W. TELFER | J.W. TELFER | N.A.A. MURPHY | N.A.A. MURPHY | A.E.I. PASK |
| A.E.I. PASK | A.E.I. PASK | A.E.I. PASK | J.W. TELFER | A.E.I. PASK | J.W. TELFER |
| N.A.A. MURPHY | N.A.A. MURPHY 1T | †R.A. LAMONT | R.A. LAMONT | R.A. LAMONT 1T | R.A. LAMONT |
| Sydney WON 11-8 | Brisbane WON 31-0 | Dunedin LOST 3-20 | Wellington LOST 12-16 | Christchurch LOST 6-19 | Auckland LOST 11-24 |
| AUST.: 1G 1PG | AUST.: NIL | NZ: 1G 2PG 1DG 2T | NZ: 2G 1PG 1T | NZ: 2G 2PG 1T | NZ: 3G 1PG 1DG 1T |
| BI: 1G 1PG 1T | BI: 5G 1PG 1DG | BI: 1PG | BI: 3PG 1DG | BI: 2T | BI: 1G 1PG 1T |
| 28 May 1966 | 4 Jun. 1966 | 16 Jul. 1966 | 6 Aug. 1966 | 27 Aug. 1966 | 10 Sep. 1966 |

The 1966 Lions made a promising start to their Australasian tour, boasting an unbeaten record in the eight matches of the Australian leg of the trip. Included in that run were two sound performances in the Tests against the Australians, and the record Test score of 31 points at Brisbane gave the tourists heart for the New Zealand part of their schedule. Stewart Wilson also set a record in the Brisbane win, landing five conversions.

But there was a rude awakening for the British as soon as they reached New Zealand. Ruthlessly efficient provincial forwards outscrummaged and outrucked the Lions in three of the first five games, and ultimately the pattern of strong forward play was to enable the All Blacks to take the series 4-0.

British rugby was at its nadir: never before had a British touring team suffered the disgrace of losing every Test of a series, and much soul-searching followed the tour. In many ways it was the analysis of British rugby which resulted from this dreadful reverse which paved the way for the British successes of the 1970s; for an increased commitment to fitness and coaching were some of the recommendations put into practice following the inquests on the tour.

## 1968

| 1st v. S.AFRICA | 2nd v. S.AFRICA | 3rd v. S.AFRICA | 4th v. S.AFRICA |
|---|---|---|---|
| *T.J. KIERNAN 5PG,1C | *T.J. KIERNAN 2PG | *T.J. KIERNAN 2PG | *T.J. KIERNAN 2PG |
| †K.F. SAVAGE | K.F. SAVAGE | K.F. SAVAGE | K.F. SAVAGE |
| †F.P.K. BRESNIHAN | F.P.K. BRESNIHAN | †T.G.R. DAVIES | J.W.C. TURNER |
| †J.W.C. TURNER | J.W.C. TURNER | J.W.C. TURNER | F.P.K. BRESNIHAN |
| †M.C.R. RICHARDS | A.J.W. HINSHELWOOD | M.C.R. RICHARDS | M.C.R. RICHARDS |
| †B. JOHN[1] | C.M.H. GIBSON | C.M.H. GIBSON | C.M.H. GIBSON |
| †G.O. EDWARDS | G.O. EDWARDS | †R.M. YOUNG | †G.C. CONNELL |
| S. MILLAR | S. MILLAR | †M.J. COULMAN[1] | W.D. THOMAS |
| †J. YOUNG | †J.V. PULLIN | J.V. PULLIN | J.V. PULLIN |
| †J.P. O'SHEA | †A.L. HORTON | A.L. HORTON | A.L. HORTON |
| †P.K. STAGG | †P.J. LARTER | P.K. STAGG | P.K. STAGG |
| W.J. McBRIDE 1T | W.J. McBRIDE | W.J. McBRIDE | W.J. McBRIDE |
| †R.J. ARNEIL | R.J. ARNEIL | R.J. ARNEIL | R.J. ARNEIL |
| †R.B. TAYLOR | J.W. TELFER | J.W. TELFER | J.W. TELFER |
| †M.G. DOYLE | R.B. TAYLOR | R.B. TAYLOR | R.B. TAYLOR |
| Pretoria LOST 20-25 | Port Elizabeth DRAWN 6-6 | Cape Town LOST 6-11 | Johannesburg LOST 6-19 |
| SA: 2G 4PG 1T | SA: 2PG | SA: 1G 2PG | SA: 2G 1DG 2T |
| BI: 1G 5PG | BI: 2PG | BI: 2PG | BI: 2PG |
| 8 Jun. 1968 | 22 Jun. 1968 | 13 Jul. 1968 | 27 Jul. 1968 |
| [1]Rep. by C.M.H. Gibson | | [1]Rep. by W.D. Thomas | |

Tom Kiernan, popular captain of the 1968 British Lions (and the fifth Irishman to lead the Lions since 1938), set a fine example by creating new British Test records. He kicked a new highest individual points record with his 17 points in the first Test, and his 35 points in the series represented the highest total ever gained by a British tourist.

Yet still the Lions were unable to make headway against overseas rivals. Although hampered by the usual spate of injuries, confused by unusual refereeing decisions, and exposed to much greater media coverage than any of their predecessors, the Lions had to concede considerable weight and power to the Springboks. And in losing the series 0-3 (with a drawn game at Port Elizabeth), a further telling statistic was that 92% of the Lions' points in the series resulted from penalties.

The lack of tries was in part due to the injuries to the side's natural runners. Gerald Davies, Barry John, Keri Jones and Billy Raybould were key backs who were expected to enjoy the fast conditons offered by the firm South African grounds. Alas none survived more than one Test. John was injured in the opening Test, where Gibson became the first British player to appear as a replacement in an international match, and the talented young Welsh fly-half did not appear on the tour again.

## 1971

| 1st v. NZ | 2nd v. NZ | 3rd v. NZ | 4th v. NZ |
|---|---|---|---|
| †J.P.R. WILLIAMS | J.P.R. WILLIAMS | J.P.R. WILLIAMS | J.P.R. WILLIAMS 1DG |
| | | | |
| T.G.R. DAVIES | T.G.R. DAVIES 2T | T.G.R. DAVIES 1T | T.G.R. DAVIES |
| *†S.J. DAWES | *S.J. DAWES | *S.J. DAWES | *S.J. DAWES |
| C.M.H. GIBSON | C.M.H. GIBSON | C.M.H. GIBSON | C.M.H. GIBSON |
| †J.C. BEVAN | †D.J. DUCKHAM | D.J. DUCKHAM | D.J. DUCKHAM |
| | | | |
| B. JOHN 2PG | B. JOHN 1PG,1DG | B. JOHN 1T,2C,1DG | B. JOHN 2PG,1C |
| G.O. EDWARDS[1] | G.O. EDWARDS | G.O. EDWARDS | G.O. EDWARDS |
| | | | |
| †J. MCLAUCHLAN 1T | J. MCLAUCHLAN | J. MCLAUCHLAN | J. MCLAUCHLAN |
| J.V. PULLIN | J.V. PULLIN | J.V. PULLIN | J.V. PULLIN |
| †J.F. LYNCH | J.F. LYNCH | J.F. LYNCH | J.F. LYNCH |
| W.D. THOMAS | W.D. THOMAS | †G.L. BROWN | G.L. BROWN[1] |
| W.J. MCBRIDE | W.J. MCBRIDE | W.J. MCBRIDE | W.J. MCBRIDE |
| †P.J. DIXON | P.J. DIXON | †D.L. QUINNELL | P.J. DIXON 1T |
| †T.M. DAVIES | T.M. DAVIES | T.M. DAVIES | T.M. DAVIES |
| †J. TAYLOR | J. TAYLOR | J. TAYLOR | J. TAYLOR |
| Dunedin | Christchurch | Wellington | Auckland |
| WON 9-3 | LOST 12-22 | WON 13-3 | DRAWN 14-14 |
| NZ: 1PG | NZ: 2G‡ 1PG 3T | NZ: 1T | NZ: 1G 2PG 1T |
| BI: 2PG 1T | BI: 1PG 1DG 2T | BI: 2G 1DG | BI: 1G 2PG 1DG |
| 26 Jun. 1971 | 10 Jul. 1971 | 31 Jul. 1971 | 14 Aug. 1971 |
| [1]Rep. by †R. Hopkins | ‡Includes penalty try | | [1]Rep. by W.D. Thomas |

"We'll win the Test series 2-1, with one match drawn," prophesied manager Dr Doug Smith at the outset of the tour. He was absolutely right. His men became the first British side to win a Test series against the All Blacks, losing just twice on tour.

After losing their key props Ray McLoughlin and Sandy Carmichael in a brutal provincial game at Canterbury, just before the first Test, the Lions opened the series with a careful win at Dunedin. There, despite injury to Gareth Edwards, the tourists had Ian McLauchlan (a try) and Barry John to thank for their narrow victory. Then, well beaten up front in the second Test, the Lions had to strengthen their scrummage by introducing Brown and the uncapped Quinnell for the third Test. Rucking effectively and counter attacking splendidly from defence, the Lions soon went into an unassailable thirteen-point lead to make the series safe.

The Lions' backs on this tour were probably the finest combination ever to represent British rugby. Calmly led by John Dawes, players such as J.P.R. Williams, Duckham, Gerald Davies, Barry John, Gareth Edwards and Mike Gibson flourished under the perceptive and imaginative guidance of Carwyn James, a man with the wisdom of a thousand coaches.

## 1974

| 1st v. S.AFRICA | 2nd v. S.AFRICA | 3rd v. S.AFRICA | 4th v. S.AFRICA |
|---|---|---|---|
| J.P.R. WILLIAMS | J.P.R. WILLIAMS | J.P.R. WILLIAMS | J.P.R. WILLIAMS |
| | | | |
| †W.C.C. STEELE | W.C.C. STEELE | †A.R. IRVINE 2PG,1C | A.R. IRVINE 1PG,1T |
| †I.R. MCGEECHAN | I.R. MCGEECHAN 1DG | I.R. MCGEECHAN | I.R. MCGEECHAN |
| †R.A. MILLIKEN | R.A. MILLIKEN 1T | R.A. MILLIKEN | R.A. MILLIKEN |
| †J.J. WILLIAMS | J.J. WILLIAMS 2T | J.J. WILLIAMS 2T | J.J. WILLIAMS |
| | | | |
| †P. BENNETT 3PG | P. BENNETT 1PG,1T,1C | P. BENNETT 2DG | P. BENNETT 1C |
| G.O. EDWARDS 1DG | G.O. EDWARDS | G.O. EDWARDS | G.O. EDWARDS |
| | | | |
| J. MCLAUCHLAN | J. MCLAUCHLAN | J. MCLAUCHLAN | J. MCLAUCHLAN |
| †R.W. WINDSOR | R.W. WINDSOR | R.W. WINDSOR | R.W. WINDSOR |
| †F.E. COTTON | F.E. COTTON | F.E. COTTON | F.E. COTTON |
| G.L. BROWN | G.L. BROWN 1T | G.L. BROWN 1T | †C.W. RALSTON |
| *W.J. MCBRIDE | *W.J. MCBRIDE | *W.J. MCBRIDE | *W.J. MCBRIDE |
| †J.F. SLATTERY | J.F. SLATTERY | J.F. SLATTERY | J.F. SLATTERY |
| T.M. DAVIES | T.M. DAVIES | T.M. DAVIES | T.M. DAVIES |
| †R.M. UTTLEY | R.M. UTTLEY | R.M. UTTLEY | R.M. UTTLEY 1T |
| Cape Town | Pretoria | Port Elizabeth | Johannesburg |
| WON 12-3 | WON 28-9 | WON 26-9 | DRAWN 13-13 |
| SA: 1DG | SA: 2PG 1DG | SA: 3PG | SA: 3PG 1T |
| BI: 3PG 1DG | BI: 1G 1PG 1DG 4T | BI: 1G 2PG 2DG 2T | BI: 1G 1PG 1T |
| 8 Jun. 1974 | 22 Jun. 1974 | 13 Jul. 1974 | 27 Jul. 1974 |

The 1974 Lions broke all British touring records. The first side to win a Test series in South Africa since 1896; the scorers of the highest points registered against the Springboks in a Test series; the highest-ever defeat (28-9 at Pretoria) inflicted on South Africa in a Test; and the most points ever scored by any touring team to South Africa: these were some of the new heights reached by the 1974 tourists. The team was unbeaten until the final Test, where the Springboks salvaged some pride with a draw.

The foundations of the Test successes were dominance up front, mobility in the loose, and immense pace across the backs. Edwards and Bennett formed the ideal link between these brilliant divisions. J.J. Williams, with four tries in the series, created a new individual record for a British player on tour.

To Willie John McBride, the captain, went the credit for welding the side into an invincible combination. He led by example at all times and set two records which are unlikely to be broken for many years: he became the first player to make five Lions tours, and with 17 international appearances (between 1962 and 1974) retired as the Lions' most-capped Test player.

## 1977

| 1st v. NZ | 2nd v. NZ | 3rd v. NZ | 4th v. NZ |
|---|---|---|---|
| A.R. Irvine 1PG | A.R. Irvine | A.R. Irvine 1PG | A.R. Irvine |
| †P.J. Squires | J.J. Williams 1T | J.J. Williams[1] | †H.E. Rees |
| †S.P. Fenwick | S.P. Fenwick | S.P. Fenwick | S.P. Fenwick |
| I.R. McGeechan | I.R. McGeechan | †D.H. Burcher | I.R. McGeechan |
| J.J. Williams | †G.L. Evans | G.L. Evans | G.L. Evans |
| *P. Bennett 3PG | *P. Bennett 3PG | *P. Bennett | *P. Bennett |
| †D.B. Williams | D.B. Williams | D.B. Williams[2] | D.W. Morgan 1T,1c,1PG |
| †P.A. Orr | F.E. Cotton | F.E. Cotton | F.E. Cotton |
| R.W. Windsor | †P.J. Wheeler | P.J. Wheeler | P.J. Wheeler |
| †G. Price | G. Price | G. Price | G. Price |
| †A.J. Martin | †W.B. Beaumont | W.B. Beaumont | W.B. Beaumont |
| †M.I. Keane | G.L. Brown | G.L. Brown | G.L. Brown |
| †T.J. Cobner | T.J. Cobner | T.J. Cobner | †J. Squire |
| †W.P. Duggan | W.P. Duggan | W.P. Duggan 1T | W.P. Duggan |
| †T.P. Evans | D.L. Quinnell | D.L. Quinnell | †A. Neary |
| Wellington | Christchurch | Dunedin | Auckland |
| LOST 12-16 | WON 13-9 | LOST 7-19 | LOST 9-10 |
| NZ: 2G 1T | NZ: 3PG | NZ: 1G 2PG 1DG 1T | NZ: 2PG 1T |
| BI: 4PG | BI: 3PG 1T | BI: 1PG 1T | BI: 1G 1PG |
| 18 Jun. 1977 | 9 Jul. 1977 | 30 Jul. 1977 | 13 Aug. 1977 |
| | | [1]Rep. by I.R. McGeechan | |
| | | [2]Rep. by †D.W. Morgan | |

Phil Bennett's side, managed by George Burrell and coached by John Dawes, hit one of New Zealand's wettest winters on record, and rarely managed to match the standards set by their predecessors of 1971. The party was largely drawn from Wales – some critics said there were far too many Welshmen in the squad – but the three outstanding British backs of the day, Gerald Davies, Gareth Edwards and J.P.R. Williams, had been unable to make the tour. For once the traditional strengths of British and New Zealand rugby were reversed: the Lions' forwards outplayed their opponents in the Tests, though the backs were unable to get into their stride in sticky conditions.

## 1980

| 1st v. S.AFRICA | 2nd v. S.AFRICA | 3rd v. S.AFRICA | 4th v. S.AFRICA |
|---|---|---|---|
| †R.C. O'Donnell | A.R. Irvine 1PG | A.R. Irvine | A.R. Irvine 1T |
| †J. Carleton[1] | J. Carleton | C.R. Woodward | J. Carleton |
| †J.M. Renwick | †C.R. Woodward | †P.W. Dodge | P.W. Dodge |
| †D.S. Richards | R.W.R. Gravell 1T | R.W.R. Gravell | R.W.R. Gravell |
| †M.A.C. Slemen | †B.H. Hay | B.H. Hay 1T | B.H. Hay |
| †A.J.P. Ward 5PG,1DG | †W.G. Davies 2PG,1C[1] | S.O. Campbell 2PG | S.O. Campbell 1PG,1C |
| †C.S. Patterson | C.S. Patterson | C.S. Patterson | †J.C. Robbie |
| †C. Williams | C. Williams | C. Williams | C. Williams 1T |
| P.J. Wheeler | P.J. Wheeler | P.J. Wheeler | P.J. Wheeler |
| G. Price 1T | G. Price | G. Price | G. Price |
| *W.B. Beaumont | *W.B. Beaumont | *W.B. Beaumont | *W.B. Beaumont |
| †M.J. Colclough | M.J. Colclough | M.J. Colclough | M.J. Colclough |
| †J.B. O'Driscoll | J.B. O'Driscoll 1T | J.B. O'Driscoll | J.B. O'Driscoll 1T |
| D.L. Quinnell | D.L. Quinnell | J. Squire | J. Squire |
| J. Squire | J. Squire | †C.C. Tucker | C.C. Tucker |
| Cape Town | Bloemfontein | Port Elizabeth | Pretoria |
| LOST 22-26 | LOST 19-26 | LOST 10-12 | WON 17-13 |
| SA: 3G 2T | SA: 2G 2PG 2T | SA: 1G 1PG 1DG | SA: 3PG 1T |
| BI: 5PG 1DG 1T | BI: 1G 3PG 1T | BI: 2PG 1T | BI: 1G 1PG 2T |
| 31 May 1980 | 14 Jun. 1980 | 28 Jun. 1980 | 12 Jul. 1980 |
| [1]Rep. by †R.W.R. Gravell | [1]Rep. by †S.O. Campbell | | |

Surely no Lions side has ever been as unlucky as the 1980 team, captained by Billy Beaumont. Injuries and other calls resulted in eight players joining the squad as replacements, and the repeated interruptions these changes necessitated among the backs deprived the side from gaining practice as an attacking unit, as well as undermining the overall defensive organisation of the team.

Beaumont, the first Englishman to lead the Lions for fifty years, was a key member of a pack which had no superior in South Africa, and it was only the unorthodoxy of the Springbok threequarters and full-back, supported by an extremely swift back row, which helped them to pip the Lions in a close series. Some fateful defensive lapses in the third Test allowed the Springboks to snatch the winning try ten minutes from the end. None denied Beaumont's men a well-merited victory in the final Test.

Tony Ward, who had flown to South Africa as replacement when Gareth Davies was injured, set a new British Test record with his 18 points at Cape Town.

## 1983

| 1st v. NZ | 2nd v. NZ | 3rd v. NZ | 4th v. NZ |
|---|---|---|---|
| †H.P. MacNeill | H.P. MacNeill | †G. Evans | G. Evans 1pg |
| | | | |
| †T.M. Ringland | J. Carleton | J. Carleton | J. Carleton |
| †D.G. Irwin | D.G. Irwin | †J.Y. Rutherford 1t | D.G. Irwin |
| †R.A. Ackerman | †M.J. Kiernan | M.J. Kiernan | M.J. Kiernan |
| †G.R.T. Baird | G.R.T. Baird | G.R.T. Baird 1t | G.R.T. Baird¹ |
| | | | |
| S.O. Campbell 1dg,3pg | S.O. Campbell | S.O. Campbell | S.O. Campbell 1pg² |
| †T.D. Holmes¹ | R.J. Laidlaw | R.J. Laidlaw | R.J. Laidlaw |
| | | | |
| †I. Stephens | †S.T. Jones | S.T. Jones | S.T. Jones |
| *†C.F. Fitzgerald | *C.F. Fitzgerald | *C.F. Fitzgerald | *C.F. Fitzgerald |
| G. Price | G. Price | G. Price | G. Price |
| M.J. Colclough | M.J. Colclough | M.J. Colclough | M.J. Colclough |
| †R.L. Norster | R.L. Norster | †S. Bainbridge | S. Bainbridge |
| J. Squire | J.B. O'Driscoll | †J.H. Calder | J.B. O'Driscoll |
| †I.A.M. Paxton | I.A.M. Paxton¹ | I.A.M. Paxton | I.A.M. Paxton |
| †P.J. Winterbottom | P.J. Winterbottom | P.J. Winterbottom | P.J. Winterbottom |
| | | | |
| Christchurch | Wellington | Dunedin | Auckland |
| LOST 12-16 | LOST 0-9 | LOST 8-15 | LOST 6-38 |
| | | | |
| NZ: 3pg 1dg 1t | NZ: 1g 1pg | NZ: 1g 3pg | NZ: 4g 2pg 2t |
| BI: 3pg 1dg | BI: nil | BI: 2t | BI: 2pg |
| | | | |
| 4 Jun. 1983 | 18 Jun. 1983 | 2 Jul. 1983 | 16 Jul. 1983 |
| ¹Rep. by †R.J. Laidlaw | ¹Rep. by †J.R. Beattie | | ¹Rep. by R.A. Ackerman |
| | | | ²Rep. by H.P. MacNeill |

Ciaran Fitzgerald, Irish captain and skipper of the 1983 Lions, had the misfortune to lead his side to a Test whitewash in New Zealand, only the second time in 100 years of tours that a British team had lost every Test of a series overseas.

In the first three Tests the story of the Lions' play was of missed chances. There were good showings by a competent pack in the first Test, but the backs completely failed to capitalise upon a stream of very good possession. In the second Test the Lions were unable to take advantage of a stiff wind in the second half, and though they actually led for a stage of the third international, the powerful New Zealanders had Hewson to fall back on to kick them to victory. At Auckland the tourists were completely outclassed, however, and defeat by 32 points was the biggest-ever losing points margin suffered by a British side in an international.

On the credit side the party was a happy one well-led by Willie John McBride, the manager. The players were good ambassadors, though McBride hit the nail on the head when he said that the tour was too brief for the itinerary set. The Lions had 18 demanding games in too short a time, with a host of serious injuries to further complicate preparations for Test matches.

# BRITISH/IRISH COMBINED MATCH RECORDS

## Match Results 1891 to 1987

| Match | Date | Opponents | For T | C | D | P | Pts | Against T | C | D | P | Pts | Result | Venue | Captain |
|---|---|---|---|---|---|---|---|---|---|---|---|---|---|---|---|
| 1 | 30.7.1891 | S.Africa | 2 | 1 | — | — | 4 | — | — | — | — | 0 | Won | Port Elizabeth | W. E. Maclagan |
| 2 | 29.8.1891 | S.Africa | — | — | ★ | — | 3 | — | — | — | — | 0 | Won | Kimberley | W. E. Maclagan |
| 3 | 5.9.1891 | S.Africa | 2 | 1 | — | — | 4 | — | — | — | — | 0 | Won | Cape Town | W. E. Maclagan |
| 4 | 30.7.1896 | S.Africa | 2 | 1 | — | — | 8 | — | — | — | — | 0 | Won | Port Elizabeth | T. J. Crean |
| 5 | 22.8.1896 | S.Africa | 3 | 2 | 1 | — | 17 | 2 | 1 | — | — | 8 | Won | Johannesburg | J. Hammond |
| 6 | 29.8.1896 | S.Africa | 1 | 1 | 1 | — | 9 | 1 | — | — | — | 3 | Won | Kimberley | T. J. Crean |
| 7 | 5.9.1896 | S.Africa | — | — | — | — | 0 | 1 | 1 | — | — | 5 | Lost | Cape Town | J. Hammond |
| 8 | 24.6.1899 | Australia | 1 | — | — | — | 3 | 3 | 2 | — | — | 13 | Lost | Sydney | M. M. Mullineaux |
| 9 | 22.7.1899 | Australia | 3 | 1 | — | — | 11 | — | — | — | — | 0 | Won | Brisbane | F. M. Stout |
| 10 | 5.8.1899 | Australia | 3 | 1 | — | — | 11 | 2 | 2 | — | — | 10 | Won | Sydney | F. M. Stout |
| 11 | 12.8.1899 | Australia | 2 | 2 | — | 1 | 13 | — | — | — | — | 0 | Won | Sydney | F. M. Stout |
| 12 | 26.8.1903 | S.Africa | 2 | 2 | — | — | 10 | 2 | 2 | — | — | 10 | Drawn | Johannesburg | M. C. Morrison |
| 13 | 5.9.1903 | S.Africa | — | — | — | — | 0 | — | — | — | — | 0 | Drawn | Kimberley | M. C. Morrison |
| 14 | 12.9.1903 | S.Africa | — | — | — | — | 0 | 2 | 1 | — | — | 8 | Lost | Cape Town | M. C. Morrison |
| 15 | 2.7.1904 | Australia | 3 | 2 | 1 | — | 17 | — | — | — | — | 0 | Won | Sydney | D. R. Bedell-Sivright |
| 16 | 23.7.1904 | Australia | 3 | — | 1★ | — | 17 | 1 | — | — | — | 3 | Won | Brisbane | E. Morgan |
| 17 | 30.7.1904 | Australia | 4 | 2 | — | — | 16 | — | — | — | — | 0 | Won | Sydney | E. Morgan |
| 18 | 13.8.1904 | N.Z. | — | — | — | 1 | 3 | 2 | — | 1 | — | 9 | Lost | Wellington | E. Morgan |
| 19 | 6.6.1908 | N.Z. | 1 | 1 | — | — | 5 | 7 | 4 | — | 1 | 32 | Lost | Dunedin | A. F. Harding |
| 20 | 27.6.1908 | N.Z. | 1 | — | — | — | 3 | 1 | — | 1 | — | 3 | Drawn | Wellington | A. F. Harding |
| 21 | 25.7.1908 | N.Z. | — | — | — | — | 0 | 9 | 1 | — | — | 29 | Lost | Auckland | A. F. Harding |
| 22 | 6.8.1910 | S.Africa | 2 | — | 1 | — | 10 | 4 | 1 | — | — | 14 | Lost | Kimberley | J. P. Jones |
| 23 | 27.8.1910 | S.Africa | 2 | 1 | — | — | 8 | 1 | — | — | — | 3 | Won | Port Elizabeth | T. Smyth |
| 24 | 3.9.1910 | S.Africa | 1 | 1 | — | — | 5 | 4 | 3 | — | 1 | 21 | Lost | Cape Town | T. Smyth |
| 25 | 16.8.1924 | S.Africa | 1 | — | — | — | 3 | 1 | — | 1 | — | 7 | Lost | Durban | R. Cove-Smith |
| 26 | 23.8.1924 | S.Africa | — | — | — | — | 0 | 4 | 1 | — | 1 | 17 | Lost | Johannesburg | R. Cove-Smith |
| 27 | 13.9.1924 | S.Africa | 1 | — | — | — | 3 | 1 | — | — | — | 3 | Drawn | Port Elizabeth | R. Cove-Smith |
| 28 | 20.9.1924 | S.Africa | 2 | — | — | 1 | 9 | 4 | — | 1 | — | 16 | Lost | Cape Town | R. Cove-Smith |
| 29 | 21.6.1930 | N.Z. | 2 | — | — | — | 6 | 1 | — | — | — | 3 | Won | Dunedin | C. D. Aarvold |
| 30 | 5.7.1930 | N.Z. | 2 | 2 | — | — | 10 | 2 | 2 | ★ | — | 13 | Lost | Christchurch | F. D. Prentice |
| 31 | 26.7.1930 | N.Z. | 2 | 2 | — | — | 10 | 3 | 1 | 1 | — | 15 | Lost | Auckland | C. D. Aarvold |
| 32 | 9.8.1930 | N.Z. | 1 | 1 | — | 1 | 8 | 6 | 2 | — | — | 22 | Lost | Wellington | C. D. Aarvold |
| 33 | 30.8.1930 | Australia | 1 | 1 | — | — | 5 | 2 | — | — | — | 6 | Lost | Sydney | F. D. Prentice |
| 34 | 6.8.1938 | S.Africa | — | — | — | 4 | 12 | 4 | 4 | — | 2 | 26 | Lost | Johannesburg | S. Walker |
| 35 | 3.9.1938 | S.Africa | 1 | — | — | — | 3 | 3 | 2 | — | 2 | 19 | Lost | Port Elizabeth | S. Walker |
| 36 | 10.9.1938 | S.Africa | 4 | 1 | 1 | 1 | 21 | 3 | 2 | — | 1 | 16 | Won | Cape Town | S. Walker |
| 37 | 27.5.1950 | N.Z. | 2 | — | — | 1 | 9 | 2 | — | — | 1 | 9 | Drawn | Dunedin | K. D. Mullen |
| 38 | 10.6.1950 | N.Z. | — | — | — | — | 0 | 2 | 1 | — | — | 8 | Lost | Christchurch | K. D. Mullen |
| 39 | 1.7.1950 | N.Z. | — | — | — | 1 | 3 | 1 | — | 1 | — | 6 | Lost | Wellington | B. L. Williams |
| 40 | 29.7.1950 | N.Z. | 1 | 1 | — | 1 | 8 | 2 | 1 | 1 | — | 11 | Lost | Auckland | B. L. Williams |
| 41 | 19.8.1950 | Australia | 2 | 2 | 1 | 2 | 19 | — | — | — | 2 | 6 | Won | Brisbane | B. L. Williams |
| 42 | 26.8.1950 | Australia | 5 | 3 | — | 1 | 24 | 1 | — | — | — | 3 | Won | Sydney | K. D. Mullen |
| 43 | 6.8.1955 | S.Africa | 5 | 4 | — | — | 23 | 4 | 2 | — | 2 | 22 | Won | Johannesburg | R. H. Thompson |
| 44 | 20.8.1955 | S.Africa | 2 | — | — | 1 | 9 | 7 | 2 | — | — | 25 | Lost | Cape Town | R. H. Thompson |
| 45 | 3.9.1955 | S.Africa | 1 | — | 1 | 1 | 9 | — | — | — | 2 | 6 | Won | Pretoria | C. I. Morgan |
| 46 | 24.9.1955 | S.Africa | 2 | 1 | — | — | 8 | 5 | 2 | 1 | — | 22 | Lost | Port Elizabeth | R. H. Thompson |
| 47 | 6.6.1959 | Australia | 2 | 1 | 1 | 2 | 17 | — | — | — | 2 | 6 | Won | Brisbane | A. R. Dawson |
| 48 | 13.6.1959 | Australia | 5 | 3 | — | 1 | 24 | — | — | — | 1 | 3 | Won | Sydney | A. R. Dawson |
| 49 | 18.7.1959 | N.Z. | 4 | 1 | — | 1 | 17 | — | — | — | 6 | 18 | Lost | Dunedin | A. R. Dawson |
| 50 | 15.8.1959 | N.Z. | 1 | 1 | — | 1 | 8 | 3 | 1 | — | — | 11 | Lost | Wellington | A. R. Dawson |
| 51 | 29.8.1959 | N.Z. | 1 | 1 | — | 1 | 8 | 4 | 2 | 1 | 1 | 22 | Lost | Christchurch | A. R. Dawson |
| 52 | 19.9.1959 | N.Z. | 3 | — | — | — | 9 | — | — | — | 2 | 6 | Won | Auckland | A. R. Dawson |
| 53 | 23.6.1962 | S.Africa | 1 | — | — | — | 3 | 1 | — | — | — | 3 | Drawn | Johannesburg | A. R. Smith |
| 54 | 21.7.1962 | S.Africa | — | — | — | — | 0 | 1 | — | — | 1 | 3 | Lost | Durban | A. R. Smith |
| 55 | 4.8.1962 | S.Africa | — | — | 1 | — | 3 | 1 | 1 | — | 1 | 8 | Lost | Cape Town | A. R. Smith |
| 56 | 25.8.1962 | S.Africa | 3 | 1 | — | 1 | 14 | 6 | 5 | — | 2 | 34 | Lost | Bloemfontein | R. E. G. Jeeps |
| 57 | 28.5.1966 | Australia | 2 | 1 | — | 1 | 11 | 1 | 1 | — | 1 | 8 | Won | Sydney | M. J. Campbell-Lamerton |
| 58 | 4.6.1966 | Australia | 5 | 5 | 1 | 1 | 31 | — | — | — | — | 0 | Won | Brisbane | M. J. Campbell-Lamerton |
| 59 | 16.7.1966 | N.Z. | — | — | — | 1 | 3 | 3 | 1 | 1 | 2 | 20 | Lost | Dunedin | M. J. Campbell-Lamerton |
| 60 | 6.8.1966 | N.Z. | — | — | 1 | 3 | 12 | 3 | 2 | — | 1 | 16 | Lost | Wellington | D. Watkins |
| 61 | 27.8.1966 | N.Z. | 2 | — | — | — | 6 | 3 | 2 | — | 2 | 19 | Lost | Christchurch | M. J. Campbell-Lamerton |
| 62 | 10.9.1966 | N.Z. | 2 | 1 | — | 1 | 11 | 4 | 3 | 1 | 1 | 24 | Lost | Auckland | D. Watkins |
| 63 | 8.6.1968 | S.Africa | 1 | 1 | — | 5 | 20 | 3 | 2 | — | 4 | 25 | Lost | Pretoria | T. J. Kiernan |
| 64 | 22.6.1968 | S.Africa | — | — | — | 2 | 6 | — | — | — | 2 | 6 | Drawn | Port Elizabeth | T. J. Kiernan |
| 65 | 13.7.1968 | S.Africa | — | — | — | 2 | 6 | 1 | 1 | — | 2 | 11 | Lost | Cape Town | T. J. Kiernan |
| 66 | 27.7.1968 | S.Africa | — | — | — | 2 | 6 | 4 | 2 | 1 | — | 19 | Lost | Johannesburg | T. J. Kiernan |

*★ in the drop-goal column denotes a goal from a mark*

| Match | Date | Opponents | T | C | D | P | Pts | T | C | D | P | Pts | Result | Venue | Captain |
|-------|------|-----------|---|---|---|---|-----|---|---|---|---|-----|--------|-------|---------|
| | | | | | *For* | | | | | *Against* | | | | | |
| 67 | 26.6.1971 | N.Z. | 1 | — | — | 2 | 9 | — | — | — | 1 | 3 | Won | Dunedin | S. J. Dawes |
| 68 | 10.7.1971 | N.Z. | 2 | — | 1 | 1 | 12 | 5 | 2 | — | 1 | 22 | Lost | Christchurch | S. J. Dawes |
| 69 | 31.7.1971 | N.Z. | 2 | 2 | 1 | — | 13 | 1 | — | — | — | 3 | Won | Wellington | S. J. Dawes |
| 70 | 14.8.1971 | N.Z. | 1 | 1 | 1 | 2 | 14 | 2 | 1 | — | 2 | 14 | Drawn | Auckland | S. J. Dawes |
| 71 | 8.6.1974 | S.Africa | — | — | 1 | 3 | 12 | — | — | 1 | — | 3 | Won | Cape Town | W. J. McBride |
| 72 | 22.6.1974 | S.Africa | 5 | 1 | 1 | 1 | 28 | — | — | 1 | 2 | 9 | Won | Pretoria | W. J. McBride |
| 73 | 13.7.1974 | S.Africa | 3 | 1 | 2 | 2 | 26 | — | — | — | 3 | 9 | Won | Port Elizabeth | W. J. McBride |
| 74 | 27.7.1974 | S.Africa | 2 | 1 | — | 1 | 13 | 1 | — | — | 3 | 13 | Drawn | Johannesburg | W. J. McBride |
| 75 | 18.6.1977 | N.Z. | — | — | — | 4 | 12 | 3 | 2 | — | — | 16 | Lost | Wellington | P. Bennett |
| 76 | 9.7.1977 | N.Z. | 1 | — | — | 3 | 13 | — | — | — | 3 | 9 | Won | Christchurch | P. Bennett |
| 77 | 30.7.1977 | N.Z. | 1 | — | — | 1 | 7 | 2 | 1 | 1 | 2 | 19 | Lost | Dunedin | P. Bennett |
| 78 | 13.8.1977 | N.Z. | 1 | 1 | — | 1 | 9 | 1 | — | — | 2 | 10 | Lost | Auckland | P. Bennett |
| 79 | 31.5.1980 | S.Africa | 1 | — | 1 | 5 | 22 | 5 | 3 | — | — | 26 | Lost | Cape Town | W. B. Beaumont |
| 80 | 14.6.1980 | S.Africa | 2 | 1 | — | 3 | 19 | 4 | 2 | — | 2 | 26 | Lost | Bloemfontein | W. B. Beaumont |
| 81 | 28.6.1980 | S.Africa | 1 | — | — | 2 | 10 | 1 | 1 | 1 | 1 | 12 | Lost | Port Elizabeth | W. B. Beaumont |
| 82 | 12.7.1980 | S.Africa | 3 | 1 | — | 1 | 17 | 1 | — | — | 3 | 13 | Won | Pretoria | W. B. Beaumont |
| 83 | 4.6.1983 | N.Z. | — | — | 1 | 3 | 12 | 1 | — | 1 | 3 | 16 | Lost | Christchurch | C. F. Fitzgerald |
| 84 | 18.6.1983 | N.Z. | — | — | — | — | 0 | 1 | 1 | — | 1 | 9 | Lost | Wellington | C. F. Fitzgerald |
| 85 | 2.7.1983 | N.Z. | 2 | — | — | — | 8 | 1 | 1 | — | 3 | 15 | Lost | Dunedin | C. F. Fitzgerald |
| 86 | 16.7.1983 | N.Z. | — | — | — | 2 | 6 | 6 | 4 | — | 2 | 38 | Lost | Auckland | C. F. Fitzgerald |

# MATCH RECORDS

## MOST CONSECUTIVE MATCHES WON

| | |
|---|---|
| 6 | *1891* SA 1,2,3   *1896* SA 1,2,3 |
| 3 | *1899* A 2,3,4 |
| 3 | *1904* A 1,2,3 |
| 3 | *1950* A 1,2   *1955* SA 1 |
| 3 | *1974* SA 1,2,3 |

## MOST CONSECUTIVE MATCHES WITHOUT DEFEAT

| Matches | Wins | Draws | Period |
|---------|------|-------|--------|
| 6 | 6 | 0 | 1891 to 1896 |
| 6 | 4 | 2 | 1971 to 1974 |
| 5 | 3 | 2 | 1899 to 1903 |

## MOST CONSECUTIVE MATCHES WITHOUT CONCEDING A TRY

| | |
|---|---|
| 4 | between 1891 and 1896 |
| 3 | in 1959 |
| 3 | in 1974 |

## MOST CONSECUTIVE MATCHES WITHOUT CONCEDING A SCORE

| | |
|---|---|
| 4 | between 1891 and 1896 |

# MOST POINTS IN A MATCH

## By the team

| Pts | Opponents | Venue | Seasons |
|---|---|---|---|
| 31 | Australia | Brisbane | 1966 |
| 28 | South Africa | Pretoria | 1974 |
| 26 | South Africa | Port Elizabeth | 1974 |
| 24 | Australia | Sydney | 1959 |
| 24 | Australia | Sydney | 1950 |
| 23 | South Africa | Johannesburg | 1955 |
| 22 | South Africa | Cape Town | 1980 |
| 21 | South Africa | Cape Town | 1938 |
| 20 | South Africa | Pretoria | 1968 |

## By a player

| Pts | Player | Opponents | Venue | Season |
|---|---|---|---|---|
| 18 | A.J.P. Ward | South Africa | Cape Town | 1980 |
| 17 | T.J. Kiernan | South Africa | Pretoria | 1968 |
| 16 | B.L. Jones | Australia | Brisbane | 1950 |
| 13 | S. Wilson | Australia | Brisbane | 1966 |
| 12 | S.O. Campbell | New Zealand | Christchurch | 1983 |
| 11 | P.F. Bush | Australia | Brisbane | 1904 |
| 10 | C.Y. Adamson | Australia | Sydney | 1899 |
| 10 | B. John | New Zealand | Wellington | 1971 |

# MOST TRIES IN A MATCH

## By the team

| T | Opponents | Venue | Season |
|---|---|---|---|
| 5 | South Africa | Pretoria | 1974 |
| 5 | Australia | Sydney | 1950 |
| 5 | South Africa | Johannesburg | 1955 |
| 5 | Australia | Sydney | 1959 |
| 5 | Australia | Brisbane | 1966 |
| 4 | Australia | Sydney | 1904 |
| 4 | South Africa | Cape Town | 1938 |
| 4 | New Zealand | Dunedin | 1959 |

## By a player

| T | Player | Opponents | Venue | Season |
|---|---|---|---|---|
| 2 | A.M. Bucher | Australia | Sydney | 1899 |
| 2 | W.M. Llewellyn | Australia | Sydney | 1904 |
| 2 | C.D. Aarvold | New Zealand | Christchurch | 1930 |
| 2 | J.E. Nelson | Australia | Sydney | 1950 |
| 2 | M.J. Price | Australia | Sydney | 1959 |
| 2 | M.J. Price | New Zealand | Dunedin | 1959 |
| 2 | D.K. Jones | Australia | Brisbane | 1966 |
| 2 | T.G.R. Davies | New Zealand | Christchurch | 1971 |
| 2 | J.J. Williams | South Africa | Pretoria | 1974 |
| 2 | J.J. Williams | South Africa | Port Elizabeth | 1974 |

# MOST CONVERSIONS IN A MATCH

## By the team

| C | Opponents | Venue | Season |
|---|---|---|---|
| 5 | Australia | Brisbane | 1966 |
| 4 | South Africa | Johannesburg | 1955 |
| 3 | Australia | Sydney | 1950 |
| 3 | Australia | Sydney | 1959 |

## By a player

| C | Player | Opponents | Venue | Season |
|---|--------|-----------|-------|--------|
| 5 | S. Wilson | Australia | Brisbane | 1966 |
| 4 | A. Cameron | South Africa | Johannesburg | 1955 |
| 2 | J.F. Byrne | South Africa | Johannesburg | 1896 |
| 2 | C.Y. Adamson | Australia | Sydney | 1899 |
| 2 | J.I. Gillespie | South Africa | Johannesburg | 1903 |
| 2 | F.D. Prentice | New Zealand | Christchurch | 1930 |
| 2 | B.L. Jones | Australia | Brisbane | 1950 |
| 2 | J.D. Robins | Australia | Sydney | 1950 |
| 2 | D. Hewitt | Australia | Sydney | 1959 |
| 2 | B. John | New Zealand | Wellington | 1971 |

# MOST DROPPED GOALS IN A MATCH

## By the team

| DG | | Opponents | Venue | Season |
|----|---|-----------|-------|--------|
| 2 | | South Africa | Port Elizabeth | 1974 |

## By a player

| DG | Player | Opponents | Venue | Season |
|----|--------|-----------|-------|--------|
| 2 | P. Bennett | South Africa | Port Elizabeth | 1974 |

# MOST PENALTY GOALS IN A MATCH

## By the team

| PG | | Opponents | Venue | Season |
|----|---|-----------|-------|--------|
| 5 | | South Africa | Pretoria | 1968 |
| 5 | | South Africa | Cape Town | 1980 |
| 4 | | South Africa | Johannesburg | 1938 |
| 4 | | New Zealand | Wellington | 1977 |
| 3 | | New Zealand | Wellington | 1966 |
| 3 | | South Africa | Cape Town | 1974 |
| 3 | | New Zealand | Christchurch | 1977 |
| 3 | | South Africa | Bloemfontein | 1980 |
| 3 | | New Zealand | Christchurch | 1983 |

## By a player

| PG | Player | Opponents | Venue | Season |
|----|--------|-----------|-------|--------|
| 5 | T.J. Kiernan | South Africa | Pretoria | 1968 |
| 5 | A.J.P. Ward | South Africa | Cape Town | 1980 |
| 3 | V.G.J. Jenkins | South Africa | Johannesburg | 1938 |
| 3 | S. Wilson | New Zealand | Wellington | 1966 |
| 3 | P. Bennett | New Zealand | Wellington | 1977 |
| 3 | P. Bennett | New Zealand | Christchurch | 1977 |
| 3 | S.O. Campbell | New Zealand | Christchurch | 1983 |

# GOALS FROM MARKS

| * | Player | Opponents | Venue | Season |
|---|--------|-----------|-------|--------|
| 1 | W.G. Mitchell | South Africa | Kimberley | 1891 |
| 1 | P.F. Bush | Australia | Brisbane | 1904 |

# TRY ON DEBUT

| Player | Opponents | Venue | Season |
|--------|-----------|-------|--------|
| R.L. Aston | South Africa | Port Elizabeth | 1891 |
| T. Whittaker | South Africa | Port Elizabeth | 1891 |
| L.Q. Bulger | South Africa | Port Elizabeth | 1896 |
| W.J. Carey | South Africa | Port Elizabeth | 1896 |
| E.G. Nicholls | Australia | Sydney | 1899 |
| W.T.C. Cave | South Africa | Johannesburg | 1903 |
| R.T. Skrimshire | South Africa | Johannesburg | 1903 |
| P.F. Bush | Australia | Sydney | 1904 |
| W.M. Llewellyn | Australia | Sydney | 1904 |
| R.A. Gibbs | New Zealand | Dunedin | 1908 |
| A.R. Foster | South Africa | Kimberley | 1910 |
| J.A. Spoors | South Africa | Kimberley | 1910 |
| H. Whitley | South Africa | Durban | 1924 |
| W. Cunningham | South Africa | Port Elizabeth | 1924 |
| J.C. Morley | New Zealand | Dunedin | 1930 |
| J.S.R. Reeve | New Zealand | Dunedin | 1930 |
| P.L. Duff | South Africa | Port Elizabeth | 1938 |
| K.J. Jones | New Zealand | Dunedin | 1950 |
| J.W. Kyle | New Zealand | Dunedin | 1950 |
| C.I. Morgan | South Africa | Johannesburg | 1955 |
| A.C. Pedlow | South Africa | Johannesburg | 1955 |
| J. Butterfield | South Africa | Johannesburg | 1955 |
| A.J.F. O'Reilly | South Africa | Johannesburg | 1955 |
| J.T. Greenwood | South Africa | Johannesburg | 1955 |
| G.K. Smith | Australia | Brisbane | 1959 |
| J.R.C. Young | New Zealand | Wellington | 1959 |
| D.K. Jones | South Africa | Johannesburg | 1962 |
| R.C. Cowan | South Africa | Bloemfontein | 1962 |
| K.W. Kennedy | Australia | Sydney | 1966 |
| R.J. McLoughlin | Australia | Sydney | 1966 |
| J. McLauchlan | New Zealand | Dunedin | 1971 |
| J.Y. Rutherford | New Zealand | Dunedin | 1983 |

# CAPTAIN ON INTERNATIONAL DEBUT

| Player | Opponents | Venue | Season |
|--------|-----------|-------|--------|
| W.E. Maclagan | South Africa | Port Elizabeth | 1891 |
| T.J. Crean | South Africa | Port Elizabeth | 1896 |
| M.C. Morrison | South Africa | Johannesburg | 1903 |
| D.R. Bedell-Sivright | Australia | Sydney | 1904 |
| T. Smyth | South Africa | Port Elizabeth | 1910 |
| R. Cove-Smith | South Africa | Durban | 1924 |
| C.D. Aarvold | New Zealand | Dunedin | 1930 |
| F.D. Prentice | New Zealand | Christchurch | 1930 |
| S. Walker | South Africa | Johannesburg | 1938 |
| K.D. Mullen | New Zealand | Dunedin | 1950 |
| R.H. Thompson | South Africa | Johannesburg | 1955 |
| A.R. Dawson | Australia | Brisbane | 1959 |
| A.R. Smith | South Africa | Johannesburg | 1962 |
| S.J. Dawes | New Zealand | Dunedin | 1971 |
| C.F. Fitzgerald | New Zealand | Christchurch | 1983 |

# TRIES BY FULL-BACKS

| Player | Opponents | Venue | Season |
|--------|-----------|-------|--------|
| A.B. O'Brien | Australia | Brisbane | 1904 |
| B.L. Jones | Australia | Brisbane | 1950 |
| A.R. Irvine | South Africa | Pretoria | 1980 |

# ALL THE POINTS FOR BRITISH/IRISH
## IN A MATCH
### (where more than one scoring action is involved)

| Pts | Player | Opponents | Venue | Season |
|-----|--------|-----------|-------|--------|
| 12 | S.O. Campbell | New Zealand | Christchurch | 1983 |
| 9 | D.W. Morgan | New Zealand | Auckland | 1977 |
| 6 | T.J. Kiernan | South Africa | Port Elizabeth | 1968 |
| 6 | T.J. Kiernan | South Africa | Cape Town | 1968 |
| 6 | T.J. Kiernan | South Africa | Johannesburg | 1968 |

# INDIVIDUAL RECORDS

## LONGEST CAREER SPAN

| Seasons | Player | Caps | Career Span |
|---|---|---|---|
| 13 | W.J. McBride | 17 | 1962-74 |

## MOST CONSECUTIVE CAPS IN A CAREER

| Caps | Player | Opponents |
|---|---|---|
| 15 | W.J. McBride | 1966 NZ 2,3,4  1968 SA 1,2,3,4  1971 NZ 1,2,3,4  1974 SA 1,2,3,4 |
| 12 | C.M.H. Gibson | 1966 NZ 1,2,3,4  1968 SA 1 (R),2,3,4  1971 NZ 1,2,3,4 |
| 12 | G. Price | 1977 NZ 1,2,3,4  1980 SA 1,2,3,4  1983 NZ 1,2,3,4 |

## MOST CAPS IN A CAREER

| Caps | Player | Career Span |
|---|---|---|
| 17 | W.J. McBride | 1962 to 1974 |
| 13 | R.E.G. Jeeps | 1955 to 1962 |
| 12 | C.M.H. Gibson | 1966 to 1971 |
| 12 | G. Price | 1977 to 1983 |
| 10 | A.J.F. O'Reilly | 1955 to 1959 |
| 10 | R.H. Williams | 1955 to 1959 |
| 10 | G.O. Edwards | 1968 to 1974 |

## MOST POINTS IN A CAREER

| Pts | Player | Matches | Career Span |
|---|---|---|---|
| 44 | P. Bennett | 8 | 1974 to 1977 |
| 35 | T.J. Kiernan | 5 | 1962 to 1968 |
| 30 | S. Wilson | 5 | 1966 |
| 30 | B. John | 5 | 1968 to 1971 |
| 28 | A.R. Irvine | 9 | 1974 to 1980 |
| 26 | B.L. Jones | 3 | 1950 |
| 26 | S.O. Campbell | 7 | 1980 to 1983 |
| 20 | P.F. Bush | 4 | 1904 |
| 20 | J.J. Williams | 7 | 1974 to 1977 |

## MOST TRIES IN A CAREER

| T | Player | Matches | Career Span |
|---|---|---|---|
| 6 | A.J.F. O'Reilly | 10 | 1955 to 1959 |
| 5 | J.J. Williams | 7 | 1974 to 1977 |
| 4 | W.M. Llewellyn | 4 | 1904 |
| 4 | M.J. Price | 5 | 1959 |

## MOST CONVERSIONS IN A CAREER

| C | Player | Matches | Career Span |
|---|---|---|---|
| 6 | S. Wilson | 5 | 1966 |
| 4 | J.F. Byrne | 4 | 1896 |
| 4 | C.Y. Adamson | 4 | 1899 |
| 4 | B.L. Jones | 3 | 1950 |
| 4 | A. Cameron | 2 | 1955 |

## MOST DROPPED GOALS IN A CAREER

| DG | Player | Matches | Career Span |
|---|---|---|---|
| 2 | P.F. Bush | 4 | 1904 |
| 2 | D. Watkins | 6 | 1966 |
| 2 | B. John | 5 | 1968 to 1971 |
| 2 | P. Bennett | 8 | 1974 to 1977 |

## MOST PENALTY GOALS IN A CAREER

| PG | Player | Matches | Career Span |
|---|---|---|---|
| 11 | T.J. Kiernan | 5 | 1962 to 1968 |
| 10 | P. Bennett | 8 | 1974 to 1977 |
| 7 | S.O. Campbell | 7 | 1980 to 1983 |
| 6 | S. Wilson | 5 | 1966 |
| 6 | A.R. Irvine | 9 | 1974 to 1980 |
| 5 | B. John | 5 | 1968 to 1971 |
| 5 | A.J.P. Ward | 1 | 1980 |
| 4 | B.L. Jones | 3 | 1950 |

## MOST MATCHES AS CAPTAIN

|   |   |   |
|---|---|---|
| 6 | A.R. Dawson | (3 victories) |

# INTERNATIONAL REFEREES

The first international matches were conducted without referees. Two umpires, one supplied by each of the participating nations, were given responsibility for patrolling the touchlines and ensuring that the game was played within the Laws. It was not until 1876 that referees joined the players on the pitch at internationals, and invariably these adjudicators, supported by two umpires, were senior members of the Rugby Union Committee of the nation hosting the match. Arthur Guillemard, for instance, refereed all of England's home internationals during the first three years of his Presidency of the RFU (1878-1881).

Following England's match against Scotland in 1881, however, Guillemard criticised the Scottish President, D.H. Watson, for some peculiar refereeing decisions in the game at Raeburn Place. Three minutes from no-side, with England leading, a Scottish forward scored a try under the posts, no player on the English side challenging him due to an impression that he was off-side. The try was converted and Scotland escaped from the match with a draw.

Guillemard's last year as President of the RFU was 1881-82, but his feelings concerning that 1881 Calcutta Cup game remained strong. Rather than pursue a pointless argument with the Scots, he took the positive (and then novel) step of asking H.L. Robinson, a former Dublin University three-quarter who was an Irish selector, to take charge of England's next home international. The first international to be controlled by a neutral referee was thus the Calcutta Cup contest at Manchester in 1882. Scotland's victory had a significant edge to it, for the result was the first win by the visiting side in an England-Scotland encounter. Every subsequent Calcutta Cup game has been controlled by a neutral referee, and it is interesting to note that until 1893 the honour was always bestowed on an Irishman.

When possible, neutral referees have always been in control for internationals in Britain, Ireland and France ever since. Mr Rowland Hill, a respected RFU Committee member for nearly fifty years, took charge of the Scotland-Wales game of 1883, the first of his eleven international appearances, and his total was only surpassed before the Great War by Billy Williams, another RFU member. Williams was the man credited for the acquisition and development of the Twickenham site which became the game's headquarters. He controlled a number of the early French home internationals during an era when former players traditionally turned out to referee big games. Such players, of course, have not always become the best referees: Gwyn Nicholls, the former Welsh centre who was first appointed to officiate at the 1909 Calcutta Cup game, for example, left the field saying "wasn't I awful", and never again took control at international level.

The tradition for former international players becoming top referees continued between the wars, and two of the game's outstanding officials in this period were Tommy Vile and Dr J.R. Wheeler, ex-international half-backs. Perhaps the skills and senses halves develop at the top level are qualities which later enable them to become appreciated as referees. Certainly the majority of former internationals who successfully made the transition to refereeing at senior level have been gifted half-backs.

Another noted referee to emerge during the period between the wars was Albert Freethy of Neath. An official respected by players and spectators, he will always be remembered as the first man to dismiss a player in an international. His action clearly did not make him unpopular, as some careless writers have previously asserted. Freethy refereed eighteen major internationals between 1923 and 1931, and his total included every English match in Paris between the wars (except 1921), as well as the France-United States Olympic final of 1924.

Cyril Gadney (whose brother captained England), M.A. Allan, Alan Bean, R.A. Beattie and Ivor David were among the leading officials of the late -1930s, and they had the unusual distinctions of refereeing at the top level both before and after the Second World War. By this time referees were graduating through various refereeing societies, which clearly defined a hierarchical progression to international level. In the 1950s and 1960s, therefore, it became extremely rare for a former leading player to succeed as a top-class referee. The societies captured their outstanding men young, usually recruiting players whose careers had been prematurely finished through injury. As a result, by the 1960s referees in internationals were relatively young men who were fitter than most of their predecessors. One of these new young men, Gwynne Walters of Wales, went on to become rugby's most "capped" referee, controlling 23 major internationals between 1959 and 1966. His contemporary, Kevin Kelleher of Ireland, also officiated in twenty-three matches and will be remembered for his dismissal of Colin Meads at Murrayfield in the Scotland-New Zealand international of 1967.

The picture in the Southern Hemisphere has been quite similar, though a major bone of contention for years was the impossibility of appointing neutral referees for overseas Test series. Matches on the early tours were often controlled by local officials appointed by the provincial or State authorities responsible for staging Tests (and thereby minimising travel expenses). Thus in Australia, for instance, it was invariably a Queensland referee who ran Tests at Brisbane, and a New South Wales official for the Sydney matches.

However, one or two interesting exceptions to this rule occurred on the pioneer tours by British sides. The first international on Australian soil, against Great Britain in 1899, was refereed by a New Zealander, "Gun" Garrard; whereas in South Africa in 1903 a Briton actually controlled the opening Test of the series. W.P. "Bill" Donaldson, who had played half-back for Scotland in the 1890s, refereed a Test in which *both* captains were also Scottish internationals! Mark Morrison was the leader of the British and a captain of Scotland, while Dr Frew, the South African skipper, had played for Scotland in 1901. Appropriately, the match was drawn.

As in Britain, many former inter-national players overseas rose to prominence as referees. H.H. Castens, former Oxford Blue and the man who captained South Africa in their first-ever Test (against Britain in 1891), went on to control the final Test of that series, while Eric Tindill, the 1936 All Black, created a record which is never likely to be equalled: in addition to playing and refereeing for New Zealand in rugby internationals, he also played Test cricket for New Zealand and umpired Test cricket matches.

The French, rugby's youngest International Board members, have figured prominently in the refereeing sphere of the game in the past twenty years. Georges Domercq and Francis Palmade have become as well known as John West and their British counterparts, but, before 1965, no French referee had been invited to control an international in Britain.

Cyril Rutherford, the Scottish-born administrator who did so much for French rugby in its infancy, appears as touch-judge in almost all French match programmes and team photographs until the late 1920s, and he did referee the France-England international of 1908. Jacques Muntz was the leading French official of the 1920s, and although he did not take charge of any Championship matches, he was invited in 1929 to referee the Four Nations match (England and Wales *v* Scotland and Ireland) at Twickenham, when the Rowland Hill Memorial Gates were opened. J-F Sampieri, Muntz's successor, was similarly honoured in 1959 when the Four Nations match at Twickenham celebrated the ground's Silver Jubilee.

It was only a fluke incident which led to French officials joining the rota for Home international matches. During the 1965 France-Wales game in Paris, Mr Gilliland was injured and unable to continue refereeing in the second half. As a result of a flip of a coin between the two touch-judges, Bernard Marie, a noted French referee, took over in the second half. Marie's calm authority and scrupulous impartiality in that half were followed by an invitation in 1966 for him to control the England-Ireland match at Twickenham. Ever since, Frenchmen have been in demand at international level.

In 1975 there was a move which was probably the most significant regarding international referees since the appointment of neutral officials in 1882. The rigid adherence to overseas referees for overseas Tests was broken in the short series between South Africa and France. Norman Sanson, the popular London Scottish referee, was invited to become the first overseas neutral official of modern times. It has now become accepted practice for neutral officials to referee in overseas Tests, and to balance the experience gained by British referees travelling to the Southern Hemisphere, since 1983 the Home Unions and France have

been happy to invite overseas officials to control matches in the Five Nations Championship. More recently too there has been an insistence that touch-judges at internationals should be top-class officials, from the same panel as the nation providing the referee for an international, just in case a referee becomes injured and is required to retire. Nowadays internationals are thus in the hands of neutral referees who are supported and helped by neutral touch-judges.

The list which follows shows the referees who have controlled major international matches (i.e. games for which a member country of the International Board has awarded caps) since 1876, when referees were first appointed.

*Note:* Internationals controlled during a Northern Hemisphere winter are labelled 1986-87, whereas the Southern Hemisphere winters are shown as 1986. Where a referee has officiated at more than one Test of a series, numbers are shown in parentheses.

| Season | Match | Referee |
|---|---|---|
| 1875-76 | I v E | Mr A. Combe (Ire.) |
| | E v S | Mr A. Rutter (Eng.) |
| 1876-77 | E v I | Mr A.G. Guillemard (Eng.) |
| | I v S | Mr A. Buchanan (Scot.) |
| | S v E | Mr W. Cross (Scot.) |
| 1877-78 | E v I | Mr A.G. Guillemard (Eng.) |
| | I v E | Mr E. Swainston (Eng.) |
| 1878-79 | I v S | Dr. J. Chiene (Scot.) |
| | S v E | Mr G.R. Fleming (Scot.) |
| | E v I | Mr A.G. Guillemard (Eng.) |
| 1879-80 | I v E | Mr G.P. Nugent (Ire.) |
| | S v I | Mr A. Buchanan (Scot.) |
| | E v S | Mr A.G. Guillemard (Eng.) |
| 1880-81 | E v I | Mr A.G. Guillemard (Eng.) |
| | E v W | Mr A.G. Guillemard (Eng.) |
| | I v S | Mr H.C. Kelly (Ire.) |
| | S v E | Mr D.H. Watson (Scot.) |
| 1881-82 | I v W | Mr W.J. Goulding (Ire.) |
| | I v E | Dr W.C. Neville (Ire.) |
| | S v I | Mr A.G. Petrie (Scot.) |
| | E v S | Mr H.L. Robinson (Ire.) |
| 1882-83 | W v E | Mr Herbert (Wales) |
| | S v W | Mr G.R. Hill (Eng.) |
| | E v I | Mr A.S. Pattison (Scot.) |
| | I v S | Mr H.C. Kelly (Ire.) |
| | S v E | Mr H.C. Kelly (Ire.) |
| 1883-84 | E v W | Mr J.A. Gardner (Scot.) |
| | W v S | Mr J.S. MacLaren (Eng.) |
| | I v E | Mr J.S. Lang (Scot.) |
| | S v I | Mr G.R. Hill (Eng.) |
| | E v S | Mr G. Scriven (Ire.) |
| | W v I | Mr G.R. Hill (Eng.) |
| 1884-85 | W v E | Mr C.P. Lewis (Wales) |
| | S v W | Mr G.R. Hill (Eng.) |
| | E v I | Mr H.S. Lyne (Wales) |
| | S v I | Mr H.C. Kelly (Ire.) |
| 1885-86 | E v W | Mr D.F. Moore (Ire.) |
| | W v S | Mr D.F. Moore (Ire.) |
| | I v E | Mr R. Mullock (Wales) |
| | S v I | Mr G.R. Hill (Eng.) |
| | S v E | Mr H.G. Cook (Ire.) |
| 1886-87 | W v E | Mr G.R. Hill (Eng.) |
| | I v E | Mr W.D. Phillips (Wales) |
| | I v S | Mr G.R. Hill (Eng.) |
| | S v W | Mr F.I. Currey (Eng.) |
| | E v S | Mr T.R. Lyle (Ire.) |
| | W v I | Mr J.A. Gardner (Scot.) |
| 1887-88 | W v S | Mr J. Chambers (Ire.) |
| | I v W | Mr G.R. Hill (Eng.) |
| | S v I | Mr J.S. MacLaren (Eng.) |
| 1888-89 | I v M | Mr J. Chambers (Ire.) |
| | W v M | Mr S. Mortimer (Eng.) |
| | S v W | Mr E. McAllister (Ire.) |
| | E v M | Mr G.R. Hill (Eng.) |
| | I v S | Mr W.D. Phillips (Wales) |
| | W v I | Mr A.R. Don Wauchope (Scot.) |
| 1889-90 | W v S | Mr E. McAllister (Ire.) |
| | E v W | Mr R.D. Rainie (Scot.) |
| | S v I | Mr H.L. Ashmore (Eng.) |
| | I v W | Mr F.W. Burnand (Eng.) |
| | S v E | Mr J. Chambers (Ire.) |
| | E v I | Mr A.R. Don Wauchope (Scot.) |
| 1890-91 | W v E | Mr R.D. Rainie (Scot.) |
| | I v E | Mr W.M. Douglas (Wales) |

| Season | Match | Referee |
|---|---|---|
| | S v W | Mr H.L. Ashmore (Eng.) |
| | I v S | Mr G.R. Hill (Eng.) |
| | E v S | Mr J. Chambers (Ire.) |
| | W v I | Mr A. Rowsell (Eng.) |
| 1891 | SA v GB | Dr Griffin (SA) |
| | SA v GB | Mr P.R. Frames (SA) |
| | SA v GB | Mr H.H. Castens (SA) |
| 1891-92 | E v W | Mr M.C. McEwan (Scot.) |
| | W v S | Mr J. Hodgson (Eng.) |
| | E v I | Mr J.A. Smith (Scot.) |
| | S v I | Mr H.L. Ashmore (Eng.) |
| | I v W | Mr E.B. Holmes (Eng.) |
| | S v E | Mr R.G. Warren (Ire.) |
| 1892-93 | W v E | Mr D.S. Morton (Scot.) |
| | I v E | Mr A.R. Don Wauchope (Scot.) |
| | S v W | Mr Humphreys (Eng.) |
| | I v S | Mr G.R. Hill (Eng.) |
| | E v S | Mr W.H. Wilkins (Wales) |
| | W v I | Mr Humphreys (Eng.) |
| 1893-94 | E v W | Mr J.A. Smith (Scot.) |
| | W v S | Mr E.B. Holmes (Eng.) |
| | E v I | Mr W.M. Douglas (Wales) |
| | I v S | Mr H.L. Ashmore (Eng.) |
| | S v E | Mr W.H. Wilkins (Wales) |
| | I v W | Mr R.D. Rainie (Scot.) |
| 1894-95 | W v E | Mr J.A. Smith (Scot.) |
| | S v W | Mr E.B. Holmes (Eng.) |
| | I v E | Mr D.G. Findlay (Scot.) |
| | S v I | Mr H.L. Ashmore (Eng.) |
| | E v S | Mr W.H. Wilkins (Wales) |
| | W v I | Mr E.B. Holmes (Eng.) |
| 1895-96 | E v W | Mr D.G. Findlay (Scot.) |
| | W v S | Mr G.H. Harnett (Eng.) |
| | E v I | Mr D.G. Findlay (Scot.) |
| | I v S | Mr E.B. Holmes (Eng.) |
| | I v W | Mr E.B. Holmes (Eng.) |
| | S v E | Mr W.M. Douglas (Wales) |
| 1896 | SA v GB | Mr H.B. Kemsley (SA) |
| | SA v GB | Mr G. Beves (SA) |
| | SA v GB | Mr W.M. Bissett (SA) |
| | SA v GB | Mr A.R. Richards (SA) |
| 1896-97 | W v E | Mr J.T. Magee (Ire.) |
| | I v E | Mr D.G. Findlay (Scot.) |
| | S v I | Mr E.B. Holmes (Eng.) |
| | E v S | Mr J.T. Magee (Ire.) |
| 1897-98 | E v I | Mr D.G. Findlay (Scot.) |
| | I v S | Mr E.T. Gurdon (Eng.) |
| | S v E | Mr J. Dodds (Ire.) |
| | I v W | Mr A. Turnbull (Scot.) |
| | E v W | Mr J.T. Magee (Ire.) |
| 1898-99 | W v E | Mr A. Turnbull (Scot.) |
| | I v E | Mr D.G. Findlay (Scot.) |
| | S v I | Mr E.T. Gurdon (Eng.) |
| | S v W | Mr M.G. Delany (Ire.) |
| | E v S | Mr J.T. Magee (Ire.) |
| | W v I | Mr A. Turnbull (Scot.) |
| 1899 | A v GB | Mr W.G. Garrard (NZ) |
| | A v GB | Mr W.H. Beattie (Aus.) |
| | A v GB(2) | Mr W.S. Corr (Aus.) |
| 1899-1900 | E v W | Mr A. Turnbull (Scot.) |
| | W v S | Mr A. Hartley (Eng.) |
| | E v I | Mr D.G. Findlay (Scot.) |
| | I v S | Dr Badger (Eng.) |
| | S v E | Mr M.G. Delany (Ire.) |
| | I v W | Mr A. Turnbull (Scot.) |

| 1900-01 | W v E | Mr A. Turnbull (Scot.) |
| | I v E | Mr D.G. Findlay (Scot.) |
| | S v W | Mr R.W. Jeffares (Ire.) |
| | S v I | Mr G.H. Harnett (Eng.) |
| | E v S | Mr R.W. Jeffares (Ire.) |
| | W v I | Mr G.H. Harnett (Eng.) |
| | | |
| 1901-02 | E v W | Mr R.W. Jeffares (Ire.) |
| | W v S | Mr P. Gilliard (Eng.) |
| | E v I | Mr R. Welsh (Scot.) |
| | I v S | Mr A. Hill (Eng.) |
| | I v W | Mr J.C. Findlay (Scot.) |
| | S v E | Mr F.M. Hamilton (Ire.) |
| | | |
| 1902-03 | W v E | Mr R. Welsh (Scot.) |
| | S v W | Mr E. Martelli (Ire.) |
| | I v E | Mr J.C. Findlay (Scot.) |
| | S v I | Mr F.H.R. Alderson (Eng.) |
| | W v I | Mr P. Coles (Eng.) |
| | E v S | Mr W.M. Douglas (Wales) |
| | | |
| 1903 | A v NZ | Dr R. Waugh (Aus.) |
| | SA v GB | Mr W.P. Donaldson (Scot.) |
| | SA v GB | Mr P.W. Day (SA) |
| | SA v GB | Mr J.H. Anderson (SA) |
| | | |
| 1903-04 | E v W | Mr J.C. Findlay (Scot.) |
| | W v S | Mr F. Nicholls (Eng.) |
| | E v I | Mr T. Williams (Wales) |
| | I v S | Mr W. Williams (Eng.) |
| | I v W | Mr J.C. Findlay (Scot.) |
| | S v E | Mr S. Lee (Ire.) |
| | | |
| 1904 | A v GB(2) | Mr T.G. Pauling (Aus.) |
| | A v GB | Mr W.H. Beattie (Aus.) |
| | NZ v GB | Mr F.T. Evans (NZ) |
| | | |
| 1904-05 | W v E | Mr C. Lefevre (Ire.) |
| | S v W | Mr G.H.B. Kennedy (Ire.) |
| | I v E | Mr R. Welsh (Scot.) |
| | S v I | Mr P. Coles (Eng.) |
| | W v I | Mr W. Williams (Eng.) |
| | E v S | Mr D.H. Bowen (Wales) |
| | | |
| 1905 | NZ v A | Mr J. Williams (NZ) |
| | | |
| 1905-06 | S v NZ | Mr W. Kennedy (Ire.) |
| | I v NZ | Mr J.C. Findlay (Scot.) |
| | E v NZ | Mr G. Evans (Eng.) |
| | W v NZ | Mr J.D. Dallas (Scot.) |
| | F v NZ | Mr L. Dedet (Fr.) |
| | E v W | Mr A. Jardine (Scot.) |
| | W v S | Mr J.W. Allen (Ire.) |
| | E v I | Mr A. Llewellyn (Wales) |
| | I v S | Mr V.H. Cartwright (Eng.) |
| | I v W | Dr J.W. Simpson (Scot.) |
| | S v E | Mr J.W. Allen (Ire.) |
| | F v E | Mr L. Dedet (Fr.) |
| | | |
| 1906-07 | S v SA | Mr H.H. Corley (Ire.) |
| | I v SA | Mr J.T. Tulloch (Scot.) |
| | W v SA | Mr A.O. Jones (Eng.) |
| | E v SA | Mr J.T. Tulloch (Scot.) |
| | E v F | Mr W. Williams (Eng.) |
| | W v E | Mr J.I. Gillespie (Scot.) |
| | S v W | Mr C. Lefevre (Ire.) |
| | I v E | Mr J.T. Tulloch (Scot.) |
| | S v I | Mr A.O. Jones (Eng.) |
| | W v I | Mr F.W. Marsh (Eng.) |
| | E v S | Mr T.D. Schofield (Wales) |
| | | |
| 1907 | A v NZ | Mr A. Brown (Aus.) |
| | A v NZ | Mr C.B. Cochrane (Aus.) |
| | A v NZ | Mr C.E. Morgan (Aus.) |
| | | |
| 1907-08 | F v E | Mr C.F. Rutherford (Scot.) |
| | E v W | Mr J.T. Tulloch (Scot.) |
| | W v S | Mr W. Williams (Eng.) |
| | E v I | Mr T.D. Schofield (Wales) |
| | I v S | Mr W. Williams (Eng.) |
| | W v F | Mr W. Williams (Eng.) |
| | I v W | Mr J.D. Dallas (Scot.) |
| | S v E | Mr H.H. Corley (Ire.) |

| 1908 | NZ v AW | Mr J. Duncan (NZ) |
| | NZ v AW(2) | Mr A. Campbell (NZ) |
| | | |
| 1908-09 | W v A | Mr G. Evans (Eng.) |
| | E v A | Mr J. Games (Wales) |
| | W v E | Mr J.D. Dallas (Scot.) |
| | E v F | Mr W. Williams (Eng.) |
| | S v W | Mr R.W. Jeffares (Ire.) |
| | I v E | Mr J.D. Dallas (Scot.) |
| | F v W | Mr W. Williams (Eng.) |
| | S v I | Mr V.H. Cartwright (Eng.) |
| | W v I | Mr F.C. Potter-Irwin (Eng.) |
| | I v F | Mr W. Williams (Eng.) |
| | E v S | Mr E.G. Nicholls (Wales) |
| | | |
| 1909-10 | W v F | Mr W. Williams (Eng.) |
| | E v W | Mr J.D. Dallas (Scot.) |
| | S v F | Mr G.A. Harris (Ire.) |
| | W v S | Mr G.H.B. Kennedy (Ire.) |
| | E v I | Mr T.D. Schofield (Wales) |
| | I v S | Mr V.H. Cartwright (Eng.) |
| | F v E | Mr G. Bowden (Scot.) |
| | I v W | Mr J.D. Dallas (Scot.) |
| | S v E | Mr G.H.B. Kennedy (Ire.) |
| | F v I | Mr V.H. Cartwright (Eng.) |
| | | |
| 1910 | A v NZ | Mr C.E. Morgan (Aus.) |
| | A v NZ(2) | Mr N.B. Martin (Aus.) |
| | SA v GB(3) | Mr R.W. Stanton (SA) |
| | | |
| 1910-11 | F v S | Mr A.O. Jones (Eng.) |
| | W v E | Mr J.I. Gillespie (Scot.) |
| | E v F | Mr E.A. Johns (Wales) |
| | S v W | Mr I.G. Davidson (Ire.) |
| | I v E | Mr J.D. Dallas (Scot.) |
| | S v I | Mr V.H. Cartwright (Eng.) |
| | F v W | Mr W. Williams (Eng.) |
| | W v I | Mr F.C. Potter-Irwin (Eng.) |
| | E v S | Mr T.D. Schofield (Wales) |
| | I v F | Mr J.C. Findlay (Scot.) |
| | | |
| 1911-12 | F v I | Mr A.O. Jones (Eng.) |
| | S v F | Mr J.J. Coffey (Ire.) |
| | E v W | Mr J.T. Tulloch (Scot.) |
| | W v S | Mr F.C. Potter-Irwin (Eng.) |
| | E v I | Mr T.D. Schofield (Wales) |
| | I v S | Mr F.C. Potter-Irwin (Eng.) |
| | I v W | Mr J.D. Dallas (Scot.) |
| | S v E | Mr F. Gardiner (Ire.) |
| | W v F | Mr A.O. Jones (Eng.) |
| | F v E | Mr T.D. Schofield (Wales) |
| | | |
| 1912 | US v A | Mr L.S. Reading (Eng.) |
| | | |
| 1912-13 | S v SA | Mr F.C. Potter-Irwin (Eng.) |
| | I v SA | Mr F.C. Potter-Irwin (Eng.) |
| | W v SA | Mr F.C. Potter-Irwin (Eng.) |
| | F v S | Mr J. Baxter (Eng.) |
| | E v SA | Mr J.T. Tulloch (Scot.) |
| | F v SA | Mr W. Williams (Eng.) |
| | W v E | Mr S.H. Crawford (Ire.) |
| | E v F | Mr J. Games (Wales) |
| | S v W | Mr S.H. Crawford (Ire.) |
| | I v E | Dr J.R.C. Greenlees (Scot.) |
| | S v I | Mr J. Baxter (Eng.) |
| | F v W | Mr J.H. Miles (Eng.) |
| | W v I | Mr J.G. Cunningham (Scot.) |
| | E v S | Mr T.D. Schofield (Wales) |
| | I v F | Mr J.H. Miles (Eng.) |
| | | |
| 1913 | NZ v A | Mr R.L. Simpson (NZ) |
| | NZ v A | Mr A.D. Downes (NZ) |
| | NZ v A | Mr G.W. Nicholson (NZ) |
| | US v NZ | Mr W.W. Hill (Aus.) |
| | | |
| 1913-14 | F v I | Mr E.W. Calver (Eng.) |
| | E v W | Dr J.R.C. Greenlees (Scot.) |
| | W v S | Mr V. Drennon (Ire.) |
| | E v I | Mr T.D. Schofield (Wales) |
| | I v S | Mr J. Baxter (Eng.) |
| | W v F | Mr J.H. Miles (Eng.) |
| | I v W | Mr J.T. Tulloch (Scot.) |
| | S v E | Mr T.D. Schofield (Wales) |
| | F v E | Mr J. Games (Wales) |

| | | |
|---|---|---|
| 1914 | A v NZ | Mr T.G. Pauling (Aus.) |
| | A v NZ | Mr P. Ferguson (Aus.) |
| | A v NZ | Mr. C.C. Butt (Aus.) |
| 1918-19 | W v NZA | Mr R. Charman (Eng.) |
| 1919-20 | F v S | Mr F.C. Potter-Irwin (Eng.) |
| | W v E | Mr J.T. Tulloch (Scot.) |
| | E v F | Mr W.A. Robertson (Scot.) |
| | S v W | Mr S.H. Crawford (Ire.) |
| | I v E | Mr W.A. Robertson (Scot.) |
| | F v W | Col W.S.D. Craven (Eng.) |
| | S v I | Mr J. Baxter (Eng.) |
| | W v I | Mr F.C. Potter-Irwin (Eng.) |
| | E v S | Mr T.D. Schofield (Eng.) |
| | I v F | Mr J.M. Tennent (Scot.) |
| 1920-21 | F v US | Mr Jeffries (Eng.) |
| | E v W | Mr J.C. Sturrock (Scot.) |
| | S v F | Mr W.P. Hinton (Ire.) |
| | W v S | Mr J. Baxter (Eng.) |
| | E v I | Mr T.D. Schofield (Wales) |
| | I v S | Mr J. Baxter (Eng.) |
| | W v F | Mr P.M.R. Royds (Eng.) |
| | I v W | Mr J.M. Tennent (Scot.) |
| | S v E | Mr J.C. Crawford (Ire.) |
| | F v E | Mr J.C. Sturrock (Scot.) |
| | F v I | Mr J.G. Cunningham (Scot.) |
| 1921 | NZ v SA | Mr E. McKenzie (NZ) |
| | NZ v SA(2) | Mr A.E. Neilson (NZ) |
| 1921-22 | F v S | Mr H.C. Harrison (Eng.) |
| | W v E | Mr J.M. Tennent (Scot.) |
| | S v W | Mr R.A. Lloyd (Ire.) |
| | I v E | Mr J.M. Tennent (Scot.) |
| | S v I | Mr T.D. Schofield (Wales) |
| | E v F | Mr J.M. Tennent (Scot.) |
| | W v I | Mr J.C. Sturrock (Scot.) |
| | E v S | Mr R.A. Lloyd (Ire.) |
| | F v W | Mr R.W. Harland (Ire.) |
| | I v F | Mr J.M. Tennent (Scot.) |
| 1922-23 | S v F | Mr T.H. Vile (Wales) |
| | E v W | Mr J.M.B. Scott (Scot.) |
| | W v S | Mr J. Baxter (Eng.) |
| | E v I | Mr T.H. Vile (Wales) |
| | I v S | Mr T.H. Vile (Wales) |
| | W v F | Mr J.B. McGowan (Ire.) |
| | I v W | Mr J.M. Tennent (Scot.) |
| | S v E | Mr T.H. Vile (Wales) |
| | F v E | Mr A.E. Freethy (Wales) |
| | F v I | Mr P.M.R. Royds (Eng.) |
| 1923-24 | F v S | Mr E. Roberts (Wales) |
| | W v E | Mr A.W. Angus (Scot.) |
| | I v F | Mr A.A. Lawrie (Scot.) |
| | S v W | Mr J.B. McGowan (Ire.) |
| | I v E | Mr T.H. Vile (Wales) |
| | E v F | Mr A.E. Freethy (Wales) |
| | S v I | Mr T.H. Vile (Wales) |
| | W v I | Mr J.T. Tulloch (Scot.) |
| | E v S | Mr T.H. Vile (Wales) |
| | F v W | Mr R.A. Roberts (Eng.) |
| | F v R | Mr J. Muntz (Fr.) |
| | F v US | Mr A.E. Freethy (Wales) |
| 1924 | SA v GB | Mr L.D. Oakley (SA) |
| | SA v GB | Mr V.H. Neser (SA) |
| | SA v GB(2) | Mr W.A. Millar (SA) |
| 1924-25 | I v NZ | Mr A.E. Freethy (Wales) |
| | W v NZ | Col J. Brunton (Eng.) |
| | F v I | Mr J. MacGill (Scot.) |
| | E v NZ | Mr A.E. Freethy (Wales) |
| | E v W | Mr A.A. Lawrie (Scot.) |
| | F v NZ | Maj H.E.B. Wilkins (Eng.) |
| | S v F | Dr E. de C. Wheeler (Ire.) |
| | W v S | Mr J. Baxter (Eng.) |
| | E v I | Mr T.H. Vile (Wales) |
| | W v F | Mr R.W. Harland (Ire.) |
| | I v S | Mr A.E. Freethy (Wales) |
| | I v W | Mr J. Baxter (Eng.) |
| | S v E | Mr A.E. Freethy (Wales) |
| | F v E | Mr A.E. Freethy (Wales) |
| 1925-26 | F v S | Mr W.J. Llewellyn (Wales) |
| | W v E | Mr W.H. Acton (Ire.) |
| | I v F | Mr A.A. Lawrie (Scot.) |
| | S v W | Mr D. Hellewell (Eng.) |
| | I v E | Mr W.J. Llewellyn (Wales) |
| | E v F | Mr A.E. Freethy (Wales) |
| | S v I | Mr B.S. Cumberlege (Eng.) |
| | W v I | Mr B.S. Cumberlege (Eng.) |
| | E v S | Mr W.H. Acton (Ire.) |
| | F v W | Mr R.W. Harland (Ire.) |
| 1926-27 | F v M | Mr W.H. Jackson (Eng.) |
| | F v I | Mr R.L. Scott (Scot.) |
| | E v W | Mr R.L. Scott (Scot.) |
| | S v F | Mr B.S. Cumberlege (Eng.) |
| | W v S | Mr W.H. Jackson (Eng.) |
| | E v I | Mr T.H. Vile (Wales) |
| | W v F | Mr W.H. Jackson (Eng.) |
| | I v S | Mr B.S. Cumberlege (Eng.) |
| | I v W | Mr B.S. Cumberlege (Eng.) |
| | S v E | Mr N.M. Purcell (Ire.) |
| | F v E | Mr A.E. Freethy (Wales) |
| | F v G | Mr W.H. Jackson (Eng.) |
| | G v F | Mr W.H. Jackson (Eng.) |
| 1927-28 | I v A | Mr A.W. Angus (Scot.) |
| | W v A | Mr D. Hellewell (Eng.) |
| | S v A | Mr W.J. Llewellyn (Wales) |
| | F v S | Mr R.M. Magrath (Ire.) |
| | E v A | Mr T.H. Vile (Wales) |
| | W v E | Mr R.W. Harland (Ire.) |
| | F v A | Mr T.J. Bradburn (Eng.) |
| | I v F | Mr J. Anderson (Scot.) |
| | S v W | Mr R.W. Harland (Ire.) |
| | I v E | Mr A.E. Freethy (Wales) |
| | S v I | Mr B.S. Cumberlege (Eng.) |
| | E v F | Mr A.E. Freethy (Wales) |
| | W v I | Mr T.H.H. Warren (Scot.) |
| | E v S | Mr T.H. Vile (Wales) |
| | G v F | Maj H.E.B. Wilkins (Eng.) |
| | F v W | Mr R.W. Harland (Ire.) |
| 1928 | SA v NZ(4) | Mr V.H. Neser (SA) |
| 1928-29 | F v I | Mr B.S. Cumberlege (Eng.) |
| | E v W | Mr R.W. Harland (Ire.) |
| | S v F | Mr B.S. Cumberlege (Eng.) |
| | W v S | Mr D. Hellewell (Eng.) |
| | E v I | Mr A.E. Freethy (Wales) |
| | W v F | Maj H.E.B. Wilkins (Eng.) |
| | I v S | Mr B.S. Cumberlege (Eng.) |
| | I v W | Mr J. MacGill (Scot.) |
| | E v S | Dr J.R. Wheeler (Ire.) |
| | F v E | Mr A.E. Freethy (Wales) |
| | F v G | Mr T.J. Bradburn (Eng.) |
| 1929 | A v NZ(2) | Mr A.V. Mayne (Aus.) |
| | A v NZ | Mr R.A. Cooney (Aus.) |
| 1929-30 | F v S | Mr D. Hellewell (Eng.) |
| | W v E | Mr R.W. Jeffares (Ire.) |
| | I v F | Mr B.S. Cumberlege (Eng.) |
| | S v W | Dr J.R. Wheeler (Ire.) |
| | I v E | Mr A.E. Freethy (Wales) |
| | E v F | Mr A.E. Freethy (Wales) |
| | S v I | Mr B.S. Cumberlege (Eng.) |
| | W v I | Mr D. Hellewell (Eng.) |
| | E v S | Mr R.W. Jeffares (Ire.) |
| | G v F | Mr D. Hellewell (Eng.) |
| | F v W | Mr D. Hellewell (Eng.) |
| 1930 | NZ v GB(3) | Mr S. Hollander (NZ) |
| | NZ v GB | Mr F.E. Sutherland (NZ) |
| | A v GB | Mr R.C. Cooney (Aus.) |
| 1930-31 | F v I | Mr T.H. Vile (Wales) |
| | E v W | Dr J.R. Wheeler (Ire.) |
| | S v F | Mr R.W. Jeffares (Ire.) |
| | W v S | Mr J.G. Bott (Eng.) |
| | E v I | Mr A.E. Freethy (Wales) |
| | W v F | Mr R.W. Harland (Ire.) |
| | I v S | Mr B.S. Cumberlege (Eng.) |
| | I v W | Mr M.A. Allan (Scot.) |
| | S v E | Dr J.R. Wheeler (Ire.) |

|  |  |  |
|---|---|---|
|  | F v E | Mr A.E. Freethy (Wales) |
|  | F v G | Mr Hollis (Eng.) |
| 1931 | M v A | Mr R.J. Paton (NZ) |
|  | NZ v A | Mr S. Hollander (NZ) |
| 1931-32 | W v SA | Mr E. Holmes (Eng.) |
|  | I v SA | Mr M.A. Allan (Scot.) |
|  | E v SA | Mr W.L. Freeman (Ire.) |
|  | S v SA | Mr B.S. Cumberlege (Eng.) |
|  | W v E | Mr F.J.C. Moffat (Scot.) |
|  | S v W | Mr T. Bell (Ire.) |
|  | I v E | Mr W. Burnet (Scot.) |
|  | S v I | Mr B.S. Cumberlege (Eng.) |
|  | W v I | Mr E. Holmes (Eng.) |
|  | E v S | Dr J.R. Wheeler (Ire.) |
|  | G v F | Mr Steyn (Ger.) |
| 1932 | A v NZ | Mr A.V. Mayne (Aus.) |
|  | A v NZ | Mr F.A. Larkin (Aus.) |
|  | A v NZ | Mr R.C. Cooney (Aus.) |
| 1932-33 | E v W | Mr T. Bell (Ire.) |
|  | W v S | Mr J.G. Bott (Eng.) |
|  | E v I | Mr M.A. Allan (Scot.) |
|  | I v W | Mr M.A. Allan (Scot.) |
|  | S v E. | Dr J.R. Wheeler (Ire.) |
|  | F v G | Mr L. Mailhan (Fr.) |
|  | I v S | Mr B.S. Cumberlege (Eng.) |
| 1933 | SA v A(4) | Mr V.H. Neser (SA) |
|  | SA v A | Mr A.W. van der Horst (SA) |
| 1933-34 | W v E | Mr F.W. Haslett (Ire.) |
|  | S v W | Mr H.L.V. Day (Eng.) |
|  | I v E | Mr M.A. Allan (Scot.) |
|  | S v I | Mr B.S. Cumberlege (Eng.) |
|  | W v I | Mr W. Burnet (Scot.) |
|  | E v S | Mr F.W. Haslett (Ire.) |
|  | G v F | Mr Lieprand (Ger.) |
| 1934 | A v NZ | Mr R.C. Cooney (Aus.) |
|  | A v NZ | Mr A.L.C. Irving (Aus.) |
| 1934-35 | E v W | Mr F.W. Haslett (Ire.) |
|  | W v S | Mr F.W. Haslett (Ire.) |
|  | E v I | Mr M.A. Allan (Scot.) |
|  | I v S | Mr J. Hughes (Eng.) |
|  | I v W | Mr M.A. Allan (Scot.) |
|  | S v E | Mr R.W. Jeffares (Ire.) |
|  | F v G | Mr L. Mailhan (Ger.) |
| 1935-36 | S v NZ | Mr C.H. Gadney (Eng.) |
|  | I v NZ | Mr R.W. Jeffares (Ire.) |
|  | W v NZ | Mr C.H. Gadney (Eng.) |
|  | E v NZ | Mr J.W. Faull (Wales) |
|  | W v E | Mr F.W. Haslett (Ire.) |
|  | S v W | Mr C.H. Gadney (Eng.) |
|  | I v E | Mr M.A. Allan (Scot.) |
|  | S v I | Mr J.W. Faull (Wales) |
|  | W v I | Mr C.H. Gadney (Eng.) |
|  | E v S | Mr T.H. Phillips (Wales) |
|  | G v F | Mr van der Moerve (Ger.) |
| 1936 | NZ v A | Mr J. Moffitt (NZ) |
|  | NZ v A | Mr H.J. McKenzie (NZ) |
|  | M v A | Mr N.R. Gilchrist (NZ) |
| 1936-37 | G v F | Mr Wiesse (Ger.) |
|  | E v W | Mr R.A. Beattie (Scot.) |
|  | W v S | Mr C.H. Gadney (Eng.) |
|  | E v I | Mr J.W. Faull (Wales) |
|  | I v S | Mr C.H. Gadney (Eng.) |
|  | E v S | Mr S. Donaldson (Ire.) |
|  | I v W | Mr M.A. Allan (Scot.) |
|  | F v G | Mr L. Mailhan (Fr.) |
| 1937 | A v SA | Mr A.L.C. Irving (Aus.) |
|  | A v SA | Mr W.F.B. Kilner (Aus.) |
|  | NZ v SA | Mr L.E. Macassey (NZ) |
|  | NZ v SA(2) | Mr J.S. King (NZ) |
| 1937-38 | F v It | Mr J. Roca (Fr.) |
|  | W v E | Mr R.A. Beattie (Scot.) |
|  | S v W | Mr C.H. Gadney (Eng.) |

|  |  |  |
|---|---|---|
|  | I v E | Mr J.C.H. Ireland (Scot.) |
|  | S v I | Mr C.H. Gadney (Eng.) |
|  | W v I | Mr J.C.H. Ireland (Scot.) |
|  | E v S | Mr I. David (Wales) |
|  | G v F | Mr Krembs (Ger.) |
|  | R v F | Mr Schwoenberg (Ger.) |
|  | G v F | Mr Herck (Rom.) |
| 1938 | A v NZ(2) | Mr W.S. Chapman (Aus.) |
|  | A v NZ | Mr P. Barnes (Aus.) |
|  | SA v GB | Mr A.T. Horak (SA) |
|  | SA v GB | Dr J.J. Strasheim (SA) |
|  | SA v GB | Mr N. Pretorius (SA) |
| 1938-39 | E v W | Mr J.C.H. Ireland (Scot.) |
|  | W v S | Mr A.S. Bean (Eng.) |
|  | E v I | Mr J.C.H. Ireland (Scot.) |
|  | I v S | Mr C.H. Gadney (Eng.) |
|  | I v W | Mr J.C.H. Ireland (Scot.) |
|  | S v E | Mr I. David (Wales |
| 1939-40 | F v B | Mr C.H. Gadney (Eng.) |
| 1944-45 | F v B | Mr H.A. Fry (Eng.) |
|  | B v F | Mr R.A. Beattie (Scot.) |
| 1945-46 | W v F | Mr A.S. Bean (Eng.) |
|  | F v B | Mr C.H. Gadney (Eng.) |
|  | I v F | Mr H.G. Lathwell (Eng.) |
|  | F v K | Col G. Warden (Eng.) |
|  | F v W | Mr A.S. Bean (Eng.) |
| 1946 | NZ v A | Mr A.S. Fong (NZ) |
|  | NZ v A | Mr A.M. Matheson (NZ) |
|  | M v A | Mr A.A. Griffiths (NZ) |
| 1946-47 | F v S | Mr C.H. Gadney (Eng.) |
|  | W v E | Mr R.A. Beattie (Scot.) |
|  | I v F | Mr J.B.G. Whittaker (Eng.) |
|  | S v W | Capt M.J. Dowling (Ire.) |
|  | I v E | Mr M.A. Allan (Scot.) |
|  | S v I | Mr C.H. Gadney (Eng.) |
|  | E v S | Mr I. David (Wales) |
|  | F v W | Mr A.S. Bean (Eng.) |
|  | W v I | Mr J.B.G. Whittaker (Eng.) |
|  | E v F | Mr T. Jones (Wales) |
| 1947 | A v NZ | Mr T. Moore (Aus.) |
|  | A v NZ | Mr L.C. Tomalin (Aus.) |
| 1947-48 | S v A | Mr N.H. Lambert (Ire.) |
|  | I v A | Mr R.A. Beattie (Scot.) |
|  | W v A | Mr A.S. Bean (Eng.) |
|  | F v I | Mr T.N. Pearce (Eng.) |
|  | E v A | Mr N.H. Lambert (Ire.) |
|  | F v A | Mr C.H. Gadney (Eng.) |
|  | E v W | Mr R.A. Beattie (Scot.) |
|  | S v F | Mr A.S. Bean (Eng.) |
|  | W v S | Mr T.N. Pearce (Eng.) |
|  | E v I | Mr T. Jones (Wales) |
|  | W v F | Mr A.S. Bean (Eng.) |
|  | I v S | Mr C.H. Gadney (Eng.) |
|  | I v W | Mr M.A. Allan (Scot.) |
|  | S v E | Mr N.H. Lambert (Ire.) |
|  | F v E | Mr T. Jones (Wales) |
| 1948-49 | F v S | Mr T.N. Pearce (Eng.) |
|  | W v E | Mr N.H. Lambert (Ire.) |
|  | I v F | Mr T.N. Pearce (Eng.) |
|  | S v W | Mr N.H. Lambert (Ire.) |
|  | I v E | Mr R.A. Beattie (Scot.) |
|  | E v F | Mr T. Jones (Wales) |
|  | S v I | Mr A.S. Bean (Eng.) |
|  | W v I | Mr T.N. Pearce (Eng.) |
|  | E v S | Mr N.H. Lambert (Ire.) |
|  | F v W | Mr N.H. Lambert (Ire.) |
| 1949 | SA v NZ(2) | Mr R.D. Burmeister (SA) |
|  | SA v NZ(2) | Mr E.W. Hofmeyr (SA) |
|  | NZ v A | Mr E.D. Hill (NZ) |
|  | NZ v A | Mr L. Walsh (NZ) |
|  | Arg v F | Mr J. Knox (Arg.) |
|  | Arg v F | Mr O. Noon (Arg.) |
|  | A v M(2) | Mr L.C. Tomalin (Aus.) |
|  | A v M | Mr W.D. Wyllie (Aus.) |

| | | |
|---|---|---|
| 1949-50 | S v F | Mr T. Jones (Wales) |
| | E v W | Mr N.H. Lambert (Ire.) |
| | F v I | Mr T.N. Pearce (Eng.) |
| | W v S | Capt M.J. Dowling (Ire.) |
| | E v I | Mr R.A. Beattie (Scot.) |
| | I v S | Mr T.N. Pearce (Eng.) |
| | F v E | Mr N.H. Lambert (Ire.) |
| | I v W | Mr R.A. Beattie (Scot.) |
| | S v E | Capt M.J. Dowling (Ire.) |
| | W v F | Capt M.J. Dowling (Ire.) |
| 1950 | NZ v BI(2) | Mr E.W.T. Tindill (NZ) |
| | NZ v BI | Mr A.S. Fong (NZ) |
| | NZ v BI | Mr G. Sullivan (NZ) |
| | A v BI | Mr L.C. Tomalin (Aus.) |
| | A v BI | Mr T.W. Moore (Aus.) |
| 1950-51 | F v S | Mr T.N. Pearce (Eng.) |
| | W v E | Capt M.J. Dowling (Ire.) |
| | I v F | Mr T.N. Pearce (Eng.) |
| | S v W | Capt M.J. Dowling (Ire.) |
| | I v E | Mr T. Jones (Wales) |
| | S v I | Mr T.N. Pearce (Eng.) |
| | E v F | Mr V.S. Llewellyn (Wales) |
| | W v I | Mr W.C.W. Murdoch (Scot.) |
| | E v S | Capt M.J. Dowling (Ire.) |
| | F v W | Capt M.J. Dowling (Ire.) |
| 1951 | A v NZ(2) | Mr H.A. Tolhurst (Aus.) |
| | A v NZ | Mr T.W. Moore (Aus.) |
| 1951-52 | S v SA | Capt M.J. Dowling (Ire.) |
| | I v SA | Mr W.C.W. Murdoch (Scot.) |
| | W v SA | Mr N.H. Lambert (Ire.) |
| | E v SA | Mr W.C.W. Murdoch (Scot.) |
| | S v F | Mr I. David (Wales) |
| | E v W | Mr N.H. Lambert (Ire.) |
| | F v I | Mr T.N. Pearce (Eng.) |
| | W v S | Capt M.J. Dowling (Ire.) |
| | F v SA | Capt M.J. Dowling (Ire.) |
| | I v S | Mr I. David (Wales) |
| | I v W | Dr P.F. Cooper (Eng.) |
| | S v E | Capt M.J. Dowling (Ire.) |
| | W v F | Mr A.W.C. Austin (Scot.) |
| | E v I | Mr I. David (Wales) |
| | F v E | Mr W.C.W. Murdoch (Scot.) |
| | It v F | Mr T.E. Priest (Eng.) |
| 1952 | A v Fj(2) | Mr D.C. Furness (Aus.) |
| | NZ v A | Mr A.A. Griffiths (NZ) |
| | NZ v A | Mr J. Frood (Aus.) |
| 1952-53 | F v S | Mr O.B. Glasgow (Ire.) |
| | W v E | Capt M.J. Dowling (Ire.) |
| | I v F | Mr T.E. Priest (Eng.) |
| | S v W | Dr P.F. Cooper (Eng.) |
| | I v E | Mr A.W.C. Austin (Scot.) |
| | E v F | Mr V.J. Parfitt (Wales) |
| | S v I | Mr I. David (Wales) |
| | W v I | Dr P.F. Cooper (Eng.) |
| | E v S | Capt M.J. Dowling (Ire.) |
| | F v W | Mr O.B. Glasgow (Ire.) |
| | F v It | Dr P.F. Cooper (Eng.) |
| 1953 | SA v A | Mr R.D. Burmeister (SA) |
| | SA v A(2) | Mr C.J. Ackermann (SA) |
| | SA v A | Mr L.L. Louw (SA) |
| 1953-54 | W v NZ | Dr P.F. Cooper (Eng.) |
| | S v F | Mr I. David (Wales) |
| | I v NZ | Dr P.F. Cooper (Eng.) |
| | E v W | Capt M.J. Dowling (Ire.) |
| | F v I | Mr A.I. Dickie (Scot.) |
| | E v NZ | Mr I. David (Wales) |
| | S v NZ | Mr I. David (Wales) |
| | E v I | Mr A.I. Dickie (Scot.) |
| | I v S | Mr V.J. Parfitt (Wales) |
| | F v NZ | Mr I. David (Wales) |
| | I v W | Mr A.W.C. Austin (Scot.) |
| | S v E | Mr O.B. Glasgow (Ire.) |
| | W v F | Mr A.I. Dickie (Scot.) |
| | F v E | Mr I. David (Wales) |
| | W v S | Dr P.F. Cooper (Eng.) |
| | It v F | Dr P.F. Cooper (Eng.) |

| | | |
|---|---|---|
| 1954 | A v Fj | Mr T.W. Moore (Aus.) |
| | A v Fj | Mr D.C. Furness (Aus.) |
| | Arg v F(2) | Mr E. Fornes (Arg.) |
| 1954-55 | F v S | Mr H.B. Elliott (Eng.) |
| | W v E | Mr O.B. Glasgow (Ire.) |
| | I v F | Mr I. David (Wales) |
| | S v W | Capt M.J. Dowling (Ire.) |
| | I v E | Mr A.I. Dickie (Scot.) |
| | S v I | Mr L.M. Boundy (Eng.) |
| | E v F | Mr R. Mitchell (Ire.) |
| | W v I | Mr A.I. Dickie (Scot.) |
| | E v S | Mr D.C. Joynson (Wales) |
| | F v W | Mr O.B. Glasgow (Ire.) |
| | F v It | Mr H.B. Elliott (Eng.) |
| 1955 | SA v BI(2) | Mr R.D. Burmeister (SA) |
| | SA v BI | Mr M.J. Slabber (SA) |
| | SA v BI | Mr C.J. Ackermann (SA) |
| | NZ v A | Mr F.G.M. Parkinson (NZ) |
| | NZ v A | Mr E.W.T. Tindill (NZ) |
| | NZ v A | Mr B.H. Wolstenholme (NZ) |
| 1955-56 | S v F | Capt M.J. Dowling (Ire.) |
| | E v W | Mr R. Mitchell (Ire.) |
| | F v I | Dr P.F. Cooper (Eng.) |
| | W v S | Mr L.M. Boundy (Eng.) |
| | E v I | Mr A.I. Dickie (Scot.) |
| | I v S | Mr H.B. Elliott (Eng.) |
| | I v W | Mr A.I. Dickie (Scot.) |
| | S v E | Capt M.J. Dowling (Ire.) |
| | W v F | Dr P.F. Cooper (Eng.) |
| | It v F | Dr P.F. Cooper (Eng.) |
| | F v E | Mr I. David (Wales) |
| 1956 | A v SA | Dr I.R. Vanderfield (Aus.) |
| | A v SA | Mr T.W. Moore (Aus.) |
| | NZ v SA(2) | Mr F.G.M. Parkinson (NZ) |
| | NZ v SA(2) | Mr W.H. Fright (NZ) |
| 1956-57 | F v Cz | Mr W.N. Gillmore (Eng.) |
| | F v S | Mr L.M. Boundy (Eng.) |
| | W v E | Mr A.I. Dickie (Scot.) |
| | I v F | Mr L.M. Boundy (Eng.) |
| | S v W | Mr R.C. Williams (Ire.) |
| | I v E | Mr A.I. Dickie (Scot.) |
| | S v I | Mr L.M. Boundy (Eng.) |
| | E v F | Mr R.C. Williams (Ire.) |
| | W v I | Mr J.A.S. Taylor (Scot.) |
| | E v S | Mr R. Mitchell (Ire.) |
| | F v W | Dr P.F. Cooper (Eng.) |
| | F v It | Mr H. Waldron (Eng.) |
| | R v F | Mr L.M. Boundy (Eng.) |
| 1957 | A v NZ | Mr A.T. Tierney (Aus.) |
| | A v NZ | Mr N.V. Haydon (Aus.) |
| 1957-58 | F v R | Mr S. Pozzi (Italy) |
| | W v A | Mr A.I. Dickie (Scot.) |
| | S v F | Mr L.M. Boundy (Eng.) |
| | I v A | Mr W.J. Evans (Wales) |
| | E v W | Mr R.C. Williams (Ire.) |
| | E v A | Mr R.C. Williams (Ire.) |
| | W v S | Dr N.M. Parkes (Eng.) |
| | E v I | Mr G. Burrell (Scot.) |
| | S v A | Mr R.C. Williams (Ire.) |
| | I v S | Mr W.N. Gillmore (Eng.) |
| | F v E | Mr W.J. Evans (Wales) |
| | F v A | Dr N.M. Parkes (Eng.) |
| | I v W | Dr N.M. Parkes (Eng.) |
| | S v E | Mr R.C. Williams (Ire.) |
| | W v F | Mr A.I. Dickie (Scot.) |
| | It v F | Mr W.N. Gillmore (Eng.) |
| | F v I | Dr N.M. Parkes (Eng.) |
| 1958 | A v M | Mr J.O'Leary (Aus.) |
| | A v M | Dr I.R. Vanderfield (Aus.) |
| | A v M | Mr A.T. Tierney (Aus.) |
| | SA v F | Dr E.A. Strasheim (SA) |
| | SA v F | Mr C.J. Ackermann (SA) |
| | NZ v A(2) | Mr C.R. Gillies (NZ) |
| | NZ v A | Mr R.A. Forsyth (NZ) |

| 1958-59 | F v S | Mr D.G. Walters (Wales) |
|---|---|---|
| | W v E | Mr R.C. Williams (Ire.) |
| | S v W | Mr R.C. Williams (Ire.) |
| | I v E | Mr D.G. Walters (Wales) |
| | S v I | Mr L.M. Boundy (Eng.) |
| | E v F | Mr R.C. Williams (Ire.) |
| | W v I | Mr G. Burrell (Scot.) |
| | E v S | Mr D.G. Walters (Wales) |
| | F v It | Dr N.M. Parkes (Eng.) |
| | F v W | Dr N.M. Parkes (Eng.) |
| | I v F | Mr D.G. Walters (Wales) |
| 1959 | A v BI | Mr B.J. O'Callaghan (Aus.) |
| | A v BI | Mr A.T. Tierney (Aus.) |
| | NZ v BI | Mr A.L. Fleury (NZ) |
| | NZ v BI(2) | Mr C.R. Gillies (NZ) |
| | NZ v BI | Mr J.P. Murphy (NZ) |
| 1959-60 | S v F | Mr D.G. Walters (Wales) |
| | E v W | Mr J.A.S. Taylor (Scot.) |
| | W v S | Mr K.D. Kelleher (Ire.) |
| | E v I | Mr D.G. Walters (Wales) |
| | I v S | Mr D.G. Walters (Wales) |
| | F v E | Mr J.A.S. Taylor (Scot.) |
| | I v W | Mr D.A. Brown (Eng.) |
| | S v E | Mr R.C. Williams (Ire.) |
| | W v F | Dr N.M. Parkes (Eng.) |
| | F v I | Mr D.G. Walters (Wales) |
| | It v F | Mr D.A. Brown (Eng.) |
| | R v F | Mr S. Pozzi (Italy) |
| 1960 | SA v S | Dr E.A. Strasheim (SA) |
| | SA v NZ | Dr E.A. Strasheim (SA) |
| | SA v NZ | Mr M.J. Slabber (SA) |
| | SA v NZ(2) | Mr R.D. Burmeister (SA) |
| | Arg v F (2) | Mr B. Marie (Fr.) |
| | Arg v F | Mr J. Camardon (Arg.) |
| 1960-61 | W v SA | Mr J.A.S. Taylor (Scot.) |
| | I v SA | Mr G.J. Treharne (Wales) |
| | F v S | Mr R.C. Williams (Ire.) |
| | E v SA | Mr G.J. Treharne (Wales) |
| | S v SA | Mr L.M. Boundy (Eng.) |
| | W v E | Mr K.D. Kelleher (Ire.) |
| | S v W | Mr R.C. Williams (Ire.) |
| | I v E | Mr G.J. Treharne (Wales) |
| | F v SA | Mr D.G. Walters (Wales) |
| | S v I | Mr M.H.R. King (Eng.) |
| | E v F | Mr D.G. Walters (Wales) |
| | W v I | Mr D.C.J. McMahon (Scot.) |
| | E v S | Mr K.D. Kelleher (Ire.) |
| | F v W | Dr N.M. Parkes (Eng.) |
| | F v It | Mr J.A.S. Taylor (Scot.) |
| | I v F | Mr G.J. Treharne (Wales) |
| 1961 | A v Fj(2) | Dr I.R. Vanderfield (Aus.) |
| | A v Fj | Mr A.K. Finlay (Aus.) |
| | SA v I | Mr M. Calitz (SA) |
| | SA v A | Mr E.W. Hofmeyr (SA) |
| | SA v A | Mr R.D. Burmeister (SA) |
| | NZ v F(3) | Mr A.B. Farquhar (NZ) |
| | A v F | Dr I.R. Vanderfield (Aus.) |
| 1961-62 | F v R | Mr R.C. Williams (Ire.) |
| | S v F | Mr R.C. Williams (Ire.) |
| | E v W | Mr J.A.S. Taylor (Scot.) |
| | W v S | Dr N.M. Parkes (Eng.) |
| | E v I | Mr D.G. Walters (Wales) |
| | I v S | Dr N.M. Parkes (Eng.) |
| | F v E | Mr D.G. Walters (Wales) |
| | S v E | Mr K.D. Kelleher (Ire.) |
| | W v F | Mr K.D. Kelleher (Ire.) |
| | F v I | Mr J.A.S. Taylor (Scot.) |
| | It v F | Mr H.B. Keenan (Eng.) |
| | I v W | Mr J.A.S. Taylor (Scot.) |
| 1962 | A v NZ | Mr A.K. Finlay (Aus.) |
| | A v NZ | Dr I.R. Vanderfield (Aus.) |
| | SA v BI(2) | Dr E.A. Strasheim (SA) |
| | SA v BI | Mr K.R.V. Carlson (SA) |
| | SA v BI | Capt P.A. Myburgh (SA) |
| | NZ v A | Mr C.J. McAuley (NZ) |
| | NZ v A(2) | Mr A.B. Farquhar (NZ) |

| 1962-63 | R v F | Mr Lacroix (Bel.) |
|---|---|---|
| | F v S | Mr R.C. Williams (Ire.) |
| | W v E | Mr K.D. Kelleher (Ire.) |
| | I v F | Mr F.G. Price (Wales) |
| | S v W | Mr R.C. Williams (Ire.) |
| | I v E | Mr H.B. Laidlaw (Scot.) |
| | E v F | Mr D.C.J. McMahon (Scot.) |
| | S v I | Mr G.J. Treharne (Wales) |
| | W v I | Mr A.C. Luff (Eng.) |
| | E v S | Mr D.G. Walters (Wales) |
| | F v W | Mr P.G. Brook (Eng.) |
| | F v It | Mr K.D. Kelleher (Ire.) |
| 1963 | NZ v E | Mr C.F. Robson (NZ) |
| | NZ v E | Mr J.P. Murphy (NZ) |
| | A v E | Mr C.F. Ferguson (Aus.) |
| | SA v A | Mr E.W. Hofmeyr (SA) |
| | SA v A(3) | Capt P.A. Myburgh (SA) |
| 1963-64 | I v NZ | Mr H.B. Keenan (Eng.) |
| | F v R | Mr D.G. Walters (Wales) |
| | W v NZ | Mr R.C. Williams (Ire.) |
| | E v NZ | Mr D.C.J. McMahon (Scot.) |
| | S v F | Mr R.C. Williams (Ire.) |
| | E v W | Mr K.D. Kelleher (Ire.) |
| | S v NZ | Mr R.C. Williams (Ire.) |
| | W v S | Mr P.G. Brook (Eng.) |
| | E v I | Mr D.G. Walters (Wales) |
| | F v NZ | Mr R.C. Williams (Ire.) |
| | I v S | Mr A.C. Luff (Eng.) |
| | F v E | Mr D.G. Walters (Wales) |
| | I v W | Mr A.C. Luff (Eng.) |
| | S v E | Mr R.C. Williams (Ire.) |
| | W v F | Mr H.B. Laidlaw (Scot.) |
| | It v F | Mr R.W. Gilliland (Ire.) |
| | F v I | Mr D.G. Walters (Wales) |
| 1964 | SA v W | Dr G.K. Engelbrecht (SA) |
| | NZ v A | Mr A.B. Farquhar (NZ) |
| | NZ v A(2) | Mr J.P. Murphy (NZ) |
| | SA v F | Dr E.A. Strasheim (SA) |
| 1964-65 | F v Fj | Mr D.G. Walters (Wales) |
| | R v F | Mr K.D. Kelleher (Ire.) |
| | F v S | Mr K.D. Kelleher (Ire.) |
| | W v E | Mr K.D. Kelleher (Ire.) |
| | I v F | Mr D.G. Walters (Wales) |
| | S v W | Mr R.W. Gilliland (Ire.) |
| | I v E | Mr H.B. Laidlaw (Scot.) |
| | S v I | Mr D.G. Walters (Wales) |
| | E v F | Mr R.W. Gilliland (Ire.) |
| | W v I | Mr P.G. Brook (Eng.) |
| | E v S | Mr D.G. Walters (Ire.) |
| | F v W | Mr R.W. Gilliland (Ire.) |
| | | replaced by |
| | | Mr B. Marie (Fr.) |
| | F v It | Mr D.M. Hughes (Wales) |
| | I v SA | Mr P.G. Brook (Eng.) |
| | S v SA | Mr D.G. Walters (Wales) |
| 1965 | A v SA | Mr C.F. Ferguson (Aus.) |
| | A v SA | Mr K.J. Crowe (Aus.) |
| | NA v SA(3) | Mr J.P. Murphy (NZ) |
| | | replaced by |
| | | Mr A.R. Taylor during the third Test |
| | NZ v SA | Mr D.H. Millar (NZ) |
| 1965-66 | F v R | Mr R.W. Gilliland (Ire.) |
| | E v W | Mr R.W. Gilliland (Ire.) |
| | S v F | Mr D.M. Hughes (Wales) |
| | F v I | Mr P.G. Brook (Eng.) |
| | W v S | Mr M.H. Titcomb (Eng.) |
| | E v I | Mr B. Marie (Fr.) |
| | I v S | Mr D.M. Hughes (Wales) |
| | F v E | Mr D.G. Walters (Wales) |
| | I v W | Mr R.P. Burrell (Scot.) |
| | S v E | Mr K.D. Kelleher (Ire.) |
| | W v F | Mr K.D. Kelleher (Ire.) |
| | It v F | Mr P.G. Brook (Eng.) |
| 1966 | A v BI | Dr I.R. Vanderfield (Aus.) |
| | A v BI | Mr K.J. Crowe (Aus.) |
| | NZ v BI | Mr J.P.G. Pring (Aus.) |
| | NZ v BI(3) | Mr J.P. Murphy (NZ) |

| | | |
|---|---|---|
| 1966-67 | R v F | Mr P.G. Brook (Eng.) |
| | W v A | Mr K.D. Kelleher (Ire.) |
| | S v A | Mr M. Joseph (Wales) |
| | E v A | Mr K.D. Kelleher (Ire.) |
| | F v S | Mr K.D. Kelleher (Ire.) |
| | I v A | Mr M. Joseph (Wales) |
| | S v W | Mr K.D. Kelleher (Ire.) |
| | F v A | Mr R.W. Gilliland (Ire.) |
| | I v E | Mr D.M. Hughes (Wales) |
| | S v I | Mr D.M. Hughes (Wales) |
| | E v F | Mr D.P. d'Arcy (Ire.) |
| | W v I | Mr M.H. Titcomb (Eng.) |
| | E v S | Mr D.P. d'Arcy (Ire.) |
| | F v It | Mr K. Morgan (Wales) |
| | F v W | Mr D.P. d'Arcy (Ire.) |
| | I v F | Mr R.P. Burrell (Scot.) |
| | W v E | Mr D.C.J. McMahon (Scot.) |
| 1967 | A v I | Dr I.R. Vanderfield (Aus.) |
| | SA v F | Dr E.A. Strasheim (SA) |
| | SA v F(2) | Mr M. Baise (SA) |
| | SA v F | Mr P. Robbertse (SA) |
| | NZ v A | Mr J.P.G. Pring (NZ) |
| 1967-68 | E v NZ | Mr D.C.J. McMahon (Scot.) |
| | W v NZ | Mr M.H. Titcomb (Eng.) |
| | F v NZ | Mr R.P. Burrell (Scot.) |
| | S v NZ | Mr K.D. Kelleher (Ire.) |
| | F v R | Mr D.P. d'Arcy (Ire.) |
| | S v F | Mr K.D. Kelleher (Ire.) |
| | E v W | Mr D.P. d'Arcy (Ire.) |
| | F v I | Air Cdr G.C. Lamb (Eng.) |
| | W v S | Air Cdr G.C. Lamb (Eng.) |
| | E v I | Mr M. Joseph (Wales) |
| | F v E | Mr H.B. Laidlaw (Scot.) |
| | I v S | Mr M. Joseph (Wales) |
| | I v W | Mr M.H. Titcomb (Eng.) |
| | S v E | Mr D.P. d'Arcy (Ire.) |
| | W v F | Mr H.B. Laidlaw (Scot.) |
| | Cz v F | Mr Tagnini (Italy) |
| 1968 | SA v BI(2) | Mr M. Baise (SA) |
| | SA v BI | Mr J.P.J. Schoeman (SA) |
| | SA v BI | Dr E.A. Strasheim (SA) |
| | A v NZ | Dr I.R. Vanderfield (Aus.) |
| | A v NZ | Mr K.J. Crowe (Aus.) |
| | NZ v F | Mr D.H. Millar (NZ) |
| | NZ v F | Mr J.P.G. Pring (NZ) |
| | NZ v F | Mr J.P. Murphy (NZ) |
| | A v F | Mr C.F. Ferguson (Aus.) |
| 1968-69 | I v A | Mr W.K.M. Jones (Wales) |
| | S v A | Mr M.H. Titcomb (Eng.) |
| | F v SA | Air Cdr G.C. Lamb (Eng.) |
| | F v SA | Mr D.P. d'Arcy (Ire.) |
| | R v F | Mr M. Joseph (Wales) |
| | F v S | Air Cdr G.C. Lamb (Eng.) |
| | I v F | Air Cdr G.C. Lamb (Eng.) |
| | S v W | Mr K.D. Kelleher (Ire.) |
| | I v E | Mr R.P. Burrell (Scot.) |
| | E v F | Mr D.P. d'Arcy (Ire.) |
| | S v I | Mr M. Joseph (Wales) |
| | W v I | Mr D.C.J. McMahon (Scot.) |
| | E v S | Mr C. Durand (Fr.) |
| | F v W | Mr R.P. Burrell (Scot.) |
| | W v E | Mr D.P. d'Arcy (Ire.) |
| 1969 | NZ v W(2) | Mr J.P. Murphy (NZ) |
| | A v W | Mr C.F. Ferguson (Aus.) |
| | SA v A | Mr P.Robbertse (SA) |
| | SA v A | Mr M. Baise (SA) |
| | SA v A | Mr S. Baise (SA) |
| | SA v A | Mr C.J. de Bruyn (SA) |
| 1969-70 | S v SA | Mr M. Joseph (Wales) |
| | F v R | Mr R.F. Johnson (Eng.) |
| | E v SA | Mr K.D. Kelleher (Ire.) |
| | S v F | Air Cdr G.C. Lamb (Eng.) |
| | I v SA | Mr T.F.E. Grierson (Scot.) |
| | F v I | Mr R.F. Johnson (Eng.) |
| | W v SA | Air Cdr G.C. Lamb (Eng.) |
| | W v S | Dr D.P. d'Arcy (Ire.) |
| | E v I | Mr A.R. Lewis (Wales) |

| | | |
|---|---|---|
| | E v W | Mr R. Calmet (Fr.) |
| | | replaced by |
| | | Mr R.F. Johnson (Eng.) |
| | I v S | Mr C. Durand (Fr.) |
| | I v W | Air Cdr G.C. Lamb (Eng.) |
| | S v E | Mr M. Joseph (Wales) |
| | W v F | Mr K.D. Kelleher (Ire.) |
| | F v E | Mr W.K.M. Jones (Wales) |
| 1970 | A v S | Dr I.R. Vanderfield (Aus.) |
| | SA v NZ(2) | Mr P. Robbertse (SA) |
| | SA v NZ | Dr W.C. Malan (SA) |
| | SA v NZ | Mr A. Woolley (SA) |
| 1970-71 | R v F | Air Cdr G.C. Lamb (Eng.) |
| | W v E | Mr D.P. d'Arcy (Ire.) |
| | F v S | Mr K.D. Kelleher (Ire.) |
| | I v F | Air Cdr G.C. Lamb (Eng.) |
| | S v W | Mr M.H. Titcomb (Eng.) |
| | I v E | Mr M. Joseph (Wales) |
| | E v F | Mr A.R. Lewis (Wales) |
| | S v I | Mr W.K.M. Jones (Wales) |
| | W v I | Mr R.F. Johnson (Eng.) |
| | E v S | Mr C. Durand (Fr.) |
| | F v W | Mr J. Young (Scot.) |
| | S v E | Mr M. Joseph (Wales) |
| | E v P | Mr M.H. Titcomb (Eng.) |
| 1971 | SA v F(2) | Dr W.C. Malan (SA) |
| | NZ v BI(4) | Mr J.P.G. Pring (NZ) |
| | A v SA(2) | Mr C.F. Ferguson (Aus.) |
| | A v SA | Dr I.R. Vanderfield (Aus.) |
| 1971-72 | F v A | Mr E.M. Lewis (Wales) |
| | F v A | Air Cdr G.C. Lamb (Eng.) |
| | F v R | Mr T.F.E. Grierson (Scot.) |
| | S v F | Mr M. Joseph (Wales) |
| | E v W | Mr J. Young (Scot.) |
| | F v I | Mr A.R. Lewis (Wales) |
| | W v S | Mr G.A. Jamison (Ire.) |
| | E v I | Mr R. Austry (Fr.) |
| | F v E | Mr T.F.E. Grierson (Scot.) |
| | S v E | Mr M. Joseph (Wales) |
| | W v F | Mr M.H. Titcomb (Eng.) |
| | I v F | Mr R.F. Johnson (Eng.) |
| 1972 | SA v E | Dr J. Moolman (SA) |
| | A v F | Mr W.M. Cooney (Aus.) |
| | A v F | Mr J.R. Reilly (Aus.) |
| | NZ v A | Mr P.A. McDavitt (NZ) |
| | NZ v A | Mr J.P.G. Pring (NZ) |
| | NZ v A | Mr A.R. Taylor (NZ) |
| | Fj v A | Mr J. Costello (Fiji) |
| 1972-73 | R v F | Mr J. Young (Scot.) |
| | W v NZ | Mr R.F. Johnson (Eng.) |
| | S v NZ | Mr G. Domercq (Fr.) |
| | E v NZ | Mr J. Young (Scot.) |
| | F v S | Mr K.A. Pattinson (Eng.) replaced by |
| | | Mr F. Palmade (Fr.) |
| | I v NZ | Mr M. Joseph (Wales) |
| | W v E | Mr G. Domercq (Fr.) |
| | S v W | Mr F. Palmade (Fr.) |
| | I v E | Mr A.M. Hosie (Scot.) |
| | F v NZ | Mr D.P. d'Arcy (Ire.) |
| | S v I | Mr A.R. Lewis (Wales) |
| | E v F | Mr K.H. Clark (Ire.) |
| | W v I | Mr T.F.E. Grierson (Scot.) |
| | E v S | Mr. J.C. Kelleher (Wales) |
| | F v W | Mr D.P. d'Arcy (Ire.) |
| | S v P | Mr M. Joseph (Wales) |
| | I v F | Mr R.F. Johnson (Eng.) |
| 1973 | A v Tg | Dr I.R. Vanderfield (Aus.) |
| | A v Tg | Mr R.T. Burnett (Aus.) |
| | NZ v E | Mr R.F. McMullen (NZ) |
| 1973-74 | F v J | Mr M. Joseph (Wales) |
| | W v A | Mr K.A. Pattinson (Eng.) |
| | F v R | Mr D.P. d'Arcy (Ire.) |
| | E v A | Mr A.R. Lewis (Wales) |
| | F v I | Mr A.M. Hosie (Scot.) |
| | W v S | Mr R.F. Johnson (Eng.) |
| | S v E | Mr J. St Guilhem (Fr.) |

|  | I v W | Mr K.A. Pattinson (Eng.) |
|  | E v I | Mr M. Joseph (Wales) |
|  | W v F | Mr N.R. Sanson (Scot.) |
|  | I v S | Mr F. Palmade (Fr.) |
|  | F v E | Mr J.C. Kelleher (Wales) |
|  | S v F | Mr K.H. Clark (Ire.) |
|  | E v W | Mr J.R. West (Ire.) |
| 1974 | A v NZ(2) | Dr I.R. Vanderfield (Aus.) |
|  | A v NZ | Mr R.T. Burnett (Aus.) |
|  | SA v BI(2) | Mr M. Baise (SA) |
|  | SA v BI(2) | Mr C.J. de Bruyn (SA) |
|  | Arg v F(2) | Mr A.R. Lewis (Wales) |
| 1974-75 | I v P | Mr N.R. Sanson (Scot.) |
|  | R v F | Mr K.A. Pattinson (Eng.) |
|  | I v NZ | Mr R.F. Johnson (Eng.) |
|  | F v SA | Mr N.R. Sanson (Scot.) |
|  | F v SA | Mr R.F. Johnson (Eng.) |
|  | I v E | Mr F. Palmade (Fr.) |
|  | F v W | Mr K.A. Pattinson (Eng.) |
|  | E v F | Mr T.F.E. Grierson (Scot.) |
|  | S v I | Mr R.F. Johnson (Eng.) |
|  | W v E | Mr A.M. Hosie (Scot.) |
|  | F v S | Mr M.S. Lewis (Wales) |
|  | I v F | Mr D.M. Lloyd (Wales) |
|  | S v W | Mr J.R. West (Ire.) |
|  | E v S | Mr D.P. d'Arcy (Ire.) |
|  | W v I | Mr J. St Guilhem (Fr.) |
| 1975 | A v E | Mr W.M. Cooney (Aus.) |
|  | A v E | Mr R.T. Burnett (Aus.) |
|  | NZ v S | Mr P.A. McDavitt (NZ) |
|  | SA v F(2) | Mr N.R. Sanson (Scot.) |
|  | A v J | Mr W.M. Cooney (Aus.) |
|  | A v J | Mr R.T. Burnett (Aus.) |
| 1975-76 | F v Arg | Mr D.P. d'Arcy (Ire.) |
|  | F v Arg | Mr M. Joseph (Wales) |
|  | F v R | Mr N.R. Sanson (Scot.) |
|  | S v A | Mr R.F. Johnson (Eng.) |
|  | W v A | Mr D.P. d'Arcy (Ire.) |
|  | E v A | Mr M. Joseph (Wales) |
|  | S v F | Mr K.A. Pattinson (Eng.) |
|  | E v W | Mr G. Domercq (Fr.) |
|  | I v A | Mr N.R. Sanson (Scot.) |
|  | US v A | Mr A.C. Pontin (USA) |
|  | F v I | Mr A. Welsby (Eng.) |
|  | W v S | Dr A. Cluny (Fr.) |
|  | S v E | Mr D.M. Lloyd (Wales) |
|  | I v W | Mr N.R. Sanson (Scot.) |
|  | E v I | Mr A.M. Hosie (Scot.) |
|  | W v F | Mr J.R. West (Ire.) |
|  | F v E | Mr K.H. Clark (Ire.) |
|  | I v S | Mr M.S. Lewis (Wales) |
| 1976 | NZ v I | Mr T.F. Doocey (NZ) |
|  | US v F | Mr J. Curnow (Can.) |
|  | A v Fj | Mr R.G. Byres (Aus.) |
|  | A v Fj | Mr K.J. Crowe (Aus.) |
|  | A v Fj | Mr W.M. Cooney (Aus.) |
|  | SA v NZ | Mr I.W. Gourlay (SA) |
|  | SA v NZ(3) | Mr G.P. Bezuidenhout (SA) |
| 1976-77 | F v A | Mr A.M. Hosie (Scot.) |
|  | F v A | Mr M. Joseph (Wales) |
|  | R v F | Mr J.C. Kelleher (Wales) |
|  | E v S | Mr M. Joseph (Wales) |
|  | W v I | Mr N.R. Sanson (Scot.) |
|  | I v E | Mr F. Palmade (Fr.) |
|  | F v W | Mr A.M. Hosie (Scot.) |
|  | E v F | Mr J.C. Kelleher (Wales) |
|  | S v I | Mr M. Joseph (Wales) |
|  | W v E | Mr D.I.H. Burnett (Ire.) |
|  | F v S | Mr M. Joseph (Wales) |
|  | I v F | Mr A.M. Hosie (Scot.) |
|  | S v W | Mr G. Domercq (Fr.) |
| 1977 | NZ v BI | Mr P.A. McDavitt (NZ) |
|  | NZ v BI | Mr B.W. Duffy (NZ) |
|  | NZ v BI(2) | Mr D.H. Millar (NZ) |
|  | Arg v F(2) | Mr R.C. Quittenton (Eng.) |
|  | SA v Wld | Dr J. Gouws (SA) |

| 1977-78 | F v NZ | Mr J.R. West (Ire.) |
|  | F v NZ | Mr C.G.P. Thomas (Wales) |
|  | F v R | Mr P.E. Hughes (Eng.) |
|  | I v S | Mr P.E. Hughes (Eng.) |
|  | F v E | Mr N.R. Sanson (Scot.) |
|  | E v W | Mr N.R. Sanson (Scot.) |
|  | S v F | Mr C.G.P. Thomas (Wales) |
|  | F v I | Mr C.G.P. Thomas (Wales) |
|  | W v S | Mr J.R. West (Ire.) |
|  | S v E | Mr J.R. West (Ire.) |
|  | I v W | Mr G. Domercq (Fr.) |
|  | E v I | Mr F. Palmade (Fr.) |
|  | W v F | Mr A. Welsby (Eng.) |
| 1978 | A v W | Mr R.T. Burnett (Aus.) |
|  | A v W | Mr R.G. Byres (Aus.) |
|  | NZ v A(3) | Mr D.H. Millar (NZ) |
| 1978-79 | I v NZ | Mr C. Norling (Wales) |
|  | W v NZ | Mr R.C. Quittenton (Eng.) |
|  | E v NZ | Mr N.R. Sanson (Scot.) |
|  | R v F | Mr M.D.M. Rea (Ire.) |
|  | S v NZ | Mr J.R. West (Ire.) |
|  | I v F | Mr R.C. Quittenton (Eng.) |
|  | S v W | Mr F. Palmade (Fr.) |
|  | E v S | Mr C. Norling (Wales) |
|  | W v I | Mr A.M. Hosie (Scot.) |
|  | I v E | Mr A.M. Hosie (Scot.) |
|  | F v W | Mr D.I.H. Burnett (Ire.) |
|  | E v F | Mr J.R. West (Ire.) |
|  | S v I | Mr C. Thomas (Wales) |
|  | F v S | Mr R.C. Quittenton (Eng.) |
|  | W v E | Mr J-P Bonnet (Fr.) |
| 1979 | A v I(2) | Mr R.G. Byres (Aus.) |
|  | NZ v F(2) | Mr J.R. West (Ire.) |
|  | A v NZ | Mr R.G. Byres (Aus.) |
|  | Arg v A(2) | Mr S. Strydom (SA) |
| 1979-80 | S v NZ | Mr R.C. Quittenton (Eng.) |
|  | E v NZ | Mr N.R. Sanson (Scot.) |
|  | F v R | Mr J.A. Short (Scot.) |
|  | E v I | Mr C. Thomas (Wales) |
|  | W v F | Mr A.M. Hosie (Scot.) |
|  | F v E | Mr C. Norling (Wales) |
|  | I v S | Mr G. Chevrier (Fr.) |
|  | E v W | Mr D.I.H. Burnett (Ire.) |
|  | S v F | Mr J.R. West (Ire.) |
|  | F v I | Mr A.M. Hosie (Scot.) |
|  | W v S | Mr L. Prideaux (Eng.) |
|  | I v W | Mr L. Prideaux (Eng.) |
|  | S v E | Mr J-P Bonnet (Fr.) |
| 1980 | SA v S Am(2) | Mr K. Rowlands (Wales) |
|  | Fj v A | Mr G.L. Harrison (NZ) |
|  | SA v BI(2) | Mr F. Palmade (Fr.) |
|  | SA v BI(2) | Mr J-P Bonnet (Fr.) |
|  | A v NZ(2) | Mr A.F. Garling (Aus.) |
|  | A v NZ | Mr R.G. Byres (Aus.) |
|  | S Am v SA(2) | Mr L. Prideaux (Eng.) |
|  | SA v F | Mr J.R. West (Ire.) |
| 1980-81 | W v NZ | Mr J.R. West (Ire.) |
|  | R v F | Mr A. Richards (Wales) |
|  | F v S | Mr K. Rowlands (Wales) |
|  | W v E | Mr J.B. Anderson (Scot.) |
|  | I v F | Mr C. Norling (Wales) |
|  | S v W | Mr D.I.H. Burnett (Ire.) |
|  | E v S | Mr D.I.H. Burnett (Ire.) |
|  | W v I | Mr F. Palmade (Fr.) |
|  | F v W | Mr A. Welsby (Eng.) |
|  | I v E | Mr J-P Bonnet (Fr.) |
|  | E v F | Mr A.M. Hosie (Scot.) |
|  | S v I | Mr L. Prideaux (Eng.) |
| 1981 | Arg v E(2) | Mr J-P Bonnet (Fr.) |
|  | NZ v S | Mr R.G. Byres (Aus.) |
|  | NZ v S | Mr C.K. Collett (Aus.) |
|  | SA v I(2) | Mr F. Palmade (Fr.) |
|  | A v F | Mr G.L. Harrison (NZ) |
|  | A v F | Mr A. Richards (Wales) |
|  | NZ v SA | Mr L. Prideaux (Eng.) |
|  | NZ v SA(2) | Mr C. Norling (Wales) |
|  | US v SA | Mr D. Morrison (USA) |

| | | |
|---|---|---|
| 1981-82 | S v R | Mr M.D.M. Rea (Ire.) |
| | R v NZ | Mr A.M. Hosie (Scot.) |
| | F v R | Mr J.A.F. Trigg (Eng.) |
| | F v NZ | Mr C. Norling (Wales) |
| | F v NZ | Mr J.R. West (Ire.) |
| | I v A | Mr J.B. Anderson (Scot.) |
| | W v A | Mr J.R. West (Ire.) |
| | S v A | Mr R.C. Quittenton (Eng.) |
| | E v A | Mr A. Richards (Wales) |
| | S v E | Mr K. Rowlands (Wales) |
| | I v W | Mr J.A. Short (Scot.) |
| | E v I | Mr A.M. Hosie (Scot.) |
| | W v F | Mr D.I.H. Burnett (Ire.) |
| | I v S | Mr C. Norling (Wales) |
| | F v E | Mr M.D.M. Rea (Ire.) |
| | E v W | Mr F. Palmade (Fr.) |
| | S v F | Mr J.A.F. Trigg (Eng.) |
| | W v S | Mr J-P Bonnet (Scot.) |
| | F v I | Mr A. Welsby (Eng.) |
| 1982 | SA v S Am | Mr S. Strydom (SA) |
| | SA v S Am | Mr F. Muller (SA) |
| | A v S(2) | Mr R.G. Byres (Aus.) |
| | NZ v A | Mr R.C. Quittenton (Eng.) |
| | NZ v A(2) | Mr A.M. Hosie (Scot.) |
| 1982-83 | R v F | Mr J.B. Anderson (Scot.) |
| | F v Arg | Mr J.R. West (Ire.) |
| | F v Arg | Mr D.I.H. Burnett (Ire.) |
| | E v F | Mr D.I.H. Burnett (Ire.) |
| | S v I | Mr J-C Yche (Fr.) |
| | W v E | Mr J.R. West (Ire.) |
| | F v S | Mr A. Richards (Wales) |
| | I v F | Mr A.M. Hosie (Scot.) |
| | S v W | Mr R.C. Quittenton (Eng.) |
| | E v S | Mr T.F. Doocey (NZ) |
| | W v I | Mr J.A.F. Trigg (Eng.) |
| | I v E | Mr J.B. Anderson (Scot.) |
| | F v W | Mr T.F. Doocey (NZ) |
| 1983 | A v US | Mr G.L. Harrison (NZ) |
| | NZ v BI(2) | Mr F. Palmade (Fr.) |
| | NZ v BI(2) | Mr R.G. Byres (Aus.) |
| | A v Arg(2) | Mr C. Norling (Wales) |
| | A v NZ | Mr J.B. Anderson (Scot.) |
| 1983-84 | It v A | Mr J-C Yche (Fr.) |
| | R v W | Mr J-C Yche (Fr.) |
| | S v NZ | Mr R. Hourquet (Fr.) |
| | F v A(2) | Mr G.L. Harrison (NZ) |
| | E v NZ | Mr A.M. Hosie (Scot.) |
| | F v R | Mr R.C. Quittenton (Eng.) |
| | W v S | Mr O.E. Doyle (Ire.) |
| | F v I | Mr C. Norling (Wales) |
| | I v W | Mr R.G. Byres (Aus.) |
| | S v E | Mr D.I.H. Burnett (Ire.) |
| | W v F | Mr R.G. Byres (Aus.) |
| | E v I | Mr R. Hourquet (Fr.) |
| | I v S | Mr F.A. Howard (Eng.) |
| | F v E | Mr A.M. Hosie (Scot.) |
| | E v W | Mr J.B. Anderson (Scot.) |
| | S v F | Mr W. Jones (Wales) |
| | R v S | Mr O.E. Doyle (Ire.) |
| 1984 | Fj v A | Mr G.L. Harrison (NZ) |
| | SA v E(2) | Mr R. Hourquet (Fr.) |
| | NZ v F(2) | Mr W. Jones (Wales) |

| | | |
|---|---|---|
| | A v NZ(2) | Mr R.C. Quittenton (Eng.) |
| | A v NZ | Mr D.I.H. Burnett (Ire.) |
| | SA v S Am(2) | Mr R. Hourquet (Fr.) |
| 1984-85 | E v A | Mr R.C. Francis (NZ) |
| | I v A | Mr R.C. Francis (NZ) |
| | R v F | Mr J.R. West (Ire.) |
| | W v A | Mr O.E. Doyle (Ire.) |
| | S v A | Mr S.R. Hilditch (Ire.) |
| | E v R | Mr W.D. Bevan (Wales) |
| | E v F | Mr D.I.H. Burnett (Ire.) |
| | S v I | Mr S. Strydom (SA) |
| | F v S | Mr L. Prideaux (Eng.) |
| | S v W | Mr R. Hourquet (Fr.) |
| | I v F | Mr K.V.J. Fitzgerald (Aus.) |
| | E v S | Mr C. Norling (Wales) |
| | W v I | Mr K.V.J. Fitzgerald (Aus.) |
| | F v W | Mr S. Strydom (SA) |
| | I v E | Mr J.M. Fleming (Scot.) |
| | W v E | Mr F. Palmade (Fr.) |
| 1985 | NZ v E(2) | Mr K.V.J. Fitzgerald (Aus.) |
| | A v C(2) | Mr K.H. Lawrence (NZ) |
| | Arg v F(2) | Mr R.C. Francis (NZ) |
| | NZ v A | Mr D.I.H. Burnett (Ire.) |
| | A v Fj(2) | Mr J-C Yche (Fr.) |
| | Arg v NZ(2) | Mr K.V.J. Fitzgerald (Aus.) |
| 1985-86 | W v Fj | Mr S.R. Hilditch (Ire.) |
| | E v W | Mr R.J. Fordham (Aus.) |
| | S v F | Mr D.I.H. Burnett (Ire.) |
| | W v S | Mr R.C. Francis (NZ) |
| | F v I | Mr R.J. Fordham (Aus.) |
| | S v E | Mr R.C. Francis (NZ) |
| | I v W | Mr F.A. Howard (Eng.) |
| | E v I | Mr C. Norling (Wales) |
| | W v F | Mr J.B. Anderson (Scot.) |
| | I v S | Mr F. Palmade (Fr.) |
| | F v E | Mr W.D. Bevan (Wales) |
| | R v S | Mr R.C. Quittenton (Eng.) |
| | F v R | Mr C.A. Waldron (Aus.) |
| 1986 | SA v Cv(4) | Mr K. Rowlands (Wales) |
| | A v It | Mr K.H. Lawrence (NZ) |
| | Arg v F(2) | Mr R.J. Fordham (Aus.) |
| | Fj v W | Mr D.J. Bishop (NZ) |
| | Tg v W | Mr B. Kinsey (Aus.) |
| | W Sm v W | Mr R.C. Francis (NZ) |
| | A v F | Mr F.A. Howard (Eng.) |
| | NZ v F | Mr F.A. Howard (Eng.) |
| | A v Arg(2) | Mr J.M. Fleming (Scot.) |
| | NZ v A(2) | Mr W.D. Bevan (Wales) |
| | NZ v A | Mr J.B. Anderson (Scot.) |
| 1986-87 | R v F | Mr D.J. Bishop (NZ) |
| | I v R | Mr D.J. Bishop (NZ) |
| | F v NZ(2) | Mr S. Strydom (SA) |
| | I v E | Mr R. Hourquet (Fr.) |
| | F v W | Mr C.J. High (Eng.) |
| | S v I | Mr R.C. Quittenton (Eng.) |
| | E v F | Mr J.M. Fleming (Scot.) |
| | F v S | Mr K.H. Lawrence (NZ) |
| | W v E | Mr R. Megson (Scot.) |
| | S v W | Mr K.H. Lawrence (NZ) |
| | I v F | Mr C. Norling (Wales) |
| | E v S | Mr O.E. Doyle (Ire.) |
| | W v I | Mr G. Maurette (Fr.) |

## MOST INTERNATIONAL APPEARANCES

| 23 | D.G. Walters | (Wales) | between 1958-59 and 1965-66 |
|---|---|---|---|
| 23 | K.D. Kelleher | (Ire.) | between 1959-60 and 1970-71 |
| 22 | M. Joseph | (Wales) | between 1966-67 and 1976-77 |
| 21 | R.C. Williams | (Ire.) | between 1956-57 and 1963-64 |
| 19 | A.M. Hosie | (Scot.) | between 1972-73 and 1983-84 |
| 18 | M.J. Dowling | (Ire.) | between 1946-47 and 1955-56 |
| 18 | J.R. West | (Ire.) | between 1973-74 and 1984-85 |

## REFEREES WHO HAVE DISMISSED PLAYERS IN INTERNATIONALS

| A.E. Freethy | dismissed | C.J. Brownlie (NZ) | E v NZ 1925 |
|---|---|---|---|
| K.D. Kelleher | dismissed | C.E. Meads (NZ) | S v NZ 1967 |
| R.T. Burnett | dismissed | M.A. Burton (Eng.) | A v E 1975 |
| W.M. Cooney | dismissed | J.Sovau (Fiji) | A v Fj 1976 |
| N.R. Sanson | dismissed | G.A.D. Wheel (Wales) | W v I 1977 |
| N.R. Sanson | dismissed | W.P. Duggan (Ire.) | W v I 1977 |
| D.I.H. Burnett | dismissed | P. Ringer (Wales) | E v W 1980 |
| C. Norling | dismissed | J-P Garuet (Fr.) | F v I 1984 |

## REFEREES WHO HAVE APPEARED IN INTERNATIONALS AS REPLACEMENTS

| B. Marie | (Fr.) | replaced R.W. Gilliland | F v W 1965 |
|---|---|---|---|
| A.R. Taylor | (NZ) | replaced J.P. Murphy | NZ v SA 1965 |
| R.F. Johnson | (Eng.) | replaced R. Calmet | E v W 1970 |
| F. Palmade | (Fr.) | replaced K.A. Pattinson | F v S 1973 |

# COMBINED INTERNATIONAL
# RECORDS AND STATISTICS

# INTERNATIONAL RECORDS

## MOST CONSECUTIVE MATCHES WON

17    by New Zealand between 1965 and 1969

## MOST CONSECUTIVE MATCHES WITHOUT DEFEAT

17    by New Zealand between 1961 and 1964
17    by New Zealand between 1965 and 1969

## MOST CONSECUTIVE MATCHES WITHOUT CONCEDING A TRY

10    by England between 1874-75 and 1878-79

## MOST CONSECUTIVE MATCHES WITHOUT CONCEDING A SCORE

7    by Scotland between 1884-85 and 1886-87

## MOST POINTS IN A MATCH
### By a team

60    by France v Italy Toulon 1966-67
60    by Ireland v Romania Dublin 1986-87

### By a player

27    by G. Camberabero for France v Italy Toulon 1966-67

## MOST TRIES IN A MATCH
### By a team

13    by England v Wales Blackheath 1880-81
13    by New Zealand v United States Berkeley 1913
13    by France v Romania Paris 1923-24

### By a player

5    by G.C. Lindsay for Scotland v Wales Edinburgh 1886-87
5    by D. Lambert for for England v France Richmond 1906-07

## MOST CONVERSIONS IN A MATCH
### By a team

9    by France v Italy Toulon 1966-67

### By a player

9    by G. Camberabero for France v Italy Toulon 1966-67

## MOST DROPPED GOALS IN A MATCH
### By a team

3    by France v Ireland Paris 1959-60
3    by Australia v England Twickenham 1966-67
3    by Scotland v Ireland Edinburgh 1972-73
3    by South Africa v South America Durban 1980
3    by South Africa v Ireland Durban 1981
3    by Australia v Ireland Dublin 1984-85
3    by France v England Twickenham 1984-85
3    by Australia v Fiji Brisbane 1985
3    by New Zealand v France Christchurch 1986
3    by France v New Zealand Christchurch 1986

### By a player

| | |
|---|---|
| 3 | by P. Albaladejo for France v Ireland Paris 1959-60 |
| 3 | by P. F. Hawthorne for Australia v England Twickenham 1966-67 |
| 3 | by H. E. Botha for South Africa v South America Durban 1980 |
| 3 | by H. E. Botha for South Africa v Ireland Durban 1981 |
| 3 | by J. P. Lescarboura for France v England Twickenham 1984-85 |
| 3 | by J. P. Lescarboura for France v New Zealand Christchurch 1986 |

## MOST PENALTY GOALS IN A MATCH
### By a team

| | |
|---|---|
| 7 | by South Africa v France Pretoria 1975 |

### By a player

| | |
|---|---|
| 6 | by D. B. Clarke for New Zealand v British Isles Dunedin 1959 |
| 6 | by G. R. Bosch for South Africa v France Pretoria 1975 |
| 6 | by J. M. Aguirre for France v Argentina Buenos Aires 1977 |
| 6 | by G. Evans for Wales v France Cardiff 1981-82 |
| 6 | by S. O. Campbell for Ireland v Scotland Dublin 1981-82 |
| 6 | by K. J. Crowley for New Zealand v England Christchurch 1985 |
| 6 | by A. G. Hastings for Scotland v France Edinburgh 1985-86 |
| 6 | by C. R. Andrew for England v Wales Twickenham 1985-86 |
| 6 | by M. P. Lynagh for Australia v France Sydney 1986 |

## MOST GOALS FROM MARKS IN A MATCH
### By a team

| | |
|---|---|
| 2 | by New Zealand v Australia Sydney 1903 |

### By a player

| | |
|---|---|
| 2 | by W. J. Wallace for New Zealand v Australia Sydney 1903 |

## MOST POINTS IN A MATCH BY A PLAYER ON DEBUT

| | |
|---|---|
| 21 | by R. Blair for South Africa v World XV Pretoria 1977 |
| 21 | by D. Knox for Australia v Fiji Brisbane 1985 |

## MOST TRIES IN A MATCH BY A PLAYER ON DEBUT

| | |
|---|---|
| 5 | by D. Lambert for England v France Richmond 1906-07 |

## MOST POINTS BY A PLAYER IN A SERIES

| | |
|---|---|
| 69 | by H. E. Botha for South Africa v NZ Cavaliers in 1986 |

## PLAYERS SCORING A FULL SET IN A MATCH

*(i.e. a try, conversion, drop-goal and penalty goal)*

J. Shea for Wales v England Swansea 1919-20
B. L. Jones for British Isles v Australia Brisbane 1950
D. B. Clarke for New Zealand v England Auckland 1963
G. Camberabero for France v Wales Paris 1966-67
J. P. Romeu for France v England Paris 1973-74
A. R. Hewson for New Zealand v Australia Auckland 1982
J. P. Lescarboura for France v Romania Toulouse 1983-84

## LONGEST CAREER SPAN IN SEASONS

| | |
|---|---|
| 16 | by G. M. Cooke for Australia between 1932 and 1947-48 |
| 16 | by A. R. Miller for Australia between 1952 and 1967 |
| 16 | by A. J. F. O'Reilly for Ireland between 1954-55 and 1969-70 |
| 16 | by C. M. H. Gibson for Ireland between 1963-64 and 1979 |

*(T. H. Vile's combined career for Britain and Wales spanned the seasons 1904 and 1920-21)*

## MOST CONSECUTIVE APPEARANCES IN A CAREER

53     by G. O. Edwards for Wales between 1966-67 and 1978-79

## MOST APPEARANCES IN A CAREER

69     by C. M. H. Gibson for Ireland between 1963-64 and 1979
69     by R. Bertranne for France between 1970-71 and 1981-82

*(Gibson's combined career for Britain and Ireland included 81 appearances in internationals)*

## MOST APPEARANCES AS CAPTAIN

34     by J. P. Rives for France between 1974-75 and 1983-84

## MOST POINTS IN A CAREER

273     by A. R. Irvine for Scotland between 1972-73 and 1982

*(Irvine's combined career for Britain and Scotland included 301 points in internationals)*

## FASTEST PLAYER TO REACH A CENTURY OF POINTS

A. G. Hastings for Scotland in his 9th international

## MOST TRIES IN A CAREER

24     by I. S. Smith for Scotland between 1923-24 and 1932-33

## MOST TRIES BY A FULL-BACK

13     by S. Blanco for France between 1980 and 1986-87

*(Blanco has scored additional tries as a wing in internationals)*

## MOST CONVERSIONS IN A CAREER

45     by M. Vannier for France between 1952-53 and 1961

## MOST DROP-GOALS IN A CAREER

14     by H. E. Botha for South Africa between 1980 and 1986
14     by J. P. Lescarboura for France between 1981-82 and 1986-87

## MOST PENALTY GOALS IN A CAREER

67     by W. H. Hare for England between 1973-74 and 1984

*(A. R. Irvine also kicked 67 in his combined international career for Scotland and Britain)*

## MOST GOALS FROM MARKS IN A CAREER

2     by W. J. Wallace for New Zealand between 1903 and 1908
2     by D. B. Clarke for New Zealand between 1956 and 1964

# INTERNATIONAL PLAYERS BIRTHS AND DEATHS

Compiled by Timothy Auty

# ENGLAND

| PLAYER | CAREER SPAN | | |
|---|---|---|---|
| AARVOLD, Carl Douglas | (1928-33) | b 7.6.1907 | |
| ADAMS, Alan Augustus | (1910) | b 8.5.1883 | d 28.7.1963 |
| ADAMS, Frank Reginald | (1875-9) | b 1853 | d 1932 |
| ADEY, Gary John | (1976) | b 13.6.1947 | |
| ADKINS, Stanley John | (1950-3) | b 2.6.1922 | |
| AGAR, Albert Eustace | (1952-3) | b 12.11.1923 | |
| ALCOCK, Arnold | (1906) | b 18.8.1882 | d 7.11.1973 |
| ALDERSON, Frederic Hodgson Rudd | (1891-3) | b 27.6.1867 | d 18.2.1925 |
| ALEXANDER, Harry | (1900-02) | b 6.1.1879 | d 17.10.1915 |
| ALEXANDER, William | (1927) | b 6.10.1905 | |
| ALLISON, Dennis Fenwick | (1956-8) | b 20.4.1931 | |
| ALLPORT, Alfred | (1892-4) | b 12.9.1867 | d 2.5.1949 |
| ANDERSON, Stanley | (1899) | | |
| ANDERSON, William Francis | (1973) | b 1945 | |
| ANDERTON, Charles | (1889) | | |
| ANDREW, Christopher Robert | (1985-  ) | b 18.2.1963 | |
| ARCHER, Herbert | (1909) | b 8.1884 | d 26.12.1946 |
| ARMSTRONG, Reginald | (1925) | b 6.12.1898 | d 17.2.1968 |
| ARTHUR, Terence Gordon | (1966) | b 5.9.1940 | |
| ASHBY, Roland Clive | (1966-7) | b 24.1.1937 | |
| ASHCROFT, Alan | (1956-9) | b 21.8.1930 | |
| ASHCROFT, Alec Hutchinson | (1909) | b 18.10.1887 | d 18.4.1963 |
| ASHFORD, William | (1897-8) | b 18.12.1871 | d 1.1.1954 |
| ASHWORTH, Abel | (1892) | b 1864 | d 10.1.1938 |
| ASKEW, John Garbutt | (1930) | b 2.9.1908 | d 31.8.1942 |
| ASLETT, Alfred Rimbault | (1926-9) | b 14.1.1901 | d 5.1980 |
| ASSINDER, Eric Walter | (1909) | b 29.8.1885 | d 11.10.1974 |
| ASTON, Randolph Littleton | (1890) | b 6.9.1869 | d 3.11.1930 |
| AUTY, Joseph Richard | (1935) | b 19.8.1910 | |
| BAILEY, Mark David | (1984-  ) | b 21.11.1960 | |
| BAINBRIDGE, Stephen | (1982-  ) | b 7.10.1956 | |
| BAKER, Douglas George Santley | (1955) | b 29.11.1929 | |
| BAKER, Edward Morgan | (1895-7) | b 12.8.1874 | d 25.11.1940 |
| BAKER, Hiatt Cowles | (1887) | b 30.6.1863 | d 19.9.1934 |
| BANCE, John Forsyth | (1954) | b 15.1.1925 | |
| BARLEY, Bryan | (1984-  ) | b 4.1.1960 | |
| BARNES, Stuart | (1984-  ) | b 22.11.1962 | |
| BARR, Robert John | (1932) | b 26.5.1907 | d 24.9.1975 |
| BARRETT, Edward Ivo Medhurst | (1903) | b 22.6.1879 | d 10.7.1950 |
| BARRINGTON, Thomas James Mountstevens | (1931) | b 8.7.1908 | |
| BARRINGTON-WARD, Lancelot Edward | (1910) | b 4.7.1884 | d 17.11.1953 |
| BARRON, James Henry | (1896-7) | b 28.8.1874 | d 2.12.1942 |
| BARTLETT, Jasper Twining | (1951) | b 17.10.1924 | d 16.1.1969 |
| BARTLETT, Richard Michael | (1957-8) | b 13.2.1929 | d 5.3.1984 |
| BARTON, John | (1967-72) | b 19.3.1943 | |
| BATCHELOR, Tremlett Brewer | (1907) | b 22.6.1884 | d 21.12.1966 |
| BATESON, Alfred Hardy | (1930) | b 10.8.1901 | d 21.2.1982 |
| BATESON, Harold Dingwall | (1879) | b 2.5.1856 | d 29.10.1927 |
| BATSON, Thomas | (1872-5) | b 1852 | d 5.2.1933 |
| BATTEN, John Maxwell | (1874) | b 28.2.1853 | d 15.10.1917 |
| BAUME, John Lea | (1950) | b 18.7.1920 | |
| BAXTER, James | (1900) | b 8.6.1870 | d 5.7.1940 |
| BAZLEY, Reginald Charles | (1952-5) | b 15.12.1929 | |
| BEAUMONT, William Blackledge | (1975-82) | b 9.3.1952 | |
| BEDFORD, Harry | (1889-90) | b 1866 | d 1.1929 |
| BEDFORD, Lawrence Leslie | (1931) | b 11.2.1903 | d 25.11.1963 |
| BEER, Ian David Stafford | (1955) | b 28.4.1931 | |
| BEESE, Michael Christopher | (1972) | b 8.10.1948 | |
| BELL, F.J. | (1900) | | |

| PLAYER | CAREER SPAN | | |
|---|---|---|---|
| BELL, Henry | (1884) | b 1860 | d 20.9.1935 |
| BELL, John Lowthian | (1878) | b 1853 | d 16.12.1916 |
| BELL, Peter Joseph | (1968) | b 28.4.1937 | |
| BELL, Robert William | (1900) | b 19.12.1875 | d 9.6.1940 |
| BENDON, Gordon John | (1959) | b 9.4.1929 | |
| BENNETT, Norman Osborn | (1947-8) | b 21.9.1922 | |
| BENNETT, William Neil | (1975-9) | b 20.4.1951 | |
| BENNETTS, Barzillia Beckerleg | (1909) | b 14.7.1883 | d 26.7.1958 |
| BENTLEY, John Edmund | (1871-2) | b 1847 | d 12.12.1913 |
| BERRIDGE, Michael John | (1949) | b 28.2.1923 | d 2.10.1973 |
| BERRY, Henry | (1910) | b 8.1.1883 | d 9.5.1915 |
| BERRY, John | (1891) | b 25.9.1866 | d 10.5.1930 |
| BERRY, Joseph Thomas Wade | (1939) | b 17.7.1907 | |
| BESWICK, Edmund | (1882) | b 1860 | d 22.1.1911 |
| BIGGS, John Maundy | (1878-9) | b 1855 | d 3.6.1935 |
| BIRKETT, John Guy Gilberne | (1906-12) | b 27.12.1884 | d 16.10.1968 |
| BIRKETT, Louis | (1875-7) | b 1.1.1853 | d 11.4.1943 |
| BIRKETT, Reginald Halsey | (1871-7) | b 28.3.1849 | d 30.6.1898 |
| BISHOP, Colin Charles | (1927) | b 5.10.1903 | d 4.3.1980 |
| BLACK, Brian Henry | (1930-3) | b 27.5.1907 | d 29.7.1940 |
| BLACKLOCK, J.H. | (1898-9) | b 20.10.1878 | d 28.6.1945 |
| BLAKEWAY, Philip John | (1980-5) | b 31.12.1950 | |
| BLAKISTON, Arthur Frederick | (1920-5) | b 16.6.1892 | d 2.1974 |
| BLATHERWICK, Thomas | (1878) | b 25.12.1855 | d 29.6.1940 |
| BODY, James Alfred | (1872-3) | b 1846 | d 9.9.1929 |
| BOLTON, Charles Arthur | (1909) | b 3.1.1882 | d 23.11.1963 |
| BOLTON, Reginald | (1933-8) | b 20.11.1909 | |
| BOLTON, Wilfred Nash | (1882-7) | b 14.9.1862 | d 12.8.1930 |
| BONAVENTURA, Maurice Sydney | (1931) | b 28.4.1902 | |
| BOND, Anthony Matthew | (1978-82) | b 3.8.1954 | |
| BONHAM-CARTER, Edgar | (1891) | b 2.4.1870 | d 24.4.1956 |
| BONSOR, Frederick | (1886-9) | b 1865 | d 2.1933 |
| BOOBBYER, Brian | (1950-2) | b 25.2.1928 | |
| BOOTH, Lewis Alfred | (1933-5) | b 26.9.1909 | d 25.6.1942 |
| BOTTING, Ian James | (1950) | b 18.5.1922 | d 9.7.1980 |
| BOUGHTON, Harold J. | (1935) | b 7.9.1910 | |
| BOYLE, Cecil William | (1873) | b 16.3.1853 | d 5.4.1900 |
| BOYLE, Stephen Brent | (1983)) | b 9.8.1953 | |
| BOYLEN, Francis | (1908) | b 1879 | d 3.2.1938 |
| BRADBY, Matthew Seymour | (1922) | b 25.3.1899 | |
| BRADLEY, Robert | (1903) | | |
| BRADSHAW, Harry | (1892-4) | b 17.4.1868 | d 31.12.1910 |
| BRAIN, Stephen Edward | (1984-  ) | b 11.11.1954 | |
| BRAITHWAITE, John | (1905) | b 21.4.1873 | d 15.11.1915 |
| BRAITHWAITE-EXLEY, Bryan | (1949) | b 30.11.1927 | |
| BRETTARGH, A.T. | (1900-5) | | |
| BREWER, J. | (1876) | | |
| BRIGGS, Arthur | (1892) | b 1871 | d 18.8.1943 |
| BRINN, Alan | (1972) | b 21.7.1942 | |
| BROADLEY, Tom | (1893-6) | b 18.8.1871 | d 26.11.1950 |
| BROMET, William Ernest | (1891-6) | b 17.5.1868 | d 23.1.1949 |
| BROOK, Peter Watts Pitt | (1930-6) | b 21.9.1906 | |
| BROOKE, Terence John | (1968) | b 8.10.1940 | |
| BROOKS, Frederick G. | (1906) | b 1.5.1883 | d 9.1947 |
| BROOKS, Marshall Jones | (1874) | b 30.5.1855 | d 5.1.1944 |
| BROPHY, Thomas John | (1964-6) | b 8.7.1942 | |
| BROUGH, James Wasdale | (1925) | b 5.11.1903 | d 16.9.1986 |
| BROUGHAM, Henry | (1912) | b 8.7.1888 | d 18.2.1923 |
| BROWN, Alan Arthur | (1938) | b 28.8.1911 | |
| BROWN, Leonard Graham | (1911-22) | b 6.9.1888 | d 23.5.1950 |
| BROWN, Thomas W | (1928-33) | b 1907 | d 14.5.1961 |
| BRUNTON, Joseph | (1914) | b 21.8.1888 | d 18.9.1971 |
| BRUTTON, Ernest Bartholomew | (1886) | b 1863 | d 19.4.1922 |
| BRYDEN, Charles Cowper | (1876-7) | b 16.6.1852 | d 20.2.1941 |
| BRYDEN, Henry Anderson | (1874) | b 3.5.1854 | d 23.9.1937 |

| PLAYER | CAREER SPAN | | |
|---|---|---|---|
| BUCKINGHAM, Ralph Arthur | (1927) | b 15.1.1907 | |
| BUCKNALL, Anthony Launce | (1969-71) | b 7.6.1945 | |
| BUDD, Arthur | (1878-81) | b 14.10.1853 | d 27.8.1899 |
| BUDWORTH, Richard Thomas Dutton | (1890-1) | b 17.10.1867 | d 7.12.1937 |
| BULL, Arthur Gilbert | (1914) | | |
| BULLOUGH, E | (1892) | | |
| BULPITT, Michael Philip | (1970) | b 12.4.1944 | |
| BULTEEL, A.J. | (1876) | | |
| BUNTING, William Louis | (1897-1901) | b 9.8.1873 | d 15.10.1947 |
| BURLAND, Donald William | (1931-3) | b 22.1.1908 | d 26.1.1976 |
| BURNS, Benjamin Henry | (1871) | b 28.5.1848 | d 3.6.1932 |
| BURTON, George William | (1879-81) | b 29.8.1955 | d 17.9.1890 |
| BURTON, Hyde Clarke | (1926) | b 10.6.1898 | |
| BURTON, Michael Alan | (1972-8) | b 18.12.1945 | |
| BUSH, James Arthur | (1872-6) | b 28.7.1850 | d 21.9.1924 |
| BUTCHER, Christopher John Simon | (1984- ) | b 19.8.1960 | |
| BUTCHER, Walter Vincent | (1903-5) | b 2.2.1878 | d 26.8.1957 |
| BUTLER, Arthur Geoffrey | (1937) | b 30.9.1914 | |
| BUTLER, Peter Edward | (1975-6) | b 23.6.1951 | |
| BUTTERFIELD, Jeffrey | (1953-9) | b 9.8.1929 | |
| BYRNE, Francis A. | (1897) | b 1873 | |
| BYRNE, James Frederick | (1894-9) | b 19.6.1871 | d 10.5.1954 |
| | | | |
| CAIN, John Joseph | (1950) | b 12.6.1920 | |
| CAMPBELL, David Alfred | (1937) | b 1915 | d 1982 |
| CANDLER, Peter Laurence | (1935-8) | b 28.1.1914 | |
| CANNELL, Lewis Bernard | (1948-57) | b 10.6.1926 | |
| CAPLAN, David William Nigel | (1978) | b 5.4.1954 | |
| CARDUS, Richard Michael | (1979) | b 23.5.1956 | |
| CAREY, Godfrey Mohun | (1895-6) | b 17.8.1872 | d 18.12.1927 |
| CARLETON, John | (1979- ) | b 24.11.1955 | |
| CARPENTER, Alfred Denzel | (1932) | b 23.7.1900 | d 18.4.1974 |
| CARR, Robert Stanley Leonard | (1939) | b 11.7.1917 | d 1977 |
| CARTWRIGHT, Vincent Henry | (1903-6) | b 10.9.1882 | d 25.11.1965 |
| CATCHESIDE, Howard Carston | (1924-7) | b 18.8.1899 | |
| CATTELL, Richard Henry Burdon | (1895-1900) | b 23.3.1871 | d 19.7.1948 |
| CAVE, John Watkins | (1889) | b 5.2.1867 | d 4.12.1949 |
| CAVE, William Thomas Charles | (1905) | b 24.11.1882 | |
| CHALLIS, Robert | (1957) | b 9.3.1932 | |
| CHAMBERS, Ernest Leonard | (1908-10) | b 24.7.1882 | d 23.11.1946 |
| CHANTRILL, Bevan Stanislaus | (1924) | b 11.2.1897 | |
| CHAPMAN, Charles Edward | (1884) | b 26.8.1860 | d 23.8.1901 |
| CHAPMAN, Frederick Ernest | (1910-14) | b 1888 | d 8.5.1938 |
| CHEESMAN, William Inkersole | (1913) | b 20.6.1889 | d 20.11.1969 |
| CHESTON, Ernest Constantine | (1873-6) | b 24.10.1848 | d 9.7.1913 |
| CHILCOTT, Gareth James | (1984- ) | b 20.11.1956 | |
| CHRISTOPHERSON, Percy | (1891) | b 31.3.1866 | d 4.5.1921 |
| CLARK, Charles William Henry | (1876) | b 19.3.1857 | d 11.5.1943 |
| CLARKE, Allan James | (1935-6) | b 21.2.1913 | d 25.9.1975 |
| CLARKE, Simon John Scott | (1963-5) | b 2.4.1938 | |
| CLAYTON, John Henry | (1871) | b 24.8.1849 | d 21.3.1924 |
| CLEMENTS, Jeffrey Woodward | (1959) | b 18.8.1932 | d 10.1986 |
| CLEVELAND, Charles Riatt | (1887) | b 2.11.1866 | d 18.1.1929 |
| CLIBBORN, W.G. | (1886-7 | | |
| CLOUGH, Francis John | (1986- ) | b 1.11.1962 | |
| COATES, Charles Hutton | (1880-2) | b 4.5.1857 | d 14.2.1922 |

| PLAYER | CAREER SPAN | | |
|---|---|---|---|
| COATES, Vincent Hope Middleton | (1913) | b 18.5.1889 | d 14.11.1934 |
| COBBY, William | (1900) | b 5.7.1877 | d 15.1.1957 |
| COCKERHAM Arthur | (1900) | | |
| COLCLOUGH, Maurice John | (1978- ) | b 2.9.1953 | |
| COLEY, Eric | (1929-32) | b 23.7.1903 | d 3.5.1957 |
| COLLINS, Philip John | (1952) | b 4.11.1928 | |
| COLLINS, William Edward | (1874-6) | b 14.10.1853 | d 11.8.1934 |
| CONSIDINE, Stanley George Ulick | (1925) | b 11.8.1901 | d 31.8.1950 |
| CONWAY, Geoffrey Seymour | (1920-7) | b 15.11.1897 | |
| COOK, John Gilbert | (1937) | b 16.5.1911 | d 9.1979 |
| COOK, Peter William | (1965) | b 8.1.1943 | |
| COOKE, David Alexander | (1976) | b 10.2.1949 | |
| COOKE, David Harold | (1981- ) | b 19.11.1955 | |
| COOKE, Paul | (1939) | b 18.12.1916 | d 1.5.1940 |
| COOP, Thomas | (1892) | b 10.3.1863 | |
| COOPER, John Graham | (1909) | b 3.6.1881 | d 26.10.1965 |
| COOPER, Martin | (1973-7) | b 23.4.1948 | |
| COOPPER, Sidney Frank | (1900-07) | b 10.1878 | d 16.1.1961 |
| CORBETT, Leonard James | (1921-7) | b 12.5.1897 | d 1.1983 |
| CORLESS, Barrie James | (1976-8) | b 7.11.1945 | |
| COTTON, Francis Edward | (1971-81) | b 3.1.1948 | |
| COULMAN, Michael John | (1967-8) | b 6.5.1944 | |
| COULSON, Thomas John | (1927-8) | b 31.12.1896 | d 26.3.1948 |
| COURT, Edward Darlington | (1885) | b 22.6.1862 | d 2.4.1935 |
| COVERDALE, Harry | (1910-20) | b 22.3.1889 | d 29.10.1965 |
| COVE-SMITH, Ronald | (1921-9) | b 26.11.1899 | |
| COWLING, Robin James | (1977-9) | b 24.3.1944 | |
| COWMAN, Alan Richard | (1971-3) | b 18.3.1949 | |
| COX, Norman Simpson | (1901) | b 3.9.1877 | d 29.3.1930 |
| CRANMER, Peter | (1934-8) | b 10.9.1914 | |
| CREED, Roger Norman | (1971) | b 19.11.1945 | |
| CRIDLAN, Arthur Gordon | (1935) | b 9.7.1909 | |
| CROMPTON, Charles Arthur | (1871) | b 21.10.1848 | d 6.7.1875 |
| CROSSE, Charles William | (1874-5) | b 13.6.1854 | d 28.5.1905 |
| CUMBERLEGE, Barry Stephenson | (1920-2) | b 5.6.1891 | d 22.9.1970 |
| CUMMING, Duncan Cameron | (1925) | b 10.8.1903 | d 10.12.1979 |
| CUNLIFFE, Foster Lionel | (1874) | b 20.4.1854 | d 15.4.1927 |
| CURREY, Frederick Innes | (1872) | b 3.5.1849 | d 18.12.1896 |
| CURRIE, John David | (1956-62) | b 3.5.1932 | |
| CUSANI, David Anthony | (1987-) | b 16.7.1959 | |
| CUSWORTH, Leslie | (1979-) | b 3.7.1954 | |
| D'AGUILAR, Francis Burton Grant | (1872) | b 11.12.1849 | d 24.7.1896 |
| DALTON, Timothy J. | (1969) | | |
| DANBY, Thomson | (1949) | b 10.8.1926 | |
| DANIELL, John | (1899-1904) | b 12.12.1878 | d 24.1.1963 |
| DARBY, Arthur John Lobert | (1899) | b 9.1.1876 | d 16.1.1960 |
| DAVENPORT, Alfred | (1871) | b 5.5.1849 | d 2.4.1932 |
| DAVEY, James | (1908-09) | b 25.12.1880 | d 21.10.1951 |
| DAVEY, Richard Frank | (1931) | b 22.9.1905 | |
| DAVIDSON, James | (1897-9) | b 28.12.1868 | d 23.12.1945 |
| DAVIDSON, Joseph | (1899) | b 5.10.1878 | d 8.10.1910 |
| DAVIES, Geoffrey Huw | (1981-) | b 18.2.1959 | |
| DAVIES, Patrick Harry | (1927) | b 17.3.1903 | d 21.2.1979 |
| DAVIES, Vivian Gordon | (1922-5) | b 22.1.1899 | d 23.12.1941 |
| DAVIES, William John Abbott | (1913-23) | b 21.6.1890 | d 26.4.1967 |
| DAVIES, William Philip Cathcart | (1953-7) | b 6.8.1928 | |
| DAVIS, Alec Michael | (1963-70) | b 23.1.1942 | |
| DAWE, Richard Graham Reed | (1987-) | b 4.9.1959 | |
| DAWSON, Ernest Frederick | (1878) | b 10.5.1858 | d 7.7.1904 |
| DAY, Harold Lindsay Vernon | (1920-6) | b 12.8.1898 | d 15.6.1972 |
| DEAN, Geoffrey John | (1931) | b 12.11.1909 | |
| DEE, John Mackenzie | (1962-3) | b 22.10.1938 | |
| DEVITT, Sir Thomas Gordon | (1926-8) | b 27.12.1902 | |
| DEWHURST, John Henry | (1887-90) | b 27.12.1863 | d 22.4.1947 |

| PLAYER | CAREER SPAN | | |
|---|---|---|---|
| DE WINTON, Robert Francis Chippini | (1893) | b 9.9.1868 | d 14.3.1923 |
| DIBBLE, Robert | (1906-12) | | |
| DICKS, John | (1934-7) | b 12.9.1912 | |
| DILLON, Edward Wentworth | (1904-5) | b 15.2.1881 | d 26.4.1941 |
| DINGLE, Arthur James | (1913-14) | b 1891 | d 22.8.1915 |
| DIXON, Peter John | (1971-8) | b 30.4.1944 | |
| DOBBS, George Eric Burroughs | (1906) | b 21.7.1884 | d 17.6.1917 |
| DOBLE, Samuel Arthur | (1972-3) | b 9.3.1944 | d 9.1977 |
| DOBSON, Denys Douglas | (1902-3) | b 28.10.1880 | d 10.7.1916 |
| DOBSON, Thomas Hyde | (1895) | b 2.1872 | d 12.11.1902 |
| DODGE, Paul William | (1978- ) | b 26.5.1958 | |
| DONNELLY, Martin Paterson | (1947) | b 17.10.1917 | |
| DOOLEY, Wade Anthony | (1985- ) | b 2.10.1957 | |
| DOVEY, Beverley Alfred | (1963) | b 24.10.1938 | |
| DOWN, Percy John | (1909) | b 14.10.1883 | d 22.7.1954 |
| DOWSON, Aubrey Osler | (1899) | b 10.11.1875 | d 5.10.1940 |
| DRAKE-LEE, Nicholas James | (1963-5) | b 7.4.1942 | |
| DUCKETT, Horace | (1893) | b 11.10.1867 | d 3.3.1939 |
| DUCKHAM, David John | (1969-76) | b 28.6.1946 | |
| DUDGEON, Herbert William | (1897-9) | | d 4.10.1935 |
| DUGDALE, John Marshall | (1871) | b 15.10.1852 | d 30.10.1918 |
| DUN, Andrew Frederick | (1984) | b 26.11.1960 | |
| DUNCAN, Robert Francis Hugh | (1922) | b 10.6.1896 | |
| DUNKLEY, Philip Edward | (1931-6) | b 9.8.1904 | d 17.6.1985 |
| DUTHIE, James | (1903) | | d 29.5.1946 |
| DYSON, John William | (1890-3) | b 6.9.1866 | d 3.1.1909 |
| EBDON, Percy John | (1897) | b 16.3.1874 | d 16.2.1943 |
| EDDISON, John Horncastle | (1912) | b 25.8.1888 | d 18.11.1982 |
| EDGAR, Charles Stuart | (1901) | b 1876 | d 26.5.1949 |
| EDWARDS, Reginald | (1921-5) | b 11.12.1887 | d 8.1951 |
| ELLIOT, Charles Henry | (1886) | b 31.5.1861 | d 1.4.1934 |
| ELLIOT, Edgar William | (1901-4) | b 9.7.1879 | d 1931 |
| ELLIOT, Walter | (1932-4) | b 17.2.1910 | |
| ELLIOTT, Albert Ernest | (1894) | b 5.3.1869 | d 1.12.1900 |
| ELLIS, Jack | (1939) | b 28.10.1912 | |
| ELLIS, Sidney S. | (1880) | b 13.3.1859 | d 1.12.1937 |
| EMMOTT, Charles | (1892) | b 1868 | d 10.3.1927 |
| ENTHOVEN, H.J. | (1878) | | |
| ESTCOURT, Noel Sidney Dudley | (1955) | b 7.1.1929 | |
| EVANS, Eric | (1948-58) | b 1.2.1925 | |
| EVANS, Geoffrey William | (1972-4) | b 10.12.1950 | |
| EVANS, Nevill Lloyd | (1932-3) | b 16.12.1908 | |
| EVANSON, Arthur Macdonell | (1883-4) | b 15.9.1859 | d 31.12.1934 |
| EVANSON, Wyndham Alleyn Daubeny | (1875-9) | b 1851 | d 30.10.1934 |
| EVERSHED, Frank | (1889-93) | b 6.9.1866 | d 29.6.1954 |
| EYRES, Wallace C.T. | (1927) | | |
| FAGAN, Arthur Robert St Leger | (1887) | b 24.11.1862 | d 15.3.1930 |
| FAIRBROTHER, Keith Eli | (1969-71) | b 8.5.1944 | |
| FAITHFULL, Charles Kirke Tindall | (1924-6) | b 6.1.1903 | d 8.8.1979 |
| FALLAS, Herbert | (1884) | | |
| FEGAN, John Herbert Crangle | (1895) | b 20.1.1872 | d 26.7.1949 |
| FERNANDES, Charles Walker Luis | (1881) | b 3.4.1857 | d 12.8.1944 |
| FIDLER, John Howard | (1981-) | b 16.9.1948 | |
| FIELD, Edwin | (1893) | b 16.12.1871 | d 9.1.1947 |
| FIELDING, Keith John | (1969-72) | b 8.7.1949 | |
| FINCH, Richard Tanner | (1880) | b 1857 | d 12.1.1921 |
| FINLAN, John Frank | (1967-73) | b 9.9.1941 | |
| FINLINSON, Horace William | (1895) | b 9.6.1871 | d 31.10.1956 |
| FINNEY, Stephen | (1872-3) | b 8.9.1852 | d 1.3.1924 |
| FIRTH, Frederick | (1894) | b 1870 | d 2.1936 |
| FLETCHER, Nigel Corbet | (1901-3) | b 23.8.1877 | d 21.12.1951 |
| FLETCHER, Thomas | (1897) | b 1874 | d 28.8.1950 |

| PLAYER | CAREER SPAN | | |
|---|---|---|---|
| FLETCHER, William Robert Badger | (1873-5) | b 10.12.1851 | d 20.4.1895 |
| FOOKES, Ernest Faber | (1896-9) | b 31.5.1874 | d 3.3.1948 |
| FORD, Peter John | (1964) | b 2.5.1932 | |
| FORREST, J.W. | (1930-4) | | |
| FORREST, Reginald | (1899-1903) | b 12.5.1878 | d 11.4.1903 |
| FOULDS, Robert Thompson | (1929) | b 27.4.1906 | |
| FOWLER, Frank Dashwood | (1878-9) | b 16.8.1855 | |
| FOWLER, Howard | (1878-81) | b 20.10.1857 | d 6.5.1934 |
| FOWLER, R. Henry | (1877) | | |
| FOX, Francis Hugh | (1890) | b 12.6.1863 | d 28.5.1952 |
| FRANCIS, Thomas Egerton Seymour | (1926) | b 21.11.1902 | d 24.2.1969 |
| FRANKCOM, Geoffrey Peter | (1965) | b 5.4.1942 | |
| FRASER, Edward Cleather | (1875) | b 1853 | d 15.10.1927 |
| FRASER, George | (1902-3) | b 9.1878 | d 20.8.1950 |
| FREAKES, Hubert Dainton | (1938-9) | b 2.2.1914 | d 3.1942 |
| FREEMAN, Harold | (1872-4) | b 15.1.1850 | d 15.7.1916 |
| FRENCH, Raymond James | (1961) | b 23.12.1939 | |
| FRY, Henry Arthur | (1934) | b 22.12.1910 | d 3.1.1977 |
| FRY, Thomas W. | (1880-1) | | |
| FULLER, Herbert George | (1882-4) | b 4.10.1856 | d 2.1.1896 |
| GADNEY, Bernard C. | (1932-8) | b 16.7.1909 | |
| GAMLIN, Herbert Temlett | (1899-1904) | b 12.2.1878 | d 12.7.1937 |
| GARDNER, Ernest Robert | (1921-3) | b 6.10.1886 | d 26.1.1954 |
| GARDNER, Herbert Prescott | (1878) | b 1855 | |
| GARNETT, Harry Wharfedale Tennant | (1877) | b 16.9.1851 | d 27.4.1928 |
| GAVINS, Michael Neil | (1961) | b 14.10.1934 | |
| GAY, David John | (1968) | b 10.3.1948 | |
| GENT, David Robert | (1905-10) | b 9.1.1883 | d 16.1.1964 |
| GENTH, J.S.M | (1874-5) | | |
| GEORGE, James Thomas | (1947-9) | b 24.8.1918 | |
| GERRARD, Ronald Anderson | (1932-6) | b 26.1.1912 | d 22.1.1943 |
| GIBBS, George Anthony | (1947-8) | b 31.3.1920 | |
| GIBBS, John Clifford | (1925-7) | b 10.3.1902 | |
| GIBBS, Nigel | (1954) | b 24.9.1922 | |
| GIBLIN, Lyndhurst Falkiner | (1896-7) | b 12.5.1872 | d 2.3.1951 |
| GIBSON, Arthur Sumner | (1871) | b 14.7.1844 | d 23.1.1927 |
| GIBSON, Charles Osborne Provis | (1901) | b 10.1876 | d 9.11.1931 |
| GIBSON, George Ralph | (1899-1901) | b 3.1878 | d 10.1939 |
| GIBSON, Thomas Alexander | (1905) | b 30.1.1880 | d 27.4.1937 |
| GILBERT, F.G. | (1923) | b 1885 | |
| GILBERT, R. | (1908) | | |
| GILES, James Leonard | (1935-8) | b 5.1.1912 | d 28.3.1967 |
| GITTINGS, William John | (1967) | b 5.10.1939 | |
| GLOVER, Peter Bernard | (1967-71) | b 25.9.1945 | |
| GODFRAY, Reginald Edmund | (1905) | b 10.5.1880 | d 4.2.1967 |
| GODWIN, Herbert O. | (1959-67) | b 21.12.1935 | |
| GORDON-SMITH, Gerald W. | (1900) | | d 23.1.1911 |
| GOTLEY, Anthony Lefroy Henniker | (1910-11) | b 2.3.1887 | d 5.1972 |
| GRAHAM, David | (1901) | b 6.1875 | d 1.1962 |
| GRAHAM, H.J. | (1875-6) | | |
| GRAHAM, John Duncan George | (1876) | b 1856 | |
| GRAY, Arthur | (1947) | b 4.9.1917 | |
| GREEN, John | (1905-07) | b 17.9.1881 | d 27.12.1968 |
| GREEN, Joseph Fletcher | (1871) | b 28.4.1846 | d 28.8.1923 |
| GREENWELL, John Henry | (1893) | b 1864 | d 1942 |
| GREENWOOD, John Eric | (1912-20) | b 23.7.1891 | d 23.7.1975 |
| GREENWOOD, John Richard Heaton | (1966-9) | b 11.9.1941 | |
| GREG, Walter | (1876) | b 14.2.1851 | d 6.2.1906 |
| GREGORY, Gordon George | (1931-4) | b 8.12.1908 | d 4.12.1963 |
| GREGORY, John Arthur | (1949) | b 22.6.1923 | |
| GRYLLS, William | (1905) | b 9.1.1885 | |
| GUEST, Richard Heaton | (1939-49) | b 12.3.1918 | |

| PLAYER | CAREER SPAN | | |
|---|---|---|---|
| GUILLEMARD, Arthur | | | |
| George | (1871-2) | b 18.12.1845 | d 7.8.1909 |
| GUMMER, Charles Henry | | | |
| Alexander | (1929) | b 20.11.1905 | |
| GUNNER, Charles | | | |
| Richards | (1876) | b 7.1.1853 | d 4.2.1924 |
| GURDON, Charles | (1880-6) | b 3.12.1855 | d 26.6.1931 |
| GURDON, Edward | | | |
| Temple | (1878-86) | b 25.6.1854 | d 12.6.1929 |
| | | | |
| HAIGH, Leonard | (1910-11) | b 19.10.1880 | d 6.8.1916 |
| HALE, Peter Martin | (1969-70) | b 12.8.1943 | |
| HALL, C. | (1901) | | |
| HALL, John | (1894) | | |
| HALL, Jon Peter | (1984-) | b 15.3.1962 | |
| HALL, Norman Macleod | (1947-55) | b 2.8.1925 | d 26.6.1972 |
| HALLIDAY, Simon John | (1986-) | b 13.7.1960 | |
| HAMERSLEY, Alfred | | | |
| St. George | (1871-4) | b 8.10.1848 | d 25.2.1929 |
| HAMILTON-HILL, | | | |
| Edward | (1936) | b 22.11.1908 | d 23.10.1979 |
| HAMILTON-WICKES, | | | |
| Richard Henry | (1924-7) | b 31.12.1901 | d 2.6.1963 |
| HAMMETT, Ernest Dyer | | | |
| Galbraith | (1920-2) | b 15.10.1891 | d 23.6.1947 |
| HAMMOND, Charles | | | |
| Edward Lucas | (1905-08) | b 3.10.1879 | d 15.4.1963 |
| HANCOCK, Andrew | | | |
| William | (1965-6) | b 19.6.1939 | |
| HANCOCK, George | | | |
| Edward | (1939) | b 21.3.1912 | |
| HANCOCK, William Jack | | | |
| Henry | (1955) | b 26.9.1932 | |
| HANCOCK, Philip Froude | (1886-90) | b 29.8.1865 | d 16.10.1933 |
| HANCOCK, Patrick | | | |
| Sortain | (1904) | b 1883 | |
| HANDFORD, Frank | | | |
| Gordon | (1909) | b 1884 | |
| HANDS, Reginald Harold | | | |
| Myburgh | (1910) | b 26.7.1888 | d 20.4.1918 |
| HANLEY, Joseph | (1927-8) | b 14.9.1901 | |
| HANNAFORD, Ronald | | | |
| Charles | (1971) | b 19.10.1944 | |
| HANVEY, Robert Jackson | (1926) | b 16.8.1899 | |
| HARDING, Ernest Harold | (1931) | b 22.5.1899 | d 25.12.1980 |
| HARDING, Richard Mark | (1985-) | b 29.8.1953 | |
| HARDING, Victor Sydney | | | |
| James | (1961-2) | b 18.6.1932 | |
| HARDWICK, Peter F. | (1902-04) | b 1878 | d 2.1925 |
| HARDY, Evan Michael | | | |
| Pearce | (1951) | b 3.11.1927 | |
| HARE, William Henry | (1974-84) | b 29.11.1952 | |
| HARPER, Charles Henry | (1899) | b 24.2.1876 | d 14.5.1950 |
| HARRIS, Stanley | | | |
| Wakefield | (1920) | b 13.12.1893 | |
| HARRIS, Thomas William | (1929-32) | b 1906 | d 11.1958 |
| HARRISON, Arthur | | | |
| Clifford | (1931) | b 10.5.1911 | |
| HARRISON, Arthur | | | |
| Leyland | (1914) | b 3.2.1886 | d 23.4.1918 |
| HARRISON, Gilbert | (1877-85) | b 13.6.1858 | d 9.11.1894 |
| HARRISON, Harold Cecil | (1909-14) | b 26.2.1889 | d 26.3.1940 |
| HARRISON, Michael | | | |
| Edward | (1985-) | b 19.4.1956 | |
| HARTLEY, Bernard | | | |
| Charles | (1901-2) | b 16.3.1879 | d 24.4.1960 |
| HASLETT, Leslie Woods | (1926) | b 5.6.1900 | |
| HASTINGS, George | | | |
| William | (1955-8) | b 7.11.1924 | |
| HAVELOCK, Harold | (1908) | | |
| HAWCRIDGE, John | | | |
| Joseph | (1885) | b 1863 | d 1.1.1905 |
| HAYWARD, Leslie | | | |
| William | (1910) | b 17.5.1886 | |
| HAZELL, David St. | | | |
| George | (1955) | b 23.4.1931 | |
| HEARN, Robert Daniel | (1966-7) | b 12.8.1940 | |
| HEATH, Arthur Howard | (1876) | b 29.5.1856 | d 24.4.1930 |
| HEATON, John | (1935-47) | b 30.8.1912 | |
| HENDERSON, A.P. | (1947-9) | | |
| HENDERSON, Robert | | | |
| Samuel Findlay | (1883-5) | b 11.12.1858 | d 5.10.1924 |

| PLAYER | CAREER SPAN | | |
|---|---|---|---|
| HEPPELL, W.G. | (1903) | | |
| HERBERT, A. John | (1958-9) | b 1.1.1933 | |
| HESFORD, Robert | (1981-) | b 26.5.1953 | |
| HETHERINGTON, James | | | |
| Gilbert George | (1958-9) | b 3.3.1932 | |
| HEWITT, Edwin Newbury | (1951) | b 22.4.1924 | |
| HEWITT, Walter W. | (1881-2) | | |
| HICKSON, John Lawrence | (1887-90) | b 1860 | d 4.8.1920 |
| HIGGINS, Reginald | (1954-9) | b 11.7.1930 | d 29.12.1979 |
| HIGNELL, Alastair James | (1975-9) | b 4.9.1955 | |
| HILL, Basil Alexander | (1903-07) | b 23.4.1880 | d 31.7.1960 |
| HILL, Richard John | (1984-) | b 4.5.1961 | |
| HILLARD, Ronald | | | |
| Johnstone | (1925) | b 6.5.1903 | |
| HILLER, Robert | (1968-72) | b 14.10.1942 | |
| HIND, Alfred Ernest | (1906) | b 7.4.1878 | d 21.3.1947 |
| HIND, Guy Reginald | (1910-11) | b 4.4.1887 | d 8.11.1970 |
| HOBBS, Reginald Francis | | | |
| Arthur | (1899-1903) | b 30.1.1878 | d 10.7.1953 |
| HOBBS, Reginald Geoffrey | | | |
| Stirling | (1932) | b 8.8.08 | |
| HODGES, Harold | | | |
| Augustus | (1906) | b 22.1.1886 | d 24.3.1918 |
| HODGSON, John | | | |
| McDonald | (1932-6) | b 13.2.1909 | d 4.1970 |
| HODGSON, Stanley | | | |
| Arthur Murray | (1960-4) | b 14.5.1928 | |
| HOFMEYR, Murray | | | |
| Bernard | (1950) | b 9.12.1925 | |
| HOGARTH, Thomas | | | |
| Bradley | (1906) | b 1877 | d 1961 |
| HOLFORD, G. | (1920) | b 1886 | |
| HOLLAND, David | (1912) | b 1886 | d 7.3.1945 |
| HOLLIDAY, Thomas E. | (1923-6) | b 13.7.1898 | d 19.7.1969 |
| HOLMES, Cyril Butler | (1947-8) | b 11.11.1915 | |
| HOLMES, Edgar | (1890) | b 1863 | |
| HOLMES, Walter Alan | (1950-3) | b 10.9.1925 | |
| HOLMES, William Barry | (1949) | b 6.1.1928 | d 10.11.1949 |
| HOOK, William Gordon | (1951-2) | b 21.12.1920 | |
| HOOPER, Charles | | | |
| Alexander | (1894) | b 6.6.1869 | d 16.9.1950 |
| HOPLEY, Frederick John | | | |
| van der Byl | (1907-8) | b 28.8.1883 | d 16.8.1951 |
| HORDERN, Peter Cotton | (1931-4) | b 13.5.1907 | |
| HORLEY, Charles Henry | (1885) | b 1861 | d 10.5.1924 |
| HORNBY, Albert Neilson | (1877-82) | b 10.2.1847 | d 17.12.1925 |
| HORROCKS-TAYLOR, | | | |
| John Philip | (1958-64) | b 27.10.1934 | |
| HORSFALL, Edward | | | |
| Luke | (1949) | b 11.8.1917 | d 1.6.1981 |
| HORTON, Anthony | | | |
| Lawrence | (1965-7) | b 13.7.1938 | |
| HORTON, John Philip | (1978-84) | b 11.4.1951 | |
| HORTON, Nigel Edgar | (1969-80) | b 13.4.1948 | |
| HOSEN, Roger Wills | (1963-7) | b 12.6.1933 | |
| HOSKING, Geoffrey | | | |
| Robert D'Aubrey | (1949-50) | b 11.3.1922 | |
| HOUGHTON, Samuel | (1892-6) | b 16.8.1870 | d 17.8.1920 |
| HOWARD, Peter | | | |
| Dunsmore | (1930-1) | b 20.12.1908 | d 25.2.1965 |
| HUBBARD, George Cairns | (1892) | b 23.11.1867 | d 18.12.1931 |
| HUBBARD, John Cairns | (1930) | b 27.6.1902 | |
| HUDSON, Arthur | (1906-10) | b 27.10.1882 | d 27.7.1973 |
| HUGHES, George Edgar | (1896) | b 24.2.1870 | d 6.10.1947 |
| HULME, Frank Croft | (1903-05) | b 31.8.1881 | |
| HUNT, James Thomas | (1882-4) | | |
| HUNT, Robert | (1880-2) | b 21.1.1856 | d 19.3.1913 |
| HUNT, William Henry | (1876-8) | b 11.5.1854 | |
| HUNTSMAN, Robert Paul | (1985-) | b 5.5.1957 | |
| HURST, Andrew Charles | | | |
| Brunel | (1962) | b 1.10.1935 | |
| HUSKISSON, Thomas | | | |
| Frederick | (1937-9) | b 1.7.1914 | |
| HUTCHINSON, Frank | (1909) | b 1885 | d 5.3.1960 |
| HUTCHINSON, James E. | (1906) | b 1884 | |
| HUTCHINSON, W. C. | (1876-7) | b 1856 | d prior to 1892 |
| HUTCHINSON, William | | | |
| Henry Heap | (1875-6) | b 31.10.1849 | d 4.7.1929 |
| HUTH, Henry | (1879) | b 1859 | d 12.1929 |
| HYDE, John Phillip | (1950) | b 8.6.1930 | |
| HYNES, William Baynard | (1912) | b 1889 | d 2.3.1968 |

| PLAYER | CAREER SPAN | | |
|---|---|---|---|
| IBBITSON, Ernest | | | |
| Denison | (1909) | b 1.2.1882 | d 1956 |
| IMRIE, Henry Marshall | (1905-07) | b 1877 | d 16.10.1938 |
| INGLIS, Rupert Edward | (1886) | b 17.5.1863 | d 18.9.1916 |
| IRVIN, Samuel Howell | (1905) | b 1880 | d 1939 |
| ISHERWOOD, Francis | | | |
| William Ramsbottom | (1872) | b 16.10.1852 | d 30.4.1888 |
| | | | |
| JACKETT, Edward John | (1905-09) | b 4.7.1882 | d 1935 |
| JACKSON, A.H. | (1878-80) | | |
| JACKSON, Barry K. | (1970) | b 9.8.1937 | |
| JACKSON, Peter Barrie | (1956-63) | b 22.9.1930 | |
| JACKSON, Walter Jesse | (1894) | b 16.3.1870 | d 1.12.1958 |
| JACOB, Frederick | (1897-9) | b 4.1.1873 | d 1.9.1945 |
| JACOB, Herbert Percy | (1924-30) | b 12.10.1902 | |
| JACOB, Philip Gordon | (1898) | b 14.5.1875 | |
| JACOBS, Charles Ronald | (1956-64) | b 28.10.1928 | |
| JAGO, Raphael Anthony | (1906-07) | b 20.1.1882 | |
| JANION, Jeremy Paul | (1971-5) | b 25.9.1946 | |
| JARMAN, J. Wallace | (1900) | b 15.7.1872 | d 9.1950 |
| JEAVONS, Nicholas Clive | (1981-) | b 12.11.1957 | |
| JEEPS, Richard Eric | | | |
| Gautrey | (1956-62) | b 25.11.1931 | |
| JEFFERY, George Luxton | (1886-7) | b 1863 | d 4.11.1937 |
| JENNINS, Christopher | | | |
| Robert | (1967) | b 5.2.1942 | |
| JEWITT, J. | (1902) | | |
| JOHNS, William | | | |
| Alexander | (1909-10) | b 1.2.1882 | |
| JOHNSTON, William R. | (1910-14) | b 1887 | |
| JONES, Frederick Phelp | (1893) | b 1873 | d 14.8.1944 |
| JONES, Herbert Arthur | (1950) | b 22.8.1918 | |
| JORDEN, Anthony | | | |
| Mervyn | (1970-5) | b 28.1.1947 | |
| JOWETT, Donald | (1889-91) | b 4.12.1866 | d 27.8.1908 |
| JUDD, Philip Edward | (1962-7) | b 8.4.1934 | |
| | | | |
| KAYLL, Henry Edward | (1878) | b 16.7.1855 | d 14.2.1910 |
| KEELING, John Hugh | (1948) | b 28.10.1925 | |
| KEEN, Brian Warwick | (1968) | b 1.6.1944 | |
| KEETON, George Haydn | (1904) | b 13.10.1878 | d 7.1.1949 |
| KELLY, Geoffrey Arnold | (1947-8) | b 9.2.1914 | |
| KELLY, Thomas Stanley | (1906-08) | b 1882 | |
| KEMBLE, Arthur Twiss | (1885-7) | b 3.2.1862 | d 13.3.1925 |
| KEMP, Dudley Thomas | (1935) | b 18.1.1910 | |
| KEMP, Thomas Arthur | (1937-48) | b 12.8.1915 | |
| KENDALL, Percy Dale | (1901-03) | b 21.8.1878 | d 25.1.1915 |
| KENDALL- | | | |
| CARPENTER, John | | | |
| MacGregor Kendall | (1949-54) | b 25.9.1925 | |
| KENDREW, Douglas | | | |
| Anthony | (1930-6) | b 22.7.1910 | |
| KENNEDY, Robert Day | (1949) | b 14.8.1925 | d 5.1979 |
| KENT, Thomas | (1891-2) | b 19.6.1864 | d 29.1.1928 |
| KENT, Charles Philip | (1977-8) | b 4.8.1953 | |
| KERSHAW, Cecil | | | |
| Ashworth | (1920-23) | b 3.2.1895 | d 1.11.1972 |
| KEWLEY, Edward | (1874-78) | b 20.6.1852 | d 17.4.1940 |
| KEWNEY, Alfred Lionel | (1906-13) | b 1883 | d 16.12.1959 |
| KEY, Alan | (1930-3) | b 4.6.1908 | |
| KEYWORTH, Mark | (1976) | b 19.2.1948 | |
| KILNER, Barron | (1880) | b 11.10.1852 | d 28.12.1922 |
| KINDERSLEY, Richard | | | |
| Stephen | (1883-5) | b 27.9.1858 | d 26.9.1932 |
| KING, Ian | (1954) | b 1923 | |
| KING, John Abbott | (1911-13) | b 21.8.1883 | d 9.8.1916 |
| KING, Quentin Eric | | | |
| Moffitt Ayres | (1921) | b 8.7.1895 | d 30.10.1954 |
| KINGSTON, Peter | (1975-9) | b 24.7.1951 | |
| KITCHING, Alfred | | | |
| Everley | (1913) | b 6.5.1889 | d 17.3.1945 |
| KITTERMASTER, Harold | | | |
| James | (1925-6) | b 7.1.1902 | d 28.3.1967 |
| KNIGHT, Frederick | (1909) | | |
| KNIGHT, Peter Michael | (1972) | b 7.10.1947 | |
| KNOWLES, Edward | (1896-7) | b 1868 | d 17.3.1945 |
| KNOWLES, Thomas | | | |
| Caldwell | (1931) | b 6.5.1908 | d 12.9.1985 |
| KRIGE, J. A. | (1920) | b 6.6.1897 | d 27.9.1946 |
| | | | |
| LABUSCHAGNE, | | | |
| Nicholas Arthur | (1953-5) | b 26.5.1931 | |

| PLAYER | CAREER SPAN | | |
|---|---|---|---|
| LAGDEN, Ronald Owen | (1911) | b 21.11.1889 | d 1.3.1915 |
| LAIRD, Henri Colin | | | |
| Campbell | (1927-9) | b 3.9.1908 | |
| LAMBERT, Douglas | (1907-11) | b 4.10.1883 | d 13.10.1915 |
| LAMPKOWSKI, Michael | | | |
| Stanley | (1976) | b 4.1.1953 | |
| LAPAGE, Walter Nevill | (1908) | b 5.2.1883 | d 17.5.1939 |
| LARTER, Peter John | (1967-73) | b 7.9.1944 | |
| LAW, Archibald Fitzgerald | (1877) | b 1853 | d 26.7.1921 |
| LAW, Douglas Edward | (1927) | b 12.10.1902 | |
| LAWRENCE, The Hon. | | | |
| Henry Arnold | (1873-5) | b 17.3.1848 | d 16.4.1902 |
| LAWRIE, Percy William | (1910-11) | b 26.9.1888 | d 27.12.1956 |
| LAWSON, Richard | | | |
| Gordon | (1925) | b 1.9.1901 | d 3.1.61 |
| LAWSON, Thomas | | | |
| Mattocks | (1928) | b 1900 | d 21.10.1951 |
| LEADBETTER, Michael | | | |
| Morris | (1970) | b 25.7.1947 | |
| LEADBETTER, Victor | (1954) | b 9.1929 | |
| LEAKE, William Robert | | | |
| Martin | (1891) | b 31.12.1865 | d 14.11.1942 |
| LEATHER, George | (1907) | b 22.2.1881 | d 2.1.1957 |
| LEE, Frederic Hugh | (1876-7) | b 14.9.1855 | d 6.2.1924 |
| LEE, Harry | (1907) | b 8.12.1882 | d 11.1.1933 |
| LE FLEMING, John | (1887) | b 23.10.1865 | d 9.10.1942 |
| LESLIE-JONES, | | | |
| Frederick Archibald | (1895) | b 9.7.1874 | d 24.1.1946 |
| LEWIS, Alec Ormonde | (1952-4) | b 20.8.1920 | |
| LEYLAND, Roy | (1935) | b 6.3.1912 | d 4.1.1984 |
| LIVESAY, Robert O'Hara | (1898-9) | b 27.6.1876 | d 23.3.1946 |
| LLOYD, Robert Hoskins | (1967-8) | b 3.3.1943 | |
| LOCKE, Harold Meadows | (1923-7) | b 1898 | d 23.3.1960 |
| LOCKWOOD, Richard | | | |
| Evison | (1887-94) | b 11.11.1867 | d 10.11.1915 |
| LOGIN, Spencer Henry | | | |
| Metcalfe | (1876) | b 24.9.1851 | d 22.1.1909 |
| LOHDEN, Frederick | | | |
| Charles | (1893) | b 13.6.1871 | d 13.4.1954 |
| LONGLAND, Raymond | | | |
| John | (1932-8) | b 29.12.1908 | d 21.9.1975 |
| LOWE, Cyril Nelson | (1913-23) | b 7.10.1891 | d 6.2.1983 |
| LOWRIE, Frederick | | | |
| William | (1889-90) | b 1.3.1868 | d 9.8.1902 |
| LOWRY, Wilfrid Malbon | (1920) | b 14.7.1900 | d 4.7.1974 |
| LOZOWSKI, Robert | | | |
| Andrew Peter | (1984-) | b 18.11.1960 | |
| LUDDINGTON, William | | | |
| George Ernest | (1923-6) | b 8.2.1894 | d 12.6.1940 |
| LUSCOMBE, Francis | (1872-6) | b 1846 | d 17.7.1926 |
| LUSCOMBE, John Henry | (1871) | b 1848 | d 3.4.1937 |
| LUXMOORE, Arthur | | | |
| Fairfax Charles | (1900-01) | b 27.2.1876 | d 25.9.1944 |
| LUYA, Humphrey | | | |
| Fleetwood | (1948-9) | b 3.2.1918 | |
| LYON, Arthur | (1871) | b 4.8.1852 | d 4.12.1905 |
| LYON, George Hamilton | | | |
| D'Oyly | (1908-09) | b 3.10.1883 | d 20.8.1947 |
| | | | |
| McCANLIS, Maurice | | | |
| Alfred | (1931) | b 17.6.1906 | |
| McFADYEAN, Colin | | | |
| William | (1966-68) | b 11.3.1943 | |
| MacILWAINE, Alfred | | | |
| Herbert | (1912-20) | b 27.3.1889 | d 1983 |
| MACKIE, Osbert | | | |
| Gadesden | (1897-8) | b 23.8.1869 | d 25.1.1927 |
| MACKINLAY, James | | | |
| Egan Harrison | (1872-5) | b 17.12.1850 | d 1.7.1917 |
| MacLAREN, William | (1871) | | |
| MacLENNAN, Roderick | | | |
| Ross Forrest | (1925) | b 23.12.1903 | |
| McLEOD, Norman F. | (1879) | b 30.6.1856 | d 20.4.1921 |
| MADGE, Richard John | | | |
| Palmer | (1948) | b 19.12.1914 | |
| MALIR, Frank William | | | |
| Stewart | (1930) | b 4.8.1905 | d 22.1.1974 |
| MANGLES, Roland Henry | (1897) | b 9.2.1874 | d 29.9.1948 |
| MANLEY, Donald Charles | (1963) | b 17.2.1932 | |
| MANN, William Edgar | (1911) | b 19.1.1885 | d 14.2.1969 |
| MANTELL, Neil | | | |
| Dennington | (1975) | b 13.10.1953 | |

| PLAYER | CAREER SPAN | | |
|---|---|---|---|
| MARKENDALE, Ellis T. | (1880) | b 11.1856 | |
| MARQUES, Reginald William David | (1956-61) | b 9.12.1932 | |
| MARQUIS, John Campbell | (1900) | b 1876 | d 28.1.1928 |
| MARRIOTT, Charles John Bruce | (1884-7) | b 15.7.1861 | d 25.12.1936 |
| MARRIOTT, Ernest Edward | (1876) | b 15.1.1857 | d 1917 |
| MARRIOTT, Victor Robert | (1963-4) | b 29.1.1938 | |
| MARSDEN, George Herbert | (1900) | b 16.10.1880 | d 7.7.1948 |
| MARSH, Henry | (1873) | b 8.9.1850 | d 25.4.1939 |
| MARSH, James | (1892) | | d 1.8.1928 |
| MARSHALL, Howard | (1893) | b 20.12.1870 | d 10.1929 |
| MARSHALL, Murray Wyatt | (1873-8) | b 1853 | d 28.7.1930 |
| MARSHALL, Robert Mackenzie | (1938-9) | b 18.5.1917 | d 12.5.1945 |
| MARTIN, Christopher Ronald | (1985-) | b 27.6.1961 | |
| MARTIN, Nicholas | (1972) | b 1946 | |
| MARTINDALE, Samuel Airey | (1929) | b 5.5.1905 | |
| MASSEY, Edward John | (1925) | b 2.7.1900 | d 30.4.1977 |
| MATHIAS, John Lloyd | (1905) | b 1878 | d 21.11.1940 |
| MATTERS, John Charles | (1899) | b 1879 | d 24.4.1949 |
| MATTHEWS, John Robert Clive | (1949-52) | b 14.6.1922 | |
| MAUD, Philip | (1893) | b 8.8.1870 | d 28.2.1947 |
| MAXWELL, Andrew William | (1975-78) | b 3.3.1951 | |
| MAXWELL-HYSLOP, John Edgar | (1922) | b 31.3.1899 | |
| MAYNARD, Alfred Frederick | (1914) | b 23.3.1894 | d 13.11.1916 |
| MEIKLE, Graham William Churchill | (1934) | b 14.10.1911 | |
| MEIKLE, Stephen Spencer Churchill | (1929) | b 6.7.1904 | d 4.6.1960 |
| MELLISH, Frank Whitmore | (1920-1) | b 26.4.1897 | d 21.8.1965 |
| MELVILLE, Nigel Donald | (1984-) | b 6.1.1961 | |
| MERRIAM, Laurence Pierce Brooke | (1920) | b 28.1.1894 | d 27.7.1966 |
| MICHELL, Arthur Thompson | (1875-6) | b 26.9.1853 | d 13.8.1923 |
| MIDDLETON, Bernard Boswell | (1882-3) | b 25.12.1858 | d 22.10.1947 |
| MIDDLETON, John Alan | (1922) | b 11.1.1894 | |
| MILES, John Henry | (1903) | b 1880 | d 23.1.1953 |
| MILLETT, Harry | (1920) | b 2.4.1892 | d 26.5.1974 |
| MILLS, Frederick William | (1872-3) | b 5.5.1849 | d 2.2.1904 |
| MILLS, Stephen Graham Ford | (1981-) | b 24.2.1953 | |
| MILLS, William Alonzo | (1906-08) | b 2.2.1879 | |
| MILMAN, Dermot Lionel Kennedy | (1937-8) | b 24.10.1912 | |
| MILTON, Cecil Henry | (1906) | b 7.1.1884 | d 1961 |
| MILTON, J. G. | (1904-07) | b 1.5.1885 | d 15.6.1915 |
| MILTON, William Henry | (1874-5) | b 3.12.1854 | d 6.3.1930 |
| MITCHELL, Frank | (1895-6) | b 3.8.1872 | d 11.10.1935 |
| MITCHELL, William Grant | (1890-3) | b 23.5.1865 | d 14.1.1905 |
| MOBBS, Edgar Roberts | (1909-10) | b 29.6.1882 | d 29.7.1917 |
| MOBERLY, William Octavius | (1872) | b 14.11.1850 | d 2.2.1914 |
| MOORE, Brian Christopher | (1987-) | b 11.1.1962 | |
| MOORE, Edward James | (1883) | b 25.5.1862 | d 7.3.1925 |
| MOORE, Norman J.N. | (1904) | b 1877 | d 8.3.1938 |
| MOORE, Philip Brian Cecil | (1951) | b 6.4.1921 | |
| MOORE, William Kenneth Thomas | (1947-50)) | b 24.2.1921 | |
| MORDELL, Robert John | (1978) | b 2.7.1951 | |
| MORFITT, Samuel | (1894-6) | b 12.1868 | d 1.1.1954 |
| MORGAN, James Rydiard | (1920) | b 1890 | d 29.4.1961 |
| MORGAN, William George Derek | (1960-61) | b 30.11.1935 | |
| MORLEY, Alan John | (1972-5) | b 25.6.1950 | |

| PLAYER | CAREER SPAN | | |
|---|---|---|---|
| MORRIS, Alfred Drummond Warrington | (1909) | b 1883 | d 24.3.1962 |
| MORRISON, Piercy Henderson | (1890-1) | b 30.7.1868 | d 12.7.1936 |
| MORSE, Sydney | (1873-5) | b 1.6.1854 | d 27.1.1929 |
| MORTIMER, William | (1899) | b 2.4.1874 | d 31.10.1916 |
| MORTON, Harold James Storrs | (1909-10) | b 31.1.1886 | d 3.1.1955 |
| MOSS, F. | (1885-6) | | |
| MYCOCK, Joseph | (1947-8) | b 17.1.1916 | |
| MYERS, Edward | (1920-5) | b 23.9.1895 | d 29.3.1956 |
| MYERS, Harry | (1898) | b 3.2.1875 | d 19.12.1906 |
| NANSON, William Moore Bell | (1907) | b 12.12.1880 | d 4.6.1915 |
| NASH, Edward Henry | (1875) | b 20.12.1854 | d 18.9.1932 |
| NEALE, Bruce Alan | (1951) | b 15.9.1923 | |
| NEALE, Maurice Edward | (1912) | b 1886 | d 9.7.1967 |
| NEAME, Stuart | (1879-80) | b 15.6.1856 | d 16.11.1936 |
| NEARY, Anthony | (1971-80) | b 25.11.1949 | |
| NELMES, Barry George | (1975-8) | b 17.4.1948 | |
| NEWBOLD, Charles Joseph | (1904-05) | b 12.1.1881 | d 26.10.1946 |
| NEWMAN, Sidney Charles | (1947-8) | b 27.7.1919 | |
| NEWTON, Arthur Winstanley | (1907) | b 12.9.1879 | |
| NEWTON, Philip Arthur | (1882) | b 11.4.1860 | d 25.12.1946 |
| NEWTON-THOMPSON, John Oswald | (1947) | b 2.12.1920 | d 3.4.1974 |
| NICHOLL, William | (1892) | b 30.10.1868 | d 10.4.1922 |
| NICHOLAS, Philip Leach | (1902) | b 30.5.1876 | d 31.1.1952 |
| NICHOLSON, Basil Ellard | (1938) | b 1.1.1913 | |
| NICHOLSON, Edward Sealy | (1935-6) | b 10.6.1912 | |
| NICHOLSON, Elliot Tennant | (1900) | b 13.12.1871 | d 1.12.1953 |
| NICHOLSON, Thomas | (1893) | | |
| NINNES, Barry Francis | (1971) | b 23.3.1948 | |
| NORMAN, Douglas James | (1932) | b 12.6.1897 | d 27.12.1971 |
| NORTH, Eustace Herbert Guest | (1891) | b 4.11.1868 | d 17.3.1942 |
| NORTHMORE, S. | (1897) | | |
| NOVAK, Michael John | (1970) | b 27.9.1947 | |
| NOVIS, Anthony Leslie | (1929-33) | b 22.9.1906 | |
| OAKELEY, Francis Eckley | (1913-4) | b 5.2.1891 | d 11.12.1914 |
| OAKES, Robert Frederick | (1897-99) | b 1873 | d 23.10.1952 |
| OAKLEY, Lionel Frederick Lightborn | (1951) | b 24.1.1926 | d 1981 |
| OBOLENSKY, Alexander | (1936) | b 17.2.1916 | d 29.3.1940 |
| OLD, Alan Gerald Bernard | (1972-8) | b 23.9.1945 | |
| OLDHAM, W.L. | (1908-09) | | |
| O'NEILL, A. | (1901) | | |
| OPENSHAW, William Edward | (1879) | b 1851 | d 15.2.1915 |
| ORWIN, John | (1985- ) | b 20.3.1954 | |
| OSBORNE, Richard | (1871) | b 20.5.1848 | d 4.11.1926 |
| OSBORNE, Sidney Herbert | (1905) | b 26.2.1880 | d 15.7.1939 |
| OUGHTRED, Bernard | (1901-03) | b 22.8.1888 | d 12.11.1949 |
| OWEN, John Ernest | (1963-7) | b 21.9.1939 | |
| OWEN-SMITH, Harold Geoffrey | (1934-7) | b 18.2.1909 | |
| PAGE, John Jackson | (1971-5) | b 16.4.1947 | |
| PALLANT, John Noel | (1967) | b 24.12.1944 | |
| PALMER, Alexander Croydon | (1909) | b 2.7.1887 | d 16.10.1963 |
| PALMER, F.H. | (1905) | b 6.8.1977 | |
| PALMER, Godfrey Vaughan | (1928) | b 21.2.1900 | d 28.4.1972 |
| PALMER, John Anthony | (1984-6) | b 13.2.1957 | |
| PARGETTER, Thomas Alfred | (1962-3) | b 21.7.1932 | |
| PARKER, Grahame Wilshaw | (1938) | b 11.2.1912 | |
| PARKER, The Hon. Sydney | (1874-5) | b 3.10.1853 | d 21.5.1897 |
| PARSONS, Ernest Ian | (1939) | b 24.10.1912 | d 14.10.1940 |
| PARSONS, Michael James | (1968) | b 13.3.1943 | |

| PLAYER | CAREER SPAN | | |
|---|---|---|---|
| PATTERSON, William Michael | (1961) | b 11.4.1936 | |
| PATTISSON, Richard Murrills | (1883) | b 5.8.1860 | d 28.11.1948 |
| PAUL, J.E. | (1875) | | |
| PAYNE, Arthur Thomas | (1935) | b 11.11.1908 | d 7.6.1968 |
| PAYNE, Colin Martin | (1964-6) | b 19.5.1937 | |
| PAYNE, John Henry | (1882-5) | b 19.3.1858 | d 24.1.1942 |
| PEARSON, A.W. | (1875-8) | b 1854 | |
| PEARCE, Gary Stephen | (1979- ) | b 2.3.1956 | |
| PEART, Thomas George Anthony Hunter | (1964) | b 10.9.1939 | |
| PEASE, Francis Ernest | (1887) | b 17.1.1864 | d 27.6.1957 |
| PENNY, Sidney Herbert | (1909) | b 1875 | d 1965 |
| PENNY, W.J. | (1878-9) | | |
| PERCIVAL, Launcelot Jefferson | (1891-3) | b 22.5.1869 | d 22.6.1941 |
| PERITON, Harold Greaves | (1925-30) | b 8.3.1901 | d 4.1980 |
| PERROTT, Edward Simcocks | (1875) | b 16.9.1852 | d 22.4.1915 |
| PERRY, David Gordon | (1963-6) | b 26.12.1937 | |
| PERRY, Samuel Victor | (1947-8) | b 16.7.1918 | |
| PETERS, James | (1906-08) | b 1880 | d 3.1954 |
| PHILLIPS, Charles | (1880-1) | b 14.8.1857 | d 11.9.1940 |
| PHILLIPS, Malcolm Stanley | (1958-64) | b 3.3.1936 | |
| PICKERING, Arthur Stanley | (1907) | b 24.3.1885 | d 17.2.1969 |
| PICKERING, Roger David Austin | (1967-8) | b 15.6.1943 | |
| PICKLES, Reginald Clarence Werrett | (1922) | b 11.12.1895 | |
| PIERCE, Richard | (1898-1903) | b 30.5.1874 | d 1905 |
| PILKINGTON, William Norman | (1898) | b 26.7.1877 | d 8.2.1935 |
| PILLMAN, Charles Henry | (1910-14) | b 1.1890 | d 13.11.1955 |
| PILLMAN, Robert Laurence | (1914) | b 19.2.1893 | d 9.7.1916 |
| PINCH, John | (1896-7) | b 1871 | d 1946 |
| PINCHING, William Wyatt | (1872) | b 24.3.1851 | d 16.8.1878 |
| PITMAN, Isaac James | (1922) | b 14.8.1901 | d 1.9.1985 |
| PLUMMER, Kenneth Clive | (1969-76) | b 17.1.1947 | |
| POOLE, Francis Oswald | (1895) | b 17.12.1870 | d 22.5.1949 |
| POOLE, Robert Watkins | (1896) | b 4.11.1874 | d 1930 |
| POPE, Edward Brian | (1931) | b 29.6.1911 | |
| PORTUS, Garnet Vere | (1908) | b 7.6.1883 | d 6.1954 |
| POULTON, Ronald William | (1909-14) | b 12.9.1889 | d 5.5.1915 |
| POWELL, David Lewes | (1966-71) | b 17.5.1942 | |
| PRATTEN, William Edgar | (1927) | b 29.5.1907 | |
| PREECE, Ivor | (1948-51) | b 15.12.1920 | d 14.3.1987 |
| PREECE, Peter Stuart | (1972-6) | b 15.11.1949 | |
| PREEDY, Malcolm | (1984- ) | b b.15.9.1960 | |
| PRENTICE, Frank Douglas | (1928) | b 1897 | d 3.10.1962 |
| PRESCOTT, Robert Edward | (1937-9) | b 3.4.1913 | d 18.5.1975 |
| PRESTON, Nicholas John | (1979-80) | b 5.4.1958 | |
| PRICE, Herbert Leo | (1922-3) | b 21.6.1899 | d 18.7.1943 |
| PRICE, John | (1961) | | |
| PRICE, P.L.A. | (1877-8) | | |
| PRICE, Thomas William | (1948-9) | b 26.7.1914 | |
| PROUT, Derek Henry | (1968) | b 10.11.1942 | |
| PULLIN, John Vivian | (1966-76) | b 1.11.1941 | |
| PURDY, Stanley John | (1962) | b 6.2.1936 | |
| PYKE, James | (1892) | b 8.2.1866 | d 17.5.1941 |
| PYM, John Alfred | (1912) | b 25.3.1891 | d 9.2.1969 |
| QUINN, James Patrick | (1954) | b 19.2.1930 | d 19.1.1986 |
| RAFTER, Michael | (1977-81) | b 31.3.1952 | |
| RALSTON, Christopher Wayne | (1971-5) | b 25.5.44 | |
| RAMSDEN, Harold E. | (1898) | | |
| RANSON, John Matthew | (1963-4) | b 26.7.1938 | |
| RAPHAEL, John Edward | (1902-06) | b 30.4.1882 | d 11.6.1917 |
| RAVENSCROFT, John | (1881) | b 11.6.1857 | d 18.8.1902 |

| PLAYER | CAREER SPAN | | |
|---|---|---|---|
| RAWLINSON, William Cecil Welsh | (1876) | b 17.12.1855 | d 14.2.1898 |
| REDFERN, Stephen Paul | (1984) | b 26.1.1958 | |
| REDMAN, Nigel Charles | (1984- ) | b 16.8.1964 | |
| REDMOND, Gerald Francis | (1970) | b 23.3.1943 | |
| REDWOOD, Brian William | (1968) | b 6.2.1939 | |
| REES, Gary William | (1984-) | b 2.5.1960 | |
| REEVE, James Stanley Roope | (1929-31) | b 12.9.1908 | d 6.11.1936 |
| REGAN, Martin | (1953-56) | b 24.9.1929 | |
| RENDALL, Paul Anthony George | (1984-) | b 18.2.1954 | |
| REW, Henry | (1929-34) | b 11.11.1906 | d 11.12.1940 |
| REYNOLDS, Frank Jeffrey | (1937-8) | b 2.1.1916 | |
| REYNOLDS, Shirley | (1900-01) | b 1874 | d 9.1.1946 |
| RHODES, John | (1896) | | |
| RICHARDS, Dean | (1986-) | b 11.7.1963 | |
| RICHARDS, Ernest Edward | (1929) | b 11.3.1905 | d 9.6.1982 |
| RICHARDS, Joseph | (1891) | | |
| RICHARDS, Stephen Brookhouse | (1965-7) | b 28.8.1941 | |
| RICHARDSON, James Vere | (1928) | b 16.12.1903 | |
| RICHARDSON, William Ryder | (1881) | b 9.1861 | d 30.7.1920 |
| RICKARDS, Cyril Henry | (1873) | b 11.1.1854 | d 25.2.1920 |
| RIMMER, Gordon | (1949-54) | b 28.2.1925 | |
| RIMMER, Laurance Ivor | (1961) | b 31.5.1935 | |
| RIPLEY, Andrew George | (1972-6) | b 1.12.1947 | |
| RISMAN, Augustus Beverley Walter | (1959-61) | b 23.11.1937 | |
| RITSON, John Anthony Sydney | (1910-13) | b 18.8.1887 | d 16.10.1957 |
| RITTSON-THOMAS, George Christopher | (1951) | b 18.12.1926 | |
| ROBBINS, Graham Leslie | (1986-) | b 24.9.1956 | |
| ROBBINS, Peter George Derek | (1956-62) | b 21.9.1933 | d 25.3.1987 |
| ROBERTS, Alan Dixon | (1911-14) | b 1888 | d 1.9.1940 |
| ROBERTS, Ernest William | (1901-07) | b 14.11.1878 | d 19.11.1933 |
| ROBERTS, Geoffrey Dorling | (1907-08) | b 27.8.1886 | d 7.3.1967 |
| ROBERTS, James | (1960-4) | b 25.6.1932 | |
| ROBERTS, Reginald Sidney | (1932) | b 4.12.1911 | |
| ROBERTS, Sam | (1887) | | |
| ROBERTS, Victor George | (1947-56) | b 6.8.1924 | |
| ROBERTSHAW, Albert Rawson | (1886-7) | b 1861 | d 17.11.20 |
| ROBINSON, Arthur | (1889-90) | b 8.11.1865 | d 9.4.1948 |
| ROBINSON, Ernest T. | (1954-61) | b 17.1.1929 | |
| ROBINSON, George Carmichael | (1897-1901) | b 1876 | d 29.5.1940 |
| ROBINSON, John James | (1893-1902) | b 28.6.1872 | d 3.1.1959 |
| ROBSON, Alan | (1924-6) | | |
| ROBSON, Matthew | (1930) | b 16.12.1908 | d 30.11.1983 |
| ROGERS, Derek Prior | (1961-9) | b 20.6.1935 | |
| ROGERS, John Henry | (1890-1) | | d 30.3.1922 |
| ROGERS, Walter Lacy Yea | (1905) | b 20.9.1878 | d 10.2.1948 |
| ROLLITT, David Malcolm | (1967-75) | b 24.3.1943 | |
| RONCORONI, Anthony Dominic Sebastian | (1933) | b 16.3.1909 | d 20.7.1953 |
| ROSE, William Marcus Henderson | (1981-) | b 12.1.1957 | |
| ROSSBOROUGH, Peter Alec | (1971-5) | b 30.6.1948 | |
| ROSSER, David William Albert | (1965-6) | b 27.3.1940 | |
| ROTHERHAM, Alan | (1883-7) | b 31.7.1862 | d 30.8.1898 |
| ROTHERHAM, Arthur | (1898-9) | b 27.5.1869 | d 3.3.1946 |
| ROUGHLEY, David | (1873-4) | b 10.12.1947 | |
| ROWELL, Robert Errington | (1964-5) | b 29.8.1939 | |
| ROWLEY, Alfred J. | (1932) | b 1908 | |
| ROWLEY, Hugh Campbell | (1879-82) | b 3.1854 | |
| ROYDS, Percy Molyneux Rawson | (1898-9) | b 1874 | d 25.3.1955 |
| ROYLE, A.V. | (1889) | | |

| PLAYER | CAREER SPAN | |
|---|---|---|
| RUDD, Edward Lawrence | (1965-6) | b 28.9.1944 |
| RUSSELL, Richard Forbes | (1905) | b 5.4.1879 d 30.5.1960 |
| RUTHERFORD, Donald | (1960-7) | b 22.9.1937 |
| RYALLS, Henry John | (1885) | b 12.12.1858 d 17.10.1949 |
| RYAN, Peter Henry | (1955) | b 1.10.1930 |
| SADLER, Edward H. | (1933) | b 1912 |
| SAGAR, John Warburton | (1901) | b 6.12.1878 d 10.1.1941 |
| SALMON, James Lionel Broome | (1985-) | b 16.10.1959 |
| SAMPLE, Charles Herbert | (1884-6) | b 22.11.1862 d 2.6.1938 |
| SANDERS, Donald Louis | (1954-6) | b 6.9.1924 |
| SANDERS, Frank Warren | (1923) | b 24.1.1893 d 22.6.1953 |
| SANDFORD, Joseph Ruscombe Poole | (1906) | b 5.3.1881 d 19.7.1916 |
| SANGWIN, Roger Dennis | (1964) | b 2.12.1937 |
| SARGENT, Gordon A.F. | (1981) | b 18.10.1950 |
| SAVAGE, Keith Frederick | (1966-8) | b 24.8.1940 |
| SAWYER, Charles Montague | (1880-1) | b 1856 d 30.3.1921 |
| SAXBY, Leslie Eric | (1932) | b 19.5.1900 |
| SCHOFIELD, John Wood | (1880) | b 3.1858 d 3.5.1931 |
| SCHOLFIELD, John Arthur | (1911) | b 6.4.1888 d 14.9.1967 |
| SCHWARZ, Reginald Oscar | (1899-1901) | b 4.5.1875 d 18.11.1918 |
| SCORFIELD, Edward Scafe | (1910) | b 21.4.1882 d 1966 |
| SCOTT, Charles Tillard | (1900-01) | b 26.8.1877 d 6.11.1965 |
| SCOTT, Edward Keith | (1947-8) | b 14.6.1918 |
| SCOTT, Frank Sholl | (1907) | b 9.1.1886 d 4.2.1952 |
| SCOTT, Harry | (1955) | b 7.11.1926 |
| SCOTT, John Philip | (1978-84) | b 28.9.1954 |
| SCOTT, John Stanley Marshall | (1958) | b 23.1.1935 |
| SCOTT, Mason Thompson | (1887-90) | b 20.12.1865 d 1.6.1916 |
| SCOTT, William Martin | (1889) | b 27.3.1870 d 26.2.1944 |
| SEDDON, Robert L. | (1887) | b 1860 d 15.8.1888 |
| SELLAR, Kenneth Anderson | (1927-8) | b 11.8.1906 |
| SEVER, Harry Sedgewick | (1936-8) | b 3.3.1910 |
| SHACKLETON, Ian Roger | (1969-70) | b 17.6.1948 |
| SHARP, Richard Adrian William | (1960-7) | b 9.9.1938 |
| SHAW, Cecil Hamilton | (1906-07) | b 1.8.1879 d 13.11.1964 |
| SHAW, Frederick | (1898) | |
| SHAW, James Fraser | (1898) | b 2.1.1878 d 23.7.1941 |
| SHEPPARD, Austin | (1981-) | b 1.5.1950 |
| SHERRARD, Charles William | (1871-2) | b 25.12.1849 d 1921 |
| SHERRIFF, George Albert | (1966-7) | b 29.5.1937 |
| SHEWRING, Harry Edward | (1905-07) | b 26.4.1882 d 27.11.1960 |
| SHOOTER, John Henry | (1899-1900) | b 25.3.1875 d 13.8.1922 |
| SHUTTLEWORTH, Dennis William | (1951-3) | b 22.7.1928 |
| SIBREE, Herbert John Hyde | (1908-9) | b 9.5.1885 d 20.8.1962 |
| SILK, Nicholas | (1965) | b 26.5.1941 |
| SIMMS, Kevin Gerard | (1985-) | b 25.12.1964 |
| SIMPSON, Colin Peter | (1965) | b 21.9.1942 |
| SIMPSON, Paul Donald | (1983-) | b 7.6.1958 |
| SIMPSON, Thomas | (1902-9) | |
| SLADEN, Geoffrey Mainwaring | (1929) | b 3.8.1904 |
| SLEMEN, Michael Anthony Charles | (1976-84) | b 11.5.1951 |
| SLOCOCK, Lancelot Andrew Noel | (1907-8) | b 25.12.1886 d 9.8.1916 |
| SLOW, Charles | (1934) | b 1911 d 15.4.1939 |
| SMALL, Harold Dudley | (1950) | b 7.1.1922 |
| SMALLWOOD, Alastair McNaughton | (1920-5) | b 18.11.1892 |
| SMART, Colin Edward | (1979-83) | b 5.3.1950 |
| SMART, Sidney | (1913-20) | b 1888 |
| SMEDDLE, Robert William | (1929-31) | b 14.7.1908 |
| SMITH, C. | (1901) | |
| SMITH, Dyne Fenton | (1910) | b 21.7.1890 d 28.8.1969 |
| SMITH, John Vincent | (1950) | b 23.5.1926 |
| SMITH, Keith | (1974-5) | b 19.11.1952 |

| PLAYER | CAREER SPAN | |
|---|---|---|
| SMITH, Michael John Knight | (1956) | b 30.6.1933 |
| SMITH, Simon Timothy | (1985-) | b 29.4.1960 |
| SMITH, Stephen James | (1973-83) | b 22.7.1951 |
| SMITH, Stephen Rider | (1959-64) | b 21.10.1934 |
| SMITH, Trellevyn Harvey | (1951) | b 3.4.1920 |
| SOANE, Frank | (1893-4) | b 12.9.1866 d 1.4.1932 |
| SOBEY, Wilfred Henry | (1930-2) | b 1.4.1905 |
| SOLOMON, Bert | (1910) | b 8.3.1885 d 30.6.1961 |
| SPARKS, Robert Henry Ware | (1928-31) | b 19.2.1899 |
| SPEED, Harry | (1894-6) | b 19.8.1871 d 3.7.1937 |
| SPENCE, Frederick William | (1890) | b 5.1867 |
| SPENCER, Jeremy | (1966) | b 27.6.1939 |
| SPENCER, John Sothern | (1969-71) | b 10.8.1947 |
| SPONG, Roger Spencer | (1929-32) | b 23.10.1906 d 27.3.1980 |
| SPOONER, Reginald Herbert | (1903) | b 21.10.1880 d 2.10.1961 |
| SPRINGMAN, Herman Henry | (1879-87) | b 1859 d 17.10.1936 |
| SPURLING, Aubrey | (1882) | b 19.7.1856 d 26.3.1945 |
| SPURLING, Norman | (1886-7) | b 15.2.1864 d 20.7.1919 |
| SQUIRES, Peter John | (1973-79) | b 4.8.1951 |
| STAFFORD, Richard Calvert | (1912) | b 23.7.1893 d 1.12.1912 |
| STAFFORD, William Francis Howard | (1874) | b 19.12.1854 d 8.8.1942 |
| STANBURY, Edward | (1926-9) | b 1897 d 1.5.1968 |
| STANDING, G. | (1883) | |
| STANGER-LEATHES, Christopher Francis | (1905) | b 9.5.1881 d 27.2.1966 |
| STARK, Kendrick James | (1927-8) | b 18.8.1904 |
| STARKS, Anthony | (1896) | b 11.8.1873 d 1.1952 |
| STARMER-SMITH, Nigel Christopher | (1969-71) | b 25.12.1944 |
| START, Sydney Philip | (1907) | b 17.5.1879 d 14.12.1969 |
| STEEDS, John Harold | (1949-50) | b 27.9.1916 |
| STEELE-BODGER, Michael Roland | (1947-8) | b 4.9.1925 |
| STEINTHAL, Francis Eric | (1913) | b 21.11.1886 |
| STEVENS, Claude Brian | (1969-75) | b 2.6.1941 |
| STILL, Ernest Robert | (1873) | b 14.7.1852 d 23.11.1931 |
| STIRLING, Robert Victor | (1951-54) | b 4.9.1919 |
| STODDART, Andrew Ernest | (1885-93) | b 11.3.1863 d 3.4.1915 |
| STODDART, Wilfrid Bowring | (1897) | b 27.4.1871 d 8.1.1935 |
| STOKES, Frederick | (1871-3) | b 12.7.1851 d 7.1.1929 |
| STOKES, Lennard | (1875-81) | b 12.2.1856 d 3.5.1933 |
| STONE, Francis le Strange | (1914) | b 1886 d 7.10.1938 |
| STOOP, Adrian Dura | (1905-12) | b 27.3.1883 d 27.11.1957 |
| STOOP, Frederick Macfarlane | (1910-13) | b 17.9.1888 d 24.11.1972 |
| STOUT, Frank Moxham | (1897-1905) | b 21.2.1877 d 30.5.1926 |
| STOUT, Percy Wyfold | (1898-9) | b 20.11.1875 d 9.10.1937 |
| STRINGER, Nicholas Courtenay | (1982-) | b 4.10.1960 |
| STRONG, Edmund Linwood | (1884) | b 12.1862 d 20.3.1945 |
| SUMMERSCALES, George Edward | (1905) | b 1879 d 31.12.1936 |
| SUTCLIFFE, John William | (1889) | b 14.4.1868 d 7.7.1947 |
| SWARBRICK, David William | (1947-9) | b 17.1.1927 |
| SWAYNE, Deneys Harald | (1931) | b 23.11.1909 |
| SWAYNE, John Walter Rocke | (1929) | b 27.5.1906 |
| SWIFT, Anthony Hugh | (1981-) | b 24.5.1959 |
| SYDDALL, James Paul | (1982-) | b 7.3.1956 |
| SYKES, A.R.V. | (1914) | |
| SYKES, Frank Douglas | (1955-63) | b 9.12.1927 |
| SYKES, Patrick William | (1948-53) | b 3.3.1925 |
| SYRETT, Ronald Edward | (1958-62) | b 5.1.1931 |
| TALLENT, John Arthur | (1931-5) | b 8.3.1911 |
| TANNER, Christopher Champain | (1930-2) | b 24.6.1908 d 22.5.1941 |
| TATHAM, William Meaburn | (1882-4) | b 30.7.1862 d 18.10.1938 |

| PLAYER | CAREER SPAN | | |
|---|---|---|---|
| TARR, Francis Nathaniel | (1909-13) | b 14.8.1887 | d 18.7.1915 |
| TAYLOR, Arthur Sneyd | (1883-6) | b 7.12.1859 | d 31.7.1917 |
| TAYLOR, Ernest William | (1892-9) | b 20.2.1869 | |
| TAYLOR, Frank | (1920) | b 4.5.1890 | d 10.1956 |
| TAYLOR, Frederick Mark | (1914) | b 18.3.1888 | d 1964 |
| TAYLOR, Henry Herbert | (1879-82) | b 1.9.1858 | d 25.5.1942 |
| TAYLOR, John T. | (1897-1905) | b 26.5.1876 | d 8.9.1951 |
| TAYLOR, Philip Joseph | (1955-62) | b 6.6.1931 | |
| TAYLOR, Robert Bainbridge | (1966-71) | b 30.4.1942 | |
| TAYLOR, William John Kirwan | (1928) | b 29.6.1905 | |
| TEAGUE, Michael Clive | (1985-) | b 8.10.1959 | |
| TEDEN, Derek Edmund | (1939) | b 19.7.1916 | d 15.10.1940 |
| TEGGIN, Alfred | (1884-7) | b 1860 | d 1941 |
| TETLEY, Thomas Spence | (1876) | b 1856 | d 15.8.1924 |
| THOMAS, Charles | (1895-9) | b 1875 | d 1935 |
| THOMPSON, Peter Humphrey | (1956-9) | b 18.1.1929 | |
| THOMSON, George Thomas | (1878-85) | b 1857 | d 31.10.1889 |
| THOMSON, W.B. | (1892-5) | b 1871 | |
| THORNE, John David | (1963) | b 1.1.1934 | |
| TINDALL, Victor Ronald | (1951) | b 1.8.1928 | |
| TOBIN, Frank | (1871) | b 23.9.1849 | d 6.2.1927 |
| TODD, Alexander Findlater | (1900) | b 20.9.1873 | d 20.4.1915 |
| TODD, R. | (1877) | b 4.1847 | d 2.1927 |
| TOFT, Henry Bert | (1936-9) | b 2.10.1909 | d 7.7.1987 |
| TOOTHILL, John James | (1890-4) | b 1866 | d 29.6.1947 |
| TOSSWILL, Leonard Robert | (1902) | b 12.1.1880 | d 3.10.1932 |
| TOUZEL, Charles John Cliff | (1877) | b 1855 | d 23.8.1899 |
| TOWELL, Allan Clark | (1948-51) | b 1924 | |
| TRAVERS, Basil Holmes | (1947-9) | b 7.7.1919 | |
| TREADWELL, William Thomas | (1966) | b 13.3.1939 | |
| TRICK, David Mark | (1983-) | b 26.10.1960 | |
| TRISTRAM, Henry Barrington | (1883-7) | b 5.9.1861 | d 1.10.1946 |
| TROOP, Carlton Lang | (1933) | b 10.6.1910 | |
| TUCKER, John Samuel | (1922-31) | b 1.6.1895 | d 4.1.1973 |
| TUCKER, William Eldon | (1894-5) | b 17.8.1872 | d 18.10.1953 |
| TUCKER, William Eldon | (1926-30) | b 6.8.1903 | |
| TURNER, Dawson Palgrave | (1871-5) | b 15.12.1846 | d 2.1909 |
| TURNER, Edward Beadon | (1876-8) | b 9.1854 | d 30.6.1931 |
| TURNER, George Robertson | (1876) | b 22.10.1855 | d 7.4.1941 |
| TURNER, H.J.C. | (1871) | | |
| TURNER, Martin Frederick | (1948) | b 1.8.1921 | |
| TURQUAND-YOUNG, David | (1928-9) | | |
| TWYNAM, Henry Thomas | (1879-84) | b 1852 | d 19.5.1899 |
| UNDERWOOD, Adrian Martin | (1962-4) | b 19.7.1940 | |
| UNDERWOOD, Rory | (1984-) | b 19.6.1963 | |
| UNWIN, Ernest James | (1937-8) | b 18.9.1912 | |
| UNWIN, Geoffrey Thomas | (1898) | b 1.6.1874 | d 12.2.1948 |
| UREN, Richard | (1948-50) | b 26.2.1926 | |
| UTTLEY, Roger Miles | (1973-80) | b 11.9.1949 | |
| VALENTINE, James | (1890-6) | b 29.7.1866 | d 25.7.1904 |
| VANDERSPAR, Charles Henry Richard | (1873) | b 1852 | d 9.4.1877 |
| VAN RYNEVELD, Clive Berrange | (1949) | b 19.3.1928 | |
| VARLEY, Harry | (1892) | b 25.11.1868 | d 21.11.1915 |
| VASSALL, Henry | (1881-3) | b 22.10.1860 | d 5.1.1926 |
| VASSALL, Henry Holland | (1908) | b 23.3.1887 | d 8.10.1949 |
| VAUGHAN, Douglas Brian | (1948-50) | b 15.7.1925 | d 19.4.1977 |
| VAUGHAN-JONES, Arthur | (1932-3) | b 25.9.1909 | |
| VERELST, Courtenay Lee | (1876-8) | b 16.11.1855 | d 9.1.1890 |
| VERNON, George Frederic | (1878-81) | b 20.6.1856 | d 10.8.1902 |
| VICKERY, George | (1905) | b 25.5.1879 | d 7.1970 |

| PLAYER | CAREER SPAN | | |
|---|---|---|---|
| VIVYAN, Elliott | (1901-4) | b 6.1.1879 | d 3.12.1935 |
| VOYCE, Anthony Thomas | (1920-6) | b 18.5.1897 | d 22.1.1980 |
| WACKETT, John Arthur Sibley | (1959) | b 27.9.1930 | |
| WADE, Charles Gregory | (1883-6) | b 26.1.1863 | d 26.9.1922 |
| WADE, Michael R. | (1962) | b 1938 | |
| WAKEFIELD, William Wavell | (1920-7) | b 10.3.1898 | d 12.8.1983 |
| WALKER, George Augustus | (1939) | b 24.8.1912 | d 11.12.1986 |
| WALKER, Harry W. | (1947-8) | b 11.2.1915 | |
| WALKER, Roger | (1874-80) | b 18.9.1846 | d 11.11.1919 |
| WALLENS, J.N.S. | (1927) | | |
| WALTON, Ernest John | (1901-02) | b 11.1879 | d 8.4.1947 |
| WALTON, William | (1894) | b 23.9.1874 | d 1.6.1940 |
| WARD, George | (1913-14) | b 19.3.1885 | d 1963 |
| WARD, Herbert | (1895) | b 1873 | d 18.2.1955 |
| WARD, James Ibbotson | (1881-2) | b 24.4.1858 | d 28.9.1924 |
| WARD, John Willie | (1896) | b 29.1.1873 | d 30.4.1939 |
| WARDLOW, Christopher Story | (1969-71) | b 12.7.1942 | |
| WARFIELD, Peter John | (1973-5) | | |
| WARR, Anthony Lawley | (1934) | b 15.5.1913 | |
| WATKINS, John Arthur | (1972-5) | b 28.11.1946 | |
| WATKINS, John Kingdon | (1939) | b 24.2.1913 | d 13.5.1970 |
| WATSON, Fischer Burges | (1908-09) | b 9.1884 | d 14.8.1960 |
| WATSON, James Henry Digby | (1914) | b 31.8.1890 | d 15.10.1914 |
| WATT, David Edward James | (1967) | b 5.7.1938 | |
| WEBB, Charles Samuel Henry | (1932-6) | b 1902 | d 28.10.1961 |
| WEBB, J.W.G. | (1926-9) | | |
| WEBB, Rodney Edward | (1967-72) | b 18.8.1943 | |
| WEBB, St Lawrence Hugh | (1959) | b 7.3.1931 | d 30.5.1978 |
| WEBSTER, Jan Godfrey | (1972-5) | b 24.8.1946 | |
| WEDGE, Thomas George | (1907-09) | | |
| WEIGHILL, Robert Harold George | (1947-8) | b 9.9.1920 | |
| WELLS, Cyril Mowbray | (1893-7) | b 21.3.1871 | d 22.8.1963 |
| WEST, Bryan Ronald | (1968-70) | b 7.6.1948 | |
| WESTON, Henry Thomas Franklin | (1901) | b 9.7.1869 | d 5.4.1955 |
| WESTON, Lionel Edward | (1972) | b 22.2.1947 | |
| WESTON, Michael Philip | (1960-8) | b 21.8.1938 | |
| WESTON, William Henry | (1933-8) | b 21.12.1905 | d 8.1.1987 |
| WHEATLEY, Arthur A. | (1937-8) | b 9.12.1908 | |
| WHEATLEY, Harold F. | (1936-9) | b 25.12.1912 | |
| WHEELER, Peter John | (1975-84) | b 26.11.1948 | |
| WHITE, Colin | (1983-) | b 31.3.1948 | |
| WHITE, Donald Frederick | (1947-53) | b 16.1.1926 | |
| WHITELEY, Eric Cyprian Perry | (1931) | b 18.7.1904 | |
| WHITELEY, W. | (1896) | b 1871 | |
| WHITLEY, Herbert | (1929) | b 26.8.1903 | d 1975 |
| WIGHTMAN, Brian John | (1959-63) | b 23.9.1936 | |
| WIGGLESWORTH, Henry John | (1884) | b 1861 | d 3.3.1925 |
| WILKINS, Dennis Thomas | (1951-3) | b 26.12.1924 | |
| WILKINSON, Edgar | (1886-7) | b 1863 | d 27.8.1896 |
| WILKINSON, Harry James | (1889) | b 1864 | d 7.6.1942 |
| WILKINSON, Harry | (1929-30) | b 22.3.1903 | |
| WILKINSON, P. | (1872) | | |
| WILKINSON, Robert Michael | (1975-6) | b 25.7.1951 | |
| WILLCOCKS, T.J. | (1902) | | |
| WILLCOX, John Graham | (1961-4) | b 16.2.1937 | |
| WILLIAM-POWLETT, Peveril Barton Reiby Wallop | (1922) | b 5.3.1898 | d 10.11.1985 |
| WILLIAMS, Cyril Stoate | (1910) | b 17.11.1887 | |
| WILLIAMS, Christopher Gareth | (1976) | b 21.12.1950 | |
| WILLIAMS, John Edward | (1954-65) | b 31.1.1932 | |
| WILLIAMS, John Michael | (1951) | b 24.8.1927 | |
| WILLIAMS, Peter Nicholas | (1987-) | b 14.12.1958 | |
| WILLIAMS, S.G. | (1902-07) | | |

| PLAYER | CAREER SPAN | | |
|---|---|---|---|
| WILLIAMS, Stanley Horatio | (1911) | b 2.11.1886 | d 30.4.1936 |
| WILLIAMSON, Rupert Henry | (1908-09) | b 22.11.1886 | d 16.3.1946 |
| WILSON, Arthur James | (1909) | b 29.12.1886 | d 1.7.1917 |
| WILSON, Charles Edward | (1898) | b 2.6.1871 | d 17.9.1914 |
| WILSON, Charles Plumpton | (1881) | b 12.5.1859 | d 9.3.1938 |
| WILSON, Dyson Stayt | (1953-5) | b 7.10.1926 | |
| WILSON, Guy Summerfield | (1929) | b 30.8.1907 | d 8.7.1979 |
| WILSON, Kenneth James | (1963) | b 25.11.1938 | |
| WILSON, Roger Parker | (1891) | b 13.5.1870 | d 12.12.1943 |
| WILSON, Walter Carandini | (1907) | b 22.6.1885 | d 12.4.1967 |
| WINN, Christopher Elliott | (1952-4) | b 13.11.1926 | |
| WINTERBOTTOM, Peter James | (1982-) | b 31.5.1960 | |
| WINTLE, Trevor Clifford | (1966-9) | b 10.1.1940 | |
| WODEHOUSE, Norman Atherton | (1910-13) | b 18.5.1887 | d 4.9.1941 |
| WOOD, Albert | (1884) | | |
| WOOD, Alfred Ernest | (1908) | b 1882 | d 15.2.1963 |
| WOOD, George William | (1914) | b 5.2.1886 | d 12.6.1969 |
| WOOD, Robert | (1894) | b 1873 | |
| WOOD, Robert Dudley | (1901-03) | b 1873 | |
| WOODGATE, Edmund Elliot | (1952) | b 2.1.1922 | |
| WOODHEAD, Ernest | (1880) | b 2.2.1857 | d 17.6.1944 |
| WOODRUFF, Charles Garfield | (1951) | b 30.10.1920 | |
| WOODS, Samuel Moses James | (1890-5) | b 14.4.1868 | d 30.4.1931 |
| WOODS, Thomas | (1908) | b 9.2.1883 | d 12.4.1955 |
| WOODS, Tom | (1920-1) | | |
| WOODWARD, Clive Ronald | (1980-) | b 6.1.1956 | |
| WOODWARD, J. Edward | (1952-6) | b 17.4.1931 | |
| WOOLDRIDGE, Charles Sylvester | (1883-5) | b 31.12.1858 | d 19.2.1941 |
| WORDSWORTH, Alan John | (1975) | b 9.11.1953 | |
| WORTON, James Robert Bute | (1926-7) | b 31.3.1901 | |
| WRENCH, David Frederick Bryan | (1964) | b 27.11.1936 | |
| WRIGHT, Cyril Carne Glenton | (1909) | b 7.3.1887 | d 15.9.1960 |
| WRIGHT, Frank Thurlow | (1881) | b 2.7.1862 | d 1934 |
| WRIGHT, Ian Douglas | (1971) | b 24.12.1945 | |
| WRIGHT, John Cecil | (1934) | b 6.8.1910 | |
| WRIGHT, James F. | (1890) | b 1.4.1863 | d 4.10.1932 |
| WRIGHT, Thomas Peter | (1960-2) | b 28.2.1931 | |
| WRIGHT, William Henry George | (1920) | b 6.6.1889 | |
| WYATT, Derek M. | (1976) | b 4.12.1949 | |
| YARRANTON, Peter George | (1954-5) | b 30.9.1924 | |
| YIEND, William | (1889-93) | b 1861 | d 22.1.1939 |
| YOUNG, Arthur Tudor | (1924-9) | b 14.10.1901 | d 26.2.1933 |
| YOUNG, John Robert Chester | (1958-61) | b 6.9.1937 | |
| YOUNG, Malcolm | (1977-9) | b 4.1.1946 | |
| YOUNG, Peter Dalton | (1954-5) | b 9.11.1927 | |
| YOUNGS, Nicholas Gerald | (1983-) | b 15.12.1959 | |

# SCOTLAND

| PLAYER | CAREER SPAN | |
|---|---|---|
| ABERCROMBIE, Cecil Halliday | (1910-13) | b 12.4.1886 d 31.5.1916 |
| ABERCROMBIE, James Gilbert | (1949-50) | b 9.5.1928 |
| AGNEW, W.C.C. | (1930) | |
| AINSLIE, Robert | (1879-82) | b 1858 d 12.5.1906 |
| AINSLIE, Thomas | (1881-5) | b 1859 d 16.3.1926 |
| AITCHISON, G.R. | (1883) | |
| AITCHISON, Thomas Graham | (1929) | d 25.12.1977 |
| AITKEN, Alexander | (1889) | d 7.7.1925 |
| AITKEN, George Gothard | (1924-9) | b 2.7.1898 d 24.8.1952 |
| AITKEN, James | (1977- ) | b 22.11.1948 |
| AITKEN, Richard | (1947) | b 29.6.1914 |
| ALLAN, Bryce | (1881) | b 1859 d 11.1922 |
| ALLAN, James Leslie | (1952-3) | b 4.3.1927 |
| ALLAN, John Lewis Forsyth | (1957) | b 20.8.1934 |
| ALLAN, John W. | (1927-34) | b 1905 d 29.12.1958 |
| ALLAN, Richard Campbell | (1969) | b 16.3.1939 |
| ALLARDICE, William Dallas | (1948-9) | b 4.11.1919 |
| ALLEN, H.W. | (1873) | |
| ANDERSON, Alexander Harvie | (1894) | b 1873 d 14.12.1939 |
| ANDERSON, Darsie Gordon | (1889-92) | d 26.12.1937 |
| ANDERSON, Ernest | (1947) | b 20.10.1918 |
| ANDERSON, John W. | (1872) | b 9.5.1850 d 26.5.1934 |
| ANDERSON, Thomas | (1882) | b 17.5.1863 d 17.6.1938 |
| ANGUS, Alexander William | (1909-20) | b 11.11.1889 d 25.3.1947 |
| ANTON, Peter A. | (1873) | b 25.6.1850 d 10.12.1911 |
| ARNEIL, Rodger James | (1968-73) | b 1.5.1944 |
| ARTHUR, Allen | (1875-6) | b 3.4.1857 d 9.10.1923 |
| ARTHUR, John William | (1871-2) | b 25.4.1848 d 15.3.1921 |
| ASHER, Augustus Gordon Grant | (1882-6) | b 18.12.1861 d 15.7.1930 |
| AULD, William | (1889-90) | b 4.1868 d 19.7.1945 |
| AULDJO, L.J. | (1878) | |
| | | |
| BAIN, David McLaren | (1911-14) | b 10.12.1891 d 3.6.1915 |
| BAIRD, Gavin Roger Todd | (1981-) | b 12.4.1960 |
| BALFOUR, Andrew | (1896-7) | b 21.3.1873 d 30.1.1931 |
| BALFOUR-MELVILLE, Leslie Melville | (1872) | b 9.3.1854 d 16.7.1937 |
| BANNERMAN, Edward Mordaunt | (1872-3) | b 14.1.1850 |
| BANNERMAN, John MacDonald | (1921-9) | b 1.9.1901 d 12.4.1969 |
| BARNES, Ian Andrew | (1972-7) | b 19.4.1948 |
| BARRIE, Robert W. | (1936) | b 7.11 |
| BEARNE, Keith Robert Fraser | (1960) | b 1937 |
| BEATTIE, John Armstrong | (1929-36) | b 5.1.1907 d 10.2.1977 |
| BEATTIE, John Ross | (1980- ) | b 27.11.1957 |
| BEDELL-SIVRIGHT, David Revell | (1900-08) | b 8.12.1880 d 5.9.1915 |
| BEDELL-SIVRIGHT, John Vandaleur | (1902) | b 10.1881 d 21.10.1920 |
| BEGBIE, Thomas Allan | (1881) | b 1862 d 26.2.1896 |
| BELL, David Lauder | (1975) | b 28.4.1949 |
| BELL, John Arthur | (1901-02) | b 1882 |
| BELL, Lewis Hay Irving | (1900-04) | b 23.10.1878 d 25.6.1924 |
| BERKELEY, William Vaughan | (1926-9) | b 14.6.1904 |
| BERRY, Charles Walter | (1884-8) | b 6.9.1863 d 11.10.1947 |
| BERTRAM, David Minto | (1922-4) | b 24.1.1899 d 10.4.1975 |
| BIGGAR, Alastair Gourlay | (1969-72) | b 4.8.1946 |
| BIGGAR, Michael Andrew | (1975-80) | b 20.11.1949 |
| BIRKETT, Graham Anthony | (1975) | |
| BISHOP, J.M. | (1893) | |
| BISSET, Alexander Anderson | (1904) | b 18.10.1883 d 14.2.1927 |
| BLACK, Angus William | (1947-50) | b 6.5.1925 |
| BLACK, William Pollock | (1948-51) | b 27.11.1921 |

| PLAYER | CAREER SPAN | |
|---|---|---|
| BLACKADDER, William Francis | (1938) | b 23.1.1913 |
| BLAIKIE, Colin Fraser | (1963-9) | b 21.11.1941 |
| BLAIR, Patrick Charles Bentley | (1913) | b 18.7.1891 d 6.7.1915 |
| BOLTON, William Henry | (1876) | b 15.3.1851 d 5.12.1896 |
| BORTHWICK, John Bishop | (1938) | |
| BOS, Frans Herman ten | (1959-63) | b 21.4.1937 |
| BOSWELL, John Douglas | (1889-94) | b 16.2.1867 d 5.1.1948 |
| BOWIE, Thomas Chalmers | (1913-14) | b 28.4.1889 d 28.11.1972 |
| BOYD, G.M. | (1926) | b 8.3.1905 |
| BOYD, J.L. | (1912) | |
| BOYLE, Allan Cameron Wilson | (1963) | b 11.11.1937 |
| BOYLE, Alasdair Hugh Wilson | (1966-8) | b 30.9.1945 |
| BRASH, John Craig | (1961) | b 5.1939 |
| BREAKEY, Richard William | (1978) | b 14.11.1956 |
| BREWIS, Nathaniel Thomas | (1876-80) | b 16.4.1856 d 21.10.24 |
| BREWSTER, Alexander Kinloch | (1977- ) | b 3.5.1954 |
| BROWN, Alexander Henderson | (1928-9) | b 12.5.1905 |
| BROWN, Arthur Robert | (1971-2) | b 10.12.1949 |
| BROWN, Charles H.C. | (1929) | d 25.10.1976 |
| BROWN, David Ian | (1933) | b 8.2.1909 |
| BROWN, Gordon Lamont | (1969-76) | b 1.11.1947 |
| BROWN, J.A. | (1908) | |
| BROWN, J.B. | (1879-86) | |
| BROWN, Peter Currie | (1964-73) | b 16.12.1941 |
| BROWN, Thomas Gow | (1929) | b 1902 |
| BROWN, William David | (1871-5) | b 29.5.1852 d 24.3.1875 |
| BROWN, William Sorley | (1880-3) | b 1859 d 15.9.1901 |
| BROWNING, Arthur | (1920-3) | b 2.7.1897 |
| BRUCE, Charles Russell | (1947-9) | b 25.4.1918 |
| BRUCE, Norman Scott | (1958-64) | b 1932 |
| BRUCE, Robert Mitchell | (1947-8) | b 19.6.1922 |
| BRUCE-LOCKHART, John Harold | (1913-20) | b 4.3.1889 d 4.6.1956 |
| BRUCE-LOCKHART, Logie | (1948-53) | b 12.10.1921 |
| BRUCE-LOCKHART, Rab Brougham | (1937-9) | b 1.12.1916 |
| BRYCE, C.C. | (1873-4) | d 2.1895 |
| BRYCE, Robert Donaldson Hamish | (1973) | b 12.11.1941 |
| BRYCE, William Erskine | (1922-4) | b 16.1.1901 d 22.2.1983 |
| BRYDON, William Ritchie Crawford | (1939) | b 6.11.1915 d 11.6.1980 |
| BUCHANAN, Angus | (1871) | b 15.1.1847 d 21.2.1927 |
| BUCHANAN, Fletcher Gordon | (1910-11) | b 23.12.1889 d 1.1967 |
| BUCHANAN, John Cecil Rankin | (1921-5) | b 18.6.1896 d 19.2.1976 |
| BUCHER, Alfred Moore | (1897) | b 22.3.1874 d 20.8.1939 |
| BUDGE, Grahame Morris | (1950) | b 7.11.1920 d 14.11.1979 |
| BULLMORE, Herbert Henry | (1902) | d 12.1937 |
| BURNET, Patrick John | (1960) | b 25.7.1939 |
| BURNET, William Alexander | (1912) | b 6.3.1886 d 25.7.1958 |
| BURNET, William Alexander | (1934-6) | b 8.7.1912 |
| BURNETT, James Niven | (1980) | 12.7.1947 |
| BURRELL, George | (1950-1) | b 21.1.1921 |
| | | |
| CAIRNS, Alexander Gordon | (1903-06) | b 26.4.1878 d 8.4.1968 |
| CALDER, Finlay | (1986-) | b 20.8.1957 |
| CALDER, James Hamilton | (1981-) | b 20.8.1957 |
| CALLANDER, Gary Jones | (1984-) | b 5.7.1959 |
| CAMERON, Angus | (1948-56) | b 24.6.1929 |
| CAMERON, Alan Douglas | (1951-4) | b 4.3.1924 |
| CAMERON, Alexander William Cumming | (1887-94) | b 3.3.1866 d 14.3.1957 |

| PLAYER | CAREER SPAN | | |
|---|---|---|---|
| CAMERON, Donald | (1953-4) | b 25.12.1927 | |
| CAMERON, Neil William | (1952-3) | b 2.9.1925 | d 1979 |
| CAMPBELL, Alister James | (1984-) | b 1.1.1959 | |
| CAMPBELL, George Theophilus | (1892-1900) | b 17.10.1872 | d 28.3.1924 |
| CAMPBELL, H.H. | (1947-8) | | |
| CAMPBELL, James Alexander | (1878-81) | b 1858 | d 20.6.1902 |
| CAMPBELL, John Argentine | (1900) | b 20.10.1877 | d 2.12.1917 |
| CAMPBELL, Norman MacDonald | (1956) | b 1931 | |
| CAMPBELL-LAMERTON, Jeremy Robert Edward | (1986-) | b 21.2.1959 | |
| CAMPBELL-LAMERTON, Michael John | (1961-6) | 1.8.1933 | |
| CARMICHAEL, Alexander Bennett | (1967-78) | b 2.2.1944 | |
| CARMICHAEL, James Howden | (1921) | b 22.3.1900 | |
| CARRICK, James Stewart | (1876-7) | b 4.9.1855 | d 2.1.1923 |
| CASSELS, David Young | (1880-3) | b 1859 | d 25.1.1923 |
| CATHCART, Charles Walker | (1872-6) | b 16.3.1853 | d 22.2.1932 |
| CAWKWELL, George Law | (1947) | b 25.10.1919 | |
| CHALMERS, Thomas | (1871-6) | b 20.3.1850 | d 25.5.1926 |
| CHAMBERS, Henry Francis Townsend | (1888-9) | b 22.5.1865 | d 12.2.1934 |
| CHARTERS, Robert Gray | (1955) | b 29.10.1930 | |
| CHISHOLM, David Hardie | (1964-8) | b 23.1.1937 | |
| CHISHOLM, Robin William Taylor | (1955-60) | b 16.10.29 | |
| CHURCH, William Campbell | (1906) | b 1884 | d 28.6.1915 |
| CLARK, Robert Lawson | (1972-3) | b 27.1.1944 | |
| CLAUSS, Paul Robert Adolph | (1891-5) | b 22.6.1868 | d 21.4.1945 |
| CLAY, Alexander Thomson | (1886-8) | b 27.9.1863 | d 29.11.1950 |
| CLUNIES-ROSS, A. | (1871) | | |
| COLTMAN, Stuart | (1948-9) | b 27.3.1920 | |
| COLVILLE, Andrew Galbraith | (1871-2) | b 1847 | d 17.4.1881 |
| CONNELL, Gordon Colin | (1968-70) | b 3.10.1944 | |
| COOPER, Malcolm McGregor | (1936) | b 17.8.1910 | |
| CORDIAL, Ian F. | (1952) | | |
| COTTER, James Logan | (1934) | b 6.1.1907 | |
| COTTINGTON, Gordon Stanley | (1934-6) | b 2.4.1911 | |
| COUGHTRIE, Stanley | (1959-63) | b 19.7.1935 | |
| COUPER, J.H. | (1896-9) | | |
| COUTTS, Frank Henderson | (1947) | b 8.7.1918 | |
| COUTTS, Ian Douglas Freeman | (1951-2) | b 27.4.1928 | |
| COWAN, Ronald C. | (1961-2) | b 26.11.1941 | |
| COWIE, William Lorn Kerr | (1953) | b 1.6.1926 | |
| COWNIE, William Brodie | (1893-5) | b 1871 | d 12.1932 |
| CRABBIE, George Ernest | (1904) | b 23.7.1882 | d 23.10.1921 |
| CRABBIE, John Edward | (1900-05) | b 11.4.1879 | d 21.8.1937 |
| CRAIG, John Binnie | (1939) | b 7.12.1918 | |
| CRANSTON, Alastair Gerald | (1976-81) | b 11.12.1949 | |
| CRAWFORD, John Archibald | (1934) | b 20.11.1910 | d 10.1.1973 |
| CRAWFORD, W.H. | (1938-9) | | |
| CRICHTON-MILLER, Donald | (1931) | b 7.12.1906 | |
| CROLE, Gerard Bruce | (1920) | b 7.6.1894 | d 31.3.1965 |
| CROSS, Malcolm | (1875-80) | b 16.6.1855 | d 20.12.1919 |
| CROSS, William | (1871-2) | b 1851 | d 16.10.1890 |
| CUMMING, Ronald Stuart | (1921) | b 4.1900 | d 17.11.1982 |
| CUNNINGHAM, George | (1908-11) | b 23.3.1888 | d 8.12.1963 |
| CUNNINGHAM, Robert Fraser | (1978-9) | b 4.1.1953 | |

| PLAYER | CAREER SPAN | | |
|---|---|---|---|
| CURRIE, L.R. | (1947-9) | | |
| CUTHBERTSON, William | (1980- ) | b 6.12.1949 | |
| DALGLEISH, Adam | (1890-4) | | d 10.1938 |
| DALGLEISH, Kenneth James | (1951-3) | b 7.6.1931 | d 1974 |
| DALLAS, John Dewar | (1903) | b 1878 | d 31.7.1942 |
| DAVIDSON, John Alexander | (1959-60) | b 6.8.1932 | |
| DAVIDSON, James Norman Grieve | (1952-4) | b 28.1.1931 | |
| DAVIDSON, J.P. | (1873-4) | b 3.9.1851 | |
| DAVIES, Douglas S. | (1922-7) | b 23.7.1899 | |
| DAVIDSON, Roger Stewart | (1893) | b 17.2.1869 | d 18.2.1955 |
| DAWSON, James Cooper | (1947-53) | b 29.10.1925 | |
| DEANS, Colin Thomas | (1978- ) | b 3.5.1955 | |
| DEANS, Derek Thomas | (1968) | b 30.4.1945 | |
| DEAS, David Wallace | (1947) | b 30.3.1919 | |
| DICK, Lewis Gibson | (1972-77) | b 20.12.1950 | |
| DICK, Robert Charles Stewart | (1934-8) | b 1913 | |
| DICKSON, Gordon | (1978-82) | b 10.12.1954 | |
| DICKSON, Maurice Rhynd | (1905) | b 2.1.1882 | d 10.1.1940 |
| DICKSON, Walter Michael | (1912-13) | b 23.11.1884 | d 26.9.1915 |
| DOBSON, John | (1911-12) | b 1887 | d 14.7.1936 |
| DOBSON, James Donald | (1910) | b 1889 | |
| DOBSON, William Goldie | (1922) | b 9.2.1894 | d 11.3.1973 |
| DOCHERTY, James Thomas | (1955-8) | b 5.6.1931 | |
| DODS, Francis Palliser | (1901) | b 23.2.1879 | d 29.6.1910 |
| DODS, John Henry | (1895-7) | b 30.9.1875 | d 30.12.1915 |
| DODS, Peter William | (1983- ) | b 6.1.1958 | |
| DONALD, David Grahame | (1914) | b 27.7.1891 | d 23.12.1976 |
| DONALD, Russell L.H. | (1921) | b 9.9.1898 | d 31.12.1932 |
| DONALDSON, William Patrick | (1893-9) | b 4.3.1871 | d 27.3.1923 |
| DON-WAUCHOPE, Andrew Ramsay | (1881-8) | b 29.4.1861 | d 16.1.1948 |
| DON-WAUCHOPE, Patrick Hamilton | (1885-7) | b 1.5.1863 | d 11.1.1939 |
| DORWARD, Arthur Fairgrieve | (1950-7) | b 3.3.1925 | |
| DORWARD, Thomas Fairgrieve | (1938-9) | b 27.3.1916 | d 5.3.1941 |
| DOUGLAS, George | (1921) | b 1897 | d 26.10.1957 |
| DOUGLAS, John | (1961-3) | b 18.12.1934 | |
| DOUTY, Peter Sime | (1927-8) | b 26.10.1903 | d 18.7.1948 |
| DREW, Daniel | (1871-6) | | d 12.1911 |
| DRUITT, William Arthur Harvey | (1936) | b 19.4.1910 | d 6.2.1973 |
| DRUMMOND, Archibald Hugh | (1938) | b 2.4.1915 | |
| DRUMMOND, Charles William | (1947-50) | b 26.5.1923 | d 5.1985 |
| DRYBROUGH, Andrew Stanley | (1902-03) | b 1879 | d 12.9.1946 |
| DRYDEN, Robert Hunter | (1937) | b 10.1.1918 | |
| DRYSDALE, Daniel | (1923-9) | b 18.5.1901 | |
| DUFF, Peter Laurence | (1936-9) | b 12.11.1912 | |
| DUFFY, Hugh | (1955) | b 1.4.1934 | |
| DUKE, Alfred | (1888-90) | b 1866 | d 11.12.1945 |
| DUNCAN, Alexander William | (1901-02) | b 19.6.1881 | d 18.11.1934 |
| DUNCAN, Denoon | (1920) | | d 1955 |
| DUNCAN, Macbeth Moir | (1888) | b 9.1866 | d 2.10.1942 |
| DUNCAN, Matthew Dominic Fletcher | (1986- ) | b 29.8.1959 | |
| DUNLOP, James | (1875) | b 16.10.54 | d 30.11.1928 |
| DUNLOP, Quintin | (1971) | b 9.3.1943 | |
| DYKES, Andrew Spenser | (1932) | b 19.6.1904 | |
| DYKES, James Carroll | (1922-9) | b 4.7.1901 | |
| DYKES, John Morton | (1898-1902) | | d 12.10.1955 |
| EDWARDS, Douglas Baxter | (1960) | b 19.3.1930 | |
| ELGIE, Michael Kelsey | (1954-5) | b 6.3.1933 | |
| ELLIOT, Christopher | (1958-65) | b 24.2.1933 | |
| ELLIOT, Matthew | (1895-98) | b 1871 | d 3.12.1945 |

| PLAYER | CAREER SPAN | | |
|---|---|---|---|
| ELLIOT, Thomas | (1905) | b 1880 | d 11.1948 |
| ELLIOT, Tom | (1955-58) | b 6.4.1926 | |
| ELLIOT, Thomas Grieve | (1968-70) | b 1.3.1941 | |
| ELLIOT, W.I.Douglas | (1947-54) | b 18.4.1923 | |
| EMSLIE, William Duncan | (1930-2) | | d 7.8.1969 |
| EVANS, Harry Loft | (1885) | | |
| EWART, E.N. | (1879-80) | | d 1902 |
| FAHMY, Ernest Chalmers | (1920) | b 28.11.1892 | d 25.8.1982 |
| FASSON, Francis Hamilton | (1900-02) | b 21.9.1877 | d 23.10.1955 |
| FELL, Alfred Nolan | (1901-03) | b 17.1.1878 | d 20.4.1953 |
| FERGUSON, James Huck | (1928) | b 19.10.1903 | |
| FERGUSON, William Gordon | (1927-8) | | d 11.12.1963 |
| FERGUSSON, Ewen Alastair John | (1954) | b 28.10.1932 | |
| FINLAY, Arthur Bannatyne | (1875) | b 21.4.1854 | d 10.9.1921 |
| FINLAY, James Fairbairn | (1871-5) | b 8.4.1852 | d 25.1.1930 |
| FINLAY, Robert | (1948) | b 9.4.1923 | |
| FINLAY, Ninian Jamieson | (1875-81) | b 31.1.1858 | d 7.3.1936 |
| FISHER, Alastair Thomson | (1947) | b 3.9.1916 | d 26.1.1983 |
| FISHER, Colin Douglas | (1975-6) | b 27.12.1949 | |
| FISHER, D. | (1893) | | |
| FISHER, James Pringle | (1963-8) | b 17.3.1939 | |
| FLEMING, Charles James Nicol | (1896-7) | b 5.4.1868 | d 13.11.1948 |
| FLEMING, G.R. | (1875-6) | | |
| FLETCHER, Hugh Nethersole | (1904-05) | b 27.4.1877 | |
| FLETT, Andrew Binny | (1901-02) | b 1875 | d 15.7.1961 |
| FORBES, John Lockhart | (1905-06) | b 1.4.1883 | d 10.2.1967 |
| FORD, Drummond St. Clair | (1930-2) | b 16.12.1907 | d 12.12.1942 |
| FORD, James R. | (1893) | | |
| FORREST, James Edmiston | (1932-5) | b 3.2.1907 | d 2.4.1981 |
| FORREST, John Gordon Scott | (1938) | b 28.4.1917 | d 9.1942 |
| FORREST, Walter Torrie | (1903-05) | b 14.11.1880 | d 19.4.1917 |
| FORSAYTH, Hector Henry | (1921-2) | b 18.12.1899 | d 7.3.1952 |
| FORSYTH, Ian William | (1972-3) | b 4.7.1946 | |
| FORSYTH, J. | (1871) | | |
| FOSTER, R.A. | (1930-2) | b 7.12.1907 | |
| FOX, John | (1952) | b 30.8.1921 | |
| FRAME, John Neil Munro | (1967-73) | b 8.10.1946 | |
| FRANCE, C. | (1903) | | |
| FRASER, C.F.P. | (1888-89) | | |
| FRASER, James William | (1881) | | |
| FRASER, Rowland | (1911) | b 10.1.1890 | d 1.7.1916 |
| FRENCH, J. | (1886-7) | | |
| FREW, Alexander | (1901) | | d 4.1947 |
| FREW, George M. | (1906-11) | b 9.9.1883 | |
| FRIEBE, John Percy | (1952) | b 9.5.1931 | |
| FULTON, Adam Kelso | (1952-4) | b 1929 | |
| FYFE, Kenneth Carmichael | (1933-9) | | d 2.1974 |
| GALLIE, George Holmes | (1939) | b 17.9.1917 | d 16.1.1944 |
| GALLIE, Robert Arthur | (1920-21) | b 1.1893 | d 25.5.1948 |
| GAMMELL, William Benjamin Bowring | (1977-8) | b 29.12.1952 | |
| GEDDES, Irvine Campbell | (1906-08) | b 9.7.1882 | d 18.5.1962 |
| GEDDES, Keith Irvine | (1947) | b 1918 | |
| GEDGE, Henry Theodore Sidney | (1894-9) | b 19.8.1870 | d 5.12.1943 |
| GEDGE, Peter Maurice Sydney | (1933) | b 18.5.1910 | |
| GEMMILL, Robert | (1950-1) | b 20.2.1930 | |
| GIBSON, William Ross | (1891-5) | b 1865 | d 2.1.1924 |
| GILBERT-SMITH, David Stuart | (1952) | b 3.12.1931 | |
| GILCHRIST, James | (1925) | b 8.12.1903 | d 1972 |
| GILL, Andrew Davidson | (1973-4) | b 30.8.1949 | |
| GILLESPIE, John Imrie | (1899-1904) | b 16.1.1879 | d 5.12.1943 |
| GILLIES, Alexander Campbell | (1924-7) | b 25.3.1900 | d 22.1.1980 |
| GILRAY, Colin Macdonald | (1908-12) | b 17.3.1885 | d 15.7.1974 |

| PLAYER | CAREER SPAN | | |
|---|---|---|---|
| GLASGOW, Ronald James Cunninghham | (1962-5) | b 5.11.1930 | |
| GLEN, William Sutherland | (1955) | b 13.3.1932 | |
| GLOAG, Lawrence Gjers | (1949) | b 3.10.1925 | d 2.1984 |
| GOODFELLOW, John | (1928) | b 1906 | d 2.4.1951 |
| GOODHUE, Frederick William Jervis | (1890-2) | b 26.4.1867 | d 30.12.1940 |
| GORDON, Richard John | (1982) | | |
| GORDON, Robert | (1951-3) | b 25.7.1930 | |
| GORDON, Roland Elphinstone | (1913) | b 22.1.1893 | d 30.8.1918 |
| GORE, A. Fraser C. | (1882) | | |
| GOSSMAN, Bryan Murray | (1980- ) | b 5.5.1951 | |
| GOSSMAN, James S. | (1980- ) | | |
| GOWANS, James Jollie | (1893-6) | b 23.4.1872 | d 27.4.1936 |
| GOWLLAND, Geoffrey Cathcart | (1908-10) | b 27.5.1885 | d 9.10.1980 |
| GRACIE, Archibald Leslie | (1921-4) | b 15.10.96 | d 2.8.1982 |
| GRAHAM, Ian N. | (1939) | b 8.5.1918 | |
| GRAHAM, James | (1926-32) | b 19.6.1902 | |
| GRAHAM, James Hope Stewart | (1876-81) | b 16.4.1856 | d 17.10.1922 |
| GRANT, Derrick | (1965-8) | b 19.4.1938 | |
| GRANT, D.M. | (1911) | b 1.1893 | |
| GRANT, Malcolm Leith | (1955-7) | b 8.11.1927 | |
| GRANT, Thomas Oliver | (1960-4) | b 5.9.1932 | |
| GRANT, William St Clair | (1873-4) | b 1853 | |
| GRAY, David | (1978-81) | b 28.3.1953 | |
| GRAY, George Leitch | (1935-7) | | d 2.9.1975 |
| GRAY, Thomas | (1950-1) | b 20.1.1917 | |
| GREENLEES, Harry Dickson | (1927-30) | b 31.7.1903 | d c.1977 |
| GREENLEES, James Robertson Campbell | (1900-03) | b 14.12.1878 | d 16.5.1951 |
| GREENWOOD, James Thomson | (1952-9) | b 1928 | |
| GREIG, A. | (1911) | b 27.10.1889 | |
| GREIG, Louis Leisler | (1905-08) | b 17.11.1880 | d 1.3.1953 |
| GREIG, Robert Coventry | (1893-7) | b 1871 | d 3.2.1951 |
| GRIEVE, Charles Frederick | (1935-6) | b 1.10.1913 | |
| GRIEVE, Robert George Moir | (1935-6) | b 1.2.1911 | |
| GUNN, Alexander William | (1912-13) | b 16.11.1890 | d 4.1980 |
| HAMILTON, Andrew Steven | (1914-20) | b 8.3.1893 | d 3.11.1975 |
| HAMILTON, Hugh Montgomerie | (1874-5) | b 26.6.1854 | d 11.8.1930 |
| HANNAH, Ronald S.M. | (1971) | | |
| HARROWER, Patrick R. | (1885) | b 19.1.1860 | |
| HART, John G.M. | (1951) | | |
| HART, Thomas Mure | (1930) | b 1.3.1909 | |
| HART, Walter | (1960) | b 30.3.1935 | |
| HARVEY, Laurence | (1899) | | |
| HASTIE, Alexander James | (1961-8) | b 29.7.1935 | |
| HASTIE, Ian Robert | (1955-9) | b 7.9.1929 | |
| HASTIE, John Dickson Hart | (1938) | b 16.3.1908 | d 19.1.1965 |
| HASTINGS, Andrew Gavin | (1986- ) | b 3.1.1962 | |
| HASTINGS, Scott | (1986- ) | b 4.12.1964 | |
| HAY, Bruce Hamilton | (1975-81) | b 23.5.1950 | |
| HAY-GORDON, John Robert | (1875-7) | b 9.11.1849 | d 1.1934 |
| HEGARTY, Charles Brian | (1978) | b 29.11.1950 | |
| HEGARTY, John Jackson | (1951-5) | b 13.4.1925 | |
| HENDERSON, Brian Carlyle | (1963-6) | b 1939 | |
| HENDERSON, Frederick William | (1900) | b 3.1.1879 | d 1950 |
| HENDERSON, Ian C. | (1939-48) | b 31.10.1918 | |
| HENDERSON, John Hamilton | (1953-4) | b 9.2.1930 | |
| HENDERSON, J.M. | (1933) | b 1.5.1907 | |
| HENDERSON, James Young Milne | (1911) | b 9.3.1891 | d 31.7.1917 |
| HENDERSON, M.M. | (1937) | | |
| HENDERSON, Nelson Faviell | (1892) | b 24.9.1865 | d 16.6.1943 |
| HENDERSON, Robert Gordon | (1924) | b 8.1.1900 | d 24.2.1977 |

| PLAYER | CAREER SPAN | | |
|---|---|---|---|
| HENDRIE, Kelvin | | | |
| Gladstone Peter | (1924) | b 2.7.1898 | d 12.1953 |
| HENDRY, T.L. | (1893-5) | | |
| HENRIKSEN, E.H. | (1953) | | |
| HEPBURN, Derek Peter | (1947-9) | b 15.3.1920 | |
| HERON, G. | (1874-5) | | |
| HILL, Colin Cecil Pitcairn | (1912) | b 7.1887 | d 8.6.1953 |
| HINSHELWOOD, | | | |
| Alexander James Watt | (1966-70) | b 23.3.1942 | |
| HODGSON, Charles | | | |
| Gordon | (1968) | b 11.5.1938 | |
| HOGG, Charles Graham | (1978) | b 2.3.1948 | |
| HOLMS, William | | | |
| Frederick | (1886-9) | b 27.8.1866 | d 30.9.1950 |
| HORSBURGH, George B. | (1937-9) | b 1910 | |
| HOWIE, David Duchie | (1912-13) | b 1888 | d 19.1.1916 |
| HOWIE, Robert A. | (1924-5) | b 11.6.1898 | |
| HOYER-MILLAR, Gurth | | | |
| Christian | (1953) | b 13.12.1929 | |
| HUGGAN, James Laidlaw | (1914) | b 11.10.1888 | d 16.9.1914 |
| HUME, John | (1912-22) | b 17.3.1890 | d 20.12.1969 |
| HUME, John William | | | |
| Gardner | (1928-30) | b 13.6.1906 | d 23.3.1976 |
| HUNTER, Frank | (1882) | b 7.1858 | d 10.1930 |
| HUNTER, Iain Gordon | (1984- ) | b 7.8.1958 | |
| HUNTER, John Murray | (1947) | b 11.1920 | |
| HUNTER, Michael | | | |
| Douglas | (1974) | b 1945 | |
| HUNTER, William John | (1964-7) | b 5.6.1934 | |
| HUTCHISON, William | | | |
| Ramsay | (1911) | b 16.1.1889 | d 22.3.1918 |
| HUTTON, Alexander | | | |
| Harry M. | (1932) | b 30.12.1907 | d 23.12.1981 |
| HUTTON, James Edward | (1930-1) | b 8.8.1906 | |
| | | | |
| INGLIS, Hamish | | | |
| MacFarlan | (1951-2) | b 3.8.1931 | |
| INGLIS, James Mercer | (1952) | b 20.3.1928 | |
| INGLIS, William Murray | (1937-8) | b 20.1.1915 | |
| INNES, John Robert | | | |
| Stephen | (1939-48) | b 16.9.1917 | |
| IRELAND, James Cecil | | | |
| Hardin | (1925-7) | b 10.12.1903 | |
| IRVINE, Andrew | | | |
| Robertson | (1972-82) | b 16.9.1951 | |
| IRVINE, Duncan | | | |
| Robertson | (1878-9) | b 2.4.1851 | d 17.3.1914 |
| IRVINE, Robert William | (1871-80) | b 19.4.1853 | d 18.4.1897 |
| IRVINE, Thomas Walter | (1885-9) | b 21.10.1865 | d 26.1.1919 |
| | | | |
| JACKSON, Kenneth Leslie | | | |
| Tattersall | (1933-4) | b 17.11.1913 | d 21.3.1982 |
| JACKSON, Thomas G.H. | (1947-9) | b 15.10.1921 | |
| JACKSON, William | | | |
| Douglas | (1964-9) | b 5.12.1941 | |
| JAMIESON, John | (1883-5) | | |
| JEFFREY, John | (1984- ) | b 25.3.1959 | |
| JOHNSTON, David Ian | (1979- ) | b 20.10.1958 | |
| JOHNSTON, Henry | | | |
| Halcro | (1877) | b 13.9.1856 | d 13.10.1939 |
| JOHNSTON, James | (1951-2) | b 17.9.1925 | |
| JOHNSTON, William | | | |
| Graham Stuart | (1935-7) | b 1913 | |
| JOHNSTON, William C. | (1922) | b 16.12.1896 | d 6.10.1983 |
| JUNOR, J.E. | (1876-81) | | |
| KEDDIE, Robert Ramsay | (1967) | b 19.7.1945 | |
| KEITH, George James | (1968) | b 1941 | |
| KELLER, Douglas | | | |
| Holcombe | (1949-50) | b 18.6.1922 | |
| KELLY, Robert Forrest | (1927-8) | b 12.3.1907 | d 23.2.1975 |
| KEMP, James William | | | |
| Young | (1954-60) | b 13.2.1933 | |
| KENNEDY, Alexander | | | |
| Euan | (1983- ) | b 30.7.1954 | |
| KENNEDY, Finlay | (1920) | b 23.1.1892 | d 8.3.1925 |
| KENNEDY, Norman | (1903) | b 17.3.1881 | d 15.1.1960 |
| KER, Hugh Torrance | (1887-90) | b 1865 | d 19.3.1938 |
| KERR, David S. | (1923-8) | b 3.2.1899 | d 3.1969 |
| KERR, Graham Carmichael | (1898-1900) | b 29.4.1872 | d 18.8.1913 |
| KERR, James Mitchell | (1935-7) | b 12.5.1910 | |
| KERR, James Reid | (1909) | b 4.12.1884 | d 19.8.1963 |
| KERR, Walter | (1953) | b 14.9.1930 | |
| KIDSTON, D.W. | (1883) | | |

| PLAYER | CAREER SPAN | | |
|---|---|---|---|
| KIDSTON, William | | | |
| Hamilton | (1874) | b 29.4.1852 | d 4.6.1929 |
| KILGOUR, Ian James | (1921) | b 23.10.1900 | d 20.4.1977 |
| KING, John Hope | | | |
| Fairbairn | (1953-4) | b 10.4.1925 | d 8.9.1982 |
| KININMONTH, Peter | | | |
| Wyatt | (1949-54) | b 23.6.1924 | |
| KINNEAR, Roy Muir | (1926) | b 3.2.1904 | d 22.9.1942 |
| KNOX, John | (1903) | b 5.8.1880 | d 20.4.1964 |
| KYLE, William Elliot | (1902-10) | b 13.7.1881 | d 11.12.1959 |
| | | | |
| LAIDLAW, Alexander | | | |
| Smith | (1897) | b 13.8.1877 | d 12.9.1933 |
| LAIDLAW, Francis | | | |
| Andrew Linden | (1965-71) | b 20.9.1940 | |
| LAIDLAW, Roy James | (1980-) | b 5.10.1953 | |
| LAING, Arthur Douglas | (1914-21) | b 1892 | d 24.11.1927 |
| LAMBIE, Ian Kerr | (1978-9) | b 13.4.1954 | |
| LAMBIE, Lindsay B. | (1934-5) | b 30.5.1910 | |
| LAMOND, George A.W. | (1899-1905) | b 1878 | d 25.2.1918 |
| LANG, D. | (1876-7) | | |
| LANGRISH, Reginald W. | (1930-1) | b 1.12.1905 | d 15.3.1986 |
| LAUDER, Wilson | (1969-77) | b 4.11.48 | |
| LAUGHLAND, Ian Hugh | | | |
| Page | (1959-67) | b 29.10.1935 | |
| LAWRIE, James Ruthven | (1922-4) | b 11.8.1900 | d 9.7.1981 |
| LAWRIE, Kenneth | | | |
| Graham | (1980) | b 31.7.1951 | |
| LAWSON, Alan James | | | |
| Macgregor | (1972-80) | b 19.5.1948 | |
| LAWTHER, Thomas | | | |
| Hope Brendan | (1932) | b 6.10.1909 | |
| LEDINGHAM, George | | | |
| Alexander | (1913) | b 8.3.1890 | d 8.11.1978 |
| LEES, James Blanch | (1947-8) | b 11.8.1919 | |
| LEGGATT, Herbert | | | |
| Thomas Owen | (1891-4) | b 1869 | d 23.5.1945 |
| LELY, William Gerald | (1909) | b 7.1886 | |
| LESLIE, David George | (1975-) | | |
| LIDDELL, Eric Henry | (1922-3) | b 16.1.1902 | d 21.1.1945 |
| LIND, Henry | (1928-36) | b 27.3.1906 | |
| LINDSAY, Andrew | | | |
| Alexander Bonar | (1910-11) | b 19.7.1885 | d 15.5.1970 |
| LINDSAY, George | | | |
| Campbell | (1884-7) | b 3.1.1863 | d 5.4.1905 |
| LINDSAY-WATSON, | | | |
| Robert Hamilton | (1909) | b 4.10.1886 | d 26.1.1956 |
| LITTLE, Anthony W. | (1905) | b 1882 | |
| LOGAN, William Ross | (1931-7) | b 24.11.1909 | |
| LORRAINE, Herbert | | | |
| Derrick Bell | (1933) | b 4.1.1913 | d 19.3.1982 |
| LOUDON-SHAND, Eric | | | |
| Gordon | (1913) | b 31.3.1893 | |
| LOWE, J. Douglas | (1934) | b 28.5.1906 | d 7.11.1936 |
| LUMSDEN, Ian James | | | |
| Michael | (1947-9) | b 6.4.1923 | |
| LYALL, George G. | (1947-8) | b 23.5.1921 | |
| LYALL, William John | | | |
| Campbell | (1871) | b 27.1.1848 | |
| | | | |
| MABON, John Thomas | (1898-1900) | b 13.2.1874 | d 2.6.1945 |
| McARTHUR, John | | | |
| Parlane | (1932) | b 12.9.1904 | |
| MacCALLUM, John | | | |
| Cameron | (1905-12) | b 1883 | d 29.11.1957 |
| McCLUNG, Thomas | (1956-60) | b 14.2.1933 | |
| McCLURE, G.B. | (1873) | | |
| McCLURE, J.H. | (1872) | | |
| McCOWAN, David | (1880-4) | b 1860 | d 15.5.1937 |
| McCOWAT, R.H. | (1905) | | |
| McCRAE, Ian George | (1967-72) | b 19.5.1941 | |
| McCROW, John William | | | |
| Stuart | (1921) | b 11.5.1899 | d 25.2.1950 |
| McDONALD, Charles | (1947) | b 19.4.1919 | |
| MacDONALD, Donald C. | (1953-8) | b 1931 | |
| MacDONALD, Donald | | | |
| Shaw Mackinnon | (1977-8) | b 25.9.1951 | |
| MacDONALD, James | | | |
| Stirling | (1903-05) | | |
| MacDONALD, John | | | |
| Donald | (1966-7) | b 5.4.1938 | |
| MacDONALD, John | | | |
| MacKinnon | (1911) | b 12.1890 | d 1.6.1980 |

| PLAYER | CAREER SPAN | | |
|---|---|---|---|
| MacDONALD, Keith Roy | (1956-7) | b 13.5.1933 | |
| MACDONALD, Ranald | (1950) | b 18.1.1928 | |
| McDONALD, William Alexander | (1889-92) | b 1862 | |
| MacDONALD, William Gordon | (1969) | b 30.12.1938 | |
| MacDOUGALL, John Bowes | (1913-21) | b 1890 | d 1967 |
| McEWAN, Matthew Clark | (1886-92) | b 5.10.1865 | d 13.4.1899 |
| McEWAN, William Maclean Clark | (1894-1900) | b 24.10.1875 | d 5.1934 |
| McEWAN, Nairn Alexander | (1971-5) | b 12.12.1941 | |
| MacEWAN, Robert Kenneth Gillespie | (1954-8) | b 25.2.1928 | |
| MACFARLAN, David James | (1883-8) | b 1.3.1862 | d 2.1.1940 |
| MACFARLANE, John L.H. | (1871-3) | b 1851 | d 2.1874 |
| McGAUGHEY, Sean K | (1984-) | | |
| McGEECHAN, Ian Robert | (1972-9) | b 30.10.1946 | |
| McGLASHAN, Thomas Perry Lang | (1947-54) | b 29.12.1925 | |
| MacGREGOR, Duncan Grant | (1907) | b 20.5.1887 | d 5.10.1971 |
| MacGREGOR, Gregor | (1890-6) | b 31.8.1869 | d 20.8.1919 |
| MacGREGOR, Ian Allan Alexander | (1955-7) | b 9.8.1931 | |
| MacGREGOR, John Roy | (1909) | b 27.8.1885 | d 24.7.1940 |
| McGUINNESS, Gerald Michael | (1982-) | b 14.9.53 | |
| McHARG, Alastair Ferguson | (1968-79) | b 17.6.1944 | |
| McINDOE, Flowerdew | (1886) | b 1867 | |
| MacINTYRE, Ian | (1890-1) | b 11.1869 | d 29.6.1946 |
| MACKAY, E.B. | (1920-2) | | |
| McKEATING, Edward | (1957-61) | b 1.9.1936 | |
| McKENDRICK, J.G. | (1889) | | |
| MACKENZIE, Alexander David Gregor | (1984-) | b 9.7.1956 | |
| McKENZIE, Cecil James Granville | (1921) | b 26.2.1889 | d 7.12.1959 |
| MACKENZIE, David Douglas | (1947-8) | b 28.12.1921 | |
| MACKENZIE, Donald Kenneth Andrew | (1939) | b 30.11.1916 | d 12.6.1940 |
| MACKENZIE, James Moir | (1905-11) | b 17.10.1886 | d 22.1.1963 |
| MACKENZIE, Robert Campbell | (1877-81) | b 12.1.1856 | d 26.5.1945 |
| MACKIE, George Yuill | (1975-8) | b 19.4.1949 | |
| MacKINNON, Andrew | (1898-1900) | b 30.4.1873 | |
| MACKINTOSH, Charles Ernest Whistler Christopher | (1924) | b 31.10.1903 | d 1974 |
| MACKINTOSH, Hugh Stewart | (1929-32) | b 19.1.1903 | |
| MacLACHLAN, Lachlan Patrick | (1954) | b 16.3.1928 | |
| MACLAGAN, William Edward | (1878-90) | b 5.4.1858 | d 10.10.1926 |
| McLAREN, Alexander | (1931) | b 29.8.1910 | d 1978 |
| McLAREN, Edward | (1923-4) | b 28.5.1902 | d 30.3.1950 |
| McLAUCHLAN, John | (1969-79) | b 14.4.1942 | |
| McLEAN, Duncan Ian | (1947) | b 1.5.1923 | d 21.3.1962 |
| MacLENNAN, William Donald | (1947) | b 4.4.1921 | |
| MACLEOD, Duncan Archibald | (1886) | b 12.6.1866 | d 9.12.1907 |
| MACLEOD, George | (1878-82) | b 1860 | |
| McLEOD, Hugh Ferns | (1954-62) | b 8.6.1932 | |
| MacLEOD, Kenneth Grant | (1905-08) | b 2.2.1888 | d 7.3.1969 |
| MacLEOD, Lewis Macdonald | (1904-05) | b 6.1885 | d 12.11.1907 |
| MACLEOD, William Mackintosh | (1886) | b 6.1861 | d 30.6.1931 |
| McMILLAN, Keith Henry Douglas | (1953) | b 1926 | |
| MacMILLAN, Robert Gordon | (1887-97) | b 3.4.1865 | d 3.4.1936 |
| MacMYN, David James | (1925-8) | b 18.2.1903 | d 16.3.1978 |
| McNEIL, Alastair Simpson Bell | (1935) | b 28.1.1915 | d 26.1.1944 |
| McPARTLIN, Joseph James | (1960-2) | b 12.6.1938 | |
| MacPHAIL, J.A.R. | (1949-51) | b 14.10.1923 | |
| MacPHERSON, Donald Gregory | (1910) | b 23.7.1882 | d 26.11.1956 |
| MacPHERSON, George Philip Stewart | (1922-32) | b 14.12.1903 | d 2.3.1981 |
| MacPHERSON, Neil Clark | (1920-3) | b 26.9.1892 | d 11.11.1957 |
| McQUEEN, Samuel Brown | (1923) | b 1896 | d 16.10.1983 |
| MACRAE, Duncan James | (1937-9) | b 4.11.1914 | |
| MADSEN, Duncan Frederick | (1974-8) | b 16.4.1947 | |
| MAIR, Norman George Robertson | (1951) | b 7.10.1928 | |
| MAITLAND, Gardyne | (1885) | | |
| MAITLAND, Robert | (1881-5) | | |
| MAITLAND, Reginald Paynter | (1872) | b 6.3.1851 | d 10.4.1926 |
| MALCOLM, A.G. | (1888) | | |
| MARSH, James | (1889) | | d 1.8.1928 |
| MARSHALL, Arthur | (1875) | b 27.4.1855 | d 9.12.1909 |
| MARSHALL, John Campbell | (1954) | b 30.1.1929 | |
| MARSHALL, Kenneth William | (1934-7) | b 23.7.1911 | |
| MARSHALL, Thomas Roger | (1871-4) | b 26.6.1849 | d 27.6.1913 |
| MARSHALL, William | (1872) | b 22.6.1852 | d 10.1907 |
| MARTIN, Hugh | (1908-09) | b 9.4.1888 | d 6.1.1970 |
| MASTERS, William Hay | (1879-80) | b 1858 | d 2.10.1897 |
| MAXWELL, F.T. | (1872) | b 10.1.1849 | d 15.1.1881 |
| MAXWELL, Georgius Henry Hope Patrick | (1913-22) | b 18.10.1892 | d 21.2.1961 |
| MAXWELL, James MacMillan | (1957) | b 30.4.1932 | |
| MEIN, James Andrew Whitelock | (1871-5) | b 1.7.1852 | d 2.3.1918 |
| MELVILLE, Christian Landale | (1937) | b 9.12.1913 | d 23.4.1984 |
| MENZIES, Henry Fisher | (1893-4) | b 6.1867 | d 31.7.1938 |
| METHUEN, Alfred | (1889) | b 15.2.1868 | d 5.3.1949 |
| MICHIE, Ernest James Stewart | (1954-7) | b 7.11.1933 | |
| MILLAR, John Neill | (1892-5) | b 9.3.1873 | d 9.11.1921 |
| MILLAR, Robert Kirkpatrick | (1924) | b 29.6.1901 | d 17.4.1981 |
| MILLICAN, John Gilbert | (1973) | b 21.8.1951 | |
| MILNE, Charles James Barclay | (1886) | b 5.1864 | d 6.5.1892 |
| MILNE, Iain Gordon | (1979-) | b 17.6.1958 | |
| MILNE, William Murray | (1904-05) | b 27.7.1883 | d 16.12.1982 |
| MILROY, Eric | (1910-14) | b 4.12.1887 | d 18.7.1916 |
| MITCHELL, George Willis Earle | (1967-8) | b 23.11.1943 | |
| MITCHELL, J. Gordon | (1885) | | |
| MONCREIFF, Hon. Francis Jeffrey | (1871-3) | b 27.8.1849 | d 30.5.1900 |
| MONTEITH, Hugh Glencairn | (1905-08) | b 11.5.1883 | |
| MONYPENNY, Douglas Blackwell | (1899) | b 5.1878 | d 22.2.1900 |
| MOODIE, Alexander Reid | (1909-11) | b 30.9.1886 | d 1968 |
| MORGAN, Douglas Waugh | (1973-8) | b 9.3.1947 | |
| MORRISON, Mark Coxon | (1896-1904) | b 2.4.1877 | d 10.5.1945 |
| MORRISON, Reginald Herbert | (1886) | | |
| MORRISON, William Henry | (1900) | b 26.12.1875 | d 9.2.1944 |
| MORTON, David Simson | (1887-90) | | d 21.5.1937 |
| MOWAT, John Gunn | (1883) | b 1859 | d 1.1.1935 |
| MUIR, Douglas E. | (1950-2) | b 17.3.1925 | |
| MUNNOCH, Norman McQueen | (1952) | b 4.1.1929 | |
| MUNRO, Patrick | (1905-11) | b 9.10.1883 | d 3.5.1942 |
| MUNRO, R. | (1871) | | |
| MUNRO, Stephen | (1980-) | b 11.6.1958 | |
| MUNRO, William Hutton | (1947) | b 28.9.1918 | d 12.9.1970 |
| MURDOCH, William Copeland Wood | (1935-48) | b 3.10.1914 | |
| MURRAY, George Macgibbon | (1921-6) | b 21.6.1900 | d 26.12.1981 |

| PLAYER | CAREER SPAN | | | PLAYER | CAREER SPAN | | |
|---|---|---|---|---|---|---|---|
| MURRAY, H.M. | (1936) | b 3.5.1912 | | ROBERTSON, Alexander | | | |
| MURRAY, Keith Tony | (1985-) | b 23.3.1962 | | Hamilton | (1871) | b 1.10.1848 | |
| MURRAY, Ronald | | | | ROBERTSON, Alexander | | | |
| Ormiston | (1935) | b 14.11.1912 | | Weir | (1897) | b 11.12.1877 | d 28.10.1941 |
| MURRAY, William | | | | ROBERTSON, Duncan | (1875) | b 30.6.1851 | d 29.9.1907 |
| Alexander Kininmonth | (1920-1) | b 17.4.1894 | | ROBERTSON, David | | | |
| | | | | Donaldson | (1893) | b 21.3.1869 | d 13.9.1937 |
| NAPIER, H.M. | (1877-9) | | | ROBERTSON, Ian | (1968-70) | b 17.1.1945 | |
| NEILL, John Brian | (1963-5) | b 28.7.1937 | | ROBERTSON, Ian Peter | | | |
| NEILL, Robert Milne | (1901-02) | b 5.9.1882 | d 14.9.1914 | Macintosh | (1910) | b 1887 | d 9.5.1949 |
| NEILSON, George | | | | ROBERTSON, J. | (1908) | b 5.5.1883 | |
| Thompson | (1891-6) | b 22.1.1872 | | ROBERTSON, Keith | | | |
| NEILSON, J.A. | (1878-9) | | | William | (1978- ) | b 5.12.54 | |
| NEILSON, Robert | | | | ROBERTSON, Lewis | (1908-13) | b 4.8.1883 | d 3.11.1914 |
| Thomson | (1898-1900) | b 17.11.1878 | d 16.7.1945 | ROBERTSON, Michael | | | |
| NEILSON, T. | (1874) | | | Alexander | (1958) | b 1929 | |
| NEILSON, William | (1891-7) | b 18.8.1873 | d 16.3.1960 | ROBERTSON, Robert | | | |
| NEILSON, Walter Gordon | (1894) | b 1.10.1876 | d 29.4.1927 | Dalrymple | (1912) | b 28.7.1891 | |
| NELSON, James Benzie | (1925-31) | b 9.2.1903 | d 10.1981 | ROBSON, Adam | (1954-60) | b 16.8.1928 | |
| NELSON, Thomas Arthur | (1898) | b 1876 | d 9.4.1917 | RODD, John Adrian | | | |
| NICHOL, James Alastair | (1955) | b 12.2.1932 | | Tremayne | (1958-65) | b 26.8.1935 | |
| NIMMO, Charles Stuart | (1920) | b 10.6.1895 | d 20.2.1943 | ROGERSON, John | (1894) | | |
| | | | | ROLAND, Ernest T. | (1884) | | d 1897 |
| OGILVY, Charles | (1911-12) | b 1889 | d 9.1958 | ROLLO, David Miller | | | |
| OLIVER, George Kenneth | (1970) | b 4.3.1946 | | Durie | (1959-68) | b 7.7.1934 | |
| ORR, Charles Edward | (1887-92) | b 21.11.1866 | d 6.4.1935 | ROSE, David M. | (1951-3) | b 20.2.1881 | |
| ORR, Hugh James | (1903-04) | b 21.1.1878 | d 16.5.1946 | ROSS, Andrew | (1924) | b 8.11.1904 | |
| ORR, John Ernest | (1889-93) | b 20.8.1865 | d 1936 | ROSS, Andrew | (1905-09) | b 1879 | d 6.4.1916 |
| ORR, John Henry | (1947) | b 13.6.1918 | | ROSS, Andrew Russell | (1911-14) | b 13.1.1892 | d 1980 |
| OSLER, F.L. | (1911) | | | ROSS, Edward Johnson | (1904) | b 2.3.1884 | d 22.6.1943 |
| PARK, Jack | (1934) | b 27.4.1913 | | ROSS, Graham Tullis | (1954) | b 5.7.1928 | |
| PATERSON, Duncan | | | | ROSS, Iain A. | (1951) | b 15.12.1928 | |
| Sinclair | (1969-72) | b 27.3.1943 | | ROSS, James | (1901-03) | b 15.2.1880 | d 31.10.1914 |
| PATERSON, George | | | | ROSS, Kenneth Innes | (1961-3) | b 15.3.1937 | |
| Quentin | (1876) | b 1854 | | ROSS, William Alexander | (1937) | b 15.11.1913 | d 28.9.1942 |
| PATERSON, John | | | | ROTTENBURG, Harry | (1899-1900) | b 6.10.1875 | d 25.3.1955 |
| Rimmer | (1924-9) | b 19.12.1900 | d 25.9.1970 | ROUGHEAD, William | | | |
| PATTERSON, David | (1896) | b 11.12.1873 | d 21.1.1945 | Nicol | (1927-32) | b 19.9.1905 | d 22.4.1975 |
| PATTULLO, Gordon L. | (1920) | b 9.1892 | d 1966 | ROWAN, Norman Arthur | (1980-) | b 17.9.1951 | |
| PEARSON, James | (1909-13) | b 24.2.1889 | d 22.5.1915 | ROWAND, Robert | (1930-4) | b 30.8.1906 | d 23.2.1974 |
| PAXTON, Eric | (1982-) | b 4.4.1957 | | ROY, Allan | (1938-9) | b 13.5.1911 | |
| PAXTON, Iain Angus | | | | RUSSELL, William L. | (1905-06) | | |
| McLeod | (1981-) | b 29.12.1957 | | RUTHERFORD, John | | | |
| PENDER, Ian MacAlister | (1914) | b 18.8.1894 | d 10.1961 | Young | (1979-) | b 4.10.1955 | |
| PENDER, Norman Ewart | | | | | | | |
| Ker | (1977-8) | b 1.2.1948 | | SAMPSON, Ralph W.F. | (1939-47) | | |
| PENMAN, William | | | | SANDERSON, George | | | |
| Mitchell | (1939) | b 12.5.1917 | d 3.10.1943 | Alfred | (1907-08) | b 9.8.1881 | d 23.11.1957 |
| PETERKIN, W.A. | (1881-5) | | | SANDERSON, James | | | |
| PETRIE, Alexander | | | | Lyon Playfair | (1873) | b 1852 | |
| Gordon | (1873-80) | b 1852 | d 4.2.1909 | SCHULZE, Douglas | | | |
| PHILP, Andrew | (1882) | | | Gordon | (1905-11) | b 15.3.1881 | d 17.5.1956 |
| POCOCK, E.I. | (1877) | | | SCOBIE, Ronald | | | |
| POLLOCK, James Alan | (1982-) | b 16.11.1958 | | Mackenzie | (1914) | b 8.6.1893 | d 23.2.1969 |
| POLSON, Adam Henry | (1930) | b 19.11.1907 | | SCOTLAND, Kenneth | | | |
| PURDIE, William | (1939) | b 24.6.1910 | | James Forbes | (1957-65) | b 29.8.1936 | |
| PURVES, Alexander | | | | SCOTT, Donald Macdonald | (1950-3) | b 15.4.1928 | |
| Buckholm Haliburton | | | | SCOTT, John Menzies | | | |
| Laidlaw | (1906-08) | b 8.1886 | d 20.9.1945 | Baillie | (1907-13) | b 6.10.1887 | d 14.1.1967 |
| PURVES, William Donald | | | | SCOTT, J.S. | (1950) | | |
| Campbell Laidlaw | (1912-13) | b 4.7.1888 | d 1964 | SCOTT, James William | (1925-30) | b 24.9.1903 | d 24.8.1949 |
| | | | | SCOTT, Robert | (1898-1900) | | |
| REA, Christopher William | | | | SCOTT, Tom | (1896-1900) | b 8.3.1875 | d 16.4.1947 |
| Wallace | (1968-71) | b 22.10.1943 | | SCOTT, Thomas Munro | (1893-1900) | b 1870 | d 1930 |
| REID, Charles | (1881-8) | b 14.1.1864 | d 25.10.1909 | SCOTT, William Patrick | (1900-07) | b 3.1880 | d 1.6.1948 |
| REID, James | (1874-7) | b 24.2.1851 | d 29.7.1908 | SCOULAR, John | | | |
| REID, John Murray | (1898-99) | b 25.7.1876 | d 25.5.1967 | Gladstone | (1905-06) | b 17.9.1885 | d 7.9.1953 |
| REID, Marshall Frederick | (1883) | b 3.8.1864 | d 20.3.1925 | SELBY, John Alexander | | | |
| RELPH, William Keith | | | | Robertson | (1920) | b 28.7.1900 | d 15.2.1951 |
| Linford | (1955) | b 21.11.1928 | | SHACKLETON, James | | | |
| RENNIE-TAILYOUR, | | | | Alexander Pirie | (1959-65) | | |
| Henry Waugh | (1872) | b 9.10.1849 | d 15.6.1920 | SHARP, Gregor | (1960-4) | b 20.4.1934 | |
| RENWICK, James | | | | SHAW, George Duncan | (1935-9) | b 29.5.1915 | |
| Menzies | (1972-84) | b 12.2.1952 | | SHAW, Ian | (1937) | b 4.8.1911 | |
| RENWICK, William | | | | SHAW, James Norrie | (1921) | b 13.9.1896 | |
| Norman | (1938-9) | b 29.11.1914 | d 15.6.1944 | SHAW, Robert Wilson | (1934-9) | b 11.4.1913 | d 23.7.1979 |
| RITCHIE, George | (1871) | b 16.4.1848 | d 31.1.1896 | SHEDDEN, David | (1972-8) | b 24.5.1944 | |
| RITCHIE, George F. | (1932) | | | SHILLINGLAW, Robert | | | |
| RITCHIE, James McPhail | (1933-4) | b 10.7.1907 | d 6.7.1942 | Brian | (1960-1) | b 1938 | |
| RITCHIE, William Traill | (1905) | b 11.3.1882 | d 22.5.1940 | SIMMERS, Brian Maxwell | (1965-71) | b 26.2.1940 | |
| ROBB, George Henry | (1881-5) | b 9.1858 | d 15.4.1927 | SIMMERS, William | | | |
| ROBERTS, George | (1938-9) | b 13.2.1914 | d 6.1943 | Maxwell | (1926-32) | b 7.8.1904 | d 14.11.1972 |

| PLAYER | CAREER SPAN | | |
|---|---|---|---|
| SIMPSON, John William | (1893-99) | b 1872 | d 11.1.1921 |
| SIMPSON, Robert Simpson | (1923) | b 28.4.1899 | |
| SIMSON, Ernest David | (1902-07) | b 13.3.1882 | d 22.7.1910 |
| SIMSON, John Thomas | (1905-11) | b 21.10.1884 | d 30.3.1976 |
| SIMSON, Ronald Francis | (1911) | b 6.9.1890 | d 14.9.1914 |
| SLOAN, Allen Thomson | (1914-21) | b 30.12.1892 | d 2.10.1952 |
| SLOAN, D.A. | (1950-3) | b 11.5.1926 | |
| SLOAN, Tennent | (1905-09) | b 9.11.1884 | d 15.10.1972 |
| SMEATON, Patrick Walker | (1881-3) | b 12.11.1857 | d 11.8.1928 |
| SMITH, Allan Ramsay | (1895-1900) | b 10.1.1875 | d 31.3.1926 |
| SMITH, Arthur Robert | (1955-62) | b 23.1.1933 | d 3.2.1975 |
| SMITH, Douglas William Cumming | (1949-53) | b 27.10.1924 | |
| SMITH, Errol Ross | (1879) | b 1860 | d 23.3.1902 |
| SMITH, George Kenneth | (1957-61) | b 2.6.1931 | |
| SMITH, Harry Oswald | (1895-1902) | b 1873 | d 31.7.1957 |
| SMITH, Ian Scott | (1924-33) | b 31.10.1903 | d 18.9.1972 |
| SMITH, Ian Sidney Gibson | (1969-71) | b 16.6.1944 | |
| SMITH, Michael Adam | (1970) | b 23.11.1945 | |
| SMITH, Robert Tait | (1929-30) | b 1908 | d 7.4.1958 |
| SMITH, S.H. | (1877-8) | | |
| SMITH, Thomas John | (1983-) | b 31.8.1953 | |
| SOLE, David Michael Barclay | (1986-) | b 8.5.1962 | |
| SOMERVILLE, D. | (1879-84) | | |
| SPEIRS, Louis Moritz | (1906-10) | b 23.10.1885 | d 4.1949 |
| SPENCE, Kenneth Magnus | (1953) | b 21.11.1929 | |
| SPENCER, E. | (1898) | | |
| STAGG, Peter Kidner | (1965-70) | b 22.11.1941 | |
| STEELE, William Charles Common | (1969-77) | b 18.4.1947 | |
| STEPHEN, A.E. | (1885-6) | | |
| STEVEN, Peter David | (1984-) | b 4.7.1959 | |
| STEVEN, Robert | (1962) | | |
| STEVENSON, A.K. | (1922-3) | | |
| STEVENSON, A.M. | (1911) | | |
| STEVENSON, George Drummond | (1956-65) | b 30.5.1933 | |
| STEVENSON, Henry James | (1888-93) | b 12.7.1867 | d 8.8.1945 |
| STEVENSON, Louis Edgar | (1888) | b 31.1.1864 | d 19.8.1931 |
| STEVENSON, Ronald Cochran | (1897-9) | b 25.7.1873 | d 12.2.1934 |
| STEVENSON, R.C. | (1910-11) | | |
| STEVENSON, W.H. | (1925) | | d 1972 |
| STEWART, Alexander Kenneth | (1874-6) | b 30.8.1852 | d 13.2.1945 |
| STEWART, Archibald Mathison | (1914) | b 27.9.1890 | d 18.9.1974 |
| STEWART, Charles Alexander Reid | (1880) | b 1858 | d 26.2.1890 |
| STEWART, Charles Edward Bell | (1960-1) | b 23.12.1936 | |
| STEWART J. | (1930) | b 20.2.1905 | d 27.5.1936 |
| STEWART, J.L. | (1921) | b 6.5.1894 | d 6.8.1971 |
| STEWART, Mark Sprot | (1932-4) | b 7.1.1905 | |
| STEWART, William Allan | (1913-14) | b 23.10.1889 | |
| STEYN, Stephen Sebastian Lombard | (1911-12) | b 10.11.1889 | d 8.12.1917 |
| STRACHAN, Gordon Matthew | (1971-3) | b 16.11.1947 | |
| STRONACH, R.S. | (1901-05) | | d 6.1930 |
| STUART, Charles Douglas | (1909-11) | b 18.5.1887 | d 15.1.1982 |
| STUART, Ludovic Mair | (1923-30) | b 22.10.1902 | d 3.3.1957 |
| SUDDON, Norman | (1965-70) | b 28.6.1943 | |
| SUTHERLAND, Walter Riddell | (1910-14) | b 19.11.1890 | d 4.10.1918 |
| SWAN, John Spence | (1953-8) | b 14.7.1930 | |
| SWAN, Malcolm William | (1958-9) | b 4.12.1934 | |
| SWEET, John Brunton | (1913-14) | b 26.3.1892 | |
| SYMINGTON, Archibald William | (1914) | b 3.1892 | d 8.5.1941 |
| TAIT, John Guthrie | (1880-5) | b 24.8.1861 | d 4.10.1945 |
| TAIT, Peter Webster | (1935) | b 19.10.1906 | d 22.4.1980 |
| TAYLOR, Edward Graham | (1927) | b 3.7.1907 | d 13.9.1959 |
| TAYLOR, Robert Capel | (1951) | b 31.8.1924 | |
| TELFER, Colin McLeod | (1968-76) | b 26.2.1947 | |
| TELFER, James William | (1964-70) | b 17.3.1940 | |

| PLAYER | CAREER SPAN | | |
|---|---|---|---|
| TENNENT, James MacWilliam | (1909-10) | b 7.9.1888 | d 19.3.1955 |
| THOM, David Alexander | (1934-5) | b 16.2.1910 | d 1982 |
| THOM, George | (1920) | | d 8.1927 |
| THOM, James Robert | (1933) | b 22.11.1910 | |
| THOMSON, A.E. | (1921) | | |
| THOMSON, A.M. | (1949) | | |
| THOMSON, Bruce Ewan | (1953) | b 19.11.1930 | |
| THOMSON, Ian Hosie Munro | (1951-3) | b 13.4.1930 | |
| THOMSON, J.S. | (1871) | | |
| THOMSON, Ronald Hew | (1960-4) | | |
| THOMSON, W.H.M. | (1906) | | |
| THOMSON, William John | (1899-1900) | b 18.4.1876 | d 10.11.1939 |
| TIMMS, Alec Boswell | (1896-1905) | b 1871 | d 5.5.1922 |
| TOD, H. Borth | (1911) | | d 31.12.1962 |
| TOD, John | (1884-6) | b 1862 | d 9.9.1935 |
| TODD, J.K. | (1874-5) | | |
| TOLMIE, James Munro | (1922) | b 20.11.1895 | d 9.3.1955 |
| TOMES, Alan James | (1976-) | b 6.11.1951 | |
| TORRIE, Thomas Jameson | (1877) | b 13.4.1857 | d 18.6.1913 |
| TUKALO, Iwan | (1985-) | b 5.3.1961 | |
| TURK, Arthur Steven | (1971) | b 9.1.1948 | |
| TURNBULL, Phipps | (1901-02) | b 3.4.1878 | d 24.8.1907 |
| TURNBULL, F. Oliver | (1951) | b 3.6.1919 | |
| TURNBULL, George Oliver | (1896-1904) | b 21.7.1877 | d 14.1.1970 |
| TURNER, Frederic Harding | (1911-14) | b 29.5.1888 | d 11.1.1915 |
| TURNER, John William Cleet | (1966-71) | b 28.9.1943 | |
| USHER, Charles Milne | (1912-22) | b 26.9.1891 | d 21.1.1981 |
| VALENTINE, Alec | (1953) | b 23.2.1928 | |
| VALENTINE, David Donald | (1947) | b 12.9.1926 | d 14.8.1976 |
| VEITCH, James Pringle | (1882-6) | b 1862 | d 22.1.1917 |
| VILLAR, Charles | (1876-7) | | |
| WADDELL, Gordon Herbert | (1957-62) | b 12.4.1937 | |
| WADDELL, Herbert | (1924-30) | b 19.9.1902 | |
| WADE, Albert Luvian | (1908) | b 20.9.1884 | d 28.4.1917 |
| WALKER, Archibald | (1881-3) | b 29.6.1858 | d 10.6.1945 |
| WALKER, A.W. | (1931-2) | | |
| WALKER, James George | (1882-3) | b 9.10.1859 | d 24.3.1923 |
| WALKER, Michael | (1952) | b 11.3.1930 | |
| WALLACE, Arthur Cooper | (1923-6) | b 5.10.1900 | d 3.11.1975 |
| WALLACE, William Middleton | (1913-14) | b 23.9.1892 | d 22.8.1915 |
| WALLS, William Alexander | (1882-6) | b 29.12.1859 | d 19.2.1936 |
| WALTER, Maurice Winn | (1906-10) | b 4.1.1888 | d 3.9.1910 |
| WARREN, J.R. | (1914) | | |
| WARREN, Ronald C. | (1922-30) | | |
| WATERS, Frank Henry | (1930-2) | b 2.12.1908 | d 18.10.1954 |
| WATERS, John Alexander | (1933-7) | b 11.11.1908 | |
| WATERS, Joseph Bow | (1904) | b 29.4.1882 | d 30.6.1954 |
| WATHERSTON, J.G. | (1934) | b 24.8.1909 | |
| WATHERSTON, William Rory Andrews | (1963) | b 5.3.1933 | |
| WATSON, D.H. | (1876-7) | | |
| WATSON, William Sinclair | (1974-9) | b 7.1.1949 | |
| WATT, Alexander Gordon Mitchell | (1947-8) | b 19.12.1916 | d 16.4.1982 |
| WEATHERSTONE, Thomas Grant | (1952-9) | b 1931 | |
| WELSH, Robin | (1895-96) | b 20.10.1869 | d 21.10.1934 |
| WELSH, Robert Brown | (1967) | b 2.2.1943 | |
| WELSH, William Berridge | (1927-33) | b 11.2.1907 | d 27.2.1987 |
| WELSH, William Halliday | (1900-02) | b 4.9.1879 | d 30.6.1972 |
| WEMYSS, Andrew | (1914-22) | b 22.5.1893 | d 21.1.1974 |
| WEST, Leonard | (1903-06) | b 5.1879 | d 26.1.1945 |
| WESTON, V.G. | (1936) | | |
| WHITE, David Mathew | (1963) | b 21.11.1943 | |
| WHITE, Derek Bolton | (1982-) | b 30.1.58 | |
| WHITE, Thomas Brown | (1888-9) | b 1.3.1866 | d 6.7.1939 |
| WHITTINGTON, Thomas Price | (1873) | b 12.8.1849 | d 7.10.1919 |

| PLAYER | CAREER SPAN | | |
|---|---|---|---|
| WHITWORTH, R.J.E. | (1936) | | |
| WHYTE, David James | (1965-7) | b 21.2.1940 | |
| WILL, John George | (1912-14) | b 2.9.1892 | d 25.3.1917 |
| WILSON, Alfred William | (1931) | | d 1985 |
| WILSON, Graham Alexander | (1949) | b 23.11.1922 | |
| WILSON, George | (1886-91) | b 1868 | d 1908 |
| WILSON, John Howard | (1953) | b 3.3.1930 | |
| WILSON, James Stewart | (1931-2) | b 4.9.1909 | |
| WILSON, John Skinner | (1908-09) | b 10.3.1884 | d 31.5.1916 |
| WILSON, Ronald | (1976-83) | b 1.7.1954 | |
| WILSON, Robert Little | (1951-3) | b 1.7.1926 | |
| WILSON, R.W. | (1873-4) | b 4.2.1854 | d 6.7.1911 |
| WILSON, Stewart | (1964-68) | b 22.10.1942 | |
| WOOD, Alexander Thomson | (1873-5) | b 30.4.1848 | d 26.10.1905 |
| WOOD, George | (1931-2) | b 19.4.1905 | |
| WOODBURN, J.C. | (1892) | | |
| WOODROW, Alexander Norie | (1887) | b 1867 | d 26.2.1916 |

| PLAYER | CAREER SPAN | | |
|---|---|---|---|
| WOTHERSPOON, William | (1891-4) | b 2.5.1868 | d 19.8.1942 |
| WRIGHT, Francis Aitken | (1932) | b 14.7.1909 | d 14.3.1959 |
| WRIGHT, Hugh Brooks | (1894) | b 1875 | |
| WRIGHT, Kenneth M. | (1929) | b 6.9.1904 | |
| WRIGHT, Ronald William James | (1973) | b 6.5.1949 | d 11.10.1983 |
| WRIGHT, S.T.H. | (1949) | | |
| WRIGHT, Thomas | (1947) | b 18.12.1924 | |
| WYLLIE, Douglas Stewart | (1984-) | b 20.5.1963 | |
| YOUNG, Arthur Henderson | (1874) | b 31.10.1854 | d 20.10.1938 |
| YOUNG, Eric Templeton | (1914) | b 5.1892 | d 28.6.1915 |
| YOUNG, Robert Graham | (1970) | b 13.9.1940 | |
| YOUNG, Thomas Eric Boswell | (1911) | b 6.2.1891 | d 12.3.1973 |
| YOUNG, W.B. | (1937-48) | | |

# IRELAND

| PLAYER | CAREER SPAN | |
|---|---|---|
| ABRAHAM, Myles | (1912-14) | b. 1887 |
| ADAMS, Charles | (1908-14) | b. 8.12.1883 d. 13.11.1965 |
| AGAR, Robert Dunlop | (1947-50) | b. 29.3.1920 |
| AGNEW, Patrick Joseph | (1974-6) | b. 18.3.1942 |
| AHEARNE, Thomas | (1899) | |
| ALEXANDER, Robert | (1936-9) | b. 24.9.1910 d. 19.7.1943 |
| ALLEN, Charles Elliot | (1900-07) | b. 14.10.1880 d. 15.1.1966 |
| ALLEN, Gerald Glyn | (1891-9) | b. 14.3.1874 d. 4.1.1949 |
| ALLEN, T.C. | (1885) | |
| ALLEN, W. | (1875) | |
| ALLISON, James Barnett | (1899-1903) | b. 28.6.1880 d. 30.3.1907 |
| ANDERSON, Frederick Edmund | (1953-5) | b. 29.8.1929 |
| ANDERSON, Henry James | (1903-06) | b. 17.3.1882 d. 9.11.1949 |
| ANDERSON, William Andrew | (1984-) | b. 3.4.1955 |
| ANDREWS, G. | (1875-6) | |
| ANDREWS, H.W. | (1888-9) | |
| ARCHER, Arthur Montfort | (1879) | |
| ARIGHO, John Edward | (1928-31) | b. 10.7.1907 |
| ARMSTRONG, William Kenneth | (1960-1) | b 22.10.1931 |
| ARNOTT, David Taylor | (1876) | b. 1855 d. 23.7.1915 |
| ASH, W.H. | (1875-7) | |
| ASTON, Herbert Reid | (1908) | d. 27.1.1968 |
| ATKINS, Alfred Patrick | (1924) | b. 9.4.1900 d. 25.3.1979 |
| ATKINSON, J. Maurice | (1927) | d. 26.7.1980 |
| ATKINSON, Joseph Richard | (1882) | b 23.9.1862 |
| BAGOT, John Christopher | (1879-81) | b. 1859 d. 27.4.1935 |
| BAILEY, Aidan Hilary | (1934-8) | b. 1.1.1916 d. 6.6.1976 |
| BAILEY, Niall | (1952) | b. 20.3.1929 |
| BARDON, Maurice Edgar | (1934) | b. 4.8.1907 |
| BARLOW, M. | (1875) | |
| BARNES, Robert James | (1933) | b. 25.3.1911 |
| BARR, Ainsworth | (1898-1901) | b. 1875 d. 19.12.1934 |
| BEAMISH, Charles E. St. J. | (1933-8) | b. 23.6.1908 d. 18.5.1984 |
| BEAMISH, George Robert | (1925-33) | b. 29.4.1905 d. 13.11.1967 |
| BEATTY, William John | (1910-12) | d. 10.2.1919 |
| BECKER, Vincent Anthony Mary | (1974) | b. 9.10.1947 |
| BECKETT, Gerald Gordon Paul | (1908) | b. 28.6.1886 d. 3.9.1950 |
| BELL, Richard Junior | (1875-6) | b 1847 d. 11.11.1885 |
| BELL, William Ewart | (1953) | b.13.11.1924 |
| BENNETT, Frank | (1913) | b. 1893 d. 5.1981 |
| BENT, Gerard C. | (1882) | |
| BERKERY, Patrick, Joseph | (1954-8) | b. 3.2.1929 |
| BERMINGHAM, Joseph Conleth | (1921) | b. 19.10.1899 d. 1961 |
| BLACKHAM, J.C. | (1909-10) | |
| BLAKE-KNOX, Stephen Ernest Fitzroy | (1976-7) | b. 9.7.1948 |
| BLAYNEY, John Joseph | (1950) | b. 13.3.1925 |
| BOND, Andrew T.W. | (1894) | b. 17.8.1871 |
| BORNEMANN, Walter William | (1960) | b. 19.1.1936 |
| BOWEN, Daniel St. James | (1977) | b. 11.2.1957 |
| BOYD, Cecil Anderson | (1900-01) | b. 1875 d. 27.2.1942 |
| BOYLE, Charles Vesey | (1935-9) | b. 2.7.1915 |
| BRABAZON, Henry | (1884-6) | |
| BRADLEY, Michael James | (1920-7) | b. 1895 |
| BRADLEY, Michael Timothy | (1984-) | b. 17.11.1962 |
| BRADSHAW, George | (1903) | |
| BRADSHAW, Robert McNevin | (1885) | b. 1860 d. 12.1907 |
| BRADY, Aidan Malachy | (1966-8) | b. 16.10.1939 |
| BRADY, Joseph Anthony | (1976) | b. 9.4.1952 |
| BRADY, James R. | (1951-7) | b. 11.2.1931 |
| BRAMWELL, Thomas | (1928) | |
| BRAND, Thomas Norman | (1924) | b. 5.1.1899 d. 6.1938 |
| BRENNAN, James Irwin | (1957) | b. 22.8.1934 |

| PLAYER | CAREER SPAN | |
|---|---|---|
| BRESNIHAN, Finbarr Patrick | (1966-71) | b. 13.3.1944 |
| BRETT, Jasper Thomas | (1914) | b. 8.8.1895 d. 4.2.1917 |
| BRISTOW, James Rippingham | (1879) | b. 10.1858 d. 4.4.1925 |
| BROPHY, Niall Henry | (1957-67) | b. 19.11.1935 |
| BROWN, Eric Lawrence | (1958) | b. 6.9.1930 |
| BROWN, G.S. | (1912) | |
| BROWN, H. | (1877) | |
| BROWN, T. | (1877) | |
| BROWN, W.H. | (1899) | |
| BROWN, William James | (1970) | b. 19.8.1943 |
| BROWN, Walter Stewart | (1893-4) | b. 1868 d. 31.1.1946 |
| BROWNE, Antony William | (1951) | |
| BROWNE, Daniel | (1920) | b. 12.1.1900 |
| BROWNE, Hugh Christopher | (1929) | b. 28.11.1905 d. 6.11.1983 |
| BROWNE, William Fraser | (1925-8) | b. 29.1.1903 d. 23.5.1931 |
| BROWNING, David R. | (1881) | |
| BRUCE, Stewart Armit Macdonald | (1883-4) | b. 17.11.1858 d. 6.6.1937 |
| BRUNKER, Alfred Arthur | (1895) | b. 1873 d. 24.8.1946 |
| BRYANT, Charles H. | (1920) | |
| BUCHANAN, Allan McMillan | (1926-7) | b. 21.5.1904 d. 24.11.1956 |
| BUCHANAN, John Whitla Blacker | (1882-4) | b. 1863 d. 1933 |
| BUCKLEY, James Henry | (1973) | b. 1944 |
| BULGER, Lawrence Quinlivan | (1896-8) | b. 5.7.1875 d. 17.3.1928 |
| BULGER, Michael Joseph | (1888) | b. 15.5.1867 d. 20.7.1938 |
| BURGES, John Hume | (1950) | b. 26.10.1928 |
| BURGESS, Robert Balderston | (1912) | b. 25.12.1890 d. 9.12.1915 |
| BURKITT, John Colley Smyth | (1881) | b. 1860 d. 23.11.1929 |
| BURNS, Ian George | (1980) | b. 7.12.1955 |
| BUTLER, Lochlann Gerard | (1960) | b. 9.10.1935 |
| BUTLER, Noel | (1920) | d. 21.1.1952 |
| BYERS, Rowland Morrow | (1928-9) | b. 18.6.1905 |
| BYRNE, Edward Michael Joseph | (1977-8) | b. 14.9.1948 |
| BRYNE, Noel Francis | (1962) | b. 18.12.1938 |
| BYRNE, Seamus Joseph | (1953-5) | b. 7.6.1931 |
| BYRON, William G. | (1896-9) | d.1961 |
| CADDELL, Ernest Duncan | (1904-08) | b. 18.11.1881 d. 27.5.1942 |
| CAGNEY, Stephen J. | (1925-9) | d. 1961 |
| CALLAN, Colum Patrick | (1947-9) | b. 6.1.1923 |
| CAMERON, Edwin Douglas | (1891) | d 1895 |
| CAMPBELL, Edward Fitzhardinge | (1899-1900) | b. 17.1.1880 d. 13.12.1957 |
| CAMPBELL, Charles Eric | (1970) | b. 12.12.1942 |
| CAMPBELL, Samuel Burnside Boyd | (1911-13) | b. 29.6.1889 d. 1.3.1971 |
| CAMPBELL, Seamus Oliver | (1976-84) | b. 5.3.1954 |
| CANNIFFE, Donal Martin | (1976) | b. 14.8.1949 |
| CANTRELL, John Leo | (1976-81) | b. 10.1.1954 |
| CARPENDALE, Maxwell John | (1886-8) | b. 1865 d. 1.1941 |
| CARR, Nigel John | (1985-) | b. 27.7.1959 |
| CARROLL, Claude | (1930) | d. 1938 |
| CARROLL, Raymond | (1947-50) | b. 9.2.1926 |
| CASEMENT, Brabazon Newcomer | (1875-9) | b. 1852 d. 1910 |
| CASEMENT, Francis | (1906) | b. 1881 d. 14.8.1967 |
| CASEY, James Christopher | (1930-2) | b. 1.12.1902 |
| CASEY, Patrick Joseph | (1963-5) | b 4.8.1941 |
| CHAMBERS, Joseph | (1886-7) | b. 1864 d. 22.9.1935 |
| CHAMBERS, Richard Rodney | (1951-2) | b. 15.8.1927 |
| CLARKE, Joseph A.B. | (1922-4) | |

| PLAYER | CAREER SPAN | | |
|---|---|---|---|
| CLEGG, Roger James | (1973-5) | b. 4.12.1948 | |
| CLIFFORD, Jeremiah Thomas | (1949-52) | b. 15.11.1923 | |
| CLINCH, Andrew Daniel | (1892-7) | b. 28.11.1867 | d. 2.1937 |
| CLINCH, James Daniel | (1923-31) | b. 28.9.1901 | d. 1.5.1981 |
| CLUNE, John Joseph | (1912-14) | b. 2.4.1890 | d. 1942 |
| COFFEY, John J. | (1900-10) | b. 6.5.1877 | d. 28.9.1945 |
| COGAN, William St. John | (1907) | | |
| COLLIER, Samuel Ruddell | (1883) | b. 1864 | d. 29.8.1941 |
| COLLIS, William Robert Fitzgerald | (1924-6) | b 16.2.1900 | d. 27.5.1975 |
| COLLIS, William Stewart | (1884) | b. 1860 | d. 2.1.1947 |
| COLLOPY, George | (1891-2) | | d. 8.1925 |
| COLLOPY, Richard J. | (1923-5) | b. 2.5.1899 | |
| COLLOPY, William P. | (1914-24) | b. 5.5.1894 | d. 4.1.1972 |
| COMBE, Abram | (1875) | b. 16.7.1852 | |
| CONDON, Hugh Charles | (1984) | b. 17.2.1955 | |
| COOK, H.G. | (1884) | | |
| COOTE, Patrick Bernard | (1933) | b. 7.1.1910 | d. 13.4.1941 |
| CORCORAN, James Michael | (1947-8) | b. 14.7.1922 | |
| CORKEN, Thomas Samuel | (1937) | b. 15.9.1910 | |
| CORLEY, Henry Hagarty | (1902-04) | b. 1879 | d. 2.1936 |
| CORMAC, Henry S.T. | (1921) | b. 18.5.1902 | |
| COSTELLO, Patrick Joseph | (1960) | b. 18.8.1931 | |
| COTTON, J. | (1889) | | |
| COULTER, Henry Herbert | (1920) | b. 1898 | d. 13.7.1965 |
| COURTNEY, Antony William | (1920-1) | b. 19.5.1899 | d. 3.1.1970 |
| COX, Henry Lawrence | (1875-7) | | d. 14.11.1881 |
| CRAIG, Ronald G. | (1938) | | |
| CRAWFORD, Ernest | (1885) | b. 26.1.1861 | d. 20.4.1923 |
| CRAWFORD, William Ernest | (1920-7) | b. 17.11.1891 | d. 12.1.1959 |
| CREAN, Thomas Joseph | (1894-6) | b. 19.4.1873 | d. 25.3.1923 |
| CRICHTON, Robert Young | (1920-5) | b. 18.8.1897 | d. 29.7.1940 |
| CROKER, E.W.D. | (1878) | | |
| CROMEY, George Ernest | (1937-9) | b. 8.5.1913 | |
| CRONYN, Abraham Prim | (1875-80) | b. 3.9.1855 | d. 26.4.1937 |
| CROSSAN, Kevin Derek | (1982-) | b. 29.12.1959 | |
| CROWE, James Fintan | (1974) | b. 21.11.1952 | |
| CROWE, Louis | (1950) | b. 1928 | d. 9.1968 |
| CROWE, Morgan Patrick | (1929-34) | b. 5.3.1907 | |
| CROWE, Philip Martin | (1935-8) | b. 24.8.1910 | |
| CULLEN, Thomas Joseph | (1949) | b. 25.9.1926 | |
| CULLEN, William John | (1920) | b. 7.12.1894 | d. 28.6.1960 |
| CULLITON, Michael Gerard | (1959-64) | b. 15.6.1936 | |
| CUMMINS, William Edward Ashley | (1879-82) | b. 1858 | d. 18.10.1923 |
| CUNNINGHAM, Dunlop McCosh | (1923-5) | b. 20.2.1901 | d. 1.1985 |
| CUNNINGHAM, Martin John | (1955-6) | b. 23.6.1933 | |
| CUNNINGHAM, William | (1920-3) | b. 27.3.1900 | d. 13.12.1959 |
| CUPPAIDGE, John Loftus | (1879-80) | b. 1858 | d. 11.1934 |
| CURRELL, J. | (1877) | | |
| CURTIS, Arthur Bryan | (1950) | b. 27.3.1924 | |
| CUSCADEN, William Andrew | (1876) | b. 1.11.1853 | d. 5.8.1936 |
| CUSSEN, Denis John | (1921-7) | b. 19.7.1901 | d. 15.12.1980 |
| DALY, John Christopher | (1947-8) | b. 12.12.1916 | |
| DALY, Maurice J. | (1938) | | |
| DARGAN, Michael James | (1952) | b. 9.10.1928 | |
| DAVIDSON, Cecil T. | (1921) | | d. 1960 |
| DAVIDSON, Ian G. | (1899-1902) | b. 10.8.1879 | d. 6.1939 |
| DAVIDSON, James Charles | (1969-76) | b. 23.10.1942 | |
| DAVIES, Frederick E. | (1892-3) | b. 1866 | d. 11.5.1951 |
| DAVIS, J.L. | (1898) | | |
| DAVIS, William John Nixon | (1890-5) | b. 1870 | d. 1.1962 |
| DAVISON, W. | (1887) | | |
| DAVY, Eugene O'Donnell | (1925-34) | b. 26.7.1904 | |
| DAWSON, Alfred Ronald | (1958-64) | b. 5.6.1932 | |
| DEAN, Paul Michael | (1981-) | b. 28.6.1960 | |
| DEANE, Ernest Cotton | (1909) | b. 4.5.1887 | d. 25.9.1915 |

| PLAYER | CAREER SPAN | | |
|---|---|---|---|
| DEERING, Mark Joseph | (1929) | b. 6.3.1900 | d. 26.4.1973 |
| DEERING, Seamus Joseph | (1935-7) | b. 18.11.1906 | |
| DEERING, Seamus Mary | (1974-8) | b. 5.8.1948 | |
| DE LACY, Hugh | (1948) | b. 20.11.1919 | d. 8.11.1979 |
| DELANY, Michael Gilbert | (1895) | b. 1872 | d. 6.1938 |
| DENNISON, Seamus Patrick | (1973-5) | b. 26.1.1950 | |
| DICK, Charles John | (1961-3) | b. 26.1.1937 | |
| DICK, James | (1962) | b. 24.10.1939 | |
| DICK, John Stavely | (1887) | b. 4.1865 | d. 1951 |
| DICKSON, James Alfred Nicholson | (1920) | b. 12.3.1897 | d. 24.11.1963 |
| DOHERTY, Alan Edward | (1974) | b. 31.7.1945 | |
| DOHERTY, William David | (1920-1) | b. 17.7.1893 | d. 31.3.1966 |
| DONALDSON, James Albert | (1958) | b. 16.9.1936 | |
| DONOVAN, Thomas Matthew | (1889) | | |
| DOOLEY, John Francis | (1959) | b. 10.8.1934 | |
| DORAN, Bertie R.W. | (1900-02) | b. 1876 | d. 22.2.1948 |
| DORAN, Edward F. | (1890) | | |
| DORAN, Gerald Percy | (1899-1904) | b. 1877 | d. 31.3.1943 |
| DOUGLAS, Arthur Coates | (1923-8) | b. 16.8.1902 | d. 27.6.1937 |
| DOWNING, Arthur Joseph | (1882) | b. 17.8.1860 | |
| DOWSE, John Cecil Alexander | (1914) | b. 16.11.1891 | d. 16.8.1964 |
| DOYLE, James Anthony Paul | (1984) | b. 26.4.1958 | |
| DOYLE, John Thomas | (1935) | b. 29.5.1915 | |
| DOYLE, Michael Gerard Martin | (1965-8) | b 13.10.1941 | |
| DOYLE, Thomas Joseph | (1968) | b 9.6.1944 | |
| DUGGAN, Alan Thomas Anthony | (1963-72) | b 11.6.1942 | |
| DUGGAN, William | (1920) | b 14.6.1890 | d 1944 |
| DUGGAN, William Patrick | (1975-84) | b 12.3.1950 | |
| DUNCAN, William Robert | (1984) | b 14.7.1957 | |
| DUNLOP, Robert | (1889-94) | | d 30.11.1935 |
| DUNN, Peter Edward | (1923) | 21.2.1894 | d 12.4.1965 |
| DUNN, Thomas Brown | (1935) | | d 22.12.1975 |
| DUNNE, Michael J. | (1929-34) | b 14.7.1906 | d 7.2.1967 |
| DWYER, Patrick Joseph | (1962-4) | b 24.5.1940 | |
| EDWARDS, H.G. | (1877-8) | | |
| EDWARDS, R.W. | (1904) | | |
| EDWARDS, T. | (1888-93) | | |
| EDWARDS, William Victor | (1912) | b 16.10.1887 | d 29.12.1917 |
| EGAN, John D. | (1922) | | d 3.1950 |
| EGAN, James T. | (1931) | | |
| EGAN, Michael Stanislaus | (1893-5) | 12.4.1872 | d 2.1.1954 |
| EKIN, William | (1888) | | |
| ELLIOTT, William Ronald Joseph | (1979) | b 20.11.1952 | |
| ENGLISH, Michael Anthony Francis | (1958-63) | b 2.6.1933 | |
| ENNIS, Francis Noel Gerard | (1979) | b 24.12.1955 | |
| ENSOR, Anthony Howard | (1973-8) | b 17.8.1949 | |
| ENTRICAN, John Cuthbertson | (1931) | b 24.9.1908 | d 19.5.1985 |
| FAGAN, William Bernard Cecil | (1956) | b 23.4.1927 | |
| FAGAN, George Lautie | (1878) | b 27.11.1859 | d 1885 |
| FARRELL, James Leo | (1926-32) | b 7.8.1903 | d 24.10.1979 |
| FEDDIS, Noel | (1956) | b 29.12.1932 | |
| FEIGHERY, Conleth Francis | (1972) | b 13.8.1946 | |
| FEIGHERY, Thomas Anthony Oliver | (1977) | b 16.1.1945 | |
| FERRIS, J.H. | (1900) | b 30.7.1876 | |
| FERRISS, Hugh H. | (1901) | | |
| FINLAY, James Ernest | (1913-20) | b 1888 | d 6.4.1966 |
| FINLAY, William | (1876-82) | | |
| FINN, Maurice Cornelius | (1979-) | b 29.3.1957 | |
| FINN, Raymond Gerard Andrew | (1977) | b 25.11.1953 | |
| FITZGERALD, Charles Conway | (1902-03) | | |

| PLAYER | CAREER SPAN | | |
|---|---|---|---|
| FITZGERALD, Ciaran Fintan | (1979-) | b 4.6.1952 | |
| FITZGERALD, Desmond Christopher | (1984- ) | b 20.12.57 | |
| FITZGERALD, J. | (1884) | | |
| FITZPATRICK, Michael Patrick | (1978-85) | b 25.11.1950 | |
| FLETCHER, W.W. | (1882-3) | | |
| FLOOD, Robert Stanislaus | (1925) | b 1903 | d 22.4.1955 |
| FLYNN, Michael Kevin | (1959-73) | b 20.3.1939 | |
| FOGARTY, Thomas | (1891) | | |
| FOLEY, Brendan Oliver | (1976-81) | b 6.8.1950 | |
| FORBES, R.E. | (1907) | b 11.12.1880 | |
| FORREST, Arthur James | (1880-3) | b 13.10.1859 | d 13.7.1936 |
| FORREST, Edmund George | (1888-97) | b 5.10.1870 | d 19.2.1902 |
| FORREST, H. | (1893) | b 4.2.1864 | |
| FORTUNE, John Joseph | (1963-4) | b 1.12.1933 | |
| FOSTER, Alexander Roulston | (1910-21) | b 22.6.1890 | d 24.8.1972 |
| FRANKS, James Gordon | (1898) | b 1878 | d 11.1941 |
| FRAZER, Edward Fitzgerald | (1891-2) | b 1869 | d 9.1943 |
| FREEAR, Arthur E. | (1901) | | |
| FULTON, John | (1895-1904) | b 1871 | d 17.4.1948 |
| GAFFIKIN, W. | (1875) | | |
| GAGE, John H. | (1926-7) | b 2.7.1907 | |
| GALBRAITH, Edward | (1875) | | |
| GALBRAITH, Hugh Tener | (1890) | | |
| GALBRAITH, Richard | (1875-7) | | |
| GANLY, James Blandford | (1927-30) | b 7.3.1904 | d 7.1976 |
| GARDINER, Frederick | (1900-09) | b 31.5.1874 | d 6.1920 |
| GARDINER, James Burnett | (1923-5) | b 27.10.1902 | d 11.4.1961 |
| GARDINER, S. | (1893) | | |
| GARDINER, William | (1892-8) | | d 21.3.1924 |
| GARRY, Michael G. | (1909-11) | b 1887 | d 17.9.1967 |
| GASTON, Joseph Tate | (1954-6) | b 28.11.1930 | |
| GAVIN, Thomas Joseph | (1949) | | |
| GIBSON, Cameron Michael Henderson | (1964-79) | b 3.12.1942 | |
| GIBSON, Michael Edward | (1979-86) | b 3.3.1954 | |
| GIFFORD, Henry Peter | (1890) | | |
| GILLESPIE, Joseph Cecil | (1922) | b 1897 | d 3.1945 |
| GILPIN, Francis Gerald | (1962) | b 20.10.1940 | |
| GLASS, Dion Caldwell | (1958-61) | b 15.5.1934 | |
| GLENNON, James Joseph | (1980) | b 7.7.1953 | |
| GODFREY, Robin Patrick | (1954) | b 16.9.1931 | |
| GOODALL, Kenneth George | (1967-70) | b 23.2.1947 | |
| GORDON, Alexander | (1884) | | |
| GORDON, Thomas Gisborne | (1877-8) | b 15.12.1851 | d 8.7.1935 |
| GOTTO, Robert Porter Corry | (1906) | b 20.1.1881 | d 5.8.1960 |
| GOULDING, William Joshua | (1879) | b 7.3.1856 | d 12.7.1925 |
| GRACE, Thomas Oliver | (1972-8) | b 24.10.1948 | |
| GRAHAM, Richard Irvine | (1911) | b 22.7.1889 | d 15.4.1912 |
| GRANT, Edwin Leslie | (1971) | b 13.4.1946 | |
| GRANT, Patrick J. | (1894) | b 12.1871 | |
| GRAVES, Charles Robert Arthur | (1934-8) | 23.5.1909 | |
| GRAY, Robert Disney | (1923-6) | b 2.1.1896 | d 1980 |
| GREGG, Robin Johnston | (1953-4) | b 28.11.1930 | |
| GREENE, Ernest | (1882-6) | b 1862 | d 11.1937 |
| GREER, R. | (1876) | | |
| GREEVES, Thomas Jackson | (1907-09) | b 1.7.1886 | d 28.8.1974 |
| GRIFFIN, Cornelius | (1951) | | |
| GRIFFIN, Leslie John | (1949) | b 14.9.1922 | |
| GRIFFITHS, W. | (1878) | | |
| GRIMSHAW, Colin | (1969) | b 20.3.1947 | |
| GUERIN, Brendan Noel | (1956) | b 2.1.1930 | |
| GWYNN, Arthur Percival | (1895) | b 11.6.1874 | d 14.2.1898 |
| GWYNN, Lucius Henry | (1893-8) | b 25.5.1873 | d 23.12.1902 |
| HAKIN, Ronald Frederick | (1976-7) | b 3.9.1950 | |
| HALL, R.O.N. | (1884) | | |
| HALL, William Herdman | (1923-4) | b 16.8.1901 | d 20.10.1983 |

| PLAYER | CAREER SPAN | | |
|---|---|---|---|
| HALLARAN, Charles Francis George Thomas | (1921-6) | b 10.6.1897 | d 21.3.1941 |
| HALPIN, Thomas | (1909-12) | b 1888 | d 12.1950 |
| HAMILTON, A.J. | (1884) | | |
| HAMILTON, Rex Lamont | (1926) | b 30.4.1898 | d 2.6.1984 |
| HAMILTON, Robert Wallace | (1893) | b 1870 | d 23.8.1946 |
| HAMILTON, Willoughby J. | (1877) | | |
| HAMLET, George Thomas | (1902-11) | b 9.4.1881 | d 10.10.1959 |
| HARBISON, Henry Thomas | (1984-) | b 19.8.1957 | |
| HANRAHAN, Charles J. | (1926-32) | | d 28.2.1969 |
| HARDY, Gerald Gabriel | (1962) | b 29.3.1937 | d 10.1963 |
| HARMAN, George Richard Uniacke | (1899) | b 6.6.1874 | d 14.12.1975 |
| HARPER, John | (1947) | b 15.8.1921 | |
| HARPUR, Thomas Gerald | (1908) | b 30.10.1887 | |
| HARRISON, Tom | (1879-81) | | |
| HARVEY, Frederick Maurice Watson | (1907-11) | b 1.9.1888 | d 21.8.1980 |
| HARVEY, George Alfred Duncan | (1903-05) | b 27.10.1882 | 22.9.1957 |
| HARVEY, Thomas Arnold | (1900-03) | b 17.4.1878 | d 25.12.1966 |
| HEADON, Thomas Aloysius | (1939) | b 21.6.1918 | d 21.8.1966 |
| HEALEY, Patrick | (1901-04) | b 1878 | d 6.1948 |
| HEFFERNAN, Michael | (1911) | | d 20.11.1970 |
| HEMPHILL, Robert | (1912) | b 26.8.1888 | d 21.4.1935 |
| HENDERSON, Noel Joseph | (1949-59) | b 10.8.1928 | |
| HENEBREY, Geoffrey Joseph | (1906-09) | b 1880 | d 22.2.1945 |
| HERON, Archibald George | (1901) | b 21.10.1875 | |
| HERON, James | (1877-9) | | |
| HERON, W.T. | (1880) | | |
| HERRICK, Robert Warren | (1886) | | |
| HEUSTON, Frederick Samuel | (1882-3) | b 1857 | d 1914 |
| HEWITT, David | (1958-65) | b 9.9.1939 | |
| HEWITT, Francis Seymour | (1924-7) | b 3.10.1906 | |
| HEWITT, John Arthur | (1981) | b 21.11.1960 | |
| HEWITT, Thomas | (1924-6) | b 12.3.1905 | |
| HEWITT, Victor Alexander | (1935-6) | b 23.3.1913 | |
| HEWITT, William John | (1954-61) | b 6.6.1928 | |
| HEWSON, Francis Thomas | (1875) | b 9.10.1852 | d 10.8.1886 |
| HICKIE, Denis Joseph | (1971-72) | b 12.4.1943 | |
| HIGGINS, J.A. Dudley | (1947-8) | | |
| HIGGINS, W.W. | (1884) | | |
| HILLARY, Michael Francis | (1952) | b 6.6.1925 | |
| HINGERTY, Daniel Joseph | (1947) | b 11.1.1920 | |
| HINTON, William Peart | (1907-12) | b 27.10.1882 | d 29.8.1953 |
| HIPWELL, Michael Louis | (1962-72) | b 15.7.1940 | |
| HOBBS, T.H.M. | (1884-5) | | |
| HOBSON, Edward Waller | (1876) | b 5.12.1851 | d 17.4.1924 |
| HOGG, W. | (1885) | | |
| HOLLAND, Jeremiah Joseph | (1981-) | b 24.11.1955 | |
| HOLMES, George William | (1912-13) | | |
| HOLMES, Luke Jackson | (1889) | b 1867 | d 1939 |
| HOOKS, Kenneth John | (1981) | b 1.1.1960 | |
| HORAN, Arthur Kevin | (1920) | b 13.10.1886 | d 15.1.1970 |
| HOUSTON, Kenneth James | (1961-5) | b 20.7.1941 | |
| HUGHES, Robert Wood | (1878-86) | | d 15.1.1927 |
| HUNT, Edward William Francis de Vere | (1930-3) | b 2.12.1908 | d 20.12.1941 |
| HUNTER, D.V. | (1885) | | |
| HUNTER, Laurence Mervyn | (1968) | b 10.10.1943 | |
| HUNTER, William Raymond | (1962-6) | b 3.4.1938 | |
| HUTTON, Samuel Allen | (1967) | b 1940 | |
| IRELAND, John | (1876-7) | | |
| IRVINE, Harry Augustus Stewart | (1901) | | d 8.10.1943 |
| IRWIN, David George | (1980-) | b 1.2.1959 | |

| PLAYER | CAREER SPAN | |
|---|---|---|
| IRWIN, John Walker Sinclair | (1938-9) | b 1913 |
| IRWIN, Samuel Thompson | (1900-03) | b 3.7.1877 d 21.6.1961 |
| | | |
| JACK, Henry Walter | (1914-21) | b 14.6.1891 d 19.12.1977 |
| JACKSON, A.R.V. | (1911-14) | b 25.8.1890 d 31.1.1969 |
| JACKSON, Finlay William | (1923) | b 22.11.1901 d 13.3.1941 |
| JACKSON, Howard W. | (1877) | |
| JAMESON, Joseph Singer | (1888-93) | |
| JEFFARES, Ernest W. | (1913) | |
| JOHNSON-SMYTH, T.R. | (1882) | |
| JOHNSTON, Jack | (1881-7) | d 1911 |
| JOHNSTON, Meredith | (1880-6) | b 1860 d 4.1944 |
| JOHNSTON, Robert | (1893) | b 13.8.1872 d 24.3.1950 |
| JOHNSTON, Ralph William | (1890) | |
| JOHNSTON, T.J. | (1892-5) | |
| JOHNSTONE, W.E. | (1884) | |
| | | |
| KAVANAGH, James Ronald | (1953-62) | b 21.1.1931 |
| KAVANAGH, Patrick Joseph | (1952-5) | b 2.9.1929 |
| KEANE, Maurice Ignatius | (1974-84) | b 27.7.1948 |
| KEARNEY, Ronan Kieran | (1982-) | b 5.3.1957 |
| KEEFFE, Ernest | (1947-8) | b 16.3.1919 |
| KELLY, Hugh Cunningham | (1877-80) | b 1849 d 11.1944 |
| KELLY, James Charles | (1962-4) | b 8.4.1940 |
| KELLY, Seamus | (1954-60) | b 15.3.1931 |
| KELLY, W. | (1884) | |
| KENNEDY, Adrian George | (1956) | b 4.11.1932 |
| KENNEDY, Anthony Paul | (1986-) | b 30.1.1957 |
| KENNEDY, F. | (1880-2) | |
| KENNEDY, Frederick Alexander | (1904) | b 2.1.1879 |
| KENNEDY, Hector | (1938) | d 15.1.1975 |
| KENNEDY, John Murray Prior | (1882-4) | |
| KENNEDY, Kenneth William | (1965-75) | b 10.5.1941 |
| KENNEDY, Terence Joseph | (1978-81) | b 19.10.1954 |
| KEOGH, Fergus Stephen | (1964) | b 28.6.1939 |
| KEON, Jack J. | (1879) | |
| KEYES, Ralph Patrick | (1986-) | b 1.8.1961 |
| KIDD, Frederick W. | (1877-8) | |
| KIELY, Matthew David | (1962-3) | b 1934 |
| KIERNAN, Michael Joseph | (1982-) | b 17.1.1961 |
| KIERNAN, Thomas Joseph | (1960-73) | b 7.1.1939 |
| KILLEEN, George Valentine | (1912-14) | b 6.1884 d 9.1933 |
| KING, Henry | (1883) | |
| KNOX, Hercules John | (1904-08) | b 2.8.1880 d 11.3.1975 |
| KYLE, John Wilson | (1947-58) | b 10.1.1926 |
| | | |
| LAMBERT, Noel Hamilton | (1934) | b 5.6.1910 |
| LAMONT, Ronald Arthur | (1965-70) | b 18.11.1941 |
| LANDERS, Maurice F. | (1904-05) | b 1871 d 7.3.1948 |
| LANE, David J. | (1934-5) | b 30.9.1913 |
| LANE, Michael Francis | (1947-53) | b 3.4.1926 |
| LANE, Patrick | (1964) | b 7.9.1934 |
| LANGAN, Daniel Joseph | (1934) | b 19.3.1910 d 9.8.1985 |
| LAVERY, Patrick | (1974-6) | b 1949 |
| LAWLER, Patrick Joseph | (1951-6) | |
| LAWLOR, Patrick Joseph | (1935-7) | d 30.10.1965 |
| LEAHY, Michael William | (1964) | b 6.6.1935 |
| LEE, Samuel | (1891-8) | b 26.9.1871 d 5.1.1944 |
| LE FANU, Victor Charles | (1886-92) | b 14.10.1866 d 9.8.1939 |
| LENIHAN, Donal Gerard | (1981-) | b 12.9.1959 |
| L'ESTRANGE, Laurence Perot Farrar | (1962) | b 1.11.1934 |
| LEVIS, F.H. | (1884) | |
| LIGHTFOOT, Edward J. | (1931-3) | b 29.11.1907 d 25.3.1981 |
| LINDSAY, Harry | (1893-8) | |
| LITTLE, Thomas Joseph | (1898-1901) | |
| LLOYD, Richard Averil | (1910-20) | b 4.8.1891 d 23.12.1950 |

| PLAYER | CAREER SPAN | |
|---|---|---|
| LYDON, Charles Thomas John | (1956) | b 31.8.1933 |
| LYLE, Robert Knox | (1910) | b 22.6.1884 d 6.1968 |
| LYLE, Thomas Ranken | (1885-7) | b 26.8.1860 d 31.3.1944 |
| LYNCH, John Francis | (1971-4) | b 22.9.1942 |
| LYNCH, Leo Michael | (1956) | b 7.5.1930 |
| LYTLE, James Hill | (1894-9) | b 18.5.1875 d 11.7.1928 |
| LYTLE, John N. | (1888-94) | |
| LYTTLE, Victor Johnston | (1938-9) | b 17.7.1911 |
| | | |
| McALLAN, George Herbert | (1896) | b 2.2.1878 d 12.1918 |
| McBRIDE, William James | (1962-75) | b 6.6.1940 |
| McCALL, Brian William | (1985-) | b 17.6.1959 |
| McCALLAN, Barton | (1960) | b 18.7.1936 |
| McCARTEN, Ronald James | (1961) | b 6.8.1935 |
| McCARTHY, Edward A. | (1882) | d 28.3.1948 |
| McCARTHY, James Stephen | (1948-55) | b 30.1.1926 |
| McCARTHY, Thomas St George | (1882) | |
| McCARTHY, T. | (1898) | |
| MACAULAY, John | (1887) | b 1866 d 17.8.1957 |
| McCLELLAND, Thomas Alexander | (1921-4) | b 1900 d 12.8.1966 |
| McCLENAHAN, Robert Orr | (1923) | b 10.5.1902 d 1957 |
| McCLINTON, Arthur Norman | (1910) | b 16.8.1886 |
| McCOMBE, William McMachan | (1968-75) | b 6.2.1949 |
| McCONNELL, Albert Arthur McGown | (1947-9) | b 29.10.1919 |
| McCONNELL, George | (1912-13) | b 1.8.1889 d 24.3.1948 |
| McCONNELL, J.W. | (1913) | |
| McCORMAC, Frederick Maxwell | (1909-10) | b 21.5.1884 |
| McCORMICK, William John | (1930) | b 18.12.1905 |
| McCOULL, H.C. | (1895-9) | b 20.11.1873 d 1917 |
| McCOURT, Desmond | (1947) | b 1923 |
| McCOY, James Joseph | (1984-) | b 28.6.58 |
| McCRACKEN, Herbert Lowry | (1954) | b 8.7.1927 |
| McDERMOTT, Sean J. | (1955) | b 28.3.1932 |
| McDONALD, James Alexander | (1875-84) | b 1849 d 23.4.1928 |
| McDONNELL, Alaster Colla | (1889-91) | b 20.1.1867 d 15.10.1950 |
| McDOWELL, John Craig | (1924) | b 8.5.1896 d 23.11.1978 |
| McFARLAND, Basil Alexander Talbot | (1920-2) | b 18.2.1898 d 5.3.1986 |
| McGANN, Barry John | (1969-76) | b 28.5.1948 |
| McGOWN, Thomas Melville Whitson | (1899-1901) | b 22.2.1876 d 15.7.1956 |
| McGRATH, Derek George | (1984-) | b 3.5.1960 |
| McGRATH, Noel Fitzgerald | (1934) | b 6.2.1909 |
| McGRATH, Patrick John | (1965-7) | b 20.8.1941 |
| McGRATH, Robert John Murray | (1977-84) | b 18.7.1951 |
| McGRATH, Timothy | (1956-61) | b 3.10.1933 d 23.9.1978 |
| McGUIRE, Eamonn Paul | (1963-4) | b 28.6.1939 |
| MacHALE, Séan | (1965-7) | b 6.4.1936 |
| McILDOWIE, George | (1906-10) | b 3.11.1886 d 28.12.1953 |
| McILWRATH, John Alexander | (1976-7) | b 10.3.1946 |
| McILWAINE, E.H. | (1895) | |
| McILWAINE, E.N. | (1875-6) | |
| McILWAINE, John Elder | (1897-9) | b 3.8.1874 |
| McINTOSH, Louis Maxwell | (1884) | |
| MacIVOR, Charles Vernon | (1912-13) | b 12.2.1891 d 18.10.1913 |
| McKAY, James William | (1947-52) | b 12.7.1921 |
| McKEE, William Desmond | (1947-51) | b 17.9.1926 d 28.1.1982 |
| McKELVEY, James Moorehead | (1956) | b 2.4.1933 |
| McKIBBIN, Alistair Richard | (1977-80) | b 13.1.1958 |
| McKIBBIN, Christopher Henry | (1976) | b 24.6.1948 |

| PLAYER | CAREER SPAN | | |
|---|---|---|---|
| McKIBBIN, Desmond | (1950-1) | | |
| McKIBBIN, Henry Roger | (1938-9) | b 13.7.1915 | |
| McKINNEY, Stewart Alexander | (1972-8) | b 20.11.1946 | |
| McLAUGHLIN, James Henry | (1887-8) | b 23.4.1864 | d 12.1942 |
| McLEAN, Robert Edward | (1881-5) | | d 10.1936 |
| MacLEAR, Basil | (1905-07) | b 7.4.1881 | d 24.5.1915 |
| McLENNAN, Alfred Charles | (1977-81) | b 8.2.1951 | |
| McLOUGHLIN, Gerard Anthony Joseph | (1979-) | b 11.6.1952 | |
| McLOUGHLIN, Phelim M. | (1976) | b 8.8.1941 | |
| McLOUGHLIN, Raymond John | (1962-75) | b 24.8.1939 | |
| McMAHON, Laurance B. | (1931-8) | b 4.12.1911 | d 5.1.1987 |
| McMASTER, Arthur Wallace | (1972-6) | b 2.12.1945 | |
| McMORDIE, J. | (1886) | | |
| McMORROW, Aengus | (1951) | b 6.11.1927 | |
| McMULLAN, Alfred Robinson | (1881) | b 1860 | d 2.1938 |
| McNAMARA, Vincent | (1914) | b 11.4.1891 | d 29.11.1915 |
| McNAUGHTON, Paul Peter | (1978-81) | b 18.11.1952 | |
| MacNEILL, Hugh Patrick | (1981-) | b 16.9.1958 | |
| MacSWEENEY, David Anthony | (1955) | b 26.1.1936 | |
| McVICKER, Hugh | (1927-8) | b 9.2.1901 | d 19.1.1931 |
| McVICKER, James | (1924-30) | b 1.10.1896 | d 18.12.1985 |
| McVICKER, Samuel | (1922) | b 12.12.1890 | d 23.7.1972 |
| MADDEN, Michael N. | (1955) | b 24.11.1929 | |
| MAGEE, Aloysius Mary ("Louis") | (1895-1904) | b 5.1874 | d 4.4.1945 |
| MAGEE, Joseph Thomas | (1895) | b 25.3.1870 | d 18.5.1924 |
| MAGINESS, R.M. | (1875-6) | | |
| MAGRATH, Richard M. | (1909) | b 1877 | d 9.10.1972 |
| MAGUIRE, J.F. | (1884) | | |
| MAHONY, Jack | (1923) | | d 14.6.1974 |
| MALCOLMSON, George Leslie | (1935-7) | b 2.5.1910 | |
| MARSHALL, Brian David Edward | (1963) | b 25.7.1940 | |
| MASSY-WESTROPP, R.H. | (1886) | | |
| MATIER, R.N. | (1878-9) | | |
| MATTHEWS, Philip Michael | (1984-) | b 24.1.1960 | |
| MATTSSON, John Alfred | (1948) | b 16.7.1917 | |
| MAYNE, Robert Blair | (1937-9) | b 11.1.1915 | d 14.12.1955 |
| MAYNE, R.H. | (1888) | | |
| MAYNE, Thomas | (1921) | | d 1960 |
| MAYS, Kevin Michael Andrew | (1973) | b 9.8.1949 | |
| MEARES, Arthur William Devenish | (1899-1900) | b 1874 | d 23.5.1935 |
| MEGAW, John | (1934-8) | b 16.11.1909 | |
| MILLAR, A. | (1880-3) | | d 1923 |
| MILLAR, Henry J. | (1904-05) | | d 4.1959 |
| MILLAR, Sidney | (1958-70) | b 23.5.1934 | |
| MILLAR, William Henry Jordan | (1951-2) | b 9.1.1924 | |
| MILLER, Francis Henry | (1886) | b 5.10.1865 | d 16.6.1936 |
| MILLIKEN, Richard Alexander | (1973-5) | b 2.9.1950 | |
| MILLIN, Terence John | (1925) | b 9.1.1903 | d 3.7.1980 |
| MINCH, John Berchmans | (1912-14) | b 29.7.1890 | d 2.1943 |
| MOFFATT, James | (1888-91) | | |
| MOFFATT, John Edward | (1904-05) | b 3.3.1882 | |
| MOFFETT, Jonathan William | (1961) | b 30.4.1937 | |
| MOLLOY, Michael Gabriel | (1966-76) | b 27.9.44 | |
| MOLONEY, John Joseph | (1972-80) | b 27.8.1949 | |
| MOLONEY, Lawrence Anthony | (1976-8) | b 14.6.1951 | |
| MOLONY, Jack | (1950) | b 21.10.1924 | |
| MONTEITH, Jack Deryk Erle | (1947) | b 24.8.1922 | |
| MONTGOMERY, A. | (1895) | b 26.9.1871 | d 1.1928 |
| MONTGOMERY, Frank Percivale | (1914) | b 10.6.1892 | d 11.8.1972 |
| MONTGOMERY, Robert | (1887-92) | b 1.2.1866 | |
| MOORE, C. Malcolm | (1887-8) | | |
| MOORE, D. Frank | (1883-4) | | |
| MOORE, Frederick William | (1884-6) | b 3.9.1857 | d 23.8.1949 |
| MOORE, Herbert | (1876-7) | | |
| MOORE, Herbert | (1910-12) | b 8.6.1890 | d 1976 |
| MOORE, Terence Anthony Patrick | (1967-74) | b 29.4.1945 | |
| MOORE, W.D. | (1878) | | |
| MORAN, Frederick George | (1936-9) | b 1913 | d 17.10.1979 |
| MORELL, Henry Brown | (1881-2) | b 1858 | d 3.1934 |
| MORGAN, George Joseph | (1934-9) | b 24.3.1912 | d 16.4.1979 |
| MORIARTY, Cecil Charles Hudson | (1899) | b 28.1.1877 | d 7.4.1958 |
| MORONEY, John Christopher M. | (1968-9) | b 28.10.1945 | |
| MORONEY, Rory Joseph Matthew | (1984-5) | b 3.10.57 | |
| MORONEY, Thomas Aloysius | (1964-7) | b 27.7.1941 | |
| MORPHY, Edward McGillicuddy | (1908) | b 28.1.1886 | |
| MORRIS, Dermot Patrick | (1931-5) | b 31.1.1908 | |
| MORROW, Robert David | (1986-) | b 24.8.1956 | |
| MORROW, Robert Whiteside | (1882-8) | | |
| MORTELL, Maurice P. | (1953-4) | b 13.3.1930 | |
| MORTON, William Andrews | (1888) | b 1865 | d 19.3.1948 |
| MOYERS, Lambert William | (1884) | | |
| MULCAHY, William Albert | (1958-65) | b 7.1.1935 | |
| MULLAN, Bernard | (1947-8) | | |
| MULLANE, Jerome P. | (1928-9) | | d 1931 |
| MULLEN, Karl Daniel | (1947-52) | b 26.11.1926 | |
| MULLIGAN, Andrew Armstrong | (1956-61) | b 4.2.1936 | |
| MULLIN, Brendan John | (1984-) | b 31.10.1963 | |
| MURPHY, Cornelius Joseph | (1939-47) | b 19.9.1914 | |
| MURPHY, John Gervase Maurice Walker | (1951-8) | b 20.8.1926 | |
| MURPHY, John Joseph | (1981-) | b 27.8.1957 | |
| MURPHY, Noel Francis | (1930-3) | b 27.12.1904 | |
| MURPHY, Noel Arthur Augustine | (1958-69) | b 22.2.1937 | |
| MURPHY-O'CONNOR, James Colman | (1954) | | |
| MURRAY, Henry Walker | (1877-9) | b 12.5.1854 | d 25.10.1942 |
| MURRAY, John Brendan | (1963) | b 3.4.1942 | |
| MURRAY, Paul Finbar | (1927-33) | b 29.6.1905 | d 1.6.1981 |
| MURTAGH, Charles William | (1977) | b 30.8.1949 | |
| MYLES, John | (1875) | b 1854 | d 4.1934 |
| NASH, L.C. | (1889-91) | | |
| NEELY, Matthew Robert | (1947) | b 24.12.1919 | |
| NEILL, Harry James | (1885-8) | b 1861 | d 27.6.1949 |
| NEILL, Joseph McFerran | (1926) | b 10.6.1905 | d 10.6.1967 |
| NELSON, James Edward | (1947-54) | b 16.9.1921 | |
| NELSON, Robert | (1882-6) | | |
| NESDALE, Thomas Jude | (1961) | b 18.8.1933 | |
| NEVILLE, William Cox | (1879) | b 1855 | d 15.11.1904 |
| NICHOLSON, Percy Claude | (1900) | b 1879 | d 8.1948 |
| NORTON, George William | (1949-51) | b 1.4.1920 | |
| NOTLEY, John Robert | (1952) | b 25.6.1926 | |
| O'BRIEN, Brian | (1893) | b 12.7.1872 | d 1916 |
| O'BRIEN, Brian Anthony Philip | (1968) | b 5.7.1939 | |
| O'BRIEN, Desmond Joseph | (1948-52) | b 22.5.1919 | |
| O'BRIEN, Kevin Anthony | (1980-1) | b 5.6.1955 | |
| O'BRIEN-BUTLER, P.E. | (1897-1900) | | d 1902 |
| O'CALLAGHAN, Cyril Tate | (1910-12) | b 9.9.1889 | |

| PLAYER | CAREER SPAN | | |
|---|---|---|---|
| O'CALLAGHAN, Michael Paul | (1962-4) | b 1936 | |
| O'CALLAGHAN, Philip | (1967-76) | b 25.3.1946 | |
| O'CONNELL, Patrick | (1913-14) | b 27.3.1892 | d 1972 |
| O'CONNELL, William Joseph | (1955) | b 22.4.1930 | |
| O'CONNOR, Hubert Stephen | (1957) | b 2.9.1933 | |
| O'CONNOR, Joseph J. | (1909) | | |
| O'CONNOR, John | (1895) | b 21.6.1873 | |
| O'CONNOR, Joseph J. | (1933-8) | b 27.10.1911 | |
| O'CONNOR, P.J. | (1887) | b 18.4.1863 | d 26.12.1919 |
| O'CONOR, John Hamilton | (1888-96) | b 1866 | d 23.5.1953 |
| ODBERT, Reginald Vere Massey | (1928) | b 9.2.1904 | d 18.7.1943 |
| O'DONNELL, Rodney Christopher | (1979-80) | b 16.8.1956 | |
| O'DONOGHUE, Patrick Joseph | (1955-8) | b 22.11.1931 | |
| O'DRISCOLL, Barry Joseph | (1971) | b 18.9.1943 | |
| O'DRISCOLL, John Brian | (1978-) | b 26.11.1953 | |
| O'FLANAGAN, Kevin Patrick | (1947) | b 6.1919 | |
| O'FLANAGAN, Michael | (1948) | b 29.9.1922 | |
| O'HANLON, Bartholomew Reginald | (1947-50) | b 23.10.1924 | |
| O'LEARY, Arthur Finbarr | (1952) | b 30.11.1929 | |
| O'LOUGHLIN, David Bonaventure | (1938-9) | b 13.7.1916 | d 17.7.1971 |
| O'MEARA, John Anthony | (1951-8) | b 26.6.1929 | |
| O'NEILL, Henry O'Hara | (1930-3) | b 1.7.1907 | |
| O'NEILL, James Bowman | (1920) | b 21.8.1895 | d 19.4.1968 |
| O'NEILL, William Arthur | (1952-4) | b 15.11.1928 | d 1.1985 |
| O'REILLY, Anthony Joseph Francis Kevin | (1955-70) | b 7.5.1936 | |
| ORR, Philip Andrew | (1976-) | b 14.12.1950 | |
| O'SULLIVAN, Alexander Charles | (1882) | b 1858 | d 1924 |
| O'SULLIVAN, John M. | (1884-7) | b 9.1865 | |
| O'SULLIVAN, Patrick Joseph Antony | (1957-63) | b 2.6.1933 | |
| O'SULLIVAN, William | (1895) | b 1874 | d 3.3.1953 |
| OWENS, Reuben H. | (1922) | | |
| PARFREY, Padraic Seosamh | (1974) | b 12.8.1950 | |
| PARKE, James Cecil | (1903-09) | b 26.7.1881 | d 27.2.1946 |
| PARR, S. John | (1914) | b 21.8.1889 | d 1959 |
| PATTERSON, Colin Stewart | (1978-80) | b 3.3.1955 | |
| PATTERSON, R. D'Arcy | (1912-13) | | d 11.1930 |
| PAYNE, Charles Trevor | (1926-30) | b 1905 | d 12.7.1980 |
| PEDLOW, Alexander Cecil | (1953-63) | b 20.1.1934 | |
| PEDLOW, Joseph | (1882-4) | | |
| PEDLOW, Robert | (1891) | b 16.8.1868 | d 10.2.1943 |
| PEDLOW, Thomas Bowen | (1889) | b 9.7.1866 | d 16.7.1952 |
| PEEL, T. | (1892) | | |
| PEIRCE, William | (1881) | b 1861 | d 3.1936 |
| PHIPPS, George C. | (1950-2) | | |
| PIKE, Theodore Ouseley | (1927-8) | b 2.8.1904 | |
| PIKE, Victor Joseph | (1931-4) | b 1.7.1907 | d 25.2.1986 |
| PIKE, William Watson | (1879-83) | b 10.3.1860 | d 22.6.1941 |
| PINION, Godfrey | (1909) | b 1883 | d 7.12.1956 |
| PIPER, Oliver James S. | (1909-10) | b 1886 | |
| POLDEN, Stanhope Ernest | (1913-20) | b 24.3.1885 | d 14.10.1958 |
| POPHAM, Ivan | (1922-3) | | |
| POTTERTON, H. Norman | (1920) | b 3.4.1897 | d 1978 |
| PRATT, Robert Henry | (1933-4) | b 24.12.1911 | |
| PRICE, Alfred Henry | (1920) | | |
| PRINGLE, John Conrad | (1902) | b 8.11.1881 | d 8.5.1952 |
| PURCELL, Noel Mary | (1921) | b 14.12.1891 | d 1962 |
| PURDON, Henry | (1879-81) | | |
| PURDON, William Brooke | (1906) | b 28.11.1881 | d 1.12.1950 |
| PURSER, Francis Carmichael | (1898) | b 16.9.1876 | d 2.1934 |
| QUINLAN, Sean Vincent Joseph | (1956-8) | b 13.10.1934 | |
| QUINN, Brendan Thomas | (1947) | b 1.8.1919 | |

| PLAYER | CAREER SPAN | | |
|---|---|---|---|
| QUINN, Joseph Patrick | (1910-14) | b 23.11.1888 | d 6.1955 |
| QUINN, Francis Peter | (1981) | b 5.9.1954 | |
| QUINN, Kevin Joseph | (1947-53) | b 14.3.1923 | |
| QUINN, Michael Anthony Mary | (1973-81) | b 31.5.1952 | |
| QUIRKE, John Michael Thornton | (1962-8) | b 26.6.1944 | |
| RAMBAUT, Daniel Frederick | (1887-8) | b 1860 | d 12.1932 |
| REA, Harold Halliday | (1967-9) | b 1946 | |
| READ, Henry Marvelle | (1910-13) | b 8.11.1888 | d 6.12.1972 |
| REARDEN, James V. | (1934) | | d 13.7.1979 |
| REID, Carl | (1899-1903) | | |
| REID, John Lewis | (1934) | b 16.4.1909 | |
| REID, Patrick Joseph | (1947-8) | b 17.3.1924 | |
| REID, Thomas Eymard | (1953-7) | b 3.3.1926 | |
| REIDY, Charles J. | (1937) | b 8.7.1912 | |
| REIDY, Gerald | (1953-4) | b 13.5.1926 | |
| RICHEY, Henry Alexander | (1889-90) | | |
| RIDGEWAY, Ernest Charles | (1932-5) | b 16.9.1911 | d 3.5.1986 |
| RINGLAND, Trevor Maxwell | (1981-) | b 13.11.1959 | |
| RIORDAN, William F. | (1910) | b 30.8.1883 | d 11.7.1939 |
| RITCHIE, James S. | (1956) | b 11.12.1926 | |
| ROBB, Campbell Glynn | (1904-06) | b 25.2.1882 | |
| ROBBIE, John Cameron | (1976-81) | b 17.11.1955 | |
| ROBINSON, Thomas Trevor Hull | (1904-07) | b 17.11.1880 | d 1962 |
| ROCHE, J. | (1890-2) | | |
| ROCHE, Richard Edwin | (1955-7) | b 22.2.1930 | |
| ROCHE, William Joseph | (1920) | b 28.3.1895 | d 26.6.1983 |
| RODDY, Patrick Joseph | (1920) | | d 19.3.1967 |
| ROE, Robin | (1952-7) | b 11.11.1928 | |
| ROOKE, Charles Vaughan | (1891-7) | b 1874 | d 6.1.1946 |
| ROSS, Daniel Joseph | (1884-6) | b 1865 | d 8.11.1951 |
| ROSS, George Robert Porter | (1955) | b 1.11.1925 | |
| ROSS, J.F. | (1886) | | |
| ROSS, J.P. | (1885-6) | | |
| ROSS, Norman G. | (1927) | | |
| ROSS, William McC. | (1932-5) | | d 7.1.1969 |
| RUSSELL, John | (1931-7) | b 30.6.1909 | d 13.5.1977 |
| RUTHERFORD, W.G. | (1884-8) | | |
| RYAN, Edmund G. | (1937-8) | | |
| RYAN, John | (1897-1904) | | d 10.1937 |
| RYAN, James Gerard | (1939) | b 1.4.1917 | d 7.1978 |
| RYAN, Michael | (1897-1904) | b 1871 | d 19.8.1947 |
| SAYERS, Herbert James Michael | (1935-9) | b 1.5.1911 | d 12.1943 |
| SCHUTE, Frederick | (1878-9) | | |
| SCHUTE, F. Godfrey | (1912-13) | | d 3.1970 |
| SCOTT, Dennis | (1961-2) | b 19.11.1933 | |
| SCOTT, Robert Desmond | (1967-8) | b 2.10.1941 | |
| SCOVELL, Rowland Hill | (1883-4) | | d 2.1939 |
| SCRIVEN, George | (1879-83) | b 9.11.1856 | d 31.3.1932 |
| SEALY, James | (1896-1900) | b 19.3.1876 | d 4.2.1949 |
| SEXTON, William | (1984-) | b 21.7.1959 | |
| SHANAHAN, T. | (1885-8) | | |
| SHAW, G.M. | (1877) | | d 12.1922 |
| SHEEHAN, Michael Danaher | (1932) | b 1909 | d 3.11.1974 |
| SHERRY, Brendan Francis | (1967-8) | b 7.6.1943 | |
| SHERRY, Michael James Aloysius | (1975) | b 21.6.1951 | |
| SIGGINS, John Allen Edgar | (1931-7) | b 28.6.1909 | |
| SLATTERY, John Fergus | (1970-84) | b 12.1.1949 | |
| SMARTT, Frank Nangle Bury | (1908-09) | b 24.12.1885 | d 2.1965 |
| SMITH, John Hartley | (1951-4) | b 27.7.1926 | |
| SMITH, R.E. | (1892) | | |
| SMITHWICK, Frederick Falkiner Standish | (1898) | b 1880 | d 4.10.1962 |
| SMYTH, John Trevor | (1920) | b 27.1.1897 | |
| SMYTH, Patrick James | (1911) | | d 12.1.1928 |
| SMYTH, Robertson Stewart | (1903-04) | b 1880 | d 5.4.1916 |
| SMYTH, Thomas | (1908-12) | b 12.1884 | d 5.1928 |

| PLAYER | CAREER SPAN | | |
|---|---|---|---|
| SMYTH, William S. | (1910-20) | | d 1.1937 |
| SOLOMONS, Bethel Albert Herbert | (1908-10) | b 27.2.1885 | d 11.9.1965 |
| SPAIN, Alexander William | (1924) | b 22.9.1897 | d 24.2.1983 |
| SPARROW, William | (1893-4) | | |
| SPILLANE, Brian Jeremiah | (1985-) | b 26.1.1960 | |
| SPRING, Donal Eugene | (1978-81) | b 23.8.1956 | |
| SPRING, Richard Martin | (1979) | b 29.8.1950 | |
| SPUNNER, H.F. | (1881-4) | | |
| STACK, C.R.R. | (1889) | | |
| STACK, George Hall | (1875) | | d 11.1876 |
| STEELE, Harold William | (1976-9) | b 4.9.1948 | |
| STEPHENSON, George Vaughan | (1920-30) | b 22.12.1901 | d 6.8.1970 |
| STEPHENSON, Henry William Vaughan | (1922-8) | b 28.11.1900 | d 18.11.1958 |
| STEVENSON, James | (1888-9) | | |
| STEVENSON, James Burton | (1958) | b 28.9.1929 | |
| STEVENSON, Robert | (1887-93) | b 27.3.1866 | d 1960 |
| STEVENSON, T.H. | (1895-7) | | |
| STEWART, Albert Lewis | (1913-14) | b 19.2.1889 | d 4.10.1917 |
| STEWART, William Joseph | (1922-9) | b 24.9.1900 | d 1959 |
| STOKER, Ernest Wilson | (1888) | b 1864 | d 1914 |
| STOKER, Frank Owen | (1886-91) | b 1866 | d 1.1939 |
| STOKES, Oliver | (1882-4) | | |
| STOKES, Patrick | (1913-22) | b 3.4.1890 | d 29.10.1970 |
| STOKES, Robert Day | (1891) | b 1866 | d 1943 |
| STRATHDEE, Ernest | (1947-9) | | d 17.7.1971 |
| STUART, Charles Parnell | (1912) | b 2.4.1886 | d 21.11.1958 |
| STUART, Ian Malcolm Bowen | (1924) | b 18.9.1902 | d 3.8.1969 |
| SUGARS, Harold Sanderson | (1905-07) | | |
| SUGDEN, Mark | (1925-31) | b 11.2.1902 | |
| SULLIVAN, Donal Bartholomew | (1922) | b 28.8.1898 | d 26.4.1974 |
| SWEENEY, James Austin | (1907) | b 29.5.1884 | d 6.9.1944 |
| SYMES, George R. | (1895) | | |
| SYNGE, John Samuel | (1929) | b 12.7.1906 | d 26.8.1982 |
| TAGGART, Thomas | (1887) | b 1866 | d 2.1945 |
| TAYLOR, Alfred Squire | (1910-12) | b 6.7.1889 | d 31.7.1917 |
| TAYLOR, David Robertson | (1903) | b 26.10.1880 | d 11.1941 |
| TAYLOR, James D. | (1914) | | |
| TAYLOR, John Wilgar | (1879-83) | b 30.6.1859 | d 16.12.1924 |
| TECTOR, William Richard | (1955) | b 16.4.1929 | |
| TEDFORD, Alfred | (1902-08) | b 7.1.1877 | d 6.1.1942 |
| TEEHAN, Charles | (1939) | b 6.5.1919 | |
| THOMPSON, Charles | (1907-10) | | |
| THOMPSON, J. | (1885) | | |
| THOMPSON, John Knox Stafford | (1921-3) | | |
| THOMPSON, Robert George | (1882) | | |
| THOMPSON, Robin Henderson | (1951-6) | b 5.5.1931 | |
| THORNHILL, Thomas | (1892-3) | | d 1939 |
| THRIFT, Harry | (1904-09) | b 24.12.1882 | d 2.2.1958 |
| TIERNEY, Dennis | (1938-9) | b 1915 | d 7.1970 |
| TILLIE, C.R. | (1887-8) | | |
| TODD, Andrew W.P. | (1913-14) | b 6.7.1892 | d 3.1942 |
| TORRENS, Desmond | (1938-9) | b 10.3.1915 | d 8.7.1981 |
| TUCKER, Colm Christopher | (1979-80) | b 22.9.1952 | |
| TUKE, Benjamin Burland | (1890-5) | b 1870 | d 5.1936 |
| TURLEY, Patrick Noel | (1962) | b 13.12.1936 | |
| TYDINGS, John Joseph | (1968) | b 26.6.1945 | |
| TYRRELL, William | (1910-14) | b 20.11.1885 | d 29.4.1968 |
| UPRICHARD, Richard J. | (1950) | | |
| WAIDE, Shaun Lockhart | (1932-3) | b 8.8.1912 | d 26.2.1984 |
| WAITES, J. | (1886-91) | | |
| WALDRON, Cornelius Oliver | (1966-68) | b 11.7.1943 | |
| WALKER, Samuel | (1934-8) | b 21.4.1912 | d 27.1.1972 |
| WALKINGTON, Dolway B. | (1887-91) | | d 18.4.1926 |
| WALKINGTON, R.B. | (1875-82) | | |
| WALL, Henry | (1965) | b 1.12.1935 | |
| WALLACE, James | (1904) | b 30.10.1876 | d 1960 |
| WALLACE, Joseph | (1903-06) | b 3.8.1878 | d 29.1.1967 |
| WALLACE, Thomas | (1920) | b 25.4.1892 | d 9.9.1954 |
| WALLIS, Arthur Knight | (1892-3) | | d 1905 |
| WALLIS, Clive O'Neill | (1935) | b 16.10.1913 | d 26.10.1981 |
| WALLIS, Thomas Gill | (1921-2) | b 2.10.1892 | |
| WALLIS, William Armstrong | (1880-3) | | d 1925 |
| WALMSLEY, George | (1894) | b 1869 | d 8.1942 |
| WALPOLE, A. | (1888) | b 26.10.1865 | d 24.6.1910 |
| WALSH, Edward J. | (1887-93) | b 1868 | d 25.3.1939 |
| WALSH, H.D. | (1875-6) | | |
| WALSH, Jeremiah Charles | (1960-7) | b 3.11.1938 | |
| WARD, Anthony Joseph Patrick | (1978- ) | b 9.10.1954 | |
| WARREN, J.P. | (1883) | | |
| WARREN, Robert Gibson | (1884-90) | b 1866 | d 19.11.1940 |
| WATSON, Richard | (1912) | | d 1960 |
| WELLS, H.G. | (1891-4) | | |
| WESTBY, A.J. | (1876) | | |
| WHEELER, George Herbert | (1884-5) | b 9.12.1864 | d 16.1.1955 |
| WHEELER, James Reid | (1922-4) | b 1898 | d 23.3.1973 |
| WHELAN, Patrick Charles | (1975-81) | b 2.5.1950 | |
| WHITE, Michael | (1906-07) | b 2.2.1882 | d 26.9.1956 |
| WHITESTONE, Augustus Mayberry | (1877-83) | | |
| WILKINSON, Richard W. | (1947) | b 24.3.1915 | |
| WILLIAMSON, Frederick William | (1930) | b 25.7.1905 | |
| WILLIS, W.J. | (1879) | | |
| WILSON, Francis | (1977) | b 1.9.1952 | |
| WILSON, Hugh Gilmer | (1905-10) | b 11.4.1879 | d 13.1.1941 |
| WILSON, William Henry | (1877) | b 25.11.1852 | d 10.2.1931 |
| WITHERS, Henry Hastings Cavendish | (1931) | b 11.10.1904 | d 6.9.1948 |
| WOLFE, E.J. | (1882) | | d 2.1933 |
| WOOD, George Harold | (1913-14) | b 6.9.1891 | d 2.1980 |
| WOOD, Benjamin Gordon Malison | (1954-61) | b 20.6.1931 | d 18.5.1982 |
| WOODS, D.C. | (1888-9) | | |
| WRIGHT, Robert Aikin | (1912) | | d 7.12.1955 |
| YEATES, R.A. | (1889) | | d 1894 |
| YOUNG, Gordon | (1913) | | |
| YOUNG, Roger Michael | (1965-71) | b 29.6.1943 | |

# WALES

| PLAYER | CAREER SPAN | |
|---|---|---|
| ACKERMAN, Robert Angus | (1980-5) | b 2.3.1961 |
| ALEXANDER, Edward Perkins | (1885-7) | b 1864 d 26.10.1931 |
| ALEXANDER, William H. | (1898-1901) | b 1878 |
| ALLEN, Charles Peter | (1884) | b 2.12.1861 d 18.9.1930 |
| ANDREWS, Frank | (1912-13) | b 1888 |
| ANDREWS, Frederick Graham | (1884) | b 15.9.1864 d 2.6.1929 |
| ANDREWS, George E. | (1926-7) | b 24.8.1904 |
| ANTHONY, Leslie | (1948) | b 21.11.1921 |
| ARNOLD, William Richard | (1903) | b 7.7.1881 d 30.7.1957 |
| ARTHUR, Charles Suckling | (1888-91) | b 21.1.1866 d 12.12.1925 |
| ARTHUR, Tom | (1927-33) | b 10.1.1906 d 1.11.1986 |
| ASHTON, Clifford I. | (1959-62) | b 1933 |
| ATTEWELL, Stephen Leonard | (1921) | b 31.12.1895 d 26.2.1983 |
| | | |
| BADGER, Owen | (1895-6) | b 3.11.1871 d 17.3.1939 |
| BAKER, Albert Melville | (1909-10) | b 1885 |
| BAKER, Ambrose | (1921-3) | b 7.7.1897 d 24.11.1976 |
| BAKER-JONES, Paul Esmond R. | (1921) | b 27.12.1894 d 5.1934 |
| BAKER-JONES, Thomas | (1882-5) | b 16.9.1862 d 26.5.1959 |
| BANCROFT, John | (1909-14) | b 1879 d 7.1.1942 |
| BANCROFT, William John | (1890-1901) | b 2.3.1870 d 3.3.1959 |
| BARLOW, Thomas Marriott | (1884) | b 1864 d 27.1.1942 |
| BARRELL, Robert | (1929-33) | b 1905 |
| BARTLETT, John Dudley | (1927-8) | b 1907 d 17.1.1967 |
| BASSETT, Arthur | (1934-8) | b 28.6.1914 |
| BASSETT, John Archibald | (1929-32) | b 11.7.1905 |
| BAYLISS, Gwyn | (1933) | b 5.1907 d 10.3.1976 |
| BEBB, Dewi Iorwerth Ellis | (1959-67) | b 7.8.1938 |
| BECKINGHAM, Geoffrey | (1953-8) | b 29.7.1924 |
| BENNETT, Ivor | (1937) | b 16.6.1913 |
| BENNETT, Percy | (1891-2) | |
| BENNETT, Philip | (1969-78) | b 24.10.1948 |
| BERGIERS, Roy Thomas Edmond | (1972-5) | b 11.11.1950 |
| BEVAN, Griffith Wilfred | (1947) | b 15.8.1914 |
| BEVAN, James Alfred | (1881) | b 1859 d 3.2.1938 |
| BEVAN, John Charles | (1971-3) | b 28.10.1950 |
| BEVAN, John David | (1975) | b 12.3.1948 d 5.6.1986 |
| BEVAN, Thomas Sydney | (1904) | b 1877 d 17.10.1933 |
| BEYNON, Benjamin | (1920) | b 14.3.1894 d 1969 |
| BEYNON, George Edward | (1925) | b 1902 d 14.10.1957 |
| BIGGS, Norman Witchell | (1888-94) | d 3.11.1870 d 27.2.1908 |
| BIGGS, Selwyn Hanam | (1895-1900) | b 1875 |
| BIRCH, James | (1911) | |
| BIRT, Frederick W. | (1911-13) | b 10.11.1886 d 5.7.1956 |
| BISHOP, David | (1984- ) | b 31.10.1960 |
| BISHOP, Edward H. | (1889) | |
| BLACKMORE, Jacob Henry | (1909) | b 1884 |
| BLACKMORE, Steven Walter | (1987-) | b 3.3.1962 |
| BLAKE, Jere | (1899-01) | b 1875 d 15.2.1933 |
| BLAKEMORE, Reginald Edward | (1947) | b 1.9.1924 |
| BLAND, Alexander Frederick | (1887-90) | b 24.11.1866 d 18.10.47 |
| BLYTH, Leonard | (1951-2) | b 20.11.1920 |
| BLYTH, William Roger | (1974-80) | b 2.4.1950 |
| BOON, Ronald Winston | (1930-3) | b 6.6.1909 |
| BOOTH, Joseph | (1898) | b 1873 d 28.4.1958 |
| BOOTS, John George | (1898-1904) | b 2.7.1874 d 30.12.1928 |
| BOUCHER, Arthur William | (1892-7) | b 29.6.1870 d 26.4.1948 |
| BOWCOTT, Henry Morgan | (1929-33) | b 30.4.1907 |
| BOWDLER, Frederick Arthur | (1927-33) | |

| PLAYER | CAREER SPAN | |
|---|---|---|
| BOWEN, Bleddyn | (1983- ) | b 16.7.1961 |
| BOWEN, Clifford Alfred | (1896-7) | b 1874 d 30.4.1929 |
| BOWEN, David Harry | (1883-7) | b 1864 d 17.8.1913 |
| BOWEN, George E. | (1887-8) | |
| BOWEN, William Arnold | (1886-91) | b 1862 d 26.9.1925 |
| BOWEN, William E | (1921-2) | b 1899 |
| BRACE, David Onllwyn | (1956-61) | b 16.11.1932 |
| BRADDOCK, Kenneth James | (1966-7) | b 1942 |
| BRADSHAW, Keith | (1964-6) | b 7.4.1939 |
| BREWER, Trevor John | (1950-5) | b 16.8.1930 |
| BRICE, Alfred | (1899-1904) | b 21.9.1872 |
| BRIDIE, R.H. | (1882) | |
| BRITTON, Gordon R | (1961) | |
| BROUGHTON, Augustus Stephen | (1927-9) | b 29.4.1904 d 9.1981 |
| BROWN, Archibald | (1921) | b 1895 |
| BROWN, James | (1925) | b 22.3.1901 d 30.7.1976 |
| BROWN, John Alfred | (1907-9) | |
| BROWN, Mark | (1983- ) | b 18.12.1958 |
| BURCHER, David Howard | (1977) | b 26.10.1951 |
| BURGESS, Robert Clive | (1977-82) | d 25.11.1950 |
| BURNETT, Roy | (1953) | b 6.10.1926 |
| BURNS, James | (1927) | b 1902 d 1971 |
| BUSH, Percy Frank | (1905-10) | b 23.6.1879 d 19.5.1955 |
| BUTLER, Edward Thomas | (1980-4) | b 8.5.1957 |
| CALE, William Ray | (1949-50) | |
| CATTELL, Alfred | (1883) | b 1857 d 10.9.1933 |
| CHALLINOR, Cyril | (1939) | b 13.5.1912 d 29.11.1976 |
| CLAPP, Thomas J.S. | (1882-8) | b 1855 d 15.11.1933 |
| CLARE, J. | (1883) | |
| CLARK, Samuel Simmonds | (1882-7) | b 1857 d 25.5.1947 |
| CLEAVER, William Benjamin | (1947-50) | b 15.9.1921 |
| CLEGG, Barry G. | (1979) | b 30.10.1952 |
| CLEMENT, William Harries | (1937-8) | b 9.4.1915 |
| COBNER, Terence John | (1974-8) | b 10.1.1946 |
| COLDRICK, Albert Percy | (1911-2) | b 1888 d 26.12.1953 |
| COLEMAN, Ernest | (1949) | |
| COLES, Fenton C. | (1960) | b 14.9.1937 |
| COLLINS, John | (1958-61) | b 1932 |
| COLLINS, Richie Graham | (1987-) | b 2.3.1962 |
| COLLINS, Tom | (1923) | |
| COOK, Terence | (1949) | b 24.6.1927 |
| COPE, William | (1896) | b 18.8.1870 d 15.7.1946 |
| CORNISH, Frederick Henry | (1897-9) | b 1876 d 27.4.1940 |
| CORNISH, Robert Arthur | (1923-6) | b 30.6.1897 d 29.7.1948 |
| COSLETT, Kelvin | (1962) | b 14.1.1942 |
| COWEY, Bernard Turing Vionnee | (1934-5) | b 20.11.1911 |
| CRESSWELL, Brian | (1960) | b 1934 |
| CUMMINS, William | (1922) | |
| CUNNINGHAM, Leonard John | (1960-4) | b 3.1.1932 |
| DACEY, Malcolm | (1983-) | b 12.7.1960 |
| DANIEL, David John | (1891-9) | b 1871 d 30.4.1948 |
| DANIEL, Laurence Thomas David | (1970) | b 5.3.1942 |
| DANIELS, Patrick Charles Thomas | (1981-2) | b 15.5.1957 |
| DARBISHIRE, Godfrey | (1881) | b 26.9.1853 d 29.10.1889 |
| DAUNCEY, Frederick Herbert | (1896) | b 1.12.1871 d 30.10.1955 |
| DAVEY, E. Claude | (1930-8) | b 14.12.1908 |
| DAVID, Richard J. | (1907) | b 1876 |
| DAVID, Thomas Patrick | (1973-6) | b 2.4.1948 |
| DAVIDGE, Glyn D. | (1959-62) | b 1934 |
| DAVIES, Abel Christmas | (1889) | b 1861 d 18.6.1914 |
| DAVIES, Alun Eirian | (1984) | b 25.3.1956 |
| DAVIES, Ben | (1895-6) | b 1874 d 6.1930 |
| DAVIES, Christmas Howard | (1939-47) | b 25.12.1916 |

| PLAYER | CAREER SPAN | | |
|---|---|---|---|
| DAVIES, Cyril Allan Harvard | (1957-61) | b 21.11.1936 | |
| DAVIES, Clifton | (1947-51) | b 12.12.1919 | d 28.1.1967 |
| DAVIES, Charles Lynn | (1956) | b 1929 | |
| DAVIES, Cecil Rhys | (1934) | | d 25.12.1941 |
| DAVIES, Daph. | (1921-5) | | d 1965 |
| DAVIES, David Bailey | (1907) | b 3.12.1884 | d 24.8.1968 |
| DAVIES, David Brian | (1962-3) | b 7.7.1941 | |
| DAVIES, David G. | (1923) | b 1897 | |
| DAVIES, D.H. | (1904) | | |
| DAVIES, David Hunt | (1924) | b 11.11.1896 | d 8.5.1979 |
| DAVIES, David Idwal | (1939) | b 10.11.1915 | |
| DAVIES, David John | (1962) | b 20.2.1941 | d 16.4.1969 |
| DAVIES, David Maldwyn | (1950-4) | b 2.5.1925 | |
| DAVIES, Eirwynne Gwynne | (1928-30) | b 23.6.1908 | |
| DAVIES, Emlyn | (1947-8) | | |
| DAVIES, Evan | (1919) | b 1892 | d 1946 |
| DAVIES, Ewan Gibson | (1912) | b 23.6.1887 | d 2.9.1979 |
| DAVIES, George | (1900-05) | b 25.12.1875 | |
| DAVIES, Howell | (1984- ) | b 6.6.1959 | |
| DAVIES, Glyn | (1947-51) | b 24.8.1927 | d 11.1976 |
| DAVIES, Hopkin | (1898-1901) | | |
| DAVIES, Harry Graham | (1921-5) | b 19.4.1899 | |
| DAVIES, Haydn J. | (1959) | b 1934 | |
| DAVIES, Harold Joseph | (1924) | b 5.12.1899 | d 29.3.1976 |
| DAVIES, Henry Stanley | (1923) | b 23.4.1895 | d 14.2.1966 |
| DAVIES, Howell J. | (1912) | | |
| DAVIES, Ivor Thomas | (1914) | b 6.4.1892 | d 1954 |
| DAVIES, Jenkin Alban | (1913-14) | b 5.9.1885 | d 8.1976 |
| DAVIES, John Henry | (1923) | | |
| DAVIES, Jonathan | (1985- ) | b 24.10.1962 | |
| DAVIES, Leonard Morris | (1954-5) | b 1930 | d 23.9.1957 |
| DAVIES, Leslie | (1939) | b 13.7.1913 | d 9.1984 |
| DAVIES, Lyn | (1966) | b 2.2.1940 | |
| DAVIES, Mark | (1981- ) | b 9.7.1958 | |
| DAVIES, Michael John | (1939) | b 7.10.1918 | d 8.7.1984 |
| DAVIES, N. Glyn | (1955) | b 1928 | |
| DAVIES, Philip Thomas | (1985- ) | b 19.10.1963 | |
| DAVIES, Robin Harvard | (1957-62) | b 12.1.1934 | |
| DAVIES, Terence John | (1953-61) | b 24.9.1933 | |
| DAVIES, Thomas Gerald Reames | (1966-78) | b 7.2.1945 | |
| DAVIES, Thomas Mervyn | (1969-76) | b 9.12.1946 | |
| DAVIES, W. | (1896) | | |
| DAVIES, William | (1931-2) | b 14.2.1906 | d 5.10.1975 |
| DAVIES, William Avon | (1912) | b 27.12.1890 | d 18.9.1967 |
| DAVIES, William Edward Norman | (1939) | b 7.9.1913 | |
| DAVIES, William Gareth | (1978-85) | b 29.9.1956 | |
| DAVIES, William Thomas Harcourt | (1936-9) | b 28.3.1916 | |
| DAVIS, Clive Enoch | (1978-81) | b 17.9.1949 | |
| DAWES, Sydney John | (1964-71) | b 29.6.1940 | |
| DAY, Harry T. | (1892-4) | | |
| DAY, Hubert Charles | (1930-1) | b 8.5.1908 | d 27.6.1977 |
| DAY, Thomas Brynmor | (1931-5) | b 29.12.1907 | d 9.1980 |
| DEACON, J. Thomas | (1891-2) | b 1868 | |
| DELAHAY, William James | (1922-7) | b 2.9.1900 | d 12.9.1978 |
| DEVEREUX, Donald | (1958) | b 1931 | |
| DEVEREUX, John Anthony | (1986- ) | b 30.3.1966 | |
| DOBSON, George | (1900) | b 1873 | |
| DOBSON, Tom | (1898-9) | b 1872 | d 4.7.1936 |
| DONOVAN, Alun John | (1978-82) | b 5.10.1955 | |
| DONOVAN, Richard | (1983- ) | | |
| DOUGLAS, Mark Henry James | (1984- ) | b 10.12.1960 | |
| DOUGLAS, William M | (1886-7) | b 2.7.1863 | d 1945 |
| DOWELL, William Henry | (1907-8) | b 21.5.1885 | |
| DYKE, John Charles Meredith | (1906) | b 20.6.1884 | d 1960 |
| DYKE, Louis Meredith | (1910-11) | b 1888 | d 12.7.1961 |
| EDWARDS, Arthur Bernard | (1955) | b 17.10.1927 | 19.9.1984 |
| EDWARDS, Benjamin Oswald | (1951) | b 29.5.1923 | 2.9.1978 |
| EDWARDS, Gareth Owen | (1967-78) | b 12.7.1947 | |
| EDWARDS, David | (1921) | b 21.3.1896 | d 24.8.1960 |
| EIDMAN, Ian Harold | (1983- ) | b 31.10.1957 | |

| PLAYER | CAREER SPAN | | |
|---|---|---|---|
| ELLIOTT, John E. | (1894-8) | | d 30.3.1938 |
| ELSEY, W.J. | (1895) | b 1871 | |
| EVANS, Arthur Candy | (1924) | b 19.2.1904 | d 7.1.1952 |
| EVANS, Brinley Samuel | (1920-2) | b 21.1.1894 | d 28.6.1964 |
| EVANS, Bryn (Llanelli) | (1933-7) | b 27.9.1905 | d 6.10.1978 |
| EVANS, Colin | (1960) | b 20.11.1936 | |
| EVANS, Daniel Brinley | (1933) | b 16.1.1902 | d 29.4.1970 |
| EVANS, David | (1896-8) | b 1872 | |
| EVANS, David Danny | (1934) | b 7.4.1909 | |
| EVANS, D.B. | (1926) | | |
| EVANS, Dennis Pritchard | (1960) | b 19.3.1936 | |
| EVANS, David William | (1889-91) | b 4.11.1866 | d 17.3.1926 |
| EVANS, Emrys | (1937-9) | b 24.4.1911 | d 6.1983 |
| EVANS, Frank | (1921) | b 3.4.1897 | d 30.11.1972 |
| EVANS, Gareth Llewellyn | (1977-8) | b 2.11.1953 | |
| EVANS, Gwyn | (1947-9) | | |
| EVANS, Gwyn | (1981-3) | b 6.9.1957 | |
| EVANS, Ieuan Cenydd | (1987-) | b 21.3.1964 | |
| EVANS, Iorwerth | (1934) | b 1906 | d 1985 |
| EVANS, Islwyn | (1922) | b 25.12.1898 | d 13.5.1974 |
| EVANS, Jack | (1904) | | |
| EVANS, Jack Elwyn | (1924) | b 1897 | d 1941 |
| EVANS, Jack H. | (1907) | | |
| EVANS, John | (1896-7) | b 1871 | d 1924 |
| EVANS, John David | (1958) | b 1928 | |
| EVANS, John R. | (1934) | b 12.9.1913 | d 2.1943 |
| EVANS, O.J. | (1887-8) | | |
| EVANS, Peter Denzil | (1951) | b 1929 | |
| EVANS, Rosser | (1889) | | |
| EVANS, Ronald | (1963) | b 6.11.1941 | |
| EVANS, Robert Thomas | (1947-51) | b 16.2.1921 | |
| EVANS, Stuart | (1985- ) | b 14.6.1963 | |
| EVANS, Tom | (1924) | | |
| EVANS, Thomas Geoffrey | (1970-2) | b 1.5.1943 | |
| EVANS, Thomas Henry | (1906-11) | b 31.12.1882 | d 3.1955 |
| EVANS, Trevor Pryce | (1975-7) | b 26.11.1947 | |
| EVANS, Vivian | (1954) | b 14.7.1919 | |
| EVANS, William Frederick | (1882-3) | b 1856 | |
| EVANS, William George | (1911) | b 1888 | d 1949 |
| EVANS, W.H. | (1914) | b 9.2.1892 | d 1979 |
| EVANS, Wilfred J. | (1947) | b 12.5.1914 | |
| EVANS, William Roderick | (1958-62) | b 19.12.1934 | |
| EVANS, Thomas Wynne | (1958) | b 13.8.1926 | d 8.5.1987 |
| EVERSON, William Aaron | (1926) | b 3.1906 | d 24.4.1966 |
| FAULKNER, Anthony George | (1975-79) | b 27.2.1941 | |
| FAULL, John | (1957-60) | b 30.6.1933 | |
| FEAR, Albert | (1934-5) | | |
| FENDER, Norman Henry | (1930-1) | b 2.9.1910 | d 24.10.1983 |
| FENWICK, Steven Paul | (1975-81) | b 23.7.1951 | |
| FINCH, Ernest | (1924-8) | b 16.7.1899 | d 1.10.1983 |
| FINLAYSON, Alex | (1974) | b 18.3.1948 | |
| FITZGERALD, Gerald David | (1894) | b 1873 | d 30.11.1951 |
| FORD, Frederick John Vivian | (1939) | b 13.10.1917 | |
| FORD, Ian | (1959) | b 6.6.1929 | |
| FORWARD, Allan | (1951-2) | | |
| FOWLER, Isaac John | (1919) | b 27.8.1894 | d 17.6.1981 |
| FRANCIS, David Gwyn | (1919-24) | b 2.2.1896 | d 7.5.1987 |
| FRANCIS, P. | (1987-) | | |
| GABE, Rhys Thomas | (1901-8) | b 22.6.1880 | d 15.9.1967 |
| GALE, Norman Reginald | (1960-9) | b 24.7.1939 | |
| GALLACHER, Ian Stuart | (1970) | b 22.5.1946 | |
| GARRETT, Richard Marks | (1888-92) | b 1865 | d 1908 |
| GEEN, William Purdon | (1912-13) | b 14.3.1891 | d 30.7.1915 |
| GEORGE, Ernest Edward | (1895-6) | b 1871 | d 29.11.1952 |
| GETHING, Glyn Ivor | (1913) | b 16.6.1892 | d 20.3.1977 |
| GIBBS, Reginald Arthur | (1906-11) | b 1882 | d 28.11.1938 |
| GILES, Raymond | (1983-5) | b 15.1.1961 | |
| GIRLING, Barry Edward | (1881) | b 1857 | d 28.10.1905 |
| GOLDSWORTHY, Samuel James | (1884-5) | b 1855 | d 28.9.1889 |
| GORE, John Henry | (1924-5) | b 16.6.1899 | d 18.3.1971 |
| GORE, William | (1947) | b 19.11.1919 | |
| GOULD, Arthur Joseph | (1885-97) | b 10.10.1864 | d 2.1.1919 |
| GOULD, George Herbert | (1892-3) | b 1870 | d 18.12.1913 |
| GOULD, Robert | (1882-7) | b 1864 | d 29.12.1931 |
| GRAHAM, Thomas Cooper | (1890-5) | b 1866 | d 1.12.1945 |

| PLAYER | CAREER SPAN | | |
|---|---|---|---|
| GRAVELL, Raymond William Robert | (1975-82) | b 12.9.1951 | |
| GRAY, Anthony John | (1968) | b 14.6.1942 | |
| GREENSLADE, Desmond | (1962) | b 11.1.1933 | |
| GREVILLE, Handel | (1947) | b 3.9.1921 | |
| GRIFFIN, A. | (1883) | | |
| GRIFFITHS, Clive Ronald | (1979) | b 2.4.1954 | |
| GRIFFITHS, Daniel | (1888-89) | b 1858 | d 29.10.1936 |
| GRIFFITHS, Griffith | (1889) | b 1864 | d 1938 |
| GRIFFITHS, Gareth M. | (1953-7) | b 27.11.1931 | |
| GRIFFITHS, Vincent M. | (1924) | b 29.5.1901 | d 7.1.1967 |
| GRONOW, Benjamin | (1910) | b 10.3.1887 | d 24.11.1967 |
| GWILLIAM, John Albert | (1947-54) | b 28.2.1923 | |
| GWYNN, David | (1883-91) | b 1860 | d 3.1910 |
| GWYNN, William Henry | (1884-5) | b 1856 | d 1.4.1897 |
| HADLEY, Adrian Michael | (1983-) | b 1.3.1963 | |
| HALL, Ian | (1967-74) | b 4.11.1946 | |
| HANCOCK, Francis Escott | (1884-6) | b 7.2.1859 | d 29.10.1943 |
| HANNAN, James | (1888-95) | b 1864 | d 22.6.1905 |
| HARDING, Arthur Flowers | (1902-08) | b 8.8.1878 | d 15.5.1947 |
| HARDING, George Frederick | (1881-3) | b 1858 | d 8.7.1927 |
| HARDING, Rowe | (1923-8) | b 10.9.1901 | |
| HARDING, Charles Theodore | (1888-89) | b 1860 | d 13.7.1919 |
| HARRIS, Daniel J.E. | (1959-61) | b 1936 | |
| HARRIS, Tal | (1927) | | |
| HATHWAY, George Frederick | (1924) | b 23.1.1897 | d 30.1.1971 |
| HAVARD, William Thomas | (1919) | b 23.10.1889 | d 17.8.1956 |
| HAWKINS, Frank | (1912) | | |
| HAYWARD, Donald James | (1949-52) | b 30.6.1925 | |
| HAYWARD, David John | (1963-4) | b 1.3.1934 | |
| HAYWARD, George | (1908-09) | b 1887 | |
| HELLINGS, Dick | (1897-1901) | b 1.12.1874 | d 9.2.1938 |
| HERRERA, Ronald C. | (1925-7) | b 16.1.1905 | d 16.3.1973 |
| HIAMS, Harry | (1912) | | |
| HICKMAN, Arthur | (1930-3) | b 6.8.1910 | |
| HIDDLESTONE, David Daniel | (1922-4) | b 14.6.1890 | d 16.11.1973 |
| HILL, Algernon Frank | (1885-94) | b 13.1.1866 | d 20.4.1927 |
| HINAM, Sidney | (1925-6) | b 29.8.1898 | d 18.8.1982 |
| HINTON, J.T. | (1884) | | |
| HIRST, George Littlewood | (1912-14) | b 5.5.1890 | d 30.7.1967 |
| HODDER, Wilfred | (1921) | b 6.5.1898 | d 12.11.1957 |
| HODGES, Jehoida Joseph | (1899-1906) | b 1877 | d 13.9.1930 |
| HODGSON, Graham Thomas Robert | (1962-7) | b 1938 | |
| HOLLINGDALE, Herbert | (1912-13) | | |
| HOLLINGDALE, Thomas Henry | (1928-30) | b 12.11.1900 | d 14.4.1978 |
| HOLMES, Terence David | (1978-85) | b 10.3.1957 | |
| HOPKIN, William H. | (1937) | b 1.7.1914 | |
| HOPKINS, Kevin | (1985-) | b 29.9.1961 | |
| HOPKINS, Philip Lewis | (1908-10) | b 21.1.1882 | d 26.9.1966 |
| HOPKINS, Raymond | (1970) | b 8.7.1948 | |
| HOPKINS, Thomas | (1926) | b 20.1.1903 | d 26.1.1980 |
| HOPKINS, William John | (1925) | b 1898 | |
| HOWELLS, Brynmor | (1934) | b 9.2.1911 | d 6.1983 |
| HOWELLS, William Geoffrey | (1957) | b 29.10.1929 | |
| HOWELLS, W.H. | (1888) | | |
| HUGHES, Dennis | (1967-70) | b 3.7.1941 | |
| HUGHES, Gomer | (1934) | b 13.5.1910 | d 14.11.1974 |
| HUGHES, Hugh | (1887-9) | | |
| HUGHES, Keith | (1970-4) | b 15.12.1949 | |
| HULLIN, William G. | (1967) | b 2.1.1942 | |
| HURRELL, John | (1959) | b 17.8.1933 | |
| HUTCHINSON, Fred | (1894-6) | b 1867 | |
| HUXTABLE, Richard | (1920) | b 13.10.1890 | d 29.8.1970 |
| HUZZEY, Henry Vivian Pugh | (1898-9) | b 1876 | d 16.8.1929 |
| HYBART, Albert John | (1887) | b 1865 | d 28.1.1945 |
| INGLEDEW, Hugh Murray | (1890-1) | b 26.10.1865 | d 1.2.1937 |
| ISAAC, Iorwerth | (1933) | b 12.10.1911 | d 25.4.1966 |

| PLAYER | CAREER SPAN | | |
|---|---|---|---|
| JACKSON, Thomas Henry | (1895) | b 1870 | d 1952 |
| JAMES, Boyo John | (1968) | b 4.9.1938 | |
| JAMES, Carwyn Rees | (1958) | b 11.1929 | d 10.1.1983 |
| JAMES, David | (1891-9) | b 1867 | d 2.1.1929 |
| JAMES, David Rees | (1931) | b 7.10.1906 | |
| JAMES, Evan | (1890-9) | b 1869 | d 1902 |
| JAMES, Maldwyn | (1947-48) | b 28.6.1913 | |
| JAMES, Thomas Owen | (1935-7) | b 6.10.1904 | d 4.1984 |
| JAMES, William John | (1983-) | b 18.7.1956 | |
| JAMES, William P. | (1925) | b 1902 | |
| JARMAN, Henry | (1910-11) | b 1883 | d 13.12.1928 |
| JARRETT, Keith Stanley | (1967-9) | b 18.5.1948 | |
| JEFFREY, John J. | (1967) | b 1945 | |
| JENKIN, Albert Mortimer | (1895-6) | b 1872 | d 3.7.1961 |
| JENKINS, Albert | (1920-8) | b 1895 | d 7.10.1953 |
| JENKINS, David Morgan | (1926) | b 1901 | d 4.1968 |
| JENKINS, David Rees | (1927-9) | b 12.4.1904 | d 13.8.1951 |
| JENKINS, Ernest | (1910) | | |
| JENKINS, Edward Macdonald | (1927-32) | b 28.7.1904 | |
| JENKINS, John Charles | (1906) | b 19.4.1880 | |
| JENKINS, John Llewellyn | (1923) | b 12.3.1903 | |
| JENKINS, Leighton H. | (1954-6) | b 1931 | |
| JENKINS, Vivian Gordon James | (1933-9) | b 2.11.1911 | |
| JENKINS, William J. | (1912-13) | b 1882 | d 1956 |
| JOHN, Barry | (1966-72) | b 6.1.1945 | |
| JOHN, David Arthur | (1925-8) | b 1905 | d 16.8.1929 |
| JOHN, David Evan | (1923-8) | b 1.3.1902 | d 20.11.1973 |
| JOHN, David Glyndwr | (1954) | b 22.2.1932 | d 7.6.1983 |
| JOHN, Ernest Raymond | (1950-4) | b 3.12.1925 | d 28.9.1981 |
| JOHN, John Howell | (1926-7) | b 31.8.1898 | d 1977 |
| JOHNSON, Thomas Albert | (1921-5) | b 1893 | d 1948 |
| JOHNSON, William Dillwyn | (1953) | b 5.12.1923 | |
| JONES, Arthur Hugh | (1933) | b 1908 | d 26.6.1964 |
| JONES, Brian James | (1960) | b 10.10.1935 | |
| JONES, Benjamin Lewis | (1950-2) | b 11.4.1931 | |
| JONES, Clifford W. | (1934-8) | b 12.3.1914 | |
| JONES, Charles W. | (1920) | b 18.6.1893 | d 1959 |
| JONES, Dan | (1927) | b 2.3.1907 | |
| JONES, Daniel | (1897) | b 1875 | d 1.1.1959 |
| JONES, David | (1902-06) | b 1881 | d 1.1933 |
| JONES, David | (1947-9) | b 30.4.1916 | |
| JONES, David Kenneth | (1962-6) | b 7.8.1941 | |
| JONES, David L. | (1926-7) | b 1901 | |
| JONES, David Phillips | (1907) | b 1882 | d 1.1936 |
| JONES, Edgar Lewis | (1930-5) | b 4.5.1910 | d 9.2.1986 |
| JONES, Elvet Lewis | (1939) | b 29.4.1913 | |
| JONES, Graham Glyn | (1930-3) | b 24.11.1906 | |
| JONES, Graham | (1963) | | |
| JONES, Harry | (1902) | b 1878 | |
| JONES, Howell | (1904) | b 1882 | d 1.12.1908 |
| JONES, Harold James | (1929) | b 18.12.1908 | d 16.10.1955 |
| JONES, Howie | (1930) | b 8.9.1907 | |
| JONES, Ian Conin | (1968) | b 2.3.1940 | |
| JONES, Iorwerth | (1927-8) | b 3.4.1903 | d 31.8.1983 |
| JONES, Ivor Egwad | (1924-30) | b 10.12.1901 | d 16.11.1982 |
| JONES, James Phillips | (1913) | b 1884 | d 1960 |
| JONES, Jim | (1919-21) | b 1893 | |
| JONES, John | (1901) | | |
| JONES, Joseph | (1924) | b 15.3.1899 | d 27.1.1960 |
| JONES, J. Arthur | (1883) | b 1857 | d 20.1.1919 |
| JONES, J. Bedwellty | (1914) | | |
| JONES, John Phillips | (1908-21) | b 2.3.1887 | d 19.3.1951 |
| JONES, Kingsley D. | (1960-3) | b 1935 | |
| JONES, Kenneth Jeffrey | (1947-57) | b 30.12.1921 | |
| JONES, Kenyon William James | (1934) | b 5.9.1911 | |
| JONES, Mark | (1987-) | b 22.6.1965 | |
| JONES, Percy | (1912-14) | | |
| JONES, Raymond Bark | (1933) | b 29.8.1911 | |
| JONES, Richard | (1901-10) | b 27.11.1879 | |
| JONES, Richard | (1929) | | |
| JONES, Robert | (1926) | | |
| JONES, Ronald Elvet | (1967-8) | b 24.2.1943 | |
| JONES, Robert | (1901) | | |
| JONES, Robert Nicholas | (1986-) | b 10.11.1965 | |
| JONES, Stephen Thomas | (1983-) | b 4.1.1959 | |
| JONES, Tom | (1922-4) | b 13.12.1895 | |
| JONES, W. | (1898) | | |

| PLAYER | CAREER SPAN | | |
|---|---|---|---|
| JONES, Wyndham | (1905) | b 1883 | d 9.4.1953 |
| JONES, Walter Idris | (1925) | b 18.1.1900 | d 5.7.1971 |
| JONES, William Desmond | (1948) | b 1925 | |
| JONES, William Herbert | (1934) | b 6.5.1906 | d 31.7.1982 |
| JONES, William John | (1924) | b 4.2.1894 | d 7.1978 |
| JONES, William Keri | (1967-8) | b 13.1.1945 | |
| JONES, William Roy | (1927-8) | b 22.2.1903 | |
| JONES-DAVIES, Thomas Ellis | (1930-1) | b 1906 | d 25.8.1960 |
| JORDAN, Henry Martyn | (1885-9) | b 7.3.1865 | |
| JOSEPH, William | (1902-06) | b 10.5.1878 | d 1959 |
| JOWETT, William Frederick | (1903) | b 1879 | d 5.10.1939 |
| JUDD, Sydney | (1953-5) | b 1929 | d 24.2.1959 |
| JUDSON, J.H. | (1883) | | |
| KEDZLIE, Quentin D. | (1888) | | |
| KEEN, Leslie | (1980) | b 13.11.1954 | |
| KNILL, Franklyn Michael David | (1976) | | |
| LANE, Stuart Morris | (1978-80) | b 12.11.1952 | |
| LANG, James | (1931-7) | b 1.10.1909 | |
| LAW, Vivian J. | (1939) | b 11.6.1910 | |
| LAWRENCE, Stephen David | (1925-7) | b 5.8.1899 | d 13.2.1978 |
| LEGGE, Walter Sydney George | (1937-8) | b 11.11.1911 | d 1984 |
| LELEU, John | (1959-60) | b 13.3.1935 | |
| LEMON, Arthur | (1929-33) | b 15.4.1905 | d 6.1982 |
| LEWIS, Arthur John | (1970-3) | b 26.9.1941 | |
| LEWIS, Alan Robert | (1966-7) | b 7.10.1942 | |
| LEWIS, Brinley Richard | (1912-13) | b 4.1.1891 | d 2.4.1917 |
| LEWIS, Charles Prydderch | (1882-4) | b 20.8.1853 | d 28.5.1923 |
| LEWIS, D.H. | (1886) | | |
| LEWIS, Edward John | (1881) | b 5.12.1859 | d 8.6.1925 |
| LEWIS, Howell | (1913-14) | b 24.5.1888 | d 1971 |
| LEWIS, Geoffrey Windsor | (1960) | b 7.4.1936 | |
| LEWIS, John Goulstone | (1887) | b 1860 | d 1935 |
| LEWIS, John Morris Clement | (1912-23) | b 22.6.1890 | d 27.10.1944 |
| LEWIS, John Rhodri | (1981-) | b 25.2.1959 | |
| LEWIS, Mark | (1913) | | |
| LEWIS, Phillip Ivor | (1984-) | b 6.1.1961 | |
| LEWIS, Thomas William | (1926-7) | b 7.6.1902 | |
| LEWIS, William | (1925) | b 14.3.1899 | d 26.1.1927 |
| LEWIS, Windsor Hopkin | (1926-8) | b 11.11.1906 | |
| LLEWELLYN, Donald Barry | (1970-2) | b 6.1.1948 | |
| LLEWELLYN, Philip | (1973-4) | b 12.5.1948 | |
| LLEWELLYN, Willie Morris | (1899-1905) | b 1.1.1879 | d 12.3.1973 |
| LLOYD, David John | (1966-73) | b 29.3.1943 | |
| LLOYD, David Percy | (1890-1) | b 1871 | d 3.1959 |
| LLOYD, Evan | (1895) | b 1871 | d 28.2.1951 |
| LLOYD, George Llewellyn | (1896-1903) | b 1877 | d 1.8.1957 |
| LLOYD, Robert | (1913-14) | b 1888 | d 18.1.1930 |
| LLOYD, Trevor | (1953) | b 5.9.1924 | |
| LLOYD, Thomas C. | (1909-14) | | |
| LOCKWOOD, T.W. | (1887) | | |
| LONG, Edgar Cecil | (1936-9) | b 1908 | d 31.1.1958 |
| LYNE, Horace Sampson | (1883-5) | b 31.12.1860 | d 1.5.1949 |
| McCALL, Barney Ernest Wilford | (1936) | b 13.5.1913 | |
| McCARLEY, Allan | (1938) | | d 1955 |
| McCUTCHEON, William Morgan | (1891-4) | b 1870 | d 3.7.1949 |
| MADDOCK, Hopkin Thomas | (1906-10) | b 1881 | d 15.12.1921 |
| MADDOCKS, Keith | (1957) | b 16.6.1927 | |
| MAIN, Derrick R. | (1959) | b 1933 | |
| MAINWARING, Haydn James | (1961) | b 10.6.1933 | |
| MAINWARING, William T. | (1967-8) | b 1941 | |
| MAJOR, Windsor Cynwyd | (1949-50) | b 5.6.1930 | |
| MALE, Benjamin Oswald | (1921-8) | b 31.12.1893 | d 23.2.1975 |
| MANFIELD, Leslie | (1939-48) | b 10.11.1915 | |
| MANN, B.B. | (1881) | | |
| MANTLE, John Thomas | (1964) | | |

| PLAYER | CAREER SPAN | | |
|---|---|---|---|
| MARGRAVE, Frederick Lofthouse | (1884) | b 25.12.1858 | d 1.1.1946 |
| MARSDEN-JONES, Douglas | (1921-4) | b 1894 | d 5.1.1955 |
| MARTIN, Allan Jeffrey | (1973-1981) | b 11.12.1948 | |
| MARTIN, Walter John | (1912-19) | b 14.5.1883 | d 30.4.1933 |
| MATHEWS, Alfred Augustus | (1886) | b 7.2.1864 | d 12.8.1946 |
| MATHIAS, Roy | (1970) | b 2.9.1949 | |
| MATTHEWS, Christopher | (1939) | b 1911 | d 1965 |
| MATTHEWS, Jack | (1947-51) | b 21.6.1920 | |
| MEREDITH, Alun | (1949) | b 1919 | |
| MEREDITH, Brinley Victor | (1954-62) | b 21.11.1930 | |
| MEREDITH, Courtenay Charles | (1953-7) | b 23.9.1929 | |
| MEREDITH, John | (1888-90) | b 1864 | d 30.9.1920 |
| MERRY, James Augustus | (1912) | b 1888 | |
| MICHAEL, Gwilym Morgan | (1923) | b 1892 | d 24.5.1941 |
| MICHAELSON, Roger Carl Brandon | (1963) | b 31.3.1941 | |
| MILLER, Fred | (1896-1901) | b 1873 | |
| MILLS, Frank | (1892-6) | b 1873 | d 17.2.1925 |
| MOORE, William John | (1933) | b 17.2.1980 | d 31.3.1976 |
| MORGAN, Charles Henry | (1957) | b 22.12.1932 | |
| MORGAN, Clifford Isaac | (1951-8) | b 7.4.1930 | |
| MORGAN, David | (1895-6) | b 1872 | d 1933 |
| MORGAN, D. | (1885-9) | | |
| MORGAN, David Robert Ruskin | (1962-3) | b 1941 | |
| MORGAN, David Edgar | (1920-1) | b 17.5.1896 | d 9.9.1983 |
| MORGAN, Edgar | (1914) | b 1882 | d 4.1962 |
| MORGAN, Edward | (1902-08) | b 7.10.1879 | d 1.9.1949 |
| MORGAN, Frederick Luther | (1938-9) | b 11.2.1915 | |
| MORGAN, Haydn John | (1958-66) | b 30.7.1936 | |
| MORGAN, Harry P. | (1956) | b 16.6.1930 | |
| MORGAN, Ivor | (1908-12) | b 8.1884 | d 12.1943 |
| MORGAN, Jack | (1912-13) | b 1892 | |
| MORGAN, Morgan Edward | (1938-9) | b 18.12.1913 | d 1978 |
| MORGAN, Norman | (1960) | b 1934 | |
| MORGAN, Peter John | (1980-1) | b 1.1.1959 | |
| MORGAN, Philip E.J. | (1961) | b 21.12.1937 | |
| MORGAN, Rhys | (1984-) | | |
| MORGAN, Thomas | (1889) | b 1866 | d 1899 |
| MORGAN, William Guy | (1927-30) | b 26.12.1907 | d 27.7.1973 |
| MORGAN, William Llewellyn | (1910) | b 1885 | |
| MORIARTY, Robert Daniel | (1981-) | b 1.5.1957 | |
| MORIARTY, William Paul | (1986-) | b 16.7.1964 | |
| MORLEY, John Cuthbert | (1929-32) | b 28.7.1909 | d 7.3.1972 |
| MORRIS, George Lockwood | (1882-4) | b 29.1.1859 | d 23.11.1947 |
| MORRIS, Haydn Thomas | (1951-5) | b 1928 | |
| MORRIS, Joseph Ifor | (1924) | b 4.8.1901 | |
| MORRIS, Martyn Stuart | (1985-) | b 23.8.1962 | |
| MORRIS, Ronald Rhys | (1933-7) | b 13.6.1913 | d 2.1983 |
| MORRIS, Stephen | (1920-5) | b 1896 | d 6.1965 |
| MORRIS, Will | (1896-7) | b 1869 | d 11.1946 |
| MORRIS, Will | (1919-21) | | |
| MORRIS, William David | (1967-74) | b 11.1.1942 | |
| MORRIS, William J. | (1963) | b 1940 | |
| MORRIS, William John | (1965-6) | b 16.6.1941 | |
| MURPHY, Cornelius Dennis | (1935) | b 3.9.1908 | d 13.7.1964 |
| NASH, David | (1960-2) | | |
| NEILL, William | (1904-08) | b 5.6.1878 | d 2.4.1955 |
| NEWMAN, Charles Henry | (1881-7) | b 28.2.1857 | d 28.9.1922 |
| NICHOLAS, David Llewellyn | (1981) | b 3.3.1955 | |
| NICHOLAS, Trevor J. | (1919) | | |
| NICHOLL, Charles Bowen | (1891-6) | b 19.6.1870 | d 9.7.1939 |
| NICHOLL, David Wilmot | (1894) | b 1871 | d 11.3.1918 |
| NICHOLLS, Erith Gwyn | (1896-1906) | b 6.1874 | d 24.3.1939 |
| NICHOLLS, F.E. | (1892) | | |
| NICHOLLS, Howard | (1958) | | |
| NICHOLLS, Sidney H. | (1888-91) | | |
| NORRIS, Charles Howard | (1963-6) | b 11.6.1934 | |

| PLAYER | CAREER SPAN | |
|---|---|---|
| NORSTER, Robert Leonard | (1982-) | b 23.6.1957 |
| NORTON, William Barron | (1882-4) | b 28.4.1862 | d 17.12.1898 |
| O'CONNOR, Anthony | (1960-2) | b 24.4.1934 |
| O'CONNOR, Rory | (1957) | | d 3.1986 |
| O'SHEA, John Patrick | (1967-8) | b 2.6.1940 |
| OLIVER, George | (1920) |
| OSBORNE, W.T. | (1902-3) | b 1880 |
| OULD, W.J. | (1924) | b 6.5.1899 |
| OWEN, Albert | (1924) | b 1901 |
| OWEN, Garfield David | (1955-6) | b 20.3.1932 |
| OWEN, Richard Morgan | (1901-12) | b 1876 | d 2.1932 |
| PACKER, Harry | (1891-7) | b 3.9.1868 | d 22.5.1946 |
| PALMER, Frank | (1922) | b 1896 | d 16.10.1925 |
| PARFITT, Frederick Charles | (1893-6) | b 12.8.1869 | d 20.3.1953 |
| PARKER, David | (1924-30) | | d 1965 |
| PARKER, Thomas | (1919-23) | b 1893 | d 1967 |
| PARKER, William | (1899) |
| PARSONS, George W. | (1947) | b 21.4.1926 |
| PASCOE, Daniel | (1923) | b 7.7.1900 | d 19.5.1971 |
| PASK, Alun Edward Islwyn | (1961-7) | b 10.9.1937 |
| PAYNE, Gareth W. | (1960) | b 8.9.1935 |
| PAYNE, Harry | (1935) | b 10.12.1907 |
| PEACOCK, Harry | (1929-30) |
| PEAKE, Edward | (1881) | b 29.3.1860 | d 3.1.1945 |
| PEARCE, Gary Peter | (1981-2) | b 11.11.1960 |
| PEARSON, Thomas William | (1891-1903) | b 10.5.1872 | d 12.9.1957 |
| PEGGE, Edward Vernon | (1891) | b 1864 | d 21.3.1915 |
| PERKINS, Sydney John | (1983-) | b 27.2.1954 |
| PERRETT, Fred Leonard | (1912-13) | b 1891 | d 1.12.1918 |
| PERRINS, Victor Charles | (1970) | b 1944 |
| PERRY, William | (1911) |
| PHILLIPS, Alan John | (1979-) | b 21.8.1955 |
| PHILLIPS, Bryn | (1925-6) | b 4.10.1900 |
| PHILLIPS, David Horace | (1952) | b 24.8.1928 |
| PHILLIPS, Henry Thomas | (1927-8) | b 22.6.1903 | d 16.12.1978 |
| PHILLIPS, Henry Percival | (1892-4) | b 1868 | d 26.2.1947 |
| PHILLIPS, Kevin | (1987-) |
| PHILLIPS, Louis Augustus | (1900-01) | b 24.2.1878 | d 14.3.1916 |
| PHILLIPS, William David | (1881-4) | b 16.8.1855 | d 15.10.1918 |
| PICKERING, David Francis | (1983-) | b 16.12.1960 |
| PLUMMER, Reginald Clifford Stanley | (1912-13) | b 29.12.1888 | d 18.6.1953 |
| POOK, Thomas | (1895) |
| POWELL, Graham | (1957) | b 17.11.1932 |
| POWELL, Jack | (1906) |
| POWELL, Jack | (1923) |
| POWELL, Richard W. | (1888) |
| POWELL, Wickham C. | (1926-35) | b 1905 | d 1973 |
| POWELL, Wickham James | (1920) | b 13.9.1892 | d 20.3.1961 |
| PRICE, Brian | (1961-9) | b 30.10.1937 |
| PRICE, Graham | (1975-83) | b 24.11.1951 |
| PRICE, Malcolm John | (1959-62) | b 8.12.1937 |
| PRICE, Ronald E. | (1939) | b 16.9.1915 |
| PRICE, Terence Graham | (1965-7) | b 1945 |
| PRIDAY, Alun James | (1958-61) | b 23.1.1933 |
| PRITCHARD Cecil | (1928-9) |
| PRITCHARD Clifford Charles | (1904-06) | b 1.10.1881 | d 14.12.1954 |
| PRITCHARD, Charles Meyrick | (1904-10) | b 30.9.1882 | d 14.8.1916 |
| PROSSER, Frederick John | (1921) | b 15.12.1892 |
| PROSSER, Glyn | (1934-6) | | d 1.1973 |
| PROSSER, David Rees | (1934) | b 13.10.1912 | d 6.5.1973 |
| PROSSER, Thomas Raymond | (1956-61) | b 2.3.1930 |
| PROTHEROE, Gareth John | (1964-6) | b 7.12.1941 |
| PRYCE-JENKINS, Thomas John | (1888) | b 1.2.1864 | d 6.8.1922 |
| PUGH, Charles Henry | (1924-5) | b 7.3.1896 | d 23.1.1951 |
| PUGSLEY, Joseph | (1910-11) | b 10.5.1885 | d 13.6.1976 |
| PULLMAN, Joseph J. | (1910) |
| PURDON, F.T. | (1881-3) |

| PLAYER | CAREER SPAN | |
|---|---|---|
| QUINNELL, Derek Leslie | (1972-80) | b 22.5.1949 |
| RADFORD, William J. | (1923) | b 4.1889 | d 1.1.1924 |
| RALPH, Albert Raymond | (1931-2) | b 21.1.1908 |
| RAMSEY, Samuel H. | (1896-1904) | b 1874 |
| RANDALL, Robert | (1924) |
| RAYBOULD, William Henry | (1967-70) | b 6.5.1944 |
| REES, Aeron | (1919) |
| REES, Alan | (1962) | b 17.2.1938 |
| REES, Arthur Morgan | (1934-8) | b 20.11.1912 |
| REES, Brian Idris | (1967) | b 28.8.1942 |
| REES, Clive Frederick William | (1974-83) | b 6.10.1951 |
| REES, Dan | (1900-05) | b 1876 |
| REES, Douglas | (1968) | b 1944 |
| REES, Evan B. | (1919) |
| REES, Harold Elgan | (1979-83) | b 5.1.1954 |
| REES, Henry | (1937-8) | | d 1.7.1976 |
| REES, John Idwal | (1934-38) | b 25.7.1910 |
| REES, John Conway | (1892-4) | b 13.1.1870 | d 30.8.1932 |
| REES, Joseph | (1920-4) | b 3.6.1893 | d 12.4.1950 |
| REES, Lewis Morgan | (1933) | b 17.1.1910 | d 21.12.1976 |
| REES, Peter | (1947) | b 8.2.1925 |
| REES, Peter M. | (1961-4) | b 1938 |
| REES, Theophilus Aneurin | (1881) | b 1858 | d 11.9.1932 |
| REES, Thomas Edgar | (1926-8) | b 22.8.1904 | d 10.11.1968 |
| REES, Thomas James | (1935-7) | b 8.5.1913 |
| REES-JONES, Geoffrey Rippon | (1934-6) | b 8.7.1914 |
| REEVES, Frederick Charles | (1920-1) | b 12.1.1892 | d 1976 |
| RHAPPS, John James | (1897) | b 7.1877 | d 23.1.1950 |
| RICE-EVANS, Walter | (1890-1) | b 10.9.1865 | d 9.6.1909 |
| RICHARDS, Bryan | (1960) | b 23.11.1932 |
| RICHARDS, Clifford | (1922-4) | b 1901 |
| RICHARDS, David Stuart | (1979-83) | b 23.5.1954 |
| RICHARDS, E.S. | (1885-7) |
| RICHARDS, Ernest Gwyn | (1927) | b 22.12.1905 | d 17.12.1985 |
| RICHARDS, Huw David | (1986-) | b 9.10.1960 |
| RICHARDS, Idris | (1925) | | d 1962 |
| RICHARDS, Kenneth Henry Llewellyn | (1960-61) | b 29.1.1934 | d 8.1.1972 |
| RICHARDS, Maurice Charles Rees | (1968-9) | b 2.2.1945 |
| RICHARDS, Rees | (1913) |
| RICHARDS, Rex | (1956) | b 4.2.1934 |
| RICHARDS, T.L. | (1923) |
| RICHARDSON, Stanley John | (1978-9) | b 1.4.1949 |
| RICKARDS, Arnold Robert | (1924) | b 17.8.1901 |
| RING, John | (1921) | b 13.11.1900 | d 10.11.1984 |
| RING, Mark Gerard | (1983-) | b 15.10.1962 |
| RINGER, Paul | (1978-80) | b 28.1.1951 |
| ROBERTS, Cyril | (1958) | b 19.12.1930 |
| ROBERTS, David Edward Arfon | (1930) | b 23.1.1909 |
| ROBERTS, Evan | (1886-7) | b 1861 | d 16.10.1927 |
| ROBERTS, Edward J. | (1888-9) | b 1868 | d 1940 |
| ROBERTS, Gareth John | (1985-) | b 15.1.1959 |
| ROBERTS, H. Meiron | (1960-3) | b 1934 |
| ROBERTS, John | (1927-9) | b 1908 | d 1968 |
| ROBERTS, Michael Gordon | (1971-9) | b 20.2.1946 |
| ROBERTS, Tom | (1921-3) | b 1897 |
| ROBERTS, William | (1929) | b 20.2.1909 |
| ROBINS, John Denning | (1950-3) | b 17.5.1926 |
| ROBINS, Russell John | (1953-7) | b 1932 |
| ROBINSON, Ian R. | (1974) | b 21.2.1946 |
| ROCYN-JONES, David Nathan | (1925) | b 17.7.1902 | d 26.1.1984 |
| RODERICK, William Buckley | (1884) | b 17.1.1862 | d 1.2.1908 |
| ROSSER, Melville A. | (1924) | b 18.4.1901 |
| ROWLAND, Ernest Melville | (1885) | b 21.9.1864 |
| ROWLANDS, Charles Foster | (1926) | b 1900 | d 10.11.1958 |
| ROWLANDS, Daniel Clive Thomas | (1963-5) | b 14.5.1938 |
| ROWLANDS, Gwyn | (1953-6) | b 19.12.1928 |

| PLAYER | CAREER SPAN | | |
|---|---|---|---|
| ROWLANDS, Keith A. | (1962-5) | b 7.2.1936 | |
| ROWLES, George R. | (1892) | | |
| | | | |
| SAMUEL, David | (1891-3) | b 1868 | d 1943 |
| SAMUEL, Fred | (1922) | | |
| SAMUEL J. | (1891) | | |
| SCOURFIELD, Thomas | (1930) | b 1909 | d 2.1976 |
| SCRINE, Frederick | | | |
| George | (1899-1901) | b 25.3.1877 | d 1962 |
| SHANKLIN, James | | | |
| Llewellyn | (1970-3) | b 11.12.1948 | |
| SHAW, Glyndwr | (1972-77) | b 11.4.1951 | |
| SHAW, Terence Windsor | (1983) | b 9.8.1962 | |
| SHEA, Jeremiah | (1919-21) | b 8.1892 | |
| SHELL, Roger Clive | (1973) | b 9.9.1947 | |
| SIMPSON, H.J. | (1884) | | |
| SKRIMSHIRE, Reginald | | | |
| Truscott | (1899) | b 30.1.1878 | d 20.9.1963 |
| SKYM, Archibald | (1928-35) | b 12.7.1906 | d 15.6.1970 |
| SMITH, J. Sidney | (1884-5) | | |
| SPARKS, Brian Anthonie | (1954-7) | b 23.6.1931 | |
| SPILLER, William John | (1910-13) | b 8.7.1886 | d 9.6.1970 |
| SQUIRE, Jeffrey | (1977-83) | b 23.9.1951 | |
| STADDEN, William James | | | |
| Wood | (1884-90) | b 1861 | d 30.12.1906 |
| STEPHENS, Glyn | (1912-19) | b 29.11.1891 | d 22.4.1965 |
| STEPHENS, Ian | (1981-) | b 25.5.1952 | |
| STEPHENS, John Griffith | (1922) | b 30.10.1893 | d 14.5.1956 |
| STEPHENS, John Rees | | | |
| Glyn | (1947-57) | b 16.4.1922 | |
| STOCK, Albert R. | (1924-6) | b 18.4.1898 | |
| STONE, Peter | (1949) | b 20.6.1924 | d 10.7.1971 |
| STRAND-JONES, John | (1902-03) | b 2.12.1877 | d 3.4.1958 |
| SUMMERS, Richard | | | |
| Henry Bowlas | (1881) | b 30.7.1860 | d 22.12.1941 |
| SUTTON, Stephen | (1982-) | b 17.2.1958 | |
| SWEET-ESCOTT, Ralph | | | |
| Bond | (1891-5) | b 11.1.1869 | d 10.11.1907 |
| | | | |
| TAMPLIN, William Ewart | (1947-8) | | |
| TANNER, Haydn | (1935-49) | b 9.1.1917 | |
| TARR, Donald James | (1935) | b 11.3.1910 | d 4.6.1980 |
| TAYLOR, Albert Russell | (1937-9) | b 20.12.1914 | d 9.10.1965 |
| TAYLOR, Charles Gerard | (1884-7) | b 1864 | d 24.1.1915 |
| TAYLOR, John | (1967-73) | b 21.7.1945 | |
| THOMAS, Alan | (1963-4) | b 1940 | |
| THOMAS, Alun Gruffydd | (1952-5) | b 1926 | |
| THOMAS, Beriah | | | |
| Melbourne Gwynne | (1919-24) | b 11.6.1896 | d 23.3.1966 |
| THOMAS, Brian Edwin | (1963-9) | b 18.5.1940 | |
| THOMAS, Charles J. | (1888-91) | | |
| THOMAS, Cyril Rhys | (1925) | b 27.3.1902 | d 1975 |
| THOMAS, David | (1961) | b 1939 | |
| THOMAS, David John | (1930-5) | b 30.3.1909 | |
| THOMAS, David J. | (1904-12) | b 1880 | d 19.10.1925 |
| THOMAS, David Leyshon | (1937) | b 3.1909 | d 28.9.1952 |
| THOMAS, Edward John | | | |
| Richard | (1906-09) | b 1881 | d 7.7.1916 |
| THOMAS, Edwin | (1904-10) | b 1878 | d 11.1961 |
| THOMAS, George | (1888-1891) | | |
| THOMAS, Harold | (1912) | | |
| THOMAS, Harold Watkin | (1936-7) | b 19.2.1914 | |
| THOMAS, Horace | | | |
| Wyndham | (1912-13) | b 1891 | d 3.9.1916 |
| THOMAS, Ivor | (1924) | b 30.4.1900 | |
| THOMAS, James Denzil | (1954) | b 21.4.1929 | |
| THOMAS, Lewis Cobden | (1885) | b 1865 | |
| THOMAS, Malcolm | | | |
| Campbell | (1949-59) | b 25.4.1929 | |
| THOMAS, Rees | (1909-13) | b 1882 | d 14.6.1926 |
| THOMAS, Richard | | | |
| Clement Charles | (1949-59) | b 28.1.1929 | |
| THOMAS, Robert | (1900-01) | b 1871 | d 2.1910 |
| THOMAS, Rowland Lewis | (1889-1892) | b 1863 | d 21.1.1949 |
| THOMAS, Samuel Gethin | (1923) | b 1898 | d 1.2.1939 |
| THOMAS, Stephen | (1890-1) | b 1865 | d 10.1937 |
| THOMAS, Watcyn Gwyn | (1927-33) | b 16.1.1906 | d 10.8.1977 |
| THOMAS, William Delme | (1966-74) | b 12.9.1942 | |
| THOMAS, William Henry | (1885-91) | b 22.3.1866 | d 10.1921 |
| THOMAS, William J. | (1961-3) | b 1.9.1933 | |
| THOMAS, William | | | |
| Llewellyn | (1894-5) | b 6.5.1872 | d 19.1.1943 |

| PLAYER | CAREER SPAN | | |
|---|---|---|---|
| THOMAS, W. Trevor | (1930) | b 1909 | |
| THOMPSON, Joseph | | | |
| Francis | (1923) | b 22.12.1902 | d 13.10.1983 |
| THORBURN, Paul Huw | (1985-) | b 24.11.1962 | |
| TITLEY, Mark Howard | (1983-) | b 3.5.1959 | |
| TOWERS, W.H. | (1887-8) | | |
| TRAVERS, George | (1903-11) | b 9.6.1877 | d 26.12.1945 |
| TRAVERS, William Henry | (1937-49) | b 2.12.1913 | |
| TREHARNE, E. | (1881-3) | | |
| TREW, William John | (1900-13) | b 1878 | d 20.8.1926 |
| TROTT, R. Frank | (1948-9) | | d 28.3.1987 |
| TRUMAN, William Harry | (1934-5) | b 11.12.1909 | d 26.7.1984 |
| TRUMP, Leonard Charles | (1912) | b 23.4.1887 | d 9.6.1948 |
| TURNBULL, Bernard | | | |
| Ruel | (1925-30) | b 16.10.1904 | d 7.4.1984 |
| TURNBULL, Maurice | | | |
| Joseph Lawson | (1933) | b 16.3.1906 | d 5.8.1944 |
| | | | |
| UZZELL, Henry | (1912-20) | b 6.1.1883 | d 20.12.1960 |
| UZZELL, John R. | (1963-5) | b 1942 | |
| | | | |
| VICKERY, Walter | (1938-9) | b 25.10.1909 | |
| VILE, Thomas Henry | (1908-21) | b 1.9.1883 | d 30.10.1958 |
| VINCENT, Hugh Corbet | (1882) | b 22.4.1862 | d 22.2.1931 |
| | | | |
| WALDRON, Ronald | (1965) | b 1934 | |
| WALLER, Philip Dudley | (1908-10) | b 28.1.1889 | d 14.12.1917 |
| WALTERS, Nathaniel | (1902) | b 23.5.1875 | d 22.2.1956 |
| WANBON, Robert | (1968) | b 1944 | |
| WARD, William | (1934) | | |
| WARLOW, John | (1962) | b 13.2.39 | |
| WATERS, David Ralph | (1986-) | b 4.6.1955 | |
| WATKINS, David | (1963-7) | b 5.3.1942 | |
| WATKINS, Edward | (1924) | b 27.3.1899 | d 12.10.1983 |
| WATKINS, Edward | (1935-9) | b 2.3.1916 | |
| WATKINS, Emlyn | (1926) | b 21.9.1904 | d 15.5.1978 |
| WATKINS, Henry | | | |
| Vaughan | (1904-06) | b 1881 | d 16.5.1945 |
| WATKINS, Leonard | (1881) | b 7.12.1859 | d 7.2.1901 |
| WATKINS, Michael John | (1984) | b 9.1.1952 | |
| WATKINS, Stuart John | (1964-70) | b 5.6.1941 | |
| WATKINS, William | (1959) | | |
| WATT, William James | (1914) | b 16.5.1890 | d 16.9.1950 |
| WATTS, David | (1914) | b 14.3.1886 | |
| WATTS, James | (1907-09) | b 1878 | d 2.1933 |
| WATTS, Wallace Howard | (1892-6) | b 25.3.1870 | d 29.4.1950 |
| WEAVER, David | (1964) | | |
| WEBB, James | (1907-12) | b 1883 | d 2.1955 |
| WEBB, James E. | (1888-9) | b 1862 | d 8.3.1913 |
| WEBBE, Glenfield Michael | | | |
| Charles | (1986-) | b 21.1.1962 | |
| WELLS, Gordon | (1955-8) | | |
| WESTACOTT, David | (1906) | b 1882 | d 28.8.1917 |
| WETTER, John James | (1914-24) | b 29.12.1889 | d 29.7.1967 |
| WETTER, William Henry | (1913) | b 1880 | d 12.1933 |
| WHEEL, Geoffrey Arthur | | | |
| Derek | (1974-82) | b 30.6.1951 | |
| WHEELER, Paul J. | (1967-8) | b 1947 | |
| WHITEFOOT, Jeffrey | (1984-) | b 18.4.1956 | |
| WHITFIELD, Jack | (1919-24) | b 23.3.1893 | d 26.12.1927 |
| WHITSON, Geoffrey | | | |
| Keith | (1956-60) | b 4.12.1930 | d 18.5.1984 |
| WILLIAMS, Bleddyn | | | |
| Llewellyn | (1947-55) | b 22.2.1923 | |
| WILLIAMS, Brinley | (1920) | b 3.4.1895 | d 5.1.1987 |
| WILLIAMS, Clifford | (1924-5) | b 20.4.1898 | d 28.5.1930 |
| WILLIAMS, Clive | (1977-) | b 2.11.1948 | |
| WILLIAMS, Charles | | | |
| Derek | (1955-6) | b 28.11.1924 | |
| WILLIAMS, David | | | |
| Brynmor | (1978-81) | b 29.10.1951 | |
| WILLIAMS, Denzil | (1963-71) | b 17.10.1939 | |
| WILLIAMS, Edwin | (1925) | b 14.10.1898 | d 31.1.1983 |
| WILLIAMS, Evan | (1924-5) | b 18.6.1906 | d 18.11.1976 |
| WILLIAMS, Frank | | | |
| Llewellyn | (1929-33) | | |
| WILLIAMS, Gareth | | | |
| Powell | (1980-2) | b 6.11.1954 | |
| WILLIAMS, Gerald | (1981-82) | b 21.10.1954 | |
| WILLIAMS, Gerwyn | (1950-4) | b 22.4.1924 | |
| WILLIAMS, Griff | (1936) | b 30.6.1907 | |

| PLAYER | CAREER SPAN | | |
|---|---|---|---|
| WILLIAMS, Henry Raymond | (1954-8) | b 3.11.1927 | |
| WILLIAMS, Jack | (1920-1) | b 1891 | d 6.12.1965 |
| WILLIAMS, John Frederick | (1905-06) | b 18.11.1882 | d 28.8.1911 |
| WILLIAMS, John James | (1973-79) | b 1.4.1948 | |
| WILLIAMS, John Lewis | (1906-11) | b 3.1.1882 | d 12.7.1916 |
| WILLIAMS, John Peter Rhys | (1969-81) | b 2.3.1949 | |
| WILLIAMS, Lloyd H. | (1957-62) | b 1932 | |
| WILLIAMS, Mapson | (1923) | b 1895 | |
| WILLIAMS, Oswald | (1947-8) | b 12.4.1921 | |
| WILLIAMS, Rhys Haydn | (1954-60) | b 14.7.1930 | |
| WILLIAMS, Richard David Garnons | (1881) | b 15.6.1856 | d 27.9.1915 |
| WILLIAMS, Robert F. | (1912-14) | | |
| WILLIAMS, Sydney Arthur | (1939) | b 17.4.1918 | d 28.8.1976 |
| WILLIAMS, Stanley | (1947-8) | b 1914 | d 21.11.1967 |
| WILLIAMS, T. | (1888) | | |
| WILLIAMS, Trevor | (1935-7) | | |
| WILLIAMS, Tom | (1882) | | d 4.2.1913 |
| WILLIAMS, Tom | (1912-14) | b 1887 | d 9.9.1927 |
| WILLIAMS, Tudor | (1921) | b 1892 | d 1922 |

| PLAYER | CAREER SPAN | | |
|---|---|---|---|
| WILLIAMS, Walter P.J. | (1974) | b 14.11.1943 | d 10.3.1985 |
| WILLIAMS, William Arthur | (1927) | b 29.12.1905 | d 4.11.1973 |
| WILLIAMS, William A. | (1952-3) | | |
| WILLIAMS, William Edward Osborne | (1887-90) | b 15.12.1866 | d 22.6.1945 |
| WILLIAMS, William Henry | (1900-01) | b 1873 | d 9.1.1936 |
| WILLIAMS, William Leslie Thomas | (1947-9) | b 1921 | |
| WILLIAMS, William Owen Gooding | (1951-6) | b 11.1929 | |
| WILLIS, William Rex | (1950-5) | b 25.10.1924 | |
| WILTSHIRE, Max | (1967-8) | b 1939 | |
| WINDSOR, Robert William | (1973-9) | b 31.1.1948 | |
| WINFIELD, Herbert Benjamin | (1903-08) | b 1879 | d 21.9.1919 |
| WINMILL, Stanley | (1921) | b 1889 | d 1940 |
| WOOLLER, Wilfred | (1933-39) | b 20.11.1912 | |
| WYATT, Mark Anthony | (1983- ) | b 12.2.1957 | |
| YOUNG, George Avery | (1886) | b 1863 | d 23.1.1900 |
| YOUNG, Jeffrey | (1968-73) | b 16.9.1943 | |

# FRANCE

| PLAYER | CAREER SPAN | | | PLAYER | CAREER SPAN | | |
|---|---|---|---|---|---|---|---|
| ABADIE, André | (1964) | b 27.7.1934 | | BIANCHI, Jérôme | (1986- ) | b 31.7.1961 | |
| ABADIE, Alain | (1965-8) | b 15.8.1946 | | BICHINDARITZ, Jean | (1954) | b 3.5.1928 | |
| ABADIE, Lucien | (1963) | | | BIDART, Laurent | (1953) | b 11.1.1930 | |
| AGUERRE, Roger | (1979) | b 13.3.1957 | | BIEMOURET, Jean-Paul | (1969-73) | b 1.4.1943 | |
| AGUILAR, David | (1937) | b 25.10.1905 | d 5.8.1967 | BIENES, René | (1950-6) | b 2.8.1923 | |
| AGUIRRE, Jean-Michel | (1971-80) | b 2.11.1951 | | BIGOT, Charles | (1930-1) | b 4.2.1906 | d 25.8.1979 |
| AINCIART, Edouard | (1933-8) | b 21.12.1908 | | BILBAO, Louis | (1978-9) | b 14.9.1956 | |
| ALBALADEJO, Pierre | (1954-64) | b 13.2.1933 | | BILLAC, Eugène | (1920-3) | b 16.3.1898 | d 29.11.1957 |
| ALVAREZ, André | (1945-51) | b 26.5.1923 | | BILLIERE, Michel | (1968) | b 16.7.1943 | |
| AMAND, Henri | (1906) | b 17.9.1873 | d 1967 | BIOUSSA, Alex | (1924-30) | b 7.3.1902 | |
| AMBERT, Albert | (1930) | | | BIOUSSA, Clovis | (1913-14) | b 1892 | |
| AMESTOY, Jean-Baptiste | (1964) | b 28.8.1936 | | BIRABEN, Maurice | (1920-2) | b 1892 | d 25.3.1963 |
| ANDRE, Géo | (1913-14) | b 13.8.1889 | d 4.5.1943 | BLAIN, Antoine | (1934) | | |
| ANDRIEU, Marc | (1986- ) | b 19.9.1959 | | BLANCO, Serge | (1980-) | b 31.8.1958 | |
| ANDURAN, Joe | (1910) | | d 1914/18 | BLOND, Jean | (1935-8) | b 11.4.1909 | |
| ARAOU, René | (1924) | b 18.10.1902 | d 1.1955 | BOFFELLI, Victor | (1971-5) | b 30.3.1947 | |
| ARCALIS, Roger | (1950-1) | b 1.6.1927 | | BONAL, Jean-Marie | (1968-70) | b 12.12.1945 | |
| ARINO, Michel | (1962) | | | BONAMY, Raoul | (1928) | b 13.12.1905 | |
| ARISTOUY, Pierre | (1948-50) | b 18.10.1920 | d 17.5.1974 | BONIFACE, André | (1954-66) | b 14.8.1934 | |
| ARNAL, Jean-Marie | (1914) | b 1892 | d 1958 | BONIFACE, Guy | (1960-66) | b 6.3.1937 | d 31.12.1967 |
| ARNAUDET, Michel | (1964-7) | b 11.3.1943 | | BONNES, Etienne | (1924) | | |
| AROTCA, René | (1938) | | | BONNEVAL, Eric | (1984-) | b 19.11.1963 | |
| ARRIETA, Julien | (1953) | b 3.9.1924 | | BONNUS, Firmin | (1950) | b 25.8.1924 | d 26.4.1970 |
| ASTRE, Richard | (1971-6) | b 28.8.1948 | | BONNUS, Michel | (1937-40) | | |
| AUGE, Joseph | (1929) | | | BONTEMPS, Dominique | (1968) | b 27.5.1946 | |
| AUGRAS-FABRE, Lucien | (1931) | b 13.8.1912 | | BORCHARD, Georges | (1908-11) | b 25.12.1885 | d 4.1962 |
| AVEROUS, Jean-Luc | (1975-81) | b 22.10.1954 | | BORDE, François | (1920-6) | b 8.12.1899 | |
| AZARETE, Jean-Louis | (1969-75) | b 8.5.1945 | | BORDENAVE, Léon | (1948-9) | b 11.5.1920 | |
| | | | | BOUBEE, Jean | (1921-5) | b 11.10.1900 | d 3.1973 |
| BADER, Edouard | (1926-7) | b 26.7.1899 | | BOUDREAU, R. | (1910) | | d 1914/18 |
| BADIN, Christian | (1973-5) | b 11.9.1949 | | BOUGUYON, Gérard | (1961) | b 24.11.1935 | |
| BAILLETTE, Marcel | (1925-32) | b 12.10.1904 | d 4.1987 | BOUJET, Christian | (1968) | b 29.8.1942 | |
| BALADIE, Georges | (1945-6) | b 20.5.1917 | | BOUQUET, Jacques | (1954-62) | b 3.7.1933 | |
| BALLARIN, Jacques | (1924-5) | | | BOURDEU, Jean-Roger | (1952-3) | b 6.1.1927 | |
| BAQUET, Jean | (1921) | | | BOURGAREL, Roger | (1969-73) | b 21.4.1947 | |
| BARBAZANGES, Antonin | (1932-3) | | | BOUSQUET, Adolphe | (1921-4) | b 14.11.1899 | |
| BARRAU, Max | (1971-4) | b 26.11.1950 | | BOUSQUET, René | (1926-30) | b 19.3.1903 | d 1960 |
| BARRERE, Paul | (1929-31) | b 1905 | | BOYAU, Maurice | (1912-13) | b 1889 | d 16.9.1918 |
| BARRIERE, Raoul | (1960) | b 3.3.1928 | | BOYER, Paul | (1935) | b 19.5.1908 | |
| BARTHE, E. | (1925) | | | BRANCA, Gérard | (1928-9) | b 29.12.1903 | |
| BARTHE, Jean | (1954-9) | b 22.7.1932 | | BRANLAT, Albert | (1906-08) | | |
| BASAURI, Robert | (1954) | b 30.8.1934 | | BREJASSOU, René | (1952-55) | b 12.8.1929 | |
| BASCOU, Paulin | (1914) | | | BRETHES, Roger | (1960) | b 31.1.1935 | |
| BASQUET, Guy | (1945-52) | b 13.7.1921 | | BRINGEON, Adolphe | (1925) | b 23.1.1898 | d 14.5.1944 |
| BASTIAT, Jean-Pierre | (1969-78) | b 11.4.1949 | | BRUN, Georges | (1950-3) | b 23.12.1922 | |
| BAUDRY, Noel | (1949) | b 1.4.1914 | | BRUNEAU, Maurice | (1910-13) | b 1.8.1883 | |
| BAULON, Robert | (1954-7) | b 22.10.1930 | | BRUNET, Yves | (1975-7) | b 25.8.1950 | |
| BAUX, Jean-Paul | (1968) | b 16.6.1946 | | BUCHET, Eric | (1980-) | b 28.11.1957 | |
| BAVOZET, Jacques | (1911) | b 1887 | | BUISSON, Henri | (1931) | b 4.8.1904 | |
| BAYARD, Jean | (1923-4) | | | BUONOMO, Yvan | (1971-2) | b 19.9.1946 | |
| BAYARDON, Jacques | (1964) | b 25.1.1934 | | BURGUN, Marcel | (1909-14) | b 1887 | d 1915 |
| BEAURIN, Charles | (1907-08) | | | BUSTAFFA, Daniel | (1977-80) | b 11.1.1956 | |
| BEGU, Jacques | (1982-84) | b 22.4.1957 | | BUZY, Eugène | (1946-9) | b 13.2.1917 | |
| BEGUERIE, Christian | (1979) | b 26.7.1951 | | | | | |
| BEGUET, Louis | (1922-24) | b 7.12.1894 | d 3.1983 | CABANIER, Jean-Michel | (1963-68) | b 13.5.1936 | |
| BEHOTEGUY, André | (1923-9) | b 19.10.1900 | d 1960 | CABROL, Henri | (1972-4) | b 11.2.1947 | |
| BEHOTEGUY, Henri | (1923-8) | b 18.10.1898 | | CADENAT, Jules | (1910-13) | b 9.1885 | d 1965 |
| BELASCAIN, Christian | (1977-83) | b 1.11.1953 | | CAHUC, François | (1922) | | |
| BELLETANTE, Guy | (1951) | b 13.3.1927 | | CALS, Robert | (1938) | b 19.3.1913 | |
| BENESIS, René | (1969-74) | b 29.8.1944 | | CALVO, Guy | (1961) | b 13.5.1933 | |
| BENETIERE, Jean | (1954) | | | CAMBERABERO, Didier | (1982-) | b 9.1.1961 | |
| BERBIZIER, Pierre | (1981- ) | b 17.6.1958 | | CAMBERABERO, Guy | (1961-68) | b 27.5.1936 | |
| BEREJNOI, Jean-Claude | (1963-7) | b 20.4.1939 | | CAMBERABERO, Lilian | (1964-68) | b 15.7.1937 | |
| BERGES, Bernard | (1926) | | | CAMBRE, Théo | (1920) | | |
| BERGES-CAU, René | (1976) | b 28.2.1949 | d 22.5.1983 | CAMEL, André | (1928-35) | b 9.1.1905 | |
| BERGEZE, Félix | (1936-8) | b 11.1.1914 | | CAMEL, Marcel | (1929) | b 9.1.1905 | |
| BERGOUGNAN, Yves | (1945-9) | b 8.5.1924 | | CAMICAS, Fernand | (1927-9) | b 7.5.1899 | d 11.5.1973 |
| BERNARD, René | (1951) | b 11.5.1925 | | CAMO, Ernest | (1931-2) | | d 10.1978 |
| BERNON, Jean | (1922-3) | | | CAMPAES, André | (1965-73) | b 30.3.1944 | |
| BEROT, Jean-Louis | (1968-74) | b 28.7.1947 | | CANTONI, Jack | (1970-5) | b 11.5.1948 | |
| BEROT, Philippe | (1986-) | b 29.1.1965 | | CAPDOUZE, Jean | (1964-5) | b 30.8.1942 | |
| BERTRAND, Pierre | (1951-53) | b 27.10.1927 | | CAPENDEGUY, Jean-Michel | (1967) | b 5.3.1944 | d 1.1.1968 |
| BERTRANNE, Roland | (1971-81) | b 6.12.1949 | | CAPITANI, Philibert | (1954) | b 1.8.1928 | |
| BESSET, Edmond | (1924) | | | CAPMAU, – | (1914) | | |
| BESSET, Lucien | (1914) | b 4.1.1892 | d 22.4.1975 | CARABIGNAC, Georges ("Jo") | (1951-3) | b 10.10.1929 | d 22.2.1973 |
| BESSON, Marcel | (1924-7) | b 1901 | | | | | |
| BESSON, Pierre, | (1963-8) | b 11.4.1940 | | | | | |

| PLAYER | CAREER SPAN | | |
|---|---|---|---|
| CARBONNE, P. | (1927) | | |
| CARMINATI, Alain | (1986-) | b 17.8.1966 | |
| CARON, Lucien | (1947-9) | b 16.12.1916 | d 12.1984 |
| CARPENTIER, Manuel | (1980-2) | b 14.10.1959 | |
| CARRERE, Christian | (1966-71) | b 27.7.1943 | |
| CARRERE, Jean | (1956-9) | b 5.4.1930 | |
| CARRERE, Robert | (1953) | b 13.3.1921 | |
| CASAUX, Louis | (1959-62) | b 15.7.1938 | |
| CASSAGNE, Paul | (1957) | b 22.1.1931 | |
| CASSAYET, Aimé | (1920-7) | b 1898 | d 26.5.1927 |
| CASSIEDE, Marcel | (1961) | b 24.8.1934 | |
| CASTETS, Jean | (1923) | b 7.9.1900 | d 3.1937 |
| CAUJOLLE, Jean | (1909-14) | b 1888 | d 1946 |
| CAUNEGRE, Robert | (1938) | | |
| CAUSSADE, Alain | (1978-81) | b 27.7.1952 | |
| CAUSSARIEU, Georges | (1929) | | d 9.1974 |
| CAYREFOURCQ, Edmond | (1921) | | |
| CAZALS, Pierre | (1961) | b 8.2.1931 | |
| CAZENAVE, Albert | (1927-8) | b 7.3.1902 | d 9.1982 |
| CAZENAVE, Fernand | (1950-4) | b 26.11.1924 | |
| CELAYA, Michel | (1953-61) | b 27.7.1930 | |
| CELHAY, Maurice | (1935-40) | b 17.5.1911 | |
| CESSIEUX, Noël | (1906) | b 22.12.1879 | d 1948 |
| CESTER, Elie | (1966-74) | b 27.7.1942 | |
| CHABAN-DELMAS, Jacques | (1945) | | |
| CHABOWSKI, Hervé | (1985-) | b 8.1959 | |
| CHADEBACH, Pierre | (1982-) | b 3.5.1959 | |
| CHAMP, Eric | (1985-) | b 8.6.1962 | |
| CHAPUY, Léon | (1926) | | |
| CHARPENTIER, Gilbert | (1911-12) | | |
| CHARTON, Pierre | (1940) | | |
| CHARVET, Denis | (1986-) | b 12.5.1962 | |
| CHASSAGNE, Jean | (1938) | | |
| CHATEAU, Albert | (1913) | | |
| CHAUD, Eugène | (1932-5) | b 2.3.1906 | |
| CHENEVAY, Claude | (1968) | b 9.2.1943 | |
| CHEVALLIER, Bernard | (1952-7) | b 7.9.1925 | |
| CHIBERRY, Jacques | (1955) | | |
| CHILO, André | (1920-5) | b 5.7.1898 | |
| CHOLLEY, Gérard | (1975-9) | b 6.6.1945 | |
| CHOY, Joseph | (1930-6) | b 19.8.1905 | |
| CIMAROSTI, Jacques | (1976) | b 23.10.1950 | |
| CLADY, André | (1929-31) | | |
| CLARAC, Henri | (1938) | b 13.10.1912 | |
| CLAUDEL, Roger | (1932-4) | | d 1945 |
| CLAUZEL, François | (1924-5) | b 19.3.1900 | d 27.10.1965 |
| CLAVE, Jean | (1936-8) | b 2.3.1915 | |
| CLAVERIE, Henri | (1954) | b 21.1.1925 | |
| CLEMENT, Jean Pierre Laurent | (1921-3) | b 25.9.1899 | d 1945 |
| CLEMENT, Pierre | (1931) | b 1906 | |
| CLEMENTE, Michel | (1978-80) | b 30.11.1955 | |
| CLUCHAGUE, Louis | (1924-5) | | d 7.1978 |
| CODERC, Jean | (1932-6) | b 10.8.1908 | |
| CODORNIOU, Didier | (1979-) | b 13.2.1958 | |
| COGNET, Lucien | (1932-7) | b 22.5.1909 | |
| COLOMBIER, Jean | (1952) | b 23.9.1928 | |
| COLOMINE, Guy | (1979) | b 11.7.1955 | |
| COMBE, Julien | (1910-11) | | |
| COMBES, Gaston | (1945) | b 29.2.1920 | |
| COMMUNEAU, Marcel | (1906-13) | b 11.9.1885 | d 26.6.1971 |
| CONDOM, Jean | (1982-) | b 15.4.1960 | |
| CONIL de BEYSSAC, Jacques | (1912-14) | b 1888 | d 11.6.1918 |
| CONSTANT, Georges | (1920) | b 13.4.1899 | d 9.6.1978 |
| COSCOLL, Gilbert | (1921) | | d 8.1921 |
| COSTANTINO, Jean | (1973) | | |
| COSTES, Frédéric | (1979-80) | b 27.6.1957 | |
| COULON, J. | (1928) | | |
| CRABOS, René | (1920-4) | b 7.2.1899 | d 17.6.1964 |
| CRAMPAGNE, Jacques | (1967) | | |
| CRANCEE, Roland | (1960-1) | b 24.9.1932 | |
| CRAUSTE, Michel | (1957-66) | b 6.7.1934 | |
| CREMASCHI, Michel | (1980-4) | b 26.4.1956 | |
| CRICHTON, W.H. | (1906) | | |
| CRISTINA, Jacques | (1979) | b 7.7.1948 | |
| CUSSAC, Pierre | (1934) | b 21.8.1909 | |
| CUTZACH, Amédée | (1929) | b 4.6.1904 | |
| DAGUERRE, Francis | (1936) | b 31.10.1908 | |

| PLAYER | CAREER SPAN | | |
|---|---|---|---|
| DAGUERRE, Jean | (1933) | b 12.9.1907 | |
| DANION, Jean | (1924) | | |
| DANOS, Pierre | (1954-60) | b 4.6.1929 | |
| DARBOS, Pierre | (1969) | | |
| DARRACQ, Roland | (1957) | b 20.1.1933 | |
| DARRIEUSSECQ, André | (1973) | b 4.6.1947 | |
| DARRIEUSSECQ, Jean | (1953) | b 6.3.1924 | |
| DARROUY, Christian | (1957-67) | b 13.1.1937 | |
| DAUDIGNON, Georges | (1928) | b 1.10.1905 | |
| DAUGA, Benoit | (1964-72) | b 8.5.1942 | |
| DAUGER, Jean, | (1945-53) | b 12.11.1919 | |
| DAULOUEDE, Pierre | (1937-40) | b 27.7.1909 | |
| DECAMPS, Paul | (1911) | | d 1914/18 |
| DEDET, Jacques | (1910-13) | b 4.3.1887 | d 4.3.1971 |
| DEDEYN, Paul | (1906) | | |
| DEDIEU, Paul | (1963-5) | b 8.5.1933 | |
| DE GREGORIO, Jean | (1960-4) | b 9.12.1935 | |
| DEHEZ, Jean-Louis | (1967-9) | b 6.5.1944 | |
| DE JOUVENCEL, Etienne | (1909) | | |
| DE LABORDERIE, Marcel | (1921-5) | b 11.1.1899 | d 1953 |
| DELAGE, Christian | (1983) | b 16.11.1954 | |
| DE MALHERBE, Henri | (1932-33) | b 9.2.1910 | |
| DE MALMANN, René | (1908-10) | | |
| DE MUISON, J. | (1910) | | |
| DELAIGUE, Gilles | (1973) | b 23.11.1949 | |
| DELQUE, Antonin | (1937-8) | | |
| DESCAMPS, Paul | (1927) | b 28.4.1903 | |
| DESCLAUX, Francis | (1949-53) | b 9.2.1926 | |
| DESCLAUX, Joseph | (1934-45) | b 1.2.1912 | |
| DESNOYER, Laurent | (1974) | b 19.5.1948 | |
| DESTARAC, Louis | (1926-7) | b 1.9.1902 | |
| DESVOUGES, Robert | (1914) | | |
| DETREZ, Pierre-Edouard | (1983-) | b 17.6.1956 | |
| DEYGAS, Marcel | (1937) | | |
| DINTRANS, Philippe | (1979-) | b 29.1.1957 | |
| DIZABO, Pierre | (1948-60) | b 4.10.1929 | |
| DOMEC, Albert | (1929) | | |
| DOMEC, Henri | (1953-8) | b 9.8.1932 | |
| DOMENECH, Amédèe | (1954-63) | b 3.5.1933 | |
| DOMERCQ, Jean | (1912) | | |
| DOROT, Jacques | (1935) | b 4.11.1906 | |
| DOSPITAL, Pierre | (1977-85) | b 15.5.1950 | |
| DOURTHE, Claude | (1966-75) | b 20.11.1948 | |
| DOUSSEAU, Emile | (1938) | b 7.3.1909 | d 28.4.1940 |
| DROITECOURT, Michel | (1972-77) | 30.10.1949 | |
| DUBERTRAND, André | (1971-6) | b 25.4.1950 | |
| DUBOIS, Daniel | (1971) | b 17.6.1944 | |
| DUBROCA, Daniel | (1979-) | b 25.4.1954 | |
| DUCHE, André | (1929) | | |
| DUCLOS, Antoine | (1931) | b 5.2.1900 | d 1979 |
| DUCOUSSO, J. | (1925) | b 12.5.1900 | |
| DUFAU, Gérard | (1948-57) | b 27.8.1924 | |
| DUFAU, Julien | (1912) | | d 1914/18 |
| DUFFAUT, Yves | (1954) | | |
| DUFOURCQ, Jacques | (1906-08) | b 19.8.1881 | d 1975 |
| DUFOUR, René | (1911) | b 13.9.1881 | d 4.2.1979 |
| DUHARD, Yves | (1980) | b 11.7.1955 | |
| DUHAU, Jean | (1928-33) | b 1.5.1906 | d 24.9.1973 |
| DULAURENS, Jacques | (1926-9) | | |
| DULUC, André | (1934) | b 2.7.1911 | |
| DU MANOIR, Yves | (1925-7) | b 11.8.1904 | d 2.1.1928 |
| DUPONT, Clément | (1923-9) | b 11.4.1899 | |
| DUPONT, Jean-Louis | (1983) | b 17.3.1956 | |
| DUPONT, Louis | (1934-8) | b 14.11.1910 | |
| DUPOUY, Albert | (1924) | | |
| DUPRAT, Bernard | (1966-72) | b 17.7.1943 | |
| DUPRE, Paul | (1909) | | d 1914/18 |
| DUPUY, Jean | (1956-64) | b 25.5.1934 | |
| DU SOUICH, Charles | (1911) | | |
| DUTIN, Bernard | (1968) | b 9.12.1944 | |
| DUTOUR, François-Xavier | (1911-13) | b 6.11.1886 | |
| DUTRAIN, Henri | (1945-9) | b 1923 | |
| DUTREY, Joseph | (1940) | b 17.9.1914 | |
| DUVAL, René | (1908-11) | b 7.10.1886 | |
| ECHAVE, Louis | (1961) | b 11.6.1934 | |
| ELISSALDE, Edmond | (1936-40) | | |
| ELISSALDE, Jean-Pierre | (1980-81) | b 31.12.1953 | |
| ERBANI, Dominique | (1981-) | b 16.8.1956 | |
| ESCAFFRE, Pierre | (1933-34) | b 1.2.1911 | |

| PLAYER | CAREER SPAN | | |
|---|---|---|---|
| ESCOMMIER, Marcel | (1955) | b 12.10.1933 | |
| ESPONDA, Jean-Michel | (1967-9) | b 24.4.1943 | |
| ESTEVE, Alain | (1971-5) | b 15.9.1946 | |
| ESTEVE, Patrick | (1982-) | b 14.2.1959 | |
| ETCHEBERRY, Jean | (1923-7) | b 27.8.1901 | |
| ETCHENIQUE, Jean-Martin | (1974-5) | b 17.1.1954 | |
| ETCHEPARE, Jean | (1922) | b 8.11.1898 | d 1970 |
| ETCHEVERRY, Marc | (1971) | b 23.8.1942 | |
| EUTROPE, A. | (1913) | | d 1914/18 |
| | | | |
| FABRE, Emile | (1937-8) | | |
| FABRE, Jean | (1963-4) | b 7.11.1935 | |
| FABRE, Lolo | (1930) | | |
| FABRE, Michel | (1981-82) | b 17.9.1956 | |
| FAILLIOT, Pierre | (1911-13) | b 21.2.1889 | d 21.12.1935 |
| FARGUES, Hector | (1923) | | |
| FAURE, Félix | (1914) | | |
| FAUVEL, Jean-Pierre | (1980) | b 9.2.1956 | |
| FAVRE, M. | (1913) | | |
| FERRAND, Lucien | (1940) | b 4.1.1909 | |
| FERRIEN, Roger | (1950) | b 9.11.1924 | |
| FINAT, René | (1932-3) | | |
| FITE, Roger | (1963) | b 13.10.1938 | |
| FORESTIER, Jacques | (1912) | b 1890 | d 27.3.1978 |
| FORGUES, Fernand | (1911-14) | b 30.11.1884 | d 12.4.1977 |
| FORT, Jacques | (1967) | b 16.1.1938 | |
| FOURCADE, Geo | (1909) | | |
| FOURES, Henri | (1951) | b 29.8.1925 | |
| FOURNET, Franck | (1950) | b 26.11.1922 | d 7.1982 |
| FOUROUX, Jacques | (1972-77) | b 24.7.1947 | |
| FRANCQUENELLE, André | (1911-13) | b 15.8.1889 | |
| FURCADE, Roger | (1952) | b 22.1.1928 | |
| | | | |
| GABERNET, Serge | (1980-83) | b 6.2.1955 | |
| GACHASSIN, Jean | (1961-9) | b 23.12.1941 | |
| GALAU, Henri | (1924) | b 17.9.1897 | d 1.2.1950 |
| GALIA, Jean | (1927-31) | b 20.3.1905 | d 18.1.1949 |
| GALLION, Jerome | (1978-) | b 4.4.1955 | |
| GALY, Joseph | (1953) | b 22.12.1929 | |
| GARUET, Jean-Pierre | (1983-) | b 15.6.1953 | |
| GASC, Jacques | (1977) | b 24.12.1949 | |
| GASPAROTTO, Guy | (1976) | b 2.6.1948 | |
| GAUBY, Georges | (1956) | b 27.6.1933 | |
| GAUDERMEN, Pierre | (1906) | | d 1948 |
| GAYRAUD, William | (1920) | b 1.5.1898 | d 9.12.1962 |
| GENESTE, Robert | (1945-9) | | |
| GENSANE, Roger | (1962-3) | b 4.2.1934 | |
| GERALD, Géo | (1927-31) | b 17.3.1904 | d 9.11.1977 |
| GERINTES, Gilbert | (1924-6) | b 16.8.1902 | d 5.1968 |
| GESCHWIND, Pierre | (1936) | | |
| GIACCARDY, Marc | (1907) | | d 1914/18 |
| GOMMES, Jacques | (1909) | | |
| GONNET, Charles Albert | (1921-7) | b 3.11.1897 | |
| GOT, Raoul | (1920-4) | b 11.10.1900 | |
| GOURDON, Jean-Francois | (1974-80) | b 8.9.1954 | |
| GOYARD, André | (1936-38) | b 27.6.1910 | d 23.8.1980 |
| GRACIET, René | (1926-30) | | |
| GRATTON, Jacques | (1984-) | b 29.11.1957 | |
| GRAULE, Vincent | (1926-31) | b 22.1.1904 | |
| GREFFE, Michel | (1968) | b 27.10.1940 | |
| GRIFFARD, Joseph | (1932-4) | b 13.11.1905 | d 13.3.1983 |
| GRUARIN, Arnaldo | (1964-8) | b 5.2.1938 | |
| GUELORGUET, Pierre | (1931) | b 10.3.1906 | d 17.4.1984 |
| GUICHEMERRE, Abel | (1920-3) | b 23.8.1889 | d 26.4.1946 |
| GUILBERT, Alain | (1975-9) | b 28.9.1950 | |
| GUILLEMIN, Pierre | (1908-11) | | d 1914/18 |
| GUILLEUX, Pierre | (1952) | b 1924 | |
| GUIRAL, Marius | (1931-3) | b 15.12.1904 | |
| | | | |
| HAGET, André | (1953-8) | b 26.4.1931 | |
| HAGET, François | (1974-) | b 1.10.1949 | |
| HAGET, Henri | (1928-30) | b 13.10.1905 | d 1968 |
| HALET, René | (1925) | b 17.3.1899 | |
| HARIZE, Dominique | (1975-7) | b 26.2.1956 | |
| HAUC, Jules | (1928-9) | b 20.5.1905 | |
| HAUSER, Michel | (1969) | b 1945 | |
| HEDEMBAIGT, Maurice | (1913-14) | | d 1914/18 |
| HERICE, Daniel | (1950) | b 7.9.1921 | |
| HERRERO, André | (1963-7) | b 28.1.1938 | |
| HERRERO, Bernard | (1983-) | b 19.9.1957 | |

| PLAYER | CAREER SPAN | | |
|---|---|---|---|
| HIQUET, Jean-Claude | (1964) | b 4.11.1939 | |
| HOCHE, Michel | (1957) | b 20.9.1932 | |
| HORTOLAND, Jean-Pierre | (1971) | | |
| HOUBLAIN, H. | (1909-10) | | |
| HOUDET, Robert | (1927-30) | | |
| HOURDEBAIGT, M. | (1909-10) | | |
| HUBERT, Albert | (1906-09) | | |
| HUTIN, Robert | (1927) | b 23.9.1903 | |
| | | | |
| ICARD, J. | (1909) | | |
| IGUINITZ, Emmanuel | (1914) | | d 1914/18 |
| IHINGOUE, Daniel | (1912) | | d 1914/18 |
| IMBERNON, Jean-François | (1976-83) | b 17.10.1951 | . |
| IRAÇABAL, Jean | (1968-74) | b 6.7.1941 | |
| ISAAC, Henri | (1907-08) | | d 1914/18 |
| ITHURRA, Etienne | (1936-7) | | |
| | | | |
| JANECZEK, Thierry | (1982-) | b 4.6.1959 | |
| JARASSE, Auguste | (1945) | b 12.2.1915 | |
| JARDEL, Jean | (1928) | | |
| JAUREGUY, Adolphe | (1920-9) | b 18.2.1898 | d 4.9.1977 |
| JAUREGUY, Pierre | (1913) | b 28.5.1891 | |
| JEANGRAND, Henri | (1921) | | |
| JEANJEAN, Pierre | (1948) | b 3.2.1924 | |
| JEROME, Georges | (1906) | | |
| JOINEL, Jean-Luc | (1977-) | b 21.9.1953 | |
| JOL, Marcel | (1947-9) | b 16.5.1923 | d 1981 |
| JUNQUAS, Louis | (1945-8) | b 11.11.1920 | |
| | | | |
| KACZOROWSKI, Daniel | (1974) | b 31.10.1952 | |
| KAEMPF, Albert | (1946) | b 30.3.1921 | |
| | | | |
| LABADIE, Paul | (1952-57) | b 27.4.1928 | |
| LABARTHETE, Robert | (1952) | b 5.10.1924 | |
| LABAZUY, Antoine | (1952-9) | b 9.2.1929 | |
| LABORDE, Claude | (1962-5) | b 25.8.1940 | |
| LACANS, Pierre | (1980-2) | b 23.4.1957 | d 30.9.1985 |
| LACASSAGNE, A. | (1906-07) | | d 1914/18 |
| LACAUSSADE, Roger | (1948) | b 30.1.1922 | |
| LACAZE, Claude | (1961-9) | b 5.3.1940 | |
| LACAZE, Henri | (1928-9) | b 11.4.1898 | |
| LACAZE, Pierre | (1958-9) | b 4.5.1934 | |
| LACAZEDIEU, Michel | (1923-9) | b 4.3.1901 | |
| LACOME, Michel | (1960) | b 28.9.1935 | |
| LACOSTE, Robert | (1914) | | |
| LACRAMPE, Félix | (1949) | b 12.12.1924 | |
| LACROIX, Pierre | (1958-63) | b 23.1.1935 | |
| LAFARGE, Yves | (1978-81) | b 16.11.1953 | |
| LAFFONT, Honoré | (1926) | | d 2.1975 |
| LAFFITTE, I.. | (1910) | | |
| LAFOND, André | (1922) | | |
| LAFOND, Jean-Baptiste | (1983-) | b 29.12.1961 | |
| LAGISQUET, Patrice | (1983-) | b 4.9.1962 | |
| LAGRANGE, Jean-Claude | (1966) | | |
| LALANDE, Max | (1923) | | |
| LANE, Gaston | (1906-13) | b 1883 | d 24.9.1914 |
| LAPORTE, Guy | (1981-) | b 15.12.1952 | |
| LARREGUY, Gilbert | (1954) | b 6.5.1931 | d 1969 |
| LARRIBEAU, Léon | (1912-14) | b 1889 | d 13.12.1916 |
| LARRIEU, Jean | (1920-3) | b 2.1.1895 | |
| LARRIEUX, Maurice | (1927) | b 18.4.1899 | d 9.7.1978 |
| LARRUE, Hervé | (1960) | b 5.7.1935 | |
| LASAOSA, Paul | (1950-5) | b 13.7.1927 | |
| LASSEGUE, Jean | (1946-9) | b 15.2.1924 | |
| LASSERRE, Jean-Claude | (1963-7) | b 12.4.1938 | |
| LASSERRE, Michel | (1967-71) | b 21.1.1940 | |
| LASSERRE, René | (1914-24) | b 9.10.1895 | d 1950 |
| LATERRADE, Guillaume | (1910-11) | b 19.5.1889 | d 13.7.1929 |
| LAUDOUAR, Jean | (1961-2) | b 3.1.1934 | |
| LAUGA, Pierre | (1950) | b 17.1.1922 | d 8.7.1984 |
| LAURENT, Auguste | (1925-6) | b 18.4.1901 | |
| LAURENT, Joseph | (1920) | | |
| LAURENT, Marcel | (1932-6) | b 17.4.1909 | |
| LAVAIL, Gilbert | (1937-40) | b 12.7.1917 | |
| LAVAUD, P. | (1914) | | |
| LAVERGNE, Pierre | (1950) | b 1923 | |
| LAVIGNE, Bernard | (1920) | | |
| LAVIGNE, Bernard | (1984-5) | b 23.8.1954 | |
| LAZIES, Henri | (1954-7) | b 1.11.1929 | |
| LE BOURHIS, René | (1961) | | |

| PLAYER | CAREER SPAN | | |
|---|---|---|---|
| LECOINTRE, Michel | (1952) | | |
| LE DROFF, Jean | (1963-71) | b 22.6.1939 | |
| LEFEVRE, Roland | (1961) | b 19.9.1936 | |
| LEFORT, Jean-Baptiste | (1938) | b 22.2.1908 | d 7.6.1982 |
| LE GOFF, Raymond | (1938) | | |
| LEGRAIN, Marcel | (1909-14) | | d 1914/18 |
| LENIENT, Jean-Jacques | (1967) | | |
| LEPATEY, Jacques | (1954-55) | b 25.9.1929 | |
| LEPATEY, Louis | (1924) | b 29.8.1898 | |
| LESCARBOURA, Jean-Patrick | (1982-) | b 12.3.1961 | |
| LESIEUR, Emile | (1906-12) | b 16.9.1885 | d 1.1985 |
| LEUVIELLE, Maurice | (1908-14) | | d 1958 |
| LEVASSEUR, Robert | (1925) | | d 1974 |
| LEVEE, Henri | (1906) | | |
| LEWIS, E.W. | (1906) | | |
| LIBAROS, Georges | (1936-40) | | |
| LIRA, Maurice | (1962-5) | b 30.4.1941 | d 26.1.1986 |
| LLARI, Roger | (1926) | b 15.3.1903 | d 20.12.1973 |
| LOBIES, Jean | (1921) | | |
| LOMBARD, François | (1934-7) | | |
| LOMBARTEIX, René | (1938) | b 22.2.1913 | |
| LONDIOS, Jacques | (1967) | b 14.1.1944 | |
| LORIEUX, Alain | (1981-) | b 26.3.1956 | |
| LOURY, André | (1927-8) | b 11.5.1900 | d 3.12.1968 |
| LOUSTEAU, Marcel | (1923) | | |
| LUBIN-LEBRERE, Marcel Frederic | (1914-25) | b 21.7.1891 | d 11.7.1972 |
| LUBRANO, André | (1972-3) | b 19.9.1946 | |
| LUX, Jean-Pierre | (1967-75) | b 9.1.1944 | |
| MACLOS, Paul | (1906-07) | | |
| MAGNANOU, Christian | (1923-30) | b 15.1.1903 | |
| MAGNOL, Louis | (1928-9) | | d 5.1979 |
| MAGOIS, Henri | (1968) | b 1.1.1947 | |
| MAJERUS, Richard | (1928-30) | b 10.6.1905 | |
| MALBET, Jean-Claude | (1967) | b 28.8.1937 | |
| MALEIG, Alain | (1979-80) | b 10.7.1952 | |
| MALQUIER, Yves | (1979) | b 7.5.1956 | |
| MANTEROLA, Thomas | (1955-7) | b 19.12.1927 | |
| MANTOULAN, Claude | (1959) | b 5.3.1936 | d 9.11.1983 |
| MARCET, Jean | (1925-6) | | |
| MARCHAL, Jean-François | (1979-80) | b 16.12.1949 | |
| MARCHAND, Robert | (1920) | | |
| MAROCCO, Philippe | (1986-) | b 14.6.1960 | |
| MAROT, Alain | (1969-76) | b 11.3.1948 | |
| MARQUESUZAA, Arnaud | (1958-60) | b 14.6.1934 | |
| MARRACQ, Henri | (1961) | | |
| MARTIN, Charles | (1909-10) | | |
| MARTIN, Henri | (1907-08) | b 29.8.1888 | |
| MARTIN, Jean-Louis | (1971-2) | b 17.4.1948 | |
| MARTIN, Lucien | (1948-50) | b 28.9.1920 | |
| MARTINE, Roger | (1952-61) | b 3.1.1930 | |
| MARTINEZ, Gérald | (1982-3) | b 30.3.1955 | |
| MAS, Francis | (1962-3) | b 8.12.1936 | |
| MASO, Joseph | (1966-73) | b 27.12.1944 | |
| MASSARE, Jean | (1945-6) | b 29.8.1922 | |
| MASSE, Alphonse | (1908-10) | | |
| MASSE, Henri | (1937) | | |
| MATHEU, Jean | (1945-51) | b 23.6.1920 | |
| MAUDUY, Gérard | (1957-61) | b 10.12.1937 | |
| MAURAN, Jacques | (1952-3) | b 1929 | |
| MAURIAT, Paul | (1907-13) | b 27.5.1887 | |
| MAURIN, | (1906) | | |
| MAURY, André | (1925-6) | | |
| MAYSONNIE, Alfred | (1908-10) | b 10.4.1884 | d 1916 |
| MENRATH, J. | (1910) | | |
| MENTHILLER, Yves | (1964-5) | b 7.12.1941 | |
| MERET, François | (1940) | | |
| MERICQ, Serge | (1959-61) | b 16.5.1937 | |
| MERQUEY, Jacques | (1950) | b 26.9.1929 | |
| MESNEL, Frank | (1986-) | b 30.6.1961 | |
| MESNY, Patrick | (1979-82) | | |
| MEYER, Gilbert-Sylvain | (1960) | b 1.6.1934 | |
| MEYNARD, Jacques | (1954-6) | b 28.9.1935 | |
| MIAS, Lucien | (1951-9) | b 28.9.1930 | |
| MILLIAND, Pierre | (1936-7) | b 27.3.1912 | d 18.5.1984 |
| MINJAT, Roger | (1945) | b 3.8.1920 | |
| MIR, Jean-Henri | (1967-8) | b 21.2.1945 | |
| MIR, Jean-Pierre | (1967) | b 6.7.1947 | |
| MOGA, Alban | (1945-9) | b 1.5.1923 | |
| MOMMEJAT, Bernard | (1958-63) | b 18.5.1934 | |

| PLAYER | CAREER SPAN | | |
|---|---|---|---|
| MONCLA, François | (1956-61) | b 1.4.1932 | |
| MONIE, René | (1956-7) | b 2.1.1934 | |
| MONNIER, Robert | (1911-12) | | |
| MONNIOT, Marcel | (1912) | | |
| MONTADE, Camille | (1925-6) | b 1.5.1901 | |
| MORAITIS, Basil | (1969) | b 2.1.1946 | |
| MOREL, André | (1954) | | |
| MORERE, Jean | (1927-8) | | |
| MOUNICQ, Paul | (1911-13) | b 9.2.1887 | d 1967 |
| MOURE, Henri | (1908) | | |
| MOUREU, Pierre | (1920-5) | b 24.8.1895 | |
| MOURNET, Adrien | (1981) | b 5.7.1953 | |
| MOURONVAL, Francis | (1909) | b 4.6.1881 | |
| MUHR, Allan H. | (1906-07) | b 1880 | d 1939/45 |
| MURILLO, Gérard | (1954) | | |
| NAMUR, René | (1931) | b 12.12.1909 | |
| NOBLE, Jean-Claude | (1968) | b 29.12.1944 | |
| NORMAND, René | (1957) | | |
| NOVES, Guy | (1977-9) | b 5.2.1954 | |
| OLIVE, Dacien | (1951-2) | b 12.7.1924 | |
| ONDARTS, Pascal | (1986-) | b 1.1.1956 | |
| ORSO, Jean-Charles | (1982-) | b 6.1.1958 | |
| OTHATS, Jean | (1960) | b 6.5.1937 | d 9.1964 |
| PACO, Alain | (1974-80) | b 1.5.1952 | |
| PALAT, Jacques | (1938) | | |
| PALMIE, Michel | (1975-8) | b 1.12.1951 | |
| PAOLI, Raoul | (1911-12) | b 24.12.1889 | |
| PAPAREMBORDE, Robert | (1975-83) | b 5.7.1948 | |
| PARDO, Laurent | (1924) | b 19.11.1897 | d 14.8.1979 |
| PARDO, Laurent | (1980-) | b 19.2.1958 | |
| PARGADE, Jean-Henri | (1953) | b 21.9.1928 | |
| PARIES, Lucien | (1968-75) | b 4.8.1947 | |
| PASCALIN, Pierre | (1950-1) | b 21.9.1926 | |
| PASCAREL, A. | (1912-13) | | |
| PASCOT, Jep | (1922-7) | | |
| PAUL, Roger | (1940) | b 14.6.1911 | |
| PAUTHE Guy | (1956) | b 24.10.1932 | |
| PEBEYRE, Elie | (1945-7) | b 27.1.1923 | |
| PEBEYRE, Michel | (1970-3) | b 21.6.1948 | |
| PECUNE, Joel | (1974-6) | b 3.3.1951 | |
| PEDEUTOUR, Pierre | (1980) | b 30.3.1955 | |
| PELLISSIER, Louis | (1928) | b 12.2.1906 | d 16.3.1973 |
| PERON, Patrice | (1975) | b 20.6.1949 | |
| PERRIER, Patrick | (1982) | b 10.1.1957 | |
| PESTEIL, Jean-Pierre | (1975-6) | b 12.11.1954 | |
| PETIT, Charles | (1931) | b 5.1.1904 | |
| PEYRELADE, Henri | (1940) | b 30.12.1917 | |
| PEYROUTOU, Georges | (1911) | b 15.8.1888 | d 1925 |
| PHLIPONNEAU, Jean-François | (1973) | b 23.11.1950 | d 8.5.1976 |
| PIAZZA, André | (1968) | b 1.12.1947 | |
| PICARD, Thierry | (1985-) | b 10.11.1956 | |
| PIERROT, Gilbert | (1914) | b 3.2.1889 | d 3.1979 |
| PILON, Jean | (1949-50) | b 14.10.1925 | |
| PIQUE, Jean | (1961-5) | b 17.9.1935 | |
| PIQUEMAL, Maixent | (1927-30) | b 18.2.1907 | |
| PIQUIRAL, Etienne | (1924-8) | b 1904 | d 1944 |
| PITEU, Roger | (1921-6) | b 14.5.1899 | |
| PLANTEFOL, Alain | (1967-9) | b 26.12.1942 | |
| PLANTEY, Serge | (1961-2) | b 14.2.1940 | |
| PODEVIN, J. | (1913) | | |
| POIRIER, G. | (1907) | | |
| POMATHIOS, Michel | (1948-54) | b 18.3.1924 | |
| PONS, Pierre | (1920-2) | | d 3.1981 |
| PORRA, M. | (1931) | | |
| PORTHAULT, Alain | (1951-3) | b 15.7.1929 | |
| PORTOLAN, Claude | (1986-) | b 16.12.1960 | |
| POTEL, Albert | (1932) | b 18.9.1903 | d 22.3.1985 |
| POYDEBASQUE, François | (1914) | | d 1914/18 |
| PRAT, Jean | (1945-55) | b 1.8.1923 | |
| PRAT, Maurice | (1951-8) | b 17.9.1928 | |
| PREVOST, Alfred | (1926-7) | b 5.5.1894 | d 10.1974 |
| PRINCLARY, Jean | (1945-7) | b 15.7.1912 | |
| PUECH, Louis | (1920-1) | b 4.12.1896 | |
| PUGET, Marcel | (1961-70) | b 28.9.1940 | |
| PUIG, Alphonse | (1926) | b 1901 | d 12.1974 |
| PUJOL, T. | (1906) | | |

| PLAYER | CAREER SPAN | |
|---|---|---|
| QUAGLIO, Aldo | (1957-9) | b 17.2.1932 |
| QUILIS, André | (1967-71) | b 28.10.1941 |
| | | |
| RAMIS, Roger | (1922-3) | b 29.3.1902 |
| RANCOULE, Henri | (1955-62) | b 6.2.1933 |
| RAPIN, André | (1938) | b 18.4.1911 |
| RAYMOND, François | (1925-8) | b 8.1.1902  d 8.7.1970 |
| RAYNAL, François | (1935-7) | b 16.2.1904 |
| RAYNAUD, Firmin | (1933) | |
| RAZAT, Jean-Pierre | (1962-3) | b 15.10.1940 |
| REBUJENT, Raymond | (1963) | |
| REVALLIER, Daniel | (1981-2) | b 20.8.1948 |
| REVILLON, Jean | (1926-7) | |
| RIBERE, Eugène | (1924-33) | b 14.6.1902 |
| RIVES, Jean-Pierre | (1975-84) | b 31.12.1952 |
| ROCHON, Aimé | (1936) | |
| RODRIGO, Marius | (1931) | b 16.3.1908 |
| RODRIGUEZ, Laurent | (1981- ) | b 28.6.1960 |
| ROGE, Lucien | (1952-60) | b 18.10.1932 |
| ROLLET, Jacques | (1960-3) | b 18.8.1934 |
| ROMERO, Henri | (1962-3) | b 21.9.1935 |
| ROMEU, Jean-Pierre | (1972-77) | b 15.4.1948 |
| ROQUES, Alfred | (1958-63) | b 17.2.1925 |
| ROQUES, Jean-Claude | (1966) | b 19.3.1943 |
| ROSSIGNOL, Jean-Claude | (1972) | b 10.8.1945 |
| ROUAN, Jean-Claude | (1953) | b 30.10.1933 |
| ROUCARIES, Gérard | (1956) | b 13.8.1932 |
| ROUFFIA, Lucien | (1945-8) | |
| ROUGERIE, Jacques | (1973) | |
| ROUJAS, R. | (1910) | |
| ROUSIE, Max | (1931-3) | b 15.7.1912  d 2.6.1959 |
| ROUSSET, Gérard | (1975-6) | b 21.1.1953 |
| RUIZ, André | (1968) | b 30.3.1937 |
| RUPERT, Jean-Joseph | (1963-8) | b 7.3.1938 |
| | | |
| SAGOT, R. | (1906-09) | |
| SAHUC, André | (1945) | b 4.8.1914 |
| SAHUC, Frantz | (1936) | b 10.2.1910  d 1970 |
| SAISSET, Olivier | (1971-5) | b 7.6.1949 |
| SALAS, Patrick | (1979-82) | b 3.3.1954 |
| SALINIE, René | (1923) | |
| SALLEFRANQUE, Marc | (1981-82) | b 6.4.1960 |
| SALUT, Jean-Pierre | (1966-9) | b 14.4.1943 |
| SAMATAN, Robert | (1930-1) | b 16.4.1907  d 6.1986 |
| SANAC, André | (1952-7) | b 4.8.1929 |
| SANGALLI, François | (1975-77) | b 8.9.1952 |
| SAPPA, Michel | (1973-77) | b 19.3.1949 |
| SARRADE, Robert | (1929) | b 19.2.1904  d 11.10.1982 |
| SAUX, Jean-Pierre | (1960-3) | b 13.11.1928 |
| SAVITSKY, Michel | (1969) | |
| SAVY, Maurice | (1931-6) | b 22.9.1906 |
| SAYROU, Joseph | (1926-9) | |
| SCOHY, Robert | (1931) | b 28.4.1909 |
| SEBEDIO, Jean | (1913-23) | b 6.12.1890  d 2.6.1951 |
| SEGUIER, Noël | (1973) | b 8.9.1949 |
| SELLA, Philippe | (1982- ) | b 14.2.1962 |
| SEMMARTIN, Jean | (1913) | |
| SENAL, Georges | (1974-5) | b 21.4.1947 |
| SENTILLES, Jean | (1912-13) | b 14.2.1886  d 14.1.1940 |
| SERIN, Lucien | (1928-31) | b 8.11.1902 |
| SERRE, Paul | (1920) | b 13.12.1895  d 14.7.1972 |
| SERRIERE, Patrick | (1986- ) | b 7.7.1960 |
| SERVOLE, Léopold | (1931-5) | b 22.9.1906 |
| SICART, Noël | (1922) | b 25.12.1899 |
| SILLIERES, Jean | (1968-72) | b 15.11.1946 |

| PLAYER | CAREER SPAN | |
|---|---|---|
| SIMAN, Maurice | (1948-50) | b 12.7.1924 |
| SITJAR, Michel | (1964-67) | b 14.9.1942 |
| SKRELA, Jean-Claude | (1971-8) | b 1.10.1949 |
| SOLER, | (1929) | |
| SORO, Robert | (1945-9) | b 28.11.1922 |
| SORRONDO, Michel | (1946-8) | b 16.7.1919  d 24.7.1976 |
| SOULIE, Eugène | (1920-2) | |
| SOURGENS, Joseph | (1926) | b 3.9.1903 |
| SPANGHERO, Claude | (1971-5) | b 5.6.1948 |
| SPANGHERO, Walter | (1964-73) | b 21.12.1943 |
| STENER, Guy | (1956-8) | b 11.2.1931  d 12.1967 |
| STRUXIANO, Philippe | (1913-20) | b 11.3.1891  d 1956 |
| SUTRA, Gérard | (1967-70) | b 22.3.1946 |
| SWIERCZINSKI, Christian | (1969-77) | b 28.7.1947 |
| | | |
| TAFFARY, Michel | (1975) | b 25.5.1950 |
| TAILLANTOU, Jean-Fernand | (1930) | b 17.2.1905 |
| TARRICQ, Pierre | (1958) | b 4.7.1929 |
| TAVERNIER, Clovis | (1913) | |
| TERREAU, Maurice | (1945-51) | b 30.1.1923 |
| THEURIET, André | (1909-13) | b 30.3.1887 |
| THEVENOT, G. | (1910) | |
| THIERRY, Robert | (1920) | b 23.6.1893  d 23.10.1973 |
| THIERS, Pierre | (1936-45) | b 16.4.1914 |
| THIL, Paul | (1912-13) | d 1935 |
| TIGNOL, Paul | (1953) | b 3.3.1933 |
| TORREILLES, Serge | (1956) | b 31.12.1931 |
| TOURTE, Robert | (1940) | |
| TRILLO, Jean | (1967-73) | b 27.10.1944 |
| TRIVIAUX, R. | (1931) | b 10.8.1902 |
| TUCOO-CHALAT, Marcel | (1940) | |
| | | |
| UGARTEMENDIA, Jean-Louis | (1975) | b 10.7.1943 |
| | | |
| VAILLS, Georges | (1928-9) | |
| VALLOT, E. | (1912) | |
| VANNIER, Michel | (1953-61) | b 21.7.1931 |
| VAQUER, Fernand | (1921-2) | b 22.6.1889  d 17.9.1979 |
| VAQUERIN, Armand | (1971-80) | b 21.2.1951 |
| VAREILLES, Charles | (1907-10) | d 1930 |
| VARENNE, François | (1952) | b 26.7.1926 |
| VARVIER, Théo | (1906-12) | d 1914/18 |
| VASSAL, Guy | (1938) | |
| VAYSSE, Jean | (1924-6) | b 28.4.1900  d 10.1974 |
| VELLAT, Edmond | (1927-8) | b 14.2.1897 |
| VERGER, André | (1927-8) | b 28.5.1906  d 4.1978 |
| VERGES, | (1906-07) | |
| VIARD, Gérard | (1969-71) | b 19.5.1945 |
| VIGERIE, Max | (1931) | b 28.11.1906  d 10.1986 |
| VIGIER, Robert | (1956-9) | b 15.12.1926  d 2.9.1986 |
| VIGNEAU, Armand | (1935) | b 2.7.1914 |
| VIGNES, Christian | (1957-8) | b 5.6.1934 |
| VILLA, Ernest | (1926) | b 7.7.1898 |
| VILLAGRA, Jean | (1945) | |
| VILLEPREUX, Pierre | (1967-72) | b 5.7.1943 |
| VIVIES, Bernard | (1978-83) | b 3.9.1955 |
| VOLOT, Marcel | (1945-6) | |
| | | |
| WOLFF, Jean-Paul | (1980-2) | b 7.11.1960 |
| | | |
| YACHVILI, Michel | (1968-75) | b 25.9.1946 |
| | | |
| ZAGO, Fernand | (1963) | b 27.2.1942 |

# SOUTH AFRICA

| PLAYER | CAREER SPAN | | |
|---|---|---|---|
| ACKERMANN, David Schalk Pienaar | (1955-8) | | |
| ALBERTYN, Pieter Kuypers | (1924) | b 27.5.1897 | |
| ALEXANDER, E. | (1891) | | |
| ALLEN, Peter B. | (1960) | b 10.4.1930 | |
| ALLPORT, Percy | (1910) | | |
| ANDERSON, J.A. | (1903) | | |
| ANDERSON, John Henry | (1896) | b 26.4.1874 | d 11.3.1926 |
| ANDREW, J.B. | (1896) | | |
| ANTELME, Joseph George Michael | (1960-1) | b 23.4.1934 | |
| APSEY, John T. | (1933-8) | | |
| ASHLEY, Sydney | (1903) | | |
| ASTON, Ferdinand T.D. | (1896) | b 1871 | |
| AUCAMP, J. | (1924) | | |
| | | | |
| BAARD, Adriaan Pieter | (1960) | b 17.5.1933 | |
| BABROW, Louis | (1937) | b 24.4.1915 | |
| BARNARD, Anton Stefanus | (1984-) | b 7.4.1958 | |
| BARNARD, Johannes Hendrikus | (1965) | b 29.1.1945 | d 3.1985 |
| BARNARD, Robert William | (1970) | b 26.11.1941 | |
| BARNARD, Willem Hendrick Minnaar | (1949-51) | b 7.8.1923 | |
| BARRY, J. | (1903) | | |
| BARTMANN, Wahl Justice | (1986-) | b 13.6.1963 | |
| BASTARD, William Eberhardt | (1937-8) | b 1912 | d 2.1949 |
| BATES, Albert Jacobus | (1969-72) | b 18.4.1941 | |
| BAYVEL, Paul Campbell Robertson | (1974-6) | b 28.3.1949 | |
| BECK, Jacobus Johannes | (1981) | b 27.3.1959 | |
| BEDFORD, Thomas Pleydell | (1963-71) | b 8.2.1942 | |
| BEKKER, Hendrick Jordaan | (1952-6) | b 11.2.1925 | |
| BEKKER, Hendrik Johannes | (1981) | b 12.9.1952 | |
| BEKKER, Martiens J. | (1960) | | |
| BEKKER, Rudolph Phillipus | (1953) | b 26.12.1926 | |
| BERGH, Willem Ferdinand | (1931-8) | b 2.11.1906 | |
| BESBIER, André | (1974) | b 31.3.1946 | |
| BESTER, J.J.N. | (1924) | | |
| BESTER, Johannes Lodewyk Augustinus | (1938) | b 1918 | |
| BESWICK, A.M. | (1896) | | |
| BEZUIDENHOUDT, C.E. | (1962) | | |
| BEZUIDENHOUDT, Nicholas Stephanus Erasmus | (1972-7) | b 4.8.1950 | |
| BIERMAN, J. Nicholas | (1931) | b 1910 | |
| BISSET, William Molteno | (1891) | b 1867 | d 2.1958 |
| BLAIR, Robert | (1977) | b 3.6.1953 | |
| BOSCH, Gerald Raymond | (1974-6) | b 12.5.1949 | |
| BOSMAN, N.J.S. | (1924) | | |
| BOTHA, Daniel Sarel | (1981) | b 26.6.1955 | |
| BOTHA, Hendrik Egnatius | (1980-) | b 27.2.1958 | |
| BOTHA, J.P. | (1903) | | |
| BOTHA, Johannes Petrus Frederick | (1962) | b 11.5.1937 | |
| BOTHA, Pieter Hendrik | (1965) | b 13.10.1935 | |
| BOYES, H.C. | (1891) | | d 1892 |
| BRAND, Gerhardt Hamilton | (1928-38) | b 8.10.1906 | |
| BREDENKAMP, M. | (1896) | | |
| BREEDT, Johannes Christoffel | (1986-) | b 4.6.1959 | |
| BREWIS, Johannes D. | (1949-53) | b 15.6.1920 | |
| BRIERS, Theunis Petrus Daniel | (1955-6) | b 11.7.1929 | |
| BRINK, Danie J. | (1906) | b 7.11.1882 | |

| PLAYER | CAREER SPAN | | |
|---|---|---|---|
| BROOKS, D. | (1906) | b 1883 | |
| BROWN, C. | (1903) | | |
| BRYNARD, Gert Steenkamp | (1965-8) | b 27.10.1938 | |
| BUCHLER, Johnny U. | (1951-6) | b 7.4.1930 | |
| BURDETT, A.F. | (1906) | b 1881 | |
| BURGER, Matthys Boshoff | (1980-81) | b 10.11.1954 | |
| BURGER, Schalk W.P. | (1984-) | b 6.10.1955 | |
| BURGER, W.A.G. | (1906-10) | b 1884 | |
| | | | |
| CARELSE, Gabriel | (1964-69) | b 21.7.1941 | |
| CARLSON, Raymond Allen | (1972) | b 2.10.1948 | |
| CAROLIN, Harold William | (1903-6) | b 1880 | |
| CASTENS, Herbert Hayton | (1891) | b 23.11.1864 | d 18.10.1929 |
| CHIGNELL, Thomas Wilson | (1891) | b 1866 | d 17.10.1952 |
| CILLIERS, Gert D. | (1963) | b 28.7.1940 | |
| CLAASSEN, Johannes Theodore | (1955-62) | b 23.9.1930 | |
| CLAASSEN, Wynand | (1981-2) | b 16.1.1951 | |
| CLARKE, W.H. | (1933) | b 11.10.1905 | |
| CLARKSON, Walter A. | (1921-4) | b 8.7.1896 | d 1973 |
| CLOETE, H.A. | (1896) | | |
| COCKRELL, Charles Herbert | (1969-70) | b 10.1.1939 | |
| COCKRELL, Robert James | (1974-81) | b 4.4.1950 | |
| COETZEE, Johannes Hermanus Hugo | (1974-6) | b 20.1.1945 | |
| COPE, David | (1896) | b 1877 | d 1898 |
| COTTY, W. | (1896) | | |
| CRAMPTON, G. | (1903) | | |
| CRAVEN, Daniel Hartman | (1931-8) | b 11.10.1910 | |
| CRONJE, Peter Arnold | (1971-4) | b 21.9.1949 | |
| CROSBY, J.H. | (1896) | | |
| CROSBY, Nicholas J. | (1910) | | |
| CURRIE, C. | (1903) | | |
| | | | |
| D'ALTON, George | (1933) | | |
| DANEEL, George M. | (1928-32) | b 29.8.1904 | |
| DANEEL, Henry J. | (1906) | | d 1946 |
| DAVIDSON, Max | (1910) | | |
| DE BRUYN, Johan | (1974) | b 12.10.1948 | |
| DE JONGH, Hermanus Paul Kruger | (1928) | | |
| DE KLERK, Izak Johannes | (1969-70) | b 28.10.1938 | |
| DE KLERK, Kevin Brian Henry | (1974-81) | b 6.6.1950 | |
| DE KOCK, Arthur | (1891) | b 11.1.1866 | d 6.7.1957 |
| DE KOCK, J.S. | (1921-4) | | |
| DELPORT, Willem Hendrik | (1951-3) | b 5.11.1920 | |
| DE MELKER, Sydney Clarence | (1903-6) | b 1884 | d 3.11.1953 |
| DEVENISH, Charles | (1896) | | |
| DEVENISH, George St Leger | (1896) | b 11.5.1872 | |
| DEVENISH, M. | (1891) | | |
| DE VILLIERS, D.I. | (1910) | | |
| DE VILLIERS, Dawid Jacobus | (1962-70) | b 10.7.1940 | |
| DE VILLIERS, H.A. | (1906) | | d 1940 |
| DE VILLIERS, Henry Oswald | (1967-70) | b 10.3.1945 | |
| DE VILLIERS, Pierre du P. | (1928-37) | b 6.1905 | |
| DEVINE, Daunce | (1924-8) | | |
| DE VOS, Dirk Johannes Jacobus | (1965-9) | b 8.4.1941 | |
| DE WAAL, Albertus Nicholas | (1967) | b 14.2.1942 | |
| DE WAAL, P. | (1896) | | |
| DE WET, André Eloff | (1969-70) | b 1.8.1946 | |
| DE WET, Piet | (1938) | | |

| PLAYER | CAREER SPAN | | |
|---|---|---|---|
| DINKELMANN, Ernst E. | (1951-3) | b 14.5.1927 | |
| DIRKSEN, Corra W. | (1963-8) | b 22.1.1938 | |
| DOBBIN, Frederick James | (1903-1913) | b 1879 | d 2.1950 |
| DOBIE, John A.R. | (1928) | b 4.8.1905 | |
| DORMEHL, Pieter J. | (1896) | | |
| DOUGLASS, Frank W. | (1896) | | |
| DRYBURGH, Royden Gladstone | (1955-60) | b 1.11.1929 | |
| DUFF, Benjamin | (1891) | | |
| DUFFY, B.A. | (1928) | | |
| DU PLESSIS, Carel Johan | (1982-) | b 4.6.1960 | |
| DU PLESSIS, Daniel Coenraad | (1977-80) | b 9.4.1948 | |
| DU PLESSIS, Felix | (1949) | | d 5.1978 |
| DU PLESSIS, Michael | (1984-) | b 4.11.1958 | |
| DU PLESSIS, Morné | (1971-80) | b 21.10.1949 | |
| DU PLESSIS, Nicholas J. | (1921-4) | | d 1949 |
| DU PLESSIS, Pieter George | (1972) | b 23.7.1947 | |
| DU PLESSIS, Thomas Dannhauser | (1980) | b 29.6.1953 | |
| DU PLESSIS, Willem | (1980-) | b 4.9.1955 | |
| DU PLOOY, Amos Johannes J. | (1955) | | d 1983 |
| DU PREEZ, Frederick Christoffel Hendrik | (1961-71) | b 28.11.1935 | |
| DU PREEZ, Jan Gysbert Hermanus | (1956) | b 6.10.1930 | |
| DU RAND, Jacobus Abraham | (1949-56) | b 16.1.1926 | d 1979 |
| DU TOIT, A.F. | (1928) | b 12.5.1899 | |
| DU TOIT, Benjamin Abraham | (1938) | b 10.11.1912 | |
| DU TOIT, Pieter Alfonso | (1949-52) | b 13.3.1920 | |
| DU TOIT, Pieter Gerhard | (1981-) | b 23.8.1952 | |
| DU TOIT, Pieter Stephanus | (1958-61) | b 9.10.1935 | |
| DUVENHAGE, Floris P. | (1949) | b 6.11.1917 | |
| EDWARDS, Pierre | (1980) | b 23.5.1953 | |
| ELLIS, Jacobus Hendrik | (1965-76) | b 5.1.1943 | |
| ELLIS, Mervyn | (1921-4) | b 1892 | |
| ENGLEBRECHT, Jan Pieter | (1960-9) | b 10.11.1938 | |
| ERASMUS, Frans Stefanus | (1986-) | b 19.6.1959 | |
| ETLINGER, T.E. | (1896) | | |
| FERREIRA, Christoffel | (1986-) | b 28.8.1960 | |
| FERREIRA, Petrus Stephanus | (1984-) | b 17.3.1959 | |
| FERRIS, Hilton H. | (1903) | | |
| FORBES, H.H. | (1896) | | |
| FOURIE, Carel | (1974-5) | b 1.8.1950 | |
| FOURIE, Teodorus Theunis | (1974) | b 19.7.1945 | |
| FOURIE, Willem L. | (1958) | b 23.7.1936 | |
| FRANCIS, Joseph A.J. | (1912-13) | b 1888 | d 1925 |
| FREDERICKSON, Cornelius Abraham | (1974-80) | b 17.8.1950 | |
| FREW, Alexander | (1903) | | d 4.1947 |
| FRONEMAN, Dirk Cornelius | (1977) | b 14.4.1954 | |
| FRONEMAN, Innes Lyndon | (1933) | b 18.12.1907 | |
| FRY, Stephen Perry | (1951-5) | b 14.7.1924 | |
| GAGE, John H. | (1933) | b 2.4.1907 | |
| GAINSFORD, John Leslie | (1960-7) | b 4.8.1938 | |
| GEEL, P.J. | (1949) | b 1910 | d 6.1971 |
| GEERE, V. | (1933) | b 9.9.1906 | |
| GEFFIN, Aaron | (1949-51) | b 28.5.1921 | |
| GELDENHUYS, Schalk Burger | (1981-2) | b 18.5.1956 | |
| GENTLES, Thomas Alexander | (1955-8) | b 31.5.1934 | |
| GERAGHTY, Edmund M. | (1949) | b 20.4.1927 | |
| GERBER, Danie Mattheus | (1980-) | b 14.4.1958 | |
| GERBER, Michael C. | (1958-60) | b 12.10.1935 | |
| GERICKE, F.W. | (1960) | b 8.6.1933 | |
| GERMISHUYS, Johannes Servaas | (1974-81) | b 29.10.1949 | |
| GIBBS, B. | (1903) | | |
| GOOSEN, Cornelius Petrus | (1965) | b 3.2.1937 | |
| GORTON, H.C. | (1896) | | |
| GOULD, Rodney Lloyd | (1968) | b 10.8.1942 | |
| GRAY, B. Geoffrey | (1931-3) | b 28.7.1909 | |
| GREENWOOD, Colin M. | (1961) | b 25.1.1936 | |
| GREYLING, Pieter Johannes Frederick | (1967-72) | b 16.5.1942 | |
| GROBLER, Cornelius Johannes | (1974-5) | b 24.8.1944 | |
| GUTHRIE, F.H. | (1891-6) | | |
| HAHN, C.H.L. | (1910) | | |
| HAMILTON, F. | (1891) | | |
| HARRIS, Terence Anthony | (1937-8) | b 27.8.1916 | |
| HARTLEY, A.J. | (1891) | | |
| HATTINGH, L.B. | (1933) | | |
| HEATLIE, Barry Heatlie | (1891-1903) | b 25.4.1872 | d 19.8.1951 |
| HEPBURN, T. | (1896) | | |
| HEUNIS, Johan Wilhelm | (1981-) | b 26.1.1958 | |
| HILL, Ronald Andrew | (1960-3) | b 20.12.1934 | |
| HIRSCH, John Gauntlett | (1906-10) | b 20.2.1883 | d 2.1958 |
| HOBSON, T.E.C. | (1903) | | |
| HOFFMAN, Richard Stephanus | (1953) | b 2.12.1931 | |
| HOLTON, Douglas Norman | (1960) | b 23.9.1932 | |
| HOPWOOD, Douglas John | (1960-5) | b 3.6.1934 | |
| HOWE, Bennett Frederick | (1956) | b 30.8.1932 | |
| HOWE-BROWNE, Noel Richard Frank George | (1910) | b 24.12.1884 | d 3.4.1943 |
| IMMELMAN, J.H. | (1913) | b 2.8.1888 | |
| JACKSON, Dirk Cloet | (1906) | b 21.4.1885 | d 17.9.1976 |
| JACKSON, J.S. | (1903) | | |
| JANSEN, Ebenhaeser | (1981) | b 5.6.1954 | |
| JANSEN, Joachim Scholtz | (1970-2) | b 5.2.1948 | |
| JENNINGS, Cecil B. | (1937) | b 16.8.1914 | |
| JOHNSTONE, Paul Geoffrey | (1951-6) | b 30.6.1930 | |
| JONES, C.H. | (1903) | | |
| JONES, Percy Sydney Twentyman | (1896) | b 13.9.1876 | d 8.3.1954 |
| JORDAAN, R.P. | (1949) | b 13.7.1920 | |
| JOUBERT, Stephen J. | (1906) | b 1887 | d 4.1939 |
| KAHTS, Wilhelm Julius Heinrich | (1980-2) | b 20.2.1947 | |
| KAMINER, J. | (1958) | b 25.1.1934 | |
| KELLY, E.W. | (1896) | | |
| KENYON, Basil James | (1949) | b 17.5.1918 | |
| KIPLING, Herbert George | (1931-3) | b 1905 | d 1981 |
| KIRKPATRICK, Alexander Ian | (1953-61) | b 25.7.1930 | |
| KNIGHT, Arnold S. | (1912-13) | b 16.12.1885 | d 2.7.1946 |
| KOCH, Augustus Christoffel | (1949-60) | b 21.9.1927 | d 4.1986 |
| KOCH, H.V. | (1949) | b 13.6.1921 | |
| KOTZE, G.J.M. | (1967) | b 12.8.1940 | |
| KRANTZ, Eduard Friedrich Wilhelm | (1976-81) | b 10.8.1954 | |
| KRIGE, Jacob Daniel | (1903-6) | b 5.7.1879 | |
| KRITZINGER, Johannes Lordewyk | (1974-6) | b 1.3.1948 | |
| KROON, Colin Maxwell | (1955) | b 22.2.1931 | |
| KRUGER, Petrus Ebersohn | (1986-) | b 11.4.1958 | |
| KRUGER, Theuns Lodewicus | (1921-8) | b 17.6.1896 | d 6.7.1957 |
| KUHN, Stephanus Petrus | (1960-5) | b 12.6.1935 | |
| LA GRANGE, J.B. | (1924) | | |
| LARARD, Arthur | (1896) | b 1871 | d 15.8.1936 |
| LATEGAN, Martinus Theunis | (1949-53) | b 9.1925 | |
| LAWLESS, Michael John | (1964-70) | b 17.9.1942 | |
| LEDGER, Septimus Heyns | (1912-13) | b 29.4.1889 | d 13.4.1917 |
| LE ROUX, Martiens | (1980-1) | b 30.3.1951 | |
| LE ROUX, Pieter A. | (1906) | b 1885 | |
| LITTLE, E.M.M. | (1891) | | d 1945 |
| LOCHNER, George Philip | (1955-58) | b 1.2.1931 | |

| PLAYER | CAREER SPAN | | | PLAYER | CAREER SPAN | | |
|---|---|---|---|---|---|---|---|
| LOCHNER, George Philippus | (1937-8) | b 11.1.1914 | | MOSS, Cecil | (1949) | b 12.2.1925 | |
| LOCKYEAR, Richard John | (1960-1) | b 26.6.1932 | | MOSTERT, Phillipus Jacobus | (1921-32) | b 30.10.1898 | |
| LOMBARD, A.C. | (1910) | | | MULLER, Gert Hendrik | (1969-74) | b 10.5.1948 | |
| LOTZ, Jan W. | (1937-8) | b 26.8.1910 | d 7.1986 | MULLER, Helgard Lourens | (1986-) | b 1.6.1963 | |
| LOUBSER, Johannes Albertus | (1903-10) | b 6.8.1884 | | MULLER, Hendrik Scholtz Vosloo | (1949-53) | b 26.3.1922 | d 5.1977 |
| LOURENS, Matthys Johann | (1968) | b 5.5.1943 | | MYBURGH, F.R. | (1896) | | |
| LOUW, J.S. | (1891) | | | MYBURGH, Johannes Lodewikus | (1962-70) | b 24.8.1936 | |
| LOUW, Marthinus Johannes | (1971) | b 20.4.1938 | | MYBURGH, W.H. | (1924) | | |
| LOUW, Matthys Michael | (1928-38) | b 21.2.1906 | | | | | |
| LOUW, Robert James | (1980-4) | b 26.3.1955 | | NAUDE, Jacobus Pieter | (1963-8) | b 2.11.1936 | |
| LOUW, Stephanus Cornelius | (1933-38) | b 1909 | d 1940 | NEETHLING, Jacobus Burger | (1967-70) | b 6.7.1938 | |
| LUYT, Frederick Pieter | (1910-13) | b 26.2.1888 | | NEL, Johannes Arnoldus | (1960-70) | b 11.8.1935 | |
| LUYT, John Douglas | (1912-13) | b 1885 | | NEL, Jeremy John | (1956-8) | | |
| LUYT, Richard Robin | (1910-13) | b 16.4.1886 | | NEL, P.A.R.O. | (1903) | | |
| LYONS, D. | (1896) | | | NEL, Phillip Jacobus | (1928-37) | b 17.6.1902 | d 12.2.1984 |
| LYSTER, Patrick James | (1933-37) | b 31.5.1913 | | NIMB, Charles Frederick | (1961) | b 6.9.1938 | |
| | | | | NOMIS, Sydney Harold | (1967-72) | b 14.11.1941 | |
| MacDONALD, Andrew William | (1965) | b 27.8.1934 | | NYKAMP, J.L. | (1933) | | d 1968 |
| MacDONALD, Dugald Alexander | (1974) | b 20.1.1950 | | OCHSE, Johannes Karl | (1951-3) | b 9.2.1925 | |
| MALAN, Avril Stefan | (1960-5) | b 9.4.1937 | | OELOFSE, Johannes S.A. | (1953) | b 16.12.1926 | d 1978 |
| MALAN, Ewoud | (1980) | b 4.7.1953 | | OLIVER, J.F. | (1928) | | d 1980 |
| MALAN, Gabriel Frederick | (1958-65) | b 18.11.1935 | | OLIVIER, Ebenhaezer | (1967-70) | b 10.4.1944 | |
| MALAN, Piet | (1949) | b 13.2.1919 | | OLVER E. | (1896) | | |
| MALLETT, Nicholas Vivian Haward | (1984-) | b 30.10.1956 | | OOSTHUIZEN, Jacobus Johannes | (1974-6) | b 4.7.1951 | |
| MANS, Wynand Jacobus | (1964-5) | b 21.2.1942 | | OOSTHUIZEN, Ockert Wessel | (1981-4) | b 1.4.1955 | |
| MARAIS, Franswa Pierre | (1949-53) | b 13.12.1927 | | OSLER, Benjamin Louwrens | (1924-33) | b 23.11.1901 | d 23.4.1960 |
| MARAIS, Johannes Frederik Klopper | (1963-74) | b 21.9.1941 | | OSLER, Stanley Gordon | (1928) | b 31.1.1907 | d 4.1980 |
| MARE, Dietlof Siegfriedt | (1906) | | d 14.10.1913 | OXLEE, Keith | (1960-5) | b 17.12.1934 | |
| MARSBERG, Arthur Frederick W. | (1906) | b 1883 | d 3.1942 | PARKER, Walter Hambly | (1965) | b 13.4.1934 | |
| MARSBERG, P.A. | (1910) | | | PARTRIDGE, Joseph Edward Crawshay | (1903) | b 13.6.1879 | d 1.7.1965 |
| MARTHEZE, W.C. | (1903-06) | b 1878 | | PAYN, Cecil | (1924) | | d 31.10.1959 |
| MARTIN, H.J. | (1937) | b 10.6.1910 | | PELSER, Hendrik Jacobus Martin | (1958-61) | b 23.3.1934 | |
| McCALLUM, Ian Duncan | (1970-74) | b 30.7.1944 | | PFAFF, Brian Desmond | (1956) | b 2.3.1930 | |
| McCALLUM, Roy James | (1974) | b 12.4.1946 | | PICKARD, Jan Albertus Jacobus | (1953-8) | b 25.12.1927 | |
| McCULLOCH, J. Duncan | (1912-13) | b 11.4.1884 | d 19.4.1953 | PIENAAR, Zacharias Mattheus Johannes | (1980-1) | b 21.12.1954 | |
| McDONALD, J. André J. | (1931-2) | b 17.2.1909 | | PITZER, Gysbertus | (1967-9) | b 8.7.1939 | |
| McEWAN, William Maclean Clark | (1903) | b 24.10.1875 | d 5.1934 | POPE, Christopher Francis | (1974-6) | b 30.9.1952 | |
| McHARDY, Evelyn Edgar | (1912-13) | b 11.6.1890 | d 1960 | POTGIETER, H.J. | (1928) | b 1903 | d 11.11.1957 |
| McKENDRICK, J.A. | (1891) | | | POTGIETER, Hermanus Lambertus | (1977) | b 11.1.1953 | |
| MELLETT, T. | (1896) | | | POWELL, Albert William | (1896) | b 18.7.1873 | d 11.9.1948 |
| MELLISH, Frank Whitmore | (1921-4) | b 26.4.1897 | d 21.8.1965 | POWELL, John Mercer | (1891-1903) | | |
| MERRY, J. | (1891) | | | PRENTIS, Richard Basil | (1980-1) | b 27.2.1947 | |
| METCALF, H.D. | (1903) | | | PRETORIUS, N.F. | (1928) | | |
| MEYER, Charles Du P. | (1921) | | d 1980 | PRINSLOO, Jan | (1958) | b 1935 | d 28.7.1966 |
| MEYER, P.J. | (1896) | | | PRINSLOO, J. | (1963) | b 11.10.1935 | |
| MICHAU, J.M. | (1921) | | d 1945 | PRINSLOO, J.P. | (1928) | | |
| MICHAU, J.P. | (1921) | | | PUTTER, D.J. | (1963) | b 13.2.1932 | |
| MILLAR, Wiliam Alexander | (1906-13) | b 6.11.1883 | | | | | |
| MILLS, Walter J. | (1910) | b 16.6.1891 | | RAAFF, J.W.E. | (1903-10) | b 1879 | d 7.1949 |
| MOLL, Toby M. | (1910) | b 20.7.1890 | d 14.7.1916 | RAS, Wouter Johannes De Wet | (1976-80) | b 28.1.1954 | |
| MONTINI, Patrick Evan | (1956) | b 15.6.1929 | | REID, Allan | (1903) | b 1.10.1877 | d 31.10.1948 |
| MOOLMAN, Louis Christian | (1977-) | b 21.1.1951 | | REID, B.C. | (1933) | | |
| MORDT, Raymond Herman | (1980-4) | b 15.2.1957 | | REINACH, Jaco | (1986-) | b 1.1.1962 | |
| MORKEL, Andrew O. | (1903) | | d 23.2.1946 | RENS, Ignatius Johannes | (1953) | b 19.7.1929 | |
| MORKEL, Douglas Francis Theodore | (1906-13) | b 1886 | d 20.2.1950 | RETIEF, Daniel François | (1955-6) | b 28.6.1925 | |
| MORKEL, Harry J. | (1921) | b 14.10.1883 | d 1956 | REYNECKE, H.J. | (1910) | | |
| MORKEL, Henry William | (1921) | b 14.7.1894 | | RICHARDS, Alfred Renfrew | (1891) | b 1868 | d 9.1.1904 |
| MORKEL, J.A. | (1921) | b 22.3.1896 | d 10.1926 | RILEY, Norman | (1963) | b 25.2.1939 | |
| MORKEL, Jan Willem Hunter | (1912-13) | b 13.11.1891 | d 15.5.1916 | RIORDAN, C.E. | (1910) | | |
| MORKEL, Pieter Gerhard | (1912-21) | b 15.10.1888 | | ROBERTSON, Ian William | (1974-6) | b 28.4.1950 | |
| MORKEL, P.K. | (1928) | | | ROGERS, Chris D. | (1984-) | b 10.10.1956 | |
| MORKEL, W.H. | (1910-21) | b 2.1.1886 | d 1954 | ROOS, Gideon D. | (1910) | | |
| MORKEL, W.S. | (1906) | b 1880 | | ROOS, Paul Johannes | (1903-06) | b 1880 | d 22.9.1948 |
| | | | | ROSENBERG, Wilfred | (1955-8) | b 18.6.1934 | |

| PLAYER | CAREER SPAN | |
|---|---|---|
| ROSSOUW, D.H. | (1953) | b 5.9.1930 |
| ROUSSEAU, Willie P. | (1928) | b 11.8.1906 |
| ROUX, François du Toit | (1960-70) | b 12.4.1939 |
| ROUX, Ockert Antonie | (1969-74) | b 22.2.1947 |
| | | |
| SAMUELS, T.A. | (1896) | |
| SAUERMANN, Johannes Theodorus | (1971-4) | b 16.11.1944 |
| SCHLEBUSCH, Johannes Jacobus | (1974-5) | b 5.5.1949 |
| SCHMIDT, Louis Ulrich | (1958-62) | b 6.2.1936 |
| SCHMIDT, Ulrich Louis | (1986-) | b 10.7.1961 |
| SCHOEMAN, Johannes | (1963-5) | b 15.3.1940 |
| SCHOLTZ, Hugo H. | (1921) | |
| SCOTT, P. | (1896) | |
| SENDIN, William D. | (1921) | b 1896 d 1977 |
| SERFONTEIN, David Jacobus | (1980-4) | b 3.8.1954 |
| SHAND, R. | (1891) | |
| SHERIFF, A.R. | (1938) | b 1912 d 1951 |
| SHUM, Ernest Hamilton | (1913) | b 17.8.1886 d 1952 |
| SINCLAIR, Desmond John | (1955) | b 14.7.1928 |
| SINCLAIR, James Hugh | (1903) | b 16.10.1876 d 23.2.1913 |
| SKENE, Alan L. | (1958) | b 2.10.1932 |
| SLATER, John T. | (1924-8) | b 16.4.1901 |
| SMAL, Gert Petrus | (1986-) | b 27.12.1961 |
| SMITH, Cornelius Michael | (1963-5) | b 8.5.1934 |
| SMITH, C.W. | (1891-6) | |
| SMITH, Daniel | (1891) | |
| SMITH, David J. | (1980) | b 9.11.1957 |
| SMITH, George A.C. | (1938) | d 1978 |
| SMOLLAN, Frederick C. | (1933) | b 20.8.1908 |
| SNEDDEN, Robert C. | (1891) | |
| SNYMAN, Dawid Stephanus Lubbe | (1972-7) | b 5.7.1949 |
| SNYMAN, Jacobus Cornelius Pauw | (1974) | b 14.4.1948 |
| SONNEKUS, Gerhardus Hermanus Henricus | (1974-84) | b 1.2.1953 |
| SPIES, Johannes Jacobus | (1970) | b 8.5.1945 |
| STANDER, Jacobus Casparus Johannes | (1974-6) | b 25.12.1945 d 8.1980 |
| STAPELBERG, Willem P. | (1974) | b 29.1.1947 |
| STARKE, James J. | (1956) | b 16.5.1931 |
| STARKE, K.T. | (1924) | d 1981 |
| STEENEKAMP, J.G.A. | (1958) | b 2.9.1935 |
| STEGMANN, Anton C. | (1906) | b 1884 |
| STEGMANN, Johannes Augustus | (1912-13) | b 21.6.1887 d 7.12.1984 |
| STEWART, David Alfred | (1960-5) | b 14.7.1935 |
| STOFBERG, Marthinus Theunis Steyn | (1976-) | b 6.6.1955 |
| STRACHAN, Louis Cornelius | (1932-8) | b 12.9.1907 d 3.1985 |
| STRAUSS, Jacobus Adriaan | (1984-) | b 2.9.1957 |
| STRAUSS, Johan Hendrik Potgieter | (1976-80) | b 27.9.1951 |
| STRAUSS, S.S.F. | (1921) | |
| STRYDOM, Coenraad Frederick | (1955-8) | b 20.1.1932 |
| STRYDOM, Louis J. | (1949) | b 27.10.1921 |
| SUTER, Melvyn R. | (1965) | b 14.12.1939 |
| SWART, Josias Johannes Nicolaas | (1955) | b 29.7.1934 |
| | | |
| TABERER, W.S. | (1896) | |
| TAYLOR, Ormonde B. | (1962) | b 5.6.1937 |
| THEUNISSEN, Daniel Johannes | (1896) | b 12.7.1862 d 1964 |
| THOMPSON, Gerald | (1912) | b 4.10.1886 d 30.6.1916 |
| TINDALL, John C. | (1924-8) | b 1901 d 3.5.1946 |
| TOBIAS, Errol George | (1981-4) | b 18.3.1950 |
| TOD, N.S. | (1928) | |
| TOWNSEND, W.H. | (1921) | |
| TRENERY, W. | (1891) | |
| TRUTER, D.R. | (1924) | |
| TRUTER, Jacobus Tredoux | (1963-5) | b 5.6.1939 |
| TURNER, Frederick G. | (1933-8) | b 18.3.1914 |
| TWIGGE, Robert John | (1960) | b 24.7.1936 |

| PLAYER | CAREER SPAN | |
|---|---|---|
| ULYATE, Clive Anthony | (1955-6) | b 11.12.1933 |
| UYS, Pieter de Waal | (1960-9) | b 10.12.1937 |
| | | |
| VAN ASWEGEN, Henning Jonathan | (1981) | b 11.2.1955 |
| VAN BROEKHUIZEN, Herman Dirk | (1896) | b 17.6.1872 d 4.8.1953 |
| VAN BUUREN, Mauritz Christian | (1891) | b 12.8.1865 d 1951 |
| VAN DE VYVER, Daniel Ferdinand | (1937) | b 1910 |
| VAN DEN BERG, Derek Sean | (1975-6) | b 2.1.1946 |
| VAN DEN BERG, Mauritz A. | (1937) | b 1910 |
| VAN DER MERWE, Albertus Johannes | (1955-60) | b 14.7.1929 d 1974 |
| VAN DER MERWE, Alfred J. | (1931) | b 14.9.1908 |
| VAN DER MERWE, B.S. | (1949) | |
| VAN DER MERWE, Hendrik Stefanus | (1960-4) | b 24.8.1936 |
| VAN DER MERWE, Johann Philmar | (1970) | b 7.12.1947 |
| VAN DE MERWE, Phillip Rudolph | (1981-) | b 8.7.1957 |
| VANDERPLANK, B.E. | (1924) | b 29.4.1894 |
| VAN DER SCHYFF, Jack Henry | (1949-55) | b 11.6.1928 |
| VAN DER WATT, Andrew Edward | (1970) | b 10.10.1946 |
| VAN DER WESTHUIZEN, J.C. | (1928-31) | b 22.11.1905 |
| VAN DER WESTHUIZEN, J.H. | (1931-2) | b 4.11.1909 |
| VAN DRUTEN, Nicholas J.V. | (1924-8) | b 12.6.1898 |
| VAN HEERDEN, Adrian Jacobus | (1921) | b 10.3.1898 |
| VAN HEERDEN, Johannes Lodewikus | (1974-80) | b 18.7.1951 |
| VAN JAARSVELD, Christoffel Jacobus | (1949) | b 21.2.1918 |
| VAN JAARSVELDT, Desmond Charles | (1960) | b 31.3.1929 |
| VAN NIEKERK, J.A. | (1928) | b 1.6.1907 |
| VAN REENEN, George L. | (1937) | b 1914 d 12.11.1968 |
| VAN RENEN, Charles Gerhard | (1891-6) | b 23.8.1868 d 1942 |
| VAN RENEN, William A. | (1903) | b 1872 d 1941 |
| VAN ROOYEN, George W. | (1921) | b 1892 d 1942 |
| VAN RYNEVELD, R. Clive B. | (1910) | |
| VAN SCHOOR, Ryk A.M. | (1949-53) | b 3.12.1921 |
| VAN VOLLENHOVEN, Karel Thomas | (1955-6) | b 29.4.1935 |
| VAN VUUREN, T.F. | (1912-3) | b 1889 d 7.1942 |
| VAN WYK, Christiaan Johannes | (1951-5) | b 5.11.1923 |
| VAN WYK, Jacobus Frederick Beatrix | (1970-6) | b 21.12.1943 |
| VAN WYK, S.P. | (1928) | |
| VAN ZYL, Ben-Piet | (1961) | |
| VAN ZYL, Christoffel Gert Petrus | (1965) | b 1.6.1932 |
| VAN ZYL, Gideon Higo | (1958-62) | b 20.8.1932 |
| VAN ZYL, Hendrik Jacobus | (1960-1) | b 31.1.1936 |
| VAN ZYL, Pieter Johannes | (1961) | b 23.7.1933 |
| VELDSMAN, Pieter Eeden | (1977) | b 11.3.1952 |
| VENTER, Floris D. | (1931-3) | b 13.4.1909 |
| VERSFELD, Charles | (1891) | |
| VERSFELD, Marthinus | (1891) | b 1868 d 1941 |
| VIGNE, J.T. | (1891) | |
| VILJOEN, Joachim Frederick | (1971-2) | b 14.5.1945 |
| VILJOEN, Johannes Theodorus | (1971) | b 21.4.1943 |
| VILLET, John Villiers | (1984-) | b 3.11.1954 |
| VISAGIE, Petrus Jacobus | (1967-71) | b 16.4.1943 |

| PLAYER | CAREER SPAN | | |
|---|---|---|---|
| VISAGIE, Rudolf | | | |
| Gerhardus | (1984-) | b 27.6.1959 | |
| VISSER, Johann de Villiers | (1981) | b 26.11.1958 | |
| VISSER, P.J. | (1933) | | d 1969 |
| VIVIERS, Stephanus | | | |
| Sebastian | (1956) | b 1.3.1927 | |
| VOGEL, Martin Leon | (1974) | b 22.10.1949 | |
| | | | |
| WAGENAAR, Christo | (1977) | b 11.3.1952 | |
| WAHL, Johannes Joubert | (1949) | | |
| WALKER, Alfred P. | (1921-4) | | |
| WALKER, H. Newton | (1953-6) | | |
| WALKER, H.W. | (1910) | | |
| WALTON, Donald | | | |
| Cameron | (1964-69) | b 5.4.1939 | |
| WARING, F.W. | (1931-3) | b 7.11.1908 | |

| PLAYER | CAREER SPAN | | |
|---|---|---|---|
| WESSELS, J.J. | (1896) | | |
| WHIPP, Peter John Milton | (1974-80) | b 22.9.1950 | |
| WHITE, James | (1931-7) | b 1912 | |
| WILLIAMS, A.E. | (1910) | | |
| WILLIAMS, Avril P. | (1984-) | b 10.2.1961 | |
| WILLIAMS, David Owen | (1937-8) | b 16.6.1913 | d 1.1976 |
| WILLIAMS, Johannes | | | |
| Gerhardus | (1971-6) | b 29.10.1946 | |
| WILSON, Lionel Geoffrey | (1960-5) | b 25.5.1933 | |
| WOLMARANS, Barend | | | |
| Johannes | (1977) | b 22.2.1953 | |
| WRIGHT, Garth Derick | (1986-) | b 9.9.1963 | |
| WYNESS, M.R.K. | (1962-3) | b 23.1.1937 | |
| | | | |
| ZELLER, William Charles | (1921) | b 18.3.1896 | |
| ZIMERMAN, Maurice | (1931-2) | b 8.6.1911 | |

# NEW ZEALAND

| PLAYER | CAREER SPAN | | |
|---|---|---|---|
| ABBOTT, Harold Louis | (1906) | b 17.6.1882 | d 16.1.1971 |
| AITKEN, George Gothard | (1921) | b 2.7.1898 | d 8.7.1952 |
| ALLEN, Frederick Richard | (1946-9) | b 9.2.1920 | |
| ALLEN, Nicholas Houghton | (1980) | b 30.8.1958 | d 7.8.1984 |
| ALLEY, Geoffrey Thomas | (1928) | b 4.2.1903 | d 25.9.1986 |
| ANDERSON, Albert | (1983- ) | b 5.2.1961 | |
| ANDERSON, Brent Leslie | (1986- ) | b 10.3.1960 | |
| ARCHER, William Roberts | (1955-6) | b 19.9.1930 | |
| ARGUS, Walter Garland | (1946-7) | b 29.5.1921 | |
| ARNOLD, Derek Austin | (1963-4) | b 10.1.1941 | |
| ARNOLD, Keith Dawson | (1947) | b 1.3.1920 | |
| ASHBY, David Lloyd | (1958) | b 15.2.1931 | |
| ASHER, Albert Arapeha | (1903) | b 3.12.1879 | d 8.1.1965 |
| ASHWORTH, Barry Graeme | (1978) | b 23.9.1949 | |
| ASHWORTH, John Charles | (1978- ) | b 15.9.1949 | |
| ATKINSON, Henry | (1913) | b 1888 | |
| AVERY, Henry Esau | (1910) | b 3.10.1885 | d 22.3.1961 |
| BADELEY, Cecil Edward Oliver | (1921) | b 7.11.1896 | d 10.11.1986 |
| BAIRD, James Alexander Steenson | (1913) | b 17.12.1893 | d 7.6.1917 |
| BALL, Nelson | (1931-6) | b 11.10.1908 | d 9.5.1986 |
| BARRETT, James | (1913) | b 8.10.1888 | d 31.8.1971 |
| BARRY, Edward Fitzgerald | (1934) | b 3.9.1905 | |
| BATTY, Grant Bernard | (1972-7) | b 31.8.1951 | |
| BATTY, Walter | (1930-1) | b 1.1.1905 | d 10.5.1979 |
| BEATTY, George Edward | (1950) | b 29.3.1925 | |
| BELL, Raymond Henry | (1951-2) | b 31.12.1925 | |
| BELLISS, Ernest Arthur | (1921) | b 1.4.1894 | d 22.4.1974 |
| BENNET, Robert | (1905) | b 23.7.1879 | d 9.4.1962 |
| BERGHAN, Trevor | (1938) | b 13.7.1914 | |
| BERRY, Martin Joseph | (1986- ) | b 13.7.1966 | |
| BEVAN, Vincent David | (1949-50) | b 24.12.1921 | |
| BIRTWISTLE, William Murray | (1965-8) | b 4.7.1939 | |
| BLACK, John Edwin | (1977-80) | b 25.7.1951 | |
| BLACK, Neville Wyatt | (1949) | b 25.4.1925 | |
| BLACK, Robert Stanley | (1914) | b 23.8.1893 | d 21.9.1916 |
| BLAKE, Alan Walter | (1949) | b 3.11.1922 | |
| BOGGS, Eric George | (1946-9) | b 28.3.1922 | |
| BOND, Jack Garth Parker | (1949) | b 24.5.1920 | |
| BOOTH, Ernest Edward | (1906-07) | b 24.2.1876 | d 18.10.1935 |
| BOROEVICH, Kevin Grant | (1986- ) | b 4.10.1960 | |
| BOTICA, Frano Michael | (1986-) | b 3.8.1963 | |
| BOWDEN, Noel James Gordon | (1952) | b 19.3.1926 | |
| BOWERS, Richard Guy | (1953-4) | b 5.11.1932 | |
| BOWMAN, Albert William | (1938) | b 5.5.1915 | |
| BRAID, Gary John | (1983) | b 25.7.1960 | |
| BREMNER, Selwyn George | (1952-6) | b 2.8.1930 | |
| BREWER, Michael Robert | (1986- ) | b 6.11.1964 | |
| BRISCOE, Kevin Charles | (1959-64) | b 20.8.1936 | |
| BROOKE-COWDEN, Mark | (1986- ) | b 12.6.1963 | |
| BROWN, Charles | (1913) | b 19.12.1887 | d 2.4.1966 |
| BROWN, Ross Handley | (1955-62) | b 8.9.1934 | |
| BROWNLIE, Cyril James | (1924-5) | b 6.8.1895 | d 7.5.1954 |
| BROWNLIE, Maurice John | (1924-8) | b 10.8.1897 | d 21.1.1957 |
| BRUCE, John Alexander | (1914) | b 11.11.1887 | d 20.10.1970 |
| BRUCE, Oliver Douglas | (1976-8) | b 23.5.1947 | |
| BRYERS, Ronald Frederick | (1949) | b 14.11.1919 | |
| BUDD, Thomas Alfred | (1946-9) | d 1.8.1922 | |
| BULLOCK-DOUGLAS, George Arthur Hardy | (1932-4) | b 4.6.1911 | d 25.8.1958 |
| BURGESS, Gregory Alexander John | (1981) | b 6.7.1954 | |
| BURGESS, George Francis | (1905) | b 20.9.1883 | d 2.7.1961 |
| BURGESS, Robert Edward | (1971-3) | b 26.3.1949 | |

| PLAYER | CAREER SPAN | | |
|---|---|---|---|
| BURKE, Peter Standish | (1955-7) | b 22.9.1927 | |
| BURNS, Patrick James | (1908-13) | b 10.3.1881 | d 24.2.1943 |
| BUSH, Ronald George | (1931) | b 3.5.1909 | |
| BUSH, William Kingita Te Pohe | (1974-9) | b 24.1.1949 | |
| BUXTON, John Burns | (1955-6) | b 31.10.1933 | |
| CAIN, Michael Joseph | (1913-14) | b 7.7.1885 | d 27.8.1951 |
| CALLESEN, John Arthur | (1974-5) | b 24.5.1950 | |
| CAMERON, Donald | (1908) | b 15.7.1887 | d 25.8.1947 |
| CAMERON, Lachlan Murray | (1980-1) | b 12.4.1959 | |
| CARLETON, Sydney Russell | (1928-9) | b 22.2.1904 | d 23.10.1973 |
| CARRINGTON, Kenneth Roy | (1971) | b 3.9.1950 | |
| CASEY, Stephen Timothy | (1905-08) | b 24.12.1882 | d 10.8.1960 |
| CATLEY, Evelyn Haswell | (1946-9) | b 23.9.1915 | d 23.3.1975 |
| CAUGHEY, Thomas Harcourt Clarke | (1932-7) | b 4.7.1911 | |
| CAULTON, Ralph Walter | (1959-64) | b 10.1.1937 | |
| CHERRINGTON, Mau Paora | (1950) | b 5.3.1924 | d 26.6.1979 |
| CHRISTIAN, Desmond Lawrence | (1949) | b 9.9.1923 | d 30.8.1977 |
| CLAMP, Michael | (1984- ) | b 26.12.1961 | |
| CLARK, Donald William | (1964) | b 22.2.1940 | |
| CLARK, William Henry | (1953-6) | b 16.11.1929 | |
| CLARKE, Adrian Hipkins | (1958-60) | b 23.2.1938 | |
| CLARKE, Donald Barry | (1956-64) | b 10.11.1933 | |
| CLARKE, Ian James | (1953-63) | b 5.3.1931 | |
| CLARKE, Ray Lancelot | (1932) | b 7.1909 | |
| COBDEN, Donald Gordon | (1937) | b 11.8.1914 | d 11.8.1940 |
| COCKERILL, Maurice Stanley | (1951) | b 8.12.1928 | |
| COCKROFT, Eric Arthur Percy | (1913-14) | b 10.9.1890 | d 2.4.1973 |
| CODLIN, Brett William | (1980) | b 29.11.1956 | |
| COLLINS, Arthur Harold | (1932-4) | b 19.7.1906 | |
| COLLINS, John Law | (1964-5) | b 1.2.1939 | |
| COLMAN, John Thomas Henry | (1907-08) | b 14.1.1887 | d 28.9.1965 |
| CONNOR, Desmond Michael | (1961-64) | b 9.8.1935 | |
| CONWAY, Richard James | (1959-65) | b 22.4.1935 | |
| COOKE, Albert Edward | (1924-30) | b 5.10.1901 | d 29.9.1977 |
| COOKE, Reuben James | (1903) | | d 10.5.1940 |
| COOPER, Gregory John Luke | (1986- ) | b 10.6.1965 | |
| CORNER, Mervyn Miles Nelson | (1930-36) | b 5.7.1908 | |
| COSSEY, Raymond Reginald | (1958) | b 21.1.1935 | d 24.5.1986 |
| COTTRELL, Anthony Ian | (1929-32) | b 10.2.1907 | |
| COTTRELL, Wayne David | (1968-71) | d 30.9.1943 | |
| COUCH, Manuera Benjamin Riwai | (1947-49) | b 27.6.1925 | |
| COUGHLAN, Thomas Desmond | (1958) | b 9.4.1934 | |
| CREIGHTON, John Neville | (1962) | b 10.3.1937 | |
| CRICHTON, Scott | (1983) | b 18.2.1956 | |
| CROSS, Thomas | (1904-05) | b 21.1.1876 | |
| CROWLEY, Kieran James | (1985- ) | b 31.8.1961 | |
| CROWLEY, Patrick Joseph Bourke | (1949-50) | b 20.10.1923 | d 9.6.1981 |
| CUMMINGS, William | (1913) | b 13.3.1889 | d 28.5.1955 |
| CUNDY, Rawi Tama | (1929) | b 15.8.1901 | d 9.2.1955 |
| CUNNINGHAM, Gary Richard | (1979-80) | b 12.5.1955 | |
| CUNNINGHAM, William | (1905-08) | b 8.7.1874 | d 3.9.1927 |
| CUPPLES, Leslie Frank | (1924) | b 8.2.1898 | d 10.8.1972 |
| CURRIE, Clive James | (1978) | b 25.12.1955 | |
| CUTHILL, John Elliot | (1913) | b 24.8.1892 | d 22.4.1970 |
| DALLEY, William Charles | (1924-28) | b 18.11.1901 | |
| DALTON, Andrew Grant | (1977- ) | b 16.11.1951 | |

| PLAYER | CAREER SPAN | |
|---|---|---|
| DALTON, Douglas | (1935-8) | b 18.1.1913 |
| DALTON, Raymond | | |
| Alfred | (1947) | b 14.7.1919 |
| DALZELL, George Nelson | (1953-4) | b 26.4.1921 |
| DAVIE, Murray Geoffrey | (1983) | b 19.9.1955 |
| DAVIES, William Anthony | (1960-2) | b 16.9.1939 |
| DAVIS, Keith | (1952-8) | b 21.5.1930 |
| DAVIS, Lyndon John | (1976-7) | b 22.12.1943 |
| DAVIS, William Leslie | (1967-70) | b 15.12.1942 |
| DEANS, Robert George | (1905-08) | b 19.2.1884 d 30.9.1908 |
| DEANS, Robert Maxwell | (1983-4) | b 4.9.1959 |
| DELAMORE, Graham | | |
| Wallace | (1949) | b 3.4.1920 |
| DEWAR, Henry | (1913) | b 13.10.1883 d 19.8.1915 |
| DIACK, Ernest Sinclair | (1959) | b 22.7.1932 |
| DICK, John | (1937-8) | b 3.10.1912 |
| DICK, Malcolm John | (1963-70) | b 3.1.1941 |
| DIXON, Maurice James | (1953-7) | b 6.2.1929 |
| DOBSON, Ronald Leslie | (1949) | b 26.3.1923 |
| DODD, Ernest Henry | (1905) | b 21.3.1880 d 11.9.1918 |
| DONALD, Andrew J. | (1983- ) | b 11.5.1957 |
| DONALD, James George | (1921) | b 4.6.1898 d 29.8.1981 |
| DONALD, Quentin | (1924-5) | b 13.3.1900 d 27.12.1965 |
| DONALDSON, Mark | | |
| William | (1977-81) | b 6.11.1955 |
| DOUGAN, John Patrick | (1972-3) | b 22.12.1946 |
| DOWNING, Albert Joseph | (1913-14) | b 12.7.1886 d 8.8.1915 |
| DRAKE, John Alan | (1986-) | b 22.1.1959 |
| DUFF, Robert Hamilton | (1951-6) | b 5.8.1925 |
| DUNCAN, James | (1903) | b 12.11.1869 d 19.10.1953 |
| DUNCAN, Michael George | (1971) | b 8.8.1947 |
| DUNCAN, William Dow | (1921) | b 11.6.1892 d 14.12.1961 |
| DUNN, Edward | (1979-81) | b 19.1.1955 |
| DUNN, Ian Thomas | | |
| Wayne | (1983) | b 11.6.1960 |
| DUNN, John Markham | (1946) | b 17.11.1918 |
| | | |
| EARL, Andrew Thomas | (1986- ) | b 12.9.1961 |
| EASTGATE, Barry Peter | (1952-4) | b 10.7.1927 |
| ELLIOTT, Kenneth | | |
| George | (1946) | b 3.3.1922 |
| ELSOM, Allan Edwin | | |
| George | (1952-5) | b 18.7.1925 |
| ELVIDGE, Ronald | | |
| Rutherford | (1946-50) | b 2.3.1923 |
| ERCEG, Charles Percy | (1951-2) | b 28.11.1928 |
| EVANS, David Alexander | (1910) | b 4.10.1886 d 12.10.1940 |
| EVELEIGH, Kevin Alfred | (1976-7) | b 8.11.1947 |
| | | |
| FANNING, Alfred Henry | | |
| Netherwood | (1913) | b 31.3.1890 d 11.3.1963 |
| FANNING, Bernard John | (1903-04) | b 11.11.1874 d 9.7.1946 |
| FARRELL, Colin Paul | (1977) | b 19.3.1956 |
| FAWCETT, Christopher | | |
| Louis | (1976) | b 28.10.1954 |
| FEA, William Rognvald | (1921) | b 5.10.1898 |
| FINLAY, Brian Edward | | |
| Louis | (1959) | b 7.11.1927 d 9.3.1982 |
| FINLAY, Jack | (1946) | b 31.1.1916 |
| FINLAYSON, Innes | (1928-30) | b 4.7.1899 d 29.1.1980 |
| FITZGERALD, James | | |
| Train | (1952) | b 6.8.1928 |
| FITZPATRICK, Brian | | |
| Bernard James | (1953-4) | b 5.3.1931 |
| FITZPATRICK, Sean | | |
| Brian Thomas | (1986- ) | b 4.6.1963 |
| FLEMING, John Kingsley | (1979-80) | b 2.5.1953 |
| FLETCHER, Charles John | | |
| Compton | (1921) | b 9.5.1894 d 9.9.1973 |
| FOGARTY, Richard | (1921) | b 12.12.1891 d 9.9.1980 |
| FORD, Brian Robert | (1977-9) | b 10.7.1951 |
| FOX, Grant James | (1985- ) | b 6.6.1962 |
| FRANCIS, Arthur | | |
| Reginald Howe | (1905-10) | b 8.6.1882 d 15.6.1957 |
| FRANCIS, William Charles | (1913-14) | b 4.2.1894 |
| FRASER, Bernard Gabriel | (1979-84) | b 21.7.1953 |
| FRAZER, Harry Frederick | (1946-9) | b 21.4.1916 |
| FRYER, Frank | | |
| Cunningham | (1907-08) | b 2.11.1886 d 22.9.1958 |
| FULLER, William Bennett | (1910) | b 9.4.1883 d 25.7.1957 |
| FURLONG, Blair Donald | | |
| Marie | (1970) | b 10.3.1945 |

| PLAYER | CAREER SPAN | |
|---|---|---|
| GALLAHER, David | (1903-06) | b 30.10.1873 d 4.10.1917 |
| GARD, Philip Charles | (1971) | b 20.11.1947 |
| GARDINER, Ashley John | (1974) | b 10.12.1946 |
| GEDDES, John Herbert | (1929) | b 9.1.1907 |
| GEDDES, William McKail | (1913) | b 13.5.1893 d 1.7.1950 |
| GEMMELL, Bruce | | |
| McLeod | (1974) | b 12.5.1950 |
| GEORGE, Victor Leslie | (1938) | b 5.6.1908 |
| GILBERT, Graham | | |
| Duncan McMillan | (1935-6) | b 1.3.1911 |
| GILLESPIE, Charles | | |
| Theodore | (1913) | b 24.6.1883 d 22.1.1964 |
| GILLESPIE, William | | |
| David | (1958) | b 6.8.1934 |
| GILLETT, George Arthur | (1905-08) | b 23.4.1877 d 12.9.1956 |
| GILLIES, Colin Cuthbert | (1936) | b 8.10.1912 |
| GILRAY, Colin | | |
| MacDonald | (1905) | b 17.3.1885 d 15.7.1974 |
| GLASGOW, Francis | | |
| Turnbull | (1905-08) | b 17.8.1880 d 20.2.1939 |
| GLENN, William Spiers | (1904-06) | b 21.2.1877 d 5.10.1953 |
| GODDARD, Maurice | | |
| Patrick | (1946-9) | b 28.9.1921 d 19.6.1974 |
| GOING, Sidney Milton | (1967-77) | b 19.8.1943 |
| GRAHAM, David John | (1958-64) | b 1.1.1935 |
| GRAHAM, James Buchan | (1913-14) | b 23.4.1884 d 15.5.1941 |
| GRAHAM, Wayne | | |
| Geoffrey | (1979) | b 13.4.1957 |
| GRANT, Lachlan Ashwell | (1947-49) | b 4.10.1923 |
| GRAY, George Donaldson | (1908-13) | b 1880 d 16.4.1961 |
| GRAY, Kenneth Francis | (1963-69) | b 24.6.1938 |
| GRAY, William | | |
| Ngataiawhio | (1955-56) | b 23.12.1932 |
| GREEN, Craig Ivan | (1983- ) | b 23.3.1961 |
| GRENSIDE, Bertram | | |
| Arthur | (1928-9) | b 9.4.1899 |
| GRIFFITHS, Jack Lester | (1934-8) | b 9.4.1912 |
| GUY, Richard Alan | (1971) | b 6.4.1941 |
| | | |
| HADEN, Andrew Maxwell | (1977-85) | b 26.9.1950 |
| HADLEY, Swinbourne | (1928) | b 19.9.1904 d 30.4.1970 |
| HADLEY, William | | |
| Edward | (1934-6) | b 11.3.1910 |
| HAIG, James Scott | (1946) | b 7.12.1924 |
| HAIG, Laurence Stokes | (1950-4) | b 18.10.1922 |
| HALES, Duncan Alister | (1972-3) | b 22.11.1947 |
| HAMILTON, Donald | | |
| Cameron | (1908) | b 19.1.1883 d 14.4.1925 |
| HAMMOND, Ian Arthur | (1952) | b 25.10.1925 |
| HARPER, Eric Tristram | (1904-06) | b 1.12.1877 d 30.4.1918 |
| HARRIS, Perry Colin | (1976) | b 11.1.1946 |
| HART, Augustine Henry | (1924) | b 28.3.1897 d 1.2.1965 |
| HART, George Fletcher | (1930-36) | b 10.2.1909 d 3.6.1944 |
| HARVEY, Brett Andrew | (1986- ) | b 6.10.1959 |
| HARVEY, Ian Hamilton | (1928) | b 1.1.1903 d 22.10.1966 |
| HARVEY, Lester Robert | (1949-50) | b 14.4.1919 |
| HARVEY, Patrick | (1904) | b 3.4.1880 d 29.10.1949 |
| HASELL, Edward William | (1913) | b 26.4.1889 d 7.4.1966 |
| HAYWARD, Harold Owen | (1908) | b 23.5.1883 d 25.7.1970 |
| HAZLETT, Edward John | (1966-7) | b 21.7.1938 |
| HAZLETT, William Edgar | (1928-30) | b 8.11.1905 d 13.4.1978 |
| HEEPS, Thomas Roderick | (1962) | b 7.3.1938 |
| HEKE, Wiremu Rika | (1929) | b 3.9.1894 |
| HEMI, Ronald Courtney | (1953-9) | b 15.5.1933 |
| HENDERSON, Peter | (1949-50) | b 18.4.1926 |
| HEREWINI, MacFarlane | | |
| Alexander | (1962-7) | b 17.10.1940 |
| HEWSON, Allan Roy | (1981-4) | b 6.6.1954 |
| HIGGINSON, Graeme | (1980-3) | b 14.12.1954 |
| HILL, Stanley Frank | (1955-9) | b 9.4.1927 |
| HINES, Geoffrey Robert | (1980) | b 10.10.1960 |
| HOBBS, Michael James | | |
| Bowie | (1983- ) | b 15.2.1960 |
| HOLDER, Edward | | |
| Catchpole | (1934) | b 26.7.1908 d 2.7.1974 |
| HOOK, Llewellyn Simpkin | (1929) | b 4.5.1905 d 4.8.1979 |
| HOOPER, John Alan | (1937) | b 20.11.1913 d 21.4.1976 |
| HOPKINSON, Alister | | |
| Ernest | (1967-70) | b 30.5.1941 |
| HORE, John | (1930-6) | b 9.8.1907 d 7.7.1979 |
| HORSLEY, Ronald Hugh | (1960) | b 4.7.1932 |
| HOTOP, John | (1952-5) | b 7.12.1929 |

| PLAYER | CAREER SPAN | | |
|---|---|---|---|
| HUGHES, Arthur Maitland | (1949-50) | b 11.10.1924 | |
| HUGHES, Edward | (1907-21) | b 26.4.1881 | d 1.5.1928 |
| HUNTER, Bruce Anthony | (1971) | b 16.9.1950 | |
| HUNTER, James | (1905-08) | b 6.3.1879 | d 14.12.1962 |
| HURST, Ian Archinbald | (1972-4) | b 27.8.1951 | |
| IFWERSEN, Karl Donald | (1921) | b 6.1.1893 | d 19.5.1967 |
| INNES, Gordon Donald | (1932) | b 8.9.1910 | |
| IRVINE, Ian Bruce | (1952) | b 6.3.1929 | |
| IRVINE, John Gilbert | (1914) | b 1.7.1888 | d 10.6.1939 |
| IRVINE, William Richard | (1924-30) | b 2.12.1898 | d 26.4.1952 |
| IRWIN, Mark William | (1955-60) | b 10.2.1935 | |
| JACKSON, Everard Stanley | (1936-8) | b 12.1.1914 | d 20.9.1975 |
| JAFFRAY, John Lyndon | (1972-9) | b 17.4.1950 | |
| JARDEN, Ronald Alexander | (1951-56) | b 14.12.1929 | d 18.2.1977 |
| JEFFERD, Andrew Charles Reeves | (1981) | b 13.6.1953 | |
| JESSEP, Evan Morgan | (1931-2) | b 11.10.1904 | d 10.1.1983 |
| JOHNSON, Lancelot Matthew | (1928) | b 9.8.1897 | d 11.1.1983 |
| JOHNSTON, William | (1907) | b 13.9.1881 | d 9.1.1951 |
| JOHNSTONE, Bradley Ronald | (1976-79) | b 30.7.1950 | |
| JOHNSTONE, Peter | (1949-51) | b 9.8.1922 | |
| JONES, Murray Gordon | (1973) | b 26.10.1942 | d 12.2.1975 |
| JONES, Peter Frederick | (1953-60) | b 24.3.1932 | |
| JOSEPH, Howard Thornton | (1971) | b 25.8.1949 | |
| KARAM, Joseph Francis | (1972-5) | b 21.11.1951 | |
| KATENE, Thomas | (1955) | b 14.8.1929 | |
| KEARNEY, James Charles | (1947-49) | b 4.4.1920 | |
| KELLY, John Wallace | (1949) | b 7.12.1926 | |
| KEMBER, Gerald Francis | (1970) | b 15.11.1945 | |
| KETELS, Rodney Clive | (1980-1) | b 11.11.1954 | |
| KIERNAN, Henry Arthur Douglas | (1903) | b 24.7.1876 | d 15.1.1947 |
| KILBY, Francis David | (1932-4) | b 24.4.1906 | d 3.9.1985 |
| KILLEEN, Brian Alexander | (1936) | b 13.4.1911 | |
| KING, Ronald Russell | (1934-8) | b 19.8.1909 | |
| KINGSTONE, Charles Napoleon | (1921) | b 2.7.1895 | d 6.5.1960 |
| KIRK, David Edward | (1985-) | b 5.10.1960 | |
| KIRKPATRICK, Ian Andrew | (1967-77) | b 24.5.1946 | |
| KIRTON, Earle Weston | (1967-70) | b 29.12.1940 | |
| KIRWAN, John Joseph | (1984-) | b 16.12.1964 | |
| KIVELL, Alfred Louis | (1929) | b 12.4.1897 | |
| KNIGHT, Arthur | (1934) | b 26.1.1906 | |
| KNIGHT, Gary Albert | (1977-) | b 26.8.1951 | |
| KNIGHT, Laurence Gibb | (1977) | b 24.9.1949 | |
| KOTEKA, Paul T. | (1981-) | b 30.9.1956 | |
| KREFT, Anthony John | (1968) | b 27.3.1945 | |
| LAIDLAW, Christopher Robert | (1964-70) | b 16.11.1943 | |
| LAIDLAW, Kevin Francis | (1960) | b 9.8.1934 | |
| LAMBERT, Kent King | (1972-7) | b 23.3.1952 | |
| LAMBOURN, Arthur | (1934-8) | b 11.1.1910 | |
| LE LIEVRE, Jules Mathew | (1962) | b 17.8.1933 | |
| LENDRUM, Robert Noel | (1973) | b 22.3.1948 | |
| LESLIE, Andrew Roy | (1974-6) | b 10.11.1944 | |
| LEYS, Eric Tiki | (1929) | b 25.5.1907 | |
| LILBURNE, Herbert Theodore | (1928-34) | b 16.3.1908 | d 12.7.1976 |
| LINDSAY, David Frederick | (1928) | b 9.12.1906 | d 7.3.1978 |
| LINEEN, Terence Raymond | (1957-60) | b 5.1.1936 | |
| LISTER, Thomas Norman | (1968-71) | b 27.10.1943 | |
| LITTLE, Paul Francis | (1961-4) | b 14.9.1934 | |
| LOADER, Colin James | (1953-4) | b 10.3.1931 | |
| LOCHORE, Brian James | (1963-71) | b 3.9.1940 | |
| LONG, A.J. | (1903) | | |
| LOVERIDGE, David Steven | (1978-85) | b 22.4.1952 | |
| LUCAS, Frederick William | (1924-30) | b 30.1.1902 | d 17.9.1957 |

| PLAYER | CAREER SPAN | | |
|---|---|---|---|
| LUNN, William Albert | (1949) | b 17.9.1926 | |
| LYNCH, Thomas William | (1913-14) | b 6.3.1892 | d 6.5.1950 |
| LYNCH, Thomas | (1951) | b 20.7.1927 | |
| McATAMNEY, Francis Stevens | (1956) | b 15.5.1934 | |
| McCAW, William Alexander | (1951-4) | b 26.8.1927 | |
| McCOOL, Michael John | (1979) | b 15.9.1951 | |
| McCORMICK, William Fergus | (1965-71) | b 24.4.1939 | |
| McCULLOUGH, John Francis | (1959) | b 8.1.1936 | |
| McDONALD, Alexander | (1905-13) | b 23.4.1883 | d 4.5.1967 |
| MACDONALD, Hamish Hugh | (1972-6) | b 11.1.1947 | |
| McDOWELL, Steven Clark | (1985-) | b 27.8.1961 | |
| McELDOWNEY, John Thompson | (1977) | b 26.10.1947 | |
| MacEWAN, Ian Neven | (1956-62) | b 1.5.1934 | |
| McGRATTAN, Brian | (1983-) | b 31.12.1958 | |
| McGREGOR, Alwin John | (1913) | b 16.12.1889 | d 15.4.1963 |
| McGREGOR, Duncan | (1903-05) | b 16.7.1881 | d 11.3.1947 |
| McGREGOR, Neil Perriam | (1924-5) | b 29.12.1901 | d 12.7.1973 |
| McGREGOR, Robert Wylie | (1903-04) | b 31.12.1874 | d 22.11.1925 |
| McHUGH, Maurice James | (1946-9) | b 19.2.1917 | |
| McINTOSH, Donald Neil | (1956-7) | b 1.4.1931 | |
| McKAY, Donald William | (1961-3) | b 7.3.1937 | |
| McKECHNIE, Brian John | (1977-81) | b 6.11.1953 | |
| McKELLAR, Gerald Forbes | (1910) | b 9.1.1884 | d 16.1.1960 |
| McKENZIE, Richard John | (1913-14) | b 15.3.1892 | d 25.9.1968 |
| McKENZIE, Roderick McCulloch | (1934-8) | b 16.9.1909 | |
| MACKRELL, William Henry Clifton | (1906) | b 20.7.1881 | d 15.7.1917 |
| MACKY, John Victor | (1913) | b 3.9.1887 | d 15.9.1951 |
| McLACHLAN, Jon Stanley | (1974) | b 23.6.1949 | |
| McLAREN, Hugh Campbell | (1952) | b 8.6.1926 | |
| McLEAN, Andrew Leslie | (1921) | b 31.10.1898 | d 18.1.1964 |
| McLEAN, Hugh Foster | (1930-6) | b 18.7.1907 | |
| McLEAN, John Kenneth | (1947-9) | b 3.10.1923 | |
| McLEOD, Bruce Edward | (1964-70) | b 30.1.1940 | |
| McMINN, Archibald Forbes | (1903-05) | b 14.8.1880 | d 23.4.1919 |
| McMINN, Francis Alexander | (1904) | b 10.11.1874 | d 8.8.1947 |
| McMULLEN, Raymond Frank | (1957-60) | b 18.1.1933 | |
| McNAB, John Ronald | (1949-50) | b 26.3.1924 | |
| McNAUGHTON, Alan Murray | (1971) | b 20.9.1950 | |
| McNEECE, James | (1913-14) | b 24.12.1885 | d 21.6.1917 |
| McPHAIL, Bruce Eric | (1959) | b 26.1.1937 | |
| MACPHERSON, Donald Gregory | (1905) | b 23.7.1882 | d 26.11.1956 |
| MACPHERSON, Gordon | (1986-) | b 9.10.1962 | |
| MacRAE, Ian Robert | (1966-70) | b 6.4.1943 | |
| McRAE, John Alexander | (1946) | b 29.4.1914 | d 24.2.1977 |
| McWILLIAMS, Reuben George | (1928-30) | b 12.6.1901 | d 27.1.1984 |
| MAGUIRE, James Richard | (1910) | b 6.2.1886 | d 1.12.1966 |
| MAHONEY, Atholstan | (1935-6) | b 15.7.1908 | d 13.7.1979 |
| MAINS, Laurence William | (1971-6) | b 16.2.1946 | |
| MAJOR, John | (1967) | b 8.8.1940 | |
| MANCHESTER, John Eaton | (1932-6) | b 29.1.1908 | d 6.9.1983 |
| MASON, David Frank | (1947) | b 21.11.1923 | |
| MASTERS, Robin Read | (1924-5) | b 10.10.1900 | d 24.8.1967 |
| MATAIRA, Hawea Karepa | (1934) | b 3.12.1910 | d 15.11.1979 |
| MATHESON, Jeffrey David | (1972-3) | b 30.3.1948 | |
| MAX, Donald Stanfield | (1931-4) | b 7.3.1907 | d 4.3.1972 |
| MEADS, Colin Earl | (1957-71) | b 3.6.1936 | |
| MEADS, Stanley Thomas | (1961-66) | b 12.7.1938 | |
| MEATES, Kevin Francis | (1952) | b 20.2.1930 | |
| MEATES, William Anthony | (1949-50) | b 26.5.1923 | |

| PLAYER | CAREER SPAN | | |
|--------|-------------|---|---|
| METCALFE, Thomas | | | |
| Charles | (1931-2) | b 13.5.1909 | d 26.5.1969 |
| MEXTED, Graham George | (1950) | b 3.2.1927 | |
| MEXTED, Murray | | | |
| Graham | (1979-) | b 5.9.1953 | |
| MILL, James Joseph | (1924-30) | b 19.11.1899 | d 29.3.1950 |
| MILLIKEN, Harold | | | |
| Maurice | (1938) | b 27.2.1914 | |
| MILNER, Henare Pawhara | (1970) | b 12.2.1946 | |
| MITCHELL, Neville | | | |
| Alfred | (1935-8) | b 22.11.1913 | d 21.5.1981 |
| MITCHELL, Terry | | | |
| William | (1976) | b 11.9.1950 | |
| MITCHELL, William | | | |
| James | (1910) | b 28.11.1890 | d 2.6.1959 |
| MITCHINSON, Frank | | | |
| Edwin | (1907-13) | b 3.9.1884 | d 27.3.1978 |
| MOFFITT, James Edward | (1921) | b 3.6.1889 | d 16.3.1964 |
| MOORE, Graham John | | | |
| Tarr | (1949) | b 18.3.1923 | |
| MORETON, Raymond | | | |
| Claude | (1962-5) | b 30.1.1942 | |
| MORGAN, Joseph | | | |
| Edmund | (1974-6) | b 7.8.1945 | |
| MORRIS, Trevor James | (1972) | b 3.1.1942 | |
| MORRISON, Terry | | | |
| Godfrey | (1973) | b 16.6.1951 | |
| MORRISON, Thomas | | | |
| Clarence | (1938) | b 28.7.1913 | d 31.8.1985 |
| MORRISSEY, Peter John | (1962) | b 18.7.1939 | |
| MOURIE, Graham Neil | | | |
| Kenneth | (1977-82) | b 8.9.1952 | |
| MULLER, Brian Leo | (1967-71) | b 11.6.1942 | |
| MUMM, William John | (1949) | b 26.3.1922 | |
| MURDOCH, Keith | (1970-3) | b 9.9.1943 | |
| MURDOCH, Peter Henry | (1964-5) | b 17.6.1941 | |
| MURRAY, Harold Vivian | (1913-14) | b 9.2.1888 | d 4.7.1971 |
| MURRAY, Peter Chapman | (1908) | b 23.1.1884 | d 6.2.1968 |
| MYERS, Richard George | (1978) | b 6.7.1950 | |
| MYNOTT, Harry Jonas | (1905-10) | b 4.6.1876 | d 2.1.1924 |
| | | | |
| NATHAN, Waka Joseph | (1962-7) | b 8.7.1940 | |
| NELSON, Keith Alister | (1962) | b 26.11.1938 | |
| NEPIA, George | (1924-30) | b 25.4.1905 | d 27.8.1986 |
| NESBIT, Steven Roberto | (1960) | b 13.2.1936 | |
| NEWTON, Frederick | (1905) | b 7.5.1881 | d 10.12.1955 |
| NICHOLLS, Harry Edgar | (1921) | b 21.1.1900 | d 1.4.1978 |
| NICHOLLS, Marcus | | | |
| Frederick | (1921-30) | b 13.7.1901 | d 10.6.1972 |
| NICHOLSON, George | | | |
| William | (1903-07) | b 3.8.1878 | d 13.9.1968 |
| NORTON, Rangitane Will | (1971-77) | b 30.3.1942 | |
| | | | |
| O'BRIEN, John Gerald | (1914) | b 9.12.1889 | d 9.1.1958 |
| O'CALLAGHAN, Michael | | | |
| William | (1968) | b 27.4.1946 | |
| O'CALLAGHAN, Thomas | | | |
| Raymond | (1949) | b 19.1.1925 | |
| O'DONNELL, Desmond | | | |
| Hillary | (1949) | b 7.10.1921 | |
| OLD, Geoffrey Haldane | (1981-2) | b 22.1.1956 | |
| O'LEARY, Michael Joseph | (1910-13) | b 29.9.1883 | d 12.12.1963 |
| OLIVER, Charles Joshua | (1929-36) | b 1.11.1905 | d 25.9.1977 |
| OLIVER, Desmond | | | |
| Oswald | (1953-4) | b 26.10.1930 | |
| OLIVER, Donald Joseph | (1930) | b 1907 | |
| OLIVER, Francis James | (1976-81) | b 24.12.1948 | |
| ORR, Rex William | (1949) | b 19.6.1924 | |
| OSBORNE, William | | | |
| Michael | (1975-82) | b 24.4.1955 | |
| O'SULLIVAN, James | | | |
| Michael | (1905-07) | b 5.2.1883 | d 21.12.1960 |
| O'SULLIVAN, Terence | | | |
| Patrick Anthony | (1960-2) | b 27.11.1936 | |
| | | | |
| PAGE, James Russell | (1931-4) | b 10.5.1908 | d 22.5.1985 |
| PALMER, Bertram Pitt | (1929-32) | b 14.11.1901 | d 4.9.1932 |
| PARKER, James Hislop | (1924-5) | b 1.2.1897 | d 11.9.1980 |
| PARKHILL, Allan | | | |
| Archibald | (1937-8) | b 22.4.1912 | d 26.8.1986 |
| PARKINSON, Ross | | | |
| Michael | (1972-3) | b 30.5.1948 | |

| PLAYER | CAREER SPAN | | |
|--------|-------------|---|---|
| PATERSON, Alexander | | | |
| Marshall | (1908-10) | b 31.10.1885 | d 29.7.1933 |
| PATON, Henry | (1910) | b 12.2.1881 | d 21.1.1964 |
| PHILLIPS, William John | (1937-8) | b 30.1.1914 | d 10.11.1982 |
| PICKERING, Ernest | | | |
| Arthur Rex | (1958-9) | b 23.11.1936 | |
| PIERCE, Murray James | (1985) | b 1.11.1957 | |
| POKERE, Steven Tahurata | (1981-) | b 11.8.1958 | |
| POLLOCK, Harold | | | |
| Raymond | (1932-6) | b 7.9.1909 | d 10.1.1984 |
| PORTER, Clifford Glen | (1925-30) | b 5.5.1899 | d 12.11.1976 |
| PROCTOR, Albert Charles | (1932) | b 22.5.1906 | |
| PURDUE, Charles Alfred | (1905) | b 10.6.1874 | d 10.10.1941 |
| PURDUE, Edward | (1905) | b 1878 | d 16.7.1939 |
| PURDUE, George | | | |
| Bambery | (1931-2) | b 4.5.1909 | |
| PURVIS, Neil Alexander | (1976) | b 31.1.1953 | |
| | | | |
| QUAID, Charles Edward | (1938) | b 17.8.1908 | d 18.12.1984 |
| | | | |
| RANGI, Ronald Edward | (1964-6) | b 4.2.1941 | |
| RANKIN, John George | (1936-7) | b 14.2.1914 | |
| REEDY, William Joseph | (1908) | b 1880 | d 1.4.1939 |
| REID, Alan Robin | (1952-7) | b 12.4.1929 | |
| REID, Hikatarewa | | | |
| Rockcliffe | (1980-) | b 8.4.1958 | |
| REID, Keith Howard | (1929) | b 25.5.1904 | d 24.5.1972 |
| REID, Sana Torium | (1935-7) | b 22.9.1912 | |
| RESIDE, Walter Brown | (1929) | b 6.10.1905 | |
| RHIND, Patrick Keith | (1946) | b 20.6.1915 | |
| RICHARDSON, Johnstone | (1921-5) | b 2.4.1899 | |
| RICKIT, Haydn | (1981) | b 1951 | |
| RIDLAND, Alexander | | | |
| James | (1910) | b 3.3.1882 | d 5.11.1918 |
| ROBERTS, Edward James | (1914-21) | b 10.5.1891 | d 27.2.1972 |
| ROBERTS, Frederick | (1905-10) | b 7.4.1881 | d 21.7.1956 |
| ROBERTS, Richard | | | |
| Williams | (1913-14) | b 23.1.1889 | d 8.3.1973 |
| ROBERTSON, Bruce John | (1972-81) | b 9.4.1952 | |
| ROBERTSON, Duncan | | | |
| John | (1974-77) | b 6.2.1947 | |
| ROBILLIARD, Alan | | | |
| Charles Compton | (1928) | b 20.12.1903 | |
| ROBINSON, Charles | | | |
| Edward | (1951-2) | b 5.4.1927 | d 4.3.1983 |
| ROLLERSON, Douglas | | | |
| Leslie | (1980-1) | b 14.5.1953 | |
| ROPER, Roy Alfred | (1949-50) | b 11.8.1923 | |
| ROWLEY, Harrison | | | |
| Cotton Banks | (1949) | b 15.6.1924 | d 16.12.1956 |
| RUTLEDGE, Leicester | | | |
| Malcolm | (1978-80) | b 12.4.1952 | |
| RYAN, James | (1910-14) | b 8.2.1887 | d 17.7.1957 |
| | | | |
| SADLER, Bernard Sydney | (1935-6) | b 28.7.1914 | |
| SALMON, James Lionel | | | |
| Broome | (1981) | b 16.10.1959 | |
| SAVAGE, Laurence | | | |
| Theodore | (1949) | b 17.2.1928 | |
| SAXTON, Charles | | | |
| Kesteven | (1938) | b 23.5.1913 | |
| SCOTT, Robert William | | | |
| Henry | (1946-54) | b 6.2.1921 | |
| SCOWN, Alistair Ian | (1972) | b 21.10.1948 | |
| SCRIMSHAW, George | (1928) | b 1.12.1902 | d 13.7.1971 |
| SEEAR, Gary Alan | (1977-9) | b 19.2.1952 | |
| SEELING, Charles Edward | (1904-08) | b 14.5.1883 | d 29.5.1956 |
| SELLARS, George | | | |
| Maurice Victor | (1913) | b 16.4.1886 | d 7.6.1917 |
| SHAW, Mark William | (1980-) | b 23.5.1956 | |
| SHELFORD, Frank N.K. | (1981-) | b 16.5.1955 | |
| SHELFORD, Wayne | | | |
| Thomas | (1986-) | b 13.12.1957 | |
| SIDDELLS, Stanley Keith | (1921) | b 16.7.1897 | d 3.3.1979 |
| SIMON, Harold James | (1937) | b 7.3.1911 | d 1.10.1979 |
| SIMPSON, John George | (1947-50) | b 18.3.1922 | |
| SIMPSON, Victor Leonard | | | |
| James | (1985-) | b 26.2.1960 | |
| SIMS, Graham S. | (1972) | b 25.6.1951 | |
| SKEEN, Jack Robert | (1952) | b 23.12.1928 | |
| SKINNER, Kevin | | | |
| Lawrence | (1949-56) | b 24.11.1927 | |

| PLAYER | CAREER SPAN | | |
|---|---|---|---|
| SKUDDER, George Rupuha | (1969) | b 10.2.1948 | |
| SLOANE, Peter Henry | (1979) | b 10.9.1948 | |
| SMITH, Alan Edward | (1969-70) | b 10.12.1942 | |
| SMITH, Bruce Warwick | (1984- ) | b 4.1.1959 | |
| SMITH, George William | (1905) | b 20.9.1894 | d 8.12.1954 |
| SMITH, Ian Stanley Talbot | (1964-6) | b 20.8.1941 | |
| SMITH, John Burns | (1946-9) | b 25.9.1922 | d 3.12.1974 |
| SMITH, Ross Mervyn | (1955) | b 21.4.1929 | |
| SMITH, Wayne Ross | (1980- ) | b 19.4.1957 | |
| SMITH, William Ernest | (1905) | b 9.3.1881 | d 25.5.1945 |
| SNOW, Eric McDonald | (1929) | b 19.4.1898 | d 24.7.1974 |
| SOLOMON, Frank | (1931-2) | b 30.5.1906 | |
| SONNTAG, William Theodore Charles | (1929) | b 3.6.1894 | |
| SPEIGHT, Michael Wayne | (1986- ) | b 24.2.1962 | |
| SPENCER, John Clarence | (1905-07) | b 27.11.1880 | d 21.5.1936 |
| SPIERS, John Edmunde | (1979-81) | b 4.8.1947 | |
| SPILLANE, Augustine Patrick | (1913) | b 10.5.1888 | d 16.9.1974 |
| STANLEY, Joseph Tito | (1986- ) | b 13.4.1957 | |
| STEAD, John William | (1904-08) | b 18.9.1877 | d 21.7.1958 |
| STEEL, Anthony Gordon | (1966-68) | b 31.7.1941 | |
| STEEL, John | (1921-5) | b 10.11.1898 | d 4.8.1941 |
| STEELE, Leo Brian | (1951) | b 19.1.1929 | |
| STEERE, Edward Richard George | (1930-2) | b 10.7.1908 | d 1.6.1967 |
| STEPHENS, Owen George | (1968) | b 9.1.1947 | |
| STEVENS, Ian Neal | (1972-4) | b 13.4.1948 | |
| STEWART, Allan James | (1963-4) | b 11.10.1940 | |
| STEWART, James Douglas | (1913) | b 3.10.1890 | d 5.5.1973 |
| STEWART, Kenneth William | (1973-81) | b 3.1.1953 | |
| STEWART, Ronald Terowie | (1928-30) | b 12.1.1904 | d 15.12.1982 |
| STOHR, Leonard | (1910) | b 13.11.1889 | d 25.7.1973 |
| STONE, Arthur M. | (1981- ) | b 19.12.1960 | |
| STOREY, Percival Wright | (1921) | b 11.2.1897 | d 4.10.1975 |
| STRAHAN, Samuel Cunningham | (1967-73) | b 25.12.1944 | |
| STRANG, William Archibald | (1928-31) | b 18.10.1906 | |
| STRINGFELLOW, John Clinton | (1929) | b 26.2.1905 | d 3.1.1959 |
| STUART, Kevin Charles | (1955) | b 19.9.1928 | |
| STUART, Robert Charles | (1949-54) | b 28.10.1920 | |
| STUART, Robert Locksdale | (1977) | b 9.1.1948 | |
| SULLIVAN, John Lorraine | (1937-8) | b 30.3.1915 | |
| SUTHERLAND, Alan Richard | (1970-3) | b 4.1.1944 | |
| SVENSON, Kenneth Sydney | (1924-5) | b 6.12.1898 | d 7.12.1955 |
| SWAIN, John Patterson | (1928) | b 1902 | d 29.8.1960 |
| TANNER, John Maurice | (1950-3) | b 11.1.1927 | |
| TANNER, Kerry John | (1974-6) | b 25.4.1945 | |
| TAYLOR, Henry Morgan | (1913-4) | b 5.2.1889 | d 20.6.1955 |
| TAYLOR, John McLeod | (1937-8) | b 12.1.1913 | d 5.5.1979 |
| TAYLOR, Murray Barton | (1979-80) | b 25.8.1956 | |
| TAYLOR, Norman Mark | (1977-82) | b 11.1.1951 | |
| TAYLOR, Reginald | (1913) | b 23.3.1889 | d 20.6.1917 |
| TAYLOR, Warwick Thomas | (1983- ) | b 11.3.1960 | |
| TETZLAFF, Percy Laurence | (1947) | b 14.7.1920 | |
| THIMBLEBY, Neil William | (1970) | b 19.6.1939 | |
| THOMAS, Barry Trevor | (1962-4) | b 21.7.1937 | |
| THOMSON, Hector Douglas | (1908) | b 20.2.1881 | d 9.8.1939 |
| THORNE, Grahame Stuart | (1968-70) | b 25.2.1946 | |
| THORNTON, Neville Henry | (1947-9) | b 12.12.1918 | |

| PLAYER | CAREER SPAN | | |
|---|---|---|---|
| TILYARD, James Thomas | (1913) | b 27.8.1889 | d 1.11.1966 |
| TINDALL, Eric William Thomas | (1936) | b 18.12.1910 | |
| TOWNSEND, Lindsay James | (1955) | b 3.3.1934 | |
| TREMAIN, Kelvin Robin | (1959-68) | b 21.2.1938 | |
| TREVATHAN, David | (1937) | b 6.5.1912 | d 11.4.1986 |
| TUCK, Jack Manson | (1929) | b 13.5.1907 | d 23.3.1967 |
| TURTILL, Hubert Sydney | (1905) | b 1.2.1880 | d 9.4.1918 |
| TWIGDEN, Timothy Moore | (1980) | b 14.5.1952 | |
| TYLER, George Alfred | (1903-06) | b 10.2.1897 | d 15.4.1942 |
| UDY, Daniel Knight | (1903) | b 21.5.1874 | d 29.7.1935 |
| URBAHN, Roger James | (1959) | b 31.7.1934 | d 27.11.1984 |
| URLICH, Ronald Anthony | (1970) | b 8.2.1944 | |
| UTTLEY, Ian Neill | (1963) | b 3.12.1941 | |
| VINCENT, Patrick Bernard | (1956) | b 6.1.1926 | d 10.4.1983 |
| VODANOVICH, Ivan Matthew Henry | (1955) | b 8.4.1930 | |
| WALLACE, William Joseph | (1903-08) | b 2.8.1878 | d 2.3.1972 |
| WALSH, Patrick Timothy | (1955-63) | b 6.5.1936 | |
| WARD, Ronald Henry | (1936-7) | b 1.12.1915 | |
| WATERMAN, Alfred Clarence | (1929) | b 31.12.1903 | |
| WATKINS, Eric Leslie | (1905) | b 18.3.1880 | d 14.4.1949 |
| WATT, Bruce Alexander | (1962-4) | b 12.3.1939 | |
| WATT, James Michael | (1936) | b 5.7.1914 | |
| WATT, James Russell | (1958-62) | b 29.12.1935 | |
| WATTS, Murray Gordon | (1979-80) | b 31.3.1955 | |
| WEBB, Desmond Stanley | (1959) | b 10.9.1934 | d 24.3.1987 |
| WELLS, John | (1936) | b 4.1.1911 | |
| WEST, Alfred Hubert | (1921) | b 6.5.1893 | d 7.1.1934 |
| WHETTON, Alan James | (1984- ) | b 15.12.1959 | |
| WHETTON, Gary W. | (1981- ) | b 15.12.1959 | |
| WHINERAY, Wilson James | (1957-65) | b 10.7.1935 | |
| WHITE, Andrew | (1921-5) | b 21.3.1894 | d 3.8.1968 |
| WHITE, Hallard Leo | (1953-5) | b 27.3.1929 | |
| WHITE, Richard Alexander | (1949-56) | b 11.6.1925 | |
| WHITE, Roy Maxwell | (1946-7) | b 18.10.1917 | d 19.1.1980 |
| WHITING, Graham John | (1972-3) | b 4.6.1946 | |
| WHITING, Peter John | (1971-6) | b 6.8.1946 | |
| WILLIAMS, Bryan George | (1970-8) | b 3.10.1950 | |
| WILLIAMS, Graham Charles | (1967-8) | b 26.1.1945 | |
| WILLIAMS, Peter | (1913) | b 22.4.1884 | d 30.8.1976 |
| WILLIMENT, Michael | (1964-7) | b 25.2.1940 | |
| WILLOCKS, Charles | (1946-9) | b 28.6.1919 | |
| WILSON, Bevan William | (1977-9) | b 22.3.1956 | |
| WILSON, Douglas Dawson | (1954) | b 30.1.1931 | |
| WILSON, Hector William | (1949-51) | b 27.1.1924 | |
| WILSON, Nathaniel Arthur | (1908-14) | b 18.5.1886 | d 11.8.1953 |
| WILSON, Norman Leslie | (1951) | b 13.12.1923 | |
| WILSON, Richard George | (1979) | b 19.5.1953 | |
| WILSON, Stuart Sinclair | (1977-83) | b 22.7.1955 | |
| WOLFE, Thomas Neil | (1961-3) | b 20.10.1941 | |
| WOOD, Morris Edwin | (1903-04) | b 9.10.1876 | d 9.8.1956 |
| WOODMAN, Freddy Akehurst | (1981) | b 10.2.1958 | |
| WRIGHT, Terence John | (1986- ) | b 21.1.1963 | |
| WRIGLEY, Edgar | (1905) | b 15.6.1886 | d 2.6.1958 |
| WYLIE, James Thomas | (1913) | b 26.10.1887 | d 19.12.1956 |
| WYLLIE, Alexander John | (1970-3) | b 30.8.1944 | |
| YATES, Victor Moses | (1961) | b 15.6.1939 | |
| YOUNG, Denis | (1956-64) | b 1.4.1930 | |

# AUSTRALIA

| PLAYER | CAREER SPAN | | |
|--------|-------------|---|---|
| ABRAHAMS, Anthony Morris Frederick | (1967-69) | b 28.3.1944 | |
| ADAMS, Neil Joseph | (1955) | b 26.8.1925 | |
| ADAMSON, Robert Wilson | (1912) | b 1889 | d 1952 |
| ALLAN, Trevor | (1946-49) | b 26.9.1926 | |
| ANLEZARK, Ernest Arthur | (1905) | b 29.12.1882 | d 1956 |
| AUSTIN, Leslie Raymond | (1963) | b 10.12.1935 | |
| BAKER, Harald William | (1914) | b 29.9.1887 | d 17.10.1962 |
| BAKER, Reginald Leslie | (1904) | b 8.2.1884 | d 2.12.1953 |
| BALLESTY, John Patrick | (1968-9) | b 20.5.1946 | |
| BANNON, Desmond Patrick | (1946) | b 1923 | |
| BARKER, Herbert Samuel | (1952-4) | b 1929 | |
| BARNETT, John Thomas | (1907-09) | b 19.1.1880 | d 1933 |
| BARRY, Michael Joseph | (1971) | b 21.10.1942 | |
| BARTON, Roger Furnivall Daranth | (1899) | | |
| BATCH, Patrick Gerard | (1975-79) | b 19.1.1953 | |
| BATTERHAM, Rodney Paul | (1967-70) | b 24.11.1947 | |
| BATTISHALL, Bruce Robert | (1973) | b 3.9.1946 | |
| BAXTER, Archibald John | (1949-52) | b 30.8.1922 | |
| BAXTER, Thomas J. | (1958) | b 28.4.1935 | |
| BEITH, Bruce McNeil | (1914) | b 28.9.1893 | d 9.1961 |
| BELL, Keith Radcliffe | (1968) | b 10.6.1948 | |
| BENNETT, Walter Gordon | (1931-3) | b 26.3.1906 | d 11.9.1979 |
| BERMINGHAM, Vincent J. | (1934-7) | b 1910 | d 7.1983 |
| BERNE, John Edward | (1975) | b 14.3.1954 | |
| BESOMO, Keith Scot | (1979) | b 1954 | |
| BETTS, Terence Neil | (1951-54) | b 13.4.1926 | |
| BIILMANN, Ronald | (1933) | b 1908 | d 16.5.1963 |
| BIRT, J. | (1914) | | |
| BLACK, James William | (1985- ) | b 10.6.1958 | |
| BLAIR, Malcolm Rignold | (1928-31) | b 1905 | d 1966 |
| BLACKWOOD, John Garven | (1927-8) | b 1899 | d 1979 |
| BLAND, Geoffrey Victor | (1932-3) | b 1906 | d 1961 |
| BLOMLEY, John | (1949-50) | b 1927 | d 1973 |
| BOLAND, Sinon Bernard | (1899-1903) | b 12.7.1875 | d 1954 |
| BONIS, Edward Tasman | (1929-38) | b 1908 | d 23.9.1984 |
| BOSLER, John Morgan | (1953) | b 4.2.1933 | |
| BOUFFLER, Robert George | (1899) | b 1874 | d 1956 |
| BOURKE, Thomas Kevin | (1947) | b 1922 | |
| BOWERS, Alan John | (1927) | b 27.10.1902 | |
| BOYCE, Edward Stewart | (1962-7) | b 14.12.1941 | |
| BOYCE, James Stewart | (1962-5) | b 14.12.1941 | |
| BOYD, Alister Forrest McClelland | (1958) | b 1935 | |
| BOYD, Archibald | (1899) | b 1872 | d 6.5.1905 |
| BRASS, John Ellis | (1966-8) | b 7.10.1946 | |
| BRECKENRIDGE, John Wylie | (1927-30) | b 22.4.1903 | |
| BRIDLE, Owen Lawman | (1931-6) | b 1909 | d 5.1983 |
| BROAD, Edmund George | (1949) | b 3.1.1921 | |
| BROCKHOFF, John David | (1949-51) | b 8.6.1928 | |
| BROWN, Bruce Robert | (1972) | b 18.8.1944 | |
| BROWN, James Vicker | (1956-8) | b 1935 | |
| BROWN, Robert Charles | (1975) | b 9.2.1953 | |
| BROWN, Spencer William | (1953) | b 1922 | d 15.1.1973 |
| BUCHAN, Arthur John | (1946-9) | b 1924 | |
| BURDON, Alexander | (1903-05) | b 31.3.1879 | d 13.12.1943 |
| BURGE, Albert Bentley | (1907-08) | b 3.6.1887 | d 1943 |
| BURGE, Peter Harold Boyne | (1907) | b 14.2.1884 | d 7.1956 |
| BURKE, Cyril Thomas | (1946-56) | b 7.11.1925 | |
| BURKE, Matthew Peter | (1984- ) | b 15.9.1964 | |
| BURNET, David Ronald | (1972) | b 8.9.1950 | |
| BUTLER, Owen Frederick | (1969-71) | b 31.5.1944 | |
| CALCRAFT, William Joseph | (1985- ) | b 23.5.1957 | |
| CAMERON, Alan Stewart | (1951-8) | b 18.11.1929 | |
| CAMPBELL, John Denison | (1910) | b 22.7.1889 | d 31.8.1966 |
| CAMPBELL, William Alexander | (1984- ) | b 28.11.1961 | |
| CAMPESE, David Ian | (1982- ) | b 21.10.1962 | |
| CANNIFFE, William Denis | (1907) | b 1885 | d 1956 |
| CARBERRY, Christopher Michael | (1973-82) | b 27.4.1951 | |
| CARDY, Alan Michael | (1966-68) | b 12.12.1945 | |
| CAREW, Patrick James | (1899) | b 10.9.1876 | d 1946 |
| CARMICHAEL, Philip P. | (1904-09) | b 25.1.1884 | d 9.1973 |
| CARPENTER, Maxwell Gordon | (1938) | | |
| CARR, Ernest Thomas A. | (1913-14) | b 11.5.1885 | |
| CARROLL, Daniel Brendan | (1908-12) | b 17.11.1888 | d 1956 |
| CARROLL, John Charles | (1953) | b 14.9.1925 | |
| CARROLL, John Hugh | (1958-9) | b 20.3.1934 | |
| CARSON, James | (1899) | b 1870 | d 1903 |
| CARSON, Peter John | (1979-80) | b 1952 | |
| CASEY, Terence Vincent | (1963-4) | b 1938 | |
| CATCHPOLE, Kenneth William | (1961-8) | b 21.6.1939 | |
| CAWSEY, Roy Milton | (1949) | b 1923 | d 6.5.1974 |
| CERUTTI, William Hector | (1929-37) | b 1909 | d 3.7.1965 |
| CHALLONER, Robert L. | (1899) | b 1872 | |
| CHAPMAN, Geoffrey Alexander | (1962) | b 2.12.1939 | |
| CLARK, John Goode | (1931-3) | b 9.9.1908 | d 19.4.1979 |
| CLARKEN, James C. | (1905-10) | b 19.7.1876 | d 31.7.1953 |
| CLEARY, Michael Arthur | (1961) | b 30.4.1940 | |
| CLEMENTS, Phillip | (1982) | b 1952 | |
| CLIFFORD, Michael | (1938) | b 1916 | d 1943 |
| COBB, Walter George | (1899) | b 1870 | d 1933 |
| COCKS, Michael Richard | (1972-5) | b 1.3.1945 | |
| CODEY, David | (1983- ) | b 7.7.1957 | |
| CODY, Ernest Austin | (1913) | b 1889 | d 1968 |
| COLBERT, Raymond | (1952-3) | b 30.5.1931 | |
| COLE, John Walter | (1968-74) | b 20.9.1946 | |
| COLLINS, Paul K. | (1937-8) | b 1916 | |
| COLTON, A.J. | (1899) | b 25.3.1875 | d 1946 |
| COLTON, Thomas | (1904) | b 1874 | d 1958 |
| CONNOR, Desmond Michael | (1958-9) | b 9.8.1935 | |
| COOK, Michael Terence | (1986- ) | | |
| COOKE, Bruce P. | (1979) | b 1953 | |
| COOKE, Graeme Morven | (1932-48) | b 3.1.1912 | |
| COOLICAN, John Edward | (1982-3) | b 1953 | |
| CORFE, Arthur Cecil | (1899) | b 12.12.1879 | d 30.7.1949 |
| CORNELSEN, Gregory | (1974-82) | b 29.8.1952 | |
| CORNES, John Reginald | (1972) | b 1947 | |
| CORNFORTH, Roger George Warcup | (1947-50) | b 19.1.1919 | d 30.3.1976 |
| COSTELLO, Paul Patrick Scott | (1950) | b 1925 | |
| COTTRELL, Neville Vincent | (1949-52) | b 16.3.1927 | |
| COWPER, Denis Lawson | (1931-33) | b 20.12.1908 | d 5.12.1981 |
| COX, Brian Philip | (1952-7) | b 24.9.1928 | |
| COX, Mitchell Hunter | (1981) | b 22.10.1958 | |
| COX, Philip Anthony | (1979-84) | b 2.8.1957 | |
| CRAIG, Robert Robertson | (1908) | b 1.9.1881 | d 5.3.1935 |
| CREMIN, John Francis | (1946-7) | b 1923 | |
| CRITTLE, Charles Peter | (1962-7) | b 21.7.1939 | |
| CROSS, James Robert | (1955) | b 27.10.1931 | |
| CROSS, Keith Austin | (1949-57) | b 8.6.1928 | |
| CROSSMAN, Owen Charles | (1929-30) | b 1903 | d 1962 |
| CROWE, Philip John | (1976-9) | b 27.10.1955 | |
| CURLEY, Terence George P. | (1957-8) | b 6.6.1938 | |
| CURRAN, Declan James | (1980- ) | b 15.4.1952 | |
| CURRIE, Ernest William | (1899) | b 9.4.1875 | |

| PLAYER | CAREER SPAN | |
|---|---|---|
| CUTLER, Stephen Arthur Geoffrey | (1982- ) | b 28.7.1960 |
| D'ARCY, Anthony Michael | (1980-2) | b 1959 |
| DARVENIZA, Paul | (1969) | b 19.9.1945 |
| DAVIDSON, Robert Alfred Lewars | (1952-8) | b 18.10.1926 |
| DAVIS, Clarence Clive | (1949-51) | b 28.3.1928 |
| DAVIS, Eric Hamilton | (1947-9) | b 1919 |
| DAVIS, Gregory Victor | (1963-72) | b 27.7.1939 d 24.7.1979 |
| DAVIS, Gordon Walter Gray | (1955) | b 19.6.1927 |
| DAVIS, Roger Andrew | (1974) | b 23.10.1951 |
| DAVIS, Walter | (1899) | |
| DAWSON, Walter Laird | (1946) | b 1924 |
| DIETT, Leonard John | (1959) | b 27.8.1939 |
| DIX, William | (1907-09) | b 19.11.1883 d 1944 |
| DIXON, Ernest Joseph | (1904) | b 1885 d 1941 |
| DONALD, Kenneth John | (1957-9) | b 8.8.1936 |
| DORE, Edmund | (1904) | b 1880 d 1964 |
| DORE, Michael Joseph | (1905) | b 1883 d 13.8.1910 |
| DORR, Rudolph William | (1936-7) | b 1910 d 1961 |
| DOUGLAS, James Alexander | (1962) | b 1939 |
| DOWSE, John Henry | (1961) | b 1935 |
| DUNBAR, A. Robert | (1910-12) | b 1888 d 1954 |
| DUNLOP, Ernest Edward | (1932-4) | b 12.7.1907 |
| DUNN, Peter Keith | (1958-9) | b 1936 |
| DUNWORTH, David Anthony | (1971-6) | b 29.8.1946 |
| DWYER, Laurence Joseph | (1910-14) | b 1884 d 1964 |
| EASTES, Charles Colbran | (1946-9) | b 12.7.1925 |
| ELLA, Gary Albert | (1982-3) | b 23.7.1960 |
| ELLA, Glen Joseph | (1982- ) | b 5.6.1959 |
| ELLA, Mark Gordon | (1980- ) | b 5.6.1959 |
| ELLEM, Michael Anthony | (1976) | b 1952 |
| ELLIOTT, Francis Maxwell | (1957) | b 20.12.1929 |
| ELLIS, Charles Seymour | (1899) | b 1.8.1879 |
| ELLIS, Keith Joseph | (1958-9) | b 30.3.1927 |
| ELLWOOD, Beresford John | (1958-66) | b 24.7.1937 |
| EMANUEL, David Maurice | (1957-8) | b 23.6.1934 |
| EMERY, Neville Allen | (1947-9) | b 1924 |
| EVANS, Llewellyn John | (1903-4) | b 19.2.1881 |
| EVANS, William Thomas | (1899) | b 9.4.1876 d 19.7.1964 |
| FAHEY, Edward Joseph | (1912-14) | b 1882 d 23.8.1950 |
| FAIRFAX, Russell Lance | (1971-3) | b 29.3.1952 |
| FARMER, E.H. | (1910) | |
| FARR-JONES, Nicholas Campbell | (1984- ) | b 18.4.1962 |
| FAY, Garrick | (1971-9) | b 11.4.1948 |
| FENWICKE, Peter Thomas | (1957-9) | b 14.11.1932 |
| FIHELLY, John Arthur | (1907) | b 7.11.1882 d 2.3.1945 |
| FINLAY, Arthur Noel | (1927-30) | b 25.12.1903 d 20.9.1981 |
| FINLAY, Francis George | (1904) | b 27.2.1884 d 1943 |
| FINNANE, Stephen Charles | (1975-8) | b 3.7.1952 |
| FLANAGAN, Peter | (1907) | b 1885 d 1952 |
| FLYNN, James P. | (1914) | b 18.6.1894 |
| FOGARTY, John Raymond Patrick | (1949) | b 1929 |
| FORBES, Colin Francis | (1953-6) | b 1932 |
| FORD, Brian William | (1957) | b 1939 |
| FORD, Eric Exell | (1927-9) | b 2.6.1904 d 1986 |
| FORD, John Alfred | (1927-30) | b 17.2.1906 d 20.2.1985 |
| FORMAN, Terry Robert | (1968-9) | b 12.1.1948 |
| FOX, Charles Leigh | (1928) | b 27.7.1898 d 1.1985 |
| FOX, Otho George | (1958) | b 1934 |
| FRANCIS, Eric | (1914) | b 17.6.1894 |
| FREEDMAN, John Edward | (1962-3) | b 25.6.1935 |
| FREEMAN, Eric | (1946) | b 1922 |
| FRENEY, Michael Ernest | (1972-3) | b 10.5.1948 |
| FURNESS, Donald Charles | (1946) | b 18.5.1920 |
| FUTTER, Frank Cuthbert | (1904) | b 1880 d 13.11.1941 |

| PLAYER | CAREER SPAN | |
|---|---|---|
| GARDNER, William Charles | (1950) | b 2.3.1929 |
| GARNER, Ralph Lindsay | (1949) | b 20.1.1927 |
| GAVIN, Kenneth A. | (1909) | b 20.1.1883 d 1956 |
| GELLING, Anthony Massey | (1972) | b 1.12.1946 |
| GEORGE, Harold W. | (1910-14) | b 1887 d 1916 |
| GIBBONS, Eric de Courcy | (1936) | b 1913 d 1962 |
| GIBBS, Paul Rodney | (1966) | b 6.12.1941 |
| GILBERT, Herbert | (1910) | b 1888 d 5.1.1972 |
| GORDON, George Campbell | (1929) | b 11.8.1903 |
| GORDON, Keith Milton | (1950) | b 29.4.1927 |
| GOULD, Roger George | (1980- ) | b 4.4.1957 |
| GRAHAM, Charles Stewart | (1899) | b 1870 d 1944 |
| GRAHAM, Ronald | (1973-6) | b 21.12.1946 |
| GRALTON, Arthur Sarsfield I. | (1899-1903) | b 9.2.1873 d 1919 |
| GRAVES, Robert Henderson | (1907) | b 1.9.1880 d 15.2.1957 |
| GREATOREX, Edward Neville | (1928) | b 1904 d 1964 |
| GREGORY, Stuart Carlton | (1968-73) | b 18.8.1946 |
| GREY, Gareth Owen | (1972) | b 29.8.1947 |
| GRIFFIN, Thomas Sydney | (1907-12) | b 1885 d 1952 |
| GRIGG, Peter Clive | (1980- ) | b 20.7.1958 |
| GRIMMOND, David Noel | (1964) | b 1944 |
| GUDSELL, Keith Eric | (1951) | b 19.10.1924 |
| GUERASSIMOFF, Jules | (1963-7) | b 28.6.1940 |
| GUNTHER, William John | (1957) | b 1934 |
| HALL, Duncan | (1980- ) | b 16.3.1956 |
| HAMALAINEN, Harry Arwit | (1929) | b 1903 d 1975 |
| HAMILTON, Bruce G. | (1946) | |
| HAMMON, John Douglas Campbell | (1937) | b 3.3.1914 |
| HAMMAND, Charles Ackroyd | (1908-09) | b 9.5.1885 |
| HANDY, Christopher Bernard | (1978-80) | b 28.3.1950 |
| HANLEY, Ross Gregory | (1983) | b 6.12.1961 |
| HARDCASTLE, Phillip Angus | (1946-9) | b 23.12.1919 d 1962 |
| HARDCASTLE, William Robert | (1899-1903) | b 30.8.1874 d 11.7.1944 |
| HARDING, Mark Anthony | (1983) | b 28.12.1955 |
| HARVEY, Patrick B. | (1949) | |
| HARVEY, Ronald Mason | (1958) | b 26.10.1934 |
| HATHERELL, William Ian | (1952) | b 1930 |
| HAUSER, Rodney Graham | (1975-9) | b 31.3.1952 |
| HARTILL, Mark Norman | (1986-) | |
| HAWKER, Michael John | (1980-4) | b 11.10.1959 |
| HAWTHORNE, Philip Francis | (1962-7) | b 24.10.1943 |
| HAYES, Edward Sautelle | (1934-8) | b 1911 d 1943 |
| HEINRICH, Edward Laurence | (1961-3) | b 25.6.1940 |
| HEINRICH, Vincent William | (1954) | b 1934 |
| HEMING, Robert John | (1961-7) | b 11.12.1937 |
| HEMINGWAY, Wilfred Hubert | (1931-2) | b 22.9.1908 |
| HENRY, Arthur R. | (1899) | |
| HERD, Harold Vincent | (1931) | b 1910 d 1961 |
| HICKEY, John Joseph | (1908-9) | b 4.1.1887 d 15.5.1950 |
| HILLHOUSE, David William | (1975-83) | b 13.7.1955 |
| HILLS, Ernest Fryers | (1950) | b 3.3.1930 |
| HINDMARSH, John A. | (1904) | |
| HINDMARSH, James Charles | (1975-6) | b 11.4.1952 |
| HIPWELL, John Noel Brian | (1968-82) | b 24.1.1948 |
| HIRSCHBERG, William Adolphus | (1905) | |
| HODGENS, Charles | (1910) | |
| HODGSON, Aubrey John | (1933-8) | b 9.3.1912 d 28.8.1982 |
| HOLT, Nigel Colin | (1984) | b 28.11.1961 |

| PLAYER | CAREER SPAN | | |
|---|---|---|---|
| HONAN, Barry David | (1968-9) | b 1947 | |
| HONAN, Robert Emmett | (1964) | b 1944 | |
| HORODAM, A. David | (1913) | | |
| HORSLEY, Gavan Rex | (1954) | b 1933 | |
| HORTON, Peter Alan | (1974-9) | b 20.7.1945 | |
| HOW, Richard Alfred | (1967) | b 1944 | |
| HOWARD, John | (1938) | b 1914 | d 1944 |
| HOWARD, John Leslie | (1970-3) | b 30.8.1946 | |
| HOWELL, Maxwell Leo | (1946-7) | b 23.7.1927 | |
| HUGHES, Brian Desmond | (1913) | b 1887 | d 1914 |
| HUGHES, James Charles | (1907) | b 1887 | d 1943 |
| HUGHES, Norman McLaurin | (1953-8) | b 18.11.1932 | |
| HUTCHINSON, Eric Ebsworth | (1937) | b 1916 | d 1942 |
| HUTCHINSON, Francis Ebsworth | (1936-8) | b 27.12.1917 | d 4.1.1943 |
| IDE, Winston Philip James | (1938) | b 17.9.1914 | d 12.9.1944 |
| IVES, Walter Norman | (1929) | b 10.11.1906 | d 1983 |
| JAMES, Peter Michael | (1958) | b 1935 | |
| JESSEP, Evan Morgan | (1934) | b 11.10.1904 | d 10.1.1983 |
| JOHNSON, Adrian Paul | (1946) | b 1924 | |
| JOHNSON, Brian Bernard | (1952-55) | b 29.4.1930 | d 29.8.1966 |
| JOHNSON, Peter George | (1959-71) | b 13.9.1937 | |
| JONES, Garth Glennie | (1952-6) | b 18.11.1931 | |
| JONES, Herbert A. | (1913) | b 1888 | d 1918 |
| JONES, Peter Anthony | (1963) | b 15.8.1942 | |
| JOYCE, James Emerton | (1903) | | |
| JUDD, Harold Augustus | (1903-05) | b 11.4.1880 | d 1965 |
| JUDD, Peter Bruce | (1927-31) | b 1907 | d 1970 |
| KASSULKE, Nigel | (1985-) | b 1961 | |
| KAY, A. Robert | (1958-9) | b 1935 | |
| KEARNEY, Kenneth Howard | (1947-8) | b 3.5.1924 | |
| KELAHER, John Desmond | (1933-8) | b 5.2.1912 | |
| KELLEHER, Rodney James | (1969) | b 8.11.1947 | |
| KELLER, Douglas Holcombe | (1947-8) | b 18.6.1922 | |
| KELLY, Alexander J. | (1899) | | d 1913 |
| KELLY, Russell Lindsay Frederick | (1936-8) | b 25.11.1909 | d 25.12.1943 |
| KENT, Allan | (1912) | b 1891 | d 1966 |
| KERR, Frederick R. | (1938) | b 1918 | d 1943 |
| KING, Sidney Charles | (1927-32) | b 21.3.1905 | d 30.3.1970 |
| KNIGHT, Martin | (1978) | | d 25.2.1984 |
| KNIGHT, Stephen Oliver | (1969-71) | b 24.7.1948 | |
| KNOX, David | (1985-) | | |
| KRAEFFT, Donald F. | (1947-8) | b 1923 | |
| KREUTZER, Samuel D. | (1914) | b 1894 | d 1971 |
| LAMBIE, John Kenneth | (1974-5) | b 27.3.1951 | |
| LANE, Timothy A. | (1985-) | b 24.11.1959 | |
| LANG, Clifford W.P. | (1938) | | |
| LARKIN, Edward Rennie | (1903) | | |
| LARKIN, Kerry Kelsall | (1958) | b 1936 | |
| LATIMER, Neil B. | (1957) | b 1932 | |
| LAWTON, Thomas | (1927-32) | b 16.1.1899 | d 1.7.1978 |
| LAWTON, Thomas Anthony | (1983-) | b 27.11.1962 | |
| LEEDS, Andrew | (1986-) | | |
| LENEHAN, James Kenneth | (1958-67) | b 29.4.1938 | |
| L'ESTRANGE, Rex David | (1971-6) | b 25.5.1948 | |
| LEWIS, Llewellyn S. | (1934-8) | b 1912 | |
| LILLICRAP, Cameron A. | (1985-) | b 19.4.1963 | |
| LINDSAY, Roy Thomas George | (1932) | b 1905 | d 1972 |
| LISLE, Ronald James | (1961) | b 19.9.1939 | |
| LIVERMORE, Alan Edward | (1946) | b 1919 | |
| LOANE, Mark Edward | (1973-82) | b 11.7.1954 | |
| LOGAN, Donald Leonard | (1958) | b 1933 | |
| LOUDON, Robert Briton | (1929-34) | b 24.3.1902 | |
| LOVE, E. William | (1932) | | |
| LOWTH, Donald R. | (1958) | b 1932 | |
| LUCAS, Basil C. | (1905) | | |

| PLAYER | CAREER SPAN | | |
|---|---|---|---|
| LUCAS, Peter William | (1982) | b 24.9.1956 | |
| LUTGE, Denis | (1903-4) | b 1879 | d 18.2.1953 |
| LYNAGH, Michael Patrick | (1984-) | b 25.10.1963 | |
| McARTHUR, Malcolm | (1909) | b 30.7.1884 | |
| McBAIN, Mark Ian | (1983-) | b 3.10.1959 | |
| MacBRIDE, John William Terence | (1946-8) | b 1927 | |
| McCABE, Arthur John Michael | (1909) | b 1887 | d 5.1925 |
| McCARTHY, Fabian Joseph Charles | (1950) | b 1924 | |
| McCOWAN, Robert H. | (1899) | b 28.2.1875 | d 1941 |
| McCue, Patrick Aloysius | (1907-09) | b 19.6.1883 | d 10.9.1962 |
| McDERMOTT, Lloyd Clive | (1962) | b 11.11.1939 | |
| McDONALD, Barry Stuart | (1969-70) | b 9.6.1940 | |
| McDONALD, John Charles | (1938) | b 1914 | |
| MACDOUGALL, Graham Donald | (1961) | b 1940 | |
| MACDOUGALL, Stuart Grant | (1971-6) | b 1.6.1947 | |
| McGHIE, Gordon H. | (1929-30) | b 1907 | d 1975 |
| McGILL, Arthur Neil | (1968-73) | b 5.12.1944 | |
| McINTYRE, Andrew John | (1982-) | b 23.12.1955 | |
| McKID, William Alexander | (1976-9) | b 27.1.1953 | |
| McKINNON, Alexander | (1904) | b 1881 | d 1944 |
| McKIVAT, Christopher Hobart | (1907-09) | b 27.11.1879 | d 4.5.1947 |
| McLAUGHLIN, Reginald Edward Millen | (1936) | b 1915 | |
| McLEAN, Alexander Douglas | (1933-6) | b 12.1912 | d 1961 |
| McLEAN, Douglas James | (1904-05) | b 15.4.1880 | d 12.1947 |
| McLEAN, Jeffrey James | (1971-4) | b 26.1.1947 | |
| McLEAN, Paul Edward | (1974-82) | b 12.10.1953 | |
| McLEAN, Peter William | (1978-82) | b 1954 | |
| McLEAN, Robert Alexander | (1971) | b 21.1.1949 | |
| McLEAN, William Malcolm | (1946-7) | b 28.2.1918 | |
| McMAHON, Michael James | (1913) | b 29.7.1889 | d 1961 |
| McMASTER, Robert Edmond | (1946-7) | b 5.1.1921 | |
| MACMILLAN, D. Ian | (1950) | b 1930 | d 1981 |
| McMULLEN, Kenneth Victor | (1962-3) | b 16.4.1941 | |
| McSHANE, Jan Melville Swain | (1937) | b 11.12.1910 | d 1975 |
| MACKNEY, Walter Arthur Reginald | (1933-4) | b 28.7.1903 | d 5.10.1975 |
| MAGRATH, Edward | (1961) | b 1939 | |
| MALCOLM, Sydney Joseph | (1927-34) | b 1903 | |
| MALONE, John H. | (1936-7) | b 1912 | d 1949 |
| MALOUF, Bruce Paul | (1982) | b 1956 | |
| MANDIBLE, Edward Francis | (1907-08) | b 11.5.1885 | d 1936 |
| MANNING, John | (1904) | | |
| MANNING, Russell Charles Sylvester | (1967) | | |
| MANSFIELD, Brian William | (1975) | b 1948 | |
| MARKS, Hyam | (1899) | b 8.6.1872 | |
| MARKS, Richard James Picket | (1962-7) | b 6.9.1942 | |
| MARSHALL, John Samuel | (1949) | b 21.3.1926 | |
| MARTIN, Michael Clayton | (1980-1) | b 5.5.1955 | |
| MASSEY WESTROPP, Montagu | (1914) | b 1891 | d 1974 |
| MATHERS, Michael John | (1980) | b 1.3.1955 | |
| MAUND, John Williams | (1903) | b 1876 | d 1962 |
| MEADOWS, John Ernest Charles | (1974-83) | b 2.2.1949 | |
| MEADOWS, Ronald W. | (1958) | b 12.2.1931 | d 9.1985 |
| MEAGHER, Francis Wallace | (1927) | b 1903 | d 1966 |
| MEIBUSCH, John Henry | (1904) | b 11.12.1878 | d 1955 |

| PLAYER | CAREER SPAN | | |
|---|---|---|---|
| MEIBUSCH, Ludwig | | | |
| Samuel | (1912) | b 1893 | d 1965 |
| MELROSE, Tony | | | |
| Christopher | (1978-9) | b 7.9.1959 | |
| MESSENGER, Henry | | | |
| Herbert | (1907) | b 12.4.1883 | d 24.11.1959 |
| MIDDLETON, Sydney | | | |
| Albert | (1909-10) | b 24.2.1884 | d 1945 |
| MILLER, Anthony Robert | (1952-67) | b 29.4.1929 | |
| MILLER, James Muir | (1962-7) | b 6.4.1939 | |
| MILLER, Jeffrey Scott | (1986-) | b 1962 | |
| MILLER, Sydney W.J. | (1899) | | d 12.1909 |
| MONAGHAN, Laurence | | | |
| Edward | (1973-9) | b 19.5.1952 | |
| MONTI, C.I.A. | (1938) | b 1914 | d 1977 |
| MOON, Brendan Joseph | (1978-) | b 10.10.1958 | |
| MOONEY, Thomas Paul | (1954) | b 1929 | |
| MORAN, Herbert Michael | (1908) | b 1885 | d 29.11.1945 |
| MORRISSEY, William | (1914) | | |
| MORTON, Alan Ridley | (1957-9) | b 10.9.1934 | |
| MOSSOP, Rex Peers | (1949-51) | b 18.2.1928 | |
| MOUTRAY, Ian Edmund | | | |
| Joseph | (1963) | b 2.7.1936 | |
| MURPHY, Patrick Joseph | (1910-14) | | |
| MURPHY, William | (1912) | b 1880 | d 1957 |
| NICHOLSON, Frederick | | | |
| Charles | (1904) | b 1885 | d 1975 |
| NICHOLSON, Frank V. | (1903-04) | b 1878 | d 1970 |
| O'BRIEN, Frank William | | | |
| H. | (1937-8) | b 1910 | |
| O'CONNOR, Michael | | | |
| David | (1979-82) | b 30.11.1960 | |
| O'DONNELL, Claude | | | |
| Augustus | (1913) | b 30.1.1886 | d 4.8.1953 |
| O'DONNELL, Ignatius | | | |
| Charles | (1899) | b 1876 | d 1946 |
| O'DONNELL, James M. | (1899) | | |
| O'GORMAN, John Francis | (1961-7) | b 1.6.1936 | |
| O'NEILL, Dallas John | (1964) | b 1943 | |
| O'NEILL, John Michael | (1952-6) | b 26.4.1932 | |
| OSBORNE, Douglas Hugh | (1975) | b 19.7.1952 | |
| OUTTERSIDE, Robert | (1959) | b 6.3.1932 | |
| OXENHAM, Anselm | | | |
| McEvoy | (1904-07) | b 20.7.1882 | d 1919 |
| OXLADE, Allen | | | |
| Martindale | (1904-07) | b 18.6.1882 | d 1932 |
| OXLADE, Boyd Davies | (1938) | b 1914 | |
| PALFREYMAN, James | | | |
| Richard Leonard | (1929-32) | b 9.5.1905 | d 9.9.1973 |
| PAPWORTH, Brett | (1985-) | | |
| PARKER, Anthony Joseph | (1983) | b 1961 | |
| PARKINSON, Charles | | | |
| Esmond | (1907) | b 3.10.1886 | |
| PASHLEY, John James | (1954-8) | b 31.8.1933 | |
| PAULING, Tom P. | (1936-7) | b 26.4.1912 | d 1979 |
| PEARSE, Gary Keith | (1975-8) | b 8.2.1953 | |
| PENMAN, Albert Percival | (1905) | b 1885 | d 1944 |
| PERRIN, Paul Douglas | (1962) | b 26.3.1940 | |
| PERRIN, Thomas | | | |
| Drummond | (1931) | b 1911 | d 1975 |
| PHELPS, Roderick | (1955-62) | b 15.6.1934 | |
| PHIPPS, James Alfred | (1953-6) | b 31.12.1931 | |
| PHIPPS, Peter Joseph | (1955) | b 24.2.1933 | |
| PILECKI, Stanislaw | (1978-83) | b 4.2.1947 | |
| PIPER, Brian James | | | |
| Charles | (1946-9) | b 16.9.1925 | |
| POIDEVIN, Simon Paul | (1980-) | b 31.10.1958 | |
| POPE, Alexander M. | (1968) | b 1945 | |
| POTTER, Robert Thomas | (1961) | b 1942 | |
| POTTS, John Maxwell | (1957-9) | b 21.2.1936 | |
| PRENTICE, Clarence | (1914) | b 1891 | d 1948 |
| PRENTICE, Warden Selby | (1908-12) | b 1886 | d 1969 |
| PRICE, Raymond Allan | (1974-6) | b 4.3.1953 | |
| PRIMMER, Colin James | (1951) | b 24.3.1924 | |
| PROCTOR, Ian J. | (1967) | b 1947 | |
| PROSSER, Roydon Barnett | (1967-72) | b 18.2.1942 | |
| PUGH, George Harold | (1912) | b 1890 | |
| PURCELL, Michael Peter | (1966-7) | b 6.9.1945 | |
| PURKISS, Edwin Maurice | (1958) | b 1934 | |

| PLAYER | CAREER SPAN | | |
|---|---|---|---|
| RAMALLI, Cecil | (1938) | b 1919 | |
| RAMSAY, Kehelm | | | |
| Mackenzie | (1936-8) | b 27.8.1914 | |
| RANKIN, Ronald | (1936-8) | b 1915 | |
| RATHIE, David Stewart | (1972) | b 29.5.1951 | |
| REDWOOD, Charles | | | |
| Edward Joseph | (1903-04) | b 19.5.1878 | d 16.2.1954 |
| REID, Terence William | (1961-2) | b 20.9.1934 | |
| REILLY, Norman Peter | (1968-9) | b 10.10.1947 | |
| REYNOLDS, Leo J. | (1910) | | |
| REYNOLDS, Ross John | (1984-) | b 27.9.1958 | |
| RICHARDS, Edward | | | |
| William | (1904-07) | | d 1928 |
| RICHARDS, Geoffrey | (1978-81) | b 1951 | |
| RICHARDS, Thomas | | | |
| James | (1908-12) | b 1883 | d 9.1935 |
| RICHARDS, Victor | (1936-8) | b 3.9.1911 | d 1983 |
| RICHARDSON, Geoffrey | | | |
| Colin | (1971-3) | b 17.4.1949 | |
| RILEY, Sidney Austin | (1903) | b 18.4.1878 | d 31.3.1964 |
| ROBERTS, Barry Thomas | (1956) | b 3.10.1933 | |
| ROBERTS, Harry | | | |
| Flaxmore | (1961) | b 1939 | |
| ROBERTSON, Ian Jeffrey | (1975) | b 26.11.1951 | |
| ROCHE, Christopher | (1982-4) | b 9.9.1958 | |
| RODRIGUEZ, Enrique | | | |
| Engardo | (1984-) | b 20.6.1952 | |
| ROSE, Hugh Alexander | (1967-70) | b 15.11.1946 | |
| ROSENBLUM, Rupert | | | |
| George | (1969-70) | b 1.1.1942 | |
| ROSEWELL, John S.H. | (1907) | b 1882 | |
| ROSS, Alexander William | (1927-34) | b 24.11.1905 | |
| ROSS, William Scott | (1979-83) | b 28.11.1956 | |
| ROTHWELL, Peter | | | |
| Ratcliffe | (1951-2) | | |
| ROW, Frank Leonard | (1899) | b 28.1.1877 | d 28.1.1950 |
| ROW, Norman Edward | (1907-10) | b 23.3.1883 | d 2.11.1968 |
| ROWLES, Peter George | (1972-3) | b 18.11.1952 | |
| ROXBURGH, James | | | |
| Russell | (1968-70) | b 28.10.1946 | |
| RUEBNER, George | (1966) | b 30.8.1942 | |
| RUSSELL, Charles Joseph | (1907-09) | b 5.12.1884 | d 5.1957 |
| RYAN, John Robert | (1975-6) | b 20.12.1949 | d 5.1982 |
| RYAN, Kevin James | (1958) | b 26.8.1934 | |
| RYAN, Peter Francis | (1963-6) | b 2.4.1940 | |
| SAMPSON, J.H. | (1899) | | |
| SAYLE, Jeffrey Leonard | (1967) | b 25.8.1942 | |
| SCHULTE, Bernard G. | (1946) | b 1918 | d 1954 |
| SCOTT, Peter Robert Ian | (1962) | b 1.1.1940 | |
| SHAMBROOK, Gregory | | | |
| George | (1976) | b 1953 | |
| SHAW, Anthony | | | |
| Alexander | (1973-82) | b 20.3.1953 | |
| SHAW, Geoffrey Arnold | (1969-79) | b 27.12.1948 | |
| SHEEHAN, William | | | |
| Beverley James | (1927) | b 1903 | d 1957 |
| SHEHADIE, Nicholas | | | |
| Michael | (1947-58) | b 15.11.1926 | |
| SHEIL, Ainslie Glenister | | | |
| Ross | (1956) | b 4.11.1933 | |
| SHEPHERD, David John | (1964-66) | b 1936 | |
| SIMPSON, Richard John | (1913) | | |
| SKINNER, Alan James | (1969-70) | b 16.7.1942 | |
| SLACK, Andrew Gerard | (1978-) | | |
| SLATER, Stephen | | | |
| Hazleton | (1910) | | |
| SMITH, Frank Bede | (1905-07) | b 1884 | d 1954 |
| SMITH, Lancelot | | | |
| Machattie | (1905) | b 1885 | d 1956 |
| SMITH, Philip Viviers | (1967-9) | b 15.7.1946 | |
| SMITH, Reginald Alan | (1971-6) | b 13.1.1948 | |
| SOLOMON, Herbert John | (1949-55) | b 15.10.1929 | |
| SPRAGG, Stephen Alonzo | (1899) | b 2.10.1879 | d 12.2.1904 |
| STAPLETON, Edgar | | | |
| Thomas | (1951-8) | b 21.11.1931 | |
| STEGGALL, John Cecil | (1931-3) | b 1909 | |
| STEGMAN, Trevor Robert | (1973) | b 1946 | |
| STEPHENS, Owen George | (1973-4) | b 9.1.1947 | |
| STEWART, Andrew Alec | (1979) | b 1952 | |
| STONE, Albert Hodsdon | (1937-8) | b 1913 | d 1968 |
| STONE, Charles Gordon | (1938) | | |

| PLAYER | CAREER SPAN | | |
|---|---|---|---|
| STONE, John Michael | (1946) | b 1921 | |
| STOREY, Geoffrey Parnell | (1927-30) | b 1905 | d 1975 |
| STOREY, Keith Parnell | (1936) | b 1912 | |
| STOREY, Norman John Daniel | (1962) | b 5.10.1936 | |
| STRACHAN, Donald John | (1955) | b 18.2.1929 | |
| STREET, Norman Ogilvie | (1899) | b 1876 | d 7.1963 |
| STREETER, Stephen Frederick | (1978) | b 1955 | |
| STUART, Robert | (1910) | b 14.6.1889 | d 1959 |
| STUMBLES, Barry Donald | (1972) | b 27.9.1948 | |
| STURTRIDGE, Gordon Short | (1929-33) | b 1907 | d 16.9.1963 |
| SULLIVAN, Peter David | (1971-3) | b 19.3.1948 | |
| SUMMONS, Arthur James | (1958-9) | b 13.12.1935 | |
| SUTTOR, Dudley Colin | (1913) | b 10.4.1892 | d 1962 |
| SWANNELL, Blair Inskip | (1905) | b 20.8.1875 | d 25.4.1915 |
| SWEENEY, Thomas Leo | (1953) | b 1929 | |
| | | | |
| TAAFE, Bruce Stanton | (1969-72) | b 13.8.1944 | |
| TANCRED, Arnold Joseph | (1927) | b 1904 | d 1963 |
| TANCRED, James Leo | (1928) | b 1903 | d 1965 |
| TANNER, William Henry | (1899) | b 27.12.1871 | |
| TASKER, William George | (1913-14) | b 1892 | d 1918 |
| TATE, Murray James | (1951-4) | b 1928 | |
| TAYLOR, David Aubrey | (1968) | b 11.11.1944 | |
| TAYLOR, John Inglis | (1971-2) | b 21.5.1949 | |
| TEITZEL, Ross Gordon | (1966-7) | b 20.3.1946 | |
| THOMPSON, Edward George | (1929-30) | b 1906 | |
| THOMPSON, Frederick | (1913-14) | b 1890 | d 1918 |
| THOMPSON, John | (1914) | b 7.1886 | d 1978 |
| THOMPSON, Peter D. | (1950) | | |
| THOMPSON, Robert John | (1971-2) | b 8.3.1947 | |
| THORNETT, John Edward | (1955-67) | b 30.3.1935 | |
| THORNETT, Richard Norman | (1961-2) | b 23.9.1940 | |
| THORPE, A.C. | (1929) | | |
| TIMBURY, Frederick Richard Vaughan | (1910) | b 1885 | d 4.1945 |
| TINDALL, Eric Norman | (1973) | b 1945 | |
| TOLHURST, Harold Ambrose | (1931) | b 4.7.1909 | |
| TONKIN, Arthur Edward Joseph | (1947-50) | b 19.10.1922 | |
| TOOTH, Richard Murray | (1951-7) | b 21.9.1929 | |
| TOWERS, Cyril Henry Thomas | (1927-37) | b 20.7.1906 | d 8.6.1985 |
| TRIVETT, Richard | (1966) | b 1942 | |
| TURNBULL, Adrian | (1961) | | |
| TURNBULL, Ross Vincent | (1968) | b 13.11.1941 | |
| TUYNMAN, Steven Norman | (1983-) | b 30.5.1963 | |
| TWEEDALE, Eric | (1946-9) | b 1922 | |

| PLAYER | CAREER SPAN | | |
|---|---|---|---|
| VAUGHAN, Dominic | (1983-) | | |
| VAUGHAN, Geoffrey Norman | (1958) | b 9.4.1933 | |
| VERGE, C. Arthur | (1904) | b 1882 | d 1915 |
| WALDEN, Ronald John | (1934-6) | b 27.8.1907 | d 3.1985 |
| WALKER, Alan Keith | (1947-50) | b 4.10.1925 | |
| WALKER, Arthur Stanley Billingsgate | (1912) | b 1893 | d 1958 |
| WALKER, Lance Robert | (1982) | b 1955 | |
| WALLACH, Clarence | (1913-14) | b 11.1889 | d 22.4.1918 |
| WALLACE, Arthur Cooper | (1927-8) | b 5.10.1900 | d 3.11.1975 |
| WALSH, James Austin | (1953) | b 1926 | |
| WALSH, Patrick Bernard | (1904) | b 1879 | d 1953 |
| WALSHAM, Keith Percival | (1962-3) | b 1941 | |
| WARD, Peter M. | (1899) | b 5.11.1876 | |
| WARD, Thomas | (1899) | | |
| WATSON, George William | (1907) | b 6.1.1885 | |
| WATSON, William Thornton | (1912-14) | b 10.11.1887 | d 9.9.1961 |
| WEATHERSTONE, Laurence John | (1975-6) | b 13.3.1950 | |
| WEBB, William | (1899) | | d 1930 |
| WELLS, Bruce G. | (1958) | | |
| WESTFIELD, Robert E. | (1929) | b 25.5.1907 | |
| WHITE, Charles J.B. | (1899-1904) | b 1874 | d 10.1941 |
| WHITE, James M. | (1904) | b 1883 | d 1935 |
| WHITE, Jonathon Parker Laidley | (1958-65) | b 27.2.1935 | |
| WHITE, Max Clarke | (1931-3) | b 1908 | d 2.11.1979 |
| WHITE, Saxon William | (1956-8) | b 9.3.1934 | |
| WHITE, William George Searle | (1933-36) | b 1913 | |
| WHITE, William James | (1932) | b 1908 | d 1977 |
| WICKHAM, Stanley Montgomery | (1903-05) | b 1.1.1876 | d 8.1960 |
| WILLIAMS, David | (1913-14) | | |
| WILLIAMS, John Lewis | (1963) | b 28.5.1940 | |
| WILLIAMS, Stephen Andrew | (1980-) | b 29.7.1958 | |
| WILSON, Bevan J. | (1949) | b 20.9.1927 | |
| WILSON, Charles Roy | (1957-8) | b 4.5.1931 | |
| WILSON, Vincent W. | (1937-8) | b 1913 | d 1945 |
| WINDON, Colin James | (1946-52) | b 8.11.1922 | |
| WINDON, Keith Stanley | (1937-46) | b 2.10.1917 | |
| WINDSOR, John Clement | (1947) | b 1924 | |
| WINNING, Keith Charles | (1951) | b 2.2.1928 | |
| WOGAN, Laurence William | (1913-14) | b 10.9.1890 | d 8.1979 |
| WOOD, Frederick | (1907-14) | b 23.1.1884 | d 7.1923 |
| WOOD, Robert N. | (1972) | b 6.5.1948 | |
| WOODS, Harold F. | (1927-8) | b 1904 | d 1971 |
| WRIGHT, Kenneth James | (1975-78) | b 11.4.1956 | |
| YANZ, Kenneth | (1958) | b 18.5.1924 | |

# COMBINED BRITISH/IRISH

(Includes only those who played in a Test for a Combined British/Irish team against an IB member.)

N.B. Births and Deaths are shown only for those who were *never* capped by an individual country. All Test players are listed, but details for those who were capped by their individual countries will be found in the relevant sections.

| PLAYER | CAREER SPAN | | |
|---|---|---|---|
| AARVOLD, C.D. | (1930) | England | |
| ACKERMAN, R.A. | (1983) | Wales | |
| ADAMSON, Charles Young | (1899) | b 1875 | d 17.9.1918 |
| ALEXANDER, R. | (1938) | Ireland | |
| ARCHER, H.A. | (1908) | England | |
| ARNEIL, R.J. | (1968) | Scotland | |
| ASHCROFT, A. | (1959) | England | |
| ASTON, R.L. | (1891) | England | |
| AYRE-SMITH, Alan | (1899) | b 19.8.1876 | d 3.11.1957 |
| BAINBRIDGE, S. | (1983) | England | |
| BAIRD, G.R.T. | (1983) | Scotland | |
| BAKER, A.M. | (1910) | Wales | |
| BAKER, D.G.S. | (1955) | England | |
| BASSETT, J.A. | (1930) | Wales | |
| BEAMISH, G.R. | (1930) | Ireland | |
| BEATTIE, J.R. | (1983) | Scotland | |
| BEAUMONT, W.B. | (1977-80) | England | |
| BEBB, D.I.E. | (1962-66) | Wales | |
| BEDELL-SIVRIGHT, D.R. | (1904) | Scotland | |
| BELL, Sydney Pyman | (1896) | b 19.12.1875 | d 23.11.1944 |
| BELSON, Frederick Charles | (1899) | b 1874 | d 10.8.1952 |
| BENNETT, P. | (1974-77) | Wales | |
| BEVAN, J.C. | (1971) | Wales | |
| BEVAN, T.S. | (1904) | Wales | |
| BLACK, A.W. | (1950) | Scotland | |
| BLACK, B.H. | (1930) | England | |
| BLAKISTON, A.F. | (1924) | England | |
| BOWCOTT, H.M. | (1930) | Wales | |
| BOYD, C.A. | (1896) | Ireland | |
| BOYLE, C.V. | (1938) | Ireland | |
| BRAND, T.N. | (1924) | Ireland | |
| BRESNIHAN, F.P.K. | (1968) | Ireland | |
| BROMET, Edward | (1891) | b 26.1.1867 | d 6.4.1937 |
| BROMET, W.E. | (1891) | England | |
| BROPHY, N.H. | (1962) | Ireland | |
| BROWN, G.L. | (1971-77) | Scotland | |
| BUCHER, A.M. | (1899) | Scotland | |
| BUDGE, G.M. | (1950) | Scotland | |
| BULGER, L.Q. | (1896) | Ireland | |
| BURCHER, D.H. | (1977) | Wales | |
| BUSH, P.F. | (1904) | Wales | |
| BUTTERFIELD, J. | (1955) | England | |
| BYRNE, J.F. | (1896) | England | |
| CALDER, J.H. | (1983) | Scotland | |
| CAMERON, A. | (1955) | Scotland | |
| CAMPBELL, S.O. | (1980-83) | Ireland | |
| CAMPBELL-LAMERTON, M.J. | (1962-66) | Scotland | |
| CAREY, Walter Julius | (1896) | b 12.7.1875 | d 17.2.1955 |
| CARLETON, J. | (1980-83) | England | |
| CAVE, W.T.C. | (1903) | England | |
| CHAPMAN, F.E. | (1908) | England | |
| CLAUSS, P.R.A. | (1891) | Scotland | |
| CLEAVER, W.B. | (1950) | Wales | |
| CLIFFORD, T. | (1950) | Ireland | |
| CLINCH, A.D. | (1896) | Ireland | |
| COBNER, T.J. | (1977) | Wales | |
| COLCLOUGH, M.J. | (1980-83) | England | |
| COLLETT, Gilbert Faraday | (1903) | b 18.7.1879 | d 26.2.1945 |
| CONNELL, G.C. | (1968) | Scotland | |
| COOKSON, George | (1899) | b 25.3.1874 | d 15.3.1950 |
| COTTON, F.E. | (1974-77) | England | |
| COULMAN, M.J. | (1968) | England | |
| COVE-SMITH, R. | (1924) | England | |
| COWAN, R.C. | (1962) | Scotland | |
| CREAN, T.J. | (1896) | Ireland | |

| PLAYER | CAREER SPAN | |
|---|---|---|
| CROMEY, G.E. | (1938) | Ireland |
| CROWTHER, S.N. | (1904) | |
| CUNNINGHAM, W. | (1924) | Ireland |
| DANCER, Gerald Thomas | (1938) | b 15.1.1911 |
| DAVEY, J. | (1908) | England |
| DAVIDSON, I.G. | (1903) | Ireland |
| DAVIES, C. | (1950) | Wales |
| DAVIES, D.M. | (1950) | Wales |
| DAVIES, D.S. | (1924) | Scotland |
| DAVIES, H.J. | (1924) | Wales |
| DAVIES, T.G.R. | (1968-71) | Wales |
| DAVIES, T.J. | (1959) | Wales |
| DAVIES, T.M. | (1971-74) | Wales |
| DAVIES, W.G. | (1980) | Wales |
| DAVIES, W.P.C. | (1955) | England |
| DAWES, S.J. | (1971) | Wales |
| DAWSON, A.R. | (1959) | Ireland |
| DIBBLE, R. | (1908) | England |
| DIXON, P.J. | (1971) | England |
| DOBSON, D.D. | (1904) | England |
| DODGE, P.W. | (1980) | England |
| DORAN, G.P. | (1899) | Ireland |
| DOWN, P.J. | (1908) | England |
| DOYLE, M.G. | (1968) | Ireland |
| DRYSDALE, D. | (1924) | Scotland |
| DUCKHAM, D.J. | (1971) | England |
| DUFF, P.L. | (1938) | Scotland |
| DUGGAN, W.P. | (1977) | Ireland |
| EDWARDS, G.O. | (1968-74) | Wales |
| EDWARDS, R.W. | (1904) | Ireland |
| EVANS, G. | (1983) | Wales |
| EVANS, G.L. | (1977) | Wales |
| EVANS, R.T. | (1950) | Wales |
| EVANS, T.P. | (1977) | Wales |
| EVANS, W.R. | (1959) | Wales |
| EVERS, G.V. | (1899) | |
| FARRELL, J.L. | (1930) | Ireland |
| FAULL, J. | (1959) | Wales |
| FENWICK, S.P. | (1977) | Wales |
| FITZGERALD, C.F. | (1983) | Ireland |
| FOSTER, A.R. | (1910) | Ireland |
| FRANCOMBE, J.S. | (1899) | |
| GABE, R.T. | (1904) | Wales |
| GIBBS, R.A. | (1908) | Wales |
| GIBSON, C.M.H. | (1966-71) | Ireland |
| GIBSON, G.R. | (1899) | England |
| GIBSON, T.A. | (1903) | England |
| GILES, J.L. | (1938) | England |
| GILLESPIE, J.I. | (1903) | Scotland |
| GOULD, J.H. | (1891) | |
| GRAVELL, R.W.R. | (1980) | Wales |
| GRAVES, C.R.A. | (1938) | Ireland |
| GRAY, H.G.S. | (1899) | |
| GREENWOOD, J.T. | (1955) | Scotland |
| GREIG, L.L. | (1903) | Scotland |
| GRIEVE, C.F. | (1938) | Scotland |
| GRIFFITHS, G.M. | (1955) | Wales |
| GRIFFITHS, V.M. | (1924) | Wales |
| HAMMOND, John | (1891-96) | b 28.7.1860 | d 21.11.1907 |
| HANCOCK, P.F. | (1891-96) | England |
| HANCOCK P.S. | (1903) | England |
| HANDFORD, F.G. | (1910) | England |
| HARDING, A.F. | (1904-08) | Wales |
| HARDING, W.R. | (1924) | Wales |
| HARRIS, S.W. | (1924) | England |
| HARRISON, E.M. | (1903) | |
| HAY, B.H. | (1980) | Scotland |

| PLAYER | CAREER SPAN | | PLAYER | CAREER SPAN | |
|---|---|---|---|---|---|
| HAYWARD, D.J. | (1950) | Wales | MAGEE, A.M. | (1896) | Ireland |
| HENDERSON, N.J. | (1950) | Ireland | MAGEE, J.T. | (1896) | Ireland |
| HENDRIE, K.G.P. | (1924) | Scotland | MARTINDALE, S.A. | (1930) | England |
| HEWITT, D. | (1959-62) | Ireland | MARSDEN-JONES, D. | (1924) | Wales |
| HIGGINS, R. | (1955) | England | MARSHALL, H. | (1891) | England |
| HIND, G.R. | (1908) | England | MARQUES, R.W.D. | (1959) | England |
| HINSHELWOOD, A.J.W. | (1966-8) | Scotland | MARTELLI, E. | (1899) | |
| HODGSON, J.M. | (1930) | England | MARTIN, A.J. | (1977) | Wales |
| HOLMES, T.D. | (1983) | Wales | MASSEY, Bernard F. | (1904) | b 1872 | d 1950 |
| HOPKINS, R. | (1971) | Wales | MATTHEWS, J. | (1950) | Wales |
| HORROCKS-TAYLOR, | | | MAXWELL, R.B. | (1924) | |
| J.P. | (1959) | England | MAYFIELD, Edwin | (1891) | b 21.7.1870 |
| HORTON, A.L. | (1968) | England | MAYNE, R.B. | (1938) | Ireland |
| HOWARD, William | | | MEARES, A.W.D. | (1896) | Ireland |
| Gordon | (1938) | b 13.7.1909 | MEREDITH, B.V. | (1955-62) | Wales |
| HOWIE, R.A. | (1924) | Scotland | MEREDITH, C.C. | (1955) | Wales |
| HULME, F.C. | (1904) | England | MILLAR, S. | (1959-68) | Ireland |
| | | | MILLIKEN, R.A. | (1974) | Ireland |
| IRVINE, A.R. | (1974-80) | Scotland | MITCHELL, W.G. | (1891) | England |
| IRWIN, D.G. | (1983) | Ireland | MORGAN, C.I. | (1955) | Wales |
| ISHERWOOD, George | | | MORGAN, D.W. | (1977) | Scotland |
| Aldwin M. | (1910) | b 3.2.1889 | MORGAN, Edward | (1904) | Wales |
| | | | MORGAN, Edgar | (1908) | Wales |
| JACKETT, E.J. | (1908) | England | MORGAN, G.J. | (1938) | Ireland |
| JACKSON, Frederick S. | (1908) | | MORGAN, H.J. | (1959-62) | Wales |
| JACKSON, P.B. | (1959) | England | MORGAN, M.E. | (1938) | Wales |
| JARMAN, H. | (1910) | Wales | MORGAN, W.L. | (1908) | Wales |
| JARMAN, J.W. | (1899) | England | MORLEY, J.C. | (1930) | Wales |
| JEEPS, R.E.G. | (1955-62) | England | MORRISON, M.C. | (1903) | Scotland |
| JENKINS, V.G.J. | (1938) | Wales | MORTIMER, W. | (1896) | England |
| JOHN, B. | (1968-71) | Wales | MULCAHY, W.A. | (1959-62) | Ireland |
| JOHN, E.R. | (1950) | Wales | MULLEN, K.D. | (1950) | Ireland |
| JOHNSTON, R. | (1896) | Ireland | MULLIGAN, A.A. | (1959) | Ireland |
| JONES, B.L. | (1950) | Wales | MULLINEUX, Mathew | (1896-99) | b 8.8.1867 | d 13.2.1945 |
| JONES, D.K. | (1962-66) | Wales | MULLINS, Reginald | | | |
| JONES, E.L. | (1938) | Wales | Cuthbert | (1896) | b 28.6.1873 | d 15.6.1938 |
| JONES, I.E. | (1930) | Wales | MURPHY, N.A.A. | (1959-66) | Ireland |
| JONES, J.P. [Jack] | (1908-10) | Wales | MURRAY, P.F. | (1930) | Ireland |
| JONES, J.P. [Tuan] | (1908) | Wales | | | |
| JONES, K.D. | (1962) | Wales | NEALE, M.E. | (1910) | England |
| JONES, K.J. | (1950) | Wales | NEARY, A. | (1977) | England |
| JONES, S.T. | (1983) | Wales | NEILL, R.M. | (1903) | Scotland |
| JUDKINS, W. | (1899) | | NELSON, J.E. | (1950) | Ireland |
| | | | NICHOLLS, E.G. | (1899) | Wales |
| KEANE, M.I. | (1977) | Ireland | NICHOLSON, B.E. | (1938) | England |
| KENNEDY, K.W. | (1966) | Ireland | NICHOLSON, E.T. | (1899) | England |
| KIERNAN, M.J. | (1983) | Ireland | NORRIS, C.H. | (1966) | Wales |
| KIERNAN, T.J. | (1962-68) | Ireland | NORSTER, R.L. | (1983) | Wales |
| KINNEAR, R.M. | (1924) | Scotland | NOVIS, A.L. | (1930) | England |
| KININMONTH, P.W. | (1950) | Scotland | | | |
| KYLE, J.W. | (1950) | Ireland | O'BRIEN, A.B. | (1904) | |
| | | | O'DONNELL, R.C. | (1980) | Ireland |
| KYRKE, Gerald Venables | (1908) | b 7.9.1882 | d 8.3.1932 | O'DRISCOLL, J.B. | (1980-3) | Ireland |
| LAIDLAW, F.A.L. | (1966) | Scotland | OLDHAM, W.L. | (1908) | England |
| LAIDLAW, R.J. | (1983) | Scotland | O'NEILL, H.O'H. | (1930) | Ireland |
| LAMONT, R.A. | (1966) | Ireland | O'REILLY, A.J.F. | (1955-59) | Ireland |
| LANE, M.F. | (1950) | Ireland | ORR, P.A. | (1977) | Ireland |
| LARTER, P.J. | (1968) | England | O'SHEA, J.P. | (1968) | Wales |
| LAXON, H. | (1908) | England | | | |
| LEWIS, A.R. | (1966) | Wales | PARKER, D. | (1930) | Wales |
| LLEWELLYN, W.M. | (1904) | Wales | PASK, A.E.I. | (1962-66) | Wales |
| LYNCH, J.F. | (1971) | Ireland | PATTERSON, C.S. | (1980) | Ireland |
| | | | PATTERSON, W.M. | (1959) | England |
| McBRIDE, W.J. | (1962-74) | Ireland | PAXTON, I.A.M. | (1983) | Scotland |
| MACDONALD, R. | (1950) | Scotland | PEDLOW, A.C. | (1955) | Ireland |
| McEVEDY, Patrick | | | PILLMAN, C.H. | (1910) | England |
| Francis | (1904-08) | b 17.3.1880 | d 2.3.1935 | PIPER, O.J.S. | (1910) | Ireland |
| McFADYEAN, C.W. | (1966) | England | POOLE, Harold | (1930) | |
| McGEECHAN, I.R. | (1974-77) | Scotland | PREECE, I. | (1950) | England |
| McGOWN, T.M.W. | (1899) | England | PRENTICE, F.D. | (1930) | England |
| McKAY, J.W. | (1950) | Ireland | PRICE, B. | (1966) | Wales |
| McKIBBIN, H.R. | (1938) | Ireland | PRICE, G. | (1977-83) | Wales |
| MACKIE, O.G. | (1896) | England | PRICE, M.J. | (1959) | Wales |
| MACLAGAN, W.E. | (1891) | Scotland | PROSSER, T.R. | (1959) | Wales |
| McLAUCHLAN, J. | (1971-74) | Scotland | PULLIN, J.V. | (1968-71) | England |
| McLEOD, H.F. | (1959) | Scotland | | | |
| McLOUGHLIN, R.J. | (1966) | Ireland | QUINNELL, D.L. | (1971-80) | Wales |
| MACMILLAN, R.G. | (1891) | Scotland | | | |
| MacNEILL, H.P. | (1983) | Ireland | RALSTON, C.W. | (1974) | England |
| MACPHERSON, N.C. | (1924) | Scotland | REES, H.E. | (1977) | Wales |
| MACRAE, D.J. | (1938) | Scotland | REEVE, J.S.R. | (1930) | England |
| McVICKER, J. | (1924) | Ireland | | | |

| PLAYER | CAREER SPAN | | |
|---|---|---|---|
| REID, T.E. | (1955) | Ireland | |
| RENWICK, J.M. | (1980) | Scotland | |
| REW, H. | (1930) | England | |
| REYNOLDS, F.J. | (1938) | England | |
| RICHARDS, D.S. | (1980) | Wales | |
| RICHARDS, M.C.R. | (1968) | Wales | |
| RICHARDS, T.J. | (1910) | Australia | |
| RIMMER, G. | (1950) | England | |
| RINGLAND, T.M. | (1983) | Ireland | |
| RISMAN, A.B.W. | (1959) | England | |
| RITSON, J.A.S. | (1908) | England | |
| ROBBIE, J.C. | (1980) | Ireland | |
| ROBINS, J.D. | (1950) | Wales | |
| ROBINS, R.J. | (1955) | Wales | |
| ROGERS, D.P. | (1962) | England | |
| ROTHERHAM, A. | (1891) | England | |
| ROWLANDS, K.A. | (1962) | Wales | |
| RUTHERFORD, D. | (1966) | England | |
| RUTHERFORD, J.Y. | (1983) | Scotland | |
| SAUNDERS, S.M. | (1904) | | |
| SAVAGE, K.F. | (1968) | England | |
| SCOTLAND, K.J.F. | (1959) | Scotland | |
| SCOTT, W.P. | (1903) | Scotland | |
| SEALY, J. | (1896) | Ireland | |
| SHARP, R.A.W. | (1962) | England | |
| SIMPSON, Clement Pearson | (1891) | b 13.6.1868 | d 19.9.1948 |
| SKRIMSHIRE, R.T. | (1903) | Wales | |
| SLATTERY, J.F. | (1974) | Ireland | |
| SLEMEN, M.A.C. | (1980) | England | |
| SMITH, A.R. | (1962) | Scotland | |
| SMITH, D.F. | (1910) | England | |
| SMITH, D.W.C. | (1950) | Scotland | |
| SMITH, G.K. | (1959) | Scotland | |
| SMITH, I.S. | (1924) | Scotland | |
| SMITH, T.W. | (1908) | | |
| SMYTH, R.S. | (1903) | Ireland | |
| SMYTH, T. | (1910) | Ireland | |
| SPONG, R.S. | (1930) | England | |
| SPOORS, J. | (1910) | | |
| SQUIRE, J. | (1977-83) | Wales | |
| SQUIRES, P.J. | (1977) | England | |
| STAGG, P.K. | (1968) | Scotland | |
| STANGER-LEATHES, C.F. | (1904) | England | |
| STEELE, W.C.C. | (1974) | Scotland | |
| STEPHENS, I. | (1983) | Wales | |
| STEPHENS, J.R.G. | (1950) | Wales | |
| STEVENSON, R.C. | (1910) | Scotland | |
| STOUT, F.M. | (1899) | England | |
| SURTEES, Aubone Alfred | (1891) | b 2.10.1865 | d 22.11.1923 |
| SWANNELL, B.I. | (1899-1904) | Australia | |
| TANNER, H. | (1938) | Wales | |
| TAYLOR, A.R. | (1938) | Wales | |
| TAYLOR, J. | (1971) | Wales | |
| TAYLOR, R.B. | (1968) | England | |
| TEDFORD, A. | (1903) | Ireland | |
| TELFER, J.W. | (1966-68) | Scotland | |
| THOMAS, M.C. | (1950-59) | Wales | |

| PLAYER | CAREER SPAN | | |
|---|---|---|---|
| THOMAS, R.C.C. | (1955) | Wales | |
| THOMAS, W.D. | (1966-71) | Wales | |
| THOMPSON, C.E.K. | (1899) | | |
| THOMPSON, Robert | (1891) | b 11.1.1869 | d 5.2.1952 |
| THOMPSON, R.H. | (1955) | Ireland | |
| TIMMS, A.B. | (1899) | Scotland | |
| TODD, A.F. | (1896) | England | |
| TRAIL, David Herbert | (1904) | | d 11.4.1935 |
| TRAVERS, W.H. | (1938) | Wales | |
| TUCKER, C.C. | (1980) | Ireland | |
| TURNER, J.W.C. | (1968) | Scotland | |
| UNWIN, E.J. | (1938) | England | |
| UTTLEY, R.M. | (1974) | England | |
| VASSALL, H.H. | (1908) | England | |
| VILE, T.H. | (1904) | Wales | |
| VOYCE, A.T. | (1924) | England | |
| WADDELL, G.H. | (1962) | Scotland | |
| WADDELL, H. | (1924) | Scotland | |
| WALKER, E.F. | (1903) | | |
| WALKER, S. | (1938) | Ireland | |
| WALLACE, Jos | (1903) | Ireland | |
| WALLACE, W. | (1924) | | |
| WALLER, P.D. | (1910) | Wales | |
| WARD, A.J.P. | (1980) | Ireland | |
| WATERS, J.A. | (1938) | Scotland | |
| WATKINS, D. | (1966) | Wales | |
| WATKINS, S.J. | (1966) | Wales | |
| WEBB, J. | (1910) | Wales | |
| WELSH, W.B. | (1930) | Scotland | |
| WESTON, M.P. | (1962-66) | England | |
| WHEELER, P.J. | (1977-80) | England | |
| WHITLEY, H. | (1924) | England | |
| WHITTAKER, T.S. | (1891) | b 26.1.1868 | |
| WILLCOX, J.G. | (1962) | England | |
| WILLIAMS, B.L. | (1950) | Wales | |
| WILLIAMS, C. | (1980) | Wales | |
| WILLIAMS, D. | (1966) | Wales | |
| WILLIAMS, D.B. | (1977) | Wales | |
| WILLIAMS, J.F. | (1908) | Wales | |
| WILLIAMS, J.J. | (1974-77) | Wales | |
| WILLIAMS, J.L. | (1908) | Wales | |
| WILLIAMS, J.P.R. | (1971-74) | Wales | |
| WILLIAMS, R.H. | (1955-59) | Wales | |
| WILLIAMS, S.H. | (1910) | England | |
| WILLIAMS, W.O.G. | (1955) | Wales | |
| WILLIS, W.R. | (1950) | Wales | |
| WILSON, S. | (1966) | Scotland | |
| WINDSOR, R.W. | (1974-77) | Wales | |
| WINTERBOTTOM, P.J. | (1983) | England | |
| WOOD, B.G.M. | (1959) | Ireland | |
| WOOD, K.B. | (1910) | | |
| WOODWARD, C.R. | (1980) | England | |
| WOTHERSPOON, W. | (1891) | Scotland | |
| YOUNG, A.T. | (1924) | England | |
| YOUNG, J. | (1968) | Wales | |
| YOUNG, J.R.C. | (1959) | England | |
| YOUNG, R.M. | (1966-68) | Ireland | |

# THE 1987 WORLD CUP

# THE 1987 WORLD CUP

Rugby Union's inaugural World Cup took place in Australasia in May/June 1987. There were sixteen competitors, divided initially into four pools of four. Each pool contained two seeded nations with two non-IB nations, and the pools were contested on a league basis with league winners and runners-up advancing to a quarter-final match. The latter stages of the competition were then fought out on a knockout scheme with the final taking place in Auckland on 20 June. The two losing semi-finalists took part in a third/fourth place play-off two days prior to the final, so that altogether the rugby world had thirty-two internationals to enjoy in the space of a month.

The competition was a resounding success, both financially and as a spectacle. For the traditionalists there were such fixtures as France-Scotland, Wales-England, Australia-Ireland, Wales-New Zealand, France-Australia, Wales-Australia and France-New Zealand to savour; while for those with broader outlooks and tastes for excitement there was nothing to beat the matches between Romania-Zimbabwe, Italy-Fiji and Japan-United States. Thanks to television the competition was seen by a huge worldwide audience, and countries in every continent received live coverage of the final. Little wonder, then, that even before the 1987 tournament was complete, there was unofficial talk (even among the leading Rugby World Cup organisers) of Britain staging the event in 1991.

In the absence of the Springboks the competition proved that the All Blacks are the fittest, best-drilled and most determined players in the world; the French are the most skilful ball-handlers in the game and capable of producing rugby's finest spectacle; while of the Home Countries Wales, despite huge limitations, can often be motivated to overcome stronger opponents.

The All Blacks began the tournament as hot favourites. Brian Lochore and Alex Wyllie, two distinguished former players, were responsible for preparing the New Zealand side which won the competition, and their insistence and dependence on a super-fit team capable of performing accurate basic skills was a signal lesson for rugby coaches throughout the world to follow. The New Zealanders were perceptively led by a scrum-half, David Kirk, who was not only a brilliant example to his men on the field but a personable and intelligent young man in his duties away from the matches. New Zealand has always produced strong leaders: none has gained so great an achievement as that which fittingly fell to Kirk in 1987. As Kirk proceeds to Oxford on a Rhodes Scholarship in the autumn of 1987, it is to be hoped that much of his knowledge of and approach to the game will benefit Britain.

France and Wales, by finishing second and third respectively, enabled the Northern Hemisphere to regain some footing near the top of the world's rugby mountain. Australia's shrewd coach, Alan Jones, had written off the Europeans prior to the tournament, and there were wide predictions (even among European critics) that the Northern Hemisphere sides would finish no higher than the foothills of rugby's Everest. But the French thoroughly deserved a cracking victory over Australia in their semi-final, and there is no doubt that Wales' exciting last-minute victory in the play-off at Rotorua will do the game a power of good in the Principality.

For the Australians there will be nothing but disappointment from a competition that they had held high (and let it be said realistic) ambitions of winning. There was little promise in the Wallabies' group match win over England, the Japanese gave them a run for their money in another group match, and it was only in the first half of their quarter-final against Ireland that one felt Australia's true strength and ability was revealed.

In the later stages of the competition the Australians were occasionally guilty of uncharacteristically indiscreet behaviour, and the incidents which led to the expulsion of David Codey in the match with Wales were extraordinary acts of indiscipline which seemed to be totally at odds with the Australian approach to rugby. His dismissal deprived his nation of third place in the tournament – no Welsh supporter could argue that Wales would have beaten the full Wallabies side. Still, Australians are a resilient nation and their understandable disappointment over their World Cup performance will soon be forgotten. If Alan Jones continues as coach, and Australia continues to select big, athletic players who can run and handle skilfully, there is no doubt that the Australians will be major contenders to topple the All Blacks in the next world competition.

# Warm-Up Match

The main part of this book covers international matches played up to 30 April 1987. Since then, but before the World Cup commenced, only one IB country played a major international. Australia beat South Korea in a match given full Test status by the Australian Rugby Union, notching a record Australian total of 65 points for an international. The details of that match follow.

## AUSTRALIA v. SOUTH KOREA

Date: 17 May 1987
Venue: Ballymore, Brisbane

| AUSTRALIA (5G,1PG,8T) | 65-18 | S. KOREA (2G,2PG) |
|---|---|---|
| R.G. GOULD | | S-C. CHO |
| P.C. GRIGG | | M-R. CHOI |
| *A.G. SLACK[1] | | K-Y. JUNG |
| M.T. COOK | | C-H. JEON |
| M.P. BURKE | | S-H. BAEK |
| †B. SMITH | | C-K. SIN |
| N.C. FARR-JONES[2] | | Y-P. JUNG |
| E.E. RODRIGUEZ | | D-C. GU |
| T.A. LAWTON | | E-J. PARK |
| M.N. HARTILL | | H-M. CHOI |
| S.A.G. CUTLER | | T-Y. YOON |
| W.A. CAMPBELL | | D-I. WOO |
| S.P. POIDEVIN | | S-U. JIN |
| S.N. TUYNMAN | | H. KIM |
| J.S. MILLER | | D-H. KIM[1] |

[1]Rep. by †A. Herbert
[2]Rep. by †S.L. James

[1]Rep. by S-C. Gang

Tries: Burke (3), Grigg (2), Slack (2), Miller, Cook, Farr-Jones, Smith, Gould, James
Cons: Smith (5)
PG: Smith
DG: –

Tries: Y-P. Jung, Baek
Cons: Sin (2)
PG: Sin (2)
DG: –

*Referee: C.A. Waldron (Australia)*

# Pool One

The final placings in Pool One, the only group to be wholly based in Australia, produced no surprises. All along it was expected that the Australians and England would be too strong for the unseeded Americans and Japanese. However, these younger rugby nations had several moments to remember: Nelson, a former Scottish schoolboy international, made many telling runs for the Americans and his place-kicking was as good as any seen in the opening rounds; Purcell scored a splendid winger's try against the English; and Hayashi's Japanese side disrupted the Australians for much of the group's final game before the Wallabies were eventually able to complete their pool matches an unbeaten side.

The key match of the group was that between Australia and England. The Englishmen, despite defeat by thirteen points, showed considerable promise, and one leading rugby critic was moved to report that this was the closest 13-point defeat ever seen in an international. Certainly Australia's win in this match was exaggerated by a try awarded to Campese which should never have been given. The winger dropped the ball over the line, failed to ground it, yet the score was allowed.

The final group table for Pool One was:

|  | P | W | D | L | For | Against | Pts |
|---|---|---|---|---|---|---|---|
| Australia | 3 | 3 | 0 | 0 | 108 | 41 | 6 |
| England | 3 | 2 | 0 | 1 | 100 | 32 | 4 |
| United States | 3 | 1 | 0 | 2 | 39 | 99 | 2 |
| Japan | 3 | 0 | 0 | 3 | 48 | 123 | 0 |

## AUSTRALIA v. ENGLAND

Date: 23 May 1987

Venue: Concord Oval, Sydney

**AUSTRALIA** (1G,3PG,1T)  **19-6**    **ENGLAND** (1G)

| R.G. GOULD[1] | W.M.H. ROSE[1] |
|---|---|
| P.C. GRIGG | *M.E. HARRISON |
| *A.G. SLACK | K.G. SIMMS |
| B. PAPWORTH | J.L.B. SALMON |
| D.I. CAMPESE | R. UNDERWOOD |
| M.P. LYNAGH | P.N. WILLIAMS |
| N.C. FARR-JONES | R.M. HARDING |
| E.E. RODRIGUEZ | P.A.G. RENDALL |
| T.A. LAWTON | B.C. MOORE |
| A.J. McINTYRE | G.S. PEARCE |
| S.A.G. CUTLER | W.A. DOOLEY |
| W.A. CAMPBELL | N.C. REDMAN |
| S.P. POIDEVIN | P.J. WINTERBOTTOM |
| †T. COKER | D. RICHARDS |
| S.N. TUYNMAN | G.W. REES |

[1]Rep. by S.L. James    [1]Rep by †J. Webb

Tries: Campese, Poidevin    Tries: Harrison
Cons: Lynagh    Cons: Webb
PG: Lynagh (3)    PG: –
DG: –    DG: –

Referee: K. H. Lawrence (NZ)

## JAPAN v. UNITED STATES

Date: 24 May 1987

Venue: Ballymore, Brisbane

**JAPAN** (2PG,3T)  **18-21**    **UNITED STATES** (3G,1PG)

| S. MUKAI | R. NELSON |
|---|---|
| N. TAUMOEFOLAU | M. PURCELL |
| K. YOSHINAGA | K. HIGGINS |
| E. KUTSUKI | R. HELU |
| S. ONUKI | G. HEIN |
| S. HIRAO | J. CLARKSON |
| H. IKUTA | M. SAUNDERS |
| H. YASUMI | R. BAILEY |
| T. FUJITA | J. EVERETT |
| K. HORAGUCHI | F. PAOLI |
| *T. HAYASHI | K. SWORDS |
| A. OYAGI | *E. BURLINGHAM |
| K. MIYAMOTO | B. WARHURST |
| M. CHIDA | B. VIZARD |
| S. LATU | G. LAMBERT |

Tries: Taumoefolau (2),    Tries: Nelson, Purcell,
  Yoshinaga    Lambert
Cons: –    Cons: Nelson (3)
PG: Yoshinaga, Kutsuki    PG: Nelson
DG: –    DG: –

Referee: G. Maurette (France)

## 13:6 The 1987 World Cup

### ENGLAND v. JAPAN

Date: 30 May, 1987
Venue: Concord Oval, Sydney

**ENGLAND** (7G,2PG,3T) **60-7** | **JAPAN** (1PG,1T)

| ENGLAND | JAPAN |
|---|---|
| J. Webb | D. Murai |
| *M.E. Harrison | N. Taumoefolau |
| K.G. Simms[1] | E. Kutsuki |
| J.L.B. Salmon | K. Matsuo |
| R. Underwood | S. Onuki |
| P.N. Williams[2] | S. Hirao |
| R.M. Harding | M. Hagimoto |
| P.A.G. Rendall | T. Kimura |
| B.C. Moore | T. Fujita |
| G.J. Chilcott | K. Horaguchi |
| N.C. Redman | S. Kurihara |
| S. Bainbridge | A. Oyagi |
| P.J. Winterbottom | K. Miyamoto |
| D. Richards | M. Chida |
| G.W. Rees | *T. Hayashi |

[1]Rep. by F.J. Clough
[2]Rep. by C.R. Andrew

Tries: Underwood (2), Rees Harrison (3), Salmon, Richards, Simms, Redman
Cons: Webb (7)
PG: Webb (2)
DG: –

Tries: Miyamato
Cons: –
PG: Matsuo
DG: –

*Referee: R. Hourquet (France)*

### AUSTRALIA v. UNITED STATES

Date: 31 May 1987
Venue: Ballymole, Brisbane

**AUSTRALIA** (6G,1PG,2T) **47-12** | **UNITED STATES** (1G,1PG,1DG)

| AUSTRALIA | UNITED STATES |
|---|---|
| A. Leeds | R. Nelson |
| D.I. Campese | K. Higgins |
| *A.G. Slack | R. Helu |
| B. Papworth | T. Vinick |
| M.P. Burke | G. Hein |
| M.P. Lynagh | D. Horton |
| B. Smith | D. Dickson[1] |
| C.A. Lillicrap | F. Horwath |
| T.A. Lawton | P. Johnson |
| A.J. McIntyre | *F. Paoli |
| T. Coker | K. Swords |
| W.A. Campbell | W. Shiflet[2] |
| D. Codey | A. Ridnell |
| S.N. Tuynman | B. Vizard |
| J.S. Miller | S. Finkel |

[1]Rep. by M. Saunders
[2]Rep. by G. Lambert

Tries: Leeds (2), Slack, Smith, Papworth, Codey, Campese, Penalty try
Cons: Lynagh (6)
PG: Lynagh
DG: –

Tries: Nelson
Cons: Nelson
PG: Nelson
DG: Horton

*Referee: J.B. Anderson (Scotland)*

### ENGLAND v. UNITED STATES

Date: 3 June, 1987
Venue: Concord Oval, Sydney

**ENGLAND** (3G,4PG,1T) **34-6** | **UNITED STATES** (1G)

| ENGLAND | UNITED STATES |
|---|---|
| J. Webb | R. Nelson |
| *M.E. Harrison | M. Purcell |
| F.J. Clough | K. Higgins |
| J.L.B. Salmon | T. Vinick |
| M.D. Bailey | G. Hein |
| C.R. Andrew | J. Clarkson |
| R.J. Hill | M. Saunders |
| G.J. Chilcott | R. Bailey |
| R.G.R. Dawe | J. Everett |
| G.S. Pearce | N. Brendel |
| W.A. Dooley | R. Causey |
| S. Bainbridge | *E. Burlingham |
| P.J. Winterbottom | G. Lambert |
| D. Richards | B. Vizard |
| G.W. Rees | S. Finkel |

Tries: Winterbottom (2), Harrison, Dooley
Cons: Webb (3)
PG: Webb (4)
DG: –

Tries: Purcell
Cons: Nelson
PG: –
DG: –

*Referee: K.V.J. Fitzgerald (Australia)*

### AUSTRALIA v. JAPAN

Date: 3 June 1987
Venue: Concord Oval, Sydney

**AUSTRALIA** (5G,3T) **42-23** | **JAPAN** (1G,1DG,2PG,2T)

| AUSTRALIA | JAPAN |
|---|---|
| D.I. Campese | S. Mukai |
| P.C. Grigg | N. Taumoefolau |
| A.G. Slack | K. Yoshinaga |
| M.T. Cook[1] | E. Kutsuki |
| M.P. Burke | M. Okidoi |
| M.P. Lynagh | S. Hirao |
| B. Smith | H. Ikuta |
| E.E. Rodriguez | T. Kimura |
| M.I. McBain | T. Fujita |
| M.N. Hartill | M. Aizawa |
| S.A.G. Cutler | *T. Hayashi |
| R.J. Reynolds | Y. Sakuraba |
| *S.P. Poidevin | K. Miyamoto |
| S.N. Tuynman[2] | S. Latu |
| D. Codey | Y. Kawase |

[1]Rep. by B. Papworth
[2]Rep. by W.A. Campbell

Tries: Slack (2), Burke (2), Grigg, Tuynman, Hartill, Campese
Cons: Lynagh (5)
PG: –
DG: –

Tries: Kutsuki (2), Fujita
Cons: Okidoi
PG: Okidoi (2)
DG: Okidoi

*Referee: J.M. Fleming (Scotland)*

# Pool Two

This was the group which produced the least exciting football of the early rounds. Wales and Ireland, the two seeded teams, made heavy weather of their games against Canada and Tonga, and the Welsh, despite an unlucky run of injuries, finished at the head of the group by virtue of an undistinguished win against the Irish. Nevertheless, there were some good displays by the Welsh backs, and Ieuan Evans equalled the Welsh match record by scoring four tries against Canada at Invercargill. Glen Webbe scored three against Tonga, despite sustaining concussion in the second half of the match.

The pool's most interesting result was Canada's 37-4 victory over Tonga. The result was regarded as sweet revenge by the Canadians, who had been trounced 14-40 by the Tongans in 1974. Canada owed much for their success to the kicking of Gareth Rees at fly-half and the leadership of Hans de Goede.

The final group table for Pool Two was:

|         | P | W | D | L | For | Against | Pts |
|---------|---|---|---|---|-----|---------|-----|
| Wales   | 3 | 3 | 0 | 0 | 82  | 31      | 6   |
| Ireland | 3 | 2 | 0 | 1 | 84  | 41      | 4   |
| Canada  | 3 | 1 | 0 | 2 | 65  | 90      | 2   |
| Tonga   | 3 | 0 | 0 | 3 | 29  | 98      | 0   |

---

## CANADA v. TONGA

Date: 24 May 1987

Venue: McLean Park, Napier

**CANADA** (3G, 1PG, 4T)  **37-4**  **TONGA** (1T)

| CANADA | TONGA |
|--------|-------|
| M. Wyatt | T. Ete'aki |
| P. Palmer | S. Asi[1] |
| P. Vaesen | S. Mohi |
| S. McTavish | T. Fukakitekei'aho |
| T. Woods | K. Fielea |
| G. Rees | A. Liava'a |
| I. Stuart | T. Fifita |
| E. Evans | S. Motu'apuaka |
| M. Cardinal | A. Afu Fungavaka |
| W. Handson | H. Tupou |
| *H. de Goede | P. Tui'halamaka[2] |
| R. van den Brink | K. Fine |
| R. Frame | V. Tu'uta Kakato |
| J. Robertsen[1] | K. Fotu |
| R. Radu | *F. Valu |

[1]Rep. by G. Ennis

[1]Rep. by L. Vaipulu
[2]Rep. by S. Tahaafe

Tries: Vaesen (2), Palmer (2), Stuart, Frame, Penalty try
Cons: Wyatt (2), Rees
PG: Rees
DG: –

Tries: Valu
Cons: –
PG: –
DG: –

*Referee: C. Norling (Wales)*

---

## IRELAND v. WALES

Date: 25 May 1987

Venue: Athletic Park, Wellington

**IRELAND** (2PG)  **6-13**  **WALES** (1PG, 2DG, 1T)

| IRELAND | WALES |
|---------|-------|
| H.P. MacNeill | P.H. Thorburn |
| T.M. Ringland | I.C. Evans |
| B.J. Mullin | J.A. Devereux |
| M.J. Kiernan | M.G. Ring |
| K.D. Crossan | A.M. Hadley |
| P.M. Dean | J. Davies |
| M.T. Bradley | R.N. Jones |
| P.A. Orr | J. Whitefoot |
| †T. Kingston | K. Phillips |
| D.C. Fitzgerald | S. Evans |
| *D.G. Lenihan | *R.D. Moriarty |
| W.A. Anderson | R.L. Norster |
| P.M. Matthews[1] | G.J. Roberts |
| B.J. Spillane | W.P. Moriarty |
| D.G. McGrath | R.G. Collins |

[1]Rep. by J.J. Glennon

Tries: –
Cons: –
PG: Kiernan (2)
DG: –

Tries: Ring
Cons: –
PG: Thorburn
DG: Davies (2)

*Referee: K.V.J. Fitzgerald (Australia)*

## WALES v. TONGA

Date: 29 May 1987

Venue: Showgrounds, Palmerston North

**WALES** (2G,2PG,1DG,2T)  **29-16**  **TONGA** (1G,2PG,1T)

| WALES | TONGA |
|---|---|
| P.H. Thorburn | T. Ete'aki |
| | |
| G.M.C. Webbe | M. Vunipola |
| M.G. Ring | S. Mohi |
| K. Hopkins | T. Fukakitekei'aho |
| A.M. Hadley | K. Fielea |
| | |
| M. Dacey[2] | A. 'Amone[2] |
| R.N. Jones | T. Fifita |
| | |
| †A. Buchanan | V. Lutua |
| K. Phillips | A. Afu Fungavaka |
| S. Evans[1] | H. Tupou[1] |
| *R.D. Moriarty | M. Tu'ungafasi |
| H.D. Richards | K. Fine |
| W.P. Moriarty | V. Tu'uta Kakato |
| P.T. Davies | M. Felise |
| G.J. Roberts | *F. Valu |

[1]Rep. by S.W. Blackmore
[2]Rep. by J. Davies

[1]Rep. by L. Va'Eno
[2]Rep. by A. Liava'a

Tries: Webbe (3), Hadley
Cons: Thorburn (2)
PG: Thorburn (2)
DG: J. Davies

Tries: Fielea, Fifita
Cons: Liava'a
PG: 'Amone, Liava'a
DG: –

*Referee: D.J. Bishop (NZ)*

## IRELAND v. CANADA

Date: 30 May, 1987

Venue: Carisbrook, Dunedin

**IRELAND** (5G,2DG,2PG,1T)  **46-19**  **CANADA** (4PG,1DG,1T)

| IRELAND | CANADA |
|---|---|
| H.P. MacNeill | M. Wyatt |
| | |
| T.M. Ringland | P. Palmer |
| B.J. Mullin | J. Lecky |
| M.J. Kiernan | S. McTavish |
| K.D. Crossan | T. Woods |
| | |
| A.J.P. Ward | G. Rees |
| M.T. Bradley | I. Stuart |
| | |
| P.A. Orr | E. Evans |
| †J.P. McDonald | M. Cardinal |
| D.C. Fitzgerald | W. Handson |
| *D.G. Lenihan | R. Hindson |
| W.A. Anderson | *H. de Goede |
| †P.C. Collins | R. Frame |
| B.J. Spillane | G. Ennis |
| D.G. McGrath | R. Radu |

Tries: Crossan (2), Bradley,
Spillane, Ringland,
MacNeill
Cons: Kiernan (5)
PG: Kiernan (2)
DG: Kiernan, Ward

Tries: Cardinal
Cons: –
PG: Rees (3), Wyatt
DG: Rees

*Referee: F.A. Howard (England)*

## WALES v. CANADA

Date: 3 June 1987

Venue: Rugby Park, Invercargill

**WALES** (4G,4T)  **40-9**  **CANADA** (3PG)

| WALES | CANADA |
|---|---|
| P.H. Thorburn | M. Wyatt |
| | |
| I.C. Evans | P. Palmer |
| J.A. Devereux | T. Woods |
| B. Bowen[1] | J. Lecky |
| A.M. Hadley | S. Gray |
| | |
| *J. Davies | G. Rees |
| R. Giles | I. Stuart[1] |
| | |
| J. Whitefoot | R. McKellar |
| A.J. Phillips | K. Svoboda |
| S.W. Blackmore | W. Handson |
| S. Sutton | R. Hindson |
| R.L. Norster | *H. de Goede |
| W.P. Moriarty[2] | B. Breen |
| P.T. Davies | G. Ennis |
| G.J. Roberts | R. Frame |

[1]Rep. by K. Hopkins
[2]Rep. by R.D. Moriarty

[1]Rep. by D. Tucker

Tries: Evans (4), Hadley,
Phillips, Devereux,
Bowen
Cons: Thorburn (4)
PG: –
DG: –

Tries: –
Cons: –
PG: Rees (3)
DG: –

*Referee: D.J. Bishop (NZ)*

## IRELAND v. TONGA

Date: 3 June 1987

Venue: Ballymore, Brisbane

**IRELAND** (3G,2PG,2T)  **32-9**  **TONGA** (3PG)

| IRELAND | TONGA |
|---|---|
| H.P. MacNeill | T. Ete'aki |
| | |
| T.M. Ringland | T. Fukakitekei'aho |
| B.J. Mullin | A. Liava'a |
| D.G. Irwin | S. Mohi |
| K.D. Crossan | K. Fielea |
| | |
| A.J.P. Ward | A. Amone |
| M.T. Bradley | T. Fifita |
| | |
| †J.A. Langbroek | V. Lutua |
| T. Kingston | A. Afu Fungavaka |
| J.J. McCoy | H. Tupou |
| *D.G. Lenihan | M. Tu'ungafasi |
| W.A. Anderson | K. Fine |
| P.M. Matthews | V. Tu'uta Kakato |
| †N. Francis | M. Felise |
| D.G. McGrath | *F. Valu |

Tries: MacNeill (2), Mullin
(3)
Cons: Ward (3)
PG: Ward (2)
DG: –

Tries: –
Cons: –
PG: Amone (3)
DG: –

*Referee: G. Maurette (France)*

# Pool Three

The only non-IB team to be seeded was Argentina, who found themselves alongside New Zealand in Pool Three. Hugo Porta's side had deservedly earned top-class recognition: the Pumas had beaten the French and drawn with the All Blacks in recent full internationals. But the Argentinians disappointed in their group matches and a surprise defeat by the unpredictable Fijians effectively concluded the Pumas' ambitions for a quarter-final place.

The All Blacks steam-rollered their way to the quarter-finals. Their 70 points against Italy in the opening match of the competition were a world record for an IB nation in a major Test, and their subsequent 74 points against Fiji a few days later improved this record (to the delight of the Italians!).

John Kirwan's powerful running, Fox's accurate goalkicking, and the weaving runs of Italy's left wing Cuttita were the abiding memories of the group.

The final group table for pool three was:

|  | P | W | D | L | For | Against | Pts |
|---|---|---|---|---|---|---|---|
| New Zealand | 3 | 3 | 0 | 0 | 190 | 34 | 6 |
| Fiji | 3 | 1 | 0 | 2 | 56 | 101 | 2 |
| Argentina | 3 | 1 | 0 | 2 | 49 | 90 | 2 |
| Italy | 3 | 1 | 0 | 2 | 40 | 110 | 2 |

---

## NEW ZEALAND v. ITALY

Date: 22 May 1987

Venue: Eden Park, Auckland

**NZ** (8G,2PG,4T)  **70-6**  **ITALY** (1PG,1DG)

| †J.A. GALLAGHER | S. GHIZZONI |
|---|---|
| J.J. KIRWAN | M. MASCIOLETTI |
| J.T. STANLEY | F. GAETANIELLO |
| W.T. TAYLOR | O. COLLODO |
| C.I. GREEN | M. CUTTITA |
| G. J. FOX | R. AMBROSIO |
| *D.E. KIRK | F. LORIGIOLA |
| †R. W. LOE | G. ROSSI |
| S.B.T. FITZPATRICK | G. MORELLI |
| S.C. McDOWELL | T. LUPINI |
| M.J. PIERCE | F. BERNI |
| G.W. WHETTON | M. GARDIN |
| A.J. WHETTON | *M. INNOCENTI |
| W.T. SHELFORD | G. ARTUSO |
| †M.N. JONES | P. FARINA |

Tries: Jones, Kirk (2), Taylor, Green (2), Kirwan (2), McDowell, Stanley, Whetton (A.J.), Penalty try

Tries: –

Cons: Fox (8)
PG: Fox (2)
DG: –

Cons: –
PG: Collodo
DG: Collodo

*Referee: R.J. Fordham (Australia)*

---

## FIJI v. ARGENTINA

Date: 24 May 1987

Venue: Rugby Park, Hamilton

**FIJI** (3G,2PG,1T)  **28-9**  **ARGENTINA** (1G,1PG)

| S. KORODUADUA | S. SALVAT |
|---|---|
| K. NALAGA | M. CAMPO |
| T. CAMA | D. CUESTA-SILVA |
| E. NAITUKU | F. TURNES |
| S. TUVULA | J. LANZA |
| E. ROKOWAILOA | *H. PORTA |
| P. TABULUTU[1] | F. GOMEZ |
| S. NAITUKU | F. MOREL |
| S. NAIVILIWASA | D. CASH |
| R. NAMORO | L. MOLINA |
| *K. RAKOROI | E. BRANCA |
| I. SAVAI | G. MILANO[1] |
| P. GALE[2] | J. ALLEN |
| J. SANDAY | G. TRAVAGLINI |
| M. QORO | J. MOSTANY |

[1]Rep. by P. Nawalu
[2]Rep. by S. Vunivalu

[1]Rep. by A. Schiavio

Tries: Gale, Rakoroi, Nalaga, Savai

Tries: Penalty try

Cons: Koroduadua (2), Rokowailoa
PG: Koroduadua (2)
DG: –

Cons: Porta
PG: Porta
DG: –

*Referee: J.M. Fleming (Scotland)*

## NEW ZEALAND v. FIJI

Date: 27 May 1987

Venue: Lancaster Park, Christchurch

**NZ** (10G,2PG,2T)     **74-13**     **FIJI** (3PG,1T)

| | |
|---|---|
| J.A. Gallagher | S. Koroduadua |
| | |
| J.J. Kirwan | T. Cama |
| J.T. Stanley | S. Lovokuro |
| W.T. Taylor | J. Kubu |
| C.I. Green | S. Tuvula |
| | |
| G.J. Fox | E. Rokowailoa |
| *D.E. Kirk | P. Nawalu |
| | |
| S.C. McDowell | P. Volavola |
| S.B.T. Fitzpatrick | E. Rakai |
| J.A. Drake | M. Taga |
| A. Anderson | J. Cama |
| G.W. Whetton | I. Savai |
| A.J. Whetton | L. Kididromo |
| W.T. Shelford | *K. Rakoroi |
| M.N. Jones | S. Vunivalu |

Tries: Green (4), Gallagher
  (4), Kirwan, Kirk,
  A. Whetton, Penalty try    Tries: J. Cama
Cons: Fox (10)      Cons: –
PG: Fox (2)      PG: Koroduadua (3)
DG: –      DG: –

*Referee: W.D. Bevan (Wales)*

## ARGENTINA v. ITALY

Date: 28 May 1987

Venue: Lancaster Park, Christchurch

**ARGENTINA** (1G,5PG,1T)    **25-16**    **ITALY** (1G,2PG,1T)

| | |
|---|---|
| S. Salvat | D. Tebaldi |
| | |
| J. Lanza | M. Mascioletti |
| R. Madero | F. Gaetaniello |
| D. Cuesta-Silva | S. Barba |
| P. Lanza | M. Cuttita |
| | |
| *H. Porta | O. Collodo |
| M. Yanguela[1] | F. Lorigiola |
| | |
| S. Dengra | G. Rossi |
| D. Cash | A. Galeazzo |
| L. Molina | T. Lupini |
| E. Branca | A. Colella |
| S. Carossio | M. Gardin |
| J. Allen | M. Pavin |
| G. Travaglini | G. Zanon |
| A. Schiavio | *M. Innocenti |

[1]Rep. by F. Gomez

Tries: J. Lanza, Gomez    Tries: Cuttita,
                       Innocenti
Cons: Porta      Cons: Collodo
PG: Porta (5)      PG: Collodo (2)
DG: –      DG: –

*Referee: R.C. Quittenton (England)*

## FIJI v. ITALY

Date: 31 May 1987

Venue: Carisbrook, Dunedin

**FIJI** (1G,1DG,2PG)    **15-18**    **ITALY** (1PG,1DG,3T)

| | |
|---|---|
| S. Koroduadua | D. Tebaldi |
| | |
| T. Cama | M. Mascioletti |
| K. Salusalu | F. Gaetaniello |
| T. Mitchell | S. Barba |
| S. Tuvula[1] | M. Cuttita |
| | |
| E. Rokowailoa | O. Collodo |
| P. Nawalu | A. Ghini |
| | |
| S. Naituku | G. Cucchiella |
| S. Naiviliwasa | S. Romagnoli |
| P. Volavola | T. Lupini |
| W. Nadolo | M. Gardin |
| I. Savai | A. Colella |
| J. Sanday | R. Dolfato |
| *K. Rakoroi | P. Farina |
| M. Qoro | *M. Innocenti |

[1]Rep. by E. Naituku[2]
[2]Rep. by J. Kubu

Tries: Naiviliwasa    Tries: Cuttita,
                      Cucchiella
                      Mascioletti
Cons: Koroduadua      Cons: –
PG: Koroduadua (2)      PG: Collodo
DG: Qoro      DG: Collodo

*Referee: K.H. Lawrence (NZ)*

## NEW ZEALAND v. ARGENTINA

Date: 1 June 1987

Venue: Athletic Park, Wellington

**NZ** (2G,6PG,4T)    **46-15**    **ARGENTINA** (1G,3PG)

| | |
|---|---|
| K.J. Crowley | G. Angaut |
| | |
| J.J. Kirwan | M. Campo |
| J.T. Stanely | R. Madero |
| †B.J. McCahill | F. Turnes[1] |
| T.J. Wright | J. Lanza |
| | |
| G.J. Fox | *H. Porta |
| *D.E. Kirk | F. Gomez |
| | |
| R.W. Loe | S. Dengra |
| S.B.T. Fitzpatrick | D. Cash |
| J.A. Drake | L. Molina |
| M.J. Pierce | E. Branca |
| G.W. Whetton | S. Carossio |
| A. J. Whetton | J. Allen |
| A.T. Earl | G. Travaglini[2] |
| †M.Z. Brooke | A. Schiavio |

[1]Rep. by P. Lanza
[2]Rep. by J. Mostany

Tries: Kirk Brooke, Stanley,    Tries: J. Lanza
  Earl, Crowley,
  A. Whetton
Cons: Fox (2)      Cons: Porta
PG: Fox (6)      PG: Porta (3)
DG: –      DG: –

*Referee: R.C. Quittenton (England)*

# Pool Four

This pool produced the most exciting of all the qualiting matches. Scotland and France, the two most enterprising sides in the competition, met on the first weekend of the tournament in a splendid game which ended in the only draw of the entire Cup. The Scots never permitted the French to dominate, despite the early loss of John Rutherford with a leg injury. By scoring more tries than the Scots, France were placed at the top of the group table, thus avoiding a quarter-final confrontation with the All Blacks.

This group also produced a world-record-equalling performance as well as a new record on the same afternoon. Gavin Hastings' 27 points against Romania equalled the IB record set by Guy Camberabero in 1967, for France against Italy. Within hours of Hastings' achievement, Frenchman Didier Camberabero (and the son of the previous world record-holder) went three better, scoring 30 points against Zimbabwe.

The final group table for Group Four was:

| | P | W | D | L | For | Against | Pts |
|---|---|---|---|---|---|---|---|
| France | 3 | 2 | 1 | 0 | 145 | 44 | 5 |
| Scotland | 3 | 2 | 1 | 0 | 135 | 69 | 5 |
| Romania | 3 | 1 | 0 | 2 | 61 | 130 | 2 |
| Zimbabwe | 3 | 0 | 0 | 3 | 53 | 151 | 0 |

## ROMANIA v. ZIMBABWE

Date: 23 May 1987
Venue: Eden Park, Auckland

| ROMANIA (3PG,3T) | 21-20 | ZIMBABWE (1G,2PG,2T) |
|---|---|---|
| M. TOADER | | A. FERREIRA |
| A. MARIN[1] | | P. KAULBACH |
| S. TOFAN | | R. TSIMBA[1] |
| A. LUNGU | | K. GRAHAM |
| V. DAVID | | E. BARRETT |
| D. ALEXANDRU[2] | | C. BROWN |
| *M. PARASCHIV | | *M. JELLICOE |
| I. BUCAN | | G. ELCOMBE |
| E. GRIGORE | | L. BRAY |
| G. LEONTE | | A. TUCKER |
| L. CONSTANTIN | | M. SAWYER |
| S. CONSTANTIN | | M. MARTIN |
| F. MURARIU | | R. GRAY |
| C. RADUCANU | | M. NEILL |
| H. DUMITRAS | | D. BUTTENDAG[2] |

[1]Rep. by L. Hodorca
[2]Rep. by V. Ion

[1]Rep. by A. Buitendag
[2]Rep. by E. Bredenkamp

Tries: Paraschiv, Toader, Hodorca
Cons: –
PG: Alexandru (3)
DG: –

Tries: Tsimba (2), Neill
Cons: Ferreira
PG: Ferreira (2)
DG: –

*Referee: S.R. Hilditch (Ireland)*

## FRANCE v. SCOTLAND

Date: 23 May 1987
Venue: Lancaster Park, Christchurch

| FRANCE (1G,2PG,2T) | 20-20 | SCOTLAND (4PG,2T) |
|---|---|---|
| S. BLANCO | | A.G. HASTINGS |
| P. LAGISQUET | | M.D.F. DUNCAN |
| P. SELLA | | K.W. ROBERTSON |
| D. CHARVET | | D.S. WYLLIE |
| P. ESTEVE | | I. TUKALO |
| F. MESNEL | | J.Y. RUTHERFORD[1] |
| P. BERBIZIER | | R.J. LAIDLAW |
| P. ONDARTS | | D.M.B. SOLE |
| *D. DUBROCA | | *C.T. DEANS |
| J-P. GARUET | | I.G. MILNE |
| A. LORIEUX | | D.B. WHITE |
| J. CONDOM | | A.J. TOMES |
| E. CHAMP | | J. JEFFREY |
| L. RODRIGUEZ | | I.A.M. PAXTON |
| D. ERBANI | | F. CALDER |

[1]Rep. by †A.V. Tait

Tries: Sella, Berbizier, Blanco
Cons: Blanco
PG: Blanco (2)
DG: –

Tries: White, Duncan
Cons: –
PG: Hastings (4)
DG: –

*Referee: F.A. Howard (England)*

## FRANCE v. ROMANIA

Date: 28 May 1987
Venue: Athletic Park, Wellington

**FRANCE** (8G,1PG,1T)  **55-12**  **ROMANIA** (4PG)

| FRANCE | ROMANIA |
|---|---|
| S. Blanco[1] | V. Ion |
| P. Lagisquet | M. Toader |
| P. Sella | S. Tofan |
| D. Charvet | V. David |
| M. Andrieu | A. Lungu |
| G. Laporte | R. Bezuscu |
| P. Berbizier | *M. Paraschiv |
| †L. Armary | F. Opris |
| *P. Dintrans | V. Ilca[1] |
| J-P. Garuet | V. Pascu |
| F. Haget | N. Veres |
| J. Condom | L. Constantin |
| E. Champ | E. Necula |
| D. Erbani | C. Raducanu |
| A. Carminati | G. Dumitru |

[1]Rep. by D. Camberabero   [1]Rep. by E. Grigore

Tries: Lagisquet (2), Charvet (2), Sella, Andrieu, Camberabero, Erbani, Laporte      Tries: –
Cons: Laporte (8)      Cons: –
PG: Laporte      PG: Bezuscu (4)
DG: –      DG: –

*Referee: R.J. Fordham (Australia)*

## SCOTLAND v. ZIMBABWE

Date: 30 May 1987
Venue: Athletic Park, Wellington

**SCOTLAND** (8G,3T)  **60-21**  **ZIMBABWE** (1G,5PG)

| SCOTLAND | ZIMBABWE |
|---|---|
| A.G. Hastings | A. Ferreira |
| M.D.F. Duncan | S. Graham |
| A.V. Tait | A. Buitendag |
| K.W. Robertson | K. Graham |
| I. Tukalo | E. Barrett |
| D.S. Wyllie | M. Grobler |
| †G.H. Oliver | *M. Jellicoe |
| D.M.B. Sole | A. Nicholls |
| *C.T. Deans | L. Bray |
| I.G. Milne | A. Tucker |
| J.R.E. Campbell-Lamerton | M. Sawyer |
| A.J. Tomes | M. Martin |
| J. Jeffrey | R. Gray |
| I.A.M. Paxton | M. Neill |
| F. Calder | D. Buitendag |

Tries: Tait (2), Duncan (2), Tukalo (2), Paxton (2), Oliver, Hastings, Jeffrey      Tries: D. Buitendag
Cons: Hastings (8)      Cons: Grobler
PG: –      PG: Grobler (5)
DG: –      DG: –

*Referee: D.I.H. Burnett (Ireland)*

## FRANCE v. ZIMBABWE

Date: 2 June 1987
Venue: Eden Park, Auckland

**FRANCE** (9G,4T)  **70-12**  **ZIMBABWE** (1G,2PG)

| FRANCE | ZIMBABWE |
|---|---|
| D. Camberabero | A. Ferreira |
| M. Andrieu | P. Kaulbach |
| E. Bonneval[1] | R. Tsimba |
| D. Charvet | K. Graham |
| P. Esteve | E. Barrett |
| F. Mesnel | M. Grobler |
| R. Modin | *M. Jellicoe |
| †J-L. Tolot | G. Elcombe[1] |
| *D. Dubroca | L. Bray |
| P. Ondarts | A. Tucker |
| A. Lorieux | M. Sawyer |
| J. Condom | M. Martin[2] |
| A. Carminati | R. Gray |
| L. Rodriguez | M. Neill |
| J-L. Joinel | D. Buitendag |

[1]Rep. by P. Sella[2]   [1]Rep. by A. Nicholls
[2]Rep. by G. Laporte   [2]Rep. by N. Kloppers

Tries: Modin (3), Camberabero (3) Charvet (2), Dubroca, Esteve, Rodriguez (2), Laporte      Tries: Kaulbach
Cons: Camberabero (9)      Cons: Grobler
PG: –      PG: Grobler (2)
DG: –      DG: –

*Referee: W.D. Bevan (Wales)*

## SCOTLAND v. ROMANIA

Date: 2 June 1987
Venue: Carisbrook, Dunedin

**SCOTLAND** (8G,1PG,1T)  **55-28**  **ROMANIA** (2G,4PG,1T)

| SCOTLAND | ROMANIA |
|---|---|
| A.G. Hastings | A. Ion |
| M.D.F. Duncan | A. Pilotschi |
| A.V. Tait | A. Lungu |
| S. Hastings[1] | S. Tofan |
| I. Tukalo | M. Toader |
| D.S. Wyllie | D. Alexandru |
| R.J. Laidlaw | *M. Paraschiv |
| D.M.B. Sole | I. Bucan |
| *C.T. Deans | E. Grigore |
| N.A. Rowan | G. Leonte |
| D.B. White | S. Constantin |
| A.J. Tomes[2] | L. Constantin |
| J. Jeffrey | F. Murariu |
| I.A.M. Paxton | C. Raducanu[1] |
| F. Calder | H. Dumitras |

[1]Rep. by †R. Cramb   [1]Rep. by G. Dumitru
[2]Rep. by J.R.E. Campbell-Lamerton

Tries: Tait (2), A.G. Hastings (2), Jeffrey (3),Duncan, Tukalo      Tries: Murariu (2), Toader
Cons: A.G. Hastings (8)      Cons: Alexandru, Ion
PG: A.G. Hastings      PG: Alexandru (3), Ion
DG: –      DG: –

*Referee: S.R. Hilditch (Ireland)*

# Knockout Rounds

The last eight matches of the tournament were the knockout stages leading to the World Cup final. The quarter-finals emphasised the superiority of New Zealand and Australia. The host nations gained comfortable wins against Scotland and Ireland respectively, and at this stage it looked certain that the Southern Hemisphere would provide the competition's two finalists. France did not have an easy passage against Fiji. The unfancied Pacific islanders played with skill and courage to score two tries, with Qoro outstanding in the loose. His subsequent loss through injury disrupted the Fijian performance in the later moments of the game, and when Koroduadua (playing out of position at fly-half) made a telling run in the second half, only to lose the ball through careless handling, Fiji's chances of victory subsided.

The tie of the quarter-finals was Wales-England. The two Home Nations met for the 93rd time, but for many this was their most important encounter in the 107-year history of the fixture. England, whose group matches had given encouragement to their followers and squad members, had the advantage of having played all of their earlier games in Australia. Wales, by contrast, had suffered cruelly from an unprecedented run of injuries, and had to cross the Tasman to meet the much-fancied English. In addition, with their first choice front row unavailable, the Welsh had to pluck a 19-year-old tight-head, David Young of Swansea, from Australian club rugby in order to field a team. But the prospect of facing the old enemy no doubt motivated the Welsh beyond their supporters' expectations and after 30 minutes of play a Welsh victory never really seemed in doubt. Despite injury problems for Norster and Jonathan Davies, the Welsh managed a comfortable win with Robert Jones at scrum-half making an impressive all-round contribution to the side's success.

Wales' win gave them the dubious privilege of a semi-final with New Zealand. The All Blacks proved to be in a class above the Welsh and imposed their authority to the extent that Wales suffered their highest-ever defeat in an international since the introduction of scoring by points in the late 1880s. And to add insult to injury, Huw Richards, one of the Welsh locks, became the first player to be ordered off in the World Cup when referee Kerry Fitzgerald expelled him for fighting during the second half. The referee was correct, but Mr Fitzgerald's failure to treat New Zealand's number-eight Wayne Shelford in the same way for an identical offence was an unfortunate lapse.

The France-Australia semi-final was the most exciting match of the tournament, with the French snatching success in the last minute of injury time. The French forwards dominated the tight play and subdued the big Australian forwards in the loose to pave the path to victory. Two notable landmarks were reached during the match: Campese became the world's leading try-scorer in internationals, passing Ian Smith's 54-year record of 24 tries in internationals, and Serge Blanco became the first player to score 15 international tries from the full-back position. In addition, Michael Lynagh took his career record of Test points past the previous Australian record held by Paul McLean.

France and New Zealand thus contested rugby's first World Cup final in Auckland on 20 June. The match was an unspectacular one with the All Blacks underlining their outstanding brilliance in a comfortable victory. Wales, through a last-minute touchline conversion from Paul Thorburn, finished third in the tournament by beating a depleted Australian side 22-21.

# QUARTER-FINALS

## NEW ZEALAND v. SCOTLAND

Date: 6 June 1987
Venue: Lancaster Park, Christchurch

| NZ (2G,6PG) | 30-3 | SCOTLAND (1PG) |
|---|---|---|
| J.A. GALLAGHER | | A.G. HASTINGS |
| J.J. KIRWAN | | M.D.F. DUNCAN |
| J.T. STANLEY | | A.V. TAIT |
| W.T. TAYLOR[1] | | K.W. ROBERTSON |
| C.I. GREEN | | I. TUKALO |
| G.J. FOX | | D.S. WYLLIE |
| *D.E. KIRK | | R.J. LAIDLAW |
| S.C. McDOWELL | | D.M.B. SOLE |
| S.B.T. FITZPATRICK | | *C.T. DEANS |
| J.A. DRAKE | | I.G. MILNE |
| M.J. PIERCE | | D.B. WHITE |
| G.W. WHETTON | | A.J. TOMES |
| A.J. WHETTON | | †D.J. TURNBULL |
| W.T. SHELFORD | | I.A.M. PAXTON |
| M.N. JONES | | F. CALDER |

[1]Rep. by B.J. McCahill

Tries: A.J.Whetton, Gallagher — Tries: –
Cons: Fox (2) — Cons: –
PG: Fox (6) — PG: Hastings
DG: – — DG: –

*Referee: D.I.H. Burnett (Ireland)*

## FRANCE v. FIJI

Date: 7 June 1987
Venue: Eden Park, Auckland

| FRANCE (3G,2PG,1DG,1T) | 31-16 | FIJI (1G,2PG,1T) |
|---|---|---|
| S. BLANCO[1] | | J. KUBU |
| D. CHARVET | | J. DAMU |
| P. SELLA | | K. SALUSALU |
| F. MESNEL | | T. CAMA |
| P. LAGISQUET | | T. MITCHELL |
| G. LAPORTE | | S. KORODUADUA |
| P. BERBIZIER | | P. NAWALU |
| P. ONDARTS | | R. NAMORO |
| * D. DUBROCA | | E. RAKAI |
| J-P GARUET | | S. NAITUKU |
| F. HAGET | | *K. RAKOROI |
| A. LORIEUX | | I. SAVAI[2] |
| E. CHAMP | | M. QORO[1] |
| L. RODRIGUEZ | | L. KIDIDROMO |
| D. ERBANI | | S. NAIVILIWASA |

[1]Rep. by D. Camberabero

[1]Rep. by S. Vunivalu
[2]Rep. by W. Nadolo

Tries: Rodriguez (2), Lorieux, Lagisquet — Tries: Qoro, Damu
Cons: Laporte (3) — Cons: Koroduadua
PG: Laporte (2) — PG: Koroduadua (2)
DG: Laporte — DG: –

*Referee: C. Norling (Wales)*

## AUSTRALIA v. IRELAND

Date: 7 June 1987
Venue: Concord, Oval, Sydney

| AUSTRALIA (4G,3PG) | 33-15 | IRELAND (2G,1PG) |
|---|---|---|
| D.I. Campese | | H.P. MacNeill |
| P.C. Grigg | | T.M. Ringland |
| *A.G. Slack | | B.J. Mullin[2] |
| B. Papworth | | M.J. Kiernan |
| M.P. Burke | | K.D. Crossan |
| M.P. Lynagh | | P.M. Dean |
| N.C. Farr-Jones[1] | | M.T. Bradley |
| C.A. Lillicrap | | P.A. Orr |
| T.A. Lawton | | T. Kingston |
| A.J. McIntyre | | D.C. Fitzgerald |
| S.A.G. Cutler | | *D.G. Lenihan |
| W.A. Campbell | | W.A. Anderson |
| S.P. Poidevin | | P.M. Matthews |
| S.N. Tuynman | | N. Francis[1] |
| J.S. Miller | | D.G. McGrath |

[1]Rep. by B. Smith

[1]Rep. by B.J. Spillane
[2]Rep. by D.G. Irwin

Tries: Smith, McIntyre, Burke (2)
Cons: Lynagh (4)
PG: Lynagh (3)
DG: –

Tries: MacNeill, Kiernan
Cons: Kiernan (2)
PG: Kiernan
DG: –

*Referee: J.B. Anderson (Scotland)*

## WALES v. ENGLAND

Date: 8 June 1987
Venue: Ballymore, Brisbane

| WALES (2G,1T) | 16-3 | ENGLAND (1PG) |
|---|---|---|
| P.H. Thorburn | | J. Webb |
| I.C. Evans | | *M.E. Harrison |
| J.A. Devereux | | K.G. Simms |
| B. Bowen | | J.L.B. Salmon |
| A.M. Hadley | | R. Underwood |
| J. Davies | | P.N. Williams |
| R.N. Jones | | R.M. Harding |
| A. Buchanan | | P.A.G. Rendall[1] |
| A.J. Phillips | | B.C. Moore |
| †D. Young | | G.S. Pearce |
| *R.D. Moriarty | | W.A. Dooley |
| R.L. Norster[1] | | N.C. Redman |
| G.J. Roberts | | P.J. Winterbottom |
| W.P. Moriarty | | D. Richards |
| R.G. Collins | | G.W. Rees |

[1]Rep. by H.D. Richards

[1]Rep. by G.J. Chilcott

Tries: Roberts, Jones, Devereux
Cons: Thorburn (2)
PG: –
DG: –

Tries: –
Cons: –
PG: Webb
DG: –

*Referee: R. Hourquet (France)*

# SEMI-FINALS

## FRANCE v. AUSTRALIA

Date: 13 June 1987
Venue: Concord Oval, Sydney

| FRANCE (4G,2PG) | 30-24 | AUSTRALIA (2G,1DG,3PG) |
|---|---|---|
| S. Blanco | | D.I. Campese |
| D. Camberabero | | P.C. Grigg |
| P. Sella | | *A.G. Slack |
| D. Charvet | | B. Papworth[1] |
| P. Lagisquet | | M. Burke |
| F. Mesnel | | M.P. Lynagh |
| P. Berbizier | | N.C. Farr-Jones |
| P. Ondarts | | C.A. Lillicrap |
| *D. Dubroca | | T.A. Lawton |
| J-P. Garuet | | A.J. McIntyre |
| A. Lorieux | | S.A.G. Cutler |
| J. Condom | | W.A. Campbell[2] |
| E. Champ | | S.P. Poidevin |
| L. Rodriguez | | T. Coker |
| D. Erbani | | J.S. Miller |

[1]Rep. by A. Herbert
[2]Rep. by D. Codey

Tries: Lorieux, Lagisquet, Sella, Blanco
Cons: Camberabero (4)
PG: Camberabero (2)
DG: –

Tries: Campese, Codey
Cons: Lynagh (2)
PG: Lynagh (3)
DG: Lynagh

*Referee: J.B. Anderson (Scotland)*

## WALES v. NEW ZEALAND

Date: 14 June 1987
Venue: Ballymore, Brisbane

| WALES (1G) | 6-49 | NEW ZEALAND (7G,1PG,1T) |
|---|---|---|
| P.H. Thorburn | | J.A. Gallagher |
| I.C. Evans | | J.J. Kirwan |
| J.A. Devereux | | J.T. Stanley[1] |
| B. Bowen | | W.T. Taylor |
| A.M. Hadley | | C.I. Green |
| J. Davies | | G.J. Fox |
| R.N. Jones | | *D.E. Kirk |
| A. Buchanan | | S.C. McDowell |
| K. Phillips | | S.B.T. Fitzpatrick |
| D. Young | | J.A. Drake |
| *R.D. Moriarty | | M.J. Pierce |
| H.D. Richards | | G.W. Whetton |
| W.P. Moriarty | | A.J. Whetton |
| P.T. Davies | | W.T. Shelford |
| R.G. Collins[1] | | M. Brooke-Cowden |

[1]Rep. by S. Sutton

[1]Rep. by B.J. McCahill

Tries: Devereux

Tries: Kirwan (2), Stanley, Drake, A. Whetton, Shelford (2), Brooke-Cowden
Cons: Thorburn
PG: –
DG: –

Cons: Fox (7)
PG: Fox
DG: –

*Referee: K.V.J. Fitzgerald (Australia)*

# THIRD/FOURTH PLACE PLAYOFF MATCH

## AUSTRALIA v. WALES

Date: 18 June 1987

Venue: International Park, Rotorua

**AUSTRALIA** (2G,2PG,1DG)  **21-22**   **WALES** (2G,2PG,1T)

| AUSTRALIA | WALES |
|---|---|
| A. Leeds | P.H. Thorburn |
| | |
| P.C. Grigg[1] | I.C. Evans |
| *A.G. Slack | J.A. Devereux |
| M.P. Burke | M.G. Ring |
| D.I. Campese | A.M. Hadley |
| | |
| M.P. Lynagh | J. Davies |
| B. Smith | R.N. Jones |
| | |
| C.A. Lillicrap[2] | A. Buchanan |
| T.A. Lawton | A.J. Phillips |
| A.J. McIntyre | S.W. Blackmore |
| S.A.G. Cutler | *R.D. Moriarty |
| T. Coker | S. Sutton |
| S.P. Poidevin | G.J. Roberts |
| S.N. Tuynman | W.P. Moriarty |
| D. Codey | †R. Webster |

[1]Rep. by N.C. Farr-Jones
[2]Rep. by E.E. Rodriguez

Tries: Burke, Grigg

Tries: Roberts, W.P. Moriarty, Hadley

Cons: Lynagh (2)   Cons: Thorburn (2)
PG: Lynagh (2)     PG: Thorburn (2)
DG: Lynagh         DG: –

*Referee: F.A. Howard (England)*

# THE FINAL

## NEW ZEALAND v. FRANCE

Date: 20 June 1987

Venue: Eden Park, Auckland

**NEW ZEALAND** (1G,1DG,4PG,2T) **29-9**   **FRANCE** (1G,1PG)

| NEW ZEALAND | FRANCE |
|---|---|
| J.A. Gallagher | S. Blanco |
| | |
| J.J. Kirwan | D. Camberabero |
| J.T. Stanley | P. Sella |
| W.T. Taylor | D. Charvet |
| C.I. Green | P. Lagisquet |
| | |
| G.J. Fox | F. Mesnel |
| *D.E. Kirk | P. Berbizier |
| | |
| S.C. McDowell | P. Ondarts |
| S.B.T. Fitzpatrick | *D. Dubroca |
| J.A. Drake | J-P. Garuet |
| M.J. Pierce | A. Lorieux |
| G.W. Whetton | J. Condom |
| A.J. Whetton | E. Champ |
| W.T. Shelford | L. Rodriguez |
| M.N. Jones | D. Erbani |

Tries: Kirwan, Jones, Kirk   Tries: Berbizier
Cons: Fox                    Cons: Camberabero
PG: Fox (4)                  PG: Camberabero
DG: Fox                      DG: –

*Referee: K.V.J. Fitzgerald (Australia)*

# WORLD CUP RECORDS

(*indicates a new world record; = indicates a world-record-equalling performance.)

## LEADING SCORERS

### MOST POINTS IN THE COMPETITION

| | | |
|---|---|---|
| 126 | G.J. Fox | New Zealand |
| 82 | M.P. Lynagh | Australia |
| 62 | A.G. Hastings | Scotland |

### MOST TRIES IN THE COMPETITION

| | | |
|---|---|---|
| 6 | C.I. Green | New Zealand |
| 6 | J.J. Kirwan | New Zealand |
| 5 | M.E. Harrison | England |
| 5 | D.E. Kirk | New Zealand |
| 5 | A.J. Whetton | New Zealand |
| 5 | J.A. Gallagher | New Zealand |

### MOST CONVERSIONS IN THE COMPETITION

| | | |
|---|---|---|
| 30 | G.J. Fox | New Zealand |
| 20 | M.P. Lynagh | Australia |
| 16 | A.G. Hastings | Scotland |

### MOST PENALTY GOALS IN THE COMPETITION

| | | |
|---|---|---|
| 21 | G.J. Fox | New Zealand |
| 12 | M.P. Lynagh | Australia |

### MOST DROPPED GOALS IN THE COMPETITION

| | | |
|---|---|---|
| 3 | J. Davies | Wales |
| 2 | O. Collodo | Italy |
| 2 | M.P. Lynagh | Australia |

## MOST POINTS IN A MATCH

### By a team

| | | |
|---|---|---|
| 74* | New Zealand v Fiji | Christchurch |
| 70 | New Zealand v Italy | Auckland |
| 70 | France v Zimbabwe | Auckland |
| 60 | England v Japan | Sydney |
| 60 | Scotland v Zimbabwe | Wellington |

### By a player

| | | | |
|---|---|---|---|
| 30* | D. Camberabero | France v Zimbabwe | Auckland |
| 27 | A.G. Hastings | Scotland v Romania | Dunedin |
| 26 | G.J. Fox | New Zealand v Fiji | Christchurch |
| 23 | G. Laporte | France v Romania | Wellington |
| 22 | G.J. Fox | New Zealand v Italy | Auckland |
| 22 | G.J. Fox | New Zealand v Argentina | Wellington |
| 22 | G.J. Fox | New Zealand v Scotland | Christchurch |

## MOST TRIES IN A MATCH

### By a team

| | | |
|---|---|---|
| 13= | France v Zimbabwe | Auckland |
| 12 | New Zealand v Italy | Auckland |
| 12 | New Zealand v Fiji | Christchurch |
| 11 | Scotland v Zimbabwe | Wellington |

### By a player

| | | | |
|---|---|---|---|
| 4 | I.C. Evans | Wales v Canada | Invercargill |
| 4 | C.I. Green | New Zealand v Fiji | Christchurch |
| 4† | J.A. Gallagher | New Zealand v Fiji | Christchurch |

(† Gallagher's four were a new world record for tries scored in a match by a full-back.)

# MOST CONVERSIONS IN A MATCH

## By a team

| | | |
|---|---|---|
| 10* | New Zealand v Fiji | Christchurch |
| 9 | France v Zimbabwe | Auckland |
| 8 | New Zealand v Italy | Auckland |
| 8 | France v Romania | Wellington |
| 8 | Scotland v Zimbabwe | Wellington |
| 8 | Scotland v Romania | Dunedin |

## By a player

| | | | |
|---|---|---|---|
| 10* | G.J. Fox | New Zealand v Fiji | Christchurch |
| 9 | D. Camberabero | France v Zimbabwe | Auckland |
| 8 | G.J. Fox | New Zealand v Italy | Auckland |
| 8 | G. Laporte | France v Romania | Wellington |
| 8 | A.G. Hastings | Scotland v Zimbabwe | Wellington |
| 8 | A.G. Hastings | Scotland v Romania | Dunedin |

# MOST PENALTY GOALS IN A MATCH

## By a team

| | | |
|---|---|---|
| 6 | New Zealand v Scotland | Christchurch |
| 6 | New Zealand v Argentina | Wellington |
| 5 | Argentina v Italy | Christchurch |
| 5 | Zimbabwe v Scotland | Wellington |

## By a player

| | | | |
|---|---|---|---|
| 6= | G.J. Fox | New Zealand v Scotland | Christchurch |
| 6= | G.J. Fox | New Zealand v Argentina | Wellington |
| 5 | H. Porta | Argentina v Italy | Christchurch |
| 5 | M. Grobler | Zimbabwe v Scotland | Wellington |

# MOST DROPPED GOALS IN A MATCH

## By a team

| | | |
|---|---|---|
| 2 | Wales v Ireland | Wellington |
| 2 | Ireland v Canada | Dunedin |

## By a player

| | | | |
|---|---|---|---|
| 2 | J. Davies | Wales v Ireland | Wellington |

# OTHER NEW WORLD RECORDS CREATED DURING THE WORLD CUP

## Fastest player to reach 100 points in internationals

| | | |
|---|---|---|
| G.J. Fox | (New Zealand) | in 6 matches |

## Most tries in a career

| | | |
|---|---|---|
| 25 | D.I. Campese | (Australia) |

## Most conversions in a career

| | | |
|---|---|---|
| 50 | M.P. Lynagh | (Australia) |

## Most tries by a full-back

| | | |
|---|---|---|
| 15 | S. Blanco | (France) |